O'CONNOR'S TEXAS RULES
CIVIL TRIALS

BY
MICHOL O'CONNOR

2004 EDITORS
MICHOL O'CONNOR
BYRON P. DAVIS

JONES MCCLURE PUBLISHING
HOUSTON, TEXAS

O'CONNOR'S LITIGATION SERIES

Suggested cite form: ***O'Connor's Texas Rules * Civil Trials*** (2004)

Jones McClure Publishing
Product List
To Order Call 800-OCONNOR

Texas Litigation Series

O'Connor's Texas Rules* ★ *Civil Trials

Texas civil pretrial, trial, and post-trial procedure explained in plain English. *O'Connor's Texas Rules* provides the entire Texas Rules of Civil Procedure and Texas Rules of Evidence, both with up-to-date quotations from relevant, controlling cases. Also included are the Texas Rules of Appellate Procedure and timetables for tracking important deadlines. Thoroughly researched and revised each year to bring you every important rule or case-law change in a clear and concise manner.

O'Connor's Texas Civil Forms

Covers pleadings and motions from the trial's beginning to end with easy-to-use, plain-English forms. Provides forms for every common motion, as well as original petition, answer, and discovery forms for cases involving breach of contract, personal injury (auto accident & slip and fall), DTPA, Texas Tort Claims Act, bill of review, and suit on account. The forms are also available on CD.

O'Connor's Texas Civil Appeals

Provides comprehensive coverage of appellate procedure. Includes the Texas Rules of Appellate Procedure annotated with case quotations, commentaries that explain every phase of the appeal, forms used for appeals, timetables for tracking all-important appellate deadlines, and helpful descriptions of local procedures for all appellate courts. The appellate forms are also available on CD.

Federal Litigation Series

O'Connor's Federal Rules* ★ *Civil Trials

Ten chapters of detailed commentaries explain Federal Civil Procedure in plain English. Provides entire Federal Rules of Civil Procedure and Federal Rules of Evidence, both with up-to-date quotations from relevant, controlling cases. Also included are the Federal Rules of Appellate Procedure and important Advisory Committee Notes, plus Title 28 of the U.S.C., and timetables for tracking deadlines.

O'Connor's Federal Civil Forms

Comprehensive collection of trial forms written in plain English and formatted for quick, efficient completion. Complete sets of forms are included for cases involving Admiralty-Jones Act, trademark infringement, Age Discrimination in Employment Act, Family and Medical Leave Act, breach of contract, the Federal Tort Claims Act, copyright infringement, employment discrimination and sexual harassment suits under Title VII and the ADA, civil rights suits under 42 U.S.C. §1983, negligence under the Federal Employer's Liability Act, and personal injury in an auto accident. The forms are also available on CD.

O'Connor's Federal Employment Codes Plus

Complete codes and statute resource for the federal employment law practitioner. Includes annotated provisions covering administrative procedure, alien employment, arbitration, garnishment, credit reports, NLRA, LMRA, ADEA, Rehabilitation Act, ERISA, agricultural workers, polygraph protection, plant closings, FMLA, mine safety, longshore worker's compensation, uniformed services, public contracts, Walsh-Healey, civil rights enforcement, Title VII, ADA, and railroad labor and retirement. Also includes a variety of charts and timetables on federal employment statutes, attorney fees, statute of limitations, and EEOC charges.

Texas Expert Series

Texas Rules of Evidence Handbook 5th edition

Evidence explained in ten detailed chapters of expert commentary citing the most recent case law and most authoritative sources, updated by Cathy Cochran, Justice on the Texas Court of Criminal Appeals and member of the Administration of the Rules of Evidence Committee of the State Bar, to reflect the current Texas Rules of Evidence.

O'Connor's Texas Causes of Action

Over 900 pages of comprehensive commentary discussing the most common causes of action pleaded by Texas attorneys. Lists and explains the elements of each cause of action, referring to the definitive authority on each point and providing cross references to both the relevant state pattern jury charges and law journal articles discussing the cause of action. Covers torts, contracts, negligence, and statutory causes of action.

O'Connor's Family Law Handbook *(forthcoming 2004-05)*

Complete resource for the family law practitioner. Detailed commentary covering all aspects of family practice, including cites to the most recent case law and expert practice tips. Incorporates the most up-to-date changes to the Texas Family Code.

Texas Annotated Codes Series

O'Connor's Probate Code Plus

Includes the Probate and Trust Codes with annotations, and all the statutes that affect probate and trust practice, including select provisions from the Family Code, Health & Safety Code, Property Code, the Texas Rules of Civil Procedure and Texas Rules of Evidence, and many more. Also included are charts on attorney fees, statutes of limitations, and citations and timetables on the administration of decedent's and guardianship estates.

O'Connor's CPRC Plus

Includes the Civil Practice & Remedies Code, annotated with case quotations, along with the full text of the DTPA, the Medical Practice Act, the Medical Liability & Insurance Act, and Insurance Code Arts. 21.21 & 21.28.

O'Connor's Criminal Codes Plus

Includes the Code of Criminal Procedure, Penal Code, and selected provisions from the Government Code, Transportation Code, and Water Code. Includes the Texas Rules of Evidence and Texas Rules of Appellate Procedure as well as timetables for criminal appeals based on the rules. Combines all commonly used criminal codes and statutes into one user-friendly volume with annotations carefully selected by George McCall "Mac" Secrest, Jr.

O'Connor's Family Code Plus

Includes the Family Code, Texas Rules of Civil Procedure, and Texas Rules of Evidence with case quotations carefully selected to explain how the courts interpret each section. Also includes selected sections from various codes that family lawyers need. The contents and quotations were carefully selected by Sydney Aaron Beckman.

O'Connor's Business Organizations Codes Plus

Complete reference manual for organizing and maintaining all varieties of corporations and partnerships. Contains the Business Corporation Act and Texas Securities Act, as well as all relevant partnership, limited liability, and nonprofit corporation statutes. Provides incorporation forms suitable for filing with the Secretary of State.

O'Connor's Business & Commerce Code Plus

Includes the Business & Commerce Code, annotated with case quotations. Contains both the new and old Chapter 9. Supplemented with helpful charts regarding secured transactions, the DTPA, and covenants not to compete.

O'Connor's Texas Employment Codes Plus

Comprehensive Texas employment law reference manual. Contains the entire Labor Code and selected provisions from other codes and statutes, including whistleblower; concealed handgun; employment contract; arbitration; access to criminal history; public health; and state, municipal, and educator employment. All are annotated with quotations from controlling cases. Also includes a variety of charts and timetables.

JONES
McCLURE
PUBLISHING

Mail to:
P.O. Box 3348
Houston, TX 77253-3348

Ship to:
1113 Vine, Suite 240
Houston, TX 77002

Tel: (713) 223-2727
(800) OCONNOR
(800) 626-6667
Fax: (713) 223-9393

Internet: www.JonesMcClure.com
E-mail: comments@JonesMcClure.com

Print date: January 29, 2004
Printed in the United States of America.

ISBN 1-884554-76-8

This publication is intended to provide lawyers with current and accurate information about Texas civil trial procedure. The information in this book, however, may not be sufficient in dealing with a client's particular legal problem, and Jones McClure Publishing, Michol O'Connor, and Byron P. Davis do not warrant or represent its suitability for this purpose. Lawyers using this publication do so with the understanding that the information published in this book should not be relied on as a substitute for independent research to original sources of authority.

Subscription Notice: This publication is updated periodically to reflect important changes in its subject matter. Upon ordering a book, customers can choose to be enrolled in our subscription program. Future editions of any books ordered are shipped to subscribers automatically. Subscribers receive confirmation cards before new editions are shipped, with the option to cancel or change the order. If no change or cancellation is requested, the books will be shipped. If a customer chooses to return the books, return postage is the customer's responsibility. If you did not purchase this publication directly from Jones McClure Publishing, you are not registered as a subscriber and will not receive this update service. Customers can change their subscription status at any time in writing.

Every year I strive to make significant changes to this book, whether it be through revisions in organization, substance, or case law. This year, House Bill 4 made the choice of what areas to revise easy. House Bill 4 changed procedural issues ranging from venue to postjudgment interest and required the Supreme Court to amend certain rules of procedure and enact new ones. All of these changes have been incorporated and explained in this year's edition of ***O'Connor's Texas Rules * Civil Trials***. In addition, the 2004 edition of ***O'Connor's Texas Causes of Action*** discusses the changes in substantive law enacted by House Bill 4, as well as the other changes from the 2003 legislative sessions.

LEGISLATIVE CHANGES

Below is a summary of the important statutory changes that affect procedure. To check the statutes, bill drafts, bill analyses, list of witnesses who testified at hearings, and summaries of committee actions, go to Texas Legislature Online, www.capitol.state.tx.us, and fill in the blank for the bill number, using "HB" or "SB," for House Bill or Senate Bill, in front of the number (e.g., HB 4 or SB 430). The website is a great source of information.

Pretrial Matters

Exemplary damages. House Bill 4 amended CPRC chapter 41, expanding its scope from exemplary damages to cover other types of damages. Under CPRC §41.003(a), exemplary damages are now available if the plaintiff proves fraud, malice, or gross negligence. The former statute permitted exemplary damages for a willful act or omission or, in wrongful death actions, for gross neglect. Subsection 41.003(d) was added to require the jury to render a unanimous verdict on both liability for and the amount of exemplary damages. These changes became effective September 1, 2003. See "Plaintiff's burden," ch. 5-H, §5.4, p. 268; "Exemplary damages cases," ch. 8-K, §4.2, p. 587.

Forum non conveniens. House Bill 4 amended CPRC §71.051, the forum non conveniens (FNC) statute, to curb foreign parties' use of Texas courts. Subsection 71.051(a) was repealed, eliminating the distinction between a plaintiff who is not a legal resident of the United States and one who is a legal resident. Subsection 71.051(b) was amended to remove the defendant's burden of proving by a preponderance of the evidence that a Texas court should not exercise jurisdiction. House Bill 4 repealed §71.052, concerning FNC in suits for personal injury or death caused by asbestos exposure. These changes became effective September 1, 2003. See "Forum Non Conveniens—Challenging the Texas Forum," ch. 3-D, p. 165.

Interlocutory appeal & stay. House Bill 4 amended CPRC §51.014 to allow interlocutory appeal of pretrial orders on expert reports in medical malpractice actions. Subsection 51.014(b) was amended to require a stay of all proceedings pending resolution of an interlocutory appeal under subsections 51.014(a)(3), (5), and (8). CPRC §15.003(b) was amended to allow interlocutory appeal of the court's determination that an intervening plaintiff did or did not establish venue. These changes became effective September 1, 2003. See "Joinder," ch. 3-C, §5.2.2, p. 163; "Stay of trial," ch. 3-F, §7.1.2, p. 186; "Stay," ch. 7-B, §15.4.3(2), p. 484.

Legislative continuance. Senate Bill 430 amended CPRC §30.003(c), which gave the court discretion to deny a continuance for a legislator employed within 10 days of trial. The amendment gives the court the discretion to deny a legislative continuance when a legislator was employed within 30 days before trial. This change became effective April 24, 2003. House Bill 1606 enacted §30.003(g) to require a member or member-elect of the Legislature to file a copy of the application for a legislative continuance with the Texas Ethics Commission. This provision became effective September 1, 2003. See "Continuance for Legislator," ch. 5-D, §12, p. 250.

Responsible third parties. House Bill 4 amended CPRC §33.004 to provide a new procedure for designating responsible third parties. The new provision eliminates the requirement that a responsible third party must be joined in the lawsuit before its liability can be submitted. This change became effective July 1, 2003. See "Responsible third party," ch. 3-E, §6.4, p. 180.

Venue. House Bill 4 amended CPRC §15.003 to modify the procedure for multiple and intervening plaintiffs to establish proper venue. This change became effective September 1, 2003. See "Choosing the Court—Venue," ch. 2-G, p. 111; "Motion to Transfer—Challenging Venue," ch. 3-C, p. 152.

Judge & Jury

Judges. House Bill 3306 amended Gov't Code §§74.053-74.055 to change the procedure for assigning judges and objecting to assignments. These changes became effective June 18, 2003. See "Objection to Assigned Judge," ch. 5-C, §3, p. 234.

Juries. Senate Bill 164 added CPRC §24.001, which prohibits recording jury deliberations. This bill was enacted in response to the controversy surrounding the case ***State ex rel. Rosenthal v. Poe***, 98 S.W.3d 194 (Tex.Crim.App. 2003), in which the Court of Criminal Appeals reversed an order by Judge Ted Poe allowing the television program *Frontline* to tape for future broadcast the jury deliberations in a capital murder case. Senate Bill 737 amended Gov't Code §62.106 to exempt from jury service members of the U.S. military on active duty who are away from their home station and out of their county of residence. House Bill 2188 added Gov't Code §62.0111, which allows prospective jurors to respond to a summons by contacting the county by computer, calling an automated telephone system, or appearing before the court in person. These provisions became effective September 1, 2003. See "Jury Selection," ch. 8-A, p. 519; "No recording," ch. 8-K, §2.2, p. 586.

Post-Trial Matters

Judgment interest. House Bill 4 amended Finance Code §304.003 to set the postjudgment interest rate at the prime rate. When the prime rate is less than 5%, the postjudgment interest rate is 5%; when the prime rate is more than 15%, the postjudgment interest rate is 15%. See "Postjudgment interest," ch. 9-C, §4.6, p. 599. House Bill 4 also enacted section 304.1045, which bars recovery of prejudgment interest on future damages. House Bill 4 repealed section 304.108, which gave the trial court discretion to order that prejudgment interest not accrue during periods of delay. These provisions became effective September 1, 2003. See "Prejudgment interest," ch. 9-C, §4.5, p. 599.

Miscellaneous

Fees for out-of-state attorney. House Bill 462 enacted Gov't Code §82.0361 to require a nonresident attorney requesting permission to appear in a Texas state court to pay a $250 fee for each case in which the attorney is requesting to participate. The nonresident attorney must pay the fee to the Board of Law Examiners before filing the motion pro hac vice and must provide proof of payment to the court in which the attorney is requesting to appear. This provision became effective September 1, 2003. See "Fees," ch. 1-H, §2.2.1(3), p. 38.

Contempt. House Bill 346 added Gov't Code §21.002(h) to limit confinement for civil or criminal contempt to a maximum of 18 months except in child support cases. This bill was enacted in reponse to a civil case in Liberty County where a defendant was confined for contempt for over four years for refusing to produce documents. This provision became effective June 20, 2003. See "Sanctions under Gov't Code," ch. 5-J, §7.5, p. 283.

Probate jurisdiction. House Bill 4 amended Probate Code §§5A, 5B, and 607 to provide that proper venue for an action by or against a personal representative for personal injury, death, or property damages is determined under CPRC §15.007. This change became effective September 1, 2003. See "Transfer of proceedings to statutory probate courts," ch. 2-F, §4.4.3(3), p. 108. For other legislative changes affecting probate, see "County courts," ch. 2-F, §4, p. 104; ***O'Connor's Probate Code Plus***, "2003 Legislative Changes," p. v (2003-04).

Proportionate responsibility & contribution. House Bill 4 substantially revised CPRC chapter 33, including amendments affecting a defendant's ability to elect the type of settlement credit that may apply. These changes became effective July 1, 2003. See "Settlement Credits Under Proportionate Responsibility," ch. 7-H, §4, p. 513. For a detailed discussion of the changes to CPRC chapter 33, see ***O'Connor's Texas Causes of Action***, "Proportionate Responsibility & Contribution," ch. 42, p. 1115 (2004).

RULES CHANGES

In 2003, the Supreme Court amended and added to the Texas Rules of Civil Procedure, the Texas Rules of Evidence, the Texas Rules of Appellate Procedure, and the Texas Rules of Judicial Administration. The new rules are included in this edition. The amendments are also published in the Texas Bar Journal (66 Tex. B.J. 774 (2003), 66 Tex. B.J. 900 (2003)), and are available on the Supreme Court's website at www.supreme.courts.state.tx.us.

TRCPs

TRCP 42. Substantial amendments were made to TRCP 42, the class action rule. TRCP 42(a) was amended to eliminate the derivative suit paragraph as redundant of Business Corporation Act article 5.14. TRCP 42(c) was amended to change the deadline and notice requirements for class certification, and to add requirements for an order granting or denying class certification. TRCP 42(e) was amended to change the settlement and dismissal procedures in class actions. TRCP 42(g) was added to provide rules for appointing class counsel. TRCP 42(h)-(i) were added to determine attorney fees. These changes became effective January 1, 2004, except that TRCP 42(i) applies only in cases filed on or after September 1, 2003.

TRCP 166. TRCP 166 was amended to provide that pretrial proceedings in multidistrict litigation are to be governed by Texas Rule of Judicial Administration 13. This change became effective September 1, 2003. For a discussion of the new multidistrict litigation rule, see "Motion for Pretrial Consolidation," ch. 5-G, p. 259.

TRCP 167. TRCP 167 was enacted to establish a procedure for offering, accepting, and rejecting settlement offers for most monetary claims. This rule also has a fee-shifting provision, awarding litigation costs to a party whose settlement offer is rejected if a later judgment award is "significantly less favorable" than the settlement offer. TRCP 167 became effective January 1, 2004. See "Offer of Settlement," ch. 7-G, p. 505.

TRAPs

TRAP 24. TRAP 24 was amended to change the standard for determining the amount of an appeal bond, deposit, or security. TRAP 24.2(c) was added to require the judgment debtor to submit an affidavit of net worth. TRAP 24.2(d) was added to allow the trial court to enjoin a judgment debtor from moving assets to avoid satisfaction of the judgment in certain circumstances. These changes became effective September 1, 2003. See ***O'Connor's Texas Civil Appeals***, "Superseding the Judgment," ch. 14-B (forthcoming 2004).

TREs

TRE 407. TRE 407(a) was amended to exclude evidence of subsequent remedial measures to prove negligence, culpable conduct, a defect in a product or its design, or the need for a warning or instruction. Evidence of subsequent remedial measures is now precluded in products liability cases that are based on strict liability. This change became effective July 1, 2003.

TRJAs

TRJA 13. Texas Rule of Judicial Administration 13 was enacted to establish a new procedure for consolidating cases involving common questions of fact for pretrial purposes. The enactment of Gov't Code §74.161 establishes a multidistrict litigation panel responsible for hearing motions to consolidate. TRJA 13 became effective September 1, 2003. See "Motion for Pretrial Consolidation," ch. 5-G, p. 259.

COMMON-LAW DEVELOPMENTS

In 2003, the Supreme Court issued a number of important opinions in the area of procedure and evidence.

Pretrial Matters

In ***Baker v. Monsanto Co.***, 111 S.W.3d 158, 160 (Tex.2003), the Court held that an intervenor is not required to serve citation on a defendant who has made a general appearance in the case. See "Citation not necessary," ch. 5-I, §2.3.1, p. 270.

In ***Roberts v. Williamson***, 111 S.W.3d 113, 124 (Tex.2003), the Court held that the purpose of a guardian ad litem under TRCP 173 is to protect the interests of an incapacitated person in a lawsuit in which the incapacitated person is a party. The Court also held that a trial court cannot split the ad litem fees between the parties unless the court makes a finding of good cause. See "Fees for Guardian Ad Litem," ch. 1-I, §5, p. 54.

In ***Sixth RMA Partners v. Sibley***, 111 S.W.3d 46, 55 (Tex.2003), the Court held that a person or business entity doing business under an assumed name must file an assumed-name certificate. A motion to abate is the procedural mechanism to challenge the lack of a certificate. Before judgment is rendered, the person or entity's correct legal name must be substituted for its assumed name by motion of a party or the court, by an amended pleading, or, if no objection, by a supplemental pleading. *Id.* at 53-54. See "Assumed name," ch. 2-B, §3.3.4, p. 70.

In ***City of San Benito v. Rio Grande Valley Gas Co.***, 109 S.W.3d 750, 755 (Tex.2003), the Court restated the proposition that to claim virtual representation, an unnamed party must show the following: (1) it is bound by the judgment; (2) its privity of estate, title, or interest is apparent from the record; and (3) there is a common interest between the named and unnamed parties. See "Virtual party," ch. 2-B, §3.1.2, p. 68.

In ***West Orange-Cove Consol. ISD v. Alanis***, 107 S.W.3d 558, 583 (Tex.2003), the Court restated the proposition that standing, which is a component of subject-matter jurisdiction, cannot be waived and may be raised for the first time on appeal. See "Standing," ch. 2-B, §3.2.1, p. 68.

In ***Spohn Hosp. v. Mayer***, 104 S.W.3d 878, 882 (Tex.2003), the Court reiterated that sanctions must be "just." A sanction must bear a direct relationship to the offensive conduct, measured by a direct nexus among the conduct, the offender, and the sanction imposed. In addition, a just sanction must be directed against the abuse and toward remedying the prejudice caused to the innocent party. See "Standards for Imposing Sanctions," ch. 5-J, §3, p. 275.

In ***Gibson v. Tolbert***, 102 S.W.3d 710, 712 (Tex.2003), the Court held that although a litigant is not entitled to appointed counsel in a civil case, a court may appoint a lawyer to represent an indigent civil litigant, under exceptional circumstances, when public and private interests are at stake. See "Purpose," ch. 2-I, §1.2, p. 132.

In ***In re Crow-Billingsley Air Park***, 98 S.W.3d 178, 179 (Tex.2003), the Court held that the Declaratory Judgment Act empowers the trial court to make supplemental rulings to aid in the enforcement of a declaratory judgment. While on appeal, the trial court may hear a motion to enforce its final judgment if the judgment was not superseded. See "Motion to enforce judgment," ch. 2-D, §3.9, p. 95.

Expert Testimony

In ***Roberts v. Williamson***, 111 S.W.3d 113, 121-22 (Tex.2003), the Court held that a medical expert, who was not a neurologist, was qualified to testify about the cause and effect of a newborn child's neurological injuries. The expert was a certified pediatrician with extensive experience and knowledge of the effects of pediatric neurological injuries, and he consulted a pediatric neurologist and numerous texts when interpreting the child's test results. See "Qualifications test," ch. 5-M, §2.1, p. 304.

In ***Marathon Corp. v. Pitzner***, 106 S.W.3d 724, 729 (Tex.2003), the Court restated the proposition that expert opinions must be supported by facts in evidence, and not be mere conjecture or speculation. See "Foundation test," ch. 5-M, §2.4, p. 307.

Discovery

In ***In re Kuntz***, ___ S.W.3d ___ (Tex.2003) (No. 02-0375; 12-19-03), the Court held that mere access to documents is not "physical possession" of the documents under "possession, custody, or control" as set forth in TRCP 192.7. See "Possession," ch. 6-A, §2.3, p. 313.

In ***In re CSX Corp.***, ___ S.W.3d ___ (Tex.2003) (No. 03-0381; 10-3-03), the Court held that interrogatories asking the defendant to identify all safety employees over a 30-year period were impermissibly overbroad. The interrogatories were not reasonably limited as to time and subject matter. Discovery orders requiring document production for an unreasonably long time period or from distant and unrelated locales are impermissibly overbroad. See "Overbroad," ch. 6-A, §19.1.3, p. 335.

In ***In re Bridgestone/Firestone***, 106 S.W.3d 730, 732 (Tex.2003), the Court held that to obtain discovery of a trade secret, the plaintiff must establish the information is necessary or essential to the fair adjudication of the case, weighing need against potential harm. The tire manufacturer's trade secret in this case was privileged from discovery because the plaintiffs did not establish it was necessary or essential to their case nor would they be hampered in their proof by not knowing it. See "Trade-secret privilege," ch. 6-B, §3.14, p. 360.

Directed Verdict

In ***Tana Oil & Gas Corp. v. McCall***, 104 S.W.3d 80, 82 (Tex.2003), the Court held that the timing of a motion for directed verdict is immaterial when the substantive law does not allow recovery on the pleaded cause of action. If the trial court grants a motion for directed verdict before the plaintiff rests, on appeal the appellant must show it was harmed because it was not able to present its evidence. See "After plaintiff rests," ch. 8-G, §2.1, p. 561.

Jury Charge

In ***Wal-Mart Stores v. Johnson***, 106 S.W.3d 718, 723-24 (Tex.2003), the Court held that the trial court's spoliation instruction to the jury, based on the defendant's inability to produce material evidence, was an abuse of discretion. The Court reiterated that an unnecessary instruction is reversible error if it, although a correct statement of law, serves to tilt or nudge the jury. The more closely contested the case, the more likely the superfluous instruction is error. *Id.* at 724. See "Good objections," ch. 8-I, §6.5, p. 573.

Judgments

In ***Naaman v. Grider***, ___ S.W.3d ___ (Tex.2003) (No. 02-0784; 10-31-03), the Court held an order that merely grants a motion for judgment is in no sense a judgment itself and adjudicates nothing. The only judgment in this case was the final judgment, which was signed one month before the trial court granted the motion for judgment. Therefore, the appellate deadlines began when the final judgment was signed. See "Order granting motion for judgment," ch. 9-C, §3.1.2(4), p. 597; "Final Judgment," ch. 9-C, §6, p. 602.

In ***Moritz v. Preiss***, ___ S.W.3d ___ (Tex.2003) (No. 01-1270; 6-12-03), the Court held that a judgment that did not name one of the defendants was final because the judgment was rendered after a full trial on the merits, the plaintiff did not request a separate trial for the unnamed defendant, and the plaintiff did not submit a jury question on that defendant's liability. There was nothing to indicate the trial court did not intend to finally dispose of the entire case. See "Judgments that are final," ch. 9-C, §6.3.1, p. 603.

In ***Sixth RMA Partners v. Sibley***, 111 S.W.3d 46, 54-55 (Tex.2003), the Court restated the proposition that, because the summary judgment procedure does not provide an opportunity to replead, it should not be used to terminate a suit based on pleading defects. See "Challenge the use of SJ," ch. 7-B, §6.6.1, p. 467.

Post-Trial Matters

In ***Moritz v. Preiss***, ___ S.W.3d ___ (Tex.2003) (No. 01-1270; 6-12-03), the Court restated the proposition that the last day a party may file an amended or supplemental motion for new trial is 30 days from the date the judgment was signed. Because TRCP 5 prohibits the trial court from enlarging the time to file a motion for new trial, the trial court cannot grant a party permission to file an amended or supplemental motion for new trial after the 30 days expire. The trial court may grant a new trial on the grounds stated in a late motion if it is filed before the court loses plenary power. But, an order denying an untimely motion for new trial does not preserve issues for appellate review, even if the trial court acts within its plenary power period. See "Deadlines for MNT," ch. 10-B, §5, p. 619; "Order denying new trial," ch. 10-B, §17.4, p. 636.

In ***In re M.S.***, 115 S.W.3d 534, 538 (Tex.2003), the Court held that even though a judge's findings of fact are not the same as testimony, the submission into evidence of findings of fact based on pretrial evidence could be a form of impermissible judicial influence. A trial court errs in admitting into evidence orders that contain fact-findings. See "Request for Findings of Fact," ch. 10-E, p. 641.

Miscellaneous

In ***In re B.L.D.***, 113 S.W.3d 340, 346 (Tex.2003), the Court held that in deciding whether there is a conflict of interest between parents opposing termination of their parental rights in the same lawsuit, the trial court must determine whether there is a substantial risk the appointed counsel's obligation to one parent would materially and adversely affect her obligations to the other parent. See "Violation of disciplinary rules," ch. 1-H, §8.2.1, p. 42.

In ***Roberts v. Williamson***, 111 S.W.3d 113, 119 (Tex.2003), the Court held that parents cannot recover for loss of consortium in nonfatal injury cases. Children can recover for loss of consortium when a parent suffers nonfatal injuries because the child is the party to the parent-child relationship who needs special protection. *Id.* at 117. Because the parent has a less dependent role than the child does in the relationship, extending consortium rights to include parents could lead to recognition of that right in other nondependent relatives, such as siblings. *Id.* at 119. See ***O'Connor's Texas Causes of Action***, "Loss of Consortium," ch. 35-B, §8, p. 962 (2004).

2004 PROPOSED RULES

TRCP 8a. In 2003, the Supreme Court approved TRCP 8a, addressing referral fees. The rule was initially scheduled to become effective on January 1, 2004. After considering extensive comments, including a letter from the State Bar's Executive Committee requesting postponement of the effective date to allow time for further study, the Court decided to suspend the effective date of TRCP 8a to allow the State Bar to appoint a special task force on referral fees and related advertising issues. See Tex.Sup.Ct. Order, Misc. Docket No. 03-9207 (12-23-03).

The State Bar's task force will conduct public hearings throughout the state and collect information through surveys and other means. The Court will identify the primary concerns raised by lawyers during the comment period as well as any other issues the Court believes should be addressed in the Bar's consideration of referral fees. The task force will report to the State Bar Board of Directors, which will then forward to the Court any recommendations with the request that the Court authorize the Bar to hold a referendum during the fall of 2004.

TRE 509. The Supreme Court Advisory Committee is discussing amendments to TRE 509, in light of the growing dispute of whether a lawyer can contact the other party's treating doctor ex parte, without notifying the patient's lawyer. See "Discovery from treating doctors," ch. 6-C, §3.1.2(3), p. 366.

CONVENTIONS

In writing this book, we have tried to produce a plain-English reference guide for lawyers and judges that is easy to use. To this end, the reader should be aware of a few things about this book that are helpful. First, the commentaries are in single columns and the rules are in double columns so that they may be instantly distinguished. Second, there are page headers and side-tabs for quick reference. Third, when other sections of this and other books are germane, we make cross-reference to them. Fourth, we have included practice tips and caution notes that are separate from the main text so that they may be easily spotted. Fifth, all legislative and rule changes are marked with 03 or 04, depending on the effective date of the legislative or rule change. Sixth, in a history note under each rule, we include references to earlier versions of the rules that are located in the first pages of the particular volume of S.W.2d (Texas Cases). Seventh, we have eliminated the criminal appellate rules and the history notes to the TRAPs to save space. See ***O'Connor's Texas Civil Appeals*** for a complete set of the appellate rules. Finally, we include timetables for certain pretrial, trial, and post-trial procedures.

Throughout this book, we will refer to forms in the companion volume, ***O'Connor's Texas Civil Forms*** (2002) as ***O'Connor's*** FORMS. The forms are numbered to match the chapter numbers in the commentaries where that topic is discussed. The next edition of ***O'Connor's Texas Civil Forms*** will be available in the spring of 2004.

To reduce gender choices, we refer to trial judges as the "trial court" and to parties as "it," as though all parties were corporations, which they often are. When necessary to use a gender (*e.g.*, when referring to a lawyer), we use the feminine. To shorten the book, we abbreviate the name of the Texas Rules of Civil Procedure to TRCP, the Texas Rules of Evidence to TRE, the Texas Rules of Appellate Procedure to TRAP, the Civil Practice & Remedies Code to CPRC, and the Texas Revised Civil Statutes to TRCS. When you use citations to rules and codes in a motion or brief, we suggest you use the more traditional citation forms. For more traditional rules for citations, see either ***O'Connor's Texas Civil Appeals***, "Simplified Citation Forms," p. 851 (2002-03), or the *Greenbook*, published by the Texas Law Review.

ABOUT THE 2004 EDITOR

For the last few years, I have been assisted in the updating of this book by Professor Byron P. Davis. Professor Byron Davis teaches at South Texas College of Law in Houston, Texas, specializing in Texas civil pretrial, trial, and appellate procedure. A summa cum laude graduate of South Texas College of Law, Professor Davis served as a briefing attorney for the First Court of Appeals and as an assistant district attorney in Harris County. He is a former examiner for the Texas Board of Legal Specialization in Civil Law and has taught a Texas Bar review course on civil procedure since 1985.

YOUR SUGGESTIONS

We appreciate your comments regarding additions, deletions, and corrections. If you have any ideas, just photocopy the page in the book, make a note in the margin, attach your card so we can contact you, and send it to the address on the copyright page. You may also fax information to the number on the copyright page or send it by e-mail to Douglas Rosenzweig, Director, Editorial Group, at doug@JonesMcClure.com.

CAVEAT

This book will provide you with citations to important opinions that interpret the Texas Rules of Civil Procedure and Texas Rules of Evidence through January 23, 2004. You may disagree with the explanations of the rules and the cases in this book. You should, therefore, use this book only as a research guide. Read the rules and the cases and make your own evaluation of them.

RESEARCH & VERIFICATION

The staff at Jones McClure Publishing devotes hundreds of hours each year in preparing this book and works especially hard in ensuring the accuracy of this publication both for substantive citation to the law and for precision of the layout and page design. The following persons worked on this 2004 update to ***O'Connor's Texas Rules * Civil Trials***:

MANAGING LEGAL EDITOR
Douglas Rosenzweig, J.D.

ASSISTANT LEGAL EDITORS
Sarah Berges, J.D.
Michael S. Ewing, J.D.
Douglas A. Haldane, J.D., LL.M.
Jeffrey C. Hunter, J.D.
Jemia L. Midget, J.D.

LEGAL INTERNS
Kathryn A. Ritcheske
Ellic Sahualla
Christopher Sullivan

PRODUCTION MANAGER
Donna E. Vass

LAYOUT EDITORS
Jack Arthur
Vivian W. Chum
Marisa Ramos
Amanda Schlatre
Katharine Southard
Victoria Thomas

COPYEDITORS
Jeffrey A. Brown
Lucky K. Sahualla
David W. Schultz, J.D.

MICHOL O'CONNOR
HOUSTON, TEXAS

Master Table of Contents

Commentaries

TRCP

TRE

TRAP

Timetables & Index

Contents
Commentaries

Contents
Rules & Timetables

TEXAS RULES OF CIVIL PROCEDURE

TEXAS RULES OF EVIDENCE

TEXAS RULES OF APPELLATE PROCEDURE

TIMETABLES

§1.3 Forms. ***O'Connor's Texas Civil Forms***, FORMS 1B.

§1.4 Other references. ***O'Connor's Texas Causes of Action*** (2004) (***O'Connor's COA***); Cochran, ***Texas Rules of Evidence Handbook*** (5th ed. 2003) (Cochran, ***Evidence Handbook***).

§2. TYPES OF PLEADINGS

It is important to distinguish the different types of pleadings and understand their functions.

§2.1 Pleading. The Texas system of pleadings is composed of petitions and answers. ***Elliott v. Elliott***, 797 S.W.2d 388, 391-92 (Tex.App.—Austin 1990, no writ). The pleadings define the suit, give notice of the facts and legal theories of the case, guide the trial court in admitting evidence and in charging the jury, restrict the trial court in rendering the judgment, and form the basis for appellate review. *See* ***Erisman v. Thompson***, 167 S.W.2d 731, 733 (Tex.1943) (pleadings define lawsuit and determine issues for trial); ***Crain v. San Jacinto Sav. Ass'n***, 781 S.W.2d 638, 639 (Tex.App.—Houston [14th Dist.] 1989, writ dism'd) (pleadings give notice of evidence to be introduced). The controversy described in the pleadings is resolved by a judgment. ***Lindley v. Flores***, 672 S.W.2d 612, 614 (Tex.App.—Corpus Christi 1984, no writ).

§2.2 Motion. A motion is a request for an order from the court. ***Elliott***, 797 S.W.2d at 392; ***Lindley***, 672 S.W.2d at 614. As such, motions are a type of pleading. ***Lindley***, 672 S.W.2d at 614. Most motions are resolved by an order. When a motion requesting a judgment (*e.g.*, a motion for summary judgment) is granted, the motion is resolved by a judgment; when it is denied, it is resolved by an order. See ***O'Connor's*** FORM 1B:01 for the general format of a motion.

§2.3 Plea. A plea is an archaic term referring to certain defensive pleadings. In most instances, the TRCPs replaced pleas with motions. Nevertheless, some of the rules continue to refer to pleas. For example, TRCP 85 lists the pleas that may be included in the defendant's answer. In this book, most pleas are cast as motions (*e.g.*, a motion to abate instead of a plea in abatement).

§2.4 Bill. A bill is a formal, written declaration, complaint, or statement of particular things (*e.g.*, a bill of review or a bill of exception).

§3. LOCAL REQUIREMENTS

In drafting and filing pleadings, the parties must comply with the requirements of local rules. Some local rules have specific requirements for the form and organization of the pleadings. For example, under Dallas County Civil Court Local Rule 2.04, pleadings must be pre-punched at the top to accommodate the clerk's 2¾-inch center-to-center, flat-filing system; the pleading must include a footer at the bottom of each page with the caption and the page number of the document; and motions and orders must be separate documents.

§4. FORMAL REQUIREMENTS

§4.1 In writing. All pleadings, motions, and other applications to the court must be in writing and filed with the clerk, unless made in open court and transcribed by the court reporter. *See* ***Pennington v. Gurkoff***, 899 S.W.2d 767, 771 (Tex.App.—Fort Worth 1995, writ denied). Written pleadings and motions must be on 8½-by-11 paper. TRCP 45(d). TRCP 45(d) "strongly" encourages lawyers to use recycled paper.

§4.2 Style. The style is the heading of the pleading. It contains the cause number, the names of the parties, the court, and the county of suit. Form books, and even courts, sometimes confuse the style with the caption. *See, e.g.*, ***Stewart v. USA Custom Paint & Body Shop***, 870 S.W.2d 18, 20 (Tex.1994) (document was described as "captionless" when it clearly had a caption—"Order of Dismissal"—but was missing a style—the cause number and the names of the parties). See ***O'Connor's*** FORM 1B:02.

1. Cause number. The cause number is assigned by the clerk. TRCP 23. The parties should make sure all pleadings and documents are filed with the correct cause number. Generally, filing a document with the wrong cause number should not be considered a jurisdictional defect. *See, e.g.*, ***Blankenship v. Robins***, 878 S.W.2d 138, 138-39 (Tex.1994) (motion for new trial with wrong cause number was effective because it was a "bona fide

A. INTRODUCTION TO THE TEXAS RULES

In 1939, the Texas Legislature gave the Supreme Court rule-making power in civil actions. The Legislature placed two limits on the Court's authority over the rules: (1) the Court cannot enact rules that "abridge, enlarge, or modify the substantive rights of a litigant"; and (2) the Legislature retains the power to disapprove of the Court's rules. Gov't Code §22.004(a), (b). The Court is required to file a copy of all rule changes with the Secretary of State and identify which statutes the rules repeal or modify. *Id.* §22.004(b), (c). The Secretary of State is required to report the rule changes to the Legislature by December 1, immediately before the next regular session. *Id.* §22.004(b).

§1. TEXAS RULES OF CIVIL PROCEDURE (TRCP)

In 1941, the Supreme Court adopted the Texas Rules of Civil Procedure. *See* Gov't Code §22.004; TRCP 2, 814. The rules of civil procedure have the same force and effect as statutes. ***Missouri Pac. R.R. v. Cross***, 501 S.W.2d 868, 872 (Tex.1973). When a rule of procedure conflicts with a statute, the statute prevails. ***Few v. Charter Oak Fire Ins. Co.***, 463 S.W.2d 424, 425 (Tex.1971).

§2. TEXAS RULES OF EVIDENCE (TRE)

In 1983, the Supreme Court adopted the Texas Rules of Evidence for civil cases. In 1986, it renamed them the "Texas Rules of Civil Evidence." See Cochran, ***Texas Rules of Evidence Handbook***, p. 27-31 (5th ed. 2003). In 1998, the Supreme Court and the Court of Criminal Appeals merged the civil and criminal rules and renamed them the "Texas Rules of Evidence." The TREs govern civil and criminal proceedings in all Texas courts except small-claims courts.

§3. TEXAS RULES OF APPELLATE PROCEDURE (TRAP)

In 1986, the Supreme Court and the Court of Criminal Appeals adopted the Texas Rules of Appellate Procedure. As part of that process, the appellate rules contained in the TRCPs were repealed. In 1997, the Supreme Court and the Court of Criminal Appeals adopted a new set of TRAPs.

§4. LOCAL RULES

TRCP 3a permits the trial courts to establish local rules consistent with the TRCPs. Local rules cannot impose restrictions on or conflict with the TRCPs. ***Jamar v. Patterson***, 868 S.W.2d 318, 318 n.2 (Tex.1993); ***Remington Arms Co. v. Caldwell***, 850 S.W.2d 167, 178 (Tex.1993).

§4.1 Notice of local rules. Litigants are charged with knowledge of local rules. ***Mayad v. Rizk***, 554 S.W.2d 835, 839 (Tex.App.—Houston [14th Dist.] 1977, writ ref'd n.r.e.). *But see* ***Kenley v. Quintana Pet. Corp.***, 931 S.W.2d 318, 321 (Tex.App.—San Antonio 1996, writ denied) (notice through imputed knowledge of local rules contradicts TRCP 165a). TRCP 3a requires the trial courts to file copies of their local rules with the Supreme Court for approval and to publish them 30 days before they become effective. TRCP 3a(3), (4).

§4.2 Effect of local rules. Litigants should pay particular attention to local rules. Some local rules automatically set a pretrial hearing on a certain date. Some local rules automatically place on the dismissal docket a case of a certain age not set for trial or hearing. ***State v. Rotello***, 671 S.W.2d 507, 508 (Tex.1984). Some local rules provide for dismissal within a specified period of time. ***Bilnoski v. Pizza Inn***, 858 S.W.2d 55, 57 (Tex.App.—Houston [14th Dist.] 1993, no writ). Some local rules provide that the failure to file a response to a motion indicates an acquiescence to the relief sought in the motion. *See* Harris Cty. Loc. R. 3.3.2 (district courts), 3.3.3 (county courts at law); ***Cummings v. Cire***, 74 S.W.3d 920, 924 (Tex.App.—Amarillo 2002, pet. granted 4-17-03).

B. RULES OF PLEADING

§1. GENERAL

§1.1 Rules. TRCP 21, 21b, 22-24, 45-71, 74-98, 166(b).

§1.2 Purpose. The purpose of the pleadings is to define the issues for trial. ***Murray v. O&A Express***, 630 S.W.2d 633, 636 (Tex.1982).

COMMENTARIES

CHAPTER 1. GENERAL

TABLE OF CONTENTS

COMMENTARIES

CHAPTER 1. GENERAL

TABLE OF CONTENTS

attempt" to invoke appellate jurisdiction); ***McRoberts v. Ryals***, 863 S.W.2d 450, 454-55 (Tex.1993) (motion for new trial with wrong cause number was effective); ***City of San Antonio v. Rodriguez***, 828 S.W.2d 417, 418 (Tex.1992) (appeal bond with wrong cause number was effective); ***Mueller v. Saravia***, 826 S.W.2d 608, 609 (Tex.1992) (motion for new trial with wrong cause number was effective); ***Curtis v. Gibbs***, 511 S.W.2d 263, 268 (Tex.1974) (mistake in cause number was "irrelevant"). *But see* ***Philbrook v. Berry***, 683 S.W.2d 378, 379 (Tex.1985) (motion for new trial ineffective because of wrong cause number). The ***Philbrook*** holding on this issue has been distinguished, explained, and questioned into irrelevance.

2. List of parties. In the style of the petition and the answer, all the parties should be listed by their full names. In other pleadings (motions, responses, bills), the list of parties in the style may be shortened by naming the first party and using the inclusive term "et al." *See* ***Abramcik v. U.S. Home Corp.***, 792 S.W.2d 822, 824 (Tex.App.—Houston [14th Dist.] 1990, writ denied).

§4.3 Caption. The caption is the title of the pleading (*e.g.*, "Motion to Extend Time").

1. Correct title. The parties should title their pleadings in a manner useful to the court, the clerk, and the lawyers' own files. The title should always identify the party who filed the pleading and the type of pleading (*e.g.*, "Defendant's Motion to Extend Time to ..."). If there are multiple parties, the title should use an abbreviated name for the party (*e.g.*, "The Bank's Motion to ..."). If a motion is an agreed motion, the title should include the word "agreed" (*e.g.*, "The Bank's Agreed Motion to ..."). If the motion has been made before, the title should so indicate (*e.g.*, "The Bank's Second Motion to ...").

2. Incorrect title. If the party makes an error in the caption of the pleading, the court will treat the pleading as if it had been properly named. TRCP 71; *see* ***Speer v. Stover***, 685 S.W.2d 22, 23 (Tex.1985). A misnomer of the pleading does not render it ineffective. ***G.M. Acceptance Corp. v. Harris Cty. MUD***, 899 S.W.2d 821, 824 n.3 (Tex.App.—Houston [14th Dist.] 1995, no writ). The court will look to the substance of the pleading to determine its nature. ***University of Houston v. Elthon***, 9 S.W.3d 351, 355 (Tex.App.—Houston [14th Dist.] 1999, pet. dism'd); *see, e.g.*, ***Speer***, 685 S.W.2d at 23 (plea in abatement was actually plea to the jurisdiction); ***State Bar v. Heard***, 603 S.W.2d 829, 833 (Tex.1980) (motion for summary judgment was actually motion to suspend law license under special statute); ***In re Bokeloh***, 21 S.W.3d 784, 790 (Tex.App.—Houston [14th Dist.] 2000, orig. proceeding) (motion to retain was not equivalent of motion to reinstate because it did not address reinstatement). The clerk will file a pleading using the caption the party gives it, but the trial court may order the document redesignated. TRCP 71.

§4.4 Parties' names. Generally, the full names of all parties should be included in the body (not just the style) of all petitions (amended and supplemental), in any other pleadings that must be served by citation, and in any motion that may resolve the lawsuit (*e.g.*, a motion for summary judgment). These pleadings should not rely on "et al." to refer to the parties. *See* TRCP 79. Normally, the omission in an amended petition of a party's name and the claims asserted against that party indicates an intent to nonsuit that party. ***American Petrofina v. Allen***, 887 S.W.2d 829, 831 (Tex.1994); ***Woodruff v. Wright***, 51 S.W.3d 727, 731 (Tex.App.—Texarkana 2001, pet. denied). If the party was omitted from an amended pleading but renamed in a later pleading, the later pleading renaming the omitted party will relate back to the earlier pleading as long as the omission was temporary, inadvertent, and not prejudicial to the other parties. ***American Petrofina***, 887 S.W.2d at 831; ***Woodruff***, 51 S.W.3d at 733.

§4.5 Parties' residences. Any pleading that must be served by citation must identify the residence of the party to be served, if known. TRCP 79; *see* ***Graham v. Huff***, 384 S.W.2d 904, 905 (Tex.App.—Dallas 1964, no writ) (petition did not include Ds' addresses or state they were unknown). The parties' residences are important for purposes of service, personal jurisdiction, venue, and forum non conveniens. *See* ***Kelly v. Demoss Owners Ass'n***, 71 S.W.3d 419, 424 (Tex. App.—San Antonio 2002, no pet.).

§4.6 Contents. The pleadings must give fair notice of the claims, defenses, and relief sought. TRCP 45(b), 47(a); ***Perez v. Briercroft Serv. Corp.***, 809 S.W.2d 216, 218 (Tex.1991); *see* TRCP 21 (pleadings must state grounds & relief sought). See "Fair notice of claim," ch. 2-B, §6.2, p. 74.

§4.7 Numbered paragraphs. The paragraphs in pleadings and motions must be numbered; each paragraph should be limited to a single set of circumstances. TRCP 50. Arabic numerals (1, 2, 3, etc.) should be used, and Roman numerals (I, II, III, etc.) avoided.

§4.8 Separate counts or defenses. The pleading should divide the allegations into counts or defenses. TRCP 50; *see also* TRCP 47 (listing statements must be included in original pleading). Headings and subheadings are useful in separating the sections of the pleading.

§4.9 Alternative claims or defenses. TRCP 48 permits parties to plead alternative or hypothetical theories, allege inconsistent claims or defenses, and allege claims or defenses based on legal or equitable grounds or both. TRCP 48; *see* TRCP 47 (last paragraph); ***Regency Advantage v. Bingo Idea-Watauga, Inc.***, 936 S.W.2d 275, 278 (Tex.1996); ***Zimmerman v. First Am. Title Ins. Co.***, 790 S.W.2d 690, 698 (Tex.App.—Tyler 1990, writ denied) (party may plead and prove inconsistent claims). Generally, if a pleading states inconsistent, contradictory facts that are material to the cause of action without alleging that those facts are part of an alternative theory, the pleading states no cause of action. ***Vinklarek v. Vinklarek***, 596 S.W.2d 197, 199 (Tex.App.—Houston [1st Dist.] 1980, writ dism'd).

§4.10 Adopting by reference. TRCP 58 permits a party to adopt statements by reference from another pleading if that pleading has not been superseded by an amended pleading. ***Chapman v. King Ranch***, 41 S.W.3d 693, 700 (Tex.App.—Corpus Christi 2001), *rev'd on other grounds*, 118 S.W.3d 742 (Tex.2003); *see* ***Texas Gas Utils. Co. v. Barrett***, 460 S.W.2d 409, 416 (Tex.1970). TRCP 59 permits a party to attach and adopt exhibits by reference or to copy them into the body of the pleading. Although a party should not adopt by reference from a superseded pleading, if it does, the adopted material is not void and must be challenged by a special exception. ***Hawkins v. Anderson***, 672 S.W.2d 293, 295 (Tex.App.—Dallas 1984, no writ).

§4.11 Prayer. At the end of the pleading, under "prayer," the party should state exactly what relief it wants. The prayer for relief should match the purpose of the pleading. *See, e.g.*, ***Finley v. J.C. Pace Ltd.***, 4 S.W.3d 319, 320 (Tex.App.—Houston [1st Dist.] 1999, order on mot.) (motion for rehearing was actually motion for new trial because relief requested was relitigation of issues); ***Mercer v. Band***, 454 S.W.2d 833, 835-36 (Tex.App.—Houston [14th Dist.] 1970, no writ) (motion for new trial was actually motion for judgment because prayer asked for different judgment, not new trial).

§4.12 Signature block.

1. Who must sign. The pleading must be signed by the lawyer or by the party if not represented by a lawyer. TRCP 45(d), 57. Lack of a signature does not alter the legal effect of the pleading. ***Frank v. Corbett***, 682 S.W.2d 587, 588 (Tex.App.—Waco 1984, no writ).

(1) Lawyer in charge. When signed by a lawyer, the pleading must identify the lawyer by name, State Bar number, address, telephone number, and fax number (if any). TRCP 57; *see* TRCP 191.3(a)(1). The signature fixes responsibility for the allegations and identifies the party the lawyer represents. CPRC §§9.011, 10.001; TRCP 13; ***Ingram v. Card Co.***, 540 S.W.2d 803, 804 (Tex.App.—Corpus Christi 1976, no writ). The lawyer whose signature first appears on the initial pleading for any party is the "attorney in charge," unless another attorney is specifically designated. TRCP 8. See "Attorney in charge," ch. 1-H, §3.1, p. 39. There is no requirement that the attorney in charge must sign and file all pleadings. *See* ***Sunbeam Envtl. Servs. v. Texas Workers' Comp. Ins. Facility***, 71 S.W.3d 846, 851 (Tex.App.—Austin 2002, no pet.).

(2) Party. A party may sign a pleading. *E.g.*, ***Brown v. Mulanax***, 808 S.W.2d 718, 720 (Tex.App.—Tyler 1991, orig. proceeding) (motion to recuse signed by party, instead of lawyer, was valid). A pro se's signature block must include its address, telephone number, and fax number (if any). TRCP 57; *see* TRCP 191.3(a)(2); ***Kelly v. Demoss Owners Ass'n***, 71 S.W.3d 419, 424 (Tex.App.—Amarillo 2002, no pet.).

2. Certification by signature. Signing a pleading or motion is a representation by the signatory that the pleading is not frivolous or groundless. The court can impose sanctions on an attorney who signs a frivolous or groundless pleading or on the party represented by the attorney. See "Groundless or Frivolous Pleadings," §5, p. 10; "Pleadings abuse," ch. 5-J, §5.2, p. 278.

(1) Under CPRC ch. 10. Under CPRC §10.001, signing a pleading or motion constitutes a certificate of the following:

(a) The matters in the pleading are not presented for an improper purpose, including to harass or to cause unnecessary delay or needless increase in the cost of litigation. CPRC §10.001(1). A pleading is "presented" to a court when the person signs it, files it, submits it, or later advocates it. *Cf.* FRCP 11(b) (representations to federal court).

(b) Each claim, defense, or other legal contention is warranted by existing law or by a nonfrivolous argument for the extension, modification, or reversal of existing law or the establishment of new law. CPRC §10.001(2). The filing of a general denial does not violate §10.001(2). *Id.* §10.004(f).

(c) Each allegation or factual contention has evidentiary support or, for a specifically identified allegation or factual contention, is likely to have evidentiary support after a reasonable opportunity for further investigation or discovery. CPRC §10.001(3).

(d) Each denial of a factual contention is warranted by the evidence or, for a specifically identified denial, is reasonably based on a lack of information or belief. CPRC §10.001(4).

(2) Under TRCP 13. Under TRCP 13, signing a pleading or motion constitutes a certificate that (1) the signatory has read the document and (2) to the signatory's best knowledge, information, and belief, formed after reasonable inquiry, the document is not groundless and was not brought in bad faith or for the purpose of harassment. TRCP 13.

(3) Under CPRC ch. 9. Under CPRC §9.011, signing a pleading constitutes a certificate that to the signatory's best knowledge, information, and belief, formed after reasonable inquiry, the pleading (1) is not groundless, (2) was not brought in bad faith or for the purpose of harassment, and (3) was not brought for any improper purpose, such as to cause unnecessary delay or expense. CPRC §9.011. CPRC chapter 9 does not alter the TRCPs. CPRC §9.003.

(4) Under TRCP 191.3. The discovery rules impose obligations on the signatory to discovery. See "Certification by signature," ch. 6-A, §3.1, p. 314.

§4.13 Exhibits. A pleading must identify and incorporate by reference the exhibits attached to it and those filed separately. TRCP 59. If a pleading does not incorporate the exhibits by reference, the exhibits do not add anything to the pleading. ***Street v. Cunningham***, 156 S.W.2d 541, 542 (Tex.App.—Fort Worth 1941, no writ). TRCP 59 lists the following exhibits that may be attached to a pleading, filed separately, or copied into the body of a pleading: notes, accounts, bonds, mortgages, records, and all other written instruments, in whole or in part, constituting the claim or defense. No other document may be attached as an exhibit to a pleading. TRCP 59; *see, e.g.*, ***Texas Elec. Serv. Co. v. Commercial Stand. Ins. Co.***, 592 S.W.2d 677, 684 (Tex.App.—Fort Worth 1979, writ ref'd n.r.e.) (improper to attach deposition as exhibit to pleading).

§4.14 Verification & affidavits. When a motion or a response contains facts outside the record of the case, the party may be required to verify the facts by sworn proof. Depending on the type of pleading, sworn proof can be made by a verification of the pleading or by an affidavit attached as an exhibit. See chart 1-2, "Summary Chart for Motions," ch. 1-F, p. 32.

1. Verification. A verification is a signed and notarized statement attached to a pleading by which a witness swears that the statements in the pleading are true and correct. See ***O'Connor's*** FORM 1B:05.

2. Affidavits. An affidavit is a written, factual statement signed by the person making it, sworn to before an officer authorized to administer oaths, and officially certified by the officer under seal of office. Gov't

Code §312.011(1); ***Ford Motor Co. v. Leggat***, 904 S.W.2d 643, 645-46 (Tex.1995); ***Exito Elecs. Co. v. Trejo***, 99 S.W.3d 360, 371-72 (Tex.App.—Corpus Christi 2003, pet. filed 5-7-03). See ***O'Connor's*** FORM 1B:07.

(1) Form of affidavit. Typically, the affidavit includes a caption ("Affidavit of ______"), the venue (county and state), the body of the instrument, the signature of the affiant, and a jurat. ***Acme Brick v. Temple Assocs.***, 816 S.W.2d 440, 441 (Tex.App.—Waco 1991, writ denied). The jurat is the certificate under seal by a competent officer (generally, a notary public) who administers the oath to the affiant; it identifies the officer, the affiant, and the date the affidavit was made. *Black's Law Dictionary* 854 (7th ed.1999); *see* Gov't Code §312.011(1) (definition of affidavit); ***Exito Elecs.***, 99 S.W.3d at 372 (document with jurat did not identify notary, state where affidavit was signed, or contain official seal was not affidavit). The jurat certifies that the writing was sworn to by the person who signed it. ***Huckin v. Connor***, 928 S.W.2d 180, 183 (Tex.App.—Houston [14th Dist.] 1996, writ denied); ***Acme Brick***, 816 S.W.2d at 441; *see* CPRC §121.005. If the instrument does not include a jurat, the statement is not sworn, and the instrument is not an affidavit. ***Coastal Cement Sand v. First Interstate Credit Alliance***, 956 S.W.2d 562, 567 (Tex.App.—Houston [14th Dist.] 1997, pet. denied); *see* ***Guinn v. Bosque Cty.***, 58 S.W.3d 194, 198 (Tex.App.—Waco 2001, pet. denied); *see also* ***Wilie v. Signature Geophysical Servs.***, 65 S.W.3d 355, 361-62 (Tex.App.—Houston [14th Dist.] 2001, pet. denied) (affidavit without notary seal is not competent evidence). In most cases, it is not necessary to authenticate a copy of the affidavit unless a question is raised about the authenticity of the original or unless the circumstances make it unfair to permit a copy instead of the original. TRE 1003; *see* ***Ford Motor***, 904 S.W.2d at 646.

(2) Competency of witness. An affidavit must show that it is made by a person who is competent to testify. *See* TRE 601. To be competent to testify, the affiant must be able to accurately perceive, recall, and recount. Cochran, ***Evidence Handbook***, p. 554. Competency is a TRE 601 issue and is resolved under TRE 104(a) without regard to the rules of evidence. Cochran, ***Evidence Handbook***, p. 553. Competency deals with the ability of the person to be a witness; for example, is the witness too young, too old, or too mentally unstable to testify? Competency does not deal with the sufficiency of the specific testimony, which is a TRE 602 issue of personal knowledge. *See id.* at 554. Unfortunately, the courts often treat the witness's competency and personal knowledge as the same. *See, e.g.*, ***Laidlaw Waste Sys. v. City of Wilmer***, 904 S.W.2d 656, 661 (Tex.1995) (sworn statement did not show witness had personal knowledge and was competent to testify about metes & bounds).

(3) Factual statements.

(a) Personal knowledge. An affidavit must be based on the affiant's personal knowledge and must state that the facts in it are true. ***Humphreys v. Caldwell***, 888 S.W.2d 469, 470 (Tex.1994); *see* TRE 602 (evidence must show witness has personal knowledge); *see, e.g.*, ***Radio Station KSCS v. Jennings***, 750 S.W.2d 760, 761-62 (Tex.1988) (affidavit did not show how witness became familiar with facts about operation of radio station). Personal knowledge, a TRE 602 issue, is whether the witness knows enough about the subject to testify, and is evaluated under TRE 104(b). Cochran, ***Evidence Handbook***, p. 565. Any qualifying statement about the affiant's personal knowledge renders the affidavit legally invalid. *See, e.g.*, ***Ryland Group v. Hood***, 924 S.W.2d 120, 122 (Tex. 1996) (affiant's statement about his "understanding" was conclusory & would not support SJ); ***Humphreys***, 888 S.W.2d at 470 (affiant's statement that information was based on personal knowledge acquired from inquiry rendered affidavit invalid); ***Geiselman v. Cramer Fin. Group***, 965 S.W.2d 532, 537 (Tex.App.—Houston [14th Dist.] 1997, no writ) (affiant's statement "to the best of my knowledge" would not support SJ). The affidavit must contain direct and unequivocal statements that, if false, would be grounds for perjury. ***Hall v. Stephenson***, 919 S.W.2d 454, 466 (Tex.App.—Fort Worth 1996, writ denied); *cf.* ***Burke v. Satterfield***, 525 S.W.2d 950, 955 (Tex.1975) (affidavit of executrix's attorney in probate proceeding). For summary judgment affidavits, see "Personal knowledge," ch. 7-B, §3.4.4, p. 459.

(b) Knowledge & belief. By statute or rule, some affidavits may be made on "knowledge and belief." *See* TRCP 18a(a) (motion to recuse), TRCP 93(8), (13) & (15) (some verified denials). An affidavit cannot be based on "knowledge and belief" unless it is authorized by a special statute or rule. ***Burke v. Satterfield***, 525 S.W.2d 950, 954-55 (Tex.1975); ***Slater v. Metro Nissan***, 801 S.W.2d 253, 254 (Tex.App.—Fort Worth 1990, writ denied). *But see* ***Noriega v. Mireles***, 925 S.W.2d 261, 263-64 (Tex.App.—Corpus Christi 1996, writ denied) (expert's affidavit made on his "best knowledge and belief" was not fatally defective because TRE 702 and 703 contemplate that experts bring more to court than their personal knowledge of the facts).

(4) Executed by party or agent. TRCP 14 provides that whenever an affidavit is required, it may be made either by the party or by the party's agent or lawyer. However, before assuming an affidavit may be made by someone else, the party should check the statutes and rules. *See* TRCP 197.2(d) & cmt. 2 (certain interrogatories must be signed by party under oath).

(5) Exhibits. If there are exhibits attached to the affidavit, the affidavit must show they are authentic and admissible.

(a) Authentic. To authenticate the exhibit, the affidavit should state that the attached exhibit is a true and correct copy of the original or that it is self-proving. *See* ***Kleven v. TDCJ***, 69 S.W.3d 341, 345 (Tex. App.—Texarkana 2002, no pet.). An exhibit attached to an affidavit is not competent summary judgment evidence unless the affidavit proves the exhibit is true or the exhibit is self-proving. *See* ***Llopa, Inc. v. Nagel***, 956 S.W.2d 82, 87 (Tex.App.—San Antonio 1997, pet. denied) (documents submitted as summary judgment proof must be sworn or certified); ***Norcross v. Conoco, Inc.***, 720 S.W.2d 627, 632 (Tex.App.—San Antonio 1986, no writ) (documents submitted as summary judgment proof must be authenticated by affidavit).

(b) Admissible. To show the admissibility of the exhibit, the affidavit should overcome any objection to the exhibit's admissibility. For example, invoices attached as exhibits are not admissible without the statements required by the Business Records Act or TRE 803(6) and 902(10). ***Norcross***, 720 S.W.2d at 632. If no objection is filed, the exhibits attached to the affidavit are uncontroverted. *See* ***Republic Nat'l Leasing Corp. v. Schindler***, 717 S.W.2d 606, 607 (Tex.1986) (statement in affidavit that attached records were true & correct copies was sufficient).

3. Unsworn declaration. When an affidavit is required from an inmate of the Texas Department of Criminal Justice or a county jail, the inmate may make an unsworn declaration. CPRC §§132.001(a), 132.002, 132.003; ***Smith v. McCorkle***, 895 S.W.2d 692, 692 (Tex.1995) (substantial compliance is sufficient). For the requirements of the declaration, see CPRC §132.002; for the form, see CPRC §132.003 and ***O'Connor's*** FORM 1B:06.

§4.15 Discovery & certificate of attempt to agree. All motions relating to discovery should contain a certificate that the party attempted to obtain discovery without court intervention but failed. TRCP 191.2. See "Certificate of attempt to agree," ch. 6-A, §3.2, p. 315; ***O'Connor's*** FORM 1B:11. Some local rules require a certificate of conference on other motions as well. *E.g.*, Tarrant Cty. Civ. Dist. Ct. Loc. R. 3.06(b) (no motion will be set for hearing without a certificate of conference).

§4.16 Certificate of service. All documents required to be served under TRCP 21 (except those served by process) must contain a certificate of service in the document itself. TRCP 21a. See ***O'Connor's*** FORMS 1B:09-10.

1. Contents. The certificate must contain the recipient's address (or fax number), a statement that on a certain date the document was served on opposing counsel (or opposing party if the party is pro se) by a certain method (*e.g.*, mail, delivery, fax), and the signature of the attorney of record (or party, if pro se). *See generally* TRCP 21 & 21a (service of pleadings & motions).

2. Method of service. The certificate should identify the method of service (*e.g.*, mail, delivery, fax). *See* ***Dunn v. Menassen***, 913 S.W.2d 621, 626 (Tex.App.—Corpus Christi 1995, writ denied). *But see* ***Smith v. Mike Carlson Motor Co.***, 918 S.W.2d 669, 673 (Tex.App.—Fort Worth 1996, no writ) (nothing in TRCP 21a requires certificate of service to identify method of service). It is important to include the method of service in the certificate of service to determine the deadline for the response. For example, when a document is served by mail, the deadline is determined by adding three days to the date the document was mailed. See "Served by mail," ch. 1-D, §6.1, p. 24. The certificate of service on appellate documents must describe the date and manner of service. TRAP 9.5(e)(1). See *O'Connor's Texas Civil Appeals*, FORMS 11C:12-13 (2002-03).

3. Documents to be served. All documents required to be served on the other party by TRCP 21 must contain a certificate of service.

(1) Pleadings. All pleadings, motions, responses, or applications to the court for an order, unless served with citation or presented during a hearing or trial, must contain a certificate of service. *See* TRCP 21.

(2) Orders & judgments. All orders and judgments sent to the court separately from a motion or response must contain a certificate of service. See "Certificate of service," ch. 1-G, §4.1.9, p. 36.

§4.17 Notice of party's name & address. Each party's name and address must be provided in writing to the clerk (1) when the party files its initial pleading, (2) within seven days after the clerk of the court requests the information, or (3) at any time the party changes its address. CPRC §30.015(c), (d). To comply with CPRC §30.015, a lawyer—when filing the first pleading in the case—should file a one-page notice, titled "Notice of Current Address," that contains the style of the case and the party's name, current address, and the lawyer's signature. See *O'Connor's* FORM 1B:12.

§5. GROUNDLESS OR FRIVOLOUS PLEADINGS

A party or lawyer who files groundless or frivolous pleadings, motions, or other papers may be sanctioned under CPRC chapter 9 (groundless pleadings), under CPRC chapter 10 (frivolous pleadings), and under TRCP 13 (groundless pleadings). In 1997, the Legislature added CPRC chapter 11, which provides a procedure for restricting filings by plaintiffs found to be vexatious litigants.

§5.1 Purpose. The purpose of CPRC chapter 9, CPRC chapter 10, and TRCP 13 is to curb abuses in the pleading process so that, when the pleading is filed, the litigant's position is factually well grounded and legally tenable. ***Falk & Mayfield LLP v. Molzan***, 974 S.W.2d 821, 827 (Tex.App.—Houston [14th Dist.] 1998, pet. denied) (TRCP 13); *see* ***Skepnek v. Mynatt***, 8 S.W.3d 377, 381-82 (Tex.App.—El Paso 1999, pet. denied) (CPRC ch. 10 & TRCP 13); ***Herrmann & Andreas Ins. Agency v. Appling***, 800 S.W.2d 312, 320 (Tex.App.—Corpus Christi 1990, no writ) (CPRC §9.012).

§5.2 Sanctions. For the motion for sanctions for frivolous or groundless pleadings, see "Motion for Sanctions," ch. 5-J, p. 275.

§5.3 Vexatious litigation. CPRC chapter 11 provides a procedure to restrict plaintiffs from filing vexatious litigation. A defendant may file a motion asking the court to (1) determine that the plaintiff is a vexatious litigant and (2) require the plaintiff to furnish security. CPRC §11.051. For a court to determine the plaintiff is a vexatious litigant, the defendant must show there is no reasonable probability that the plaintiff will prevail in the litigation. *See* CPRC §11.054. The defendant must file the motion within 90 days after it files its original answer or makes its special appearance. *Id.* §11.051; ***Spiller v. Spiller***, 21 S.W.3d 451, 454 (Tex.App.—San Antonio 2000, no pet.).

§6. DEFECTIVE PLEADINGS

§6.1 Effect of pleadings. The pleadings determine what issues are relevant to the lawsuit. ***Jobe v. Lapidus***, 874 S.W.2d 764, 765 (Tex.App.—Dallas 1994, writ denied). Generally, a party cannot obtain discovery of, prove at trial, or submit jury questions on issues that were not pleaded. *See* ***Bedgood v. Madalin***, 600 S.W.2d 773, 775-76 (Tex.1980) (party could not introduce evidence or submit jury question on unpleaded theory). If a party attempts to prove unpleaded issues or asks for jury findings on them, the opponent should object. See "Making & Preserving Objections," ch. 1-F, p. 29. If the pleadings are defective, the party should immediately move to amend. See §7, below; "Special Exceptions—Challenging the Pleadings," ch. 3-G, p. 187.

§6.2 Waiver of pleading defect. There are two types of pleading defects that the opponent must object to: (1) defects in form (*e.g.*, failure to include a verification) and (2) defects in substance (*e.g.*, failure to plead with sufficient specificity a cause of action or defense). If the opponent does not object to these pleading defects by special exception before the charge to the jury, or in nonjury cases before the judgment is signed, these defects are waived. TRCP 90; ***Shoemake v. Fogel, Ltd.***, 826 S.W.2d 933, 937 (Tex.1992). For example, when a plaintiff claims the action of a defendant caused injury but does not use the term "negligence," the error is waived unless the defendant specially excepts to the petition. ***Roark v. Allen***, 633 S.W.2d 804, 810 (Tex.1982).

§6.3 Trial by consent. An issue is "tried by consent" if, though not raised by the pleadings, evidence was presented and a jury question was submitted on the issue without objection. *See* TRCP 67; ***Murray v. O&A Express***, 630 S.W.2d 633, 636-37 (Tex.1982); ***Harkey v. TEIA***, 208 S.W.2d 919, 922 (Tex.1948). If the opponent objects to evidence on the ground that the issue was not pleaded, or objects to the submission of the jury question for the same reason, the issue is not tried by consent. ***Libhart v. Copeland***, 949 S.W.2d 783, 797 (Tex.App.—Waco 1997, no writ); *see also* ***Sherrod v. Bailey***, 580 S.W.2d 24, 26 (Tex.App.—Houston [1st Dist.] 1979, writ ref'd n.r.e.) (when objection and specific complaints are made to issues outside pleadings, and court makes an adverse ruling, there is no implied consent). If the opponent objects to the submission of an issue because of lack of pleadings, the party offering the jury question must amend its pleadings before the jury question can be submitted on the issue. *See* ***Matthews v. General Acc. Fire & Life Assur. Corp.***, 343 S.W.2d 251, 254-55 (Tex.1961). See "Motion for Leave to Amend Trial Pleadings," ch. 8-F, §4, p. 557.

§6.4 No waiver in default. A defendant against whom a no-answer default judgment is rendered does not waive pleading defects. TRCP 90. See "Variance between pleadings & judgment," ch. 7-A, §3.2.2, p. 444.

§7. AMENDING THE PLEADINGS

§7.1 Two methods. The rules permit the parties to change the issues by amending and supplementing the pleadings.

1. Amended pleadings. An amended pleading adds or withdraws matters to correct or change the previous pleading. TRCP 62; ***J.M. Huber Corp. v. Santa Fe Energy Res.***, 871 S.W.2d 842, 844 (Tex.App.—Houston [14th Dist.] 1994, no writ). It completely replaces and supersedes the previous pleading. TRCP 65; ***Phifer v. Nacogdoches Cty. Cent. Appr. Dist.***, 45 S.W.3d 159, 172 (Tex.App.—Tyler 2000, pet. denied); ***Hill v. Heritage Res.***, 964 S.W.2d 89, 142 (Tex.App.—El Paso 1997, pet. denied). Once an amended pleading is filed, the previous pleading is no longer part of the proceedings. TRCP 65; ***Drake Ins. Co. v. King***, 606 S.W.2d 812, 817 (Tex.1980). The last amended pleading filed is called the "live" pleading. After an amendment, statements in the earlier pleadings are no longer judicial admissions. ***Sosa v. Central Power & Light***, 909 S.W.2d 893, 895 (Tex.1995). The amended pleading must comply with the rules of the original pleading (*e.g.*, if the original pleading was verified, the amended pleading must also be verified).

2. Supplemental pleadings. A supplemental or reply pleading is made in response to the last pleading of an adverse party. TRCP 69; ***Sixth RMA Partners v. Sibley***, 111 S.W.3d 46, 53 (Tex.2003); ***J.M. Huber***, 871 S.W.2d at 844. It adds to, but does not supersede or replace, the previous pleading. The plaintiff's supplemental petition may contain the following matters in reply to what is alleged by the defendant: special exceptions, general denials, and the allegations of new matter not already alleged. TRCP 80. A supplemental pleading should restate only the things from the previous pleading that are necessary as an introduction to the things that are changed, added, or challenged. *See* TRCP 69; ***Sibley***, 111 S.W.3d at 53. When a supplemental pleading contains matters outside the scope of TRCP 69, the adverse party must object or else it waives the error. *See* ***Sibley***, 111 S.W.3d at 54.

PRACTICE TIP

Avoid using supplemental pleadings. By amending pleadings instead of supplementing them, the lawsuit file will contain fewer live pleadings and thus will be less confusing.

---

§7.2 Procedure for amending pleadings. The procedure for amending pleadings at various stages of the trial is discussed in other sections of this book.

1. Amending pleadings in summary judgment case. See "Amending the Petition or Answer," ch. 7-B, §9, p. 473.

2. Amending pleadings before trial. See "Motion to Amend Pleadings—Pretrial," ch. 5-F, p. 255.

3. Amending pleadings during trial & after verdict. See "Motion to Amend Pleadings—Trial & Post-Trial," ch. 8-F, p. 557.

§7.3 Appellate review of amended pleadings. On appeal, the court reviews the trial court's rulings on amendments under the abuse of discretion standard. ***Ohio Med. Prods. v. Suber***, 758 S.W.2d 870, 872 (Tex.App.—Houston [14th Dist.] 1988, writ denied). Whether an amendment is appropriate is a function of three factors: the nature of the amendment, the evidence introduced at trial, and the timeliness of the amendment.

1. Nature of amendment.

(1) Amendment is procedural. If the amendment corrected a procedural defect in the pleadings, it was less likely to cause surprise and should have been permitted late in the trial. *See* ***Chapin & Chapin v. Texas Sand & Gravel Co.***, 844 S.W.2d 664, 665 (Tex.1992) (trial court should have permitted defendant to add verified denial to its answer); ***Stephenson v. LeBoeuf***, 16 S.W.3d 829, 839 (Tex.App.—Houston [14th Dist.] 2000, pet. denied) (court has no discretion to refuse amendment that is merely procedural in nature).

(2) Amendment is substantive. If the amendment made a substantive change and altered the nature of the trial itself, the trial court had the discretion to deny leave to amend. ***Chapin***, 844 S.W.2d at 665; *see, e.g.*, ***Hardin v. Hardin***, 597 S.W.2d 347, 349-50 (Tex.1980) (court had discretion to deny amendment offered on day of trial to add affirmative defenses). On appeal, an appellant who objected to the amendment must show (1) surprise or prejudice, or (2) the amendment asserted a new cause of action or defense, and thus was prejudicial on its face. ***State Bar v. Kilpatrick***, 874 S.W.2d 656, 658 (Tex.1994); ***Chapin***, 844 S.W.2d at 665; ***Stephenson***, 16 S.W.3d at 839.

2. Evidence introduced at trial. If the party offered an amendment that conformed the pleadings to the evidence, the trial court should have permitted it. See "Amendment to add allegations," ch. 8-F, §5.2, p. 557.

3. Timeliness of amendment. If the party filed an amendment as soon as it realized an amendment was necessary, the court should have been inclined to permit the amendment.

§8. PLEADINGS AS JUDICIAL ADMISSIONS

§8.1 Pleading assertions of fact. Assertions of fact in a party's live pleadings that are not pleaded in the alternative are regarded as formal judicial admissions. ***Houston First Am. Sav. v. Musick***, 650 S.W.2d 764, 767 (Tex.1983). For a statement in a pleading to be a judicial admission, it must be clear, deliberate, and unequivocal. ***Regency Advantage v. Bingo Idea-Watauga, Inc.***, 936 S.W.2d 275, 278 (Tex.1996); ***Mapco, Inc. v. Carter***, 817 S.W.2d 686, 687 (Tex.1991). A party may plead alternative theories without judicially admitting them. ***Dowling v. NADW Mktg.***, 631 S.W.2d 726, 729 (Tex.1982); *see* TRCP 48.

1. Effect. A judicial admission is conclusive against the party making it, relieves the opposing party of the burden of proving the admitted fact, and bars the admitting party from disputing it. ***Mendoza v. Fidelity & Guar. Ins. Underwriters***, 606 S.W.2d 692, 694 (Tex.1980); ***Frazer v. Texas Farm Bureau Mut Ins. Co.***, 4 S.W.3d 819, 825 (Tex.App.—Houston [1st Dist.] 1999, no pet.). Once a fact is conclusively established by judicial admission, jury questions concerning the fact do not need to be submitted. ***Horizon v. Auld***, 34 S.W.3d 887, 905 (Tex.2000).

2. Waiver of judicial admission. A party relying on an opponent's pleadings as judicial admissions of fact must protect the record by objecting to the introduction of controverting evidence and to the submission of a jury question on the admitted fact. ***Marshall v. Vise***, 767 S.W.2d 699, 700 (Tex.1989); ***Musick***, 650 S.W.2d at 769;

see, e.g., ***Hurlbut v. Gulf Atl. Life Ins. Co.***, 749 S.W.2d 762, 765 (Tex.1987) (Ds did not object to submission of jury question). See "Making & Preserving Objections," ch. 1-F, p. 29.

3. Not in superseded pleadings. Statements in superseded pleadings are not conclusive or indisputable judicial admissions. ***Sosa v. Central Power & Light***, 909 S.W.2d 893, 895 (Tex.1995); ***Drake Ins. Co. v. King***, 606 S.W.2d 812, 817 (Tex.1980).

§8.2 Compared to testimonial admissions. A party's testimonial declarations that are contrary to its position are quasi-admissions, but they are not conclusive. ***Mendoza***, 606 S.W.2d at 694. Quasi-admissions are distinguishable from true judicial admissions, which are a formal waiver of proof usually found in pleadings or the stipulations of the parties. *Id.* For a party's testimonial quasi-admission to be treated as a conclusive judicial admission, the statement must be deliberate, clear, and unequivocal, and the hypothesis of mere mistake or slip of the tongue must be eliminated. ***Hennigan v. I.P. Pet. Co.***, 858 S.W.2d 371, 372 (Tex.1993).

C. RULES FOR FILING DOCUMENTS

§1. GENERAL

§1.1 Rules. TRCP 4, 5, 21, 21a, 21b, 23-27, 45(d), 74. See Gov't Code §311.014; TRAP 4.1, 5, 9.

§1.2 Purpose. Documents are filed to get them into the court's record of the lawsuit. Filing documents should not be confused with serving documents. Documents are *filed* with the clerk; they are *served* on the other parties in the lawsuit. The rules for filing and serving differ. *Compare* TRCP 21 (filing and serving of pleadings and motions), *with* TRCP 21a (methods of service). See "Rules for Serving Documents," ch. 1-D, p. 21.

§1.3 Forms. ***O'Connor's Texas Civil Forms***, FORMS 1C.

§2. WHAT TO FILE

§2.1 Almost everything. File all pleadings, motions, and other documents unless a rule explicitly states otherwise. *E.g.*, TRCP 191.4(a) (list of discovery materials that must not be filed).

§2.2 Original or copy. Usually, the signed original should be filed with the court. Under TRCP 45(d), a copy of a document may be filed instead of the original. When a copy is filed, the party is required to maintain the original for inspection should a question be raised about its authenticity. TRCP 45.

§3. WITH WHOM TO FILE

Documents are considered filed when they reach the court. *See* ***Stokes v. Aberdeen Ins. Co.***, 917 S.W.2d 267, 268 (Tex.1996) (mailing document to proper court address controls over who is named as court's representative).

§3.1 Clerk. Generally, documents should be presented to the clerk of the court for filing. Documents must be filed with the clerk, unless they are presented during a trial or hearing (TRCP 21) or given to the judge for filing (TRCP 74). When the courthouse is closed, documents may be filed with the clerk wherever the clerk can be located, generally at the clerk's residence. *See* ***Miller Brewing Co. v. Villarreal***, 829 S.W.2d 770, 771 (Tex.1992).

§3.2 Judge. Documents may be filed with the trial judge during a trial or hearing. TRCP 21, 74. When the courthouse is closed, documents may be filed with the trial judge wherever the judge can be located, generally at the judge's residence. *See* ***Miller Brewing***, 829 S.W.2d at 771. When the trial judge is not available, documents may be filed with another judge occupying the same type of bench in the same county. *See, e.g.*, ***In re Cuban***, 24 S.W.3d 381, 383 (Tex.App.—Dallas 2000, orig. proceeding) (motion to recuse judge in County Court at Law No. 2 filed with judge of County Court at Law No. 3). The judge must note the date and time on the document and forward it to the clerk's office. TRCP 74.

§4. HOW TO FILE

Local rules cannot impose additional restrictions on what constitutes a "filing" under the TRCPs (or the TRAPs). ***Jamar v. Patterson***, 868 S.W.2d 318, 318 n.2 (Tex.1993).

§4.1 By mail. A party may file a document by mailing it to the clerk on or before the last day it is due. TRCP 5; *see, e.g.*, ***Beard v. Beard***, 49 S.W.3d 40, 54 (Tex.App.—Waco 2001, pet. denied) (motion for new trial deposited in mail on day it was due was timely). When a party files a document by mail, it invokes the "mailbox rule" in TRCP 5, and the document is considered filed on the day it is postmarked by the post office. When a party uses the mail, a document will be considered timely filed on the day of the postmark if it meets the criteria listed below.

PRACTICE TIP

When attempting to establish the mailbox rule, the party must prove each element of the rule. For example, in ***Arnold v. Shuck****, 24 S.W.3d 470, 472-73 (Tex.App.—Texarkana 2000, pet. denied), the court found the affidavit did not establish the elements of the mailbox rule because the affidavit stated only that the petition was mailed, postage prepaid, and did not state that the petition was sent by first-class mail, affixed with proper postage, and addressed to the proper clerk.*

1. The document was sent by first-class U.S. mail and properly stamped. TRCP 5. When a document is sent by FedEx, UPS, or any other private delivery service, the mailbox rule in TRCP 5 does not apply. ***Fountain Parkway, Ltd. v. Tarrant Appr. Dist.***, 920 S.W.2d 799, 802-03 (Tex.App.—Fort Worth 1996, writ denied). Therefore, when a document sent by private delivery service is received by the clerk after the due date, it is not timely filed. *Id.* at 802; ***Carpenter v. Town & Country Bank***, 806 S.W.2d 959, 960 (Tex.App.—Eastland 1991, writ denied).

2. The document was addressed to the proper clerk or the proper court and sent to the correct address. TRCP 5; ***Stokes***, 917 S.W.2d at 268. An incorrect or omitted zip code does not render the address improper. ***Judkins v. Davenport***, 59 S.W.3d 689, 691 (Tex.App.—Amarillo 2000, no pet.).

3. The document was mailed on or before the due date. TRCP 5; *e.g.*, ***Milam v. Miller***, 891 S.W.2d 1, 2 (Tex.App.—Amarillo 1994, writ ref'd) (answer mailed at post office at 8:30 a.m. on due date, only 90 minutes before deadline for answer, was filed timely).

4. The document arrived at the court within ten days. TRCP 5. The document or a copy of the document must reach the court no later than ten days after it is due. *E.g.*, ***Stokes***, 917 S.W.2d at 268 (party mailed motion to judge and copy to clerk; clerk's copy was received within 10 days and considered timely filed). If the document arrives on the 11th day, it is not considered timely filed unless the party files a motion to extend the time for filing. TRCP 5. See "Motion to extend," §9.1, p. 18.

5. The document bears a U.S. Postal Service postmark, which is prima facie evidence of the date of mailing. TRCP 5; *see* ***Carpenter***, 806 S.W.2d at 960 (document sent by UPS did not qualify). See "Proving filing," §10.1, p. 18.

PRACTICE TIP

To be sure a document mailed to the clerk is received on time, send it to the clerk by certified mail. The postal service will give you a signed receipt ("Domestic Return Receipt") showing the date the document was received by the clerk. USPS Form 3811 (the "green card"). Another possibility is mailing the document with a certificate of mailing, which costs less than certified mail. USPS Form 3817. However, a certificate of mailing proves only that the document was mailed, not that it was received.

§4.2 By delivery. A party may file a document by delivering it to the clerk of the trial court. TRCP 21, 74. Anyone—the lawyer, the lawyer's office staff, or a private delivery service (*e.g.*, FedEx or UPS)—may deliver a document, as long as it is delivered on or before the date it is due. A party may also file a document with the judge; for example, while in court, a lawyer may personally hand a document to the judge for filing. TRCP 74.

§4.3 By fax. A party may file a document with the clerk by fax transfer under the authority of Gov't Code §51.803, which permits the Supreme Court to adopt rules to regulate the use of electronic devices for filing in the courts. *See* Gov't Code §51.807. The Supreme Court has approved local rules for fax filing in most counties. Because no rule in the TRCPs addresses fax filing, it is not clear when a faxed document is considered filed. The lawyer should refer to a court's local rules for fax filing to determine when a document is considered filed. For example, the rules governing fax filing for the Bexar County District Clerk's office consider a document filed on the day it is received if the transmission is completed before midnight on a business day. See *Electronically Transmitted Court Documents-Fax Filing*, Rule 4.15 (Bexar Cty.), www.co.bexar.tx.us/dclerk/e-Services/Attorney_Services/Local_Rules/local_rules.htm. The lawyer's fax machine should be set to produce a transmission verification report confirming the date and time the document was sent and received. The report should be attached to the lawyer's file copy of the document, just in case it becomes necessary to prove the date of filing.

1. When court accepts filing by fax. If the court is one of those with approved local rules for fax filing, a party may file the document over the fax line. *Cf.* ***Strawder v. Thomas***, 846 S.W.2d 51, 58 (Tex.App.—Corpus Christi 1992, no writ) (even though county was not yet approved for fax filing, document was filed when clerk accepted fax, put file mark on it, and entered it into court's minutes).

2. When court does not accept filing by fax. If a court does not accept a document filed by fax, a party can still use the fax technology to get a document filed on time. TRCP 45(d) permits parties to file photocopies of original pleadings. A party can send a document by fax to someone in the city where the courthouse is located and have that person deliver a copy of the faxed document to the clerk. See §4.2, above.

§5. WHEN TO FILE

Documents must be filed by the deadlines provided in statutes, TRCPs, local rules, pretrial docketing orders, or other orders of the court.

§5.1 By deadline. A document is filed timely if it is filed on or before the deadline. See §7, below.

§5.2 Premature. Occasionally, a document is filed before the filing period begins. A prematurely filed document is deemed filed on the date of, but after the event that begins the filing period. *See* TRCP 306c (motion for new trial, request for findings of fact); TRAP 27.1 (notice of appeal); ***Padilla v. LaFrance***, 907 S.W.2d 454, 458 (Tex.1995) (motion to modify judgment); ***In re Estate of Ayala***, 19 S.W.3d 477, 479-80 (Tex.App.—Corpus Christi 2000, orig. proceeding) (creditor suit filed before claim rejected by representative of estate); ***Perez v. TEIA***, 926 S.W.2d 425, 427 (Tex.App.—Austin 1996, order on mot.) (verified motion to reinstate).

§6. FILING FEES

§6.1 Due when filed. Some filing fees must be paid when a document is filed. A fee is required for filing a suit, a cross-claim, a counterclaim, an intervention, a motion for contempt, a motion for new trial, or a third-party petition, or for requesting issuance of a citation or other writ. Gov't Code §51.317(b).

§6.2 Filing complete when paid. If a document is filed without the payment of the required fee, it is considered "conditionally filed" on the date it was tendered to the clerk. ***Tate v. E.I. DuPont de Nemours & Co.***, 934 S.W.2d 83, 84 (Tex.1996); ***Jamar v. Patterson***, 868 S.W.2d 318, 319 (Tex.1993). If the filing fee is paid before the trial court loses plenary jurisdiction over the case, the conditional filing date is valid for purposes of the appellate timetable. ***Tate***, 934 S.W.2d at 84. If the filing fee is paid after the trial court loses plenary jurisdiction, the filing date is retroactively invalidated. *Id.*

NOTE

In ***Tate****, the Supreme Court refused to answer two related questions about the late payment of filing fees for a motion for new trial: (1) will the payment after loss of plenary power extend appellate deadlines, and (2) will the payment after loss of plenary power preserve the error in the motion for new trial?* ***Tate****, 934 S.W.2d at 84 n.1. Some courts of appeals have addressed these questions. See "Paid after loss of jurisdiction," ch. 10-B, §4.2.2, p. 619.*

§7. COMPUTING DEADLINES TO FILE

A document that is filed or served late is not effective. Calculating the time limits, therefore, is extremely important. There are two rules on computation of time: TRCP 4, "Computation of Time," and TRCP 5, "Enlargement of Time." See also Gov't Code §311.014 (computation of time).

§7.1 Computing time limits – days.

1. First day. Begin counting the day *after* the period starts. Gov't Code §311.014(a); TRCP 4. The day the time period begins (*e.g.*, the date of filing, the date of service) is not counted. For example, if a plaintiff is served with interrogatories on Friday and has 30 days to answer, Friday is "day 0," Saturday is "day 1," and Sunday is "day 2."

2. Counted days. Count every day after the first day—even Saturdays, Sundays, and legal holidays—until the last day. Gov't Code §311.014(a); TRCP 4.

3. Last day. Count the last day unless it is a Saturday, Sunday, or legal holiday. ***Lewis v. Blake***, 876 S.W.2d 314, 315-16 (Tex.1994). If the last day falls on a Saturday, Sunday, or legal holiday, the deadline is the next day that is not a Saturday, Sunday, or legal holiday. Gov't Code §311.014(b); TRCP 4; ***Melendez v. Exxon Corp.***, 998 S.W.2d 266, 275 (Tex.App.—Houston [14th Dist.] 1999, no pet.); *e.g.*, ***Williams v. Flores***, 88 S.W.3d 631, 632 (Tex.2002) (motion for new trial timely filed on 32nd day after judgment because 30th day was Sunday & 31st day was legal holiday). Continuing with the example above, if day 30 falls on a Saturday, the plaintiff's answers to interrogatories are due on Monday. If Monday is a legal holiday, the plaintiff's answers are due on Tuesday or the next day that is not a legal holiday.

4 Exception. There is an exception to the general rules for computing deadlines—and to make matters more confusing, the exception has its own exception.

(1) Period to act is 5 days or less. If the period to act is five days or less, the intervening Saturdays, Sundays, and legal holidays are not counted for any purpose. TRCP 4. That is, start counting the day after the period begins, skip any Saturday, Sunday, or legal holiday, and count the last day that is not a Saturday, Sunday, or legal holiday.

CAUTION

Unlike TRCP 4, Gov't Code §311.014 has no provision for calculating time periods of five days or less. When computing statutory deadlines involving five days or less, ignore TRCP 4—that is, start counting the day after the period begins, do not skip a Saturday, Sunday, or legal holiday, and file on the last day that is not a Saturday, Sunday, or legal holiday. ***Peacock v. Humble****, 933 S.W.2d 341, 342 (Tex.App.—Austin 1996, no writ).*

(2) Exception to the exception. The three-day extensions of time in TRCP 21 and 21a and the five-day periods for forcible entry and detainer actions in TRCP 748, 749, 749a, 749b, and 749c are counted in the same manner as under the general rules. That is, Saturdays, Sundays, and legal holidays are counted for purposes of these rules unless the last day falls on them. Gov't Code §311.014(b); TRCP 4.

§7.2 Computing time limits – months. Some deadlines are computed in terms of months, not days. *E.g.*, TRCP 190.3(b)(1)(B)(ii) (discovery period in Level 2 non-family cases). If a number of months is to be computed, the period ends on the same numerical day in the concluding month as the day in the beginning month, unless there are fewer days in the concluding month, in which case the period ends on the last day of the month. Gov't Code §311.014(c). Thus, if the discovery period in a Level 2 non-family case began on December 31st, the period would end on September 30th, the last day of the ninth, concluding month, regardless of the number of days in the period.

§7.3 Problems in computing deadlines. Determining deadlines is confusing. The problem lies with the rules because they do not describe the deadlines with uniform phrasing, and some rules apply the deadline to both filing and service, some to only filing, and some to only service. For example, TRCP 166a(c) requires a party to file and serve a motion for summary judgment "at least" 21 days before the hearing; TRCP 197.2(a) requires a party to serve responses to interrogatories "within" 30 days after service; TRCP 93(13) requires a party to file a verified denial of an Industrial Accident Board award "not less than" seven days before the case proceeds to trial.

§8. HOLIDAYS

Deadlines for filing and serving documents are extended when the last day of the period falls on a Saturday, Sunday, or legal holiday. TRCP 4.

§8.1 Definition of "legal holiday." A legal holiday, as used in TRCP 4, includes all days the courthouse is officially closed. This includes days the Legislature designates as general holidays, days the commissioners court in the county where the case is pending designates as a holiday, and days the clerk's office is officially closed. ***Miller Brewing Co. v. Villarreal***, 829 S.W.2d 770, 772 (Tex.1992); *see also* ***Walles v. McDonald***, 889 S.W.2d 236, 237 (Tex.1994) (when courthouse closed for local holiday, time to file under Election Code extended); ***Martinez v. Windsor Park Dev. Co.***, 833 S.W.2d 950, 951 (Tex.1992) (interpreting "holiday" for purposes of statute of limitations). Many of the legal holidays that extend the time to file documents are listed in Gov't Code §662.003.

PRACTICE TIP

Some trial courts are open for business on some legal holidays, and others close but leave a skeleton staff to file documents. See, e.g., ***Lowe v. Rivera****, 60 S.W.3d 366, 370 n.3 (Tex.App.—Dallas 2001, no pet.) (Dallas County courts open on Presidents' Day, a legal holiday). If the court is open for filing documents on a legal holiday, a party should consider it a regular business day and file any documents due on that day. See id. at 369-70 (statute of limitations not extended by Presidents' Day). Do not rely on assurances from the courthouse personnel that a certain day is an official holiday. If the information is wrong and you file one day late, your late filing will not be excused. See, e.g.,* ***Seismic & Digital Concepts v. Digital Res. Corp.****, 583 S.W.2d 442, 442 (Tex.App.—Houston [1st Dist.] 1979, no writ) (mistake of courthouse switchboard operator, who told lawyer courthouse would be closed, did not extend time for filing).*

§8.2 After hours. If a lawyer is facing a nonextendable deadline to file a document (*e.g.*, a motion for new trial), and it is after 5:00 p.m., there are three ways to file the document timely.

1. The easiest way to file a document when the courthouse is closed, but the post office is open, is to mail it. ***Miller Brewing***, 829 S.W.2d at 771. Remember that a document is considered filed the day it is mailed if it is sent to the proper clerk at the correct address, is sent by first-class U.S. mail, and gets to the courthouse within ten days of the day it was due. TRCP 5. The postmark date will be prima facie evidence of the day it was mailed.

See "By mail," §4.1.5, p. 14. Even without a postmark, a party can prove the date of mailing by filing an affidavit of a lawyer, the clerk, or some other person. See §10.1.1, below.

2. Some courts have a drop box for filing after hours or on holidays.

3. A lawyer may call the clerk of the court and take the document to the clerk's home to file. See "Clerk," §3.1, p. 13. If the lawyer cannot locate the clerk, the lawyer can call the trial judge and take the document to the judge's home to file. If neither the clerk nor the trial judge is available, the lawyer can file the document with another judge in the same county sitting on the same type of bench. See "Judge," §3.2, p. 13.

§9. SECURING ADDITIONAL TIME

If a party needs more time to file a document or to prepare for a hearing, the party should ask for it in advance.

§9.1 Motion to extend. A motion to extend is a request to extend the time to do some act required by the rules or the court to be done within a specified time. See ***O'Connor's*** FORM 1C:01. TRCP 5 governs motions to extend for all matters except discovery, which is governed by TRCP 191.1. For motions to extend in discovery matters, see "Extending Time to Respond to Discovery," ch. 6-A, §14, p. 324, and ***O'Connor's*** FORM 6A:01. A motion to extend should be filed as soon as it becomes apparent that more time is necessary. For non-discovery motions, the longer a party waits to ask for an extension, the harder it is to get one.

1. **Before deadline.** When the party asks for additional time before the deadline, TRCP 5 permits the court to grant an extension of time for "cause shown," with or without a motion or notice. The party is not required to show "good cause," a higher burden, if the party files the motion before the deadline. TRCP 5; *cf.* TRCP 191.1 (all motions to extend discovery deadlines require "good cause"). Even though a motion is not required, the party should always file a motion or make the request in open court on the record.

2. **After deadline.** When the party asks for additional time after the deadline, TRCP 5 requires the party to file a motion and show "good cause" for not acting before the deadline. ***Remington Arms Co. v. Canales***, 837 S.W.2d 624, 625 (Tex.1992).

§9.2 Agreement to extend. To extend the time for responding to a motion, the party seeking an extension should secure a signed agreement from the other party. TRCP 11. See "Agreements Between Lawyers – Rule 11," ch. 1-H, §9, p. 44; "Modifying discovery by agreement," ch. 6-A, §5.1, p. 316.

NOTE

The deadline to file a motion for new trial cannot be extended, even by agreement. TRCP 5.

---

§9.3 Motion for continuance. TRCP 252 governs a motion for a continuance, which is a motion to postpone or delay a trial or hearing. See "Motion for Continuance," ch. 5-D, p. 242.

§10. PROVING DATE OF FILING

§10.1 Proving filing. When a dispute arises about the filing date of a document, the date the instrument was tendered to the clerk controls, even over the file-stamp date on the document. ***Coastal Banc SSB v. Helle***, 988 S.W.2d 214, 216 (Tex.1999); ***Jamar v. Patterson***, 868 S.W.2d 318, 319 (Tex.1993).

1. **By affidavit.** To prove the date a document was filed by mail, delivery, or fax, the party can file an affidavit of a lawyer, the clerk of the court, or some other person. *See, e.g.*, ***Coastal Banc***, 988 S.W.2d at 216 (date of filing established by uncontroverted affidavits of court clerk & lawyer, even though file-stamp on document indicated it was filed on a different date); ***Lofton v. Allstate Ins. Co.***, 895 S.W.2d 693, 693-94 (Tex.1995) (date of filing established by affidavit of lawyer); *cf.* ***Thomas v. Ray***, 889 S.W.2d 237, 238 (Tex.1994) (date of service, not filing, established by affidavit of lawyer). When relying on office routine or custom to support an inference a document

was sent, the party must provide corroborating evidence that the practice was actually carried out. ***Wembley Inv. Co. v. Herrera***, 11 S.W.3d 924, 928 (Tex.1999).

2. By mail. When a document is mailed with the correct address and with proper postage, there is a presumption it was received. *Cf.* ***Thomas***, 889 S.W.2d at 238 (case involved service of document, not filing).

(1) U.S. postmark. To prove filing by mail, a party may introduce a copy of the envelope with the postmark affixed. The date of the postmark put on an envelope by the U.S. Postal Service when canceling stamps is prima facie proof of filing. TRCP 5; *cf.* ***Texas Beef Cattle Co. v. Green***, 862 S.W.2d 812, 813 (Tex.App.—Beaumont 1993, order on mot.) (interpreting former TRAP 4(b), now TRAP 9.2(b)). Some clerks keep the envelopes in which documents are filed.

PRACTICE TIP

When you use a private postage meter instead of stamps, you must introduce some evidence besides the envelope to support the date it was mailed. The date marked by a private postage meter is not prima facie proof of the date a document was mailed. See ***Doyle v. Grady****, 543 S.W.2d 893, 894 (Tex.App.—Texarkana 1976, no writ) (party filed affidavit from post office employee that envelope was processed on postage meter date). But see* ***Ector Cty. ISD v. Hopkins****, 518 S.W.2d 576, 583 n.1 (Tex.App.—El Paso 1974, no writ) (private postage meter is some evidence of date of mailing).*

---

(2) Green card. To prove filing by certified mail, a party may introduce the "green card" returned from the post office and the bar-coded, white and green postal receipt bearing the postal service cancellation. USPS Forms 3800, 3811. See "Return receipt – green card," ch. 1-D, §7.1.2(1), p. 25.

(3) Yellow card. To prove filing when the green card is lost or not returned, a party may introduce a domestic mail return receipt, the "yellow card." USPS Form 3811-A ("Request for Return Receipt"). The yellow card establishes the date of delivery and to whom the mail was delivered based on the post office's records. *Id.*

(4) White slip. To prove the document was mailed (not received), a party may introduce a U.S. Postal Service certificate of mailing, the "white slip." USPS Form 3817. See "Certificate of mailing – white slip," ch. 1-D, §7.1.2(3), p. 25.

3. By delivery. To prove filing by delivery, a party may introduce a copy of the pleading presented to the clerk when the original was filed, with the clerk's date-stamp on it, or a signed receipt from a delivery service such as UPS.

4. By fax. To prove filing by fax transfer, a party may introduce the transmission verification report. See "By fax," §4.3, p. 15. Evidence showing a fax transfer to the recipient's current fax number raises a presumption the document was received by the addressee. ***American Paging v. El Paso Paging***, 9 S.W.3d 237, 240 (Tex. App.—El Paso 1999, pet. denied).

§10.2 Proving untimely filing. The presumption of receipt in TRCP 21a vanishes when verified evidence is introduced that the document was not received. *See, e.g.*, ***Thomas***, 889 S.W.2d at 238 (party claiming nonreceipt did not present verified evidence).

1. Testimony of clerk. To prove a document was not filed, the party should present sworn testimony from the clerk that the document was not received. If the clerk's office has any procedure for logging documents as they are received, the log should be produced.

2. Affidavit by U.S. Postal Service claims clerk. To disprove a date on a green card, it is possible to get an affidavit from the claims clerk of the U.S. Postal Service. The postal service keeps a record of each certified mail delivery by date and number. *See* ***Ogunboyejo v. Prudential Prop. & Cas. Co.***, 844 S.W.2d 860, 862 (Tex. App.—Texarkana 1992, writ denied).

§11. THE FILED DOCUMENT

§11.1 Clerk's endorsement. The clerk is required to endorse each document presented for filing with the file number, the date and time it was presented, and the clerk's name. *See* TRCP 24. If for any reason the clerk believes a document should not be filed, the clerk still must accept the document and note on it the date it was presented for filing. If a party files a document with the judge instead of the clerk, the judge must endorse it, sign it, and give it to the clerk. *See* TRCP 21, 24, 74.

§11.2 Deemed filed. An instrument is deemed filed when it is placed in the custody and control of the clerk. ***Jamar v. Patterson***, 868 S.W.2d 318, 319 (Tex.1993); ***Standard Fire Ins. Co. v. LaCoke***, 585 S.W.2d 678, 680 (Tex.1979). If the clerk refuses to file a document or file-marks it late, the document is considered filed on the date it was presented for filing. ***Jamar***, 868 S.W.2d at 318-19; ***Mr. Penguin Tuxedo Rental & Sales v. NCR Corp.***, 787 S.W.2d 371, 372 (Tex.1990). If the date of filing becomes an issue, the party relying on the document must prove the date the document was tendered to the clerk. *See* ***Biffle v. Morton Rubber Indus.***, 785 S.W.2d 143, 144 (Tex.1990) (affidavit stating date document was delivered to clerk's office). If a document is mailed to the clerk and the party meets all requirements of TRCP 5, the document is considered filed on the day it was mailed.

PRACTICE TIP

When you present a document to the clerk for filing, the clerk cannot refuse to file it because of a procedural shortcoming. ***Jamar****, 868 S.W.2d at 318-19. The clerk must file whatever document you present as long as it is in writing and properly identifies the suit in which it should be filed. If a clerk refuses to file a document, insist that the clerk take the document, note on the document that it was presented for filing, state the date and the time, and sign it. Once the clerk makes a notation on the document that it was presented for filing, address the issue of whether it should be filed with the judge, not the clerk.* See ***In re Bernard****, 993 S.W.2d 453, 455 (Tex.App.—Houston [1st Dist.] 1999, orig. proceeding) (O'Connor, J., concurring).*

---

§11.3 Withdrawing pleadings. The clerk will not permit a party to withdraw a pleading from the court's file without a court order. TRCP 75.

§11.4 Lost pleadings. If a pleading is lost or destroyed during the prosecution of the suit, the parties can replace it with a copy. TRCP 77; TRE 1004(a); ***Coke v. Coke***, 802 S.W.2d 270, 275 (Tex.App.—Dallas 1990, writ denied). Replacing lost or destroyed papers or documents requires notice, a sworn motion, and a hearing. TRCP 77; ***In re Taylor***, 113 S.W.3d 385, 390 (Tex.App.—Houston [1st Dist.] 2003, orig. proceeding). However, the court can order a document replaced even if one of the parties does not agree to the replacement. *See* TRCP 77(b) (lost papers or records during suit); TRAP 34.5(e) (clerk's record lost or destroyed); *see also* ***Hackney v. First State Bank***, 866 S.W.2d 59, 61-62 (Tex.App.—Texarkana 1993, no writ) (refusal of one party to agree to replace exhibits does not automatically require a new trial). *But see* ***Hidalgo, Chambers & Co. v. FDIC***, 790 S.W.2d 700, 703 (Tex.App.—Waco 1990, writ denied) (under former TRAP 50(e), when the record is lost on appeal and appellant refuses to agree to a substitute, court will order new trial).

§12. COURT'S DOCKETS

The TRCPs require the clerk to keep five dockets.

§12.1 Clerk's file docket – TRCP 25. The clerk's file docket must show the number of the suit, the names of the attorneys, the names of the parties, the nature of the suit, the officer's return on the process (in brief form), and all proceedings in the case with the dates of each proceeding. TRCP 25.

1. **Order of cases.** The clerk must place cases on the docket as they are filed. TRCP 27. A case is "docketed" when the clerk places the case on the list of cases pending in the court. ***Bigham v. Dempster***, 901 S.W.2d 424, 431 (Tex.1995).

2. **Order of pleadings.** The clerk must note on the docket every pleading, plea, motion, or application to the court for an order, regardless of its form. TRCP 21. The clerk must docket pleadings according to the title designated by the parties (*e.g.*, motion for new trial). TRCP 71. If the court orders a pleading to be redesignated, the clerk must modify the docket and all other records to reflect the redesignation. TRCP 71. See "Incorrect title," ch. 1-B, §4.3.2, p. 5.

§12.2 Clerk's court docket – TRCP 26. Each clerk must keep a court docket in a permanent record that includes the number of the case and the names of the parties, the names of the attorneys, the nature of the action, the pleas, the motions, and the rulings of the court. TRCP 26. The clerk's docket entries of rulings are made only for the clerk's convenience and are not considered rulings of the court. ***Miller v. Kendall***, 804 S.W.2d 933, 944 (Tex.App.—Houston [1st Dist.] 1990, no writ). Only in a few situations can the appellate courts consider docket entries to determine a trial court's ruling. *See, e.g.*, ***Escobar v. Escobar***, 711 S.W.2d 230, 232 (Tex.1986) (to determine whether court had authority to correct judgment by nunc pro tunc); ***Pruet v. Coastal States Trading***, 715 S.W.2d 702, 705 (Tex.App.—Houston [1st Dist.] 1986, no writ) (to determine clerical error in nunc pro tunc proceeding); ***Buffalo Bag Co. v. Joachim***, 704 S.W.2d 482, 484 (Tex.App.—Houston [14th Dist.] 1986, writ ref'd n.r.e.) (to determine if motion for new trial lost by clerk had been filed).

§12.3 Jury docket – TRCP 218. The clerk of the court must keep a docket, styled "The Jury Docket," where the clerk lists the cases in which jury fees were paid or affidavits were filed instead of fees. TRCP 218; ***Higginbotham v. Collateral Protection***, 859 S.W.2d 487, 488 n.1 (Tex.App.—Houston [1st Dist.] 1993, writ denied).

§12.4 Nonjury docket – TRCP 249. The cases that are not set on the jury docket are set on the nonjury docket. TRCP 249.

§12.5 Dismissal docket – TRCP 165a(2). Any case not disposed of within the time standards set by the Supreme Court under its Administrative Rules may be placed on a dismissal docket. TRCP 165a(2); ***In re Seals***, 83 S.W.3d 870, 874 (Tex.App.—Texarkana 2002, no pet.).

§12.6 Unofficial dockets. A clerk cannot establish unofficial dockets outside the rules of procedure and base dismissals on information in those dockets. *See* ***Osterloh v. Ohio Decorative Prods.***, 881 S.W.2d 580, 582 (Tex. App.—Houston [1st Dist.] 1994, no writ) (clerk could not establish "register of lawyers" for purposes of dismissal notices).

D. RULES FOR SERVING DOCUMENTS

§1. GENERAL

§1.1 Rules. TRCP 21, 21a.

§1.2 Purpose. The purpose of serving documents is to give the other party a copy of the documents filed with the court. Recall the distinction between filing and serving: documents are *filed* with the clerk and *served* on other parties. This section applies only to serving documents after the suit has been filed. It does not apply to serving citation. TRCP 21 and 21a, which govern service of all documents other than citation, provide less formal service requirements than the rules for service of citation. ***Texas Nat. Res. Conserv. Comm'n v. Sierra Club***, 70 S.W.3d 809, 813 (Tex.2002). For service of citation, see "Serving the Defendant with Suit," ch. 2-H, p. 118.

§1.3 Forms. ***O'Connor's Texas Civil Forms***, FORMS 1B:09-10.

§2. WHAT TO SERVE

A lawyer should serve all parties with a copy of each document filed with the court and all other communications with the court about the lawsuit. TRCP 21. Any communication with the court about the lawsuit that is not served on opposing counsel is an improper ex parte communication, unless there is a specific exception. *See* Tex. Disc. R. Prof. Conduct 3.05(b)(2).

§3. WHOM TO SERVE

§3.1 Party or lawyer? If the party is represented by a lawyer, all documents must be served on the lawyer. *See* TRCP 8; ***Gem Vending v. Walker***, 918 S.W.2d 656, 658 (Tex.App.—Fort Worth 1996, orig. proceeding). The rules of ethics prohibit a lawyer from communicating about a lawsuit with a party who is represented by counsel. Tex. Disc. R. Prof. Conduct 4.02. Only when a party is not represented by counsel should a lawyer serve documents on the party. Despite the prohibitions in Rule 4.02, two courts have held that service of documents on the party may be proper even if a party is represented by a lawyer. ***Trevino v. Hidalgo Publ'g Co.***, 805 S.W.2d 862, 863 (Tex. App.—Corpus Christi 1991, no writ); ***Krchnak v. Fulton***, 759 S.W.2d 524, 527-28 (Tex.App.—Amarillo 1988, writ denied).

§3.2 Which lawyer? If the party is represented by more than one lawyer, the document should be served on the lawyer in charge, generally the lawyer who signed the first pleading or who has been specifically designated as the attorney in charge. *See* TRCP 8, 21, 21a. Service on an attorney other than the attorney in charge is not considered service. *See* TRCP 8; ***Reichhold Chems. v. Puremco Mfg. Co.***, 854 S.W.2d 240, 245-46 (Tex.App.—Waco 1993, writ denied); *cf.* ***Kenley v. Quintana Pet. Corp.***, 931 S.W.2d 318, 321 (Tex.App.—San Antonio 1996, writ denied) (clerk's notice of dismissal to local counsel did not comply with TRCP 8, which requires notice to attorney in charge). See "Attorney in charge," ch. 1-H, §3.1, p. 39.

§3.3 How many parties? A copy of each document filed with the trial court should be sent to lead counsel for each party, no matter how many parties there are. TRCP 21. If there are so many parties that serving them all is burdensome, a party can ask the court for relief under TRCP 166, the pretrial conference rule. The court may then designate certain key parties to receive documents on behalf of other parties. *See* TRCP 166.

§4. HOW TO SERVE

§4.1. Who can serve. The following persons can serve documents: the attorney of record, the party, a sheriff, a constable, or any other person competent to testify. TRCP 21a; ***State v. Bristol Hotel Asset Co.***, 65 S.W.3d 638, 642 (Tex.2001).

§4.2 Methods of service. TRCP 21a provides four ways to serve documents.

1. Service by mail. A party may serve documents by mail. TRCP 21a; TRAP 9.5(b). Service by mail is complete upon mailing. TRCP 21a; TRAP 9.5(c)(1). When a party serves a document by mail, it invokes the "mailbox rule" in TRCP 21a. A document is considered served on the day it is dropped in the mailbox as long as the following conditions are met:

(1) The document was sent by certified or registered mail. CPRC §136.001(a); TRCP 21a. Delivery by regular U.S. mail is not sufficient; it must be certified or registered. ***Dunn v. Menassen***, 913 S.W.2d 621, 626 (Tex.App.—Corpus Christi 1995, writ denied). Delivery by any service other than the U.S. Postal Service (*e.g.*, Federal Express, UPS) does not invoke the "mailbox rule." See §4.2.2, below.

(2) The document was properly addressed to the other party at the party's last known address. TRCP 21a. Under TRCP 21a, a document that is properly addressed and mailed with postage paid is presumed to be received by the addressee. ***Thomas v. Ray***, 889 S.W.2d 237, 238 (Tex.1994).

(3) The document was mailed on or before the due date. *See* TRCP 21a. If there is no postmark, an attorney's uncontroverted affidavit may establish the date of mailing. *Cf.* ***Lofton v. Allstate Ins. Co.***, 895 S.W.2d 693, 693-94 (Tex.1995) (case involved filing, not serving, documents).

(4) The attorney of record or the party signed a certificate of service stating the filed instrument was served in compliance with TRCP 21a. The certificate is prima facie evidence of the date of service. TRCP 21a; ***Bristol Hotel***, 65 S.W.3d at 642; ***Mosser v. Plano Three Venture***, 893 S.W.2d 8, 11 (Tex.App.—Dallas 1994, no writ).

CAUTION

*The mailbox rule for **filing** with the clerk differs in several ways from the mailbox rule for **serving** a document on the other party. See "By mail," ch. 1-C, §4.1.4, p. 14. The most important difference is that the ten-day grace period for receipt in TRCP 5 does not apply to service of documents on parties. **Salazar v. Canales**, 85 S.W.3d 859, 864 (Tex.App.—Corpus Christi 2002, no pet.). Thus, when a party mails a document to the other party on the date it is due, it is considered served on the other party on the date it was mailed, no matter when the other party receives it. But see id. (applying the ten-day grace period to served documents).*

---

2. Service by delivery. A party may serve documents by personal delivery or receipted delivery service. TRCP 21a. See ***O'Connor's*** FORM 1B:09. Service by delivery may be accomplished by the party, the lawyer, a member of the lawyer's office staff, an agent for the lawyer, or a receipted commercial delivery service (*e.g.*, FedEx or UPS). *See* TRCP 21a. Service of documents by delivery (either by private person or by commercial delivery service) is complete when the documents are delivered to the person or office to which they are addressed. *See id.*; *see also* ***Carpenter v. Town & Country Bank***, 806 S.W.2d 959, 960 (Tex.App.—Eastland 1991, writ denied) (interpreting TRCP 5, not TRCP 21a; motion for new trial sent by UPS was late, counting from date UPS delivered it to court), *cf.* TRAP 9.5(c)(2) (for appeals, documents served when placed in control of commercial delivery service).

3. Service by fax. A party may serve documents by fax transfer. TRCP 21a. See ***O'Connor's*** FORM 1B:09. Service by fax of documents is complete when the fax is sent, as long as it is received before 5:00 p.m. local time of the recipient. *See* TRCP 21a; *cf.* TRAP 9.5(c)(3) (for appeals, service by fax complete upon receipt). If the document is received after 5:00 p.m. local time of the recipient, it is considered served on the next day. TRCP 21a. The sender's fax machine should be set to produce a transmission verification report confirming the date and time the document was sent and received. The report should be attached to the lawyer's file copy of the document, just in case it becomes necessary to prove the date and time of service.

4. Service according to order. A party may use some other type of service if it can prove to the court some other method is necessary, and the court signs an order to that effect. TRCP 21a.

§4.3 Certificate of service. Once the defendant has been served with process and is before the court, all other documents filed with the court and served on other parties or nonparties should contain a certificate of service, signed by the attorney of record or the party, identifying the manner by which the document was served (*e.g.*, mail, personal delivery, fax) and the person on whom it was served. TRCP 21a; *see* ***Bristol Hotel***, 65 S.W.3d at 642. For what must be included in the certificate, see "Certificate of service," ch. 1-B, §4.16, p. 9, and ***O'Connor's*** FORM 1B:09.

CAUTION

*An attorney has a duty to review mail and other documents received in a case. An attorney who does not do so places the client's case in peril. **Clemons v. Denson**, 981 S.W.2d 941, 944 (Tex.App.—Houston [1st Dist.] 1998, pet. denied).*

---

§5. WHEN TO SERVE

§5.1 By deadline. A party should serve a document before the deadline as established by the TRCPs, statutes, or court order. See §6, below.

§5.2 Before hearing on motion. Motions presented to the court for an order (unless presented during a hearing or trial) must be served on the party at least three days before the hearing. TRCP 21. Saturdays, Sundays, and legal holidays are counted for purposes of calculating the three-day notice of hearings in TRCP 21. TRCP 4. Some rules require more than three days' notice. *E.g.*, TRCP 12 (motion for attorney to show authority, 10 days before hearing), TRCP 76a(4) (motion to seal court records, not less than 14 days after motion is filed and notice is posted), TRCP 166a(c) (motion for summary judgment, 21 days before hearing).

§6. COMPUTING DEADLINES TO RESPOND

If the served document requires a response within a certain period of time, the recipient calculates the date the response is due from the date of service. The date to respond depends on the type of service used. For the general rules for computing deadlines, see "Computing Deadlines to File," ch. 1-C, §7, p. 16.

§6.1 Served by mail. For a document served by mail, the party is considered served on the date the document is mailed. TRCP 21a. To determine the date to respond, add three days to whatever time the party is permitted to respond to the document, counting from the date of mailing. *Id.* For example, TRCP 21a extends the minimum notice for a hearing on a motion for summary judgment from 21 to 24 days when the motion is served by mail. ***Lewis v. Blake***, 876 S.W.2d 314, 315-16 (Tex.1994); *see also* ***Cherry v. North Am. Lloyds***, 770 S.W.2d 4, 5 (Tex.App.—Houston [1st Dist.] 1989, writ denied) (when party receives request for admissions by mail, TRCP 21a adds three days to 30 days permitted by TRCP 198.2(a) to serve answers). The three-day grace period presumes that the post office delivered the document within three days after it was mailed. If there is an unusual delay, the recipient should file a motion with the court before the response is due, stating the recipient did not receive the document within three days and needs additional time to respond. *See* TRCP 5, 21a; ***Cudd v. Hydrostatic Transmission***, 867 S.W.2d 101, 103 (Tex.App.—Corpus Christi 1993, no writ).

§6.2 Served by delivery. For a document served by delivery, service is complete when the document is delivered. To determine the date to respond, the recipient starts counting from the day the document was delivered. TRCP 21a.

§6.3 Served by fax. For a document served by fax, service is complete on the day it is received if received before 5:00 p.m. local time of the recipient. TRCP 21a. When a fax is received after 5:00 p.m., the document is deemed served on the next day. *Id.* When a party is served by fax, TRCP 21a adds three days to the time to respond, just as if the document had been sent by mail. See §6.1, above. To determine the date to respond, count from the date the document was served and add three days.

1-1. COMPUTING DEADLINES TO RESPOND

	DOCUMENT SERVED BY	DEADLINE
1	Mail	Date of mailing (generally, the postmark) + 3 days + number of days to perform
2	Delivery	Date of delivery + number of days to perform
3	Fax before 5 p.m.	Date of fax + 3 days + number of days to perform
4	Fax after 5 p.m.	Date of fax + 4 days + number of days to perform

§7. PROVING SERVICE

TRCP 21a creates a presumption that a document properly sent was received by the addressee. ***Thomas v. Ray***, 889 S.W.2d 237, 238 (Tex.1994); ***Cliff v. Huggins***, 724 S.W.2d 778, 780 (Tex.1987). The presumption vanishes when opposing evidence is introduced. ***Wembley Inv. Co. v. Herrera***, 11 S.W.3d 924, 927 (Tex.1999); ***Cliff***, 724 S.W.2d at 780.

§7.1 Proving receipt.

1. Proving all methods of service.

(1) Certificate of service. To prove the date of service by mail, delivery, or fax, a party should call the court's attention to the certificate of service attached to the served document, signed by the attorney of record or the party. TRCP 21a; *see* ***State v. Bristol Hotel Asset Co.***, 65 S.W.3d 638, 642 (Tex.2001). The certificate of service on the document is prima facie evidence of service. TRCP 21a; ***Smith v. Mike Carlson Motor Co.***, 918 S.W.2d 669, 672 (Tex.App.—Fort Worth 1996, no writ).

(2) Affidavit. To prove the date of service by mail, delivery, or fax, a party can file the affidavit of any person, describing the type and date of service. ***Bristol Hotel***, 65 S.W.3d at 642; *see* ***Thomas***, 889 S.W.2d at 238. When relying on office routine or custom to support an inference the document was sent, the party must provide corroborating evidence that the practice was actually carried out. ***Wembley***, 11 S.W.3d at 928; ***Mocega v. Urquhart***, 79 S.W.3d 61, 65 (Tex.App.—Houston [14th Dist.] 2002, pet. denied).

2. Proving service by mail. When proving service by mail by relying on one of the cards or slips provided by the U.S. Postal Service, the party must verify the contents of the card or slip by either attaching it to an affidavit or presenting sworn proof at a hearing.

(1) Return receipt – green card. To prove the date of service by mail, a party can introduce a domestic mail return receipt, the "green card," which establishes the date of delivery and to whom the mail was delivered. USPS Form 3811; *see* ***Ruiz v. Nicolas Trevino Forwarding Agency***, 888 S.W.2d 86, 88 (Tex.App.—San Antonio 1994, no writ) (when green card was not produced and other party swore document was not received, presumption of service was rebutted); *cf.* TRAP 9.2(b)(2)(B) (appellate courts will accept USPS's receipt for registered or certified mail as conclusive proof of date of mailing). To obtain return-receipt service, the party must send the document by certified mail, which provides the party with a certified mail receipt. USPS Form 3800. Although certified mail can be placed in a post office mail drop, it is best to present the document to a U.S. Postal Service employee and have a round-date applied to the form to show the date the article was accepted.

PRACTICE TIP

When sending documents through the U.S. Postal Service, make sure to use the most current postal forms. For example, certified mail must now bear a bar-coded white and green form. USPS Form 3800 ("Certified Mail Receipt").

---

(2) Return receipt after mailing – yellow card. To prove the date of service by mail when the green card is lost or not returned, a party can introduce a domestic mail return receipt, the "yellow card." USPS From 3811-A ("Request for Return Receipt"). The yellow card establishes the date of delivery and to whom the mail was delivered based on the post office's records. *Id.*

(3) Certificate of mailing – white slip. To prove the date of service by mail, a party can introduce a U.S. Postal Service certificate of mailing. *See* TRCP 21a; *cf.* TRAP 9.2(b)(2)(C) (appellate courts will accept USPS's certificate of mailing as conclusive proof of date of mailing). The certificate of mailing provides evidence that a document was presented to the U.S. Postal Service for mailing; it does not provide proof of delivery. USPS Form 3817.

3. Proving service by delivery. To prove the date of service by delivery, a party can introduce the signed, dated receipt.

4. Proving service by fax. To prove the date of service by fax, a party can introduce the transmission verification report. *See* ***American Paging v. El Paso Paging***, 9 S.W.3d 237, 240 (Tex.App.—El Paso 1999, pet. denied) (evidence showing fax transfer to recipient's current fax number raises presumption document was received by addressee). See "Service by fax," §4.2.3, p. 23. The report must be attached to an affidavit.

5. Proving constructive service. To prove constructive service, a party can prove the other party refused to accept service. *See, e.g.*, ***Roberts v. Roberts***, ___ S.W.3d ___ (Tex.App.—Corpus Christi 2003, no pet.) (No. 13-02-00025-CV; 2-13-03) (court found P had constructive notice of judgment because she had refused to accept certified mail).

PRACTICE TIP

An addressee cannot obstruct service by refusing to accept delivery of or refusing to retrieve certified mail after notice by the post office. ***Gonzales v. Surplus Ins. Servs.***, *863 S.W.2d 96, 102 (Tex.App.—Beaumont 1993, writ denied); see* ***Osborn v. Osborn***, *961 S.W.2d 408, 412-13 (Tex.App.—Houston [1st Dist.] 1997, pet. denied).*

---

§7.2 Proving nonreceipt. The presumption of receipt in TRCP 21a vanishes when verified evidence is introduced that the document was not received. *E.g.*, ***Wembley Inv. Co. v. Herrera***, 11 S.W.3d 924, 927 (Tex.1999) (lawyers provided affidavits stating they never received nonsuit motion or judgment); ***Thomas v. Ray***, 889 S.W.2d 237, 238-39 (Tex.1994) (party claiming nonreceipt did not present any verified evidence); ***Cliff v. Huggins***, 724 S.W.2d 778, 779 (Tex.1987) (party and lawyer swore they did not receive notice of trial setting).

1. Affidavit by U.S. Postal Service. To disprove a date on a green card, a party can secure an affidavit from the claims clerk of the U.S. Postal Service. *E.g.*, ***Ogunboyejo v. Prudential Prop. & Cas. Co.***, 844 S.W.2d 860, 862 (Tex.App.—Texarkana 1992, writ denied) (after D introduced such an affidavit, court concluded P's attorney had altered a number on green card to reflect earlier mailing date). The postal service keeps a record of each certified mail delivery by date and number.

2. Testimony of lawyer & party. To prove a document was not received, a party can present sworn testimony that neither the lawyer nor the party received the document. *See, e.g.*, ***Smith v. Holmes***, 53 S.W.3d 815, 817-18 (Tex.App.—Austin 2001, no pet.) (pro se inmate submitted declaration denying he received document). The lawyer in charge of the case at the time the document was sent should testify the document was not received. *See* TRCP 8. The testimony of a lawyer in the same firm, but not the lawyer in charge, will not rebut the presumption that the document was received. ***Gonzalez v. Stevenson***, 791 S.W.2d 250, 252 (Tex.App.—Corpus Christi 1990, no writ).

§8. SANCTIONS FOR FAILURE TO SERVE

TRCP 21b authorizes sanctions under TRCP 215.2(b) for failure to serve copies of pleadings and motions. See "Failure to serve – TRCP 21b," ch. 5-J, §5.3, p. 279; ***O'Connor's*** FORM 5J:03.

E. TYPES OF HEARINGS

§1. GENERAL

§1.1 Rule. TRCP 21.

§1.2 Purpose. A hearing serves the purpose of bringing the parties before the court to argue and sometimes to present evidence.

§1.3 Forms. ***O'Connor's Texas Civil Forms***, FORMS 1E.

§2. NOTICE OF HEARING

§2.1 First setting. The party scheduling a hearing on a motion for an order must serve notice of the hearing on all parties at least three days before the hearing, unless the rules provide otherwise or the court shortens the period. TRCP 21.

CAUTION

TRCP 4 seems to say that Saturdays, Sundays, and legal holidays "shall be counted for purposes of the three-day periods in rules 21 and 21a...." If the courts interpret it that way, a party may give notice on a Friday for a hearing the next Monday. Note, however, the ambiguity created by the qualifying phrase in TRCP 4 after the reference to the three-day periods in TRCP 21 and 21a—"extending other periods by three days when service is made by registered or certified mail or by telephonic document transfer...."

§2.2 Resetting. When a hearing on a motion is reset, the three-day notice requirement in TRCP 21 does not apply. ***Magnuson v. Mullen***, 65 S.W.3d 815, 824 (Tex.App.—Fort Worth 2002, pet. denied).

§3. DUTIES OF COURT REPORTER

TRAP 13 prescribes the duties of the court reporter. For a detailed description of the court reporter's duties, see ***O'Connor's Texas Civil Appeals***, "The Reporter's Record," ch. 16-C, p. 182 (2002-03).

§3.1 Attend court. The court reporter must attend all sessions of the court. TRAP 13.1(a); *see* Gov't Code §52.046(a)(1).

§3.2 Make record. The court reporter must make a full record of the proceedings, unless excused by the agreement of the parties. TRAP 13.1(a); *see also* Fam. Code §105.003(c) (court reporter must record all suits affecting the parent-child relationship, unless record waived by parties with court's consent). *Compare* TRAP 13.1(a) (court reporter must make full record), *with* Gov't Code §52.046(a)(2) & (d) (court reporter must record oral testimony only on request of the parties or in a contested probate matter).

PRACTICE TIP

*Even though TRAP 13.1 requires the court reporter to make a full record, if a court reporter does not record a hearing or part of a trial, the party must object to preserve error. The request should be in writing. See **O'Connor's** FORM 1E:02. In a no-answer default judgment case when the defendant is not present at the hearing, the plaintiff should object if the court reporter does not make a record. See "Ask for court reporter," ch. 7-A, §3.12.2(2)(a), p. 449.*

§3.3 Accept exhibits. The court reporter must accept and mark all exhibits offered as evidence during a hearing or trial and file them with the court clerk. TRAP 13.1(b).

§3.4 Preserve notes. Upon request, a court reporter must preserve the notes from a hearing or trial for three years from the date they were taken. Gov't Code §52.046(a)(4). See ***O'Connor's*** FORM 1E:02. After three years, even if the case is still pending, the court reporter can destroy stale notes if no party has requested that they be preserved or transcribed. ***Piotrowski v. Minns***, 873 S.W.2d 368, 371 (Tex.1993); ***Ganesan v. Vallabhaneni***, 96 S.W.3d 345, 349 (Tex.App.—Austin 2002, pet. denied). Once a lawsuit has been pending for three years, a party should either ask the court reporter to transcribe the record or file a motion with the court to require the court reporter to preserve all notes from hearings and the trial. ***Piotrowski***, 873 S.W.2d at 371. See ***O'Connor's*** FORM 1E:03.

§3.5 Prepare appellate record. The court reporter must prepare the reporter's record for appeal when requested by a party. TRAP 13.1(d); *see also* Gov't Code §52.046(a)(5) (if requested, court reporter must furnish transcript of evidence); TRAP 35.3(b) (responsibility for filing reporter's record).

§4. HEARING ON MOTION

The court will not always hold a hearing before ruling on a motion. The term "hearing" does not necessarily contemplate a personal appearance before the court or an oral presentation to the court. ***Martin v. Martin, Martin & Richards***, 989 S.W.2d 357, 359 (Tex.1998). If the court conducts a hearing, it will not always permit the parties to introduce evidence. Some rules provide for a hearing or submission date as a way of creating a deadline for filing the response (*e.g.*, motion for summary judgment).

§4.1 Hearing for argument only. If a rule prohibits oral testimony at the hearing, the hearing is for argument only. When the hearing is for argument only, the party can submit a motion for the court's decision without actually making an appearance to argue the motion in court. For example, the summary judgment rule states: "No oral testimony shall be received...." TRCP 166a(c). Because no evidence is presented at a summary judgment hearing, the court can decide the motion on the pleadings, without an appearance by the attorneys before the court. A hearing for argument only does not need to be recorded by a court reporter.

§4.2 Hearing for evidence. When a hearing is for the receipt of evidence, it should be recorded.

1. Hearing required. A few rules require the trial court to hold a hearing to receive evidence before ruling. For example, TRCP 165a, which governs the procedure to reinstate a case after dismissal for want of prosecution, requires the court to conduct a hearing even if the party does not ask for one. See "Hearing," ch. 10-F, §7, p. 653.

2. Hearing requested. If a rule authorizes a hearing for the receipt of evidence and the party asks for a hearing, the court must conduct one. For example, when a party objects to a legislative continuance on due process grounds, the trial court cannot refuse the party a hearing. ***Waites v. Sondock***, 561 S.W.2d 772, 776 (Tex.1977).

§4.3 Submitted on pleadings & proof. The Rules of Judicial Administration approve the submission of motions on written pleadings instead of a personal appearance for a hearing. *See* Tex.R.Jud.Admin. 7(a)(6)(b); ***Koslow's v. Mackie***, 796 S.W.2d 700, 703 (Tex.1990). Some motions that require evidence may be submitted on a verified motion and affidavits, without oral testimony. See §5, below.

PRACTICE TIP

If in doubt whether a particular motion may be submitted on the pleadings, file a written agreement stating that the parties agree to submit the motion for a ruling based on the motion, the response, and the evidence attached to the motion and response. Make sure the agreement meets the requirements of TRCP 11. See "Agreements Between Lawyers – Rule 11," ch. 1-H, §9, p. 44.

---

§4.4 Telephone hearing. The Rules of Judicial Administration permit a telephone hearing on a motion instead of a personal appearance. Tex.R.Jud.Admin. 7(a)(6)(b); ***Gulf Coast Inv. Corp. v. Nasa 1 Bus. Ctr.***, 754 S.W.2d 152, 153 (Tex.1988). Some courts have adopted local rules permitting telephone hearings on motions that do not require evidence. *See* ***Xu v. Davis***, 884 S.W.2d 916, 918 n.2 (Tex.App.—Waco 1994, orig. proceeding) (Brazos County).

§5. EVIDENCE FOR MOTIONS

§5.1 Live testimony. When a motion requires live testimony at the hearing, the parties must present evidence with all the formalities of a trial—the witnesses must be sworn, and the documents must be identified on the record, authenticated, and admitted into evidence. Statements made by a lawyer during the hearing are not evidence. See "Lawyer's appearance before court," ch. 1-H, §5.2, p. 40.

§5.2 Affidavit & other sworn proof. Some motions that require evidence and are generally supported with live testimony (*e.g.*, motion to abate) can be submitted on a motion and sworn proof, without live testimony.

Motions that do not permit live testimony must be submitted on pleadings and sworn proof (*e.g.*, motion for summary judgment).

§6. WAIVER

§6.1 Type of hearing. If a party appears for what it assumes is a hearing for argument only but instead is a hearing to receive evidence, the party must object on the record to preserve the error for appeal. ***Lemons v. EMW Mfg. Co.***, 747 S.W.2d 372, 373 (Tex.1988). Similarly, if a party appears for what it assumes is a hearing for evidence but instead is a hearing for argument only, the party must object on the record. *See, e.g.*, ***Union Carbide Corp. v. Moye***, 798 S.W.2d 792, 793 (Tex.1990) (D's lawyer filed motion for continuance & asked for additional time to file affidavits when he discovered no evidence would be received). The party should tell the trial court on the record that it expected to present argument (or evidence) and is not prepared to go forward. The party should file a handwritten, verified motion for continuance and describe the type of notice sent. *See* ***Lemons***, 747 S.W.2d at 373. See "Making & Preserving Objections," ch. 1-F, below; "Motion for Continuance," ch. 5-D, p. 242.

§6.2 Order signed without hearing. If the trial court signs an order without holding a hearing when a party who is entitled to a hearing has properly requested one, to preserve error the party must file a motion asking the court to set aside the order and hold a hearing. *See* ***State ex rel. Latty v. Owens***, 907 S.W.2d 484, 486 (Tex.1995) (party waived right to hearing to contest master's recommendations). See "Making & Preserving Objections," ch. 1-F, below.

§6.3 Motion waived. If the movant does not present evidence when a rule permits it, in some cases the movant waives the motion. For example, when a party files a sworn motion to abate and attaches affidavits, the party still must ask for a hearing and present testimony. ***Atkinson v. Reid***, 625 S.W.2d 64, 67 (Tex.App.—San Antonio 1981, no writ). If the party does not ask for a hearing and present evidence, the court will overrule the motion.

§7. SECURING ATTENDANCE OF WITNESS

When a party plans to introduce evidence at a hearing on a motion, the party may subpoena a witness to attend the hearing. TRCP 176.2. See "Subpoenas," ch. 1-K, p. 58.

F. MAKING & PRESERVING OBJECTIONS

§1. GENERAL

§1.1 Rules. TRE 103; TRAP 33.1, 44.

§1.2 Purpose. There are two reasons to make objections. The first and most important reason is to convince the trial court of the merits of the party's position. The second reason is to make a record of the objection so that on appeal the party will be able to argue the objection as a ground for error. *See generally* TRAP 33.1 (preservation of complaints).

§1.3 Forms. None.

§2. GROUNDS FOR OBJECTION

Almost every rule of procedure can be a ground for an objection. When rule requires action by a party or by the court, the beneficiary of the rule may object to nonperformance or inadequate performance of the required action.

§3. TYPES OF ERROR

The type of objection and the timing of the objection depend on the type of error. If the error is committed by the jury in evaluating the facts, the objection must be made in writing, in either a motion for new trial or a motion for judgment notwithstanding the verdict. TRCP 300, 320. If the error is committed by the trial judge in applying the law, the party may complain by oral objection in open court or in a written motion. Thus, the first problem in objecting is to decide who made what type of error.

§3.1 Role of jury. The jury's task is simple: it listens to the evidence and answers the questions the trial court submits to it by returning a verdict. The jury is the fact-finder. ***Chitsey v. National Lloyds Ins. Co.***, 738 S.W.2d 641, 643 (Tex.1987). Thus, a mistake by the jury is a mistake in evaluating the evidence.

§3.2 Role of trial judge. The trial judge can make mistakes in applying the law or in evaluating the evidence.

1. In jury trial. The trial judge plays two roles in a jury trial. During the trial, the judge acts as an umpire and decides which facts are admissible into evidence. After the judge admits the evidence, and the jury resolves the fact issues by the verdict, the judge announces the winner by rendering judgment. Neither as umpire nor as announcer does the judge have fact-finding power. The judge is authorized only to apply appropriate law to the established facts and sign the appropriate judgment. The judge has no discretion when applying the law.

2. In nonjury trial. In a nonjury trial, the judge is the substitute for the jury and has the same fact-finding power as the jury. Thus, in a nonjury trial the judge plays three roles: (1) the judge acts as an umpire and decides which facts are admissible into evidence; (2) relying on the admitted evidence, the judge resolves the fact issues; and (3) relying on the resolution of the fact issues, the judge applies the law, announces the winner, and signs the appropriate judgment.

§3.3 Appealable error. In broad terms, there are two kinds of error made during a trial. One is error in applying the law, and the other is error in weighing the evidence. A third type of error, the trial court's abuse of discretion, is the most difficult to reverse on appeal.

1. Error in applying law. The trial court errs in applying the law when it misinterprets the law, applies the wrong law, ignores the law, exercises power it does not possess, or refuses to exercise power it is required to exercise. *See* ***Walker v. Packer***, 827 S.W.2d 833, 840 (Tex.1992) (trial court has no discretion to decide what the law is or how to apply it to the facts). Because the trial court has no discretion in these matters, appellate courts review these rulings with little deference to the trial court's legal determinations. See "Review of legal issues," ch. 1-G, §5.2.1, p. 37.

2. Error in weighing evidence.

(1) Evaluating evidence. The fact-finder—either the jury or, in a nonjury trial, the judge—errs when it misevaluates the evidence. On appeal, this error is challenged by allegations that the evidence is legally and factually insufficient. See "MNT to Challenge the Evidence," ch. 10-B, §9, p. 623.

(2) Deciding if fact issue exists. The trial court errs when it does not recognize that a fact issue exists. A fact issue exists when a party has introduced some evidence on an issue but has not proved it conclusively as a matter of law. Deciding if there is a fact issue is one of the most difficult issues for the trial court.

(a) Fact issue. When there is a fact issue, the trial court must submit the contested issue to the jury and cannot grant a motion for summary judgment, a motion for directed verdict, or a motion for judgment notwithstanding the verdict. *See* ***White v. Southwestern Bell Tel. Co.***, 651 S.W.2d 260, 262 (Tex.1983).

(b) No fact issue. When the facts on an issue are not in contest, they are established conclusively. Thus, there are no contested issues to submit to the jury, and the trial court should grant a motion for summary judgment, a motion for directed verdict, or a motion for judgment notwithstanding the verdict. *See* ***Massey v. Houston Baptist Univ.***, 902 S.W.2d 81, 83 (Tex.App.—Houston [1st Dist.] 1995, writ denied).

For example, assume fact A is important to the outcome of a case. Before the trial starts, there is no evidence of A. After the plaintiff begins presenting evidence on A, there is some evidence of that fact, perhaps somewhere between no evidence and a preponderance of the evidence. Once the plaintiff makes a good, solid case of fact A, the plaintiff crosses the line marking preponderance of the evidence and is headed toward the great weight of the evidence. If the plaintiff produces evidence of A that is indisputable, fact A has been proved as a matter of law.

The evidence of fact A went from one absolute (no evidence) through all the sufficiency stages to the other absolute (as a matter of law). When we graph the progress of fact A, it looks like this:

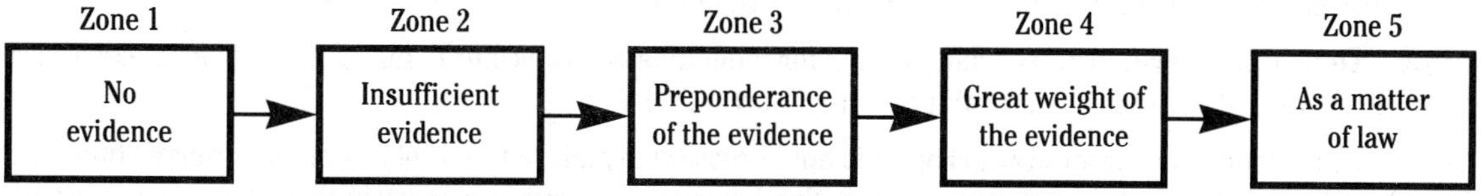

Think of the trial as a modified football game. A party scores in this game by taking the football, which represents the party's burden of proof on each one of its fact issues, beyond the 50-yard line, Zone 3. The party and its opponent face each other from opposite ends of the field, and both have the same objective: (1) take the ball as far as it can past the 50-yard line, and (2) prevent the opponent from carrying the ball past the 50-yard line. The farther the party carries the ball down the field, the stronger the party proves its case. Each party wants to establish all the facts it needs by the strongest evidence it can produce, and it wants to prevent its opponent from crossing the 50-yard line, Zone 3. If a party reaches its opponent's end zone, the party has proved an issue as a matter of law, Zone 5, and there is no longer a fact issue.

As the appellant, the party should think of the trial as a football game that it lost. Its objective on appeal is to convince the appellate court of two things: (1) it carried the ball farther than the jury believed, far beyond the 50-yard line, and (2) its opponent never made it to the 50-yard line, as the jury thought it did. The appellant wants to demonstrate to the appellate court that the jury misunderstood the sufficiency of the evidence.

3. Abuse of discretion. The most nebulous type of error, and the most difficult to reverse on appeal, is the trial court's abuse of discretion. A trial court abuses its discretion when it (1) renders an arbitrary and unreasonable decision, or (2) acts without reference to any guiding rules and principles. ***Walker***, 827 S.W.2d at 839(#1); ***Beaumont Bank v. Buller***, 806 S.W.2d 223, 226 (Tex.1991)(#2). A mere error in judgment is not an abuse of discretion. ***Loftin v. Martin***, 776 S.W.2d 145, 146 (Tex.1989). Appellate courts will not reverse the trial court simply because they disagree with the trial court; they will reverse only if they find the trial court acted in an unreasonable or arbitrary manner. See "Review of court's discretion," ch. 1-G, §5.2.3, p. 37.

§4. PRESERVING ERROR

Preserving error is governed by TRAP 33.1, an appellate rule.

§4.1 Make proper objection.
To make a proper objection, the party must do the following:

1. Assert valid complaint. The party must make a valid, timely, and specific request, motion, or objection. TRAP 33.1(a); TRE 103(a)(1); ***In re Bates***, 555 S.W.2d 420, 432 (Tex.1977); ***Till v. Thomas***, 10 S.W.3d 730, 734 (Tex.App.—Houston [1st Dist.] 1999, no pet.). If the party does not make an objection during trial, it cannot make the objection for the first time on appeal. ***City of Ft. Worth v. Zimlich***, 29 S.W.3d 62, 73 (Tex.2000); *see, e.g.*, ***Jones v. LaFargue***, 758 S.W.2d 320, 324 (Tex.App.—Houston [14th Dist.] 1988, writ denied) (complaint of defect in parties could not be made for first time on appeal). *But see* TRAP 33.1(d) (in nonjury case, complaint about legal or factual sufficiency of evidence may be made for first time on appeal). The complaint must comply with the TREs, TRCPs, or TRAPs. TRAP 33.1(a)(1)(B).

2. Properly support it. When necessary, the party must support its objection or motion with evidence. Many motions and some objections require that the party support them with evidence in the form of affidavits or sworn testimony. *See, e.g.*, ***Dillard Dept. Stores v. Hall***, 909 S.W.2d 491, 491-92 (Tex.1995) (when objecting to discovery request for all complaints filed within five-year period, Dillard filed affidavit that it had 227 stores).

3. Make it timely. The party must request relief within the time permitted by the rules and case law. TRAP 33.1(a)(1); *see, e.g.*, ***Zimlich***, 29 S.W.3d at 73 (City waived pleading error because it did not object before case submitted to jury); ***Vaughan v. Walther***, 875 S.W.2d 690, 690-91 (Tex.1994) (party waived disqualification of opposing counsel because she did not make objection as soon as conflict of interest became apparent); ***Bushell v. Dean***, 803 S.W.2d 711, 712 (Tex.1991) (party waived objection to testimony of witness by making objection before witness testified, instead of contemporaneously with testimony).

§4.2 Get ruling on record. The party asking for relief must get the court to make a ruling and make a record of the ruling. TRAP 33.1(a)(2). See "Rulings of the Court," ch. 1-G, p. 33.

§4.3 Exception – fundamental error. It is not necessary to make a timely objection to preserve "fundamental error," which is an extremely rare form of error. Fundamental error survives today in those rare instances where the record shows that the court lacked jurisdiction or that the public interest, as declared in the statutes or the Constitution of Texas, is directly and adversely affected. ***Pirtle v. Gregory***, 629 S.W.2d 919, 920 (Tex.1982).

§5. SUMMARY CHART FOR MOTIONS

Chart 1-2 summarizes some of the requirements for motions—when a motion must be in writing, when it must be verified, when affidavits should be attached, and what type of hearing should be requested. The last column indicates where in this book the motions are discussed.

1-2. SUMMARY CHART FOR MOTIONS

	MOTION	FILE WRITTEN MOTION	VERIFY MOTION	ATTACH AFFIDAVITS	HEARING FOR EVIDENCE OR ARGUMENT	CHAPTER & PAGE
1	Special appearance	yes	yes	yes	evidence	3-B, p. 143
2	Motion to transfer venue	yes	no	yes	argument	3-C, p. 152
3	Motion to change venue, local prejudice	yes	no	yes	uncertain	3-C, p. 161
4	Motion to transfer venue, Family Code	yes	no	yes	evidence	3-C, p. 164
5	Forum non conveniens	yes	yes	yes	argument	3-D, p. 165
6	Plea to the jurisdiction	yes	no	sometimes	either	3-F, p. 181
7	Special exceptions	yes	no	no	argument	3-G, p. 187
8	Motion to abate	yes	yes	yes	evidence	3-H, p. 194
9	Motion for continuance	yes	yes	yes	evidence	5-D, p. 242
10	Motion in limine	yes	no	no	argument	5-E, p. 252
11	Motion for sanctions	yes	yes	yes	evidence	5-J, p. 275
12	Motion for no-answer default judgment	not necessary	no	for damages	evidence for unliquidated damages	7-A, p. 443
13	Motion for summary judgment, TRCP 166a(a), (b)	yes	no	yes, in most cases	argument	7-B, p. 456
14	No-evidence motion for summary judgment, TRCP 166a(i)	yes	no	no	argument	7-C, p. 485
15	Motion for nonsuit	not necessary	no	no	neither	7-E, p. 493
16	Motion for JNOV	yes	no	no	argument	9-B, p. 591
17	Unsworn motion for new trial	yes	no	no	argument	10-B, p. 617
18	Sworn motion for new trial	yes	yes	yes	evidence	10-B, p. 617
19	Motion to reinstate after DWOP	yes	yes	yes	evidence	10-F, p. 649

G. RULINGS OF THE COURT

§1. GENERAL

§1.1 Rule. TRAP 33.1.

§1.2 Purpose. The purpose of a ruling is to announce the court's decision on a matter pending for resolution. The party seeking a ruling on a motion or objection must get the court to (1) make a ruling and (2) make a record of the ruling. TRAP 33.1(a)(2); *see* ***Greater Houston Transp. Co. v. Zrubeck***, 850 S.W.2d 579, 585 (Tex.App.—Corpus Christi 1993, writ denied).

§1.3 Forms. ***O'Connor's Texas Civil Forms***, FORM 1G:01.

§2. COURT'S RULING

§2.1 Judgment vs. order. A judgment is the documentation of the court's ruling that resolves the lawsuit. *See* ***Lindley v. Flores***, 672 S.W.2d 612, 614 (Tex.App.—Corpus Christi 1984, no writ). In contrast, an order is the documentation of the court's ruling that resolves a motion or objection. *See id.* If, however, an order resolves all the issues in a lawsuit, the order is a "judgment." *See* ***Stewart v. USA Custom Paint & Body Shop***, 870 S.W.2d 18, 20 (Tex.1994) (order of dismissal is a judgment). Judgments are discussed in "The Judgment," ch. 9-C, p. 595.

§2.2 Types of rulings. Under TRAP 33.1(a)(2), error is preserved by an express ruling, an implicit ruling, or a refusal to rule. TRAP 33.1 relaxed the requirement in former TRAP 52(a) for express rulings and codified case law recognizing implied rulings. ***Frazier v. Yu***, 987 S.W.2d 607, 610 (Tex.App.—Fort Worth 1999, pet. denied).

1. Express ruling. A party should attempt to secure an express ruling (*i.e.*, a ruling on the record, either in open court or in writing, that specifically states the court's ruling) on its motions, objections, or offers of evidence. *See* TRAP 33.1(a)(2)(A). If an express ruling is ambiguous, the party should ask the court to clarify it. When a ruling is susceptible to two constructions, the appellate court will adopt the construction that correctly applies the law. ***MacGregor v. Rich***, 941 S.W.2d 74, 75 (Tex.1997).

2. Implicit ruling. If the court does not make an express ruling but takes other action that implicitly overrules the motion or objection, error is preserved. *See* TRAP 33.1(a)(2)(A); ***In re Z.L.T.***, ___ S.W.3d ___ (Tex. 2003) (No. 02-0474; 11-21-03); *see, e.g.*, ***Chilkewitz v. Hyson***, 22 S.W.3d 825, 828 (Tex.1999) (by rendering judgment on verdict, court "impliedly" overruled motion for JNOV); ***Salinas v. Rafati***, 948 S.W.2d 286, 288 (Tex.1997) (ruling granting one party's motion, which was opposite of other party's motion, "automatically" denied other party's motion); ***Lopez v. Lopez***, 55 S.W.3d 194, 201 (Tex.App.—Corpus Christi 2001, no pet.) (ruling granting divorce implicitly overruled motion to reopen); ***Clemons v. Citizens Med. Ctr.***, 54 S.W.3d 463, 468 (Tex.App.—Corpus Christi 2001, no pet.) (order granting motion for summary judgment implicitly overruled request to continue summary judgment hearing); ***Amalgamated Acme Affiliates v. Minton***, 33 S.W.3d 387, 392 n.2 (Tex.App.—Austin 2000, no pet.) (constitutional arguments in motion to dissolve injunction were implicitly overruled when court refused to consider motion); ***Wal-Mart Stores v. Reece***, 32 S.W.3d 339, 347-48 (Tex.App.—Waco 2000) (D's objection to sidebar comments not preserved because court's response requesting parties abide by motion in limine was too indefinite to constitute an implicit ruling), *rev'd on other grounds*, 81 S.W.3d 812 (Tex.2002); ***Hardman v. Dault***, 2 S.W.3d 378, 381 (Tex.App.—San Antonio 1999, no pet.) (motion to strike nonjury setting preserved without express ruling). For the conflict between the courts of appeals on implicit rulings in summary judgment cases, see "Implicit ruling sufficient," ch. 7-B, §6.8.1, p. 472.

3. Refusal to rule + objection. If the trial court refuses to rule, the party must (1) object to the court's refusal to rule and (2) make sure all of the following appear in the appellate record: (a) the request for a ruling, (b) the court's refusal to rule, and (c) the objection to the court's refusal to rule. *See* TRAP 33.1(a)(2)(B), 33.2; *see, e.g.*, ***Upchurch v. Albear***, 5 S.W.3d 274, 286 (Tex.App.—Amarillo 1999, pet. denied) (record showed parties attempted to secure rulings on objections, but court refused to rule); ***O'Donnell v. Roger Bullivant, Inc.***, 940 S.W.2d 411, 416 (Tex.App.—Fort Worth 1997, writ denied) (because P objected to court's refusal to rule, error preserved), *overruled on other grounds*, ***Perry Homes v. Alwattari***, 33 S.W.3d 376 (Tex.App.—Fort Worth 2000, pet. denied). See "Offer of Proof & Bill of Exceptions," ch. 8-E, p. 553.

PRACTICE TIP

Another way to secure a ruling from an intransigent judge is to reurge the objection in a motion for new trial, along with an objection to the judge's refusal to rule. Even if the judge refuses to rule on the motion for new trial, the motion will be automatically overruled by operation of law. See TRCP 329b(c). See "Deadline to deny new trial," ch. 10-B, §8.4.2, p. 622; "Order denying new trial," ch. 10-B, §17.4, p. 636.

4. Nonruling.

(1) Ruling deferred. If the trial court says it will rule on the objection later or invites the party to reurge the objection later, the statement is not a ruling and does not preserve error. *See* ***Bushell v. Dean***, 803 S.W.2d 711, 712 (Tex.1991); ***TEIA v. Moore***, 284 S.W.2d 175, 178 (Tex.App.—Amarillo 1955, writ ref'd n.r.e.).

(2) No ruling. If the trial court does not rule on a motion or objection and no ruling can be implied (see §2.2.2, above), no error is preserved. *See, e.g.*, ***Goodchild v. Bombardier-Rotax GMBH***, 979 S.W.2d 1, 6-7 (Tex.App.—Houston [14th Dist.] 1998, pet. denied) (because P did not object to court's refusal to rule, error waived); ***Martin v. Uvalde S&L Ass'n***, 773 S.W.2d 808, 814 (Tex.App.—San Antonio 1989, no writ) (because D did not get ruling on motion to strike, error waived).

§2.3 Timing of ruling. A trial court is required to consider and rule on a motion or objection within a reasonable time. ***In re Kleven***, 100 S.W.3d 643, 644 (Tex.App.—Texarkana 2003, orig. proceeding); *see* ***Kissam v. Williamson***, 545 S.W.2d 265, 266-67 (Tex.App.—Tyler 1976, orig. proceeding) (mandamus will issue if trial court refuses to act within reasonable time). The trial court does not have the discretion to refuse to rule. ***Barnes v. State***, 832 S.W.2d 424, 426 (Tex.App.—Houston [1st Dist.] 1992, orig. proceeding). When a motion is pending before a trial court, the act of giving it consideration and ruling on it is a ministerial act, and mandamus may issue to compel the trial judge to act. ***Kleven***, 100 S.W.3d at 644; ***Safety-Kleen Corp. v. Garcia***, 945 S.W.2d 268, 270 (Tex.App.—San Antonio 1997, orig. proceeding); *see also* **Eli Lilly & Co. v. Marshall**, 829 S.W.2d 157, 158 (Tex.1992) (trial court abuses its discretion by refusing to conduct hearing and render decision on motion); ***Chiles v. Schuble***, 788 S.W.2d 205, 207 (Tex.App.—Houston [14th Dist.] 1990, orig. proceeding) (mandamus is appropriate to require trial judge to hold hearing and exercise discretion).

PRACTICE TIP

If, after the judgment is signed, you realize the court did not make a record of some ruling, you can ask the court to reduce the ruling to writing before its plenary power expires. ***Crocker v. Paulyne's Nursing Home****, 95 S.W.3d 416, 421 (Tex.App.—Dallas 2002, no pet.).*

§3. RECORD OF RULING

To be effective, all orders and rulings must be made on the record, either in writing or in open court transcribed by the court reporter. *See* TRAP 33.1(a)(2); ***State Farm Ins. Co. v. Pults***, 850 S.W.2d 691, 693 (Tex.App.—Corpus Christi 1993, no writ). The type of ruling required generally depends on the type of motion or objection. If the motion is in writing, the party should always ask the court to sign a written order. If the motion or objection is made orally during the trial, in most cases an oral ruling is sufficient.

§3.1 In writing.

1. Written order. The trial court should sign a written order that clearly reflects the ruling. *See* ***McAdams v. Capitol Prods.***, 810 S.W.2d 290, 292 (Tex.App.—Fort Worth 1991, writ denied) (court's notations on motion that sections were "or." or "sus." were not effective as rulings).

(1) Required by law. When the rules place a deadline on the court's jurisdiction to act on a matter, the court must make a written ruling; an oral ruling is not effective. ***Walker v. Harrison***, 597 S.W.2d 913, 915 (Tex.1980); *see, e.g.*, ***Faulkner v. Culver***, 851 S.W.2d 187, 188 (Tex.1993) (oral order granting new trial was ineffective); ***Emerald Oaks Hotel v. Zardenetta***, 776 S.W.2d 577, 578 (Tex.1989) (oral order reinstating case was ineffective); ***In re Montemayor***, 2 S.W.3d 542, 546 (Tex.App.—San Antonio 1999, orig. proceeding) (same); *see also* TRCP 165a(3) (order granting motion to reinstate must be in writing), TRCP 329b(c) (order granting new trial or modifying, correcting, or reforming judgment must be in writing).

(2) Not transcribed by reporter. When the trial court makes an oral ruling that the court reporter does not transcribe, the party must insist the judge sign a written order.

2. Signature. The trial judge should sign her name to her orders and judgments. However, the trial judge may direct a person who is under the judge's immediate authority to affix the judge's signature using a rubber stamp. ***In re Barber***, 982 S.W.2d 364, 366-67 (Tex.1998).

§3.2 In open court. When the trial court makes an oral ruling in open court that is transcribed by the court reporter, the statement of the court's ruling in the reporter's record preserves the ruling for appeal. ***Pride Pet. Servs. v. Criswell***, 924 S.W.2d 720, 721 (Tex.App.—El Paso 1996, writ denied) (construing former TRAP 52, now 33.1); *see* TRAP 33.2(b), (c); ***State Farm***, 850 S.W.2d at 693.

§3.3 Docket entries. A party should not rely on a docket entry as a ruling on a motion; a party should always get the trial court to sign an order. Docket entries are inherently unreliable. ***Guyot v. Guyot***, 3 S.W.3d 243, 246 (Tex.App.—Fort Worth 1999, no pet.); ***Energo Int'l Corp. v. Modern Indus. Heating***, 722 S.W.2d 149, 151 n.2 (Tex.App.—Dallas 1986, no writ). Most judges use their own shorthand for their rulings, and their docket notations are often unintelligible to others. In some cases, the clerk of the court makes the docket entries. *See* ***State Farm***, 850 S.W.2d at 693. The function of the docket sheet is limited to correcting clerical mistakes. *See* ***Energo***, 722 S.W.2d at 151 n.2.

1. Not an order. A docket entry cannot contradict or take the place of a written order or judgment. *See, e.g.*, ***Smith v. McCorkle***, 895 S.W.2d 692, 692 (Tex.1995) (docket entry indicating affidavit of indigence was denied was not effective as order); ***Faulkner***, 851 S.W.2d at 188 (docket entry granting new trial was not effective); ***Taack v. McFall***, 661 S.W.2d 923, 924 (Tex.1983) (docket entry & oral granting of motion for new trial were not effective); ***N-S-W Corp. v. Snell***, 561 S.W.2d 798, 799 (Tex.1977) (docket entry granting motion to reinstate could not contradict order); ***First Nat'l Bank v. Birnbaum***, 826 S.W.2d 189, 190 (Tex.App.—Austin 1992, no writ) (docket entry denying turnover relief was not order); ***Grant v. American Nat'l Ins. Co.***, 808 S.W.2d 181, 184 (Tex.App.—Houston [14th Dist.] 1991, no writ) (docket notation dismissing case was not appealable order); ***Miller v. Kendall***, 804 S.W.2d 933, 943-44 (Tex.App.—Houston [1st Dist.] 1990, no writ) (docket entry denying motion was not order & did not preserve error).

2. Supplement to order. The trial court's notation on the docket sheet can sometimes be used as evidence to support the trial court's testimony that judgment was orally rendered on a certain date. *See* Fam. Code §101.026 (rendition of judgment may be accomplished by docket notation for suits affecting parent-child relationship); *see, e.g.*, ***Dearing v. Johnson***, 947 S.W.2d 641, 643 (Tex.App.—Texarkana 1997, no writ) (judge's affidavit that he orally rendered judgment and docket sheet notation that "divorce granted" amounted to rendition of judgment); ***Oak Creek Homes v. Jones***, 758 S.W.2d 288, 290-91 (Tex.App.—Waco 1988, no writ) (judge's announcement that "I'll grant all the relief you've asked for" and docket notation of "default judgment," followed by judge's signature, amounted to rendition). See "Rendering, Signing, & Entering Judgment," ch. 9-C, §3, p. 596, for the distinction between rendition of judgment and the signing of a written judgment.

§3.4 Letters.

1. Not an order. A letter from the trial court announcing the ruling is not the equivalent of a signed order or judgment. *See* ***Goff v. Tuchscherer***, 627 S.W.2d 397, 398-99 (Tex.1982); *see, e.g.*, ***G.E. Capital Auto Fin. Leasing Servs. v. Stanfield***, 71 S.W.3d 351, 355-56 (Tex.App.—Tyler 2001, no pet.) (circumstances surrounding letter announcing default judgment indicated letter not intended as judgment); *see also* ***In re Fuentes***, 960 S.W.2d 261, 264-65 (Tex.App.—Corpus Christi 1997, orig. proceeding) (letter granting new trial was not valid because it was not filed with clerk); ***Hailey v. KTBS, Inc.***, 935 S.W.2d 857, 859 (Tex.App.—Texarkana 1996, no writ) (letter outlining some of grounds on which court based its order was not part of order); ***Ex parte Gnesoulis***, 525 S.W.2d 205, 209 (Tex.App.—Houston [14th Dist.] 1975, orig. proceeding) (letter to parties was not rendition because it was not filed with clerk).

2. Letter = order. In a few cases, a letter has been held to be the equivalent of a signed order or judgment. *See, e.g.*, ***Shubert v. J.C. Penney Co.***, 956 S.W.2d 634, 635 n.4 (Tex.App.—Texarkana 1997, pet. denied) (letter granting venue transfer was valid as order because it contained language of command), *overruled on other grounds*, ***Surgitek v. Abel***, 997 S.W.2d 598 (Tex.1999); ***Schaeffer Homes v. Esterak***, 792 S.W.2d 567, 569 (Tex.App.—El Paso 1990, no writ) (filed letter stating new trial "is" granted complied with requisites of formal decision); ***Abarca v. Roadstar Corp.***, 647 S.W.2d 327, 327-28 (Tex.App.—Corpus Christi 1982, no writ) (filed letter announcing ruling on motion for summary judgment and asking parties to prepare the judgment was rendition of judgment).

§4. ORDER

§4.1 Form of order. See *O'Connor's* FORM 1G:01. When a party submits an order to the trial court, the order should contain the following items:

1. Party names. The order should contain the full names of the parties. TRCP 306.

2. Identification of motion. The order should identify the motion, the party that made the motion, whether the court held a hearing, and whether the hearing was for the receipt of evidence or merely argument by the lawyers.

3. Ruling. The order should resolve the issues presented by the motion.

4. Findings. Some rules require findings to be included in the order. *E.g.*, TRCP 13 (order must contain findings of good cause for sanctions). Other rules prohibit findings from being included in the order or judgment. *E.g.,* TRCP 299a (findings of fact cannot be included in the judgment).

5. Costs. Some rules permit the trial court to award costs as part of the relief granted on a motion. *E.g.*, TRCP 138 (trial court can tax costs against the party granted the new trial).

6. Date. The order should include a line that reads, "Signed on _________, 200__," which appears immediately above the signature line for the trial court. The Supreme Court has asked authors of legal form books to tell lawyers to draft orders and judgments that say "signed" on a certain date, not rendered or entered. ***Burrell v. Cornelius***, 570 S.W.2d 382, 384 (Tex.1978).

7. Signature line for judge. The order must contain a signature line for the trial judge.

8. Signature line for lawyers. Traditionally, the order contains signature lines for the lawyers to approve the form of the order. Approving the form of the order does not waive complaints about the ruling in the order. See "Signature line for lawyers," ch. 9-C, §4.13, p. 601.

9. Certificate of service. If the order is not signed by both lawyers (see §4.1.8, above), it must contain a certificate of service. *See* TRCP 21 & 21a (all documents must contain certificate of service unless filed during open court). If the order was served on the other party with a motion or response, it is not necessary for the order to have a separate certificate of service. However, the certificate of service on the motion or response must list the order as one of the documents served on the other party. See "Certificate of service," ch. 1-B, §4.16, p. 9.

§4.2 Changing the order. For the time limits for changing orders, see "Power to Change Judgment," ch. 9-C, §7, p. 608, and "Deadline to sign order on MNT," ch. 10-B, §8.4, p. 622.

§5. REVIEW

§5.1 Challenging the ruling. There are three ways to challenge a ruling of the trial court.

1. Appeal after final judgment. Most rulings are challenged after the trial court renders a final judgment. See ***O'Connor's Texas Civil Appeals***, "Appealing from a final judgment," ch. 11-B, §2.1, p. 4 (2002-03).

2. Interlocutory appeal. The only orders that can be challenged before the rendition of a final judgment are those that are interlocutory by statute or subject to a successful motion for interlocutory appeal. See ***O'Connor's Texas Civil Appeals***, "Motion for Interlocutory Appeal & Stay of Trial," ch. 13-P, p. 131.

3. Mandamus. Any ruling that cannot be reviewed by either an appeal after final judgment or an interlocutory appeal can be challenged by mandamus. See ***O'Connor's Texas Civil Appeals***, "Writ of Mandamus," ch. 20-B, p. 280.

§5.2 Standards of review.

1. Review of legal issues. Legal issues are reviewed de novo, without any deference to the trial court's decision. ***Trinity Indus. v. Ashland, Inc.***, 53 S.W.3d 852, 868 (Tex.App.—Austin 2001, pet. denied). The trial court has no discretion to decide what the law is or how to apply it to the facts. ***Walker v. Packer***, 827 S.W.2d 833, 840 (Tex.1992).

2. Review of fact issues. Appellate courts will defer to the trial court's discretionary rulings when reviewing issues of fact. *See* ***Walker***, 827 S.W.2d at 839-40; ***Williams v. Chisolm***, 111 S.W.3d 811, 815 (Tex.App.—Houston [1st Dist.] 2003, n.p.h.). The appellate court cannot substitute its judgment for that of the trial court. ***Walker***, 827 S.W.2d at 839. See "MNT to Challenge the Evidence," ch. 10-B, §9, p. 623; ***O'Connor's Texas Civil Appeals***, "Fact-finder error," ch. 11-F, §5.2, p. 33.

3. Review of court's discretion. When the ruling was one within the trial court's discretion, the inquiry on appeal is (1) did the trial court have sufficient information to exercise its discretion; and if it did, (2) did the trial court err in its application of discretion. ***Heritage Res. v. Hill***, 104 S.W.3d 612, 618 (Tex.App.—El Paso 2003, no pet.). Appellate courts will not reverse the trial court simply because they disagree with the trial court; they will reverse only if they find the trial court acted in an unreasonable or arbitrary manner. ***Beaumont Bank v. Buller***, 806 S.W.2d 223, 226 (Tex.1991).

H. THE LAWYER

§1. GENERAL

§1.1 Rules. TRCP 7-14. See Gov't Code §81.102 (requirement of state bar membership).

§1.2 Purpose. A party has the right to be represented by counsel of choice. ***Spinks v. Brown***, 103 S.W.3d 452, 459 (Tex.App.—San Antonio 2002, pet. denied); *see* TRCP 7. Unless there is a compelling reason, courts should not deprive litigants of this right. ***Keller Indus. v. Blanton***, 804 S.W.2d 182, 185 (Tex.App.—Houston [14th Dist.] 1991, orig. proceeding).

§1.3 Forms. ***O'Connor's Texas Civil Forms***, FORMS 1H.

§1.4 Other references. ***O'Connor's Texas Causes of Action***, "Attorney Fees," ch. 38, p. 1041 (2004) (***O'Connor's COA***).

§2. APPEARING BEFORE TEXAS COURTS

§2.1 Requirements. To practice law in Texas state courts, a lawyer must be a member of the State Bar of Texas, which is governed by the State Bar Act and administratively controlled by the Texas Supreme Court. Gov't Code §81.102; ***Jimison v. Mann***, 957 S.W.2d 860, 861 (Tex.App.—Amarillo 1997, no writ); ***Daves v. State Bar***, 691 S.W.2d 784, 786 (Tex.App.—Amarillo 1985, writ ref'd n.r.e.). The Board of Law Examiners, appointed by the

Supreme Court, is empowered to investigate the fitness and moral character of each license applicant. Gov't Code §82.028(a); *see id.* §82.001; ***Board of Law Exam'rs v. Stevens***, 868 S.W.2d 773, 776 (Tex.1994).

§2.2 Limited practice of law. The Supreme Court has the authority to make rules prescribing the procedure for limited practice of law by lawyers licensed in another jurisdiction, law students, and unlicensed graduate students who are attending or have attended a law school approved by the Supreme Court. Gov't Code §81.102(b); *see id.* §82.036.

1. Out-of-state attorneys.

(1) Definition. A nonresident attorney is a person who resides in and is licensed to practice law in a state other than Texas and is not a member of the State Bar of Texas. Gov't Code §82.0361(a).

(2) Appearance in Texas court. A nonresident attorney may apply for permission to appear in a Texas state court by a sworn motion requesting admission to the court "pro hac vice," which means "for this one particular occasion." *See* ***Keller Indus.***, 804 S.W.2d at 184; ***Commercial Credit & Control Data Corp. v. Wheeler***, 756 S.W.2d 769, 770-71 (Tex.App.—Corpus Christi 1988, writ denied). The procedure is governed by the Rules Governing Admission to the Bar of Texas, Rule XIX, "Requirements for Participation in Texas Proceedings by a Non-Resident Attorney." See ***O'Connor's CPRC Plus***, p. 891 (2003-04). The nonresident attorney must file two motions. ***O'Connor's*** FORMS 1H:02-03.

(a) Motion by nonresident attorney. The nonresident attorney must state under oath that she (1) will be associated in the trial with a resident, practicing lawyer who is a member of the State Bar of Texas; (2) is a member in good standing of the bar of her state and has not been the subject of disciplinary action by the bar or courts during the last five years; (3) has not been denied admission to the courts of any state or to any federal court during the last five years; and (4) is familiar with the rules of the State Bar of Texas governing the conduct of its members and will comply with those rules as long as the trial or hearing is pending. Tex. R. Govern. Bar Adm'n XIX(a); ***Keller Indus.***, 804 S.W.2d at 184.

(b) Motion by Texas attorney. The Texas attorney must state under oath that she (1) is associated with the nonresident attorney on this case, is employed as an attorney on the case, and will personally participate in the hearings and trial; (2) is a practicing attorney and a member in good standing of the State Bar of Texas; and (3) finds the nonresident attorney to be a reputable attorney and recommends the nonresident attorney be permitted to practice in this proceeding before the court. Tex. R. Govern. Bar Adm'n XIX(b).

03 **(3) Fees.** A nonresident attorney requesting permission to appear in a Texas state court must pay a $250 fee for each case in which the attorney is requesting to participate. Gov't Code §82.0361(b). The nonresident attorney must pay the fee to the Board of Law Examiners before filing the pro hac vice motion and must provide proof of payment to the court in which the attorney is requesting to participate. *Id.* §82.0361(b), (f). The fee may be waived or reduced for a nonresident attorney who represents an indigent. *Id.* §82.0361(e).

2. Law students & unlicensed law graduates. Under Gov't Code §81.102(b) and the Rules Governing Participation of Qualified Law Students and Qualified Unlicensed Law School Graduates, law students and unlicensed law school graduates have a limited ability to participate in the practice of law. See ***O'Connor's*** FORM 1H:04.

§2.3 Pro se representation.

1. Individual. An individual litigant has the right to represent herself without a lawyer. TRCP 7; ***Ayres v. Canales***, 790 S.W.2d 554, 557 (Tex.1990); ***Thomas v. Anderson***, 861 S.W.2d 58, 61 n.1 (Tex.App.—El Paso 1993, no writ); ***Nichols v. Martin***, 776 S.W.2d 621, 623 (Tex.App.—Tyler 1989, no writ). A court cannot deny a party the right to self-representation, nor can it order a party to be represented by a lawyer unless the lack of an attorney is used to abuse the continuance privilege. ***Ex parte Shaffer***, 649 S.W.2d 300, 302 (Tex.1983). A party acting pro se must comply with substantive law and procedural rules. ***In re Caldwell***, 918 S.W.2d 9, 10 (Tex.App.—Amarillo 1995, order on mot.). A party represented by an attorney cannot also proceed pro se. ***Posner v. Dallas Cty. Child Welfare Unit***, 784 S.W.2d 585, 588 (Tex.App.—Eastland 1990, writ denied). A person unlicensed as a lawyer cannot represent another person as "next friend" under TRCP 44. ***Jimison v. Mann***, 957 S.W.2d 860, 861 (Tex.App.—Amarillo 1997, no writ).

2. Corporation. A corporation cannot represent itself pro se by an officer who is not a lawyer. ***Kunstoplast, Inc. v. Formosa Plastics Corp.***, 937 S.W.2d 455, 456 (Tex.1996); ***Dell Dev. Corp. v. Best Indus. Uniform Sup. Co.***, 743 S.W.2d 302, 303 (Tex.App.—Houston [14th Dist.] 1987, writ denied). A corporation must appear and be represented by a lawyer. ***Electronic Data Sys. v. Tyson***, 862 S.W.2d 728, 737 (Tex.App.—Dallas 1993, orig. proceeding). The one exception is that a corporation may represent itself pro se in a small-claims court. Gov't Code §28.003(e).

3. Unincorporated business. A business entity that is not incorporated (*e.g.*, a sole proprietorship or partnership) may represent itself pro se by an owner who is not a lawyer. *See* ***Holberg & Co. v. Citizens Nat'l Assur. Co.***, 856 S.W.2d 515, 518 (Tex.App.—Houston [1st Dist.] 1993, no writ) (unincorporated sole proprietorship has no existence apart from its owner).

§3. DESIGNATION OF ATTORNEYS

§3.1 Attorney in charge. The lawyer whose signature appears first on a party's first pleading is the "attorney in charge," unless another lawyer is specifically designated. TRCP 8; ***Joyner v. Commission For Lawyer Discipline***, 102 S.W.3d 344, 347 (Tex.App.—Dallas 2003, no pet.); ***Dreisbach v. Reed***, 780 S.W.2d 901, 902-03 (Tex. App.—El Paso 1989, no writ). The attorney in charge, also called lead counsel, is responsible for the lawsuit. TRCP 8, 21; ***Palmer v. Cantrell***, 747 S.W.2d 39, 41 (Tex.App.—Houston [1st Dist.] 1988, no writ); *see, e.g.*, ***Reichhold Chems. v. Puremco Mfg. Co.***, 854 S.W.2d 240, 246 (Tex.App.—Waco 1993, writ denied) (service on co-counsel to attorney in charge was not effective). Only three rules of procedure refer to the attorney in charge: TRCP 8, 10, and 21. All communications from the court or other counsel must be sent to the attorney in charge. See "Lawyer," §6.2.1, p. 41.

§3.2 Attorneys of record. The attorneys of record are all the attorneys who have made an appearance in the case or whose names appear in the pleadings, including the attorney in charge. Thirteen rules of procedure refer to the attorney of record: TRCP 21a, 44, 57, 119a, 130, 165a, 176.6, 306a, 315, 572, 655, 749a, and 791.

NOTE

There is a difference between "attorney in charge" and "attorney of record." While there can be only one attorney in charge for each party, a party may be represented by many attorneys of record. See TRCP 21a.

---

§4. AUTHORITY OF LAWYER

§4.1 Representing an individual. A party must authorize a lawyer to bring suit. *See* TRCP 12; ***Vela v. Vela***, 763 S.W.2d 601, 602 (Tex.App.—San Antonio 1988, writ denied).

§4.2 Representing a corporation. A corporation must authorize the hiring of a lawyer through its board of directors. ***Square 67 Dev. Corp. v. Red Oak State Bank***, 559 S.W.2d 136, 138 (Tex.App.—Waco 1977, writ ref'd n.r.e.). Unless permitted by the bylaws or a director's resolution, the president has no authority to conduct litigation for the corporation. ***Kaspar v. Thorne***, 755 S.W.2d 151, 154 (Tex.App.—Dallas 1988, no writ); ***Valley Int'l Props. v. Brownsville S&L Ass'n***, 581 S.W.2d 222, 227 (Tex.App.—Corpus Christi 1979, no writ); *see* Bus. Corp. Act arts. 2.31, 2.42.

§4.3 Representing other entities. The authority to represent other business entities (*e.g.*, joint ventures) depends largely on the agreements that formed the entity. *See* ***Miller v. Stout***, 706 S.W.2d 785, 787 (Tex.App.—San Antonio 1986, no writ) (joint venture agreement did not require all members to approve filing of suit).

§4.4 Representing a municipal corporation. A city attorney has the authority to represent the city. ***City of San Antonio v. Aguilar***, 670 S.W.2d 681, 684 (Tex.App.—San Antonio 1984, writ dism'd).

§4.5 Challenging authority. To challenge the authority of a lawyer to represent the other party, see "Disqualification," §8, p. 42.

§5. COMMUNICATIONS WITH THE COURT

§5.1 No ex parte communications. Ex parte communications with the judge are those that involve fewer than all of the parties. ***In re Thoma***, 873 S.W.2d 477, 496 (Tex.Rev.Trib.1994). A judge cannot directly or indirectly initiate, permit, or consider ex parte or other private communications concerning the merits of a pending or impending judicial proceeding, except in limited circumstances. Code Jud. Conduct, Canon 3(B)(8); ***U.S. Gov't v. Marks***, 949 S.W.2d 320, 325 (Tex.1997); ***Barnes v. Whittington***, 751 S.W.2d 493, 495 n.1 (Tex.1988); ***Thoma***, 873 S.W.2d at 496. A judge cannot conduct private proceedings involving the adjudication of causes. ***Thoma***, 873 S.W.2d at 496. The prohibition regarding communications about the merits of the case extends to communications with the court's staff. *See, e.g.*, ***In re J.B.K.***, 931 S.W.2d 581, 584 (Tex.App.—El Paso 1996, op. on order) (lawyer should not have asked staff person what the chances were and if he should settle case).

§5.2 Lawyer's appearance before court. An attorney's unsworn statements are not evidence. ***Marks***, 949 S.W.2d at 326-27. However, on appeal, a lawyer's unsworn statement can be considered evidence if the other side did not object at trial. ***Banda v. Garcia***, 955 S.W.2d 270, 272 (Tex.1997). Texas Disciplinary Rule of Professional Conduct 3.03 forbids a lawyer from making false statements of material fact or law to a tribunal.

1. To argue. It is not necessary for the lawyer to be sworn when the lawyer is merely arguing the facts or the law.

2. To present evidence. An attorney's statement of fact must be under oath to be considered as evidence. ***Banda***, 955 S.W.2d at 272; *see, e.g.*, ***Casino Magic Corp. v. King***, 43 S.W.3d 14, 20 (Tex.App.—Dallas 2001, pet. denied) (in garnishment action, attorney's unsworn statement that D was former husband's employer and thus liable for failing to withhold child support was not evidence). *But see* ***Goode v. Shoukfeh***, 943 S.W.2d 441, 451 (Tex.1997) (counsel may explain reason for exercising peremptory challenge against panelist without being put under oath).

(1) Objection to lack of oath. When a lawyer who is not under oath presents facts to the court, the other party should object and ask that the lawyer be sworn and subjected to cross-examination. ***Banda***, 955 S.W.2d at 272.

(2) Waiver of oath. When the other party is aware the lawyer is testifying and does not object, the administration of the oath is waived. ***Banda***, 955 S.W.2d at 272; ***Knie v. Piskun***, 23 S.W.3d 455, 463 (Tex.App.—Amarillo 2000, pet. denied); *see* ***Fullenwider v. American Guar. & Liab. Ins. Co.***, 821 S.W.2d 658, 662 (Tex.App.—San Antonio 1991, writ denied) (when issue was timely supplementation of interrogatory answers, lawyer's statements were clearly regarded as evidence). However, if the other party is not in the position to object (*e.g.*, in a default judgment case), the administration of the oath is not waived. *See* ***De La Garza v. Salazar***, 851 S.W.2d 380, 383 (Tex.App.—San Antonio 1993, no writ).

§6. COMMUNICATIONS FROM THE COURT

§6.1 Service of notice.

1. Most notices. Notices must be given by one of the following methods: (1) by delivery to the person, (2) by courier with receipted delivery, (3) by certified or registered mail, (4) by fax, or (5) as directed by court order. TRCP 21a; *see, e.g.*, ***DePue v. Henderson***, 801 S.W.2d 178, 179 (Tex.App.—Houston [14th Dist.] 1990, no writ) (notice of filing fee sent by regular mail did not meet requirements of TRCP 21a).

2. Exceptions. Some rules permit notices to be sent by regular, first-class mail. *E.g.*, TRCP 165a(1) (clerk must mail notice of intent to dismiss & must send notice of dismissal according to TRCP 306a(3)), TRCP 239a (clerk must mail notice of default judgment), TRCP 306a(3) (clerk must use first-class mail to send notice of judgment).

§6.2 Sent to lawyer or party.

1. Lawyer. When a party is represented by a lawyer, the notice must be sent to the lawyer. *See* TRCP 21a. If the party is represented by more than one lawyer, most notices must be sent to the attorney in charge. *See* TRCP 8 (all communications must be sent to attorney in charge), TRCP 21 (copy of pleadings must be sent to attorney in charge); ***Loffland Bros. v. Downey***, 822 S.W.2d 249, 251 (Tex.App.—Houston [1st Dist.] 1991, orig. proceeding) (all communications must be sent to attorney in charge). Two rules require notices to be sent to *all attorneys of record*, not just the attorney in charge: TRCP 165a, notice of dismissal, and TRCP 306a, notice of signing of a final judgment or appealable order. ***Cannon v. ICO Tubular Servs.***, 905 S.W.2d 380, 388 (Tex.App.—Houston [1st Dist.] 1995, no writ).

2. Party. When a party is pro se, the notice must be sent to the party. *See* TRCP 21a; ***G.E. Co. v. Falcon Ridge Apts.***, 811 S.W.2d 942, 943 (Tex.1991) (notice to dismiss).

§6.3 Address. The lawyer's address (or party's, if pro se) must be included in the signature block to all pleadings and discovery. See "Signature block," ch. 1-B, §4.12, p. 6. The rules do not state how the clerk or other parties are to determine the lawyer's or party's current address. *See* TRCP 21, 21a.

1. Attorney's address. One court has interpreted TRCP 165a(1) as requiring notices of intent to dismiss to be sent to the attorney's address shown on the docket or the pleadings on file with the court. *See* ***Osterloh v. Ohio Decorative Prods.***, 881 S.W.2d 580, 582 (Tex.App.—Houston [1st Dist.] 1994, no writ) (clerk could not use register of attorneys' addresses for purposes of dismissal notices); *see, e.g.*, ***Dickerson v. Sonat Expl. Co.***, 975 S.W.2d 339, 341-42 (Tex.App.—Tyler 1998, pet. denied) (dismissal reversed because court sent notice to attorney's previous address; letters in court's file had current address).

2. Party's address. Notices to pro se parties must be sent to their "last known address." TRCP 21a. Under CPRC §30.015, a party's current address must be provided to the court. See "Notice of party's name & address," ch. 1-B, §4.17, p. 10.

§7. WITHDRAWAL

The parties must give the trial court specific and unambiguous notice when an attorney withdraws or is substituted. ***Palkovic v. Cox***, 792 S.W.2d 743, 745 (Tex.App.—Houston [14th Dist.] 1990, writ denied) (signing amended petition is not a substitution of counsel).

§7.1 Termination by client. A client may discharge its lawyer at any time, even without cause. ***Rogers v. Clinton***, 794 S.W.2d 9, 10 n.1 (Tex.1990). Once a lawyer is discharged, the lawyer must withdraw from the case and cannot continue to appear or file motions for the party. *See, e.g.*, ***Bloom v. Graham***, 825 S.W.2d 244, 248 (Tex. App.—Fort Worth 1992, writ denied) (lawyer sanctioned under TRCP 13 for filing groundless pleadings because he filed motions after discharge).

§7.2 Termination by lawyer. A lawyer cannot withdraw from a case without satisfying the requirements of TRCP 10. ***Rogers***, 794 S.W.2d at 10 n.1; ***Moss v. Malone***, 880 S.W.2d 45, 49-50 (Tex.App.—Tyler 1994, writ denied). To withdraw, the lawyer must file a written motion showing good cause. TRCP 10. See ***O'Connor's*** FORM 1H:05.

1. Substitute lawyer. If another lawyer is to be substituted, the motion must state (1) the identity of the new lawyer (name, address, telephone and fax numbers, and State Bar of Texas number), (2) that the client approves of the substitution, and (3) that the withdrawal is not for delay only. TRCP 10; *see* ***Spinks v. Brown***, 103 S.W.3d 452, 459-60 (Tex.App.—San Antonio 2002, pet. denied).

2. No substitute lawyer. If no lawyer is to be substituted, the motion must state (1) that a copy of the motion was delivered to the client, (2) that the client was notified in writing of its right to object to the motion, (3) whether the client consents to the motion, (4) the client's last known address, and (5) all pending settings and deadlines. TRCP 10; ***Moss***, 880 S.W.2d at 49. *But see* ***Williams v. Bank One***, 15 S.W.3d 110, 113-14 (Tex.App.—Waco 1999, no pet.) (lawyer's failure to inform client of right to object was harmless when court gave party additional 42 days to hire new counsel).

§8. DISQUALIFICATION

Because the disqualification of a party's attorney is a severe remedy, the courts must adhere to exacting standards when considering motions to disqualify. ***In re Nitla***, 92 S.W.3d 419, 422 (Tex.2002); ***Spears v. 4th Ct. of Appeals***, 797 S.W.2d 654, 656 (Tex.1990).

§8.1 Timely-filed motion. A motion to disqualify a lawyer must be timely filed. ***In re George***, 28 S.W.3d 511, 513 (Tex.2000); *see, e.g.*, ***In re American Home Prods.***, 985 S.W.2d 68, 73 (Tex.1998) (2-month delay did not constitute waiver); ***Vaughan v. Walther***, 875 S.W.2d 690, 691 (Tex.1994) (6-month delay was too long).

§8.2 Grounds to disqualify.

1. Violation of disciplinary rules. Although the Texas Disciplinary Rules of Professional Conduct do not control the standards governing motions to disqualify, they are considered guidelines. ***Nitla***, 92 S.W.3d at 422; ***In re Users Sys. Servs.***, 22 S.W.3d 331, 334 (Tex.1999); ***In re Meador***, 968 S.W.2d 346, 350 (Tex.1998); ***Spears***, 797 S.W.2d at 656; *see* Wise, *The Lawyer-Witness Rule*, 31 S.Tex.L.Rev. 651, 663 (1990) (disciplinary rules allow client to determine disqualification in many situations). When moving to disqualify based on a disciplinary rule, the movant must show actual prejudice requiring disqualification. ***Nitla***, 92 S.W.3d at 422.

2. Lawyer represented other party. To determine whether a lawyer or firm should be disqualified for having represented the adverse party in an earlier suit, the court must decide if the two suits are "substantially related." ***Metropolitan Life Ins. Co. v. Syntek Fin. Corp.***, 881 S.W.2d 319, 320 (Tex.1994); ***NCNB Tex. Nat'l Bank v. Coker***, 765 S.W.2d 398, 399-400 (Tex.1989); *see* ***Ghidoni v. Stone Oak, Inc.***, 966 S.W.2d 573, 578-80 (Tex. App.—San Antonio 1998, pet. denied) (disqualification may be based on a single preliminary consultation); *see also* Tex. Disc. R. Prof. Conduct 1.06-1.10 (conflict of interest). To satisfy the substantial relationship test, the movant must prove the facts of the previous representation are so related to those in the pending litigation that there is a genuine threat the confidences revealed to former counsel will be divulged to a present adversary. ***Metropolitan Life***, 881 S.W.2d at 320-21; ***Coker***, 765 S.W.2d at 400.

(1) Partner. A firm must be disqualified if a partner of the firm worked for another firm representing an opposing party in a substantially related matter. ***Texaco, Inc. v. Garcia***, 891 S.W.2d 255, 257 (Tex.1995) (later case involved similar liability, scientific theories, defenses, and strategies); *see also* Tex. Disc. R. Prof. Conduct 1.09(a)(3) (same or substantially related matter), 1.09(b) (conflict of interest as member of law firm). A firm must be disqualified if a partner worked on a matter for joint clients, and the matter is subject to dispute in later litigation between the clients. ***In re Taylor***, 67 S.W.3d 530, 533-34 (Tex.App.—Waco 2002, orig. proceeding).

(2) Associate. A firm must be disqualified if an associate of the firm personally represented an opposing party in a substantially related matter. Tex. Disc. R. Prof. Conduct 1.09(a)(3), (b); ***Henderson v. Floyd***, 891 S.W.2d 252, 253-54 (Tex.1995). An associate personally represents a party if the associate is exposed to the client's case and confidential information. ***Henderson***, 891 S.W.2d at 254.

(3) Nonlawyer employee. A firm must be disqualified if a nonlawyer employee presently working on the lawsuit had previously worked on the same suit at another firm representing the opposing party. ***American Home Prods.***, 985 S.W.2d at 74; *see* ***Grant v. 13th Ct. of Appeals***, 888 S.W.2d 466, 467-68 (Tex.1994). If the law firm screens the employee from any contact with the lawsuit, disqualification is not required. ***Phoenix Founders v. Marshall***, 887 S.W.2d 831, 834 (Tex.1994) (paralegal); ***Rubin v. Enns***, 23 S.W.3d 382, 384 (Tex.App.—Amarillo 2000, orig. proceeding) (same); ***Arzate v. Hayes***, 915 S.W.2d 616, 620 (Tex.App.—El Paso 1996, writ dism'd) (same).

3. Lawyer participated in joint representation. In a multiparty case in which a group of parties conduct a joint defense, the lawyers cannot later represent parties who are adverse to any of the parties who participated in the joint defense. *See* ***National Med. Enters. v. Godbey***, 924 S.W.2d 123, 131 (Tex.1996); ***In re Skiles***, 102 S.W.3d 323, 327 (Tex.App.—Beaumont 2003, orig. proceeding). For example, if a lawyer represents defendant D1 in a suit against D1, D2, and D3 where the defendants shared information about their joint defense, that lawyer cannot later represent a plaintiff against D2 or D3 in a suit substantially related to the earlier suit. The disqualification could extend to the lawyer's firm, even if the lawyer does not work on the later suit. ***National Med. Enters.***, 924 S.W.2d at 131; *see also* TRE 503(b)(1)(C) (common-defense privilege).

4. Lawyer received privileged materials. When a lawyer receives an opponent's privileged materials, the lawyer can be disqualified from continuing to represent the client. ***Nitla***, 92 S.W.3d at 422-23; ***In re Meador***, 968 S.W.2d 346, 351 (Tex.1998).

(1) Outside discovery process. When a lawyer receives privileged material outside the normal discovery process, the lawyer may be disqualified, based on the following factors: (1) whether the attorney knew or should have known the material was privileged, (2) the promptness with which the attorney notified opposing counsel, (3) the extent to which the attorney reviewed and digested the information, (4) the significance of the privileged information, (5) the extent to which the movant may be at fault, and (6) the extent to which the nonmovant will suffer prejudice from the disqualification. ***Meador***, 968 S.W.2d at 351-52.

(2) Through discovery process. When a lawyer receives privileged material through the normal discovery process (*e.g.*, from the trial court after in camera review), the movant seeking to disqualify the lawyer must show the following: (1) the lawyer's review of the privileged material caused the movant actual harm, and (2) the lawyer's disqualification is necessary because there are no lesser means to remedy the harm. ***Nitla***, 92 S.W.3d at 423.

5. Lawyer as witness.

(1) Fact witness. When a lawyer foresees the possibility she will be called to testify about a disputed fact issue (not attorney fees), the lawyer should resolve all doubts in favor of preserving the integrity of the evidence and decide against continued participation as trial counsel. ***Warrilow v. Norrell***, 791 S.W.2d 515, 523 n.10 (Tex.App.—Corpus Christi 1989, writ denied); *see* Tex. Disc. R. Prof. Conduct 3.08. Lead counsel who will testify about an essential element of the case should be disqualified from serving as trial counsel if the dual role as advocate-witness would prevent the jury from properly evaluating the case on the merits. ***In re Bahn***, 13 S.W.3d 865, 874 (Tex.App.—Fort Worth 2000, orig. proceeding); *see* ***In re Anchor, Inc.***, ___ S.W.3d ___ (Tex.App.—Houston [14th Dist.] 2002, orig. proceeding) (No. 14-02-00760-CV; 9-27-02) (court required proof of prejudice when attorney acted as advocate-witness).

(2) Expert witness. An attorney who will testify as an expert witness is not disqualified from serving as an attorney in the same case as long as her participation is limited to out-of-court matters relating to preparing and signing pleadings, planning strategy, and settlement negotiations. ***Anderson Prod'g v. Koch Oil Co.***, 929 S.W.2d 416, 422 (Tex.1996); ***Bahn***, 13 S.W.3d at 875. Another lawyer in the expert lawyer's firm may act as trial counsel if the client gives informed consent. ***Anderson***, 929 S.W.2d at 424; *see* ***Bahn***, 13 S.W.3d at 875-76.

PRACTICE TIP

Even though an attorney can testify as an expert in the case in which she is involved, it is not a good idea. Everything an expert reviews is subject to discovery. See "Securing Discovery from Experts," ch. 6-C, p. 363. The attorney-client privilege will probably shield some of the information the expert-attorney reviewed, but other information may need to be turned over to the opposing party.

---

6. Lawyer not authorized. If a party believes that a suit is being prosecuted or defended without authority, the party should challenge the authority of the lawyer under TRCP 12. The rules require the party to file a sworn motion, before the parties announce ready for trial, alleging the suit is being prosecuted or defended without authority of the party. TRCP 12. The challenged lawyer is entitled to ten days' notice before the hearing. *Id.* At the hearing, the burden is on the challenged lawyer to show sufficient authority to prosecute or defend the suit on behalf of the party. *Id.*; ***City of San Antonio v. Aguilar***, 670 S.W.2d 681, 684 (Tex.App.—San Antonio 1984, writ dism'd). The testimony of the challenged lawyer is sufficient to support a ruling that the lawyer has the authority to represent the party. ***McCarthy v. George***, 623 S.W.2d 772, 775 (Tex.App.—Fort Worth 1981, writ ref'd n.r.e.). See ***O'Connor's*** FORM 1H:07.

§8.3 Disqualified lawyer's file. When an attorney is disqualified, the successor lawyer will want access to two types of information in the file.

1. Public materials. The successor lawyer is entitled to access and use of the pleadings, discovery, correspondence, and other public materials from the disqualified lawyer's file. ***In re George***, 28 S.W.3d 511, 514 (Tex.2000).

2. Work product. A successor lawyer's access to the disqualified lawyer's work product is restricted or denied "to the extent that such a remedy furthers the purposes underlying the disqualification." ***George***, 28 S.W.3d at 512. A presumption that the work product contains confidential information arises once the former client establishes the two representations are substantially related. *Id.* at 518. The burden then shifts to the current client to rebut the presumption by demonstrating there is not a substantial likelihood the work product contains confidential information. *Id.* Once the successor lawyer moves for access to the work product, or the former client moves to restrict access, the court should order the disqualified lawyer to produce an inventory of the work product describing (1) the type of work, (2) the subject matter of the items, (3) the claims they relate to, and (4) any other relevant factors. *Id.* The court may also conduct an in camera inspection. *Id.* at 519.

§9. AGREEMENTS BETWEEN LAWYERS – RULE 11

The purpose of TRCP 11 is to avoid disputes over the terms of oral agreements made between lawyers in a pending lawsuit. *See* ***Padilla v. LaFrance***, 907 S.W.2d 454, 461 (Tex.1995); ***Kennedy v. Hyde***, 682 S.W.2d 525, 529-30 (Tex.1984). See "Settlement of the Suit," ch. 7-H, p. 510.

§9.1 Agreements in pending suits. To be enforceable, an agreement about any matter in a pending lawsuit must meet the requirements of TRCP 11. ***London Mkt. Cos. v. Schattman***, 811 S.W.2d 550, 552 (Tex.1991); ***J.B. Custom Design & Bldg. v. Clawson***, 794 S.W.2d 38, 41 (Tex.App.—Houston [1st Dist.] 1990, no writ). The agreement may be written or oral.

1. Written agreement. An enforceable written agreement about a pending lawsuit must be in writing, signed, and filed with the court. TRCP 11; ***Padilla***, 907 S.W.2d at 459-60 (written settlement agreement); ***London Mkt.***, 811 S.W.2d at 552 (oral agreement to extend time for discovery unenforceable). The "in writing" requirement may be satisfied by a series of documents as long as the agreement can be ascertained from the documents without resorting to oral testimony. ***Padilla***, 907 S.W.2d at 460. The "filed with the court" requirement may be satisfied by filing the agreement with the court any time before it is to be enforced. *Id.* at 461; *see, e.g.*, ***Southwestern Bell Tel. Co. v. Perez***, 904 S.W.2d 817, 822 (Tex.App.—San Antonio 1995, orig. proceeding) (letter agreement extending deadlines filed as an exhibit to party's motion to compel met filing requirement of TRCP 11).

2. Oral agreement in court. An enforceable oral agreement about a pending lawsuit must be made in open court and entered into the record. TRCP 11; ***Ronin v. Lerner***, 7 S.W.3d 883, 886 (Tex.App.—Houston [1st Dist.] 1999, no pet.) (oral settlement agreement met requirements of TRCP 11); *see* ***Kennedy***, 682 S.W.2d at 529-30.

3. Oral agreement recorded in deposition. An agreement between lawyers about a pending lawsuit that is made part of the record of a deposition is enforceable as it affects the oral deposition. TRCP 191.1. An agreement recorded in a deposition and filed with the court may be enforceable as a TRCP 11 agreement regarding other matters. *Compare* ***Kosowska v. Khan***, 929 S.W.2d 505, 508 (Tex.App.—San Antonio 1996, writ denied) (settlement agreement dictated during deposition, not signed by parties or lawyers, was enforceable under TRCP 11), *with* ***Tindall v. Bishop, Peterson & Sharp, P.C.***, 961 S.W.2d 248, 251 (Tex.App.—Houston [1st Dist.] 1997, no writ) (settlement agreement dictated during deposition was not enforceable under TRCP 11, but was enforceable as exception to statute of frauds).

§9.2 Agreements before suit filed. There is no requirement that an agreement about a lawsuit that has not been filed be in writing. TRCP 11 applies only to agreements about pending suits. ***Estate of Pollack v. McMurrey***, 858 S.W.2d 388, 393 (Tex.1993) (oral presuit agreement to settle enforceable as a contract but not under TRCP 11). *But see* ***Belleza-Gonzalez v. Villa***, 57 S.W.3d 8, 12 (Tex.App.—Houston [14th Dist.] 2001, no pet.) (presuit agreement to postpone service not enforceable because it should have been reduced to writing once suit filed). See "Presuit settlement agreement," ch. 7-H, §5.1.1, p. 514.

§10. ATTORNEY FEES FROM ADVERSE PARTY

A party cannot recover attorney fees from an adverse party unless permitted by a statute or a rule of procedure, by a contract between the parties, or under equity. *See* TRCP 215.2(b)(8) (attorney fees as sanctions); ***Holland v. Wal-Mart Stores***, 1 S.W.3d 91, 95 (Tex.1999) (recovery of attorney fees allowed if permitted by statute or contract between parties); ***Travelers Indem. Co. v. Mayfield***, 923 S.W.2d 590, 593 (Tex.1996) (same); ***Knebel v. Capital Nat'l Bank***, 518 S.W.2d 795, 799 (Tex.1974) (recognizing attorney fees can be awarded under equity). For a more detailed discussion of attorney fees from an adverse party, see ***O'Connor's COA***, "Attorney Fees," ch. 38, p. 1041. For a list of statutes authorizing attorney fees, see ***O'Connor's CPRC Plus***, "Statutory Attorney Fees Chart," p. 148 (2003-04).

§10.1 Pleadings required. Unless attorney fees are mandated by statute, the party must plead for attorney fees to be entitled to them. ***Swate v. Medina Comm. Hosp.***, 966 S.W.2d 693, 701 (Tex.App.—San Antonio 1998, pet. denied); ***R. Conrad Moore & Assocs. v. Lerma***, 946 S.W.2d 90, 96 (Tex.App.—El Paso 1997, writ denied). Although a party should identify the authority for attorney fees in its pleadings, if it does not, the party is still entitled to them if it pleads facts supporting attorney fees. *See* ***O'Connell v. Hitt***, 730 S.W.2d 16, 18 (Tex.App.—Corpus Christi 1987, no writ).

§10.2 Attorney fees by contract.

1. Hourly fees. In a suit for breach of a contract that provides for attorney fees, the party seeking attorney fees should prove the base amount and, if any adjustment is sought, the adjustment factors. See "Elements of proof for attorney fees," §10.4, p. 47.

2. Contingent fees. A contingent-fee contract between the plaintiff and the attorney on its own cannot support an award of attorney fees. ***Arthur Andersen & Co. v. Perry Equip. Corp.***, 945 S.W.2d 812, 818-19 (Tex. 1997) (DTPA case); ***Lubbock Cty. v. Strube***, 953 S.W.2d 847, 858 (Tex.App.—Austin 1997, pet. denied) (whistle-blower suit). The attorney must prove the fees were reasonable and necessary (see §10.4, below) and ask the court for attorney fees in a specific amount, not a percentage of the total award. ***Arthur Andersen***, 945 S.W.2d at 818-19.

§10.3 Attorney fees under CPRC.

1. Requirements under §38.001. To be entitled to attorney fees under CPRC §38.001, a party must show the following:

(1) The plaintiff pleaded for attorney fees. See ***O'Connor's COA***, "Plaintiff pleaded for attorney fees," ch. 38-B, §2.1, p. 1055.

(2) The underlying claim is a CPRC §38.001 claim. *See* ***Coward v. Gateway Nat'l Bank***, 525 S.W.2d 857, 858-59 (Tex.1975) (citing former TRCS art. 2226); ***London v. London***, 94 S.W.3d 139, 147-48 (Tex. App.—Houston [14th Dist.] 2002, no pet.). Section 38.001 lists the following claims that qualify for attorney fees: (1) rendered services, (2) performed labor, (3) furnished material, (4) freight or express overcharges, (5) lost or damaged freight or express, (6) killed or injured stock, (7) a sworn account, or (8) an oral or written contract. See ***O'Connor's COA***, "Suit involved Section 38.001 claim," ch. 38-B, §2.2, p. 1055.

(3) The party was represented by an attorney. CPRC §38.002(1); ***Great Am. Ins. Co. v. North Austin MUD***, 908 S.W.2d 415, 427 n.10 (Tex.1995). Generally, a pro se litigant is not entitled to attorney fees. However, both a corporation represented by in-house counsel and a lawyer appearing pro se are entitled to attorney fees. See ***O'Connor's COA***, "Plaintiff represented by attorney," ch. 38-A, §2.3, p. 1043.

(4) The party against whom attorney fees are to be assessed is an individual or a corporation. CPRC §38.001; *e.g.*, ***Harris Cty. MUD v. Mitchell***, 915 S.W.2d 859, 865-66 (Tex.App.—Houston [1st Dist.] 1995, writ denied) (a MUD is not a corporation or an individual and therefore is not liable for attorney fees under CPRC §38.001); ***Base-Seal, Inc. v. Jefferson Cty.***, 901 S.W.2d 783, 786-87 (Tex.App.—Beaumont 1995, writ denied) (same, for a county). See ***O'Connor's COA***, "Defendant was individual or corporation," ch. 38-B, §2.4, p. 1058.

(5) The §38.001 claim was presented to the opposing party or its agent. CPRC §38.002(2); ***Great Am. Ins.***, 908 S.W.2d at 427 n.10. The demand should include (1) the assertion of a debt or a claim and (2) a request for compliance. ***Jones v. Kelley***, 614 S.W.2d 95, 100 (Tex.1981). The demand may be made orally or in writing. *Id.*; ***Honeycutt v. Billingsley***, 992 S.W.2d 570, 581 (Tex.App.—Houston [1st Dist.] 1999, pet. denied). See ***O'Connor's COA***, "Plaintiff presented claim to defendant," ch. 38-B, §2.5, p. 1058.

(6) The opposing party did not tender payment within 30 days after the claim was presented. CPRC §38.002(3); ***Great Am. Ins.***, 908 S.W.2d at 427 n.10. See ***O'Connor's COA***, "Defendant did not tender payment," ch. 38-B, §2.6, p. 1058.

(7) The party prevailed on a cause of action for which attorney fees are recoverable. *See* ***London***, 94 S.W.3d at 148; ***Energen Res. MAQ, Inc. v. Dalbosco***, 23 S.W.3d 551, 558 (Tex.App.—Houston [1st Dist.] 2000, pet. denied). A net recovery is not required. See ***O'Connor's COA***, "Plaintiff prevailed," ch. 38-B, §2.7, p. 1059.

(8) The party requesting attorney fees established the elements of proof for the recovery of attorney fees, either by judicial notice or by evidence. See §§10.3.2, 10.4, below; ***O'Connor's COA***, "Plaintiff incurred reasonable attorney fees," ch. 38-B, §2.8, p. 1059.

2. Judicial notice. Judicial notice of attorney fees can be taken only when (1) the claim is a CPRC §38.001 claim, and (2) the claim is tried on the merits. The trial court, without receiving evidence, can take judicial notice of (1) the usual and customary attorney fees and (2) the content of the file. CPRC §38.004. Under CPRC §38.003, the usual and customary fees are presumed reasonable.

(1) Section 38.001 claims. The claim must be a CPRC §38.001 claim. ***Hasty, Inc. v. Inwood Buckhorn Jt.V.***, 908 S.W.2d 494, 503 (Tex.App.—Dallas 1995, writ denied); *see* CPRC §38.004; ***Coward v. Gateway Nat'l Bank***, 525 S.W.2d 857, 859 (Tex.1975) (analyzing predecessor statute). If the claim is not one included in CPRC §38.001, the court cannot take judicial notice of the fees. ***In re T.L.K.***, 90 S.W.3d 833, 841 (Tex.App.—San Antonio 2002, no pet.) (no judicial notice in family law case); ***Gorman v. Gorman***, 966 S.W.2d 858, 866-67 (Tex.App.—Houston [1st Dist.] 1998, pet. denied) (no judicial notice in declaratory judgment case); ***Richards v. Mena***, 907 S.W.2d 566, 574 (Tex.App.—Corpus Christi 1995, writ dism'd) (no judicial notice in redistricting & voting rights case); ***Smith v. Smith***, 757 S.W.2d 422, 425 (Tex.App.—Dallas 1988, writ denied) (no judicial notice in DTPA case).

(2) Section 38.004 hearings. The hearing must be either (1) "a proceeding before the court" or (2) a jury case in which the amount of attorney fees is submitted to the court by agreement. CPRC §38.004. The term "proceeding before the court" is not defined in CPRC §38.004. The Supreme Court has said the trial judge may take judicial notice of attorney fees only "in his role of trier of fact in the conventional trial of a non-jury case but not in passing on a motion for summary judgment." ***Coward***, 525 S.W.2d at 859; *see* ***Garcia v. Martinez***, 894 S.W.2d 806, 807 (Tex.App.—Corpus Christi 1994, no writ) (dicta, stating trial court cannot adjudicate attorney fees based on judicial notice without hearing evidence); ***General Elec. Sup. Co. v. Gulf Electroquip***, 857 S.W.2d 591, 601 (Tex.App.—Houston [1st Dist.] 1993, writ denied) (in summary judgment case, fact issue about attorney fees cannot be resolved by judicial notice). *But see* ***Purvis Oil Corp. v. Hillin***, 890 S.W.2d 931, 939 (Tex.App.—El Paso 1994, no writ) (in summary judgment case, fact issue about attorney fees can be resolved by judicial notice).

§10.4 Elements of proof for attorney fees. To support a claim for attorney fees from the adverse party, the party must offer the following proof:

1. Fees were necessary & incurred. The record must show that attorney fees were necessary and that they were incurred. ***Arthur Andersen & Co. v. Perry Equip. Corp.***, 945 S.W.2d 812, 818-19 (Tex.1997) (discussing reasonable & necessary attorneys fees under DTPA). See ***O'Connor's COA***, "Plaintiff incurred attorney fees," ch. 39-A, §2.6, p. 839; "Requirement of necessity," ch. 38-A, §2.7.1, p. 1046.

2. Fees were reasonable. In most cases, the plaintiff must prove the attorney fees were reasonable. ***Arthur Andersen***, 945 S.W.2d at 818; *see* ***Smith v. Smith***, 757 S.W.2d 422, 424 (Tex.App.—Dallas 1988, writ denied) (except where reasonableness may be presumed, it must be supported by evidence). For a CPRC §38.001 claim, the court can take judicial notice of attorney fees. See §10.3.2, above. The following are the steps to proving reasonable attorney fees:

(1) Base amount. The party should prove the base amount (also called the "lodestar") by providing the hours worked, the amount charged per hour, a description of the work performed, a statement that the work was necessary to the prosecution of the case, and a statement that the fees were reasonable. A party should use the following factors to determine the reasonableness of attorney fees:

(a) The time and labor required, the novelty and difficulty of the questions involved, and the skill required to perform the legal service properly. Tex. Disc. R. Prof. Conduct 1.04(b)(1); ***Arthur Andersen***, 945 S.W.2d at 818; *see* ***Ragsdale v. Progressive Voters League***, 801 S.W.2d 880, 881 (Tex.1990).

(b) The likelihood that the acceptance of the particular employment prevented other employment by the lawyer. Tex. Disc. R. Prof. Conduct 1.04(b)(2); ***Arthur Andersen***, 945 S.W.2d at 818. *But see* ***Stuart v. Bayless***, 964 S.W.2d 920, 921-22 (Tex.1998) (lost contingent fees from other cases are not reasonably foreseeable).

(c) The fee customarily charged in the locality for similar legal services. Tex. Disc. R. Prof. Conduct 1.04(b)(3); ***Arthur Andersen***, 945 S.W.2d at 818.

(d) The amount involved and the results obtained. Tex. Disc. R. Prof. Conduct 1.04(b)(4); ***Arthur Andersen***, 945 S.W.2d at 818.

(e) The time limitations imposed by the client or by the circumstances. Tex. Disc. R. Prof. Conduct 1.04(b)(5); ***Arthur Andersen***, 945 S.W.2d at 818.

(f) The nature and length of the professional relationship with the client. Tex. Disc. R. Prof. Conduct 1.04(b)(6); ***Arthur Andersen***, 945 S.W.2d at 818.

(g) The experience, reputation, and ability of the lawyer performing the services. Tex. Disc. R. Prof. Conduct 1.04(b)(7); ***Arthur Andersen***, 945 S.W.2d at 818.

(h) Whether the fee is fixed or contingent on results obtained or the uncertainty of collection before the legal services have been rendered. Tex. Disc. R. Prof. Conduct 1.04(b)(8); ***Arthur Andersen***, 945 S.W.2d at 818.

(2) Adjustment of base amount. Once the base amount is determined, the court may adjust the amount up or down depending on other factors used to determine the reasonableness of the fee. See ***O'Connor's COA***, "Adjustment of lodestar figure," ch. 38-A, §4.1.3(5), p. 1050.

3. Fees were segregated. When a party is entitled to attorney fees from the adverse party on one cause of action but not another (or against one party but not another), the party claiming attorney fees must segregate the nonrecoverable fees from the recoverable fees and segregate the fees owed by different parties. ***Stewart Title Guar. Co. v. Sterling***, 822 S.W.2d 1, 10-11 (Tex.1991); ***Stamp-Ad, Inc. v. Barton Raben, Inc.***, 915 S.W.2d 932, 937 (Tex.App.—Houston [1st Dist.] 1996, no writ). Segregation is not necessary if the claims are dependent on the same set of facts or circumstances and thus are intertwined to the point of being inseparable. ***Stewart Title Guar. Co. v. Aiello***, 941 S.W.2d 68, 73 (Tex.1997); ***Sterling***, 822 S.W.2d at 11; ***Pegasus Energy Group v. Cheyenne Pet. Co.***, 3 S.W.3d 112, 129 (Tex.App.—Corpus Christi 1999, pet. denied). If the party against whom attorney fees are claimed does not object on the record, the failure to segregate attorney fees is waived. ***Green Int'l v. Solis***, 951 S.W.2d 384, 389 (Tex.1997); ***Aero Energy v. Circle C Drilling Co.***, 699 S.W.2d 821, 823 (Tex.1985). An award of attorney fees erroneously based on evidence of unsegregated fees should be remanded for a hearing on attorney fees, even if at trial the party refused to segregate after an objection. *See* ***Sterling***, 822 S.W.2d at 12; ***Aetna Cas. & Sur. v. Wild***, 944 S.W.2d 37, 41 (Tex.App.—Amarillo 1997, writ denied); ***Panizo v. YMCA***, 938 S.W.2d 163, 171 (Tex. App.—Houston [1st Dist.] 1996, no writ).

§10.5 Proof of attorney fees. For a detailed discussion of proof of attorney fees, see ***O'Connor's COA***, "Proving Attorney Fees," ch. 38-A, §4, p. 1049. Testimony by an interested witness may establish attorney fees as a matter of law only if (1) the testimony could be readily contradicted if untrue, (2) it is clear, direct, and positive, and (3) there are no circumstances tending to discredit or impeach it. ***Lofton v. Texas Brine Corp.***, 777 S.W.2d 384, 386 (Tex.1989); ***Cale's Clean Scene Carwash v. Hubbard***, 76 S.W.3d 784, 787 (Tex.App.—Houston [14th Dist.] 2002, no pet.).

1. Affidavits. The court can award attorney fees based on affidavit testimony. ***Texas Commerce Bank v. New***, 3 S.W.3d 515, 517-18 (Tex.1999). Unless there is an objection, an affidavit is probative. *Id.* at 517; *see also* TRE 802 (unobjected-to hearsay cannot be denied probative value merely because it is hearsay).

2. Other evidence. Attorney fees are often proved by deposition or in-court testimony of the lawyer in the case.

§11. REVIEW

§11.1 Disqualification.

1. Standard of review. The standard of review on a disqualification motion is abuse of discretion. *See* ***In re Meador***, 968 S.W.2d 346, 351 (Tex.1998) (mandamus); ***Metropolitan Life Ins. Co. v. Syntek Fin. Corp.***, 881 S.W.2d 319, 321 (Tex.1994) (appeal).

2. Appeal. Disqualification issues are subject to review on appeal. *See* ***Metropolitan Life***, 881 S.W.2d at 320-21; *see also* ***Hall v. Birchfield***, 718 S.W.2d 313, 322 n.1 (Tex.App.—Texarkana 1986) (mandamus would be a better procedure than awaiting the outcome of the main trial), *rev'd on other grounds sub nom.* ***Birchfield v. Texarkana Mem'l Hosp.***, 747 S.W.2d 361 (Tex.1987).

3. Mandamus. Mandamus is often appropriate when a trial judge erroneously grants or denies a motion to disqualify a lawyer or law firm. See ***O'Connor's Texas Civil Appeals***, "Disqualification of lawyer," ch. 20-B, §4.3.5, p. 285 (2002-03).

§11.2 Attorney fees. A party can preserve error by complaining for the first time in a motion for judgment notwithstanding the verdict that the other party is not entitled to attorney fees. *See* ***Holland v. Wal-Mart Stores***, 1 S.W.3d 91, 94 (Tex.1999) (statute did not permit attorney fees).

I. GUARDIANS AD LITEM UNDER TRCP 173

§1. GENERAL

§1.1 Rules. TRCP 44, 173.

§1.2 Purpose. The purpose of appointing a guardian ad litem under TRCP 173 is to protect the interests of an incapacitated person in a lawsuit in which the incapacitated person is a party. ***American Gen. Fire & Cas. Co. v. Vandewater***, 907 S.W.2d 491, 493 n.2 (Tex.1995); *see* ***Roberts v. Williamson***, 111 S.W.3d 113, 124 (Tex.2003). The term "ad litem" means "for the suit." *Black's Law Dictionary* 43 (7th ed. 1999). The term "incapacitated person" refers to a person who is a minor, a lunatic, or non compos mentis. TRCP 173.

§1.3 Forms. ***O'Connor's Texas Civil Forms***, FORMS 1I.

§1.4 Other references. Anton, *The Ambiguous Role & Responsibilities of a Guardian Ad Litem in Texas in Personal Injury Litigation*, 51 SMU L. Rev. 161 (1997) (hereafter, *Role of Guardian Ad Litem*); Wood, *The Duties of Guardians & Attorneys Ad Litem*, State Bar of Texas, The New Guardianship Laws in Texas: A Course of Instruction, at F (1994) (hereafter, *Duties*); Litman, *The Defendant's Perspective*, Dallas Bar Ass'n, The Role of the Guardian Ad Litem in Personal Injury Litigation, at IV (1992); Solls & Hendrix, *The Guardian Ad Litem's Perspective*, Dallas Bar Ass'n, The Role of the Guardian Ad Litem in Personal Injury Litigation, at V (1992); Garcia, *Guardians Ad Litem: Feast or Famine?*, 30 Hous. Lawyer 2, p. 44 (Sept.-Oct.1992).

§2. COMPARISON OF GUARDIANS & ATTORNEYS AD LITEM

The term "guardian ad litem" is often confused with the term "attorney ad litem" because both terms are used in the TRCPs, the Probate Code, the Family Code, and other statutes. *See, e.g.*, ***Estate of Catlin v. G.M. Corp.***, 936 S.W.2d 447, 452 (Tex.App.—Houston [14th Dist.] 1996, no writ) (court used terms interchangeably); ***Brownsville-Valley Reg'l Med. Ctr. v. Gamez***, 871 S.W.2d 781, 784 (Tex.App.—Corpus Christi 1994) (referred to guardian ad litem as attorney ad litem), *rev'd on other grounds*, 894 S.W.2d 753 (Tex.1995). Because the roles of a guardian ad litem and an attorney ad litem are very different, lawyers should understand the differences and insist on correct references in all court documents. Wood, *Duties*, at F-9.

§2.1 Guardian ad litem. A guardian ad litem is an officer appointed by the court as the personal representative of an incapacitated person to assist in protecting the person's interests in a lawsuit in which the person is a party. ***Vandewater***, 907 S.W.2d at 493 n.2; ***Dawson v. Garcia***, 666 S.W.2d 254, 265 (Tex.App.—Dallas 1984, no writ). Although a guardian ad litem may be a licensed attorney, she is not an attorney for the incapacitated person. *See* ***Garcia v. Martinez***, 988 S.W.2d 219, 222 n.2 (Tex.1999); ***Vandewater***, 907 S.W.2d at 493 n.2; ***Brownsville-Valley Reg'l Med. Ctr. v. Gamez***, 894 S.W.2d 753, 755 (Tex.1995).

§2.2 Attorney ad litem. An attorney ad litem performs the same services as any attorney, such as giving legal advice, doing research, and conducting litigation for an incapacitated person. ***duPont v. Southern Nat'l Bank***, 771 F.2d 874, 882 (5th Cir.1985); ***Coleson v. Bethan***, 931 S.W.2d 706, 713 (Tex.App.—Fort Worth 1996, no writ); *see* Fam. Code §107.003 (duties of attorney ad litem for child in family cases include, among other things, investigation, review of medical and psychological records, interviewing all parties to the suit, and participating in litigation as would an attorney for a party). Unlike a guardian ad litem, the attorney ad litem does not act as an officer of the court; the attorney ad litem simply performs the ordinary services of an attorney. ***duPont***, 771 F.2d at 882. 03

1-3. COMPARISON OF AD LITEMS

GUARDIAN AD LITEM	ATTORNEY AD LITEM
TRCP	
In civil litigation, guardian ad litem must be appointed to represent an incapacitated person who (1) is a D and has no guardian in Texas or (2) is a P, D, or intervenor represented by a next friend or guardian that has an interest adverse to the incapacitated person. TRCP 173.	In default judgment proceedings against a D who was served by publication but did not answer or appear, the court must appoint an attorney ad litem to represent D. TRCP 244.
PROBATE CODE	
In guardianship proceedings, guardian ad litem can be appointed to represent best interests of incapacitated person. Prob. Code §§601(12), 645(a).	In guardianship proceedings, attorney ad litem can be appointed to represent & advocate for a proposed ward, an incapacitated person, or an unborn person. Prob. Code §§601(1), 646(a).
In heirship proceedings, guardian ad litem may be appointed to represent known heirs whose whereabouts or names are unknown, if the appointment is necessary to protect that person's interest. Prob. Code §53(b).	In heirship proceedings, attorney ad litem must be appointed to represent the interests of a minor, an incompetent, or the living heir whose name or address is unknown, if the appointment is necessary to protect that person's interest. Prob. Code §53(b), (c).
	In any probate proceeding, attorney ad litem can be appointed to represent person having a legal disability, a nonresident, an unborn or unascertained person, or an unknown heir. Prob. Code §34A.
FAMILY CODE	
In suit seeking order granting a minor permission to marry, guardian ad litem must be appointed for minor. Fam. Code §2.103(e).	In any case in which the court deems an attorney ad litem is necessary to protect the interests of a child who is the subject of the suit. Fam. Code §107.011.
In suit seeking order removing the disability of minority, guardian ad litem must be appointed for minor. Fam. Code §31.004.	In any suit brought by a governmental entity seeking termination of the parent-child relationship or seeking to be named as a conservator of a child, attorney ad litem must be appointed for the child. Fam. Code §107.012.
In suit seeking authorization for minor to have abortion without notice to parents, guardian ad litem must be appointed for minor. Fam. Code §33.003(e).	In suit seeking termination of the parent-child relationship, attorney ad litem must be appointed to represent the interest of (1) an indigent parent of the child if the parent opposes the termination, (2) a parent served with citation by publication, (3) an alleged father who did not register with the paternity registry, or (4) an alleged father who has registered with the paternity registry but cannot be personally served. Fam. Code §107.013.
In suit seeking termination of the parent-child relationship, guardian ad litem must be appointed for minor. Fam. Code §107.001.	In suit to determine parentage, attorney ad litem must be appointed to represent a minor or incapacitated child if the interests of the child are not adequately represented. Fam. Code §160.612(b).

§3. MOTION TO APPOINT GUARDIAN AD LITEM UNDER TRCP 173

§3.1 Movant.

1. Party. Any party in the suit can request the appointment of a guardian ad litem under TRCP 173. *See, e.g.*, ***Enochs v. Brown***, 872 S.W.2d 312, 317 (Tex.App.—Austin 1994, no writ) (father had right to request appointment of guardian ad litem for minor son).

2. Court. The trial court can appoint a guardian ad litem under TRCP 173 on its own motion. ***Smith v. Smith***, 720 S.W.2d 586, 591 (Tex.App.—Houston [1st Dist.] 1986, no writ). However, most guardians ad litem are appointed at the request of one of the parties. Litman, *The Defendant's Perspective* at IV, p. 3.

§3.2 Grounds. A motion for the appointment of a guardian ad litem should state that (1) an incapacitated person is a defendant or (2) there is a conflict of interest between the incapacitated person and the next friend or guardian. *See* TRCP 173. The appointment of a guardian ad litem for a ground provided in TRCP 173 is mandatory. ***Kennedy v. Missouri Pac. R.R.***, 778 S.W.2d 552, 555 (Tex.App.—Beaumont 1989, writ denied).

COMMENTARIES

CHAPTER 1. GENERAL

I. GUARDIANS AD LITEM UNDER TRCP 173

1. Incapacitated person as defendant. A guardian ad litem must be appointed for any incapacitated person who is a defendant. TRCP 173; *see* ***Wright v. Jones***, 52 S.W.2d 247, 251 (Tex.Comm'n App.1932, holding approved); ***Jaynes v. Lee***, 306 S.W.2d 182, 184-85 (Tex.App.—Texarkana 1957, no writ); *see also* ***In re Faubus***, 498 S.W.2d 21, 23 (Tex.App.—Amarillo 1973, no writ) (appointment of guardian ad litem under TRCP 173 is mandatory in juvenile delinquency proceedings). If the court does not appoint a guardian ad litem for the incapacitated defendant, any judgment taken against that person is voidable. *See* ***Wallis v. Stuart***, 50 S.W. 567, 569 (Tex.1899) (under former TRCS art. 1211, judgment taken against minor without appointment of guardian ad litem can be vacated at later date); ***Miller v. Miller***, 487 S.W.2d 382, 387 (Tex.App.—Fort Worth 1972, writ ref'd n.r.e.) (rule established by ***Wallis*** applies to incompetents); *see, e.g.*, ***TEIA v. Williams***, 522 S.W.2d 549, 551 (Tex.App.—Waco 1975, writ ref'd n.r.e.) (court had jurisdiction to sign judgment because minor D was represented by guardian appointed under Prob. Code). *But see* ***Horton v. Mills Cty.***, 468 S.W.2d 876, 879 (Tex.App.—Austin 1971, no writ) (although guardian ad litem should have been appointed for minor, error was harmless because no proceedings affecting minor's rights occurred before he appeared as an adult).

2. Conflict of interest. A guardian ad litem must be appointed for any incapacitated person who is represented by a next friend or guardian if it appears there is a conflict between the interests of the incapacitated person and the next friend or guardian. TRCP 173; ***Brownsville-Valley Reg'l Med. Ctr. v. Gamez***, 894 S.W.2d 753, 755 (Tex.1995); ***Gibson v. Blanton***, 483 S.W.2d 372, 374 (Tex.App.—Houston [1st Dist.] 1972, no writ); *see, e.g.*, ***Kennedy***, 778 S.W.2d at 555 (denial of motion to appoint guardian ad litem was not abuse of discretion when there was no indication next friend sought to compromise minor's recovery for her own benefit); ***Leigh v. Bishop***, 678 S.W.2d 572, 573 (Tex.App.—Houston [14th Dist.] 1984, no writ) (trial court abused its discretion in appointing guardian ad litem when father requested that entire settlement award be placed in court's registry for son's benefit). The court has broad discretion to determine whether there is a conflict. ***Borden, Inc. v. Martinez***, 19 S.W.3d 469, 472 (Tex.App.—San Antonio 2000, no pet.); ***TEIA v. Keenom***, 716 S.W.2d 59, 67 (Tex.App.—Houston [1st Dist.] 1986, writ ref'd n.r.e.). The following are some examples of when a guardian ad litem can be appointed on the grounds of conflict of interest:

(1) After suit is filed. In the context of tort litigation, the appearance of a conflict of interest often arises when the next friend, usually a parent, sues on her own behalf and as a representative of a minor child for injuries arising out of the same occurrence. ***Philips Pet. Co. v. Welch***, 702 S.W.2d 672, 674 (Tex.App.—Houston [14th Dist.] 1985, writ ref'd n.r.e.). In some cases, it may be necessary to appoint a guardian ad litem early in the litigation to ensure the case is developed in the best interest of the incapacitated person. Solls & Hendrix, *The Guardian Ad Litem's Perspective* at V, p. 3. For example, in a suit for damages arising out of a motor vehicle accident where a parent-driver and her minor-child-passenger sue the driver of another vehicle, a conflict of interest may arise when there is a dispute regarding proportionate responsibility between the two drivers. *Id.* The plaintiff's attorney representing both the parent and the child may focus solely on proving liability of the other driver. *Id.* The guardian ad litem representing the child, however, should be concerned with liability against both drivers and seek to recover under the insurance policies of both drivers. *Id.*

(2) During settlement negotiations. In a personal injury suit where the next friend seeks damages for herself and for the incapacitated person, a conflict of interest often arises during settlement negotiations because both parties are competing for part of the same fund. ***Byrd v. Woodruff***, 891 S.W.2d 689, 705 (Tex.App.—Dallas 1994, writ denied); ***Welch***, 702 S.W.2d at 674; *see, e.g.*, ***Clark v. McFerrin***, 760 S.W.2d 822, 828 (Tex.App.—Corpus Christi 1988, writ denied) (guardian ad litem necessary to appraise settlement offers made to children and to evaluate claims before trial).

(3) After judgment. A conflict of interest between the incapacitated person and next friend can arise after judgment if the next friend continues to have a personal interest in the handling of the settlement funds while the court's judgment is on appeal. *See, e.g.*, ***McGough v. 1st Ct. of Appeals***, 842 S.W.2d 637, 640 (Tex.1992) (postjudgment appointment of guardian ad litem necessary because grandparents would receive compensation for services as managing conservators and had inheritance interest should minor predecease them); ***Sosa v. Koshy***, 961 S.W.2d 420, 425 (Tex.App.—Houston [1st Dist.] 1997, pet. denied) (postjudgment appointment of guardian ad litem reasonable because, during the appeal, parents could have attempted to settle their own claims against Ds to detriment of minor P).

§3.3 Duration of guardianship.

1. When incapacitated person is defendant. When an incapacitated person is a defendant in a suit, the guardian ad litem's appointment lasts until the incapacitated person's disability is removed or a final, nonappealable judgment is signed, whichever occurs first. *See, e.g.*, ***Members Mut. Ins. Co. v. Randolph***, 477 S.W.2d 315, 319 (Tex.App.—Houston [1st Dist.] 1972, writ ref'd n.r.e.) (guardian ad litem discharged after minor D married); *cf.* ***Barrow v. Durham***, 574 S.W.2d 857, 860 (Tex.App.—Corpus Christi 1978) (in suit to terminate parental rights, guardian ad litem's appointment ended when judgment became final), *aff'd*, 600 S.W.2d 756 (Tex.1980).

2. When conflicting interests. When there is a conflict between the interests of an incapacitated person and the next friend or guardian, the guardian ad litem's appointment lasts until the conflict no longer exists. ***Brownsville-Valley Reg'l Med. Ctr.***, 894 S.W.2d at 755; *see* ***Davenport v. Garcia***, 834 S.W.2d 4, 24 (Tex.1992); ***Estate of Catlin v. G.M. Corp.***, 936 S.W.2d 447, 452 (Tex.App.—Houston [14th Dist.] 1996, no writ).

§4. QUALIFICATIONS & DUTIES OF GUARDIAN AD LITEM

§4.1 Qualifications. The trial court has complete discretion regarding whom to appoint as a guardian ad litem. ***Borden***, 19 S.W.3d at 475 (Rickhoff, J., concurring). There is no list of qualifications. *Id.* Although Probate Code §681 does not apply to a person appointed as a guardian ad litem under TRCP 173, the statute does furnish broad guidelines for determining when a person is unqualified. *Cf.* ***Gallegos v. Clegg***, 417 S.W.2d 347, 352 (Tex.App.—Corpus Christi 1967, writ ref'd n.r.e.) (former Prob. Code §110, now §681, applied to decide if next friend was disqualified). Because the guardian ad litem's main function is to evaluate the case and any settlement offer, the court should appoint a person who has the experience to properly investigate and evaluate the incapacitated person's case. When evaluating a person to determine if she is qualified to act as a guardian ad litem in a personal injury suit, the court should consider, among other things, whether she has experience in personal injury litigation. *See* Anton, *Role of Guardian Ad Litem*, 51 SMU L. Rev. at 170; *see also* Wood, *Duties*, at F-13 (detailing pitfalls associated with personal injury suits).

§4.2 Duties. The guardian ad litem is required to participate in the case to the extent necessary to protect the interests of the incapacitated person. ***Garcia v. Martinez***, 988 S.W.2d 219, 222 n.2 (Tex.1999); ***Borden***, 19 S.W.3d at 476 (Rickhoff, J., concurring). As a fiduciary, the ad litem is empowered to make decisions for, and act on behalf of, the incapacitated person. ***Byrd***, 891 S.W.2d at 708. The responsibilities of a guardian ad litem appointed under TRCP 173 are not defined by the rule, but case law and CLE papers offer some useful guidelines to assist the guardian ad litem in carrying out her duties.

1. Generally. Once appointed, a guardian ad litem should usually assume the following responsibilities:

(1) The guardian ad litem should contact all the parties and inform them of the appointment. Wood, *Duties*, at F-13.

(2) The guardian ad litem should obtain the following information from the incapacitated person's attorney: (1) contingent fee contract; (2) guardian or next friend's address, home phone, and work phone numbers; (3) incapacitated person's date of birth and social security number; (4) latest pleadings; (5) medical records and bills; (6) any documents reflecting third-party liens, such as hospital liens; and (7) all automobile or homeowner's insurance policies. Solls & Hendrix, *The Guardian Ad Litem's Perspective*, at V, p. 10 (Guardian Ad Litem Check List).

(3) The guardian ad litem should make a preliminary investigation of the case including estimates on liability exposure and damages. Wood, *Duties*, at F-13.

(4) The guardian ad litem should ensure that all court documents refer to her as "guardian ad litem" and not "attorney ad litem." Anton, *Role of Guardian Ad Litem*, 51 SMU L. Rev. at 193.

PRACTICE TIP

Generally, a guardian ad litem appointed under TRCP 173 should not take any action that requires a bar card. When a guardian ad litem starts acting like a lawyer, the other parties should object. A guardian ad litem cannot be paid for work performed outside the role of an ad litem. ***Marshall Investigation & Sec. Agency v. Whitaker****, 962 S.W.2d 62, 63 (Tex.App.—Houston [1st Dist.] 1997, no pet.);* ***Roark v. Mother Frances Hosp.****, 862 S.W.2d 643, 647 (Tex. App.—Tyler 1993, writ denied). If the guardian ad litem believes the incapacitated person needs a lawyer, the ad litem should petition the court to appoint one. Wood, Duties, at F-21.*

2. During settlement negotiations. When a settlement is proposed, a guardian ad litem should assume the following responsibilities:

(1) The guardian ad litem must determine if the settlement is fair and reasonable to the incapacitated person. Wood, *Duties*, at F-13. To determine the adequacy of a settlement agreement, the guardian ad litem should evaluate (1) the damages suffered by the incapacitated person, (2) the adequacy of the settlement, (3) the proposed apportionment of the settlement proceeds among the interested parties, (4) the proposed manner of disbursement of the settlement proceeds, and (5) the amount of attorney fees charged by the incapacitated person's attorney. ***Byrd v. Woodruff***, 891 S.W.2d 689, 707 (Tex.App.—Dallas 1994, writ denied); *see* ***Delcourt v. Silverman***, 919 S.W.2d 777, 784 (Tex.App.—Houston [14th Dist.] 1996, writ denied) (dicta).

(2) The guardian ad litem should attend the hearing to prove up the settlement agreement. Wood, *Duties*, at F-19.

(3) The guardian ad litem must make a recommendation to the trial court on the incapacitated person's behalf. ***Byrd***, 891 S.W.2d at 707.

(4) The guardian ad litem should review the final settlement documents and judgment submitted to the court. Wood, *Duties*, at F-19.

3. When no settlement. When no settlement is proposed, a guardian ad litem should assume the following responsibilities:

(1) The guardian ad litem should become familiar with the plaintiff's attorney's trial preparation and strategy as well as all court scheduling and docket control orders. Wood, *Duties*, at F-20.

(2) The guardian ad litem should participate in the case to the extent necessary to protect the interest of the incapacitated person. ***Roark***, 862 S.W.2d at 647; ***Pleasant Hills Children's Home v. Nida***, 596 S.W.2d 947, 951 (Tex.App.—Fort Worth 1980, no writ); *see* ***Coastal States Gas Prod'g Co. v. Locker***, 436 S.W.2d 592, 596 (Tex.App.—Houston [14th Dist.] 1968, no writ). However, the guardian ad litem cannot assume the duties reserved for lawyers.

4. After judgment signed. A guardian ad litem is appointed for the case only. After the judgment is signed, the guardian ad litem usually has no further obligations or responsibilities. *See* ***Brownsville-Valley Reg'l Med. Ctr. v. Gamez***, 894 S.W.2d 753, 755 (Tex.1995) (once conflict ends, guardian ad litem should be removed). However, at the conclusion of the case, the guardian ad litem should be expected to do the following:

(1) The guardian ad litem should provide her address and telephone number to the incapacitated person and the next friend or guardian if the incapacitated person needs help in the future. Anton, *Role of Guardian Ad Litem*, 51 SMU L. Rev. at 193.

(2) The guardian ad litem should retain her file. Anton, *Role of Guardian Ad Litem*, 51 SMU L. Rev. at 193; Solls & Hendrix, *The Guardian Ad Litem's Perspective*, at V, p. 7.

(3) The guardian ad litem should expect, on a no-fee basis, to assist the minor in securing funds from the court registry when the minor becomes an adult. Wood, *Duties*, at F-20; *see* ***Gamez***, 894 S.W.2d at 756-57 (guardian ad litem cannot recover fees for services rendered after resolution of conflict for which she was appointed).

§4.3 Breach of duties. A guardian ad litem appointed under TRCP 173 to represent an incapacitated person can be liable in a civil action for damages resulting from a breach of duties as the incapacitated person's personal representative. ***Borden, Inc. v. Martinez***, 19 S.W.3d 469, 476 (Tex.App.—San Antonio 2000, no pet.) (Rickhoff, J., concurring); ***Byrd***, 891 S.W.2d at 708; *see* ***Grunewald v. Technibilt Corp.***, 931 S.W.2d 593, 597 (Tex.App.—Dallas 1996, writ denied). *But see* ***Delcourt***, 919 S.W.2d at 786 (guardian ad litem for minor appointed in custody suit under Fam. Code §107.001 is entitled to absolute judicial immunity).

§5. FEES FOR GUARDIAN AD LITEM

§5.1 Liability for fees.

1. Unsuccessful party. The guardian ad litem fees should be taxed as costs against the unsuccessful party in the suit. *See* TRCP 141, 173; ***Borden***, 19 S.W.3d at 471; ***Estate of Catlin v. G.M. Corp.***, 936 S.W.2d 447, 452 (Tex.App.—Houston [14th Dist.] 1996, no writ).

2. Prevailing party. As a rule, the guardian ad litem fees should not be taxed against the prevailing party. *See* TRCP 141, 173. Only when the court finds good cause and states it on the record can the court tax costs against the prevailing party. TRCP 141; *e.g.*, ***Rogers v. Walmart Stores***, 686 S.W.2d 599, 601 (Tex.1985) (good cause to assess part of ad litem costs against prevailing party for prolonging trial); ***Davis v. Henley***, 471 S.W.2d 883, 885 (Tex.App.—Houston [1st Dist.] 1971, writ ref'd n.r.e.) (good cause to assess ad litem fee against prevailing party because unsuccessful party had no assets or income). Without evidence of good cause, the court abuses its discretion in assessing the ad litem's costs against the prevailing party. ***Suiter v. Woodard***, 635 S.W.2d 639, 641 (Tex.App.—Waco 1982, writ ref'd n.r.e.) (court could not tax costs against P, who was neither adverse to nor on the same side as minor Ps).

3. Both parties. Without a finding of good cause, the court cannot split the ad litem fees between the parties. *See* ***Roberts v. Williamson***, 111 S.W.3d 111, 124 (Tex.2003).

§5.2 Hearing on fees. The trial court must conduct a hearing and receive evidence to determine the amount of fees for the guardian ad litem. *See* ***Garcia v. Martinez***, 988 S.W.2d 219, 221-22 (Tex.1999); ***DaimlerChrysler Corp. v. Brannon***, 67 S.W.3d 294, 299 (Tex.App.—Texarkana 2001, no pet.).

§5.3 Amount of fees. The determination of guardian ad litem fees rests within the sound discretion of the trial court. ***Garcia***, 988 S.W.2d at 222; ***Cherne Indus. v. Magallanes***, 763 S.W.2d 768, 773 (Tex.1989); ***Simon v. York Crane & Rigging Co.***, 739 S.W.2d 793, 794 (Tex.1987); ***Borden***, 19 S.W.3d at 471. However, the court's discretion is not unbridled. In general, the same factors used to determine the reasonableness of attorney fees are controlling. ***Garcia***, 988 S.W.2d at 222; ***Borden***, 19 S.W.3d at 472. See "Fees were reasonable," ch. 1-H, §10.4.2, p. 47; ***O'Connor's Texas Causes of Action***, "Attorney fees reasonable & necessary," ch. 38-A, §2.7, p. 1046 (2004). Such factors include the difficulty and complexity of the case, the amount of time spent by the guardian, the benefit derived by the client, and the skill and experience reasonably needed to perform the service. ***Garcia***, 988 S.W.2d at 222; ***Simon***, 739 S.W.2d at 794. The guardian ad litem is never entitled to a contingent fee because the ad litem does not undertake the risk of an unsuccessful outcome. *See* ***Garcia***, 988 S.W.2d at 223. The trial court cannot award fees for services to be performed by the ad litem after the conflict of interest that necessitated the ad litem's appointment has been resolved. ***Frank A. Smith Sales v. Flores***, 907 S.W.2d 487, 488 (Tex.1995); ***Gamez***, 894 S.W.2d at 757; *see, e.g.*, ***DaimlerChrysler***, 67 S.W.3d at 302 (court could not award fee based on ad litem's potential liability for 30+ years).

§5.4 Separate order. The fee to the guardian ad litem should not be included in the order appointing the guardian ad litem; instead, it must be recorded in a separate written order. Tex.Sup.Ct. Order 94-9143, §2, 890-891 S.W.2d (Tex.Cases) xlvii (1994). The district and county court clerk must report to the Supreme Court all fees of $250 or more by listing the amount of the fees and the names of the persons receiving them. *Id.* §5 at xlviii.

§5.5 Preserving error. To complain about the ad litem fees on appeal, a party must make its objection known to the trial court, either by oral objection on the record or in some post-trial motion. ***Samco Props. v. Cheatham***, 977 S.W.2d 469, 479 (Tex.App.—Houston [14th Dist.] 1998, pet. denied); *see, e.g.*, ***Torrington Co. v. Stutzman***, 46 S.W.3d 829, 852 (Tex.2000) (D waived objection that fees were awarded without supporting evidence).

J. MASTER IN CHANCERY

§1. GENERAL

§1.1 Rule. TRCP 171.

§1.2 Purpose. A master in chancery is a person designated by a judicial officer to hear certain matters. ***Simpson v. Canales***, 806 S.W.2d 802, 806 (Tex.1991) (master appointed for discovery). The theory underlying the use of masters is that, by delegating certain matters to them, the trial judge is free to devote more time to trials and substantive decisions, thus expediting the trial docket. *Id.* at 809 n.9. For a discussion of the historical development of the office of masters and an explanation for the courts' inherent distrust of them, read ***Simpson***.

§1.3 Forms. ***O'Connor's Texas Civil Forms***, FORMS 1J.

§2. AUTHORITY FOR REFERRAL TO MASTER

There are three sources of authority for a master: TRCP 171, statutes, and the consent of the parties.

§2.1 TRCP 171. Every referral to a master must comply with TRCP 171, unless authorized by statute or consented to by the parties. ***Simpson***, 806 S.W.2d at 810; ***Hansen v. Sullivan***, 886 S.W.2d 467, 469 (Tex.App.—Houston [1st Dist.] 1994, orig. proceeding).

§2.2 Statutes. The Legislature has created certain types of masters, limited to specific subjects and counties. For example, the following matters may be referred to a master: family law matters—Family Code §§201.101-201.113; juvenile matters in certain counties—*e.g.*, Gov't Code §§54.801-54.820 (Harris County); and criminal matters in certain counties—*e.g.*, Gov't Code §§54.301-54.313 (Dallas County). These provisions for the appointment of masters contain their own procedures for appointing and compensating masters and for appealing their decisions.

§2.3 Consent. The parties may consent to the referral of a case to a master, even when there is no authority under TRCP 171 or any statute. ***Simpson***, 806 S.W.2d at 810-11; ***In re Polybutylene Plumbing Litig.***, 23 S.W.3d 428, 439 (Tex.App.—Houston [1st Dist.] 2000, pet. dism'd). Consent to the referral of a matter to a master demonstrates a party's intent to be bound on the matters referred. ***In re Sheets***, 971 S.W.2d 745, 747 (Tex.App.—Dallas 1998, orig. proceeding).

§3. MOTION FOR REFERRAL TO MASTER UNDER TRCP 171

§3.1 Written. A request for a master should be in writing. See ***O'Connor's*** FORM 1J:01.

§3.2 Grounds. A motion for referral to a master under TRCP 171 should include the following allegations:

1. Specific, pending matter. The motion should identify a specific, pending matter that the party requests to be referred to a master. The motion should not ask the trial court to refer all present and future issues of a particular type to a master. *See* ***Academy of Model Aeronautics. v. Packer***, 860 S.W.2d 419, 419 (Tex.1993).

2. Exceptional matter. The matter should be referred to a master because it is exceptional. TRCP 171; ***Simpson***, 806 S.W.2d at 811. For example, the court may appoint a master with technical knowledge to conduct a comprehensive analysis of highly technical data. *E.g.*, ***TransAmerican Nat. Gas Corp. v. Mancias***, 877 S.W.2d 840, 843 (Tex.App.—Corpus Christi 1994, orig. proceeding) (geologist appointed to assist in review of documents); *see also* ***Chapa v. Garcia***, 848 S.W.2d 667, 668 (Tex.1992) (court suggested trial court appoint a master with special expertise to assist in review of documents). Just because a case is complicated or time-consuming, or the court is busy, does not justify referral to a master. ***Simpson***, 806 S.W.2d at 811-12; ***Sheets***, 971 S.W.2d at 747; ***Owens-Corning Fiberglas Corp. v. Caldwell***, 830 S.W.2d 622, 626 (Tex.App.—Houston [1st Dist.] 1991, orig. proceeding).

3. **Good cause.** The court has good cause to refer the matter to a master. TRCP 171; ***Simpson***, 806 S.W.2d at 811; ***Owens-Corning***, 830 S.W.2d at 626. The "good cause" requirement has not been precisely defined. *See generally* ***Simpson***, 806 S.W.2d at 811-12 (discussing difficulty in defining "good cause" requirement of TRCP 171).

§4. ORDER OF REFERRAL TO MASTER

The decision to appoint a master is in the discretion of the trial court. ***Simpson***, 806 S.W.2d at 811; ***Tollett v. Carmona***, 915 S.W.2d 562, 564 (Tex.App.—Houston [14th Dist.] 1995, orig. proceeding). See *O'Connor's* FORM 1J:03.

§4.1 Findings. To refer a case to a master without the consent of the parties, the trial court must find (1) the case is an exceptional one, and (2) there is good cause for the appointment. TRCP 171; ***Simpson***, 806 S.W.2d at 810; ***Sheets***, 971 S.W.2d at 747.

§4.2 Scope of referral. The order referring a matter to a master should identify the scope and limits of the master's authority. TRCP 171. The order should specify the powers of the master and direct the master to report only on particular matters, perform particular acts, or receive and report evidence only. *Id.*

§4.3 No blanket referral. The court cannot make a blanket referral of all discovery matters to a master. *See* ***Academy of Model Aeronautics***, 860 S.W.2d at 419 (trial court could not refer all present and future discovery disputes to master); ***Simpson v. Canales***, 806 S.W.2d 802, 812 (Tex.1991) (even in an exceptional case, court would be reluctant to refer all discovery matters to master); ***Owens-Corning***, 830 S.W.2d at 626 (same).

§4.4 Appointee. The master must be a citizen of Texas and cannot be related to or an attorney for either party. TRCP 171.

§4.5 Time & place. The order of referral may fix the time and place for the hearings and the time for the filing of the master's report. TRCP 171.

§5. OBJECTION TO MASTER'S APPOINTMENT

§5.1 Types of objections. When the court refers a matter to a master, a party must make its objections or waive them. *See, e.g.*, ***In re Xeller***, 6 S.W.3d 618, 624 (Tex.App.—Houston [14th Dist.] 1999, orig. proceeding) (17-month delay in objecting to appointment waived issue). See "Making & Preserving Objections," ch. 1-F, p. 29. Objections include the following:

1. This is not the type of matter that should be referred to a master because it is not exceptional, and the referral is without good cause. TRCP 171; ***Simpson v. Canales***, 806 S.W.2d 802, 811 (Tex.1991); *see* ***AIU Ins. Co. v. Mehaffy***, 942 S.W.2d 796, 803 (Tex.App.—Beaumont 1997, orig. proceeding) (trial court was not authorized to appoint master to go to N.Y. to investigate discovery abuse). See §3.2, above.

2. The scope of the appointment and the master's duties are not clearly defined in the order of referral. TRCP 171.

3. The referral is a blanket referral, in violation of TRCP 171. ***Academy of Model Aeronautics***, 860 S.W.2d at 419; ***Simpson***, 806 S.W.2d at 812; ***Owens-Corning***, 830 S.W.2d at 626.

4. The person appointed to serve as a master is objectionable.

(1) The appointee is not qualified to serve because he or she is not a citizen of Texas, is related to one of the parties, or is an attorney for one of the parties. TRCP 171.

(2) The parties already objected to the same person serving as a visiting judge in the case. *See **Tollett***, 915 S.W.2d at 563.

§5.2 Deadline to object. TRCP 171 does not specify the time for a party to object to the appointment of a master. A party must object to the appointment either before participating in any proceedings in front of the master or before the parties, master, and trial court act in reliance on the appointment. ***Tollett***, 915 S.W.2d at 564-65; ***Owens-Corning***, 830 S.W.2d at 624-25.

§6. HEARING BEFORE MASTER

§6.1 Record of hearing. When requested, the master must make a record of the evidence just as if the case were tried before the court. TRCP 171. When a party wants the proceeding recorded, the party should file a written request as soon as the appointment is made. See ***O'Connor's*** FORM 1J:04. If a court reporter is not present, any party who wants the hearing recorded should object in writing.

§6.2 Attendance of witnesses. The parties may procure the attendance of witnesses by the issuance and service of process as provided by the same rules for a trial before a judge. TRCP 171. See "Subpoenas," ch. 1-K, p. 58.

§6.3 Scope of hearing. The scope of the hearing is determined by the trial court's order referring the matter to the master. See §4.2, above.

§6.4 Authority of master. Subject to the limitations stated in the order, the master may regulate the hearing and take all measures necessary or proper for the efficient performance of the duties specified in the order. The master may require the production of evidence, including books, papers, vouchers, documents, and other writings; rule on the admissibility of evidence; and place parties and witnesses under oath and examine them. TRCP 171.

§7. MASTER'S REPORT

§7.1 Report. The master's report should conform to the instructions in the order of referral. If the order instructed the master to receive evidence and settle factual disputes, the master should file findings of fact just as if the case were tried to a court without a jury. The master does not have the authority to render judgment. ***Hansen v. Sullivan***, 886 S.W.2d 467, 469 (Tex.App.—Houston [1st Dist.] 1994, orig. proceeding).

§7.2 Notice. Once the master files the report with the trial court, the parties are entitled to notice and an opportunity to object.

§8. OBJECTION TO MASTER'S REPORT

§8.1 No objection. When issues are referred to a master under TRCP 171, the master's report is conclusive on all issues to which the parties do not object. ***Young v. Young***, 854 S.W.2d 698, 701 (Tex.App.—Dallas 1993, writ denied); ***Minnich v. Jones***, 799 S.W.2d 327, 328 (Tex.App.—Texarkana 1990, orig. proceeding).

§8.2 Objection. To the extent a party objects to the master's report, the report is not binding. ***Young***, 854 S.W.2d at 701.

1. **Timely.** A party must object to the master's report before the report is adopted by the trial court. ***Robles v. Robles***, 965 S.W.2d 605, 612 (Tex.App.—Houston [1st Dist.] 1998, pet. denied). However, if the trial court adopts the report before a party has notice of the report, the party does not waive its objections. ***Republic Ins. Co. v. Davis***, 856 S.W.2d 158, 160 (Tex.1993).

2. **Specific.** An objection to the report must be specific. *See, e.g.*, ***Young***, 854 S.W.2d at 700-01 (wife objected to finding that she executed agreement voluntarily). It is not necessary for a party to support its objection with evidence; only a formal objection is necessary. *Id.* at 703. See "Making & Preserving Objections," ch. 1-F, p. 29.

3. Effect of objection. An objection to the master's findings raise a fact issue. ***Young***, 854 S.W.2d at 701.

§9. TRIAL COURT REVIEW OF MASTER'S REPORT

§9.1 Court review of report. The court may confirm, modify, correct, reject, reverse, or recommit the report after it is filed. TRCP 171. If the court makes a finding without specifically rejecting a master's finding on the same issue, the court's finding supersedes the master's. ***Hyundai Motor Am. v. O'Neill***, 839 S.W.2d 474, 481 (Tex. App.—Dallas 1992, orig. proceeding). *But see* ***In re Polybutylene Plumbing Litig.***, 23 S.W.3d 428, 439-42 (Tex. App.—Houston [1st Dist.] 2000, pet. dism'd) (trial court had no jurisdiction to modify terms of fully performed attorney-fee agreement when master was appointed solely to implement agreement & determine whether parties' proposed formula accomplished parties' agreement).

§9.2 Trial de novo. The issues of fact raised by the objections are tried de novo (*i.e.*, the trial court must receive evidence anew on the issues to which a party objected). ***Hyundai***, 839 S.W.2d at 480. When objections are made to the master's report, each party has the right to present evidence on the issues specified in the objections. ***Young***, 854 S.W.2d at 701; ***Hyundai***, 839 S.W.2d at 480-81.

§9.3 Jury or nonjury? If one of the parties properly requested a jury, the court must conduct a jury trial on the fact issues raised by the objections to the master's report. ***Young***, 854 S.W.2d at 701; ***Minnich***, 799 S.W.2d at 328-29; *cf.* ***Mann v. Mann***, 607 S.W.2d 243, 246 (Tex.1980) (request for jury trial in divorce proceeding does not preclude appointment of a master). If no jury was requested, the court will conduct a nonjury trial on those issues.

§10. PAYMENT OF MASTER

§10.1 Reasonable compensation. The trial court will award the master reasonable compensation, which will be taxed as a cost of the suit. TRCP 171; ***TransAmerican Nat. Gas Corp. v. Mancias***, 877 S.W.2d 840, 844 (Tex. App.—Corpus Christi 1994, orig. proceeding). Fees for masters are not necessarily determined by the stringent requirements of proof of attorney fees. ***Frost v. Frost***, 695 S.W.2d 279, 282 (Tex.App.—San Antonio 1985, no writ). A fee awarded to the master will be reversed only on a showing of a clear abuse of discretion. ***Mann***, 607 S.W.2d at 246; ***Texas Bank & Trust Co. v. Moore***, 595 S.W.2d 502, 511 (Tex.1980).

§10.2 Not in advance. The trial court cannot require the parties to deposit funds into the court's registry to cover the master's fee. ***TransAmerican***, 877 S.W.2d at 844. In ***Simpson***, the Supreme Court ducked this issue. ***Simpson v. Canales***, 806 S.W.2d 802, 812 n.14 (Tex.1991).

§11. REVIEW

§11.1 Appeal. If the court overrules an objection to the master's report, the party may appeal and challenge the ruling after the rendition of a final judgment.

§11.2 Mandamus. If the court improperly overrules a party's objection to the order of referral to a master, the party can file a petition for writ of mandamus. *See* ***Simpson***, 806 S.W.2d at 812; ***Tollett v. Carmona***, 915 S.W.2d 562, 564 (Tex.App.—Houston [14th Dist.] 1995, orig. proceeding).

K. SUBPOENAS

§1. GENERAL

§1.1 Rules. TRCP 176, 199.3, 205. See CPRC §§22.001, 22.002.

§1.2 Purpose. A subpoena is a process or writ that commands a person to appear and give testimony, or orders a person to produce or permit inspection and copying of documents or other tangible things. *See* CPRC §22.002; TRCP 176.2, 199.3, 205.3.

§1.3 Forms. ***O'Connor's Texas Civil Forms***, FORMS 1K.

§1.4 Other references. Griesel, *The "New" Texas Discovery Rules: Three Years Later*, Advanced Evidence & Discovery Course, State Bar of Texas, ch. 2, §IV, p. 3 (2002); *Texas Trial Handbook* §8:14 (3d ed. 1999); 97 C.J.S. Witnesses §25.

§2. TYPES OF SUBPOENAS

Subpoenas may be issued to command a person (1) to attend and give testimony, (2) to produce and permit inspection of the books, papers, documents, or tangible things designated in the subpoena, or (3) to do both. TRCP 176.2.

§2.1 Discovery subpoena. A discovery subpoena is a writ by which a court, at the request of a party, commands a person to appear or produce documents or other things for discovery. TRCP 176.2. A person commanded to produce documents or other things does not need to appear in person unless the subpoena commands the person to attend and give testimony. TRCP 176.6(c). A subpoena cannot be used for discovery in a manner or time other than as provided by the rules of discovery. TRCP 176.3(b); *see* ***Prestige Ford Co. v. Gilmore***, 56 S.W.3d 73, 80 (Tex.App.—Houston [14th Dist.] 2001, pet. denied) (no evidence party used trial subpoena for discovery when it requested documents a few days before trial). In most cases, a discovery subpoena is issued to compel a nonparty to attend a deposition and produce documents. See "Securing Things from a Nonparty," ch. 6-H, §5, p. 428.

§2.2 Trial subpoena. A subpoena for a hearing or trial commands a witness to attend and give testimony or to produce documents or things at a hearing or trial, and to remain there from day to day until discharged by either the court or the party issuing the subpoena. TRCP 176.6(a), (f); *see* ***Electronic Data Sys. v. Tyson***, 862 S.W.2d 728, 731 n.3 (Tex.App.—Dallas 1993, orig. proceeding). See ***O'Connor's*** FORMS 1K:01-02. Lawyers may issue their own trial subpoenas. TRCP 176.4(b). See §3.3, below. A party cannot secure a trial subpoena by making an oral request to the court. ***Holleman v. West End Cab Co.***, No. 07-99-0232-CV (Tex.App.—Amarillo 2000, pet. denied) (no pub.; 7-6-00).

PRACTICE TIP

If the witness to be subpoenaed can be characterized as "friendly," the lawyer may want to include in the trial subpoena a request that the witness call the lawyer to set up a time and date for the witness to appear at trial.

---

1. Time for issuance. TRCP 176 does not state how much advance notice should be allowed for issuing a subpoena for a hearing or trial. The only rule is the party who issued the subpoena should be "diligent" in procuring the witness's testimony. *See, e.g.*, ***Hatteberg v. Hatteberg***, 933 S.W.2d 522, 526 (Tex.App.—Houston [1st Dist.] 1994, no writ) (continuance denied; attempted service of subpoena 9 days before trial was not diligent); ***Victor M. Solis Underground Util. & Paving Co. v. City of Laredo***, 751 S.W.2d 532, 537 (Tex.App.—San Antonio 1988, writ denied) (continuance denied; subpoena issued for out-of-town witness only 3 days before trial); ***Dairyland Cty. Mut. Ins. Co. v. Keys***, 568 S.W.2d 457, 460 (Tex.App.—Tyler 1978, writ ref'd n.r.e.) (continuance denied; party waited to have subpoena issued on day of trial rather than two weeks earlier at time of docket call).

2. Discharging the witness. The court or the summoning party may discharge a witness summoned for a hearing or trial. TRCP 176.6(a). A discharged witness may be re-subpoenaed to appear and give testimony. ***Burttschell v. Sheppard***, 69 S.W.2d 402, 404 (Tex.1934).

§3. FORMAL REQUIREMENTS FOR SUBPOENAS

The subpoena must meet the formal requirements of TRCP 176.1 and any additional requirements imposed by local district or county rules. Parties should check with the district or county court where the case is pending for any additional requirements for the subpoena.

§3.1 Form of subpoena. The subpoena must (1) be issued in the name of "The State of Texas"; (2) include the style of the suit and its cause number; (3) identify the court in which the suit is pending; (4) state the date on which the subpoena is issued; (5) identify the person to whom the subpoena is directed; (6) state the time, place, and nature of the action required of the person being subpoenaed; (7) identify the party who secured the subpoena; (8) include the text of TRCP 176.8(a) regarding contempt; (9) be signed by the person issuing the subpoena; and (10) command a person (a) to attend and give testimony, (b) to produce and permit inspection of the books, papers, documents, or tangible things designated in the subpoena, or (c) to do both. TRCP 176.1, 176.2. See ***O'Connor's*** FORMS 1K:01-02.

§3.2 Range of subpoena. Both TRCP 176.3 and CPRC §22.002 limit the geographical reach of subpoenas to 150 miles, but the range of a subpoena under TRCP 176.3 is broader than the one under CPRC §22.002.

1. TRCP 176.3. A witness may be required by subpoena to appear or produce documents in any county within 150 miles from the place where the witness resides or was served. TRCP 176.3(a). To determine the range of a subpoena under TRCP 176.3, trace a circle with a radius of 150 miles from the place where the witness resides or was served. The witness may be required to attend or produce at any place in any county that is even partially in that circle. TRCP 176.3 does not restrict the places for deposition listed in TRCP 199.2(b)(2) for parties and other witnesses who can be compelled to appear by notice alone. TRCP 176.3.

2. CPRC §22.002. A witness may be required by subpoena to appear for a trial or hearing in the county of suit if the witness resides or was served within 150 miles from that county. CPRC §22.002. To determine the range under CPRC §22.002, trace a circle around the county of suit with a radius of 150 miles out from the county line. If the witness resides or was served within that circle, the witness can be compelled to attend.

1-4. DISTANCE NONPARTY CAN BE COMPELLED TO TRAVEL

AUTHORITY	RESIDENCE	WHERE SERVED
TRCP 176.3	To any county, if part of county is within radius of 150 miles from witness's residence	To any county, if part of county is within radius of 150 miles from place served
CPRC §22.002	To county of suit, if witness's residence within 150 miles of county of suit	To county of suit, if witness was served within 150 miles of county of suit

§3.3 Who may issue subpoenas. Subpoenas may be issued by (1) the clerk of the court where the case is pending, (2) a lawyer, or (3) a deposition officer. TRCP 176.4. For the definition of deposition officer, see "Deposition Officer," ch. 6-E, §3, p. 386. When issued by the clerk, the clerk must provide the party requesting the subpoena with an original and a copy (both to be completed by the party) for each witness. TRCP 176.4(a).

§3.4 Who may serve subpoenas. Subpoenas may be served by the sheriff, constable, or any other person who is not a party and is at least 18 years old. TRCP 176.5(a); *see also* TRCP 103 (includes "other person authorized by law or written court order"). Generally, when a party subpoenas a witness for a deposition, the court reporter serves the subpoena and notice of deposition. *See* TRCP 176.4(c).

§3.5 Who may be subpoenaed. Subpoenas may require the attendance of parties and nonparties (*e.g.*, witness, custodian of records). TRCP 176.2, 199.3, 205.1; ***St. Luke's Episcopal Hosp. v. Garcia***, 928 S.W.2d 307, 311 (Tex.App.—Houston [14th Dist.] 1996, orig. proceeding) (a subpoena is the instrument that compels nonparties to respond to a deposition); ***Cheatham v. Rogers***, 824 S.W.2d 231, 234 (Tex.App.—Tyler 1992, orig. proceeding) (nonparty witness can be subpoenaed to attend a deposition). When securing documents from a custodian of records, it is not necessary to name the person in the subpoena; the subpoena can be addressed to the "custodian of records" of the business entity. When securing documents from a party, it is not necessary to serve a subpoena. See "Securing Things from a Party," ch. 6-H, §3, p. 424.

§3.6 Notice to other parties. A party is not required to give other parties notice of its trial subpoenas, but it must give other parties notice of its discovery subpoenas. *See* TRCP 191.5. See "Notice," ch. 6-H, §5.1, p. 428. A party cannot secure discovery by using a trial subpoena to avoid the notice requirements of TRCP 191.5. *See* TRCP 176.3(b) (prohibiting use of subpoena to circumvent discovery rules); ***Prestige Ford Co. v. Gilmore***, 56 S.W.3d 73, 80 (Tex.App.—Houston [14th Dist.] 2001, pet. denied) (same).

§3.7 Manner of service. A subpoena is served by delivering a copy of the subpoena, with the subpoena fee, to the witness. TRCP 176.5(a). If the witness is a party and is represented by an attorney, the subpoena and fee may be served on the witness's attorney of record. *Id.* When a discovery subpoena requires the witness to attend a deposition, the notice of deposition may be served with the subpoena. TRCP 176.4(c).

§3.8 Subpoena fee. The subpoena fee is $10 for each day the witness is required to attend trial or discovery. CPRC §22.001(a); Op. Tex. Att'y Gen. No. DM-342 (1995). When a person is subpoenaed to attend, the person is entitled to the payment of one day's witness fee when the subpoena is served. CPRC §22.001 ($10 per day, first day payable at service). Subpoena fees are recoverable as court costs. CPRC §22.001(c); *see* ***Shenandoah Assocs. v. J&K Props.***, 741 S.W.2d 470, 487 (Tex.App.—Dallas 1987, writ denied).

§3.9 Proof of service. Proof of service must be made by filing with the court (1) the witness's signed written memorandum or (2) a statement by the person who served the subpoena stating the date, time, and manner of service and the name of the person served. TRCP 176.5(b).

§4. OBJECTING TO TRIAL & DISCOVERY SUBPOENAS

§4.1 Who can challenge. The subpoena can be challenged by the person being subpoenaed, the parties, or any other person affected by the subpoena. TRCP 176.6(d)-(f). The subpoena may be challenged by an objection or a motion for protective order.

1. Nonparty subject to subpoena. A nonparty who has been subpoenaed may challenge the subpoena by filing (1) objections to the subpoena or (2) a motion for protective order. TRCP 176.6(d)-(e), 192.6; ***In re Diversicare Gen. Partner***, 41 S.W.3d 788, 794 (Tex.App.—Corpus Christi 2001, orig. proceeding).

2. Party or other person. A party or "any other person affected by the subpoena" may challenge the subpoena by filing a motion for protective order. TRCP 176.6(e), 192.6. See "Motion for Protective Order," ch. 6-A, §19, p. 334.

§4.2 Deadline to challenge.

1. Trial subpoena.

(1) Before trial. If possible, a witness subpoenaed to attend a hearing or trial should object or move for a protective order before the time specified for appearing in court. TRCP 176.6(d), (e).

(2) At trial. A witness subpoenaed to attend a hearing or trial may wait to object or move for a protective order until the witness appears in court. TRCP 176.6(f).

2. Discovery subpoena. Any challenge to the subpoena must be made before the time specified for compliance in the subpoena. TRCP 176.6(d), (e).

§4.3 Types of challenges.

1. Making objections.

(1) To subpoena. To avoid being cited for contempt and having a writ of attachment (a type of civil arrest) issued, the subpoenaed person should file written objections or a motion for protective order alleging one or more of the following: • The subpoena was not dated and signed by a person authorized under TRCP 176.4 to issue subpoenas. TRCP 176.1(h). • The subpoena was not served by a sheriff, constable, or other person authorized by law. TRCP 176.5. • There was no witness fee attached to the subpoena. CPRC §22.001; TRCP 176.8(b); ***Kieffer v. Miller***, 560 S.W.2d 431, 432 (Tex.App.—Beaumont 1977, writ ref'd n.r.e.). • When the subpoena was issued, the nonparty witness did not reside and was not served within 150 miles of the county where the suit is pending. CPRC §22.002; *see* TRCP 176.3(a). • Only one subpoena was issued for two or more witnesses, including the summoned person. TRCP 176.1(d).

(2) To undue burden or expense. The subpoenaed person should file objections or a motion for protective order to a subpoena that imposes an undue burden or expense. TRCP 176.7. The objections or motion must be filed within a reasonable time before the deadline for complying with the subpoena. ***St. Luke's Episcopal Hosp. v. Garcia***, 928 S.W.2d 307, 310 (Tex.App.—Houston [14th Dist.] 1996, orig. proceeding). See "Undue burden," ch. 6-A, §19.1.1, p. 334.

2. Asserting privileges. A subpoenaed person may withhold any material or information claimed to be privileged, but must comply with TRCP 193.3. TRCP 176.6(c). For the procedure for asserting a privilege, see "Asserting privileges," ch. 6-A, §17.2, p. 329. The privilege claim must be asserted before the deadline for complying with the subpoena. *See* ***St. Luke's***, 928 S.W.2d at 311.

§5. ENFORCING SUBPOENAS

The court may impose a fine or confine the subpoenaed person for contempt of court for not complying with a subpoena. TRCP 176.8(a). The court cannot impose a fine or issue a writ of attachment in a civil suit until the subpoenaing party provides an affidavit stating that all lawful fees were paid or tendered to the witness. TRCP 176.8(b); ***Kieffer***, 560 S.W.2d at 432; Op. Tex. Att'y Gen. No. DM-342 (1995). The trial court has no authority to issue a writ of attachment for a witness discharged by the party summoning the witness. ***Alcocer v. Travelers Ins. Co.***, 446 S.W.2d 927, 928-29 (Tex.App.—Houston [14th Dist.] 1969, no writ).

COMMENTARIES

CHAPTER 2. THE PLAINTIFF'S LAWSUIT
TABLE OF CONTENTS

COMMENTARIES

CHAPTER 2. THE PLAINTIFF'S LAWSUIT

TABLE OF CONTENTS

A. PREFILING CONSIDERATIONS

§1. GENERAL

§1.1 Rule. TRCP 54.

§1.2 Purpose. Before filing suit, the plaintiff should check appropriate statutes and any document on which the suit is based to determine if there are any prerequisites to filing suit.

§1.3 Forms. *O'Connor's Texas Civil Forms*, FORMS 2A.

§1.4 Other references. *O'Connor's Texas Causes of Action* (2004) (*O'Connor's COA*); Guiberteau & Motheral, *The Changing Role of Guardian & Attorney Ad Litems*, 58 Tex.B.J. 955 (1995).

§2. NOTICES & DEMANDS

The plaintiff should consider whether it must give the defendant notice or make a pretrial demand before filing suit.

§2.1 Statutory notice. Before plaintiffs can file certain types of suits against certain defendants, they must give written notice. For example, under the Texas Tort Claims Act, a plaintiff must give written notice to a state entity within six months of the date of the incident giving rise to the claim. CPRC §101.101(a). See ***O'Connor's COA***, "Most governmental units," ch. 23-A, §5.1.1, p. 678. The time limits for most statutory notices are substantially shorter than limitations periods. In some cases, the suit is barred if the plaintiff does not give the required statutory notice. *See, e.g.*, ***Cathey v. Booth***, 900 S.W.2d 339, 340 (Tex.1995) (suit barred because Ps did not give written notice and governmental entity did not have actual notice). In others, the plaintiff's failure to give notice is merely a reason to abate, not dismiss. *See, e.g.*, Bus. & Com. Code §17.505(c) (DTPA claim). See ***O'Connor's*** FORMS 2A.

§2.2 Statutory demand. Under some statutes, before filing suit, a plaintiff must make a written demand stating the extent of the plaintiff's damages, attorney fees, and costs. *See* Bus. & Com. Code §17.505(a) (60 days before filing DTPA suit); Ins. Code, art. 21.21, §16(e) (60 days before filing suit for deceptive acts). See ***O'Connor's*** FORMS 2A.

§2.3 Medical malpractice suit. Before filing a suit against a health care provider, the plaintiff must give written notice of the claim. CPRC §74.051(a). If the plaintiff does not give proper notice, and the statute of limitations runs, the suit is barred. ***Kimball v. Brothers***, 741 S.W.2d 370, 371-72 (Tex.1987). The plaintiff must serve on each party or the party's attorney an expert report (not just an affidavit) for each health care defendant against whom a liability claim is asserted. CPRC §74.351(a). See ***O'Connor's COA***, "Expert report," ch. 18-A, §7.2, p. 441.

§2.4 Conditions precedent in contracts. Many contracts contain provisions that are conditions precedent to filing suit. Typically, the provisions require the plaintiff to give notice of the claim and notice of its intent to sue. See "Conditions Precedent," ch. 2-B, §10, p. 78; ***O'Connor's*** FORM 2B:02.

§2.5 Consent to sue. In some instances, a party must obtain consent to sue. *E.g.*, ***Federal Sign v. Texas S. Univ.***, 951 S.W.2d 401, 404-05 (Tex.1997) (party who contracts with state must secure consent to sue state); ***State Farm Mut. Auto. Ins. Co. v. Azima***, 896 S.W.2d 177, 177-78 (Tex.1995) (some insurance contracts require consent to sue from insurer before filing suit against uninsured motorist).

§3. FILING CONSIDERATIONS

Before filing suit, the plaintiff should determine where it may file suit, whether it must first seek an administrative remedy, and whether the suit is subject to alternative dispute resolution.

§3.1 State vs. federal court. Some cases must be filed in federal court (*e.g.*, patent and copyright), some may be filed only in state court (*e.g.*, suits with no federal question or diversity), and others may be filed in either state or federal court. The plaintiff should decide where it has an advantage and file in that jurisdiction. If the plaintiff wants to avoid removal to federal court, it should consider including a local defendant. For information about federal jurisdiction and removal to federal court, see ***O'Connor's Federal Rules * Civil Trials***, ch. 2-F, p. 85, and ch. 4-A, p. 182 (2004).

§3.2 Administrative procedure requirements. Before filing a claim against a governmental entity, the plaintiff should determine if it must first submit the dispute to an administrative procedure. *See* ***Texas DOT v. Jones Bros. Dirt & Paving Contractors***, 92 S.W.3d 477, 484 (Tex.2002); ***General Servs. Comm'n v. Little-Tex Insulation Co.***, 39 S.W.3d 591, 597 (Tex.2001). When an agency has exclusive jurisdiction (not just primary jurisdiction) over a dispute, a party must exhaust all administrative remedies before seeking judicial review of the agency's action. ***Subaru, Inc. v. David McDavid Nissan***, 84 S.W.3d 212, 221 (Tex.2002); *see* ***Cash Am. Int'l Inc. v. Bennett***, 35 S.W.3d 12, 17 (Tex.2000).

§3.3 ADR. Sometimes, by statute or by contract, the plaintiff is required to submit a dispute to some form of dispute resolution. See "The ADR System," ch. 4-A, p. 204.

§4. MISCELLANEOUS

Before filing suit, the plaintiff should consider other miscellaneous matters.

§4.1 Internet research. Information about a defendant can be found on the Internet. For example, to find information about a corporation (registered agent, officers, directors, etc.), go to the site of the Texas Office of the Comptroller, http://ecpa.cpa.state.tx.us/coa/Index.html; to locate real property in the U.S., go to www.iaao.org. To find the address and telephone number for an individual, go to www.anywho.com. Other Internet companies can, for a fee, provide comprehensive information about individuals, including location, family members, nearest neighbors with listed telephone numbers, judgments, and bankruptcies. See, for example, www.ussearch.com.

§4.2 Presuit discovery. A plaintiff may secure discovery before filing suit. A plaintiff can file a verified motion and obtain an order authorizing the taking of a deposition before suit. TRCP 202.1, 202.2; *see also* TRCP 205 (discovery from nonparty). Presuit discovery is useful to preserve evidence when a critical witness is old, infirm, or about to leave the jurisdiction. It can also be used to investigate a case before filing suit to avoid penalties under TRCP 13 and CPRC §§9.012 and 10.004 for groundless and frivolous lawsuits. See "Deposition Before Suit," ch. 6-E, §16, p. 403; ***O'Connor's*** FORMS 6E:09-12.

§4.3 Appointment of legal representative. When the plaintiff or defendant is incompetent to represent herself in court (*e.g.*, an incapacitated person), the plaintiff's attorney should determine if the party has a legal representative with the capacity to file or defend the suit. See "Guardians Ad Litem Under TRCP 173," ch. 1-I, p. 49.

§4.4 Lis pendens notice. In some cases involving an interest in real property, the plaintiff may file a lis pendens notice. *See* Prop. Code §§12.007, 13.004. The filing of a lis pendens notice puts the public on notice that the property is involved in litigation. ***Prappas v. Meyerland Cmty. Imprv. Ass'n***, 795 S.W.2d 794, 795 (Tex.App.—Houston [14th Dist.] 1990, writ denied). The notice does not prevent transfer of the property during the litigation; it merely prevents the purchaser from claiming ignorance of the litigation. ***Cherokee Water Co. v. Advance Oil & Gas Co.***, 843 S.W.2d 132, 135 (Tex.App.—Texarkana 1992, writ denied).

B. PLAINTIFF'S ORIGINAL PETITION

§1. GENERAL

§1.1 Rules. TRCP 45-61; 78-82.

§1.2 Purpose. The plaintiff's petition defines the issues for trial. ***Murray v. O&A Express***, 630 S.W.2d 633, 636 (Tex.1982). The petition should give the defendant fair notice of the facts relied on, enabling it to prepare a defense. ***Horizon v. Auld***, 34 S.W.3d 887, 897 (Tex.2000); ***Garvey v. Vawter***, 795 S.W.2d 741, 742 (Tex.1990); ***Roark v. Allen***, 633 S.W.2d 804, 810 (Tex.1982); *see* TRCP 45.

§1.3 Forms. ***O'Connor's Texas Civil Forms***, FORMS 2B.

§1.4 Other references. ***O'Connor's Texas Causes of Action*** (2004) (***O'Connor's COA***); Reese, *Misnomer & Misidentification: Suing the Wrong Defendant*, 60 Tex.B.J. 548 (1997).

§2. DISCOVERY CONTROL PLAN

In the first numbered paragraph of its petition, the plaintiff must allege whether discovery is intended to be conducted under Level 1, 2, or 3 of TRCP 190. TRCP 190.1. See "Discovery Control Plans," ch. 6-A, §7, p. 318. The level designated for the discovery control plan must relate to the type of suit and the amount of damages. See "Damages," §8, p. 76. The plaintiff must also include the statement about the discovery level in any amended pleading. If the plaintiff does not plead a discovery level as required by TRCP 190.1, the defendant may file special exceptions. *See* TRCP 190, cmt. 1. See ***O'Connor's*** FORM 3G:01.

§2.1 Level 1. If the plaintiff intends discovery to be conducted under Level 1, its petition should allege one of the following:

1. Suits involving monetary damages. "Plaintiff intends that discovery be conducted under Level 1 and affirmatively pleads that it seeks only monetary relief aggregating $50,000 or less, excluding costs, prejudgment interest, and attorney fees." TRCP 190.2(a)(1); *see* TRCP 190, cmt. 2.

2. Suits for divorce. "Plaintiff intends that discovery be conducted under Level 1 and affirmatively pleads this is a suit for divorce in which there are no children and the value of the marital estate is more than zero but less than $50,000." TRCP 190.2(a)(2); *see* TRCP 190, cmt. 2.

§2.2 Level 2. If the plaintiff intends discovery to be conducted under Level 2, its petition should allege one of the following:

1. Suits involving monetary damages. "Plaintiff intends that discovery be conducted under Level 2 and affirmatively pleads that it seeks monetary relief aggregating more than $50,000." *See* TRCP 190.2(a)(1), 190.3(a) & cmt. 2.

2. Suits for divorce.

(1) Children. "Plaintiff intends that discovery be conducted under Level 2 and affirmatively pleads this is a suit for divorce in which there are children." Discovery for a divorce involving children cannot be conducted under Level 1. *See* TRCP 190.2(a)(2), 190.3(a) & cmt. 2.

(2) Estate over $50,000. "Plaintiff intends that discovery be conducted under Level 2 and affirmatively pleads this is a suit for divorce in which the value of the marital estate is more than $50,000." *See* TRCP 190.2(a)(2), 190.3(a).

3. Suits involving injunctive relief. "Plaintiff intends that discovery be conducted under Level 2 and affirmatively pleads that it seeks injunctive relief." *See* TRCP 190, cmt. 2.

§2.3 Level 3. If the plaintiff intends that discovery be conducted under Level 3, its petition should allege the following: "Plaintiff intends that discovery be conducted under Level 3." *See* TRCP 190.4. A plaintiff should plead Level 3 when a discovery control plan must be tailored to the circumstances of the specific suit. TRCP 190.4(a). A plaintiff's allegation that the case is to be governed by Level 3 does not make Level 3 applicable; a case can be conducted under Level 3 only by court order. TRCP 190, cmt. 1.

§3. PARTIES

§3.1 General rule.

1. Named party. A person or entity is not a party to a lawsuit unless named as a party. ***Mapco, Inc. v. Carter***, 817 S.W.2d 686, 687 (Tex.1991); *see* TRCP 79. See "Parties & Claims," ch. 2-E, p. 96; ***O'Connor's*** FORMS 2B:11-21. A suit may be maintained only by and against parties who have an actual or legal existence.

Bailey v. Vanscot Concrete Co., 894 S.W.2d 757, 759 (Tex.1995), *overruled on other grounds*, ***Chilkewitz v. Hyson***, 22 S.W.3d 825 (Tex.1999).

2. Virtual party. Under the virtual representation doctrine, persons who are not joined by name as parties may still be parties in substance and legal effect. ***New Boston Gen. Hosp. v. Texas Workforce Comm'n***, 47 S.W.3d 34, 39 (Tex.App.—Texarkana 2001, no pet.). To claim virtual representation, an unnamed party must show the following: (1) it is bound by the judgment; (2) its privity of estate, title, or interest is apparent from the record; and (3) there is a common interest between the named and unnamed parties. ***City of San Benito v. Rio Grande Valley Gas Co.***, 109 S.W.3d 750, 755 (Tex.2003); ***Motor Vehicle Bd. of the Tex. DOT v. El Paso Indep. Auto. Dealers Ass'n***, 1 S.W.3d 108, 110 (Tex.1999); ***New Boston***, 47 S.W.3d at 40. An unnamed party cannot appeal unless it is virtually represented. *E.g.*, ***City of San Benito***, 109 S.W.3d at 754-55 (unnamed class members who would be bound by judgment approving settlement were "parties" for purposes of appeal); *see* ***Motor Vehicle Bd.***, 1 S.W.3d at 110 (generally, appeal available only to parties of record).

§3.2 Standing & capacity. Before filing suit, the plaintiff should determine that (1) it has standing and capacity to file the suit, and (2) the correct defendant is sued in the correct capacity.

1. Standing. A plaintiff has standing to bring suit if (1) it has a justiciable interest in the suit, (2) standing is conferred by statute, or (3) the plaintiff is a taxpayer seeking to enjoin the illegal expenditure of public funds. ***Williams v. Lara***, 52 S.W.3d 171, 178-79 (Tex.2001); *see* ***Brown v. Todd***, 53 S.W.3d 297, 305 (Tex. 2001) (councilman & citizen lacked standing to challenge lawfulness of mayor's executive order). Standing, which is a component of subject-matter jurisdiction, cannot be waived and can be raised for the first time on appeal. ***West Orange-Cove Consol. ISD v. Alanis***, 107 S.W.3d 558, 583 (Tex.2003); ***Texas Ass'n of Bus. v. Texas Air Control Bd.***, 852 S.W.2d 440, 445 (Tex.1993). When a plaintiff has standing because it has a justiciable interest in the suit, standing limits subject-matter jurisdiction to cases involving (1) a distinct injury to the plaintiff and (2) a real controversy between the parties that will be decided by the suit. ***Brown***, 53 S.W.3d at 305; ***Wilson v. Andrews***, 10 S.W.3d 663, 669 (Tex.1999). A plaintiff who files suit as a class representative must have standing as an individual. ***M.D. Anderson Cancer Ctr. v. Novak***, 52 S.W.3d 704, 708 (Tex.2001).

2. Capacity. A party has capacity to file or defend a suit if it has the legal authority to act, regardless of whether it has a justiciable interest. ***Coastal Liquids Transp. v. Harris Cty. Appr. Dist.***, 46 S.W.3d 880, 884 (Tex.2001); ***Nootsie, Ltd. v. Williamson Cty. Appr. Dist.***, 925 S.W.2d 659, 661 (Tex.1996). A court can render judgment for or against a party only in the capacity in which the party sued or was sued. *See, e.g.*, ***Werner v. Colwell***, 909 S.W.2d 866, 870 (Tex.1995) (because D was sued only in individual capacity, judgment could not be rendered against her as trustee); ***Gracia v. RC Cola-7-Up Bottling Co.***, 667 S.W.2d 517, 519-20 (Tex.1984) (because P brought suit only as next friend, judgment mistakenly rendered for her individually was not res judicata to a second suit by her individually). Unlike standing, an objection to a party's capacity to file or defend a suit can be waived. ***Nootsie***, 925 S.W.32 at 662.

3. Distinction between standing & capacity. It is sometimes difficult to distinguish between a party's standing to sue and its capacity to sue. *See* ***City of Ft. Worth v. Groves***, 746 S.W.2d 907, 913 (Tex.App.—Fort Worth 1988, no writ). A person has standing when she is personally aggrieved; a person has capacity when she has the authority to file suit. One way of looking at the distinction between standing and capacity is this: When a party to a suit has an interest in the suit but needs a surrogate to bring or defend the suit, the party does not have capacity. For example, capacity is a problem for a minor who attempts to file suit. *See* ***Byrd v. Woodruff***, 891 S.W.2d 689, 704 (Tex.App.—Dallas 1994, writ dism'd). Even though the minor has an interest in the litigation, the suit must be filed by a surrogate.

§3.3 Party identification.

1. Full name. The petition should state the full names of the parties and allege the suing party's capacity in one of the early paragraphs under a section entitled "Parties." *See* TRCP 79.

(1) Misspelled name. Under the rule of *idem sonans*, a misspelled name is sufficient identification if it sounds practically identical to the correct name. *E.g.*, ***Mantis v. Resz***, 5 S.W.3d 388, 391 & n.5 (Tex.App.—Fort Worth 1999, pet. denied) (Mantis sounds like Mantas), *overruled on other grounds*, ***Sheldon v. Emergency Med. Consultants***, 43 S.W.3d 701 (Tex.App.—Fort Worth 2001, no pet.); ***Chumney v. Craig***, 805 S.W.2d 864, 866 (Tex.App.—Waco 1991, writ denied) (Damond sufficiently similar to Damon).

(2) Misnomer vs. misidentification. Getting the defendant's correct name determines whether the court has jurisdiction over the person and whether the statute of limitations is tolled. *See* ***Matthews Trucking Co. v. Smith***, 682 S.W.2d 237, 239 (Tex.1984). See ***O'Connor's COA***, "Misnomer & misidentification," ch. 43, §2.5.6, p. 1147.

(a) Misnomer. If a plaintiff sues and serves the correct defendant but misnames the defendant, the error is misnomer. ***Chilkewitz v. Hyson***, 22 S.W.3d 825, 828 (Tex.1999); *see also* ***Pierson v. SMS Fin. II, LLC***, 959 S.W.2d 343, 347-48 (Tex.App.—Texarkana 1998, no pet.) (misnomer when P mistakenly named a related corporate entity rather than itself as P). A misnomer can be corrected by amendment even after the statute of limitations expires. ***Enserch Corp. v. Parker***, 794 S.W.2d 2, 4-5 (Tex.1990).

(b) Misidentification. When there are two separate legal entities, and a plaintiff mistakenly sues the wrong entity with a name similar to that of the correct entity, the error is misidentification. ***Chilkewitz***, 22 S.W.3d at 828; *see, e.g.*, ***Continental S. Lines v. Hilland***, 528 S.W.2d 828, 830-31 (Tex.1975) (P sued Continental Trailways, Inc., a different corporation from Continental Southern Lines, Inc., which did business as "Continental Trailways"); ***Cortinas v. Wilson***, 851 S.W.2d 324, 327 (Tex.App.—Dallas 1993, no writ) (P sued & served mother of intended D). A misidentification can be corrected by amendment after limitations expires only if (1) there were two separate but related entities that used a similar name, (2) the correct entity had notice of the suit, and (3) it was not misled or disadvantaged by the mistake. ***Chilkewitz***, 22 S.W.3d at 830; ***Diamond v. Eighth Ave. 92***, 105 S.W.3d 691, 695 (Tex.App.—Fort Worth 2003, no pet.); ***Wright v. TDCJ-ID***, 68 S.W.3d 788, 791 (Tex.App.—Houston [14th Dist.] 2001, no pet.); *see also* TRCP 28 (permits suits against those using assumed name which in effect permits amendment to add misidentified D after limitations expires).

2. Estate. Because an estate of a decedent is not a legal entity, a suit by or against an estate must be brought in the name of its personal representative. ***Embrey v. Royal Ins. Co.***, 22 S.W.3d 414, 415 n.2 (Tex. 2000); ***Henson v. Estate of Crow***, 734 S.W.2d 648, 649 (Tex.1987); ***Price v. Estate of Anderson***, 522 S.W.2d 690, 691 (Tex.1975). The personal representative is the plaintiff or defendant. ***Sarny Holdings v. Letsos***, 896 S.W.2d 274, 276 (Tex.App.—Houston [1st Dist.] 1995, writ denied). If a suit names the estate rather than the personal representative, the trial court may still have jurisdiction if the personal representative is served with citation and participates in the suit. ***Miller v. Estate of Self***, 113 S.W.3d 554, 557 (Tex.App.—Texarkana 2003, n.p.h.); *see* ***Embrey***, 22 S.W.3d at 415 n.2 (if unnamed personal representative participated in case, judgment involving estate may be valid).

(1) Personal representative qualified in Texas. A personal representative of an estate must be qualified by a Texas court to bring or defend a suit relating to the estate in a Texas court. ***Minga v. Perales***, 603 S.W.2d 240, 242 (Tex.App.—Corpus Christi 1980, no writ); *see, e.g.*, ***McAdams v. Capitol Prods. Corp.***, 810 S.W.2d 290, 293 (Tex.App.—Fort Worth 1991, writ denied) (administrator appointed by an Arkansas court was not qualified to bring suit in Texas until she was appointed by a Texas court); *see also* Prob. Code §105 (qualification of foreign executor).

(2) Death of plaintiff during suit. When a plaintiff dies after suit is filed, the personal representative of that person's estate (or the heirs, if there is no personal representative) should file a "suggestion of death" with the court, stating that the person has died and naming the personal representative (or the heirs) of the person's estate. TRCP 151. If the cause of action survives the plaintiff's death, the personal representative or heirs may then enter an appearance and prosecute the suit in their own names. TRCP 150, 151. If, within a reasonable time, the personal representative or heirs do not file a suggestion of death and appear to prosecute the suit, the defendant should file a suggestion of death and ask the court clerk to issue and have served a writ of scire facias—similar to a citation—on the personal representative or heirs. TRCP 151, 154. If the personal representative or heirs do not appear and prosecute the suit by 10:00 a.m. on the Monday following 20 days after the scire facias is served, the defendant can ask the court to dismiss the suit for want of prosecution. TRCP 151, 154; *see* ***Gracey v. West***, 422 S.W.2d 913, 918 (Tex.1968) (D cannot ask for dismissal until scire facias is issued & personal representative does not appear).

(3) Death of defendant during suit. When a defendant dies after suit is filed, if the cause of action survives the defendant's death, the plaintiff must amend the suit to name the estate's personal representative or, if the representative is unavailable, the estate's heirs. TRCP 152; ***Rooke v. Jenson***, 838 S.W.2d 229, 230 (Tex.1992); ***Price***, 522 S.W.2d at 691. Once the plaintiff has amended the petition, or if a suggestion of death is filed, the court clerk must issue a writ of scire facias, requiring the personal representative or heirs to appear and defend the suit. TRCP 152. On the return of service, the plaintiff may proceed with the suit against the personal representative or heirs. *Id.*

(4) Death or replacement of personal representative. If a personal representative dies, resigns, or is removed while party to a suit, the suit then proceeds in the name of the successor personal representative (or the heirs, if there is no successor). TRCP 153. The procedure for substituting the successor personal representative or heirs into the suit is similar to that for the death of a plaintiff or defendant, as appropriate. *Id.*

(5) Real property. In a suit against an estate of a decedent that involves title to real property, the executor or administrator of the estate, if any, and the heirs to the estate must be made party-defendants. CPRC §17.002.

3. Corporation. A corporation must sue as a corporate entity. Except for derivative actions, a stockholder cannot file suit individually for damages owed to the corporation because the stockholder lacks both standing (the stockholder was not personally aggrieved) and capacity (the stockholder is not the right surrogate) to bring suit for damages to a corporation. *See* ***White v. Independence Bank***, 794 S.W.2d 895, 898 n.3 (Tex.App.—Houston [1st Dist.] 1990, writ denied).

4. Assumed name. A person or business entity (partnership, unincorporated association, or private corporation) doing business under an assumed name may sue or be sued in its assumed or common name. TRCP 28; ***Chilkewitz***, 22 S.W.3d at 828-29; *see* TRCS art. 6133. A person or business entity doing business under an assumed name must file an assumed-name certificate. Bus. & Com. Code §36.25; ***Sixth RMA Partners v. Sibley***, 111 S.W.3d 46, 55 (Tex.2003). The court may abate an action until the certificate is filed. ***Sibley***, 111 S.W.3d at 55. Before judgment is rendered, the person or entity's correct legal name must be substituted for its assumed name. ***Sibley***, 111 S.W.3d at 53; *see* TRCP 28. The correct name may be substituted by motion of a party or the court, by an amended pleading, or, if there is no objection, by a supplemental pleading. *See* TRCP 28; ***Sibley***, 111 S.W.3d at 53. When a person is doing business under an assumed name, a judgment rendered against the unincorporated association is binding on that person. ***Holberg & Co. v. Citizens Nat'l Assur. Co.***, 856 S.W.2d 515, 517 (Tex. App.—Houston [1st Dist.] 1993, no writ).

(1) Unincorporated for-profit association. Members of an unincorporated association are individually liable for acts of agents or employees of the association if the act is committed within the scope of their authority. ***Hutchins v. Grace Tabernacle United Pentecostal Ch.***, 804 S.W.2d 598, 599 (Tex.App.—Houston [1st Dist.] 1991, no writ).

(2) Unincorporated nonprofit association. Under the Texas Uniform Unincorporated Nonprofit Association Act (TUNA), unincorporated nonprofit associations are legal entities liable for their contracts and torts. TRCS art. 1396-70.01, §7(a). TUNA relieves the members of an unincorporated nonprofit association from individual responsibility. *Id.* §7(b)-(c). Associations that benefit from TUNA are churches and property owner's groups.

5. County or city. A suit by or against a county or incorporated city must be in the entity's corporate name. TRCP 33.

§3.4 Plaintiff.

1. P's residence. The petition should state the residence of each party. TRCP 79. When the plaintiff is relying on a venue provision that depends on the plaintiff's residence, the plaintiff should plead the county of its residence, but a street address is not necessary. Unless the county of the plaintiff's residence is relevant to venue or some other issue in the case, it is not necessary for the plaintiff to include its residence in the petition.

2. Minor as P. In Texas, a minor is an unmarried person younger than 18 years of age. CPRC §129.001; *see* Prob. Code §3(t). A minor does not have the legal capacity to employ an attorney or anyone else to watch over her interests. ***Byrd v. Woodruff***, 891 S.W.2d 689, 704 (Tex.App.—Dallas 1994, writ dism'd). A minor cannot bring a cause of action on her own behalf unless her disability has been removed. ***Sax v. Votteler***, 648 S.W.2d 661, 666 (Tex.1983); *see* CPRC §16.001(b) (tolling limitations period while person is under legal disability). However, a lawsuit may be filed on behalf of a minor by the guardian of the estate of the minor appointed by a probate court, or, if the minor has no guardian, by a next friend or guardian ad litem appointed by a district court. *See* Fam. Code §102.003(a)(2), (4); Prob. Code §773; TRCP 44, 173. See "Motion to Appoint Guardian Ad Litem Under TRCP 173," ch. 1-I, §3, p. 50. A parent is a proper "next friend," although any competent adult may act as next friend. *See* Fam. Code §102.003(a)(1) (parent may file suit for child). See §3.5.4, below.

3. Death actions. The proper plaintiff in a survival action is the legal representative of the decedent's estate. CPRC §71.021. See ***O'Connor's COA***, "Survival," ch. 7-A, p. 138. The proper plaintiffs in a wrongful death case are the decedent's spouse, children, and parents. CPRC §71.004(b). See ***O'Connor's COA***, "Wrongful Death," ch. 7-B, p. 146.

§3.5 Defendant. The petition (and the citation) should designate as the defendant the person or entity against whom the plaintiff can collect the judgment. See ***O'Connor's*** FORMS 2B:12-21. This is confusing when the defendant must be sued through a representative. For example, because an estate is not a legal entity, the petition, citation, and judgment should name the representative of the estate as the defendant on behalf of the estate, not the decedent. See "Estate," §3.3.2, p. 69. A judgment is void if the trial court did not have personal jurisdiction over the defendant. ***American Gen. Fire & Cas. Co. v. Vandewater***, 907 S.W.2d 491, 492 (Tex.1995).

1. D's address for service. For purposes of service, the petition should identify the address of the defendant or the defendant's agent. *See* TRCP 79. See "Address for service," ch. 2-H, §2.5.1(3), p. 119.

2. D's agent for service. When the defendant is a corporation or another entity served through an agent, the petition must identify the defendant's agent for service and its address. *See* ***Harmon & Reid v. Quin***, 258 S.W.2d 441, 442 (Tex.App.—San Antonio 1953, orig. proceeding); *see also* ***Interaction, Inc. v. State***, 17 S.W.3d 775, 779-80 (Tex.App.—Austin 2000, pet. denied) (corporation doing business in Texas must maintain current name & address of its registered agent on file with Secretary of State).

3. Agency. If a principal is liable for the acts of its agent, the plaintiff should sue the principal and allege the agency relationship. *See* ***Southern Cty. Mut. Ins. Co. v. First Bank & Trust***, 750 S.W.2d 170, 172 (Tex. 1988).

4. Minor as D. A minor may be sued and served through the guardian of the estate of the minor appointed by a probate court; or, if the minor has no guardian, she may be sued and served in her own name. *See* TRCP 173; ***Vandewater***, 907 S.W.2d at 492; ***Wright v. Jones***, 52 S.W.2d 247, 251 (Tex.Comm'n App.1932, holding approved); ***Peek v. DeBerry***, 819 S.W.2d 217, 218 (Tex.App.—San Antonio 1991, writ denied). Once a minor without a probate-court-appointed guardian is before a trial court as a defendant, the trial court must appoint a guardian ad litem for the minor. *See* TRCP 173; ***Wright***, 52 S.W.2d at 251; ***Jaynes v. Lee***, 306 S.W.2d 182, 184-85 (Tex.App.—Texarkana 1957, no writ). See "Motion to Appoint Guardian Ad Litem Under TRCP 173," ch. 1-I, §3,

p. 50. When a minor is named as a defendant in a suit but is actually a claimant, the minor may be represented by her parent as next friend. ***Vandewater***, 907 S.W.2d at 492. See §3.4.2, above.

5. Partnership. A petition against a partnership should allege that a partnership exists, state the name of the partnership, list all the partners, and state that the partners are sued as members of the partnership. ***Ben Fitzgerald Rlty. Co. v. Muller***, 846 S.W.2d 110, 115 (Tex.App.—Tyler 1993, writ denied) (petition did not allege partnership or that Ds were partners). By naming and individually serving all the partners, a judgment may be entered against the partnership and each partner. CPRC §31.003; *see also* TRCS art. 6132b-3.04 (all partners are liable for debts of partnership unless otherwise agreed by claimant or provided by law). If the petition names only the partnership, a judgment may be entered against the partnership and any partner actually served. CPRC §17.022; ***Fincher v. B&D Air Conditioning & Heating Co.***, 816 S.W.2d 509, 512 (Tex.App.—Houston [1st Dist.] 1991, writ denied); *see also* TRCS art. 6132b-3.04 (partners jointly & severally liable for partnership debts). Once the liability of the partnership is established, each partner is jointly and severally liable as a matter of law. ***Fincher***, 816 S.W.2d at 513.

6. Corporation.

(1) Privileges forfeited. In a suit against a corporation whose right to sue was forfeited for nonpayment of taxes, the plaintiff should name the corporation and all the stockholders. *See* ***M&M Constr. Co. v. Great Am. Ins. Co.***, 747 S.W.2d 552, 555 (Tex.App.—Corpus Christi 1988, no writ) (when corporation's charter forfeited, stockholders may defend actions to protect their property rights). If a domestic or foreign corporation does not pay its assessed franchise tax within 45 days after notice of forfeiture is mailed, the comptroller will forfeit its corporate privileges. Tax Code §171.251(2). Upon forfeiture of corporate privileges, the corporation is denied the right to sue or defend in a Texas court. *Id.* §171.252(1); ***G. Richard Goins Constr. Co. v. S.B. McLaughlin Assocs.***, 930 S.W.2d 124, 127-28 (Tex.App.—Tyler 1996, writ denied). For the difference between forfeiture of privilege to sue and forfeiture of corporate charter, see "Stages of Corporate Decay" in ***El T. Mexican Rests. v. Bacon***, 921 S.W.2d 247, 252-53 (Tex.App.—Houston [1st Dist.] 1995, writ denied).

(2) Corporate merger. In a suit against a corporation that was merged with another corporation, the plaintiff should name the surviving corporation and, to be safe, the merged corporation. When a merger takes effect, the separate existence of the corporations ceases, except for any surviving or new domestic corporation. Bus. Corp. Act art. 5.06(A)(1); ***Bailey v. Vanscot Concrete Co.***, 894 S.W.2d 757, 759 (Tex.1995), *overruled on other grounds*, ***Chilkewitz v. Hyson***, 22 S.W.3d 825 (Tex.1999). In a merger, the privileges, powers, rights, and duties of the corporation are transferred to the surviving corporation. ***Bailey***, 894 S.W.2d at 759.

7. Governmental entity. For the substantive law on suits against the State of Texas or other governmental unit, see ***O'Connor's COA***, "The Doctrine of Sovereign Immunity," ch. 22-A, p. 621.

§3.6 Necessary parties. The plaintiff should sue all defendants for all claims necessary to avoid the preclusive effects of res judicata. See "Multiple Defendants," ch. 2-E, §4, p. 97; "Res Judicata & Collateral Estoppel," ch. 9-D, p. 609.

§4. JURISDICTION

The Texas rules of pleading do not require a plaintiff to allege the court has jurisdiction over the case, as do the federal rules. However, the plaintiff must plead enough facts to affirmatively demonstrate the trial court has jurisdiction to entertain the suit. ***Texas Dept. of Crim. Justice v. Miller***, 51 S.W.3d 583, 587 (Tex.2001); ***Texas Ass'n of Bus. v. Texas Air Control Bd.***, 852 S.W.2d 440, 446 (Tex.1993). See ***O'Connor's*** FORM 2B:22. To render a binding judgment, the trial court must have (1) jurisdiction of the parties or property, (2) jurisdiction of the subject matter of the suit, (3) jurisdiction to enter the particular judgment, and (4) capacity to act as a court. ***State Bar v. Gomez***, 891 S.W.2d 243, 245 (Tex.1994); *see* ***State ex rel. Latty v. Owens***, 907 S.W.2d 484, 485 (Tex.1995). Before filing suit, the plaintiff should examine its petition to determine whether it has made sufficient jurisdictional allegations to satisfy due process requirements under the U.S. Constitution to require the defendant to answer. *See* ***Paramount Pipe & Sup. Co. v. Muhr***, 749 S.W.2d 491, 496 (Tex.1988). Unless the pleadings demonstrate the absence of jurisdiction, the court will assume it has jurisdiction over the case. ***Peek v. Equipment Serv. Co.***, 779 S.W.2d 802, 804 (Tex. 1989); ***Beacon Nat'l Ins. Co. v. Montemayor***, 86 S.W.3d 260, 266 (Tex.App.—Austin 2002, no pet.).

§4.1 Personal jurisdiction. Jurisdiction over the defendant concerns whether the defendant is properly before the court, as authorized by procedural statutes and rules, within the limits of due process. ***Perry v. Ponder***, 604 S.W.2d 306, 322 (Tex.App.—Dallas 1980, no writ). See CPRC, ch. 17. The plaintiff should draft its petition to support a default judgment in the event the defendant does not file an answer. See ***O'Connor's*** FORM 2B:01.

1. Over a resident. When the petition states the defendant is a resident of Texas and provides an address in Texas where the defendant can be served, it satisfies the threshold requirement for jurisdiction over a resident defendant.

2. Over a nonresident. The plaintiff has the burden of pleading sufficient facts to bring a nonresident defendant within the provisions of the Texas long-arm statute. ***American Type Culture Collection v. Coleman***, 83 S.W.3d 801, 807 (Tex.2002); ***BMC Software v. Marchand***, 83 S.W.3d 789, 793 (Tex.2002); *see* CPRC ch. 17 (long-arm statute). The petition must allege facts that, if true, would make the nonresident defendant subject to in personam jurisdiction of a Texas court. ***Paramount Pipe***, 749 S.W.2d at 496; *see, e.g.*, ***Frank A. Smith Sales v. Atlantic Aero***, 31 S.W.3d 742, 746 (Tex.App.—Corpus Christi 2000, no pet.) (P did not allege facts showing actions in Texas); ***Biotrace Int'l v. Wilwerding***, 937 S.W.2d 146, 147 (Tex.App.—Houston [1st Dist.] 1997, no writ) (default judgment reversed because P did not allege any activity in Texas). *But see* ***Temperature Sys. v. Bill Pepper, Inc.***, 854 S.W.2d 669, 673 (Tex.App.—Dallas 1993, writ dism'd) (judgment affirmed even though P did not allege facts to support general jurisdiction because issue was tried by consent). The plaintiff must allege facts to show the defendant "purposefully availed" itself of the privilege of conducting activities in Texas. ***Guardian Royal Exch. Assur. v. English China Clays***, 815 S.W.2d 223, 226 (Tex.1991). The petition should state how, when, and where each nonresident defendant made itself subject to the jurisdiction of Texas courts. See "Long-arm service," ch. 2-H, §5.3, p. 124; "Special Appearance—Challenging Personal Jurisdiction," ch. 3-B, p. 143.

§4.2 Subject-matter jurisdiction. Subject-matter jurisdiction concerns the kinds of controversies a court has the authority to resolve. ***Davis v. Zoning Bd.***, 865 S.W.2d 941, 942 (Tex.1993). Subject-matter jurisdiction requires that the party bringing suit have standing, that there be a live controversy between the parties, and that the case be justiciable. ***Gomez***, 891 S.W.2d at 245. See "Choosing the Court—Jurisdiction," ch. 2-F, p. 101.

1. If dependent on amount in controversy. In most cases, a court's jurisdiction is based on the allegations in the petition about the amount in controversy. ***Continental Coffee Prods. Co. v. Cazarez***, 937 S.W.2d 444, 449 (Tex.1996). When jurisdiction depends on the amount in controversy, the plaintiff's petition must allege facts showing that the court has jurisdiction. *See* ***Richardson v. First Nat'l Life Ins. Co.***, 419 S.W.2d 836, 839 (Tex.1967). This is often accomplished in the allegations regarding damages.

2. If statutory. If a particular statute creates a cause of action, the court's jurisdiction depends on that statute. *See, e.g.*, ***In re Burlington N. & S. Ry.***, 12 S.W.3d 891, 899 (Tex.App.—Houston [14th Dist.] 2000, orig. proceeding) (when court had jurisdiction over subject matter by statute, P not required to allege an amount in controversy to obtain auxiliary injunctive relief). In such a case, the plaintiff should plead the statute. For example, a suit filed under the Whistleblower Act should cite the Whistleblower Act, Gov't Code §554.002.

3. If nonremovable. If, by statute, a case filed in state court is not removable to federal court (*e.g.*, FELA or Jones Act case), the plaintiff should expressly plead the suit is not removable. If a defendant attempts to remove a case to federal court that is not removable, and the plaintiff's pleadings state the case is not removable, the defendant could face sanctions in federal court under FRCP 11 or in state court under TRCP 13 and CPRC §9.012 and §10.004. To prevent a suit from being removed to federal court when filing suit against a non-Texas corporation doing business in Texas, the plaintiff should consider suing one of the corporation's employees who resides in Texas. See ***O'Connor's Federal Rules * Civil Trials***, "Plaintiff's Motion to Remand," ch. 4-B, p. 197 (2004).

§5. VENUE

The Texas rules of pleading do not require a plaintiff to plead the basis for venue in the county of suit. ***Electronic Data Sys. Corp. v. Pioneer Elec.***, 68 S.W.3d 254, 260 (Tex.App.—Fort Worth 2002, no pet.). However, the plaintiff's original petition should state enough facts about the cause of action to establish venue in the county where the suit is filed. Pleading specific venue facts in the petition, with citation to the venue statute, may prevent a defendant from pursuing a fruitless motion to transfer venue. *See* CPRC ch. 15; TRCP 86, 87. If a particular venue statute is cited in the petition, it does not limit the plaintiff to that ground. ***Electronic Data***, 68 S.W.3d at 260. See "Choosing the Court—Venue," ch. 2-G, p. 111; "Motion to Transfer—Challenging Venue," ch. 3-C, p. 152; ***O'Connor's*** FORM 2B:23.

§6. PLEADING A CAUSE OF ACTION

A cause of action consists of a plaintiff's primary right and the defendant's act or omission that violated that right. ***Jones v. Ray***, 886 S.W.2d 817, 821 (Tex.App.—Houston [1st Dist.] 1994, orig. proceeding). For a cause of action to be adequately pleaded, the trial court must be able to determine with reasonable certainty the elements of the cause of action and the relief sought. ***Stoner v. Thompson***, 578 S.W.2d 679, 683 (Tex.1979). For a list of elements for many common causes of action, see ***O'Connor's COA***.

§6.1 Essential allegations. At a minimum, the pleaded facts must show (1) the plaintiff's right and the defendant's duty, (2) the defendant's breach of its duty, and (3) the plaintiff's injury as a result of the defendant's breach. *See, e.g.*, ***Greater Houston Transp. Co. v. Phillips***, 801 S.W.2d 523, 525 (Tex.1990) (elements of common-law negligence).

§6.2 Fair notice of claim. The pleadings must give a short statement of the cause of action sufficient to give the defendant fair and adequate notice of the claim involved and to enable it to prepare a defense. TRCP 45(b), 47(a); ***Garvey v. Vawter***, 795 S.W.2d 741, 742 (Tex.1990); ***Roark v. Allen***, 633 S.W.2d 804, 810 (Tex.1982); *see* ***Smithkline Beecham Corp. v. Doe***, 903 S.W.2d 347, 354 (Tex.1995). Texas follows the "fair notice" standard for pleading, which looks to whether the opposing party can ascertain from the pleading the nature and basic issues of the controversy and what testimony will be relevant. ***Horizon v. Auld***, 34 S.W.3d 887, 896 (Tex.2000). The "fair notice" requirement does not require the pleader to plead evidentiary matters with meticulous particularity. ***Trinity Universal Ins. Co. v. Cowan***, 945 S.W.2d 819, 825 n.4 (Tex.1997).

1. Alleging facts. The petition must state enough facts to inform the defendant of the nature of the claim. The petition does not need to include the evidence on which the plaintiff intends to rely. ***Paramount Pipe & Sup. Co. v. Muhr***, 749 S.W.2d 491, 494-95 (Tex.1988). The petition is sufficient if it alleges facts generally. *See* TRCP 45(b), 47(a); ***Willock v. Bui***, 734 S.W.2d 390, 392 (Tex.App.—Houston [1st Dist.] 1987, no writ). The plaintiff should evaluate its petition to determine if it would support a default judgment in the event the defendant does not answer. See "Sufficiency of plaintiff's petition," ch. 7-A, §3.2, p. 444.

PRACTICE TIP

The allegation that an event occurred "on or about" a certain date means generally in the time around that date. ***Winfield v. Renfro****, 821 S.W.2d 640, 646-47 (Tex.App.—Houston [1st Dist.] 1991, writ denied);* ***Fortner v. Merrill Lynch, Pierce, Fenner & Smith****, 687 S.W.2d 8, 11 (Tex.App.—Dallas 1984, writ ref'd n.r.e.). The courts have upheld as much as a three month variance in dates between a plaintiff's allegation of when the event occurred and the proof of when the event occurred.* ***Winfield****, 821 S.W.2d at 647.*

---

2. Alleging legal theories. The plaintiff must identify the legal basis for the defendant's liability for the injury. A plaintiff has no right to recover against a defendant if the defendant did not breach a legal duty it owed to the plaintiff. *See, e.g.*, ***El Chico Corp. v. Poole***, 732 S.W.2d 306, 311 (Tex.1987) (duty in negligence suit).

A duty represents a legally enforceable obligation to conform to a particular standard of conduct. Keeton, *Prosser and Keeton on the Law of Torts*, §53 at 356 (5th ed.1984).

3. Inferring legal theories from facts. A court may infer a legal theory from the facts presented, but the facts must be expressly stated. *See, e.g.*, ***Troutman v. Traeco Bldg. Sys.***, 724 S.W.2d 385, 387 (Tex.1987) (P cited section of DTPA & alleged facts that made obvious its theory that D made a false representation). A court, however, cannot infer facts from legal theories. *See, e.g.*, ***White v. Jackson***, 358 S.W.2d 174, 178 (Tex.App.—Waco 1962, writ ref'd n.r.e.) (court would not infer facts to support bare allegation that D was negligent).

§6.3 General vs. specific allegations. A petition may allege a cause of action generally or specifically. Often, plaintiffs will plead a cause of action generally and follow it with specific allegations. A specific allegation controls over a general allegation. ***Monsanto Co. v. Milam***, 494 S.W.2d 534, 536 (Tex.1973); *see also* ***Chuck Wagon Feeding Co. v. Davis***, 768 S.W.2d 360, 364 (Tex.App.—El Paso 1989, writ denied) (specific pleadings of a contract precluded proof on a collateral note). If a petition contains specific causes of action, the court will not infer another cause of action if the petition does not give fair notice of it. *See* ***Boyles v. Kerr***, 855 S.W.2d 593, 601 (Tex.1993).

PRACTICE TIP

As a plaintiff, always describe your cause of action with general allegations. If you plead specific acts of breach of duty, you will be limited at trial to proving those specific acts. ***Mobil Chem. Co. v. Bell****, 517 S.W.2d 245, 254 (Tex.1974). If you plead breach of duty generally, however, you are not limited to proving specific acts. Id. As a defendant, consider filing special exceptions to limit the plaintiff's proof at trial.*

1. Tort cases.

(1) Negligence per se. Negligence per se is a common-law doctrine in which a duty is imposed based on a standard of conduct created by a penal statute rather than on the "reasonably prudent person" test used in common-law negligence claims. ***Smith v. Merritt***, 940 S.W.2d 602, 607 (Tex.1997). See ***O'Connor's COA***, "Degree of care established by statute," ch. 19-A, §2.2.4(1), p. 504. A plaintiff relying on negligence per se must specifically plead it and should identify the specific statute. ***Daugherty v. Southern P.T. Co.***, 772 S.W.2d 81, 83 (Tex.1989). If the plaintiff does not specifically plead negligence per se and makes only a general allegation of negligence, the defendant should challenge the pleading by a special exception. *See* ***Murray v. O&A Express***, 630 S.W.2d 633, 636-37 (Tex.1982). Under the doctrine of negligence per se, the unexcused violation of a statute setting the standard of care constitutes negligence as a matter of law if the statute was designed to prevent injuries to a class of persons to which the plaintiff belongs. ***El Chico Corp.***, 732 S.W.2d at 312.

(2) Res ipsa loquitur. A general allegation of negligence includes an allegation of res ipsa loquitur. *See* ***Farm Serv. v. Gonzales***, 756 S.W.2d 747, 751 (Tex.App.—Corpus Christi 1988, writ denied). The doctrine of res ipsa loquitur is applicable only when (1) the character of the injury is such that it would not have occurred in the absence of negligence, and (2) the instrumentality that caused the injury is under the sole management and control of the defendant. ***Gaulding v. Celotex Corp.***, 772 S.W.2d 66, 68 (Tex.1989). See ***O'Connor's COA***, "Res ipsa loquitur," ch. 19-A, §6.3, p. 512.

2. Contract cases. Certain types of relief must be specifically pleaded in a contract case. See ***O'Connor's COA***, "Contract Actions," ch. 5, p. 47.

(1) Rescission. Rescission must be specifically pleaded, or the trial court cannot grant it. ***Burnett v. James***, 564 S.W.2d 407, 409 (Tex.App.—Dallas 1978, writ dism'd). *But see* ***Perez v. Briercroft Serv. Corp.***, 809 S.W.2d 216, 217-18 (Tex.1991) (because D raised rescission as a defense, it was not necessary for P to plead it). See ***O'Connor's COA***, "Rescission," ch. 5-B, §3.5.2, p. 73.

(2) **Modification.** New consideration to support modification of a contract must be pleaded. ***Barnhill v. Moore***, 630 S.W.2d 817, 820 (Tex.App.—Corpus Christi 1982, no writ). See ***O'Connor's COA***, "New consideration for modification," ch. 5-A, §2.5.2, p. 54.

(3) **Quantum meruit.** Quantum meruit is an equitable theory of recovery based on an implied agreement to pay for benefits received. ***Heldenfels Bros. v. City of Corpus Christi***, 832 S.W.2d 39, 41 (Tex.1992). Quantum meruit is often pleaded in the alternative to a contract claim. *See* ***Centex Corp. v. Dalton***, 840 S.W.2d 952, 955 (Tex.1992). In most cases, a party cannot recover under quantum meruit when there is an express contract covering the services or materials furnished. ***Truly v. Austin***, 744 S.W.2d 934, 936 (Tex.1988); ***Ludlow v. DeBerry***, 959 S.W.2d 265, 274 (Tex.App.—Houston [14th Dist.] 1997, no writ). Construction contracts are an exception to this rule. ***Murray v. Crest Constr.***, 900 S.W.2d 342, 345 (Tex.1995). See ***O'Connor's COA***, "Quantum meruit," ch. 5, §3.2.1(3)(b)[1], p. 70.

§6.4 Notice allegation. Some causes of action require the plaintiff to plead and prove notice. See ***O'Connor's*** FORMS 2A. For example, a DTPA plaintiff must plead that it gave the defendant notice before filing suit. ***Hines v. Hash***, 843 S.W.2d 464, 467-68 (Tex.1992). See "Statutory notice," ch. 2-A, §2.1, p. 65.

§6.5 Alternative claims. The plaintiff may plead alternative theories of recovery, even if they are inconsistent. *See* TRCP 47, 48. See "Alternative claims or defenses," ch. 1-B, §4.9, p. 6.

§6.6 Joinder of multiple claims. See "Parties & Claims," ch. 2-E, p. 96.

§7. ANTICIPATING DEFENSES

Before filing the original petition, the plaintiff should check the affirmative defenses listed in TRCP 94 to see if they are necessary to support its cause of action. See "Affirmative Defenses," ch. 3-E, §5, p. 175. TRCP 94 applies to plaintiffs as well as to defendants. ***Simmons v. Compania Financiara Libano***, 830 S.W.2d 789, 792 (Tex. App.—Houston [1st Dist.] 1992, writ denied). For example, if the plaintiff must rely on estoppel to establish its cause of action, the plaintiff must plead it. ***Nicholson v. Memorial Hosp. Sys.***, 722 S.W.2d 746, 749 (Tex.App.—Houston [14th Dist.] 1986, writ ref'd n.r.e.). If the plaintiff knows the defendant will challenge the suit based on limitations, it should plead the discovery rule in its original petition. ***Woods v. William M. Mercer, Inc.***, 769 S.W.2d 515, 518 (Tex.1988). See ***O'Connor's COA***, "Discovery rule," ch. 43, §2.4.1, p. 1139.

§8. DAMAGES

The damages alleged in the petition must be within the level designated for the discovery control plan. See "Discovery Control Plan," §2, p. 67. The pleadings limit the damages a party may recover. A party is not entitled to damages not requested in its pleadings. *See, e.g.*, ***Fubar, Inc. v. Turner***, 944 S.W.2d 64, 66 (Tex.App.—Texarkana 1997, no writ) (P, who pleaded for net profits, waived recovery for gross profits).

§8.1 Definition. Damages are defined as compensation in money imposed by law for loss or injury. ***Geters v. Eagle Ins. Co.***, 834 S.W.2d 49, 50 (Tex.1992). Damages are also defined as the "legal injury" itself that is an invasion of the plaintiff's legally protected interests. ***American Med. Elec. v. Korn***, 819 S.W.2d 573, 577 n.3 (Tex. App.—Dallas 1991, writ denied). If a plaintiff pleads a cause of action but does not plead damages, the omission is a pleading defect that the defendant may challenge by a special exception. ***Peek v. Equipment Serv. Co.***, 779 S.W.2d 802, 805 (Tex.1989).

§8.2 Unliquidated damages. The plaintiff must not state the amount of unliquidated damages in its original petition. ***Capitol Brick v. Fleming Mfg. Co.***, 722 S.W.2d 399, 401 (Tex.1986); *see* TRCP 47(b); *see also* CPRC §74.053 (same in medical malpractice cases). Instead, the plaintiff must allege that the unliquidated damages are within the jurisdictional limits of the court. TRCP 47(b); ***Sears, Roebuck & Co. v. Big Bend Motor Inn***, 818 S.W.2d 542, 546 (Tex.App.—Fort Worth 1991, writ denied). The defendant may file special exceptions to require the plaintiff to specify the maximum amount claimed. TRCP 47; *see also* CPRC §74.053 (same in medical malpractice cases); ***Cruz v. Morris***, 877 S.W.2d 45, 47 (Tex.App.—Houston [14th Dist.] 1994, no writ) (specificity of damages not required without proper special exception).

§8.3 Types of damages. For a detailed discussion of damages, see ***O'Connor's COA***, "Damages," ch. 35, p. 939.

1. Actual damages. Actual damages are those damages recoverable under common law. ***Arthur Andersen & Co. v. Perry Equip. Corp.***, 945 S.W.2d 812, 816 (Tex.1997). At common law, damages are either direct (general damages) or consequential (special damages). *Id.* The distinction is important because general damages need not be specifically pleaded, but special damages must be. TRCP 56.

PRACTICE TIP

Because the courts are not always in agreement as to what damages are special (and must be specifically pleaded), the plaintiff should consider pleading all damages, general and special.

---

(1) General damages. General damages are those that naturally and necessarily flow from a wrongful act and would normally compensate for the loss, damage, or injury that is presumed to have been foreseen or contemplated by the party as a consequence of its wrongful act. ***Arthur Andersen***, 945 S.W.2d at 816. General damages are not required to be specifically pleaded. ***Green v. Allied Interests***, 963 S.W.2d 205, 208 (Tex.App.—Austin 1998, pet. denied).

Examples of general damages. • In a breach of contract case, the difference between the cost of a substitute product from another company and the original contract price. ***Hess Die Mold v. American Plasti-Plate Corp.***, 653 S.W.2d 927, 929 (Tex.App.—Tyler 1983, no writ). • In a negligent misrepresentation case, damages for benefit-of-the-bargain and out-of-pocket expenses. ***Airborne Freight v. C.R. Lee Enters.***, 847 S.W.2d 289, 296 (Tex.App.—El Paso 1992, writ denied). • In a personal injury suit, damages for pretrial pain and suffering. ***Pecos & N.T. Ry. v. Huskey***, 166 S.W. 493, 494 (Tex.App.—Amarillo 1914, writ ref'd).

(2) Special damages. Special damages are those foreseeable damages that are directly traceable to and result from the defendant's wrongful act. ***Arthur Andersen***, 945 S.W.2d at 816; *see* ***Stuart v. Bayless***, 964 S.W.2d 920, 921 (Tex.1998); ***Haynes & Boone v. Bowser Bouldin, Ltd.***, 896 S.W.2d 179, 182 (Tex.1995). Because special damages vary from person to person, a party must specifically plead for them. TRCP 56; *see* ***Harkins v. Crews***, 907 S.W.2d 51, 61 (Tex.App.—San Antonio 1995, writ denied). See ***O'Connor's COA***, chart 35-1, "When Damages Must Be Specifically Pleaded," Ch. 35-A, p. 942.

Examples of special damages. • Loss of family companionship. ***Reagan v. Vaughn***, 804 S.W.2d 463, 466 (Tex.1990) (loss of parental companionship); ***Sanchez v. Schindler***, 651 S.W.2d 249, 252-53 (Tex.1983) (loss of companionship of child). • Loss of earning capacity. ***Peshak v. Greer***, 13 S.W.3d 421, 427 (Tex.App.—Corpus Christi 2000, no pet.); ***Weingartens, Inc. v. Price***, 461 S.W.2d 260, 264 (Tex.App.—Houston [14th Dist.] 1970, writ ref'd n.r.e.). • Credit damages. ***Mead v. Johnson Group***, 615 S.W.2d 685, 688 (Tex.1981); ***Boat Superstore v. Haner***, 877 S.W.2d 376, 379 (Tex.App.—Houston [1st Dist.] 1994, no writ). • Cost of repairs. ***Kissman v. Bendix Home Sys.***, 587 S.W.2d 675, 677 (Tex.1979). • Loss of investment. ***Haynes & Boone***, 896 S.W.2d at 182. • Loss of profits. ***Naegeli Transp. v. Gulf Electroquip***, 853 S.W.2d 737, 739 (Tex.App.—Houston [14th Dist.] 1993, writ denied).

2. Exemplary damages. Exemplary (or punitive) damages are designed to penalize and deter conduct that is outrageous, malicious, or morally culpable. *See* CPRC §41.001(5); ***Owens-Corning Fiberglas Corp. v. Malone***, 972 S.W.2d 35, 39-40 (Tex.1998); ***Transportation Ins. Co. v. Moriel***, 879 S.W.2d 10, 16 (Tex.1994). Exemplary damages are not compensatory. CPRC §41.001(5); *see* ***Malone***, 972 S.W.2d at 39-40. Exemplary damages, like special damages, must be pleaded. ***K-Mart Apparel Fashions Corp. v. Ramsey***, 695 S.W.2d 243, 247 (Tex.App.—Houston [1st Dist.] 1985, writ ref'd n.r.e.). For a detailed discussion of exemplary damages, see ***O'Connor's COA***, "Exemplary Damages," ch. 35-G, p. 1004.

3. Court costs & interest. The plaintiff should always plead for court costs and prejudgment and postjudgment interest, even though pleading for them is not always necessary. See "Prejudgment interest" and "Postjudgment interest," ch. 9-C, §§4.5, 4.6, p. 599; ***O'Connor's COA***, "Interest," ch. 36, p. 1027; "Court Costs," ch. 37, p. 1033.

§8.4 Damages not permitted. Some claims do not entitle the plaintiff to damages, only to equitable relief. *See, e.g.*, ***City of Beaumont v. Bouillion***, 896 S.W.2d 143, 149 (Tex.1995) (no monetary damages for violation of Texas Constitution). See "Plaintiff's Pleadings for Injunctive Relief," ch. 2-C, p. 80.

§9. ATTORNEY FEES

See "Attorney Fees from Adverse Party," ch. 1-H, §10, p. 45. For a list of statutes that authorize attorney fees, see ***O'Connor's CPRC Plus***, "Statutory Attorney Fees Chart," p. 148 (2003-04). For a detailed discussion of attorney fees, see ***O'Connor's COA***, "Attorney Fees," ch. 38, p. 1041.

§10. CONDITIONS PRECEDENT

In its petition, the plaintiff should always allege "all conditions precedent have been performed or have occurred." TRCP 54. A condition precedent is an event that must be performed or occur before a plaintiff can sue to enforce an obligation. ***Centex Corp. v. Dalton***, 840 S.W.2d 952, 956 (Tex.1992). A plaintiff who makes the TRCP 54 allegation is not required to prove it complied with any conditions precedent unless the defendant specifically denies them. TRCP 54; ***Associated Indem. Corp. v. CAT Contracting***, 964 S.W.2d 276, 283 n.6 (Tex.1998); *see* ***Greathouse v. Charter Nat'l Bank***, 851 S.W.2d 173, 176-77 (Tex.1992) (TRCP 54 allegation prevails against a general denial); ***Knupp v. Miller***, 858 S.W.2d 945, 955 (Tex.App.—Beaumont 1993, writ denied) (in suit that provided for statutory attorney fees, unchallenged TRCP 54 allegation was sufficient to support attorney fees). See "Denial of conditions precedent," ch. 3-E, §5.4, p. 178. The TRCP 54 allegation shifts the burden of pleading (not of proof) to the defendant to specifically deny those conditions precedent that have not occurred. ***Trevino v. Allstate Ins. Co.***, 651 S.W.2d 8, 11 (Tex.App.—Dallas 1983, writ ref'd n.r.e.). If a plaintiff does not include the TRCP 54 allegation in its petition, the defendant's general denial will require the plaintiff to prove the performance of all conditions precedent. *See* ***Grimm v. Grimm***, 864 S.W.2d 160, 162 (Tex.App.—Houston [14th Dist.] 1993, no writ).

PRACTICE TIP

The TRCP 54 allegation should be pleaded generally and not identify any specific claim. When pleaded specifically as to a claim, the allegation is limited to that claim. ***Cook Composites v. Westlake Styrene Corp.****, 15 S.W.3d 124, 138 (Tex.App.—Houston [14th Dist.] 2000, pet. dism'd).*

---

§11. JURY DEMAND

If the plaintiff wants a jury trial, it should include a request for a jury in its petition. For the request to be effective, the plaintiff must pay the appropriate jury fees. See "Request for Jury Trial," ch. 5-B, p. 229.

§12. REQUEST FOR DISCLOSURE

The plaintiff should consider including a request for disclosure in its original petition. The only statement necessary for a request for disclosure is the following: "Pursuant to Rule 194, you are requested to disclose, within [*30 or 50*] days of the service of this request, the information or material described in Rule [*identify rule, e.g., 194.2; 194.2(a), (c), and (f); 194.2(d)-(g)*]." TRCP 194.1; *see* TRCP 194.3(a). See "Requests for Disclosure," ch. 6-D, p. 375. If the plaintiff includes the request in the petition, it should change the title of the pleading to "Plaintiff's Original Petition and Request for Disclosure."

§13. PRAYER

The plaintiff's petition should include a demand for judgment for all the relief sought. TRCP 47(c).

§13.1 General prayer. A general prayer for relief requests "all relief, in law and in equity, to which plaintiff may be entitled." A general prayer authorizes a judgment for any relief within the court's jurisdiction, justified by the proof and consistent with the claims asserted in the petition. ***Kissman v. Bendix Home Sys.***, 587 S.W.2d 675, 677 (Tex.1979); *see* ***Stoner v. Thompson***, 578 S.W.2d 679, 683-84 (Tex.1979); ***Daniels v. Allen***, 811 S.W.2d 278, 280 (Tex.App.—Tyler 1991, no writ). A general prayer for relief for other "sums as shall be found due" does not enlarge a specific allegation of damages. *See* ***Richardson v. First Nat'l Life Ins. Co.***, 419 S.W.2d 836, 839 (Tex.1967).

§13.2 Special prayer. If a party wants relief different from or in addition to damages, the party must specifically plead for it in the prayer (*e.g.*, injunctive relief, rescission of a contract, attorney fees, costs of court, appointment of a receiver).

§14. SIGNATURE

The lawyer (or party if pro se) must sign the pleading, which must contain an address and telephone number and, if available, a fax number. TRCP 45(d), 57. See "Signature block," ch. 1-B, §4.12, p. 6.

§15. EXHIBITS

If exhibits are attached to the petition, the petition must identify them and incorporate them by reference. TRCP 59. TRCP 59 lists the types of documents that may be properly attached as exhibits to pleadings. See "Exhibits," ch. 1-B, §4.13, p. 7.

§16. VERIFICATION & AFFIDAVITS

Some pleadings must be verified, and some require affidavits. If a plaintiff forgets to verify a pleading, the trial court should permit an amendment to add the verification. *See, e.g.*, ***Chapin & Chapin v. Texas Sand & Gravel Co.***, 844 S.W.2d 664, 665 (Tex.1992) (D permitted to amend to add verification). See "Verification & affidavits," ch. 1-B, §4.14, p. 7.

§17. RESPONDING TO DEFENDANT'S PLEADINGS

Once the defendant files its answer, the plaintiff should review the answer to determine if it needs to file any additional pleadings.

§17.1 Defense to defense. The plaintiff should determine if it needs to plead a defense to the defendant's defense. For example, to avoid the defendant's defense of statute of limitations, a plaintiff must plead the discovery rule. ***Woods v. William M. Mercer, Inc.***, 769 S.W.2d 515, 518 (Tex.1988). The plaintiff is not required to plead affirmative defenses when a defendant files merely a general denial. *See* ***Berry v. Berry***, 786 S.W.2d 672, 673 n.3 (Tex.1990).

§17.2 Response to counterclaim. The plaintiff is not required to file a general denial in response to a counterclaim. However, the plaintiff must file an appropriate answer if it intends to assert an affirmative defense (TRCP 94) or a defensive theory that must be verified (TRCP 93). ***Greater Ft. Worth & Tarrant Cty. Cmty. Action Agency v. Mims***, 627 S.W.2d 149, 152 (Tex.1982); ***$191,452 v. State***, 827 S.W.2d 430, 432 (Tex.App.—Corpus Christi 1992, writ denied). See "Verified Pleas," ch. 3-E, §4, p. 172; "Affirmative Defenses," ch. 3-E, §5, p. 175. The compulsory-counterclaim rule applies to a plaintiff against whom a defendant files a counterclaim. If the defendant asserts an affirmative claim against the plaintiff, the plaintiff must assert all of its compulsory counterclaims. See "Compulsory Joinder of Claims," ch. 2-E, §6, p. 98.

§17.3 Special exceptions. The plaintiff must obey the same special exception rules in objecting to pleading defects in the defendant's answer as the defendant follows in objecting to the plaintiff's petition. *See, e.g.*, ***Shoemake v. Fogel***, 826 S.W.2d 933, 937 (Tex.1992) (counter-P failed to specially except to affirmative defense that counter-D was not liable "as a matter of law," and thus waived objection to defense of parental immunity). See "Special Exceptions—Challenging the Pleadings," ch. 3-G, p. 187.

C. PLAINTIFF'S PLEADINGS FOR INJUNCTIVE RELIEF

§1. GENERAL

§1.1 Rules. TRCP 680-693a. See CPRC ch. 65.

§1.2 Purpose. There are two general types of injunctive relief: prohibitory and mandatory. ***RP&R, Inc. v. Territo***, 32 S.W.3d 396, 400 (Tex.App.—Houston [14th Dist.] 2000, no pet.). Most injunctions are prohibitory in nature; that is, they prohibit a party from continuing certain conduct. Shannon, et al., *Temporary Restraining Orders & Temporary Injunctions in Texas—A Ten Year Survey, 1975-1985*, 17 St. Mary's L.J. 689, 736 (1986). In some cases, a party may need a mandatory injunction that requires another party to act affirmatively rather than merely to refrain from certain conduct. *Id.*; *e.g.*, ***Territo***, 32 S.W.2d at 400 (injunction required P to pay weekly paychecks to D). There are three types of injunctive orders: temporary restraining orders, temporary injunctions, and permanent injunctions.

1. Temporary restraining order (TRO). The purpose of a TRO is to preserve the status quo of the subject matter of the litigation until a preliminary hearing can be held on an application for a temporary injunction. *See* ***Cannan v. Green Oaks Apts.***, 758 S.W.2d 753, 755 (Tex.1988); Moore, *The Ingenious Use of Injunctive Remedies in Texas*, 18 S. Tex. L.J. 87, 88 (1977). The status quo is the last, actual, peaceable, noncontested status that preceded the controversy. ***Big Three Indus. v. Railroad Comm'n***, 618 S.W.2d 543, 548 (Tex.1981); ***State v. Southwestern Bell Tel. Co.***, 526 S.W.2d 526, 528 (Tex.1975).

2. Temporary injunction. The purpose of a temporary injunction is to preserve the status quo of the subject matter of the litigation until a final hearing can be held on the merits of the case. ***Butnaru v. Ford Motor Co.***, 84 S.W.3d 198, 204 (Tex.2002); ***Walling v. Metcalfe***, 863 S.W.2d 56, 58 (Tex.1993).

3. Permanent injunction. The purpose of a permanent injunction is to grant the injunctive relief to which the applicant is entitled as part of the final judgment after a trial on the merits. ***NMTC Corp. v. Conarroe***, 99 S.W.3d 865, 868 (Tex.App.—Beaumont 2003, no pet.); *see* ***Elizondo v. Williams***, 643 S.W.2d 765, 767 (Tex. App.—San Antonio 1982, orig. proceeding).

§1.3 Forms. *O'Connor's Texas Civil Forms*, FORMS 2C.

§1.4 Other references. Shannon, et al., *Temporary Restraining Orders & Temporary Injunctions in Texas—A Ten Year Survey, 1975-1985*, 17 St. Mary's L.J. 689 (1986); Urquhart, *The Most Extraordinary Remedy: The Injunction*, 45 Tex. B.J. 358 (1982); Moore, *The Ingenious Use of Injunctive Remedies in Texas*, 18 S. Tex. L.J. 87 (1977).

§2. INJUNCTIVE REMEDY PROCESS

To understand how the TRCPs affect the issuance of injunctions, it is necessary to have a general idea of how an injunctive order is obtained. Because injunction procedure varies somewhat from county to county, the following is not intended to be representative of every county but instead is a general guide to the process for obtaining injunctive relief—from the ex parte TRO to the permanent injunction.

Step 1 – Check local rules. Many local rules require the plaintiff to attempt to notify the defendant or the defendant's attorney of the filing of the application. In those counties, the plaintiff must certify in writing before the hearing on the TRO that (1) to the best of its knowledge the defendant is unrepresented, (2) the defendant is represented but does not want to be heard or could not be reached, or (3) notifying the defendant or its counsel would cause irreparable harm to the plaintiff. Bexar Cty. L.R. 6(C); *see* Dallas Cty. L.R. 2.02; Tarrant Cty. L.R. 3.30(c). When the certification is required, it should be part of the application. *See* Tarrant Cty. L.R. 3.30(c) (application for ex parte TRO must contain certificate).

Step 2 – Present ex parte TRO application to court. The plaintiff must present the original petition and TRO application to the presiding judge. Whether the petition and application can be presented to the judge without first filing the papers with the clerk's office depends on the local rules and customary practice for each county. In some counties, the plaintiff can present the petition and application directly to a designated presiding judge without first filing the papers with the clerk. *See* Bexar Cty. L.R. 6(C). In other counties, the plaintiff must file the petition and application with the clerk who will then assign the case to a court and forward the papers to the presiding judge of that court. *See* Collin Cty. L.R. 2.2(a) (unless courthouse is closed, petition & application must first be filed and assigned to a court); Dallas Cty. L.R. 2.01(a) (same); El Paso Cty. L.R. 1.05(a) (same); Tarrant Cty. L.R. 3.30(a) (unless impossible, no application can be presented to judge unless first filed with clerk and assigned to a court). In Harris County, the attorney must present the petition and application to an ancillary court that has been established solely for the purpose of hearing TRO applications. *See* Harris Cty. L.R. 3.5.1.

Step 3 – Court grants TRO application. Once the petition and application have been presented to the trial court, the court will review the application and either grant or deny the requested ex parte temporary relief. If the court grants the application, the court will set the bond in an amount that will protect the defendant from any harm it may sustain as a result of the TRO. See "Bond," §5.4, p. 86. The court must set the hearing on the temporary injunction at the earliest date possible, but no later than 14 days after the TRO is signed. *See* TRCP 680.

Step 4 – Serve defendant with citation, precept, & writ. Usually the court coordinator will deliver the original petition and TRO application and a signed TRO to the district or county clerk's office for service of process, precept (notice of TRO injunction), and writ. Once the plaintiff deposits the bond into the registry of the court, the clerk will issue a citation for the original petition, the notice of TRO injunction, and the writ of injunction. See "Serving the TRO," §5.3.3, p. 86.

Step 5 – Notify defendant of temporary injunction hearing. The defendant must be notified before the temporary injunction hearing and must be given an opportunity to present evidence, raise defenses, and be heard. See "Notice," §6.3, p. 87.

Step 6 – Court holds temporary injunction hearing. At the temporary injunction hearing, the court will hear arguments and receive evidence regarding the issuance of a temporary injunction. If the court grants the injunction, the court will set an amount for a bond for the temporary injunction (usually a continuation of the bond set for the TRO). Unless the petitioner needs to post a new bond, the clerk will issue the writ of injunction when it receives the temporary injunction order. The temporary injunction order must specify a date for trial. TRCP 683. See "Hearing," §6.4, p. 87.

Step 7 – Court conducts trial on permanent injunction. If the plaintiff pleaded for permanent injunctive relief, the court may grant the relief after a complete trial on the merits. If permanent injunctive relief is granted, a bond is no longer required, and the applicant may request return of its bond. See "Bond," §7.4, p. 89. Although not necessary, the petitioner can ask the court to instruct the clerk to issue a writ of permanent injunction. *See* TRCP 688 (does not list permanent injunction as requiring a writ).

§3. WHERE TO FILE

§3.1 Jurisdiction. The district and county courts have jurisdiction to hear applications for injunctions. *See* Tex. Const. art. 5, §8 (district court), Tex. Const. art. 5, §16 (county court); CPRC §65.021(a) (district & county courts); Gov't Code §24.007 (district courts), Gov't Code §25.0026 (statutory probate courts), Gov't Code §26.051 (county courts). See "Choosing the Court—Jurisdiction," ch. 2-F, p. 101. An application for injunctive relief invokes a court's equity jurisdiction. ***In re Gamble***, 71 S.W.3d 313, 317 (Tex.2002).

§3.2 Venue. The venue of the suit depends on whether the request for injunctive relief is incidental to the lawsuit or is the primary reason for it. ***Brown v. Gulf TV Co.***, 306 S.W.2d 706, 708 (Tex.1957). See "Choosing the Court—Venue," ch. 2-G, p. 111.

1. Ancillary relief. When injunctive relief is ancillary to the lawsuit, venue is determined by the lawsuit, not by the request for injunction. ***O'Quinn v. Hall***, 77 S.W.3d 452, 456 (Tex.App.—Corpus Christi 2002, orig.

proceeding); ***Hogg v. Professional Pathology Assocs.***, 598 S.W.2d 328, 330-31 (Tex.App.—Houston [14th Dist.] 1980, writ dism'd).

2. Primary relief. When injunctive relief is the primary relief requested in the petition, CPRC §65.023 determines venue. ***In re Continental Airlines***, 988 S.W.2d 733, 736 (Tex.1998); *e.g.*, ***Karagounis v. Bexar Cty. Hosp. Dist.***, 70 S.W.3d 145, 147 (Tex.App.—San Antonio 2001, pet. denied) (because primary relief was specific performance of contract, not injunctive relief, venue not governed by §65.023); ***Billings v. Concordia Heritage Ass'n***, 960 S.W.2d 688, 693 (Tex.App.—El Paso 1997, pet. denied) (because primary relief was to prevent Ds from exhuming body of John Wesley Hardin, a famous outlaw, venue was governed by §65.023). Generally, a suit for injunctive relief against a resident of Texas must be tried in the county of the defendant's domicile. CPRC §65.023(a). If the writ is to stay either a proceeding in a suit or the execution of a judgment, it must be tried in the court where the suit is pending or the judgment was rendered. CPRC §§15.012, 15.013, 65.023(b).

§4. GROUNDS FOR INJUNCTIVE RELIEF

To determine if a party is entitled to injunctive relief, two questions must be answered: (1) What are the grounds for the injunctive relief sought? And, (2) has the party made the appropriate showing of each prerequisite for obtaining injunctive relief?

§4.1 Grounds for injunctive relief. Several statutes authorize injunctive relief.

1. CPRC §65.011. The most common statutory grounds for injunctive relief are found in CPRC §65.011, the general injunction statute, which authorizes injunctive relief in the following instances:

(1) When the applicant is entitled to the relief demanded, and all or part of the relief requires the restraint of some act prejudicial to the applicant. CPRC §65.011(1); *see* ***Coastal Mar. Serv. v. City of Port Neches***, 11 S.W.3d 509, 515 (Tex.App.—Beaumont 2000, no pet.); *see, e.g.*, ***Dallas Cty. v. Sweitzer***, 881 S.W.2d 757, 769 (Tex.App.—Dallas 1994, writ denied) (P sought injunction to prevent enforcement of unconstitutional fee-collection statute). Although earlier cases suggested CPRC §65.011(1) does not require a showing of lack of an adequate legal remedy, the Supreme Court held it does. ***Town of Palm Valley v. Johnson***, 87 S.W.3d 110, 111 (Tex.2001).

(2) When a party performs or is about to perform, or is procuring or allowing the performance of, an act relating to the subject of pending litigation, in violation of the rights of the applicant, and the act would tend to render the judgment in that litigation ineffectual. CPRC §65.011(2). Types of injunctions under CPRC §65.011(2) include the following:

(a) An injunction to preserve the subject matter of the suit until the suit is resolved by a judgment. ***City of Dallas v. Wright***, 36 S.W.2d 973, 975 (Tex.1931); *see, e.g.*, ***PILF Invs. v. Arlitt***, 940 S.W.2d 255, 258-59 (Tex.App.—San Antonio 1997, no writ) (to prevent a forced sale of property); ***Vannerson v. Vannerson***, 857 S.W.2d 659, 674 (Tex.App.—Houston [1st Dist.] 1993, writ denied) (to safeguard property during a divorce).

(b) An anti-suit injunction to (1) address a threat to the court's jurisdiction, (2) prevent the evasion of important public policy, (3) prevent a multiplicity of suits, or (4) protect a party from vexatious or harassing litigation. ***Golden Rule Ins. Co. v. Harper***, 925 S.W.2d 649, 651 (Tex.1996). There is a conflict between the courts of appeals on whether the ***Golden Rule*** test applies only during the trial court's plenary power or applies after the trial court's loss of plenary power. *Compare* ***Panda Energy Corp. v. Allstate Ins. Co.***, 91 S.W.3d 29, 35 (Tex.App.—Dallas 2002, pet. granted w.r.m.) (applies only while the court has plenary jurisdiction), *with* ***Bridas Corp. v. Unocal Corp.***, 16 S.W.3d 887, 890 (Tex.App.—Houston [14th Dist.] 2000, pet. dism'd) (applies while case is on appeal).

(3) When the applicant is entitled to a writ of injunction under the principles of equity and the laws of Texas relating to injunctions. CPRC §65.011(3); ***Butnaru v. Ford Motor Co.***, 84 S.W.3d 198, 210 (Tex.2002).

(4) When a cloud would be placed on the title of real property being sold under an execution, against a party having no interest in the real property, irrespective of any remedy at law. CPRC §65.011(4); ***Stein v. Frieberg, Klein & Co.***, 64 Tex. 271, 272 (1885).

(5) When irreparable injury to real or personal property is threatened, irrespective of any remedy at law. CPRC §65.011(5).

2. Other statutory grounds. Other statutes that authorize injunctive relief include the following: Business & Commerce Code §15.51(a) (injunction to enforce covenant not to compete), ***Butler v. Arrow Mirror & Glass***, 51 S.W.3d 787, 795 (Tex.App.—Houston [1st Dist.] 2001, no pet.); Business & Commerce Code §24.008(a)(3)(A) (injunction to prevent further disposition of assets in suit for fraudulent transfer); and Property Code §21.064(a) (injunctive relief in eminent domain suits).

§4.2 Prerequisites for injunctive relief. Unless excepted by statute, the following prerequisites must be pleaded and proved before a party can obtain injunctive relief:

1. Permanent relief. The applicant must plead for some form of permanent relief, either a cause of action (*e.g.*, suit for damages) or, if injunctive relief is the only relief sought, a permanent injunction. *See* ***Butnaru***, 84 S.W.3d at 204; ***Walling v. Metcalfe***, 863 S.W.2d 56, 57 (Tex.1993). For the elements of various causes of action, see ***O'Connor's Texas Causes of Action*** (2004) (***O'Connor's COA***). If the applicant pleads a cause of action that is not recognized in Texas, the trial court cannot grant an injunction. *See, e.g.*, ***Valenzuela v. Aquino***, 853 S.W.2d 512, 513 (Tex.1993) (because Texas has no cause of action for negligent infliction of emotional distress, trial court could not enjoin picketers).

2. Probable right to relief. The applicant must show it has a probable right to the relief it seeks on final hearing. ***Butnaru***, 84 S.W.3d at 204; ***Walling***, 863 S.W.2d at 58; ***Sun Oil Co. v. Whitaker***, 424 S.W.2d 216, 218 (Tex.1968). That is, the applicant must prove it is likely to succeed on the merits of its lawsuit. ***DeSantis v. Wackenhut Corp.***, 793 S.W.2d 670, 686 (Tex.1990); ***Southwestern Bell Tel. Co. v. Public Util. Comm'n***, 571 S.W.2d 503, 506 (Tex.1978). It is not necessary for the applicant to prove it will ultimately prevail. ***Walling***, 863 S.W.2d at 58; ***Sun Oil***, 424 S.W.2d at 218.

3. Probable injury. The applicant must plead it will suffer a probable injury. ***Butnaru***, 84 S.W.3d at 204; ***Universal Health Servs. v. Thompson***, 24 S.W.3d 570, 577 (Tex.App.—Austin 2000, no pet.). Probable injury requires a showing that the harm is imminent, the injury would be irreparable, and that the applicant has no other adequate legal remedy. ***Harbor Perfusion v. Floyd***, 45 S.W.3d 713, 716 (Tex.App.—Corpus Christi 2001, no pet.).

(1) Imminent harm. The applicant must plead the harm is imminent. *See* ***Operation Rescue–Nat'l v. Planned Parenthood***, 975 S.W.2d 546, 554 (Tex.1998) (permanent injunction); ***Bell v. Texas Workers Comp. Comm'n***, 102 S.W.3d 299, 302 (Tex.App.—Austin 2003, no pet.) (temporary injunction); *see also* ***Surko Enters. v. Borg-Warner Acceptance Corp.***, 782 S.W.2d 223, 225 (Tex.App.—Houston [1st Dist.] 1989, no writ) (in suit over collateral, P showed imminent harm because D was insolvent & was transferring property to another). An injunction will not be issued unless it is shown that the respondent will engage in the activity enjoined. ***State v. Morales***, 869 S.W.2d 941, 946-47 (Tex.1994). An applicant's fear or apprehension of the possibility of injury is not sufficient; the applicant must prove the respondent has attempted or intends to harm the applicant. ***Jones v. Jefferson Cty.***, 15 S.W.3d 206, 213 (Tex.App.—Texarkana 2000, pet. denied); ***In re City of Dallas***, 977 S.W.2d 798, 804 (Tex.App.—Fort Worth 1998, orig. proceeding).

(2) Irreparable injury. The applicant must plead that, if the injunction is not issued, the harm that will occur is irreparable. ***Butnaru***, 84 S.W.3d at 204 (temporary injunction); ***Town of Palm Valley v. Johnson***, 87 S.W.3d 110, 111 (Tex.2001) (permanent injunction). An injury is irreparable if the injured party cannot be adequately compensated in damages or if the damages cannot be measured by any certain pecuniary standard. ***Butnaru***, 84 S.W.3d at 204; *see, e.g.*, ***Haq v. America's Favorite Chicken Co.***, 921 S.W.2d 728, 730 (Tex.App.—Corpus Christi 1996, writ dism'd) (P did not prove damages it might suffer pending trial were different than damages recoverable for breach of contract); *see also* ***Liberty Mut. Ins. Co. v. Mustang Tractor & Equip. Co.***, 812 S.W.2d 663, 666 (Tex.App.—Houston [14th Dist.] 1991, no writ) (disruption of business can be irreparable harm). *Compare* ***Estate of Dilasky***, 972 S.W.2d 763, 767 (Tex.App.—Corpus Christi 1998, orig. proceeding) (costs & delay can be factors of irreparable harm), *with* ***Reynolds, Shannon, Miller, Blinn, White & Cook v. Flanary***, 872 S.W.2d 248, 252 (Tex.App.—Dallas 1993, no writ) (costs & delay alone were not sufficient injuries). The following are some exceptions to the irreparable injury requirement:

(a) Restrictive covenant. An applicant seeking an injunction to enforce a restrictive covenant is not required to prove irreparable injury. ***Jim Rutherford Invs. v. Terramar Beach Cmty. Ass'n***, 25 S.W.3d 845, 849 (Tex.App.—Houston [14th Dist.] 2000, pet. denied); ***Munson v. Milton***, 948 S.W.2d 813, 815 (Tex.App.—San Antonio 1997, pet. denied).

(b) Zoning violation. A city seeking to enjoin the violation of a zoning ordinance is not required to prove the violation would cause injury to it or its residents. ***San Miguel v. City of Windcrest***, 40 S.W.3d 104, 108 (Tex.App.—San Antonio 2000, no pet.).

(c) Covenants not to compete. An applicant seeking to enforce a covenant not to compete is not required to prove an irreparable injury. ***Butler v. Arrow Mirror & Glass***, 51 S.W.3d 787, 795 (Tex.App.—Houston [1st Dist.] 2001, no pet.); *see* Bus. & Com. Code §15.51(a).

(3) Inadequate remedy. The applicant must plead there is no adequate remedy at law. ***Synergy Ctr. v. Lone Star Franchising***, 63 S.W.3d 561, 567 (Tex.App.—Austin 2001, no pet.); ***Fasken v. Darby***, 901 S.W.2d 591, 592 (Tex.App.—El Paso 1995, no writ). A court will not issue a temporary injunction when there is a plain and adequate remedy at law. ***McGlothlin v. Kliebert***, 672 S.W.2d 231, 232 (Tex.1984). For a legal remedy to be adequate, it must give the applicant complete, final, and equal relief. *See* ***Universal Health***, 24 S.W.3d at 577; ***Henderson v. KRTS, Inc.***, 822 S.W.2d 769, 773 (Tex.App.—Houston [1st Dist.] 1992, no writ). For purposes of injunctive relief, there is no adequate remedy at law if (1) damages cannot be calculated, (2) damages cannot be measured by any certain pecuniary standard, or (3) the defendant will be unable to pay damages. *See* ***Butnaru v. Ford Motor Co.***, 84 S.W.3d 198, 204 (Tex.2002) (reasons 1 & 2); ***Texas Indus. Gas v. Phoenix Metallurgical Corp.***, 828 S.W.2d 529, 533 (Tex.App.—Houston [1st Dist.] 1992, no writ) (reasons 1 & 3); ***Surko Enters.***, 782 S.W.2d at 225 (reason 3). The following are some exceptions to the requirement of no adequate remedy at law.

(a) Statutory right. An applicant who has a statutory right to an injunction does not have to prove there is no adequate remedy at law. ***Butnaru***, 84 S.W.3d at 210.

(b) Cloud on title. An applicant seeking to prevent a cloud from being cast on the title to real property does not have to prove there is no adequate remedy at law. CPRC §65.011(4).

(c) Irreparable injury to property. An applicant seeking to prevent irreparable injury to real or personal property does not have to prove there is no adequate remedy at law. CPRC §65.011(5).

(d) Covenants not to compete. An applicant seeking to enforce a covenant not to compete is not required to prove there is no adequate remedy at law. ***Butler***, 51 S.W.3d at 795; *see* Bus. & Com. Code §15.51(a).

§5. REQUEST FOR TEMPORARY RESTRAINING ORDER (TRO)

§5.1 Application.

1. Grounds. The application for a TRO must identify one or more of the grounds for injunction. See "Grounds for injunctive relief," §4.1, p. 82.

2. Prerequisites. The application for a TRO must plead the prerequisites for injunctive relief. See §4.2, above. The applicant must plead all of the necessary facts supporting the issuance of injunctive relief; legal conclusions are not sufficient. ***Texas State Bd. of Medical Exam'rs v. McKinney***, 315 S.W.2d 387, 390 (Tex. App.—Waco 1958, no writ).

3. Request for injunction. The application for a TRO must include a request for a temporary injunction. *See* TRCP 680; Urquhart, *The Most Extraordinary Remedy*, 45 Tex. B.J. at 359.

4. Ex parte allegations. If an applicant is seeking a TRO without notice to the other party, the application must identify specific facts that show why the order should be entered ex parte. TRCP 680. The application must show (1) the applicant will suffer irreparable injury, loss, or damage if the TRO is not granted, and (2) there is not enough time to serve notice on the respondent and hold a hearing. *See id.* Some local rules may require an additional written certificate. See "Step 1 – Check local rules," §2, p. 80.

5. Bond. The application for a TRO must state the applicant's willingness to post bond. TRCP 684.

6. Relief. The application for a TRO must identify the relief sought. A trial court may grant only the injunctive relief an applicant specifically requests. ***Fairfield v. Stonehenge Ass'n***, 678 S.W.2d 608, 611 (Tex. App.—Houston [14th Dist.] 1984, no writ); *see* TRCP 682. A general prayer for relief does not warrant relief other than that specifically requested. ***Fairfield***, 678 S.W.2d at 611; ***Colorado River Valley Co. v. Schiarone***, 476 S.W.2d 368, 370 (Tex.App.—Austin 1972, writ ref'd n.r.e.).

7. Verified. The application for a TRO must be verified or supported with affidavits. TRCP 680, 682. Affidavits must be based on the personal knowledge of the affiant. *See* ***Williams v. Bagley***, 875 S.W.2d 808, 810 (Tex.App.—Beaumont 1994, no writ).

§5.2 Hearing. The court should conduct a hearing on the TRO, but the TRO can be granted ex parte, without a hearing. *See* TRCP 680.

§5.3 TRO.

1. Form. A temporary restraining order must be in writing. *See* TRCP 680 & 683 (both rules assume, but do not state, that order must be in writing); ***Ex parte Lesikar***, 899 S.W.2d 654, 654 (Tex.1995) (TRO extension order must be in writing). Until the TRO is signed by the judge, it is not enforceable by contempt. ***Ex parte Price***, 741 S.W.2d 366, 367 (Tex.1987). The order must make certain specific statements. *See* TRCP 680, 683. In its order, the court must do the following:

(1) Identify the person or entity to be restrained. *See* TRCP 683.

(2) State why the TRO was granted without notice if it is granted ex parte. TRCP 680.

(3) State the reasons for the issuance of the TRO by defining the injury and describing why it is irreparable. TRCP 680, 683.

(4) Define, in reasonable detail, the act to be restrained. TRCP 683. The act to be restrained cannot be described by reference to the pleadings or other documents. *Id.* See "Order," §6.5.2, p. 88.

(5) State the date and hour of issuance. TRCP 680. The trial court cannot hold a party in contempt for an act that occurred before the date and time of issuance of the order. *See* ***Ex parte Guetersloh***, 935 S.W.2d 110, 111 (Tex.1996) (appeal of temporary injunction).

(6) State the date the order expires. TRCP 680. The court can grant a TRO for only 14 days. *Id.* The 14-day limitation period does not consist of 14 twenty-four hour periods that begin running from the time the TRO is signed; the TRO expires at midnight 14 calendar days after it is signed. ***In re Walkup***, ___ S.W.3d ___ (Tex. App.—Houston [1st Dist.] 2003, orig. proceeding) (No. 01-03-00131-CV; 8-7-03) (TRO granted on 1-30-03 at 2:30 p.m. expired at midnight, not at 2:30 p.m., on 2-13-03).

(7) State the date for the hearing on the temporary injunction. TRCP 680. The injunction hearing must be set at the earliest practicable time. *Id.* The hearing on the temporary injunction takes precedence over other matters. *Id.*

(8) Fix the amount of the TRO bond. TRCP 684. See §5.4, below.

2. Extending the TRO. An order extending a TRO must be in writing. An oral order extending a TRO is not effective. ***Lesikar***, 899 S.W.2d at 654.

(1) On motion & order. The applicant may ask the trial court to extend the TRO by filing a motion, before the TRO expires, showing good cause. TRCP 680; ***In re Texas Nat. Res. Conserv. Comm'n***, 85 S.W.3d 201, 203 (Tex.2002). The court can grant one extension of the TRO for an additional 14 days. TRCP 680; ***Tex. Nat. Res.***, 85 S.W.3d at 203.

(2) By agreement. If the respondent agrees, the TRO may be extended for more than 14 days. TRCP 680.

3. Serving the TRO. Once the clerk has received the original petition and application for TRO, and the bond has been filed into the registry of the court, the clerk will issue a precept for the TRO and a notice of the hearing on the temporary injunction. The precept will be served with the citation and writ of injunction. All of the documents are served on the defendant by the sheriff or constable or by a private process server. *See* TRCP 686, 688; *see also* ***In re Poe***, 996 S.W.2d 281, 282-83 (Tex.App.—Amarillo 1999, orig. proceeding) (if request for injunction is not ancillary to pending suit, citation must be served).

§5.4 Bond. The order for temporary injunctive relief must set the amount for the bond. TRCP 684. If the order does not set the bond, the order is void and not enforceable. ***Qwest Comm. Corp. v. AT&T Corp.***, 24 S.W.3d 334, 337 (Tex.2000) (temporary injunction); ***Ex parte Jordan***, 787 S.W.2d 367, 368 (Tex.1990) (TRO). The bond protects the respondent from any harm it may sustain as a result of the TRO. *See* ***DeSantis v. Wackenhut Corp.***, 793 S.W.2d 670, 686 (Tex.1990). To protect the respondent, the amount of the bond must have some relation to the potential damages in the lawsuit. *See, e.g.*, ***Franklin Sav. Ass'n v. Reese***, 756 S.W.2d 14, 16 (Tex.App.—Austin 1988, no writ) ($10,000 bond was not adequate for debt of $34 million); ***El Paso Dev. Co. v. Berryman***, 729 S.W.2d 883, 888-89 (Tex.App.—Corpus Christi 1987, no writ) ($15,000 was adequate for debt of over $7 million because there was sufficient collateral).

1. Posting the bond. The applicant must post the bond before the clerk issues the writ. *See* ***Goodwin v. Goodwin***, 456 S.W.2d 885, 885 (Tex.1970) (temporary injunction); ***Williams***, 875 S.W.2d at 810 (TRO). There are exceptions that permit the applicant not to post a bond.

(1) Against the government. If the suit is against the state, its agency, its subdivisions, or against a city in its governmental capacity, and the governmental entity has no pecuniary interest in the suit and no monetary damages can be shown, the court may fix the amount in its discretion. TRCP 684.

(2) For an indigent. Certain indigent parties are not required to post a bond for a TRO or an injunction. CPRC §§65.041, 65.042. The court may not require a bond if (1) the applicant submits an affidavit that meets the requirements of CPRC §65.043, and (2) the court finds the order is intended to restrain the adverse party from foreclosing on the applicant's residence. CPRC §§65.041, 65.042(a).

2. Challenging the bond. The party restrained by the injunction may challenge the adequacy of the bond by filing a motion to increase the bond. *See* TRCP 684; ***Maples v. Muscletech, Inc.***, 74 S.W.3d 429, 430 (Tex.App.—Amarillo 2002, no pet.). The party must make a "clear showing" that its potential losses are greater than the amount of the bond. ***Maples***, 74 S.W.3d at 432.

§5.5 Writ.

1. Form. The clerk of the court will prepare the writ of injunction for issuance. The clerk is responsible for ensuring the form of the writ complies with TRCP 687.

2. Service. The writ of injunction must be served on the respondent by a sheriff or constable of the county of the respondent's residence. TRCP 688, 689. The applicant should ensure that copies of the writ are also served on any other persons acting in concert with the respondent or the respondent's officers, agents, servants, employees, or attorneys. *See* TRCP 683.

§6. REQUEST FOR TEMPORARY INJUNCTION

§6.1 Parties. Before the court can grant temporary injunctive relief, the applicant must join all indispensable parties under TRCP 39. See "Parties to be joined," ch. 2-E, §6.2, p. 99. The following parties have been held to be indispensable to an injunction proceeding:

1. Those whose rights will be directly affected by the writ. ***Ladner v. Reliance Corp.***, 293 S.W.2d 758, 764-65 (Tex.1956); ***Scott v. Graham***, 292 S.W.2d 324, 327 (Tex.1956).

2. All parties to a contract if the applicant is seeking to restrain enforcement of the contract. ***McCharen v. Bailey***, 87 S.W.2d 284, 285 (Tex.App.—Eastland 1935, no writ).

3. Any state, county, or city if the applicant is seeking to restrain a public official acting on behalf of the state, county, or city. ***Davis v. Wildenthal***, 241 S.W.2d 620, 622 (Tex.App.—El Paso 1951, writ ref'd n.r.e.).

§6.2 Application. When the applicant's original petition includes a request for a TRO, its request for a temporary injunction is merely an additional paragraph asking the court to set a hearing for a temporary injunction. When the applicant seeks a temporary injunction without a TRO, its petition must meet all the pleading requirements for a TRO except the request for ex parte relief. That is, the petition for a temporary injunction must be verified and must allege the following: (1) a cause of action; (2) a probable right to relief; (3) a probable injury in the interim (which includes proof of imminent and irreparable injury and no adequate remedy at law); and (4) a willingness to post bond. *See* TRCP 682 (verified petition), TRCP 684 (bond). See "Prerequisites for injunctive relief," §4.2, p. 83.

§6.3 Notice. The party to be enjoined is entitled to notice and an opportunity to be heard. TRCP 681; ***PILF Invs. v. Arlitt***, 940 S.W.2d 255, 259-60 (Tex.App.—San Antonio 1997, no writ); ***City of Houston v. Houston Lighting & Power Co.***, 530 S.W.2d 866, 869 (Tex.App.—Houston [14th Dist.] 1975, writ ref'd n.r.e.). The party must be given three days' notice of the temporary injunction hearing. *See* TRCP 21.

§6.4 Hearing.

1. **Scope of proceeding.** The only issue presented at the temporary injunction hearing is the need for immediate relief pending the trial on the merits. ***Transport Co. v. Robertson Transps.***, 261 S.W.2d 549, 552 (Tex.1953); *see* ***Coastal Mar. Serv. v. City of Port Neches***, 11 S.W.3d 509, 515 (Tex.App.—Beaumont 2000, no pet.).

2. **Appearance.**

(1) Applicant does not appear. If the applicant does not appear for the hearing on the temporary injunction, any TRO granted earlier will be dissolved, and the injunction will be denied.

(2) Respondent does not appear. If the respondent does not appear for the hearing on the temporary injunction, the petitioner is not entitled to a default judgment; a full evidentiary hearing is required. *See* ***Millwrights Local Un. No. 2484 v. Rust Eng'g Co.***, 433 S.W.2d 683, 686-87 (Tex.1968).

3. **Evidence.**

(1) Applicant's burden. At the hearing, the applicant must introduce competent evidence to support a probable right to recovery and a probable injury. ***Letson v. Barnes***, 979 S.W.2d 414, 417 (Tex.App.—Amarillo 1998, pet. denied). See "Prerequisites for injunctive relief," §4.2, p. 83. An injunction cannot be upheld without evidence. ***Atkinson v. Arnold***, 893 S.W.2d 294, 297 (Tex.App.—Texarkana 1995, no writ). The court cannot consider the affidavits attached to the application for temporary injunction unless the parties agree or no one objects. ***Millwrights Local Un.***, 433 S.W.2d at 686 (no agreement); ***Ahmed v. Shimi Ventures***, 99 S.W.3d 682, 684 n.2 (Tex.App.—Houston [1st Dist.] 2003, no pet.) (no objection).

(2) **Limitation on evidence.** The trial court can impose reasonable limits on the parties' presentation of evidence in a temporary injunction hearing. ***Reading & Bates Constr. Co. v. O'Donnell***, 627 S.W.2d 239, 244 (Tex.App.—Corpus Christi 1982, writ ref'd n.r.e.); ***City of Houston***, 530 S.W.2d at 869; *see, e.g.*, ***Birds Constr. v. Gonzales***, 595 S.W.2d 926, 928-29 (Tex.App.—Corpus Christi 1981, no writ) (court did not abuse discretion in granting temporary injunction based on stipulated facts, argument, & summary of other expected evidence from both parties). The court's limitations, however, cannot deprive the parties of their right to be heard. *E.g.*, ***City of Houston***, 530 S.W.2d at 869 (court's ruling deprived D of right to offer any evidence at hearing); ***Oertel v. Gulf States Abrasive Mfg.***, 429 S.W.2d 623, 623 (Tex.App.—Houston [1st Dist.] 1968, no writ) (court refused to allow D to call any witnesses).

§6.5 Order. A valid order for an injunction must be in writing, signed by the judge, and entered into the minutes of the court. ***Ex parte Price***, 741 S.W.2d 366, 367 (Tex.1987). The order must make certain specific statements. TRCP 683. The requirements of TRCP 683 are mandatory and must be strictly followed. ***Qwest Comm. Corp. v. AT&T Corp.***, 24 S.W.3d 334, 337 (Tex.2000). An injunction order that does not comply with TRCP 683 is subject to being declared void and dissolved. *Id.* In its order, the court must do the following:

1. State the reasons for the issuance of the injunction by defining the injury and describing why it is irreparable. TRCP 683; ***State v. Cook United, Inc.***, 464 S.W.2d 105, 106 (Tex.1971). TRCP 683 requires the injunction order to state the reasons an injury will be suffered if the interlocutory relief is not granted. ***Cook United***, 464 S.W.2d at 106 ("under Rule 683 ... it is necessary to give the reasons why injury will be suffered"); *see* ***IBEW Local 479 v. Becon Constr.***, 104 S.W.3d 239, 243 (Tex.App.—Beaumont 2003, no pet.) (order void if it does not state reasons injury will be suffered); ***Fasken v. Darby***, 901 S.W.2d 591, 593 (Tex.App.—El Paso 1995, no writ) (same); ***Moreno v. Baker Tools***, 808 S.W.2d 208, 210 (Tex.App.—Houston [1st Dist.] 1991, no writ) (same). *Contra* ***Pinebrook Props. v. Brookhaven Lake Prop. Owners Ass'n***, 77 S.W.3d 487, 504 (Tex.App.—Texarkana 2002, pet. denied) (TRCP 683 does not require court to state reasons injury would be suffered). The appellate court cannot infer the reasons from the evidence, the pleadings, or the court's oral pronouncement at the hearing. ***Moreno***, 808 S.W.2d at 211.

2. Define, in reasonable detail, the act to be enjoined. TRCP 683. The act to be enjoined cannot be described by reference to the pleadings or other documents. *Id.*; *see* ***Maloy v. City of Lewisville***, 848 S.W.2d 380, 385 (Tex.App.—Fort Worth 1993, no writ) (when order described acts to be enjoined in reasonable detail, it was not error to refer to a city ordinance). When an injunction is granted to protect confidential information and trade secrets, the order can refer to sealed exhibits as long as the activity to be enjoined is described in reasonable detail. ***Rugen v. Interactive Bus. Sys.***, 864 S.W.2d 548, 553 (Tex.App.—Dallas 1993, no writ).

3. Include an order setting the case for a trial on the merits. TRCP 683; ***Qwest***, 24 S.W.3d at 337; ***InterFirst Bank San Felipe v. Paz Constr. Co.***, 715 S.W.2d 640, 641 (Tex.1986). If the injunction does not set the case for a trial on the merits, it is void. ***Qwest***, 24 S.W.3d at 337; ***InterFirst Bank***, 715 S.W.2d at 641; ***EOG Res., Inc. v. Gutierrez***, 75 S.W.3d 50, 52-53 (Tex.App.—San Antonio 2002, no pet.); ***Wyatt v. Cowley***, 74 S.W.3d 576, 577 (Tex.App.—Corpus Christi 2002, pet. dism'd).

4. Fix the amount of the bond. TRCP 684; ***Qwest***, 24 S.W.3d at 337. See "Bond," §5.4, p. 86.

§6.6 Writ. See "Writ," §5.5, p. 86.

§7. REQUEST FOR PERMANENT INJUNCTION

§7.1 Application. When the applicant's original petition includes pleadings for other injunctive relief (a TRO or a temporary injunction), its request for a permanent injunction is merely an additional paragraph asking the court to grant a permanent injunction after the trial on the merits. When the applicant seeks a permanent injunction without other injunctive relief, its petition must meet all of the requirements for a TRO except (1) a request for ex parte relief, (2) a statement of willingness to post bond, and (3) verification or affidavits. *See* ***Town of Palm Valley v. Johnson***, 17 S.W.3d 281, 288 (Tex.App.—Corpus Christi 2000) (verification not necessary), *pet. denied*, 87

S.W.3d 110 (Tex.2001). That is, the petition for a permanent injunction must allege the following: (1) a cause of action; (2) a probable right to the relief; and (3) a probable injury (which includes imminent and irreparable injury and no adequate remedy at law). See "Prerequisites for injunctive relief," §4.2, p. 83.

§7.2 Hearing. The hearing on the permanent injunction is a full trial of the issues in the applicant's petition. The applicant is entitled to a jury trial at the hearing. ***Citizens State Bank v. Caney Invs.***, 746 S.W.2d 477, 478 (Tex.1988).

§7.3 Judgment. A judgment for a permanent injunction must describe in reasonable detail the acts to be restrained, but need not describe in detail the reasons for its issuance. ***Adust Video v. Nueces Cty.***, 996 S.W.2d 245, 249-50 (Tex.App.—Corpus Christi 1999, no pet.). The requirement in TRCP 683—that the order contain detailed explanations of the reasons for the issuance of the injunction—does not apply to a permanent injunction when the injunction is the sole relief sought by the action. ***Adust Video***, 996 S.W.2d at 249; ***City of Houston v. Morgan Guar. Int'l Bank***, 666 S.W.2d 524, 536 (Tex.App.—Houston [1st Dist.] 1983, writ ref'd n.r.e.).

§7.4 Bond. No bond is required for a permanent injunction. ***Citizens State Bank v. Caney Invs.***, 733 S.W.2d 581, 585 (Tex.App.—Houston [1st Dist.] 1987), *rev'd on other grounds*, 746 S.W.2d 477 (Tex.1988); *see* ***Canteen Corp. v. Republic of Tex. Props.***, 773 S.W.2d 398, 400 (Tex.App.—Dallas 1989, no writ).

§7.5 Writ. No writ of injunction is issued after a permanent injunction. *See* TRCP 688 (refers only to writs for TROs & temporary injunctions).

§8. RESPONDENT'S RESPONSE

§8.1 Reply to request for injunction.

1. Defenses. Defenses to injunctive relief include the following: (1) the applicant has an adequate remedy at law; (2) a temporary injunction would accomplish the whole object of the suit; (3) a temporary injunction will destroy, rather than preserve, the status quo; (4) the applicant is not entitled to equitable relief because it is guilty of inequitable conduct (*e.g.*, laches, unclean hands); (5) the respondent is unable to comply with the injunction because the order does not set forth the respondent's duties in clear, specific, and unambiguous terms; (6) the respondent would not be able to purge itself of contempt; and (7) the applicant's verification is insufficient. ***Ex parte Hudson***, 917 S.W.2d 24, 26 (Tex.1996) (#5, 6); ***McGlothlin v. Kliebert***, 672 S.W.2d 231, 232 (Tex.1984) (#1); ***Texas Foundries v. International Moulders & Foundry Workers' Un.***, 248 S.W.2d 460, 464 (Tex.1952) (#2); ***Crystal Media v. HCI Acquisition Corp.***, 773 S.W.2d 732, 734 (Tex.App.—San Antonio 1989, no writ) (#7); ***Foxwood Homeowners Ass'n v. Ricles***, 673 S.W.2d 376, 379 (Tex.App.—Houston [1st Dist.] 1984, writ ref'd n.r.e.) (#4); ***Ballenger v. Ballenger***, 668 S.W.2d 467, 469-70 (Tex.App.—Corpus Christi 1984, writ dism'd) (#3).

2. Waiver. There is a split of authority whether the respondent waives its objection to an order that does not identify the reasons for the order and the harm it will preclude. *Compare* ***Big D Props. v. Foster***, 2 S.W.3d 21, 23 (Tex.App.—Fort Worth 1999, no writ) (error not waived), ***360 Degree Comm. Co. v. Grundman***, 937 S.W.2d 574, 575 (Tex.App.—Texarkana 1996, no writ) (same), *and* ***Fasken***, 901 S.W.2d at 592-93 (same), *with* ***Texas Tech Univ. Health Sci. Ctr. v. Rao***, 105 S.W.3d 763, 768 (Tex.App.—Amarillo 2003, no pet.) (error waived), *and* ***Emerson v. Fires Out, Inc.***, 735 S.W.2d 492, 493-94 (Tex.App.—Austin 1987, no writ) (same).

§8.2 Motion to dissolve or modify.

1. Ex parte TRO. If the TRO was obtained ex parte, the respondent can move to dissolve or modify the TRO. TRCP 680. The respondent must give the applicant at least two days' notice, unless shortened by court order, of the hearing on the motion to dissolve or modify. *Id.*; *see, e.g.*, ***Forestier v. San Antonio Sav. Ass'n***, 564 S.W.2d 160, 163-64 (Tex.App.—El Paso 1978, writ ref'd n.r.e.) (hearing on motion to dissolve held same day TRO was issued).

2. TRO & temporary injunction. The respondent can move to dissolve a temporary injunction on the grounds the order granting the injunction is void. A temporary injunction is void if it does not comply with the procedural prerequisites. ***Qwest Comm. Corp. v. AT&T Corp.***, 24 S.W.3d 334, 337 (Tex.2000); *see, e.g.*, ***Inter-First Bank San Felipe v. Paz Constr. Co.***, 715 S.W.2d 640, 641 (Tex.1986) (injunction void because it did not set case for trial on merits); ***Goodwin v. Goodwin***, 456 S.W.2d 885, 885 (Tex.1970) (injunction void because bond was not filed before temporary injunction issued); ***Beckham v. Beckham***, 672 S.W.2d 41, 43 (Tex.App.—Houston [14th Dist.] 1984, no writ) (injunction void because it did not set out reasons for issuance).

3. Temporary & permanent injunction. The motion to dissolve or modify an injunction must plead and prove either (1) changed circumstances or (2) fundamental error. ***Tober v. Turner, Inc.***, 668 S.W.2d 831, 835 (Tex.1984); ***Universal Health Servs. v. Thompson***, 24 S.W.3d 570, 580 (Tex.App.—Austin 2000, no pet.); ***Murphy v. McDaniel***, 20 S.W.3d 873, 877 (Tex.App.—Dallas 2000, no pet.); *see* ***City of San Antonio v. Singleton***, 858 S.W.2d 411, 412 (Tex.1993) (changed circumstances for permanent injunction); ***Smith v. O'Neill***, 813 S.W.2d 501, 502 (Tex.1991) (same). A motion to dissolve or modify cannot be used to relitigate the basis for the injunction when that basis has not changed. ***Chase Manhattan Bank v. Bowles***, 52 S.W.3d 871, 879 (Tex.App.—Waco 2001, no pet.).

(1) Changed circumstances. Changed circumstances are conditions that either alter the status quo following the issuance of the temporary injunction or make the injunction unnecessary or improper. ***Bowles***, 52 S.W.3d at 879; ***Henke v. Peoples State Bank***, 6 S.W.3d 717, 721 (Tex.App.—Corpus Christi 1999, pet. dism'd). Changed circumstances can include changes in the law, newly revealed facts, or an agreement of the parties. ***Murphy v. McDaniel***, 20 S.W.3d 873, 878 (Tex.App.—Dallas 2000, no pet.); *see* ***Bowles***, 52 S.W.3d at 878-79; ***Henke***, 6 S.W.3d at 721.

(2) Fundamental error. Fundamental error, which is rare, occurs when the record shows either (1) the trial court did not have jurisdiction or (2) the error directly and adversely affects the public interest as that interest is declared in a statute or the Texas Constitution. ***In re C.O.S.***, 988 S.W.2d 760, 765 (Tex.1999).

§8.3 Answer to the lawsuit.

1. Special appearance & venue. If the temporary injunction hearing was held before the respondent's deadline under TRCP 99 to answer the suit, the respondent does not waive any objection to personal jurisdiction or venue by participating at the hearing or filing an answer to the application for temporary injunction or a motion for continuance of the hearing. *See, e.g.*, ***Valsangiacomo v. Americana Juice Import***, 35 S.W.3d 201, 204 n.3 (Tex.App.—Corpus Christi 2000, no pet.) (participation in temporary injunction hearing did not waive special appearance); ***Gentry v. Tucker***, 891 S.W.2d 766, 768 (Tex.App.—Texarkana 1995, no writ) (filing motion for continuance did not waive venue challenge); ***Perkola v. Koelling & Assocs.***, 601 S.W.2d 110, 111-12 (Tex.App.—Dallas 1980, writ dism'd) (appearance at temporary injunction hearing did not waive venue challenge); ***Gibson v. State***, 288 S.W.2d 577, 578 (Tex.App.—Waco 1956, writ dism'd) (answer to application for temporary injunction did not waive venue challenge).

2. Answer. The respondent should remember to file an answer to the underlying suit. Once the deadline to file an answer has expired, the petitioner can take a default judgment against a nonanswering respondent, even if the respondent appeared at the injunction hearing. ***Borrego v. del Palacio***, 445 S.W.2d 620, 621 (Tex.App.—El Paso 1969, no writ).

§9. ENFORCING THE INJUNCTION

An injunction is binding on (1) the parties, (2) the parties' officers, agents, servants, employees, and attorneys, and (3) any other person acting in concert with the parties or their agents who receives actual notice of the order. TRCP 683.

§9.1 Motion for contempt. The trial court may enforce an injunction by holding the enjoined party in contempt for violating the injunction order. TRCP 692; ***Ex parte Blasingame***, 748 S.W.2d 444, 447 (Tex.1988); *see also*

Credit Bureau, Inc. v. State, 515 S.W.2d 706, 710-11 (Tex.App.—San Antonio 1974) (distinguishing between proceedings for contempt & civil penalty), *aff'd*, 530 S.W.2d 288 (Tex.1975). The order cannot punish the contemnor for actions taken before the court signed its order. ***Ex parte Guetersloh***, 935 S.W.2d 110, 111 (Tex.1996). The trial court may punish the violation of an injunction by imposing a fine or imprisonment. ***Blasingame***, 748 S.W.2d at 447; ***Southwest Prof. Indem. Corp. v. Texas Dept. of Ins.***, 914 S.W.2d 256, 265 (Tex.App.—Austin 1996, writ denied). A fine for contempt cannot exceed $500. Gov't Code §21.002(b); ***Ex parte Hudson***, 917 S.W.2d 24, 26 (Tex.1996).

§9.2 Suit to enforce penalty in injunction. The party who obtained the injunction may enforce it by filing a suit to enforce a penalty within the injunctive order. ***Transcontinental Gas Pipe Line Corp. v. American Nat'l Pet. Co.***, 763 S.W.2d 809, 824 (Tex.App.—Texarkana 1988), *rev'd on other grounds*, 798 S.W.2d 274 (Tex.1990); *see also* ***Credit Bureau***, 515 S.W.2d at 710-11 (distinguishing between proceedings for contempt & civil penalty).

§9.3 Other means of enforcement. It is uncertain whether the party who obtained the injunction may sue the enjoined party, even if there is a cause of action for damages for the violation of an injunction. *See* ***Cannan v. Green Oaks Apts.***, 758 S.W.2d 753, 755 (Tex.1988); ***Transcontinental Gas***, 763 S.W.2d at 824.

§10. RELIEF FROM WRONGFUL INJUNCTION

A person who wrongfully obtained a TRO or temporary injunction is liable for damages caused by the injunction. ***DeSantis v. Wackenhut Corp.***, 793 S.W.2d 670, 686 (Tex.1990). There are two types of actions for wrongful injunction.

§10.1 Suit on the bond. To prevail on a cause of action on a bond, the claimant must prove the injunction was issued or perpetuated when it should not have been and that it was later dissolved. ***DeSantis***, 793 S.W.2d at 685-86. The damages are limited to the amount of the bond. *Id.*

§10.2 Malicious prosecution. To prevail on a cause of action for malicious prosecution of an injunction, the claimant must prove that the injunction suit was (1) prosecuted maliciously, (2) prosecuted without probable cause, and (3) terminated in its favor. ***DeSantis***, 793 S.W.2d at 686; ***Sweezy Constr. v. Murray***, 915 S.W.2d 527, 531 (Tex.App.—Corpus Christi 1995, orig. proceeding). The suit should be brought as a counterclaim in the same lawsuit. ***Sweezy Constr.***, 915 S.W.2d at 531. The claimant is entitled to all actual damages. ***DeSantis***, 793 S.W.2d at 686. See ***O'Connor's COA***, "Malicious Civil Prosecution," ch. 17-A, p. 381.

§11. REVIEW

§11.1 TRO. A TRO cannot be appealed. ***In re Texas Nat. Res. Conserv. Comm'n***, 85 S.W.3d 201, 205 (Tex.2002); ***Ex parte Tucci***, 859 S.W.2d 1, 2 n.4 (Tex.1993); ***Henke***, 6 S.W.3d at 720; *see* TRCP 680 (TRO "shall expire by its terms").

§11.2 Temporary injunction. An order that grants or denies a temporary injunction, or grants or overrules a motion to dissolve a temporary injunction as provided by CPRC chapter 65, is an appealable interlocutory order. CPRC §51.014(a)(4); *see* ***Texas Nat. Res.***, 85 S.W.3d at 205; ***Qwest***, 24 S.W.3d at 338; ***Wyatt v. Cowley***, 74 S.W.3d 576, 577 (Tex.App.—Corpus Christi 2002, pet. dism'd); ***Cellular Mktg. v. Houston Cellular Tel. Co.***, 784 S.W.2d 734, 735 (Tex.App.—Houston [14th Dist.] 1990, no writ). If the trial court modifies the temporary injunction order during the appeal of the original order, the appellate court has jurisdiction to review the modified order if it concerns the same subject matter as the original order. TRAP 29.6(a)(1); ***Ahmed v. Shimi Ventures***, 99 S.W.3d 682, 689 (Tex.App.—Houston [1st Dist.] 2003, no pet.). The interlocutory appeal of any order under CPRC §51.014(a)(4) does not stay the commencement of the trial. CPRC §51.014(b). See ***O'Connor's Texas Civil Appeals***, "Stay of Trial Pending Appeal," ch. 13-P, §3, p. 132 (2002-03). Appellate review of a temporary injunction cannot be used to secure an advance ruling on the merits. ***Iranian Muslim Org. v. City of San Antonio***, 615 S.W.2d 202, 208 (Tex.1981).

1. Accelerated appeal. Appeals from interlocutory orders are accelerated appeals. TRAP 28.1; ***In re Gorman***, 1 S.W.3d 894, 895 (Tex.App.—Fort Worth 1999, orig. proceeding). The deadlines for perfecting the appeal (20 days), filing the record (10 days after filing the notice of appeal), and filing the briefs (20 days after filing the record) are much shorter than regular appeals. *See* TRAP 26.1(b), 35.1(b), 38.6(a). The deadlines in TRAP 26.1(b) are mandatory and jurisdictional. ***State v. Gibson's Distrib. Co.***, 436 S.W.2d 122, 123 (Tex.1968) (discussing TRCP 385, the predecessor to TRAP 42). See ***O'Connor's Texas Civil Appeals***, "Motion to Accelerate the Appeal," ch. 13-C, p. 68.

2. Motion for new trial. A party may file a motion for new trial after an interlocutory order. *See* TRAP 28.1. The motion does not extend the time to file the notice of appeal, which is only 20 days. TRAP 26.1(b), 28.1.

3. Necessity of brief. Although TRAP 28.3 permits the appellate court to proceed without a brief, the courts are reluctant to do so. ***Lagrone v. John Robert Powers Sch.***, 841 S.W.2d 34, 36 (Tex.App.—Dallas 1992, no writ).

4. Standard of review. Appellate review of the temporary injunction is limited to deciding whether the trial court clearly abused its discretion. ***Butnaru v. Ford Motor Co.***, 84 S.W.3d 198, 204 (Tex.2002); ***Davis v. Huey***, 571 S.W.2d 859, 861-62 (Tex.1978). If the parties presented conflicting evidence at the injunction hearing, the appellate court will affirm the trial court's order. ***Davis***, 571 S.W.2d at 862. The appellate court should not substitute its judgment for that of the trial court unless the court's action was so arbitrary that it exceeded the bounds of reasonable discretion. ***Butnaru***, 84 S.W.3d at 204. The trial court abuses its discretion when it misapplies the law to established facts or when it concludes the applicant has a probable right of recovery and the conclusion is not reasonably supported by the evidence. ***State v. Southwestern Bell Tel. Co.***, 526 S.W.2d 526, 538 (Tex.1975).

5. Mootness. The appellate courts cannot review a temporary injunction that is moot; such a review constitutes an impermissible advisory opinion. ***National Collegiate Athletic Ass'n v. Jones***, 1 S.W.3d 83, 86 (Tex.1999); ***Camarena v. TEC***, 754 S.W.2d 149, 151 (Tex.1988). A temporary injunction becomes moot when a change in the status of the parties or the passage of time makes the injunction inoperative or when the objective of the injunction is accomplished. *See* ***Jones***, 1 S.W.3d at 86; *see, e.g.*, ***Reagan Nat'l Adver. v. Vanderhoof Fam. Trust***, 82 S.W.3d 366, 371 (Tex.App.—Austin 2002, no pet.) (threat of loss of property to P was no longer an issue). If the trial court renders a final judgment during the pendency of the appeal of the temporary injunction, the case on appeal becomes moot. ***Isuani v. Manske-Sheffield Radiology Group***, 802 S.W.2d 235, 236 (Tex.1991); ***Jordan v. Landry's Seafood Rest.***, 89 S.W.3d 737, 741 (Tex.App.—Houston [1st Dist.] 2002, pet. denied). When a case becomes moot on appeal, the appellate court must set aside all orders pertaining to the temporary injunction and dismiss the case. ***Isuani***, 802 S.W.2d at 236.

6. Review by Supreme Court. As a general rule, the court of appeals should have the last word on injunctions. *See* Gov't Code §22.225(b)(4) (appeal not permitted to Supreme Court in cases in which temporary injunction was granted or refused); ***Butnaru***, 84 S.W.3d at 202 (jurisdiction over order granting or denying temporary injunction is final in court of appeals). See ***O'Connor's Texas Civil Appeals***, "Review by Supreme Court," ch. 13-P, §4, p. 133.

§11.3 Permanent injunction. Unlike with temporary injunctions, the appellate court does not review the trial court's decision to grant a permanent injunction for abuse of discretion. *See* ***Texas Foundries v. International Moulders & Foundry Workers' Un.***, 248 S.W.2d 460, 462 (Tex.1952). Instead, the appellate court reviews all the evidence to determine whether the trial court's ruling was correct. ***Texas Commerce Bank-Irving v. McCreary***, 677 S.W.2d 643, 644 (Tex.App.—Dallas 1984, no writ); ***Diesel Injection Sales & Servs. v. Renfro***, 656 S.W.2d 568, 571 (Tex.App.—Corpus Christi 1983, writ ref'd n.r.e.). The distinction lies in the purpose of the two injunctions—a temporary injunction is issued to preserve the status quo or to prevent irreparable injury pending final determination of the case on the merits; a permanent injunction is the final determination on the merits. Some courts, however, without taking notice of the distinction, have erroneously applied the abuse-of-discretion standard when reviewing permanent injunctions. *See* ***Crain v. Unauthorized Practice of Law Comm.***, 11 S.W.3d 328, 332 (Tex.App.—Houston [1st Dist.] 1999, pet. denied); ***Harris Cty. Emerg. Serv. Dist. v. Harris Cty. Emerg. Corps***, 999 S.W.2d 163, 167

(Tex.App.—Houston [14th Dist.] 1999, no pet.); ***Adust Video v. Nueces Cty.***, 996 S.W.2d 245, 252 (Tex.App.—Corpus Christi 1999, no pet.); ***Risk Managers Int'l v. State***, 858 S.W.2d 567, 569-70 (Tex.App.—Austin 1993, writ denied); ***Priest v. Texas Animal Health Comm'n***, 780 S.W.2d 874, 875 (Tex.App.—Dallas 1989, no writ).

D. PLAINTIFF'S REQUEST FOR DECLARATORY RELIEF

§1. GENERAL

§1.1 Rules. No rule of procedure deals directly with declaratory judgments; only a few rules even mention them. See TRCP 42(b)(2), 166a(a), 166a(b). The authority for declaratory actions is found in the Declaratory Judgments Act (DJ Act), which is located in CPRC chapter 37.

§1.2 Purpose. The DJ Act is a procedural device for deciding cases that are within the trial court's jurisdiction. ***Chenault v. Phillips***, 914 S.W.2d 140, 141 (Tex.1996); ***State v. Morales***, 869 S.W.2d 941, 947 (Tex.1994). The purpose of a declaratory action is to establish existing rights, status, or other legal relationships. ***City of Garland v. Dallas Morning News***, 22 S.W.3d 351, 357 (Tex.2000); ***Bonham State Bank v. Beadle***, 907 S.W.2d 465, 467 (Tex.1995); ***Republic Ins. Co. v. Davis***, 856 S.W.2d 158, 164 (Tex.1993). A declaratory action is an additional and cumulative remedy and does not supplant any existing remedy. ***Creative Thinking Sources v. Creative Thinking***, 74 S.W.3d 504, 513 (Tex.App.—Corpus Christi 2002, no pet.) (presence of another adequate remedy does not bar declaratory action). A declaratory action cannot be used as an affirmative ground of recovery to alter rights, status, or relationships. ***Republic Ins.***, 856 S.W.2d at 164. The DJ Act is "remedial" only. CPRC §37.002(b); ***Texas Nat. Res. Conserv. Comm'n v. IT-Davy***, 74 S.W.3d 849, 855 (Tex.2002); ***Bonham State Bank***, 907 S.W.2d at 467.

§1.3 Forms. *O'Connor's Texas Civil Forms*, FORM 2D:01.

§2. AVAILABILITY OF DECLARATORY JUDGMENT

An action for declaratory judgment is neither legal nor equitable, but is *sui generis*, that is, the only one of its kind. ***Texas Liquor Control Bd. v. Canyon Creek Land Corp.***, 456 S.W.2d 891, 895 (Tex.1970).

§2.1 When available. A declaratory judgment is appropriate only when there is a justiciable controversy about the rights and status of the parties, and the declaration would resolve the controversy. ***Bonham State Bank***, 907 S.W.2d at 467. The controversy must be real and substantial, involving a genuine conflict of tangible interests and not merely a theoretical dispute. *Id.*; *see, e.g.*, ***Farmers Tex. Cty. Mut. Ins. Co. v. Griffin***, 955 S.W.2d 81, 84 (Tex.1997) (whether insurance carrier had duty to defend when pedestrian shot from insured vehicle); ***Holmes v. Morales***, 924 S.W.2d 920, 921 (Tex.1996) (whether DA was required to turn over "closed" criminal litigation files under Open Records Act); ***Davis v. Shanks***, 898 S.W.2d 285, 286 (Tex.1995) (construction of a will); ***Harwell v. State Farm Mut. Auto. Ins. Co.***, 896 S.W.2d 170, 173 (Tex.1995) (whether insurer was responsible for judgment against insured); ***R Comm., Inc. v. Sharp***, 875 S.W.2d 314, 317-18 (Tex.1994) (controversy over issue of whether assessed taxes were owed). When a counterclaim for declaratory relief will have greater ramifications than the original suit, declaratory relief is appropriate. ***BHP Pet. Co. v. Millard***, 800 S.W.2d 838, 842 (Tex.1990); ***Georgiades v. Di Ferrante***, 871 S.W.2d 878, 880 (Tex.App.—Houston [14th Dist.] 1994, writ denied); *e.g.*, ***Winslow v. Acker***, 781 S.W.2d 322, 328 (Tex.App.—San Antonio 1989, writ denied) (in Ps' suit for recovery of royalty interests assigned to Ds, Ds' counterclaim for declaratory relief was appropriate because it would settle all future royalty disputes). Although the CPRC lists suits that are appropriate for declaratory relief in §37.004 and §37.005, the list is not exhaustive. CPRC §37.003(c).

§2.2 When not available. A declaratory judgment is not available in the following instances:

1. **No justiciable conflict.** A declaratory judgment is not available when there is no justiciable conflict. ***Bonham State Bank***, 907 S.W.2d at 467; *see, e.g.*, ***Paulsen v. Texas Equal Access to Justice Found.***, 23 S.W.3d 42, 44-45 (Tex.App.—Austin 1999, pet. denied) (parties agreed on the constitutionality of challenged statute & desired the same result); ***Barcroft v. State***, 900 S.W.2d 370, 371-72 (Tex.App.—Texarkana 1995, no writ) (P could not bring suit to be declared a Private State Citizen of Texas).

2. Potential tort liability. Generally, a defendant cannot use a declaratory judgment action to determine potential tort liability. ***Abor v. Black***, 695 S.W.2d 564, 566 (Tex.1985) (personal injury suit); ***Stein v. First Nat'l Bank***, 950 S.W.2d 172, 174 (Tex.App.—Austin 1997, no writ) (fraud & conspiracy growing out of a note); *see* ***Texas State Bank v. Amaro***, 87 S.W.3d 538, 545 (Tex.2002) (personal injury suit).

3. Future controversy. A declaratory judgment is not available to resolve issues that are not yet mature and are subject to change. *See, e.g.*, ***City of Garland v. Louton***, 691 S.W.2d 603, 605 (Tex.1985) (parties not entitled to declaratory judgment on constitutionality of referendum statute before election); ***California Prods. v. Puretex Lemon Juice***, 334 S.W.2d 780, 783 (Tex.1960) (P not entitled to advisory opinion on whether bottle design would violate injunction); ***Paulsen***, 23 S.W.3d at 47 (parties not entitled to advisory opinion on how broadly a U.S. Supreme Court opinion could be read); ***Lane v. Baxter Healthcare Corp.***, 905 S.W.2d 39, 41 (Tex. App.—Houston [1st Dist.] 1995, no writ) (P not entitled to resolve issue of ownership of trade secrets before any dispute). The DJ Act does not permit litigants to fish in judicial ponds for legal advice. ***California Prods.***, 334 S.W.2d at 781.

4. In another court. Generally, a declaratory judgment is not available to resolve an issue that will be adjudicated by a separate proceeding involving the same parties. ***Texas Liquor***, 456 S.W.2d at 895; ***Creative Thinking***, 74 S.W.3d at 513.

5. In same suit. Generally, a declaratory judgment is not available to resolve issues that are already pending in the same suit before the court. *See, e.g.*, ***Musgrave v. Owen***, 67 S.W.3d 513, 520 (Tex.App.—Texarkana 2002, no pet.) (claims in DJ action to determine rights of parties under restrictive covenant arose from same subject matter as underlying suit); ***Boatman v. Lites***, 970 S.W.2d 41, 43 (Tex.App.—Tyler 1998, no pet.) (DJ action to determine rights under Water Code §11.086 requested no greater or different relief from that requested in pending suit); ***Staff Indus. v. Hallmark Contracting***, 846 S.W.2d 542, 547-48 (Tex.App.—Corpus Christi 1993, no writ) (counterclaim for declaratory relief concerning amount due under purchase order presented no issues beyond those in underlying suit).

6. No jurisdiction over underlying dispute. A declaratory judgment is not available if the court does not have jurisdiction over the underlying cause of action. ***Chenault v. Phillips***, 914 S.W.2d 140, 141 (Tex.1996); ***Southwest Airlines Co. v. Texas High-Speed Rail Auth.***, 863 S.W.2d 123, 125-26 (Tex.App.—Austin 1993, writ denied); *see, e.g.*, ***State Bar v. Gomez***, 891 S.W.2d 243, 246 (Tex.1994) (district court had no jurisdiction over suit to compel mandatory pro bono).

7. Earlier judgment. A declaratory judgment is not available to seek a judicial interpretation of an earlier judgment. ***Samedan Oil Corp. v. Louis Dreyfus Nat. Gas Corp.***, 52 S.W.3d 788, 792 (Tex.App.—Eastland 2001, pet. denied); ***Martin v. Dosohs I, Ltd.***, 2 S.W.3d 350, 353 (Tex.App.—San Antonio 1999, pet. denied); ***Cohen v. Cohen***, 632 S.W.2d 172, 173 (Tex.App.—Waco 1982, no writ).

8. Criminal issues. A declaratory judgment is not available to determine the rights, status, or other legal relationships arising under a penal statute. *E.g.*, ***State v. Morales***, 869 S.W.2d 941, 947 (Tex.1994) (court could not decide constitutionality of sodomy law).

§3. PROCEDURE

§3.1 Court. Only a court of record may hear an action for declaratory relief. CPRC §37.003(a); ***Wilson v. Wilson***, 378 S.W.2d 156, 160 (Tex.App.—Tyler 1964, no writ).

§3.2 Parties. The petition should name as parties all persons or entities who have a claim or interest that would be affected by the declaration. CPRC §37.006(a); ***Musgrave***, 67 S.W.3d at 521; ***Dahl v. Hartman***, 14 S.W.3d 434, 436 (Tex.App.—Houston [14th Dist.] 2000, pet. denied). When a suit challenges the validity of a municipal ordinance or franchise, the municipality must be made a party. CPRC §37.006(b). When a suit challenges the constitutionality of a statute, an ordinance, or a franchise, the Attorney General must be served. *Id.*

§3.3 Jurisdiction. The DJ Act does not enlarge the existing jurisdiction of the court or create new jurisdiction. ***Texas Nat. Res. Conserv. Comm'n v. IT-Davy***, 74 S.W.3d 849, 855 (Tex.2002); ***Morales***, 869 S.W.2d at 947; ***Kadish v. Pennington Assocs.***, 948 S.W.2d 301, 304 (Tex.App.—Houston [1st Dist.] 1995, no writ). The DJ Act is not a grant of jurisdiction, but merely a procedural device for deciding cases already within the court's jurisdiction. ***Chenault***, 914 S.W.2d at 141; *see* ***Frasier v. Yanes***, 9 S.W.3d 422, 427 (Tex.App.—Austin 1999, no pet.).

§3.4 Venue. Venue for a declaratory judgment action is governed by the rules relating to civil actions generally. ***Bonham State Bank v. Beadle***, 907 S.W.2d 465, 471 (Tex.1995); ***Stiba v. Bowers***, 756 S.W.2d 835, 837 (Tex. App.—Corpus Christi 1988, no writ). Thus, to determine venue of a suit requesting a declaratory judgment, a party must look to the facts of the underlying cause of action. See "Choosing the Court—Venue," ch. 2-G, p. 111.

§3.5 Relief. The petition may ask for affirmative or negative relief. CPRC §37.003(b). The declaratory action may ask for relief in questions of construction or validity arising under a deed, will, written contract, or other instrument, or arising under another relation affected by a statute, municipal ordinance, contract, or franchise. *Id.* §37.004(a). The declaratory action may also ask for relief regarding a trust or estate. *Id.* §37.005. The lists in §37.004 and §37.005 do not limit the power of the court to grant declaratory relief. *Id.* §37.003(c).

§3.6 Jury trial. The parties are entitled to a jury trial, as in other civil cases. CPRC §37.007.

§3.7 Judgment. The declaration has the force and effect of a final judgment or decree. CPRC §37.003(b).

§3.8 Costs & attorney fees. The trial court has the discretion to award costs and attorney fees as part of a declaratory judgment. CPRC §37.009; ***Kenedy Mem'l Found. v. Dewhurst***, 90 S.W.3d 268, 289 (Tex.2002); ***Bocquet v. Herring***, 972 S.W.2d 19, 20 (Tex.1998); ***Barshop v. Medina Cty. Underground Water Conserv. Dist.***, 925 S.W.2d 618, 637 (Tex.1996). The DJ Act imposes four limitations on that discretion: the fees must be (1) reasonable, (2) necessary, (3) equitable, and (4) just. CPRC §37.009; ***Bocquet***, 972 S.W.2d at 21. The issue of the amount of attorney fees is an issue for the trier of fact (judge or jury); the issue of whether to award attorney fees is within the trial court's discretion. ***Bocquet***, 972 S.W.2d at 21; ***Russell v. City of Bryan***, 919 S.W.2d 698, 709 (Tex.App.—Houston [14th Dist.] 1996, writ denied). Attorney fees under CPRC §37.009 can be awarded to any party, not just the prevailing party. *See* ***Bocquet***, 972 S.W.2d at 20; ***Barshop***, 925 S.W.2d at 637; ***McCarthy Bros. v. Continental Lloyds Ins. Co.***, 7 S.W.3d 725, 731 (Tex.App.—Austin 1999, no pet.); ***Templeton v. Dreiss***, 961 S.W.2d 645, 671 (Tex.App.—San Antonio 1998, pet. denied). If the suit is not appropriate for a declaratory judgment, attorney fees cannot be awarded under the DJ Act. ***Brainard v. State***, 12 S.W.3d 6, 29 (Tex.1999); ***Amerman v. Martin***, 83 S.W.3d 858, 863 (Tex.App.—Texarkana 2002, pet. granted 5-1-03).

§3.9 Motion to enforce judgment. The DJ Act empowers the trial court to make supplemental rulings to aid in the enforcement of a declaratory judgment. CPRC §37.011; ***In re Crow-Billingsley Air Park***, 98 S.W.3d 178, 179 (Tex.2003). While on appeal, the trial court may hear a motion to enforce its final judgment if the judgment was not superseded. ***Crow-Billingsley***, 98 S.W.3d at 179.

§4. REVIEW

§4.1 Standard of review. Declaratory judgments are reviewed under the same standards as other judgments and decrees. ***Roberts v. Squyres***, 4 S.W.3d 485, 488 (Tex.App.—Beaumont 1999, pet. denied); ***FDIC v. Projects Am. Corp.***, 828 S.W.2d 771, 772 (Tex.App.—Texarkana 1992, writ denied). Thus, if the declaratory judgment was granted on a motion for summary judgment, the review is governed by the rules for summary judgment; if the declaratory judgment was granted on an agreed statement of facts under TRCP 263, review is governed by the rules for agreed statement of facts. *See, e.g.*, ***Roberts***, 4 S.W.3d at 488 (case submitted on agreed statement); ***Unauthorized Practice of Law Comm. v. Jansen***, 816 S.W.2d 813, 814 (Tex.App.—Houston [14th Dist.] 1991, writ denied) (case submitted on agreed statement and on summary judgment).

§4.2 Conclusion of law. The trial court's decision, which is a conclusion of law, will be upheld on appeal if it can be sustained on any legal theory supported by the evidence. ***Alma Invs. v. Bahia Mar Co-Owners Ass'n***, 999 S.W.2d 820, 823 (Tex.App.—Corpus Christi 1999, pet. denied); ***Projects Am.***, 828 S.W.2d at 772.

§4.3 Relief. If reversal is warranted, the appellate court can render the judgment the trial court should have rendered, unless a remand is necessary for further proceedings. ***Projects Am.***, 828 S.W.2d at 772.

E. PARTIES & CLAIMS

§1. GENERAL

§1.1 Rules. TRCP 28-44, 51, 174. See CPRC ch. 33 (proportionate responsibility).

§1.2 Purpose. For the sake of judicial economy, the rules encourage parties to bring multiple claims and parties into a single lawsuit. There are, however, limits to what claims and parties can be joined.

§1.3 Forms. *O'Connor's Texas Civil Forms*, FORMS 2B:11-21, 3E:01, 3E:12-15, 5G, 5H, 5I.

§1.4 Other references. ***O'Connor's Texas Causes of Action*** (2004) (***O'Connor's COA***).

§2. JOINING PARTIES & CLAIMS

Parties and claims are brought into a lawsuit by one of the following pleadings:

§2.1 Petition. The plaintiff initially decides who are the parties and what are the claims. *See* TRCP 22. See "Plaintiff's Original Petition," ch. 2-B, p. 66. A plaintiff may sue all the defendants responsible for an indivisible injury in one suit or sue them separately. ***Lone Star Salt Water Disposal Co. v. Railroad Comm'n***, 800 S.W.2d 924, 930 (Tex.App.—Austin 1990, no writ).

§2.2 Cross-actions. The term "cross-action" is used only once in the TRCPs, in TRCP 85.

1. Counterclaim. A counterclaim is an affirmative claim for relief filed against an opposing party. TRCP 97. A counterclaim is most often raised by the defendant, although it may be raised by a plaintiff in response to a defendant's or other party's pleading. Counterclaims are either compulsory or permissive. TRCP 97(a), (b). For the difference between them, see "Compulsory Joinder of Claims," §6, p. 98, and "Permissive Joinder of Claims," §7, p. 100.

2. Cross-claim. A cross-claim is an affirmative claim for relief filed by a party against a co-party. TRCP 92, 97(e). For example, if a counterclaim is brought against a plaintiff, the plaintiff may cross-claim against another plaintiff. See "Cross-claims," ch. 3-E, §6.2, p. 179.

3. Third-party action. Third-party practice, also called impleader, is the procedure by which a defendant can bring an additional party into the suit who may be liable to the defendant or to the plaintiff for all or part of the plaintiff's claim. TRCP 38. See "Third-party suit," ch. 3-E, §6.3, p. 179. A plaintiff may implead an additional party in response to a counterclaim by the defendant. TRCP 38(b).

03 **4. Responsible third party.** Under CPRC §33.004, the defendant can designate a person as a responsible third party who is alleged to have caused or contributed to causing the harm for which recovery of damages is sought. See "Responsible third party," ch. 3-E, §6.4, p. 180.

§2.3 Intervention. A plea in intervention is the procedure for a person to join a lawsuit already in progress. TRCP 60, 61. See "Petition in Intervention," ch. 5-I, §2, p. 269.

§2.4 Interpleader. A bill of interpleader is the procedure for a person in possession of property claimed by others to transfer the property and the dispute to the court. *See* TRCP 43. See "Interpleader Suit," ch. 5-I, §3, p. 272.

§2.5 Consolidation. A motion to consolidate asks the court to consolidate two or more suits with a common question of law or fact. TRCP 174(a). The consolidated suit will have one cause number and be resolved by a single judgment. See "Motion to Consolidate," ch. 5-I, §4, p. 273.

§2.6 Joint trial. A motion for joint trial asks the court to hold one trial for two or more suits. TRCP 41, 174(a). The cases are joined for trial only, are tried at the same time but under separate cause numbers, and are resolved by separate judgments.

§3. GENERAL RULES FOR JOINDER OF CLAIMS

§3.1 Single plaintiff & single defendant. There can be no misjoinder of claims when there is only one plaintiff and one defendant. *See* TRCP 51(a); *see, e.g.*, ***Twyman v. Twyman***, 855 S.W.2d 619, 625 (Tex.1993) (tort claims could be joined with divorce). The plaintiff can bring as many claims as it may have against the defendant, and the defendant can bring as many claims as it may have against the plaintiff. The claims need not arise from the same transaction or occurrence and may be entirely unrelated. *See* TRCP 51(a).

§3.2 Multiple parties. When there are multiple parties in the suit, the parties can bring as many claims as they may have against each other as long as the claims arise from the same transaction or occurrence or series of transactions or occurrences and have a common question of law or fact. *See* TRCP 39(a), 40(a), 43, 51(a). In joining other plaintiffs in a pending suit, the plaintiff should consider the effect of the venue provisions that require each plaintiff to justify venue in the county. *See* CPRC §15.003.

§4. MULTIPLE DEFENDANTS

Multiple defendants may be joined in a suit when (1) a right to relief relating to or arising out of the same transaction or occurrence is asserted against them jointly, severally, or in the alternative, and (2) if any questions of law or fact common to all of them will arise in the action. TRCP 40(a); ***In re Caballero***, 53 S.W.3d 391, 397 (Tex. App.—Amarillo 2001, pet. denied).

§4.1 Joint liability. Joint liability is when a defendant is liable with others for damages to the plaintiff.

§4.2 Several liability. Several liability is when a defendant is liable separately and distinctly from another defendant. The term "several" implies that each defendant is liable alone. *See Black's Law Dictionary* 1378 (7th ed. 1999).

§4.3 Joint & several liability. Joint and several liability refers to a defendant who is liable both jointly with other defendants and separately. When the acts of two or more wrongdoers join to produce an indivisible injury, all of the wrongdoers are jointly and severally liable for the entire damages. ***Amstadt v. U.S. Brass Corp.***, 919 S.W.2d 644, 654 (Tex.1996); ***Landers v. East Tex. Salt Water Disposal Co.***, 248 S.W.2d 731, 734 (Tex.1952). A plaintiff may sue all the defendants responsible for an indivisible injury in one suit or sue them separately. ***Lone Star Salt Water Disposal Co. v. Railroad Comm'n***, 800 S.W.2d 924, 930 (Tex.App.—Austin 1990, no writ); *see also* ***Jones v. Ray***, 886 S.W.2d 817, 822 (Tex.App.—Houston [1st Dist.] 1994, orig. proceeding) (forcing P to sue Ds separately would be inequitable because suits were intertwined). There can be only one recovery for one injury. ***Stewart Title Guar. Co. v. Sterling***, 822 S.W.2d 1, 8 (Tex.1991); *see* ***Crown Life Ins. Co. v. Casteel***, 22 S.W.3d 378, 390 (Tex.2000). The fact that more than one defendant may have caused the injury or that there may be more than one theory of liability does not modify this rule. ***Casteel***, 22 S.W.3d at 390; ***Sterling***, 822 S.W.2d at 8.

§5. PROPORTIONATE RESPONSIBILITY FOR DAMAGES

For a more detailed discussion of proportionate responsibility, see ***O'Connor's COA***, "Proportionate Responsibility & Contribution," ch. 42, p. 1115.

§5.1 Plaintiff's bar. The claimant (usually the plaintiff) is barred from recovering damages if its responsibility is found to be greater than 50% in any cause of action based on tort. CPRC §§32.001(a), 33.001.

§5.2 Among the defendants.

1. Most cases. In most cases, a defendant will be held jointly and severally liable when its responsibility with respect to the cause of action is found to be greater than 50%. CPRC §33.013(b)(1).

2. Intentional criminal acts. If the jury finds the defendant engaged in intentional conduct constituting any of the Penal Code offenses listed in CPRC §33.013(b)(2), the defendant will be held jointly and severally liable. CPRC §33.013(b)(2). The list in CPRC §33.013(b)(2) does not include two of the offenses that are grounds for exemplary damages: intoxication assault and intoxication manslaughter. CPRC §41.008(c)(14), (15); *see id.* §33.002(c)(2).

03 **§5.3 Third-party responsibility.** The defendant can designate a person as a responsible third party who is alleged to have caused or contributed to causing the harm for which recovery of damages is sought. See "Responsible third party," ch. 3-E, §6.4, p. 180.

§6. COMPULSORY JOINDER OF CLAIMS

The parties should join all claims that are compulsory to the suit. If a compulsory claim is not brought in the suit, the party with the claim is barred from asserting it in a later suit. TRCP 97(a); ***Wyatt v. Shaw Plumbing Co.***, 760 S.W.2d 245, 247 (Tex.1988); ***Tindle v. Jackson Nat'l Life Ins. Co.***, 837 S.W.2d 795, 800 (Tex.App.—Dallas 1992, no writ).

§6.1 Compulsory-counterclaim rule. The compulsory-counterclaim rule is designed to avoid piecemeal or duplicative litigation. ***Bard v. Charles R. Myers Ins. Agency***, 839 S.W.2d 791, 796 (Tex.1992). The sole compelling interest underlying the rule is judicial economy (*i.e.*, to prevent multiple suits arising out of the same transactions or occurrences). *Id.* A claim is compulsory only if it meets all the criteria in TRCP 97(a) and (d). ***Ingersoll-Rand Co. v. Valero Energy Corp.***, 997 S.W.2d 203, 207 (Tex.1999); ***Wyatt***, 760 S.W.2d at 247.

NOTE

Although this rule is called the "compulsory-counterclaim rule," it is not limited to defendants. The rule also applies against plaintiffs, cross-claim defendants, and third-party defendants. Although initially the plaintiff may choose the claims it wants to bring against the defendant, if the defendant asserts claims against the plaintiff, the plaintiff must then assert all of its compulsory counterclaims, or they will be barred in a later suit.

1. Criteria.

(1) Within jurisdiction. The claim must be within the court's subject-matter jurisdiction. ***Ingersoll-Rand***, 997 S.W.2d at 207; ***Wyatt***, 760 S.W.2d at 247; ***Compass Expl. v. B-E Drilling Co.***, 60 S.W.3d 273, 277 (Tex.App.—Waco 2001, no pet.). A court can reach below its minimum jurisdictional limits if the claim arises from the same transaction or occurrence as the plaintiff's claim. If the damages are above the court's maximum jurisdictional limits, the claim is not compulsory, only permissive. TRCP 97(a); ***Pinckard v. Associated Popcorn Distrib.***, 611 S.W.2d 491, 492 (Tex.App.—Dallas 1981, no writ). The counterclaims of defendants are not aggregated to determine if the amount in controversy exceeds the court's maximum statutory jurisdictional limit and divests it of jurisdiction. ***Smith v. Clary Corp.***, 917 S.W.2d 796, 797 (Tex.1996).

(2) Not filed elsewhere. The claim must not be pending as a suit in another court. ***Ingersoll-Rand***, 997 S.W.2d at 207; ***Wyatt***, 760 S.W.2d at 247; ***Compass Expl.***, 60 S.W.3d at 277.

(3) Mature. The claim must be mature and owned when the pleader files its answer. ***Ingersoll-Rand***, 997 S.W.2d at 207; ***Wyatt***, 760 S.W.2d at 247; ***Compass Expl.***, 60 S.W.3d at 277. Claims that are speculative and premature at the time the answer is filed are not considered compulsory counterclaims. *See, e.g.*, ***Ingersoll-Rand***, 997 S.W.2d at 208 (claim for indemnity did not mature until date of judgment). Claims for attorney fees, however, are compulsory even though they are contingent on the outcome of the suit. ***Fidelity Mut. Life Ins. Co. v. Kaminsky***, 820 S.W.2d 878, 882 (Tex.App.—Texarkana 1991, writ denied).

(4) Same transaction or occurrence. The claim must arise out of the same transaction or occurrence as the opposing party's claim. ***Ingersoll-Rand***, 997 S.W.2d at 207; ***Wyatt***, 760 S.W.2d at 247; ***Compass Expl.***, 60 S.W.3d at 277-78. Texas applies the "logical relationship" test to determine whether claims arise from the same transaction or occurrence. ***Community State Bank v. NSW Invs.***, 38 S.W.3d 256, 258 (Tex.App.—Texarkana 2001, pet. dism'd); ***Jack H. Brown & Co. v. Northwest Sign Co.***, 718 S.W.2d 397, 399 (Tex.App.—Dallas 1986, writ ref'd n.r.e.). Under this test, a transaction is flexible and may be a series of many occurrences logically related to one another. ***Community State Bank***, 38 S.W.3d at 258; ***Tindle***, 837 S.W.2d at 798. To arise from the same transaction, at least some of the facts must be relevant to both claims. ***Community State Bank***, 38 S.W.3d at 258; ***Tindle***, 837 S.W.2d at 798. The Supreme Court has drawn a parallel between the transactional approach embodied in the compulsory-counterclaim rule and the transactional approach to res judicata. ***Barr v. RTC***, 837 S.W.2d 627, 628-30 (Tex.1992); ***Weiman v. Addicks-Fairbanks Rd. Sand Co.***, 846 S.W.2d 414, 419 (Tex.App.—Houston [14th Dist.] 1992, writ denied). Under ***Barr***, factors to consider in determining whether events constitute the same transaction include (1) whether they are related in time, space, origin, or motivation; (2) whether, taken together, they form a convenient unit for trial purposes; and (3) whether their treatment as a trial unit conforms to the parties' expectations or business understanding or usage. ***Barr***, 837 S.W.2d at 631; *see* ***Getty Oil Co. v. Insurance Co. of N. Am.***, 845 S.W.2d 794, 798-99 (Tex.1992); *see also* Restatement (2d) of Judgments §24, cmt. b. (1982) (transaction connotes a natural grouping or common nucleus of operative facts).

CAUTION

A default judgment bars any claim the defendant could have asserted as a compulsory counterclaim had the defendant answered. ***Jack H. Brown***, *718 S.W.2d at 400.*

(5) In same capacity. The claim must be against the opposing party in the same capacity in which that party filed its claim. ***Ingersoll-Rand***, 997 S.W.2d at 207; ***Wyatt***, 760 S.W.2d at 247; ***Compass Expl.***, 60 S.W.3d at 277-78. For example, when the plaintiff files suit in only a representative capacity, any claim against the plaintiff in its individual capacity is not compulsory. For a discussion of capacity, see "Capacity," ch. 2-B, §3.2.2, p. 68.

(6) All parties available. The claim must not require the presence of additional parties over whom the court cannot acquire personal jurisdiction. ***Ingersoll-Rand***, 997 S.W.2d at 207; ***Wyatt***, 760 S.W.2d at 247; ***Compass Expl.***, 60 S.W.3d at 277-78.

2. Cross-claim. When parties are co-parties rather than opposing parties, the compulsory-counterclaim rule acts as a bar to a co-party's claim in a later suit only if the co-parties had "issues drawn between them" in the first suit. ***State & Cty. Mut. Fire Ins. Co. v. Miller***, 52 S.W.3d 693, 696 (Tex.2001); ***Getty Oil***, 845 S.W.2d at 800. For the purposes of res judicata, co-parties have issues drawn between them and become adverse when one co-party files a cross-action against another co-party. ***Miller***, 52 S.W.3d at 696.

§6.2 Parties to be joined. The parties should join all persons and entities needed for the just adjudication of the claims, if feasible. TRCP 39(a). Before the 1971 amendment to TRCP 39, the courts used the phrase "necessary parties"; now, the preferred phrase is "parties to be joined if feasible." ***Wyatt***, 760 S.W.2d at 248 n.2.

1. General rule. A party subject to service of process should be joined if either one of the following applies:

(1) Without the absent party, complete relief cannot be given to those who are already parties. TRCP 39(a); ***Barraza v. Smith & Gopin***, 918 S.W.2d 608, 611 (Tex.App.—El Paso 1996, no writ).

(2) The absent party claims an interest in the subject matter of the action and its absence from the suit may either (1) prevent it from protecting this interest or (2) leave the parties already joined subject to a substantial risk of multiple liability or inconsistent obligations to the absent party. TRCP 39(a); ***Barraza***, 918 S.W.2d at 611; *see also* ***Cooper v. Texas Gulf Indus.***, 513 S.W.2d 200, 204 (Tex.1974) (no precise standard for determining whether a person falls within provisions of TRCP 39(a)).

NOTE

If a party were truly indispensable, it would be fundamental error to proceed in its absence. ***Vondy v. Commissioners Ct.***, *620 S.W.2d 104, 106 (Tex.1981). Seldom will a person's presence in a suit be so indispensable that the person's absence will deprive the court of jurisdiction to adjudicate an issue between the parties already joined.* ***Cooper***, *513 S.W.2d at 204; see,* *e.g., **Allison v. National Un. Fire Ins. Co.**, 703 S.W.2d 637, 638 (Tex.1986) (failure of plaintiffs-attorneys to join their clients in declaratory judgment action against insurance companies who insured clients was not fundamental error); **Cox v. Johnson**, 638 S.W.2d 867, 868 (Tex.1982) (failure to join joint payee in suit on a note was not fundamental error).*

2. Persons secondarily liable. The rules and statutes provide for compulsory joinder of primary obligors except in certain situations.

(1) Sureties. A surety cannot be sued without suing the principal, unless judgment already has been taken against the principal or a statute authorizes the suit (such as the CPRC or the UCC). TRCP 31; *see* CPRC §17.001.

(2) Contracts with several obligors. A judgment cannot be rendered against a person who is not primarily liable on a contract unless judgment is also rendered against the principal obligor. CPRC §17.001(a). There are four exceptions. An assignor, endorser, guarantor, or surety on a contract may be sued individually if the principal obligor (1) is a nonresident or resides where he cannot be reached by the ordinary process of law, (2) resides in an unknown place that cannot be ascertained by reasonable diligence, (3) is dead, or (4) is actually or notoriously insolvent. *Id.* §17.001(b).

(3) Under the UCC. Assignors, endorsers, and other parties not primarily liable on commercial paper may be sued with the principal obligor or sued alone when permitted by statute. TRCP 30; *see* Bus. & Com. Code ch. 3.

§7. PERMISSIVE JOINDER OF CLAIMS

§7.1 General. Any claim that involves some or all of the same parties to an ongoing suit and has common issues of fact and law, but does not satisfy the compulsory-counterclaim test, is a permissive claim in that suit. *See* TRCP 40, 174(a); *see, e.g.*, ***Valley Forge Ins. Co. v. Ryan***, 824 S.W.2d 236, 239 (Tex.App.—Fort Worth 1992, no writ) (because claim between same parties was not compulsory, it was permissive); *see also* ***Getty Oil Co. v. Insurance Co. of N. Am.***, 845 S.W.2d 794, 800 (Tex.1992) (cross-claim under TRCP 97(e) against co-party is permissive). The compulsory-counterclaim rule does not bar the assertion of a permissive counterclaim in a later lawsuit. *See, e.g.*, ***Brown Lex Real Estate Dev. Corp. v. American Nat'l Bank***, 736 S.W.2d 205, 206-07 (Tex.App.—Corpus Christi 1987, writ ref'd n.r.e.) (because D admitted counterclaim was permissive, he conceded that denial of leave to file it was not error).

§7.2 Joining & separating permissive claims. There are four rules of procedure to consider in determining whether permissive claims should be tried together or separately: TRCP 40 (permissive joinder of parties), TRCP 41 (misjoinder and nonjoinder of parties), TRCP 51 (joinder of claims and remedies), and TRCP 174 (consolidation and separate trials). The relevant inquiry is whether a joint (or separate) trial of the claims will prevent manifest injustice and will not prejudice the rights of the parties. ***Womack v. Berry***, 291 S.W.2d 677, 683 (Tex. 1956); *see* TRCP 40(b) (prevent embarrassment, delay, or additional expense), TRCP 174(b) (further convenience and avoid prejudice); *see also* ***Jones v. Ray***, 886 S.W.2d 817, 822 (Tex.App.—Houston [1st Dist.] 1994, orig. proceeding) (separate trials would permit Ds to make "empty chair" argument); ***Dal-Briar Corp. v. Baskette***, 833 S.W.2d 612, 616 (Tex.App.—El Paso 1992, orig. proceeding) (joint trial would create unacceptable probability of an unfair result). The judicial economy and convenience that may be gained by consolidation must be weighed against the likelihood that consolidation may result in delay, prejudice, or jury confusion. ***Dal-Briar***, 833 S.W.2d at 616-17.

§8. REMEDIES

§8.1 For misjoinder. If there is misjoinder of claims or parties (*e.g.*, in a multiparty action, if claims are added that are not part of the same transaction or occurrence), the court should drop or add parties, consolidate separate actions, sever actions improperly joined, or order separate trials within the same case. TRCP 40(b), 41. The court cannot dismiss all or part of the suit. TRCP 41.

1. Severance. Severance of claims makes two or more suits from what was originally one suit. *See* TRCP 41. Each suit will be given its own cause number and be resolved by a separate judgment. See "Motion for Severance," ch. 5-H, §3, p. 263.

2. Separate trials. A court may order separate trials of issues in one case for reasons of convenience or to avoid prejudice or embarrassment. TRCP 40(b), 174(b). The claims remain part of the same suit and are resolved by a single judgment. See "Motion for Separate (Bifurcated) Trial," ch. 5-H, §4, p. 266.

§8.2 For absent party. To raise the issue of the absence of a party that should be joined, the complaining party should file a motion to abate. See "Motion to Abate—Challenging the Suit," ch. 3-H, p. 194.

F. CHOOSING THE COURT—JURISDICTION

§1. GENERAL

§1.1 Rules. None. See Tex. Const., art. 5; CPRC ch. 51, 61-64; Gov't Code ch. 24-28; Prob. Code §§4, 5, 5A; Prop. Code §115.001.

§1.2 Purpose. Before filing the suit, the plaintiff must decide in which of the Texas trial courts the lawsuit should be filed. That decision is made by choosing the court with both jurisdiction and venue over the dispute. For venue, see "Choosing the Court—Venue," ch. 2-G, p. 111.

NOTE

To challenge the subject-matter jurisdiction of the court, see "Plea to the Jurisdiction—Challenging the Court," ch. 3-F, p. 181.

§1.3 Forms. ***O'Connor's Texas Civil Forms***, FORM 2B:22.

§1.4 Other references. Gorham, *The Jurisdiction of Statutory Probate Courts*, 59 Tex.B.J. 240 (1996).

§2. JURISDICTION OF TEXAS TRIAL COURTS

The jurisdiction of Texas courts is conferred solely by the Texas Constitution and state statutes. ***Chenault v. Phillips***, 914 S.W.2d 140, 141 (Tex.1996).

§2.1 Types of trial courts. In Texas, there are district, county, justice of the peace, and various other courts established by legislative enactment. Each type of court has jurisdiction over specific types of cases and amounts in controversy. See "CPRC Courts" at www.JonesMcClure.com/Resources. Although all courts can render a judgment for damages, not all courts can render a judgment for other types of relief (*e.g.*, injunctive relief).

PRACTICE TIP

The easiest way to determine whether a particular court has subject-matter jurisdiction is to check the amount in controversy. If the amount in controversy is within the court's jurisdictional limits, it has jurisdiction unless the particular type of controversy is excluded from its jurisdiction or another court has exclusive jurisdiction over the controversy. Then check whether the court can grant the type of relief you are requesting.

§2.2 Computing amount in controversy. The amount in controversy is determined by the plaintiff's good-faith pleadings. ***Peek v. Equipment Serv. Co.***, 779 S.W.2d 802, 804 (Tex.1989); ***Smith Detective Agency v. Stanley Smith Sec.***, 938 S.W.2d 743, 747 (Tex.App.—Dallas 1996, writ denied); *see also* ***Tune v. Texas DPS***, 23 S.W.3d

358, 362 (Tex.2000) (amount in controversy determined by subjective value of rights asserted by P, if asserted in good faith).

1. Single plaintiff vs. single defendant. When one plaintiff asserts multiple claims against the same defendant, jurisdiction is determined by adding the amounts together. ***Texas City Tire Shop v. Alexander***, 333 S.W.2d 690, 693 (Tex.App.—Houston [1st Dist.] 1960, no writ); *see also* ***Tejas Toyota, Inc. v. Griffin***, 587 S.W.2d 775, 776 (Tex.App.—Waco 1979, writ ref'd n.r.e.) (sum of damages in cross-action exceeded jurisdiction of trial court). When a plaintiff asserts claims based on alternative theories, jurisdiction is determined according to the theory that would yield the highest award. ***Lucey v. Southeast Tex. Emerg. Physicians Assocs.***, 802 S.W.2d 300, 302 (Tex.App.—El Paso 1990, writ denied).

2. Multiple parties.

(1) By multiple plaintiffs. When multiple plaintiffs assert claims against a defendant, their claims are aggregated to determine the amount in controversy. Gov't Code §24.009; ***Dubai Pet. Co. v. Kazi***, 12 S.W.3d 71, 75 n.4 (Tex.2000). Thus, a class action with 100 plaintiffs each suing for $10 would have $1,000 in controversy and could be filed in district court.

(2) Against multiple defendants. When a plaintiff asserts separate, independent, and distinct claims against multiple defendants, jurisdiction is determined by looking at the claims separately, and the amounts are not aggregated. ***Borrego v. del Palacio***, 445 S.W.2d 620, 622 (Tex.App.—El Paso 1969, no writ). Thus, one plaintiff suing 100 defendants for $10 each would have only $10 in controversy and would file the suit in justice court.

3. Counterclaims. Counterclaims, whether permissive or compulsory, are judged on their own merits and must be within the court's jurisdiction. ***Color Tile v. Ramsey***, 905 S.W.2d 620, 623 (Tex.App.—Houston [14th Dist.] 1995, no writ); *see* TRCP 97; ***Smith v. Clary Corp.***, 917 S.W.2d 796, 798 (Tex.1996). A permissive or compulsory counterclaim can be for an amount within or below the court's minimum jurisdiction, but it cannot be for an amount above the court's maximum jurisdiction. ***Kitchen Designs v. Wood***, 584 S.W.2d 305, 307 (Tex.App.—Texarkana 1979, writ ref'd n.r.e.) (compulsory counterclaim above jurisdictional limit); ***Andel v. Eastman Kodak Co.***, 400 S.W.2d 584, 586 (Tex.App.—Houston [1st Dist.] 1966, no writ) (compulsory counterclaim below jurisdictional limit). If a counterclaim is above the jurisdictional limit of the court, the trial court should dismiss the counterclaim. ***Kitchen Designs***, 584 S.W.2d at 307. Counterclaims of multiple defendants are not aggregated under the aggregating statute. Gov't Code §24.009; ***Smith***, 917 S.W.2d at 798.

4. Actions other than for damages. When the action is to recover or foreclose on personal property, the amount in controversy is either the fair market value of the property or the amount of the underlying debt, whichever is higher. If the suit is for injunctive relief, and there is no amount in controversy, jurisdiction is in the district court based on residual jurisdiction. ***Super X Drugs v. State***, 505 S.W.2d 333, 336 (Tex.App.—Houston [14th Dist.] 1974, no writ); *see* ***Martin v. Victoria ISD***, 972 S.W.2d 815, 818 (Tex.App.—Corpus Christi 1998, pet. denied) (county court cannot hold injunction hearing unless amount in controversy is alleged). See "Special types of case," §3.1.2, p. 104.

5. Other related claims. A court can assert jurisdiction over claims that are below its minimum jurisdictional limits if those claims arise from the same transaction or occurrence as a claim over which the court has jurisdiction. ***Andel***, 400 S.W.2d at 586. A court cannot assert jurisdiction over a claim that is above its maximum jurisdictional limits. ***Hawkins v. Anderson***, 672 S.W.2d 293, 296 (Tex.App.—Dallas 1984, no writ).

6. Amendments in excess of jurisdictional limits. Generally, once jurisdiction is properly acquired, no later fact or event can defeat the court's jurisdiction. ***Continental Coffee Prods. Co. v. Cazarez***, 937 S.W.2d 444, 449 (Tex.1996); ***Dallas ISD v. Porter***, 709 S.W.2d 642, 643 (Tex.1986); ***Weidner v. Sanchez***, 14 S.W.3d 353, 360-61 (Tex.App.—Houston [14th Dist.] 2000, no pet.). If the plaintiff's original petition was properly brought in a particular court, but an amendment increases the amount in controversy above the court's jurisdictional limits, the court will continue to have jurisdiction if the additional damages accrued as a result of the passage of time.

Continental Coffee, 937 S.W.2d at 449; ***Mr. W. Fireworks v. Mitchell***, 622 S.W.2d 576, 577 (Tex.1981); ***Weidner***, 14 S.W.3d at 361. If an amendment adds a claim for damages that existed at the time the suit was filed but was not included in the original petition, and if the additional claim is outside the court's jurisdiction, the additional claim should be dismissed on a plea to the jurisdiction. ***Hawkins***, 672 S.W.2d at 296.

7. Interest. Interest is seldom included in the amount in controversy. The courts distinguish between interest *eo nomine* (interest as interest), which is excluded, and interest "as damages," which is included. ***Weidner***, 14 S.W.3d at 362; *see also* Gov't Code §25.0003(c)(1) (specifically excludes *eo nomine* interest in determining the amount in controversy in suits filed in county courts at law); ***Smith***, 917 S.W.2d at 798 (same). Interest *eo nomine* is interest as provided for by agreement or by statute; it is part of the debt. Interest as damages is interest that is added to the debt for not paying a sum certain at the time the debt was due. This calculation includes equitable prejudgment interest, unless prejudgment interest is provided for by contract or statute. ***Weidner***, 14 S.W.3d at 362; *see* ***Barnes v. U.S. Fid. & Guar. Co.***, 279 S.W.2d 919, 921 (Tex.App.—Waco 1955, no writ).

8. Attorney fees & exemplary damages. Attorney fees are generally included in the amount in controversy. ***Johnson v. Universal Life & Acc. Ins. Co.***, 94 S.W.2d 1145, 1146 (Tex.1936); ***Long v. Fox***, 625 S.W.2d 376, 378 (Tex.App.—San Antonio 1981, writ ref'd n.r.e.). *But see* Gov't Code §25.0003(c)(1) (specifically excludes attorney fees, penalties, and statutory or punitive damages from the amount in controversy in suits filed in county courts at law); ***Smith***, 917 S.W.2d at 798 (same).

9. Costs. Costs of court are not included in the amount in controversy.

§2.3 Amending to correct amount in controversy. If a pleading makes a claim for nonseverable liquidated damages that are outside the trial court's jurisdiction (either above or below), the party cannot amend its damages to state an amount within the court's jurisdiction. ***Smith Detective Agency v. Stanley Smith Sec.***, 938 S.W.2d743, 747 (Tex.App.—Dallas 1996, writ denied). However, if the claim is for unliquidated damages, a party may amend its damages to state an amount within the court's jurisdiction if the party pleads in good faith. *Id.*

2-1. OVERLAPPING MONETARY JURISDICTION OF TRIAL COURTS

	District courts	Constitutional county courts	County courts at law	Justice courts	Small claims courts
$100,000.01 +					
$100,000					
$5,000					
$500.01 +					
$200.01 +	See §3.1.1, below	See §4.1.1, below	See §4.2.1, p. 106	See §5.1, p. 108	See §6.2, p. 109
$.01 +					

§3. DISTRICT COURTS

§3.1 Constitutional district courts. The district courts are the primary trial courts of Texas. ***Dubai***, 12 S.W.3d at 75. The Constitution gives them exclusive, appellate, and original jurisdiction of all actions, proceedings, and remedies, except in cases where exclusive, appellate, or original jurisdiction is conferred by the Texas Constitution or other law on some other court, tribunal, or administrative body. Tex. Const. art. 5, §8; ***Dubai***, 12 S.W.3d at 75; *see* Gov't Code §§24.007, 24.008, 24.011. If a case cannot be filed anywhere else, it can be filed in a district court under the residual clause. *See* Gov't Code §24.008.

1. Amount in controversy. District courts have no upper limit to their amount in controversy jurisdiction. *See generally* Tex. Const. art. 5, §8 (jurisdiction of district court); Gov't Code §§24.007 & 24.008 (same). Regarding their lower limit, it is uncertain if they have a minimum limit and, if they do, what it is. The Supreme Court has suggested there may no longer be a jurisdictional minimum for district courts. ***Dubai***, 12 S.W.3d at 75 n.4; *see also* ***Peek v. Equipment Serv. Co.***, 779 S.W.2d 802, 803-04 n.4 (Tex.1989) (discussed constitutional and statutory amendments that deleted reference to $500 floor for district court's jurisdiction). Two courts of appeals have held that the district court's minimum jurisdictional amount is $200.01. ***Arteaga v. Jackson***, 994 S.W.2d 342, 343 (Tex.App.—Texarkana 1999, pet. denied) (district court begins at $200.01 because justice court has exclusive jurisdiction from $200 down); ***Arnold v. West Bend Co.***, 983 S.W.2d 365, 366 n.1 (Tex.App.—Houston [1st Dist.] 1998, no pet.) (same). One court of appeals has held that the district court's minimum jurisdictional amount is $500.01. ***Chapa v. Spivey***, 999 S.W.2d 833, 836 (Tex.App.—Tyler 1999, no pet.) (district court begins at $500.01 because the 1985 amendment to Tex. Const. art 5, §8 and recodification of Gov't Code §24.007 did not change the minimum jurisdictional amount); *see also* ***Gordon v. Scott***, 6 S.W.3d 365, 370 (Tex.App.—Beaumont 1999, pet. denied) (Walker, C.J., dissenting) (assumed ***Chapa*** correct). See chart 2-1, above.

2. Special types of cases. District courts have jurisdiction over all types of claims over which justice and county courts do not. This type of jurisdiction is called "residual" jurisdiction. Thus, it is often difficult to determine the jurisdiction of the district courts because it can be determined only by looking through the laws establishing the jurisdiction of the other Texas courts.

3. Relief available. All types of relief are available in the district courts.

§3.2 Legislative district courts. The Constitution gives the Legislature the power to "establish such other courts as it may deem necessary," to prescribe the jurisdiction of those legislative courts, and to "conform the jurisdiction of the district and other inferior courts thereto." Tex. Const. art. 5, §1. The Legislature has the power to create statutory courts that have concurrent jurisdiction with constitutional district and county courts. ***Fleming v. Fleming***, 595 S.W.2d 199, 202 (Tex.App.—Waco 1980, writ dism'd); ***Clark v. Tarrant Cty. Child Welfare Unit***, 509 S.W.2d 378, 380 (Tex.App.—Fort Worth 1974, no writ).

1. Family district courts. The Legislature created family district courts with jurisdiction equal to that of constitutional district courts and with primary responsibility for family law matters such as divorce, annulment, child conservatorship, and support. All district courts have jurisdiction over family law matters. The family district courts have the same jurisdiction as other district courts in the county in which they are located. Gov't Code §24.601(a); ***Beach v. Beach***, 912 S.W.2d 345, 347 n.3 (Tex.App.—Houston [14th Dist.] 1995, no writ). In counties with family law courts, family law matters are filed in those courts, and those courts can decide other controversies that arise from the family law matters.

2. Juvenile courts. A district court that exercises constitutional jurisdiction may be designated as a juvenile court. Gov't Code §23.001(a); Fam. Code §51.04(b). Juvenile courts have exclusive original jurisdiction over proceedings under the Juvenile Justice Code, except that in a county with a population of less than 100,000, the juvenile court has concurrent jurisdiction with the justice and municipal courts for conduct by a child that violates Education Code §25.094 (failure to attend school). Fam. Code §51.04(a), (h).

§4. COUNTY COURTS

There are various types of county courts with different types of jurisdiction. The most complicated aspect of county court jurisdiction is probate jurisdiction. As the Supreme Court noted, "Texas probate jurisdiction is, to say the least, somewhat complex." ***Palmer v. Coble Wall Trust Co.***, 851 S.W.2d 178, 180 n.3 (Tex.1992). See "Probate jurisdiction between courts," §4.4, p. 107.

§4.1 Constitutional county courts. Every county has a constitutional county court, which is the office of the chief administrator of the county. *See* Tex. Const. art. 5, §§15, 16. In some counties the constitutional county judge exercises probate jurisdiction, and in others the judge acts only as the county's administrator and takes no action as a trial judge. The Texas Constitution states that the jurisdiction of the constitutional county court is "as provided by law." Tex. Const. art. 5, §16. Its jurisdiction, therefore, is governed by statutes. *See* CPRC §§51.001, 51.002, 61.021; Gov't Code §§26.041-26.044, 26.048, 26.050, 26.051.

1. Amount in controversy. The constitutional county courts have concurrent jurisdiction with the justice courts in civil cases in which the amount in controversy is $200.01 through $5,000, excluding interest.

Gov't Code §26.042(a). The amount in controversy does not limit the court's probate jurisdiction. ***Womble v. Atkins***, 331 S.W.2d 294, 299 (Tex.1960). See chart 2-1, "Overlapping Monetary Jurisdiction of Trial Courts," p. 103.

2. Probate & guardianship matters. Except in those counties where probate jurisdiction rests exclusively in other courts, constitutional county courts have original jurisdiction of probate and guardianship. Prob. Code §§4 & 5(b) (probate), §605 (guardianship). See "Probate jurisdiction between courts," §4.4, p. 107. If the constitutional county court retains probate jurisdiction in a particular county, and a party contests any matter in a probate or guardianship case before that court, the contested matter may be assigned or transferred. The constitutional county court retains jurisdiction over the estate or guardianship, except as to the contested matter. Prob. Code §§5(b-4), 606(b-4). The contested matter may be assigned or transferred as follows:

(1) If any party moves for a statutory probate judge to be assigned to hear the contested matter, the constitutional county court must grant the motion. Prob. Code §§5(b), 606(b). The presiding statutory probate judge then assigns a current or former statutory probate judge to hear the contested matter. *See* Gov't Code §25.0022(h). The statutory probate judge has available all the jurisdictional tools of a statutory probate court when hearing the contested matter, including the power to transfer other pending matters under Probate Code §5B and §608. Prob. Code §§5(b-2), 606(b-2); Gov't Code §25.0022(i). Unless a party objects, the statutory probate judge can hear ancillary motions in that judge's home county, but the trial on the merits must be conducted in the county where the probate proceeding is pending. Gov't Code §25.0022(n).

(2) If any party moves to transfer the contested matter to the district court (or a county court at law in the county with probate jurisdiction), the constitutional county court must grant the motion. Prob. Code §§5(b)(2), (c), 606(b)(2), (c). The district court (or county court at law) then hears the contested matter as if originally filed there. Prob. Code §§5(b)(2), (c), 606(b)(2), (c). A motion to assign a statutory probate judge to the contested matter, however, controls over a motion to transfer the matter to district court. Thus, a motion to assign a statutory probate judge must be granted, unless the motion is withdrawn or the constitutional county court has already transferred the contested matter to district court. *Id.* §§5(b-1), 606(b-1).

(3) Even if no party moves to assign the contested matter to a statutory probate judge or transfer it to district court or county court at law, the constitutional county court may assign or transfer the contested matter on its own initiative. Prob. Code §§5(b), 606(b).

(4) Once the statutory probate judge, district court, or county court at law resolves the contested matter, including any appeals, the matter is transferred back to the constitutional county court for further proceedings. Prob. Code §§5(b-2), (b-3), 606(b-2), (b-3); *see id.* §§5(c), 606(c).

3. Appellate jurisdiction. Constitutional county courts have appellate jurisdiction over cases originating in the justice or small claims courts where the amount in controversy or the judgment exceeds $20, exclusive of costs. Gov't Code §26.042(e); *see* ***Weeks v. Hobson***, 877 S.W.2d 478, 480 n.1 (Tex.App.—Houston [1st Dist.] 1994, orig. proceeding) (appellate jurisdiction includes forcible entry and detainer suits). Review is by trial de novo. *See* Tex. Const. art. 5, §6(a); CPRC §51.001.

4. Additional jurisdiction. The Legislature has given some constitutional county courts limited jurisdiction over other matters. *See, e.g.*, Gov't Code §26.134 (Cass County constitutional county court has the power to receive and enter guilty pleas in misdemeanor cases).

5. Relief available. Constitutional county courts may issue writs of injunction, mandamus, certiorari, sequestration, and all other writs necessary to enforce their jurisdiction. Tex. Const. art. 5, §16; CPRC §§61.021, 62.021, 63.002, 65.021; Gov't Code §§26.044, 26.051; ***Martin v. Victoria ISD***, 972 S.W.2d 815, 817 (Tex. App.—Corpus Christi 1998, pet. denied).

6. Cases excluded. Constitutional county courts do not have jurisdiction over the following suits: (1) for recovery of damages for defamation or slander of character; (2) for enforcement of liens on land; (3) for escheat on behalf of the state; (4) for divorce; (5) for forfeiture of a corporate charter; (6) for the trial of the right to property valued at $500 or more and levied under a writ of execution, sequestration, or attachment; (7) for eminent domain; or (8) for recovery of land. Gov't Code §26.043.

§4.2 County courts at law. Every county court at law (statutory county court) has the same jurisdiction as the constitutional county court in that county, Gov't Code §§25.0003(a), 25.0004(c), unless modified by (1) the statute that created the statutory county court or (2) a statute that applies to all statutory county courts. *See* Gov't Code §25.0001(a); *see also* Tex. Const. art. 5, §1 (legislature may establish other courts as it deems necessary). To determine the jurisdiction of a particular county court at law, consult the specific Government Code provision for that county's courts at law and the general code provisions that apply to more than one legislative court. *See* Gov't Code ch. 25. See "CPRC Courts" at www.JonesMcClure.com/Resources. Some county courts at law have very limited jurisdiction, but others have about the same jurisdiction as the district courts. *See* Gov't Code §25.0222(a) (Brazoria County), Gov't Code §25.0592(a) (Dallas County); *see, e.g.*, ***Schuld v. Dembrinski***, 12 S.W.3d 485, 489 (Tex. App.—Dallas 2000, no pet.) (because Dallas county court at law had concurrent jurisdiction with district court in civil cases regardless of amount in controversy, county court had jurisdiction over partition suit); ***Underwood v. Underwood***, 902 S.W.2d 152, 154 (Tex.App.—Houston [1st Dist.] 1995, no writ) (because Brazoria statutory county court had jurisdiction over family law cases, it had jurisdiction over family law claim over $100,000).

1. Amount in controversy. Gov't Code §25.0003(c)(1) provides that the county courts at law have concurrent jurisdiction with the district courts where the amount in controversy exceeds $500 but does not exceed $100,000, excluding mandatory damages and penalties, attorney fees, interest, and costs. ***Smith v. Clary Corp.***, 917 S.W.2d 796, 798 (Tex.1996). Because county courts at law have the same jurisdiction as constitutional county courts, the actual dollar range of the amount in controversy for county courts at law starts as low as $200.01 and goes as high as $100,000, depending on which statute controls that court's jurisdiction. *See* Gov't Code §§25.0003(a), 26.042(a). See chart 2-1, "Overlapping Monetary Jurisdiction of Trial Courts," p. 103.

2. Probate & guardianship matters. Gov't Code §25.0003(d) authorizes county courts at law to exercise probate jurisdiction, except when there is a statutory probate court in the same county. Gov't Code §25.0003(e). However, the county court at law does not have the same jurisdiction granted to statutory probate courts under the Texas Probate Code. Gov't Code §25.0003(f); *see* ***In re G.C.***, 66 S.W.3d 517, 522 (Tex.App.—Fort Worth 2002, no pet.) (county court at law does not become statutory probate court merely by exercising its probate jurisdiction). Instead, the county court at law has the general probate jurisdiction of a constitutional county court. Gov't Code §25.0003(d); *see* Prob. Code §5A(a).

3. Civil & criminal. County courts at law have jurisdiction over all civil and criminal causes prescribed by law for county courts. Gov't Code §25.0003(a); ***Weeks***, 877 S.W.2d at 480 n.1.

4. Extraordinary relief. County courts at law may issue writs of injunction, mandamus, sequestration, attachment, garnishment, certiorari, supersedeas, and other writs necessary to enforce the court's jurisdiction. Gov't Code §25.0004(a); ***In re Burlington N. & S. Ry.***, 12 S.W.3d 891, 896 (Tex.App.—Houston [14th Dist.] 2000, orig. proceeding); ***Martin***, 972 S.W.2d at 817.

5. Matters excluded. A county court at law does not have jurisdiction over county business of the commissioners court or over matters excluded from the jurisdiction of the constitutional county court. *See* Gov't Code §25.0003(b) (county business exclusion), *id.* §26.043 (exclusions for constitutional county courts); *see, e.g.*, ***Matherne v. Carre***, 7 S.W.3d 903, 906 (Tex.App.—Beaumont 1999, pet. denied) (county court at law does not have jurisdiction of suit for enforcement of lien on land); ***Loville v. Loville***, 944 S.W.2d 818, 819 (Tex.App.—Beaumont 1997, writ denied) (like constitutional county court, statutory county court does not have jurisdiction in suit to recover land). *But see* Gov't Code §25.1032(c)(1) (Harris County Civil Court at Law has jurisdiction over issue of title to real property). See §4.1.6, above.

§4.3 Statutory probate court. 03

1. Probate & guardianship matters. In certain counties, the Legislature has established statutory probate courts with exclusive probate jurisdiction. Statutory probate courts have general probate jurisdiction as set forth in the Probate Code. *See* Gov't Code §25.0021(b)(1); ***Schuld***, 12 S.W.3d at 487; ***Green v. Watson***, 860 S.W.2d 238, 242 (Tex.App.—Austin 1993, no writ). Gov't Code §25.0021(a) does, however, limit statutory probate court jurisdiction to matters in probate, guardianship, mental health, and eminent domain, superseding any other Government Code provisions that give statutory probate courts in specific counties additional jurisdiction.

2. Appertaining or incident to an estate. Unless the statutory probate court's jurisdiction is concurrent with that of another court, all matters appertaining or incident to an estate must be brought in a statutory probate court. Prob. Code §§5A(b), 607(b); *see id.* §5(e) (granting concurrent jurisdiction to district courts in certain cases). See §4.4.3(1), below. A suit is appertaining to or incident to an estate when the controlling issue is the collection, settlement, partition, or distribution of the estate. *See* Prob. Code §§5A(a)-(b), 607(a)-(b); ***In re SWEPI, L.P.***, 85 S.W.3d 800, 805 (Tex.2002); ***In re Graham***, 971 S.W.2d 56, 58 (Tex.1998); ***Palmer v. Coble Wall Trust Co.***, 851 S.W.2d 178, 181 (Tex.1992). In addition, any proceeding filed against or on behalf of any decedent's estate or guardianship is appertaining to or incident to the estate. Prob. Code §§5A(b), 607(b); *see id.* §§5(h), 606(i). Thus, in a statutory probate court, a proceeding is appertaining or incident to the estate if the personal representative or a guardian is a party, regardless of whether the controlling issue in the proceeding is the collection, settlement, partition, or distribution of the estate. *See* Prob. Code §§5(h), 5A(b), 606(i), 607(b).

3. Trust matters. A statutory probate court has concurrent jurisdiction with the district court in actions involving inter vivos and charitable trusts. Prob. Code §5(e); *see* Prop. Code §115.001(d); ***Schuele v. Schuele***, 119 S.W.3d 822, 825 (Tex.App.—San Antonio 2003, n.p.h.). As a result of the 2003 amendments to Probate Code §5, whether a statutory probate court has jurisdiction in actions involving testamentary and constructive trusts is now in question. *Compare* Prob. Code §5(e) (statutory probate court has concurrent jurisdiction over inter vivos and charitable trusts), *with id.* §5A(b) (matters appertaining and incident to estates include testamentary and constructive trusts). See ***O'Connor's Probate Code Plus***, "Statutory Probate Court Jurisdiction Gets Even More Complicated," 2003 Legislative Comment, §1.5, pp. XIX-XXI (2003-04).

4. Pendent & ancillary jurisdiction. Statutory probate courts may exercise pendent and ancillary jurisdiction necessary to promote judicial efficiency and economy. Prob. Code §§5(i), 606(j). Other courts exercising probate jurisdiction do not have pendent and ancillary jurisdiction.

§4.4 Probate jurisdiction between courts. In some counties, the Legislature has established statutory probate courts or given probate jurisdiction to a county court at law or another statutory court. Probate jurisdiction differs depending on whether the county has one of these probate courts. *See* Prob. Code §5(b). 03

1. Counties with no statutory probate court or county court at law. In counties with no statutory probate court, county court at law, or other statutory court exercising probate jurisdiction, all probate matters are filed in the constitutional county court. Prob. Code §§5(b), 606(b). If the constitutional county court retains probate jurisdiction in a particular county, and a party contests some matter in a pending probate or guardianship case, the court may on its own motion, and must on any party's motion, either transfer the contest to a district court or ask to have a statutory probate judge assigned to hear the contest. *Id.* §§5(b), 606(b). See "Probate & guardianship matters," §4.1.2, p. 105.

2. Counties with no statutory probate court but with county court at law. In counties with no statutory probate court but with a county court at law or other statutory court exercising probate jurisdiction, the county court at law has concurrent jurisdiction with the constitutional county court in probate and guardianship matters. Prob. Code §§5(c), 606(c). In contested matters, the constitutional county court may on its own motion, and must on the motion of any party, transfer the proceeding to the county court at law. *Id.* §§5(c), 606(c). See "Probate & guardianship matters," §4.1.2, p. 105.

3. Counties with statutory probate court. Statutory probate courts are those courts designated as "statutory probate courts" under Gov't Code chapter 25. Gov't Code §21.009(4); Prob. Code §3(ii). In a county with a statutory probate court, all probate matters must be heard in the statutory probate court. Prob. Code §§5(d), 606(d).

(1) Concurrent jurisdiction. Statutory probate courts have concurrent jurisdiction with district courts in (1) all personal injury, survival, or wrongful death actions by or against a person in her capacity as a personal representative or a guardian and (2) all actions involving a personal representative of an estate or a guardian in which each other party aligned with the personal representative or guardian is not an interested person in that estate or guardianship. Prob. Code §§5(e), 606(h). Statutory probate courts also have concurrent jurisdiction with district courts in actions involving inter vivos trusts and charitable trusts. See §4.3.3, above. Constitutional county courts and county courts at law do not have jurisdiction over trusts. *See* Prop. Code §115.001(a) (district court has exclusive jurisdiction over trusts); ***Schuele***, 119 S.W.3d at 825 (same).

(2) Dominant jurisdiction. If the suit was filed first in the probate court, its jurisdiction is dominant over any other court's jurisdiction. ***Bailey v. Cherokee Cty. Appr. Dist.***, 862 S.W.2d 581, 586 (Tex.1993); *see also* ***Garza v. Rodriguez***, 18 S.W.3d 694, 699 (Tex.App.—San Antonio 2000, no pet.) (district court did not have jurisdiction over action that sought to undo probate order entered by constitutional county court); ***Green v. Watson***, 860 S.W.2d 238, 242-43 (Tex.App.—Austin 1993, no writ) (because statutory county court in Williamson County had jurisdiction over estate, district court in Travis County did not have jurisdiction to void a sale of estate property in Travis County). A cause of action filed in another court that pertains to or is incident to an estate pending in the probate court can be dismissed on a plea to the jurisdiction. ***Speer v. Stover***, 685 S.W.2d 22, 23 (Tex.1985).

(3) Transfer of proceedings to statutory probate courts. On a party's motion, a statutory probate court may transfer to itself from a district court, constitutional county court, or county court at law, a cause of action appertaining or incident to an estate or guardianship or a cause of action in which the personal representative or guardian is a party. Prob. Code §§5B(a), 608; ***In re Houston Nw. Partners***, 98 S.W.3d 777, 779 (Tex.App.—Austin 2003, orig. proceeding); ***In re Azle Manor***, 83 S.W.3d 410, 412 (Tex.App.—Fort Worth 2002, orig. proceeding); *see* ***Graham***, 971 S.W.2d at 57 (§608). However, for an action by or against a personal representative for personal injury, death, or property damage, proper venue is determined under CPRC §15.007. Prob. Code §§5B(b), 607(e); *see* CPRC §15.007 (in suits for personal injury, death, or property damage brought by or against executor, administrator, or guardian, CPRC venue provisions control over Prob. Code); ***Reliant Energy v. Gonzalez***, 102 S.W.3d 868, 873 (Tex.App.—Houston [1st Dist.] 2003, pet. granted 9-11-03) (same). *But see* ***Houston Nw. Partners***, 98 S.W.3d at 779 (transfer provisions of Prob. Code §§5B & 608 are jurisdictional statutes, not venue statutes governed by CPRC §15.007).

§5. JUSTICE COURTS

The justice courts were created by the Texas Constitution. *See* Tex. Const. art. 5, §19. Jury trials are available in justice courts. Gov't Code §28.035.

§5.1 Amount in controversy. Justice courts have jurisdiction over cases in which the amount in controversy is not more than $5,000, excluding interest. Gov't Code §27.031(a)(1). They have exclusive original jurisdiction over civil cases in which the amount in controversy is $200 or less. Tex. Const. art. 5, §19. Their original jurisdiction is concurrent with the district and county courts in civil cases in which the amount in controversy exceeds $200 but does not exceed $5,000. *See* Gov't Code §27.031(a)(1). See chart 2-1, "Overlapping Monetary Jurisdiction of Trial Courts," p. 103.

§5.2 Special cases – FED. Justice courts in the precinct where the real property is located have original, exclusive jurisdiction over forcible entry and detainer (FED) cases. Gov't Code §27.031(a)(2); Prop. Code §24.004;

Aguilar v. Weber, 72 S.W.3d 729, 731 (Tex.App.—Waco 2002, no pet.); ***Goggins v. Leo***, 849 S.W.2d 373, 375 (Tex. App.—Houston [14th Dist.] 1993, no writ). The only issue tried and determined in an FED suit is the right to possession. TRCP 746; ***Aguilar***, 72 S.W.3d at 732; ***Carlson's Hill Country Beverage v. Westinghouse Rd. Jt.V.***, 957 S.W.2d 951, 954 (Tex.App.—Austin 1997, no pet.). A claim for unpaid rent or other damages is not part of the FED case and therefore cannot be heard by the justice court unless the amount is within the jurisdictional limits and the claim is joined in the suit. TRCP 738; ***Haginas v. Malbis Mem'l Found.***, 354 S.W.2d 368, 371 (Tex.1962). An FED suit cannot be used to determine title to real property. ***Aguilar***, 72 S.W.3d at 732; ***Martinez v. Daccarett***, 865 S.W.2d 161, 163 (Tex.App.—Corpus Christi 1993, no writ).

§5.3 Relief available. Justice courts have jurisdiction to (1) foreclose mortgages and enforce liens on personal property when the amount in controversy is within their jurisdictional limits, Gov't Code §27.031(a)(3); (2) issue writs of attachment, garnishment, and sequestration in cases within their jurisdiction, *id.* §27.032; and (3) enforce deed restrictions that do not involve a structural change to a dwelling, *id.* §27.034. When a statute provides that the jurisdiction of the justice court is concurrent with that of a superior court, the justice court has all the authority of the superior court. *See, e.g.*, ***Malmgren v. Inverness Forest Residents Civic Club***, 981 S.W.2d 875, 879 (Tex.App.—Houston [1st Dist.] 1998, no pet.) (because Gov't Code §27.034 states justice court's jurisdiction is concurrent with jurisdiction of district court, justice court can issue injunctions).

§5.4 Cases excluded. Justice courts do not have jurisdiction over the following suits: (1) on behalf of the state to recover penalties, forfeitures, and escheats; (2) for divorce; (3) for slander or defamation; (4) for title to land; or (5) to enforce liens on land. Gov't Code §27.031(b). Unless expressly permitted by the Legislature, justice courts cannot issue writs of mandamus or injunction. *See* ***Bowles v. Angelo***, 188 S.W.2d 691, 693 (Tex.App.—Galveston 1945, no writ).

§6. SMALL CLAIMS COURT

Jury trials are available in small claims courts. Gov't Code §28.035(a). The parties (even corporations) may represent themselves or may choose to be represented by lawyers. *Id.* §28.003(c), (e). Small claims courts use a less formal procedure than the justice courts.

§6.1 Presiding judge. The justice of the peace is the judge of the small claims court. Gov't Code §28.002.

§6.2 Amount in controversy. Small claims courts have concurrent jurisdiction with the justice courts in actions by any person for the recovery of money in which the amount involved does not exceed $5,000, exclusive of costs. Gov't Code §28.003(a). Thus, small claims courts have jurisdiction over claims from $.01 to $5,000. See chart 2-1, "Overlapping Monetary Jurisdiction of Trial Courts," p. 103.

§6.3 Matters excluded. An action cannot be brought by (1) an assignee of the claim or other person seeking to bring an action on an assigned claim, (2) a person primarily engaged in the business of lending money at interest, or (3) a collection agency or collection agent. Gov't Code §28.003(b).

§6.4 Right to appeal. If the amount in controversy exceeds $20, a party may appeal from a small claims court judgment to the constitutional county court or county court at law. Gov't Code §28.052(a). The judgment of the county court acting as an appellate court is final. *Id.* §28.053(d). Several courts of appeals have interpreted the word "final" in Gov't Code §28.053(d) to mean there is no further appeal beyond the constitutional county court or county court at law. ***Woodlands Plumbing Co. v. Rodgers***, 47 S.W.3d 146, 148 (Tex.App.—Texarkana 2001, pet. denied); ***Howell Aviation Servs. v. Aerial Ads***, 29 S.W.3d 321, 323 (Tex.App.—Dallas 2000, no pet.); ***Williamson v. A-1 Elec. Auto Serv.***, 28 S.W.3d 731, 731 (Tex.App.—Corpus Christi 2000, pet. dism'd); ***Lederman v. Rowe***, 3 S.W.3d 254, 256 (Tex.App.—Waco 1999, no pet.); ***Gaskill v. Sneaky Enters.***, 997 S.W.2d 296, 297 (Tex. App.—Fort Worth 1999, pet. denied); ***Davis v. Covert***, 983 S.W.2d 301, 303 (Tex.App.—Houston [1st Dist.] 1998, pet. dism'd). *But see* ***Texas DOT v. Jones***, 983 S.W.2d 90, 91 (Tex.App.—Corpus Christi 1999), *rev'd on other grounds*, 8 S.W.3d 636 (Tex.1999) (Supreme Court reversed case, without discussing jurisdiction, that began in small claims court & was appealed to court of appeals & then to Supreme Court). Note that in the Supreme

Court's opinion in ***Jones***, it incorrectly stated that the case was filed in the justice of the peace court, when in fact it was filed in small claims court. ***Jones***, 8 S.W.3d at 637.

§7. SUMMARY CHART OF JURISDICTION

Chart 2-2, below, shows the various levels of civil courts in Texas and their jurisdiction. This chart is derived from the Office of Court Administration, *Texas Judicial System Annual Report* (2003). For a comprehensive chart showing the jurisdiction of Texas trial courts by county, see "CPRC Courts," www.JonesMcClure.com/Resources.

2-2. CIVIL JURISDICTION OF TEXAS COURTS

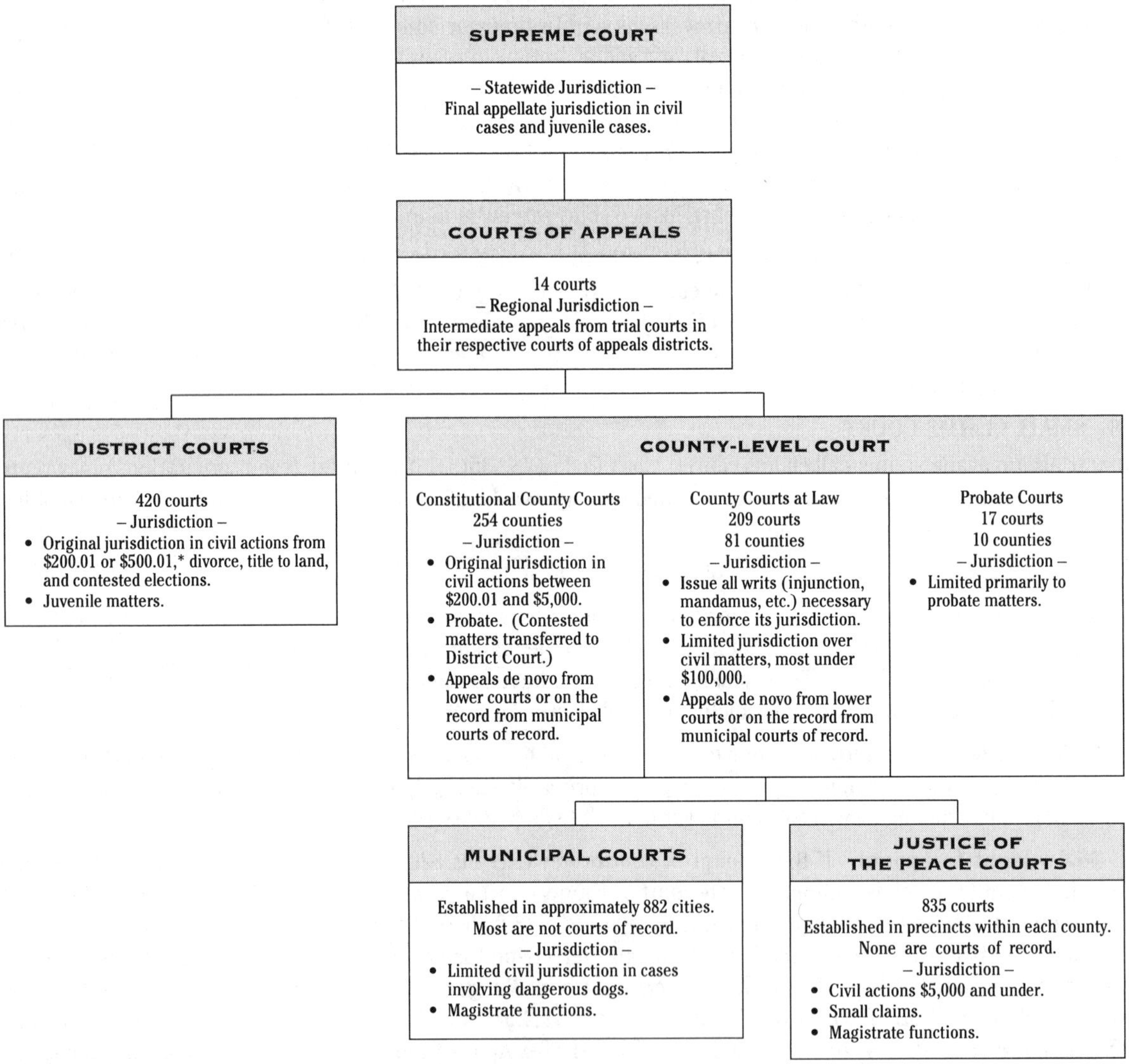

* The dollar amount is currently unclear. See "Amount in controversy," §3.1.1, p. 103.

G. CHOOSING THE COURT—VENUE

In the last 20 years, the Texas Legislature twice reversed the bias in the venue scheme: from one that favored the defendant's choice to one that favored the plaintiff's choice (1983 revisions), then back to one that favored the defendant's choice (1995 revisions). When researching the issue of venue, avoid venue cases based on the 1983 revisions that were in effect until 1995.

§1. GENERAL

§1.1 Rules. TRCP 85-89. See CPRC ch. 15.

§1.2 Purpose. Before filing the suit, the plaintiff must decide in which of the 254 Texas counties the lawsuit should be filed. Venue is different from jurisdiction—it deals with the propriety of prosecuting a suit in a particular county, not the power of a court to determine the dispute and render judgment.

§1.3 Forms. ***O'Connor's Texas Civil Forms***, FORM 2B:23.

§1.4 Other references. For a discussion of the 1995 amendments to the venue provisions in CPRC, see Dwyer, Colleluori & Graves, *Texas Civil Procedure*, 49 SMU L.Rev. 1371, 1375-78 (1996).

NOTE

To challenge the venue of the suit, see "Motion to Transfer—Challenging Venue," ch. 3-C, p. 152.

---

§2. DEFINITIONS

§2.1 Principal office. Principal office means a Texas office of a corporation, unincorporated association, or partnership, in which the decision-makers for the organization within Texas conduct the daily affairs of the organization. CPRC §15.001(a). The mere presence of an organization's agency or representative in a county does not establish a principal office in that county. *Id.*; *see, e.g.*, ***In re Missouri Pac. R.R.***, 998 S.W.2d 212, 221 (Tex.1999) (Ps did not show D's office in Tarrant County was a principal office as compared to responsibility and authority exercised by company officials in Harris County office). A business may have more than one principal office in Texas. *See* CPRC §15.001(a) (code says "a" principal office, not "the" principal office).

§2.2 Residence. A person may have more than one residence for venue purposes. ***GeoChem Tech Corp. v. Verseckes***, 962 S.W.2d 541, 543-44 (Tex.1998). However, venue is fixed at whichever residence the party was occupying at the time the cause of action accrued. *See* CPRC §15.002(a)(2) (residence of defendant at time of accrual), *id.* §15.002(a)(4) (residence of plaintiff at time of accrual), *id.* §15.006 (court shall determine venue on facts existing at time of accrual). Residence is established if the party (1) possessed a fixed place of abode and (2) occupied or intended to occupy it over a substantial period of time in a permanent, rather than temporary, manner. ***Snyder v. Pitts***, 241 S.W.2d 136, 140 (Tex.1951); ***In re S.D.***, 980 S.W.2d 758, 760 (Tex.App.—San Antonio 1998, pet. denied); ***Rosales v. H.E. Butt Grocery Co.***, 905 S.W.2d 745, 749 (Tex.App.—San Antonio 1995, writ denied). The element of permanency is critical to establish venue residence. ***Tieuel v. Southern P.T. Co.***, 654 S.W.2d 771, 774 (Tex.App.—Houston [14th Dist.] 1983, no writ). However, the intent to make the residence a permanent home is not necessary to establish venue residence. ***Snyder***, 241 S.W.2d at 139; *e.g.*, ***Mijares v. Paez***, 534 S.W.2d 435, 436 (Tex. App.—Amarillo 1976, no writ) (Texas Tech student was resident of Lubbock County for venue purposes even though he was in Lubbock County only to complete degree).

§2.3 When cause accrues. Venue is determined by facts as they existed at the time the cause of action accrued. CPRC §15.006. As a rule, a cause of action accrues when a wrongful act causes a legal injury, even if the fact of injury is not discovered until later and all resulting damages have not yet occurred. *See* ***S.V. v. R.V.***, 933 S.W.2d 1, 4 (Tex.1996) (limitations case).

§2.4 Where cause accrues. A cause of action accrues in a county in which all or a substantial part of the events or omissions that gave rise to the claim occurred. CPRC §15.002(a)(1); *see* ***Jackson v. Biotectronics, Inc.***, 937 S.W.2d 38, 43 (Tex.App.—Houston [14th Dist.] 1996, no writ). A substantial part of the act or omission may occur in more than one county. ***Southern Cty. Mut. Ins. Co. v. Ochoa***, 19 S.W.3d 452, 458-59 (Tex.App.—Corpus Christi 2000, no pet.). The phrase "a substantial part" restricts venue choices to fewer counties than other venue provisions. *Compare* CPRC §15.002(a)(1) ("in the county in which all or a substantial part of the events or omissions giving rise to the claim occurred"), *with* CPRC §101.102(a) ("in the county in which the cause of action or a part of the cause of action arises"). In cases predating CPRC §15.002, the Supreme Court interpreted "occurred" to mean where the negligent act—not the results of the occurrence—took place. *E.g.*, ***Leonard v. Abbott***, 366 S.W.2d 925, 927 (Tex.1963) (in suit for damages to crops from aerial spraying, venue was in county where aerial spraying occurred, not in county where crops where damaged); ***Kirtley v. Morriss***, 496 S.W.2d 954, 955 (Tex.App.—Dallas 1973, no writ) (in suit for negligent entrustment, venue was in county where entrustment occurred, not in county where collision occurred).

§3. COUNTY OF PROPER VENUE

The venue scheme describes "proper venue" in hierarchical terms. CPRC §15.001(b). All lawsuits must be brought according to the following venue scheme:

§3.1 Mandatory venue provisions. A suit must be filed in the county of mandatory venue, as required by CPRC chapter 15, subchapter B, or other statutes prescribing mandatory venue. *See generally* CPRC §§15.011-15.020 (mandatory venue provisions). See §4, below.

§3.2 General venue rule. If there is no mandatory venue, the general venue rule applies. See "General Venue Rule," §5, p. 115.

§3.3 Permissive venue provisions. The permissive venue provisions come into play if no mandatory provision applies. CPRC §15.001(b)(2). The permissive venue provisions provide venue alternatives to the general venue rule. See "Permissive Venue Provisions," §6, p. 116.

§4. MANDATORY VENUE PROVISIONS

Mandatory venue is compulsory only if a defendant properly objects to the plaintiff's choice of venue. Most of the mandatory venue provisions are listed in CPRC chapter 15, subchapter B.

§4.1 Mandatory venue in CPRC ch. 15.

1. Suit affecting title to land. A suit involving title to land must be filed in the county where all or part of the land is located. CPRC §15.011; ***Bristol v. Placid Oil Co.***, 74 S.W.3d 156, 158 & n.1 (Tex.App.—Amarillo 2002, no pet.). A suit involving title to land includes the following types of suits: to recover real property, to recover an estate or interest in real property, to partition real property, to remove encumbrances on title to real property, to recover damages to real property, or to quiet title to real property. CPRC §15.011. Two venue facts must be established to invoke the mandatory venue section for land: (1) all or part of the land is located in the county of suit, and (2) the nature of the claim is enumerated in CPRC §15.011. ***In re Stroud Oil Props.***, 110 S.W.3d 18, 24 (Tex. App.—Waco 2002, orig. proceeding); *see* ***Stiba v. Bowers***, 756 S.W.2d 835, 839 (Tex.App.—Corpus Christi 1988, no writ). The dominant purpose of the suit determines which venue section controls. ***Stiba***, 756 S.W.2d at 839. The claim must directly involve a question of title to land. *See, e.g.*, ***Kilgore v. Black Stone Oil Co.***, 15 S.W.3d 666, 670 (Tex.App.—Beaumont 2000, pet. denied) (suit for conversion of oil & gas and title to minerals was suit for recovery of land); ***Midland Nat'l Life Ins. Co. v. Bridges***, 889 S.W.2d 17, 19 (Tex.App.—Eastland 1994, writ denied) (suit involved breach of contract on note for property, not title to land); ***Trafalgar House Oil & Gas v. De Hinojosa***, 773 S.W.2d 797, 798 (Tex.App.—San Antonio 1989, no writ) (suit to recover liquidated damages for breach of notice requirements of lease was not suit for recovery of land); ***Stiba***, 756 S.W.2d at 839-40 (suit for construction of a will, even though it disposed of land, did not involve title to land); *see also* ***Caldwell Nat'l Bank v. O'Neil***, 785 S.W.2d

840, 843 (Tex.App.—El Paso 1990, writ denied) (venue was proper in county where land was located because purpose of suit was to quiet title).

2. Landlord-tenant suit. A suit between a landlord and tenant arising under a lease must be brought in the county where all or part of the real property is located. CPRC §15.0115(a). If another provision prescribes mandatory venue, that provision controls over the landlord-tenant provision in CPRC §15.0115(a). The term "lease" includes any written or oral agreement between the landlord and tenant that establishes or modifies the terms, conditions, or other provisions relating to the use and occupancy of the real property. *Id.* §15.0115(b).

3. Injunction against suit. An action to stay a proceeding in a suit must be filed in the county where the suit is pending. CPRC §15.012; ***O'Quinn v. Hall***, 77 S.W.3d 452, 455 (Tex.App.—Corpus Christi 2002, orig. proceeding); *see also* CPRC §65.023(b) (writ of injunction to stay proceedings must be tried in the court where suit is pending or judgment was rendered).

4. Injunction against execution of judgment. An action to restrain the execution of a judgment or a writ, based on the invalidity of that judgment or writ, must be filed in the county where the judgment was rendered. CPRC §15.013; *see also* CPRC §65.023(b) (execution on judgment must be tried in the court in which suit is pending or judgment was rendered).

5. Mandamus against State. A mandamus against the head of a department of the State of Texas must be filed in Travis County. CPRC §15.014.

6. Action against county. A suit against a county must be filed in that county. CPRC §15.015; ***Wichita Cty. v. Hart***, 917 S.W.2d 779, 781 (Tex.1996); *see also* CPRC §101.102(a) (venue under Tort Claims Act). A suit against a county official only in that person's individual capacity is not a suit against the county for purposes of CPRC §15.015. *See* ***McIntosh v. Copeland***, 894 S.W.2d 60, 63-64 (Tex.App.—Austin 1995, writ denied).

7. Suit against political subdivisions. A suit filed against a political subdivision that is located in a county with a population of 100,000 or less must be brought in the county where the political subdivision is located. CPRC §15.0151(a).

8. Suit involving defamation or invasion of privacy. A suit for libel, slander, or invasion of privacy must be filed in one of the following counties: (1) the county where the plaintiff resided at the time the action accrued, (2) the county where the defendant resided when the suit was filed, (3) the county where any of the defendants reside, or (4) the domicile of any corporate defendant. CPRC §15.017; ***Rodriguez v. Printone Color Corp.***, 982 S.W.2d 69, 71 (Tex.App.—Houston [1st Dist.] 1998, pet. denied); ***Acker v. Denton Publ'g Co.***, 937 S.W.2d 111, 114 (Tex.App.—Fort Worth 1996, no writ); *see* ***Marshall v. Mahaffey***, 974 S.W.2d 942, 950 (Tex.App.—Beaumont 1998, pet. denied). See ***O'Connor's Texas Causes of Action***, "Venue," ch. 16-A, §6.2, p. 366 (2004).

9. FELA & Jones Act suits. A suit brought under the Federal Employers' Liability Act (45 U.S.C. §51) or the Jones Act (46 U.S.C. §688) must be brought in one of the following counties: (1) the county where all or a substantial part of the events or omissions giving rise to the claim occurred, (2) the county where the defendant's principal office in Texas is located, or (3) the county where the plaintiff resided at the time the cause of action accrued. CPRC §15.018; ***In re Missouri Pac. R.R.***, 998 S.W.2d 212, 214 (Tex.1999).

10. Inmate litigation. A suit brought by an inmate for an action that accrued while the inmate was in a Texas prison operated by the Texas Department of Criminal Justice must be filed in the county where the facility is located. CPRC §15.019(a).

11. Contractual agreement for venue. Under CPRC §15.020, parties may agree to venue in writing in a "major transaction." That is, the suit must be filed in a certain county determined according to a written agreement signed before suit. *See* CPRC §15.020(a)-(c). A major transaction is one in which the consideration has an aggregate value of at least $1 million. *Id.* §15.020(a). By definition, it does not include a transaction for personal, family, or household purposes or for settlement of a personal injury or wrongful death suit. *Id.* Except for major transactions, the parties cannot contractually agree before suit to a venue contrary to a mandatory venue provision or a specific venue statute. *See, e.g.*, ***Leonard v. Paxson***, 654 S.W.2d 440, 441-42 (Tex.1983) (settlement agreement could not contravene venue in Family Code); ***Fidelity Un. Life Ins. Co. v. Evans***, 477 S.W.2d 535, 537 (Tex.1972) (contract agreement on venue could not override venue provision in injunction statute).

§4.2 Other CPRC provisions governing mandatory venue.

1. TTCA suit. The Texas Tort Claims Act (TTCA) provides that a suit under the TTCA "shall" be brought in the county where "the cause of action or a part of the cause of action arises." CPRC §101.102(a); *e.g.*, ***Wilson v. Texas Parks & Wildlife Dept.***, 886 S.W.2d 259, 262 (Tex.1994) (suit should not have been transferred from county where negligence was alleged to have occurred to county of accident).

2. Injunction against party. CPRC §65.023(a) provides that, except as mandated by subsection (b), injunction suits against a resident must be tried in a district or county court in the county where the party is domiciled. CPRC §65.023(a); ***In re Continental Airlines***, 988 S.W.2d 733, 736 (Tex.1998). See "Injunction against suit" and "Injunction against execution of judgment," §§4.1.3, 4.1.4, above.

§4.3 Other mandatory venue statutes. An action governed by any other statute prescribing mandatory venue must be brought in the county required by that statute. CPRC §15.016. The following are some mandatory venue provisions in other codes.

04 **1. Attorney disciplinary action.** In a suit against a lawyer for disciplinary action, venue is in the district court (1) in the county of the attorney's principal place of practice, (2) in the county of the attorney's residence, or (3) in the county where the misconduct occurred in whole or in part. Tex. R. Disc. P. 3.03; *see* ***State Bar v. McGee***, 972 S.W.2d 770, 774 (Tex.App.—Corpus Christi 1998, no pet.) (proper venue was county where attorney had principal place of practice). In all other instances, venue is in Travis County. Tex. R. Disc. P. 3.03.

2. Condemnation suit. In a condemnation proceeding, if the owner resides in a county in which part of the property is located, venue is in the county in which the owner resides. Prop. Code §21.013(a). Otherwise, venue is in any county in which at least part of the property is located. *Id.*

03 **3. Probate matters.** Probate Code §§6, 8, and 610 establish venue for the probate of wills, administration of estates, and appointments of guardians. Prob. Code §§6, 8, 610; *see also* Prob. Code. §48(a) (proceeding to declare heirship), *id.* §88(a)(2) (letters testamentary), *id.* §137(a)(4) (small estates), *id.* §433(a) (recovery of funds paid to state), *id.* §684(b)(1) (appointment of guardian). However, in suits brought by or against a personal representative for personal injury, death, or property damage, proper venue is determined under CPRC §15.007. Prob. Code §§5B(b), 607(e); *see* CPRC §15.007. See "Transfer of proceedings to statutory probate courts," ch. 2-F, §4.4.3(3), p. 108. Venue for probate largely depends on where the applicant resides, where the decedent was domiciled, or where the majority of the estate is located. In general, the court with venue over probate matters has venue over all similar matters if two or more courts have jurisdiction. Venue for guardianship of a minor largely depends on where the parents reside. Prob. Code §610.

4. Trust matters. For suits involving a trust, venue is in any county where, during the four-year period before the suit was filed, the trustee resided or the trust was administered. Prop. Code §115.002(b), (c). An action against a corporate trustee may also be brought in the county of the trustee's principal office. *Id.* §115.002(c). Venue may be transferred to another county for the convenience of the parties and witnesses, or if all parties agree. *Id.* §115.002(d), (e).

5. Family law proceedings. The Family Code has its own rules and procedures governing mandatory venue. For example, in an original suit affecting the parent-child relationship (SAPCR), venue is in the county where the child resides, unless an exception applies. Fam. Code §103.001.

6. Suit on insurance contract. Suits on an insurance policy are governed by mandatory venue provisions in the Insurance Code and permissive venue provisions in the CPRC.

(1) Mandatory venue. In a suit against an insurance company regarding coverage, Insurance Code article 5.06-1(8) provides two mandatory venues: (1) in the county where the policyholder or beneficiary who instituted the suit resided at the time of the accident or (2) in the county where the accident involving the uninsured or underinsured motorist's vehicle occurred. Ins. Code art. 5.06-1(8).

(2) Permissive venue. See §6.1.4, below.

§4.4 Miscellaneous rules governing mandatory venue.

1. Two counties of mandatory venue. When there are two counties of mandatory venue, the plaintiff's choice between the two is controlling. ***Marshall v. Mahaffey***, 974 S.W.2d 942, 947 (Tex.App.—Beaumont 1998, pet. denied); *see* ***Wilson***, 886 S.W.2d at 261 (reversible error to transfer venue from a county of proper venue to another county of proper venue).

2. Permissive & mandatory counties. When there is a county of mandatory venue and a county of permissive venue, the suit should be brought in, and on motion must be transferred to, the county of mandatory venue. *See* CPRC §15.004; TRCP 86(3)(b); *see, e.g.*, ***Wichita Cty. v. Hart***, 917 S.W.2d 779, 781 (Tex.1996) (suit against county was governed by mandatory provision, not by permissive venue provision in Whistleblower suit).

3. Multiple claims. If any claim in a suit is controlled by a mandatory venue provision, all properly joined claims arising from the same transaction, occurrence, or series of transactions or occurrences are controlled by the same provision. CPRC §15.004; ***Madera Prod. Co. v. Atlantic Richfield Co.***, 107 S.W.3d 652, 658 (Tex.App.—Texarkana 2003, no pet.). See "Multiple Parties & Claims," §7, p. 117.

§5. GENERAL VENUE RULE

§5.1 Selecting venue if no mandatory venue. If no mandatory venue provision applies, the plaintiff must decide where to file the suit according to the general venue rule. Under the general venue rule, a suit must be brought in one of the following counties:

1. In the county where all or a substantial part of the events giving rise to the claim occurred. CPRC §15.002(a)(1).

2. In the county of the defendant's residence at the time the cause of action accrued, if the defendant is a natural person. *Id.* §15.002(a)(2).

3. In the county of the defendant's principal office in Texas, if the defendant is not a natural person (*i.e.*, if defendant is a corporation). *Id.* §15.002(a)(3). There is no distinction between domestic and foreign corporations; both are governed by the same venue provisions. *See id.* §§15.001(a), 15.002.

4. If none of the other provisions applies, in the county where the plaintiff resided at the time the action accrued. *Id.* §15.002(a)(4). The purpose of CPRC §15.002(a)(4) is to provide venue for a plaintiff's suit against a nonresident defendant when the cause of action arose outside of Texas.

§5.2 Other considerations. The present venue system does not favor the plaintiff's choice of venue. Thus, in choosing the county for suit, the plaintiff should consider the counties to which the trial court may transfer the case "for convenience" and "in the interest of justice." CPRC §15.002(b). When the defendant makes a timely motion to transfer venue based on CPRC §15.002(b), the court may transfer a suit from a county of proper venue to any other county of proper venue if the court finds all of the following:

1. Maintenance in the county of suit will work an economic and personal hardship on the defendant. CPRC §15.002(b)(1).

2. The balance of interests of all the parties predominates in favor of the action being brought in the other county. *Id.* §15.002(b)(2).

3. The transfer will not work an injustice on any other party. *Id.* §15.002(b)(3).

NOTE

The court's decision on a convenience transfer is not appealable and is not reversible error. CPRC §15.002(c). See "Review," ch. 3-C, §5, p. 163.

§6. PERMISSIVE VENUE PROVISIONS

The permissive venue provisions provide venue alternatives to the general venue rule. Most of the permissive venue provisions are listed in CPRC chapter 15, subchapter C.

§6.1 Permissive venue in CPRC ch. 15.

1. Suit against executor, administrator, or guardian. CPRC §15.031 is a permissive venue provision that governs suits against an executor, administrator, or guardian. The provisions in CPRC §15.031 control over any conflicting venue provisions in the Probate Code in a suit against an executor, administrator, or guardian for personal injury, death, or property damage. CPRC §15.007.

(1) Negligent act. In a suit against an executor, administrator, or guardian for a negligent act or omission of the person whose estate is being represented, venue is permissive in the county where the negligent act or omission occurred. CPRC §15.031.

(2) Debt of an estate. In a suit for a debt of an estate, venue is permissive in the county where the estate is being administered. CPRC §15.031.

2. Breach of warranty. In a suit against a manufacturer of consumer goods for breach of warranty, venue is permissive in any of the following counties: (1) the county where all or a substantial part of the events or omissions giving rise to the claim occurred, (2) the county where the manufacturer has its principal office in Texas, or (3) the county where the plaintiff resided at the time the cause of action accrued. CPRC §15.033.

3. Written contract.

(1) County of performance. In a suit on a written contract that states the contract is to be performed in a certain county or a definite place in that county, venue is permissive either in the specified county or in the county of the defendant's domicile. CPRC §15.035(a); *see also* ***Midland Nat'l Life Ins. Co. v. Bridges***, 889 S.W.2d 17, 19 (Tex.App.—Eastland 1994, writ denied) (promissory note); ***Trafalgar House Oil & Gas v. De Hinojosa***, 773 S.W.2d 797, 798 (Tex.App.—San Antonio 1989, no writ) (oil lease). See §6.1.3(2), below, for an exception to CPRC §15.035(a).

(2) Contract in consumer transaction. In a suit by a creditor involving a consumer transaction, venue is permissive in the county where the defendant signed the contract or where the defendant resided when the suit was filed. CPRC §15.035(b). Subsection (b) of CPRC §15.035 controls over subsection (a) and cannot be waived. *See id.* §15.035(b). Thus, if a consumer contract identifies the creditor's home county as the place of payment, the creditor cannot sue there unless it is also the county where the defendant signed the contract or the county of the defendant's residence.

NOTE

Under the DTPA, it is a false, misleading, or deceptive act to file suit based on a consumer transaction involving a written contract signed by the defendant-consumer in any county other than the county (1) where the defendant-consumer resides at the time the suit is brought or (2) where the defendant-consumer signed the contract. Bus. & Com. Code §17.46(b)(23).

4. Suit on insurance contract. CPRC §15.032 provides two permissive venues for suits on insurance policies: (1) in a suit against a fire, marine, or inland insurance company, venue is permissive in the county where the insured property is located; or (2) in a suit against any life, accident, or health insurance company, venue is permissive in the county where the insurance company's principal office is located, in the county where the loss occurred, or in the county where the policyholder or beneficiary resided at the time the cause of action accrued. CPRC §15.032. Suits against an insurance company regarding coverage are governed by mandatory venue provisions in the Insurance Code. See "Mandatory venue," §4.3.6(1), p. 114.

§6.2 Other permissive venue statutes. An action governed by any other statute prescribing permissive venue may be brought in the county allowed by that statute. CPRC §15.038. The following are some permissive venue provisions in other codes.

1. Suit under DTPA. A suit under the DTPA may be filed only in a county (1) where venue is proper under CPRC chapter 15 (except in a suit against an insurer relating to uninsured motorist coverage) or (2) where the defendant or its authorized agent solicited the transaction that forms the basis of the suit. Bus. & Com. Code §17.56.

2. Whistleblower suit. A whistleblower suit brought by a state employee may be filed in the county in which the cause of action arose or in Travis County. Gov't Code §554.007(a). The venue provision in a whistleblower suit is permissive. ***City of Ft. Worth v. Zimlich***, 29 S.W.3d 62, 72 (Tex.2000); ***Wichita Cty. v. Hart***, 917 S.W.2d 779, 782 (Tex.1996). For whistleblower suits filed by local government employees, see Gov't Code §554.007(b).

§7. MULTIPLE PARTIES & CLAIMS

§7.1 Multiple plaintiffs. In a suit with multiple plaintiffs, a plaintiff or intervenor may remain in the suit only if it is able to establish one of the following: 03

1. Proper venue. Venue in the county of suit is proper as to that plaintiff independently of every other plaintiff. CPRC §15.003(a); ***Surgitek v. Abel***, 997 S.W.2d 598, 602 (Tex.1999); ***O'Quinn v. Hall***, 77 S.W.3d 438, 448 (Tex.App.—Corpus Christi 2002, no pet.).

2. Proper joinder. Though the plaintiff cannot establish that venue is proper, it meets the requirements of CPRC §15.003(a)(1)-(4). CPRC §15.003(a); ***Surgitek***, 997 S.W.2d at 602; ***O'Quinn***, 77 S.W.3d at 448. See "Joinder proper under §15.003(a)," ch. 3-C, §2.6.4(2), p. 155.

§7.2 Multiple claims. If a plaintiff properly joins two or more claims arising from the same transaction, occurrence, or series of transactions or occurrences, and one of the claims is governed by a mandatory venue provision in CPRC chapter 15, subchapter B, the mandatory venue provision controls venue for the suit. CPRC §15.004; ***In re Stroud Oil Props.***, 110 S.W.3d 18, 23 (Tex.App.—Waco 2002, orig. proceeding). CPRC chapter 15 venue provisions control over conflicting venue provisions in the Probate Code. See "Probate matters," §4.3.3, p. 114; §6.1.1, above.

§7.3 Multiple defendants.

1. Venue against all. In a suit against multiple defendants, if the plaintiff establishes proper venue against one defendant, the court also has venue of all defendants in all claims arising out of the same transaction, occurrence, or series of transactions or occurrences. CPRC §15.005; ***American Home Prods. Corp. v. Clark***, 38 S.W.3d 92, 94 (Tex.2000).

2. No waiver. A wavier of venue by one defendant does not prevent another defendant from appropriately challenging venue. CPRC §15.0641; ***WTFO, Inc. v. Braithwaite***, 899 S.W.2d 709, 718 (Tex.App.—Dallas 1995, no writ); *see, e.g.*, ***Pearson v. Jones Co.***, 898 S.W.2d 329, 331-32 (Tex.App.—Eastland 1994, no writ) (waiver of venue by two Ds by filing answers does not waive third D's venue objection).

§7.4 Counter, cross-, or third-party claims. Venue for the main action establishes venue for a defendant's counterclaim or cross-claim or for a third-party claim if the claim is properly joined under the TRCPs or any applicable statute. CPRC §15.062(a). When the original defendant joins a third-party defendant, venue for the main action establishes venue for any claim by the plaintiff against that third-party defendant arising out of the same transaction, occurrence, or series of transactions or occurrences. *Id.* §15.062(b).

H. SERVING THE DEFENDANT WITH SUIT

§1. GENERAL

§1.1 Rules. TRCP 15-17, 99, 103, 105-108, 108a, 109a, 118-119, 119a, 120, 120a, 121-124, 237. See CPRC ch. 17; Business Corp. Act arts. 2.11, 8.10.

§1.2 Purpose. Service of citation is a term that describes the formal process by which a plaintiff gives a defendant notice that it has been sued. ***Texas Nat. Res. Conserv. Comm'n v. Sierra Club***, 70 S.W.3d 809, 813 (Tex.2002). The purpose of the citation is to give the court jurisdiction over the defendant, to satisfy due process requirements, and to give the defendant the opportunity to appear and defend. ***Cockrell v. Estevez***, 737 S.W.2d 138, 140 (Tex.App.—San Antonio 1987, no writ). A judgment cannot be rendered against a defendant unless the defendant was served with process, accepted or waived service, or entered an appearance. TRCP 124; ***Werner v. Colwell***, 909 S.W.2d 866, 869-70 (Tex.1995); ***Mapco, Inc. v. Carter***, 817 S.W.2d 686, 687 (Tex.1991). The citation and a copy of the plaintiff's petition, which is attached, are collectively referred to as the "process." Service of process is accomplished when the citation and a copy of the petition are delivered to the defendant, or the defendant is given notice of the suit through some other authorized means.

The rules concerning the issuance of citation, service of process, and the return of process are especially important when the court renders a default judgment. Because the ordinary presumptions of valid service do not apply in an appeal of a no-answer default judgment, the judgment will be reversed unless there is strict compliance with the rules. ***Primate Constr. v. Silver***, 884 S.W.2d 151, 152 (Tex.1994). See "Sufficiency of the service," ch. 7-A, §3.4, p. 445.

§1.3 Forms & timetables. ***O'Connor's Texas Civil Forms***, FORMS 2H; Timetables, this book, Pretrial Motions, p. 998, Default Judgment, p. 1007.

§1.4 Other references. Miller, *Misnomer: Default Judgments & Strict Compliance with Service of Process Rules*, 46 Baylor L.Rev. 633 (1994); Anderson, *Transnational Litigation Involving Mexican Parties*, 25 St. Mary's L.J. 1059 (1994).

§2. REQUIREMENTS FOR THE CITATION

The citation must comply with TRCP 15 and 99. The citation is issued by the clerk of the court upon payment of a fee.

§2.1 Style of process. The style of the process must be "The State of Texas." TRCP 15, 99(b)(1). The process must be directed to any sheriff or any constable within the State of Texas. TRCP 15.

§2.2 Information about suit. The citation must identify the suit by showing the cause number. TRCP 99(b)(6) (called "file" number). If the citation omits the cause number or contains the wrong number, the citation is fatally defective. ***Martinez v. Wilber***, 810 S.W.2d 461, 463 (Tex.App.—San Antonio 1991, writ denied). Service of process with one cause number will not support a suit with a different cause number. *See, e.g.*, ***Finlay v. Jones***, 435 S.W.2d 136, 137 (Tex.1968) (D was served under cause number 144,608 instead of 144,607).

§2.3 Information about court. The citation must contain the following information about the court:

1. Identification of court. The citation must contain the name and location of the court and the address of the clerk who issued the citation. TRCP 99(b)(3), (11).

2. Signature & seal. The citation must be signed by the clerk and issued under the seal of the court. TRCP 15, 99(b)(2); ***Verlander Enters. v. Graham***, 932 S.W.2d 259, 262 (Tex.App.—El Paso 1996, no writ).

§2.4 Information about P. The citation must contain the following information about the plaintiff:

1. Identification of P. The citation must contain the name of the plaintiff. TRCP 99(b)(7). If pro se, the citation must contain the plaintiff's address. TRCP 99(b)(9).

2. P's lawyer. The citation must contain the name and address of the plaintiff's lawyer. TRCP 99(b)(9).

§2.5 Information about D.

1. Identification of D.

(1) Name. The citation must contain the defendant's correct name. TRCP 99(b)(7); *see* ***Amato v. Hernandez***, 981 S.W.2d 947, 949 (Tex.App.—Houston [1st Dist.] 1998, pet. denied). If the correct defendant was incorrectly named in the petition, the error is a misnomer, and a default judgment against that defendant will be affirmed if (1) the correct defendant was actually served, and (2) the petition describes the facts in such a way that the correct defendant knows it is the intended defendant. ***Union Pac. Corp. v. Legg***, 49 S.W.3d 72, 78 (Tex.App.—Austin 2001, no pet.). If the wrong defendant was named in the petition, the error is a misidentification, and a default judgment must be reversed. *See, e.g.*, ***Union Pac.***, 49 S.W.3d at 78 (P named & served Union Pacific Railroad, not Union Pacific Corp.). See "Misnomer vs. misidentification," ch. 2-B, §3.3.1(2), p. 69.

(2) Capacity. When the defendant is sued in a representative capacity, the defendant must be identified in the petition by that capacity (*e.g.*, trustee, executor). *See, e.g.*, ***Werner***, 909 S.W.2d at 870 (judgment could not be rendered against D as a trustee when she was sued only as an individual). See "Capacity," ch. 2-B, §3.2.2, p. 68.

(3) Address for service. The citation must include the defendant's address for service of process. When the defendant is a nonresident, the petition should use the exact language from the long-arm statute, TRCP 108, or other applicable statute to describe the place for service. The long-arm statute requires that the documents to be served on the Secretary of State (the petition and citation) must include a statement of the nonresident's name and home or home office address where the process is to be served. CPRC §17.045(a).

2. Citation directed to D. The citation must "be directed to the defendant." TRCP 99(b)(8); *see, e.g.*, ***Plains Chevrolet v. Thorne***, 656 S.W.2d 631, 633 (Tex.App.—Waco 1983, no writ) (service void because citation directed to G.M. Corporation, not Plains Chevrolet). TRCP 15, however, requires the process "to be directed to any sheriff or any constable within the State of Texas." The inclusion of directions to the sheriff or constable to serve the defendant does not invalidate the citation under TRCP 99(b)(8). *See* ***Barker CATV Constr. v. Ampro, Inc.***, 989 S.W.2d 789, 792-93 (Tex.App.—Houston [1st Dist.] 1999, no pet.) (overruling other 1st court cases that held citation defective because it was directed to sheriff as well as D).

§2.6 Identification of D's agent for service. If the defendant must be served through an agent, the citation must name the agent for service and state the address for service on the agent. Even though an agent is to be served for the defendant, the citation must be directed to the defendant and not to the agent. *See* ***Barker CATV***, 989 S.W.2d at 792. If the citation is directed to the agent, it does not confer jurisdiction over the defendant. ***Dan Edge Motors v. Scott***, 657 S.W.2d 822, 823 (Tex.App.—Texarkana 1983, no writ); *see, e.g.*, ***Verlander Enters.***, 932 S.W.2d at 261 (citation was directed to a vice-president instead of the corporation). When the citation names one person as agent for service, but the return of the citation shows it was served on another person, the trial court does not acquire jurisdiction over the defendant. ***Pharmakinetics Labs. v. Katz***, 717 S.W.2d 704, 706 (Tex.App.—San Antonio 1986, no writ).

1. Corporation. When the defendant is a corporation, the citation should be directed to the corporation and name as agent for service the president, any vice-president, or the registered agent. ***Dan Edge Motors***, 657 S.W.2d at 823.

2. **Partnership.** When the defendant is a partnership, the citation must be directed to the defendant-partnership and name the individual partners for service. CPRC §17.022; ***ISO Prod. Mgmt. 1982 v. M&L Oil & Gas Expl.***, 768 S.W.2d 354, 356 (Tex.App.—Waco 1989, no writ).

§2.7 Critical dates. The citation must contain the following dates:

1. **Date petition filed.** The citation must state the date the plaintiff filed the petition. TRCP 99(b)(4). If the filing date of the plaintiff's petition is omitted, the defect is fatal. ***Hance v. Cogswell***, 307 S.W.2d 277, 278-79 (Tex.App.—Austin 1957, no writ). If the citation states an impossible date for filing, the defect is fatal. *E.g.*, ***McGraw-Hill, Inc. v. Futrell***, 823 S.W.2d 414, 417 (Tex.App.—Houston [1st Dist.] 1992, writ denied) (date of service was 17 days before suit filed); ***George v. Elledge***, 261 S.W.2d 201, 201 (Tex.App.—San Antonio 1953, no writ) (date of service was 7 months before suit filed).

2. **Date citation issued.** The citation must state the date it was issued. TRCP 15, 99(b)(5); ***London v. Chandler***, 406 S.W.2d 203, 204 (Tex.1966). The date the citation is issued may be different from the date the clerk signs and seals the citation. ***London***, 406 S.W.2d at 204. The citation is issued when it is sent forth from the clerk's office under the clerk's authority and given to an officer or other authorized person for service. *Id.* If the date the citation was issued is omitted, the citation can be amended. TRCP 118; ***London***, 406 S.W.2d at 204.

3. **Time to answer.** The citation for district and county courts must state the defendant is required to file a written answer on or before 10:00 a.m. on the Monday next after the expiration of 20 days from the date of service. TRCP 15, 99(b), (c). This requirement must be stated in the exact language of TRCP 99(c). If the 20th day falls on a Monday, the answer must be filed by the next Monday. The citation for justice courts must make the same statement as the citation for district and county courts, but it has a shorter deadline—10 days. TRCP 534(b).

§2.8 Warning of default. The citation must notify the defendant that if it does not file an answer, judgment by default may be rendered for the relief demanded in the petition. TRCP 99(b)(12). This requirement must be stated in the exact language of TRCP 99(c).

§2.9 Attachment of petition. The plaintiff's original petition must be attached to the citation. *See* TRCP 99(a), 106. If the plaintiff amends the petition before service by adding parties, claims, or damages, the amended petition must be attached to the citation. *See, e.g.*, ***Primate Constr. v. Silver***, 884 S.W.2d 151, 152-53 (Tex.1994) (default judgment reversed because D served with original petition, which did not name it as D, instead of amended petition); ***Seeley v. KCI USA, Inc.***, 100 S.W.3d 276, 277-78 (Tex.App.—San Antonio 2001, no pet.) (same). See "What was served," §9.2.2, p. 127; "Amending the petition," §10.1, p. 130.

§3. WHO MAY SERVE PROCESS

The plaintiff should make sure that service is accomplished by a person who is authorized by rule, statute, or court order to serve process. Service of process by a person who is not authorized to accomplish service is invalid and will not support a default judgment.

§3.1 Clerk of court. The clerk of the court is authorized to serve process by registered or certified mail and to serve citation by publication. TRCP 103.

§3.2 Authorized officer. A sheriff, constable, or other person authorized by law may serve process in Texas. Local Gov't Code §85.021(a) (sheriff), §86.021(c) (constable); TRCP 103. Nothing in Local Gov't Code §85.021 limits sheriffs to serving process in their own counties. Under Local Gov't Code §86.021(c) and (d), however, constables are limited to serving process only in their own and contiguous counties.

§3.3 Private process server. A person who has no interest in the lawsuit, is at least 18 years old, and is authorized by a written court order may serve process. TRCP 103; *see* ***Mayfield v. Dean Witter Fin. Servs.***, 894 S.W.2d 502, 505 (Tex.App.—Austin 1995, writ denied); *cf.* Ins. Code art. 1.36, §3(a) (service on insurance company). A plaintiff or member of its lawyer's staff cannot serve process. The process must include a copy of the court order that authorized the disinterested person to serve process; without it, the disinterested person cannot effectuate service. *See, e.g.*, ***HB & WM, Inc. v. Smith***, 802 S.W.2d 279, 281 (Tex.App.—San Antonio 1990, no writ) (no order authorizing commercial process server). The Secretary of State's office will not accept service of process from a private process server unless the process includes a copy of the order appointing the server.

§3.4 Not interested person. No person who is a party or who is interested in the outcome of the suit may serve process. TRCP 103.

§4. METHODS OF SERVICE

Service of process is accomplished by providing the person or entity to be served with a copy of both the citation and the petition. *See* TRCP 99(a). If a defendant cannot be served by one of the methods below, and it does not waive service, it may not be subject to service of process regardless of it having minimum contacts with the forum. If the citation restricts service to a particular method, service must be made according to the citation's terms. *See, e.g.*, ***Smith v. Commercial Equip. Leasing Co.***, 678 S.W.2d 917, 917-18 (Tex.1984) (service invalid because citation was restricted to personal service & process was served by certified mail). Process may be served on the defendant according to any of the following methods.

NOTE

A citation cannot be served on Sunday, except in cases of injunction, attachment, garnishment, sequestration, or distress proceedings. TRCP 6; ***Nichols v. Nichols,*** *857 S.W.2d 657, 659 (Tex.App.—Houston [1st Dist.] 1993, no writ).*

§4.1 Service by U.S. Mail. Service by certified mail, return receipt requested is the most popular method of serving most defendants. It is much less expensive and time-consuming than any other method of service. Service by certified mail may be made by (1) the clerk of the court, (2) the sheriff or constable or any other person authorized by law, or (3) any person 18 years of age or older, authorized by law or by order of court. TRCP 103, 106(a)(2); ***P&H Transp. v. Robinson***, 930 S.W.2d 857, 859 (Tex.App.—Houston [1st Dist.] 1996, writ denied) (authorized private process server can serve by mail); *cf.* Gov't Code §28.013(c) (service in small claims courts). Under CPRC §17.026(a), the clerk of the court, or a party or its representative, may serve process on the Secretary of State by certified mail, return receipt requested.

§4.2 Service by personal delivery. Any person who has the authority to serve process (by law or court order) may serve the defendant by delivering the process to the defendant personally. TRCP 106(a)(1); *see* ***Woodall v. Lansford***, 254 S.W.2d 540, 541 (Tex.App.—Fort Worth 1953, no writ). When the authorized person hands the citation to the defendant, the defendant must understand that it is a lawsuit and that the defendant is being served. *See* ***Texas Indus. v. Sanchez***, 521 S.W.2d 133, 135-36 (Tex.App.—Dallas 1975), *writ ref'd n.r.e.*, 525 S.W.2d 870 (Tex. 1975).

§4.3 Service by court order. If personal service or service by mail was attempted but was unsuccessful, the court may authorize another method of service. TRCP 106(b); ***State Farm Fire & Cas. Co. v. Costley***, 868 S.W.2d 298, 299 (Tex.1993); ***Rivers v. Viskozki***, 967 S.W.2d 868, 870 (Tex.App.—Eastland 1998, no pet.). When a court orders substituted service under TRCP 106, the only authority for the service is the order itself. ***Dolly v. Aethos Comm. Sys.***, 10 S.W.3d 384, 388 (Tex.App.—Dallas 2000, no pet.). Due process is the minimum requirement for alternative service.

1. Motion & affidavit. The plaintiff must file a motion for substituted service supported by an affidavit describing the unsuccessful attempts at service under TRCP 106(a)(1) or (a)(2), and stating a place where the defendant can probably be found (*e.g.*, usual place of residence or business). TRCP 106(b); ***Costley***, 868 S.W.2d at 299; *e.g.*, ***Lewis v. Ramirez***, 49 S.W.3d 561, 565 (Tex.App.—Corpus Christi 2001, no pet.) (affidavit lacked the necessary specificity because it only said service on D attempted "on several occasions"). If the plaintiff does not file an affidavit verifying the unsuccessful efforts to serve the defendant, the trial court cannot order substitute service. ***Wilson v. Dunn***, 800 S.W.2d 833, 836 (Tex.1990). A party need show only that attempts failed under either TRCP 106(a)(1) or (a)(2). ***Costley***, 868 S.W.2d at 299 n.2.

2. Types of service. Under TRCP 106(b), the following types of service are permissible:

(1) Delivery of process to any authorized person over 16 years of age at the location of the defendant's usual place of residence or business, or any other place where the defendant may be found, as stated in the affidavit. TRCP 106(b)(1); ***Walker v. Brodhead***, 828 S.W.2d 278, 280 (Tex.App.—Austin 1992, writ denied); *see* ***Olympia Marble & Granite v. Mayes***, 17 S.W.3d 437, 444-45 (Tex.App.—Houston [1st Dist.] 2000, no pet.).

(2) Service of process in any other manner that the affidavit or other evidence shows will be reasonably effective to give the defendant notice of the suit. TRCP 106(b)(2); ***Costley***, 868 S.W.2d at 299 (first-class mail service); *see, e.g.*, ***Dolly***, 10 S.W.3d at 388-89 (posting copy on D's front door).

§4.4 Service by publication. Citation by publication is authorized for use in actions against a defendant whose residence is unknown (TRCP 109), against unknown heirs or stockholders of defunct corporations (TRCP 111), against unknown owners or claimants of an interest in land (TRCP 112), or for delinquent ad valorem taxes (TRCP 117a). Citation by publication also may be authorized by order of the court under TRCP 106(b)(2). The form of citation and technicalities of service are set out in TRCP 114-117. *See, e.g.*, ***Wiebusch v. Wiebusch***, 636 S.W.2d 540, 542 (Tex.App.—San Antonio 1982, no writ) (notice of nature of suit is necessary for service by publication); *see also* ***Wood v. Brown***, 819 S.W.2d 799, 800 (Tex.1991) (attorney's affidavit did not satisfy TRCP 109). Service by publication is not favored because it is unlikely to provide the defendant with notice of suit. ***Mullane v. Central Hanover Bank & Trust Co.***, 339 U.S. 306, 315, 70 S.Ct. 652, 658 (1950). A defendant served by publication who does not answer or appear must be represented by an attorney appointed by the court. TRCP 244. A defendant served by publication can challenge a motion for default judgment by a motion for new trial up to two years after the judgment. TRCP 329(a). See "MNT After Service by Publication" ch. 10-B, §16, p. 634.

§5. SERVICE ON SECRETARY OF STATE

Thirty-eight separate statutory provisions designate the Secretary of State as an agent for service of process. For the list of the statutes, see www.sos.state.tx.us/statdoc/forms/2401.pdf. The two most important of these involve service on a nonresident and service on a corporation. See "Long-arm service," §5.3, p. 124; "Service on corporation," §5.4, p. 124. Some of the other statutes include CPRC §101.102(c) (Tort Claims Act), CPRC §17.091 (nonresident in a delinquent tax case); Insurance Code article 1.36, §8(d) & (e) and article 21.21, §19(b) (insurance company); and Probate Code §105A(b) (foreign corporate fiduciary). For information about serving the Secretary of State, call the Citations Unit at (512) 463-5560.

§5.1 General rules. When serving the Secretary of State with process, the plaintiff should consult the specific statutes and observe the following general rules:

1. Service on Secretary. The plaintiff may accomplish service on the Secretary of State by certified mail, CPRC §17.026(a) (sent by clerk or party); by delivery by a qualified officer or a private process server; or by any other means permitted by rule or statute. Personal service on the Secretary of State is not necessary. *See* ***Capitol Brick v. Fleming Mfg. Co.***, 722 S.W.2d 399, 401 (Tex.1986) (service under long-arm statute). Two copies of the process must be served on the Secretary of State. 1 Tex.Admin. Code §71.21(a). When process is served by a sheriff or constable, the plaintiff must include an additional copy of the process for the return. When process is served by a private process server, the plaintiff must include copies of the order appointing the process server. When process is served by mail, the citation should be sent to the Secretary of State's post office address; when process is served by delivery, it should be sent to the street address of the Citations Unit.

2. Necessary information. The citation must contain the following information: (1) the identity of the statute authorizing service, (2) the defendant's name, (3) the defendant's address for service, and (4) when specified in the statute, the proper identification of the address. *See* CPRC §17.045(a); 1 Tex.Admin. Code §71.21(a). The plaintiff should check the statute under which the Secretary is being served and, if it identifies the address by name, use the same language. For example, for service on a nonresident under CPRC §17.045(a), the plaintiff must identify the address as that of the "home" or "home office"; if not, service is invalid. *E.g.*, ***Seeley v. KCI USA, Inc.***, 100 S.W.3d 276, 278-79 (Tex.App.—San Antonio 2001, no pet.) (citation stated D's "office address"); ***World Distribs. v. Knox***, 968 S.W.2d 474, 477-78 (Tex.App.—El Paso 1998, no pet.) (no allegation that address was home or home office); ***Chaves v. Todaro***, 770 S.W.2d 944, 946 (Tex.App.—Houston [1st Dist.] 1989, no writ) (no allegation that address was home address). *But see* ***Mahon v. Caldwell, Haddad, Skaggs***, 783 S.W.2d 769, 771 (Tex.App.—Fort Worth 1990, no writ) ("place of business" was sufficient instead of "home office").

Chart 2-3, below, lists some of the statutory identifications of the addresses for service on defendants through the Secretary of State.

2-3. SERVICE THROUGH SECRETARY OF STATE

	STATUTE	IDENTIFY ADDRESS AS THE
1	Business Corporation Act art. 2.11(B) art. 8.10(B) art. 8.14(A)(4) & (5)	Registered office Principal office Post office address
2	Long-Arm Statute CPRC §17.045(a) CPRC §17.045(c)	Home or home office Principal place of business
3	Insurance Code art. 1.36, §8(e)	Last known home office or principal place of business
4	Non-Profit Corporation Act TRCS art. 1396-2.07(B) TRCS art. 1396-8.09(B) TRCS art. 1396-8.13(A)(4) & (5)	Registered office Principal office Street or post office address
5	Limited Partnership Act TRCS art. 6132a-1, §1.08(b) TRCS art. 6132a-1, §9.10(b)	Address of general partner on file or partnership's last registered office Principal office in state where formed
6	Limited Liability Company TRCS art. 1528n, art. 2.08(B) TRCS art. 1528n, art. 7.09(A)(4) & (5)	Registered office Post office address

3. Fees. The fee payable to the Secretary of State is $40 for each defendant for maintaining a record of service of process and $10 for the issuance of a certificate of service. Gov't Code §405.031(a)(1), (4).

4. Secretary forwards process. Once served, the Secretary of State will mail a copy of the citation and petition to the defendant by registered or certified mail, return receipt requested. *See* CPRC §17.045(b)-(d) (notice to nonresident). Service is complete on the defendant when the Secretary of State is served, not when the defendant receives notice. ***Bonewitz v. Bonewitz***, 726 S.W.2d 227, 230 (Tex.App.—Austin 1987, writ ref'd n.r.e.); *see also* ***Whitney v. L&L Rlty. Corp.***, 500 S.W.2d 94, 96 (Tex.1973) (service under long-arm statute).

§5.2 Proof of service. Proof the citation was served on the Secretary of State is not enough to support jurisdiction over the defendant; the plaintiff must prove the Secretary of State forwarded the process to the defendant. ***Whitney***, 500 S.W.2d at 96. To prove the Secretary forwarded the process, the plaintiff should secure a certificate (sometimes referred to as a "Whitney certificate") from the Secretary of State. ***Capitol Brick v. Fleming Mfg. Co.***, 722 S.W.2d 399, 401 (Tex.1986). Before taking a default judgment, the plaintiff should contact the Secretary of State's Citations Unit at (512) 463-5560 and request a certificate of service. The certificate will show the date the Secretary of State's office received the process, the date it forwarded the process to the defendant, and the date it received the return receipt. Once the Secretary of State forwards process to the defendant, the defendant is considered served even if the process is returned to the Secretary of State. ***Zuyus v. No'Mis Comm.***, 930 S.W.2d 743, 746 (Tex.App.—Corpus Christi 1996, no writ) (process returned with notation "unclaimed"); ***BLS Limousine Serv. v. Buslease, Inc.***, 680 S.W.2d 543, 546 (Tex.App.—Dallas 1984, writ ref'd n.r.e.) (process returned with notation "refused"); *see also* ***Mahon***, 783 S.W.2d at 772 (D's agent signed return receipt, instead of D). *But see* ***GMR Gymnastics Sales v. Walz***, 117 S.W.3d 57, 59 (Tex.App.—Fort Worth 2003, pet. filed 11-12-03) (return labeled "not deliverable as addressed, unable to forward" was prima facie evidence address P provided to Secretary of State was incorrect; thus D not served). If the Secretary of State forwards the process to the wrong address because of a typographical error, the service is invalid. *E.g.*, ***Royal Surplus Lines Ins. Co. v. Samaria Baptist Ch.***, 840 S.W.2d 382, 383 (Tex.1992) (citation mailed to 1201 Bassie, instead of 1201 Bessie, was invalid).

§5.3 Long-arm service.

1. Minimum contacts. The test for service on a nonresident is whether the state has provisions for service on a defendant under the facts presented and, if so, whether service on the defendant violates the due process clause of the U.S. Constitution. See "Special Appearance," ch. 3-B, §2, p. 144.

2. Long-arm allegations in petition. When serving a nonresident defendant by service on the Secretary of State, the face of the plaintiff's petition must support long-arm service. ***McKanna v. Edgar***, 388 S.W.2d 927, 929 (Tex.1965). Thus, the petition must allege (1) the Secretary of State is the agent for service on the nonresident, (2) the nonresident engaged in business in Texas, (3) the nonresident does not maintain a regular place of business in Texas, (4) the nonresident does not have a designated agent for service of process, and (5) the lawsuit arises out of the nonresident's business in Texas. CPRC §17.044(b); ***Lozano v. Hayes Wheel Int'l***, 933 S.W.2d 245, 247-48 (Tex.App.—Corpus Christi 1996, no writ); ***South Mill Mushrooms Sales v. Weenick***, 851 S.W.2d 346, 350 (Tex.App.—Dallas 1993, writ denied). For other allegations regarding service on a nonresident, see CPRC §17.044(a), (c), (d). See ***O'Connor's*** FORMS 2B:16-20.

§5.4 Service on corporation. Domestic and foreign corporations who do business in Texas are required to designate and maintain registered agents for service in Texas. Bus. Corp. Act arts. 2.09, 2.10, 8.05(A)(5), 8.08, 8.09; ***Ingram Indus. v. U.S. Bolt Mfg.***, 121 S.W.3d 31, 34 (Tex.App.—Houston [1st Dist.] 2003, n.p.h.); *see* ***Interaction, Inc. v. State***, 17 S.W.3d 775, 779 (Tex.App.—Austin 2000, pet. denied).

1. Diligence. The record must show on its face that the plaintiff used reasonable diligence to serve the corporation's president, vice-president, or registered agent at its registered office. Bus. Corp. Act art. 2.11(A), (B); ***Wright Bros. Energy v. Krough***, 67 S.W.3d 271, 274 (Tex.App.—Houston [1st Dist.] 2001, no pet.); ***Maddison Dual Fuels v. Southern Un. Co.***, 944 S.W.2d 735, 738 (Tex.App.—Corpus Christi 1997, no writ); *see* ***National Multiple Sclerosis Soc'y v. Rice***, 29 S.W.3d 174, 176 (Tex.App.—Eastland 2000, no pet.) (construing TRCS art. 1396-2.07, which is identical to Bus. Corp. Act art. 2.11). To establish reasonable diligence, the record must reflect more than that there was some problem with the address. ***Wright Bros.***, 67 S.W.3d at 274-75 (return citation must explain why service was not accepted); *see, e.g.*, ***Ingram Indus.***, 121 S.W.3d at 34 (return stated that registered agent was not at registered address and the location had been occupied by another person for the past 10 years; one attempt at service constituted reasonable diligence). If the corporation's president, vice-president, or registered agent cannot be found through reasonable diligence, only then can the plaintiff serve the Secretary of State. ***Interaction***, 17 S.W.3d at 779.

2. Secretary forwards process. Once served, the Secretary of State will immediately mail a copy of the citation and petition to the defendant by registered mail or certified mail, return receipt requested. Bus. Corp. Act arts. 2.11(B), 8.10(B). If the Secretary of State forwards the process to the wrong address because the corporation did not notify the Secretary of State of a change of address of its registered office, the service is still valid. ***Tankard-Smith, Inc. Gen. Contractors v. Thursby***, 663 S.W.2d 473, 475-76 (Tex.App.—Houston [14th Dist.] 1983, writ ref'd n.r.e.).

§6. WHO MAY BE SERVED

There are two issues regarding the proper person to serve: (1) when the defendant is not an individual, who is the person that is authorized to receive service of process for the defendant; and (2) when service on the defendant is not possible, who can be served as a substitute for the defendant? Chart 2-4, below, should help.

2-4. PROPER SERVICE IS MADE ON

	IF DEFENDANT IS	ACTUAL SERVICE IS MADE ON	CONSTRUCTIVE SERVICE MAY BE MADE ON
1	Individual	The defendant. TRCP 106(a).	Various persons by court order, TRCP 106(b), 109a; by publication, TRCP 109; agent or clerk at defendant's office, CPRC §17.021; TRCP 106(b); Sec'y of State, CPRC §17.044.
2	Partnership	Partners. CPRC §§17.022, 31.003.	Agent or clerk at partnership office, CPRC §17.021(a); Sec'y of State, *id.* §17.044.
3	Corporation	President, vice-president, or registered agent. Bus. Corp. Act art. 2.11(A).	Sec'y of State. CPRC §17.044; Bus. Corp. Act art. 2.11(B).
4	Authorized foreign corporation	President, vice-president, or registered agent. Bus. Corp. Act art. 8.10(A).	Sec'y of State. CPRC §17.044; Bus. Corp. Act art. 8.10(B).
5	Non-profit corporation	President, vice-president, registered agent, or members of executive committee. TRCS art. 1396-2.07(A).	Sec'y of State. TRCS art. 1396-2.07(B).
6	Insurance company	President, active vice-president, secretary, or attorney-in-fact at home office or principal place of business, or by leaving copy of process at home office or principal place of business during business hours. Ins. Code art. 1.36, §2(a).	Commissioner of Insurance. Ins. Code art. 1.36, §2(b).
7	Foreign insurance company	Attorney for service. Ins. Code art. 1.36, §4(a).	Commissioner of Insurance. Ins. Code arts. 1.36, §§4(b), 15.14(c).
8	Unincorporated business association	President, secretary, treasurer, or general agent. TRCS art. 6134.	Agent or clerk at association's office, CPRC §17.021(a); Sec'y of State, *id.* §17.044.
9	Minor	Minor & legal guardian or next friend. ***Am. Gen. v. Vandewater***, 907 S.W.2d 491, 492 (Tex.1995).	Same as permitted on an individual, see Individual, above.
10	Estate	Executor or administrator. *See* Prob. Code §33. If suit involves title to land, executor or administrator and heirs must be served. CPRC §17.002.	Sec'y of State (only for estate of nonresident defendant). CPRC §17.044.
11	Trust	Trustee. Prop. Code §§114.083, 114.084. If charitable trust, also serve Att'y Gen. Prop. Code §115.011(c).	Sec'y of State (only for nonresident trustee). CPRC §17.044.
12	United States	U.S. Att'y Gen., D.C.; and Assistant U.S. Attorney (AUSA) for district where suit brought, or designated AUSA or clerk.	
13	State of Texas	Sec'y of State. CPRC §101.102(c).	
14	County	County judge. CPRC §17.024(a).	
15	Incorporated city, town, or village	Mayor, clerk, secretary, or treasurer. CPRC §17.024(b).	
16	School district	President of school board or superintendent. CPRC §17.024(c).	
17	Nonresident or out-of-state defendant	The defendant. TRCP 108.	Person in charge of Texas office, CPRC §17.043; Sec'y of State, *id.* §17.044.
18	Out-of-U.S. defendant	The defendant. TRCP 108a.	Person in charge of Texas office, CPRC §17.043; Sec'y of State, *id.* §17.044. Service in foreign country depends on Hague Convention, U.S. treaties, & laws of foreign country. *See* TRCP 108a.

2-4. PROPER SERVICE IS MADE ON

	IF DEFENDANT IS	ACTUAL SERVICE IS MADE ON	CONSTRUCTIVE SERVICE MAY BE MADE ON
19	Foreign railway	The defendant. *See* TRCP 108.	Some train conductors, CPRC §17.093(1); agent in Texas who arranges transport on railway, *id.* §17.093(2); person in charge of Texas office, *id.* §17.043; Sec'y of State, *id.* §17.044.
20	Out-of-state defendant driver	The defendant. *See* CPRC §17.065; TRCP 108.	Chair of the State Transportation Commission. CPRC §17.062.
21	Foreign country	Depends on U.S. treaties & laws of foreign country.	

§7. DEADLINE FOR SERVICE

§7.1 Within limitations. The process should be served on the defendant within the limitations period.

§7.2 Outside limitations. Service outside the limitations period is valid only if both of the following conditions are met:

1. **Petition filed.** The petition was filed within the limitations period. ***Gant v. DeLeon***, 786 S.W.2d 259, 260 (Tex.1990).

2. **Diligence in service.** The plaintiff exercised diligence in procuring service of process on the defendant. ***Gant***, 786 S.W.2d at 260; ***Harrell v. Alvarez***, 46 S.W.3d 483, 485 (Tex.App.—El Paso 2001, no pet.); ***Roberts v. Padre Island Brewing Co.***, 28 S.W.3d 618, 621 (Tex.App.—Corpus Christi 2000, pet. denied). When a plaintiff serves the defendant after limitations, the date of service relates back to the date of filing the suit if the plaintiff exercised diligence in effecting service. ***Gant***, 786 S.W.2d at 260; ***Brown v. Shores***, 77 S.W.3d 884, 887 (Tex.App.—Houston [14th Dist.] 2002, no pet.). The test for diligence is whether the plaintiff (1) acted as an ordinary prudent person would act under the same circumstances and (2) was diligent up until the time the defendant was served. ***Parsons v. Turley***, 109 S.W.3d 804, 808-09 (Tex.App.—Dallas 2003, n.p.h.); ***Zacharie v. U.S. Nat. Res.***, 94 S.W.3d 748, 754 (Tex.App.—San Antonio 2002, no pet.); ***$6,453.00 v. State***, 63 S.W.3d 533, 536 (Tex. App.—Waco 2001, no pet.); *see* ***Tarrant Cty. v. Vandigriff***, 71 S.W.3d 921, 925 (Tex.App.—Fort Worth 2002, pet. denied) (delay of service for over 2 years showed no due diligence as a matter of law). Repeated ineffective attempts at service do not constitute due diligence if easily available and more effective alternatives are ignored. ***Carter v. MacFadyen***, 93 S.W.3d 307, 314-15 (Tex.App.—Houston [14th Dist.] 2002, pet. denied). If the plaintiff learns, or through the exercise of due diligence should have learned, that the clerk has not fulfilled her duty to issue citation in compliance with TRCP 99, the plaintiff must ensure that the defendant is served. *E.g.*, ***Tarrant Cty.***, 71 S.W.3d at 926 (although error in clerk's office was reason for 28-month delay in serving D, P should have discovered through diligence that D was not properly served); ***Boyattia v. Hinojosa***, 18 S.W.3d 729, 734 (Tex. App.—Dallas 2000, pet. denied) (after 3 months, clerk's duty to serve citation is replaced by P's duty to ensure that service actually was completed).

PRACTICE TIP

To prove diligence, the plaintiff should keep a log of its attempts to serve the defendant. The log must show constant and continuous attempts at service. Any period in which there are no attempts to serve the defendant will negate diligence. See, e.g., ***Webster v. Thomas****, 5 S.W.3d 287, 291 (Tex.App.—Houston [14th Dist.] 1999, no pet.) (4-month delay, where efforts to procure service were careless & not persistent, negated diligence);* ***Butler v. Ross****, 836 S.W.2d 833, 835-36 (Tex.App.—Houston [1st Dist.] 1992, no writ) (no activity for 5-1/2 months after return of unserved original citation);* ***Hansler v. Mainka****, 807 S.W.2d 3, 5 (Tex.App.—Corpus Christi 1991, no writ) (no request for process for 5 months after suit filed).*

§8. WAIVER OF SERVICE

§8.1 Voluntary appearance. A defendant who is legally competent may appear in open court and waive service of process in person, by an attorney, or by an authorized agent. TRCP 120; ***Gonzalez v. Phoenix Frozen Foods***, 884 S.W.2d 587, 589 (Tex.App.—Corpus Christi 1994, no writ); *see also* ***Shamrock Oil Co. v. Gulf Coast Nat. Gas***, 68 S.W.3d 737, 739 (Tex.App.—Houston [14th Dist.] 2001, pet. denied) (appearance by corporate lawyer did not waive service on corporate officers). Once a defendant makes a voluntary appearance, the court must note the appearance on the docket and enter it in the minutes. TRCP 120.

§8.2 Written waiver. A defendant who is legally competent may waive service of process in writing. TRCP 119. To be effective, the waiver must (1) expressly state the defendant waives service, (2) acknowledge that the defendant received a copy of the plaintiff's petition, (3) be in writing, (4) be signed by the defendant or its authorized agent or attorney, (5) be verified before someone other than an attorney in the case, (6) be dated after the suit was filed, and (7) be filed among the papers of the case. TRCP 119; *see, e.g.*, ***Deen v. Kirk***, 508 S.W.2d 70, 71 (Tex.1974) (waiver ineffective because it was signed before suit filed); ***Dunn v. Wilson***, 752 S.W.2d 15, 17 (Tex. App.—Fort Worth 1988) (document ineffective because it did not state D waived service), *aff'd*, 800 S.W.2d 833 (Tex. 1990). In a divorce action, the waiver must include the defendant's mailing address. TRCP 119; ***Travieso v. Travieso***, 649 S.W.2d 818, 820 (Tex.App.—San Antonio 1983, no writ) (default judgment). *But see* ***Spivey v. Holloway***, 902 S.W.2d 46, 48 (Tex.App.—Houston [1st Dist.] 1995, no writ) (address can be waived by consent judgment).

§8.3 Presuit waiver. There is one statutorily created exception that permits a presuit waiver of service. A waiver of service in an affidavit to relinquish parental rights, signed before suit is filed, effectively waives service of process. Fam. Code §§102.009(a)(7), 161.103(c), 161.106(a); ***Brown v. McLennan Cty. C.P.S.***, 627 S.W.2d 390, 393 (Tex.1982).

§9. PROOF OF SERVICE – THE RETURN

The return of service is not a trivial, formulaic document. ***Primate Constr. v. Silver***, 884 S.W.2d 151, 152 (Tex. 1994); ***Rivers v. Viskozki***, 967 S.W.2d 868, 870 (Tex.App.—Eastland 1998, no pet.). Unless the plaintiff observes strict compliance with the rules relating to proper service, the service is invalid. ***Primate Constr.***, 884 S.W.2d at 152; ***Union Pac. Corp. v. Legg***, 49 S.W.3d 72, 77 (Tex.App.—Austin 2001, no pet.). Strict compliance is determined by whether the exact procedural requirements have been met, not whether the intended party received notice of the lawsuit. ***Union Pac.***, 49 S.W.3d at 78. Strict compliance, however, does not require "obeisance to the minutest detail." ***Westcliffe, Inc. v. Bear Creek Constr.***, 105 S.W.3d 286, 290 (Tex.App.—Dallas 2003, no pet.); ***Herbert v. Greater Gulf Coast Enters.***, 915 S.W.2d 866, 871 (Tex.App.—Houston [1st Dist.] 1995, no writ).

§9.1 Endorsed or attached. The return must be endorsed on or attached to the citation. TRCP 107; ***Verlander Enters. v. Graham***, 932 S.W.2d 259, 262 (Tex.App.—El Paso 1996, no writ). If it is not, service does not confer jurisdiction on the court. ***Verlander***, 932 S.W.2d at 262.

§9.2 Recitation of due service. The plaintiff must make sure the court's record of the case reflects the defendant was properly served. ***Primate Constr.***, 884 S.W.2d at 153. That responsibility involves checking the statements on the return, including the preprinted statements on the form used by the sheriff's or constable's office. *Id.*

1. Date process received by server. The return must show when the officer or other authorized person received the process for service, and the process must be endorsed with the day and hour on which it was received. TRCP 16, 105; ***TAC Americas v. Boothe***, 94 S.W.3d 315, 319 (Tex.App.—Austin 2002, no pet.); *see, e.g.*, ***Melendez v. John R. Schatzman, Inc.***, 685 S.W.2d 137, 138 (Tex.App.—El Paso 1985, no writ) (officer did not endorse day & hour he received process).

2. What was served. The return must state that a copy of the citation and a copy of the petition were served on the defendant. TRCP 106(a)(1), 107; ***Woodall v. Lansford***, 254 S.W.2d 540, 541 (Tex.App.—Fort Worth 1953, no writ). The return must correctly identify the petition served on the defendant. *See, e.g.*, ***Primate Constr.***,

884 S.W.2d at 152 (recitation that original petition was served, instead of second petition, was fatal); ***Shamrock Oil***, 68 S.W.3d at 738-39 (recitation that "[blank] petition" served was fatal); ***Ortiz v. Avante Villa***, 926 S.W.2d 608, 612 (Tex.App.—Corpus Christi 1996, writ denied) (recitation that "petition attached" was served was sufficient); ***Herbert***, 915 S.W.2d at 871 (recitation that "complaint" was served was sufficient); ***Woodall***, 254 S.W.2d at 542 (recitation that "copy of the citation" was served instead of petition was fatal). The return must show that the defendant was named as a defendant in the petition with which it was served. *See, e.g.*, ***Primate Constr.***, 884 S.W.2d at 152-53 (default judgment reversed because return showed D served with original petition but not named as D until amended petition); ***Seeley v. KCI USA, Inc.***, 100 S.W.3d 276, 277-78 (Tex.App.—San Antonio 2001, no pet.) (same).

3. Who was served. The return must identify the exact person who was served. ***Uvalde Country Club v. Martin Linen Sup. Co.***, 690 S.W.2d 884, 885 (Tex.1985).

(1) Fatal errors. The following mistakes in the name on the return made the return invalid: • The return did not include "Jr." ***Uvalde***, 690 S.W.2d at 885. • The citation named one person as agent for service on the defendant, but the return showed service on another person. ***All Commercial Floors v. Barton & Rasor***, 97 S.W.3d 723, 726-27 (Tex.App.—Fort Worth 2003, no pet.). • The return did not identify the defendant-corporation as the entity served. ***Benefit Planners v. Rencare, Ltd.***, 81 S.W.3d 855, 861 (Tex.App.—San Antonio 2002, pet. denied). • The return did not give the complete and correct name of the defendant. ***Hercules Concrete Pumping Serv. v. Bencon Mgmt. & Gen. Contracting Corp.***, 62 S.W.3d 308, 310-11 (Tex.App.—Houston [1st Dist.] 2001, pet. denied). • The return contained only the surname. ***Exposition Apts. Co. v. Barba***, 630 S.W.2d 462, 465 (Tex.App.—Austin 1982, no writ) ("Mr. Thompson"). • The return did not include the correct middle initial. ***Zaragoza v. Morales***, 616 S.W.2d 295, 296 (Tex.App.—Eastland 1981, writ ref'd n.r.e.). • The return did not identify the defendant as a corporation, as it was identified in the petition and citation. ***Brown-McKee, Inc. v. J.F. Bryan & Assocs.***, 522 S.W.2d 958, 959 (Tex.App.—Texarkana 1975, no writ). • The return receipt was signed by a person other than the addressee. *See, e.g.*, ***American Universal Ins. Co. v. D.B.&B., Inc.***, 725 S.W.2d 764, 765 (Tex. App.—Corpus Christi 1987, writ ref'd n.r.e.) (record did not show person who signed return was agent of D).

(2) Nonfatal errors. The following mistakes in the name of the return did not make the return invalid: • The return omitted "Ltd." after "Co." ***Stephenson v. Corporate Servs.***, 650 S.W.2d 181, 183 (Tex.App.—Tyler 1983, writ ref'd n.r.e.); *see also* ***Ortiz v. Avante Villa***, 926 S.W.2d 608, 613 (Tex.App.—Corpus Christi 1996, writ denied) (omission of "Inc." on return did not invalidate service). • The return misspelled the defendant's name. *See, e.g.*, ***Popkowsi v. Gramza***, 671 S.W.2d 915, 917-18 (Tex.App.—Houston [1st Dist.] 1984, no writ) (return substituted an "r" for a "k" in D's name).

4. Where D was served. The return must show the place where service was made. TRCP 16; ***Jacksboro Nat'l Bank v. Signal Oil & Gas Co.***, 482 S.W.2d 339, 341-42 (Tex.App.—Tyler 1972, no writ). In most cases, the citation should contain a statement identifying the address as either the defendant's residence or its usual place of business. When service is by order under TRCP 106, the order is considered part of the record; if the order identifies the address as the defendant's residence or usual place of business, the citation need not contain the same statement. ***Brown v. Magnetic Media***, 795 S.W.2d 41, 43 (Tex.App.—Houston [1st Dist.] 1990, no writ).

5. How D was served. The return must identify "the manner of service." TRCP 107; ***Wohler v. La Buena Vida***, 855 S.W.2d 891, 892 (Tex.App.—Fort Worth 1993, no writ). Manner of service requires the showing of two things: (1) how the citation was served (*e.g.*, delivered or mailed) and (2) that the citation was served on a person capable of accepting service. ***Faggett v. Hargrove***, 921 S.W.2d 274, 277 (Tex.App.—Houston [1st Dist.] 1995, no writ), *overruled on other grounds*, ***Barker CATV Constr. v. Ampro, Inc.***, 989 S.W.2d 789 (Tex.App.—Houston [1st Dist.] 1999, no pet.); *see, e.g.*, ***Cox Mktg. v. Adams***, 688 S.W.2d 215, 217 (Tex.App.—El Paso 1985, no writ) (return did not show person served was authorized to accept service); ***Curry Motor Freight v. Ralston***

Purina Co., 565 S.W.2d 105, 106-07 (Tex.App.—Amarillo 1978, no writ) (return merely said service was accomplished by "serving" a person); *see also* ***Dolly v. Aethos Comm. Sys.***, 10 S.W.3d 384, 388 (Tex.App.—Dallas 2000, no pet.) (return that stated D was served "in person," but also noted that process was "posted to front door," was inherently inconsistent).

6. Who served D. The return must identify who served the defendant. *See* TRCP 16, 107. When public officials such as sheriffs, constables, and clerks are authorized to effect service, they may personally serve process, or they may serve process through their deputies. ***Pratt v. Moore***, 746 S.W.2d 486, 487 (Tex.App.—Dallas 1988, no writ). When citation is served by a deputy, the deputy must indicate who employed him as a deputy. ***Houston Pipe Coating Co. v. Houston Freightways***, 679 S.W.2d 42, 45 (Tex.App.—Houston [14th Dist.] 1984, writ ref'd n.r.e.). If the trial court appointed a disinterested person to serve the citation, the return must show service by that person, and the name of the person in the order must match the name of the person who served the citation. *See, e.g.*, ***Cates v. Pon***, 663 S.W.2d 99, 102 (Tex.App.—Houston [14th Dist.] 1983, writ ref'd n.r.e.) (invalid service because order appointed disinterested adult to serve process & return was signed by deputy constable); ***Mega v. Anglo Iron & Metal Co.***, 601 S.W.2d 501, 504 (Tex.App.—Corpus Christi 1980, no writ) (invalid service because order appointed "A.R. 'Tony' Martinez" to serve process & the return was signed by "A.R. Martinez, Jr.").

7. Date D was served. The return must show the date and time of service. TRCP 16, 107; ***Conseco Fin. Servicing Corp. v. Klein ISD***, 78 S.W.3d 666, 672 (Tex.App.—Houston [14th Dist.] 2002, no pet.); ***Melendez v. John R. Schatzman, Inc.***, 685 S.W.2d 137, 138 (Tex.App.—El Paso 1985, no writ); *e.g.*, ***TAC Americas v. Boothe***, 94 S.W.3d 315, 320-22 (Tex.App.—Austin 2002, no pet.) (service was invalid when return indicated process server delivered documents before receiving them). When service is made by certified mail, the postmark is sufficient to show the latest date of delivery. ***Nelson v. Remmert***, 726 S.W.2d 171, 172 (Tex.App.—Houston [14th Dist.] 1987, writ ref'd n.r.e.).

8. Date return filed. The return must state the date on which it was filed; if it does not, the record cannot establish that the return was on file for ten days, which is necessary before a default judgment may be granted. TRCP 107; ***HB & WM, Inc. v. Smith***, 802 S.W.2d 279, 281-82 (Tex.App.—San Antonio 1990, no writ); *see, e.g.*, ***Melendez***, 685 S.W.2d at 138 (because clerk did not include date and filemark on citation, it was impossible to determine how long return had been on file).

§9.3 Addressee's signature. When the return is served by mail, it must contain the return receipt with the addressee's signature. TRCP 107; ***All Commercial Floors***, 97 S.W.3d at 726; ***Fowler v. Quinlan ISD***, 963 S.W.2d 941, 944 (Tex.App.—Texarkana 1998, no pet.); *e.g.*, ***Union Pac. Corp. v. Legg***, 49 S.W.3d 72, 79 (Tex.App.—Austin 2001, no pet.) (return invalid because it was stamped with signature & no proof was offered to show signature was authorized). If the defendant is a corporation, the return receipt must be signed by the corporation's president, vice-president, or registered agent. *See* Bus. Corp. Act art. 2.11(A); ***Cox Mktg.***, 688 S.W.2d at 217; *see also* ***Harmon Truck Lines v. Steele***, 836 S.W.2d 262, 264 (Tex.App.—Texarkana 1992, writ dism'd) (when signature was not plainly the agent's, service was not adequate). When a return recites that the person served is a corporation's registered agent, it is prima facie evidence of that person's status. ***Primate Constr. v. Silver***, 884 S.W.2d 151, 152 n.1 (Tex.1994). ***Primate*** overruled those cases that held the record must affirmatively show that the person served was in fact the registered agent.

§9.4 Signature of server. The signature of the server must appear on the return. TRCP 107; ***Hot Shot Messenger Serv. v. State***, 818 S.W.2d 905, 907 (Tex.App.—Austin 1991, no writ); ***American Bankers Ins. Co. v. State***, 749 S.W.2d 195, 197 (Tex.App.—Houston [14th Dist.] 1988, no writ). A stamped or printed signature of the officer satisfies the requirement of TRCP 107. ***Payne & Keller Co. v. Word***, 732 S.W.2d 38, 40 (Tex.App.—Houston [14th Dist.] 1987, writ ref'd n.r.e.) (constable). If served by a deputy, the deputy's signature may be applied with a stamp under the printed name of the constable. ***Houston Pipe Coating***, 679 S.W.2d at 45.

§9.5 Verification by private process server. When process is served by an "authorized person" (private process server), that person must verify the return of citation. TRCP 107; ***Carmona v. Bunzl Distrib.***, 76 S.W.3d 566, 569 (Tex.App.—Corpus Christi 2002, no pet.); ***Bautista v. Bautista***, 9 S.W.3d 250, 251 (Tex.App.—San Antonio 1999, no pet.); ***McGraw-Hill, Inc. v. Futrell***, 823 S.W.2d 414, 416 (Tex.App.—Houston [1st Dist.] 1992, writ denied); *see also* TRCP 108 (out-of-state service). The verification must be on or attached to the citation. ***Carmona***, 76 S.W.3d at 569; *see also* ***Garza v. Zavala***, 905 S.W.2d 312, 313 (Tex.App.—El Paso 1995, no writ) (certificate of delivery by itself was not a verification); ***McGraw-Hill***, 823 S.W.2d at 416 (same). The verification must verify the facts relating to the act of service. ***Dolly***, 10 S.W.3d at 389 (verification with statement that citation executed pursuant to TRCPs is defective). In contrast, when process is served by an officer, it is not necessary for the officer to verify the return. ***14.9 Grams of Methamphetamine v. State***, 28 S.W.3d 146, 148 (Tex.App.—Texarkana 2000, no pet.). The return may be amended by adding the verification, even after a default judgment. TRCP 118; ***Walker v. Brodhead***, 828 S.W.2d 278, 282 (Tex.App.—Austin 1992, writ denied). Under TRCP 108 (service outside of Texas), the server must swear in the return that she is a disinterested person and that she is competent to make an oath of that fact. ***Scucchi v. Woodruff***, 503 S.W.2d 356, 358-59 (Tex.App.—Fort Worth 1973, no writ).

§10. AMENDING THE SERVICE DOCUMENTS

§10.1 Amending the petition. When the plaintiff amends the petition after service but before the defendant files an answer, if the amended petition asks for a more onerous judgment, the defendant must be served with citation and the amended petition. See "Service of amended pleadings," ch. 5-F, §3.3, p. 257; "Adding claims or damages – service required," ch. 7-A, §3.2.1(1), p. 444.

§10.2 Amending citation & return. The trial court may allow the process or proof of service to be amended at any time in the court's discretion and on such notice and terms as it deems just. TRCP 118. No other person has the authority to amend the citation or the return. *See, e.g.*, ***Barker CATV Constr. v. Ampro, Inc.***, 989 S.W.2d 789, 793-94 (Tex.App.—Houston [1st Dist.] 1999, no pet.) (no proof trial court authorized amended return; amended return disallowed); ***Plains Chevrolet v. Thorne***, 656 S.W.2d 631, 633 (Tex.App.—Waco 1983, no writ) (serving officer cannot correct D's name in citation; amended citation disallowed). If the court signs an order permitting amendment of the citation or the return, the plaintiff does not need to re-serve the defendant with process.

1. **Amending the citation.** The court may permit the citation to be amended. TRCP 118; ***London v. Chandler***, 406 S.W.2d 203, 204 (Tex.1966).

2. **Amending the return.** The court, at any time during its plenary power, may permit proof of service to be amended to reflect the actual service on the defendant. *See* TRCP 118; ***Higginbotham v. General Life & Acc. Ins. Co.***, 796 S.W.2d 695, 696 (Tex.1990); ***Dawson v. Briggs***, 107 S.W.3d 739, 747 (Tex.App.—Fort Worth 2003, no pet.); *see, e.g.*, ***Brodhead***, 828 S.W.2d at 282 (verification of return added; amendment permitted); ***Bavarian Autohaus v. Holland***, 570 S.W.2d 110, 113 (Tex.App.—Houston [1st Dist.] 1978, no writ) (return amended and filed before judgment to reflect service on corporation by delivery to vice-president; amendment permitted). The return cannot be amended without court approval. ***Barker CATV***, 989 S.W.2d at 793-94. The amended return must be attached to a valid citation. ***Verlander Enters. v. Graham***, 932 S.W.2d 259, 262 (Tex. App.—El Paso 1996, no writ). A properly amended return relates back to and is considered filed on the date the original return was filed. ***Brodhead***, 828 S.W.2d at 282; ***Bavarian Autohaus***, 570 S.W.2d at 113.

§11. SERVICE OUTSIDE THE UNITED STATES

Service of process in a foreign country must give the defendant actual notice of the proceeding in time to answer and defend. TRCP 108a.

§11.1 Limitations on foreign service.

1. **Comity.** Comity is the extent to which the laws of one nation are allowed to operate within the territory of another nation. ***Hilton v. Guyot***, 159 U.S. 113, 163, 16 S.Ct. 139, 143 (1895). No nation can demand that

its laws have effect beyond the limits of its sovereignty. *Id.* Some countries consider service of judicial documents as requiring the performance of a judicial or "sovereign" act, and thus view service of judicial documents from another country within their borders as offensive to their sovereignty. *See* ***O'Connor's Federal Rules * Civil Trials***, 1993 *Notes of Adv. Comm. to FRCP 4*, ¶20, p. 1072 (2004).

2. Constitution. If a defendant has no contact with Texas, it cannot be required to appear in a Texas court. See "Special Appearance—Challenging Personal Jurisdiction," ch. 3-B, p. 143. Before a court exercises jurisdiction over a foreign defendant, the U.S. Constitution requires that the defendant have affiliating contacts with the United States sufficient to justify the exercise of personal jurisdiction. ***Helicopteros Nacionales de Colombia, S.A. v. Hall***, 466 U.S. 408, 414, 104 S.Ct. 1868, 1872 (1984). In addition, a plaintiff's choice of forum might be so inconvenient to a defendant that it would be a denial of "fair play and substantial justice," as required by due process, to require the defendant to defend the suit even though the defendant had significant affiliating contacts with the United States. ***World-Wide Volkswagen Corp. v. Woodson***, 444 U.S. 286, 291-92, 100 S.Ct. 559, 564 (1980).

§11.2 Methods of service permitted. A person outside the United States may be served by any method permitted by TRCP 108a. A nonresident defendant may be served with process outside the United States as provided by (1) foreign law, (2) foreign authority in response to a letter rogatory, (3) TRCP 106, (4) a treaty, (5) the U.S. Department of State, or (6) any other means directed by the court that is not prohibited by law in the country where service is to be made. TRCP 108a(1); ***Commission of Contracts v. Arriba, Ltd.***, 882 S.W.2d 576, 584 & n.6 (Tex.App.—Houston [1st Dist.] 1994, no writ).

CAUTION

Unless a plaintiff uses the appropriate method of service in a foreign country as required by a treaty with that country, a judgment rendered for the plaintiff may not be enforceable in that country. ***Kreimerman v. Casa Veerkamp, S.A.***, *22 F.3d 634, 640-41 (5th Cir.1994).*

§11.3 Preference for service according to international agreements. The preferred method of serving a defendant in another country is under the Hague Convention on the Service Abroad of Judicial & Extrajudicial Documents (Hague Convention), or under any other applicable treaty. Service abroad must be made under a treaty if (1) there is a treaty and (2) the treaty requires service to be made according to its terms. A treaty does not necessarily preempt all other methods of service on a defendant who resides in a signatory country; preemption depends on the language, history, and purpose of the treaty. ***Kreimerman***, 22 F.3d at 637-38. The Hague Convention by its terms preempts inconsistent methods of service prescribed by state law in all cases to which it applies. ***Volkswagenwerk Aktiengesellschaft v. Schlunk***, 486 U.S. 694, 699, 108 S.Ct. 2104, 2108 (1988); *see* ***Ackerman v. Levine***, 788 F.2d 830, 838-39 (2d Cir.1986). In contrast, the Inter-American Convention on Letters Rogatory does not. ***Kreimerman***, 22 F.3d at 647.

PRACTICE TIP

To determine if a particular country has signed the Hague Convention or any other treaty, contact the Treaty Affairs Section, Department of State, Washington, D.C. at (202) 647-1345, or refer to the Hague Conference website, www.hcch.net/e/status.

For the procedure for service under the Hague Convention, see ***O'Connor's Federal Rules * Civil Trials***, "Serving Process Abroad," ch. 2-H, §6, p. 119 (2004).

I. SUIT BY INDIGENT

§1. GENERAL

§1.1 Rules. TRCP 145, 217; in forcible entry and detainer cases, see TRCP 749a, 749b; TRAP 20. See CPRC chs. 13, 14.

§1.2 Purpose. The Texas Constitution and the rules of procedure recognize that courts must be open to all persons with legitimate disputes, not just those who can afford to pay the fees to get in. Tex. Const. art. 1, §13; TRCP 145, 217; ***Griffin Indus. v. 13th Ct. of Appeals***, 934 S.W.2d 349, 353 (Tex.1996). TRCP 145 gives an indigent access to the courthouse without the payment of costs. ***Spellmon v. Sweeney***, 819 S.W.2d 206, 208 (Tex.App.—Waco 1991, no writ). TRCP 217 gives an indigent the right to a jury trial without the payment of the jury fee. Although a litigant is not entitled to appointed counsel in a civil case, under exceptional circumstances, when public and private interests are at stake, the court may appoint a lawyer to represent an indigent civil litigant. ***Gibson v. Tolbert***, 102 S.W.3d 710, 712 (Tex.2003) (Gov't Code §24.016); *see* ***In re A.N.***, ___ S.W.3d ___ (Tex.App.—Amarillo 2003, order on mot.) (07-03-0124-CV; 4-30-03) (Fam. Code §107.013(a)).

§1.3 Forms & timetables. ***O'Connor's Texas Civil Forms***, FORMS 2I; Timetable, ***O'Connor's Texas Civil Appeals***, Appeal by Indigent to Court of Appeals, p. 964 (2002-03).

§1.4 Other references. ***O'Connor's Texas Civil Appeals***, "Appealing as an Indigent," ch. 12, p. 45 (2002-03); Hewitt & Warton, *Dismissing Pauper Suits in Texas Courts*, 26 Tex.Tech L.Rev. 123 (1995).

§2. WHO IS INDIGENT?

An indigent is a person who has no ability to pay the costs for the suit. TRCP 145. Generally, an individual receiving a governmental entitlement or public assistance may proceed as an indigent. *See id.*; ***Griffin Indus.***, 934 S.W.2d at 351; ***Baughman v. Baughman***, 65 S.W.3d 309, 315 (Tex.App.—Waco 2001, pet. denied).

§2.1 Parties who are indigent. The following parties are considered indigent: • A personal injury plaintiff who has a contingency-fee contract with an attorney who cannot or will not advance the costs. ***Griffin Indus.***, 934 S.W.2d at 354. • A prisoner at the Texas Department of Criminal Justice (TDCJ) who has no money or property. ***Allred v. Lowry***, 597 S.W.2d 353, 355 (Tex.1980). • A person who has been living on welfare, has not been regularly employed, and has not been able to obtain loans to pay for court costs. ***Goffney v. Lowry***, 554 S.W.2d 157, 159-60 (Tex.1977). • A corporation in bankruptcy. *See* ***Modern Living, Inc. v. Alworth***, 730 S.W.2d 444, 445-46 (Tex. App.—Beaumont 1987, orig. proceeding).

§2.2 Parties who are not indigent. The following parties are not considered indigent: • A person who remains voluntarily unemployed and lives on the generosity of relatives. ***Keller v. Walker***, 652 S.W.2d 542, 544 (Tex.App.—Dallas 1983, orig. proceeding). • An inmate who has funds in his trust account. *See* CPRC §14.006(b)(1) (prisoner must pay costs from trust account according to specific formula).

§3. AFFIDAVIT OF INDIGENCE

An affidavit of indigence does not need to strictly comply with the requirements of the rules of procedure; substantial compliance is sufficient. ***Walker v. Blue Water Garden Apts.***, 776 S.W.2d 578, 580-81 (Tex.1989). See ***O'Connor's*** FORM 2I:01.

§3.1 The contents of the affidavit. The affidavit must contain the complete information about the party's identity, nature and amount of income (governmental entitlement, employment, or other income, *e.g.*, interest and dividends), spouse's income (if available to the party), property owned (other than homestead), cash or checking account, dependents, debts, and monthly expenses. TRCP 145(2). In addition, the affidavit must state the following:

1. The indigent desires to prosecute the lawsuit without paying costs. TRCP 145.

2. The indigent is unable to pay the costs required by the rules. The indigent must make the statements, "I am unable to pay the court costs. I verify that the statements made in this affidavit are true and correct."

TRCP 145(2). The indigent must state facts that support the statement that he is unable to pay costs, *e.g.*, plaintiff is on welfare; plaintiff is unemployed and looking for work; plaintiff's expenses exceed income (itemizing both); plaintiff has no other available sources of money (*e.g.*, cannot get a loan, no income available from spouse); plaintiff owns no real property; plaintiff's only personal property consists of his clothes and other personal items; plaintiff's only asset is a truck, and if it were sold, plaintiff could not keep a job and support a family. *See* TRCP 145(2). For a comprehensive list of facts to cover in an affidavit of indigence, see TRAP 20.1(b). See ***O'Connor's Texas Civil Appeals***, "Affidavit of Indigence," ch. 12-B, p. 49.

3. If the indigent is an inmate, the inmate must file a separate affidavit or unsworn declaration that provides specific information about other suits previously brought by him and attach to it a certified copy of the inmate's trust account statement. CPRC §14.004; *see* ***Obadele v. Johnson***, 60 S.W.3d 345, 348 (Tex.App.—Houston [14th Dist.] 2001, no pet.); *see also* ***Thomas v. Wichita Gen. Hosp.***, 952 S.W.2d 936, 939-40 (Tex.App.—Fort Worth 1997, pet. denied) (CPRC §14.004 is not unconstitutional). See §4, below.

§3.2 Verification.

1. **Most indigents.** The affidavit of indigence must be sworn before a notary public. TRCP 145(2).

2. **Inmate indigents.** Inmates of the TDCJ or county jail may make unsworn declarations instead of affidavits. CPRC §132.001; ***Smith v. McCorkle***, 895 S.W.2d 692, 692 (Tex.1995). An unsworn declaration must be in writing and subscribed as true under the penalty of perjury. CPRC §132.002; ***Smith***, 895 S.W.2d at 692; *see* ***Teixeira v. Hall***, 107 S.W.3d 805, 808 (Tex.App.—Texarkana 2003, no pet.). See ***O'Connor's*** FORM 1B:06.

§3.3 Time to file. The affidavit should be filed along with the original petition and served on the defendant along with the citation. *See* TRCP 145(1); ***Baughman***, 65 S.W.3d at 312. If the affidavit is not filed with the original petition, it must be served on the other parties under TRCP 21a.

§3.4 Amending the affidavit. A party may amend a defective affidavit of indigence. ***In re J.W.***, 52 S.W.3d 730, 732 (Tex.2001); ***American Comm. Telecomm. v. Commerce N. Bank***, 660 S.W.2d 570, 571 (Tex.App.—San Antonio 1983, order on mot.).

§3.5 Attorney's supporting affidavit. An attorney who represents an indigent may file an affidavit supporting the affidavit of indigence stating that legal services are being provided for free, without contingency, because of the party's indigence. TRCP 145(3). A contingent-fee arrangement does not nullify a plaintiff's indigent status. ***Griffin Indus.***, 934 S.W.2d at 354. See ***O'Connor's*** FORM 2I:02.

§4. SUIT BY INDIGENT INMATE

§4.1 Declaration of indigence. An indigent inmate must file the affidavit of indigence required by TRCP 145. See §3 above.

§4.2 Declaration relating to previous filings. An indigent inmate must file the declaration required by CPRC §14.004. See ***O'Connor's*** FORM 2I:03. In the declaration, the inmate must provide the following:

1. A list of all suits (other than those under the Family Code) brought by the inmate in which the inmate was not represented by an attorney. CPRC §14.004(a)(1); *see* ***Light v. Womack***, 113 S.W.3d 872, 874 (Tex. App.—Beaumont 2003, n.p.h.) (must disclose all pro se suits, not just suits filed as indigent). The inmate must include the following information: (1) the operative facts for which relief was sought; (2) the case name, cause number, and court in which suit was brought; (3) the identity of each party named in the suit; (4) the results of the suit, including whether it was dismissed as frivolous or malicious; and (5) if a previous suit was dismissed as frivolous or malicious, the date of the final order affirming the dismissal. CPRC §14.004(a)(2), (b); *see, e.g.*, ***Obadele***, 60 S.W.3d at 348 (affidavit that did not identify parties or operative facts was not in substantial compliance with CPRC §14.004(a)); ***Clark v. Unit***, 23 S.W.3d 420, 421-22 (Tex.App.—Houston [1st Dist.] 2000, pet. denied) (inmate did not include operative facts in affidavit; dismissal affirmed).

2. A certified copy of the inmate's trust account statement. CPRC §14.006(f); ***Bonds v. Texas Dept. of Crim. Justice***, 953 S.W.2d 233, 233 (Tex.1997) (if statement not certified, court must request that inmate file certified copy before ordering inmate to pay full amount of court fees and costs).

3. When a claim is subject to the grievance system established under Gov't Code §501.008, the inmate must file (1) an affidavit or unsworn declaration stating the date the grievance was filed and the date the written decision was received by the inmate and (2) a copy of the written decision. CPRC §14.005(a); ***Draughon v. Cockrell***, 112 S.W.3d 775, 776 (Tex.App.—Beaumont 2003, no pet.); *see* ***Spurlock v. Schroedter***, 88 S.W.3d 733, 737 (Tex.App.—Corpus Christi 2002, no pet.).

§4.3 Other miscellaneous information. For additional information about the hearing, costs, the submission of evidence, and the order of dismissal, see CPRC §§14.006-14.014.

§5. SUMMARY DISMISSAL ON COURT'S MOTION

Under CPRC §13.001(c) (indigents) and CPRC §14.003(a) (indigent inmates), the trial court has the authority to dismiss an indigent's suit even before process is served. ***Pedraza v. Tibbs***, 826 S.W.2d 695, 698 (Tex.App.—Houston [1st Dist.] 1992, writ dism'd). This action spares the prospective defendant the inconvenience and expense of answering a frivolous complaint.

§5.1 Hearing. The trial court may dismiss a lawsuit without a hearing on factual issues only when there is no arguable basis in law for the suit. ***Denson v. TDCJ–ID***, 63 S.W.3d 454, 459 (Tex.App.—Tyler 1999, pet. denied); ***Leon Springs Gas Co. v. Restaurant Equip. Leasing***, 961 S.W.2d 574, 579 (Tex.App.—San Antonio 1997, no pet.); ***Hector v. Thaler***, 862 S.W.2d 176, 178 (Tex.App.—Houston [1st Dist.] 1993, no writ). Before a court can dismiss a suit for having no arguable basis in fact, it must hold a hearing. ***Hector***, 862 S.W.2d at 178. *But see* ***Timmons v. Luce***, 840 S.W.2d 582, 586 (Tex.App.—Tyler 1992, no writ) (court is not required to hold hearing if action is frivolous); ***Kendrick v. Lynaugh***, 804 S.W.2d 153, 154 (Tex.App.—Houston [14th Dist.] 1990, no writ) (same).

§5.2 No amendment. The trial court is not required to give the indigent an opportunity to amend its petition before dismissing under CPRC §13.001 or §14.003. *See* ***Kendrick***, 804 S.W.2d at 156 (case involved §13.001). However, if the court gives an indigent the opportunity to amend his pleadings and the indigent does not amend, the trial court can dismiss the indigent's suit with prejudice. ***Lentworth v. Trahan***, 981 S.W.2d 720, 722-23 (Tex. App.—Houston [1st Dist.] 1998, no pet.); *see* ***Hughes v. Massey***, 65 S.W.3d 743, 746 (Tex.App.—Beaumont 2001, no pet.) (if indigent not given opportunity to amend, dismissal should be "without prejudice").

§5.3 No notice. Neither CPRC §13.001 nor §14.003 requires the trial court to give the indigent notice that it intends to dismiss the suit for "no arguable basis in law." *See* ***Timmons***, 840 S.W.2d at 586 (CPRC §13.001). See §5.2, above. However, if there is a hearing, the indigent must be given notice.

§5.4 Grounds for dismissal. The trial court has the authority to dismiss a suit filed by an indigent if the trial court finds any of the following:

1. **Not indigent.** The allegation of poverty in the affidavit is false. CPRC §§13.001(a)(1), 14.003(a)(1).

2. **No arguable basis.** The action or claim is frivolous or malicious. CPRC §13.001(a)(2) (uses term "action"), *id.* §14.003(a)(2) (uses term "claim"); ***Johnson v. Lynaugh***, 796 S.W.2d 705, 706 (Tex.1990); ***McDonald v. Houston Dairy***, 813 S.W.2d 238, 238 (Tex.App.—Houston [1st Dist] 1991, no writ). To determine if an action is frivolous or malicious, the court is limited to CPRC §13.001(b)(2), which permits the court to dismiss if the claim has no arguable basis in law or in fact. ***Johnson***, 796 S.W.2d at 706 (dismissal under CPRC §13.001(b)(3) not appropriate); ***Pedraza***, 826 S.W.2d at 698 (dismissal under CPRC §13.001(b)(1) & (3) is discouraged). A claim that has no arguable basis in law or in fact does not constitute a cause of action and has no value as a property right. ***Pedraza***, 826 S.W.2d at 698; ***Spellmon v. Sweeney***, 819 S.W.2d 206, 210 (Tex.App.—Waco 1991, no writ).

3. Inmate – false filing. The indigent inmate filed an affidavit or unsworn declaration required by CPRC chapter 14 that the inmate knew was false. CPRC §14.003(a)(3); *see id.* §14.004 (affidavit regarding previous filings).

4. Inmate – substantially similar claim. The indigent inmate filed a claim that was substantially similar to a previous claim and was based on the same operative facts. CPRC §14.003(a)(2), (b)(4); ***Vacca v. Farrington***, 85 S.W.3d 438, 440 (Tex.App.—Texarkana 2002, no pet.).

§5.5 Order on summary dismissal. The court's order summarily dismissing the indigent's suit must state the reasons for the dismissal. ***Dillon v. Ousley***, 890 S.W.2d 500, 502 (Tex.App.—Corpus Christi 1994, no writ). The trial court's order dismissing an inmate's suit should be based on CPRC chapter 14, not CPRC chapter 13. ***Thompson v. Henderson***, 927 S.W.2d 323, 324 (Tex.App.—Houston [1st Dist.] 1996, no writ) (remanded for trial court to consider provisions of CPRC ch. 14).

§6. DUTIES OF THE CLERK

§6.1 Issue citation. Once the indigent files an affidavit under TRCP 145, the clerk must docket the action, issue a citation, and provide other customary services as are provided to any other party. The clerk must issue a citation even though the court has not yet ruled on the affidavit of indigence. ***McDonald***, 813 S.W.2d at 238; *see* ***Downs v. Trevathan***, 783 S.W.2d 689, 690 (Tex.App.—Houston [1st Dist.] 1989, orig. proceeding).

§6.2 Give notice. The clerk will give the defendant notice of the filing of the affidavit along with the service of the citation. TRCP 145(1). There is no requirement for the indigent plaintiff to give the defendant notice of the suit and the affidavit.

§7. CONTESTING THE AFFIDAVIT

Once the citation is served, the defendant may contest the affidavit by filing a written contest giving notice to all parties. TRCP 145(1); *see* ***Holt v. F.F. Enters.***, 990 S.W.2d 756, 758 (Tex.App.—Amarillo 1998, pet. denied). If a contest is not filed, the uncontested affidavit is conclusive as a matter of law. ***Equitable Gen. Ins. Co. v. Yates***, 684 S.W.2d 669, 671 (Tex.1984). The defendant's contest cannot delay any temporary hearing. TRCP 145(1).

§8. HEARING ON THE CONTEST

§8.1 Notice of hearing. The indigent must be given notice of the hearing or submission of the contest to the affidavit of indigence. ***Aguilar v. Stone***, 68 S.W.3d 1, 2 (Tex.App.—Houston [1st Dist.] 1997, orig. proceeding).

§8.2 Hearing for indigents. The court should conduct a hearing on the contest to the affidavit at the first regular hearing in the suit. TRCP 145(1). At that hearing, the indigent should provide proof of indigence. The proper consideration is the present ability to pay costs rather than a future, more speculative ability. ***Brown v. Clapp***, 613 S.W.2d 78, 80 (Tex.App.—Tyler 1981, orig. proceeding).

§8.3 Hearing for indigent inmates. A court may hold a hearing by video communications for indigent inmates at a jail facility. CPRC §14.008(a). A court may also consider the case on submission, by requiring that written statements be submitted and copies be provided to the inmate. *Id.* §14.009.

§9. ORDER ON THE CONTEST

§9.1 Indigent. If the court finds the plaintiff is indigent, the suit will proceed, and the plaintiff will not be liable for costs. TRCP 145(1). If the plaintiff recovers a monetary judgment from the defendant, the court may order the indigent to pay costs from the award. *Id.*

§9.2 Not indigent. If the court finds the plaintiff is not indigent, the court must state the reasons in the order. TRCP 145(1); ***Varkonyi v. Troche***, 802 S.W.2d 63, 65 (Tex.App.—El Paso 1990, orig. proceeding).

1. Valid grounds. A court may dismiss if it finds (1) the allegations of poverty are false or (2) the action is frivolous or malicious. ***Creel v. District Atty.***, 818 S.W.2d 45, 46 n.2 (Tex.1991).

2. No further action. If the court signs an order sustaining the contest, the indigent may take no further action in the suit until the indigent makes payment. TRCP 145(1).

§10. REVIEW

§10.1 To file suit as indigent. If the trial court dismisses the indigent's suit because the allegations of poverty are false or the claim is frivolous or malicious, the indigent can challenge the order by filing a notice of appeal. *See* ***In re Arroyo***, 988 S.W.2d 737, 738 (Tex.1998) (appeal, not mandamus, is the proper vehicle to challenge order sustaining contest to affidavit of indigence).

§10.2 To appeal as indigent. To challenge the order of dismissal on appeal, the indigent who claimed indigence for purposes of the trial must claim indigence for the appeal and file an affidavit of indigence. See ***O'Connor's Texas Civil Appeals***, "Affidavit of Indigence," ch. 12-B, p. 49. Indigence provisions are liberally construed in favor of the right to appeal. ***Jones v. Stayman***, 747 S.W.2d 369, 370 (Tex.1987).

COMMENTARIES

CHAPTER 3. THE DEFENDANT'S RESPONSES & PLEADINGS
TABLE OF CONTENTS

COMMENTARIES

CHAPTER 3. THE DEFENDANT'S RESPONSES & PLEADINGS
TABLE OF CONTENTS

A. DEFENDANT'S PLEADINGS

§1. GENERAL

§1.1 Rules. TRCP 83-98.

§1.2 Purpose. Initially, the most important function of the defendant's pleadings in response to the lawsuit is to avoid a default judgment. After that, the defendant's pleadings challenge the plaintiff's petition and answer its allegations.

§1.3 Forms & timetables. *O'Connor's Texas Civil Forms*, FORMS 3; Timetables, this book, Special Appearance, p. 992, Motions to Transfer Venue, p. 993-94, Motions to Dismiss—Forum Non Conveniens, pp. 995-96, Motion to Abate, p. 997, Pretrial Motions, p. 998.

§2. PREFILING CONSIDERATIONS

§2.1 Notice to carrier. If the claim is covered by insurance, the defendant should read its policy and give its insurance carrier all required notices. *See* ***Harwell v. State Farm Mut. Auto. Ins. Co.***, 896 S.W.2d 170, 173-74 (Tex.1995) (D must notify carrier; notice of claim sent to carrier by P's lawyer was not sufficient); ***Struna v. Concord Ins. Servs.***, 11 S.W.3d 355, 359 (Tex.App.—Houston [1st Dist.] 2000, no pet.) (D must notify carrier whenever claim is made & forward papers). Unless the carrier receives proper notice of the suit, the carrier is not bound by the judgment. ***Harwell***, 896 S.W.2d at 175.

§2.2 Offer to settle. If the defendant receives a demand notice before the suit is filed, it should consider making a reasonable offer to settle. For cases filed on or after January 1, 2004, a defendant can recover litigation costs under CPRC ch. 42 if the other party rejected an offer of settlement that was significantly more favorable than the judgment. See "Offer of Settlement," ch. 7-G, p. 505. Under other statutes, a defendant's offer to settle can limit the damages. *See, e.g.*, CPRC §38.002(3) (tender limits attorney fees); Ins. Code art. 21.21, §16A(g) (tender limits actual damages); Bus. & Com. Code §17.5052(a) & (h) (tender limits actual damages & attorney fees).

§2.3 State vs. federal court. Once the defendant is served with the suit, it should consider whether it would prefer trying the case in federal court and, if so, whether the case is removable. For information about removing a case to federal court, see ***O'Connor's Federal Rules * Civil Trials***, "Removal & Remand," ch. 4, p. 181 (2004).

§2.4 Alternative dispute resolution (ADR). If the parties are required by statute or contract to submit a dispute to a form of alternative dispute resolution, the defendant should file a motion to abate and a motion to compel ADR after filing its answer. See "The ADR System," ch. 4-A, p. 204.

§3. DUE ORDER OF PLEADINGS

§3.1 Filing order. Even though strict "due order" of pleading was abolished in 1950, a defendant still must file the special appearance and the motion to transfer venue in a specific order. *See History of TRCP 84*, p. 688, this book. If the defendant files them out of order, it will waive them. ***Bluebonnet Farms v. Gibraltar Sav. Ass'n***, 618 S.W.2d 81, 83 (Tex.App.—Houston [1st Dist.] 1980, writ ref'd n.r.e.); *see, e.g.*, ***Allianz Risk Transfer Ltd. v. S.J. Camp & Co.***, 117 S.W.3d 92, 97 (Tex.App.—Tyler 2003, n.p.h.) (D filed motion to transfer venue & original answer one minute before filing special appearance; special appearance waived). The order of defendant's pleadings is as follows:

1. **Special appearance.** When challenging personal jurisdiction, the defendant must file a special appearance before any other pleading. TRCP 120a(1); *see* TRCP 86(1).

2. **Motion to transfer venue.** When challenging venue, the defendant must file a motion to transfer venue after a special appearance (if any) and before any other pleading. TRCP 86(1), 120a(1); *see* ***Massey v. Columbus State Bank***, 35 S.W.3d 697, 700 (Tex.App.—Houston [1st Dist.] 2000, pet. denied); ***Antonio v. Rico Marino, S.A.***, 910 S.W.2d 624, 630 (Tex.App.—Houston [14th Dist.] 1995, no writ).

3. Motion for forum non conveniens (FNC). When challenging the forum under CPRC §71.051, the defendant must file a motion for FNC after filing a special appearance (if any) or a motion to transfer venue (if any) and within 180 days from the last day to file a motion to transfer venue. CPRC §71.051(d); TRCP 86(1). See "Deadline," ch. 3-D, §3.2.4, p. 166. There is no deadline for filing a common-law FNC motion. See "Deadline to file," ch. 3-D, §4.1.3, p. 170.

4. Answer. After filing a special appearance or a motion to transfer venue or both, the defendant should file its answer and any other pleadings in response or to the plaintiff's petition.

§3.2 Exceptions to filing order. There are only a few exceptions to the rules on the order of filing. A defendant can take the following actions without waiving the special appearance or the motion to transfer venue.

1. Removal to federal court. The defendant may file a notice of removal to federal court before the special appearance without waiving the special appearance or the motion to transfer venue. ***Antonio***, 910 S.W.2d at 629.

2. Other pleadings. The defendant may file motions that are not related to the merits of the suit and do not invoke the court's general jurisdiction before the special appearance without waiving the special appearance or the motion to transfer venue. *See, e.g.*, ***Gentry v. Tucker***, 891 S.W.2d 766, 768 (Tex.App.—Texarkana 1995, no writ) (D did not waive venue by filing motion to continue temporary injunction hearing before answer date); ***Perkola v. Koelling & Assocs.***, 601 S.W.2d 110, 112 (Tex.App.—Dallas 1980, writ dism'd) (D did not waive venue by contesting temporary injunction). See "No waiver," ch. 3-B, §3.4, p. 148.

3. Correspondence with court. The defendant may correspond with the court without waiving the special appearance or the motion to transfer venue. *See, e.g.*, ***N803RA, Inc. v. Hammer***, 11 S.W.3d 363, 367 (Tex. App.—Houston [1st Dist.] 2000, no pet.) (letter to court was answer, but because letter also challenged jurisdiction, special appearance not waived); ***Moore v. Elektro-Mobil Technik GmbH***, 874 S.W.2d 324, 327 (Tex. App.—El Paso 1994, writ denied) (German company did not waive special appearance when it wrote to court stating service was improper, requesting case be dismissed, & making objections to interrogatories).

§3.3 Ruling order.

1. General rule – due order of pleading. The defendant should ask the court to rule first on the special appearance, then on venue, and then on other motions. *See* CPRC §15.063; TRCP 86(1), 120a(2); *see, e.g.*, ***Landry v. Daigrepont***, 35 S.W.3d 265, 267 (Tex.App.—Corpus Christi 2000, no pet.) (special appearance waived because D asked for ruling on motion for new trial first).

2. Exceptions. Without violating the due-order-of-pleading rule, the defendant may secure a ruling on the following:

(1) Motion for continuance. The defendant may secure a ruling on a motion for continuance of the hearing on special appearance, venue, or FNC, or on a motion to continue some preliminary motion filed by the plaintiff. *See* TRCP 120a(3) (rule permits continuance in special appearance); ***Dawson-Austin v. Austin***, 968 S.W.2d 319, 323 (Tex.1998) (special appearance not waived by filing motion for continuance after special appearance).

(2) P's motions. The defendant may ask the court to rule on the plaintiff's preliminary motions or on pleadings filed by the defendant in response to the plaintiff's pleadings. *See* ***Gentry***, 891 S.W.2d at 768; ***Perkola***, 601 S.W.2d at 112.

§4. CONSTRUCTING THE ORIGINAL ANSWER

§4.1 Options. There are three ways for a defendant to file its answer and other pleas and motions: (1) the answer and all other initial pleas and motions may be filed in one document; (2) the answer and each of the other pleas and motions may be filed separately; or (3) the answer and some of the pleas and motions may be filed in one document, with the other pleas and motions filed separately. When filed separately, the documents must be filed in the appropriate order; when included in one document, they should be listed in the appropriate order.

§4.2 Inclusive answer + motions. For practical reasons, the best procedure is to file an original answer containing some of the defendant's pleas and motions, and file other pleas and motions separately.

1. Original answer. The following is a series of considerations that will help construct the defendant's original answer in one document.

Part 1: Is the defendant a nonresident of Texas claiming it has not done business in Texas? If so, the first part of the answer must be a special appearance. See "Special Appearance—Challenging Personal Jurisdiction," ch. 3-B, p. 143.

Part 2: Is there another county in Texas where the defendant contends the suit should or could have been filed? If so, the next part of the answer must be a motion to transfer venue. See "Motion to Transfer—Challenging Venue," ch. 3-C, p. 152.

Part 3: Is there a court in another jurisdiction outside Texas that the defendant contends has jurisdiction over the lawsuit and is a more appropriate forum? If so, the defendant must file a motion for FNC. See "Forum Non Conveniens—Challenging the Texas Forum," ch. 3-D, p. 165.

Part 4: The next part of the answer is the general denial. See "General Denial," ch. 3-E, §3, p. 172.

Part 5: Does the defendant want to assert any of the pleas listed in TRCP 93? If so, the defendant must specifically plead them and verify the answer. See "Verified Pleas," ch. 3-E, §4, p. 172.

Part 6: Does the defendant want to plead a defense establishing an independent reason why the plaintiff cannot prevail? If so, the defendant must affirmatively plead those defenses. See "Affirmative Defenses," ch. 3-E, §5, p. 175.

Part 7: Did the plaintiff plead "all conditions precedent have been performed" according to TRCP 54? If so, to challenge this allegation the defendant must specifically deny the statement, identify the specific conditions with which the plaintiff did not comply, and verify the allegations. See "Denial of conditions precedent," ch. 3-E, §5.4, p. 178.

Part 8: Does the defendant have claims against the plaintiff or other persons? If so, the next part of the answer should identify the counterclaims, cross-claims, or third-party claims. TRCP 38, 97. See "Cross-actions," ch. 2-E, §2.2, p. 96.

Part 9: The next part of the answer is the request for disclosure. See "Request for Disclosure," ch. 3-E, §7, p. 181.

Part 10: The last part of the answer is the conclusion, prayer, signature block, and, when necessary, verification and affidavits.

2. Separate motions. There are often other pleadings the defendant may want to file. The following are the considerations for those pleadings.

Motion 1: Are there responsible third parties (as defined in CPRC §33.011(6)) that the defendant should designate? If so, the defendant should file a motion for leave to designate a person as an RTP. The motion must be filed at least 60 days before trial. See "Responsible third party," ch. 3-E, §6.4, p. 180. 03

Motion 2: Are there defects in the court's subject-matter jurisdiction that prevent this particular court from hearing the case? If so, the defendant should file a plea to challenge the jurisdiction. See "Plea to the Jurisdiction—Challenging the Court," ch. 3-F, p. 181.

Motion 3: Are there defects in the plaintiff's lawsuit that are apparent from the face of the plaintiff's petition? If so, the defendant should file special exceptions to object to the pleading defects and, if necessary, a motion for summary judgment. See "Special Exceptions—Challenging the Pleadings," ch. 3-G, p. 187.

Motion 4: Are there defects in the plaintiff's lawsuit that are not apparent from the petition itself? That is, must the defendant inform the court of facts not in the petition to illustrate the defect? If so, the defendant should file a verified motion to abate. Many of the matters the defendant files as part of a verified answer should also be the subject of a motion to abate. See "Motion to Abate—Challenging the Suit," ch. 3-H, p. 194.

§5. DEADLINE TO FILE DEFENDANT'S ANSWER & MOTIONS

See each subchapter for deadlines to file. For example, for the deadline to file an answer, see "Deadline to Answer," ch. 3-E, §2, p. 171.

§6. SUMMARY OF DEFENDANT'S PLEADINGS

Chart 3-1, below, matches the challenges defendants may make with the proper procedural steps.

3-1. SUMMARY OF DEFENDANT'S PLEADINGS

IF YOU WANT TO URGE THIS	FILE THIS
Challenging jurisdiction	
The defendant, a nonresident, has never conducted business in Texas & Texas courts do not have jurisdiction over it or its property.	A special appearance with a prayer to dismiss.
The court does not have jurisdiction over the subject matter of this suit.	A plea to the jurisdiction with a prayer to dismiss.
Challenging the court where the suit was filed	
The case should be tried in another county because this county is not a county of proper venue.	A motion to transfer venue.
The case should be tried in another county that is more convenient.	A motion to transfer venue.
The case should be tried in another county because of local prejudice.	A motion to change venue.
Another court outside Texas has jurisdiction & is more appropriate.	A motion for forum non conveniens with a prayer to stay or dismiss.
The same dispute between the same parties is pending in another court.	A verified denial & a motion to abate. After other suit is litigated, if nothing is left to litigate in this suit, file a motion to dismiss.
Challenging the pleadings	
The plaintiff did not plead notice or proof of the claim, as required by statute.	Special exceptions.
The plaintiff should amend to delete an unspecified claim for damages & plead damages specifically.	Special exceptions.
The plaintiff did not verify its petition.	Special exceptions.
The pleadings do not state a cause of action (*e.g.*, for fraud) because they do not include the element of injury.	Special exceptions.
The pleadings do not state a viable cause of action (*e.g.*, no cause of action for death of unborn child).	Special exceptions & a motion to dismiss, and, if necessary, a motion for summary judgment.
Challenging the suit	
The government is immune from suit.	A plea to the jurisdiction & a motion to dismiss.
The government is immune from liability.	An affirmative defense & a motion for summary judgment.
The suit is barred by a statute of limitations.	An affirmative defense & a motion for summary judgment.
The suit is barred by laches.	An affirmative defense & a motion for summary judgment.
The same dispute was litigated & resolved by final judgment.	An affirmative defense & a motion for summary judgment.

3-1. SUMMARY OF DEFENDANT'S PLEADINGS

IF YOU WANT TO URGE THIS	FILE THIS
The dispute is subject to arbitration.	A motion to abate & to compel arbitration.
The plaintiff's TRCP 54 conditions precedent were not met.	A verified denial listing conditions with which the plaintiff did not comply.
Challenging the parties	
The plaintiff (defendant) cannot sue (be sued) in that capacity.	A verified denial & a motion to abate. If the matter cannot be cured by an amendment, file a motion for summary judgment.
The plaintiff lacks standing to bring suit.	A plea to the jurisdiction.
Another entity is a necessary party to this suit.	A verified denial & a motion to abate.
The defendant is secondarily liable, & the plaintiff has not sued the principal.	A verified denial & a motion to abate.
The plaintiff is a foreign corporation doing business in Texas, has not registered with the Secretary of State, & cannot bring a suit for relief.	A verified denial & a motion to dismiss.
The plaintiff did not file an assumed name certificate.	A verified denial & a motion to abate.
The death of a party requires the substitution of a representative.	A motion to abate. If a representative is not substituted, the defendant must get a *scire facias* before moving to dismiss.
The plaintiff (or defendant) is not a corporation (or partnership), as pleaded.	A verified denial & a motion to abate. If the matter cannot be cured by amendment, file a motion for summary judgment.
The death of a party extinguished the cause of action.	A verified plea to the jurisdiction with a prayer to dismiss.
The defendant is a debtor in bankruptcy.	The bankruptcy order acts as an automatic stay. File a notice of bankruptcy with a copy of the bankruptcy petition.
Misnomer of the defendant.	A motion to abate alleging the defendant was sued in wrong name.
Wrong defendant.	A verified denial & a motion for summary judgment.
Challenging liability	
The defendant is not responsible for the plaintiff's injury.	A general denial & a motion for summary judgment.
Other persons are responsible for some or all of the plaintiff's injury.	A motion for leave to designate a responsible third party.
The defendant did not execute the contract as the plaintiff alleges.	A verified denial & a motion for summary judgment.
The endorsement on the note was not genuine.	A verified denial & a motion for summary judgment.
There was no consideration for the contract subject to the suit; the contract is usurious.	A verified denial & a motion for summary judgment.
A contingency in the contract precludes liability; the contract was modified; failure of consideration; mutual mistake.	An affirmative defense & a motion for summary judgment.
The defendant's debts were discharged in bankruptcy.	An affirmative defense & a motion for summary judgment.
Duress; estoppel; illegality; license; payment; waiver.	An affirmative defense & a motion for summary judgment.
The loss was within a specific exclusion to an insurance contract.	An affirmative defense & a motion for summary judgment.
Any other matter constituting avoidance.	An affirmative defense & a motion for summary judgment.

B. SPECIAL APPEARANCE—CHALLENGING PERSONAL JURISDICTION

§1. GENERAL

§1.1 Rule. TRCP 120a. See CPRC ch. 17.

§1.2 Purpose. A special appearance permits a nonresident defendant to challenge the court's personal jurisdiction over the defendant without becoming subject to the jurisdiction of Texas courts. TRCP 120a; ***Kawasaki Steel Corp. v. Middleton***, 699 S.W.2d 199, 201 (Tex.1985). The due process clause of the U.S. Constitution guarantees that a party cannot be bound by the judgment of a forum with which the party has established no meaningful contacts, ties, or relations. ***National Indus. Sand Ass'n v. Gibson***, 897 S.W.2d 769, 772 (Tex.1995). The only question addressed in the special appearance is whether a Texas court can constitutionally exercise jurisdiction over the defendant. ***Kawasaki***, 699 S.W.2d at 202.

§1.3 Forms & timetables. ***O'Connor's Texas Civil Forms***, FORMS 3B; Timetables, this book, Special Appearance, p. 992, Pretrial Motions, p. 998.

§1.4 Other references. Muldrow & Gray, *Treading the Mine Field: Suing and Defending Non-Residents in Texas State Courts*, 46 Baylor L.Rev. 581 (1994); Comment, *Personal Jurisdiction in Cyberspace*, 35 Hous. L.Rev. 453 (1998).

§2. SPECIAL APPEARANCE

§2.1 Deadline to file special appearance. The special appearance must be filed within the same time as the answer. See "Deadline to Answer," ch. 3-E, §2, p. 171.

§2.2 Due order of pleadings. The special appearance must be the first pleading the defendant files. See "Due Order of Pleadings," ch. 3-A, §3, p. 139. Every other pleading or motion is presumed to be subject to the court's ruling on the special appearance. ***Dawson-Austin v. Austin***, 968 S.W.2d 319, 322 (Tex.1998). See "No waiver," §3.4, p. 148.

§2.3 Allegations. The defendant must negate all grounds of personal jurisdiction included in the plaintiff's petition. ***BMC Software v. Marchand***, 83 S.W.3d 789, 793 (Tex.2002); ***CSR Ltd. v. Link***, 925 S.W.2d 591, 596 (Tex.1996); ***Siskind v. Villa Found. for Educ.***, 642 S.W.2d 434, 438 (Tex.1982); ***Tuscano v. Osterberg***, 82 S.W.3d 457, 462 (Tex.App.—El Paso 2002, no pet.). The defendant should plead and prove (1) it is not a Texas resident, (2) it did not have minimum contacts with Texas, and (3) even if it had some contacts with Texas, the exercise of jurisdiction will offend the traditional notions of fair play and substantial justice. ***BMC Software***, 83 S.W.3d at 795; ***Guardian Royal Exch. Assur. v. English China Clays***, 815 S.W.2d 223, 226 (Tex.1991). If the defendant produces evidence negating jurisdiction, the burden shifts to the plaintiff to show that the court has jurisdiction over the defendant. ***M.G.M. Grand Hotel v. Castro***, 8 S.W.3d 403, 408 (Tex.App.—Corpus Christi 1999, no pet.).

1. Not Texas resident. The defendant should state that it is not a resident of Texas. If a plaintiff does not allege the defendant did an act or conspired to do an act in Texas, the defendant's pleading and proof that it is a nonresident is enough to meet its burden of negating all potential bases of jurisdiction. ***Siskind***, 642 S.W.2d at 437-38; ***Frank A. Smith Sales v. Atlantic Aero***, 31 S.W.3d 742, 746 (Tex.App.—Corpus Christi 2000, no pet.); ***Hotel Partners v. KPMG Peat Marwick***, 847 S.W.2d 630, 634 (Tex.App.—Dallas 1993, writ denied).

CAUTION

The Corpus Christi Court of Appeals, relying on ***Kawasaki****, said in dicta that a defendant must challenge a defective allegation of personal jurisdiction in a motion to quash or else it waives the complaint, which is contrary to* ***Siskind*** *and the cases cited above. See* ***Exito Elecs. v. Trejo****, 99 S.W.3d 360, 367 (Tex.App.—Corpus Christi 2003, pet. filed 5-7-03).* ***Kawasaki*** *does not support the* ***Exito*** *holding. It is the plaintiff's burden to plead facts that confer jurisdiction over a nonresident. The defendant is required to negate any theory of jurisdiction pleaded by the plaintiff; it is not required to negate unpleaded theories of jurisdiction. See* ***Siskind****, 642 S.W.2d at 438. If a defendant follows the advice of* ***Exito*** *and challenges a defective allegation of personal jurisdiction in a motion to quash, it will subject itself to the trial court's jurisdiction. See TRCP 122.*

---

2. No minimum contacts. The defendant should state that Texas courts do not have jurisdiction over the defendant because the defendant did not purposefully establish minimum contacts with Texas. ***CSR***, 925 S.W.2d at 594-95; ***Guardian Royal***, 815 S.W.2d at 226-27; ***Schlobohm v. Schapiro***, 784 S.W.2d 355, 358 (Tex.1990); *cf.* ***Asahi Metal Indus. Co. v. Superior Ct. of Cal.***, 480 U.S. 102, 112-13, 107 S.Ct. 1026, 1032 (1987) (Japanese company that sold valve to Taiwanese tire company that sold tires in the U.S. was not subject to personal jurisdiction in California). The defendant faces the task of alleging and proving a negative—it did not have any (or enough) contacts with Texas to justify a Texas court claiming personal jurisdiction over the defendant or the property subject to the suit. *See* ***BMC Software***, 83 S.W.3d at 795; ***Siskind***, 642 S.W.2d at 438. The defendant's contacts with Texas can give rise to either specific or general jurisdiction. *See* ***BMC Software***, 83 S.W.3d at 795; ***Hoffmann-La Roche, Inc. v. Kwasnik***, 109 S.W.3d 21, 25 (Tex.App.—El Paso 2003, no pet.).

(1) Specific jurisdiction. To negate specific jurisdiction, the defendant should plead and prove the plaintiff's cause of action did not arise from or relate to the defendant's contacts with Texas. *See* ***BMC Software***, 83 S.W.3d at 796-97; ***Guardian Royal***, 815 S.W.2d at 227-28; ***Schlobohm***, 784 S.W.2d at 358.

(a) Sufficient. The following contacts were sufficient to establish specific jurisdiction: • Defendant put products into the "stream of commerce" with the reasonable expectation the products would enter Texas. ***Keen v. Ashot Ashkelon, Ltd.***, 748 S.W.2d 91, 93 (Tex.1988) (Israeli company that manufactured trailer supports knew its product might be used anywhere in the U.S. after being assembled as part of a trailer), *overruled on other grounds*, ***G.M. Corp. v. Sanchez***, 997 S.W.2d 584 (Tex.1999); ***Kawasaki Steel Corp. v. Middleton***, 699 S.W.2d 199, 201 (Tex.1985) (D annually sold $40-48 million dollars worth of steel that reached Texas consumers). • Joint venture between Florida company and Texas company, where both shared control, contracted for elevators to be delivered to Texas. ***Zac Smith & Co. v. Otis Elevator Co.***, 734 S.W.2d 662, 664-65 (Tex.1987). • Defendant purchased promissory notes executed by Texas parties, with the knowledge that the notes were the subject of litigation in Texas. ***Kelly Inv. v. Basic Capital Mgmt.***, 85 S.W.3d 371, 373-74 (Tex.App.—Dallas 2002, no pet.). • Defendant, over a five-year period, audited a Texas investment firm managed entirely in San Antonio that later was the subject of a securities fraud class action. ***Gutierrez v. Deloitte & Touche***, 100 S.W.3d 261, 272-73 (Tex.App.—San Antonio 2002, pet. dism'd). • Defendant repeatedly shipped its product to its Texas distributor. ***SPA Giacomini v. Lamping***, 42 S.W.3d 265, 273 (Tex.App.—Corpus Christi 2001, no pet.). • Defendant, an attorney, had four contracts with clients in Texas and corresponded with them about the progress of lawsuits. ***Cartlidge v. Hernandez***, 9 S.W.3d 341, 348 (Tex.App.—Houston [14th Dist.] 1999, no pet.). • Defendant, a sales agent who contracted with a Texas corporation, sent orders to Texas, received payments from Texas, and cashed checks drawn on a Texas bank. ***Billingsley Parts & Equip. v. Vose***, 881 S.W.2d 165, 169-70 (Tex.App.—Houston [1st Dist.] 1994, writ denied). • Defendant initiated negotiations over the telephone with a Texas resident, executed and returned to Texas a contract requiring payment in Texas, and wired the money to the plaintiff's account in Texas. ***Bissbort v. Wright Printing & Publ'g Co.***, 801 S.W.2d 588, 589 (Tex.App.—Fort Worth 1990, no writ).

(b) Insufficient. The following contacts were not sufficient to establish specific jurisdiction: • Chairman and CEO of wholly-owned subsidiary of defendant discussed in Texas offer of employment and stock options to plaintiff who was not present during the conversations. ***BMC Software***, 83 S.W.3d at 797. • Foreign manufacturer knew product would be shipped to Texas but did not design product for use or market it in Texas. ***CMMC v. Salinas***, 929 S.W.2d 435, 439 (Tex.1996). • An allegation of conspiracy between a Maryland lobbying organization and a Texas corporation. ***National Indus. Sand Ass'n v. Gibson***, 897 S.W.2d 769, 774-76 (Tex.1995). • Defendant, a foreign reinsurer, contracted with a foreign primary insurer to pay the primary insurer for claims paid to its insureds, some of whom lived in Texas. ***Malaysia British Assur. v. El Paso Reyco, Inc.***, 830 S.W.2d 919, 921 (Tex.1992). • Defendant initiated contract discussions with Texas corporation, entered into a contract with the corporation that was to be performed entirely in New York, and forwarded payment to Texas. ***Blair Comm. v. SES Survey Equip. Servs.***, 80 S.W.3d 723, 730 (Tex.App.—Houston [1st Dist.] 2002, no pet.). • Passive website that provided information and advertising. ***Gessmann v. Stephens***, 51 S.W.3d 329, 339 (Tex.App.—Tyler 2001, no pet.). • One of the plaintiffs traveled to Texas for reasons unrelated to suit and made one telephone call to defendants' agent to confirm a transaction unrelated to suit. ***Al-Turki v. Taher***, 958 S.W.2d 258, 262 (Tex.App.—Eastland 1997, pet. denied).

(2) General jurisdiction. To negate general jurisdiction, the defendant should plead and prove it did not have continuous or systematic contacts with Texas. *See* ***BMC Software v. Marchand***, 83 S.W.3d 789, 796 (Tex.2002); ***Guardian Royal Exchange Assur. v. English China Clays***, 815 S.W.2d 223, 228 (Tex.1991); ***Schlobohm***, 784 S.W.2d at 358. General jurisdiction requires a showing of substantial contacts with the forum, a more demanding minimum-contacts analysis than for specific jurisdiction. ***BMC Software***, 83 S.W.3d at 797; ***Schlobohm***, 784 S.W.2d at 357; ***Kwasnik***, 109 S.W.3d at 25. For example, a plaintiff cannot rely on the "stream of commerce" doctrine to establish general jurisdiction in Texas. ***Kwasnik***, 109 S.W.3d at 26; ***Lonza AG v. Blum***, 70 S.W.3d 184, 191 (Tex.App.—San Antonio 2001, pet. denied).

(a) Sufficient. The following contacts were sufficient to establish general jurisdiction: • Defendant made frequent trips to Texas to visit his children and, while in the state, conducted a job search. ***In re S.A.V.***, 837 S.W.2d 80, 86 (Tex.1992). • Defendant, who loaned money to a Texas corporation in exchange for stock, became the corporation's sole director, conducted the corporation's first meeting in Dallas, and personally guaranteed leases for the corporation. ***Schlobohm***, 784 S.W.2d at 356. • Defendant had a bank account in Texas used to exchange currency, invest money, deposit loans, and provide profits to subsidiary corporations. ***El Puerto de Liverpool v. Servi Mundo Llantero***, 82 S.W.3d 622, 633 (Tex.App.—Corpus Christi 2002, pet. dism'd). • Defendant company had 9,000 Texans as members, used an interactive website as part of its marketing efforts in Texas, and entered into a contract with a Texas company to be performed in Texas. ***Experimental Aircraft Ass'n v. Doctor***, 76 S.W.3d 496, 505-08 (Tex.App.—Houston [14th Dist.] 2002, no pet.). • Defendant company continuously used its trademarks and service marks in Texas to identify its cars and related parts and services. ***Daimler-Benz v. Olson***, 21 S.W.3d 707, 725 (Tex.App.—Austin 2000, pet. dism'd). • Defendant conducted business from a permanent office in Texas. ***James v. Illinois Cent. R.R.***, 965 S.W.2d 594, 598-99 (Tex.App.—Houston [1st Dist.] 1998, no pet.). • Defendant attorney who lived in Colorado was licensed to practice in Texas and handled Texas cases. ***Nikolai v. Strate***, 922 S.W.2d 229, 239 (Tex.App.—Fort Worth 1996, writ denied). • Defendant owned real estate in Texas that was involved in the lawsuit. ***Potkovick v. Regional Ventures***, 904 S.W.2d 846, 850 (Tex.App.—Eastland 1995, no writ). • Defendant, who lived in California, was director of two Texas corporations. ***Thorpe v. Volkert***, 882 S.W.2d 592, 596 (Tex.App.—Houston [1st Dist.] 1994, no writ). • Defendant signed a contract with a Texas company and made routine sales to Texas companies. ***G.E. Co. v. Brown & Ross Int'l Distrib.***, 804 S.W.2d 527, 531 (Tex.App.—Houston [1st Dist.] 1990, writ denied).

(b) Insufficient. The following contacts were not sufficient to establish general jurisdiction: • Defendant purchased helicopters, negotiated contracts, and trained its pilots in Texas. ***Helicopteros Nacionales de Colombia, S.A. v. Hall***, 466 U.S. 408, 413-16, 104 S.Ct. 1868, 1872-73 (1984). Nonprofit research organization sold products to Texas residents mostly by phone or written orders received in Maryland, purchased supplies from Texas vendors, and had representatives set up exhibit booths and distribute corporate publications at science conferences in Texas. ***American Type Culture Collection v. Coleman***, 83 S.W.3d 801, 807-08 (Tex.2002). • Defendant purchased products from wholly-owned subsidiary in Texas to distribute in Europe. ***BMC Software***, 83 S.W.3d at 797. • Australian company sold goods F.O.B. Australia and did not own property or solicit business in Texas. ***CSR Ltd. v. Link***, 925 S.W.2d 591, 595 (Tex.1996). • A Maryland lobbying organization mailed letters and publications to its membership, some of whom lived in Texas. ***National Indus.***, 897 S.W.2d at 774. • Chinese corporation shipped goods to Texas at the direction of a third party with whom it had contracted. ***Hitachi Shin Din Cable v. Cain***, 106 S.W.3d 776, 784-85 (Tex.App.—Texarkana 2003, no pet.). • German corporation owned indirect interests in six companies doing business in Texas. ***Preussag v. Coleman***, 16 S.W.3d 110, 123 (Tex.App.—Houston [1st Dist.] 2000, pet. dism'd).

3. Exercise of jurisdiction unfair. The defendant should state that the court's exercise of jurisdiction over the defendant and its property will offend traditional notions of fair play and substantial justice and is inconsistent with the constitutional requirements of due process. ***International Shoe Co. v. Washington***, 326 U.S. 310, 316, 66 S.Ct. 154, 158 (1945); ***Guardian Royal***, 815 S.W.2d at 232-33. The defendant should allege it would be better for the Texas court to forgo jurisdiction over the defendant, considering the following factors: (1) the burden on the defendant; (2) the interest of Texas in adjudicating the dispute; (3) the plaintiff's interest in obtaining convenient and effective relief; (4) the interstate judicial system's interest in obtaining the most efficient resolution of controversies; and (5) the shared interest of the states in furthering fundamental and substantive social policies. ***Guardian Royal***, 815 S.W.2d at 232; ***General Refractories Co. v. Martin***, 8 S.W.3d 818, 822-24 (Tex.App.—Beaumont 2000, pet. denied); *see* ***EMI Music Mex. v. Rodriguez***, 97 S.W.3d 847, 859 (Tex.App.—Corpus Christi 2003, no pet.) (only in rare cases will exercise of jurisdiction be deemed unfair when D has established minimum contacts with state); ***Minucci v. Sogevalor, S.A.***, 14 S.W.3d 790, 798-99 (Tex.App.—Houston [1st Dist.] 2000, no pet.) (same).

§2.4 Verification. The special appearance motion must be sworn. TRCP 120a(1); ***Casino Magic Corp. v. King***, 43 S.W.3d 14, 18 (Tex.App.—Dallas 2001, pet. denied); ***International Turbine Serv. v. Lovitt***, 881 S.W.2d 805, 808 (Tex.App.—Fort Worth 1994, writ denied). The motion cannot be verified based on information and belief. *See* ***International Turbine***, 881 S.W.2d at 808. An unverified special appearance may be amended to cure the defect, even after the trial court has ruled on the special appearance, as long as the amendment is filed before the defendant enters a general appearance. ***Dawson-Austin v. Austin***, 968 S.W.2d 319, 322 (Tex.1998). If the plaintiff does not object to an unverified special appearance, and sworn proof is presented at the hearing, the issue is tried by consent. ***General Refractories***, 8 S.W.3d at 820 n.1. If the special appearance motion is not verified, and no sworn proof attests to the veracity of the statements in the motion (either by affidavit or at the hearing), the court should deny the motion. *See* ***Casino***, 43 S.W.3d at 18.

§2.5 Affidavits. The defendant should file affidavits with the special appearance to provide evidentiary support for the factual allegations. See "Affidavits," §8.3.3, p. 150.

§2.6 Request hearing. The defendant must ask for and secure a hearing. ***Bruneio v. Bruneio***, 890 S.W.2d 150, 154 (Tex.App.—Corpus Christi 1994, no writ). If a defendant proceeds to trial without a ruling on the special appearance, it has made a general appearance and waives the issue of lack of personal jurisdiction. *Id.*; ***Seeley v. Seeley***, 690 S.W.2d 626, 627-28 (Tex.App.—Austin 1985, no writ).

§2.7 Amending the special appearance. A defendant may amend a special appearance. TRCP 120a(1); *see* ***Dawson-Austin***, 968 S.W.2d at 322 (amendment to add verification permitted after hearing but before entering a general appearance).

§3. WAIVER OF SPECIAL APPEARANCE

§3.1 Consent to jurisdiction. A defendant waives its objection to personal jurisdiction by executing a contract with a forum-selection clause selecting Texas as the forum. ***Abacan Tech. Servs. Ltd. v. Global Mar. Int'l Servs. Corp.***, 994 S.W.2d 839, 843-44 (Tex.App.—Houston [1st Dist.] 1999, no pet.).

§3.2 Failure to observe due order of pleadings. A defendant waives its objection to personal jurisdiction if it files its special appearance after any other pleading. See "Due Order of Pleadings," ch. 3-A, §3, p. 139.

§3.3 Making a general appearance. A defendant waives its objection to personal jurisdiction by making a general appearance. ***Von Briesen, Purtell & Roper v. French***, 78 S.W.3d 570, 575 (Tex.App.—Amarillo 2002, pet. dism'd). Every appearance before judgment that does not comply with TRCP 120a is a general appearance. TRCP 120a(1); ***Gutierrez v. Deloitte & Touche***, 100 S.W.3d 261, 267 (Tex.App.—San Antonio 2002, pet. dism'd); *e.g.*, ***Exito Elecs. v. Trejo***, 99 S.W.3d 360, 368-69 (Tex.App.—Corpus Christi 2003, pet. filed 5-7-03) (unconditional Rule 11 agreement filed before special appearance is general appearance). *But see* ***Angelou v. African Overseas Un.***, 33 S.W.3d 269, 275-76 (Tex.App.—Houston [14th Dist.] 2000, no pet.) (even though Rule 11 agreement to extend answer date was filed before special appearance, it was not general appearance because agreement did not seek affirmative action from court). If an appearance invokes the trial court's judgment on any question other than the court's jurisdiction, it is a general appearance. ***Gutierrez***, 100 S.W.3d at 267; ***Moore v. Elektro-Mobil Technik GmbH***, 874 S.W.2d 324, 327 (Tex.App.—El Paso 1994, writ denied).

§3.4 No waiver. A defendant does not make a general appearance (and does not waive its objection to personal jurisdiction) if it asks for intermediate relief by filing other pleadings and motions after the special appearance, as long as the documents neither acknowledge the trial court's jurisdiction nor seek court action other than a dismissal for lack of jurisdiction. *See, e.g.*, ***GFTA Trendanalysen v. Varme***, 991 S.W.2d 785, 786-87 (Tex.1999) (D did not consent to personal jurisdiction by challenging service in its special appearance).

PRACTICE TIP

In a pleading filed after the special appearance, the defendant is not required to include the statement that the pleading filed is "subject to the ruling on the special appearance" as long as the pleading does not acknowledge jurisdiction or ask for some action other than dismissal for lack of jurisdiction. See ***Dawson-Austin****, 968 S.W.2d at 322-23.*

---

1. Notice of removal. A defendant may file a notice of removal to federal court before the special appearance without waiving the special appearance or the motion to transfer venue. ***Antonio v. Rico Marino, S.A.***, 910 S.W.2d 624, 629 (Tex.App.—Houston [14th Dist.] 1995, no writ).

2. Motion for continuance. The defendant may file a motion for continuance without waiving its special appearance. ***Dawson-Austin***, 968 S.W.2d at 323.

3. Motion for new trial after default judgment. See §4, below.

4. Correspondence with court. See "Correspondence with court," ch. 3-A, §3.2.3, p. 140.

5. Discovery. See "Discovery," §6, below.

§4. SPECIAL APPEARANCE AFTER DEFAULT JUDGMENT

If a nonresident defendant discovers a default judgment was rendered against it before the deadline for filing a motion for new trial, the nonresident defendant should preserve the due order of pleading while challenging the default judgment by filing the documents in the following order: a special appearance, a motion for new trial, and an answer. *See* TRCP 120a(1) (special appearance must be filed before any other pleading or motion); *see, e.g.*, ***Lang v. Capital Res. Invs.***, 102 S.W.3d 861, 864 (Tex.App.—Dallas 2003, no pet.) (D filed special appearance and, subject to that, motion for new trial); ***Puri v. Mansukhani***, 973 S.W.2d 701, 706-07 (Tex.App.—Houston [14th Dist.] 1998, no pet.) (same); ***Koch Graphics v. Avantech, Inc.***, 803 S.W.2d 432, 433 (Tex.App.—Dallas 1991, no writ) (D filed special appearance and, subject to that, motion to quash, motion for new trial, and answer). The defendant must request a ruling on the special appearance before a ruling on any other motion. ***Landry v. Daigrepont***, 35 S.W.3d 265, 267 (Tex.App.—Corpus Christi 2000, no pet.). A motion for new trial and a motion to quash service, filed with or after a special appearance, do not waive the special appearance; matters in the same or a later instrument are subject to the special appearance. TRCP 120a(1); ***Dawson-Austin***, 968 S.W.2d at 322. The defendant may include language in the motion for new trial that it is ready to proceed to trial without waiving the special appearance as long as the motion does not acknowledge jurisdiction or ask for some action other than dismissal for lack of jurisdiction. *See* ***Lang***, 102 S.W.3d at 864; ***Puri***, 973 S.W.2d at 707.

§5. RESPONSE

The plaintiff may file a response challenging the defendant's allegations of lack of personal jurisdiction. The response should be verified and supported with affidavits. The plaintiff may respond to the defendant's special appearance in the following ways.

§5.1 Amend petition. If the defendant filed a bare-bones response and affidavit, alleging simply that it is a nonresident, the plaintiff should check its petition. See "Not Texas resident," §2.3.1, p. 144. If the plaintiff finds it did not allege any actions by the defendant in Texas, it should amend its pleading to include them. See "Over a nonresident," ch. 2-B, §4.1.2, p. 73.

§5.2 Object to procedural errors. The plaintiff should object to any procedural errors in the defendant's special appearance. If the plaintiff does not object, it will waive the error. *See, e.g.*, ***International Turbine Serv. v. Lovitt***, 881 S.W.2d 805, 808 (Tex.App.—Fort Worth 1994, writ denied) (P waived error in inadequate affidavit).

§5.3 Allege waiver by defendant. The plaintiff should be on the alert for any action the defendant takes that is inconsistent with a special appearance and can be construed as a general appearance. In the response, the plaintiff should allege the defendant waived its special appearance because (as is appropriate to the case) the defendant did not observe the "due order" of pleadings, the defendant made a general appearance, or the defendant did not limit the special appearance to the issue of personal jurisdiction.

§5.4 Challenge defendant's allegations. The plaintiff should challenge the defendant's factual grounds for denying jurisdiction and the defendant's legal interpretation of the factors that constitute jurisdiction over a nonresident.

1. Minimum contacts. The plaintiff should state that the court has jurisdiction over the defendant because the defendant purposefully established minimum contacts with Texas. ***Schlobohm v. Schapiro***, 784 S.W.2d 355, 358 (Tex.1990); *see* ***Guardian Royal Exchange Assur. v. English China Clays***, 815 S.W.2d 223, 232 (Tex.1991).

(1) Specific jurisdiction. To establish specific jurisdiction, the plaintiff should plead and prove its cause of action arose from or relates to the nonresident defendant's contacts with Texas. ***Schlobohm***, 784 S.W.2d at 358. Even a single act can support jurisdiction, as long as it is substantial. ***EMI Music Mex. v. Rodriguez***, 97 S.W.3d 847, 859 (Tex.App.—Corpus Christi 2003, no pet.); ***Royal Mortg. Corp. v. Montague***, 41 S.W.3d 721, 731 (Tex.App.—Fort Worth 2001, no pet.). See "Sufficient," §2.3.2(1)(a), p. 145.

(2) General jurisdiction. To establish general jurisdiction, the plaintiff should plead and prove the nonresident defendant had continuous and systematic contacts with Texas. ***Schlobohm***, 784 S.W.2d at 358. See "Sufficient," §2.3.2(2)(a), p. 146.

2. No issue of fair play. The plaintiff should plead and prove that the court's exercise of jurisdiction over the defendant and its property will not offend traditional notions of fair play and substantial justice and is consistent with the constitutional requirements of due process. ***Schlobohm***, 784 S.W.2d at 358-59.

§6. DISCOVERY

The parties may engage in discovery before the hearing on the special appearance. *See* TRCP 120a(1). The defendant does not waive its special appearance by engaging in discovery. *E.g.*, ***Silbaugh v. Ramirez***, ___ S.W.3d ___ (Tex.App.—Houston [1st Dist.] 2002, no pet.) (No. 01-02-01129-CV; 12-19-02) (filing discovery objections does not waive special appearance); ***Gutierrez v. Deloitte & Touche***, 100 S.W.3d 261, 267 (Tex.App.—San Antonio 2002, pet. dism'd) (filing mandamus to challenge discovery order does not waive special appearance); ***International Turbine***, 881 S.W.2d at 808-09 (filing motion for protective order to limit discovery to jurisdictional matters does not waive special appearance). Discovery conducted before the special appearance is resolved should be limited to issues related to the special appearance. *See* ***Dawson-Austin v. Austin***, 968 S.W.2d 319, 323-24 (Tex.1998). However, even if discovery involves the merits of the case, it does not waive the special appearance. ***Minucci v. Sogevalor, S.A.***, 14 S.W.3d 790, 801 (Tex.App.—Houston [1st Dist.] 2000, no pet.); ***Hotel Partners v. Craig***, 993 S.W.2d 116, 123 (Tex.App.—Dallas 1994, writ denied).

§7. CONTINUANCE

Although TRCP 120a does not identify the contents of a motion for continuance for a hearing on a special appearance, the party asking for a continuance should probably follow the outline for a continuance based on the need for additional evidence. See "Continuance for Additional Discovery," ch. 5-D, §8, p. 244.

§7.1 Plaintiff. TRCP 120a authorizes the court to grant the plaintiff's sworn motion for a continuance if the plaintiff cannot present facts by affidavit to respond to the special appearance and needs time to secure affidavits, take depositions, or engage in other discovery. TRCP 120a(3).

§7.2 Defendant. A defendant also may file a motion for continuance. *See, e.g.*, ***Dawson-Austin***, 968 S.W.2d at 323 (D filed motion for continuance on day of hearing on grounds that she had been given inadequate notice, her counsel had just been hired & was in trial, and discovery was necessary).

§8. HEARING

The hearing on a special appearance is for the receipt of evidence. ***Jack B. Anglin Co. v. Tipps***, 842 S.W.2d 266, 269 n.4 (Tex.1992).

§8.1 Nonjury. The hearing on a special appearance is before the court, not the jury. ***Roquemore v. Roquemore***, 431 S.W.2d 595, 601 (Tex.App.—Corpus Christi 1968, no writ).

§8.2 Defendant's burden. At the hearing on a special appearance, the nonresident defendant must disprove jurisdiction by negating all alleged grounds of personal jurisdiction. ***Kawasaki Steel Corp. v. Middleton***, 699 S.W.2d 199, 203 (Tex.1985); ***Siskind v. Villa Found. for Educ.***, 642 S.W.2d 434, 438 (Tex.1982).

§8.3 Evidence. TRCP 120a(3) lists the types of proof that are permitted at the hearing on a special appearance.

1. Stipulations. Stipulations must meet the requirements of TRCP 11; that is, they must be in writing and signed by the attorneys or parties and filed with the court, or made in open court and entered in the record. See "Agreements Between Lawyers – Rule 11," ch. 1-H, §9, p. 44.

2. Discovery. Discovery submitted to the court at the special appearance hearing may include requests for disclosure, interrogatories, depositions, requests for admissions, and documents produced through discovery. See "Discovery," ch. 6, p. 305.

3. Affidavits. Affidavits and attachments must meet certain requirements. They must be filed at least seven days before the hearing on the special appearance. TRCP 120a(3); ***Potkovick v. Regional Ventures***, 904 S.W.2d 846, 850 (Tex.App.—Eastland 1995, no writ). They must be made on personal knowledge, set forth specific facts that would be admissible as evidence, and affirmatively show the affiant is competent to testify. TRCP 120a(3); *see* ***SPA Giacomini v. Lamping***, 42 S.W.3d 265, 270 (Tex.App.—Corpus Christi 2001, no pet.); ***International Turbine***, 881 S.W.2d at 808. See "Affidavits," ch. 1-B, §4.14.2, p. 7.

4. Oral testimony. The trial court has the authority to consider live testimony from witnesses at the hearing. TRCP 120a(3); ***Anglin***, 842 S.W.2d at 269 n.4.

PRACTICE TIP

When the court is going to rely on both affidavits and oral testimony, to object to any of the statements in an affidavit, you should file objections to the affidavits on the ground that you will not have an opportunity to cross-examine the witness at the hearing. The court may require you to take the deposition of the witness. By objecting before the hearing, you will give the court and the other party notice that you intend to assert your right to cross-examine the witness.

---

§9. RULING

After the court rules on a special appearance, it should sign the appropriate order. TRCP 120a(4). Without a ruling on the special appearance, the party cannot preserve error for review. ***Wilson v. Chemco Chem. Co.***, 711 S.W.2d 265, 266 (Tex.App.—Dallas 1986, no writ).

§9.1 Sustains motion. If the court sustains the special appearance, it will sign an order of dismissal. TRCP 120a(4). If the court hears other motions and sustains them at the same time it sustains the special appearance, the order should state that the other rulings are made in the alternative. *See, e.g.*, ***Antonio v. Rico Marino, S.A.***, 910 S.W.2d 624, 626 (Tex.App.—Houston [14th Dist.] 1995, no writ) (court ordered dismissal based on special appearance & forum non conveniens and sustained D's venue challenge). If the order sustains and dismisses the special appearance first, with the other rulings as alternate reasons to dismiss or transfer, on appeal the plaintiff is forced to challenge each ruling in a domino-like fashion.

§9.2 Overrules motion. If the court overrules the special appearance, it will sign an order overruling the motion and continue with the trial of the case. Once the court overrules the defendant's special appearance, the defendant's participation in the trial does not waive its objection to jurisdiction. TRCP 120a(4); ***N.H. Helicopters v. Brown***, 841 S.W.2d 424, 425 (Tex.App.—Dallas 1992, orig. proceeding).

§9.3 Sanctions. The court may impose sanctions for affidavits that violate TRCP 13 and CPRC chapter 10. *See* TRCP 120a(3); *see, e.g.*, ***Skepnek v. Mynatt***, 8 S.W.3d 377, 381-82 (Tex.App.—El Paso 1999, pet. denied) (attorney fined $30,000 for filing special appearance that was groundless, presented for improper purposes, & based on false affidavit of president of corporation).

§10. FINDINGS OF FACT

The party who receives an adverse ruling on the special appearance should request findings of fact. ***Goodenbour v. Goodenbour***, 64 S.W.3d 69, 75 (Tex.App.—Austin 2001, pet. denied); *see* TRCP 296; *see also* TRAP 28.1 (trial court may file findings of fact after rendering interlocutory order). When no findings of fact are filed, all facts necessary to support the judgment and supported by the evidence are implied. ***BMC Software v. Marchand***, 83 S.W.3d 789, 795 (Tex.2002); *see* ***American Type Culture Collection v. Coleman***, 83 S.W.3d 801, 806 (Tex.2002). See "Jurisdictional challenge," ch. 10-E, §2.3.2(2), p. 643.

§11. REVIEW

§11.1 Record. If the trial court received evidence at a hearing, the reporter's record is necessary on appeal. If the trial court did not hear evidence and the court's order reflects that the motion was considered on the filed evidence, the reporter's record is not necessary. ***Antonio***, 910 S.W.2d at 626.

§11.2 Interlocutory review.

1. Appeal. An order granting or denying a special appearance may be immediately appealed (except in a suit brought under the Family Code). CPRC §51.014(a)(7). See ***O'Connor's Texas Civil Appeals***, "Special appearance," ch. 11-B, §2.2.1(6), p. 11 (2002-03). For an interlocutory review of the special appearance, the appellant must file a notice of appeal within 20 days after the trial court signs the order. ***Raymond Overseas Holding v. Curry***, 955 S.W.2d 470, 471 (Tex.App.—Fort Worth 1997, orig. proceeding). See ***O'Connor's Texas Civil Appeals***, "Appeals That Must Be Accelerated," ch. 13-C, §4, p. 69.

2. Stay of trial. The interlocutory appeal of an order granting a special appearance automatically stays the commencement of trial during the appeal. *See* CPRC §51.014(b). The interlocutory appeal of an order denying a special appearance does not automatically stay the commencement of trial during the appeal. *Id.* §51.014(c). For a discussion of when the defendant may be entitled to a stay after the denial of a special appearance, see ***O'Connor's Texas Civil Appeals***, "Automatic stay after motion denied," ch. 13-P, §3.2, p. 133. For the requirements of an agreed stay, see ***O'Connor's Texas Civil Appeals***, "Stay by agreed motion," ch. 13-P, §3.3, p. 133.

§11.3 Mandamus. Generally, mandamus is not an appropriate method to review orders denying a special appearance. ***K.D.F. v. Rex***, 878 S.W.2d 589, 592 (Tex.1994); *see* ***Raymond Overseas***, 955 S.W.2d at 471. However, a party may be entitled to mandamus relief from the denial of a special appearance when "exceptional circumstances" make appeal an inadequate remedy. *E.g.*, ***CSR Ltd. v. Link***, 925 S.W.2d 591, 596 (Tex.1996) (Supreme Court could review denial of special appearance in mass tort case by mandamus); *see also* ***National Indus. Sand Ass'n v. Gibson***, 897 S.W.2d 769, 771 (Tex.1995) (mandamus appropriate to review denial of special appearance when harm to D becomes irreparable).

§11.4 Standard of review. The issue on appeal is whether the nonresident defendant negated all possible grounds of personal jurisdiction. ***Kawasaki Steel Corp. v. Middleton***, 699 S.W.2d 199, 203 (Tex.1985); ***Minucci v. Sogevalor, S.A.***, 14 S.W.3d 790, 794 (Tex.App.—Houston [1st Dist.] 2000, no pet.). The courts of appeals should review the trial court's factual findings for legal and factual sufficiency and review the trial court's legal conclusions de novo. ***American Type***, 83 S.W.3d at 806; *see* ***BMC Software***, 83 S.W.3d at 794.

C. MOTION TO TRANSFER—CHALLENGING VENUE

§1. GENERAL

§1.1 Rules. TRCP 85-89, 255-261. See Tex. Const. art. 3, §45; CPRC ch. 15.

§1.2 Purpose. A motion to transfer venue is the procedure to transfer the case to another county in Texas. There are three types of motions to transfer: (1) improper county, (2) convenience of the parties and witnesses, and (3) local prejudice. Only the defendant can file the first and second types; either the plaintiff or the defendant can file the third type. *See* ***Tenneco, Inc. v. Salyer***, 739 S.W.2d 448, 449 (Tex.App.—Corpus Christi 1987, orig. proceeding).

§1.3 Forms & timetables. ***O'Connor's Texas Civil Forms***, FORMS 3C; Timetables, this book, Motion to Transfer Venue—Wrong or Inconvenient County, p. 993, Motion to Change Venue—Local Prejudice, p. 994.

NOTE

For the rules governing selection of venue, see "Choosing the Court—Venue," ch. 2-G, p. 111.

---

§2. IMPROPER COUNTY

Venue selection presupposes the parties to the lawsuit have choices and preferences about where the case will be tried. ***Wilson v. Texas Parks & Wildlife Dept.***, 886 S.W.2d 259, 260 (Tex.1994). "Proper venue" means venue under the mandatory venue provisions, or, if none apply, venue under the general venue rule or the permissive venue provisions. CPRC §15.001(b); ***O'Quinn v. Hall***, 77 S.W.3d 438, 448-49 (Tex.App.—Corpus Christi 2002, no pet.).

§2.1 Plaintiff's choice of venue. The plaintiff has the first choice to fix venue in a proper county; the plaintiff does this by filing the suit in the proper county of its choice. ***In re Masonite Corp.***, 997 S.W.2d 194, 197 (Tex.1999).

§2.2 Defendant's procedure. A defendant raises the question of proper venue by challenging the plaintiff's choice through a motion to transfer venue. TRCP 86(1); ***Wichita Cty. v. Hart***, 917 S.W.2d 779, 781 (Tex.1996); ***Wilson***, 886 S.W.2d at 260. Without a motion, the court cannot transfer venue, even to a county of proper venue. ***Masonite***, 997 S.W.2d at 198.

1. **Deadline to file motion to transfer.** The deadline for the motion to transfer venue is the same as the deadline for filing the answer. *See* CPRC §15.063; TRCP 86(1). See "Deadline to Answer," ch. 3-E, §2, p. 171.

2. **Due order of pleading.** The defendant must file a motion to transfer venue before or along with all other pleadings or motions except the special appearance, which must be filed first. TRCP 86(1). See "Due Order of Pleadings," ch. 3-A, §3, p. 139. The defendant will waive its objection to improper venue if it files a motion to

transfer after it files an answer. ***Sutton v. State Bar***, 750 S.W.2d 853, 855 (Tex.App.—El Paso 1988, writ denied); *see* ***Kshatrya v. Texas Workforce Comm'n***, 97 S.W.3d 825, 832 (Tex.App.—Dallas 2003, no pet.). The due-order-of-pleading rule does not apply to a motion to transfer based on local prejudice under TRCP 257-259. See "Local Prejudice," §4, p. 161.

3. Form. The motion to transfer venue must be in writing and may be made either as part of the defendant's first responsive pleading or as a separate document. TRCP 86(1), (2). See ***O'Connor's*** FORMS 3C:01-02.

4. No affidavit necessary. The defendant may, but is not required to, support the motion with affidavits when it is filed. TRCP 86(3) (last paragraph); ***GeoChem Tech Corp. v. Verseckes***, 962 S.W.2d 541, 543 (Tex. 1998). The question of proper venue is raised by simply objecting to a plaintiff's venue choice through a motion to transfer venue. ***Billings v. Concordia Heritage Ass'n***, 960 S.W.2d 688, 692 (Tex.App.—El Paso 1997, pet. denied). However, once the plaintiff responds to the motion and denies the defendant's venue facts, the defendant must provide proof as required by TRCP 87(3). *See* TRCP 87(2).

5. Request hearing. The defendant must request a hearing, give the plaintiff notice of the hearing, and press the court to hold a hearing. *See* TRCP 87(1); *see, e.g.*, ***Grozier v. L-B Sprinkler & Plumbing Repair***, 744 S.W.2d 306, 311 (Tex.App.—Fort Worth 1988, writ denied) (although D asked for hearing, he did not ask for setting); *see also* ***Bristol v. Placid Oil Co.***, 74 S.W.3d 156, 159 (Tex.App.—Amarillo 2002, no pet.) (32-month delay between motion to transfer & ruling not attributable to D because D's motion asked for hearing). See "Procedure for hearing," §2.11, p. 157.

6. No codefendant waiver. Although a defendant can waive its own venue rights, it cannot waive the venue rights of a codefendant. No act or omission constituting waiver by one defendant impairs the rights of any other defendant to challenge venue. CPRC §15.0641; ***WTFO, Inc. v. Braithwaite***, 899 S.W.2d 709, 718 (Tex.App.—Dallas 1995, no writ); *e.g.*, ***Pearson v. Jones Co.***, 898 S.W.2d 329, 331-32 (Tex.App.—Eastland 1994, no writ) (waiver of venue by 2 Ds by filing answers does not waive other D's venue objection).

§2.3 Defendant's grounds. The defendant should allege that the county where the plaintiff filed the suit is not the proper venue for one of the following reasons:

1. Parties agreed to transfer.

(1) Contractual venue before suit is filed. The parties signed a written agreement in a "major transaction" that included an agreement on venue, and the suit must be transferred according to that agreement. CPRC §15.020(a)-(c). See "Contractual agreement for venue," ch. 2-G, §4.1.11, p. 113.

(2) Written consent after suit is filed. The parties signed a written consent to transfer the case to another county of proper venue. CPRC §15.063(3); TRCP 255. There is no deadline for the parties to file a written consent. TRCP 86(1); *see* ***Glover v. Glover***, 287 S.W.2d 287, 288 (Tex.App.—Eastland 1956, writ dism'd). The agreement should be filed in the court where the case is pending. *See* ***Farris v. Ray***, 895 S.W.2d 351, 352 (Tex. 1995).

2. Venue is mandatory elsewhere. A mandatory venue provision requires transfer to a county other than the county of suit. *See* CPRC §15.001(b)(1). The defendant must identify the mandatory venue provision that requires transfer to a specific county. For a list of mandatory venue provisions, see "Mandatory Venue Provisions," ch. 2-G, §4, p. 112.

3. Venue under general venue rule is elsewhere. No mandatory venue provision applies, but venue is not proper in the county of suit because the general venue rule requires transfer to another county. *See* CPRC §15.002. The defendant must identify the specific part of the statute that was violated when the plaintiff filed suit and the specific county to which the suit should be transferred. For a discussion of the general venue rule, see "General Venue Rule," ch. 2-G, §5, p. 115.

4. Venue is permissive elsewhere. No mandatory venue provision applies, venue is not proper in the county of suit, and venue is permissive in another county. The defendant must state why the plaintiff's choice of venue is not proper and identify the permissive venue provision that permits transfer to a specific county. For a list of permissive venue provisions, see "Permissive Venue Provisions," ch. 2-G, §6, p. 116.

5. Venue is improper for some plaintiffs. Venue is improper for one plaintiff but not for the others, and that specific plaintiff cannot establish venue under a mandatory venue provision, the general venue rule, or a permissive venue provision. *See* CPRC §15.003. See "Multiple plaintiffs," ch. 2-G, §7.1, p. 117.

6. Venue is more convenient elsewhere. No mandatory venue provision applies, and although suit is proper in the county of suit, venue is more convenient in another county of proper venue. CPRC §15.002(b). A defendant probably should include a request for transfer based on convenience in every motion because a ruling granting a convenience transfer is not subject to review. *Id.* §15.002(c). See "Convenience Transfer," §3, p. 160.

§2.4 Defendant's other allegations.

1. Specifically deny plaintiff's venue facts. The defendant must specifically deny the venue facts in the plaintiff's petition; if not, they are taken as true. TRCP 87(3)(a). See "Specific denial of venue facts," §2.11.4(1), p. 158. The following are some of the matters the defendant may wish to deny:

(1) The accident did not happen in this county as the plaintiff alleges; it happened in [*identify other county*]. CPRC §15.002(a)(1).

(2) The defendant did not reside in this county at the time of the accident. CPRC §15.002(a)(2). A statement that the defendant resides in another county is not equivalent to a statement that the defendant does not reside in the county of suit. ***Garcia v. Garza***, 70 S.W.3d 362, 370 (Tex.App.—Corpus Christi 2002, pet. granted 10-10-02). A person may have more than one residence. *Id.*

(3) The defendant does not have a principal office in this county because the decision-makers for the defendant do not conduct the organization's daily affairs within Texas from its office in this county. CPRC §§15.001(a), 15.002(a)(3); ***In re Missouri Pac. R.R.***, 998 S.W.2d 212, 220 (Tex.1999). The defendant can add that it merely has an agent or representative in this county and should supply facts showing that the daily affairs of the organization are conducted elsewhere.

(4) This county is not a county of proper or mandatory venue as the plaintiff alleges because [*identify reasons*]. CPRC §15.001(b).

(5) Another defendant is not a properly joined defendant; once the other defendant is severed, venue is not proper in this county because [*identify reasons*]. *See* ***Bleeker v. Villarreal***, 941 S.W.2d 163, 175 (Tex. App.—Corpus Christi 1996, writ dism'd).

2. Allege specific county. The motion to transfer venue must ask the court to transfer the case to a specific county and provide facts showing why venue is proper in that county. *See* TRCP 86(3). Nothing in the venue rule or the CPRC prevents a defendant from alleging two or more counties are counties of proper venue. *See* ***GeoChem Tech***, 962 S.W.2d at 543-44; ***Rosales v. H.E. Butt Grocery Co.***, 905 S.W.2d 745, 748 (Tex.App.—San Antonio 1995, writ denied). By filing a motion to transfer to a county where the cause of action accrued, the defendant does not admit the plaintiff has a valid claim. TRCP 87(2)(b). See "Prima facie proof," §2.11.4(2), p. 158.

3. File motion to sever & transfer. Severance is contemplated as part of venue procedure. *See* TRCP 89. Before a suit can be divided into two parts and one part transferred to another county, the court must apply the following three-part test: (1) the controversy must involve more than one cause of action, (2) the severed cause must be one that would be the proper subject of a lawsuit if independently asserted, and (3) the severed and the remaining causes must not be so intertwined as to involve the same facts and issues. ***Guaranty Fed. Sav. Bank v. Horseshoe Oper. Co.***, 793 S.W.2d 652, 658 (Tex.1990). See "Motion for Severance," ch. 5-H, §3, p. 263.

NOTE

Because each plaintiff must be able to maintain suit in the county of suit (see CPRC §15.003(a)), when a defendant is sued by two plaintiffs and venue for one of the plaintiffs is not proper in that county, the defendant may move to sever and transfer that plaintiff's cause of action to a proper venue.

§2.5 Plaintiff's procedure. The plaintiff is not required to file a response to a motion to transfer, unless proof is necessary. TRCP 86(4). As a general rule, the plaintiff should file a response and address the grounds asserted in the defendant's motion. See §2.7, below.

1. Deadline. The deadline to file a response to the motion to transfer is 30 days before the venue hearing, unless the plaintiff secures permission to file it later. TRCP 87(1); ***Moriarty v. Williams***, 752 S.W.2d 610, 611 (Tex.App.—El Paso 1988, writ denied). See "Continuance," §2.10.3, p. 157.

2. Form. The response to the motion to transfer venue must be in writing. *See* TRCP 86(1). See *O'Connor's* FORMS 3C:05-06.

3. Affidavits & attachments. To establish its factual allegations by prima facie proof once the defendant has specifically denied the plaintiff's venue facts, the plaintiff must file affidavits and, when necessary, discovery products. The discovery products should be attached to affidavits verifying their authenticity. See "Procedure for securing evidence," §2.10, p. 157.

§2.6 Plaintiff's response to defendant's grounds.

1. Venue proper under general rule. If the defendant alleged that the general venue rule requires a transfer, the plaintiff should argue that the plaintiff's choice of county complies with the requirements of the general venue rule because (1) a substantial part of the events or omissions occurred in this county; (2) the defendant, a natural person, resides in this county; (3) the defendant, a corporation or other organization, has a principal office in this county in Texas; or (4) if no other provision in CPRC §15.002(a) applies, the suit is proper in this county because it is where the plaintiff resided when the cause of action accrued. CPRC §15.002(a); *see, e.g.*, ***Missouri Pac.***, 998 S.W.2d at 221 (Ps did not show D's office in county of suit was a principal office as compared to responsibility and authority exercised by company officials in another county in Texas).

2. Venue not mandatory elsewhere. If the defendant alleged that a mandatory venue provision requires transfer to another county, the plaintiff should argue that the defendant's choice of county is not a mandatory county for venue. *See* CPRC §15.001(b)(1).

3. Venue not permissive elsewhere. If the defendant alleged that venue is not proper in the county of suit and is permissive in another county, the plaintiff should argue that (1) venue is proper and (2) the defendant's choice of county is not a permissive county for venue.

4. Venue or joinder proper to all plaintiffs. If the defendant alleged that venue was improper for one of the plaintiffs, that plaintiff has two options.

(1) Venue proper. The plaintiff can establish proper venue under the general venue rule, a mandatory venue provision, or a permissive venue provision. ***O'Quinn v. Hall***, 77 S.W.3d 438, 448-49 (Tex.App.—Corpus Christi 2002, no pet.); *see* CPRC §§15.001(b), 15.003.

(2) Joinder proper under §15.003(a). If the plaintiff cannot establish proper venue, that plaintiff's part of the suit, including its claims and causes of action, must be transferred to a county of proper venue or dismissed, whichever is appropriate, unless that plaintiff establishes, independently of every other plaintiff, all of the following:

(a) Joinder of that plaintiff or intervention by that plaintiff is proper under the TRCPs. CPRC §15.003(a)(1); *see also* TRCP 40 (permissive joinder), TRCP 43 (interpleader), TRCP 60 & 61 (intervention), TRCP 174 (consolidation).

(b) Maintaining venue for that plaintiff in the county of suit does not unfairly prejudice another party to the suit. CPRC §15.003(a)(2).

(c) There is an essential need to have that plaintiff's claim tried in the county where the suit is pending. *Id.* §15.003(a)(3). The "essential need" requirement means that each plaintiff must demonstrate it is "indispensably necessary" to try its claims in that county; "essential" means that it is "necessary, such that one cannot do without it." ***Surgitek v. Abel***, 997 S.W.2d 598, 604 (Tex.1999); *see* ***O'Quinn***, 77 S.W.3d at 451; ***American Home Prods. Corp. v. Burrough***, 998 S.W.2d 696, 699-700 (Tex.App.—Eastland 1999, no pet.). It is not sufficient for the plaintiff to prove it must pool resources against common experts and issues. ***Surgitek***, 997 S.W.2d at 604; *see* ***American Home Prods. Corp. v. Bernal***, 5 S.W.3d 344, 347-48 (Tex.App.—Corpus Christi 1999, no pet.).

(d) The county where the suit is pending is a fair and convenient venue for that plaintiff seeking to join in or maintain venue and for all persons against whom the suit is brought. CPRC §15.003(a)(4).

5. Deny defendant's venue facts. When appropriate, the plaintiff should specifically deny the venue facts pleaded by the defendant. Unless the plaintiff specifically denies them, the defendant's venue facts will be taken as true. TRCP 87(3)(a). See "Specific denial of venue facts," §2.11.4(1), p. 158.

6. Allege waiver. When appropriate, the plaintiff should allege the defendant waived a change of venue (*e.g.*, the defendant waived venue by filing its motion to transfer after filing its answer). See "Due order of pleading," §2.2.2, p. 152.

§2.7 Plaintiff's proof.

1. Proof of denied venue facts. If the defendant specifically denied the plaintiff's venue facts, the plaintiff must make a prima facie case of those facts through sworn proof. TRCP 87(3)(a); ***In re Missouri Pac. R.R.***, 998 S.W.2d 212, 216 (Tex.1999); ***GeoChem Tech Corp. v. Verseckes***, 962 S.W.2d 541, 543 (Tex.1998); ***Rosales v. H.E. Butt Grocery Co.***, 905 S.W.2d 745, 748-49 (Tex.App.—San Antonio 1995, writ denied); *see, e.g.*, ***Maranatha Temple v. Enterprise Prods. Co.***, 833 S.W.2d 736, 740 (Tex.App.—Houston [1st Dist.] 1992, writ denied) (because Ds did not deny venue facts specifically, P was not required to make prima facie proof).

2. Proof of joinder elements. The plaintiff is required to offer prima facie proof of each of the four joinder elements of CPRC §15.003(a). ***Surgitek***, 997 S.W.2d at 602. See §2.6.4(2), above.

3. No proof of cause of action. The plaintiff is not required to prove the existence of a cause of action. TRCP 87(2)(b), (3)(a). By its pleading, the plaintiff establishes all the elements of its cause of action, which the defendant cannot controvert for venue purposes.

§2.8 Plaintiff's other options.

1. Amend petition. The plaintiff may add or subtract claims to establish proper venue. The plaintiff must file an amended petition at least seven days before the hearing on the motion to transfer. TRCP 63. If the plaintiff is timely in amending its petition, the court must consider the amended petition at the hearing. *See* ***Watson v. City of Odessa***, 893 S.W.2d 197, 199-200 (Tex.App.—El Paso 1995, writ denied) (P amended petition to delete claim on which motion to transfer was based); ***Moriarty v. Williams***, 752 S.W.2d 610, 611 (Tex.App.—El Paso 1988, writ denied) (P amended petition to add claims not addressed by D's motion to transfer).

2. Take nonsuit. In some circumstances, the plaintiff may be able to avoid an unfavorable venue ruling by taking a nonsuit of the entire case and refiling the case in another county. *See* ***GeoChem Tech***, 962 S.W.2d at 543. If the plaintiff nonsuits a case after the defendant files a motion to transfer and before the court rules on the motion, the dismissal does not fix venue in the county designated in the defendant's motion. *See id.* at 544. Upon refiling, the plaintiff does not lose the right to choose between two counties where mandatory venue is proper by filing its first suit in a county where venue was improper. *Id.* The court must consider the state of the record at the time the nonsuit was filed. *Id.* at 543; *see, e.g.*, ***Peysen v. Dawson***, 974 S.W.2d 377, 379-80 (Tex. App.—San Antonio 1998, no pet.) (venue not fixed in Bexar County because Ds had not challenged venue at time of nonsuit). After the nonsuit, the court in which the case is pending must sign the order of nonsuit; that court cannot transfer the suit to the defendant's choice of county. ***Zimmerman v. Ottis***, 941 S.W.2d 259, 263 (Tex. App.—Corpus Christi 1996, orig. proceeding).

§2.9 Procedure for defendant's reply. The defendant does not need to file a reply to the plaintiff's response; the reply is optional. TRCP 87(1).

1. Deadline. The deadline to file a reply to the plaintiff's response is seven days before the venue hearing, unless the defendant secures permission to file it later. TRCP 87(1). See §2.10.3, below.

2. Affidavits & attachments. If the plaintiff specifically denied the defendant's venue facts, the defendant must file affidavits and, if necessary, discovery establishing those facts by prima facie proof. TRCP 87(3)(a). See §2.10, below.

§2.10 Procedure for securing evidence.

1. Affidavits. The parties may support their factual allegations with affidavits and sworn proof attached to the affidavits. Affidavits must be made on personal knowledge, set forth specific facts that would be admissible in evidence, and show that the affiant is competent to testify. TRCP 87(3)(a). For the requirements of the affidavit, see "Affidavits," ch. 1-B, §4.14.2, p. 7.

2. Discovery. The parties may engage in discovery for the motion to transfer venue and for the case-in-chief without waiving the issue of venue. TRCP 88. Reasonable discovery is permitted to support or oppose the motion. TRCP 88, 258; ***Beard v. Gonzalez***, 924 S.W.2d 763, 765 (Tex.App.—El Paso 1996, orig. proceeding) (motion under TRCP 257); ***City of La Grange v. McBee***, 923 S.W.2d 89, 91 (Tex.App.—Houston [1st Dist.] 1996, writ denied) (same). The parties must be given reasonable time to conduct discovery before the venue hearing. ***Union Carbide Corp. v. Moye***, 798 S.W.2d 792, 793 (Tex.1990) (motion under TRCP 257); *see also* ***Bridgestone/Firestone, Inc. v. 13th Ct. of Appeals***, 929 S.W.2d 440, 442 (Tex.1996) (5 months & 1 continuance of hearing was reasonable time). To be considered at the hearing on the motion to transfer, the discovery must be attached to, or incorporated by reference in, an affidavit of a party, witness, or attorney who has knowledge of the discovery. TRCP 88. See TRCP 87(3)(a) for the requirements for these affidavits.

3. Continuance. If one of the parties needs additional time to collect affidavits and conduct discovery on the issue of venue, it should file a motion for continuance. ***Beard***, 924 S.W.2d at 765 (motion under TRCP 257); *see* ***McBee***, 923 S.W.2d at 91 (same). See "Continuance for Additional Discovery," ch. 5-D, §8, p. 244.

§2.11 Procedure for hearing. The court cannot rule on the motion without a hearing. ***Henderson v. O'Neill***, 797 S.W.2d 905, 905 (Tex.1990). The hearing must be held promptly and in a reasonable time before the beginning of the trial on the merits. TRCP 87(1).

1. Burden to ask for hearing. The defendant must request a hearing on its motion within a reasonable time. TRCP 87(1); *e.g.*, ***Whitworth v. Kuhn***, 734 S.W.2d 108, 111 (Tex.App.—Austin 1987, no writ) (1-year delay between filing motion to transfer & requesting hearing showed lack of diligence); *see also* ***Accent Energy Corp. v. Gillman***, 824 S.W.2d 274, 276-77 (Tex.App.—Amarillo 1992, writ denied) (3-year delay reasonable because P asked for continuance & filed amended pleadings after motion set for hearing).

2. Notice of hearing. The court must give the parties at least 45 days' notice of the hearing on the motion. TRCP 87(1); ***HCA Health Servs. v. Salinas***, 838 S.W.2d 246, 247-48 (Tex.1992); ***Henderson***, 797 S.W.2d at 905; ***Orion Enters. v. Pope***, 927 S.W.2d 654, 657 (Tex.App.—San Antonio 1996, orig. proceeding); *cf.* ***Beard***, 924 S.W.2d at 765 (45 days' notice required for motion under TRCP 257); ***McBee***, 923 S.W.2d at 91 (same). To preserve an objection to lack of sufficient notice, the party must file a written objection and a motion for continuance. ***Beard***, 924 S.W.2d at 765; ***Gonzalez v. Nielson***, 770 S.W.2d 99, 101 (Tex.App.—Corpus Christi 1989, writ denied).

3. Hearing. The motion may be submitted for an oral hearing before the court or may be submitted on written documents. *See* TRCP 87(1); ***Orion Enters.***, 927 S.W.2d at 657. The hearing is without a jury. TRCP 87(4); ***Eddins v. Parker***, 63 S.W.3d 15, 18 (Tex.App.—El Paso 2001, pet. denied).

(1) Most cases. The hearing on a motion to transfer venue is for argument only, and no evidence may be received. *See* CPRC §15.064(a); ***Jack B. Anglin Co. v. Tipps***, 842 S.W.2d 266, 269 n.4 (Tex.1992); ***Eddins***, 63 S.W.3d at 18.

(2) Joinder cases. In cases under CPRC §15.003(a) regarding joinder determination, the trial court may limit the scope of evidence to pleadings and affidavits, but it has discretion to consider a broad range of evidence, including live testimony. ***Surgitek v. Abel***, 997 S.W.2d 598, 602 (Tex.1999).

4. Burden of proof.

(1) Specific denial of venue facts. The court must take as true any pleaded venue facts that are not specifically denied by the other party. TRCP 87(3)(a); ***GeoChem Tech Corp. v. Verseckes***, 962 S.W.2d 541, 543 (Tex.1998); ***Garcia v. Garza***, 70 S.W.3d 362, 368 (Tex.App.—Corpus Christi 2002, pet. granted 10-10-02); ***Sanes v. Clark***, 25 S.W.3d 800, 803 (Tex.App.—Waco 2000, pet. denied). When a party's venue facts are not specifically denied, there is no burden on the party to submit proof of those facts. ***Bleeker v. Villarreal***, 941 S.W.2d 163, 175 (Tex.App.—Corpus Christi 1996, writ dism'd). A global denial (*e.g.*, "I specifically deny the venue facts") is not a specific denial. *See* ***Garcia***, 70 S.W.3d at 369 (specific denial requires more than just the words "We specifically deny"); ***Maranatha Temple v. Enterprise Prods. Co.***, 833 S.W.2d 736, 740 (Tex.App.—Houston [1st Dist.] 1992, writ denied) (same); *see also* ***Bleeker***, 941 S.W.2d at 175 (denying "the fact that venue is proper" is not a specific denial).

(2) Prima facie proof. Once a venue fact has been specifically denied, the burden of proof is placed on the party pleading the venue fact to make prima facie proof of that fact. ***GeoChem Tech***, 962 S.W.2d at 543; *see* ***Bleeker***, 941 S.W.2d at 175. Prima facie proof is made when the venue facts are properly pleaded and are supported by proper affidavit proof. TRCP 87(3)(a); *see* ***O'Quinn v. Hall***, 77 S.W.3d 438, 449 (Tex.App.—Corpus Christi 2002, no pet.).

(a) No rebuttal – most cases. Prima facie proof is not subject to rebuttal, cross-examination, impeachment, or disproof. ***Ruiz v. Conoco, Inc.***, 868 S.W.2d 752, 757 (Tex.1993); ***Garcia***, 70 S.W.3d at 370. The trial court should not weigh the credibility of the affiants when it evaluates the venue proof. ***Humphrey v. May***, 804 S.W.2d 328, 329 (Tex.App.—Austin 1991, writ denied).

(b) Rebuttal – joinder cases. Because the four elements a plaintiff must establish under CPRC §15.003(a)—joinder is proper under the TRCPs, unfair prejudice, essential need, and fairness and convenience—do not lend themselves readily to the prima facie standard applied in venue hearings, the defendant must be given the opportunity to rebut the plaintiff's prima facie proof. ***Surgitek***, 997 S.W.2d at 603; ***American Home Prods. Corp. v. Bernal***, 5 S.W.3d 344, 346-47 (Tex.App.—Corpus Christi 1999, no pet.). To the extent that a defendant's joinder evidence rebuts the plaintiff's prima facie proof on any of the joinder elements, the court has discretion to consider all available evidence to resolve any disputes that the parties' proof creates. ***Surgitek***, 997 S.W.2d at 603.

§2.12 Order. The court will decide venue based on the pleadings, the motion, the response, the affidavits, and discovery filed in support of the defendant's motion to transfer and the plaintiff's response. CPRC §15.064(a); TRCP 87(3)(b), 87(4), 88. The defendant has the burden to secure a ruling, or else it will waive its venue challenge. *See* ***Marathon Corp. v. Pitzner***, 55 S.W.3d 114, 138 (Tex.App.—Corpus Christi 2001), *rev'd on other grounds*, 106 S.W.3d 724 (Tex.2003).

1. Transfer denied. If the court denies the motion to transfer, the case should proceed to trial.

2. Transfer granted. If the court sustains the motion to transfer, the clerk will begin the process of transferring the case to the other county; the case will not be dismissed. TRCP 89.

PRACTICE TIP

If the court grants a motion to transfer venue that included a request to transfer for convenience, the order should state that the court granted the motion for that reason only. See "Order," §3.3, p. 161.

---

§2.13 Rehearing & later motions. An original timely motion to transfer venue may be amended to cure defects in the original motion if the amended motion is filed before the court rules on the original motion. ***In re Pepsico, Inc.***, 87 S.W.3d 787, 794 (Tex.App.—Texarkana 2002, orig. proceeding) (amended motion relates back to and supersedes original motion). Once the court rules on the motion to transfer, it must not consider any further motions to transfer, regardless of whether the movant was a party when the motion was heard. TRCP 87(5); *see* ***Marathon***, 55 S.W.3d at 137 n.6. This rule does not preclude a second motion made on grounds of mandatory venue by a later-added defendant, if the ground was not available to the earlier defendants, or on grounds of an impartial trial under TRCP 257-259. TRCP 87(5). See §2.13.2, below.

1. Rehearing of initial motion. The court may reconsider its ruling granting the motion to transfer before the case is transferred to another county and while it still has plenary power. *See* ***U.S. Res., Inc. v. Placke***, 682 S.W.2d 403, 405 (Tex.App.—Austin 1984, orig. proceeding). The court retains plenary power over the order transferring the case to another county for 30 days after it signs the order of transfer. ***In re Southwestern Bell Tel. Co.***, 35 S.W.3d 602, 605 (Tex.2000); ***HCA Health Servs. v. Salinas***, 838 S.W.2d 246, 248 (Tex.1992). Thirty days after the trial court signs an order transferring a case, that order is final as to the transferring court, even though it is interlocutory as to the parties. ***Southwestern Bell***, 35 S.W.3d at 605.

2. Motion by new defendant. Under TRCP 87(5), a new defendant is limited to motions to transfer based on (1) local prejudice or (2) a mandatory ground of venue not available to the other defendants. TRCP 87(5). However, under CPRC §15.0641 no act or omission by one defendant impairs the rights of another defendant. Thus, it is uncertain whether a defendant is limited in its venue objections when it is brought into the suit after the court ruled on another defendant's motion to transfer venue.

3. Motion by third-party defendant. Venue for the main action establishes venue for a defendant's third-party claim as long as the claim is properly joined under the TRCPs or other applicable statutes. CPRC §15.062(a). When an original defendant joins a third-party defendant, venue for the main action establishes venue for any claim by the plaintiff against that third-party defendant arising out of the same transaction, occurrence, or series of transactions or occurrences. *Id.* §15.062(b). The third-party defendant can object that the claim was not properly joined and, on that ground, move to transfer to another county.

4. Motion by substituted defendant. A defendant substituted for another defendant is bound by the actions of its predecessor and cannot change the venue status of the case. ***First Heights Bank v. Gutierrez***, 852 S.W.2d 596, 618 (Tex.App.—Corpus Christi 1993, writ denied); *see* TRCP 87(5).

5. Motion by intervening defendant. An intervening defendant has the status of a plaintiff and is in no better position to contest venue. ***First Heights***, 852 S.W.2d at 618.

§3. CONVENIENCE TRANSFER

A court can transfer a case to another county based on the convenience of the parties and witnesses. CPRC §15.002(b). Only the defendant may make this kind of motion to transfer. *Id.* A motion to transfer for convenience is governed by the same procedure as a motion to transfer to a county of proper venue. See "Improper County," §2, p. 152. However, a convenience transfer is unique because the trial court's ruling cannot be challenged by appeal or by mandamus, and if it is challenged, the trial court's decision is not reversible error. CPRC §15.002(c). See "No appeal of convenience transfer," §5.1, p. 163.

§3.1 Defendant's motion. A defendant may file a motion to transfer venue to another county of proper venue based on convenience whenever venue is not controlled by a mandatory venue provision. CPRC §15.002(b). See ***O'Connor's*** FORM 3C:03. Before the adoption of §15.002(b), a defendant was not entitled to have venue transferred from one permissive venue to another permissive venue.

1. Deadline. The deadline to file a motion to transfer under CPRC §15.002(b) is the same as for a motion to transfer based on improper venue—the motion must be filed before or at the time of the answer. *See* CPRC §15.063(1); TRCP 86(1). See "Deadline to file motion to transfer," §2.2.1, p. 152; "Due order of pleading," §2.2.2, p. 152.

2. Grounds. The defendant should allege that in the interest of justice, and for the convenience of the parties and witnesses, the court should transfer the suit to another specific county of proper venue. CPRC §15.002(b). The defendant should show how the parties and the witnesses will be inconvenienced by maintaining the suit in the county where suit was filed because of the following:

(1) Hardship on D. Maintenance of the suit in the original county of suit will impose an economic and personal hardship on the defendant. CPRC §15.002(b)(1). The defendant should state why litigation in the other county will not impose an economic and personal hardship.

(2) Balance of interests. The balance of interests of all the parties weighs in favor of the action being brought in the other county. CPRC §15.002(b)(2). The defendant should list the factors that weigh in favor of the county of its choice.

(3) No hardship on P. The transfer will not impose a hardship or injustice on any other party. CPRC §15.002(b)(3). The defendant should state why the move would not impose a hardship or injustice on the plaintiff or any other parties.

(4) Proper county. The other county is a county of proper venue. CPRC §15.002(b).

3. Affidavit. The defendant should support all its factual allegations with affidavits or other sworn proof. The general rule is that a defendant is not required to support a motion to transfer with affidavits when it is filed. See "No affidavit necessary," §2.2.4, p. 153. However, because a motion to transfer for convenience is based on facts outside the plaintiff's petition, the defendant is probably required to file sworn proof with its motion. Because the ruling on a motion to transfer is not appealable, the courts may never resolve this issue.

§3.2 Plaintiff's response.

1. Deadline. The deadline to file a response to the motion to transfer is 30 days before the venue hearing, unless the plaintiff secures permission to file it later. TRCP 87(1). See "Continuance," §2.10.3, p. 157.

2. Response to motion. The plaintiff's response should include the following:

(1) Waiver. The defendant filed the motion after the deadline. See "Allege waiver," §2.6.6, p. 156.

(2) Mandatory venue. Venue is mandatory in the county of suit. CPRC §15.001(b)(1).

(3) Interest of justice. In the interest of justice, and for the convenience of the parties and the witnesses, the suit must be maintained in the county where suit was originally filed. CPRC §15.002(b). The plaintiff should show how the parties and the witnesses will be inconvenienced by the move. The plaintiff should identify those witnesses who will probably testify by deposition and thus cannot be inconvenienced by maintaining the suit in the current county.

(a) No hardship on D. Maintaining the suit in the county of suit will not impose an economic or personal hardship on the defendant. CPRC §15.002(b)(1). The plaintiff should include reasons why the suit will be no more inconvenient for the defendant in the county of suit than in the defendant's county of choice.

(b) Balance of interests. The balance of interests of all the parties weighs in favor of the suit remaining in the county of suit. CPRC §15.002(b)(2). The plaintiff should list the factors that weigh in favor of the county of suit.

(c) Hardship on P. The transfer to the other county will impose an injustice on the plaintiff and other parties. CPRC §15.002(b)(3). The plaintiff should include specific examples of the hardship.

(d) Improper county for transfer. The county to which the defendant seeks transfer is not a county of proper venue. CPRC §15.002(b).

3. Affidavit. The plaintiff should support all factual allegations with affidavits or other sworn proof.

§3.3 Order. The order based on a convenience motion should state it is made under CPRC §15.002(b). To be exempt from appellate review, the order must expressly state that the case was or was not transferred for the convenience of the parties under §15.002(b), or the record must contain express findings of fact in accordance with §15.002(b). ***Garcia v. Garza***, 70 S.W.3d 362, 368 (Tex.App.—Corpus Christi 2002, pet. granted 10-10-02).

§4. LOCAL PREJUDICE

A motion to change venue because of local prejudice is different from a motion to transfer under the CPRC. A motion to change because of local prejudice is governed by TRCP 257-259, which were not altered by the 1983 codification of the venue statute or the 1995 revisions to the CPRC.

§4.1 Purpose. The motion to change venue because of local prejudice allows the court to transfer a case from a county if trial in that county would be unfair for one or both parties. The allegation that a party cannot get a fair trial implicates the due process clause in the 14th Amendment of the U.S. Constitution and the due course of law provision in Texas Constitution article 1, §19. Most motions to change venue arising under TRCP 257-259 involve prejudice generated by extensive pretrial publicity.

§4.2 Motion. Either party—plaintiff or defendant—may make a motion to change venue because of local prejudice, even though the plaintiff chose the venue. TRCP 257; *e.g.*, ***Carrasco v. Goatcher***, 623 S.W.2d 769, 771 (Tex.App.—El Paso 1981, no writ) (plaintiff filed motion). See ***O'Connor's*** FORM 3C:04.

NOTE

The "due order" rule regarding filing venue motions before most other pleadings does not apply to the motion to change venue based on local prejudice for two reasons: (1) the local prejudice might arise or become known after the answer is due; and (2) even a plaintiff may file such a motion.

§4.3 Grounds. The grounds to transfer based on local prejudice include the following:

1. Prejudice. The prejudice in the county of suit is so great that the party cannot get a fair trial. TRCP 257(a).

2. Combination. There is a combination against the party instigated by influential persons in the county of suit that would prevent a fair trial. TRCP 257(b).

3. No impartial trial. An impartial trial cannot be had in the county of suit. TRCP 257(c); *see* ***Dorchester Gas Prod'g Co. v. Harlow Corp.***, 743 S.W.2d 243, 253 n.6 (Tex.App.—Amarillo 1987, no writ). The movant should also allege that local prejudice will deprive the movant of its due process rights to a fair trial under both the U.S. and Texas Constitutions.

4. Other reason. The motion may assert any other relevant reasons. TRCP 257(d).

§4.4 Deadline. The motion to change venue should be filed as soon as the local prejudice becomes known. *See, e.g.*, ***City of Abilene v. Downs***, 367 S.W.2d 153, 155-56 (Tex.1963) (motion to change venue filed after case reset for trial); ***Lone Star Steel Co. v. Scott***, 759 S.W.2d 144, 146 (Tex.App.—Texarkana 1988, writ denied) (motion to change venue filed after D announced ready for trial). Although CPRC §15.063 includes the motion to transfer venue on grounds of local prejudice among those that must be filed before or with the defendant's answer, its inclusion is generally acknowledged as an error. *See* ***Union Carbide Corp. v. Moye***, 798 S.W.2d 792, 797 & n.5 (Tex.1990) (Gonzalez, J., concurring) (CPRC §15.063 does not establish exclusive circumstances for transfer based on local prejudice).

§4.5 Affidavits. The movant must file its own affidavit and the affidavits of at least three credible residents of the county where the suit is pending to support the grounds for change of venue because of local prejudice. TRCP 257; ***Acker v. Denton Publ'g Co.***, 937 S.W.2d 111, 118 (Tex.App.—Fort Worth 1996, no writ).

§4.6 Discovery & continuance. Discovery is permitted to support or oppose the motion. See "Procedure for securing evidence," §2.10, p. 157.

§4.7 Response. By filing the affidavit of a credible person, the nonmovant may challenge the credibility of the movant's affiants and their means of knowing the truth of the facts stated in the motion. TRCP 258. If the party needs additional time to respond, it must file a motion for continuance. See "Continuance," §2.10.3, p. 157.

§4.8 Waiver. If the nonmovant does not file affidavits controverting the claim of local prejudice, the court must transfer the case. ***Downs***, 367 S.W.2d at 155; ***Scott***, 759 S.W.2d at 146. If the movant waits too long to ask for a hearing, the motion can be waived. *See, e.g.*, ***Whitworth v. Kuhn***, 734 S.W.2d 108, 111 (Tex.App.—Austin 1987, no writ) (1-year delay in asking for hearing is inconsistent with purpose of TRCP 87(1)).

§4.9 Notice of hearing. Each party is entitled to at least 45 days' notice of the hearing. See "Notice of hearing," §2.11.2, p. 158.

§4.10 Hearing. If the credibility of the movant's affiants is attacked, the issue of local prejudice must be tried by the court. TRCP 258. The movant should ask for a hearing to present evidence. The hearing to determine local prejudice is probably for the presentation of evidence, although that is uncertain. *See* CPRC §15.064(a) (court must determine venue on pleadings and affidavits). The Supreme Court dodged the issue in ***Moye***. *See* ***Moye***, 798 S.W.2d at 793 n.1. *But see id.* at 794-95 (Hecht, J., concurring) (trial court has discretion to hear live testimony or decide motion on affidavits); *id.* at 795-98 (Gonzalez, J., concurring) (trial court must hear live testimony).

PRACTICE TIP

Until the Texas Supreme Court resolves the issue of whether a hearing under TRCP 258 is for the receipt of evidence or merely for argument, support a motion to transfer for local prejudice with affidavits and discovery, but also ask for a hearing to present evidence. If the trial court refuses to give you one, make a bill of exceptions and create the record you would have made if the trial court had given you the opportunity to present evidence. See "Offer of Proof & Bill of Exceptions," ch. 8-E, p. 553.

---

§4.11 Ruling. If the court grants a motion to change venue under TRCP 257, it should transfer the suit according to the following rules. First, if the transfer is from a district court, the court should transfer to any county of proper venue in the same or an adjoining district. TRCP 259(a). Second, if the transfer is from a county court, the court should transfer to any adjoining county of proper venue. TRCP 259(b). Third, if neither TRCP 259(a) nor (b) applies, the court should transfer to any county of proper venue. TRCP 259(c). Fourth, when there is no county of proper venue other than the county where suit was originally filed, the court should transfer according to the following guidelines: (1) when the transfer is from district court, the court should transfer to any county in the same or an adjoining district or to any district where an impartial trial can be had, TRCP 259(d)(1); (2) when the transfer is from a county court, the court should transfer to any adjoining county or to any district where an impartial trial can be had, TRCP 259(d)(2); or (3) when the parties agree to some other county, the court should transfer to that county, TRCP 259(d).

§5. REVIEW

§5.1 No appeal of convenience transfer. The court's decision on a motion to transfer based on convenience is not subject to review by appeal or mandamus and, if appealed, the decision is not reversible error. CPRC §15.002(c); ***Garcia v. Garza***, 70 S.W.3d 362, 367 (Tex.App.—Corpus Christi 2002, pet. granted 10-10-02); *see* ***In re Continental Airlines***, 988 S.W.2d 733, 735 (Tex.1998); ***Lopez v. Texas Workers' Comp. Ins. Fund***, 11 S.W.3d 490, 494 (Tex.App.—Austin 2000, pet. denied). Thus, there is no review of the decision to transfer for convenience—not during the trial, not by mandamus, and not after final judgment. *See* ***Armstrong v. Lindsay***, 934 S.W.2d 784, 785 (Tex.App.—Houston [1st Dist.] 1996, orig. proceeding) (constitutionality of CPRC §15.002(c) could not be challenged by mandamus).

§5.2 Interlocutory appeal. For the rules on interlocutory appeal, see ***O'Connor's Texas Civil Appeals***, "Motion for Interlocutory Appeal & Stay of Trial," ch. 13-P, p. 131 (2002-03).

1. Ruling on venue. Generally, there is no interlocutory appeal from trial court rulings on venue motions. CPRC §15.064(a); TRCP 87(6); ***Electronic Data Sys. Corp. v. Pioneer Elec.***, 68 S.W.3d 254, 257 (Tex. App.—Fort Worth 2002, no pet.). However, CPRC §51.014(d) allows parties to agree to an interlocutory appeal. See ***O'Connor's Texas Civil Appeals***, "Appealable orders by agreed motion," ch. 13-P, §2.2, p. 131.

2. Joinder. CPRC §15.003 allows an interlocutory appeal to contest the trial court's decision that (1) a plaintiff did or did not independently establish proper venue, or (2) a plaintiff who did not independently establish proper venue did or did not establish the elements of CPRC §15.003(a)(1)-(4). CPRC §15.003(b); ***Ramirez v. Collier, Shannon, Scott, PLLC***, ___ S.W.3d ___ (Tex.App.—Houston [1st Dist.] 2003, no pet.) (No. 01-01-00752-CV; 9-11-03). See "Joinder proper under §15.003(a)," §2.6.4(2), p. 155. CPRC §15.003(c) suggests that any affected party may take an interlocutory appeal from an order granting or denying intervention or joinder. CPRC §15.003(c); *see* ***Surgitek v. Abel***, 997 S.W.2d 598, 601 (Tex.1999); ***Electronic Data***, 68 S.W.3d at 257. The court of appeals will make an independent determination—without any deference to the trial court's decision—of whether the trial court's order was proper. *See* CPRC §15.003(c)(1). An interlocutory appeal under CPRC §15.003(b) stays the commencement of trial until the appeal has been resolved. CPRC §15.003(d).

§5.3 Appeal after trial on merits. Most venue rulings should be appealed after a judgment is rendered on the merits. *See* ***Mauro v. Banales***, 858 S.W.2d 651, 653 (Tex.App.—Corpus Christi 1993, orig. proceeding).

1. Record.

(1) Entire reporter's record. To appeal the venue ruling, the appellant must bring forward the reporter's record from the trial and from the hearing on venue. See §5.3.2, below.

(2) Limited reporter's record. One court of appeals has approved the appeal of the issue of venue with a limited reporter's record under TRAP 34.6(c). ***Steger & Bizzell, Inc. v. VandeWater Constr.***, 811 S.W.2d 687, 689 (Tex.App.—Austin 1991, writ denied) (analysis under former TRAP 53(d)). Under this procedure, the appellant serves the court reporter and the appellee with a request for the preparation of part of the record along with a statement of points or issues to be presented on appeal. TRAP 34.6(c)(1). The appellee can designate any additions from the testimony to be incorporated into the reporter's record. TRAP 34.6(c)(2). If the appellant complies with the procedure, there is a presumption that nothing omitted from the reporter's record is relevant to the appeal. TRAP 34.6(c)(4). In ***Steger***, the court noted that the trial on the merits lasted 22 days, and the limited record for venue was an appropriate use of the TRAP 53(d) procedure. ***Steger***, 811 S.W.2d at 689. For a description of the procedure for limited appeals, see ***O'Connor's Texas Civil Appeals***, "Requesting a Partial Record Under TRAP 34.6(c)," ch. 16-C, §8, p. 192.

2. Scope of review. When the trial court's ruling on venue is challenged on appeal after a trial on the merits, the appellate court conducts an independent review of the entire record to determine if the evidence introduced during the trial on the merits supports the venue ruling. CPRC §15.064(b); ***Wilson v. Texas Parks & Wildlife Dept.***, 886 S.W.2d 259, 261 (Tex.1994); ***Ruiz v. Conoco, Inc.***, 868 S.W.2d 752, 758 (Tex.1993); *see* ***Ford Motor Co. v. Miles***, 967 S.W.2d 377, 380 (Tex.1998). The appellate court may reverse a decision that was correct when it was made at the venue hearing but was erroneous in light of the evidence introduced at the trial on the merits. ***Bleeker v. Villarreal***, 941 S.W.2d 163, 167 (Tex.App.—Corpus Christi 1996, writ dism'd). The requirement for the appellate court to review the entire record was designed to prevent fraud in pleading venue facts that might not be discoverable until after the trial on the merits. ***Humphrey v. May***, 804 S.W.2d 328, 330 (Tex.App.—Austin 1991, writ denied).

§5.4 Mandamus. Most venue determinations are correctable on appeal and cannot be challenged by mandamus. ***Montalvo v. 4th Ct. of Appeals***, 917 S.W.2d 1, 2 (Tex.1995). But mandamus is appropriate in the following instances:

1. Mandatory venue in CPRC. A party may file a writ of mandamus to enforce a mandatory venue provision in CPRC chapter 15. CPRC §15.0642; ***In re Missouri Pac. R.R.***, 998 S.W.2d 212, 215 (Tex.1999); ***In re Continental Airlines***, 988 S.W.2d 733, 735 (Tex.1998). Under CPRC §15.0642, the relator is not required to show it lacks an adequate remedy on appeal. ***Missouri Pac. R.R.***, 998 S.W.2d at 216; ***KJ Eastwood Invs. v. Enlow***, 923 S.W.2d 255, 258 (Tex.App.—Fort Worth 1996, orig. proceeding). The application for writ of mandamus must be filed before the later of the following dates: (1) the 90th day before the trial starts, or (2) the tenth day after the party receives notice of the trial setting. CPRC §15.0642.

2. Mandatory venue in Family Code. When a court has a mandatory duty to transfer a case under the Family Code, a party may seek mandamus relief to enforce the transfer. *See* ***Proffer v. Yates***, 734 S.W.2d 671, 673 (Tex.1987) (under former Fam. Code §11.06(b), now §155.201); ***In re Knotts***, 62 S.W.3d 922, 923 n.1 (Tex.App.—Texarkana 2001, orig. proceeding) (under Fam. Code §155.201); ***In re Kramer***, 9 S.W.3d 449, 450 (Tex.App.—San Antonio 1999, orig. proceeding) (same).

3. Exceptional circumstances. Occasionally, a party may be entitled to mandamus relief from a venue order when "exceptional circumstances" make appeal an inadequate remedy. ***In re Masonite Corp.***, 997 S.W.2d 194, 197 (Tex.1999); *see, e.g.*, ***HCA Health Servs. v. Salinas***, 838 S.W.2d 246, 247-48 (Tex.1992) (order transferring venue signed by mistake); ***Union Carbide Corp. v. Moye***, 798 S.W.2d 792, 793 (Tex.1990) (mandamus appropriate when trial court misled party about acceptable form of venue proof); ***Henderson v. O'Neill***, 797 S.W.2d 905, 905 (Tex.1990) (no notice of hearing); ***Dorchester Master L.P. v. Anthony***, 734 S.W.2d 151, 152 (Tex.App.—Houston [1st Dist.] 1987, orig. proceeding) (order granting second motion was void); *see also* ***In re City of Irving***, 45 S.W.3d 777, 779 (Tex.App.—Texarkana 2001, orig. proceeding) (trial court's erroneous venue order that eventually would be reversed on appeal was not exceptional circumstance warranting mandamus).

§5.5 Standard of review. The standard of review for venue rulings depends on the type of venue ruling being challenged.

1. **Most venue rulings.**

(1) **Venue proper.** If the record contains any probative evidence that venue was proper, even if the preponderance of the evidence is to the contrary, the appellate court must uphold the trial court's venue determination. ***Bonham State Bank v. Beadle***, 907 S.W.2d 465, 471 (Tex.1995); ***Ruiz***, 868 S.W.2d at 758; *see* CPRC §15.064(b).

(2) **Venue improper.**

(a) **No harmless-error analysis.** If there is no evidence that venue was proper, the appellate court must reverse the trial court's erroneous venue ruling and remand for a new trial without conducting the usual harm analysis. ***Wichita Cty. v. Hart***, 917 S.W.2d 779, 781 (Tex.1996); ***Bleeker***, 941 S.W.2d at 167; *see* CPRC §15.064(b). Thus, venue is one of the few situations where the harmless-error rule, TRAP 44.1(a), does not apply. If the trial court makes an erroneous venue ruling, the case must be reversed even if the appellant cannot show harm. ***Wilson***, 886 S.W.2d at 261; ***Maranatha Temple v. Enterprise Prods. Co.***, 833 S.W.2d 736, 740-41 (Tex. App.—Houston [1st Dist.] 1992, writ denied). The Legislature intended venue rulings to be exempt from the harmless-error rule to discourage the prosecution of meritless venue claims. ***Maranatha Temple***, 833 S.W.2d at 741.

(b) **Rendition error.** If the defendant presents other arguments on appeal that entitle it to rendition of judgment—not just remand—the appellate court should consider those points first and, if it sustains them, reverse and render judgment for the defendant without reaching the venue issues. ***Bradleys' Elec. v. Cigna Lloyds Ins. Co.***, 995 S.W.2d 675, 677 (Tex.1999); *see* ***CMH Homes v. Daenen***, 15 S.W.3d 97, 99 (Tex.2000).

2. **Mandamus under §15.0642.** The standard of review for mandatory venue under CPRC §15.0642 is whether the trial court abused its discretion. ***Missouri Pac. R.R.***, 998 S.W.2d at 215; ***Continental Airlines***, 988 S.W.2d at 735.

3. **Joinder under §15.003.** The standard of review for the trial court's order under CPRC §15.003 is de novo. *See* CPRC §15.003(c)(1); ***Surgitek v. Abel***, 997 S.W.2d 598, 603 (Tex.1999). If a party contends that it was improperly denied the opportunity to present proof, the standard of review for that complaint is abuse of discretion. ***Surgitek***, 997 S.W.2d at 603.

4. **Local prejudice.** The standard of review for local prejudice is abuse of discretion. *See, e.g.*, ***Moye***, 798 S.W.2d at 793 (court did not permit reasonable opportunity to supplement venue record); ***Beard v. Gonzalez***, 924 S.W.2d 763, 764 (Tex.App.—El Paso 1996, orig. proceeding) (court did not permit reasonable discovery); ***City of La Grange v. McBee***, 923 S.W.2d 89, 90 (Tex.App.—Houston [1st Dist.] 1996, writ denied) (same).

D. FORUM NON CONVENIENS—CHALLENGING THE TEXAS FORUM

§1. GENERAL

§1.1 Rules. None. See CPRC §71.051.

§1.2 Purpose. A forum non conveniens motion asks the court to dismiss or stay a suit because a court outside of Texas has jurisdiction over the dispute and is a more appropriate forum. ***A.P. Keller Dev. v. One Jackson Place***, 890 S.W.2d 502, 505 (Tex.App.—El Paso 1994, no writ). The doctrine presumes at least two forums have jurisdiction over the dispute. ***Sarieddine v. Moussa***, 820 S.W.2d 837, 841 (Tex.App.—Dallas 1991, writ denied). Forum non conveniens is an equitable doctrine exercised by courts to avoid the imposition of an inconvenient jurisdiction on a litigant, even if jurisdiction is supported by the long-arm statute and would not violate due process. ***Tullis v. Georgia-Pacific Corp.***, 45 S.W.3d 118, 122 (Tex.App.—Fort Worth 2000, no pet.). A motion to stay or dismiss on grounds of forum non conveniens is appropriate only when the defendant wants to defend the suit in another state or country.

§1.3 Forms & timetables. ***O'Connor's Texas Civil Forms***, FORMS 3D; Timetables, this book, Motion to Dismiss—Code Forum Non Conveniens, p. 995, Motion to Dismiss—Common-Law Forum Non Conveniens, p. 996.

§1.4 Other references. Robertson & Speck, *Access to State Courts in Transnational Personal Injury Cases: Forum Non Conveniens & Antisuit Injunctions*, 68 Tex.L.Rev. 937 (1990); Scherz, Comment, *Section 71.051 of the [CPRC]—The Texas Legislature's Answer to Alfaro*, 46 Baylor L.Rev. 99 (1994); Restatement (Second) of Conflicts of Laws, §84 & cmts. (a)-(f) (1971).

§2. TYPES OF MOTIONS FOR FORUM NON CONVENIENS (FNC)

There are three types of motions for forum non conveniens in Texas courts: (1) a motion under the CPRC when the plaintiff asserts a claim for personal injury or death; (2) a motion for common-law forum non conveniens when the plaintiff asserts almost any other cause of action; and (3) a motion to enforce a forum selection clause in a contract. Forum non conveniens under CPRC §71.051 will be referred to as "Code FNC." Forum non conveniens for cases not covered by CPRC §71.051 will be referred to as "common-law FNC."

§3. CODE FNC MOTION

§3.1 Definitions under §71.051.

1. Plaintiff. CPRC §71.051(h)(2) defines a plaintiff as a party seeking to recover damages for personal injury or wrongful death. The term "plaintiff" includes both the person who was injured and the party seeking recovery. CPRC §71.051(h)(2). "Plaintiff" does not include a counterclaimant, a cross-claimant, a third-party plaintiff, a person who is assigned a cause of action for personal injury, or a person who accepts an appointment as a personal representative in a wrongful-death action in bad faith for purposes of affecting the application of this section. *Id.*

2. Legal resident. CPRC §71.051(h)(1) defines a legal resident as an individual who intends a specified political subdivision to be her permanent residence and who intends to return to that political subdivision despite temporary residence elsewhere or despite temporary absences. The individual's country of citizenship or national origin is irrelevant. CPRC §71.051(h)(1). The term does not include an individual who adopts a residence in bad faith for purposes of avoiding this section. *Id.*

§3.2 General requirements for motion.

1. Written. The defendant must make a written Code FNC motion. CPRC §71.051(b).

2. Verified. Because most of the defendant's factual allegations are outside the record, the defendant should probably verify the motion. However, nothing in CPRC §71.051 requires verification. By comparison, CPRC §71.051(f) requires the party opposing the motion (the plaintiff) to submit verified evidence. See "Verified," §3.4.1(2), p. 168.

3. Request hearing. The defendant must request a hearing on the motion. CPRC §71.051(d). See "Hearing on motion," §3.8, p. 169.

4. Deadline. The deadline to file the motion for Code FNC is 180 days from the last date for filing a motion to transfer venue. CPRC §71.051(d). Because the deadline to file a motion to transfer venue is the same as the deadline to file an answer, the deadline to file a Code FNC motion is approximately 200 days (180 days plus 20+ days). See "Deadline to Answer," ch. 3-E, §2, p. 171.

5. Statute of limitations. A nonresident plaintiff whose cause of action for personal injury or wrongful death accrued in another state or country with a shorter statute of limitations than Texas's must file the suit within the limitations period imposed by that law. CPRC §71.031(a)(3); ***Owens Corning v. Carter***, 997 S.W.2d 560, 566 (Tex.1999); ***Tullis v. Georgia-Pacific Corp.***, 45 S.W.3d 118, 123 (Tex.App.—Fort Worth 2000, no pet.).

§3.3 Defendant's grounds. If the plaintiff is not a Texas resident, the defendant may file a motion to stay or dismiss under §71.051(b). *See* CPRC §71.051(e). Specifically, the motion must allege the following:

1. Plaintiff not Texas resident. If the suit involves a single plaintiff, the defendant must allege the plaintiff is not a Texas resident. *See* CPRC §71.051(e). See §3.1, above. If the suit involves multiple plaintiffs, some who are legal residents of Texas and others who are not, the defendant must show by a preponderance of the evidence that (1) the Texas plaintiffs were joined solely for the purpose of obtaining or maintaining jurisdiction in Texas, and (2) the party's claim would be more properly heard in a forum outside Texas. CPRC §71.051(e).

2. No Texas injury. The act or omission that the plaintiff alleges was a proximate or producing cause of the injury or death occurred outside Texas. *See* CPRC §71.051(f).

3. Interest of justice. In the interest of justice and for the convenience of the parties, the claim or action would be more properly heard in a forum outside Texas. CPRC §71.051(b). "Interest of justice" is an issue of fundamental fairness to be determined on a case-by-case basis. ***Baker v. Bell Helicopter Textron***, 985 S.W.2d 272, 277 (Tex.App.—Fort Worth 1999, pet. denied) (under former CPRC §71.051(a), discussing plaintiffs who are not legal residents of U.S.). 03

4. Alternate forum. The defendant should plead and prove the suit should be heard in a forum outside Texas. In its motion, the defendant should state the following:

(1) Available. There is an alternate forum in which the claim may be tried. CPRC §71.051(b)(1). The defendant must identify the alternate forum. 03

(2) Adequate. The alternate forum provides an adequate remedy. CPRC §71.051(b)(2).

(3) Substantial injustice. Maintenance of the action in Texas would impose a substantial injustice on the defendant. CPRC §71.051(b)(3).

(4) Jurisdiction. The alternate forum, as a result of the submission of the parties or otherwise, can exercise jurisdiction over all the defendants properly joined to the plaintiff's claim. CPRC §71.051(b)(4).

(5) Balance of interests. The balance of private interests of the parties and public interests of the state weighs in favor of the claim or action being brought in an alternate forum. CPRC §71.051(b)(5); ***Tullis***, 45 S.W.3d at 132. The private and public interests referred to in CPRC §71.051(b)(5) originated in ***Gulf Oil Corp. v. Gilbert***, 330 U.S. 501, 508, 67 S.Ct. 839, 843 (1947), and are called the ***Gilbert*** factors.

(a) Private interests. The private interests of the litigants will be better served in the other forum because (1) access to sources of proof will be easier in the other forum than in Texas; (2) compulsory process for the attendance of unwilling witnesses is available in the other forum; (3) the costs of obtaining the presence of willing witnesses will be lower in the other forum than in Texas; (4) if a view of the premises is necessary to the suit, the possibility of obtaining a view of the premises is better in the other forum than in Texas; and (5) the enforceability of the judgment is just as good or better in the other forum than in a Texas court. ***Gulf Oil***, 330 U.S. at 508, 67 S.Ct. at 843.

(b) Public interests. The public interests favor the other forum because (1) the administrative burden (*e.g.*, congested docket, jury duty of citizens) on the other court is not as great as the burden on the Texas court; (2) there is an interest in deciding the case in the other forum, and there is none in Texas; and (3) the law of the other forum will control the disposition of the case. ***Gulf Oil***, 330 U.S. at 508-09, 67 S.Ct. at 843. The court should consider whether the foreign law must be applied to the facts of the case and, if so, whether it is so dissimilar to the laws of Texas that it will be difficult or incapable of enforcement here. ***Gurvich v. Tyree***, 694 S.W.2d 39, 46 (Tex.App.—Corpus Christi 1985, no writ).

(6) No duplication or proliferation. The stay or dismissal will not result in unreasonable duplication or proliferation of litigation. CPRC §71.051(b)(6).

§3.4 Plaintiff's response.

1. Form.

(1) Written. The plaintiff should file a written response to challenge the allegations in the defendant's motion.

(2) Verified. The plaintiff must produce credible evidence in support of its response. *See* CPRC §71.051(f). The plaintiff's evidence must be verified, even though it does not need to be in admissible form. *Id.*; ***Berg v. AMF, Inc.***, 29 S.W.3d 212, 220 (Tex.App.—Houston [14th Dist.] 2000, no pet.).

(3) Deadline. There is no deadline stated in CPRC §71.051 for filing the plaintiff's response.

2. Objections to motion. The plaintiff must negate the defendant's allegations and identify any exceptions to the application of CPRC §71.051.

(1) Plaintiff is Texas resident. When the action involves just one plaintiff, the plaintiff can allege that, contrary to the defendant's allegation, the plaintiff is a legal resident of Texas. CPRC §71.051(e). When the action involves multiple plaintiffs, some who are Texas residents and others who are not, the plaintiff can allege that the plaintiffs who are Texas residents are properly joined in the action and the action arose out of a single occurrence. *Id.*

(2) Texas injury. The plaintiff can allege that an act or omission that was a proximate or producing cause of the injury or death occurred in Texas. CPRC §71.051(f). The plaintiff must make a prima facie showing that an act or omission that was a proximate or producing cause of the injury occurred in whole or in part in Texas. *Id.*; *see, e.g.*, ***Berg***, 29 S.W.3d at 219-20 (Ps did not prove chemicals mixed in Houston & shipped to Canada caused P's type of lung damage). The plaintiff satisfies the requirement for a prima facie showing if it produces credible evidence, which does not need to be in admissible form. See §3.8.3, below.

03 **(3) Alternate forum.** The plaintiff can allege that the defendant did not identify an alternate forum, or if it did, that the alternate forum is not adequate. *See* CPRC §71.051(b)(1), (2).

(4) No substantial injustice. The plaintiff can allege that maintaining the suit in Texas would not impose a substantial injustice on the defendant. *See* CPRC §71.051(b)(3).

(5) No jurisdiction. The plaintiff can allege that the alternate forum does not have jurisdiction over the claim. *See* CPRC §71.051(b)(4). The plaintiff can argue that the defendant has not submitted itself to the jurisdiction of the alternate forum and that the alternate forum has no other means of exercising personal jurisdiction over the defendant. *See id.*

(6) Balance of interests. The plaintiff can allege the private and public interests favor the Texas forum. *See* CPRC §71.051(b)(5). The plaintiff should construct its argument around the ***Gilbert*** factors. See §3.3.4(5), above.

(7) Duplication or proliferation. The plaintiff can allege the alternate forum's stay or dismissal would result in unreasonable duplication or proliferation of litigation. *See* CPRC §71.051(b)(6).

(8) Improper notice of hearing. If the defendant did not give proper notice, the plaintiff must challenge the notice or waive the issue. The plaintiff can assert that the defendant set the hearing within 30 days of trial or the defendant did not give the plaintiff 21 days' notice of the hearing. CPRC §71.051(d). See §3.8, below.

(9) Waiver. If the defendant filed its Code FNC motion after the deadline to file, the plaintiff should allege the defendant waived the motion. See "Deadline," §3.2.4, p. 166.

§3.5 Defendant's reply. If the plaintiff meets its burden of proving its allegations, the defendant should respond by supplying verified evidence to support its motion. *See generally* CPRC §71.051(f) (burden of proof). See §3.8.3, below.

§3.6 Motion to extend time. The court may extend any time limit established under CPRC §71.051 at the request of any party for good cause. CPRC §71.051(g). If any of the parties need additional time for filing the response, they should file a motion for continuance. See "Motion for Continuance," ch. 5-D, p. 242.

§3.7 Discovery. The court must give the parties "ample opportunity" to obtain discovery before the hearing on the motion. CPRC §71.051(d). See "Discovery," ch. 6, p. 311. If additional time is necessary for discovery, the parties should file a motion for continuance. See "Motion for Continuance," ch. 5-D, p. 242.

§3.8 Hearing on motion. The court must hold a hearing before ruling on a Code FNC motion. CPRC §71.051(d). The hearing is similar to the hearing on a motion for summary judgment. See "Summary Judgment Hearing," ch. 7-B, §12, p. 481.

1. Notice. The court cannot rule on a motion unless the parties have at least 21 days' notice of the hearing. CPRC §71.051(d).

2. Deadline. The hearing must be held a reasonable time before trial—at least 30 days. CPRC §71.051(d).

3. Evidence. The parties should produce evidence in the form of affidavits, deposition testimony, discovery responses, or other verified evidence. *See* CPRC §71.051(f). The evidence does not need to be in admissible form. *Id.*

4. For argument. At the hearing, the court will consider the pleadings and discovery produced by the parties. *See* CPRC §71.051(f). Nothing in CPRC §71.051 explicitly prohibits the introduction of oral testimony at the hearing.

5. Burden of proof. The 2003 amendments to CPRC §71.051 removed the defendant's burden of proving by a preponderance of the evidence that the court should not exercise jurisdiction. *See* CPRC §71.051(b). The amendments do not explicitly place the burden of proof on either the plaintiff or the defendant. *See id.* 03

§4. COMMON-LAW FNC MOTION

Because no rules or statutes govern the procedure for motions for common-law FNC the courts presumably will follow some of the procedures described in CPRC §71.051, except for the deadline provisions.

§4.1 Motion.

1. Grounds. The motion should allege the following:

(1) No plaintiff is Texas resident. None of the plaintiffs is a Texas resident. *See* ***Sarieddine v. Moussa***, 820 S.W.2d 837, 842 (Tex.App.—Dallas 1991, writ denied).

(2) Other forum available & more appropriate. Another forum is available and is more appropriate. ***Sarieddine***, 820 S.W.2d at 841-42. Even when the plaintiff is a corporation authorized to do business in Texas, the case may be dismissed because of forum non conveniens if the suit has no significant connection with Texas. ***In re Smith Barney, Inc.***, 975 S.W.2d 593, 597-98 (Tex.1998); *see, e.g.*, ***Seguros Comercial Am., S.A. v. American President Lines***, 966 S.W.2d 652, 656 (Tex.App.—San Antonio 1998, no pet.) (suit brought by foreign insurance company authorized to do business in Texas could be dismissed on FNC grounds).

(3) Private & public interests favor other forum. The private and public interests favor the other forum. The defendant should argue the ***Gilbert*** factors. See "Balance of interests," §3.3.4(5), p. 167. Unless the ***Gilbert*** factors strongly favor the alternate forum, the plaintiff's choice of forum will rarely be disturbed. ***Gulf Oil Corp. v. Gilbert***, 330 U.S. 501, 508, 67 S.Ct. 839, 843 (1947); ***A.P. Keller Dev. v. One Jackson Place***, 890 S.W.2d 502, 505 (Tex.App.—El Paso 1994, no writ); ***Sarieddine***, 820 S.W.2d at 842.

(4) Grounds similar to those under Code FNC. If any of the grounds under a Code FNC motion are relevant, the defendant can assert those grounds. *See* CPRC §71.051(b)(1)-(6).

2. Stipulation. The doctrine of forum non conveniens assumes that the defendant agrees to be sued in another jurisdiction. Thus, the defendant should file some agreement, probably stipulations, to be sued in the other jurisdiction. *See* ***Seguros***, 966 S.W.2d at 656 (D was willing to submit to jurisdiction of Mexican court); *see also* CPRC §71.051(c)(1) (pre-1997 version).

3. Deadline to file. There is no deadline for filing the motion for common-law FNC. *See* ***Direct Color Servs. v. Eastman Kodak Co.***, 929 S.W.2d 558, 567 (Tex.App.—Tyler 1996, writ denied) (motion may be filed anytime before trial).

§4.2 Response. The plaintiff should file a response to challenge the allegations in the defendant's common-law FNC motion.

1. Plaintiff is Texas resident. The plaintiff can allege that one of the plaintiffs is a Texas resident.

2. Other forum not available or appropriate. The plaintiff should challenge the defendant's assertions that the other forum is available and is more appropriate.

3. Private & public interests favor Texas. The plaintiff should allege that the private and public interests favor the Texas forum. See "Balance of interests," §3.3.4(5), p. 167.

4. Arguments similar to those under Code FNC. If any of the exceptions under Code FNC are relevant, the plaintiff should make the same arguments under the common-law FNC response. See "Objections to motion," §3.4.2, p. 168.

§4.3 Hearing. There are no rules on the notice and deadline for the common-law FNC hearing. At the hearing, the court will consider the pleadings, affidavits, depositions, discovery responses, and other verified evidence on file. See §§3.8.3, 3.8.4, above.

§5. FORUM SELECTION BY CONTRACT

Contractual forum selection clauses are valid in Texas. ***CMS Partners v. Plumrose USA, Inc.***, 101 S.W.3d 730, 732 (Tex.App.—Texarkana 2003, no pet.); ***Barnett v. Network Solutions***, 38 S.W.3d 200, 203 (Tex.App.—Eastland 2001, pet. denied); *see also* CPRC §15.020 (parties involved in "major transactions" may contractually agree to venue & jurisdiction). When a party contractually consents to the jurisdiction of a particular state, that state will have jurisdiction over that party if it enforces the type of forum selection clause signed by the parties. ***CMS Partners***, 101 S.W.3d at 732; ***Barnett***, 38 S.W.3d at 203. A forum selection clause does not bind a Texas court if the interests of the witnesses and the public strongly favor jurisdiction in a forum other than the one the parties agreed to in the contract. ***Accelerated Christian Educ. v. Oracle Corp.***, 925 S.W.2d 66, 71 (Tex.App.—Dallas 1996, no writ); ***Greenwood v. Tillamook Country Smoker***, 857 S.W.2d 654, 656 (Tex.App.—Houston [1st Dist.] 1993, no writ). Forum selection clauses do not apply when the suit alleges the plaintiff was induced by misrepresentations to sign the contract. ***Busse v. Pacific Cattle Feeding Fund***, 896 S.W.2d 807, 813 (Tex.App.—Texarkana 1995, writ denied). Dismissal is the appropriate remedy after granting a motion based on a forum selection clause that identifies another state as the proper forum. ***Accelerated Christian***, 925 S.W.2d at 70; *see* ***Greenwood***, 857 S.W.2d at 657.

§6. ORDER

The court must sign a written order sustaining or overruling the motion.

§6.1 Dismissal or stay under Code. When the court sustains a motion for Code FNC, it can grant either a dismissal or a stay. The court has continuing jurisdiction over the suit, even after granting a motion to dismiss. The court may set terms and conditions for dismissing or staying a claim, as the interest of justice requires. CPRC §71.051(c). If a defendant violates the terms or conditions of the order of dismissal or stay, the court can withdraw the order, notwithstanding any other law on jurisdiction. *Id.*

NOTE

A Texas court does not have the power to transfer a case to another state's court. See ***Accelerated Christian****, 925 S.W.2d at 70; Restatement (Second) of Conflicts of Laws §84, cmt. e (1971). Thus, a Texas court can only dismiss or stay the suit.*

§6.2 Stay under common law. When dealing with a motion for common-law FNC, the court should probably not grant a dismissal, but instead only grant a stay. If the court grants a dismissal under common-law, it cannot later withdraw the order of dismissal, as it can under CPRC §71.051(c). By granting a stay, the court can reclaim the case if the defendant does not comply with its agreement to be sued in the other forum.

§7. REVIEW

§7.1 Interlocutory review. As a rule, there is no interlocutory appeal of the denial of a motion for forum non conveniens. However, CPRC §51.014(d) allows parties to agree to an interlocutory appeal. See ***O'Connor's Texas Civil Appeals***, "Appealable orders by agreed motion," ch. 13-P, §2.2, p. 131 (2002-03).

§7.2 Appeal after judgment. An order that dismisses a suit based on an FNC order is a final, appealable order, even if the Texas court has continuing jurisdiction over the case under CPRC §71.051(c). *See, e.g.*, ***VE Corp. v. Ernst & Young***, 860 S.W.2d 83, 84 (Tex.1993) (Code FNC order, P was U.S. citizen); ***Feltham v. Bell Helicopter Textron***, 41 S.W.3d 384, 386-87 (Tex.App.—Fort Worth 2001, no pet.) (Code FNC order, Ps were Canadians); *see also* ***Sarieddine***, 820 S.W.2d at 841 (common-law FNC order). *But see* ***Martinez v. Bell Helicopter Textron***, 49 S.W.3d 890, 891 (Tex.App.—Fort Worth 2001, pet. denied) (Code FNC order dismissing suit, pending resolution in foreign country, was not appealable).

1. Standard of review. An order dismissing a suit because of forum non conveniens is reviewed for abuse of discretion. ***Tullis v. Georgia-Pacific Corp.***, 45 S.W.3d 118, 121 (Tex.App.—Fort Worth 2000, no pet.); ***A.P. Keller Dev. v. One Jackson Place***, 890 S.W.2d 502, 505 (Tex.App.—El Paso 1994, no writ); ***Sarieddine***, 820 S.W.2d at 841. To determine whether the trial court abused its discretion, the appellate court must decide whether the trial court acted without reference to any guiding rules or principles—in other words, whether the act was arbitrary or unreasonable. ***Feltham***, 41 S.W.3d at 387. If the factors are not heavily weighted toward either jurisdiction, the court will not abuse its discretion by either sustaining or overruling the FNC motion. ***New Process Steel Corp. v. Steel Corp.***, 638 S.W.2d 522, 525 (Tex.App.—Houston [1st Dist.] 1982, no writ).

2. Filing suit in another jurisdiction. After a dismissal based on a Code FNC order, the plaintiff can file the suit in another jurisdiction while pursuing an appeal in Texas. ***VE Corp.***, 860 S.W.2d at 84.

E. THE ANSWER—DENYING LIABILITY

§1. GENERAL

§1.1 Rules. TRCP 38, 83-85, 90-95, 97-98.

§1.2 Purpose. By its answer, the defendant enters an appearance, denies the allegations in the plaintiff's petition, identifies its defenses, and avoids a default judgment. Once the defendant files an answer, it is entitled to notice of all proceedings in the case.

§1.3 Forms & timetable. ***O'Connor's Texas Civil Forms***, FORMS 3E; Timetable, this book, Pretrial Motions, p. 998.

§1.4 Other references. ***O'Connor's Texas Causes of Action*** (2004) (***O'Connor's COA***).

§2. DEADLINE TO ANSWER

§2.1 In most cases. In district and county courts, the defendant must file its answer by 10:00 a.m. on the Monday next after the expiration of 20 days from the date the defendant was served with the citation. TRCP 99(b);

Solis v. Garcia, 702 S.W.2d 668, 671 (Tex.App.—Houston [14th Dist.] 1985, no writ). An answer is timely if the defendant puts it in the custody of the U.S. Postal Service before 10:00 a.m. on the day it is due as long as the clerk receives it no later than ten days after the due date. ***Milam v. Miller***, 891 S.W.2d 1, 2 (Tex.App.—Amarillo 1994, writ ref'd). If the 20th day after service falls on a Monday, the answer is due on the next Monday. ***Proctor v. Green***, 673 S.W.2d 390, 392 (Tex.App.—Houston [1st Dist.] 1984, no writ). If the first Monday after 20 days is a legal holiday, the answer is due on Tuesday. *See* TRCP 4; ***Conaway v. Lopez***, 880 S.W.2d 448, 450 (Tex.App.—Austin 1994, writ ref'd); ***Solis***, 702 S.W.2d at 671; ***Proctor***, 673 S.W.2d at 392. The defendant has until the end of the next day that is not a legal holiday to file an answer, not just until 10:00 a.m. *E.g.*, ***Conaway***, 880 S.W.2d at 450 (default judgment granted on Tuesday afternoon was reversed).

NOTE

Although it has not been addressed by the Supreme Court, there is some authority stating that the deadline for filing the answer is delayed until after the court rules on the motion to transfer venue. ***Glover v. Moser****, 930 S.W.2d 940, 943-44 (Tex.App.—Beaumont 1996, writ denied); 2 McDonald, Texas Civil Practice §7:16 (1992).*

§2.2 Service through Secretary of State. When a defendant is served through the Secretary of State, service on the Secretary is constructive service on the defendant and triggers the defendant's answer date. ***Bonewitz v. Bonewitz***, 726 S.W.2d 227, 230 (Tex.App.—Austin 1987, writ ref'd n.r.e.). Thus, if the Secretary receives the process on May 8, forwards it to the defendant on May 12, and the defendant receives it on May 16, the defendant starts counting from the day the Secretary received the process—May 8 is "day 0," May 9 is "day 1," May 10 is "day 2," etc. See "Computing time limits – days," ch. 1-C, §7.1, p. 16.

§2.3 After bankruptcy. When a case is in bankruptcy, the automatic stay tolls the time for a bankruptcy defendant to answer. The time for a bankruptcy defendant to answer in state court resumes running 30 days after the bankruptcy court lifts the stay or dismisses or closes the case. 11 U.S.C. §108(c); *see* ***HBA East, Ltd. v. JEA Boxing Co.***, 796 S.W.2d 534, 536 (Tex.App.—Houston [1st Dist.] 1990, writ denied).

§2.4 After remand. Once a case has been remanded to state court after removal to federal court, TRCP 237a give the defendant 15 days to file an answer, counting from the date the defendant receives notice of the federal court's remand notice. *See* ***HBA East***, 796 S.W.2d at 538. TRCP 237a places the burden on the plaintiff to file a copy of the remand order with the clerk of the state court and give the defendant written notice of the remand. ***HBA East***, 796 S.W.2d at 538. Actual notice of the remand is not relevant. *Id.* at 537. Until the plaintiff gives the defendant notice of the remand, the defendant's deadline to answer does not begin to run. *Id.* at 538. If the defendant filed an answer in federal court during removal, that answer will suffice in state court once the case is remanded. *See* TRCP 237a.

§3. GENERAL DENIAL

All answers should contain a general denial. A general denial puts at issue all matters not required to be denied under oath or specially denied. TRCP 92; ***Shell Chem. Co. v. Lamb***, 493 S.W.2d 742, 744 (Tex.1973); ***Cadle Co. v. Castle***, 913 S.W.2d 627, 631 (Tex.App.—Dallas 1995, writ denied). By comparison, a special denial is a denial that must be specifically pleaded (*i.e.*, when a general denial is not sufficient). *See, e.g.*, TRCP 52 (denial of corporate status), TRCP 93 (verified pleas), TRCP 94 (affirmative defenses). A general denial does not permit the defendant to submit any jury questions. ***Luther Transfer & Storage v. Walton***, 296 S.W.2d 750, 754 (Tex.1956); *see also* TRCP 278 (court must submit questions raised by written pleadings & evidence).

§4. VERIFIED PLEAS

A general denial cannot put all the plaintiff's allegations into issue. Some matters must be specifically pleaded and verified. If the defendant does not verify a denial that the rules require to be verified, the plaintiff must object to the defect or waive the error. *See* ***Werner v. Colwell***, 909 S.W.2d 866, 870 (Tex.1995); ***Southern Cty. Mut. Ins. Co. v. Ochoa***, 19 S.W.3d 452, 461 (Tex.App.—Corpus Christi 2000, no pet.). A pleading may usually be amended to include a verification, even during trial. *E.g.*, ***Chapin & Chapin, Inc. v. Texas Sand & Gravel Co.***, 844 S.W.2d 664, 664-65 (Tex.1992) (trial court should have permitted amendment the day of trial).

PRACTICE TIP

If you need to file a verified plea under TRCP 93, you may also need to file a motion to abate on the same ground to avoid waiving the error. See "Motion to Abate—Challenging the Suit," ch. 3-H, p. 194.

§4.1 Verified pleas in TRCP 93. TRCP 93 contains a list of defenses, pleas, and other matters that must be verified "unless the truth of such matters appear of record." ***Montemayor v. Chapa***, 61 S.W.3d 758, 762 (Tex. App.—Corpus Christi 2001, no pet.). Verification, therefore, is necessary to assert certain defenses when the issue is not apparent on the face of the plaintiff's pleadings. *See* ***Pledger v. Schoellkopf***, 762 S.W.2d 145, 146 (Tex.1988); *see also* ***City of Ft. Worth v. Robles***, 51 S.W.3d 436, 444-45 (Tex.App.—Fort Worth 2001, pet. denied) (even if facts in P's petition were true, verified plea was not necessary to challenge jurisdiction because P's pleading was insufficient to invoke court's jurisdiction). If there is any doubt, the defendant should verify its answer. As a rule, the following pleas must be verified:

1. An attack on the legal capacity of either the plaintiff to sue or the defendant to be sued. TRCP 93(1); ***Sixth RMA Partners v. Sibley***, 111 S.W.3d 46, 56 (Tex.2003); ***Nootsie, Ltd. v. Williamson Cty. Appr. Dist.***, 925 S.W.2d 659, 662 (Tex.1996); ***Prostok v. Browning***, 112 S.W.3d 876, 921 (Tex.App.—Dallas 2003, pet. filed 10-24-03). See "Capacity," ch. 2-B, §3.2.2, p. 68; "Defects in the parties," ch. 3-H, §3.1.1, p. 195.

2. An allegation that the plaintiff is not entitled to recover in the capacity in which it sues or that the defendant is not liable in the capacity in which it is sued. TRCP 93(2); ***Pledger***, 762 S.W.2d at 146; ***W.O.S. Constr. Co. v. Hanyard***, 684 S.W.2d 675, 676 (Tex.1985). Even though the failure to file a verified plea waives any complaint about a judgment rendered in the capacity in which the party was sued, such failure does not authorize a court to render a judgment against the party in a capacity in which it was not sued. ***Werner***, 909 S.W.2d at 870. See "Defects in the parties," ch. 3-H, §3.1.1, p. 195.

3. An allegation that another suit is pending in Texas between the same parties and involves the same claim. TRCP 93(3); ***Southern Cty. Mut. Ins.***, 19 S.W.3d at 461. See "Abate – same dispute in another Texas court," ch. 3-H, §3.2, p. 196.

4. An allegation of any other defect of the parties. TRCP 93(4); ***Cantu v. Holiday Inns***, 910 S.W.2d 113, 115 (Tex.App.—Corpus Christi 1995, writ denied). Any defect of the parties not covered by some other section of TRCP 93 must be denied under oath under this section. *See, e.g.*, ***Allison v. National Un. Fire Ins. Co.***, 703 S.W.2d 637, 638 (Tex.1986) (D should have filed verified denial that necessary parties were not joined); ***Beacon Nat'l Ins. Co. v. Reynolds***, 799 S.W.2d 390, 395 (Tex.App.—Fort Worth 1990, writ denied) (D should have filed verified denial that it was not the correct insurance company); *see also* ***CHCA E. Houston, L.P. v. Henderson***, 99 S.W.3d 630, 632-33 (Tex.App.—Houston [14th Dist.] 2003, no pet.) (misidentification must be raised by verified pleading).

5. A denial of a partnership alleged in a pleading for any party to the suit. TRCP 93(5); ***Cadle Co. v. Bankston & Lobingier***, 868 S.W.2d 918, 922-23 (Tex.App.—Fort Worth 1994), *writ denied*, 893 S.W.2d 949 (Tex. 1994); *e.g.*, ***Champion v. Wright***, 740 S.W.2d 848, 851 (Tex.App.—San Antonio 1987, writ denied) (D did not file verified denial that P did not have authority to recover damages to partnership). The failure to deny partnership status is an admission of the partnership that cannot be controverted at trial. ***Washburn v. Krenek***, 684 S.W.2d 187, 191 (Tex.App.—Houston [14th Dist.] 1984, writ ref'd n.r.e.).

6. A denial that a party is incorporated as alleged. TRCP 93(6); *see* ***Panama Ref. Co. v. Crouch***, 124 S.W.2d 988, 989 (Tex.1939); *see also* TRCP 52 (alleging a corporation).

7. A denial that the defendant or a person under its authority executed a written instrument that is the subject of the suit. TRCP 93(7); ***Methodist Hosps. v. Corporate Communicators***, 806 S.W.2d 879, 882 (Tex. App.—Dallas 1991, writ denied). To deny the execution of a document alleged to have been executed by a person now deceased, a party may state that it "has reason to believe and does believe that such instrument was not executed by the decedent or by his authority." TRCP 93(7). Without a verified denial, the document is fully proved. *Id.*; *e.g.*, ***Boyd v. Diversified Fin. Sys.***, 1 S.W.3d 888, 891 (Tex.App.—Dallas 1999, no pet.) (documents were admissible regardless of their hearsay status because no verified denial was filed).

8. A denial of the genuineness of an indorsement or assignment of a written instrument that is the subject of the suit. TRCP 93(8). The denial may be made on information and belief. *Id.* If no verified denial is filed, the indorsement is fully proved. *Id.*; *see also* ***Overall v. Southwestern Bell Yellow Pages***, 869 S.W.2d 629, 632 (Tex.App.—Houston [14th Dist.] 1994, no writ) (evidence contesting genuineness of contract excluded because no verified denial was filed).

9. An allegation a written instrument that is the subject of the suit either is without consideration or the consideration failed in whole or in part. TRCP 93(9), 94; ***Brown v. Aztec Rig Equip.***, 921 S.W.2d 835, 845 (Tex.App.—Houston [14th Dist.] 1996, writ denied); ***Champion***, 740 S.W.2d at 851-52. If no verified plea is filed, the plaintiff is not required to prove consideration. See ***O'Connor's COA***, "Failure of consideration," ch. 5-B, §5.1.7, p. 80.

10. A denial of an account, supported by an affidavit. TRCP 93(10), 185; ***Powers v. Adams***, 2 S.W.3d 496, 498 (Tex.App.—Houston [14th Dist.] 1999, no pet.); ***Cooper v. Scott Irrigation Constr.***, 838 S.W.2d 743, 745 (Tex. App.—El Paso 1992, no writ). A general denial, even if verified, does not comply with the requirements of TRCP 93(10) and 185. ***Andrews v. East Tex. Med. Center-Athens***, 885 S.W.2d 264, 268 (Tex.App.—Tyler 1994, no writ). If no verified denial is filed, the plaintiff is not required to introduce further evidence. ***Northeast Wholesale Lumber v. Leader Lumber***, 785 S.W.2d 402, 407 (Tex.App.—Dallas 1989, no writ); *see* TRCP 185.

11. An allegation that the contract is usurious. TRCP 93(11); ***Powers***, 2 S.W.3d at 498. See ***O'Connor's COA***, "Usury," ch. 27, p. 763.

12. An allegation that notice and proof of the loss or claim were not given as alleged. TRCP 93(12); *see also* TRCP 54 (conditions precedent). The denial must be made with specificity. If a verified denial is not filed, notice and proof are presumed, and no evidence to the contrary may be admitted. TRCP 93(12); ***Sanchez v. Jary***, 768 S.W.2d 933, 936 (Tex.App.—San Antonio 1989, no writ).

13. A denial of specific matters in an appeal from the Industrial Accident Board. TRCP 93(13). TRCP 93(13) lists the allegations that must be denied. A defendant may make a denial under TRCP 93(13)(g)—that the plaintiff did not have good cause for filing the claim outside the one-year deadline—based on information and belief. ***National Un. Fire Ins. Co. v. Reyna***, 897 S.W.2d 777, 779 (Tex.1995).

14. A denial that a party is doing business under an assumed or trade name. TRCP 93(14); ***Hyson v. Chilkewitz***, 971 S.W.2d 563, 569 (Tex.App.—Dallas 1998), *rev'd on other grounds*, 22 S.W.3d 825 (Tex.1999).

15. A denial of the occurrence or performance of a condition precedent in a suit by an insured against an auto insurer. TRCP 93(15). The denial may be made on information and belief. *Id.*

16. An allegation of any other matter required by statute to be pleaded under oath. TRCP 93(16).

§4.2 Verified pleas in other rules. Other matters that must be verified include the following: a confession of judgment, TRCP 314; a writ of certiorari to a county court, TRCP 577; the answer of a garnishee, TRCP 665; a complaint seeking an injunction, TRCP 680, 682; a request to dissolve an injunction before a final hearing, TRCP 690; a claimant's oath by a third party to reclaim personal property that has been levied, TRCP 717; and a claim of right of property, TRCP 717.

§5. AFFIRMATIVE DEFENSES

A general denial does not include affirmative defenses. If a defendant wants to rely on an affirmative defense, it must specifically plead it. TRCP 94. An affirmative defense is an independent reason why the plaintiff should not recover. ***Texas Beef Cattle Co. v. Green***, 921 S.W.2d 203, 212 (Tex.1996); ***Gorman v. Life Ins. Co. of N. Am.***, 811 S.W.2d 542, 546 (Tex.1991). An affirmative defense allows the defendant to avoid liability even if the allegations in the plaintiff's petition are true.

NOTE

The defendant does not waive an affirmative defense by not pleading it if the plaintiff anticipated the defense in its pleading, and if the defense is established at trial as a matter of law. ***Shoemake v. Fogel, Ltd.****, 826 S.W.2d 933, 937 (Tex.1992) (parental immunity);* ***Phillips v. Phillips****, 820 S.W.2d 785, 789 (Tex.1991) (illegality).*

§5.1 Affirmative defense vs. counterclaim. Some claims can be raised as either an affirmative defense or a counterclaim (*e.g.*, fraud). *See* ***Kuehnhoefer v. Welch***, 893 S.W.2d 689, 692 (Tex.App.—Texarkana 1995, writ denied); ***Adams v. Tri-Continental Leasing Corp.***, 713 S.W.2d 152, 153 (Tex.App.—Dallas 1986, no writ). The test to determine if a claim should be raised as an affirmative defense or a counterclaim is whether the defendant asks for affirmative relief. If the defendant does not ask for affirmative relief as part of the claim, it is an affirmative defense; if the defendant asks for affirmative relief, it is a counterclaim. For example, if a defendant alleges fraud and asks for damages, fraud is a counterclaim. ***Kuehnhoefer***, 893 S.W.2d at 692. If a defendant does not ask for damages, fraud is an affirmative defense.

§5.2 Affirmative defenses in TRCP 94. Many, but not all, of the affirmative defenses are listed in TRCP 94. The following are the affirmative defenses in that rule:

1. Accord and satisfaction. ***Hunt, Hopkins & Mitchell v. Facility Ins.***, 78 S.W.3d 564, 568 (Tex.App.—Austin 2002, pet. denied).

2. Arbitration and award. ***Transwestern Pipeline Co. v. Horizon Oil & Gas Co.***, 809 S.W.2d 589, 593 (Tex.App.—Dallas 1991, writ dism'd).

3. Assumption of the risk. The Supreme Court abolished the affirmative defense of assumption of the risk in negligence actions. ***Farley v. M M Cattle Co.***, 529 S.W.2d 751, 758 (Tex.1975). In product liability cases, assumption of the risk is subsumed under the defense of contributory negligence. ***Duncan v. Cessna Aircraft Co.***, 665 S.W.2d 414, 428 (Tex.1984). Assumption of the risk retains limited viability in the following instances:

(1) When the plaintiff was injured while committing a felony or attempting suicide. CPRC §93.001(a)(1), (2).

(2) When the plaintiff knowingly and expressly consented (orally or in writing) to the dangerous activity or condition. ***Farley***, 529 S.W.2d at 758; *see, e.g.*, ***Newman v. Tropical Visions***, 891 S.W.2d 713, 718-19 (Tex.App.—San Antonio 1994, writ denied) (by written agreement, assumed risk of scuba diving). Participants in certain sports activities are deemed to accept the risk of being injured. *See, e.g.*, ***Hathaway v. Tascosa Country Club***, 846 S.W.2d 614, 616-17 (Tex.App.—Amarillo 1993, no writ) (golfers assume risk of being hit by golf ball); *see also* ***Moore v. Phi Delta Theta Co.***, 976 S.W.2d 738, 741 (Tex.App.—Houston [1st Dist.] 1998, pet. denied) (only participants, not sponsors of event or nonparticipants, are immunized by the competitive contact sports doctrine). *But see* ***Greer v. Davis***, 921 S.W.2d 325, 328 (Tex.App.—Corpus Christi 1996) (players do not

assume risk of intentional assault), *writ denied*, 940 S.W.2d 582 (Tex.1996). See ***O'Connor's COA***, "Competitive sports doctrine," ch. 19-A, §5.5.1(2), p. 508.

4. Contributory negligence. ***McFadden v. Hale***, 615 S.W.2d 345, 348 (Tex.App.—Waco 1981, no writ). See ***O'Connor's COA***, "Proportionate Responsibility & Contribution," ch. 42, p. 1115.

5. Discharge in bankruptcy. ***Burnam v. Patterson***, 119 S.W.3d 12, 15 (Tex.App.—Amarillo 2003, pet. denied). An allegation that the defendant filed for bankruptcy is not sufficient; the defendant must plead that it was discharged from bankruptcy. ***Seiffert v. Bowden***, 556 S.W.2d 406, 409 (Tex.App.—Corpus Christi 1977, no writ).

6. Duress. ***Gooch v. American Sling Co.***, 902 S.W.2d 181, 186 (Tex.App.—Fort Worth 1995, no writ). See ***O'Connor's COA***, "Duress," ch. 5-B, §5.1.8, p. 80.

7. Estoppel. ***In re Estate of Dillard***, 98 S.W.3d 386, 396 (Tex.App.—Amarillo 2003, pet. denied) (judicial estoppel); ***Hennessey v. Vanguard Ins. Co.***, 895 S.W.2d 794, 798 (Tex.App.—Amarillo 1995, writ denied) (equitable estoppel); ***Huddleston v. Texas Commerce Bank***, 756 S.W.2d 343, 346-47 (Tex.App.—Dallas 1988, writ denied) (estoppel by deed).

8. Failure of consideration. ***Murphy v. Canion***, 797 S.W.2d 944, 949 (Tex.App.—Houston [14th Dist.] 1990, no writ); *see also* TRCP 93(9) (verified plea). See ***O'Connor's COA***, "Failure of consideration," ch. 5-B, §5.1.7, p. 80.

9. Fraud. ***Texas Farmers Ins. Co. v. Murphy***, 996 S.W.2d 873, 879-80 (Tex.1999). See ***O'Connor's COA***, "Fraud," ch. 11, p. 221.

10. Illegality. ***Phillips v. Phillips***, 820 S.W.2d 785, 789 (Tex.1991). If illegality is apparent on the face of the plaintiff's pleadings because the plaintiff anticipated the defense, and if the defense is proved as a matter of law at trial, the defendant is not required to plead illegality as a defense. *Id.*; ***Lewkowicz v. El Paso Apparel Corp.***, 625 S.W.2d 301, 303 (Tex.1981). See ***O'Connor's COA***, "Illegality," ch. 5-B, §5.1.5, p. 78.

11. Injury by a fellow servant. ***City of San Antonio v. Mendoza***, 532 S.W.2d 353, 360 (Tex.App.—San Antonio 1975, writ ref'd n.r.e.).

12. Laches. ***Murray v. Murray***, 611 S.W.2d 172, 173 (Tex.App.—El Paso 1981, no writ). See ***O'Connor's COA***, "Determining whether claim is barred by laches," ch. 43, §2.8, p. 1150.

13. License. *See* ***Moore v. Sedig***, 791 S.W.2d 556, 561 (Tex.App.—Dallas 1990, no writ) (absence of a license is an affirmative defense).

14. Loss within an exception to general liability. *See* ***Venture Encoding Serv. v. Atlantic Mut. Ins. Co.***, 107 S.W.3d 729, 733 (Tex.App.—Fort Worth 2003, no pet.). When a plaintiff sues to collect on a general hazards insurance policy that has provisions limiting general liability, the insurer-defendant must specifically allege the loss was within a particular exception to general liability. *Id.* If the carrier pleads an exclusion under the policy, the plaintiff must then prove the loss was not within the exclusion. ***Southern Ins. Co. v. Progressive Cty. Mut. Ins. Co.***, 708 S.W.2d 549, 551 (Tex.App.—Houston [1st Dist.] 1986, writ ref'd n.r.e.).

15. Payment. ***Southwestern Fire & Cas. Co. v. Larue***, 367 S.W.2d 162, 163 (Tex.1963); ***Equitable Trust Co. v. Roland***, 644 S.W.2d 46, 53 (Tex.App.—San Antonio 1982, no writ); *see also* TRCP 93(10) (verified denial), TRCP 95 (plea of payment). When a defendant claims it paid the sums sued upon, it should either (1) file with its answer an account that distinctly states the details of payment or (2) describe the payment in the answer so plainly and particularly as to give the plaintiff full notice of the character of the payment. TRCP 95. If the defendant does not do either, it will not be allowed to prove the payment at trial. *See* ***Jack Parker Indus. v. FDIC***, 769 S.W.2d 700, 702 (Tex.App.—El Paso 1989, no writ).

16. Release. ***Dresser Indus. v. Page Pet.***, 853 S.W.2d 505, 508 (Tex.1993) (pre-injury); ***Williams v. Glash***, 789 S.W.2d 261, 264 (Tex.1990) (post-injury). See "Provisions in a Settlement Agreement," ch. 7-H, §3.1, p. 510.

17. Res judicata. ***Texas Beef Cattle Co. v. Green***, 921 S.W.2d 203, 206-07 (Tex.1996); ***Dardari v. Texas Commerce Bank***, 961 S.W.2d 466, 470 (Tex.App.—Houston [1st Dist.] 1997, no pet.). See "Res Judicata & Collateral Estoppel," ch. 9-D, p. 609.

18. Statute of frauds. ***First Nat'l Bank v. Zimmerman***, 442 S.W.2d 674, 675-76 (Tex.1969); ***Adams v. H&H Meat Prods.***, 41 S.W.3d 762, 776 (Tex.App.—Corpus Christi 2001, no pet.). See ***O'Connor's COA***, "Statute of frauds," ch. 5-B, §5.1.10, p. 83.

19. Statute of limitations. ***Woods v. William M. Mercer, Inc.***, 769 S.W.2d 515, 517 (Tex.1988). See ***O'Connor's COA***, "Limitations," ch. 43, p. 1135.

20. Waiver. ***Tenneco Inc. v. Enterprise Prods. Co.***, 925 S.W.2d 640, 643 (Tex.1996); *see* ***T.O. Stanley Boot Co. v. Bank of El Paso***, 847 S.W.2d 218, 223 (Tex.1992) (by not pleading waiver, P waived affirmative defense of waiver).

§5.3 Other affirmative defenses. Any other matter constituting an avoidance may be pleaded as an affirmative defense. TRCP 94. The following are some other affirmative defenses:

1. Contract-related actions.

(1) Ambiguity. See ***O'Connor's COA***, "Ambiguity," ch. 5-B, §6.1.2(3), p. 93.

(2) Justification. See ***O'Connor's COA***, "Justification," ch. 5-C, §5.4.2, p. 104.

(3) Mistake. See ***O'Connor's COA***, "Mistake," ch. 5-B, §5.1.9, p. 82.

(4) Penalty. See ***O'Connor's COA***, "Penalty," ch. 5-B, §5.1.18, p. 92.

(5) Ratification. See ***O'Connor's COA***, "Ratification," ch. 5-B, §5.1.15, p. 91.

(6) Rescission. See ***O'Connor's COA***, "Rescission," ch. 5-B, §3.5.2, p. 73.

2. Criminal acts.

(1) By plaintiff. If the plaintiff was injured while committing an offense for which she was convicted, neither the plaintiff nor those with derivative claims are entitled to recover for the plaintiff's injuries. CPRC §§86.001-86.003; *see also* CPRC §93.001(a) (P cannot recover if injured while attempting to commit felony or suicide). See ***O'Connor's COA***, "Felony or suicide," ch. 19-A, §5.5.2, p. 509. The defense in CPRC chapter 86 does not apply to injuries arising from traffic offenses and certain other conduct. *See* CPRC §§86.005, 86.007.

(2) By third person. As a general rule, a person has no duty to protect another from the criminal acts of a third person. *See* ***Walker v. Harris***, 924 S.W.2d 375, 377 (Tex.1996). If the defendant is negligent but the plaintiff is actually injured as a result of a criminal act of a third person, the criminal conduct is a superseding cause that relieves the defendant of liability unless the criminal act was a foreseeable result of the defendant's negligence.

3. DTPA. See ***O'Connor's COA***, "Defenses," ch. 8, §5, p. 190.

4. Disclaimer. See ***O'Connor's COA***, "Disclaimers of Warranty," ch. 28-A, §4, p. 785.

5. ERISA. The claim is preempted by the Employee Retirement Income Security Act of 1974, 29 U.S.C. §1001. ***Gorman v. Life Ins. Co. of N. Am.***, 811 S.W.2d 542, 546 (Tex.1991).

6. Failure to mitigate. The defendant may assert that the plaintiff did not make reasonable efforts to mitigate its damages. *E.g.*, ***Gunn Infiniti, Inc. v. O'Byrne***, 996 S.W.2d 854, 856-57 (Tex.1999) (claimant in DTPA suit); ***Austin Hill Country Rlty. v. Palisades Plaza***, 948 S.W.2d 293, 296-97 (Tex.1997) (landlord's duty to mitigate); ***Gulf Consol. Int'l v. Murphy***, 658 S.W.2d 565, 566 (Tex.1983) (discharged employee's duty to mitigate).

But see ***Moulton v. Alamo Ambulance Serv.***, 414 S.W.2d 444, 448 (Tex.1967) (failure to mitigate damages by not treating personal injuries is not affirmative defense, but is admissible under general denial). See ***O'Connor's COA***, "Mitigation of damages," ch. 5-B, §5.1.17, p. 92.

7. First Amendment. When a plaintiff's suit implicates a defendant's free exercise of rights, the defendant may assert the First Amendment as an affirmative defense. See ***O'Connor's COA***, "Libel & Slander Actions," ch. 16-A, p. 335.

8. Immunity.

(1) Charitable. See ***O'Connor's COA***, "Charitable organizations & volunteers," ch. 40, §1.6, p. 1107.

(2) Governmental. The defendant may be immune from liability because it is a governmental entity. ***Kinnear v. Texas Comm'n on Human Rights***, 14 S.W.3d 299, 300 (Tex.2000); ***Tarrant Cty. v. Denton Cty.***, 87 S.W.3d 159, 176-77 (Tex.App.—Fort Worth 2002, pet. denied). See ***O'Connor's CPRC Plus***, "Waivers of Governmental Immunity Chart," p. 341 (2003-04); ***O'Connor's COA***, "Suits Against the Government," ch. 22, p. 621. When the defendant is immune from suit, it should file a plea to the jurisdiction. See "Governmental immunity from suit," ch. 3-F, §3.6, p. 183.

(3) Judicial. See ***O'Connor's COA***, "Judicial Immunity," ch. 39-C, p. 1097.

(4) Legislative. See ***O'Connor's COA***, "Legislative Immunity," ch. 39-B, p. 1088.

(5) Official. The common-law defense of official immunity protects individual officials from personal liability when they perform discretionary duties in good faith within the scope of their authority. See ***O'Connor's COA***, "Official Immunity," ch. 39-A, p. 1075.

(6) Parental. See ***O'Connor's COA***, "Parental Immunity," ch. 41, p. 1111.

03 (7) Professional employee of school district. A professional employee of a school district is immune from liability for any discretionary act committed within the scope of the employee's duties. Educ. Code §22.0511(a); *see* ***Downing v. Brown***, 935 S.W.2d 112, 114 (Tex.1996); ***Chesshir v. Sharp***, 19 S.W.3d 502, 504 (Tex.App.—Amarillo 2000, no pet.). See ***O'Connor's COA***, "Employee immunity," ch. 40, §2.1, p. 1108.

9. Negligence.

(1) Unavoidable accident. See ***O'Connor's COA***, "Unavoidable accident," ch. 19-A, §5.10.3, p. 512.

(2) Sudden emergency. See ***O'Connor's COA***, "Sudden emergency," ch. 19-A, §5.10.4, p. 512.

10. Suicide. It is an affirmative defense to a suit for personal injury or death that the plaintiff's suicide or attempted suicide was the sole cause of the injury. CPRC §93.001(a)(2); ***Kassen v. Hatley***, 887 S.W.2d 4, 12 (Tex.1994).

11. Truth. In defamation suits brought by private individuals, truth is an affirmative defense. See ***O'Connor's COA***, "Substantial truth," ch. 16-A, §5.4, p. 362.

§5.4 Denial of conditions precedent. If the plaintiff alleged that "all conditions precedent have been performed or have occurred," the defendant must specifically deny any conditions that were not performed or have not occurred. TRCP 54; ***Greathouse v. Charter Nat'l Bank***, 851 S.W.2d 173, 174 (Tex.1992); *see also* TRCP 93(12) (requires specific denial for notice and proof of loss or claim for damages). The defendant cannot simply plead that it denies some conditions precedent have occurred. ***Hill v. Thompson & Knight***, 756 S.W.2d 824, 826 (Tex.App.—Dallas 1988, no writ). By specifically denying the plaintiff's TRCP 54 allegations, the defendant forces the plaintiff to prove those conditions specifically denied. ***Betty Leavell Rlty. Co. v. Raggio***, 669 S.W.2d 102, 104 (Tex.1984); ***Phifer v. Nacogdoches Cty. Cent. Appr. Dist.***, 45 S.W.3d 159, 174 (Tex.App.—Tyler 2000, pet. denied); ***Love of God Holiness Temple Ch. v. Union Stand. Ins. Co.***, 860 S.W.2d 179, 180 (Tex.App.—Texarkana 1993, writ denied). A specific denial under TRCP 54 should be verified, just like specific pleas under TRCP 93.

§6. DEFENDANT'S CLAIMS

TRCP 97 permits parties to file counterclaims and cross-claims; TRCP 38 permits parties to bring in third parties who may be liable for all or part of the claims involved in the suit; and CPRC §33.004 permits a defendant to designate a person as a responsible third party.

PRACTICE TIP

If a defendant asserts a counterclaim or cross-claim that changes the discovery control level, the defendant should probably allege a new discovery control level in the first paragraph of its pleading. TRCP 190 does not mention defendants. See "Discovery Control Plans," ch. 6-A, §7, p. 318.

§6.1 Counterclaims. A defendant may file a claim against the plaintiff by way of counterclaim. TRCP 97(a), (b). A counterclaim is an affirmative claim for relief filed against an opposing party. Generally, the term "counterclaim" denotes a defendant's claim against a plaintiff that will, in some way, defeat or reduce a judgment for the plaintiff. ***Doyer v. Pitney Bowes, Inc.***, 80 S.W.3d 215, 218 (Tex.App.—Austin 2002, pet. denied). A counterclaim can be either compulsory or permissive.

1. Compulsory counterclaim. For the test for a compulsory counterclaim, see "Compulsory Joinder of Claims," ch. 2-E, §6, p. 98.

2. Permissive counterclaim. Any counterclaim that does not satisfy the compulsory-counterclaim test is a permissive counterclaim. For the test for joinder of permissive claims, see "Permissive Joinder of Claims," ch. 2-E, §7, p. 100.

3. Service of process not necessary. Service of process is not necessary when a counterclaim is filed against a party who has already made an appearance in the case; service under TRCP 21a is sufficient. TRCP 124; ***In re A.L.H.C.***, 49 S.W.3d 911, 916-17 (Tex.App.—Dallas 2001, pet. denied); *see* ***Houston Crushed Concrete v. Concrete Recycling Corp.***, 879 S.W.2d 258, 261 (Tex.App.—Houston [14th Dist.] 1994, no writ) (counter-plaintiff—the original defendant—may serve counterclaim on counter-defendant—the original plaintiff—through service of process or under TRCP 21a). If the party has not made an appearance, service of process is necessary.

§6.2 Cross-claims. A cross-claim is an affirmative claim for relief filed against a coparty. A defendant may file a cross-claim against a codefendant if the claim arises out of the same transaction or occurrence as the original action or any counterclaim. TRCP 97(e). The cross-defendant must assert its compulsory claims against the cross-claimant, or its claims will be barred. *See* ***Getty Oil Co. v. Insurance Co. of N. Am.***, 845 S.W.2d 794, 800 (Tex. 1992). In such a case, the parties are no longer merely coparties but are opposing parties, and the compulsory-counterclaim rule applies. For example, if A sues B and C, and B files a cross-claim against C, C must file its compulsory counterclaims against A and B, or the claims will be barred in a later suit. Service of process is not necessary when a cross-claim is filed against a party who has already made an appearance in the case; service under TRCP 21a is sufficient. TRCP 124; ***Mays v. Perkins***, 927 S.W.2d 222, 227 (Tex.App.—Houston [1st Dist.] 1996, no writ); *see* ***Von Briesen, Purtell & Roper v. French***, 78 S.W.3d 570, 575 (Tex.App.—Amarillo 2002, pet. dism'd). If the party has not made an appearance, service of process is necessary.

§6.3 Third-party suit. Third-party practice is the procedure by which a defendant brings additional parties into the lawsuit. ***Heard v. Moore***, 101 S.W.3d 726, 728-29 (Tex.App.—Texarkana 2003, pet. denied). Third-party practice is sometimes called impleader. A defendant, as a third-party plaintiff, may bring into the suit any third party who is or may be liable to it or to the plaintiff for all or part of the plaintiff's claim. TRCP 38(a); ***Goose Creek Consol. ISD v. Jarrar's Plumbing***, 74 S.W.3d 486, 492 (Tex.App.—Texarkana 2002, pet. denied). This is more restrictive than the "same transaction or occurrence" test used for counterclaims and cross-claims, and thus is limited to contribution and indemnification claims.

1. Leave of court. The defendant may file a third-party action without leave of court within 30 days after filing its answer; after that, leave of court is required. TRCP 38(a); ***Bilek & Purcell Indus. v. Paderwerk Gebr. Benteler GmbH & Co.***, 694 S.W.2d 225, 227 (Tex.App.—Houston [1st Dist.] 1985, no writ).

2. Service of citation. The defendant, as third-party plaintiff, must serve the third-party defendant with citation and petition. TRCP 38(a).

03 **§6.4 Responsible third party.** In 2003, the Legislature eliminated the requirement that a third party who bears some responsibility for the plaintiff's injuries must be joined in the lawsuit before its liability can be submitted to the jury. *See* H.B. 4, 78th Leg., §4.03, eff. July 1, 2003. The old joinder practice was replaced with a more lenient "designation" practice. *See id.* The 2003 amendments affect only those cases filed after June 30, 2003. *See id.* §23.02(c) (savings provision). For rules on joinder of a responsible third party for cases filed before July 1, 2003, see ***O'Connor's COA***, "Responsible third party," ch. 42, §3.4.1, p. 1122.

1. Who is an RTP. A responsible third party (RTP) is anyone who is alleged to have caused or contributed to the harm for which recovery of damages is sought, whether by negligent act or omission, by any defective or unreasonably dangerous product, or by other conduct or activity that violates an applicable legal standard. CPRC §33.011(6). A defendant can designate an unknown person as an RTP. *See id.* §33.004(j). See §6.4.3, below. An RTP does not include a seller eligible for indemnity in a products liability action under CPRC §82.002. CPRC §33.011(6).

2. Motion for leave to designate. The defendant may designate a person as an RTP by filing a motion for leave to designate that person as an RTP. CPRC §33.004(a). The court must grant leave to designate the named person as an RTP unless an objection is filed. See §6.4.6, below. If the RTP is an unknown criminal, the defendant must first file an amended answer before seeking leave to designate. See §6.4.3, below. The filing or granting of a motion for leave to designate a person as an RTP or a finding of fault against the person does not by itself impose liability on the RTP in that suit or in any other proceeding. CRPC §33.004(i). The designation allows the jury to consider the third party's percentage of responsibility. CPRC §33.003(a). By designating an RTP who shares the blame for the injury, the defendant can reduce its own percentage of responsibility.

3. RTP – unknown criminal. If the RTP is an unknown person alleged to have committed a criminal act, the defendant must designate that person in an amended answer before filing a motion for leave to designate the person as an RTP. *See* CPRC §33.004(j). The RTP must be designated in an amended answer no later than 60 days after the defendant filed its original answer. *Id.* In the amended answer, the defendant must do the following:

(1) Allege the person committed a criminal act that caused the loss or injury that is the subject of the suit. *Id.*

(2) Plead sufficient facts to show a reasonable probability that the act was criminal. *Id.* §33.004(j)(1).

(3) Plead all identifying characteristics of the unknown person at the time the amended answer is filed. *Id.* §33.004(j)(2).

(4) Plead sufficient facts about the alleged responsibility of the third party to satisfy the pleading requirements of the TRCPs. *Id.* §33.004(j)(3).

(5) Refer to the RTP as "Jane Doe" or "John Doe." *Id.* §33.004(k).

4. Deadline for motion. A defendant must file a motion for leave to designate an RTP at least 60 days before the trial date. CPRC §33.004(a). On a finding of good cause, the court may allow the motion for leave to designate an RTP to be filed at a later date. *Id.*

5. Plaintiff's joinder. If the defendant designates an RTP, the plaintiff may join the RTP as a defendant no later than 60 days after that person is designated as an RTP, even if the plaintiff's claim against the RTP would otherwise be barred by limitations. CPRC §33.004(e). If the RTP is joined by the plaintiff, the RTP becomes a defendant and can be liable to the plaintiff.

6. Objection. If a party does not object to the motion for leave, the court must grant leave to designate the named person as an RTP. CPRC §33.004(f). A party must file the objection within 15 days after the date the motion is served. *Id.* To defeat the motion for leave, the objecting party must establish that (1) the defendant did not plead sufficient facts about the RTP to satisfy the pleading requirements of the TRCPs, and (2) after being given the opportunity to replead, the defendant still did not satisfy the pleading requirements of the TRCPs concerning the alleged responsibility of the third party. *Id.* §33.004(g)

7. Ruling on motion. If the court grants the motion for leave to designate a person as an RTP, the person named in the motion is designated as an RTP without any further action by the court or the party. CPRC §33.004(h).

8. Strike designation. After an adequate time for discovery, a party may move to strike the designation of an RTP because there is no evidence the designated person is responsible for any part of the plaintiff's injury or damage. CPRC §33.004(*l*). The court should grant the motion to strike unless the defendant presents sufficient evidence to raise a fact issue about the designated person's responsibility for the plaintiff's injury or damage. *Id.*

9. Jury charge. If the plaintiff does not join the RTP as a defendant, the charge will be submitted to the jury inquiring about the responsibility for the injury as between the plaintiff, the defendant, the RTP, and any settling person. *See* CPRC §33.003(a). A question regarding the conduct of any person cannot be submitted to the jury without sufficient evidence to support the submission. *Id.* §33.003(b). The defendant is liable for the percentage of responsibility attributed to it by the trier of fact, as well as for those amounts for which the defendant is jointly and severally liable. *Id.* §33.013(a), (b). See ***O'Connor's COA***, "Determining What Each Defendant Owes," ch. 42, §6, p. 1129.

§7. REQUEST FOR DISCLOSURE

The defendant should consider including a request for disclosure in its original answer. The only statement necessary for a request for disclosure is the following: "Pursuant to Rule 194, you are requested to disclose, within 30 days of the service of this request, the information or material described in Rule [*identify rule, e.g., 194.2; 194.2(a), (c), and (f); 194.2(d)-(g)*]." TRCP 194.1. See "Requests for Disclosure," ch. 6-D, p. 375. If the defendant includes the request in the answer, the defendant must change the title of the instrument to "Defendant's Original Answer and Request for Disclosure."

§8. DRAFTING THE ANSWER

For a series of considerations that will help the defendant construct its original answer, see "Constructing the Original Answer," ch. 3-A, §4, p. 140.

F. PLEA TO THE JURISDICTION—CHALLENGING THE COURT

§1. GENERAL

§1.1 Rule. TRCP 85. See CPRC §16.064.

§1.2 Purpose. The purpose of a plea to the jurisdiction is to defeat a cause of action without regard to whether the claim has merit. ***Bland ISD v. Blue***, 34 S.W.3d 547, 554 (Tex.2000). The plea challenges the court's power to determine the subject matter of the controversy. ***In re Brilliant***, 86 S.W.3d 680, 683 (Tex.App.—El Paso 2002, no pet.); ***Axtell v. University of Tex.***, 69 S.W.3d 261, 263 (Tex.App.—Austin 2002, no pet.); ***Godley ISD v. Woods***, 21 S.W.3d 656, 658 (Tex.App.—Waco 2000, pet. denied). Subject-matter jurisdiction is essential to the authority of a court to decide a case. ***Bland ISD***, 34 S.W.3d at 553-54; ***Texas Ass'n of Bus. v. Texas Air Control Bd.***, 852 S.W.2d 440, 443 (Tex.1993). Without subject-matter jurisdiction, a court cannot render a valid judgment. ***Dubai Pet. Co. v. Kazi***, 12 S.W.3d 71, 74-75 (Tex.2000); ***Liberty Mut. Ins. Co. v. Sharp***, 874 S.W.2d 736, 739 (Tex.App.—Austin 1994, writ denied). Subject-matter jurisdiction cannot be presumed and cannot be waived.

Continental Coffee Prods. Co. v. Cazarez, 937 S.W.2d 444, 449 n.2 (Tex.1996). Lack of subject-matter jurisdiction makes a judgment void, not just voidable. ***Mapco, Inc. v. Forrest***, 795 S.W.2d 700, 703 (Tex.1990).

§1.3 Forms & timetable. *O'Connor's Texas Civil Forms*, FORMS 3F; Timetable, this book, Pretrial Motions, p. 998.

§2. PLEA TO THE JURISDICTION

NOTE

For the rules governing the selection of a court, see "Choosing the Court—Jurisdiction," ch. 2-F, p. 101.

§2.1 Form. The plea to the jurisdiction may be included in the general answer or filed as a separate motion. TRCP 85. If filed as a motion, it should be captioned as a motion to dismiss for lack of jurisdiction. See ***O'Connor's*** FORM 3F:01.

§2.2 Evidence. The trial court can consider evidence on a plea to the jurisdiction when evidence is necessary to determine jurisdictional facts. ***Bland ISD***, 34 S.W.3d at 555; ***In re Brilliant***, 86 S.W.3d at 684; *see, e.g.*, ***Texas Dept. of Crim. Justice v. Miller***, 51 S.W.3d 583, 586 (Tex.2001) (in TTCA suit, court considered deposition testimony); ***F/R Cattle Co. v. State***, 866 S.W.2d 200, 201 (Tex.1993) (in suit under Clean Air Act, court conducted evidentiary hearing to determine whether odors were produced by natural processes); ***State v. Sledge***, 36 S.W.3d 152, 155 (Tex.App.—Houston [1st Dist.] 2000, pet. denied) (in condemnation suit, court considered affidavits & other evidence at hearing); ***Diocese of Galveston-Houston v. Stone***, 892 S.W.2d 169, 176-77 (Tex.App.—Houston [14th Dist.] 1994, orig. proceeding) (in suit against church by employee, discovery permitted to determine whether church could assert ecclesiastical privilege). The court should limit the evidence to what is relevant to the jurisdictional issue and avoid considering evidence that goes to the merits. ***Bland ISD***, 34 S.W.3d at 555; ***Harris Cty. v. Progressive Nat'l Bank***, 93 S.W.3d 381, 384 (Tex.App.—Houston [14th Dist.] 2002, pet. denied); *see, e.g.*, ***Texas Dept. of Parks & Wildlife v. Miranda***, 55 S.W.3d 648, 651-52 (Tex.App.—San Antonio 2001, pet. dism'd) (trial court not authorized to examine P's gross negligence claim because D did not allege claim was pleaded as means for wrongfully obtaining jurisdiction).

§2.3 No verification. No rule or statute requires the plea to the jurisdiction to be verified. ***Ab-Tex Bev. Co. v. Angelo State Univ.***, 96 S.W.3d 683, 688 (Tex.App.—Austin 2003, no pet.); *see* ***City of Ft. Worth v. Robles***, 51 S.W.3d 436, 444-45 (Tex.App.—Fort Worth 2001, pet. denied). If jurisdictional evidence is necessary, affidavits and other sworn proof should be attached to the plea.

§2.4 No deadline. There is no deadline for the plea to the jurisdiction. Lack of subject-matter jurisdiction can be raised at any time. ***Sivley v. Sivley***, 972 S.W.2d 850, 855 (Tex.App.—Tyler 1998, orig. proceeding). The challenge can be raised for the first time on appeal. ***Waco ISD v. Gibson***, 22 S.W.3d 849, 851 (Tex.2000); ***Tullos v. Eaton Corp.***, 695 S.W.2d 568, 568 (Tex.1985). A court can inquire into its jurisdiction on its own initiative at any time, without a motion. *See* ***Texas Workers' Comp. Comm'n v. Garcia***, 893 S.W.2d 504, 517 n.15 (Tex.1995).

§3. GROUNDS

NOTE

Unless it is clear from the pleadings that the court does not have jurisdiction over the controversy, the court should retain the case. See ***Peek v. Equipment Serv. Co.***, *779 S.W.2d 802, 804 (Tex.1989). If the jurisdictional defect is a pleading defect that can be cured by amendment, it should be challenged by special exceptions. See "Curable defects in jurisdiction," ch. 3-G, §2.2.4, p. 188.*

§3.1 No justiciable issue. A plea to the jurisdiction is proper to challenge the lack of a justiciable issue. To present a justiciable issue, a lawsuit must involve a real controversy that will be resolved by the judicial relief sought. *E.g.*, ***State Bar v. Gomez***, 891 S.W.2d 243, 245-46 (Tex.1994) (district court did not have authority to compel State Bar or Supreme Court to implement mandatory pro bono); *see, e.g.*, ***In re Nolo Press***, 991 S.W.2d 768, 778 (Tex.1999) (district court did not have authority to modify order of Supreme Court).

§3.2 No standing. A plea to the jurisdiction is proper to challenge a party's lack of standing. *See* ***M.D. Anderson Cancer Ctr. v. Novak***, 52 S.W.3d 704, 710-11 (Tex.2001); ***Waco ISD***, 22 S.W.3d at 850. Standing focuses on who is the correct party to bring the suit. ***Patterson v. Planned Parenthood***, 971 S.W.2d 439, 442 (Tex.1998). See "Standing & capacity," ch. 2-B, §3.2, p. 68.

§3.3 Not ripe. A plea to the jurisdiction is proper to challenge the lack of "ripeness." *See* ***Waco ISD***, 22 S.W.3d at 851-52. Ripeness focuses on when an action may be brought. ***Patterson***, 971 S.W.2d at 442; ***American Nat'l Ins. Co. v. Cannon***, 86 S.W.3d 801, 806 (Tex.App.—Beaumont 2002, no pet.); ***Texas Dept. of Banking v. Mount Olivet Cemetery Ass'n***, 27 S.W.3d 276, 282 (Tex.App.—Austin 2000, pet. denied).

§3.4 Another court has exclusive jurisdiction. A plea to the jurisdiction is proper to challenge a suit brought in one court when another court has continuing and exclusive jurisdiction. ***Jansen v. Fitzpatrick***, 14 S.W.3d 426, 430-31 (Tex.App.—Houston [14th Dist.] 2000, no pet.); *see also* ***Speer v. Stover***, 685 S.W.2d 22, 23 (Tex.1985) (district court did not have jurisdiction over case pending in probate court); ***Howe State Bank v. Crookham***, 873 S.W.2d 745, 747-48 (Tex.App.—Dallas 1994, no writ) (same); *cf.* ***Geary v. Peavy***, 878 S.W.2d 602, 604-05 (Tex.1994) (Minnesota court had exclusive jurisdiction over child custody case). When two courts have concurrent jurisdiction, the issue of dominant jurisdiction should be challenged by a plea in abatement, not a plea to the jurisdiction. ***Tovias v. Wildwood Props. Prtshp.***, 67 S.W.3d 527, 529 (Tex.App.—Houston [1st Dist.] 2002, no pet.) (county court & district court had concurrent jurisdiction). See "Abate – same dispute in another Texas court," ch. 3-H, §3.2, p. 196.

§3.5 Administrative agency has exclusive jurisdiction. A plea to the jurisdiction is proper to allege that an administrative agency has exclusive jurisdiction over the dispute. *See* ***Subaru, Inc. v. David McDavid Nissan, Inc.***, 84 S.W.3d 212, 221 (Tex.2002). When an agency's jurisdiction is exclusive, courts defer to the agency as a matter of subject-matter jurisdiction, and a dismissal is mandatory. *Id.*; *see* ***City of Galveston v. Flagship Hotel***, 73 S.W.3d 422, 427 (Tex.App.—Houston [1st Dist.] 2002, no pet.). By comparison, when an agency has primary jurisdiction, abatement is appropriate. See "Abate – administrative agency has primary jurisdiction," ch. 3-H, §3.4, p. 197.

§3.6 Governmental immunity from suit. A plea to the jurisdiction is proper to challenge a suit filed against a governmental entity when it is apparent from the pleadings that the government is immune from suit. ***Texas DOT v. Jones***, 8 S.W.3d 636, 638-39 (Tex.1999); *see, e.g.*, ***Federal Sign v. Texas S. Univ.***, 951 S.W.2d 401, 404 (Tex.1997) (TSU was immune from suit without State's consent); ***Liberty Mut. Ins. Co. v. Sharp***, 874 S.W.2d 736, 739 (Tex.App.—Austin 1994, writ denied) (P did not have State's consent to sue comptroller of public accounts & director of TDCJ). When filing suit for damages against the government, the plaintiff must affirmatively demonstrate the court's jurisdiction to hear the lawsuit under the Texas Tort Claims Act or some other statute that waives the government's immunity from suit. ***Miller***, 51 S.W.3d at 587. For the elements in a suit against a governmental entity, see ***O'Connor's Texas Causes of Action***, "The issues," ch. 22-A, §1.1, p. 623 (2004); for the allegations to include in the petition, see ***O'Connor's*** FORM 2B:08. If the government has immunity from suit but the plaintiff can cure the defect (*e.g.*, obtain legislative consent to sue), the case should be abated until the defect is remedied. *See* ***Federal Sign***, 951 S.W.2d at 403-04.

§3.7 Federal preemption. A plea to the jurisdiction is proper to challenge a suit preempted by federal law. *See* ***Southland Life Ins. Co. v. Estate of Small***, 806 S.W.2d 800, 801 (Tex.1991) (ERISA).

§3.8 Death.

1. Claim extinguished. A plea to the jurisdiction is proper to challenge the continuation of a suit when the cause is extinguished by a party's death. For example, a suit for usury should be dismissed if either party dies before the trial court renders judgment. ***Orr v. International Bank of Commerce***, 649 S.W.2d 769, 772 (Tex. App.—San Antonio 1983, no writ). When a party in a divorce suit dies before the trial court renders judgment on the merits, the suit should be dismissed. ***Whatley v. Bacon***, 649 S.W.2d 297, 299 (Tex.1983); ***Turner v. Ward***, 910 S.W.2d 500, 503 (Tex.App.—El Paso 1994, no writ).

2. Claim not extinguished. If the claim survives the party's death, dismissal is not appropriate, and the suit should proceed to judgment. *See* TRCP 150. For example, a suit for wrongful acquisition of property by fraud survives the death of either party. ***Pace v. McEwen***, 574 S.W.2d 792, 800 (Tex.App.—El Paso 1978, writ ref'd n.r.e.). Once a judgment is rendered, the death of one of the parties does not extinguish the claim. *See* TRAP 7.1(a)(1) (when party dies after trial court renders judgment, case may be appealed). See "Rendition," ch. 9-C, §3.1, p. 596.

§3.9 Statutory causes of action. A plea to the jurisdiction is proper to challenge a suit when the plaintiff did not comply with the statute on which the claim is based, and that statute defines, enlarges, or restricts the class of claims the court may decide or the relief it may award. *See* ***Sierra Club v. Texas Nat. Res. Conserv. Comm'n***, 26 S.W.3d 684, 688 (Tex.App.—Austin 2000), *aff'd*, 70 S.W.3d 809 (Tex.2002). This concept of jurisdiction in statutory causes of action is the result of ***Dubai Pet. Co. v. Kazi***, 12 S.W.3d 71, 76 (Tex.2000), an opinion that is not easy to understand. Under ***Dubai***, if the trial court has authority to adjudicate the type of controversy alleged in the suit, the plaintiff's failure to comply with some statutory requirement is not a jurisdictional defect that can be cured. *See* ***Dubai***, 12 S.W.3d at 75; ***Kshatrya v. Texas Workforce Comm'n***, 97 S.W.3d 825, 831-32 (Tex.App.—Dallas 2003, no pet.); ***Sierra Club***, 26 S.W.3d at 688.

§3.10 Fabricated jurisdiction. A plea to the jurisdiction is proper to challenge fraudulent allegations of an amount in controversy. *See, e.g.*, ***Delk v. City of Dallas***, 560 S.W.2d 519, 520 (Tex.App.—Texarkana 1977, no writ) (in suit to foreclose lien, D alleged P made fraudulent allegation of value of property); *see also* ***Denton Cty. v. Howard***, 22 S.W.3d 113, 119 (Tex.App.—Fort Worth 2000, no pet.) (in TTCA suit, D alleged P made fraudulent allegation he was public employee of D). The defendant must plead and prove that the allegations of the amount in controversy in the plaintiff's pleadings are false and were made fraudulently for the purpose of conferring jurisdiction. ***Delk***, 560 S.W.2d at 520.

§3.11 Religious matters. A plea to the jurisdiction is proper when the dispute clearly involves ecclesiastical matters over which the courts have no jurisdiction. *See* ***Hawkins v. Friendship Missionary Baptist Ch.***, 69 S.W.3d 756, 758-59 (Tex.App.—Houston [14th Dist.] 2002, no pet.); ***Green v. United Pentecostal Ch. Int'l***, 899 S.W.2d 28, 30 (Tex.App.—Austin 1995, writ denied); ***Patterson v. Southwestern Baptist Theological Seminary***, 858 S.W.2d 602, 604-05 (Tex.App.—Fort Worth 1993, no writ); *see also* ***Williams v. Gleason***, 26 S.W.3d 54, 55-56 (Tex.App.—Houston [14th Dist.] 2000, pet. denied) (resolved issue by motion for summary judgment). Secular courts cannot constitutionally determine the truth or falsity of religious matters. ***Tilton v. Marshall***, 925 S.W.2d 672, 678-79 (Tex.1996); *see also* ***Serbian E. Orthodox Diocese v. Milivojevich***, 426 U.S. 696, 723, 96 S.Ct. 2372, 2387 (1976) (religious controversies are not proper subject of civil court inquiry).

§3.12 Estate as defendant. A plea to the jurisdiction is proper when the plaintiff names an estate as the defendant without any reference to the personal representative. *See* ***Henson v. Estate of Crow***, 734 S.W.2d 648, 649 (Tex.1987); ***Miller v. Estate of Self***, 113 S.W.3d 554, 557 (Tex.App.—Texarkana 2003, n.p.h.); ***Estate of C.M. v. S.G.***, 937 S.W.2d 8, 10 (Tex.App.—Houston [14th Dist.] 1996, no writ). *But see* ***Estate of Crawford v. Town of Flower Mound***, 933 S.W.2d 727, 731 (Tex.App.—Fort Worth 1996, writ denied) (claim that estate lacks legal capacity to be sued must be raised in verified pleading). See "Estate," ch. 2-B, §3.3.2, p. 69.

§4. RESPONSE

If the defendant's plea to the jurisdiction is valid, the plaintiff should admit it and do whatever is necessary to get the lawsuit into a court that has jurisdiction. If the limitations period has run, however, the plaintiff must be careful to avoid losing the tolling benefits of CPRC §16.064. See §6.2, below. If the plea to the jurisdiction is not valid, the plaintiff should file a response and contest the factual allegations in the plea. The response should follow the format of the plea. If the plea includes evidence and is verified, the response should include evidence and be verified.

§5. HEARING

The trial court can rule on a plea to the jurisdiction by submission or after a hearing. When a trial court holds an evidentiary hearing, it may receive evidence in the form of oral testimony, discovery, and exhibits. *See, e.g.*, ***Bland ISD v. Blue***, 34 S.W.3d 547, 550 (Tex.2000) (trial court conducted evidentiary hearing & received oral testimony); ***State v. Sledge***, 36 S.W.3d 152, 155 (Tex.App.—Houston [1st Dist.] 2000, pet. denied) (trial court conducted hearing & received oral testimony, affidavits, exhibits, & stipulations). See "Evidence," §2.2, p. 182.

§6. RULING

§6.1 Order. If a claim is not within a court's jurisdiction and the impediment to jurisdiction cannot be removed, the claim must be dismissed; in contrast, if the impediment to jurisdiction can be removed, the court should abate the proceedings to allow a reasonable opportunity for the jurisdictional problem to be cured. ***American Motorists Ins. Co. v. Fodge***, 63 S.W.3d 801, 805 (Tex.2001).

1. Opportunity to amend. If the jurisdictional defect can be cured by an amendment, the court must permit the plaintiff to amend. ***County of Cameron v. Brown***, 80 S.W.3d 549, 555 (Tex.2002); ***Peek v. Equipment Serv. Co.***, 779 S.W.2d 802, 805 (Tex.1989). A plaintiff is not entitled to amend if its petition affirmatively negates jurisdiction. ***Cameron***, 80 S.W.3d at 555.

2. Dismiss without prejudice. If the court does not have jurisdiction over the subject matter of the suit, it must dismiss the suit without prejudice. ***Black v. Jackson***, 82 S.W.3d 44, 56 (Tex.App.—Tyler 2002, no pet.); ***Jansen v. Fitzpatrick***, 14 S.W.3d 426, 431 (Tex.App.—Houston [14th Dist.] 2000, no pet.).

3. No transfer. The court does not have the power to transfer the case to the appropriate court. ***State v. Benavides***, 772 S.W.2d 271, 273 (Tex.App.—Corpus Christi 1989, writ denied). After the case is dismissed, the plaintiff may refile it in the proper court.

§6.2 Dismissal & limitations. If the statute of limitations expired after the filing of the suit in the first court and before the case was dismissed, the plaintiff may refile the suit in the proper court within 60 days after the dismissal in the first suit becomes final. CPRC §16.064(a). CPRC §16.064(a) tolls the statute of limitations for the period between the date the plaintiff filed the suit in the first court and the date the plaintiff refiles the suit in the correct court. If the plaintiff filed the suit in the first court with intentional disregard for proper jurisdiction, CPRC §16.064(a) does not toll limitations. *Id.* §16.064(b). To defeat the plaintiff's use of CPRC §16.064(a), a defendant must show that either (1) the first suit was not dismissed for want of jurisdiction or (2) the causes of action are not the same for purposes of the tolling provision. ***Turner v. Texas Dept. of MHMR***, 920 S.W.2d 415, 418 (Tex.App.—Austin 1996, writ denied); *see, e.g.*, ***Malmgren v. Inverness Forest Residents Civic Club***, 981 S.W.2d 875, 879 (Tex.App.—Houston [1st Dist.] 1998, no pet.) (because P voluntarily dismissed suit, §16.064 did not apply).

§6.3 Findings. Findings of fact are not necessary when the trial court rules on a motion to dismiss based on the face of the pleadings. ***Awde v. Dabeit***, 938 S.W.2d 31, 32 (Tex.1997). However, when the trial court considers evidence (*e.g.*, plea based on fabricated jurisdiction), findings of fact are helpful on appeal. See "Jurisdictional challenge," ch. 10-E, §2.3.2(2), p. 643.

§7. REVIEW

§7.1 Interlocutory review.

1. Appeal. A party may appeal an interlocutory order that grants or denies a plea to the jurisdiction by a governmental unit. CPRC §51.014(a)(8). No other order on a plea to the jurisdiction may be appealed before final judgment. However, CPRC §51.014(d) allows parties to agree to an interlocutory appeal. See ***O'Connor's Texas Civil Appeals***, "Appealable orders by agreed motion," ch. 13-P, §2.2, p. 131 (2002-03). This procedure may reduce the need for mandamus discussed in §7.3.2, below.

03 **2. Stay of trial.** The interlocutory appeal of an order granting a plea to the jurisdiction by a governmental unit automatically stays the commencement of trial during the appeal. *See* CPRC §51.014(b). The interlocutory appeal under CPRC §51.014(a)(8) also stays all other proceedings in the trial court pending resolution of that appeal. *Id.* §51.014(b). The interlocutory appeal of an order denying a plea to the jurisdiction by a governmental unit does not automatically stay the commencement of trial during the appeal. *Id.* §51.014(c). To determine when the defendant may be entitled to a stay after the denial of a plea to the jurisdiction by a governmental unit, see ***O'Connor's Texas Civil Appeals***, "Automatic stay after motion denied," ch. 13-P, §3.2, p. 133.

§7.2 Appeal after final judgment.

1. Standard of review. The appellate court's standard of review of a trial court's ruling on a plea to the jurisdiction is de novo. ***Mayhew v. Town of Sunnyvale***, 964 S.W.2d 922, 928 (Tex.1998).

(1) Jurisdictional facts. In the appeal of a case dismissed for want of jurisdiction based on facts that were primarily jurisdictional, the appellate court reviews both the plaintiff's petition and the evidence introduced below. ***Bland ISD***, 34 S.W.3d at 554-55.

(2) Jurisdictional allegations. In the appeal of a case dismissed for want of jurisdiction based on the plaintiff's petition, the appellate court must accept as true all the factual allegations in the plaintiff's petition. ***Axtell v. University of Tex.***, 69 S.W.3d 261, 264 (Tex.App.—Austin 2002, no pet.); ***Jansen***, 14 S.W.3d at 431. The court looks to the pleader's intent and construes the pleadings in the plaintiff's favor. ***County of Cameron v. Brown***, 80 S.W.3d 549, 555 (Tex.2002); ***Texas Ass'n of Bus. v. Texas Air Control Bd.***, 852 S.W.2d 440, 446 (Tex.1993).

2. Record. The reporter's record is not necessary to appeal the trial court's ruling on subject-matter jurisdiction, unless the trial court held an evidentiary hearing.

§7.3 Mandamus.

1. Mandamus not available. In most cases, a party cannot challenge the trial court's lack of subject-matter jurisdiction by mandamus. ***Bell Helicopter Textron v. Walker***, 787 S.W.2d 954, 955 (Tex.1990); ***In re Liberty Mut. Ins. Co.***, 24 S.W.3d 637, 639 (Tex.App.—Texarkana 2000, orig. proceeding); ***Brown v. Herman***, 852 S.W.2d 91, 92 (Tex.App.—Austin 1993, orig. proceeding). Typically, the remedy by appeal is adequate.

2. Mandamus available.

(1) Child custody. A party is entitled to challenge the trial court's lack of subject-matter jurisdiction by mandamus when two trial courts issue conflicting child custody orders. ***Geary v. Peavy***, 878 S.W.2d 602, 603-05 (Tex.1994).

(2) Constitutional challenges to suit. If a constitutional issue is not resolved by the trial court, mandamus may be available to resolve the issue before a trial on the merits. *See, e.g.*, ***Tilton v. Marshall***, 925 S.W.2d 672, 676 & n.4 (Tex.1996) (D challenged trial court's refusal to dismiss and refusal to bar discovery on grounds of free exercise of religion).

(3) Court lacks authority. If the court erroneously concludes it has subject-matter jurisdiction, its order is void, and the party may challenge the order by mandamus. ***Qwest Microwave v. Bedard***, 756 S.W.2d 426, 434 (Tex.App.—Dallas 1988, orig. proceeding).

G. SPECIAL EXCEPTIONS—CHALLENGING THE PLEADINGS

§1. GENERAL

§1.1 Rules. TRCP 90, 91.

§1.2 Purpose. The purpose of special exceptions is to inform the opposing party of defects in its pleadings so the party can cure them, if possible, by amendment. ***Horizon v. Auld***, 34 S.W.3d 887, 897 (Tex.2000). By filing special exceptions, the opposing party identifies defects that should be remedied before a substantive response is required. ***O'Neal v. Sherck Equip. Co.***, 751 S.W.2d 559, 562 (Tex.App.—Texarkana 1988, no writ). Unless a party challenges pleading defects by special exceptions, the defects are waived. See "Waiver," §6, p. 189.

§1.3 Forms & timetable. *O'Connor's Texas Civil Forms*, FORMS 3G; Timetable, this book, Pretrial Motions, p. 998.

§2. TYPES OF PLEADINGS TO CHALLENGE BY SPECIAL EXCEPTIONS

There are two types of pleading defects to which the opponent must object before trial: (1) defects in form and (2) defects in substance. ***Aquila Sw. Pipeline v. Harmony Expl.***, 48 S.W.3d 225, 233 (Tex.App.—San Antonio 2001, pet. denied).

§2.1 Defects in form.

1. Lack of verification. If the plaintiff did not verify its petition when necessary, the defendant may file special exceptions to require the plaintiff to correct the defect. ***Huddleston v. Western Nat'l Bank***, 577 S.W.2d 778, 781 (Tex.App.—Amarillo 1979, writ ref'd n.r.e.).

2. Failure to plead discovery level. If the plaintiff did not plead the discovery level in its original petition as required by TRCP 190.1, the defendant may file special exceptions to require the plaintiff to do so. *See* TRCP 190, cmt. 1.

§2.2 Defects in substance.

1. General allegations. If the plaintiff pleaded a cause of action in general terms, the defendant may file special exceptions to require the plaintiff to plead specifically. ***Subia v. Texas Dept. of Human Servs.***, 750 S.W.2d 827, 829 (Tex.App.—El Paso 1988, no writ). Texas follows the "fair notice" standard for pleading, which looks to whether the opposing party can ascertain from the pleading the nature and basic issues of the controversy and what testimony will be relevant. ***Horizon***, 34 S.W.3d at 896; *see also* TRCP 45(b) (action must be stated in plain and concise language), TRCP 47(a) (action must be sufficient to give fair notice of the claim). TRCP 45 does not require the plaintiff to detail the evidence in its petition. ***Paramount Pipe & Sup. Co. v. Muhr***, 749 S.W.2d 491, 494-95 (Tex.1988). If the plaintiff's petition does not give fair notice of the facts, the trial court can either require the plaintiff to amend its petition or require the defendant to obtain additional facts through discovery.

2. Inadequate allegations. If the plaintiff did not plead all the elements of its cause of action, the defendant may file special exceptions to require the plaintiff to plead specifically. *See* ***Mowbray v. Avery***, 76 S.W.3d 663, 677 (Tex.App.—Corpus Christi 2002, pet. denied). The defendant must specifically identify the missing element. *See* ***Spencer v. City of Seagoville***, 700 S.W.2d 953, 957 (Tex.App.—Dallas 1985, no writ). The plaintiff's omission of an element of the cause of action does not deprive the court of jurisdiction; it is merely a defect in pleading subject to special exceptions and amendment. *E.g.*, ***Peek v. Equipment Serv. Co.***, 779 S.W.2d 802, 805 (Tex.1989) (P did not allege amount of damages). For lists of the elements for various causes of action, see ***O'Connor's Texas Causes of Action*** (2004).

3. No viable cause of action. If the plaintiff's suit is not permitted by law, the defendant may file special exceptions and a motion to dismiss. ***Duddlesten v. Highland Ins.***, 110 S.W.3d 85, 96-97 (Tex.App.—Houston [1st Dist.] 2003, pet. denied); *see, e.g.*, ***Trevino v. Ortega***, 969 S.W.2d 950, 951 (Tex.1998) (no cause of action for spoliation of evidence); ***Friesenhahn v. Ryan***, 960 S.W.2d 656, 658 (Tex.1998) (no cause of action for social host liability); ***Krishnan v. Sepulveda***, 916 S.W.2d 478, 479 (Tex.1995) (parents do not have cause of action for negligence to fetus; mother may have action for mental anguish).

4. Curable defects in jurisdiction. If a jurisdictional defect is a pleading defect that can be cured by amendment, it should be challenged by special exceptions, not by a plea to the jurisdiction or a motion for summary judgment. ***Texas Dept. of Corr. v. Herring***, 513 S.W.2d 6, 9-10 (Tex.1974); *see* ***Texas DOT v. Beckner***, 74 S.W.3d 98, 104 (Tex.App.—Waco 2002, no pet.); ***Washington v. Fort Bend ISD***, 892 S.W.2d 156, 159 (Tex.App.—Houston [14th Dist.] 1994, writ denied). For example, when a party's allegation of unliquidated damages is above or below the trial court's limits of jurisdiction, it may be amended. ***Smith Detective Agency & Nightwatch Serv. v. Stanley Smith Sec.***, 938 S.W.2d 743, 747 (Tex.App.—Dallas 1996, writ denied).

5. Unliquidated damages. If the plaintiff pleaded for unliquidated damages as required by TRCP 47(b) ("the damages sought are within the jurisdictional limits of the court"), the defendant may specially except and require the plaintiff to state the maximum amount of its damages. Pleading for damages that are "at least" a certain amount is the same as pleading for unliquidated damages, and unless the defendant specially excepts, the plaintiff can recover more than its "at least" pleadings. *See, e.g.*, ***City of Wichita Falls v. Dye***, 517 S.W.2d 680, 682 (Tex.App.—Fort Worth 1974, writ ref'd n.r.e.) (P did not specially except to Ds' cross-action that sought relief for sum of "at least $900.00"; trial court's award of $1007.50 was proper).

§3. FORM

§3.1 Written. Special exceptions must be in writing. TRCP 90. An oral objection to pleadings does not comply with the rules. ***Nassar v. Hughes***, 882 S.W.2d 36, 38 (Tex.App.—Houston [1st Dist.] 1994, writ denied); ***Hawkins v. Anderson***, 672 S.W.2d 293, 295 (Tex.App.—Dallas 1984, no writ).

§3.2 Specific. When drafting special exceptions, the party must identify the particular part of the opposing party's pleading it challenges and point out the particular defect, omission, obscurity, duplicity, generality, or other insufficiency. TRCP 91; ***Muecke v. Hallstead***, 25 S.W.3d 221, 224 (Tex.App.—San Antonio 2000, no pet.); ***Gutierrez v. Karl Perry Enters.***, 874 S.W.2d 103, 105 (Tex.App.—El Paso 1994, no writ). The party should identify the defective paragraph by number, state why it is defective, and explain how it can be corrected. General allegations that the petition is vague, is indefinite, or does not state a cause of action are not sufficient to identify the defect. ***Spillman v. Simkins***, 757 S.W.2d 166, 168 (Tex.App.—San Antonio 1988, no writ); ***Farrar v. Farrar***, 620 S.W.2d 801, 802 (Tex.App.—Houston [14th Dist.] 1981, no writ). If the special exception is not specific, it is a prohibited general demurrer and should be overruled. *See* TRCP 90; ***Fuentes v. McFadden***, 825 S.W.2d 772, 778 (Tex.App.—El Paso 1992, no writ); ***Spillman***, 757 S.W.2d at 168.

§3.3 Limited to pleadings. When drafting special exceptions, the party cannot challenge pleading defects by relying on facts outside the plaintiff's petition. ***O'Neal v. Sherck Equip. Co.***, 751 S.W.2d 559, 562 (Tex.App.—Texarkana 1988, no writ) (called a "speaking demurrer"); ***Augustine v. Nusom***, 671 S.W.2d 112, 114 (Tex.App.—Houston [14th Dist.] 1984, writ ref'd n.r.e.) (same). If a party must rely on facts that are not in the petition to demonstrate the defect, the party should file some other type of pleading (*e.g.*, a motion to abate or a motion for summary judgment). ***Bader v. Cox***, 701 S.W.2d 677, 686-87 (Tex.App.—Dallas 1985, writ ref'd n.r.e.); ***Augustine***, 671 S.W.2d at 114.

§3.4 Not verified. Special exceptions should not be verified. *See* TRCP 90, 91.

§3.5 Request hearing. The party challenging the pleadings must secure a hearing on the special exceptions, or else the exceptions are waived. ***Brooks v. Housing Auth.***, 926 S.W.2d 316, 322 (Tex.App.—El Paso 1996, no writ).

§4. DEADLINE

As a general rule, special exceptions should be filed by the defendant either with its answer or shortly thereafter and by the plaintiff shortly after the defendant files its answer. Special exceptions may also be raised during trial. In a jury trial, a party must bring the special exceptions to the trial court's attention before the charge is read to the jury; in a nonjury trial, before the judgment is signed. TRCP 90; *see, e.g.*, ***Hudspeth v. Hudspeth***, 756 S.W.2d 29, 34 (Tex.App.—San Antonio 1988, writ denied) (party waived error in pleadings by not objecting until after trial court signed judgment).

§5. GROUNDS

§5.1 Proper objections to pleadings. For examples of special exceptions that are valid objections to the pleadings, see ***O'Connor's*** FORM 3G:01.

§5.2 Improper objections to pleadings. The following are examples of special exceptions that are not valid objections to the pleadings.

1. The pleadings do not set out enough factual details. *See, e.g.*, ***Roark v. Allen***, 633 S.W.2d 804, 810 (Tex.1982) (P not required to plead exactly how doctor used forceps; general allegation of negligent delivery was sufficient).

2. The pleadings do not state a cause of action. ***Martin v. Hunter***, 233 S.W.2d 354, 355 (Tex.App.—San Antonio 1950, writ ref'd n.r.e.). The complaint that the pleadings do not state a cause of action is a general demurrer and is prohibited by TRCP 90.

3. The pleadings do not allege all the elements necessary to support a cause of action. *See* ***Spencer v. City of Seagoville***, 700 S.W.2d 953, 957 (Tex.App.—Dallas 1985, no writ). When a defendant objects that the plaintiff did not plead a complete cause of action, the defendant must list the specific elements the plaintiff omitted.

4. The plaintiff's pleadings allege matters that are immaterial, prejudicial, and inflammatory. ***Pargas of Canton, Inc. v. Clower***, 434 S.W.2d 192, 196 (Tex.App.—Tyler 1968, no writ). These objections are too general.

5. The plaintiff did not attach a copy of the contract to its pleadings. ***Randolph Junior Coll. v. Isaacks***, 113 S.W.2d 628, 629 (Tex.App.—Eastland 1938, no writ). The plaintiff is not required to attach documents to its petition. *See id.*

6. The damages allegations do not enumerate the specific dollar value for each element of special damages. *See* ***Phillips v. Vinson Sup. Co.***, 581 S.W.2d 789, 791 (Tex.App.—Houston [14th Dist.] 1979, no writ). TRCP 47 does not require the plaintiff to designate how much money is attributable to each element of damages, only the maximum amount claimed. ***Phillips***, 581 S.W.2d at 791.

§6. WAIVER

§6.1 Waiver of pleading defects. If a party does not file special exceptions, it waives any error in the other party's pleadings. TRCP 90; ***Sixth RMA Partners v. Sibley***, 111 S.W.3d 46, 55-56 (Tex.2003); ***Shoemake v. Fogel, Ltd.***, 826 S.W.2d 933, 937 (Tex.1992); *see, e.g.*, ***Troutman v. Traeco Bldg. Sys.***, 724 S.W.2d 385, 387 (Tex.1987) (D waived error in P's failure to plead DTPA violation properly). If no special exceptions are filed to challenge the pleadings, the court will construe the pleadings liberally in favor of the pleader. ***Horizon v. Auld***, 34 S.W.3d 887, 896 (Tex.2000); ***Boyles v. Kerr***, 855 S.W.2d 593, 601 (Tex.1993). The court will look to the pleader's intent and will supply every fact "that can reasonably be inferred from what is specifically stated." ***Roark***, 633 S.W.2d at 809. Without special exceptions, the court will uphold the pleading even if an element of a cause of action is omitted. *Id.*

§6.2 Reversal on appeal. Before the jury is charged or, in a nonjury case, before the judgment is signed, every defect not specifically pointed out by a special exception is waived "by the party seeking reversal." TRCP 90. This rule means that a party may waive a defect in the pleadings and not be able to rely on it as a ground for reversal. For example, if the plaintiff pleads "all conditions precedent have … occurred" under TRCP 54, and the defendant responds with a general statement that the plaintiff did not meet all conditions precedent, the plaintiff should challenge the general statement by filing a special exception. If the general statement goes unchallenged, the plaintiff will waive any right to reverse on appeal for the defendant's failure to specifically state which conditions precedent were not met. *See* ***Dairyland Cty. Mut. Ins. Co. v. Roman***, 498 S.W.2d 154, 158-59 (Tex.1973) (because D was urging reversal, P did not waive defects in D's general response to TRCP 54 allegation).

§7. RESPONSE

If the party whose pleadings were challenged agrees the exceptions are valid, the party should amend its pleadings without contesting the exceptions at a hearing. If the party whose pleadings were challenged does not agree the exceptions are valid, the party should file a response arguing why the exceptions should be denied.

§8. HEARING

§8.1 Argument only. The hearing on special exceptions is for argument only. No evidence may be presented.

§8.2 Standard. When ruling on special exceptions, the court must accept as true all material factual allegations and all factual statements reasonably inferred from the allegations in the pleadings being challenged. ***Sorokolit v. Rhodes***, 889 S.W.2d 239, 240 (Tex.1994) (appellate court); ***City of Austin v. H.L.&P. Co.***, 844 S.W.2d 773, 783 (Tex.App.—Dallas 1992, writ denied) (trial court). The trial court has wide discretion in ruling on special exceptions. ***LaRue v. GeneScreen, Inc.***, 957 S.W.2d 958, 961 (Tex.App.—Beaumont 1997, pet. denied); ***City of Austin***, 844 S.W.2d at 783.

§9. RULING

§9.1 Written order. The party who filed the special exceptions must obtain a written ruling, or else the exceptions are waived. *See* TRCP 90; ***Smith v. Grace***, 919 S.W.2d 673, 678 (Tex.App.—Dallas 1996, writ denied); ***In re Moore***, 890 S.W.2d 821, 826-27 (Tex.App.—Amarillo 1994, no writ). When making its ruling, the court should not merely make margin notations on the special exceptions. *E.g.*, ***McAdams v. Capitol Prods. Corp.***, 810 S.W.2d 290, 292 (Tex.App.—Fort Worth 1991, writ denied) (unclear whether notations "OR," "Sus.," or "withdrawn" constituted court's ruling on special exceptions). The party must insist that the judge sign a written order. *Id.*

§9.2 Options for court.

1. Court overrules special exceptions. When the court overrules the special exceptions, it will proceed with other matters. When exceptions are overruled, error regarding the defective pleadings is preserved. *See, e.g.*, ***Johnson v. Willis***, 596 S.W.2d 256, 260 (Tex.App.—Waco 1980, writ ref'd n.r.e.) (court held special exceptions were improperly overruled because pleading did not provide proper notice under DTPA).

2. Court sustains special exceptions.

(1) Curable defect. When the court sustains the special exceptions, it must give the party a chance to amend its pleadings by ordering the party to replead. ***Friesenhahn v. Ryan***, 960 S.W.2d 656, 658-59 (Tex.1998); ***Texas Dept. of Corr. v. Herring***, 513 S.W.2d 6, 10 (Tex.1974); ***Mowbray v. Avery***, 76 S.W.3d 663, 677 (Tex.App.—Corpus Christi 2002, pet. denied). The court cannot dismiss the case at the same time it sustains the special exceptions. *See* ***Herring***, 513 S.W.2d at 10; ***Mowbray***, 76 S.W.3d at 678. To dismiss without giving the party the opportunity to amend is the functional equivalent of a general demurrer, long prohibited by TRCP 90. ***Hunter v. Johnson***, 25 S.W.3d 247, 249 (Tex.App.—El Paso 2000, no pet.).

(2) Incurable defect. The court is not required to give the party an opportunity to amend if the pleading defect is the type that cannot be cured by amendment (*i.e.*, a pleading that asserts an unrecognized cause of action). ***Mowbray***, 76 S.W.3d at 678. See "No viable cause of action," §2.2.3, p. 188.

§9.3 Options for party with objectionable pleadings. When special exceptions are sustained, the party with objectionable pleadings may do any of the following:

1. Amend. The party may amend its pleadings to correct the defect. ***Mowbray***, 76 S.W.3d at 677; ***Butler Weldments v. Liberty Mut. Ins. Co.***, 3 S.W.3d 654, 658 (Tex.App.—Austin 1999, no pet.); ***Cameron v. University of Houston***, 598 S.W.2d 344, 345 (Tex.App.—Houston [14th Dist.] 1980, writ ref'd n.r.e.). In the amended pleading, the party may include new allegations.

2. Refuse to amend. The party may challenge the trial court's ruling by refusing to amend. ***Mowbray***, 76 S.W.3d at 677; ***Muecke v. Hallstead***, 25 S.W.3d 221, 223-24 (Tex.App.—San Antonio 2000, no pet.); ***Butler Weldments***, 3 S.W.3d at 658. When a party believes it is entitled to the claim or defense, the party should ask the trial court to sign an order striking the paragraphs; the party should not voluntarily amend its pleadings to delete the allegations. By refusing to amend, the party can test the validity of the trial court's ruling on appeal. ***Mowbray***, 76 S.W.3d at 677; ***Muecke***, 25 S.W.3d at 223-24; ***Butler Weldments***, 3 S.W.3d at 658. If the party amends its pleadings to delete the allegations, the party waives its right to raise the issue on appeal. ***Long v. Tascosa Nat'l Bank***, 678 S.W.2d 699, 703 (Tex.App.—Amarillo 1984, no writ).

3. Partially comply. If the trial court sustains a number of special exceptions, the party may agree to make some changes but refuse to make others. For example, assume the trial court sustained two special exceptions: the first, to the plaintiff's petition for a bad-faith claim, and the second, that the plaintiff did not plead all the elements of fraud against the defendant. If the plaintiff believes it has a cause of action for bad faith, it should amend the defective allegations of fraud but refuse to delete the bad-faith allegation. By reasserting the bad-faith allegation in the amended petition and having the court strike that part of the petition, the plaintiff preserves for appeal the issue of whether it has such a cause of action. ***Fuentes v. TEIA***, 757 S.W.2d 31, 33 (Tex.App.—San Antonio 1988, no writ).

4. Request time to amend & obtain ruling. If the trial court sustained the special exceptions but did not give the party an opportunity to replead, the party must ask the court for time to amend and obtain a ruling on the record denying the requested opportunity to amend. ***Inglish v. Prudential Ins. Co.***, 928 S.W.2d 702, 705 (Tex.App.—Houston [1st Dist.] 1996, writ denied); *see* TRAP 33.1(a). If the court's ruling denying the party the opportunity to amend is not reflected in the record, the party should file a motion for new trial to preserve the error for appeal. ***Inglish***, 928 S.W.2d at 705.

§9.4 Options for party who filed exceptions.

1. If defect not cured. When special exceptions are sustained, and the other party was given an opportunity to amend but refused to amend, the party who filed the exceptions has three options.

(1) Move to dismiss. The party objecting to the pleadings may file a motion to dismiss based on the other party's failure to cure the defect. If the request for a dismissal was included in the special exceptions, the party may need only to set a hearing on the request to dismiss.

(2) Move to strike. If only part of the pleading was subject to a special exception, the party objecting to the pleading may file a motion to strike certain paragraphs in the pleading, instead of a motion to dismiss the entire pleading.

(3) File a motion for summary judgment. Instead of seeking a dismissal, the party whose special exceptions were sustained may file a motion for summary judgment. *See* ***Friesenhahn***, 960 S.W.2d at 658. A summary judgment is preferable over a dismissal without prejudice because it is a resolution on the merits and invokes res judicata. See "Special Exceptions & Summary Judgments," §10, p. 193.

2. If original defect cured but others created. When amended pleadings are filed after special exceptions are sustained, the opposing party should review the new allegations to determine if any additional special exceptions to the pleadings are required. ***Humphreys v. Meadows***, 938 S.W.2d 750, 753 (Tex.App.—Fort Worth 1996, writ denied).

§9.5 Options for court after party given opportunity to replead.

1. Party amended & cured defect. If the party amended the pleadings and cured the defect, the trial court should permit the suit to go forward. If the party added other allegations that are objectionable, before the court can strike them the other party must file special exceptions to the new allegations, the court must order the party to replead, and the party must be given the opportunity to amend. *See* ***Geochem Labs. v. Brown & Ruth Labs.***, 689 S.W.2d 288, 290 (Tex.App.—Houston [1st Dist.] 1985, writ ref'd n.r.e.).

2. Party amended but did not cure defect.

(1) Good-faith attempt to cure. If the party amended the pleadings and made a good-faith attempt to cure the defect, the court cannot strike the objectionable allegations. ***Humphreys***, 938 S.W.2d at 753. The other party must file new special exceptions, the court must sustain them, and the party must be given another opportunity to amend before the court can dismiss. *Id.* However, the party's right to amend may be limited in the face of repeated grants of special exceptions. ***Mowbray v. Avery***, 76 S.W.3d 663, 678 (Tex.App.—Corpus Christi 2002, pet. denied) (if no reasonable probability that further amendment would disclose facts legally sufficient to sustain cause of action, court may deny leave to amend).

(2) Lack of good faith. If the party amended the pleadings but did not cure the objectionable allegations, the court can strike the objectionable allegations if the party did not make a good-faith effort to cure the defect. *Cf.* ***Cruz v. Morris***, 877 S.W.2d 45, 47 (Tex.App.—Houston [14th Dist.] 1994, no writ) (if party refuses to amend, court can strike). If the party added other allegations that are objectionable, before the court can strike them the other party must file special exceptions, the court must order the party to replead, and the party must be given the opportunity to amend. *See* ***Geochem Labs.***, 689 S.W.2d at 290.

3. Party refused to amend. If the party refused to amend, the trial court should strike the objectionable allegations. *E.g.*, ***Cruz***, 877 S.W.2d at 47 (court struck damages allegations after P refused to replead).

(1) Proceed on remainder of petition. The party may proceed to trial based on the rest of its pleadings.

(2) No cause of action remains. If no cause of action is stated in the remainder of the petition, the trial court will dismiss the suit. ***Mowbray***, 76 S.W.3d at 678; ***Cruz***, 877 S.W.2d at 47. The issue then is whether the court should dismiss with or without prejudice.

(a) Without prejudice. In most cases, the dismissal after a refusal to amend is without prejudice. ***Kutch v. Del Mar Coll.***, 831 S.W.2d 506, 508 (Tex.App.—Corpus Christi 1992, no writ). If the defect can be cured by amendment, dismissal should be without prejudice. ***Hajdik v. Wingate***, 753 S.W.2d 199, 202 (Tex.App.—Houston [1st Dist.] 1988), *aff'd*, 795 S.W.2d 717 (Tex.1990); ***Atkinson v. Reid***, 625 S.W.2d 64, 66 (Tex.App.—San Antonio 1981, no writ).

(b) With prejudice. If the defect cannot be cured by amendment, dismissal may be with prejudice. *See, e.g.*, ***Joseph E. Seagram & Sons, Inc. v. McGuire***, 814 S.W.2d 385, 386 (Tex.1991) (with prejudice; no duty to warn of alcoholism); ***Hickman v. Myers***, 632 S.W.2d 869, 869-70 (Tex.App.—Fort Worth 1982, writ ref'd n.r.e.) (with prejudice; no recovery for healthy, but unplanned, child).

§9.6 Amendments after pleadings struck. If, after the court strikes a claim or defense in the pleadings, the party finds it necessary to amend its pleadings for some reason unrelated to the special exceptions, the party should not include the struck paragraphs in its amended pleading. Once the court strikes allegations in the pleadings, a party is not required to violate the court's order and include them in its amended pleadings. ***Melendez v. Exxon Corp.***, 998 S.W.2d 266, 272 & n.1 (Tex.App.—Houston [14th Dist.] 1999, no pet.). In fact, there is some danger in repleading struck allegations. In ***Duncan v. Cessna Aircraft Co.***, 665 S.W.2d 414, 433 (Tex.1984), after the trial court struck allegations in the defendant's pleadings, the defendant repleaded them in an amended pleading. On appeal, the court said the defendant waived the issues because it had not introduced evidence to support them. ***Duncan***, 665 S.W.2d at 433.

§10. SPECIAL EXCEPTIONS & SUMMARY JUDGMENTS

§10.1 No viable cause of action. If the plaintiff has no viable cause of action and refuses to amend after special exceptions are sustained, the defendant has two options. First, it may ask the court to dismiss the case with prejudice. See §9.5.3(2)(b), above. Second, it may move for summary judgment on the pleadings. ***Friesenhahn v. Ryan***, 960 S.W.2d 656, 658 (Tex.1998); ***Pietila v. Crites***, 851 S.W.2d 185, 186 n.2 (Tex.1993); ***Massey v. Armco Steel Co.***, 652 S.W.2d 932, 934 (Tex.1983); *see, e.g.*, ***Castleberry v. Goolsby Bldg. Corp.***, 617 S.W.2d 665, 666 (Tex. 1981) (affirmed summary judgment on pleadings when P's pleadings showed suit was barred by statute).

§10.2 Defective pleading of cause of action. When the plaintiff has a viable cause of action but pleaded it defectively, the defendant should file special exceptions, not a motion for summary judgment. ***Friesenhahn***, 960 S.W.2d at 659; ***Pietila***, 851 S.W.2d at 186 n.2; *see* ***Natividad v. Alexsis, Inc.***, 875 S.W.2d 695, 699 (Tex.1994). Because the summary judgment procedure does not provide an opportunity to replead, it should not be used to terminate a suit based on pleading defects. ***Sixth RMA Partners v. Sibley***, 111 S.W.3d 46, 54-55 (Tex.2003); ***Saenz v. Southern Un. Gas Co.***, 916 S.W.2d 703, 705 (Tex.App.—El Paso 1996, writ denied); *see also* ***Friesenhahn***, 960 S.W.2d at 658-59 (reversed summary judgment when Ps were not given an opportunity to amend their claims for wrongful death of a minor); ***Peek v. Equipment Serv. Co.***, 779 S.W.2d 802, 804-05 (Tex.1989) (failure to plead for damages in the jurisdictional amount should have been challenged by special exception, not summary judgment); ***Texas Dept. of Corr. v. Herring***, 513 S.W.2d 6, 9-10 (Tex.1974) (reversed summary judgment when P did not correctly plead requirements of TTCA).

§10.3 Uncertain if no viable cause of action or defective pleading of cause of action. If the defendant is uncertain whether the plaintiff has a viable cause of action or merely pleaded a cause of action defectively, the defendant should first file special exceptions and then, if the plaintiff is not able to plead a viable cause of action, file a motion for summary judgment. ***Freisenhahn***, 960 S.W.2d at 658; ***Pietila***, 851 S.W.2d at 186 n.2. Summary judgment based on a pleading deficiency is proper if a party has had an opportunity to amend after a special exception and refuses to do so. ***Natividad***, 875 S.W.2d at 699; *see* ***Friesenhahn***, 960 S.W.2d at 658; ***Pietila***, 851 S.W.2d at 186 & n.2.

§10.4 Waiver. If the defendant files a motion for summary judgment when it should have first filed special exceptions, the plaintiff must object to the defendant's motion for summary judgment on the ground that it is an attempt to circumvent the special exception practice. ***Vawter v. Garvey***, 786 S.W.2d 263, 264 (Tex.1990); ***San Jacinto River Auth. v. Duke***, 783 S.W.2d 209, 209 (Tex.1990); ***Dickey v. Jansen***, 731 S.W.2d 581, 583 (Tex.App.—Houston [1st Dist.] 1987, writ ref'd n.r.e.). If not, the plaintiff waives the issue. ***Duke***, 783 S.W.2d at 209-10.

§11. SPECIAL EXCEPTIONS & DEFAULT JUDGMENTS

Special exceptions are not required to preserve pleading errors in default judgment cases. TRCP 90; ***Stoner v. Thompson***, 578 S.W.2d 679, 684-85 (Tex.1979); ***Rose v. Burton***, 614 S.W.2d 651, 652 (Tex.App.—Texarkana 1981, writ ref'd n.r.e.).

§12. REVIEW

§12.1 Appeal. When the trial court makes an erroneous ruling on special exceptions, the aggrieved party has a remedy by appeal. ***Low v. King***, 867 S.W.2d 141, 142 (Tex.App.—Beaumont 1993, orig. proceeding); ***Hill v. Lopez***, 858 S.W.2d 563, 565 (Tex.App.—Amarillo 1993, orig. proceeding).

1. Complaint on appeal. An appellant who complains of the dismissal of a cause of action following special exceptions must first attack the trial court's decision to sustain the special exceptions and then attack the court's decision to dismiss the cause of action. ***Mowbray v. Avery***, 76 S.W.3d 663, 678 (Tex.App.—Corpus Christi 2002, pet. denied); ***Cole v. Hall***, 864 S.W.2d 563, 566 (Tex.App.—Dallas 1993, writ dism'd). The appellant must challenge both rulings or face waiver of the unchallenged issue. ***Mowbray***, 76 S.W.3d at 678.

2. Standard of review. The appellate court reviews the trial court's ruling on special exceptions for abuse of discretion. ***Muecke v. Hallstead***, 25 S.W.3d 221, 224 (Tex.App.—San Antonio 2000, no pet.); ***LaRue v. GeneScreen, Inc.***, 957 S.W.2d 958, 961 (Tex.App.—Beaumont 1997, pet. denied). The appellate court must construe the pleadings liberally and accept as true all factual allegations in the pleadings. ***Aranda v. Insurance Co. of N. Am.***, 748 S.W.2d 210, 213 (Tex.1988). The appellate court must ignore any factual propositions outside the petition that tend to contradict the petition. ***Hur v. City of Mesquite***, 893 S.W.2d 227, 233 (Tex.App.—Amarillo 1995, writ denied).

3. Record. To appeal a dismissal based on refusal to amend pleadings after special exceptions, the appellant must request the clerk's record but does not need the reporter's record. The appropriateness of the dismissal will be judged on the pleadings, not on evidence. ***Holt v. Reproductive Servs.***, 946 S.W.2d 602, 604 (Tex.App.—Corpus Christi 1997, writ denied); *see* ***Cole***, 864 S.W.2d at 566.

§12.2 No mandamus. Mandamus is not available to review the trial court's rulings on special exceptions. ***Hill***, 858 S.W.2d at 566.

H. MOTION TO ABATE—CHALLENGING THE SUIT

§1. GENERAL

§1.1 Rules. TRCP 85, 150-160, 175.

§1.2 Purpose. A defendant uses a motion to abate, also called a plea in abatement, to challenge the plaintiff's pleadings by alleging facts outside the pleadings that prove the suit cannot go forward in its present condition. ***Martin v. Dosohs I, Ltd.***, 2 S.W.3d 350, 354 (Tex.App.—San Antonio 1999, pet. denied). By a motion to abate, the defendant identifies some impediment to the continuation of the suit, identifies an effective cure, and asks the court to suspend the suit until the plaintiff corrects the defect. *Id.*; *see* ***American Motorists Ins. Co. v. Fodge***, 63 S.W.3d 801, 805 (Tex.2001). By granting the motion to abate, the court gives the plaintiff an opportunity to correct the defect. ***Speer v. Stover***, 685 S.W.2d 22, 23 (Tex.1985). If the plaintiff corrects the defect, the court will permit the suit to continue; if not, the court will dismiss the suit. *See* ***Garcia-Marroquin v. Nueces Cty. Bail Bond Bd.***, 1 S.W.3d 366, 374 (Tex.App.—Corpus Christi 1999, no pet.).

§1.3 Forms & timetable. *O'Connor's Texas Civil Forms*, FORMS 3H; Timetable, this book, Motion to Abate, p. 997.

§2. MOTION

§2.1 Separate instrument. For practical reasons, it is best to ask for an abatement in a separate instrument from the answer. If a motion to abate is included in the answer, it is called a plea in abatement. *See* TRCP 85; ***Southwestern Life Ins. Co. v. Sanguinet***, 231 S.W.2d 727, 730 (Tex.App.—Fort Worth 1950, no writ).

§2.2 Specific allegations. A motion to abate must specify the grounds on which a suit is improperly brought and show how it should have been brought. ***Bryce v. Corpus Christi Area Convention & Tourist Bureau***, 569 S.W.2d 496, 499 (Tex.App.—Corpus Christi 1978, writ ref'd n.r.e.). The motion must inform the court and the other party exactly what is wrong and how to cure it. ***M&M Constr. Co. v. Great Am. Ins. Co.***, 747 S.W.2d 552, 554 (Tex. App.—Corpus Christi 1988, no writ).

§2.3 Verified. The motion to abate must be verified. ***Sparks v. Bolton***, 335 S.W.2d 780, 785 (Tex.App.—Dallas 1960, no writ); *see* TRCP 93. *But see* ***Southern Cty. Mut. Ins. Co. v. Ochoa***, 19 S.W.3d 452, 461-62 (Tex.App.—Corpus Christi 2000, no pet.) (verification requirement excused when D filed verified answer & verified motion to transfer venue with plea in abatement). The movant may also file affidavits if necessary to support the allegations in the motion.

§2.4 Deadline to file. A motion to abate must be raised in a timely manner, or it is waived. ***Wyatt v. Shaw Plumbing Co.***, 760 S.W.2d 245, 248 (Tex.1988); ***Lopez v. Texas Workers' Comp. Ins. Fund***, 11 S.W.3d 490, 493 (Tex.App.—Austin 2000, pet. denied). The motion must be made while the purpose of the motion remains viable. *See* ***Hines v. Hash***, 843 S.W.2d 464, 469 (Tex.1992) (when objecting to lack of notice, D must request abatement with filing of answer or soon thereafter); ***Garcia-Marroquin***, 1 S.W.3d at 374 (same); *see also* ***Bluebonnet Farms v. Gibraltar Sav. Ass'n***, 618 S.W.2d 81, 83-84 (Tex.App.—Houston [1st Dist.] 1980, writ ref'd n.r.e.) (motion to abate filed 4 years after suit filed & after limitations ran was too late).

§3. TYPES OF MOTIONS TO ABATE

PRACTICE TIP

In deciding whether to file a motion to abate, a defendant should look at the verified denials in its original answer. Many of the matters that a party is required to deny under oath, listed in TRCP 93, are also matters that should be made the subject of a verified motion to abate. See "Verified pleas in TRCP 93," ch. 3-E, §4.1, p. 173.

§3.1 Abate – defect in pleadings. A defendant should file a motion to abate when there is a defect in the pleadings. If the pleading defect depends on extrinsic evidence for support, it can be challenged by a motion to abate; if the defect is apparent from the face of the pleadings, it can be challenged by special exceptions. See "Limited to pleadings," ch. 3-G, §3.3, p. 188. Below are the types of pleading defects that can be challenged by a motion to abate.

1. Defects in the parties. A motion to abate is appropriate to challenge the following defects in the parties:

(1) Minor & incapacitated person. To challenge a minor who files suit in his or her own name, instead of the next friend or guardian's name. ***Sax v. Votteler***, 648 S.W.2d 661, 666 (Tex.1983). See "Minor as P," ch. 2-B, §3.4.2, p. 71.

(2) Estate of decedent. • To challenge a suit brought by an individual for an estate, instead of by the representative of the estate. ***Coakley v. Reising***, 436 S.W.2d 315, 317 (Tex.1968). • To contest the authority of an administrator to represent the estate, who must then file proof of authority (the bond and oath). ***Shiffers v. Estate of Ward***, 762 S.W.2d 753, 755 (Tex.App.—Fort Worth 1988, writ denied). See "Estate," ch. 2-B, §3.3.2, p. 69.

(3) Death action beneficiary. To challenge the plaintiff in its representative capacity under the Texas Survival Statute and the Texas Wrongful Death Act. *See* ***Ford Motor Co. v. Aguiniga***, 9 S.W.3d 252, 259 (Tex.App.—San Antonio 1999, pet. denied). See ***O'Connor's Texas Causes of Action***, "Legal representative of estate," ch. 7-A, §2.1.2, p. 139; "Statutory beneficiaries," ch. 7-B, §2.1.2, p. 147 (2004).

(4) Wrong representative of corporation. To challenge whether the stockholder, suing for damages to a corporation, has standing and capacity to bring suit. A stockholder lacks both standing (the stockholder was not personally aggrieved) and capacity (the stockholder is not the right surrogate) to bring suit for damages to a corporation. *See* ***White v. Independence Bank***, 794 S.W.2d 895, 898 n.3 (Tex.App.—Houston [1st Dist.] 1990, writ denied). See "Corporation," ch. 2-B, §3.3.3, p. 70.

(5) Not corporation or partnership. To challenge whether the plaintiff is a corporation or partnership, as it alleges. TRCP 52, 93(5), 93(6); *see* ***Lighthouse Ch. v. Texas Bank***, 889 S.W.2d 595, 600 (Tex.App.—Houston [14th Dist.] 1994, writ denied); ***Mercantile Mortg. Co. v. University Homes***, 663 S.W.2d 45, 47 (Tex. App.—Houston [14th Dist.] 1983, no writ).

(6) Unauthorized foreign corporation. To challenge whether a foreign corporation is registered with the Secretary of State and may maintain an action for affirmative relief. *See* ***Jay-Lor Textiles v. Pacific Compress Whs. Co.***, 547 S.W.2d 738, 740 (Tex.App.—Corpus Christi 1977, writ ref'd n.r.e.).

(7) No assumed name certificate. To challenge the lack of an assumed name certificate. ***Sixth RMA Partners v. Sibley***, 111 S.W.3d 46, 55 (Tex.2003); *see* Bus. & Com. Code §36.25 (party is prohibited from prosecuting suit until it files assumed name certificate).

(8) Necessary party is absent. To challenge the absence of a necessary party and force the plaintiff to add the missing party. *See, e.g.*, ***Allison v. National Un. Fire Ins. Co.***, 703 S.W.2d 637, 638 (Tex. 1986) (to challenge absence of necessary parties from contract dispute); ***Dahl v. Hartman***, 14 S.W.3d 434, 435-36 (Tex.App.—Houston [14th Dist.] 2000, pet. denied) (to challenge absence of necessary parties in declaratory judgment action); ***Wolfe v. Schuster***, 591 S.W.2d 926, 931 (Tex.App.—Dallas 1979, no writ) (to challenge P's failure to sue principal when D is surety and P has not already taken judgment against principal); *see also* TRCP 31-32 (surety).

(9) Improper party. To challenge the party. *Cf.* ***Bailey v. Vanscot Concrete Co.***, 894 S.W.2d 757, 759 (Tex.1995) (company that merged into another ceased to exist; P should have sued the merged company), *overruled on other grounds*, ***Chilkewitz v. Hyson***, 22 S.W.3d 825 (Tex.1999).

(10) Misnomer of defendant. To challenge the name under which the defendant was sued. *See* ***Matthews Trucking Co. v. Smith***, 682 S.W.2d 237, 238-39 (Tex.1984) (if correct D sued in wrong name, D should file motion to abate).

2. Defects in the allegations. A motion to abate is appropriate to challenge the following defects in the allegations:

(1) Lack of notice. The lack of notice or the allegation that the plaintiff gave proper presuit notice. *See, e.g.*, Educ. Code §22.0513(c) (notice of suit against professional employee of school district); ***De Checa v. Diagnostic Ctr. Hosp.***, 852 S.W.2d 935, 939 (Tex.1993) (notice for medical malpractice suit under former TRCS art. 4590i, §4.01, now CPRC §74.051); ***Hines v. Hash***, 843 S.W.2d 464, 467 (Tex.1992) (notice under DTPA). Under the DTPA, a defendant must move to abate for lack of notice within 30 days of filing its answer. Bus. & Com. Code §17.505(c); ***America Online v. Williams***, 958 S.W.2d 268, 277 (Tex.App.—Houston [14th Dist.] 1997, no pet.). The abatement under Bus. & Com. Code §17.505(d) is automatic when a verified plea in abatement is filed and lack of presuit notice is not controverted. ***America Online***, 958 S.W.2d at 273. In some cases, lack of notice subjects the suit to dismissal, not abatement. *See, e.g.*, ***Reese v. Texas State Dept. of Highways & Pub. Transp.***, 831 S.W.2d 529, 530-31 (Tex.App.—Tyler 1992, writ denied) (lack of notice under TTCA was not subject to abatement; suit was perpetually barred).

(2) Lack of residency. The lack of residency, when there is a residency requirement for filing suit. ***Cook v. Mayfield***, 886 S.W.2d 840, 841 (Tex.App.—Waco 1994, orig. proceeding); *see* Fam. Code §6.301(2) (one of the parties to a divorce must be resident of county for 90 days); *see, e.g.*, ***Reynolds v. Reynolds***, 86 S.W.3d 272, 277 (Tex.App.—Austin 2002, no pet.) (divorce petition did not properly allege residency requirements under Fam. Code §6.301).

§3.2 Abate – same dispute in another Texas court. When two lawsuits involving the same subject matter are filed in courts of concurrent jurisdiction, a party may file a motion to abate in one court, claiming the other court has dominant jurisdiction. *See* ***Wyatt v. Shaw Plumbing Co.***, 760 S.W.2d 245, 248 (Tex.1988); ***In re Sims***, 88 S.W.3d 297, 302 (Tex.App.—San Antonio 2002, orig. proceeding); *cf.* ***Miles v. Ford Motor Co.***, 914 S.W.2d 135, 139 (Tex.1995) (appeals filed by different parties in different courts of appeals). If the movant can prove the grounds for abatement as set out below, the court should abate the suit because the other court has dominant jurisdiction. *See* ***Curtis v. Gibbs***, 511 S.W.2d 263, 267 (Tex.1974); ***Hartley v. Coker***, 843 S.W.2d 743, 746 (Tex.App.—Corpus Christi 1992, no writ).

1. Dominant jurisdiction. To be entitled to an abatement based on dominant jurisdiction, the movant must file a motion to abate in the court where the second suit was filed and allege and prove the following.

(1) Commenced. The movant's suit (the "first suit") was "commenced" first. *See* ***Sims***, 88 S.W.3d at 303. Even though TRCP 22 states that a civil suit is commenced by filing a petition with the clerk, the mere filing of a petition does not fulfill the requirement for "commencement" of a suit for purposes of abatement. ***Russell v. Taylor***, 49 S.W.2d 733, 737 (Tex.Comm'n App. 1932); ***Grimes v. Harris***, 695 S.W.2d 648, 651 (Tex.App.—Dallas 1985, orig. proceeding). The movant must show citation in that suit was timely served. See §3.2.2(2), below.

(2) Pending. The first suit is still pending in the other court. ***Sims***, 88 S.W.3d at 303; ***Southern Cty. Mut. Ins. Co. v. Ochoa***, 19 S.W.3d 452, 468 (Tex.App.—Corpus Christi 2000, no pet.).

(3) Same parties & issues. The two suits involve the same parties and the same controversy. ***Sims***, 88 S.W.3d at 303; *see* ***Wyatt***, 760 S.W.2d at 248; ***Southern Cty.***, 19 S.W.3d at 468. The exact issues and all the parties do not need to be included in the first suit as long as the petition in the first suit can be amended to bring in all necessary parties and issues. ***Wyatt***, 760 S.W.2d at 247; ***Sims***, 88 S.W.3d at 303.

2. Exceptions to dominant jurisdiction. There are three exceptions to the dominant jurisdiction of the first court. ***Wyatt***, 760 S.W.2d at 248; ***In re McCall***, 967 S.W.2d 934, 936 (Tex.App.—Corpus Christi 1998, orig. proceeding).

(1) Estoppel. A party can be estopped from asserting the dominant jurisdiction of the first court. ***Wyatt***, 760 S.W.2d at 248. A party can be estopped by a variety of conduct, including representing to a second court that it has jurisdiction, not requesting abatement in a timely fashion, and not acting while different courts issue conflicting orders. ***Sweezy Constr. v. Murray***, 915 S.W.2d 527, 532 (Tex.App.—Corpus Christi 1995, orig. proceeding). A party can be estopped from asserting dominant jurisdiction if it files a claim, by either an original or an amended pleading, that is not ripe. ***Perry v. Del Rio***, 66 S.W.3d 239, 252-53 (Tex.2001).

(2) Lack of intent to prosecute. A party's lack of intent to prosecute a suit deprives the first court of dominant jurisdiction. ***Wyatt***, 760 S.W.2d at 248. The first suit does not confer dominant jurisdiction if the plaintiff delayed service of process. *See* ***Russell***, 49 S.W.2d at 737 (suit is not commenced if P directs clerk not to issue service of citation); *see, e.g.*, ***Curtis***, 511 S.W.2d at 268 (delay of 26 days in service was not unreasonable; abatement of second suit should have been sustained); ***Reed v. Reed***, 311 S.W.2d 628, 631 (Tex.1958) (delay of service for almost 15 months was unreasonable; second suit should not have been abated); ***Southern Cty.***, 19 S.W.3d at 468 (delay of service for 4 months unreasonable; denial of abatement of second suit affirmed).

(3) Lack of necessary parties. The lack of necessary parties deprives the first court of dominant jurisdiction. ***Wyatt***, 760 S.W.2d at 248; ***McCall***, 967 S.W.2d at 936.

3. Strategy. When two suits involving the same parties and the same dispute are on file in two counties, each party will want to abate the other party's suit. A party must make a strategic decision—whether to file a motion to abate the suit in which it is a defendant or to move the other suit forward and force the defendant in that suit to file a motion to abate.

§3.3 Abate – same dispute is subject to arbitration. A defendant may file a motion to abate requesting a suspension of the suit when the dispute should have been submitted to arbitration. See "Motion to Compel ADR Arbitration," ch. 4-C, §2, p. 213.

§3.4 Abate – administrative agency has primary jurisdiction. A defendant may file a motion to abate requesting a suspension of the suit when an administrative agency has primary jurisdiction over the dispute. *See* ***Subaru, Inc. v. David McDavid Nissan, Inc.***, 84 S.W.3d 212, 221 (Tex.2002). When an agency shares jurisdiction of a dispute with the courts, courts defer to the agency for policy reasons. *See id.* (agency is staffed with experts trained to handle complex issues presented and is better able to uniformly interpret its laws & regulations than the courts); ***City of Galveston v. Flagship Hotel***, 73 S.W.3d 422, 425 (Tex.App.—Houston [1st Dist.] 2002, no pet.)

(same). By comparison, when an administrative agency has exclusive jurisdiction, dismissal is mandatory. See "Administrative agency has exclusive jurisdiction," ch. 3-F, §3.5, p. 183.

§3.5 Stay – same dispute in another state's court. Instead of a motion to abate, a defendant may file a motion to stay requesting a suspension when the same case is pending in another state's court. *See* ***Crown Leasing Corp. v. Sims***, 92 S.W.3d 924, 927 (Tex.App.—Texarkana 2002, no pet.) (distinguishing between motion to stay & motion to abate; the first is discretionary, the second is a matter of right); ***Evans v. Evans***, 186 S.W.2d 277, 279 (Tex.App.—San Antonio 1945, no writ) (same). The court that first takes and maintains jurisdiction of a controversy should be allowed to dispose of it without the interference of any other court of coordinate jurisdiction. The mere pendency of an action in one state is not a reason to abate a suit in another state between the same parties and involving the same subject matter. ***Crown Leasing***, 92 S.W.3d at 927; *see, e.g.*, ***VE Corp. v. Ernst & Young***, 860 S.W.2d 83, 84 (Tex.1993) (appeal of dismissal not rendered moot because of pendency of suit in another state). As a matter of comity, however, it is the custom for the court in which the later action is filed to stay proceedings until the earlier-filed action is determined. ***VE Corp.***, 860 S.W.2d at 84. If the other court has continuing and exclusive jurisdiction, however, the issue should be challenged by a plea to the jurisdiction. See "Another court has exclusive jurisdiction," ch. 3-F, §3.4, p. 183.

§3.6 Stay – same dispute in federal court. Instead of a motion to abate, a defendant may file a motion to stay requesting a suspension when the same case is pending in federal court. The mere pendency of a suit in federal court involving the same parties and similar issues is not a reason to abate a later-filed state court proceeding. ***Taiwan Shrimp Farm Village Ass'n v. U.S.A. Shrimp Farm Dev.***, 915 S.W.2d 61, 68 (Tex.App.—Corpus Christi 1996, writ denied); ***Williamson v. Tucker***, 615 S.W.2d 881, 885 (Tex.App.—Dallas 1981, writ ref'd n.r.e.). As a matter of comity, however, it is the custom for the court in which the later action is filed to stay proceedings until the earlier-filed action is determined. ***Space Master Int'l v. Porta-Kamp Mfg. Co.***, 794 S.W.2d 944, 946 (Tex.App.—Houston [1st Dist.] 1990, no writ); ***Alpine Gulf, Inc. v. Valentino***, 563 S.W.2d 358, 359 (Tex.App.—Houston [14th Dist.] 1978, writ ref'd n.r.e.).

§4. RESPONSE

§4.1 Cure. The plaintiff may agree with the motion to abate and cure the defect. For example, when a motion to abate is filed in the second court on the ground of dominant jurisdiction of the first court, if the plaintiff dismisses the first suit, there is no longer a reason to abate. *See* ***Pleasants v. Emmons***, 871 S.W.2d 296, 298 (Tex.App.—Eastland 1994, no writ).

§4.2 Object. The plaintiff may file a response that challenges the factual matters alleged by the defendant. The response should follow the format of the motion to abate. It should be verified, and, if necessary, it should include affidavits.

§5. HEARING

§5.1 Evidence. The hearing on a motion to abate is for the receipt of evidence, not just argument of counsel. *See* ***Upchurch v. Albear***, 5 S.W.3d 274, 277 & n.4 (Tex.App.—Amarillo 1999, pet. denied); ***Kriegel v. Scott***, 439 S.W.2d 445, 447 (Tex.App.—Houston [14th Dist.] 1969, writ ref'd n.r.e.). The defendant must introduce evidence at the hearing. ***Bernal v. Garrison***, 818 S.W.2d 79, 82 (Tex.App.—Corpus Christi 1991, writ denied). When a defendant does not introduce evidence to support its motion to abate, the court must overrule it, unless the matters alleged in the motion appear on the face of the plaintiff's pleadings. *See id.* at 83; *see also* ***Brazos Elec. Power Coop. v. Weatherford ISD***, 453 S.W.2d 185, 189 (Tex.App.—Fort Worth 1970, writ ref'd n.r.e.) (reversible error for abatement to be sustained without any evidence).

§5.2 No jury. The hearing is before the court, not a jury. ***Union Pac. Fuels v. Johnson***, 909 S.W.2d 130, 135 (Tex.App.—Houston [14th Dist.] 1995, orig. proceeding); ***Miller v. Stout***, 706 S.W.2d 785, 787 (Tex.App.—San Antonio 1986, no writ).

§5.3 Waiver. A motion to abate is waived if it is not set for a hearing before the trial. ***Shiffers v. Estate of Ward***, 762 S.W.2d 753, 755 (Tex.App.—Fort Worth 1988, writ denied).

§5.4 Burden of proof. The defendant has the burden of proof on the allegations in its motion to abate. ***Flowers v. Steelcraft Corp.***, 406 S.W.2d 199, 199 (Tex.1966); ***Southern Cty. Mut. Ins. Co. v. Ochoa***, 19 S.W.3d 452, 469 (Tex.App.—Corpus Christi 2000, no pet.); ***Lopez v. Texas Workers' Comp. Ins. Fund***, 11 S.W.3d 490, 493 (Tex.App.—Austin 2000, pet. denied). The defendant must prove the relevant facts by a preponderance of the evidence. ***Lopez***, 11 S.W.3d at 493; ***Bernal***, 818 S.W.2d at 82; ***Brazos Elec.***, 453 S.W.2d at 188. If the defendant does not disprove the facts in the plaintiff's petition, the court must accept those facts as true. ***Bernal***, 818 S.W.2d at 82; ***Seth v. Meyer***, 730 S.W.2d 884, 885 (Tex.App.—Fort Worth 1987, no writ).

§6. ORDER

§6.1 Motion overruled. The first court to overrule a motion to abate becomes vested with dominant jurisdiction; the case will proceed to trial in that court. ***4M Linen & Uniform Sup. Co. v. W.P. Ballard & Co.***, 793 S.W.2d 320, 322 (Tex.App.—Houston [1st Dist.] 1990, writ denied). The other court cannot enjoin the court that overruled the motion to abate from proceeding to trial. ***Johnson v. Avery***, 414 S.W.2d 441, 442-43 (Tex.1966). If the other court continues to issue conflicting orders in the case, that court is subject to mandamus. ***Hall v. Lawlis***, 907 S.W.2d 493, 494 (Tex.1995). See §7.3, below.

§6.2 Motion sustained. If the motion to abate is sustained, the case is abated until the obstacle to its prosecution is removed. ***Texas Highway Dept. v. Jarrell***, 418 S.W.2d 486, 488 (Tex.1967). A court must set the terms for the abatement; a case cannot be abated indefinitely. ***Gebhardt v. Gallardo***, 891 S.W.2d 327, 332 (Tex.App.—San Antonio 1995, orig. proceeding).

1. Suspending suit. The order sustaining a motion to abate suspends all action in the suit until the cause of the abatement is cured. *See* ***America Online v. Williams***, 958 S.W.2d 268, 272 (Tex.App.—Houston [14th Dist.] 1997, no pet.); ***Permanente Med. Ass'n v. Johnson***, 917 S.W.2d 515, 517 (Tex.App.—Waco 1996, orig. proceeding). The parties should not attempt to engage in discovery while an abatement is in effect; discovery requests filed during abatement are a legal nullity and are not revived when the case is revived. ***Lumbermens Mut. Cas. Co. v. Garza***, 777 S.W.2d 198, 198-99 (Tex.App.—Corpus Christi 1989, orig. proceeding). The abatement prevents both the court and the parties from taking any action in the case. ***In re Kimball Hill Homes Tex.***, 969 S.W.2d 522, 527 (Tex.App.—Houston [14th Dist.] 1998, orig. proceeding). An exception to this rule is that the abatement does not prevent the plaintiff from dismissing claims or taking a nonsuit. ***United Oil & Minerals v. Costilla Energy***, 1 S.W.3d 840, 846 (Tex.App.—Corpus Christi 1999, no pet.).

PRACTICE TIP

When the trial court drafts an abatement order, if you want to continue with discovery, ask that the order state that discovery is exempt from the abatement. In other words, ask for a partial abatement.

2. Reviving suit. When the cause for the abatement is cured, the suit may be revived if anything remains to be litigated. ***TEIA v. Baeza***, 584 S.W.2d 317, 321 (Tex.App.—Amarillo 1979, no writ).

3. Dismissing suit. If the trial court grants a motion to abate and the plaintiff refuses to cure the defect, the suit may be dismissed. The dismissal should be "without prejudice." *See* ***M&M Constr. Co. v. Great Am. Ins. Co.***, 747 S.W.2d 552, 555 (Tex.App.—Corpus Christi 1988, no writ). The trial court cannot dismiss a lawsuit immediately after granting the motion to abate; the party whose pleadings are attacked must be given the opportunity to amend to cure the defect. ***Martin v. Dosohs I, Ltd.***, 2 S.W.3d 350, 354 (Tex.App.—San Antonio 1999, pet. denied); ***Lighthouse Ch. v. Texas Bank***, 889 S.W.2d 595, 600 (Tex.App.—Houston [14th Dist.] 1994, writ denied); ***Polk v. Braddock***, 864 S.W.2d 78, 80 (Tex.App.—Dallas 1992, no writ).

§7. REVIEW

§7.1 Interlocutory appeal.

1. Order denying arbitration. An order that denies a motion to abate for arbitration in a suit that is subject to the Texas Arbitration Act can be appealed before final judgment. See "Order denying arbitration – TAA," ch. 4-C, §5.2.2(1), p. 220.

2. Other orders. As a rule, there is no interlocutory appeal from most rulings on a motion to abate. However, CPRC §51.014(d) allows parties to agree to an interlocutory appeal. See ***O'Connor's Texas Civil Appeals***, "Appealable orders by agreed motion," ch. 13-P, §2.2, p. 131 (2002-03). This procedure may reduce the need for review by mandamus discussed in §7.3, below.

§7.2 Appeal after final judgment. In most cases, the order on a motion to abate is reviewable on appeal only after the case is terminated by a final judgment. ***Johnson v. Avery***, 414 S.W.2d 441, 443 (Tex.1966); *see also* ***Wyatt v. Shaw Plumbing Co.***, 760 S.W.2d 245, 248 (Tex.1988) (Supreme Court reversed judgment from Nueces County court that denied D's plea in abatement with instructions not to abate until after suit was completed in Duval County).

1. Standard of review. On appeal, the standard of review on a motion to abate is for abuse of discretion. ***Dolenz v. Continental Nat'l Bank***, 620 S.W.2d 572, 575 (Tex.1981); ***Dahl v. Hartman***, 14 S.W.3d 434, 436 (Tex.App.—Houston [14th Dist.] 2000, pet. denied).

2. Record. To review an allegation that the trial court erred in its ruling on a motion to abate, the complaining party must present the court of appeals with a record of the hearing on the motion. ***4M Linen***, 793 S.W.2d at 322-23. The reporter's record must contain the evidence from the hearing on the motion to abate, as well as from the trial. *See* ***Hartley v. Coker***, 843 S.W.2d 743, 748 (Tex.App.—Corpus Christi 1992, no writ).

§7.3 Mandamus. The appellate courts have granted mandamus to review abatement orders in the following situations: • The trial court refused to compel arbitration when the parties executed an agreement that required arbitration. See "Contractual arbitration," ch. 4-C, §5.2, p. 220. • The trial court abated the case indefinitely. ***Gebhardt v. Gallardo***, 891 S.W.2d 327, 333 (Tex.App.—San Antonio 1995, orig. proceeding). • The trial court refused to acknowledge another court's ruling on an abatement and interfered with the jurisdiction of that court. ***Hall v. Lawlis***, 907 S.W.2d 493, 494 (Tex.1995); ***Abor v. Black***, 695 S.W.2d 564, 567 (Tex.1985); ***Curtis v. Gibbs***, 511 S.W.2d 263, 267 (Tex.1974); *see* ***In re Mendoza***, 83 S.W.3d 233, 236 (Tex.App.—Corpus Christi 2002, orig. proceeding). • The trial court sustained a plea in abatement that suspended the suit, but no other court was willing to go forward. ***Trapnell v. Hunter***, 785 S.W.2d 426, 429 (Tex.App.—Corpus Christi 1990, orig. proceeding); *see* ***In re Sims***, 88 S.W.3d 297, 306 (Tex.App.—San Antonio 2002, orig. proceeding) (by granting plea in abatement, court effectively refused to proceed to trial). • The plaintiff did not give notice of the claim before suit was filed as required by statute. ***Hines v. Hash***, 843 S.W.2d 464, 469 (Tex.1992) (DTPA); ***Kimball Hill Homes***, 969 S.W.2d at 526-27 (Residential Construction Liability Act); ***Permanente Med. Ass'n***, 917 S.W.2d at 517 (medical malpractice).

I. MOTION TO QUASH—CHALLENGING THE SERVICE

§1. GENERAL

§1.1 Rule. TRCP 122.

§1.2 Purpose. A motion to quash is used to challenge defects in the citation or the service of process. ***Kawasaki Steel Corp. v. Middleton***, 699 S.W.2d 199, 203 (Tex.1985); ***Texas DPS v. Kreipe***, 29 S.W.3d 334, 336 (Tex.App.—Houston [14th Dist.] 2000, pet. denied). A successful motion to quash service merely delays the date when the defendant must answer the plaintiff's suit. ***Kawasaki***, 699 S.W.2d at 202; ***Kreipe***, 29 S.W.3d at 336; *see* TRCP 122. The motion to quash service is like the motion to abate in that it delays but does not end the suit. A motion to quash cannot be used to challenge the court's jurisdiction over the defendant. *See* ***Wheat v. Toone***, 700 S.W.2d 915, 915 (Tex.1985); ***Kawasaki***, 699 S.W.2d at 202-03. In fact, because a party makes a general appearance when it files a motion to quash, the motion actually confers jurisdiction. ***Onda Enters. v. Pierce***, 750 S.W.2d 812, 814 (Tex.App.—Tyler 1988, orig. proceeding).

CAUTION

The Corpus Christi Court of Appeals, relying on ***Kawasaki***, *said in dicta that a defendant should challenge defective allegations of personal jurisdiction by a motion to quash. See* ***Exito Elecs. v. Trejo***, *99 S.W.3d 360, 367 (Tex.App.—Corpus Christi 2003, pet. filed 5-7-03). A party should not do so until the Supreme Court clarifies the issue. By challenging a defective allegation of personal jurisdiction in a motion to quash, the defendant will subject itself to the court's jurisdiction. See TRCP 122.* ***Kawasaki*** *does not support* ***Exito***. *The holding in* ***Kawasaki*** *is that a nonresident cannot challenge curable jurisdictional defects (e.g., defects in service, citation, jurisdictional allegations in petition) in a special appearance.* ***Kawasaki***, *699 S.W.2d at 203. The only jurisdictional defect discussed in* ***Kawasaki*** *was the failure to bring a suit under the correct statute. See* ***Kawasaki***, *699 S.W.2d at 202 (quoting from Professor Thode, "an attempt to bring the defendant before the court under the wrong statute does not authorize the use of the special appearance"). See "Not Texas resident," ch. 3-B, §2.3.1, p. 144.*

§1.3 Forms. None.

§2. MOTION TO QUASH

A defendant may challenge defective service of citation with a motion to quash or a motion for new trial, depending on whether a no-answer default judgment was rendered.

§2.1 Motion to quash – no default judgment.

1. Resident defendant. If, before filing an answer, a defendant discovers that service of process was defective, the defendant may file a motion to quash service. *See* ***Onda Enters.***, 750 S.W.2d at 814. The effect of the motion to quash is to make an appearance before the court and, when the motion is granted, to delay the filing of the answer. ***Alcala v. Williams***, 908 S.W.2d 54, 56 (Tex.App.—San Antonio 1995, no writ); *see* ***Allright, Inc. v. Roper***, 478 S.W.2d 245, 247-48 (Tex.App.—Houston [14th Dist.] 1972, writ dism'd).

2. Nonresident defendant. A nonresident defendant who intends to challenge personal jurisdiction should not file a motion to quash. *See* ***Onda Enters.***, 750 S.W.2d at 814 (D should have filed special appearance, not motion to quash). A special appearance is the correct motion to challenge personal jurisdiction. If, as a back-up argument, the defendant contends that service of process was technically defective, it should file a motion to quash after it files the special appearance. If the court overrules the special appearance but sustains the motion to quash, the ruling on the motion to quash confers jurisdiction on the court.

§2.2 Motion for new trial after default judgment. Once a no-answer default judgment is rendered, any challenge to service can be made in a motion for new trial, with affidavits attached proving defective service. See "MNT After Default Judgment," ch. 10-B, §15, p. 631. A motion for new trial must be filed within 30 days of the date of the default judgment. TRCP 329b(a). If the court grants the motion for new trial, the defendant will have additional time to answer, counting from the date of the ruling on the motion for new trial. See §4.2.1, below. If the court denies the motion for new trial, the defendant should perfect its appeal.

1. Resident defendant. If—after a no-answer default judgment was rendered but before the expiration of the deadline to file a motion for new trial—a resident defendant discovers the service of process was defective, the defendant should file a motion for new trial to challenge service. See "Improper service + no-answer default," ch. 10-B, §15.1.1, p. 631.

2. Nonresident defendant. If—after a no-answer default judgment was rendered but before the expiration of the deadline to file a motion for new trial—a nonresident defendant discovers the service of process was defective, the defendant should first file a special appearance (alleging no personal jurisdiction) and then a motion for new trial (alleging defective service). *See* TRCP 120a(1); *see, e.g.*, ***Puri v. Mansukhani***, 973 S.W.2d 701, 707 (Tex.App.—Houston [14th Dist.] 1998, no pet.) (D filed motion for new trial subject to special appearance); *see also* ***Koch Graphics v. Avantech, Inc.***, 803 S.W.2d 432, 433 (Tex.App.—Dallas 1991, no writ) (D filed special appearance and then filed motion to quash, motion for new trial, and answer, all subject to special appearance). The defendant must request a ruling on the special appearance before a ruling on the motion for new trial. ***Landry v. Daigrepont***, 35 S.W.3d 265, 267 (Tex.App.—Corpus Christi 2000, no pet.). See "Due Order of Pleadings," ch. 3-B, §2.2, p. 144.

§3. RESPONSE

In most cases, the plaintiff should keep quiet, not contest the defendant's motion to quash service, encourage the trial court to grant the motion, and see if the defendant files an answer as required. If the defendant does not file an answer by the new answer date, the plaintiff may take a default judgment. TRCP 122; ***Kawasaki Steel Corp. v. Middleton***, 699 S.W.2d 199, 202 (Tex.1985).

§4. ORDER

§4.1 Court denies motion. If the court denies the motion to quash, the time for the defendant to file its answer is not extended.

§4.2 Court grants motion.

1. Time to answer. If the court grants the defendant's motion to quash or a motion for new trial challenging service, the defendant must file an answer on the Monday after the expiration of 20 days from the date of the order. TRCP 122; *see* ***Kawasaki***, 699 S.W.2d at 202 (remedy for defective service is additional time to answer). The plaintiff is not required to re-serve the defendant. ***Boreham v. Hartsell***, 826 S.W.2d 193, 197 (Tex.App.—Dallas 1992, no writ); *see* ***Allright***, 478 S.W.2d at 248. The defendant is deemed served when the trial court quashes the service or citation. TRCP 122.

2. No dismissal. The court will not grant a motion to dismiss after granting a motion to quash. ***Texas DPS v. Kreipe***, 29 S.W.3d 334, 336 (Tex.App.—Houston [14th Dist.] 2000, pet. denied); *see* TRCP 122; ***Kawasaki***, 699 S.W.2d at 202.

§5. REVIEW

If the trial court denies the motion to quash, the defendant can appeal that order after a final judgment. If the appellate court decides the trial court erred in denying the motion to quash, the appellate court will reverse the judgment and remand the case to the trial court, which will give the defendant additional time to answer the suit. ***Boreham***, 826 S.W.2d at 197. On remand, the plaintiff does not need to reissue service. *Id.*

COMMENTARIES

CHAPTER 4. ALTERNATIVE DISPUTE RESOLUTION

TABLE OF CONTENTS

COMMENTARIES

CHAPTER 4. ALTERNATIVE DISPUTE RESOLUTION
A. THE ADR SYSTEM

A. THE ADR SYSTEM

The alternative dispute resolution system (ADR) is a method of privatizing justice. The parties are taken out of the public justice system by agreement or by court order and sent to resolve their dispute before a private tribunal.

§1. GENERAL

§1.1 Rules. None. See CPRC ch. 154.

§1.2 Purpose. The purpose of ADR is to encourage the peaceable resolution of civil disputes and the early settlement of litigation through voluntary settlement procedures. CPRC §154.002; ***Keene Corp. v. Gardner***, 837 S.W.2d 224, 232 (Tex.App.—Dallas 1992, writ denied); ***Downey v. Gregory***, 757 S.W.2d 524, 525 (Tex.App.—Houston [1st Dist.] 1988, orig. proceeding).

§1.3 Forms. ***O'Connor's Texas Civil Forms***, FORMS 4A.

§1.4 Other references. Alderman, *Pre-dispute Mandatory Arbitration in Consumer Contracts: A Call for Reform*, 38 Hous.L.Rev. 1237 (2001); Huber & Trachte-Huber, *International ADR in the 1990's: The Top Ten Developments*, 1 Hous. Bus. & Tax L.J. 184 (2001); Galton & Kovach, *Texas ADR: A Future So Bright We Gotta Wear Shades*, 31 St. Mary's L.J. 949 (2000); *Rau & Sherman's Texas ADR and Arbitration Statutes: Commentary & Annotations* (1994 & Supp. 1997); Trachte-Huber & Huber, *Alternative Dispute Resolution: Strategies for Law & Business* (1997); Trachte-Huber, *Negotiation: Strategies for Law & Business* (1995); White Dispute Resolution Inst., *Texas Registry of ADR Professionals* (1994); Roth, Wulff & Cooper, *The Alternative Dispute Resolution Practice Guide* (1993); State Bar of Texas, *Handbook for Alternative Dispute Resolution* (2d ed. 1990).

§2. TYPES OF ADR

§2.1 By agreement, motion, or order. The following types of ADR are available by agreement of the parties, by motion of one of the parties, or by order of the court.

1. Mediation. Most cases referred to ADR are referred to mediation. Mediation is a procedure in which an impartial person (the mediator) facilitates communication between the parties to promote reconciliation, settlement, or understanding. CPRC §154.023(a). See "Mediation," ch. 4-B, p. 210; ***O'Connor's*** FORMS 4B.

2. Moderated settlement conference. A moderated settlement conference is a nonbinding procedure in which the case is submitted to a panel of three impartial third parties for an evaluation of the case and realistic settlement negotiations. This procedure requires each party and its counsel to present the party's position before a panel of impartial third parties (often three lawyers); after deliberations, the panel may issue a nonbinding advisory opinion on liability, damages, or both. CPRC §154.025(b)-(d). The parties may be asked to provide a written memorandum of the issues to the panel before the proceeding begins. The typical conference starts with an introduction from the panel and a presentation from each party. The panel will ask questions, and each party will be given an opportunity to summarize its case. After the panel deliberates, it will issue an advisory opinion, often in the form of ranges based on the panel's experience with similar suits. See ***O'Connor's*** FORMS 4A:01, 4A:05.

3. Summary jury trial. A summary jury trial is a nonbinding procedure in which the case is submitted to a panel of jurors drawn from the county's jury pool. See Judge Brown, *The Summary Jury Trial*, Part I & II, 38 Hous. Lawyer 5, p. 32 (Mar.-Apr. 2001) & 38 Hous. Lawyer 6, p. 16 (May-June 2001). The jury is not told it is not providing a binding verdict. This procedure requires each party and its counsel to present the party's position before a panel of six jurors (unless the parties agree otherwise). CPRC §154.026(b), (c). After deliberations, the panel may issue a nonbinding advisory opinion on liability, damages, or both. *Id.* §154.026(d), (e). The summary jury trial uses a format similar to a regular jury trial, but the rules of procedure and evidence are relaxed. *See* CPRC §154.073(a), (b); TRCP 76a(2)(a)(2). The supervising court will establish guidelines for voir dire, opening statements, summary of admissible evidence, closing arguments, jury deliberations, verdict, and final discussion. The final discussion takes place between the jurors and the parties outside the presence of the judge. See ***O'Connor's*** FORMS 4A:01, 4A:06.

4. County-sponsored ADR center. A county may establish an ADR system. CPRC §152.002(a). "ADR system" means an informal forum using mediation, conciliation, or nonbinding arbitration. *Id.* §152.001. Each county has the authority to collect money, which may be taxed as a cost of suit (up to $10 per case). *Id.* §152.004(a). Each county may contract with a private nonprofit corporation, a political subdivision, or another organization to establish a dispute resolution center (DRC). *Id.* §152.002(b)(1). CPRC §152.002(b)(3) vests management of the ADR system in a committee selected by the county bar association. For example, in Harris County, the Harris County Dispute Resolution Center is supervised by the Houston Bar Association and provides free services for controversies involving no more than $100,000 and no more than three parties. There are 17 DRCs in Texas: Amarillo, Austin, Beaumont, Bryan-College Station, Conroe, Corpus Christi, Dallas, Denton, El Paso, Fort Worth, Houston, Kerrville, Lubbock, Paris, Richmond, San Antonio, and Waco. See ***O'Connor's*** FORM 4A:01.

5. Binding arbitration. There are two types of binding arbitration: (1) contractually where the parties agree as part of a contract to refer all disputes to arbitration, and (2) agreed, where the parties agree to settle a particular dispute by binding arbitration. CPRC §154.027(b). In binding arbitration, each party and its counsel present the party's position to an impartial third party, who renders a specific award. The award is binding and enforceable in the same manner as any contract obligation. *Id.* See "Arbitration," ch. 4-C, p. 213; ***O'Connor's*** FORMS 4C.

6. Nonbinding arbitration. Nonbinding arbitration is a forum in which each party and its counsel present the party's position to an impartial third party, who renders a specific award. CPRC §154.027(a). The parties do not agree in advance that the award is binding. *Id.* §154.027(b). The award is advisory only and functions as the basis for further settlement negotiations between the parties. *Id.* See "Nonbinding," ch. 4-C, §2.1, p. 213; ***O'Connor's*** FORMS 4A.

§2.2 By agreement only. The court can order the following types of ADR only when both parties agree to participate.

1. Mini-trial. A mini-trial is a nonbinding settlement procedure that uses several dispute resolution processes. In a mini-trial, each party and its counsel present the party's position to an impartial third party or selected representatives of the parties. The impartial third party may issue a nonbinding advisory opinion on the merits of the case. CPRC §154.024(c), (d). The advisory opinion becomes binding if the parties agree and enter into a written settlement agreement. *Id.* §154.024(d). In most cases, the procedure for the mini-trial is as follows: each party makes an opening statement summarizing the facts and legal arguments; each party has an opportunity to respond to the other party's opening statement; the parties are questioned by the impartial third party or the selected representatives; the parties negotiate; and, if necessary, an advisory opinion is issued. See ***O'Connor's*** FORMS 4A:07-08.

2. Special judge trial. In a trial by a special judge, the parties try their case before a retired or former judge who is selected by the parties to hear the case. The procedure is described in CPRC chapter 151. See "Special Judge," ch. 4-D, p. 221; ***O'Connor's*** FORMS 4D.

3. Expert panel. Many cases hinge on issues involving highly technical, scientific, medical, or other specialized concepts or theories that cannot be established without the use of expert testimony. An expert panel provides an ADR forum in which one expert or a panel of experts serves as a neutral third party decision maker to review and evaluate the merits of a case and make a determination based on the factual information and evidence presented to the expert panel. *See* Kovach, *Mediation: Principles & Practice* 13 (2d ed.2000). The expert determination may be either binding or advisory. *See id.* If the parties decide to be bound by the expert panel's opinions, the parties must agree in advance that the expert panel's evaluation of the issues presented is conclusive. *Id.* If the expert panel's opinion is merely advisory, the parties can agree that a trial court or subsequent decision-maker is free to reach new, independent conclusions about the evidence and that the expert panel's decision is not controlling. *See id.*

4. Jury determined settlement. Jury determined settlement (JDS) combines the ADR procedures of a summary jury trial and arbitration into one proceeding. Kovach, *Mediation: Principles & Practice* at 15. Under a JDS approach, a jury is impaneled, and the trial moves forward like to a summary jury trial. *Id.* at 15. The JDS participants retain some control over the outcome of the process by structuring exposure limits through a high-low settlement agreement. *Id.* at 16. Once the JDS proceeding is completed, the jury does not render a verdict; instead, the jury issues a settlement decision that is binding on the JDS participants. *Id.* at 15-16.

5. Collaborative law procedure. In suits for dissolution of marriage or suits affecting the parent-child relationship, the parties may agree to enter into a collaborative law agreement. Fam. Code §§6.603, 153.0072. Collaborative law agreements must be in writing and signed by the parties and their attorneys. *Id.* §§6.603(a), 153.0072(a). In a collaborative law procedure, the parties and their counsel agree to use their best efforts and make a good-faith attempt at resolving their dispute without judicial intervention. *Id.* §§6.603(b), 153.0072(b). The only role the court plays is approving the settlement agreement, making the legal pronouncements, and signing the order to effectuate the agreement. *Id.* §§6.603(b), 153.0072(b).

§3. REFERRAL PROCEDURES FOR ADR

§3.1 Procedure for proposing ADR.

1. By agreement. The parties may agree to submit a dispute to ADR.

(1) Presuit agreements. The parties may agree by contract to submit a dispute to ADR.

(2) Pretrial agreements. Once parties are in litigation, they may agree to take all or part of the dispute out of litigation and submit it to another form of dispute resolution. *See* ***Massey v. Galvan***, 822 S.W.2d 309, 318 (Tex.App.—Houston [14th Dist.] 1992, writ denied). The ADR agreement should be signed by the parties and their lawyers, should identify which part of the lawsuit is subject to the agreement, and should state whether the ADR result is binding or nonbinding. See, for example, Family Code §153.0071(a), which permits the parties to execute a binding agreement to submit a suit affecting the parent-child relationship to arbitration.

2. On motion of a party. A party may ask the court to refer the suit to ADR. CPRC §154.021(a); ***Downey v. Gregory***, 757 S.W.2d 524, 525 (Tex.App.—Houston [1st Dist.] 1988, orig. proceeding).

3. On motion of the court. The court may, on its own initiative, refer a suit to ADR. CPRC §154.021(a); *see* ***In re Acceptance Ins. Co.***, 33 S.W.3d 443, 451 (Tex.App.—Fort Worth 2000, orig. proceeding); ***In re Daley***, 29 S.W.3d 915, 918 (Tex.App.—Beaumont 2000, orig. proceeding); *see, e.g.*, ***Decker v. Lindsay***, 824 S.W.2d 247, 251-52 (Tex.App.—Houston [1st Dist.] 1992, orig. proceeding) (court referred case to ADR without motion of either party). The court may refer a case to ADR at any time during the trial. ***Downey***, 757 S.W.2d at 525. Even an appellate court can refer a case to ADR. *See, e.g.*, ***In re Cassey D.***, 783 S.W.2d 592, 598 (Tex.App.—Houston [1st Dist.] 1990, no writ) (after court of appeals reversed trial court's denial of visitation privileges to parent, it referred case to ADR).

§3.2 Pre-referral issues for the court.

1. Considerations for referral. Some of the things the court may consider in deciding whether to refer a case to ADR are (1) the nature of the dispute, (2) the complexity of the issues, (3) the number of parties, (4) the extent of past settlement discussions, (5) the positions of the parties, and (6) whether there has been sufficient discovery to permit an accurate case evaluation. ***Walton v. Canon, Short & Gaston, P.C.***, 23 S.W.3d 143, 150 (Tex.App.—El Paso 2000, no pet.); ***Downey***, 757 S.W.2d at 525.

2. Consultation with parties. The court must "confer" with the parties to determine the most appropriate ADR procedure. CPRC §154.021(b). This does not mean the court must give the parties an oral hearing. *See* ***Downey***, 757 S.W.2d at 525 (trial court may, but is not required to, hold a hearing before making a decision about referral to ADR).

3. Notice of intent to refer. When the court decides that a case should go to ADR, it must notify the parties that it intends to send the case to ADR. *See* CPRC §154.022(a). The trial court cannot require ADR without giving at least ten days' notice. ***Keene Corp. v. Gardner***, 837 S.W.2d 224, 232 (Tex.App.—Dallas 1992, writ denied) (24 hours' notice to mediate violated the statute); *see* CPRC §154.022(b).

§4. OBJECTING TO ADR

§4.1 Written. An objection to ADR must be in writing. CPRC §154.022(b). See ***O'Connor's*** FORMS 4A:02-03. If the objection includes any statement of facts outside the record, it should be verified.

§4.2 Deadline. To object to ADR, a party must file its objections within ten days of the referral. CPRC §154.022(b); ***Keene Corp.***, 837 S.W.2d at 232.

§4.3 Grounds. To avoid ADR, the objections must state a "reasonable basis." CPRC §154.022(c). Nothing in the ADR statute provides any guidance for making objections that have a "reasonable basis." The following are some possible objections to a referral to ADR:

1. Too broad. If the trial court's order is too broad and goes beyond the statute, the party should object. ***Decker***, 824 S.W.2d at 251-52. For example, while a court may compel parties to participate in mediation, it cannot compel the parties to negotiate in good faith or to settle their dispute. ***Avary v. Bank of Am.***, 72 S.W.3d 779, 797 (Tex.App.—Dallas 2002, pet. denied); ***Texas Parks & Wildlife Dept. v. Davis***, 988 S.W.2d 370, 375 (Tex.App.—Austin 1999, no pet.); *see* ***Decker***, 824 S.W.2d at 251-52.

2. No conference with parties. A party may challenge the court's referral if the court did not "confer" with the parties to determine the most appropriate ADR procedure, as required by CPRC §154.021(b). *See* ***Decker***, 824 S.W.2d at 248 (parties did not object to lack of conference).

3. Less than ten days' notice. A party may challenge the court's referral if the court did not give the parties at least ten days' notice of the referral. ***Keene Corp.***, 837 S.W.2d at 232.

4. Case not appropriate. A party may challenge the court's referral if the case is not appropriate for ADR. So far, this challenge has not been successful. *See* ***Decker***, 824 S.W.2d at 249 (parties did not want to mediate a simple car-accident case; trial would probably last only 2 days).

5. Other ADR procedure. A party may challenge the court's choice of ADR procedure and suggest a more appropriate procedure. ***Paul v. Paul***, 870 S.W.2d 349, 350 (Tex.App.—Waco 1994, no writ).

6. Multiple referrals in same case. A party may challenge the court's referral if the case has already been submitted to ADR. Some trial courts repeatedly send the same case to ADR, probably to avoid trying it.

§5. ORDER FOR ADR

§5.1 Ruling on objection. If the trial court finds there is a reasonable basis for an objection, the court cannot refer the dispute for ADR. CPRC §154.022(c).

§5.2 Order. The court may require the parties to attend ADR; however, the court cannot force the parties to negotiate in good faith because this violates the "open courts" provision of the Texas Constitution. ***Hansen v. Sullivan***, 886 S.W.2d 467, 469 (Tex.App.—Houston [1st Dist.] 1994, orig. proceeding); ***Decker***, 824 S.W.2d at 251. An order requiring good-faith negotiations is void. ***Acceptance Ins. Co.***, 33 S.W.3d at 452.

§5.3 ADR providers. Under CPRC §154.021(a), a court is authorized to refer a case to the following ADR providers:

1. County dispute resolution center. A county-sponsored ADR system established under CPRC ch. 152. CPRC §154.021(a)(1). See "County-sponsored ADR center," §2.1.4, p. 205.

2. Dispute resolution organization. A dispute resolution organization as defined in CPRC §154.001(2). CPRC §154.021(a)(2).

3. Impartial third party. A nonjudicial and informally conducted forum for the voluntary settlement of citizens' disputes through the intervention of an impartial third party. CPRC §154.021(a)(3).

4. Other ADR providers. Any other ADR provider the court deems appropriate. *See* CPRC §154.021(a) (uses the term "including" before list of ADR providers).

§6. APPOINTMENT OF IMPARTIAL THIRD PARTY

If the court refers a dispute to ADR, the court may appoint one or more impartial third parties on whom the parties agree to facilitate the ADR. CPRC §154.051.

§6.1 Qualifications.

1. Generally. To qualify for appointment as an impartial third party, the person must have completed 40 classroom hours of training provided by an ADR system or other organization approved by the court. CPRC §154.052(a).

2. For parent-child disputes. To qualify for appointment in a dispute relating to the parent-child relationship, a person must have 24 hours of training in the fields of family dynamics, child development, and family law in addition to the 40 classroom hours of general ADR training. CPRC §154.052(b).

3. Exceptions. A court has the discretion to appoint a person who does not otherwise qualify, as long as the court bases its appointment on legal or other professional training or experience. CPRC §154.052(c). For example, the court could appoint a former judge who has not satisfied the training requirement.

§6.2 Standards & duties. A person appointed as an impartial third party must encourage and assist the parties in reaching a settlement but cannot compel or coerce the parties to settle. CPRC §154.053(a). The job of the third party is to facilitate communication between the parties, to encourage reconciliation, settlement, and understanding, and to avoid further litigation. ***In re Ames***, 860 S.W.2d 590, 592 (Tex.App.—Amarillo 1993, no writ). Impartial third parties cannot alter the agreement between the parties, nor can they interject their own terms into the agreements. ***In re McIntosh***, 918 S.W.2d 87, 88 (Tex.App.—Amarillo 1996, no writ).

§6.3 Fees. The court may set a reasonable fee for the services of an impartial third party appointed to facilitate an ADR procedure. CPRC §154.054(a); ***Decker v. Lindsay***, 824 S.W.2d 247, 249-50 (Tex.App.—Houston [1st Dist.] 1992, orig. proceeding). Unless otherwise agreed by the parties, the court must tax the fee as a cost of the suit. CPRC §154.054(b); ***Paul***, 870 S.W.2d at 350.

§6.4 Confidentiality. Any communication about the subject matter of the dispute (civil or criminal) made by any participant in an ADR procedure is confidential, is not subject to disclosure, and cannot be used as evidence against the participant in any judicial or administrative proceeding. CPRC §154.073(a); ***In re Cartwright***, 104 S.W.3d 706, 713-14 (Tex.App.—Houston [1st Dist.] 2003, orig. proceeding); *see* TRE 408 (evidence of statements in compromise negotiations is not admissible).

1. No disclosure by impartial third party. The impartial third party cannot disclose the following:

(1) To either party, the information given in confidence by the other party, unless authorized by the disclosing party. CPRC §154.053(b).

(2) To any person, including the court, any matters relating to the settlement process, including the conduct and demeanor of the parties and their counsel, unless the parties agree otherwise. CPRC §154.053(c); *see also* ***Cartwright***, 104 S.W.3d at 714 (improper for mediator to later serve as arbitrator of same or related dispute between same parties). Mediators, in most cases, cannot testify about the bargaining sessions they attend. ***In re Anonymous***, 283 F.3d 627, 639-40 (4th Cir.2002); ***NLRB v. Joseph Macaluso, Inc.***, 618 F.2d 51, 53 (9th Cir.1980).

The complete exclusion of mediator testimony is necessary to preserve an effective system of mediation. ***NLRB***, 618 F.2d at 56; *see also* ***Wilson v. Attaway***, 757 F.2d 1227, 1245 (11th Cir.1985) (trial court did not abuse its discretion by refusing to admit report of community mediator who witnessed a riot).

2. Confidential record. Any record made at an ADR procedure is confidential; the participants and the third party facilitating the procedure cannot be required to testify in any proceeding relating to or arising out of the matter in dispute or be subject to process requiring disclosure of confidential information or data relating to or arising out of the matter in dispute. CPRC §154.073(b).

3. Exceptions. There are several exceptions to the general rule of confidentiality for communications made in an ADR procedure.

(1) Independently discoverable. A communication used in an ADR procedure is discoverable and admissible if the same information is discoverable independently of the ADR procedure. CPRC §154.073(c); ***In re Learjet Inc.***, 59 S.W.3d 842, 845 (Tex.App.—Texarkana 2001, orig. proceeding).

(2) Legal requirements for disclosure. If CPRC §154.073 conflicts with other legal requirements for disclosure of communications or materials, the confidential information may be presented to the court having jurisdiction to determine, in camera, whether it is discoverable. CPRC §154.073(e); ***Avary v. Bank of Am.***, 72 S.W.3d 779, 796 (Tex.App.—Dallas 2002, pet. denied); ***In re Acceptance Ins. Co.***, 33 S.W.3d 443, 453 (Tex. App.—Fort Worth 2000, orig. proceeding); *see* Said, Comment, *The Mediator's Dilemma: The Legal Requirements Exception to Confidentiality Under the Texas ADR Statute*, 36 S.Tex.L.Rev. 579, 586-87 (1995); *see also* TRE 408 (permits in-court disclosure of evidence of settlement if evidence is offered for another purpose listed in TRE 408).

(3) Report of abuse. CPRC §154.073 does not affect the requirements for reporting abuse under Family Code chapter 261 or Human Resources Code chapter 48. CPRC §154.073(f).

(4) Unrelated to dispute. When a communication does not relate to or arise out of the subject matter of a dispute, it may not be confidential under CPRC §154.073(a) and (b). ***Avary***, 72 S.W.3d at 794; *see, e.g.*, ***In re Daley***, 29 S.W.3d 915, 918 (Tex.App.—Beaumont 2000, orig. proceeding) (deposition questions regarding whether participant attended mediation & whether he had permission to leave did not concern subject matter of underlying suit & thus were not confidential).

§7. SANCTIONS

§7.1 Sanctions. The trial court may impose sanctions for refusal to participate in court-ordered mediation. *See, e.g.*, ***Roberts v. Rose***, 37 S.W.3d 31, 34-35 (Tex.App.—San Antonio 2000, no pet.) (because lawyer misinformed client about need to appear at ADR, lawyer was sanctioned, not client); ***Texas DOT v. Pirtle***, 977 S.W.2d 657, 658 (Tex.App.—Fort Worth 1998, pet. denied) (sanctions assessed against the prevailing party for not filing written objections to ADR & for refusing to participate); ***Gleason v. Lawson***, 850 S.W.2d 714, 717 (Tex.App.—Corpus Christi 1993, no writ) (judge may hold party in contempt for not appearing at ADR meeting); ***Luxenberg v. Marshall***, 835 S.W.2d 136, 141 (Tex.App.—Dallas 1992, orig. proceeding) (trial court struck D's pleadings because D did not comply with numerous pretrial orders, including an order to mediate). The court cannot dismiss or default a case for failure to observe court-imposed ADR deadlines unless it first applies the test for death penalty sanctions. ***Wal-Mart Stores v. Butler***, 41 S.W.3d 816, 818 (Tex.App.—Dallas 2001, no pet.). See "To impose death penalty sanctions," ch. 5-J, §3.2, p. 276.

§7.2 No sanctions. The trial court cannot impose sanctions for refusal to settle a case in court-ordered mediation. ***Hansen v. Sullivan***, 886 S.W.2d 467, 469 (Tex.App.—Houston [1st Dist.] 1994, orig. proceeding). Nor can the court compel a party to negotiate in good faith. ***Avary***, 72 S.W.3d at 797; ***Texas Parks & Wildlife Dept. v. Davis***, 988 S.W.2d 370, 375 (Tex.App.—Austin 1999, no pet.); ***Gleason***, 850 S.W.2d at 717. Once the case is settled, the trial court cannot impose sanctions for failure to pay the settlement agreement. ***Island Entm't, Inc. v. Castaneda***, 882 S.W.2d 2, 5 (Tex.App.—Houston [1st Dist.] 1994, writ denied) (written settlement agreement after mediation).

§8. SETTLEMENT WEEKS

In every county with a population of at least 150,000, the ADR statute requires two weeks—law week and judicial conference week—to be set aside each year for the courts to facilitate the voluntary settlement of pending cases. CPRC §155.001. Any licensed attorney may serve as a mediator during settlement weeks under terms, conditions, and training as required by the administrative judge of the judicial district. *Id.* §155.003.

§9. SETTLEMENT AGREEMENT

§9.1 Agreement reached. If the parties execute a written agreement disposing of the dispute in ADR, the agreement is enforceable like any other written contract. CPRC §154.071(a); ***Mantas v. 5th Ct. of Appeals***, 925 S.W.2d 656, 658 (Tex.1996); ***Hardman v. Dault***, 2 S.W.3d 378, 380 (Tex.App.—San Antonio 1999, no pet.); ***Davis v. Wickham***, 917 S.W.2d 414, 416 (Tex.App.—Houston [14th Dist.] 1996, no writ); ***Stevens v. Snyder***, 874 S.W.2d 241, 243 (Tex.App.—Dallas 1994, writ denied). If the agreement complies with TRCP 11 or contract law, one of the parties can enforce it without the other party's consent. ***Davis***, 917 S.W.2d at 416; ***Stevens***, 874 S.W.2d at 243. As with any enforceable contract, a party who signs a settlement agreement disposing of a dispute through ADR cannot unilaterally repudiate the agreement. ***In re Banks***, 887 S.W.2d 160, 163 (Tex.App.—Texarkana 1994, no writ); ***In re Ames***, 860 S.W.2d 590, 591 (Tex.App.—Amarillo 1993, no writ). See "Settlement of the Suit," ch. 7-H, p. 510.

§9.2 Action to enforce. The court cannot take action on a settlement agreement without a request to do so, such as an amended pleading requesting relief or proposing a defense based on the agreement, or a motion for summary judgment based on the agreement. ***Pickell v. Guaranty Nat'l Life Ins. Co.***, 917 S.W.2d 439, 441-42 (Tex.App.—Houston [14th Dist.] 1996, no writ). The court may incorporate the terms of the agreement into the final decree disposing of the case. CPRC §154.071(b). The terms of the settlement agreement may be enforced as contract rights regardless of whether they have been incorporated into the judgment. ***McFarland v. Bridges***, 104 S.W.3d 906, 910-11 (Tex.App.—El Paso 2003, no pet.). The court cannot modify the agreement reached in ADR without the consent of both parties. See "Enforcing the settlement agreement," ch. 7-H, §5.2, p. 515.

§9.3 Parent-child cases. A party in a suit affecting the parent-child relationship is entitled to judgment on a mediated settlement agreement if the agreement meets the requirements of Family Code §153.0071(d), even when the agreement does not meet the requirements of TRCP 11. ***In re Calderon***, 96 S.W.3d 711, 718 (Tex.App.—Tyler 2003, orig. proceeding); ***Alvarez v. Reiser***, 958 S.W.2d 232, 233 (Tex.App.—Eastland 1997, pet. denied); *see* ***Boyd v. Boyd***, 67 S.W.3d 398, 402 (Tex.App.—Fort Worth 2002, no pet.). To be enforceable, the agreement must (1) include a prominently displayed statement, in boldfaced type or in capital letters or underlined, that the agreement is not subject to revocation, (2) be signed by each party to the agreement, and (3) be signed by the party's attorney, if any, who is present when the agreement is signed. Fam. Code §153.0071(d)-(e); ***Calderon***, 96 S.W.3d at 717; ***Boyd***, 67 S.W.3d at 402; *see* ***In re Kasschau***, 11 S.W.3d 305, 310 (Tex.App.—Houston [14th Dist.] 1999, orig. proceeding); ***Spinks v. Spinks***, 939 S.W.2d 229, 230 (Tex.App.—Houston [1st Dist.] 1997, no writ). A party cannot avoid rendition of a judgment on the mediated settlement agreement by withdrawing consent after the requirements of Family Code §153.0071(d) have been met. ***Alvarez***, 958 S.W.2d at 234.

B. MEDIATION

§1. GENERAL

§1.1 Rules. None. See CPRC §154.023.

§1.2 Purpose. The purpose of mediation is to provide a forum in which an impartial person—the mediator—facilitates communication between the parties to promote reconciliation, settlement, or understanding. CPRC §154.023(a); *see* ***In re Jones***, 55 S.W.3d 243, 247 (Tex.Spec.Ct.Rev.2000) (CPRC contemplates mediation in family or civil context only).

§1.3 Forms. ***O'Connor's Texas Civil Forms***, FORMS 4B.

§1.4 Other references. Butler, *Ethics in Mediation: Protecting the Integrity of the Mediation Process*, 38 Hous. Lawyer 5, p. 40 (Mar.-Apr. 2001); Stradley, Wright, & Murto, "Settlement Negotiations & Mediation," State Bar, Advanced Personal Injury Law Course, ch. 29 (2000); Galton, *Representing Clients in Mediation* (1994); Kovach, *Mediation: Principles & Practice* (2d ed.2000); Friedman, *A Guide to Divorce Mediation* (1993).

§2. AGREEMENTS TO MEDIATE

See "By agreement," ch. 4-A, §3.1.1, p. 206.

§3. COMPULSORY MEDIATION

§3.1 DTPA claims. A party can compel mediation by filing a motion to compel mediation within 90 days after service of a pleading requesting relief under the DTPA. Bus. & Com. Code §17.5051(a). A claim for damages less than $15,000 cannot be forced into mediation unless the party moving for mediation agrees to pay the costs of the mediation. *Id.* §17.5051(f). Section 17.5051 does not apply to a suit for a restraining order brought by the Texas Attorney General. *Id.* §17.5051(h). See ***O'Connor's Texas Causes of Action***, "Compelled mediation," ch. 8, §6.4, p. 195 (2004).

1. Order. The court must sign an order setting the time and place of the mediation not later than the 30th day after the date the motion is filed. Bus. & Com. Code §17.5051(b). The mediation must be held within 30 days of the date the order is signed, unless the parties agree otherwise or the court determines that additional time, not to exceed an additional 30 days, is warranted. *Id.* §17.5051(d).

2. Fees. Unless the parties agree otherwise, the parties share the mediation fees. Bus. & Com. Code §17.5051(e).

§3.2 By local rule. Some courts require mediation by local rule. For example, the Harris County family courts require all disputed custody or visitation matters that are set for a temporary hearing to be submitted for mediation to Family Court Services or another private mediator, as agreed by the parties and their attorneys. Harris Cty. Fam. Ct. L.R. 7.1; *see also* Travis Cty. Dist. Ct. L.R. 17.4(a) (provides for automatic referral of civil cases to pretrial mediation).

§4. MEDIATOR

§4.1 Appointment. Most of the rules governing mediation are contained in the general ADR statutes. *See* CPRC §§154.001-154.073. For rules on the appointment, qualifications, standards, duties, and compensation of the mediator, see "Appointment of Impartial Third Party," ch. 4-A, §6, p. 208.

§4.2 Resolution. The mediator cannot impose her own judgment on the issues for that of the parties. CPRC §154.023(b); ***Decker v. Lindsay***, 824 S.W.2d 247, 251 (Tex.App.—Houston [1st Dist.] 1992, orig. proceeding). The mediator cannot alter any resulting agreement, nor can the mediator interject her own terms into the agreement. ***In re McIntosh***, 918 S.W.2d 87, 88-89 (Tex.App.—Amarillo 1996, no writ).

§5. PREPARING FOR MEDIATION

§5.1 Have authority to settle. Mediation can be successful only if a party or its representative with settlement authority attends the mediation. *See, e.g.*, ***Suarez v. Jordan***, 35 S.W.3d 268, 273 (Tex.App.—Houston [14th Dist.] 2000, no pet.) (mediated settlement agreement signed by son did not bind father). While the ADR statute is silent on the issue of who must attend, there are cases that address this issue. *See, e.g.*, ***In re Stone***, 986 F.2d 898, 904-05 (5th Cir.1993) (court recommended a "practical approach" to settlement-authority requirements imposed on government bodies, such as allowing the official with ultimate authority to be fully prepared & available by telephone at the time of the conference); ***Nueces Cty. v. De Pena***, 953 S.W.2d 835, 836-37 (Tex.App.—Corpus Christi 1997, orig. proceeding) (county judge could not be ordered to attend mediation because he had no authority to settle the case without agreement of commissioner's court); ***Hur v. City of Mesquite***, 893 S.W.2d 227, 232-34 (Tex. App.—Amarillo 1995, writ denied) (during mediation, the city agreed to settle for a specific amount, but later claimed the agreement was subject to approval of city council; the court of appeals held that P could sue the city for breach of an oral agreement to settle).

§5.2 **Send documents to mediator.** Most mediations begin when the parties supply the mediator with copies of the pleadings and other important documents and copies of any legal authority necessary to resolve the issues. In some cases, the parties also supply the mediator with a short position paper explaining their version of the issues.

§5.3 **Send documents to other party.** Each party should send the other party copies of all materials it sent to the mediator, except for confidential materials.

§5.4 **Review file.** The attorneys should review their files and be thoroughly prepared to argue the facts, the issues, and the law.

§5.5 **Prepare the party.** The attorneys should explain the mediation process to the parties and explain their roles. Galton, *Representing Clients in Mediation*, 69-72 (1994). The attorneys should review both sets of documents the parties sent to the mediator. *Id.* The attorneys must make each party aware of the other party's position. *Id.*

§5.6 **Take documents to mediation.** If possible, the attorney should take the entire file to mediation. The documents a party will most likely need will be those sent to the mediator, but there are additional documents and discovery that a party may want to refer to during mediation. As the parties review their positions in the mediation, it is sometimes necessary to refer to the documents and discovery to verify the accuracy of the party's memory of events and discovery concessions.

§6. MEDIATION SESSION

§6.1 **Opening statement of mediator.** The mediator will begin the session by explaining the procedure for mediation. In most cases, the mediator will require the parties to sign an acknowledgment that the mediation procedure is confidential.

§6.2 **Opening statement of parties.** Each party is given an opportunity to make an opening statement explaining its position on the issues. The lawyers, as well as the parties, may make an opening statement. A party's opening statement permits the opposition to assess that party's understanding of the lawsuit and its determination to proceed with settlement or trial, and it helps the lawyers evaluate the party as a witness should mediation fail. An attorney should determine whether allowing the party to make the opening statement will enhance the presentation of the case. If the party is strong and articulate and will make a good witness, it is probably useful to allow the party to participate in the opening statement.

§7. CAUCUSING

After the joint session, the parties will normally separate into different rooms, and "shuttle diplomacy" begins. The mediator will spend time with each party, learning about the case and conveying ideas for settlement back and forth without disclosing confidential information. *See* CPRC §§154.053(b), (c), 154.073. Some mediators ask each party to submit a written "wish list" and a list of non-negotiable matters. From that point, the mediator tries to move the parties toward settlement.

§8. DURATION

Most mediations are set for one day. Mediation seldom ends at 5:00 p.m., and it can go on into the night. Often, it is late in the afternoon before the parties start making serious efforts to settle the case, just as exhaustion begins to take its toll. In cases involving child custody and visitation, several shorter sessions are probably more appropriate than a single extended one. In such cases it is not advisable to push the parties to exhaustion because financial issues are not the most important issues to be resolved.

C. ARBITRATION

§1. GENERAL

§1.1 Rules. None. See the Federal Arbitration Act, 9 U.S.C. §§4-16 (FAA); the Texas Arbitration Act (TAA), CPRC ch. 171; and the Alternative Dispute Resolution Code, CPRC title 7 (ADR Act).

§1.2 Purpose. Arbitration is a method of settling a dispute outside the courtroom. Federal and state laws strongly favor arbitration. ***In re FirstMerit Bank***, 52 S.W.3d 749, 753 (Tex.2001); ***EZ Pawn Corp. v. Mancias***, 934 S.W.2d 87, 90 (Tex.1996); ***Cantella & Co. v. Goodwin***, 924 S.W.2d 943, 944 (Tex.1996). There are three kinds of arbitration: ADR arbitration, contractual arbitration, and statutory arbitration.

§1.3 Forms. ***O'Connor's Texas Civil Forms***, FORMS 4C.

§1.4 Other references. Sheldon, Bland & Quirk, *Consumer Arbitration Agreements* (2001); Ho, Comment, *Discovery in Commercial Arbitration Proceedings*, 34 Hous.L.Rev. 199 (1997).

§2. MOTION TO COMPEL ADR ARBITRATION

§2.1 Nonbinding. A party may file a motion to refer its case to arbitration as part of an ADR procedure, even if the parties have no contractual obligation to arbitrate. CPRC §§152.003, 154.021. The parties should follow the procedure described in "Referral Procedures for ADR," ch. 4-A, §3, p. 206.

NOTE

Agreements to arbitrate suits affecting the parent-child relationship must state whether arbitration is to be binding or nonbinding. Fam. Code §153.0071(a). If the parties agree to binding arbitration, the court must sign an order on the arbitrator's award unless the court determines the award is not in the best interest of the child. Id. §153.0071(b).

§2.2 Binding. If, after the suit is filed, the parties agree to submit the case to binding arbitration, the agreement to arbitrate must meet the requirements of TRCP 11. *See* CPRC §154.027(b). Courts will enforce the arbitration agreement, even if it does not meet the requirements of TRCP 11, when the parties have fulfilled the agreement by performance. *See **Massey v. Galvan***, 822 S.W.2d 309, 317 (Tex.App.—Houston [14th Dist.] 1992, writ denied).

§3. MOTION TO COMPEL CONTRACTUAL ARBITRATION

§3.1 Federal Arbitration Act (FAA). Under federal law, parties can be compelled to attend arbitration by their contractual agreement to arbitrate. *See **Circuit City Stores v. Adams***, 532 U.S. 105, 118-19, 121 S.Ct. 1302, 1311 (2001). See ***O'Connor's Federal Rules * Civil Trials***, "Compelling Arbitration," ch. 7-E, §2, p. 466 (2004).

1. Written agreement. Under the FAA, a court must direct the parties to proceed to arbitration when they have a written agreement to do so. ***Dean Witter Reynolds, Inc. v. Byrd***, 470 U.S. 213, 218, 105 S.Ct. 1238, 1241 (1985). Texas courts have the power to compel arbitration under the FAA. ***USX Corp. v. West***, 781 S.W.2d 453, 455 (Tex.App.—Houston [1st Dist.] 1989, orig. proceeding); *see also **Jack B. Anglin Co. v. Tipps***, 842 S.W.2d 266, 268 (Tex.1992) (when Texas courts decide if disputed claims fall within scope of arbitration clause under FAA, Texas procedure controls).

2. Interstate commerce. The FAA applies to an arbitration agreement in a contract for a transaction involving "commerce." ***American Rlty. Trust v. JDN Real Estate–McKinney***, 74 S.W.3d 527, 530 (Tex.App.—Dallas 2002, pet. denied); *see, e.g.*, ***In re Nasr***, 50 S.W.3d 23, 25 (Tex.App.—Beaumont 2001, orig. proceeding) (contract to build residence in Texas using, among other things, items purchased from Walmart was a transaction involving commerce); ***Palm Harbor Homes v. McCoy***, 944 S.W.2d 716, 720 (Tex.App.—Fort Worth 1997, orig. proceeding) (purchase of mobile home manufactured & delivered in Texas affected interstate commerce because it included components purchased or manufactured in other states). The FAA does not require a substantial effect on interstate commerce; it requires only that commerce be involved or affected. ***In re L & L Kempwood Assocs.***, 9 S.W.3d 125, 127 (Tex.1999). If the parties agree to arbitrate under the FAA, they are not required to prove the transaction involved or affected interstate commerce. ***In re Kellogg Brown & Root***, 80 S.W.3d 611, 617 (Tex.App.—Houston [1st Dist.] 2002, orig. proceeding).

3. Arbitrable dispute. When the FAA applies, federal law determines whether a dispute is arbitrable. ***In re First Tex. Homes***, ___ S.W.3d ___ (Tex.2003) (No. 02-0876; 11-14-03); ***Prudential Sec. v. Marshall***, 909 S.W.2d 896, 899 (Tex.1995); ***Hou-Scape, Inc. v. Lloyd***, 945 S.W.2d 202, 205 (Tex.App.—Houston [1st Dist.] 1997, orig. proceeding).

§3.2 Texas Arbitration Act (TAA). The procedure to compel contractual arbitration under the TAA is outlined in CPRC §§171.021-171.026 and 171.096(d).

1. Arbitration clause.

(1) Binding. A general, broad-form arbitration clause is binding if it contains language stating that any controversy or claim arising out of or relating to the contract or a breach of the contract will be settled by arbitration and that any court having jurisdiction over the case may enter a judgment upon the award rendered by the arbitrator. ***Belmont Constructors v. Lyondell Pet. Co.***, 896 S.W.2d 352, 358 n.2 (Tex.App.—Houston [1st Dist.] 1995, no writ); *see* ***American Rlty.***, 74 S.W.3d at 531. If the contract to arbitrate specifically forecloses certain relief, that relief cannot be granted; if the contract does not, the relief can be awarded. ***Mastrobuono v. Shearson Lehman Hutton, Inc.***, 514 U.S. 52, 59-60, 115 S.Ct. 1212, 1217-18 (1995) (punitive damages); ***J.J. Gregory Gourmet Servs. v. Antone's Import Co.***, 927 S.W.2d 31, 36 (Tex.App.—Houston [1st Dist.] 1995, no writ) (injunctive relief).

(2) Nonbinding. To provide for nonbinding arbitration under the TAA, a contract must specifically state that arbitration will be nonbinding. ***Porter & Clements v. Stone***, 935 S.W.2d 217, 221 (Tex.App.—Houston [1st Dist.] 1996, orig. proceeding). When a contract does not state whether arbitration is binding or nonbinding, the courts assume it is binding. *See id.* at 221-22.

2. Both parties want arbitration. If both parties want arbitration, they should initiate an arbitration proceeding according to the terms of the arbitration agreement.

3. Presuit request by one party. Before a lawsuit is filed, if one party wants arbitration but the other party does not, the party seeking arbitration can file suit and ask the court to order the parties to arbitration.

4. Defendant wants arbitration. Once the plaintiff files suit, a defendant that wants to arbitrate should file its answer along with a verified motion to abate. See "Motion to Abate—Challenging the Suit," ch. 3-H, p. 194. In the motion to abate, the defendant should ask the court to order the parties to arbitration and stay the proceedings. *See* ***Shearson Lehman Bros. v. Kilgore***, 871 S.W.2d 925, 926-27 (Tex.App.—Corpus Christi 1994, orig. proceeding). To be entitled to arbitration, the defendant must establish that (1) the parties agreed to arbitrate in a written contract and (2) the scope of the contract covers the dispute. ***Phillips v. ACS Mun. Brokers***, 888 S.W.2d 872, 875 (Tex.App.—Dallas 1994, no writ); ***Merrill Lynch, Pierce, Fenner & Smith v. Eddings***, 838 S.W.2d 874, 878 (Tex.App.—Waco 1992, writ denied). On proof of these two matters, the court must order the parties to arbitrate, despite the opposing party's unwillingness to arbitrate. *See* CPRC §171.021(a); ***In re Noteboom***, 111 S.W.3d 794, 796 (Tex.App.—Fort Worth 2003, orig. proceeding).

(1) Agreement to arbitrate. There must be a valid arbitration agreement for the court to compel arbitration. ***In re Oakwood Mobile Homes***, 987 S.W.2d 571, 573 (Tex.1999); ***Dalton Contractors v. Bryan Autumn Woods***, 60 S.W.3d 351, 353 (Tex.App.—Houston [1st Dist.] 2001, no pet.); *see* ***Freis v. Canales***, 877 S.W.2d 283, 284 (Tex.1994); *see also* ***Weekley Homes v. Jennings***, 936 S.W.2d 16, 18 (Tex.App.—San Antonio 1996, writ denied) (condition precedent was not fulfilled). The issue of whether the parties are bound by an arbitration clause is determined by state law principles of contract law. ***First Options v. Kaplan***, 514 U.S. 938, 944, 115 S.Ct.

1920, 1924 (1995); ***American Rlty. Trust v. JDN Real Estate–McKinney***, 74 S.W.3d 527, 531 (Tex.App.—Dallas 2002, pet. denied); ***In re Alamo Lumber Co.***, 23 S.W.3d 577, 579 (Tex.App.—San Antonio 2000, orig. proceeding); *see also* ***Tri-Star Pet. Co. v. Tipperary Corp.***, 107 S.W.3d 607, 613-14 (Tex.App.—El Paso 2003, pet. filed 8-21-03) (just as material breach is ground for revoking a contract, it is also ground for revoking arbitration agreement; once revoked, agreement effectively does not exist). Thus, valid consideration must be given for an arbitration agreement to be enforceable. *See, e.g.*, ***In re Tenet Healthcare***, 84 S.W.3d 760, 766 (Tex.App.—Houston [1st Dist.] 2002, orig. proceeding) (mutual promises to relinquish right to litigate constitutes valid consideration); ***Labor Ready Cent. v. Gonzalez***, 64 S.W.3d 519, 522-24 (Tex.App.—Corpus Christi 2001, no pet.) (arbitration agreement was unenforceable when party had unilateral right to pursue judicial action in the event of breach); ***Alamo Lumber***, 23 S.W.3d at 579 (arbitration agreement was enforceable when both parties gave up rights to jury trial).

(a) Written. The TAA requires the terms of the agreement between the parties to be written. CPRC §171.001(a); ***Burlington N. R.R. v. Akpan***, 943 S.W.2d 48, 52 (Tex.App.—Fort Worth 1996, no writ). Persons who are not parties to the agreement sometimes may be subject to or may enforce an arbitration clause. *See, e.g.*, ***In re FirstMerit Bank***, 52 S.W.3d 749, 755-56 (Tex.2001) (adult children who brought suit with parents were bound by parents' arbitration agreement); ***In re Rolland***, 96 S.W.3d 339, 345 (Tex.App.—Austin 2001, orig. proceeding) (D was assigned contract with arbitration clause); ***McMillan v. Computer Translation Sys. & Support***, 66 S.W.3d 477, 481-82 (Tex.App.—Dallas 2001, no pet.) (Ds were agents of signatories of arbitration agreement).

(b) No signature required. The TAA does not require the agreement to be signed by either party. ***Akpan***, 943 S.W.2d at 52; *see* CPRC §171.001. When another law requires a signature on the agreement, the agreement must be signed for the arbitration clause to be enforceable. *See, e.g.*, ***In re Godt***, 28 S.W.3d 732, 738 (Tex.App.—Corpus Christi 2000, orig. proceeding) (arbitration clause in contingency fee agreement could not be enforced because agreement was not signed by both parties as required by Gov't Code §82.065(a)).

(c) Clear intent. The agreement must clearly demonstrate the intention of the parties to arbitrate the dispute. ***In re ACG Cotton Mktg.***, 985 S.W.2d 632, 633 (Tex.App.—Amarillo 1999, orig. proceeding). The issue is a factual question. ***Shearson Lehman Hutton v. McKay***, 763 S.W.2d 934, 937 (Tex.App.—San Antonio 1989, orig. proceeding). Courts must resolve any doubts about an agreement to arbitrate in favor of arbitration. ***Cantella & Co. v. Goodwin***, 924 S.W.2d 943, 944 (Tex.1996); ***In re Scott***, 100 S.W.3d 575, 580 (Tex.App.—Fort Worth 2003, orig. proceeding).

(2) Scope of agreement. The factual allegations in the plaintiff's petition must fall within the scope of the arbitration agreement. *See* ***Oakwood Mobile Homes***, 987 S.W.2d at 573; ***Prudential Sec.***, 909 S.W.2d at 900; ***In re Nestle USA***, 82 S.W.3d 767, 776 (Tex.App.—Corpus Christi 2002, orig. proceeding); ***Dalton Contractors***, 60 S.W.3d at 353. If the facts alleged have a "significant relationship" to or are "factually intertwined" with the contract that is subject to the arbitration agreement, the claim is arbitrable. ***Nestle USA***, 82 S.W.3d at 776. If an arbitration clause is broad, arbitration should not be denied unless the particular dispute is positively not covered. ***Emerald Tex., Inc. v. Peel***, 920 S.W.2d 398, 403 (Tex.App.—Houston [1st Dist.] 1996, no writ). If an arbitration clause covers all controversies arising out of one agreement, it does not necessarily cover controversies arising out of other agreements between the same parties. ***Weber v. Hall***, 929 S.W.2d 138, 143 (Tex.App.—Houston [14th Dist.] 1996, orig. proceeding). The controversy subject to arbitration may encompass different causes of action and claims for different types of damages. For example, an agreement to arbitrate all controversies arising out of a contract may encompass some tort claims. ***Merrill Lynch, Pierce, Fenner & Smith v. Wilson***, 805 S.W.2d 38, 39 (Tex.App.—El Paso 1991, no writ); *see* ***Fridl v. Cook***, 908 S.W.2d 507, 511 (Tex.App.—El Paso 1995, writ dism'd). The test is whether the particular tort claim is so interwoven with the contract that it could not stand alone. ***Merrill Lynch***, 805 S.W.2d at 39; *see* ***Gerwell v. Moran***, 10 S.W.3d 28, 31 (Tex.App.—San Antonio 1999, no pet.) (label of claim is not controlling; instead, focus lies on factual allegations and their relationship to subject matter encompassed by arbitration clause).

5. Objections to arbitration. If the party opposing arbitration files a response denying the existence of an agreement to arbitrate, the court must summarily resolve that issue. CPRC §171.021(b); *see* ***Jack B. Anglin Co. v. Tipps***, 842 S.W.2d 266, 268-69 (Tex.1992); ***Belmont Constructors v. Lyondell Pet. Co.***, 896 S.W.2d 352, 355 (Tex.App.—Houston [1st Dist.] 1995, no writ). The party opposing arbitration bears the burden of defeating the existence of an agreement. ***Cantella & Co. v. Goodwin***, 924 S.W.2d 943, 944 (Tex.1996). If the arbitration agreement encompasses the claim at issue, and the party opposing arbitration does not present any defenses to the enforcement of the agreement itself, the trial court must compel arbitration. ***In re J.D. Edwards World Solutions Co.***, 87 S.W.3d 546, 549 (Tex.2002); ***In re H2O Plumbing***, 115 S.W.3d 79, 80-81 (Tex.App.—San Antonio 2003, orig. proceeding). Because public policy strongly favors arbitration, the court must presume the matter is subject to arbitration unless the party opposing arbitration proves otherwise. ***U.P.S. v. McFall***, 940 S.W.2d 716, 719 (Tex.App.—Amarillo 1997, orig. proceeding). For a comprehensive discussion of the arguments used to defeat arbitration, see Sheldon, Bland, & Quirk, *Consumer Arbitration Agreements* (2001) (to order, call 202-797-8600). The following are some of the valid objections to arbitration:

(1) No agreement. There is no agreement to arbitrate the dispute. See "Agreement to arbitrate," §3.2.4(1), p. 214.

(2) Outside scope of agreement. The dispute is outside the scope of the arbitration agreement. See §3.2.4(2), above.

(3) Fraud. The arbitration agreement (not the contract as a whole) was induced or procured by fraud. ***FirstMerit Bank***, 52 S.W.3d at 756; *see* ***In re Oakwood Mobile Homes***, 987 S.W.2d 571, 573-74 (Tex.1999) (no fraud present because P could not prove D-seller made any material representations that were false). Defenses pertaining to the entire contract can be arbitrated. ***FirstMerit Bank***, 52 S.W.3d at 756; *see* ***J.D. Edwards***, 87 S.W.3d at 550-51 (fraudulent inducement claim constitutes dispute relative to the contract & is subject to arbitration).

(4) Unconscionable. The arbitration agreement (not the contract as a whole) was unconscionable at the time it was made and is not subject to arbitration. CPRC §171.022; ***FirstMerit Bank***, 52 S.W.3d at 756; ***American Employers' Ins. Co. v. Aiken***, 942 S.W.2d 156, 160 (Tex.App.—Fort Worth 1997, no writ). Unconscionability includes two aspects: (1) procedural unconscionability, which refers to the circumstances surrounding the actual making of the arbitration provision, and (2) substantive unconscionability, which refers to the fairness of the terms and conditions of the arbitration provision itself. ***In re Halliburton Co.***, 80 S.W.3d 566, 571 (Tex.2002). Courts may consider complaints of both procedural and substantive unconscionability in reviewing the validity of an arbitration provision. ***Halliburton***, 80 S.W.3d at 571. *But see* ***Oakwood Mobile Homes***, 987 S.W.2d at 573 n.3 (dicta; complaints of substantive unconscionability should be submitted to designated arbitrator for determination, not to the court as objection to arbitration).

(5) Waiver. The party waived its right to arbitration. There is a presumption against the waiver of a contractual right to arbitration. ***In re Service Corp. Int'l***, 85 S.W.3d 171, 174 (Tex.2002); ***In re Bruce Terminix Co.***, 988 S.W.2d 702, 704 (Tex.1998); ***EZ Pawn Corp. v. Mancias***, 934 S.W.2d 87, 89 (Tex.1996); ***Prudential Sec. v. Marshall***, 909 S.W.2d 896, 898 (Tex.1995). For a party to waive its right to arbitration, that party must take action inconsistent with its right to arbitration and prejudicial to the other party. ***Oakwood Mobile Homes***, 987 S.W.2d at 574; ***EZ Pawn Corp.***, 934 S.W.2d at 89; ***In re Certain Underwriters at Lloyd's***, 18 S.W.3d 867, 876-77 (Tex.App.—Beaumont 2000, orig. proceeding); *see* ***In re Weekly Homes***, 985 S.W.2d 111, 114 (Tex.App.—San Antonio 1998, orig. proceeding) (waiver cannot be inferred from party's conduct when party continues to act consistently with the right to arbitrate). A party waives arbitration if it substantially invokes the judicial process to the detriment and prejudice of the other party. ***Service Corp.***, 85 S.W.3d at 174; ***EZ Pawn***, 934 S.W.2d at 89; ***Prudential Sec.***, 909 S.W.2d at 899; ***Menna v. Romero***, 48 S.W.3d 247, 251 (Tex.App.—San Antonio 2001, pet. dism'd); ***Sedillo v. Campbell***, 5 S.W.3d 824, 827 (Tex.App.—Houston [14th Dist.] 1999, no pet.); *e.g.*, ***Bruce Terminix***, 988 S.W.2d at 704 (party did not substantially invoke the judicial process by filing an answer and propounding discovery). Mere delay in seeking arbitration does not necessarily demonstrate prejudice. ***EZ Pawn***, 934 S.W.2d at 89-90; ***Prudential Sec.***, 909 S.W.2d at 898-99. A party against whom a claim is asserted does not waive its right to arbitration by not initiating arbitration proceedings. ***Bruce Terminix***, 988 S.W.2d at 706.

(6) Dispute not arbitrable. The dispute is not arbitrable by law. Under the TAA, the following matters cannot be submitted to arbitration: (1) a contract subject to arbitration that is unconscionable when it is made, CPRC §171.022; (2) a collective bargaining agreement between an employer and a labor union, *id.* §171.002(a)(1); (3) a contract for acquisition by an individual (not a corporation or other business entity) of real property, services, money, or credit where the total consideration is $50,000 or less, unless the agreement is in writing and signed by both parties and their attorneys, *id.* §171.002(a)(2); (4) a claim for personal injuries, unless each party, on the advice of counsel, agrees in writing to arbitrate and the agreement is signed by each party and each party's attorney, *id.* §171.002(a)(3); (5) a claim for workers' compensation benefits, *id.* §171.002(a)(4); and (6) an agreement made before January 1, 1966, *id.* §171.002(a)(5). Most disputes, however, are arbitrable. *See, e.g.*, ***In re FirstMerit Bank***, 52 S.W.3d 749, 755 (Tex.2001) (loan agreement, which had broad arbitration agreement, made all issues of purchase, even revocation of contract, arbitrable); ***In re American Homestar***, 50 S.W.3d 480, 490-91 (Tex.2001) (nothing in the Magnuson-Moss Act or the FTC rules prohibit the use of binding arbitration clauses in written warranties); *see also* ***Circuit City Stores v. Adams***, 532 U.S. 105, 112, 121 S.Ct. 1302, 1307 (2001) (FAA requires enforcement of arbitration agreements in all employment categories except for transportation workers exempted by the FAA).

NOTE

The courts are in disagreement whether a mandatory arbitration clause in an attorney-client agreement is enforceable if not signed by each party on the advice of counsel and signed by each party's attorney, as required by §171.002(c). See ***O'Connor's Texas Causes of Action***, *"Mandatory arbitration," ch. 15-B, §6.3, p. 332 (2004).*

---

6. Hearing. If material facts are uncontroverted, the trial court may decide whether to compel arbitration based on the affidavits, pleadings, discovery, and stipulations. ***Jack B. Anglin Co.***, 842 S.W.2d at 269. If material facts are controverted by admissible evidence, the trial court must conduct an evidentiary hearing to resolve the disputed facts. *Id.* When the court holds a hearing to resolve fact questions, the parties should introduce evidence with all the formalities of a nonjury trial, that is, with witnesses and a court reporter.

7. Trial court's order.

(1) Arbitration.

(a) Grant motion. If no objection is filed to a motion to compel arbitration, the court must order the parties to proceed to arbitration. CPRC §171.021(a). If an objection is filed to a motion to compel, but the court overrules the objection, the court must order the parties to proceed to arbitration. *Id.* §171.021(b).

(b) Deny motion. If the court sustains an objection to arbitration, the court must deny the arbitration application. CPRC §171.021(b).

(2) Stay. When a case is ordered to arbitration under CPRC §§171.021-171.026, the court must sign an order that stays the proceedings during the arbitration. CPRC §171.025(a); *see* ***Cash Am. Int'l v. Exchange Servs.***, 83 S.W.3d 183, 187 (Tex.App.—Amarillo 2002, no pet.). If the matter referred to arbitration is severable from the rest of the proceeding, the order must stay only the matter referred to arbitration. CPRC §171.025(b); ***Cash Am. Int'l***, 83 S.W.3d at 186-87.

8. Trial court review of award. The TAA requires the court to confirm an arbitrator's award unless a party offers grounds for modifying, correcting, or vacating the award. CPRC §171.087; ***Callahan & Assocs. v. Orangefield ISD***, 92 S.W.3d 841, 844 (Tex.2002).

(1) Motion to confirm award. Once the arbitration results in an award, either party may file a motion with the trial court to confirm the award. CPRC §171.087; ***City of Baytown v. C.L. Winter, Inc.***, 886 S.W.2d 515, 520 (Tex.App.—Houston [1st Dist.] 1994, writ denied).

(2) Motion to modify or correct award. A party can apply to the court to modify or correct the award with proof of (1) an evident miscalculation of numbers or a mistake in the description of any person, thing, or property referred to in an award, (2) an award on a matter not submitted, or (3) an error in the form of the award not affecting the merits of the controversy. CPRC §171.091(a); ***Barsness v. Scott***, ___ S.W.3d ___ (Tex.App.—San Antonio 2003, n.p.h.) (No. 04-02-00928-CV; 11-5-03); ***Powell v. Gulf Coast Carriers***, 872 S.W.2d 22, 24 (Tex.App.—Houston [14th Dist.] 1994, no writ). Upon application, the trial court must either confirm the original award or correct the arbitrator's miscalculation or mistake in the description of a person, thing, or property referred to in the award. *See* ***Callahan***, 92 S.W.3d at 844 (appellate court could not award damages when arbitrator refused).

(3) Motion to vacate award. To set aside an arbitration award, a party must allege a statutory or common-law ground to vacate the award. ***Koch v. Koch***, 27 S.W.3d 93, 96 (Tex.App.—San Antonio 2000, no pet.); ***Anzilotti v. Gene D. Liggin, Inc.***, 899 S.W.2d 264, 266 (Tex.App.—Houston [14th Dist.] 1995, no writ); *see also* ***Blue Cross Blue Shield v. Juneau***, 114 S.W.3d 126, 135-36 (Tex.App.—Austin 2003, n.p.h.) (motion to vacate award because of arbitrator's evident partiality is exclusive remedy under TAA; suit against individual arbitrator not allowed).

(a) Statutory grounds. A party can apply to the trial court to vacate an arbitration award on any of the following grounds:

[1] Corruption of the process. The award was procured by corruption, fraud, or other undue means. CPRC §171.088(a)(1).

[2] Evident partiality. The party's rights were prejudiced by the evident partiality of the arbitrator who was appointed as a neutral arbitrator. CPRC §171.088(a)(2)(A). A court must vacate an award if a neutral arbitrator exhibits "evident partiality." ***Burlington N. R.R. v. TUCO, Inc.***, 960 S.W.2d 629, 636 (Tex.1997). Evident partiality is shown when a neutral arbitrator does not disclose facts that might create a reasonable impression of the arbitrator's partiality to an objective observer. *E.g., id.* (nondisclosure of arbitrator's referral to represent co-arbitrator's law firm in federal lawsuit was evident partiality); ***J.D. Edwards World Solutions Co. v. Estes, Inc.***, 91 S.W.3d 836, 840 (Tex.App.—Fort Worth 2002, pet. denied) (nondisclosure of arbitrator's ongoing representation of D was evident partiality); ***Thomas James Assocs. v. Owens***, 1 S.W.3d 315, 320-21 (Tex.App.—Dallas 1999, no pet.) (no evident partiality when arbitrator did not disclose involvement in earlier, unrelated arbitration for which he was later sued); ***Texas Commerce Bank v. Universal Tech. Inst.***, 985 S.W.2d 678, 680-81 (Tex.App.—Houston [1st Dist.] 1999, pet. dism'd) (nondisclosure of arbitrator's earlier representation of the bank in a $1.5 million lawsuit was evident partiality); *see also* ***Mariner Fin. Group v. Bossley***, 79 S.W.3d 30, 35 (Tex.2002) (although Ps have ultimate burden of proving arbitrator's partiality, summary judgment improper because D did not establish as a matter of law that arbitrator was not evidently partial). Evident partiality is shown by the nondisclosure itself, regardless of whether the undisclosed information establishes bias. ***TUCO***, 960 S.W.2d at 636.

[3] Corruption or misconduct by arbitrator. The party's rights were prejudiced by the arbitrator's corruption, misconduct, or willful misbehavior. CPRC §171.088(a)(2)(B), (C).

[4] Procedural misconduct. The arbitrators exceeded their powers, refused to postpone the hearing, refused to hear evidence material to the controversy, or otherwise conducted the hearing in a way that substantially prejudiced the rights of a party. CPRC §171.088(a)(3).

[5] No arbitration agreement. There was no arbitration agreement, the issue was not adversely determined in proceedings to compel arbitration, and the party did not participate in the arbitration hearing without raising the objection. CPRC §171.088(a)(4).

(b) Common-law grounds. Under the common law, a trial court can vacate an arbitrator's award if the award (1) violates public policy or the law, (2) exceeds the scope of the arbitrator's authority, or (3) appears to be tainted with fraud, misconduct, or gross mistake that would imply bad faith and lack of honest judgment. *See* ***Goodyear Tire & Rubber Co. v. Sanford***, 540 S.W.2d 478, 483 (Tex.App.—Houston [14th Dist.] 1976, no writ) (public policy); *see, e.g.*, ***IPCO-G.&C. Jt.V. v. A.B. Chance Co.***, 65 S.W.3d 252, 258 (Tex.App.—Houston [1st Dist.] 2001, pet denied) (ex parte telephone call by arbitrator to P's attorney did not deprive P of right to fair hearing); ***Lee v. El Paso Cty.***, 965 S.W.2d 668, 672 (Tex.App.—El Paso 1998, pet. denied) (arbitrator exceeded his jurisdiction by ordering the county to violate the Texas Constitution).

(4) Deadline to challenge award. When the motion is made on any ground in CPRC §171.088(a)(1) (corruption, fraud, or other undue means), it must be filed 90 days from the date the party learned or should have learned of the ground. CPRC §171.088(b); ***Louisiana Nat. Gas Pipeline v. Bludworth Bond Shipyard***, 875 S.W.2d 458, 462 (Tex.App.—Houston [1st Dist.] 1994, writ denied); *see* ***Hou-Scape, Inc. v. Lloyd***, 945 S.W.2d 202, 204 (Tex.App.—Houston [1st Dist.] 1997, orig. proceeding). When a motion is made on any other grounds in CPRC §171.088(a), it must be filed within 90 days after the party receives a copy of the award. CPRC §171.088(b). If the motion is filed later than 90 days after delivery of the award, it is waived. ***Teleometrics Int'l v. Hall***, 922 S.W.2d 189, 192 (Tex.App.—Houston [1st Dist.] 1995, writ denied); *cf.* ***Eurocapital Group, Ltd. v. Goldman Sachs & Co.***, 17 S.W.3d 426, 430 (Tex.App.—Houston [1st Dist.] 2000, no pet.) (under the FAA, notice of motion to vacate award must be served within 3 months after delivery of award).

§4. MOTION TO COMPEL STATUTORY ARBITRATION

§4.1 Statutes requiring arbitration. A number of statutes require parties to arbitrate controversies instead of litigating them. *See, e.g.*, Agric. Code ch. 64 (arbitration of seed performance disputes); Alco. Bev. Code §102.77 (intra-industry disputes); Local Gov't Code §143.057 (matters affecting firefighters & police officers), Local Gov't Code §212.902 (school district land development standards); Tax Code §42.225 (property owner's right to appeal through binding arbitration). *But see* ***City of League City v. Blevins***, 821 S.W.2d 212, 215 (Tex.App.—Houston [14th Dist.] 1991, no writ) (arbitration under Local Gov't Code §143.001 is not really arbitration, even though that is what it is called).

§4.2 Procedure for statutory arbitration. When a case is referred to arbitration under a specific code provision, the lawyer should check the provisions in that code for the procedures to follow in arbitration.

§5. REVIEW

§5.1 Standard of review.

1. To challenge arbitration award. To set, modify, or correct an arbitration award, the trial court must determine whether the award contains an "evident miscalculation of figures" or an "evident mistake in the description of a person, thing, or property referred to in the award." CPRC §171.091(a)(1); ***Callahan & Assocs. v. Orangefield ISD***, 92 S.W.3d 841, 844 (Tex.2002). To set aside an arbitration award, the trial court must determine that the award is "tainted with fraud, misconduct, or such gross mistake as would imply bad faith and failure to exercise honest judgment." ***Powell***, 872 S.W.2d at 23-24 (common-law standard); *see* CPRC §171.088(a); *cf.* ***Cooper v. Bushong***, 10 S.W.3d 20, 24-25 (Tex.App.—Austin 1999, pet. denied) (construing 4 statutory grounds to set aside an arbitration award). A mere mistake of fact or law alone is insufficient to set aside an arbitration award. ***Riha v. Smulcer***, 843 S.W.2d 289, 294 (Tex.App.—Houston [14th Dist.] 1992, no writ).

2. To challenge denial of arbitration. The standard of review used to challenge the trial court's order denying arbitration is the "no evidence" standard. ***Certain Underwriters at Lloyd's v. Celebrity***, 950 S.W.2d 375, 377 (Tex.App.—Tyler 1996), *writ dism'd*, 988 S.W.2d 731 (Tex.1998); ***Phillips v. ACS Mun. Brokers***, 888 S.W.2d 872, 874 (Tex.App.—Dallas 1994, no writ); ***Hearthshire Braeswood Plaza L.P. v. Bill Kelly Co.***, 849 S.W.2d 380, 384 (Tex.App.—Houston [14th Dist.] 1993, writ denied); *cf.* ***Henry v. Gonzalez***, 18 S.W.3d 684, 689 (Tex.App.—San Antonio 2000, pet. dism'd) (when court decides matter involving both factual issues & legal conclusions, standard of review is abuse of discretion). The Texas Supreme Court does not have jurisdiction over an order denying a motion to compel arbitration unless there is (1) a dissent in the court of appeals or (2) a conflict between the courts of appeals. ***Certain Underwriters***, 988 S.W.2d at 732-33.

3. To challenge a SAPCR order. In a suit affecting the parent-child relationship, the standard of review is whether the award is in the best interest of the child. *See* Fam. Code §153.0071(b); ***Cooper***, 10 S.W.3d at 25-26.

§5.2 Contractual arbitration. Appeals of arbitration orders may be taken in the same manner and to the same extent as all other civil appeals. CPRC §171.098(b).

1. Final order on the award. A party may appeal a trial court's order that confirms, denies confirmation of, vacates, modifies, or corrects an award after a final judgment is rendered. CPRC §171.098(a); ***City of Baytown v. C.L. Winter, Inc.***, 886 S.W.2d 515, 518 (Tex.App.—Houston [1st Dist.] 1994, writ denied). A party cannot appeal a court's order that vacates an award but orders a new arbitration. ***Stolhandske v. Stern***, 14 S.W.3d 810, 813-15 (Tex.App.—Houston [1st Dist.] 2000, pet. denied) (order vacating arbitration award & directing a rehearing is the functional equivalent of an order granting new trial); ***Prudential Sec. v. Vondergoltz***, 14 S.W.3d 329, 331 (Tex.App.—Houston [14th Dist.] 2000, no pet.) (same); *see* CPRC §171.098(a)(5); *cf.* 9 U.S.C. §16(a)(1)(E) (no limitation under the FAA; all orders vacating arbitration awards are immediately appealable).

2. Interlocutory review. Generally, interlocutory orders regarding arbitration are not appealable unless made appealable by statute. However, CPRC §51.014(d) allows parties to agree to an interlocutory appeal. See ***O'Connor's Texas Civil Appeals***, "Appealable orders by agreed motion," ch. 13-P, §2.2, p. 131 (2002-03). This procedure may reduce the need for review by mandamus discussed in §5.2.3, below.

(1) Order denying arbitration – TAA. If a suit is subject to arbitration under the TAA, and the court denies an application to compel arbitration made under CPRC §171.021, the party may file an interlocutory appeal. CPRC §171.098(a)(1); ***Certain Underwriters***, 988 S.W.2d at 732; ***In re MacGregor***, ___ S.W.3d ___ (Tex. App.—Houston [1st Dist.] 2003, orig. proceeding) (No. 01-02-01318-CV; 7-10-03); ***Phillips***, 888 S.W.2d at 874; ***American Physicians Serv. Group v. Port Lavaca Clinic Assocs.***, 843 S.W.2d 675, 677 (Tex.App.—Corpus Christi 1992, writ denied).

(2) Other orders. If the court signs some other order, but does not deny an application to compel arbitration or grant an application to stay arbitration, the order is not an appealable interlocutory order. *See* CPRC §171.098(a)(1), (2); ***In re MHI Prtshp.***, 7 S.W.3d 918, 920 (Tex.App.—Houston [1st Dist.] 1999, orig. proceeding); ***Batton v. Green***, 801 S.W.2d 923, 926-27 (Tex.App.—Dallas 1990, no writ); *see e.g.*, ***In re O'Quinn***, ___ S.W.3d ___ (Tex.App.—Tyler 2003, orig. proceeding) (No. 12-02-00352-CV; 6-25-03) (order compelling arbitration is not appealable interlocutory order); ***Elm Creek Villas Homeowner Ass'n v. Beldon Roofing & Remodeling Co.***, 940 S.W.2d 150, 153 (Tex.App.—San Antonio 1996, no writ) (same). When the trial court denies a motion to abate and a motion to stay, but does not deny an application to compel arbitration or grant an application to stay arbitration, the denial is not an appealable order. *See* ***Batton***, 801 S.W.2d at 926-27.

3. Mandamus.

(1) Order denying arbitration – FAA. If a suit is subject to arbitration under the FAA, a party denied a request for arbitration has no adequate remedy by appeal but is entitled to review by mandamus. ***In re L & L Kempwood Assocs.***, 9 S.W.3d 125, 128 (Tex.1999); ***In re Oakwood Mobile Homes***, 987 S.W.2d 571, 574-75 (Tex.1999).

(2) Order granting arbitration. If a party is compelled to arbitrate without having agreed to do so, the party is entitled to review by mandamus. ***Freis v. Canales***, 877 S.W.2d 283, 284 (Tex.1994); ***In re Rolland***, 96 S.W.3d 339, 341 & n.1 (Tex.App.—Austin 2001, orig. proceeding); ***In re Godt***, 28 S.W.3d 732, 738 (Tex.App.—Corpus Christi 2000, orig. proceeding).

(3) Other orders. If the court abuses its discretion in making an order that neither denies an application to compel arbitration nor grants an application to stay arbitration, a party may be entitled to mandamus relief. *See, e.g.*, ***In re MHI Prtshp.***, 7 S.W.3d 918, 920-21 (Tex.App.—Houston [1st Dist.] 1999, orig. proceeding) (court had no discretion to defer ruling on arbitration motion until after completion of discovery).

D. SPECIAL JUDGE

§1. GENERAL

§1.1 Rules. None. See CPRC ch. 151.

§1.2 Purpose. A trial by a special judge is a forum in which the parties try their case to a retired or former judge (not a sitting judge) who is selected by the parties to hear the case. This type of ADR is sometimes called "rent-a-former-judge" ADR. It is expensive and rarely used.

§1.3 Forms. ***O'Connor's Texas Civil Forms***, FORMS 4D.

§2. AGREED MOTION FOR TRIAL BY SPECIAL JUDGE

A case may be referred to a special judge only by agreement of the parties. CPRC §151.001. Before a court will refer a case to a special judge, both parties must file a motion that (1) requests the referral, (2) waives the right to a jury, (3) states the issues to be referred, (4) states the time and place for the agreed trial, and (5) states the name of the special judge, the fact that the special judge has agreed to hear the case, and the fee the judge is to receive as agreed by the parties. *Id.* §151.002. See ***O'Connor's*** FORM 4D:01.

§3. THE SPECIAL JUDGE

§3.1 Qualifications. The special judge must be a retired or former state district, statutory county court, or appellate judge who (1) served as a judge for at least four years in district, statutory county court, or appellate court; (2) developed substantial experience in her area of specialty; (3) was not removed from office or did not resign while under investigation for discipline or removal; and (4) annually completes at least five days of continuing legal education in courses approved by the state bar or the Supreme Court. CPRC §151.003.

§3.2 Powers. While trying the case, the special judge has the same powers as a district judge, except the special judge cannot hold a person in contempt of court unless the person is a witness before her. CPRC §151.006(b); ***NCF, Inc. v. Harless***, 846 S.W.2d 79, 82-83 (Tex.App.—Dallas 1992, orig. proceeding) (special judge could not enforce turnover order by contempt).

§4. ORDER OF REFERRAL

§4.1 Contents of order. The order of referral must specify the issues referred and the name of the special judge. CPRC §151.004. The order may designate the time and place for trial and the time for filing the special judge's report. *Id.* The clerk of the court will send the special judge a copy of the order. *Id.* See ***O'Connor's*** FORM 4D:02.

§4.2 Effect of referral. The referral will stay all proceedings until after the conclusion of the special trial. CPRC §151.001.

§5. PROCEDURE FOR THE TRIAL

§5.1 Rules for special trial. The case will be conducted in the same manner as a bench trial under the TRCPs and the TREs. CPRC §§151.005, 151.006(a). A party has the right to be represented by a lawyer. *Id.* §151.007.

§5.2 Court reporter. A court reporter is required. CPRC §151.008.

§5.3 No public courtroom. The trial cannot be held in a public courtroom, and public employees cannot be involved during regular work hours. CPRC §151.010.

§5.4 Costs & fees. The parties will divide all the costs related to the trial: the special judge's fee, the court reporter's fee, and other administrative costs. CPRC §151.009(a). Each party must pay the costs of its witnesses and any other cost related only to its case. *Id.* §151.009(b). Neither the state nor the local government may pay any costs related to trial by a special judge. *Id.* §151.009(c).

§5.5 Special judge's verdict. The verdict of the special judge must comply with the requirements for a verdict by the court in which the action was filed. *See* CPRC §151.011. The verdict will stand as a verdict of the district court. *Id.* Unless otherwise specified in the order of referral, the special judge must submit the verdict within 60 days of the day the trial adjourns. *Id.*

§5.6 Motion for new trial. If the special judge does not file a verdict within the time specified by CPRC §151.011, the court may grant a new trial if (1) a party files a motion requesting a new trial, (2) notice is given to all parties of the time and place of the hearing on the motion, and (3) the hearing is held. CPRC §151.012. See ***O'Connor's*** FORM 4D:03.

§6. REVIEW

The parties have a right to appeal. CPRC §151.013. The right to appeal cannot be invoked until (1) the special judge submits a verdict to the trial court, (2) all claims are resolved, and (3) the trial court signs an order memorializing the finality of the case. ***Baroid Equip., Inc. v. Odeco Drilling, Inc.***, 64 S.W.3d 504, 505 (Tex.App.—Houston [1st Dist.] 2001, no pet.).

COMMENTARIES

CHAPTER 5. PRETRIAL MOTIONS
TABLE OF CONTENTS

COMMENTARIES
CHAPTER 5. PRETRIAL MOTIONS
TABLE OF CONTENTS

A. THE PRETRIAL CONFERENCE

§1. GENERAL

§1.1 Rule. TRCP 166. See Gov't Code §21.001(a) (courts have power to enforce their orders); Tex.R. Jud.Admin. 7(a)(6) (courts shall "utilize methods to expedite the disposition of cases on the docket").

§1.2 Purpose. TRCP 166 gives trial judges the power to control pretrial matters and to assist in settling cases. ***Lindley v. Johnson***, 936 S.W.2d 53, 55 (Tex.App.—Tyler 1996, writ denied). The purpose of a pretrial conference is to narrow the issues and to dispose of other matters, thus aiding final disposition of the case. ***Walden v. Affiliated Computer Servs.***, 97 S.W.3d 303, 322 (Tex.App.—Houston [14th Dist.] 2003, pet. denied); ***Griffin v. Wolfe***, 626 S.W.2d 895, 897 (Tex.App.—Fort Worth 1981, no writ).

§1.3 Forms & timetables. ***O'Connor's Texas Civil Forms***, FORM 5A:01; Timetables, this book, Pretrial Motions, p. 998, Discovery Schedule for Level 1, p. 1001, Discovery Schedule for Level 2, p. 1003.

§2. PROCEDURE

§2.1 Automatic pretrial calendar. The court may establish a pretrial calendar "by rule." TRCP 166. Attorneys should always check the local rules to see if they create automatic deadlines for discovery, pleadings, motions, or any other matters.

§2.2 Initiating a pretrial conference. A pretrial conference can be scheduled by the court either on its own initiative or on motion of a party. To request a pretrial conference, the party should file a motion stating the reasons for the conference. Whether the trial court conducts a pretrial conference is a matter within its discretion, and a party cannot force the trial court to conduct one. ***Taiwan Shrimp Farm Village Ass'n v. U.S.A. Shrimp Farm Dev.***, 915 S.W.2d 61, 69 (Tex.App.—Corpus Christi 1996, writ denied); ***Ryland Group v. White***, 723 S.W.2d 160, 163 (Tex.App.—Houston [1st Dist.] 1986, orig. proceeding).

§3. SCOPE OF THE PRETRIAL CONFERENCE

§3.1 Outside scope of conference. A court cannot resolve contested issues of fact at a pretrial conference. ***Provident Life & Acc. Ins. Co. v. Hazlitt***, 216 S.W.2d 805, 807 (Tex.1949); ***McCreight v. City of Cleburne***, 940 S.W.2d 285, 288 (Tex.App.—Waco 1997, writ denied); ***Masterson v. Cox***, 886 S.W.2d 436, 439 (Tex.App.—Houston [1st Dist.] 1994, no writ); *see also* ***Walden***, 97 S.W.3d at 323 (court may receive evidence and hear expert testimony to identify & rule on legal issues only). It is a violation of due process for a court to convert a pretrial conference into a trial on the merits. ***Murphree v. Ziegelmair***, 937 S.W.2d 493, 495 (Tex.App.—Houston [1st Dist.] 1995, no writ); *see, e.g.*, ***Ulloa v. Davila***, 860 S.W.2d 202, 204 (Tex.App.—San Antonio 1993, no writ) (at settlement conference, court could not sua sponte dismiss counterclaim).

§3.2 Matters that aid disposition. TRCP 166 contains a catch-all provision that allows the court to consider any matter that "may aid in the disposition of the action." TRCP 166(p); *see* ***Williams v. Akzo Nobel Chems.***, 999 S.W.2d 836, 842 (Tex.App.—Tyler 1999, no pet.).

§3.3 Trial setting. Although not specifically listed in TRCP 166, setting the date for trial is commonly done by pretrial order. *See, e.g.*, ***Loffland Bros. v. Downey***, 822 S.W.2d 249, 251 (Tex.App.—Houston [1st Dist.] 1991, orig. proceeding) (docket control order set deadlines for discovery, amending pleadings, & trial date). The trial court must give the parties 45 days' notice of the first trial setting. TRCP 245; ***Smith v. Lippmann***, 826 S.W.2d 137, 138 n.1 (Tex.1992). However, if the case has been previously set for trial, and the parties received 45 days' notice of the original trial setting, the court may reset the trial to a later date on any reasonable notice. TRCP 245; ***Arkla, Inc. v. Harris***, 846 S.W.2d 623, 628 (Tex.App.—Houston [14th Dist.] 1993, orig. proceeding). See "Deadline begins – notice of trial," ch. 5-B, §4.1.1, p. 230.

§3.4 Pleading deadlines. By a pretrial order, the court can set deadlines for amendments to pleadings that supersede the deadlines in TRCP 63. TRCP 166; *see* ***Wilson v. Korthauer***, 21 S.W.3d 573, 577-78 (Tex.App.—Houston

[14th Dist.] 2000, pet. denied); ***Texas Commerce Bank v. Lebco Constructors***, 865 S.W.2d 68, 79 (Tex.App.—Corpus Christi 1993, writ denied). Once the court signs an order setting pleading deadlines, parties must secure leave of court to amend after those deadlines. ***Texas Commerce Bank***, 865 S.W.2d at 79. See "After deadline in pretrial order," ch. 5-F, §3.2.1, p. 256.

§3.5 Discovery deadlines. The pretrial conference is most often used to determine what discovery has been completed and what discovery has yet to be undertaken. *See* TRCP 166(c) (court can consider discovery schedule at pretrial conference). Every case must be governed by a discovery control plan, which sets the deadlines for discovery. TRCP 190.1. See "Discovery Periods," ch. 6-A, §6, p. 317; "Discovery Control Plans," ch. 6-A, §7, p. 318. The court can change the deadlines set by the discovery rules only for good cause. TRCP 191.1.

§3.6 Pending motions. At the pretrial conference, the trial court may require the parties to argue pending motions—dilatory pleas, motions, and exceptions. TRCP 166(a). A dilatory plea, most commonly a plea in abatement, asks the court to abate or dismiss the proceeding because of a fundamental defect in the manner in which the action was brought. The court can set an abbreviated discovery schedule to resolve pretrial motions. *See* ***Montalvo v. 4th Ct. of Appeals***, 917 S.W.2d 1, 2 (Tex.1995).

§3.7 Joint pretrial status report. The trial court has the authority to require the parties to confer and file a joint pretrial status report. *See* ***Koslow's v. Mackie***, 796 S.W.2d 700, 703 (Tex.1990).

§3.8 Contentions & admissions of the parties. The court may require the parties to confer and narrow the factual and legal issues of the trial. TRCP 166(d), (g), (j); ***Koslow's***, 796 S.W.2d at 703.

1. Facts. The court may require the parties to submit written statements of their contentions, to consider the contested issues of fact and simplification of the issues, and to discuss the possibility of stipulations of fact. TRCP 166(d)-(f).

2. Law. The court may require the parties to identify the legal issues for the court and to agree to the application of law and the contested issues of law. TRCP 166(g), (j).

§3.9 Trial witnesses & exhibits.

1. Identification of experts. The court may require the parties to appear for a pretrial conference to exchange information about experts—names, addresses, telephone numbers, and the subject of each expert's testimony. TRCP 166(i). The schedule for designating experts is determined with reference to the end of the discovery period and according to whether the party is seeking affirmative relief. TRCP 195.2. When a court signs an order setting the deadline for the parties to identify experts, the order controls over the deadlines in TRCP 195.2(a) and (b). TRCP 195.2; ***State Farm Fire & Cas. Co. v. Price***, 845 S.W.2d 427, 434 (Tex.App.—Amarillo 1992, writ dism'd). The court cannot set a deadline for the disclosure of expert witnesses that is unreasonable. *See, e.g.*, ***Loffland Bros.***, 822 S.W.2d at 252 (8 months before trial was unreasonable). If the court does not sign an order setting the deadline for disclosure of experts, the parties must designate experts according to the schedule in TRCP 195.2. See "Deadlines for Securing Discovery from Experts," ch. 6-C, §6, p. 372. When the court signs a pretrial order on the discovery of experts, it cannot disregard its own order at trial. *See* ***Dennis v. Haden***, 867 S.W.2d 48, 51 (Tex.App.—Texarkana 1993, writ denied) (court should not have admitted testimony of expert whose report had not been provided).

2. Witness list. The court may require the parties to exchange lists of direct fact witnesses who will be called to testify at trial and the rebuttal and impeachment witnesses whose testimony can reasonably be anticipated before trial, along with their addresses, telephone numbers, and the subject of each witness's testimony. TRCP 166(h). A party also may obtain discovery of the names, addresses, and telephone numbers of the other party's trial witnesses by way of interrogatory. *See* TRCP 192.3(d). See "Trial witnesses," ch. 6-B, §2.9, p. 344.

3. Exhibits & objections. The court may require the parties to mark and exchange exhibits and stipulate to their authenticity and admissibility. TRCP 166(*l*), 192.5(c)(2); *see also* ***British Am. Ins. Co. v. Howarton***, 877 S.W.2d 347, 350 (Tex.App.—Houston [1st Dist.] 1994, writ dism'd) (because videotape was not listed as an exhibit, it was excluded at trial). The court also may require the parties to make written objections to the other parties' exhibits, stating the ground for each objection. TRCP 166(m); ***Owens-Corning Fiberglas Corp. v. Malone***, 916 S.W.2d 551, 557 (Tex.App.—Houston [1st Dist.] 1996), *aff'd*, 972 S.W.2d 35 (Tex.1998). Unlike rulings on a motion in limine, rulings on pretrial objections preserve error on appeal. ***Huckaby v. A.G. Perry & Son***, 20 S.W.3d 194, 203 (Tex.App.—Texarkana 2000, pet. denied); ***Owens-Corning***, 916 S.W.2d at 557. See "Motion in Limine," ch. 5-E, p. 252.

PRACTICE TIP

There are two reasons to request a pretrial exchange of trial exhibits. First, if a privileged document has been inadvertently produced, the producing party may utilize the snap-back provisions of TRCP 193.3(d) to assert a privilege. See TRCP 193, cmt. 4. See "Use snap-back provision," ch. 6-A, §17.2.4, p. 330. Second, if a party identifies a document produced in discovery, the producing party may prevent the self-authentication of the document by objecting to its authenticity. TRCP 193.7 & cmt. 7; see TRCP 176.6(c) (production by nonparties). See "Authenticity," ch. 8-C, §8.4, p. 540.

§3.10 Jury questions. The court may require the parties to prepare proposed jury questions, instructions, definitions, and, for a nonjury trial, proposed findings of fact and conclusions of law. TRCP 166(k).

§3.11 Master or auditor. The court may consider the advisability of referring issues to a master or auditor for findings to be used as evidence in a jury trial. TRCP 166(n), 171. See "Master in Chancery," ch. 1-J, p. 55.

§3.12 Settlement. The court may encourage the parties to settle the case. TRCP 166(o). See "Alternative Dispute Resolution," ch. 4, p. 203.

§4. HEARING ON THE PRETRIAL CONFERENCE

§4.1 Type of hearing. The pretrial conference may be held by telephone, by mail, in the judge's chambers, or in the courtroom. *See* ***Koslow's***, 796 S.W.2d at 703 (court required a written status report to be mailed).

§4.2 Attendance. The court can require the attorneys for the parties, the parties themselves, or the parties' authorized agents to attend a pretrial conference. TRCP 166; *see* ***Koslow's***, 796 S.W.2d at 703 (pleadings struck after Ds did not submit status report & appear at hearing).

§4.3 Evidence. If a pending motion is one that must be supported by evidence (*e.g.*, a motion to abate), the parties should be prepared to present evidence at the pretrial conference.

§4.4 Objections. In most instances, objections at the pretrial conference regarding rulings required to be made at trial are premature and do not preserve error. *See* ***Clark v. Trailways, Inc.***, 774 S.W.2d 644, 648 n.2 (Tex. 1989) (dictum); *see, e.g.*, ***Texas Commerce Bank v. Lebco Constructors***, 865 S.W.2d 68, 78 (Tex.App.—Corpus Christi 1993, writ denied) (objection at pretrial conference to allocation of peremptory challenges did not preserve error); ***Barras v. Monsanto Co.***, 831 S.W.2d 859, 864 (Tex.App.—Houston [14th Dist.] 1992, writ denied) (objection to pretrial ruling that certain agreements between the parties could be discussed did not preserve error because party did not obtain ruling); *see also* ***Reveal v. West***, 764 S.W.2d 8, 10 (Tex.App.—Houston [1st Dist.] 1988, orig. proceeding) (pretrial ruling that document was privileged was merely a ruling similar to motion in limine). But, under TRCP 166(m), the trial court has the authority to rule on objections to exhibits at a pretrial conference, and one court has held those rulings will preserve error. ***Owens-Corning***, 916 S.W.2d at 557.

CAUTION

Do not rely on an objection made at a pretrial conference to preserve error. If the matter is one that will arise at trial (e.g., the introduction of evidence), remember to object on the record during the trial.

§5. ORDER ON PRETRIAL CONFERENCE

§5.1 In writing. The pretrial order must be in writing. ***Palacios v. Winters***, 26 S.W.3d 734, 735 (Tex.App.—Corpus Christi 2000, no pet.); ***FDIC v. Finlay***, 832 S.W.2d 158, 162 (Tex.App.—Houston [1st Dist.] 1992), *writ denied*, 849 S.W.2d 344 (Tex.1993).

§5.2 Contents. The pretrial order must recite the actions taken and rulings made at the pretrial conference. TRCP 166; ***Finlay***, 832 S.W.2d at 160. The pretrial order will control the suit unless it is modified at trial to prevent manifest injustice. In most cases, the pretrial order includes the following: (1) the actions taken at the pretrial conference, (2) the pleadings that can be amended and the deadline to amend, (3) any agreements made by the parties, (4) the rulings of the court on any pleas or motions, and (5) whether the case will be tried to the court or to a jury. *See* TRCP 166.

§5.3 Notice. The parties are entitled to notice of pretrial or docket control orders. *See* ***Loffland Bros. v. Downey***, 822 S.W.2d 249, 251 (Tex.App.—Houston [1st Dist.] 1991, orig. proceeding). The court must send the pretrial order to the attorney in charge for each party. TRCP 8; ***Loffland Bros.***, 822 S.W.2d at 251.

§5.4 Discretion to modify order. Under TRCP 166, the court can modify its pretrial order to prevent "manifest injustice." ***Trevino v. Trevino***, 64 S.W.3d 166, 170 (Tex.App.—San Antonio 2001, no pet.); *see* ***Griffin v. Wolfe***, 626 S.W.2d 895, 897 (Tex.App.—Fort Worth 1981, no writ) (court's refusal to permit amendment was not abuse of discretion). If the court modifies the pretrial order, it must do so by written order or oral statement on the record. ***Susanoil, Inc. v. Continental Oil Co.***, 516 S.W.2d 260, 264 (Tex.App.—San Antonio 1973, no writ). *But see* ***Trevino***, 64 S.W.3d at 170 (court implicitly modified docket control order by overruling Ps' motion to strike & setting Ds' summary judgment motion for submission).

§6. BINDING EFFECT OF PRETRIAL ORDER

§6.1 On procedure for trial. A pretrial order controls the procedure for the case. To the extent that the order changes the deadlines in the rules of procedure, the order prevails. ***Lindley v. Johnson***, 936 S.W.2d 53, 55 (Tex.App.—Tyler 1996, writ denied); *see* ***ForScan Corp. v. Dresser Indus.***, 789 S.W.2d 389, 393 (Tex.App.—Houston [14th Dist.] 1990, writ denied) (deadline for amending pleadings in pretrial order prevailed over deadline in TRCP 63).

§6.2 On trial judge. The trial court cannot disregard its own pretrial order. ***Mercedes-Benz Credit Corp. v. Rhyne***, 925 S.W.2d 664, 666 (Tex.1996). For example, if the trial court signed an order setting the case on the jury docket, the court cannot ignore that order on the eve of trial, even if no jury fee was paid. *Id.* The parties are entitled to rely on the trial court's pretrial order. ***Dennis v. Haden***, 867 S.W.2d 48, 51 (Tex.App.—Texarkana 1993, writ denied). *But see* ***Trevino***, 64 S.W.3d at 170 (court implicitly modified docket control order by overruling Ps' motion to strike & setting Ds' motion for summary judgment for submission).

§6.3 On parties. The parties must comply with the pretrial order. *See, e.g.*, ***British Am. Ins. Co. v. Howarton***, 877 S.W.2d 347, 350-51 (Tex.App.—Houston [1st Dist.] 1994, writ dism'd) (party could not introduce videotape because it was not listed as an exhibit as required by pretrial order); ***Dennis***, 867 S.W.2d at 51 (party could not call expert to testify because expert's report was not produced as required by pretrial order); ***ForScan Corp.***, 789 S.W.2d at 393 (party could not amend pleadings after deadline in pretrial order).

§6.4 On rescheduled trial. A pretrial or docket control order setting discovery deadlines does not survive if the trial is rescheduled for a date that is more than three months after the discovery period ends. *See* TRCP 190.5(b).

§6.5 On retrial. The discovery deadlines in a pretrial order do not survive the granting of a new trial. ***State Dept. of Highways & Pub. Transp. v. Ross***, 718 S.W.2d 5, 11 (Tex.App.—Tyler 1986, orig. proceeding) (order closing discovery did not remain in effect after mistrial). After a new trial is ordered, a suit stands upon the docket as if it had not been tried. *Id.*

§7. SANCTIONS

The trial court has the power to enforce its orders with sanctions. ***In re Patton***, 47 S.W.3d 825, 827 (Tex.App.—Fort Worth 2001, no pet.); *see* Gov't Code §21.001(a) (court has all powers necessary to enforce its orders); ***Woodall v.***

Clark, 802 S.W.2d 415, 418 (Tex.App.—Beaumont 1991, no writ) (Gov't Code §21.001(a) gives court power to dismiss suit for repeated refusal to comply with pretrial order). Courts may impose the sanctions listed in TRCP 215 for violations of pretrial orders. *See* ***Koslow's v. Mackie***, 796 S.W.2d 700, 703-04 (Tex.1990) (sanctions for not appearing at pretrial conference). Any sanctions imposed for violation of a pretrial order must be just and appropriate. ***Koslow's***, 796 S.W.2d at 703 n.1; ***In re Bledsoe***, 41 S.W.3d 807, 812 (Tex.App.—Fort Worth 2001, no pet.); *see* ***Roberts v. Golden Crest Waters***, 1 S.W.3d 291, 292-93 (Tex.App.—Corpus Christi 1999, no pet.) (court abused its discretion by imposing death penalty sanctions for failure to file pretrial statement). See "Motion for Sanctions," ch. 5-J, p. 275.

§8. REVIEW

§8.1 Standard of review. In most cases, the standard of review for a pretrial order is abuse of discretion. ***TransAmerican Nat. Gas Corp. v. Powell***, 811 S.W.2d 913, 916-17 (Tex.1991) (pretrial discovery order). However, if the trial court summarily disposes of a party's claim or defense, the standard of review would be the same as in the appeal of a summary judgment. ***McCreight v. City of Cleburne***, 940 S.W.2d 285, 287 (Tex.App.—Waco 1997, writ denied).

§8.2 Appeal. A pretrial order may be appealed after the entry of a final judgment. *See* ***Finlay***, 832 S.W.2d at 161.

§8.3 Mandamus. A pretrial order can be the subject of an application for writ of mandamus if an appeal would not provide effective relief. *See* ***Loffland Bros.***, 822 S.W.2d at 251-52 (party missed deadline for naming experts because it did not receive docket control order).

B. REQUEST FOR JURY TRIAL

§1. GENERAL

§1.1 Rules. TRCP 216-220, 245. See U.S. Const. amend. 7; Tex. Const. art. 1, §15, art. 5, §10; Gov't Code §51.604 (jury fee); Fam. Code §6.703 (right to jury in divorce action); Prob. Code §21 (contested issues tried by jury).

§1.2 Purpose. A request for a jury trial invokes the party's right to a jury trial.

§1.3 Forms. ***O'Connor's Texas Civil Forms***, FORMS 5B.

§2. RIGHT TO A JURY TRIAL

The U.S. and Texas Constitutions guarantee a jury trial. U.S. Const. amend. 7; Tex. Const. art. 1, §15. In civil matters, a party has a right to a trial by jury of any action that is the same or analogous to those actions that could have been submitted to a jury in 1876, the year the Texas Constitution was adopted. ***Barshop v. Medina Cty. Underground Water Conserv. Dist.***, 925 S.W.2d 618, 636 (Tex.1996). To be entitled to a jury trial, a party must have a right to a jury trial and properly request a jury under TRCP 216. ***Huddle v. Huddle***, 696 S.W.2d 895, 895 (Tex.1985); ***In re J.N.F.***, 116 S.W.3d 426, 431 (Tex.App.—Houston [14th Dist.] 2003, n.p.h.).

§3. REQUIREMENTS

To make a proper request for a jury trial, a party must do two things at least 30 days before the date trial is set: (1) make a written request for a jury trial and (2) pay the jury fee. TRCP 216; ***Huddle***, 696 S.W.2d at 895; ***Universal Printing Co. v. Premier Victorian Homes***, 73 S.W.3d 283, 289 (Tex.App.—Houston [1st Dist.] 2001, pet. denied). When one party requests a jury and pays a fee, all other parties in the suit acquire the right to a jury. Thus, any party in the suit can rely on any other party's jury request. ***White Motor Co. v. Loden***, 373 S.W.2d 863, 865 (Tex. App.—Dallas 1963, no writ).

§3.1 Request.

1. In writing. The request for a jury trial (also called a jury demand) must be in writing and must be filed with the clerk. TRCP 216(a); ***Grossnickle v. Grossnickle***, 865 S.W.2d 211, 212 (Tex.App.—Texarkana 1993, no writ).

It can be included in the plaintiff's petition, in the defendant's answer, or filed as a separate document. One court held that a request for a setting on the jury docket was a sufficient request for a jury trial under TRCP 216. ***Sheth v. White***, 722 S.W.2d 805, 805 (Tex.App.—Houston [14th Dist.] 1987, orig. proceeding). A party should not rely on a request for a jury trial in a cover letter to the clerk. ***ForScan Corp. v. Dresser Indus.***, 789 S.W.2d 389, 392 (Tex. App.—Houston [14th Dist.] 1990, writ denied).

2. Allegations.

(1) For a timely request. In the request, the party should state that it wants a jury trial and that it tenders the jury fee to the clerk. *See* TRCP 216. See ***O'Connor's*** FORM 5B:01.

(2) For an untimely request. If the case is set for trial on the nonjury docket, the party should file the request for a jury and a motion to strike the nonjury setting. See ***O'Connor's*** FORMS 5B:01-02. In the motion to strike the nonjury setting, the party should allege the following under oath (and attach affidavits if necessary):

(a) A jury is available. The attorney should contact the clerk to determine if a jury is available. If a jury is not available, the party should file a motion for continuance so the case can be reset on the jury docket. *See* ***McCrann v. Tandy Computer Leasing***, 737 S.W.2d 10, 11 (Tex.App.—Corpus Christ 1987, no writ).

(b) A jury trial can be had without any additional delay or inconvenience to the trial court's docket.

(c) There is a disputed fact in the case, and an instructed verdict would not be proper. ***Halsell v. Dehoyos***, 810 S.W.2d 371, 372 (Tex.1991); ***In re V.R.W.***, 41 S.W.3d 183, 194 (Tex.App.—Houston [14th Dist.] 2001, no pet.).

(d) The reason the jury request was not made earlier.

(e) The Texas Constitution guarantees a jury trial in this type of case. Tex. Const. art. 1, §15.

§3.2 Jury fee. To make a proper request for a jury trial, in addition to filing a written request for a jury, the party must pay the jury fee or file an affidavit of inability to pay the fee. ***J.N.F.***, 116 S.W.3d at 431; *see* ***Huddle***, 696 S.W.2d at 895; ***Walton v. Canon, Short & Gaston***, 23 S.W.3d 143, 149 (Tex.App.—El Paso 2000, no pet.).

1. Amount. The jury fee is $30 in district court and $22 in county court. Gov't Code §51.604(a). This fee includes the amount required under TRCP 216. Gov't Code §51.604(c).

PRACTICE TIP

When paying the filing fees and the jury fee, give the clerk separate checks. If you give the clerk one check and it is not sufficient to cover both fees, the clerk will apply it to the filing fees and you will not have paid the jury fee. See, e.g., ***Universal Printing Co.****, 73 S.W.3d at 289-90 ($105 paid by Ds did not cover jury fee after filing costs deducted).*

---

2. Indigent. An indigent is not required to pay a jury fee. TRCP 217. Instead, the indigent must file a jury request within the deadline in TRCP 217 and file an affidavit of inability to pay within the deadline for paying the fee. See §4, below. In the affidavit, the indigent must swear that she cannot obtain the money necessary for the fee, by pledge of property or otherwise. TRCP 217. See "Suit by Indigent," ch. 2-I, p. 132.

§4. DEADLINES

§4.1 Deadline to file jury request.

1. Deadline begins – notice of trial. The event that triggers the party's deadline to request a jury trial is the notice it receives from the trial court that the case is set for trial. The reason TRCP 245 requires the trial court to give the parties 45 days' notice of the first trial setting is to permit a party to make a timely request for a jury trial. *See **In re J.C.***, 108 S.W.3d 914, 916-17 (Tex.App.—Texarkana 2003, n.p.h.); ***Hardin v. Hardin***, 932 S.W.2d 566, 567 (Tex.App.—Tyler 1995, no writ). If the trial court notifies the parties that a case is set on the nonjury docket without giving the parties enough time to request a jury trial, the appellate court will consider a late request as being timely. ***In re J.C.***, 108 S.W.3d at 916-17; ***In re V.R.W.***, 41 S.W.3d at 195; *see **Simpson v. Stem***, 822 S.W.2d 323, 324 (Tex.App.—Waco 1992, orig. proceeding) (less than 30 days' notice of trial setting was not sufficient); *see also **Martin v. Black***, 909 S.W.2d 192, 197-98 (Tex.App.—Houston [14th Dist.] 1995, writ denied) (no notice of trial setting given, late request timely).

2. Reasonable time before trial. TRCP 216 states that the request for a jury should be made at a "reasonable time before" the date the case is set for trial on the nonjury docket, but at least 30 days in advance. TRCP 216(a); ***Halsell***, 810 S.W.2d at 371; ***Southern Farm Bureau Cas. Ins. Co. v. Penland***, 923 S.W.2d 758, 760 (Tex.App.—Corpus Christi 1996, no writ).

(1) 30 days – presumed reasonable. A request for a jury made at least 30 days before trial is presumed to have been made a reasonable time before the trial. ***Halsell***, 810 S.W.2d at 371; ***Penland***, 923 S.W.2d at 760.

(2) Less than 30 days – no presumption. If the request is made less than 30 days before trial, there is no presumption the request is reasonable. In such a case, the decision to permit a jury trial is strictly within the trial court's discretion.

3. Reschedule trial after late request. If the case is reset, the final trial date is the date that controls the 30-day deadline. ***Halsell***, 810 S.W.2d at 371; ***Whiteford v. Baugher***, 818 S.W.2d 423, 425 (Tex.App.—Houston [1st Dist.] 1991, writ denied). Thus, when a case is reset for trial, an untimely request can become timely. ***Halsell***, 810 S.W.2d at 371; *see also **Ricardo N., Inc. v. Turcios de Argueta***, 907 S.W.2d 423, 429 (Tex.1995) (untimely request for 1987 trial was timely for 1991 trial after remand from federal court).

4. Retrial after waiver. If a party waived a jury on the first trial, but the case is reversed and remanded for another trial, the party may request a jury trial for the retrial. ***Gordon v. Gordon***, 704 S.W.2d 490, 492 (Tex.App.—Corpus Christi 1986, writ dism'd).

§4.2 Deadline to pay jury fee.

1. Deadline in TRCP 216. Under TRCP 216, the deadlines for paying the jury fee and filing the written jury request are the same—30 days before the date the case is set for trial. TRCP 216(a), (b); ***Huddle v. Huddle***, 696 S.W.2d 895, 895 (Tex.1985); ***Universal Printing Co. v. Premier Victorian Homes***, 73 S.W.3d 283, 289 (Tex. App.—Houston [1st Dist.] 2001, pet. denied). Even if a jury fee is not timely paid, the trial court has discretion to permit a jury trial if it will not interfere with the court's docket, delay the trial, or prejudice the opposing party. ***G.M. Corp. v. Gayle***, 951 S.W.2d 469, 476 (Tex.1997). See §4.1.2, above.

2. Deadline in §51.604. Under Gov't Code §51.604, the deadline to pay the jury fee is "not later than the 10th day before the jury trial is scheduled to begin." Gov't Code §51.604(b); ***Universal Printing***, 73 S.W.3d at 292.

CAUTION

*The jury fee paid under Gov't Code §51.604 includes the fee paid under TRCP 216. Gov't Code §51.604(c). Thus, the deadline to file the jury fee under Gov't Code §51.604(b) should control. But see **Universal Printing**, 73 S.W.3d at 292 (concluding that §51.604 does not supplant the 30-day deadline imposed by TRCP 216). Out of caution, pay the fee at the same time you make your request, at least 30 days before the date set for trial. See §4.2.1, above.*

§5. RESPONSE

§5.1 Request timely. The trial court may deny a timely request for a jury only if the party opposing it can rebut the presumption that the request was reasonable. ***Halsell v. Dehoyos***, 810 S.W.2d 371, 371 (Tex.1991); ***Penland***, 923 S.W.2d at 760. To oppose a timely request for a jury trial, the response must show that a jury trial will (1) injure the party, (2) disrupt the court's docket, or (3) impede the ordinary handling of the court's business. ***Halsell***, 810 S.W.2d at 371; ***In re J.N.F.***, 116 S.W.3d 426, 436 (Tex.App.—Houston [14th Dist.] 2003, n.p.h.). Considering that the right to a jury trial is guaranteed by the Texas Constitution, a court should seldom deny a party a jury trial if the request for a jury was timely. *See* Tex. Const. art. 1, §15. *But see* ***Crittenden v. Crittenden***, 52 S.W.3d 768, 770 (Tex.App.—San Antonio 2001, pet. denied) (wife's timely request for jury was denied because she had earlier agreed to settlement, no jury was available for 6 months, & she had engaged in tactics to delay divorce).

§5.2 Request untimely. To oppose a request for a jury trial made after the deadline, the party should file a motion to strike, stating that the request was made too late. *See, e.g.*, ***Wright v. Brooks***, 773 S.W.2d 649, 650 (Tex. App.—San Antonio 1989, writ denied) (P filed motion to strike jury demand made 23 days before trial).

§6. ORDER

§6.1 Clerk's duty. Generally the court does not sign an order on a request for a jury trial. ***Mercedes-Benz Credit Corp. v. Rhyne***, 925 S.W.2d 664, 666 (Tex.1996). The court clerk simply enters a notation on the court's docket sheet that the jury fee was paid. Gov't Code §51.604(a); TRCP 216(b). When the court actually signs an order setting the case for a jury trial, it cannot disregard the order and withdraw the case from the jury docket just before trial, even if no jury fee was paid. ***Mercedes-Benz***, 925 S.W.2d at 666.

§6.2 Issue contested. The court will make a ruling on the request for a jury trial only if the request is contested.

PRACTICE TIP

If the trial court denies you a trial by jury, immediately file a verified motion for continuance, even if handwritten, asking that the case be continued so that it may be reset on the jury docket. See "Motion for Continuance," ch. 5-D, p. 242.

---

§6.3 Withdrawing the request for a jury. A party may withdraw its request for a jury trial so that the case may be heard by the court. If the party who requested the jury withdraws its request, the other party may prevent the withdrawal by either making a timely objection or filing its own request for a jury. ***Lambert v. Coachmen Indus.***, 761 S.W.2d 82, 85 (Tex.App.—Houston [14th Dist.] 1988, writ denied). The trial court cannot withdraw a case from the jury docket over the objection of a party, even if the party making the objection did not request a jury or pay the fee. *See* TRCP 220; ***J.N.F.***, 116 S.W.3d at 434-35.

§6.4 No sua sponte withdrawal. A trial court cannot withdraw a case from the jury docket on its own initiative. ***Bank of Houston v. White***, 737 S.W.2d 387, 388 (Tex.App.—Houston [14th Dist.] 1987, orig. proceeding). If the court signed an order setting the case for a jury trial—even if the order was signed by mistake—the court cannot disregard its own order and force the parties to try the case without a jury. ***Rhyne***, 925 S.W.2d at 666; ***Texas Valley Ins. Agency v. Sweezy Constr.***, 105 S.W.3d 217, 221 (Tex.App.—Corpus Christi 2003, no pet.).

§7. WAIVER OF JURY

§7.1 Failure to appear at trial. A party will waive its request for a jury if it does not appear for a scheduled trial. TRCP 220; ***Bradley Motors v. Mackey***, 878 S.W.2d 140, 141 (Tex.1994); ***In re W.B.W.***, 2 S.W.3d 421, 422-23 (Tex.App.—San Antonio 1999, no pet.) (party, though not personally present, appears for trial when her attorney is present).

§7.2 Failure to object to nonjury. A party will waive its request for a jury trial if it does not object when the trial court begins a nonjury trial. ***Sunwest Reliance Acquisitions Group v. Provident Nat'l Assur. Co.***, 875 S.W.2d 385, 387 (Tex.App.—Dallas 1993, no writ).

§7.3 Failure to object to discharge of jury. A party will waive a jury trial if it does not object when the trial court dismisses the jury, resolves the case by summary disposition, and signs a judgment. ***Rodriguez v. Texas Dept. of MHMR***, 942 S.W.2d 53, 55-56 (Tex.App.—Corpus Christi 1997, no writ).

§7.4 Waiver by contract. It is uncertain whether a contractual waiver of a jury trial is constitutional. ***Rivercenter Assocs. v. Rivera***, 858 S.W.2d 366, 368 n.2 (Tex.1993). However, a contractual jury waiver provision can be waived if the party does not assert it timely. *Id.* at 367-68.

§8. REVIEW

§8.1 Standard on appeal. When the trial court erroneously refuses to grant a jury trial, the error is always harmful, unless there are no material issues of fact and the court could have granted an instructed verdict. ***Rhyne***, 925 S.W.2d at 667; ***Halsell***, 810 S.W.2d at 372; ***Weng Enters. v. Embassy World Travel***, 837 S.W.2d 217, 222 (Tex. App.—Houston [1st Dist.] 1992, no writ). If the party was entitled to a jury trial, and there were material fact issues in the case, the appellate courts will reverse for a retrial. ***Halsell***, 810 S.W.2d at 372; ***In re V.R.W.***, 41 S.W.3d 183, 196 (Tex.App.—Houston [14th Dist.] 2001, no pet.); ***Grossnickle v. Grossnickle***, 865 S.W.2d 211, 212 (Tex. App.—Texarkana 1993, no writ).

§8.2 Burden. Some courts of appeals put the burden on the trial court to explain why it denied a jury trial to a party that made a request for a jury more than 30 days before trial. *See* ***M.M.M. v. Central State Depository of Crim. Records***, 681 S.W.2d 908, 910 (Tex.App.—Fort Worth 1984, no writ). Other courts put the burden on the party that wants the jury trial. *See* ***Olson v. Texas Commerce Bank***, 715 S.W.2d 764, 767 (Tex.App.—Houston [1st Dist.] 1986, writ ref'd n.r.e.).

C. MOTION TO CHALLENGE THE JUDGE

§1. GENERAL

Judges may be removed from a case for one of three reasons: (1) they are subject to a statutory strike as an assigned judge, (2) they are constitutionally disqualified, or (3) they are recused under rules promulgated by the Supreme Court. Tex. Const. art. 5, §11 (constitutional disqualifications); Gov't Code §74.053(d) (statutory strike); TRCP 18a-18b (recusal rules promulgated by court); ***In re Union Pac. Res. Co.***, 969 S.W.2d 427, 428 (Tex.1998).

§1.1 Rules. TRCP 18a, 18b. See Tex. Const. art. 5, §11 (disqualification); CPRC §30.016 (tertiary motion to recuse or disqualify); Gov't Code §25.00255 (recusal of statutory probate judge), Gov't Code §74.053 (objection to assigned judge); TRAP 16.2 & 16.3 (recusal of appellate justice).

§1.2 Purpose. A motion to challenge the trial judge seeks to remove the judge from the case so that another judge may be assigned to preside over the case.

§1.3 Forms. ***O'Connor's Texas Civil Forms***, FORMS 5C.

§2. TYPES OF MOTIONS

There are four types of challenges to the trial judge.

§2.1 Objection to assigned judges. An objection to an assigned judge is a peremptory challenge that, if timely made, results in the automatic removal of the assigned judge. Gov't Code §74.053(b); ***In re Perritt***, 992 S.W.2d 444, 446 (Tex.1999). Various code provisions refer to a judge assigned to serve as an "assigned" or a "visiting" judge. *See* Gov't Code §§74.053-74.054 (use term "assigned" judge), *id.* §74.060(b) (uses term "visiting" judge).

§2.2 Motion to disqualify. A motion to disqualify seeks to prevent a judge from hearing a case for a constitutional or statutory disqualification. ***Union Pac. Res.***, 969 S.W.2d at 428. When a judge is disqualified under the constitution, she has no jurisdiction in the case. ***Gulf Maritime Whs. Co. v. Towers***, 858 S.W.2d 556, 559 (Tex. App.—Beaumont 1993, writ denied); *see* ***Spigener v. Wallis***, 80 S.W.3d 174, 179-80 & n.5 (Tex.App.—Waco 2002, no pet.) (constitutional disqualification deprives judge of authority to act). TRCP 18b(1) incorporates the grounds for disqualification from the Texas Constitution. *See* Tex. Const. art. 5, §11.

§2.3 Motion to recuse. A motion to recuse seeks to prevent a judge from hearing a case for a non-constitutional reason. Recusal can be waived if not raised by a proper motion. ***Gulf Maritime***, 858 S.W.2d at 559-60. TRCP 18b(2) identifies the grounds for recusal.

§2.4 Tertiary motion to recuse. The third (or later) motion to recuse or disqualify a judge in the same case by the same party is called a "tertiary" motion. CPRC §30.016. Although the substantive law is the same as for motions to recuse, separate rules govern the procedure for tertiary motions. See "Tertiary Motion to Recuse or Disqualify," §5, p. 240.

5-1. COMPARISON OF DISQUALIFICATION, RECUSAL, & OBJECTION TO ASSIGNED JUDGE

		DISQUALIFICATION	RECUSAL	OBJECTION TO ASSIGNED JUDGE
1	Source of challenge	Constitution, statutes, & rules	Statutes & rules	Statute
2	Discretionary or mandatory	Mandatory	Discretionary	Mandatory if timely
3	Waivable	No	Yes	Yes
4	Parties may consent to judge	No	Yes	Yes
5	Effect if judge serves after valid challenge	Judgment void	Reversible error	Judgment void
6	Requires written motion	No, judge must recuse on own motion	Yes	Yes
7	Judgment subject to collateral attack	Yes	No	No

03

§3. OBJECTION TO ASSIGNED JUDGE

§3.1 Who may make assignment. Most assignments of judges are made by the presiding judge of the administrative region, who has the authority to assign judges residing within the region. Gov't Code §74.056(c); ***Chandler v. Chandler***, 991 S.W.2d 367, 379 (Tex.App.—El Paso 1999, pet. denied). However, assignments of judges can be made by the Chief Justice of the Texas Supreme Court when (1) the assigned judge does not reside within the administrative region to which she is assigned, *see* Gov't Code §§74.052(a), 74.057(a); or (2) the presiding judge of the administrative region is incapacitated, dies, or resigns, or is disqualified in the matter, *id.* §74.049; ***State v. Preslar***, 751 S.W.2d 477, 479 (Tex.1988).

§3.2 Who may be assigned. A visiting judge is a person who is assigned under Gov't Code chapter 74 to sit temporarily for the regular judge of the court. *See* Gov't Code §74.052 (assignment of judges), *id.* §74.053 (objection to assigned judges), *id.* §74.054 (judges who may be assigned as visiting judges). Judges assigned to hear a TRCP 18a motion (disqualification or recusal) are appointed under Government Code chapter 74—not under TRCP 18a—and are subject to challenge as an assigned judge. ***Perritt***, 992 S.W.2d at 447. There are four types of judges who may be assigned as visiting judges, and the assignment order must state which type of judge is being assigned. Gov't Code §74.053(a)(1).

1. Active judge. An "active judge" is a person who is a current judicial officeholder. Gov't Code §74.041(4). The term includes the following judges: a district judge, a constitutional or statutory county court judge, or an active appellate justice (Supreme Court, Court of Criminal Appeals, or court of appeals) who has had trial court experience. Gov't Code §74.054(a)(1), (5); *see* ***O.C.S., Inc. v. Pi Energy Corp.***, 24 S.W.3d 548, 551 (Tex. App.—Houston [1st Dist.] 2000, no pet.) (district judge assigned to hear motion to recuse in another court).

2. Retired judge. A "retired judge" is a person who (1) is a retiree or (2) served as an active judge for at least 8 years in a district, statutory probate, statutory county, or appellate court and has retired under the Texas County and District Retirement System. Gov't Code §§74.041(6), 74.055(c)(1); *see id.* §74.054(a)(3), (4); *see also* ***Mitchell Energy Corp. v. Ashworth***, 943 S.W.2d 436, 438-39 (Tex.1997) (retired judge is one receiving annuity under judicial retirement system); ***Chandler***, 991 S.W.2d at 380 (same). To be eligible for assignment, a retired judge must meet the qualifications listed in Gov't Code §74.055(c).

3. Former judge. A "former judge" is a person who served for at least 8 years as an active judge in a district, statutory probate, statutory county, or appellate court but is not a retired judge. Gov't Code §§74.041(5), 74.055(c)(1); *see id.* §74.054(a)(3), (4). To be eligible for assignment, a former judge must meet the qualifications listed in Gov't Code §74.055(c). A judge's status as a former judge is fixed when the judge leaves office. ***Mitchell Energy***, 943 S.W.2d at 439.

4. Senior judge. A "senior judge" is a retiree who has elected to be a judicial officer. Gov't Code §74.041(7); *see id.* §§74.054(a)(2), 75.001.

§3.3 Notice of assignment. If time permits, and if it is practical, the presiding judge of the administrative region must give the parties notice of the assignment of a visiting judge. Gov't Code §74.053(a)(2); ***In re Canales***, 52 S.W.3d 698, 701 (Tex.2001); ***Tivoli Corp. v. Jewelers Mut. Ins. Co.***, 932 S.W.2d 704, 709 (Tex.App.—San Antonio 1996, writ denied). Notice of assignment may be given by e-mail. Gov't Code §74.053(f).

§3.4 Deadline to object. An objection to an assigned judge must be filed before the date of the first hearing (including pretrial hearings) or trial over which the assigned judge is to preside, or at least seven days after receiving actual notice of the assignment, whichever is earlier. Gov't Code §74.053(c); ***In re Approximately $17,239.00***, ___ S.W.3d ___ (Tex.App.—Houston [14th Dist.] 2003, orig. proceeding) (No. 14-03-01177-CV; 10-24-03). The presiding judge may extend the deadline for good cause on a party's written motion. Gov't Code §74.053(c). An objection to an assignment may be filed by e-mail. *Id.* §74.053(f). If an assigned judge who heard part of the case is reassigned to hear an additional part of the case by a new order of assignment, the reassignment does not permit the parties to make another objection. ***Canales***, 52 S.W.3d at 704. The requirement in TRCP 18a(a) that the objection must be filed at least ten days before the hearing or trial does not apply to objections to assigned judges. *See* Gov't Code §74.053(c); TRCP 18a(e).

CAUTION

The objection must be the first matter presented to the assigned judge for a ruling. ***Chandler****, 991 S.W.2d at 383; see* ***Approximately $17,239.00****, ___ S.W.3d at ___. If the objection is filed after the assigned judge makes a ruling, even on a pretrial motion submitted without a hearing, the objection is too late.* ***Perkins v. Groff****, 936 S.W.2d 661, 666-67 (Tex.App.—Dallas 1996, writ denied);* ***Tivoli****, 932 S.W.2d at 709. An objection after ordinary docket call is timely.* ***Lee v. Bachus****, 900 S.W.2d 390, 392 (Tex.App.—Texarkana 1995, orig. proceeding).*

---

§3.5 Challenges.

1. Single challenge. Each party is entitled to make one challenge in a case to an assigned judge who is a retired, former, or senior judge appointed under Gov't Code §74.054. *See* Gov't Code §74.053(b); *see, e.g.*, ***In re Perritt***, 992 S.W.2d 444, 446 n.2 (Tex.1999) (former judge); ***Flores v. Banner***, 932 S.W.2d 500, 501 (Tex.1996) (retired judge). For definitions of retired, former, and senior judges, see §§3.2.2-3.2.4, above. Under Gov't Code §74.053, "party" includes multiple parties aligned in a case as determined by the presiding judge. Gov't Code §74.053(g).

2. Multiple challenges. An assigned judge who was defeated in the last primary or general election for which the judge was seeking re-election cannot sit in a case if either party objects. Gov't Code §74.053(d).

3. Active judge—no challenge. An active judge assigned under Gov't Code chapter 74 is not subject to a §74.053 objection. Gov't Code §74.053(e).

PRACTICE TIP

If the judge of the court discusses possible appointments for an assigned judge, and the parties voice an objection to one of the judges mentioned, the oral objection does not count as a formal objection to an assigned judge. ***Kellogg v. Martin****, 810 S.W.2d 302, 304-05 (Tex.App.—Texarkana 1991, orig. proceeding).*

§3.6 Automatic removal. A proper and timely objection to an assigned judge is a peremptory objection; the removal is mandatory and automatic. Gov't Code §74.053(b); ***Canales***, 52 S.W.3d at 701; ***In re Union Pac. Res. Co.***, 969 S.W.2d 427, 428 (Tex.1998); ***Flores***, 932 S.W.2d at 501.

§3.7 How to object to an assigned judge.

1. In writing. The objection must be in writing. ***Wolfe v. Wolfe***, 918 S.W.2d 533, 541 (Tex.App.—El Paso 1996, writ denied). Gov't Code §74.053(b) does not state an objection must be in writing, but the use of the words "files" presupposes it will be. ***Kellogg***, 810 S.W.2d at 305. If a party learns at docket call that a visiting judge was assigned to the case, an oral objection at the hearing is not enough. ***Money v. Jones***, 766 S.W.2d 307, 308 (Tex.App.—Dallas 1989, writ denied). The party must file a written objection to an assigned judge, even if it is a handwritten one. ***Morris v. Short***, 902 S.W.2d 566, 569 (Tex.App.—Houston [1st Dist.] 1995, writ denied).

2. Identify challenged judge. The objection should identify the assigned judge by name. *See* ***Texas Empl. Comm'n v. Alvarez***, 915 S.W.2d 161, 164 (Tex.App.—Corpus Christi 1996, orig. proceeding) (because TEC did not name judge in objection, and did not reurge objection when case was reset, judge was unaware of objection). However, if the identity of the challenged judge can be determined from the objection, the lack of a name is not critical. *See* ***Flores***, 932 S.W.2d at 501-02 (because Flores did not know the name of the judge to be assigned, she filed an objection to "any" assigned judge; objection was effective).

3. Grounds.

(1) Standard objection. An objection under Gov't Code §74.053 to an assigned judge should state that the party objects to the assignment of the judge. Because a §74.053 objection depends on the judge's status, the judge's status should be identified in the objection. It is not necessary to provide a reason for the objection. ***Perritt***, 992 S.W.2d at 446.

(2) Objections to procedural errors in assignment. A party must object to any procedural errors in the assignment or waive the error. *See, e.g.*, ***In re General Elec. Capital Corp.***, 63 S.W.3d 568, 572 (Tex. App.—El Paso 2001, orig. proceeding) (waived objection that assigned judge did not take required oath); ***Lopez v. State***, 57 S.W.3d 625, 629 (Tex.App.—Corpus Christi 2001, pet. ref'd) (waived objection that record did not contain a copy of order of assignment).

(3) Recusal or disqualification challenges. When a party has exhausted its objections to assigned judges, the party can assert any recusal or disqualification challenges that are available. See §4, below.

4. Identify number of challenges. Although not required by statute, the party should state the number of objections to other assigned judges, if any, that it has made in the same case. *See* ***Amateur Athletic Found. v. Hoffman***, 893 S.W.2d 602, 604 (Tex.App.—Dallas 1994, orig. proceeding) (Whittington, J., dissenting).

5. Verification.

(1) Standard objection. There is no statutory requirement that a standard objection to an assigned judge be verified. ***O'Connor v. Lykos***, 960 S.W.2d 96, 99 (Tex.App.—Houston [1st Dist.] 1997, orig. proceeding). Verification for the standard objection is unnecessary because a party need not assert any facts in an objection to an assee signed judge. *Id.* However, one court of appeals has held the objection must be verified. *See* ***Hawkins v. Volkmann***, 898 S.W.2d 334, 343-44 (Tex.App.—San Antonio 1994, writ denied) (court overruled unverified challenge to assigned judge). Until the issue is resolved by the Supreme Court, parties should verify objections to assigned judges.

(2) Other challenges. If facts are necessary to support other challenges to the assigned judge (see §3.7.3(2), above), the motion should be verified. See §4.1.2, below.

§3.8 No hearing. When a party files a timely objection under Gov't Code §74.053(b) to an assigned judge, no hearing is necessary because the removal is automatic. The only fact issue that could arise is whether the objection was timely, and for that reason, the judge and the parties should make a record. If the assigned judge is challenged for other reasons (see §3.7.3(2), above), a hearing is necessary. See "Hearing before another judge," §4.7, p. 239.

§3.9 Termination of assignment. The term for an assignment depends on the language used in the order of assignment. ***In re Republic Parking Sys.***, 60 S.W.3d 877, 879 (Tex.App.—Houston [14th Dist.] 2001, orig. proceeding). Generally, judges are assigned either for a period of time or for a particular case. *Id.* Typical orders of assignment contain the language that the assignment is to continue until the assigned judge completes the trial of any case begun during the period of assignment, passes on motions for new trial, and completes all other matters growing out of any cause heard by the assigned judge. *See* ***Davis v. Crist Indus.***, 98 S.W.3d 338, 341 (Tex.App.—Fort Worth 2003, pet. denied). The following is a representative sample of cases determining when an assignment ends: • Power expires on the date set in the order, if the judge does not begin the trial by that date. ***Republic Parking Sys.***, 60 S.W.3d at 880. • Power expires when the court loses plenary power over the case. ***Ex parte Eastland***, 811 S.W.2d 571, 572 (Tex.1991). • Power expires when the appeal is perfected. ***Starnes v. Chapman***, 793 S.W.2d 104, 106 (Tex.App.—Dallas 1990, orig. proceeding). • Power expires when the assigned judge grants a new trial. ***Lykos***, 960 S.W.2d at 98. • Power extends to postjudgment discovery after the trial court loses plenary power, unless limited by language in the assignment. ***O'Connor v. Smith***, 815 S.W.2d 338, 346 (Tex.App.—Houston [1st Dist.] 1991, orig. proceeding).

§4. MOTION TO RECUSE OR DISQUALIFY

§4.1 The motion to recuse or disqualify.

1. Written.

(1) Motion to recuse. A motion to recuse must be in writing. TRCP 18a(a); *cf.* ***Kellogg v. Martin***, 810 S.W.2d 302, 304-05 (Tex.App.—Texarkana 1991, orig. proceeding) (objection to assigned judge under Gov't Code §74.053 must be in writing).

(2) Motion to disqualify. A motion to disqualify should be in writing. Although a party may make an oral motion to disqualify, it should be followed by a written motion to preserve error. See ***O'Connor's Texas Civil Appeals***, "Standard requirements," ch. 13-J, §5.1.1, p. 113 (2002-03).

2. Verified. A motion to recuse must be verified. TRCP 18a(a); *see* ***McElwee v. McElwee***, 911 S.W.2d 182, 186 (Tex.App.—Houston [1st Dist.] 1995, writ denied) (motion must state particular grounds for recusal).

3. Facts. A motion to recuse or disqualify must state facts that support the challenge. TRCP 18a(a). Facts may be stated on information and belief if the grounds that support the belief are specifically stated. *Id.*

4. Grounds. The grounds for recusal or disqualification are included in a companion to this book, ***O'Connor's Texas Civil Appeals*** (2002-03), to conserve space in this book and avoid duplication and possible inconsistencies with the same sections in that book. For the forms for recusal and disqualification see ***O'Connor's***, FORMS 5C:03-04.

(1) Recusal. A motion to recuse must identify the specific legal grounds for recusal. TRCP 18a(a). For the grounds for recusal, see ***O'Connor's Texas Civil Appeals***, "Grounds for Recusal," ch. 13-J, §4, p. 109.

(2) Disqualification. For the grounds for disqualification, see ***O'Connor's Texas Civil Appeals***, "Grounds for Disqualification," ch. 13-J, §3, p. 104.

5. Defects in motion. Even if a motion to recuse is procedurally defective, it should still be referred to another judge for that judge to make the determination. ***Johnson v. Pumjani***, 56 S.W.3d 670, 672 (Tex.App.—Houston [14th Dist.] 2001, no pet.) *But see* ***Barron v. State Att'y Gen.***, 108 S.W.3d 379, 382 (Tex.App.—Tyler 2003, no pet.) (challenged judge may make initial decision of whether motion conforms with TRCP 18a).

§4.2 Notice to other parties. Upon filing the motion, the party must send the other parties copies of the motion with notice that the movant expects the motion to be presented to the judge within three days of filing. TRCP 18a(b).

§4.3 Deadline to file. A motion to recuse must be filed at least ten days before the date set for the trial or other hearing. TRCP 18a(a); ***Waste Water, Inc. v. Alpha Finishing & Dev. Corp.***, 874 S.W.2d 940, 944 (Tex. App.—Houston [14th Dist.] 1994, no writ); *see also* ***CNA Ins. Co. v. Scheffey***, 828 S.W.2d 785, 793 (Tex.App.—Texarkana 1992, writ denied) (10 days before hearing on motion for new trial). There are three instances in which a motion to recuse or disqualify may be filed after the ten-day deadline in TRCP 18a(a).

1. Late motion to recuse. A movant can file a motion to recuse after the ten-day deadline only if the movant learns of the reason for recusal after that deadline and files the motion immediately after learning of the reason. ***Keene Corp. v. Rogers***, 863 S.W.2d 168, 172 (Tex.App.—Texarkana 1993, no writ); *see also* ***Sun Expl. & Prod. Co. v. Jackson***, 783 S.W.2d 202, 206 (Tex.1989) (Spears, J., concurring) (petitioner should be allowed to present recusal motion on remand when petitioner was unaware of judge's disability to hear case until after trial); ***Stafford v. State***, 948 S.W.2d 921, 925 n.6 (Tex.App.—Texarkana 1997, pet. ref'd) (criminal case; TRCP 18a does not contemplate situation where party could not know of basis for recusal until deadline had passed).

2. Late motion to disqualify. A motion to disqualify based on a constitutional ground can be presented at any time; the motion is not limited by the ten-day deadline. *See* ***Buckholts ISD v. Glaser***, 632 S.W.2d 146, 148 (Tex.1982); ***Spigener v. Wallis***, 80 S.W.3d 174, 180 (Tex.App.—Waco 2002, no pet.).

3. After remand. When a case is reversed for retrial, the parties may make a motion to recuse after remand. *See* ***Winfield v. Daggett***, 846 S.W.2d 920, 922 (Tex.App.—Houston [1st Dist.] 1993, orig. proceeding) (when new trial is granted, case stands on the docket as if it had not been tried).

§4.4 Waiver.

1. By agreement. The parties may waive a ground for recusal after it is fully disclosed on the record. TRCP 18b(5). Parties cannot waive a constitutional ground for disqualification. *See* ***Buckholts ISD***, 632 S.W.2d at 148; ***Jennings v. Garner***, 721 S.W.2d 445, 446 (Tex.App.—Tyler 1986, no writ).

2. By default. Noncompliance with the procedural requirements of TRCP 18a results in waiver of recusal. ***Spigener***, 80 S.W.3d at 180; ***Hall v. Treon***, 39 S.W.3d 722, 723 (Tex.App.—Beaumont 2001, no pet.); *see, e.g.*, ***Parker v. Parker***, ___ S.W.3d ___ (Tex.App.—Fort Worth 2003, n.p.h.) (No. 2-02-312-CV; 8-14-03) (parties waived recusal by not filing written motion after judge retracted oral recusal); ***Gill v. TDCJ***, 3 S.W.3d 576, 579 (Tex. App.—Houston [1st Dist.] 1999, no pet.) (inmate's objection not verified by affidavit or unsworn declaration).

§4.5 Response by other party. The other party in the suit may file an opposing or concurring statement to the motion at any time before the motion is heard. TRCP 18a(b). If a motion to recuse or disqualify was brought solely for the purpose of delay, the other party may ask for sanctions under TRCP 215.2(b). See "Sanctions," §4.8.3, below.

§4.6 Response by challenged judge. The challenged judge should not voluntarily participate in the recusal hearing or a mandamus proceeding regarding the recusal. Active participation in the recusal proceedings can lead to the judge's recusal. ***Blanchard v. Krueger***, 916 S.W.2d 15, 19 n.9 (Tex.App.—Houston [1st Dist.] 1995, orig. proceeding).

1. Two options. When a motion to disqualify or recuse is filed, the trial judge has only two options—grant the motion or refer the motion for a hearing before another judge. ***Johnson***, 56 S.W.3d at 672.

(1) The judge grants motion. When a challenged judge grants a motion to recuse or disqualify, she must sign an order to that effect and request that the presiding judge of the administrative judicial district assign another judge to the case. TRCP 18a(c); *see* Gov't Code §74.059(c)(3); ***McLeod v. Harris***, 582 S.W.2d 772, 774 (Tex.1979) (interpreting predecessor to Gov't Code §74.059(c)(3)); ***In re Rio Grande Valley Gas Co.***, 987 S.W.2d 167, 179 (Tex.App.—Corpus Christi 1999, orig. proceeding).

(2) The judge refuses to recuse – the referral. When a challenged judge denies a motion to recuse or disqualify, she must ask the presiding judge of the administrative judicial district to assign another judge to hear the motion. TRCP 18a(d); ***In re Perritt***, 992 S.W.2d 444, 447 (Tex.1999); ***McLeod***, 582 S.W.2d at 775; ***Winfield***, 846 S.W.2d at 922; *see* Gov't Code §74.059(c)(3). The trial judge cannot deny the motion without referring the motion to the presiding judge for a hearing. ***Winfield***, 846 S.W.2d at 922; *see* ***Perritt***, 992 S.W.2d at 447. The challenged judge must send the presiding judge the order of referral, the motion, and all opposing and concurring statements. TRCP 18a(d).

2. Prohibited actions.

(1) Ignore or overrule. The judge does not have the option to ignore the motion or overrule it and proceed to trial. *See* ***Johnson***, 56 S.W.3d at 672; ***Rio Grande Valley***, 987 S.W.2d at 178.

(2) Transfer. Once a motion to recuse has been filed, the challenged judge cannot transfer the case to another district court to avoid recusal. The transfer of a case after the filing of a motion to recuse must comply with local rules governing transfers. *See, e.g.*, ***Rio Grande Valley***, 987 S.W.2d at 179-80 (transfer of case by district judge of another court to that judge's court was void because not authorized by local rules). If the local rules give the administrative judge the authority to transfer a case after a recusal motion, the case may be transferred. *See, e.g.*, ***In re PG&E Reata Energy***, 4 S.W.3d 897, 901 (Tex.App.—Corpus Christi 1999, orig. proceeding.) (administrative judge had authority under local rule to transfer case despite pending recusal motion).

(3) Orders pending resolution. Once challenged, a judge cannot take any action in the case until the motion to disqualify or recuse is resolved. TRCP 18a(c), (d). Any order signed by the challenged judge while the motion is pending is void. ***Rio Grande Valley***, 987 S.W.2d at 179; ***Brosseau v. Ranzau***, 911 S.W.2d 890, 893 (Tex.App.—Beaumont 1995, no writ). There is one exception—a judge may sign an order while the motion for recusal is pending if the judge identifies "good cause" in the order. TRCP 18a(d); ***Carson v. McAdams***, 908 S.W.2d 228, 228-29 (Tex.App.—Houston [1st Dist.] 1993, orig. proceeding).

§4.7 Hearing before another judge. The party that filed the motion to recuse or disqualify is entitled to a hearing on the motion. Gov't Code §74.059(c)(3); TRCP 18a(d); ***Rio Grande Valley***, 987 S.W.2d at 179; ***Winfield***, 846 S.W.2d at 922; *see also* TRCP 18a(f) (provides appellate review of denied motion after final judgment). The hearing affords the movant an opportunity to develop a record to support its motion. ***Rio Grande Valley***, 987 S.W.2d at 179; ***Winfield***, 846 S.W.2d at 922. See "Hearing requested," ch. 1-E, §4.2.2, p. 28.

1. Notice of hearing. All parties must receive notice of the hearing on a motion to recuse or disqualify. TRCP 18a(d).

2. Designated judge. Once the trial judge declines to recuse or disqualify herself, the presiding judge of the administrative judicial district must immediately set the motion for a hearing before herself or another judge she designates. TRCP 18a(d); ***CNA Ins. Co. v. Scheffey***, 828 S.W.2d 785, 793 (Tex.App.—Texarkana 1992, writ denied).

3. Objection to designated judge. Either party may file an objection to the judge who is assigned to hear the motion to recuse or disqualify. Gov't Code §74.053(b); ***Perritt***, 992 S.W.2d at 446; *see* ***In re Flores***, 53 S.W.3d 428, 431 (Tex.App.—San Antonio 2001, orig. proceeding). See "Objection to Assigned Judge," §3, p. 234.

4. Burden of proof. The burden of proof at the hearing on the motion to recuse or disqualify is on the movant, who must be prepared to present sworn evidence. A judge is presumed to be qualified until the contrary is shown. ***Sparkman v. Peoples Nat'l Bank***, 553 S.W.2d 680, 681 (Tex.App.—Waco 1977, writ ref'd n.r.e.).

§4.8 Order on the motion to recuse or disqualify.

1. Denying the motion. If the judge assigned to hear the motion to recuse or disqualify denies it, the case will be returned to the challenged judge for a trial on the merits. *See* TRCP 18a(f).

2. Granting the motion. If the judge assigned to hear the motion to recuse or disqualify grants the motion, the presiding judge must appoint another judge to hear the case on the merits. ***District Judges of Collin Cty. v. Commissioner's Ct. of Collin Cty.***, 677 S.W.2d 743, 745 (Tex.App.—Dallas 1984, writ ref'd n.r.e.). The phrase "another judge" in TRCP 18a(f) does not exclude the judge assigned to hear the motion to recuse or disqualify. ***District Judges***, 677 S.W.2d at 745.

NOTE

The Texas Constitution provides that if a district court judge is disqualified on constitutional grounds, the parties may, by consent, appoint a proper person to try the case. If they are unable to do so, a competent person may be appointed to try the case in the same county where it is pending. Tex. Const. art. 5, §11.

3. Sanctions. If a motion to recuse was brought solely for the purpose of delay, the judge may impose any sanctions authorized by TRCP 215.2(b). TRCP 18a(h); ***Sommers v. Concepcion***, 20 S.W.3d 27, 44-45 (Tex. App.—Houston [14th Dist.] 2000, pet. denied); ***Palais Royal, Inc. v. Partida***, 916 S.W.2d 650, 654 (Tex.App.—Corpus Christi 1996, orig. proceeding); ***Enterprise-Laredo Assocs. v. Hachar's, Inc.***, 839 S.W.2d 822, 841 (Tex.App.—San Antonio 1992), *writ denied*, 843 S.W.2d 476 (Tex.1992); *see also* ***Waddell v. Huckabee***, 807 S.W.2d 455, 459 (Tex.App.—Houston [1st Dist.] 1991, orig. proceeding) (issue regarding sanctions should be considered on appeal, not by mandamus).

§5. TERTIARY MOTION TO RECUSE OR DISQUALIFY

§5.1 Definition. A tertiary motion to recuse is a party's third or later motion filed in the same case to recuse or disqualify a judge in a district court, statutory probate court, or statutory county court. CPRC §30.016(a).

§5.2 Differences in procedure. With the exceptions noted below, the procedure for a tertiary motion to recuse or disqualify a judge is the same as in other motions to recuse or disqualify. *Id.* §30.016(b).

1. Judge declines to recuse. When a judge declines to recuse after a tertiary motion, the judge shall continue to (1) preside over the case, (2) sign orders in the case, and (3) move the case to final disposition as though a motion had not been filed. *Id.* §30.016(b).

2. Attorney fees & costs. If the judge hearing the tertiary motion denies it, attorney fees and costs shall be awarded to the party opposing the motion. *Id.* §30.016(c). Both the party making the motion and its attorney are jointly and severally liable for the attorney fees and costs. *Id.* The fees and costs must be paid within 30 days of the date the order is rendered, unless the order is superseded. *Id.*

3. Review. The denial of a tertiary recusal motion is reviewable only on appeal from a final judgment. *Id.* §30.016(d).

4. If reversed. If a tertiary motion ultimately is sustained, the new judge for the case shall vacate all orders signed by the sitting judge during the pendency of the motion. *Id.* §30.016(e).

§6. VOLUNTARY RECUSAL

A judge should voluntarily recuse herself in any proceeding in which her impartiality might reasonably be questioned. TRCP 18b(2)(a); ***Dunn v. County of Dallas***, 794 S.W.2d 560, 562 (Tex.App.—Dallas 1990, no writ); *see also* ***Sao Paulo State v. American Tobacco Co.***, 535 U.S. 229, 230, 122 S.Ct. 1290, 1291 (2002) (interpreting 28 U.S.C. 455(a)). A judge should observe the following procedure.

§6.1 Timely. The judge should recuse herself before the trial starts. If the judge recuses herself on a discretionary ground after the trial starts, the order of recusal is void. ***Logic Sci., Inc. v. Smith***, 798 S.W.2d 394, 395 (Tex. App.—Houston [1st Dist.] 1990, orig. proceeding). The judge may recuse herself on a constitutional or other mandatory ground even after the trial starts. *See* ***Buckholts ISD v. Glaser***, 632 S.W.2d 146, 148 (Tex.1982) (constitutional disqualification can be raised at any point in the proceeding).

§6.2 Order. The judge must sign an order of recusal. *See* ***Dunn***, 794 S.W.2d at 562 (letter of recusal satisfied the requirement of a written, signed order of recusal).

§6.3 Referral. When a judge voluntarily recuses herself, the judge must refer the case to the presiding judge of the administrative district to assign another judge to hear the case. ***Dunn***, 794 S.W.2d at 562.

§6.4 Other orders. Except for good cause stated in an order, a judge who voluntarily recuses herself cannot enter any order in the case other than the order of recusal. Thus, a judge cannot render a summary judgment after recusing herself. ***Dunn***, 794 S.W.2d at 563.

§7. REVIEW

§7.1 Appeal. In most cases, an appeal is an adequate remedy to challenge an erroneous ruling on a motion to recuse. ***In re Union Pac. Res. Co.***, 969 S.W.2d 427, 428-29 (Tex.1998). A party can appeal an order refusing the motion to recuse; however, a party cannot appeal an order granting the motion to recuse. TRCP 18a(f); ***District Judges***, 677 S.W.2d at 745.

1. The record. For a proper review of the trial court's decision, the party must present the appellate court with a record of the motion and proceedings. ***Ceballos v. El Paso Health Care Sys.***, 881 S.W.2d 439, 445 (Tex.App.—El Paso 1994, writ denied).

2. Standard of review. The standard of review for an order denying a motion to recuse is abuse of discretion. TRCP 18a(f); ***In re M.C.M.***, 57 S.W.3d 27, 33 (Tex.App.—Houston [1st Dist.] 2001, pet. denied); ***Chandler v. Chandler***, 991 S.W.2d 367, 385 (Tex.App.—El Paso 1999, pet. denied).

3. Effect of erroneous denial. When a case is reversed because of an erroneous ruling denying a motion to disqualify or recuse or an objection to the trial judge, the issue on appeal is the status of the rulings the judge made after the motion or objection was denied.

(1) Disqualification. All orders of a judge who was constitutionally disqualified are void. ***Union Pac. Res.***, 969 S.W.2d at 428; ***Buckholts ISD***, 632 S.W.2d at 148.

(2) **Recusal.** The orders of judge who should have been recused as a result of a valid motion to recuse are not void. ***Union Pac. Res.***, 969 S.W.2d at 428. Even though a judgment rendered by a judge subject to a valid motion for recusal may be reversed on appeal, it is not fundamental error. ***Union Pac. Res.***, 969 S.W.2d at 428.

(3) **Objection to assigned judge.** The orders of an assigned judge who should have been removed after an objection under Gov't Code §74.053 are void. ***In re Canales***, 52 S.W.3d 698, 701 (Tex.2001); ***Dunn v. Street***, 938 S.W.2d 33, 34-35 (Tex.1997); ***Flores v. Banner***, 932 S.W.2d 500, 501 (Tex.1996); ***In re Flores***, 53 S.W.3d 428, 430 (Tex.App.—San Antonio 2001, orig. proceeding).

§7.2 Mandamus. Mandamus is appropriate when a trial judge refuses to sustain a proper motion to disqualify or a timely challenge to an assigned judge. ***Union Pac. Res.***, 969 S.W.2d at 428.

D. MOTION FOR CONTINUANCE

§1. GENERAL

§1.1 Rules. TRCP 247, 251-254, 330(d).

§1.2 Purpose. A motion for continuance is a request to postpone or delay a case that has been set for trial. By comparison, a motion to extend is a request for more time to file a document. TRCP 5. See "Motion to extend," ch. 1-C, §9.1, p. 18.

§1.3 Forms. *O'Connor's Texas Civil Forms*, FORMS 5D.

§2. MOTION

If a motion for continuance does not comply with the rules, the appellate court will presume the trial court did not abuse its discretion in denying the motion. ***Villegas v. Carter***, 711 S.W.2d 624, 626 (Tex.1986); *see* TRCP 251-254.

§2.1 Written. A motion for continuance must be in writing. ***Green v. Texas Dept. of Protective & Reg. Servs.***, 25 S.W.3d 213, 218 (Tex.App.—El Paso 2000, no pet.); ***Favaloro v. Commission for Lawyer Discipline***, 13 S.W.3d 831, 838 (Tex.App.—Dallas 2000, no pet.). An oral request for a continuance does not preserve error. ***Phifer v. Nacogdoches Cty. Cent. Appr. Dist.***, 45 S.W.3d 159, 173 (Tex.App.—Tyler 2000, pet. denied). In an emergency, a handwritten motion is sufficient. *See* ***Higginbotham v. Collateral Protection***, 859 S.W.2d 487, 490 (Tex.App.—Houston [1st Dist.] 1993, writ denied).

PRACTICE TIP

If a party made only an oral motion for continuance during trial, on appeal, the party should attempt to circumvent the requirement for a written and verified motion by arguing that the attorney's unsworn statement should be considered as sworn evidence because the other party did not object. See ***Banda v. Garcia****, 955 S.W.2d 270, 272 (Tex.1997).*

§2.2 Specific. The motion must state the specific facts supporting the motion. ***Blake v. Lewis***, 886 S.W.2d 404, 409 (Tex.App.—Houston [1st Dist.] 1994, no writ). General allegations (*e.g.*, that the attorney is busy with personal matters and other cases or that the attorney has not had time to prepare for the trial or hearing) are not enough to support a motion. *Id.*; ***Cronen v. Nix***, 611 S.W.2d 651, 653 (Tex.App.—Houston [1st Dist.] 1980, writ ref'd n.r.e.).

§2.3 Affidavits & verification. The facts in the motion must be verified or supported by an affidavit. TRCP 251, 252; ***Taherzadeh v. Ghaleh-Assadi***, 108 S.W.3d 927, 928 (Tex.App.—Dallas 2003, pet. denied); ***Hawthorne v. Guenther***, 917 S.W.2d 924, 929 (Tex.App.—Beaumont 1996, writ denied). *But see* ***Villegas***, 711 S.W.2d at 626 (it was unreasonable to require lay litigant, whose attorney withdrew two days before trial, to file sworn proof). If the motion is not verified or supported by affidavit, the appellate courts presume the trial court did not abuse its discretion in denying the motion. ***Waste Water, Inc. v. Alpha Finishing & Dev. Corp.***, 874 S.W.2d 940, 942 (Tex.App.—Houston [14th Dist.] 1994, no writ). See "Verification & affidavits," ch. 1-B, §4.14, p. 7; ***O'Connor's*** FORM 5D:04.

§2.4 Request hearing. As a general rule, a hearing is not required on a motion for continuance. Most motions for continuance are resolved on affidavits. However, a movant may want to request a hearing to bring live witnesses to support the allegations in the motion.

§3. DEADLINE

A motion for continuance may be filed any time after the defendant files an answer. TRCP 251.

§3.1 Before announcement of ready. A party should file a continuance before making an unconditional announcement of ready. ***Reyna v. Reyna***, 738 S.W.2d 772, 775 (Tex.App.—Austin 1987, no writ); *see* ***E.C. ex rel. Gonzales v. Graydon***, 28 S.W.3d 825, 828 (Tex.App.—Corpus Christi 2000, no pet.) (announcement of ready waived motion for continuance).

§3.2 During trial. A party may file a written motion for continuance during trial if an unforeseeable emergency arises through no fault of that party. ***Butcher v. Tinkle***, 183 S.W.2d 227, 230 (Tex.App.—Beaumont 1944, writ ref'd). A motion for continuance made during trial is extremely hard to get, and if the trial court denies the motion, it is difficult to reverse on appeal.

§4. RESPONSE

If the nonmovant disagrees with the request for continuance, it should file a response, and when necessary attach affidavits to controvert the allegations in the motion for continuance. See ***O'Connor's*** FORM 5D:03. Uncontroverted statements in a sworn motion for continuance must be accepted as true. See §5.3, below.

§5. RULING

§5.1 Obtain a ruling. To preserve error when the trial court refuses to grant a motion for continuance, the party should ask the trial court to make a ruling, either on the record in open court or by a written order. ***Direkly v. ARA Devcon, Inc.***, 866 S.W.2d 652, 656 (Tex.App.—Houston [1st Dist.] 1993, writ dism'd). See "Record of Ruling," ch. 1-G, §3, p. 34. When a motion for continuance is presented in open court, an oral ruling on the record is sufficient to preserve error. See "Express ruling," ch. 1-G, §2.2.1, p. 33. If the record does not contain an express ruling on the motion but shows the court took some other action that implicitly overruled the motion, error is preserved. *See* TRAP 33.1(a)(2)(A). See "Implicit ruling," ch. 1-G, §2.2.2, p. 33.

§5.2 Court's discretion. The trial court may grant a motion for continuance if the motion is supported by an affidavit and states sufficient cause. TRCP 247, 251, 252. The trial court's ruling on a motion for continuance is within its discretion. ***State v. Wood Oil Distrib.***, 751 S.W.2d 863, 865 (Tex.1988); ***Villegas***, 711 S.W.2d at 626.

§5.3 Uncontested motion. If a motion for continuance is in substantial compliance with the rule, is properly verified, and is not controverted, the trial court must accept the statements in the motion as true. ***Verkin v. Southwest Ctr. One, Ltd.***, 784 S.W.2d 92, 94 (Tex.App.—Houston [1st Dist.] 1989, writ denied); ***Garza v. Serrato***, 699 S.W.2d 275, 281 (Tex.App.—San Antonio 1985, writ ref'd n.r.e.). The trial court has no discretion to reject uncontroverted facts in a sworn motion for continuance. ***Roob v. Von Beregshasy***, 866 S.W.2d 765, 766 (Tex.App.—Houston [1st Dist.] 1993, writ denied); ***Verkin***, 784 S.W.2d at 96.

§6. CONTINUANCE ON AGREED MOTION

The court should respect agreements to postpone or continue a case unless the delay would unreasonably interfere with other business of the court. TRCP 330(d). The parties should prepare a written agreement to pass or continue, have the attorneys for all parties sign it, and file it with the court on or before docket call. TRCP 11, 247, 251. See "Agreements Between Lawyers – Rule 11," ch. 1-H, §9, p. 44. A party may orally announce the agreement to pass at docket call, but it should also file a written agreement. An agreement to pass, postpone, or continue a case pending in a district court is not binding on the court when the case has been reached for trial on two or more occasions. TRCP 330(d). See *O'Connor's* FORM 5D:02, §C, ¶¶9-10.

§7. CONTINUANCE BASED ON INSUFFICIENT NOTICE OF TRIAL

§7.1 Notice of trial. The trial court must give the parties reasonable notice of the first trial setting of "not less than 45 days." TRCP 245; ***Smith v. Lippmann***, 826 S.W.2d 137, 138 n.1 (Tex.1992). If the trial court does not give the party reasonable notice of a trial setting, it is a violation of due process. ***Hardin v. Hardin***, 932 S.W.2d 566, 567 (Tex.App.—Tyler 1995, no writ). The language of TRCP 245 is mandatory. *Id.*

§7.2 The motion. When a party seeks a continuance because of insufficient notice of trial, the motion must state (1) the party received less than 45 days' notice of trial, (2) the notice given was not reasonable, (3) the notice was not adequate to permit the party to prepare for trial, (4) the lack of reasonable notice violated the party's right of due process, and (5) the lack of 45 days' notice violated TRCP 245. ***Hardin***, 932 S.W.2d at 567. The allegations must be supported by sworn proof. TRCP 251. See "Affidavits & verification," §2.3, p. 242. See *O'Connor's* FORM 5D:02, §C, ¶¶11-14.

§8. CONTINUANCE FOR ADDITIONAL DISCOVERY

When a party requests additional time for discovery, it must fulfill the requirements of TRCP 252 under oath. ***Verkin***, 784 S.W.2d at 94. See *O'Connor's* FORM 5D:01.

PRACTICE TIP

All cases have a discovery control plan that sets limits for the discovery period, interrogatories, and depositions. See "Discovery Control Plans," ch. 6-A, §7, p. 318. TRCP 190 permits the court to extend the time for discovery. TRCP 190.5. See "Modification of discovery periods," ch. 6-A, §6.2, p. 318. Thus, before you file a motion for continuance for additional discovery, check whether you also need to file a motion to modify the discovery control plan. See "Modifying Discovery Procedures & Limitations," ch. 6-A, §5, p. 316.

---

§8.1 Description of necessary evidence. The motion must identify (1) the specific discovery necessary, (2) the person from whom the discovery is sought, and (3) the type of information sought. ***Gabaldon v. G.M. Corp.***, 876 S.W.2d 367, 370 (Tex.App.—El Paso 1993, no writ); *see, e.g.*, ***Martinez v. Flores***, 865 S.W.2d 194, 197 (Tex.App.—Corpus Christi 1993, writ denied) (request for more time "to complete discovery" was not sufficient). Although not required, a party should attach outstanding discovery requests as exhibits to the motion for continuance. *See* ***Verkin***, 784 S.W.2d at 96 (not required to attach copies of discovery requests); *see, e.g.*, ***Gabaldon***, 876 S.W.2d at 370 (among other problems, no discovery requests attached).

1. Procedure for discovery. The motion should describe the procedure the party intends to utilize to secure discovery, and the person from whom the discovery will be sought. For example, the motion should state that the party intends to depose a certain person on a certain date.

(1) Deposition witness. If a continuance is sought to depose a witness, the motion must include the following information: (1) the witness's name and address (street, county, and state of residence); and (2) a description of the testimony the witness will probably give and what the party expects the testimony to prove. TRCP 252.

(2) Discovery period. The motion should state whether the discovery period has expired.

2. Substance of discovery. The motion should state that at the deposition of a witness, the party intends to seek discovery of certain evidence, and the motion should describe that evidence.

§8.2 Materiality. The motion must state that the testimony it seeks is material and show why it is material. TRCP 252; ***J.E.M. v. Fidelity & Cas. Co.***, 928 S.W.2d 668, 676 (Tex.App.—Houston [1st Dist.] 1996, no writ); *see,* *e.g.*, ***Celotex Corp. v. Gracy Meadow Owners Ass'n***, 847 S.W.2d 384, 388 (Tex.App.—Austin 1993, writ denied) (appellate court decided evidence was immaterial). The party must show its case will be injured if it is not permitted to obtain the evidence. ***Commercial Stand. Ins. Co. v. Merit Clothing Co.***, 377 S.W.2d 179, 181 (Tex.1964); *see, e.g.*, ***Garza v. Serrato***, 699 S.W.2d 275, 281 (Tex.App.—San Antonio 1985, writ ref'd n.r.e.) (court should have granted continuance to prepare rebuttal evidence when P's doctor changed diagnosis 2 days before trial).

§8.3 Diligence. The party must present affidavit evidence showing due diligence. ***Risner v. McDonald's Corp.***, 18 S.W.3d 903, 909 (Tex.App.—Beaumont 2000, pet. denied); ***Rhima v. White***, 829 S.W.2d 909, 912 (Tex. App.—Fort Worth 1992, writ denied). Conclusory statements about diligence do not satisfy the requirements of TRCP 252. ***Gregg v. Cecil***, 844 S.W.2d 851, 853 (Tex.App.—Beaumont 1992, no writ).

1. Statement of diligence. The party must state it was not able to obtain the testimony earlier even though it diligently used the discovery procedures. The party should explain why it was unable to obtain the testimony earlier. *See* TRCP 252 (cause of failure, if known). If a party does not diligently use the discovery procedures, it can seldom claim reversible error when the trial court refuses the continuance. ***State v. Wood Oil Distrib.***, 751 S.W.2d 863, 865 (Tex.1988); *see also* ***Risner***, 18 S.W.3d at 909 (summary judgment hearing set 18 months after suit was filed; party did not state why affidavits could not have been obtained timely); ***Hatteberg v. Hatteberg***, 933 S.W.2d 522, 527 (Tex.App.—Houston [1st Dist.] 1994, no writ) (case pending more than a year; discovery was sent out close to trial date); ***Central Nat'l Gulfbank v. Comdata Network***, 773 S.W.2d 626, 628 (Tex.App.—Corpus Christi 1989, no writ) (case pending for 2 years; movant had not served or taken deposition of witness).

2. Description of diligence. The party must describe its attempts to secure discovery of the evidence. If other discovery was necessary before the party could embark on this discovery, the party should state in detail the reasons. ***Rhima***, 829 S.W.2d at 912 (party did not describe diligence).

§8.4 Not otherwise available. In a second (or later) motion for continuance, the party must state that the missing testimony cannot be procured from any other source. TRCP 252. This statement is not necessary in the first motion for continuance based on the need for additional testimony. *Id.*

§8.5 Not for delay. The motion should always include the statement, "The continuance is not sought for delay only, but so that justice may be done." TRCP 252.

§8.6 Affidavits. The party must attach affidavits to support all factual allegations. TRCP 251; *see* ***Rhima***, 829 S.W.2d at 912 (did not file affidavit describing diligence). The person with the knowledge of the facts stated in the motion (either the party or the attorney) should state the facts supporting the motion in an affidavit. See "Affidavits & verification," §2.3, p. 242.

§8.7 Exhibits. All attachments to the motion should be verified by affidavit. See "Exhibits," ch. 1-B, §4.14.2(5), p. 9.

§9. CONTINUANCE IN SUMMARY JUDGMENT CASE

A party who needs additional time to respond to a motion for summary judgment must ask for it. ***Tenneco Inc. v. Enterprise Prods. Co.***, 925 S.W.2d 640, 647 (Tex.1996).

§9.1 Continuance by agreement. The parties may change the summary judgment deadlines by agreement. See "Continuance on Agreed Motion," §6, p. 243.

§9.2 Motion to reset SJ hearing for lack of 21 days' notice. When requesting a resetting of the hearing on a motion for summary judgment because the movant did not provide the nonmovant with the required 21 days' notice, the motion should rely on TRCP 166a(c). See "Deadlines for Summary Judgment," ch. 7-B, §10, p. 474. The 21-day notice requirement is waived if the nonmovant does not object in writing. ***Nguyen v. Short, How, Frels & Heitz***, 108 S.W.3d 558, 560 (Tex.App.—Dallas 2003, pet. denied); ***Veal v. Veterans Life Ins. Co.***, 767 S.W.2d 892, 895 (Tex.App.—Texarkana 1989, no writ). The objection that the movant did not provide the full 21 days' notice should be made before the hearing, but can be made as late as a motion for new trial. *See* ***Nickerson v. E.I.L. Instr.***, 817 S.W.2d 834, 835-36 (Tex.App.—Houston [1st Dist.] 1991, no writ) (objection in motion for new trial). The nonmovant should object to lack of the 21 days' notice, file a motion to reset or delay the hearing, present sworn proof, and make a record. *See* ***Nguyen***, 108 S.W.3d at 560; *see, e.g.*, ***Roob v. Von Beregshasy***, 866 S.W.2d 765, 766 (Tex.App.—Houston [1st Dist.] 1993, writ denied) (appellant should have made and filed a reporter's record in appellate court).

Some cases hold that a nonmovant must comply with the requirements of TRCP 166a(g) when the movant does not give 21 days' notice. *See, e.g.*, ***Pankow v. Colonial Life Ins. Co.***, 932 S.W.2d 271, 275 (Tex.App.—Amarillo 1996, writ denied) (court required motion for continuance to explain need for additional evidence even though nonmovant did not get the required 21 days' notice). However, a nonmovant should file a request for continuance under TRCP 166a(g) only when it needs more than 21 days to prepare for the hearing, not when it seeks the 21 days it is entitled to under TRCP 166a(c). All that is necessary to preserve error when the nonmovant does not get the required 21 days' notice is an objection and proof the nonmovant did not get proper notice. *See, e.g.*, ***Guinn v. Zarsky***, 893 S.W.2d 13, 17 (Tex.App.—Corpus Christi 1994, no writ) (because less than 21 days' notice received, court reversed SJ without requiring nonmovant to show need for time to obtain affidavits or discovery). See ***O'Connor's*** FORM 7B:07.

PRACTICE TIP

The reason a nonmovant should not file a motion for continuance under TRCP 166a(g) when it objects that it did not get the notice required by TRCP 166a(c) is because the trial court has the discretion to deny a motion for continuance under TRCP 166a(g). However, the court does not have the discretion to refuse a request to reset the hearing when the nonmovant received less than the full 21 days' notice required by TRCP 166a(c). When the trial court improperly overrules an objection to inadequate notice, it commits an error of law, not an abuse of discretion.

§9.3 Motion to continue SJ hearing. When requesting a continuance for additional time to secure affidavits or discovery for a summary judgment hearing, the motion should blend all the requirements of TRCP 166a(g) and TRCP 252. ***Tenneco Inc.***, 925 S.W.2d at 647; *see* ***Kahanek v. Rogers***, 900 S.W.2d 131, 134 (Tex.App.—San Antonio 1995, no writ) (court noted the motion complied with both TRCP 166a(g) and 251). See ***O'Connor's*** FORM 7B:09.

1. Grounds. The party should allege it cannot present, by affidavits, facts essential to justify its opposition to the motion for summary judgment and that it needs additional time to secure affidavits or conduct discovery. TRCP 166a(g); ***Green v. City of Friendswood***, 22 S.W.3d 588, 594 (Tex.App.—Houston [14th Dist.] 2000, pet. denied).

2. Factors to cover in motion. The request for additional time should cover the following:

(1) Discovery period. The motion should identify the end of the discovery period.

(a) Motion during discovery period. When a motion for summary judgment is filed during the discovery period, the motion for continuance should (1) state that the discovery period has not expired, (2) identify the date it expires, and (3) argue that the motion for summary judgment addresses complex fact issues that require full discovery. When a case is complex, and the motion for summary judgment challenges the merits of the case, full discovery is probably necessary. *See* ***McClure v. Attebury***, 20 S.W.3d 722, 729 (Tex.App.—Amarillo 1999, no pet.) (when threshold issue is a question of law, discovery requirements are minimal).

(b) Motion after discovery period. When a motion for summary judgment is filed after the discovery period, the party who wants a continuance must also ask the court to enlarge the discovery period. *See* TRCP 190.5, 191.1. See "Modification of discovery periods," ch. 6-A, §6.2, p. 318.

(2) **Description of specific discovery or affidavits.** See "Description of necessary evidence," §8.1, p. 244.

(3) **Materiality.** See "Materiality," §8.2, p. 244.

(4) **Diligence.** See "Diligence," §8.3, p. 245.

(5) **Length of time suit on file.** The motion for continuance should state how long the case has been on file.

(a) **Fact issues.** When a motion for summary judgment based on facts is filed shortly after the lawsuit is commenced, the trial court should grant a motion for a continuance. *See, e.g.*, ***Two Thirty Nine Jt.V. v. Joe***, 60 S.W.3d 896, 902-03 (Tex.App.—Dallas 2001, pet. granted 2-13-03) (P's motion for continuance should have been granted because D filed for SJ 2 months after P filed lawsuit & discovery necessary on issue of official immunity); ***Levinthal v. Kelsey-Seybold Clinic, P.A.***, 902 S.W.2d 508, 512 (Tex.App.—Houston [1st Dist.] 1994, no writ) (P's motion for continuance should have been granted because D filed for SJ 3 months after P filed lawsuit & before D responded to discovery); ***Verkin v. Southwest Ctr. One, Ltd.***, 784 S.W.2d 92, 96 (Tex.App.—Houston [1st Dist.] 1989, writ denied) (D's motion for continuance should have been granted because P filed for SJ 50 days after filing lawsuit and before D responded to discovery).

(b) **Legal issues.** When a motion for summary judgment is based on a legal issue and facts are unnecessary, the court can overrule a motion for continuance even though the motion for summary judgment was filed shortly after the suit was commenced. *See, e.g.*, ***White v. Mellon Mortg. Co.***, 995 S.W.2d 795, 803-04 (Tex. App.—Tyler 1999, no pet.) (because discovery unnecessary & irrelevant to the determination of the legal issues, P's motion for continuance denied, even though D filed for SJ 3 months after suit filed); *see also* ***National Un. Fire Ins. Co. v. CBI Indus.***, 907 S.W.2d 517, 520-22 (Tex.1995) (additional time for discovery unnecessary because contract was unambiguous); ***J.E.M. v. Fidelity & Cas. Co.***, 928 S.W.2d 668, 676-77 (Tex.App.—Houston [1st Dist.] 1996, no writ) (no discovery necessary on issue of duty to defend, which was controlled by contract); ***Mayhew v. Town of Sunnyvale***, 774 S.W.2d 284, 298 (Tex.App.—Dallas 1989, writ denied) (no discovery necessary to review legislation).

(6) **Abuse of discovery.** If the movant for summary judgment abused the discovery process by withholding key evidence, the nonmovant is entitled to a continuance to complete the discovery before the court considers the motion for summary judgment. ***Tempay, Inc. v. TNT Concrete & Constr.***, 37 S.W.3d 517, 522-23 (Tex.App.—Austin 2001, pet. denied).

(7) **Not for delay.** See "Not for delay," §8.5, p. 245.

3. **Affidavits.** The grounds for the continuance must be supported by affidavit. TRCP 166a(g). See "Affidavits," ch. 7-B, §3.4, p. 459. The affidavit must be specific. See "Specific," §2.2, p. 242. All exhibits to the motion must be verified by affidavit. See "Exhibits to affidavits," ch. 7-B, §3.4.7, p. 460.

4. **Response to the motion.** The movant for summary judgment may either agree or disagree with the nonmovant's request for the continuance. By agreeing with the request for a continuance, the movant denies the nonmovant the argument on appeal that, if it had had more time, it would have been able to secure evidence to prove a fact issue. If the movant disagrees with the request for a continuance, it should attempt to negate the grounds in the nonmovant's motion for continuance.

5. **Order on the motion.** The court may grant the party additional time to secure affidavits or discovery, deny the motion for summary judgment, or "make such other order as is just." TRCP 166a(g). To preserve error, the party requesting a continuance must get a ruling on the record. See "Obtain a ruling," §5.1, p. 243.

§10. CONTINUANCE WHEN WITNESS OR PARTY UNAVAILABLE

If a witness or party is unavailable for trial, and the party cannot proceed to trial without that person, the party should move for a continuance. A trial court is not required to grant a motion for continuance just because a party is unable to be present at trial. ***Humphrey v. Ahlschlager***, 778 S.W.2d 480, 483 (Tex.App.—Dallas 1989, no writ). The motion for continuance must include the following information. See ***O'Connor's*** FORM 5D:02, §C, ¶¶15-23.

§10.1 Name & address of witness. The party should provide the witness's name and residence (street, county, and state), not office address. TRCP 252; *see* ***Hatteberg v. Hatteberg***, 933 S.W.2d 522, 526-27 (Tex.App.—Houston [1st Dist.] 1994, no writ) (motion did not identify home address, only office); ***Gabaldon v. G.M. Corp.***, 876 S.W.2d 367, 370 (Tex.App.—El Paso 1993, no writ) (motion did not identify witnesses to be deposed).

§10.2 Unavailable. The party should explain why the party or witness is not available to testify at trial. Conflicting business plans of the party or witness will seldom constitute sufficient grounds for continuance. *See* ***Echols v. Brewer***, 524 S.W.2d 731, 734 (Tex.App.—Houston [14th Dist.] 1975, no writ).

§10.3 Description of testimony. The motion should describe the party's or witness's testimony and what it is expected to prove. ***Richards v. Schion***, 969 S.W.2d 131, 133 (Tex.App.—Houston [1st Dist.] 1998, no pet.) (motion did not describe testimony of party who could not attend trial); ***Lynd v. Wesley***, 705 S.W.2d 759, 764 (Tex.App.—Houston [14th Dist.] 1986, no writ) (motion did not describe testimony of witness).

§10.4 Materiality. The party must state that the party's or witness's testimony is material and show how it is material. TRCP 252; ***Aguilar v. Alvarado***, 39 S.W.3d 244, 249 (Tex.App.—Waco 1999, pet. denied); ***Richards***, 969 S.W.2d at 133. The party must show that proceeding without the party or witness will prejudice the party's case. ***Richards***, 969 S.W.2d at 133.

§10.5 Diligence.

1. Statement of diligence. To support a motion for continuance based on the absence of a party or witness, the movant must show diligence in attempting to obtain the required testimony of the party or witness. ***Aguilar***, 39 S.W.3d at 249; ***Humphrey***, 778 S.W.2d at 483.

2. Description of diligence. The motion must describe the party's diligence in procuring the attendance of the party or witness.

(1) Witness lives within 100 miles of courthouse.

(a) Deposition not necessary. If the witness lives within 100 miles of the courthouse where suit is pending, the party can prove diligence for a continuance based on that witness's absence by showing that the party subpoenaed the witness for trial but the witness did not appear. *See* TRCP 252. See "Subpoenas," ch. 1-K, p. 58. For purposes of a continuance based on an absent witness who lives within 100 miles of the courthouse, the party does not need to have taken the witness's deposition. TRCP 252. A last-minute attempt at service does not constitute diligence. ***Hatteberg***, 933 S.W.2d at 526-27.

(b) Deposition necessary. The party's failure to depose a witness who lives within 100 miles of the courthouse where the suit is pending shows a lack of diligence if (1) the party could have anticipated the witness would not be able to attend the trial because of age, infirmity, sickness, or official duty; or (2) the witness is about to leave or has left the state or county of suit and will not be present for the trial. TRCP 252.

(2) Witness lives more than 100 miles from courthouse. If the witness lives more than 100 miles from the courthouse where suit is pending, the party should take the witness's deposition and not rely on a promise to attend the trial. If the witness lives more than 100 miles from the courthouse, the witness's absence is not a ground for a continuance. *See* TRCP 252.

§10.6 Medical excuse affidavit. If a party or witness is unavailable because of illness, the party must attach to the motion the affidavit of a doctor for the party or witness. TRCP 251; ***Hawthorne v. Guenther***, 917 S.W.2d 924, 930 (Tex.App.—Beaumont 1996, writ denied); *see, e.g.*, ***Burke v. Scott***, 410 S.W.2d 826, 827 (Tex.App.—Austin 1967, writ ref'd n.r.e.) (court should have granted the continuance because 2 doctors' affidavits confirmed party & critical witness were too ill to attend trial). The doctor's affidavit should state the nature and severity of the illness, that the witness is too ill to attend the trial, that the witness's health will be jeopardized if the witness is forced to attend the trial, and the prognosis for recovery. *See* ***Olivares v. State***, 693 S.W.2d 486, 490 (Tex.App.—San Antonio 1985, writ dism'd); *see, e.g.*, ***Humphrey***, 778 S.W.2d at 484 (court denied fourth motion for continuance based on witness's health problems because party did not attempt to depose witness & the motion did not contain any prognosis of witness's recovery or ability to testify); *see also* ***American Trendex Corp. v. Ultradyne Corp.***, 490 S.W.2d 205, 207 (Tex.App.—Austin 1973, writ ref'd n.r.e.) (court denied third motion for continuance when one of several parties was ill because motion did not state that a deposition could not be taken).

§10.7 Testimony not available. In a second (or later) motion for continuance, the party must state that the party's or witness's testimony cannot be procured from any other source. TRCP 252.

§10.8 Not for delay. See "Not for delay," §8.5, p. 245.

§10.9 Verified. See "Affidavits & verification," §2.3, p. 242.

§11. CONTINUANCE WHEN ATTORNEY UNAVAILABLE

§11.1 Attorney vacation letter. When a local rule mandates that the lead attorney is entitled to a continuance when a case is set for trial within the period designated by the attorney in a vacation letter, the court must grant the continuance. ***In re North Am. Refractories Co.***, 71 S.W.3d 391, 394 (Tex.App.—Beaumont 2001, orig. proceeding). The trial court has a ministerial duty to grant the continuance in compliance with the local rules of procedure, unless the other party proves a due process exception. *Id.*

§11.2 Attorney not available. Absence of counsel is not a ground for a continuance except at the discretion of the trial court. TRCP 253; ***Rehabilitation Facility v. Cooper***, 962 S.W.2d 151, 155 (Tex.App.—Austin 1998, no pet.); ***Rabe v. Guaranty Nat'l Ins. Co.***, 787 S.W.2d 575, 578 (Tex.App.—Houston [1st Dist.] 1990, writ denied). When an attorney is unavailable for trial, the record must show good cause or that the judge had knowledge of good cause for the continuance. ***Rabe***, 787 S.W.2d at 578. The motion for continuance should include the information described below. See *O'Connor's* FORM 5D:02, §C, ¶¶24-27.

1. Attorney is necessary. The motion should state that the attorney's presence is necessary for the proper representation of the case and give the reasons. TRCP 253; *see, e.g.*, ***Rabe***, 787 S.W.2d at 579 (continuance denied because no explanation what P's attorney could have accomplished at hearing after P did not file response to motion for summary judgment).

2. Reason attorney unavailable. The motion should state why the attorney is not available for trial. If the attorney is in another case, the motion should state why that case has precedence. *See* ***Smith v. Babcock & Wilcox Constr. Co.***, 913 S.W.2d 467, 468 (Tex.1995) (attorney was in trial in another county); ***Dancy v. Daggett***, 815 S.W.2d 548, 549 (Tex.1991) (attorney had a hearing on a criminal case in federal court, and under local rules, criminal case had priority). The motion must show some attempt to avoid the conflict in settings. *See* ***Smock v. Fischel***, 207 S.W.2d 891, 892 (Tex.1948); ***Rehabilitation Facility***, 962 S.W.2d at 155-56.

3. No substitute possible. The motion should state why another attorney in the firm could not handle the case. For a trial, the motion should state that no other attorney could try the case; for a hearing, it should state the hearing is important and involves difficult questions of law as applied to the facts of the case. If two attorneys signed the pleadings, the trial court can presume that either attorney can represent the party. *See* ***Rehabilitation Facility***, 962 S.W.2d at 155-56 (continuance denied because no explanation why attorney who signed pleadings could not conduct trial); ***Rabe***, 787 S.W.2d at 579 (continuance denied because no explanation why another attorney at firm could not represent P at summary judgment hearing); ***Echols v. Brewer***, 524 S.W.2d 731, 734 (Tex.App.—Houston [14th Dist.] 1975, no writ) (continuance denied because another attorney's name appeared on pleadings). If the attorney has no associates, the motion should so state.

4. Not for delay. See "Not for delay," §8.5, p. 245.

§11.3 Party not represented. If a party discovers shortly before trial that it is without an attorney, the trial court should grant a motion for continuance in the following cases:

1. The party is not at fault for not having an attorney. ***State v. Crank***, 666 S.W.2d 91, 94 (Tex.1984); *e.g.*, ***Wayne C. Holden Corp. v. Verheul***, 769 S.W.2d 629, 632 (Tex.App.—Corpus Christi 1989, writ denied) (settlement fell apart at last minute & attorney was ill).

2. The trial court permitted the attorney to withdraw. If the trial court permitted the attorney to withdraw before trial, the court should allow the party time to get another attorney. ***Villegas v. Carter***, 711 S.W.2d 624, 626 (Tex.1986); ***Kahanek v. Rogers***, 900 S.W.2d 131, 133-34 (Tex.App.—San Antonio 1995, no writ). *But see* ***St. Gelais v. Jackson***, 769 S.W.2d 249, 254 (Tex.App.—Houston [14th Dist.] 1988, no writ) (court granted attorney's motion to withdraw 1 month before trial; denial of continuance not abuse of discretion because withdrawal was party's fault).

§11.4 Verified. See "Affidavits & verification," §2.3, p. 242.

03 **§12. CONTINUANCE FOR LEGISLATOR**

A party is entitled to a legislative continuance while the Legislature is in session if either the party or the attorney is unavailable because the party or attorney is a member or member-elect of the Legislature. CPRC §30.003(b); TRCP 254. When properly requested, a legislative continuance is mandatory, unless the continuance violates the other party's due process rights. ***In re Starr Produce Co.***, 988 S.W.2d 808, 811 (Tex.App.—San Antonio 1999, orig. proceeding); ***First Interstate Bank v. Burns***, 951 S.W.2d 237, 240 (Tex.App.—Austin 1997, no writ). See ***O'Connor's*** FORM 5D:02, §C, ¶¶29-33.

§12.1 Motion. To obtain a legislative continuance, the party must file a sworn motion for continuance supported by an affidavit. CPRC §30.003(d); TRCP 251, 254. The motion must be filed within 30 days of the date the Legislature is to be in session, or during the legislative session. CPRC §30.003(b).

1. **Grounds.** The motion and affidavit must state the following:

(1) **Status of attorney.** A party or its attorney is a member or member-elect of the Legislature and is or will be in actual attendance of the session of the Legislature. CPRC §30.003(b); TRCP 254.

(2) **Legislator statements.** If the continuance is based on the attorney's participation in the Legislature, the motion and affidavit must also make these statements:

(a) The attorney intends to participate actively in the preparation or presentation of the case. CPRC §30.003(e); TRCP 254; ***Burns***, 951 S.W.2d at 240.

(b) The attorney did not take the case for purposes of a continuance. CPRC §30.003(e); ***Burns***, 951 S.W.2d at 240.

(3) **Trial date.** The motion should identify the date the case is set for trial; the timing of the motion in relation to the trial date determines whether the court has discretion to deny the motion.

(a) **Mandatory.** When the attorney was employed more than 30 days before the date set for trial, the court must grant the continuance. CPRC §30.003(c); *see* ***In re CNA Holdings***, 102 S.W.3d 280, 282 (Tex. App.—Beaumont 2003, orig. proceeding) (in case predating 2003 amendment to §30.003, applying 10-day rule). Although TRCP 254 provides that the continuance is mandatory if the attorney was employed more than ten days before trial, the Legislature's amendment of CPRC §30.003(c) overrides the rule. *See* Gov't Code §22.004(b) (rules adopted by Supreme Court remain in effect until disapproved by the Legislature).

(b) **Discretionary.** When the attorney was employed within 30 days of the date set for trial, the court has the discretion to deny the continuance. CPRC §30.003(c); *see* ***CNA Holdings***, 102 S.W.3d at 281 (applying 10-day rule).

(4) No TRO. The case is not set for a temporary restraining order (TRO). CPRC §30.003(a); TRCP 254.

2. File with Ethics Commission. If the attorney for a party seeking a continuance is a member or member-elect of the Legislature, the attorney must file a copy of the motion for continuance with the Texas Ethics Commission. CPRC §30.003(g). The copy must be sent to the commission no later than three business days after the date the motion is filed. *Id.*

§12.2 Response. To contest a legislative continuance, a party should file a sworn motion supported by affidavits that challenge the allegations in the motion. See *O'Connor's* FORM 5D:03, §F.

1. The movant's attorney was employed within 30 days of the trial and the court has the discretion to deny the motion for continuance. CPRC §30.003(c); *see* ***CNA Holdings***, 102 S.W.3d at 281 (applying 10-day rule).

2. The movant's attorney was employed for the purpose of getting a continuance.

3. The movant's attorney has no intention of participating in the preparation or presentation of the case.

4. Irreparable injury and harm will occur if the continuance is granted. This is the due process exception to a legislative continuance. The open-courts provision of the Texas Constitution prohibits a continuance when a party can show irreparable harm by the delay. *See* ***Waites v. Sondock***, 561 S.W.2d 772, 776 (Tex.1977); *see also* Tex. Const. art. I, §13 (remedy by due course of law).

§12.3 Hearing. The party opposing the continuance should move for a hearing. When a party claims a legislative continuance will result in the loss of a substantial existing right, the trial court must hold a hearing. ***Waites***, 561 S.W.2d at 775. At the hearing, the party opposing the continuance must present evidence. *See* ***Amoco Prod. Co. v. Salyer***, 814 S.W.2d 211, 213 (Tex.App.—Corpus Christi 1991, orig. proceeding).

§12.4 Ruling.

1. Court grants continuance. If the court grants the motion for a legislative continuance, the trial court must continue the case until 30 days after the Legislature adjourns. CPRC §30.003(b); TRCP 254.

2. Mandatory denial of continuance. The trial court must overrule the motion in the following instances:

(1) TRO hearing. If a party makes a motion to continue a hearing on a temporary restraining order on legislative continuance grounds, the court has no discretion and must overrule it. CPRC §30.003(a); TRCP 254.

(2) Due process. If the due process exception to the legislative continuance rule applies, the court must overrule the motion for continuance. ***Waites***, 561 S.W.2d at 776 (mother filed a contempt hearing for enforcement of child support claiming to be unable to feed her children). If after a hearing, the court does not believe the party opposing the motion will suffer irreparable harm, the court should grant the legislative continuance. ***Cryer v. West***, 771 S.W.2d 5, 7 (Tex.App.—Houston [1st Dist.] 1989, orig. proceeding). *Compare* ***Condovest Corp. v. John St. Builders***, 662 S.W.2d 138, 141 (Tex.App.—Austin 1983, no writ) (court denied continuance because party proved substantial right would be harmed by the continuance; loss of a $400,000 sale), *with* ***Amoco Prod.***, 814 S.W.2d at 213 (court granted continuance because party did not prove irreparable harm; no proof of loss of business opportunity in sale of oil from disputed property).

(3) Reason for hiring legislator. The attorney took the case for purposes of a continuance or does not intend to participate in the case. CPRC §30.003(e); TRCP 254.

3. Discretionary ruling. The trial court may overrule the motion for a legislative continuance if the attorney was employed within 30 days of the date the case is set for trial. CPRC §30.003(c); *see* ***CNA Holdings***, 102 S.W.3d at 281 (applying 10-day rule).

§13. CONTINUANCE FOR RELIGIOUS HOLY DAY

§13.1 The motion. A party or attorney who wishes a continuance for a religious holy day must file an affidavit stating (1) the grounds for continuance and (2) that the party or attorney holds religious beliefs that prohibit him from taking part in court proceedings on the day he is required to appear in court. CPRC §30.005(c). See ***O'Connor's*** FORM 5D:02, §C, ¶¶34-37.

§13.2 Verified. See "Affidavits & verification," §2.3, p. 242.

§14. REVIEW

§14.1 Standard of review. The ruling on a motion for continuance is reviewed for abuse of discretion. ***Villegas v. Carter***, 711 S.W.2d 624, 626 (Tex.1986); ***State v. Crank***, 666 S.W.2d 91, 94 (Tex.1984).

§14.2 Record. If the trial court conducted a hearing on the motion for continuance, the appellate record consists of the reporter's record of the hearing and the clerk's record with the motion, affidavits, response, and order. *See* ***Roob v. Von Beregshasy***, 866 S.W.2d 765, 766 (Tex.App.—Houston [1st Dist.] 1993, writ denied). If no hearing was held, the reporter's record is not required.

§14.3 Appeal. As a general rule, the trial court's ruling on a motion for continuance can be reviewed only after the case is tried and appealed.

1. **First motion.** The trial court does not have the discretion to reject the uncontroverted facts established in a party's first motion for continuance. ***Roob***, 866 S.W.2d at 766; ***Garza v. Serrato***, 699 S.W.2d 275, 281 (Tex.App.—San Antonio 1985, writ ref'd n.r.e.).

2. **Second motion.** Appellate courts seldom reverse a trial court for overruling a second (or later) motion for continuance for additional time for discovery. *See* ***Eckman v. Centennial Sav. Bank***, 757 S.W.2d 392, 395 (Tex.App.—Dallas 1988, writ denied); ***Employers Mut. Cas. Co. v. Gifford***, 723 S.W.2d 811, 812-13 (Tex.App.—Fort Worth 1987, no writ). If a party states sufficient good cause, however, the trial court should grant a second motion for continuance. *See* ***Garza***, 699 S.W.2d at 281 (D should have been given more time to find rebuttal evidence after P produced last-minute medical evidence different from earlier evidence).

§14.4 Mandamus. When a continuance is within the discretion of the trial court, mandamus is not generally available to review the trial court's ruling. ***G.M. Corp. v. Gayle***, 924 S.W.2d 222, 227 (Tex.App.—Houston [14th Dist.] 1996, orig. proceeding). When the trial court has no discretion, mandamus may be available. *See, e.g.*, ***Amoco Prod.***, 814 S.W.2d at 213 (legislative continuance).

E. MOTION IN LIMINE

§1. GENERAL

§1.1 Rule. None. See TRE 103, 104.

§1.2 Purpose. A motion in limine is a procedural device that permits a party to identify, before trial, certain evidentiary rulings that the court may be asked to make. ***Lohmann v. Lohmann***, 62 S.W.3d 875, 881 (Tex.App.—El Paso 2001, no pet.); ***Weidner v. Sanchez***, 14 S.W.3d 353, 363 (Tex.App.—Houston [14th Dist.] 2000, no pet.). The purpose of this procedure is to prevent the presentation of potentially prejudicial information in front of a jury before a ruling on admissibility can be obtained. ***Hartford Acc. & Indem. Co. v. McCardell***, 369 S.W.2d 331, 335 (Tex.1963); ***Lohmann***, 62 S.W.3d at 881. It avoids the injection of irrelevant, inadmissible, and prejudicial information in the trial. ***Wilkins v. Royal Indem. Co.***, 592 S.W.2d 64, 66 (Tex.App.—Tyler 1979, no writ). A motion in limine is optional; it is not a required procedural step for objections to evidence. ***Bridges v. City of Richardson***, 354 S.W.2d 366, 367-68 (Tex.1962).

§1.3 Forms. ***O'Connor's Texas Civil Forms***, FORMS 5E.

§1.4 Other references. Cochran, ***Texas Rules of Evidence Handbook***, p. 88-89 (5th ed. 2003).

PRACTICE TIP

Do not file a motion in limine when you want a pretrial ruling that actually excludes evidence. Instead, file a motion to exclude evidence. See, e.g., "Motion to Exclude Expert," ch. 5-M, p. 303.

§2. MOTION

Because no rule or statute provides for a motion in limine, the procedures for such motions have developed through case law.

§2.1 Procedure. A motion in limine must be in writing, and copies must be served on all parties. *See* TRCP 21. The motion should state (1) exactly what evidence the party anticipates its opponent will attempt to introduce, or the question the opponent will ask in front of the jury; and (2) why the evidence or the question is inadmissible.

§2.2 Deadline. A motion in limine should be filed and presented for a ruling before voir dire. *See* ***City of Houston v. Watson***, 376 S.W.2d 23, 33 (Tex.App.—Houston 1964, writ ref'd n.r.e.) (after parties announce ready). However, because error cannot be based on the motion itself (only on a ruling on evidence during trial), the timing of the motion is not critical.

§2.3 Grounds. Before drafting a motion in limine, the attorney should review the rules of evidence that govern the exclusion of evidence, TRE 401-610. Any evidence the rules classify as inadmissible may be made the subject of a motion in limine. For a collection of grounds for motions in limine, see ***O'Connor's*** FORM 5E:01.

§3. RESPONSE

It is not generally necessary to file a response to a motion in limine, although the party may file a response to address the issue of the admissibility of the evidence.

§4. HEARING

If the court holds a hearing on a motion in limine, it is not for evidence, but merely for argument of counsel. If the court regularly schedules a pretrial conference, the party may ask the court to consider the motion at that time. *See* TRCP 166(g).

§5. RULING ON THE MOTION

§5.1 Written order. The party should present a written order for the trial court's signature and file it with the court. *See* TRE 103(a)(1); TRAP 33.1(a)(1); ***Wilkins***, 592 S.W.2d at 67. See ***O'Connor's*** FORM 5E:02.

§5.2 Function of order. The trial court's ruling on a motion in limine is not a ruling that excludes or admits evidence. ***Fort Worth Hotel L.P. v. Enserch Corp.***, 977 S.W.2d 746, 757 (Tex.App.—Fort Worth 1998, no pet.). It is merely a tentative ruling that prohibits a party from asking a certain question or offering certain evidence in front of the jury without first approaching the bench for a ruling. *Id.*; ***Chavis v. Director***, 924 S.W.2d 439, 446 (Tex.App.—Beaumont 1996, no writ). A limine order also may prevent parties from referring to matters during voir dire or the opening statement without first approaching the bench for a ruling. *See, e.g.*, ***Babcock v. Northwest Mem'l Hosp.***, 767 S.W.2d 705, 708-09 (Tex.1989) (P could mention the "lawsuit crisis" or "liability insurance crisis" in voir dire).

§6. OFFER & OBJECTION AT TRIAL

§6.1 When motion denied. When a trial court denies a motion in limine, the court has refused to require the person who intends to offer the evidence to approach the bench before offering it.

1. Offer. At trial, the party seeking to introduce the evidence must offer the evidence. The denial of the motion in limine does not admit the evidence.

2. Objection. If the evidence is offered at trial, the party that wants to exclude it must object when it is offered. ***Hartford Acc. & Indem.***, 369 S.W.2d at 335; ***Sims v. State***, 816 S.W.2d 502, 504 (Tex.App.—Houston [1st Dist.] 1991, writ denied). The denial of the motion in limine does not preserve error.

§6.2 When motion granted. When a trial court grants a motion in limine, its ruling is that the person offering the evidence must approach the bench for a ruling on the admissibility of the evidence before offering it in front of the jury.

1. Offer. When a motion in limine is granted, the party who wants to introduce the evidence must (1) approach the bench and ask for a ruling, (2) formally offer the evidence, and (3) obtain a ruling on the offer. *See* ***Johnson v. Garza***, 884 S.W.2d 831, 834 (Tex.App.—Austin 1994, writ denied); ***Tempo Tamers, Inc. v. Crow-Houston Four, Ltd.***, 715 S.W.2d 658, 662-63 (Tex.App.—Dallas 1986, writ ref'd n.r.e.). The court's ruling granting the motion in limine does not exclude the evidence. *See* ***Johnson***, 884 S.W.2d at 834. If necessary, the party offering the evidence should ask the court to remove the jury for a hearing on the admissibility of the evidence. Whether the offer takes place at a bench conference or in a hearing outside the presence of the jury, the party should make sure the court reporter records the offer and the ruling.

2. Objection. If a party introduces evidence in violation of the ruling on the motion in limine (*i.e.*, without first asking for a bench conference), the party that made the motion in limine must object. ***Pool v. Ford Motor Co.***, 715 S.W.2d 629, 637 (Tex.1986). If the party does not object, the evidence will be considered by the jury, and the error in its admission is waived. *Id.* The court's ruling granting the motion in limine does not preserve error. *Id.*

3. Bill of exceptions. If the trial court rules the evidence is not admissible, the party that wants to introduce the evidence must preserve it in a bill of exceptions (or offer of proof). ***Johnson***, 884 S.W.2d at 834. See "Offer of Proof & Bill of Exceptions," ch. 8-E, p. 553.

§7. RULING ON THE OFFER

Once the party offers the evidence, and the opposing party makes an objection, both parties should ensure the court makes a ruling on the record, either admitting or excluding the evidence. See "Court's Ruling," ch. 1-G, §2, p. 33.

§8. WHEN LIMINE ORDER VIOLATED

§8.1 Pursue an adverse ruling. If an order on a motion in limine is violated, and prejudicial information is revealed to the jury, the party that wanted the evidence excluded must object immediately after the information is revealed or waive the error. ***Weidner v. Sanchez***, 14 S.W.3d 353, 364-65 (Tex.App.—Houston [14th Dist.] 2000, no pet.). That party must make a series of objections, called "pursuing an adverse ruling." See "When jury hears inadmissible evidence," ch. 8-D, §6.6, p. 548. By making the appropriate objections, the issue is preserved for appeal. ***Dove v. Director***, 857 S.W.2d 577, 579-80 (Tex.App.—Houston [1st Dist.] 1993, writ denied) (party objected, asked for instruction, and made a motion for mistrial); *see also* ***Kendrix v. Southern P.T. Co.***, 907 S.W.2d 111, 112-14 (Tex.App.—Beaumont 1995, writ denied) (disclosure of workers' compensation & other lawsuit); ***Cody v. Mustang Oil Tool Co.***, 595 S.W.2d 214, 216 (Tex.App.—Eastland 1980, writ ref'd n.r.e.) (disclosure of receipt of traffic ticket).

§8.2 Sanction. A court may strike pleadings as a sanction for a violation of a motion in limine if the circumstances warrant harsh sanctions. *See* ***Lassiter v. Shavor***, 824 S.W.2d 667, 669-70 (Tex.App.—Dallas 1992, no writ) (sanction was an abuse of discretion because no evidence of direct relationship between sanctions & offensive conduct). A court may impose a fine or hold a party or witness in contempt of court for violating an order on a motion in limine. *See* ***Onstad v. Wright***, 54 S.W.3d 799, 802 (Tex.App.—Texarkana 2001, pet. denied) (attorney fined $32,198); ***Kidd v. Lance***, 794 S.W.2d 586, 588 (Tex.App.—Austin 1990, no writ) (attorney & party held in contempt; fine limited to $500 by statute).

§9. REVIEW

§9.1 Court's ruling on motion. The trial court's ruling on a motion in limine is never reversible error. ***Hartford Acc. & Indem. Co. v. McCardell***, 369 S.W.2d 331, 335 (Tex.1963); *see also* ***State v. Wood Oil Distrib.***, 751 S.W.2d 863, 866 (Tex.1988) (appellate complaint of ruling on motion in limine presents nothing for review).

Even if the trial court makes an erroneous ruling on a motion in limine, there is no reversible error unless the court, during the trial, erroneously admits or excludes evidence over a proper objection. ***Acord v. G.M. Corp.***, 669 S.W.2d 111, 116 (Tex.1984). The right to appeal an erroneous ruling on the admission or exclusion of evidence does not depend on a motion in limine. ***Hartford Acc. & Indem.***, 369 S.W.2d at 335.

§9.2 Violation of order. The violation of an order on the motion in limine is reversible if the harm resulting from the violation is incurable. ***Lohmann. v. Lohmann***, 62 S.W.3d 875, 881 (Tex.App.—El Paso 2001, no pet.); ***Weidner***, 14 S.W.3d at 363; *see, e.g.*, ***National Un. Fire Ins. Co. v. Kwiatkowski***, 915 S.W.2d 662, 664-65 (Tex. App.—Houston [14th Dist.] 1996, no writ) (reversed because jury argument violated motion in limine, even though no objection to some of comments); ***Kendrix***, 907 S.W.2d at 112-14 (reversed because no instructions could cure the improper impression the statement left in minds of jurors); ***Dove***, 857 S.W.2d at 580 (reversed because repeated violations of order to first approach the bench permitted jury to hear prejudicial matters not curable by instruction to disregard).

F. MOTION TO AMEND PLEADINGS—PRETRIAL

§1. GENERAL

§1.1 Rules. TRCP 63-65. See TRCP 66-67 (trial amendments).

§1.2 Purpose. A party amends its pleadings to correct errors and defects in the pleadings.

§1.3 Forms. *O'Connor's Texas Civil Forms*, FORMS 5F.

§2. GENERAL RULES FOR AMENDING PLEADINGS

There are three sections in this book regarding amending pleadings: "Amending the Pleadings," ch. 1-B, §7, p. 11; this subchapter, "Motion to Amend Pleadings—Pretrial"; and "Motion to Amend Pleadings—Trial & Post-Trial," ch. 8-F, p. 557.

§3. RULES REGARDING AMENDING PLEADINGS BEFORE TRIAL

TRCP 63 does not allow a party the unlimited right to amend its pleadings before trial. ***Stevenson v. Koutzarov***, 795 S.W.2d 313, 321 (Tex.App.—Houston [1st Dist.] 1990, writ denied).

§3.1 No leave to amend required. In the following instances, a party is not required to secure leave of court to amend its pleadings:

1. **Before deadline in pretrial order.** When a pretrial order establishes deadlines to amend, a party must file amendments according to those deadlines. ***Mackey v. U.P. Enters.***, 935 S.W.2d 446, 461 (Tex.App.—Tyler 1996, no writ); ***ForScan Corp. v. Dresser Indus.***, 789 S.W.2d 389, 393 (Tex.App.—Houston [14th Dist.] 1990, writ denied). TRCP 166, the rule governing pretrial orders, prevails over TRCP 63, the rule governing pretrial amendments. ***ForScan***, 789 S.W.2d at 393.

2. **At least 7 days before trial.** When no pretrial order establishes deadlines to amend, the following rules govern amendments made at least seven days before trial.

(1) **No surprise.** A party has the right to amend pleadings at least seven days before trial, as long as the amendment does not operate as a surprise to the opposing party. TRCP 63; ***Sosa v. Central Power & Light***, 909 S.W.2d 893, 895 (Tex.1995); *see also* TRCP 63, cmt., 785-786 S.W.2d (Tex.Cases) xlii (1990) (requires all pleadings to be on file at least 7 days before trial). The trial setting from which to count the seven days is the original trial date; that is, the date the case is set for trial, not the date trial actually begins. ***Taiwan Shrimp Farm Village Ass'n v. U.S.A. Shrimp Farm Dev.***, 915 S.W.2d 61, 69 (Tex.App.—Corpus Christi 1996, writ denied); ***AmSav Group v. American S&L Ass'n***, 796 S.W.2d 482, 490 (Tex.App.—Houston [14th Dist.] 1990, writ denied). If the case actually goes to trial at a later date, the new setting does not enlarge the time to amend pleadings. *See* ***Taiwan Shrimp***, 915 S.W.2d at 69-70; ***AmSav Group***, 796 S.W.2d at 490.

NOTE

Compare the cases (see §3.1.2(1), above) suggesting that a limited resetting of the trial does not enlarge the time to file amended pleadings to those cases holding that a resetting of more than 30 days extends the discovery deadlines and the time to request a jury. See ***H.B. Zachry Co. v. Gonzalez****, 847 S.W.2d 246, 246 (Tex.1993) (discovery);* ***Halsell v. Dehoyos****, 810 S.W.2d 371, 371 (Tex.1991) (jury request).*

(2) Surprise. The court has the discretion to strike an amendment filed at least seven days before trial if the party opposing the amendment shows the amendment was a surprise. *See, e.g.*, ***Flo Trend Sys. v. Allwaste, Inc.***, 948 S.W.2d 4, 7 (Tex.App.—Houston [14th Dist.] 1997, no writ) (no abuse of discretion in striking amendment filed 7 days before trial because it added new theory of liability); ***Favor v. Hochheim Prairie Farm Mut. Ins. Ass'n***, 939 S.W.2d 180, 181-82 (Tex.App.—San Antonio 1996, writ denied) (same); ***Stevenson***, 795 S.W.2d at 321 (court abused discretion in refusing to strike amendment filed 8 days before trial because it was a wholesale revision of lawsuit).

3. At least 45 days before trial. A party may amend its pleadings, changing the case from a Level 1 discovery control plan to Level 2 or 3, without filing a motion for leave to file if the amendment is filed at least 45 days before trial. TRCP 190.2(b) (last paragraph).

§3.2 Leave to amend required. In the following instances, a party must secure leave of court to amend pleadings.

1. After deadline in pretrial order. To amend its pleadings after the deadline in a pretrial order, the party must secure leave of court. ***Hart v. Moore***, 952 S.W.2d 90, 95 (Tex.App.—Amarillo 1997, pet. denied); ***Texas Commerce Bank v. Lebco Constructors***, 865 S.W.2d 68, 78-79 (Tex.App.—Corpus Christi 1993, writ denied). The rules that govern late amendments addressed in §3.2.2, below, also control late amendments filed after the deadline in a pretrial order. ***Texas Commerce***, 865 S.W.2d at 79; *see* ***Brown v. State***, 984 S.W.2d 348, 350 (Tex.App.—Fort Worth 1999, pet. denied) (court abused its discretion in permitting amendment that changed nature of case 18 days after deadline in pretrial order).

2. Less than 7 days before trial. All pleadings, responses, or pleas offered for filing less than seven days from the date of trial can be filed only with leave of court, which the court must grant unless the party resisting the amendment objects and shows surprise. TRCP 63; ***Chapin & Chapin v. Texas Sand & Gravel Co.***, 844 S.W.2d 664, 665 (Tex.1992); ***Guereque v. Thompson***, 953 S.W.2d 458, 463-64 (Tex.App.—El Paso 1997, pet. denied) (because party did not file motion for leave, pleading not "filed"); *see* ***Burrow v. Arce***, 997 S.W.2d 229, 246 (Tex. 1999).

(1) Procedural change. If the change to the pleading is merely procedural and it does not change any substantive issues in the trial, the court must permit the amendment. TRCP 63; ***Chapin & Chapin***, 844 S.W.2d at 665. For example, adding a verified denial to an answer. ***Chapin & Chapin***, 844 S.W.2d at 665.

(2) Substantive change. If the change to the pleading is substantive and alters the nature of the trial, the trial judge retains discretion to deny leave to amend. ***Chapin & Chapin***, 844 S.W.2d at 665; *see, e.g.*, ***Hardin v. Hardin***, 597 S.W.2d 347, 349-50 (Tex.1980) (court had discretion to deny amendment offered on day of trial to add affirmative defenses); ***Bekins Moving & Storage Co. v. Williams***, 947 S.W.2d 568, 574 (Tex.App.—Texarkana 1997, no writ) (same). When a party offers an amendment that makes a substantive change, the burden is on the party opposing the amendment to object and show surprise. TRCP 63; ***Burrow***, 997 S.W.2d at 246; ***Chapin & Chapin***, 844 S.W.2d at 665.

3. Less than 45 days before trial. If an amendment changes a case from a Level 1 discovery control plan to Level 2 or 3, and it is filed less than 45 days before trial, the party must file a motion for leave to amend, showing that good cause to file the pleading outweighs any prejudice to the other party. TRCP 190.2(b) (last paragraph). The effect of a late amendment that changes the discovery level upward is that (1) it reopens the discovery period, (2) any person previously deposed may be redeposed, and (3) the trial date should be reset if necessary to permit completion of discovery. TRCP 190.2(d).

§3.3 Service of amended pleadings. Service of process of amended pleadings is not necessary on parties who have filed petitions or answers in the case; service of the amended pleading need only comply with the requirements of TRCP 21 and 21a. *See* ***Arce v. Burrow***, 958 S.W.2d 239, 257 (Tex.App.—Houston [14th Dist.] 1997), *modified on other grounds*, 997 S.W.2d 229 (Tex.1999). However, service of an amended petition on a nonanswering defendant must be by service of process if the petition includes more claims or more damages. See "Amending the petition," ch. 7-A, §3.2.1, p. 444.

§4. MOTION FOR LEAVE TO AMEND PLEADINGS BEFORE TRIAL

§4.1 Written motion for leave. When a motion for leave is required, the motion should be in writing, unless made in open court and dictated into the record. ***Pennington v. Gurkoff***, 899 S.W.2d 767, 771 (Tex.App.—Fort Worth 1995, writ denied); *see* TRCP 45(d). The better practice is to file a written motion, even when an oral motion was made on the record. In the motion for leave to amend, the party should state why the amendment is appropriate and necessary. See ***O'Connor's*** FORM 5F:01.

§4.2 The amended pleading. The amended pleading must be in writing and signed by the attorney or the party. TRCP 45(d), 63; ***Pennington***, 899 S.W.2d at 771; *see also* ***First Nat'l Indem. Co. v. First Bank & Trust***, 753 S.W.2d 405, 407 (Tex.App.—Beaumont 1988, no writ) (error not preserved when amendment to pleadings was not reduced to writing). The amended pleading should be filed along with (but not attached to) the motion for leave to amend.

§5. RESPONSE TO MOTION FOR PRETRIAL AMENDMENT

To prevent an amendment to the pleadings, a party must object either by filing a motion to strike the pleading or by opposing the motion for leave to amend in open court.

§5.1 Motion to strike. The motion to strike the pleadings should contain the following allegations. See ***O'Connor's*** FORM 5F:02.

1. **Claim surprise.** The party opposing the amendment must show surprise. Unless the party opposing the amendment shows surprise, the court should grant leave to file the amended pleading. TRCP 63. Courts must construe TRCP 63 liberally. ***Goswami v. Metropolitan S&L Ass'n***, 751 S.W.2d 487, 490 (Tex.1988).

2. **Claim prejudice.** Although TRCP 63 requires only a showing of surprise, not prejudice, the party opposing the amendment should attempt to convince the trial court the amendment would prejudice its claim or defense on the merits. *Compare* TRCP 63 (surprise), *with* TRCP 66 (prejudice).

3. **Show lack of diligence.** Some courts consider the lack of diligence of the party offering the amendment as a factor, even though TRCP 63 does not mention it. *See, e.g.*, ***AmSav Group v. American S&L Ass'n***, 796 S.W.2d 482, 490 (Tex.App.—Houston [14th Dist.] 1990, writ denied) (pretrial amendment adding defense of ambiguity was properly denied because it was known earlier); ***Stevenson v. Koutzarov***, 795 S.W.2d 313, 321 (Tex. App.—Houston [1st Dist.] 1990, writ denied) (pretrial amendment adding causes of action should have been struck because it was not based on newly discovered matters). Other courts refuse to consider lack of diligence. ***Zavala v. Trujillo***, 883 S.W.2d 242, 249 (Tex.App.—El Paso 1994, writ denied).

§5.2 Continuance. If the court permits a late amendment to the pleadings, and the party opposing the amendment needs additional time for discovery, that party should request a continuance. TRCP 190.5 (modification of discovery control plan); *see also* TRCP 70 (court may order cost of continuance be paid by party causing the surprise). See "Motion for Continuance," ch. 5-D, p. 242.

1. **Request continuance to preserve error.** There is some disagreement between courts whether a party who objects to a late amendment must file a motion for continuance to preserve error. Most courts say the party must (1) object, (2) claim surprise, and (3) move for a continuance. ***Wingate v. Hajdik***, 795 S.W.2d 717, 721 & n.1 (Tex.1990); ***Fletcher v. Edwards***, 26 S.W.3d 66, 74 (Tex.App.—Waco 2000, pet. denied); ***Louisiana & Ark. Ry. v. Blakely***, 773 S.W.2d 595, 597 (Tex.App.—Texarkana 1989, writ denied); ***H.O. Dyer, Inc. v. Steele***, 489 S.W.2d 686, 688 (Tex.App.—Houston [1st Dist.] 1972, no writ). Other courts say that a party opposing an amendment must do two of the three: (1) object and (2) either claim surprise or move for a continuance. ***In re Loftis***, 40 S.W.3d 160, 164 n.3 (Tex.App.—Texarkana 2001, no pet.); ***Howard v. Phillips***, 728 S.W.2d 448, 451 (Tex.App.—Fort Worth 1987, no writ); *see also* ***Stevenson***, 795 S.W.2d at 321 (party opposing amendment not required to move for continuance because amendment filed 8 days before trial was a wholesale revision of the lawsuit).

2. **Refusal of continuance = waiver.** When a party objects to a late amendment and then refuses an offer of continuance, the party waives its right to complain of the late amendment on appeal. ***Kaufman Nw. v. Bi-Stone Fuel Co.***, 529 S.W.2d 281, 288 (Tex.App.—Tyler 1975, writ ref'd n.r.e.).

PRACTICE TIP

For the party filing a late amendment, the lesson is this: If the other party objects to the late amendment, you may want to get the trial court to offer a continuance, knowing the other party will refuse it. On appeal, you can claim the other party waived its objection to the late amendment. For the party objecting to a late amendment, the lesson is this: If you are offered a continuance, you may want to accept it if you need time for additional discovery. If not, you may waive your objection to the late amendment.

§5.3 Preserve error. The party opposing the amendment must ensure the record on appeal reflects its objection to the late amendment and the court's ruling denying the amendment. If the record does not affirmatively show the trial court denied leave to file the late amendment, the appellate court will presume leave was granted. ***Lee v. Key W. Towers***, 783 S.W.2d 586, 588 (Tex.1989) (assumed trial court considered a verified denial filed 3 days before trial); ***Goswami***, 751 S.W.2d at 490 (assumed trial court considered amendment filed 4 days before summary judgment hearing).

§6. RULINGS ON PRETRIAL AMENDMENTS

§6.1 Amendments permitted. The following pretrial amendments were allowed: • Six days before trial, to add a verified denial of allegations of open account. ***Chapin & Chapin v. Texas Sand & Gravel Co.***, 844 S.W.2d 664, 665 (Tex.1992). • Assumed trial court permitted amendment four days before summary judgment hearing because appellate record did not show amendment had been refused. ***Goswami***, 751 S.W.2d at 490; ***Wilson v. Korthauer***, 21 S.W.3d 573, 578 (Tex.App.—Houston [14th Dist.] 2000, pet. denied). • In personal injury suit, to amend petition seven days before summary judgment hearing to delete factual allegations on which motion for summary judgment was based and to add lack of discovery of injury. ***Sosa v. Central Power & Light***, 909 S.W.2d 893, 894 (Tex.1995).

§6.2 Amendments not permitted. The following pretrial amendments were denied: • In suit for damages, amendment that completely revised lawsuit, even though filed seven days before trial. ***Stevenson***, 795 S.W.2d at 321. • In suit for promissory note, to amend on day of trial to add claims for duress, failure of consideration, fraud, illegality, and unjust enrichment. *See* ***Hardin v. Hardin***, 597 S.W.2d 347, 350 (Tex.1980). • Amended answer raising new defense less than seven days before trial. ***Phifer v. Nacogdoches Cty. Cent. Appr. Dist.***, 45 S.W.3d 159, 171 (Tex.App.—Tyler 2000, pet. denied).

§7. COSTS

If the trial court allows the filing of a late-amended or supplemental pleading that causes surprise to the other party, the trial court may charge the cost of a continuance to the party causing the surprise. TRCP 70.

§8. REVIEW

See "Appellate review of amended pleadings," ch. 1-B, §7.3, p. 12.

G. MOTION FOR PRETRIAL CONSOLIDATION

§1. GENERAL

In 2003, the Legislature enacted rules establishing the new multidistrict litigation (MDL) procedure for consolidating individual cases involving common factual issues for pretrial purposes. *See* Gov't Code §§74.161-74.164; *see also id.* §74.024(c)(10) (S.Ct. may adopt rules for transfer of related cases for consolidated pretrial proceedings). Texas Rule of Judicial Administration (TRJA) 13 applies to civil actions involving one or more common questions of fact filed in a constitutional county court, county court at law, probate court, or district court on or after September 1, 2003. Gov't Code §74.162; TRJA 13.1(b). For cases filed before September 1, 2003, TRJA 11 applies. TRJA 13.1(b). See ***O'Connor's Texas Rules * Civil Trials***, "Motion for Pretrial Consolidation Between Counties," ch. 5-G, p. 256 (2003). For cases filed before September 1, 2003, the parties may agree in writing to the application of TRJA 13 if (1) no pretrial judge has been appointed or (2) a pretrial judge has been appointed and the parties in all related cases to which the same pretrial judge has been assigned have agreed to the application of TRJA 13. TRJA 11.7(b).

§1.1 Rules. Gov't Code §§74.161-74.164; TRJA 11.7, 13

§1.2 Purpose. Under TRJA 13, cases pending in different counties involving the same material questions of fact may be consolidated for pretrial purposes, including summary judgment. *See* CPRC §74.162; TRJA 13.3(a)(1).

§1.3 Forms. ***O'Connor's Texas Civil Forms***, FORMS 5G (forthcoming 2004).

§2. JUDICIAL PANEL ON MULTIDISTRICT LITIGATION

The MDL procedure is governed by a judicial panel (MDL Panel) consisting of five members, who must be active court of appeals justices or administrative judges, designated by the Supreme Court Chief Justice. Gov't Code §74.161(a). The judicial panel includes temporary members designated by the Supreme Court Chief Justice when regular members are unable to sit. TRJA 13.2(a). Any action taken by the panel must have a concurrence of three panel members. Gov't Code §74.161(b). The panel may prescribe any rules for conducting its business as long as they are not inconsistent with the law or the rules adopted by the Supreme Court. *Id.* §74.163(b).

§3. MOTION TO CONSOLIDATE FOR PRETRIAL PURPOSES

§3.1 Who may file.

1. Party. A party in the case may file a motion to transfer the case and related cases to a pretrial court. TRJA 13.3(a).

2. Judge. A trial court judge or a presiding judge of an administrative judicial region may file a written request listing related cases to be transferred. TRJA 13.3(b).

§3.2 Motion.

1. In writing. The motion must be in writing and must conform with TRAP 9.4. TRJA 13.3(a), (e). Unless leave of the MDL Panel is requested, the portions of the motion required by TRJA 13.3(a)(1) & (2) must not exceed 20 pages. TRJA 13.3(e).

2. Common issues. The motion must identify the common questions of fact involved in the cases. TRJA 13.3(a)(1).

3. Reasons to consolidate. The motion must state why the consolidation would be convenient for the parties and witnesses and would promote the just and efficient conduct of the action. TRJA 13.3(a)(2); *see* Gov't Code §74.163(a)(2).

4. Agreement of parties. The motion must state whether all parties agree to the motion. TRJA 13.3(a)(3).

5. Appendix. The motion must contain an appendix that lists the following:

(1) Related cases. The cause number, style, and trial court of the related cases for which transfer is sought. TRJA 13.3(a)(4)(A).

(2) Parties. A list of all parties in those cases, along with their attorney's names, addresses, telephone and fax numbers, and e-mail addresses. TRJA 13.3(a)(4)(B).

§3.3 Brief. The MDL Panel may request additional briefing from any party. TRJA 13.3(e).

§3.4 Notice. A party must file a notice with the trial court that a motion for transfer has been filed. TRJA 13.3(i). If a judge files a request for transfer, the MDL Panel Clerk (Clerk of the Supreme Court) must file the notice with the trial court. TRJA 13.3(i), (n).

§3.5 Stay. Filing a motion to transfer does not automatically limit the trial court's jurisdiction or suspend proceedings or orders in that court. TRJA 13.4(a). However, the trial court or MDL Panel may stay all or a part of any proceedings until a ruling by the MDL Panel. TRJA 13.4(b).

§3.6 Retransfer. On a party's motion, at the request of the pretrial court, or on its own initiative, the MDL Panel may transfer cases from one pretrial court to another when the pretrial judge has died, resigned, been replaced, or been disqualified, or in any other situation when retransfer would promote the just and efficient conduct of the cases. TRJA 13.3(o).

§3.7 Show-cause order. The MDL Panel may, on its own initiative, issue an order to show cause why related cases should not be transferred to a pretrial court. TRJA 13.3(c).

§4. RESPONSE

§4.1 Who may respond. Any other party in the cases to be consolidated may file the following:

1. A response to a motion or request for transfer within 20 days after service of the motion or request. TRJA 13.3(d)(1).

2. A response to an MDL Panel show-cause order within the time provided in the order. TRJA 13.3(d)(2). See §3.7, above.

3. A reply to a response within ten days of service of the response. TRJA 13.3(d)(3).

§4.2 Form of response. The response or reply must be in writing and must conform with TRAP 9.4. TRJA 13.3(e). Unless leave of the MDL Panel is requested, the response or reply must not exceed 20 pages. *Id.*

§4.3 Brief. The MDL Panel may request additional briefing from any party. TRJA 13.3(e).

§5. FILING & SERVICE

§5.1 Filing. A motion, request, response, or reply must be filed with the MDL Panel Clerk. TRJA 13.3(f); *see* TRJA 13.2(c) (MDL Panel Clerk is clerk of Supreme Court). Copies of the document must be sent to each member of the MDL Panel. TRJA 13.3(f). The MDL Panel Clerk may also require the documents to be sent electronically. *Id.*

§5.2 Service. All papers filed under TRJA 13.3 must be served on all parties to the cases to be consolidated in accordance with TRAP 9.5. TRJA 13.3(h). The MDL Panel Clerk may designate a party to serve a request on all other parties. *Id.*

§5.3 Filing fees. The MDL Panel Clerk may set reasonable fees approved by the Supreme Court for filing and other services. TRJA 13.3(g).

§6. HEARING

§6.1 Hearing. The MDL Panel is not required to hold a hearing; it may decide the matter on the written submission. TRJA 13.3(k). The MDL Panel may hold an oral hearing at a time and place of its choosing, and the clerk must give notice of the date of submission or the time and place of the hearing to all parties. TRJA 13.3(k), (n). The MDL Panel Clerk may determine the manner in which notice is given, including whether notice should be given by e-mail or fax. TRJA 13.3(n).

§6.2 Evidence. A party may file evidence only with leave of the MDL Panel. TRJA 13.3(j). The panel will accept as true facts stated in a motion, response, or reply, unless another party contradicts them. *Id.* If the panel decides to accept evidence, it may order the parties to submit affidavits or deposition evidence and to file documents, discovery, or stipulations from the related cases. *Id.*

§7. ORDER

The MDL Panel must issue a written order to transfer the case. TRJA 13.3(*l*). The written order must have a concurrence of at least three members of the panel and contain a finding that (1) the related cases involve one or more common questions of fact and (2) the transfer will be for the convenience of the parties and will promote the just and efficient conduct of the related cases. *Id.* The order must be signed by either the MDL Panel chair or the clerk and must identify the members who concurred in the ruling. TRJA 13.3(m). If the MDL Panel refuses to rule, the movant may file an original mandamus proceeding in the Supreme Court. *See* TRJA 13.3(n) (clerk must give notice to all parties of MDL Panel actions, including decisions). See §10.1, below.

§8 TRANSFER

§8.1 When effective. A case is deemed transferred when the transfer notice is filed with the trial and pretrial courts. TRJA 13.5(a). After the notice is filed, the trial court cannot take any further action in the case except for good cause stated in the order and after conferring with the pretrial court. TRJA 13.5(b). Any service of process issued by the trial court may be completed and the return filed in the pretrial court. *Id.*

§8.2 Contents of notice. The transfer notice must include the following:

1. A list of all parties who have appeared and remain in the case, along with the names, addresses, telephone and bar numbers of their attorneys, or if pro se, the party's name, address, and telephone number. TRJA 13.5(a)(1).

2. A list of the parties who have not yet appeared in the case. TRJA 13.5(a)(2).

3. A copy of the MDL transfer order. TRJA 13.5(a)(3). See §7, above.

§8.3 Transfer of files. If the trial and pretrial courts are in different counties, the trial court clerk must transmit the case file to the pretrial court clerk. TRJA 13.5(c). If the trial court and pretrial court are in the same county, the trial court must transfer the case file to the pretrial court according to the local rules of the courts of that county. *Id.* The pretrial court may direct the manner in which the pretrial documents are filed, including electronic filing. *Id.*

§8.4 Fees. The party moving for transfer must pay the costs of refiling the transferred cases in the pretrial court, including filing fees and other reasonable costs, unless the MDL Panel decides otherwise. TRJA 13.5(d).

§8.5 Tag-along cases. A tag-along case is one that is related to the transferred cases but is not subject to the transfer order. TRJA 13.2(g). Tag-along cases are deemed transferred when the transfer notice is filed in both the trial and pretrial court. TRJA 13.5(e). Within 30 days after the transfer notice is served, a party to the tag-along case or any of the related cases may move for the pretrial court to remand on the ground the case is not a tag-along case. *Id.* If the motion to remand is granted, the case must be returned to the trial court, and the pretrial court may assess costs, including attorney fees, in the remand order. *Id.* The remand order may be appealed to the MDL Panel by filing a motion for rehearing with the clerk. *Id.*

§9. PRETRIAL PROCEEDINGS

§9.1 Assignment of pretrial judge. The MDL Panel may assign any active district judge, or any former or retired district or appellate judge approved by the Supreme Court Chief Justice as the pretrial judge. TRJA 13.6(a); *see* Gov't Code §74.164. For definitions of active, former, and retired judges, see "Who may be assigned," ch. 5-C, §3.2, p. 234. A pretrial judge appointed under TRJA 13 is not subject to an objection to an assigned judge under Gov't Code §74.053. TRJA 13.6(a); *see* ***In re Perritt***, 992 S.W.2d 444, 447 n.4 (Tex.1999) (TRJA 11).

§9.2 Authority of pretrial court. The pretrial court has the authority to decide all pretrial matters (*e.g.*, jurisdiction, joinder, venue) in the related cases transferred to the court. TRJA 13.6(b). This includes disposition by means other than trial on the merits (*e.g.*, default judgment, summary judgment, settlement). TRJA 13.6(b); *see* Gov't Code §§74.162, 74.163(a)(3). The pretrial court may set aside or modify any pretrial ruling made by the trial court before transfer over which the trial court would not have lost plenary power. TRJA 13.6(b). After transfer, the pretrial court should, at the earliest practical date, conduct a hearing and enter a case management order. TRJA 13.6(c). The case management order should address all matters pertinent to the conduct of the litigation. *Id.* For a list of matters the case management order should address, see TRJA 13.6(c).

§9.3 Trial settings. The pretrial court must confer, or order the parties to confer, with the trial court regarding trial settings or matters regarding remand. TRJA 13.6(d). The pretrial court must defer appropriately to the trial court's docket. *Id.* The trial court must not continue or postpone a trial setting without the pretrial court's concurrence. *Id.*

§9.4 Remand. The pretrial court may order remand of cases or separable triable portions of cases when pretrial proceedings are sufficiently completed. TRJA 13.7(b). However, remand is required for a trial on the merits. Gov't Code §74.163(a)(3). The pretrial court will not remand a case in which it has rendered a final and appealable judgment. TRJA 13.7(a).

§9.5 Orders after remand.

1. **Concurrence required.** The trial court cannot, over an objection, vacate, set aside, or modify pretrial court orders without the written concurrence of the pretrial court. TRJA 13.8(b). If the pretrial court is unavailable for any reason, the concurrence of the MDL Panel Chair must be obtained. TRJA 13.8(d).

2. **Exception.** The trial court does not need a written concurrence to vacate, set aside, or modify pretrial court orders regarding the admissibility of evidence at trial (other than expert evidence) when the ruling is necessary because of changed circumstances, to correct an error of law, or to prevent manifest injustice. TRJA 13.8(c). The trial court must support its action with specific findings and conclusions in a written order or stated on the record. *Id.*

§10. REVIEW

§10.1 MDL Panel orders. Orders of the MDL Panel, including orders granting or denying a motion for transfer, may be reviewed only by the Supreme Court in an original mandamus proceeding. TRJA 13.9(a); *see* Gov't Code §74.163(a)(4).

§10.2 Pretrial & trial court orders. Orders and judgments of the pretrial and trial courts may be reviewed by the appellate court that normally reviews orders of the court in which the case is pending, whether or not that court issued the order or judgment to be reviewed. TRJA 13.9(b).

H. MOTIONS FOR SEVERANCE & SEPARATE TRIALS

§1. GENERAL

§1.1 Rules. TRCP 41 (severance), TRCP 174(b) (separate trials). See CPRC §41.009 (bifurcated trial for exemplary damages).

§1.2 Purpose. The rules permit a court to divide a lawsuit into separate lawsuits or separate parts.

§1.3 Forms. ***O'Connor's Texas Civil Forms***, FORMS 5H.

§1.4 Other references. Page & Sigel, *Bifurcated Trials in Texas Practice*, 53 Tex.B.J. 318 (1990); ***O'Connor's Texas Causes of Action***, "Exemplary Damages," ch. 35-G, p. 1004 (2004) (***O'Connor's COA***).

§2. DISTINCTION BETWEEN MOTIONS TO SEVER & FOR SEPARATE TRIALS

§2.1 Severance. When a court grants a motion for severance, it divides a lawsuit into two or more independent lawsuits, each of which will terminate with a separate, final, and enforceable judgment. See §3, below.

§2.2 Separate trials – bifurcation. When the court orders separate trials under TRCP 174, the court bifurcates the case into two (or more) parts, which are tried separately to the same jury and resolved by one final judgment. An order for a separate trial leaves the lawsuit intact but enables the court to determine some issues separately from others. See "Motion for Separate (Bifurcated) Trial," §4, p. 266. For a separate trial for exemplary damages under CPRC chapter 41, see "Motion to Bifurcate Exemplary Damages," §5, p. 267.

NOTE

For the rules that govern joining and separating permissive claims, see "Permissive Joinder of Claims," ch. 2-E, §7, p. 100.

§3. MOTION FOR SEVERANCE

The purpose of a motion to sever is to divide a lawsuit into independent suits that may be resolved separately. A severance splits a single suit into two or more independent lawsuits, each resulting in a separate judgment. ***Van Dyke v. Boswell, O'Toole, Davis & Pickering***, 697 S.W.2d 381, 383 (Tex.1985). See ***O'Connor's*** FORM 5H:01.

§3.1 Motion. For allegations supporting severance, the movant should review ***Liberty Nat'l Fire Ins. Co. v. Akin***, 927 S.W.2d 627, 629 (Tex.1996), and ***Guaranty Fed. Sav. Bank v. Horseshoe Operating Co.***, 793 S.W.2d 652, 658 (Tex.1990). The motion should allege the following:

1. **More than one cause.** The controversy involves more than one cause of action. ***Liberty Nat'l***, 927 S.W.2d at 629; ***Guaranty Fed.***, 793 S.W.2d at 658; *e.g.*, ***McGuire v. Commercial Un. Ins. Co.***, 431 S.W.2d 347, 351 (Tex.1968) (one P's wrongful death suit & other P's suit for PI); ***In re Trinity Universal Ins. Co.***, 64 S.W.3d 463, 468 (Tex.App.—Amarillo 2001, orig. proceeding) (prompt-payment claim & claim for underinsured motorist benefits); ***Black v. Smith***, 956 S.W.2d 72, 75 (Tex.App.—Houston [14th Dist.] 1997, orig. proceeding) (PI claims & claims against D's insurer for invasion of privacy); ***U.S. Fire Ins. Co. v. Millard***, 847 S.W.2d 668, 672 (Tex.App.—Houston [1st Dist.] 1993, orig. proceeding) (claims for uninsured motorist benefits & bad-faith claims).

2. **Independent claim.** The severed claim could be independently asserted in a separate lawsuit. ***Liberty Nat'l***, 927 S.W.2d at 629; ***Guaranty Fed.***, 793 S.W.2d at 658; ***Trinity Universal***, 64 S.W.3d at 468; ***Black***, 956 S.W.2d at 75; *e.g.*, ***H.E. Butt Grocery Co. v. Currier***, 885 S.W.2d 175, 177 (Tex.App.—Corpus Christi 1994, no writ) (discovery order could not be severed because it was not a claim). To be severable, the causes must be capable of being brought as separate suits with separate, final judgments. ***Martinez v. Humble Sand & Gravel***, 875 S.W.2d 311, 312 (Tex.1994).

3. **Not interwoven.** The severed cause is not so interwoven with the remaining action that it involves the same facts and issues. ***Liberty Nat'l***, 927 S.W.2d at 629; ***Guaranty Fed.***, 793 S.W.2d at 658; *e.g.*, ***State Dept. of Highways & Pub. Transp. v. Cotner***, 845 S.W.2d 818, 819 (Tex.1993) (severance of Ps' claims was improper because facts & issues relating to their injuries were interwoven); ***Pilgrim Enters. v. Maryland Cas. Co.***, 24 S.W.3d 488, 491-92 (Tex.App.—Houston [1st Dist.] 2000, no pet.) (severance of P's claims was proper because insurer's duties to defend and to indemnify are separate and, thus, not inextricably interwoven).

4. For justice. Granting the motion to sever will do justice, avoid prejudice, and further the convenience of the parties and the court. ***Guaranty Fed.***, 793 S.W.2d at 658; ***Adams v. Baxter Healthcare Corp.***, 998 S.W.2d 349, 357 (Tex.App.—Austin 1999, no pet.); ***Black***, 956 S.W.2d at 75.

PRACTICE TIP

In a motion to sever, you can ask the trial court, as an alternative, to grant a separate trial as to the party or issue that you want severed. TRCP 174(b). A severable cause of action may be tried separately under the provisions of TRCP 174(b). ***Kansas Univ. Endowment Ass'n v. King****, 350 S.W.2d 11, 19 (Tex.1961). See "Motion for Separate (Bifurcated) Trial," §4, p. 266.*

§3.2 Objection. To object to a motion to sever, the party must make a specific and timely objection. TRAP 33.1(a)(1); ***Shank, Irwin v. Durant, Mankoff***, 748 S.W.2d 494, 501 (Tex.App.—Dallas 1988, no writ).

§3.3 Hearing & evidence. It is uncertain whether the trial court should receive and consider evidence in ruling on a severance. In ***Jones v. Ray***, 886 S.W.2d 817, 820 (Tex.App.—Houston [1st Dist.] 1994, orig. proceeding), the court held that the trial court should look exclusively to the live pleadings on file and should not consider evidence. Other courts have made statements that indicate evidence should be considered. *See, e.g.*, ***Allstate Ins. Co. v. Hunter***, 865 S.W.2d 189, 194 (Tex.App.—Corpus Christi 1993, orig. proceeding) (D did not carry its burden of proof on the motion to sever); ***Progressive Cty. Mut. Ins. Co. v. Parks***, 856 S.W.2d 776, 780 (Tex.App.—El Paso 1993, orig. proceeding) (pleadings alone are insufficient to require severance); ***Geophysical Data Processing Ctr. v. Cruz***, 576 S.W.2d 666, 667 (Tex.App.—Beaumont 1978, no writ) (propriety of severance not always dependent on pleadings).

§3.4 Order on motion to sever. TRCP 41 vests the trial court with broad discretion to sever a lawsuit into separate suits. ***Liberty Nat'l***, 927 S.W.2d at 629; ***Guaranty Fed.***, 793 S.W.2d at 658. The trial court's discretion is not, however, unlimited. ***Womack v. Berry***, 291 S.W.2d 677, 683 (Tex.1956). The court must exercise "a sound and legal discretion within limits created by the circumstances of the particular case." *Id.*

1. Immediately effective. The order severing part of a lawsuit is effective when it is signed. ***McRoberts v. Ryals***, 863 S.W.2d 450, 452-53 (Tex.1993). When a lawsuit is severed, the clerk assigns the severed cause a new number. If the clerk delays in assigning a cause number, it does not delay the effectiveness of the severance, but it can sometimes cause problems for the parties. *See id.* at 453 n.3. The trial court should assign a cause number to the severed action at the same time it signs the order of severance. *Id.* As an alternative, the trial court can condition the effectiveness of the order of severance on the clerk's assignment of a cause number and the party's payment of fees for the severance. *Id.*

2. Separate file. It is not necessary for the clerk to create a separate physical file for a severed cause of action. ***McRoberts***, 863 S.W.2d at 453 n.4; ***Darden v. Kitz Corp.***, 997 S.W.2d 388, 391 (Tex.App.—Beaumont 1999, pet. denied).

§3.5 Deadline for motion to sever. The trial court cannot sever a case after the case has been submitted to the trier of fact. TRCP 41; ***Cotner***, 845 S.W.2d at 819 (jury trial); ***In re El Paso Cty. Hosp.***, 979 S.W.2d 10, 12 (Tex. App.—El Paso 1998, orig. proceeding) (nonjury trial on stipulated facts). Despite the prohibition in TRCP 41 against post-submission severances, the trial court may order a partial new trial. *See* TRCP 320. TRCP 320 is an exception to TRCP 41. ***Cotner***, 845 S.W.2d at 819. See "Partial new trial," ch. 10-B, §8.3, p. 622.

§3.6 Severance proper, but not required.

1. Interlocutory summary judgment. The trial court may sever from the rest of the lawsuit a partial summary judgment granted on a claim or defense or granted to one of the parties, allowing the summary judgment to be appealed. *See, e.g.*, ***Cherokee Water Co. v. Forderhause***, 641 S.W.2d 522, 525 (Tex.1982) (SJ on suit to declare rights under a deed could be severed from suit to reform deed); ***Pilgrim Enters. v. Maryland Cas. Co.***, 24 S.W.3d 488, 491-92 (Tex.App.—Houston [1st Dist.] 2000, no pet.) (SJ on duty to defend claims severed from remaining claims); ***Guidry v. National Freight***, 944 S.W.2d 807, 812 (Tex.App.—Austin 1997, no writ) (SJ in favor of one D severed from claims against other Ds). The trial court cannot be forced to sever an interlocutory summary judgment. ***Marshall v. Harris***, 764 S.W.2d 34, 35 (Tex.App.—Houston [1st Dist.] 1989, orig. proceeding).

PRACTICE TIP

If you discover on appeal that what you thought was a final summary judgment is really a partial judgment, under the authority of TRAP 27.2, you may be able to convert it to a final summary judgment while the appeal is abated. For the procedure, see ***Iacono v. Lyons****, 6 S.W.3d 715, 717 (Tex.App.—Houston [1st Dist.] 1999, no pet.).*

2. Attorney fees. The trial court should not sever a claim for attorney fees without making a distinction between a claim for attorney fees that is an independent lawsuit (*e.g.*, an attorney's suit against the client for not paying fees), and a claim that is dependent on another claim (*e.g.*, claim for attorney fees as part of a suit on a note). If the claim for attorney fees is an independent cause of action, it may be severed and resolved by a separate judgment. If the claim is dependent on another claim, it should not be severed because it cannot be resolved by a separate judgment. Trial courts, however, seldom make this distinction. Though it cannot be severed, a dependent claim for attorney fees can be bifurcated for a separate trial and all issues resolved by one judgment. See §4, below.

3. Third-party action. The court may sever a third party's claims from the rest of the suit. ***Guaranty Fed. Sav. Bank v. Horseshoe Operating Co.***, 793 S.W.2d 652, 658 (Tex.1990) (fraud severed from wrongful dishonor of check).

4. Permissive counterclaim. The trial court may sever a permissive counterclaim. TRCP 41 (any claim may be severed); *see also* ***Straughan v. Houston Citizens Bank & Trust Co.***, 580 S.W.2d 29, 33 (Tex.App.—Houston [1st Dist.] 1979, no writ) (trial court did not abuse discretion in severing permissive counterclaim). For the rules governing permissive counterclaims, see "Permissive Joinder of Claims," ch. 2-E, §7, p. 100.

5. Separate cause of action. The trial court may, and in some cases must, sever a lawsuit if it involves two or more separate and distinct causes of action. See §3.7, below.

§3.7 Severance required. If the joint trial of multiple claims will prejudice one of the claims, the trial court should sever the lawsuit into separate trials or bifurcate the trial (see §4, below). This type of prejudice occurs when evidence is admissible on one claim but is prejudicial to the other claim. ***Liberty Nat'l Fire Ins. Co. v. Akin***, 927 S.W.2d 627, 630 (Tex.1996). For example, when a plaintiff sues an insurer for breach of contract and for bad faith, evidence of a settlement offer could prejudice the insurer's defense to the coverage dispute. *Id.*; ***Mid-Century Ins. Co. v. Lerner***, 901 S.W.2d 749, 752 (Tex.App.—Houston [14th Dist.] 1995, orig. proceeding); ***U.S. Fire Ins. Co. v. Millard***, 847 S.W.2d 668, 672-73 (Tex.App.—Houston [1st Dist.] 1993, orig. proceeding). *But see* ***In re Republic Lloyds***, 104 S.W.3d 354, 359-60 (Tex.App.—Houston [14th Dist.] 2003, orig. proceeding) (offer to settle undisputed part of contract claim did not require severance of contract & bad-faith claims).

§3.8 Severance not permitted. In the following instances, when a party makes a proper objection, severance is not permitted.

1. Indivisible injury. The court cannot sever claims against several defendants when the injury is indivisible. ***Landers v. East Tex. Salt Water Disposal Co.***, 248 S.W.2d 731, 734 (Tex.1952). *But see* ***Morgan v. Compugraphic Corp.***, 675 S.W.2d 729, 733-34 (Tex.1984) (severance of case involving indivisible injury was harmless). When the torts of two or more parties cause an indivisible injury, the claims should be tried together. If not, each tortfeasor could make the "empty chair" argument. ***Jones v. Ray***, 886 S.W.2d 817, 821-22 (Tex.App.—Houston [1st Dist.] 1994, orig. proceeding).

2. Dividing a cause of action. The trial court cannot sever a single cause of action into multiple claims. *E.g.*, ***Pierce v. Reynolds***, 329 S.W.2d 76, 79 n.1 (Tex.1959) (court should not have divided one claim into two lawsuits based on dates the damages accrued); ***Duncan v. Calhoun Cty. Nav. Dist.***, 28 S.W.3d 707, 711-12 (Tex.App.—Corpus Christi 2000, pet. denied) (in condemnation suit, issues of right-to-take & just compensation are components of one cause of action, not separate claims); ***Ryland Group v. White***, 723 S.W.2d 160, 162 (Tex. App.—Houston [1st Dist.] 1986, orig. proceeding) (court should not have severed negligence from contribution issue); ***Garrison v. Texas Commerce Bank***, 560 S.W.2d 451, 453 (Tex.App.—Houston [1st Dist.] 1977, writ ref'd n.r.e.) (court cannot sever property issues from divorce).

3. Compulsory counterclaim. The court cannot sever a compulsory counterclaim arising out of the same transaction or occurrence as the issue in the main suit. *E.g.*, ***Rucker v. Bank One Tex.***, 36 S.W.3d 649, 651-52 (Tex.App.—Waco 2000, pet. denied) (counterclaim for fraudulent inducement was intertwined with suit for breach of contract); ***Fuentes v. McFadden***, 825 S.W.2d 772, 779 (Tex.App.—El Paso 1992, no writ) (claim for attorney fees was intertwined with counterclaim for breach of contract); ***Mathis v. Bill De La Garza & Assocs.***, 778 S.W.2d 105, 106 (Tex.App.—Texarkana 1989, no writ) (suit for payment on a contract was intertwined with counterclaim for breach of contract). *But see* ***In re Occidental Permian, Ltd.***, ___ S.W.3d ___ (Tex.App.—Amarillo 2003, orig. proceeding) (No. 07-03-0016-CV; 4-7-03) (as long as court complies with TRCP 41, it is not error to sever and proceed with counterclaim). For the rules governing compulsory counterclaims, see "Compulsory Joinder of Claims," ch. 2-E, §6, p. 98.

4. Same liability. The court cannot sever a cause of action against the maker of a note (*e.g.*, the partnership) from the cause of action against the guarantors of the note (*e.g.*, the individual partners). ***McRoberts v. Tesoro S&L Ass'n***, 781 S.W.2d 705, 706 (Tex.App.—San Antonio 1989, writ denied).

5. Prejudice. If separate trials of a party's claims would prejudice the other party, the trial court should not sever. *See, e.g.*, ***Whataburger, Inc. v. Rutherford***, 642 S.W.2d 30, 35 (Tex.App.—Dallas 1982, no writ) (contract & fraud claims could not be separated without unfairness to D).

§4. MOTION FOR SEPARATE (BIFURCATED) TRIAL

The purpose of a motion for separate trials between the parties or on issues is to avoid prejudice and promote the ends of justice. ***In re Ethyl Corp.***, 975 S.W.2d 606, 610 (Tex.1998); ***Womack v. Berry***, 291 S.W.2d 677, 683 (Tex. 1956). A separate trial of issues leaves the lawsuit intact but bifurcates the case into two or more parts that are tried separately to the same jury. *See* ***Transportation Ins. Co. v. Moriel***, 879 S.W.2d 10, 30 (Tex.1994) (liability & damages should have been tried separately). See "Separate trials – bifurcation," §2.2, p. 263. See ***O'Connor's*** FORM 5H:04.

§4.1 Motion. Although TRCP 174(b) gives the trial court the power to conduct bifurcated trials, as a general rule, the courts should not try cases piecemeal. ***Moriel***, 879 S.W.2d at 30 n.29. TRCP 174(b) permits the trial court to bifurcate the trial of any claim, cross-claim, counterclaim, third-party claim, or any separate issue.

1. Grounds in most cases. The trial court may bifurcate the case (1) for convenience or (2) to avoid prejudice. TRCP 174(b). The following are some examples of when bifurcation is proper: • Bifurcated trials on the issues of marriage and divorce. *See* ***Winfield v. Renfro***, 821 S.W.2d 640, 652 (Tex.App.—Houston [1st Dist.] 1991, writ denied). • In suit for recovery under uninsured motorist provision of contract, bifurcated trial on issue of whether the plaintiff released the insurance company. ***Johnson v. State Farm Mut. Auto. Ins.***, 762 S.W.2d 267, 268-69 (Tex.App.—San Antonio 1988, writ denied). • In a suit against insurance company where there was a settlement offer, bifurcated trial on contractual and bad-faith claims. *See* ***Liberty Nat'l***, 927 S.W.2d at 630. • Bifurcated trial on defendant's issue of limitations from plaintiff's personal injury suit. ***Phipps v. Miller***, 597 S.W.2d 458, 460

(Tex.App.—Dallas 1980, writ ref'd n.r.e.). • Bifurcated exemplary damages from the issues of liability and actual damages. ***Moriel***, 879 S.W.2d at 30; *see* CPRC §41.009. See §5, below.

NOTE

In a personal injury case, the trial court cannot bifurcate the trial on liability from actual damages. ***Iley v. Hughes****, 311 S.W.2d 648, 651 (Tex.1958).*

2. Grounds in mass torts. For mass tort litigation (*e.g.*, asbestos litigation), the Supreme Court expanded on the TRCP 174(b) grounds (convenience & prejudice) by adopting the "Maryland factors." *See* ***Ethyl Corp.***, 975 S.W.2d at 614-17.

§4.2 Response. If any party objects to a motion to bifurcate, the party must make a specific and timely objection or it waives error. *See* TRAP 33.1(a)(1); ***Winkle v. Tullos***, 917 S.W.2d 304, 312-13 (Tex.App.—Houston [14th Dist.] 1995, writ denied). The party that opposes a motion to bifurcate should file a response stating its objections. See ***O'Connor's*** FORM 5H:05. Some of the objections a party may assert are as follows:

1. Bifurcating the trial will not be convenient. ***Guaranty Fed. Sav. Bank v. Horseshoe Operating Co.***, 793 S.W.2d 652, 658 (Tex.1990).

2. Bifurcating the trial will not avoid prejudice. ***Greater Houston Transp. Co. v. Zrubeck***, 850 S.W.2d 579, 587 (Tex.App.—Corpus Christi 1993, writ denied).

3. The court should not try the case piecemeal. ***Moriel***, 879 S.W.2d at 30 n.29.

4. Liability and damages are elements of an indivisible cause of action and cannot be tried separately. ***Iley***, 311 S.W.2d at 651; ***Waples-Platter Co. v. Commercial Stand. Ins. Co.***, 294 S.W.2d 375, 377 (Tex.1956).

§4.3 Hearing to bifurcate. Unless there is a reason to present evidence, a hearing for the receipt of evidence is not necessary. The motion can be resolved either by submission or at a hearing for argument only.

§4.4 One judgment. After one part of a bifurcated case is tried, any order the court signs is an interlocutory order that is not appealable; the court cannot sign a final, appealable judgment until all parts of the case have been tried. ***Hall v. City of Austin***, 450 S.W.2d 836, 838 (Tex.1970).

§5. MOTION TO BIFURCATE EXEMPLARY DAMAGES

§5.1 Motion of defendant. Only the defendant may move to bifurcate the issue of exemplary damages from the suit. CPRC §41.009(a). When there are multiple defendants, any one of them may make the motion. *Id.* §41.009(b). See ***O'Connor's*** FORM 5H:06.

1. Deadline. The defendant must make a motion to bifurcate the trial before the voir dire examination of the jury or the time specified in a pretrial order. CPRC §41.009(a).

2. Grounds. The motion should state the defendant requests a bifurcated trial on exemplary damages, as provided by CPRC §41.009(c)(1).

§5.2 Plaintiff's response. If the defendant makes a timely request under CPRC §41.009, the trial court must grant the motion. The only ground for objecting is that the defendant's motion is untimely. *See* CPRC §41.009(a).

§5.3 Trial procedure. For more information about the jury questions and the burdens of proof for the issues in an exemplary damage case, see ***O'Connor's COA***, "Bifurcated Trial on Exemplary Damages," ch. 35-G, §4, p. 1021.

1. Phase one. In phase one, the jury will resolve the issues of liability for actual damages, the amount of actual damages, and liability for exemplary damages. CPRC §41.009(c); ***Moriel***, 879 S.W.2d at 30. The jury is presented with evidence and jury questions on all the issues except the amount of exemplary damages.

Transportation Ins. Co. v. Moriel, 879 S.W.2d 10, 30 (Tex.1994). Evidence that is relevant only to the amount of exemplary damages is not admissible during the first part of a bifurcated trial. CPRC §41.011(b).

2. Phase two. If the jury found the defendant was liable for actual damages, awarded actual damages, and was unanimous in finding liability for exemplary damages, in phase two the jury will determine the amount of exemplary damages. CPRC §§41.003(d), 41.009(d). The jury is given questions to determine the proper amount of exemplary damages, considering the evidence presented during both parts of the trial. ***Moriel***, 879 S.W.2d at 30. In determining the amount of exemplary damages, the jury must consider evidence relating to the following issues: (1) the nature of the wrong, (2) the character of the conduct involved, (3) the degree of culpability of the wrongdoer, (4) the situation and sensibilities of the parties concerned, (5) the extent to which such conduct offends a public sense of justice and propriety, and (6) the net worth of the defendant. CPRC §41.011(a). A claimant who elects to have her recovery multiplied under another statute cannot be awarded exemplary damages. *Id.* §41.004(b).

§5.4 Plaintiff's burden.

1. Preponderance of the evidence. The phase one issues of liability for actual damages and the amount of actual damages must be decided by a preponderance of the evidence. See ***O'Connor's COA***, "Issues on actual damages," ch. 35-G, §4.3.1(1), p. 1022. Preponderance of the evidence means the greater weight and degree of credible evidence. ***Upjohn Co. v. Freeman***, 847 S.W.2d 589, 591 (Tex.App.—Dallas 1992, no writ).

2. Clear & convincing evidence. Exemplary damages may be awarded only if the plaintiff proves by clear and convincing evidence that the harm for which the plaintiff seeks recovery of exemplary damages resulted from one of the following: (1) fraud, (2) malice, or (3) gross negligence. CPRC §41.003(a)(1)-(3); *see also* Tex. Const. art. 16, §26 (liability for exemplary damages when D by willful act or omission or gross neglect causes death). Clear and convincing evidence is that degree of proof that will produce in the mind of the factfinder a firm belief or conviction about the truth of the allegations. ***State v. Addington***, 588 S.W.2d 569, 570 (Tex.1979). The burden of proof cannot be shifted to the defendant or satisfied by evidence of ordinary negligence, bad faith, or deceptive practice. CPRC §41.003(b).

3. Actual, not nominal damages. As a rule, the plaintiff must recover actual damages; nominal damages are not sufficient to support an award of exemplary damages. *See* CPRC §41.004(a). See ***O'Connor's COA***, "Actual damages required," ch. 35-G, §2.3.2, p. 1011. For cases filed after August 31, 2003, nominal damages are not sufficient to support an award of exemplary damages even if the plaintiff proves malice. See ***O'Connor's COA***, "Malice," ch. 35-G, §2.3.2(2), p. 1012. Actual damages, however, are not required to recover exemplary damages in a wrongful death suit brought by the employee's surviving spouse or heirs under Labor Code §408.001 for the death of the employee caused by the intentional act or omission or the gross negligence of the employer. *See* ***Wright v. Gifford-Hill & Co.***, 725 S.W.2d 712, 714 (Tex.1987). See ***O'Connor's COA***, "Wrongful death of employee," ch. 35-G, §2.3.2(3), p. 1012.

§5.5 Unanimous jury. The jury must render a unanimous verdict on liability for and the amount of exemplary damages. CPRC §41.003(d). Thus, all 12 jurors must agree on both phase one and phase two issues. *See id.* See "Exemplary damages cases," ch. 8-K, §4.2, p. 587.

§5.6 One judgment. After a bifurcated trial under CPRC chapter 41, the trial court will enter one judgment that resolves all the issues.

§6. REVIEW

§6.1 Motion to sever.

1. Appeal. On appeal, the appellate court will not disturb the trial court's decision to grant a severance unless the trial court abused its discretion. ***Guaranty Fed.***, 793 S.W.2d at 658. If the appellate court finds error in the ruling on severance, the court will reverse and remand. ***Nicor Expl. Co. v. Florida Gas Transmission Co.***, 911 S.W.2d 479, 482-83 (Tex.App.—Corpus Christi 1995, writ denied).

2. Mandamus. When the trial court has a duty either to grant or to deny severance, it has no discretion, and its order can be reviewed by mandamus. *See, e.g.*, ***Lusk v. Puryear***, 896 S.W.2d 377, 380-81 (Tex.App.—Amarillo 1995, orig. proceeding) (trial court improperly granted severance); ***F.A. Richard & Assocs. v. Millard***, 856 S.W.2d 765, 767 (Tex.App.—Houston [1st Dist.] 1993, orig. proceeding) (trial court improperly denied severance). Mandamus is appropriate to review the issue of severance only when there is no adequate remedy by appeal. ***Liberty Nat'l Fire Ins. Co. v. Akin***, 927 S.W.2d 627, 629 (Tex.1996) (mandamus denied); ***McLain v. Smith***, 899 S.W.2d 412, 414 (Tex.App.—Amarillo 1995, orig. proceeding) (same).

3. Severance on appeal. The rules that prohibit severance by the trial court of part of a cause of action do not apply to appellate courts. Under TRCP 320, an appellate court can grant a new trial on points that affect only a part of the case if that part is clearly separable without unfairness to the parties; however, an appellate court cannot grant a new trial on damages if liability was contested. TRCP 320. A partial new trial may be ordered notwithstanding the prohibition in TRCP 41 against post-submission severance. ***State Dept. of Highways & Pub. Transp. v. Cotner***, 845 S.W.2d 818, 819 (Tex.1993). An appellate court may affirm part of a case and sever part for remand, even though the trial court could not have. *See, e.g.*, ***Collins v. Collins***, 904 S.W.2d 792, 795 (Tex.App.—Houston [1st Dist.] 1995) (appellate court can affirm divorce and remand property issues), *writ denied*, 923 S.W.2d 569 (Tex.1996). Appellate courts regularly sever and remand attorney fees from the rest of the case, even when the attorney fees are dependent on another claim. *See, e.g.*, ***Woods Expl. & Prod'g Co. v. Arkla Equip. Co.***, 528 S.W.2d 568, 571 (Tex.1975) (claim for attorney fees for suit on a note was severed on appeal); ***Permian Report v. Lacy***, 817 S.W.2d 175, 178 (Tex.App.—El Paso 1991, writ denied) (claim for attorney fees for declaratory judgment action was severed on appeal).

§6.2 Motion to bifurcate. The trial court's decision regarding bifurcation is reviewed for abuse of discretion. ***Johnson v. State Farm Mut. Auto. Ins.***, 762 S.W.2d 267, 269 (Tex.App.—San Antonio 1988, writ denied).

I. JOINING AN ONGOING LAWSUIT

§1. GENERAL

§1.1 Rules. TRCP 43 (interpleader), TRCP 60-61 (intervention), TRCP 174 (consolidation).

§1.2 Purpose. The rules of joinder permit additional parties and claims to be brought into a lawsuit. Joinder may be accomplished through intervention, interpleader, or consolidation.

§1.3 Forms. ***O'Connor's Texas Civil Forms***, FORMS 5I.

§2. PETITION IN INTERVENTION

The purpose of a petition in intervention is to join a lawsuit that is already in progress.

§2.1 Filing the petition. The rules of pleading apply to intervenors just as they do to other parties. TRCP 61.

1. In writing. To intervene, a party must file a written pleading. ***Diaz v. Attorney Gen.***, 827 S.W.2d 19, 22 (Tex.App.—Corpus Christi 1992, no writ). See ***O'Connor's*** FORM 5I:01.

2. No motion for leave. An intervenor is not required to receive the court's permission to intervene. TRCP 60; ***Guaranty Fed. Sav. Bank v. Horseshoe Operating Co.***, 793 S.W.2d 652, 657 (Tex.1990); ***Intermarque Automotive Prods. v. Feldman***, 21 S.W.3d 544, 549 (Tex.App.—Texarkana 2000, no pet.). A nonparty may intervene in a suit as a plaintiff or a defendant without leave of court. *See* TRCP 60.

3. Interest of intervenor. The interest the intervenor asserts in the lawsuit may be legal or equitable. ***Guaranty Fed.***, 793 S.W.2d at 657; ***Gracida v. Tagle***, 946 S.W.2d 504, 506 (Tex.App.—Corpus Christi 1997, orig. proceeding). The interest must be more than a mere contingent or remote interest. ***Feldman***, 21 S.W.3d at 549.

4. Sufficiency of the pleadings. The sufficiency of the intervention is tested by the allegations of fact on which the right to intervene depends. ***Serna v. Webster***, 908 S.W.2d 487, 492 (Tex.App.—San Antonio 1995, no writ); ***H. Tebbs, Inc. v. Silver Eagle Distrib.***, 797 S.W.2d 80, 84 (Tex.App.—Austin 1990, no writ).

(1) Justiciable interest. The intervening party must have a justiciable interest in the suit. ***Mendez v. Brewer***, 626 S.W.2d 498, 499 (Tex.1982). To intervene as a plaintiff, the party must be entitled to some recovery; to intervene as a defendant, the party must be able to defeat some recovery. ***Guaranty Fed.***, 793 S.W.2d at 657; *see, e.g.*, ***Law Offices of Windle Turley v. Ghiasinejad***, 109 S.W.3d 68, 70-71 (Tex.App.—Fort Worth 2003, no pet.) (attorney with contingency fee contract had justiciable interest in plaintiff's suit); ***Feldman***, 21 S.W.3d at 551 (corporate policy owner could not intervene to claim right to defense costs paid by insurer to additional insured); ***Gracida***, 946 S.W.2d at 506 (third-party claimant could not intervene in declaratory judgment action to determine if insurer had duty to defend); ***Live Oak Resort v. T.A.B. Comm'n***, 920 S.W.2d 795, 798 (Tex.App.—Houston [1st Dist.] 1996, no writ) (protesters could not intervene in suit involving denial of TABC license because Alco. Bev. Code §11.67 provides that in such suit TABC is the only D); ***Beutel v. Dallas Cty. Flood Control Dist.***, 916 S.W.2d 685, 692 (Tex.App.—Waco 1996, writ denied) (lienholder, who did not have interest in property at time of taking, could not intervene in condemnation).

(2) Same transaction or occurrence. The intervening party must assert a claim that arises from the same transaction or occurrence and that has a common question of law or fact with the original claim. TRCP 40(a).

5. Venue. Each intervening plaintiff must, independently of every other plaintiff, establish proper venue. CPRC §15.003(a). See "Joinder proper under §15.003(a)," ch. 3-C, §2.6.4(2), p. 155.

6. For all purposes. Once a party intervenes, the intervenor becomes a party to the suit for all purposes.

§2.2 Deadline to file.

1. Before judgment. A petition in intervention generally may be filed at any time before judgment is rendered. *See* ***First Alief Bank v. White***, 682 S.W.2d 251, 252 (Tex.1984); ***Comal Cty. Rural High Sch. Dist. v. Nelson***, 314 S.W.2d 956, 957 (Tex.1958). A petition in intervention is not subject to the seven-day requirement in TRCP 63 concerning amendments and responses to pleadings. ***In re Estate of York***, 951 S.W.2d 122, 124-25 (Tex. App.—Corpus Christi 1997, no writ).

2. After judgment. A petition in intervention is too late if it is filed after judgment is rendered. ***First Alief Bank***, 682 S.W.2d at 252; ***Preston v. American Eagle Ins. Co.***, 948 S.W.2d 18, 20 (Tex.App.—Dallas 1997, no writ); *see also* ***Keim v. Anderson***, 943 S.W.2d 938, 943 (Tex.App.—El Paso 1997, no writ) (intervention filed after oral rendition of judgment was too late). *But see* ***Breazeale v. Casteel***, 4 S.W.3d 434, 436 (Tex.App.—Austin 1999, pet. denied) (intervention filed after final judgment rendered is not barred when intervenor does not attack existing judgment but instead seeks protection of property interests under CPRC §31.002). An intervention filed after rendition of judgment may be considered only if the trial court sets aside the judgment. ***First Alief Bank***, 682 S.W.2d at 252; ***Comal Cty.***, 314 S.W.2d at 957; ***State & Cty. Mut. Fire Ins. Co. v. Kelly***, 915 S.W.2d 224, 227 (Tex. App.—Austin 1996, orig. proceeding).

3. Laches. The intervention must be timely. *See, e.g.*, ***Armstrong v. Tidelands Life Ins. Co.***, 466 S.W.2d 407, 412 (Tex.App.—Corpus Christi 1971, no writ) (intervention filed 3 years & 9 months after suit filed was too late).

§2.3 Notice of the petition.

1. Citation not necessary. An intervenor may serve a petition in intervention on the parties in the suit under TRCP 21 and 21a. TRCP 61; ***McWilliams v. Snap-Pac Corp.***, 476 S.W.2d 941, 949 (Tex.App.—Houston [1st Dist.] 1971, writ ref'd n.r.e.); *see* TRCP 60, cmt., 785-786 S.W.2d (Tex.Cases) xlii (1990) ("Rules 21 and 21a control notice and service of pleadings of intervenors."). It is not necessary for the intervenor to serve citation on the parties that are before the court or on a defendant who makes a general appearance before limitations expires. ***Baker v. Monsanto Co.***, 111 S.W.3d 158, 160 (Tex.2003); *see* ***McWilliams***, 476 S.W.2d at 949-50; 1 McDonald, *Texas Civil Practice* §5:81 (1992). An intervenor's claim against a defendant served under TRCP 21 and 21a is barred if limitations runs before the defendant makes a general appearance. ***Baker***, 111 S.W.3d at 160-61.

2. Citation necessary. An intervenor must serve citation on (1) any defendant that has not made a general appearance and from whom the intervenor seeks affirmative relief, and (2) any third party brought into the lawsuit by the intervenor. ***Baker***, 111 S.W.3d at 160; 1 McDonald, *Texas Civil Practice* §5:81 (1992).

§2.4 Motion to strike. If any party in the suit opposes the intervention, that party must challenge it by filing a motion to strike the petition in intervention. TRCP 60; ***Guaranty Fed. Sav. Bank v. Horseshoe Operating Co.***, 793 S.W.2d 652, 658 (Tex.1990); ***Feldman***, 21 S.W.3d at 548-49. See ***O'Connor's*** FORM 5I:02. A court cannot strike an intervention on its own initiative. ***Guaranty Fed.***, 793 S.W.2d at 657; ***Flores v. Melo-Palacios***, 921 S.W.2d 399, 404 (Tex.App.—Corpus Christi 1996, writ denied). If the party opposing the intervention does not move to strike, that party waives any right to complain. ***Ghidoni v. Stone Oak, Inc.***, 966 S.W.2d 573, 587 (Tex.App.—San Antonio 1998, pet. denied) (motions to abate or sever are not substitutes for a motion to strike). The motion to strike should allege the following:

1. The intervenor could not have brought all or part of the same action in its own name; or, if the action had been brought against it, the intervenor would not have been able to defeat recovery. ***Guaranty Fed.***, 793 S.W.2d at 657.
2. The intervention will complicate the case by an excessive multiplication of the issues. *Id.*
3. The intervention is not essential to protect the intervenor's interest. *Id.*

§2.5 Hearing on motion to strike.

1. Make a record. If the trial court conducts a hearing to receive evidence on the motion to strike, the parties should request a court reporter. Without a reporter's record of the hearing, an appellant cannot challenge the ruling on appeal. ***Saldana v. Saldana***, 791 S.W.2d 316, 320 (Tex.App.—Corpus Christi 1990, no writ).

2. Burden on intervenor. At the hearing, the burden is on the intervenor to show it has a justiciable interest in the lawsuit. ***Mendez v. Brewer***, 626 S.W.2d 498, 499 (Tex.1982); ***Intermarque Automotive Prods. v. Feldman***, 21 S.W.3d 544, 549 (Tex.App.—Texarkana 2000, no pet.). The intervenor should be given the opportunity to respond to the motion, but the issue of whether it has a justiciable interest may be resolved by reference to the petition in intervention. ***Potash Corp. v. Mancias***, 942 S.W.2d 61, 64 (Tex.App.—Corpus Christi 1997, orig. proceeding). To establish the right to intervene as a plaintiff, the intervenor must show that it could have brought all or part of the same action in its own name; to establish the right to intervene as a defendant, the intervenor must show it would be able to defeat all or part of the suit had the suit been brought against it. ***Guaranty Fed.***, 793 S.W.2d at 657; ***Feldman***, 21 S.W.3d at 549.

§2.6 Order on the motion to strike.

1. Trial court standard. The trial court has broad discretion to rule on the motion to strike the intervention. ***Guaranty Fed.***, 793 S.W.2d at 657. The trial court should not strike a petition in intervention if (1) the intervenor meets the test for intervention (see §2.1.4(1), above); (2) the intervention will not complicate the case by an excessive multiplication of the issues; and (3) the intervention is almost essential to protect the intervenor's interest effectively. *Id.*; *see, e.g.*, ***Ghiasinejad***, 109 S.W.3d at 71 (intervention struck because it would have injected new issues into already complicated case).

2. Options. The trial court has a number of options regarding a petition in intervention. It may (1) try the intervention claim, (2) sever the intervention claim, (3) order a separate trial on the intervention claim, or (4) strike the intervention for good cause. ***Saldana***, 791 S.W.2d at 320.

§3. INTERPLEADER SUIT

By filing an interpleader, a party may protect itself from multiple liability by interpleading the funds that are subject to conflicting claims. TRCP 43; *see* ***Davis v. East Tex. S&L Ass'n***, 354 S.W.2d 926, 930 (Tex.1962); ***Tri-State Pipe & Equip. v. Southern Mut. Ins. Co.***, 8 S.W.3d 394, 402 (Tex.App.—Texarkana 1999, no pet.). This procedure is useful when two or more persons claim insurance proceeds, escrow accounts, or trust funds that are in the hands of a disinterested party. *E.g.*, ***Great Am. Reserve Ins. Co. v. Sanders***, 525 S.W.2d 956, 958 (Tex.1975) (insurance proceeds claimed by widow & former wife). A suit filed as an interpleader is a suit in equity. ***Northshore Bank v. Commercial Credit Corp.***, 668 S.W.2d 787, 790 (Tex.App.—Houston [14th Dist.] 1984, writ ref'd n.r.e.). See *O'Connor's* FORM 5I:04.

§3.1 Interpleader-party.

1. Plaintiff-stakeholder. A party that is subject to multiple liability because several claims have been or may be asserted against the same property may file a petition in interpleader, joining the competing claimants to the lawsuit as defendants. TRCP 43.

2. Defendant-stakeholder. A defendant already in a suit may file an interpleader as a cross-claim or counterclaim. When multiple claims are made for the same property, TRCP 43 authorizes a defendant to join all claimants in the lawsuit and deposit the disputed property into the registry of the court. ***Olmos v. Pecan Grove Mun. Util. Dist.***, 857 S.W.2d 734, 741 (Tex.App.—Houston [14th Dist.] 1993, no writ).

3. Garnishee. A garnishee subject to conflicting claims may file an interpleader. ***Northshore Bank***, 668 S.W.2d at 789.

§3.2 Petition. A party is entitled to relief by interpleader if it establishes the following:

1. Rival claims. The interpleader must show it is subject to (or has reasonable grounds to anticipate) rival claims to the same fund or property. ***Olmos***, 857 S.W.2d at 741; *see* ***Davis***, 354 S.W.2d at 930 (claims must place interpleader in some real doubt or hazard); .

2. Timely filing. The interpleader must show it did not unreasonably delay filing the action for interpleader. ***Union Gas Corp. v. Gisler***, ___ S.W.3d ___ (Tex.App.—Corpus Christi 2003, n.p.h.) (No. 13-01-734-CV; 8-29-03); ***Serna v. Webster***, 908 S.W.2d 487, 491 (Tex.App.—San Antonio 1995, no writ); *see* ***Savings & Profit Sharing Fund of Sears Employees v. Stubbs***, 734 S.W.2d 76, 79 (Tex.App.—Austin 1987, no writ) (3-year delay was unreasonable).

3. Unconditional tender. The interpleader must show it unconditionally tendered the disputed money or property into the registry of the court. ***Tri-State Pipe***, 8 S.W.3d at 402-03; ***Serna***, 908 S.W.2d at 491; *see, e.g.*, ***Rapp v. Mandell & Wright***, ___ S.W.3d ___ (Tex.App.—Corpus Christi 2003, n.p.h.) (No. 13-01-255-CV; 8-28-03) (deposit was not unconditional because it was made without waiver of rights & there was no disinterested person to qualify as stakeholder). Only an unconditional tender, not a deposit, is required. ***Security Nat'l Bank v. Washington Loan & Fin. Corp.***, 570 S.W.2d 40, 43 n.4 (Tex.App.—Dallas 1978, writ dism'd); *see* ***Tri-State Pipe***, 8 S.W.3d at 403. The interpleader must tender or deposit the money or property so the court can allocate it among the parties as part of the judgment. The deposit of the money or property discharges the interpleader. ***Stubbs***, 734 S.W.2d at 79.

4. Discharge. The interpleader should ask the court to sign an order of discharge.

5. Costs & attorney fees. A disinterested stakeholder is entitled to recover attorney fees if it had reasonable doubts as to which party was entitled to the funds and it interpleaded the claimants in good faith. ***U.S. v. Ray Thomas Gravel Co.***, 380 S.W.2d 576, 580 (Tex.1964); ***Olmos***, 857 S.W.2d at 741; ***Salazar v. San Benito Bank & Trust Co.***, 730 S.W.2d 21, 24 (Tex.App.—Corpus Christi 1987, no writ). However, if the stakeholder was responsible for the conflicting claims to the funds, the stakeholder is not entitled to attorney fees. ***Olmos***, 857 S.W.2d at 742; *see*

Brown v. Getty Reserve Oil, 626 S.W.2d 810, 815 (Tex.App.—Amarillo 1981, writ dism'd) (stakeholder improperly created fund that became subject of conflicting claims).

§3.3 Response. The following are some of the allegations a party opposing the interpleader may assert.

1. No rival claims. The interpleader is not subject to and has no reasonable grounds to anticipate rival claims to the same property. *See* ***Davis***, 354 S.W.2d at 930; ***Olmos***, 857 S.W.2d at 741.

2. Unreasonable delay. The interpleader has unreasonably delayed filing the action for interpleader. ***Petro Source Partners v. 3-B Rattlesnake Ref., Ltd.***, 905 S.W.2d 371, 377 (Tex.App.—El Paso 1990, writ denied).

3. No unconditional tender. The interpleader has not unconditionally tendered the fund or property into the registry of the court. ***Rapp***, ___ S.W.3d at ___; ***Tri-State Pipe***, 8 S.W.3d at 402-03.

4. Not disinterested. The interpleader is not a disinterested stakeholder, is responsible for the conflicting claims, and should not recover costs and attorney fees. ***Brown***, 626 S.W.2d at 815.

§3.4 Hearing on interpleader. The court must conduct a hearing on the initial issue of whether interpleader is appropriate. *See* ***Taliaferro v. Texas Commerce Bank***, 669 S.W.2d 172, 174 (Tex.App.—Fort Worth 1984, no writ). The interpleader must introduce evidence to support the petition in interpleader and, if appropriate, attorney fees. *Id.*

§3.5 Order on interpleader.

1. Interpleader is appropriate. If the court determines the suit is properly an interpleader action, it will ordinarily order the following:

(1) Require the interpleader to deposit the funds or property into the registry of the court (if not already on deposit).

(2) Discharge the interpleader from the suit.

(3) Enjoin the rival claimants from taking any action against the interpleader.

(4) Grant costs and attorney fees to the innocent interpleader. ***Ray Thomas Gravel***, 380 S.W.2d at 581.

(5) Continue the suit on the merits between the rival claimants to determine their respective rights to the money or property.

2. Interpleader is not appropriate. If the suit is not properly brought as an interpleader action, the court will dismiss it.

§3.6 Trial on the merits. During the trial on the merits, each claimant has the burden to prove its own claim to the funds; a claimant cannot merely disprove the other's right. ***McBryde v. Curry***, 914 S.W.2d 616, 620 (Tex. App.—Texarkana 1995, writ denied); ***Northshore Bank v. Commercial Credit Corp.***, 668 S.W.2d 787, 789 (Tex. App.—Houston [14th Dist.] 1984, writ ref'd n.r.e.).

§4. MOTION TO CONSOLIDATE

Consolidation of separate suits is the opposite of separating lawsuits into distinct parts, and thus the same legal principles apply in ordering consolidation under TRCP 174(a) as in ordering separate trials under TRCP 174(b). ***Dal-Briar Corp. v. Baskette***, 833 S.W.2d 612, 615 (Tex.App.—El Paso 1992, orig. proceeding). See "Motion for Separate (Bifurcated) Trial," ch. 5-H, §4, p. 266.

§4.1 Motion. TRCP 174(a) gives the trial court broad discretion to consolidate cases with common issues of law or fact. ***Owens-Corning Fiberglas Corp. v. Martin***, 942 S.W.2d 712, 716 (Tex.App.—Dallas 1997, no writ). See ***O'Connor's*** FORM 5I:07.

1. Standards to apply. Suits to be consolidated should relate to substantially the same subject matter, and the same evidence should be material, relevant, and admissible in both suits. ***Owens-Corning***, 942 S.W.2d at 716; ***Lone Star Ford v. McCormick***, 838 S.W.2d 734, 737 (Tex.App.—Houston [1st Dist.] 1992, writ denied). If consolidation would result in prejudice, the cases should not be joined. ***Lone Star***, 838 S.W.2d at 738.

2. Pending before the court. A court may consolidate lawsuits that are pending in different district courts within the same county. ***Starnes v. Holloway***, 779 S.W.2d 86, 96 (Tex.App.—Dallas 1989, writ denied). A court in one county cannot order a matter pending in another county to be transferred out of that county and into its court, unless there is some specific statutory authority. ***Flores v. Peschel***, 927 S.W.2d 209, 213 (Tex.App.—Corpus Christi 1996, orig. proceeding). See "Motion for Pretrial Consolidation," ch. 5-G, p. 259.

3. Local rules. Some local rules require that the motion to consolidate be filed in whichever case was filed first. *See* ***Starnes***, 779 S.W.2d at 96 (Dallas County); ***Santa Fe Drilling Co. v. O'Neill***, 774 S.W.2d 423, 424 (Tex.App.—Houston [14th Dist.] 1989, orig. proceeding) (Harris County).

§4.2 Objection. If any party objects to a motion to consolidate, the party must make a specific and timely objection. TRAP 33.1(a)(1).

§4.3 Order. In deciding whether to consolidate, the trial court must weigh the judicial economy and convenience that may be gained by the consolidation against the risk of an unfair outcome because of prejudice or jury confusion. ***In re Ethyl Corp.***, 975 S.W.2d 606, 610 (Tex.1998); ***Owens-Corning***, 942 S.W.2d at 716.

§5. REVIEW

§5.1 Intervention.

1. Interlocutory appeal. As a general rule, when the trial court strikes the petition in intervention, the order cannot be appealed until after the court renders a final judgment in the case. ***Metromedia Long Distance v. Hughes***, 810 S.W.2d 494, 499 (Tex.App.—San Antonio 1991, writ denied). However, there are exceptions. If venue is at issue, CPRC §15.003(b) allows an interlocutory appeal of an intervention decision. See "Joinder," ch. 3-C, §5.2.2, p. 163. Under CPRC §51.014(d), the parties may agree to an interlocutory appeal even when it is not made specifically available by statute. See ***O'Connor's Texas Civil Appeals***, "Appealable orders by agreed motion," ch. 13-P, §2.2, p. 131 (2002-03).

2. Standard. The appellate court will review the trial court's ruling for abuse of discretion. ***Guaranty Fed. Sav. Bank v. Horseshoe Operating Co.***, 793 S.W.2d 652, 657 (Tex.1990). The trial court abuses its discretion in denying an intervention if (1) the intervenor could have brought all or part of the same action in its own name, or if the action had been brought against it, the intervenor could have defeated all or part of the recovery; (2) the intervention would not complicate the case by an excessive multiplication of issues; and (3) the intervention was almost essential to protecting the intervenor's interest. *Id.*; ***City of Port Arthur v. Southwestern Bell Tel. Co.***, 13 S.W.3d 841, 843 (Tex.App.—Austin 2000, no pet.). If the appellate court finds the trial court's ruling was wrong, the court applies the harmless error rule in TRAP 44.1 and 61.1.

§5.2 Interpleader. If the order granting interpleader disposes of all issues involving the interpleader, it is a final order and is appealable. ***K&S Interests v. Texas Am. Bank/Dallas***, 749 S.W.2d 887, 889-90 (Tex.App.—Dallas 1988, writ denied); ***Taliaferro v. Texas Commerce Bank***, 660 S.W.2d 151, 155 (Tex.App.—Fort Worth 1983, no writ). If the order is final, any party wishing to appeal must perfect its appeal from the date the court signs the order granting the interpleader.

§5.3 Consolidation. The same standards that control separation of issues control the consolidation of issues. See "Motion to bifurcate," ch. 5-H, §6.2, p. 269.

J. MOTION FOR SANCTIONS

§1. GENERAL

§1.1 Rules. CPRC §§9.011-9.014 (groundless pleadings), CPRC §§10.001-10.006 (frivolous pleadings); TRCP 13 (groundless pleadings), TRCP 21b (failure to serve copies), TRCP 215 (discovery abuse). See Gov't Code §21.002 (officer of court can be held in contempt), Gov't Code §82.061 (attorney may be fined or imprisoned for misbehavior or contempt).

§1.2 Purpose. A motion for sanctions is a request to the trial court to impose sanctions on the other party. ***Tri-M Erectors v. Clearwater Constructors***, 788 S.W.2d 906, 908 (Tex.App.—Austin 1990, writ denied). The purpose of sanctions is to secure the parties' compliance with the rules, punish those that violate the rules, and deter other litigants from violating the rules. ***Chrysler Corp. v. Blackmon***, 841 S.W.2d 844, 849 (Tex.1992); ***Bodnow Corp. v. City of Hondo***, 721 S.W.2d 839, 840 (Tex.1986). In most cases, the imposition of sanctions should not prevent a decision on the merits of the case. ***Chrysler***, 841 S.W.2d at 850; ***TransAmerican Nat. Gas Corp. v. Powell***, 811 S.W.2d 913, 918 (Tex.1991).

§1.3 Forms. *O'Connor's Texas Civil Forms*, FORMS 5J.

§2. AUTHORITY FOR SANCTIONS

§2.1 Rule or statute. Most sanctions are imposed under the authority of a specific statute or rule that permits the court to order sanctions. See CPRC §9.012, chs. 10, 13; TRCP 13, 166(a)(h), 215.

§2.2 Inherent power. Sanctions may also be imposed under the court's inherent power. A trial court has inherent power to sanction for abuses of the judicial process not covered by rule or statute. ***Kutch v. Del Mar Coll.***, 831 S.W.2d 506, 510 (Tex.App.—Corpus Christi 1992, no writ). For the court to exercise this inherent power, the conduct complained about must significantly interfere with the court's legitimate exercise of one of its core functions. *Id.*; *see, e.g.*, ***Kennedy v. Kennedy***, ___ S.W.3d ___ (Tex.App.—Austin 2002, pet. denied) (No. 03-02-00025-CV; 12-5-02) (court could not punish spouse under inherent power by granting interlocutory divorce).

§3. STANDARDS FOR IMPOSING SANCTIONS

Sanctions must be "just." TRCP 215.2(b); ***Spohn Hosp. v. Mayer***, 104 S.W.3d 878, 882 (Tex.2003); ***Chrysler Corp.***, 841 S.W.2d at 849; ***TransAmerican***, 811 S.W.2d at 917. In other words, the punishment should fit the crime. ***TransAmerican***, 811 S.W.2d at 917.

§3.1 To impose sanctions. There is a two-part test to determine whether sanctions are just:

1. **Direct relationship.** The sanction must bear a direct relationship to the offensive conduct, measured by a direct nexus among the conduct, the offender, and the sanction imposed. ***Spohn Hosp.***, 104 S.W.3d at 882; ***TransAmerican***, 811 S.W.2d at 917; *e.g.*, ***Remington Arms Co. v. Caldwell***, 850 S.W.2d 167, 171 (Tex.1993) (striking pleadings is not appropriate sanction for failure to designate witness; proper sanction is to exclude witness); ***Magnuson v. Mullen***, 65 S.W.3d 815, 828 (Tex.App.—Fort Worth 2002, pet. denied) (direct relationship between P's conduct & dismissal when P frustrated all attempts to define the cause of action & investigate defenses). A just sanction must be directed against the abuse and toward remedying the prejudice caused to the innocent party. ***Spohn Hosp.***, 104 S.W.3d at 882; ***TransAmerican***, 811 S.W.2d at 917.

2. **Necessary severity.** The sanction must not be excessive; it should be no more severe than necessary to promote full compliance. ***Spohn Hosp.***, 104 S.W.3d at 882; ***Chrysler Corp.***, 841 S.W.2d at 849; ***Braden v. Downey***, 811 S.W.2d 922, 929-30 (Tex.1991); ***TransAmerican***, 811 S.W.2d at 917; *see, e.g.*, ***Zappe v. Zappe***, 871 S.W.2d 910, 913 (Tex.App.—Corpus Christi 1994, no writ) (incomplete answers to discovery did not justify default judgment in child custody suit). Discovery sanctions that are so severe as to inhibit presentation of the merits of a case should be reserved for a party's flagrant bad faith or an attorney's callous disregard for the discovery rules.

Spohn Hosp., 104 S.W.3d at 883; ***TransAmerican***, 811 S.W.2d at 918. The courts should consider the least stringent sanction necessary to promote compliance. ***Spohn Hosp.***, 104 S.W.3d at 882.

§3.2 To impose death penalty sanctions. A death penalty sanction is one that has the effect of adjudicating the dispute. ***TransAmerican***, 811 S.W.2d at 918. Death penalty sanctions should be imposed only in exceptional cases when they are clearly justified and it is apparent that no lesser sanctions would promote compliance with the rules. ***Spohn Hosp.***, 104 S.W.3d at 882; ***GTE Comm. Sys. v. Tanner***, 856 S.W.2d 725, 729 (Tex.1993). Death penalty sanctions include dismissal, default judgment, excluding evidence, and jury instructions resolving fact issues in favor of one party. *See* ***Spohn Hosp.***, 104 S.W.3d at 883 (jury instructions); ***In re Adkins***, 70 S.W.3d 384, 391 (Tex.App.—Fort Worth 2002, orig. proceeding) (same); ***Adkins Servs. v. Tisdale Co.***, 56 S.W.3d 842, 846 (Tex.App.—Texarkana 2001, no pet.) (order excluding evidence). There is a four-part test to determine whether death penalty sanctions are appropriate.

1. **Direct relationship.** See §3.1.1, above.

2. **Necessary severity.** See §3.1.2, above.

3. **Lesser sanction first.** The trial court must use a lesser sanction first to determine if it is adequate to secure compliance, deterrence, and punishment of the offender. ***Chrysler Corp.***, 841 S.W.2d at 849; ***Kugle v. DaimlerChrysler Corp.***, 88 S.W.3d 355, 364 (Tex.App.—San Antonio 2002, pet. denied); *see* ***Williams v. Akzo Nobel Chems.***, 999 S.W.2d 836, 844 (Tex.App.—Tyler 1999, no pet.) (threat of sanctions, without more, was not sufficient). The order cannot just say the court "considered" a lesser sanction before imposing death penalty sanctions. ***Adkins***, 70 S.W.3d at 391; ***Humphreys v. Meadows***, 938 S.W.2d 750, 752 (Tex.App.—Fort Worth 1996, writ denied); *see also* ***In re N.R.C.***, 94 S.W.3d 799, 812 (Tex.App.—Houston [14th Dist.] 2002, pet. denied) (silent record does not support conclusion court considered lesser sanctions). An order compelling discovery is not a lesser sanction. ***In re Western Star Trucks US***, 112 S.W.3d 756, 766 (Tex.App.—Eastland 2003, orig. proceeding); ***In re Polaris Indus.***, 65 S.W.3d 746, 753 (Tex.App.—Beaumont 2001, orig. proceeding). *But see* ***Andras v. Memorial Hosp. Sys.***, 888 S.W.2d 567, 572-73 (Tex.App.—Houston [1st Dist.] 1994, writ denied) (order to compel under threat of sanctions met requirement of "lesser" sanction).

4. **No merit to claims or defenses.** For death penalty sanctions to be appropriate, the party's conduct must justify the presumption that its claims or defenses lack merit. ***Hamill v. Level***, 917 S.W.2d 15, 16 (Tex.1996); ***TransAmerican***, 811 S.W.2d at 918; *see, e.g.*, ***Chasewood Oaks Condo. Homeowners Ass'n v. Amatek Holdings***, 977 S.W.2d 840, 844-45 (Tex.App.—Fort Worth 1998, pet. denied) (lawsuit properly dismissed because P abused discovery process); ***Andras***, 888 S.W.2d at 573 (lawsuit against hospital for overcharging was properly dismissed because P's attorney refused to produce canceled checks).

§4. PERSONS WHO MAY BE SANCTIONED

The trial court should impose the sanctions against the offender. ***Spohn Hosp.***, 104 S.W.3d at 882-83; ***TransAmerican***, 811 S.W.2d at 917. Before imposing sanctions that severely inhibit the presentation of a party's claim, the court should make a record identifying who was responsible for the sanctionable conduct—the party, the attorney, or both. ***Spohn Hosp.***, 104 S.W.3d at 882.

§4.1 Party. The court may impose sanctions on the party. *See* TRCP 215.1(d), 215.2(b), 215.3; ***TransAmerican***, 811 S.W.2d at 917. A party should not be punished for conduct in which it is not implicated. ***TransAmerican***, 811 S.W.2d at 917; *see, e.g.*, ***In re Harvest Cmtys.***, 88 S.W.3d 343, 348 (Tex.App.—San Antonio 2002, orig. proceeding) (no evidence party was guilty of anything but hiring offensive attorney); ***Smith v. Nguyen***, 855 S.W.2d 263, 266-67 (Tex.App.—Houston [14th Dist.] 1993, writ denied) (nothing in record implicated party in late designation of witnesses). The trial court cannot impose a sanction on a party that adversely affects other parties who were not implicated in the abuse. ***Arkla, Inc. v. Harris***, 846 S.W.2d 623, 628-29 (Tex.App.—Houston [14th Dist.] 1993, orig. proceeding).

§4.2 Attorney. If the attorney was responsible for the sanctionable conduct and the party was unaware of it, the court should sanction the attorney, not the party. *See* TRCP 215.1(d), 215.2(b)(8); ***TransAmerican Nat. Gas Corp. v. Powell***, 811 S.W.2d 913, 917 (Tex.1991); ***In re Barnes***, 956 S.W.2d 746, 748 (Tex.App.—Corpus Christi 1997, orig. proceeding); *see, e.g.*, ***Jones v. Andrews***, 873 S.W.2d 102, 106 (Tex.App.—Dallas 1994, no writ) (party should not be punished by death penalty sanctions because attorney did not timely ask for extension). When multiple attorneys are involved in the sanctionable conduct, they can be held jointly and severally liable. *See, e.g.*, ***Kugle***, 88 S.W.3d at 364-65 (3 attorneys jointly & severally liable for fraud in PI suit).

§4.3 Both party & attorney. When both the attorney and the party are implicated in sanctionable conduct, the court may sanction both of them. *See* TRCP 215.1(d); *see, e.g.*, ***Kugle***, 88 S.W.3d at 366 (lawyers liable for monetary sanctions & suit dismissed); ***In re Zenergy***, 968 S.W.2d 1, 11 (Tex.App.—Corpus Christi 1997, orig. proceeding) (party & attorney jointly & severally liable for monetary sanctions).

§4.4 Nonparty.

1. Discovery abuse. When a nonparty refuses to comply with a subpoena (to produce documents or to appear) or a court order (*e.g.*, to appear for a deposition, permit inspection of land), the court can treat the noncompliance as contempt. TRCP 176.8(a), 196.7, 205.3(a), 215.2(a), (c); ***City of Houston v. Chambers***, 899 S.W.2d 306, 309 (Tex.App.—Houston [14th Dist.] 1995, orig. proceeding) (addressed former TRCP 215(2)(a)). Neither TRCP 215.2(b) nor TRCP 215.3 authorizes other sanctions against a nonparty. ***Pope v. Davidson***, 849 S.W.2d 916, 920 (Tex.App.—Houston [14th Dist.] 1993, orig. proceeding); *see* ***Chambers***, 899 S.W.2d at 309 (because nonparty had not violated order in resisting discovery, court could not impose monetary sanctions); ***Texas A.G.'s Office v. Adams***, 793 S.W.2d 771, 775 (Tex.App.—Fort Worth 1990, no writ) (court could not sanction nonparty to pay attorney fees of $9,628 for refusing to comply with subpoena). When a person is found guilty of contempt, the court is limited to a monetary fine ($500 limit) or incarceration. *See* Gov't Code §21.002; ***In re Acceptance Ins. Co.***, 33 S.W.3d 443, 450 (Tex.App.—Fort Worth 2000, orig. proceeding); *see, e.g.*, ***Pope***, 849 S.W.2d at 920 (court could not require nonparty to perform community service).

2. Pleading abuse. A nonparty cannot be sanctioned for pleading abuse under TRCP 13. ***Chambers***, 899 S.W.2d at 309; *see also* CPRC §9.012 (addresses pleading abuse by party). TRCP 13 applies only to parties and their attorneys. ***Chambers***, 899 S.W.2d at 309; *see, e.g.*, ***Jimenez v. Transwestern Prop. Co.***, 999 S.W.2d 125, 130 (Tex.App.—Houston [14th Dist.] 1999, no pet.) (paralegal could not be sanctioned under TRCP 13); ***Adams***, 793 S.W.2d at 775 (nonparty's claims of privilege could not be punished under TRCP 13).

§5. CONDUCT THAT JUSTIFIES SANCTIONS

§5.1 Discovery abuse.

1. Designation of witness. The court can impose sanctions on a corporation or other entity that does not make a designation of a witness under TRCP 199.2(b)(1) or TRCP 200.1(b). TRCP 215.1(b)(1). See "When organization deposed," ch. 6-E, §4.6.3, p. 392.

2. Oral discovery. The court can impose sanctions on a party, other deponent, or person designated to testify on behalf of a party or other deponent. See "Grounds for sanctions," ch. 6-E, §10.1, p. 397.

3. Written discovery. The court can impose sanctions on a party for any of the following:

(1) Not serving answers or objections to interrogatories submitted under TRCP 197. TRCP 215.1(b)(3)(A); ***Swain v. Southwestern Bell Yellow Pages***, 998 S.W.2d 731, 732-33 (Tex.App.—Fort Worth 1999, no pet.); ***Drozd Corp. v. Capitol Glass & Mirror Co.***, 741 S.W.2d 221, 222 (Tex.App.—Austin 1987, no writ).

(2) Not answering an interrogatory submitted under TRCP 197. TRCP 215.1(b)(3)(B); ***Able Sup. Co. v. Moye***, 898 S.W.2d 766, 771 (Tex.1995).

(3) Not serving a written response to a request for inspection submitted under TRCP 196, after proper service of the request. TRCP 215.1(b)(3)(C).

(4) Not responding that discovery will be permitted as requested or not permitting discovery as requested in response to a request for inspection submitted under TRCP 196. TRCP 215.1(b)(3)(D).

(5) Not responding to a request for disclosures. ***Magnuson v. Mullen***, 65 S.W.3d 815, 828 (Tex. App.—Fort Worth 2002, pet. denied).

4. Evasive or incomplete answer. For purposes of sanctions, an evasive or incomplete answer is treated as a failure to answer. TRCP 215.1(c).

5. Frivolous objections. The court can impose sanctions when an attorney files frivolous objections to discovery. *See, e.g.*, ***Childs v. Argenbright***, 927 S.W.2d 647, 649 (Tex.App.—Tyler 1996, no writ) (attorney filed 9 pages of objections to interrogatories without answering any of them).

6. False discovery certification. The court can impose sanctions under CPRC chapter 10 on an attorney who signed a discovery disclosure, request, notice, response, or objection in violation of TRCP 191.3(b) or (c). TRCP 191.3(e). For the representations certified by the signer of discovery under TRCP 191.3, see "Certification by signature," ch. 6-A, §3.1, p. 314. The sanction can be imposed on the person who made the certification or the party on whose behalf it was made, or on both. TRCP 191.3(e). See "Sanctions under CPRC §10.004(c)," §7.2, p. 283.

7. False testimony. The court can impose sanctions when a party gives false testimony. *See, e.g.*, ***Schaver v. British Am. Ins. Co.***, 795 S.W.2d 875, 877-78 (Tex.App.—Beaumont 1990, no writ) (because P did not disclose post-injury work history, causing extra depositions of doctors, court imposed monetary sanctions; when P did not pay, court dismissed suit).

8. Improper discovery methods. The court can impose sanctions when an attorney engages in improper discovery procedures. *See, e.g.*, ***Sanchez v. Brownsville Sports Ctr.***, 51 S.W.3d 643, 659 (Tex.App.—Corpus Christi 2001, pet. granted w.r.m.) (attorney went to D's store & pretended to be interested in buying vehicle).

9. Pattern of abuse. The court can consider a pattern of discovery abuse to justify sanctions. ***Downer v. Aquamarine Operators***, 701 S.W.2d 238, 242-43 (Tex.1985); *see, e.g.*, ***Chasewood Oaks Condo. Homeowners Ass'n v. Amatek Holdings***, 977 S.W.2d 840, 844-45 (Tex.App.—Fort Worth 1998, pet. denied) (P actively frustrated D's legitimate attempts to investigate potential defenses).

§5.2 Pleadings abuse. When seeking sanctions for pleadings abuse, the party can choose between CPRC §10.004, CPRC §9.012, and TRCP 13. Of the three, CPRC §10.004 is usually the best choice. First, CPRC §9.012 does not apply in any proceeding to which CPRC §10.004 or TRCP 13 applies. CPRC §9.012(h). Second, TRCP 13 is narrower in scope than CPRC §10.004 and imposes a greater burden of proof on the party seeking sanctions. TRCP 13 requires a showing that a pleading was (1) groundless and (2) brought in bad faith or for the purpose of harassment. ***Skepnek v. Mynatt***, 8 S.W.3d 377, 382 (Tex.App.—El Paso 1999, pet. denied). By comparison, CPRC §10.004 allows sanctions when pleadings are brought for an improper purpose, including harassment, delay, or increasing the cost of litigation. *See* CPRC §§10.001, 10.004. When in doubt, a party should seek sanctions under both CPRC §10.004 and TRCP 13. *See* ***Alexander v. Alexander***, 956 S.W.2d 712, 713 (Tex.App.—Houston [14th Dist.] 1997, pet. denied).

1. Frivolous pleadings – CPRC chapter 10. The court can impose sanctions on the attorney who signed the pleading or the party represented by the attorney, if the pleading, motion, or other paper was signed in violation of CPRC §10.001. See "Order under CPRC chapter 10," §11.2, p. 288; ***O'Connor's*** FORM 5J:01, §D. For the representations certified by the signer of the pleadings under CPRC §10.001, see "Under CPRC chapter 10," ch. 1-B, §4.12.2(1), p. 7.

2. Groundless pleadings – TRCP 13. The court can impose sanctions on the person who signed the pleading (party or attorney) if the pleading, motion, or other paper was signed in violation of TRCP 13. For the representations certified by the signer of the pleadings under TRCP 13, see "Under TRCP 13," ch. 1-B, §4.12.2(2), p. 7. See *O'Connor's* FORM 5J:01, §C.

(1) Objective test – groundless. A groundless pleading is one that has no basis in law or fact and is not warranted by a good-faith argument for the extension, modification, or reversal of existing law. TRCP 13; ***GTE Comm. Sys. v. Tanner***, 856 S.W.2d 725, 730 (Tex.1993). The standard is objective: Did the party and attorney make a "reasonable inquiry" into the legal and factual basis of the claim? To decide whether the investigation was reasonable, the court looks to the facts available to the litigant and the circumstances at the time the party filed the pleading. ***Griffin Indus. v. Grimes***, ___ S.W.3d ___ (Tex.App.—San Antonio 2003, no pet.) (No. 04-02-00430-CV; 4-23-03); ***Skepnek***, 8 S.W.3d at 382-83. In some cases, the court must also determine whether, at the time the pleading was filed, the legal arguments asserted in the pleading were warranted by a good-faith argument for the extension of existing law. *Compare* ***McIntyre v. Wilson***, 50 S.W.3d 674, 687 (Tex.App.—Dallas 2001, pet. denied) (sanction reversed; P offered arguable legal basis for extension of law), *with* ***Bradt v. Sebek***, 14 S.W.3d 756, 766 (Tex.App.—Houston [1st Dist.] 2000, pet. denied) (sanctions affirmed; P offered no arguable legal basis for extension of law), *and* ***Stites v. Gillum***, 872 S.W.2d 786, 792 (Tex.App.—Fort Worth 1994, writ denied) (same).

(2) Subjective test – bad faith, harassment. A groundless pleading is not sanctionable unless it was brought in bad faith or for the purpose of harassment. ***GTE***, 856 S.W.2d at 731; *see also* ***In re Estate of Davis v. Cook***, 9 S.W.3d 288, 298 (Tex.App.—San Antonio 1999, no pet.) (to prove bad faith, party must show claim was motivated by malicious or discriminatory purpose). Thus, the party seeking sanctions must prove the pleading party's subjective state of mind.

3. Groundless pleadings – CPRC chapter 9. The court can impose sanctions on the attorney or party represented by the attorney who signed a pleading, motion, or other paper in violation of CPRC §9.011. For the representations certified by the signer of the pleadings under CPRC §9.011, see "Under CPRC Chapter 9," ch. 1-B, §4.12.2(3), p. 7. Sanctions under CPRC §9.012 are not available in any proceeding in which sanctions are available under CPRC §10.004 or TRCP 13. CPRC §9.012(h). Under CPRC §9.011, the court may sanction a party for filing pleadings that are (1) groundless and (2) brought in bad faith, brought for the purposes of harassment, or interposed for any improper purpose (*e.g.*, to cause delay or needless increase in cost of litigation). ***Elkins v. Stotts-Brown***, 103 S.W.3d 664, 668 (Tex.App.—Dallas 2003, no pet.); ***Herrmann & Andreas Ins. Agency v. Appling***, 800 S.W.2d 312, 320 (Tex.App.—Corpus Christi 1990, no writ). CPRC §9.012(d) gives the party a 90-day grace period to withdraw, amend, or move to dismiss the offending pleading. See *O'Connor's* FORM 5J:01, §E.

§5.3 Failure to serve – TRCP 21b. The court can impose sanctions on a party that does not serve on or deliver to other parties copies of pleadings, motions, or other papers as required by TRCP 21 and TRCP 21a. TRCP 21b; ***Union City Body Co. v. Ramirez***, 911 S.W.2d 196, 200 (Tex.App.—San Antonio 1995, orig. proceeding). See *O'Connor's* FORM 5J:03.

§5.4 Contempt under Gov't Code. Under Gov't Code §21.002, a court can punish an attorney or other person for contempt of court; under Gov't Code §82.061, a court can punish an attorney for misbehavior or contempt of court. See "Sanctions under Gov't Code," §7.5, p. 283.

§5.5 Violation of limine order. See "Sanction," ch. 5-E, §8.2, p. 254.

5-2. SUMMARY OF SANCTIONS

	SANCTIONABLE CONDUCT	AUTHORITY	PERSON TO BE SANCTIONED	AVAILABLE RELIEF
1	Frivolous pleadings	CPRC §§10.001-10.006	Lawyer & party	Reasonable expenses (including attorney fees), penalty to be paid into court, and directive to perform or refrain from performing act
2	Groundless pleadings	CPRC §§9.011-9.014	Lawyer & party	Striking of pleadings, dismissal of party, and order to pay reasonable expenses (including attorney fees) incurred because of filing of pleadings
3	Groundless pleadings brought in bad faith or for harassment	TRCP 13	Lawyer & party	Sanctions under TRCP 215.2(b)—ranging from reasonable expenses (including attorney fees) to dismissal with prejudice or default judgment against offending party
4	Failure to serve or deliver pleadings and motions	TRCP 21b	Lawyer & party	Sanctions under TRCP 215.2(b)—for list of sanctions under TRCP 215, see "Types of Sanctions," §7.1, below
5	Bad-faith affidavits in summary judgment proceedings	TRCP 166a(h)	Lawyer & party	Reasonable expenses, including attorney fees
6	Discovery abuses	TRCP 191.3, 199.5, 215	Lawyer & party	See "Motion for Discovery Sanctions," ch. 6-A, §22, p. 337
7	Contempt of court	Gov't Code §21.002	Lawyer & party	*Justice or municipal court*: confinement up to 3 days or fine up to $100, or both *Other courts*: confinement up to 6 months or fine up to $500, or both
8	Contempt of court or related misbehavior	Gov't Code §82.061	Lawyer	Confinement or fine
9	Any improper conduct related to trial	Inherent power	Lawyer & party	Sanction necessary to deter, alleviate, and counteract abuse

§6. CONDUCT THAT DOES NOT JUSTIFY SANCTIONS

The rules do not permit sanctions in the following circumstances: • A court cannot impose a sanction when there has been no conduct justifying sanctions in the matter before the court. *See, e.g.*, ***Thompson v. Davis***, 901 S.W.2d 939, 940 (Tex.1995) (court could not extend sanction from earlier motion to modify child support to later motion to modify custody). • A court cannot sanction a party for filing a motion for summary judgment claiming there is no fact issue about a disputed issue, unless the motion is groundless. ***GTE***, 856 S.W.2d at 730. • A court cannot sanction a party or attorney for a groundless affidavit filed by the party but signed by a witness. *Id.* at 730. • A court cannot impose sanctions under TRCP 13 for a plaintiff's failure to give the defendant the required notice of intention to file suit; the appropriate remedy is abatement, not dismissal. ***Trimble v. Itz***, 898 S.W.2d 370, 374 (Tex.App.—San Antonio 1995), *writ denied*, 906 S.W.2d 481 (Tex.1995). • A court cannot impose sanctions under TRCP 13 on a plaintiff for lacking sufficient proof of its claim. *Id.* • A court cannot strike all of a party's pleadings because the party filed an amended petition after the deadline in the pretrial order. ***Granado v. Madsen***, 729 S.W.2d 866, 869-70 (Tex.App.—Houston [14th Dist.] 1987, writ ref'd n.r.e.). • A court cannot impose sanctions under TRCP 13 for the continuation of a suit after it is shown to be baseless. ***Karagounis v. Property Co. of Am.***, 970 S.W.2d 761, 765 (Tex.App.—Amarillo 1998, pet. denied).

§7. TYPES OF SANCTIONS

The choice of sanctions is within the discretion of the court. ***Bodnow Corp. v. City of Hondo***, 721 S.W.2d 839, 840 (Tex.1986).

NOTE

The ultimate sanctions of dismissal or default are limited by constitutional considerations. When a trial court imposes the ultimate sanction, it is adjudicating the party's claims without regard to the merits. ***TransAmerican Nat. Gas Corp. v. Powell****, 811 S.W.2d 913, 918 (Tex. 1991). A court may dismiss or default a party only when a party's actions justify the presumption that its claims or defenses lack merit. Id.*

§7.1 Sanctions for discovery abuse.

1. Disallow discovery. The court may disallow further discovery of any kind or of a particular kind by the disobedient party. TRCP 215.2(b)(1).

2. Award costs & expenses. The court may charge all or part of the expenses of discovery, taxable court costs, or both against the disobedient party or the attorney advising the party. TRCP 215.2(b)(2); ***Chrysler Corp. v. Blackmon***, 841 S.W.2d 844, 850 (Tex.1992); *see also* ***Onstad v. Wright***, 54 S.W.3d 799, 804-05 (Tex.App.—Texarkana 2001, pet. denied) (fine of $32,198 on P's attorney was to compensate D for mistrial for violation of limine order). If the disobedient party is not able to pay, the trial court cannot enforce its order by jailing the party and conditioning release from jail on payment. ***Ex parte Dolenz***, 893 S.W.2d 677, 680-81 (Tex.App.—Dallas 1995, orig. proceeding).

3. Establish facts. The court may order that the discovery matters the disobedient party did not produce will be taken to be established for the purposes of the suit according to the claims of the other party. TRCP 215.2(b)(3); ***Spohn Hosp. v. Mayer***, 104 S.W.3d 878, 881-82 & n.2 (Tex.2003).

4. Limit or exclude evidence. The court may refuse to allow the disobedient party to support or oppose designated claims or defenses or prohibit it from introducing designated matters in evidence. TRCP 215.2(b)(4); *see also* TRCP 193.6(a) (party who does not timely respond to discovery request cannot introduce material into evidence).

(1) Sanctions. Whether the court should limit or exclude evidence the party refused to produce or attempted to conceal depends on whether the evidence is beneficial or detrimental to that party's case. ***CRSS, Inc. v. Montanari***, 902 S.W.2d 601, 610 (Tex.App.—Houston [1st Dist.] 1995, writ denied).

(a) Undisclosed evidence beneficial. When the evidence the disobedient party did not disclose is beneficial to the disobedient party, the court may prohibit the party from introducing it, may establish those facts against the party, and may prohibit the party from supporting or opposing designated claims or defenses. TRCP 215.2(b)(3), (4); *see, e.g.*, ***Adkins Servs. v. Tisdale Co.***, 56 S.W.3d 842, 843 (Tex.App.—Texarkana 2001, no pet.) (court excluded P's evidence because P did not answer interrogatories & requests for admissions); ***CRSS***, 902 S.W.2d at 610 (court should have prevented disobedient party from offering witnesses & prohibited it from cross-examining those witnesses offered by opposing party). See "Objecting to Unidentified Witness," ch. 6-D, §10, p. 383.

(b) Undisclosed evidence detrimental. When the evidence the disobedient party did not disclose is detrimental to that party, the court should permit the other party to introduce the evidence. As a sanction to the disobedient party, the court may prohibit it from supporting or opposing designated claims or defenses and may establish the facts in the concealed evidence against that party. TRCP 215.2(b)(3), (4); *see, e.g.*, ***City of San Antonio v. Fulcher***, 749 S.W.2d 217, 220 (Tex.App.—San Antonio 1988, writ denied) (disobedient party should not be permitted to offer evidence that contradicts nondisclosed evidence). See §7.1.3, above.

(2) Exceptions. There are four exceptions that permit the court to admit evidence even though the party did not timely make, amend, or supplement a discovery response.

(a) **Named party.** A named party did not identify herself as a witness. TRCP 193.6(a).

(b) **Good cause.** The party had good cause for the failure to timely make, amend, or supplement the discovery response. TRCP 193.6(a)(1), (b); ***Northwestern Nat'l Cty. Mut. Ins. Co. v. Rodriguez***, 18 S.W.3d 718, 721-22 (Tex.App.—San Antonio 2000, pet. denied).

(c) **No unfair surprise.** The party's failure to timely make, amend, or supplement the discovery response will not unfairly surprise or prejudice the other party. TRCP 193.6(a)(2), (b); ***Mares v. Ford Motor Co.***, 53 S.W.3d 416, 419 (Tex.App.—San Antonio 2001, no pet.).

(d) **Trial reset 30 days.** The date for trial was reset at least 30 days beyond the original trial date. Because the purpose of a sanction that excludes evidence for not responding to discovery is to require complete responses and prevent trial by ambush, when the date for trial is postponed the sanction does not survive to the next trial. *See, e.g.*, ***Thompson v. Davis***, 901 S.W.2d 939, 940 (Tex.1995) (sanction that prohibited discovery on issue of child support could not remain in effect months later when husband sought to modify child custody); ***Schein v. American Rest. Group***, 852 S.W.2d 496, 497 (Tex.1993) (sanctions for untimely response did not survive nonsuit). See "When trial reset," ch. 6-A, §16.4.3, p. 327.

5. **Strike pleadings.** The court may (1) strike all or part of the disobedient party's pleadings, (2) dismiss (with or without prejudice) all or part of the disobedient party's suit or proceedings, or (3) render a default judgment against the disobedient party. TRCP 215.2(b)(5). See "To impose death penalty sanctions," §3.2, p. 276.

6. **Stay proceedings.** The court may stay further proceedings until the order is obeyed. TRCP 215.2(b)(5).

7. **Hold in contempt.** Instead of or in addition to any of the sanctions in TRCP 215.2(b)(1)-(5), the court may treat a party's refusal to obey an order as a contempt of court. TRCP 215.2(b)(6). However, the court cannot hold a party or person in contempt for refusing to submit to a physical or mental examination under TRCP 204. TRCP 215.2(b)(6).

8. **Sanctions for refusal to comply with TRCP 204.** When a party refuses to comply with an order under TRCP 204 requiring the person to appear or to produce another person for a physical or mental examination, the court may impose the sanctions listed in TRCP 215.2(b)(1)-(5) (see §7.1.1 through §7.1.5, above), unless the person who did not comply shows that she was unable to appear or to produce the person for examination. TRCP 215.2(b)(7).

9. **Loss of privilege.** When a party refuses to comply with discovery, the trial court may permit privileged information (non-core work product) to be produced as a sanction. ***Occidental Chem. Corp. v. Banales***, 907 S.W.2d 488, 490 (Tex.1995).

10. **Any sanctions under TRCP 215.2(b).** If the court finds a party is abusing the discovery process in seeking, making, or resisting discovery, or if the court finds that any interrogatory or request for inspection or production is unreasonably frivolous, oppressive, or harassing or that a response or answer is unreasonably frivolous or made for purposes of delay, then the court may, after notice and hearing, impose any appropriate sanction authorized by TRCP 215.2(b)(1)-(5), and (8). TRCP 215.3.

11. **Deem admissions.** For sanctions for failure to comply with a request for admissions, see "Challenging Response," ch. 6-G, §5, p. 419.

12. **Strike expert testimony.** The trial court may strike the testimony of a disobedient party's expert witness. *See* ***State Farm Fire & Cas. Co. v. Rodriguez***, 88 S.W.3d 313, 325-26 (Tex.App.—San Antonio 2002, pet. denied). As long as the exclusion of testimony only impairs the presentation of a party's case and does not preclude a trial on the merits, the striking of the testimony is within the court's discretion and is not a death penalty sanction. *Id.* at 326.

13. Other sanctions that are "just." The Supreme Court encourages creative sanctions. For example, even though TRCP 215.2(b) does not mention community service, the trial court can impose it as a sanction under the rule. ***Braden v. Downey***, 811 S.W.2d 922, 930 (Tex.1991) (order to perform community service must be deferred until it can be challenged on appeal); *e.g.*, ***Cap Rock Elec. Coop. v. Texas Util. Elec. Co.***, 874 S.W.2d 92, 98 (Tex.App.—El Paso 1994, no writ) (court ordered officers & directors of corporation, who attempted to hide documents, to perform 200 hours of community service); ***Braden v. South Main Bank***, 837 S.W.2d 733, 742 (Tex. App.—Houston [14th Dist.] 1992, writ denied) (attorney who filed frivolous objections to interrogatories ordered to perform 10 hours of community service).

§7.2 Sanctions under CPRC §10.004. The following sanctions are available under CPRC §10.004: (1) a directive to perform or refrain from performing an act, (2) an order for a monetary sanction, and (3) an order to pay the other party the amount of reasonable expenses incurred because of the filing of the frivolous pleading, including attorney fees. CPRC §10.004(c).

§7.3 Sanctions under TRCP 13. Under TRCP 13, the court can impose any appropriate sanction in TRCP 215.2(b). ***Bradt v. Sebek***, 14 S.W.3d 756, 762 (Tex.App.—Houston [1st Dist.] 2000, pet. denied). The rules leave the choice of sanctions to the trial court. See "Sanctions for discovery abuse," §7.1, p. 281.

§7.4 Sanctions under CPRC §9.012. The following sanctions are available under CPRC §9.012: (1) striking the pleadings or the offending part of the pleadings, (2) dismissing the party, or (3) ordering the party to pay the other party the amount of reasonable expenses incurred because of the filing of the pleading, including costs, reasonable attorney fees, witness fees, fees of experts, and deposition expenses. CPRC §9.012(e).

§7.5 Sanctions under Gov't Code. A court may impose fines and imprisonments as sanctions for a person held in contempt of court under Gov't Code §21.002 or §82.061. The maximum time a person can be confined for civil contempt is 18 months. Gov't Code §21.002(h)(2). The 18-month limit does not apply to contempt under Family Code chapter 157, when a person disobeys a court order to make child support payments. Gov't Code §21.002(f). 03

1. Section 21.002. If the contemptuous conduct takes place in a county or district court, the court may impose a fine up to $500 or order confinement up to six months, or both. Gov't Code §21.002(b); ***In re Long***, 984 S.W.2d 623, 625 (Tex.1999); ***Cadle Co. v. Lobingier***, 50 S.W.3d 662, 667-68 (Tex.App.—Fort Worth 2001, pet. denied); *see also* Gov't Code §21.002(c) (for contemptuous conduct in justice or municipal courts, the limit is $100 & three days imprisonment). The monetary limit of $500 for contempt in Gov't Code §21.002(b) does not limit monetary sanctions imposed for attorney misconduct in violation of the TRCPs, court orders, or other statutes. *See* ***Onstad v. Wright***, 54 S.W.3d 799, 804-05 (Tex.App.—Texarkana 2001, pet. denied) (attorney fined $32,198 for violating motion in limine). See ***O'Connor's Texas Civil Appeals***, "Contempt sentence," ch. 20-E, §2.3, p. 296 (2002-03).

2. Section 82.061. Gov't Code §82.061 does not provide limits for monetary fines or imprisonment for contempt. However, under the 2003 amendments to Gov't Code §21.002, an attorney cannot be confined for civil contempt for a period greater than 18 months. *See* Gov't Code §21.002(h)(2) ("notwithstanding any other law," person cannot be confined for civil contempt for more than 18 months).

§7.6 Improper sanctions. There are limits to the types of sanctions a trial court may impose, even when the conduct justifies sanctions.

1. Prohibit access to court. A trial court cannot sanction a party by prohibiting it from filing pleadings. ***Glass v. Glass***, 826 S.W.2d 683, 687 (Tex.App.—Texarkana 1992, writ denied); ***Kahn v. Garcia***, 816 S.W.2d 131, 133 (Tex.App.—Houston [1st Dist.] 1991, orig. proceeding); *see also* Tex. Const. art. 1, §13 (open courts provision); *cf.* CPRC §11.101(a) (court may prohibit pro se litigant from filing suit if court determines, after notice & hearing, that the person is a vexatious litigant). Such a prohibition denies the party the means to communicate with the trial court. ***Kahn***, 816 S.W.2d at 133.

2. Prevent review. A trial court cannot sanction a party by striking post-trial motions, thereby foreclosing the appeal. ***Lehtonen v. Clarke***, 784 S.W.2d 945, 946-47 (Tex.App.—Houston [14th Dist.] 1990, writ denied). TRAP 42.3 does not authorize an appellate court to dismiss a party's appeal as punishment. ***O'Connor v. Sam Houston Med. Hosp.***, 807 S.W.2d 574, 576 (Tex.1991).

3. Dismiss a separate lawsuit. A trial court cannot dismiss a separate lawsuit as a discovery sanction. ***McKellar Dev. Group v. Fairbank***, 827 S.W.2d 579, 581 (Tex.App.—San Antonio 1992, no writ).

4. Sanctions after special exceptions. A trial court cannot impose a monetary sanction for refusal to amend pleadings after special exceptions are sustained. ***D.A. Buckner Constr. v. Hobson***, 793 S.W.2d 74, 75-76 (Tex.App.—Houston [14th Dist.] 1990, orig. proceeding). When special exceptions are sustained, the party has the option to amend the pleadings or refuse to amend and test the validity of the court's ruling. *Id.* at 75. See "Special Exceptions—Challenging the Pleadings," ch. 3-G, p. 187.

5. Security for costs. A court cannot require a party to post bond as security for the suit as a sanction. ***Johnson v. Smith***, 857 S.W.2d 612, 615-16 (Tex.App.—Houston [1st Dist.] 1993, orig. proceeding).

6. Charity work by nonparty. A court cannot require a nonparty to perform indigent medical care as a sanction. ***Pope v. Davidson***, 849 S.W.2d 916, 920 (Tex.App.—Houston [14th Dist.] 1993, orig. proceeding). Contempt is the only sanction that a court may impose on a nonparty.

7. Arbitrary monetary fine under TRCP 215.3. TRCP 215.3 does not permit the trial court to impose an arbitrary monetary fine against a party for discovery abuse. ***Ford Motor Co. v. Tyson***, 943 S.W.2d 527, 532-33 (Tex.App.—Dallas 1997, orig. proceeding) (fine of $10 million set aside); ***Owens-Corning Fiberglas Corp. v. Caldwell***, 807 S.W.2d 413, 415-16 (Tex.App.—Houston [1st Dist.] 1991, orig. proceeding) (fine of $2.3 million set aside). A sanction under TRCP 215.3 must be compensatory or remedial; an arbitrary fine cannot be imposed solely for the purpose of punishment. ***Tyson***, 943 S.W.2d at 533. Monetary sanctions under TRCP 215.3 must be related to the expenses caused by the abuse. ***Clone Component Distribs. v. State***, 819 S.W.2d 593, 597 (Tex.App.—Dallas 1991, no writ) (reversed $50,000 fine). A fine for discovery abuse is arbitrary if it is unrestrained by law or statute and unrelated to any damages or expenses incurred by the injured party. ***Tyson***, 943 S.W.2d at 534. Arbitrariness is a characteristic of a violation of substantive due process. *Id.*

8. Arbitrary amount for expenses. When a court awards expenses under TRCP 215.2(b)(2), or awards expenses and attorney fees under TRCP 215.2(b)(8), the amount of the award cannot be arbitrary; the amount must be related to the harm suffered by the other party. ***Hanley v. Hanley***, 813 S.W.2d 511, 522 (Tex.App.—Dallas 1991, no writ); *see, e.g.*, ***Kugle v. DaimlerChrysler Corp.***, 88 S.W.3d 355, 364-65 (Tex.App.—San Antonio 2002, pet. denied) (monetary sanction of $865,000 assessed against P's attorney's upheld as cost for defense of fraudulent PI suit).

9. Discovery of attorney notes. The privilege for core work product, which relates to an attorney's thought processes, is absolute, and the trial court cannot sanction a party by ordering production as a sanction. ***Occidental Chem. Corp. v. Banales***, 907 S.W.2d 488, 490 (Tex.1995). The court can order non-core work product produced as a sanction. *See id.* See "Loss of privilege," §7.1.9, p. 282.

10. Trial setting. An early trial setting is not an appropriate sanction for discovery abuse. ***Arkla, Inc. v. Harris***, 846 S.W.2d 623, 629 (Tex.App.—Houston [14th Dist.] 1993, orig. proceeding).

11. Penalty paid to litigant. When a statute authorizes a monetary penalty as sanctions, the trial court cannot require a party to pay the penalty into the court registry for the benefit of the other party. ***Sterling v. Alexander***, 99 S.W.3d 793, 799-800 (Tex.App.—Houston [14th Dist.] 2003, pet. denied).

12. Death penalty sanctions. Sanctions that terminate the lawsuit are proper only under certain conditions. See "To impose death penalty sanctions," §3.2, p. 276.

§8. MOTION FOR SANCTIONS

§8.1 On court's initiative. A court may impose sanctions under CPRC chapter 10, TRCP 13, or TRCP 191.3 on its own initiative without a motion. *See* CPRC §10.002(b); TRCP 13, 191.3(e); ***Koslow's v. Mackie***, 796 S.W.2d 700, 704 (Tex.1990). The party against whom the sanctions are imposed is entitled to notice and a hearing. ***Aldine ISD v. Baty***, 946 S.W.2d 851, 852-53 (Tex.App.—Houston [14th Dist.] 1997, no writ) (sanctions under TRCP 13); *see* CPRC §10.002(b) (person to be sanctioned under §10.001 must receive show-cause hearing), *id.* §10.003 (court must provide notice and reasonable opportunity to respond). The trial court cannot on its own initiative impose monetary sanctions after a voluntary dismissal or settlement, unless the court issued the show-cause order before the dismissal or settlement. CPRC §10.004(e); ***In re Bennett***, 960 S.W.2d 35, 40 n.5 (Tex.1997); ***Scott & White Mem'l Hosp. v. Schexnider***, 940 S.W.2d 594, 596 n.1 (Tex.1996).

§8.2 By a party.

1. Identify sanctionable conduct. The motion for sanctions must identify the specific conduct that deserves sanction. Because the trial court may consider other matters that have occurred in the litigation, the motion for sanctions may include other earlier conduct that warrants sanctions. *See* ***Downer v. Aquamarine Operators***, 701 S.W.2d 238, 241 (Tex.1985); ***Medical Protective Co. v. Glanz***, 721 S.W.2d 382, 388 (Tex.App.—Corpus Christi 1986, writ ref'd).

2. Identify authority for sanction. The motion for sanctions must identify the specific statute, rule, or order the party violated. A court cannot grant sanctions under a statute or rule that is not identified in the motion. *E.g.*, ***Ball v. Rao***, 48 S.W.3d 332, 338 (Tex.App.—Fort Worth 2001, pet. denied) (court could not grant sanctions under CPRC §9.011 because it was not included as ground for sanctions in motion).

3. Request sanction. The movant should identify the sanction it requests the court to impose (*e.g.*, monetary sanctions, default, dismissal) and argue the sanction (1) has a direct relationship to the offensive conduct and (2) is not excessive. A party should not ask for a death penalty sanction in its first motion for sanctions unless it is apparent that a lesser sanction will not promote compliance. ***GTE Comm. Sys. v. Tanner***, 856 S.W.2d 725, 729 (Tex.1993); ***Sanchez v. Brownsville Sports Ctr.***, 51 S.W.3d 643, 659 (Tex.App.—Corpus Christi 2001, pet. granted w.r.m.). See "Standards for Imposing Sanctions," §3, p. 275.

4. Be verified. If the motion for sanctions contains evidence that does not appear in the court's record, the motion should be verified and affidavits attached as necessary.

5. Deadline to file.

(1) Pretrial conduct. To be entitled to sanctions based on pretrial conduct, the party must secure a pretrial hearing and ruling on that conduct or waive any claim for sanctions based on that conduct. ***Remington Arms Co. v. Caldwell***, 850 S.W.2d 167, 170 (Tex.1993); ***Finlay v. Olive***, 77 S.W.3d 520, 526 (Tex.App.—Houston [1st Dist.] 2002, no pet.). However, if the grounds for pretrial sanctions are not known until after the trial has begun, the claim for sanctions is not waived. ***Remington Arms***, 850 S.W.2d at 170.

(2) Trial conduct. To be entitled to sanctions based on trial conduct, the motion for sanctions must be filed before the court loses plenary power over its judgment. ***Schexnider***, 940 S.W.2d at 596; *see* ***Laboratory Corp. v. Compton***, ___ S.W.3d ___ (Tex.App.—San Antonio 2003, n.p.h.) (No. 04-02-00629-CV; 9-24-03). Neither the filing of a nonsuit nor the removal of a case to federal court deprives the trial court of jurisdiction to sanction attorneys for conduct before the nonsuit or removal. ***Bennett***, 960 S.W.2d at 38-40; *see* ***Ex parte Durham***, 921 S.W.2d 482, 487-88 (Tex.App.—Corpus Christi 1996, orig. proceeding) (sanctions to punish discovery abuses survives nonsuit). When sanctions are imposed after removal, the sanctions cannot affect the merits of the litigation pending in federal court. ***Bennett***, 960 S.W.2d at 39.

§8.3 Proper court. Ordinarily, a motion for sanctions should be filed in the court where the action is pending. When sanctions are sought against a nonparty who refuses to answer questions propounded at a deposition, the motion should be filed in the court in the district where the deposition is being taken. TRCP 215.1(a); ***Latham v. Thornton***, 806 S.W.2d 347, 349-50 (Tex.App.—Fort Worth 1991, orig. proceeding).

§9. RESPONSE

When a party is notified that a motion for sanctions is pending against it, the party should take the following steps.

§9.1 File response. The party charged with sanctionable conduct should file a response to the motion for sanctions and inform the trial court, under oath, why sanctions should not be imposed. The response should make the following arguments, as appropriate: (1) no sanctionable conduct occurred; (2) there is no relationship between the offensive conduct and the sanction requested; (3) the sanction requested is excessive; and, if death penalty sanctions are requested, (4) the court did not impose a lesser sanction first, and (5) the party's claims or defenses in the underlying suit are meritorious. See "Standards for Imposing Sanctions," §3, p. 275. The party should attach as many affidavits as necessary.

§9.2 Ask for hearing. The party charged with sanctionable conduct should follow the procedure in the local rules for securing a hearing to present evidence.

§10. HEARING

§10.1 Necessity of hearing. CPRC §10.003, TRCP 13, 21b, 215.2(b)-(c), and due process require the court to hold a hearing before imposing sanctions. A court cannot strike a party's pleadings, render a default judgment, or impose monetary sanctions without giving the party an opportunity to be heard. ***Sears, Roebuck & Co. v. Hollingsworth***, 293 S.W.2d 639, 642 (Tex.1956) (sanctions for disregarding subpoena duces tecum); ***Bisby v. Dow Chem. Co.***, 931 S.W.2d 18, 21 (Tex.App.—Houston [1st Dist.] 1996, no writ) (sanctions under TRCP 13 for frivolous pleadings); ***First Dallas Pet. v. Hawkins***, 727 S.W.2d 640, 648 (Tex.App.—Dallas 1987, no writ) (sanctions under TRCP 215 for not obeying court order regarding discovery). *Contra* ***Cummings v. Cire***, 74 S.W.3d 920, 924 (Tex.App.—Amarillo 2002, pet. granted 4-17-03) (discovery sanction). Without a hearing to receive evidence supporting the allegations that sanctions are warranted, the trial court has no evidence to impose sanctions. ***Bedding Component Manufactors, Ltd. v. Royal Sleep Prods.***, 108 S.W.3d 563, 564 (Tex.App.—Dallas 2003, n.p.h.) (sanctions under TRCP 13); ***Bisby***, 931 S.W.2d at 21 (same). At the hearing, the trial court must permit the party to introduce evidence before imposing sanctions. ***Davila v. World Car Five Star***, 75 S.W.3d 537, 544 (Tex.App.—San Antonio 2002, no pet.).

§10.2 Necessity of adequate notice. CPRC §9.012(a), §10.003, TRCP 13, 21b, and due process require the court to give the party notice of the hearing on sanctions. ***Mills v. Ghilain***, 68 S.W.3d 141, 146 (Tex.App.—Corpus Christi 2001, no pet.); ***In re L.A.M. & Assocs.***, 975 S.W.2d 80, 83 (Tex.App.—San Antonio 1998, orig. proceeding); *see* ***Pope v. Davidson***, 849 S.W.2d 916, 920-21 (Tex.App.—Houston [14th Dist.] 1993, orig. proceeding) (nonparty subject to sanctions is entitled to notice of hearing on sanctions). The notice of the hearing on sanctions must be adequate. ***Plano S&L Ass'n v. Slavin***, 721 S.W.2d 282, 284 (Tex.1986). One day's notice of the hearing is not adequate. *Id.* Oral notice is not adequate; the party must be given written notice of the hearing. ***In re Acceptance Ins. Co.***, 33 S.W.3d 443, 451 (Tex.App.—Fort Worth 2000, orig. proceeding).

§10.3 Make a record. The party charged with sanctionable conduct should treat the hearing on sanctions as one for evidence, not just for argument. The party should make sure the court reporter is present and transcribes the entire hearing, including arguments. Once the hearing starts, the attorneys and parties should be sworn and should formally offer evidence on the issue of sanctions. One court has said the party, not the attorney, should testify at the hearing on sanctions. ***Walsh v. Mullane***, 725 S.W.2d 263, 264 (Tex.App.—Houston [1st Dist.] 1986, writ ref'd n.r.e.). But, if the attorney knows about the failure to comply with discovery (when the fault lies with the attorney), the attorney should testify.

§10.4 Burden.

NOTE

Under TRCP 13, the trial court begins with the presumption that all pleadings are filed in good faith. ***GTE Comm. Sys. v. Tanner,*** *856 S.W.2d 725, 731 (Tex.1993);* ***Trimble v. Itz,*** *898 S.W.2d 370, 374 (Tex.App.—San Antonio 1995), writ denied, 906 S.W.2d 481 (Tex.1995). There is no such presumption under CPRC §10.001.*

1. **On court's initiative.** When the court sets a matter for sanctions on its own initiative, the party seeking to avoid sanctions must prove that sanctions should not be imposed. *See* CPRC §10.002(b) (show-cause hearing).

2. **On party's motion.** At a hearing on sanctions, the party that filed the motion for sanctions must first prove the allegations in its motion for sanctions. ***GTE***, 856 S.W.2d at 729. Once the movant proves the other party's conduct justifies sanctions, the other party must produce evidence demonstrating why sanctions should not be imposed.

3. **Burden on party to be sanctioned.** To avoid sanctions, the party or attorney charged with sanctionable conduct should prove the allegations in its response. See §9.1, above. The party and the attorney subject to the motion for sanctions should introduce testimonial and documentary proof, not just argument. ***Lopez v. Foremost Paving***, 796 S.W.2d 473, 477 (Tex.App.—San Antonio 1990, writ dism'd). See "Lawyer's appearance before court," ch. 1-H, §5.2, p. 40.

§10.5 Entire case. The trial court is not limited to considering the specific violation committed in imposing sanctions but may consider other matters that have occurred in the litigation. ***Downer v. Aquamarine Operators***, 701 S.W.2d 238, 241 (Tex.1985); ***Medical Protective Co. v. Glanz***, 721 S.W.2d 382, 388 (Tex.App.—Corpus Christi 1986, writ ref'd).

§10.6 Violations by both parties. The trial court is justified in refusing to impose sanctions if both sides are equally guilty. *See* ***Larson v. H.E. Butt Grocery Co.***, 769 S.W.2d 694, 695-96 (Tex.App.—Corpus Christi 1989, writ denied) (record was full of inferences & indications of lack of candor & attempts at gamesmanship on both sides).

§11. ORDER FOR SANCTIONS

The court may impose sanctions on a person who abused the discovery process or signed a pleading in violation of CPRC §10.001, TRCP 13, or CPRC §9.011. The court's discretion is limited by a requirement that the sanction be "just." TRCP 215.2(b); ***Spohn Hosp. v. Mayer***, 104 S.W.3d 878, 882 (Tex.2003); ***TransAmerican Nat. Gas Corp. v. Powell***, 811 S.W.2d 913, 917 (Tex.1991). See ***O'Connor's*** FORM 5J:05.

§11.1 Order for discovery sanctions.

1. **Sanctions.** See "Sanctions for discovery abuse," §7.1, p. 281.

2. **Attorney fees & costs.** The court may require the offending party, the attorney advising the party, or both to pay reasonable expenses, including attorney fees, caused by the discovery abuse. TRCP 215.2(b)(8). The court should not impose sanctions under subsection (b)(8) if the court finds the noncompliance was substantially justified or if other circumstances make an award of expenses unjust. *Id.*

3. **Explanation.** The court must explain the reason for imposing sanctions by providing the following information: (1) a description of the sanctionable conduct; (2) the relationship between the conduct and the sanctions; (3) the necessity for the severity of the sanctions; and, if death penalty sanctions are imposed, (4) a lesser sanction was imposed without effect, and (5) the party's conduct justifies the presumption its claims or defenses lack merit. *See* ***GTE***, 856 S.W.2d at 729-30. See "Standards for Imposing Sanctions," §3, p. 275.

4. Separate findings. When judgment is rendered as a sanction for discovery abuse, the court should file separate findings of fact. See "After hearing on sanctions under TRCP 215," ch. 10-E, §2.3.1, p. 643.

§11.2 Order under CPRC chapter 10.

1. Sanctions. The court may impose sanctions on the party, the attorney, or both. CPRC §10.004(a). The sanction should be sufficient to deter repetition of the conduct by other persons. *Id.* §10.004(b); ***University of Tex. v. Bishop***, 997 S.W.2d 350, 357 (Tex.App.—Fort Worth 1999, pet. denied). When a party is represented by an attorney, the court cannot impose monetary sanctions on the party for violating CPRC §10.001(2) (pleadings not supported by existing law or argument to extend existing law). CPRC §10.004(d); ***Bishop***, 997 S.W.2d at 357. If a party appears pro se, the court may impose sanctions on the party for violating CPRC §10.001(2). *See* CPRC §10.004(d).

2. Attorney fees & costs. The court may award attorney fees and costs to the prevailing party. CPRC §§10.002(c), 10.004(b)(3). Costs include inconvenience, harassment, and out-of-pocket expenses incurred or caused by the litigation. *Id.* §10.002(c).

3. Explanation. When the court imposes sanctions, it must include in the order a description of the conduct that violated CPRC §10.001 and explain the basis for the sanctions imposed. CPRC §10.005; ***Bishop***, 997 S.W.2d at 355. When imposing death penalty sanctions, the court should explain why it imposed the sanction on the party and not just the attorney. *See* ***TransAmerican***, 811 S.W.2d at 917.

4. Not separate findings. The court should not file separate findings of fact to support sanctions under CPRC chapter 10. See "After hearing on groundless pleadings," ch. 10-E, §2.3.2(3), p. 643.

§11.3 Order under TRCP 13.

1. Sanctions. The trial court has the discretion to determine the severity of the sanctions, but the rule requires the court to impose punishment for a violation. *See* TRCP 13.

2. Explanation.

(1) Identify sanctionable conduct. The order must identify the specific acts or omissions on which the court based the sanctions. ***Jimenez v. Transwestern Prop. Co.***, 999 S.W.2d 125, 130 (Tex.App.—Houston [14th Dist.] 1999, no pet.); ***Luxenberg v. Marshall***, 835 S.W.2d 136, 140-41 (Tex.App.—Dallas 1992, orig. proceeding); *see* ***Tarrant Cty. v. Chancey***, 942 S.W.2d 151, 155 (Tex.App.—Fort Worth 1997, no writ) (statement that pleading filed to harass & cause unnecessary delays was too general). When imposing death penalty sanctions, the court should explain why it imposed the sanction on the party and not just the attorney. *See* ***TransAmerican***, 811 S.W.2d at 917.

(2) State good cause. No sanctions may be imposed under TRCP 13 "except for good cause ... stated in the sanction order." ***Toles v. Toles***, 45 S.W.3d 252, 266 (Tex.App.—Dallas 2001, pet. denied); ***Murphy v. Friendswood Dev. Co.***, 965 S.W.2d 708, 709 (Tex.App.—Houston [1st Dist.] 1998, no pet.). Thus, the court must include a statement of good cause in the order to support the imposition of sanctions. ***Chancey***, 942 S.W.2d at 155; ***Kahn v. Garcia***, 816 S.W.2d 131, 133 (Tex.App.—Houston [1st Dist.] 1991, orig. proceeding).

PRACTICE TIP

Make an objection on the record if the order does not identify the sanctionable conduct or does not make a statement of good cause. See ***Jimenez****, 999 S.W.2d at 130-31. If no objection is made, the error is waived.* ***Appleton v. Appleton****, 76 S.W.3d 78, 85 (Tex.App.—Houston [14th Dist.] 2002, no pet.);* ***Texas-Ohio Gas v. Mecom****, 28 S.W.3d 129, 135-36 (Tex.App.—Texarkana 2000, no pet.). The objection can be preserved in a motion for new trial, if not made earlier.* ***Thomas v. Thomas****, 917 S.W.2d 425, 433 (Tex.App.—Waco 1996, no writ).*

3. Not separate findings. The court should not file separate findings of fact to support sanctions under TRCP 13. See "After hearing on groundless pleadings," ch. 10-E, §2.3.2(3), p. 643.

§11.4 Order under CPRC chapter 9.

1. Withdraw or amend. Before imposing sanctions, the court must give the attorney or party 90 days to withdraw or amend the offending pleadings. CPRC §9.012(c), (d); ***Elkins v. Stotts-Brown***, 103 S.W.3d 664, 668 (Tex.App.—Dallas 2003, no pet.).

2. Sanctions. The court may impose sanctions on the party, the attorney, or both. CPRC §9.012(c). The court may strike the pleadings or dismiss the offending party. *Id.* §9.012(e)(1), (2).

3. Attorney fees & costs. The court may award the objecting party reasonable expenses incurred because of the filing, including attorney fees, witness fees, expert fees, and deposition expenses. CPRC §9.012(e)(3). If the objecting party has been sanctioned in the same matter, that party cannot be awarded costs and fees. *Id.* §9.012(f).

§12. REVIEW

§12.1 Standard of review. Sanction orders are reviewed for abuse of discretion. ***Chrysler Corp. v. Blackmon***, 841 S.W.2d 844, 852 (Tex.1992); ***Walker v. Packer***, 827 S.W.2d 833, 839 (Tex.1992). If the trial court makes findings of fact to support the sanction order, on appeal, the appellate court should not treat the findings as findings of fact made under TRCP 296, which are reviewable under legal and factual insufficiency standards. ***IKB Indus. v. Pro-Line Corp.***, 938 S.W.2d 440, 442 (Tex.1997); ***Chrysler Corp.***, 841 S.W.2d at 852. The findings filed by the trial court after sanctions are merely to assist the appellate court in deciding whether the trial court abused its discretion. ***Chrysler Corp.***, 841 S.W.2d at 852.

§12.2 Method of review.

1. By appeal. A party is entitled to challenge the sanctions on appeal after a final judgment is rendered in the case. TRCP 215.1(d), 215.2(b)(8), 215.3. When a sanction can be appealed, mandamus is not appropriate. *See, e.g.*, ***Street v. 2d Ct. of Appeals***, 715 S.W.2d 638, 639 (Tex.1986) (sanction of attorney fees should be challenged on appeal); ***Keller Indus. v. Blanton***, 804 S.W.2d 182, 186 (Tex.App.—Houston [14th Dist.] 1991, orig. proceeding) (challenge to sanctions for costs of out-of-state depositions should be by appeal). Even when a case is settled or dismissed by a nonsuit, sanctions can be reviewed on appeal. ***See Felderhoff v. Knauf***, 819 S.W.2d 110, 111 (Tex.1991) (appeal after nonsuit); ***Braden v. South Main Bank***, 837 S.W.2d 733, 741 (Tex.App.—Houston [14th Dist.] 1992, writ denied) (appeal after settlement).

2. By mandamus. Ordinarily, sanctions are not reviewable by mandamus because the party has an adequate remedy by appeal. ***Street***, 715 S.W.2d at 639. However, mandamus is appropriate in some cases.

(1) Sanction terminates litigation. When the trial court imposes severe sanctions that, in effect, preclude a decision on the merits of a party's claims, the appellate remedy may be inadequate. When such an order is not immediately appealable, the party can seek review by mandamus. ***TransAmerican Nat. Gas Corp. v. Powell***, 811 S.W.2d 913, 920 (Tex.1991).

(2) Monetary sanction threatens litigation. The imposition of monetary sanctions can so threaten a party's ability to continue with the litigation that an eventual appeal would not provide an adequate remedy. ***Braden v. Downey***, 811 S.W.2d 922, 929 (Tex.1991); *see also* ***In re Ford Motor Co.***, 988 S.W.2d 714, 723 (Tex. 1998) (appeal is not adequate remedy when court imposes a monetary penalty on a party's exercise of its legal rights). In most situations, however, the trial court can prevent this either (1) by providing that the sanction is payable only at a date that coincides with or follows the rendition of a final order terminating the litigation or (2) by making express written findings after a hearing as to why the monetary sanctions do not have a preclusive effect. ***Braden***, 811 S.W.2d at 929; ***Prime Group v. O'Neill***, 848 S.W.2d 376, 379 (Tex.App.—Houston [14th Dist.] 1993, orig. proceeding); ***Susman Godfrey, L.L.P. v. Marshall***, 832 S.W.2d 105, 108 (Tex.App.—Dallas 1992, orig. proceeding). *But see* ***Onstad v. Wright***, 54 S.W.3d 799, 802-03 (Tex.App.—Texarkana 2001, pet. denied) (attorney fined $32,198 was required to place it into registry of court until appeal). In reviewing the trial court's order of sanctions, the appellate court cannot substitute its judgment for that of the trial court. ***Carr v. Harris Cty.***, 745 S.W.2d 531, 532 (Tex.App.—Houston [1st Dist.] 1988, no writ).

§12.3 The record. The record should include the order imposing sanctions, the motion for sanctions, the response, findings of fact and conclusions of law (if filed), and a transcription of the hearing on the motion. If the trial court does not hear evidence and states that it bases its opinion on the papers on file and argument of counsel, the parties are not required to produce a reporter's record. ***Otis Elevator Co. v. Parmelee***, 850 S.W.2d 179, 180-81 (Tex.1993). See "Findings of fact are helpful," ch. 10-E, §2.3, p. 643.

§12.4 Abate appeal for good cause statement. If the sanctioned party objected to the lack of particularized findings as required by TRCP 13, on appeal, the court may abate the appeal and order the trial court to state properly the particulars of good cause. ***Campos v. Ysleta Gen. Hosp.***, 879 S.W.2d 67, 70-71 (Tex.App.—El Paso 1994, writ denied). *But see* ***Murphy v. Friendswood Dev. Co.***, 965 S.W.2d 708, 710 (Tex.App.—Houston [1st Dist.] 1998, no pet.) (abatement not feasible because new judge elected; case remanded for new hearing).

K. MOTION TO SEAL COURT RECORDS

§1. GENERAL

§1.1 Rule. TRCP 76a.

§1.2 Purpose. TRCP 76a recognizes the public's right to have access to judicial records. In response to a Legislative directive, the Supreme Court adopted TRCP 76a to establish a system to control the sealing of court records. Gov't Code §22.010; ***General Tire v. Kepple***, 970 S.W.2d 520, 523 & n.8 (Tex.1998); ***Boardman v. Elm Block Dev. L.P.***, 872 S.W.2d 297, 298-99 (Tex.App.—Eastland 1994, no writ).

§1.3 Forms. ***O'Connor's Texas Civil Forms***, FORMS 5K.

§1.4 Other references. Doggett & Mucchetti, *Public Access to Public Courts*, 69 Tex.L.Rev. 643 (1991).

§2. WHAT DOCUMENTS ARE "COURT RECORDS"

§2.1 Presumption of openness. All court records, except certain unfiled discovery, are presumed to be open to the general public and can be sealed only after all the requirements set out in TRCP 76a are satisfied. ***Kepple***, 970 S.W.2d at 523; ***Burlington N. R.R. v. Southwestern Elec. Power Co.***, 905 S.W.2d 683, 684 (Tex.App.—Texarkana 1995, no writ).

§2.2 Documents that are court records. All documents that relate to the lawsuit, with few exceptions, are considered court records and are presumed to be open to the general public for inspection.

1. Court orders. Court orders are court records and cannot be sealed under any circumstance. TRCP 76a(1); ***Fox v. Anonymous***, 869 S.W.2d 499, 503 (Tex.App.—San Antonio 1993, writ denied).

2. Filed documents. All documents filed with the court in connection with any civil matter are court records. TRCP 76a(2)(a). The exceptions are noted in §2.3, below.

3. Some settlement agreements. Settlement agreements filed with the court are considered court records. TRCP 76a(2)(a). Unfiled settlement agreements, excluding any reference to monetary consideration, are court records only if they "seek to restrict disclosure of information concerning matters that have a probable adverse effect on the general public health or safety, or the administration of public office, or the operation of government." TRCP 76a(2)(b). The financial portions of all settlement agreements, however, can be redacted. *See* ***Fox***, 869 S.W.2d at 503. A settlement agreement cannot change the effect of what is a court record. *See* TRCP 76a(2)(b) (unfiled settlement agreements are defined as court records).

4. The trial record. The entire record of trial proceedings is "public" and cannot be sealed. *Cf. **Burlington***, 905 S.W.2d at 684 n.2 (declined to decide whether TRCP 76a allows sealing of entire record).

5. Discovery products.

(1) Filed discovery. Filed discovery products are court records. TRCP 76a(2)(a).

(2) Unfiled discovery. TRCP 76a does not presume unfiled discovery products are "court records." ***Eli Lilly & Co. v. Biffle***, 868 S.W.2d 806, 808 (Tex.App.—Dallas 1993, no writ). Unfiled discovery products are court records only if they concern matters that have a probable adverse effect on (1) the general public health or safety, (2) the administration of public office, or (3) the operation of government. TRCP 76a(2)(c); ***Kepple***, 970 S.W.2d at 523; ***Upjohn Co. v. Freeman***, 906 S.W.2d 92, 95 (Tex.App.—Dallas 1995, no writ). If a court attempts to limit the disclosure or distribution of unfiled discovery (*e.g.*, by a protective order), it must comply with TRCP 76a. ***Chandler v. Hyundai Motor Co.***, 829 S.W.2d 774, 774-75 (Tex.1992).

§2.3 Documents that are not court records. TRCP 76a does not apply to documents that are not "court records" as defined in TRCP 76a(2). ***Kepple***, 970 S.W.2d at 523; ***Wood v. Moriarty***, 940 S.W.2d 359, 361 (Tex. App.—Dallas 1997, no writ). Documents that are not court records under TRCP 76a may be sealed only if another rule or statute permits. See "Protecting Documents That Are Not Court Records," §8, p. 294.

1. In camera discovery. Documents that are filed for in camera inspection, solely for the purpose of getting a ruling on their discoverability, are not court records. TRCP 76a(2)(a)(1); ***Texans United Educ. Fund v. Texaco, Inc.***, 858 S.W.2d 38, 40 (Tex.App.—Houston [14th Dist.] 1993, writ denied); *see also **U.S. Gov't v. Marks***, 949 S.W.2d 320, 324 (Tex.1997) (transcript of certain statements concerning grand jury investigation made by federal prosecutor during ex parte hearing was not court record under TRCP 76a(2)(a)(2)).

2. Restricted by other law. Documents to which another law restricts access (*e.g.*, certain employment records, financial information, medical records) are not court records. TRCP 76a(2)(a)(2); Doggett & Mucchetti, *Public Access*, 69 Tex.L.Rev. at 658-59.

PRACTICE TIP

*The Dallas Court of Appeals has held that the confidentiality provisions for summary jury trials in CPRC §154.073(a), (b), trump the disclosure requirements of TRCP 76a. See **In re Kaiser Found. Health Plan**, 997 S.W.2d 605, 606 (Tex.App.—Dallas 1998, orig. proceeding). If this interpretation is correct, summary jury trials should be attractive to defendants who want to keep court records out of the public domain. See "Summary jury trial," ch. 4-A, §2.1.3, p. 204.*

3. Family Code cases. Documents filed in a suit that originally arose under the Family Code (*e.g.*, divorce, adoption, termination of parental rights, paternity, juvenile delinquency cases) are not court records. TRCP 76a(2)(a)(3); ***P.I.A., Inc. v. Sullivan***, 837 S.W.2d 844, 845-46 (Tex.App.—Fort Worth 1992, orig. proceeding).

4. Unfiled discovery.

(1) Trade-secret suit. Unfiled discovery products in a case initiated to preserve bona fide trade secrets or other intangible property rights are not court records. TRCP 76a(2)(c); ***Eli Lilly & Co. v. Marshall***, 829 S.W.2d 157, 158 (Tex.1992) (trade-secret interest can justify restricting access to documents). A trade secret is a formula, pattern, device, or compilation of information that is used in one's business and presents an opportunity to obtain an advantage over competitors. ***Computer Assocs. Int'l v. Altai, Inc.***, 918 S.W.2d 453, 455 (Tex.1996).

(2) No adverse effect on public. Unfiled discovery products are not court records if they do not have a probable adverse effect on the general public health or safety, administration of public office, or operation of government. TRCP 76a(2)(c). See §2.2.5(2), above. There is no presumption in TRCP 76a that unfiled discovery products are court records. ***Kepple***, 970 S.W.2d at 523 & n.8; ***Biffle***, 868 S.W.2d at 808. For the procedure to limit the dissemination of unfiled discovery, see "Protecting Documents That Are Not Court Records," §8, p. 294.

5. Settlement agreement + no adverse effect on public. Unfiled settlement agreements are not court records if they do not seek to restrict disclosure of information concerning matters that have a probable adverse effect on the general public health or safety, the administration of public office, or the operation of government. TRCP 76a(2)(b).

§3. SEALING COURT RECORDS

§3.1 Motion to seal records under TRCP 76a.

PRACTICE TIP

*If a party wants to limit dissemination of documents it believes are not court records, the party should file a motion for protective order under TRCP 192.6(b)(5), not a motion under TRCP 76a. See **General Tire v. Kepple**, 970 S.W.2d 520, 525 (Tex.1998). See "Protecting Documents That Are Not Court Records," §8, p. 294.*

---

1. In writing. The party who wants court records sealed must file a written motion to seal. TRCP 76a(3). See ***O'Connor's*** FORM 5K:01. The motion itself must be open to public inspection. TRCP 76a(3).

2. Grounds. When a party seeks to have documents protected from disclosure under TRCP 76a, it should allege the following:

(1) There is a serious, specific, and substantial interest in sealing the records that outweighs (1) the presumption of openness and (2) any probable adverse effect on the general welfare. TRCP 76a(1)(a); ***Fox v. Doe***, 869 S.W.2d 507, 512 (Tex.App.—San Antonio 1993, writ denied) (minor's right to privacy in suit alleging sexual assault by AIDS-infected employee).

(2) There are no other less-restrictive means that will adequately protect the specific interest asserted. TRCP 76a(1)(b).

§3.2 Agreement not to disclose under TRCP 11. A TRCP 11 agreement not to disclose unfiled discovery cannot protect court documents from disclosure without the procedural protections of TRCP 76a. *Cf.* ***Kepple***, 970 S.W.2d at 524 (before court can protect discovery from dissemination under TRCP 166b(5)(c), now TRCP 192.6(b)(5), it must observe the requirements of TRCP 76a). *But see* ***In re Kaiser Found. Health Plan***, 997 S.W.2d 605, 606 (Tex.App.—Dallas 1998, orig. proceeding) (because parties limited disclosure by a TRCP 11 agreement, they did not invoke TRCP 76a). The Supreme Court obliquely addressed the issue regarding TRCP 11 agreements limiting disclosure of documents in the case of ***In re Dallas Morning News***, 10 S.W.3d 298, 299 (Tex.1999), which dealt with appellate jurisdiction over a TRCP 11 order that protected documents from disclosure. In that case, the court reversed the mandamus granted by the court of appeals, presumably because an appeal was an adequate remedy to challenge the decision to hold a hearing on the TRCP 11 agreement, long after the trial court's plenary power expired. *See* ***Dallas Morning News***, 10 S.W.3d at 299. If the TRCP 11 agreement could prevent disclosure of documents, the Supreme Court could have decided the issue by mandamus.

§4. PUBLIC NOTICE

Court records may be sealed only after public notice and a hearing. TRCP 76a(3), (4).

§4.1 Public notice. The party that seeks to seal court records must post a public notice wherever meetings of county governmental bodies are required to be posted. ***Kepple***, 970 S.W.2d at 523. TRCP 76a(3) requires the notice to state the following:

1. The hearing will be in open court.

2. Any person may intervene and be heard.

3. The specific time and place of the hearing.

4. The style and number of the case.

5. A brief description of the nature of the case and the records sought to be sealed. *E.g.*, ***Doe***, 869 S.W.2d at 510-11 (ad litem's description of suit as one brought to settle minor's claim of sexual abuse was sufficient).

6. The identity of the movant. *E.g.*, *id.* (ad litem's description of P as anonymous was sufficient).

§4.2 Filed with two clerks. Immediately after posting the notice, the movant must file a verified copy of the notice with the clerk of the trial court and the clerk of the Supreme Court. TRCP 76a(3).

§5. HEARING ON MOTION TO SEAL

Court records may be sealed only after a public hearing. TRCP 76a(4); ***Chandler v. Hyundai Motor Co.***, 844 S.W.2d 882, 884-85 (Tex.App.—Houston [1st Dist.] 1992, no writ).

§5.1 Open court. A hearing to seal court records must be open to the public. TRCP 76a(4). At the hearing, the court may inspect documents in camera when necessary. *Id.*

§5.2 Deadline. A public hearing must be held as soon as practical, but not less than 14 days after a motion to seal is filed and public notice is posted. TRCP 76a(4).

§5.3 Participants. Both parties and any nonparty intervenor may participate in the hearing on a motion to seal court records. TRCP 76a(4).

§5.4 Burden. The burden of proof is on the movant seeking to seal the records to establish the standards by a preponderance of the evidence. ***Roberts v. West***, ___ S.W.3d ___ (Tex.App.—San Antonio 2003, n.p.h.) (No. 04-02-00414-CV; 8-29-03); ***Wood v. Moriarty***, 940 S.W.2d 359, 361 (Tex.App.—Dallas 1997, no writ); *see* TRCP 76a(1). The party with the burden must show the following:

1. There is a specific, serious, and substantial interest that clearly outweighs both (1) the presumption of openness and (2) any probable adverse effect that sealing would have on the general public health or safety. TRCP 76a(1)(a); *e.g.*, ***Doe***, 869 S.W.2d at 512 (public health & safety would not be adversely affected by nondisclosure of names in settlement agreement of sexual abuse claim by minor against employee of corporation).

2. There are no other less-restrictive means that will adequately protect the specific interest asserted. TRCP 76a(1)(b); *e.g.*, ***Compaq Computer Corp. v. Lapray***, 75 S.W.3d 669, 674 (Tex.App.—Beaumont 2002, no pet.) (that documents were trade secrets was insufficient to establish element of no other less-restrictive means).

§5.5 Procedure. TRCP 76a(4) provides that the same procedure as in TRCP 120a (special appearance) is to be followed in motions to seal or unseal cases. ***Doe***, 869 S.W.2d at 512. TRCP 120a allows proof by way of pleadings, stipulations, discovery, affidavits, and oral testimony. See "Special Appearance—Challenging Personal Jurisdiction," ch. 3-B, p. 143.

§6. ORDERS ON MOTION TO SEAL

§6.1 Temporary orders. The trial court may enter a temporary sealing order after motion and notice to the parties. TRCP 76a(5). The order must be in writing. TRCP 76a(6).

1. **Notice.** Notice for a temporary sealing order may be given under TRCP 21 and 21a.

2. **Requirements.** The movant must show a compelling need for a temporary sealing order based on specific facts; that is, the movant must show that a temporary order is necessary because a specific interest of the movant will suffer an immediate and irreparable injury before notice can be posted and a hearing held.

3. The order. A temporary sealing order must (1) state the time for a hearing and (2) direct the movant to post the necessary public notice. TRCP 76a(5).

§6.2 The sealing order.

1. Written. The order sealing court records must be a written order that is separate from any other order or the judgment in the case. TRCP 76a(6). A trial court cannot evade the requirements of TRCP 76a by closing the record with an unwritten order. ***Davenport v. Garcia***, 834 S.W.2d 4, 24 (Tex.1992).

2. Contents. The sealing order must include (1) the style and number of the case, (2) the specific reasons for the court's findings and conclusions, (3) the specific portions of the records to be sealed, and (4) the time period for which the records are to be sealed. TRCP 76a(6).

§7. CONTINUING JURISDICTION

An order sealing court records is subject to challenge by any person, at any time, even after the trial court loses plenary power over the case. The order is never final and is always appealable. It is always subject to challenge by nonparty intervenors, even after the court has held a hearing to order the records sealed. There is no finality to the order, no res judicata, no law of the case, and no judicial estoppel. TRCP 76a(7).

§7.1 Intervenors. Any person has the right to intervene any time before or after an order is entered to seal or unseal court records. TRCP 76a(7).

§7.2 Jurisdiction. The trial court that issued the sealing order will maintain continuing jurisdiction to enforce, alter, or vacate the order sealing or unsealing court records. TRCP 76a(7); ***Boyles v. Kerr***, 815 S.W.2d 545, 545 (Tex.1991).

§7.3 Rehearing. No party or intervenor who had actual notice of the hearing preceding the sealing or unsealing order may ask the court to reconsider the order without first showing a change in circumstances that materially affects the order. TRCP 76a(7). The changed circumstances need not relate to the case. A nonparty who was represented at the TRCP 76a hearing is "a party with actual notice" and is precluded from obtaining a reconsideration without showing a change of circumstances. ***Public Citizen v. Insurance Servs. Office***, 824 S.W.2d 811, 813 (Tex. App.—Austin 1992, no writ).

§7.4 Burden. The burden of proof under TRCP 76a(1) is always on the party seeking to seal records, even after an order is signed sealing the records. TRCP 76a(7).

§8. PROTECTING DOCUMENTS THAT ARE NOT COURT RECORDS

§8.1 Motion for protective order. A party who wants to restrict the dissemination of unfiled discovery documents or other documents that are not "court records" should file a motion for a protective order under TRCP 192.6(a). ***General Tire v. Kepple***, 970 S.W.2d 520, 524-25 (Tex.1998); ***Roberts***, ___ S.W.3d at ___. See ***O'Connor's*** FORM 6A:08. It is not necessary for the party to invoke TRCP 76a. If no person (another party, intervenor, or the court) makes the claim that the unfiled discovery documents are court records, TRCP 76a does not apply. ***Kepple***, 970 S.W.2d at 525.

§8.2 Response to motion for protective order. To trigger the requirements of TRCP 76a, the other party or an intervenor must show, in response to the motion for protective order or at a later date, that the documents are court records. ***Kepple***, 970 S.W.2d at 525. The burden is on the person attempting to benefit from the presumption of openness in TRCP 76a to prove the documents are court records. ***Upjohn Co. v. Freeman***, 906 S.W.2d 92, 96 (Tex.App.—Dallas 1995, no writ).

§8.3 Decision on court records allegations. Before the court addresses the issue of whether TRCP 76a prevents sealing, the court must decide whether the documents are court records. ***Kepple***, 970 S.W.2d at 525; *see* ***Compaq Computer***, 75 S.W.3d at 673-74 (called a "***Kepple*** inquiry"). For purposes of that decision, the trial court is not required to post a notice or hold a hearing. ***Kepple***, 970 S.W.2d at 525. The court should not give an intervenor access to the records before deciding whether the records are court records. *Id.* at 524-25.

1. Not court records. If the court determines the documents are not court records, dissemination can be restricted under TRCP 192.6(a) without reference to TRCP 76a. ***Kepple***, 970 S.W.2d at 525.

2. Court records. If the court determines the documents are court records, the party seeking to restrict dissemination must comply with the requirements of TRCP 76a. ***Kepple***, 970 S.W.2d at 525; ***Chandler v. Hyundai Motor Co.***, 829 S.W.2d 774, 774-75 (Tex.1992). That means the party seeking to limit distribution of the records must comply with the procedures discussed in "Sealing Court Records," §3, p. 292; "Public Notice," §4, p. 292; and "Hearing on Motion to Seal," §5, p. 293.

§9. GAG ORDER

§9.1 Constitutional limitations. Any restraint on speech is presumptively unconstitutional, even if imposed by court order. *E.g.*, ***Davenport***, 834 S.W.2d at 10 (trial court could not prevent guardian ad litem, who had been dismissed from case, from discussing case); ***Low v. King***, 867 S.W.2d 141, 142 (Tex.App.—Beaumont 1993, orig. proceeding) (trial court could not prevent party from placing ad in newspaper seeking witnesses); *see also* ***Star-Telegram v. Walker***, 834 S.W.2d 54, 56-58 (Tex.1992) (trial court could not prevent newspaper from using the rape victim's name, even though it had been expunged from court records). A gag order in a civil proceeding is valid only when (1) an imminent and irreparable harm to the judicial process will deprive litigants of a just resolution of their dispute, and (2) the judicial action represents the least-restrictive means to prevent that harm. ***Grigsby v. Coker***, 904 S.W.2d 619, 620 (Tex.1995); ***Davenport***, 834 S.W.2d at 10; *see* ***In re Houston Chronicle Publ'g Co.***, 64 S.W.3d 103, 107-08 (Tex.App.—Houston [14th Dist.] 2001, orig. proceeding) (gag order in Yates criminal trial, which restricted parties & attorneys from making statements to press, did not violate constitutional rights of publisher).

§9.2 Motion. The party moving for a gag order should file a motion stating the specific reasons a gag order should be imposed and the limits of the gag order. *See* ***Grigsby***, 904 S.W.2d at 620-21. See ***O'Connor's*** FORM 5K:09.

§9.3 Notice & hearing. The court must hold a hearing at which evidence is received. ***Grigsby***, 904 S.W.2d at 620-21.

§9.4 Findings. The court must make written findings supported by the evidence. ***Grigsby***, 904 S.W.2d at 620-21. The findings must state both of the following: (1) an imminent and irreparable harm to the judicial process will deprive litigants of a just resolution of their dispute, and (2) the judicial action represents the least-restrictive means to prevent that harm. ***Davenport***, 834 S.W.2d at 10.

§10. REVIEW

§10.1 The record. To review an error in a sealing or gag order, the appellant must file a reporter's record from the hearing. Without the reporter's record, the appellate court must presume that sufficient evidence was produced at the trial court level to support the order. ***Wood v. Moriarty***, 940 S.W.2d 359, 362-63 (Tex.App.—Dallas 1997, no writ).

§10.2 Motion to seal.

1. Standard of review. TRCP 76a decisions are reviewed for abuse of discretion. ***Kepple***, 970 S.W.2d at 526.

2. Sufficiency of evidence. The appellate courts review the trial court's order restricting access to documents on grounds of factual and legal sufficiency of the evidence. ***Chandler***, 829 S.W.2d at 775.

3. Appeal. Any party or intervenor who participated in the hearing preceding the order may seek review by appeal. TRCP 76a(8); ***Eli Lilly & Co. v. Marshall***, 829 S.W.2d 157, 158 (Tex.1992); *see* ***Wood v. James R. Moriarty, P.C.***, 940 S.W.2d 359, 360-61 (Tex.App.—Dallas 1997, no writ). The appeal is not considered an interlocutory appeal, but is an appeal from a final judgment. *See* TRCP 76a(8).

(1) **Severed.** Any order sealing or unsealing court records is deemed to be severed from the case and is a final judgment that may be appealed. TRCP 76a(8).

(2) **Expedited.** The appellate court may expedite the appeal of a TRCP 76a order. ***Dallas Morning News v. 5th Ct. of Appeals***, 842 S.W.2d 655, 657 n.2 (Tex.1992).

(3) **Abatement.** The appellate court may abate the appeal and order the trial court to give further notice or to hold additional hearings. TRCP 76a(8); ***Chandler***, 829 S.W.2d at 775 n.1.

(4) **Other orders.** During the appeal of a TRCP 76a order sealing records, the court may limit access to the records subject to the order. ***Dallas Morning News***, 842 S.W.2d at 657-58.

4. **Mandamus not necessary.** Mandamus is not necessary to challenge a TRCP 76a order because TRCP 76a(8) deems such an order severed and final. *See* TRCP 76a(8); ***Chandler***, 829 S.W.2d at 775; ***Marshall***, 829 S.W.2d at 158. Mandamus may be appropriate to challenge an interim order that causes harm that cannot be remedied by appeal. ***In re Dallas Morning News***, 10 S.W.3d 298, 306 (Tex.1999) (Gonzales, J., concurring).

§10.3 Gag order. A party may challenge a gag order by mandamus. ***Grigsby***, 904 S.W.2d at 621. The test on review is (1) whether an imminent and irreparable harm to the judicial process will deprive litigants of a just resolution of their dispute, and (2) whether the judicial action represents the least-restrictive means to prevent that harm. *Id.* at 620-21.

L. MOTION FOR JUDICIAL NOTICE

§1. GENERAL

§1.1 Rules. TRE 201-204.

§1.2 Purpose. Judicial notice promotes judicial efficiency by avoiding the expenditure of time and effort involved in adducing unnecessary evidence. Cochran, ***Texas Rules of Evidence Handbook***, p. 129 (5th ed. 2003) (Cochran, ***Evidence Handbook***). It dispenses with formal proof of a fact that is either known throughout the jurisdiction or easily determinable from reliable sources. *See id.* at 129-30.

§1.3 Forms. *O'Connor's Texas Civil Forms*, FORMS 5L.

§1.4 Other references. For a comprehensive discussion of judicial notice, see Cochran, ***Evidence Handbook***, p. 129-70. Other references include: Wellborn, *Judicial Notice Under Article II of the Texas Rules of Evidence*, 19 St. Mary's L.J. 1, 17 (1987); Hardberger, *Texas Courtroom Evidence*, ch. 29 (5th ed. 2003).

§2. TYPES OF JUDICIAL NOTICE

Matters that may be judicially noticed are often divided into three categories: adjudicative facts, legislative facts, and law. Cochran, ***Evidence Handbook***, p. 131. Different rules of proof or procedure apply to each.

§2.1 Adjudicative facts. Adjudicative facts are those facts that go to the jury and are proved by the introduction of evidence. *See* Cochran, ***Evidence Handbook***, p. 132. They relate to the parties, their activities, their properties, and their businesses. *Id.* When an adjudicative fact is not subject to reasonable dispute, TRE 201 dispenses with the need for evidence. See "Adjucative facts," §4.1, p. 298.

§2.2 Legislative facts. Legislative facts are those that help the tribunal to determine the content of law and policy and to exercise its judgment or discretion in determining what judicial course of action to take. ***Emerson v. State***, 880 S.W.2d 759, 764 (Tex.Crim.App.1994); Cochran, ***Evidence Handbook***, p. 133. Legislative facts are relevant to legal reasoning and the law-making process. ***O'Connell v. State***, 17 S.W.3d 746, 749 (Tex.App.—Austin 2000, no pet.). Generally, legislative facts can be determined without an adversarial proceeding, although an opportunity for open debate in a public hearing or in a notice and comment procedure is probably appropriate, if not essential. ***Tarrant Cty. v. Ashmore***, 635 S.W.2d 417, 423 (Tex.1982).

§2.3 Law. A court must take judicial notice of the law of the forum and may take notice of the law of the U.S., sister states, and foreign countries. Cochran, ***Evidence Handbook***, p. 134. When the content or applicability of the law of the forum is to be judicially noticed, the court is unrestricted in its investigation and conclusion. *Id.* Some statutes provide mandatory and permissive judicial notice provisions.

§3. MOTION FOR JUDICIAL NOTICE

§3.1 Court's motion. A court may take judicial notice on its own motion, without a request from the parties, under TRE 201(c) (adjudicative facts), TRE 202 (laws of other states), and TRE 204 (city & county ordinances, contents of Texas Register, published agency rules). *See, e.g.*, ***In re Houston Chronicle Publ'g Co.***, 64 S.W.3d 103, 105 (Tex.App.—Houston [14th Dist.] 2001, orig. proceeding) (on its own, trial court in Yates criminal trial judicially noticed that parties were discussing case with media & issued gag order); ***Int'l Ass'n of Firefighters v. City of San Antonio***, 822 S.W.2d 122, 127 (Tex.App.—San Antonio 1991, writ denied) (on its own, appellate court judicially noticed city charter even though trial court was not asked to do so). It is uncertain whether the court can inquire into the law of a foreign jurisdiction on its own initiative. Cochran, ***Evidence Handbook***, p. 167.

§3.2 Party's motion.

1. In writing. In most cases, a motion for judicial notice should be in writing, although there is no such requirement in the TREs. During trial, a motion may be oral. *See, e.g.*, ***Cutler v. Cutler***, 543 S.W.2d 1, 2 (Tex. App.—Dallas 1976, writ ref'd n.r.e.) (oral motion made on the record during trial); ***Utica Mut. Ins. Co. v. Bennett***, 492 S.W.2d 659, 663-64 (Tex.App.—Houston [1st Dist.] 1973, writ dism'd) (oral motion requesting notice of Mississippi law, along with copies of cases, was sufficient).

2. Type of information. The type of information required depends on the type of judicial notice requested. *See, e.g.*, TRE 201(d) (for adjudicative facts, "necessary information"), TRE 202 (for laws of U.S. & sister states, "sufficient information"), TRE 204 (for ordinances, "sufficient information"). The parties should attach to the motion copies of the information that supports the request for judicial notice. The trial court has discretion to determine if the party has complied with this requirement. ***Daugherty v. Southern P.T. Co.***, 772 S.W.2d 81, 83 (Tex. 1989); *see* Cochran, ***Evidence Handbook***, p. 162. For adjudicative facts, see §4.1.2, below. For city or county ordinances, see "City & county ordinances," §4.3, p. 299. For Texas Register or codified rules of the agencies published in the Administrative Code, see "Texas Register & Administrative Code," §4.4, p. 299. For laws of sister states, see "Sufficient information for laws of other states," §4.5.1, p. 300. For federal laws, see "Federal laws," §4.6, p. 300.

3. Verification. Whenever the party furnishes the court with factual information outside the record, and the information is not universally known, the information must be supported by an affidavit. For example, the movant should verify the laws of foreign jurisdictions and statements of experts on laws of foreign jurisdictions. *See, e.g.*, ***Holden v. Capri Lighting***, 960 S.W.2d 831, 833 (Tex.App.—Amarillo 1997, no pet.) (copy of California case without affidavit from California attorney was insufficient). Although TRE 204 does not require it, some appellate courts require municipal ordinances to be verified. See "City & county ordinances," §4.3, p. 299.

§3.3 Notice. A party is entitled to notice of the request to take judicial notice. If the court takes judicial notice on its own motion without notice to the parties, either party may request an opportunity to be heard after judicial notice has been taken. TRE 201(e) (adjudicative facts), TRE 202 (laws of sister states), TRE 204 (city and county ordinances). See §3.4, below.

§3.4 Request hearing. Upon timely request, a party is entitled to an opportunity to be heard as to the propriety of taking judicial notice and the tenor of the matter noticed. TRE 201(e) (adjudicative facts), TRE 202 (laws of sister states), TRE 204 (city and county ordinances).

§3.5 Deadlines.

1. Before or during trial. The motion for judicial notice should be made as early as possible, preferably before trial. Courts may take judicial notice of most matters at any stage of the proceeding. TRE 201(f) (adjudicative facts), TRE 202 (laws of other states, of U.S. territories, or other U.S. jurisdiction); *see, e.g.*, ***City of Dallas v. Moreau***, 718 S.W.2d 776, 781 (Tex.App.—Corpus Christi 1986, writ ref'd n.r.e.) (request for judicial notice of city charter at JNOV hearing was timely).

2. On appeal. Courts may take judicial notice for the first time during the appeal. ***Office of Pub. Util. Counsel v. PUC***, 878 S.W.2d 598, 600 (Tex.1994); *see, e.g.*, ***Harper v. Killion***, 348 S.W.2d 521, 523 (Tex.1961) (court of appeals properly took judicial notice of geographic fact); ***Prostok v. Browning***, 112 S.W.3d 876, 924 (Tex.App.—Dallas 2003, pet. filed 10-24-03) (court of appeals took judicial notice of earlier federal judgments). However, some courts of appeals limit the matters about which they will take judicial notice to those involving their jurisdiction or matters ancillary to decisions that are mandated by law (*e.g.*, prejudgment interest calculations). ***City of Glenn Heights v. Sheffield Dev. Co.***, 55 S.W.3d 158, 162-63 (Tex.App.—Dallas 2001, pet. denied) (court of appeals refused to take judicial notice of ordinance).

§4. GROUNDS FOR JUDICIAL NOTICE

§4.1 Adjudicative facts.

1. Types of facts. For a court to take judicial notice of an adjudicative fact, the fact must not be subject to reasonable dispute because either (1) it is generally known within the territorial jurisdiction of the trial court (a notorious fact), or (2) it is capable of accurate and ready determination by resort to sources whose accuracy cannot reasonably be questioned (a verifiable fact). TRE 201(b).

(1) Notorious fact. If a fact is generally known within the territorial jurisdiction of the court, it is a notorious fact. TRE 201(b)(1); *see, e.g.*, ***Barber v. Intercoast Jobbers & Brokers***, 417 S.W.2d 154, 158 (Tex. 1967) (city of Odessa is in Ector County); ***Harper***, 348 S.W.2d at 523 (Jacksonville is in Cherokee County); ***Apostolic Ch. v. American Honda Motor Co.***, 833 S.W.2d 553, 555-56 (Tex.App.—Tyler 1992, writ denied) (highway 96 is known as Tenaha Highway & is in Shelby City); ***Settlers Village Cmty. Imprv. Ass'n v. Settlers Village***, 828 S.W.2d 182, 184 (Tex.App.—Houston [14th Dist.] 1992, no writ) (term $0.015 commonly understood to mean one and one-half cents). See Cochran, ***Evidence Handbook***, p. 138-40. It is not necessary to provide any documentation or extrinsic documentation of a "notorious" fact. Notorious facts do not include facts known personally by the trial judge or known to a specially informed group of people. *Id.* at 140.

(2) Verifiable fact. If a fact is capable of easy and accurate determination from a reliable source, it is a verifiable fact. TRE 201(b)(2); *see, e.g.*, ***Concord Oil Co. v. Pennzoil Expl. & Prod. Co.***, 966 S.W.2d 451, 459 (Tex.1998) (judicial notice of standard royalty in oil & gas leases around 1937); ***PUC***, 878 S.W.2d at 600 (judicial notice of published order of the PUC); ***City of Houston v. Todd***, 41 S.W.3d 289, 301 (Tex.App.—Houston [1st Dist.] 2001, pet. denied) (judicial notice that railroads supplied transportation to all developed sections of Texas by 1900, by consulting history sources); ***Texas DPS v. Ackerman***, 31 S.W.3d 672, 676 (Tex.App.—Waco 2000, pet. denied) (judicial notice of population, by consulting the federal census); ***J. Weingarten, Inc. v. Tripplett***, 530 S.W.2d 653, 656 (Tex.App.—Beaumont 1975, writ ref'd n.r.e.) (judicial notice of weather for a particular day, by consulting weather bureau records). See Cochran, ***Evidence Handbook***, p. 140-46.

(3) Reasoning facts. Some "reasoning" facts are so universally known that they are not subject to the requirements of judicial notice. *See* Cochran, ***Evidence Handbook***, p. 136-37, *see, e.g.*, ***El Chico Corp. v. Poole***, 732 S.W.2d 306, 311 (Tex.1987) (common knowledge that alcohol distorts perception, slows reaction, and impairs motor skills); ***City of Austin v. Selter***, 415 S.W.2d 489, 501 (Tex.App.—Austin 1967, writ ref'd n.r.e.) (death by drowning is painful).

2. Necessary information for "verifiable" adjudicative facts. For judicial notice of "verifiable" adjudicative facts, a party is required to furnish the court with "necessary information." TRE 201(d). Necessary information includes documentation that qualifies as a source whose accuracy cannot reasonably be questioned. ***PUC***, 878 S.W.2d at 600 (published PUC order); *see, e.g.*, ***Magee v. Ulery***, 993 S.W.2d 332, 338-39 (Tex.App.—Houston [14th Dist.] 1999, no pet.) (when court supplied with information from Medical Examiners Board, it should have taken judicial notice of physician's age & practice status); ***Drake v. Holstead***, 757 S.W.2d 909, 911 (Tex. App.—Beaumont 1988, no writ) (when court was supplied with computation, it should have taken judicial notice of the distance a car would travel at a given speed); ***Wagner & Brown v. E.W. Moran Drilling Co.***, 702 S.W.2d 760, 772-73 (Tex.App.—Fort Worth 1986, no writ) (court may take judicial notice of the discount rate on 90-day commercial paper in effect at a Federal Reserve bank if provided with the appropriate Federal Reserve bulletins); ***J. Weingarten***, 530 S.W.2d at 656 (court may consult weather bureau records to judicially notice a weather report for a particular day); *see also* Cochran, ***Evidence Handbook***, p. 150 (industry source routinely used & relied on by those in same industry qualifies as necessary information). A movant should attach verified copies of the information to the motion. Once the court has been given the motion and necessary information, judicial notice of the adjudicative fact is mandatory. TRE 201(d); ***Drake***, 757 S.W.2d at 910-11.

§4.2 Texas statutes. A party is not required to provide the court with information about the laws of the state of Texas. Texas courts are required to take judicial notice of the public statutes of this state. ***Kish v. Van Note***, 692 S.W.2d 463, 467 (Tex.1985).

1. Unambiguous statute. If a statute is clear and unambiguous, a party should not provide the court with legislative facts to explain its meaning. In such case, the court should give the statute its common meaning. ***St. Luke's Episcopal Hosp. v. Agbor***, 952 S.W.2d 503, 505 (Tex.1997).

2. Ambiguous statute. When a statute is ambiguous, the party should provide the court with information about the following: (1) the object sought to be attained, (2) the circumstances under which the statute was enacted, (3) the legislative history, (4) the common law or former statutory provisions, (5) the consequences of a particular construction, (6) the administrative construction of the statute, and (7) the effect of the title (caption), preamble, and emergency provisions. Gov't Code §311.023. The court may take judicial notice of these sources. *See* ***Bally Total Fitness Corp. v. Jackson***, 53 S.W.3d 352, 365 (Tex.2001) (court considered object sought to be attained & consequences of particular construction). The party should argue it seeks an interpretation (1) to obtain a just and reasonable result, as intended by the Legislature, (2) to make execution of the statute reasonably feasible, as intended by the Legislature, and (3) that favors the public interest over any private interest. *See* Gov't Code §311.021.

§4.3 City & county ordinances. For judicial notice of the ordinances of municipalities and counties of Texas, the party must furnish the court with "sufficient information" to enable it to comply with the request. TRE 204. The movant must attach copies of the ordinance, which probably should be certified or verified even though TRE 204 does not specifically impose such a requirement. *See, e.g.*, ***City of Houston v. Southwest Concrete Constr.***, 835 S.W.2d 728, 733 n.5 (Tex.App.—Houston [14th Dist.] 1992, writ denied) (refused to take judicial notice because ordinance not verified); ***Hollingsworth v. King***, 810 S.W.2d 772, 774 (Tex.App.—Amarillo 1991) (refused to take judicial notice of unauthorized municipal ordinances), *writ denied*, 816 S.W.2d 340 (Tex.1991).

§4.4 Texas Register & Administrative Code. The provisions of TRE 204 that refer to taking judicial notice of the contents of the Texas Register and Texas Administrative Code duplicate provisions in the Administrative Procedure and Texas Register Acts. ***Metro Fuels v. City of Austin***, 827 S.W.2d 531, 532 (Tex.App.—Austin 1992, no writ); *see* Gov't Code §2002.022(a) (contents of Texas Register are to be judicially noticed), *id.* §2002.054(1) (state agency rules published in Administrative Code are to be judicially noticed). Because Gov't Code §2002.022(a) and §2002.054(1) require the court to take judicial notice, it is probably not necessary for the party to file a written motion or supply sufficient information, as stated in TRE 204. However, for the convenience of a court that does not regularly deal with matters in the Texas Register or the Texas Administrative Code, the party should file a motion and provide copies of the information about which it wishes the court to take notice. As a source of law, agency regulations are like statutes or the decisions of a higher court to which a lower court owes obedience under the doctrine of stare decisis. ***Eckmann v. Des Rosiers***, 940 S.W.2d 394, 399 (Tex.App.—Austin 1997, no writ).

§4.5 Laws of sister state. For judicial notice of the constitutions, public statutes, rules, regulations, ordinances, court decisions, and common law of other states, territories, or any jurisdiction of the U.S., a party must furnish the court with "sufficient information" before the court is required to take judicial notice. TRE 202; ***Pittsburgh Corning Corp. v. Walters***, 1 S.W.3d 759, 769 (Tex.App.—Corpus Christi 1999, pet. denied).

1. Sufficient information for laws of other states. The party requesting notice should attach sufficient information to its motion so that the court can determine the applicability of the law of another state to the case. ***Daugherty v. Southern P.T. Co.***, 772 S.W.2d 81, 83 (Tex.1989); *see* ***Knops v. Knops***, 763 S.W.2d 864, 867 (Tex.App.—San Antonio 1988, no writ) (broad request without any information is not sufficient); *see also* ***Wickware v. Session***, 538 S.W.2d 466, 469 (Tex.App.—Tyler 1976, writ ref'd n.r.e.) (photocopy of statute & oral motion requesting notice of California probate code were sufficient). The movant should attach copies of the law to be judicially noticed and include citations to the law in its motion and notice. *See, e.g.*, ***Burns v. RTC***, 880 S.W.2d 149, 151 (Tex.App.—Houston [14th Dist.] 1994, no writ) (copies of relevant Colorado statutes attached to request); ***Cal Growers v. Palmer Whs. & Transfer Co.***, 687 S.W.2d 384, 386 (Tex.App.—Houston [14th Dist.] 1985, no writ) (even though copy of California statute was not provided, court could take judicial notice because motion cited statute). In some instances, it might be helpful to supply the court with an affidavit from a practicing attorney in the sister state to prove the documentary evidence—such as a copy of the statute or case law—is still controlling law in that jurisdiction. Cochran, ***Evidence Handbook***, p. 162-63.

2. When no request made. If no one makes a request for judicial notice of the laws of another state, or if no one submits proper proof, Texas courts presume the laws of that state are the same as the laws of Texas. ***Walters***, 1 S.W.3d at 769; ***Burns***, 880 S.W.2d at 151; ***Mathis v. Wachovia Bank & Trust Co.***, 583 S.W.2d 800, 802 (Tex.App.—Houston [1st Dist.] 1979, writ ref'd n.r.e.).

§4.6 Federal laws. For judicial notice of federal laws, a party should attach sufficient information to its motion so that the court can determine the law's applicability to the case. On the motion of a party supported by sufficient information, a court must take judicial notice of federal laws. TRE 202; ***Daugherty***, 772 S.W.2d at 83 (OSHA regulation). TRE 202 does not permit judicial notice of private orders. ***Centex Corp. v. Dalton***, 810 S.W.2d 812, 824 (Tex.App.—San Antonio 1991), *rev'd on other grounds*, 840 S.W.2d 952 (Tex.1992).

§4.7 Foreign laws. The procedure for judicial notice of foreign laws is more complicated than that for other types of laws. TRE 203 is considered a "hybrid rule"; the presentation of the law to the court resembles the presentment of evidence, but it is ultimately decided as a question of law. ***Long Distance Int'l v. Telefonos de Mex., S.A.***, 49 S.W.3d 347, 351 (Tex.2001); ***Bridas Corp. v. Unocal Corp.***, 16 S.W.3d 893, 896 (Tex.App.—Houston [14th Dist.] 2000, pet. denied). For more detailed information about proving laws of foreign countries, see Cochran, ***Evidence Handbook***, p. 164-67.

1. Pleading. To raise an issue about the laws of a foreign country, a party must plead the law in its petition, its answer, or a written motion. TRE 203.

2. Proof of foreign law – 30 days before trial. The party must provide the proof of foreign law at least 30 days before the date of trial. TRE 203.

(1) Foreign law. The movant must provide copies of the foreign law on which it intends to rely. TRE 203.

(2) Expert opinion. TRE 203 permits the movant to provide proof from an expert in the form of affidavits or deposition testimony explaining the foreign law. *See, e.g.*, ***Reading & Bates Constr. Co. v. Baker Energy Res. Corp.***, 976 S.W.2d 702, 707 (Tex.App.—Houston [1st Dist.] 1998, pet. denied) (parties provided affidavits of law professors explaining Canadian law); ***Trailways, Inc. v. Clark***, 794 S.W.2d 479, 484 (Tex.App.—Corpus Christi 1990, writ denied) (P provided letter explaining Mexican law with copies of law).

3. Translation of foreign law – 45 days. If the foreign laws, the expert's opinion explaining the laws, or other sources of information are in a language other than English, the movant must, at least 45 days before trial, provide the following information to the court and other parties: (1) a copy of the foreign language text, (2) a copy of the English translation, and (3) an affidavit from a qualified translator that sets forth the translator's qualifications and certifies that the translation is fair and accurate. TRE 203, 1009(a); *see* ***In re Estates of Garcia-Chapa***, 33 S.W.3d 859, 862 (Tex.App.—Corpus Christi 2000, no pet.); *see, e.g.*, ***Clark***, 794 S.W.2d at 484 (P provided certified translation). The 45-day deadline can be enlarged or shortened, on motion showing good cause. TRE 1009(f).

4. Challenging translation – 15 days before trial.

(1) Objection. To challenge the accuracy of the translation of a foreign law, a party must serve objections to the translation at least 15 days before trial. TRE 1009(b). The 15-day deadline can be enlarged or shortened, on motion showing good cause. TRE 1009(f). The objection must identify specific inaccuracies of the translation and state with specificity a fair and accurate translation. TRE 1009(b).

(2) Effect of objection. The trial court must determine whether there is a genuine issue, to be resolved by the trier of fact, about the accuracy of a material part of the translation. TRE 1009(d). If necessary, the trial court may appoint a qualified translator to translate the foreign law. TRE 1009(g). The reasonable value of the translator's services are taxed as court costs. *Id.*

(3) When no objection made. When no objection or conflicting translation is served timely, the trial court must admit a translation if it complies with TRE 1009(a) and the underlying foreign language documents are otherwise admissible under the TREs. TRE 1009(c). A party who does not serve a conflicting translation or objections cannot attack or offer evidence contradicting the accuracy of the translation at trial. *Id.*

5. Court's sources of proof. If the court considers sources other than those submitted by a party, the court must give all parties notice and a reasonable opportunity to comment on the sources and to submit further materials to the court. ***Lawrenson v. Global Mar.***, 869 S.W.2d 519, 525 (Tex.App.—Texarkana 1993, writ denied); *see also* ***Ossorio v. Leon***, 705 S.W.2d 219, 221-22 (Tex.App.—San Antonio 1985, no writ) (after introduction of foreign law in motion for summary judgment, court granted postponement to comply with requirements in TRE 203).

6. Court's ruling. The court, not the jury, determines the laws of foreign countries. TRE 203. The court's determination is reviewed on appeal as a question of law. *Id.*

§4.8 Other matters that may be judicially noticed.

1. Attorney fees. The court can take judicial notice of the reasonableness of attorney fees in some cases. See "Judicial notice," ch. 1-H, §10.3.2, p. 46.

2. Learned treatises. Particular sources, such as treatises, periodicals, or pamphlets on a subject of history, medicine, other science, or art may be established as a reliable authority by judicial notice. TRE 803(18); *see, e.g.*, ***King v. Bauer***, 767 S.W.2d 197, 199 (Tex.App.—Corpus Christi 1989, writ denied) (textbook on radiotherapy).

3. Records of the same court. A court may take judicial notice of its own records and judgments. ***Texas Real Estate Comm'n v. Nagle***, 767 S.W.2d 691, 694 (Tex.1989); ***In re J.G.W.***, 54 S.W.3d 826, 833 (Tex.App.—Texarkana 2001, no pet.); *see also* ***McDaniel v. Hale***, 893 S.W.2d 652, 673 (Tex.App.—Amarillo 1994, writ denied) (because bill-of-review proceeding is before the same judge who presided at trial, that judge can take judicial notice of underlying trial). The court's use of its own records is circumscribed by the doctrines of res judicata and collateral estoppel. ***Nagle***, 767 S.W.2d at 694.

4. Records of another court. To prove the records of another court (*e.g.*, for purposes of collateral estoppel) the party must provide the court with sworn or certified copies of the records. ***Krishnan v. Ramirez***, 42 S.W.3d 205, 222-23 (Tex.App.—Corpus Christi 2001, pet. denied); ***Bhalli v. Methodist Hosp.***, 896 S.W.2d 207, 210 (Tex.App.—Houston [1st Dist.] 1995, writ denied); *see also* ***Bekins Moving & Storage Co. v. Williams***, 947 S.W.2d

568, 575 (Tex.App.—Texarkana 1997, no writ) (appellate court took judicial notice of records from county court of same case that was dismissed & refiled in district court).

5. Local court rules. Appellate courts can take judicial notice of the local rules of the trial courts. ***Cummings v. Cire***, 74 S.W.3d 920, 924 (Tex.App.—Amarillo 2002, pet. granted 4-17-03); ***Hilal v. Gatpandan***, 71 S.W.3d 403, 407 (Tex.App.—Corpus Christi 2001, no pet.). Some appellate courts refuse to take judicial notice of local rules unless a party provides a certified copy of the rules. *See* ***Seigle v. Hollech***, 892 S.W.2d 201, 202 (Tex. App.—Houston [14th Dist.] 1994, no writ).

§5. RESPONSE

If the motion for judicial notice was in writing, the response should be in writing. The following is a list of objections to judicial notice.

§5.1 Fact not commonly known. The adjudicative fact to be judicially noticed is not indisputable, commonly known, or easily ascertainable. TRE 201(b).

§5.2 Personally known facts. The adjudicative fact to be judicially noticed is based on personal knowledge possessed by the other party or the trial judge, but is disputed. *E.g.*, ***Eagle Trucking Co. v. Texas Bitulithic Co.***, 612 S.W.2d 503, 506 (Tex.1981) (court could not take judicial notice that certain land was outside residential or business district); ***1.70 Acres v. State***, 935 S.W.2d 480, 489 (Tex.App.—Beaumont 1996, no writ) (court could not take judicial notice of time to drive a certain 9.2 miles).

§5.3 Known by special class. The adjudicative fact to be judicially noticed is commonly known by only a specially informed class of persons. *See, e.g.*, ***Soto v. Texas Indus.***, 820 S.W.2d 217, 220 (Tex.App.—Fort Worth 1991, no writ) (fact that concrete walls do not fall in the absence of negligence was not within general knowledge).

§5.4 Lack of sufficient information. The movant did not present sufficient information for the court to take judicial notice. *See, e.g.*, ***Pittsburgh Corning Corp. v. Walters***, 1 S.W.3d 759, 769-70 (Tex.App.—Corpus Christi 1999, pet. denied) (D's motion did not contain significant recitation of California law or where such law could be located).

§5.5 Disputed fact issue. The adjudicative fact to be judicially noticed requires a determination of a contested fact issue. ***First Nat'l Bank v. Jarnigan***, 794 S.W.2d 54, 62 (Tex.App.—Amarillo 1990, writ denied).

§5.6 Foreign law. Some objections to a motion to take judicial notice of foreign laws include the following: (1) the movant did not provide a copy of the foreign language text or an English translation, as required by TRE 203; (2) the movant did not provide the proof 30 days before the date for trial, as required by TRE 203; or (3) the movant's expert did not properly interpret the law of the foreign jurisdiction. When objecting to the interpretation, the nonmovant must provide its own expert testimony to counter the movant's expert's interpretation. *See* TRE 1009(c).

§6. HEARING

Most motions for judicial notice can be resolved without a formal hearing to receive evidence.

§7. RULING

§7.1 Order. After the hearing, the court should make a determination whether the matter requested is to be judicially noticed. To preserve error, the party should make sure the court signs a written order.

1. When mandatory. The court must take judicial notice of adjudicative facts or laws when properly requested and supplied with the necessary information. TRE 201(d), 202, 204; ***Office of Pub. Util. Counsel v. PUC***, 878 S.W.2d 598, 600 (Tex.1994).

2. When discretionary. A court may take judicial notice of adjudicative facts or laws, whether requested or not. TRE 201(c), 202, 204; *see* ***Daugherty v. Southern P.T. Co.***, 772 S.W.2d 81, 83 (Tex.1989) (court is not required to take judicial notice of federal law).

§7.2 Established fact. Once the court has judicially noticed a fact, that fact is established as a matter of law. ***Langdale v. Villamil***, 813 S.W.2d 187, 190 (Tex.App.—Houston [14th Dist.] 1991, no writ).

§7.3 Jury instruction. Once the court has judicially noticed an adjudicative fact, it must instruct the jury in a civil case to accept that fact as conclusive. TRE 201(g); *see, e.g.*, ***Hoechst Celanese Corp. v. Arthur Bros.***, 882 S.W.2d 917, 930 (Tex.App.—Corpus Christi 1994, writ denied) (dicta; trial court took judicial notice of & instructed jury on D's net worth); ***Allied Gen. Agency v. Moody***, 788 S.W.2d 601, 607 (Tex.App.—Dallas 1990, writ denied) (court took judicial notice of & instructed jury on definition of "promotion" from three dictionaries); *see also* ***O'Connell v. State***, 17 S.W.3d 746, 749 (Tex.App.—Austin 2000, no pet.) (error for court to instruct jury on a legislative, rather than an adjudicative, fact).

§8. REVIEW

§8.1 The record. The appellate record must contain (1) the motion for judicial notice, (2) all supporting information, and (3) the court's ruling. *See* ***Metro Fuels v. City of Austin***, 827 S.W.2d 531, 532 n.2 (Tex.App.—Austin 1992, no writ) (court of appeals refused to take judicial notice of ordinance because it was not included in record).

§8.2 Standard of review. When a court erroneously takes or refuses to take judicial notice of a matter, the error is reversible only if it probably caused the rendition of an improper judgment. TRAP 44.1(a)(1); ***Daugherty***, 772 S.W.2d at 83; ***Magee v. Ulery***, 993 S.W.2d 332, 339 (Tex.App.—Houston [14th Dist.] 1999, no pet.); ***Hill v. Heritage Res.***, 964 S.W.2d 89, 137 (Tex.App.—El Paso 1997, pet. denied).

M. MOTION TO EXCLUDE EXPERT

A 1998 federal study of the use of experts revealed that the most frequent types of trials that rely on experts are tort cases (comprising 45%), primarily personal injury and medical malpractice. Johnson, Krafka & Cecil, *Expert Testimony in Federal Civil Trials: A Preliminary Analysis, Federal Judicial Center*, p. 1 (2000). Next are civil rights cases (23%); contract cases (11%); intellectual property cases, primarily patent cases (10%); labor cases (2%); prisoner cases (2%); and other civil cases (8%). *Id.*

§1. GENERAL

§1.1 Rules. TRE 104, 401-403, 702-705.

§1.2 Purpose. Under TRE 702, the trial court must act as a "gatekeeper" to determine the qualifications of an expert and whether the expert's opinion is admissible. ***E.I. du Pont de Nemours & Co. v. Robinson***, 923 S.W.2d 549, 556 (Tex.1995).

§1.3 Forms. ***O'Connor's Texas Civil Forms***, FORMS 5M.

§1.4 Other references. ***O'Connor's Texas Causes of Action***, "Expert testimony," ch. 18-A, §8, p. 444 (2004) (***O'Connor's COA***); Cochran, ***Texas Rules of Evidence Handbook***, p. 665 (5th ed. 2003) (Cochran, ***Evidence Handbook***); Blend, *Using Expert Witnesses in Employment Litigation*, 17 Rev. Litig. 27 (1998); Baker, *"Gatekeeping" in Texas*, 27 St. Mary's L.J. 237 (1996); Black, Ayala, & Saffran-Brinks, *Science & the Law in the Wake of Daubert: A New Search for Scientific Knowledge*, 72 Tex.L.Rev. 715 (1994).

§2. THE *DAUBERT-ROBINSON* TEST FOR EXPERT TESTIMONY

The language of TRE 702 and 705(c) suggest four distinct but interrelated tests for the admissibility of expert testimony: qualifications, knowledge, helpfulness, and foundation data. The four cases to read about experts are the following: ***Kumho Tire Co. v. Carmichael***, 526 U.S. 137, 119 S.Ct. 1167 (1999); ***Daubert v. Merrell Dow Pharms.***, 509 U.S. 579, 113 S.Ct. 2786 (1993); ***Gammill v. Jack Williams Chevrolet***, 972 S.W.2d 713 (Tex.1998); and ***E.I. du Pont de Nemours & Co. v. Robinson***, 923 S.W.2d 549 (Tex.1995).

§2.1 Qualifications test. The expert must be qualified to give an opinion as an expert "by knowledge, skill, experience, training, or education." TRE 702. In deciding if an expert is qualified, trial courts must ensure that those who purport to be experts truly have expertise concerning the actual subject about which they are offering an opinion. ***Roberts v. Williamson***, 111 S.W.3d 113, 121 (Tex.2003); ***Broders v. Heise***, 924 S.W.2d 148, 153 (Tex. 1996). When a subject is substantially developed in more than one field, testimony can come from a qualified expert in any of those fields. ***Broders***, 924 S.W.2d at 154.

1. Education or training. The first inquiry is whether the expert is qualified by education or training to give an expert opinion.

(1) Qualified. The following experts were qualified: • Pediatrician, who was not a neurologist but was certified in pediatric advanced life support and studied and advised parents of the effects of pediatric neurological injuries, was qualified to testify about a newborn child's neurological injuries. ***Roberts***, 111 S.W.3d at 121-22. • An officer with training and experience in investigating accidents was qualified to testify that the driver's inattention caused the accident. ***Ter-Vartanyan v. R&R Freight***, 111 S.W.3d 779, 781 (Tex.App.—Dallas 2003, n.p.h.). • Otolaryngologist was qualified to testify about plastic surgery on the face. ***Keo v. Vu***, 76 S.W.3d 725, 732-33 (Tex. App.—Houston [1st Dist.] 2002, pet. denied). • Neurologist was qualified to testify as to standard of care and treatment of strokes even though he admitted no knowledge of the standard of care applied to cardiologists. ***Blan v. Ali***, 7 S.W.3d 741, 746 (Tex.App.—Houston [14th Dist.] 1999, no pet.). • Nonphysician with doctorate in neuroscience, who conducted research on the causes of neurological injuries and taught doctors how the brain works, could testify as expert about the cause of brain damage. ***Ponder v. Texarkana Mem'l Hosp.***, 840 S.W.2d 476, 477-78 (Tex.App.—Houston [14th Dist.] 1991, writ denied).

(2) Not qualified. The following experts were not qualified: • Expert with degrees in bacteriology and public health was not qualified to testify regarding transmission of AIDS virus through blood transfusion because he had no medical training or experience relating to blood transfusions. ***United Blood Servs. v. Longoria***, 938 S.W.2d 29, 30-31 (Tex.1997). • Emergency room doctor was not qualified to testify in death case about cause of brain injury. ***Broders***, 924 S.W.2d at 153. • Psychiatrist was not qualified to give opinion about postoperative care following neurosurgery. ***Tomasi v. Liao***, 63 S.W.3d 62, 66 (Tex.App.—San Antonio 2001, no pet.).

2. Specialized knowledge, skill, & experience. If an expert is not qualified by education or training to give an opinion as an expert, the second inquiry is whether the expert is qualified by specialized knowledge, skill, or experience. *See* ***Guadalupe-Blanco River Auth. v. Kraft***, 77 S.W.3d 805, 807 (Tex.2002) (appraisal expertise is a form of specialized knowledge).

(1) Qualified. The following experts were qualified: • Expert with experience in conducting grain performance trials was qualified to testify about suitability of a particular seed to dry-land farming even though he was not a plant pathologist. ***Helena Chem. Co. v. Wilkins***, 47 S.W.3d 486, 500 (Tex.2001). • Surgeon with 11 years of surgical practice was qualified to testify that foreign body he removed from patient was a surgical sponge. ***Mitchell v. Baylor Univ. Med. Ctr.***, 109 S.W.3d 838, 842 (Tex.App.—Dallas 2003, n.p.h.). • Trooper with 16 years of experience in accident investigation was qualified to testify as to highway design. ***Huckaby v. A.G. Perry & Son***, 20 S.W.3d 194, 208 (Tex.App.—Texarkana 2000, pet. denied). • Appraiser with 20 years of experience was qualified to testify that ranch could not be partitioned. ***Egan v. Egan***, 8 S.W.3d 1, 4 (Tex.App.—San Antonio 1999, pet. denied).

(2) Not qualified. The following experts were not qualified: • Engineer who had experience in designing & testing fighter planes, but had no experience regarding cars, could not testify about design defects in cars. ***Gammill***, 972 S.W.2d at 718-19. • Co-worker was not qualified to testify that lift belt would have prevented back injury. ***Leitch v. Hornsby***, 935 S.W.2d 114, 119 (Tex.1996). • Railroad engineer was not qualified because nothing connected engineer's experience and training with the matter at issue. ***Houghton v. Port Terminal R.R.***, 999 S.W.2d 39, 47-49 (Tex.App.—Houston [14th Dist.] 1999, no pet.).

3. License. The courts disagree whether an expert may testify about the standard of care in a particular profession without a license in the same profession. *Compare* ***Harnett v. State***, 38 S.W.3d 650, 659 (Tex.App.—Austin 2000, pet. ref'd) (license unnecessary), ***State v. Northborough Ctr.***, 987 S.W.2d 187, 194 (Tex.App.—Houston [14th Dist.] 1999, pet. denied) (same), *and* ***Southland Lloyd's Ins. Co. v. Tomberlain***, 919 S.W.2d 822, 827 (Tex. App.—Texarkana 1996, writ denied) (same), *with* ***Prellwitz v. Cromwell, Truemper, Levy, Parker & Woodsmale***, 802 S.W.2d 316, 317 (Tex.App.—Dallas 1990, no writ) (license necessary). Before an expert can testify about the standard of care in a medical malpractice suit, the expert must meet the requirements of CPRC §§74.401-74.403. See ***O'Connor's COA***, "Expert's qualifications," ch. 18-A, §8.3, p. 445.

§2.2 Knowledge test. The subject of the testimony must be "scientific, technical, or other specialized knowledge." TRE 702; ***Helena Chem.***, 47 S.W.3d at 499. An expert cannot proffer an opinion based on a discipline that itself lacks reliability (*e.g.*, astrology). ***Kumho Tire Co. v. Carmichael***, 526 U.S. 137, 151, 119 S.Ct. 1167, 1175 (1999). Valid knowledge consists of facts, as well as conclusions or ideas inferred from facts "on good grounds." ***Daubert v. Merrell Dow Pharms.***, 509 U.S. 579, 590, 113 S.Ct. 2786, 2795 (1995); *e.g.*, ***GTE Sw. v. Bruce***, 998 S.W.2d 605, 619-20 (Tex.1999) (in suit for emotional distress, expert could not testify that certain conduct was extreme & outrageous; issue did not involve specialized knowledge); ***Warren v. Hartnett***, 561 S.W.2d 860, 863 (Tex.App.—Dallas 1977, writ ref'd n.r.e.) (in probate case, expert could not testify from handwriting sample that testatrix lacked testamentary capacity).

§2.3 Helpfulness test. The knowledge must "assist the trier of fact to understand the evidence or to determine a fact in issue." TRE 702; *see, e.g.*, ***K-Mart Corp. v. Honeycutt***, 24 S.W.3d 357, 360-61 (Tex.2000) (human factors expert excluded as not helpful to the jury; opinions were within the average juror's common knowledge). Under TRE 702, it is the court's duty to determine if the expert's testimony is sufficiently reliable and relevant to assist a jury. ***Gammill v. Jack Williams Chevrolet***, 972 S.W.2d 713, 725 (Tex.1998). Thus, there are two parts of the helpfulness test.

1. Reliability of opinion. The opinion of the expert must be reliable. TRE 702; ***E.I. du Pont de Nemours & Co. v. Robinson***, 923 S.W.2d 549, 557 (Tex.1995). All expert testimony—not just scientific expert testimony—must be shown to be reliable before it is admitted. ***Kumho Tire***, 526 U.S. at 147, 119 S.Ct. at 1174; ***Gammill***, 972 S.W.2d at 726. An expert's opinion is not admissible if it is based on flawed reasoning and methodology. ***Merrell Dow Pharms. v. Havner***, 953 S.W.2d 706, 714 (Tex.1997); ***Austin v. Kerr-McGee Ref. Corp.***, 25 S.W.3d 280, 288 (Tex.App.—Texarkana 2000, no pet.).

(1) Scientific expert. In the area of hard science, experts are qualified to give an opinion according to the rules of scientific discipline as provided in ***Daubert-Robinson***. ***Gammill***, 972 S.W.2d at 725-26. Some of the factors that are relevant are listed below. Of those, the first four (a)-(d) were initially set out by the U.S. Supreme Court in ***Daubert***; the last two (e)-(f) were added by the Texas Supreme Court in ***Robinson***.

(a) The extent to which the theory has been or can be tested. ***Daubert***, 509 U.S. at 593, 113 S.Ct. at 2796; ***Robinson***, 923 S.W.2d at 557; *see, e.g.*, ***Texas Workers' Comp. Ins. Fund v. Lopez***, 21 S.W.3d 358, 364 (Tex.App.—San Antonio 2000, pet. denied) (P's expert introduced articles demonstrating that his theory had been subjected to reliable testing); ***Purina Mills v. Odell***, 948 S.W.2d 927, 934 (Tex.App.—Texarkana 1997, pet. denied) (P's experts conducted no testing); ***America W. Airlines v. Tope***, 935 S.W.2d 908, 919 (Tex.App.—El Paso 1996, no writ) (mental health worker's opinion could not be tested).

(b) The technique's potential rate of error. ***Daubert***, 509 U.S. at 594, 113 S.Ct. at 2797; ***Robinson***, 923 S.W.2d at 557; *e.g.*, ***Lopez***, 21 S.W.3d at 364-65 (confidence level in studies cited by P was 95%; within the acceptable range required under ***Havner***); ***America W. Airlines***, 935 S.W.2d at 919 (the potential rate of error in mental health worker's opinion was "wholly unexplored").

(c) Whether the theory has been or could be subjected to peer review or publication. ***Daubert***, 509 U.S. at 593, 113 S.Ct. at 2797; *see, e.g.*, ***America W. Airlines***, 935 S.W.2d at 919 (mental health worker's opinion could not be subjected to peer review). Publication and other peer review are significant indicators of the reliability of scientific evidence when the expert's testimony is in an area in which peer review or publication would not be uncommon. ***Havner***, 953 S.W.2d at 726; ***Robinson***, 923 S.W.2d at 557. Publication in reputable, established scientific journals and other forms of peer review increases the likelihood that substantive flaws in methodology will be detected. ***Havner***, 953 S.W.2d at 726-27. Publication is not a prerequisite for scientific reliability in every case. *Id.* at 727.

(d) Whether the underlying theory or technique has been generally accepted as valid by the relevant scientific community. ***Daubert***, 509 U.S. at 594, 113 S.Ct. at 2797; ***Robinson***, 923 S.W.2d at 557; *see* ***Neal v. Dow Agrosciences, L.L.C.***, 74 S.W.3d 468, 473-74 (Tex.App.—Dallas 2002, no pet.) (causation testimony stricken; scientific literature relied on by expert did not support expert's conclusion).

(e) The extent to which the technique relies on the subjective interpretation of the expert. ***Robinson***, 923 S.W.2d at 557; *e.g.*, ***Lopez***, 21 S.W.3d at 364-65 (expert's causation testimony was based on objective criteria); ***America W. Airlines***, 935 S.W.2d at 919 (mental health worker's opinion was entirely subjective).

(f) The nonjudicial uses that have been made of the theory or technique. ***Robinson***, 923 S.W.2d at 557; *e.g.*, ***Lopez***, 21 S.W.3d at 364-66 (expert's theory had been used to develop better clothing to protect workers from lung disease); ***Waring v. Wommack***, 945 S.W.2d 889, 892 (Tex.App.—Austin 1997, no writ) (test performed by accident reconstruction engineer had nonjudicial uses).

(2) Nonscientific expert. In the area outside of hard science, analysis under the ***Daubert-Robinson*** rules of scientific discipline does not always help evaluate the reliability of the opinion. ***Kumho Tire***, 526 U.S. at 150, 119 S.Ct. at 1175; ***Gammill***, 972 S.W.2d at 720. When the ***Daubert-Robinson*** factors are not helpful, the expert's opinion must be evaluated according to the rules governing that expert's discipline. *See* ***Gammill***, 972 S.W.2d at 725-26. For example, even though beekeepers do not publish for peer review, a beekeeper could testify that bees take off into the wind based on the beekeeper's observations. *Id.* at 726; *see also* ***JCPenney Life Ins. Co. v. Baker***, 33 S.W.3d 417, 428 (Tex.App.—Fort Worth 2000, no pet.) (internist's opinion, based largely on his experience & observation in the medical field, was reliable). The trial court must review the general methodology used by a nonscientific expert and its application to the particular matter at issue. *See* ***Kumho Tire***, 526 U.S. at 152-53, 119 S.Ct. at 1176-77. If the "analytical gap" between the data relied on by the expert and the testimony offered is too great, the testimony is unreliable. ***Exxon Pipeline Co. v. Zwahr***, 88 S.W.3d 623, 629 (Tex.2002); ***Gammill***, 972 S.W.2d at 727.

2. Relevance of opinion. The opinion of the expert must be relevant. ***Daubert***, 509 U.S. at 597, 113 S.Ct. at 2799; ***Robinson***, 923 S.W.2d at 555; *see* TRE 702; *see also* TRE 401 (definition of relevant evidence), TRE 402 (admissibility of relevant evidence). To be relevant, the testimony must be "sufficiently tied to the facts of the case that it will aid the jury in resolving a factual dispute." ***Robinson***, 923 S.W.2d at 556. Evidence that has no relationship to any of the issues in the case is irrelevant and does not satisfy TRE 702's requirement that the testimony be of assistance to the jury. *Id;* ***U.S. Rest. Props. Oper. v. Motel Enters.***, 104 S.W.3d 284, 292 (Tex.App.—Beaumont 2003, pet. denied). Thus, it is inadmissible under TRE 702 as well as under TRE 401 and 402. ***Robinson***, 923 S.W.2d at 555.

NOTE

An expert witness may offer an opinion on a mixed question of law and fact as long as the opinion is confined to the relevant issues and based on proper legal concepts. ***Birchfield v. Texarkana Mem'l Hosp.***, *747 S.W.2d 361, 365 (Tex.1987). An expert cannot testify regarding an opinion on a pure question of law.* ***Upjohn Co. v. Rylander***, *38 S.W.3d 600, 611 (Tex. App.—Austin 2000, pet. denied).*

---

§2.4 Foundation test. The expert's opinion must be based on sufficient "underlying facts or data" under TRE 702 (testimony by experts) and TRE 703 (bases of opinion testimony by experts). TRE 705(c). An expert's opinion is not admissible if it is based on unreliable foundation evidence. ***Merrell Dow Pharms. v. Havner***, 953 S.W.2d 706, 714 (Tex.1997); *see, e.g.*, ***Marathon Corp. v. Pitzner***, 106 S.W.3d 724, 729 (Tex.2003) (expert opinion was speculation not based on evidence); ***E.I. du Pont de Nemours & Co. v. Robinson***, 923 S.W.2d 549, 558-59 (Tex.1995) (expert's testimony was not based on reliable foundation because he did not conduct test to exclude other possible causes); ***Martinez v. City of San Antonio***, 40 S.W.3d 587, 594-95 (Tex.App.—San Antonio 2001, pet. denied) (expert's testimony properly excluded; expert did not rule out other plausible causes of contamination); ***Austin v. Kerr-McGee Ref. Corp.***, 25 S.W.3d 280, 292-93 (Tex.App.—Texarkana 2000, no pet.) (foundation evidence unreliable; expert could not exclude other plausible causes with reasonable certainty).

§3. GATEKEEPER HEARING ON QUALIFICATIONS & OPINIONS OF EXPERTS

If specialized knowledge will assist the fact-finder to understand the evidence or decide a fact issue, a witness who qualifies as an expert may testify in the form of an opinion "or otherwise." TRE 702; *see* ***Louder v. De Leon***, 754 S.W.2d 148, 149 (Tex.1988); *see, e.g.*, ***GTE Sw. v. Bruce***, 998 S.W.2d 605, 620 (Tex.1999) (in suit for intentional infliction of emotional distress, expert could not testify that certain conduct was extreme and outrageous; issue involved only general knowledge & experience rather than expertise).

§3.1 Deadline to object to expert. Issues regarding the admissibility of the expert's opinion should be resolved as early as possible, preferably as a pretrial matter. ***Maritime Overseas Corp. v. Ellis***, 971 S.W.2d 402, 412 (Tex.1998) (Gonzalez, J., concurring). That is, the movant should file a written motion before trial challenging the expert. *But see* ***North Dallas Diagnostic Ctr. v. Dewberry***, 900 S.W.2d 90, 96 (Tex.App.—Dallas 1995, writ denied) (expert challenged on voir dire).

§3.2 Objection to expert. To object to an expert, the party should make a written pretrial objection to the admissibility of the expert's opinion under TRE 104(c). See the procedures used in ***Havner***, 953 S.W.2d at 709, and ***Robinson***, 923 S.W.2d at 552. For more details on the procedures for making the motion, see Baker, *"Gatekeeping" in Texas*, 27 St. Mary's L.J. 237, 282-83 (1996) and ***O'Connor's*** FORMS 5M:01, 5M:04.

1. Allegations. The party must identify each expert and each expert's opinion and conclusion that it seeks to exclude. The motion should challenge the expert on some or all of the following grounds:

(1) The expert is not qualified to give the opinion. See "Qualifications test," §2.1, p. 304.

(2) The subject of the testimony is not specialized knowledge. See "Knowledge test," §2.2, p. 305.

(3) The opinion of the expert is not reliable. See "Reliability of opinion," §2.3.1, p. 305.

(4) The opinion of the expert is not relevant. See §2.3.2, above.

(5) The underlying facts of the expert's opinion do not provide a sufficient basis for the expert's opinion. See §2.4, above. An objection to an expert's qualifications does not preserve error regarding the foundation for the expert's opinion. ***City of Paris v. McDowell***, 79 S.W.3d 601, 605 (Tex.App.—Texarkana 2002, no pet.).

(6) The probative value of the opinion is substantially outweighed by the danger of unfair prejudice, confusion, or delay. TRE 403; ***State v. Malone Serv. Co.***, 829 S.W.2d 763, 767 (Tex.1992); ***North Dallas Diagnostic***, 900 S.W.2d at 95-96. Once the court finds that the expert's opinion is admissible, the court has the additional duty to weigh the expert's testimony against the danger of unfair prejudice, confusion of the issues, or possibility of misleading the jury. TRE 403; ***Texas Workers' Comp. Ins. Fund v. Lopez***, 21 S.W.3d 358, 363-64 (Tex.App.—San Antonio 2000, pet. denied).

2. Challenger's evidence. Because the party challenging the expert initially bears no burden to undermine the expert or the expert's opinion, that party bears no burden to provide evidence to support its challenges.

But see "Gatekeeping" in Texas, 27 St. Mary's L.J. at 282-83 (suggesting motion be accompanied by evidence supporting the objections to the expert).

§3.3 Sponsor's response to objection. Once a party objects to the expert's testimony, the party sponsoring the expert bears the burden of responding to each objection and showing that the testimony is admissible by a preponderance of the evidence. *See **Robinson***, 923 S.W.2d at 557; ***Frias v. Atlantic Richfield Co.***, 104 S.W.3d 925, 927 (Tex.App.—Houston [14th Dist.] 2003, no pet.); ***Purina Mills v. Odell***, 948 S.W.2d 927, 933 (Tex.App.—Texarkana 1997, pet. denied).

1. Motion for gatekeeper hearing under TRE 104. Because the expert's sponsor has the burden to show the expert is qualified, the sponsor should ask the court to set the objections for a hearing. *But see **Piro v. Sarofim***, 80 S.W.3d 717, 720 (Tex.App.—Houston [1st Dist.] 2002, no pet.) (no error for court to refuse to hold live gatekeeper hearing). If the challenge to an expert is made as part of a motion for summary judgment, the nonmovant should also ask for a continuance so that the hearing under TRE 104 can resolve the issue of admissibility of the expert's opinion. *See, e.g.*, ***Weiss v. Mechanical Associated Servs.***, 989 S.W.2d 120, 124 n.6 (Tex.App.—San Antonio 1999, pet. denied) (nonmovant had burden to bring forward competent evidence in a no-evidence summary judgment proceeding).

PRACTICE TIP

Do not include an objection to an expert in a motion in limine. A ruling on a motion in limine does not preserve error for either party. See §3.7, below.

---

2. Allegations. If the party challenging the expert made specific complaints about the qualifications of the expert or the relevance or the reliability of the opinion, the sponsor of the expert should respond to just those complaints. If, however, the movant made only a general complaint under ***Robinson***, the sponsor of the expert should assume the full burden and allege the following:

(1) The expert is qualified. The party offering the expert must show that the expert's knowledge, experience, skill, training, or education qualifies the expert to give an opinion regarding the specific issue before the court. See "Qualifications test," §2.1, p. 304.

(2) The subject of the testimony is specialized knowledge that is appropriate for an expert's opinion. See "Knowledge test," §2.2, p. 305.

(3) The expert's opinion is reliable. See "Reliability of opinion," §2.3.1, p. 305.

(4) The expert's opinion is relevant. See "Relevance of opinion," §2.3.2, p. 306.

(5) The underlying facts of the expert's opinion provide a sufficient basis for the expert's opinion. See §2.4, above.

(6) The probative value of the opinion is not substantially outweighed by the danger of unfair prejudice, confusion, or delay. TRE 403; ***Robinson***, 923 S.W.2d at 557. See §3.2.1(6), above.

3. Sponsor's evidence. To meet its burden of showing that the opinion is admissible, the party sponsoring the expert should attach verified proof to the response, either by affidavit or deposition testimony. To bolster the expert's testimony, qualifications, relevance, and reliability, the party may also submit other evidence, including the affidavit or deposition of another expert, the published works of the challenged expert or other experts, and learned treatises. The evidence should show (1) the expert is qualified, (2) the expert's opinion is relevant, and (3) the expert's opinion is reliable.

§3.4 Reply by party challenging expert. If the sponsor's response seems to meet its burden of showing that its expert's opinion is admissible, the party challenging the expert should probably file a reply with verified proof showing that (1) the expert is not qualified, (2) the expert's opinion is not relevant, or (3) the expert's opinion is not reliable. If the court resolves the issue on the pleadings without holding a hearing to receive evidence, the party challenging the expert would want to have its proof on file.

§3.5 TRE 104 hearing. In making the determination of admissibility, the court is not bound by the rules of evidence except those with respect to privileges. TRE 104(a). In most cases, the court should conduct a pretrial hearing to determine the admissibility of the expert's opinion. The hearing should be conducted with all the formalities of trial and should be recorded by the court reporter. Without a record from the hearing, the appellant will not be able to show harm. See §5.1, below. For suggestions on preparing for the hearing, see *"Gatekeeping" in Texas*, 27 St. Mary's L.J. at 283-85.

1. Sponsor. To meet its burden of showing the opinion is admissible, the expert's sponsor should offer the testimony of the challenged expert, either live or by deposition. To bolster the expert's testimony, qualifications, relevance, and reliability, the sponsor may offer other evidence, including another expert, the published works of the challenged expert or other experts, and learned treatises.

2. Challenger. If the sponsor meets its burden of showing the opinion is admissible, the party challenging the expert should attempt to undermine the expert by providing testimony of its own expert that challenges (1) the qualifications of the sponsor's expert and (2) the scientific validity of the other party's expert. The challenger's expert should show why the sponsor's expert's opinion fails the ***Daubert-Robinson*** test.

§3.6 Ruling. After receiving evidence, the trial court must rule on each objection raised by the motion. If the party offering the expert does not meet its required burden of proof, the trial court should exclude the expert. To exclude the expert witness, the order should state unequivocally that the expert and the expert's evidence are excluded.

§3.7 Preserving error. To preserve a complaint that an expert's testimony is unreliable and thus no evidence, a party must object to the testimony before trial or when it is offered. See §5.2, below. The court's order after a gatekeeper hearing should be considered a pretrial ruling on the admissibility of the expert's opinion, not a ruling on a motion in limine. A ruling on a motion in limine does not preserve error. See "Function of order," ch. 5-E, §5.2, p. 253. Whether the ruling after the gatekeeper hearing preserves error depends on the wording of the order. If the order unequivocally states that the expert's testimony will or will not be admitted at trial, the ruling is a pretrial ruling on the admissibility of the evidence and preserves error. *See* TRE 103(a)(2); ***Huckaby v. A.G. Perry & Son***, 20 S.W.3d 194, 205-06 (Tex.App.—Texarkana 2000, pet. denied). If the ruling is tentative and requires the parties to approach the bench or to reurge their objections at trial, the ruling is a motion in limine ruling and does not preserve error. See "Offer & Objection at Trial," ch. 5-E, §6, p. 253.

§4. EXPERTS IN MEDICAL MALPRACTICE SUITS

This section has been removed because the information about experts in medial malpractice suits is covered in detail in ***O'Connor's COA***, "Expert testimony," ch. 18-A, §8, p. 444.

§5. REVIEW

§5.1 Record. When appealing from a final judgment rendered in a trial in which the trial court ruled on a motion to exclude an expert at an evidentiary hearing, the appellant should include the record of the hearing in the appellate record. *See* ***Exxon Corp. v. Makofski***, 116 S.W.3d 176, 196 (Tex.App.—Houston [14th Dist.] 2003, n.p.h.) (Seymore, J., dissenting). *But see id.* at 180 (D did not waive error by not submitting record of pretrial hearing because P waived complaint on appeal). For example, if the trial court excluded an expert in a gatekeeper hearing and later rendered a summary judgment, the appellant should request the clerk's record, which includes all the pleadings necessary to challenge the summary judgment and the ruling on the expert, and request the reporter's record from the gatekeeper hearing.

§5.2 Preserving error. To preserve a complaint that scientific evidence is unreliable, a party must object to the evidence before trial or when the evidence is offered. ***Guadalupe-Blanco River Auth. v. Kraft***, 77 S.W.3d 805, 807 (Tex.2002); ***Maritime Overseas Corp. v. Ellis***, 971 S.W.2d 402, 409 (Tex.1998). The objecting party cannot wait until the appeal to argue for the first time that the scientific evidence is unreliable and should be ignored. ***Maritime Overseas***, 971 S.W.2d at 409. Without a timely objection, the offering party is not given an opportunity to cure the defect that may exist and thus would be subject to trial and appeal by ambush. *Id.*

§5.3 Standard of review. The decision of the trial court to admit expert testimony is reviewed for abuse of discretion. ***Exxon Pipeline Co. v. Zwahr***, 88 S.W.3d 623, 629 (Tex.2002); ***Kraft***, 77 S.W.3d at 807; ***Gammill v. Jack Williams Chevrolet***, 972 S.W.2d 713, 727 (Tex.1998).

COMMENTARIES

CHAPTER 6. DISCOVERY
TABLE OF CONTENTS

COMMENTARIES

CHAPTER 6. DISCOVERY

TABLE OF CONTENTS

Before engaging in discovery, the parties should prepare a draft of the jury charge based on all the pleadings. Only when the parties know what questions the jury will be asked can they design an intelligent discovery plan.

A. GENERAL RULES FOR DISCOVERY

§1. GENERAL

§1.1 Rules. TRCP 176, 190-205, 215.

§1.2 Purpose. The purpose of discovery is to allow the parties to obtain full knowledge of the issues and facts of the lawsuit before trial. ***West v. Solito***, 563 S.W.2d 240, 243 (Tex.1978). The objective of the Texas discovery rules is to prevent trial by ambush. ***Gutierrez v. Dallas ISD***, 729 S.W.2d 691, 693 (Tex.1987).

§1.3 Forms & timetables. ***O'Connor's Texas Civil Forms***, FORMS 6A. See Timetables, this book, Discovery Schedule for Level 1, p. 1001, Discovery Schedule for Level 2, p. 1003.

§1.4 Other references. Griesel, *The "New" Texas Discovery Rules: Three Years Later*, Advanced Evidence & Discovery Course, State Bar of Texas, ch. 2 (2002).

§2. TERMS & DEFINITIONS

The discovery rules define several key terms used throughout chapter 6.

§2.1 Discovery periods. Discovery periods determine the length of time the parties have to conduct discovery. See "Discovery Periods," §6, p. 317.

§2.2 Documents & tangible things. The phrase "documents and tangible things" includes papers, books, accounts, drawings, graphs, charts, photographs, electronic or videotape recordings, data, and data compilations. TRCP 192.3(b).

§2.3 Possession. Possession, custody, or control of an item means the person either has physical possession of the item or has a right to possession that is equal or superior to that of the person who has physical possession. TRCP 192.7(b); ***In re Kuntz***, ___ S.W.3d ___ (Tex.2003) (No. 02-0375; 12-19-03); ***GTE Comm. Sys. v. Tanner***, 856 S.W.2d 725, 729 (Tex.1993). Mere access to documents is not "physical possession" of the documents under TRCP 192.7(b). ***Kuntz***, ___ S.W.3d at ___. The right to obtain possession is a legal right based on the relationship between the party responding to discovery and the person or entity that has actual possession of the document or thing. ***GTE***, 856 S.W.2d at 729; *see* ***State v. Lowry***, 802 S.W.2d 669, 673-74 (Tex.1991) (request to Attorney General was sufficient to require production of documents held by all divisions of office); ***In re Diversicare Gen. Partner***, 41 S.W.3d 788, 794 (Tex.App.—Corpus Christi 2001, orig. proceeding) (nonparty's legal representatives had right to possession equal or superior to that of nursing facility, which had physical possession of records). A party is required to produce only those documents or tangible things within its "possession, custody, or control." TRCP 192.3(b); ***GTE***, 856 S.W.2d 728-29; *see also* ***In re U-Haul Int'l***, 87 S.W.3d 653, 656-57 (Tex.App.—San Antonio 2002, orig. proceeding) (P did not meet burden of proving D had the right to obtain possession of documents from D's related subsidiary).

§2.4 Privilege & confidentiality. Although the terms privilege and confidentiality are used interchangeably in many rules and statutes to limit the scope of discovery, they represent different legal concepts. An evidentiary privilege is part of a body of evidence law that deals with what evidence is discoverable for purposes of litigation (*e.g.*, communications & records between a dentist and patient, under Occupations Code §258.102). By comparison, confidentiality is part of a body of law that defines the ethical responsibilities of a certain person or entity to certain other persons (*e.g.*, HIV test results are confidential under Health & Safety Code §81.103).

§2.5 Side. "Side" refers to all the litigants with generally common interests in the litigation. TRCP 190.3(b)(2). The concept of "side" in TRCP 190.3(b)(2) was borrowed from TRCP 233, which governs the allocation of peremptory strikes, and from FRCP 30(a)(2). TRCP 190, cmt. 6. In most cases there are only two sides—plaintiffs and defendants. *Id.* In complex cases, however, there may be more than two sides, such as when defendants have sued third parties not named by plaintiffs or when defendants have sued each other. *Id.*

§2.6 Withholding statement. A withholding statement is a statement by which a party claims that information responsive to written discovery is privileged. TRCP 193.3(a). See "Withholding statement," §17.2.1(2), p. 329.

§2.7 Work product. Work product includes (1) material prepared or mental impressions developed in anticipation of litigation or for trial by or for a party or its representatives, including the party's attorneys, consultants, sureties, indemnitors, insurers, employees, or agents; or (2) a communication made in anticipation of litigation or for trial if made between a party and its representatives or among a party's representatives, including the party's attorneys, consultants, sureties, indemnitors, insurers, employees, or agents. TRCP 192.5(a). Work product replaced the "attorney work product" and "party communication" discovery exemptions in former TRCP 166b. TRCP 192, cmt. 8.

1. Core work product. Core work product is the work product of an attorney or an attorney's representative containing the attorney's or the representative's mental impressions, opinions, conclusions, or legal theories. TRCP 192.5(b)(1).

2. Non-core work product. Non-core work product, which is not specifically defined in the TRCPs, is all work product except the work product of an attorney or an attorney's representative containing the attorney's or the representative's mental impressions, opinions, conclusions, or legal theories. *See* TRCP 192.5(b)(1). Non-core work product includes party communications. TRCP 192.5(a)(2).

§2.8 Written discovery. Written discovery means (1) requests for disclosure, (2) requests for production and inspection of documents and tangible things, (3) requests for entry onto property, (4) interrogatories, and (5) requests for admission. TRCP 192.7(a). It does not include depositions on written questions. *See id.*

§3. DISCOVERY CERTIFICATES

§3.1 Certification by signature. All written discovery—including disclosures, discovery requests, notices, objections, and responses—must be signed. TRCP 191.3(a). The signature must be of the attorney, unless the party is pro se. *Id.* TRCP 191.3(a) applies to documents used to satisfy a discovery request, response, or objection (*e.g.*, a withholding statement). TRCP 191, cmt. 3. See "Who must sign," ch. 1-B, §4.12.1, p. 6.

1. Effect of signature on disclosure. The signature of an attorney (or party when pro se) on a disclosure made under TRCP 194 constitutes a certification that, to the best of the signer's knowledge, information, and belief, formed after a reasonable inquiry, the disclosure is complete and correct at the time it is made. TRCP 191.3(b).

2. Effect of signature on other discovery. The signature of an attorney (or party when pro se) on a discovery request, notice, response, or objection constitutes a certification that, to the best of the signer's knowledge, information, and belief, formed after a reasonable inquiry, the discovery (1) is consistent with the TRCPs or presents a good-faith argument for the extension, change, or reversal of existing law, (2) has a good-faith factual basis, (3) is not made for an improper purpose (such as delay, harassment, or expense), and (4) is not unreasonable, unduly burdensome, or expensive, given the needs of the case. TRCP 191.3(c); *see also* CPRC §9.011 (signing of pleadings), *id.* §10.001 (signing of pleadings & motions).

3. Effect of no signature. If a discovery request, notice, response, or objection is not signed, it must be struck. TRCP 191.3(d). The omission can be remedied by providing a signature as soon as the omission is called to the attention of the party. *Id.* A party who receives an unsigned request or notice is not required to respond to it. *Id.*

4. Effect of false signature. The court can impose sanctions under CPRC chapter 10 on a person who signs a false certification on a discovery disclosure, request, notice, response, or objection. TRCP 191.3(e).

§3.2 Certificate of attempt to agree.

1. Under TRCP 191. Parties and their attorneys are expected to cooperate in discovery and to make any agreements reasonably necessary for the efficient disposition of the case. TRCP 191.2 & cmt. 2; ***In re Alford Chevrolet-Geo***, 997 S.W.2d 173, 184 (Tex.1999). All discovery motions or requests for hearings relating to discovery must contain a certificate by the party filing the document that a reasonable effort was made to resolve the dispute without the need for court intervention and that the effort failed. TRCP 191.2; ***United Serv. Auto. Ass'n v. Thomas***, 893 S.W.2d 628, 629 (Tex.App.—Corpus Christi 1994, writ denied). Because TRCP 191.2 is for the benefit of the trial court, the failure to include a certificate is not grounds for mandamus. ***Groves v. Gabriel***, 874 S.W.2d 660, 661 n.3 (Tex.1994).

2. Some counties. In some counties (*e.g.*, Harris, Dallas, Tarrant), courts require a more detailed certificate. See the local rules for each county. See ***O'Connor's*** FORM 1B:11.

§3.3 Certificate of written discovery. Some local rules require parties to file a certificate of written discovery with the court when serving discovery requests or responses. See ***O'Connor's*** FORM 6A:03. TRCP 191.4 contains no such requirement. Unless a local rule requires such a certificate, it is not required.

§4. FORMS OF DISCOVERY

The discovery rules provide the only permissible forms of discovery. *See* TRCP 192.1. However, a court may order, or the parties may agree to, discovery methods other than those provided in the discovery rules. TRCP 191, cmt. 1. The written forms of discovery may be combined in the same document and may be taken in any order or sequence. TRCP 192.2.

§4.1 Request for disclosure. Disclosures are standard written questions designed to afford parties discovery of specific types of information. They are answered on request, without preparation of a lengthy inquiry, and without objection. TRCP 194 & cmt. 1. See "Requests for Disclosure," ch. 6-D, p. 375.

§4.2 Deposition on oral examination. A deposition on oral examination allows a party to question a witness under oath before trial. Depositions can be used to acquire information from both parties and nonparties. TRCP 199-203, 205. Depositions are expensive and time-consuming. They should be used only after a party knows something about the case. See "Depositions," ch. 6-E, p. 386.

§4.3 Deposition on written questions. A deposition on written questions allows a party to propound written questions to a witness who answers orally under oath. TRCP 200. Depositions on written questions can be used to acquire information from both parties and nonparties. Although by name they sound like depositions on oral examination, they are similar to interrogatories because they are written and are relatively inexpensive. Depositions on written questions are most often used to obtain records from a nonparty (*e.g.*, a hospital) and, at the same time, to ask the custodian of the records the necessary questions to "prove up" the records. See "Deposition on Written Questions," ch. 6-E, §15, p. 402.

§4.4 Interrogatories. Interrogatories are written questions used to acquire information from another party. TRCP 197. Most interrogatory answers are signed by the party under oath. See "Form of answers," ch. 6-F, §4.1.1(4)-(5), p. 411. Interrogatories are a relatively inexpensive method of discovery, but they are a slower form of discovery than depositions. They should be used to narrow the issues and identify the legal theories and factual bases of the parties' claims or defenses. The rule governing discovery limitations specifies the number of interrogatories a party may propound. TRCP 190. See "Interrogatories," ch. 6-F, p. 408.

§4.5 Request for admissions. A request for admissions is used to force the other party to admit or deny specific facts, thus narrowing the fact issues for trial. TRCP 198. Responses to requests for admissions are signed by the lawyer. The rule governing requests for admissions does not limit the number of requests. *See id.* See "Requests for Admissions," ch. 6-G, p. 416.

§4.6 Request for production & inspection. A request for production is used to obtain documents, records, and other tangible things in the possession of a party. TRCP 196. To obtain or inspect documents or tangible things from a nonparty, a party must file a notice of production and subpoena, not a request. TRCP 176, 205.3. See "Securing Documents & Tangible Things," ch. 6-H, p. 423.

§4.7 Request for medical records. A party may obtain the medical records of another party or nonparty by a request for disclosure or by use of a medical authorization. TRCP 194.2(j), (k), 196.1(c). See "Medical Records," ch. 6-I, p. 434.

§4.8 Motion for physical or mental examination. A motion for physical or mental examination may be used to obtain an examination of a party, someone in the party's custody, or someone under the party's legal control. TRCP 204.1. See "Motion to Examine the Person," ch. 6-I, §5, p. 436.

§4.9 Request for entry on land. A request to enter land may be used to gain entry on land owned by a party to inspect the land or anything on it. TRCP 196.7. To gain entry on land of a nonparty, the party must file a motion (not a request), ask for a hearing, and get a court order. TRCP 196.7(a)(2), (b). See "Entry on Land," ch. 6-J, p. 438.

§4.10 Subpoena. A subpoena may be used to secure documents from a party or nonparty. TRCP 176, 205. In most cases, a subpoena is issued to compel a nonparty to attend a deposition and produce documents. See "Securing Things from a Nonparty," ch. 6-H, §5, p. 428.

§4.11 Expert's report. An expert's report includes the discoverable factual observations, tests, supporting data, calculations, photographs, and opinions of the expert. TRCP 195.5. If a retained testifying expert has not reduced her report to tangible form, the court may order the expert to reduce it to tangible form and produce it. *Id.* See "Expert's Report," ch. 6-C, §7, p. 374; ***O'Connor's*** FORM 6C:01.

§5. MODIFYING DISCOVERY PROCEDURES & LIMITATIONS

§5.1 Modifying discovery by agreement. The parties may agree to modify discovery procedures and limitations as long as the modification is not specifically prohibited. TRCP 191.1. To be enforceable, an agreement on discovery must comply with TRCP 11, or if it affects a deposition, it must be made part of the record of the deposition. TRCP 191.1; *see* ***Remington Arms Co. v. Canales***, 837 S.W.2d 624, 625 (Tex.1992) (written agreement must comply with TRCP 11). An agreement that does not comply with TRCP 191.1 is not enforceable. ***London Mkt. Cos. v. Schattman***, 811 S.W.2d 550, 552 (Tex.1991) (oral agreement to extend time to respond to discovery was not enforceable because it did not meet requirements of TRCP 11). See "Agreements Between Lawyers – Rule 11," ch. 1-H, §9, p. 44; ***O'Connor's*** FORM 1H:12 (Rule 11 agreement), FORM 6A:02 (agreement to extend time to respond to discovery).

§5.2 Modifying discovery by court order. The court may modify discovery procedures and limitations if (1) there is "good cause," and (2) the modification is not specifically prohibited by some other rule. TRCP 191.1. See ***O'Connor's*** FORM 6A:01 (motion to extend time to respond to discovery). In most rules, the parties—not the courts—are held to the standard of good cause. Under the old rules, discovery orders were reviewed to determine if they were so unreasonable that they showed a clear abuse of discretion. *See, e.g.*, ***Wal-Mart Stores v. Cordova***, 856 S.W.2d 768, 771 (Tex.App.—El Paso 1993, writ denied). None of the cases ever inquired into the trial court's good cause to sign the order. The stated intent of TRCP 191.1 is to limit the trial court's ability to bypass the requirements for discovery control plans. *See* TRCP 191, cmt. 1 (trial court cannot simply "opt out" of the discovery rules by form orders or approve a discovery control plan that does not contain the matters specified in TRCP 190.4). However, because TRCP 191.1 covers all orders modifying discovery, the new good-cause requirement may have unintended consequences. See "Court order to extend," §14.2, p. 324.

Although the trial court has great latitude in managing discovery, the court cannot abate discovery and prevent a party from obtaining basic information that goes to the heart of the litigation. *See **In re Van Waters & Rogers, Inc.***, 62 S.W.3d 197, 200 (Tex.2001); ***In re Colonial Pipeline Co.***, 968 S.W.2d 938, 941-42 (Tex.1998).

§5.3 Chart summary. Chart 6-1, below, provides a summary of the various types of enforceable agreements on discovery and whether agreement of the parties is sufficient or a court order is required.

6-1. ENFORCEABLE AGREEMENTS REGARDING DISCOVERY

	TYPE OF AGREEMENT	CAN AGREE UNDER TRCP 11?	CAN AGREE DURING DEPOSITION?	NEED COURT ORDER?	TRCP
1	To modify any court order	No	No	Yes	191, cmt. 1
2	To extend discovery deadlines	Yes	Yes*	No	191, cmt. 1
3	To extend time to supplement	Yes	Yes*	No	191.1, 193.5(b)
4	To modify deposition procedure	Yes	Yes*	No	191, cmt. 1
5	To modify time to designate experts	Yes	No	No	191.1, 195.2
6	To adopt new method of discovery	Yes	Yes*	No	191, cmt. 1
7	To serve request less than 30 days before end of discovery period	Yes	No	No	190, cmt. 4
8	To modify any discovery procedure that is not prohibited by TRCPs	Yes	Yes*	No	191.1
9	To produce documents or tangible things at a different time and place than stated in the request for discovery	Yes	Yes*	No	194.4, 196.3(a), 197.2(c)
10	To take deposition outside discovery period	Yes	Yes*	No	199.2(a), 200.1(a)
11	To be controlled by Level 3	No	No	Yes	190, cmt. 1
12	In Level 1 – To extend time for depositions to 10 hours	Yes	Yes*	No	190.2(c)(2)
13	In Level 1 – To extend time for depositions to more than 10 hours	No	No	Yes	190.2(c)(2)
14	In Level 1 – To agree to be controlled by Level 2	Yes	No	No	190.2(b)(1)
15	In Level 3 – To modify discovery	No	No	Yes	190.4(a)

* Lawyers can make an enforceable agreement on the record during a deposition only as it affects the deposition. TRCP 191.1.

§6. DISCOVERY PERIODS

The purpose of discovery periods is to speed the resolution of trials. Parties are advised to begin discovery as soon as they file their original pleadings. Some courts have held that any delay in beginning discovery shows a lack of diligence. *E.g.*, ***Broom v. Arvidson***, No. 04-00-00214-CV (Tex.App.—San Antonio 2001, no pet.) (no pub.; 3-7-01) (continuance denied; P waited 3 months before initiating discovery).

§6.1 Discovery periods. Every case must be assigned to one of three levels, depending on the amount in controversy and the issues involved. The party seeking discovery must serve requests for discovery far enough in advance of the end of the discovery period so that the responding party can serve its response within the discovery period. TRCP 190, cmt. 4; ***Pape v. Guadalupe-Blanco River Auth.***, 48 S.W.3d 908, 913 (Tex.App.—Austin 2001, pet. denied). For purposes of defining discovery periods, "trial" does not include summary judgment. TRCP 190, cmt. 8. The trial court may change a deadline for sending discovery requests. TRCP 190, cmt. 4.

1. Discovery period for Level 1.

(1) Original period. The discovery period in a Level 1 case begins when the suit is filed and continues until 30 days before the date set for trial. TRCP 190.2(c)(1).

(2) Period reopens. The discovery period in a Level 1 case reopens if, within 45 days of the date set for trial, a party files a pleading that transforms the case into a Level 2 or 3 case, rendering TRCP 190.2 inapplicable. TRCP 190.2(b)(3), (d). Discovery must then be completed within the limitations of TRCP 190.3 (Level 2) or TRCP 190.4 (Level 3), whichever is applicable. TRCP 190.2(d). Any person already deposed may be redeposed. *Id.* The court should continue the trial date if necessary to permit the completion of discovery. *Id.*

2. Discovery period for Level 2.

(1) Most cases. Discovery in a Level 2 case begins when the suit is filed and continues until the earliest of the following: (1) 30 days before trial, (2) nine months after the date of the first oral deposition, or (3) nine months after the due date of the first response to written discovery. TRCP 190.3(b)(1)(B); ***Ersek v. Davis & Davis***, 69 S.W.3d 268, 273 (Tex.App.—Austin 2002, pet. denied); ***Pape***, 48 S.W.3d at 913.

(2) Family Code cases. In Family Code cases, discovery begins when the suit is filed and continues until 30 days before the date set for trial. TRCP 190.3(b)(1)(A).

3. Discovery period for Level 3. Discovery in a Level 3 case must be conducted during the discovery period for Level 1 or Level 2, whichever is applicable, unless the court orders a different period. TRCP 190.4(b).

§6.2 Modification of discovery periods. The court may modify a discovery period at any time; it must do so when justice requires it. TRCP 190.5. See *O'Connor's* FORM 6A:06.

1. Amended or supplemental pleadings. When pleadings are amended or supplemented, or new information is disclosed in a discovery response, the court must allow additional related discovery if the movant shows both of the following:

(1) After deadline. The pleadings or responses were made after the deadline for discovery or so close to the deadline that the opposing party did not have an adequate opportunity to conduct discovery related to the new matters. TRCP 190.5(a)(1).

(2) Unfair prejudice. The movant would be unfairly prejudiced without the additional discovery. TRCP 190.5(a)(2).

2. Material changes. The court must allow additional discovery on matters that have changed materially after the discovery cutoff when there is more than a three-month gap between the trial date and the end of the discovery period. TRCP 190.5(b).

§6.3 Certain discovery excepted. The limits on discovery under TRCP 190 do not apply to discovery conducted under TRCP 202 ("Depositions Before Suit or to Investigate Claims") or TRCP 621a ("Discovery and Enforcement of Judgment"). TRCP 190.6. However, TRCP 202 cannot be used to circumvent the limitations of TRCP 190. TRCP 190.6.

§7. DISCOVERY CONTROL PLANS

The purpose of discovery control plans is to promote the efficient resolution of cases by assigning each case to one of three levels, depending on the amount in controversy and the issues involved in the case.

§7.1 Discovery control plan required. Every case filed after January 1, 1999, must be governed by a discovery control plan. TRCP 190.1. A plaintiff must allege in the first numbered paragraph of the original petition whether discovery is intended to be conducted under Level 1, 2, or 3 of TRCP 190. TRCP 190.1. See "Discovery Control Plan," ch. 2-B, §2, p. 67. For cases filed before January 1, 1999, the court may adopt an appropriate discovery control plan. Tex.Sup.Ct. Order, Misc. Docket No. 98-9196, §4(b), 977-978 S.W.2d (Tex.Cases) xxxiii (1998).

§7.2 Level 1. Level 1 discovery is designed as a "safe haven," enabling plaintiffs with small cases to avoid being overtaxed by the defendant's discovery. Griesel, *The "New" Texas Discovery Rules*, §V(A), p. 4.

1. Application. The Level 1 discovery control plan governs cases in which the amount in controversy is no more than $50,000. TRCP 190.2(a). TRCP 190.2 does not conflict with TRCP 47(b) (which limits the plaintiff's statement of damages to "within the jurisdictional limits of the court") because the purpose of TRCP 190.2 is to bind the pleader to a maximum claim. TRCP 190, cmt. 2.

(1) $50,000 or less. A suit in which all plaintiffs plead they seek only monetary relief totaling $50,000 or less (excluding costs, prejudgment interest, and attorney fees) will be governed by the Level 1 discovery control plan. TRCP 190.2(a)(1).

PRACTICE TIP

The plaintiff should not choose Level 1 unless it wants to limit its damages to $50,000. In a Level 1 case, the court cannot award more than $50,000 in damages (excluding costs, prejudgment interest, and attorney fees) even if the jury returns a verdict for more than that amount. TRCP 190, cmt. 2.

(2) Divorce suits. A suit for divorce not involving children in which a party pleads that the value of the marital estate is not more than $50,000 will be governed by the Level 1 discovery control plan. TRCP 190.2(a)(2).

2. Exceptions. The Level 1 discovery control plan does not apply in the following instances:

(1) Suit for injunctive relief or divorce involving children. When a party files a petition for injunctive relief or for a divorce involving children. TRCP 190, cmt. 2.

(2) Parties agree. When the parties agree to be governed by the Level 2 discovery control plan. TRCP 190.2(b)(1).

(3) Court order. When the trial court orders a Level 3 discovery control plan. TRCP 190.2(b)(2).

(4) Supplemental pleading. If a party files an amended or supplemental pleading that seeks more than $50,000 in damages. TRCP 190.2(b)(3). A pleading that renders a Level 1 plan inapplicable must be filed at least 45 days before trial, unless the party secures leave of court by showing that good cause outweighs any prejudice to the other party. *Id.* See §6.1.1(2), above.

3. Discovery limitations. In Level 1 cases, discovery is subject to the following limitations:

(1) Discovery period. See §6.1.1, above.

(2) Oral depositions. Each party may take no more than six hours to examine and cross-examine all witnesses in oral depositions. TRCP 190.2(c)(2). The parties may agree to expand this time, but they cannot expand it beyond ten hours without a court order. *Id.* The court may modify the deposition hours so that no party is given an unfair advantage. *Id.*

(3) Interrogatories. A party may serve no more than 25 interrogatories on any other party. TRCP 190.2(c)(3). Each discrete subpart of an interrogatory is considered a separate interrogatory. *Id.* However, not every separate factual inquiry is a discrete subpart. TRCP 190, cmt. 3. The limit of 25 does not include interrogatories that ask a party to identify or authenticate specific documents. TRCP 190.2(c)(3). See "Interrogatories," ch. 6-F, p. 408.

(4) Other written discovery. TRCP 190 does not limit other written discovery. However, depositions on written questions cannot be used to circumvent the limits on interrogatories. TRCP 190, cmt. 5.

§7.3 Level 2. Level 2 discovery is the basic "default" discovery track that governs discovery in most cases. Griesel, *The "New" Texas Discovery Rules*, §V(A), p. 4. If the plaintiff does not plead a discovery level in its original petition, the case is automatically a Level 2 case. TRCP 190, cmt. 1.

1. Application. Unless a suit is governed by Level 1 under TRCP 190.2 or Level 3 under TRCP 190.4, discovery will be governed by Level 2 under TRCP 190.3. TRCP 190.3(a). Most lawsuits will be conducted under a Level 2 discovery control plan.

2. Discovery limitations. In Level 2 cases, discovery is subject to the following limitations:

(1) Discovery period. See "Discovery period for Level 2," §6.1.2, p. 318.

(2) Oral depositions. Each side is limited to 50 hours of oral depositions to examine and cross-examine parties on the opposing side, experts designated by those parties, and persons who are subject to those parties' control. TRCP 190.3(b)(2). For the definition of "side," see "Side," §2.5, p. 314. TRCP 190.3(b)(2) does not limit the time for deposing witnesses who are not subject to either party's control (*e.g.*, an eyewitness to an accident). In using the 50 hours, the parties should consider another rule, TRCP 199.5(c), which limits to six hours the time each side may examine or cross-examine an individual witness. TRCP 199.5(c). See "Time Limitations on Oral Depositions," ch. 6-E, §6, p. 394.

(a) If one side designates more than two experts, the opposing side may have an additional six hours of total deposition time for each additional expert designated. TRCP 190.3(b)(2). The rule does not state whether the additional six hours must be used for the expert's deposition.

(b) The court has discretion to modify the deposition hours and must do so when a side or party would be given an unfair advantage. TRCP 190.3(b)(2).

(3) Interrogatories. The limitation on interrogatories for Level 2 discovery is the same as for Level 1. TRCP 190.3(b)(3). See §7.2.3(3), above.

(4) Other written discovery. See §7.2.3(4), above.

§7.4 Level 3. Level 3 discovery is court-managed discovery, similar to federal court practice. Griesel, *The "New" Texas Discovery Rules*, §V(A), p. 4. Level 3 is designed for more complex cases that will not easily fit into the framework of Level 1 or 2. *Id.* Once a suit is designated as Level 3, all changes to the basic default provisions must be made by court order. *See* TRCP 191, cmt. 1; *see also* Griesel, *The "New" Texas Discovery Rules*, §VI(A)(1), p. 6 (court may modify any discovery procedure or limitation by order for good cause). Level 3 discovery cannot be changed by agreement of the parties without a court order.

1. Application. The court must on a party's motion, and may on its own initiative, order that discovery be conducted as a Level 3 case with a discovery control plan tailored to the specific suit. TRCP 190.4(a). The court should act on a party's motion or agreed order as soon as reasonably possible. *Id.* See ***O'Connor's*** FORMS 6A:04-05.

2. Discovery limitations. In Level 3 cases, discovery is subject to the following limitations:

(1) By court order. When the court signs an order instituting a discovery control plan for a Level 3 suit, that plan will control the outlines of discovery. The court-ordered discovery control plan may address any issue concerning discovery or the matters listed in TRCP 166, and may change any limitations on the time for or amount of discovery set forth in TRCP 190. TRCP 190.4(b); *see* ***In re Alford Chevrolet-Geo***, 997 S.W.2d 173, 181 (Tex. 1999) (trial court may limit discovery pending resolution of threshold issues like venue, jurisdiction, forum non conveniens, & official immunity). The plan must include the following information: (1) a date for trial or for a conference to determine a trial date; (2) a discovery period during which, for the entire case or an appropriate phase of it, (a) all discovery must be conducted or (b) all discovery requests must be sent; (3) appropriate limits on the amount of discovery; and (4) deadlines for joining additional parties, amending or supplementing pleadings, and designating expert witnesses. TRCP 190.4(b).

(2) Default discovery limitations. When the court does not sign an order adopting a discovery plan for a Level 3 case, the default discovery limitations are as follows:

(a) Amount of discovery. The amount of discovery is controlled by the provisions for Level 1 or 2, depending on the amount of damages and the type of suit. TRCP 190.4(b). See "Level 1," §7.2, p. 319; §7.3, above.

(b) Discovery period. The length of the discovery is controlled by the provisions for Level 1 or 2, depending on the amount of damages and the type of suit. TRCP 190.4(b). See "Discovery period for Level 1," §6.1.1, p. 318; "Discovery period for Level 2," §6.1.2, p. 318.

§8. SECURING DISCOVERY

Chart 6-2, below, provides a summary of the various types of discovery, whether a motion and order are needed to secure the discovery, who signs the response to the discovery, and whether the response must be verified.

6-2. SECURING & RESPONDING TO DISCOVERY

		NEED MOTION & ORDER?	RESPONSE SIGNED BY	RESPONSE VERIFIED?	SEE INFRA AT
A. PARTY DISCOVERY					
1	Disclosures	No	Lawyer	No	ch. 6-D, p. 375
2	Deposition (oral or written questions)	No	Party	Yes	ch. 6-E, p. 386
3	Interrogatories about fact & trial witnesses or legal contentions	No	Lawyer	No	ch. 6-F, §4.1.1(4)-(5), p. 411
4	Interrogatories about other matters	No	Lawyer & party	Yes, by party	ch. 6-F, §4.1.1(4)-(5), p. 411
5	Request for admissions	No	Lawyer	No	ch. 6-G, p. 416
6	Request to produce documents	No	Lawyer	No	ch. 6-H, p. 423
7	Authorization for medical records	No	Party	No	ch. 6-I, p. 434
8	Physical or mental examination	Yes	Lawyer	No	ch. 6-I, §5, p. 436
9	Request to inspect land	No	Lawyer	No	ch. 6-J, p. 438
B. NONPARTY DISCOVERY					
1	Deposition (oral or written questions)	No, just notice & subpoena	Nonparty	Yes	ch. 6-E, p. 386
2	Notice to produce documents	No, just notice & subpoena	Nonparty	No	ch. 6-H, §5, p. 428
3	Deposition before lawsuit	Yes	Nonparty	Yes	ch. 6-E, §16, p. 403
4	Medical records	Yes	Nonparty	No	ch. 6-I, §4, p. 435
5	Motion to inspect land	Yes	Nonparty	No	ch. 6-J, §4, p. 439

§8.1 Securing discovery from parties.

1. By discovery procedures. All forms of discovery can be used to secure discovery from parties. See "Forms of Discovery," §4, p. 315.

2. By agreement. Parties are expected to cooperate in discovery. TRCP 191.2; *see* ***Alford Chevrolet-Geo***, 997 S.W.2d at 184. To this end, parties may make any agreement reasonably necessary to dispose of the case efficiently. TRCP 191.2. This includes using a form of discovery not provided for in the TRCPs. TRCP 191, cmt. 1. However, there are limits on what the parties can change by agreement. For example, the parties cannot agree to be abusive toward a witness. *Id.* See "Modifying discovery by agreement," §5.1, p. 316.

§8.2 Securing discovery from nonparties. The only discovery procedures a party can use to obtain discovery from a nonparty are those outlined in TRCP 205.1. ***In re Guzman***, 19 S.W.3d 522, 524 (Tex.App.—Corpus Christi 2000, orig. proceeding). See chart 6-2, above.

1. Court order. A party may obtain a court order for (1) entry on land under TRCP 196.7, (2) taking a deposition before suit under TRCP 202, or (3) a physical or mental examination under TRCP 204. TRCP 205.1.

2. Subpoena. A party may serve a subpoena on a nonparty to compel (1) an oral deposition; (2) a deposition on written questions; (3) the production of documents or tangible things, served with a notice of deposition on oral examination (under TRCP 199.2(b)(5)) or written questions (under TRCP 200.1(b)); or (4) the production of documents and tangible things under TRCP 205. TRCP 205.1(a)-(d).

§9. PRETRIAL CONFERENCE

Generally, the trial court uses the pretrial conference to oversee discovery—to determine what discovery has been completed and what discovery remains to be undertaken. See "The Pretrial Conference," ch. 5-A, p. 225.

§10. SPECIAL MASTER FOR DISCOVERY

The theory underlying the use of masters in discovery disputes is that it frees the trial judge to devote more time to substantive decisions, thus expediting the trial docket. See "Master in Chancery," ch. 1-J, p. 55.

§11. FILING & RETAINING DISCOVERY

§11.1 Filing discovery. Most discovery is not filed until needed. This rule was adopted to resolve storage problems encountered by the court clerks. Griesel, *The "New" Texas Discovery Rules*, §VI(A)(4), p. 6.

1. Discovery materials to be filed. TRCP 191.4(b) lists the discovery documents that must be filed.

(1) Discovery requests, deposition notices, and subpoenas required to be served on nonparties. TRCP 191.4(b)(1). For rules on filing deposition materials, see chart 6-8, "Filing Deposition Documents," ch. 6-E, p. 387.

(2) Motions and responses to motions relating to discovery matters. TRCP 191.4(b)(2).

(3) Agreements concerning discovery matters, to the extent necessary to comply with TRCP 11. TRCP 191.4(b)(3).

2. Discovery materials not to be filed. TRCP 191.4(a) lists the discovery documents that must not be filed.

(1) Discovery requests, deposition notices, and subpoenas required to be served only on parties. TRCP 191.4(a)(1).

(2) Responses and objections to discovery requests and deposition notices from parties or nonparties. TRCP 191.4(a)(2).

(3) Documents and tangible things produced in discovery. TRCP 191.4(a)(3).

(4) Withholding statements prepared in compliance with TRCP 193.3(b) and TRCP 193.3(d). TRCP 191.4(a)(4).

3. Exceptions. TRCP 191.4(c) lists the exceptions to the do-not-file rule.

(1) The court may order that discovery materials be filed. TRCP 191.4(c)(1). This provision is an additional safeguard against destruction of discovery in cases where it should be preserved, such as in cases involving TRCP 76a. Griesel, *The "New" Texas Discovery Rules*, §VI(A)(4), p. 6.

(2) A person may file discovery materials in support of or in opposition to a motion or for other use in a court proceeding. TRCP 191.4(c)(2).

(3) A person may file discovery materials necessary for a proceeding in an appellate court. TRCP 191.4(c)(3).

§11.2 Retaining discovery. When a person (party or nonparty) serves discovery materials not required to be filed under TRCP 191.4, that person must retain the original or a copy of the materials during the pendency of the case, including any appeals begun within six months after the judgment is signed. TRCP 191.4(d); ***National Fam. Care Life Ins. Co. v. Fletcher***, 57 S.W.3d 662, 667 n.6 (Tex.App.—Beaumont 2001, pet. denied). The court may modify this requirement. TRCP 191.4(d). The clerk of the court must retain and dispose of deposition transcripts and depositions on written questions as directed by the Supreme Court. TRCP 191.4(e).

§12. SERVICE OF DISCOVERY MATERIALS

§12.1 Service on all parties. When a party serves discovery materials (*i.e.*, disclosures, discovery requests, notices, responses, objections), it must serve a copy of those materials on all other parties of record. TRCP 191.5.

§12.2 Serving discovery with original pleadings. Plaintiffs and defendants may serve discovery requests with their original pleadings. *See, e.g.*, TRCP 194.3(a) (provides 50 days for D to respond to requests for disclosure when D served before answer date).

PRACTICE TIP

Many plaintiffs include a request for disclosures as part of their original petition, changing the name of the petition to "Plaintiff's Original Petition & Request for Disclosures," and noting the full name of the document on the citation. If the plaintiff serves discovery with the petition but in a separate document, the citation must identify the discovery as one of the documents being served on the defendant. ***Sosa v. Williams***, *936 S.W.2d 708, 710 (Tex.App.—Waco 1996, writ denied).*

§13. DEADLINE TO RESPOND TO DISCOVERY

For the general rules for computing deadlines, see "Computing Deadlines to Respond," ch. 1-D, §6, p. 24.

§13.1 Deadline to serve the response. The party responding to the discovery must serve its response (answers, objections and assertions of privilege) on the other party before the deadline for the discovery.

1. Standard time to answer – 30 days. When parties are served with requests for written discovery, the request must provide at least 30 days to respond. TRCP 194.3 (request for disclosure), TRCP 196.2(a) (request for production), TRCP 196.7(c)(1) (request for entry on land), TRCP 197.2(a) (interrogatories), TRCP 198.2(a) (request for admissions). A discovery request can provide more than 30 days to answer, but it cannot provide less than 30 days. Depending on the type of service (mail or fax), the party may have an additional three or four days to respond. TRCP 21a. See "Computing Deadlines to Respond," ch. 1-D, §6, p. 24; chart 6-3, below.

2. Served before answer date – 50 days. When a defendant is served with requests for written discovery before its answer is due, the defendant must serve its response within 50 days from the date of service of the discovery request. TRCP 194.3(a) (request for disclosure), TRCP 196.2(a) (request for production), TRCP 196.7(c)(1) (request for entry on land), TRCP 197.2(a) (interrogatories), TRCP 198.2(a) (request for admissions). This is true, regardless of when the defendant actually files its answer. For example, if a request for written discovery is filed at the same time as the petition, the defendant has 50 days to answer even if it files its answer before the date it is due. Depending on the type of service (mail or fax), the defendant may have an additional three or four days to respond. TRCP 21a. See "Computing Deadlines to Respond," ch. 1-D, §6, p. 24; chart 6-3, below.

6-3. DEADLINES TO RESPOND TO DISCOVERY		
1	Service by U.S. Mail	Date of mailing (generally, the postmark) + 3 days + 30 days = 33 days
2	Service by delivery	Date of delivery + 30 days = 30 days
3	Service by fax before 5 p.m.	Date of fax + 3 days + 30 days = 33 days
4	Service by fax after 5 p.m.	Date of fax + 4 days + 30 days = 34 days
5	Service on defendant before answer date—request for disclosure, request for entry, interrogatories, request for admissions, request for production	Date of service + 50 days = 50 to 54 days, depending on type of service, see rows 1-4, above

3. Discovery deadline in pretrial orders. If the court signs a pretrial order governing discovery, the parties must comply with its terms. ***Werner v. Miller***, 579 S.W.2d 455, 456 (Tex.1979). However, the trial court cannot arbitrarily shorten discovery deadlines by pretrial order. ***G.E. Co. v. Salinas***, 861 S.W.2d 20, 23 (Tex.App.—Corpus Christi 1993, orig. proceeding). See "Discovery deadlines," ch. 5-A, §3.5, p. 226.

4. Discovery deadline when trial reset. When the date for trial is reset more than 30 days beyond the original trial date, the resetting nullifies the original discovery deadlines. See "When trial reset," §16.4.3, p. 327.

§13.2 Deadlines regarding experts. See "Deadlines for Securing Discovery from Experts," ch. 6-C, §6 p. 372.

§14. EXTENDING TIME TO RESPOND TO DISCOVERY

To secure additional time to respond to discovery, a party must secure either an agreement or a court order. Unless the court orders or the parties agree to an extension, all untimely objections to the discovery request are waived. *See* ***Hobson v. Moore***, 734 S.W.2d 340, 341 (Tex.1987).

§14.1 Agreement to extend. See "Modifying discovery by agreement," §5.1, p. 316. See ***O'Connor's*** FORM 6A:02.

§14.2 Court order to extend. To secure additional time to respond to discovery, the party must file a motion to extend time showing "good cause" for the late response. TRCP 191.1. See ***O'Connor's*** FORM 6A:01. Because TRCP 191.1 states that the court can modify discovery procedures (including the deadlines to respond) only on "good cause," the rule seems to be in conflict with TRCP 5, which requires only "cause shown" for a motion to extend that is filed before the deadline sought to be extended, and with TRCP 193.6, which permits a party to introduce evidence not produced in discovery if it shows either good cause or no unfair surprise or prejudice. Until this apparent conflict is clarified by the courts, all motions to extend time in discovery matters—even if filed before the deadline to respond—should include a showing of good cause. See "Modifying discovery by court order," §5.2, p. 316.

§15. PRODUCING WRITTEN DISCOVERY

§15.1 Form of response.

1. In writing. The party must provide written answers to discovery requests. TRCP 193.1, 196.2(a) (request for production), TRCP 197.2(a) (interrogatories), TRCP 198.2(a) (request for admissions). A party cannot answer written discovery requests orally. *See* TRCP 193.1; *see, e.g.*, ***Sharp v. Broadway Nat'l Bank***, 784 S.W.2d 669, 671 (Tex.1990) (oral identification of witness was not proper). When responding to written requests for discovery, the answers, objections, and other responses must be preceded by the request to which they apply. TRCP 193.1.

2. Signed. The responses to written discovery must be signed by the lawyer (or party when pro se). TRCP 191.3(a). See "Certification by signature," §3.1, p. 314; chart 6-2, "Securing & Responding to Discovery," p. 321.

3. Verified. It is not necessary to verify most responses to written discovery. See chart 6-2, "Securing & Responding to Discovery," p. 321. For interrogatory answers, see "Signed & verified by party," ch. 6-F, §4.1.1(4), p. 411.

§15.2 Service on attorney in charge. Discovery responses must be served on the attorney in charge. *See* TRCP 8 (all communications about lawsuit must be sent to attorney in charge); ***Reichhold Chems. v. Puremco Mfg. Co.***, 854 S.W.2d 240, 246 (Tex.App.—Waco 1993, writ denied) (response to discovery served on co-counsel, instead of attorney in charge, was not timely). See "Attorney in Charge," ch. 1-H, §3.1, p. 39.

§15.3 Timely. A party must timely respond to discovery requests. TRCP 193.1. Discovery responses must be served within the time permitted by the rules, ordered by the court, or agreed to by the parties. To compute time, see "Deadline to serve the response," §13.1, p. 323.

§15.4 Discovery that must be produced.

1. Information requested. A party is required to produce all information requested, unless the party serves timely objections or assertions of privilege. TRCP 193.2, 193.3. See "Burden to partially comply," §17.9, p. 333.

2. Information in possession. A party is required to produce all documents or things requested that are in its possession, custody, or control. TRCP 196.3(a). See "Possession," §2.3, p. 313.

§15.5 Discovery not required to be produced. A party who makes a proper and timely objection or assertion of privilege is not required to produce the following:

1. Evidence subject to objection or privilege. A party is not required to produce evidence that is subject to an objection or an assertion of privilege. See "Burden to partially comply," §17.9, p. 333.

2. Information not reasonably available. A party is not required to produce information that, at the time the response is made, is not reasonably available to the party or its attorney. TRCP 193.1.

3. Impeachment or rebuttal evidence. A party is not required to anticipate the other party's case and produce impeachment or rebuttal evidence in response to a general request for information. TRCP 192.3(d) implicitly acknowledges this by stating that the parties may obtain discovery of trial witnesses but not witnesses who will testify for rebuttal or impeachment if the necessity for their testimony cannot reasonably be anticipated before trial.

§15.6 Organization of discovery products. Discovery must be produced either (1) as the material is kept in the usual course of business or (2) organized and labeled to correspond with the categories of the request. TRCP 196.3(c). See "Organization of documents," ch. 6-H, §3.4.1(2), p. 426.

§15.7 Authenticity of produced documents. See "Using Requested Documents," ch. 6-H, §8, p. 433.

§16. SUPPLEMENTING DISCOVERY RESPONSES

§16.1 When supplementation required. The burden to supplement is on the party responding to discovery; the party requesting discovery has no burden to request supplementation. TRCP 193.5(a). When in doubt whether to supplement, a party should lean in favor of supplementing because the court may exclude the information if it is not properly supplemented. TRCP 193.6(a); *see* ***Alvarado v. Farah Mfg. Co.***, 830 S.W.2d 911, 913-14 (Tex.1992); ***Boothe v. Hausler***, 766 S.W.2d 788, 789 (Tex.1989). See ***O'Connor's*** FORMS 6A:22-23. A party must supplement a discovery response in the following instances:

1. The party obtains information that reveals its response to discovery was incomplete or incorrect when made. TRCP 193.5(a).

2. The party discovers its response to discovery, though complete and correct when made, is no longer complete and correct. TRCP 193.5(a); *see* ***Boothe***, 766 S.W.2d at 789; *see also* ***Alvarado***, 830 S.W.2d at 917 (P could not show good cause for calling unlisted witness for rebuttal).

§16.2 Extent of supplementation.

1. Written discovery.

(1) Identity of witnesses. Supplementation of written discovery is required to the extent the discovery sought the identification of persons with knowledge of relevant facts, trial witnesses, or expert witnesses. TRCP 193.5(a)(1); ***Vingcard A.S. v. Merrimac Hospitality Sys.***, 59 S.W.3d 847, 855 (Tex.App.—Fort Worth 2001, pet. denied); *see, e.g.*, ***Sharp v. Broadway Nat'l Bank***, 784 S.W.2d 669, 671 (Tex.1990) (expert witness not disclosed); ***Yeldell v. Holiday Hills Retirement & Nursing Ctr.***, 701 S.W.2d 243, 246-47 (Tex.1985) (party learned of fact witness whose identity it did not disclose).

(2) Other information. Supplementation of written discovery is required to the extent the discovery sought information other than the identification of witnesses, unless the information was made known in writing, on the record at a deposition, or through other discovery responses. TRCP 193.5(a)(2). See §16.3.2, below.

2. Discovery from retained testifying expert. To the extent a party's retained testifying expert changes or modifies her opinion, the party must supplement the expert's deposition testimony or written report with the expert's mental impressions or opinions and the bases for them. TRCP 195.6; ***Vingcard***, 59 S.W.3d at 856; *see, e.g.*, ***Aluminum Co. of Am. v. Bullock***, 870 S.W.2d 2, 4 (Tex.1994) (Ps should have supplemented interrogatory answers to show material change in their expert's testimony; in deposition, expert stated D was not consciously indifferent, but at trial expert testified D was grossly negligent). See "Supplementing discovery of retained testifying expert," ch. 6-C, §5.1, p. 371.

3. Order or agreement. Supplementation is required when the court orders it or the parties agree to it. *See* TRCP 191.1; ***Cole v. Huntsville Mem'l Hosp.***, 920 S.W.2d 364, 376 (Tex.App.—Houston [1st Dist.] 1996, writ denied) (failure to supplement as required by order contributed to imposition of death penalty sanctions).

§16.3 When supplementation not required.

1. Deposition testimony of fact witness. A party is not required to supplement deposition testimony of fact witnesses. See "Deposition of fact witnesses," ch. 6-E, §11.1, p. 398.

2. Information provided by other means. It is not necessary to supplement responses to written discovery requests for most discovery matters if the additional or corrective information was made known to the other party (1) in writing, (2) on the record at a deposition, or (3) through other discovery responses. TRCP 193.5(a)(2); ***City of Paris v. McDowell***, 79 S.W.3d 601, 606 (Tex.App.—Texarkana 2002, no pet.). Supplementation by other means does not apply to supplementation of witness information listed in TRCP 193.5(a)(1). The phrase in TRCP 193.5(a)(2), "unless the additional or corrective information has been made known to the other parties in writing, on the record at a deposition, or through other discovery responses," applies only to "other information," not to the identity of witnesses. *See, e.g.*, ***City of Paris***, 79 S.W.3d at 606 (qualifications of expert witness). See §16.2.1(2), above.

3. Lapse of request. A party is not required to supplement discovery if the requesting party does not maintain a valid request for information. ***Kawasaki Motors v. Thompson***, 872 S.W.2d 221, 224 (Tex.1994) (parties' agreement inadvertently eliminated question about experts).

4. For summary judgment witnesses. A party should, but is not required to, supplement answers to written discovery requesting the designation of witnesses before using an affidavit of a witness in support of, or in response to, a motion for summary judgment. *See* ***Johnson v. Fuselier***, 83 S.W.3d 892, 897 (Tex.App.—Texarkana 2002, no pet.) (timeliness of discovery supplementation, including experts, is controlled by the trial date, which cannot be determined at SJ proceeding). *But see* ***Ersek v. Davis & Davis***, 69 S.W.3d 268, 270-71 (Tex.App.—Austin 2002, pet. denied) (timeliness for expert discovery is determined by discovery cut-off date in TRCP 195.2, even in SJ proceedings).

§16.4 Deadline to supplement answers.

1. Under the TRCPs.

(1) After discovering need to supplement. A party must supplement or amend its answers to written discovery "reasonably promptly" after the party discovers the need to do so. TRCP 193.5(b); ***Snider v. Stanley***, 44 S.W.3d 713, 716 (Tex.App.—Beaumont 2001, pet. denied). Although there is a presumption that a supplemented discovery response made less than 30 days before trial was not reasonably prompt (see §16.4.1(3), below), the converse is not true—a supplemented discovery response made more than 30 days before trial is not necessarily reasonably prompt. ***Snider***, 44 S.W.3d at 715. The following supplementations were not reasonably prompt: • Disclosure of witness statements 41 days before trial, on last day for discovery, 9 months after discovery request. ***Matagorda Cty. Hosp. v. Burwell***, 94 S.W.3d 75, 81 (Tex.App.—Corpus Christi 2002, pet. filed 2-3-03). • Plaintiff's designation of expert eight months after request, after defendant filed motion for summary judgment. ***Ersek***, 69 S.W.3d at 271 n.2. • Defendants' designation of expert 30 days before trial. ***Snider***, 44 S.W.3d at 715.

CAUTION

One court has held that if a party responded to a request for disclosure of experts with "no experts at this time," the party cannot designate an expert for the first time after the deadline in TRCP 195.2 (90 days before end of discovery period for plaintiff, 60 days for defendant). ***Ersek***, *69 S.W.3d at 270-71.*

---

(2) At least 30 days before trial. A party may supplement its discovery responses as late as 30 days before trial. TRCP 193.5(b); *see* ***Aluminum Co.***, 870 S.W.2d at 3-4 (experts under former TRCP 166b(6)(b)). If a case is set for trial "for the week of" instead of a certain date, the 30 days run from the actual date of trial, not the Monday of that week. *See* TRCP 193.5(b) (says "before trial," not "before the week set for trial").

(3) Less than 30 days before trial. To supplement discovery responses less than 30 days before trial, a party must show good cause for the late supplementation or show the late supplementation will not unfairly surprise or prejudice the other parties. TRCP 193.6(a), (b); ***Rutledge v. Staner***, 9 S.W.3d 469, 472 (Tex.App.—Tyler 1999, pet. denied); *see, e.g.*, ***Forman v. Fina Oil & Chem. Co.***, 858 S.W.2d 373, 374 (Tex.1993) (good cause for late designation of expert because P designated same doctor D designated, 3 days after receiving D's designation). There is a presumption that a supplemental or amended response made less than 30 days before trial is not made "reasonably promptly." TRCP 193.5(b). If the party does not carry its burden, the court may exclude the evidence or grant a continuance to allow the other parties to conduct discovery on new information disclosed in the supplementation. TRCP 193.6(a), (c).

2. By court order or agreement. A party must supplement its answers to written discovery according to the modified deadlines in any court order or agreement between the parties. *See* TRCP 191.1 (discovery procedures can be modified by court order or agreement); ***Mack v. Suzuki***, 6 S.W.3d 732, 733 (Tex.App.—Houston [1st Dist.] 1999, no pet.) (expert report struck because P served it after deadline in agreed scheduling order).

3. When trial reset. When the trial setting is rescheduled, a party may supplement its answers to discovery. ***H.B. Zachry Co. v. Gonzalez***, 847 S.W.2d 246, 246 (Tex.1993); ***Coastal Mart v. Hernandez***, 76 S.W.3d 691, 699 (Tex.App.—Corpus Christi 2002, pet. dism'd); *see, e.g.*, ***Ricardo N., Inc. v. Turcios de Argueta***, 907 S.W.2d 423, 429 (Tex.1995) (late witness designations became timely after case was removed to federal court & then remanded); ***Texas Tech Univ. Health Sci. Ctr. v. Apodaca***, 876 S.W.2d 402, 410 (Tex.App.—El Paso 1994, writ denied) (during continuance, party supplemented answers with new witness). The automatic exclusion of the evidence and witnesses under TRCP 193.6 does not continue beyond the original trial date when the trial is reset for a date more than 30 days after the original trial setting. ***H.B. Zachry***, 847 S.W.2d at 246.

§16.5 Not filed. Most supplemental or amended answers to written discovery are not filed with the court. See "Filing Discovery," §11.1, p. 322.

§16.6 Form of supplemental discovery. Supplemental or amended answers to written discovery should be made in the same form as the original answers. TRCP 193.5(b); ***State Farm Fire & Cas. Co. v. Morua***, 979 S.W.2d 616, 618 (Tex.1998); *see* ***Varner v. Howe***, 860 S.W.2d 458, 462-63 (Tex.App.—El Paso 1993, no writ) (witness identified by letter should have been excluded). See ***O'Connor's*** FORMS 6A:22-23.

1. In writing. The party should provide the supplemental or amended answer in writing. *See* TRCP 193.5(b). For the exceptions, see "Information provided by other means," §16.3.2, p. 326.

2. Verified. A supplemental or amended response must be verified by the party if the original response was required to be verified by the party. TRCP 193.5(b); *see* ***Morua***, 979 S.W.2d at 618 (former TRCP 166b required verification of responses if original answer required to be verified). For a list of written discovery that must be verified, see chart 6-2, "Securing & Responding to Discovery," p. 321.

3. Objections to form of response. A supplemental or amended response that is not in the correct form or is not verified when required is not deemed untimely, unless the party making the response refuses to correct the defect within a reasonable time after it is pointed out. TRCP 193.5(b).

§16.7 Review. If a party supplements discovery less than 30 days before trial, and the trial court admits the untimely disclosed evidence over the opposing party's objection, to obtain a reversal on appeal the objecting party must show that the trial court's error probably caused the rendition of an improper judgment. TRAP 44.1(a)(1); ***Bott v. Bott***, 962 S.W.2d 626, 628 (Tex.App.—Houston [14th Dist.] 1997, no pet.).

§17. RESISTING DISCOVERY

6-4. BURDENS IN DISCOVERY PROCEDURE

	BURDEN	DISCOVERY FROM PARTY	DISCOVERY FROM NONPARTY *
		BURDEN IS ON—	
1	To plead objection	Party resisting discovery, §17.1, below	
2	To assert privilege	Party resisting discovery, §17.2, below	
3	To request privilege log	Party seeking discovery, §17.2.2, p. 330	
4	To secure hearing	Party seeking discovery, §17.5.1, p. 331	Party resisting discovery, §17.4.1, p. 331
5	To produce evidence at hearing	Party resisting discovery, §17.6, p. 331	
6	To ask for in camera inspection	Party resisting discovery, §17.7, p. 332	
7	To secure ruling	Party seeking discovery, §17.5.1, p. 331	Party resisting discovery, §17.4.1, p. 331

* Assumes the nonparty does not object to producing discovery but one of the parties does.

The discovery rules provide two procedures for resisting discovery: (1) the procedure for making most discovery objections, and (2) the procedure for asserting claims of privilege.

NOTE

Even though TRCP 196.2(b) seems to say that a party responding to discovery must make its objections and assert its privileges at the same time, if the same information is subject to an objection and a privilege, the discovery rules permit a party to file its objections first and wait until after the court rules on the objections to file its assertions of privilege. ***In re Lincoln Elec. Co.****, 91 S.W.3d 432, 437 (Tex.App.—Beaumont 2002, orig. proceeding).*

COMMENTARIES

CHAPTER 6. DISCOVERY
A. GENERAL RULES FOR DISCOVERY

§17.1 Making objections. The burden is on the party resisting discovery to plead its objection to discovery. ***State v. Lowry***, 802 S.W.2d 669, 671 (Tex.1991). No matter how improper the discovery request, the party to whom it is addressed must object, or it waives its objections. ***Young v. Ray***, 916 S.W.2d 1, 3 (Tex.App.—Houston [1st Dist.] 1995, orig. proceeding).

1. Timely objection. The party resisting discovery must object at or before the time to respond to discovery or the objection is waived, unless the party obtained an extension of time by agreement or court order, or can show good cause for not timely objecting. TRCP 193.2(e); *see* ***Remington Arms Co. v. Canales***, 837 S.W.2d 624, 625 (Tex.1992); ***Hobson v. Moore***, 734 S.W.2d 340, 341 (Tex.1987). After the deadline to respond, a party may amend its objection or response to include a ground that was initially inapplicable or was unknown after reasonable inquiry. TRCP 193.2(d).

2. Specific objection. The party resisting discovery must make a specific objection for each item it wishes to exclude from discovery. TRCP 193.2(a); *see, e.g.*, ***In re Alford Chevrolet-Geo***, 997 S.W.2d 173, 181 (Tex. 1999) (party made general allegations of undue burden & harassment); ***National Un. Fire Ins. Co. v. Hoffman***, 746 S.W.2d 305, 307 n.3 (Tex.App.—Dallas 1988, orig. proceeding) (party made general objections by merely reciting particular privileges). Valid objections obscured by unfounded objections are automatically waived unless the party shows good cause. TRCP 193.2(e).

§17.2 Asserting privileges. To protect privileged information from written discovery, a party must "assert" a privilege under TRCP 193.3. ***In re Shipmon***, 68 S.W.3d 815, 822 (Tex.App.—Amarillo 2001, orig. proceeding); ***In re Monsanto Co.***, 998 S.W.2d 917, 924 (Tex.App.—Waco 1999, orig. proceeding); *see also* TRCP 176.6(c) (nonparty objecting to subpoena requesting documents must follow provisions of TRCP 193.3). A party should not "object" to discovery that asks for privileged information. TRCP 193.2(f); ***Shipmon***, 68 S.W.3d at 822; ***Monsanto***, 998 S.W.2d at 924. However, a party will not waive a privilege if it mistakenly objects to a request for privileged information instead of complying with TRCP 193.3. TRCP 193.2(f); ***In re University of Tex. Health Ctr.***, 33 S.W.3d 822, 826 (Tex.2000).

1. Claiming privilege. A privilege against written discovery must be asserted as follows:

(1) Withhold information. The party must withhold the privileged information from the discovery it produces. TRCP 193.3(a). The party can withhold only the information sought to be protected; it cannot withhold other information requested in the same discovery request. See "Burden to partially comply," §17.9, p. 333.

(2) Withholding statement. The party must serve a withholding statement. TRCP 193.3(a). A withholding statement is a statement in a response to discovery in which a party claims that information responsive to written discovery is privileged. *Id.* A withholding statement may be included in the response or filed separately. *Id.* The withholding statement must (1) state that information responsive to the written discovery request is being withheld, (2) identify the request to which the information or material relates, and (3) identify the privilege asserted. *Id.*; ***Monsanto***, 998 S.W.2d at 924; Griesel, *The "New" Texas Discovery Rules*, §VII(A)(2), p. 13. See ***O'Connor's*** FORM 6B:01.

(3) Exemption for litigation materials. A party is not required to assert a privilege in the withholding statement for materials created by or for lawyers for purposes of the litigation. TRCP 193.3(c). It is assumed such materials will be withheld on the grounds of attorney-client privilege or core work product. TRCP 193, cmt. 3. A party may withhold a privileged communication to or from a lawyer or lawyer's representative or a privileged document of a lawyer or lawyer's representative if—

(a) the communication was created when the party consulted a lawyer to obtain professional legal services from the lawyer in the prosecution or defense of a specific claim in the litigation in which discovery is requested; and

(b) the communication concerned the litigation in which the discovery is requested. TRCP 193.3(c).

NOTE

TRCP 193.3(c) does not prohibit a party from specifically requesting information that may be subject to an attorney-client privilege or core-work-product exemption if the party has a good-faith basis for asserting the information is discoverable. TRCP 193, cmt. 3. For example, a party can request information described by TRE 503(d)(1), the crime-fraud exception.

2. Request privilege log. After receipt of a withholding statement, the party seeking discovery may request in writing that the withholding party identify the information or material withheld. TRCP 193.3(b); ***Monsanto***, 998 S.W.2d at 924. The document listing the information withheld from discovery is called a privilege log. See ***O'Connor's*** FORM 6B:02.

3. Serve privilege log. Within 15 days of service of the request for the privilege log, the withholding party must serve a response. TRCP 193.3(b); ***Spohn Hosp. v. Mayer***, 72 S.W.3d 52, 62 (Tex.App.—Corpus Christi 2001), *rev'd on other grounds*, 104 S.W.3d 878 (Tex.2003). See ***O'Connor's*** FORM 6B:03. The response must include the following information:

(1) Assert privilege. The party must assert a specific privilege for each item or group of items withheld. TRCP 193.3(b)(2); ***Monsanto***, 998 S.W.2d at 924.

(2) Describe information or material withheld. The party must specify the nature of the information or material withheld, without revealing the privileged information itself. TRCP 193.3(b)(1); ***Spohn Hosp.***, 72 S.W.3d at 62. The withheld information or material must be described in a way that allows the party seeking discovery to assess the applicability of the privilege. TRCP 193.3(b)(1); ***Monsanto***, 998 S.W.2d at 925 n.8. A description of documents should include the document number ("Bates number"), author or source, recipient, persons receiving copies, date, document title, document type, number of pages, and any other relevant information. *See* ***Monsanto***, 998 S.W.2d at 925.

4. Use snap-back provision. An inadvertent production of privileged information is considered involuntary. TRCP 193.3(d); *see* ***Monsanto***, 998 S.W.2d at 921 n.2. A party may claim a privilege on inadvertently produced information by following the snap-back provision of TRCP 193.3(d). *See also* TRCP 193, cmt. 4 (snap-back provision in TRCP 193.3 overrules ***Granada Corp. v. 1st Ct. of Appeals***, 844 S.W.2d 223 (Tex.1992), on inadvertent production). The purpose of the snap-back provision is to reduce costs and risks in large document productions. TRCP 193, cmt. 4. The focus of TRCP 193.3(d) is on the intent to waive the privilege, not the intent to produce the information or material. TRCP 193, cmt. 4; ***In re AEP Tex. Cent. Co.***, ___ S.W.3d ___ (Tex.App.—San Antonio 2003, orig. proceeding) (No. 04-03-00253-CV; 7-16-03). A party who does not diligently screen documents before producing them does not waive a claim of privilege. TRCP 193, cmt. 4; ***AEP Tex.***, ___ S.W.3d at ___. To claim a privilege after inadvertent production, the party must, within ten days of discovering the accidental production, serve on the other parties an amended withholding statement that (1) identifies the information produced, (2) identifies the privilege asserted for that information, and (3) requests that all copies of the privileged information be returned. TRCP 193.3(d). See ***O'Connor's*** FORM 6B:04. The ten-day period allowed for an amended response (which may be shortened by the court) does not run from the production of the material or information but from the party's first awareness of the mistake. TRCP 193, cmt. 4.

PRACTICE TIP

To avoid complications at trial about inadvertently disclosed documents, a party may ask the court to require all parties to make pretrial identification of documents that they intend to offer. This will trigger the obligation to assert any overlooked privileges under TRCP 193.3. TRCP 193, cmt. 4.

§17.3 Objecting to amended discovery requests. When a party receives an amended discovery request, the party is not required to restate its objections and reassert its privileges to the requests that are the same as those already objected to in response to the earlier discovery request. *See* ***In re University of Tex. Health Ctr.***, 33 S.W.3d 822, 826 (Tex.2000) (hospital not required to reassert privileges when deposition reset).

§17.4 Objections regarding discovery & nonparties.

1. Party information from nonparty. When discovery about a party is sought from a nonparty, to prevent disclosure of the information the party should file a motion for protective order. Only a protective order—not an objection—will prevent the nonparty from producing the discovery. *See* TRCP 192.6(b). When both the party and the nonparty object to the discovery, the party and the nonparty can coordinate their efforts, and the nonparty will withhold the requested information. When only the party objects and the nonparty is willing to produce the information, the party must quickly file a motion for protective order, set the motion for a hearing, and get a ruling before the nonparty produces the information requested. *See* TRCP 176.6(e) (party affected by subpoena may move for protective order before time to respond), TRCP 192.6(a) (party affected by discovery request may file motion for protective order within time to respond). However, when the information is produced by the nonparty, the party may recover any information that is privileged. *See* TRCP 193.3(d). See §17.2.4, above.

2. Nonparty information from party. The discovery rules do not require notice to nonparties when a party seeks information about a nonparty from another party. *See* ***In re CI Host, Inc.***, 92 S.W.3d 514, 517 (Tex. 2002). The party from whom the discovery is sought should inform the court when the information sought is the privileged information of a nonparty. The court should give serious considerations to the interest of a nonparty whose information is sought in discovery. *See id.*

§17.5 Burden to secure hearing & ruling. Either party may ask for a hearing on objections, on claims of privilege, or on motions for protective orders, to quash, or to compel. *See* TRCP 176.6(d), (e), 192.6, 193.4.

1. Most discovery. If neither party asks for a hearing, the party who sent the request for discovery waives the requested discovery. Thus, once objections or claims of privilege have been served, the burden to secure a hearing on a discovery dispute is on the party seeking the discovery. *See* TRCP 193.4(a); ***McKinney v. National Un. Fire Ins. Co.***, 772 S.W.2d 72, 75 (Tex.1989).

2. Discovery involving nonparty. When a party wants to block a nonparty from producing information about the party requested from the nonparty in discovery, the party should secure a hearing and ruling before the nonparty produces the information. See §17.4.1, above.

§17.6 Burden to provide evidence. Once a hearing is set, generally the person who resists discovery needs to produce evidence to support a claim of privilege or an objection to discovery.

1. When necessary. Generally, when a party makes an objection or asserts a claim of privilege, that party has the burden to produce evidence at the hearing necessary to support its objection or claim of privilege. TRCP 193.4(a), 199.6; *e.g.*, ***CI Host***, 92 S.W.3d at 516-17 (evidence necessary to support objection that information on computer tapes was protected); ***Huie v. DeShazo***, 922 S.W.2d 920, 926 (Tex.1996) (evidence necessary to support privilege); ***G.M. Corp. v. Tanner***, 892 S.W.2d 862, 863 (Tex.1995) (evidence necessary to support objection that testing would destroy evidence); ***Humphreys v. Caldwell***, 888 S.W.2d 469, 470 (Tex.1994) (evidence necessary to support privilege); ***Axelson, Inc. v. McIlhany***, 798 S.W.2d 550, 553 n.6 (Tex.1990) (documents necessary for in camera inspection to support objection of relevance). When evidence is necessary, it must be produced at or before the hearing. TRCP 193.4(a). Evidence at the hearing can include the following:

(1) Affidavits. When a party relies on affidavits, the affidavits must be served at least seven days before the hearing. TRCP 193.4(a), 199.6; ***In re Monsanto Co.***, 998 S.W.2d 917, 924, 933 n.24 (Tex.App.—Waco 1999, orig. proceeding). The affidavits must be based on the affiant's personal knowledge and must show that the facts in it are true. See "Personal knowledge," ch. 1-B, §4.14.2(3)(a), p. 8. The affidavits must contain something more than global allegations that the documents are privileged or a recitation of facts ascertainable from the documents themselves. ***Barnes v. Whittington***, 751 S.W.2d 493, 495 (Tex.1988). The affidavits should be offered into evidence at the hearing. *See* ***Monsanto***, 998 S.W.2d at 926 (even though not offered, record showed court considered them).

(2) Live testimony. If a party intends to rely on live testimony at the hearing, it should proceed with all the formalities of trial—make sure a court reporter is present, have the witnesses sworn, introduce exhibits, and make objections to the other party's evidence. *See* TRCP 193.4(a), 199.6. The witness should explain why specific documents are exempt from discovery. *See, e.g.*, ***Conrad v. Wilson***, 873 S.W.2d 467, 469-70 (Tex.App.—Beaumont 1994, orig. proceeding) (testimony of hospital's general counsel was not specific).

(3) Documents for inspection. When a party is resisting discovery on the grounds of privilege or relevance, the documents themselves may be the only adequate evidence to support the claim. *See* ***Humphreys***, 888 S.W.2d at 470-71 (work-product privilege); ***State v. Lowry***, 802 S.W.2d 669, 673 (Tex.1991) (investigative privilege); ***Axelson***, 798 S.W.2d at 553 (claim of relevance). See §17.7, below.

2. When not necessary. In some cases, an objection or claim of privilege does not need to be supported by evidence. *See, e.g.*, ***In re Union Pac. Res. Co.***, 22 S.W.3d 338, 341 (Tex.1999) (evidence not necessary to support objection of relevance); ***Loftin v. Martin***, 776 S.W.2d 145, 148 (Tex.1989) (request was so vague & overbroad party did not know how to respond); ***Garner, Lovell & Stein, P.C. v. Burnett***, 911 S.W.2d 108, 112-13 (Tex.App.—Amarillo 1995, orig. proceeding) (request for documents created after lawsuit filed was clearly not proper discovery); ***Texas Tech Univ. Health Sci. Ctr. v. Schild***, 828 S.W.2d 502, 504 (Tex.App.—El Paso 1992, orig. proceeding) (request obviously asked for attorney's thought processes). When in doubt, a party should file an affidavit that explains the reasons for the objection or claim of privilege.

§17.7 In camera inspection. The court must decide whether an in camera inspection is necessary. TRCP 193.4(a), 199.6; ***CI Host***, 92 S.W.3d at 516. When an inspection is necessary, it is an abuse of discretion for the trial court to rule without first examining the documents. ***Lowry***, 802 S.W.2d at 674; ***Avary v. Bank of Am.***, 72 S.W.3d 779, 803 (Tex.App.—Dallas 2002, pet. denied).

1. Make prima facie case. The party resisting discovery should initially attempt to establish its privileges by producing evidence (affidavits or live testimony). ***Monsanto***, 998 S.W.2d at 924; *see, e.g.*, ***Garcia v. Peeples***, 734 S.W.2d 343, 345 (Tex.1987) (court ruled documents were trade secret based on affidavit).

2. Identify documents to be inspected. Once a party makes a prima facie case for its claim of privilege, the party seeking discovery should, based on the privilege log, identify which documents or groups of documents it believes the court should inspect in camera. ***Monsanto***, 998 S.W.2d at 925.

3. Produce documents for inspection. The party resisting discovery should mark each document with the appropriate privilege claimed for that document, and file them in a sealed wrapper with the court for an in camera inspection. TRCP 193.4(a), 199.6; ***Axelson***, 798 S.W.2d at 553 n.6.

§17.8 Nonparty objections to discovery. Parties must follow the applicable rules of procedure governing obtaining nonparty records. ***In re Diversicare Gen. Partner***, 41 S.W.3d 788, 794 (Tex.App.—Corpus Christi 2001, orig. proceeding). As a general rule, a nonparty (*e.g.*, a witness subpoenaed for a deposition) who objects to discovery must follow the same procedures as a party. TRCP 176.6(c)-(e); ***Diversicare***, 41 S.W.3d at 794; *see, e.g.*, ***State ex rel. Curry v. Walker***, 873 S.W.2d 379, 380 (Tex.1994) (DA's office, a nonparty, filed motion to quash and for protective order); ***Olinger v. Curry***, 926 S.W.2d 832, 835 (Tex.App.—Fort Worth 1996, orig. proceeding) (nonparty objected at deposition). See "Objecting to Trial & Discovery Subpoenas," ch. 1-K, §4, p. 61; "Challenging nonparty discovery subpoena," ch. 6-H, §5.5, p. 429.

§17.9 Burden to partially comply.

1. Partial compliance necessary. A party is required to comply with written discovery to the extent no objection is made. TRCP 192.6 (motion for protective order), TRCP 193.2(b) & cmt. 2 (objections to written discovery), TRCP 193.3(a) (assertions of privilege). For example, when a party objects to producing documents from a remote time period, it must produce documents from a more recent period. TRCP 193, cmt. 2.

2. No compliance necessary. A party is not required to partially comply if (1) it is unreasonable to comply before obtaining a ruling, (2) the production would be burdensome and duplicative if the objection is sustained, or (3) the request asks for "all documents relevant to the lawsuit," which is overbroad and not in compliance with the rule requiring specific requests for documents. *See* TRCP 192.6, 193.2(b) & cmt. 2. See §19.1.1, below; "Overbroad," §19.1.3, p. 335.

§18. TYPES OF OBJECTIONS TO DISCOVERY

§18.1 Reasons to object to discovery requests.

See ***O'Connor's*** FORM 6A:07. A party may object to a request for discovery for the following reasons:

1. Not within scope of discovery. A party may object to a discovery request that asks for information outside the scope of discovery. The scope of discovery is any unprivileged information that is relevant to the subject matter of the lawsuit, even if it would be inadmissible at trial, as long as the information sought is reasonably calculated to lead to the discovery of admissible evidence. TRCP 192.3(a); ***In re CSX Corp***, ___ S.W.3d ___ (Tex.2003) (No. 03-0381-CV; 10-3-03); ***Axelson, Inc. v. McIlhany***, 798 S.W.2d 550, 553 (Tex.1990). A discovery request is outside the scope of discovery when it asks for information that is not relevant and the information requested will not lead to admissible evidence. TRCP 192.3(a).

(1) Is not relevant. For example, the amounts paid by the defendant to settle other suits, sought for use in settlement discussions, was not relevant to the subject matter of the suit. ***Ford Motor Co. v. Leggat***, 904 S.W.2d 643, 649 (Tex.1995); *see also* ***Martin v. Khoury***, 843 S.W.2d 163, 165-67 (Tex.App.—Texarkana 1992, orig. proceeding) (membership list of nonparty organization for use in voir dire was not discoverable). For the form of objections based on relevance, see the charts produced by Ford in ***Ford Motor Co. v. Ross***, 888 S.W.2d 879, 900-02 (Tex.App.—Tyler 1994, orig. proceeding).

(2) Would not lead to admissible evidence. For example, when a suit does not include a claim for exemplary damages, a defendant may object to a request for information about its net worth on the grounds that it is not within the scope of discovery because it is not calculated to lead to admissible evidence. ***Al Parker Buick Co. v. Touchy***, 788 S.W.2d 129, 130-31 (Tex.App.—Houston [1st Dist.] 1990, orig. proceeding).

2. Not a permissible form of discovery. A party may object when a discovery request asks for a type of discovery not permitted by the rules of discovery. *See, e.g.*, TRCP 195.1 & 197.1 (party is prohibited from learning identity of other party's testifying expert witness through interrogatories); ***In re Guzman***, 19 S.W.3d 522, 524-25 (Tex.App.—Corpus Christi 2000, orig. proceeding) (court cannot require party to execute authorization for nonparty to produce information; nonparty discovery must comply with TRCP 205.1). *But see* TRCP 191, cmt. 1 (court may order, or parties may agree, to use discovery methods other than those prescribed in the rules).

3. Not reasonably available. A party is not required to produce information that, at the time the response is made, is not reasonably available to the party or its attorney. TRCP 193.1. When information is not available to answer a request for admissions, see "Lack of information," ch. 6-G, §4.2.4, p. 418.

4. Request lacks specificity. A party may object when a request lacks specificity or is so vague and unclear that the party has no means to identify the information requested. ***Davis v. Pate***, 915 S.W.2d 76, 79 n.2 (Tex.App.—Corpus Christi 1996, orig. proceeding) (distinguishing requests that are overbroad from those that lack specificity).

5. Improper procedure. When a party makes an improper request for discovery, the other party may file either an objection or a motion for a protective order, whichever is appropriate, before the response is due, stating why the request is improper. TRCP 192.6, 193.2. For example, a party may object when the other party serves more than 25 written interrogatories in Level 1 or 2 discovery. TRCP 190.2(c)(3). The responding party should answer the first 25 interrogatories and object to the others. TRCP 193.2(b) & cmt. 2.

6. Same information already provided. A party may object if the information has already been provided in response to other discovery in another form. *See, e.g.*, ***Sears, Roebuck & Co. v. Ramirez***, 824 S.W.2d 558, 559 (Tex.1992) (Sears not required to produce tax returns to prove net worth because it had produced audited, certified annual report).

7. Burdensome, harassing, or overbroad. A party may object that a discovery request is unduly burdensome, harassing, or overbroad. See §§19.1.1-19.1.3, below.

§18.2 Invalid objections to discovery requests. The following are some objections to discovery that are not valid: • The information requested is privileged. A party must follow the procedure for asserting a privilege under TRCP 193.3. See "Asserting privileges," §17.2, p. 329. • The evidence will not be admissible at trial. As long as information appears reasonably calculated to lead to the discovery of admissible evidence, it is discoverable. TRCP 192.3(a). • The evidence is not relevant. It is not a valid objection that information is not relevant, unless the information will not lead to admissible evidence. *See id.* • The other party combined two forms of discovery. Different forms of discovery may be combined in the same document and may be taken in any order or sequence. TRCP 192.2.

§19. MOTION FOR PROTECTIVE ORDER

A person who resists discovery (party or nonparty) may file a motion for protective order in response to a discovery request or a motion to compel. TRCP 192.6; *see* ***In re Alford Chevrolet-Geo***, 997 S.W.2d 173, 180-81 (Tex.1999). See ***O'Connor's*** FORMS 6A:08-09. A person should not seek a protective order when it is more appropriate to make an objection or a claim of privilege. TRCP 192.6(a).

§19.1 Grounds to limit scope of discovery. Under TRCP 192.4, the trial court has the authority to limit the scope of discovery. TRCP 192, cmt. 7. A person may file a motion for protective order for the following reasons:

1. Undue burden. A person may ask for protection from a discovery request that is unduly burdensome, annoying to produce, or unnecessarily expensive. TRCP 176.7 (undue burden of subpoena), TRCP 192.4(a) & (b) (limitations on scope of discovery), TRCP 192.6(b) (order to protect movant from undue burden, expense, annoyance); ***Alford Chevrolet-Geo***, 997 S.W.2d at 181 (same). The person resisting discovery has the burden to plead and prove the request will impose an undue burden. ***ISK Biotech Corp. v. Lindsay***, 933 S.W.2d 565, 568-69 (Tex.App.—Houston [1st Dist.] 1996, orig. proceeding); ***Tjernagel v. Roberts***, 928 S.W.2d 297, 302 (Tex.App.—Amarillo 1996, orig. proceeding). To prove undue burden, the person cannot simply make conclusory allegations that the requested discovery is unduly burdensome. ***Alford Chevrolet-Geo***, 997 S.W.2d at 181; *see* ***In re Amaya***, 34 S.W.3d 354, 358 (Tex.App.—Waco 2001, orig. proceeding) (no evidence produced to show burden). The discovery must be unduly burdensome, not merely burdensome. ***In re Energas Co.***, 63 S.W.3d 50, 55 (Tex.App.—Amarillo 2001, orig. proceeding). The person resisting discovery cannot rely on problems in retrieving documents caused by the way it filed them in its own records. ***ISK Biotech***, 933 S.W.2d at 569. Once the person resisting discovery proves the request for discovery is an undue burden, the person requesting discovery must show the request is not so burdensome. ***Forward v. Housing Auth.***, 864 S.W.2d 167, 169 (Tex.App.—Tyler 1993, no writ); *see also* TRCP 191.3(c)(4) (signature on discovery request is certification that request is not unduly burdensome). Undue burden occurs when discovery is any of the following:

(1) Duplicative. The discovery is unreasonably cumulative or duplicative. TRCP 192.4(a); *see* ***Walker v. Packer***, 827 S.W.2d 833, 843 (Tex.1992) (discovery that compels production of patently irrelevant or duplicative documents can constitute undue burden).

(2) Obtainable from alternate source. The discovery is obtainable from some other source that is more convenient, less burdensome, or less expensive. TRCP 192.4(a); ***In re Arras***, 24 S.W.3d 862, 864 (Tex. App.—El Paso 2000, orig. proceeding) (deposition of nonparty for addresses of other parties was inconvenient & burdensome).

(3) Unduly expensive. The burden or expense of the proposed discovery outweighs its likely benefit, taking into account the needs of the case, the amount in controversy, the parties' resources, the importance of the issues at stake in the litigation, and the importance of the proposed discovery in resolving the issues. TRCP 192.4(b); *see also* TRCP 176.7 (subpoena).

2. Harassing. A person may ask for protection from a discovery request that is harassing. *See* TRCP 192.6. By signing discovery requests, lawyers certify the discovery is not sought for purposes of harassment. TRCP 191.3(c)(3); *see also* TRCP 199.5(h) (attorney cannot ask deposition questions solely to harass or mislead the witness), TRCP 215.3 (harassing discovery is grounds for sanctions).

3. Overbroad. A person may ask for protection from a discovery request that is overbroad. A request for all documents without limitation as to time, place, or subject matter is overbroad. ***Texaco, Inc. v. Sanderson***, 898 S.W.2d 813, 815 (Tex.1995); *see, e.g.*, ***In re CSX Corp.***, ___ S.W.3d ___ (Tex.2003) (No. 03-0381-CV; 10-3-03) (request to identify all safety employees of D over 30-year period was overbroad); ***In re American Optical***, 988 S.W.2d 711, 713 (Tex.1998) (request for all documents about all asbestos products for 50 years was overbroad); ***K-Mart Corp. v. Sanderson***, 937 S.W.2d 429, 431 (Tex.1996) (request for all information about criminal conduct at location for 7 years overbroad); ***Dillard Dept. Stores v. Hall***, 909 S.W.2d 491 (Tex.1995) (request for all similar claims from every store was overbroad); ***Loftin v. Martin***, 776 S.W.2d 145, 148 (Tex.1989) (request for all documents that supported allegations was overbroad & vague). When a request asks for "all documents," the party may object to the request and refuse to comply with it entirely, TRCP 193, cmt. 2; or, the party may file a motion for a protective order, TRCP 192.6(a). Generally, a request for "all documents" is merely a fishing expedition into the other party's files, which is prohibited. ***American Optical***, 988 S.W.2d at 713; ***Dillard***, 909 S.W.2d at 492; ***Loftin***, 776 S.W.2d at 148. A trial court cannot permit a party to search through the other party's records to make sure the other party produced all documents requested. ***Texaco, Inc. v. Dominguez***, 812 S.W.2d 451, 455-56 (Tex.App.—San Antonio 1991, orig. proceeding).

4. Invades protected rights. A person may ask for protection from a discovery request that is an invasion of personal, constitutional, or property rights. TRCP 192.6(b); ***Hoffman v. 5th Ct. of Appeals***, 756 S.W.2d 723, 723 (Tex.1988).

5. Temporary protection. A person may ask for temporary protection from discovery pending the resolution of threshold issues like venue, jurisdiction, forum non conveniens, and official immunity. ***Alford Chevrolet***, 997 S.W.2d at 181.

§19.2 Procedure for motion.

1. File timely. A motion for a protective order should be filed as soon as the person recognizes a protective order is necessary and before the deadline to produce the requested discovery. TRCP 192.6(a); *see* ***Bohmfalk v. Linwood***, 742 S.W.2d 518, 520 (Tex.App.—Dallas 1987, no writ) (party waived inadequate notice of deposition because party did not file motion for protective order to reschedule it). See "Timely objection," §17.1.1, p. 329.

2. Withhold information. The person must withhold the information subject to the motion for protection. In most cases, a party must partially comply with a written discovery request. See "Burden to partially comply," §17.9, p. 333.

3. Attach evidence. To support the motion, the person should attach affidavits, discovery pleadings, or other necessary documents. *See* TRCP 193.4(a), 199.6. See "Burden to provide evidence," §17.6, p. 331; "In camera inspection," §17.7, p. 332. The person "must show particular, specific and demonstrable injury by facts sufficient to justify a protective order." ***Masinga v. Whittington***, 792 S.W.2d 940, 940 (Tex.1990); ***In re Amaya***, 34 S.W.3d 354, 356-57 (Tex.App.—Waco 2001, orig. proceeding).

§19.3 Order. The general rule is that the person seeking discovery should secure a hearing and a ruling on an objection to discovery. There are exceptions. See "Burden to secure hearing & ruling," §17.5, p. 331. The trial court has broad discretion to protect a person with a protective order. *See* TRCP 192.6(b); ***Axelson, Inc. v. McIlhany***, 798 S.W.2d 550, 553 (Tex.1990). The court may protect the person by ordering any of the things listed in TRCP 192.6(b), but it is not limited by that list.

1. Limit scope of discovery. The protective order may provide that the requested discovery not be sought in whole or in part, or may limit the extent or subject matter of discovery. TRCP 192.6(b)(1), (2). For example, the trial court can strike certain subject areas from a notice of deposition if it determines they are not relevant. ***Lindsey v. O'Neill***, 689 S.W.2d 400, 403 (Tex.1985). The court can also redact privileged or sensitive information from documents to be produced. ***R.K. v. Ramirez***, 887 S.W.2d 836, 843 (Tex.1994); ***M.A.W. v. Hall***, 921 S.W.2d 911, 916 (Tex.App.—Houston [14th Dist.] 1996, orig. proceeding).

2. Specify procedure for discovery. The protective order may provide that the discovery not be undertaken at the time or place specified. TRCP 192.6(b)(3). The protective order may specify the terms, conditions, methods, and time and place of the discovery. TRCP 192.6(b)(4).

3. Seal or limit distribution of discovery. The protective order may seal or limit the distribution of discovery to the parties. TRCP 192.6(b)(5); *see* ***In re Temple-Inland***, 8 S.W.3d 459, 462-63 (Tex.App.—Beaumont 2000, orig. proceeding) (court should have included sealing & limiting distribution provisions in order protecting privacy rights of nonparties named in documents).

4. Limits of protective order.

(1) Sealing court records. A trial court cannot use a protective order to bypass the requirements of TRCP 76a. TRCP 192.6(b)(5). An order sealing or limiting the distribution of documents must be made on a showing of good cause and in accordance with the provisions of TRCP 76a. *See* TRCP 192.6(b)(5); ***Chandler v. Hyundai Motor Co.***, 829 S.W.2d 774, 774-75 (Tex.1992); *see also* ***Stroud v. VBFSB Holding***, 917 S.W.2d 75, 83 (Tex. App.—San Antonio 1996, writ denied) (stipulation and protective order did not constitute sealing order). The person requesting the order to seal or limit distribution has the burden of proving the elements of TRCP 76a. ***General Tire v. Kepple***, 970 S.W.2d 520, 523 (Tex.1998). See "Motion to Seal Court Records," ch. 5-K, p. 290.

(2) Shared discovery doctrine. A trial court cannot render a protective order so broad that it prevents sharing discovery products with other litigants in other lawsuits. ***Garcia v. Peeples***, 734 S.W.2d 343, 348-49 (Tex.1987). Under the doctrine of shared discovery, the products of discovery may be disseminated to other litigants and potential litigants. ***Eli Lilly & Co. v. Marshall***, 850 S.W.2d 155, 160 (Tex.1993).

§20. MOTION TO QUASH OR MODIFY SUBPOENA

See "Objecting to Trial & Discovery Subpoenas," ch. 1-K, §4, p. 61; "Challenging nonparty discovery subpoena," ch. 6-H, §5.5, p. 429; ***O'Connor's*** FORM 6A:10.

§21. MOTION TO COMPEL DISCOVERY

A party is entitled to secure discovery from another party without court intervention. When a party refuses to comply with proper discovery requests, the party seeking discovery may file a pretrial motion to secure an order compelling the other party to respond. TRCP 215.1(b). See ***O'Connor's*** FORM 6A:16.

§21.1 Grounds. A party may file a motion to compel discovery and request a hearing in the following instances:

1. Inadequate responses to request for disclosure. See "Objecting to Answers," ch. 6-O, §7, p. 382.

2. Refusal to appear or answer at deposition. See "Motion to compel answer," ch. 6-E, §9.4, p. 397.

3. **Inadequate answers to interrogatories.** See "Objecting to Answers," ch. 6-F, §8, p. 414.

4. **Inadequate responses to request for admissions.** See "Challenging Response," ch. 6-G, §5, p. 419.

5. **Inadequate responses to request for production.** See "Compelling Production & Sanctions," ch. 6-H, §6, p. 430.

6. **Refusal to follow agreed schedule.** When a party does not comply with a TRCP 11 agreement setting deadlines for discovery, the other party should file a motion to compel compliance. *See* ***Sullivan v. Bickel & Brewer***, 943 S.W.2d 477, 484 (Tex.App.—Dallas 1995, writ denied).

7. **After objection to discovery.** When a party serves objections or claims of privileges to a discovery request, or files a motion to quash or a motion for protective order, the party seeking discovery can either move for a hearing on the objections or file a motion to compel production, or both. TRCP 193.4(a), 215.1(b); ***McKinney v. National Un. Fire Ins. Co.***, 772 S.W.2d 72, 75 (Tex.1989); *see, e.g.*, ***Pace v. Jordan***, 999 S.W.2d 615, 622 (Tex. App.—Houston [1st Dist.] 1999, pet. denied) (Ps waived deposition because they did not get ruling on Ds' motion for protective order and did not file motion to compel).

PRACTICE TIP

The advantage of filing a motion to compel, instead of merely asking for a hearing on the other party's objections, is that in a motion to compel the movant can ask for expenses and attorney fees. See TRCP 215.1(d).

---

§21.2 Request for sanctions. The trial court can impose sanctions against a party for refusing to comply with proper discovery requests, regardless of whether the party has disobeyed an order compelling discovery. *See* TRCP 215.1(b). Thus, the party seeking discovery can include a motion for sanctions in its first motion to compel discovery. ***Lewis v. Illinois Employers Ins. Co.***, 590 S.W.2d 119, 120 (Tex.1979). A party may pursue sanctions instead of filing a motion to compel. ***Adkins Servs. Inc. v. Tisdale Co.***, 56 S.W.3d 842, 845 (Tex.App.—Texarkana 2001, no pet.).

§21.3 Request for expenses. After ruling on a motion to compel, the court may award attorney fees and other expenses to the party or person who prevails. TRCP 215.1(d). If the court grants the motion in part and denies it in part, the court may apportion the expenses. *Id.* If the court finds the conduct was substantially justified or finds other reasons that make the award of expenses unjust, the court is not required to award them. *Id.*

§21.4 Response to motion to compel. The party against whom the motion to compel was filed should always file a response. Under some local rules, the failure to file a response permits the trial court to conclude there is no opposition to the relief sought in the motion. ***Cummings v. Cire***, 74 S.W.3d 920, 924 (Tex.App.—Amarillo 2002, pet. granted 4-17-03); *see* Harris Cty. L.R. 3.3.2 (district courts).

§22. MOTION FOR DISCOVERY SANCTIONS

Sanctions for discovery abuse are imposed (1) to secure compliance with the rules of discovery, (2) to deter other litigants from violating the discovery rules, (3) to punish parties that violate the rules of discovery, and (4) to promote settlements. ***Schein v. American Rest. Group***, 852 S.W.2d 496, 497 (Tex.1993); ***Chrysler Corp. v. Blackmon***, 841 S.W.2d 844, 849 (Tex.1992). See "Motion for Sanctions," ch. 5-J, p. 275; ***O'Connor's*** FORM 6A:19.

§22.1 Standard for sanctions. See "Standards for Imposing Sanctions," ch. 5-J, §3, p. 275.

§22.2 Motion.

1. **Grounds.** See "Discovery abuse," ch. 5-J, §5.1, p. 277.

2. **Persons against whom discovery sanctions may be imposed.** See "Persons Who May Be Sanctioned," ch. 5-J, §4, p. 276.

3. Permissible discovery sanctions. See "Sanctions for discovery abuse," ch. 5-J, §7.1, p. 281.

4. Impermissible sanctions. See "Improper sanctions," ch. 5-J, §7.6, p. 283.

§22.3 Response. See *O'Connor's* FORM 6A:20.

§22.4 Order for sanctions. See "Order for discovery sanctions," ch. 5-J, §11.1, p. 287; ***O'Connor's*** FORM 6A:21.

§23. WAIVER OF SANCTIONS, DISCOVERY, & OBJECTIONS

§23.1 Waiver of sanctions. If a party does not obtain a pretrial ruling on known discovery misconduct that occurred before the trial, the party waives any claim for sanctions based on that misconduct. ***Remington Arms Co. v. Caldwell***, 850 S.W.2d 167, 170 (Tex.1993); *see* ***Kramer v. Lewisville Mem'l Hosp.***, 858 S.W.2d 397, 407 (Tex. 1993). However, if the misconduct involves failure to disclose information requested in discovery, the trial court can impose suitable trial sanctions, such as excluding the testimony of an undisclosed witness. *See* ***Remington***, 850 S.W.2d at 170-71.

§23.2 Waiver of discovery.

1. Discovery proponent. If a party seeking discovery does not ask for a hearing on the other party's objections, motion for protection, or its own motion to compel, it waives its right to the requested discovery. *See* ***Pace v. Jordan***, 999 S.W.2d 615, 622 (Tex.App.—Houston [1st Dist.] 1999, pet. denied) (party did not get ruling on other party's objections and did not file motion to compel).

2. Discovery opponent. A party resisting discovery is not required to request a ruling to preserve its own objections or assertions of privilege. TRCP 193.4(b). However, a party cannot use information it withheld from discovery under a claim of privilege at a hearing or trial without first amending or supplementing its responses to the discovery. TRCP 193.4(c). By contrast, if a party refuses to respond to discovery pending the resolution of its objections to a request for discovery, nothing prohibits it from relying on the withheld discovery.

§23.3 Waiver of objections & privileges.

1. Failure to comply with procedures. If a party does not comply with the procedures for resisting discovery, the party waives its objections to the discovery, and the trial court should compel production. TRCP 193.2(e); *see, e.g.*, ***Hobson v. Moore***, 734 S.W.2d 340, 341 (Tex.1987) (police officer waived law enforcement privilege because he filed late objections to interrogatories); ***Villarreal v. Dominguez***, 745 S.W.2d 570, 572 (Tex.App.—Corpus Christi 1988, orig. proceeding) (city waived its privileges from discovery by not objecting); ***Dunn Equip. v. Gayle***, 725 S.W.2d 372, 374-75 (Tex.App.—Houston [14th Dist.] 1987, orig. proceeding) (party objecting to discovery of its insurance company's file waived privilege because it did not prove elements of privilege). However, a party does not waive a privilege if it mistakenly objects to a request for privileged information instead of complying with TRCP 193.3. See "Asserting privileges," §17.2, p. 329.

2. Failure to object to inadequate responses. If a party does not object before trial to the other party's responses to discovery that it knows are inadequate, it waives the objection. ***Interceramic, Inc. v. South Orient R.R.***, 999 S.W.2d 920, 930 (Tex.App.—Texarkana 1999, pet. denied) (inadequate supplemental responses to discovery).

3. Failure to respond to motion to compel. Under some local rules, if a party does not file a response to the motion to compel, the trial court can conclude the party does not oppose the relief sought in the motion. See §21.4, above.

4. Sanctions. If a party abuses discovery, the court may find that the party waived its discovery privileges and objections. ***Occidental Chem. v. Banales***, 907 S.W.2d 488, 490 (Tex.1995); *e.g.*, ***In re Lavernia Nursing Facility***, 12 S.W.3d 566, 571 (Tex.App.—San Antonio 1999, orig. proceeding) (court found D concealed records).

5. No ruling. If the party seeking discovery does not secure a ruling on the objections or assertions of privilege, the party waives the discovery. *See* TRCP 193.4(b), 199.6. The party resisting discovery does not waive its objections if they are not resolved before trial. TRCP 199.6.

6. Obscured objections. If a party obscures valid objections with unfounded objections, the party waives its valid objections unless it can show good cause. TRCP 193.2(e).

7. Deliberate disclosure. If a party makes a voluntary and deliberate disclosure of "any significant part" of the privileged matter, it waives the privilege. TRE 511(1); *see, e.g.*, ***In re Cooper***, 47 S.W.3d 206, 209 (Tex. App.—Beaumont 2001, orig. proceeding) (D's assignment of Stowers claim to P did not waive attorney-client privilege); ***In re Monsanto Co.***, 998 S.W.2d 917, 925-26 (Tex.App.—Waco 1999, orig. proceeding) (oral description of documents did not waive privilege).

(1) Inadvertent disclosure. An inadvertent production of privileged information or material is considered involuntary and does not waive a claim of privilege under the TRCPs or TREs if, within ten days of discovering the inadvertent disclosure, the producing party amends its response, identifies the material produced, identifies the privilege asserted, and requests the return of the material. TRCP 193.3(d); TRE 512. The issue is whether the producing party intended to waive the particular privilege, not whether it intended to produce the information. TRCP 193.3(d) & cmt. 4. See "Use snap-back provision," §17.2.4, p. 330.

(2) In camera inspection. Tendering the documents for an in camera inspection does not waive a privilege. ***M.A.W. v. Hall***, 921 S.W.2d 911, 915-16 (Tex.App.—Houston [14th Dist.] 1996, orig. proceeding); ***Johnson v. Casseb***, 722 S.W.2d 253, 256 (Tex.App.—San Antonio 1986, orig. proceeding).

8. Use of document to refresh recollection. If a party uses documents to refresh the memory of a witness, under certain circumstances the documents are discoverable.

(1) If the witness uses a document while testifying, the adverse party has a right to see it. TRE 612(1); *see* ***Goode v. Shoukfeh***, 943 S.W.2d 441, 449 (Tex.1997); ***City of Denison v. Grisham***, 716 S.W.2d 121, 123 (Tex.App.—Dallas 1986, orig. proceeding). See Cochran, ***Texas Rules of Evidence Handbook***, p. 630 (5th ed. 2003) (Cochran, ***Evidence Handbook***).

(2) If the witness uses a document before testifying, the trial court has discretion to require that the document be produced. TRE 612(2); ***Goode***, 943 S.W.2d at 449; ***Portland S&L Ass'n v. Bernstein***, 716 S.W.2d 532, 541 (Tex.App.—Corpus Christi 1985, writ ref'd n.r.e.), *overruled on other grounds*, ***Dawson-Austin v. Austin***, 968 S.W.2d 319 (Tex.1998). The waiver applies to those parts of the document that relate to the witness's testimony. TRE 612. See Cochran, ***Evidence Handbook***, p. 630.

9. Waiver by offensive use. Under the doctrine of waiver by offensive use, a party cannot "use one hand to seek affirmative relief and with the other lower an iron curtain of silence" around the facts of the case. *E.g.*, ***Ginsberg v. 5th Ct. of Appeals***, 686 S.W.2d 105, 108 (Tex.1985) (P could not claim psychotherapist privilege to exclude information that would assist D). The Supreme Court set out the test for the application of the offensive-use doctrine in ***Republic Ins. Co. v. Davis***, 856 S.W.2d 158, 163 (Tex.1993) (attorney-client privilege), and restated it in ***Texas DPS Officers Ass'n v. Denton***, 897 S.W.2d 757, 761 (Tex.1995) (5th Amendment privilege). Before a party waives a privilege by offensive use, the court must determine that (1) the party is seeking affirmative relief, (2) the evidence the party refuses to produce is outcome-determinative, and (3) there is no alternative source for the evidence. ***Denton***, 897 S.W.2d at 761 (party seeking evidence met all three elements); ***Trans-American Nat. Gas v. Flores***, 870 S.W.2d 10, 11-12 (Tex.1994) (party seeking evidence met only first element); ***Republic Ins.***, 856 S.W.2d at 164 (party seeking evidence did not meet first element because declaratory judgment action is not request for affirmative relief). If the party seeking evidence proves all three elements, the court must take some remedial action. As a remedy, the court may limit the discovery inquiry, restrict the evidence the party asserting the privilege introduces on the subject, delay the trial (when 5th Amendment privilege is asserted), and ultimately, if the party asserting the privilege is the plaintiff, dismiss the suit. ***Denton***, 897 S.W.2d at 763. The trial court must consider a number of factors before forcing the party resisting discovery to elect between its privilege and the lawsuit. *Id.* For a list of factors affecting the choice of remedies, see ***Denton***, 897 S.W.2d at 763.

10. Failure to timely respond.

(1) Waiver. When a party does not timely respond to a discovery request, the party waives its objections to the request and must produce the discovery. *See* TRCP 193.1, 193.2(e).

(2) Exceptions. There are four exceptions to the rule of mandatory waiver for not timely responding to a discovery request.

(a) The parties agree to an extension, and the agreement meets the requirements of TRCP 11. TRCP 191.1; ***Remington Arms Co. v. Canales***, 837 S.W.2d 624, 625 (Tex.1992); ***Young v. Ray***, 916 S.W.2d 1, 3 (Tex. App.—Houston [1st Dist.] 1995, orig. proceeding).

(b) The parties agree to an extension that affects an oral deposition, and the agreement is made part of the record of the deposition. TRCP 191.1.

(c) The trial court signs an order extending the time to respond to discovery. TRCP 191.1; ***Remington Arms***, 837 S.W.2d at 625; ***Young***, 916 S.W.2d at 3.

(d) The party proves good cause for not timely objecting. TRCP 193.2(e); ***Remington Arms***, 837 S.W.2d at 625; ***Young***, 916 S.W.2d at 3.

§24. REVIEW OF DISCOVERY ORDERS

For the rules and forms for prosecuting or responding to an appeal or original proceeding, see ***O'Connor's Texas Civil Appeals*** (2002-03).

§24.1 Review by appeal. In most cases, discovery orders should be reviewed on appeal after final judgment. ***Walker v. Packer***, 827 S.W.2d 833, 842 (Tex.1992); *see* ***Vega v. Davila***, 31 S.W.3d 376, 378 (Tex.App.—Corpus Christi 2000, no pet.) (court had jurisdiction to hear appeal from order overruling motion to quash subpoena for deposition). The standard for review of a discovery order is abuse of discretion. ***TransAmerican Nat. Gas v. Powell***, 811 S.W.2d 913, 917 (Tex.1991). A trial court abuses its discretion when it reaches a result that is so arbitrary and unreasonable as to amount to a clear and prejudicial error of law. ***Johnson v. 4th Ct. of Appeals***, 700 S.W.2d 916, 917 (Tex.1985).

§24.2 Review by mandamus. Most orders relating to discovery disputes cannot be reviewed by mandamus. The appellate courts will grant a petition for writ of mandamus only if the following conditions are met:

1. The relator has a clear right to the relief requested and clearly demands that right.

2. The trial court had a clear legal duty to perform the act the relator seeks to compel. That is, (a) the trial court refused to perform a ministerial act that the court is required to perform, or (b) the trial court clearly abused its discretion in making a discretionary ruling. ***Johnson***, 700 S.W.2d at 917. The party must show the trial court's decision on discovery was "so arbitrary and unreasonable as to amount to a clear and prejudicial error of law." *Id.* That is, the party must show the appellate court that the trial court acted without reference to any guiding rules and principles.

3. The trial court clearly refused to grant the relief requested. The party must prove it asked the court to rule, and the court either ruled adversely or refused to rule. In most cases, the party must file a copy of the court's order with exhibits attached to the petition for writ.

4. There is no other adequate legal remedy available to rectify the improper action or inaction. ***Montalvo v. 4th Ct. of Appeals***, 917 S.W.2d 1, 2 (Tex.1995); ***Walker***, 827 S.W.2d at 842; *see* ***In re Continental Gen. Tire***, 979 S.W.2d 609, 615 (Tex.1998); *see also* ***In re Bay Area Citizens Against Lawsuit Abuse***, 982 S.W.2d 371,

375 (Tex.1998) (no adequate remedy by appeal because discovery order violated 1st Amendment rights); ***Pope v. Stephenson***, 787 S.W.2d 953, 954 (Tex.1990) (mandamus is not necessarily a "timely" remedy for wrongful denial of discovery). In ***Walker***, the Court identified three discovery situations where a party does not have an adequate appellate remedy for an erroneous ruling by the trial court. ***Walker***, 827 S.W.2d at 843-44.

(1) When the appellate court cannot cure the trial court's discovery error. ***Walker***, 827 S.W.2d at 843. This happens when the trial court erroneously orders the disclosure of privileged information that will materially affect the rights of the aggrieved party, such as attorney-client privileged information. *Id.*; *see also* ***In re Perry***, 60 S.W.3d 857, 858 (Tex.2001) (mandamus appropriate to prevent disclosure of information protected by legislative immunity).

(2) When the party's ability to present a viable claim or defense at trial is severely compromised by the trial court's discovery error. ***Montalvo***, 917 S.W.2d at 2; ***Walker***, 827 S.W.2d at 843; ***J.G. v. Murray***, 915 S.W.2d 548, 549 (Tex.App.—Corpus Christi 1995, orig. proceeding). The party seeking mandamus must show harm to prove lack of adequate remedy by appeal. ***Montalvo***, 917 S.W.2d at 2. The delay, inconvenience, or expense of an appeal is not sufficient harm. ***Walker***, 827 S.W.2d at 843. Denial of discovery that goes to the heart of the party's case may be sufficient harm. *Id.*; *see, e.g.*, ***Revco, D.S., Inc. v. Cooper***, 873 S.W.2d 391, 395 (Tex.App.—El Paso 1994, orig. proceeding) (mandamus available when court struck experts who were designated late); ***Peters v. Moore***, 835 S.W.2d 764, 767 (Tex.App.—Houston [14th Dist.] 1992, orig. proceeding) (mandamus available when court refused to permit experts to testify).

(3) When the trial court disallows discovery, the missing discovery cannot be made part of the appellate record, and the reviewing court is unable to evaluate the effect of the trial court's error. ***Walker***, 827 S.W.2d at 843-44. If the procedures of TRCP 193.4 are followed, this situation should seldom arise. *Id.* (former TRCP 166b(4)).

§24.3 Record. If evidence was received at the hearing on discovery, the party challenging the trial court's order must provide the appellate court with a reporter's record from the hearing. *See* TRAP 34.6, 52.7(a)(2). For the record in an appeal, see ***O'Connor's Texas Civil Appeals***, "The Record on Appeal," ch. 16, p. 171; for the record in a mandamus proceeding, see ***O'Connor's Texas Civil Appeals***, "Record for the Petition," ch. 20-A, §6, p. 277. A reporter's record is not necessary if the trial court clearly based its order on the papers on file and the arguments of counsel. ***Otis Elevator Co. v. Parmelee***, 850 S.W.2d 179, 181 (Tex.1993). When a reporter's record is not necessary, the petitioner may file an affidavit with the petition, attesting that no evidence was heard. See ***O'Connor's Texas Civil Appeals***, "Hearing," ch. 20-A, §6.1.2(2), p. 278.

§24.4 Findings of fact. Findings of fact are helpful but not required when challenging the trial court's findings on discovery sanctions. See "Findings of fact are helpful," ch. 10-E, §2.3, p. 643.

B. SCOPE OF DISCOVERY

§1. GENERAL

§1.1 Rule. TRCP 192.3.

§1.2 Purpose. The scope of discovery controls what information can and cannot be discovered. This subchapter deals with what is discoverable (see §2, below) and what is not discoverable (see §3, p. 352).

§1.3 Forms. ***O'Connor's Texas Civil Forms***, FORMS 6B.

§1.4 Other references. Griesel, *The "New" Texas Discovery Rules: Three Years Later*, Advanced Evidence & Discovery Course, State Bar of Texas, ch. 2, §VII, p. 7 (2002); Cochran, ***Texas Rules of Evidence Handbook*** (5th ed. 2003) (Cochran, ***Evidence Handbook***).

§2. WHAT IS DISCOVERABLE?

TRCP 192.3 is the principal rule that identifies things that are discoverable.

§2.1 General rule. Discovery is permitted of any unprivileged information relevant to the subject of the lawsuit, including inadmissible evidence, so long as the request is reasonably calculated to lead to the discovery of admissible evidence. TRCP 192.3(a); ***In re CSX Corp.***, ___ S.W.3d ___ (Tex.2003) (No. 03-0381-CV; 10-3-03); ***In re American Optical***, 988 S.W.2d 711, 713 (Tex.1998); ***Eli Lilly & Co. v. Marshall***, 850 S.W.2d 155, 160 (Tex.1993); *see* TRE 501. While the scope of discovery is quite broad, it is confined by the subject matter of the case and the reasonable expectations of obtaining information that will aid resolution of the dispute. TRCP 192, cmt. 1; ***CSX Corp.***, ___ S.W.3d at ___; *see* ***American Optical***, 988 S.W.2d at 713 (court must impose reasonable discovery limits); ***K-Mart Corp. v. Sanderson***, 937 S.W.2d 429, 431 (Tex.1996) (discovery cannot be used to "fish" for evidence). There are five principal questions relating to the scope of discovery:

1. *Is the information relevant, as defined in TRE 401, to the suit?* Discovery is limited to matters relevant to the case. TRCP 192.3(a); ***Texaco, Inc. v. Sanderson***, 898 S.W.2d 813, 814 (Tex.1995). Information is relevant if it tends to make the existence of a fact that is of consequence to the determination of the action more or less probable than it would be without the information. TRE 401; ***R.K. v. Ramirez***, 887 S.W.2d 836, 842 (Tex.1994).

2. *Will the information lead to the discovery of admissible evidence?* A party cannot object to discovery on the ground that the information sought is not admissible at trial. TRCP 192.3(a); ***Axelson, Inc. v. McIlhany***, 798 S.W.2d 550, 553 (Tex.1990). If the information will lead to the discovery of admissible evidence, it is discoverable.

3. *Is there an exemption from discovery that precludes the discovery of the information?* If so, the information is not discoverable. See "What Is Not Discoverable?," §3, p. 352.

4. *Do the discovery rules permit the type of discovery procedure necessary to secure the information?* If no discovery rule permits the type of discovery procedure involved, the information is not discoverable unless the court orders or the parties agree to the discovery procedure. TRCP 191, cmt. 1 (trial court may order or parties may agree to use discovery methods other than those prescribed in the rules). See "General Rules for Discovery," ch. 6-A, p. 313.

5. *Should the court limit discovery because it is cumulative, too expensive, or too burdensome?* The court's power to limit discovery based on the needs and circumstances of the case is expressly stated in TRCP 192.4. TRCP 192, cmt. 7. Courts should limit discovery under this rule only to prevent unwarranted delay and expense as stated in the rule. *Id.* See "Grounds to limit scope of discovery," ch. 6-A, §19.1, p. 334.

§2.2 Potential parties. The names, addresses, and telephone numbers of potential parties to the suit are discoverable. TRCP 192.3(i) (scope of discovery), TRCP 192.5(c)(3) (exception to work product), TRCP 194.2(b) (request for disclosure); ***Helfand v. Coane***, 12 S.W.3d 152, 157 n.3 (Tex.App.—Houston [1st Dist.] 2000, pet. denied).

§2.3 Party contentions. An opinion or contention relating to a fact or the application of the law to a fact is discoverable. TRCP 192.3(j), 194.2(c), 197.1. A party may request by disclosure or interrogatory the opinion or contention of the other party. See "Contentions," ch. 6-D, §3.2.1(3), p. 377; "Party contentions," ch. 6-F, §3.2.5, p. 410.

§2.4 Party admissions. A party's statement of opinion, of fact, or of the application of law to fact, or the genuineness of a document that is described in the request (and attached or made available for inspection and copying), is discoverable through a request for admissions. TRCP 198.1. See "Requests for Admissions," ch. 6-G, p. 416.

§2.5 Party statements. Some party statements are discoverable. TRCP 192.3(h). These statements, even if made or prepared in anticipation of litigation, are not protected by the work-product privilege. TRCP 192.5(c)(1).

1. **Party as witness.** A party's statement as a witness is discoverable. See §2.6, below.

2. Party statements from another suit. A party's statements contained in non-core work product in one suit may be discoverable in another suit. ***Republic Ins. Co. v. Davis***, 856 S.W.2d 158, 164-65 (Tex.1993). To be privileged, work product must be made in the same suit. *Id.*; *see* TRCP 192.5(a)(2) (communication made in anticipation of litigation or trial).

§2.6 Witness statements. A witness statement is (1) a written statement signed, adopted, or approved in writing by the person making it, or (2) a stenographic, mechanical, electrical, or other type of recording of a witness's oral statement, or any substantially verbatim transcription of such a recording. TRCP 192.3(h). Notes taken by another person during a conversation or interview with a witness are not considered a witness statement. *Id.*

1. Discoverable. Witness statements, even when made or prepared in anticipation of litigation, are not protected from discovery by the work-product privilege. TRCP 192.5(c)(1); *see* ***Spohn Hosp. v. Mayer***, 72 S.W.3d 52, 62 (Tex.App.—Corpus Christi 2001), *rev'd on other grounds*, 104 S.W.3d 878 (Tex.2003); ***In re Team Transp.***, 996 S.W.2d 256, 259 (Tex.App.—Houston [14th Dist.] 1999, orig. proceeding). For example, a letter to a party's insurance carrier describing an accident, prepared by an employee who witnessed the accident, is discoverable. ***Team Transport***, 996 S.W.2d at 259; *see also* ***In re Learjet Inc.***, 59 S.W.3d 842, 846 (Tex.App.—Texarkana 2001, orig. proceeding) (edited & unedited versions of videotaped witness statements, which were used in mediation, were discoverable).

Most insurance companies call witnesses immediately after an accident and record their statements over the telephone. Those statements are discoverable. *See* ***In re Jimenez***, 4 S.W.3d 894, 896 (Tex.App.—Houston [1st Dist.] 1999, orig. proceeding) (D's statement to carrier was discoverable); ***In re W&G Trucking***, 990 S.W.2d 473, 475 (Tex. App.—Beaumont 1999, orig. proceeding) (same); *see also* ***In re Ford Motor Co.***, 988 S.W.2d 714, 719 (Tex.1998) (in case predating 1999 discovery rules, P's statement to carrier was not protected from discovery because no attorney-client relationship between them). An insurance company cannot avoid producing those statements by hiring a lawyer to conduct post-accident interviews. The work-product privilege does not permit an attorney to hide facts from discovery that were acquired by the attorney. ***Owens-Corning Fiberglas v. Caldwell***, 818 S.W.2d 749, 750 n.2 (Tex. 1991); *see also* ***In re Texas Farmers Ins. Exch.***, 990 S.W.2d 337, 340 (Tex.App.—Texarkana 1999, orig. proceeding) (carrier required to produce report of attorney hired to investigate claim). The purpose of work product is to shelter the mental processes of the attorney, not the facts about the case. ***Caldwell***, 818 S.W.2d at 750.

PRACTICE TIP

When a lawyer sends an investigator to talk to a witness, the lawyer should instruct the investigator not to take a statement (recorded or signed) if the information is not favorable. When the information is not favorable, the investigator can simply prepare a memo stating the substance of the interview. That memo is not discoverable as a witness statement. TRCP 192.3(h).

---

2. Not discoverable. Witness statements are protected from discovery if they are shielded by some other objection or privilege (*e.g.*, the attorney-client privilege). *See* TRCP 192, cmt. 9; ***In re Fontenot***, 13 S.W.3d 111, 113 (Tex.App.—Fort Worth 2000, orig. proceeding). For example, a party's statement provided to its attorney is not discoverable because it is protected under TRE 503. *See, e.g.*, ***Fontenot***, 13 S.W.3d at 114 (written narrative by P sent to his attorney in another suit & P's confidential claim questionnaire with same narrative sent to his attorney & carrier after receipt of presuit notice were not discoverable).

§2.7 Person's own statements. If a person (party or witness) made a statement about the subject matter of the litigation, that person is entitled to receive a copy from any party who has possession of it. TRCP 192.3(h). The person must make a written request for a copy of the statement. *Id.* See ***O'Connor's*** FORM 6B:05.

§2.8 Fact witnesses. A party may obtain discovery of persons having knowledge of relevant facts. TRCP 192.3(c); *see* ***Smith v. Southwest Feed Yards***, 835 S.W.2d 89, 90 (Tex.1992). The purpose for requiring the disclosure of the names, addresses, and telephone numbers is to allow the opposing party to locate, interview, and depose the witnesses. ***$23,900 v. State***, 899 S.W.2d 314, 316-17 (Tex.App.—Houston [14th Dist.] 1995, no writ). The plain language of TRCP 192.3(c) and 192.5(c)(3) clearly indicates that information about the identity and location of persons with knowledge of relevant facts can never be protected from discovery. *See* ***Giffin v. Smith***, 688 S.W.2d 112, 113 (Tex.1985) (predecessor rules).

1. Who is a fact witness. A person has knowledge of relevant facts when that person has or may have knowledge of discoverable matters. TRCP 192.3(c); ***Jamail v. Anchor Mortg. Servs.***, 809 S.W.2d 221, 223 (Tex. 1991). The person need not have admissible information. TRCP 192.3(c); *see* ***Team Transport***, 996 S.W.2d at 259. Personal knowledge is not required. TRCP 192.3(c); ***Team Transport***, 996 S.W.2d at 259.

2. What is discoverable about fact witnesses. Information about fact witnesses is discoverable. TRCP 192.3(c) (scope of discovery), TRCP 192.5(c)(1) (exception to work product), TRCP 194.2(e) (request for disclosure).

(1) Identity. A party is entitled to the names, addresses, and telephone numbers of persons having knowledge of relevant facts. TRCP 192.3(c), 194.2(e); *see* ***$23,900 v. State***, 899 S.W.2d 314, 316-17 (Tex.App.—Houston [14th Dist.] 1995, no writ) (address of police headquarters was sufficient for officer, even though interrogatory also asked for residential address). See "Identify witness," ch. 6-D, §4.2.5(1), p. 380.

(2) Connection with case. A party is entitled to a brief description of the person's connection with the suit. TRCP 192.3(c), 194.2(e). See "Identify connections with case," ch. 6-D, §4.2.5(2), p. 380.

(3) Witness statements. A party is entitled to any witness statements made by fact witnesses. TRCP 192.3(h). See §2.6, above.

(4) Matters not privileged. A party is entitled to any information in the possession of the witness that is not privileged and is relevant to the subject matter of the pending action, whether it relates to the claim or defense of the party seeking discovery or to the claim or defense of any other party. TRCP 192.3(a).

§2.9 Trial witnesses. The discovery rules permit a party to obtain discovery of the name, address, and telephone number of any person who is expected to be called to testify at trial. TRCP 192.3(d), 192.5(c)(1) (exception to work product). A party is not entitled to secure information about rebuttal or impeaching witnesses, unless the necessity of the testimony can reasonably be anticipated before trial. TRCP 192.3(d). Because TRCP 194 does not mention trial witnesses, information about trial witnesses cannot be discovered through a request for disclosure. Therefore, parties should seek this information through interrogatories. See "Trial witnesses," ch. 6-F, §3.2.3, p. 409.

PRACTICE TIP

In interrogatories, a party should always ask for (1) trial witnesses and (2) rebuttal and impeachment witnesses whose testimony can reasonably be anticipated before trial. See TRCP 192.3(d).

---

§2.10 Experts. See "Types of Information Discoverable from Experts," ch. 6-C, §4, p. 367.

§2.11 Documents & tangible things. A party can discover the existence, description, nature, custody, condition, location, and contents of documents and tangible things that constitute or contain relevant information and are in the possession, custody, or control of the other party. TRCP 192.3(b); *see* TRCP 196 (request for production). See "Documents & tangible things," ch. 6-A, §2.2, p. 313; "Possession," ch. 6-A, §2.3, p. 313. To be discoverable, the document or thing must exist. ***Smith v. O'Neal***, 850 S.W.2d 797, 799 (Tex.App.—Houston [14th Dist.] 1993, no writ). A request for production does not require a party to create a document to satisfy the request. *Id.* See "Securing Documents & Tangible Things," ch. 6-H, p. 423. The following types of documents are discoverable.

1. Income tax returns. Income tax returns are discoverable if relevant and material. ***Hall v. Lawlis***, 907 S.W.2d 493, 494-95 (Tex.1995). If the tax return duplicates other evidence, the trial court may refuse to require its production. *E.g.*, ***Sears, Roebuck & Co. v. Ramirez***, 824 S.W.2d 558, 559 (Tex.1992) (Sears had already produced audited, certified annual report).

2. Financial statements. The defendant's net worth is discoverable when a plaintiff sues for exemplary damages. ***Lunsford v. Morris***, 746 S.W.2d 471, 473 (Tex.1988) (P not required to make a prima facie case). If the pleadings do not request exemplary damages, the defendant's net worth is outside the scope of discovery. ***Al Parker Buick Co. v. Touchy***, 788 S.W.2d 129, 131 (Tex.App.—Houston [1st Dist.] 1990, orig. proceeding).

3. Photographs. "Photographs" are defined in the TREs to include still photographs, X-ray films, videotapes, and motion pictures. TRE 1001(b). *But see* ***County of Dallas v. Harrison***, 759 S.W.2d 530, 531 (Tex. App.—Dallas 1988, no writ) (request for production of all "photographs" did not require production of videotapes). Photographs and other electronic images are discoverable. TRCP 192.3(b). Photographs are not "communications" that are exempt from discovery under TRCP 192.5(a) (work product). TRCP 192.5(c)(4); ***Terry v. Lawrence***, 700 S.W.2d 912, 913 (Tex.1985). See "Photographs," §2.13.3(4), p. 347.

4. Insurance & indemnity agreements. Generally, insurance policies and indemnity agreements are discoverable. TRCP 192.3(f). By permitting the discovery of insurance and indemnity agreements, the plaintiff can determine the settlement value of the case. ***Carroll Cable Co. v. Miller***, 501 S.W.2d 299, 299 (Tex.1973). The discovery of an insurance policy or an indemnity agreement does not make it admissible. TRCP 192.3(f). TRCP 192.3(f) does not preclude other discovery on insurance issues. ***In re Senior Living Props.***, 63 S.W.3d 594, 597 (Tex.App.—Tyler 2002, orig. proceeding).

5. Settlement agreements. The existence and contents of relevant portions of a settlement agreement are discoverable. TRCP 192.3(g). A settlement agreement made in another dispute may be discoverable if it is relevant to the pending litigation. TRCP 192.3(g) & cmt. 4; ***Ford Motor Co. v. Leggat***, 904 S.W.2d 643, 649 (Tex. 1995); ***In re Frank A. Smith Sales***, 32 S.W.3d 871, 874 (Tex.App.—Corpus Christi 2000, orig. proceeding). In most cases, the settlement amounts are not relevant. *See, e.g.*, ***Leggat***, 904 S.W.2d at 649 (settlement amounts not relevant to determine D's net worth or motives); ***Palo Duro Pipeline Co. v. Cochran***, 785 S.W.2d 455, 457 (Tex.App.—Houston [14th Dist.] 1990, orig. proceeding) (settlement amounts not relevant to issue of conspiracy). *But see* ***Collier Servs. v. Salinas***, 812 S.W.2d 372, 377 (Tex.App.—Corpus Christi 1991, orig. proceeding) (D's receipt of funds in settlement of unrelated suit was relevant to creditor's search for assets). The discovery of a settlement agreement does not make it admissible to prove liability. TRCP 192.3(g); TRE 408; ***Leggat***, 904 S.W.2d at 649; ***McGuire v. Commercial Un. Ins. Co.***, 431 S.W.2d 347, 352 (Tex.1968). Settlement negotiations, as opposed to settlement agreements, are not discoverable. *See* TRCP 192.3(g).

6. Claim files.

(1) Claim file in same suit. The claim file of a party's insurance company is generally discoverable in the same suit. *See, e.g.*, ***In re Ford Motor Co.***, 988 S.W.2d 714, 719 (Tex.1998) (D entitled to claim file from P's carrier); ***Dunn Equip. v. Gayle***, 725 S.W.2d 372, 374-75 (Tex.App.—Houston [14th Dist.] 1987, orig. proceeding) (P entitled to claim file from D's carrier). However, if the claim file is exempt from discovery under one cause of action (*e.g.*, contract), the party cannot get it for another cause in the same suit (*e.g.*, bad faith). ***Maryland Am. Gen. Ins. Co. v. Blackmon***, 639 S.W.2d 455, 457-58 (Tex.1982).

(2) Claim file in separate suit. The claim file of an insurance company is sometimes discoverable in another suit. *Compare* ***Turbodyne Corp. v. Heard***, 720 S.W.2d 802, 804 (Tex.1986) (documents from claim file in main suit were discoverable in subrogation action), ***Lewis v. Wittig***, 877 S.W.2d 52, 58 (Tex.App.—Houston

[14th Dist.] 1994, orig. proceeding) (claim files of client companies were discoverable in suit against lawyers for malpractice), *and* ***Eddington v. Touchy***, 793 S.W.2d 335, 337 (Tex.App.—Houston [1st Dist.] 1990, orig. proceeding) (documents from claim file were discoverable by lawyer who sued insurance company for settling with lawyer's client without lawyer's permission), *with* ***Humphreys v. Caldwell***, 888 S.W.2d 469, 471 (Tex.1994) (after first suit, D in that suit sued P's carrier; claim file in first suit was not discoverable).

7. Investigative reports. Investigative reports are discoverable when not prepared in anticipation of litigation. *See, e.g.,* ***Axelson, Inc. v. McIlhany***, 798 S.W.2d 550, 552-53 (Tex.1990) (internal kickback investigation, unrelated to the matter that gave rise to litigation, was discoverable); ***In re Weeks Mar., Inc.***, 31 S.W.3d 389, 391 (Tex.App.—San Antonio 2000, orig. proceeding) (D's investigative report made after P hired lawyer was not discoverable). See "Work-product privilege," §3.3, p. 352.

8. Computer data. If discoverable information is contained in a party's computer databases or files, it is discoverable upon a specific request. *See* TRCP 192.3(b) (any data compilations), TRCP 196.4 (electronic or magnetic data). Computer data can be requested in hard copy (printed version) or in computer files. TRCP 196.4.

9. Personnel files. When relevant, a party may discover the documents in the personnel file of a party or witness. *See* ***In re Lavernia Nursing Facility***, 12 S.W.3d 566, 570 (Tex.App.—San Antonio 1999, orig. proceeding). A personnel file includes all matters about the employee, even if filed separately under a different name. *Id.* (personnel file included disciplinary actions filed separately).

10. Ongoing studies. Status reports of ongoing clinical studies and the identities of clinical research organizations are discoverable. ***In re American Home Prods.***, 980 S.W.2d 506, 510 (Tex.App.—Waco 1998, orig. proceeding).

§2.12 Entry on land. A party has a right of entry on land when it is relevant to the lawsuit. The purpose of the entry must be to inspect, measure, survey, photograph, conduct nondestructive tests, or sample the land or a designated object or operation on the land. TRCP 196.7(a). See "Entry on Land," ch. 6-J, p. 438.

§2.13 Discoverable work product. For definition of work product see "Work product," ch. 6-A, §2.7, p. 314. Most work product is not discoverable. See "Work-product privilege," §3.3, p. 352. However, some work product is discoverable.

1. Facts. The facts about the case are discoverable. The work-product privilege does not permit the attorney to hide facts from discovery that were acquired by the attorney and are relevant and not exempt from discovery by some other privilege. ***Owens-Corning Fiberglas v. Caldwell***, 818 S.W.2d 749, 750 n.2 (Tex.1991); *see,* ***In re Ford Motor Co.***, 988 S.W.2d 714, 719 (Tex.1998); *see also* ***Hickman v. Taylor***, 329 U.S. 495, 511, 67 S.Ct. 385, 394 (1947) (relevant & nonexempt information in a lawyer's file may be discovered); ***Leede Oil & Gas v. McCorkle***, 789 S.W.2d 686, 687 (Tex.App.—Houston [1st Dist.] 1990, orig. proceeding) (neutral facts about case in lawyer's file were discoverable because lawyer obtained information from fact witness who died after interview). A lawyer cannot classify a document as work product by simply including it in a litigation file. ***National Un. Fire Ins. Co. v. Valdez***, 863 S.W.2d 458, 460 (Tex.1993); ***Lewis v. Wittig***, 877 S.W.2d 52, 57-58 (Tex.App.—Houston [14th Dist.] 1994, orig. proceeding).

2. Need & hardship exception. A party may secure non-core work product under the need and hardship exception in TRCP 192.5(b)(2). ***In re Monsanto Co.***, 998 S.W.2d 917, 930 (Tex.App.—Waco 1999, orig. proceeding). If the court permits discovery of non-core work product under this exception, it must prevent the disclosure of mental impressions, opinions, conclusions, or legal theories, which are not discoverable. TRCP 192.5(b)(4). To meet the need and hardship exception, the party seeking discovery must show the following:

(1) Non-core work product. The information is not core work product. *See* TRCP 192.5(b)(1); ***In re Team Transp.***, 996 S.W.2d 256, 259 (Tex.App.—Houston [14th Dist.] 1999, orig. proceeding) (need & hardship exception applies only to "other work product"). For a definition, see "Non-core work product," ch. 6-A, §2.7.2, p. 314.

(2) Substantial need. The party has a substantial need for the information in the preparation of its case. TRCP 192.5(b)(2); ***Flores v. 4th Ct. of Appeals***, 777 S.W.2d 38, 42 (Tex.1989), *modified on other grounds*, ***National Tank Co. v. Brotherton***, 851 S.W.2d 193 (Tex.1993); *see, e.g.*, ***State v. Lowry***, 802 S.W.2d 669, 673 (Tex. 1991) (Ds had substantial need because State collected information during investigation that led to lawsuit & could provide evidence for defense); ***Dillard Dept. Stores v. Sanderson***, 928 S.W.2d 319, 321-22 (Tex.App.—Beaumont 1996, orig. proceeding) (issues of witness credibility & failing memory of witness were sufficient to show substantial need); ***Leede Oil & Gas***, 789 S.W.2d at 687 (neutral facts about case in lawyer's file were discoverable because lawyer obtained information from fact witness who died after interview).

(3) Undue hardship. The party is unable, without undue hardship, to obtain the substantial equivalent of the information by other means. TRCP 192.5(b)(2); ***Flores***, 777 S.W.2d at 42; *e.g.*, ***Lowry***, 802 S.W.2d at 673 (party argued it would be extremely difficult & costly to duplicate material that State had gathered).

3. Exceptions in TRCP 192.5(c). The following information is discoverable even if it was collected or prepared in anticipation of litigation:

(1) Witness information. Information discoverable under TRCP 192.3 (scope of discovery) concerning experts, trial witnesses, witness statements, and contentions. TRCP 192.5(c)(1). See "Witness statements," §2.6, p. 343.

(2) Trial exhibits. Trial exhibits required to be disclosed by court order under TRCP 166 (pretrial order) or by TRCP 190.4 (Level 3 discovery control plan). TRCP 192.5(c)(2).

(3) Party & fact witnesses. The name, address, and telephone number of any potential party or any person with knowledge of relevant facts. TRCP 192.5(c)(3).

(4) Photographs. Photographs and other electronic images containing images of underlying facts (*e.g.*, a photograph of the accident scene) or that the party intends to offer into evidence. TRCP 192.5(c)(4); *see also* TRCP 192.3(b) (scope of discovery). See "Photographs," §2.11.3, p. 345.

(5) TRE 503(d) exceptions. Any work product created under circumstances within an exception to the attorney-client privilege in TRE 503(d) (crime-fraud & other exceptions). TRCP 192.5(c)(5); ***Goode v. Shoukfeh***, 943 S.W.2d 441, 448 (Tex.1997). The same exceptions that apply to attorney-client communications apply to work product. TRCP 192.5(c)(5). See §2.14.1, below.

4. Waiver by offensive use. Information classified as non-core work product may be discoverable under the offensive-use doctrine. *See* ***Occidental Chem. v. Banales***, 907 S.W.2d 488, 490 (Tex.1995) (dicta; case involved sanctions). See "Waiver by offensive use," ch. 6-A, §23.3.9, p. 339.

§2.14 Discoverable attorney-client communications. For a definition of the attorney-client privilege, see "Attorney-client privilege," §3.4, p. 354. The following communications between a lawyer and client are not privileged and are discoverable.

1. TRE 503(d) exceptions. If the communication falls within one of the five exceptions listed in TRE 503(d), it is discoverable.

(1) Crime or fraud. Communications made in furtherance of a crime or fraud are discoverable. TRE 503(d)(1); TRCP 192.5(c)(5); *see* ***Granada Corp. v. 1st Ct. of Appeals***, 844 S.W.2d 223, 227 (Tex.1992), *overruled on other grounds*, TRCP 193.3 & cmt. 4 (TRCP 193.3(d) overrules ***Granada*** to the extent the two conflict). This exception applies only if the party seeking the information (1) makes a prima facie case of contemplated fraud, and (2) the information sought is related to the prima facie proof. ***Granada***, 844 S.W.2d at 227; *see*

Volcanic Gardens Mgmt. Co. v. Paxson, 847 S.W.2d 343, 347 (Tex.App.—El Paso 1993, no writ). The prima facie proof must show a violation serious enough to defeat the privilege. ***In re Monsanto Co.***, 998 S.W.2d 917, 934 (Tex.App.—Waco 1999, orig. proceeding).

(2) Claimants through same deceased client. Communications that are relevant to an issue between parties who assert claims through the same deceased client are discoverable. TRE 503(d)(2); TRCP 192.5(c)(5); ***In re Texas A&M–Corpus Christi Found.***, 84 S.W.3d 358, 361 (Tex.App.—Corpus Christi 2002, orig. proceeding). Other than this narrow exception, communications between a lawyer and client survive the death of the client. See "Duration," §3.4.4, p. 355.

(3) Breach of duty. Communications relevant to a breach of a duty either by a lawyer to the client or by a client to the lawyer are discoverable. TRE 503(d)(3); TRCP 192.5(c)(5); ***Scrivner v. Hobson***, 854 S.W.2d 148, 152 (Tex.App.—Houston [1st Dist.] 1993, orig. proceeding).

(4) Attestation by lawyer. Communications relevant to an issue about a document to which the lawyer was an attesting witness are discoverable. TRE 503(d)(4); TRCP 192.5(c)(5).

(5) Joint clients. In a suit between clients who jointly consulted or retained a lawyer, communications with the lawyer that are common to the interests of both clients and are relevant to the dispute are discoverable. TRE 503(d)(5); TRCP 192.5(c)(5); *see* ***Scrivner***, 854 S.W.2d at 152.

2. Preexisting document. Documents that preexisted the attorney-client relationship, delivered to the lawyer by the client, are discoverable. ***MortgageAmerica Corp. v. American Nat'l Bank***, 651 S.W.2d 851, 858 (Tex.App.—Austin 1983, writ ref'd n.r.e.).

3. Conditions of employment. Nonconfidential matters of employment, such as the terms, conditions, and purpose of the lawyer's employment, are discoverable. ***Allstate Tex. Lloyds v. Johnson***, 784 S.W.2d 100, 105 (Tex.App.—Waco 1989, orig. proceeding); ***Borden, Inc. v. Valdez***, 773 S.W.2d 718, 720-21 (Tex.App.—Corpus Christi 1989, orig. proceeding).

4. Discussions with employee. Communications with the client's employees are discoverable unless the discussion falls within the provisions of TRE 503(a) (definition of client & representative) and TRE 503(b) (attorney-client privilege). See "Who is included," §3.4.1, p. 354.

5. Identity of witnesses. The names and locations of the persons with knowledge of relevant facts are discoverable. See "Fact witnesses," §2.8, p. 344.

6. Offensive use. Information classified as attorney-client privilege may be discoverable under the offensive-use doctrine. *E.g.*, ***In re Tjia***, 50 S.W.3d 614, 617 (Tex.App.—Amarillo 2001, orig. proceeding) (in breach of contract suit, attorney's letter to P, his client, was discoverable by D, when P said it relied on advice of counsel in making decision not to sublease). See "Waiver by offensive use," ch. 6-A, §23.3.9, p. 339.

§2.15 Discoverable accountant-client communications. Information transferred between an accountant and a client is usually not discoverable. See "Accountant-client privilege," §3.7, p. 356. Accountant-client information is discoverable in the following instances:

1. When the client or its representative gives permission to disclose the information. Occ. Code §901.457(a).

2. When required by the professional standards for reporting on the examination of a financial statement. *Id.* §901.457(b)(1).

3. To respond to a summons under the provisions of the Internal Revenue Code, the 1933 Securities Act, the 1934 Securities Exchange Act, or a court order if the summons or order meets the requirements of Occupations Code §901.457(b)(2)(A)-(C). *Id.* §901.457(b)(2).

4. In an investigation conducted by the Texas State Board of Public Accountancy. *Id.* §901.457(b)(3).

5. In an ethical investigation conducted by a professional organization of CPAs. *Id.* §901.457(b)(4).

6. In the course of a peer review proceeding under Occupations Code §901.159. *Id.* §901.457(b)(5).

§2.16 Discoverable husband-wife communications. Most communications between spouses are not discoverable. See "Husband-wife privilege," §3.9, p. 356. The husband-wife privilege does not protect the following information from disclosure. TRE 504.

1. Nonconfidential communications. There is no husband-wife communication privilege for communications made in the presence of another person (*e.g.*, a spouse's mother). Such communications are not privileged and are discoverable. ***Bear v. State***, 612 S.W.2d 931, 931-32 (Tex.Crim.App.1981) (criminal case interpreting Code of Crim. Proc. art. 38.11). If one spouse discusses the other spouse with a third person, that conversation is not privileged. ***Gibbons v. State***, 794 S.W.2d 887, 892 (Tex.App.—Tyler 1990, no pet.) (interpreting former TRCrE 504).

2. Nonverbal communications. There is no husband-wife communication privilege for nonverbal communications. ***Freeman v. State***, 786 S.W.2d 56, 59 (Tex.App.—Houston [1st Dist.] 1990, no pet.) (criminal case interpreting former TRCrE 504(2)(a)); *see also* ***Pereira v. U.S.***, 347 U.S. 1, 6, 74 S.Ct. 358, 361 (1954) (actions are not communications, thus not privileged).

3. Crime or fraud. There is no husband-wife communication privilege for communications made in furtherance of a crime or fraud; such communications are discoverable. TRE 504(a)(4)(A). See "Crime or fraud," §2.14.1(1), p. 347.

4. Suits between spouses. There is no husband-wife communication privilege in a civil suit between spouses or in a proceeding between a surviving spouse and a person who makes a claim through the deceased spouse. TRE 504(a)(4)(B); *see, e.g.*, ***Earthman's, Inc. v. Earthman***, 526 S.W.2d 192, 206 (Tex.App.—Houston [1st Dist.] 1975, no writ) (discussions between spouses were admissible in lawsuit between them). *But see* ***Lanham v. Lanham***, 145 S.W. 336, 338 (Tex.1912) (wife violated privilege by testifying in probate hearing about husband's mental condition when he executed will).

5. Crime against spouse or minor child. There is no husband-wife communication privilege in a proceeding in which the party is accused of a criminal act against the spouse, any minor child, or any member of the household of either spouse. TRE 504(a)(4)(C).

6. Commitment proceedings. There is no husband-wife communication privilege at a proceeding to commit either spouse or to place the property of one spouse under the control of the other because of a mental or physical condition. TRE 504(a)(4)(D).

7. Competence hearings. There is no husband-wife communication privilege in a hearing brought by or on behalf of either spouse to establish competence. TRE 504(a)(4)(E).

8. Communications made before marriage. There is no husband-wife communication privilege for communications made before marriage. *See* TRE 504(a)(1) (communication is confidential if made to "person's spouse").

§2.17 Discoverable parent-child communications. There is no privilege for communications between parent and child. *See, e.g.*, ***Port v. Heard***, 764 F.2d 423, 428-30 (5th Cir.1985) (in criminal case, parent spent 6 months in jail for refusing to divulge communications by child accused of murder); *see also* ***Diehl v. State***, 698 S.W.2d 712, 712-14 (Tex.App.—Houston [1st Dist.] 1985, pet. ref'd) (search warrant based on affidavit of D's 11-year-old child).

§2.18 Discoverable physician-patient information. Medical information about a patient is usually not discoverable. See "Physician-patient privilege," §3.10, p. 356. There are seven exceptions to the physician-patient privilege. TRE 509(e).

1. **Patient vs. physician.** Medical information is discoverable if (1) the patient sues the physician or if the patient is the complainant in a license revocation proceeding, and (2) disclosure is relevant to the claims against or defenses of the physician. TRE 509(e)(1); ***Mutter v. Wood***, 744 S.W.2d 600, 600-01 (Tex.1988).

2. **Written consent.** Medical information is discoverable if the patient or an agent signs a written consent, as provided in TRE 509(f), to release privileged information. TRE 509(e)(2); ***Mutter***, 744 S.W.2d at 600-01. A patient's authorization for doctors to release information to an insurance company does not authorize the insurance company to release the information in a lawsuit in which the patient is not a party. ***Alpha Life Ins. Co. v. Gayle***, 796 S.W.2d 834, 836 (Tex.App.—Houston [14th Dist.] 1990, orig. proceeding); *see* TRE 509(f)(3).

3. **Suit for debt.** Medical information is discoverable in a suit to substantiate and collect on a claim for medical services rendered to the patient. TRE 509(e)(3).

4. **Relevant to claim or defense.** Medical information is discoverable if the communication or record is relevant to an issue of the physical, mental, or emotional condition of a patient in a proceeding in which any party relies on the condition as part of its claim or defense, even when the patient is not a party to the litigation. TRE 509(e)(4); ***Mutter***, 744 S.W.2d at 600-01; *see, e.g.*, ***Rios v. MHMR***, 58 S.W.3d 167, 169 (Tex.App.—San Antonio 2001, no pet.) (in PI suit, D could depose doctor that P consulted for second opinion); *see also* ***In re Whiteley***, 79 S.W.3d 729, 733-34 (Tex.App.—Corpus Christi 2002, orig. proceeding) (other patients' redacted medical records discoverable because D relied on defense that same surgical procedure was successful on them). For discoverable mental health information relevant to suit, see §2.19.5, below.

5. **Disciplinary investigation.** Medical information is discoverable in a disciplinary investigation of a physician under the Medical Practice Act, Occupations Code §159.003(a)(5), or of a registered nurse under Occupations Code chapter 301. *See* TRE 509(e)(5).

6. **Involuntary commitment.** Medical information is discoverable in an involuntary commitment proceeding, a proceeding for court-ordered treatment, or a probable-cause hearing under various statutes. TRE 509(e)(6).

7. **Institutional abuse or neglect.** Medical information is discoverable in a suit regarding abuse or neglect of a resident in an "institution," as defined by Health & Safety Code §242.002(10). TRE 509(e)(7).

§2.19 Discoverable mental health information. Most mental health information about a patient is not discoverable. TRE 510(b). See "Mental health information privilege," §3.11, p. 357. There are six exceptions to the mental health information privilege that make mental health information discoverable. TRE 510(d).

1. **Patient vs. professional.** Mental health information is discoverable if (1) the patient sues the professional for malpractice or if the patient is the complainant in a license revocation proceeding, and (2) disclosure is relevant to the claims against or defenses of the professional. TRE 510(d)(1).

2. **Written waiver.** Mental health information is discoverable if a patient waives the right to the privilege in writing. TRE 510(d)(2).

3. **Suit for debt.** Mental health information is discoverable if the professional sues to collect on a claim for mental or emotional health services rendered to the patient. TRE 510(d)(3).

4. **Communication made without privilege.** Mental health information is discoverable if the patient made the disclosure in the course of a court-ordered examination, and the judge makes a finding that the patient was told the communication would not be privileged. TRE 510(d)(4); ***Subia v. Texas Dept. of Human Servs.***, 750 S.W.2d 827, 830 (Tex.App.—El Paso 1988, no writ); ***Dudley v. State***, 730 S.W.2d 51, 54 (Tex.App.—Houston [14th Dist.] 1987, no writ).

5. Relevant to claim or defense. Mental health information is discoverable when any party relies on the patient's physical, mental, or emotional condition as part of its claim or defense. TRE 510(d)(5); *e.g.*, ***R.K. v. Ramirez***, 887 S.W.2d 836, 842-44 (Tex.1994) (P claimed hospital was negligent because its doctor was physically & emotionally impaired); ***Groves v. Gabriel***, 874 S.W.2d 660, 661 (Tex.1994) (P's allegation of severe emotional distress waived her privilege relating to her mental health records); ***M.A.W. v. Hall***, 921 S.W.2d 911, 913-14 (Tex. App.—Houston [14th Dist.] 1996, orig. proceeding) (Ps claimed doctor was impaired by drugs); ***Easter v. McDonald***, 903 S.W.2d 887, 890-91 (Tex.App.—Waco 1995, orig. proceeding) (P claimed mental health counselor was negligent). Whether the condition of the patient is part of a claim or defense is determined from the face of the pleadings. ***R.K.***, 887 S.W.2d at 843 n.7; *see* ***Easter***, 903 S.W.2d at 891 n.1. See §2.18.4, above.

6. Institutional abuse or neglect. Mental health information is discoverable in a suit regarding abuse or neglect of a resident in an "institution," as defined by the Health & Safety Code §242.002(10). TRE 510(d)(6).

§2.20 Medical matters under TRCP 204. If the mental or physical condition of a party or a person under the party's control is in controversy, on a motion showing good cause, the person may be compelled to submit to an examination. TRCP 204.1; *see also* ***Coates v. Whittington***, 758 S.W.2d 749, 750-51 (Tex.1988) (mental exam); ***In re Caballero***, 36 S.W.3d 143, 144 (Tex.App.—Corpus Christi 2000, orig. proceeding) (physical exam). For more details on TRCP 204, see "Motion to Examine the Person," ch. 6-I, §5, p. 436.

§2.21 Medical requests under Family Code. In a suit affecting the parent-child relationship under Family Code Title 2 or 5, the court, on its own initiative or on a motion, may appoint (1) psychiatrists or psychologists to examine children who are the subject of a lawsuit, or (2) non-physician experts who are qualified to take blood and other samples to conduct tests in paternity disputes. TRCP 204.4(a), (b); *see* Fam. Code §§160.501-160.511 (genetic testing). See "Examination," ch. 6-I, §5.4, p. 437.

§2.22 Discoverable information about informants. The United States, Texas, and its political subdivisions have a privilege to refuse to disclose the identity of informants. TRE 508(a). See "Identity of informant," §3.22, p. 362. However, information about informants is discoverable in the following situations:

1. The informant's identity or interest in the subject matter of the communication was disclosed to those who would have cause to resent the communication by the holder of the privilege or by the informant's own action. TRE 508(c)(1).

2. The informant appears as a witness for the public entity. *Id.*

3. The informant can testify about a material issue on the merits of a civil case. TRE 508(c)(2). The court must permit the entity with the privilege to present the matter for an in camera hearing, generally by affidavit, to determine whether the informant can supply the testimony. *Id.*

4. The information from an informant is relied on to establish the legality of the means by which evidence was obtained, and the trial court does not believe the evidence is reliable or credible. TRE 508(c)(3); Harris & Androphy, *Informers in Civil Cases*, 31 Hous. Lawyer, 5, p. 32 (Mar.-Apr. 1994).

§2.23 Shared discovery. The doctrine of shared discovery allows litigants access to discovery in other lawsuits that they can use in their own suits. ***Eli Lilly & Co. v. Marshall***, 850 S.W.2d 155, 160 (Tex.1993); *see* TRCP 192.3(a) ("any matter that is not privileged").

§2.24 Information in possession of journalist. There is conflicting authority whether journalists have a qualified privilege to protect confidential information from discovery. *Compare* ***Dallas Morning News Co. v. Garcia***, 822 S.W.2d 675, 678 (Tex.App.—San Antonio 1991, orig. proceeding) (journalists have privilege), *with* ***Dolcefino v. Ray***, 902 S.W.2d 163, 164-65 (Tex.App.—Houston [1st Dist.] 1995, orig. proceeding) (no authority for privilege, but court did not rule whether there is such a privilege). Even if there is such a privilege, if the discovery seeks information that is not confidential, there is no issue of privilege, and discovery must be allowed. ***In re***

Union Pac. R.R., 6 S.W.3d 310, 312 (Tex.App.—Houston [14th Dist.] 1999, orig. proceeding); *see* ***De La Paz v. Henry's Diner***, 946 F.Supp. 484, 485 (N.D. Tex.1996) (no privilege for non-confidential information). *See generally* Sherwin, Comment, *"Source" of Protection: The Status of the Reporter's Privilege in Texas ...*, 32 Tex. Tech L.Rev. 137 (2000) (discussion of reporter's privilege in Texas).

§2.25 Any matter subject to waiver. A party is entitled to discover anything it requested if the other party waived its objections or claims of privilege. See "Waiver of Sanctions, Discovery, & Objections," ch. 6-A, §23, p. 338.

§3. WHAT IS NOT DISCOVERABLE?

To determine what is not discoverable, lawyers should read TRCP 192, which outlines the scope of discovery and, by inference, the matters outside discovery, and then should consult the evidence rules that list the privileges from discovery, TRE 501-513.

§3.1 Outside scope of discovery. Information is not discoverable if it is not relevant to the subject matter of the pending action or, even if relevant, it will not lead to the discovery of admissible evidence. TRCP 192.3(a); *see* TRE 501. The scope of discovery is confined by the subject matter of the case and reasonable expectations of obtaining information that will aid resolution of the dispute. TRCP 192, cmt. 1.

§3.2 Limitation on scope of discovery. TRCP 192.4 gives the court power to limit discovery if it determines (1) the discovery is cumulative, (2) the discovery is obtainable from a more convenient source, or (3) the burden or expense of the discovery outweighs its benefits. TRCP 192.4; *see* ***In re Colonial Pipeline Co.***, 968 S.W.2d 938, 941-42 (Tex.1998) (scope of discovery is largely within the trial court's discretion). See "Grounds to limit scope of discovery," ch. 6-A, §19.1, p. 334.

§3.3 Work-product privilege. For the definition of work product, see "Work product," ch. 6-A, §2.7, p. 314. The work product of a party or its representatives—including the party's attorneys, consultants, sureties, indemnitors, insurers, employees, or agents—is exempt from discovery. TRCP 192.5(a), (b); ***Goode v. Shoukfeh***, 943 S.W.2d 441, 448 (Tex.1997); ***National Tank Co. v. Brotherton***, 851 S.W.2d 193, 201 (Tex.1993). Work product replaced the "attorney work product" and "party communication" exemptions from former TRCP 166b. TRCP 192, cmt. 8. The work-product privilege is essential to the attorney-client relationship. ***Occidental Chem. v. Banales***, 907 S.W.2d 488, 490 (Tex.1995). The term "work product" applies only to materials prepared, mental impressions developed, or communications made in anticipation of litigation or for trial. TRCP 192.5(a); ***Huie v. DeShazo***, 922 S.W.2d 920, 927 (Tex.1996); ***National Tank***, 851 S.W.2d at 200. The primary purpose of the work-product privilege is to protect the mental processes, conclusions, and legal theories of the lawyer and provide a privileged area so the lawyer can analyze and prepare the case for trial. *See* TRCP 192.5(b)(1) (defining "core work product"); ***Owens-Corning Fiberglas v. Caldwell***, 818 S.W.2d 749, 750 (Tex.1991); *see also* ***National Tank***, 851 S.W.2d at 202 n.11 (explanation of work-product rule under former TRCP 166b(3)(a)). The work-product privilege promotes the adversary system by safeguarding the fruits of an attorney's trial preparations from the other party. ***Wiley v. Williams***, 769 S.W.2d 715, 717 (Tex.App.—Austin 1989, orig. proceeding).

NOTE

The work-product privilege and the attorney-client privilege are often confused. They cover much of the same material, but with some important differences. The work-product privilege covers work relating to the preparation of the client's lawsuit; the attorney-client privilege covers the communications with the client. See ***National Tank****, 851 S.W.2d at 200;* ***Owens-Corning****, 818 S.W.2d at 750. The work-product privilege depends on proof that the materials were prepared in anticipation of litigation; the attorney-client privilege does not.* ***National Tank****, 851 S.W.2d at 202;* ***Boring & Tunneling Co. v. Salazar****, 782 S.W.2d 284, 288 (Tex. App.—Houston [1st Dist.] 1989, orig. proceeding).*

1. Date of "occurrence." To qualify as work product, material must have been prepared or mental impressions developed in anticipation of litigation, that is, after the occurrence or transaction on which the suit is based. *See* TRCP 192.5(a). In most cases, the date of the occurrence is easy to determine—it is the date of the injury. Sometimes, however, it is more difficult. *See, e.g.*, ***Jackson v. Downey***, 817 S.W.2d 858, 860 (Tex.App.—Houston [1st Dist.] 1991, orig. proceeding) (in suit against insurance company for refusal to pay medical claim, the "occurrence" was date insurance company denied coverage, not date of surgery); ***National Sur. Corp. v. Dominguez***, 715 S.W.2d 67, 68-69 (Tex.App.—Corpus Christi 1986, orig. proceeding) (in suit to recover on surety bond, the "occurrence" was date surety denied coverage).

2. Anticipation of litigation. The materials must have been prepared or the mental impressions developed in anticipation of litigation or for trial. TRCP 192.5(a); ***National Tank***, 851 S.W.2d at 202-03. The "litigation" referred to in TRCP 192.5(a)(1) refers to the proceedings in which the work-product privilege is claimed. *See* ***Flores v. 4th Ct. of Appeals***, 777 S.W.2d 38, 41-42 (Tex.1989) (discussing former TRCP 166b(3)(d)), *modified on other grounds*, ***National Tank Co. v. Brotherton***, 851 S.W.2d 193 (Tex.1993). The test to determine whether the party asserting the privilege had good cause to anticipate litigation has two parts:

(1) Objective test. First, the court must determine whether a reasonable person, based on the circumstances at the time of the investigation, would have anticipated litigation. ***National Tank***, 851 S.W.2d at 203. "Imminence" of litigation is not a factor; the objective prong is satisfied when a reasonable person would conclude from the severity of the accident and other circumstances surrounding it that there is a substantial chance that litigation will ensue. *Id.* at 203-04.

(2) Subjective test. Second, the court must make a subjective determination whether the party resisting discovery believed in good faith there was a substantial chance that litigation would follow and conducted the investigation for the purpose of preparing for the litigation. ***National Tank***, 851 S.W.2d at 204. This part of the test looks to the defendant-to-be's reaction to circumstances surrounding the occurrence.

NOTE

Reports prepared in the ordinary course of business may be exempt from discovery under the "anticipation of litigation" exception. There is no specific rule that makes ordinary course of business documents discoverable. ***National Tank****, 851 S.W.2d at 206. The courts must consider the reasons that gave rise to the defendant's ordinary business practice. Id. This does not mean, however, that all the claim files of an insurance company are privileged. Id. at 206 n.13.*

---

3. Prepared by or for party. To qualify as work product, the materials assembled for litigation must have been prepared by or for a party or a party's representatives, including the party's attorneys, consultants, sureties, indemnitors, insurers, employees, or agents. TRCP 192.5(a)(1); *see* ***Humphreys v. Caldwell***, 888 S.W.2d 469, 471 (Tex.1994); *see, e.g.*, ***Marshall v. Hall***, 943 S.W.2d 180, 183 (Tex.App.—Houston [1st Dist.] 1997, orig. proceeding) (interview notes prepared by lawyer's employee were protected); ***Bearden v. Boone***, 693 S.W.2d 25, 28 (Tex. App.—Amarillo 1985, orig. proceeding) (investigator's work conducted for lawyer was protected). In a criminal prosecution, the work-product privilege extends only to a litigation file that is still active. See "Law enforcement privilege," §3.21.1(4), p. 362.

4. For same litigation. An investigation conducted after a suit was filed or before the suit was filed but in anticipation of litigation is protected only if it was conducted for the same suit in which the privilege is asserted. *See, e.g.*, ***Allen v. Humphreys***, 559 S.W.2d 798, 802-03 (Tex.1977) (tests were discoverable even though conducted after P filed suit, because D admitted they were not conducted in connection with P's suit), *overruled on other grounds*, ***Walker v. Packer***, 827 S.W.3d 833 (Tex.1992). If the work was done to prepare for another suit arising from the same occurrence, it is not protected. ***Turbodyne Corp. v. Heard***, 720 S.W.2d 802, 804 (Tex.1986); ***Robinson v. Harkins & Co.***, 711 S.W.2d 619, 621 (Tex.1986).

5. Work product exempt from discovery.

(1) Core work product. Core work product—the work product of an attorney or an attorney's representative that contains the attorney's or the attorney's representative's mental impressions, opinions, conclusions, or legal theories—is not discoverable. TRCP 192.5(b)(1). The protection for the attorney's thought processes is absolute. ***Occidental Chem. v. Banales***, 907 S.W.2d 488, 490 (Tex.1995). The privilege protects the litigation file, ***National Un. Fire Ins. Co. v. Valdez***, 863 S.W.2d 458, 460 (Tex.1993); indexes, notes, and memoranda prepared by a lawyer, ***Garcia v. Peeples***, 734 S.W.2d 343, 348 (Tex.1987); the lawyer's notes and correspondence prepared in connection with the lawsuit, ***Occidental Chem.***, 907 S.W.2d at 490, ***Humphreys***, 888 S.W.2d at 471; and the lawyer's notes made during trial, ***Goode v. Shoukfeh***, 943 S.W.2d 441, 449 (Tex.1997). Core work product is not subject to the "need and hardship" exception.

(2) Non-core work product. Non-core work product—work product that does not reflect the attorney's thought processes—is also exempt from discovery. However, if the party seeking discovery proves the "need and hardship" exception, non-core work product is discoverable. See "Discoverable work product," §2.13, p. 346.

6. Duration of work-product privilege. The work-product privilege is perpetual. ***Occidental Chem.***, 907 S.W.2d at 490; ***Owens-Corning***, 818 S.W.2d at 751-52. This means the mental impressions and opinions of the lawyer from one suit are not discoverable in another suit. ***Humphreys***, 888 S.W.2d at 471; ***Owens-Corning***, 818 S.W.2d at 751-52; ***Cigna Corp. v. Spears***, 838 S.W.2d 561, 564 (Tex.App.—San Antonio 1992, orig. proceeding).

§3.4 Attorney-client privilege. The purpose of the attorney-client privilege is to foster the client's confidence in the lawyer and to encourage free communication between them. ***Maryland Am. Gen. Ins. Co. v. Blackmon***, 639 S.W.2d 455, 458 (Tex.1982); ***West v. Solito***, 563 S.W.2d 240, 245 (Tex.1978). The attorney-client privilege, a creation of common law now codified in TRE 503(b), ensures that confidential communications between the attorney and the client, made for the purpose of rendering legal services, will not be disclosed. ***In re Ford Motor Co.***, 988 S.W.2d 714, 718 (Tex.1998); ***Huie v. DeShazo***, 922 S.W.2d 920, 922 (Tex.1996); ***Republic Ins. Co. v. Davis***, 856 S.W.2d 158, 160 (Tex.1993). The attorney-client privilege is the oldest of the privileges for confidential communications known to the common law. ***In re City of Georgetown***, 53 S.W.3d 328, 332 (Tex.2001); ***Ford Motor Co. v. Leggat***, 904 S.W.2d 643, 647 (Tex.1995). For attorney-client information that is discoverable, see "Discoverable attorney-client communications," §2.14, p. 347.

1. Who is included. The attorney-client privilege covers attorney-client communications between the following persons:

(1) Attorney. Under TRE 503(a)(1), there must be a professional relationship between the attorney and the client. ***Huie***, 922 S.W.2d at 925 (no attorney-client relationship between trustee's attorney & beneficiary); *see also* ***Parker v. Carnahan***, 772 S.W.2d 151, 156 (Tex.App.—Texarkana 1989, writ denied) (signing tax return in lawyer's office did not create attorney-client relationship).

(2) Attorney's representatives. A representative of the lawyer includes a person "employed by the lawyer to assist the lawyer in the rendition of professional legal services." TRE 503(a)(4)(A); ***National Tank Co. v. Brotherton***, 851 S.W.2d 193, 197 (Tex.1993). Those persons include secretaries, paralegals, accountants, and investigators. ***Bearden***, 693 S.W.2d at 27-28.

(3) Client. A "client" is a person, public officer, or corporation, association, or other organization or entity, either public or private. TRE 503(a)(1); *see* ***Markowski v. City of Marlin***, 940 S.W.2d 720, 726-27 (Tex. App.—Waco 1997, writ denied) (city council's consultation with its attorney in closed session was protected by privilege).

(4) Client's representatives. A client's representative includes (1) a person having the authority to obtain legal services or to act on legal advice rendered on behalf of the client, and (2) any other person who, for purposes of effectuating legal representation for the client, makes or receives a confidential communication while acting in the scope of employment for the client. TRE 503(a)(2); ***In re Monsanto Co.***, 998 S.W.2d 917, 922 (Tex. App.—Waco 1999, orig. proceeding) (element 2). TRE 503(a)(2) was amended in 1998, by adding (a)(2)(B), to adopt the "subject matter" test. *See* TRE 503, cmt.; ***Monsanto***, 998 S.W.2d at 922. The subject-matter test covers more types of communications by more people at different levels within a corporation than does the control-group test. ***Leggat***, 904 S.W.2d at 646. For an in-depth discussion of the subject-matter test, see Cochran, ***Evidence Handbook***, pp. 419-22.

2. What is protected. The attorney-client privilege will protect information when the communication meets the following test:

(1) Attorney-client communication. There must be a communication between the lawyer and the client. *See* TRE 503(b). See §3.4.1, above. The attorney-client privilege attaches to the complete communication, including legal advice, opinions, mental analysis, and the specific facts on which they are based. ***Pittsburgh Corning Corp. v. Caldwell***, 861 S.W.2d 423, 425 (Tex.App.—Houston [14th Dist.] 1993, orig. proceeding) (attorney-client privilege covers the whole document, not just parts relating to legal advice). Not all statements and communications made between a client and a lawyer are privileged. ***Borden, Inc. v. Valdez***, 773 S.W.2d 718, 720-21 (Tex.App.—Corpus Christi 1989, orig. proceeding) (client's lawyer can be deposed, but cannot be questioned about privileged matters). A communication made to an attorney after a person was told no attorney-client relationship would be accepted is not a privileged communication. ***McGrede v. Rembert Nat'l Bank***, 147 S.W.2d 580, 584 (Tex. App.—Texarkana 1941, writ dism'd).

(2) Confidential communication. The communication must be confidential. TRE 503(a)(5). A communication is confidential if it is not intended to be disclosed to third persons. *Id.*; *see* ***Huie***, 922 S.W.2d at 925 (trustee had expectation that communication to lawyer would be confidential). If the communication between the client and the lawyer is made in the presence of a third person who is not an agent or representative of the lawyer, no privilege attaches. ***Ledisco Fin. Servs. v. Viracola***, 533 S.W.2d 951, 959 (Tex.App.—Texarkana 1976, no writ).

(3) For legal assistance. The communication must be made to facilitate the rendition of professional legal services. TRE 503(b)(1); ***Huie***, 922 S.W.2d at 923. The attorney-client privilege does not apply if the attorney is acting in a capacity other than that of an attorney. ***In re Texas Farmers Ins. Exch.***, 990 S.W.2d 337, 340 (Tex.App.—Texarkana 1999, orig. proceeding); *see, e.g.*, ***Clayton v. Canida***, 223 S.W.2d 264, 266 (Tex.App.—Texarkana 1949, no writ) (no privilege because attorney was acting as accountant). A person cannot cloak a material fact with the privilege merely by communicating it to an attorney. ***Huie***, 922 S.W.2d at 923.

3. Who may assert. The attorney-client privilege belongs to the client, not the lawyer. ***West v. Solito***, 563 S.W.2d 240, 244 n.2 (Tex.1978). The attorney-client privilege may be claimed by the client, the client's guardian, the personal representative of a deceased client, or other successor representative of the client. TRE 503(c). The lawyer is presumed to have the authority to claim the privilege on behalf of the client. *Id.*; ***Cole v. Gabriel***, 822 S.W.2d 296, 296 (Tex.App.—Fort Worth 1991, orig. proceeding) (lawyer had no standing to assert attorney-client privilege in his individual capacity).

4. Duration. The attorney-client privilege continues for as long as the client asserts it. *See* ***Maryland Am. Gen. Ins. Co. v. Blackmon***, 639 S.W.2d 455, 458 (Tex.1982); ***Bearden v. Boone***, 693 S.W.2d 25, 27-28 (Tex. App.—Amarillo 1985, orig. proceeding). It does not terminate at the conclusion of the employment or the end of the dispute for which the client hired the lawyer. ***Bearden***, 693 S.W.2d at 27-28. The privilege survives the death of the client. ***Swidler & Berlin v. U.S.***, 524 U.S. 399, 410, 118 S.Ct. 2081, 2088 (1998); *see* TRE 503(c). See "Discoverable work product," §2.13, p. 346.

§3.5 Joint-defense privilege ("common interest rule"). Defendants who are coordinating their legal strategy can share information protected by the attorney-client privilege without waiving the privilege. *See* TRE 503(b)(1)(C). This is an exception to the rule that disclosure of privileged information to third parties waives the privilege. To be entitled to the joint-defense privilege, the defendants must share a common legal interest and must be (1) parties in the same suit, or if only one of them is in the suit, the communication must be made in anticipation of litigation; or (2) parties with common defenses against a plaintiff. ***Ryals v. Canales***, 767 S.W.2d 226, 228 (Tex.App.—Dallas 1989, orig. proceeding); *see* Cochran, ***Evidence Handbook***, p. 404; *see also* ***Rio Hondo Implement Co. v. Euresti***, 903 S.W.2d 128, 132 (Tex.App.—Corpus Christi 1995, orig. proceeding) (not a discovery case). As long as the parties share an actual common interest, even if the parties are adversarial, they may invoke the privilege. *See* ***Ryals***, 767 S.W.2d at 228-229.

§3.6 Confidential client information. A client's confidential information is protected from discovery because a lawyer is prohibited from disclosing it. *See* Tex. Disc. R. Prof. Conduct 1.05(b); ***Perez v. Kirk & Carrigan***, 822 S.W.2d 261, 265 (Tex.App.—Corpus Christi 1991, writ denied). Confidential information includes both privileged and unprivileged information. Tex. Disc. R. Prof. Conduct 1.05(a). Rule 1.05 expands privilege from discovery in TRE 503 to include unprivileged information. A lawyer may reveal confidential client information only as permitted under Rule 1.05(b), (c), (d), and other rules. ***Duncan v. Board of Disciplinary Appeals***, 898 S.W.2d 759, 761 (Tex.1995).

§3.7 Accountant-client privilege. A communication made by a client to an accountant or to a partner, member, officer, shareholder, or employee of the accountant or the accountant's firm in connection with services provided to the client is confidential and is not discoverable. Occ. Code §901.457(a). However, no accountant-client privilege is recognized under federal law. ***U.S. v. Arthur Young & Co.***, 465 U.S. 805, 817, 104 S.Ct. 1495, 1503 (1984). For when accountant-client information is discoverable, see "Discoverable accountant-client communications," §2.15, p. 348.

§3.8 Nondiscoverable consulting expert. Purely consulting experts are protected from discovery as part of the work-product privilege. *See* TRCP 195, cmt. 1. See "Consulting-only expert," ch. 6-C, §2.2.1, p. 364.

§3.9 Husband-wife privilege. The purpose of the husband-wife communication privilege is to preserve the integrity of the marital relationship. Communications between spouses are privileged and not subject to discovery. TRE 504.

1. Existence of marriage. The person claiming the husband-wife privilege must prove a marriage. *See* ***Lara v. State***, 740 S.W.2d 823, 837 (Tex.App.—Houston [1st Dist.] 1987, pet. ref'd) (applying former TRCrE 504; held no common-law marriage).

2. Who may assert. The husband-wife communication privilege may be asserted by the person who made the statement, her guardian or representative, or her spouse on her behalf. TRE 504(a)(3). There is a presumption that one spouse has the authority to claim the privilege on behalf of the other spouse. *Id.*

3. Duration. The husband-wife communication privilege survives a divorce or the death of one of the spouses. ***Wiggins v. Tiller***, 230 S.W. 253, 254 (Tex.App.—San Antonio 1921, no writ).

4. What is protected. The privilege exempts from discovery any husband-wife communication made privately and not intended for disclosure. TRE 504(a)(1). For a list of discoverable matters between spouses, see "Discoverable husband-wife communications," §2.16, p. 349.

§3.10 Physician-patient privilege. A confidential communication between a physician and a patient about the professional services rendered by the physician is privileged and is not discoverable. TRE 509(c); Occ. Code §159.002(b); Health & Safety Code §241.152; ***Mutter v. Wood***, 744 S.W.2d 600, 600 (Tex.1988); ***Kavanaugh v. Perkins***, 838 S.W.2d 616, 621 (Tex.App.—Dallas 1992, no writ). The rationale for the physician-patient privilege (as well as the mental health privilege, see §3.11, below) is twofold: (1) to encourage the full communication necessary for effective treatment, and (2) to prevent unnecessary disclosure of highly personal information. ***R.K. v. Ramirez***, 887 S.W.2d 836, 840 (Tex.1994).

1. Physician. A physician is a person licensed to practice medicine in any state or nation, or a person the patient reasonably believes to be licensed. TRE 509(a)(2).

2. Patient. A patient is any person who consults or is seen by a physician to receive medical care. TRE 509(a)(1); *see* ***Tarrant Cty. Hosp. Dist. v. Hughes***, 734 S.W.2d 675, 677 (Tex.App.—Fort Worth 1987, orig. proceeding) (because blood donors were not patients, their identities were not protected by physician-patient privilege). Generally, the physician-patient relationship is voluntary and wholly contractual, created by an express or implied agreement. ***Garay v. County of Bexar***, 810 S.W.2d 760, 764 (Tex.App.—San Antonio 1991, writ denied) (even though person was unconscious, physician-patient relationship was established). However, a physician may agree in advance to the creation of a physician-patient relationship, such as when a physician's agreement with a hospital leaves the physician no discretion to decline treatment of the hospital's patients. ***Lection v. Dyll***, 65 S.W.3d 696, 704 (Tex.App.—Dallas 2001, pet. denied); *see, e.g.*, ***Hand v. Tavera***, 864 S.W.2d 678, 680 (Tex.App.—San Antonio 1993, no writ) (when patient enrolled in prepaid medical plan goes to hospital emergency room and plan's designated doctor is consulted, there is a physician-patient relationship).

3. Who may assert. The physician-patient privilege may be asserted by the patient, a representative of the patient, or the physician on behalf of the patient. TRE 509(d); ***Bristol-Myers Squibb Co. v. Hancock***, 921 S.W.2d 917, 920 (Tex.App.—Houston [14th Dist.] 1996, orig. proceeding). There is a presumption the doctor has the authority to claim the privilege on behalf of the patient. TRE 509(d)(2).

4. What is protected. The privilege protects from discovery confidential communications by the patient and records of the patient's identity, diagnosis, evaluation, or treatment that are created or maintained by a physician in connection with professional services rendered by the physician to the patient. TRE 509(c); *see* ***In re Columbia Valley Reg'l Med. Ctr.***, 41 S.W.3d 797, 801 (Tex.App.—Corpus Christi 2001, orig. proceeding) (privilege covers whole document, not just parts relating to patient's identity, diagnosis, evaluation & treatment). For information that is discoverable, see "Discoverable physician-patient information," §2.18, p. 349.

§3.11 Mental health information privilege. A confidential communication made to a mental health professional is privileged. TRE 510(b)(1); ***R.K.***, 887 S.W.2d at 839-40.

1. Professional. A mental health professional is a person authorized to practice medicine in any state or nation; a person licensed or certified by Texas in the diagnosis, evaluation, or treatment of mental or emotional disorders; a person involved in the treatment or examination of drug abusers; or a person the patient reasonably believes is in one of the above categories. TRE 510(a)(1). The definition includes clinical psychologists.

2. Patient. A patient is any person who consults or is seen by a professional to receive diagnosis, evaluation, or treatment of any mental or emotional condition, including alcoholism and drug addiction, or who is being treated voluntarily for drug abuse. TRE 510(a)(2).

3. Who may assert. The mental health information privilege may be asserted by the patient, a representative of the patient, or the professional on behalf of the patient. TRE 510(c). There is a presumption the professional has the authority to claim the privilege on behalf of the patient. TRE 510(c)(2).

4. What is protected. The privilege protects from discovery communications by the patient and records of the patient's identity, diagnosis, evaluation, and treatment. TRE 510(b). For discoverable mental health information, see "Discoverable mental health information," §2.19, p. 350.

§3.12 Other medical privileges. A number of other statutes protect a patient's medical records.

1. Chiropractor records. The communications and records of a chiropractor's patient are confidential and privileged. Occ. Code §201.402.

2. Podiatrist records. The communications and records of a podiatrist's patient are confidential and privileged. Occ. Code §202.402.

3. Dentist records. The communications and records of a dentist's patient are privileged. Occ. Code §258.102.

4. Results of AIDS tests. The results of a person's AIDS test are confidential and not subject to discovery. Health & Safety Code §81.103(a); ***Wadley Research Inst. v. Whittington***, 843 S.W.2d 77, 85-86 (Tex.App.—Dallas 1992, orig. proceeding).

5. Blood bank records. The medical and donor records of a blood bank are confidential and cannot be disclosed except as permitted under Health & Safety Code chapter 162. Health & Safety Code §162.003; *see* ***Tarrant Cty. Hosp. Dist. v. Curry***, 907 S.W.2d 445, 445-46 (Tex.1995) (donor's birthday is confidential).

6. EMS-patient communications & records. The communications and records of a patient treated by emergency medical services personnel or by a physician providing medical supervision are confidential and privileged. Health & Safety Code §773.091.

§3.13 Peer review & medical committee privileges. The Medical Practice Act, Occupations Code §160.007(e) (for peer review), and Health & Safety Code §161.032 (for medical committee) limit the discovery of documents from medical institutions. In analyzing these two statutory exemptions from discovery, lawyers should read four Supreme Court cases: ***In re University of Tex. Health Ctr.***, 33 S.W.3d 822, 824-27 (Tex.2000) (discovery requested by third party); ***Brownwood Reg'l Hosp. v. 11th Ct. of Appeals***, 927 S.W.2d 24, 26-27 (Tex.1996) (same); ***Irving Healthcare Sys. v. Brooks***, 927 S.W.2d 12, 16-17 (Tex.1996) (discovery requested by doctor); ***Memorial Hosp. v. McCown***, 927 S.W.2d 1, 12 (Tex.1996) (discovery requested by third party). *See generally* Friend et al., *The New Rules of Show & Tell: Identifying & Protecting the Peer Review & Medical Committee Privileges*, 49 Baylor L.Rev. 607 (1997) (tracks history & development of peer review & medical committee privileges).

1. Information exempt from discovery.

(1) Peer review committee. Peer review proceedings are confidential, and communications to a peer review committee are privileged. Occ. Code §160.007(a). The peer review privilege in the Occupations Code applies to professional review action or medical peer review conducted by a professional review body or medical peer review committee. *Id.* §160.001.

(a) Protected entities. The term "medical peer review committee" or "professional review body" means a committee of a health care entity, of the governing board of a health care entity, or of the medical staff of a health care entity, which (1) operates under written bylaws approved by the policy-making body or the governing board of the health care entity and (2) is authorized to evaluate the quality of medical and health care services or the competence of physicians, including evaluation of the performance of those functions specified by Health & Safety Code §85.204. Occ. Code §151.002(a)(8). For a list of persons and entities included in the "medical peer review committee," see Occupations Code §151.002(a)(8).

(b) The privilege. The peer review privilege provides that medical peer review records are (1) not subject to subpoena or discovery and (2) not admissible as evidence in any civil, judicial, or administrative proceeding without a written waiver of the privilege of confidentiality, "unless disclosure is required or authorized by law." Occ. Code §160.007(e); ***UT Health Ctr.***, 33 S.W.3d at 827; ***Memorial Hosp.***, 927 S.W.2d at 4; *see* ***Irving Healthcare***, 927 S.W.2d at 16-17. Records, reports, evaluations, and recommendations received, maintained, or developed by a peer review committee are privileged from discovery. Occ. Code §160.007(e); *e.g.*, ***Brownwood***, 927 S.W.2d at 27 (peer review documents were privileged even though patient sued hospital for malpractice); ***Irving Healthcare***, 927 S.W.2d at 16-17 (peer review documents were privileged even though doctor sued other doctor for maliciously providing false information to peer review committee); ***Memorial Hosp.***, 927 S.W.2d at 4 (peer review documents privileged even though media-D in libel case sought peer review documents to defend itself).

(c) Waiver of privilege. The privilege may be waived in writing by the chair, vice chair, or secretary of the peer review committee. Occ. Code §160.007(e), (g); *see* ***UT Health Ctr.***, 33 S.W.3d at 827; ***Irving Healthcare***, 927 S.W.2d at 16-17.

(2) Medical committee.

(a) Protected entities. The term "medical committee" means any committee of a hospital, medical organization, university medical school or health science center, HMO, extended care facility, hospital district, or hospital authority, including ad hoc and joint committees. Health & Safety Code §161.031(a), (b).

(b) The privilege. The medical committee privilege provides that records and proceedings of medical committees are confidential and not subject to court subpoena. Health & Safety Code §161.032(a); ***UT Health Ctr.***, 33 S.W.3d at 827; ***Memorial Hosp.***, 927 S.W.2d at 8.

2. What is not exempt. Not all information reviewed by the committee is exempt from discovery.

(1) Disclosure required by law. Medical peer review records are discoverable and admissible into evidence when their "disclosure is required or authorized by law." Occ. Code §160.007(e); ***UT Health Ctr.***, 33 S.W.3d at 827; ***Memorial Hosp.***, 927 S.W.2d at 4; *see* ***Irving Healthcare***, 927 S.W.2d at 16-17. When disclosure is required by law and that disclosure is itself privileged, the privilege is not waived by the disclosure. Occ. Code §160.007(d)-(g); *see* ***UT Health Ctr.***, 33 S.W.3d at 827. When a protected entity responds to discovery with privileged information, that limited waiver does not extend to other privileged information. *See* ***UT Health Ctr.***, 33 S.W.3d at 827 (voluntary production of information about committee recommendations does not waive privilege protecting committee documents themselves). For a list of disclosures authorized by law, see Occupations Code §§160.002 and 160.007.

(2) Business records & other documents. The business records of a hospital, HMO, medical organization, university medical center or health science center, hospital district, hospital authority, or extended care facility are discoverable. Health & Safety Code §161.032(f); ***Irving Healthcare***, 927 S.W.2d at 18; *see* ***Memorial Hosp.***, 927 S.W.2d at 10-11 (business records must be treated the same under both Health & Safety Code §161.032 & Occupations Code §160.007); *see, e.g.*, ***In re Osteopathic Med. Ctr.***, 16 S.W.3d 881, 886 (Tex.App.—Fort Worth 2000, orig. proceeding) (incident report on slip-and-fall submitted to peer review committee was discoverable). For other exceptions, see chart 6-5, below.

3. Application of exemption. The extent of the exemption from discovery depends on whether the party seeking discovery from the committee is the doctor who was investigated by the committee or a third party, generally a plaintiff in a medical malpractice suit. See chart 6-5, below.

6-5. MEDICAL COMMITTEE PRIVILEGES

	INFORMATION SOUGHT IN DISCOVERY	IS INFORMATION DISCOVERABLE BY —	
		Doctor who was investigated?	Party who sued doctor?
1	Committee's final decision to censure, revoke, etc., membership or privileges in health care entity	Yes. Occ. §160.007(d); ***Irving***, 927 S.W.2d at 18.	No. *See* Occ. §160.007(d), (e); ***Irving***, 927 S.W.2d at 18.
2	Committee documents relating to peer review, other than those in 1, above	No. *See* Occ. §160.007(a); H&S §161.032(a); ***Irving***, 927 S.W.2d at 18.	No. *See* Occ. §160.007(a); H&S §161.032(a); ***Irving***, 927 S.W.2d at 18.
3	Committee's initial credentialing of doctor	No. ***Brownwood***, 927 S.W.2d at 26-27; ***Memorial***, 927 S.W.2d at 11; *see* H&S §161.032(a).	No. ***Brownwood***, 927 S.W.2d at 26-27; ***Memorial***, 927 S.W.2d at 11; *see* H&S §161.032(a).
4	Committee's minutes of meetings	No. ***Brownwood***, 927 S.W.2d at 27; ***Memorial***, 927 S.W.2d at 10; *see* H&S §161.032(a).	No. ***Brownwood***, 927 S.W.2d at 27; ***Memorial***, 927 S.W.2d at 10; *see* H&S §161.032(a).
5	Documents created by or at request of committee to evaluate medical care	No. ***UT Health***, 33 S.W.3d at 825; *see* ***Brownwood***, 927 S.W.2d at 27.	No. ***UT Health***, 33 S.W.3d at 825; *see* ***Brownwood***, 927 S.W.2d at 27.
6	Documents provided by doctor to committee, including application	Yes. ***Irving***, 927 S.W.2d at 21.	No. ***Irving***, 927 S.W.2d at 21.
7	Patient medical records, generated by doctor or hospital, in possession of committee	Yes. ❶ ***Irving***, 927 S.W.2d at 18; ***Memorial***, 927 S.W.2d at 9-10; *see* H&S §161.032(c).	Yes. ❶ ***Irving***, 927 S.W.2d at 18; ***Memorial***, 927 S.W.2d at 9-10; *see* H&S §161.032(c).
8	Business records of health care facility in possession of committee	Yes. ❷ H&S §161.032(c); ***Irving***, 927 S.W.2d at 18; ***Memorial***, 927 S.W.2d at 9.	Yes. ❷ H&S §161.032(c); ***Irving***, 927 S.W.2d at 18; ***Memorial***, 927 S.W.2d at 9.
9	Documents in public domain reviewed by committee	Yes. ***Irving***, 927 S.W.2d at 18.	Yes. ***Irving***, 927 S.W.2d at 18.
10	Committee's documents when doctor waives privilege	No. *See* Occ. §160.007(e); ***Irving***, 927 S.W.2d at 16-17.	No. *See* Occ. §160.007(e); ***Irving***, 927 S.W.2d at 16-17.
11	Committee documents when committee waives privilege in writing	Yes. Occ. §160.007(e); ***Irving***, 927 S.W.2d at 16-17.	Yes. Occ. §160.007(e); ***Irving***, 927 S.W.2d at 16-17.
12	Documents provided to committee shared with persons not covered by privilege	Yes. ❷ ***Irving***, 927 S.W.2d at 18.	Yes. ❷ ***Irving***, 927 S.W.2d at 18.
13	Committee documents sought in anti-competitive actions or in civil rights suits brought under 42 U.S.C. §1983	Yes. Occ. §160.007(b); ***Irving***, 927 S.W.2d at 16.	Yes. Occ. §160.007(b); ***Irving***, 927 S.W.2d at 16.
14	Bylaws, rules, and regulations of hospital's medical staff or board of trustees	Yes. ***Brownwood***, 927 S.W.2d at 27.	Yes. ***Brownwood***, 927 S.W.2d at 27.
15	Deposition of person on committee about committee deliberations	No. ***Irving***, 927 S.W.2d at 18.	No. ***Irving***, 927 S.W.2d at 18.

❶ The information is discoverable unless subject to some other privilege (*e.g.*, physician-patient) and must be obtained from some source other than the committee.
❷ The information is discoverable but must be obtained from some source other than the committee.

4. Other peer review committees. There are a number of other peer review discovery exemptions that protect records created by peer review committees of nonphysicians. *E.g.*, Occ. Code §202.454 (podiatric peer review), Occ. Code §261.051 (dental peer review), Occ. Code §303.006 (nursing peer review).

§3.14 Trade-secret privilege. A person has a qualified privilege to refuse to disclose and to prevent other persons from disclosing a trade secret that the person owns. TRE 507; ***In re Continental Gen. Tire***, 979 S.W.2d 609, 613

(Tex.1998); *see also* TRCP 76a(2)(c) (court records open to public do not include discovery in cases initiated to preserve bona fide trade secrets). A trade secret is a formula, pattern, device, or compilation of information that is used in one's business and presents an opportunity to obtain an advantage over competitors. ***In re Bass***, 113 S.W.3d 735, 739 (Tex.2003); ***Computer Assocs. Int'l v. Altai, Inc.***, 918 S.W.2d 453, 455 (Tex.1996); *see* Penal Code §31.05(a)(4). If the information is material and necessary to the litigation and unavailable from any other source, a witness may be required to disclose it. ***Continental***, 979 S.W.2d at 615; ***Automatic Drilling Machs. v. Miller***, 515 S.W.2d 256, 259 (Tex.1974); *see* ***In re Bridgestone/Firestone***, 106 S.W.3d 730, 732 (Tex.2003). A party cannot assert the trade secret privilege if the privilege will tend to conceal fraud or work an injustice. TRE 507; ***In re Leviton Mfg. Co.***, 1 S.W.3d 898, 902 (Tex.App.—Waco 1999, orig. proceeding). If the court requires disclosure, the court must take measures to protect the information. ***Automatic Drilling***, 515 S.W.2d at 260; ***Leviton***, 1 S.W.3d at 902. Discoverable documents cannot be shielded from discovery by placing them in a file with trade secrets. ***Chapa v. Garcia***, 848 S.W.2d 667, 668 (Tex.1992).

§3.15 Privilege against self-incrimination. A person cannot be compelled to give evidence that will be self-incriminating in a criminal proceeding. U.S. Const. amend. 5; Tex. Const. art. 1, §10. A party has the right to assert the Fifth Amendment privilege to avoid civil discovery if the party has a reasonable fear the answers would tend to be incriminating. ***Texas DPS Officers Ass'n v. Denton***, 897 S.W.2d 757, 760 (Tex.1995); ***Gebhardt v. Gallardo***, 891 S.W.2d 327, 330 (Tex.App.—San Antonio 1995, orig. proceeding). The person asserting the Fifth Amendment privilege must raise it in response to each specific inquiry, or waive the privilege. A trial court can ultimately dismiss a plaintiff's lawsuit or grant a default judgment if a party does not comply with an order for discovery. In a civil proceeding, TRE 513(c) allows a comment on or an inference to be made on a witness's claim of Fifth Amendment privilege and permits a party to force a witness to invoke the Fifth Amendment in front of a jury. Cochran, ***Evidence Handbook***, p. 547-48; *see also* ***In re L.S.***, 748 S.W.2d 571, 576 (Tex.App.—Amarillo 1988, no writ) (witness's selective invocation of Fifth Amendment precluded invoking privilege outside presence of jury); ***Smith v. Smith***, 720 S.W.2d 586, 594-95 (Tex.App.—Houston [1st Dist.] 1986, no writ) (deposition testimony containing witness's assertion of Fifth Amendment rights could be read into evidence).

§3.16 Clergy privilege. Confidential communications are privileged if made to a member of the clergy "in the member's professional character as a spiritual advisor." TRE 505(b).

1. Member of clergy. Clergy includes a minister, priest, rabbi, accredited Christian Science Practitioner, or an individual that a party reasonably believes is a member of the clergy. TRE 505(a)(1).

2. Who may assert. An individual, her guardian or conservator, or her personal representative (if she is deceased) may assert the clergy privilege. TRE 505(c).

3. What is protected. The privilege protects confidential communications made privately and not intended for further disclosure except to other persons present in furtherance of the purpose of the communication. TRE 505(a)(2); *see* ***Nicholson v. Wittig***, 832 S.W.2d 681, 685 (Tex.App.—Houston [1st Dist.] 1992, orig. proceeding) (clergy privilege includes all conversations with hospital chaplain, even secular ones conducted when other people are present). The clergy privilege may protect the identity of the communicant. ***Simpson v. Tennant***, 871 S.W.2d 301, 306 (Tex.App.—Houston [14th Dist.] 1994, orig. proceeding).

§3.17 Journalist's privilege. There is conflicting authority whether journalists have a qualified privilege to protect confidential information from discovery. See "Information in possession of journalist," §2.24, p. 351.

§3.18 Political vote. No person can be forced to disclose his or her vote in a political election conducted by secret ballot, unless the vote was cast illegally. TRE 506. A person who casts an illegal vote does not have a privilege to refuse to disclose the vote; an illegal voter is not considered a "voter" for any purpose. ***Oliphint v. Christy***, 299 S.W.2d 933, 939 (Tex.1957); ***Simmons v. Jones***, 838 S.W.2d 298, 300 (Tex.App.—El Paso 1992, no writ).

§3.19 Reports required by law. Any person or entity required by law to make a report has a privilege to refuse to disclose the contents of the report if the law requiring the report permits the person to refuse to disclose it. TRE 502. The purpose of this privilege is to enhance the government's ability to obtain self-reporting information. The rule protects reports "required by law to be made" if the law requiring the report to be made makes such a report privileged. *See* ***Star-Telegram v. Schattman***, 784 S.W.2d 109, 111 (Tex.App.—Fort Worth 1990, orig. proceeding) (EEOC sexual harassment guidelines in 29 C.F.R. §1604.11 do not require a report, and thus an internal investigation was not exempt from discovery under TRE 502).

§3.20 Social security information. The Social Security Act provides that information obtained by the Secretary of Health and Human Services or the Secretary of Labor or any employee of either must not be disclosed, except as provided by regulation. 42 U.S.C. §1306(a). The statute does not say who can claim the privilege or how it is waived. ***TEIA v. Jackson***, 719 S.W.2d 245, 247 (Tex.App.—El Paso 1986, writ ref'd n.r.e.).

§3.21 Law enforcement privilege.

1. Information regarding crime. Information regarding detection, investigation, or prosecution of a crime and records or notations maintained for internal use in matters relating to law enforcement or prosecution are not discoverable if the law enforcement agency or prosecutor can show one of the following:

(1) The release of information would interfere with the detection, investigation, or prosecution of a crime, Gov't Code §552.108(a)(1); or the release of internal records or notations would interfere with law enforcement or prosecution, *id.* §552.108(b)(1).

(2) The information relates only to an investigation that did not result in conviction or deferred adjudication. *Id.* §552.108(a)(2), (b)(2).

(3) The information relates to a threat against a peace officer collected or distributed under Government Code §411.048. *Id.* §552.108(a)(3).

(4) The information was prepared by an attorney for the state in anticipation of or in the course of preparing for criminal litigation. *Id.* §552.108(a)(4)(A), (b)(3)(A). In a criminal prosecution, the work-product privilege extends only to a litigation file that is still active. *See, e.g.*, ***State ex rel. Curry v. Walker***, 873 S.W.2d 379, 380-81 (Tex.1994) (case still active where Ds received deferred adjudication and probation).

(5) The information reflects the mental impressions or legal reasoning of an attorney representing the state. Gov't Code §552.108(a)(4)(B), (b)(3)(B). See "Work-product privilege," §3.3, p. 352.

2. What is not exempt. Basic information about an arrested person, an arrest, or a crime is considered public information. Gov't Code §552.108(c). "Basic information" includes an arrestee's name, alias, social security number, race, sex, age, occupation, physical condition, name of arresting officer, and the charge, as well as a detailed description of the offense. *See* ***Thomas v. Cornyn***, 71 S.W.3d 473, 479 (Tex.App.—Austin 2002, no pet.). "Basic information" is not defined in the Government Code.

§3.22 Identity of informant. The United States, Texas, and its political subdivisions have the privilege to refuse to disclose the identity of a person who has furnished information about an investigation of a possible violation of the law. TRE 508(a); ***Roviaro v. U.S.***, 353 U.S. 53, 59-60, 77 S.Ct. 623, 627 (1957); *see also* ***State v. Lowry***, 802 S.W.2d 669, 673 (Tex.1991) (discussing informant & investigative privileges). For discoverable information about an informant, see "Discoverable information about informants," §2.22, p. 351.

§3.23 Disclosure of membership list. The First Amendment protects the right of association, which in turn protects from discovery the membership list of an organization engaged in the advocacy of particular beliefs. ***NAACP v. Alabama***, 357 U.S. 449, 462-63, 78 S.Ct. 1163, 1171-72 (1958); ***Ex parte Lowe***, 887 S.W.2d 1, 2 (Tex. 1994). Before a court may order disclosure of the membership list of an organization engaged in the advocacy of particular beliefs, the party seeking the list must show a compelling state interest. ***Lowe***, 887 S.W.2d at 3; ***Tilton v. Moye***, 869 S.W.2d 955, 956 (Tex.1994); ***Martin v. Khoury***, 843 S.W.2d 163, 167 (Tex.App.—Texarkana 1992, orig. proceeding).

§3.24 Environmental audit privilege. The Environmental, Health, & Safety Audit Privilege Act creates a documentary privilege for environmental audits and assessments conducted at real property operations and facilities in Texas. TRCS art. 4447cc, §5. The privilege may be waived only by the owner or operator of the land. *Id.* §6(a). See the EPA's policy statement on audit privileges, "Voluntary Environmental Self-Policing & Self-Disclosure Interim Policy Statement," 60 Fed. Reg. 16875 (4-3-95).

§3.25 Public Information Act. If documents or other information are privileged or confidential under the TRCPs or the TREs, they are confidential under the Public Information Act (formerly known as the Open Records Act). Gov't Code §552.022; ***In re City of Georgetown***, 53 S.W.3d 328, 331 (Tex.2001).

§3.26 Legislative privilege. Persons acting in a legislative capacity generally cannot be compelled to testify about their legislative activities. ***In re Perry***, 60 S.W.3d 857, 860 (Tex.2001).

§3.27 Privileges of foreign jurisdictions. When the laws of a foreign jurisdiction protect relevant information from discovery, the court must balance the interest of the Texas court with those of the foreign nation. ***Volkswagen, A.G. v. Valdez***, 909 S.W.2d 900, 902 (Tex.1995). The court must weigh the following factors: (1) the importance of the discovery request to the investigation or litigation, (2) the degree of specificity of the request, (3) whether the information originated in the U.S., (4) the availability of alternative means of securing the information, and (5) the extent to which noncompliance with the request would undermine important interests of the U.S., or the extent to which compliance would undermine important interests of the foreign jurisdiction where the information is located. *Id.*; *see* Restatement (3d) of Foreign Relations Law §442(1)(c) (1987).

C. SECURING DISCOVERY FROM EXPERTS

§1. GENERAL

§1.1 Rules. TRCP 192.3, 192.7, 194.2(f), 195; see TRCP 197.1 (interrogatories cannot be used to secure information covered by TRCP 195).

§1.2 Purpose. This section discusses discovery about and from expert witnesses.

§1.3 Forms. *O'Connor's Texas Civil Forms*, FORMS 6C.

§1.4 Other references. Griesel, *The "New" Texas Discovery Rules: Three Years Later*, Advanced Evidence & Discovery Course, State Bar of Texas, ch. 2, §IX, p. 22 (2002); Gold, *"So, Who Died & Made You King?"* State Bar, Advanced Medical Malpractice, Tab K (2000).

§2. TYPES OF EXPERTS

For purposes of litigation, an expert witness is a person with specialized knowledge who is consulted in anticipation of litigation or in preparation for trial and who renders opinions concerning the matters at issue. *See* TRCP 192.3(e); TRE 702-704. TRCP 192.3(e) recognizes two categories of experts: (1) testifying experts, which can be subdivided into retained and nonretained; and (2) consulting experts, which can be subdivided into "consulting-only" and "consulting-plus."

§2.1 Testifying experts. A testifying expert is an expert who may be called to testify as an expert witness at trial. TRCP 192.7(c). Testifying experts are either retained or nonretained. Different discovery rules apply depending on whether the expert is retained. See "Testifying experts," §3.1, p. 365.

1. Retained testifying expert. A retained testifying expert is an expert who is retained by, employed by, or otherwise subject to the control of the party. *See* TRCP 194.2(f)(4), 195.3. Examples include a doctor employed to give an opinion in a breast-implant case and an accident reconstructionist retained in a car accident case. Retained testifying experts are discoverable. See "Discovery about retained expert," §3.1.1, p. 365.

PRACTICE TIP

In medical malpractice cases, plaintiff and defense lawyers are sure to argue about the phrase "retained by, employed by" in TRCP 194.2(f)(4). Does it include an emergency room doctor the plaintiff did not choose and perhaps did not even pay? Probably not. Whether it includes treating doctors, who are seldom under a party's control and are often hostile to being called as witnesses, is an open question. Until clarified by the courts, retained experts should probably be limited to those doctors employed for purposes of litigation or subject to a party's control.

2. **Nonretained testifying expert.** A nonretained expert is an expert who is not retained by, employed by, or otherwise subject to the control of the party. *See* TRCP 194.2(f)(3). Examples include an emergency room doctor, an accident investigator for the DPS, and the other party's expert who the party intends to call to testify. Nonretained testifying experts are discoverable. See §3.1.2, below.

§2.2 Consulting experts. A consulting expert is an expert who has been consulted, retained, or specially employed by a party in anticipation of litigation or in preparation for trial, but who is not a testifying expert. TRCP 192.7(d). Consulting experts can be conveniently classified as either "consulting-only" or "consulting-plus" experts.

1. **Consulting-only expert.** A consulting-only expert is an expert (1) who is hired as a trial consultant only, (2) who is not expected to testify, (3) who has no firsthand factual knowledge about the case and no secondhand factual knowledge except for knowledge acquired through the consultation, and (4) whose work product, opinions, or mental impressions are not reviewed by the testifying expert. TRCP 192.3(c), (e), 192.7(d); ***In re Ford Motor Co.***, 988 S.W.2d 714, 719 (Tex.1998); ***Lindsey v. O'Neill***, 689 S.W.2d 400, 402 (Tex.1985); *see, e.g.*, ***Castellanos v. Littlejohn***, 945 S.W.2d 236, 239 (Tex.App.—San Antonio 1997, orig. proceeding) (because P's lawyer hired doctor to examine, not to treat P or testify, doctor was not discoverable); ***Teran v. Longoria***, 703 S.W.2d 300, 301 (Tex.App.—Corpus Christi 1985, orig. proceeding) (because treating doctor had facts, he could not be consulting-only expert). The consulting-only expert privilege grants the party and its attorney a sphere of protection and privacy in which to develop their case. ***G.M. Corp. v. Gayle***, 951 S.W.2d 469, 474 (Tex.1997). A party's employee can be a consulting-only expert if she was not employed in the area that is the subject of litigation and was reassigned to that area specifically to assist her employer in anticipation of litigation or in preparation for trial. ***Axelson, Inc. v. McIlhany***, 798 S.W.2d 550, 555 (Tex.1990); *see* TRCP 192.7(d). Consulting-only experts are not discoverable. ***Axelson***, 798 S.W.2d at 554 n.8. See "Consulting-only experts – no discovery," §3.2.1, p. 367.

PRACTICE TIP

To protect the status of a consulting-only expert, do not let the consulting expert view the site of the accident or examine or test the physical evidence in the case; do not let the consulting expert's work be reviewed by the testifying expert; and do not let the consulting expert interact with the testifying expert. Keep separate, segregated files for each expert, and keep a log of all documents reviewed by each expert.

2. **Consulting-plus experts.** A consulting-plus expert is an expert who was hired as a trial consultant but lost her status as a consulting-only expert because her work was reviewed by a testifying expert or because she became a fact witness. TRCP 192.3(c), (e).

(1) **Consulting expert + work reviewed = testifying expert.** A consulting expert whose mental impressions and opinions were reviewed by a testifying expert is considered to be, and is treated just like, a testifying expert. TRCP 192.3(e); ***Ford Motor Co.***, 988 S.W.2d at 719; ***Martin v. Boles***, 843 S.W.2d 90, 92 (Tex.App.—Texarkana 1992, orig. proceeding). A consulting expert whose work was reviewed by the testifying expert is discoverable

to the same extent as a testifying expert. ***Beam v. A.H. Chaney, Inc.***, 56 S.W.3d 920, 925 (Tex.App.—Fort Worth 2001, pet. denied). Because employees of the testifying expert are not considered consulting experts if they did not form an opinion reviewed by the testifying expert, their disclosure is not required. *See, e.g., id.* 925-26 (employee of testifying expert who did not form opinions or mental impressions in the case and simply functioned as an assistant was not a consulting expert). See "Consulting expert + work reviewed," §3.2.2(1), p. 367.

(2) Consulting expert + facts = fact witness. A consulting expert who obtained knowledge about the case either firsthand or in some way other than in consultation about the case is discoverable as a fact witness. TRCP 192.3(c). For example, when a consulting expert visits the accident site to measure skid marks, the expert acquires firsthand information about the case; thus, that expert's identity and factual knowledge must be disclosed, just as for other fact witnesses. *See, e.g.,* ***Axelson***, 798 S.W.2d at 555 (consultants hired after accident to examine wellhead equipment were discoverable as fact witnesses; employees cannot be consulting-only experts if employed in area that became subject of litigation). By comparison, when a consulting expert, at the request of the party, examines a photograph of the accident site, that expert does not become discoverable as a fact witness. See "Consulting expert + facts," §3.2.2(2), p. 367.

§3. TYPES OF DISCOVERY PROCEDURES AVAILABLE

6-6. PROCEDURES FOR SECURING DISCOVERY ABOUT & FROM EXPERTS

	TYPE OF DISCOVERY	TESTIFYING EXPERT WHO IS –		CONSULTING EXPERT –	
		Retained	Nonretained	Whose work was reviewed	With facts
1	Request for disclosure, TRCP 192.1(a)	Yes TRCP 194.2(f)	Yes TRCP 194.2(f)	No	Yes TRCP 194.2(e)
2	Oral depositions, TRCP 192.1(f)	Yes TRCP 195.4	Yes TRCP 205.1(a)	Yes TRCP 205.1(a)	Yes TRCP 205.1(a)
3	Court-ordered expert report, TRCP 195.5	Yes	No	No	No
4	Request for documents, separate from deposition, TRCP 176, 192.1(b)	No	Yes	Yes	Yes
5	Deposition on written questions, TRCP 192.1(f), 200, 205.1(b)	No	Yes	Yes	Yes
6	Interrogatories, TRCP 192.1(d), 197.1	No	No	Yes	Yes
7	Requests for admissions, TRCP 192.1(e), 198.1	No	No	Yes	Yes

§3.1 Testifying experts.
TRCP 195 is the principal rule governing discovery from testifying experts.

1. Discovery about retained expert. There are four discovery procedures that may be used to secure information about or from a retained testifying expert: (1) a request for disclosure, (2) an expert report, (3) an oral deposition, and (4) a request for production with oral deposition. TRCP 194.2(f), 195.1, 195.4, 195.5. A party may not seek information about a retained testifying expert through depositions on written questions, interrogatories, or other forms of discovery not listed in TRCP 195.1. For the scope of discovery about retained testifying experts, see "Information about retained testifying experts," §4.1.1, p. 367; for the scope of discovery about retained nontestifying experts, see "Information about consulting-plus experts," §4.2.2, p. 370.

2. Discovery about nonretained expert. There are four discovery procedures that may be used to secure information about or from a nonretained testifying expert: (1) a request for disclosure, (2) an oral deposition, (3) a deposition on written questions, and (4) a subpoena. TRCP 176, 194.2(f)(1)-(3), 205.1. Although TRCP 195.1 lists the permissible discovery tools for testifying experts, Comment 2 to TRCP 195 overrides TRCP 195.1 regarding nonretained experts by stating that TRCP 195 does not address depositions of nonretained testifying experts nor the production from them of the materials listed in TRCP 192.3(e)(5) (bias of the witness) and TRCP 192.3(e)(6) (documents provided to or reviewed by the expert). TRCP 195, cmt. 2. For the scope of discovery from nonretained experts, see "Information about nonretained experts," §4.1.2, p. 369.

(1) Discovery from party. To secure information from the party about a designated, nonretained testifying expert, the other party should first secure the basic information available through a request for disclosure and then use the other discovery procedures (*e.g.*, oral depositions of the party) to obtain more specific information.

(2) Discovery from nonretained expert. To secure information from the nonretained testifying expert, a party can use a subpoena and deposition (oral or written) to secure the following: (1) detailed information about those matters listed in TRCP 194.2(f)(2) & (3) (the subject of testimony and substance of opinion); (2) information outlined in TRCP 194.2(f)(4) & 192.3(e)(7) (things used or prepared by the expert in anticipation of testimony, and the expert's résumé and bibliography); and (3) any other discoverable information outlined in TRCP 192.3(e)(1)-(6) (scope of discovery). For example, to secure information about a nonretained testifying expert's bias, the party may depose the expert or subpoena records from her.

(3) Discovery from treating doctors. There is a growing dispute whether a lawyer can contact the other party's treating doctor ex parte, without notifying the patient's lawyer. Under the Health Insurance Portability & Accountability Act (HIPAA), medical providers are limited to the kinds of information they may disclose about a patient's health care. HIPAA provides for fines up to $25,000 for violations of a patient's privacy. For more information about HIPAA, go to www.hhs.gov/ocr/hipaa.

(a) Ex parte contact not permitted. Lawyers arguing that ex parte contact with a doctor is not permitted cite the following cases: ***Perkins v. U.S.***, 877. F.Supp. 330, 333 (E.D. Tex.1995) (privately contacting doctor could expose doctor to civil liability & professional sanctions); ***Horner v. Rowan Cos.***, 153 F.R.D. 597, 601 (S.D. Tex.1994) (when treating doctor is interviewed ex parte by defense counsel, there are no safeguards against revelation of matters irrelevant to lawsuit & personally damaging to patient, & potential for breaches in confidentiality can have chilling effect on underlying relationship); ***Mutter v. Wood***, 744 S.W.2d 600, 600 (Tex.1988) (allowing lawyer to question doctor ex parte does not balance competing interests of parties); ***Travelers Ins. Co. v. Woodard***, 461 S.W.2d 493, 496 (Tex.App.—Tyler 1970, writ ref'd n.r.e.) (nothing requires patient to grant other party right to interrogate medical personnel outside of patient's presence); ***In re Trostel***, No. 05-00-02059-CV (Tex. App.—Dallas 2001, orig. proceeding) (no pub.; 6-15-01) (by protective order, trial court prevented D from talking ex parte with P's treating doctor).

(b) Ex parte contact permitted. Lawyers arguing that ex parte contact with a doctor is permitted cite the following cases: ***James v. Kloos***, 75 S.W.3d 153, 160 (Tex.App.—Fort Worth 2002, no pet.) (no proof of prejudice from D's attorney meeting ex parte with P's treating doctor); ***Durst v. Hill Country Mem'l Hosp.***, 70 S.W.3d 233, 238 (Tex.App.—San Antonio 2001, no pet.) (court refused to strike testimony of doctor because of ex parte contact with other party's lawyer); ***Hogue v. Kroger Store***, 875 S.W.2d 477, 480-81 (Tex.App.—Houston [1st Dist.] 1994, writ denied) (court did not permit cross-examination on issue of ex parte contact).

To prevent ex parte contact with a treating doctor, the lawyer should take the following steps:

1. The lawyer should notify the doctor that the doctor's patient (the lawyer's client) does not authorize the doctor to discuss the patient's treatment or condition outside the presence of the patient's lawyer, and that divulging any confidential information is a violation of the physician-patient privilege.

2. The lawyer should draft a medical authorization to expressly prohibit any ex parte communication. See "No ex parte discovery," ch. 6-I, §3.2.2, p. 435.

3. The lawyer should, at the outset of the case, seek a protective order to prevent ex parte contact with the doctor. ***Trostel***, No. 05-00-02059-CV (no pub.). See "Motion for Protective Order," ch. 6-A, §19, p. 334.

§3.2 Consulting experts.

1. Consulting-only experts – no discovery. Because no information about a consulting-only expert is discoverable, there are no discovery tools that can be used to secure information about them or from them.

2. Discovery about consulting-plus experts.

(1) Consulting expert + work reviewed. A party cannot use TRCP 194.2(f) (request for disclosures about testifying experts) or TRCP 195 (discovery from testifying experts) to secure information about a consulting expert whose work was reviewed by the testifying expert. *See* TRCP 195, cmt. 1. However, a party may use any other discovery rule to secure such information. *See id.* (methods of securing discovery about a consulting expert whose work was reviewed by testifying expert is not limited by TRCP 195). Thus, a party may use interrogatories, requests for admissions, and any other type of discovery.

(2) Consulting expert + facts. The discovery procedures available to secure information about a consulting expert who has firsthand knowledge about the facts or secondhand knowledge gained outside the consultation are the same as those for securing information about fact witnesses. *See* TRCP 192.3(c). Thus, to secure information about these consulting experts, a party may use requests for disclosures in TRCP 194.2(e) (for fact witnesses), interrogatories, requests for admissions, and any other type of discovery.

§4. TYPES OF INFORMATION DISCOVERABLE FROM EXPERTS

6-7. SCOPE OF DISCOVERY FROM EXPERTS

	INFORMATION TO BE DISCOVERED	TESTIFYING EXPERT WHO IS –		CONSULTING EXPERT –	
		Retained	Non-retained	Whose work was reviewed	With facts
1	Identity of expert, TRCP 192.3(e)(1)	Yes	Yes	Yes	Yes
2	Subject matter of testimony, TRCP 192.3(e)(2)	Yes	Yes	N/A	N/A
3	Facts learned through consultation, TRCP 192.3(e)(3)	Yes	Yes	Yes	No
4	Firsthand facts acquired directly from evidence, TRCP 192.3(e)(3)	Yes	Yes	Yes	Yes
5	Secondhand facts learned outside of consultation, TRCP 192.3(e)(3)	Yes	Yes	Yes	Yes
6	Mental impressions, opinions, & methods used to derive opinions, TRCP 192.3(e)(4)	Yes	Yes	Yes	No
7	Bias of witness, TRCP 192.3(e)(5)	Yes	Yes	Yes	Maybe ❶
8	Materials & documents created or used by expert, TRCP 192.3(e)(6)	Yes	Yes	Yes	No
9	Written report, TRCP 192.3(e)(6)	Yes	Maybe ❷	Yes	N/A
10	Expert résumé & bibliography, TRCP 192.3(e)(7)	Yes	Yes	Yes	No

❶ When a party is entitled to bias information from a consulting expert with facts, it cannot obtain that information under TRCP 192.3(e), which outlines the scope of discovery for testifying experts.
❷ If the nonretained expert did not create a written report, a party cannot force the expert to prepare one.

§4.1 Testifying experts.

1. Information about retained testifying experts. Parties are entitled to full discovery of each other's retained testifying experts. TRCP 192.3(e), 192.5(c)(1), 194.2(f); ***Aluminum Co. of Am. v. Bullock***, 870 S.W.2d 2, 4 (Tex.1994); ***Collins v. Collins***, 904 S.W.2d 792, 800 (Tex.App.—Houston [1st Dist.] 1995), *writ denied*, 923 S.W.2d 569 (Tex.1996). The following is a list of the discoverable information about retained testifying experts.

(1) **Identity.** A party is entitled to the names, addresses, and telephone numbers of the retained testifying expert witnesses. TRCP 192.3(e)(1); *see* ***Morrow v. H.E.B., Inc.***, 714 S.W.2d 297, 297 (Tex.1986) (duty to supplement if witness acquires new address). This information can be secured through a request for disclosure. TRCP 194.2(f)(1).

(2) **Subject of testimony.** A party is entitled to discover the subject matter on which the retained testifying expert will testify. TRCP 192.3(e)(2); *see* ***Aluminum Co.***, 870 S.W.2d at 4. A brief form of this information may be obtained from the other party through a request for disclosure, TRCP 194.2(f)(2); more detailed information can be secured through an oral deposition or an expert's report, *see* TRCP 195.1, 195.4, 195.5.

(3) **Facts.** A party is entitled to discover the facts known by the retained testifying expert that relate to or form the basis of the expert's mental impressions and opinions formed or made in connection with the case in which the discovery is sought, regardless of when and how the factual information was acquired. TRCP 192.3(e)(3). A brief form of this information may be obtained from the other party through a request for disclosure, TRCP 194.2(f)(3); more detailed information can be secured through an oral deposition or an expert's report, *see* TRCP 195.1, 195.4, 195.5.

(4) **Opinions.** A party is entitled to discover the mental impressions and opinions of the retained testifying expert and any methods used to derive them. TRCP 192.3(e)(4); ***Yarborough v. Tarrant Appr. Dist.***, 846 S.W.2d 552, 553 (Tex.App.—Fort Worth 1993, no writ). Any information regarding the testifying expert's mental impressions or opinions are discoverable. TRCP 192.3(e)(4); *see, e.g.*, ***In re Family Hospice***, 62 S.W.3d 313, 316 (Tex.App.—El Paso 2001, orig. proceeding) (expert's notes made while reviewing interrogatories were discoverable). The general substance of the retained testifying expert's mental impressions and opinions and a brief summary of the basis for them may be obtained from the other party through a request for disclosure, TRCP 194.2(f)(3); more detailed information can be secured through an oral deposition or an expert's report, *see* TRCP 195.1, 195.4, 195.5.

PRACTICE TIP

TRCP 192.3(e)(4) permits discovery of, among other things, the expert's method in arriving at her opinion. However, TRCP 194.2(f) does not include this among the matters that must be disclosed in response to a request for disclosure. A responding party should include the expert's methodology, even though not required by TRCP 194.2(f), because that party will have the burden to show the expert's methodology is sound if the expert's opinion is challenged as inadmissible under TRE 702. See ***Merrell Dow Pharms. v. Havner****, 953 S.W.2d 706, 714 (Tex.1997) (an expert's opinion is not admissible if it is based on flawed methodology). See "Motion to Exclude Expert," ch. 5-M, p. 303.*

---

(5) **Evidence of bias.** A party is entitled to discover information about the retained testifying expert's potential bias. TRCP 192.3(e)(5); ***In re Doctors' Hosp.***, 2 S.W.3d 504, 507 (Tex.App.—San Antonio 1999, orig. proceeding); *see also* TRE 613(b) (evidence of witness's bias is considered relevant & admissible). See Cochran, ***Texas Rules of Evidence Handbook***, p. 644 (5th ed. 2003). It is not necessary to put the expert's credibility at issue before seeking evidence of the expert's potential bias. *See* TRCP 192.3(e)(5) (party may discover any bias of testifying witness); ***Russell v. Young***, 452 S.W.2d 434, 436 (Tex.1970) (expert may be cross-examined about number of times she was paid for testifying); *see also* ***Walker v. Packer***, 827 S.W.2d 833, 838-39 (Tex.1992) (in case that predated TRCP 192.3(e)(5), court held once evidence raised possibility of bias, information about potential bias was discoverable). Discovery of bias information from a retained testifying expert can be secured through a targeted request for disclosure, questions during an oral deposition, a request for production of documents sent with a notice of an oral deposition, and as part of the expert's report. *See* TRCP 194.2(f), 195.1, 195.4, 195.5.

(a) List of expert's other cases. A party should always ask the expert to produce a list of all other cases in which she testified as an expert—at trial or by deposition—within the last four years, and the amount of money paid for each appearance. *Cf.* FRCP 26(a)(2)(B) (in federal cases, rule requires, as part of expert's written report, a list of all other cases in which witness testified as expert at trial or by deposition within last four years). This information can be sought through a targeted request for disclosure asking for the information as part of the résumé of the retained expert, or by deposition, or as part of a court-ordered report.

(b) Personal financial records. When information about bias is not available by less intrusive means, a party may be able to obtain the financial records of an expert to prove bias. *See **Doctors' Hosp.***, 2 S.W.3d at 507 (Hardberger, C.J., concurring) (court abuses its discretion by requiring disclosure of tax returns when same information is available through less intrusive reasons); ***Kern v. Gleason***, 840 S.W.2d 730, 737-38 (Tex. App.—Amarillo 1992, orig. proceeding) (party seeking personal financial records must show information unavailable from another source); *see, e.g.*, ***Olinger v. Curry***, 926 S.W.2d 832, 834-35 (Tex.App.—Fort Worth 1996, orig. proceeding) (D's expert's tax returns not discoverable because expert admitted to potential bias in deposition); *see also **In re Dolezal***, 970 S.W.2d 650, 653 (Tex.App.—Corpus Christi 1998, orig. proceeding) (D could not get list from P's chiropractor of all lawyers who referred patients to chiropractor).

(6) Materials used by expert. A party is entitled to all documents, tangible things, physical models, reports, compilations of data, or other material provided to, reviewed by, or prepared by or for the retained testifying expert in anticipation of trial. TRCP 192.3(e)(6), 194.2(f)(4)(A). Almost everything the retained testifying expert reviewed or produced as part of her participation in the case is discoverable, including drafts of reports prepared by the expert and even the expert's file. This information can be secured from the party through a request for disclosure and an oral deposition with a request for documents. TRCP 194.2(f)(4)(A), 195.4.

(7) Expert's report. A party is entitled to copies of reports prepared by or for the retained testifying expert in anticipation of trial. TRCP 192.3(e)(6), 194.2(f)(4)(A). A report prepared by a retained testifying expert can be secured as part of a request for disclosure. TRCP 194.2(f)(4). When the retained testifying expert has not prepared a written report, the trial court may order a report be reduced to writing, or other tangible form, and produced. TRCP 195.5; ***Loftin v. Martin***, 776 S.W.2d 145, 147 (Tex.1989); *see **Dennis v. Haden***, 867 S.W.2d 48, 51-52 (Tex.App.—Texarkana 1993, writ denied) (because party did not provide expert's report as required by pretrial order, expert should have been excluded). See "Expert's Report," §7, p. 374; ***O'Connor's*** FORM 6C:01.

(8) Résumé & bibliography. A party is entitled to the current résumé and bibliography of retained testifying experts. TRCP 192.3(e)(7), 194.2(f)(4)(B). The résumé and bibliography can be secured through a request for disclosure. TRCP 194.2(f)(4)(B). If the facts on the résumé change before trial, the party has a duty to supplement. *See, e.g.*, ***City of Paris v. McDowell***, 79 S.W.3d 601, 606 (Tex.App.—Texarkana 2002, no pet.) (expert earned a master's degree between initial disclosure & trial, which was not reflected on résumé).

2. Information about nonretained experts. The following is a list of the information discoverable about and from nonretained testifying experts.

(1) Identity. A party is entitled to the name, address, and telephone number of the nonretained testifying expert witnesses. TRCP 192.3(e)(1). See §4.1.1(1), above.

(2) Subject of testimony. A party is entitled to discover the subject matter of the nonretained testifying expert's testimony. TRCP 192.3(e)(2). A brief form of this information may be obtained from the other party through a request for disclosure. TRCP 194.2(f)(2). A more detailed form of this information may be obtained from the nonretained expert through an oral deposition, a deposition on written questions, or a subpoena. TRCP 176, 205; TRCP 195, cmt. 2.

(3) Facts. A party is entitled to discover the facts known by the nonretained testifying expert that relate to or form the basis of the expert's mental impressions and opinions. TRCP 192.3(e)(3). A brief form of this information may be obtained from the other party through a request for disclosure. TRCP 194.2(f)(3). A more detailed form of this information may be obtained from the nonretained expert through an oral deposition, a deposition on written questions, or a subpoena. TRCP 176, 205; TRCP 195, cmt. 2.

(4) Opinions. A party is entitled to discover the general substance of the nonretained testifying expert's mental impressions and opinions and the basis for them. TRCP 192.3(e)(4). A brief form of this information or documents that reflect this information may be obtained from the other party through a request for disclosure. TRCP 194.2(f)(3). A more detailed form of this information may be obtained from the nonretained expert through an oral deposition, a deposition on written questions, or a subpoena. TRCP 176, 205; TRCP 195, cmt. 2.

(5) Evidence of bias. A party is entitled to discover information about the nonretained testifying expert's potential bias. TRCP 192.3(e)(5). See "Evidence of bias," §4.1.1(5), p. 368. This information can be secured from the nonretained expert through an oral deposition, a deposition on written questions, or a subpoena for documents. TRCP 176, 205; TRCP 195, cmt. 2. Bias evidence about a nonretained testifying expert cannot be secured through TRCP 194 or 195. TRCP 195, cmt. 2.

(6) Materials used by expert. A party is entitled to all documents, tangible things, physical models, reports, compilations of data, or other materials provided to, reviewed by, or prepared by or for the nonretained testifying expert in anticipation of trial. TRCP 192.3(e)(6). This information can be secured from the nonretained expert through an oral deposition, a deposition on written questions, or a subpoena for documents. TRCP 176, 205; TRCP 195, cmt. 2. Materials used by a nontestifying expert cannot be secured through TRCP 194 or 195. TRCP 195, cmt. 2.

(7) Expert's report. A report prepared by a nonretained testifying expert may be secured from the expert through TRCP 176 or TRCP 205. A nonretained expert's report cannot be secured through TRCP 194 or TRCP 195. TRCP 195, cmt. 2. See "Expert's Report," §7, p. 374.

(8) Résumé & bibliography. A party is entitled to the current résumé and bibliography of nonretained testifying experts. TRCP 192.3(e)(7). The nonretained expert's résumé and bibliography can be secured from the nonretained expert through an oral deposition, a deposition on written questions, or a subpoena. TRCP 176, 205; TRCP 195, cmt. 2.

§4.2 Consulting experts.

1. Consulting-only expert – no discovery. Consulting-only experts are protected from discovery as part of the work-product privilege. *See* TRCP 195, cmt. 1. No information about a consulting-only expert is discoverable, not the expert's identity, mental impressions, opinions, or work product. TRCP 192.3(e); ***In re City of Georgetown***, 53 S.W.3d 328, 334 (Tex.2001); ***In re Ford Motor Co.***, 988 S.W.2d 714, 719 (Tex.1998). Tests conducted by a consulting expert are protected from discovery as long as the tests are not conducted on the physical evidence in the case and the results are not reviewed by a testifying expert. TRCP 192.3(e); *see* ***G.M. Corp. v. Gayle***, 951 S.W.2d 469, 474-75 (Tex.1997) (consulting experts could conduct crash tests). Materials protected by the privilege for the nondiscoverable consulting-only expert are protected from discovery, and the privilege is not qualified by the "need and hardship" exception stated in TRCP 192.5(b)(2).

2. Information about consulting-plus experts.

(1) Consulting expert + work reviewed. A party is entitled to obtain the same information about a consulting expert whose work was reviewed by a testifying expert as it can obtain about the testifying expert. TRCP 192.3(e). See "Information about retained testifying experts," §4.1.1, p. 367.

PRACTICE TIP

Although TRCP 195 limits the procedures for securing discovery about testifying experts, it does not limit the procedures for securing discovery about discoverable consulting experts. TRCP 195, cmt. 1. Discovery about discoverable consulting experts can be obtained through any means permitted by the TRCPs (interrogatories, requests for production, depositions, etc.).

(2) Consulting expert + facts. A consulting expert with facts about the case is treated as a fact witness. See "Consulting expert + facts = fact witness," §2.2.2(2), p. 365. A party is entitled to obtain the same information about a consulting expert who has knowledge of facts as it can obtain about a fact witness. TRCP 192.3(c) (scope of discovery), TRCP 192.5(c)(1) (exception to work product), TRCP 194.2(e) (request for disclosure). A party may obtain this discovery through TRCP 194.2(e) and any other discovery rule except TRCP 195. The information discoverable about the consultant with facts includes the following:

(a) Identity. A party is entitled to the name, address, and telephone number of an expert who has firsthand knowledge of facts or secondhand knowledge of facts obtained outside of the consultation. TRCP 192.3(c) (scope of discovery), TRCP 194.2(e) (request for disclosure of fact witnesses).

(b) Connection with the case. A party is entitled to obtain a brief description of the consulting expert's connection with the case. TRCP 192.3(c), 194.2(e). This does not mean the party must provide a narrative statement of the facts the expert knows. TRCP 192, cmt. 3. For example, the description could be "examined wellhead after accident." *Id.*

(c) Facts known by consultant. A party is entitled to obtain the following information known by the consultant:

[1] Firsthand facts. The consultant's firsthand knowledge about information in the case. TRCP 192.3(c).

[2] Secondhand facts. The consultant's secondhand knowledge (*i.e.*, hearsay) about facts in the case learned in some way other than in consultation about the case (*i.e.*, not in anticipation of litigation or in preparation for trial). TRCP 192.3(c).

(d) Witness statements. A party is entitled to obtain a witness statement given by a consulting expert who has knowledge of the facts. TRCP 192.3(h).

§5. SUPPLEMENTING EXPERT DISCOVERY

A party has a duty to amend and supplement discovery about its testifying experts. TRCP 195.6. See ***O'Connor's*** FORMS 6C:02-03.

§5.1 Supplementing discovery of retained testifying expert. An expert cannot give an opinion at trial that was not provided in response to discovery, unless there is good cause to permit it or the opinion would not unfairly surprise or prejudice the other parties. TRCP 193.6(a); *see* ***Mares v. Ford Motor Co.***, 53 S.W.3d 416, 419 (Tex.App.—San Antonio 2001, no pet.); *see, e.g.*, ***Vingcard A.S. v. Merrimac Hospitality Sys.***, 59 S.W.3d 847, 856 (Tex.App.—Fort Worth 2001, pet. denied) (court did not find good cause but found admission of expert's opinion harmless error); *see also* ***Ersek v. Davis & Davis***, 69 S.W.3d 268, 271 (Tex.App.—Austin 2002, pet. denied) (court did not find good cause for designating expert after deadline, more than a year after filing suit).

1. Written discovery responses. A party's duty to amend and supplement written discovery about a retained testifying expert is governed by TRCP 193.5. TRCP 195.6; ***Vingcard***, 59 S.W.3d at 855. See "Supplementing Discovery Responses," ch. 6-A, §16, p. 325.

2. Deposition testimony.

(1) Supplementation required. To the extent a party's retained testifying expert changes or modifies her opinion, the party must amend and supplement the expert's deposition testimony regarding the expert's mental impressions, opinions, and the basis for them. TRCP 195.6; *see* ***Collins v. Collins***, 923 S.W.2d 569, 569 (Tex. 1996); *see, e.g.*, ***Farm Servs. v. Gonzales***, 756 S.W.2d 747, 750 (Tex.App.—Corpus Christi 1988, writ denied) (testimony of expert who changed her opinion after deposition should have been excluded); *see also* ***Titus Cty. Hosp. Dist. v. Lucas***, 988 S.W.2d 740, 740 (Tex.1998) (acknowledging a narrow duty to supplement certain expert testimony); ***Collins v. Collins***, 904 S.W.2d 792, 801 (Tex.App.—Houston [1st Dist.] 1995) (in divorce proceeding, husband could not testify about value of business because he did not identify himself as an expert & said in deposition that he would not testify as expert), *writ denied*, 923 S.W.2d 569 (Tex.1996).

(2) Supplementation not required. An expert can modify her testimony based on refinements in her calculations made shortly before trial without invoking the need to supplement. ***Exxon Corp. v. West Tex. Gathering Co.***, 868 S.W.2d 299, 304 (Tex.1993); *see, e.g.*, ***Koko Motel v. Mayo***, 91 S.W.3d 41, 51 (Tex.App.—Amarillo 2002, pet. denied) (change in opinion was merely a refinement because data & formula were already in record). An expert can also modify her testimony without supplementation if the opinion expands on a subject that has already been disclosed. ***Norfolk S. Ry. v. Bailey***, 92 S.W.3d 577, 581 (Tex.App.—Austin 2002, no pet.); *see* ***Navistar Int'l Transp. v. Crim Truck & Tractor Co.***, 883 S.W.2d 687, 691 (Tex.App.—Texarkana 1994, writ denied). The testimony of an expert should not be barred because a change in some minor detail of the person's work has not been disclosed a month before trial. ***Exxon Corp.***, 868 S.W.2d at 304.

3. Expert's report. A party has a duty to amend and supplement the report of the retained testifying expert regarding the expert's mental impressions, opinions, and the basis for them. TRCP 195.6.

§5.2 Supplementing discovery of nonretained testifying expert. A party has a duty to amend and supplement discovery about a nonretained testifying expert as set out in TRCP 193.5. Under that rule, a party has a duty to supplement its written responses to discovery relating to a nonretained expert. See "When supplementation required," ch. 6-A, §16.1, p. 325. A party has no burden to supplement the deposition testimony of a nonretained testifying expert. *See* TRCP 193.5(a) (duty to supplement written discovery, not oral discovery). The nonretained testifying expert has no burden to supplement her own responses to discovery. *See* TRCP 205 (discovery from nonparties).

PRACTICE TIP

Instruct your experts to promptly inform you of any change in their responses (oral or written) so you can timely supplement or amend your discovery responses.

§6. DEADLINES FOR SECURING DISCOVERY FROM EXPERTS

The deadline for securing discovery from experts depends on the designation of experts.

§6.1 Deadlines to designate testifying experts. The designation of testifying experts is accomplished by furnishing the information about the experts requested under TRCP 194.2(f). TRCP 195.2.

1. Making designation. TRCP 195.2 establishes a schedule for responding to requests for disclosure about testifying experts. The schedule may be modified by court order (for good cause) or by agreement of the parties. TRCP 191.1, 195.2. A party must designate its testifying experts and supply the information required by TRCP 194.2(f) within the following time periods:

(1) Plaintiff's expert. A party seeking affirmative relief (generally, the plaintiff) must identify its testifying experts within 30 days after service of the request for disclosures or 90 days before the end of the discovery period, whichever is later. TRCP 195.2(a); ***Ersek v. Davis & Davis***, 69 S.W.3d 268, 270 (Tex.App.—Austin 2002, pet. denied); ***Snider v. Stanley***, 44 S.W.3d 713, 715 (Tex.App.—Beaumont 2001, pet. denied).

(2) Defendant's expert. A party who is not seeking affirmative relief (generally, the defendant) must identify its testifying experts within 30 days after service of the request for disclosures or 60 days before the end of the discovery period, whichever is later. *See* TRCP 195.2(b).

NOTE

Even though TRCP 195.2 and 195.3 require the plaintiff to designate and present its experts for deposition first, the trial court may alter this schedule under TRCP 191. TRCP 195, cmt. 3; Griesel, The "New" Texas Discovery Rules, §IX(A), p. 22. For example, the court could modify the schedule if a contested issue on which expert testimony is required is raised by an affirmative defense rather than by the primary liability claim. Griesel, The "New" Texas Discovery Rules, §IX(A), p. 22.

2. Changing designation. Once an expert is designated as a testifying expert, the expert can be redesignated as a consulting expert as long as there is no bargain to suppress testimony or some other improper purpose behind the redesignation. ***In re Doctors' Hosp.***, 2 S.W.3d 504, 506 (Tex.App.—San Antonio 1999, orig. proceeding); *see, e.g.*, ***Tom L. Scott, Inc. v. McIlhany***, 798 S.W.2d 556, 560 (Tex.1990) (redesignation was improper because it was part of bargain between adversaries to suppress testimony); ***Lopez v. Martin***, 10 S.W.3d 790, 794 (Tex.App.—Corpus Christi 2000, pet. denied) (nothing in record indicated redesignation was made for improper purpose); ***Castellanos v. Littlejohn***, 945 S.W.2d 236, 239 (Tex.App.—San Antonio 1997, orig. proceeding) (party who accidentally listed consulting expert as testifying expert could redesignate); ***Harnischfeger Corp. v. Stone***, 814 S.W.2d 263, 265 (Tex.App.—Houston [14th Dist.] 1991, orig. proceeding) (D could not designate same expert as testifying expert in one case and nontestifying expert in companion case).

§6.2 Deadlines to depose testifying experts.

1. Deposing retained testifying experts. TRCP 195.3 establishes a schedule for deposing testifying experts retained by, employed by, or otherwise subject to the control of a party.

(1) Plaintiff did not furnish report. If the party seeking affirmative relief (generally, the plaintiff) did not furnish a report when it designated its retained testifying expert, it must tender the expert for deposition reasonably promptly after designation and before the other party is required to designate its experts. TRCP 195.3(a)(1) & cmt. 3; ***Vaughn v. Ford Motor Co.***, 91 S.W.3d 387, 392 (Tex.App.—Eastland 2002, pet. filed 3-14-03). When, through the actions of the plaintiff, the deposition cannot be concluded more than 15 days before the deadline for designating other experts, the deadline must be extended for other experts testifying on the same subject. TRCP 195.3(a)(1); *see also* Gold, *"So, Who Died & Made You King?"* State Bar, Advanced Medical Malpractice Course, IV.D.1(a)(3) at K-10 to 11 (2000) (under TRCP 195.3, deadline should not be extended if P attempted in good faith to schedule expert's deposition before deadline expired).

(2) Plaintiff furnished report. If the party seeking affirmative relief (generally, the plaintiff) produced a report when it designated its retained testifying expert, the burden shifts to the other party to designate its experts testifying on the same subject before the plaintiff is required to tender its expert for deposition. TRCP 195.3(a)(2) & cmt. 3. This provision is a compromise designed to allow defendants to obtain sufficient information from plaintiffs to enable them to obtain appropriate experts, yet prevent plaintiffs from being unfairly surprised or "sandbagged." Griesel, *The "New" Texas Discovery Rules*, §IX(A), p. 22.

(3) Defendant's experts. A party not seeking affirmative relief (generally, the defendant) must tender its expert for deposition "reasonably promptly" after it designates its expert and after the plaintiff's experts have been deposed on the same subject. TRCP 195.3(b).

2. **Deposing nonretained testifying experts.** A party is not required to "tender" a nonretained testifying expert for a deposition. TRCP 195, cmt. 2 (TRCP 195 does not address depositions of nonretained testifying experts). The deposition of a nonretained testifying expert may be taken according to the same rules for deposing nonparties. *See* TRCP 199 (oral depositions), TRCP 205 (discovery from nonparties). See "Procedure for the Standard Oral Deposition," ch. 6-E, §4, p. 387.

§6.3 Deadlines to supplement. See "Deadline to supplement answers," ch. 6-A, §16.4, p. 327.

§6.4 Discovery deadline after trial reset. When the date for trial is reset more than 30 days beyond the original trial date, the resetting nullifies the original discovery deadlines. See "Discovery deadline when trial reset," ch. 6-A, §13.1.4, p. 324.

§7. EXPERT'S REPORT

There is no requirement that parties automatically produce expert reports.

§7.1 Contents of expert's report. An expert's report includes the discoverable factual observations, tests, supporting data, calculations, photographs, and opinions of the expert. TRCP 195.5. The report must provide the expert's opinion and the underlying basis for it. *See* ***Mauzey v. Sutliff***, ___ S.W.3d ___ (Tex.App.—Austin 2003, pet. denied) (No. 03-02-00188-CV; 4-17-03) (trial courts must ensure that expert report fully discloses substance of and basis for expert's mental impressions). For example, a report in a medical malpractice suit might contain a medical history, diagnosis, prognosis, opinions, impressions, and causation. ***Tibbetts v. Gagliardi***, 2 S.W.3d 659, 663 n.1 (Tex.App.—Houston [14th Dist.] 1999, pet. denied); *see* CPRC §74.351(j), (r)(6). The expert's report can be secured through a request for disclosure or by court order.

§7.2 Securing reports from retained testifying experts.

1. **By request for disclosure.**

(1) **Request.** A party can ask for a report from the other party's retained testifying expert in a request for disclosure. TRCP 194.2(f)(4)(A).

(2) **Response.** The party responding to a request for disclosure under TRCP 194.2(f)(4)(A) has two choices:

(a) **Produce report.** The party may ask its retained expert to produce a report to be provided to the requesting party. TRCP 195, cmt. 3. The production of the report will trigger the designation of the other party's expert. *Id.*

(b) **Tender expert.** A party who does not wish to incur the expense of creating a report may simply tender its retained expert for deposition. TRCP 195, cmt. 3.

2. **By court order.** A party can file a motion asking for a court order requiring the other party to produce an expert report from its retained testifying experts. TRCP 195.5. See ***O'Connor's*** FORM 6C:01. The court can order the report of a retained expert be reduced to a tangible form and produced. TRCP 195.5. The court may order a report from a testifying expert in addition to a deposition. *Id.*

§7.3 Securing reports from nonretained experts. A nonretained expert's report cannot be secured through TRCP 194 (request for disclosures) or TRCP 195.5 (court-ordered report). TRCP 195, cmt. 2.

1. **From nonretained expert.**

(1) **By deposition & subpoena.** If the nonretained expert prepared a report, a copy may be secured from the expert through a discovery subpoena to appear and produce at a deposition or simply to produce. TRCP 176, 205. See "Securing Things from a Nonparty," ch. 6-H, §5, p. 428.

(2) By request for medical records. In a suit alleging physical or mental injury, a party may request that the injured party produce medical records or furnish an authorization permitting disclosure of medical records. TRCP 194.2(j). See "Request for Party's Medical Records or Authorization," ch. 6-I, §3, p. 435.

(3) By payment. A party may offer to pay a nonretained expert to prepare a report. However, if the nonretained expert had a privileged relationship with the other party (*e.g.*, doctor-patient), a party cannot offer to pay the nonretained expert to prepare a report without the patient's consent.

2. From other party.

(1) By request for disclosure. If the nonretained expert's report was provided to, reviewed by, or prepared for the retained testifying expert, the party can secure it as part of the request for information about the retained expert. TRCP 194.2(f)(4)(A).

(2) By request for production. If a party has a copy of a nontestifying expert's report that was not provided to its retained testifying expert, other parties can secure a copy of it by a request for production. TRCP 196.1(a).

(3) By witness statement request. If a party has a copy of a witness statement made by the nonretained testifying expert, other parties are entitled to obtain a copy of it. TRCP 192.3(h).

3. Under Public Information Act. If the nonretained expert is a police officer or other public official, a party may be able to secure a copy of the officer's report under the Public Information Act. *See* Gov't Code §§552.021, 552.022.

§8. PAYING THE EXPERT

§8.1 Expert fees for most discovery. As a rule, a party pays the fees charged by its expert. The amount of the fees is established by the contract between the party and the expert.

§8.2 Expert fees for depositions.

1. Retained expert of opposing party. When a party takes the oral deposition of an expert witness retained by the opposing party, all reasonable fees charged by the expert for time spent in preparing for, giving, reviewing, and correcting the deposition must be paid by the party that retained the expert. TRCP 195.7. If the party that retained the expert feels the other side is purposefully running up the costs and abusing TRCP 195.7, that party can seek relief under TRCP 191.1 (trial court has the power to modify discovery procedures and limitations) and TRCP 192.6 (the party can seek protective order). TRCP 191.1 permits a trial court, for good cause, to modify the allocation of fees and expenses. *See* TRCP 191.1 & cmt. 1. See "Modifying discovery by court order," ch. 6-A, §5.2, p. 316.

2. Nonretained expert. The TRCPs do not address the issue of who pays for the deposition of the nonretained expert. The nonretained expert's fees for the deposition should probably be paid by the party who notices the deposition. For example, if the defendant notices the deposition of an emergency room doctor who treated the plaintiff after the accident, the defendant should pay for the expert's fees, not the plaintiff.

D. REQUESTS FOR DISCLOSURE

§1. GENERAL

§1.1 Rule. TRCP 194.

§1.2 Purpose. A request for disclosure is a written request for information designed to produce basic discovery of specific categories of information. TRCP 194, cmt. 1. This procedure is borrowed from the federal discovery rules. Griesel, *The "New" Texas Discovery Rules: Three Years Later*, Advanced Evidence & Discovery Course, State

Bar of Texas, ch. 2, §VIII(A), p. 19 (2002). Unlike interrogatories, disclosure responses are not verified, and no objections are permitted. TRCP 194.5. Requests for disclosure will likely be the first form of discovery in a lawsuit.

§1.3 Forms. See *O'Connor's Texas Civil Forms*, FORMS 6D.

§1.4 Other references. Griesel, *The "New" Texas Discovery Rules*, §VIII, p. 19; Pemberton, *The First Year Under the New Discovery Rules* (1-1-00), www.supreme.courts.state.tx.us/rules/tdr/ (*The First Year*).

§2. SCOPE

The scope of discovery for disclosures is governed by TRCP 192 as limited by TRCP 194. See §3.2, below.

§3. PROPOUNDING DISCLOSURES

§3.1 Procedure.

1. Format. The request for disclosure should be typed on letter-size paper. Some lawyers include the request in their first pleading, either the original petition or the original answer. See "Request for Disclosure," ch. 2-B, §12, p. 78.

2. Served on party. A request for disclosure can be served only on another party. TRCP 194.1. It cannot be served on a nonparty.

3. Time to serve request for disclosure.

(1) How early. A request for disclosure may be served any time after suit is filed. TRCP 190.2(c)(1), 190.3(b)(1). The rules contemplate that a plaintiff may serve the initial set of discovery with its original petition. See "Serving discovery with original pleadings," ch. 6-A, §12.2, p. 323.

(a) With or as part of P's original petition. The plaintiff should consider serving the request for disclosure along with the original petition or as part of the original petition. If the plaintiff includes the request in the petition, the plaintiff must change the title of the instrument to "Plaintiff's Original Petition and Request for Disclosure." If the plaintiff serves a request for disclosure as a separate document but with the original petition, the plaintiff must list the request as one of the documents served in both the citation and the return for the citation.

(b) Along with D's answer. The defendant can serve a request for disclosure when it serves its answer on the plaintiff.

(2) How late. The deadline to serve the request is 30 days before the end of the discovery period. TRCP 194.1. See "Discovery Periods," ch. 6-A, §6, p. 317. When served by mail or fax, the request should be served at least 34 days before the end of the discovery period. See "Deadline to Respond to Discovery," ch. 6-A, §13, p. 323.

4. Specify time to answer. The person serving the request for disclosure should specify when the answers are due, but it must allow at least 30 days after service of the request. TRCP 194.1, 194.3.

(1) Most cases. In most cases, a party will ask the other party to answer a request for disclosure within the shortest time permitted by TRCP 194.1, that is, "within 30 days of service."

(2) Disclosures served before answer date. When the plaintiff serves a request for disclosure on the defendant before the defendant's answer is due, the defendant has 50 days from the date of service of the request to respond. TRCP 194.3(a). See "Deadline to Respond to Discovery," ch. 6-A, §13, p. 323.

(3) Disclosure of testifying experts. The time to respond to a request asking for disclosure of the other party's testifying experts is governed by TRCP 195.2. See "Deadlines to designate testifying experts," ch. 6-C, §5.1, p. 372.

(4) By agreement or court order. The parties may vary the deadlines in TRCP 194.3 by agreement or with a court order. TRCP 191.1. See "Modifying Discovery Procedures & Limitations," ch. 6-A, §5, p. 316.

§3.2 Content of request.

1. Standard requests. A party may make the request in the language suggested by TRCP 194.1, by stating the following: "Pursuant to Rule 194, you are requested to disclose, within [*30 or 50*] days of the service of this request, the information or material described in Rule [*identify rule, e.g., 194.2; 194.2(a), (c), and (f); 194.2(d)-(g)*]." See ***O'Connor's*** FORM 6D:01. Or, a party may make requests for the individual items in the subparts of TRCP 194.2.

PRACTICE TIP

The problem with the request provided in TRCP 194.1 and the more specific requests below is that the party receiving it might not be aware that a consulting expert with knowledge of facts is discoverable as a fact witness. Thus, you should use targeted requests to ask for experts. See §3.2.2, below.

TRCP 194.2 permits a party to ask for the following information:

(1) Correct party names. The correct names of the parties to the lawsuit. TRCP 194.2(a); *see* ***Bailey v. Vanscot Concrete Co.***, 894 S.W.2d 757, 761 n.3 (Tex.1995), *overruled on other grounds*, ***Chilkewitz v. Hyson***, 22 S.W.3d 825 (Tex.1999).

(2) Potential parties. The name, address, and telephone number of any potential party. TRCP 194.2(b). Potential parties can be a good source of information, just like fact witnesses.

(3) Contentions. The legal theories and, in general, the factual bases of the responding party's claims or defenses. TRCP 192.3(j), 194.2(c). These requests are similar to so called "contention interrogatories," and may be used for the same purpose. TRCP 194, cmt. 2.

(4) Damages. The amount and any method of calculating economic damages. TRCP 194.2(d).

(5) Fact witnesses. The name, address, and telephone number of any person having knowledge of relevant facts, and a brief statement of each identified person's connection with the case. TRCP 194.2(e). See "Fact witnesses," ch. 6-B, §2.8, p. 344.

(6) Retained testifying experts. See "Information about retained testifying experts," ch. 6-C, §4.1.1, p. 367. A request may ask the other party to disclose the following information about a retained testifying expert:

(a) The expert's name, address, and telephone number. TRCP 194.2(f)(1).

(b) The subject matter on which the expert will testify. TRCP 194.2(f)(2).

(c) The general substance of the expert's mental impressions and opinions and a brief summary of the basis for them. TRCP 194.2(f)(3).

(d) All documents, tangible things, reports, models, or data compilations that have been provided to, reviewed by, or prepared by or for the expert in anticipation of the expert's testimony. TRCP 194.2(f)(4)(A); ***Vingcard A.S. v. Merrimac Hospitality Sys.***, 59 S.W.3d 847, 855 (Tex.App.—Fort Worth 2001, pet. denied).

(e) The expert's current résumé and bibliography. TRCP 194.2(f)(4)(B). The request should ask that the expert produce as part of her résumé, a list of all other cases in which she has testified as an expert at trial or by deposition within the last four years. See "List of expert's other cases," ch. 6-C, §4.1.1(5)(a), p. 369.

(7) Nonretained testifying experts. See "Information about nonretained experts," ch. 6-C, §4.1.2, p. 369. A request may ask the other party to disclose the following information about a nonretained testifying expert:

(a) The expert's name, address, and telephone number. TRCP 194.2(f)(1).

(b) The subject matter on which the expert will testify. TRCP 194.2(f)(2).

(c) Either the general substance of the expert's mental impressions and opinions and a brief summary of the basis for them, or documents reflecting such information. TRCP 194.2(f)(3).

(8) Documents. A request may ask the other party to disclose the following documents: (1) discoverable indemnity and insuring agreements, (2) discoverable settlement agreements, and (3) discoverable witness statements. TRCP 194.2(g)-(i).

(9) Medical records. See "Medical Records," ch. 6-I, p. 434. In a suit alleging physical or mental injury and damages from the occurrence that is the subject of the suit, the request may ask for medical records as follows:

(a) From the party who alleges injury, (1) all medical records and bills that are reasonably related to the injuries or damages asserted or (2) as an alternative, an authorization permitting the disclosure of those medical records and bills. TRCP 194.2(j); ***In re Shipmon***, 68 S.W.3d 815, 820 (Tex.App.—Amarillo 2001, orig. proceeding).

(b) From the party who obtained the injured party's medical records with an authorization furnished by the injured party, a copy of all the records it obtained. TRCP 194.2(k).

2. Targeted request. To secure specific information, the party should consider using a "targeted" request that identifies, in a separate sentence, the discoverable information sought under TRCP 194.2. For example, if a party wants a business entity to name others who may be potential parties because of their ownership interest in the entity, the request could state, "You are requested to disclose the information or material described in Rule 194.2(b). Please answer to the full extent authorized by the rules, which should include the names of all individuals and entities with an ownership interest in the business." For other targeted requests, see ***O'Connor's*** FORM 6D:02.

NOTE

Some lawyers believe that TRCP 194.2 requires a request for disclosure to be stated in the language quoted in TRCP 194.1, without any elaboration. See Pemberton, The First Year, II.I.1 (S.Ct. intended requests for disclosure to "precisely track" the language of TRCP 194.1). That certainly was the intent of the Supreme Court Advisory Committee (SCAC), which drafted Rule 9 (the SCAC'S predecessor to TRCP 194.2) in 1995 to include the directive that the request for disclosure "shall state." See Appendix G, SCAC Report, Handbook on Texas Discovery Practice, p. 626, 637 (1999). However, the Supreme Court deleted "shall state" in the June 1998 draft. Compare Discovery Rules - Tentative Draft No. 2, Rule 5.1 (6-9-98) (deletion of "shall state"), with Tentative Draft No. 1, Rule 9 (1-19-98) (inclusion of "shall state"), at www.supreme.courts.state.tx.us/rules/tdr/.

§4. RESPONDING TO REQUESTS FOR DISCLOSURE

§4.1 Procedure.

1. Time to respond. Generally, a party has 30 days from the date of service to respond to a request for disclosure, depending on the type of service. TRCP 21, 21a, 194.3. See "Deadline to Respond to Discovery," ch. 6-A, §13, p. 323. There are two exceptions.

(1) Served before answer is due. When a request for disclosure is served on a defendant before the defendant's answer is due, the defendant has 50 days after service of the request to respond. TRCP 194.3(a). See "Deadline to Respond to Discovery," ch. 6-A, §13, p. 323. To extend the time, see "Extending Time to Respond to Discovery," ch. 6-A, §14, p. 324.

(2) Testifying experts. TRCP 195.2 establishes the schedule for furnishing information regarding testifying experts. TRCP 194.2(f), 194.3(b), 195.2. See "Deadlines for Securing Discovery from Experts," ch. 6-C, §6, p. 372.

2. Not filed. The responding party's disclosures are not filed with the court. TRCP 191.4(a)(2); ***National Fam. Care Life Ins. Co. v. Fletcher***, 57 S.W.3d 662, 667 n.6 (Tex.App.—Beaumont 2001, pet. denied). For exceptions, see "Discovery materials not to be filed," ch. 6-A, §11.1.2, p. 322.

3. Form of responses. To respond to requests for disclosure properly, the answers, objections, and other responses must be made in the form required by the rules. See "Producing Written Discovery," ch. 6-A, §15, p. 324; ***O'Connor's*** FORM 6D:03.

(1) In writing. The response must be in writing. TRCP 193.1, 194.3; ***Vingcard***, 59 S.W.3d at 855. Each answer must follow the question to which the answer responds. TRCP 193.1.

(2) Signed. The response must be signed by a lawyer (or party when pro se). TRCP 191.3(a).

(3) Not verified. The response should not be verified.

(4) Separate answers. The response must provide separate answers for each request.

(5) Separate set of answers. In most cases, each set of requests for disclosure should be answered separately. In a multi-party case, a party responding to the same disclosures from different opposing parties may file one response that is sufficient to answer all sets. *See, e.g.*, ***Ward v. O'Connor***, 816 S.W.2d 446, 446 (Tex.App.—San Antonio 1991, no writ) (Ps filed one list of fact and expert witnesses in response to interrogatories from two Ds). *But see* ***Clark Equip. Co. v. Pitner***, 923 S.W.2d 117, 121-22 (Tex.App.—Houston [14th Dist.] 1996, writ denied) (answer to one party's interrogatory regarding subject matter of expert's testimony could not serve as answer to another party's interrogatory regarding substance of expert's testimony).

(6) Produce documents. The responding party must serve copies of documents and other tangible items with the response, unless the responsive items are voluminous, in which case the response must state a reasonable time and place for the production of documents. TRCP 194.4. The responding party must produce the documents at the time and place stated in the request, unless otherwise agreed by the parties or ordered by the court. *Id.* The requesting party must have a reasonable opportunity to inspect the documents or other items. *Id.*

§4.2 Content of response. The party must provide a complete response, based on all information reasonably available to the responding party or its attorney at the time the response is made. TRCP 193.1. When asked, a party must produce the following information:

1. Correct party name. A party is required to provide its correct name. TRCP 194.2(a); *see* ***Bailey v. Vanscot Concrete Co.***, 894 S.W.2d 757, 761 n.3 (Tex.1995), *overruled on other grounds*, ***Chilkewitz v. Hyson***, 22 S.W.3d 825 (Tex.1999).

2. Potential parties. A party is required to identify any potential parties and provide their names, addresses, and telephone numbers. TRCP 194.2(b); *see* ***Helfand v. Coane***, 12 S.W.3d 152, 157 n.3 (Tex.App.—Houston [1st Dist.] 2000, pet. denied).

3. Contentions. A party must disclose its legal theories and, in general, the factual bases of its claims or defenses. TRCP 194.2(c). The party is not required to marshal all evidence that may be offered at trial or to brief legal issues. TRCP 194.2(c) & cmt. 2. For example, a plaintiff would be required to disclose that it claimed damages suffered in a car wreck caused by the defendant's negligence in speeding but would not be required to state the speed at which the defendant was driving; and, a defendant in the same suit would be required to disclose its denial of the speeding allegation. TRCP 194, cmt. 2. TRCP 194.2(c) is intended to require disclosure of a party's basic assertions made in prosecution or defense of claims. TRCP 194, cmt. 2. A defendant cannot respond to a request for contentions by reurging its general denial. Pemberton, *The First Year*, II.I.2.

PRACTICE TIP

When responding to a contention request, the parties should review their pleadings and include all of their legal theories and the factual bases for them. If a legal theory or factual basis is omitted, the court may limit the subject matter on which the party can present evidence. See ***National Fam. Care****, 57 S.W.3d at 668 (in limiting evidence, trial court was too restrictive in interpreting D's response).*

4. Damages. A party must disclose the amount and any method of calculating economic damages. TRCP 194.2(d). For example, a plaintiff would be required to state how loss of past earnings and future earning capacity was calculated, and a defendant in the same suit would be required to disclose any grounds for contesting the damage calculations. TRCP 194, cmt. 2. If a plaintiff cannot demonstrate its method of calculation, the court may limit the damages the plaintiff can recover. *See* ***Butan Valley v. Smith***, 921 S.W.2d 822, 832 (Tex.App.—Houston [14th Dist.] 1996, no writ). A party is not required to state a method of calculating noneconomic damages, such as for mental anguish. TRCP 194, cmt. 2.

5. Fact witnesses. A party must identify persons who have knowledge of relevant facts and provide a brief statement of each person's connection with the case. TRCP 194.2(e). See "Who is a fact witness," ch. 6-B, §2.8.1, p. 344; "What is discoverable about fact witnesses," ch. 6-B, §2.8.2, p. 344.

(1) Identify witness. A party must identify all persons who have knowledge of relevant facts by name, address, and telephone number. TRCP 194.2(e); *see* ***Apresa v. Montfort Ins. Co.***, 932 S.W.2d 246, 248 (Tex. App.—El Paso 1996, no writ) (witnesses excluded at trial because answers did not provide addresses & telephone numbers). Even when a party answering the request for disclosure has little or no use for a witness's testimony, the party must still identify the witness as a source of relevant facts. *See* ***Walsh v. Mullane***, 725 S.W.2d 263, 265 (Tex.App.—Houston [1st Dist.] 1986, writ ref'd n.r.e.). The other party may have an important use for that witness's testimony. ***Stevenson v. Koutzarov***, 795 S.W.2d 313, 318 (Tex.App.—Houston [1st Dist.] 1990, writ denied). Fact witnesses typically include eyewitnesses; parties and their spouses, employers, and co-workers; treating doctors; other medical personnel; lawyers (for attorney fees); nonretained experts (*e.g.*, police officers); and consulting experts who have firsthand knowledge about the facts in the case or secondhand knowledge of the facts, learned outside the consultation. TRCP 192.3(c) (definition of fact witness). See "Consulting expert + facts = fact witness," ch. 6-C, §2.2.2(2), p. 365.

(2) Identify connections with case. A party is entitled to a brief description of the person's connection with the suit. TRCP 192.3(c), 194.2(e); ***Beam v. A.H. Chaney, Inc.***, 56 S.W.3d 920, 922 (Tex.App.—Fort Worth 2001, pet. denied). See "Connection with case," ch. 6-B, §2.8.2(2), p. 344. This does not mean the party must provide a narrative statement of the facts the person knows. TRCP 192, cmt. 3. The description could be "treating physician," "eyewitness," "chief financial officer," or "plaintiff's mother and eyewitness to accident." *Id.*

6. Testifying experts. The party must provide information about the experts it plans to call as witnesses. *See* TRCP 194.2(f). The requirement to identify experts does not depend on whether the expert is compensated for her time as a witness. ***Baylor Med. Plaza Servs. v. Kidd***, 834 S.W.2d 69, 73 (Tex.App.—Texarkana 1992, writ denied).

(1) Retained testifying experts. For retained testifying experts, a party must provide (1) the identity and location, including the name, address, and telephone number of its expert witness; (2) the subject matter of the expert's testimony; (3) the expert's mental impressions and opinions, including facts known by the expert that relate to or form the basis of those mental impressions and opinions; (4) all documents, reports, or compilations provided to, reviewed by, or prepared by or for the expert in anticipation of the expert's testimony; and (5) the expert's current résumé and bibliography. TRCP 194.2(f); *see* ***Mares v. Ford Motor Co.***, 53 S.W.3d 416, 418-19 (Tex.App.—San Antonio 2001, no pet.). A list of specific facts known by the expert is not required; a general description of the categories of facts known will suffice. *See* ***J.G. v. Murray***, 915 S.W.2d 548, 550-51 (Tex.App.—Corpus Christi 1995, orig. proceeding). For the definition of retained experts, see "Retained testifying expert," ch. 6-C, §2.1.1, p. 363.

(a) Name of retained experts. A party should list the names of all experts it has retained to testify on its behalf and those that are subject to the party's control. For example, the party should list a doctor who was hired to give an opinion in a medical malpractice case or an accident reconstructionist who was hired to give an opinion in a car accident case.

(b) Parties. A party should always list the name of any party who might testify as an expert witness. *See* ***Collins v. Collins***, 904 S.W.2d 792, 799-800 (Tex.App.—Houston [1st Dist.] 1995) (in divorce suit, husband could not testify about value of business because he was not identified as expert witness), *writ denied*, 923 S.W.2d 569 (Tex.1996); ***Tinkle v. Henderson***, 777 S.W.2d 537, 539 (Tex.App.—Tyler 1989, writ denied) (because defendant-doctors did not list themselves as experts, they could not testify as experts).

(c) Lawyer. If there is a claim for attorney fees, the party should list the lawyer as an expert to testify about attorney fees. *See* ***E.F. Hutton & Co. v. Youngblood***, 741 S.W.2d 363, 364 (Tex.1987) (because lawyer was not listed, he could not testify about attorney fees); ***Campos v. State Farm Gen. Ins. Co.***, 943 S.W.2d 52, 54-55 (Tex.App.—San Antonio 1997, writ denied) (same); *see also* ***Northwestern Nat'l Cty. Mut. Ins. Co. v. Rodriguez***, 18 S.W.3d 718, 721-22 (Tex.App.—San Antonio 2000, pet. denied) (good cause permitted undesignated lawyer to testify about fees because he was identified as fact witness on damages). The answer should state that the lawyer will testify about attorney fees for trial and appeal.

(2) Nonretained testifying experts. For nonretained testifying experts, a party must provide (1) the identity and location, including the name, address, and telephone number of its expert; (2) the subject matter of the expert's testimony; and (3) either (a) the general substance of the expert's mental impressions and opinions, including facts known by the expert that relate to or form the basis of those mental impressions and opinions, or (b) documents reflecting such information. TRCP 194.2(f). A list of specific facts known by the expert is not required; a general description of the categories of facts known will suffice. For the definition of nonretained experts, see "Nonretained testifying expert," ch. 6-C, §2.1.2, p. 364. The list of nonretained testifying experts could include the following:

(a) Treating doctor. A party should list the treating doctor as a nonretained testifying expert if the party intends to call the doctor to testify and the doctor is not retained by, employed by, or otherwise subject to the control of the party. For example, if the party was treated by an emergency room doctor, the doctor is a nonretained expert as long as the doctor is not paid for his or her "expert" opinion and is not "otherwise" subject to the party's control. Not all treating doctors are nonretained. For example, if the lawyer referred the party to a doctor for purposes of treatment and litigation, the doctor would be a retained doctor.

(b) Accident investigator. A party should list an accident investigator who is employed by a local police department or some state agency (*e.g.*, the DPS) as a nonretained testifying expert if the party intends to call the person to testify as an expert.

7. Documents. A party must produce the following documents in response to a request for disclosure: (1) discoverable indemnity and insuring agreements, (2) discoverable settlement agreements, and (3) discoverable witness statements. TRCP 194.2(g)-(i).

8. Medical records. In a suit alleging physical or mental injury, the parties must produce the following medical records:

(1) The party alleging injury must produce (a) medical records and bills reasonably related to the injuries or damages asserted, or (b) an authorization permitting disclosure of those medical records and bills. TRCP 194.2(j). For medical authorization under Health & Safety Code §241.152, see "Medical authorization," ch. 6-I, §3.2, p. 435.

(2) The other party must produce medical records and bills that it obtained by virtue of an authorization furnished by the party alleging injury. TRCP 194.2(k).

§5. OBJECTING TO REQUESTS

A party abuses the discovery process if it does not respond fully to a request for disclosure. TRCP 194, cmt. 1.

§5.1 No objections. No objections are permitted to requests for disclosure. TRCP 194.5. The procedure for requests for disclosure is designed to afford parties basic discovery without objection. TRCP 194, cmt. 1; *see* TRCP 194.5.

§5.2 Asserting privileges.

1. Most privileges. A party may assert privileges to protect information requested in a request for disclosure (other than work product, see §5.2.2, below). TRCP 194, cmt. 1. See "Asserting privileges," ch. 6-A, §17.2, p. 329.

2. Work product. A party cannot assert work-product privilege in response to a request for disclosure. TRCP 194.5 & cmt. 1; *e.g.*, ***In re Jimenez***, 4 S.W.3d 894, 896 (Tex.App.—Houston [1st Dist.] 1999, orig. proceeding) (D's statement to his insurer was not protected under work product).

§5.3 Moving for protection. Only in extremely rare cases will a party be able to protect information requested in disclosures. For example, a party could file a motion for protective order to prevent disclosure of a person's residential address if the disclosure might result in harm to that person. TRCP 194, cmt. 1. See "Motion for Protective Order," ch. 6-A, §19, p. 334; ***O'Connor's*** FORM 6A:08.

§6. SUPPLEMENTING OR AMENDING DISCLOSURES

§6.1 Deadline to supplement answers. See "Deadline to supplement answers," ch. 6-A, §16.4, p. 327.

§6.2 Deadlines to designate experts. See "Deadlines to designate testifying experts," ch. 6-C, §6.1, p. 372.

§6.3 Substance of supplemental response. For the substance of what additional information must be provided, see "Extent of supplementation," ch. 6-A, §16.2, p. 326.

§7. OBJECTING TO ANSWERS

§7.1 Technical errors. If a party makes a technical error in responding to requests for disclosure (*e.g.*, response not signed), the party propounding the requests must raise the issue as soon as possible. *See* TRCP 191.3(d) (unsigned discovery response will be stricken unless signed after party is made aware of omission); *cf.* ***State Farm Fire & Cas. Co. v. Morua***, 979 S.W.2d 616, 617 (Tex.1998) (verification of interrogatories under former TRCP 168); ***Kramer v. Lewisville Mem'l Hosp.***, 858 S.W.2d 397, 407 (Tex.1993) (same). See "Effect of no signature," ch. 6-A, §3.1.3, p. 314. A party waives any technical defect it does not raise before trial. ***Morua***, 979 S.W.2d at 619.

§7.2 Procedure. The procedure for objecting to answers filed in response to requests for disclosure is similar to that for objecting to answers to interrogatories. See "Objecting to Answers," ch. 6-F, §8, p. 414.

§8. USING DISCLOSURES AS EVIDENCE

§8.1 Similar to interrogatories. The procedures for using disclosures as evidence is similar to that for using answers to interrogatories. See "Using Interrogatories as Evidence," ch. 6-F, §9, p. 415.

§8.2 Superseded responses. A response to a request for disclosure under TRCP 194.2(c) (legal theories) or TRCP 194.2(d) (damages) that has been changed by an amended or supplemental response is not admissible and cannot be used for impeachment. TRCP 194.6. The purpose of this provision is to encourage parties to disclose and discuss their basic legal and factual assertions early in the case. Griesel, *The "New" Texas Discovery Rules*, §VIII(A), p. 19.

§9. OBJECTING TO LATE OR PARTIAL DISCLOSURES

§9.1 Tardy disclosure. When a party's response to the requests is late, the trial court can exclude the witness. TRCP 193.6(a); ***Ersek v. Davis & Davis***, 69 S.W.3d 268, 273 (Tex.App.—Austin 2002, pet. denied). If a party serves a late response to the requests, the trial court can also look to TRCP 215.3 for sanctions—that is, postpone the trial and impose appropriate sanctions to compensate the non-offending party for any wasted expenses in preparing for trial. *See* TRCP 215.3; *see also* TRCP 193.6(c) (court may grant a continuance). At a hearing on a motion for sanctions, the party objecting to the untimely designated expert witness has the burden to produce evidence showing that the designation was not timely. *See* ***Mentis v. Barnard***, 870 S.W.2d 14, 16 (Tex.1994); ***Sims v. Brackett***, 885 S.W.2d 450, 454 (Tex.App.—Corpus Christi 1994, writ denied).

§9.2 Partial disclosure. When a party's response to the requests does not furnish all the information required by TRCP 194, the trial court can exclude the testimony regarding the omitted information. *See, e.g.*, ***Vingcard A.S. v. Merrimac Hospitality Sys.***, 59 S.W.3d 847, 856 (Tex.App.—Fort Worth 2001, pet. denied) (although P identified its expert, it did not provide mental impressions & opinions; thus, court should have excluded expert's opinion).

§10. OBJECTING TO UNIDENTIFIED WITNESS

To exclude the testimony of a witness not identified in disclosures, a party must make a timely objection. The objection should be made either in a pretrial motion to exclude or when the witness is first offered at trial. ***Clark v. Trailways, Inc.***, 774 S.W.2d 644, 647 (Tex.1989). Once an objection is made, the exclusion is automatic unless the other party proves good cause or lack of unfair surprise or prejudice. See §10.2, below.

§10.1 Form of objection. The party should object that the witness should not be permitted to testify because the witness was not disclosed in response to a request asking for the identity of fact or expert witnesses.

§10.2 Exclude witness. On objection, the court must exclude a witness (other than a named party) from testifying if the witness was not listed in response to the requests, unless the court finds (1) there was good cause for the failure to timely respond or (2) the failure to timely respond will not unfairly surprise or prejudice the other parties. TRCP 193.6(a); ***Snider v. Stanley***, 44 S.W.3d 713, 715 (Tex.App.—Beaumont 2001, pet. denied); ***Northwestern Nat'l Cty. Mut. Ins. Co. v. Rodriguez***, 18 S.W.3d 718, 722 n.1 (Tex.App.—San Antonio 2000, pet. denied); *see* ***Alvarado v. Farah Mfg. Co.***, 830 S.W.2d 911, 914 (Tex.1992). The purpose of the exclusion rule is to require complete responses to discovery, promote responsible assessment of settlement, and prevent trial by ambush. ***Alvarado***, 830 S.W.2d at 914.

§10.3 Continuance. Even if the party offering the witness does not carry its burden under TRCP 193.6(b), the court may grant a continuance to allow the party to make, amend, or supplement the response and to allow discovery regarding any new information presented. TRCP 193.6(c); *see* ***Henderson v. Wellmann***, 43 S.W.3d 591, 598 (Tex.App.—Houston [1st Dist.] 2001, no pet.).

§10.4 Appropriate sanctions. See "Sanctions for discovery abuse," ch. 5-J, §7.1, p. 281.

§10.5 Preserving error when witness excluded.

1. Hearing on exclusion. If an objection is made to an unidentified witness, the party offering the witness should ask the court to conduct a hearing on its failure to identify the witness. The burden is on the party offering an unidentified witness to prove good cause, lack of unfair surprise, or lack of unfair prejudice. TRCP 193.6(b); *see* ***Sharp v. Broadway Nat'l Bank***, 784 S.W.2d 669, 671 (Tex.1990); ***Morrow v. H.E.B., Inc.***, 714 S.W.2d 297, 298 (Tex.1986). If the party offering the witness can show good cause for not listing the witness or no unfair surprise or prejudice to the other party, the court may permit the witness to testify. *See* ***Gee v. Liberty Mut. Fire Ins. Co.***, 765 S.W.2d 394, 395 (Tex.1989) (good cause under former TRCP 168); ***Rodriguez***, 18 S.W.3d at 722 n.1 (no unfair surprise under TRCP 193.6(a)). The trial court has discretion to determine whether there is good cause or no unfair surprise or prejudice to permit the witness to testify. *See* ***Morrow***, 714 S.W.2d at 298. The trial court's findings must be supported by the record. TRCP 193.6(b); ***Rodriguez***, 18 S.W.3d at 722 n.1. The hearing must be conducted out of the presence of the jury.

(1) Unidentified witness permitted to testify. The following are some examples of when an unidentified witness was or should have been permitted to testify: • D's experts permitted to give same opinions given in earlier trial, even though D did not disclose the opinions of the experts in response to request for disclosure. ***Mares v. Ford Motor Co.***, 53 S.W.3d 416, 419 (Tex.App.—San Antonio 2001, no pet.). • P's unidentified witness should have been permitted to testify because she was P's employee who was a substitute for another of P's employees who had been identified as witness but who had left P's employment. ***Best Indus. Unif. Sup. Co. v. Gulf Coast Alloy Welding***, 41 S.W.3d 145, 148-49 (Tex.App.—Amarillo 2000, pet. denied).

NOTE

Under the discovery rules, a named party cannot be excluded as a fact witness because the party was not listed as a fact witness in response to a request for disclosure. See TRCP 193.6(a) (party cannot offer the testimony of a witness "other than a named party" who was not listed). Even though an unlisted party may testify as a fact witness, nothing in the rules or case law permits a party not designated as a testifying expert to testify as an expert. ***Collins v. Collins****, 904 S.W.2d 792, 801 (Tex.App.—Houston [1st Dist.] 1995), writ denied, 923 S.W.2d 569 (Tex.1996).*

---

(2) Unidentified witness excluded. The following are some examples of when the unidentified witness was not or should not have been permitted to testify: • P's expert should have been excluded, even though deposed, because he was not identified in response to interrogatories. ***Sharp v. Broadway Nat'l Bank***, 784 S.W.2d 669, 670-72 (Tex.1990). • D's expert should have been excluded because he was not identified in response to interrogatories, and counsel's inadvertence was not good cause. *Id.*; ***E.F. Hutton & Co. v. Youngblood***, 741 S.W.2d 363, 364 (Tex.1987). • Other party's ability to cross-examine the witness at trial is not good cause. ***E.F. Hutton***, 741 S.W.2d at 364. • D's expert should have been excluded because D did not provide the expert's opinions, but the error was harmless. ***Vingcard***, 59 S.W.3d at 856-57. • State's witnesses should have been excluded because state did not file a response to the request for disclosures and did not prove good cause. ***F & H Invs. Inc. v. State***, 55 S.W.3d 663, 669-70 (Tex.App.—Waco 2001, no pet.). • Witness who had been a party to the suit but settled before trial, and had identified himself as expert witness, could not testify as expert for another party who had not identified him as expert. ***Codner v. Arellano***, 40 S.W.3d 666, 675 (Tex.App.—Austin 2001, no pet.). • The expectation that the case would settle is not good cause for not identifying a witness. ***Rainbo Baking Co. v. Stafford***, 787 S.W.2d 41, 41 (Tex.1990); ***Cruz v. Furniture Technicians***, 949 S.W.2d 34, 36 (Tex.App.—San Antonio 1997, writ denied). • Designated fact witness cannot testify as an expert witness. ***Collins***, 904 S.W.2d at 802 (party); ***Baylor Med. Plaza Servs. v. Kidd***, 834 S.W.2d 69, 73 (Tex.App.—Texarkana 1992, writ denied) (witness).

2. Present evidence. A party offering an unidentified witness must present sworn testimony to explain the reason the witness was not listed. The court reporter should transcribe the proceeding. To prove good cause or lack of unfair surprise or prejudice for not listing unidentified witness, the party should establish the following:

(1) The party made a good-faith effort to locate the witness. *See* ***Clark v. Trailways, Inc.***, 774 S.W.2d 644, 647 (Tex.1989) (inability to locate witness despite good-faith efforts might support a finding of good cause).

(2) The party did not know of the existence of the witness or did not know the witness had knowledge about the case. To prove this, both the attorney and the party should testify at the hearing that they did not know of the witness. If either the party or the attorney had the information, it should have been disclosed. ***Yeldell v. Holiday Hills Retirement & Nursing Ctr.***, 701 S.W.2d 243, 246 (Tex.1985) (attorney knew of witness); ***Williams v. Union Carbide Corp.***, 734 S.W.2d 699, 701 (Tex.App.—Houston [1st Dist.] 1987, writ ref'd n.r.e.) (party knew of witness).

(3) The other parties were aware of the unidentified witness and her testimony. To prove this, the party should demonstrate that the identity of the witness was certain and her personal knowledge of relevant facts was communicated to all other parties through timely response to other written discovery or deposition. TRCP 193.5(a)(2); *see* ***Northwestern Nat'l Cty. Mut. Ins. Co. v. Rodriguez***, 18 S.W.3d 718, 722-23 (Tex.App.—San Antonio 2000, pet. denied).

3. Get ruling on record. The party attempting to overcome the automatic exclusion of the witness should ask the court to (1) state on the record whether good cause, lack of unfair surprise, or lack of unfair prejudice was proved, and (2) identify the particulars of its ruling.

4. Make offer of proof. If the court excludes any evidence, the party must make an offer of proof to preserve the testimony of the witness so the appellate courts can determine whether the erroneous exclusion was harmful. TRE 103(a)(2). If a party presents the witness's testimony as part of the good-cause or unfair-surprise hearing, and the court reporter transcribes it, the court reporter's record will include the evidence. If the witness's testimony is not presented at the hearing, the party should ask the court for permission to make an offer of proof during the trial. If, for some reason the court does not permit the party to make an offer of proof, the evidence may be preserved in a formal bill of exceptions. TRE 103; TRAP 33.2. See "Offer of Proof & Bill of Exceptions," ch. 8-E, p. 553; ***O'Connor's*** FORMS 8E.

§10.6 Offering witness for impeachment or rebuttal. A party may ask the trial court for permission to offer an undesignated witness for impeachment or rebuttal. See "Impeachment & rebuttal evidence not produced in discovery," ch. 8-C, §5.3, p. 536.

§11. REVIEW

For the rules and forms for prosecuting or responding to an appeal or original proceeding, see ***O'Connor's Texas Civil Appeals*** (2002-03).

§11.1 Appeal or mandamus? See "Review of Discovery Orders," ch. 6-A, §24, p. 340.

§11.2 Undisclosed witness. On appeal, the party objecting to the exclusion or admission of the testimony of an unidentified witness must show the court abused its discretion. ***Mentis v. Barnard***, 870 S.W.2d 14, 16 (Tex. 1994) (objection to exclusion under former TRCP 166b); ***Henry S. Miller Co. v. Bynum***, 836 S.W.2d 160, 162 (Tex. 1992) (objection to admission). Obtaining a reversal on the admission or exclusion of an undisclosed witness is a two-step process: the party must show (1) it proved good cause or lack of unfair surprise or prejudice (or the other party did not prove good cause or lack of unfair surprise or prejudice), and (2) the trial court's erroneous ruling was harmful. *See* ***Mentis***, 870 S.W.2d at 16 (testimony excluded at trial); ***Alvarado v. Farah Mfg. Co.***, 830 S.W.2d 911, 916-17 (Tex.1992) (testimony admitted at trial). Once error in the trial court's ruling is demonstrated, the appellate court must review the entire record to determine the harm. To determine whether the erroneous admission or exclusion of the testimony of an undisclosed witness was harmful, the appellate court must determine whether the error "probably caused the rendition of an improper judgment." TRAP 44.1(a)(1).

1. Undisclosed witness permitted to testify. If the court admitted the testimony of an undisclosed witness, to challenge that ruling on appeal, the appellant must show that the admitted testimony (1) disputed a material allegation in the case and (2) was not cumulative. ***Boothe v. Hausler***, 766 S.W.2d 788, 789 (Tex.1989). If the testimony of the undisclosed witness was cumulative of other evidence, the courts will hold it was harmless error to admit it. *Id.*; ***Beam v. A.H. Chaney, Inc.***, 56 S.W.3d 920, 924 (Tex.App.—Fort Worth 2001, pet. denied). The test of whether the evidence was cumulative is whether other similar evidence was offered at trial, not whether other similar evidence was available in discovery. ***Jamail v. Anchor Mortg. Servs.***, 809 S.W.2d 221, 223 (Tex.1991).

2. Undisclosed witness excluded. If the court excluded the testimony of an undisclosed witness, to challenge that ruling on appeal, the appellant must show that the excluded testimony (1) was preserved by an offer of proof or a formal bill of exceptions, (2) was controlling on a material issue in the case, and (3) was not cumulative. ***Williams Distrib. Co. v. Franklin***, 898 S.W.2d 816, 817 (Tex.1995) (element 2); ***Mentis***, 870 S.W.2d at 16 (elements 2 & 3); ***McInnes v. Yamaha Motor Corp.***, 673 S.W.2d 185, 187 (Tex.1984) (element 1). To prove the "controlling" element, it is not necessary for the party to show no other controlling evidence could have been introduced through another witness. ***Williams Distrib.***, 898 S.W.2d at 817.

E. DEPOSITIONS

§1. GENERAL

§1.1 Rules. TRCP 176, 199-203, 205, 215.5. See CPRC §7.011 (attorney's liability for costs), CPRC §§20.001 & 20.002 (persons who may take depositions); Gov't Code §52.021 (certification of court reporter), Gov't Code §52.059 (charges for depositions).

§1.2 Purpose. The purpose of depositions is to elicit and preserve sworn testimony for use in trial.

§1.3 Forms. See ***O'Connor's Texas Civil Forms***, FORMS 6E.

§1.4 Other references. Griesel, *The "New" Texas Discovery Rules: Three Years Later*, Advanced Evidence & Discovery Course, State Bar of Texas, ch. 2, §XIII-XVII, pp. 26-30 (2002); Uniform Format Manual for Texas Court Reporters, §11, cmt. (May 1, 1999), www.supreme.courts.state.tx.us/rules/reporter; Cochran, ***Texas Rules of Evidence Handbook*** (5th ed. 2003) (Cochran, ***Evidence Handbook***); Corr & Madden, *Don't Answer that Question,* For the Defense, 11 (Mar.1995).

§2. SCOPE

The scope of discovery for depositions is governed by TRCP 192. See "Scope of Discovery," ch. 6-B, p. 341.

§3. DEPOSITION OFFICER

The deposition officer is a person who is authorized by law to administer an oath and who is in charge of the stenographic or nonstenographic recording of the deposition. *See* TRCP 199.1(c). The deposition officer is responsible for the amount of time each party or side uses during the deposition. For definition of "side," see "Side," ch. 6-A, §2.5, p. 314.

§3.1 Stenographic depositions. Stenographic oral depositions taken in Texas must be recorded by a certified shorthand reporter. Gov't Code §52.021(b), (f).

§3.2 Nonstenographic depositions. Audio or video depositions may be recorded by any person who is qualified to administer an oath. TRCP 199.1(c); *see* Gov't Code §602.002(4) (notary public may administer oath). A court reporter or any person authorized to administer oaths may act as the deposition officer at a nonstenographic deposition. See "Deposition by Nonstenographic Recording Device," §13, p. 401.

§3.3 Deposition on written questions. Depositions by written questions may be taken by (1) a clerk of the district court, (2) a judge or clerk of the county court, (3) a court reporter, or (4) a notary public. CPRC §20.001(a) (persons 1, 2 & 4).

§4. PROCEDURE FOR THE STANDARD ORAL DEPOSITION

The most common type of deposition is the oral deposition recorded stenographically by a court reporter or by a mechanical recording device operated by a notary public. The deposition consists of a series of questions by one lawyer, answers by the deponent, and objections and cross-examination by the other lawyers.

§4.1 Agreements for scheduling deposition. Most depositions are taken by agreement. TRCP 191.1 permits the parties to modify the deposition procedure by agreement and take the deposition before any person, at any time or place, and on any notice. If the parties make an agreement regarding the taking of the deposition, it should be recorded in the deposition transcript. TRCP 191.1. To be enforceable when not recorded in the transcript, the agreement must comply with TRCP 11. TRCP 191.1. See "Oral agreement recorded in deposition," ch. 1-H, §9.1.3, p. 45; "Modifying discovery by agreement," ch. 6-A, §5.1, p. 316; ***O'Connor's*** FORM 6E:01.

§4.2 Scheduling expert's deposition. TRCP 195.3 establishes a schedule for depositions of testifying experts retained by, employed by, or otherwise subject to the control of a party. See "Deadlines for Securing Discovery from Experts," ch. 6-C, §6, p. 372. Depositions of experts who are not retained by a party are controlled by TRCP 176, 205, and the deposition rules. TRCP 195, cmt. 2.

§4.3 Deadline to take deposition. An oral deposition must be taken during the discovery period unless the parties agree otherwise or a party obtains leave of court. TRCP 199.2(a). See "Discovery Periods," ch. 6-A, §6, p. 317; ***O'Connor's*** FORM 6E:08. For expert depositions, see "Deadlines to depose testifying experts," ch. 6-C, §6.2, p. 373.

§4.4 Filing deposition documents. Chart 6-8, below, summarizes the filing requirements for deposition documents.

6-8. FILING DEPOSITION DOCUMENTS

	DOCUMENT	FILE?	TRCP
1	Notice of deposition & subpoena required to be served only on a party	No	191.4(a)(1)
2	Notice of deposition & subpoena required to be served on nonparty	Yes	191.4(b)(1)
3	Motions for protection & to quash	Yes	191.4(b)(2)
4	Agreements regarding depositions	Yes	11, 191.4(b)(3)
5	The deposition	No	191.4(a)(3)
6	The response & objections to deposition notices	No	191.4(a)(2)
7	Any document that the trial court orders to be filed	Yes	191.4(c)(1)
8	Any document necessary to support or oppose a motion or other matter in the trial or appellate court	Yes	191.4(c)(2), (3)

§4.5 Notice of oral deposition. See ***O'Connor's*** FORM 6E:02.

1. Contents of notice. The notice of intent to take a deposition must be in writing. TRCP 199.2(a).

(1) Addressed to other parties. The notice of deposition is addressed to the other parties in the lawsuit. TRCP 199.2(a). The purpose of the notice is to notify the other parties of the deposition so they may attend. The notice serves as a subpoena when parties are to be deposed. TRCP 199.3.

(2) Identity of deponent. The notice of deposition must identify the witness to be deposed. TRCP 199.2(b)(1).

(a) Nonparty witness. When the deponent is not a party, the notice should include the deponent's address so the officer or court reporter who issues the subpoena can locate the witness. *See* TRCP 176.5. See "Subpoenas," ch. 1-K, p. 58; "Challenging nonparty discovery subpoena," ch. 6-H, §5.5, p. 429.

(b) Unknown corporate witness. When the deposition notice is sent to a corporation or other entity and the identity of a person in the organization with knowledge of a certain subject is unknown, the notice can require the organization to identify a witness to be deposed. TRCP 199.2(b)(1); ***Allstate Tex. Lloyds v. Johnson***, 784 S.W.2d 100, 104 (Tex.App.—Waco 1989, orig. proceeding). The notice must describe the subjects about which testimony is requested and direct the organization to designate the person who will testify on its behalf. TRCP 199.2(b)(1); ***Lindsey v. O'Neill***, 689 S.W.2d 400, 402 (Tex.1985). This procedure does not limit a party's right to depose other employees of the entity. ***Hospital Corp. v. Farrar***, 733 S.W.2d 393, 395 (Tex.App.—Fort Worth 1987, orig. proceeding).

2. Date for oral deposition. The notice of deposition must state the day and time for the oral deposition. TRCP 199.2(b)(2); *cf.* ***St. Luke's Episcopal Hosp. v. Garcia***, 928 S.W.2d 307, 312 (Tex.App.—Houston [14th Dist.] 1996, orig. proceeding) (because notice & subpoena did not identify date for deposition on written questions, nonparty did not waive its objections). After stating the date, the notice should include the phrase, "and continuing from day to day until the deposition is completed." The date for the deposition depends on how much notice a party must give the other party and the deponent, which in turn depends on whether the deponent is a party or nonparty and whether the deponent is required to bring documents or other things to the deposition. See chart 6-9, "Deadlines to Serve Notice & Subpoena," p. 391.

(1) For deposition with documents.

(a) Party deposition with documents. For a deposition of a party when production of documents or tangible things is requested, the notice of deposition must be served on the witness at least 30 days before the deposition. *See* TRCP 199, cmt. 1. TRCP 199.2(b)(5) incorporates into deposition procedures the procedures for requests for production under TRCP 196, including the 30-day deadline for responses. TRCP 199, cmt. 1; *see* TRCP 196.2(a) (response to request for production must be served within 30 days). See "Deadline to respond," ch. 6-H, §3.3.2, p. 426. The date for the deposition should probably be set at least 40 days from the date the notice is served, so the party noticing the deposition can reschedule it if the witness files a response on the last day refusing to produce.

When rescheduling the deposition of a party with documents or tangible things, the party noticing the deposition is not required to provide an additional 30 days' notice as long as no additional documents or things are requested. Because it is the request for documents that triggers the 30 days' notice requirement, the purpose of the 30 days' notice—to provide the deponent time to file a response to the request for documents—is satisfied by the first notice. *See* TRCP 199.2(b)(5).

(b) Nonparty deposition with documents. For a deposition of a nonparty when production of documents or tangible things is requested, the notice of deposition must be served on the nonparty a reasonable time before the date for compliance. TRCP 199.2(a); Pemberton, *First Year Under the New Discovery Rules*, §II(D) (1-1-00), www.supreme.courts.state.tx.us/rules/tdr/. The party must also serve a subpoena to appear and produce with or after the notice of deposition. TRCP 205.2. Although a document request to a party requires a 30-day response period, there is no similar requirement for a document request to a nonparty. Pemberton, *First Year*, §II(D).

(2) For deposition without documents.

(a) Party deposition without documents. To take a deposition of a party without a request for production of documents or tangible things, the notice of the deposition must be served a reasonable time before the date of the deposition. TRCP 199.2(a), (b)(2). Neither TRCP 199.2(a) nor 199.2(b)(2) state how much notice is reasonable. As a general rule, ten days' notice should be reasonable, but depending on the circumstances, a shorter time might also be reasonable. *See, e.g.*, ***Gutierrez v. Walsh***, 748 S.W.2d 27, 28 (Tex.App.—Corpus Christi 1988, no writ) (6 days reasonable). *But see* ***Hycarbex, Inc. v. Anglo-Suisse, Inc.***, 927 S.W.2d 103, 111 (Tex. App.—Houston [14th Dist.] 1996, no writ) (4 days unreasonable); ***Bloyed v. G.M. Corp.***, 881 S.W.2d 422, 437 (Tex. App.—Texarkana 1994) (Thursday notice of Monday deposition unreasonable), *aff'd*, 916 S.W.2d 949 (Tex. 1996).

(b) Nonparty deposition without documents. To take a deposition of a nonparty without a request for documents or tangible things, the party must serve the notice and the subpoena a reasonable time before the date for the deposition. TRCP 199.2(a), 205.2. However, the notice must be served before or at the same time as the subpoena; the subpoena cannot be served before the notice. TRCP 205.2.

3. Alternative means for conducting deposition. If the deposition is to be taken by telephone, other remote electronic means, or by a nonstenographic recording (audio recording or videotape), the notice must identify the means for conducting the deposition. TRCP 199.2(b)(3). To take a deposition by alternative means, the party must observe additional notice requirements.

(1) For telephonic deposition. For a deposition by telephone, the notice must be served a reasonable time before the deposition. TRCP 199.1(b). See "Deposition by Telephone," §14, p. 401.

(2) For electronically recorded deposition. For a deposition by nonstenographic means, the notice must be served at least five days before the deposition. TRCP 199.1(c). See "Deposition by Nonstenographic Recording Device," §13, p. 401.

4. Place for deposition. The notice of deposition must identify the location for the deposition. TRCP 199.2(b)(2). The place must be reasonable. *Id.* Where the deposition may be taken depends on a number of factors, including the residence of the deponent, whether the deponent is a party or a nonparty, and whether one of the parties is a corporation. *Id.*

(1) Deposition of most witnesses. The deposition of most witnesses may be taken in the following places: (1) the county of the witness's residence, (2) the county where the witness is employed or regularly transacts business in person, or (3) any convenient place, as directed by the court in which the case is pending. TRCP 199.2(b)(2)(A), (B), (E); *see, e.g.*, ***In re Rogers***, 43 S.W.3d 20, 29 (Tex.App.—Amarillo 2001, orig. proceeding) (court could not order depositions in Dallas when nothing in record showed Dallas was reasonable or convenient for any of the witnesses); ***First State Bank v. Chappell & Handy, P.C.***, 729 S.W.2d 917, 922 (Tex.App.—Corpus Christi 1987, writ ref'd n.r.e.) (court can order deposition in county other than one provided for in rule when deponent is being difficult about scheduling deposition).

(2) Deposition of party & representative. In addition to the places listed above, the deposition of a party, or a person designated by a party under TRCP 199.2(b)(1), may be taken in the county of suit. TRCP 199.2(b)(2)(C); ***Davis v. Ruffino***, 881 S.W.2d 186, 187 (Tex.App.—Houston [1st Dist.] 1994, orig. proceeding); *see also* ***Wal-Mart Stores v. Street***, 754 S.W.2d 153, 155 (Tex.1988) (when deponent was associated with party but was not designated representative, his deposition could not be taken in county of suit over his objection); ***Borden, Inc. v. Valdez***, 773 S.W.2d 718, 721 (Tex.App.—Corpus Christi 1989, orig. proceeding) (same). *But see* ***Prudential Prop. & Cas. Co. v. Dow Chevrolet-Olds***, 10 S.W.3d 97, 103 (Tex.App.—Texarkana 1999, pet. dism'd) (when carrier filed subrogation suit in insureds' names, insureds could not be forced to come to Texas for deposition).

(3) Deposition of nonresident or transient. The deposition of a person who is either a nonresident of Texas or a transient may be taken (1) in the county where the witness was served with subpoena, (2) within 150 miles of the place of service; or (3) in any convenient place, as directed by the court in which the case is pending. TRCP 199.2(b)(2)(D), (E); *see, e.g.*, ***Wal-Mart***, 754 S.W.2d at 154 (deposition of chairman of the board, who was not a designated witness, had to be taken in Arkansas, his county of residence); ***Butan Valley v. Smith***, 921 S.W.2d 822, 829 (Tex.App.—Houston [14th Dist.] 1996, no writ) (deposition of corporate director, who was not a designated witness, had to be taken in his country of residence, Saudi Arabia).

5. Additional attendee. The notice of deposition, or a separate notice, must identify any person who will attend the deposition who is not listed in TRCP 199.5(a)(3); that is, any person who is not the deponent, one of the parties, the spouse of one of the parties, the lawyers, an employee of one of the lawyers, or the officer taking the deposition. TRCP 199.2(b)(4), 199.5(a)(3); *see, e.g.*, ***Burrhus v. M&S Sup.***, 933 S.W.2d 635, 640-41 (Tex.App.—San Antonio 1996, writ denied) (party attending deposition required to give notice before bringing an expert to deposition of other party's expert). If a party other than the party who set the deposition intends to bring to the deposition a person not listed in TRCP 199.5(a)(3), that party must give the other parties reasonable notice. TRCP 199.5(a)(3); ***Burrhus***, 933 S.W.2d at 641. To exclude a person from the deposition, a party must secure a protective order. ***Burrhus***, 933 S.W.2d at 641.

6. Request for documents. The notice of deposition may include a request that the witness produce at the deposition documents or tangible things within the scope of discovery and within the witness's possession, custody, or control. TRCP 199.2(b)(5).

(1) Documents from parties. A notice of deposition to a party or its agents that includes a request for documents or tangible things has the same effect as a subpoena. TRCP 199.3.

(2) Documents from nonparties. To compel a nonparty to bring documents or tangible things to a deposition, the nonparty must be served with the notice of deposition and a subpoena. TRCP 199.2(b)(5). The subpoena and the notice of deposition must include the list of documents or things to be produced at the deposition. *See* TRCP 176.2(b) (subpoena must command person to produce "designated" documents), TRCP 199.2(b)(5) (list of materials to be produced by nonparty that are identified in subpoena must be attached to or included in deposition notice), TRCP 200.1(b) (same).

7. Signed. The notice of deposition must be signed by the attorney (or party when pro se). TRCP 191.3(a). See "Certification by signature," ch. 6-A, §3.1, p. 314.

PRACTICE TIP

Before the adoption of the 1999 discovery rules, court reporters issued subpoenas and notices of depositions over their own signatures. Now, because discovery must be signed by the lawyer, court reporters are sending subpoenas and notices to the lawyers for their signatures, which is burdensome. Therefore, the lawyers could agree that all deposition discovery requests may be signed by the court reporter as the lawyer's agent, and this would have the same effect as if signed by the lawyer. See "Modifying discovery by agreement," ch. 6-A, §5.1, p. 316; ***O'Connor's FORM 6E:01, ¶5.***

8. Certificate of service. The notice of deposition must contain a certificate of service stating that it was served on all parties. TRCP 199.2(a); *see* TRCP 21. If it is not served on all parties, the deposition cannot be used at trial. ***Shenandoah Assocs. v. J & K Props.***, 741 S.W.2d 470, 492-93 (Tex.App.—Dallas 1987, writ denied). See "Certificate of service," ch. 1-B, §4.16, p. 9.

6-9. DEADLINES TO SERVE NOTICE & SUBPOENA

PURPOSE OF DISCOVERY	TYPE OF DISCOVERY		PARTY OR NONPARTY	TIME FOR NOTICE	TIME FOR SUBPOENA	CROSS REFERENCE
To secure testimony	Oral deposition	1	Party	Reasonable time TRCP 199.2(a)		Ch. 6-E, §4.5.2(2)(a), p. 388
		2	Nonparty	Reasonable time TRCP 199.2(a)	With or after notice TRCP 205.2	Ch. 6-E, §4.5.2(2)(b), p. 389
	Deposition on written questions	3	Party	20 days TRCP 200.1(a)		Ch. 6-E, §15.3.2, p. 402
		4	Nonparty	20 days TRCP 200.1(a)	With or after notice TRCP 205.2	Ch. 6-E, §15.3.2, p. 402
To secure testimony & tangible things	Oral deposition & request for documents	5	Party	30 days TRCP 196.2(a), 199.2(b)(5) & cmt. 1		Ch. 6-E, §4.5.2(1)(a), p. 388
		6	Nonparty	Reasonable time TRCP 199.2(b)(5), 205.2	With or after notice TRCP 205.2	Chs. 6-E, §4.5.2(1)(b), p. 388
	Deposition on written questions & request for documents	7	Party	30 days TRCP 196.2(a), 199.2(b)(5), 200.1(b)		Ch. 6-E, §15.3.2, p. 402
		8	Nonparty	20 days TRCP 199.2(b)(5), 200.1(a)	With or after notice TRCP 205.2	Ch. 6-E, §15.3.2, p. 402
To secure tangible things (not testimony)	Request for production	9	Party	30 days TRCP 196.2(a)		Ch. 6-H, §3.1.2, p. 424
	Subpoena for production	10	Nonparty	Reasonable time TRCP 205.3	10 days after notice TRCP 205.2	Ch. 6-H, §5.3.1, p. 429

§4.6 Responding to notice of deposition.

1. When no documents requested. When no documents are requested, no response is necessary unless the party objects to the time, place, or other conditions of the deposition. See "Objecting Before Oral Deposition," §7, p. 394.

2. When documents requested. For the procedure to object to production of documents, see "Making objections," ch. 6-A, §17.1, p. 329. For the procedure to assert privileges, see "Asserting privileges," ch. 6-A, §17.2, p. 329. To object to the time, place, or other conditions of the deposition, see "Objecting Before Oral Deposition," §7, p. 394.

(1) Party's response. When a party, or a witness subject to its control, is served with a deposition notice that requests the production of documents or tangible things, the party's response, objections, and privilege claims are governed by the request for production rule, TRCP 196, as well as the procedures and duties imposed by TRCP 193. TRCP 199.2(b)(5), TRCP 199, cmt. 1. When a party is requested to produce documents at a deposition, it must file a response to the request, just as if it had been served with a request for production of documents. For parties and witnesses subject to the party's control, TRCP 199.2(b)(5) incorporates the procedures for responding that are applicable to requests for production under TRCP 196. TRCP 199, cmt. 1. For the procedure to respond, see "Procedure to respond," ch. 6-H, §3.3, p. 425.

(2) Nonparty's response. When a nonparty is served with a notice and subpoena to appear at a deposition and produce documents or tangible things, the nonparty's response, objections, motion for protective order, and privilege claims are governed by TRCP 176, the subpoena rule, as well as TRCP 205, the rule governing discovery from nonparties. TRCP 199.2(b)(5); *see also* TRCP 176.6(c) (production of documents), TRCP 193.3 (asserting a privilege). See "Subpoenas," ch. 1-K, p. 58; "Securing Things from a Nonparty," ch. 6-H, §5, p. 428; "Challenging nonparty discovery subpoena," ch. 6-H, §5.5, p. 429. When a nonparty objects to a subpoena to produce documents at a deposition, it must make its objections and assertions of privilege in writing before the time specified for compliance in the subpoena. TRCP 176.6(d). If the nonparty contends the subpoenaed documents are privileged, it must comply with TRCP 193.3 and file a withholding statement. See "Making objections," ch. 6-A, §17.1, p. 329; "Asserting privileges," ch. 6-A, §17.2, p. 329. The nonparty must comply with the subpoena to the extent that it does not object or assert privileges to the documents. TRCP 176.6(d).

3. When organization deposed. When a deposition notice directs a corporation or other entity to identify a person with knowledge of a certain subject, the organization must (1) designate the persons who will testify on behalf of the organization and (2) identify the matters on which each person will testify. TRCP 199.2(b)(1); *see also* TRCP 176.6(b) (when subpoena directed to an organization). The organization's response must be served on the other party a "reasonable time before the deposition." TRCP 199.2(b)(1).

§4.7 Oath. Before beginning the deposition, the deponent must be sworn. TRCP 199.5(b); TRE 603. The oath must be administered by the deposition officer. TRCP 203.2(a). See "Deposition Officer," §3, p. 386. When a deposition is taken outside of Texas, the person administering the oath must have the power to administer an oath in that jurisdiction. TRCP 201.1(b); *see also* CPRC §20.001(b) & (c) (persons who may take deposition).

§4.8 Interrogation. The scope of the examination is governed by TRCP 192. See "Scope of Discovery," ch. 6-B, p. 341.

1. First question. No matter who noticed the deponent to appear, the lawyer who asks the first question at the deposition is the lawyer who (1) will get the deposition from the court reporter, TRCP 203.3(a)(1); and (2) is personally responsible, along with her firm, for the cost of taking the deposition, Gov't Code §52.059(a), (d)(2)(C). See §4.13, below.

2. Oral examination. The lawyer who noticed the deponent to appear will most often begin the interrogation. If the deponent was called as an adverse witness, the deposition will begin with cross-examination. That lawyer should finish all questions before any other lawyer attempts to question the deponent. After the examination by the lawyer who noticed the deposition, the other lawyers, one at a time, have the opportunity to examine the deponent.

3. Written questions. A party may, in lieu of participating in the examination, serve written questions in a sealed envelope on the party noticing the oral deposition, who must then deliver them to the deposition officer, who must open the envelope and propound the questions to the witness at the deposition. TRCP 199.5(b).

4. Documents. When required to bring documents, the deponent may provide copies of the documents if the originals are made available for inspection. TRCP 203.4. If the deponent brings the originals, the court reporter will make copies, attach them to the deposition, and return the originals to the deponent. *Id.* The originals must be available for production for a hearing or for the trial on seven days' notice from any party. *Id.*

PRACTICE TIP

When a witness provides documents as part of a deposition, and the witness is not going to appear in person at trial, you must "prove up" the documents during the deposition. The documents are not admissible simply because they were produced during a deposition. See ***James v. Hudgins****, 876 S.W.2d 418, 422 (Tex.App.—El Paso 1994, writ denied).*

§4.9 Signing deposition. Once the deposition is prepared, the deponent must review and sign it under oath, unless the parties and the deponent agree to waive the signature. TRCP 203.1(a), (c). The court reporter usually handles the signature in one of the following ways:

1. Party deposition. If the deponent is a party or an agent of a party, TRCP 203.1 requires the court reporter to send the deposition to the party's lawyer, along with a sheet to note corrections. *See* TRCP 203.1. The lawyer arranges for the deponent to review the deposition and sign the original signature page under oath; then, the lawyer returns the deposition to the court reporter. TRCP 203.1(b). If the deposition is not returned in 20 days, the deponent's right to make changes is waived. *Id.*

2. Unaligned witness. If the deponent is not aligned with any party, TRCP 203.1 requires the court reporter to send the deposition, along with a sheet to note corrections, to the deponent to be signed and notarized. *See* TRCP 203.1. If the deposition is not returned in 20 days, the deponent's right to make changes is waived. TRCP 203.1(b).

§4.10 Changing answers. The deponent may submit changes to the deposition and the reasons for the changes in writing and under oath to the court reporter within 20 days of the submission of the deposition to the deponent or counsel. TRCP 203.1(b). The court reporter attaches the deponent's changes to the deposition; the original transcription is not retyped. *See id.*

§4.11 Refusing to sign deposition. When a party files a motion to suppress the deposition under TRCP 203.5 because the deponent refused to sign the deposition, the court must determine if the reason the witness refused to sign impugns the reliability of the deposition. ***Hill v. Rich***, 522 S.W.2d 597, 600 (Tex.App.—Austin 1975, writ ref'd n.r.e.). Suppression is not justified by the mere lack of a signature. ***Smith v. Smith***, 720 S.W.2d 586, 599 (Tex. App.—Houston [1st Dist.] 1986, no writ). Unless the deposition is suppressed, it may be used at trial. *See* TRCP 203.5, 203.6.

§4.12 Not filed. Depositions are not filed with the court. They are kept by the custodial lawyer. *See* TRCP 203.3(a). After the court reporter receives the signed deposition, the court reporter must (1) attach any corrections, (2) send the deposition to the lawyer who asked the first question (unless the parties agreed otherwise) with notice to the other lawyers, and (3) file a sworn certificate with the trial court that meets the requirements of TRCP 203.2. TRCP 203.1(b), 203.2, 203.3. If the deposition is taken by nonstenographic means, the original record of the deposition is sent to the party that requested the nonstenographic recording, not the party who asked the first question. *See* TRCP 203.3(a).

§4.13 Paying for deposition.

1. Cost of original. The lawyer who takes the deposition and that lawyer's firm are jointly and severally liable for the court reporter's charges for reporting the deposition, for transcribing it, and for providing the copies of it requested by that lawyer. Gov't Code §52.059(a). A lawyer "takes" a deposition if the lawyer secures the deponent's appearance through formal or informal means or asks the first question. Gov't Code §52.059(d)(2); *see* TRCP 203.3(a) (original deposition transcript is delivered to the lawyer "who asked the first question"). The attorney (and the attorney's firm) who asks for a copy of the deposition is personally responsible for the court reporter's charges for that copy. Gov't Code §52.059(b); *cf.* CPRC §7.011 (lawyer who is not a party is not liable for the costs of the proceedings). If the attorneys refuse to be bound by the provisions of Gov't Code §52.059(a) and (b), they must state on the record who will pay the cost of the deposition. Gov't Code §52.059(c).

2. Cost of copy. The custodial attorney must make the original deposition available to other parties for copying. TRCP 203.3(c). It is not necessary for the parties to pay the court reporter for more than the original transcript of the deposition; the court reporter's charge for a copy of a deposition is much higher than the photocopy cost. The parties can agree to split the cost of the original deposition and the cost of the photocopy.

§5. SUBPOENAS FOR DEPOSITION

See "Subpoenas," ch. 1-K, p. 58; "Securing Things from a Nonparty," ch. 6-H, §5, p. 428.

§6. TIME LIMITATIONS ON ORAL DEPOSITIONS

§6.1 Limits under discovery control plans. A party or side's total deposition time depends on the discovery limitations for the case. For the definition of "side," see "Side," ch. 6-A, §2.5, p. 314; for discovery limitations for the case, see "Discovery limitations," ch. 6-A, §7.2.3, p. 319; "Discovery limitations," ch. 6-A, §7.3.2, p. 320; "Discovery limitations," ch. 6-A, §7.4.2, p. 320.

§6.2 Limits on witness deposition. No side may examine or cross-examine a witness for more than six hours, excluding breaks. TRCP 199.5(c). For purposes of this rule, each person designated by an organization under TRCP 199.2(b)(1) is a separate witness. TRCP 199, cmt. 2. The time credited to a party includes ordinary pauses by the interrogator or the witness, but not off-the-record discussion or protracted lapses (*e.g.*, when a witness is reviewing a stack of documents). Uniform Format Manual for Texas Court Reporters, §12, cmt., ¶3, www.supreme.courts.state.tx.us/rules/reporter.

PRACTICE TIP

Because each witness can be deposed for only six hours, a party should prepare for the deposition by conducting its written discovery first.

§6.3 Breaks. Breaks do not count against the time limitations. TRCP 199.5(c). Even though private conferences between the witness and the witness's attorney during the actual taking of the deposition are improper (except for the purpose of determining whether a privilege should be asserted), during agreed recesses and adjournments, the witness may confer privately with the lawyers. TRCP 199.5(d).

§6.4 Timekeeper. The deposition officer, generally the court reporter, is the timekeeper for purposes of the time limits on discovery. *See* TRCP 203.2(e). When a deposition is recorded without a court reporter, the person administering the oath to the witness, generally a notary public, must act as the timekeeper. *See* TRCP 199.1(c), 203.2(e); *see also* Gov't Code §602.002(4) (notary public may administer oaths). The deposition officer can use a time-stamping machine, a stopwatch, or other time-keeping device. Uniform Format Manual for Texas Court Reporters, §12, cmt., ¶3. The sworn certificate filed with the court must state the amount of time used by each party at the deposition. TRCP 203.2(e).

§7. OBJECTING BEFORE ORAL DEPOSITION

To object to the time, place, manner of proceeding, or scope of a deposition, the party should file a written objection to the deposition, a motion to quash the deposition, or a motion for protective order. TRCP 192.6, 199.4. See "Objecting to Trial & Discovery Subpoenas," ch. 1-K, §4, p. 61; "Motion for Protective Order," ch. 6-A, §19, p. 334; ***O'Connor's*** FORM 6E:03. The objection or motion should be filed as soon as possible—certainly before the date of the deposition unless filing the motion earlier is not feasible. ***Bohmfalk v. Linwood***, 742 S.W.2d 518, 520 (Tex. App.—Dallas 1987, no writ); *see, e.g.*, ***Siegel v. Smith***, 836 S.W.2d 193, 194 (Tex.App.—San Antonio 1992, writ denied) (P filed motion day of deposition with evidence of medical reason for inability to attend).

§7.1 To object to time or place. To object to the time or place designated for an oral deposition, the party or witness must file a motion for protective order or a motion to quash the notice of deposition. TRCP 192.6(a), 199.4; *see, e.g.*, ***Bohmfalk***, 742 S.W.2d at 520 (party waived inadequate notice of deposition because it did not file motion for protective order to reschedule it). The motion must identify a reasonable time or place for the deposition with which the party or witness will comply. TRCP 192.6(a). See "Date for oral deposition," §4.5.2, p. 388; "Place for deposition," §4.5.4, p. 389. If the motion is filed within three business days after service of the notice of deposition, the deposition is automatically stayed until the motion can be determined. TRCP 199.4. A TRCP 199.4 objection does not delay the time for compliance with a document request served with a deposition notice; it only delays the time of the deposition itself.

§7.2 To cancel or limit because of privilege. To prevent a deposition or limit the scope of the interrogation because of a particular privilege, the party objecting should file a motion to quash the subpoena or a motion for protective order, with affidavits, that proves it is entitled to the privilege. See "Scope of Discovery," ch. 6-B, p. 341. For example, if a consulting-only expert is noticed for deposition, the party seeking to prevent the deposition should file a motion for protective order or motion to quash the subpoena and attach an affidavit swearing the expert was hired in anticipation of litigation, the expert will not testify, and the expert's work was not reviewed by the testifying expert. *See* ***Essex Crane Rental v. Kitzman***, 723 S.W.2d 241, 242-43 (Tex.App.—Houston [1st Dist.] 1986, orig. proceeding).

§7.3 To cancel an apex deposition. To cancel the deposition of a corporate president or other high-level corporate official (an "apex deposition"), the corporation must file a motion for protective order accompanied by the official's affidavit denying any personal knowledge of relevant facts. ***In re Alcatel USA, Inc.***, 11 S.W.3d 173, 175 (Tex.2000); ***Crown Cent. Pet. Corp. v. Garcia***, 904 S.W.2d 125, 128 (Tex.1995). Once the motion is filed, the trial court must determine whether the party seeking the deposition has shown the official has any unique or superior personal knowledge of discoverable information. ***Alcatel***, 11 S.W.3d at 175-76; ***Crown Cent.***, 904 S.W.2d at 128. If the party cannot establish the official has such knowledge, the trial court should grant the motion for protective order and require the party to attempt to obtain the discovery through less-intrusive methods. ***Alcatel***, 11 S.W.3d at 176; ***Crown Cent.***, 904 S.W.2d at 128; *see* ***AMR Corp. v. Enlow***, 926 S.W.2d 640, 644 (Tex.App.—Fort Worth 1996, orig. proceeding) (highest ranking officer could not be deposed simply because he had ultimate responsibility). After making a good-faith effort at less-intrusive discovery, the party seeking the apex deposition may attempt to show that (1) there is a reasonable indication the official's deposition will lead to the discovery of admissible evidence, and (2) the less-intrusive discovery was unsatisfactory, insufficient, or inadequate. ***Alcatel***, 11 S.W.3d at 176; ***Crown Cent.***, 904 S.W.2d at 128; *see* ***In re Daisy Mfg. Co.***, 17 S.W.3d 654, 658 (Tex.2000) (merely completing some less-intrusive discovery does not trigger automatic right to depose apex official). The apex doctrine does not protect from deposition a corporate officer who is a named party in the suit. ***Simon v. Bridewell***, 950 S.W.2d 439, 443 (Tex.App.—Waco 1997, orig. proceeding).

§7.4 To exclude extra person. To object to an extra person attending the deposition who was identified under TRCP 199.5(a)(3), the party should file an objection before the deposition and ask the court to exclude that person.

§7.5 Other objections. See "Reasons to object to discovery requests," ch. 6-A, §18.1, p. 333.

§8. CONDUCT DURING ORAL DEPOSITION

If the lawyers and witnesses do not comply with TRCP 199.5(d), the court may allow into evidence at trial the statements, objections, discussions, and other occurrences during the oral deposition that reflect on the credibility of the witness or the testimony. TRCP 199.5(d).

§8.1 Conduct of lawyers. Lawyers should cooperate with and be courteous to each other and the witness. TRCP 199.5(d). The oral deposition must be conducted in the same manner as if the testimony were being elicited in open court. *Id.* An attorney must not ask a question at an oral deposition solely to harass or mislead the witness, for any other improper purpose, or without a good-faith legal basis. TRCP 199.5(h). An attorney must not object to a question at an oral deposition, instruct the witness not to answer a question, or suspend the deposition unless there is a good-faith factual and legal basis to do so. *Id.*

§8.2 Conduct of witness. The witness should not be evasive and should not unduly delay the examination. TRCP 199.5(d).

§8.3 Conferring with witness. Private conferences between the witness and the witness's attorney during the actual taking of the deposition are improper except for determining whether a privilege should be asserted. TRCP 199.5(d). Private conferences may be held during agreed recesses and adjournments. *Id.*

§8.4 Conduct of court reporter. The court reporter or other officer taking the oral deposition does not rule on objections, but records them for a ruling by the court. TRCP 199.5(e). The officer taking the oral deposition cannot stop recording the testimony because an objection has been made. *Id.*

§9. OBJECTING DURING ORAL DEPOSITION

§9.1 Procedure to object. Objections are made and recorded in the deposition and reserved for a ruling by the trial court. *See* TRCP 199.5(e).

1. Permissible objections. TRCP 199.5(e) governs the type of objections and limits the exact words that may be used in an objection. The only objections the parties can make during the deposition are (1) "Objection, leading"; (2) "Objection, form"; and (3) "Objection, nonresponsive." TCRP 199.5(e). If these objections are not stated as phrased, they are waived. *Id.* All other objections should be made at trial, unless the parties agree to another method. TRCP 199.5(e); *see* TRCP 191.1. The parties can agree to reserve all objections, including those stated in TRCP 199.5(e), until the time of trial. TRCP 191.1.

2. Request for explanation of objections. If requested by the party interrogating the deponent, the objecting party must give a clear and concise explanation of its objection, or the objection is waived. TRCP 199.5(e).

(1) Objections to form of question. Objections to the form of the question include the following: (1) the question assumes facts that are in dispute or are not in evidence; (2) the question is argumentative; (3) the question misquotes the deponent; (4) the question calls for speculation; (5) the question is vague, ambiguous, or confusing; (6) the question is compound; (7) the question is too general; (8) the question calls for a narrative answer; and (9) the question has been asked and answered. TRCP 199, cmt. 4; ***St. Luke's Episcopal Hosp. v. Garcia***, 928 S.W.2d 307, 309 (Tex.App.—Houston [14th Dist.] 1996, orig. proceeding).

(2) Objections to nonresponsiveness of answer. If the deponent's response addresses issues not raised by a question or states more than is strictly required to answer the question, the lawyer must object or waive any complaint. *See* TRCP 199.5(e).

3. Sanctionable objections. Argumentative or suggestive objections or explanations waive the objection and may be grounds for terminating the oral deposition or assessing costs or other sanctions. TRCP 199.5(e).

§9.2 Instructions not to answer. There are very few instances when it is proper for a lawyer to instruct the deponent not to answer. When requested by the opposing party, the lawyer who instructed the witness not to answer must give a concise, nonargumentative, and nonsuggestive explanation of the grounds for the instruction. TRCP 199.5(f). After giving the requested explanation, if the lawyer who asked the question insists that it is a proper line of inquiry, the objecting lawyer may suspend the deposition to get a court ruling. See §9.3, below. If the objecting lawyer does not suspend the deposition but refuses to permit the deponent to answer, the lawyer who asked the question may suspend the deposition and file a motion to compel the deponent to answer. *See generally* ***Huie v. DeShazo***, 922 S.W.2d 920, 922 (Tex.1996) (Supreme Court stayed deposition while considering writ of mandamus regarding motion to compel testimony over assertion of attorney-client privilege). An attorney may object and instruct a witness not to answer a question during an oral deposition only for one of the following reasons.

1. Preserve privileges. To prevent the discovery of privileged information, the lawyer may object and instruct the witness not to answer. TRCP 199.5(f). If the witness answers and discloses privileged information, the privilege may be waived. *See* ***Delaporte v. Preston Square***, 680 S.W.2d 561, 564 (Tex.App.—Dallas 1984, writ ref'd n.r.e.) (party who answered question about privileged matter in deposition waived privilege; however, trial court excluded answer at trial); *see also* ***Eloise Bauer & Assocs. v. Electronic Rlty. Assocs.***, 621 S.W.2d 200, 204 (Tex. App.—Texarkana 1981, writ ref'd n.r.e.) (party who voluntarily produced document waived privilege because no evidence its production was accidental). If necessary for an in camera review, the deposition questions can be answered in front of the court reporter in the absence of the party seeking discovery and be submitted to the court in camera. TRCP 199.6.

2. Comply with court order or rules. A lawyer may instruct a witness not to answer a question if necessary to comply with a court order or "these rules." TRCP 199.5(f). For example, if a deponent is asked for "net worth" information in a suit that involves only actual damages, the deponent should be instructed not to answer because the information is not relevant under "these rules." If the deponent is asked for information the court has already ruled is not discoverable, the deponent should be instructed not to answer. *See* TRCP 199.5(f).

3. Protect a witness. A lawyer may instruct a witness not to answer if one of the parties asks the deponent questions that are abusive or for which any answer would be misleading. TRCP 199.5(f). For example, a lawyer could instruct a witness not to answer when the question incorporates such unfair assumptions or is so worded that any answer would necessarily be misleading—the when-did-you-stop-beating-your-spouse sort of question. TRCP 199, cmt. 4. Abusive questions include questions that inquire into matters clearly beyond the scope of discovery or that are argumentative, repetitious, or harassing. *Id.*

4. Stopwatch objection. When a party exceeds the deposition time limits, the other party should object and suspend the deposition to obtain a court ruling. TRCP 199.5(g).

§9.3 Suspending deposition. A party or witness may suspend the deposition for the time necessary to obtain a court ruling if the time limitations for the deposition have expired or the deposition is being conducted or defended in violation of the rules. TRCP 199.5(g).

§9.4 Motion to compel answer. When a witness refuses to answer a question at a deposition, the party asking the question may file a motion to compel along with a copy of the deposition (or the certified question) and request a hearing. TRCP 199.6, 215.1(b)(2)(B); *see, e.g.*, ***Huie***, 922 S.W.2d at 922 (after witness refused to answer questions based on privilege, P filed motion to compel with certified questions); ***Koepp v. Utica Mut. Ins. Co.***, 833 S.W.2d 514, 514 (Tex.1992) (after P refused to answer questions about drug use, D filed motion to compel). The certified question is an excerpt from the deposition prepared by the court reporter to be used when a party intends to ask for an immediate court ruling. See "Motion to Compel Discovery," ch. 6-A, §21, p. 336.

§9.5 Motion to suppress. To object to errors or irregularities in the taking or the preparation of a deposition—how the deposition was prepared, transcribed, signed, certified, sealed, endorsed, or delivered—the party must file a written motion to suppress and serve it on all other parties. TRCP 203.5; *see* TRCP 202.3(b)(2). The motion to suppress must be served before the trial commences if the deposition officer delivered the deposition at least one entire day before the day of trial. TRCP 203.5; ***Klorer v. Block***, 717 S.W.2d 754, 759 (Tex.App.—San Antonio 1986, writ ref'd n.r.e.). See ***O'Connor's*** FORM 6E:04.

§10. DEPOSITION SANCTIONS

§10.1 Grounds for sanctions. A party or a deponent can be sanctioned for violating deposition procedures. For the standards for imposing sanctions, see "Motion for Sanctions," ch. 5-J, p. 275.

1. Refusal to attend deposition.

(1) By party-deponent. If the party to be deposed does not attend a noticed or court-ordered deposition, the trial court can impose the ultimate sanction of dismissal or default. TRCP 215.2(b)(5); *see, e.g.*, ***Greater Houston Transp. Co. V. Wilson***, 725 S.W.2d 427, 431 (Tex.App.—Houston [14th Dist.] 1987, writ ref'd n.r.e.) (D did not attend deposition; default judgment entered); ***Petitt v. Laware***, 715 S.W.2d 688, 691-92 (Tex.App.—Houston [1st Dist.] 1986, writ ref'd n.r.e.) (P refused to attend court-ordered deposition; case dismissed). *But see* ***Hogan v. Beckel***, 783 S.W.2d 307, 308 (Tex.App.—San Antonio 1989, writ denied) (dismissal was improper when P did not appear for one noticed deposition). There is no requirement that the failure to attend be willful. ***Meek v. Bishop, Peterson & Sharp***, 919 S.W.2d 805, 809 (Tex.App.—Houston [14th Dist.] 1996, writ denied); *see* TRCP 215.1(b)(2)(A).

(2) By party who noticed deposition. If the party giving notice of the deposition does not attend the deposition, and if another party or that party's lawyer does attend, the court may award the attending party reasonable expenses, including attorney fees. TRCP 215.5(a); ***Hlavinka v. Griffin***, 721 S.W.2d 521, 523-24 (Tex. App.—Corpus Christi 1986, no writ).

(3) By nonparty witness-deponent.

(a) If the witness does not attend a deposition, and the fault lies with the party giving notice, the court may order that party to pay reasonable expenses, including attorney fees, to any party that does attend. TRCP 215.5(b); *see also* ***Downer v. Aquamarine Operators***, 701 S.W.2d 238, 242-43 (Tex.1985) (court struck D's answer because D, who was noticed for deposition, sent witnesses out of town, left P waiting at deposition for an hour, and then requested that deposition be taken the next day in another city).

(b) If a nonparty witness does not attend a deposition after being ordered by the trial court to attend, the court may hold the nonparty witness in contempt. TRCP 176.8(a), 215.2(a).

2. Refusal to answer questions. A deponent is subject to sanctions for refusing to answer a proper question asked in a deposition. TRCP 215.1(b)(2)(B). A deponent's evasive or incomplete answer can be treated as a refusal to answer a question. TRCP 215.1(c). When a trial court orders a deponent to answer a question and the deponent refuses, the court can impose sanctions.

(1) Contempt. The court can hold the deponent (party or nonparty) in contempt and punish with a fine or confinement. TRCP 176.8(a), 215.2(a).

(2) Strike pleadings. The court can strike a party's pleadings. *See, e.g.*, ***First State Bank v. Chappell & Handy, P.C.***, 729 S.W.2d 917, 921 (Tex.App.—Corpus Christi 1987, writ ref'd n.r.e.) (court struck D corporation's counterclaim & defensive pleadings because D's officer refused to answer questions after being ordered to answer).

(3) Award expenses. The court can require a party or deponent whose conduct necessitated the motion for sanctions or the attorney advising such conduct, or both, to pay the moving party's reasonable expenses, including attorney fees. TRCP 215.2(b)(8); *see also* TRCP 215.3 (sanctions may be imposed for abusing discovery process).

§10.2 Appropriate court to hear objections & motions. TRCP 215.1(a) determines the appropriate court to hear and determine objections and motions about a deposition.

1. Party deponent. The court where the suit is filed should hear and determine objections made about a deposition of a party. TRCP 215.1(a). Any district court in the district where a party's deposition is being taken may also hear a motion relating to the taking of a deposition. *Id.*

2. Nonparty deponent. A district court in the district where the deposition is being taken should hear and determine the objections made about the deposition of a nonparty. ***Latham v. Thornton***, 806 S.W.2d 347, 349 (Tex.App.—Fort Worth 1991, orig. proceeding).

§11. SUPPLEMENTING DEPOSITION TESTIMONY

§11.1 Deposition of fact witnesses. A party does not have a general duty to supplement the deposition testimony of fact witnesses who change their minds about facts disclosed in a deposition. TRCP 193, cmt. 5; ***Titus Cty. Hosp. Dist. v. Lucas***, 988 S.W.2d 740, 740 (Tex.1998); *see* ***Collins v. Collins***, 923 S.W.2d 569, 569 (Tex.1996).

PRACTICE TIP

To avoid the surprise at trial that the other party's witnesses have changed their minds about the facts of the case, the parties could enter into a Rule 11 agreement to supplement the deposition testimony of fact witnesses who are aligned with each party.

§11.2 Deposition testimony of retained expert. See "Supplementing discovery of retained testifying expert," ch. 6-C, §5.1, p. 371.

§11.3 Deposition testimony of nonretained expert. See "Supplementing discovery of nonretained testifying expert," ch. 6-C, §5.2, p. 372.

§12. USING DEPOSITION AT TRIAL

§12.1 Admissibility. A deposition is admissible at trial according to the rules of evidence. TRCP 203.6(b), (c); *see* ***Jones v. Colley***, 820 S.W.2d 863, 866 (Tex.App.—Texarkana 1991, writ denied) (party is entitled to offer deposition testimony into evidence in most effective manner, provided it does not convey false impression).

1. Deposition taken in same proceeding. A deposition taken in the same proceeding as the trial is not hearsay, and the deponent does not need to be unavailable before the deposition can be used as evidence. TRCP 203.6(b)(1); TRE 801(e)(3). The deposition can be used instead of live testimony or in addition to live testimony. "Same proceeding" includes any other suit involving the same subject matter and between the same parties or their representatives or successors in interest. TRCP 203.6(b).

(1) Party not present at deposition. Depositions taken in the absence of a party may be used at trial if the party received notice but chose not to attend. ***Bohmfalk v. Linwood***, 742 S.W.2d 518, 520 (Tex.App.—Dallas 1987, no writ).

(2) Not party at time of deposition. A deposition may not be used against a party that was joined after the deposition was taken, unless the late party had a reasonable opportunity to redepose the deponent after being joined and did not exercise that opportunity. TRCP 203.6(b)(2); ***Stevenson v. Koutzarov***, 795 S.W.2d 313, 317 (Tex.App.—Houston [1st Dist.] 1990, writ denied). If a deposition was taken before a party was joined, it can be used at trial if the late party has a similar interest with any party already in the suit at the time the deposition was taken.

PRACTICE TIP

If you took a deposition before a party was added, and if the late party does not have similar interests with any other party, you should redepose the witness to give the late party the opportunity for cross-examination. See ***Elizondo v. Tavarez****, 596 S.W.2d 667, 671 (Tex.App.—Corpus Christi 1980, writ ref'd n.r.e.). You can satisfy the requirement to redepose the witness by deposing the witness with written questions. If you represent a late party, and one of the parties sends a deposition on written questions to a witness who was deposed before your client was added, you should file objections to the deposition on written questions, and notice the witness to appear for an oral deposition.* ***Stevenson****, 795 S.W.2d at 316 n.1.*

2. Deposition from other proceeding. A deposition from another proceeding is admissible, subject to the rules of evidence. TRCP 203.6(c).

(1) Party deposition. The deposition of a party taken in another proceeding is admissible as a party-admission or as former testimony. TRE 801(e)(2); *see, e.g.*, ***Worley v. Butler***, 809 S.W.2d 242, 245 (Tex. App.—Corpus Christi 1990, no writ) (client's testimony at first trial about employment contract with his lawyer was admissible against him in later lawsuit over attorney fees); *see also* TRE 801(e)(1) (prior statement by witness).

(2) **Nonparty deposition.** The deposition of a nonparty taken in another proceeding is admissible as former testimony if the deponent is unavailable to testify. TRE 804(b)(1); ***Smith v. Smith***, 720 S.W.2d 586, 599 (Tex.App.—Houston [1st Dist.] 1986, no writ); *see* TRCP 203.6(c); *see, e.g.*, ***Celotex Corp. v. Tate***, 797 S.W.2d 197, 205 (Tex.App.—Corpus Christi 1990, writ dism'd) (deposition of claimant in workers' compensation case, who died, was admissible in another case). TRE 804(a) defines unavailability of a witness as a (a) claim of privilege, (b) refusal to testify, (c) lack of memory, (d) death or physical or mental illness or infirmity, or (e) absence from the hearing and inability of the proponent to procure attendance or testimony. TRE 804(a); Cochran, ***Evidence Handbook***, p. 873; *see* ***Keene Corp. v. Rogers***, 863 S.W.2d 168, 177-78 (Tex.App.—Texarkana 1993, writ filed, bankruptcy stay granted) (because party did not prove unavailability, court should have excluded expert's deposition from another case). The party against whom the deposition is offered, or a person with a similar interest, must have had an opportunity and similar motive to develop the former testimony by direct, cross-, or redirect examination. TRE 804(b)(1).

§12.2 Procedure. Deposition testimony is introduced at trial as follows:

1. **Read into evidence.** The party offering deposition testimony must read a transcribed deposition (or play a videotape deposition) before the jury. *See* TRCP 203.6(b). When introducing a written deposition, one lawyer reads the questions and another lawyer, sitting in the witness stand, reads the answers given by the deponent.

CAUTION

When you read a deposition into evidence (or play a videotape deposition), insist that the court reporter transcribe the testimony as the jury hears it. If the court reporter does not transcribe the deposition testimony as it is presented at trial, the appellate record will not contain the deposition testimony of the witness. If you do not object on the record during the trial, you will waive the issue of an incomplete record on appeal. ***Lascurain v. Crowley***, *917 S.W.2d 341, 344-45 (Tex.App.—El Paso 1996, no writ) (court reporter left courtroom during deposition testimony with permission of parties). If the court reporter appeared to be transcribing the testimony, but was not, you may be able to reconstruct the record.* ***State Farm Fire & Cas. Ins. Co. v. Vandiver***, *941 S.W.2d 343, 347-48 (Tex.App.—Waco 1997, no writ).*

2. **Submit deposition as offer of proof.** If the court rules a deposition is not admissible, the party may submit the deposition as an offer of proof, have it marked as an exhibit, identify the portions offered by line and page number, and file it with the court reporter. *See* TRE 103(a)(2); ***Soefje v. Stewart***, 847 S.W.2d 311, 313 (Tex.App.—San Antonio 1992, writ denied). The offer of proof should be made before the charge is read to the jury. If, for some reason, the deposition is not immediately offered as an offer of proof, it may be filed as a formal bill of exceptions after the trial. TRAP 33.2. See "Offer of Proof & Bill of Exceptions," ch. 8-E, p. 553.

§12.3 Trial objections to deposition testimony. At trial, a party may urge (1) those objections to leading, form, and nonresponsiveness that were made during the deposition and (2) all other objections. TRCP 199.5(e). See "Procedure to object," §9.1, p. 396.

§12.4 Objection to trial testimony. A party may object to the trial testimony of a witness if it is materially different from the witness's deposition testimony. See "Impeaching a Witness," ch. 8-C, §6, p. 539.

§12.5 Use in summary judgment cases. When a deposition is used as summary judgment evidence, it is not necessary for the deposition to be authenticated by an affidavit that certifies the truthfulness and correctness of the copied material. *See* TRCP 166a(d); TRE 901(a); ***McConathy v. McConathy***, 869 S.W.2d 341, 342 (Tex.1994). See "Unverified," ch. 7-B, §3.5.3, p. 462.

§13. DEPOSITION BY NONSTENOGRAPHIC RECORDING DEVICE

A party may take a deposition by videotape or other recording device. TRCP 199.1(c). A video deposition has a more powerful effect on the jury than a deposition that is read to the jury. ***Ochs v. Martinez***, 789 S.W.2d 949, 956 (Tex.App.—San Antonio 1990, writ denied).

§13.1 Deposition officer. When a deposition is to be recorded by video or audio recording without a simultaneous stenographic recording by a court reporter, the party noticing the deposition is responsible for obtaining a person authorized by law to act as the deposition officer and administer the oath. TRCP 199.1(c), 203.2. See Uniform Format Manual for Texas Court Reporters, §11, cmt.

§13.2 Notice. To take a videotape deposition, the party must give the witness and the other parties at least five days' notice in writing. TRCP 199.1(c). The notice must state that the deposition (1) will be recorded by other than stenographic means, (2) will be recorded by videotape or audiotape (or by some other means), and (3) will or will not be recorded stenographically. *Id.* The notice may be included in the deposition notice or served separately. *Id.* See "Date for oral deposition," §4.5.2, p. 388. See ***O'Connor's*** FORM 6E:02, ¶3.

PRACTICE TIP

TRCP 199.1(c) is a significant improvement over its predecessor because it eliminates the requirement that a videotaped deposition be accompanied by a stenographic transcript. Unless one of the parties elects to pay for a court reporter to transcribe the testimony, or the court orders the deposition to be transcribed for trial, no stenographic transcript is necessary. TRCP 199.1(c), 203.6(a).

§13.3 Response. After a party gives notice of its intent to take a nonstenographic deposition, any other party may serve written notice designating another method of recording (usually stenographic) at its own expense. TRCP 199.1(c); *see also* TRCP 203.6(a) (court may require nonstenographic recording be reduced to writing by certified court reporter).

§13.4 Recording. The party taking the deposition is responsible for ensuring the recording is intelligible, accurate, and trustworthy. TRCP 199.1(c). See "Deposition Officer," §3, p. 386.

§13.5 Copies. The original video recording must be available for inspection. TRCP 203.3(c). All parties must have reasonable access to the video deposition and may obtain a duplicate copy at their own expense. *Id.*

§13.6 Use at trial. A party may play a recording of a nonstenographic deposition at trial, instead of reading the deposition. TRCP 203.6(a). A party may use a written transcription of a nonstenographic deposition to the same extent as one taken by stenographic means. *Id.*; ***Wrenn v. G.A.T.X. Logistics***, 73 S.W.3d 489, 499 (Tex.App.—Fort Worth 2002, no pet.). The court, on a motion showing good cause, may order the party to provide a transcript of the deposition. TRCP 203.6(a).

§14. DEPOSITION BY TELEPHONE

A deposition by telephone is useful when the deponent is far away and the parties need only limited information.

§14.1 Notice. A written notice to take a deposition by telephone or other remote electronic means must be served on the witness and all parties a reasonable time before the deposition is to be taken. TRCP 199.1(b). See "Notice of oral deposition," §4.5, p. 387. To take a telephone deposition without a request for documents, see "For deposition without documents," §4.5.2(2), p. 388. To take a telephone deposition that requests the production of documents, see "For deposition with documents," §4.5.2(1), p. 388. See ***O'Connor's*** FORM 6E:02, ¶5.

§14.2 Location of witness. A deposition by telephone is considered as having been taken "in the district and at the place where the witness is located when answering the questions." TRCP 199.1(b). The person administering the oath to the witness must have the power to administer an oath in the jurisdiction where the witness is located. *Id.*; *see* CPRC §20.001(b), (c).

§14.3 Location of deposition officer. The deposition officer may be located with the party who noticed the deposition or with the witness. TRCP 199.1(b); *see* ***Clone Component Distribs. v. State***, 819 S.W.2d 593, 598 (Tex. App.—Dallas 1991, no writ).

§14.4 Exhibits. If it is necessary to question the witness about exhibits, and the deposition officer is not physically in the same room with the witness, the parties should send premarked exhibits to the witness before the deposition. Another option is to use a fax machine to transfer copies of exhibits during the deposition. *See* ***Clone Component***, 819 S.W.2d at 599-600.

§15. DEPOSITION ON WRITTEN QUESTIONS

Depositions on written questions are useful for securing testimony from a deponent with limited relevant information—for example, a custodian of business records. A deposition on written questions is relatively inexpensive when compared to an oral deposition. Depositions on written questions are similar to interrogatories in that the questions are drafted in advance. They are unlike interrogatories in other ways—depositions on written questions can be served on nonparties (interrogatories can be served only on parties), and depositions on written questions are not limited in number (interrogatories are limited). Depositions on written questions cannot be used to circumvent the limits on interrogatories. TRCP 190, cmt. 5.

§15.1 Procedure. A deposition on written questions proceeds much like the standard oral deposition that is transcribed by a court reporter. See "Procedure for the Standard Oral Deposition," §4, p. 387, for most of the requirements. This section will focus on the differences between the two procedures.

§15.2 Deposition officer. The only persons who can take a deposition on written questions are a court reporter, a clerk of a county or district court, a judge, or a notary public. CPRC §20.001(a).

§15.3 Notice of deposition on written questions. The notice to take a deposition on written questions must include the following:

1. Name & address. The notice must state the name of the deponent (if known) and the deponent's address (if known). TRCP 200.1(b). The name of the deponent might not be known if the deponent is a custodian of records, or the party has asked an organization to provide a deponent to give testimony about a certain subject. TRCP 199.2(b), 200.1(b). The notice of a deposition on written questions to a nonparty business association or business entity can require the nonparty to designate a deponent to testify on a particular subject. TRCP 199.2(b), 200.1(b).

2. Date for deposition by written questions. The notice to take a deposition on written questions of a witness (a party or nonparty) must be served on the witness and all parties 20 days before the deposition is to be taken. TRCP 200.1(a). If the notice requests a party (not a nonparty) to produce documents, the notice must be served at least 30 days before the deposition. *See* TRCP 200.1(b). See "For deposition with documents," §4.5.2(1), p. 388; chart 6-9, "Deadlines to Serve Notice & Subpoena," p. 391; ***O'Connor's*** FORM 6E:05.

3. Designation of documents & things. The notice must identify those items the deponent is required to produce. TRCP 200.1(b).

4. Extra persons in attendance. The notice must identify any person not listed in TRCP 199.5(a)(3) who will attend the deposition. TRCP 200.1(b). See "Additional attendee," §4.5.5, p. 390.

5. Signed. The notice must be signed by the attorney (or party when pro se). TRCP 191.3(a). See "Certification by signature," ch. 6-A, §3.1, p. 314.

6. Subpoena. When the deponent is a nonparty, a subpoena must be issued. TRCP 200.2, 205.1(b); ***St. Luke's Episcopal Hosp. v. Garcia***, 928 S.W.2d 307, 311 (Tex.App.—Houston [14th Dist.] 1996, orig. proceeding). If the nonparty deponent is required to produce documents, the subpoena must meet the requirements of TRCP 176. TRCP 176, 199.2(b)(5), 200.1(b). See "Subpoenas," ch. 1-K, p. 58; "Securing Things from a Nonparty," ch. 6-H, §5, p. 428.

7. Direct questions. The questions the deponent is required to answer must be attached to the notice. TRCP 200.3(a). See *O'Connor's* FORM 6E:06.

8. Provide to deposition officer. The party that noticed the deposition must send a copy of the notice and copies of all questions to the officer designated to take the deposition, generally the court reporter. TRCP 200.1(a). If the deponent is a nonparty, the court reporter will issue a subpoena.

§15.4 Cross-questions. Any other party in the suit may serve cross-questions within ten days after the notice and the direct questions are served. TRCP 200.3(b). See ***O'Connor's*** FORM 6E:07.

§15.5 Redirect question. The propounder of the direct questions may serve redirect questions within five days after being served cross-questions. TRCP 200.3(b).

§15.6 Recross question. The other parties may serve recross questions within three days after being served redirect questions. TRCP 200.3(b).

§15.7 Objections to form of question. Objections to the form of questions must be served on the party propounding them within the time allowed for serving the succeeding cross- or other questions and within five days after service of the last authorized questions. TRCP 200.3(b); *see* ***St. Luke's***, 928 S.W.2d at 310. The deadline for objections applies only to objections to form, not objections to substantive issues or privileges. ***St. Luke's***, 928 S.W.2d at 310. Objections to the form of the question are waived unless asserted in accordance with TRCP 200.3(b). TRCP 200.3(c). See *O'Connor's* FORM 6E:07.

§15.8 Objections to substance. To lodge objections to substance or privileges, the deponent or a party should file a motion to quash or a motion for protective order. If the deponent is a nonparty, the movant should press for a hearing before the date of the deposition. See "Subpoenas," ch. 1-K, p. 58; "Objecting Before Oral Deposition," §7, p. 394.

§15.9 Taking deposition. At the time of the deposition, the deposition officer administers the oath, asks the questions, receives any documents produced, and transcribes the deponent's testimony. The officer then prepares the questions and answers and certifies and delivers them to the deponent for examination and signature. TRCP 200.4. When necessary, the officer has authority to summon and administer an oath to an interpreter. *Id.*

§15.10 Filing deposition. Nonparty deposition notices and subpoenas must be filed with the court. TRCP 191.4(b)(1). No other deposition documents should be filed. TRCP 191.4(a)(1). For exceptions, see "Filing discovery," ch. 6-A, §11.1.3, p. 322.

§16. DEPOSITION BEFORE SUIT

A deposition before suit or to investigate a claim is an examination by oral or written questions taken by court order before a lawsuit is filed. TRCP 202.1. The proceeding is not, in itself, a separate lawsuit but is incident to and in anticipation of a suit. ***Office Employees Int'l Un. v. Southwestern Drug***, 391 S.W.2d 404, 406 (Tex.1965) (former TRCP 187); ***Valley Baptist Med. Ctr. v. Gonzalez***, 18 S.W.3d 673, 675 (Tex.App.—Corpus Christi 1999), *vacated as moot*, 33 S.W.3d 821 (Tex.2000). It is an ancillary proceeding. ***Valley Baptist***, 18 S.W.3d at 676. TRCP 202 applies to all discovery before suit covered by the former rules governing depositions to perpetuate testimony (former TRCP 187) and bills of discovery (former TRCP 737). TRCP 202, cmt. 1.

§16.1 Petition. The requirements for the petition are stated in TRCP 202.2.

1. Form. The petition must be in the name of the petitioner and must be verified. TRCP 202.2(a), (c). See ***O'Connor's*** FORM 6E:09.

2. Grounds. The petition must state either one of two grounds for a deposition before suit. TRCP 202.2(d)(1), (2); ***In re Sw. Sec.***, No. 05-99-01836-CV (Tex.App.—Dallas 2000, orig. proceeding) (no pub.; 6-14-00).

(1) Anticipation of another suit. A petition for a TRCP 202 deposition may be filed in anticipation of another suit. TRCP 202.2(d)(1). Such a petition must include the statement: "The petitioner anticipates the institution of a suit in which the petitioner may be a party." *Id.* In addition, the petition must do the following:

(a) Identify subject. The petition must identify the subject matter of the anticipated action and the petitioner's interest in it. TRCP 202.2(e).

(b) Identify adverse persons. The petition must either (1) include the names, addresses, and telephone numbers of the persons whom the petitioner expects to have interests adverse to the petitioner's in the anticipated suit or (2) state that the information cannot be ascertained through diligent inquiry and describe those persons. TRCP 202.2(f); ***U.S. Gov't v. Marks***, 949 S.W.2d 320, 322 (Tex.1997) (former TRCP 187).

(2) Investigate claim. A petition for a TRCP 202 deposition may be filed to investigate a claim. TRCP 202.2(d)(2). Such a petition must include the statement: "The petitioner seeks to investigate a potential claim by or against the petitioner." *Id.* Under TRCP 202.2(d)(2), there is no expectation of another suit. This ground can help plaintiffs comply with TRCP 13 and CPRC §9.011, which require plaintiffs to make a good-faith inquiry before deciding whether to file suit. *See also* CPRC §10.001 (certificate by signature). When investigating a claim, unlike a deposition in anticipation of suit, the petitioner is not required to notify those who may have an adverse interest. Fineberg & Shore, *Discovery Update*, Advanced Civil Trial Course, State Bar of Texas, ch. 1, §I(A)(3), p. 3 (2001).

3. Deponent information. The petition must identify the persons to be deposed by name, address, and telephone number, the substance of the testimony the petitioner expects to elicit from each, the documents the persons will be requested to bring to the deposition, and the petitioner's reasons for desiring to obtain the testimony of each. TRCP 202.2(g).

4. Prayer. The petition must request an order authorizing the petitioner to take the depositions of the persons named in the petition. TRCP 202.2(h).

§16.2 Where to file. A petition under TRCP 202 must be filed where venue of the anticipated suit may lie, if suit is anticipated, or where the witness resides, if no suit is anticipated. TRCP 202.2(b); ***In re Akzo Nobel Chem.***, 24 S.W.3d 919, 920 (Tex.App.—Beaumont 2000, orig. proceeding).

PRACTICE TIP

As courts begin to impose serious financial sanctions for groundless and frivolous lawsuits under TRCP 13, CPRC §9.012, and CPRC §10.001, lawyers may begin to use the deposition before suit to investigate the facts before filing suit. ***Valley Baptist***, *18 S.W.3d at 676.*

§16.3 Notice & service.

1. Persons named in petition. At least 15 days before the hearing, the petition and the notice of the hearing must be served on the deponent and any potential adverse party named in the petition. TRCP 202.3(a); ***Marks***, 949 S.W.2d at 322. See ***O'Connor's*** FORM 6E:10. The petitioner may request a shorter period of notice if "justice or necessity" requires that the deposition be taken on shorter notice. TRCP 202.3(d). TRCP 202.3(a) provides that service can be accomplished under TRCP 21a. However, to secure the attendance of the witness at the hearing, the witness must be served with a subpoena.

2. Persons not named in petition. Unnamed persons described in the petition whom the petitioner expects to have interests adverse to petitioner's in the anticipated suit, may be served by publication with the petition and notice of the hearing. See *O'Connor's* FORM 6E:11. The notice must state the place for the hearing and the time it will be held, which must be more than 14 days after the first publication of the notice. TRCP 202.3(b)(1). The petition and notice must be published once each week for two consecutive weeks in the newspaper of broadest circulation in the county in which the petition is filed, or if no such newspaper exists, in the newspaper of broadest circulation in the nearest county where a newspaper is published. *Id.* Any interested party may move, in the proceeding or by bill of review, to suppress any deposition, in whole or in part, taken on notice by publication, and may also attack or oppose the deposition by any other means available. TRCP 202.3(b)(2).

3. In probate cases. A petition to take a deposition in anticipation of an application for probate of a will, and a notice of the hearing on the petition, may be served by posting as prescribed by Probate Code §33(f)(2). TRCP 202.3(c). The notice and petition must be directed to all parties interested in the testator's estate and must comply with the requirements of Probate Code §33(c), to the extent it is applicable. TRCP 202.3(c).

§16.4 Response.

1. Objecting to deposition. If the deponent or any potential adverse party objects to the taking of the deposition, it should file a motion to vacate the order for the deposition and ask for a hearing. *See* ***Marks***, 949 S.W.2d at 322 (former TRCP 187). If a potential adverse party did not receive notice and wants to object to the deposition, that party should file a motion to intervene as an interested party. *See id.* at 322-23.

2. Not removable to federal court. A TRCP 202 proceeding is not removable to federal court. *See* ***Texas v. Real Parties in Interest***, 259 F.3d 387, 394 (5th Cir.2001) (when TRCP 202 is used as investigatory tool for potential claims, claim is not subject to removal); ***Mayfield-George v. Texas Rehab. Comm'n***, 197 F.R.D. 280, 283 (N.D. Tex.2000) (TRCP 202 proceeding is not a "civil action" under 28 U.S.C. §1441(b) because it does not assert a claim on which relief can be granted); ***McCrary v. Kansas City S. R.R.***, 121 F.Supp.2d 566, 569 (E.D. Tex. 2000) (same). The All Writs Act, 28 U.S.C. §1651(a), does not provide an independent ground to remove a TRCP 202 claim from state court. ***Real Parties***, 259 F.3d at 392. For a TRCP 202 proceeding to be enjoined under the All Writs Act, it must develop into a claim that threatens an earlier federal court judgment. *Id.* at 395. For a detailed discussion of the use of the All Writs Act to support removal, see Hoffman, *Removal Jurisdiction & the All Writs Act*, 148 U.Pa.L.Rev. 401 (1999).

§16.5 Hearing.

1. Subpoena witness. The petitioner should issue and serve a subpoena on the witness to appear at the hearing.

2. Proof. The petitioner should show (1) that allowing the deposition may prevent a failure or delay of justice in an anticipated suit or (2) that the likely benefits of allowing the deposition to investigate a potential claim outweigh the burden or expense of the procedure. TRCP 202.4(a).

§16.6 Order. See *O'Connor's* FORM 6E:12.

1. Required findings. The order must contain one of the following findings: (1) allowing the deposition may prevent a failure or delay of justice in an anticipated suit or (2) the likely benefits of allowing the deposition to investigate a potential claim outweigh the burden or expense of the procedure. TRCP 202.4(a); ***Valley Baptist Med. Ctr. v. Gonzalez***, 18 S.W.3d 673, 678 (Tex.App.—Corpus Christi 1999), *vacated as moot*, 33 S.W.3d 821 (Tex.2000).

2. Discovery permitted.

(1) Deposition. The order must state the type of deposition (oral or written) to be conducted and may also state the time and place for the deposition. TRCP 202.4(b). The time and place may be stated in the notice of the deposition instead of in the order. *Id.* Depositions are the only form of discovery that may be ordered under TRCP 202. ***In re Akzo Nobel Chem.***, 24 S.W.3d 919, 921 (Tex.App.—Beaumont 2000, orig. proceeding).

(2) Subpoena for documents. As part of the deposition, the court may permit the issuance of a subpoena to produce documents at the deposition. Fineberg & Shore, *Discovery Update*, ch. 1, §I(A)(4), p. 4.

3. Protection for others. The order must also contain any provisions the court deems necessary to protect the witness or any other person that might be affected by the deposition. TRCP 202.4(b); ***Valley Baptist***, 18 S.W.3d at 678 (suggested court could order bond to protect D from costs); ***In re Fernandez***, No. 04-99-00841-CV (Tex.App.—San Antonio 1999, orig. proceeding) (no pub.; 12-30-99).

§16.7 Taking deposition. The rules apply just as in other depositions. TRCP 202.5.

§16.8 Use at trial.

1. Impeachment. Testimony from a presuit deposition is admissible to impeach a witness, even if the other parties were not notified of the deposition. *See* Fineberg & Shore, *Discovery Update*, ch. 1, §I(A)(4), p. 4.

2. Restricted use. The court may restrict or prohibit the use of a deposition taken under TRCP 202 in a later lawsuit to protect a person who was not served with notice of the deposition from unfair prejudice. TRCP 202.5. If a party objects to the use of a TRCP 202 deposition, the party must show that it (1) did not receive notice of the deposition and (2) will be unfairly prejudiced by the use of the deposition. To show unfair prejudice, the party would probably have to prove the deponent gave false testimony. *See* Fineberg & Shore, *New Investigative Discovery*, Advanced Civil Trial Course, State Bar of Texas, Tab A, p. A-5 (1999).

§16.9 Appellate review. The issue of the finality of a TRCP 202 order has not been resolved. Thus, a party should challenge a TRCP 202 order by filing both an appeal and a petition for mandamus.

§17. DEPOSITION IN ANOTHER STATE

§17.1 Deposition officer. A deposition may be taken before a person authorized to administer oaths in the place where the deposition is being taken, either by the law of that state or of Texas. TRCP 201.1(b).

§17.2 Procedure. A deposition in another state may be taken by notice, letter rogatory, letter of request, agreement of the parties, or court order. TRCP 201.1. Parties may also take the deposition of a witness in another state by telephone or video conference while the parties and their lawyers are in Texas. TRCP 199.1(b), 201.1(g). *See* ***Clone Component Distribs. v. State***, 819 S.W.2d 593, 598 (Tex.App.—Dallas 1991, no writ). See "Deposition by Telephone," §14, p. 401.

PRACTICE TIP

The easiest way to arrange for a deposition in another state is to contact a lawyer or court reporter in the other state and make arrangements through that person.

§18. DEPOSITION IN A FOREIGN COUNTRY

Obtaining discovery in foreign countries is extremely complicated. Most foreign countries are hostile to the American form of pretrial discovery.

PRACTICE TIP

Before taking a deposition in a foreign country, call the Bureau of Consular Affairs, Office of American Citizens Services, Department of State, Washington, D.C. at (202) 647-5225 or refer to the Bureau's website at http://travel.state.gov/judicial_assistance.html.

§18.1 Procedure. The procedure for foreign discovery is outlined in TRCP 201. ***Smith v. Smith***, 720 S.W.2d 586, 598-99 (Tex.App.—Houston [1st Dist.] 1986, no writ) (substantial compliance with former TRCP 188, now TRCP 201, is sufficient). A deposition in a foreign jurisdiction may be taken by notice, letter rogatory, letter of request, agreement of the parties, or court order. TRCP 201.1. A deposition may also be taken by any other means and terms of any applicable treaty or convention. TRCP 201.1(d). The Hague Evidence Convention is the most well-known treaty for obtaining evidence abroad. *See* Martikan, Note, *The Boundaries of the Hague Convention*, 68 Tex.L.Rev. 1003, 1004-05 (1990).

1. **Notice.** Parties may take by notice the deposition of a witness in a foreign jurisdiction before a person authorized to administer oaths, either under the law of the place where the examination is held or under Texas law. TRCP 201.1(b). There are two serious drawbacks to taking depositions in foreign countries by notice: (1) the parties have no power to compel the attendance of a witness; and (2) taking testimony in some countries violates local laws and, in some cases, can result in criminal penalties. Bishop, *International Litigation in Texas*, 19 Hous.L.Rev. 361, 364-65 (1982).

2. **Letter of request.** Generally, if the foreign country subscribes to the Hague Evidence Convention, the method to obtain discovery is by letter of request under the Convention. Bishop, 19 Hous.L.Rev. at 371. The Hague Evidence Convention supplements, but does not replace, other means of obtaining evidence located abroad. ***Societe Nationale Industrielle Aerospatiale v. U.S. Dist. Ct.***, 482 U.S. 522, 534-39, 107 S.Ct. 2542, 2551-53 (1987); ***Sandsend Fin. Consultants v. Wood***, 743 S.W.2d 364, 365-66 (Tex.App.—Houston [1st Dist.] 1988, orig. proceeding). The procedure for discovery under the Hague Evidence Convention can be found in 28 U.S.C. chapter 117.

3. **Letter rogatory.** If a country does not subscribe to the Hague Evidence Convention, a party must use a letter rogatory to take the deposition in a foreign country. A letter rogatory is a judicial request addressed to a foreign authority asking it to use its compulsive powers to require evidence to be obtained from a person within its territory. Bishop, 19 Hous.L.Rev. at 383. In some countries, only the judicial officer can ask the witness questions, not the attorneys. *Id.* at 384. The letter rogatory must be addressed to the appropriate authority in the jurisdiction. TRCP 201.1(c)(1).

§18.2 Officer to conduct deposition. A deposition may be taken in a foreign country by one of the following:

1. A U.S. minister, commissioner, or charge d'affaires who is a resident of and is accredited in the country where the deposition is taken. CPRC §20.001(c)(1).

2. A U.S. consul general, consul, vice-consul, commercial agent, vice-commercial agent, deputy consul, or consular agent who is a resident of and is accredited in the country where the deposition is taken. *Id.* §20.001(c)(2).

3. Any notary public. *Id.* §20.001(c)(3); *e.g.*, ***Kugle v. DaimlerChrysler Corp.***, 88 S.W.3d 355, 362 (Tex. App.—San Antonio 2002, pet. denied) (deponent in Mexico permitted to be sworn by Texas notary); *see also* TRCP 201.1(b) (deposition officer may be a person authorized to administer oaths in place where deposition taken).

4. If the deponent is a witness who is a member of the U.S. Armed Forces or Auxiliary or a civilian employed by such forces or auxiliary outside the U.S., the deposition may be taken by a commissioned officer in the Armed Forces or Auxiliary or Reserve. CPRC §20.001(d).

§18.3 Depositions in Texas for use in foreign jurisdictions. If a court of record of any other state or foreign jurisdiction issues an order that requires a witness's oral or written deposition testimony in Texas, the witness may be compelled to appear and testify in the same manner and by the same process used for taking testimony in a proceeding pending in Texas. TRCP 201.2.

F. INTERROGATORIES

§1. GENERAL

§1.1 Rules. TRCP 197.

§1.2 Purpose. Interrogatories are written questions served on a party that require the party to file written answers, generally under oath. Interrogatories are used to narrow the issues.

§1.3 Forms. See ***O'Connor's Texas Civil Forms***, FORMS 6F.

§1.4 Other references. Griesel, *The "New" Texas Discovery Rules: Three Years Later*, Advanced Evidence & Discovery Course, State Bar of Texas, ch. 2, §XI, p. 24 (2002).

§2. SCOPE

The scope of discovery for interrogatories is governed principally by TRCP 192. See "Scope of Discovery," ch. 6-B, p. 341. Interrogatories may ask broad questions to find out what the other party knows.

§2.1 Party contentions. An interrogatory may ask whether the party makes specific legal or factual contentions and may ask the party to state its legal theories and to describe, in general, the factual bases for the party's claims or defenses. See "Party contentions," §3.2.5, p. 410.

§2.2 Trial witnesses. An interrogatory may ask the other party to provide a list of its trial witnesses. See §3.2.3, below. Formerly, a party could secure a list of trial witnesses only by court order.

§2.3 Limits of interrogatories.

1. **Not for testifying expert information.** An interrogatory cannot be used to request information about another party's testifying expert witnesses. TRCP 197.1 (interrogatories cannot be used to secure information covered by TRCP 195).

2. **No fishing.** An interrogatory may not be used to "fish" for information or to require the responding party to provide a statement of all its available proof. TRCP 197.1; ***K-Mart Corp. v. Sanderson***, 937 S.W.2d 429, 431 (Tex.1996).

§3. PROPOUNDING INTERROGATORIES

§3.1 Procedure. The interrogatories must be in writing. TRCP 197.1. See ***O'Connor's*** FORMS 6F:01-02.

PRACTICE TIP

Ask the other party to the lawsuit to agree to supply a copy by e-mail of any request for written discovery. It will make responding to interrogatories and other discovery much simpler.

---

1. **Serve on party.** Interrogatories can be served only on another party. TRCP 197.1. They cannot be served on nonparty witnesses. TRCP 205.1.

2. **Time to serve interrogatories.** Interrogatories may be served any time after suit is filed. *See* TRCP 190.2(c)(1), 190.3(b)(1). The discovery rules permit the plaintiff to serve the initial set of discovery with its original petition. See "Serving discovery with original pleadings," ch. 6-A, §12.2, p. 323. The deadline to serve interrogatories is 30 days before the end of the discovery period. TRCP 197.1. See "Discovery Periods," ch. 6-A, §6, p. 317. When served by mail or fax, interrogatories should be served up to 34 days before the end of the discovery period. See chart 6-3, "Deadlines to Respond to Discovery," ch. 6-A, p. 324.

PRACTICE TIP

Although parties may serve interrogatories with their original pleadings, the only interrogatories they should serve that early in the discovery process are ones that do not count against their limit of 25 questions; that is, interrogatories asking about documents. See §3.1.3(1), below.

3. Number of interrogatories. Although there are some limits to the number of interrogatories, there are no limits to the number of sets of interrogatories that can be sent. TRCP 190, cmt. 3.

(1) Unlimited interrogatories. There is no limit to the number of interrogatories a party may serve asking for the identification or authentication of specific documents. TRCP 190.2(c)(3), 190.3(b)(3).

(2) Limited interrogatories. The number of interrogatories each party is permitted to serve (other than those about documents) is governed by the discovery control plan in effect. See "Discovery Control Plans," ch. 6-A, §7, p. 318. Parties in all three levels are limited to 25 interrogatories, unless expressly changed by court order. TRCP 190.2(c)(3), 190.3(b)(3), 190.4(b). Each discrete subpart of an interrogatory is considered a separate interrogatory. TRCP 190.2(c)(3), 190.3(b)(3). Not every separate factual inquiry is a discrete subpart. TRCP 190, cmt. 3. If a party needs more than the number of interrogatories allotted, it should either get an agreement with the other party or file a motion to modify the discovery control plan and ask for a court order. TRCP 190.5, 191.1. See "Modifying discovery by agreement," ch. 6-A, §5.1, p. 316.

4. Specify time to answer. The interrogatories must specify when the answers are due, but the date must be at least 30 days after service of the interrogatories. *See* TRCP 197.2(a). In most cases, a party asks the other party to answer interrogatories within the shortest time permitted by TRCP 197.2(a), that is, "within 30 days after service." When the plaintiff serves interrogatories on the defendant before the defendant's answer is due, the interrogatories should state the answers are due "within 50 days after service." *Id.* See "Deadline to serve the response," ch. 6-A, §13.1.2, p. 323.

5. Combine with request for production. The discovery rules permit a party to combine different forms of discovery requests in the same document. TRCP 192.2. Thus, if an interrogatory asks for the identification of documents, it can be followed by a request to produce those documents.

§3.2 Standard interrogatories. The following are interrogatories that seek information not subject to a request for disclosure under TRCP 194. See ***O'Connor's*** FORM 6F:02.

1. Documents.

(1) Existence & location. An interrogatory may ask about the existence, description, nature, custody, condition, location, and contents of documents that are relevant or will lead to relevant evidence. TRCP 192.3(b). See "Possession," ch. 6-A, §2.3, p. 313; ***O'Connor's*** FORM 6F:02, §A. An interrogatory that asks for information about documents can be followed by a request to produce those documents. TRCP 192.2.

(2) Authentication. An interrogatory can ask for the authentication of specific documents. TRCP 190.2(c)(3), 190.3(b)(3).

2. Person answering. An interrogatory may ask the other party to identify the persons answering the interrogatories, supplying information, or in any way assisting with the preparation of the answers. A party may want to depose anyone who provided information for the answers. See ***O'Connor's*** FORM 6F:02, §B, ¶1.

3. Trial witnesses. An interrogatory may ask the other party to identify its trial witnesses (fact and expert). TRCP 192.3(d). Because the only information that is authorized by TRCP 192.3(d) is the identity of trial witnesses, it should not conflict with the limitations in TRCP 195.1 and 197.1, which limit the discovery tools a party can use to seek information about the testifying experts. See "Trial witnesses," ch. 6-B, §2.9, p. 344; ***O'Connor's*** FORM 6F:02, §B, ¶2.

4. Discoverable consulting experts. An interrogatory may ask for information about discoverable consulting expert witnesses.

(1) Consultant's work reviewed. When the consulting expert's opinions, mental impressions, or work product were reviewed by a testifying expert, a party is entitled to discover the same information about the consulting expert as about the testifying expert. TRCP 192.3(e). See "Consulting expert + work reviewed," ch. 6-C, §3.2.2(1), p. 367; ***O'Connor's*** FORM 6F:02, §B, ¶3.

(2) Consultant with facts. When a consulting expert has firsthand knowledge about the case or secondhand knowledge gained outside the consultation, a party is entitled to discover the same information about the consulting expert as about other fact witnesses. See "Consulting expert + facts," ch. 6-C, §3.2.2(2), p. 367; ***O'Connor's*** FORM 6F:02, §B, ¶4.

5. Party contentions. An interrogatory may ask whether the party makes specific legal or factual contentions and may ask the party to state its legal theories and to describe, in general, the factual bases for the party's claims or defenses. TRCP 197.1; *see also* TRCP 194.2(c) (disclosure request). For example, an interrogatory may ask whether the party claims a breach of implied warranty, or when the party contends that limitations began to run. TRCP 197, cmt. 1. However, an interrogatory may not ask the party to state all its legal and factual assertions or to marshal all of its proof or the proof the party intends to offer at trial. TRCP 197.1 & cmt. 1. See ***O'Connor's*** FORM 6F:02, §B, ¶6.

6. Impeachment & rebuttal evidence. The party should consider asking for the other party's rebuttal and impeachment evidence and witnesses. TRCP 192.3(d); *see* TRCP 166(h). Rebuttal and impeachment evidence is discoverable only if the party responding to the request has enough information to anticipate its use at trial. TRCP 192.3(d); ***Alvarado v. Farah Mfg. Co.***, 830 S.W.2d 911, 916-17 (Tex.1992). Unless specifically asked, a party is not required to anticipate the other party's case and identify witnesses to be used for impeachment or rebuttal. *See* TRCP 192.3(d) (party may not obtain discovery of rebuttal or impeaching witnesses whose testimony cannot reasonably be anticipated before trial). See "Impeachment & rebuttal evidence not produced in discovery," ch. 8-C, §5.3, p. 536; ***O'Connor's*** FORM 6F:02, §B, ¶¶7, 8.

7. Elements of claim or defense. The interrogatories may ask for information based on the elements of the claim or defense. See ***O'Connor's*** FORMS 6F for interrogatories in the following types of lawsuits: breach of contract (FORMS 6F:04-05), suit on a sworn account (FORMS 6F:06-07), automobile accident (FORMS 6F:08-09), slip and fall (FORMS 6F:10-11), and suit under the DTPA (FORMS 6F:12-13).

§4. RESPONDING TO INTERROGATORIES

§4.1 Procedure.

1. Form of answers. The answers to interrogatories must be made in the form required by TRCP 197.2. See ***O'Connor's*** FORM 6F:03.

(1) In writing. The party must respond to interrogatories in writing. TRCP 197.2(a). Oral information is not a substitute for written answers. *See* ***Sharp v. Broadway Nat'l Bank***, 784 S.W.2d 669, 671 (Tex. 1990) (oral identification of witness was not sufficient). Each answer, objection, or other response must follow the question to which it applies. TRCP 193.1.

(2) Separate answers. Each interrogatory must be answered separately. ***Orkin Exterm. Co. v. Williamson***, 785 S.W.2d 905, 910 (Tex.App.—Austin 1990, writ denied). If an interrogatory asks a question already answered in response to another interrogatory, the answer to that interrogatory may refer to the other answer.

(3) Separate answer set. In most cases, a party should file a separate set of answers for each set of interrogatories. In a multiple-party case, a party responding to the same interrogatories from different opposing parties may file one response that is sufficient to answer all sets. *See, e.g.*, ***Ward v. O'Connor***, 816 S.W.2d 446, 447

(Tex.App.—San Antonio 1991, no writ) (Ps filed one list of fact and expert witnesses in response to requests from 2 Ds). *But see* ***Clark Equip. Co. v. Pitner***, 923 S.W.2d 117, 121-22 (Tex.App.—Houston [14th Dist.] 1996, writ denied) (dicta, even though P provided complete information to D-1, because incomplete information was provided to D-2, D-1 could have asked to limit testimony).

(4) Signed & verified by party. The party must sign most answers to interrogatories under oath. TRCP 197.2(d). An affidavit verifying the answers to interrogatories must be unqualified and cannot be made "to the best of my knowledge." *See* ***Ebeling v. Gawlik***, 487 S.W.2d 187, 189 (Tex.App.—Houston [1st Dist.] 1972, no writ). There are two exceptions to the rule that requires a party to sign and verify its answers under oath: (1) a party is not required to verify its answer when the answer states it is based on information obtained from other persons; and (2) a party is not required to sign or verify its answer to an interrogatory that asks about persons with knowledge of relevant facts, trial witnesses, and legal contentions. TRCP 197.2(d).

(5) Signed by attorney. The party's attorney must sign the answers to interrogatories. TRCP 191.3(a)(1), 197, cmt. 2. An attorney is not required to verify answers to interrogatories. TRCP 197.2(d).

2. Time to respond. Generally, a party has 30 days from the date of service of the interrogatories to respond, depending on the type of service. TRCP 21, 21a, 197.2(a). When interrogatories are served on a defendant before the defendant's answer is due, the defendant has 50 days after service to respond. TRCP 197.2(a). See "Deadline to serve the response," ch. 6-A, §13.1.2, p. 323. To extend the time, see "Extending Time to Respond to Discovery," ch. 6-A, §14, p. 324.

3. Not filed. The answers to interrogatories are not filed with the court. TRCP 191.4(a). For exceptions, see "Filing discovery," ch. 6-A, §11.1.3, p. 322.

§4.2 Answers. Each interrogatory must be answered fully. The party must make a complete response, based on all information reasonably available to the responding party or its attorney at the time the response is made. TRCP 193.1. The sufficiency of the answers to any set of interrogatories must be decided on a case-by-case basis. ***Alexander v. Barlow***, 671 S.W.2d 531, 533 (Tex.App.—Houston [1st Dist.] 1983, writ ref'd n.r.e.). The court will treat an evasive or incomplete answer as a failure to answer. TRCP 215.1(c). When the interrogatory asks for information permitted by the rules of discovery, the information must be disclosed. When the interrogatory asks for more information than the rules permit, the party must file an objection.

1. Existence & location of documents. When asked in an interrogatory, a party is required to supply information about the existence, description, nature, custody, condition, location, and contents of documents that are relevant or will lead to relevant evidence. TRCP 192.3(b). See "Possession," ch. 6-A, §2.3, p. 313.

2. Evidence equally available. When an interrogatory asks for information that is available from public records, from the business records of the responding party, or from a compilation, abstract, or summary of the responding party's business records, the responding party is not obligated to give a narrative answer to the interrogatory if the burden of ascertaining the answer is substantially the same for both parties. TRCP 197.2(c). In such a case, the responding party may answer the interrogatory by specifying and, when applicable, producing the records or a compilation, abstract, or summary of the records. *Id.*; *see* ***Clear Lake City Water Auth. v. Winograd***, 695 S.W.2d 632, 641 (Tex.App.—Houston [1st Dist.] 1985, writ ref'd n.r.e.). The records from which the answer may be derived must be specified in sufficient detail to permit the requesting party to locate and identify them as readily as can the responding party. TRCP 197.2(c). If the responding party has specified business records, it must state a reasonable time and place for examination of the documents. *Id.* The responding party must produce the documents at the time and place stated and must provide the requesting party a reasonable opportunity to inspect them. *Id.* The rule requires a balancing test of the relative burden imposed on the two parties. *See, e.g.*, ***State Farm Mut. Auto. Ins. Co. v. Engelke***, 824 S.W.2d 747, 752 (Tex.App.—Houston [1st Dist.] 1992, orig. proceeding) (because State Farm's witness testified information was available from its computer, it was less burdensome for State Farm to produce information).

3. Witnesses. When asked in an interrogatory, a party is required to identify the following witnesses:

(1) Person answering. The party should identify any person answering the interrogatories, supplying information, or assisting with the preparation of the answers.

(2) Trial witnesses. The party should list all persons the party plans to call as witnesses at trial, no matter what the subject of their testimony. TRCP 192.3(d); *see, e.g.*, ***Jamail v. Anchor Mortg. Servs.***, 809 S.W.2d 221, 223 (Tex.1991) (witness, called to testify about lending regulations of mortgage company, should have been listed as fact witness, even though witness did not know facts of case). The response should list the following persons as trial witnesses:

(a) Fact witnesses for trial. The party should list all persons who have knowledge of relevant facts that it might call as witnesses at trial. See "Fact witnesses," ch. 6-B, §2.8, p. 344. Along with its own witnesses, the party should consider including the following: (1) any person who was deposed, (2) the other party, (3) the other party's fact witnesses, and (4) the other party's consulting expert with knowledge of facts. A party should err on the side of inclusion. At trial, the court will not permit a party to call a witness that the party did not specifically identify.

PRACTICE TIP

If a named party is not listed in response to an interrogatory asking for trial witnesses, the unlisted party can still testify. See TRCP 193.6(a).

(b) Expert witnesses for trial. The party should list all experts that it intends to call to testify, which could include (1) retained testifying experts, (2) nonretained testifying experts, (3) the party (if the party intends to testify as an expert), (4) the party's attorney (for attorney fees), (5) the opposing party's testifying experts (if the party intends to call them), and (6) the opposing party's consulting experts who lost their status of consulting-only. *See* ***Baylor Med. Plaza Servs. v. Kidd***, 834 S.W.2d 69, 73 (Tex.App.—Texarkana 1992, writ denied) (party could not call witness it did not designate but who was designated by another party). The party should compare this list to the list of testifying experts it produced in response to a request for disclosures. If any of the experts listed in response to an interrogatory asking for trial witnesses is not listed in response to a request for experts under TRCP 194.2(f), the party should amend its response to the request.

(c) Character witnesses. When character evidence is necessary, the party should list all persons who will testify about the party's character. ***Clayton v. First State Bank***, 777 S.W.2d 577, 580 (Tex.App.—Fort Worth 1989, writ denied).

(d) Impeachment & rebuttal witnesses. When an interrogatory asks for impeachment and rebuttal information, and the responding party knows it can and will impeach or rebut the other party's witness or evidence, the responding party must list that evidence. See "Impeachment & rebuttal evidence," §3.2.6, p. 410; "Impeachment & rebuttal evidence not produced in discovery," ch. 8-C, §5.3, p. 536.

4. Discoverable consulting experts. When asked in an interrogatory, a party is required to identify the following expert witnesses:

(1) Consultant's work reviewed. If any opinions, mental impressions, or work product of an informally consulted expert were reviewed by a testifying expert, the other party is entitled to obtain the same information about the consulting expert as about the testifying expert. TRCP 192.3(e). See "Consulting expert + work reviewed," ch. 6-C, §3.2.2(1), p. 367; "Types of Information Discoverable from Experts," ch. 6-C, §4, p. 367.

(2) Consultant with facts. A consulting expert who obtained knowledge about the case either firsthand or in some way other than in consultation about the case is discoverable as a fact witness. TRCP 192.3(c). When a consulting expert has firsthand knowledge of facts or secondhand knowledge acquired in some way other than in consultation about the case, the other party is entitled to obtain the same information about the expert as about other fact witnesses. See "Consulting expert + facts," ch. 6-C, §3.2.2(2), p. 367.

5. Contentions. When asked in an interrogatory, a party is required to provide information about specific factual or legal assertions. *See* TRCP 197.1 & cmt. 1. See "Party contentions," §3.2.5, p. 410. The use of the answers to these "contention interrogatories" is limited, just as is the use of similar disclosures under TRCP 194.6. TRCP 197, cmt. 1.

§5. SUPPLEMENTING OR AMENDING ANSWERS TO INTERROGATORIES

§5.1 What to supplement. When a party discovers additional information after responding to discovery, the party must supplement or amend its response. TRCP 193.5(a) (duty to supplement), TRCP 193.6 (sanctions for failure to supplement). For the substance of what additional information to provide, see "Supplementing Discovery Responses," ch. 6-A, §16, p. 325.

§5.2 Deadline to supplement. A party must serve supplemental or amended answers to interrogatories reasonably promptly after the party discovers the need for such a response, but no later than 30 days before trial. TRCP 193.5(b). See "Deadline to supplement answers," ch. 6-A, §16.4, p. 327.

§5.3 Form of supplement. Supplemental or amended answers to interrogatories must be made in the same form as the original answers. TRCP 193.5(b). See "Form of supplemental discovery," ch. 6-A, §16.6, p. 328. For the exceptions, see "Information provided by other means," ch. 6-A, §16.3.2, p. 326.

§6. OBJECTING TO QUESTIONS

§6.1 Procedure to object. See "Making objections," ch. 6-A, §17.1, p. 329.

1. When to serve. Objections to interrogatories must be served on the other party on or before the date the answers to the interrogatories are due. TRCP 193.2(a). See "Timely objection," ch. 6-A, §17.1.1, p. 329.

2. Objection defers answer. When a party objects to an interrogatory, the answer to that interrogatory is deferred until the court rules on the objection. TRCP 193.2(b). The party must answer all other interrogatories by the answer deadline. *Id.*

3. Form of objections. In the response or in a separate document, the party should state the specific objection to the interrogatory. TRCP 193.2(a).

4. Partial compliance. The party must comply with each part of the request to which the party has not objected or not asserted a privilege. See "Burden to partially comply," ch. 6-A, §17.9, p. 333. The party should withhold from the information it produces the material subject to an objection or an assertion of privilege. TRCP 192.3(a), 193.3(a).

5. Not filed. The objections to interrogatories are not filed with the court. TRCP 191.4(a). See "Not filed," ch. 6-A, §16.5, p. 328.

§6.2 Valid objections. See the list of objections in "Types of Objections to Discovery," ch. 6-A, §18, p. 333. See ***O'Connor's*** FORM 6F:03. The following are some additional objections that are specific for interrogatories.

1. Number of questions. "The interrogatories ask more than 25 questions." *See* TRCP 190.2(c)(3), 190.3(b)(3). See "Number of interrogatories," §3.1.3, p. 409. When a party asks more than 25 questions, the responding party cannot merely object and refuse to answer any of them. The party's options are (1) to answer the first 25 and object to the rest of them, or (2) to file objections and a motion for protective order to stay the deadline to answer until the set of interrogatories is redrafted to comply with the rules. ***Childs v. Argenbright***, 927 S.W.2d 647, 652 (Tex.App.—Tyler 1996, no writ); ***Owens v. Wallace***, 821 S.W.2d 746, 749 (Tex.App.—Tyler 1992, orig. proceeding).

2. Improper request. "The interrogatory requests information about testifying experts, which is obtainable only through requests for disclosure under TRCP 194 or through depositions." *See* TRCP 197.1. See "Requests for Disclosure," ch. 6-D, p. 375.

3. Premature request. "The interrogatory is premature because it requests information that will not be known until after additional discovery is completed. This interrogatory will be answered promptly once additional discovery is completed." *See* TRCP 193.1 (responding party must make complete response based on information available).

§6.3 Invalid objections. See "Invalid objections to discovery requests," ch. 6-A, §18.2, p. 334.

§6.4 Waiver of objections. A party waives any error in the form or substance of the interrogatories if the party does not object within the time provided to answer. TRCP 193.2(e). When a party answers an interrogatory without making an objection, the party must answer fully, even if the interrogatory is objectionable. ***In re Striegler***, 915 S.W.2d 629, 641 (Tex.App.—Amarillo 1996, writ denied).

§7. ASSERTING A PRIVILEGE

A party may not "object" to an interrogatory on the grounds that it calls for privileged information. Instead, a party must "assert a privilege" under TRCP 193.3. See "Asserting privileges," ch. 6-A, §17.2, p. 329.

§8. OBJECTING TO ANSWERS

§8.1 Move to compel answers. A party may file a motion to compel answers when the interrogatories are not answered, when they are not answered properly, or when objections are served. TRCP 215.1(b), 215.2(b), 215.3. See "Motion to Compel Discovery," ch. 6-A, §21, p. 336.

§8.2 Object to formal defects. A party must object to formal (*i.e.*, technical) defects in the answer so that the responding party has the opportunity to correct them before trial. *See* ***State Farm Fire & Cas. Co. v. Morua***, 979 S.W.2d 616, 620 (Tex.1998) (court should not exclude witness based on technical defect in answer when no objection was made before trial); ***$23,900 v. State***, 899 S.W.2d 314, 317 (Tex.App.—Houston [14th Dist.] 1995, no writ) (party should file pretrial objections or motion to compel compliance with rules). Formal defects do not impair the integrity of the answers unless the party refuses to cure the defect after it is identified by the other party. *See* TRCP 197, cmt. 2; *see also* TRCP 193.5(b) (failure to properly supplement discovery does not make response untimely unless party refused to correct defect).

§8.3 Challenge privileges after withholding statement. After receiving a withholding statement indicating that information is being withheld on grounds of privilege, the party seeking discovery should ask the withholding party to provide a privilege log. TRCP 193.3(b). See "Request privilege log," ch. 6-A, §17.2.2, p. 330.

§8.4 Move for sanctions. See "Motion for Discovery Sanctions," ch. 6-A, §22, p. 337.

1. Late or inadequate answer. When an answer to an interrogatory is inadequate, the party seeking discovery can ask the court to impose reasonable sanctions. *See, e.g.*, ***Hamill v. Level***, 917 S.W.2d 15, 16 (Tex.1996) (even though P was repeatedly late in answering interrogatories, dismissal not warranted because no less severe sanction had been imposed); ***Clark Equip. Co. v. Pitner***, 923 S.W.2d 117, 121-22 (Tex.App.—Houston [14th Dist.] 1996, writ denied) (because P's answer to D-1's interrogatory provided everything but substance of expert's testimony, D-2 could have asked to limit testimony, not exclude expert); ***Orkin Exterm. Co. v. Williamson***, 785 S.W.2d 905, 910-11 (Tex.App.—Austin 1990, writ denied) (because D's answer was not sufficient to identify witness, witness not permitted to testify). If an answer is evasive or incomplete, the court will treat it as a failure to answer. TRCP 215.1(c).

2. No answers. When a party refuses to file answers to interrogatories, the party seeking discovery may ask the court to dismiss the suit, render a default judgment, exclude evidence, or impose other sanctions. *See* TRCP 215.1(b)(3)(A) (failure to serve response), TRCP 215.1(b)(3)(B) (failure to answer particular interrogatory); *see,* *e.g.*, ***Swain v. Southwestern Bell Yellow Pages***, 998 S.W.2d 731, 732-33 (Tex.App.—Fort Worth 1999, no pet.) (P not permitted to testify about damages because he refused to respond to interrogatory about damages); ***Fears v. Mechanical & Indus. Technicians***, 654 S.W.2d 524, 529 (Tex.App.—Tyler 1983, writ ref'd n.r.e.) (default rendered because D did not file answers to interrogatories). When a party wholly fails to answer, the party seeking discovery is not required to file a motion to compel before filing a motion for sanctions. ***Swain***, 998 S.W.2d at 733.

§8.5 Request hearing. The party seeking discovery must request a hearing on the objection or on the motion to compel, or it will waive its objections to the answers to the interrogatories. TRCP 193.4; ***McKinney v. National Un. Fire Ins. Co.***, 772 S.W.2d 72, 75 (Tex.1989). See "Burden to secure hearing & ruling," ch. 6-A, §17.5, p. 331.

§9. USING INTERROGATORIES AS EVIDENCE

§9.1 By whom, against whom.

1. Against answering party. Generally, the answers to interrogatories cannot be used as evidence by the party that answered them. TRCP 197.3; ***Morgan v. Anthony***, 27 S.W.3d 928, 929 (Tex.2000); ***Yates v. Fisher***, 988 S.W.2d 730, 731 (Tex.1998). However, when a party is questioned under oath about an answer, is subject to cross-examination, and affirms that everything contained in the answer is true, the interrogatory answer becomes competent evidence. ***Morgan***, 27 S.W.3d at 929; *see* ***Price Pfister, Inc. v. Moore & Kimmey, Inc.***, 48 S.W.3d 341, 348-49 (Tex.App.—Houston [14th Dist.] 2001, pet. denied).

2. By any other party. In a multiparty case, even if the parties do not have common causes of action, all parties can rely on the answers to interrogatories by any other party. *E.g.*, ***Ticor Title Ins. Co. v. Lacy***, 803 S.W.2d 265, 265-66 (Tex.1991) (non-settling D was entitled to rely on P's failure to designate witnesses in response to settling D's interrogatories); ***Smith v. Christley***, 755 S.W.2d 525, 529-30 (Tex.App.—Houston [14th Dist.] 1988, writ denied) (same).

(1) Motion to strike witness. Any party may move to strike a witness if the party offering the witness did not list the witness in answer to an interrogatory requesting the identity of trial witnesses. ***Smith***, 755 S.W.2d at 529.

(2) No continuing duty to supplement. If the party that served the interrogatory is dismissed from the suit, the party that answered the interrogatory no longer has a duty to supplement its answers to the dismissed party's interrogatories. ***Austin Ranch Enters. v. Wells***, 760 S.W.2d 703, 710 (Tex.App.—Fort Worth 1988, writ denied). Thus, the remaining parties cannot object to the responding party's failure to supplement answers to interrogatories propounded by the dismissed party. *Id.*

§9.2 Using answers in trial. Interrogatories are considered evidence once they are admitted into evidence by a ruling of the court. ***Cornell v. Cornell***, 570 S.W.2d 22, 23 (Tex.App.—San Antonio 1978, no writ). A party's answers to interrogatories are not hearsay. *See* TRE 801(e)(1)(A) (inconsistent with trial testimony), TRE 801(e)(2) (admission by party-opponent). There are three steps to introducing the answers to interrogatories.

1. Identify. The interrogatories and answers must be identified. The best procedure is to mark the interrogatories with an exhibit number.

2. Offer. The interrogatories and answers must be formally offered into evidence.

3. Admit. The court must admit them into evidence. Once the answers are read into evidence, they become testimonial evidence. ***Eubanks v. Eubanks***, 892 S.W.2d 181, 181-82 (Tex.App.—Houston [14th Dist.] 1994, no writ). Interrogatories that are not admitted into evidence cannot be considered in support of the judgment. ***Sammons Enters. v. Manley***, 540 S.W.2d 751, 757 (Tex.App.—Texarkana 1976, writ ref'd n.r.e.).

§9.3 Using supplanted answers. Supplanted answers to interrogatories are not valid answers and cannot be used as evidence. They can, in some cases, be used to impeach the new answers. *See* ***Thomas v. International Ins. Co.***, 527 S.W.2d 813, 820 (Tex.App.—Waco 1975, writ ref'd n.r.e.). However, supplanted answers that inquire about either a party's legal theories or damages cannot be used for impeachment. TRCP 197.3.

§9.4 Using answers in summary judgment. Interrogatory answers can be used in a motion for summary judgment proceeding. ***Judwin Props. v. Griggs & Harrison***, 911 S.W.2d 498, 503-04 (Tex.App.—Houston [1st Dist.] 1995, no writ). Because answers can be used only against the party answering them, a party cannot rely on its own answers to raise a fact issue. *See* TRCP 197.3; ***Yates***, 988 S.W.2d at 731; *see also* ***Garcia v. National Eligibility Express***, 4 S.W.3d 887, 890 (Tex.App.—Houston [1st Dist.] 1999, no pet.) (answers cannot be used in favor of answering party even if other party puts them in evidence and does not timely challenge them on appeal).

§10. OBJECTING TO AN UNIDENTIFIED TRIAL WITNESS

See "Objecting to Unidentified Witness," ch. 6-D, §10, p. 383.

§11. REVIEW

For the rules and forms for prosecuting or responding to an appeal or original proceeding, see ***O'Connor's Texas Civil Appeals*** (2002-03).

G. REQUESTS FOR ADMISSIONS

§1. GENERAL

§1.1 Rule. TRCP 198.

§1.2 Purpose. Requests for admissions are narrowly drawn questions that call for the responding party to either admit or deny a specific fact. They seldom lead to the discovery of additional evidence. Their primary function is to simplify trials by eliminating matters about which there is no real controversy, but which may be difficult or expensive to prove. ***Natural Gas Pipeline Co. v. Pool***, 30 S.W.3d 639, 652 (Tex.App.—Amarillo 2000), *rev'd on other grounds*, 121 S.W.3d 317 (Tex.2003).

§1.3 Forms. See ***O'Connor's Texas Civil Forms***, FORMS 6G.

§1.4 Other references. Griesel, *The "New" Texas Discovery Rules: Three Years Later*, Advanced Evidence & Discovery Course, State Bar of Texas, ch. 2, §XII, p. 25 (2002).

§2. SCOPE

The scope of discovery by requests for admissions is governed principally by TRCP 192. See "Scope of Discovery," ch. 6-B, p. 341. Requests for admissions are often used to prove the genuineness of documents and may be used to ask a party to admit an opinion or fact or the application of law to facts. TRCP 198.1.

§3. REQUESTS FOR ADMISSIONS

Before drafting requests for admissions, the attorney should examine the live pleadings of both parties. The requests for admissions should be used to affirm evidence of incidental but important issues in the pleadings (*e.g.*, the identity of the owner of the premises, the validity of the signatures on the contract, that notice was timely).

§3.1 Procedure. Requests for admissions must be in writing. TRCP 198.1. See ***O'Connor's*** FORMS 6G:01-02.

1. Serve on party. Requests for admissions may be served only on other parties. TRCP 198.1. A party's duty to respond to requests for admissions is dependent on receipt of the requests. ***Payton v. Ashton***, 29 S.W.3d 896, 898 (Tex.App.—Amarillo 2000, no pet.).

2. Time to serve requests for admissions. Requests for admissions may be served any time after suit is filed. TRCP 190.2(c)(1), 190.3(b)(1). The discovery rules permit the plaintiff to serve the initial set of discovery with its original petition. See "Serving discovery with original pleadings," ch. 6-A, §12.2, p. 323. The deadline to serve requests for admissions is 30 days before the end of the discovery period. TRCP 198.1. See "Discovery Periods," ch. 6-A, §6, p. 317. When served by mail or fax, the requests should be served up to 34 days before the end of the discovery period. See chart 6-3, "Deadlines to Respond to Discovery," ch. 6-A, p. 324.

3. Number of requests. There is no limit on the number of requests for admissions or the number of sets of requests a party may serve.

4. Specify time to answer. The request must specify the time to answer, generally 30 days after the service of the request. TRCP 198.2(a). If the request is to be served on a defendant before its answer was due, the request must state that the defendant has 50 days after service of the request to respond. *Id.* See "Deadline to Respond to Discovery," ch. 6-A, §13, p. 323.

§3.2 Typical requests. The requests for admissions should begin with a request that the party "admit the truth of the following statements." TRCP 198.1. The requests should be made in short, simple, declarative sentences. For example, admit or deny the following: The promissory note, a copy of which is attached to this request and marked Exhibit A, is a genuine copy of the note that is the subject of this litigation. See ***O'Connor's*** FORMS 6G for requests for admissions in the following types of lawsuits: breach of contract (FORMS 6G:04-05), suit on a sworn account (FORMS 6G:06-07), automobile accident (FORMS 6G:08-09), slip and fall (FORMS 6G:10-11), and suit under the DTPA (FORMS 6G:12-13).

§4. RESPONDING TO REQUESTS FOR ADMISSIONS

§4.1 Procedure.

1. Form of answers. The answers to requests for admissions must be made in the form required by TRCP 198.2. See ***O'Connor's*** FORM 6G:03.

(1) In writing. The party must respond to requests for admissions in writing. TRCP 198.2(a). Each answer, objection, or other response must be preceded by the request to which it applies. TRCP 193.1.

(2) Signed. The response to the requests for admissions must be signed by the lawyer (or party when pro se). TRCP 191.3(a); *see* ***In re Estate of Herring***, 970 S.W.2d 583, 588-89 (Tex.App.—Corpus Christi 1998, no pet.) (unsigned responses were deemed admitted). *But see* TRCP 191.3(d) (failure to sign can be corrected).

(3) Not verified. The answers to the requests for admissions do not need to be verified. ***Guzman v. Carnevale***, 964 S.W.2d 311, 313-14 (Tex.App.—Corpus Christi 1998, no pet.).

2. Time to respond. Generally, a party has 30 days from the date of service of the requests for admissions to serve a response, depending on the type of service. TRCP 198.2(a). When requests for admissions are served on a defendant before the defendant's answer is due, the defendant has 50 days after service to respond. *Id.* See "Deadline to Respond to Discovery," ch. 6-A, §13, p. 323.

3. Extending time to respond. A party may ask the court to extend the time to respond to requests for admissions only if the motion is made before the date to answer. See "Extending Time to Respond to Discovery," ch. 6-A, §14, p. 324. Once the time to respond expires, it is too late to ask the court for more time to serve answers to requests for admissions. ***Cherry v. North Am. Lloyds***, 770 S.W.2d 4, 5 (Tex.App.—Houston [1st Dist.] 1989, writ denied). The answers are automatically deemed admitted against the defaulting party the day after the answers are due. *Id.* To avoid the effect of the deemed answers, the defaulting party must file a motion to strike, withdraw, or amend the deemed admissions. *Id.* See "Avoiding Deemed Admissions," §7, p. 420.

4. Amending or withdrawing answers. The court has the authority to permit a party to amend or withdraw its admissions. ***Marshall v. Vise***, 767 S.W.2d 699, 700 (Tex.1989). The court may permit amendment or withdrawal when the moving party shows (1) good cause, (2) that the party relying on the responses will not be unduly prejudiced, and (3) that the withdrawal will serve the purpose of legitimate discovery and the merits of the case. TRCP 198.3; ***Stelly v. Papania***, 927 S.W.2d 620, 622 (Tex.1996); *e.g.*, ***Texas Capital Sec., Inc v. Sandefer***, 58 S.W.3d 760, 770-71 (Tex.App.—Houston [1st Dist.] 2001, pet. denied) (motion to withdraw did not show good cause).

§4.2 Response. The response to a request for admissions must (1) admit, (2) specifically deny, (3) set forth in detail the reasons why the answering party cannot truthfully admit or deny the matter, (4) object, or (5) assert a privilege. TRCP 198.2(b). If the court determines that a response does not comply with the requirements of TRCP 198, it may (1) deem the matter admitted or (2) require an amended answer. TRCP 215.4(a).

1. Admissions. To admit, the party simply states it admits the request. TRCP 198.2(b). Evasive or incomplete answers are treated as a failure to answer, and the request is deemed admitted. TRCP 215.4(a).

2. Denials. To deny, the party simply states it denies the request. TRCP 198.2(b). A denial must "fairly meet the substance of the request." *Id.* A party may qualify an answer or deny part of a request. *Id.*

3. Cannot admit or deny. If the party claims it cannot admit or deny the request, it must explain in detail the reasons it cannot admit or deny. TRCP 198.2(b).

4. Lack of information. A party can refuse to admit or deny on the ground it lacks information or knowledge to admit or deny only if the party states (1) it made a reasonable inquiry, and (2) the information known or easily obtained by the party is insufficient to enable the party to admit or deny the request. TRCP 198.2(b); *see* ***Montes v. Lazzara Shipyard***, 657 S.W.2d 886, 888-89 (Tex.App.—Corpus Christi 1983, no writ). Once the party acquires information responsive to the answer, it must supplement its answer. See "Motion to deem," §6.2, p. 420.

5. Objections & privileges. The party must make its objections and assert its privileges before the time expires to serve the answers. TRCP 193.2, 193.3, 198.2. Objections and privileges served after the deadline are waived, and the requests are deemed admitted. See "Answer deemed admitted," §6.1, p. 420.

(1) Objections. Objections must be specific. To object to only part of the matter in a request, the party must identify the specific part and admit or deny the remainder. TRCP 193.2, 198.2(b).

(a) Valid objections. These are examples of valid objections to requests for admissions: • The request asks the party to admit a proposition of law. ***Humble Sand & Gravel v. Gomez***, 48 S.W.3d 487, 505-06 (Tex.App.—Texarkana 2001, pet. granted 5-30-02); ***Esparza v. Diaz***, 802 S.W.2d 772, 775 (Tex.App.—Houston [14th Dist.] 1990, no writ). Answers which constitute admissions of law are not binding on a court and do not preclude a party from proving fact issues. ***Esparza***, 802 S.W.2d at 775. • The request asks the party to admit matters that are hearsay. ***Gaynier v. Ginsberg***, 715 S.W.2d 749, 759 (Tex.App.—Dallas 1986, writ ref'd n.r.e.) (it is improper to ask whether certain documents were those of treating doctor, now deceased). • The request is premature because the party will not know the answer until discovery is completed. *See* TRCP 193.1. • The party cannot admit or deny the genuineness of the document attached to the request because the copy is illegible. The party must be able to inspect the original before responding. • When the state is a party, it may object before trial that the requests for admissions will prejudice the rights of the state under the provisions of Gov't Code §402.004. *See* ***Lowe v. Texas Tech Univ.***, 540 S.W.2d 297, 300-01 (Tex.1976); ***Carrasco v. Texas Transp. Inst.***, 908 S.W.2d 575, 578-79 (Tex.App.—Waco 1995, no writ); *see also* ***Employees Ret. Sys. v. Bass***, 840 S.W.2d 710, 713-14 (Tex.App.—Eastland 1992, no writ) (Gov't Code §402.004 prevents deemed admissions against the state).

(b) Invalid objections. These are examples of invalid objections to requests for admissions: • The request relates to statements or opinions of fact. TRCP 198.1. • The request relates to the application of law to fact, or to mixed questions of law and fact. *Id.*; ***Laycox v. Jaroma, Inc.***, 709 S.W.2d 2, 4 (Tex.App.—Corpus Christi 1986, writ ref'd n.r.e.). • The request relates to a document that will not be admissible at trial. TRCP 192.3(a). The general rule is that as long as information appears reasonably calculated to lead to the discovery of admissible evidence, it is discoverable. • The request presents a genuine issue for the trial. TRCP 198.2(b). If the party believes the request presents a genuine issue for the trial, the party cannot, on that ground alone, object to the request. *Id.*

(2) Privileges. A party must assert its privileges in a withholding statement. TRCP 193.3(a). See "Asserting privileges," ch. 6-A, §17.2, p. 329.

§5. CHALLENGING RESPONSE

§5.1 Challenging response to requests. The requesting party can move to determine the sufficiency of the responding party's answers or objections. TRCP 215.4(a).

1. Challenging answers. If the court decides an answer does not comply with TRCP 198, the court may deem the request admitted or order that an amended answer be served. TRCP 215.4(a); ***Taylor v. Taylor***, 747 S.W.2d 940, 945 (Tex.App.—Amarillo 1988, writ denied). See ***O'Connor's*** FORM 6G:14.

(1) Evasive answer. The party who served the requests should challenge answers that do not specifically deny or affirm the requests. *See* TRCP 198.2(b). The court may treat an evasive answer as a failure to answer and deem the request admitted. TRCP 215.4(a); ***State v. Carrillo***, 885 S.W.2d 212, 216 (Tex.App.—San Antonio 1994, no writ).

(2) Quibbling. The party who served the requests should challenge answers that quibble over the meaning of simple words. If an answer quibbles over the meaning of a word, the court may hold that the answer is evasive and deem the request admitted. *See* ***McPeak v. Texas DPS***, 346 S.W.2d 138, 140 (Tex.App.—Dallas 1961, no writ).

(3) Refusal to answer. The party who served the requests should challenge a refusal to answer made on the ground that the responding party did not have sufficient information. The refusal to answer is not valid unless the party also states that it made a reasonable effort to ascertain the requested matters. ***U.S. Fire Ins. Co. v. Maness***, 775 S.W.2d 748, 749 (Tex.App.—Houston [1st Dist.] 1989, writ ref'd); ***Stewart v. Vaughn***, 504 S.W.2d 600, 602 (Tex.App.—Houston [14th Dist.] 1974, no writ).

2. Challenging objections. If the court determines that an objection is not justified, it may order the request to be answered or deem it admitted. For example, a party should challenge an objection made on the grounds that the request was confusing, when it was not. *See, e.g.*, ***Gray v. Armstrong***, 364 S.W.2d 485, 488 (Tex. App.—Dallas 1962, no writ) (because request was not confusing, court deemed it admitted).

3. Challenging privileges. After receiving a withholding statement in response to a request for admission indicating that information has been withheld on grounds of privilege, the party seeking the discovery may ask the withholding party to provide a privilege log. TRCP 193.3(b). See "Request privilege log," ch. 6-A, §17.2.2, p. 330.

§5.2 Expenses for failure to admit. If the responding party refuses to admit the truth of a matter asked or the genuineness of a document, and the party who served the request later proves the matter is true or the document is genuine, the requesting party may be entitled to reasonable expenses incurred in making that proof, including reasonable attorney fees. TRCP 215.4(b); ***City of Austin v. Miller***, 767 S.W.2d 284, 290-91 (Tex.App.—Austin 1989, writ denied) ($4,164 awarded); *see also* ***Tharp v. Blackwell***, 570 S.W.2d 154, 158 (Tex.App.—Texarkana 1978, no writ) (attorney fees available for failure to comply with predecessor to TRCP 198.2). The award of costs is mandatory unless the court finds one of the following: (1) the request was objectionable, (2) the admission sought was of no substantial importance, (3) the responding party had a reasonable ground to believe that it would prevail on the matter, or (4) there was another good reason for the refusal to admit. TRCP 215.4(b); *see* ***Natural Gas Pipeline Co. v. Pool***, 30 S.W.3d 639, 652 (Tex.App.—Amarillo 2000) (award of expenses reversed, request was improper), *rev'd on other grounds*, 121 S.W.3d 317 (Tex.2003).

§6. DEEMED ADMISSIONS

§6.1 Answer deemed admitted. Requests are automatically deemed admitted as a matter of law on the day after the answers are due if no answers, objections, or assertions of privilege are served. TRCP 198.2(c); *see* ***Marshall v. Vise***, 767 S.W.2d 699, 700 (Tex.1989); ***Payton v. Ashton***, 29 S.W.3d 896, 897-98 (Tex.App.—Amarillo 2000, no pet.); ***In re Estate of Herring***, 970 S.W.2d 583, 588 (Tex.App.—Corpus Christi 1998, no pet.). The trial court does not have the discretion to refuse to deem the requests admitted. ***Barker v. Harrison***, 752 S.W.2d 154, 155 (Tex.App.—Houston [1st Dist.] 1988, writ dism'd).

§6.2 Motion to deem.

1. Not necessary. Once the answers are overdue and no response has been served, it is not necessary for the requesting party to file a motion to ask the court to deem unanswered requests for admissions admitted. TRCP 198.2(c); *see* ***Marshall***, 767 S.W.2d at 700.

2. Necessary. When a party responding to requests for admissions serves timely but evasive answers or invalid objections, the party who sent the requests should file a motion asking the court to deem the requests admitted. TRCP 215.4(a); *see* ***Carrillo***, 885 S.W.2d at 216; ***Taylor***, 747 S.W.2d at 945. See ***O'Connor's*** FORM 6G:14.

§6.3 Response to motion to deem. When a party files a motion to deem answers admitted, the other party should file a response, challenging the grounds in the motion or asking the court for permission to amend its answers. TRCP 215.4(a). See ***O'Connor's*** FORM 6G:15.

§7. AVOIDING DEEMED ADMISSIONS

§7.1 Take a nonsuit. If the statute of limitations has not run, a plaintiff can avoid the effect of deemed admissions by taking a nonsuit and refiling the case. The deemed admissions in one suit are not effective in another. TRCP 198.3; ***Osteen v. Glynn Dodson, Inc.***, 875 S.W.2d 429, 431 (Tex.App.—Waco 1994, writ denied). See ***O'Connor's*** FORM 7E:01.

§7.2 Strike deemed admissions. A party may move to withdraw or amend the admissions deemed against it. In many cases, a party first realizes the requests for admissions were deemed admitted when the propounding party files a motion for summary judgment based on deemed admissions. *See* ***Cherry v. North Am. Lloyds***, 770 S.W.2d 4, 5-6 (Tex.App.—Houston [1st Dist.] 1989, writ denied). When this occurs, the party should follow the procedure outlined here.

1. Motion for continuance. If a motion for summary judgment (or any other motion that depends on the deemed admissions) is pending, the party against whom the admissions were deemed should file a motion to continue the summary judgment hearing. The party attempting to challenge the deemed findings will need more time than permitted under TRCP 166a to respond to the motion for summary judgment. See "Motion for Continuance," ch. 5-D, p. 242; ***O'Connor's*** FORMS 5D:01-02, 7B:09.

2. Motion to strike deemed admissions. The party against whom the admissions were deemed should file a motion to strike the deemed admissions. See ***O'Connor's*** FORM 6G:17. TRCP 198.3 permits the trial court to allow a party to withdraw or amend its admissions. The motion must include the following:

(1) Good cause. The party must state good cause, explaining why it did not timely serve its answers to the requests for admissions. TRCP 198.3(a); ***Wal-Mart Stores v. Deggs***, 968 S.W.2d 354, 356-57 (Tex. 1998); ***In re Kellogg-Brown & Root***, 45 S.W.3d 772, 775 (Tex.App.—Tyler 2001, orig. proceeding). Good cause can be mere accident or mistake. ***Cudd v. Hydrostatic Transmission***, 867 S.W.2d 101, 104 (Tex.App.—Corpus Christi 1993, no writ) (mistake in counting the days permitted to serve answers); *see, e.g.*, ***North River Ins. Co. v. Greene***, 824 S.W.2d 697, 701 (Tex.App.—El Paso 1992, writ denied) (mistaken calendar entry).

(2) No prejudice. The party must state that the other party will not be unduly prejudiced by the striking of the deemed admission. TRCP 198.3(b); *see* ***Deggs***, 968 S.W.2d at 357 (trial court should have permitted withdrawal of admissions; P did not depend on admissions to develop case); ***Morgan v. Timmers Chevrolet***, 1 S.W.3d 803, 806-07 (Tex.App.—Houston [1st Dist.] 1999, pet. denied) (trial court should not have permitted withdrawal of deemed admissions in middle of trial; Ps had relied on admissions to limit discovery); ***Cudd***, 867 S.W.2d at 105 (trial court should have permitted withdrawal of deemed admissions; would not have delayed trial on merits).

(3) Case tried on the merits. The party against whom the admissions were deemed should state that by striking the admissions the case will be tried on the merits. TRCP 198.3(b); *see* ***Kellogg-Brown & Root***, 45 S.W.3d at 777 (trial court's denial of motion to withdraw deemed admissions precluded D from presenting any viable defense at trial).

3. Attachments to motion to strike. The party against whom the admissions were deemed should attach the following to the motion to strike.

(1) Affidavits. In affidavits, the party should state detailed facts that support the excuses and explanations for all three elements: good cause, no prejudice, presentation of merits. *See* ***Ramsey v. Criswell***, 850 S.W.2d 258, 259-60 (Tex.App.—Texarkana 1993, no writ) (court denied motion because it was unverified and no affidavits or other proof was attached or offered).

(2) Answers. The party should attach the answers it would have served in response to the requests for admissions if it had not missed the deadline.

4. Response to motion to strike. When a party files a motion to strike deemed admissions, the other party should file a response, challenging the grounds in the motion. See ***O'Connor's*** FORM 6G:18.

5. Hearing.

(1) Request hearing. The party who filed the motion to strike deemed admissions should request a hearing on the motion.

(2) Present evidence. The party who filed the motion to strike the deemed admissions should present the testimony of as many witnesses as are necessary to convince the trial court to permit withdrawal of the admissions. The hearing should be treated as a full trial on the issues of good cause and no prejudice. See §7.2.2, above.

(3) Record hearing. The party should make sure the court reporter transcribes the hearing. Without a record of the hearing, it is impossible to prove good cause and lack of prejudice on appeal. *See* ***Ruiz v. Nicolas Trevino Forwarding Agency***, 888 S.W.2d 86, 89 (Tex.App.—San Antonio 1994, no writ).

6. Secure ruling. The party attempting to set aside the deemed admissions must make sure the court rules on its motion to strike. ***Laycox v. Jaroma, Inc.***, 709 S.W.2d 2, 3 (Tex.App.—Corpus Christi 1986, writ ref'd n.r.e.).

(1) Deemed admissions set aside. The courts have set aside deemed admissions in the following instances: • When the requests were not answered because of some confusion caused by the party serving the request. *See, e.g.*, ***City of Houston v. Riner***, 896 S.W.2d 317, 319-20 (Tex.App.—Houston [1st Dist.] 1995, writ denied) (P left requests with building guard, who was not a representative of D, and D never received them); ***Birdo v. Holbrook***, 775 S.W.2d 411, 413 (Tex.App.—Fort Worth 1989, writ denied) (pro se P sent multiple requests for same information). • When the party shows diligence in attempting to resolve the problem as soon as it was discovered. *See, e.g.*, ***Kellogg-Brown & Root***, 45 S.W.3d at 776 (attorney immediately prepared & delivered responses after she realized she never received requests & could not find them in her office); ***Esparza v. Diaz***, 802 S.W.2d 772, 776 (Tex.App.—Houston [14th Dist.] 1990, no writ) (D filed answers 6 months before trial, P was not injured, and trial not delayed); ***Employers Ins. of Wausau v. Hilton***, 792 S.W.2d 462, 467 (Tex.App.—Dallas 1990, writ denied) (attorney drafted answers immediately after receiving requests for admissions, but they were not typed and served; attorney filed motion to set aside deemed answers as soon as he realized the problem); ***Boone v. TEIA***, 790 S.W.2d 683, 688-89 (Tex.App.—Tyler 1990, no writ) (attorney immediately filed motion to withdraw deemed admissions). • When the error is clerical. *See, e.g.*, ***Burden v. John Watson Landscape Illumination***, 896 S.W.2d 253, 255-56 (Tex.App.—Eastland 1995, writ denied) (lawyer did not see letter from court shortening time to respond to 14 days); ***Cudd v. Hydrostatic Transmission***, 867 S.W.2d 101, 104 (Tex.App.—Corpus Christi 1993, no writ) (mistake in counting days to answer); ***North River Ins. Co. v. Greene***, 824 S.W.2d 697, 701 (Tex.App.—El Paso 1992, writ denied) (incorrect diary entry regarding date answers were due).

(2) Deemed admissions not set aside. In the following instances, the court refused to set aside deemed answers: • The party's failure to respond to requests for admissions was the result of a disputed oral agreement to extend time. ***Hoffman v. Texas Commerce Bank***, 846 S.W.2d 336, 339-40 (Tex.App.—Houston [14th Dist.] 1992, writ denied). • The party did not attach affidavits to unverified motion to withdraw deemed admissions or offer other evidence to support its allegations that he was sick and his lawyer was out of town on the day of filing. ***Ramsey***, 850 S.W.2d at 259-60.

§8. ADMISSIONS AS EVIDENCE

§8.1 Admissions as evidence. Admissions may be used by all parties in the lawsuit, including parties joined after the admissions were made. *See* ***Grimes v. Jalco, Inc.***, 630 S.W.2d 282, 284 (Tex.App.—Houston [1st Dist.] 1981, writ ref'd n.r.e), *overruled on other grounds*, ***Medina v. Herrera***, 927 S.W.2d 597 (Tex.1996).

1. Only in same suit. Answers to requests for admissions are admissible only in the same suit. TRCP 198.3; ***Osteen v. Glynn Dodson, Inc.***, 875 S.W.2d 429, 431 (Tex.App.—Waco 1994, writ denied).

2. Only against party addressed. Answers to requests for admissions and deemed admissions are admissible only against the party to whom the admissions were addressed. TRCP 198.3; ***Thalman v. Martin***, 635 S.W.2d 411, 414 (Tex.1982); ***Hartman v. Trio Transp.***, 937 S.W.2d 575, 578 (Tex.App.—Texarkana 1996, writ denied). An admission by an agent or servant is admissible against the principal only if (1) the statement concerns a matter within the scope of the agency or employment, and (2) it was made during the existence of that relationship. TRE 801(e)(2)(D); ***Hartman***, 937 S.W.2d at 579-80.

3. Not against other parties. Admissions of a party are not admissible against a third party and do not bind co-parties. ***Wal-Mart Stores v. Deggs***, 968 S.W.2d 354, 357 (Tex.1998) (allowing party to fall into trap produced by another party's failure to respond runs contrary to intent of rules); *see* ***Bleeker v. Villarreal***, 941 S.W.2d 163, 168-69 (Tex.App.—Corpus Christi 1996, writ dism'd); ***USX Corp. v. Salinas***, 818 S.W.2d 473, 479 (Tex.App.—San Antonio 1991, writ denied).

4. Not by addressed party. The party to whom the requests were addressed cannot use its own self-serving answers. ***Sympson v. Mor-Win Prods.***, 501 S.W.2d 362, 364 (Tex.App.—Fort Worth 1973, no writ); *see also* TRE 801(e)(2) (admission by party-opponent).

5. Not the denial. A party cannot introduce into evidence a party's denial or refusal to admit a fact. *See* ***Americana Motel v. Johnson***, 610 S.W.2d 143, 143 (Tex.1980) (denial of request for admission cannot be used as summary judgment evidence). When a party denies or refuses to make an admission of fact, it is nothing more than a refusal to admit a fact; it is not evidence of any fact except the fact of refusal. ***Newman v. Utica Nat'l Ins. Co.***, 868 S.W.2d 5, 8 (Tex.App.—Houston [1st Dist.] 1993, writ denied).

§8.2 Using admissions in trial. When a party intends to use the other party's response to requests for admissions in trial, that party should file them with the clerk. *See* TRCP 191.4(c)(2). Admissions made by parties in response to requests for admissions that are on file with the court do not need to be introduced into evidence to be properly before the trial and appellate courts. ***Red Ball Motor Freight v. Dean***, 549 S.W.2d 41, 43 (Tex.App.—Tyler 1977, writ dism'd). If the trier of fact returns findings contradictory to a judicial admission, the admission must be accepted as controlling. ***Beutel v. Dallas Cty. Flood Control Dist.***, 916 S.W.2d 685, 694 (Tex.App.—Waco 1996, writ denied).

PRACTICE TIP

*For dramatic effect, a party may introduce the admissions into evidence by formally reading the specific admissions to the jury. See **Deggs**, 968 S.W.2d at 356; **Parkway Hosp. v. Lee**, 946 S.W.2d 580, 587 (Tex.App.—Houston [14th Dist.] 1997, writ denied).*

1. **No contradictory proof.** A request for admission, once admitted or deemed, is a judicial admission, and a party cannot introduce conflicting testimony. ***Marshall v. Vise***, 767 S.W.2d 699, 700 (Tex.1989); ***Beutel***, 916 S.W.2d at 694; ***Bay Area Thoracic & Cardiovascular Surgical Ass'n v. Nathanson***, 908 S.W.2d 10, 11 (Tex. App.—Houston [1st Dist.] 1995, no writ).

2. **Waiver of admissions.** A party can waive its right to rely on the other party's admissions. When the admitting party attempts to offer evidence that contradicts the admissions, the party relying on the admissions must object, or it will waive its right to rely on the binding effect of the admissions. ***Marshall***, 767 S.W.2d at 700; *e.g.*, ***RTC v. Thurlow***, 820 S.W.2d 51, 53 (Tex.App.—San Antonio 1991, no writ) (admissions were not waived because party objected to contradictory evidence). If controverting evidence is introduced without objection, the admissions are no longer conclusive, but they are still evidence. ***Parkway Hosp.***, 946 S.W.2d at 587-88.

§8.3 Using admissions in summary judgment. The same rules apply when relying on admissions in a summary judgment procedure as at trial—answers to requests for admissions and deemed admissions are admissible only against the party to whom the admissions were addressed. *See* ***Americana Motel***, 610 S.W.2d at 143 (cannot use denials to request for admissions); ***Schulz v. State Farm Mut. Auto. Ins. Co.***, 930 S.W.2d 872, 876 (Tex. App.—Houston [1st Dist.] 1996, no writ) (cannot use own answers to admissions). The trial court cannot consider affidavits to contradict deemed admissions. ***Beasley v. Burns***, 7 S.W.3d 768, 770-71 (Tex.App.—Texarkana 1999, pet. denied). See §8.2, above.

§9. REVIEW

For the rules and forms for prosecuting or responding to an appeal or original proceeding, see ***O'Connor's Texas Civil Appeals*** (2002-03).

§9.1 Standard on appeal. The trial court has broad discretion to grant or refuse a party leave to withdraw deemed admissions and substitute answers. ***Stelly v. Papania***, 927 S.W.2d 620, 622 (Tex.1996); ***In re Kellogg-Brown & Root***, 45 S.W.3d 772, 775 (Tex.App.—Tyler 2001, orig. proceeding). The trial court's decision will be set aside on appeal only on a showing of a clear abuse of discretion. ***Stelly***, 927 S.W.2d at 622; ***Rosenthal v. National Terrazzo Tile & Marble***, 742 S.W.2d 55, 57 (Tex.App.—Houston [14th Dist.] 1987, no writ).

§9.2 Appeal or mandamus. Generally, mandamus relief is not available to review a trial court's action relating to deemed admissions. *See* ***Sutherland v. Moore***, 716 S.W.2d 119, 121 (Tex.App.—El Paso 1986, orig. proceeding) (mandamus not available to review trial court's withdrawal of deemed admissions). See "Review of Discovery Orders," ch. 6-A, §24, p. 340.

H. SECURING DOCUMENTS & TANGIBLE THINGS

§1. GENERAL

§1.1 Rules. TRCP 176, 196, 205.

§1.2 Purpose. TRCP 196 provides the discovery procedure for obtaining documents and other tangible things from a party, and TRCP 176 provides the procedure for obtaining documents and other tangible things from a non-party.

§1.3 Forms. See ***O'Connor's Texas Civil Forms***, FORMS 6H.

§1.4 Other references. Griesel, *The "New" Texas Discovery Rules: Three Years Later*, Advanced Evidence & Discovery Course, State Bar of Texas, ch. 2, §X, p. 22 (2002).

§2. SCOPE

A party may secure the production of any document, tangible item, or information in electronic or magnetic form that is not privileged and is relevant or reasonably calculated to lead to relevant evidence. TRCP 192.3(a). See "Documents & tangible things," ch. 6-B, §2.11, p. 344. A party may also request the production of an item for inspection, sampling, testing, photographing, and copying. TRCP 196.1(a); *see, e.g.*, ***G.M. Corp. v. Tanner***, 892 S.W.2d 862, 863 (Tex.1995) (GM wanted to examine item under microscope); ***G.E. Co. v. Salinas***, 861 S.W.2d 20, 23 (Tex.App.—Corpus Christi 1993, orig. proceeding) (GE wanted to test materials involved in residential fire).

§3. SECURING THINGS FROM A PARTY

To obtain documents from another party, a party serves a request for production. TRCP 196.1(a). No motion is necessary.

§3.1 Procedure.

1. Form of request. The request for production must be in writing. TRCP 192.7(a); *see* ***City of San Antonio v. Vela***, 762 S.W.2d 314, 319 (Tex.App.—San Antonio 1988, writ denied). There is no limit in TRCP 196 to the number of items a party can ask to have produced or the number of sets of requests it can serve. See ***O'Connor's*** FORMS 6H:01-02.

2. Specify place & time to respond. The request must state the place and date for production. TRCP 196.1(b), 196.2(a). The date to respond to the request is generally 30 days from the date the request was served. TRCP 196.2(a). When a request is served on a defendant before the defendant's answer is due, the defendant has until 50 days after service to respond. *Id.* See "Deadline to serve the response," ch. 6-A, §13.1.2, p. 323.

3. Deadline to serve. A request for production may be served any time after the suit is filed. TRCP 190.2(c)(1), 190.3(b)(1). The deadline for serving a request is 30 days before the end of the discovery period. TRCP 196.1(a). See "Discovery Periods," ch. 6-A, §6, p. 317. When served by mail or fax, the request should be served up to 34 days before the end of the discovery period. See "Deadline to Respond to Discovery," ch. 6-A, §13, p. 323.

4. Not filed. The request for production is not filed with the court. TRCP 191.4(a)(3). For exceptions, see "Filing Discovery," ch. 6-A, §11.1.3, p. 322.

§3.2 Request. A request for documents or things must be reasonably tailored to request only matters relevant to the case. ***Texaco, Inc. v. Sanderson***, 898 S.W.2d 813, 815 (Tex.1995).

1. Items to produce. The request for production must identify items, either individually or by category, and describe each item and category with reasonable particularity. TRCP 196.1(b); *see, e.g.*, ***Texaco***, 898 S.W.2d at 815 (request for all documents generally too broad); ***County of Dallas v. Harrison***, 759 S.W.2d 530, 531 (Tex.App.—Dallas 1988, no writ) (request for photographs did not include videotape). A request for production cannot be used as a fishing expedition for information. ***In re American Optical***, 988 S.W.2d 711, 713 (Tex.1998); ***Dillard Dept. Stores v. Hall***, 909 S.W.2d 491, 492 (Tex.1995).

(1) Electronic information. To obtain discovery of magnetic or electronic information, the requesting party must (1) specifically request the data, (2) specify the form in which the data should be produced, and (3) specify any extraordinary steps necessary for retrieval and translation. TRCP 196.4 & cmt. 3.

(2) Other things. The request for production should ask for documents and other things based on the elements of the claim or defense. See ***O'Connor's*** FORMS 6H for suggested requests for production in the following types of lawsuits: breach of contract (FORM 6H:04), suit on a sworn account (FORM 6H:05), automobile accident (FORMS 6H:06-07), slip and fall (FORMS 6H:08-09), and suit under the DTPA (FORMS 6H:10-11).

2. Items to be tested. If the requesting party intends to test or sample the requested item, the party must describe with specificity the means, manner, and procedure for testing or sampling. TRCP 196.1(b). The requesting party should identify to what extent, if any, the testing or sampling will destroy or alter the item. If the testing will destroy or materially alter the item, the requesting party must secure a court order before conducting the test. *See* TRCP 196.5.

3. Particulars for compliance. The request for production should state the particulars for compliance: the deadline (generally 30 days after service of the request), the place to produce documents (generally the office of the lawyer), and the way to produce the documents (organized as they are kept in the ordinary course of business or organized and labeled to correspond with each particular request). TRCP 196.1(b), 196.3(c). See "Deadline to serve the response," ch. 6-A, §13.1, p. 323.

4. Appropriate requests. The following requests were held proper: • Request for all documents relating to incident in which plaintiff was injured, excluding work product. ***K-Mart Corp. v. Sanderson***, 937 S.W.2d 429, 430-31 (Tex.1996). • Request for personnel file. ***Tri-State Wholesale Associated Grocers v. Barrera***, 917 S.W.2d 391, 399 (Tex.App.—El Paso 1996, writ dism'd). See "Personnel files," ch. 6-B, §2.11.9, p. 346. • Request for "any and all" lease agreements between the parties since 1974. ***Chamberlain v. Cherry***, 818 S.W.2d 201, 204 (Tex. App.—Amarillo 1991, orig. proceeding).

PRACTICE TIP

If you believe the other party is going to hide documents, skip the request for production. Instead, as early as possible in the lawsuit, subpoena for an oral deposition the lowest-level employee of the party who keeps the documents and request a list of documents as part of the deposition notice. You have a better chance to get the documents if a lay person (not a lawyer) is subpoenaed (not noticed) for deposition and swears under oath (not just states in response to a request for production) that the documents produced are all the documents that were requested.

---

5. Inappropriate requests.

(1) Trial exhibits. A party should not request copies of the other party's trial exhibits in a request for production. ***Texas Tech Univ. Health Sci. Ctr. v. Schild***, 828 S.W.2d 502, 504 (Tex.App.—El Paso 1992, orig. proceeding). Trial exhibits may be secured before trial if a pretrial or discovery control order requires their production. TRCP 166(*l*), 190.4. See "Exhibits & objections," ch. 5-A, §3.9.3, p. 226.

(2) To create a document. A party should not ask a party to create a document. ***In re Colonial Pipeline Co.***, 968 S.W.2d 938, 942 (Tex.1998); ***McKinney v. National Un. Fire Ins. Co.***, 772 S.W.2d 72, 73 n.2 (Tex. 1989); *see also* ***In re Guzman***, 19 S.W.3d 522, 525 (Tex.App.—Corpus Christi 2000, orig. proceeding) (court cannot require nonparty to create document). To be subject to discovery, the thing or document must exist in the custody, control, or possession of a party on whom the request is served. ***Colonial Pipeline***, 968 S.W.2d at 942; ***Smith v. O'Neal***, 850 S.W.2d 797, 799 (Tex.App.—Houston [14th Dist.] 1993, no writ).

(3) Overbroad request. A party should not ask for "all documents" without limiting the request as to time, place, or subject matter. See "Overbroad," ch. 6-A, §19.1.3, p. 335. When a request asks for "all documents," the party can object to the request and refuse to comply with it entirely, TRCP 193, cmt. 2; or the party can file a motion for a protective order, TRCP 192.6(a).

§3.3 Procedure to respond.

1. Form of response. See *O'Connor's* FORM 6H:03.

(1) In writing. The party responding to a request for production must serve a written response on the requesting party. TRCP 196.2(a); *see* ***Cellular Mktg. v. Houston Cellular Tel. Co.***, 838 S.W.2d 331, 333 n.2

(Tex.App.—Houston [14th Dist.] 1992, writ denied). Each answer, objection, or other response must be preceded by the request to which it applies. TRCP 193.1.

(2) Not verified. The response does not need to be verified. *See* TRCP 191.3(a).

(3) Signed. The response must be signed by the lawyer (or party when pro se). TRCP 191.3(a).

2. Deadline to respond. Generally, a party has 30 days from the date of service of the request for documents to respond, depending on the type of service. TRCP 196.2(a); *see* ***Schein v. American Rest. Group***, 852 S.W.2d 496, 497 n.2 (Tex.1993). *But see* TRCP 196.2(a) (D has 50 days if request served before D's answer is due). See "Deadline to Respond to Discovery," ch. 6-A, §13, p. 323. The party must file its answers, its objections, and assert its privileges by this deadline; if not, the party waives its objections and privileges. See "Waiver of objections & privileges," ch. 6-A, §23.3, p. 338. Once a party's objections and privileges are waived, the requested documents must be produced. To extend the time, see "Extending Time to Respond to Discovery," ch. 6-A, §14, p. 324.

3. Not filed. The written response and the documents produced in response to the request are not filed with the court. TRCP 191.4(a). The documents should be kept by the party that requested their production. Other parties should be provided with copies of the documents.

4. Costs of producing. The cost of producing materials is the responsibility of the responding party. TRCP 196.6. The cost of inspecting, sampling, testing, photographing, or copying materials is the responsibility of the requesting party. *Id.*; ***Limas v. De Delgado***, 770 S.W.2d 953, 954 (Tex.App.—El Paso 1989, no writ). For good cause, the court can order that costs be borne differently than provided for in TRCP 196.6. TRCP 196.6.

§3.4 Contents of response. See *O'Connor's* FORM 6H:03. With respect to each item or category of items, the responding party must make one of the following responses:

1. Party will comply. When complying with the request, the party should state that production, inspection, or other requested action will be permitted as requested. TRCP 196.2(b)(1).

(1) Production of things. A party must produce all the documents and things that are requested, discoverable, in its possession (actual or constructive), and not subject to an objection. TRCP 196.3(a). For discussion of constructive possession, see "Possession," ch. 6-A, §2.3, p. 313. See "Burden to partially comply," ch. 6-A, §17.9, p. 333.

(2) Organization of documents. Documents must be produced either (1) organized as they are kept in the ordinary course of business or (2) organized and labeled to correspond to each particular request. TRCP 196.3(c); *see, e.g.*, ***Steenbergen v. Ford Motor Co.***, 814 S.W.2d 755, 758-59 (Tex.App.—Dallas 1991, writ denied) (D could produce documents as kept in course of business because P's request did not seek to organize or label according to categories). A party producing documents cannot collect the documents requested and shuffle them before turning them over to the party requesting the documents.

(3) Electronic or magnetic data. When a request for production asks for electronic or magnetic information, the responding party must produce the data responsive to the request. TRCP 196.4. If the responding party cannot reasonably retrieve the requested information or produce it in the form requested, the responding party must object to the request. TRCP 196.4; *see* TRCP 193.2(b).

2. Party objects to procedure to respond. When a party intends to comply with the request but objects to the time, place, or method identified in the request for compliance, the response should state both the objection and the solution.

(1) Objection to time & place. When a party objects to the time or place of production or inspection, the response should state that it would be more reasonable to produce or inspect the documents at a different time or place and describe the suggested terms (*e.g.*, at the corporate office instead of the lawyer's office, or produce all copies instead of permitting inspection first). TRCP 193.2(b), 196.2(b). The party must comply without further request or order. TRCP 193.2(b).

(2) Objection to method of compliance. When a party objects to a request for production because it asks the party to produce a large number of documents, the responding party may notify the other party in its response that the documents are available in its office for inspection and copying. *See* ***Overall v. Southwestern Bell Yellow Pages***, 869 S.W.2d 629, 631 (Tex.App.—Houston [14th Dist.] 1994, no writ). When a request for production asks for a manageable number of documents, the responding party should attach them to the response. *See* ***Overall***, 869 S.W.2d at 631 (documents excluded from trial for failure to provide copies with response).

3. Party objects to production. When objecting to the production of documents and things, the objection must be in writing, contained either in the response or in a separate document, and must provide specific reasons why the discovery should not be permitted. TRCP 193.2(a). A party's objections must be supported by a good-faith factual or legal basis. TRCP 193.2(c). A party must comply with the requests to which it does not object. TRCP 193.2(b) & cmt. 2. See "Burden to partially comply," ch. 6-A, §17.9, p. 333.

(1) Destruction by testing. A party may object when testing or sampling the thing to be produced will destroy or materially alter the condition of it. TRCP 196.5; ***G.M. Corp. v. Tanner***, 892 S.W.2d 862, 863-64 (Tex. 1995) (must support objection with evidence).

(2) Other objections. For other objections, see "Reasons to object to discovery requests," ch. 6-A, §18.1, p. 333; "Grounds to limit scope of discovery," ch. 6-A, §19.1, p. 334.

4. Party asserts privileges. When asserting privileges in response to the request, the party must comply with TRCP 193.3. TRCP 193.2(f); *see* 196.2(b). See "Asserting privileges," ch. 6-A, §17.2, p. 329. A party must comply with the requests to which it does not assert a privilege. TRCP 193.2(b) & cmt. 2. See "Burden to partially comply," ch. 6-A, §17.9, p. 333.

5. Party unable to locate things. If a party is not able to locate documents or things responsive to the request, it must state that after a diligent search no items were identified that are responsive to the request. TRCP 196.2(b)(4).

§3.5 Hearing on objections & privileges. Generally, the burden to secure a hearing, to present evidence, and to secure a ruling on objections or assertions of privileges is on the party seeking discovery. See "Burden to secure hearing & ruling," ch. 6-A, §17.5, p. 331; "Burden to provide evidence," ch. 6-A, §17.6, p. 331.

§3.6 Supplementing or amending responses. When a party discovers additional information after responding to discovery, the party must supplement or amend its response. TRCP 193.5 (duty to supplement), TRCP 193.6 (sanctions for failure to supplement). For the substance of what additional information to provide, see "Supplementing Discovery Responses," ch. 6-A, §16, p. 325.

1. Time to serve supplemental or amended responses. A party should serve supplemental or amended responses to requests for production reasonably promptly after the party discovers the need for such a response. TRCP 193.5(b).

2. Form of response. Supplemental or amended responses must be made in the same form as the original responses. TRCP 193.5(b). See "Form of supplemental discovery," ch. 6-A, §16.6, p. 328.

§4. SECURING THINGS FROM A PARTY ABOUT A NONPARTY

§4.1 Nonparty information. When a party seeks information from another party about a nonparty, the production can affect the privacy interests of the nonparty. ***In re Temple-Inland***, 8 S.W.3d 459, 462-63 (Tex.App.—Beaumont 2000, orig. proceeding). The court can restrict the dissemination of discoverable information about nonparties, even when no privilege is involved. *See, e.g., id.* (court limited dissemination of list of former employees which ascribed criminal and other embarrassing conduct to them). For nonparty medical records in the possession of a party, see "Request to Party for Nonparty's Medical Records," ch. 6-I, §4, p. 435.

§4.2 Who can object. Any person affected by the discovery request can object to the discovery request—including other parties and the nonparties. TRCP 192.6.

§5. SECURING THINGS FROM A NONPARTY

To secure documents and other tangible things from a nonparty, the party serves a notice to produce or appear and a discovery subpoena. TRCP 205.3(a); *see* TRCP 196, cmt. 6; ***In re Diversicare Gen. Partner***, 41 S.W.3d 788, 794 (Tex.App.—Corpus Christi 2001, orig. proceeding). A party is not required to file a motion for production to obtain documents from a nonparty in an ongoing suit. TRCP 205, cmt. By comparison, a party is required to file a motion and secure a court order to depose a nonparty before suit under TRCP 202, to secure a physical or mental examination of a nonparty under TRCP 204, and to secure entry on a nonparty's land under TRCP 196.7. TRCP 205.1.

§5.1 Notice.

1. Contents of notice.

(1) For documents only. When a nonparty is required to produce documents or things without appearing for a deposition, the notice of production must provide: (1) the name of the person from whom production is sought, (2) a reasonable time and place for production, (3) a description of the items to be produced, and (4) if testing or sampling is requested, information about the means, manner, and procedure. TRCP 205.3(b).

(2) For documents at deposition. When a nonparty is required to produce documents at an oral deposition, the notice for the deposition must comply with TRCP 199.2. TRCP 205.1(c). See "Contents of notice," ch. 6-E, §4.5.1, p. 387.

2. Filing. Discovery notices served on nonparties must be filed with the clerk. TRCP 191.4(b)(1).

§5.2 The discovery subpoena. The subpoena is the instrument that compels a nonparty to comply with a notice for discovery. *See* ***St. Luke's Episcopal Hosp. v. Garcia***, 928 S.W.2d 307, 312 (Tex.App.—Houston [14th Dist.] 1996, orig. proceeding). For general information about subpoenas, see "Subpoenas," ch. 1-K, p. 58. The scope of production of a discovery subpoena is governed by TRCP 192.3. *See* ***Martin v. Khoury***, 843 S.W.2d 163, 166 (Tex.App.—Texarkana 1992, orig. proceeding). A subpoena cannot be used to secure information that is not discoverable by other forms of discovery requests. *See* TRCP 176.3(b) (prohibits use of subpoena to circumvent discovery rules); ***Prestige Ford Co. v. Gilmore***, 56 S.W.3d 73, 80 (Tex.App.—Houston [14th Dist.] 2001, pet. denied) (same).

1. Types of discovery subpoenas. There are three types of discovery subpoenas.

(1) To produce. A nonparty may be subpoenaed to produce documents or things, without requiring the nonparty to appear for a deposition. TRCP 176.6(c), 205.3(a). When the subpoena commands a witness to produce documents or other things but not to give testimony, the witness need not appear in person at the time and place of production. TRCP 176.6(c).

(2) To appear. A nonparty may be subpoenaed to appear for a deposition without producing any documents. TRCP 205.1(a), (b). The discovery subpoena should direct the witness to appear for deposition at the time and place stated in the notice of deposition. TRCP 176.1(e), 176.2.

(3) To appear & produce. A nonparty may be subpoenaed to appear for a deposition and produce documents or other things. TRCP 205.1(c), 205.3(a), (b); *see* ***In re Amaya***, 34 S.W.3d 354, 356-57 (Tex.App.—Waco 2001, orig. proceeding) (nonparty could not refuse to appear & produce documents). See "Documents from nonparties," ch. 6-E, §4.5.6(2), p. 390.

2. Filing. Subpoenas required to be served on nonparties must be filed with the clerk. TRCP 191.4(b)(1).

§5.3 Time to serve notice & subpoena. The notice (either of intent to take the nonparty's deposition or to compel the nonparty to produce documents and things, or both) and the subpoena compelling the nonparty to comply must be served on the nonparty and the other parties. TRCP 205.2. See "Proof of service," ch. 1-K, §3.9, p. 61; chart 6-9, "Deadlines to Serve Notice & Subpoena," ch. 6-E, p. 391.

1. Nonparty documents without deposition. To compel the production of documents from a nonparty without requiring the nonparty to appear for an oral deposition, the notice to produce and the subpoena must be served a reasonable time before the response is due. TRCP 205.3(a). The notice to produce must be served at least ten days before service of the subpoena. TRCP 205.2. The ten-day gap between service of the notice and the subpoena gives anyone (party or nonparty) who objects to the production of the documents time to move for a protective order before the nonparty produces the documents.

2. Nonparty deposition with documents. To compel the production of documents from a nonparty at a deposition, the notice of deposition and the subpoena must be served a reasonable time before the deposition. See "Nonparty deposition with documents," ch. 6-E, §4.5.2(1)(b), p. 388.

3. Nonparty deposition without documents. To compel the appearance of a nonparty at a deposition without requiring the production of documents, the notice of deposition and the subpoena must be served a reasonable time before the deposition; the subpoena cannot be served before the notice. See "Nonparty deposition without documents," ch. 6-E, §4.5.2(2)(b), p. 389.

§5.4 Nonparty's response to discovery subpoena. A nonparty must respond to the discovery subpoena and notice as required by TRCP 176.6. TRCP 205.3(d). The rules governing a nonparty's response to a notice and subpoena to produce documents are similar to the rules governing a party's response to a request for production. See "Procedure to respond," §3.3, p. 425.

1. No appearance necessary. A nonparty requested to produce documents or other things is not required to appear in person at the time and place of production unless the person is also subpoenaed to attend and give testimony. TRCP 176.6(c).

2. Organization of documents. A nonparty must produce the documents either as they are (1) kept in the ordinary course of business or (2) organized and labeled to correspond to each request. TRCP 176.6(c). See "Organization of documents," §3.4.1(2), p. 426.

§5.5 Challenging nonparty discovery subpoena. See "Objecting to Trial & Discovery Subpoenas," ch. 1-K, §4, p. 61; ***O'Connor's*** FORMS 6A:10-11.

1. Who can challenge. The subpoena can be challenged by the person subpoenaed, a party to the suit, or any person affected by the subpoena. TRCP 176.6(d), (e).

2. Deadline to challenge. Any challenge to the subpoena must be made before the time specified for compliance in the subpoena. TRCP 176.6(d), (e).

3. How to challenge subpoena.

(1) Objections & privileges. A nonparty may make written objections to production and may assert privileges and withhold documents by complying with TRCP 193.3. *See* TRCP 176.6(c), (d). See "Types of challenges," ch. 1-K, §4.3, p. 61; "Asserting privileges," ch. 6-A, §17.2, p. 329.

(2) Protective order. A nonparty, a party, or any person affected by the discovery subpoena may file a motion for protective order under TRCP 192.6. TRCP 176.6(e). See "Motion for Protective Order," ch. 6-A, §19, p. 334.

4. Effect of challenge to discovery.

(1) Objection to time & place. When a nonparty or party objects to the time or place of an oral deposition of a nonparty by filing a motion for protection or motion to quash within three business days after service of the notice of deposition, the motion stays the deposition until the motion can be decided by the court. TRCP 199.4.

(2) Other objections by nonparty. When the nonparty challenges the subpoena by filing objections, assertions of privileges, or a motion for protection, the nonparty should produce all requested information not subject to its challenges. *See* TRCP 192.6(a), (b).

(3) Other objections by parties & third persons. When a party or a third person affected by the discovery challenges the discovery sought from a nonparty by filing a motion for protection or motion to quash, the motion does not prevent the nonparty from producing the discovery. *See* TRCP 176.6(e) (although subpoenaed witness "need not" produce documents for which protection is sought, rule does not prohibit production). The party or affected person must secure a court order staying production of the discovery, or the nonparty may produce it. See §5.5.5(2), below.

5. Burden to get ruling.

(1) On objection by nonparty. The burden to get a ruling on a nonparty's objections is on the party that issued the subpoena. ***Olinger v. Curry***, 926 S.W.2d 832, 835 (Tex.App.—Fort Worth 1996, orig. proceeding). Although TRCP 176.6(d) and (e) require the subpoenaed person to object to a discovery subpoena or seek a protective order before the time specified for compliance, they do not require the witness to get a ruling before the time for compliance. The party who issued the subpoena may move for an order any time after an objection is made or a motion for protection is filed. TRCP 176.6(d), (e).

(2) On objections by other persons. The burden to get a ruling on objections filed by a party or third person affected by the subpoena is on the party or third person that filed the motion objecting to production. The reason the burden is on the party or third person is that, unless prevented by a court order, a nonparty may produce documents even though a motion for protection was filed. *See* TRCP 176.6(e) (rule does not prohibit subpoenaed witness from producing after objection filed).

6. Ruling on objections. The court may sustain objections, grant a protective order, or impose reasonable conditions on compliance with a subpoena, including compensation to the nonparty for undue hardship. *See* TRCP 176.7.

§5.6 Cost of document production. The party who issues the subpoena requiring production of documents or other things must reimburse the nonparty for the reasonable costs of production. TRCP 205.3(f).

§5.7 Copies for other parties. The party who issued the subpoena must make the produced materials available to the other parties for inspection on reasonable notice. TRCP 205.3(e). At their own expense, the other parties may obtain copies of the documents from the party who issued the subpoena. *Id.*

§6. COMPELLING PRODUCTION & SANCTIONS

§6.1 Motion to compel & for sanctions. If the party or nonparty responding to the request for or notice of production refuses to produce documents, the party requesting documents can move to compel production and move for sanctions or an order of contempt. *See* TRCP 215.2. See "Motion to Compel Discovery," ch. 6-A, §21, p. 336; "Motion for Discovery Sanctions," ch. 6-A, §22, p. 337.

1. Sanctions against party. When a party refuses to produce a document that was properly requested, the trial court can exclude the document, limit the testimony about the document or the issue, or impose any other sanction listed in TRCP 215.2(b). See "Sanctions for discovery abuse," ch. 5-J, §7.1, p. 281.

2. Sanctions against nonparty. The only sanction the court may impose on a nonparty for not complying with an order under TRCP 205.3 is contempt. TRCP 176.8(a), 215.2(a), (c). See "Nonparty," ch. 5-J, §4.4, p. 277.

§6.2 Other remedies. When the party requesting documents believes the responding party has overlooked or ignored relevant documents in responding to the request, the requesting party has a number of options: (1) it can ask the court to appoint a master, (2) it can take depositions, or (3) it can send written interrogatories. ***Texaco, Inc. v. Dominguez***, 812 S.W.2d 451, 456 (Tex.App.—San Antonio 1991, orig. proceeding). The party cannot ask the court for permission to go through the other party's files. *Id.* at 455-56.

§7. SECURING DOCUMENTS FROM A FINANCIAL INSTITUTION

§7.1 Exclusive discovery procedure. To secure a customer's records from a bank or other financial institution, a party must comply with Finance Code §59.006, which is the exclusive method to compel discovery of a customer's records. Fin. Code §59.006(a); *see* CPRC §30.007; ***Enviro Protection v. National Bank***, 989 S.W.2d 454, 455 (Tex.App.—El Paso 1999, no pet.) (applying provisions from former CPRC §30.007).

§7.2 Definitions under Finance Code §59.001.

1. Financial institution. A "financial institution" is defined as any of the following but does not include an entity organized under the laws of another state or under federal law, which has its main office in another state, and does not maintain a branch or other office in Texas. Fin. Code §59.001(5).

(1) A bank, whether chartered under the laws of this state, another state, the United States, or another country. Fin. Code §201.101(1)(A).

(2) A savings and loan association chartered under Finance Code chapter 62 or similar laws of another state. *Id.* §201.101(1)(B).

(3) A federal savings and loan association, federal savings bank, federal credit union, or credit union chartered under Finance Code chapter 122 or similar laws of another state. *Id.* §201.101(1)(C), (D).

(4) A trust company chartered under the laws of this state or another state. *Id.* §201.101(1)(E).

2. Record. "Record" means financial or other information of a customer maintained by a financial institution. Fin. Code §59.001(7).

3. Record request. "Record request" means a valid and enforceable subpoena, request for production, or other instrument issued under authority of a tribunal that compels production of a customer record. Fin. Code §59.001(8).

4. Tribunal. "Tribunal" means a court or other adjudicatory tribunal with jurisdiction to issue a request for records, including a government agency exercising adjudicatory functions and an alternative dispute resolution mechanism, voluntary or required, under which a party may compel the production of records. Fin. Code §59.001(10).

§7.3 Procedure to secure party-customer records.

1. Requesting records. The party requesting records from a financial institution about one of its customers who is a party to the suit must do the following:

(1) Serve the bank with a record request that gives the financial institution at least 24 days to comply with the request. Fin. Code §59.006(b)(1); *see, e.g.*, ***Enviro Protection***, 989 S.W.2d at 456 (subpoena to produce records from bank not valid because it was not issued with 24 days' notice).

(2) Pay the financial institution's reasonable costs of complying with the record request or post a cost bond in an amount estimated by the financial institution to cover the costs before the financial institution

complies with the record request. Fin. Code §59.006(b)(2). Costs include costs of reproduction, postage, research, delivery, and attorney fees. *Id.*

2. Objecting to request. The bank's customer bears the burden of preventing or limiting the financial institution's compliance with a record request by seeking an appropriate remedy, including filing a motion to quash the record request or a motion for a protective order. Fin. Code §59.006(e). Any motion must be served on the financial institution and the requesting party before the date that compliance with the request is required. *Id.*

§7.4 Procedure to secure nonparty-customer records.

1. Requesting records. When the financial institution's customer is not a party to the proceeding in which the request was issued, the requesting party must do the following:

(1) Serve the financial institution with a record request. See §7.3.1(1), above.

(2) Pay the financial institution's reasonable costs. See §7.3.1(2), above.

(3) Give notice to the nonparty-customer, stating the customer's rights under Finance Code §59.006(e), and serve a copy of the request to the customer under TRCP 21a. Fin. Code §59.006(c)(1).

(4) File with the tribunal and the financial institution a certificate of service indicating that the nonparty-customer was mailed or served with the notice and a copy of the record request. *Id.* §59.006(c)(2).

(5) Request the nonparty-customer's written consent authorizing the financial institution to comply with the request. *Id.* §59.006(c)(3).

2. Objecting to request. The nonparty-customer's procedure to object is to withhold written consent authorizing the financial institution to comply with the request. *See* Fin. Code §59.006(d) (sole means of obtaining access to records of nonparty is to file motion seeking in camera inspection).

3. Procedure to compel disclosure for nonparty-customer records.

(1) File motion for in camera review. When a nonparty-customer refuses to execute the consent or does not respond to the request under Finance Code §59.006(c)(3) by the date for compliance, the sole means of obtaining access to the requested record is for the requesting party to file a written motion seeking an in camera inspection of the requested record by the court. Fin. Code §59.006(d).

(2) Court inspection. In response to a motion for in camera inspection, the court may inspect the record requested to determine its relevance to the matter before the tribunal. Fin. Code §59.006(d). The tribunal may order redaction of parts of the record that it determines should not be produced. *Id.* The court must sign a protective order preventing the record it orders produced from being disclosed to a person who is not a party to the proceeding and from being used for any purpose other than resolving the dispute before the court. *Id.*

§7.5 Deadline to produce.

1. Party-customer. The financial institution must produce the records of a party by the 24th day after the date of receipt of the record request, as provided by Finance Code §59.006(b). Fin. Code §59.006(f)(1).

2. Nonparty-customer. The financial institution must produce the records of a nonparty before the later of the following:

(1) The 15th day after the date of receipt of a customer consent to disclose a record. Fin. Code §59.006(f)(2).

(2) If the nonparty-customer did not sign a consent, the 15th day after the date a court ordered production of the records. *Id.* §59.006(f)(3).

§7.6 No interlocutory appeal. By statute, an order to quash or for protection or other remedy granted or denied by the tribunal under Finance Code §59.006(d) or (e) is not a final order and is not subject to an interlocutory appeal. Fin. Code §59.006(g).

§7.7 Exemptions. Finance Code §59.006 does not create a right of privacy in a customer record. Fin. Code §59.006(a); ***Martin v. Darnell***, 960 S.W.2d 838, 843 (Tex.App.—Amarillo 1997, orig. proceeding) (citing statutory language from former CPRC §30.007(b)). Section 59.006 does not apply to and does not require or authorize a financial institution to give a customer notice of the following:

1. A demand or inquiry from a state or federal government agency authorized by law to conduct an examination of the financial institution. Fin. Code §59.006(a)(1).

2. A record request from a state or federal government agency or instrumentality under statutory or administrative authority that provides for, or is accompanied by, a specific mechanism for discovery and protection of a customer record of a financial institution, including a record request from a federal agency subject to the Right to Financial Privacy Act of 1978, 12 U.S.C. §3401 et seq., or from the IRS under §1205, Internal Revenue Code of 1986. Fin. Code §59.006(a)(2).

3. A record request from or report to a government agency arising out of the investigation or prosecution of a criminal offense. Fin. Code §59.006(a)(3); ***State of Texas v. Rutherford***, 18 S.W.3d 666, 670 (Tex.App.—San Antonio 1999, pet. ref'd).

4. A record request in connection with a garnishment proceeding in which the financial institution is garnishee and the customer is debtor. Fin. Code §59.006(a)(4).

5. A record request by a duly appointed receiver for the customer. *Id.* §59.006(a)(5).

6. An investigative demand or inquiry from a state legislative investigating committee. *Id.* §59.006(a)(6).

7. An investigative demand or inquiry from the attorney general of Texas as authorized by law other than the procedural law governing discovery in civil cases. *Id.* §59.006(a)(7).

8. The voluntary use or disclosure of a record by a financial institution subject to other applicable state or federal law. *Id.* §59.006(a)(8).

§8. USING REQUESTED DOCUMENTS

§8.1 Offering documents. To use a document produced in response to a request for or notice of production, the party offering the document must prove its authenticity and its admissibility.

1. Self-authenticating. A party's production of a document in response to written discovery authenticates the document for use against that party in any pretrial proceeding or at trial, unless the producing party timely objects to the authenticity of the document. TRCP 193.7. See §8.3, below. Authentication, however, does not establish admissibility. TRCP 193, cmt. 7; *see* TRE 901(a). See §8.1.2, below.

2. Admissibility. To use a document produced in response to a request for or notice of production, the party offering the document must prove it is admissible, lay the proper predicate for its admission, offer it into evidence, and get the court to rule on its admissibility. *See* TRE 104, 105, 402. Just because a document was produced by the other party in discovery does not mean the document is admissible. For example, although an insurance policy is discoverable, it generally is not admissible. TRE 411. See "Introducing Evidence," ch. 8-C, p. 534.

§8.2 Using the response. When relevant to the suit, a party may read into evidence the other party's response to the request for documents. *See, e.g.*, ***Wal-Mart Stores v. Cordova***, 856 S.W.2d 768, 772 (Tex.App.—El Paso 1993, writ denied) (on rebuttal, P read into evidence Wal-Mart's response that it had no safety manual at the time of the accident).

§8.3 Objections to documents.

1. Objection to authenticity. A party may object, either in writing or on the record, to the authenticity of all or part of a document it produced in discovery. TRCP 193.7. The objection must be made within ten days after the party had actual notice the document would be used. *Id.* In appropriate circumstances, the court can alter the ten-day period. TRCP 193, cmt. 7. The objection to authenticity must specify the basis for the objection and must have a good-faith, factual and legal basis. TRCP 193.7. An objection made to the authenticity of part of a document does not affect the authenticity of the remainder. *Id.* Once an objection is made, the court must permit the party attempting to use the document a reasonable opportunity to establish its authenticity. *Id.*

PRACTICE TIP

To avoid complications about authenticity at trial, a party should ask the court to require in its pretrial order that the parties identify all the documents they intend to offer at trial. This will trigger the obligation to object to authenticity and the ability to "snap-back" an inadvertently produced privileged document. TRCP 193, cmt. 7; see TRCP 193.3(d). See FORM 5A:01, §J, ¶12.

2. Other objections to documents. To object to a document produced in response to a request for or notice of production, see "Objecting to Evidence," ch. 8-D, p. 544.

§9. REVIEW

For the rules and forms for prosecuting or responding to an appeal or original proceeding, see ***O'Connor's Texas Civil Appeals*** (2002-03).

§9.1 The record. If the court rules that documents presented for an in camera inspection under seal are not discoverable, the party that was denied discovery of the documents must make sure the documents are transferred under seal to the appellate court to permit the appellate court to evaluate them. ***Pope v. Stephenson***, 787 S.W.2d 953, 954 (Tex.1990).

§9.2 Appeal or mandamus? See "Review of Discovery Orders," ch. 6-A, §24, p. 340.

I. MEDICAL RECORDS

§1. GENERAL

§1.1 Rules. TRCP 194.2(j), (k), 204; TRE 509(e)(4), 510(d)(5). See Occ. Code §159.002(b); Health & Safety Code §§241.151(2), 241.152.

§1.2 Purpose. The discovery rules provide two procedures that are specific to the discovery of medical records—a written request for disclosure, and a motion to examine the person. The parties also may use all the other traditional methods of discovery: request for production, a notice of deposition with a notice to the party to bring the medical records, and a deposition on written questions of a records custodian.

§1.3 Forms. See ***O'Connor's Texas Civil Forms***, FORMS 6I.

§1.4 Other references. Fineberg & Shore, *Discovery Update*, Advanced Civil Trial Course, State Bar of Texas, ch. 1, §IV.A.2, p. 24 (2001); Griesel, *The "New" Texas Discovery Rules: Three Years Later*, Advanced Evidence & Discovery Course, State Bar of Texas, ch. 2, §XVIII, p. 31 (2002).

§2. SCOPE

A party may discover the medical records of any person who is claiming physical or mental injury arising from the event that is the subject of the suit. TRCP 194.2(j). See "What is Discoverable?," ch. 6-B, §§2.18-2.21, pp. 349-51.

§3. REQUEST FOR PARTY'S MEDICAL RECORDS OR AUTHORIZATION

§3.1 Request for disclosure of medical records or for authorization. In a suit alleging physical or mental injury and damages, a party may request the injured party either produce all relevant medical records and bills or furnish an authorization permitting the disclosure of those medical records. TRCP 194.2(j). The request should be made as part of a TRCP 194 request for disclosure. TRCP 194.1. See "Medical records," ch. 6-D, §3.2.1(9), p. 378.

§3.2 Medical authorization. A party may serve a written request for the injured party to sign a medical authorization. *See* Health & Safety Code §241.152. A medical authorization is valid for 180 days from the date it is signed, unless it provides otherwise or is revoked. *Id.* §241.152(c), (d).

1. Requirements. An authorization under Health & Safety Code §241.152(b) must (1) be in writing, (2) be dated and signed by the patient or legal representative, (3) identify the information to be disclosed, (4) identify the person or entity to whom the information is to be disclosed, and (5) be contained in a separate document from the one that contains the consent to medical treatment obtained from the patient. Health & Safety Code §241.152(b).

2. No ex parte discovery. A party should consider adding a statement to a medical authorization that the patient does not authorize any health care professional to discuss the patient's treatment with anyone outside the presence of the patient's attorney. *See* ***In re Trostel***, No. 05-00-02059-CV (Tex.App.—Dallas 2001, orig. proceeding) (no pub.; 6-15-01). See "Discovery from treating doctors," ch. 6-C, §3.1.2(3), p. 366.

3. Providing records. The hospital or its agent must provide copies of the medical records not later than 15 days after the request and payment for reasonable fees are received. Health & Safety Code §241.154(a). The hospital or its agent is permitted to charge fees as set out in Health & Safety Code §241.154(b).

§3.3 Health care liability claim. In a suit asserting a health care liability claim, the parties are entitled to obtain copies of the claimant's medical records from any other party in possession of the records within 45 days of receipt of a written request for the records. CPRC §74.051(d). 03

§3.4 Order compelling production. An order compelling the release of medical records must be restricted to maintain the confidentiality of records not relevant to the underlying suit. ***Groves v. Gabriel***, 874 S.W.2d 660, 661 (Tex.1994); *see* TRCP 196.1(c)(3). The order must meet the standard set out in ***Mutter v. Wood***, 744 S.W.2d 600, 601 (Tex.1988). Depending on the circumstances, ***Mutter*** may require a time limitation on disclosure. ***Groves***, 874 S.W.2d at 661.

§4. REQUEST TO PARTY FOR NONPARTY'S MEDICAL RECORDS

§4.1 Service on nonparty required. When a party requests that another party produce a nonparty's medical records, the requesting party must serve the nonparty with the request for production under TRCP 21a. TRCP 196.1(c)(1), 205.3(c).

§4.2 Service on nonparty not required. When a party requests that another party produce a nonparty's medical records, the party is not required to serve the request on the nonparty if (1) the nonparty signed a release that is effective as to the requesting party, (2) the identity of the nonparty will not be disclosed, either directly or indirectly, by production of the records, or (3) on good cause shown, the court orders that service is not required. TRCP 196.1(c)(2), 205.3(c); *see* ***In re Columbia Valley Reg'l Med. Ctr.***, 41 S.W.3d 797, 800 (Tex.App.—Corpus Christi 2001, orig. proceeding) (redaction of information did not defeat medical privilege).

§4.3 Confidentiality. Production of medical records about a nonparty under TRCP 196.1(c) is subject to the laws concerning confidentiality of medical and mental health records. TRCP 196.1(c)(3); ***Columbia Valley***, 41 S.W.3d at 800; *see, e.g.*, ***In re Diversicare Gen. Partner***, 41 S.W.3d 788, 795 (Tex.App.—Corpus Christi 2001, orig. proceeding) (TRCP 196.1(c) cannot be used to circumvent confidentiality laws governing nursing home records).

TRCP 196.1(c) does not expand the scope of discovery of a nonparty's medical records. TRCP 196, cmt. 8; ***Columbia Valley***, 41 S.W.3d at 800. See "Discoverable physician-patient information," ch. 6-B, §2.18, p. 349; "Physician-patient privilege," ch. 6-B, §3.10, p. 356.

§5. MOTION TO EXAMINE THE PERSON

§5.1 Motion. To request a mental or physical examination under TRCP 204.1, the movant must file a motion for an order compelling the examination of the person. The examination under TRCP 204.1 is limited to a party or a person in the custody or under the legal control of a party. TRCP 204.1(a).

1. Elements. The court may issue an order for examination only when (1) the movant shows good cause and (2) either (a) the mental or physical condition of a party, or of a person under the legal control of a party, is in controversy or (b) the party responding to the motion designated a psychologist as a testifying expert or disclosed a psychologist's records for possible use at trial. TRCP 204.1(c).

(1) Good cause. There must be good cause for the examination. TRCP 204.1(c); ***Coates v. Whittington***, 758 S.W.2d 749, 753 (Tex.1988). "Good cause" requires a showing of the following components:

(a) The examination is relevant to the genuine issues. ***Coates***, 758 S.W.2d at 753. The movant must show that the examination will produce or is likely to lead to evidence relevant to the case. *Id.*; *see, e.g.*, ***In re Caballero***, 36 S.W.3d 143, 145 (Tex.App.—Corpus Christi 2000, orig. proceeding) (mandamus to compel physical examination denied because Ds were unable to articulate why examination would shed any light on P's condition before hysterectomy).

(b) There is a reasonable connection between the condition in controversy and the examination sought. ***Coates***, 758 S.W.2d at 753.

(c) It is not possible to obtain the information sought through some other, less-intrusive, means. *Id.*; *e.g.*, ***Caballero***, 36 S.W.3d at 145 (mandamus denied because Ds did not show information was not available through less intrusive means).

(2) In controversy. The movant may show that the mental or physical condition (including the blood group) of a party, or of a person in the custody, conservatorship, or under the legal control of a party, is in controversy. TRCP 204.1(c)(1); ***In re Transwestern Publ'g Relators Co.***, 96 S.W.3d 501, 504-05 (Tex.App.—Fort Worth 2002, orig. proceeding); *see* ***Coates***, 758 S.W.2d at 750-51.

(a) Objecting party put issue in controversy by pleading. The condition may be in controversy if the party objecting to the examination put it in issue by pleading the condition in support of or in defense of its position. *See, e.g.*, ***Laub v. Millard***, 925 S.W.2d 363, 364-65 (Tex.App.—Houston [1st Dist.] 1996, orig. proceeding) (suit to set aside gifts, P pleaded statute of limitations was tolled because she was incompetent); ***Crouch v. Gleason***, 875 S.W.2d 738, 740 (Tex.App.—Amarillo 1994, orig. proceeding) (in contract dispute, P alleged D exploited his mental weakness); ***Beamon v. O'Neill***, 865 S.W.2d 583, 586 (Tex.App.—Houston [14th Dist.] 1993, orig. proceeding) (in personal injury suit, P put physical condition in controversy); ***Exxon Corp. v. Starr***, 790 S.W.2d 883, 887 (Tex.App.—Tyler 1990, orig. proceeding) (P claimed severe mental injury & designated psychological experts). A party's mental condition is not "in controversy" just because the party makes a routine request for damages for mental anguish or emotional distress. ***Coates***, 758 S.W.2d at 752; *see* ***In re Doe***, 22 S.W.3d 601, 607-08 (Tex.App.—Austin 2000, orig. proceeding) (court abused discretion in ordering mental examination in PI suit alleging sexual assault). A party's state of mind is not equivalent to a mental condition. ***Amis v. Ashworth***, 802 S.W.2d 374, 378 (Tex.App.—Tyler 1990, orig. proceeding) (mental health professional not permitted to examine party based on pleadings of self-defense).

(b) Movant put issue in controversy by pleading. The condition may be in controversy if the movant put it in controversy by pleading the condition in support of or in defense of its position. *See* ***Coates***,

758 S.W.2d at 752 (D's allegations of contributory negligence did not justify examination of P); ***Spear v. Gayle***, 857 S.W.2d 122, 125 (Tex.App.—Houston [1st Dist.] 1993, orig. proceeding) (P's allegations that D was negligent in failing to seek help to cure psycho-sexual disorder did not put D's mental health in controversy).

(c) Proof of "in controversy." If the parties' pleadings did not put a party's mental or physical condition in controversy, the movant must provide evidence to show it is in controversy. *E.g.*, ***Walsh v. Ferguson***, 712 S.W.2d 885, 887 (Tex.App.—Austin 1986, orig. proceeding) (examination not permitted in divorce because husband did not assert his mental or physical condition in support or in defense of his position, and wife did not offer any proof at hearing).

(3) Designation of psychologist as expert or disclosure of psychologist's records. The movant may show that the other party identified a psychologist as a testifying expert or disclosed a psychologist's records for possible use at trial. TRCP 204.1(c)(2). This provision does not apply in cases under Family Code Title 2 or 5. TRCP 204.1(c)(2). See §5.4.1(2), below.

2. Doctor. The motion should suggest a physician or psychologist to conduct the examination. *See* TRCP 204.1(d) (order must identify person to perform examination).

3. Time to serve motion for examination. A motion requesting a physical or mental examination may be served any time after suit is filed. TRCP 190.2(c)(1), 190.3(b). The deadline to serve the motion is 30 days before the end of the discovery period. TRCP 204.1(a). See "Discovery Periods," ch. 6-A, §6, p. 317. When served by mail or fax, the motion should be served up to 34 days before the end of the discovery period. See "Deadline to Respond to Discovery," ch. 6-A, §13, p. 323. If the trial date is reset, it extends the discovery deadline for a medical examination. See "When trial reset," ch. 6-A, §16.4.3, p. 327.

4. Notice. The party seeking the examination must give notice to all parties and to the person to be examined. TRCP 204.1(b).

5. Hearing request. The party seeking discovery must ask for and secure a hearing on the motion. TRCP 204.1 (requires motion, notice, showing of good cause, and order). If there is no hearing, the request is waived. *See* ***Von Behren v. Von Behren***, 800 S.W.2d 919, 924 (Tex.App.—San Antonio 1990, writ denied) (party seeking examination did not present motion).

§5.2 Hearing. The court must conduct a hearing on a motion made under TRCP 204. At the hearing, the movant must present evidence. ***Walsh***, 712 S.W.2d at 887. If the court grants the motion without receiving evidence at the hearing, the appellate court will find the trial court abused its discretion and will reverse. *See id.*

§5.3 Order. The order must (1) be in writing; (2) identify the person to be examined; (3) specify the time, place, manner, conditions, and scope of the examination; and (4) identify the person or persons to make the examination. TRCP 204.1(d).

§5.4 Examination.

1. Medical professional.

(1) In most cases. A qualified physician may conduct a mental or physical examination. TRCP 204.1(a)(1). A psychologist may conduct a mental examination if the party responding to the motion identified a psychologist as a testifying expert or disclosed a psychologist's records for possible use at trial. TRCP 204.1(c)(2). A vocational rehabilitation specialist is not a physician or a psychologist and cannot conduct an examination. *See* TRCP 204.5; ***Moore v. Wood***, 809 S.W.2d 621, 624 (Tex.App.—Houston [1st Dist.] 1991, orig. proceeding) (construing former TRCP 167a(a)). *But see* TRCP 191, cmt. 1 (trial court may order, or parties may agree to, discovery methods other than those prescribed in these rules).

(2) **In Family Code matters.** In cases arising under Title 2 or 5 of the Family Code, TRCP 204.4 provides that the court on motion or on its own may appoint the following:

(a) A psychiatrist or psychologist to make mental examinations of any children who are the subject of the suit, or of any other parties. TRCP 204.4(a).

(b) A nonphysician expert qualified in paternity testing to take blood and other bodily fluids to conduct tests in paternity disputes. TRCP 204.4(b); *see also* Fam. Code §§160.501-160.511 (genetic testing).

2. **Attendance of lawyer.** The trial court has the discretion to permit or prohibit a party's lawyer from attending the person's examination. ***Simmons v. Thompson***, 900 S.W.2d 403, 404 (Tex.App.—Texarkana 1995, orig. proceeding) (physical examination). Because the medical professional conducting the examination is chosen by the adverse party, the party's lawyer should probably be permitted to attend. *See id.* (Grant, J., dissenting).

§6. USING MEDICAL RECORDS

§6.1 Medical records. Medical records may be introduced into evidence by a custodian who testifies by affidavit or in person that the records are kept in the course of regularly conducted business activity. TRE 803(6), (7), 902(10). See "Business record by witness," ch. 8-C, §8.4.3(7), p. 542; "Business record by affidavit," ch. 8-C, §8.4.4(1), p. 543.

§6.2 Physical or mental examination. If a physical or mental examination was ordered under TRCP 204, the parties may introduce the testimony of the doctor or medical professional who conducted the examination, either by deposition or as a live witness. *See* TRCP 204.2(b). Mental health information disclosed by a patient during a court-ordered examination is discoverable if the patient was told the communication would not be privileged. See "Communication made without privilege," ch. 6-B, §2.19.4, p. 350.

§6.3 Refusal to make a report. If a physician or psychologist does not make a report required by court order, the court may exclude the testimony if offered at trial. TRCP 204.2(a).

§6.4 Effect of no examination. If no examination is sought under TRCP 204, the party whose condition is in controversy cannot comment to the fact-finder that she was willing to submit to an examination or that the other party did not seek an examination. TRCP 204.3. The primary purpose of TRCP 204.3 is to ensure that the defendant is not penalized for not seeking a physical examination. ***Parkway Hosp. v. Lee***, 946 S.W.2d 580, 585 (Tex.App.—Houston [14th Dist.] 1997, writ denied) (interpreting former TRCP 167a(c)).

§7. REVIEW

See "Review of Discovery Orders," ch. 6-A, §24, p. 340. For the rules and forms for prosecuting or responding to an appeal or original proceeding, see ***O'Connor's Texas Civil Appeals*** (2002-03).

J. ENTRY ON LAND

§1. GENERAL

§1.1 Rules. TRCP 196.7.

§1.2 Purpose. A request or motion for entry on land allows a party to gain entry to land to inspect, measure, survey, photograph, test, and sample the property or any designated object or operation on the property. TRCP 196.7(a).

§1.3 Forms. See ***O'Connor's Texas Civil Forms***, FORMS 6J.

§1.4 Other references. Griesel, *The "New" Texas Discovery Rules: Three Years Later*, Advanced Evidence & Discovery Course, State Bar of Texas, ch. 2, §X, p. 22 (2002).

§2. SCOPE

The scope of discovery for entry on land is governed by TRCP 196.7. The rules of discovery do not entitle a party to gain entry to another's property to reenact an event made the basis of the suit. ***Amis v. Ashworth***, 802 S.W.2d 374, 377 (Tex.App.—Tyler 1990, orig. proceeding). See "Scope of Discovery," ch. 6-B, p. 341.

§3. REQUEST TO ENTER LAND OF A PARTY

A party may gain entry on the land of another party by serving a request on all parties. TRCP 196.7(a)(1). A party is not entitled to trespass on another party's property to conduct an investigation or inspection without first serving a request under TRCP 196.7(a). ***Schenck v. Ebby Halliday Real Estate***, 803 S.W.2d 361, 372 (Tex.App.—Fort Worth 1990, no writ).

§3.1 The request. To gain entry on land of another party, the party must serve a request, which should include the following: (1) the identification of the land or other property in the possession or control of the party; (2) the particulars about the inspection—the time, place, manner, condition, and scope of the inspection; (3) a specific description of the desired means, manner, and procedure for testing or sampling (*i.e.*, to inspect, measure, survey, photograph, test, or sample property); and (4) the identity of the person or persons who are to conduct the inspection, testing, or sampling. TRCP 196.7(a), (b). The test cannot materially alter or destroy the thing to be examined. TRCP 196.5; ***G.M. Corp. v. Tanner***, 892 S.W.2d 862, 863-64 (Tex.1995).

§3.2 Time to serve request for entry. A request for entry on land may be served any time after suit is filed. TRCP 190.2(c)(1), 190.3(b). The deadline to serve the request is 30 days before the end of the discovery period. TRCP 196.7(a). See "Discovery Periods," ch. 6-A, §6, p. 317. When served by mail or fax, the request should be served up to 34 days before the end of the discovery period. TRCP 196.7(a). See "Deadline to Respond to Discovery," ch. 6-A, §13, p. 323.

§3.3 Response.

1. Time to respond. Generally, a party has 30 days from the date of service of a request to enter land to respond to the request, depending on the type of service. TRCP 196.7(c)(1). When a request is served on a defendant before the defendant's answer is due, the defendant has 50 days after service of the request to respond. TRCP 196.7(c)(1). See "Deadline to Respond to Discovery," ch. 6-A, §13, p. 323. To extend the time, see "Extending Time to Respond to Discovery," ch. 6-A, §14, p. 324.

2. Contents of response. In response to a request for entry on land, a party must assert its objections and claims of privilege and then state one of the following: (1) entry will be permitted as requested; (2) entry will be permitted at a different time or place, as specified in the response; or (3) entry will not be permitted. TRCP 196.7(c)(2). If entry will not be permitted, the party must state its reasons in the response. TRCP 196.7(c)(2)(C).

§4. MOTION TO ENTER LAND OF A NONPARTY

A party may gain entry on the land of a nonparty by filing a motion, requesting a hearing, and obtaining an order. TRCP 196.7(a)(2), (b).

§4.1 Motion. To gain entry on land of a nonparty, the party must file a motion. The motion should include the following: (1) good cause; (2) the relevance of entry to the lawsuit; (3) the scope of the inspection; (4) the desired means, manner, and procedure for testing or sampling; (5) who will conduct the inspection, testing, or sampling; and (6) a request for a hearing. TRCP 196.7(a)(2), (b), (d). See ***O'Connor's*** FORM 6J:01.

§4.2 Notice & hearing. The party seeking entry on land of a nonparty must give notice to the nonparty and all the parties and request a hearing. TRCP 196.7(a)(2).

§4.3 Response. The nonparty has the following options.

1. Comply. The nonparty may inform the party requesting entry that it has no objection to the motion.

2. Object. The nonparty may inform the party requesting entry that it objects to the motion requesting entry. Once the requesting party learns the nonparty will not permit entry, the party must request a hearing.

3. Move for protective order. The nonparty may file a motion for protective order under TRCP 192.6 to protect itself from undue burden, unnecessary expense, harassment, annoyance, or invasion of personal, constitutional, or property rights. See "Motion for Protective Order," ch. 6-A, §19, p. 334.

§4.4 Hearing. The court cannot sign an order requiring inspection of the property of a nonparty without a hearing. TRCP 196.7(a)(2). At the hearing, the parties and the nonparty may assert objections. *See* TRCP 176.6(d).

§4.5 Order. The order for entry on a nonparty's property should include the following: (1) identification of the property and its owner; (2) good cause; (3) statement that the land, property, or object on it is relevant to the subject matter of the action; (4) the time, place, manner, conditions and scope of the inspection; (5) a description of any desired means, manner, and procedure for testing or sampling; and (6) a list of the persons performing the inspection, testing, or sampling. TRCP 196.7(b), (d). See ***O'Connor's*** FORM 6J:02.

§5. USING EVIDENCE AT TRIAL

To introduce the inspection, measurement, survey, photograph, results of a test, or samples of the land, the party offering the evidence must prove that it is admissible, lay the proper predicate for its admission, offer it into evidence, and get the court to rule on its admissibility. *See* TRE 104, 105, 402. Just because information was gained in response to a request or motion for entry on land does not mean it is admissible.

NOTE

If a party attempts to introduce evidence about property gained by trespass, the court should exclude it. ***Schenck,*** *803 S.W.2d at 372-73 (testimony of an appraiser);* ***Day & Zimmermann, Inc. v. Strickland,*** *483 S.W.2d 541, 546-47 (Tex.App.—Texarkana 1972, writ ref'd n.r.e.) (testimony of an architect).*

§6. REVIEW

See "Review of Discovery Orders," ch. 6-A, §24, p. 340. For the rules and forms for prosecuting or responding to an appeal or original proceeding, see ***O'Connor's Texas Civil Appeals*** (2002-03).

COMMENTARIES

CHAPTER 7. DISPOSITION WITHOUT TRIAL

TABLE OF CONTENTS

COMMENTARIES

CHAPTER 7. DISPOSITION WITHOUT TRIAL

TABLE OF CONTENTS

A. DEFAULT JUDGMENT

§1. GENERAL

§1.1 Rules. TRCP 239-241, 243. See TRAP 30 (restricted appeals).

§1.2 Purpose. A default judgment permits the trial court to render judgment for the plaintiff on its petition without a trial. Only a plaintiff is entitled to a default judgment; a default judgment cannot be rendered for a defendant on the merits of its answer. ***Freeman v. Freeman***, 327 S.W.2d 428, 431 (Tex.1959), *overruled on other grounds*, ***Mapco, Inc. v. Forrest***, 795 S.W.2d 700 (Tex.1990); ***State v. Herrera***, 25 S.W.3d 326, 327 (Tex.App.—Austin 2000, no pet.). When a plaintiff does not appear at trial, the proper remedy is dismissal of the suit, not default judgment. ***Smock v. Fischel***, 207 S.W.2d 891, 892 (Tex.1948); ***Slaughter v. Clement***, 64 S.W.3d 448, 450 (Tex.App.—El Paso 2001, no pet.). See "Involuntary Dismissal," ch. 7-F, p. 499.

§1.3 Forms & timetables. ***O'Connor's Texas Civil Forms***, FORMS 7A; Timetables, this book, Pretrial Motions, p. 998, Default Judgment, p. 1007.

§1.4 Other references. Miller, *Misnomer: Default Judgments & Strict Compliance with Service of Process Rules*, 46 Baylor L.Rev. 633 (1994).

§2. TYPES OF DEFAULT JUDGMENTS

Default judgments can be conveniently divided into two types—those rendered before the defendant files an answer to the lawsuit (no-answer default), and those rendered after the defendant files an answer (post-answer default). No-answer defaults are covered in §3, below, and post-answer defaults are covered in §4, p. 450.

7-1. COMPARISON OF DEFAULT JUDGMENTS

	NO-ANSWER DEFAULT	POST-ANSWER DEFAULT
1	Court can grant default judgment on the pleadings, except for unliquidated damages.	Court cannot grant default judgment on the pleadings.
2	Default constitutes admission by D of allegations in P's pleadings, except for unliquidated damages.	Default does not constitute admission by D of P's claims or abandonment of D's defenses.
3	P must prove unliquidated damages and causal nexus.	P must prove all elements of cause of action and damages, as in a trial on the merits.
4	D does not waive pleading defects.	D waives pleading defects unless D filed special exceptions.
5	D has no right to notice of hearing unless D files answer before final judgment rendered.	D has right to notice of hearing or trial.
6	D has no right to participate, unless D files answer or makes appearance before hearing on unliquidated damages.	D has right to participate if D appears.
7	If D files answer requesting jury after default judgment rendered but before hearing on damages, D is entitled to jury trial on damages alone; if D does not appear, D waives right to jury.	If jury trial was requested before default, D has right to jury if D appears; if D does not appear, D waives right to jury.
8	P must file certificate of last known address & soldiers' & sailors' affidavit.	P is not required to file certificate of last known address or soldiers' & sailors' affidavit.
9	Sufficiency of service of process on D is an issue; default judgment will be set aside if service defective.	Sufficiency of service is not an issue because D has answered.

§3. THE NO-ANSWER DEFAULT

Before taking a default judgment, the plaintiff should check the petition, the citation, the service, and the return. If they are inadequate to support a default judgment, they can be amended. If they are amended, the plaintiff may need to re-serve the defendant before taking a default. After discovering a default judgment, the defendant should check the plaintiff's petition, the citation, the service, and the return for sufficiency. If they are inadequate to support a default judgment, they can be challenged.

§3.1 Effect of defendant's failure to answer. The court may render a default judgment on the pleadings against a defendant that has not filed an answer. A defendant who defaults admits all allegations of facts in the plaintiff's petition except unliquidated damages. ***Jackson v. Biotectronics, Inc.***, 937 S.W.2d 38, 41 (Tex.App.—Houston [14th Dist.] 1996, no writ); ***Norton v. Martinez***, 935 S.W.2d 898, 901 (Tex.App.—San Antonio 1996, no writ). After a no-answer default, the only claim the plaintiff is required to prove is its claim for unliquidated damages. TRCP 243; *see* ***Zuyus v. No'Mis Comm.***, 930 S.W.2d 743, 747 (Tex.App.—Corpus Christi 1996, no writ); ***Herbert v. Greater Gulf Coast Enters.***, 915 S.W.2d 866, 872 (Tex.App.—Houston [1st Dist.] 1995, no writ).

§3.2 Sufficiency of plaintiff's petition. The plaintiff's petition will support a default judgment if the petition (1) attempts to state a cause of action within the jurisdiction of the court, (2) gives fair notice to the defendant of the claim asserted, and (3) does not affirmatively disclose the invalidity of the claim on its face. ***Paramount Pipe & Sup. Co. v. Muhr***, 749 S.W.2d 491, 494 (Tex.1988); ***Jackson***, 937 S.W.2d at 42-43.

1. Amending the petition.

(1) Adding claims or damages – service required. When, after service of the original petition, the plaintiff amends to ask for a more onerous judgment by adding claims or increasing damages, the plaintiff must serve the defendant with a new citation and the amended petition before taking a default judgment. *See* ***Weaver v. Hartford Acc. & Indem. Co.***, 570 S.W.2d 367, 370 (Tex.1978); *see, e.g.*, ***Atwood v. B & R Sup. & Equip. Co.***, 52 S.W.3d 265, 268 (Tex.App.—Corpus Christi 2001, no pet.) (amended petition for suit on sworn account was more onerous than original suit for breach of contract); ***Caprock Constr. Co. v. Guaranteed Floorcovering, Inc.***, 950 S.W.2d 203, 205 (Tex.App.—Dallas 1997, no writ) (amended petition added another P, which increased D's liability); ***Harris v. Shoults***, 877 S.W.2d 854, 855 (Tex.App.—Fort Worth 1994, no writ) (amended petition deleted damages of $5,443 & stated damages in an unspecified amount, which permitted P to secure default judgment for $40,443). *Contra* ***In re R.D.C.***, 912 S.W.2d 854, 855 (Tex.App.—Eastland 1995, no writ) (service of amended petition under TRCP 21 & 21a, without a new citation, was sufficient, even though it asked for more onerous judgment).

(2) No additional claims or damages – no service required. If the amended petition does not add claims or increase damages, it does not need to be re-served. ***Palomin v. Zarsky Lumber Co.***, 26 S.W.3d 690, 694 (Tex.App.—Corpus Christi 2000, pet. denied) (amended petition made minor change in D's name); ***Halligan v. First Heights, F.S.A.***, 850 S.W.2d 801, 802-03 (Tex.App.—Houston [14th Dist.] 1993, no writ) (amended petition in intervention did not assert new claims or seek additional damages). When the plaintiff amends its petition to specify the amount of damages and deletes the TRCP 47(b) allegation (damages are within the jurisdictional limits of the court), the amended petition does not increase damages; thus, the plaintiff does not need to serve the defendant with a new citation and the amended petition. ***Henry S. Miller Co. v. Hamilton***, 813 S.W.2d 631, 636 (Tex. App.—Houston [1st Dist.] 1991, no writ).

2. Variance between pleadings & judgment. A default judgment must be based on the pleadings. The judgment, therefore, cannot rely on causes of action that are not adequately pleaded or award damages in excess of the damages specifically pleaded. ***Capitol Brick, Inc. v. Fleming Mfg. Co.***, 722 S.W.2d 399, 401 (Tex. 1986); ***Simon v. BancTexas Quorum***, 754 S.W.2d 283, 286 (Tex.App.—Dallas 1988, writ denied). There is no variance between the pleadings and the judgment when the court awards damages based on a TRCP 47(b) allegation (damages are within the jurisdictional limits of the court). ***Continental Sav. Ass'n v. Gutheinz***, 718 S.W.2d 377, 383 (Tex.App.—Amarillo 1986, writ ref'd n.r.e.).

§3.3 Sufficiency of the citation. The citation must strictly comply with TRCP 99. See "Requirements for the Citation," ch. 2-H, §2, p. 118.

§3.4 Sufficiency of the service. The record must show strict compliance with the type of service used. See "Serving the Defendant with Suit," ch. 2-H, p. 118. A default judgment cannot withstand a direct attack by a defendant who was not served in strict compliance with the appropriate service rules. ***Wood v. Brown***, 819 S.W.2d 799, 800 (Tex.1991); *see* ***Uvalde Country Club v. Martin Linen Sup. Co.***, 690 S.W.2d 884, 885 (Tex.1985). Actual notice of suit is not a substitute for proper service. ***Wilson v. Dunn***, 800 S.W.2d 833, 836 (Tex.1990). If a default judgment is not based on proper service, it is void. ***Westcliffe, Inc. v. Bear Creek Constr.***, 105 S.W.3d 286, 290 (Tex.App.—Dallas 2003, no pet.); ***Ackerly v. Ackerly***, 13 S.W.3d 454, 458 (Tex.App.—Corpus Christi 2000, no pet.). A default judgment is void unless the defendant was served with process in strict compliance with the law, the defendant accepted or waived service, or the defendant made an appearance. TRCP 124; ***Min v. Avila***, 991 S.W.2d 495, 500 (Tex.App.—Houston [1st Dist.] 1999, no pet.).

PRACTICE TIP

Before taking a no-answer default judgment against a defendant who is covered by insurance, the plaintiff should encourage the defendant to notify its carrier according to the notice-of-suit provision in the policy. See ***Liberty Mut. Ins. Co. v. Cruz****, 883 S.W.2d 164, 165-66 (Tex. 1993). Compliance with the notice provision is a condition precedent to the carrier's liability.* ***Harwell v. State Farm Mut. Auto. Ins. Co.****, 896 S.W.2d 170, 173-74 (Tex.1995). If the carrier is not notified about the suit until after a judgment becomes final and nonappealable, the carrier is prejudiced as a matter of law. Id. at 174.*

---

§3.5 Sufficiency of the return. There is a long list of requirements for the return. See "Proof of Service – the Return," ch. 2-H, §9, p. 127.

§3.6 Amending citation & return. The court can permit an amendment to the citation and the return. See "Amending citation & return," ch. 2-H, §10.2, p. 130.

§3.7 Sufficiency of defendant's answer. An answer, even if defective, places the merits of the plaintiff's case at issue and will prevent a default judgment if it is filed before the rendition (announcement) of judgment. When an answer is defective, the plaintiff's remedy is to file special exceptions. See "Special Exceptions—Challenging the Pleadings," ch. 3-G, p. 187.

1. Filing that constituted an answer. In the following cases, the court found the defendant's filing sufficient to constitute an answer: • Pauper's affidavit, instead of a written answer. ***Hughes v. Habitat Apts.***, 860 S.W.2d 872, 873 (Tex.1993). • Answer that was not signed by either the party or the lawyer. ***Frank v. Corbett***, 682 S.W.2d 587, 588 (Tex.App.—Waco 1984, no writ). • Answer for corporation that was signed by a nonlawyer. ***Custom-Crete, Inc. v. K-Bar Servs.***, 82 S.W.3d 655, 658 (Tex.App.—San Antonio 2002, no pet.); ***Handy Andy, Inc. v. Ruiz***, 900 S.W.2d 739, 741-42 (Tex.App.—Corpus Christi 1994, writ denied). • Letter from a pro se defendant to the district clerk in which the defendant confirmed that he received the citation and provided his current address. ***Smith v. Lippmann***, 826 S.W.2d 137, 138 (Tex.1992); *see also* ***Terehkov v. Cruz***, 648 S.W.2d 441, 443 (Tex.App.—San Antonio 1983, no writ) (letter to clerk returning citation, denying the accident happened). • Letter to the court from the secretary-treasurer of the corporation that contained the defendant's address, admitted the debt, and made an arguable counterclaim. ***Santex Roofing & Sheet Metal v. Venture Steel***, 737 S.W.2d 55, 57 (Tex.App.—San Antonio 1987, no writ). • Plea in abatement. ***Alcala v. Williams***, 908 S.W.2d 54, 56 (Tex.App.—San Antonio 1995, no writ); ***Schulz v. Schulz***, 726 S.W.2d 256, 258 (Tex.App.—Austin 1987, no writ). • Motion to dismiss suggesting that the plaintiff sued the wrong entity. ***LBL Oil Co. v. International Power Servs.***, 777 S.W.2d 390, 390-91 (Tex.1989).

2. Filing that did not constitute an answer. In the following cases, the court did not find the defendant's filing sufficient to constitute an answer: • Letter from a pro se defendant to the plaintiff's attorney that did not have a case heading or certificate of service. ***Cotton v. Cotton***, 57 S.W.3d 506, 511-12 (Tex.App.—Waco 2001, no pet.). • A motion for new trial. ***First State Bldg. & Loan Ass'n v. B.L. Nelson & Assocs.***, 735 S.W.2d 287, 289 (Tex.App.—Dallas 1987, no writ); ***Gonzalez v. Regalado***, 542 S.W.2d 689, 691 (Tex.App.—Waco 1976, writ ref'd n.r.e.). • The defendant's motion to transfer venue. ***Duplantis v. Noble Toyota***, 720 S.W.2d 863, 866 (Tex.App.—Beaumont 1986, no writ).

§3.8 Moving for no-answer default judgment.

1. Documents to file.

(1) Motion for default judgment. Most default judgments are granted upon motion. However, it is not necessary to file a motion for default judgment. The plaintiff is entitled to have the judge or clerk call the cause for default judgment on appearance day. TRCP 238, 239; ***Maldonado v. Puente***, 694 S.W.2d 86, 90 (Tex. App.—San Antonio 1985, no writ); *see* ***Texas Prop. & Cas. Ins. Guar. Ass'n v. Johnson***, 45 S.W.3d 328, 332, n.2 (Tex.App.—Austin 1999, pet. denied). When the case is called, as long as the citation has been on file with the clerk for ten days and the defendant has not filed an answer, the court can grant a default judgment. TRCP 107, 238, 239. See ***O'Connor's*** FORM 7A:01.

(2) Proposed default judgment. The plaintiff should file a proposed default judgment, even if the plaintiff does not file a motion for default. If the plaintiff's claim is for unliquidated damages, the plaintiff can file an order granting the default on liability and setting the date for a hearing to determine the amount of unliquidated damages. If the plaintiff is prepared to prove the unliquidated damage claim at the same time the court renders the judgment, the court may sign a final default judgment. *See* ***Long v. McDermott***, 813 S.W.2d 622, 624 (Tex.App.—Houston [1st Dist.] 1991, no writ). For an order, see ***O'Connor's*** FORM 7A:05; for a judgment, see ***O'Connor's*** FORM 9C:02.

(3) Affidavits to prove damages. The court can award unliquidated damages based on affidavit testimony. See "Unliquidated damages," §3.12.2(2), p. 449. If the plaintiff relies solely on affidavit evidence, the affidavit must establish a causal nexus. See "Establish causal nexus," §3.12.2(2)(b), p. 449; ***O'Connor's*** FORM 7A:04.

(4) Certificate of last known address. At the time or immediately before a default judgment is rendered, the plaintiff must certify to the clerk in writing the last known mailing address of the defendant. TRCP 239a; ***Xu v. Davis***, 884 S.W.2d 916, 917 (Tex.App.—Waco 1994, orig. proceeding). The certificate must be filed in the papers of the court. TRCP 239a. The clerk must mail written notice to the defaulting party at the address shown in the certificate. *Id.*; ***John v. State***, 826 S.W.2d 138, 139 n.1 (Tex.1992). The notice must contain the style and the number of the case. TRCP 239a. The plaintiff's failure to comply with this requirement does not affect the finality of the judgment. *Id.* Failure to comply with TRCP 239a can be grounds for reversal in a bill of review proceeding setting up lack of notice, but not in a restricted appeal (formerly called appeal by writ of error). ***Jordan v. Jordan***, 36 S.W.3d 259, 264 (Tex.App.—Beaumont 2001, pet. denied). See ***O'Connor's*** FORM 7A:02.

(5) Servicemembers' affidavit. The Servicemembers Civil Relief Act, 50 U.S.C. app. §501 et seq., provides protection from civil litigation to members of the armed services. *See* ***Hawkins v. Hawkins***, 999 S.W.2d 171, 174 (Tex.App.—Austin 1999, no pet.). Before a court can render a default judgment, the plaintiff must file an affidavit setting forth facts that show either (1) the defendant is not in the military, (2) the defendant is in the military, or (3) the plaintiff is unable to determine if the defendant is in the military. 50 U.S.C. app. §521(b)(1). If the defendant is not in the military, the court can render a default judgment. If the defendant is in the military, the court must appoint a lawyer to represent the defendant. *Id.* §521(b)(2). If the court is unable to determine whether the defendant is in the military, the plaintiff may be required to file a bond. *Id.* §521(b)(3). The bond is available to indemnify the defendant for any loss suffered as a result of a judgment against the defendant, if the defendant is later found to be in the military and the judgment is set aside. *Id.* If a default judgment is rendered against a defendant while in the military or within 60 days after discharge, the defendant may, within 90 days after termination of military service, ask the court to vacate it. *Id.* §521(g). See ***O'Connor's*** FORM 7A:03.

(6) Motion for severance. If a plaintiff is taking a default judgment against one defendant in a multiple-defendant case, the plaintiff should consider filing a motion for severance so that the default judgment can become final. ***Castano v. Foremost Cty. Mut. Ins. Co.***, 31 S.W.3d 387, 388 (Tex.App.—San Antonio 2000, no pet.). See "Final judgment," §5.3, p. 452.

(7) No notice to defendant. The plaintiff is not required to give the defendant notice before securing a no-answer default judgment. ***Novosad v. Cunningham***, 38 S.W.3d 767, 772-73 (Tex.App.—Houston [14th Dist.] 2001, no pet.). The defendant received all the notice to which it is entitled when it was served with process. ***Continental Carbon Co. v. Sea-Land Serv.***, 27 S.W.3d 184, 189 (Tex.App.—Dallas 2000, pet. denied). The Texas Lawyer's Creed, which states, "I will not take advantage, by causing any default ... to be rendered, when I know the identity of an opposing counsel, without first inquiring about that counsel's intention to proceed," does not create any additional duty enforceable by the courts. ***Continental Carbon***, 27 S.W.3d at 189.

2. When to move for default.

(1) In most cases. The plaintiff can ask for a default judgment after the defendant's deadline to file an answer has expired and the citation and proof of service have been on file with the clerk at least ten days, excluding the day of filing and the day of the judgment. TRCP 107; ***Union Pac. Corp. v. Legg***, 49 S.W.3d 72, 78 (Tex. App.—Austin 2001, no pet.); ***Onyx TV v. TV Strategy Group***, 990 S.W.2d 427, 429-30 (Tex.App.—Texarkana 1999, no pet.). See "Deadline to Answer," ch. 3-E, §2, p. 171.

(2) After appearance. If a defendant makes an appearance in a case, the appearance gives the court jurisdiction over the defendant. Appearance is the submission by the defendant to the jurisdiction of the court in which it is sued. ***Bass v. Duffey***, 620 S.W.2d 847, 850 (Tex.App.—Houston [14th Dist.] 1981, no writ). An appearance, as contemplated by TRCP 120 and 330(a), is entered by appearing in open court and having the appearance noted on the court's docket. ***Freeman v. Freeman***, 327 S.W.2d 428, 430 (Tex.1959), *overruled on other grounds*, ***Mapco, Inc. v. Forrest***, 795 S.W.2d 700 (Tex.1990). Before taking a default against a defendant who has appeared but not answered, the plaintiff must give the defendant notice, as a matter of due process. ***Coastal Banc SSB v. Helle***, 48 S.W.3d 796, 801 (Tex.App.—Corpus Christi 2001, pet. denied).

(3) After Secretary of State served. If the Secretary of State was served as the defendant's agent, the period for filing the answer runs from the date the Secretary of State was served, not from the date the Secretary of State forwarded the process to the defendant. ***Bonewitz v. Bonewitz***, 726 S.W.2d 227, 229-30 (Tex. App.—Austin 1987, writ ref'd n.r.e.). The Secretary of State is considered the agent of the defendant for service of process, and service on the Secretary is constructive service on the defendant. *Id.* at 230. Before taking a default, the plaintiff must obtain a certificate (referred to as a "***Whitney*** Certificate") from the Secretary of State certifying compliance with the statute that authorizes substituted service—that is, certifying that process was forwarded to the defendant by certified mail, return receipt requested. ***Whitney v. L&L Rlty. Corp.***, 500 S.W.2d 94, 96 (Tex. 1973). The defendant is considered served even if the process is returned to the Secretary of State with a notation that it was refused or unclaimed. See "Proof of service," ch. 2-H, §5.2, p. 123.

(4) After notice to Attorney General. In some suits against the State, the plaintiff must send a notice of intent to take a default to the Attorney General by certified mail, return receipt requested, at least ten days before the entry of the default judgment. CPRC §§30.004(b), 39.001. Before taking a default judgment against the State, any state agency, or any state official or employee, the plaintiff should check the list of persons and entities in CPRC chapter 104 that must be represented by the Attorney General. If the plaintiff does not give the Attorney General notice, the default judgment will be set aside without costs. CPRC §§30.004(d), 39.002. Whether a plaintiff must give the Attorney General ten days' notice before taking a post-answer default judgment against the State has not been decided. *See* ***Director v. Evans***, 889 S.W.2d 266, 267 n.1 (Tex.1994).

(5) After service by publication. If the defendant was served by publication, the court must appoint an attorney ad litem to represent the defendant. TRCP 244. See "MNT After Service by Publication," ch. 10-B, §16, p. 634.

§3.9 The response to the motion for default – the answer. If the defendant gets notice that a motion for no-answer default is pending, it should immediately file an answer. The clerk should note on the answer the date and the exact minute it was filed. If the answer is filed after the deadline to answer but before the trial court announces (renders) a default judgment in open court or signs a judgment, the court cannot render a default judgment. TRCP 239; *e.g.*, ***Davis v. Jefferies***, 764 S.W.2d 559, 560 (Tex.1989) (answer filed 1 day after deadline, but more than 2 hours before default judgment was rendered); ***Dowell Schlumberger, Inc. v. Jackson***, 730 S.W.2d 818, 819-20 (Tex.App.—El Paso 1987, writ ref'd n.r.e.) (answer filed during default hearing but before court announced judgment). If an answer is mailed to the clerk before a default judgment is announced, it is considered filed before the judgment is rendered, even if it is not received until after the judgment is signed. ***Thomas v. Gelber Group***, 905 S.W.2d 786, 788-89 (Tex.App.—Houston [14th Dist.] 1995, no writ); ***Milam v. Miller***, 891 S.W.2d 1, 2 (Tex.App.—Amarillo 1994, writ ref'd). See "By mail," ch. 1-C, §4.1, p. 14.

§3.10 Hearing on no-answer default. When the defendant does not file an answer or make an appearance, the plaintiff is not required to give the defendant notice of the hearing before the court renders the default judgment. ***Long v. McDermott***, 813 S.W.2d 622, 624 (Tex.App.—Houston [1st Dist.] 1991, no writ); ***Olivares v. Cauthorn***, 717 S.W.2d 431, 434 (Tex.App.—San Antonio 1986, writ dism'd).

§3.11 Rendition of default judgment. The court renders a no-answer default judgment either by announcing in open court that it renders judgment or by signing a judgment to that effect. See "Rendition," ch. 9-C, §3.1, p. 596.

§3.12 Hearing on damages. Once the court renders a no-answer default judgment, whether a hearing is necessary for damages depends on the type of damages the plaintiff requested in its petition.

1. Type of damages.

(1) Liquidated damages. "Liquidated damages," as the term is used in TRCP 241, are damages that can be accurately calculated from (1) the factual (as opposed to the conclusory) allegations in the petition and (2) the written instrument attached to the petition. ***Novosad v. Cunningham***, 38 S.W.3d 767, 773 (Tex.App.—Houston [14th Dist.] 2001, no pet.); ***Willacy Cty. Appr. Rev. Bd. v. South Padre Land Co.***, 767 S.W.2d 201, 204 (Tex.App.—Corpus Christi 1989, no writ).

(2) Unliquidated damages. "Unliquidated damages" are damages that cannot be accurately calculated from (1) the factual allegations in the petition and (2) any attached instruments. ***Atwood v. B & R Sup. & Equip. Co.***, 52 S.W.3d 265, 268 (Tex.App.—Corpus Christi 2001, no pet.). Unliquidated damages are disputed or uncertain. ***Fogel v. White***, 745 S.W.2d 444, 446 (Tex.App.—Houston [14th Dist.] 1988, orig. proceeding). When liquidated claims are inadequately described in the plaintiff's petition, or if no written instrument is attached to the petition, the damages are considered unliquidated. *See, e.g.*, ***Atwood***, 52 S.W.3d at 268 (because written instrument was not attached, claim was unliquidated); ***Kelley v. Southwestern Bell Media***, 745 S.W.2d 447, 448-49 (Tex. App.—Houston [1st Dist.] 1988, no writ) (because petition did not allege date of default, claim was unliquidated).

2. Necessity for hearing.

(1) Liquidated damages. When damages are liquidated, it is not necessary to hold a hearing to present evidence of damages. The trial court can assess the damages for a liquidated damage claim that is proved by an instrument in writing. TRCP 241; ***Aavid Thermal Tech. v. Irving ISD***, 68 S.W.3d 707, 711 (Tex.App.—Dallas 2001, no pet.); ***Pentes Design v. Perez***, 840 S.W.2d 75, 79 (Tex.App.—Corpus Christi 1992, writ denied). The written instrument must be attached to the petition. ***Abcon Paving v. Crissup***, 820 S.W.2d 951, 953 (Tex.App.—Fort Worth 1991, no writ).

(2) Unliquidated damages. When damages are unliquidated, the court must receive evidence on damages before the court can render a final default judgment. TRCP 243; ***Holt Atherton Indus. v. Heine***, 835 S.W.2d 80, 83 (Tex.1992); ***Arenivar v. Providian Nat'l Bank***, 23 S.W.3d 496, 498 (Tex.App.—Amarillo 2000, no pet.). TRCP 243 does not prescribe either the manner in which to conduct the hearing or the type of evidence required. ***Arenivar***, 23 S.W.3d at 498. Thus, the court can award unliquidated damages based on affidavits. ***Ingram Indus. v. U.S. Bolt Mfg.***, 121 S.W.3d 31, 37 (Tex.App.—Houston [1st Dist.] 2003, n.p.h.) (award of damages based on affidavit testimony satisfied TRCP 243's hearing requirement without the need for holding evidentiary hearing); *see* ***Texas Commerce Bank v. New***, 3 S.W.3d 515, 517 (Tex.1999) (unobjected-to hearsay evidence in affidavit can support damages).

(a) Ask for court reporter. When the defendant is not present for the no-answer default hearing on damages, and evidence is introduced, the plaintiff should make sure the court reporter transcribes the hearing. If a defendant, through no fault of its own, is unable to procure a record of the evidence introduced, in most cases a new trial will be required. ***Smith v. Smith***, 544 S.W.2d 121, 123 (Tex.1976); ***Alvarado v. Reif***, 783 S.W.2d 303, 304-05 (Tex.App.—Eastland 1989, no writ). Thus, it is in the plaintiff's best interest to make a record.

(b) Establish causal nexus. When damages are unliquidated, the plaintiff must present evidence of the "causal nexus" between the event sued on and the plaintiff's injuries. ***Morgan v. Compugraphic Corp.***, 675 S.W.2d 729, 732 (Tex.1984). By the default, the defendant admits only that it caused the event that led to the suit, not that there is a connection between the event and the damages. *Id.* Thus, the plaintiff must both offer proof of its damages and connect its damages to the defendant's conduct. *Id.* Courts have required plaintiffs to prove a causal nexus in the following types of suits: • Personal injury, *id.*; ***Transport Concepts v. Reeves***, 748 S.W.2d 302, 305 (Tex.App.—Dallas 1988, no writ). • Breach of warranty of title to real estate, ***Gibraltar Sav. Ass'n v. Kilpatrick***, 770 S.W.2d 14, 18 (Tex.App.—Texarkana 1989, writ denied). • Breach of warranty and violation of the DTPA, ***Capitol Brick, Inc. v. Fleming Mfg. Co.***, 722 S.W.2d 399, 402 (Tex.1986).

(c) Prove damages. At the hearing, the plaintiff must present evidence of its damages. For example, in a personal injury case, the plaintiff must present evidence of pain, suffering, lost wages, medical expenses, and the reasonableness and necessity of the medical expenses. ***Transport Concepts***, 748 S.W.2d at 305. Hearsay evidence that is not objected to is sufficient to support an award for damages. *See* TRE 802.

PRACTICE TIP

When the trial court awards unliquidated damages after a default, the defendant should ask for findings of fact and conclusions of law. ***IKB Indus. v. Pro-Line Corp.****, 938 S.W.2d 440, 443 (Tex.1997).*

(d) Prove attorney fees.

[1] Evidence. A demand for reasonable attorney fees is a claim for unliquidated damages, and the award must be based on evidence. ***Higgins v. Smith***, 722 S.W.2d 825, 827-28 (Tex.App.—Houston [14th Dist.] 1987, no writ); ***Nettles v. Del Lingco***, 638 S.W.2d 633, 636 (Tex.App.—El Paso 1982, no writ). Attorney fees can be proved by affidavit. See "Proof of attorney fees," ch. 1-H, §10.5, p. 48. The court should not consider the unsworn testimony of the plaintiff's attorney to support attorney fees. ***Bloom v. Bloom***, 767 S.W.2d 463, 471 (Tex. App.—San Antonio 1989, writ denied). However, if the court awards attorney fees based on unsworn testimony at a hearing where the defendant was present but did not object, the defendant waives that issue on appeal. See "Lawyer's appearance before court," ch. 1-H, §5.2, p. 40.

[2] No judicial notice. Attorney fees in a default judgment case cannot be established by the judicial notice provision in CPRC §38.004. That provision permits judicial notice of attorney fees only when a case is tried on the merits. See "Judicial notice," ch. 1-H, §10.3.2, p. 46.

3. The defendant's rights in a no-answer default.

(1) Right to notice. Ordinarily, a defendant against whom a no-answer default judgment was rendered does not have a right to notice of a hearing on unliquidated damages. ***Long v. McDermott***, 813 S.W.2d 622, 624 (Tex.App.—Houston [1st Dist.] 1991, no writ). But once a defendant makes an appearance or files an answer, the defendant is entitled to notice of all later hearings. ***Bradford v. Bradford***, 971 S.W.2d 595, 597 (Tex.App.—Dallas 1998, no pet.).

(2) Right to jury. If the defendant filed an answer requesting a jury after the court rendered a default judgment on liability but before the hearing on damages, the defendant is entitled to a jury trial on damages. TRCP 241, 243. TRCP 243 calls this limited jury trial on damages a "writ of inquiry." ***Maywald Trailer Co. v. Perry***, 238 S.W.2d 826, 828 (Tex.App.—Galveston 1951, writ ref'd n.r.e.).

(3) Right to participate. If the defendant appears at the hearing on damages, it has the right to cross-examine witnesses and to present evidence on unliquidated damages only. ***Northeast Wholesale Lumber v. Leader Lumber***, 785 S.W.2d 402, 407 (Tex.App.—Dallas 1989, no writ); ***Bass v. Duffey***, 620 S.W.2d 847, 849-50 (Tex.App.—Houston [14th Dist.] 1981, no writ); *see* ***Maywald Trailer***, 238 S.W.2d at 828. The defendant may introduce evidence to mitigate the plaintiff's damages and evidence to negate the causal nexus. ***Morgan v. Compugraphic Corp.***, 675 S.W.2d 729, 732 (Tex.1984) (causation); ***Maywald Trailer***, 238 S.W.2d at 828 (damages). The defendant cannot offer evidence or call witnesses to contravene its liability. *See* ***Fiduciary Mtg. Co. v. City Nat'l Bank***, 762 S.W.2d 196, 200-02 (Tex.App.—Dallas 1988, writ denied) (default as sanction). The defendant cannot introduce evidence to support its defenses. *See, e.g.*, ***Downer v. Aquamarine Operators***, 701 S.W.2d 238, 243 (Tex.1985) (once its answer was struck, D was not entitled to introduce evidence of contributory negligence).

§3.13 Waiver. The plaintiff waives the right to default if it proceeds to trial as though the defendant had filed an answer. ***Artripe v. Hughes***, 857 S.W.2d 82, 87 (Tex.App.—Corpus Christi 1993, writ denied). Once the parties announce ready for trial and the jury has been selected, it is too late to ask for a default judgment. ***Dodson v. Citizens State Bank***, 701 S.W.2d 89, 94 (Tex.App.—Amarillo 1986, writ ref'd n.r.e.).

§4. THE POST-ANSWER DEFAULT

§4.1 Effect of defendant's answer. The court cannot render a default judgment on the pleadings against a defendant that filed an answer. When a defendant files an answer but does not appear at trial, the defendant neither abandons its answer nor confesses by implication to any issues joined by its answer. ***Frymire Eng'g Co. v. Grantham***, 524 S.W.2d 680, 681 (Tex.1975); ***Flores v. Brimex Ltd.***, 5 S.W.3d 816, 820 (Tex.App.—San Antonio 1999, no pet.).

§4.2 Sufficiency of plaintiff's pleadings. A post-answer default, like a no-answer default, must be supported by the plaintiff's petition. *See* ***Stoner v. Thompson***, 578 S.W.2d 679, 684 (Tex.1979). See "Sufficiency of plaintiff's petition," §3.2, p. 444.

§4.3 Notice of the trial or dispositive hearing. A post-answer default is valid only if the defendant received notice of the setting for trial or other dispositive hearing at which the default was rendered. ***$429.30 v. State***, 896 S.W.2d 363, 366 (Tex.App.—Houston [1st Dist.] 1995, no writ); ***Matsushita Elec. Corp. v. McAllen Copy Data***, 815 S.W.2d 850, 853 (Tex.App.—Corpus Christi 1991, writ denied); *see* TRCP 21a, 245. A court cannot render a default judgment if the defendant does not appear at just any type of hearing; only if the hearing is a dispositive hearing can the court render default for failure to appear. ***Masterson v. Cox***, 886 S.W.2d 436, 438 (Tex. App.—Houston [1st Dist.] 1994, no writ). Before rendering a default judgment against a defendant that answered but did not appear for trial or a dispositive hearing, the trial court should determine if the defendant received notice. *See, e.g.*, ***Cliff v. Huggins***, 724 S.W.2d 778, 779 (Tex.1987) (reversed; D did not receive notice of trial setting); ***Murphree v. Ziegelmair***, 937 S.W.2d 493, 495 (Tex.App.—Houston [1st Dist.] 1995, no writ) (reversed; Ds did not have notice that failure to attend pretrial conference could result in immediate disposition).

1. Due process. A defendant that answered has a constitutional right to notice of all hearings. ***LBL Oil Co. v. International Power Servs.***, 777 S.W.2d 390, 390-91 (Tex.1989); ***Smith v. Holmes***, 53 S.W.3d 815, 817 (Tex.App.—Austin 2001, no pet.). The right of a party to be heard in a contested case is fundamental. ***LBL Oil***, 777 S.W.2d at 390-91; ***Bloom v. Bloom***, 767 S.W.2d 463, 472 (Tex.App.—San Antonio 1989, writ denied).

2. TRCP 245. A defendant that answered must have received 45 days' notice of the setting that results in a post-answer default judgment. *See* TRCP 245; ***Burress v. Richardson***, 97 S.W.3d 806, 807 (Tex.App.—Dallas 2003, no pet.); ***Custom-Crete, Inc. v. K-Bar Servs.***, 82 S.W.3d 655, 659 (Tex.App.—San Antonio 2002, no pet.). Because the notice is mandatory and involves constitutional rights, a post-answer default must be set aside when the court's notice is sent but is returned as undeliverable. ***Burress***, 97 S.W.3d at 807 (appeal, no motion for new trial); ***Transoceanic Shipping Co. v. General Universal Sys.***, 961 S.W.2d 418, 419-20 (Tex.App.—Houston [1st Dist.] 1997, no writ) (appeal by writ of error). *Contra* ***Withrow v. Schou***, 13 S.W.3d 37, 41-42 (Tex.App.—Houston [14th Dist.] 1999, pet. denied) (disagreeing with ***Transoceanic***; trial court is not required to find D's lawyer & send another notice of trial setting after first notice was returned as undeliverable).

§4.4 The motion. A motion for post-answer default is not always necessary. Generally, when a defendant does not appear for trial or a dispositive hearing, the court decides to go forward with a post-answer default hearing on its own initiative. For the form for a motion for post-answer default, see ***O'Connor's*** FORM 7A:06.

§4.5 The trial. If the trial court grants a post-answer default against the defendant for not appearing at a scheduled trial, the court can conduct the trial without the defendant, although the plaintiff must still put on evidence and prove its case. ***Bradley Motors v. Mackey***, 878 S.W.2d 140, 141 (Tex.1994).

1. Right to jury. When the defendant does not appear for a scheduled trial, the case can be tried to the court, even though the defendant requested a jury. When the defendant does not appear at trial, it waives its right to a jury trial. ***Bradley Motors***, 878 S.W.2d at 141; ***Hanners v. State Bar***, 860 S.W.2d 903, 911 (Tex.App.—Dallas 1993, no writ). If the defendant requested a jury trial before its answer was struck, and if the defendant appears for trial, it is entitled to a jury trial. *See* ***Brantley v. Etter***, 662 S.W.2d 752, 756 (Tex.App.—San Antonio 1983) (after D's answer was struck as a sanction, D was still entitled to jury trial on damages), *writ ref'd n.r.e.*, 677 S.W.2d 503 (Tex.1984); *see also* ***Otis Elevator Co. v. Parmelee***, 850 S.W.2d 179, 181 (Tex.1993) (trial court could not award unliquidated damages without a hearing after imposing sanction equivalent to default judgment).

2. Ask for court reporter. The plaintiff should ask the court reporter to record the hearing. If the defendant is unable to get the court reporter to prepare a record because the reporter did not transcribe the hearing, in most cases the defendant is entitled to a new trial. ***Smith v. Smith***, 544 S.W.2d 121, 122-23 (Tex.1976); ***CarStar Collision v. Mercury Fin. Co.***, 23 S.W.3d 368, 370 (Tex.App.—Houston [1st Dist.] 1999, pet. denied). See ***O'Connor's Texas Civil Appeals***, "Default judgment," ch. 16-C, §4.1.6, p. 186 (2002-03).

3. Prove liability & damages. At trial, the plaintiff must carry its burden to prove all the elements of its cause of action; the defendant has admitted nothing by its default. ***Stoner***, 578 S.W.2d at 682; ***Flores***, 5 S.W.3d at 820; ***Onwuteaka v. Gill***, 908 S.W.2d 276, 281 (Tex.App.—Houston [1st Dist.] 1995, no writ); ***Holberg v. Short***, 731 S.W.2d 584, 587 (Tex.App.—Houston [14th Dist.] 1987, no writ). The plaintiff's evidence must be sufficient to support both the liability finding and the damages award. *See* ***Stone Res. v. Barnett***, 661 S.W.2d 148, 151 (Tex.App.—Houston [1st Dist.] 1983, no writ).

§5. DRAFTING THE DEFAULT JUDGMENT

For a no-answer default judgment, see ***O'Connor's*** FORM 9C:02; for a post-answer default judgment, see FORM 9C:03.

§5.1 General terms. The default judgment, like any judgment, should identify the parties and the relief granted. See "The Judgment," ch. 9-C, p. 595.

§5.2 Service & jurisdiction. The no-answer default judgment should recite all the jurisdictional requisites: (1) the citation was duly served with process, (2) the return of service was on file for ten days before the default was rendered, and (3) the defendant failed to answer and appear.

§5.3 Final judgment.

1. No-answer default. To be final and appealable, a no-answer default judgment must dispose of all issues and parties in the plaintiff's petition. ***Houston Health Clubs v. 1st Ct. of Appeals***, 722 S.W.2d 692, 693 (Tex.1986); *see* ***Castano v. Foremost Cty. Mut. Ins. Co.***, 31 S.W.3d 387, 388 (Tex.App.—San Antonio 2000, no pet.) (default judgment against one D was not final because order to sever other Ds not signed). There is no presumed disposition of issues in a no-answer default judgment case. ***Houston Health Clubs***, 722 S.W.2d at 693. See "Summary disposition," ch. 9-C, §6.3.2(2), p. 604.

2. Post-answer default. Because a post-answer default judgment can be rendered only after notice to the defendant (see §4.3, p. 450) and a trial of the issues (see §4.5, above), a post-answer default judgment is presumed to dispose of all issues. *See* ***Strut Cam Dimensions v. Sutton***, 896 S.W.2d 799, 801-02 (Tex.App.—Corpus Christi 1994, writ denied) (post-answer default disposes of all claims by implication); ***Thomas v. DuBovy-Longo***, 786 S.W.2d 506, 507 (Tex.App.—Dallas 1990, writ denied) (post-answer default judgment is presumed to be final). A post-answer default is not a summary disposition of the claims, as is a no-answer default.

§6. NOTICE OF DEFAULT JUDGMENT

§6.1 Notice after no-answer default. The clerk of the trial court is required to send to the defendant, at the mailing address certified by the plaintiff, written notice that a no-answer default judgment has been rendered against it. TRCP 239a. The clerk must note on the docket that it mailed the notice to the defendant immediately after the default judgment was signed. *Id.* The purpose of TRCP 239a is to give the defendant an opportunity to file a motion for new trial after a no-answer default judgment. ***Bloom***, 767 S.W.2d at 468. Because nothing in TRCP 239a discusses the type of notice, the notice must be sent as required by TRCP 21a—either by personal delivery, receipted delivery, or certified or registered mail. The clerk's failure to give notice does not affect the finality of the judgment. TRCP 239a; ***Campbell v. Fincher***, 72 S.W.3d 723, 724-25 (Tex.App.—Waco 2002, no pet.).

§6.2 Notice after post-answer default. Notice of a post-answer default judgment is governed by the rule that governs notice of judgments generally. See "TRCP 306a," ch. 9-C, §5.2.1, p. 602.

§7. ATTACKING THE DEFAULT JUDGMENT

There are two ways to attack a default judgment: directly or collaterally. If the default judgment is void, it can be challenged by a direct or collateral attack; if it is merely voidable, it can be challenged only by a direct attack. The purpose of a direct attack is to change the judgment and secure the entry of a correct judgment. *See* ***Cadle Co. v. Lobingier***, 50 S.W.3d 662, 672 (Tex.App.—Fort Worth 2001, pet. denied). The purpose of a collateral attack is to avoid the judgment, not to change it. *Id.*

§7.1 Direct attacks on default judgment. Direct attacks at the trial court level include a motion for new trial and a bill of review; direct attacks in the appellate court level include an ordinary appeal, a restricted appeal (formerly called an appeal by writ of error), and an appeal of a denial of a bill of review. ***Glunz v. Hernandez***, 908 S.W.2d 253, 255 n.3 (Tex.App.—San Antonio 1995, writ denied). When a no-answer default judgment is challenged by a direct attack, the judgment's recitals regarding service do not raise a presumption of proper service; every step of the proceeding from service of process to final judgment is open to examination. *See* ***Primate Constr. v. Silver***, 884 S.W.2d 151, 152 (Tex.1994) (restricted appeal); ***Min v. Avila***, 991 S.W.2d 495, 499-500 (Tex.App.—Houston [1st Dist.] 1999, no pet.) (bill of review); ***Webb v. Oberkampf Sup.***, 831 S.W.2d 61, 64 (Tex.App.—Amarillo 1992, no writ) (appeal following denial of motion for new trial). Only if the record affirmatively shows strict compliance with the manner and mode of service of process will a no-answer default judgment withstand a challenge based on a claim of invalid service. ***Primate Constr.***, 884 S.W.2d at 152.

1. Motion for new trial. A defendant that has suffered a default judgment may ask the trial court to overturn the default by granting a motion for new trial. TRCP 329b. This is the easiest way to invalidate the default judgment and obtain a new trial. See "MNT After Default Judgment," ch. 10-B, §15, p. 631. If the trial court denies relief, the defendant can appeal to the court of appeals. See ***O'Connor's Texas Civil Appeals*** (2002-03).

2. Bill of review. A defendant may attack a default judgment by a bill of review after the time for filing a motion for new trial has expired and when a restricted appeal is not available. ***King Ranch v. Chapman***, 118 S.W.3d 742, 751 (Tex.2003); ***Caldwell v. Barnes***, 975 S.W.2d 535, 537-38 (Tex.1998); ***State v. 1985 Chevrolet Pickup Truck***, 778 S.W.2d 463, 464 (Tex.1989); *see* TRCP 329b(f). A bill of review is an independent suit in equity filed by a party to an earlier suit, in the trial court that rendered the judgment in that suit, after it is too late to appeal. ***Wembley Inv. Co. v. Herrera***, 11 S.W.3d 924, 926-27 (Tex.1999); ***1985 Chevrolet***, 778 S.W.2d at 464; ***Hernandez v. Koch Mach. Co.***, 16 S.W.3d 48, 57 (Tex.App.—Houston [1st Dist.] 2000, pet. denied).

(1) Deadline. A petition for bill of review must be filed after the trial court's plenary power expires, TRCP 329b(f), but within the residual four-year statute of limitations, CPRC §16.051; ***Caldwell***, 975 S.W.2d at 538; ***Law v. Law***, 792 S.W.2d 150, 153 (Tex.App.—Houston [1st Dist.] 1990, writ denied). The only exception to the four-year limitation is when the defendant can show extrinsic fraud. ***Defee v. Defee***, 966 S.W.2d 719, 722 (Tex. App.—San Antonio 1998, no pet.); ***Law***, 792 S.W.2d at 153. Extrinsic fraud prevents a losing party from fully litigating rights or defenses and prevents a real trial on the issues involved. ***King Ranch***, 118 S.W.3d at 752; ***Martindale v. Reno***, ___ S.W.3d ___ (Tex.App.—Eastland 2003, no pet.) (No. 11-02-00256-CV; 5-22-03).

(2) Grounds. The defendant must file a sworn pleading that states the grounds for the bill of review. ***Beck v. Beck***, 771 S.W.2d 141, 141-42 (Tex.1989). For a defendant to be entitled to a hearing, it must make a prima facie showing of the elements it is required to prove. ***1985 Chevrolet***, 778 S.W.2d at 464.

(a) Sufficient cause. The bill must state sufficient cause, which is not defined by TRCP 329b(f).

[1] Meritorious defense. The defendant must present a prima facie meritorious defense to the action and show that it did not have an opportunity to present the defense. ***1985 Chevrolet***, 778 S.W.2d at 464-65; ***Beck***, 771 S.W.2d at 142; ***Alexander v. Hagedorn***, 226 S.W.2d 996, 998 (Tex.1950). A defendant establishes a meritorious defense when it proves that (1) its defense is not barred as a matter of law and (2) it will be entitled to judgment on retrial if no contrary evidence is offered. ***Ortmann v. Ortmann***, 999 S.W.2d 85, 88 (Tex.App.—Houston [14th Dist.] 1999, pet. denied).

[2] Justification for failure to assert defense. The defendant must justify its failure to make a defense by alleging fraud, accident, wrongful act of the plaintiff, or official mistake. ***Wembley***, 11 S.W.3d at 927; ***Caldwell***, 975 S.W.2d at 538; ***1985 Chevrolet***, 778 S.W.2d at 464; ***Alexander***, 226 S.W.2d at 998; *see, e.g.*, ***Baker v. Goldsmith***, 582 S.W.2d 404, 407 (Tex.1979) (letter that constituted answer was misplaced at the courthouse).

[3] No fault or negligence. The defendant must show the default judgment was not rendered as a result of its own fault or negligence. ***Caldwell***, 975 S.W.2d at 537; ***Texas Mach. & Equip. Co. v. Gordon Knox Oil & Expl. Co.***, 442 S.W.2d 315, 317-18 (Tex.1969); ***Alexander***, 226 S.W.2d at 998; *see* ***King Ranch***, 118 S.W.3d at 752 (allegations of fraud or negligence by party's own attorney insufficient to support bill of review).

(b) Due process violation. When a party claims a due process violation in a bill of review (*e.g.*, defective service or no notice) or claims that the judgment is void for some other reason, the party is not required to prove the "sufficient cause" elements set out above in §7.1.2(2)(a). *See* ***Peralta v. Heights Med. Ctr.***, 485 U.S. 80, 86, 108 S.Ct. 896, 899-900 (1988) (no service); ***Caldwell***, 975 S.W.2d at 537 (no service); ***Lopez v. Lopez***, 757 S.W.2d 721, 723 (Tex.1988) (no notice).

(3) Defenses.

(a) Laches. Because a bill of review is an equitable remedy, laches may be raised as a defense. ***Caldwell***, 975 S.W.2d at 538. The two elements of laches are (1) unreasonable delay by one having legal or equitable rights in asserting them, and (2) a good-faith change of position by another to its own detriment because of the delay. *Id.*; ***Rogers v. Ricane Enters.***, 772 S.W.2d 76, 80 (Tex.1989). Generally, laches will not bar a suit before the limitations period expires unless some extraordinary circumstance rendered it inequitable to permit the petitioner to assert its rights. ***Caldwell***, 975 S.W.2d at 538-39 (laches did not bar bill of review filed almost 2 years after petitioner first learned of judgment).

(b) Failure to exhaust other remedies. The petitioner is not entitled to relief by way of bill of review unless it exhausted all other remedies available in Texas courts at the time it filed the bill of review. ***Wembley***, 11 S.W.3d at 927; ***Caldwell***, 975 S.W.2d at 537. For example, a petitioner is not entitled to relief by way of bill of review if it could have but did not file a motion for new trial, an appeal, or a restricted appeal. *See* ***Lawrence v. Lawrence***, 911 S.W.2d 443, 448 (Tex.App.—Texarkana 1995, writ denied); *see, e.g.*, ***Gold v. Gold***, 111 S.W.3d 799, 803 (Tex.App.—Dallas 2003, n.p.h.) (6-month deadline to file restricted appeal had not expired).

(4) Trial. If the defendant's petition meets the standards of prima facie proof, the court will hold a trial on two issues: (1) the bill-of-review plaintiff (defendant in earlier suit) must prove the elements of the bill of review by a preponderance of the evidence, and (2) the bill-of-review defendant (plaintiff in earlier suit) must prove the merits of the underlying cause of action. ***1985 Chevrolet***, 778 S.W.2d at 464-65; ***Baker***, 582 S.W.2d at 409. Once the trial is finished, the court will render a new final judgment. ***1985 Chevrolet***, 778 S.W.2d at 465.

3. Restricted appeal. A defendant who did not participate in the trial of a cause of action may obtain review of the judgment in the court of appeals by a restricted appeal (formerly called an appeal by writ of error). TRAP 30; ***Quaestor Invs. v. Chiapas***, 997 S.W.2d 226, 227 (Tex.1999); ***Norman Comm. v. Texas Eastman Co.***, 955 S.W.2d 269, 270 (Tex.1997); *see also* ***Texaco, Inc. v. Central Power & Light Co.***, 925 S.W.2d 586, 588 (Tex.1996) (not a default judgment case). The issue on appeal is whether a lack of jurisdiction is apparent on the face of the record, thus invalidating the trial court's judgment. ***Dezso v. Harwood***, 926 S.W.2d 371, 373 (Tex.App.—Austin 1996, writ denied).

(1) Deadline. The restricted appeal must be filed within six months of the date the judgment was signed. CPRC §51.013; TRAP 26.1(c); ***Quaestor***, 997 S.W.2d at 227; ***Primate Constr. v. Silver***, 884 S.W.2d 151, 152 (Tex.1994).

(2) Grounds. To appeal by restricted appeal, the defendant must show the following:

(a) It filed the restricted appeal timely (within six months of the judgment). CPRC §51.013; TRAP 26.1(c); ***Norman Comm.***, 955 S.W.2d at 270; *see also* ***Quaestor***, 997 S.W.2d at 229 (removal suspends 6-month timetable; time clock restarts when federal court executes remand order and mails certified copy to state court).

(b) It was a party in the suit being challenged. ***Norman Comm.***, 955 S.W.2d at 270. A restricted appeal is also available to (1) a person whose privity of estate, title, or interest appears from the record in the trial court or (2) a person who is a party under the doctrine of virtual representation. ***Gunn v. Cavanaugh***, 391 S.W.2d 723, 725 (Tex.1965). See "Virtual party," ch. 2-B, §3.1.2, p. 68.

(c) It did not timely file a postjudgment motion, a request for findings of fact, or a notice of appeal within the time permitted by TRAP 26.1(a). TRAP 30; *see* ***Laboratory Corp. v. Mid-Town Surgical Ctr.***, 16 S.W.3d 527, 528 (Tex.App.—Dallas 2000, no pet.).

(d) It did not participate, either in person or through counsel, in the actual trial of the case. TRAP 30; ***Norman Comm.***, 955 S.W.2d at 270; ***Texaco***, 925 S.W.2d at 588; ***Stubbs v. Stubbs***, 685 S.W.2d 643, 644 (Tex.1985). If the record shows the defendant participated in the decision-making event producing the final judgment adjudicating the defendant's rights, the defendant cannot proceed by restricted appeal. ***Texaco***, 925 S.W.2d at

589. "Participation" means taking part in a hearing in open court that leads to the rendition of judgment on questions of law (if the case was disposed of on the questions of law) or on questions of fact (if the final judgment was rendered on the facts). ***Withem v. Underwood***, 922 S.W.2d 956, 957 (Tex.1996); *see also* ***Stubbs***, 685 S.W.2d at 645 (party who signed waiver of citation was not precluded from appealing by writ of error). The policy behind the nonparticipation requirement is to deny review by restricted appeal to those who should have resorted to the quicker method of appeal. ***Texaco***, 925 S.W.2d at 590.

(e) The trial court erred, and the error is apparent from the face of the record. ***Norman Comm.***, 955 S.W.2d at 270; ***G.E. Co. v. Falcon Ridge Apts.***, 811 S.W.2d 942, 943 (Tex.1991); ***Stubbs***, 685 S.W.2d at 644. The "face of the record" includes the clerk's record and the reporter's record, if any. ***Norman Comm.***, 955 S.W.2d at 270. The appellate court cannot consider evidence outside the record. ***G.E.***, 811 S.W.2d at 944. For example, if the petition, citation, or return of service is inadequate on its face to support a no-answer default judgment, the court of appeals will reverse the default judgment. *See, e.g.*, ***Autozone, Inc. v. Duenes***, 108 S.W.3d 917, 920-21 (Tex.App.—Corpus Christi 2003, n.p.h.) (invalid service on foreign corporation); ***Dolly v. Aethos Comm. Sys.***, 10 S.W.3d 384, 388-89 (Tex.App.—Dallas 2000, no pet.) (return of service was inherently inconsistent and lacked recitations to demonstrate citation was served according to trial court's order of substituted service); ***Laidlaw Waste Sys. v. Wallace***, 944 S.W.2d 72, 73 (Tex.App.—Waco 1997, writ denied) (court could not consider affidavit filed by clerk of trial court); ***Whiskeman v. Lama***, 847 S.W.2d 327, 329 (Tex.App.—El Paso 1993, no writ) (petition did not allege facts necessary to support service on nonresident).

§7.2 Collateral attacks on default judgment. If a defendant is not able to attack a default judgment directly by one of the above methods, it may be able to attack the judgment collaterally. A collateral attack seeks to avoid the effect of an earlier judgment by showing that the court rendering it had no jurisdiction over the parties or property, no jurisdiction over the subject matter, no capacity to enter that particular judgment, or no capacity to act as a court, or by showing that the order did not meet the requisites of a valid judgment. ***Browning v. Placke***, 698 S.W.2d 362, 363 (Tex.1985); ***Austin ISD v. Sierra Club***, 495 S.W.2d 878, 881-82 (Tex.1973); *see* ***Stewart v. USA Custom Paint & Body Shop***, 870 S.W.2d 18, 20 (Tex.1994) (order of dismissal was so uncertain it did not act as a dismissal order). A judgment of a court of general jurisdiction is not subject to collateral attack in another court of equal jurisdiction unless the judgment is void. ***Browning***, 698 S.W.2d at 363; *see* Hodges, *Collateral Attacks on Judgments*, 41 Tex.L.Rev. 163, 164 (1962). In a collateral proceeding, the judgment under attack is presumed to be valid. ***Stewart***, 870 S.W.2d at 20; *see* ***McKanna v. Edgar***, 388 S.W.2d 927, 929 (Tex.1965).

1. General rule. When a defendant attacks a judgment collaterally, the lack of jurisdiction must appear from the recitals in the judgment. *See* ***Stewart***, 870 S.W.2d at 20 (captionless sheet was not a properly executed order of dismissal); ***Solomon, Lambert, Roth & Assocs. v. Kidd***, 904 S.W.2d 896, 901 (Tex.App.—Houston [1st Dist.] 1995, no writ) (default judgment must affirmatively show lack of jurisdiction on face of judgment). The defendant cannot rely on either the record of the proceeding in which the judgment was rendered or extrinsic evidence to prove lack of jurisdiction. *See* ***Empire Gas & Fuel Co. v. Albright***, 87 S.W.2d 1092, 1096 (Tex.1935); ***Glunz v. Hernandez***, 908 S.W.2d 253, 256 (Tex.App.—San Antonio 1995, writ denied); ***Burrows v. Miller***, 797 S.W.2d 358, 359-60 (Tex.App.—Tyler 1990, no writ); *cf.* Hodges, 41 Tex.L.Rev. at 169 (extrinsic evidence inappropriate; only the record may be considered).

2. Attack on personal jurisdiction by a nonresident. A nonresident is not limited to the judgment recitals when attacking a judgment on grounds of lack of personal jurisdiction. The nonresident may present extrinsic evidence of lack of proper service or lack of amenability for service, even if the judgment recitals state otherwise. *See* ***Hicks v. Sias***, 102 S.W.2d 460, 464 (Tex.App.—Beaumont 1937, writ ref'd). However, once a defendant has unsuccessfully litigated the issue of personal jurisdiction in the court that issued the default judgment, it may not relitigate that issue by collaterally attacking the judgment. *See, e.g.*, ***Layton v. Layton***, 538 S.W.2d 642, 647 (Tex.App.—San Antonio 1976, writ ref'd n.r.e.) (Texas court refused to review Maryland court's determination of personal jurisdiction over a Texas resident because resident had litigated issue in Maryland & lost).

§7.3 Mandamus. Mandamus is not an appropriate means of reviewing a final default judgment if the trial court had jurisdiction when it rendered the default judgment. ***In re Barber***, 982 S.W.2d 364, 368 (Tex.1998); *see* ***Thursby v. Stovall***, 647 S.W.2d 953, 954 (Tex.1983). In certain unique circumstances, however, mandamus relief may be appropriate. *See, e.g.*, ***Barber***, 982 S.W.2d at 368 (mandamus appropriate to review trial court's refusal to acknowledge validity of its own order setting aside default).

B. MOTION FOR SUMMARY JUDGMENT

§1. GENERAL

§1.1 Rule. TRCP 166a.

§1.2 Purpose. The purpose of the summary judgment procedure is to permit the trial court to promptly dispose of cases that involve unmeritorious claims or untenable defenses. ***City of Houston v. Clear Creek Basin Auth.***, 589 S.W.2d 671, 678 n.5 (Tex.1979). Summary judgment procedure should not deprive litigants of their right to a trial by jury or to try a case by affidavit and deposition testimony. ***Collins v. County of El Paso***, 954 S.W.2d 137, 145 (Tex.App.—El Paso 1997, pet. denied).

§1.3 Forms & timetable. ***O'Connor's Texas Civil Forms***, FORMS 7B; Timetable, this book, Motion for Summary Judgment, p. 1008.

§1.4 Other references. ***O'Connor's Texas Causes of Action*** (2004) (***O'Connor's COA***).

§2. TYPES OF MOTIONS FOR SUMMARY JUDGMENT

There are two types of motions for summary judgment. The first type of motion (discussed in this subchapter) is the traditional motion, which depends on summary judgment evidence. TRCP 166a(c). The second type of motion (discussed in subchapter 7-C, p. 485) is a no-evidence summary judgment, which is made without summary judgment evidence. TRCP 166a(i). When a motion contains grounds that are appropriate for both the traditional summary judgment and the no-evidence summary judgment, it is sometimes called a hybrid motion for summary judgment. *See* ***Young Ref. Corp. v. Pennzoil***, 46 S.W.3d 380, 385 (Tex.App.—Houston [1st Dist.] 2001, pet. denied).

7-2. COMPARISON OF SUMMARY JUDGMENT PROCEDURES

		REGULAR MSJ, TRCP 166a(a)-(b)	NO-EVIDENCE MSJ, TRCP 166a(i)
1	Initial assumption	The nonmovant has a supportable claim or defense.	The nonmovant does not have a supportable claim or defense.
2	Movant's burden	Movant must prove its claim or defense or disprove element of nonmovant's claim or defense as a matter of law.	Movant must allege there is no evidence to prove a specific element of nonmovant's claim or defense.
3	Nonmovant's burden	Nonmovant does not have burden until movant offers proof it is entitled to SJ as a matter of law.	Nonmovant has the burden to raise fact issue on its claim or defense.
4	Shifting of burden to nonmovant	Burden shifts to nonmovant when movant produces SJ evidence proving as a matter of law it is entitled to SJ.	Burden shifts to nonmovant when movant alleges nonmovant has no evidence.
5	Earliest time to file MSJ	Any time after lawsuit filed.	After adequate time for discovery.

§3. SUMMARY JUDGMENT EVIDENCE

Summary judgment evidence must be admissible under the rules of evidence. ***United Blood Servs. v. Longoria***, 938 S.W.2d 29, 30 (Tex.1997); *see* TRCP 166a(f) ("affidavits ... shall set forth such facts as would be admissible in evidence"). That is, facts must be proved by the same type of evidence that would be introduced at trial, except that facts are proved by affidavits, depositions, interrogatories, and other discovery, rather than by oral testimony.

See TRCP 166a(c); ***Jensen Constr. Co. v. Dallas Cty.***, 920 S.W.2d 761, 768 (Tex.App.—Dallas 1996, writ denied), *overruled on other grounds*, ***Travis Cty. v. Pelzel & Assocs.***, 77 S.W.3d 246 (Tex.2002).

§3.1 Pleadings as proof.

1. General rule. As a general rule, pleadings are not summary judgment evidence. ***Laidlaw Waste Sys. v. City of Wilmer***, 904 S.W.2d 656, 660 (Tex.1995); ***Hidalgo v. Surety S&L Ass'n***, 462 S.W.2d 540, 545 (Tex. 1971).

(1) Petition or answer. A party cannot rely on factual statements contained in its own petition or answer as summary judgment proof. ***Hidalgo***, 462 S.W.2d at 545; ***Flameout Design & Fabrication v. Pennzoil Caspian Corp.***, 994 S.W.2d 830, 838 (Tex.App.—Houston [1st Dist.] 1999, no pet.).

(2) Motion or response. A party cannot rely on factual statements contained in its own motion for summary judgment or response as summary judgment proof, even if the motion or response is verified. ***Quanaim v. Frasco Rest. & Catering***, 17 S.W.3d 30, 42 (Tex.App.—Houston [14th Dist.] 2000, pet. denied) (response); ***Barrow v. Jack's Catfish Inn***, 641 S.W.2d 624, 625 (Tex.App.—Corpus Christi 1982, no writ) (motion).

(3) Pleadings as exhibits. A party cannot rely on other pleadings attached as exhibits to its own motion or response as summary judgment evidence, even if the pleadings are verified. *E.g.*, ***Laidlaw Waste***, 904 S.W.2d at 660 (P could not rely on its own verified petition attached as an exhibit to its response).

2. Exceptions.

(1) Other party's pleadings. When a party's pleadings contain statements admitting facts or conclusions directly contrary to the party's theory of recovery or defense, the pleadings may constitute summary judgment proof for the other party. *See* ***Lyons v. Lindsey Morden Claims Mgmt.***, 985 S.W.2d 86, 92 (Tex.App.—El Paso 1998, no pet.) (if a party's pleadings contain judicial admissions negating a cause of action, SJ may be granted on the basis of those pleadings). Although pleadings are not "evidence," when the motion for summary judgment is based on the nonmovant's pleadings, the court assumes the facts in the nonmovant's pleadings are true. See "Moving on the pleadings," §4.5.2, p. 464.

(2) Suit on sworn account. When the underlying claim is a suit on a sworn account, the plaintiff's pleadings establish a prima facie case if the defendant does not file a verified denial. ***Powers v. Adams***, 2 S.W.3d 496, 498 (Tex.App.—Houston [14th Dist.] 1999, no pet.).

§3.2 Organizing the evidence. If a party intends to rely on a few affidavits, it can attach them to the motion or the response. If the party is going to rely on an assortment of evidence, it should organize the evidence in an appendix. *See* TRCP 166a(d); *see also* ***Upchurch v. Albear***, 5 S.W.3d 274, 284-85 (Tex.App.—Amarillo 1999, pet. denied) (evidence consisting of 3,000 pages was not properly before the court; it was not indexed, nor did it refer to or cite the motion). If all the summary judgment proof is presented in an appendix, here are the items to include:

1. Table of contents. Include a table of contents with references to the tabs where the different items are located.

2. Incorporation by reference. Include a statement that all the summary judgment proof in the appendix is incorporated by reference into the motion or response. The same statement should be included in the motion or response.

3. Verification of proof. Include a verification for all evidence that is required to be verified. It is not necessary to separately authenticate each piece of documentary evidence. ***Llopa, Inc. v. Nagel***, 956 S.W.2d 82, 87 (Tex.App.—San Antonio 1997, writ denied).

§3.3 Types of witnesses. For a witness to present testimony by affidavit, the witness must be competent, have personal knowledge, and present admissible evidence. TRCP 166a(f).

1. Disinterested witness. The best summary judgment proof is the uncontradicted testimony of a disinterested witness. *See, e.g.*, ***Hunsucker v. Omega Indus.***, 659 S.W.2d 692, 696 (Tex.App.—Dallas 1983, no writ) (testimony of disinterested witnesses, who identified truck that left accident scene as belonging to defendant, raised fact issue that driver was in scope of employment).

2. Interested witness. To establish the facts through an interested witness, the testimony must be uncontroverted, clear, positive, direct, credible, free from contradiction, and susceptible to being readily controverted. TRCP 166a(c); ***McIntyre v. Ramirez***, 109 S.W.3d 741, 749 (Tex.2003); ***Trico Tech. Corp. v. Montiel***, 949 S.W.2d 308, 310 (Tex.1997). If the testimony does not meet these requirements, it will not support a summary judgment. ***Casso v. Brand***, 776 S.W.2d 551, 558 (Tex.1989). The phrase "could have been readily controverted" in TRCP 166a(c) does not simply mean the party's summary judgment proof could have been easily and conveniently rebutted; instead, it means the testimony is of a nature that can be effectively countered by opposing evidence. ***Trico***, 949 S.W.2d at 310; ***Casso***, 776 S.W.2d at 558. If the credibility of the affiant is likely to be a dispositive factor in the resolution of the case, summary judgment is not appropriate. ***Casso***, 776 S.W.2d at 558; ***CEBI Metal v. Garcia***, 108 S.W.3d 464, 465 (Tex.App.—Houston [14th Dist.] 2003, no pet.).

3. Expert witness. An expert's opinion testimony can establish or defeat a claim as a matter of law. *See* ***Burrow v. Arce***, 997 S.W.2d 229, 235 (Tex.1999). For purposes of summary judgment proof, experts are considered interested witnesses. *See* TRCP 166a(c) (last sentence). An expert's testimony (fact or opinion) must be uncontroverted, clear, positive, direct, credible, free from contradiction, and it must be susceptible to being readily controverted by another expert. TRCP 166a(c); ***Wadewitz v. Montgomery***, 951 S.W.2d 464, 466 (Tex.1997); ***Anderson v. Snider***, 808 S.W.2d 54, 55 (Tex.1991). The expert's opinion must meet the test for expert testimony. See "The *Daubert-Robinson* Test for Expert Testimony," ch. 5-M, §2, p. 303. If an expert's testimony meets the test for expert testimony under TRE 702 and the requirements of TRCP 166a(c) and (f), it will support a summary judgment even when the expert is a party to the suit. *See* ***Anderson***, 808 S.W.2d at 55; ***Shook v. Herman***, 759 S.W.2d 743, 746-47 (Tex.App.—Dallas 1988, writ denied). The testimony of an expert should include (1) the expert's qualifications, (2) the expert's opinion, (3) the facts on which the opinion is based, and (4) the reasoning on which the expert's opinion is based. *See* ***United Blood Servs. v. Longoria***, 938 S.W.2d 29, 30-31 (Tex.1997) (qualifications of expert); ***Anderson***, 808 S.W.2d at 55 (expert's reasoning). The expert's testimony cannot merely state unsubstantiated legal conclusions. ***Burrow***, 997 S.W.2d at 235; ***Wadewitz***, 951 S.W.2d at 466; ***Anderson***, 808 S.W.2d at 55; ***Barraza v. Eureka Co.***, 25 S.W.3d 225, 230 (Tex.App.—El Paso 2000, pet. denied). If the expert's opinion is based on records, the records should be attached to the affidavit or included in the other summary judgment evidence. TRCP 166a(f); ***Ceballos v. El Paso Health Care Sys.***, 881 S.W.2d 439, 445 (Tex.App.—El Paso 1994, writ denied). See "Failure to attach exhibits," §6.7.1(6), p. 470.

CAUTION

If you use an expert's affidavit in a summary judgment hearing, you cannot later claim purely consulting status for that expert. ***Hardesty v. Douglas****, 894 S.W.2d 548, 551 (Tex.App.—Waco 1995, orig. proceeding). That expert's opinion will be subject to discovery. See "Consulting-plus experts," ch. 6-C, §2.2.2, p. 364.*

(1) Attorney expert. If unchallenged, the movant's affidavit by a lawyer as an expert on attorney fees is sufficient to support a summary judgment for fees. See "Proof of attorney fees," ch. 1-H, §10.5, p. 48. If the nonmovant believes the amount of attorney fees the movant claims is unreasonable, the nonmovant should challenge the attorney fees in the response and file a controverting affidavit by a lawyer as an expert on attorney fees. *See* ***Guity v. C.C.I. Enter., Co.***, 54 S.W.3d 526, 528 (Tex.App.—Houston [1st Dist.] 2001, no pet.). If the movant's affidavit is controverted, the court cannot award attorney fees without holding a hearing. *Id.* See ***O'Connor's COA***, "Attorney Fees," ch. 38, p. 1041.

(2) Medical expert. CPRC chapter 74 limits the persons who can testify as experts in a medical malpractice case against doctors and other health care providers. *See* CPRC §§74.401-74.403. See ***O'Connor's COA***, "In claims against physicians," ch. 18-A, §8.3.2(1), p. 446.

§3.4 Affidavits. The most common form of summary judgment evidence is the affidavit. It is easy to prepare and inexpensive.

1. Must be an affidavit. The affidavit must meet the minimum requirements of an affidavit—that is, it must be sworn. See "Affidavits," ch. 1-B, §4.14.2, p. 7. An unsworn statement that purports to be an affidavit will not support a summary judgment, even if unchallenged. ***Perkins v. Crittenden***, 462 S.W.2d 565, 568 (Tex.1970); *see* ***Medford v. Medford***, 68 S.W.3d 242, 247 (Tex.App.—Fort Worth 2002, no pet.) (no notarization); ***Laman v. Big Spring State Hosp.***, 970 S.W.2d 670, 672 (Tex.App.—Eastland 1998, pet. denied) (defective jurat).

2. Admissible evidence. The affidavit must contain facts that would be admissible at a conventional trial on the merits. ***Longoria***, 938 S.W.2d at 30; *see* TRCP 166a(f) ("affidavits ... shall set forth such facts as would be admissible in evidence"); *see, e.g.*, ***Beasley v. Burns***, 7 S.W.3d 768, 770 (Tex.App.—Texarkana 1999, pet. denied) (party cannot offer affidavit that contradicts deemed admissions).

3. Competent witness. The affidavit must affirmatively show the witness is competent to testify about the matters in the affidavit. TRCP 166a(f). See "Competency of witness," ch. 1-B, §4.14.2(2), p. 8.

PRACTICE TIP

The courts often treat a witness's competence and personal knowledge as the same issue, but they are not. Competence, a TRE 601 issue, is whether the witness has the ability to testify—can the witness accurately perceive, recall, and recount?—and it is evaluated under TRE 104(a) without regard to the rules of evidence. See Cochran, ***Texas Rules of Evidence Handbook****, p. 553 (5th ed. 2003). Personal knowledge, a TRE 602 issue, is whether the witness knows enough about the subject to testify, and it is evaluated under TRE 104(b). See id. at 564-65.*

---

4. Personal knowledge. A summary judgment affidavit must state that it is based on the affiant's personal knowledge and that the facts in it are true. TRCP 166a(f); ***Garner v. Long***, 106 S.W.3d 260, 267 (Tex.App.—Fort Worth 2003, no pet.); ***Geiselman v. Cramer Fin. Group***, 965 S.W.2d 532, 537 (Tex.App.—Houston [14th Dist.] 1997, no writ). Statements based merely on the affiant's "best knowledge" are insufficient to raise a fact issue and are improper summary judgment evidence. ***Price v. American Nat'l Ins. Co.***, 113 S.W.3d 424, 429-30 (Tex.App.—Houston [1st Dist.] 2003, no pet.). See "Personal knowledge," ch. 1-B, §4.14.2(3)(a), p. 8; "Lack of personal knowledge," §6.7.1(3), p. 470.

5. Not legal conclusions. The affidavit must state facts and cannot merely recite legal conclusions. ***Brownlee v. Brownlee***, 665 S.W.2d 111, 112 (Tex.1984). Legal conclusions not supported by facts will not support a summary judgment. ***Anderson v. Snider***, 808 S.W.2d 54, 55 (Tex.1991). Legal conclusions in affidavits have no probative force. ***Life Ins. Co. v. Gar-Dal, Inc.***, 570 S.W.2d 378, 381-82 (Tex.1978); ***801 Nolana, Inc. v. RTC Mtg. Trust***, 944 S.W.2d 751, 754 (Tex.App.—Corpus Christi 1997, writ denied). The following are examples of legal conclusions when no underlying facts were stated: • The assault had nothing to do with work; it occurred for reasons personal to the physician. ***Walls Reg'l Hosp. v. Bomar***, 9 S.W.3d 805, 807 (Tex.1999). • The defendant did not commit legal malpractice, was not negligent, and did not breach the contract. ***Anderson***, 808 S.W.2d at 55. • The indebtedness was renewed and extended. ***Mercer v. Daoran Corp.***, 676 S.W.2d 580, 583 (Tex.1984). • The parties modified the contractual obligations. ***Brownlee***, 665 S.W.2d at 112. • The party held adverse possession to the property. ***Ellis v. Jansing***, 620 S.W.2d 569, 571 (Tex.1981). • Not all offsets and payments were credited. ***Gar-Dal***, 570 S.W.2d at 381-82.

• The note was purchased for valuable consideration, in good faith, and without notice of default or dishonor. ***Hidalgo v. Surety S&L Ass'n***, 487 S.W.2d 702, 703 (Tex.1972).

6. Not factual conclusions. The affidavit must be based on facts and cannot merely recite factual conclusions. Conclusory statements that are not supported by facts are not proper as summary judgment proof. *See* ***McIntyre v. Ramirez***, 109 S.W.3d 741, 749-50 (Tex.2003); ***Purcell v. Bellinger***, 940 S.W.2d 599, 602 (Tex.1997); ***Ryland Group v. Hood***, 924 S.W.2d 120, 122 (Tex.1996). Unsupported conclusory statements are not credible and are not susceptible to being readily controverted. ***Ryland Group***, 924 S.W.2d at 122; *see* TRCP 166a(c).

(1) By expert witness. Unsupported conclusory statements by an expert witness will not support a summary judgment. *See, e.g.*, ***Ryland Group***, 924 S.W.2d at 122 (statement that D's failure to notify anyone of use of untreated wood on P's deck violated industry practice was conclusory); ***Karen Corp. v. Burlington***, 107 S.W.3d 118, 126 (Tex.App.—Fort Worth 2003, pet. denied) (statement that attorney fees were excessive was conclusory); ***Griffin v. Methodist Hosp.***, 948 S.W.2d 72, 75 (Tex.App.—Houston [14th Dist.] 1997, no writ) (statement that nurses properly assessed patient's condition was conclusory). Opinion testimony cannot be based on the assumption of an unproven fact. ***Sipes v. G.M. Corp.***, 946 S.W.2d 143, 148 (Tex.App.—Texarkana 1997, writ denied). Opinion testimony can rise no higher than the facts on which it is based. *Id.*

(2) By lay witness. Unsupported conclusory statements by a lay witness will not support a summary judgment. *See, e.g.*, ***Purcell***, 940 S.W.2d at 602 (statement by mother about child's interest in pursuing paternity suit was conclusory); ***Laidlaw Waste Sys. v. City of Wilmer***, 904 S.W.2d 656, 661 (Tex.1995) (statements that area exceeded statutory minimum size & that boundary did not close were conclusory); ***Continental Casing Corp. v. Samedan Oil Corp.***, 751 S.W.2d 499, 501 (Tex.1988) (statement about offset was conclusory because it did not expressly state whether it was taken before or after bankruptcy).

7. Exhibits to affidavits. The affidavit must show that any exhibits attached to the affidavit are authentic and admissible. See "Exhibits," ch. 1-B, §4.14.2(5), p. 9; "Party's own discovery responses," §3.5.3(1)(b), p. 462.

8. Filing the affidavits.

(1) Attach to motion or response. The affidavits should be incorporated by reference in and filed with the motion or response. Affidavits attached to the original petition or the answer, but not included as part of the motion or response, are not competent summary judgment proof. ***Boeker v. Syptak***, 916 S.W.2d 59, 61-62 (Tex. App.—Houston [1st Dist.] 1996, no writ) (copy of petition & its affidavits attached to motion); ***Sugarland Bus. Ctr. v. Norman***, 624 S.W.2d 639, 642 (Tex.App.—Houston [14th Dist.] 1981, no writ) (affidavit was attached to pleadings but not to motion).

(2) Affidavit & amended motion or response. An amended motion or response should expressly incorporate by reference the affidavits attached to the earlier motion or response. However, failure to incorporate by reference the affidavits attached to the earlier motion or response is not fatal. ***Vaughn v. Burroughs Corp.***, 705 S.W.2d 246, 248 (Tex.App.—Houston [14th Dist.] 1986, no writ); *see* ***R.I.O. Sys. v. Union Carbide Corp.***, 780 S.W.2d 489, 492 (Tex.App.—Corpus Christi 1989, writ denied) (SJ proof attached to earlier motion was proper proof for later motion). *But see* ***Corpus Christi Mun. Gas Corp. v. Tuloso-Midway ISD***, 595 S.W.2d 203, 204 (Tex. App.—Eastland 1980, writ ref'd n.r.e.) (evidence attached to an earlier motion could not support SJ).

9. Affidavits made in bad faith. If a party relies on an affidavit made in bad faith or solely for the purpose of delay, the court must award the other party reasonable expenses caused by the affidavit, including reasonable attorney fees. TRCP 166a(h). Any offending party or attorney may be adjudged guilty of contempt. *Id.*

10. "Sham" affidavit. A "sham" affidavit is one that contradicts the affiant's earlier testimony for the purpose of creating a fact issue to avoid summary judgment. ***Farroux v. Denny's Rests.***, 962 S.W.2d 108, 111 (Tex. App.—Houston [1st Dist.] 1997, no pet.). There is a split in authority about whether a fact issue is created when a party submits an affidavit that conflicts with earlier deposition testimony. *Compare* ***Trostle v. Trostle***, 77 S.W.3d

908, 915 (Tex.App.—Amarillo 2002, no pet.) (party cannot defeat motion for SJ with affidavit contradicting earlier testimony without explaining reason for the change), ***Elson Thermoplastics v. Dynamic Sys.***, 49 S.W.3d 891, 901 (Tex.App.—Austin 2001, no pet.) (same), ***Burkett v. Wellborn***, 42 S.W.3d 282, 286 (Tex.App.—Texarkana 2001, no pet.) (same), *and* ***Farroux***, 962 S.W.2d at 111 (same), *with* ***Randall v. Dallas Power & Light Co.***, 752 S.W.2d 4, 5 (Tex.1988) (fact issue is presented when conflicting inferences are drawn from deposition testimony and affidavit), ***Larson v. Family Violence & Sexual Assault Prevention Ctr.***, 64 S.W.3d 506, 513 (Tex.App.—Corpus Christi 2001, pet. denied) (same), *and* ***Thompson v. City of Corsicana Hous. Auth.***, 57 S.W.3d 547, 557 (Tex.App.—Waco 2001, no pet.) (same). If the affiant was confused at the deposition or discovered additional, relevant materials after the deposition, the sham affidavit rule does not apply. *See* ***Farroux***, 962 S.W.2d at 111 n.1. For more information on the sham affidavit rule, see Wilson, *The Sham Affidavit Doctrine in Texas*, 66 Tex. B.J. 962 (2003).

§3.5 Discovery products. Discovery products used to support a summary judgment motion or a response can be filed separately or attached to the motion or response. ***McConathy v. McConathy***, 869 S.W.2d 341, 342 n.2 (Tex.1994).

NOTE

Two types of discovery products cannot be used as summary judgment evidence: a party's own answers to interrogatories and a party's own denials in response to requests for admissions. See "Using answers in summary judgment," ch. 6-F, §9.4, p. 416; "Using admissions in summary judgment," ch. 6-G, §8.3, p. 423.

1. On file. To rely on discovery on file with the court, the motion or response must refer to it. TRCP 166a(c); *see, e.g.*, ***Steinkamp v. Caremark***, 3 S.W.3d 191, 194-95 (Tex.App.—El Paso 1999, pet. denied) (party made court aware of the particular evidence on which she was relying by referring to portions of it and stating that it was already before the court).

2. Not on file. TRCP 166a(d) permits discovery not on file with the court to be used as summary judgment evidence as long as the party files and serves the following on all parties:

(1) Statement of intent. As part of the motion or response, the party should file a statement of intent to use unfiled discovery products as summary judgment proof. TRCP 166a(d). The requirement for "statement of intent" is satisfied when the party relies on evidence attached to its motion or response. ***McConathy***, 869 S.W.2d at 342 n.2; *see* ***Schauer v. Memorial Care Sys.***, 856 S.W.2d 437, 452 (Tex.App.—Houston [1st Dist.] 1993, no writ) (separate pleading called "statement of intent" not necessary), *overruled on other grounds*, ***Huckabee v. Time Warner Entm't Co.***, 19 S.W.3d 413 (Tex.2000).

(2) Unfiled discovery products. The party should attach one of the following to the statement of intent: (1) copies of the unfiled discovery, (2) appendixes containing the unfiled discovery, or (3) a notice containing specific references to and quotes from the unfiled discovery. TRCP 166a(d); *see, e.g.*, ***Barraza v. Eureka Co.***, 25 S.W.3d 225, 228 (Tex.App.—El Paso 2000, pet. denied) (attaching unfiled discovery & making specific reference to some of it in SJ response was sufficient); ***Guthrie v. Suiter***, 934 S.W.2d 820, 826 (Tex.App.—Houston [1st Dist.] 1996, no writ) (attaching deposition to motion was not sufficient; party should have identified evidence in the deposition on which it relied); ***E.B. Smith Co. v. U.S. Fid. & Guar. Co.***, 850 S.W.2d 621, 623 (Tex.App.—Corpus Christi 1993, writ denied) (broad statements about unfiled discovery were not sufficient; quotes from unfiled discovery were necessary). Objections to unfiled discovery are waived if not made before the court rules on the motion for summary judgment. ***Grainger v. Western Cas. Life Ins. Co.***, 930 S.W.2d 609, 613-14 (Tex.App.—Houston [1st Dist.] 1996, writ denied). *But see* ***Gomez v. Tri City Cmty. Hosp.***, 4 S.W.3d 281, 283-84 (Tex.App.—San Antonio 1999, no pet.) (CA refused to consider deposition testimony not on file with the trial court before entry of SJ).

CAUTION

The provision in TRCP 166a(d) relating to filing a statement of intent to use unfiled discovery seems to say that you do not need to file the discovery and other instruments, but merely refer to them in the statement of intent. Until the courts clarify TRCP 166a(d), do not rely on a "statement of intent" to use unfiled discovery without providing the court with extensive quotes from or copies of the discovery. ***Gomez****, 4 S.W.3d at 283-84;* ***E.B. Smith****, 850 S.W.2d at 624.*

3. Unverified. It is not necessary to verify by affidavit the authenticity of most discovery products.

(1) Discovery responses.

(a) Other party's discovery responses. When relying on another party's discovery responses (*e.g.*, documents that are not self-authenticating, answers to interrogatories), a party does not need to authenticate them unless the producing party filed timely objections to their authenticity. TRCP 193.7; ***Blanche v. First Nationwide Mortg. Corp.***, 74 S.W.3d 444, 451 (Tex.App.—Dallas 2002, no pet.).

(b) Party's own discovery responses. When relying on its own discovery responses, a party must authenticate them. ***Blanche***, 74 S.W.3d at 451-52; *see, e.g.*, ***Banowsky v. State Farm Mut. Auto. Ins. Co.***, 876 S.W.2d 509, 513 (Tex.App.—Amarillo 1994, no writ) (D should have authenticated release from its file). The affidavit authenticating a party's own documents must be made by a person with knowledge of the document's authenticity. ***Closs v. Goose Creek Consol. ISD***, 874 S.W.2d 859, 868 (Tex.App.—Texarkana 1994, no writ).

(2) Deposition excerpts. When relying on deposition excerpts, it is not necessary to authenticate them. ***McConathy***, 869 S.W.2d at 341.

§3.6 Stipulations. A party may rely on the parties' stipulations in a summary judgment motion or response. TRCP 166a(c)(ii). The stipulations must be in writing, signed by both parties, and filed with the court. TRCP 11. See "Agreements Between Lawyers – Rule 11," ch. 1-H, §9, p. 44. Typical stipulations in summary judgment proceedings include stipulations to the terms of a contract in dispute, to the agreed facts, and to the legal issues in dispute. *See* ***Francis v. International Serv. Ins. Co.***, 546 S.W.2d 57, 58-59 (Tex.1976).

§3.7 Reporter's record.

1. From another hearing in same suit. If the trial court conducts some other hearing in the same case before the hearing on the motion for summary judgment, the reporter's record from that hearing may be used as summary judgment proof. On appeal, the record must reflect that the reporter's record was considered at the summary judgment hearing. ***Munoz v. Gulf Oil Co.***, 693 S.W.2d 372, 373 (Tex.1984) (reporter's record from hearing, which did not bear a file mark, could not be considered on appeal); ***Munoz v. Gulf Oil Co.***, 732 S.W.2d 62, 64 (Tex.App.—Houston [14th Dist.] 1987, writ ref'd n.r.e.) (reporter's record from hearing, which bore a file mark, was proper SJ proof).

2. From another case. Sworn testimony from another case between the same parties can be used as summary judgment proof. ***Austin Bldg. Co. v. National Un. Fire Ins. Co.***, 432 S.W.2d 697, 698-99 (Tex.1968); *see also* ***Murillo v. Valley Coca-Cola Bottling Co.***, 895 S.W.2d 758, 761-62 (Tex.App.—Corpus Christi 1995, no writ) (reporter's record from another trial was admissible because D was sued for same incident by another P). See "Deposition from other proceeding," ch. 6-E, §12.1.2, p. 399.

§3.8 Public records. A party may rely on authenticated or certified public records as summary judgment evidence. TRE 902 lists documents that are self-authenticating. The document must be properly authenticated. See "Introducing Documents," ch. 8-C, §8, p. 540.

§3.9 Conflicts in SJ proof. Conflicting statements in summary judgment evidence made by the same witness raise a fact issue. ***Randall v. Dallas Power & Light Co.***, 752 S.W.2d 4, 5 (Tex.1988) (conflict between affidavit & deposition); ***Gaines v. Hamman***, 358 S.W.2d 557, 562 (Tex.1962) (same); ***Waldmiller v. Continental Express***, 74 S.W.3d 116, 125 (Tex.App.—Texarkana 2002, no pet.) (conflict between affidavits); *see* TRCP 166a(c) ("free from contradictions"). When the first statement is confusing, a statement made later that is more specific is not in conflict with it. *See* ***Gold v. City of Coll. Station***, 40 S.W.3d 637, 647 n.6 (Tex.App.—Houston [1st Dist.] 2001, pet. granted w.r.m.). A court cannot strike an affidavit of a party because it is inconsistent with an earlier affidavit from the same party. ***Thompson v. City of Corsicana Housing Auth.***, 57 S.W.3d 547, 557 (Tex.App.—Waco 2001, no pet.). Instead, after the trial on the merits, the court may impose sanctions for filing an affidavit in bad faith. *See* 3 McDonald & Carlson, *Texas Civil Practice* §18.19[f] (2d ed.2000). See "Affidavits made in bad faith," §3.4.9, p. 460.

§3.10 No oral testimony. No oral testimony may be considered in support of a motion for summary judgment or response. TRCP 166a(c). See "Hearing or submission," §12.2, p. 481.

§4. MOTION FOR SUMMARY JUDGMENT UNDER TRCP 166a(c)

§4.1 When to file. A plaintiff may move for summary judgment anytime after the defendant answers the lawsuit. TRCP 166a(a). A defendant may move for summary judgment at any time. TRCP 166a(b); *see* ***Zimmelman v. Harris Cty.***, 819 S.W.2d 178, 181 (Tex.App.—Houston [1st Dist.] 1991, no writ).

§4.2 In writing. The motion for summary judgment must be in writing. ***City of Houston v. Clear Creek Basin Auth.***, 589 S.W.2d 671, 677 (Tex.1979).

§4.3 Unverified. The motion for summary judgment should not be verified. A factual statement in a verified motion for summary judgment is not summary judgment proof. ***Hidalgo v. Surety S&L Ass'n***, 462 S.W.2d 540, 545 (Tex.1971). If a party needs sworn evidence to support its motion for summary judgment, it must attach affidavits or other sworn evidence.

PRACTICE TIP

After you draft your motion for summary judgment, check your pleadings and amend them if necessary. If you assert a ground for summary judgment that is not contained in your pleadings (e.g., an affirmative defense), the nonmovant can defeat your motion for summary judgment by objecting to the lack of pleadings. See "Challenge the pleadings," §6.6.2, p. 468.

§4.4 Grounds.

1. Stated in motion. The motion for summary judgment must state the grounds on which it is made. TRCP 166a(c); ***McConnell v. Southside ISD***, 858 S.W.2d 337, 341 (Tex.1993); ***Travis v. City of Mesquite***, 830 S.W.2d 94, 99-100 (Tex.1992). A party cannot rely on its brief to state the grounds for a summary judgment. ***McConnell***, 858 S.W.2d at 339. The trial court cannot grant a summary judgment on grounds not presented in the motion. ***Johnson v. Brewer & Pritchard, P.C.***, 73 S.W.3d 193, 204 (Tex.2002); *see, e.g.*, ***Science Spectrum v. Martinez***, 941 S.W.2d 910, 912 (Tex.1997) (D's motion for SJ did not raise issue that D had created dangerous condition); ***Sysco Food Servs. v. Trapnell***, 890 S.W.2d 796, 805 (Tex.1994) (D waived issue of collateral estoppel because it raised issue only in its brief); ***Teer v. Duddlesten***, 664 S.W.2d 702, 704 (Tex.1984) (court could not grant SJ for party that did not file motion for SJ). If a ground that may support a summary judgment is not stated in the motion, the ground cannot be supplied by a prayer for general relief. ***Golden Triangle Energy v. Wickes Lumber***, 725 S.W.2d 439, 441 (Tex.App.—Beaumont 1987, no writ). On appeal, the summary judgment cannot be affirmed on a ground not presented to the trial court in the motion. ***Stiles v. RTC***, 867 S.W.2d 24, 26 (Tex.1993); ***Travis v. City of Mesquite***, 830 S.W.2d 94, 100 (Tex.1992).

PRACTICE TIP

First, never file a trial brief to support a motion for summary judgment; instead, include in the motion all arguments supporting the grounds. See ***McConnell****, 858 S.W.2d at 339-40. Second, begin each ground for summary judgment by incorporating by reference all the facts from other parts of the motion that are necessary to that ground. See* ***Johnson****, 73 S.W.3d at 204.*

2. Specificity = fair notice. The grounds in the motion are sufficiently specific if they give "fair notice" to the nonmovant. ***Thomas v. Cisneros***, 596 S.W.2d 313, 316 (Tex.App.—Austin 1980, writ ref'd n.r.e.); *see* ***Upchurch v. Albear***, 5 S.W.3d 274, 284-85 (Tex.App.—Amarillo 1999, pet. denied) (general reference to voluminous record, which did not direct attention to evidence relied on, did not satisfy "fair notice" requirement). If the grounds are vague, the nonmovant should file special exceptions. See "Summary Judgment *and* Special Exceptions," §8, p. 473; ***O'Connor's*** FORM 7B:06.

§4.5 SJ based on facts or pleadings.

1. Moving on the facts. When a movant files a motion for summary judgment based on the summary judgment evidence, the court can grant the motion only when the movant's evidence, as a matter of law, either proves all the elements of the movant's claim or defense or disproves the facts of at least one element of the nonmovant's claim or defense. ***Park Place Hosp. v. Estate of Milo***, 909 S.W.2d 508, 511 (Tex.1995) (doctor proved affirmative defense that patient had less than 50% chance of survival, in spite of malpractice); ***Lear Siegler, Inc. v. Perez***, 819 S.W.2d 470, 471-72 (Tex.1991) (causation disproved as a matter of law). When evaluating a motion for summary judgment based on summary judgment proof, the trial court must do the following:

(1) Assume all the nonmovant's proof is true. ***Limestone Prods. Distrib. v. McNamara***, 71 S.W.3d 308, 311 (Tex.2002); ***Shah v. Moss***, 67 S.W.3d 836, 842 (Tex.2001); ***M.D. Anderson Hosp. v. Willrich***, 28 S.W.3d 22, 23 (Tex.2000); ***Nixon v. Mr. Prop. Mgmt. Co.***, 690 S.W.2d 546, 548-49 (Tex.1985).

(2) Indulge every reasonable inference in favor of the nonmovant. ***M.D. Anderson***, 28 S.W.3d at 23; ***Science Spectrum***, 941 S.W.2d at 911; ***Walker v. Harris***, 924 S.W.2d 375, 377 (Tex.1996); ***Nixon***, 690 S.W.2d at 549.

(3) Resolve all doubts about the existence of a genuine issue of a material fact against the movant. ***M.D. Anderson***, 28 S.W.3d at 23; ***Johnson Cty. Sheriff's Posse v. Endsley***, 926 S.W.2d 284, 285 (Tex.1996); ***Nixon***, 690 S.W.2d at 548-49.

2. Moving on the pleadings. The movant may file a motion for summary judgment that shows the nonmovant has no viable cause of action or defense based on the nonmovant's pleadings. *See, e.g.*, ***National Un. Fire Ins. Co. v. Merchants Fast Motor Lines***, 939 S.W.2d 139, 141 (Tex.1997) (no duty to defend insurance claim based on allegations in pleadings & terms of policy); ***Trinity River Auth. v. URS Consultants***, 889 S.W.2d 259, 261 (Tex.1994) (petition showed statute of repose had run); ***Helena Lab. Corp. v. Snyder***, 886 S.W.2d 767, 768-69 (Tex.1994) (no cause of action for negligent interference with family relationship); ***City of Houston v. Clear Creek Basin Auth.***, 589 S.W.2d 671, 681 (Tex.1979) (under the Water Code, P had no cause of action against D for discharging polluted wastes outside P's boundaries). In some cases when the motion is based on the pleadings, the parties may include summary judgment proof. *See, e.g.*, ***St. John v. Pope***, 901 S.W.2d 420, 424 (Tex.1995) (no malpractice action against doctor who was "on call" at hospital; doctor filed affidavit). When evaluating a motion for summary judgment based on the nonmovant's pleadings, the trial court must do the following:

(1) Assume all allegations and facts in the nonmovant's pleading are true. ***Natividad v. Alexsis, Inc.***, 875 S.W.2d 695, 699 (Tex.1994); ***Valles v. Texas Comm'n on Jail Stand.***, 845 S.W.2d 284, 286 (Tex.App.—Austin 1992, writ denied); *see also* ***American Tobacco Co. v. Grinnell***, 951 S.W.2d 420, 434 (Tex.1997) (not incumbent on nonmovant-P to produce evidence supporting allegations made in her pleadings).

(2) Indulge all inferences in the nonmovant's pleadings in the light most favorable to the nonmovant. ***Medina v. Herrera***, 927 S.W.2d 597, 602 (Tex.1996); ***Natividad***, 875 S.W.2d at 699; ***Valles***, 845 S.W.2d at 286.

(3) Ensure that any defects in the pleadings cannot be cured by amendment. ***In re B.I.V.***, 870 S.W.2d 12, 13 (Tex.1994).

PRACTICE TIP

Before the court grants a "no cause of action" summary judgment, it should give the nonmovant adequate opportunity to amend to plead a viable cause of action. See ***Friesenhahn v. Ryan***, *960 S.W.2d 656, 659 (Tex.1998). See "Defective pleading of cause of action," ch. 3-G, §10.2, p. 193.*

---

§4.6 Motion for final SJ. If the movant intends for the summary judgment to be final, it must ask the court to dispose of all issues and all parties. ***Continental Airlines v. Kiefer***, 920 S.W.2d 274, 276-77 (Tex.1996); ***Teer v. Duddlesten***, 664 S.W.2d 702, 703 (Tex.1984). If the motion does not dispose of everything, the judgment will not be final.

1. All parties. The motion should ask for relief for and against all parties in the suit and name all the parties. *See* ***Continental Airlines***, 920 S.W.2d at 276-77.

2. All issues. The motion should ask the court to dispose of all the issues (claims, counterclaims, cross-claims, third-party claims), all theories of damages (actual, exemplary), and all other claims (attorney fees, costs, interest). The motion should identify all the issues on which it seeks summary judgment. *See* ***Continental Airlines***, 920 S.W.2d at 276 (motion "on all claims" did not encompass issues outside of the motion). If the movant accidentally overlooks including one of its claims in its motion for summary judgment, it cannot contend on appeal that it intended to abandon that claim; the unadjudicated claim makes what was intended to be a final judgment interlocutory. *See, e.g.*, ***McNally v. Guevara***, 52 S.W.3d 195, 196 (Tex.2001) (D's motion for SJ forgot to ask for attorney fees, which made it a partial SJ).

3. Request for final SJ. The motion should ask the court to render a final, appealable judgment. See "Statement of finality," ch. 9-C, §4.3, p. 598.

4. Sever or dismiss other claims. A summary judgment on some of the claims can be transformed into a final judgment by severing or dismissing the remaining claims.

§4.7 Motion for partial SJ. A party may file a motion for summary judgment asking the court to dispose of some but not all of the issues or parties in the case.

1. Parties & claims. The motion should identify the parties against whom, and the claims on which, the movant wants a partial summary judgment.

2. Request for interlocutory SJ. The motion should ask the court to render a partial judgment. The order granting a partial summary judgment is interlocutory and cannot be appealed until a final judgment is rendered. To convert a partial summary judgment into a final judgment, see "To make a partial SJ final," §13.4, p. 483.

§4.8 Supporting evidence. Most motions for summary judgment require supporting evidence. The summary judgment proof should be incorporated by reference in and attached to the motion or the response. See "Summary Judgment Evidence," §3, p. 456.

§4.9 Attorney fees. If the movant is entitled to attorney fees, it should include a request for attorney fees in its original pleading and in the motion for summary judgment.

1. Proof of attorney fees. The movant should support the request for attorney fees with an affidavit by a lawyer proving the amount, the necessity, and the reasonableness of the fees. See "Attorney Fees from Adverse Party," ch. 1-H, §10, p. 45; ***O'Connor's COA***, "Attorney Fees," ch. 38, p. 1041; ***O'Connor's*** FORMS 1H:13; 7B:01, §E.

2. No judicial notice. Attorney fees in a summary judgment case cannot be established using the judicial notice provision in CPRC §38.004. That provision permits judicial notice of attorney fees only when a case is tried on the merits. See "Judicial notice," ch. 1-H, §10.3.2, p. 46.

§4.10 Successive motions. TRCP 166a does not place a limit on the number of motions for summary judgment that may be filed. ***Cameron Cty. v. Carrillo***, 7 S.W.3d 706, 709 (Tex.App.—Corpus Christi 1999, no pet.).

§5. THE NOTICE

§5.1 For the hearing. The nonmovant is entitled to receive sufficient notice of the hearing date on the summary judgment motion so that it knows when its response is due. ***Martin v. Martin, Martin & Richards***, 989 S.W.2d 357, 359 (Tex.1998); ***Aguirre v. Phillips Props.***, 111 S.W.3d 328, 332-33 (Tex.App.—Corpus Christi 2003, n.p.h.).

1. The first setting. The movant is required to give the nonmovant 21 days' notice of the hearing or submission of a summary judgment motion. TRCP 166a(c); ***Lewis v. Blake***, 876 S.W.2d 314, 316 (Tex.1994). To compute the 21 days, see "Deadlines for Summary Judgment," §10, p. 474.

2. Resetting the hearing. Once a nonmovant is given 21 days' notice of the hearing, if the hearing date is reset, the nonmovant is not entitled to another 21 days' notice of the new date. ***Birdwell v. Texins Credit Un.***, 843 S.W.2d 246, 250 (Tex.App.—Texarkana 1992, no writ).

§5.2 In writing. The movant must give the nonmovant written notice of the hearing on the motion for summary judgment. *See* TRCP 21a ("every notice required by these rules ... may be served by delivering...."), TRCP 166a(c) (does not specify written notice). The notice must include the fact that a hearing has been set, and it must give the date and time for the hearing. ***Mosser v. Plano Three Venture***, 893 S.W.2d 8, 11 (Tex.App.—Dallas 1994, no writ). If the movant does not provide timely notice, the summary judgment will be reversed. ***Guinn v. Zarsky***, 893 S.W.2d 13, 17 (Tex.App.—Corpus Christi 1994, no writ). Without notice of the date for the hearing, the nonmovant cannot calculate the date the response is due. ***Courtney v. Gelber***, 905 S.W.2d 33, 34 (Tex.App.—Houston [1st Dist.] 1995, no writ). See "Deadlines for Summary Judgment," §10, p. 474.

§5.3 Included in SJ motion. The notice of the hearing may be included in the motion for summary judgment. ***Guinn***, 893 S.W.2d at 16. The notice must state the date and time actually set for the hearing; a movant's written request for a certain date for the hearing is not notice of the date set for the hearing. ***Veal v. Veterans Life Ins. Co.***, 767 S.W.2d 892, 895 (Tex.App.—Texarkana 1989, no writ).

§5.4 Separate notice. If the notice of the hearing is filed separately from the motion for summary judgment, the notice must contain a certificate of service because TRCP 21a requires all notices to contain a certificate of service. ***Guinn***, 893 S.W.2d at 16-17 (notice of hearing, which was on a separate sheet in same envelope with SJ motion, was not sufficient because it was not certified). If the motion is filed before the hearing date is set, and the notice of the hearing is filed later, the movant must give the nonmovant 21 days' notice of the hearing, counting from the date of the notice, not the motion. ***Chadderdon v. Blaschke***, 988 S.W.2d 387, 388 (Tex.App.—Houston [1st Dist.] 1999, no pet.). Regardless of how long the motion is on file, when the movant sets the motion for a hearing, it must give the nonmovant 21 days' notice of the date for the hearing. *Id.*

§6. NONMOVANT'S RESPONSE TO THE MOTION UNDER TRCP 166a(c)

The response to the motion for summary judgment serves two functions: (1) it identifies defects in the motion, and (2) it presents reasons the summary judgment should not be granted. The only defect that does not need to be specifically raised in the response is an attack on the legal sufficiency of the grounds for the judgment. ***City of***

Houston v. Clear Creek Basin Auth., 589 S.W.2d 671, 678 (Tex.1979). Every other defect must be raised in the response.

§6.1 In writing. The response to the motion for summary judgment must be made in writing. ***Clear Creek***, 589 S.W.2d at 677.

§6.2 Unverified. The response should not be verified; a verified response does not present summary judgment evidence. *See* ***Quanaim v. Frasco Rest. & Catering***, 17 S.W.3d 30, 42 (Tex.App.—Houston [14th Dist.] 2000, pet. denied); ***Webster v. Allstate Ins. Co.***, 833 S.W.2d 747, 748-49 (Tex.App.—Houston [1st Dist.] 1992, no writ).

§6.3 Deadline. The response must be filed and served at least seven days before the hearing. See "For the response – 7 days before hearing," §10.4, p. 475.

§6.4 The grounds. To defeat a motion for summary judgment, the nonmovant should show one of the following:

1. The nonmovant's evidence raises a fact issue on a vital fact that must be submitted to a jury. See §6.5, below.

2. The movant's evidence offered to prove a vital fact is no more than a mere scintilla. *See* ***Duckstein v. General Dynamics Corp.***, 499 S.W.2d 907, 910 (Tex.App.—Fort Worth 1973, writ ref'd n.r.e.); *cf.* ***Merrell Dow Pharms. v. Havner***, 953 S.W.2d 706, 711 (Tex.1997) (jury trial).

3. The court is barred by rules of law or evidence from giving weight to the movant's evidence offered to prove a vital fact. See "Objections to the SJ evidence," §6.7, p. 469.

4. The movant has no cause of action or defense. See "Moving on the pleadings," §4.5.2, p. 464.

§6.5 Nonmovant's SJ evidence. In most cases, the nonmovant should file summary judgment evidence to raise a fact issue. See "Summary Judgment Evidence," §3, p. 456.

1. File counter-affidavits. If the movant's motion is based on summary judgment evidence, the nonmovant should file counter-affidavits. See "Moving on the facts," §4.5.1, p. 464. The purpose of counter-affidavits is to create fact issues that preclude summary judgment.

2. Support affirmative defenses. If the nonmovant wishes to assert an affirmative defense to the motion for summary judgment, it must urge the defense in its response and provide enough summary judgment evidence to create a fact issue on each element of the defense. ***Jones v. Texas Pac. Indem. Co.***, 853 S.W.2d 791, 795 (Tex.App.—Dallas 1993, no writ); *see* ***Beathard Jt.V. v. West Houston Airport Corp.***, 72 S.W.3d 426, 434 (Tex. App.—Texarkana 2002, pet. denied). For example, the allegation that the movant did not credit the nonmovant with offsets will not preclude summary judgment; the nonmovant must present proof. *See* ***Keenan v. Gibraltar Sav. Ass'n***, 754 S.W.2d 392, 394 (Tex.App.—Houston [14th Dist.] 1988, no writ). The nonmovant is not required to prove the affirmative defense by a preponderance of the evidence or as a matter of law—raising a fact issue is enough. *See* ***American Petrofina v. Allen***, 887 S.W.2d 829, 830 (Tex.1994) (P asserted affirmative defense as nonmovant); ***Brownlee v. Brownlee***, 665 S.W.2d 111, 112 (Tex.1984) (D asserted affirmative defense as nonmovant). See "Burden of Proof," §11, p. 477.

§6.6 Objections to SJ motion. In the response to the motion for summary judgment, the nonmovant must object to any defect in the form or substance of the motion or pleadings. If the nonmovant does not make any objections in its response, on appeal it can argue only that the grounds presented to the trial court are insufficient as a matter of law to support the summary judgment. ***Roadside Stations v. 7HBF, Ltd.***, 904 S.W.2d 927, 932 (Tex. App.—Fort Worth 1995, no writ).

1. Challenge the use of SJ. As a general rule, a party should not use a motion for summary judgment to attack a deficiency in the other party's pleadings that could be cured by amendment. ***Sixth RMA Partners v.***

Sibley, 111 S.W.3d 46, 54-55 (Tex.2003); ***In re B.I.V.***, 870 S.W.2d 12, 13 (Tex.1994); *see also* ***Friesenhahn v. Ryan***, 960 S.W.2d 656, 659 (Tex.1998) (not affording P an opportunity to plead a viable cause of action before granting a "no cause of action" SJ was error); ***Peek v. Equipment Serv. Co.***, 779 S.W.2d 802, 805 (Tex.1989) (failure to plead jurisdictional amount in controversy should have been challenged by special exceptions, not SJ); ***Texas Dept. of Corr. v. Herring***, 513 S.W.2d 6, 9 (Tex.1974) (failure to plead requirements of Tort Claims Act should have been challenged by special exceptions, not SJ). There are two situations in which a summary judgment based on a pleading deficiency is proper: (1) if the party had the opportunity to amend after special exceptions and did not do so, ***Natividad v. Alexsis, Inc.***, 875 S.W.2d 695, 699 (Tex.1994); or (2) when the party affirmatively pleads itself out of court, *see* ***Castleberry v. Goolsby Bldg. Corp.***, 617 S.W.2d 665, 666 (Tex.1981) (negligence action was precluded by workers' compensation); *see also* ***Vaughn v. Hughes***, 917 S.W.2d 477, 480 (Tex.App.—Fort Worth 1996, no writ) (rule applies to live pleadings only). If the pleadings show on their face that the plaintiff has no viable cause of action, summary judgment is proper; if the pleadings are merely defective, summary judgment is improper. *See* ***Toles v. Toles***, 113 S.W.3d 899, 909 (Tex.App.—Dallas 2003, n.p.h.). See "Special Exceptions & Summary Judgments, ch. 3-G, §10, p. 193. If the nonmovant does not object to the movant's motion for summary judgment on the ground that it is an attempt to circumvent the special exception practice, or does not request additional time to amend, the nonmovant waives the error. ***Kassen v. Hatley***, 887 S.W.2d 4, 13 n.10 (Tex.1994); ***Vawter v. Garvey***, 786 S.W.2d 263, 264 (Tex.1990).

2. Challenge the pleadings. If the movant's pleadings do not support the motion for summary judgment, the nonmovant must object or waive the error. An unpleaded claim or defense included in the motion for summary judgment is tried by consent if the nonmovant does not object in its response. ***Roark v. Stallworth Oil & Gas***, 813 S.W.2d 492, 495 (Tex.1991) (D moved for SJ on unpleaded affirmative defense, but because P did not object, P waived error); ***Webster v. Thomas***, 5 S.W.3d 287, 289 n.1 (Tex.App.—Houston [14th Dist.] 1999, no pet.) (nonmovant did not object to unpleaded affirmative defense). When a nonmovant objects to the variance between the movant's motion for summary judgment and the movant's pleadings, the movant should immediately file an amended pleading conforming the pleadings to the motion.

3. Challenge the motion. The nonmovant should challenge all legal and procedural shortcomings in the motion for summary judgment. See "Motion for Summary Judgment Under TRCP 166a(c)," §4, p. 463.

4. Challenge the notice. If the movant did not file and serve the motion, the evidence, and the notice of hearing 21 days before the hearing, the nonmovant must object to the lack of notice in writing. *See* TRCP 166a(c). The 21-day notice requirement for the motion is waived if the nonmovant does not make an objection—in writing and under oath—before or at the hearing. ***Nguyen v. Short, How, Frels & Heitz***, 108 S.W.3d 558, 560 (Tex.App.—Dallas 2003, pet. denied); ***Veal v. Veterans Life Ins. Co.***, 767 S.W.2d 892, 895 (Tex.App.—Texarkana 1989, no writ). The nonmovant should file a motion to reset the date of the hearing, along with an affidavit that identifies the date it received the motion and notice of hearing and a request that the hearing on the motion be reset to allow the full 21 days' notice. See §6.6.6(2), below; ***O'Connor's*** FORM 7B:07.

5. File special exceptions. If the motion is unclear or ambiguous, the nonmovant should challenge it by special exceptions. See "Summary Judgment *and* Special Exceptions," §8, p. 473.

6. Motions for more time.

(1) Motion to continue hearing. When a nonmovant needs additional time to secure affidavits or discovery, it should file a motion for continuance. See "Motion to continue SJ hearing," ch. 5-D, §9.3, p. 246; ***O'Connor's*** FORM 7B:09. The trial court has the discretion to deny a motion for continuance under TRCP 251. A motion for continuance is not the correct motion to file when the nonmovant did not get the required 21 days' notice. See §6.6.6(2), below.

(2) Motion to reset SJ hearing. When a nonmovant did not get 21 days' notice of the hearing, it should file a motion to reset the hearing date. The trial court does not have the discretion to refuse a motion to reset the hearing when the nonmovant was not given the full 21 days' notice required by TRCP 166a(c). See "Motion to reset SJ hearing for lack of 21 days' notice," ch. 5-D, §9.2, p. 245; ***O'Connor's*** FORM 7B:07.

(3) Motion for leave to file late SJ response. A nonmovant who needs permission to file the response less than seven days before the hearing should file a motion for leave to file a late summary judgment response. The court should grant the motion when the nonmovant establishes good cause by sworn proof (1) that its failure to timely respond was not intentional or the result of conscious indifference, but the result of an accident or mistake, and (2) that allowing the late response will not unduly delay or otherwise injure the party seeking summary judgment. ***Carpenter v. Cimarron Hydrocarbons Corp.***, 98 S.W.3d 682, 688 (Tex.2002). As an alternative, the nonmovant should ask for a continuance of the hearing. See §6.6.6(1), above.

§6.7 Objections to the SJ evidence. If the movant's affidavits (or other summary judgment proof) contain evidence that would not be admissible at trial, the nonmovant should object and move to strike the inadmissible evidence. *See* TRCP 166a(f) ("affidavits ... shall set forth such facts as would be admissible in evidence"). As a general rule, unless a party objects in writing (in a response, reply, special exceptions, separate objections, or motion to strike) to the deficiencies in the summary judgment proof, the party waives the objection. *See* ***City of Houston v. Clear Creek Basin Auth.***, 589 S.W.2d 671, 677 (Tex.1979). However, that rule applies only if the defect is one of form; if the defect is one of substance, no objection is necessary to preserve the error. *See id.*; ***Rizkallah v. Conner***, 952 S.W.2d 580, 585 (Tex.App.—Houston [1st Dist.] 1997, no writ). It is not always easy to determine when the defect is one of substance (and thus not waivable) or one of form (and thus waivable). Even the Texas Supreme Court confuses the two. See "Errors in substance," §6.7.2, p. 471; ***O'Connor's*** FORMS 7B:11-13. Therefore, parties should always object in writing to all defects in the evidence.

1. Waivable objections to evidence. TRCP 166a(f) requires a party to object to formal defects in the affidavits or their attachments (*i.e.*, other evidence). Formal defects in the affidavits or attachments are not grounds to reverse unless the objecting party (generally, the appellant-nonmovant) specifically objected and the other party (generally, the appellee-movant) was given, but refused, the opportunity to amend. TRCP 166a(f); ***Bauer v. Jasso***, 946 S.W.2d 552, 556-57 (Tex.App.—Corpus Christi 1997, no writ). This rule inures to the benefit of the successful movant for summary judgment—generally, the appellee. *See* ***Knetsch v. Gaitonde***, 898 S.W.2d 386, 389-90 (Tex.App.—San Antonio 1995, no writ). The only occasions where the appellant would be the movant for summary judgment are in those few instances when a party is permitted to appeal the denial of a summary judgment. See "Appeal when SJ denied," §15.4, p. 484. Thus, on appeal, when an appellant-nonmovant discovers that its own affidavit was defective in form, the appellant cannot argue that the appellee-movant should have objected to the affidavit and, because it did not, the defect was waived. ***Ceballos v. El Paso Health Care Sys.***, 881 S.W.2d 439, 444-45 (Tex.App.—El Paso 1994, writ denied). These are some of the objections to evidence that a party must make or waive:

(1) Defects in affidavits. If the affidavits meet the minimum requirements of an affidavit, any formal defects in the movant's affidavits are not grounds for reversal unless the nonmovant specifically objected and the movant was given the opportunity to amend, but refused. TRCP 166a(f). However, if the document that purports to be an affidavit is not an affidavit, the defect is one of substance, and no objection is necessary to preserve error. See "Must be an affidavit," §3.4.1, p. 459. The party objecting to an affidavit must identify the specific statements in the affidavit that are objectionable. *See* ***Jensen Constr. Co. v. Dallas Cty.***, 920 S.W.2d 761, 769 (Tex. App.—Dallas 1996, writ denied), *overruled on other grounds*, ***Travis Cty. v. Pelzel & Assocs.***, 77 S.W.3d 246 (Tex. 2002). An entire affidavit cannot be excluded if only part of it is inadmissible. When the trial court sustains a general objection to the entire affidavit, the party offering the affidavit should either ask to amend it or ask that only the objectionable part be struck. See "Request for limited admissibility," ch. 8-D, §7.1.3(1), p. 551.

(2) Witness not competent. TRCP 166a(f) states that the affidavit must show affirmatively that the witness is competent. See "Competency of witness," ch. 1-B, §4.14.2(2), p. 8. Lack of competence is waived if no objection is made. *See* ***Rizkallah***, 952 S.W.2d at 586.

PRACTICE TIP

Although courts often treat competence and lack of personal knowledge as the same thing, they are not. See "Competent Witness," §3.4.3, p. 459; "Personal Knowledge," §3.4.4, p. 459.

(3) Lack of personal knowledge. The objection that the affidavit (or deposition) is not based on the personal knowledge of the affiant must be made, or it is waived. ***Grand Prairie ISD v. Vaughan***, 792 S.W.2d 944, 945 (Tex.1990); ***Grotjohn Precise Connexiones Int'l v. JEM Fin.***, 12 S.W.3d 859, 866 (Tex.App.—Texarkana 1999, no pet.); ***Rizkallah***, 952 S.W.2d at 585; ***Bauer***, 946 S.W.2d at 557. *But see* ***Dailey v. Albertson's, Inc.***, 83 S.W.3d 222, 226 (Tex.App.—El Paso 2002, no pet.) (lack of personal knowledge, shown by affiant's testimony itself, was defect of substance that could be raised for the first time on appeal). See "Personal knowledge," ch. 1-B, §4.14.2(3)(a), p. 8.

(4) Not readily controvertible. The objection that an affidavit contains declarations that are not easily controverted must be made before the summary judgment is granted, or the objection is waived. *See* ***Patterson v. Mobiloil Fed. Credit Un.***, 890 S.W.2d 551, 554 (Tex.App.—Beaumont 1994, no writ). See "Interested witness," §3.3.2, p. 458.

(5) Hearsay evidence. Unless a party objects to hearsay evidence, the evidence will support a summary judgment. TRE 103(a)(1), 802; *see, e.g.*, ***Southland Corp. v. Lewis***, 940 S.W.2d 83, 85 (Tex.1997) (hearsay excluded because party objected); ***Columbia Rio Grande Reg'l Hosp. v. Stover***, 17 S.W.3d 387, 396 (Tex. App.—Corpus Christi 2000, no pet.) (nonmovant whose hearsay objections were not specific enough waived objection); ***In re J.A.M.***, 945 S.W.2d 320, 322 (Tex.App.—San Antonio 1997, no writ) (nonmovant who did not object to hearsay waived objection); *cf.* ***Texas Commerce Bank v. New***, 3 S.W.3d 515, 517 (Tex.1999) (unobjected-to hearsay can support default judgment).

(6) Failure to attach exhibits. A party should object when an affidavit relies on facts contained in an exhibit that is not attached to the affidavit. *See, e.g.*, ***Guthrie v. Suiter***, 934 S.W.2d 820, 824-25 (Tex.App.—Houston [1st Dist.] 1996, no writ) (trial court excluded expert's affidavit that did not include the documents expert reviewed in reaching opinion). Determining whether a missing exhibit is a formal defect (objection required to preserve error) or a substantive defect (no objection required) depends on whether the information in the missing exhibit is supplied elsewhere in the summary judgment evidence.

(a) Formal defect. When an affidavit relies on facts contained in a missing exhibit but the same information is supplied elsewhere in the summary judgment evidence, the missing exhibit is a formal defect, and the error is waived if not objected to before the summary judgment. *See* ***Sunsinger v. Perez***, 16 S.W.3d 496, 501 (Tex.App.—Beaumont 2000, pet. denied); ***Martin v. Durden***, 965 S.W.2d 562, 565 (Tex.App.—Houston [14th Dist.] 1997, pet. denied); ***Watts v. Hermann Hosp.***, 962 S.W.2d 102, 105 (Tex.App.—Houston [1st Dist.] 1997, no pet.); ***Noriega v. Mireles***, 925 S.W.2d 261, 265 (Tex.App.—Corpus Christi 1996, writ denied).

(b) Substantive defect. When an affidavit relies on facts contained only in a missing exhibit, the missing exhibit is a substantive defect and is reversible error even without objection. *See* ***Galindo v. Dean***, 69 S.W.3d 623, 627 (Tex.App.—Eastland 2002, no pet.) (failure to attach medical records was substantive defect); ***Nat. Gas Clearinghouse v. Midgard Energy Co.***, 23 S.W.3d 372, 380 (Tex.App.—Amarillo 1999, pet. denied) (consultant's opinion on damages based on records not attached was substantive defect); ***Mincron SBC Corp. v. Worldcom, Inc.***, 994 S.W.2d 785, 795-96 (Tex.App.—Houston [1st Dist.] 1999, no pet.) (failure to attach invoices supporting disputed damages was substantive defect); ***Gorrell v. Texas Utils. Elec. Co.***, 915 S.W.2d 55, 60 (Tex.App.—Fort Worth

1995, writ denied) (failure to attach exhibits was substantive defect); ***Ceballos v. El Paso Health Care Sys.***, 881 S.W.2d 439, 445 (Tex.App.—El Paso 1994, writ denied) (nontreating doctor's opinions based on records not attached was substantive defect); ***Sorrells v. Giberson***, 780 S.W.2d 936, 938 (Tex.App.—Austin 1989, writ denied) (in suit on a note, failure to attach note was reversible error because affidavit did not prove elements of suit).

(7) Failure to lay predicate. The objection that an affidavit does not lay the proper predicate for admissibility is a defect of form and is waived if not pointed out to the trial court before summary judgment is rendered. ***Life Ins. Co. v. Gar-Dal, Inc.***, 570 S.W.2d 378, 380-81 (Tex.1978); ***Cottrell v. Carrillon Assocs.***, 646 S.W.2d 491, 494 (Tex.App.—Houston [1st Dist.] 1982, writ ref'd n.r.e.).

(8) Not "best evidence." The nonmovant must object that the affidavit is not the best evidence of the contents of the document, or else it waives the objection. *See* TRE 1002 (an original writing is required to prove its contents unless otherwise provided); ***Jensen Constr. Co. v. Dallas Cty.***, 920 S.W.2d 761, 768 (Tex.App.—Dallas 1996, writ denied) (same), *overruled on other grounds*, ***Travis Cty. v. Pelzel & Assocs.***, 77 S.W.3d 246 (Tex.2002). A copy of the document is not admissible if the original document is not produced, its content is disputed, and its absence is not explained. *See* ***Mercer v. Daoran Corp.***, 676 S.W.2d 580, 584 (Tex.1984) (court should have sustained objection to unsigned copy of note). The best-evidence rule applies only when a party seeks to prove the contents of a disputed document not in evidence. ***Osuna v. Quintana***, 993 S.W.2d 201, 206 (Tex.App.—Corpus Christi 1999, no pet.); ***White v. Bath***, 825 S.W.2d 227, 231 (Tex.App.—Houston [14th Dist.] 1992, writ denied).

(9) Opinion of expert. The nonmovant should object if the sworn testimony of the expert is not admissible expert testimony under TRE 702 (testimony by experts) or TRCP 193.6(a) (exclusion of evidence for not timely responding to discovery). See "The *Daubert-Robinson* Test for Expert Testimony," ch. 5-M, §2, p. 303; "Expert witness," §3.3.3, p. 458.

2. Errors in substance. Substantive errors in the summary judgment evidence are not waivable. However, a party should object to all errors in the summary judgment evidence, even to errors of substance. Here are some objections to errors in substance. This list is helpful on appeal once a party realizes that an objection was not made in the trial court.

(1) Unsubstantiated legal conclusion. Legal conclusions, unsupported by evidence, are defects in substance, and no objection is necessary to preserve error. ***Hou-Tex, Inc. v. Landmark Graphics***, 26 S.W.3d 103, 112 (Tex.App.—Houston [14th Dist.] 2000, no pet.); ***Rizkallah v. Conner***, 952 S.W.2d 580, 587 (Tex.App.—Houston [1st Dist.] 1997, no writ); ***Lara v. Tri-Coastal Contractors***, 925 S.W.2d 277, 279 n.3 (Tex.App.—Corpus Christi 1996, no writ). See "Not legal conclusions," §3.4.5, p. 459.

(2) Unsubstantiated factual conclusion. Factual conclusions, opinions, and subjective beliefs, unsupported by evidence, are defects in substance, and no objection is necessary to preserve error. ***Rizkallah***, 952 S.W.2d at 586; ***Harley-Davidson Motor Co. v. Young***, 720 S.W.2d 211, 213 (Tex.App.—Houston [14th Dist.] 1986, no writ). See "Not factual conclusions," §3.4.6, p. 460.

(3) Conflict in movant's SJ proof. If the affidavit for the movant contains conflicting statements that raise a fact issue, they preclude summary judgment even when no objection is made. *See* TRCP 166a(c); ***Dillard v. NCNB Tex. Nat'l Bank***, 815 S.W.2d 356, 360-61 (Tex.App.—Austin 1991, no writ), *overruled on other grounds*, ***Amberboy v. Societe de Banque Privee***, 831 S.W.2d 793 (Tex.1992).

§6.8 Secure ruling on objections. The nonmovant should ask the court to make written rulings on its objections to the summary judgment evidence. Although the trial court has a duty to make written rulings on objections to summary judgment evidence, some courts—perhaps to ensure their judgment is affirmed on appeal—refuse to do so. There is a conflict between the courts of appeals—sometimes even within the same court—on whether error is preserved if the trial court does not make an express ruling in writing overruling the nonmovant's objections.

1. **Implicit ruling sufficient.** Five courts of appeals hold that if the trial court does not explicitly rule on the nonmovant's objections to the motion for summary judgment, the granting of the summary judgment implicitly overrules the objections. *See* ***Clement v. City of Plano***, 26 S.W.3d 544, 550 n.5 (Tex.App.—Dallas 2000, no pet.), *overruled on other grounds*, ***Telthorster v. Tennell***, 92 S.W.3d 457 (Tex.2002); ***Dagley v. Haag Eng'g Co.***, 18 S.W.3d 787, 795 n.9 (Tex.App.—Houston [14th Dist.] 2000, no pet.); ***Columbia Rio Grande Reg'l Hosp. v. Stover***, 17 S.W.3d 387, 395-96 (Tex.App.—Corpus Christi 2000, no pet.); ***Williams v. Bank One***, 15 S.W.3d 110, 114-15 (Tex.App.—Waco 1999, no pet.); ***Frazier v. Yu***, 987 S.W.2d 607, 610 (Tex.App.—Fort Worth 1999, pet. denied). TRAP 33.1 relaxes the requirement in former TRAP 52(a) for an express ruling. ***Frazier***, 987 S.W.2d at 610. The burden to get a ruling on an objection is satisfied if (1) the record affirmatively indicates the trial court ruled on the objections in granting the summary judgment, or (2) the granting of the summary judgment necessarily implies a ruling on the objections. ***Trusty v. Strayhorn***, 87 S.W.3d 756, 760 (Tex.App.—Texarkana 2002, no pet.); *see, e.g.*, ***Mowbray v. Avery***, 76 S.W.3d 663, 689 n.45 (Tex.App.—Corpus Christi 2002, pet. denied) (because order said court considered response, it implicitly overruled objections in response). For implicit rulings that preserve error in other contexts, see "Implicit ruling," ch. 1-G, §2.2.2, p. 33.

2. **Express ruling required.** Six courts of appeals (some of the same ones listed above) hold the nonmovant must secure a written ruling on its objections or else the objections are waived. *See* ***Sunshine Mining & Ref. Co. v. Ernst & Young***, 114 S.W.3d 48, 51 (Tex.App.—Eastland 2003, n.p.h.); ***Allen v. Albin***, 97 S.W.3d 655, 663 (Tex.App.—Waco 2002, no pet.); ***In re Estate of Loveless***, 64 S.W.3d 564, 573 (Tex.App.—Texarkana 2001, no pet.); ***Montemayor v. Chapa***, 61 S.W.3d 758, 763 (Tex.App.—Corpus Christi 2001, no pet.); ***Rodriguez v. Wal-Mart Stores***, 52 S.W.3d 814, 823 (Tex.App.—San Antonio 2001), *rev'd in part on other grounds*, 92 S.W.3d 502 (Tex.2002); ***Hou-Tex, Inc. v. Landmark Graphics***, 26 S.W.3d 103, 112 (Tex.App.—Houston [14th Dist.] 2000, no pet.).

PRACTICE TIP

To preserve error when a court refuses to overrule your objections to the motion for summary judgment, file a motion for new trial within 30 days of the judgment, re-urge the objections, and include an objection to the court's refusal to rule. See ***Alejandro v. Bell**, 84 S.W.3d 383, 388 (Tex.App.—Corpus Christi 2002, no pet.). When the motion for new trial is overruled, either by order or by operation of law, your objections are preserved for appeal. See "Refusal to rule + objection," ch. 1-G, §2.2.3, p. 33.*

§6.9 Waiver. The nonmovant should assert all of its challenges to the summary judgment in its response. On appeal, the appellate courts will not consider any issues as grounds for reversal that were not presented to the trial court by written response. ***City of Houston v. Clear Creek Basin Auth.***, 589 S.W.2d 671, 675 (Tex.1979); ***Thompson v. Chrysler First Bus. Credit Corp.***, 840 S.W.2d 25, 34 (Tex.App.—Dallas 1992, no writ).

§6.10 Consider amending the pleadings. Amending the pleadings to add new issues or to delete factual admissions can sometimes be the easiest and most effective way to avoid a final summary judgment. See §9, below. Once the pleadings are amended to add or delete issues, the movant may respond by amending its motion for summary judgment. ***Smith v. Atlantic Richfield Co.***, 927 S.W.2d 85, 88 (Tex.App.—Houston [1st Dist.] 1996, writ denied).

§6.11 Consider a nonsuit. If the statute of limitations has not run, a plaintiff may avoid a summary judgment by taking a nonsuit. The plaintiff can take a nonsuit after the defendant files a motion for summary judgment, but the nonsuit must be filed before the court rules on the motion for summary judgment. See "Deadlines for Nonsuit," ch. 7-E, §3, p. 495.

§7. SUMMARY JUDGMENT *OR* SPECIAL EXCEPTIONS

Defects in the other party's petition, counterclaim, or cross-claim can be challenged by special exceptions (which can lead to an order of dismissal) or by a motion for summary judgment (which can lead to a judgment). It is not always clear whether a party should challenge defects in the other party's pleadings by special exceptions or a motion for summary judgment. See "Special Exceptions & Summary Judgments," ch. 3-G, §10, p. 193.

§8. SUMMARY JUDGMENT *AND* SPECIAL EXCEPTIONS

The purpose of special exceptions in the summary judgment procedure is to ensure that the parties and the trial court are focused on the same grounds. ***McConnell v. Southside ISD***, 858 S.W.2d 337, 342 (Tex.1993); *see also* ***Harwell v. State Farm Mut. Auto. Ins. Co.***, 896 S.W.2d 170, 175 (Tex.1995).

§8.1 When necessary. If the motion or response states grounds that are unclear or ambiguous, it is "prudent trial practice" to file special exceptions. ***McConnell***, 858 S.W.2d at 342-43 & n.7; *see* ***Pettitte v. SCI Corp.***, 893 S.W.2d 746, 748 (Tex.App.—Houston [1st Dist.] 1995, no writ).

§8.2 When not necessary. It is not necessary to file special exceptions in the following situations: (1) when the grounds for the motion or response are stated only in a brief or other document but not in the motion or response, (2) when the motion or response presents no grounds, or (3) when the motion or response clearly presents some grounds but not others. ***McConnell***, 858 S.W.2d at 342.

§8.3 In writing. The special exceptions must be in writing. ***McConnell***, 858 S.W.2d at 343 n.7.

§8.4 The ruling. The party who files special exceptions in a summary judgment proceeding should ask the trial court to sign a written order overruling or sustaining the special exceptions at or before the hearing on the motion for summary judgment. ***McConnell***, 858 S.W.2d at 343 n.7. The ruling on the special exceptions can be included in the summary judgment.

§8.5 Deadlines for special exceptions. See "For special exceptions," §10.7, p. 475.

§9. AMENDING THE PETITION OR ANSWER

The filing requirements and deadlines for amending the pleadings (petition and answer) are different from the filing requirements and deadlines for amending the motion for summary judgment and response. By understanding the differences, a nonmovant may be able to preclude a final summary judgment.

§9.1 Procedure to amend. The trial court must render a summary judgment on the pleadings on file at the time of the hearing. TRCP 166a(c). A party may file an amended pleading after it files its motion or response. *See, e.g.*, ***Cluett v. Medical Protective Co.***, 829 S.W.2d 822, 825-26 (Tex.App.—Dallas 1992, writ denied) (movant filed amended petition after SJ motion but 4 months before hearing).

1. Amending pleadings before hearing. A party should file an amended petition or answer as soon as it becomes aware it is necessary, and no later than seven days before the hearing. TRCP 63; ***Sosa v. Central Power & Light***, 909 S.W.2d 893, 895 (Tex.1995). In computing the seven-day period, the day the party files the amended pleading is not counted, but the day of the hearing on the motion for summary judgment is counted. ***Sosa***, 909 S.W.2d at 895. If the party decides to amend after the seven-day deadline (*e.g.*, six days before the hearing), it should file its amended pleading before the hearing without filing a motion for leave to amend. *See* TRCP 166a(c). Unless the record shows that the court denied leave to file, the appellate courts will assume the trial court considered the amended pleading. ***Goswami v. Metropolitan S&L Ass'n***, 751 S.W.2d 487, 490-91 (Tex.1988) (nonmovant filed amended petition 4 days before hearing). *But see* ***Honea v. Morgan Drive Away***, 997 S.W.2d 705, 707 (Tex.App.—Eastland 1999, no pet.) (when order said it considered all "timely" pleadings, court presumably did not consider late-amended pleadings). Leave to file within seven days of the hearing is presumed granted when (1) the summary judgment states that all pleadings were considered, (2) the record does not show that an amended pleading was not considered, and (3) the opposing party does not show surprise. ***Continental Airlines v. Kiefer***, 920 S.W.2d 274, 276 (Tex.1996) (amended pleading filed 5 days before hearing). If the late amendment creates a fact issue, the appellate courts will reverse the summary judgment. ***Goswami***, 751 S.W.2d at 491.

2. Amending pleadings after the hearing. Once the hearing date for the motion for summary judgment has passed, a party may file an amended pleading before the court signs a judgment if the party secures a written order granting leave to file. TRCP 166a(c); *see* ***Hussong v. Schwan's Sales Enters.***, 896 S.W.2d 320, 323 (Tex.App.—Houston [1st Dist.] 1995, no writ) (nonmovant did not get permission to file amended petition one month after hearing & before court granted SJ); ***Leinen v. Buffington's Bayou City Serv. Co.***, 824 S.W.2d 682, 685 (Tex.App.—Houston [14th Dist.] 1992, no writ) (nonmovant filed amended petition two weeks after hearing). Unless the record shows that the court granted leave to file, the appellate courts will assume it was denied. ***Leinen***, 824 S.W.2d at 685.

§9.2 Objecting to an amendment.

1. Amendment filed before hearing. Under TRCP 63, the party opposing the amendment bears the burden to show surprise. If a party objects to a late amendment, it should make sure the record reflects its objection and the court's ruling. Unless the record shows the court denied leave to file the late amendment, the appellate courts will assume it was granted. ***Goswami***, 751 S.W.2d at 490.

2. Amendment filed after hearing. The party opposing an amendment filed after the hearing has no burden to object unless the party filing the amendment asks for leave to file.

§10. DEADLINES FOR SUMMARY JUDGMENT

§10.1 By rule – 21 days before hearing. The nonmovant is entitled to 21 days' notice of the date set for the hearing or submission of the motion, counting from the date the motion and notice of hearing are served. TRCP 166a(c); ***Lewis v. Blake***, 876 S.W.2d 314, 316 (Tex.1994). The nonmovant is entitled to 21 days' notice of each motion. TRCP 21a, 166a(c); *see* ***Luna v. Estate of Rodriguez***, 906 S.W.2d 576, 582 (Tex.App.—Austin 1995, no writ).

1. Filing & serving motion & notice. In computing the number of days before the hearing, the day the motion and notice of hearing are served is not counted (it is "day 0"), but the day of the hearing is counted (it is "day 21" or "day 24"). TRCP 4, 166a(c); ***Lewis***, 876 S.W.2d at 316. See "Computing time limits – days," ch. 1-C, §7.1, p. 16; chart 1-1, "Computing Deadlines to Respond," ch. 1-D, p. 24.

(1) By delivery – 21 days. When the motion and notice of hearing are served by delivery, they must be served at least 21 days before the hearing. TRCP 166a(c); *see* ***Lewis***, 876 S.W.2d at 316.

(2) By mail – 24 days. When the motion and notice of hearing are served by mail, they must be mailed at least 24 days before the hearing because TRCP 21a extends the minimum notice by 3 days. ***Lewis***, 876 S.W.2d at 315; ***Chadderdon v. Blaschke***, 988 S.W.2d 387, 388 (Tex.App.—Houston [1st Dist.] 1999, no pet.); *see* TRCP 4, 21a. Thus, when the motion and notice are mailed, the day they are mailed is "day 0," the next day is "day 1," and the day of the hearing is "day 24" or later. ***Lewis***, 876 S.W.2d at 316.

(3) By fax – 24 days. When the motion and notice of hearing are served by fax, they must be faxed at least 24 days before the hearing. ***Lewis***, 876 S.W.2d at 315; *see* TRCP 21a, 166a(c).

2. Form for notice of hearing. If the date for the hearing is known before the motion for summary judgment is served, the notice of the hearing can be included in the motion itself or it can be served as a separate document from the motion with its own certificate of service. See "Included in SJ motion," §5.3, p. 466. If the date for the hearing is not known at the time the motion for summary judgment is served, the 21 (or 24) days must be calculated from the service of the notice of hearing, and the notice must contain a certificate of service. See "Separate notice," §5.4, p. 466.

§10.2 By agreement. The parties may change the deadlines by agreement. If the agreement meets the requirements of TRCP 11, the court should enforce it. *See, e.g.*, ***EZ Pawn Corp. v. Mancias***, 934 S.W.2d 87, 91 (Tex. 1996) (because parties made Rule 11 agreement to permit the nonmovant to file response a week before the hearing, trial court should have disregarded response filed after that deadline). See "Agreements Between Lawyers – Rule 11," ch. 1-H, §9, p. 44.

§10.3 By court order. The court may permit the hearing to be set with less than 21 days' notice, with advance notice to the parties. TRCP 166a(c); *see, e.g.*, ***Hall v. Stephenson***, 919 S.W.2d 454, 461 (Tex.App.—San Antonio 1996, writ denied) (with advance notice, court reduced 21 days' notice to 17 days). *But see* ***Stephens v. Turtle Creek Apts.***, 875 S.W.2d 25, 26-27 (Tex.App.—Houston [14th Dist.] 1994, no writ) (even with advance notice, court cannot reduce 21 days' notice to 6 days). A court cannot grant leave for a shorter hearing period to excuse the movant's inadequate notice after the nonmovant complains of the inadequate notice. *See* TRCP 166a(c).

§10.4 For the response – 7 days before hearing. The nonmovant must file its response and affidavits at least seven days before the hearing. TRCP 166a(c); ***Carpenter v. Cimarron Hydrocarbons Corp.***, 98 S.W.3d 682, 686 (Tex.2002); ***K-Six TV v. Santiago***, 75 S.W.3d 91, 96 (Tex.App.—San Antonio 2002, no pet.); *see also* ***Alford v. Thornburg***, 113 S.W.3d 575, 586 (Tex.App.—Texarkana 2003, n.p.h.) (court did not consider opposing affidavit filed timely but served late because P did not ask to serve late affidavit or request continuance). *But see* ***Hammonds v. Thomas***, 770 S.W.2d 1, 2 (Tex.App.—Texarkana 1989, no writ) (court should have considered nonmovant's affidavits filed 6 days before hearing because 7th day before hearing was July 4th, a national holiday). See "Computing time limits – days," ch. 1-C, §7.1, p. 16. The response may be filed by mailing it on the day it is due, and it is timely filed even if it reaches the court less than seven days before the hearing, as long as it is received by the clerk no more than ten days after the due date. TRCP 5, 21a; ***Geiselman v. Cramer Fin. Group***, 965 S.W.2d 532, 535 (Tex. App.—Houston [14th Dist.] 1997, no writ); ***Clendennen v. Williams***, 896 S.W.2d 257, 259 (Tex.App.—Texarkana 1995, no writ). The three-day rule for mailing in TRCP 21a does not require the nonmovant to mail the response 10 days before the hearing. ***Holmes v. Ottawa Truck***, 960 S.W.2d 866, 869 (Tex.App.—El Paso 1997, pet. denied). The seven-day deadline gives the nonmovant at least 14 days to obtain and file summary judgment evidence. ***Extended Servs. Program v. First Extended Serv. Corp.***, 601 S.W.2d 469, 470 (Tex.App.—Dallas 1980, writ ref'd n.r.e.) (21 days' notice of hearing minus the 7-day deadline to file response before the hearing = 14 days to file response & SJ evidence).

§10.5 For the SJ evidence. The deadline to file affidavits, unfiled discovery, and other summary judgment evidence is the same deadline that applies to the motion or response. TRCP 166a(c), (d). No evidence can be filed after the court rules on the motion, even if the motion was a partial motion. *See* TRCP 166a(c); ***Valores Corporativos v. McLane Co.***, 945 S.W.2d 160, 162 (Tex.App.—San Antonio 1997, writ denied). See §10.9.5, below.

§10.6 For the movant's reply to the response. If the nonmovant filed a response to the motion for summary judgment, the movant may want to reply to the response. There is no deadline in TRCP 166a for a movant's reply to a response. ***Callaghan Ranch v. Killam***, 53 S.W.3d 1, 4 (Tex.App.—San Antonio 2000, pet. denied); ***Knapp v. Eppright***, 783 S.W.2d 293, 296 (Tex.App.—Houston [14th Dist.] 1989, no writ). However, the local rules of some courts prescribe time limits for responsive pleadings. *See, e.g.*, Harris Cty. Loc. R. 3.3.3 (in county courts at law, replies must be filed at least three working days before submission). If the movant needs time to cure defects in its motion, pleadings, or summary judgment evidence, it should request a continuance of the hearing.

§10.7 For special exceptions.

1. For the nonmovant. If the nonmovant challenges the motion for summary judgment by special exceptions, it must file and serve them at least seven days before the hearing. ***McConnell v. Southside ISD***, 858 S.W.2d 337, 343 n.7 (Tex.1993).

2. For the movant. If the movant challenges the response to the motion for summary judgment by special exceptions, it must file and serve them at least three days before the hearing. *Id.*

§10.8 For filing an amendment to pleadings. The filing deadlines for amendments to the pleadings (petition and answer) are different from the filing deadlines for amendments to the summary judgment motion and response. See "Procedure to amend," §9.1, p. 473.

§10.9 Late filing.

1. Filing a late motion. TRCP 166a(c) requires the movant to obtain leave of court to file a motion for summary judgment with less than 21 days' notice. Nevertheless, if the nonmovant does not object to the late motion, the error is waived. ***Ajibade v. Edinburg Gen. Hosp.***, 22 S.W.3d 37, 40 (Tex.App.—Corpus Christi 2000, no pet.); ***Luna v. Estate of Rodriguez***, 906 S.W.2d 576, 582 (Tex.App.—Austin 1995, no writ).

2. Filing after the hearing. If the movant amends or supplements its motion for summary judgment to add additional grounds after the hearing, the movant must give the nonmovant another full 21 days to respond. ***Sams v. N.L. Indus.***, 735 S.W.2d 486, 488 (Tex.App.—Houston [1st Dist.] 1987, no writ).

3. Filing a late response. The nonmovant must file its response and evidence at least seven days before the summary judgment hearing, unless it gets permission to file it later. TRCP 166a(c). If a nonmovant files a late response to the summary judgment, it must get permission from the court in writing, or the response will not be before the court. ***INA v. Bryant***, 686 S.W.2d 614, 615 (Tex.1985); ***Neely v. Coleman Enters.***, 62 S.W.3d 802, 806 (Tex.App.—Waco 2001, pet. denied); ***Lazaro v. University of Tex. Health Sci. Ctr.***, 830 S.W.2d 330, 331-32 (Tex. App.—Houston [14th Dist.] 1992, writ denied). If the record does not contain some indication the trial court granted the nonmovant leave to file a late response, the nonmovant waives the issues raised in the late response. ***Goswami v. Metropolitan S&L Ass'n***, 751 S.W.2d 487, 490 n.1 (Tex.1988); *see* ***K-Six TV***, 75 S.W.3d at 96.

4. Filing a late amendment to the response. If an amended response is filed after the deadline, and if the record does not contain a ruling by the court, the appellate court will assume the response was not before the trial court. ***INA***, 686 S.W.2d at 615; ***Mello v. A.M.F., Inc.***, 7 S.W.3d 329, 332 (Tex.App.—Beaumont 1999, pet. denied).

5. Filing late evidence. TRCP 166a(c) permits the late filing of summary judgment evidence but requires leave of court. ***Benchmark Bank v. Crowder***, 919 S.W.2d 657, 663 (Tex.1996). When filing late evidence, the party should file a motion requesting leave to file and make sure the trial court signs an order granting leave. If either the movant or the nonmovant files late summary judgment evidence or a late amendment to the evidence, and if no order appears in the record granting leave to file, the evidence will not be considered as being before the court. *See id.* (affidavit filed two days before hearing was too late); ***Basin Credit Consultants v. Obregon***, 2 S.W.3d 372, 374 (Tex.App.—San Antonio 1999, pet. denied) (affidavit filed by nonmovant after SJ hearing was filed too late); ***Luna***, 906 S.W.2d at 582 (deposition filed by movant at SJ hearing was too late); ***Texas Airfinance Corp. v. Lesikar***, 777 S.W.2d 559, 561 (Tex.App.—Houston [14th Dist.] 1989, no writ) (affidavit filed by movant 12 days before hearing was too late). If the court does not make a separate ruling granting leave to file the late evidence, it can state in the summary judgment that it granted or denied leave to file it. ***Daniell v. Citizens Bank***, 754 S.W.2d 407, 409 (Tex.App.—Corpus Christi 1988, no writ). TRCP 166a(c) permits the parties to amend the summary judgment evidence, even after the hearing, with the court's permission. For example, the court permitted a defective affidavit to be amended to add the notary's signature almost two months after the summary judgment hearing. ***Marek v. Tomoco Equip. Co.***, 738 S.W.2d 710, 713 (Tex.App.—Houston [14th Dist.] 1987, no writ) (court noted on the late-filed affidavit that it was filed "by Court").

7-3. FILING DEADLINES IN SUMMARY JUDGMENT CASES

		DEADLINE TO FILE BEFORE HEARING	ASK FOR LEAVE TO FILE LATE	OBJECTION NECESSARY IF LATE	IF NO OBJECTION, IS COMPLAINT WAIVED?
A. MOVANT					
1	Motion for SJ	21 days	yes	yes	yes
2	SJ evidence to support motion	21 days	yes	no	no
3	Amended motion with new ground	21 days	yes	yes	yes
4	Amended pleading (*e.g.*, answer)	7 days	no	yes	yes
5	Special exceptions to the response	3 days	yes	?	?
B. NONMOVANT					
1	Response to motion for SJ	7 days	yes	no	no
2	SJ evidence to support response	7 days	yes	no	no
3	Amended response	7 days	yes	no	no
4	Amended pleading (*e.g.*, petition)	7 days	no	yes	yes
5	Special exceptions to the motion	7 days	yes	?	?

§11. BURDEN OF PROOF

The most complicated part of the traditional summary judgment procedure is the burden of proof. In a simple case, the burden on the movant is easily stated. Complications arise when one of the parties asserts affirmative defenses or counterclaims. The burden also is complicated by reference to cases that predate ***City of Houston v. Clear Creek Basin Auth.***, 589 S.W.2d 671, 678 (Tex.1979). TRCP 166a was substantially revised in 1978 to require the nonmovant to provide some assistance to the trial judge. ***Clear Creek***, 589 S.W.2d at 675.

§11.1 Burden on the movant. The movant for summary judgment must show there is no genuine issue as to a material fact and that the movant is entitled to judgment as a matter of law. TRCP 166a(c); ***M.D. Anderson Hosp. v. Willrich***, 28 S.W.3d 22, 23 (Tex.2000); ***Lear Siegler, Inc. v. Perez***, 819 S.W.2d 470, 471 (Tex.1991). Even if the nonmovant does not file a response and the motion for summary judgment is uncontroverted, the movant must still carry the burden of proof. ***Clear Creek***, 589 S.W.2d at 678.

§11.2 Burden on the nonmovant. When the movant does not meet its burden of proof, the burden does not shift to the nonmovant. ***M.D. Anderson***, 28 S.W.3d at 23; ***Clear Creek***, 589 S.W.2d at 678. The burden shifts to the nonmovant only after the movant has established it is entitled to summary judgment as a matter of law. ***Casso v. Brand***, 776 S.W.2d 551, 556 (Tex.1989). Only then must the nonmovant produce any summary judgment evidence to raise a fact issue.

§11.3 When plaintiff moves for SJ. See flowchart 7-4, "Motion for Summary Judgment Under TRCP 166a(a), (b)," p. 480.

1. Plaintiff's motion. See *O'Connor's* FORM 7B:01.

(1) Prove plaintiff's cause of action. When the plaintiff moves for summary judgment on its own cause of action, the plaintiff must prove it is entitled to summary judgment by establishing each element of its claim as a matter of law. ***MMP, Ltd. v. Jones***, 710 S.W.2d 59, 60 (Tex.1986); ***Fry v. Commission for Lawyer Discipline***, 979 S.W.2d 331, 334 (Tex.App.—Houston [14th Dist.] 1998, pet. denied). If the plaintiff does not conclusively establish all the elements necessary to its cause of action, summary judgment is improper. *See, e.g.*, ***Wesson v. Jefferson S&L Ass'n***, 641 S.W.2d 903, 905-06 (Tex.1982) (because P did not prove it was D's duty to procure insurance, an essential element, SJ was improper). When the damages are unliquidated, the court may grant an interlocutory summary judgment on liability and hold a hearing on damages. TRCP 166a(a); *see* ***State v. Roberts***, 882 S.W.2d 512, 514 (Tex.App.—Austin 1994, no writ) (SJ rarely appropriate in cases with unliquidated damages).

(2) Ignore defendant's affirmative defense. When a defendant pleads an affirmative defense in its original answer, the plaintiff may ignore it in the motion for summary judgment. ***Bauer v. Jasso***, 946 S.W.2d 552, 555-56 (Tex.App.—Corpus Christi 1997, no writ). The defendant's affirmative defense will not, without summary judgment evidence, defeat the plaintiff's motion for summary judgment. ***Brownlee v. Brownlee***, 665 S.W.2d 111, 112 (Tex.1984); ***Brown v. Aztec Rig Equip.***, 921 S.W.2d 835, 845 (Tex.App.—Houston [14th Dist.] 1996, writ denied). If the plaintiff wants to force the defendant to prove its affirmative defense, the plaintiff may move for a summary judgment under TRCP 166a(i). See "No-Evidence Motion for Summary Judgment," ch. 7-C, §3, p. 486.

NOTE

The distinction between an affirmative defense and a counterclaim is important in summary judgment practice because the two place different burdens on the movant and afford different protections to the nonmovant. Recall the distinction: an affirmative defense is merely a defensive claim and does not seek damages; a counterclaim seeks damages. See "Affirmative defense vs. counterclaim," ch. 3-E, §5.1, p. 175.

(3) Challenge defendant's counterclaim under TRCP 166a(i). When the defendant asserts a counterclaim in its original answer, for the plaintiff to be entitled to a final summary judgment under TRCP 166a(c), the plaintiff must prove, as a matter of law, all the elements of the plaintiff's cause of action and disprove at least one element of the defendant's counterclaim. *See* ***Taylor v. GWR Operating Co.***, 820 S.W.2d 908, 910 (Tex. App.—Houston [1st Dist.] 1991, writ denied). Instead of moving for summary judgment under TRCP 166a(c), it is easier for the plaintiff to seek a no-evidence summary judgment on the counterclaim under TRCP 166a(i). See "No-Evidence Motion for Summary Judgment," ch. 7-C, §3, p. 486. There is no reason the two motions cannot be combined in one motion for summary judgment, but they should be argued separately in the motion.

2. Defendant's response to plaintiff's motion. See *O'Connor's* FORM 7B:04. To preclude the trial court from granting the plaintiff's motion for summary judgment, the defendant can do the following:

(1) Create fact issue about plaintiff's cause. The defendant can defeat the plaintiff's motion for summary judgment by creating a fact issue about one element of the plaintiff's cause of action. To do that, the defendant must file a response that either identifies a fact issue in the summary judgment evidence already in the record or includes summary judgment evidence that creates a fact issue. *See, e.g.*, ***Geiselman v. Cramer Fin. Group***, 965 S.W.2d 532, 534 (Tex.App.—Houston [14th Dist.] 1997, no writ) (D's response identified defects in P's affidavits, which made them incompetent).

(2) Support its counterclaim under TRCP 166a(i). If the plaintiff moved for a no-evidence summary judgment under TRCP 166a(i) on the defendant's counterclaim, the defendant should follow the procedures outlined in "The Movant's Reply to the Nonmovant's Response," ch. 7-C, §5, p. 489.

(3) Create fact issue about defendant's affirmative defense. To avoid the plaintiff's motion for summary judgment, the defendant may create fact issues about its own affirmative defense. To do that, the defendant must file a response that identifies its affirmative defense and provides summary judgment evidence that raises a fact issue on each element. ***Brownlee***, 665 S.W.2d at 112; ***Brown***, 921 S.W.2d at 845. The defendant is not required to prove its affirmative defense as a matter of law; it is required only to raise a fact issue about each element of its affirmative defense. ***Brownlee***, 665 S.W.2d at 112. If the defendant did not plead an affirmative defense in its answer, it can still assert one in its response if the plaintiff does not object. See "Challenge the pleadings," §6.6.2, p. 468. If the plaintiff moved for summary judgment under TRCP 166a(i) on the defendant's affirmative defense, the defendant is required to produce evidence to support its defense. See "Nonmovant's Response to No-Evidence Motion for Summary Judgment," ch. 7-C, §4, p. 486.

3. Plaintiff's reply to defendant's response. If the defendant, by its response and summary judgment evidence, challenged the plaintiff's right to summary judgment, the plaintiff should file a reply to assure the court that summary judgment in its favor is still warranted.

(1) Negate fact issues about plaintiff's cause. If the defendant identified or raised fact issues about the plaintiff's right to a summary judgment on its cause of action, for the plaintiff to salvage its right to a summary judgment, it must show, as a matter of law, there are no fact issues.

(2) Negate fact issues about defendant's affirmative defenses. If the defendant raised fact issues to support its affirmative defense, for the plaintiff to salvage its right to a summary judgment, it must negate, as a matter of law, the existence of at least one element of the affirmative defense.

§11.4 When defendant moves for SJ on its affirmative defense. See flowchart 7-4, below.

1. Defendant's motion. The defendant may move for summary judgment on its affirmative defense. *See* ***Randall's Food Mkts. v. Johnson***, 891 S.W.2d 640, 644 (Tex.1995). A defendant that relies on an affirmative defense must plead the defense either in its answer to the suit or in a motion for summary judgment. ***Roark v. Stallworth Oil & Gas***, 813 S.W.2d 492, 494 (Tex.1991) (unpleaded affirmative defense may serve as basis for SJ when raised in motion for SJ & nonmovant does not object). When a defendant moves for summary judgment on its affirmative defense, it must prove each element of its defense as a matter of law, leaving no issues of material fact. ***Johnson & Johnson Med. v. Sanchez***, 924 S.W.2d 925, 927 (Tex.1996); *see* ***McIntyre v. Ramirez***, 109 S.W.3d 741, 748 (Tex.2003) (when moving for SJ on affirmative defense, D has burden to conclusively establish defense). For example, when a defendant moves for summary judgment on a statute of limitations defense, the defendant must conclusively (1) prove when the cause of action accrued and (2) if the plaintiff pleaded a tolling provision, negate its application as a matter of law. ***Rhone-Poulenc, Inc. v. Steel***, 997 S.W.2d 217, 224 (Tex.1999); ***Velsicol Chem. Corp. v. Winograd***, 956 S.W.2d 529, 530 (Tex.1997); ***Jennings v. Burgess***, 917 S.W.2d 790, 793 (Tex.1996); *see, e.g.*, ***In re Matejek***, 960 S.W.2d 650, 651 (Tex.1997) (when P does not raise discovery rule in pleadings, D is not required to negate it in motion for SJ). See ***O'Connor's CPRC Plus***, "Statutes of Limitations Chart," p. 71 (2003-04); ***O'Connor's*** FORM 7B:02.

2. Plaintiff's response. The plaintiff, as the nonmovant, does not have any burden of proof unless the defendant conclusively proves all elements of its affirmative defense. See ***O'Connor's*** FORM 7B:05. If the defendant establishes its right to an affirmative defense as a matter of law, the defendant is entitled to a summary judgment unless the plaintiff can do one of the following:

(1) Challenge the pleadings. If the defendant moved for summary judgment on an affirmative defense that it did not plead in its original answer, the plaintiff can challenge the motion for summary judgment on that ground. See "Challenge the pleadings," §6.6.2, p. 468.

(2) Create fact issue. The plaintiff can create a fact issue by producing controverting evidence on one of the elements of the defendant's affirmative defense. *See, e.g.*, ***McFadden v. American United Life Ins. Co.***, 658 S.W.2d 147, 148 (Tex.1983) (P created fact issue about insurance company's defense that medical procedure was not covered by policy); ***Woodbine Elec. Serv. v. McReynolds***, 837 S.W.2d 258, 261-62 (Tex.App.—Eastland 1992, no writ) (P created fact issue about statute of limitations).

(3) Create fact issue about a counter-affirmative defense. The plaintiff can create a fact issue on each element of its own affirmative defense that counters the defendant's affirmative defense. *See, e.g.*, ***Ryland Group v. Hood***, 924 S.W.2d 120, 121 (Tex.1996) (to defeat SJ based on statute of repose, P who asserts fraudulent concealment has burden to create fact issue); ***American Petrofina v. Allen***, 887 S.W.2d 829, 830 (Tex.1994) (same); ***Williams v. Glash***, 789 S.W.2d 261, 264 (Tex.1990) (to defeat SJ based on release, P produced evidence to create fact issue about mutual mistake).

§11.5 When defendant moves for SJ on its own counterclaim. See flowchart 7-4, below.

1. Defendant's motion. When the defendant moves for summary judgment on its counterclaim, the defendant's burden is the same as for a plaintiff moving for summary judgment on its cause of action—the defendant must prove each element of its counterclaim as a matter of law. *See, e.g.*, ***Daniell v. Citizens Bank***, 754 S.W.2d 407, 409-10 (Tex.App.—Corpus Christi 1988, no writ) (bank moved for SJ on its counterclaim regarding the collateral). See the procedure under "Plaintiff's motion," §11.3.1, p. 477; ***O'Connor's*** FORM 7B:02.

2. Plaintiff's response. If the defendant established its right to a summary judgment on its counterclaim as a matter of law, to defeat the summary judgment, the plaintiff must either (1) create a fact issue about at least one element of the counterclaim or (2) create a fact issue on each element of the plaintiff's own affirmative defense to the defendant's counterclaim. See the procedure under "Defendant's response to plaintiff's motion," §11.3.2, p. 478; ***O'Connor's*** FORM 7B:05.

7-4. MOTION FOR SUMMARY JUDGMENT UNDER TRCP 166a(a), (b)

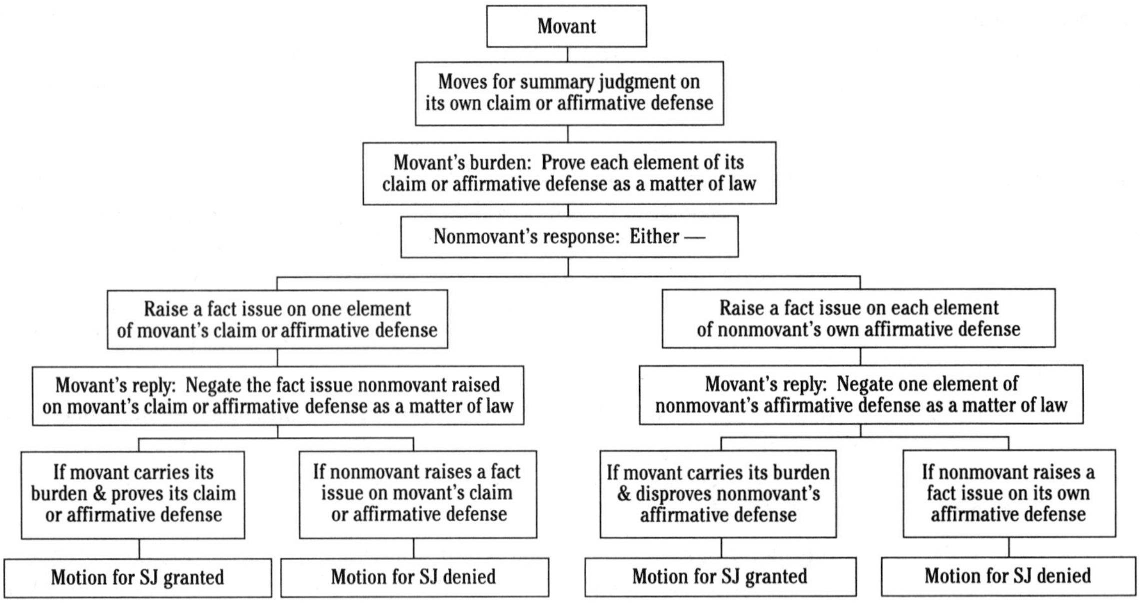

§11.6 When defendant moves for SJ on plaintiff's cause of action. Although a defendant can move for summary judgment on the plaintiff's cause of action under TRCP 166a(c)—that is, by proving with summary judgment evidence that the plaintiff has no cause of action—a defendant can accomplish the same thing under TRCP 166a(i) without providing summary judgment evidence. See "No-Evidence Motion for Summary Judgment," ch. 7-C, p. 485.

§11.7 When both parties move for SJ.

1. Burdens. When both parties move for summary judgment, each party must carry its own burden as the movant and, in response to the other party's motion, as the nonmovant. ***Martin v. Harris Cty. Appr. Dist.***, 44 S.W.3d 190, 193 (Tex.App.—Houston [14th Dist.] 2001, pet. denied); ***James v. Hitchcock ISD***, 742 S.W.2d 701, 703 (Tex.App.—Houston [1st Dist.] 1987, writ denied).

2. Evidence. When both motions are before the court, the court may consider all the summary judgment evidence in deciding whether to grant either motion. ***Martin***, 44 S.W.3d at 193; ***Rose v. Baker & Botts***, 816 S.W.2d 805, 810 (Tex.App.—Houston [1st Dist.] 1991, writ denied). The court can rely on one party's evidence to supply missing evidence in the other party's motion. ***Seaman v. Seaman***, 686 S.W.2d 206, 210 (Tex.App.—Houston [1st Dist.] 1984, writ ref'd n.r.e.).

3. SJ not automatic. Simply because both parties move for summary judgment does not mean the litigation can be resolved as a matter of law. ***Calhoun v. Killian***, 888 S.W.2d 51, 54 (Tex.App.—Tyler 1994, writ denied). There may be fact issues that preclude both motions for summary judgment.

§12. SUMMARY JUDGMENT HEARING

§12.1 Notice. The nonmovant is entitled to receive sufficient notice of a hearing date on the motion so that it knows when its response is due. See "The Notice," §5, p. 466.

§12.2 Hearing or submission. The hearing for summary judgment is for argument only; no oral testimony may be presented. TRCP 166a(c); ***Jack B. Anglin Co. v. Tipps***, 842 S.W.2d 266, 269 n.4 (Tex.1992); ***Martin v. Cohen***, 804 S.W.2d 201, 203 (Tex.App.—Houston [14th Dist.] 1991, no writ). A party is not entitled to a hearing to present argument for a motion for summary judgment. ***In re American Media Consol.***, ___ S.W.3d ___ (Tex. App.—San Antonio 2003, orig. proceeding) (No. 04-03-00545-CV; 9-10-03). The court can decide the motion for summary judgment on submission, without an appearance by the attorneys before the court. ***Martin v. Martin, Martin & Richards***, 989 S.W.2d 357, 359 (Tex.1998).

§12.3 Hearing on expert. If a movant files a motion for summary judgment that includes objections to the nonmovant's expert, the court should hold a ***Daubert-Robinson*** hearing separate from the hearing on the motion for summary judgment. *See, e.g.*, ***Heller v. Shaw Indus.***, 167 F.3d 146, 151 (3d Cir.1999) (before considering motion for SJ, court held a ***Daubert*** hearing to determine admissibility of expert's opinion). *But see* ***Weiss v. Mechanical Assoc. Servs.***, 989 S.W.2d 120, 124 & n.6 (Tex.App.—San Antonio 1999, pet. denied) (when trial court granted motion for SJ, which included objection to nonmovant's expert, appellate court assumed trial court found expert's opinion inadmissible). The ***Daubert-Robinson*** ("DR") and summary judgment ("SJ") hearings should be held separately for the following reasons: (1) the trial burdens are different (DR – preponderance of the evidence; SJ – as a matter of law); (2) the purposes of the hearings are different (DR – for testimony; SJ – for argument); (3) the appellate standards are different (DR – abuse of discretion; SJ – de novo); and (4) the appellate records are different (DR – reporter's record required; SJ – no reporter's record required). Beneke, *Experts & Summary Judgments*, 4 The Appellate Lawyer 6, 7 (1999).

§13. THE SUMMARY JUDGMENT

§13.1 Not sua sponte. The trial court does not have the authority to grant summary judgment on its own initiative. ***Daniels v. Daniels***, 45 S.W.3d 278, 282 (Tex.App.—Corpus Christi 2001, no pet.). When granting a summary judgment, the court is limited to the grounds stated in the motion for summary judgment. See "Stated in motion," §4.4.1, p. 463.

§13.2 Judgment or order?

1. Judgment. If the trial court grants the motion for summary judgment and no other issues remain, the court should sign a final judgment.

2. Order. See *O'Connor's* FORM 7B:14.

(1) Denies SJ. If the trial court denies the motion for summary judgment, the court should sign an order denying the motion.

(2) Grants partial SJ. If the trial court grants the motion for summary judgment but other issues remain pending, the court should sign an order granting the partial summary judgment.

(a) Nonsuit or severance. If the case is not fully adjudicated on the motion, the court may nonsuit or sever the unadjudicated part of the case, in which case the order granting the summary judgment becomes final. If, after granting a partial summary judgment, the court signs an order of nonsuit or severance that disposes of or severs all remaining claims, the appellate deadlines for the summary judgment begin to run on the date the court signs the order of nonsuit or severance. *See* ***Park Place Hosp. v. Estate of Milo***, 909 S.W.2d 508, 510 (Tex.1995). See Motion for Severance," ch. 5-H, §3, p. 263; "Voluntary Dismissal—Nonsuit," ch. 7-E, p. 493.

(b) Unadjudicated issues. Claims not adjudicated by the motion for summary judgment are preserved for disposition by the trial court after resolution of the motion. TRCP 166a(e); *see* ***McNally v. Guevara***, 52 S.W.3d 195, 196 (Tex.2001) (no presumption that SJ motion addresses all of movant's claims).

§13.3 Drafting the summary judgment. See *O'Connor's* FORM 9C:04.

1. Identify grounds. Although it is helpful on appeal for the summary judgment to include the grounds on which it was granted, it is not necessary. On appeal, the court will consider all grounds for summary judgment included in the motion for summary judgment. See §15.3.1, below. The appellate court will not affirm a summary judgment on a ground not presented to the trial court in the motion. See "Stated in motion," §4.4.1, p. 463.

2. State whether final or partial. The judgment should state whether it is intended to be a final or partial summary judgment. In ***Lehmann v. Har-Con Corp.***, 39 S.W.3d 191, 192 (Tex.2001), the Supreme Court overruled ***Mafrige v. Ross***, 866 S.W.2d 590 (Tex.1993), to the extent that ***Mafrige*** held a Mother Hubbard clause ("all relief not granted in this judgment is denied") transformed a partial summary judgment into a final one. Instead of the Mother Hubbard language, the Court suggested that each summary judgment intended to be final should include a statement on finality.

(1) Final summary judgment. If the parties intend the summary judgment to be a final, appealable judgment, the judgment should (1) actually dispose of all claims and parties or (2) state with unmistakable clarity that it is a final judgment as to all claims and all parties. ***Lehmann***, 39 S.W.3d at 192-93. See "Statement of finality," ch. 9-C, §4.3, p. 598; "What judgments are final," ch. 9-C, §6.3, p. 603.

(2) Partial summary judgment. If the parties intend the summary judgment to be a partial judgment, the judgment should so state. A summary judgment is a partial, interlocutory order if it does not dispose of all claims and all parties. ***Lehmann***, 39 S.W.3d at 205. The following orders are not final orders:

(a) An order that adjudicates the plaintiff's claims but not a counterclaim, cross-claim, or third party claim. *Id.* Or the converse, an order that adjudicates a counterclaim, cross-claim, or third party claim but not the plaintiff's claims. *Id.*

(b) An order that disposes of the claims by only one of multiple plaintiffs. *Id.*; ***Liu v. Yang***, 69 S.W.3d 225, 228 (Tex.App.—Corpus Christi 2001, no pet.). Or the converse, an order that disposes of the claims against only one of multiple defendants. ***Lehmann***, 39 S.W.3d at 205.

3. Resolve issues on the merits. A summary judgment should not state that the case is dismissed. ***Martinez v. Southern P.T. Co.***, 951 S.W.2d 824, 830 (Tex.App.—San Antonio 1997, no writ); ***Heibel v. Bermann***, 407 S.W.2d 945, 947 (Tex.App.—Houston [1st Dist.] 1966, no writ). A summary judgment should dispose of claims on the merits, not by dismissal. *See, e.g.*, ***Martinez***, 951 S.W.2d at 830 (appellate court reformed judgment to delete "dismissal with prejudice" language, leaving "take nothing" language).

4. Overrule objections. The nonmovant should make sure the summary judgment includes a statement that all of its objections and any special exceptions were overruled. See "Secure ruling on objections," §6.8, p. 471. If the court refuses to rule, the nonmovant should object to the refusal in writing. By objecting to the court's refusal to rule, the nonmovant will preserve error on the objection. TRAP 33.1(a)(2)(B). See "Refusal to rule + objection," ch. 1-G, §2.2.3, p. 33.

§13.4 To make a partial SJ final. To convert a partial summary judgment into a final one, the unadjudicated claims can be resolved on the merits by another summary judgment or at trial, dismissed from the case, or severed from the partial summary judgment. See "What judgments are final," ch. 9-C, §6.3, p. 603.

PRACTICE TIP

If you discover on appeal that what you thought was a final summary judgment is really a partial judgment, you may be able to convert it to a final judgment by asking the trial court to sever it from the rest of the suit, allowing you to continue with the appeal. See TRAP 27.2, 27.3; ***State Farm Mut. Auto. Ins. Co. v. Leeds****, 981 S.W.2d 693, 693 (Tex.App.—Houston [1st Dist.] 1998, no pet.).*

§14. MOTION FOR NEW TRIAL

See "MNT After Summary Judgment," ch. 10-B, §11, p. 624; ***O'Connor's*** FORM 10B:06.

§15. REVIEW

§15.1 Appellate record. The appellate record for summary judgment is limited to the clerk's record. As a rule, no reporter's record is necessary because no oral testimony can be received at the hearing. TRCP 166a(c). However, a reporter's record may be necessary if the court made rulings about the summary judgment that are reflected only in the reporter's record. ***Aguilar v. LVDVD, L.C.***, 70 S.W.3d 915, 917 (Tex.App.—El Paso 2002, order on mot.) (hearing preserved ruling on written objections). See ***O'Connor's Texas Civil Appeals***, "Summary judgment," ch. 16-C, §4.2.1, p. 187 (2002-03).

§15.2 Final summary judgment. As a general rule, only final summary judgments can be appealed. See "Final Judgment," ch. 9-C, §6, p. 602. If a summary judgment leaves some claims unresolved, it is an interlocutory order and cannot be appealed until after the rendition of a final judgment. ***Lehmann***, 39 S.W.3d at 205. In ***Lehmann***, the Supreme Court distinguished between the finality that makes a judgment appealable and the issue of finality that is reviewed on appeal. See "Finality for purposes of appeal," ch. 9-C, §6.4, p. 605.

§15.3 Appeal when SJ granted. A summary judgment becomes final and appealable when the trial court disposes of all the parties and issues in the lawsuit. ***Park Place Hosp. v. Estate of Milo***, 909 S.W.2d 508, 510 (Tex. 1995). Once the trial court grants a final summary judgment, the nonmovant may appeal.

1. Grounds for review. The appellate court may review and affirm on any ground the movant presented to the court in its motion for summary judgment, regardless of whether the trial court identified the ground relied on to grant the summary judgment. ***Cincinnati Life Ins. Co. v. Cates***, 927 S.W.2d 623, 625 (Tex.1996). In addition, the appellate court may review grounds in earlier summary judgment motions, even though they were denied. See §15.4.2, below.

2. SJ grants more relief than requested. When a summary judgment disposes of more claims than the motion requested, the appellate court should affirm the grounds on which it was properly granted and reverse the unaddressed grounds for further proceedings. ***Bandera Elec. Coop. v. Gilchrist***, 946 S.W.2d 336, 337 (Tex. 1997) (P's motion for SJ did not address counterclaim); ***Page v. Geller***, 941 S.W.2d 101, 102 (Tex.1997) (motion for SJ granted more relief than requested). The appellate court should not reverse the entire case. ***Bandera***, 946 S.W.2d at 337; ***Page***, 941 S.W.2d at 102.

3. SJ appealed by agreed motion. Some interlocutory orders granting summary judgment may be appealable by agreed motion to the trial court and the court of appeals. See ***O'Connor's Texas Civil Appeals***, "Appealable orders by agreed motion," ch. 13-P, §2.2, p. 131.

§15.4 Appeal when SJ denied. In most cases, an order denying a motion for summary judgment is not a final judgment and thus is not appealable. *See* ***Ackerman v. Vordenbaum***, 403 S.W.2d 362, 365 (Tex.1966); ***Cummings v. Cire***, 74 S.W.3d 920, 923-24 (Tex.App.—Amarillo 2002, pet. granted 4-17-03). There are exceptions:

1. **Both parties move for SJ.** When both parties move for summary judgment and the trial court grants one motion but denies the other, the result is a final judgment. The party that did not prevail may appeal on both the summary judgment granted against it and on its motion for summary judgment that was denied. ***Commissioners Ct. v. Agan***, 940 S.W.2d 77, 81 (Tex.1997); ***Holmes v. Morales***, 924 S.W.2d 920, 922 (Tex.1996); ***Jones v. Strauss***, 745 S.W.2d 898, 900 (Tex.1988). If the appellate court finds the summary judgment was erroneously granted, the court will review the ruling on the opposing motion and grant summary judgment based on that motion if it finds the trial court should have granted it. ***Agan***, 940 S.W.2d at 81; ***Holmes***, 924 S.W.2d at 922; ***Jones***, 745 S.W.2d at 900. The reviewing court should review the summary judgment evidence presented by both sides and determine all questions presented. ***Agan***, 940 S.W.2d at 81; ***Samms v. Autumn Run Cmty. Imprv. Ass'n***, 23 S.W.3d 398, 401 (Tex.App.—Houston [1st Dist.] 2000, pet. denied). Before the appellate court can reverse and render for the other party, that party must be entitled to a final—not partial—summary judgment as a matter of law. ***CU Lloyd's v. Feldman***, 977 S.W.2d 568, 569 (Tex.1998); ***Jones***, 745 S.W.2d at 900; *see* ***Bowman v. Lumberton ISD***, 801 S.W.2d 883, 889 (Tex.1990). See "When both parties move for SJ," §11.7, p. 480.

2. **Denial of earlier SJ.** In the appeal of a summary judgment, the appellate court may review grounds in earlier summary judgment motions that the trial court denied. ***Baker Hughes, Inc. v. Keco R.&D., Inc.***, 12 S.W.3d 1, 5 (Tex.1999).

3. **Denial of official-immunity SJ.**

(1) **Appeal.** Under CPRC §51.014(a)(5), an officer or employee of a state or political subdivision who asserts a qualified immunity may appeal the denial of a motion for summary judgment to the court of appeals before the entry of a final judgment. See ***O'Connor's Texas Civil Appeals***, "Denies official-immunity SJ," ch. 11-B, §2.2.1(5), p. 10; ***O'Connor's COA***, "Summary judgment," ch. 22-A, §4.1.1(2), p. 641.

03 (2) **Stay.** The interlocutory appeal of an order denying a summary judgment based on an assertion of immunity does not automatically stay the commencement of trial during the appeal. CPRC §51.014(c). For when the defendant may be entitled to a stay after the denial of a summary judgment based on an assertion of immunity, see ***O'Connor's Texas Civil Appeals***, "Orders resulting in automatic stay," ch. 13-P, §3.1.1, p. 132. An interlocutory appeal under CPRC §51.014(a)(5), however, does stay all other proceedings in the trial court pending resolution of that appeal. CPRC §51.014(b).

4. **Denial of free-speech SJ.** Under CPRC §51.014(a)(6), a defendant in a defamation case may appeal the denial of a motion for summary judgment to the court of appeals if (1) the defendant is a member of the electronic or print media or a person whose communication was published by the electronic or print media, and (2) the defendant asserted a claim or defense involving free speech or free press under the U.S. Constitution 1st Amendment, the Texas Constitution article I, §8, or CPRC chapter 73. See ***O'Connor's Texas Civil Appeals***, "Denies free-speech SJ," ch. 11-B, §2.2.1(4), p. 10; ***O'Connor's COA***, "Interlocutory appeal," ch. 16-A, §6.5, p. 367. An interlocutory appeal of an order denying a motion for summary judgment under CPRC §51.014(a)(6) automatically stays the commencement of trial during the appeal. *See* CPRC §51.014(b).

§15.5 Mandamus – refusal to rule. Mandamus is appropriate when the trial court refuses to rule on a timely submitted motion for summary judgment to prevent the movant from perfecting a statutory interlocutory appeal. *See* ***In re American Media Consol.***, ___ S.W.3d ___ (Tex.App.—San Antonio 2003, orig. proceeding) (No. 04-03-00545-CV; 9-10-03) (mandamus denied); ***Grant v. Wood***, 916 S.W.2d 42, 45 (Tex.App.—Houston [1st Dist.] 1995, orig. proceeding) (mandamus granted). If the record does not reflect a refusal to rule but rather shows only a failure to rule, mandamus is not appropriate. *See* ***American Media Consol.***, ___ S.W.3d at ___.

C. NO-EVIDENCE MOTION FOR SUMMARY JUDGMENT

The no-evidence summary judgment is a procedural device designed to help the party who does not have the burden of proof at trial, generally the defendant. *See* ***Nowak v. DAS Inv. Corp.***, 110 S.W.3d 677, 680 (Tex.App.—Houston [14th Dist.] 2003, n.p.h.) (party cannot file no-evidence SJ motion on claim or defense on which it has burden of proof); ***Keszler v. Memorial Med. Ctr.***, 105 S.W.3d 122, 125 (Tex.App.—Corpus Christi 2003, no pet.) (no-evidence SJ motion is fundamentally flawed when used against party who would not have burden of proof at trial on element or issue raised). The only instance in which a no-evidence motion can help the plaintiff is when the burden of proof is on the defendant (*e.g.*, to challenge a defendant's affirmative defense or counterclaim).

§1. GENERAL

§1.1 Rule. TRCP 166a(i).

§1.2 Purpose. The purpose of the no-evidence summary judgment procedure, which is modeled after federal summary judgment practice, is to pierce the pleadings and evaluate the evidence to see if a trial is necessary. ***Benitz v. Gould Group***, 27 S.W.3d 109, 112 (Tex.App.—San Antonio 2000, no pet.). To accomplish this, the no-evidence summary judgment procedure is designed to isolate and dispose of claims or defenses not supported by facts. *Cf.* ***Celotex Corp. v. Catrett***, 477 U.S. 317, 323-24, 106 S.Ct. 2548, 2553 (1986) (purpose of FRCP 56(e) is to dispose of unsupported claims). A no-evidence summary judgment does not violate the right to a jury trial. ***Springer v. American Zurich Ins. Co.***, 115 S.W.3d 582, 585 (Tex.App.—Waco 2003, pet. denied).

§1.3 Forms & timetable. ***O'Connor's Texas Civil Forms***, FORMS 7C; Timetable, this book, Motion for Summary Judgment, p. 1008.

§1.4 Other references. Patton, *Summary Judgments in Texas*, §5.06, p. 6 (2d ed. Supp. 2002).

§2. DISCOVERY & THE NO-EVIDENCE MOTION FOR SUMMARY

§2.1 Adequate time for discovery. The no-evidence motion for summary judgment should be filed after the nonmovant has had "an adequate time for discovery." TRCP 166a(i); ***Morehouse v. Chase Manhattan Bank***, 76 S.W.3d 608, 612 (Tex.App.—San Antonio 2002, no pet.); ***In re Mohawk Rubber Co.***, 982 S.W.2d 494, 498 (Tex. App.—Texarkana 1998, orig. proceeding). The rule does not require that discovery be completed. ***Specialty Retailers v. Fuqua***, 29 S.W.3d 140, 145 (Tex.App.—Houston [14th Dist.] 2000, pet. denied).

1. After discovery period. When a no-evidence motion for summary judgment is filed after the discovery period for the case, the motion is presumed timely. *See* Notes & Comments to TRCP 166a(i) (discovery period set by pretrial order should be adequate opportunity for discovery unless there is a contrary showing).

2. During discovery period. When a no-evidence motion for summary judgment is filed before the end of the discovery period, it is considered timely as long as the nonmovant had adequate time for discovery. See §4.2.2, below.

§2.2 Factors. To determine whether the nonmovant had an adequate time for discovery, the courts examine some of the following factors: (1) the nature of the claim, (2) the evidence necessary to controvert the motion, (3) the length of time the case was on file, (4) the length of time the no-evidence motion was on file, (5) whether the movant requested stricter deadlines for discovery, (6) the amount of discovery already conducted, and (7) whether the discovery deadlines in place were specific or vague. ***Restaurant Teams Int'l v. MG Sec. Corp.***, 95 S.W.3d 336, 339 (Tex.App.—Dallas 2002, no pet.) (7-month old case); ***Martinez v. City of San Antonio***, 40 S.W.3d 587, 591 (Tex. App.—San Antonio 2001, pet. denied) (5-year old case); ***Specialty Retailers***, 29 S.W.3d at 145 (16-month old case); *see* ***Carter v. MacFadyen***, 93 S.W.3d 307, 311 (Tex.App.—Houston [14th Dist.] 2002, pet. denied) (8-month old case); *see also* ***McClure v. Attebury***, 20 S.W.3d 722, 729 (Tex.App.—Amarillo 1999, no pet.) (need for discovery minimal because issue was a question of law). Only one no-evidence summary judgment has been reversed on the ground the nonmovant did not have adequate time for discovery. *See* ***Tempay, Inc. v. TNT Concrete & Constr.***, 37

S.W.3d 517, 522-23 (Tex.App.—Austin 2001, pet. denied) (motion for continuance should have been granted to allow P to complete discovery).

§3. NO-EVIDENCE MOTION FOR SUMMARY JUDGMENT

§3.1 Form of motion. The motion for no-evidence summary judgment must follow the general summary judgment rules. That is, it must be in writing and should not be verified. See "In writing," ch. 7-B, §4.2, p. 463; "Unverified," ch. 7-B, §4.3, p. 463; ***O'Connor's*** FORM 7C:01. If the motion does not unambiguously state that it is filed under TRCP 166a(i) and does not strictly comply with the rule's requirements, the motion will be treated as a traditional summary judgment motion. ***Keszler***, 105 S.W.3d at 125.

§3.2 The allegations. The no-evidence motion for summary judgment should be organized as follows:

1. Discovery statement. The motion should include the statement that an adequate time for discovery has passed. See §2, above. The movant probably should identify the date the suit was filed and describe the discovery completed and any pending discovery.

2. Nonmovant's claim. The motion should identify the nonmovant's claims or defenses and list their elements.

3. Specific element challenged. The motion must state there is no evidence to support one or more specific elements of a claim or defense on which the nonmovant has the burden of proof at trial. ***Callaghan Ranch v. Killam***, 53 S.W.3d 1, 3 (Tex.App.—San Antonio 2000, pet. denied); Notes & Comments to TRCP 166a(i). The motion cannot generally allege there is no evidence to support the nonmovant's claim or defense. Notes & Comments to TRCP 166a(i). The specificity requirement is designed to avoid conclusory no-evidence challenges to the nonmovant's cause of action. ***Specialty Retailers***, 29 S.W.3d at 147. When a no-evidence motion for summary judgment does not challenge specific elements, it should be treated as a traditional motion for summary judgment under TRCP 166a(c), which imposes the burden of proof on the movant, not as a motion under TRCP 166a(i), which imposes the burden on the nonmovant. *See* ***Michael v. Dyke***, 41 S.W.3d 746, 751-52 (Tex.App.—Corpus Christi 2001, no pet.); ***Amouri v. Southwest Toyota***, 20 S.W.3d 165, 168 (Tex.App.—Texarkana 2000, pet. denied); ***Weaver v. Highlands Ins. Co.***, 4 S.W.3d 826, 829 n.2 (Tex.App.—Houston [1st Dist.] 1999, no pet.).

PRACTICE TIP

For a list of the elements for various causes of action, see ***O'Connor's Texas Causes of Action*** *(2004).*

---

4. Relief. The motion should include a prayer for relief—either final or partial summary judgment. See "Motion for final SJ," ch. 7-B, §4.6, p. 465; "Motion for partial SJ," ch. 7-B, §4.7, p. 465.

§3.3 No supporting evidence. A no-evidence motion for summary judgment does not require supporting evidence. *See* ***McClure***, 20 S.W.3d at 727; ***Moore v. K Mart Corp.***, 981 S.W.2d 266, 269 (Tex.App.—San Antonio 1998, pet. denied).

§3.4 Attorney fees. If the movant is entitled to attorney fees, it should include a request for attorney fees in the motion. See "Attorney fees," ch. 7-B, §4.9, p. 465. Because the movant has the burden of proof on its attorney fees, the movant must support its claim for attorney fees with summary judgment evidence.

§3.5 The notice. The movant must give the nonmovant written notice of the hearing on the motion. See "The Notice," ch. 7-B, §5, p. 466.

§4. NONMOVANT'S RESPONSE TO NO-EVIDENCE MOTION FOR SUMMARY JUDGMENT

The nonmovant's response to a no-evidence motion for summary judgment serves three functions: (1) it supplies evidence to raise a fact issue on the challenged element, (2) it identifies any procedural defect in the motion, and

(3) it presents any other reasons why the summary judgment should not be granted. Because TRCP 166a(i) requires the trial court to grant the no-evidence motion for summary judgment if the nonmovant does not produce evidence that raises a genuine issue of material fact, the court may grant a no-evidence summary judgment by default if the nonmovant does not file a response and the motion warrants rendition of a final summary judgment. ***Roventini v. Ocular Sci.***, 111 S.W.3d 719, 722 (Tex.App.—Houston [1st Dist.] 2003, n.p.h.). See "Mandatory," §7.1, p. 490.

§4.1 Form of response. The response to the no-evidence motion for summary judgment must follow the general summary judgment rules. That is, it must be in writing and should not be verified. See "In writing," ch. 7-B, §6.1, p. 467; "Unverified," ch. 7-B, §6.2, p. 467; ***O'Connor's*** FORM 7C:02.

§4.2 Objections. In the response to the motion for summary judgment, the nonmovant should object to any defect in the form or substance of the motion or pleadings. The nonmovant will waive most objections to the summary judgment not included in its response. See "Waiver," ch. 7-B, §6.9, p. 472. The record should contain written rulings on the objections. See "Secure ruling on objections," ch. 7-B, §6.8, p. 471; ***O'Connor's*** FORMS 7B:11-13.

1. Challenge the notice. If the movant did not file and serve the motion, the notice of hearing, and the evidence 21 days in advance of the hearing, the nonmovant must object. *See* TRCP 166a(d). See "Challenge the notice," ch. 7-B, §6.6.4, p. 468; ***O'Connor's*** FORM 7B:07.

2. Challenge timing of motion. If the no-evidence motion was filed before the end of the discovery period, the nonmovant may allege the motion was premature because the nonmovant did not have adequate time for discovery. See "Factors," §2.2, p. 485.

3. Challenge the motion. The nonmovant should challenge all legal and procedural shortcomings in the motion.

(1) Lacks specificity. When a no-evidence motion globally challenges the nonmovant's claim or defense, the nonmovant should object. *See* Notes & Comments to TRCP 166a(i) ("paragraph (i) does not authorize conclusory motions or general no-evidence challenges"). However, the failure to object does not waive the error. ***In re Estate of Swanson***, ___ S.W.3d ___ (Tex.App.—El Paso 2003, n.p.h.) (No. 08-02-00154-CV; 9-25-03); ***Crocker v. Paulyne's Nursing Home***, 95 S.W.3d 416, 419 (Tex.App.—Dallas 2002, no pet.); ***Cuyler v. Minns***, 60 S.W.3d 209, 213 (Tex.App.—Houston [14th Dist.] 2001, pet. denied); ***Callaghan Ranch***, 53 S.W.3d at 3. *Contra* ***Williams v. Bank One***, 15 S.W.3d 110, 117 (Tex.App.—Waco 1999, no pet.) (treated no-evidence motion challenging 5 causes of action in 2 sentences as TRCP 166a(i) motion & affirmed for failure to object to lack of specificity). When a no-evidence motion for summary judgment does not challenge specific elements, it should be treated as a traditional motion for summary judgment under TRCP 166a(c), which imposes the burden of proof on the movant. See §3.2.3, above.

(2) Other challenges. See "Objections to SJ motion," ch. 7-B, §6.6, p. 467.

4. Challenge use of SJ. If the motion for summary judgment is based on a pleading defect in the nonmovant's petition or answer, the nonmovant should (1) object on the ground that the movant is required to challenge pleadings by special exceptions and (2) move to correct the defect. See "Special Exceptions & Summary Judgments," ch. 3-G, §10, p. 193; "Challenge the use of SJ," ch. 7-B, §6.6.1, p. 467.

§4.3 Burden of proof. The nonmovant has the entire burden of proof once the movant files a no-evidence motion. TRCP 166a(i). The burden of proof in a summary judgment proceeding is on the same party who would bear the burden of proof at trial. ***Marsaglia v. UTEP***, 22 S.W.3d 1, 3 (Tex.App.—El Paso 1999, pet. denied); ***Esco Oil & Gas v. Sooner Pipe & Sup. Corp.***, 962 S.W.2d 193, 197 n.3 (Tex.App.—Houston [1st Dist.] 1998, pet. denied). The burden on the nonmovant is to raise a genuine issue of material fact about the element challenged by the motion for summary judgment. TRCP 166a(i); ***Dow Chem Co. v. Francis***, 46 S.W.3d 237, 242 (Tex.2001); ***Praytor v. Fort Motor Co.***, 97 S.W.3d 237, 241 (Tex.App.—Houston [14th Dist.] 2002, no pet.). The trial court must resolve all reasonable doubts about the facts in favor of the nonmovant. ***Lehrer v. Zwernemann***, 14 S.W.3d 775, 777 (Tex. App.—Houston [1st Dist.] 2000, pet. denied).

7-5. NO-EVIDENCE MOTION FOR SUMMARY JUDGMENT UNDER TRCP 166a(i)

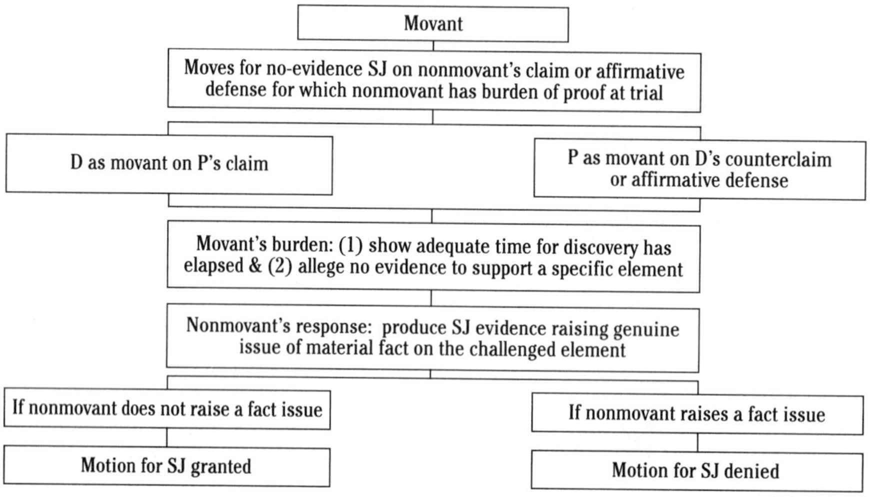

§4.4 Grounds for response. To defeat a no-evidence motion for summary judgment, the nonmovant must prove there is a genuine issue of material fact on the elements challenged by the movant as having no evidence. *See* TRCP 166a(i). The response should include a heading for each element that was challenged and under that heading a discussion of the evidence that creates a fact issue for that element. If the nonmovant discusses all the facts under one general heading called "Facts," the nonmovant may forget to address one of the elements. *Cf.* ***Johnson v. Brewer & Pritchard, P.C.***, 73 S.W.3d 193, 204 (Tex.2002) (although movant addressed issue of fiduciary relationship, it did not address issue of breach).

PRACTICE TIP

When a no-evidence motion challenges all the elements of the cause of action, the nonmovant should remember to support its damages with evidence. The court will grant a no-evidence motion for summary judgment when a nonmovant forgets to support a challenged damage element with evidence. ***Dow Chem. Co. v. Francis****, 46 S.W.3d 237, 242 (Tex.2001).*

§4.5 How to produce SJ evidence under TRCP 166a(i). The Notes & Comments to TRCP 166a(i) state that, to defeat a no-evidence motion, the nonmovant "is not required to marshal its proof; its response need only point out evidence that raises a fact issue on the challenged elements." Notes & Comments to TRCP 166a(i); ***Saenz v. Southern Un. Gas Co.***, 999 S.W.2d 490, 493-94 (Tex.App.—El Paso 1999, pet. denied). The nonmovant should prepare summary judgment evidence in the same form as would be admissible at trial. See "Summary Judgment Evidence," ch. 7-B, §3, p. 456.

§4.6 Sufficiency of evidence. TRCP 166a(i) states that the court should grant the motion unless the nonmovant presents summary judgment evidence that raises a genuine issue of material fact on each element challenged. ***In re Mohawk Rubber Co.***, 982 S.W.2d 494, 498 (Tex.App.—Texarkana 1998, orig. proceeding). A no-evidence motion is essentially a motion for a pretrial directed verdict. ***Ridgway v. Ford Motor Co.***, 82 S.W.3d 26, 29 (Tex.App.—San Antonio 2002, pet. granted 3-27-03). To defeat a no-evidence motion for summary judgment, the nonmovant must produce more than a scintilla of evidence to raise a genuine issue of material fact on the challenged elements. TRCP 166a(i); ***Forbes, Inc. v. Granada Biosciences***, ___ S.W.3d ___ (Tex.2003) (No. 01-0788; 12-19-03); ***Boales v. Brighton Builders***, 29 S.W.3d 159, 164 (Tex.App.—Houston [14th Dist.] 2000, pet. denied). If the nonmovant presents more than a scintilla of evidence on the challenged elements, it is entitled to a trial on the merits. ***Ridgway***, 82 S.W.3d at 29. A nonmovant produces more than a scintilla when the evidence "rises to a level that would enable reasonable and fair-minded people to differ in their conclusions." *Id.* at 29; ***Marsaglia v. UTEP***, 22 S.W.3d 1, 4 (Tex.App.—El Paso 1999, pet. denied); *cf.* ***Merrell Dow Pharms. v. Havner***, 953 S.W.2d 706, 711 (Tex.1997) (jury trial). A nonmovant produces less than a scintilla when the evidence is "so weak as to do no more than create a mere surmise or suspicion" of a fact. ***Forbes***, ___ S.W.3d ___; ***Marsaglia***, 22 S.W.3d at 4; *cf.* ***Kindred v. Con/Chem, Inc.***, 650 S.W.2d 61, 63 (Tex.1983) (jury trial).

§4.7 Expert testimony. If expert testimony is required to defeat a no-evidence motion for summary judgment, the nonmovant must produce evidence that meets the test for expert testimony. *See* ***Praytor v. Ford Motor Co.***, 97 S.W.3d 237, 242-43 (Tex.App.—Houston [14th Dist.] 2002, no pet.) (nonmovant did not produce TRE 702 proof for expert's opinion about causation). See "The *Daubert-Robinson* Test for Expert Testimony," ch. 5-M, §2, p. 303.

§4.8 File motion for continuance. When a nonmovant needs additional time to secure affidavits or discovery, it should file a motion for continuance. See "Motion to continue SJ hearing," ch. 5-D, §9.3, p. 246; ***O'Connor's*** FORM 7B:09.

§4.9 Other responsive pleadings. When appropriate, the nonmovant may file any of the following:

1. An amended petition or answer. See "Amending the Petition or Answer," ch. 7-B, §9, p. 473.
2. A cross-motion for summary judgment. See "When both parties move for SJ," ch. 7-B, §11.7, p. 480.
3. A nonsuit. See "Consider a nonsuit," ch. 7-B, §6.11, p. 472.

§5. THE MOVANT'S REPLY TO THE NONMOVANT'S RESPONSE

§5.1 Deadline. There is no deadline in TRCP 166a for a movant to file a reply to the nonmovant's response. ***Callaghan Ranch v. Killam***, 53 S.W.3d 1, 4 (Tex.App.—San Antonio 2000, pet. denied). See "For the movant's reply to the response," ch. 7-B, §10.6, p. 475.

§5.2 Negate nonmovant's evidence. In the reply, the movant can attempt to negate the nonmovant's claim that there is evidence of a triable fact regarding its claims or defenses. *Cf.* ***Irby v. Bittick***, 44 F.3d 949, 953 (11th Cir.1995) (under FRCP 56(e), nonmovant must do more than assert there is some doubt about the material facts).

§5.3 Object to nonmovant's SJ evidence. The movant should object to any of the nonmovant's summary judgment evidence that would not be admissible at trial. *See* TRCP 166a(f). See "Objections to the SJ evidence," ch. 7-B, §6.7, p. 469.

§5.4 Produce SJ evidence. When a nonmovant produces summary judgment evidence supporting the challenged element of its claim or defense, the movant can produce summary judgment evidence to attempt to disprove or discredit the nonmovant's evidence. See "Summary Judgment Evidence," ch. 7-B, §3, p. 456.

§5.5 Respond to motion for continuance. See "Response to the motion," ch. 5-D, §9.3.4, p. 247.

§5.6 File special exceptions. If the claims in the response are vague, unintelligible, unclear, or ambiguous, the movant should challenge them by special exceptions. See "Summary Judgment *and* Special Exceptions," ch. 7-B, §8, p. 473.

§5.7 No additional grounds. In its reply, the movant cannot add challenges to the nonmovant's claims or defenses. ***Callaghan Ranch***, 53 S.W.3d at 4; *see* ***Specialty Retailers v. Fuqua***, 29 S.W.3d 140, 148 (Tex.App.—Houston [14th Dist.] 2000, pet. denied) (nonmovant had no burden to present evidence to support claims challenged for the first time in the reply).

§6. THE NONMOVANT'S TIME TO CURE

The court should give the nonmovant the opportunity to cure any defects in its summary judgment evidence identified by the movant in its reply. *See* TRCP 166a(f) (party should be given opportunity to cure defects in form of affidavits & attachments).

§6.1 Deadline to cure. Nothing in TRCP 166a provides a deadline to cure defects in a party's evidence once objections have been filed. Under the TRCP 166a(a)-(b) summary judgment procedure, the time to cure is built in because an adverse ruling is not fatal to the party with the summary judgment burden of proof. Under TRCP 166a(a)-(b), if the trial court rules adversely to the movant (the party with the summary judgment burden of proof) based on defects in its evidence, the court merely denies the motion, which is in effect an opportunity to cure because the movant can file another motion. By comparison, in a no-evidence summary judgment under TRCP 166a(i), if the trial court rules adversely to the nonmovant (the party with the burden of proof) based on defects in the response or the evidence, the court grants the motion for summary judgment, which is fatal to the nonmovant's case. The opportunity to cure in TRCP 166a(f) should apply to both the movant and nonmovant in both types of summary judgments. *See, e.g.*, ***Webster v. Allstate Ins. Co.***, 833 S.W.2d 747, 750 (Tex.App.—Houston [1st Dist.] 1992, no writ) (trial court should not have sustained objections to party's evidence on day of hearing without giving party chance to amend).

§6.2 Motion for continuance. If the movant identified defects in the nonmovant's pleading, response, or evidence, the nonmovant should file a motion for continuance asking the court for time to cure the defects. *See* ***Peerenboom v. HSP Foods***, 910 S.W.2d 156, 160 (Tex.App.—Waco 1995, no writ); ***Webster***, 833 S.W.2d at 750. See §4.8, above. The nonmovant will need additional time because the movant's reply, if filed by the three-day deadline recommended for the movant's special exceptions in ***McConnell v. Southside ISD***, 858 S.W.2d 337, 343 n.7 (Tex. 1993), will not provide the nonmovant with sufficient time to cure the defect. The nonmovant should ask the court to state a deadline to cure the defects and a date for the hearing. *See* ***Peerenboom***, 910 S.W.2d at 160 (appellate court did not consider evidence because party did not file it 7 days before new hearing date).

§7. TRIAL COURT'S RULING UNDER TRCP 166a(i)

§7.1 Mandatory. TRCP 166a(i) requires the trial court to grant the motion for no-evidence summary judgment if the nonmovant does not produce summary judgment evidence that raises a genuine issue of material fact. *See* ***Dolcefino v. Randolph***, 19 S.W.3d 906, 917 (Tex.App.—Houston [14th Dist.] 2000, pet. denied); ***Saenz v. Southern Un. Gas Co.***, 999 S.W.2d 490, 492-93 (Tex.App.—El Paso 1999, pet. denied).

§7.2 The judgment. See "The Summary Judgment," ch. 7-B, §13, p. 481.

§8. OTHER SUMMARY JUDGMENT PROCEDURES

§8.1 Deadlines. See "Deadlines for Summary Judgment," ch. 7-B, §10, p. 474.

§8.2 Hearing. See "The Summary Judgment Hearing," ch. 7-B, §12, p. 481.

§8.3 Summary judgment or order. See "The Summary Judgment," ch. 7-B, §13, p. 481.

§8.4 Motion for new trial. See "MNT After Summary Judgment," ch. 10-B, §11, p. 624.

§8.5 Review. The appellate courts should apply the same legal sufficiency standard in reviewing a no-evidence summary judgment as they apply in reviewing a directed verdict. ***Garcia v. National Eligibility Express***, 4 S.W.3d 887, 889 (Tex.App.—Houston [1st Dist.] 1999, no pet.); ***Moore v. K Mart Corp.***, 981 S.W.2d 266, 269 (Tex. App.—San Antonio 1998, pet. denied). The review of judgments granted under TRCP 166a(i) is the same as under TRCP 166a(a)-(b). See "Review," ch. 7-B, §15, p. 483.

§8.6 Sanctions. The Notes & Comments state that a motion under TRCP 166a(i) is subject to sanctions provided by existing law and refer parenthetically to CPRC §9.001, §10.006, and TRCP 13. Notes & Comments to TRCP 166a(i). See "Groundless or Frivolous Pleadings," ch. 1-B, §5, p. 10.

D. MOTION FOR JUDGMENT ON AGREED STATEMENT OF FACTS

§1. GENERAL

§1.1 Rules. TRCP 263. See TRCP 11.

§1.2 Purpose. The purpose of a motion for judgment on an agreed statement of facts under TRCP 263 is to ask the trial court to render a decision on the law when the facts are not in controversy. ***State Bar v. Faubion***, 821 S.W.2d 203, 205 (Tex.App.—Houston [14th Dist.] 1991, writ denied). TRCP 263 requires the parties to agree on all ultimate facts essential for determination of the lawsuit, leaving to the court the function of deciding questions of law.

§1.3 Forms. ***O'Connor's Texas Civil Forms***, FORMS 7D.

§2. DISTINCTION BETWEEN AGREED STATEMENT & STIPULATIONS

An agreed case under TRCP 263 is not the same thing as a case tried on stipulated facts. *See* ***Perry v. Aetna Life Ins. Co.***, 380 S.W.2d 868, 875 (Tex.App.—Tyler 1964, writ ref'd n.r.e.). Parties may stipulate to some undisputed facts without submitting the case as an agreed case. The ordinary stipulation permits the trial court to make any findings and indulge in any inferences supported by the evidence. ***Farah v. First Nat'l Bank***, 624 S.W.2d 341, 345 (Tex.App.—Fort Worth 1981, writ ref'd n.r.e.); ***Parsons v. Watley***, 492 S.W.2d 61, 63 (Tex.App.—Eastland 1973, no writ); ***Perry***, 380 S.W.2d at 875. A case submitted on an agreed statement of facts does not permit the court to make inferences from the facts, unless the parties so stipulate. ***City of Galveston v. Giles***, 902 S.W.2d 167, 171-72 (Tex.App.—Houston [1st Dist.] 1995, no writ); ***Cummins & Walker Oil Co. v. Smith***, 814 S.W.2d 884, 886 (Tex.App.—San Antonio 1991, no writ); ***Perry***, 380 S.W.2d at 875.

To determine whether a stipulation of facts is an agreed statement of facts under TRCP 263, answer the following questions. If the answers are mostly "yes," the case probably falls under TRCP 263. • Does the instrument denote itself as an agreed statement of facts and refer to TRCP 263? *See* ***Abbott v. Blue Cross & Blue Shield***, 113 S.W.3d 753, 759 (Tex.App.—Austin 2003, n.p.h.). • Does it purport to contain all the facts to decide the case? If it is clear from the record that the trial court considered other facts outside the stipulation, the case was not an agreed case under TRCP 263. ***Peterson v. NCNB Texas Nat'l Bank***, 838 S.W.2d 263, 265 (Tex.App.—Dallas 1992, no writ); ***Farah***, 624 S.W.2d at 345; *see* ***Parsons***, 492 S.W.2d at 63. • Did the judge certify and approve the agreed statement of facts? ***Peterson***, 838 S.W.2d at 265. • Does the instrument place the ultimate facts that are essential to determination of the case beyond the need for adjudication? • Does the judgment show the case was tried as an agreed case?

§3. MOTION

§3.1 In writing. The motion for judgment on an agreed statement of facts must be in writing. *See* TRCP 11; ***Beddall v. Reader's Wholesale Distribs.***, 408 S.W.2d 237, 238 (Tex.App.—Houston 1966, no writ) (oral stipulation in open court was not an agreed case under TRCP 263). *But see* ***Lambda Constr. Co. v. Chamberlin Waterproofing & Roofing Sys.***, 784 S.W.2d 122, 125 (Tex.App.—Austin 1990, writ denied) (telephone conference was considered an agreed case under TRCP 263). See ***O'Connor's*** FORM 7D:01.

§3.2 Identify all necessary facts. The motion for judgment must state specific facts on which the parties agree and on which the parties seek a judgment. *See* ***Cummins & Walker Oil***, 814 S.W.2d at 886 (presumption that all facts are included in the agreed statement). The motion must expressly state that the case is to be tried on the agreed facts and that those are all the facts of the case. *See id.* Parties can agree only to the facts and cannot stipulate the law. See ***O'Connor's*** FORM 7D:02.

§3.3 Request for judgment. The agreed statement should ask the court to resolve the controversy on the agreed statement of facts.

§3.4 Signatures of parties. The parties or their lawyers must sign the agreed statement of facts. *See* TRCP 11, 263.

§3.5 Certificate for judge. The agreed statement should contain a certificate for the court to sign, certifying and approving the agreed facts. TRCP 263; ***Davis v. State***, 904 S.W.2d 946, 949 n.3 (Tex.App.—Austin 1995, no writ). The certification shows the appellate court the facts on which the trial court based its judgment. ***State Farm Lloyds v. Kessler***, 932 S.W.2d 732, 735 (Tex.App.—Fort Worth 1996, writ denied). See ***O'Connor's*** FORM 7D:02.

§3.6 Proposed judgment. The parties should submit a proposed judgment for the court to sign, and they should file it with the agreed statement. The judgment can be a simple, one-sentence judgment: "On the agreed statement of facts, judgment is rendered for…."

§3.7 Filed with court. The agreed statement must be filed with the court. TRCP 263.

§3.8 Strict requirements not required. When parties stipulate to all the facts in a case, the stipulation may be treated as a submission of an agreed statement even though it does not strictly comply with TRCP 263. ***Giles***, 902 S.W.2d at 169 & n.1; ***Reed v. Valley Fed. S&L Co.***, 655 S.W.2d 259, 264 (Tex.App.—Corpus Christi 1983, writ ref'd n.r.e.). Even if the parties did not follow the technical requirements of TRCP 263, if the final judgment appears to be the product of a TRCP 263 agreed case, the appellate court will treat it as one. ***Port Arthur ISD v. Port Arthur Teachers Ass'n***, 990 S.W.2d 955, 957-58 (Tex.App.—Beaumont 1999, pet. denied) (court did not sign or certify agreed statement); ***Giles***, 902 S.W.2d at 169 & n.1 (same); ***Jim Sowell Constr. Co. v. Dallas Cent. Appr. Dist.***, 900 S.W.2d 82, 84 (Tex.App.—Dallas 1995, writ denied) (same).

§4. HEARING

§4.1 Argument only. The hearing under TRCP 263 is not for evidence; all material evidence must be included in the agreed statement. If the court holds a hearing, it is for argument only.

§4.2 Presumption of all facts. All facts necessary to the presentation of the case are conclusively presumed to have been brought before the court. The court may not draw any inference or find any facts not embraced in the agreement. ***Diamond Shamrock Ref. & Mktg. Co. v. Nueces Cty. Appr. Dist.***, 876 S.W.2d 298, 300-01 & n.2 (Tex. 1994); ***Lawler v. Lomas & Nettleton Mortg. Investors***, 691 S.W.2d 593, 595 (Tex.1985); ***Jim Sowell Constr.***, 900 S.W.2d at 84. *But see* ***Davis v. State***, 904 S.W.2d 946, 950 (Tex.App.—Austin 1995, no writ) (inferential findings beyond agreed facts may be compelled by the facts as a matter of law).

§4.3 Binding effect. The court is bound by the agreed statement of facts. ***Tarrant Appr. Rev. Bd. v. Martinez Bros. Invs.***, 946 S.W.2d 914, 917 (Tex.App.—Fort Worth 1997, no writ); ***Crow Southland Jt.V. v. North Ft. Worth Bank***, 838 S.W.2d 720, 723 (Tex.App.—Dallas 1992, writ denied); ***Trinity Universal Ins. Co. v. Fidelity & Cas. Co.***, 837 S.W.2d 202, 203 (Tex.App.—Dallas 1992, no writ).

§5. JUDGMENT

§5.1 Court certification. Once a case is submitted on an agreed statement, the court must sign and certify the statement as correct. ***Perry***, 380 S.W.2d at 875. If the court does not sign or certify the statement as required by TRCP 263, the appellate court will consider it as a TRCP 263 case only if it is clear that the case was tried on agreed facts. ***Crow Southland***, 838 S.W.2d at 723; ***Trinity Universal Ins.***, 837 S.W.2d at 203 n.1; *see* ***Abbott v. Blue Cross & Blue Shield***, 113 S.W.3d 753, 758-59 (Tex.App.—Austin 2003, n.p.h.) (court refused to certify stipulations & considered evidence outside stipulations).

§5.2 The judgment. The court should sign a judgment, based on its interpretation of the law applicable to the agreed statement of facts. TRCP 263. The court's judgment must declare only the law necessarily arising from the agreed facts. ***Harris Cty. Appr. Dist. v. Transamerica Container Leasing***, 920 S.W.2d 678, 680 (Tex.App.—Houston [1st Dist.] 1995, writ denied); ***State Bar v. Faubion***, 821 S.W.2d 203, 205 (Tex.App.—Houston [14th Dist.] 1991, writ denied). See ***O'Connor's*** FORM 9C:05.

§5.3 No findings of fact. The court cannot make fact findings in addition to those agreed to by the parties. ***International UAW Un. v. G.M. Corp.***, 104 S.W.3d 126, 129-30 (Tex.App.—Fort Worth 2003, no pet.); ***Crow Southland***, 838 S.W.2d at 725. Findings of fact are not appropriate in the trial of an agreed case. ***Port Arthur ISD***, 990 S.W.2d at 957; ***City of Galveston v. Giles***, 902 S.W.2d 167, 170 & n.2 (Tex.App.—Houston [1st Dist.] 1995, no writ).

§5.4 Object to judgment. If the trial court interprets a statement by the parties as an agreement to submit the issue on agreed facts, a party not intending such an agreement must object to preserve error. ***Lambda Constr. Co. v. Chamberlin Waterproofing & Roofing Sys.***, 784 S.W.2d 122, 125 (Tex.App.—Austin 1990, writ denied).

§6. REVIEW

§6.1 The record. The agreed statement signed and certified by the court, along with the court's judgment, is the record of the case for the appeal. TRCP 263; ***Henry S. Miller Co. v. Wood***, 584 S.W.2d 302, 304 (Tex.App.—Texarkana 1979), *aff'd*, 597 S.W.2d 332 (Tex.1980).

§6.2 No presumptions. On appeal, the courts make no presumed findings in favor of the judgment. ***State Farm Lloyds v. Kessler***, 932 S.W.2d 732, 735 (Tex.App.—Fort Worth 1996, writ denied).

§6.3 Limited scope. The appeal is limited to the single issue of whether the law applied to the agreed facts is correct. ***Roberts v. Squyres***, 4 S.W.3d 485, 488 (Tex.App.—Beaumont 1999, pet. denied); ***Tarrant Appr. Rev. Bd.***, 946 S.W.2d at 917; ***Crow Southland***, 838 S.W.2d at 723; ***Reed***, 655 S.W.2d at 264. The appellate court does not review the legal or factual sufficiency of the evidence. ***City of Harlingen v. Avila***, 942 S.W.2d 49, 51 (Tex.App.—Corpus Christi 1997, writ denied); ***Crow Southland***, 838 S.W.2d at 723. The review is de novo. ***Orange Cty. Appr. Dist. v. Agape Neighborhood Imprv.***, 57 S.W.3d 597, 601 (Tex.App.—Beaumont 2001, pet. denied).

§6.4 Render or remand. If the appellate court determines that the trial court erred, in most cases it should render the judgment the trial court should have rendered. If, however, the appellate court decides there are factual issues unresolved by the agreed statement that preclude a judgment, the court should remand the case to the trial court. *See* ***Cameron Cty. Appr. Rev. Bd. v. Creditbanc Sav. Ass'n***, 763 S.W.2d 577, 578 (Tex.App.—Corpus Christi 1988, writ denied).

E. VOLUNTARY DISMISSAL—NONSUIT

§1. GENERAL

§1.1 Rules. TRCP 96, 162, 163.

§1.2 Purpose. A nonsuit is a voluntary dismissal of the party's claims.

§1.3 Forms. ***O'Connor's Texas Civil Forms***, FORMS 7E.

§2. MOTION

A party has an absolute right to a nonsuit at the moment it makes a timely oral or written request for nonsuit, as long as the defendant has not made a claim for affirmative relief. ***Hooks v. 4th Ct. of Appeals***, 808 S.W.2d 56, 59 (Tex.1991); ***BHP Pet. Co. v. Millard***, 800 S.W.2d 838, 840 (Tex.1990); ***Greenberg v. Brookshire***, 640 S.W.2d 870, 872 (Tex.1982). See "Effect on defendant's claims," §6.3, p. 497.

§2.1 Oral or written. To take a nonsuit, the party can either file a written motion for nonsuit (sometimes called a notice of nonsuit) or make an oral announcement of the nonsuit in open court. ***Greenberg***, 640 S.W.2d at 872. In this section, "motion for nonsuit" refers to both an oral request and a written motion for nonsuit.

§2.2 The grounds. There are no formal requirements for the motion for nonsuit. ***Greenberg***, 640 S.W.2d at 872. The motion does not need to state a reason for taking the nonsuit. *See id.* See ***O'Connor's*** FORM 7E:01.

§2.3 With or without prejudice. The motion should state whether the party requests a dismissal with or without prejudice. If the case is dismissed with prejudice, the order is a final adjudication on the merits and the lawsuit cannot be refiled. ***Mossler v. Shields***, 818 S.W.2d 752, 754 (Tex.1991); *see also* ***Galvan v. America's Favorite Chicken Co.***, 934 S.W.2d 409, 410 (Tex.App.—San Antonio 1996, writ denied) (when party mistakenly filed for nonsuit with prejudice, it was res judicata in later suit).

§2.4 The movant.

1. The plaintiff. In most cases, the party taking a nonsuit is the plaintiff.

2. The defendant. A defendant may nonsuit its counterclaims. *See* ***Mackie v. McKenzie***, 890 S.W.2d 807, 808 (Tex.1994); ***Mossler***, 818 S.W.2d at 753.

§2.5 Partial nonsuit. The movant may choose to nonsuit some parties and claims without nonsuiting the other parties and claims. *See* TRCP 162, 163; ***Shadowbrook Apts. v. Abu-Ahmad***, 783 S.W.2d 210, 211 (Tex.1990); *see, e.g.*, ***Mainland Sav. Ass'n v. Wilson***, 545 S.W.2d 491, 493 (Tex.App.—Houston [1st Dist.] 1976, no writ) (plaintiff, suing on 3 notes, nonsuited 1).

§2.6 Service of notice. TRCP 162 requires the movant to serve notice of the nonsuit in accordance with TRCP 21a on any party that has answered or has been served with process. ***Novosad v. Cunningham***, 38 S.W.3d 767, 772 (Tex.App.—Houston [14th Dist.] 2001, no pet.). A certificate of service creates a presumption that the nonsuit was received; the presumption vanishes when opposing evidence is introduced. ***Wembley Inv. Co. v. Herrera***, 11 S.W.3d 924, 927 (Tex.1999). Nevertheless, lack of a certificate of service on a motion for nonsuit does not affect the finality of the judgment. ***McGrew v. Heard***, 779 S.W.2d 455, 458 (Tex.App.—Houston [1st Dist.] 1989, orig. proceeding).

§2.7 Costs. The clerk must tax the court costs of the nonsuit against the party moving for dismissal, unless the court orders otherwise. TRCP 162; ***Leon Springs Gas Co. v. Restaurant Equip. Leasing Co.***, 961 S.W.2d 574, 580 (Tex.App.—San Antonio 1997, no pet.).

§2.8 Alternatives to nonsuit. There are other ways to eliminate parties or claims from the suit.

1. Nonsuit by amendment. Because an amended pleading supersedes and supplants all previous pleadings, an amendment of the pleading can work as a nonsuit of parties and claims. ***Randolph v. Jackson Walker, L.L.P.***, 29 S.W.3d 271, 274 (Tex.App.—Houston [14th Dist.] 2000, pet. denied); *see* TRCP 65 (substituted instrument is no longer regarded as part of the pleadings). See "Amended pleadings," ch. 1-B, §7.1.1, p. 11.

(1) Omitted parties. As a general rule, the omission of a party from an amended petition indicates an intent to nonsuit that party. ***American Petrofina v. Allen***, 887 S.W.2d 829, 831 (Tex.1994) (omitted Ps); ***Webb v. Jorns***, 488 S.W.2d 407, 409 (Tex.1972) (omitted D); ***Randolph***, 29 S.W.3d at 274 (omitted Ds); *see also* ***Green v. Vidlak***, 76 S.W.3d 117, 119-20 (Tex.App.—Amarillo 2002, no pet.) (even though D listed in style of amended petition, omission of D's name from text of amended petition was nonsuit). If a petition omits a party by mistake but the party is renamed in a later petition, the omission does not operate as a nonsuit. ***American Petrofina***, 887 S.W.2d at 831; ***Woodruff v. Wright***, 51 S.W.3d 727, 733 (Tex.App.—Texarkana 2001, pet. denied). In such a case, the party seeking to exclude the temporarily dismissed party has the burden to show it was prejudiced when the omitted party was later renamed. ***American Petrofina***, 887 S.W.2d at 831. When a defendant is omitted from the preamble of the petition but is named in the body of the petition, the omission is not a nonsuit. ***Cox v. Union Oil Co.***, 917 S.W.2d 524, 527 (Tex.App.—Beaumont 1996, no writ). By including the generic term "et al." in the style of the case of an amended petition, a party negates the intent to nonsuit any of the parties named in the earlier petition. ***American Petrofina***, 887 S.W.2d at 831; ***Abramcik v. U.S. Home Corp.***, 792 S.W.2d 822, 824 (Tex.App.—Houston [14th Dist.] 1990, writ denied).

(2) Omitted claims. The omission of a claim from an amended petition indicates an intent to nonsuit that claim. *See, e.g.*, ***Dolenz v. All Saints Episcopal Hosp.***, 638 S.W.2d 141, 142 (Tex.App.—Fort Worth 1982, writ ref'd n.r.e.) (P abandoned claim because he went to trial on amended petition that did not contain the claim).

2. TRCP 165 – abandonment. A party may abandon any part of its claim and have that fact noted on the record. TRCP 165; *see* ***Jones v. Nightingale***, 900 S.W.2d 87, 90 (Tex.App.—San Antonio 1995, writ ref'd) (claims abandoned under TRCP 165 barred from relitigation by compulsory-counterclaim rule).

§3. DEADLINES FOR NONSUIT

§3.1 Before resting. A plaintiff may take a nonsuit at any time before introducing all of its evidence other than rebuttal (*i.e.*, before resting). TRCP 162; ***In re Bennett***, 960 S.W.2d 35, 38 (Tex.1997); ***O'Brien v. Stanzel***, 603 S.W.2d 826, 828 (Tex.1980); ***United Oil & Minerals v. Costilla Energy***, 1 S.W.3d 840, 845 (Tex.App.—Corpus Christi 1999, no pet.); *see also* ***Martini v. Tatum***, 776 S.W.2d 666, 669 (Tex.App.—Amarillo 1989, writ denied) (it was too late for nonsuit after parties closed & court granted an instructed verdict for D).

§3.2 Before SJ. A plaintiff has a right to take a nonsuit after the defendant files a motion for summary judgment, up until the time the court grants a summary judgment. ***Pace Concerts, Ltd v. Resendez***, 72 S.W.3d 700, 702 (Tex.App.—San Antonio 2002, pet. denied); ***Leon Springs Gas Co.***, 961 S.W.2d at 577; ***Taliaferro v. Smith***, 804 S.W.2d 548, 550 (Tex.App.—Houston [14th Dist.] 1991, no writ).

§4. OBJECTIONS TO NONSUIT

There are not many legitimate objections to a nonsuit. See *O'Connor's* FORM 7E:02.

§4.1 Request too late. A defendant should object when the request for nonsuit is too late, that is when (a) the plaintiff asks for a nonsuit after it introduced all of its evidence (other than rebuttal), see §3.1, above; or (b) the plaintiff asks for a nonsuit on a claim already resolved by a summary judgment. *See* ***Hyundai Motor Co. v. Alvarado***, 892 S.W.2d 853, 855 (Tex.1995) (once SJ is granted, P cannot take nonsuit on any claim resolved by SJ).

§4.2 Order too inclusive. A party must object when the order of nonsuit dismisses more claims or parties than requested in the nonsuit. *See* ***Shadowbrook Apts.***, 783 S.W.2d at 211.

§5. ORDER OF NONSUIT

§5.1 Court's authority. A trial court cannot nonsuit parties without a motion for nonsuit of those parties by the plaintiff. ***Shadowbrook Apts.***, 783 S.W.2d at 211. When properly requested, the court does not have the authority to deny a nonsuit. ***Zimmerman v. Ottis***, 941 S.W.2d 259, 261 (Tex.App.—Corpus Christi 1996, orig. proceeding); ***Baldwin v. Klanke***, 877 S.W.2d 879, 881 (Tex.App.—Houston [1st Dist.] 1994, no writ). *But see* ***Bennett***, 960 S.W.2d at 38 (court can defer signing nonsuit until disposition of sanctions issue).

§5.2 Written order. When the court signs an order granting a nonsuit, it is simply a ministerial act. ***Greenberg v. Brookshire***, 640 S.W.2d 870, 872 (Tex.1982).

1. Most cases. Once a nonsuit is requested (in open court or in writing), the court should sign an order granting the dismissal. The signing of the order of dismissal—not the filing of the nonsuit—triggers the appellate deadlines. ***Bennett***, 960 S.W.2d at 38; ***Park Place Hosp. v. Estate of Milo***, 909 S.W.2d 508, 510 (Tex. 1995); ***Farmer v. Ben E. Keith Co.***, 907 S.W.2d 495, 496 (Tex.1995); ***Harris Cty. Appr. Dist. v. Wittig***, 881 S.W.2d 193, 194 (Tex.App.—Houston [1st Dist.] 1994, orig. proceeding); *see, e.g.*, ***Coastal Banc SSB v. Helle***, 48 S.W.3d 796, 800 (Tex.App.—Corpus Christi 2001, pet. denied) (oral rendition of nonsuit did not begin appellate timetables); ***Iacono v. Lyons***, 6 S.W.3d 715, 716 (Tex.App.—Houston [1st Dist.] 1999, no pet.) (docket notation that nonsuit was "entered" did not begin appellate timetables).

2. After conventional trial on merits. There is one exception to the rule that a nonsuit must be memorialized in a written order. A separate order on the nonsuit is not necessary when the nonsuit is filed before the court signs a judgment after a conventional trial on the merits (*i.e.*, a jury or nonjury trial). After a conventional trial on the merits, the judgment is presumed to be final and dispositive. See "Judgment after conventional trial," ch. 9-C, §6.3.1(2), p. 603. A default judgment, summary judgment, or judgment of dismissal is not a conventional trial on the merits for purposes of transforming a nonsuit into a final judgment. *See* ***In re Bro Bro Props.***, 50 S.W.3d

528, 530-31 (Tex.App.—San Antonio 2000, orig. proceeding) (nonsuit announced before default judgment did not become effective by rendition of default judgment).

PRACTICE TIP

To avoid problems about the finality of the judgment, insist the court sign an order of nonsuit or memorialize the nonsuit in the final judgment.

---

§5.3 Without prejudice. In most cases, the court should sign an order dismissing the nonsuited claims without prejudice to the refiling of the nonsuited claims. *See* TRCP 162.

1. To plaintiff. The dismissal after a nonsuit is not an adjudication of the plaintiff's rights; the nonsuit merely places the plaintiff in the position it was in before filing the lawsuit. ***In re T.N.V.***, 855 S.W.2d 102, 103 (Tex. App.—Corpus Christi 1993, no writ); ***KT Bolt Mfg., Co. v. Texas Elec. Coop.***, 837 S.W.2d 273, 275 (Tex.App.—Beaumont 1992, writ denied).

2. To defendant. If, at the time the plaintiff files a nonsuit, the defendant has already filed a counterclaim, motion for sanctions, or any other request for affirmative relief, the nonsuit does not preclude their consideration by the court. TRCP 96, 162. See §6.3, below.

§5.4 With prejudice. A dismissal with prejudice constitutes an adjudication on the merits. ***Mossler v. Shields***, 818 S.W.2d 752, 754 (Tex.1991).

PRACTICE TIP

Check the order before the time expires to challenge it by a motion for new trial or motion to modify the judgment. If the order states the dismissal is with prejudice when it should have been without prejudice, you must challenge it within 30 days of the date it was signed, or the order will be final. ***America's Favorite Chicken Co. v. Galvan****, 897 S.W.2d 874, 876 (Tex. App.—San Antonio 1995, writ denied).*

---

§6. EFFECT OF THE NONSUIT

§6.1 Effect on plaintiff's suit. The nonsuit is effective as soon as the plaintiff files a motion for nonsuit or asks for one in open court. ***Greenberg***, 640 S.W.2d at 872; ***Avmanco, Inc. v. City of Grand Prairie***, 835 S.W.2d 160, 163 (Tex.App.—Fort Worth 1992, writ dism'd). Pleadings filed by the defendant after the nonsuit will not continue the suit. *See* ***Ault v. Mulanax***, 724 S.W.2d 824, 828 (Tex.App.—Texarkana 1986, orig. proceeding).

§6.2 Effect on refiling the suit.

1. The rule. In most cases, when the court signs an order on the plaintiff's nonsuit dismissing the suit without prejudice, the plaintiff is not precluded from refiling the same suit. ***Aetna Cas. & Sur. Co. v. Specia***, 849 S.W.2d 805, 806 (Tex.1993); *see* ***Osteen v. Glynn Dodson, Inc.***, 875 S.W.2d 429, 431 (Tex.App.—Waco 1994, writ denied).

2. The exceptions.

(1) After statute of limitations. An attempt to litigate a claim that was earlier dismissed on a nonsuit (or a compulsory counterclaim to the nonsuited claim) is barred if, at the time the second suit is filed, the statute of limitations has run on the claim. *See* ***Weiman v. Addicks-Fairbanks Rd. Sand Co.***, 846 S.W.2d 414, 421 (Tex.App.—Houston [14th Dist.] 1992, writ denied) (compulsory counterclaim); ***Guaranty Cty. Mut. Ins. Co. v. Reyna***, 700 S.W.2d 325, 327 (Tex.App.—San Antonio 1985) (nonsuit), *writ ref'd n.r.e.*, 709 S.W.2d 647 (Tex.1986).

(2) After summary judgment. A plaintiff cannot escape the effect of a summary judgment on a claim by taking a nonsuit. ***Hyundai Motor Co. v. Alvarado***, 892 S.W.2d 853, 854-55 (Tex.1995). When a plaintiff takes a nonsuit on a claim that was resolved by a partial summary judgment, the claim is considered dismissed with prejudice. *Id.* After the court grants a partial summary judgment, the plaintiff may take a nonsuit only on the unadjudicated claims.

§6.3 Effect on defendant's claims. When the court signs an order on the plaintiff's nonsuit, the dismissal does not preclude the defendant from being heard on its own claims for affirmative relief. TRCP 96, 162; ***BHP Pet. Co. v. Millard***, 800 S.W.2d 838, 840-41 (Tex.1990); *see also* ***Klein v. Dooley***, 949 S.W.2d 307, 308 (Tex.1997) (nonsuit does not affect D's derivative DTPA claim for costs & attorney fees). Not all counterclaims are claims for affirmative relief under TRCP 162.

1. Independent of P's claim. For a counterclaim to qualify as a claim for affirmative relief under TRCP 162, it must allege the defendant has a cause of action on which it can recover independent of the plaintiff's claim, even if the plaintiff abandons its claims. ***General Land Office v. OXY U.S.A., Inc.***, 789 S.W.2d 569, 570 (Tex.1990); *see* ***Quanto Int'l Co. v. Lloyd***, 897 S.W.2d 482, 487 (Tex.App.—Houston [1st Dist.] 1995, orig. proceeding) (request to compel arbitration is an independent claim for relief); ***Ulloa v. Davila***, 860 S.W.2d 202, 204 (Tex.App.—San Antonio 1993, no writ) (counterclaim did more than resist Ps' suit). The following are examples of independent claims: • A defendant's request for a declaratory judgment if it seeks resolution of continuing issues. ***BHP Pet.***, 800 S.W.2d at 842. • A request for attorney fees if the defendant pleads a claim for which damages and attorney fees are recoverable. ***Leon Springs Gas Co. v. Restaurant Equip. Leasing Co***., 961 S.W.2d 574, 578 (Tex. App.—San Antonio 1997, no pet.).

2. Derivative of P's claim. A counterclaim that mirrors the controlling issues in a case is not an independent claim for affirmative relief. ***In re Estate of Kidd***, 812 S.W.2d 356, 359 (Tex.App.—Amarillo 1991, writ denied). The following are examples of derivative claims: • A defendant's request for a declaratory judgment that seeks a finding of no liability. ***BHP Pet.***, 800 S.W.2d at 841. • A counterclaim that asks for indemnity, contribution, or costs. ***Pleasants v. Emmons***, 871 S.W.2d 296, 298 (Tex.App.—Eastland 1994, no writ). • A request for attorney fees when a defendant claims them for defense of the plaintiff's suit. ***Smith v. Texas Farmers Ins. Co.***, 82 S.W.3d 580, 588-89 (Tex.App.—San Antonio 2002, pet. denied). *Contra* ***In re Frost Nat'l Bank***, 103 S.W.3d 647, 650 (Tex. App.—Corpus Christi 2003, orig. proceeding) (claim for attorney fees for defense is independent claim).

§6.4 Effect on venue. Whether a motion to transfer venue fixes venue in the county of the defendant's choice when the plaintiff's case is dismissed on a nonsuit depends on the state of the record at the time the nonsuit was filed. ***GeoChem Tech Corp. v. Verseckes***, 962 S.W.2d 541, 543 (Tex.1998). The venue facts in the plaintiff's petition, the motion to transfer venue, and any response must be examined to determine if the defendant established a prima facie case of venue. *Id.*

1. Before D files venue motion. If the plaintiff takes a nonsuit before the defendant filed a motion to transfer venue, the dismissal does not fix venue in the county where the plaintiff first filed suit unless the plaintiff's petition alleged facts invoking a mandatory venue provision. *See* ***Peysen v. Dawson***, 974 S.W.2d 377, 380 (Tex.App.—San Antonio 1998, no pet.) (because only venue fact in P's petition was that one of Ds lived in Bexar County, it was a county of permissive venue, not mandatory venue). Venue is not fixed merely by filing suit. ***Hyman Farm Serv. v. Earth Oil & Gas Co.***, 920 S.W.2d 452, 456 (Tex.App.—Amarillo 1996, no writ).

2. Before court rules on D's motion. If the plaintiff takes a nonsuit after the defendant files a motion to transfer venue but before the court rules on the motion, the motion to transfer fixes venue in the county of the defendant's choice if the uncontradicted venue facts compel venue in that county. *See* ***GeoChem Tech***, 962 S.W.2d at 544 (venue facts in Ds' motions permitted P to refile in either of two counties of mandatory venue).

3. After court rules on D's motion. If the plaintiff takes a nonsuit after the trial court grants the defendant's motion to transfer venue, the ruling fixes venue if the suit is later refiled. ***Le v. Kilpatrick***, 112 S.W.3d

631, 633-34 (Tex.App.—Tyler 2003, n.p.h.); ***Hendrick Med. Ctr. v. Howell***, 690 S.W.2d 42, 44 (Tex.App.—Dallas 1985, orig. proceeding).

§6.5 Effect on injunction. When the underlying suit is dismissed by a nonsuit, a temporary injunction is automatically dissolved and any appeal becomes moot. ***OXY U.S.A.***, 789 S.W.2d at 571.

§6.6 Effect on sanctions.

1. Discovery sanctions. Whether a discovery sanction survives a nonsuit depends on the nature of the sanction involved. ***Aetna Cas. & Sur. Co. v. Specia***, 849 S.W.2d 805, 807 (Tex.1993). In most cases, when an order excludes evidence as a sanction for failing to respond to discovery, the sanction does not survive the dismissal and refiling of the same suit. *See* ***Schein v. American Rest. Group***, 852 S.W.2d 496, 497 (Tex.1993) (failure to respond to interrogatories and request for production); ***Specia***, 849 S.W.2d at 807 (failure to supplement discovery).

2. Motion for sanctions. A trial court has the power to impose sanctions after a nonsuit, as long as the motion for sanctions is filed before the court loses plenary power over the judgment. ***In re Bennett***, 960 S.W.2d 35, 38 (Tex.1997); ***Scott & White Mem'l Hosp. v. Schexnider***, 940 S.W.2d 594, 596 (Tex.1996). Once the court's plenary power expires, the court can no longer impose sanctions. ***Schexnider***, 940 S.W.2d at 596.

§6.7 Effect on finality of judgment. If the nonsuit disposes of the last remaining claim in the suit, the order on the nonsuit is a final, appealable judgment. *See* ***Coastal Banc SSB v. Helle***, 48 S.W.3d 796, 799-800 (Tex. App.—Corpus Christi 2001, pet. denied). See "Last claim resolved = merger," ch. 9-C, §6.3.1(3)(a), p. 603. If the nonsuit disposes of some claims but other, unadjudicated claims remain, the order on the nonsuit is interlocutory. *See, e.g.*, ***Law Office of Windle Turley v. French***, 109 S.W.3d 599, 601 (Tex.App.—Dallas 2003, n.p.h.) (nonsuit order that did not specifically state it was a final judgment or dispose of all claims was interlocutory); ***In re Romero***, 956 S.W.2d 659, 662 (Tex.App.—San Antonio 1997, orig. proceeding) (because nonsuit order dismissing P's claim against D did not dispose of the insurer's subrogation claim, it was interlocutory).

§7. REINSTATEMENT OF NONSUITED CASE

While the trial court has plenary power over its judgment, a party may ask the court to set aside the nonsuit and reinstate the case. ***Missouri Pac. R.R. v. Whitaker***, 815 S.W.2d 348, 349 n.2 (Tex.App.—Tyler 1991, orig. proceeding). The nonsuit does not divest the trial court of jurisdiction. ***Quanto Int'l Co. v. Lloyd***, 897 S.W.2d 482, 485 (Tex.App.—Houston [1st Dist.] 1995, orig. proceeding); ***Missouri Pac. R.R.***, 815 S.W.2d at 349 n.2. A motion to reinstate a nonsuited case is not a motion to reinstate under TRCP 165a, which governs reinstatement of cases dismissed for want of prosecution. ***In re Simon Prop. Group***, 985 S.W.2d 212, 214 (Tex.App.—Corpus Christi 1999, orig. proceeding); *see* TRCP 165a(3) (authorizing reinstatement upon finding that party's failure to prosecute cause of action was reasonably explained). The motion to set aside a nonsuited case can be labeled a motion to reinstate after nonsuit, a motion to set aside the nonsuit, a motion to withdraw the nonsuit, or even a motion for new trial. *See, e.g.*, ***Osborne v. St. Luke's Episcopal Hosp.***, 915 S.W.2d 906, 909 (Tex.App.—Houston [1st Dist.] 1996, writ denied) (motion to set aside nonsuit); ***Quanto Int'l***, 897 S.W.2d at 484 (motion to reinstate); ***Golodetz Trading Corp. v. Curland***, 886 S.W.2d 503, 504 (Tex.App.—Houston [1st Dist.] 1994, no writ) (motion to withdraw nonsuit). See *O'Connor's* FORM 7E:03.

§8. REVIEW

§8.1 Appeal.

1. Plaintiff's right to appeal. Taking a nonsuit does not preclude the plaintiff from challenging any action of the trial court before the nonsuit was taken. *E.g.*, ***Felderhoff v. Knauf***, 819 S.W.2d 110, 111 (Tex.1991) (after nonsuit, P appealed sanctions imposed by trial court before nonsuit). *But see* ***United Oil & Minerals v. Costilla Energy***, 1 S.W.3d 840, 844 (Tex.App.—Corpus Christi 1999, no pet.) (party nonsuited by amended petition had no standing to appeal judgment); ***Preston v. American Eagle Ins. Co.***, 948 S.W.2d 18, 21 (Tex.App.—Dallas 1997, no writ) (persons nonsuited before SJ had no standing to appeal judgment).

2. Appellate deadlines. The date the court signs the order of nonsuit triggers the appellate deadlines if no other claims remain in the case. ***Bennett***, 960 S.W.2d at 38; ***Farmer v. Ben E. Keith Co.***, 907 S.W.2d 495, 496 (Tex.1995). The period within which a party must perfect an appeal is calculated from the time the judgment is signed, not from the filing of the notice of nonsuit. ***Farmer***, 907 S.W.2d at 496.

3. Plenary power. The court retains plenary power over an order of dismissal for 30 days from the date it signs the order. ***America's Favorite Chicken Co. v. Galvan***, 897 S.W.2d 874, 876 (Tex.App.—San Antonio 1995, writ denied); ***Harris Cty. Appr. Dist. v. Wittig***, 881 S.W.2d 193, 194 (Tex.App.—Houston [1st Dist.] 1994, orig. proceeding). If certain post-trial motions are filed, the court retains plenary power for as long as 105 days after the judgment is signed. See chart 9-1, "Plenary Power Deadlines," ch. 9-C, p. 607.

§8.2 Mandamus. If a trial court refuses to grant a plaintiff's timely motion for nonsuit, the plaintiff may seek mandamus relief. ***Hooks v. 4th Ct. of Appeals***, 808 S.W.2d 56, 59 (Tex.1991); ***Greenberg v. Brookshire***, 640 S.W.2d 870, 872 (Tex.1982). If a trial court reinstates a nonsuited case over the plaintiff's objection, the plaintiff may seek mandamus relief. ***Johnson v. Harless***, 651 S.W.2d 259, 260 (Tex.1983); ***Quanto Int'l***, 897 S.W.2d at 485.

F. INVOLUNTARY DISMISSAL

§1. GENERAL

§1.1 Rules. TRCP 165a.

§1.2 Purpose. The purpose of a dismissal is to dispose of the case without a trial.

§1.3 Forms & timetables. ***O'Connor's Texas Civil Forms***, FORM 7F:01; Timetables, ***O'Connor's Texas Civil Appeals***, Appeal After Late Notice of Judgment, p. 972, Appeal of Dismissal for Want of Prosecution, p. 979 (2002-03).

§1.4 Other references. Merritt, *Rule 165a Dismissal for Want of Prosecution*, 60 Tex. B.J. 555 (1997).

§2. GROUNDS FOR DISMISSAL

To be entitled to a dismissal in a Texas court, the defendant must make some complaint about the plaintiff's lawsuit or conduct that, if not cured, entitles the defendant to move for a dismissal. By comparison, in federal court a defendant can ask the court to dismiss the plaintiff's suit because the plaintiff's pleadings do not state a cause of action. ***Fort Bend Cty. v. Wilson***, 825 S.W.2d 251, 253 (Tex.App.—Houston [14th Dist.] 1992, no writ) (discussing FRCP 12(b)(6), which permits federal courts to dismiss for failure to state a claim). In Texas, such a complaint is considered a general demurrer and is prohibited by TRCP 90. ***Wilson***, 825 S.W.2d at 253.

§2.1 Bar to the suit. Most requests to dismiss are made as part of another motion that alleges the plaintiff cannot maintain the suit as filed. The defendant must prove there is a bar to the plaintiff's suit or a defect in the pleadings, the court, the parties, or the claim for liability that cannot be cured by amendment. The following are some of the grounds that bar a suit:

1. The case is moot. See "Motion to Abate—Challenging the Suit," ch. 3-H, p. 194.

2. The trial court does not have jurisdiction over the defendant or its property. See "Special Appearance—Challenging Personal Jurisdiction," ch. 3-B, p. 143.

3. The trial court does not have subject-matter jurisdiction. See "Plea to the Jurisdiction—Challenging the Court," ch. 3-F, p. 181.

4. The plaintiff's petition does not state a cause of action against the defendant. See "Special Exceptions—Challenging the Pleadings," ch. 3-G, p. 187; "Motion to Abate—Challenging the Suit," ch. 3-H, p. 194.

5. A Texas court is not the appropriate forum for the lawsuit. See "Forum Non Conveniens—Challenging the Texas Forum," ch. 3-D, p. 165. If the court sustains a motion to dismiss on the ground of forum non conveniens, it may either dismiss or stay the suit.

§2.2 Failure to prosecute. The trial court's authority to dismiss for want of prosecution stems from two sources, TRCP 165a and the court's inherent power. ***Villarreal v. San Antonio Truck & Equip.***, 994 S.W.2d 628, 630 (Tex.1999).

1. TRCP 165a. A trial court may dismiss a suit under TRCP 165a for (1) the failure to appear or (2) for failure to dispose of the case within the time standards. ***Villarreal***, 994 S.W.2d at 630. See ***O'Connor's*** FORM 7F:01.

(1) Failure to appear. The court has the authority under TRCP 165a(1) to dismiss a suit when a party seeking affirmative relief (generally the plaintiff) does not appear at trial or other hearing after receiving notice of the setting. TRCP 165a(1); ***Villarreal***, 994 S.W.2d at 630; ***Texas Sting, Ltd. v. R.B. Foods***, 82 S.W.3d 644, 648 (Tex.App.—San Antonio, 2002, pet. denied); ***Johnson-Snodgrass v. KTAO, Inc.***, 75 S.W.3d 84, 87 (Tex.App.—Fort Worth 2002, pet. filed 7-29-02). A dismissal for failure to appear under TRCP 165a(1) is appropriate only when the plaintiff had notice of (1) a trial on the merits, (2) a dispositive hearing, or (3) a non-dispositive hearing that stated the failure to appear could result in dismissal. For example, failure to appear at docket call does not constitute a failure to appear unless the party was given notice that its failure to appear would result in the disposition of the suit. *See* ***Degen v. General Coatings***, 705 S.W.2d 734, 735 (Tex.App.—Houston [14th Dist.] 1986, no writ); *cf.* ***Masterson v. Cox***, 886 S.W.2d 436, 439 (Tex.App.—Houston [1st Dist.] 1994, no writ) (post-answer default reversed because D did not have notice that pretrial conference was for hearing on the merits). See "Dismissal for failure to appear," ch. 10-F, §3.4.1, p. 650.

(2) Failure to comply with time standards. The court has the authority under TRCP 165a(2) to dismiss a suit that was not disposed of within the time limits in the Rules of Judicial Administration. ***Johnson-Snodgrass***, 75 S.W.3d at 87; ***Hosey v. County of Victoria***, 832 S.W.2d 701, 704-05 (Tex.App.—Corpus Christi 1992, no writ). Rule 6 of the Rules of Judicial Administration provides that civil jury cases (other than family law cases) should be brought to trial or final disposition within 18 months from the appearance date, and civil nonjury cases within 12 months from the appearance date. Tex.R.Jud.Admin. 6b. Contested family law cases should be disposed of within six months, and uncontested family law cases should be disposed of within three months. Tex.R.Jud. Admin. 6c. See "Failure to comply with time standards," ch. 10-F, §3.4.2(2), p. 651.

2. Inherent power. Under the common law, the trial court has the inherent power to dismiss—independent of its authority under TRCP 165a—when a plaintiff does not prosecute its case with diligence. ***Villarreal***, 994 S.W.2d at 630; *see* ***Rizk v. Mayad***, 603 S.W.2d 773, 776 (Tex.1980); ***Veterans' Land Bd. v. Williams***, 543 S.W.2d 89, 90 (Tex.1976); ***Lopez v. Harding***, 68 S.W.3d 78, 80 (Tex.App.—Dallas 2001, no pet.). See "Inherent power," ch. 10-F, §3.4.2(3), p. 651.

§2.3 Sanctions. Some rules and code provisions permit the trial court to strike pleadings or dismiss a suit as a sanction. *See, e.g.*, CPRC §9.012(e) (groundless suit); TRCP 13 (frivolous pleadings), TRCP 215.2(b)(5) (discovery abuse). See "Defective Pleadings," ch. 1-B, §6, p. 10; "Conduct that Justifies Sanctions," ch. 5-J, §5, p. 277; "Motion for Discovery Sanctions," ch. 6-A, §22, p. 337.

§2.4 Frivolous indigent suit. The trial court has the authority to dismiss a suit filed by an indigent if the trial court finds (1) the allegation of poverty in the affidavit is false or (2) the action is frivolous or malicious. See "Suit by Indigent," ch. 2-I, p. 132.

§2.5 Objections to med-mal suit. When a plaintiff in a medical malpractice suit does not comply with the provisions for filing an expert report under CPRC §74.351(a), the defendant may move to dismiss under CPRC

§74.351(b)(2). See ***O'Connor's Texas Causes of Action***, "Expert report," ch. 18-A, §7.2, p. 441 (2004); ***O'Connor's*** FORM 7F:01.

§2.6 Improper grounds for dismissal.

1. Conflict in trial settings. The trial court cannot dismiss a suit if the party informs the court that its attorney is in another trial. ***Dancy v. Daggett***, 815 S.W.2d 548, 549 (Tex.1991) (criminal trial in federal court); ***Seigle v. Hollech***, 892 S.W.2d 201, 203-04 (Tex.App.—Houston [14th Dist.] 1994, no writ) (criminal trial in state court). *But see* ***Burton v. Hoffman***, 959 S.W.2d 351, 353-54 (Tex.App.—Austin1998, no pet.) (dismissal upheld when attorney knew of conflicting trial settings yet waited until Friday before Monday setting to seek continuance, sent associate to argue motion when case was called, and refused to put on evidence when given opportunity).

2. Special exceptions. A court cannot dismiss a party's suit after sustaining special exceptions without giving the party permission to amend its pleadings to cure the defect. See "Options for court," ch. 3-G, §9.2, p. 190; ***O'Connor's*** FORM 7F:01.

3. Summary judgment. A summary judgment should not state that the case is dismissed. See "Resolve issues on the merits," ch. 7-B, §13.3.3, p. 482.

§3. NOTICE OF INTENT TO DISMISS

A trial court cannot dismiss a suit without giving the plaintiff notice of its intent to dismiss. ***Villarreal***, 994 S.W.2d at 630; ***Creel v. District Atty.***, 818 S.W.2d 45, 46 (Tex.1991); ***Texas Sting***, 82 S.W.3d at 648. A dismissal without notice violates the party's due process rights and requires reversal. ***Villarreal***, 994 S.W.2d at 630; ***Hubert v. Illinois State Assistance Comm'n***, 867 S.W.2d 160, 163 (Tex.App.—Houston [14th Dist.] 1993, no writ). For the exception, see §3.2, below. The notice of intent to dismiss must identify the specific grounds for dismissal. ***Villarreal***, 994 S.W.2d at 630. The trial court cannot give notice of intent to dismiss on one ground and dismiss on another ground. *E.g.*, *id.* (notice under TRCP 165a(1) does not support dismissal under 165a(2) or inherent power); ***Johnson-Snodgrass***, 75 S.W.3d at 88 (notice under TRCP 165a does not support dismissal under inherent power); ***Lopez***, 68 S.W.3d at 80-81 (same).

§3.1 Requirements.

1. Identify grounds for dismissal. The notice to dismiss must state whether the dismissal is (1) under TRCP 165a(1) for failure to appear, (2) under TRCP 165a(2) for failure to comply with the Supreme Court's time standards, or (3) under the court's inherent power for failure to diligently prosecute the suit. ***Villarreal***, 994 S.W.2d at 630.

2. Sent to party or lawyer. TRCP 165a(1) requires the clerk of the trial court to mail a notice of the court's intention to dismiss the suit to either the attorneys of record or the parties (if pro se). See "Sent to lawyer or party," ch. 1-H, §6.2, p. 41.

(1) Notice to attorneys. TRCP 165a(1) requires the clerk to send a notice of the court's intent to dismiss to "each attorney of record." ***Cannon v. ICO Tubular Servs.***, 905 S.W.2d 380, 388 (Tex.App.—Houston [1st Dist.] 1995, no writ) (dismissal reversed because notices were not sent to all attorneys of record); *see also* ***Kenley v. Quintana Pet. Corp.***, 931 S.W.2d 318, 320-21 (Tex.App.—San Antonio 1996, writ denied) (dismissal reversed because notice sent to attorney of record but not attorney in charge).

(2) Notice to pro se. When a party is not represented by counsel, the notice must be sent to the party. TRCP 165a(1); ***G.E. Co. v. Falcon Ridge Apts.***, 811 S.W.2d 942, 943 (Tex.1991).

3. State when & where. The notice of intent to dismiss must identify the date and place of the dismissal hearing. TRCP 165a(1); ***Brown v. Brookshires Grocery Store***, 10 S.W.3d 351, 353 (Tex.App.—Dallas 1999, pet. denied); ***Rohus v. Licona***, 942 S.W.2d 111, 112 (Tex.App.—Houston [1st Dist.] 1997, no writ). The notice cannot merely state the case will be dismissed if a timely motion to retain is not filed. ***Cannon***, 905 S.W.2d at 388.

§3.2 Dismissal without notice. When an indigent's claim has "no arguable basis in law," some courts of appeal have held the trial court can dismiss without notice of its intent to dismiss. See "Suit by Indigent," ch. 2-I, p. 132.

§4. RESPONSE TO THREAT OF DISMISSAL

§4.1 Motion to retain. When a case is set on the court's dismissal docket for want of prosecution, the plaintiff should file a verified motion to retain. *See* TRCP 165a(1). The motion must provide "good cause for the case to be maintained on the docket." *Id.* If the court retains the case, it must assign a trial date, and any continuances must be by court order. TRCP 165a(1). If the court dismisses the case, the plaintiff should file a motion to reinstate. See "Motion to Reinstate After DWOP," ch. 10-F, p. 649; ***O'Connor's*** FORM 10F:01.

PRACTICE TIP

The motion to retain informs the court why the case should not be dismissed. The motion to reinstate informs the court why the dismissal was wrong. Therefore, the motion to retain and the motion to reinstate will state similar grounds. See "Grounds to reinstate," ch. 10-F, §3.4, p. 650.

§4.2 Response to motion. When the dismissal is based on the defendant's motion to dismiss, the plaintiff should file a response to the motion challenging the grounds for dismissal; if the defendant's motion was verified and included affidavits, so should the plaintiff's response.

§5. HEARING

If the trial court dismisses a lawsuit without a hearing, the lack of a hearing raises due process concerns. *See* ***Creel***, 818 S.W.2d at 46 (no notice or hearing). In a few situations, a motion to dismiss may be submitted for the trial court's ruling without a hearing.

§5.1 Bar to suit. If the trial court sustains a challenge to the continuation of the suit by motion to abate, special exceptions, or some other motion, and the plaintiff fails to correct the problem, the case is ripe for dismissal. In some cases, the hearing on the initial motion satisfies the requirements of due process (*e.g.*, the hearing on a motion to abate). In other cases, another hearing is necessary to determine if the plaintiff's attempt to correct the problem was sufficient to satisfy the court's order (*e.g.*, if the plaintiff amends after special exceptions).

§5.2 DWOP. Before dismissing a case for want of prosecution, the court should conduct an oral hearing and give the plaintiff the opportunity to present evidence. TRCP 165a(1) (notice of court's intention to dismiss and date and place of dismissal hearing shall be sent); ***Villarreal v. San Antonio Truck & Equip.***, 994 S.W.2d 628, 630 (Tex.1999) (before dismissing, court must give party opportunity to be heard); ***Brookshires Grocery***, 10 S.W.3d at 354 (same); ***Collier Mfg. & Sup. v. Interfirst Bank***, 749 S.W.2d 560, 564-65 (Tex.App.—Austin 1988, no writ) (same).

§5.3 Sanctions. The court must hold a hearing before dismissing a case as a sanction. See "Motion for Sanctions," ch. 5-J, p. 275.

§5.4 Frivolous indigent suit. The courts of appeals disagree on whether a hearing is necessary before the court can dismiss a suit filed by an indigent under TRCP 145. See "Hearing," ch. 2-I, §5.1, p. 134.

§6. THE ORDER OF DISMISSAL

§6.1 Language of dismissal. When a court dismisses a case, the order should be drafted to dismiss the suit and do nothing else. If the order purports to make any decision on the merits, it is reversible error. ***Alvarado v.***

Magic Valley Elec. Co-op, 784 S.W.2d 729, 733 (Tex.App.—San Antonio 1990, writ denied) (dismissal for failure to appear). Even the statement "all other relief is expressly denied" constitutes a decision on the merits, *id.*, as does the statement "plaintiff take nothing," ***De La Garza v. Express-News Corp.***, 722 S.W.2d 251, 253 (Tex.App.—San Antonio 1986, no writ) (dismissal as sanctions). Neither statement is appropriate in an order of dismissal.

§6.2 Type of dismissal. There are two types of dismissals: with and without prejudice. If the order of dismissal does not state the case is dismissed with prejudice, the case is presumed to be dismissed without prejudice. ***Greenwood v. Tillamook Country Smoker***, 857 S.W.2d 654, 656 (Tex.App.—Houston [1st Dist.] 1993, no writ). See §6.3, below.

1. Without prejudice. In most cases, the trial court can dismiss only without prejudice.

(1) Failure to prosecute. The trial court should dismiss without prejudice for a failure to appear or prosecute under TRCP 165a or under the court's inherent power. *See* ***Attorney Gen. v. Rideaux***, 838 S.W.2d 340, 342 (Tex.App.—Houston [1st Dist.] 1991, no writ) (failure to prosecute or to appear does not support dismissal with prejudice); ***Almanara World Class Rest. v. Caspian Enters.***, ___ S.W.3d ___ (Tex.App.—Houston [14th Dist.] 2003, no pet.) (No. 14-02-00347-CV; 3-6-03) (failure to appear does not support dismissal with prejudice). Because a dismissal for want of prosecution is not a trial on the merits, a "take nothing" judgment, which is the equivalent of a dismissal with prejudice, is inappropriate. ***Attorney Gen. v. Abbs***, 812 S.W.2d 605, 608 (Tex.App.—Dallas 1991, no writ).

(2) No jurisdiction. The trial court should dismiss without prejudice after it sustains a plea to the jurisdiction. See "Dismiss without prejudice," ch. 3-F, §6.1.2, p. 185.

(3) Special exceptions. In most cases, if a party refuses to amend after the court sustains special exceptions, the court should dismiss without prejudice. See "Party refused to amend," ch. 3-G, §9.5.3(2)(a), p. 192.

(4) Case moot. A dismissal for mootness is not a ruling on the merits; thus, a case dismissed for mootness should be dismissed without prejudice. ***Ritchey v. Vasquez***, 986 S.W.2d 611, 612 (Tex.1999).

2. With prejudice. In some cases, the trial court may dismiss all or part of a plaintiff's suit with prejudice. See §6.3.1, below.

(1) Sanctions. For groundless pleadings, TRCP 13 and TRCP 215.2(b)(5) permit a court to dismiss a suit or strike pleadings as a sanction. *See also* CPRC §9.012(e) (permits court to dismiss a party or strike pleadings for groundless suit). For frivolous pleadings, CPRC §10.004 does not list dismissal as one of the sanctions available. When a case is dismissed as a sanction, the sanction is referred to as a "death penalty" sanction. See "Motion for Sanctions," ch. 5-J, p. 275.

(2) Special exceptions. In a few cases, if a party refuses to amend after the court sustains special exceptions, the court can dismiss with prejudice. See "Party refused to amend," ch. 3-G, §9.5.3(2)(b), p. 192.

§6.3 Effect of dismissal.

1. Dismissal with prejudice. A dismissal with prejudice to refiling is a final determination on the merits. ***Mossler v. Shields***, 818 S.W.2d 752, 754 (Tex.1991); *see also* ***Almanara World Class Rest.***, ___ S.W.3d at ___ ("take nothing" judgment is equivalent to dismissal with prejudice). Such a dismissal has full res judicata and collateral estoppel effect, barring relitigation of the same cause of action or issues between the same parties. ***Almanara World Class Rest.***, ___ S.W.3d at ___; *see* ***Hammonds v. Holmes***, 559 S.W.2d 345, 346-47 (Tex.1977) (P argued 2nd suit brought in different capacity). The plaintiff can appeal the dismissal but cannot refile the lawsuit unless the dismissal is reversed on appeal. *See* ***Mossler***, 818 S.W.2d at 754.

NOTE

The notation "with prejudice to refiling" is not appropriate when the trial court dismisses a motion, as opposed to a lawsuit. ***Republic Royalty Co. v. Evins****, 931 S.W.2d 338, 344 (Tex. App.—Corpus Christi 1996, orig. proceeding). Such a notation does not prevent the party from refiling the motion. Id. At most, it is an indication that the trial court will not look favorably on another motion asking for the same relief. Id.*

2. **Dismissal without prejudice.** A dismissal without prejudice to refiling is not a final determination on the merits. Thus, if the statute of limitations has not run, the case may be refiled without appealing the order of dismissal. *See* ***Webb v. Jorns***, 488 S.W.2d 407, 409 (Tex.1972); ***Denton v. Texas DPS Officers Ass'n***, 862 S.W.2d 785, 787 (Tex.App.—Austin 1993), *aff'd*, 897 S.W.2d 757 (Tex.1995); ***Palmer v. Cantrell***, 747 S.W.2d 39, 40 (Tex. App.—Houston [1st Dist.] 1988, no writ).

§6.4 Preservation of error. If the trial court's order dismisses a suit with prejudice when only a dismissal without prejudice was appropriate, the notation of "with prejudice" must be challenged in some postjudgment motion (*e.g.*, a motion for new trial, motion to modify the judgment, or as part of a motion to reinstate); otherwise, the error is waived and the suit cannot be refiled. ***El Paso Pipe & Sup. v. Mountain States Leasing***, 617 S.W.2d 189, 190 (Tex.1981). See "MNT After Dismissal," ch. 10-B, §12, p. 625.

§7. REQUEST FOR FINDINGS OF FACT

If the trial court holds a hearing and receives evidence before dismissing the case, the plaintiff should ask the court to file findings of fact and conclusions of law. To determine when findings should be requested, see "After dismissal hearings," ch. 10-E, §2.3.2, p. 643.

§8. NOTICE OF DISMISSAL ORDER

§8.1 Notice of order. The clerk must send notice that the court signed an order of dismissal by first class mail; certified mail is not required. TRCP 165a(1), 306a(3). The clerk is not required to send a copy of the dismissal order; a postcard notice of the dismissal is sufficient. See "Notice of Judgment," ch. 9-C, §5, p. 601. If the clerk does not send the notice, the beginning of the postjudgment periods listed in TRCP 306a(1) are not affected, except as provided by TRCP 306a(4). TRCP 165a(1). If a party gets late notice of the judgment, TRCP 306a(4) permits the party to file a motion that effectively extends the time for post-trial motions. See "Motion to Extend Postjudgment Deadlines," ch. 10-G, p. 654.

§8.2 Notice to attorneys. The clerk must send the notice of the dismissal to the "attorneys of record," which includes all lawyers of record for the parties. TRCP 165a(1), 306(a)(3); *see* ***Cannon v. ICO Tubular Servs.***, 905 S.W.2d 380, 388 (Tex.App.—Houston [1st Dist.] 1995, no writ); *cf.* TRCP 8 ("attorney in charge" includes only one lawyer for each party). See "Lawyer," ch. 1-H, §6.2.1, p. 41.

§8.3 Notice to pro se party. The clerk must send the notice of the dismissal to any party who is not represented by counsel. TRCP 165a(1), 306a(3). See "Party," ch. 1-H, §6.2.2, p. 41.

§9. REINSTATEMENT

§9.1 Appealing a DWOP. See "Motion to Reinstate After DWOP," ch. 10-F, p. 649.

§9.2 Appealing other dismissals. See "Motion for New Trial," ch. 10-B, p. 617.

§9.3 Appealing late notice of dismissal order. See "Motion to Extend Postjudgment Deadlines," ch. 10-G, p. 654.

§10. REVIEW

The order dismissing a case is a final, appealable order. *See* ***Stewart v. USA Custom Paint & Body Shop***, 870 S.W.2d 18, 20 (Tex.1994) (properly executed order of dismissal is a judgment).

G. OFFER OF SETTLEMENT

§1. GENERAL

In 2003, the Texas Legislature enacted CPRC chapter 42, creating the "offer of settlement" (also called "offer of judgment") procedure. The Texas Supreme Court then adopted TRCP 167, implementing this procedure.

§1.1 Rule. TRCP 167; CPRC ch. 42.

§1.2 Purpose. The purpose of the offer-of-settlement procedure is to encourage early settlements by shifting litigation costs to the party that rejected a fair settlement offer.

§1.3 Forms & timetable. ***O'Connor's Texas Civil Forms***, FORMS 7G (forthcoming 2004); Timetable, this book, Offer of Settlement, p. 1010.

§1.4 Other references. Carlson, *Offers of Settlement: Understanding the New Rules*, Law Practice After HB4: What Every Practitioner Needs to Know, University of Texas School of Law, Tab 3 (2003) ("*Offers of Settlement*"); Quinn, *Statutorily Regulated Offers of Settlement in Texas 2003*, Law Practice After HB4: What Every Practitioner Needs to Know, University of Texas School of Law, Tab 5 (2003).

§1.5 Similar provisions in other jurisdictions. Other jurisdictions have cost-shifting procedures; of those, TRCP 167 most closely resembles Florida's procedure. Carlson, *Offers of Settlement*, at 2; *see* Fla. Stat. ch. 768.79 (1997 & Supp. 2004). FRCP 68 contains a somewhat different procedure, which can shift post-offer costs (but not attorney fees) to a party who rejects a settlement offer.

§2. AVAILABILITY & ELECTION OF THE SETTLEMENT PROCEDURE

§2.1 Availability.

1. Available. The offer-of-settlement procedure can be used only for claims seeking monetary damages in cases filed on or after January 1, 2004. CPRC §42.002(a); TRCP 167.1, 167.2(d); *see* CPRC §42.001(1) (definition of claim).

2. Not available. The offer-of-settlement procedure cannot be used in the following cases:

(1) Class actions. CPRC §42.002(b)(1); TRCP 167.1(a).

NOTE

Neither CPRC chapter 42 nor TRCP 167 makes clear whether "class action" includes all cases filed as class actions, or only those cases certified as class actions.

---

(2) Shareholder derivative actions. CPRC §42.002(b)(2); TRCP 167.1(b).

(3) Actions by or against a governmental unit. CPRC §42.002(b)(3); TRCP 167.1(c); *see* CPRC §42.001(4).

(4) Family Code actions. CPRC §42.002(b)(4); TRCP 167.1(d).

(5) Workers' compensation actions. CPRC §42.002(b)(5); TRCP 167.1(e).

(6) Actions filed in justice of the peace court, including small claims proceedings. CPRC 42.002(b)(6); TRCP 167.1(f).

(7) Mediation, arbitration, or other ADR proceedings. TRCP 167.7.

(8) Suits seeking equitable relief only. CPRC §42.001(1) ("claim" is limited to suit for monetary relief); TRCP 167.1 (same).

(9) Cases filed before January 1, 2004. H.B. 4, 78th Leg., §2.02, eff. September 1, 2003.

§2.2 Other settlement offers. TRCP 167 does not affect other settlement offers. Parties can make settlement offers in cases to which TRCP 167 does not apply, in cases where TRCP 167 has not been invoked, and in cases that do not comply with TRCP 167's requirements. CPRC §42.002(d), (e); TRCP 167.7. A settlement offer made outside of TRCP 167 cannot be the basis for cost-shifting under TRCP 167. CPRC §42.002(e); TRCP 167.7.

§3. DEFENDANT'S DECLARATION

The offer-of-settlement procedure is not automatically available. Before either party (plaintiff or defendant) can make a settlement offer under TRCP 167, the defendant must file a declaration invoking the rule. CPRC §42.002(c); TRCP 167.2(a).

§3.1 Invoking the procedure. Only a defendant can invoke the offer-of-settlement procedure. CPRC §42.002(c); TRCP 167.2(a).

1. Definition of defendant. A defendant is a person from whom a party seeks monetary damages, including a counterdefendant (*i.e.*, a plaintiff subject to monetary damages in a counterclaim), cross-defendant, or third-party defendant. CPRC §42.001(3); TRCP 167.1, 167.2(a).

2. Multiple defendants. In a case with multiple defendants, each defendant must file a separate declaration for the procedure to apply to that defendant. *See* CPRC §42.002(c).

PRACTICE TIP

When a defendant files a counterclaim or a TRCP 167 declaration, it may end up paying the plaintiff's litigation costs. A defendant should therefore consider the case with care before filing a counterclaim or a declaration.

§3.2 Deadline. The defendant must file a TRCP 167 declaration at least 45 days before trial. TRCP 167.2(a). On motion based on good cause, the court may sign a pretrial order modifying this time limit. TRCP 167.5(a). See Timetable, this book, Offer of Settlement, p. 1010.

§4. SETTLEMENT OFFER

Once the defendant has invoked TRCP 167 by filing a declaration, either party may make a settlement offer under the offer-of-settlement procedure.

§4.1 In writing. A settlement offer must be in writing and must state that it is made under CPRC chapter 42 and TRCP 167. CPRC §42.003(1), (2); TRCP 167.2(b)(1), (2).

§4.2 Parties. A settlement offer must identify the party or parties making the offer and the party or parties to whom the offer is made. TRCP 167.2(b)(3).

§4.3 Terms.

1. Monetary claims. A settlement offer must state the amount for which the monetary claims—including attorney fees, interest, and costs—between the parties may be settled. CPRC §42.003(3); TRCP 167.3(b)(4).

2. No nonmonetary claims. A settlement offer must not include nonmonetary claims or other claims that fall outside TRCP 167. TRCP 167.2(d); *see also* TRCP 167.1 (listing claims that fall outside TRCP 167).

3. Other conditions. A settlement offer may require the offeree to meet other reasonable conditions, including executing releases, indemnities, or other documents. TRCP 167.2(c). A condition is presumed reasonable unless an offeree objects in writing to the condition before the deadline for acceptance. *Id.* If an offeree objects to an offer's condition, that offer cannot be the basis for cost-shifting unless the trial court determines the condition was reasonable. *Id.*

§4.4 Deadlines.

1. Making the offer. A settlement offer must be made as follows:

(1) After the defendant files a TRCP 167 declaration. TRCP 167.2(e)(1). See §3, above.

(2) At least 60 days after both the plaintiff and defendant have appeared in the case. TRCP 167.2(e)(2).

(3) At least 14 days before the case is set for a conventional trial on the merits (not summary judgment), unless the settlement offer answers an earlier offer and is made within seven days of the earlier offer. TRCP 167.2(e)(3).

2. Accepting the offer. The settlement offer must state an acceptance deadline. CPRC §42.003(4); TRCP 167.2(b)(5). The acceptance deadline must be at least 14 days after the offer is served. TRCP 167.2(b)(5).

3. Modifying the deadlines. On motion based on good cause, the court may sign a pretrial order modifying the time limits for making an offer. TRCP 167.5(a).

§4.5 Service. A settlement offer must be served on all parties to whom it is made. CPRC §42.003(5); TRCP 167.2(b)(6); *see* TRCP 21a. The offer is not filed with the court, nor must it be served on other parties to whom it is not made. *See* TRCP 21, 167.3(b).

§4.6 Designating or joining additional party. An offeror may designate a responsible third party or join another party after making a TRCP 167 offer. TRCP 167.3(d). See "Third-party suit," ch. 3-E, §6.3, p. 179; "Responsible third party," ch. 3-E, §6.4, p. 180.

§5. WITHDRAWAL, ACCEPTANCE, OBJECTIONS & REJECTION

§5.1 Withdrawing the offer. Before a settlement offer is accepted, an offeror may withdraw it by serving written notice of the withdrawal on the offeree. TRCP 167.3(a). The withdrawal takes effect when the notice is served. *Id*; *see* TRCP 21a. Once the offer is withdrawn, it cannot be accepted and cannot be the basis for cost-shifting. TRCP 167.3(a).

§5.2 Objecting to the offer.

1. To the conditions. An offeree may object to a settlement offer's conditions by serving written notice on the offeror on or before the acceptance deadline. TRCP 167.2(c). If the offeree objects to the offer on this ground, the offer cannot be the basis for cost-shifting, unless the court finds the conditions were reasonable. *Id.*

2. To additional parties. If an offeror joins another party or designates a responsible third party after making an offer, the offeree may file an objection to the offer within 15 days after service of the pleading or designation. TRCP 167.3(d). If the offeree objects to the offer on this ground, the offer cannot be the basis for cost-shifting. *Id.*

§5.3 Accepting the offer. An offeree may accept a settlement offer by serving written notice on the offeror on or before the offer's acceptance deadline and before the offer is withdrawn. TRCP 167.3(b). When the offer is accepted, either party may file the offer and acceptance and ask the court to enforce the settlement. *Id.* See "Consent judgment," ch. 7-H, §5.2.1, p. 515.

§5.4 Rejecting the offer. An offeree may reject a settlement offer by serving written notice on the offeror on or before the acceptance deadline. TRCP 167.3(c). An offer that is not withdrawn or accepted on or before the acceptance deadline is deemed rejected. *Id.*

§5.5 Making successive offers. A party may make another offer after having made or rejected an earlier offer. TRCP 167.2(f). Only an offeror's best offer exposes the offeree to possible cost-shifting. *Id.*

§6. LITIGATION COSTS

Litigation costs are defined as the money spent and the obligations incurred that directly relate to the claims in a settlement offer. CPRC §42.001(5); TRCP 167.4(c). Litigation costs include (1) court costs, (2) reasonable fees for not more than two testifying expert witnesses, and (3) reasonable attorney fees. CPRC §42.001(5); TRCP 167.4(c). See ***O'Connor's Texas Causes of Action***, "Court Costs," ch. 37, p. 1033; "Attorney Fees," ch. 38, p. 1041 (2004). An offeror can recover litigation costs from a rejecting offeree if the judgment to be rendered on the claim is significantly less favorable to the offeree than the rejected offer. CPRC §42.004(a); TRCP 167.4(a).

§6.1 Significantly less favorable. A judgment is significantly less favorable in either of the following situations:

1. Plaintiff rejected offer. The judgment is significantly less favorable to the plaintiff if the plaintiff rejected the defendant's offer and the award is less than 80 percent of the rejected offer. CPRC 42.004(b)(1); TRCP 167.4(b)(1).

2. Defendant rejected offer. The judgment is significantly less favorable to the defendant if the defendant rejected the plaintiff's offer and the award is more than 120 percent of the rejected offer. CPRC 42.004(b)(2); TRCP 167.4(b)(2).

EXAMPLE

Assume that the jury awards the plaintiff $120,000 in damages. If the plaintiff rejected a settlement offer from the defendant that was over $150,000 (80% of $150,000 = $120,000), the verdict is "significantly less favorable" to the plaintiff than the defendant's settlement offer, and the plaintiff must pay the defendant's litigation costs. On the other hand, if the defendant rejected a settlement offer from the plaintiff that was under $100,000 (120% of $100,000 = $120,000), the verdict is "significantly less favorable" to the defendant than the plaintiff's settlement offer, and the defendant must pay the plaintiff's litigation costs.

§6.2 Calculating costs.

1. After rejection. The offeror may recover only those litigation costs it incurred between the date of rejection and the date of judgment. CPRC §42.004(c); TRCP 167.4(a).

2. Cap on costs. The judgment damages limit the recoverable litigation costs. The recoverable litigation costs cannot exceed the following: the total of 50% of the plaintiff's economic damages; plus 100% of the plaintiff's noneconomic, exemplary, and additional damages; minus any statutory or contractual liens connected to the occurrences or incidents giving rise to the claim. CPRC §42.004(d); TRCP 167.4(d).

3. No double recovery. An offeror that recovers litigation costs under another law (*e.g.*, CPRC chapter 38) cannot recover the same litigation costs under TRCP 167. CPRC §42.004(e); TRCP 167.4(e).

4. No costs to rejecting party. If a party is entitled to litigation costs under another law (*e.g.*, CPRC chapter 38), but that party rejects a TRCP 167 settlement offer and litigation costs are imposed against it, the party cannot recover under the other law the litigation costs it incurred after rejecting the offer. CPRC §42.004(f); TRCP

167.4(f). In other words, a party that rejects a fair settlement offer may lose some of its own litigation costs as well as having to pay those of the other side.

5. Defendant's costs awarded as offset. If the defendant recovers litigation costs, those costs are awarded in the judgment as an offset against the plaintiff's recovery. CPRC §42.004(g); TRCP 167.4(g).

EXAMPLE

Assume the defendant makes a $200,000 settlement offer, which the plaintiff rejects. The plaintiff then receives a verdict for $100,000 in economic damages and $20,000 in noneconomic damages. This verdict is significantly less favorable to the plaintiff than the settlement offer ($120,000 is less than $160,000, which is 80% of $200,000). The defendant may therefore recover up to $70,000 in litigation costs (50% of $100,000 = $50,000, plus 100% of $20,000). If the defendant had at least $70,000 in litigation costs, the plaintiff's total recovery would be $50,000 ($120,000 less a $70,000 offset).

---

§6.3 Awarding costs. The court will award TRCP 167 litigation costs by incorporating them with the jury's verdict into the final judgment. *See* TRCP 167.4(a).

1. Post-trial hearing. The court should hold a post-trial hearing on the amount and reasonableness of the litigation costs and on the reasonableness of any conditions in the rejected offer.

(1) Amount & reasonableness of litigation costs. On request, the court must hold a post-trial hearing for evidence before awarding litigation costs. TRCP 167.5(c). The court should determine the amount of litigation costs to be awarded, as well as consider any challenge to their reasonableness. *See* TRCP 167.4, 167.5. The court should determine reasonableness using the factors in ***Arthur Andersen & Co. v. Perry Equip. Corp.***, 945 S.W.2d 812, 818 (Tex.1997), and Rule 1.04 of the Texas Disciplinary Rules of Professional Conduct. See "Attorney Fees from Adverse Party," ch. 1-H, §10, p. 45. If the reasonableness of the litigation costs is challenged, and the court finds them to be reasonable, the court must award an additional amount to cover any attorney fees and expenses incurred in responding to post-trial discovery on reasonableness. TRCP 167.5(b).

(2) Reasonableness of conditions. When an offeree properly objected to an offer's condition (*e.g.*, that the offeree execute a release, indemnity, or other document as part of the settlement), no award of litigation costs can be based on that offer unless the court determines the condition was reasonable. TRCP 167.2(c). Thus, before the court awards litigation costs based on an offer with conditions to which the offeree properly objected, the court must conduct a hearing for evidence to determine the reasonableness of the conditions. *Id.* See "To the conditions," §5.2.1, p. 507.

2. Post-trial discovery. On a motion based on good cause, the rejecting party may conduct post-trial discovery on the reasonableness of the offeror's costs. TRCP 167.5(b).

3. Admissibility of evidence. Evidence relating to a settlement offer is admissible only as needed to enforce the settlement agreement or to obtain litigation costs. TRCP 167.6; *see* TRE 408. TRCP 167's provisions cannot be made known to the jury. TRCP 167.6.

4. Award mandatory. Normally, to recover attorney fees, a party must plead for their recovery in a petition or answer. *See* ***Swate v. Medina Cmty. Hosp.***, 966 S.W.2d 693, 701 (Tex.App.—San Antonio 1998, pet. denied) (unless mandatory statute says otherwise, court's jurisdiction to render judgment for attorney fees must be invoked by pleadings). But TRCP 167's award of attorney fees (and other litigation costs) is mandatory once TRCP 167 is properly invoked. Thus, even when a party's petition or answer does not ask for attorney fees or other litigation costs, the court must award litigation costs against the party rejecting a TRCP 167 offer. TRCP 167.4(a).

H. SETTLEMENT OF THE SUIT

§1. GENERAL

§1.1 Rules. TRCP 11, 76a, 97(a). See CPRC §§32.001-32.003.

§1.2 Purpose. When parties settle a lawsuit, they resolve the dispute according to the terms of a private contract. *See* ***Montanaro v. Montanaro***, 946 S.W.2d 428, 431 (Tex.App.—Corpus Christi 1997, no writ). The settlement brings the lawsuit to a conclusion, preventing the expense and uncertainty of litigation. Public policy favors the amicable settlement of controversies. ***Transport Ins. Co. v. Faircloth***, 898 S.W.2d 269, 280 (Tex.1995).

§1.3 Forms. ***O'Connor's Texas Civil Forms***, FORM 7G:01.

§1.4 Other references. ***O'Connor's Texas Causes of Action***, "Proportionate Responsibility & Contribution," ch. 42, p. 1115 (2004) (***O'Connor's COA***); Quinley & Khin, *We Love Settlements: An Insurer's Perspective*, For the Defense, 26 (Jan.1991); Rubendall, *I Hate Settlements: A Defense Lawyer's Lament*, For the Defense, 11 (Feb. 1990); Shanahan, *The High-Low Agreement*, For the Defense, 25 (July 1991); Williams, *A Comment on Williams v. Glash*, 24 Texas Trial Lawyers Forum, p. 27 (11-4-90); Hogan & Barger, *Contribution, Indemnity, Joint & Severed Liability, & Pitfalls of Multi-Party Settlements*, State Bar of Texas, Advanced Personal Injury Law Course, Tab GG (1998).

§2. ADVANTAGES OF SETTLEMENT VS. TRIAL

Some of the advantages of settlement over trial are the following: a trial will delay the resolution of the dispute; all trials are expensive, even short ones; a trial leaves the outcome of the dispute in the hands of the judge and jury; a trial affords limited types of relief—money damages and injunctive relief; by settlement, the parties may be able to construct remedies that give both parties something and permit both parties to avoid the possibility of a total loss. *See* ***Transport Ins.***, 898 S.W.2d at 280. For contrasting views, compare the two articles *We Love Settlements* and *I Hate Settlements*, cited in §1.4, above.

§3. PROVISIONS IN A SETTLEMENT AGREEMENT

Settlement agreements are governed by the law of contracts. ***Schlumberger Tech. Corp. v. Swanson***, 959 S.W.2d 171, 178 (Tex.1997); ***Williams v. Glash***, 789 S.W.2d 261, 264 (Tex.1990). See ***O'Connor's*** FORM 7G:01.

§3.1 The release. A release is a contractual surrender by one party of its cause of action against the other party. ***Lloyd v. Ray***, 606 S.W.2d 545, 547 (Tex.App.—San Antonio 1980, writ ref'd n.r.e.). A release extinguishes a claim or cause of action, as would a judgment. ***Dresser Indus. v. Page Pet.***, 853 S.W.2d 505, 508 (Tex.1993); ***Derr Constr. Co. v. City of Houston***, 846 S.W.2d 854, 858 (Tex.App.—Houston [14th Dist.] 1992, no writ). A release must meet the fair notice requirements—it must be conspicuous and specific. ***Dresser Indus.***, 853 S.W.2d at 507.

1. Identity of the parties. To be effective, a release must identify the parties to the release.

(1) The releasing party. A release binds only the person or entity specifically identified or named in the release as the releasing party. Both parties and nonparties may release claims by settlement agreements. For example, spouses and other family members may relinquish possible causes of action that have not been asserted. When a minor child releases rights, if there is a conflict of interest on the part of the child's parents or guardians, the minor should be represented by a guardian ad litem, who has authority to approve or reject the settlement agreement. See "Motion to Appoint Guardian Ad Litem Under TRCP 173," ch. 1-I, §3, p. 50.

PRACTICE TIP

The settlement agreement should always provide that both parties release each other, instead of just providing that the plaintiff releases the defendant. See TRCP 97(a) (agreed judgment between some parties before final disposition on the merits of other claims does not bar the claims of any other party if there is no written consent that the judgment will act as a bar).

---

(2) The released party. A release discharges only the person or entity specifically identified or named in the release. *E.g.*, ***Angus Chem. Co. v. IMC Fertilizer***, 939 S.W.2d 138, 139 (Tex.1997) (release of tortfeasor did not release tortfeasor's insurer); ***McMillen v. Klingensmith***, 467 S.W.2d 193, 196 (Tex.1971) (release of one doctor did not release other doctors); *see also* ***Knutson v. Morton Foods***, 603 S.W.2d 805, 806 (Tex.1980) (release of employee did not release principal under doctrine of respondeat superior). A person is identified when the language is sufficiently particular so that a stranger to the release could readily identify the released party even though the party's name is missing. *E.g.*, ***Duncan v. Cessna Aircraft Co.***, 665 S.W.2d 414, 419-20 (Tex.1984) (release of "any other corporations ... responsible" in a settlement with the pilot did not release the manufacturer of the aircraft); ***Frazer v. Texas Farm Bureau Mut. Ins. Co.***, 4 S.W.3d 819, 823-24 (Tex.App.—Houston [1st Dist.] 1999, no pet.) (release of insurer "and its affiliated companies" sufficiently identified insurer's underwriters); ***Lloyd***, 606 S.W.2d at 546-47 & n.1 (release of one doctor and "all other persons, firms and corporations" did not release a second, unnamed doctor). In a few situations, a release also releases entities not specifically named. *See, e.g.*, ***Winkler v. Kirkwood Atrium Office Park***, 816 S.W.2d 111, 113-14 (Tex.App.—Houston [14th Dist.] 1991, writ denied) (release of a health club from any injuries suffered while participating in its programs released all individuals & entities involved in its operation, maintenance, & administration).

(3) The attorneys. Attorneys representing parties in a consent judgment are bound by that judgment. ***Newman v. Link***, 889 S.W.2d 288, 289 (Tex.1994). If the attorneys have complaints about attorney fees and ad litem costs, they must object before the judgment becomes final. *Id.*

(4) The insurer. If the parties intend to release the defendant's insurer, the insurer should be named as a released party in the settlement papers. In Texas, if the injured party cannot sue the tortfeasor, it cannot sue the tortfeasor's insurer. ***Angus Chem.***, 939 S.W.2d at 138. Thus, when an injured party releases the tortfeasor, it can no longer sue the tortfeasor's insurer in Texas. *Id.* However, the release of the tortfeasor does not prevent the injured party from suing the tortfeasor's insurer in another jurisdiction. *Id.* at 139 (Louisiana law permits direct suits against insurers).

2. The dispute & the released claim. The settlement agreement should describe the dispute and the extent to which the release is intended to settle it. A release discharges only the claims specifically identified in the release. ***Victoria Bank & Trust Co. v. Brady***, 811 S.W.2d 931, 938 (Tex.1991). If the claim is not clearly within the subject matter of the release, it is not discharged. *Id.* When a release does not name one of the claims involved in the litigation, it "strongly suggests" the parties did not intend to release that claim. ***Baty v. Protech Ins. Agency***, 63 S.W.3d 841, 854-55 (Tex.App.—Houston [14th Dist.] 2001, pet. denied). General categorical releases are narrowly construed. ***Brady***, 811 S.W.2d at 938. The release may be broad (releasing all claims, known or unknown) or narrow (releasing only the particular claims asserted in the lawsuit). *See, e.g.*, ***Memorial Med. Ctr. v. Keszler***, 943 S.W.2d 433, 435 (Tex.1997) (release of all claims "relating to P's relationship with D" released all claims between parties, even ones unknown at time of release); ***Torchia v. Aetna Cas. & Sur. Co.***, 804 S.W.2d 219, 222 (Tex.App.—El Paso 1991, writ denied) (release of workers' compensation claim & all claims "arising out of the manner in which" D handled the settlement released claim for bad faith); ***Izaguirre v. TEIA***, 749 S.W.2d 550, 555 (Tex.App.—Corpus Christi 1988, writ denied) (release, which recognized carrier's liability was "indefinite" & "uncertain," released breach of duty of good faith). *But see* ***Transportation Ins. Co. v. Moriel***, 879 S.W.2d 10, 14-16 (Tex.1994) (release, which recognized that extent of injuries, liability, & medical expenses was "uncertain," did not preclude claim for punitive damages).

PRACTICE TIP

If the release is a separate instrument from the settlement agreement, make sure the description of the released claims is stated in identical language in both the release and the settlement agreement. In ***Memorial Med. Ctr.***, *943 S.W.2d at 434, the terms were much broader in the release than in the settlement agreement, and the court held the defendant was released according to the terms stated in the release, not in the settlement agreement.*

---

3. The consideration. The settlement agreement should recite consideration for the release. *See* ***Torchia***, 804 S.W.2d at 223 (release recited consideration & identified claims released). The financial inadequacy of the compensation is not a sufficient reason to set aside a release. *Id.* Although in most cases the consideration is the payment of money damages, the settlement of a contested lawsuit is itself sufficient consideration to support a settlement agreement. ***Schuh v. Schuh***, 453 S.W.2d 203, 204 (Tex.App.—Dallas 1970, no writ); *see also* ***Adams v. Petrade Int'l***, 754 S.W.2d 696, 723 (Tex.App.—Houston [1st Dist.] 1988, writ denied) (release is surrender of cause of action, which may be given for inadequate or no consideration).

PRACTICE TIP

When the recovery for some of the plaintiff's claims is not taxable as income, the plaintiff should consider having the settlement agreement attribute the bulk of the recovery to those claims.

§3.2 Other provisions.

1. Assignment of causes of action. If the identity of persons to be released is unknown, the plaintiff may assign any unreleased claims to the released parties. Such an assignment prevents the plaintiff from later suing any other persons without authority from the owner of the claim. ***Duke v. Brookshire Grocery Co.***, 568 S.W.2d 470, 472 (Tex.App.—Texarkana 1978, no writ). A settling defendant that is jointly responsible for the plaintiff's personal injuries, however, cannot preserve contribution rights against codefendants by purchasing the plaintiff's claim. ***Beech Aircraft Corp. v. Jinkins***, 739 S.W.2d 19, 22 (Tex.1987); *see* ***International Proteins Corp. v. Ralston-Purina Co.***, 744 S.W.2d 932, 934 (Tex.1988); ***Filter Fab v. Delauder***, 2 S.W.3d 614, 617 (Tex.App.—Houston [14th Dist.] 1999, no pet.).

2. Indemnity. Settlement agreements may contain provisions by which the plaintiff agrees to indemnify the defendant. An indemnity agreement is a promise by the indemnitor to safeguard or hold the indemnitee harmless against existing or future loss or liability, or both. ***Dresser Indus. v. Page Pet.***, 853 S.W.2d 505, 508 (Tex. 1993); ***Wallerstein v. Spirt***, 8 S.W.3d 774, 779 (Tex.App.—Austin 1999, no pet.). Unlike a release, which bars a cause of action, an indemnity provision creates a potential cause of action between the indemnitee and the indemnitor. ***Wallerstein***, 8 S.W.3d at 779. By the agreement, the plaintiff accepts liability for any claims that third parties may assert against the settling defendant arising out of the matter being settled. Thus, the indemnity protects that defendant against liability on cross-claims and other claims. The agreement creates a circular pattern of indemnity that extinguishes the plaintiff's cause of action. For example, in ***Bonniwell v. Beech Aircraft Corp.***, 663 S.W.2d 816, 819 (Tex.1984), the plaintiffs settled with Metro and agreed to indemnify it from any further liability. As the court explained, any judgment the plaintiffs obtained against the defendant would be collected from Metro, which would be reimbursed by the plaintiffs. ***Bonniwell***, 663 S.W.2d at 819; *see also* ***Phillips Pipe Line Co. v. McKown***, 580 S.W.2d 435, 440 (Tex.App.—Tyler 1979, writ ref'd n.r.e.) (when landowner released the contractor, he also released the pipeline owner because the contractor had a duty to indemnify the pipeline owner). A defendant who is not a party to a judgment but is a party to a settlement agreement cannot then seek indemnity from its codefendants. ***Trussway, Inc. v. Wetzel***, 928 S.W.2d 174, 176 (Tex.App.—Beaumont 1996, writ denied).

3. Covenants not to execute. Settlement agreements may contain covenants not to execute on the judgment against the settling defendant. Covenants not to execute are often made between a plaintiff and a defendant when the defendant's insurer has refused to provide a defense. These covenants are usually given in exchange for an assignment to the plaintiff of the defendant's rights against its insurer. Covenants not to execute are invalid if (1) they are made before the plaintiff's claim is adjudicated in a full adversarial trial, (2) the defendant's insurer tendered a defense, and (3) the insurer has either accepted coverage or made a good-faith effort to adjudicate coverage issues before adjudication of the plaintiff's claim. ***State Farm Fire & Cas. Co. v. Gandy***, 925 S.W.2d 696, 714 (Tex.1996).

4. Confidentiality. Settlement agreements may contain confidentiality provisions. These agreements, however, are subject to the restrictions in TRCP 76a(2)(b). Under TRCP 76a(2)(b), the parties cannot, by their settlement agreements, without notice and hearing, seal information that relates to matters that may adversely affect the general public health or safety, the administration of public office, or the operation of government. See "Motion to Seal Court Records," ch. 5-K, p. 290.

5. Structured payment. Settlement agreements may contain a provision for structured payment of damages by which the plaintiff receives deferred payments rather than one lump sum. The benefit to the plaintiff is the assurance of support for a number of years; the benefit to the defendant is the reduced cost of settlement because of delayed payments. CPRC chapter 139 covers structured settlements in personal injury cases.

(1) Offer must be in writing. If a plaintiff is either incapacitated, as defined by Probate Code §601(14), or substantially disabled as a result of the personal injury, an offer of structured settlement must be in writing and presented to the plaintiff's attorney. *See* CPRC §139.101.

(2) Offer must be explained. Before the offer expires, the plaintiff's attorney must explain to the plaintiff or the plaintiff's representative the terms, conditions, and other attributes of the settlement agreement and the appropriateness of the settlement under the circumstances. CPRC §139.102(b).

6. Agreement to vacate judgment. Settlement agreements may contain an agreement to vacate the judgments of the trial court and the court of appeals in the case. ***Houston Cable TV v. Inwood W. Civic Ass'n***, 860 S.W.2d 72, 73 (Tex.1993). A settlement agreement does not require an appellate court to vacate its opinion. ***Crown Life Ins. Co. v. Casteel***, 22 S.W.3d 378, 392 (Tex.2000). In most cases, the opinion will not be vacated, just the judgment. ***Houston Cable***, 860 S.W.2d at 73. A private agreement between litigants does not operate to vacate a court's writing on matters of public importance. *Id.*

7. Reservation of right to appeal. Settlement agreements may contain a reservation of the right to appeal some issues. *See* ***Ruiz v. Conoco, Inc.***, 868 S.W.2d 752, 754 (Tex.1993). An opinion issued in an appeal from a judgment rendered on a settlement agreement does not constitute an advisory opinion. *See id.*

8. Reservation of other claims. Settlement agreements may contain a reservation of the right to pursue other claims. *See, e.g.*, ***Transportation Ins. Co. v. Moriel***, 879 S.W.2d 10, 14-16 (Tex.1994) (settlement release preserved right to sue for bad faith & punitive damages); ***Indiana Lumbermen's Mut. Ins. Co. v. State***, 1 S.W.3d 264, 268 (Tex.App.—Fort Worth 1999, pet. denied) (party reserved its right to defend against another lawsuit by the state).

9. Judgment or dismissal order. The settlement agreement can provide that the parties will ask the court to render an agreed judgment or dismiss the case. *See* ***Compania Financiara Libano v. Simmons***, 53 S.W.3d 365, 368 (Tex.2001). If the parties agree to memorialize the settlement by an agreed judgment, the judgment should accurately state the terms of the settlement. ***Vickrey v. American Youth Camps***, 532 S.W.2d 292, 292 (Tex.1976). However, it is not necessary for the judgment to incorporate all the terms of the settlement agreement; even unincorporated terms can be enforced. ***Simmons***, 53 S.W.3d at 368.

10. Relationships between settling parties. Once a settlement agreement is executed, it extinguishes any duty of good faith and fair dealing that existed between the parties before settlement. ***Stewart Title Guar. Co. v. Aiello***, 941 S.W.2d 68, 71-72 (Tex.1997) (insurer no longer had duties to insured after settlement). The parties become judgment-creditor and judgment-debtor, with all remedies for enforcing the judgment. *Id.*

§4. SETTLEMENT CREDITS UNDER PROPORTIONATE RESPONSIBILITY

03

The Texas proportionate responsibility statute provides rules for apportioning liability for damages among the plaintiff and multiple defendants. This apportionment scheme also provides rules for applying a settlement "credit" (or a reduction of damages) based on a plaintiff's settlement with one of the defendants in a lawsuit. See §4.1, below. In 2003, CPRC chapter 33 was substantially revised by the Legislature. The 2003 amendments affect only cases filed after June 30, 2003, and thus many cases will still be governed by the 1995 version of CPRC chapter 33. *See* H.B. 4, 78th Leg., §23.02(c), eff. July 1, 2003 (savings provision). For more information about the 2003 amendments to proportionate responsibility and contribution, see ***O'Connor's COA***, "Proportionate Responsibility & Contribution," ch. 42, p. 1115.

§4.1 Settlement credits. In most cases (not medical malpractice cases), if the plaintiff settles with one or more persons, only one type of settlement credit applies—the percentage credit. The settlement credit is the sum of each settling person's percentage of responsibility. CPRC §33.012(b). In medical malpractice cases, the defendants can elect which type of settlement credit applies—either a dollar-for-dollar credit or a percentage credit. *Id.* §33.012(c). See ***O'Connor's COA***, "Filed after 6-30-03," ch. 42, §5.2.2, p. 1128. For rules on settlement credits for cases filed before July 1, 2003, see ***O'Connor's COA***, "Filed before 7-01-03," ch. 42, §5.2.1, p. 1125.

§4.2 One-satisfaction rule. The one-satisfaction rule provides that a party is entitled to recover damages only once for the same injury. ***Crown Life Ins. Co. v. Casteel***, 22 S.W.3d 378, 390 (Tex.2000); *see* ***Stewart Title Guar. Co. v. Sterling***, 822 S.W.2d 1, 5 (Tex.1991); ***Buccaneer Homes v. Pelis***, 43 S.W.3d 586, 589 (Tex.App.—Houston [1st Dist.] 2001, no pet.). The rule prevents a party from recovering more than the amount required for the full satisfaction of its damages. ***First Title Co. v. Garrett***, 860 S.W.2d 74, 78 (Tex.1993). The one-satisfaction rule applies whether the defendants committed joint or separate acts that resulted in the injury. ***Crown Life***, 22 S.W.3d at 390. The nonsettling defendant is entitled to offset any liability for joint and several damages by the amount of common damages paid by the settling defendant. *Id.* at 391-92. See ***O'Connor's COA***, "One Satisfaction Rule," ch. 35-A, §4, p. 944.

§5. ENFORCEABLE SETTLEMENT AGREEMENTS

§5.1 Agreement to settle.

1. Presuit settlement agreement. An oral agreement to settle a dispute before a lawsuit is filed is not governed by TRCP 11. *See* ***Estate of Pollack v. McMurrey***, 858 S.W.2d 388, 393 (Tex.1993) (TRCP 11 applies only to agreements in pending suits). An oral agreement to settle before suit is filed is governed by the law of contracts and by Business & Commerce Code §26.01, the statute of frauds. *See* ***Carter v. Allstate Ins. Co.***, 962 S.W.2d 268, 270-71 (Tex.App.—Houston [1st Dist.] 1998, pet. denied) (agreement by insurer to settle before suit was enforceable); *see also* ***Banda v. Garcia***, 955 S.W.2d 270, 272 (Tex.1997) (court assumed without discussion that oral pretrial settlement agreement was enforceable).

2. Settlement agreement after suit filed. To be enforceable, a settlement agreement must comply with TRCP 11. ***Padilla v. LaFrance***, 907 S.W.2d 454, 460 (Tex.1995); ***Roeglin v. Daves***, 83 S.W.3d 326, 330 (Tex. App.—Austin 2002, pet. denied). The agreement must be in writing, signed, and filed with the papers as part of the record, or it must be made in open court and entered of record. ***Padilla***, 907 S.W.2d at 459; ***Neasbitt v Warren***, 105 S.W.3d 113, 116 (Tex.App.—Fort Worth 2003, no pet.); ***Ronin v. Lerner***, 7 S.W.3d 883, 886 (Tex.App.—Houston [1st Dist.] 1999, no pet.). The Supreme Court does not require "slavish adherence" to the literal requirements of TRCP 11. ***Kennedy v. Hyde***, 682 S.W.2d 525, 529 (Tex.1984). See "Agreements Between Lawyers – Rule 11," ch. 1-H, §9, p. 44.

(1) In writing, signed, & filed. A written settlement agreement must contain all the essential terms of the settlement, be signed by the parties, and be filed with the papers as part of the record of the case. ***Padilla***, 907 S.W.2d at 461. It is not necessary for the entire agreement to be contained in one document. *Id.* at 460 (series of faxes). The agreement may be filed with the court even after one of the parties withdraws consent to the settlement; however, it must be filed before one of the parties attempts to enforce it. *Id.* at 461. See "Oral agreement recorded in deposition," ch. 1-H, §9.1.3, p. 45.

(2) In open court. An oral settlement agreement is enforceable if it is made in open court and entered of record, satisfying the requirements of TRCP 11. *See* ***Padilla***, 907 S.W.2d at 459; ***Neasbitt***, 105 S.W.3d at

116; ***Ronin***, 7 S.W.3d at 886-87. The TRCP 11 requirement for "entered of record" is satisfied if the agreement is noted in the judgment or in an order of the court. ***City of Houston v. Clear Creek Basin Auth.***, 589 S.W.2d 671, 677 (Tex.1979).

§5.2 Enforcing the settlement agreement. A binding settlement agreement may be enforced by the entry of a consent judgment or by a lawsuit.

1. Consent judgment. When the parties reach a settlement agreement in pending litigation, the court may render a judgment based on the agreement as long as no party has withdrawn consent. ***S&A Rest. Corp. v. Leal***, 892 S.W.2d 855, 857 (Tex.1995) (party withdrew consent before court rendered judgment); ***Kennedy v. Hyde***, 682 S.W.2d 525, 528 (Tex.1984) (same); ***Kelley v. Pirtle***, 826 S.W.2d 653, 654 (Tex.App.—Texarkana 1992, writ denied) (court orally rendered judgment in open court before party withdrew consent). If the parties agree to the terms of a settlement agreement, but one of them revokes consent before the court renders judgment, the agreement cannot be enforced as a consent judgment. ***S&A Rest.***, 892 S.W.2d at 857; ***Able Cabling Servs. v. Aaron-Carter Elec.***, 16 S.W.3d 98, 100 (Tex.App.—Houston [1st Dist.] 2000, pet. denied).

PRACTICE TIP

Once you reach a settlement, immediately ask the court to render judgment on the settlement agreement to prevent the other party from revoking the agreement. If the agreement is dictated into the record, ask the trial court to state on the record that "I now render judgment on the agreement." ***Galerie D'Tile v. Shinn****, 792 S.W.2d 792, 794 (Tex.App.—Houston [14th Dist.] 1990, no writ). Make sure the judge uses the present tense and not the future. See, e.g.,* ***Tinney v. Willingham****, 897 S.W.2d 543, 545 n.2 (Tex.App.—Fort Worth 1995, no writ) (because court said "I will" approve, it did not render judgment). The judge can sign the written judgment later.*

---

2. Suit to enforce as contract. Although a court cannot render a valid judgment based on a settlement agreement without consent at the time the judgment is rendered, the court may enforce the agreement as a contract if the agreement complies with TRCP 11, even after one party has withdrawn consent. ***Padilla***, 907 S.W.2d at 461; ***City of Roanoke v. Town of Westlake***, 111 S.W.3d 617, 626 (Tex.App.—Fort Worth 2003, pet. filed 8-18-03). A settlement agreement is enforceable as a contract even if its terms are not incorporated into a judgment. ***Compania Financiara Libano v. Simmons***, 53 S.W.3d 365, 368 (Tex.2001); ***Padilla***, 907 S.W.2d at 461; *see also* CPRC §154.071(a) (settlement agreements reached in ADR are enforceable like other contracts). If the suit that gave rise to the settlement agreement is still pending in the trial court, a party seeking to enforce the agreement may amend its pleadings in the suit to add a claim for breach of contract. ***Mantas v. 5th Ct. of Appeals***, 925 S.W.2d 656, 658 (Tex.1996). If the suit is not pending in the trial court, a party seeking to enforce the settlement agreement must file a separate breach of contract suit under a new cause number. *Id.* at 658-59.

COMMENTARIES

CHAPTER 8. THE TRIAL
TABLE OF CONTENTS

COMMENTARIES

CHAPTER 8. THE TRIAL
TABLE OF CONTENTS

A. JURY SELECTION

§1. GENERAL

§1.1 Rules. TRCP 221-236. See Gov't Code §§62.001-62.501 (petit juries).

§1.2 Purpose. The purpose of jury selection is to seat a fair and impartial jury. ***Hallett v. Houston Northwest Med. Ctr.***, 689 S.W.2d 888, 889 (Tex.1985).

§1.3 Forms. ***O'Connor's Texas Civil Forms***, FORMS 8A.

§1.4 Other references. Ballesteros, Comment, *Don't Mess with Texas Voir Dire*, 39 Hous.L.R. 201 (2002); Hart & Cawyer, *A Practitioner's Guide for Requesting a Civil Batson Hearing*, 26 Tex.Tech L.Rev. 109 (1995); Wright, Comment, *Challenges for Cause Due to Bias or Prejudice*, 46 Baylor L.Rev. 825 (1994); Godfrey, *Civil Voir Dire in Texas*, 31 S.Tex.L.Rev. 409 (1990); Perdue, *Jury Bias*, 28 Hous. Lawyer 2, p. 38 (Sept.-Oct.1990); Sheehan & Hollingsworth, *Allocation of Peremptory Challenges Among Multiple Parties*, 10 St. Mary's L.J. 511 (1979).

§2. QUALIFICATIONS & EXEMPTIONS OF JURORS

The statutory exemptions from jury service reflect a recognition that some persons are incapable of effectively performing a juror's function.

§2.1 General qualifications. All individuals are considered competent jurors unless disqualified by statute. Gov't Code §62.101. To be qualified to serve as a juror, a person must:

1. Be at least 18 years of age. *Id.* §62.102(1).

2. Be a citizen of Texas and the county where she is to serve. *Id.* §62.102(2).

3. Be qualified to vote in the county where she is to serve. *Id.* §62.102(3). A person who is not registered to vote is not disqualified from serving as a juror. *Id.* §62.1031.

4. Be of sound mind and good moral character. *Id.* §62.102(4).

5. Be able to read and write. *Id.* §62.102(5); ***Jenkins v. Chapman***, 636 S.W.2d 238, 240 (Tex.App.—Texarkana 1982, writ dism'd). The trial court may suspend this requirement if there are not enough jurors in the county who can read and write. Gov't Code §62.103(a).

6. Have not served as a juror for six or more days during the preceding three months in the county court or during the preceding 6 months in the district court. *Id.* §62.102(6). The court may suspend this restriction if the county's sparse population makes it seriously inconvenient to enforce. *Id.* §62.103(b).

7. Have not been convicted of a felony. *Id.* §62.102(7); ***Dempsey v. Beaumont Hosp.***, 38 S.W.3d 287, 289 (Tex.App.—Beaumont 2001, pet. dism'd); *see* ***Volkswagen of Am. v. Ramirez***, 79 S.W.3d 113, 119-21 (Tex. App.—Corpus Christi 2002, pet. granted 3-6-03) (dismissal of felony conviction after community supervision restored right of felon to serve on jury).

NOTE

Even though a person convicted of a felony cannot serve on a jury, TRCP 230 prohibits asking a panelist if she was convicted of one of the disqualifying offenses or if she has been charged with theft or any felony.

---

8. Not be under indictment or other legal accusation of a misdemeanor or felony. Gov't Code §62.102(8); ***Palmer Well Servs. v. Mack Trucks***, 776 S.W.2d 575, 576 (Tex.1989). The parties may waive the error by agreeing to continue with a juror who is under indictment. ***Mendoza v. Varon***, 563 S.W.2d 646, 648 (Tex.App.—Dallas 1978, writ ref'd n.r.e.). If a juror's indictment is discovered after the verdict is rendered, and that juror's vote is required for a verdict of ten jurors, the judgment must be reversed. ***Palmer Well Servs.***, 776 S.W.2d at 577.

§2.2 Physical qualifications. A blind or deaf person is not disqualified solely because of the disability, unless the disability renders the person unfit in that particular case. Gov't Code §62.104(b) (blindness), *id.* §62.1041(b) (deafness). The court is required to provide an interpreter for a deaf juror during the trial and the deliberations. CPRC §§21.002(a); 21.009; *cf.* ***Saunders v. State***, 49 S.W.3d 536, 539-40 (Tex.App.—Eastland 2001, pet. ref'd) (criminal case; juror entitled to interpreter during deliberations).

CAUTION

The Americans with Disabilities Act (ADA) prohibits the courts from automatically excluding persons from a jury on the grounds of disabilities. 42 U.S.C. §12132; ***Galloway v. Superior Ct.****, 816 F.Supp. 12, 18 (D.D.C.1993) (ADA prevented court from automatically excluding blind persons from juries).*

§2.3 Statutory disqualifications. The right to a fair and impartial trial is codified in Gov't Code §62.105. ***Babcock v. Northwest Mem'l Hosp.***, 767 S.W.2d 705, 708 (Tex.1989). If a person is disqualified by statute, the court must excuse that person from service. ***Compton v. Henrie***, 364 S.W.2d 179, 182 (Tex.1963). Under Gov't Code §62.105, a panelist is disqualified to serve as a juror on a particular case in the following instances.

1. **Witness.** The person is a witness in the case. Gov't Code §62.105(1).

2. **Interest.** The person has a direct or indirect interest in the case. *Id.* §62.105(2).

(1) **Examples of disqualifying interests.** • The employee of a party. ***Galveston H. & S.A. Ry. v. Thornsberry***, 17 S.W. 521, 522 (Tex.1891); ***Preston v. Ohio Oil Co.***, 121 S.W.2d 1039, 1041-42 (Tex.App.—Eastland 1938, writ ref'd). • Stockholders of a party corporation. ***Texas Power & Light Co. v. Adams***, 404 S.W.2d 930, 943 (Tex.App.—Tyler 1966, no writ). • Insureds of a party insurer. ***TEIA v. Lane***, 251 S.W.2d 181, 182 (Tex.App.—Fort Worth 1952, writ ref'd n.r.e.). • A warm, grateful friend of one of the parties. *E.g.*, ***Texas Cent. R.R. v. Blanton***, 81 S.W. 537, 538 (Tex.App.—Houston 1904, no writ) (P, a lawyer, had represented panelist and won lawsuit for him; panelist had named child after lawyer).

(2) **Examples of interests too remote to disqualify.** • Social relationship with employee of governmental entity-party. *E.g.*, ***Pharo v. Chambers Cty.***, 922 S.W.2d 945, 949 n.4 (Tex.1996) (juror dating a deputy sheriff in suit against county for negligence of sheriff). • Members of a cooperative buying club belonging to a party. *E.g.*, ***Guerra v. Wal-Mart Stores***, 943 S.W.2d 56, 59 (Tex.App.—San Antonio 1997, writ denied) (members of "Sam's Club" in suit against Wal-Mart). • Taxpayer residents of a city-party. ***City of Hawkins v. E.B. Germany & Sons***, 425 S.W.2d 23, 26 (Tex.App.—Tyler 1968, writ ref'd n.r.e.). • A casual friend who had former business relationship with one of the parties. ***Gant v. Dumas Glass & Mirror***, 935 S.W.2d 202, 208-09 (Tex.App.—Amarillo 1996, no writ).

3. **Relative.** The person is related by consanguinity or affinity within the third degree to a party in the case. Gov't Code §§62.105(3), 573.022-573.025. Degrees of relationship are determined according to the civil law system. See the charts in ***O'Connor's CPRC Plus***, pp. 529-30 (2003-04), showing which relatives are within the third degree.

4. **Same case.** The person has served as a juror in an earlier trial of the same case or in another case involving the same questions of fact. Gov't Code §62.105(5).

5. **Bias or prejudice.** The person has a bias or prejudice in favor of or against a party in the case. Gov't Code §62.105(4). A bias is an inclination toward one side of an issue over the other. ***Goode v. Shoukfeh***, 943 S.W.2d 441, 453 (Tex.1997); ***Compton***, 364 S.W.2d at 182. For a bias to disqualify a panelist, the panelist's state of mind leads to the inference she will not or cannot act with impartiality. ***Compton***, 364 S.W.2d at 182. Prejudice is the prejudgment of an issue. *Id.* Prejudice includes bias. *Id.*; ***Buls v. Fuselier***, 55 S.W.3d 204, 209 (Tex.App.—Texarkana 2001, no pet.). A panelist who is biased or prejudiced against the parties or the type of lawsuit should be disqualified. ***Compton***, 364 S.W.2d at 182. If bias or prejudice is established as a matter of law, the prospective juror

is automatically disqualified. ***Goode***, 943 S.W.2d at 452-53; ***Compton***, 364 S.W.2d at 182. If bias or prejudice is not established as a matter of law, the trial court must make a factual determination whether the panelist's bias or prejudice merits disqualification. ***Malone v. Foster***, 977 S.W.2d 562, 564 (Tex.1998); ***Swap Shop v. Fortune***, 365 S.W.2d 151, 154 (Tex.1963); ***Buls***, 55 S.W.3d at 209.

(1) Examples of bias or prejudice. • Juror was prejudiced against personal injury lawsuits. ***Compton***, 364 S.W.2d at 182. • Juror placed higher burden on juvenile than required by law. ***W.D.A. v. State***, 835 S.W.2d 227, 229 (Tex.App.—Waco 1992, no writ). • Juror was prejudiced against drinking and said this would affect her judgment. ***Flowers v. Flowers***, 397 S.W.2d 121, 123-24 (Tex.App.—Amarillo 1965, no writ).

(2) No rehabilitation. When a panelist admits bias or prejudice, the panelist is disqualified, must be excused from service, and cannot be rehabilitated. ***Sullemon v. U.S. Fid. & Guar. Co.***, 734 S.W.2d 10, 14 (Tex. App.—Dallas 1987, no writ); *see* ***Shepherd v. Ledford***, 962 S.W.2d 28, 34 (Tex.1998); *see also* ***W.D.A.***, 835 S.W.2d at 229 (criminal case). The court must disregard any declaration from the panelist that she will set aside the bias or prejudice and render a verdict on the evidence. ***White v. Dennison***, 752 S.W.2d 714, 718 (Tex.App.— Dallas 1988, writ denied); ***Gum v. Schaefer***, 683 S.W.2d 803, 808 (Tex.App.—Corpus Christi 1984, no writ).

§2.4 Exemptions from jury service. A person qualified to be a juror may be exempted from jury service as permitted by statute. Gov't Code §62.106 allows the following persons to claim exemptions: (1) a person over 70; (2) a person with legal custody of a child younger than ten if jury service would require leaving the child without adequate supervision; (3) a student in secondary school or an institution of higher education; (4) an officer or employee of the legislative branch of state government; (5) the primary caretaker of an invalid; (6) in a county with a population over 200,000, a person who has served as a juror during the preceding 24-month period; (7) in a county with a population over 250,000, a person who served as a juror during the preceding 36-month period if the county's jury wheel has not been reconstituted since the person served as a juror; or (8) a member of the United States military serving on active duty and deployed to a location away from the person's home station and out of her county of residence. Gov't Code §62.106. 03

§3. ASSEMBLING PROSPECTIVE JURORS

§3.1 Jury source. The Secretary of State compiles a list of prospective jurors by combining the lists of licensed drivers and registered voters. Gov't Code §62.001(a). The Secretary of State sends each county its combined list of prospective jurors before the end of each year. *Id.* §62.001(g).

§3.2 Counties with interchangeable juries. Counties with at least three district courts are governed by the laws for interchangeable juries, which require the judges of the county to determine the approximate number of prospective jurors necessary for each week of the year for the general panel. Gov't Code §62.016(a). The names are drawn from the jury wheel or compiled by a mechanical device. When impaneled, the prospective jurors constitute a general panel for service in all courts of the county. *Id.* §62.016(e). The district judge who impanels the jury for the week inquires as to the jurors' general qualifications for jury duty. *See* ***Benavides v. Soto***, 893 S.W.2d 69, 70-71 (Tex.App.—Corpus Christi 1994, no writ). When one of the courts in the county needs a jury, the presiding judge, acting through the clerk, sends about 32 prospective jurors to a district court or 18 to a county court. If the lawyers in the case believe additional prospective jurors will be necessary because they anticipate the case will result in a number of challenges for cause, they can ask the trial court judge to request a larger panel.

§3.3 Other counties. In counties not governed by the laws providing for interchangeable juries, the clerk assembles a panel for a particular court by randomly drawing slips of paper with names on them from a container and listing them in the order selected. TRCP 224. In those counties, the clerk is authorized to select 24 panelists for the district court and 12 for the county court. *Id.*

§3.4 Objection to prospective jurors. There are two kinds of objections to the selection of prospective jurors.

1. Challenge the array. A party may challenge the array, which is an objection that challenges the procedure for selecting and summoning prospective jurors or asserts a violation of the jury-wheel statute. ***Martinez v. City of Austin***, 852 S.W.2d 71, 73 (Tex.App.—Austin 1993, writ denied); *see* Gov't Code §§62.001-62.021. The challenge must be by written motion, supported by affidavit, and filed with the particular judge in charge of the local jury system. TRCP 221; ***State v. Smith***, 671 S.W.2d 32, 36 (Tex.1984); ***TEIA v. Burge***, 610 S.W.2d 524, 525 (Tex.App.—Beaumont 1980, writ ref'd n.r.e.). Noncompliance with TRCP 221 waives any objection to the array, unless there was fundamental error. ***Mann v. Ramirez***, 905 S.W.2d 275, 278 (Tex.App.—San Antonio 1995, writ denied). An objection to the array may be made to the trial judge only if the party had no opportunity to object at the time the impaneling judge assembled the array. ***Mendoza v. Ranger Ins. Co.***, 753 S.W.2d 779, 780-81 (Tex.App.—Fort Worth 1988, writ denied) (lack of randomness of panel did not become apparent until voir dire). If the movant successfully challenges the array, the entire array is dismissed, and a new one is summoned. ***Martinez***, 852 S.W.2d at 73.

2. Request jury shuffle. After the panel is assigned to a court and before voir dire, a party may demand a jury shuffle. TRCP 223; ***Martinez***, 852 S.W.2d at 73. When a juror questionnaire is used, the phrase "before voir dire" means before the responses to the questionnaire are examined by the parties. ***Carr v. Smith***, 22 S.W.3d 128, 133-34 (Tex.App.—Fort Worth 2000, pet. denied). The order in which the panelists are listed on the jury list is important because the first 12 (or six in county court) unchallenged panelists will sit on the jury. When requested, the names of the members of the panel must be placed in a receptacle, shuffled, drawn, and transcribed on the jury list in the order drawn. TRCP 223; *see* ***Whiteside v. Watson***, 12 S.W.3d 614, 618 (Tex.App.—Eastland 2000, pet. denied) (shuffle of jury cards did not comply with rule). It is not necessary for the judge to draw the names from the receptacle; the bailiff can perform that task. ***Whiteside***, 12 S.W.3d at 618-19 n.1. Only one jury shuffle is allowed in each case. TRCP 223; ***Martinez***, 852 S.W.2d at 73. *But see* ***Whiteside***, 12 S.W.3d at 618-19 (second shuffle was harmless error because first shuffle did not comply with rule).

§4. VOIR DIRE EXAMINATION

§4.1 Purpose. During voir dire, each party is given the opportunity to examine the members of the panel to determine if any of them are disqualified or should not serve on the case. *See* ***Implement Dealers Mut. Ins. Co. v. Castleberry***, 368 S.W.2d 249, 254 (Tex.App.—Beaumont 1963, writ ref'd n.r.e.). The right to conduct a proper voir dire is linked to the constitutional right to a fair trial. ***Babcock v. Northwest Mem'l Hosp.***, 767 S.W.2d 705, 709 (Tex.1989).

§4.2 Right to initiate voir dire. Except for good cause shown on the record, the party with the burden of proof on the whole case should be allowed to initiate voir dire, make the initial opening statement, open and close the evidence, and open and close the final summation. TRCP 265, 266, 269; *see* ***Ocean Transp. v. Greycas, Inc.***, 878 S.W.2d 256, 268-69 (Tex.App.—Corpus Christi 1994, writ denied). See "Right to Make First Opening Statement," ch. 8-B, §2, p. 533.

§4.3 Control of voir dire. The trial court has broad discretion in ruling on the propriety of the voir dire. ***Dickson v. Burlington N. R.R.***, 730 S.W.2d 82, 85 (Tex.App.—Fort Worth 1987, writ ref'd n.r.e.).

1. Scope of examination. A party is entitled to inquire into matters reasonably related to the kinds of issues presented by the case. *See* ***Babcock***, 767 S.W.2d at 709; ***TEIA v. Loesch***, 538 S.W.2d 435, 440 (Tex.App.—Waco 1976, writ ref'd n.r.e.). The trial court is more likely to be reversed on appeal if it prevents a party from asking a question than if it allows a question. *See, e.g.*, ***Babcock***, 767 S.W.2d at 708-09 (trial court abused its discretion by refusing to allow Ps to question jurors about "lawsuit crisis"). The court should give the attorneys broad latitude during the examination of the jury panel. *Id.*; ***Loesch***, 538 S.W.2d at 440.

2. Time for examination. The trial court has the right to reasonably limit the time permitted for questioning the jurors. *See* ***McCarter v. State***, 837 S.W.2d 117, 119 (Tex.Crim.App.1992) (criminal case). The Court of Criminal Appeals has adopted a test for criminal trials that can be helpful in civil trials to determine when the trial court errs in limiting voir dire. To preserve error when the trial court limits the time for voir dire, the party making an objection must show all of the following: (1) the party did not attempt to prolong voir dire; (2) the party was prevented from asking proper and relevant voir dire questions because the court imposed unreasonable time limitations; and (3) the party was not permitted to examine prospective jurors who actually served on the jury. *Id.* The party must identify the specific questions it was not permitted to ask. *Compare* ***S.D.G. v. State***, 936 S.W.2d 371, 380 (Tex.App.—Houston [14th Dist.] 1996, writ denied) (identifying general topics for questions was not sufficient), *with* ***Clemments v. State***, 940 S.W.2d 207, 210 (Tex.App.—San Antonio 1996, pet. ref'd) (identifying specific questions preserved error). The specific questions must be identified to the court before the jury is selected. ***S.D.G.***, 936 S.W.2d at 380-81.

§4.4 Error in panelist's answer.

1. Types of errors.

(1) Erroneous answer. A panelist's erroneous or incorrect material answer to a question on voir dire may be a ground for a new trial. TRCP 327(a). See "Erroneous juror answer on voir dire," ch. 10-B, §13.5.2, p. 628.

(2) No response. When a panelist does not respond to a question, the courts generally find it was not juror misconduct and hold there was no harm to the complainant. *See* ***Kiefer v. Continental Airlines***, 10 S.W.3d 34, 40 (Tex.App.—Houston [14th Dist.] 1999, pet. denied); ***Durbin v. Dal-Briar Corp.***, 871 S.W.2d 263, 272-73 (Tex.App.—El Paso 1994, writ denied), *disapproved on other grounds*, ***Golden Eagle Archery v. Jackson***, 24 S.W.3d 362 (Tex.2000); ***Missouri Pac. R.R. v. Cunningham***, 515 S.W.2d 678, 685 (Tex.App.—San Antonio 1974, writ dism'd).

(3) Prejudicial statement. If a panelist makes a spontaneous, prejudicial statement that is curable by an instruction, the party must object and, if the objection is sustained, ask for an instruction to disregard. *See, e.g.*, ***Brentwood Fin. Corp. v. Lamprecht***, 736 S.W.2d 836, 840 (Tex.App.—San Antonio 1987, writ ref'd n.r.e.) (instruction was sufficient to cure adverse effect of panelist's statement). See "When jury hears inadmissible evidence," ch. 8-D, §6.6, p. 548. If the statement poisons the panel, the party must make a motion to strike the entire panel. *See, e.g.*, ***Reviea v. Marine Drilling Co.***, 800 S.W.2d 252, 256 (Tex.App.—Corpus Christi 1990, writ denied) (panelist's spontaneous remark about excessive insurance rates did not require that trial court strike panel). In most cases, the party moving to strike the entire panel must ask follow-up questions of the panel to establish that the panel was affected by the statement. *See* ***Brentwood***, 736 S.W.2d at 840.

2. Preserving error. To preserve error regarding the answers of the panelists during voir dire, the attorney should take the following steps:

(1) Make a record. The attorney should always ask the court reporter to record the complete voir dire, including bench conferences. *See* TRAP 13.1(a) (duties of court reporter include making a full record of all proceedings); ***Soto v. Texas Indus.***, 820 S.W.2d 217, 219 (Tex.App.—Fort Worth 1991, no writ) (court of appeals could not consider a ***Batson*** objection because no record was made of voir dire); ***Loesch***, 538 S.W.2d at 441 (D could not complain of error in P's voir dire because record did not include its own voir dire). *But see* ***McCoy v. Wal-Mart Stores***, 59 S.W.3d 793, 796 (Tex.App.—Texarkana 2001, no pet.) (court of appeals permitted case to be abated for hearing on what transpired at unrecorded bench conferences during voir dire). See "Duties of Court Reporter," ch. 1-E, §3, p. 27. The record must contain the question the party wanted to ask and the court's ruling that prevented the question. If the nature of the question is apparent from the context, it is not necessary to state the specific questions on the record. ***Babcock v. Northwest Mem'l Hosp.***, 767 S.W.2d 705, 708 (Tex.1989) (language in motion in limine & recorded voir dire made it obvious what questions P wanted to ask).

(2) Conduct complete voir dire. The attorney must conduct a complete voir dire. Without a complete voir dire, the party waives the right to complain of prejudice. ***City of San Antonio v. Willinger***, 345 S.W.2d 577, 578 (Tex.App.—San Antonio 1961, no writ). A complete voir dire includes (1) inquiry about the subject on voir dire, (2) specific rather than general questions, (3) questions that are clear and unambiguous, and (4) pursuit of inquiries suggested by the answers of the panelists. *Id.* at 578-79.

(3) Ask specific questions of individuals. The attorney should direct specific questions to each panelist. Because individual panelists often are reluctant to respond to general questions, general questions are not a good predicate for complaints of concealment of information, incorrect answers, or a failure to answer. *See* ***Durbin***, 871 S.W.2d at 273 (question whether anyone had a problem with large jury verdicts did not preserve error); ***Soliz v. Saenz***, 779 S.W.2d 929, 933 (Tex.App.—Corpus Christi 1989, writ denied) (question whether they could follow the law did not preserve error); ***Barron v. State***, 378 S.W.2d 144, 145-46 (Tex.App.—San Antonio 1964, no writ) (question whether any person knew the State's witnesses did not preserve error).

(4) Keep panelists' attention. The attorney must ensure that the members of the jury panel hear the questions and understand them. ***Burton v. R.E. Hable Co.***, 852 S.W.2d 745, 746 (Tex.App.—Tyler 1993, no writ) (panelist did not understand the question); ***Barron***, 378 S.W.2d at 146 (panelist did not pay attention to questions).

(5) Object to improper question or statement. When an attorney asks an objectionable question or makes an objectionable statement that is curable, the other attorney must make an objection, and if the objection is sustained, the attorney must request an instruction to disregard the question or statement. ***TEIA v. Loesch***, 538 S.W.2d 435, 441 (Tex.App.—Waco 1976, writ ref'd n.r.e.). If the court sustains the objection and instructs the jury to disregard, the attorney must then ask for a mistrial to preserve error for appeal. This is called "pursuing an adverse ruling." See chart 8-1, "Pursuing an Adverse Ruling," ch. 8-D, p. 550. If counsel makes no objection, does not request an instruction, and does not make a motion for mistrial, the error is waived. ***General Res. Org. v. Deadman***, 907 S.W.2d 22, 29 (Tex.App.—San Antonio 1995), *writ denied*, 932 S.W.2d 485 (Tex.1996).

§4.5 Proper questions & comments. The following matters are proper subjects of inquiry on voir dire. • The panelist's bias or prejudice in favor of or against a party in the case. Gov't Code §62.105(4); ***American Cyanamid Co. v. Frankson***, 732 S.W.2d 648, 653 (Tex.App.—Corpus Christi 1987, writ ref'd n.r.e.). • The panelist's bias or prejudice against the type of lawsuit. ***Compton v. Henrie***, 364 S.W.2d 179, 182 (Tex.1963). • Questions to determine if the panelist is biased in favor of or against a party because of nationality, wealth, or status. ***Haryanto v. Saeed***, 860 S.W.2d 913, 918 (Tex.App.—Houston [14th Dist.] 1993, writ denied). • The panelist's relationship with the other lawyer. ***Anderson v. Owen***, 269 S.W. 454, 455 (Tex.App.—Galveston 1924, no writ). • The panelist's relationship with an organization to which the other lawyer belongs. ***Lopez v. Allee***, 493 S.W.2d 330, 335 (Tex.App.—San Antonio 1973, writ ref'd n.r.e.). • A panelist's representation by one of the lawyers. ***Implement Dealers Mut. Ins. Co. v. Castleberry***, 368 S.W.2d 249, 254 (Tex.App.—Beaumont 1963, writ ref'd n.r.e.). • The panelist's relationship to a party. *See* Gov't Code §§62.105(3), 573.022-573.025. • The panelist's financial interest in the litigation. ***Carey v. Planters' State Bank***, 280 S.W. 251, 252 (Tex.App.—San Antonio 1926, writ dism'd); *see also* Gov't Code §62.105(2) (panelist's direct or indirect interest in the subject matter of the case). • The panelist's acquaintance with potential witnesses. ***Employers Mut. Liab. Ins. Co. v. Butler***, 511 S.W.2d 323, 325-26 (Tex.App.—Texarkana 1974, writ ref'd n.r.e.). • The panelist's interest in the "lawsuit crisis" or the "insurance crisis." ***Babcock***, 767 S.W.2d at 708-09; *see* ***National Cty. Mut. Fire Ins. Co. v. Howard***, 749 S.W.2d 618, 621 (Tex.App.—Fort Worth 1988, writ denied). • The panelist's bias against the use of intoxicants. ***Flowers v. Flowers***, 397 S.W.2d 121, 122-23 (Tex.App.—Amarillo 1965, no writ). • The panelist's ability to award a certain sum of money if warranted by the evidence. ***Cavnar v. Quality Control Parking***, 678 S.W.2d 548, 555 (Tex.App.—Houston [14th Dist.] 1984), *rev'd in part on other grounds*, 696 S.W.2d 549 (Tex.1985).

PRACTICE TIP

In exemplary damage cases, lawyers cannot question panelists about exemplary damages based on a preponderance of the evidence because the burden for exemplary damages is clear and convincing. CPRC §41.003(a). See "Motion to Bifurcate Exemplary Damages," ch. 5-H, §5, p. 267.

§4.6 Improper questions & comments. The following matters have been found to be improper on voir dire. • For a plaintiff, telling the jury the defendant has insurance or that the plaintiff has no insurance; for a defendant, telling the jury the plaintiff has insurance. ***Ford v. Carpenter***, 216 S.W.2d 558, 559 (Tex.1949). • Discussing evidence that will be inadmissible at trial. *See, e.g.*, ***Travelers Ins. Co. v. DeLeon***, 456 S.W.2d 544, 545 (Tex.App.—Amarillo 1970, writ ref'd n.r.e.) (in workers' compensation case, weekly compensation benefits); ***Christie v. Brewer***, 374 S.W.2d 908, 911-12 (Tex.App.—Austin 1964, writ ref'd n.r.e.) (in suit on a contract, that the other party was indicted for matters relating to the same transaction). • Advising the jury of the effect of their answers. ***Loesch***, 538 S.W.2d at 442; ***Robinson v. Lovell***, 238 S.W.2d 294, 298 (Tex.App.—Galveston 1951, writ ref'd n.r.e.). • Getting the jury to commit to certain views or conclusions. ***Campbell v. Campbell***, 215 S.W. 134, 137 (Tex.App.—Dallas 1919, writ ref'd). • Asking a question in which the prejudicial effect outweighs the probative value. ***Gulf States Util. Co. v. Reed***, 659 S.W.2d 849, 855-56 (Tex.App.—Houston [14th Dist.] 1983, writ ref'd n.r.e.); *see* ***Loesch***, 538 S.W.2d at 440.

§5. CHALLENGES FOR CAUSE

§5.1 Purpose. A challenge for cause is an objection to a panelist, alleging some fact that by law disqualifies the person from serving as a juror or renders the person unfit to sit on the jury. TRCP 228; ***Wooten v. Southern P.T. Co.***, 928 S.W.2d 76, 80 (Tex.App.—Houston [14th Dist.] 1995, no writ). The challenge for cause permits the parties to eliminate from the panel those panelists who are disqualified from serving on the jury for that case. As soon as it becomes apparent that a panelist may be disqualified, the attorney should ask the panelist to approach the bench for questioning outside the hearing of the rest of the panel.

§5.2 Grounds for challenges for cause.

1. **General qualifications.** See list in "Qualifications & Exemptions of Jurors," §2, p. 519.

2. **Statutory disqualification.** See list in "Statutory disqualifications," §2.3, p. 520.

3. **Other grounds for disqualification.** The court may exercise its discretion and excuse a panelist for cause even when there is no statutory ground for disqualification. TRCP 228 ("or which in the opinion of the court, renders him an unfit person to sit on the jury").

§5.3 Preserving error. To complain about error when the trial court refuses to permit a challenge for cause, the attorney must follow the procedure set out in ***Hallett v. Houston Northwest Med. Ctr.***, 689 S.W.2d 888, 890 (Tex.1985). To preserve error, the attorney must take the following steps:

1. **During voir dire.** During voir dire, the attorney must challenge a panelist for cause (the "for-cause panelist"). The record must reflect the court overruled the challenge for cause. If there is a discussion with the for-cause panelist at the bench, the attorney must make sure the court reporter records it.

2. **After deciding strikes, but before giving to clerk.** The timing of the objection to the exhaustion of the peremptory strikes is critical. The record must show the attorney objected to the exhaustion of peremptory strikes before the attorney gave its peremptory strikes to the clerk. See §5.3.3, below. To properly object, the party must do all of the following:

(1) Inform the court that, as a result of the court's refusal to strike the for-cause panelist, the party will exhaust its peremptory challenges before striking an objectionable panelist on the list. ***Lucas v. Titus Cty. Hosp. Dist.***, 964 S.W.2d 144, 157-58 (Tex.App.—Texarkana 1998), *pet. denied*, 988 S.W.2d 740 (Tex.1998); ***Wooten***, 928 S.W.2d at 81.

(2) Identify the objectionable panelist who will remain on the jury list once the party uses its last peremptory strike. The objectionable panelist can be either the panelist who should have been struck for cause or another objectionable panelist, and the objectional panelist actually serves on the jury. *See, e.g.*, ***Shepherd v. Ledford***, 962 S.W.2d 28, 34 (Tex.1998) (for-cause panelist left on list); ***Hallett***, 689 S.W.2d at 889-90 (same); ***Operation Rescue v. Planned Parenthood***, 937 S.W.2d 60, 69 (Tex.App.—Houston [14th Dist.] 1996) (same), *modified on*

other grounds, 975 S.W.2d 546 (Tex.1998); ***Pharo v. Chambers Cty.***, 893 S.W.2d 264, 268 (Tex.App.—Houston [1st Dist.] 1995) (panelist other than for-cause panelist left on list), *aff'd*, 922 S.W.2d 945 (Tex.1996); ***Beavers v. Northrup Worldwide Aircraft Servs.***, 821 S.W.2d 669, 673 (Tex.App.—Amarillo 1991, writ denied) (for-cause panelists left on list). In most appeals, the error is waived because the party did not identify the objectionable panelist who remained on the panel. *See, e.g.*, ***Pharo***, 893 S.W.2d at 268 (statement that "I object to this juror" did not identify panelist).

To determine if a panelist will probably remain on the panel, the attorney should count 12 panelists, skipping the party's own peremptory strikes and any strikes the attorney believes the other party will make. The attorney should identify someone within those 12 panelists as the objectionable panelist. The rationale for identifying someone who could remain on the panel is the harmless error rule—the objectionable panelist might be struck by the other party, or the objectionable panelist might be so far down the list that the panelist could not have been picked for the jury. *See* ***Carpenter v. Wyatt Constr. Co.***, 501 S.W.2d 748, 750-51 (Tex.App.—Houston [14th Dist.] 1973, writ ref'd n.r.e.) (by requiring the objectionable panelist to be identified before strikes exercised, other party may strike the objectionable panelist).

(3) Ask the court to reconsider its ruling on the strike for cause or, as an alternative, to grant the party an additional peremptory strike to compensate for the erroneous ruling on the challenge for cause. *See* ***Hallett***, 689 S.W.2d at 890 (harm occurs when the court is made aware that objectionable jurors will be chosen because the party has no additional peremptory strikes); ***Sullemon v. U.S. Fid. & Guar. Co.***, 734 S.W.2d 10, 13-14 (Tex. App.—Dallas 1987, no writ) (party is not required to ask for additional peremptory strike to preserve error); ***Red River Pipeline v. Amonett***, 695 S.W.2d 802, 807 (Tex.App.—Amarillo 1985, no writ) (party waived error because it neither asked for additional strikes nor objected that it was forced to take objectionable panelists), *overruled on other grounds*, ***Callejo v. Brazos Elec. Power Coop.***, 755 S.W.2d 73 (Tex.1988).

3. After court overrules request. Once the court overrules the request, only then should the attorney give the clerk the peremptory strikes. The record must show the court overruled the party's objection to the exhaustion of its peremptory strikes before the party gave the clerk its peremptory strikes. ***Beavers***, 821 S.W.2d at 681 (record was ambiguous, error not preserved). If the attorney does not make the objection before it turns in its peremptory strikes, it waives the error. ***Operation Rescue***, 937 S.W.2d at 68-69; ***Goode v. Shoukfeh***, 915 S.W.2d 666, 673 (Tex.App.—Amarillo 1996), *aff'd*, 943 S.W.2d 441 (Tex.1997); ***Lopez v. Southern P.T. Co.***, 847 S.W.2d 330, 332-33 (Tex.App.—El Paso 1993, no writ).

PRACTICE TIP

To preserve error, counsel should state on the record: "Because the court refused to remove Mr. Smith for cause, the defendant will have no peremptory strikes left to challenge an objectionable panelist, [identify either Mr. Smith or another objectionable panelist on the jury list]. To cure the error, the defendant asks the court to strike Mr. Smith for cause or, in the alternative, to grant the defendant an additional peremptory strike." If the request is denied, counsel should state, "Having stated my objection on the record, I now hand my list of peremptory challenges to the clerk." After the jury is selected, ask the court reporter to take possession of the juror information sheets and the strike lists so they can be included in the record.

§6. PEREMPTORY CHALLENGES

Peremptory challenges are made after the panel has been interviewed by both sides and after all challenges for cause have been resolved.

§6.1 Purpose. A peremptory challenge, commonly referred to as a "strike," is a challenge to a panelist without assigning a reason. TRCP 232; ***Patterson Dental Co. v. Dunn***, 592 S.W.2d 914, 917 (Tex.1979). Peremptory strikes permit the parties to reject certain panelists who may be unsympathetic to their position; the strikes do not permit the parties to select the members for the panel. ***Patterson Dental***, 592 S.W.2d at 919.

§6.2 Size of panel. In a two-party case, after the parties make their challenges for cause, at least 24 persons must remain on the panel in district court (12 in county court). If the jury panel has fewer than those numbers, the trial court must direct the clerk to call other panelists to complete the jury. TRCP 231, 235; ***Thomas v. City of O'Donnell***, 811 S.W.2d 757, 759 (Tex.App.—Amarillo 1991, no writ). *But see* ***McRae v. Echols***, 8 S.W.3d 797, 798-99 (Tex.App.—Waco 2000, pet. denied) (harmless error to begin voir dire with 23 jurors). The burden is on the trial court, not the parties, to summon additional panelists. TRCP 231, 235; ***Thomas***, 811 S.W.2d at 759.

§6.3 Allocation of strikes. The purpose of allocating strikes is to ensure no party or "side" has an unfair advantage because of its peremptory challenges. TRCP 233; ***Patterson Dental***, 592 S.W.2d at 919.

1. In most cases. In a two-party case, each side is entitled to six peremptory strikes in district court (three in county court). TRCP 233; ***Perkins v. Freeman***, 518 S.W.2d 532, 533 (Tex.1974).

2. Motion to equalize in multiparty cases. In a multiparty case, a party may file a motion to equalize the peremptory strikes if parties on one side of the case are antagonistic to each other on an issue going to the jury. ***Van Allen v. Blackledge***, 35 S.W.3d 61, 64 (Tex.App.—Houston [14th Dist.] 2000, pet. denied). See ***O'Connor's*** FORM 8A:01. The motion must be filed before the parties exercise their peremptory strikes. TRCP 233; ***Van Allen***, 35 S.W.3d at 64. If such a motion is made, the following procedure is used.

(1) Conduct hearing. The trial court should conduct a hearing and consider the pleadings, pretrial discovery, statements made during voir dire examination, and any other information brought to its attention. ***Scurlock Oil Co. v. Smithwick***, 724 S.W.2d 1, 5 (Tex.1986); ***Garcia v. Central Power & Light Co.***, 704 S.W.2d 734, 737 (Tex.1986); *see also* TRCP 233 (court should consider any matter brought to its attention to eliminate any unfair advantage). A cross-claim alone will not support a finding of antagonism. *See* ***Central Power***, 704 S.W.2d at 737. Antagonism must be decided after voir dire and before the parties exercise their peremptory strikes. ***Central Power***, 704 S.W.2d at 737 (statements made on voir dire established no antagonism); *see* ***Patterson Dental***, 592 S.W.2d at 919.

(2) Align parties according to antagonism. The trial court must determine if the litigants on the same side of the litigation are antagonistic with respect to any issue to be submitted to the jury. TRCP 233; ***Scurlock Oil***, 724 S.W.2d at 5; ***Central Power***, 704 S.W.2d at 736. A "side" is defined as litigants with a common interest on an issue to be submitted to the jury. TRCP 233; ***"Y" Propane Serv. v. Garcia***, 61 S.W.3d 559, 569 (Tex.App.—San Antonio 2001, no pet.). The term side is not synonymous with "party," "litigant," or "person." TRCP 233; ***"Y" Propane***, 61 S.W.3d at 569. The parties must be antagonistic on an issue of fact that will be submitted to the jury, not on a matter that constitutes a pure question of law. ***Patterson Dental***, 592 S.W.2d at 918; *see* ***"Y" Propane***, 61 S.W.3d at 570 (antagonism in a future contribution suit did not establish antagonism in the primary suit). The antagonism must be between litigants on the same side vis-à-vis each other, not because they each have differing conflicts with the other side. ***Patterson Dental***, 592 S.W.2d at 918. For example, defendants are antagonistic with each other when they contend the other is solely responsible for the plaintiff's injuries. *Id.* Whether there is antagonism between multiple litigants on the same side of a lawsuit is a question of law. ***Central Power***, 704 S.W.2d at 736.

(a) No antagonism. If the court decides the parties on the same side are not antagonistic, each side must receive the same number of strikes. ***Central Power***, 704 S.W.2d at 736; *see also* ***American Cyanamid Co. v. Frankson***, 732 S.W.2d 648, 652 (Tex.App.—Corpus Christi 1987, writ ref'd n.r.e.) (D was not aligned with P just because he offered to settle); ***Diamond Shamrock Corp. v. Wendt***, 718 S.W.2d 766, 769 (Tex.App.—Corpus Christi 1986, writ ref'd n.r.e.) (P was not aligned with one D just because he was more hostile to the other D). If there is no antagonism between parties on one side of the litigation, that side gets only six strikes in district court (three in county court). TRCP 233; *see also* ***Wendt***, 718 S.W.2d at 770 (error to give P 12 strikes, and each of 2 Ds, 6).

(b) Antagonism – equalize the strikes. If the court decides the parties on the same side are antagonistic, it has the discretion to determine the number of strikes to give each side so neither side has an unfair advantage. ***Patterson Dental***, 592 S.W.2d at 919. The court may proportion the strikes by increasing the strikes on one side or decreasing the strikes on the other, or both. *Id.* at 920. If the parties on one side are antagonistic to each other, they each get their own strikes. *See* ***Frank B. Hall & Co. v. Beach***, 733 S.W.2d 251, 256-57 (Tex.App.—Corpus Christi 1987, writ ref'd n.r.e.) (court gave intervenor 3 strikes and equalized strikes of other parties). If antagonistic parties are given additional strikes, they should not be permitted to coordinate their strikes. *See* ***Van Allen***, 35 S.W.3d at 65.

3. Objections. To preserve error when the court refuses to realign or erroneously realigns, the party must object to the allocation of strikes after voir dire and before the exercise of the strikes. ***In re T.E.T.***, 603 S.W.2d 793, 798 (Tex.1980); ***Van Allen***, 35 S.W.3d at 65; ***Texas Commerce Bank v. Lebco Constructors***, 865 S.W.2d 68, 77 (Tex.App.—Corpus Christi 1993, writ denied).

4. Alternate jurors. When the trial court impanels alternate jurors under Gov't Code §62.020, the sides must be given additional peremptory strikes. ***Temple EasTex, Inc. v. Old Orchard Creek Partners***, 848 S.W.2d 724, 738 (Tex.App.—Dallas 1992, writ denied). If the trial court impanels one or two alternate jurors, the sides are each entitled to one additional peremptory strike. Gov't Code §62.020(e). If the trial court impanels three or four alternate jurors, the sides are each entitled to two additional peremptory strikes. *Id.*

§6.4 *Batson* limitations on peremptory strikes. The objection that a panelist was excluded because of some prohibited classification is called a ***Batson*** challenge, after the first criminal case that held racially based challenges were unconstitutional. ***Batson v. Kentucky***, 476 U.S. 79, 96, 106 S.Ct. 1712, 1723 (1986). *But see* ***Goode v. Shoukfeh***, 943 S.W.2d 441, 450 (Tex.1997) (calls it ***Edmonson*** challenge). A party in a civil case has standing to assert the equal protection rights of a panelist who was excluded from the jury because of a protected classification. ***Edmonson v. Leesville Concrete Co.***, 500 U.S. 614, 630, 111 S.Ct. 2077, 2088 (1991); *see* ***Powers v. Palacios***, 813 S.W.2d 489, 490-91 (Tex.1991). The TRCPs have not been amended to incorporate the ***Batson*** holding. ***Goode***, 943 S.W.2d at 450. Therefore, the courts look to criminal procedure for guidance. *Id.*

1. Protected classifications. Litigants cannot exercise peremptory strikes to exclude panelists solely for the following characteristics:

- *Race.* ***Batson***, 476 U.S. at 96, 106 S.Ct. at 1723; *e.g.*, ***Palacios***, 813 S.W.2d at 491 (only black panelist struck & race "figured into" strike).

NOTE

It is not necessary for the struck panelist and the party challenging the strike to be a member of the same cognizable group. A party may challenge any peremptory strike that violates a panelist's equal protection rights. ***Powers v. Ohio***, *499 U.S. 400, 415-16, 111 S.Ct. 1364, 1373-74 (1991).*

- *Ethnicity.* ***Hernandez v. New York***, 500 U.S. 352, 362, 111 S.Ct. 1859, 1867 (1991) (Hispanic); ***Benavides v. American Chrome & Chems.***, 893 S.W.2d 624, 626-27 (Tex.App.—Corpus Christi 1994) (same), *writ denied*, 907 S.W.2d 516 (Tex.1995).

- *Gender.* ***J.E.B. v. Alabama***, 511 U.S. 127, 143, 114 S.Ct. 1419, 1429 (1994); ***Fritz v. State***, 946 S.W.2d 844, 850 (Tex.Crim.App.1997). Strikes based on characteristics that are disproportionately associated with one gender are not necessarily prohibited. *See, e.g.*, ***J.E.B.***, 511 U.S. at 143 n.16, 114 S.Ct. at 1429 n.16 (challenge to all nurses is not gender-based even though it would disproportionately affect women).

2. Others may be protected. Other "cognizable" groups under ***Batson*** may include the following:

- *Native Americans.* *See* ***U.S. v. Childs***, 5 F.3d 1328, 1337 (9th Cir.1993); ***U.S. v. Iron Moccasin***, 878 F.2d 226, 229 (8th Cir.1989); ***U.S. v. Chalan***, 812 F.2d 1302, 1313-14 (10th Cir.1987).

- *Italian-Americans. See* ***U.S. v. Biaggi***, 853 F.2d 89, 95-96 (2d Cir.1988). *But see* ***U.S. v. Bucci***, 839 F.2d 825, 832-33 (1st Cir.1988) (whether Italian-Americans are a cognizable group is a question of fact). A list of cases involving ***Batson*** challenges to Italian-Americans can be found in ***U.S. v. Campione***, 942 F.2d 429, 432-33 (7th Cir.1991).

- *Asian-Americans. See* ***U.S. v. Sneed***, 34 F.3d 1570, 1578-79 (10th Cir.1994).

- *Disabled persons.* Protections similar to ***Batson*** may prevent litigants from striking disabled persons from the jury panel solely because of their disability. The Americans with Disabilities Act (ADA) and the Texas Gov't Code prohibit the automatic exclusion of a person on the grounds of disability. *See* 42 U.S.C. §12132 (any disability); Gov't Code §62.104(a) (blindness), *id.* §62.1041(a) (deafness). The ADA applies to everything the State does, including acts of the judiciary. ***Galloway v. Superior Ct.***, 816 F.Supp. 12, 18-19 (D.D.C.1993) (ADA prevented federal court from automatically excluding blind persons from juries).

- *Religious affiliation.* No civil court has addressed this issue. The Court of Criminal Appeals held ***Batson*** does not prohibit strikes based on religion. ***Casarez v. State***, 913 S.W.2d 468, 495-96 (Tex.Crim.App. 1994) (op. on reh'g). The Fifth Circuit has held that no current precedent clearly dictates that ***Batson*** should be extended to religion. ***Fisher v. Texas***, 169 F.3d 295, 305 (5th Cir.1999). *But see* ***Davis v. Minnesota***, 511 U.S. 1115, 1117, 114 S.Ct. 2120, 2121 (1994) (Thomas, J., dissenting from denial of certiorari) ("***J.E.B.*** would seem to have extended ***Batson's*** equal protection analysis to all strikes based on ... religion."); ***U.S. v. Stafford***, 136 F.3d 1109, 1114 (7th Cir.1998) (improper to strike a juror because he is a Jew, Catholic, or Muslim), *modified on other grounds*, 136 F.3d 1115 (7th Cir.1998).

3. Unprotected classifications. Litigants may exercise peremptory strikes to exclude panelists based on the following • Appearance, ***Purkett v. Elem***, 514 U.S. 765, 769, 115 S.Ct. 1769, 1771 (1995) (long, unkempt hair, mustache, & beard), ***Mayr v. Lott***, 943 S.W.2d 553, 556-57 (Tex.App.—Waco 1997, no writ) (large, flamboyant hat). • Age or employment status, ***Brumfield v. Exxon Corp.***, 63 S.W.3d 912, 916 (Tex.App.—Houston [14th Dist.] 2002, pet. denied), ***Dominguez v. State Farm Ins. Co.***, 905 S.W.2d 713, 716-17 (Tex.App.—El Paso 1995, writ dism'd). • Medical treatment received by panelist, ***Mayr***, 943 S.W.2d at 556.

4. Procedure for *Batson* challenge. After voir dire, if one party believes the other party used its peremptory strikes in a discriminatory manner, the party should follow the three-step procedure set out in ***Goode***, 943 S.W.2d at 445-46.

(1) Step 1 – prima facie case. The opponent of the challenge must make a prima facie case of discriminatory use of peremptory challenges. ***Goode***, 943 S.W.2d at 445. A prima facie case is established by a suspect pattern of strikes against members of a protected class. ***Dominguez***, 905 S.W.2d at 715. To challenge possible discriminatory selection, the movant must show (1) the other lawyer exercised peremptory challenges to remove from the venire a member of a protected class, and (2) that and other relevant circumstances raise an inference that the other lawyer excluded a person from the venire because of the person's status. *See* ***Lott v. City of Ft. Worth***, 840 S.W.2d 146, 150 (Tex.App.—Fort Worth 1992, no writ). A prima facie case requires a party to come forward with facts, not just numbers. *See, e.g.,* ***Brown v. Kinney Shoe Corp.***, 237 F.3d 556, 562-63 (5th Cir. 2001) (standing alone, fact that P used 4 peremptory challenges to strike white jurors did not make a prima facie case). If the movant makes a prima facie case, it creates a rebuttable presumption of discriminatory use of strikes. ***Lott***, 840 S.W.2d at 150.

(a) Make objection timely. A party must make a ***Batson*** challenge before the court impanels the jury and dismisses the excluded panel members. Code Crim. Proc. art. 35.261(a); ***In re K.M.B.***, 91 S.W.3d 18, 27 (Tex.App.—Fort Worth 2002, no pet.); ***Pierson v. Noon***, 814 S.W.2d 506, 508 (Tex.App.—Houston [14th Dist.] 1991, writ denied). If the party makes an objection for the first time in a motion for new trial, it is too late. ***Jones v. Martin K. Eby Constr. Co.***, 841 S.W.2d 426, 428-29 (Tex.App.—Dallas 1992, writ denied).

(b) Make record of objection. The movant must make a record that illustrates the trial court abused its discretion. *See* ***Goode v. Shoukfeh***, 943 S.W.2d 441, 446 (Tex.1997). There are two parts of the record for a ***Batson*** objection. First, the lawyer should introduce into evidence the information cards provided by the panelists. ***Goode***, 943 S.W.2d at 451 (juror information cards can be included in the clerk's record or formally introduced into evidence); *see* ***In re A.D.E.***, 880 S.W.2d 241, 245 (Tex.App.—Corpus Christi 1994, no writ). Although the cards do not contain information about the race of the panelists, they can be used to show pretext of the strike. Second, the lawyer should (1) ask the court to take judicial notice of the racial composition of the panel, (2) state the composition on the record, and (3) identify the panelists who were excluded by name, race or other status, and their position on the panel. For example, the lawyer should state the panel was composed of 24 persons, including 16 white, five African-American, and three Mexican-American; identify the panel number of each minority member; and list those who were excluded—panel member number three, Mrs. Smith, who is an African-American, etc.

(2) Step 2 – response. After the movant makes a prima facie case, the burden shifts to the party who exercised the strike to come forward with a neutral explanation for the strike. ***Goode***, 943 S.W.2d at 445. The issue at this stage is the facial validity of the explanation. *Id.* The attorney who made the strike should rebut the inference that the strikes were discriminatory by offering a neutral explanation for the strikes. ***In re A.D.E.***, 880 S.W.2d at 243. A neutral explanation is one based on something other than the race, gender, or other discriminatory characteristic of the panelist. ***Goode***, 943 S.W.2d at 445. The explanation need not be plausible. ***Purkett***, 514 U.S. at 768, 115 S.Ct. at 1771; ***Molina v. Pigott***, 929 S.W.2d 538, 545 (Tex.App.—Corpus Christi 1996, writ denied). If the nonmovant admits the discriminatory characteristic played any role in making its strike, the peremptory strike is constitutionally defective. ***Benavides v. American Chrome & Chems.***, 893 S.W.2d 624, 626-27 (Tex.App.—Corpus Christi 1994), *writ denied*, 907 S.W.2d 516 (Tex.1995). For purposes of step two, the reason offered will be considered neutral unless a discriminatory intent is inherent in the explanation. ***Goode***, 943 S.W.2d at 445. If the explanation is race-neutral, the issue does not terminate at step two, even if the party offers a "silly or superstitious" explanation for the strike. *Id.* At this stage, the trial court must assume that the reasons given for the peremptory challenge are true. *Id.* Only in step three does the persuasiveness of the justification become an issue. *Id.*

A neutral explanation may be the lawyer's hunch, the panelist's failure to make eye contact, inattentiveness, appearance, or employment status. *See, e.g.*, ***Mayr***, 943 S.W.2d at 556-57 (large gold hat sufficient reason to strike juror). However, when a peremptory strike is based on a panelist's nonverbal conduct, the party must describe that conduct, or the court will infer the strike was discriminatory. ***Price v. Short***, 931 S.W.2d 677, 682 (Tex.App.—Dallas 1996, no writ).

(3) Step 3 – pretext. Once the challenged lawyer explains the strikes, the burden shifts back to the challenging lawyer to prove by a preponderance of the evidence that the challenged lawyer's explanation was a mere pretext for discrimination. *See* ***Goode***, 943 S.W.2d at 445-46; ***Molina***, 929 S.W.2d at 545. The challenging lawyer has the right to offer rebuttal testimony and to cross-examine the challenged lawyer regarding the motivation for the strikes. ***Goode***, 943 S.W.2d at 451-52. The courts have identified five factors that weigh against the legitimacy of a race-neutral explanation. ***Lott v. City of Ft. Worth***, 840 S.W.2d 146, 151 (Tex.App.—Fort Worth 1992, no writ). It is at this stage that the trial court may find that an implausible justification for striking a panelist was a pretext for purposeful discrimination. ***Goode***, 943 S.W.2d at 446. The challenging lawyer should attempt to prove at least one of the following:

(a) The reasons the challenged lawyer gave for the peremptory challenge are not related to the facts of the case. ***Lott***, 840 S.W.2d at 151; *see, e.g.*, ***Mayr v. Lott***, 943 S.W.2d 553, 556 (Tex.App—Waco 1997, no writ) (in PI case, striking a juror because she had undergone chiropractic treatment was related to case).

(b) There was little or no questioning directed to the challenged juror or the questions were not meaningful. ***Lott***, 840 S.W.2d at 151; *see* ***Short***, 931 S.W.2d at 684-85 (unless panelist was questioned, court may assume the lawyer's explanation for a strike is a pretext for a racially discriminatory strike).

(c) Disparate treatment (*i.e.*, the challenged lawyer did not strike persons with the same or similar characteristics as the challenged juror). ***Lott***, 840 S.W.2d at 151.

(d) Disparate examination of members of the venire (*i.e.*, the challenged lawyer questioned the challenged juror so as to evoke a certain response without asking the same question of other panel members). ***Lott***, 840 S.W.2d at 151. *But see* ***Mayr***, 943 S.W.2d at 558 (even though court found disparate treatment, court affirmed).

(e) The challenged lawyer offered an explanation based on a group bias where the group trait was not shown to apply to the challenged juror. ***Lott***, 840 S.W.2d at 151.

5. *Batson* hearing. A ***Batson*** hearing must be held in open court. *See* ***Goode v. Shoukfeh***, 943 S.W.2d 441, 451 (Tex.1997). The challenged attorney need not be put under oath; unsworn statements may be offered to explain peremptory challenges. *Id.* The juror information cards should be introduced into evidence or made a part of the clerk's record. *Id.* The challenging lawyer has the right to cross-examine the challenged lawyer. *Id.* at 452. For introducing other evidence, the TRCPs and TREs apply. *Id.* at 451.

PRACTICE TIP

If the challenged lawyer uses voir dire notes to refresh her recollection while giving sworn or unsworn testimony during the hearing, the other lawyer is entitled to examine the notes. ***Goode****, 943 S.W.2d at 449; see TRE 612(1). If the challenged lawyer uses voir dire notes only before the hearing, the issue whether to require the production of the notes is within the trial court's discretion.* ***Goode****, 943 S.W.2d at 449; see TRE 612(2).*

---

6. Court's ruling. After both parties present their positions, the court must determine if the explanations were neutral or if they were merely a pretext for discriminatory strikes. ***In re A.D.E.***, 880 S.W.2d at 243; ***Lott***, 840 S.W.2d at 150. The court must evaluate the challenge and the response to determine whether the ***Batson*** claimant proved purposeful discrimination. *See* ***Purkett v. Elem***, 514 U.S. 765, 768, 115 S.Ct. 1769, 1771 (1995); ***Lott***, 840 S.W.2d at 150.

7. Trial remedies. The civil courts look to criminal cases to determine remedies for a ***Batson*** violation. ***Texas Tech Univ. Health Sci. Ctr. v. Apodaca***, 876 S.W.2d 402, 406 (Tex.App.—El Paso 1994, writ denied). Once the trial court decides a panelist was improperly excluded, the court may reinstate the challenged panelist to the panel, or the court may dismiss the panel and call a new one. ***Batson v. Kentucky***, 476 U.S. 79, 99 n.24, 106 S.Ct. 1712, 1725 n.24 (1986) (criminal case); *see* ***Short***, 931 S.W.2d at 681 (trial court reinstated 4 panelists).

§7. JUROR NOTE-TAKING

Historically, jurors were prohibited from taking notes. *See* ***Price v. State***, 887 S.W.2d 949, 953-54 (Tex.Crim. App.1994). Today, the vast majority of states and most of the federal circuits permit jurors to take notes. Annotation, *Taking & Use of Trial Notes by Jury*, 14 A.L.R.3d 831, 834 (1967). In 1994, the Court of Criminal Appeals approved note-taking in criminal cases. ***Price***, 887 S.W.2d at 954. See ***O'Connor's*** FORM 8A:07.

§7.1 No rule. There is no prohibition in the TRCPs against the taking of notes by jurors. ***Manges v. Willoughby***, 505 S.W.2d 379, 383 (Tex.App.—San Antonio 1974, writ ref'd n.r.e.). Nothing in TRCP 226a, the approved instructions to the jury, mentions jury notes. ***Manges***, 505 S.W.2d at 383. The chief objection to note-taking is the possibility the jurors might rely on the notes as evidence or place undue emphasis on them and not merely use the notes as a device to refresh their recollection of the evidence. *See* ***English v. American & Foreign Ins. Co.***, 529 S.W.2d 810, 813 (Tex.App.—Texarkana 1975, no writ).

§7.2 Criminal procedure. In ***Price***, the Court of Criminal Appeals created a four-step procedure to control juror note-taking. ***Price***, 887 S.W.2d at 954-55. The trial court should (1) determine if juror note-taking would be beneficial in light of the factual and legal issues to be presented at trial; (2) inform the parties, before voir dire, that jurors will be permitted to take notes; (3) admonish the jury at the time it is impaneled; and (4) instruct the jury in the jury charge as to the proper use of its notes during deliberation. *Id.*

§8. JURY PANEL

After the parties deliver their peremptory challenges to the clerk, the clerk calls the names of those panelists who have not been stricken by either party, and those persons comprise the jury panel. Once the jury is called, the court cannot add or subtract jurors. ***Dunlap v. Excel Corp.***, 30 S.W.3d 427, 433 (Tex.App.—Amarillo 2000, no pet.). See "Verdict by Fewer Than 12 Jurors," ch. 8-K, §3, p. 586.

§8.1 District court. In the district court, the first 12 persons not stricken comprise the jury panel. TRCP 234; ***Dunlap***, 30 S.W.3d at 433; *see* Tex. Const. art. 5, §13; Gov't Code §62.201.

§8.2 County court. In the county court, the first six persons not stricken comprise the jury panel. TRCP 234; *see* Tex. Const. art. 5, §17; Gov't Code §62.301.

§9. REVIEW

§9.1 Voir dire. The trial court's rulings on voir dire are reviewed for abuse of discretion. ***TEIA v. Loesch***, 538 S.W.2d 435, 440 (Tex.App.—Waco 1976, writ ref'd n.r.e.).

§9.2 Allocation of strikes. The standard of review to challenge the court's erroneous allocation of strikes is the "relaxed" harmless error rule. ***Lopez v. Foremost Paving***, 709 S.W.2d 643, 644 (Tex.1986). The complaining party must show only that the resulting trial was materially unfair. *Id.*; *see* ***Garcia v. Central Power & Light Co.***, 704 S.W.2d 734, 737 (Tex.1986); ***Patterson Dental Co. v. Dunn***, 592 S.W.2d 914, 920 (Tex.1979). *But see* ***Torrington Co. v. Stutzman***, 46 S.W.3d 829, 851 (Tex.2000) (dicta; party must show erroneous allocation probably caused rendition of improper judgment). The appellate court looks at the record to determine if the trial was hotly contested and if the evidence was sharply conflicting. If it was, the court will find the trial was materially unfair as a matter of law. ***Lopez***, 709 S.W.2d at 644; ***Central Power***, 704 S.W.2d at 737; ***Patterson Dental***, 592 S.W.2d at 921. The existence of antagonism between the parties is a question of law reviewable de novo. ***Central Power***, 704 S.W.2d at 736; ***Patterson Dental***, 592 S.W.2d at 919.

§9.3 *Batson* ruling. The standard to review the trial court's decision of a ***Batson*** challenge is "abuse of discretion." ***Goode***, 943 S.W.2d at 446. In Federal courts and in Texas criminal courts, the standard is "clearly erroneous." ***Hernandez v. New York***, 500 U.S. 352, 365, 111 S.Ct. 1859, 1869 (1991); ***Whitsey v. State***, 796 S.W.2d 707, 726 (Tex.Crim.App.1989) (op. on reh'g). Under both standards, a court is not bound to accept a justification for a peremptory strike if it is "simply too incredible to be accepted." ***Goode***, 943 S.W.2d at 446.

§9.4 Error in selecting jury. If there was error in the process of selecting the jurors, it is not necessary for the party challenging the error to show injury. ***Compton v. Henrie***, 364 S.W.2d 179, 182 (Tex.1963) (statutory disqualification); ***Mann v. Ramirez***, 905 S.W.2d 275, 280 (Tex.App.—San Antonio 1995, writ denied) (error in excusing persons from service).

B. OPENING STATEMENT

§1. GENERAL

§1.1 Rules. TRCP 265(a), 266. See TRCP 269 (closing argument).

§1.2 Purpose. Immediately after the jury is impaneled, the parties make opening statements in which they briefly tell the jury the nature of their claims or defenses, the relief sought, and what they expect to prove. TRCP 265(a). Assertions made during opening argument are not evidence and are not judicial admissions. ***Weslaco Fed'n of Teachers v. Texas Educ. Agency***, 27 S.W.3d 258, 263 (Tex.App.—Austin 2000, no pet.) (not judicial admissions); ***Carrasco v. Texas Transp. Inst.***, 908 S.W.2d 575, 580 (Tex.App.—Waco 1995, no writ) (not evidence).

§1.3 Forms. ***O'Connor's Texas Civil Forms***, FORMS 8B.

§2. RIGHT TO MAKE FIRST OPENING STATEMENT

The right to make the first opening statement is an important advantage—the party that makes the first opening statement gets to summarize its case to the jury before its opponent. TRCP 265(a). The right to make the first opening statement is related to the right to initiate voir dire, the right to open and close the evidence, and the right to open and close the final argument. See "Right to initiate voir dire," ch. 8-A, §4.2, p. 522; "Right to Open Evidence," ch. 8-C, §2, p. 534; "Right to Open & Close Final Argument," ch. 8-J, §2, p. 581.

§2.1 The rule – P goes first. The party with the burden of proof on the whole case has the right to make the first opening statement to the jury (and introduce evidence first). TRCP 265(a), (b). Most often, that means the plaintiff has the right to make the first opening statement (and introduce its evidence first).

§2.2 The exceptions – D goes first. There are exceptions to the rule that the plaintiff has the right to make the first opening statement.

1. **Burden of proof.** A defendant has the right to make the first opening statement (and introduce evidence first) if it has the burden of proof for the entire case under the pleadings. TRCP 265(a), (b). To determine who has the burden of proof on the whole case, ask which party would lose if no evidence were introduced. If the defendant would lose, then the defendant has the burden of proof. ***Union City Transfer v. Adams***, 248 S.W.2d 256, 260 (Tex.App.—Fort Worth 1952, writ ref'd n.r.e.); *see, e.g.*, ***Ocean Transp. v. Greycas, Inc.***, 878 S.W.2d 256, 269 (Tex.App.—Corpus Christi 1994, writ denied) (in suit on a note, D did not have right to make first opening statement because P had burden to prove deficiency & attorney fees).

2. **Admission under TRCP 266.** A defendant has the right to make the first opening argument (and introduce evidence first) if, before the trial begins, the defendant admits the plaintiff is entitled to recover, subject to proof of defensive allegations in the answer. TRCP 266; *cf.* ***First State Bank v. Fatheree***, 847 S.W.2d 391, 397 (Tex.App.—Amarillo 1993, writ denied) (right to open & close final argument). The admission must relieve the plaintiff from the necessity of offering any evidence in support of its case. *Cf.* ***Trice v. Stamford Builders Sup.***, 248 S.W.2d 213, 215 (Tex.App.—Eastland 1952, no writ) (right to open & close final argument). A defendant cannot secure the right to open merely by voluntarily assuming the burden of proof; the defendant must unequivocally admit liability and damages or establish them as a matter of law and remove them as issues from the case. *See, e.g.*, ***Seigler v. Seigler***, 391 S.W.2d 403, 404 (Tex.1965) (contestants of will could not voluntarily assume burden; they had to remove issue of testamentary capacity from case); *see also* ***4M Linen & Uniform Sup. Co. v. W.P. Ballard & Co.***, 793 S.W.2d 320, 324-25 (Tex.App.—Houston [1st Dist.] 1990, writ denied) (even though D stipulated liability, P had burden on attorney fees).

§3. LIMITS OF OPENING STATEMENT

The trial court has broad discretion to limit opening statements. ***Tacon Mech. Contractors v. Grant Sheet Metal***, 889 S.W.2d 666, 675 (Tex.App.—Houston [14th Dist.] 1994, writ denied).

§3.1 Brief statement of case. The party permitted to open briefly states to the jury the nature of its claim or defense, what it expects to prove, and the relief sought. TRCP 265(a). After the opening statement, the other parties may make similar statements.

§3.2 No details of evidence. TRCP 265(a) does not permit a party in its opening statement to describe the evidence in detail or to read, describe, or display documents to the jury. ***Guerrero v. Smith***, 864 S.W.2d 797, 799 (Tex.App.—Houston [14th Dist.] 1993, no writ); ***Ranger Ins. Co. v. Rogers***, 530 S.W.2d 162, 170 (Tex.App.—Austin 1975, writ ref'd n.r.e.).

§3.3 Improper argument by both parties. If both parties make improper comments in their opening statements, the error in one cancels the other and on appeal will be considered harmless error. ***Wells v. HCA Health Servs.***, 806 S.W.2d 850, 855 (Tex.App.—Fort Worth 1990, writ denied); ***Ranger Ins.***, 530 S.W.2d at 170-71. If one party discusses a certain issue, that party cannot object if the other party also discusses it. ***Smith v. Smith***, 720

S.W.2d 586, 593 (Tex.App.—Houston [1st Dist.] 1986, no writ) (wife's attorney referred to criminal proceedings after husband's attorney referred to it).

§3.4 Response to opening statement. The party adverse to the party who opened may make a statement about the case either before any evidence is introduced or before introducing its own evidence. TRCP 265(a), (c). In a multiple-defendant case, the trial court may require all the defendants to make their opening statement together, either after the plaintiff's opening statement or before introducing their own evidence. ***Fibreboard Corp. v. Pool***, 813 S.W.2d 658, 691 (Tex.App.—Texarkana 1991, writ denied).

§4. OBJECTING & PRESERVING ERROR

§4.1 Timely. A complaint about an improper comment during the opening statement is waived unless an objection is timely made, which means the objection must be made at the earliest practical moment. ***City of Corsicana v. Herod***, 768 S.W.2d 805, 816 (Tex.App.—Waco 1989, no writ). If the party does not object to the first reference, it waives any error. *Id.* To preserve error, the party must distinctly point out the error and state the grounds of the objection. *Id.*

§4.2 Incurable error. Although the rule is that a party must object to improper opening statements, if the cumulative effect of the improper statements is so prejudicial that an instruction to disregard would not remove the prejudice produced, the error is not waived. ***Mapco, Inc. v. Jenkins***, 476 S.W.2d 55, 61-62 (Tex.App.—Amarillo 1971, writ ref'd n.r.e.). The same rules regarding incurable error in the final argument apply to the opening statement. See "Types of Error in Argument," ch. 8-J, §5, p. 584.

C. INTRODUCING EVIDENCE

§1. GENERAL

§1.1 Rules. TRCP 265-267; TRE 103, 403, 614, 701-705, 1008; TRAP 33.1.

§1.2 Purpose. The parties prove their case for the jury (or the judge in a nonjury trial) by introducing evidence. Most evidence is introduced in the form of the testimony of witnesses, who, under oath, relate facts within their knowledge. ***Goudeau v. Marquez***, 830 S.W.2d 681, 683 (Tex.App.—Houston [1st Dist.] 1992, no writ); ***Bloom v. Bloom***, 767 S.W.2d 463, 470 (Tex.App.—San Antonio 1989, writ denied). The decision to admit evidence—as opposed to the task of evaluating it—is within the exclusive authority of the trial court. ***City of Brownsville v. Alvarado***, 897 S.W.2d 750, 753 (Tex.1995).

§1.3 Forms & timetable. ***O'Connor's Texas Civil Forms***, FORMS 8C; Timetable, this book, Offer of Proof & Bill of Exceptions, p. 1005.

§1.4 Other references. Cochran, ***Texas Rules of Evidence Handbook*** (5th ed. 2003) (Cochran, ***Evidence Handbook***).

§2. RIGHT TO OPEN EVIDENCE

The party with the burden of proof on the entire case has the right to present its evidence first. TRCP 265(b), 266; ***Amis v. Ashworth***, 802 S.W.2d 374, 384 (Tex.App.—Tyler 1990, orig. proceeding). In most cases, the opening party is the plaintiff, not because the plaintiff filed the suit, but because the plaintiff is usually the party asking for relief, and the other party is happy with the status quo. ***Pace Corp. v. Jackson***, 284 S.W.2d 340, 350 (Tex.1955). See "Right to Make First Opening Statement," ch. 8-B, §2, p. 533.

§3. INVOKING THE RULE

To exclude witnesses from the courtroom during the trial, a party must invoke "the Rule" at the beginning of the trial. TRCP 267(a) and TRE 614 require the trial court, at the request of either party, to administer the oath to the witnesses and remove them from the courtroom so they cannot hear the testimony given by other witnesses. ***Drilex Sys. v. Flores***, 1 S.W.3d 112, 117 (Tex.1999). Neither TRCP 267 nor TRE 614 can be invoked to prevent a witness from talking about the case before trial. ***Kennedy v. Eden***, 837 S.W.2d 98, 98 (Tex.1992).

§3.1 Court's instructions. The court must instruct the witnesses that they are not to converse about the case with each other or with any person other than the attorneys in the case (except by permission of the court) and that they are not to read any reports of or comments on the testimony in the case while under the Rule. TRCP 267(d); *see* TRE 614; ***Drilex***, 1 S.W.3d at 117. The parties are obligated to ensure that their witnesses either comply with the Rule or are exempted from it. ***Drilex***, 1 S.W.3d at 120.

§3.2 Persons not excluded. The following persons may not be excluded from the courtroom during trial: (1) a party who is a natural person or spouse, (2) an officer or employee of a party that is not a natural person and who is designated as its representative by its attorney, or (3) a person whose presence is shown by a party to be essential to the presentation of the cause. TRCP 267(b); TRE 614; *see also* ***Century 21 Real Estate Corp. v. Hometown Real Estate Co.***, 890 S.W.2d 118, 129 (Tex.App.—Texarkana 1994, writ denied) (trial court should have required corporation to name representative & excluded other officers); ***Fazzino v. Guido***, 836 S.W.2d 271, 277 (Tex.App.—Houston [1st Dist.] 1992, writ denied) (parties could remain in courtroom).

§3.3 Exemption. Once the Rule is invoked, the parties should ask the court to exempt any witnesses whose presence is essential to the presentation of the cause. ***Drilex***, 1 S.W.3d at 120. Witnesses who the trial court exempts are not placed under the Rule. *Id.* To exempt an expert from the Rule under the "essential presence" exception, the party must show the expert needs to be present in the courtroom to form an opinion based on more accurate factual assumptions. TRE 703; *see* ***Drilex***, 1 S.W.3d at 119.

§3.4 Violation of Rule. A nonexempt witness violates the Rule by remaining in the courtroom during the testimony of another witness, by learning about another's trial testimony through discussions with persons other than the attorneys, or by reading comments about the testimony. ***Drilex***, 1 S.W.3d at 117. When the Rule is violated, the trial court may allow or exclude the testimony of the potential witness or hold the violator in contempt. TRCP 267(e); ***Drilex***, 1 S.W.3d at 117; ***In re K.M.B.***, 91 S.W.3d 18, 28 (Tex.App.—Fort Worth 2002, no pet.); ***In re D.T.C.***, 30 S.W.3d 43, 49 (Tex.App.—Houston [14th Dist.] 2000, no pet.). A court may also exclude the testimony of a witness who arrived after the Rule was invoked, even though the witness was never actually placed under the Rule. *See* ***Drilex***, 1 S.W.3d at 118 (nonexempt witness's testimony was excluded because he discussed case with another witness).

§4. SCOPE OF EXAMINATION

§4.1 Direct examination. The scope of direct examination is limited by the pleadings. *See* Cochran, ***Evidence Handbook***, pp. 205-06. When evidence is not relevant under the pleadings, it should not be admitted. TRE 402. The court should admit all relevant evidence unless some rule or principle requires its exclusion. TRE 402; ***Stokes v. Puckett***, 972 S.W.2d 921, 926 (Tex.App.—Beaumont 1998, pet. denied). When evidence is relevant, but its probative value is substantially outweighed by its prejudicial effect, the evidence should be excluded. TRE 403. Rules excluding relevant evidence bearing on the truth sought must be supported by good cause and solid policy reasons. *See* ***Davis v. Davis***, 521 S.W.2d 603, 607 (Tex.1975).

§4.2 Cross-examination. A witness may be cross-examined on any matter relevant to any issue in the case, including credibility. TRE 611(b); Cochran, ***Evidence Handbook***, p. 623; *see* TRE 405(a) (cross-examination allowed on relevant specific instances of conduct). Due process requires that a party be given the opportunity to confront and cross-examine adverse witnesses. ***Davidson v. Great Nat'l Life Ins. Co.***, 737 S.W.2d 312, 314 (Tex. 1987); ***National Fam. Care Life Ins. Co. v. Fletcher***, 57 S.W.3d 662, 666 (Tex.App.—Beaumont 2001, pet. denied). Texas jurisprudence recognizes the right of full and complete cross-examination. TRE 611(b); ***Davidson***, 737 S.W.2d at 314. Texas follows the so-called "English rule," which allows cross-examination in all phases of the case. ***Continental Cas. Co. v. Thomas***, 463 S.W.2d 501, 506-07 (Tex.App.—Beaumont 1971, no writ). Texas does not limit a litigant's cross-examination to the matters covered by direct examination. ***CPS Int'l v. Harris & Westmoreland***, 784 S.W.2d 538, 543 (Tex.App.—Texarkana 1990, no writ). A party's cross-examination may be limited by its response to a contention in a request for disclosure. *See* ***National Fam. Care***, 57 S.W.3d at 668 (in limiting cross-examination, trial court was too restrictive in interpreting D's response to contention request). See "Contentions," ch. 6-D, §4.2.3, p. 379.

§4.3 Redirect examination. On redirect examination, the party may ask the witness to explain answers given on cross-examination and to amplify new material elicited for the first time. ***Sims v. Brackett***, 885 S.W.2d 450, 455 (Tex.App.—Corpus Christi 1994, writ denied). The purpose of redirect is to prevent the jury from being left with a false and incomplete picture created by cross-examination and counsel's ability to use leading questions. *Id.*

§4.4 Recross examination. On recross examination, the party may ask the witness to explain answers given on redirect examination and to amplify new material elicited for the first time. *See* TRE 611(b).

§4.5 Rebuttal evidence. Once the plaintiff or the defendant rests, the other party may introduce evidence to rebut the last round of evidence. On rebuttal, a party is limited to evidence that directly answers or disproves the last round of the other party's evidence. ***In re Bledsoe***, 41 S.W.3d 807, 813 (Tex.App.—Fort Worth 2001, orig. proceeding); ***Gendke v. Travelers Ins. Co.***, 368 S.W.2d 3, 5 (Tex.App.—Waco 1963, no writ).

§4.6 Questions by jurors. It is not clear whether the trial court in a civil case should permit jurors to ask questions. The courts that have addressed this question have held that if it is error to permit questions by jurors, the error must be preserved by an objection. ***Hudson v. Markum***, 948 S.W.2d 1, 3 (Tex.App.—Dallas 1997, writ denied); ***Fazzino***, 836 S.W.2d at 275-76. The Court of Criminal Appeals has held that questions by jurors compromise a fair trial by modifying the jury's role as a neutral fact-finder. ***Morrison v. State***, 845 S.W.2d 882, 889 (Tex. Crim.App.1992). For an article that recommends permitting jurors to ask questions and outlines the procedures currently used in civil courts, see Curry & Krugler, *The Sound of Silence: Are Silent Juries the Best Juries?*, 62 Tex.B.J. 441 (1999).

§5. INTRODUCING TESTIMONY

§5.1 Discovery products. See "Using Disclosures as Evidence," ch. 6-D, §8, p. 383; "Using Deposition at Trial," ch. 6-E, §12, p. 399; "Using Interrogatories as Evidence," ch. 6-F, §9, p. 415; "Admissions as Evidence," ch. 6-G, §8, p. 422; "Using Requested Documents," ch. 6-H, §8, p. 433; "Using Medical Records," ch. 6-I, §6, p. 438; "Using Evidence at Trial," ch. 6-J, §5, p. 440.

§5.2 Over closed-circuit TV. If a witness was deposed before trial, the parties may file an agreed motion asking the court to permit that witness to be examined over closed-circuit television or other two-way electronic communication that is capable of visually and audibly recording the proceedings. CPRC §30.012(a), (b).

§5.3 Impeachment & rebuttal evidence not produced in discovery. A party may introduce rebuttal or impeachment evidence, even though it was not produced in discovery, if (1) the evidence is solely for impeachment or rebuttal, (2) its use could not have been anticipated, and (3) the evidence is not responsive to a direct discovery request. *See, e.g.*, ***Aluminum Co. of Am. v. Bullock***, 870 S.W.2d 2, 4 (Tex.1994) (party should have been permitted to use undesignated expert to rebut unexpected change in material testimony of the other party's expert); ***Emery v. Rollins***, 880 S.W.2d 237, 239-40 (Tex.App.—Houston [14th Dist.] 1994, writ denied) (documents could be used as rebuttal evidence because their need was unanticipated); ***Dennis v. Haden***, 867 S.W.2d 48, 51-52 (Tex.App.—Texarkana 1993, writ denied) (when D did not supply expert's report as required, P should have been permitted to use deposition of undesignated witness on rebuttal); ***Munoz v. Missouri Pac. R.R.***, 823 S.W.2d 766, 769 (Tex.App.—Corpus Christi 1992, no writ) (D did not learn of impeachment witness until trial-time deposition of another witness); ***Tinkle v. Henderson***, 777 S.W.2d 537, 540 (Tex.App.—Tyler 1989, writ denied) (fact witness offered to rebut matter that arose during trial); ***Ellsworth v. Bishop Jewelry & Loan Co.***, 742 S.W.2d 533, 534 (Tex.App.—Dallas 1987, writ denied) (party had good cause to use undisclosed medical expert to rebut the testimony of a medical expert who testified beyond the subject matter identified in the interrogatory); *see also* TRCP 166(h) (exchange of list of fact witnesses at pretrial conference does not include rebuttal or impeaching witnesses the necessity of whose testimony cannot be anticipated before trial).

§5.4 Testimony of a fact witness. The testimony of a fact witness is limited to the facts within the witness's personal knowledge. ***United Way v. Helping Hands Lifeline Found.***, 949 S.W.2d 707, 713 (Tex.App.—San Antonio 1997, writ denied). A non-expert witness cannot give opinion testimony. However, a non-expert witness may testify in the form of opinion or inference if the opinion or inference is (1) rationally based on the perception of the witness and (2) helpful to a clear understanding of the witness's testimony or the determination of a fact in issue. TRE 701; Cochran, ***Evidence Handbook***, p. 668.

PRACTICE TIP

If a witness refers to notes while on the stand, TRE 612(1) grants the adverse party access to the notes; if a witness uses notes to refresh her recollection before taking the stand, TRE 612(2) gives the trial court discretion to allow the adverse party access to the notes. ***Goode v. Shoukfeh****, 943 S.W.2d 441, 449 (Tex.1997); Cochran,* ***Evidence Handbook****, p. 632.*

§5.5 Testimony from expert. If specialized knowledge will assist the fact-finder to understand the evidence or decide a fact issue, a witness who qualifies as an expert may testify in the form of an opinion. TRE 702; ***Broders v. Heise***, 924 S.W.2d 148, 152-53 (Tex.1996); Cochran, ***Evidence Handbook***, p. 682. See "The *Daubert-Robinson* Test for Expert Testimony," ch 5-M, §2, p. 303. Opinion testimony from an expert "can rise no higher than the facts upon which it is based." ***Sipes v. G.M. Corp.***, 946 S.W.2d 143, 148 (Tex.App.—Texarkana 1997, writ denied). Once an expert is challenged, the party offering the expert has the burden to respond to each objection and show the testimony is admissible by a preponderance of the evidence. ***E.I. du Pont de Nemours & Co. v. Robinson***, 923 S.W.2d 549, 557 (Tex.1995). That party must prove the reliability of the underlying tests on which the expert's opinion is based. ***Merrell Dow Pharms. v. Havner***, 953 S.W.2d 706, 712-14 (Tex.1997). To prove admissibility, see "Sponsor's response to objection," ch. 5-M, §3.3, p. 308.

For the qualifications of and objections to an expert who testifies in a medical liability suit against doctors (not other health care providers), see ***O'Connor's Texas Causes of Action***, "Expert testimony," ch. 18-A, §8, p. 444 (2004).

§5.6 Testimony from expert about learned treatise. To use a "learned treatise" on direct examination, a party must take the following steps: (1) prove the treatise was published, (2) prove the expert relied on it as authority (by admission or judicial notice) before trial to corroborate her opinion, and then (3) read the statement in the treatise to the jury. *See* TRE 803(18). See Cochran, ***Evidence Handbook***, pp. 855-57. To use a "learned treatise" on cross-examination, a party must take the following steps: (1) prove the treatise was published, (2) prove the treatise is authoritative, and then (3) read the statement in the treatise to the jury. *See* TRE 803(18). See Cochran, ***Evidence Handbook***, pp. 855-57. Statements from the learned treatise are admissible only when used in the direct or cross-examination of an expert. ***Owens-Corning Fiberglas Corp. v. Malone***, 916 S.W.2d 551, 559 (Tex.App.—Houston [1st Dist.] 1996), *aff'd*, 972 S.W.2d 35 (Tex.1998). The treatise itself cannot be introduced into evidence as an exhibit or taken by the jury to the jury room. TRE 803(18); *e.g.*, ***Kahanek v. Rogers***, 12 S.W.3d 501, 504 (Tex.App.—San Antonio 1999, pet. denied) (because physician's desk reference was learned treatise it could not be taken into jury room).

§5.7 Proving a dying declaration. To introduce a dying declaration, a party must prove the following: (1) the declarant made a statement when she believed death was imminent; (2) the statement was about the cause or circumstances of what the declarant believed to be her impending death; (3) the declarant was physically and mentally capable to recollect and narrate accurately the cause or circumstances; and (4) the declarant is unavailable at the time of trial. TRE 804(b)(2); *see* Cochran, ***Evidence Handbook***, p. 881.

§5.8 Audio or video recording. If a recording is a fair representation of a transaction, conversation, or occurrence, it is admissible. ***Seymour v. Gillespie***, 608 S.W.2d 897, 898 (Tex.1980). To introduce a recording, a party must establish the following: (1) the recording machine can accurately record and reproduce sounds or images; (2) the operator was experienced and qualified to operate the recording machine; (3) the authenticity or the correctness of the recording—the witness heard (or saw) what was being recorded; (4) no changes, additions, or deletions were made to the tape; (5) the manner in which the tape was preserved; (6) the witness recognizes and can identify the voices heard (and the locations and persons seen) on the tape; and (7) if the subject of the tape is a conversation, the testimony elicited was voluntarily made without any kind of inducement. *Id.* Some of these elements may be inferred from the evidence and are not required to be proved. *Id.*

PRACTICE TIP

When introducing orally recorded testimony (video or tape recorded), make sure the court reporter stays in the courtroom and transcribes the testimony as it is heard by the jury. Court reporters often take a coffee break while taped testimony is played and simply type into the record, "The tape was played for the jury." Thus, that part of the evidence is not included in the appellate record. If you do not object to the court reporter's absence, you will waive the issue of an incomplete record. ***Lascurain v. Crowley****, 917 S.W.2d 341, 344-45 (Tex.App.—El Paso 1996, no writ) (court reporter left courtroom during deposition testimony with permission of parties). If the court reporter appeared to be transcribing the testimony, but was not, you may be able to reconstruct the record.* ***State Farm Fire & Cas. Ins. Co. v. Vandiver****, 941 S.W.2d 343, 347-49 (Tex.App.—Waco 1997, no writ).*

§5.9 Results of experiment. To introduce the results of an experiment that the other party was not invited to attend, the offering party must prove the following: (1) the party conducted an out-of-court experiment, and (2) the circumstances surrounding the experiment were substantially similar to the conditions that gave rise to the litigation. ***Fort Worth & D.R. Co. v. Williams***, 375 S.W.2d 279, 281-82 (Tex.1964); ***Horn v. Hefner***, 115 S.W.3d 255, 256-57 (Tex.App.—Texarkana 2003, n.p.h.); *see, e.g.*, ***Ford Motor Co. v. Miles***, 967 S.W.2d 377, 388-89 (Tex.1998) (because party never contended tests were conducted under similar conditions, videotapes of tests should have been excluded); ***Alice Leasing Corp. v. Castillo***, 53 S.W.3d 433, 446 (Tex.App.—San Antonio 2001, pet. denied) (because videotaped demonstration was substantially similar to conditions of accident, it was admissible). It is not necessary that the conditions be identical. ***Williams***, 375 S.W.2d at 282; ***Horn***, 115 S.W.3d at 256; *see* ***Mottu v. Navistar Int'l Transp. Corp.***, 804 S.W.2d 144, 148 (Tex.App.—Houston [14th Dist.] 1990, writ denied) (if major dissimilarities, videotapes of tests excluded).

§5.10 Similar accident. To introduce evidence of earlier, similar accidents, the party must show with specificity that earlier accidents occurred in a similar manner and could be attributed to a similar causation. ***Huckaby v. A.G. Perry & Son***, 20 S.W.3d 194, 202 (Tex.App.—Texarkana 2000, pet. denied). If the party does not establish the factors listed below, evidence of similar accidents is neither relevant nor material and is prejudicial. *Id.*

1. The conditions surrounding the earlier accidents were reasonably similar. *Id.*; ***Fredericksburg Indus. v. Franklin Int'l***, 911 S.W.2d 518, 521-22 (Tex.App.—San Antonio 1995, writ denied); ***Henry v. Mrs. Baird's Bakeries***, 475 S.W.2d 288, 294 (Tex.App.—Fort Worth 1971, writ ref'd n.r.e.).

2. The conditions of the earlier accidents and the party's accident were connected in some special way. ***Huckaby***, 20 S.W.3d at 202; ***Henry***, 475 S.W.2d at 294; *see, e.g.*, ***Dallas Ry. & Terminal Co. v. Farnsworth***, 227 S.W.2d 1017, 1019-20 (Tex.1950) (evidence street car operator started car too quickly at each of three stops before P got off was closely related to issue of whether operator gave P enough time to get off car before starting it).

3. The earlier accidents were attributable to the same condition that caused the party's accident. *See* ***Huckaby***, 20 S.W.3d at 202; ***Henry***, 475 S.W.2d at 294; *see, e.g.*, ***Bell v. Buddies Super-Mkt.***, 516 S.W.2d 447, 450 (Tex.App.—Tyler 1974, writ ref'd n.r.e.) (cause of earlier "near-falls"—ramp's rough concrete—was not attributable to same condition causing P's fall—ramp's steep slope).

§6. IMPEACHING A WITNESS

The credibility of a witness may be attacked by any party, including the party calling the witness. TRE 607; *e.g.*, ***Owens-Corning Fiberglas Corp. v. Malone***, 916 S.W.2d 551, 567 (Tex.App.—Houston [1st Dist.] 1996) (court permitted Ps to call D's expert in their case-in-chief & impeach him), *aff'd*, 972 S.W.2d 35 (Tex.1998). See Cochran, ***Evidence Handbook***, p. 588.

§6.1 Impeaching by reputation for truthfulness. There are two questions to ask a witness about the reputation of another witness: (1) Does the witness know the general character or reputation for truthfulness of the witness intended to be impeached? (2) If so, what is the character of the witness, good or bad? ***International Sec. Life Ins. Co. v. Melancon***, 463 S.W.2d 762, 767 (Tex.App.—Beaumont 1971, writ ref'd n.r.e.); *see* TRE 404(a)(3), 608. Once the court determines the impeaching witness is qualified to speak on the general reputation of the other witness, the other party has the right to cross-examine the impeaching witness about her means of knowledge before she answers the question about reputation for truthfulness. *See* ***Melancon***, 463 S.W.2d at 767. See Cochran, ***Evidence Handbook***, p. 594.

§6.2 Impeaching by earlier inconsistent statement. To impeach a witness with an earlier statement (whether oral or written) that is inconsistent with the witness's trial statement, the lawyer must (1) tell the witness about the contents of the earlier statement and when, where, and to whom it was made and (2) give the witness an opportunity to explain or deny it. TRE 613(a). If the statement is in writing, it does not need to be shown to the witness, but, on request, it must be shown to opposing counsel. *Id.* If the witness unequivocally admits having made the statement, extrinsic evidence of the earlier statement is not admissible. *Id.*; ***Downen v. Texas Gulf Shrimp Co.***, 846 S.W.2d 506, 512 (Tex.App.—Corpus Christi 1993, writ denied). Extrinsic evidence is admissible only if the witness denies the statement. *See* TRE 613(a). This provision does not apply to admissions of a party-opponent as defined in TRE 801(e)(2). TRE 613(a). See Cochran, ***Evidence Handbook***, p. 637.

§6.3 Impeaching by bias. To impeach a witness by proof of circumstances or statements showing bias or interest, the lawyer must (1) tell the witness about the circumstances supporting the claim of bias or the details of the statement, including the contents and when, where, and to whom it was made and (2) give the witness an opportunity to explain or deny the circumstances or statement. TRE 613(b). If the statement is in writing, it does not need to be shown to the witness, but, on request, it must be shown to opposing counsel. *Id.* If the witness unequivocally admits to the bias or interest, extrinsic evidence of the earlier statement is not admissible. *Id.*; ***Walker v. Packer***, 827 S.W.2d 833, 839 n.5 (Tex.1992). Extrinsic evidence is admissible only if the witness denies bias or interest. *See* TRE 613(b). See Cochran, ***Evidence Handbook***, p. 643.

§6.4 Impeaching by conviction. Before attempting to attack the credibility of a witness by proving a conviction, the party must give the other party advance written notice (if the other party timely requested it) of the intent to use the conviction. TRE 609(f). The credibility of a witness may be attacked on the ground the witness was convicted of a crime if (1) the witness admits the conviction on the stand or the conviction is of public record, (2) the crime was a felony or it involved moral turpitude, and (3) the court determines the probative value of admitting the evidence outweighs its prejudicial effect. TRE 609(a); *see* ***Porter v. Nemir***, 900 S.W.2d 376, 382 (Tex.App.—Austin 1995, no writ). To impeach by conviction, a party must prove the following: (1) the witness was convicted of a felony or a crime that involved moral turpitude; (2) the conviction is not over ten years old; (3) the witness has not been pardoned, the conviction has not been annulled, or a certificate of rehabilitation has not been issued; (4) the conviction was not the result of a juvenile adjudication; and (5) no appeal is pending on the conviction. TRE 609; *see* ***In re G.M.P.***, 909 S.W.2d 198, 209 (Tex.App.—Houston [14th Dist.] 1995, no writ); *see, e.g.*, ***Reviea v. Marine Drilling Co.***, 800 S.W.2d 252, 258 (Tex.App.—Corpus Christi 1990, writ denied) (20-year-old conviction too remote to impeach). See Cochran, ***Evidence Handbook***, pp. 603-21.

§7. REHABILITATING A WITNESS

§7.1 Proving truthfulness. In most civil cases, supporting evidence of a party's good character is not admissible. ***Commonwealth Lloyd's Ins. Co. v. Thomas***, 678 S.W.2d 278, 294 (Tex.App.—Fort Worth 1984, writ ref'd n.r.e.); *see* TRE 608(a)(2); ***Rose v. Intercontinental Bank***, 705 S.W.2d 752, 757 (Tex.App.—Houston [1st Dist.] 1986, writ ref'd n.r.e.). Testimony of a witness's good character for truth or honesty, however, is admissible when the character of the witness is directly at issue, after a witness is impeached, or when one party (in its pleadings or by the evidence) charges the other party with a crime of moral turpitude. ***Commonwealth***, 678 S.W.2d at 294; *see, e.g.*, ***State Bar v. Evans***, 774 S.W.2d 656, 658 (Tex.1989) (lawyer charged with conduct involving moral turpitude was permitted to offer evidence of pertinent character trait). To rehabilitate a witness's character for truth, the lawyer must introduce evidence through another witness as follows: (1) prove the witness has knowledge of the character of the witness who was attacked (*i.e.*, establish facts that show how the witness knows of the character of the person); (2) prove the witness has an opinion about that person's character for truthfulness; and (3) have the witness state her opinion regarding that person's character for truthfulness. *See* TRE 404(a)(3), 608(a).

§7.2 Rebutting charge of recent fabrication or improper influence. When a witness who testified at a trial or hearing is accused of recent fabrication or improper influence during cross-examination, a party may introduce an earlier consistent statement to prove through a second witness that (1) the first witness made an out-of-court statement consistent with testimony before testifying, and (2) the statement was made before a reason to fabricate arose. TRE 801(e)(1)(B); ***Skillern & Sons v. Rosen***, 359 S.W.2d 298, 301-02 (Tex.1962); ***Reviea***, 800 S.W.2d at 257; *cf.* ***Tome v. U.S.***, 513 U.S. 150, 156-58, 115 S.Ct. 696, 701 (1995) (criminal case interpreting FRE 801(d)).

§8. INTRODUCING DOCUMENTS

Every exhibit must meet certain threshold requirements before it can be admitted into evidence: (1) the qualifying witness must be competent; (2) the witness must have personal knowledge sufficient to authenticate the exhibit; (3) the exhibit must be relevant to the trial; and (4) the exhibit must be authenticated. *See* TRE 401 (relevance), TRE 601 (competence), TRE 602 (personal knowledge), TRE 901(a) (authentication). However, just because an exhibit is relevant and authentic does not make it admissible; the exhibit may be excluded on other grounds (*e.g.*, hearsay). ***Director v. Lara***, 901 S.W.2d 635, 638 (Tex.App.—El Paso 1995, writ denied).

§8.1 Competence. The witness must be competent to testify, which means the witness must be able to accurately perceive, recall, and recount. *See* TRE 601. See "Competency of witness," ch. 1-B, §4.14.2(2), p. 8. Courts often confuse competence with personal knowledge.

§8.2 Personal knowledge. The witness must have personal knowledge on which to base the authentication. TRE 602; *see, e.g.*, ***City of Dallas v. GTE Southwest***, 980 S.W.2d 928, 935 (Tex.App.—Fort Worth 1998, pet. denied) (witness did not have personal knowledge about exhibit); ***Savage v. Psychiatric Inst.***, 965 S.W.2d 745, 753-54 (Tex.App.—Fort Worth 1998, pet. denied) (attorney's affidavit did not establish his personal knowledge about documents); *see also* ***Davidson v. Great Nat'l Life Ins. Co.***, 737 S.W.2d 312, 314-15 (Tex.1987) (although court said witness was competent to authenticate photographs, court discussed personal knowledge). See "Personal knowledge," ch. 1-B, §4.14.2(3)(a), p. 8; Cochran, ***Evidence Handbook***, pp. 562-66.

§8.3 Relevance. To be relevant, the exhibit must tend to make the existence of a material fact more or less probable than it would have otherwise been. TRE 401; ***Edwards v. TEC***, 936 S.W.2d 462, 466-67 (Tex.App.—Fort Worth 1996, no writ); *see, e.g.*, ***Prestige Ford Co. v. Gilmore***, 56 S.W.3d 73, 80 (Tex.App.—Houston [14th Dist.] 2001, pet. denied) (report made existence of material fact less probable). See Cochran, ***Evidence Handbook***, pp. 203-20.

§8.4 Authenticity. Authentication is a prerequisite to admissibility. TRE 901(a); ***In re G.F.O.***, 874 S.W.2d 729, 731 (Tex.App.—Houston [1st Dist.] 1994, no writ). See Cochran, ***Evidence Handbook***, pp. 889-939.

1. Proof of authenticity. Authentication is established by evidence that the matter in question is what its proponent claims it to be. TRE 901(b)(1); ***G.F.O.***, 874 S.W.2d at 731. A document is considered authentic if (1) the document is being used against the party or nonparty who produced it in response to written discovery, (2) a sponsoring witness vouches for the document's authenticity, or (3) the document meets the requirements of self-authentication. *See* TRCP 176.6(c), 193.7; TRE 901(b)(10), 902; ***G.F.O.***, 874 S.W.2d at 731.

2. Presumption of authenticity. Documents produced in response to written discovery are presumed authentic and may be used in a pretrial proceeding or at trial against the producing party or nonparty. TRCP 176.6(c), 193.7; *see also* TRE 901(b)(10) (any method of authentication provided by rule meets requirements of TRE 901(a)). See "Using Requested Documents," ch. 6-H, §8, p. 433; "Other party's discovery responses," ch. 7-B, §3.5.3(1)(a), p. 462. To use a discovery document against someone other than the producing party, a witness must vouch for the document's authenticity, or the document must satisfy the requirements for self-authentication. *See* ***G.F.O.***, 874 S.W.2d at 731. *But see* ***Lection v. Dyll***, 65 S.W.3d 696, 702-03 (Tex.App.—Dallas 2001, pet. denied) (in case involving by-laws produced by D-hospital, it was not necessary to authenticate them for use against D-doctor). See §§8.4.3, 8.4.4, below.

3. Documents authenticated by witness.

(1) Signed instrument. To introduce a signed document, a party must do one of the following: (1) call the signing person (as an adverse witness, if necessary) to identify the signature as being her own, (2) call a witness who saw the person sign the document, (3) call a witness who is familiar with the person's signature and can identify it, or (4) call a handwriting expert who can testify that, based on handwriting comparisons, the signature was made by the person. *See* TRE 901(b); Cochran, ***Evidence Handbook***, p. 900 & n.71.

(2) Copy of document. A duplicate is admissible as an original, unless a question is raised as to the authenticity of the original, or it would be unfair to introduce the duplicate. TRE 1003; ***ESIS, Inc. v. Johnson***, 908 S.W.2d 554, 561 (Tex.App.—Fort Worth 1995, no writ); Cochran, ***Evidence Handbook***, p. 945; *see also* ***Owens-Corning Fiberglas Corp. v. Malone***, 916 S.W.2d 551, 558 (Tex.App.—Houston [1st Dist.] 1996) (copy admissible despite extraneous markings), *aff'd*, 972 S.W.2d 35 (Tex.1998). If a question is raised regarding the authenticity of the original, to introduce a copy, the party must prove the following: (1) the original was lost, destroyed, is not obtainable, is outside of Texas, or is in the possession of the opponent; (2) a copy of the original was made; and (3) the offered document is a true and accurate copy of the original. TRE 1003, 1004.

PRACTICE TIP

Do not object to a witness discussing the contents of a document in evidence with the "best evidence" objection. The best evidence rule comes into play only when a witness is asked to discuss the contents of a disputed document that is not in evidence. ***White v. Bath****, 825 S.W.2d 227, 231 (Tex.App.—Houston [14th Dist.] 1992, writ denied). Once the document is introduced, a witness may discuss it or read from it.*

---

(3) Summary. To introduce a summary, a party must prove the following: (1) the chart, summary, or calculation is a summary of other records; (2) the other records are voluminous writings, recordings, or photographs that are admissible; (3) the other records cannot be conveniently examined in court; and (4) the other records were made available to the other party for inspection and copying. TRE 1006; *see* ***Aquamarine Assocs. v. Burton Shipyard***, 659 S.W.2d 820, 821 (Tex.1983) (because underlying business records were not shown to be admissible, summary was not admissible); ***Duncan Dev. v. Haney***, 634 S.W.2d 811, 812-13 (Tex.1982) (summary of invoices received from subcontractors was admissible as summary of business records of contractor). The court may order the other records be produced in court. TRE 1006. See Cochran, ***Evidence Handbook***, pp. 969-72.

(4) Computer printout. To introduce a computer record, a party must prove the following: (1) the witness is a competent computer operator; (2) the computer used is accepted as standard and efficient equipment; (3) appropriate procedures were followed regarding data entry and checks for accuracy; (4) the computer was operated and programmed properly; and (5) the record has the significance that the witness claims it has. Cochran, ***Evidence Handbook***, p. 950. If data is stored in a computer, any printout or other output readable by sight and shown to reflect the data accurately is an "original." TRE 1001(c); *see* Cochran, ***Evidence Handbook***, p. 950.

(5) Photograph. To introduce a photograph, a party must prove the following: (1) the witness saw the subject of the photograph at or near the time of the event in issue; (2) the witness recognizes the exhibit as a representation of the subject seen; and (3) the exhibit is a true and accurate representation of the subject as it appeared at the relevant time. ***State v. City of Greenville***, 726 S.W.2d 162, 168 (Tex.App.—Dallas 1986, writ ref'd n.r.e.). An "original" of a photograph includes the negative or any print made from it. TRE 1001(c). If a verbal description of the matter is admissible, generally a photograph of it is also admissible. ***City of Greenville***, 726 S.W.2d at 168. A court should exclude a photograph if its probative value is substantially outweighed by the danger of unfair prejudice. TRE 403; ***Castro v. Sebesta***, 808 S.W.2d 189, 193 (Tex.App.—Houston [1st Dist.] 1991, no writ). *But see* ***Fibreboard Corp. v. Pool***, 813 S.W.2d 658, 671 (Tex.App.—Texarkana 1991, writ denied) (if relevant, a photograph is admissible, even if gruesome). See Cochran, ***Evidence Handbook***, p. 958.

(6) Public records by witness. To introduce public records, reports, statements, or data compilations of public offices or agencies, the records must show on their face (or it must be proved by a witness) that they contain reports of (1) the activities of the office or agency, (2) matters observed under a duty imposed by law and for which there was a duty to report, or (3) factual findings resulting from an investigation made under authority granted by law. TRE 803(8); *see* ***State v. Foltin***, 930 S.W.2d 270, 272 (Tex.App.—Houston [14th Dist.] 1996, writ denied). The court should admit records that meet the requirements of TRE 803(8) unless the circumstances indicate a lack of trustworthiness. TRE 803(8) (last phrase). Conclusions and opinions contained in an investigatory report, which is admissible under TRE 803(8)(C), are admissible if they are based on the factual investigation and satisfy TRE 803's requirement of trustworthiness. ***McRae v. Echols***, 8 S.W.3d 797, 800 (Tex.App.—Waco 2000, pet. denied) (police accident report); *see* ***Ter-Vartanyan v. R&R Freight***, 111 S.W.3d 779, 784 (Tex.App.—Dallas 2003, pet. denied) (same). Not everything in an official record is exempt from the hearsay rule. For example, a statement of an eyewitness included in a police report is not admissible under TRE 803(8). ***Kratz v. Exxon Corp.***, 890 S.W.2d 899, 905 (Tex.App.—El Paso 1994, no writ). See Cochran, ***Evidence Handbook***, pp. 843-51.

(7) Business record by witness. To introduce a business record through a witness, a party must prove the following: (1) the record is a memorandum, report, record, or other compilation of data; (2) the witness is the custodian or other qualified witness; (3) the record was made from information transmitted by a person with knowledge of the facts; (4) the record was made at or near the time of the acts, events, conditions, opinions, or diagnoses appearing on it; (5) the record was made as part of the regular practice of that business activity; and (6) the record was kept in the course of a regularly conducted business activity. TRE 803(6); *see* ***Freeman v. American Motorists Ins. Co.***, 53 S.W.3d 710, 715 (Tex.App.—Houston [1st Dist.] 2001, no pet.) (letter from doctor to P's lawyer about P's condition was inadmissible as business record because it did not qualify as a routine entry); ***Brooks v. Housing Auth.***, 926 S.W.2d 316, 322 (Tex.App.—El Paso 1996, no writ) (security guard records admissible as business records); ***Connor v. Wright***, 737 S.W.2d 42, 44-45 (Tex.App.—San Antonio 1987, no writ) (business records of lawyer admissible to prove attorney fees). The business records of one company can contain business records received from another company. ***GT&MC, Inc. v. Texas City Ref.***, 822 S.W.2d 252, 257-58 (Tex.App.—Houston [1st Dist.] 1991, writ denied); *see, e.g.*, ***Duncan***, 634 S.W.2d at 812-13 (summary of invoices received from subcontractors was admissible as summary of business records of contractor). See Cochran, ***Evidence Handbook***, pp. 834-42.

PRACTICE TIP

Never rely on a live witness to prove business records, if you can avoid it. Most witnesses will stumble over the questions, and the other party's employee will never answer the questions properly. You should always file a business records affidavit. See §8.4.4(1), below.

---

4. Documents that are self-authenticating. If a document can overcome the hearsay objection, it can be admitted into evidence without a sponsoring witness as long as it is self-authenticating. TRE 902; *see* ***Larson***

v. Family Violence & Sexual Assault Prevention Ctr., 64 S.W.3d 506, 511 (Tex.App.—Corpus Christi 2001, pet. denied). A self-proving document under TRE 902 must satisfy the requirements of TRE 901. Cochran, ***Evidence Handbook***, p. 920. A party can object to a self-proving document on grounds other than authentication, such as relevancy, hearsay, or unfair prejudice. *Id.* at 920-21.

(1) Business record by affidavit. To introduce a business record by affidavit of a custodian or other qualified witness, a party must show the following: (1) the record is admissible under TRE 803(6) or 803(7); (2) the affidavit required by TRE 902(10)(b) is attached to the record; (3) the record and the affidavit were filed with the clerk 14 days before trial; (4) the other parties were given prompt notice of the filing of the affidavit; and (5) the notice includes the name and employer of the person making the affidavit and the statement that the records were available for inspection and copying. TRE 902(10); *see* ***Fullick v. City of Baytown***, 820 S.W.2d 943, 945-46 (Tex.App.—Houston [1st Dist.] 1991, no writ) (tax statements from school districts were self authenticated); ***March v. Victoria Lloyds Ins. Co.***, 773 S.W.2d 785, 789 (Tex.App.—Fort Worth 1989, writ denied) (test of alcohol level in blood was admissible as business record with affidavit); ***National Stand. Ins. Co. v. Gayton***, 773 S.W.2d 75, 76 (Tex.App.—Amarillo 1989, no writ) (doctor's records, with factual observations and diagnosis, were admissible as business record with affidavit). If the affidavit is the same as or substantially complies with the sample provided in TRE 902(10)(b), it will satisfy the requirement of authentication. ***March***, 773 S.W.2d at 789. The 14-day requirement is necessary only if the party offering the records relies on the affidavit to prove them; if, instead, the party relies on a qualified witness to prove them, the other party cannot object that the records were not on file with the court 14 days before trial. ***Chemical Bank v. Commercial Indus. Serv. Co.***, 668 S.W.2d 336, 337 (Tex.1984). See Cochran, ***Evidence Handbook***, pp. 834-42; ***O'Connor's*** FORM 8C:03.

(2) Affidavit for past expenses. CPRC §18.001 permits a party to prove the reasonableness and necessity of past expenses with an affidavit from either the person who provided the service or the person in charge of records, showing the service provided and the charge made. CPRC §18.001(c); *see id.* §18.002 (form of affidavit). If an opposing party wants to controvert the affidavit concerning cost and necessity of services, a counter-affidavit must be filed showing (1) the affiant is qualified as an expert to contravene the particular service and charge involved and (2) the specific reason why the service was not necessary or the charge was unreasonable. ***Turner v. Peril***, 50 S.W.3d 742, 747-48 (Tex.App.—Dallas 2001, pet. denied). See ***O'Connor's*** FORMS 8C:05-07. *But see* ***City of El Paso v. PUC***, 916 S.W.2d 515, 524 (Tex.App.—Austin 1995, writ dism'd) (in case involving affidavits of audit fees before PUC, court said CPRC §18.001 does not address admissibility of affidavit but only sufficiency of affidavit to support finding of fact that expense was reasonable or service was necessary). See ***O'Connor's Texas Causes of Action***, "Affidavit of past expenses," ch. 35-B, §6.3.1(1)(b), p. 958 (2004).

(3) Domestic public record under seal. To introduce a domestic record under seal, a party must show the following: (1) the document bears a seal of the U.S., a state, or any other political subdivision listed in TRE 902(1); and (2) the document bears a signature purporting to be an attestation or execution. TRE 902(1), 1005. The document must also meet the requirements of TRE 803(8)(A), (B), or (C). See §8.4.3(6), above.

(4) Domestic public record not under seal. To introduce a public record that is not under seal, a party must show the following: (1) the document bears the signature in the official capacity of an officer or employee of an entity listed in TRE 902(1); and (2) a public officer having a seal and having official duties in the district or political subdivision of the officer or employee certifies that the signer of the document has the official capacity and that the person's signature is genuine. TRE 902(2), 1005; ***Shaw v. Kennedy, Ltd.***, 879 S.W.2d 240, 246 (Tex.App.—Amarillo 1994, no writ) (copies of application for and order accepting the closing of bankruptcy proceedings, certified by bankruptcy court).

(5) Foreign public documents. To introduce public documents from other countries, see TRE 902(3) and Cochran, ***Evidence Handbook***, pp. 925-27.

(6) Excerpt from commercial publications. To introduce an excerpt from a commercial publication, a party must show the following: (1) the document is the original or photocopy of a market quotation, tabulation, list, directory, or other published compilation; and (2) the publication is generally used and relied on by the public or by persons in particular occupations. TRE 803(17) (market reports & commercial publications), TRE 902(6) (newspapers & periodicals); *see, e.g.*, ***Lewis v. Southmore Sav. Ass'n***, 480 S.W.2d 180, 186 (Tex.1972) (market reports); ***Curran v. Unis***, 711 S.W.2d 290, 296-97 (Tex.App.—Dallas 1986, no writ) (photocopies of pages from Dunn & Bradstreet regarding ownership of a partnership were admissible).

D. OBJECTING TO EVIDENCE

§1. GENERAL

§1.1 Rules. TRCP 166(m), 267; TRE 103-106, 403, 614; TRAP 33.1, 43.3, 44.1.

§1.2 Purpose. The primary reason to object to evidence is to prevent it from being introduced in the trial and heard by the jury. A secondary reason to object is to preserve the issue for appellate review. *See* TRE 103(a); TRAP 33.1(a).

§1.3 Forms & timetable. ***O'Connor's Texas Civil Forms***, FORMS 5E, 8E; Timetable, this book, Offer of Proof & Bill of Exceptions, p. 1005.

§1.4 Other references. Cochran, ***Texas Rules of Evidence Handbook*** (5th ed. 2003) (Cochran, ***Evidence Handbook***).

§2. TIME TO MAKE OBJECTIONS

§2.1 Pretrial objections.

1. Motion in limine. A party can object to evidence before trial in a motion in limine. A ruling on a motion in limine is not a ruling on the admissibility of the evidence. See "Motion in Limine," ch. 5-E, p. 252.

2. Motion to exclude. A party can object to evidence before trial in a motion to exclude. *See* ***Owens-Corning Fiberglas Corp. v. Malone***, 916 S.W.2d 551, 557 (Tex.App.—Houston [1st Dist.] 1996), *aff'd*, 972 S.W.2d 35 (Tex.1998). At trial, the court may reconsider its pretrial rulings on the admissibility of evidence. ***Reveal v. West***, 764 S.W.2d 8, 11 (Tex.App.—Houston [1st Dist.] 1988, orig. proceeding). Unlike rulings on a motion in limine, rulings on motions to exclude evidence preserve error on appeal. *See* ***Malone***, 916 S.W.2d at 557.

3. Objections to exhibits. A trial court may require parties to submit written pretrial objections to tendered exhibits. TRCP 166(m); *see* TRCP 193, cmt. 7.

§2.2 Trial objections. When objectionable evidence is offered at trial, the party that believes the evidence is not admissible must object. ***Clark v. Trailways, Inc.***, 774 S.W.2d 644, 647 (Tex.1989). If a party does not object to the evidence, it waives any error in its admission. TRE 103(a)(1); TRAP 33.1(a); ***Stein v. American Residential Mgmt.***, 793 S.W.2d 1, 1 (Tex.1990). To preserve error, the party must state the substance of the objection on the record. TRAP 33.1(a)(1)(A). If the objection is apparent from the context, however, the objection alone will preserve error. *Id.*; ***Ramirez v. Volkswagen, Inc.***, 788 S.W.2d 700, 705 (Tex.App.—Corpus Christi 1990, writ denied).

§2.3 Timing of objections. A trial objection to evidence must be made as soon as the reason for the objection becomes apparent. TRE 103(a)(1); ***Wolfe v. East Tex. Seed Co.***, 583 S.W.2d 481, 482 (Tex.App.—Houston [1st Dist.] 1979, writ dism'd).

1. Too early. If an objection is premature, it does not preserve error. *See, e.g.*, ***Bushell v. Dean***, 803 S.W.2d 711, 712 (Tex.1991) (although D objected before the witness testified, D did not reurge objection during testimony); ***Correa v. G.M. Corp.***, 948 S.W.2d 515, 518 (Tex.App.—Corpus Christi 1997, no writ) (general objection to anticipated evidence does not preserve error).

2. On time. In most cases, the objection must be made at the time the evidence is offered. ***MBank Dallas v. Sunbelt Mfg.***, 710 S.W.2d 633, 638 (Tex.App.—Dallas 1986, writ ref'd n.r.e.). For testimonial evidence, the objection must be made after the question is asked and before the witness answers. An objection made after the witness answers is timely in some situations, such as when the witness makes an objectionable answer to a proper question, the witness answers an objectionable question too quickly for the objection to be made, or the witness volunteers an objectionable statement. *See, e.g.*, ***Beall v. Ditmore***, 867 S.W.2d 791, 794 (Tex.App.—El Paso 1993, writ denied) (in response to D's question, P mentioned insurance). In these instances, the party must also make other objections. See "When jury hears inadmissible evidence," §6.6, p. 548.

3. Too late. An objection is not timely if it is not made as soon as the question is asked or shortly thereafter. *E.g.*, ***Miles v. Ford Motor Co.***, 922 S.W.2d 572, 591 (Tex.App.—Texarkana 1996) (objection to expert's testimony regarding previously undisclosed theory of recovery was untimely when made after theory was completely introduced), *rev'd in part on other grounds*, 967 S.W.2d 377 (Tex.1998); ***Seneca Res. Corp. v. Marsh & McLennan, Inc.***, 911 S.W.2d 144, 152 (Tex.App.—Houston [1st Dist.] 1995, no writ) (objection made after lengthy testimony in violation of motion in limine was untimely). *But see* ***Beall***, 867 S.W.2d at 795 (when P mentioned insurance in response to D's question, objection lodged after next question and answer was timely). An objection is not timely if it is made the second time the evidence is offered. ***In re A.V.***, 849 S.W.2d 393, 396 (Tex.App.—Fort Worth 1993, no writ).

§3 SPECIFIC VS. GENERAL OBJECTIONS

§3.1 Specific objections. An objection must be specific. TRE 103(a)(1); TRAP 33.1(a)(1)(A); ***Sciarrilla v. Osborne***, 946 S.W.2d 919, 924 (Tex.App.—Beaumont 1997, pet. denied); ***McCormick v. Texas Commerce Bank***, 751 S.W.2d 887, 890 (Tex.App.—Houston [14th Dist.] 1988, writ denied). There are at least three reasons the courts require a specific objection. A specific objection (1) enables the court to understand the challenge, (2) permits the court to make an informed ruling, and (3) affords the party offering the evidence the opportunity to remedy the defect and re-offer it in admissible form. ***McKinney v. National Un. Fire Ins. Co.***, 772 S.W.2d 72, 74 (Tex.1989).

1. How to make specific objections. There are two parts to an objection. First, the objection must identify the exact part of the question or the evidence that is objectionable. ***Speier v. Webster Coll.***, 616 S.W.2d 617, 619 (Tex.1981). Second, the objection must identify the legal principle the court will violate if it admits the evidence (if it is not apparent from the context). TRE 103(a)(1); ***United Cab Co. v. Mason***, 775 S.W.2d 783, 785 (Tex. App.—Houston [1st Dist.] 1989, writ denied).

2. Rulings on specific objections on appeal.

(1) Untenable specific objection sustained. If the trial court sustains an untenable specific objection (and excludes the evidence), the appellate court should uphold the ruling if there was any valid ground for excluding the evidence. ***State Bar v. Evans***, 774 S.W.2d 656, 658 n.5 (Tex.1989); *see* Cochran, ***Evidence Handbook***, p. 87 & n.131. That is, if a party urged the wrong objection and the court sustained it, on appeal, the party can urge a different objection to support the ruling.

(2) Untenable specific objection overruled. If the trial court overrules an untenable specific objection (and admits the evidence), the appellate court will uphold the ruling even if there were valid objections to the evidence. ***Wilkerson v. Pic Rlty. Corp.***, 590 S.W.2d 780, 782 (Tex.App.—Houston [14th Dist.] 1979, no writ); *see* Cochran, ***Evidence Handbook***, p. 87 & n.131; *see, e.g.*, ***Smith v. Levine***, 911 S.W.2d 427, 436 (Tex.App.—San Antonio 1995, writ denied) (party objected to photos as inaccurate depiction of condition but did not object that photos were not produced in discovery); ***Richard Gill Co. v. Jackson's Landing Owners' Ass'n***, 758 S.W.2d 921, 927-28 (Tex.App.—Corpus Christi 1988, writ denied) (party incorrectly objected that expert was not designated and did not object to failure to specify subject matter about which expert was expected to testify).

§3.2 General objections. A general objection is one that merely challenges the admissibility of the evidence or objects to evidence for vague or inexact reasons. *See* ***Sciarrilla***, 946 S.W.2d at 924; ***Mayfield v. Employers***

Reinsurance Corp., 539 S.W.2d 398, 400 (Tex.App.—Tyler 1976, writ ref'd n.r.e.); *see, e.g.*, ***Lege v. Jones***, 919 S.W.2d 870, 874 (Tex.App.—Houston [14th Dist.] 1996, no writ) (objection that evidence is "immaterial and irrelevant" is a general objection); ***Ramirez v. Johnson***, 601 S.W.2d 149, 151 (Tex.App.—San Antonio 1980, writ ref'd n.r.e.) ("note our exception" does not preserve objection).

1. Reason to avoid general objections. A general objection is no objection at all. ***Murphy v. Waldrip***, 692 S.W.2d 584, 591 (Tex.App.—Fort Worth 1985, writ ref'd n.r.e.).

2. Rulings on general objections on appeal.

(1) General objection sustained. When the trial court sustains a general objection (and excludes the evidence), the appellate court will uphold the objection if there was a valid ground for excluding the evidence and the proponent of the evidence did not request a more specific objection. 1 McCormick on Evidence, §52 (5th ed. 1999); 1 Wigmore, §18 (1983). The appellate court will deem the valid ground for the objection was apparent to the trial court when neither the trial court nor the proponent of the evidence asked for a more specific objection. ***General Acc. Fire & Life Assur. Corp. v. Camp***, 348 S.W.2d 782, 784 (Tex.App.—Houston [1st Dist.] 1961, no writ); *see, e.g.*, ***Hannum v. General Life & Acc. Ins. Co.***, 745 S.W.2d 500, 502 (Tex.App.—Corpus Christi 1988, no writ) (because document was not properly authenticated, no error to exclude it on a general objection).

(2) General objection overruled. When the trial court overrules a general objection (and admits the evidence), the appellate court will hold that the general objection did not preserve error. ***Speier***, 616 S.W.2d at 619; ***Lege***, 919 S.W.2d at 874. Normally, a party cannot complain on appeal that the trial court erred in overruling a general objection by raising a ground it did not raise with the trial court. *See* ***Pfeffer v. Southern Tex. Laborers' Pension Trust Fund***, 679 S.W.2d 691, 693 (Tex.App.—Houston [1st Dist.] 1984, writ ref'd n.r.e.) (appellant may not enlarge ground for error with objection not asserted at trial). There are two exceptions: (1) if the ground for exclusion is so obvious that it is indicated by a general phrase, TRE 103(a)(1), ***Ramirez***, 601 S.W.2d at 151; and (2) if the evidence was not admissible for any purpose, ***Mueller v. Central Power & Light Co.***, 403 S.W.2d 901, 904 (Tex. App.—Corpus Christi 1966, no writ).

§4. OBJECTING TO WITNESS

§4.1 Taking witness on voir dire. If a party believes a witness is not able to testify because of lack of knowledge, the party should object; if the objection is overruled, the party should ask to take the witness on voir dire before the witness testifies. *See* ***Marling v. Maillard***, 826 S.W.2d 735, 739 (Tex.App.—Houston [14th Dist.] 1992, no writ). This technique is essentially a cross-examination of the witness during the proponent's direct examination, on the limited issue of knowledge.

1. Scope of examination. The purpose of a voir dire examination is to test the personal knowledge of a witness. *See* ***Celotex Corp. v. Tate***, 797 S.W.2d 197, 206 (Tex.App.—Corpus Christi 1990, writ dism'd) (either cross-examination or voir dire can be used to challenge knowledge of witness).

2. Repeat objection after voir dire. After completing the voir dire of the witness, the party should repeat its objection to the testimony. When the party does not object after voir dire, the court will assume the party decided not to challenge the witness. ***Marling***, 826 S.W.2d at 739.

3. No right to voir dire. The party does not have an absolute right to conduct a voir dire examination. TRE 705(b); ***Brook v. Brook***, 865 S.W.2d 166, 172 (Tex.App.—Corpus Christi 1993), *aff'd*, 881 S.W.2d 297 (Tex. 1994). When the trial court permits voir dire, it is within the court's discretion to require the party to conduct voir dire in front of the jury. ***State v. Sunland Sup. Co.***, 404 S.W.2d 316, 318 (Tex.1966).

§4.2 Objection to opinion of expert. To object to the opinion of an expert, the party should object that the expert is not qualified or that the opinion is not relevant or reliable or that the probative value of the opinion is substantially outweighed by the danger of unfair prejudice, confusion, or delay. TRE 104(a), 401-403, 702, 703, 705;

E.I. du Pont de Nemours & Co. v. Robinson, 923 S.W.2d 549, 556-57 (Tex.1995). See "Motion to Exclude Expert," ch. 5-M, p. 303.

§4.3 Objection to witness who violated "the Rule." If a witness violates the Rule, the trial court must determine whether it will permit the witness to testify. *See, e.g.*, ***Drilex Sys. v. Flores***, 1 S.W.3d 112, 117-18 (Tex. 1999) (court struck expert for violating the Rule); ***In re D.T.C.***, 30 S.W.3d 43, 49-50 (Tex.App.—Houston [14th Dist.] 2000, no pet.) (court struck three witnesses for violating the Rule); ***Guerrero v. Smith***, 864 S.W.2d 797, 800-01 (Tex.App.—Houston [14th Dist.] 1993, no writ) (witness who heard D's testimony was permitted to testify). See "Invoking the Rule," ch. 8-C, §3, p. 520.

§4.4 Failing to supplement discovery. If a party attempts to introduce evidence that was not disclosed even though a pretrial order or a discovery request required disclosure, the other party should object. *See* TRCP 193.6. To exclude evidence that was required to be disclosed by a pretrial order, see "Order on Pretrial Conference," ch. 5-A, §5, p. 228. To exclude the testimony of a witness not disclosed in discovery, see "Objecting to Unidentified Witness," ch. 6-D, §10, p. 383; see also "Limit or exclude evidence," ch. 5-J, §7.1.4, p. 281.

§4.5 Preserving error. When evidence is excluded, the party must make an offer of proof (or, after trial, a bill of exception) to preserve the testimony of the witness so the appellate courts can determine whether the erroneous exclusion was harmful. See "Offer of Proof & Bill of Exceptions," ch. 8-E, p. 553; ***O'Connor's*** FORM 8E:01.

§5. OBJECTING TO A QUESTION

Generally, an improper question that is not answered by the witness does not constitute reversible error. *See* ***Luna v. North Star Dodge Sales***, 667 S.W.2d 115, 119-20 (Tex.1984). In most cases, the error in asking a prejudicial question can be cured by an instruction to the jury to disregard the question. When the trial court sustains the objection, to preserve error, the party should "pursue an adverse ruling." See §6.6, below. Whether the error is reversible is judged by the same standard as for improper jury argument, set out in ***Standard Fire Ins. Co. v. Reese***, 584 S.W.2d 835, 839-40 (Tex.1979). ***Luna***, 667 S.W.2d at 120. See "Test for reversible jury argument," ch. 8-J, §6.2, p. 585.

§6. OBJECTING TO THE EVIDENCE

§6.1 Outside presence of jury. Objections to evidence made during the trial but outside the presence of the jury do not need to be repeated in front of the jury to preserve error. TRE 103(a)(1); ***Clark v. Trailways, Inc.***, 774 S.W.2d 644, 647 n.2 (Tex.1989); ***Huckaby v. A.G. Perry & Son***, 20 S.W.3d 194, 204 (Tex.App.—Texarkana 2000, pet. denied); *see also* TRAP 33.1(c) (no formal exception or separate order is required to preserve complaint for appeal).

§6.2 Multiple parties. In a multiparty case, each party has the obligation and the right to make its own objections to the admission and exclusion of evidence. ***Bohls v. Oakes***, 75 S.W.3d 473, 477 (Tex.App.—San Antonio 2002, pet. denied); ***Wolfe v. East Tex. Seed Co.***, 583 S.W.2d 481, 482 (Tex.App.—Houston [1st Dist.] 1979, writ dism'd). One party's objection does not preserve error for any other party. *E.g.*, ***Beutel v. Dallas Cty. Flood Control Dist.***, 916 S.W.2d 685, 694 (Tex.App.—Waco 1996, writ denied) (offer of proof by one D did not preserve error for other D); ***HOW Ins. Co. v. Patriot Fin. Servs.***, 786 S.W.2d 533, 544 (Tex.App.—Austin 1990, writ denied) (objection to evidence by one D did not preserve error for other Ds), *overruled on other grounds*, ***Hines v. Hash***, 843 S.W.2d 464 (Tex.1992); ***Howard v. Phillips***, 728 S.W.2d 448, 451 (Tex.App.—Fort Worth 1987, no writ) (offer of proof by one D did not preserve error for other D); ***Wolfe***, 583 S.W.2d at 482 (objection to evidence by one D did not preserve error for another D). There is an exception to this rule—one party's objection may preserve error for another party if the trial court has ruled that objections made by one party preserve error for the other parties on the same side. ***Owens-Corning Fiberglas Corp. v. Malone***, 916 S.W.2d 551, 556-57 (Tex.App.—Houston [1st Dist.] 1996), *aff'd*, 972 S.W.2d 35 (Tex.1998); ***Celotex Corp. v. Tate***, 797 S.W.2d 197, 201-02 (Tex.App.—Corpus Christi 1990, writ dism'd).

§6.3 Repeating the objection. A party should object every time inadmissible evidence is offered. If a party objects to certain evidence, but later does not object when the same evidence is introduced, the party waives its objection. ***Richardson v. Green***, 677 S.W.2d 497, 501 (Tex.1984); ***Marling v. Maillard***, 826 S.W.2d 735, 739 (Tex. App.—Houston [14th Dist.] 1992, no writ). For a limited exception to this rule, see §6.4, below.

§6.4 Running objection. A party can preserve error to repeated offers of the same evidence by asking the court for a running objection. ***State v. Baker***, 574 S.W.2d 63, 65 (Tex.1978); *see also* TRE 611(a) (court has control over the interrogation of witnesses). A running objection protects the objecting party from annoying the jury by restating an objection that has already been overruled. When a party relies on a running objection, it may accidentally waive the objection if the later evidence is slightly different from the evidence that the running objection challenges. *See* ***Huckaby***, 20 S.W.3d at 203 (running objection did not apply to all witnesses pertaining to the same type of evidence where party limited its objection to one witness's testimony); *cf.* ***Davis v. Stallones***, 750 S.W.2d 235, 238 (Tex.App.—Houston [1st Dist.] 1987, no writ) (objection to improper jury argument was waived because running objection applied only to questions). In a jury trial, the safest procedure is to object each time the evidence is offered. *See* ***Schindler Elevator Corp. v. Anderson***, 78 S.W.3d 392, 404 (Tex.App.—Houston [14th Dist.] 2001, pet. granted w.r.m.) (error not preserved because party did not ask for running objection & did not object every time the evidence was offered).

PRACTICE TIP

If you rely on a running objection, you should get the court to permit the objection to run against each witness's testimony on the same issue. See ***Huckaby****, 20 S.W.3d at 203 (properly framed running objection extends to testimony of all witnesses pertaining to same type of evidence);* ***Commerce, Crowdus & Canton v. DKS Constr.****, 776 S.W.2d 615, 620 (Tex.App.—Dallas 1989, no writ) (in nonjury trial, running objection is effective for similar evidence from other witnesses).*

§6.5 Rule of optional completeness. A party may object on the ground of optional completeness when the other party attempts to introduce part of a document or written statement. *See* TRE 106, 107; ***Jones v. Colley***, 820 S.W.2d 863, 866 (Tex.App.—Texarkana 1991, writ denied). To rely on TRE 106 or 107 to introduce omitted parts of a document, the party offering the remainder of the document must show that (1) the other party introduced only part of a document or written statement, and (2) the remainder of the document or written statement should be admitted so that in fairness it can be considered contemporaneously with the original part introduced. *See* TRE 106, 107. TRE 106 and 107 also apply to depositions. *See* ***Jones***, 820 S.W.2d at 866.

§6.6 When jury hears inadmissible evidence. Occasionally evidence is presented to a jury before the party can object; for example, when a witness blurts out an answer or gives an answer that is not responsive to the question. To preserve error after the jury hears inadmissible evidence (or an improper statement from a lawyer), the party must make a number of objections in sequential order until the court makes an adverse ruling. ***One Call Sys. v. Houston Lighting & Power***, 936 S.W.2d 673, 677 (Tex.App.—Houston [14th Dist.] 1996, writ denied); ***Hur v. City of Mesquite***, 893 S.W.2d 227, 231 (Tex.App.—Amarillo 1995, writ denied). This procedure is called "pursuing an adverse ruling." The order of making the objections is as follows:

Step 1 – Make objection. The party must make a proper and specific objection.

- **Objection overruled – error preserved.** If the court overrules the objection, the error is preserved. *See* ***Lone Star Ford v. Carter***, 848 S.W.2d 850, 854 (Tex.App.—Houston [14th Dist.] 1993, no writ) (improper jury argument). When a court overrules an objection, the party has secured an adverse ruling, and it is not necessary to request an instruction to disregard or move for a mistrial.

• **Objection sustained – pursue adverse ruling.** If the court sustains the objection, to preserve error the party must "pursue an adverse" ruling by making the objections listed below in steps 2 through 4. ***One Call Sys.***, 936 S.W.2d at 677. If the party stops before receiving an adverse ruling, the error is not preserved. ***Hur***, 893 S.W.2d at 231; ***Ortiz v. Ford Motor Credit Co.***, 859 S.W.2d 73, 77-78 (Tex.App.—Corpus Christi 1993, writ denied). A party cannot complain on appeal after it received all the relief it requested from the trial court. ***Cook v. Caterpillar, Inc.***, 849 S.W.2d 434, 442 (Tex.App.—Amarillo 1993, writ denied). Therefore, to preserve error once the objection is sustained, the party must continue with the following steps:

Step 2 – Request instruction. The party must ask the court to instruct the jury to disregard the evidence. ***State Bar v. Evans***, 774 S.W.2d 656, 658 n.6 (Tex.1989); ***Peshak v. Greer***, 13 S.W.3d 421, 424-25 (Tex. App.—Corpus Christi 2000, no pet.); ***Chavis v. Director***, 924 S.W.2d 439, 447 (Tex.App.—Beaumont 1996, no writ). If the party makes no other objection or skips the request for an instruction to disregard and asks for a mistrial, the party waives any objection to curable error. ***Evans***, 774 S.W.2d at 658 n.6; ***Peshak***, 13 S.W.3d at 424-25. The party must press the court to instruct the jury to disregard or to deny the request. If the court instructs the jury, the party must continue with steps 3 and 4, below, to preserve error.

PRACTICE TIP

*If the error is incurable by an instruction to disregard, it is not necessary to request an instruction. See **Evans**, 774 S.W.2d at 658 n.6. However, do not assume the error is incurable. Ask for an instruction even if you think the error is incurable.*

Step 3 – Motion to strike. It is not certain whether a motion to strike the evidence must be made in addition to the other objections. TRE 103(a)(1), entitled "Objection," refers to an objection *or* a motion to strike. *See* ***Ortiz***, 859 S.W.2d at 77 (opinion did not list motion to strike as one of necessary objections). Most courts use the two terms interchangeably. *See* ***Smith Motor Sales v. Texas Motor Vehicle Comm'n***, 809 S.W.2d 268, 272 (Tex.App.—Austin 1991, writ denied) (to challenge evidence on appeal, party must make a timely objection or motion to strike). However, two courts said a motion to strike is necessary in addition to the other objections. *See* ***Parallax Corp. v. City of El Paso***, 910 S.W.2d 86, 90 (Tex.App.—El Paso 1995, writ denied) (party waived error because it did not make motion to strike); ***Hur***, 893 S.W.2d at 231 (mentions motion to strike as one of the necessary objections). The court's ruling on a motion to strike is a ruling that purports to, but does not, strike the information from the court reporter's record. If the court grants the motion to strike, the party must continue with step 4, below, to preserve error.

Step 4 – Motion for mistrial. If the court sustains the objections and instructs the jury to disregard, the party must make a motion for mistrial to preserve error. ***Hur***, 893 S.W.2d at 231-32; ***Ortiz***, 859 S.W.2d at 77. *But see* ***Condra Funeral Home v. Rollin***, 314 S.W.2d 277, 279-80 (Tex.1958) (not necessary for P to move for mistrial after trial court sustained objection & instructed jury to disregard); ***Hur v. City of Mesquite***, 916 S.W.2d 510, 511-12 (Tex.App.—Amarillo 1995, no writ) (on motion for rehearing, court reviewed evidence of error, seeming to back off from position that motion for mistrial is necessary to preserve error).

8-1. PURSUING AN ADVERSE RULING

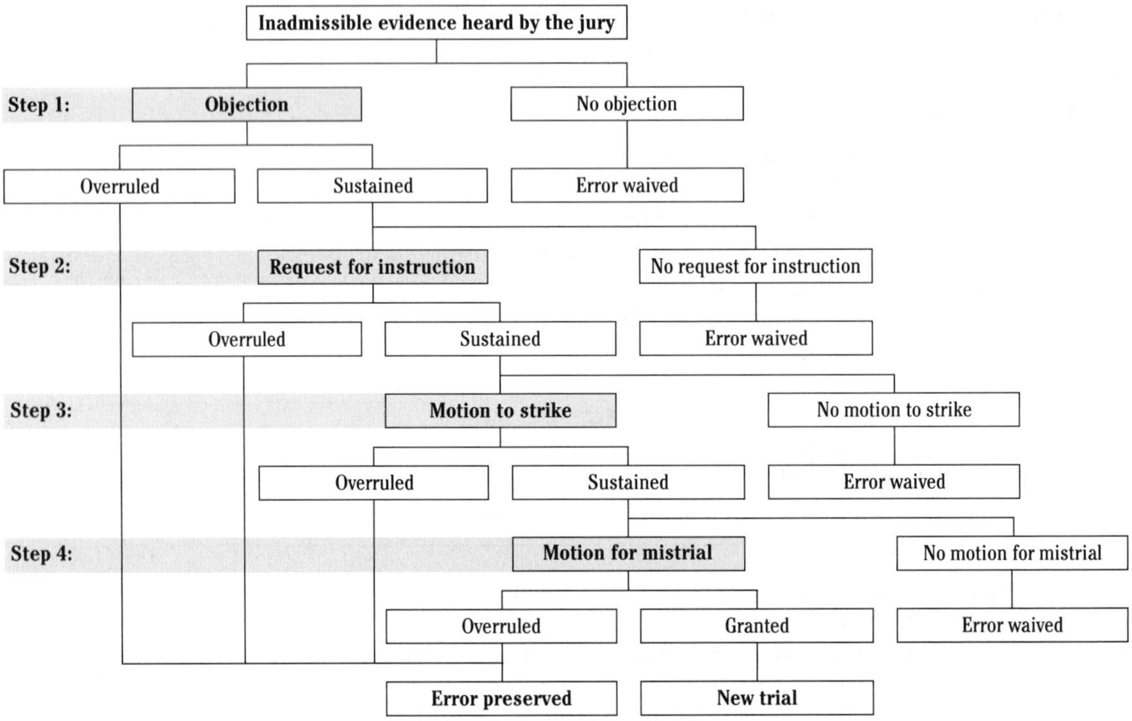

§6.7 Waiver.

1. Different forms of same evidence. An objection to evidence is waived if the same evidence was previously admitted without objection, even though the evidence is in a different form. *See, e.g.*, ***Texaco, Inc. v. Pennzoil Co.***, 729 S.W.2d 768, 842 (Tex.App.—Houston [1st Dist.] 1987, writ ref'd n.r.e.) (no error in admitting magazine article over objection because same evidence was admitted through author's testimony).

2. Withdrawn objection. If an objection is withdrawn, it does not preserve error. ***Beken v. Elstner***, 503 S.W.2d 408, 410 (Tex.App.—Houston [14th Dist.] 1973, no writ).

3. No adverse ruling. If the jury hears objectionable evidence, the error is waived if the party does not pursue an adverse ruling through an objection, a motion to instruct the jury to disregard, a motion to strike, and a motion for mistrial. ***Hur v. City of Mesquite***, 893 S.W.2d 227, 231 (Tex.App.—Amarillo 1995, writ denied). See "When jury hears inadmissible evidence," §6.6, p. 548.

4. After conditional admissibility. When a proponent's evidence is subject to the objection of relevance (and therefore admissibility), the trial court may admit the evidence subject to the condition that the proponent later "prove up" the relevance. If the proponent does not prove up the relevance before it closes, the opposing party must repeat the objection and pursue an adverse ruling (objection, instruction, request to strike, and then a motion for mistrial). *See* ***Owens-Corning Fiberglas Corp. v. Keeton***, 922 S.W.2d 658, 661 (Tex.App.—Austin 1996, writ denied) (opposing party waived error because it made only a motion for mistrial).

§7. RULING ON OBJECTION

The trial court has the discretion to admit or exclude evidence; the appellate courts will reverse only for an abuse of discretion. *See* ***National Liab. & Fire Ins. Co. v. Allen***, 15 S.W.3d 525, 527-28 (Tex.2000); ***City of Brownsville v. Alvarado***, 897 S.W.2d 750, 753 (Tex.1995).

§7.1 Ruling.

1. Sustains objection. If the trial court sustains the objection, it will not admit the evidence. The party who offered the evidence still has other options that it must exercise, or it waives the error. See §7.1.3, below.

2. Overrules objection. If the trial court overrules the objection, it will admit the evidence. The party whose objection was overruled still has other options that it must exercise, or it waives the error. See §7.1.3, below.

3. Next objection & request.

(1) Request for limited admissibility. After the trial court rules on the admissibility of evidence, whichever party received an adverse ruling—either the party offering it or the party objecting to it—may ask the court to limit the admissibility of the evidence by instructing the jury to consider it only for a certain purpose. *See* ***Larson v. Cactus Util. Co.***, 730 S.W.2d 640, 642 (Tex.1987). If the court ruled the evidence was inadmissible, the party that offered it should re-offer the evidence by asking the court to admit it for limited purposes. TRE 105(b); ***In re K.S.***, 76 S.W.3d 36, 40 (Tex.App.—Amarillo 2002, no pet.); ***Bean v. Baxter Healthcare Corp.***, 965 S.W.2d 656, 660 (Tex.App.—Houston [14th Dist.] 1998, no pet.). If the court ruled the evidence was admissible, the party that objected to it should ask the court to limit the purpose for which the evidence may be considered. *See* TRE 105(a); ***Horizon v. Auld***, 34 S.W.3d 887, 906 (Tex.2000); ***City of Austin v. H.L.&P. Co.***, 844 S.W.2d 773, 793 (Tex.App.—Dallas 1992, writ denied). Unless a party requests that the court instruct the jury to consider the evidence only for a limited purpose, the party waives a complaint to the general admission of the evidence. ***Horizon***, 34 S.W.3d at 906; ***Birchfield v. Texarkana Mem'l Hosp.***, 747 S.W.2d 361, 365 (Tex.1987); ***K.S.***, 76 S.W.3d at 40.

(2) Request for partial admission of evidence. If the trial court ruled the evidence was inadmissible, the party offering it can re-offer the evidence with the objectionable part excised. The party that offers the evidence that is admitted subject to the deletion of specifically identified information has a duty to redact or sanitize the document before submitting the evidence to the jury. ***American Gen. Fire & Cas. Co. v. McInnis Book Store***, 860 S.W.2d 484, 488 (Tex.App.—Corpus Christi 1993, no writ); *see also* ***Olson v. Bayland Publ'g***, 781 S.W.2d 659, 665 (Tex.App.—Houston [1st Dist.] 1989, writ denied) (court did not abuse discretion by excluding evidence that offering party did not attempt to redact), *overruled on other grounds*, ***Sage St. Assocs. v. Northdale Constr.***, 863 S.W.2d 438 (Tex.1993).

§7.2 Types of rulings. Under TRAP 33.1(a)(2), error is preserved by an express ruling, an implicit ruling, or a refusal to rule. See "Types of rulings," ch. 1-G, §2.2, p. 33.

§8. REVIEW

§8.1 Admissibility. In making the preliminary decision concerning the admissibility of evidence, the trial court is not bound by the TREs, except those that relating to privileges. TRE 104(a). Thus, the review of an erroneous decision on privilege is probably a review of a legal error, not abuse of discretion. Other decisions on admissibility are reviewed for abuse of discretion. *See, e.g.*, ***Crescendo Invs. v. Brice***, 61 S.W.3d 465, 477 (Tex.App.—San Antonio 2001, pet. denied) (compensation information); ***Southwestern Bell Tel. Co. v. Sims***, 615 S.W.2d 858, 862 (Tex.App.—Houston [1st Dist.] 1981, no writ) (qualifications of expert).

§8.2 Record on appeal. To challenge successfully a ruling regarding the admissibility of evidence, the appellant must request the court reporter's record. See ***O'Connor's Texas Civil Appeals***, "Rulings on evidence," ch. 16-C, §4.1.3, p. 184 (2002-03). If evidence was excluded, the record must contain an offer of proof or a bill of exceptions. See "Offer of Proof & Bill of Exceptions," ch. 8-E, p. 553; ***O'Connor's*** FORM 8E:01.

§8.3 Evidence rulings & harmless error rule. If evidence is erroneously admitted or excluded, the appellate courts will apply the harmless error test in TRAP 44.1(a) to determine whether the error probably caused the rendition of an improper verdict. ***Owens-Corning Fiberglas Corp. v. Malone***, 972 S.W.2d 35, 43 (Tex.1998); *see* ***Dow Chem. Co. v. Francis***, 46 S.W.3d 237, 241 (Tex.2001) (remanded because court of appeals did not conduct harm analysis under TRAP 44.1(a)).

1. Types of error regarding evidence.

(1) Error in admitting evidence. To obtain a reversal based on the erroneous admission of evidence, the appellant must show three elements: (1) the trial court erroneously admitted evidence, (2) no other similar evidence was admitted, and (3) the error probably caused the rendition of an improper judgment. *See* TRAP 44.1(a)(1); ***Interstate Northborough Prtshp. v. State***, ___ S.W.3d ___ (Tex.2001) (No. 00-0070; 10-25-01) (element 3); ***Alvarado v. Farah Mfg. Co.***, 830 S.W.2d 911, 917 n.8 (Tex.1992) (elements 2 & 3); ***Texas Dept. of Human Servs. v. White***, 817 S.W.2d 62, 63 (Tex.1991) (elements 1 & 3).

(2) Error in excluding evidence. To obtain a reversal based on the erroneous exclusion of evidence, the appellant must show four elements: (1) the trial court erroneously excluded evidence; (2) what evidence was excluded (generally, in an offer of proof); (3) the excluded evidence (a) was controlling on a material issue and (b) was not cumulative of other evidence; and (4) the error probably caused the rendition of an improper judgment. *See* TRAP 44.1(a)(1); ***Texas DOT v. Able***, 35 S.W.3d 608, 617 (Tex.2000) (elements 3 & 4); ***Williams Distrib. Co. v. Franklin***, 898 S.W.2d 816, 817 (Tex.1995) (element 3); ***Mentis v. Barnard***, 870 S.W.2d 14, 16 (Tex.1994) (element 3); ***McCraw v. Maris***, 828 S.W.2d 756, 757 (Tex.1992) (elements 1 & 4). To show that the evidence is controlling does not require a showing that it was the only evidence of its kind. *See* ***Williams Distrib.***, 898 S.W.2d at 817.

2. Not the "but for" test. Over the years, the Supreme Court has developed two conflicting lines of authority regarding the appellant's burden when challenging the erroneous ruling admitting or excluding evidence. The Supreme Court has vacillated between the heavy burden of requiring the appellant to show that "but for" the court's ruling a different judgment would have resulted, and the less onerous burden of requiring the appellant to show that the error "probably" resulted in an improper judgment. In the 1992 ***McCraw*** opinion, the Supreme Court seemed to settle the issue when it held the appellant is not required to show that but for the erroneous ruling on evidence a different judgment would have resulted; rather, the Court held the appellant is required to show only that the exclusion of evidence probably resulted in the rendition of an improper judgment. ***McCraw***, 828 S.W.2d at 758. However, three years later the Supreme Court confused the issue again by stating that a successful challenge to a ruling on evidence usually requires the appellant to show that the judgment "turns on" the evidence excluded or admitted. ***City of Brownsville v. Alvarado***, 897 S.W.2d 750, 753-54 (Tex.1995). The "turns on" test from ***Alvarado*** appears to conflict with the "probably" test in ***McCraw***. ***$18,000 in U.S. Currency v. State***, 961 S.W.2d 257, 266 & n.3 (Tex.App.—Houston [1st Dist.] 1997, no writ). To the extent there is a conflict between the ***McCraw*** and ***Alvarado*** lines of authority, the issue is resolved in favor of ***McCraw*** because TRAP 44.1(a), adopted after the two cases were issued, requires the appellant to show the error probably caused the rendition of an improper judgment. Because ***McCraw*** is consistent with TRAP 44.1(a) and both are inconsistent with ***Alvarado***, the "turns on" test in ***Alvarado*** should be dismissed as a mistake.

CAUTION

Because of the conflicting lines of authority in the Supreme Court opinions, you can find the courts of appeals making the same error. On appeal, when error is alleged in the admission or exclusion of evidence, make sure your opponent, and ultimately the court, uses the correct standard of review.

---

§8.4 Reversing judgment. If the appellate court sets aside a verdict because of an erroneous ruling excluding evidence, the court cannot render a judgment contrary to the verdict. ***Transport Ins. Co. v. Faircloth***, 898

S.W.2d 269, 275 (Tex.1995); *see* ***Hyundai Motor Co. v. Chandler***, 882 S.W.2d 606, 620 (Tex.App.—Corpus Christi 1994, writ denied). Instead, the court must remand for a trial to give the opposing party an opportunity to impeach the evidence or to respond with rebuttal evidence. ***Transport Ins.***, 898 S.W.2d at 275. If, however, the court can exclude the improperly admitted evidence, the record may be sufficient to support a rendition. *See, e.g.*, ***McElroy v. Fitts***, 876 S.W.2d 190, 199 (Tex.App.—El Paso 1994, writ dism'd) (court subtracted amounts attributable to evidence that should have been excluded and, as modified, affirmed that part of the judgment).

E. OFFER OF PROOF & BILL OF EXCEPTIONS

§1. GENERAL

§1.1 Rules. TRE 103(a)(2) (offer of proof); TRAP 33.2 (bill of exceptions). See TRCP 75a (exhibits tendered on bill of exceptions).

§1.2 Purpose. The primary purpose of an offer of proof and a bill of exceptions is to include excluded evidence in the record so the appellate court can determine if the trial court erred in excluding it. ***Ludlow v. DeBerry***, 959 S.W.2d 265, 269-70 (Tex.App.—Houston [14th Dist.] 1997, no writ); ***Sullivan v. Bickel & Brewer***, 943 S.W.2d 477, 484 (Tex.App.—Dallas 1995, writ denied); *see* TRE 103(a)(2), (b), (c); TRAP 33.1, 33.2. Another purpose is to permit the trial court to reconsider its ruling in light of the actual evidence. ***Ludlow***, 959 S.W.2d at 270.

§1.3 Forms & timetable. ***O'Connor's Texas Civil Forms***, FORMS 8E; Timetable, this book, Offer of Proof & Bill of Exceptions, p. 1005.

§1.4 Other references. Cochran, ***Texas Rules of Evidence Handbook***, pp. 98-100 (5th ed. 2003) (Cochran, ***Evidence Handbook***).

§2. DIFFERENCE BETWEEN OFFER & BILL

To preserve error when the trial court excludes evidence, the party must comply with TRE 103(a)(2), which states that error cannot be predicated on the exclusion of evidence unless the substance of the evidence was made known to the court by an offer. ***Ludlow***, 959 S.W.2d at 269-70. There are two types of offers, one made during trial (an offer of proof) and one made after trial (a formal bill of exceptions). ***Clone Component Distribs. v. State***, 819 S.W.2d 593, 596 (Tex.App.—Dallas 1991, no writ).

§2.1 Offer of proof. An offer of proof (formerly called an informal bill of exceptions) is a trial-time offer of evidence the court excluded. *See* TRE 103(a)(2); TRAP 33.1(a)(1)(B). A party makes an offer of proof by presenting the excluded evidence in the form of a summary or in question-and-answer form, out of the presence of the jury.

§2.2 Formal bill of exceptions. A formal bill of exceptions is a post-trial offer of evidence in written form. *See* TRAP 33.2; ***Clone Component Distribs.***, 819 S.W.2d at 596. A formal bill is necessary only when the complaint or evidence is not preserved in an offer of proof. *See* TRAP 33.2.

§3. WHEN AN OFFER OR BILL IS NECESSARY

§3.1 To preserve excluded evidence. When the trial court rules evidence is not admissible and excludes it, the party who offered the evidence should make an offer of proof to get the evidence into the record for the appeal. TRE 103(a)(2); ***Akin v. Santa Clara Land Co.***, 34 S.W.3d 334, 339 (Tex.App.—San Antonio 2000, pet. denied); ***Wade v. Commission for Lawyer Discipline***, 961 S.W.2d 366, 374 (Tex.App.—Houston [1st Dist.] 1997, no writ); *see, e.g.*, ***E.I. du Pont de Nemours & Co. v. Robinson***, 923 S.W.2d 549, 552 (Tex.1995) (after trial court excluded expert, party preserved expert's testimony in bill of exceptions). If the substance of the evidence is apparent from the record, an offer of proof is not necessary. TRE 103(a)(2); ***Marathon Corp. v. Pitzner***, 55 S.W.3d 114, 143 (Tex.App.—Corpus Christi 2001), *rev'd on other grounds*, 106 S.W.3d 724 (Tex.2003). See "Preserving error," ch. 5-M, §3.7, p. 309.

§3.2 To preserve off-the-record matters. When the trial court refuses to permit testimony about matters outside the record that affect a party's case, the lawyer must preserve the error in an offer of proof or bill of exceptions.

See, e.g., ***Ricardo N., Inc. v. Turcios de Argueta***, 870 S.W.2d 95, 104 (Tex.App.—Corpus Christi 1993) (party made bill to preserve testimony from clerk about time necessary to provide additional venirepersons), *rev'd in part on other grounds*, 907 S.W.2d 423 (Tex.1995); ***McLaughlin v. First Nat'l Bank***, 858 S.W.2d 511, 515 (Tex.App.—Texarkana 1993, writ denied) (party made bill to preserve fact that it was dismissed from lawsuit before charge conference & did not have chance to object to charge).

§4. OFFER OF PROOF

A party should preserve excluded evidence in an offer of proof, not in a formal bill of exceptions. An offer of proof is easier to make than a formal bill.

§4.1 Offer evidence. Before a party is entitled to make an offer of proof, it must offer the evidence at trial. ***Estate of Veale v. Teledyne Indus.***, 899 S.W.2d 239, 242 (Tex.App.—Houston [14th Dist.] 1995, writ denied). The party cannot rely on a motion in limine ruling. *But see* ***Durbin v. Dal-Briar Corp.***, 871 S.W.2d 263, 270 (Tex.App.—El Paso 1994, writ denied) (formal offer was not necessary because D stipulated that P could submit depositions as bill of exceptions), *disapproved on other grounds*, ***Golden Eagle Archery v. Jackson***, 24 S.W.3d 362 (Tex.2000).

§4.2 Specify purpose. When an objection is lodged, the party offering the evidence should specify the purpose for which the evidence is offered and the reason it is admissible. ***Sanchez v. Brownsville Sports Ctr.***, 51 S.W.3d 643, 663 (Tex.App.—Corpus Christi 2001, pet. granted w.r.m.); ***Estate of Veale***, 899 S.W.2d at 242.

§4.3 Get a ruling excluding evidence. Before a party is entitled to make an offer of proof, the court must make a ruling that the evidence is inadmissible. TRAP 33.1(a)(2); ***Estate of Veale***, 899 S.W.2d at 242; ***Ramirez v. Ramirez***, 873 S.W.2d 735, 741 (Tex.App.—El Paso 1994, no writ); *see* ***Waldon v. City of Longview***, 855 S.W.2d 875, 880 (Tex.App.—Tyler 1993, no writ) (ruling on city's motion in limine was not ruling on admissibility of evidence).

§4.4 Make an offer. Once the court rules the evidence is inadmissible, the party must make an offer of proof. ***Estate of Veale***, 899 S.W.2d at 242. The offer must show the substance of the evidence that was offered and excluded. ***In re N.R.C.***, 94 S.W.3d 799, 806 (Tex.App.—Houston [14th Dist.] 2002, pet. denied); ***Sullivan v. Bickel & Brewer***, 943 S.W.2d 477, 484 (Tex.App.—Dallas 1995, writ denied). Formal proof is not required, and courts prefer a concise statement over a lengthy presentation. ***N.R.C.***, 94 S.W.3d at 806.

1. Oral testimony. To preserve testimonial evidence, the party offering it must make an offer of proof in the presence of the judge, the court reporter, and the opposing counsel, but outside the presence of the jury. The offer of proof is conducted out of the hearing of the jury to prevent the jury from hearing inadmissible evidence. TRE 103(c). When making an offer of proof, the lawyer should make a concise statement of what testimony would be elicited from the witness. ***Babcock v. Northwest Mem'l Hosp.***, 767 S.W.2d 705, 708 (Tex.1989); ***N.R.C.***, 94 S.W.3d at 806. At the request of either party, the trial court should permit the offer to be made in question-and-answer form. TRE 103(b). *But see* ***Chance v. Chance***, 911 S.W.2d 40, 51 (Tex.App.—Beaumont 1995, writ denied) (no error to refuse question-and-answer form of offer). The trial court may add a comment to the offer to show the character of the evidence, the form in which it was offered, the objection, and the ruling. TRE 103(b).

2. Documents & things. To preserve documentary evidence, the party should, at the time the document is excluded, say, "I make an offer of proof of this document and ask that it be filed with the record." An offer of proof to preserve an excluded document may be made in the presence of the jury because the jury is not prejudiced by evidence in an excluded document that it cannot see. The court reporter should mark the document as an offer of proof and identify it with an exhibit number. The document will be filed with the court clerk so that it will be included with the exhibits in the reporter's record. TRCP 75a; *see* ***Owens-Illinois, Inc. v. Chatham***, 899 S.W.2d 722, 731 (Tex.App.—Houston [14th Dist.] 1995, writ dism'd).

(1) Filed discovery. Even when a document is already on file with the court—for example, a deposition—if the court refuses to permit it to be introduced into evidence, the party should submit it as an offer of proof and get the court to rule on the offer. *See, e.g.*, ***McInnes v. Yamaha Motor Corp.***, 673 S.W.2d 185, 187 (Tex.

1984) (excluded deposition that was not offered as bill did not preserve error); ***Malone v. Foster***, 956 S.W.2d 573, 577 (Tex.App.—Dallas 1997) (same), *aff'd*, 977 S.W.2d 562 (Tex.1998).

(2) Taped evidence. To preserve tape-recorded evidence ruled inadmissible by the trial court, the party should, at the time the tape is excluded, say, "I make an offer of proof of this tape and ask that it be filed with the record." As part of the offer, the party must describe the excluded evidence on the tape and specify the purpose of the evidence. *See, e.g.*, ***Chubb Lloyds Ins. Co. v. Kizer***, 943 S.W.2d 946, 949 (Tex.App.—Fort Worth 1997, writ denied) (error waived because party did not make bill to preserve audio portion of tape when court permitted only the video portion). If a transcript of the tape is available, the party should file it as part of the offer; if not, the party should ask permission to file a transcript as part of the offer of proof as soon as one can be made.

§4.5 Get ruling. Error is preserved by the court's explicit ruling that the evidence in the offer of proof is not admissible during trial. *See, e.g.*, ***Greenstein, Logan & Co. v. Burgess Mktg.***, 744 S.W.2d 170, 181 (Tex.App.—Waco 1987, writ denied) (error was not preserved because reporter's record did not show what was refused). However, under TRAP 33, error can also be preserved if the trial court implicitly overrules the offer, or refuses to rule on the offer and the complaining party objects to the refusal. TRAP 33.1(a)(B)(2). See "Types of rulings," ch. 1-G, §2.2, p. 33.

§4.6 Deadline. An offer of proof must be made before the court reads the charge to the jury. TRE 103(b) (offer of proof shall be made "as soon as practicable, but before the court's charge is read to the jury"). Although nothing in TRAP 33 states a deadline for making an offer of proof, under TRAP 33.1(a)(1)(B), the record must show the parties complied with the TREs. Making the offer before the charge is read to the jury gives the trial court the opportunity to correct the error.

§5. FORMAL BILL OF EXCEPTIONS

The formal bill of exceptions is an archaic leftover from a different era of trial practice. There is no equivalent to a formal bill in federal procedure. Because the requirements for a formal bill are so strict, it can be a trap. On the other hand, a formal bill may be the last chance, and sometimes the only chance, to preserve some kinds of error.

§5.1 In writing. The formal bill of exceptions must be in writing. *See* TRAP 33.2(a). It should state the party's objection and the trial court's ruling or action, together with the circumstances or evidence needed to explain the situation. *See* TRAP 33.2. All factual statements contained in the bill must be verified by affidavit.

§5.2 Presented to court. The formal bill must be presented to the trial judge for a ruling. TRAP 33.2(c)(1).

§5.3 Judge signs bill. If the court decides the bill is correct, the court should sign the bill and file it with the clerk. TRAP 33.2(c)(2)(A). The bill is then complete.

§5.4 Judge suggests corrections. If the court decides the bill is incorrect, the court may suggest a correction or amendment. TRAP 33.2(c)(2)(B). If the party agrees with the suggestion, the changes can be made, and the amended bill is signed and filed with the clerk. *Id.* The bill is then complete.

§5.5 Judge refuses to sign bill. If the court disagrees with the bill, and the party rejects the suggested corrections, the court should endorse the bill "refused" and return it to the party for filing. TRAP 33.2(c)(2)(C).

1. Judge's bill. The judge should prepare and sign a bill that, in the judge's opinion, correctly reflects what was said or what happened. TRAP 33.2(c)(2)(C); ***H.L.&P. Co. v. Russo Props.***, 710 S.W.2d 711, 717 (Tex. App.—Houston [1st Dist.] 1986, no writ). In most instances, the other party in the case probably will prepare a proposed judge's bill for the trial court's signature.

NOTE

When the trial court disagrees with the party's bill, TRAP 33.2(c)(2)(C) contemplates two bills will be filed, one by the party and one by the judge. See ***H.L.&P.***, *710 S.W.2d at 717.*

2. Bystanders' bill. The party attempting to make a bill must file the refused bill and a "bystanders' bill," in which at least three bystanders, who are not interested in the outcome of the case, state they were present and observed the matter that the bill addresses. TRAP 33.2(c)(3); ***Circle Y v. Blevins***, 826 S.W.2d 753, 755 (Tex. App.—Texarkana 1992, writ denied) (attorneys in the case cannot submit bystanders' affidavits). Filing the bystanders' affidavits without the bill of exceptions does not preserve error. ***Citizens Law Inst. v. State***, 559 S.W.2d 381, 383 (Tex.App.—Dallas 1977, no writ). Filing the refused bill without the bystanders' affidavits does not preserve error. ***Boddy v. Canteau***, 441 S.W.2d 906, 914 (Tex.App.—San Antonio 1969, writ ref'd n.r.e.).

§5.6 Additional affidavits. Any party may file affidavits to controvert or maintain the judge's or party's bill of exceptions within ten days of the filing of the bill. TRAP 33.2(c)(3).

§5.7 Objections to bill. The other parties in the case must be given the opportunity to review the bill and make objections and file affidavits. TRAP 33.2(c)(3); ***McLaughlin v. First Nat'l Bank***, 858 S.W.2d 511, 516 (Tex. App.—Texarkana 1993, writ denied).

§5.8 Deadline. The deadline for filing the complete formal bill of exceptions is 30 days after the party's notice of appeal is filed. TRAP 33.2(e)(1). The court of appeals may extend the time to file a formal bill if, within 15 days of the date the bill is due, the party files a motion to extend time that complies with TRAP 10.5(b). TRAP 33.2(e)(3).

§6. REFUSAL TO PERMIT OFFER OR BILL

It is reversible error for the trial court to refuse to permit a party to make an offer of proof or a bill of exceptions. ***State v. Biggers***, 360 S.W.2d 516, 517 (Tex.1962); ***In re Goodwin***, 562 S.W.2d 532, 533 (Tex.App.—Texarkana 1978, no writ). However, if the appellate court can determine from the record what evidence would have been preserved, the trial court's refusal to permit a party to make a bill is not reversible error. ***Pennington v. Brock***, 841 S.W.2d 127, 131 (Tex.App.—Houston [14th Dist.] 1992, no writ); ***Ledisco Fin. Servs. v. Viracola***, 533 S.W.2d 951, 959 (Tex.App.—Texarkana 1976, no writ). If the evidence the party attempted to preserve in a bill was immaterial to the outcome of the suit, the court's refusal to permit the party to make a bill is not reversible error. ***4M Linen & Uniform Sup. Co. v. W.P. Ballard & Co.***, 793 S.W.2d 320, 328 (Tex.App.—Houston [1st Dist.] 1990, writ denied); ***Dorn v. Cartwright***, 392 S.W.2d 181, 186 (Tex.App.—Dallas 1965, writ ref'd n.r.e.).

§7. REVIEW

An appellate court cannot reach the question of whether evidence was erroneously excluded unless the excluded evidence is included in the record for its review. ***McInnes v. Yamaha Motor Corp.***, 673 S.W.2d 185, 187 (Tex. 1984); ***Hartford Ins. Co. v. Jiminez***, 814 S.W.2d 551, 552-53 (Tex.App.—Houston [1st Dist.] 1991, no writ).

§7.1 Record. Testimonial and documentary evidence in an offer of proof will be included in the reporter's record. ***Owens-Illinois, Inc. v. Chatham***, 899 S.W.2d 722, 729 (Tex.App.—Houston [14th Dist.] 1995, writ dism'd). Testimonial and documentary evidence included in a formal bill of exceptions will be included in the clerk's record. TRAP 33.2 (f).

§7.2 Standard of review. To challenge evidence erroneously excluded, see "Evidence rulings & harmless error rule," ch. 8-D, §8.3, p. 552.

§7.3 Conflict between record & bill. On appeal, if the appellate court finds a conflict between the provisions of a bill of exceptions and the reporter's record, the bill will control. TRAP 33.2(d); ***Mea v. Mea***, 464 S.W.2d 201, 204 (Tex.App.—Tyler 1971, no writ).

§7.4 Another party's bill. A party cannot rely on another party's bill of exceptions unless the party specifically adopts the other party's bill or joins in making it. ***Howard v. Phillips***, 728 S.W.2d 448, 451 (Tex.App.—Fort Worth 1987, no writ).

F. MOTION TO AMEND PLEADINGS—TRIAL & POST-TRIAL

§1. GENERAL

§1.1 Rules. TRCP 62-67.

§1.2 Purpose. A party amends its pleadings to correct errors and defects, to add or delete claims or defenses, and to make the pleadings conform to the evidence. TRCP 66, 67.

§1.3 Forms. *O'Connor's Texas Civil Forms*, FORMS 8F.

§2. GENERAL RULES FOR AMENDING PLEADINGS

There are three sections in this book regarding amending pleadings: "Amending the Pleadings," ch. 1-B, §7, p. 11; "Motion to Amend Pleadings—Pretrial," ch. 5-F, p. 255; and this subchapter, "Motion to Amend Pleadings—Trial & Post-Trial."

§3. RULES REGARDING AMENDING PLEADINGS DURING TRIAL

§3.1 General rule. During trial, the trial court must permit a request to amend the pleadings when the party seeking the amendment (1) asks the court's permission to amend and (2) tenders the written amendment. TRCP 63, 66.

§3.2 Exceptions. The only circumstances in which the court may refuse to permit an amendment is when the party opposing the amendment objects and presents evidence of surprise or prejudice or shows the amendment presents a new cause of action or defense and, thus, is prejudicial on its face. TRCP 66; ***State Bar v. Kilpatrick***, 874 S.W.2d 656, 658 (Tex.1994); ***Greenhalgh v. Service Lloyds Ins. Co.***, 787 S.W.2d 938, 939 (Tex.1990); ***Hardin v. Hardin***, 597 S.W.2d 347, 349 (Tex.1980).

§4. MOTION FOR LEAVE TO AMEND TRIAL PLEADINGS

§4.1 Oral motion. The motion for leave to amend pleadings during trial may be dictated into the record. In the motion, the party should state why the amendment is appropriate and necessary.

§4.2 Written pleadings. The amended pleading should be in writing, signed by the attorney or the party, and tendered to the court for filing. TRCP 45(d), 63; ***City of Fort Worth v. Zimlich***, 29 S.W.3d 62, 73 (Tex.2000) (must be in writing); *see* ***Hunt v. Baldwin***, 68 S.W.3d 117, 134-35 (Tex.App.—Houston [14th Dist.] 2001, no pet.) (record must reflect that written trial amendment was offered). If the court accepts an oral amendment and the other party does not object before the case is submitted to the jury, the error is waived. TRAP 33.1; ***Zimlich***, 29 S.W.3d at 73. See "Motion for Leave to Amend Pleadings Before Trial," ch. 5-F, §4, p. 257.

§5. GROUNDS TO AMEND – TRIAL & POST-TRIAL

Trial amendments may be made only with leave of court, but must be freely permitted when they serve the presentation of the merits of the case. TRCP 66, 67. Trial amendments are usually offered in response to an objection that the evidence or the jury question is not supported by the pleadings.

§5.1 Amendment to correct procedural defects. If, after trial begins, a party discovers its pleadings are procedurally defective, the party should ask for leave to amend. ***Chapin & Chapin v. Texas Sand & Gravel Co.***, 844 S.W.2d 664, 665 (Tex.1992) (amendment added verified denial to petition); ***Smith Detective Agency v. Stanley Smith Sec.***, 938 S.W.2d 743, 749 (Tex.App.—Dallas 1996, writ denied) (same). Amendments that correct formal, procedural defects and do not change the substantive issues should almost always be granted. *See* ***Chapin***, 844 S.W.2d at 665; ***Francis v. Coastal Oil & Gas Corp.***, ___ S.W.3d ___ (Tex.App.—Houston [1st Dist.] 2003, no pet.) (No. 01-01-00457-CV; 5-29-03).

§5.2 Amendment to add allegations. If, after trial begins, a party discovers its pleadings are substantively defective, whether the pleadings may be amended depends on whether the issue sought to be added was tried by implied consent. An issue is tried by consent when (1) a party introduces evidence to support an unpleaded issue, and (2) the other party does not object to the admission of that evidence and, if a jury trial, to a jury question on that issue. The rule of trial by implied consent is intended to apply only to exceptional cases where it is clear from the record the parties tried an unpleaded issue by consent. ***Mastin v. Mastin***, 70 S.W.3d 148, 154 (Tex.App.—San Antonio 2001, no pet.); ***In re Walters***, 39 S.W.3d 280, 289 (Tex.App.—Texarkana 2001, no pet.).

1. Trial by consent. No amendment of the pleadings is necessary—but should be permitted if requested—when an unpleaded issue was fully developed at trial without objection, and thus was tried by consent. TRCP 66, 67; *see* ***Bell v. Meeks***, 725 S.W.2d 179, 179-80 (Tex.1987) (Ps permitted to add DTPA-misrepresentation claim after verdict); ***Ranger Ins. Co. v. Robertson***, 707 S.W.2d 135, 142 (Tex.App.—Austin 1986, writ ref'd n.r.e.) (P not required to plead issue because it was tried by consent). An unpleaded issue tried by consent is treated as if it had been raised by the pleadings. TRCP 67; ***Roark v. Stallworth Oil & Gas***, 813 S.W.2d 492, 495 (Tex.1991) (discussing trial by consent in summary judgment case). A party who allows an issue to be tried by consent and then does not challenge the lack of a pleading before submission of the case cannot later raise the pleading deficiency for the first time on appeal. ***Roark***, 813 S.W.2d at 495; ***National Convenience Stores v. Erevia***, 73 S.W.3d 518, 522 (Tex.App.—Houston [1st Dist.] 2002, pet. denied).

2. No trial by consent.

(1) Amendment permitted. When the other party objects to either the introduction of evidence or the submission of a jury question on the ground the evidence or the question is not supported by the pleadings, the issue is not tried by consent. ***Texas Indus., Inc v. Vaughan***, 919 S.W.2d 798, 803 (Tex.App.—Houston [14th Dist.] 1996, writ denied) (objection to jury question); ***Hirsch v. Hirsch***, 770 S.W.2d 924, 926 (Tex.App.—El Paso 1989, no writ) (objection to jury question); *see* ***Bedgood v. Madalin***, 600 S.W.2d 773, 775-76 (Tex.1980) (objection to evidence & jury question); ***Northwest Otolaryngology Assocs. v. Mobilease, Inc.***, 786 S.W.2d 399, 402-03 (Tex. App.—Texarkana 1990, writ denied) (objection to lack of pleadings waived in nonjury trial because no objection). When an objection is raised to the lack of pleadings, a party should ask for leave to amend and file an amended pleading. TRCP 66, 67.

(2) Amendment not permitted. Even when some evidence is introduced on an unpleaded issue, a party is not always entitled to amend its pleadings.

(a) Issue not developed. When a party introduces some evidence on an unpleaded issue but does not develop it, the party is not entitled to amend its pleadings to add the unpleaded issue. ***Whatley v. City of Dallas***, 758 S.W.2d 301, 306-07 (Tex.App.—Dallas 1988, writ denied); ***Realtex Corp. v. Tyler***, 627 S.W.2d 441, 443-44 (Tex.App.—Houston [1st Dist.] 1981, no writ).

(b) Evidence relevant to pleaded issue. When a party introduces evidence that is relevant to both pleaded and unpleaded issues, the party is not entitled to amend its pleadings to add the unpleaded issue. *See* ***Boyles v. Kerr***, 855 S.W.2d 593, 601 (Tex.1993); ***Integrated Title Data Sys. v. Dulaney***, 800 S.W.2d 336, 339 (Tex.App.—El Paso 1990, no writ); ***Harrison v. City of San Antonio***, 695 S.W.2d 271, 278 (Tex.App.—San Antonio 1985, no writ).

§6. RESPONSE TO MOTION TO AMEND TRIAL PLEADINGS

§6.1 Object. The party opposing an amendment must object. If the party does not object, and the court and the parties act as if leave was granted, on appeal, the court will presume leave was granted. ***Diesel Fuel Injection Serv. v. Gabourel***, 893 S.W.2d 610, 611 (Tex.App.—Corpus Christi 1994, no writ) (nonjury trial).

§6.2 Prove amendment is prejudicial. The party opposing the amendment must prove prejudice or show prejudice on the face of the amendment.

1. Prove prejudice. The party must produce evidence of surprise or prejudice. TRCP 63 (surprise), TRCP 66 (prejudice); ***Hardin v. Hardin***, 597 S.W.2d 347, 349-50 (Tex.1980). For example, the party may show that its pretrial preparation was made in reliance on the pleadings on file, or that it decided not to pursue other avenues

of pretrial investigation it would have pursued under the proposed amended pleading. ***Whole Foods Mkt. Southwest, L.P. v. Tijerina***, 979 S.W.2d 768, 777 (Tex.App.—Houston [14th Dist.] 1998, pet. denied).

2. Show prejudice on its face. The party must show the amendment presents a new cause of action or defense, and thus it is prejudicial on its face. TRCP 66; *e.g.*, ***Hardin***, 597 S.W.2d at 348-50 (on day of trial, D could not add 5 affirmative defenses). However, not all amendments that add a new cause of action are prejudicial on their face. ***State Bar v. Kilpatrick***, 874 S.W.2d 656, 658 (Tex.1994); ***Francis v. Coastal Oil & Gas Corp.***, ___ S.W.3d ___ (Tex.App.—Houston [1st Dist.] 2003, n.p.h.) (No. 01-01-00457-CV; 5-29-03); ***Stephenson v. LeBoeuf***, 16 S.W.3d 829, 839 (Tex.App.—Houston [14th Dist.] 2000, pet. denied). A pleading that asserts a new claim or defense is prejudicial on its face if it does all of the following:

(1) Reshapes lawsuit. The pleading asserts a new substantive matter that reshapes the nature of the lawsuit. ***Smith Detective Agency v. Stanley Smith Sec.***, 938 S.W.2d 743, 749 (Tex.App.—Dallas 1996, writ denied). When an amendment asserts a new cause of action or defense that alters the nature of the trial itself, the trial judge has the discretion to deny leave to amend. ***Chapin & Chapin v. Texas Sand & Gravel Co.***, 844 S.W.2d 664, 665 (Tex.1992); *see also* ***Hardin***, 597 S.W.2d at 350 (court had discretion to deny amendment offered on day of trial to add affirmative defenses); ***In re Loftis***, 40 S.W.3d 160, 163-64 (Tex.App.—Texarkana 2001, no pet.) (trial amendment adding resulting trust did not alter nature of trial).

(2) Was not anticipated. The new matter could not have been anticipated by the opposing party in light of the development of the case. ***Hardin***, 597 S.W.2d at 350; ***Smith Detective Agency***, 938 S.W.2d at 749.

(3) Will have adverse effect. If the amendment is permitted, the other party's presentation of the case will be adversely affected. ***Hardin***, 597 S.W.2d at 350; ***Smith Detective Agency***, 938 S.W.2d at 749.

§6.3 Motion for continuance. If the court grants the motion for leave to amend, the nonmovant may ask for a continuance. *See* TRCP 66 (court may grant postponement to enable nonmovant to meet trial amendment); ***Deutsch v. Hoover, Bax & Slovacek***, 97 S.W.3d 179, 185-86 (Tex.App.—Houston [14th Dist.] 2002, no pet.) (postponement may cure prejudice resulting from trial amendment). See "Motion for Continuance," ch. 5-D, p. 242.

§6.4 Motion for additional discovery. If the court grants the motion for leave to amend, the nonmovant may be entitled to ask for additional discovery on the unpleaded issue. *See* TRCP 66.

§6.5 Sworn proof. In most cases, the response to an oral motion to amend is also made orally. If the response is oral, and the lawyer states facts outside the record, the lawyer should ask to be sworn; if the response is written and includes facts outside the record, it should be verified by affidavit. See "Lawyer's appearance before the court," ch. 1-H, §5.2, p. 40.

§7. RULINGS ON AMENDMENTS DURING TRIAL

§7.1 Amendments permitted during trial. • To add verified denial. ***Chapin***, 844 S.W.2d at 665 (denying P's open-account allegations); ***Kirby Forest Indus. v. Dobbs***, 743 S.W.2d 348, 352 (Tex.App.—Beaumont 1987, writ denied) (denying partnership). • To add claim of negligence per se. ***Zavala v. Trujillo***, 883 S.W.2d 242, 246 (Tex.App.—El Paso 1994, writ denied). • To add damages for mental anguish. *E.g.*, ***Yowell v. Piper Aircraft Corp.***, 703 S.W.2d 630, 634 (Tex.1986) (after trial court permitted D to introduce evidence on a new defense, court permitted Ps to amend to add mental anguish damages); *see also* ***Texas Indus. v. Vaughan***, 919 S.W.2d 798, 804 (Tex.App.—Houston [14th Dist.] 1996, writ denied) (trial court should have allowed trial amendment on mental anguish). • To add request for attorney fees. ***Jess v. Libson***, 742 S.W.2d 90, 92 (Tex.App.—Austin 1987, no writ). • To add a cause of action that shares elements and evidence with the causes pleaded. ***Kilpatrick***, 874 S.W.2d at 658 (adding barratry to suit for disbarment). • To add a claim to conform the pleadings to the evidence. ***Campbell v. Salazar***, 960 S.W.2d 719, 730-31 (Tex.App.—El Paso 1997, pet. denied) (past lost income); ***H.O. Dyer, Inc. v. Steele***, 489 S.W.2d 686, 688-89 (Tex.App.—Houston [1st Dist.] 1972, no writ) (negligence). • To add an affirmative defense. ***Deutsch***, 97 S.W.3d at 185-86 (statute of limitations); ***Diesel Fuel***, 893 S.W.2d at 611 (same).

§7.2 Amendments refused during trial. • To assert "Stowers" claim, when some evidence came in without objection, but the issue was not developed. ***Whatley v. City of Dallas***, 758 S.W.2d 301, 307 (Tex.App.—Dallas 1988, writ denied). • To add new and separate cause of action when the facts were known to the plaintiff ahead of time. ***Sosa v. City of Corpus Christi***, 739 S.W.2d 397, 400 (Tex.App.—Corpus Christi 1987, no writ). • To add new defensive theory after the close of evidence. ***White v. Sullins***, 917 S.W.2d 158, 161 (Tex.App.—Beaumont 1996, writ denied); ***Tuck v. Tuck***, 509 S.W.2d 656, 657-58 (Tex.App.—Austin 1974, writ ref'd n.r.e.). • To add cross-action and additional defense of unavoidable accident during the preparation of the charge. ***Leong v. Wright***, 478 S.W.2d 839, 846-47 (Tex.App.—Houston [14th Dist.] 1972, writ ref'd n.r.e.). • To add new theory of the case after close of the evidence. ***Burroughs Corp. v. Farmers Dairies***, 538 S.W.2d 809, 811 (Tex.App.—El Paso 1976, writ ref'd n.r.e.). • To add substantive matter in response to a defense known to the party since pretrial discovery. ***Miller v. Wal-Mart Stores***, 918 S.W.2d 658, 666 (Tex.App.—Amarillo 1996, writ denied).

§8. RULINGS ON AMENDMENTS AFTER VERDICT

The court must grant leave to amend the pleadings after the evidence is concluded to conform the pleadings to the verdict. ***Greenhalgh v. Service Lloyds Ins. Co.***, 787 S.W.2d 938, 939 (Tex.1990).

§8.1 Amendments permitted after verdict. • To conform the pleadings to the damages awarded. ***Greenhalgh***, 787 S.W.2d at 939 (granting amendment was mandatory because no surprise or prejudice); ***Weidner v. Sanchez***, 14 S.W.3d 353, 376-77 (Tex.App.—Houston [14th Dist.] 2000, no pet.) (no evidence of surprise or prejudice). • To conform the pleadings to the evidence. *E.g.*, ***Krishnan v. Ramirez***, 42 S.W.3d 205, 225 (Tex.App.—Corpus Christi 2001, pet. denied) (after verdict, P permitted to amend to clarify his capacity as guardian of minor who was both heir & assignee). • To add claim for prejudgment interest. ***Benavidez v. Isles Constr. Co.***, 726 S.W.2d 23, 26 (Tex.1987); ***Firefighters' & Police Officers' Civil Serv. Comm'n v. Herrera***, 981 S.W.2d 728, 734-35 (Tex.App.—Houston [1st Dist.] 1998, pet. denied). • To add claim for attorney fees. ***Swate v. Medina Cmty. Hosp.***, 966 S.W.2d 693, 701-02 (Tex.App.—San Antonio 1998, pet. denied). • To add a party in a nonjury trial before judgment signed. *E.g.*, ***Fincher v. B&D Air Conditioning & Heating Co.***, 816 S.W.2d 509, 514 (Tex.App.—Houston [1st Dist.] 1991, writ denied) (D-partner who was served as partnership representative, but not named individually, was added individually); ***Lloyd's of London v. Walker***, 716 S.W.2d 99, 103-04 (Tex.App.—Dallas 1986, writ ref'd n.r.e.) (P added). • To add prayer for mental anguish. ***Centroplex Ford v. Kirby***, 736 S.W.2d 261, 265 (Tex.App.—Austin 1987, no writ). • To add cause of action. *E.g.*, ***Bell v. Meeks***, 725 S.W.2d 179, 179-80 (Tex.1987) (after verdict, Ps permitted to add DTPA-misrepresentation claim, which was similar to DTPA-warranty claim they pleaded and proved); ***Group Hosp. Servs. v. Daniel***, 704 S.W.2d 870, 876 (Tex.App.—Corpus Christi 1985, no writ) (in DTPA case, Ps permitted to amend to add allegation of unconscionable conduct).

§8.2 Amendments refused after verdict. • To include all damages found by the jury, when the trial court already had permitted an amendment at the close of evidence. ***Capital Title Co. v. Donaldson***, 739 S.W.2d 384, 393 (Tex.App.—Houston [1st Dist.] 1987, no writ). • To add the defense of breach of contract one month after the verdict. ***Nance v. RTC***, 803 S.W.2d 323, 332 (Tex.App.—San Antonio 1990), *writ denied*, 813 S.W.2d 154 (Tex.1991). • To add new theory of recovery nine days after the verdict. ***Arnold D. Kamen & Co. v. Young***, 466 S.W.2d 381, 386-87 (Tex.App.—Dallas 1971, writ ref'd n.r.e.). • To add new cause of action three months after the verdict. ***Dorchester Gas Prod'g Co. v. Harlow Corp.***, 743 S.W.2d 243, 259-60 (Tex.App.—Amarillo 1987, no writ).

§9. AMENDMENTS AFTER JUDGMENT

§9.1 No new claims. After the trial court renders judgment, it is too late to ask to amend the pleadings to add new parties or claims. ***Mitchell v. LaFlamme***, 60 S.W.3d 123, 132 (Tex.App.—Houston [14th Dist.] 2000, no pet.); ***Cantu v. Martin***, 934 S.W.2d 859, 860-61 (Tex.App.—Corpus Christi 1996, no writ). See "Rendering, Signing, & Entering Judgment," ch. 9-C, §3, p. 596.

§9.2 Conform pleadings to evidence. After the court renders judgment, it may be possible to amend the pleadings to conform them to the evidence as long as the court still has plenary power. *See* ***Cantu***, 934 S.W.2d at 861

(dicta); ***Boarder to Boarder Trucking v. Mondi, Inc.***, 831 S.W.2d 495, 500 (Tex.App.—Corpus Christi 1992, no writ) (Hinojosa, J., concurring). To determine if the court has plenary power, see chart 9-1, "Plenary Power Deadlines," ch. 9-C, p. 607.

§10. REVIEW

See "Appellate review of amended pleadings," ch. 1-B, §7.3, p. 12.

G. MOTION FOR DIRECTED VERDICT

§1. GENERAL

§1.1 Rules. TRCP 268; TRAP 33.1.

§1.2 Purpose. The motion for directed verdict is a procedural device to ask the court to render judgment without submitting the charge to the jury because there is nothing for the jury to decide. A directed verdict is also called an instructed verdict. Compare the title to TRCP 268, which calls it a motion for *instructed* verdict, with the body of the rule, which calls it a motion for *directed* verdict.

A motion for directed verdict may be made in a nonjury trial, even though the name of the motion is technically incorrect because there is no jury to "direct." ***Carrasco v. Texas Transp. Inst.***, 908 S.W.2d 575, 576 (Tex.App.—Waco 1995, no writ). In a nonjury trial, the correct procedure is to make a "motion for judgment." *See* ***McKinley Iron Works v. TEC***, 917 S.W.2d 468, 469-70 (Tex.App.—Fort Worth 1996, no writ).

§1.3 Forms. ***O'Connor's Texas Civil Forms***, FORMS 8G.

§2. WHO CAN MAKE THE MOTION & WHEN

There are several times during a trial when the parties can move for a directed verdict.

§2.1 After plaintiff rests. After the plaintiff rests (*i.e.*, completes the presentation of its evidence), only the defendant may make a motion for directed verdict. *See* ***Wedgeworth v. Kirskey***, 985 S.W.2d 115, 116 (Tex.App.—San Antonio 1998, pet. denied) (court cannot render directed verdict before P rests); ***Nassar v. Hughes***, 882 S.W.2d 36, 38 (Tex.App.—Houston [1st Dist.] 1994, writ denied) (same); ***Buckner v. Buckner***, 815 S.W.2d 877, 878 (Tex. App.—Tyler 1991, no writ) (directed verdict before trial is premature). *But see* ***Tana Oil & Gas Corp. v. McCall***, 104 S.W.3d 80, 82 (Tex.2003) (timing of motion immaterial when substantive law does not allow recovery on pleaded cause of action). If the court grants a motion before the plaintiff rests, on appeal the appellant must show it was harmed because it was not able to present its evidence. *See* ***Tana Oil***, 104 S.W.3d at 82.

§2.2 After defendant rests. After the defendant rests, either party may make a motion for directed verdict. *See* ***Cecil Pond Constr. Co. v. Ed Bell Invs.***, 864 S.W.2d 211, 214 (Tex.App.—Tyler 1993, no writ) (P's motion for directed verdict, made before D presented evidence, was premature).

§2.3 After both sides close. After both sides close (*i.e.*, offer their rebuttal testimony), either party may make a motion for directed verdict. To preserve error in the overruling of an earlier motion for directed verdict, the party must reurge the motion at the close of the evidence. See "Reurging Motion at End of Evidence," §6, p. 563.

§2.4 If jury unable to reach verdict. If the trial court discharges the jury because it is not able to reach a verdict but does not grant a mistrial, the court may reconsider one of the party's motions for directed verdict. ***Encina Prtshp. v. Corenergy, L.L.C.***, 50 S.W.3d 66, 69 (Tex.App.—Corpus Christi 2001, pet. denied); ***Nelson v. Data Terminal Sys.***, 762 S.W.2d 744, 748-49 (Tex.App.—San Antonio 1988, writ denied).

§2.5 On court's motion. The court may on its own initiative grant a motion for directed verdict. ***Adams v. Houston Nat'l Bank***, 1 S.W.2d 878, 879 (Tex. Comm'n App. 1928, holding approved); ***Valero Eastex Pipeline Co. v. Jarvis***, 926 S.W.2d 789, 792 (Tex.App.—Tyler 1996, writ denied). Before granting a motion on its own initiative, the court must give the parties notice that it intends to consider granting a directed verdict sua sponte. The party against whom the motion may be granted should be given the opportunity to amend its pleadings or introduce additional evidence before the court grants a motion sua sponte. See "Motion to Amend Pleadings—Trial & Post-Trial," ch. 8-F, p. 557; "Motion to Reopen for Additional Evidence," ch. 8-H, p. 564.

§3. MOTION

§3.1 Oral or written. A motion for directed verdict may be in writing or may be made orally. ***Dillard v. Broyles***, 633 S.W.2d 636, 645 (Tex.App.—Corpus Christi 1982, writ ref'd n.r.e.); *see also* TRCP 268 ("shall state the specific grounds"). If made orally, the grounds are preserved only if recorded by the court reporter and included in the reporter's record.

§3.2 Partial directed verdict. Although a partial directed verdict is not expressly contemplated by TRCP 268, the device can be used to remove certain parts of a case from the fact-finder. ***Johnson v. Swain***, 787 S.W.2d 36, 36 n.1 (Tex.1989) (court granted partial directed verdict, holding D liable for damages caused by vicious animal).

§3.3 Specific reasons. The motion for directed verdict should state the specific reasons for the motion. TRCP 268. If, however, the court grants a directed verdict on a ground that is not specified in the motion, and there are no fact issues for the jury to resolve, it is not reversible error. ***TEIA v. Page***, 553 S.W.2d 98, 102 (Tex.1977); ***Deutsch v. Hoover, Bax & Slovacek***, 97 S.W.3d 179, 195 (Tex.App.—Houston [14th Dist.] 2002, no pet.); ***Crescendo Invs. v. Brice***, 61 S.W.3d 465, 472 (Tex.App.—San Antonio 2001, no pet.).

§4. GROUNDS FOR DIRECTED VERDICT

A directed verdict is proper only under limited circumstances. ***Delp v. Douglas***, 948 S.W.2d 483, 492 (Tex.App.—Fort Worth 1997), *rev'd on other grounds*, 987 S.W.2d 879 (Tex.1999). A party is entitled to a directed verdict in the following instances:

§4.1 No evidence. The evidence does not raise a fact issue on one or more elements that the nonmovant must establish to be entitled to judgment. ***Cherqui v. Westheimer St. Festival***, 116 S.W.3d 337, 343 (Tex.App.—Houston [14th Dist.] 2003, n.p.h.); ***Koepke v. Martinez***, 84 S.W.3d 393, 395 (Tex.App.—Corpus Christi 2002, pet. denied); *e.g.*, ***Hyman Farm Serv. v. Earth Oil & Gas Co.***, 920 S.W.2d 452, 455-57 (Tex.App.—Amarillo 1996, no writ) (no evidence of offer & acceptance).

§4.2 Conclusive evidence. The evidence conclusively proves a fact that establishes the movant's right to judgment as a matter of law. ***Cherqui***, 116 S.W.3d at 343; ***Koepke***, 84 S.W.3d at 395; ***Orozco v. Orozco***, 917 S.W.2d 70, 73 (Tex.App.—San Antonio 1996, writ denied). That is, the court should direct a verdict when reasonable minds can draw only one conclusion from the evidence. ***Vance v. My Apt. Steak House***, 677 S.W.2d 480, 483 (Tex.1984); ***Collora v. Navarro***, 574 S.W.2d 65, 68 (Tex.1978); *see, e.g.*, ***Shelton v. Swift Motors***, 674 S.W.2d 337, 341 (Tex. App.—San Antonio 1984, writ ref'd n.r.e.) (evidence showed P sued wrong party; D was not liable to P). If there is any conflicting, probative evidence, the trial court must submit the issue to the jury. ***Air Conditioning, Inc. v. Harrison-Wilson-Pearson***, 253 S.W.2d 422, 425 (Tex.1952); ***Facciolla v. Linbeck Constr. Corp.***, 968 S.W.2d 435, 440 (Tex.App.—Texarkana 1998, no pet.); ***Nelson v. American Nat'l Bank***, 921 S.W.2d 411, 415 (Tex.App.—Corpus Christi 1996, no writ).

§4.3 Legal bar in pleadings. The substantive law does not permit the plaintiff to recover on its cause of action or does not permit the defendant to assert its defense. *See, e.g.*, ***Dietrich v. Goodman***, ___ S.W.3d ___ (Tex. App.—Houston [14th Dist.] 2003, n.p.h.) (No. 14-01-01168-CV; 7-24-03) (court directed verdict because, under Water Code, flood water did not qualify as "surface water"); ***Arguelles v. UT Fam. Med. Ctr.***, 941 S.W.2d 255, 258 (Tex.App.—Corpus Christi 1996, no writ) (court directed verdict because Texas does not recognize the "lost chance doctrine" in medical malpractice suits); ***Anderson v. Vinson Expl.***, 832 S.W.2d 657, 665 (Tex.App.—El Paso 1992, no writ) (court directed verdict because, under DTPA, an investor is not a "consumer"); *see also* ***Southwestern Bell Tel. Co. v. DeLanney***, 809 S.W.2d 493, 494-95 (Tex.1991) (court could have directed verdict on negligence claim because P was limited to breach of contract).

PRACTICE TIP

To avoid a directed verdict based on failure to prove part of the cause of action or defense, the party should prepare a draft of the charge before trial. During the trial, the party should use the draft of the charge as a checklist of the elements that must be supported with evidence.

§5. RESPONSE

§5.1 Objections. Generally, the party opposing the motion should respond to the motion and state the converse of the movant's allegations: (1) a fact issue was raised on all material issues in the case, (2) the evidence does not conclusively prove anything, and (3) no legal theory precludes a judgment. The party should argue that all the issues should be submitted to the jury.

§5.2 Leave to amend. If the motion for directed verdict is based on a defect in the pleadings that is curable by amendment, the nonmovant should ask for permission to amend the pleadings. See "Motion to Amend Pleadings—Trial & Post-Trial," ch. 8-F, p. 557.

§5.3 Motion to reopen. If the motion for directed verdict is based on a lack of evidence of an essential element, the nonmovant should ask to reopen the evidence. *See* ***MCI Telecomm. Corp. v. Tarrant Cty. Appr. Dist.***, 723 S.W.2d 350, 353 (Tex.App.—Fort Worth 1987, no writ). See "Motion to Reopen for Additional Evidence," ch. 8-H, p. 564.

§6. REURGING MOTION AT END OF EVIDENCE

§6.1 Rule. If the court overrules a motion for directed verdict during the trial, the movant has two options: (1) stand on the motion and test the ruling on appeal or (2) introduce additional evidence. If the movant chooses to introduce evidence, the movant must make a second motion at the close of all the evidence; if it does not, it waives the grounds stated in the first motion. ***Horton v. Horton***, 965 S.W.2d 78, 86 (Tex.App.—Fort Worth 1998, no pet.); ***Cliffs Drilling Co. v. Burrows***, 930 S.W.2d 709, 712 (Tex.App.—Houston [1st Dist.] 1996, no writ). This rule applies in both jury and nonjury trials. *See* ***Horton***, 965 S.W.2d at 86 (jury); ***Wenk v. City Nat'l Bank***, 613 S.W.2d 345, 348 (Tex.App.—Tyler 1981, no writ) (nonjury). To preserve error, all grounds in the first motion must be restated in the second motion.

§6.2 Criticism & exceptions. The application of the rule requiring the motion to be reurged after the introduction of additional evidence has been criticized. ***Sipco Servs. Mar. v. Wyatt Field Serv. Co.***, 857 S.W.2d 602, 609-10 (Tex.App.—Houston [1st Dist.] 1993, no writ) (Cohen, J., concurring). Federal courts, which work under the same rule that requires the motion to be reurged at the close of the evidence, have developed exceptions that ameliorate the harshness of the rule. In federal courts, a motion for directed verdict (called a motion for judgment as a matter of law) made during the trial preserves error even though additional evidence is introduced after the motion when (1) the trial court reserved a ruling on the motion, (2) little or no evidence was presented to rebut the motion, or (3) considering all the circumstances, the purposes of FRCP 50 were satisfied. See ***O'Connor's Federal Rules * Civil Trials***, "Reurging the Motion at End of Evidence," ch. 8-G, §6, p. 518 (2004).

§7. ORDER

The order sustaining or overruling the motion for directed verdict can be made in writing and filed with the clerk or made orally on the record. *See* TRAP 33.1(c) (a signed order is not required to preserve a complaint for appeal).

§8. REVIEW

§8.1 Record on appeal. To challenge successfully the granting or denial of a directed verdict, the appellant must file a complete reporter's record in the appellate court. ***McDonald v. State***, 936 S.W.2d 734, 737 (Tex.App.—Waco 1997, no writ).

§8.2 Directed verdict denied. In reviewing the denial of a directed verdict, the appellate court is limited to the specific grounds stated in the motion. ***Cooper v. Lyon Fin. Servs.***, 65 S.W.3d 197, 207 (Tex.App.—Houston [14th Dist.] 2001, no pet.); ***American Petrofina Co. v. Panhandle Pet. Prod.***, 646 S.W.2d 590, 593 (Tex.App.—Amarillo 1983, no writ). The denial of a motion for directed verdict lays the foundation for challenging the evidence on appeal by issues or points of error contending there was "no evidence" of a certain fact or the fact was established "as a matter of law." *See, e.g.*, ***Weidner v. Sanchez***, 14 S.W.3d 353, 366 (Tex.App.—Houston [14th Dist.] 2000, no pet.) (no evidence); ***White v. Liberty Eylau ISD***, 920 S.W.2d 809, 813 (Tex.App.—Texarkana 1996, writ denied) (as a matter of law).

§8.3 Directed verdict granted. In reviewing a directed verdict, the appellate court can consider any reason the directed verdict should have been granted, even if not stated in the order. ***Reyna v. First Nat'l Bank***, 55 S.W.3d 58, 69 (Tex.App.—Corpus Christi 2001, no pet.); ***Gonzales v. Willis***, 995 S.W.2d 729, 740 (Tex.App.—San Antonio 1999, no pet.). The appellate court must consider all the evidence in the light most favorable to the party against whom the verdict was directed, disregarding all contrary evidence and inferences. ***S.V. v. R.V.***, 933 S.W.2d 1, 8 (Tex. 1996); ***Szczepanik v. First S. Trust Co.***, 883 S.W.2d 648, 649 (Tex.1994); ***Mills v. Angel***, 995 S.W.2d 262, 267 (Tex. App.—Texarkana 1999, no pet.). The appellate court must determine if there is any probative evidence to raise a fact issue. ***Porterfield v. Brinegar***, 719 S.W.2d 558, 559 (Tex.1986). If the record contains any probative and conflicting evidence on a material issue, the issue should have been resolved by the jury, and the appellate court must reverse. *See* ***White v. Southwestern Bell Tel. Co.***, 651 S.W.2d 260, 262 (Tex.1983); ***Rente Co. v. Truckers Express***, 116 S.W.3d 326, 330 (Tex.App.—Houston [14th Dist.] 2003, n.p.h.); ***Mills***, 995 S.W.2d at 267.

§8.4 Nonjury trial. In reviewing the trial court's granting of a motion for judgment in a nonjury case, the appellate court examines the record as if the trial court had granted a motion for judgment based on all the facts and does not just rule on whether there was no evidence or whether a proposition was established as a matter of law. ***Qantel Bus. Sys. v. Custom Controls Co.***, 761 S.W.2d 302, 303-04 (Tex.1988).

H. MOTION TO REOPEN FOR ADDITIONAL EVIDENCE

§1. GENERAL

§1.1 Rule. TRCP 270.

§1.2 Purpose. A party should move to reopen the evidence when it is necessary to include additional evidence in the record. When a party completes the presentation of its evidence, it announces that it "rests." When all parties have rested, the parties proceed to offer their rebuttal evidence. After a party offers its rebuttal testimony, the party announces that it "closes." When all parties have closed, the evidence part of the trial is over, unless the court reopens the case for more evidence.

§1.3 Forms. ***O'Connor's Texas Civil Forms***, FORM 8H:01.

§2. MOTION TO REOPEN

Reopening is particularly important when the trial court excluded evidence the party attempted to introduce, and after the party closed, the other party introduced evidence making the excluded evidence relevant. Reopening is also important when the trial court announces it intends to grant a directed verdict for lack of evidence. *See* ***MCI Telecomm. Corp. v. Tarrant Cty. Appr. Dist.***, 723 S.W.2d 350, 353 (Tex.App.—Fort Worth 1987, no writ).

§2.1 Form. An oral motion to reopen is sufficient, but if the party has the opportunity, it should file a written motion. *See* TRCP 270. Most of the time, however, motions to reopen are made orally in open court when the party suddenly realizes it should offer additional testimony.

§2.2 Grounds. When asking the court to reopen, the party should show all of the following:

1. The party was diligent in obtaining evidence. ***Lopez v. Lopez***, 55 S.W.3d 194, 201 (Tex.App.—Corpus Christi 2001, no pet.); ***In re A.F.***, 895 S.W.2d 481, 484 (Tex.App.—Austin 1995, no writ); *see* ***Ex parte Stiles***, 950 S.W.2d 444, 446 (Tex.App.—Waco 1997, no writ).

2. The additional evidence is decisive. ***Lopez***, 55 S.W.3d at 201; ***Stiles***, 950 S.W.2d at 446-47; ***In re A.F.***, 895 S.W.2d at 484.

3. The receipt of additional evidence will not cause undue delay. ***Lopez***, 55 S.W.3d at 201; ***Stiles***, 950 S.W.2d at 446-47; ***In re A.F.***, 895 S.W.2d at 484.

4. The receipt of additional evidence will not cause an injustice. ***Lopez***, 55 S.W.3d at 201; ***Stiles***, 950 S.W.2d at 446-47; ***In re A.F.***, 895 S.W.2d at 484.

§2.3 Verification. Although not required by TRCP 270 to be in writing, when the motion to reopen is in writing, it should be verified if it contains factual allegations outside the record.

§3. RESPONSE

A party must object to the other party's motion to reopen, or waive error in the reopening. ***MCI Telecomm.***, 723 S.W.2d at 353.

§4. STANDARD

§4.1 Sound discretion. A trial court should permit a party to reopen the evidence when it clearly appears necessary to the administration of justice. TRCP 270. The decision to reopen is within the trial court's sound discretion. ***Lopez***, 55 S.W.3d at 201; ***In re Hawk***, 5 S.W.3d 874, 876-77 (Tex.App.—Houston [14th Dist.] 1999, no pet.); ***C.F. v. State***, 897 S.W.2d 464, 473 (Tex.App.—El Paso 1995, no writ). The trial court should liberally exercise its discretion to permit both sides to fully develop the case. ***Lopez***, 55 S.W.3d at 201.

§4.2 Duty to reopen. The court may have the duty to reopen the evidence when the party moving to reopen has been diligent, the receipt of additional evidence would not cause undue delay or injustice, and the evidence would be decisive. ***In re H.W.***, 85 S.W.3d 348, 357-58 (Tex.App.—Tyler 2002, no pet.); ***Word of Faith World Outreach Ctr. Ch. v. Oechsner***, 669 S.W.2d 364, 367 (Tex.App.—Dallas 1994, no writ); *see* ***Alkas v. United Sav. Ass'n***, 672 S.W.2d 852, 860 (Tex.App.—Corpus Christi 1984, writ ref'd n.r.e.); *see also* ***Hill v. Melton***, 311 S.W.2d 496, 500 (Tex.App.—Dallas 1958, writ dism'd) (because party had right to reopen, abuse of discretion was not the correct standard of review).

§5. DEADLINE

After the jury returns the verdict, the court cannot admit evidence on a controversial matter. TRCP 270.

§5.1 Party permitted to reopen. In the following cases, the trial court permitted or should have permitted the party to reopen. • After the defendant's motion for directed verdict. ***MCI Telecomm.***, 723 S.W.2d at 353. • After argument, but before judgment. ***Word of Faith***, 669 S.W.2d at 368 (case was submitted on stipulated evidence). • After the jury began considering the evidence, the trial court permitted the introduction of an invoice that was part of a series of invoices introduced during the trial. ***Turner v. Lone Star Indus.***, 733 S.W.2d 242, 244-45 (Tex.App.—Houston [1st Dist.] 1987, writ ref'd n.r.e.). • After case was submitted to the jury, court permitted party to reopen to establish standing. ***Krishnan v. Ramirez***, 42 S.W.3d 205, 223 (Tex.App.—Corpus Christi 2001, pet. denied). • After verdict was returned, court should have permitted party to reopen to introduce into evidence written demand letter submitted 30 days before trial. ***Pratt v. Trinity Projects***, 26 S.W.3d 767, 769 (Tex.App.—Beaumont 2000, pet. denied). • Before judgment, court should have permitted party to reopen to test the correctness of a plat prepared after trial that the court wanted attached to the judgment. ***Templeton v. Dreiss***, 961 S.W.2d 645, 663-65 (Tex.App.—San Antonio 1998, pet. denied). • Court should have reopened evidence when, just after the close of evidence, plaintiffs realized they had not proven damages. ***Hill***, 311 S.W.2d at 499-500. • Before the trial court rendered judgment more than two years after the trial (delay caused by an appeal), trial court should have permitted the party to reopen. ***Greater Ft. Worth & Tarrant Cty. Cmty. Action Agency v. Mims***, 627 S.W.2d 149, 151 (Tex.1982).

§5.2 Party not permitted to reopen. In the following cases, the trial court did not permit the party to reopen. • After resting, the plaintiff was not permitted to reopen to prove notice, which the defendant had denied by verified plea. ***Apresa v. Montfort Ins. Co.***, 932 S.W.2d 246, 250 (Tex.App.—El Paso 1996, no writ). • Several months after closing and after the trial court announced its judgment. ***Fisher v. Kerr Cty.***, 739 S.W.2d 434, 437 (Tex.App.—San Antonio 1987, no writ) (movant did not show diligence in presenting evidence at trial). • To ask for attorney fees under the Open Records Act after close of hearing. ***McNamara v. Fulks***, 855 S.W.2d 782, 784 (Tex.App.—El Paso 1993, no writ). • After the close of evidence in a nonjury trial, two or three weeks before judgment. ***Alkas***, 672 S.W.2d at 860 (evidence was not decisive). • After the jury sent out a question about the evidence. ***Walton Neon Co. v. Travel-Tex Corp.***, 482 S.W.2d 934, 936-37 (Tex.App.—Corpus Christi 1972, writ ref'd n.r.e.). • On date divorce decree was signed. ***Lopez v. Lopez***, 55 S.W.3d 194, 201-02 (Tex.App.—Corpus Christi 2001, no pet.) (movant did not show diligence; evidence not decisive).

§6. REVIEW

§6.1 Record. When a party is prevented from reopening, the party should make an offer of proof setting out the evidence the party tried to introduce. *See* ***Word of Faith***, 669 S.W.2d at 366 (error preserved by bill of exceptions); ***Walton Neon***, 482 S.W.2d at 937 (error not preserved because no bill of exceptions). See "Offer of Proof & Bill of Exceptions," ch. 8-E, p. 553.

§6.2 Standard of review. The trial court's action in ruling on a motion to reopen the evidence should not be disturbed unless it clearly appears the court has abused its discretion. ***In re H.W.***, 85 S.W.3d at 358; ***In re T.V.***, 27 S.W.3d 622, 624 (Tex.App.—Waco 2000, no pet.); ***Word of Faith***, 669 S.W.2d at 367. The error is reversible only if it probably caused the rendition of an improper judgment—if the evidence could have had an impact on the decision. *See* ***Word of Faith***, 669 S.W.2d at 367.

I. THE CHARGE

§1. GENERAL

§1.1 Rules. TRCP 271-279, 285-289.

§1.2 Purpose. The charge is the collection of questions, definitions, and instructions the court submits to the jury to resolve the factual disputes in the case. It is the trial court's responsibility to submit a proper charge. ***Spencer v. Eagle Star Ins. Co.***, 876 S.W.2d 154, 157 (Tex.1994).

§1.3 Forms. ***O'Connor's Texas Civil Forms***, FORMS 8I.

§1.4 Other references. Texas Pattern Jury Charges (State Bar of Texas): General Negligence & Intentional Personal Torts (2002), Malpractice, Premises & Products (2002), Business, Consumer, Insurance & Employment (2002), Family (2002).

§2. PREPARING A DRAFT OF THE CHARGE

Each party should have prepared a complete version of the charge—including its opponent's jury questions, instructions, and definitions—before engaging in discovery. Then, just before trial, each party should review and revise the proposed charge. After the introduction of evidence is completed and before the informal charge conference, the parties should again review and revise their proposed charge.

§2.1 Broad-form questions.

1. Broad form required. The trial court must use broad-form submissions whenever feasible. TRCP 277; ***Golden Eagle Archery v. Jackson***, 116 S.W.3d 757, 776 (Tex.2003); ***Hyundai Motor Co. v. Rodriguez***, 995 S.W.2d 661, 663-64 & n.8 (Tex.1999); *see* ***H.E. Butt Grocery Co. v. Bilotto***, 985 S.W.2d 22, 24-25 (Tex.1998).

2. Broad form not required. A broad-form submission is not always feasible when the governing law is unsettled or when there is doubt about the legal sufficiency of the evidence. ***Harris Cty. v. Smith***, 96 S.W.3d 230,

235-36 (Tex.2002); *see* ***Crown Life Ins. Co. v. Casteel***, 22 S.W.3d 378, 390 (Tex.2000); ***Westgate, Ltd. v. State***, 843 S.W.2d 448, 455 n.6 (Tex.1992). When there is doubt about the governing law or the legal sufficiency of the evidence, the party should object and ask the court to either (1) eliminate the doubtful element or (2) submit the doubtful element as a separate question. *See* ***Smith***, 96 S.W.3d at 236. If the court overrules the objection, and the appellate court finds no support for the doubtful element, it will reverse for a new trial. See "Challenging charge," §11.2.2, p. 580.

§2.2 Proper tender of requests. Each party should reexamine the live pleadings and the evidence before preparing the draft charge.

1. Controlling & disputed fact issues. The litigants are entitled to have controlling and disputed fact issues submitted to the jury. ***Bel-Ton Elec. Serv. v. Pickle***, 915 S.W.2d 480, 481 (Tex.1996); ***Aero Energy v. Circle C Drilling Co.***, 699 S.W.2d 821, 823 (Tex.1985). A controlling issue is one that requires a factual determination to render judgment in the case. ***Lehmann v. Wieghat***, 917 S.W.2d 379, 382 (Tex.App.—Houston [14th Dist.] 1996, writ denied). A fact issue that is established with uncontroverted evidence and is not in dispute should not be submitted to the jury. ***T.O. Stanley Boot Co. v. Bank of El Paso***, 847 S.W.2d 218, 223 (Tex.1992).

2. Supported by pleadings & evidence. The litigants are entitled to have controlling issues submitted to the jury if they are properly pleaded and supported by the evidence. TRCP 278; ***Union Pac. R.R. v. Williams***, 85 S.W.2d 162, 166 (Tex.2002); ***Triplex Comm. v. Riley***, 900 S.W.2d 716, 718 (Tex.1995); ***Samedan Oil Corp. v. Intrastate Gas Gathering***, 78 S.W.3d 425, 446 (Tex.App.—Tyler 2001, pet. granted w.r.m.). For evidence to support the submission, see "Questions," §8.3, p. 576.

3. Form of requests. The draft of the charge must be in writing. TRCP 272; ***Woods v. Crane Carrier Co.***, 693 S.W.2d 377, 379 (Tex.1985). The written request must be separate from the oral objections. TRCP 273; ***Alaniz v. Jones & Neuse, Inc.***, 907 S.W.2d 450, 451 (Tex.1995).

§2.3 Cluster of related requests. The parties should submit the proposed charge in clusters of related requests. Each cluster should include the name of the party submitting the request and a space for the judge's ruling and signature and the date. By organizing the requests in clusters of related questions, instructions, and definitions, the request will preserve error if the trial court does not submit all or part of the request. *See, e.g.*, ***Lester v. Logan***, 907 S.W.2d 452, 453 (Tex.1995) (disapproved of court of appeals' opinion that held request on one piece of paper that included 5 related matters—1 question, 2 instructions, and 2 definitions—was improper); ***Aetna Cas. & Sur. Co. v. Moore***, 361 S.W.2d 183, 187 (Tex.1962) (request for question as part of series of 9 related questions was proper and did not mislead or confuse trial court). A single request with a large number of questions, instructions, and definitions is as weak as its most vulnerable part; when a request includes an objectionable question, instruction, or definition, the court can deny the entire request. *See* ***Tempo Tamers v. Crow-Houston Four, Ltd.***, 715 S.W.2d 658, 666-67 (Tex.App.—Dallas 1986, writ ref'd n.r.e.) (20 questions in a single request); ***Hoover v. Barker***, 507 S.W.2d 299, 305 (Tex.App.—Austin 1974, writ ref'd n.r.e.) (54 questions in a single request).

1. Each cluster must be complete. All the elements—questions, instructions, definitions—necessary for each cluster must be included in that cluster. *See, e.g.*, ***Owens-Corning Fiberglas Corp. v. Keeton***, 922 S.W.2d 658, 662 (Tex.App.—Austin 1996, writ denied) (failure to submit proper instructions with broad-form question waived error); *see also* TRCP 279 (omissions from the charge). When a request contains a word or phrase that requires an instruction or definition, the appropriate instruction or definition must be included as part of the request. *See, e.g.*, ***Select Ins. Co. v. Boucher***, 561 S.W.2d 474, 479-80 (Tex.1978) (requested instruction on partial incapacity did not include definition of "earning capacity"); ***Griffin v. Eakin***, 656 S.W.2d 187, 189-90 (Tex.App.—Austin 1983, writ ref'd n.r.e.) (request contained reference to "negligence, as that term is defined herein," but did not include definition of negligence). A party cannot complain on appeal if the trial court did not submit an instruction or definition with one cluster when it was not requested as part of that cluster but as part of another cluster. *See* ***Universal Servs. Co. v. Ung***, 904 S.W.2d 638, 640 (Tex.1995).

2. Each request in cluster must be correct. The party must tender the requests in "substantially correct wording." TRCP 278; ***Willis v. Maverick***, 760 S.W.2d 642, 647 (Tex.1988); ***Harris Cty. Flood Control Dist. v. Glenbrook Patiohome Owners Ass'n***, 933 S.W.2d 570, 580 (Tex.App.—Houston [1st Dist.] 1996, writ denied). If any part of the cluster is defective, the entire request is not "substantially correct." The trial court may refuse the whole request if it finds any part of the request defective. *See* ***Willis***, 760 S.W.2d at 647 (question was not substantially correct because phrase "should have discovered" was omitted); ***Greenstein, Logan & Co. v. Burgess Mktg.***, 744 S.W.2d 170, 182 (Tex.App.—Waco 1987, writ denied) (request did not place burden of proof). There is no clear-cut rule to determine when a request meets the "substantially correct" standard. As long as a request falls somewhere between absolutely correct and affirmatively incorrect, it should be sufficient. *See* ***Southwestern Bell Tel. Co. v. John Carlo Tex., Inc.***, 843 S.W.2d 470, 472 (Tex.1992) (although definition was not exactly correct, it was substantially correct); ***Exxon Corp. v. Perez***, 842 S.W.2d 629, 630 n.1 (Tex.1992) (question was not affirmatively incorrect); ***Placencio v. Allied Indus. Int'l***, 724 S.W.2d 20, 22 (Tex.1987) (question was "affirmatively incorrect" because it was not conditioned on the affirmative answer to another question).

§2.4 Proper burden of persuasion. The party must tender each question with the proper placement of the burden of persuasion. ***TEIA v. Olivarez***, 694 S.W.2d 92, 93-94 (Tex.App.—San Antonio 1985, no writ). Generally, to place the burden of persuasion properly, the question should be asked so the party with the burden will benefit from an affirmative answer. ***Turk v. Robles***, 810 S.W.2d 755, 759 (Tex.App.—Houston [1st Dist.] 1991, writ denied). In cases where a party must prove a negative, it is sometimes difficult to determine who has the burden of persuasion and how to word the question so as not to confuse the jury. *See id.* (instruction on testamentary capacity to revoke will). If in doubt about who has the burden of persuasion on a question, include instructions for the jury to answer the question with a complete statement, not just a yes or no. *See* ***Walker v. Eason***, 643 S.W.2d 390, 391 (Tex.1982). For example, when a jury is required to fill in the blank with either "She did have sufficient mental capacity" or "She did not have sufficient mental capacity," any error in misplacing the burden is harmless. *Id.* In cases submitted with broad-form questions, it is sometimes impossible to determine which party has the burden for each part of the charge. ***State Dept. of Highways & Pub. Transp. v. Payne***, 838 S.W.2d 235, 240 (Tex.1992).

§2.5 Proper condition. When the answer to a follow-up question is conditioned on the jury's answer to an earlier question, the follow-up question must be preceded by an instruction telling the jury to answer the next question only if it responds in a certain way to the earlier question. ("If you have answered 'Yes' to Question 3, then answer Question 4; otherwise, do not answer Question 4.") A request for a jury question is not correct if it conditions a question on the wrong question. If a party does not object to an erroneous conditional submission, the party waives the error. ***Wilgus v. Bond***, 730 S.W.2d 670, 672 (Tex.1987); ***Matthews v. Candlewood Builders***, 685 S.W.2d 649, 650 (Tex.1985). If an erroneous conditional submission deprives a party of the submission of an issue raised by the pleadings and evidence, it constitutes reversible error. ***Varme v. Gordon***, 881 S.W.2d 877, 881 (Tex. App.—Houston [14th Dist.] 1994, writ denied); *see, e.g.*, ***Washington v. Reliable Life Ins. Co.***, 581 S.W.2d 153, 160 (Tex.1979) (remanded for new trial because conditioned question was not reached); ***Byrne v. Harris Adacom Network Servs.***, 11 S.W.3d 244, 248-49 (Tex.App.—Texarkana 1999, pet. denied) (improper conditioning was harmless error); ***Owens-Corning Fiberglas Corp. v. Martin***, 942 S.W.2d 712, 723 (Tex.App.—Dallas 1997, no writ) (same). The submission of a conditional damage question is expressly permitted by TRCP 277, even though it incidentally informs the jury of the legal effect of its answers. ***H.E. Butt Grocery Co. v. Bilotto***, 985 S.W.2d 22, 24 (Tex.1998).

§2.6 Proper damage questions. The damage questions must be submitted so they reflect the following:

1. Proper measure. The party must tender a damage question that asks the jury to consider the correct legal measure of damages. ***Jackson v. Fontaine's Clinics***, 499 S.W.2d 87, 90 (Tex.1973); ***Browning Oil Co. v. Luecke***, 38 S.W.3d 625, 642-43 (Tex.App.—Austin 2000, pet. denied). A jury question that does not guide the jury to a finding on any proper legal measure of damages is fatally defective. ***Jackson***, 499 S.W.2d at 90; ***Samedan Oil Corp.***, 78 S.W.3d at 452.

2. Proper segregation. The party must tender damage questions that properly segregate the damages due to each plaintiff, due from each defendant, and due on each individual claim. *See, e.g.*, ***Minnesota Mining & Mfg. Co. v. Nishika, Ltd.***, 953 S.W.2d 733, 739 (Tex.1997) (damages were not segregated between Ps); ***Green Int'l v. Solis***, 951 S.W.2d 384, 389-90 (Tex.1997) (attorney fees were not segregated according to claims); ***Wingate v. Hajdik***, 795 S.W.2d 717, 719-20 (Tex.1990) (damages were not segregated between those due to corporation & those due to stockholder). Unless the injury is indivisible, the party must tender damage questions that segregate the damages between multiple parties. ***Stewart & Stevenson Servs. v. Serv-Tech, Inc.***, 879 S.W.2d 89, 101 (Tex. App.—Houston [14th Dist.] 1994, writ denied).

3. Proper tie. The party must tender the damage question that properly ties to the liability question. *See* ***Wilgus***, 730 S.W.2d at 672 (damage claims were not properly related to the theories of recovery).

4. Alternative theories of damages. A party is entitled to seek damages on alternative theories of liability. ***Waite Hill Servs. v. World Class Metal Works***, 959 S.W.2d 182, 184 (Tex.1998). Once the jury's verdict is in, the plaintiff must elect its remedy. ***Waite Hill***, 959 S.W.2d at 184-85; ***Birchfield v. Texarkana Mem'l Hosp.***, 747 S.W.2d 361, 367 (Tex.1987).

§3. INFORMAL CHARGE CONFERENCE

The informal charge conference is held whenever the local rules provide or the judge prefers. Normally, the judge calls a recess after both sides close, and the attorneys meet with the judge in chambers to assemble the charge.

§3.1 Deadline for requests. Each party must submit its requested questions, instructions, and definitions to the court by whatever deadline the court imposes. Under TRCP 166(k), the court can require the parties to submit the requests at or before the pretrial conference. Local rules often require the attorneys to submit their requests before trial.

§3.2 Proposed charge. The court compiles the proposed charge during the informal charge conference by assembling questions, instructions, and definitions from those the attorneys provide and making any changes it believes necessary. The court then gives the proposed charge to the attorneys to examine.

§3.3 Time to examine. The trial court must allow the parties a reasonable amount of time to examine the proposed charge. TRCP 272. The court has the discretion to determine how much time to give the parties to examine the charge. *E.g.*, ***Bekins Moving & Storage Co. v. Williams***, 947 S.W.2d 568, 575 (Tex.App.—Texarkana 1997, no writ) (32 minutes to review 51-page charge was reasonable; charge was largely in same form as before charge conference). If the trial court refuses to allow reasonable time to examine the charge, a party must make an objection on the record to preserve error. The objection must state the following: (1) that the party was not given adequate time to examine the charge, (2) how much time was given, (3) how much time was necessary, (4) that the charge was too complex and lengthy to examine in the amount of time given, and (5) that the lack of adequate time to examine the charge caused harm because the party was not able to make a proper record for appeal. *See* ***Dillard v. Dillard***, 341 S.W.2d 668, 675 (Tex.App.—Austin 1960, writ ref'd n.r.e.) (although 15 minutes was not enough time to examine the charge, appellant did not show harm). The evidence of the harm can be included in a bill of exceptions if any error is discovered later, after a closer examination of the charge. See "Offer of Proof & Bill of Exceptions," ch. 8-E, p. 553.

§4. FORMAL CHARGE CONFERENCE

After the informal charge conference, the trial court will hold a formal charge conference with a court reporter present to record the parties' comments on the charge. The parties must make all their objections to the charge, present any requests for additional questions and instructions, and get rulings on all objections and requests.

CAUTION

At the formal charge conference, you must make a record of all the objections, requests for questions, instructions, and definitions that you have to the proposed charge, even if you discussed the same requests at the informal charge conference. To preserve the objections and requests you made during the informal charge conference, restate the objections on the record, have the court overrule them orally, and ask the court to mark your written requests "refused" and sign them. See ***Alaniz v. Jones & Neuse, Inc.****, 907 S.W.2d 450, 451 (Tex.1995).*

§4.1 Challenging charge. To preserve error in the charge, the party must make objections to defective submissions in the court's charge or submit written requests for additional questions, definitions, or instructions that are omitted from the charge. Under the rules relating to the charge, objections and requests are not interchangeable. *See* TRCP 273. An objection to the charge can be made orally or in writing and must be specific. A request is a written question, definition, or instruction, submitted in substantially correct form.

For years, the Supreme Court strictly applied the rules for challenging the charge. However, in ***State Dept. of Highways & Pub. Transp. v. Payne***, 838 S.W.2d 235, 241 (Tex.1992), the Court liberalized the procedure for objecting to the charge. The Court said there should be only one test to determine whether a party has preserved error in the jury charge: Did the party make the trial court "aware of the complaint, timely and plainly," and obtain a ruling? *Id.*; *see also* ***Galveston Cty. Fair & Rodeo v. Glover***, 940 S.W.2d 585, 586 (Tex.1996) (complaint preserved although party did not separately request in writing any definitions or instructions); ***Alaniz***, 907 S.W.2d at 451 (party preserved complaint even though request was not separate from completed charge).

PRACTICE TIP

When you are making your objections and requests, obey the old rules, which are set out below. When you are appealing and are worried you did not preserve error for appeal, use the test from ***Payne****.*

1. When to object – defects in charge. Object, no matter who has the burden of proof, when the court submits an erroneous or defective question, instruction, or definition. ***St. Joseph Hosp. v. Wolff***, 94 S.W.3d 513, 525 (Tex.2002) (erroneous definition); ***Spencer v. Eagle Star Ins. Co.***, 876 S.W.2d 154, 157 (Tex.1994) (defective instruction); ***Religious of the Sacred Heart v. City of Houston***, 836 S.W.2d 606, 613-14 (Tex.1992) (defective question). *But see* ***Payne***, 838 S.W.2d at 241 (request for a question preserved error in defective instruction); ***Matthiessen v. Schaefer***, 900 S.W.2d 792, 797 (Tex.App.—San Antonio 1995, writ denied) (request for a question preserved error in defective question).

2. When to request – omission in charge.

(1) Court omits question. A party must submit a request when it has the burden of proof and the court omits a question. ***W.O. Bankston Nissan v. Walters***, 754 S.W.2d 127, 128 (Tex.1988); ***Wright Way Constr. Co. v. Harlingen Mall Co.***, 799 S.W.2d 415, 419 (Tex.App.—Corpus Christi 1990, writ denied). In ***Alaniz***, the court held that when a party submits a written request before trial, if the court omits part of it from the charge, the party can preserve error merely by objecting and identifying the portion of its written request that the court omitted. ***Alaniz***, 907 S.W.2d at 451. The party should probably locate its copy of the written request and ask the court to include it in the charge or write "refused" on it. *See* ***Munoz v. Berne Group***, 919 S.W.2d 470, 472 (Tex.App.—San Antonio 1996, no writ).

(2) Court omits any party's definition or instruction. A party must make a written request, no matter who has the burden of proof, when the court omits an instruction or definition. TRCP 274, 278; ***Jarrin v. Sam White Oldsmobile Co.***, 929 S.W.2d 21, 25 (Tex.App.—Houston [1st Dist.] 1996, writ denied). A party cannot dictate a requested instruction into the record. ***Fairfield Estates L.P. v. Griffin***, 986 S.W.2d 719, 724 (Tex.App.—Eastland 1999, no pet.); ***Jarrin***, 929 S.W.2d at 25; ***Hartnett v. Hampton Inns***, 870 S.W.2d 162, 165 (Tex.App.—San Antonio 1993, writ denied).

3. When to either object or request.

PRACTICE TIP

It may seem odd to object to errors made by the other party in its jury questions, but if you don't, you may be bound by adverse express findings. See "Incomplete claim or defense submitted," §9.2, p. 577.

(1) Court omits opponent's question. A party may object or submit a request when its opponent has the burden of proof and the court omits part of the opponent's cause or defense. *See, e.g.*, ***Payne***, 838 S.W.2d at 239 (state preserved error by submitting the missing element of a question, even though it did not have the burden of proof); ***Religious of the Sacred Heart***, 836 S.W.2d at 613-14 (city preserved error by objecting to the omission of a proper damage question, on which P had burden); ***Ramos v. Frito-Lay***, 784 S.W.2d 667, 668 (Tex.1990) (D should have objected when court did not submit element of P's cause of action).

(2) Court places erroneous burden of persuasion. A party may object to a question or submit a request when the court improperly places the burden of persuasion. *See* ***Morris v. Holt***, 714 S.W.2d 311, 312-13 (Tex.1986) (preserved by request); ***Turk v. Robles***, 810 S.W.2d 755, 759 (Tex.App.—Houston [1st Dist.] 1991, writ denied) (preserved by objection).

4. Short-hand rule to challenge charge. Challenging the charge is confusing. When in doubt as to whether to object or request, a party should always object. If a party has the burden of proof on a question, it should also (not instead) submit a request. If a definition or instruction is omitted, the party should object and make a request, no matter who has the burden. Finally, the party should analyze its objections and requests in light of ***Payne***: Did the party make the trial court "aware of the complaint, timely and plainly," and obtain a ruling? ***Payne***, 838 S.W.2d at 241.

§4.2 Deadline to object & request.

1. The charge. The parties must make all objections and requests to amend the language of the charge before the court reads the charge to the jury. TRCP 272; ***Missouri Pac. R.R. v. Cross***, 501 S.W.2d 868, 873 (Tex.1973). The parties will waive any objections to errors in the charge that are made after the jury retires. TRCP 272; ***Cross***, 501 S.W.2d at 873. A party cannot preserve error by a late objection, even if the trial court permits it and the other party agrees. ***Cross***, 501 S.W.2d at 873; ***Sudderth v. Howard***, 560 S.W.2d 511, 516 (Tex.App.—Amarillo 1977, writ ref'd n.r.e.).

PRACTICE TIP

The only objection to the charge that is not necessary to make before the charge is submitted is an objection to the legal sufficiency of evidence to support the submission of a claim or defense. A legal sufficiency challenge can be made for the first time in a motion for JNOV or in a motion for new trial. See "Preserving legal sufficiency point," ch. 10-B, §9.1.3, p. 623.

2. Supplemental instructions. The trial court may, on its own motion or at the request of the parties or the jury, give the jury additional instructions after it has retired to deliberate. TRCP 285, 286. The parties must make any objections or requests to the supplemental charge before the court reads the supplemental charge to the jury.

3. Presumption of timeliness. On appeal, the court will presume the parties objected timely, unless the record shows otherwise. TRCP 272; ***Acord v. G.M. Corp.***, 669 S.W.2d 111, 114 (Tex.1984) (court's statement of "overruled" following objections of both parties was held to be a timely ruling on P's objections). If the record shows that a party did not object timely, the party waives error. ***Morales v. Morales***, 98 S.W.3d 343, 346 (Tex. App.—Corpus Christi 2003, pet. denied); ***Ruff v. Christian Servs.***, 627 S.W.2d 799, 801 (Tex.App.—Tyler 1982, no writ).

§5. MAKING FORMAL REQUEST FOR ADDITIONS TO CHARGE

§5.1 In writing. Once the court submits the proposed charge to the parties at the formal charge conference, if either party wants the court to include any additional questions, definitions, or instructions, the party must tender the additional request in writing or object to the omission of a written request that was made at the informal charge conference. ***Alaniz v. Jones & Neuse, Inc.***, 907 S.W.2d 450, 451 (Tex.1995) (objection at formal charge conference to exclusion of request offered before informal charge conference preserved error).

§5.2 Separate from objections. A party must tender the requests separate and apart from the objections. TRCP 273, 278; ***Woods v. Crane Carrier Co.***, 693 S.W.2d 377, 379 (Tex.1985); ***TEIA v. Eskue***, 574 S.W.2d 814, 818 (Tex.App.—El Paso 1978, no writ).

§6. MAKING FORMAL OBJECTIONS TO CHARGE

§6.1 Orally or in writing. A party may object to the charge orally by dictating objections to the court reporter or in writing. TRCP 272. At the formal charge conference, the parties will probably dictate the objections to the court reporter. The objections must be made in the presence of the trial judge, opposing counsel, and the court reporter. ***Brantley v. Sprague***, 636 S.W.2d 224, 225 (Tex.App.—Texarkana 1982, writ ref'd n.r.e.). If the trial judge is not present, the objections are waived. *Id.*

§6.2 Specific objections. A party must make specific objections to the charge. TRCP 274; *see* TRAP 33.1(a)(1)(A). The objection must clearly identify the error and explain the grounds for the complaint. TRCP 274; ***Castleberry v. Branscum***, 721 S.W.2d 270, 276 (Tex.1986); ***Brown v. American Transfer & Storage Co.***, 601 S.W.2d 931, 938 (Tex.1980). If the objection does not meet both requirements, it will not preserve error. ***Castleberry***, 721 S.W.2d at 276. A specific objection enables the trial court to understand the precise grounds and make an informed ruling. *Id.* It also affords the trial court an opportunity to remedy the defect. *Id.* An objection is properly specific if it gives the trial court a fair opportunity to correct the error or deficiency. ***Osteen v. Crumpton***, 519 S.W.2d 263, 264 (Tex.App.—Dallas 1975, writ ref'd). If a general objection is paired with a written request that clearly reflects the error, the objection will be preserved. ***Universal Underwriters Ins. Co. v. Pierce***, 795 S.W.2d 771, 773 (Tex.App.—Houston [1st Dist.] 1990, no writ).

PRACTICE TIP

When you object: (1) identify the defect; (2) specify how the question, definition, or instruction is defective; (3) state why it is defective; and (4) state the exact correction you wish the court to make.

§6.3 Obscured by other objections. A party should not obscure a correct objection among voluminous, unfounded, and stock objections. TRCP 274; ***Monsanto Co. v. Milam***, 494 S.W.2d 534, 536 (Tex.1973). There is no rule of thumb for when an objection has been "obscured." Generally, it is not the number of objections, but the use of repetitious or "stock" objections, that obscures a valid complaint. *See, e.g.*, ***Monsanto Co.***, 494 S.W.2d at 536-37 (42 pages of stock objections concealed valid objection); ***Hinote v. Oil, Chem. & Atomic Workers Int'l Un.***, 777 S.W.2d 134, 143-45 (Tex.App.—Houston [14th Dist.] 1989, writ denied) (30 pages of invalid & stock objections concealed valid objection); ***Baker Material Handling Corp. v. Cummings***, 692 S.W.2d 142, 145-46 (Tex.App.—Dallas 1985) (17 objections did not obscure valid objection because there were no stock objections), *writ dism'd*, 713 S.W.2d. 96 (Tex.1986).

§6.4 No adoption by reference. A party cannot adopt an objection from one question or instruction and apply it by reference to other questions or objections; TRCP 274 specifically prohibits this practice. ***Samedan Oil Corp. v. Intrastate Gas Gathering***, 78 S.W.3d 425, 452 (Tex.App.—Tyler 2001, pet. granted w.r.m.); ***Robinson Drilling Co. v. Thomas***, 385 S.W.2d 725, 728 (Tex.App.—Eastland 1964, no writ). A party cannot adopt another party's objections; each party must state its own objections to the charge. ***Wright Way Constr. Co. v. Harlingen Mall Co.***, 799 S.W.2d 415, 420-21 (Tex.App.—Corpus Christi 1990, writ denied). However, the trial court in its discretion may permit joint objections to save time. *See* ***Owens-Corning Fiberglas Corp. v. Malone***, 916 S.W.2d 551, 556 (Tex.App.—Houston [1st Dist.] 1996), *aff'd*, 972 S.W.2d 35 (Tex.1998).

§6.5 Good objections. A valid objection is one that is appropriate to the charge in the case. The following are some good objections, if relevant to the case. Each of the statements below should be preceded with the statement "the party objects because."

1. The charge submits an issue established as a matter of law. It is not necessary to submit [*identify issue*] to the jury because it was judicially admitted in the other party's pleadings. Once a fact is conclusively established by judicial admission, a jury question concerning the fact should not be submitted. ***Horizon v. Auld***, 34 S.W.3d 887, 905 (Tex.2000).

2. The charge omits an element from the cause of action [*or defense*], in that the element of [*identify the missing element*] is required to be submitted. [*Submit a written request for the missing element.*]

3. Because there is no evidence to support the submission of question number ___, that question should not be submitted to the jury.

4. Because there is no evidence to support the submission of [*identify element in broad-form submission that has no support*], the court should either submit individual questions for each element in the broad-form question or delete that element from the broad-form question. See "Broad form not required," §2.1.2, p. 566.

5. The only evidence to support the submission of question number ___ is circumstantial evidence, and, because the evidence is equally consistent with either of two facts, neither fact can be inferred, and the issue cannot be submitted to the jury. See "Circumstantial evidence," §8.3.2, p. 577.

6. Question number ___, which inquires about ___ cause of action, is improper because there are no pleadings to support its submission, and the issue was not tried by consent. [*Identify the variance between the pleading and the proof.*] See "Amendment to add allegations," ch. 8-F, §5.2, p. 557.

7. Question number ___ is not conditioned [*or is improperly conditioned*] on an affirmative answer to question ___.

8. Question number ___ should not be submitted to the jury because it is not a controlling question. [*State reason*].

9. Question number ___ is immaterial to the outcome of the case. *See* ***Oliver v. Oliver***, 889 S.W.2d 271, 273-74 (Tex.1994) (because court disregarded immaterial question without proper objection, uncertain if objection necessary to preserve error).

10. The charge does not contain an instruction [*or definition*] necessary to the submission of the question of ___, which is [*state the instruction or definition*]. [*Submit a written request for the omitted instruction or definition.*]

11. Question number ___ duplicates question number ___.

12. Question number ___ does not properly place the burden of persuasion because [*state the reason*].

13. The following language in question number ___ [*or instruction or definition*], [*quote the language*], is a comment on the weight of the evidence because it suggests the trial court's opinion that [*state exactly why it is*

a comment on the evidence]. TRCP 277; ***Alvarez v. Missouri, K. T. R.R.***, 683 S.W.2d 375, 377 (Tex.1984); ***Garza v. Southland Corp.***, 836 S.W.2d 214, 220 (Tex.App.—Houston [14th Dist.] 1992, no writ).

14. Question number ___ presents an inferential rebuttal defense. TRCP 277. An inferential rebuttal issue is permitted only as an instruction. *Id.* [*Submit the inferential rebuttal instruction.*]

15. The instruction regarding ___ should not be included because (1) the other party did not plead it, (2) the case was not tried on that theory, and (3) the jury questions do not rely on it. ***Texas Workers' Comp. Ins. Fund v. Mandlbauer***, 34 S.W.3d 909, 912 (Tex.2000).

16. The instruction regarding ___ is defective because [*state why*].

17. Definition number ___ is an improper statement of the law in that [*state why*]. *See* ***St. Joseph Hosp. v. Wolff***, 94 S.W.3d 513, 529 (Tex.2002).

18. The instruction regarding ___ is unnecessary, and even though it is a correct statement of the law, it amounts to a comment on the weight of the evidence that tilts or nudges the jury by [*state exactly how and why it nudges the jury*]. ***Wal-Mart Stores v. Johnson***, 106 S.W.3d 718, 723-24 (Tex.2003); ***Lone Star Gas Co. v. Lemond***, 897 S.W.2d 755, 756 (Tex.1995); ***Lemos v. Montez***, 680 S.W.2d 798, 801 (Tex.1984). The more closely contested the case, the greater the chance that a superfluous instruction is error. ***Johnson***, 106 S.W.3d at 724; *see* ***Timberwalk Apts. v. Cain***, 972 S.W.2d 749, 756 n.25 (Tex.1998); ***Ford Motor Co. v. Miles***, 967 S.W.2d 377, 387 (Tex.1998).

19. The charge, which is based on a statutory cause of action, does not track the language of the statute. *See* ***Borneman v. Steak & Ale***, 22 S.W.3d 411, 413 (Tex.2000).

20. The damage question is not properly related to the cause of action to which it must be tied. Question ___ must be tied to question ___. See "Proper tie," §2.6.3, p. 569.

21. The causes of action have different types of damages [*or the damages are owed to different plaintiffs*], and the damages must be segregated. Question ___ must be tied to question ___; and question ___ must be tied to question ___.

22. Question number ___ on attorney fees does not segregate the reasonable and necessary attorney fees incurred for prosecuting the causes of action on which attorney fees are recoverable from the causes of action on which no attorney fees may be recovered. Or, the question does not segregate the reasonable and necessary attorney fees incurred for prosecuting the cause of action against this party from the other parties. See "Proper segregation," §2.6.2, p. 569.

§6.6 Meritless objections. The following are not good objections in any case.

1. There is factually insufficient evidence to support the submission of question number ___; or, question number ___ is against the great weight of the evidence. A lawyer should never object that the question should not be submitted because the evidence is "factually insufficient" or "against the great weight and preponderance" of the evidence. Such complaints are totally without merit at the charge conference. ***Long Island Owner's Ass'n v. Davidson***, 965 S.W.2d 674, 680 (Tex.App.—Corpus Christi 1998, pet. denied); ***Hinote v. Oil, Chem. & Atomic Workers Int'l Un.***, 777 S.W.2d 134, 143 (Tex.App.—Houston [14th Dist.] 1989, writ denied). The trial court determines whether to submit a question to the jury on "no evidence" grounds, not on factual sufficiency grounds. The court has a duty to submit the question if there is any probative evidence to support it. ***American Home Assur. Co. v. Brandt***, 778 S.W.2d 141, 144 (Tex.App.—Texarkana 1989, writ denied). When a party makes factual sufficiency objections to the charge, it undermines the party's valid objections to the charge and the lawyer's credibility with the court. ***Hinote***, 777 S.W.2d at 143.

2. Question number ___ is unsupported by the pleadings. If there is a variance between the pleading and the proof, the party must identify the variance in the objection. ***Brown v. American Transfer & Storage Co.***,

601 S.W.2d 931, 938 (Tex.1980); ***Ron Craft Chevrolet v. Davis***, 836 S.W.2d 672, 675 (Tex.App.—El Paso 1992, writ denied).

3. Question number ___ "should read" a particular way. The objection is not proper because it does not identify the error. ***Garza***, 836 S.W.2d at 218.

4. Question number ___ could not form "a basis of liability" or "the basis of any judgment." Such objections do not call to the court's attention the failure of the charge to submit a proper question. ***Anderson v. Broome***, 233 S.W.2d 901, 904 (Tex.App.—El Paso 1950, writ ref'd n.r.e.).

5. The instruction on ___ "may confuse the jury" or "prejudice the defendant." Such complaints are too general because they do not explain how the instruction would confuse the jury or how it would prejudice the defendant. ***Castleberry v. Branscum***, 721 S.W.2d 270, 277 (Tex.1986).

6. The charge contains two (or more) theories of damages, and will give the plaintiff a double recovery. Because a party is entitled to seek damages on alternative theories, this is not a valid objection. See "Alternative theories of damages," §2.6.4, p. 569.

§7. COURT'S RULINGS ON REQUESTS & OBJECTIONS

§7.1 Deadline for rulings. The court should announce its ruling on the requests and objections before it reads the charge to the jury. TRCP 272. The trial court's rulings on the objections should appear in the record. ***Reliance Ins. Co. v. Dahlstrom Corp.***, 568 S.W.2d 733, 734 (Tex.App.—Eastland 1978, writ ref'd n.r.e.). However, if the court submits proposed questions or instructions over objections without a ruling, the court implicitly overrules the objections. ***Acord v. G.M. Corp.***, 669 S.W.2d 111, 114 (Tex.1984); *see also* TRAP 33.1(a)(2)(A) (the trial court can make ruling on request or objection either expressly or implicitly). For the rule in ***Acord*** to apply, the record must show the court in some manner acknowledged receiving the requested questions. ***Anderson v. Vinson Expl.***, 832 S.W.2d 657, 668 (Tex.App.—El Paso 1992, no writ).

PRACTICE TIP

If the court overruled your requested questions, instructions, or definitions at the charge conference, but the record from the charge conference does not clearly show it, while the trial court still has plenary power, you may ask the court to sign an order reflecting its rulings and stating they were made before the charge was submitted to the jury.

---

§7.2 Method of ruling.

1. **Oral rulings.** If the objections are dictated into the record, the court should state its ruling on the objections immediately after each party makes its objections. TRCP 272, 276. On appeal, the trial court's ruling can be inferred from the record. For example, if a party makes an objection, and the trial court makes no change in the charge, the objection is overruled. ***Acord***, 669 S.W.2d at 114; *see* TRAP 33.1(a)(2)(A). If a "common sense reading of the objection and the court's ruling" shows that the trial court necessarily overruled the objection, the appellate courts will hold that the objection was overruled. ***Betty Leavell Rlty. Co. v. Raggio***, 669 S.W.2d 102, 104 (Tex.1984).

2. **Written rulings.** When the court refuses or modifies a request, it should endorse the request as either "refused" or "modified" and sign it. TRCP 272, 276. When the court endorses "modified" on a request, the judge should also state how it has been modified. TRCP 276. If the court does not indicate its ruling on the request, the request does not preserve error. ***Munoz v. Berne Group***, 919 S.W.2d 470, 472 (Tex.App.—San Antonio 1996, no writ); ***Anderson***, 832 S.W.2d at 667. If, however, the record clearly shows the request was refused, even if the trial court did not sign the refused instruction as required by TRCP 276, the error is preserved. *See* TRAP 33.1(a)(2)(A);

Dallas Mkt. Ctr. Dev. Co. v. Liedeker, 958 S.W.2d 382, 386 (Tex.1997), *overruled on other grounds*, ***Torrington Co. v. Stutzman***, 46 S.W.3d 829 (Tex.2000); ***F.S. New Prods. v. Strong Indus.***, ___ S.W.3d ___ (Tex.App.—Houston [1st Dist.] 2003, n.p.h.) (No. 01-01-00086-CV; 9-11-03); ***Chemical Express Carriers v. Pina***, 819 S.W.2d 585, 589 (Tex.App.—El Paso 1991, writ denied). When there are several pages of requests, the record must show that the court endorsed and signed the requests, either separately or as a group; otherwise, the requests will not preserve error. ***Greenstein, Logan & Co. v. Burgess Mktg.***, 744 S.W.2d 170, 181 (Tex.App.—Waco 1987, writ denied).

§8. CHARGE SUBMITTED TO JURY

The trial court is required to read the charge to the jury before the lawyers make their final argument. TRCP 275.

§8.1 Instructions. TRCP 226a prescribes the admonitory instructions the court must give the jury, both oral and written. After the admonitory instructions, the court should give the special instructions for the case. TRCP 277 requires the trial court to submit such explanatory instructions as are necessary to enable the jury to reach a verdict. ***Wichita Cty. v. Hart***, 917 S.W.2d 779, 783-84 (Tex.1996); ***Exxon Pipeline Co. v. Zwahr***, 35 S.W.3d 705, 714 (Tex.App.—Houston [1st Dist.] 2000), *rev'd on other grounds*, 88 S.W.3d 623 (Tex.2002). Trial courts have considerable discretion in deciding what instructions are necessary. ***State Farm Lloyds v. Nicolau***, 951 S.W.2d 444, 451 (Tex.1997); ***Mobil Chem. Co. v. Bell***, 517 S.W.2d 245, 256 (Tex.1974).

1. Misstatement of law. An instruction that misstates the law as applied to the facts of the case is reversible error. ***Wakefield v. Bevly***, 704 S.W.2d 339, 350 (Tex.App.—Corpus Christi 1985, no writ).

2. Improper burden of proof. An instruction that imposes a greater burden than the law requires is reversible error. ***American Home Assur. Co. v. Brandt***, 778 S.W.2d 141, 143 (Tex.App.—Texarkana 1989, writ denied); *see* ***Marathon Oil Co. v. Salazar***, 682 S.W.2d 624, 628 (Tex.App.—Houston [1st Dist.] 1984, writ ref'd n.r.e.) (misstatement of probable cause).

§8.2 Definitions. A definition defines a term used in the charge. The purpose of definitions is to enable jurors to understand legal words or phrases so that they may properly answer the jury questions and render a verdict. ***Oadra v. Stegall***, 871 S.W.2d 882, 890 (Tex.App.—Houston [14th Dist.] 1994, no writ). Only legal or technical terms need to be defined. *E.g.*, ***Whiteside v. Watson***, 12 S.W.3d 614, 624 (Tex.App.—Eastland 2000, pet. denied) ("earning capacity" & "physical impairment" have specific legal definitions); ***Allen v. Allen***, 966 S.W.2d 658, 660 (Tex.App.—San Antonio 1998, pet. denied) ("cohabitation" did not need to be defined); ***Turner v. Roadway Express***, 911 S.W.2d 224, 227 (Tex.App.—Fort Worth 1995, writ denied) ("recklessly" did not need to be defined). TRCP 277 requires the trial court to submit such definitions as are necessary to enable the jury to reach a verdict. ***St. James Transp. Co. v. Porter***, 840 S.W.2d 658, 664 (Tex.App.—Houston [1st Dist.] 1992, writ denied); ***Lumbermens v. Mut. Cas. Co. v. Garcia***, 758 S.W.2d 893, 894 (Tex.App.—Corpus Christi 1988, writ denied). The sufficiency of the explanations is left to the discretion of the trial court. ***Porter***, 840 S.W.2d at 664; *see also* ***Mobil Chem. Co.***, 517 S.W.2d at 256 (trial court has considerable discretion in deciding what instructions are necessary and proper for submission to jury). If a term is used more than once in the charge, and the term requires a definition, the definition should follow the general instructions. ***Woods v. Crane Carrier Co.***, 693 S.W.2d 377, 379 (Tex.1985).

§8.3 Questions. TRCP 278 requires the trial court to submit a requested question to the jury if the pleadings and any evidence support it. ***Elbaor v. Smith***, 845 S.W.2d 240, 243 (Tex.1992); ***Komet v. Graves***, 40 S.W.3d 596, 603 (Tex.App.—San Antonio 2001, no pet.). The court can refuse to submit a question if (1) there is no evidence, (2) there are no pleadings, or (3) the issue is uncontroverted. *See* ***Alaniz v. Jones & Neuse, Inc.***, 907 S.W.2d 450, 452 (Tex.1995) (no pleadings or evidence for lost future profits); ***T.O. Stanley Boot Co. v. Bank of El Paso***, 847 S.W.2d 218, 222-23 (Tex.1992) (no evidence of intention not to perform; uncontroverted evidence on amount of notes).

1. Direct evidence. When a material fact is supported by direct evidence, the issue must be submitted to the jury. ***Farley v. M M Cattle Co.***, 529 S.W.2d 751, 754 (Tex.1975).

2. **Circumstantial evidence.** When a material fact is supported by circumstantial evidence, the issue may be submitted to the jury if the material fact can be reasonably inferred from the facts proved. ***Russell v. Russell***, 865 S.W.2d 929, 933 (Tex.1993). When circumstantial evidence supports more than one reasonable inference, it is for the jury to decide which inference is more reasonable, subject only to review to assure the evidence is factually sufficient. ***Lozano v. Lozano***, 52 S.W.3d 141, 148 (Tex.2001). The jury has the power to choose between competing reasonable inferences. *Id.* at 149. Properly applied, the equal inference rule is a type of "no evidence" rule: when circumstantial evidence is so slight that any plausible inference is purely a guess, it is in effect no evidence. *Id.* at 148.

§9. WAIVER OF GROUNDS & OMITTED ELEMENTS

§9.1 Entire claim or defense omitted. A party waives an entire theory of recovery or defense by not objecting to its omission from the charge. TRCP 279; ***Gulf States Utils. Co. v. Low***, 79 S.W.3d 561, 565 (Tex.2002); ***Harmes v. Arklatex Corp.***, 615 S.W.2d 177, 179 (Tex.1981); *see, e.g.*, ***American Physicians Ins. Exch. v. Garcia***, 876 S.W.2d 842, 848 n.12 (Tex.1994) (D waived estoppel defense); ***Southwestern Bell Tel. Co. v. DeLanney***, 809 S.W.2d 493, 495 (Tex.1991) (P waived breach of contract claim). If, however, the complete theory of recovery or defense was proved as a matter of law there is no waiver because a jury question is not required. *See* ***Brown v. Bank of Galveston***, 963 S.W.2d 511, 515 (Tex.1998).

§9.2 Incomplete claim or defense submitted. TRCP 279 describes the procedure when an element of a ground of recovery or defense is omitted from the jury charge. *See* ***In re J.F.C.***, 96 S.W.3d 256, 262-63 (Tex.2002).

1. **Neither party objected.** The trial court may make an express finding in support of the judgment when the charge was submitted with an element missing from a claim or defense and (1) the party with the burden of proof on the incomplete claim or defense did not request the missing element, (2) the opposing party did not object to the missing element, (3) the claim or defense consisted of more than one element, (4) the missing element is "necessarily referable" to the claim or defense, and (5) there is factually sufficient evidence to support a finding on the missing element. TRCP 279; *see* ***Gulf States***, 79 S.W.3d at 564; ***Clayton W. Williams, Jr., Inc. v. Olivo***, 952 S.W.2d 523, 529 (Tex.1997); ***Ramos v. Frito-Lay***, 784 S.W.2d 667, 668 (Tex.1990); ***Wal-Mart Stores v. Renteria***, 52 S.W.3d 848, 850 (Tex.App.—San Antonio 2001, pet. denied). By not objecting, the parties waive a jury trial on the omitted element and agree to submit the issue to the trial court. ***Gulf States***, 79 S.W.3d at 565. If the trial court does not make an express finding on the omitted element, the appellate court will deem a finding on the omitted element that supports the trial court's judgment if there is some evidence that supports the issue. ***State Farm Life Ins. Co. v. Beaston***, 907 S.W.2d 430, 437 (Tex.1995); *see, e.g.*, ***Ramos***, 784 S.W.2d at 668 (Supreme Court deemed findings in support of trial court's judgment); ***Cielo Dorado Dev. v. Certainteed Corp.***, 744 S.W.2d 10, 11 (Tex.1988) (same).

2. **Opposing party objected.** The trial court must render judgment against the party who had the burden of proof on a missing element when (1) the opposing party objected to the missing element, (2) an affirmative finding on the missing element is essential to the claim or defense, and (3) the missing element is not established as a matter of law in favor of the party with the burden of proof. ***McKinley v. Stripling***, 763 S.W.2d 407, 410 (Tex.1989); ***Physicians & Surgeons Gen. Hosp. v. Koblizek***, 752 S.W.2d 657, 660 (Tex.App.—Corpus Christi 1988, writ denied). When the opposing party objects to a missing element, a court cannot deem the missing element in favor of the party with the burden of proof on that element. *See* ***Physicians & Surgeons***, 752 S.W.2d at 660; ***Cameron Cty. v. Velasquez***, 668 S.W.2d 776, 781 (Tex.App.—Corpus Christi 1984, writ ref'd n.r.e.). In such a case, the party with the burden of proof did not secure a finding on the omitted element, which forecloses that claim or defense. ***Olivo***, 952 S.W.2d at 529; ***Dallas Cty. Med. Soc'y v. Ubiñas-Brache***, 68 S.W.3d 31, 40 (Tex.App.—Dallas 2001, pet. denied).

§9.3 How trial court makes express findings. The trial court may make an express finding any time before it renders the judgment. *See* TRCP 279.

1. The party who will benefit from an express finding should ask the court to make an express, written finding. The trial court cannot make an express finding without a request from one of the parties. *Id.*

2. The other parties must be given notice of the request. *Id.*

3. The court must conduct a hearing on the request. *Id.*

4. The court must make an express finding in writing. *Id.* When the court makes an express finding, it will render a judgment on the complete verdict. For example, assume that in a simple negligence case no proximate cause question was submitted, and the jury found negligence and damages. If the court makes an express finding that the negligence was a proximate cause of the plaintiff's injury, the court will render judgment for the plaintiff. However, if the court makes an express finding that the negligence was not a proximate cause of the plaintiff's injury, the court will render judgment for the defendant.

§9.4 How appellate courts make deemed findings. The appellate courts may make a deemed finding only in the following circumstances.

1. The trial court did not make an express finding in writing. TRCP 279; ***J.F.C.***, 96 S.W.3d at 262-63.

2. The appellate court makes a finding to support the trial court's judgment. TRCP 279; ***Gulf States***, 79 S.W.3d at 564; *see* ***J.F.C.***, 96 S.W.3d at 262-63. The appellate court cannot deem a finding that requires a different judgment from that rendered by the trial court. ***Gulf States***, 79 S.W.3d at 564; *see also* ***Logan v. Mullis***, 686 S.W.2d 605, 609 (Tex.1985) (court of appeals erred by deeming a finding in support of verdict instead of final judgment).

§10. SUPPLEMENTAL INSTRUCTIONS TO JURY

§10.1 Jury's questions to trial court. If the jury has a question or needs to communicate with the court, the presiding juror will tell the officer in charge of the jury, who will inform the trial court. TRCP 285; ***Ross v. TEIA***, 267 S.W.2d 541, 542 (Tex.1954). See "Questions by jurors," ch. 8-C, §4.6, p. 536. The trial court should assemble the jury and the lawyers in the courtroom, where the presiding juror will communicate with the court, either orally or in writing. TRCP 285, 286; ***Mid-South Bottling Co. v. Cigainero***, 799 S.W.2d 385, 387 n.1 (Tex.App.—Texarkana 1990, writ denied). If the jury asks for additional instructions on the law, its request must be in writing. TRCP 286.

§10.2 Supplemental instructions to jury. After the jury retires, the trial court may give the jury additional instructions on any matters of law, either at the request of the jury, on the court's own initiative, or on motion of a party. *See, e.g.*, ***Lochinvar Corp. v. Meyers***, 930 S.W.2d 182, 187 (Tex.App.—Dallas 1996, no writ) (party made late objection to error in charge, which court corrected by supplemental instruction). When the jury is assembled for a supplemental charge, the court must give the instruction in writing. TRCP 286. The court must give the attorneys an opportunity to object to the supplementary instructions. ***Scroggs v. Morgan***, 130 S.W.2d 283, 285 (Tex.1939). The trial court may allow additional argument, at its discretion. ***Geesbright v. Geesbright***, 570 S.W.2d 427, 433 (Tex.App.—Fort Worth 1978, writ dism'd).

§10.3 Verdict-urging instructions. TRCP 289 permits the trial court to discharge a jury without a verdict when (1) the jurors cannot agree and the parties consent to their discharge, (2) the jurors have been kept together for such time as to render it altogether improbable that they can agree, or (3) a calamity or accident that, in the opinion of the court, requires discharge. ***Shaw v. Greater Houston Transp. Co.***, 791 S.W.2d 204, 205 (Tex.App.—Corpus Christi 1990, no writ). To determine if the jurors will be able to reach a verdict, the trial court can ask them, and, in some circumstances, the court can instruct them to resume deliberations and attempt to reach a verdict. The supplemental charge is sometimes called an "Allen" charge, after ***Allen v. U.S.***, 164 U.S. 492, 17 S.Ct. 154 (1896), or the "dynamite charge," because it is used to "blast" a jury out of deadlock to reach a verdict. ***Stevens v. Travelers Ins. Co.***, 563 S.W.2d 223, 226 (Tex.1978). The trial court cannot keep the jurors captive once they have announced they cannot reach a verdict. *See* ***Shaw***, 791 S.W.2d at 210 (court's refusal to release jury was coercive & reversible).

1. Propriety of supplemental charge. There are two questions to consider when a jury has been unable to reach a verdict: (1) what kind of supplemental charge is permissible, and (2) how long should the jury be held?

(1) Supplemental charge. A supplemental charge should not be coercive. To determine if a particular charge is coercive, it must be broken down into its parts and analyzed for possible coercive statements. ***Stevens***, 563 S.W.2d at 229; ***Firestone Tire & Rubber Co. v. Battle***, 745 S.W.2d 909, 916-17 (Tex.App.—Houston [1st Dist.] 1988, writ denied). A potentially coercive statement will not invalidate the charge, unless it retains its coercive nature as a whole when all of the circumstances surrounding its rendition are considered. ***Stevens***, 563 S.W.2d at 229; *see* ***Golden v. First City Nat'l Bank***, 751 S.W.2d 639, 642 (Tex.App.—Dallas 1988, no writ); *see, e.g.*, ***Souris v. Robinson***, 725 S.W.2d 339, 343 (Tex.App.—Houston [14th Dist.] 1987, no writ) (supplemental charge that asked jury to return a verdict "today" was not coercive). The supplemental charge should not be addressed to the jurors who do not agree with the majority. ***Stevens***, 563 S.W.2d at 228. It must not suggest that the court will confine the jury until it reaches a verdict. *Id.* at 232; ***Shaw***, 791 S.W.2d at 209. It must not tell the jury that it breached its responsibility by not reaching a verdict. ***Shaw***, 791 S.W.2d at 209. Each trial judge has a copy of the *Bench Book for the Texas Judiciary* (2001), provided by the Texas Center for the Judiciary. The approved verdict-urging instruction is located on page 2-31 of the *Bench Book*. See ***O'Connor's*** FORM 8I:02.

(2) Length of deliberation. The length of time the jury is held in an effort to secure a verdict is left to the discretion of the trial court. ***Conrey v. McGehee***, 473 S.W.2d 617, 620 (Tex.App.—Houston [14th Dist.] 1971, writ ref'd n.r.e.). Once it becomes clear the jury is deadlocked, either by their notes or the passage of time, the trial court must release them. For example, the trial judge in ***Shaw*** should have released the jury after three days of deliberation when the jury repeatedly said it was deadlocked and even said it was unable to abide by the instruction. ***Shaw***, 791 S.W.2d at 209-10; *see also* ***Conrey***, 473 S.W.2d at 620 (holding jury for seven hours was not error).

2. Preserve error. To preserve error regarding the supplemental charge, the party must object.

(1) To supplemental charge. The party must object to the supplemental charge and identify each statement in the supplemental charge that is coercive and state why. The objection must be made before the court submits the supplemental charge to the jury. *E.g.*, ***Golden***, 751 S.W.2d at 642 (D waived error by not objecting at the time the court submitted verdict-urging instruction to jury).

(2) To continuation of deliberations. In addition to objecting to the supplemental charge, the party should object to continued confinement of the jury by making a motion for mistrial. *See* ***Shaw***, 791 S.W.2d at 206-07.

§11. REVIEW

§11.1 Show error caused harm. For the appellate court to reverse on a jury charge error, the appellant must show harmful error. ***Boatland, Inc. v. Bailey***, 609 S.W.2d 743, 749-50 (Tex.1980). Error in the jury charge is reversible only if it probably caused the rendition of an improper judgment or probably prevented the appellant from properly presenting the case on appeal. TRAP 44.1(a); *see* ***Wal-Mart Stores v. Johnson***, 106 S.W.3d 718, 723 (Tex .2003); ***Timberwalk Apts. v. Cain***, 972 S.W.2d 749, 756 (Tex.1998); ***Reinhart v. Young***, 906 S.W.2d 471, 473 (Tex. 1995). A misunderstanding of the court's charge by the jury is not grounds for reversible error. ***Stephens Cty. Museum v. Swenson***, 517 S.W.2d 257, 260 (Tex.1974); ***Holiday Inns v. State***, 931 S.W.2d 614, 621 (Tex.App.—Amarillo 1996, writ denied). To determine harm, the appellate court must consider the entire record—the parties' pleadings, the evidence, and the charge. ***Timberwalk Apts.***, 972 S.W.2d at 756; ***Reinhart***, 906 S.W.2d at 473; ***Island Recreational Dev. Corp. v. Republic of Tex. Sav. Ass'n***, 710 S.W.2d 551, 555 (Tex.1986). When the error in the charge relates to a contested issue in the case, the erroneous instruction will probably be considered reversible error. *E.g.*, ***Johnson***, 106 S.W.3d at 724 (in negligence case, unnecessary spoliation instruction was reversible error); ***Quantum Chem. Corp. v. Toennies***, 47 S.W.3d 473, 480 (Tex.2001) (in age discrimination case, erroneous instruction on causation was reversible error); ***Timberwalk Apts.***, 972 S.W.2d at 756 (in premises case, surplus instruction on tenant's requirement to give written request for repairs, a contested issue, was reversible error); ***Ford Motor Co. v. Miles***, 967 S.W.2d 377, 385-88 (Tex.1998) (dicta; submission of global instruction that imposed duty not to subject vehicle occupants to unnecessary & unavoidable injuries was not harmless because case was closely contested); ***Southwestern Bell Tel. Co. v. John Carlo Tex., Inc.***, 843 S.W.2d 470, 472 (Tex.1992) (failure to define justification, defensive issue, was not harmless). *But see* ***Reinhart***, 906 S.W.2d at 474 (when erroneous instruction submitted, other instruction to which P did not object could justify verdict); ***City of Brownsville v. Alvarado***, 897 S.W.2d 750, 752 (Tex.1995) (submission of improper question was harmless because jury's answers to other questions rendered it immaterial). When a party proves a submission was erroneous and meets the harm analysis, the issue will then be whether to reverse and remand for a new trial or to render judgment for the other party. See §11.5, below.

§11.2 Broad-form questions.

1. Challenging evidence. On appeal, broad-form questions reduce the chances of successfully challenging the evidence to support a jury question. To successfully challenge a finding on a broad-form question containing multiple theories of liability, the appellant must show there was inadequate evidence to support at least one element of each cause of action. ***Prudential Ins. Co. v. Jefferson Assocs.***, 896 S.W.2d 156, 160 (Tex.1995). To successfully challenge a broad-form question on damages containing multiple elements, the appellant must show there was inadequate evidence to support the entire damage award considering all of the elements. ***Price v. Short***, 931 S.W.2d 677, 688 (Tex.App.—Dallas 1996, no writ); ***Greater Houston Transp. Co. v. Zrubeck***, 850 S.W.2d 579, 589 (Tex.App.—Corpus Christi 1993, writ denied).

2. Challenging charge. When a trial court submits broad-form questions with multiple theories of liability or damages, some of which are invalid or have no evidence to support them, the error is harmful, and a new trial is required if the appellate court cannot determine whether the jury based its verdict on an invalid theory. ***Harris Cty. v. Smith***, 96 S.W.3d 230, 234 (Tex.2002); ***Crown Life Ins. Co. v. Casteel***, 22 S.W.3d 378, 388 (Tex. 2000); *see also* TRAP 61.1(b) (judgment cannot be reversed unless appellate court concludes error prevented petitioner from presenting case to appellate court).

§11.3 Challenge findings on omitted elements. A party should treat the court's findings on omitted elements—either the trial court's express findings or the court of appeals' deemed findings—as jury findings. The findings, express or deemed, should be challenged with factual and legal sufficiency points of error in both the motion for new trial and the brief on appeal. The court of appeals will review deemed findings by the factual sufficiency test and the legal sufficiency test. ***Crosbyton Seed Co. v. Mechura Farms***, 875 S.W.2d 353, 364 (Tex. App.—Corpus Christi 1994, no writ). The Supreme Court can review deemed findings only by the legal sufficiency test. ***American Nat'l Pet. Co. v. Transcontinental Gas Pipe Line Corp.***, 798 S.W.2d 274, 278-79 (Tex.1990); ***Crosbyton***, 875 S.W.2d at 364 n.9.

§11.4 Jury notations. On appeal, the courts will not consider the jury's margin notations regarding its findings. ***Thomas v. Oldham***, 895 S.W.2d 352, 359 (Tex.1995). The jury's notes are not the jury's verdict. *Id.* at 360; ***Wal-Mart Stores v. Alexander***, 868 S.W.2d 322, 328 (Tex.1993).

§11.5 Remedy for error.

1. Defective submission.

(1) Objection – remand. If a defective question was submitted over the objection of the party without the burden of proof, and the jury returns a verdict in favor of the party with the burden of proof, the party who objected is entitled to a new trial (not rendition) if there is any evidence supporting the defective question. ***Borneman v. Steak & Ale***, 22 S.W.3d 411, 413 (Tex.2000) (remanding because of defective question); ***Minnesota Mining & Mfg. Co. v. Nishika, Ltd.***, 953 S.W.2d 733, 739 (Tex.1997) (remanding because damage issue did not segregate between Ps); ***Spencer v. Eagle Star Ins. Co.***, 876 S.W.2d 154, 157 (Tex.1994) (remanding because of defective instruction). In some cases, the court does not mention whether the party objected to the defective charge. ***Arthur Andersen & Co. v. Perry Equip. Corp.***, 945 S.W.2d 812, 817 (Tex.1997) (remanding because of defective instruction); ***Jackson v. Fontaine's Clinics***, 499 S.W.2d 87, 90 (Tex.1973) (remanding because of defective damages question).

(2) No objection – affirm. If neither party objected to the submission of a defective question, the party in whose favor the verdict was returned is entitled to affirmance. The other party waived the opportunity to have the case submitted under the correct substantive law. ***Green Int'l v. Solis***, 951 S.W.2d 384, 389-90 (Tex.1997) (party failed to object that attorney fee question did not segregate attorney fees); ***Allen v. American Nat'l Ins. Co.***, 380 S.W.2d 604, 609 (Tex.1964) (jury found against P under erroneous submission); ***Casteel-Diebolt v. Diebolt***, 912 S.W.2d 302, 304 (Tex.App.—Houston [14th Dist.] 1995, no writ) (when party agrees to charge as submitted, it may not complain about its contents on appeal).

NOTE

The Texas Pattern Jury Charge is not always correct. See, e.g., ***State v. Williams****, 940 S.W.2d 583, 584 (Tex.1996) (erroneous premises liability charge). When a case is submitted on an erroneous charge from the PJC, the appellate court should reverse and remand, not render.* ***City of San Antonio v. Rodriguez****, 931 S.W.2d 535, 536 (Tex.1996).*

2. Incomplete submission.

(1) Objection – render. If an incomplete question was submitted over the objection of the party without the burden of proof, and the jury returned a verdict for the party with the burden of proof, the party who objected is entitled to a rendition. ***State Dept. of Highways & Pub. Transp. v. Payne***, 838 S.W.2d 235, 241 (Tex. 1992); ***Cosgrove v. Grimes***, 774 S.W.2d 662, 666 (Tex.1989).

(2) No objection – affirm. If an incomplete question was submitted, and neither party objected, the party in whose favor the court rendered judgment is entitled to an affirmance. *See* ***State Farm Life Ins. Co. v. Beaston***, 907 S.W.2d 430, 436-37 (Tex.1995); ***Ramos v. Frito-Lay***, 784 S.W.2d 667, 668 (Tex.1990).

J. FINAL ARGUMENT

§1. GENERAL

§1.1 Rules. TRCP 266, 269.

§1.2 Purpose. After all the evidence is introduced, the lawyers summarize their case to the jury and argue the effect of the evidence.

§1.3 Forms. *O'Connor's Texas Civil Forms*, FORM 8J:01.

§2. RIGHT TO OPEN & CLOSE FINAL ARGUMENT

§2.1 Rule – P opens & closes. As a general rule, the plaintiff has the right to open and close the final argument. TRCP 266.

§2.2 Exceptions – D opens & closes.

1. Burden of proof. A defendant has the right to open and close the final argument if it had the burden of proof in the whole case. TRCP 269(a). To determine who had the burden of proof on the whole case, ask which party would lose if no evidence were introduced. If the defendant would lose, then the defendant had the burden. ***Union City Transfer v. Adams***, 248 S.W.2d 256, 260 (Tex.App.—Fort Worth 1952, writ ref'd n.r.e.); *see, e.g.,* ***Ocean Transp. v. Greycas, Inc.***, 878 S.W.2d 256, 269 (Tex.App.—Corpus Christi 1994, writ denied) (in suit on a note, D did not have right to open & close final argument because P had burden to prove deficiency & attorney fees).

2. **Burden in the charge.** A defendant has the right to open and close the final argument if it has the burden on all matters submitted to the jury in the court's charge. TRCP 269(a); ***First State Bank v. Fatheree***, 847 S.W.2d 391, 397 (Tex.App.—Amarillo 1993, writ denied); ***Horton v. Dental Capital Leasing Corp.***, 649 S.W.2d 655, 657 (Tex.App.—Texarkana 1983, no writ). Because TRCP 269 does not become applicable until after the evidence is closed and the charge is read to the jury, it does not affect the right to make the opening statement or introduce evidence. *See* ***Amis v. Ashworth***, 802 S.W.2d 379, 383 (Tex.App.—Tyler 1990, orig. proceeding).

§2.3 Other considerations. When there are several parties that have separate claims or defenses, the court "shall" determine the order of the argument. TRCP 269(a). The court must assign an intervenor a position in the argument according to the nature of its claim. TRCP 269(c).

§3. MANAGEMENT OF ARGUMENT

§3.1 Court's authority. The trial court has the duty to supervise the scope of jury argument and to limit arguments to the evidence. ***City of Dallas v. Andrews***, 236 S.W.2d 609, 611 (Tex.1951); ***National Un. Fire Ins. Co. v. Soto***, 819 S.W.2d 619, 623-24 (Tex.App.—El Paso 1991, writ denied). The court should control the argument, even without an objection by opposing counsel. TRCP 269(g); ***TEIA v. Guerrero***, 800 S.W.2d 859, 867-68 (Tex. App.—San Antonio 1990, writ denied).

§3.2 Time to argue. The court has discretion in allotting time for the arguments. ***Aultman v. Dallas Ry. & Terminal***, 260 S.W.2d 596, 600 (Tex.1953). To complain on appeal that the court did not permit sufficient time for argument, the party must show the following: (1) it objected, (2) it requested additional time, (3) the court denied the request, and (4) the error caused the rendition of an improper judgment. ***Aetna Cas. & Sur. Co. v. Shiflett***, 593 S.W.2d 768, 772 (Tex.App.—Texarkana 1979, writ ref'd n.r.e.); *see* TRAP 44.1(a)(1).

§3.3 Nonjury trial. In a nonjury trial, the court has discretion in deciding whether it will hear oral arguments. ***City of Corpus Christi v. Krause***, 584 S.W.2d 325, 330 (Tex.App.—Corpus Christi 1979, no writ).

§4. LIMITS OF FINAL ARGUMENT

§4.1 Order of argument. See "Right to Make First Opening Statement," ch. 8-B, §2, p. 533.

1. **Concluding argument.** The party with the burden on the case or on all matters submitted to the jury (generally the plaintiff) is entitled to make the concluding argument. TRCP 269(a). The plaintiff should present its entire case in the concluding argument. TRCP 269(b).

2. **Responsive argument.** The other party (generally the defendant) is entitled to present its case to the jury.

3. **Rebuttal argument.** The plaintiff's rebuttal is limited to matters in reply to the defendant's argument. TRCP 269(b).

§4.2 What lawyers may argue. Lawyers have great latitude to indulge in "flights of oratory." ***Southwestern Greyhound Lines v. Dickson***, 236 S.W.2d 115, 119 (Tex.1951).

1. **Questions of fact.** Lawyers should argue the facts to the jury. TRCP 269(e); ***Circle Y v. Blevins***, 826 S.W.2d 753, 758 (Tex.App.—Texarkana 1992, writ denied). Lawyers should discuss the reasonableness of the evidence and the probative effect or lack of probative effect of the evidence. ***Texas Sand Co. v. Shield***, 381 S.W.2d 48, 57-58 (Tex.1964).

2. **Inferences from facts.** Lawyers may argue reasonable deductions and inferences from the facts. ***Anderson v. Vinson Expl.***, 832 S.W.2d 657, 667 (Tex.App.—El Paso 1992, no writ). The argument that the jury should "send a message" is permissible when it is based on the facts. ***Schindler Elevator Corp. v. Anderson***, 78 S.W.3d 392, 405 (Tex.App.—Houston [14th Dist.] 2001, pet. granted w.r.m.).

3. Fair criticism. Lawyers may make fair and reasonable criticism of a witness's testimony, may comment on bias or interest of parties and witnesses, and may discuss the reasonableness or the unreasonableness of the evidence. ***Dyer v. Hardin***, 323 S.W.2d 119, 127 (Tex.App.—Amarillo 1959, writ ref'd n.r.e.).

4. Effect of answer under evidence. Lawyers may argue the effect of the jury's answer only if the lawyer qualifies it with a request to make the finding "under the evidence." ***Cavnar v. Quality Control Parking***, 678 S.W.2d 548, 554-55 (Tex.App.—Houston [14th Dist.] 1984), *rev'd in part on other grounds*, 696 S.W.2d 549 (Tex. 1985). But see §4.3.2, below.

5. Concluding argument. In the concluding argument, lawyers are permitted to reply only to the argument of the opposing party. TRCP 269(b).

§4.3 What lawyers cannot argue. There are limits to a lawyer's jury arguments. ***Dickson***, 236 S.W.2d at 119.

1. Questions of law. Lawyers cannot argue questions of law to the jury. The lawyers must address arguments on the law to the court. TRCP 269(d). A lawyer cannot embellish or mischaracterize the charge given by the court. ***Timberwalk Apts. v. Cain***, 972 S.W.2d 749, 755 (Tex.1998).

2. Legal effect of answer. Lawyers should not tell the jury the legal effect of its answers. ***Magic Chef, Inc. v. Sibley***, 546 S.W.2d 851, 857 (Tex.App.—San Antonio 1977, writ ref'd n.r.e.). *But see* ***Louisiana & Ark. Ry. v. Capps***, 766 S.W.2d 291, 295 (Tex.App.—Texarkana 1989, writ denied) (it was not reversible error because same information was in the jury questions). See §4.2.4, above.

3. Outside the record. Lawyers are required to stay inside the evidence presented at trial. TRCP 269(e); *e.g.*, ***Texas Sand Co. v. Shield***, 381 S.W.2d 48, 57-58 (Tex.1964) (D's lawyer should not have argued that P's lawyer also represented the infamous Billy Sol Estes, not a party in the suit); ***Lone Star Ford v. Carter***, 848 S.W.2d 850, 853 (Tex.App.—Houston [14th Dist.] 1993, no writ) (in a suit for contract damages, lawyer should not have argued about persons killed in the Ford Pinto).

4. Matters covered by order in limine. Lawyers should not comment on matters in violation of a court's order in limine. ***National Un. Fire Ins. Co. v. Kwiatkowski***, 915 S.W.2d 662, 664 (Tex.App.—Houston [14th Dist.] 1996, no writ). See "Motion in Limine," ch. 5-E, p. 252.

5. Improper viewpoint. Even though lawyers may argue the "Golden Rule," they cannot ask the jury to consider the case from an improper viewpoint. *E.g.*, ***World Wide Tire Co. v. Brown***, 644 S.W.2d 144, 145-46 (Tex. App.—Houston [14th Dist.] 1982, writ ref'd n.r.e.) (argument asked jury to award what would satisfy them as Ps, instead of basing award on the evidence).

6. Side-bar remarks. Lawyers cannot engage in side-bar remarks while the other lawyer is making argument (or examining a witness). *See* ***Davis v. Southern P.T. Co.***, 585 S.W.2d 801, 803-04 (Tex.App.—Houston [1st Dist.] 1979, no writ). TRCP 269(f) requires the trial court to repress side-bar remarks. ***Wal-Mart Stores v. Reece***, 32 S.W.3d 339, 347 (Tex.App.—Waco 2000), *rev'd on other grounds*, 81 S.W.3d 812 (Tex.2002).

7. Personal criticism. Lawyers should not criticize each other during jury argument. TRCP 269(e); *see, e.g.*, ***Circle Y***, 826 S.W.2d at 758-59 (improper to argue lawyer manufactured evidence); ***Beavers v. Northrop Worldwide Aircraft Servs.***, 821 S.W.2d 669, 680 (Tex.App.—Amarillo 1991, writ denied) (improper to argue lawyer misrepresented facts); ***American Petrofina v. PPG Indus.***, 679 S.W.2d 740, 755 (Tex.App.—Fort Worth 1984, writ dism'd) (improper to attack lawyer's integrity); *see also* ***Amelia's Auto. v. Rodriguez***, 921 S.W.2d 767, 773 (Tex. App.—San Antonio 1996, no writ) (reversible error for Ps attorney to mention during examination of witness that D's trial attorney had been disbarred for five years for filing frivolous lawsuit); ***Byas v. State***, 906 S.W.2d 86, 87 (Tex.App.—Fort Worth 1995, pet. ref'd) (reversible error in criminal case for prosecutor to refer to defense counsel as "very slick attorney").

8. Passion or prejudice. Lawyers cannot make arguments that appeal to the jury's racial, religious, or other passions or prejudices. ***Southwestern Greyhound Lines v. Dickson***, 236 S.W.2d 115, 119 (Tex.1951); *see, e.g.*, ***TEIA v. Haywood***, 266 S.W.2d 856, 858 (Tex.1954) (reversed because D argued that P's witnesses were not as believable as white people); ***TEIA v. Jones***, 361 S.W.2d 725, 726-27 (Tex.App.—Waco 1962, writ ref'd n.r.e.) (reversed because, among other things, P referred to religion of D's witness in derogatory fashion).

9. Credibility of witness. Lawyers cannot argue that, in their opinion, a witness is credible or not. Tex. Disc. R. Prof. Conduct 3.04(c)(3); *see* ***Howell Pipeline Tex. v. ExxonMobil Pipeline***, ___ S.W.3d ___ (Tex. App.—Houston [14th Dist.] 2003, n.p.h.) (No. 14-02-00387-CV; 8-28-03); *cf.* ***Menefee v. State***, 614 S.W.2d 167, 168 (Tex.Crim.App.1981) (criminal case reversed because attorney argued "I don't believe I have ever seen anybody that I thought was any more honest than she is.").

10. Invocation of privilege. Lawyers cannot comment on the other party's invocation of a privilege. TRE 513(a). For exceptions, see TRE 504(b)(2), 513(c). See Cochran, ***Texas Rules of Evidence Handbook***, pp. 543-50 (5th ed. 2003).

11. Failure to seek medical exam. When the defendant does not seek a medical examination of the plaintiff under TRCP 204, the plaintiff's lawyer cannot comment that (1) the plaintiff was willing to submit to a medical examination, (2) the defendant had the right to such an examination, or (3) the defendant did not seek an examination. TRCP 204.3. See "Effect of no examination," ch. 6-I, §6.4, p. 438.

§5. TYPES OF ERROR IN ARGUMENT

There are two types of error in jury argument, curable and incurable. ***Otis Elevator v. Wood***, 436 S.W.2d 324, 333 (Tex.1968); ***Gannett Outdoor Co. v. Kubeczka***, 710 S.W.2d 79, 86 (Tex.App.—Houston [14th Dist.] 1986, no writ).

§5.1 Curable argument. Most improper jury arguments can be cured of its harmful effects by an objection and the court's instruction to the jury to disregard what it has just heard. ***Otis Elevator***, 436 S.W.2d at 333.

1. Preserving error. If an improper argument is curable, the party must object promptly. ***Standard Fire Ins. Co. v. Reese***, 584 S.W.2d 835, 840-41 (Tex.1979); ***Isern v. Watson***, 942 S.W.2d 186, 198 (Tex.App.—Beaumont 1997, pet. denied). The party must make sure the trial court rules on the objection, either sustaining or overruling it. TRAP 33.1(a)(2). Without a ruling on the objection, no error is preserved. ***G.M. Corp. v. Iracheta***, 90 S.W.3d 725, 745 (Tex.App.—San Antonio 2002, pet. granted 9-25-03); ***Marling v. Maillard***, 826 S.W.2d 735, 740-41 (Tex.App.—Houston [14th Dist.] 1992, no writ). When the trial court sustains the objection, to preserve error, the party should pursue an adverse ruling through a request to instruct the jury to disregard, a motion to strike, and a motion for mistrial. See "When jury hears inadmissible evidence," ch. 8-D, §6.6, p. 548.

2. Examples of curable jury argument. The errors in the following arguments were not so egregious that they were preserved without an objection. • Mention of insurance. ***Isern***, 942 S.W.2d at 198. • Asking the jury to place itself in the shoes of the party. ***Goswami v. Thetford***, 829 S.W.2d 317, 320-21 (Tex.App.—El Paso 1992, writ denied). • Going outside the record to tell the jury that the other party's lawyer represented a reprehensible party in another suit. ***Texas Sand Co. v. Shield***, 381 S.W.2d 48, 57-58 (Tex.1964). • Suggesting fraud by arguing a close connection between the plaintiff's lawyer and the doctor who treated the plaintiff. ***Reese***, 584 S.W.2d at 840-41. • In a products liability case, reference to previous litigation such as Ford Pintos, asbestos, and Dalkon shields. ***Schindler Elevator Corp. v. Anderson***, 78 S.W.3d 392, 406 (Tex.App.—Houston [14th Dist.] 2001, pet. granted w.r.m.). • Collateral benefits mentioned in personal injury action. ***Macias v. Ramos***, 917 S.W.2d 371, 375 (Tex.App.—San Antonio 1996, no writ).

§5.2 Incurable argument. Incurable argument is argument so prejudicial or inflammatory that an instruction to the jury to disregard it cannot eliminate its harm. ***Otis Elevator***, 436 S.W.2d at 333; ***Gannett Outdoor***, 710 S.W.2d at 86.

1. **Preserving error.** When the harmful effects of an incurable jury argument cannot be cured by an instruction to disregard, the failure to object at trial does not waive the error for appeal. ***Otis Elevator***, 436 S.W.2d at 333; ***TEIA v. Guerrero***, 800 S.W.2d 859, 863 (Tex.App.—San Antonio 1990, writ denied); ***Mapco, Inc. v. Jenkins***, 476 S.W.2d 55, 61-62 (Tex.App.—Amarillo 1971, writ ref'd n.r.e.). *But see* ***Cockrell v. State***, 933 S.W.2d 73, 89 (Tex.Crim.App.1996) (in criminal cases, incurable jury argument is waived if no objection made at trial). If the lawyer did not object to the argument during trial, to preserve error, the lawyer must complain about the argument in a motion for new trial. TRCP 324(b)(5) (point in motion for new trial is necessary to complain on appeal of incurable jury argument only "if not otherwise ruled on by the trial court"); ***Austin v. Shampine***, 948 S.W.2d 900, 906 (Tex. App.—Texarkana 1997, no writ) (same).

PRACTICE TIP

Always object to improper jury argument. Never assume a jury argument is so prejudicial that no objection is necessary. If you do not object, and the appellate court decides the error was curable, you will have waived the error.

2. **Examples of incurable jury argument.** The errors in the following arguments were so egregious that no objection was necessary to preserve them, and even when an objection was made and the court instructed the jury to disregard, the error was not cured. • Charges that opposing counsel manufactured evidence. ***Circle Y v. Blevins***, 826 S.W.2d 753, 758-59 (Tex.App.—Texarkana 1992, writ denied) (there was an objection). • Personal attacks on opposing counsel. ***American Petrofina v. PPG Indus.***, 679 S.W.2d 740, 754-55 (Tex.App.—Fort Worth 1984, writ dism'd) (there was an objection). • Appeals to ethnic solidarity. ***Guerrero***, 800 S.W.2d at 866. • Appeals to racial prejudice. *E.g.*, ***Haywood***, 266 S.W.2d at 858 (D argued that P's witnesses were not as believable as white people). • Appeals to religious prejudice. ***Jones***, 361 S.W.2d at 727. • Argument by plaintiff's counsel that defendant's counsel had characterized plaintiff as a liar, fraud, cheat, and impostor. ***Dickson***, 236 S.W.2d at 118.

§6. REVIEW

§6.1 Record of argument. To show error in improper argument, the appellant must prove the improper argument was not invited or provoked. ***Standard Fire Ins. Co. v. Reese***, 584 S.W.2d 835, 839 (Tex.1979). To establish this, the appellant must provide the appellate court with the entire record—the jury's voir dire, the opening statements, the evidence, and the final argument. *See* ***Central Nat'l Gulfbank v. Comdata Network***, 773 S.W.2d 626, 628 (Tex.App.—Corpus Christi 1989, no writ); *see also* ***Iracheta***, 90 S.W.3d at 743-44 (although P's statement to jury in Spanish during closing argument was not transcribed, judge noted content of statement on record and copy of interpretation was filed with court; court could review impropriety of statement).

§6.2 Test for reversible jury argument. In ***Reese***, the Supreme Court outlined the elements of improper, reversible jury argument.

1. The attorney made an improper argument. ***Reese***, 584 S.W.2d at 839.

2. The improper argument was not invited or provoked. *Id.*

3. The error was preserved by proper trial predicate (objection, motion to instruct, motion to strike, motion for mistrial). *Id.*

4. The error was not curable by instruction, prompt withdrawal of the statement, or reprimand by the court. *Id.* An appellant is required to show the error was incurable only if the trial court gave a curative instruction or the appellant did not ask for one. An appellant is not required to show the error was incurable if the appellant's objection to the argument was overruled or its request for a curative instruction was denied. ***Lone Star Ford v. Carter***, 848 S.W.2d 850, 854 (Tex.App.—Houston [14th Dist.] 1993, no writ).

5. The argument, by its nature, degree, and extent, constituted reversible error. ***Reese***, 584 S.W.2d at 839. Relevant factors include the duration of the argument, whether it was repeated or abandoned, and whether such errors were cumulative. *Id.* at 839-40; *see, e.g.*, ***Clark Equip. Co. v. Pitner***, 923 S.W.2d 117, 125 (Tex.App.—Houston [14th Dist.] 1996, writ denied) (counsel's comments about other lawsuits not harmful error because it was a single sentence & not repeated); ***Brown v. Hopkins***, 921 S.W.2d 306, 319 (Tex.App.—Corpus Christi 1996, no writ) (improper comments were isolated & later corrected); ***National Un. Fire Ins. Co. v. Kwiatkowski***, 915 S.W.2d 662, 665 (Tex.App.—Houston [14th Dist.] 1996, no writ) (based on the trial's short duration & the number of prejudicial remarks, error harmful).

6. The court must review the entire record to determine if the argument had a probable effect on a material finding. ***Reese***, 584 S.W.2d at 840. The court reviews the evidence to determine if the verdict was based on the evidence or the improper argument. ***Texas Sand Co. v. Shield***, 381 S.W.2d 48, 58-59 (Tex.1964); ***Wooten v. Southern P.T. Co.***, 928 S.W.2d 76, 80 (Tex.App.—Houston [14th Dist.] 1995, no writ). If a juror of ordinary intelligence could have been persuaded by the improper argument to agree to a verdict contrary to what he would have agreed to without the argument, the error was harmful. ***Wells v. HCA Health Servs.***, 806 S.W.2d 850, 854 (Tex. App.—Fort Worth 1990, writ denied); ***Gannett Outdoor Co. v. Kubeczka***, 710 S.W.2d 79, 86-87 (Tex.App.—Houston [14th Dist.] 1986, no writ). To obtain a reversal for abuse of discretion, a complaining party must make an affirmative showing of injury. ***Aetna Cas. & Sur. Co. v. Shiflett***, 593 S.W.2d 768, 772 (Tex.App.—Texarkana 1979, writ ref'd n.r.e.).

K. THE VERDICT

§1. GENERAL

§1.1 Rules. TRCP 290-295.

§1.2 Forms. None.

§2. JURY DELIBERATIONS

§2.1 Kept together. When the jury retires for deliberation, the jurors must be kept together under the charge of an officer until they agree on a verdict or are discharged by the court. TRCP 282. The court may permit the jurors to separate for the night, for meals, and for other proper purposes. *Id.*

03 **§2.2 No recording.** No person may use a device to produce or make any recording (audio, visual, still photograph) of a jury while it is deliberating. CPRC §24.001 (civil jury); Code of Crim. Proc. art. 36.215 (criminal jury).

§3. VERDICT BY FEWER THAN 12 JURORS

In district court, a jury consists of 12 persons. TRCP 234. See "Jury Panel," ch. 8-A, §8, p. 532. A trial cannot proceed with fewer than 12 jurors unless the juror is constitutionally "disabled" or the parties agree. ***Dempsey v. Beaumont Hosp.***, 38 S.W.3d 287, 289 (Tex.App.—Beaumont 2001, pet. dism'd) (mid-trial discovery that juror was ineligible to serve because of felony conviction required a mistrial).

§3.1 Juror disabled.

1. **Definition of disabled.** The term "disabled," as used in Texas Constitution article 5, §13, encompasses physical or mental incapacity, and any other condition or circumstance rendering a person incapable of fulfilling the function of a juror. ***McDaniel v. Yarbrough***, 898 S.W.2d 251, 253 (Tex.1995). The juror must become mentally incompetent, sick, or suffer some other physical or mental incapacity to be considered disabled. *Id.*; *see* ***Fiore v. Fiore***, 946 S.W.2d 436, 438 (Tex.App.—Fort Worth 1997, writ denied) (juror's prejudice against a party is not a disqualification, even if prejudice results in physical manifestations); ***City of Jersey Village v. Campbell***, 920 S.W.2d 694, 698 (Tex.App.—Houston [1st Dist.] 1996, writ denied) (juror's bias or prejudice is not the same as loss of mental faculties). If the death or serious illness of a family member renders a juror unable to discharge her

responsibilities, the trial may proceed with fewer than 12 jurors. ***Yanes v. Sowards***, 996 S.W.2d 849, 852 (Tex. 1999); ***Summit Mach. Tool Mfg. Corp. v. Great N. Ins. Co.***, 997 S.W.2d 840, 852 (Tex.App.—Austin 1999, no pet.). Temporary detention by flooding does not rise to the level of constitutional disability. ***McDaniel***, 898 S.W.2d at 253.

2. Effect of disability. If as many as three jurors on a 12-person jury die or become disabled, and only nine of the original 12 remain, those remaining may render and return a verdict, but it must be unanimous. Tex. Const. art. 5, §13; TRCP 292; ***Yanes***, 996 S.W.2d at 850; ***Palmer Well Servs. v. Mack Trucks***, 776 S.W.2d 575, 576 n.2 (Tex.1989). If four or more persons die or become disabled, the court must declare a mistrial.

§3.2 Agreement. The parties may agree to proceed with a jury composed of fewer than 12 jurors. Gov't Code §62.201.

§4. JURY VERDICT

§4.1 Most trials. A verdict may be rendered by the concurrence, as to each answer, of the same ten members of a 12-person jury (or five members of a six-person jury). TRCP 292; ***Palmer Well Servs.***, 776 S.W.2d at 576; ***Dunlap v. Excel Corp.***, 30 S.W.3d 427, 432 (Tex.App.—Amarillo 2000, no pet.); *see* TRCP 226a, "Written Instructions," III(6). If the same ten jurors did not agree on the same questions, the court may require the jury to continue its deliberations. ***Gonzalez v. Gutierrez***, 694 S.W.2d 384, 390 (Tex.App.—San Antonio 1985, no writ). The plaintiff must prove most issues by a preponderance of the evidence, which means the greater weight and degree of credible evidence. ***Upjohn Co. v. Freeman***, 847 S.W.2d 589, 591 (Tex.App.—Dallas 1992, no writ).

§4.2 Exemplary damages cases. The issues of liability for and amount of actual damages must be decided by a preponderance of the evidence; the issues of liability for and amount of exemplary damages must be decided by clear and convincing evidence. See "Plaintiff's burden," ch. 5-H, §5.4, p. 268; ***O'Connor's Texas Causes of Action***, "Trial procedure," ch. 35-G, §4.3, p. 1022 (2004) (***O'Connor's COA***). 03

1. Cases after 8-31-03 – unanimous jury verdict. For exemplary damages cases filed after August 31, 2003, CPRC §41.003 requires a jury to render a unanimous verdict on both liability for and the amount of exemplary damages. CPRC §41.003(d). Thus, all 12 jurors must agree on both phase one issues (liability and amount of actual damages) and the phase two issue (amount of exemplary damages).

PRACTICE TIP

The current charge instructing the jury that they "may render [a] verdict upon the vote of ten or more members" will no longer be correct for cases involving exemplary damages filed after August 31, 2003. See TRCP 226a, "Written Instructions," III(6). Until the Supreme Court or Legislature resolves this problem, lawyers will have to modify the charge to avoid misleading the jury about how many jurors must agree to impose actual damages compared to how many must agree to impose exemplary damages. See ***O'Connor's COA***, *"Jury instructions," ch. 35-G, §4.2, p. 1022.*

2. Cases before 9-1-03 – ten jurors. For exemplary damages cases filed before September 1, 2003, only ten jurors are required to agree on phase one and phase two issues. TRCP 292. It is uncertain whether the same ten jurors must agree on both phase one issues and the phase two issue. *Compare* ***Hyman Farm Serv. v. Earth Oil & Gas Co.***, 920 S.W.2d 452, 458 (Tex.App.—Amarillo 1996, no writ) (same 10 jurors must agree), *with* ***Merrell Dow Pharms. v. Havner***, 907 S.W.2d 535, 559-60 (Tex.App.—Corpus Christi 1995) (not necessary for same 10 jurors to agree), *rev'd on other grounds*, 953 S.W.2d 706 (Tex.1997), *and* ***Greater Houston Transp. Co. v. Zrubeck***, 850 S.W.2d 579, 588 (Tex.App.—Corpus Christi 1993, writ denied) (dicta; not necessary for same 10 jurors to agree).

§5. REQUEST TO POLL JURY

§5.1 Request. As soon as the verdict is returned, the parties should examine it for clerical and other errors and promptly ask the court to poll the jury before it is discharged. ***Pate v. Texline Feed Mills Inc.***, 689 S.W.2d 238, 243 (Tex.App.—Amarillo 1985, writ ref'd n.r.e.). The parties should always ask for a poll when the jury returns less than a unanimous verdict to determine if the same jurors agreed on their answers to each question. *See* ***Gonzalez***, 694 S.W.2d at 390-91. The right to poll the jury can be waived and must be requested to be invoked. ***Suggs v. Fitch***, 64 S.W.3d 658, 660 (Tex.App.—Texarkana 2001, no pet.). To preserve error, the party must secure a ruling refusing to poll. ***Greater Houston Transp.***, 850 S.W.2d at 585 (court never ruled it would not poll).

§5.2 Procedure. To poll the jury, the court should read each question and the corresponding answer, call the name of each juror, and ask if that is the verdict of that juror. TRCP 294. *But see* ***J.D. Abrams, Inc. v. McIver***, 966 S.W.2d 87, 95 (Tex.App.—Houston [1st Dist.] 1998, pet. denied) (judge did not read the questions & answers, only asked "whether this was his/her answers").

§6. DISCHARGING JURY

§6.1 Objections to verdict. If there is a conflict or inconsistency in the jury's verdict, the parties must object before the court discharges the jury; if not, the error is waived. ***Norwest Mortg. v. Salinas***, 999 S.W.2d 846, 865 (Tex.App.—Corpus Christi 1999, pet. denied); *see, e.g.*, ***Rice Food Mkts. v. Ramirez***, 59 S.W.3d 726, 730 (Tex. App.—Amarillo 2001, no pet.) (D did not object to jury's breakdown of damages in separate components, as opposed to lump sum).

§6.2 No recall. Once the court receives the jury verdict, the court will discharge the jury. Once it discharges the jury, it cannot recall the jury for additional deliberations. ***Archer Daniels Midland Co. v. Bohall***, 114 S.W.3d 42, 46 (Tex.App.—Eastland 2003, n.p.h.); ***Branham v. Brown***, 925 S.W.2d 365, 368 (Tex.App.—Houston [1st Dist.] 1996, no writ).

§7. POSTVERDICT CONTACT WITH JURORS

Communication between parties, counsel, and discharged jurors can be a valuable experience for all concerned. ***Commission for Lawyer Discipline v. Benton***, 980 S.W.2d 425, 433 (Tex.1998). In particular, a lawyer who has lost the case may ask the jurors why they were not persuaded and thus learn something that will help her in the future. *Id.* Federal courts generally disfavor postverdict interviewing of jurors, even when leave is sought to educate counsel and not to impeach the verdict. ***Haeberle v. Texas Int'l Airlines***, 739 F.2d 1019, 1021 (5th Cir.1984). In state court, a lawyer's postverdict contact with jurors is limited by the Texas Disciplinary Rules of Professional Conduct. Rule 3.06(d) prohibits lawyers connected with the case from asking "questions of or mak[ing] comments to a member of that jury that are calculated merely to harass or embarrass the juror or to influence his actions in future jury service." Tex. Disc. R. Prof. Conduct 3.06(d). The Supreme Court has limited Rule 3.06(d) by striking the term "embarrass" and narrowing the term "harass" by defining it to include four elements: "(1) a course of conduct, (2) directed at a specific person or persons, (3) causing or tending to cause substantial distress, and (4) having no legitimate purpose." ***Commission for Lawyer Discipline***, 980 S.W.2d at 439-40.

§8. REVIEW

To ask the court to disregard some or all of the jury findings, see "Motion for JNOV," ch. 9-B, p. 591. To ask the court for a new trial based on jury misconduct, see "MNT Based on Jury or Bailiff Misconduct," ch. 10-B, §13, p. 626.

COMMENTARIES

CHAPTER 9. THE JUDGMENT

TABLE OF CONTENTS

A. MOTION FOR JUDGMENT

§1. GENERAL

§1.1 Rules. TRCP 300-316.

§1.2 Purpose. The motion for judgment is a request for the court to sign the draft of the judgment prepared by the movant.

§1.3 Forms. *O'Connor's Texas Civil Forms*, FORMS 9A.

§1.4 Other references. *O'Connor's Texas Causes of Action*, "Damages," chs. 35-38, p. 937 (2004) (*O'Connor's COA*).

§2. MOTION

§2.1 Motion for judgment on the verdict. A motion for rendition of judgment should include a proposed judgment for the court to sign.

1. By the winner. A party who wants a judgment on the jury's verdict (or in a nonjury trial, on the decision announced by the court) should file a motion to render judgment. ***O'Connor's*** FORM 9A:01.

(1) Damages & interest. If the fact-finder found that one of the parties is entitled to damages, the motion should request damages and interest (prejudgment and postjudgment). See "Damages," ch. 9-C, §4.4, p. 598; "Prejudgment interest," ch. 9-C, §4.5, p. 599; "Postjudgment interest," ch. 9-C, §4.6, p. 599.

(2) Attorney fees. The motion should request attorney fees when appropriate. See "Attorney Fees from Adverse Party," ch. 1-H, §10, p. 45.

(3) Costs. The motion should make a general request for costs. Itemization is not necessary. The clerk of the court will prepare a bill of costs. See "Costs," ch. 9-C, §4.9, p. 600.

(4) Other relief. The motion should request any other relief appropriate to the case.

2. By the loser. A party who lost the case often wants the court to sign a judgment so it can begin the appeal process. ***O'Connor's*** FORM 9A:02.

(1) On the verdict. The losing party can ask the court to render judgment on the verdict without losing the right to challenge the judgment on appeal. To preserve the right to appeal, the motion for judgment should state that the party (1) disagrees with the content and result of the proposed judgment, (2) agrees only to the form of the proposed judgment, and (3) plans to challenge the judgment on appeal. ***First Nat'l Bank v. Fojtik***, 775 S.W.2d 632, 633 (Tex.1989). If the losing party asks the court to render judgment without reserving the right to appeal, the party cannot complain about the judgment on appeal. ***Casu v. Marathon Ref. Co.***, 896 S.W.2d 388, 389-90 (Tex.App.—Houston [1st Dist.] 1995, writ denied); *see* ***Green v. Texas Workers' Comp. Ins. Facility***, 993 S.W.2d 839, 843 (Tex.App.—Austin 1999, pet. denied) (party cannot, after moving for rendition of J, take a position on appeal inconsistent with that J). The reservation of the right to appeal must be contained in the motion for judgment; it is not effective if contained in some other motion. ***Fojtik***, 775 S.W.2d at 633; *see* ***Litton Indus. Prods. v. Gammage***, 668 S.W.2d 319, 322 (Tex.1984) (reservation of right to appeal in brief accompanying motion disapproved). *But see* ***Chappel Hill Bank v. Lane Bank Equip. Co.***, 38 S.W.3d 237, 247 (Tex.App.—Texarkana 2001, pet. denied) (objection in oral argument made before motion for J was filed preserved error).

(2) To limit damages. If the defendant is entitled to limit damages, the motion should so state. Damages are limited under a number of statutes: • In suits seeking exemplary damages. See ***O'Connor's COA***, "Damages Act cap," ch. 35-G, §2.6.1, p. 1017. • In DTPA suits, the plaintiff is limited to economic damages unless the defendant committed the act knowingly or intentionally. See ***O'Connor's COA***, "Additional damages," ch. 8, §3.2, p. 188.

(3) To force election of remedies. When a plaintiff prevails on two theories of recovery for the same wrong, the defendant should ask the trial court to require the plaintiff to elect damages. A plaintiff is not entitled to a double recovery for the same injury. *See* ***Waite Hill Servs. v. World Class Metal Works***, 959 S.W.2d 182, 184 (Tex.1998) (before rendition of judgment, D requested that trial court require P to elect its remedy).

§2.2 Motion for judgment contrary to the verdict. If the party seeks a judgment contrary to the jury's verdict, the party should prepare a motion for judgment notwithstanding the verdict. See "Motion for JNOV," ch. 9-B, below.

§2.3 Motion for judgment on agreement. A party who wants the court to sign a judgment on a settlement agreement should file a motion to render judgment on the agreement and attach a verified copy of the settlement agreement. See "Agreements Between Lawyers – Rule 11," ch. 1-H, §9, p. 44. A judgment rendered on the agreement of the parties cures all non-jurisdictional defects. ***Mailhot v. Mailhot***, ___ S.W.3d ___ (Tex.App.—Houston [1st Dist.] 2003, n.p.h.) (No. 01-02-00808-CV; 11-20-03).

§3. DRAFT OF THE JUDGMENT

Often, the trial court will ask the attorneys to prepare the judgment to reflect its decision, and it will sign the judgment at a later date. In most cases, the prevailing party will prepare a draft of the judgment for the trial court's signature and send copies to the other parties. Any party, however, may prepare a draft of the judgment. TRCP 305.

§4. MOTION TO SEVER, DISMISS, OR NONSUIT

If the court is rendering judgment on only part of the lawsuit, a party may file a motion to sever, dismiss, or nonsuit the remaining claims, making the judgment final and appealable. See "What judgments are final," ch. 9-C, §6.3, p. 603.

§5. RESPONSE

As a general rule, it is not necessary to file a response to the motion for judgment. However, if the motion asks for relief to which the party is not entitled, the other party should file a response objecting to the relief. *See, e.g.*, ***Wal-Mart Stores v. McKenzie***, 997 S.W.2d 278, 280 (Tex.1999) (D preserved error by objecting in its response to damages sought in motion for judgment). See ***O'Connor's*** FORM 9A:03.

§6. HEARING

It is not necessary to hold a hearing on the motion to sign the judgment. If a party wants a hearing, it should request one in writing.

§7. PRESERVATION OF ERROR

The motion for judgment preserves error should the trial court modify or reject the proposed judgment. *See, e.g.*, ***Emerson v. Tunnell***, 793 S.W.2d 947, 947-48 (Tex.1990) (P's motion for J on verdict for $238,000 preserved error when trial court rendered J for only $208,000); ***Texas Commerce Bank v. Lebco Constructors***, 865 S.W.2d 68, 81 (Tex.App.—Corpus Christi 1993, writ denied) (request to render J, which included all parties, preserved error when court did not include one of them). It is not necessary for the trial court to overrule the motion for judgment; the motion is overruled if the trial court enters a judgment different from the one proposed by the motion. *See, e.g.*, ***Salinas v. Rafati***, 948 S.W.2d 286, 288 (Tex.1997) (when court granted motion to disregard jury findings it automatically overruled motion for J on findings, thus preserving error); *see also* TRAP 33.1(a)(2)(A) (trial court may rule on motion expressly or implicitly).

B. MOTION FOR JNOV

§1. GENERAL

§1.1 Rule. TRCP 301.

§1.2 Purpose. A motion for judgment notwithstanding the verdict (JNOV) and a motion to disregard a jury answer ask the trial court to disregard all or some of the jury's answers to the jury questions and to render judgment for the movant. The only distinction between the two motions is that the motion for JNOV asks the trial court to disregard all the jury findings and render a judgment contrary to the jury's findings; the motion to disregard asks the trial court to disregard only some of the jury answers and render judgment on the remaining ones. *See* ***Teston v. Miller***, 349 S.W.2d 296, 299 (Tex.App.—Beaumont 1961, writ ref'd n.r.e.). Motions for JNOV and to disregard preserve the "no evidence" and "as a matter of law" points for appeal. Here, both motions will be referred to as a motion for JNOV.

§1.3 Forms. ***O'Connor's Texas Civil Forms***, FORMS 9B.

§1.4 Other references. ***O'Connor's Texas Causes of Action*** (2004).

§2. MOTION

§2.1 Written motion. The trial court cannot disregard a jury finding on its own initiative but can do so only on written motion. TRCP 301; ***Rush v. Barrios***, 56 S.W.3d 88, 93 (Tex.App.—Houston [14th Dist.] 2001, pet. denied); ***Lamb v. Franklin***, 976 S.W.2d 339, 343 (Tex.App.—Amarillo 1998, no pet.). The requirement for a motion is jurisdictional. ***Olin Corp. v. Cargo Carriers, Inc.***, 673 S.W.2d 211, 214 (Tex.App.—Houston [14th Dist.] 1984, no writ). One court has held that once a party files a motion for JNOV, the court can grant a JNOV on a ground not included in the motion. *See* ***McDade v. Texas Commerce Bank***, 822 S.W.2d 713, 717-18 (Tex.App.—Houston [1st Dist.] 1991, writ denied) (D's motion asserted there was no evidence to support two jury answers; court granted JNOV on statute of limitations).

§2.2 Specific reasons. The motion must specifically identify the findings to be disregarded, present the reasons and authority to disregard them, and request the court to render either a judgment on the remaining findings or, if all the findings are to be disregarded, a judgment contrary to all the findings. ***Dupree v. Piggly Wiggly Shop Rite Foods***, 542 S.W.2d 882, 892 (Tex.App.—Corpus Christi 1976, writ ref'd n.r.e.).

§2.3 Attach proposed judgment. The party should attach a draft of the proposed judgment to the motion for JNOV. See ***O'Connor's*** FORMS 9B:01, 9B:03.

§2.4 Effect of motion on plenary power & appellate deadlines. See "Motion for JNOV," ch. 9-C, §6.5.1(1)(c)[3], p. 606; "Changing judgment during plenary power," ch. 9-C, §7.1, p. 608.

§3. GROUNDS FOR JNOV

A JNOV is proper only when a directed verdict would have been proper. TRCP 301; ***Fort Bend Cty. Drainage Dist. v. Sbrusch***, 818 S.W.2d 392, 394 (Tex.1991); ***Wal-Mart Stores v. Bolado***, 54 S.W.3d 837, 841 (Tex.App.—Corpus Christi 2001, no pet.). See "Grounds for Directed Verdict," ch. 8-G, §4, p. 562. A motion for JNOV is used to present the following types of complaints to the trial court:

§3.1 No evidence. The jury's answer to a question should be disregarded because there is no evidence to support it. ***Tiller v. McLure***, ___ S.W.3d ___ (Tex.2003) (No. 02-0136; 5-8-03); ***Wal-Mart Stores v. Miller***, 102 S.W.3d 706, 709 (Tex.2003); ***Brown v. Bank of Galveston***, 963 S.W.2d 511, 513 (Tex.1998). When the evidence is no more than a scintilla, it is no evidence. ***Rush***, 56 S.W.3d at 94.

§3.2 Conclusive evidence. The jury's answer to a question should be disregarded because a fact was established to the contrary as a matter of law. *See, e.g.*, ***TRT Dev. Co. v. Meyers***, 15 S.W.3d 281, 287 (Tex.App.—Corpus Christi 2000, no pet.) (JNOV was proper when statements were protected by qualified privilege); ***Gallas v. Car Biz, Inc.***, 914 S.W.2d 592, 593 (Tex.App.—Dallas 1995, writ denied) (JNOV was proper because sale was void); ***John Masek Corp. v. Davis***, 848 S.W.2d 170, 174 (Tex.App.—Houston [1st Dist.] 1992, writ denied) (JNOV was proper because D had unilateral right to liquidate business & Ps could not sue for liquidation).

PRACTICE TIP

In a motion for JNOV, never argue that the evidence was factually insufficient. A motion for JNOV will not preserve a complaint that the evidence was factually insufficient. ***Kratz v. Exxon Corp.****, 890 S.W.2d 899, 902 (Tex.App.—El Paso 1994, no writ). To preserve a complaint that the evidence was factually insufficient, the party must file a motion for new trial. See "MNT to Challenge the Evidence," ch. 10-B, §9, p. 623.*

§3.3 Legal bar. Even when a party proves all the allegations in its pleadings, if a legal principle prevents that party from prevailing on its claim or defense, the court should grant a motion for JNOV. ***UPS, Inc. v. Tasdemiroglu***, 25 S.W.3d 914, 916 n.4 (Tex.App.—Houston [14th Dist.] 2000, pet. denied); *see, e.g.*, ***Rush***, 56 S.W.3d at 94 (JNOV was proper, based on equity, to reduce fee of discharged attorney); ***Farias v. Laredo Nat'l Bank***, 985 S.W.2d 465, 473-74 (Tex.App.—San Antonio 1997, pet. denied) (JNOV should have been granted because statute of limitations expired); ***Franklin Nat'l Bank v. Boser***, 972 S.W.2d 98, 106 (Tex.App.—Texarkana 1998, pet. denied) (JNOV should have been granted because D had a perfected security interest).

§3.4 Answer immaterial. An immaterial jury question is one that was improperly submitted or, even though properly submitted, was rendered immaterial by other findings. ***Salinas v. Rafati***, 948 S.W.2d 286, 288 (Tex.1997); ***Spencer v. Eagle Star Ins. Co.***, 876 S.W.2d 154, 157 (Tex.1994); *see* ***Quick v. City of Austin***, 7 S.W.3d 109, 116 (Tex.1998) (court may disregard as immaterial a jury's finding on a question of law). The trial court may, without a motion, disregard the answer to an immaterial jury question. ***Lamb***, 976 S.W.2d at 343; ***Brown v. Armstrong***, 713 S.W.2d 725, 728 (Tex.App.—Houston [14th Dist.] 1986, writ ref'd n.r.e.). Disregarding a jury's finding on an immaterial issue is not a JNOV. ***Anderson, Greenwood & Co. v. Martin***, 44 S.W.3d 200, 216-17 (Tex.App.—Houston [14th Dist.] 2001, pet. denied). Although a party is not required to challenge an immaterial jury finding in a motion for JNOV, it should bring the error to the court's attention in some postverdict motion, either a motion for JNOV or a motion for new trial. *See, e.g.*, ***City of Dallas v. Moreau***, 718 S.W.2d 776, 779 (Tex.App.—Corpus Christi 1986, writ ref'd n.r.e.) (court should have rendered JNOV because governmental immunity rendered jury's answers immaterial).

§4. DEADLINES

§4.1 To file motion. TRCP 301 does not identify a filing deadline for a motion for JNOV. ***Kirschberg v. Lowe***, 974 S.W.2d 844, 846 (Tex.App.—San Antonio 1998, no pet.). For years, courts have disagreed about the deadline for a motion for JNOV. *Compare* ***Commonwealth Lloyd's Ins. Co. v. Thomas***, 825 S.W.2d 135, 141 (Tex. App.—Dallas 1992) (motion for JNOV must be filed within 30 days of signing of J), *writ granted w.r.m.*, 843 S.W.2d 486 (Tex.1993), *with* ***Needville ISD v. S.P.J.S.T. Rest Home***, 566 S.W.2d 40, 42 (Tex.App.—Beaumont 1978, no writ) (motion for JNOV can be filed as long as trial court has jurisdiction over case). No matter what the actual filing deadline, for a motion for JNOV to extend the appellate deadlines and the court's plenary power, the motion for JNOV must be filed within the same deadlines as a motion for new trial—30 days from the date the court signed the judgment. See "Motion for JNOV," ch. 9-C, §6.5.1(1)(c)[3], p. 606; "Deadlines for MNT," ch. 10-B, §5, p. 619.

PRACTICE TIP

Until settled by the Supreme Court, always file your motion for JNOV within the deadlines for the motion for new trial and ask the trial court to rule on the motion no later than 75 days after the trial court signed the judgment.

§4.2 For ruling. TRCP 301 does not identify a deadline for the trial court to sign an order on the motion for JNOV. The best practice is for the movant to request that the court sign a written order on the motion for JNOV before the deadline for overruling the motion for new trial—75 days from signing the judgment. Some courts have held that a motion for JNOV does not preserve error unless the court overrules it within the same time limits for ruling on a motion for new trial. ***Spiller v. Lyons***, 737 S.W.2d 29, 29 (Tex.App.—Houston [14th Dist.] 1987, no writ); ***Commercial Stand. Ins. Co. v. Southern Farm Bureau Cas. Ins. Co.***, 509 S.W.2d 387, 392 (Tex.App.—Corpus Christi 1974, writ ref'd n.r.e.). Other courts have held that the motion for JNOV will preserve error if it is overruled before the judgment becomes final—105 days from the signing of the judgment. ***Eddings v. Black***, 602 S.W.2d 353, 357 (Tex.App.—El Paso 1980), *writ ref'd n.r.e.*, 615 S.W.2d 168 (Tex.1981); ***Needville ISD***, 566 S.W.2d at 42.

§5. RESPONSE

If there is any chance the trial court may seriously consider the movant's motion for JNOV, the nonmovant should file a response and point out why the JNOV would be improper. Some local rules presume that not responding to a motion is an acquiescence. See ***O'Connor's*** FORMS 9B:02, 9B:04.

§6. ORDER

§6.1 Hearing. No hearing is necessary. If there is a hearing, it is for argument only, not evidence.

§6.2 Written order. The order granting or denying the motion for JNOV should be in writing. However, an oral ruling made on the record or an implicit ruling will also preserve error. See "Types of rulings," ch. 1-G, §2.2, p. 33.

§6.3 Order or judgment. If the trial court grants the motion for JNOV, it should sign a final judgment. If the trial court denies the motion for JNOV, it should sign an order denying the motion. For the form of the judgment, see ***O'Connor's*** FORMS 9C.

§7. REVIEW

§7.1 Standard of review. To test whether the trial court erred in granting or denying a motion for JNOV, the appellate court must consider only the evidence and the reasonable inferences supporting the jury's answers, disregarding all contrary evidence and inferences. ***Tiller v. McLure***, ___ S.W.3d ___ (Tex.2003) (No. 02-0136; 5-8-03); ***Johnson & Johnson Med. v. Sanchez***, 924 S.W.2d 925, 929 (Tex.1996); ***Best v. Ryan Auto Group***, 786 S.W.2d 670, 671 (Tex.1990). To uphold a JNOV, an appellate court must decide that no evidence supports the jury's findings. ***Mancorp, Inc. v. Culpepper***, 802 S.W.2d 226, 227 (Tex.1990). If there is more than a scintilla of competent evidence to support the jury's finding, the JNOV will be reversed. ***Wal-Mart Stores v. Miller***, 102 S.W.3d 706, 709 (Tex.2003); ***Mancorp***, 802 S.W.2d at 228.

§7.2 Trial court denied JNOV. If the trial court denied the motion for JNOV, on appeal the movant will challenge the trial court's ruling with a "no evidence" point of error or with a point that the issue is established to the contrary as a matter of law.

1. Render for appellant. In most cases, when an appellate court reverses the trial court for denying a motion for JNOV, the court renders judgment for the appellant.

2. Remand for new trial. In some cases, when the interest of justice requires, the appellate court can reverse the judgment and remand for a new trial. ***Stephens v. Felix Mexican Rest.***, 899 S.W.2d 309, 314 (Tex.App.—Houston [14th Dist.] 1995, writ denied) (if "no evidence" objection had been sustained, appellee would have submitted other theory of liability to the jury); *see also* ***Jackson v. Ewton***, 411 S.W.2d 715, 718 (Tex.1967) (remand only in unusual cases).

§7.3 Trial court granted JNOV. If the trial court rendered a JNOV, on appeal the parties will take the following positions.

1. Appellant. The appellant (verdict winner but judgment loser) must challenge each ground for the JNOV. If the JNOV does not state a ground, the appellant must challenge all grounds stated in the motion. ***Fort Bend Cty. Drainage Dist. v. Sbrusch***, 818 S.W.2d 392, 394 (Tex.1991); ***Miga v. Jensen***, 25 S.W.3d 370, 375 (Tex.App.—Fort Worth 2000), *rev'd in part on other grounds*, 96 S.W.3d 207 (Tex.2002). The appellant should argue that the trial court erred in signing the JNOV because the evidence was not conclusive (arguing there was enough evidence to create a fact issue for the jury), or if the JNOV was granted because of a preclusive legal theory, that the law did not preclude judgment on the verdict. The JNOV should be reversed when there is more than a scintilla of competent evidence to support the jury's finding. ***Farias v. Laredo Nat'l Bank***, 985 S.W.2d 465, 470 (Tex.App.—San Antonio 1997, pet. denied). The appellant will argue that the court properly submitted the case to the jury and that the jury properly resolved the factual issues. ***Mancorp***, 802 S.W.2d at 227.

2. Appellee. The appellee (verdict loser but judgment winner) can make a number of defensive arguments to support the JNOV. *See* ***O'Connor's Texas Civil Appeals***, "Appellee's reply & cross-points," ch. 17-C, §6.6, p. 214 (2002-03).

3. Relief. If the appellate court sustains the appellant's points challenging the JNOV, the court will then consider the appellee's cross-points of error. If there are no cross-points, or if the court overrules them, the court should enter a judgment on the jury's verdict or remand in the interest of justice. *See, e.g.*, ***Kenneco Energy v. Johnson & Higgins***, 921 S.W.2d 254, 267-68 (Tex.App.—Houston [1st Dist.] 1995) (J rendered for appellant), *modified on other grounds*, 962 S.W.2d 507 (Tex.1998). When the appellate court reverses a JNOV and directs the trial court to render judgment on the verdict, the appellee can file a motion for new trial after the trial court renders the judgment on the verdict. ***Lawson v. Lawson***, 828 S.W.2d 158, 162 (Tex.App.—Texarkana 1992, writ denied). When the appellate court sustains the appellant's challenges to the JNOV and also sustains one of the appellee's cross-points listed in TRCP 324(c), the court will either affirm the JNOV or reverse and remand for a new trial. *See* ***De Los Santos v. Alamo Lumber Co.***, 683 S.W.2d 48, 51 (Tex.App.—San Antonio 1984, no writ). *See* ***O'Connor's Texas Civil Appeals***, "Appellee's reply & cross-points," ch. 17-C, §6.6, p. 214.

C. THE JUDGMENT

§1. GENERAL

§1.1 Rules. TRCP 300-316.

§1.2 Purpose. The judgment is the official document announcing the resolution of the issues in the lawsuit. ***Comet Aluminum Co. v. Dibrell***, 450 S.W.2d 56, 58 (Tex.1970). The judgment grants the winning party the relief earned by its victory. ***Jones v. Springs Ranch Co.***, 642 S.W.2d 551, 553 (Tex.App.—Amarillo 1982, no writ). The purpose of a signed judgment under TRCP 306a is to fix a date certain from which appellate deadlines can be determined. ***Burrell v. Cornelius***, 570 S.W.2d 382, 383 (Tex.1978).

§1.3 Forms & timetables. ***O'Connor's Texas Civil Forms***, FORMS 9C; Timetables, this book, Motion to Extend Postjudgment Deadlines, p. 1014, Appeal to the Court of Appeals, p. 1016.

§1.4 Other references. ***O'Connor's Texas Civil Appeals***, "Can This Case Be Appealed?", ch. 11-A, §2, p. 4 (2002-03); ***O'Connor's Texas Causes of Action*** (2004) (***O'Connor's COA***); Carlson & Dunn, *Navigating Procedural Minefields: Nuances in Determining Finality of Judgments, Plenary Power, & Appealability*, 41 S.Tex.L.Rev. 953 (2000).

§2. ESSENTIALS OF A VALID JUDGMENT

§2.1 Conform to pleadings. The judgment must conform to the pleadings. TRCP 301; ***City of Austin v. Castillo***, 25 S.W.3d 309, 314 (Tex.App.—Austin 2000, pet. denied); ***Soto v. Sea-Road Int'l***, 942 S.W.2d 67, 75 (Tex.App.—Corpus Christi 1997, writ denied). See "Grounds to Amend – Trial & Post-Trial," ch. 8-F, §5, p. 557. When a final judgment results from a settlement agreement, it must strictly comply with the terms of the agreement. ***Keim v. Anderson***, 943 S.W.2d 938, 946 (Tex.App.—El Paso 1997, no writ). See ***O'Connor's*** FORMS 9C.

§2.2 Definite & certain. The judgment must be sufficiently definite and certain so as to define and protect the rights of the litigants. ***Stewart v. USA Custom Paint & Body Shop***, 870 S.W.2d 18, 20 (Tex.1994). If a judgment is not definite, it must provide a means of determining rights so the ministerial officers can execute on the judgment. *Id.*; ***Olympia Marble & Granite v. Mayes***, 17 S.W.3d 437, 440 (Tex.App.—Houston [1st Dist.] 2000, no pet.); ***Kimsey v. Kimsey***, 965 S.W.2d 690, 694 (Tex.App.—El Paso 1998, pet. denied). If a judgment is not definite and its meaning is not capable of being ascertained, it is not a final judgment. *See* ***Hatton v. Burgess***, 167 S.W.2d 260, 262-63 (Tex.App.—Beaumont 1942, writ ref'd) (J was void because it did not provide sufficient information to identify land awarded to prevailing party); *see also* ***American Cas. & Life Ins. Co. v. Boyd***, 394 S.W.2d 685, 688 (Tex.App.—Tyler 1965, no writ) (unintelligible order has no legal effect).

§2.3 Jurisdiction over party. The trial court must have jurisdiction over the parties; if not, the judgment is void. ***State ex rel. Latty v. Owens***, 907 S.W.2d 484, 485 (Tex.1995); ***Browning v. Placke***, 698 S.W.2d 362, 363 (Tex.1985).

§2.4 Jurisdiction over subject matter. The trial court must have jurisdiction over the subject matter of the suit; if not, the judgment is void. ***Owens***, 907 S.W.2d at 485; ***Browning***, 698 S.W.2d at 363; *see* ***Dubai Pet. Co. v. Kazi***, 12 S.W.3d 71, 74-75 (Tex.2000); *see, e.g.*, ***Parker v. Veterans Admin.***, 786 S.W.2d 516, 518 (Tex.App.—Houston [14th Dist.] 1990, no writ) (court did not have jurisdiction of suit against the VA, a federal agency).

§2.5 Jurisdiction to render judgment. The trial court must have jurisdiction to render a particular judgment; if not, the judgment is void. ***Owens***, 907 S.W.2d at 485; *see, e.g.*, ***Texas Prop. & Cas. Ins. Guar. Ass'n v. De Los Santos***, 47 S.W.3d 584, 588 (Tex.App.—Corpus Christi 2001, no pet.) (court did not have jurisdiction to render second J 54 days after signing first J when no MNT was filed); ***Glunz v. Hernandez***, 908 S.W.2d 253, 257 (Tex. App.—San Antonio 1995, writ denied) (court did not have jurisdiction to render second J when parties did not appeal first J, which was final).

§2.6 Qualified judge. The trial judge must be qualified by law to sit in the court; if not, the trial judge cannot render a valid judgment. ***Buckholts ISD v. Glaser***, 632 S.W.2d 146, 148 (Tex.1982); ***Lone Star Indus. v. Ater***, 845 S.W.2d 334, 336 (Tex.App.—El Paso 1992, orig. proceeding).

§3. RENDERING, SIGNING, & ENTERING JUDGMENT

A judgment routinely goes through three stages: (1) rendition, (2) signing, and (3) entry. ***G.E. Capital Auto Fin. Leasing Servs. v. Stanfield***, 71 S.W.3d 351, 354 (Tex.App.—Tyler 2001, no pet.); ***Oak Creek Homes v. Jones***, 758 S.W.2d 288, 290 (Tex.App.—Waco 1988, no writ). The judgment becomes effective once it is "rendered." ***G.E. Capital***, 71 S.W.3d at 354. The timetables for the appeal begin to run once the judgment is reduced to writing and signed by the court. *Id.* When the judgment is "entered," it is noted in the court's records by the clerk of the court. The entry of the judgment has no legal significance for the parties or for the appellate timetables. *Id.*

§3.1 Rendition. A judgment is rendered when the court makes an official announcement—either orally in open court or by written memorandum filed with the clerk—of its decision on the matter submitted for adjudication. ***S&A Rest. v. Leal***, 892 S.W.2d 855, 857 (Tex.1995); ***Comet Aluminum Co. v. Dibrell***, 450 S.W.2d 56, 58 (Tex.1970); ***In re Guerra & Moore***, 35 S.W.3d 210, 217 (Tex.App.—Corpus Christi 2000, orig. proceeding). Rendition is a present act, either by spoken word or by signed memorandum, that resolves the issues on which the ruling is made. ***Reese v. Piperi***, 534 S.W.2d 329, 330 (Tex.1976); ***Becker v. Becker***, 997 S.W.2d 394, 395 (Tex.App.—Beaumont 1999, no pet.). The announcement of a judgment, either in open court or by an official document of the court, is the critical moment when the judgment becomes effective. ***Verret v. Verret***, 570 S.W.2d 138, 139-40 (Tex.App.—Houston [1st Dist.] 1978, no writ).

1. Methods of rendition.

(1) Written. Of the two methods of announcing or rendering a judgment, the written judgment is preferred. If possible, the parties should prepare a written judgment before the hearing where the judgment will be announced. For example, the party filing a motion for summary judgment should prepare a summary judgment to submit along with its motion.

(2) Oral. When it is not possible to prepare a written judgment in advance of the hearing, the alternative method of rendering the judgment is to have the court announce the judgment in open court on the record. The judge must announce the rendition as a present act, not as an intention to perform a future act. ***Reese***, 534 S.W.2d at 330; ***Burns v. Bishop***, 48 S.W.3d 459, 464 n.3 (Tex.App.—Houston [14th Dist.] 2001, no pet.); *see* ***In re Wilburn***, 18 S.W.3d 837, 840-41 (Tex.App.—Tyler 2000, pet. denied) (words indicated a present intent to render J); ***Able Cabling Servs. v. Aaron-Carter Elec.***, 16 S.W.3d 98, 101 (Tex.App.—Houston [1st Dist.] 2000, pet. denied) (words did not indicate a present intent to render J).

PRACTICE TIP

The winning party should make sure the trial judge makes an effective oral rendition of the judgment on the record. On the record, the judge should say "I now render the following judgment: (state the result)." Listen carefully. If the judge uses the future tense ("I plan to sign a judgment that will provide...."), ask the judge to restate the rendition as a present act, not a future one.

---

2. Not rendition.

(1) Docket entry. Docket sheet entries, which are inherently unreliable, are seldom specific enough to satisfy the requirements for a rendition. See "Docket entries," ch. 1-G, §3.3, p. 35.

(2) Letter from court. A letter from the trial court announcing the ruling is generally not a rendition or the equivalent of a signed judgment and does not begin the appellate timetables. See "Letters," ch. 1-G, §3.4, p. 35.

(3) Approval of settlement. When the trial court indicates its understanding the parties have agreed to settle and will prepare an order for a ruling, the court has not rendered judgment. ***Leal***, 892 S.W.2d at 857-58; ***In re Kasschau***, 11 S.W.3d 305, 311 (Tex.App.—Houston [14th Dist.] 1999, orig. proceeding); ***Formby's KOA v. BHP Water Sup. Corp.***, 730 S.W.2d 428, 430 (Tex.App.—Dallas 1987, no writ).

(4) Order granting motion for judgment. An order merely granting a motion for judgment is not a rendition of judgment and adjudicates nothing. ***Naaman v. Grider***, ___ S.W.3d ___ (Tex.2003) (No. 02-0784; 10-31-03) (appellate deadlines began when final J signed, not one month later when motion for J granted).

§3.2 Signing. When the trial judge signs a judgment without first making an oral announcement in open court, the act of signing the judgment is the official act of rendering the judgment; when the trial judge makes an oral announcement of the judgment in open court, the act of signing the judgment is only a ministerial act. *See* TRCP 306a(2); ***Dunn v. Dunn***, 439 S.W.2d 830, 832 (Tex.1969); ***In re Bland***, 960 S.W.2d 123, 124 (Tex.App.—Houston [1st Dist.] 1997, orig. proceeding). The signature may be made by the judge personally or through someone authorized by the judge. See "Signature," ch. 1-G, §3.1.2, p. 35. The signing of the judgment is significant because the appellate deadlines start on the date the trial court signs a judgment or appealable order. ***Farmer v. Ben E. Keith Co.***, 907 S.W.2d 495, 496 (Tex.1995); ***Martinez v. Humble Sand & Gravel***, 875 S.W.2d 311, 313 (Tex.1994); ***Reese***, 534 S.W.2d at 331; ***Coastal Bank v. Helle***, 48 S.W.3d 796, 799-800 (Tex.App.—Corpus Christi 2001, pet. denied).

§3.3 Entry. A judgment is entered when the clerk of the court performs the ministerial act of entering the judgment in the minutes of the court. ***Oak Creek Homes v. Jones***, 758 S.W.2d 288, 290 (Tex.App.—Waco 1988, no writ); *see also* ***Keim v. Anderson***, 943 S.W.2d 938, 942 (Tex.App.—El Paso 1997, no writ) (distinguishing entry of J from rendition of J). Once the judgment is signed by the trial court, it should be given to the clerk to file with the other documents of the case, and the clerk should make an entry in the minutes of the court. A signed judgment is valid whether or not it is filed or entered in the record. *See* ***In re Barber***, 982 S.W.2d 364, 367 (Tex.1998) (date of signing, not date of entry, controls); ***Prinz v. Dutschmann***, 678 S.W.2d 256, 258 (Tex.App.—Corpus Christi 1984, no writ) (divorce decree was rendered when signed, not when entered in the record).

§4. FORM OF THE JUDGMENT

§4.1 Parties. The judgment must contain the full names of the parties as stated in the pleadings. TRCP 306; ***City of Austin v. Castillo***, 25 S.W.3d 309, 314 (Tex.App.—Austin 2000, pet. denied); ***Crystal City ISD v. Wagner***, 605 S.W.2d 743, 747 (Tex.App.—San Antonio 1980, writ ref'd n.r.e.). The judgment must identify the parties in their correct capacities, that is, the same capacities in which the plaintiff brought suit and the defendant was sued. *See, e.g.*, ***Werner v. Colwell***, 909 S.W.2d 866, 869-70 (Tex.1995) (court could not render J against D as trustee, when D was sued only as individual).

§4.2 Declaration of legal effects of facts. The judgment should determine the rights of all the parties and dispose of all the issues. The judgment must state for whom and against whom it is rendered. TRCP 306.

§4.3 Statement of finality. The judgment should state whether it is intended to be a final or partial judgment. The inclusion of any of the following statements will indicate the judgment is intended to be final.

1. "This judgment finally disposes of all claims and all parties and is appealable." ***Lehmann v. Har-Con Corp.***, 39 S.W.3d 191, 206 (Tex.2001). This is the preferred statement to include in any judgment intended to be final.

2. "The plaintiff takes nothing." ***Ritzell v. Espeche***, 87 S.W.3d 536, 538 (Tex.2002); ***Lehmann***, 39 S.W.3d at 205. The statement "plaintiff takes nothing" constitutes a decision on the merits as to the plaintiff. *See* ***Clark v. Pimienta***, 47 S.W.3d 485, 486 (Tex.2001); ***De La Garza v. Express-News Corp.***, 722 S.W.2d 251, 253 (Tex. App.—San Antonio 1986, no writ).

3. "The case is dismissed." ***Lehmann***, 39 S.W.3d at 205. This language should not be used in a proceeding that resolves the case on the merits (*e.g.*, summary judgment). See "Resolve issues on the merits," ch. 7-B, §13.3.3, p. 482. A dismissal resolves a case on procedural grounds. Dismissal language should be used only in cases where dismissal is appropriate. See "Grounds for Dismissal," ch. 7-F, §2, p. 499.

PRACTICE TIP

In a case tried to a jury or to the court, it is not necessary to include a statement of finality in the judgment because such judgments are presumed to be final. See "Judgment after conventional trial," §6.3.1(2), p. 603. However, if any of the claims were disposed of outside the trial proceeding (e.g., by summary or default judgment or dismissal), the inclusion of a statement of finality will assure that the judgment is final and appealable.

---

§4.4 Damages. A money judgment should either state with certainty the amount to be recovered or furnish a means by which the amount can be determined. ***Beam v. Southwestern Bell Tel. Co.***, 164 S.W.2d 412, 416 (Tex. App.—Waco 1942, writ ref'd). If the amount of money awarded is uncertain, the judgment will be considered interlocutory. *E.g.*, ***Olympia Marble & Granite v. Mayes***, 17 S.W.3d 437, 440 (Tex.App.—Houston [1st Dist.] 2000, no pet.) (J not final because questions remained about date on which prejudgment interest would accrue); ***H.E. Butt Grocery Co. v. Bay, Inc.***, 808 S.W.2d 678, 680-81 (Tex.App.—Corpus Christi 1991, writ denied) (default J not final because it did not specify which interest rate applied for prejudgment interest); ***Jones v. Liberty Mut. Ins. Co.***, 733 S.W.2d 240, 242 (Tex.App.—El Paso 1987, no writ) (subrogation J was not final because medical payments, for which insurance company was to be reimbursed, had no termination date). See ***O'Connor's COA***, "General Concepts," ch. 35-A, p. 939.

1. **Proportionate responsibility.** In tort cases, proportionate responsibility is the method for determining the percentage of damages each party to a lawsuit must pay. *See* CPRC ch. 33. If a plaintiff is partially responsible for its own damages, the plaintiff's recovery is reduced or barred by the percentage of those damages attributed to the plaintiff. See ***O'Connor's COA***, "Proportionate Responsibility & Contribution," ch. 42, p. 1115.

2. Alternative theories of recovery & defense.

(1) Alternative recoveries. When a plaintiff's petition contains alternative grounds for recovery, the court cannot render judgment on all the grounds. ***Waite Hill Servs. v. World Class Metal Works***, 959 S.W.2d 182, 184 (Tex.1998); ***Southern Cty. Mut. Ins. Co. v. First Bank & Trust***, 750 S.W.2d 170, 173-74 (Tex.1988). When the jury returns favorable findings on alternative theories, the plaintiff is entitled to recover on the theory permitting the largest or most favorable recovery. ***Boyce Iron Works v. Southwestern Bell Tel. Co.***, 747 S.W.2d 785, 787 (Tex.1988); ***Woodlands Land Dev. Co. v. Jenkins***, 48 S.W.3d 415, 419 (Tex.App.—Beaumont 2001, no pet.). If the plaintiff does not make the election, the trial court should render a judgment allowing the greatest recovery. ***Birchfield v. Texarkana Mem'l Hosp.***, 747 S.W.2d 361, 367 (Tex.1987); ***Hill v. Heritage Res.***, 964 S.W.2d 89, 128 (Tex.App.—El Paso 1997, pet. denied).

(2) Alternative defenses. A court can render a judgment sustaining all the defendant's alternative defenses. By rendering a judgment for the defendant on all its defensive theories, the trial court can avoid a remand if one of the grounds is reversed on appeal. ***Oak Park Townhouses v. Brazosport Bank***, 851 S.W.2d 189, 190 (Tex.1993).

§4.5 Prejudgment interest. When prejudgment interest is allowed, the judgment should include the exact amount of prejudgment interest due. If the calculation is not available, the judgment must include the appropriate interest rate and the date of accrual. See ***O'Connor's COA***, "Prejudgment Interest," ch. 36, §2, p. 1027.

1. Accrual. Prejudgment interest begins to accrue either (1) 180 days after the date the defendant received written notice of the claim or (2) the date the suit in which judgment is rendered was filed, whichever is earlier. Fin. Code §304.104 (statutory); ***Johnson & Higgins v. Kenneco Energy***, 962 S.W.2d 507, 531 (Tex.1998) (common law); ***Town of Flower Mound v. Teague***, 111 S.W.3d 742, 763 (Tex.App.—Fort Worth 2003, pet. denied) (statutory). Prejudgment interest stops accruing the day before the judgment is signed. Fin. Code §304.104. Different rules apply to calculate interest if a settlement offer was extended. *See id.* §304.105. See ***O'Connor's COA***, "Settlement offer," ch. 36, §2.3.3(2)(b), p. 1030.

2. Rate. Prejudgment interest is computed as simple interest and does not compound. Fin. Code §304.104; ***Johnson & Higgins***, 962 S.W.2d at 532.

(1) Most cases. The rate for prejudgment interest is the same as for postjudgment interest. Fin. Code §304.103; ***Johnson & Higgins***, 962 S.W.2d at 532. See §4.6.2(1), below. Although Finance Code §304.103 sets the rate only for prejudgment interest for cases involving wrongful death, personal injury, and property damage, the Supreme Court has adopted the same rules of calculating prejudgment interest in all other cases. ***Johnson & Higgins***, 962 S.W.2d at 530-31.

(2) Some contract cases. In breach of contract cases where no rate of interest is specified and damages can be ascertained from the contract, prejudgment interest accrues at a rate of 6%. Fin. Code §302.002; ***Aquila Sw. Pipeline v. Harmony Expl.***, 48 S.W.3d 225, 243 (Tex.App.—San Antonio 2001, pet. denied).

3. Prejudgment interest not permitted. A party is not entitled to prejudgment interest on the following: • Future damages. Fin. Code §304.1045. • Exemplary damages. CPRC §41.007; ***C&H Nationwide v. Thompson***, 903 S.W.2d 315, 325 (Tex.1994); ***Ellis Cty. State Bank v. Keever***, 888 S.W.2d 790, 797 (Tex.1994). • Attorney fees and costs. ***Ellis Cty.***, 888 S.W.2d at 797 n.13. • Prejudgment interest itself. *Id.* See ***O'Connor's COA***, "When not recoverable," ch. 36, §2.1.2, p. 1028. 03

§4.6 Postjudgment interest. All money judgments must specify the postjudgment interest rate applicable to that judgment. Fin. Code §304.001. See ***O'Connor's COA***, "Postjudgment Interest," ch. 36, §3, p. 1030.

1. Accrual. Postjudgment interest on a money judgment accrues beginning on the date the judgment is signed and ends on the date the judgment is satisfied. Fin. Code §304.005(a).

2. Rate. Postjudgment interest is compounded annually. *Id.* §304.006.

(1) Most cases. Finance Code §304.003 controls the postjudgment interest rate in most cases. For exceptions, see §4.6.2(2), below. The postjudgment interest rate is the prime rate as published by the Federal Reserve Bank of New York on the date of computation. Fin. Code §304.003(c)(1). If the prime rate is less than 5%, then the postjudgment interest rate is 5%; if the prime rate is more than 15%, the postjudgment interest rate is 15%. *Id.* §304.003(c)(2), (3). Currently, the postjudgment interest rate is 5% per year. To check the current interest rate, call the Public Information Officer at the Office of Consumer Credit Commissioner, (512) 936-7600. The rate is published each month and can be checked online at www.occc.state.tx.us, by selecting "News Releases & Publications," then "Texas Credit Letter," and then "Current Judgment Rate."

(2) Some contract cases. If a contract provides for interest or time price differential, the judgment earns postjudgment interest at a rate equal to the lesser of (1) the rate specified in the contract, which may be a variable rate, or (2) 18% a year. Fin. Code §304.002; *see, e.g.*, ***AU Pharm. v. Boston***, 986 S.W.2d 331, 336 (Tex. App.—Texarkana 1999, no pet.) (because contract provided for a zero post-J interest rate, no post-J interest could be awarded).

§4.7 Attorney fees. When appropriate, the judgment should include a provision awarding attorney fees. See "Attorney Fees from Adverse Party," ch. 1-H, §10, p. 45; ***O'Connor's COA***, "Attorney Fees," ch. 38, p. 1041.

§4.8 Guardian ad litem fees. See "Liability for fees," ch. 1-I, §5.1, p. 54.

§4.9 Costs. The judgment should state that costs are awarded against a certain party, not the amount of the costs awarded. After the judgment is signed, the clerk will send a cost bill to the party taxed with the costs. A trial court, however, is not required to assess costs for its judgment to be final. ***City of Marshall v. Gonzales***, 107 S.W.3d 799, 803 (Tex.App.—Texarkana 2003, no pet.); ***Thompson v. Beyer***, 91 S.W.3d 902, 904-05 (Tex.App.—Dallas 2002, no pet.). See "What judgments are final," §6.3, p. 603; ***O'Connor's COA***, "Court Costs," ch. 37, p. 1033.

1. Who is entitled to costs.

(1) Successful party. The successful party to a suit is entitled to recover from the other party all taxable court costs it incurred. TRCP 131; ***Roberts v. Williamson***, 111 S.W.3d 113, 124 (Tex.2003); ***Furr's Supermkts. v. Bethune***, 53 S.W.3d 375, 378 (Tex.2001); ***Rogers v. Walmart Stores***, 686 S.W.2d 599, 601 (Tex.1985). Taxing costs against the successful party is contrary to TRCP 131. ***Martinez v. Pierce***, 759 S.W.2d 114, 114 (Tex.1988). A "successful party" is one who obtains a judgment of a competent court vindicating a civil claim of right. See ***O'Connor's COA***, "Successful party," ch. 37, §2.2.1(1), p. 1034. Whether a party is successful must be based on success on the merits, and not on whether damages were awarded. ***Johns v. Ram-Forwarding, Inc.***, 29 S.W.3d 635, 638 (Tex.App.—Houston [1st Dist.] 2000, no pet.). When both parties are successful, the trial court may tax costs against both. ***Niemeyer v. Tana Oil & Gas Corp.***, 39 S.W.3d 380, 389-90 (Tex.App.—Austin 2001, pet. denied); ***Building Concepts, Inc. v. Duncan***, 667 S.W.2d 897, 905-06 (Tex.App.—Houston [14th Dist.] 1984, writ ref'd n.r.e.).

(2) Unsuccessful party. For the court to award costs to the unsuccessful party, the court must (1) find good cause and (2) state the reasons on the record. TRCP 141; ***Roberts***, 111 S.W.3d at 124; ***Furr's***, 53 S.W.3d at 378; ***Rogers***, 686 S.W.2d at 601; *see* ***Marshall Investigation & Sec. Agency v. Whitaker***, 962 S.W.2d 62, 63 (Tex.App.—Houston [1st Dist.] 1997, no pet.) (case remanded for trial court to state good cause). See ***O'Connor's COA***, "'Good cause' exception," ch. 37, §2.2.2, p. 1036. As a matter of law, the potential harm to the unsuccessful party's emotional state is not good cause to tax costs against the successful party. ***Furr's***, 53 S.W.3d at 378.

2. Taxable court costs. Each party to a suit is responsible for accurately recording all costs and fees incurred during the lawsuit if the judgment provides for adjudication of such costs. CPRC §31.007(a). For a list of costs taxable as court costs, see ***O'Connor's COA***, "Taxable court costs," ch. 37, §2.3.1, p. 1036. For a list of costs not taxable as court costs, see ***O'Connor's COA***, "Nontaxable costs," ch. 37, §2.3.2, p. 1038.

§4.10 No findings of fact. The judgment in a nonjury case should not contain findings of fact. The findings of fact must be filed separately and should not be recited in the judgment. TRCP 299a. See "Not in judgment," ch. 10-E, §3.4.1, p. 645.

§4.11 Date signed. The judgment should have a line, immediately above the signature line for the trial judge, that reads: "Signed on ___________, 200__." ***Burrell v. Cornelius***, 570 S.W.2d 382, 384 (Tex.1978). The date the judgment is signed is important because it begins the appellate timetables. ***Farmer v. Ben E. Keith Co.***, 907 S.W.2d 495, 496 (Tex.1995); ***Reese v. Piperi***, 534 S.W.2d 329, 331 (Tex.1976); *see* ***Coinmach, Inc. v. Aspenwood Apt.***, 98 S.W.3d 377, 382 (Tex.App.—Houston [1st Dist.] 2003, no pet.) (signature date of judgment, not filing date, is relevant for determining appellate deadlines). The absence of a date on the judgment does not invalidate the judgment. TRCP 306a(2); ***Hammett v. Lee***, 730 S.W.2d 350, 351 (Tex.App.—Dallas 1987, writ dism'd). If the date is omitted and it is an issue on appeal, the appellate court can ask the trial court to certify the date the judgment was signed. ***Hammett***, 730 S.W.2d at 351.

§4.12 Signature line for judge. The judgment must contain a signature line for the trial judge.

§4.13 Signature line for lawyers. Traditionally, the judgment contains signature lines for the lawyers to approve the form of the judgment. To ensure the judgment is not construed as a consent judgment, the lawyer representing the losing party should sign under the statement "approved as to form only," not "approved as to form and substance." ***Transmission Exch. v. Long***, 821 S.W.2d 265, 275 (Tex.App.—Houston [1st Dist.] 1991, writ denied). However, even when a lawyer signs under the statement "approved as to form and substance," the appellate courts will look to the circumstances surrounding the judgment to determine if the parties intended to enter into a consent judgment. ***First Am. Title Ins. Co. v. Adams***, 829 S.W.2d 356, 364 (Tex.App.—Corpus Christi 1992, writ denied); ***Hill v. Bellville Gen. Hosp.***, 735 S.W.2d 675, 678 (Tex.App.—Houston [1st Dist.] 1987, no writ).

§5. NOTICE OF JUDGMENT

The clerk should send a notice of the judgment to the parties immediately after receiving the judgment from the judge. ***Board of Trustees of Bastrop ISD v. Toungate***, 958 S.W.2d 365, 367 (Tex.1997).

NOTE

*In **Lehmann v. Har-Con Corp.**, 39 S.W.3d 191, 206 (Tex.2001), the Supreme Court seemed to suggest that the clerk of the court is required to send the parties a copy of the judgment, citing TRCP 306a(3). However, by its very language, TRCP 306a(3) only requires the clerk to give notice that a judgment or an appealable order was signed. See TRCP 306a(3); see also TRCP 165a(1) (notice of signing, not a copy of the order), TRCP 239a (notice of the judgment, not a copy of the judgment). It is a good idea to require the clerk to send a copy of the judgment to the parties, but to accomplish that, the Supreme Court must amend the TRCPs.*

§5.1 Clerk's duty to give notice. The clerk has the duty to give the parties immediate notice, by first-class mail, that the court signed a judgment or an appealable order. *See* ***Hubert v. Illinois State Assistance Comm'n***, 867 S.W.2d 160, 163 (Tex.App.—Houston [14th Dist.] 1993, no writ) (TRCP 306a(3)). The clerk must provide notice (1) that a judgment was signed and (2) the date it was signed. ***Winkins v. Frank Winther Invs.***, 881 S.W.2d 557, 558 (Tex.App.—Houston [1st Dist.] 1994, no writ). If the clerk does not give notice of judgment, it is a violation of the party's right to due process—not merely a violation of a rule of procedure—because it deprives the party of its right to be heard by the court. ***Hubert***, 867 S.W.2d at 163. However, the lack of notice does not affect the beginning of the time periods listed in TRCP 306a(3) (except as provided by TRCP 306a(4) and TRAP 4.2), and does not constitute reversible error. *See* ***Campbell v. Fincher***, 72 S.W.3d 723, 724 (Tex.App.—Waco 2002, no pet.) (notice of default judgment).

§5.2 Rules requiring notice. There are three rules requiring the clerk to notify the parties that the court signed a judgment or appealable order: TRCP 306a(3), 165a(1), and 239a. These rules are for the administrative convenience of the parties. *See* ***Campbell***, 72 S.W.3d at 724 (TRCP 239a).

1. TRCP 306a. Under TRCP 306a(3), the clerk of the trial court is required to give the parties or their attorneys of record immediate notice by first-class mail that the court signed a judgment or an appealable order. ***John v. Marshall Health Servs.***, 58 S.W.3d 738, 740 (Tex.2001). The notice must be sent to all attorneys of record, not just lead counsel. TRCP 306a(3); ***Cannon v. ICO Tubular Servs.***, 905 S.W.2d 380, 388 (Tex.App.—Houston [1st Dist.] 1995, no writ).

2. TRCP 165a. Under TRCP 165a(1), the clerk must give the parties notice that the court signed an order of dismissal. See "Notice of Dismissal Order," ch. 7-F, §8, p. 504.

3. TRCP 239a. Under TRCP 239a, the clerk must give the defendant notice that the court signed a no-answer default judgment. See "Notice after no-answer default," ch. 7-A, §6.1, p. 452.

§5.3 Time periods run from judgment. The date the judgment is signed is the date from which to calculate the time periods for the court's plenary power and for filing postjudgment motions. TRCP 306a(1), 329b(d); ***Texas Prop. & Cas. Ins. Guar. Ass'n v. De Los Santos***, 47 S.W.3d 584, 587 n.3 (Tex.App.—Corpus Christi 2001, no pet.). When a party receives late notice of the judgment and files a motion to extend postjudgment deadlines, the date of actual notice becomes the date from which to calculate time periods. See "Motion to Extend Postjudgment Deadlines," ch. 10-G, p. 654.

§5.4 Time periods & the modified judgment. If the trial court changes the judgment while it still has plenary power over the judgment, the modified judgment extends the time to file postjudgment motions and the appellate timetables. See "Motion to Modify the Judgment," ch. 10-D, p. 639. If the court changes the judgment after it loses plenary power, only in a few cases are the appellate timetables extended. See "Motion for Judgment Nunc Pro Tunc," ch. 10-H, p. 659.

§6. FINAL JUDGMENT

Whether a judgment is final has important implications to both parties. An appeal can be prosecuted only from a final judgment (with certain statutory exceptions). *See* CPRC §§51.012, 51.014. The date of signing the judgment or final order disposing of the case begins the deadlines for filing postjudgment motions and for perfecting the appeal. TRCP 306a(1), 329b(a), (b), (g); ***In re Bennett***, 960 S.W.2d 35, 38 (Tex.1997); ***Farmer v. Ben E. Keith Co.***, 907 S.W.2d 495, 496 (Tex.1995); ***Martinez v. Humble Sand & Gravel***, 875 S.W.2d 311, 313 (Tex.1994). The period of the court's plenary power to change the judgment is calculated from the date the final judgment is signed. *See* TRCP 329b(e). See "Changing judgment during plenary power," §7.1, p. 608. Only a final judgment is given preclusive effect in later suits. Most importantly, only a final judgment can be enforced. *See, e.g.*, ***Enis v. Smith***, 883 S.W.2d 662, 663 (Tex.1994) (when Nevada court set aside its default J, that J could not be enforced in Texas). For more extensive treatment of issues relating to finality of judgments, see ***O'Connor's Texas Civil Appeals***, "Can This Case Be Appealed?", ch. 11-A, §2, p. 4.

§6.1 One-final-judgment rule.

1. Rule. As a general rule, only one final judgment may be rendered in a lawsuit. TRCP 301; ***Logan v. Mullis***, 686 S.W.2d 605, 609 (Tex.1985); ***Quanaim v. Frasco Rest. & Catering***, 17 S.W.3d 30, 35 (Tex.App.—Houston [14th Dist.] 2000, pet. denied); ***Tindall v. Bishop, Peterson & Sharp***, 961 S.W.2d 248, 252 (Tex.App.—Houston [1st Dist.] 1997, no writ). A final judgment is one disposing of all parties and all claims. ***North E. ISD v. Aldridge***, 400 S.W.2d 893, 895 (Tex.1966). By limiting the number of judgments to one per case, the one-final-judgment rule limits the number of appeals to one per case.

2. Exceptions. There are a number of exceptions to the rule that only one final, appealable judgment can be rendered in each case. The following are types of proceedings in which multiple final judgments can be rendered.

(1) Family & probate cases. In certain family and probate cases, a number of orders are appealable. See ***O'Connor's Texas Civil Appeals***, "Does the one-final judgment rule apply?", ch. 11-B, §2.1.2, p. 4.

(2) Order sealing records. An order sealing records under TRCP 76a(8) is considered a final and appealable order. See "Motion to Seal Court Records," ch. 5-K, p. 290; ***O'Connor's Texas Civil Appeals***, "Does the one-final judgment rule apply?", ch. 11-B, §2.1.2(1)(b), p. 4.

(3) Other exceptions. See ***O'Connor's Texas Civil Appeals***, "Appealing from an interlocutory order," ch. 11-B, §2.2, p. 7.

§6.2 Replacement judgment. When the court signs a judgment within its plenary power that is intended to replace the earlier judgment, it should specifically state the first judgment is vacated. ***Hammett v. Lee***, 730 S.W.2d 350, 351 (Tex.App.—Dallas 1987, writ dism'd). If the second judgment does not expressly vacate the first judgment, the second judgment will be presumed to vacate the first judgment unless the record indicates a contrary intent. ***Quanaim***, 17 S.W.3d at 39-40; *see, e.g.*, ***Tindall***, 961 S.W.2d at 252 (trial court signed two SJs on the same day, one for P and one for D; a month later, while court still had plenary power, it signed SJ for P, which was the final J); ***Owens-Corning Fiberglas Corp. v. Wasiak***, 883 S.W.2d 402, 411 (Tex.App.—Austin 1994, no writ) (signing second, identical J six days after the first J presumptively vacated first J); *see also* ***Wang v. Hsu***, 899 S.W.2d 409, 411-12 (Tex.App.—Houston [14th Dist.] 1995, writ denied) (there was no final J to appeal when trial court set aside second J). See "Second judgment problems," ch. 10-B, §5.6, p. 620; ***O'Connor's Texas Civil Appeals***, "Second judgment problems," ch. 15-A, §6.1, p. 167.

§6.3 What judgments are final. A judgment is not final just because it is captioned a "final judgment," or because the word "final" appears somewhere in the order, or because it awards costs, or because it says it is appealable. ***Lehmann v. Har-Con Corp.***, 39 S.W.3d 191, 205 (Tex.2001).

1. Judgments that are final.

(1) Judgment resolves all claims. A judgment is final if it resolves all claims in the lawsuit. ***Lehmann***, 39 S.W.3d at 200; ***Park Place Hosp. v. Estate of Milo***, 909 S.W.2d 508, 510 (Tex.1995). If the judgment resolves all claims, it is final even if it says it is not final. ***Lehmann***, 39 S.W.3d at 200.

(2) Judgment after conventional trial. There is a presumption that a judgment rendered after a conventional trial on the merits disposes of all claims and is final. ***John***, 58 S.W.3d at 740; ***Aldridge***, 400 S.W.2d at 897-98; *see also* ***Moritz v. Preiss***, ___ S.W.3d ___ (Tex.2003) (No. 01-1270; 6-12-03) (even though J named all Ds but one, finality presumption was appropriate because P did not request separate trial for that D and did not submit jury question on that D's liability).

(3) Merger or severance. An interlocutory judgment can be converted into a final judgment by merger or severance. ***City of Beaumont v. Guillory***, 751 S.W.2d 491, 492 (Tex.1988); ***Teer v. Duddlesten***, 664 S.W.2d 702, 704 (Tex.1984). A judgment becomes final on the date the judgment or order is signed disposing of the last claim, or on the date the last unadjudicated claim is severed from the adjudicated claims.

(a) Last claim resolved = merger. A judgment or order becomes final when the last claim in the lawsuit is resolved by a judgment or order. An interlocutory judgment is merged into a final judgment when all the remaining claims are resolved, either on the merits or by dismissal. *See, e.g.*, ***Parking Co. v. Wilson***, 58 S.W.3d 742, 742 (Tex.2001) (J rendered after trial of last claim made earlier partial SJ final); ***John***, 58 S.W.3d at 740 (J rendered after directed verdict made earlier nonsuit & partial SJ final); ***Clark v. Pimienta***, 47 S.W.3d 485, 486 (Tex. 2001) (last partial SJ made earlier partial SJs final); ***Wembley Inv. Co. v. Herrera***, 11 S.W.3d 924, 926 (Tex.1999) (order nonsuiting last Ds made earlier default J as to other Ds final); ***Webb v. Jorns***, 488 S.W.2d 407, 408-09 (Tex. 1972) (order dismissing hospital became final when it was merged into final J); ***Texas Sting, Ltd. v. R.B. Foods, Inc.***, 82 S.W.3d 644, 648 n.4 (Tex.App.—San Antonio, 2002, pet. denied) (post-answer default made earlier dismissal final); ***Campbell v. Kosarek***, 44 S.W.3d 647, 649 (Tex.App.—Dallas 2001, pet. denied) (J disposing of remaining Ds made earlier dismissal order against other Ds final). Under the merger doctrine, interlocutory judgments and orders are merged into the final judgment, even when they are not memorialized in the final judgment. ***Webb***, 488 S.W.2d at 408-09; ***Radelow-Gittens Real Prop. Mgmt. v. Pamex Foods***, 735 S.W.2d 558, 560 (Tex. App.—Dallas 1987, writ ref'd n.r.e.).

(b) Unresolved claim severed. An interlocutory judgment becomes final when the trial court severs the interlocutory judgment from the unadjudicated claims. *See* TRCP 41; *see, e.g.*, ***Harris Cty. Flood Control Dist. v. Adam***, 66 S.W.3d 265, 266 (Tex.2001) (when order of severance signed, SJ for two Ds became final); ***Cherokee Water Co. v. Ross***, 698 S.W.2d 363, 365-66 (Tex.1985) (when order severing P's SJ from D's counterclaim signed, SJ became final); ***Castano v. Foremost Cty. Mut. Ins. Co.***, 31 S.W.3d 387, 388 (Tex.App.—San Antonio 2000, no pet.) (because no-answer default J against one D was not severed, it was not final). *But see* ***Diversified Fin. Sys. v. Hill, Heard, O'Neal, Gilstrap & Goetz***, 63 S.W.3d 795, 795 (Tex.2001) (partial SJ was not final at severance because order said partial SJ was "to proceed as such to final judgment"); ***Martinez v. Humble Sand & Gravel***, 875 S.W.2d 311, 313 (Tex.1994) (partial SJ was not final at severance because order said other Ds were to be added). To be severable, a cause must be capable of becoming a separate suit with a separate, final judgment. ***Martinez***, 875 S.W.2d at 312. See "Motion for Severance," ch. 5-H, §3, p. 263.

(4) Summary disposition + statement of finality. When a trial court resolves some claims by summary disposition, leaving other claims unresolved, the judgment is final if it unequivocally states it finally disposes of all claims. ***Lehmann***, 39 S.W.3d at 205; *see, e.g.*, ***Ritzell v. Espeche***, 87 S.W.3d 536, 538 (Tex.2002) (SJ that said P "take nothing" was final); ***Jacobs v. Satterwhite***, 65 S.W.3d 653, 655 (Tex.2001) (same). When a judgment expressly states it disposes of all claims, it is final even if it does not actually dispose of all claims. *See* ***Lehmann***, 39 S.W.3d at 205. For example, if a defendant moves for summary judgment on only one of the plaintiff's four claims, but the trial court renders judgment that the plaintiff take nothing, the judgment is final. A judgment granting more relief than a party is entitled is not interlocutory for that reason alone. *Id.* When a judgment says it is final even though it does not resolve all claims, the issue of finality must be resolved on appeal. See §6.4.2, below.

(5) Some partial judgments = final judgments. There are some proceedings in which more than one "final" judgment can be rendered in the same case. See §6.1.2, above. In those cases, the resolution of certain discrete claims is considered a final judgment.

2. Judgments that are not final.

(1) Conventional trial + separate claims. When a trial court separates (but does not sever) an issue for later disposition, the judgment or order rendered after the first trial is not a final judgment. ***Hall v. City of Austin***, 450 S.W.2d 836, 838 (Tex.1970).

(2) Summary disposition. There is no presumption a judgment rendered after a summary disposition (*e.g.*, summary judgment, no-answer default judgment) resolves all claims and is final. ***Lehmann***, 39 S.W.3d at 199; *see, e.g.*, ***McNally v. Guevara***, 52 S.W.3d 195, 196 (Tex.2001) (SJ was not final because no presumption Ds abandoned claims not included in their SJ motion). When a trial court resolves some claims by summary disposition but leaves other claims unresolved, the judgment is not final. ***Lehmann***, 39 S.W.3d at 199; *see, e.g.*, ***Nash v. Harris Cty.***, 63 S.W.3d 415, 416 (Tex.2001) (SJ interlocutory because it did not dispose of all Ds); ***Parking Co.***, 58 S.W.3d at 742 (SJ interlocutory because it did not dispose of all claims); ***Bobbitt v. Stran***, 52 S.W.3d 734, 735 (Tex. 2001) (SJ interlocutory because it did not dispose of all parties & claims); ***McNally***, 52 S.W.3d at 196 (SJ interlocutory because it did not dispose of claim for attorney fees); ***Guajardo v. Conwell***, 46 S.W.3d 862, 864 (Tex.2001) (SJ interlocutory because it did not dispose of claims by & against intervenor). However, if an interlocutory judgment clearly and unequivocally states it finally disposes of all claims, it is final even though it does not resolve all claims. See §6.3.1(4), above.

PRACTICE TIP

If a party discovers on appeal that a final judgment is actually an interlocutory judgment, the party can ask the appellate court to abate the appeal for the trial court to sign an order of severance from the rest of the suit. See TRAP 27.2, 27.3; ***State Farm Mut. Auto. Ins. Co. v. Leeds****, 981 S.W.2d 693, 693 (Tex.App.—Houston [1st Dist.] 1998, no pet.). If an appellate court is uncertain about the intent of an order—whether the trial court intended a final or interlocutory order—it can abate the appeal to permit the trial court to clarify the finality of the order.* ***Lehmann v. Har-Con Corp.****, 39 S.W.3d 191, 206 (Tex.2001).*

§6.4 Finality for purposes of appeal. There is a difference between the finality of a judgment that starts the appellate deadlines and the issue of finality that is reviewed on appeal.

1. Finality for appeal. If a judgment actually disposes of all claims and parties or if it purports to dispose of all claims and parties, it is a final judgment for purposes of filing the notice of appeal. ***Lehmann***, 39 S.W.3d at 192-93. Even if the parties do not intend the judgment to dispose of all parties and issues but the judgment erroneously says it does, the judgment begins the appellate deadlines. *Id.* at 204. For example, if a defendant moves for summary judgment on one of the plaintiff's four claims, but the trial court renders judgment that the plaintiff take nothing, the judgment is final—erroneous, but final. *Id.* at 200. The error—that the judgment purported to be final but was not—must be resolved by the appellate courts by reviewing the record. *Id.*; *see, e.g.*, ***Jacobs***, 65 S.W.3d at 655 (SJ stating P "take nothing" was final for purposes of appeal); ***Taub v. Dedman***, 56 S.W.3d 83, 87 (Tex. App.—Houston [14th Dist.] 2001, pet. denied) (specific enumeration in SJ order of some of the Ds indicated court did not intend to dispose of all parties). If the appellant does not file a timely notice of appeal from a judgment that purports to be final but is not, the judgment becomes final.

2. Finality for review. If an appellant files a timely notice of appeal to challenge a judgment that purports to be final but is not, the appellate court will review the appellate record to determine if the judgment was a final judgment. ***Lehmann***, 39 S.W.3d at 205-06; *see, e.g.*, ***Jacobs***, 65 S.W.3d at 655 (because motion for SJ asked for SJ on only one of two claims, SJ was not final on review). If a judgment did not resolve all claims, the appellate court should state why in its opinion the judgment was not final and either dismiss the appeal or abate and remand to the trial court to decide whether to render a final judgment. *See, e.g.*, ***Bobbitt***, 52 S.W.3d at 735 (Supreme Court affirmed dismissal of appeal by court of appeals); ***McNally***, 52 S.W.3d at 196 (Supreme Court remanded to court of appeals to determine whether to abate the appeal to allow the trial court to render a final judgment or to dismiss the appeal for want of jurisdiction); *see also* TRAP 27.2 (appellate court may permit an interlocutory order to be modified to make it final).

§6.5 When judgment becomes final. A judgment becomes final and appealable when the trial court loses plenary power to change it. *See* TRCP 306a(1); ***Thomas v. Oldham***, 895 S.W.2d 352, 356 (Tex.1995). The date the court loses plenary power depends on the date the judgment was signed, whether one of the postjudgment motions extending the court's plenary power was filed, and if filed, whether the motion was overruled or granted.

1. Post-trial motions & finality. Some post-trial motions extend the trial court's plenary power over its judgment.

(1) PPE motions. The following plenary-power-extending motions (PPE motions) extend the court's plenary power over the judgment (and, in most cases, the appellate deadlines) if filed within 30 days of the date the judgment was signed:

NOTE

*To compare the effect of these motions on the court's plenary power and the appellate deadlines, see **O'Connor's Texas Civil Appeals**, chart 11-2, "Comparing Effect of Postjudgment Motions on Appellate Deadlines & Plenary Power," ch. 11-G, p. 39 (2002-03).*

(a) MNT. A motion for new trial. TRCP 329b(a), (e); ***Lane Bank Equip. Co. v. Smith S. Equip., Inc.***, 10 S.W.3d 308, 310 (Tex.2000). See "Motion for New Trial," ch. 10-B, p. 617.

(b) Motion to reinstate. A verified motion to reinstate after dismissal for want of prosecution. TRCP 165a; ***3V, Inc. v. JTS Enters., Inc.***, 40 S.W.3d 533, 538-39 (Tex.App.—Houston [14th Dist.] 2000, no pet.). See "Motion to Reinstate After DWOP," ch. 10-F, p. 649.

(c) Motion to modify J. A motion to modify, correct, or reform the judgment. *See* TRCP 329b(g); ***Lane Bank***, 10 S.W.3d at 310; ***Padilla v. LaFrance***, 907 S.W.2d 454, 458 (Tex.1995). Any motion—no matter what it is called—will extend plenary power if (1) it seeks a substantive change in the judgment, and (2) it was filed within the time limits for a motion for new trial. ***Lane Bank***, 10 S.W.3d at 314; ***Gomez v. Texas Dept. of Crim. Justice***, 896 S.W.2d 176, 176-77 (Tex.1995). See "Motion to Modify the Judgment," ch. 10-D, p. 639. For example:

[1] Motion for sanctions. A motion for sanctions to be incorporated in the judgment. ***Lane Bank***, 10 S.W.3d at 309-10; ***In re T.G.***, 68 S.W.3d 171, 176 (Tex.App.—Houston [1st Dist.] 2002, pet. denied); ***Estate of Davis v. Cook***, 9 S.W.3d 288, 296 (Tex.App.—San Antonio 1999, no pet.). See "Motion for Sanctions," ch. 5-J, p. 275.

[2] Motion for remittitur. No court has considered whether a motion for remittitur filed separately from a motion for new trial extends the court's plenary power, but under ***Lane Bank*** it should. A request for remittitur can be made in a motion for new trial, and when filed separately it should extend the court's plenary power. *Cf.* ***Landmark Am. Ins. Co. v. Pulse Ambulance Serv.***, 813 S.W.2d 497, 498 (Tex.1991) (order granting remittitur extends post-J deadlines). See "Motion for Remittitur," ch. 10-C, p. 636.

[3] Motion for JNOV. No court has considered whether a motion for JNOV extends the court's plenary power, but under ***Lane Bank*** it should. By comparison, one court has held a motion for JNOV will extend the appellate deadlines if filed within the deadlines for a motion for new trial. ***Kirschberg v. Lowe***, 974 S.W.2d 844, 847-48 (Tex.App.—San Antonio 1998, no pet.). See "Motion for JNOV," ch. 9-B, p. 591.

(2) Motions that do not extend plenary power. The following post-trial motions do not extend the court's plenary power.

(a) Request for FoF. A proper request for findings of fact does not extend the court's plenary power. ***In re Gillespie***, ___ S.W.3d ___ (Tex.App.—Houston [14th Dist.] 2003, orig. proceeding) (No. 14-03-00137-CV; 10-20-03); ***Pursley v. Ussery***, 982 S.W.2d 596, 599 (Tex.App.—San Antonio 1998, pet. denied). The only motions that extend the court's plenary power are motions seeking a substantive change in the judgment, which a request for findings of fact does not do. *See* ***Lane Bank***, 10 S.W.3d at 313-14; ***Gillespie***, ___ S.W.3d at ___. By comparison, TRAP 26.1(a)(4) specifically states a request for findings of fact extends appellate deadlines. See "Effect of request for FoF on appellate timetables," ch. 10-E, §6.1, p. 647.

(b) Unverified motion to reinstate. An unverified motion to reinstate does not extend the court's plenary power. ***3V***, 40 S.W.3d at 538.

(c) Motion to enforce J. A motion for sanctions for failure to comply with the judgment does not extend the court's plenary power. ***Guajardo v. Conwell***, 30 S.W.3d 15, 16 (Tex.App.—Houston [14th Dist.] 2000), *aff'd*, 46 S.W.3d 862 (Tex.2001).

(d) Motion for nonsubstantive change in judgment. A postjudgment motion asking for a nonsubstantive change in the judgment does not affect the trial court's plenary power over its judgment. *Cf.* ***Lane Bank***, 10 S.W.3d at 314 (post-J motion seeking substantive change in J extends trial court's plenary power). However, if the trial court modifies the judgment, even if the change is nonsubstantive, the court's plenary power is affected. See "Time periods & the modified judgment," §5.4, p. 602.

2. Effect of PPE motions.

(1) No PPE motion filed. The trial court has plenary power to change its judgment for 30 days after it signs the judgment, if no PPE motion was filed. TRCP 329b(d); ***Lane Bank***, 10 S.W.3d at 310; ***Board of Trustees of Bastrop ISD v. Toungate***, 958 S.W.2d 365, 367 (Tex.1997); ***Sadeghian v. Shaw***, 76 S.W.3d 229, 231 (Tex.App.—Texarkana 2002, no pet.).

(2) PPE motion denied. When a party files a timely PPE motion, the trial court's plenary power over its judgment is extended until 30 days after the motion is overruled, either by written order or by operation of law, whichever occurs first. TRCP 329b(e), (g); TRAP 4.3(a); ***Lane Bank***, 10 S.W.3d at 310; ***Faulkner v. Culver***, 851 S.W.2d 187, 188 (Tex.1993). Such motions are overruled by operation of law on the 75th day after the judgment is signed, if not overruled earlier by a written order. TRCP 329b(c). When a PPE motion is overruled on the 75th day after judgment (by written order or by operation of law), the trial court has plenary power over the judgment for 105 days, counting from the date it signed the judgment. *See* ***L.M. Healthcare v. Childs***, 929 S.W.2d 442, 444 (Tex. 1996); ***Harris Cty. Hosp. Dist. v. Estrada***, 831 S.W.2d 876, 879 (Tex.App.—Houston [1st Dist.] 1992, order on mot.).

(3) PPE motion granted. When the trial court grants a PPE motion, the judgment becomes final when the court's plenary power expires. *See* ***Porter v. Vick***, 888 S.W.2d 789, 789-90 (Tex.1994) (motion for new trial). When the court grants a PPE motion, its plenary power expires 75 days after the judgment was signed. ***In re Luster***, 77 S.W.3d 331, 334-35 (Tex.App.—Houston [14th Dist.] 2002, orig. proceeding); ***In re Steiger***, 55 S.W.3d 168, 170-71 (Tex.App.—Corpus Christi 2001, orig. proceeding); *see* ***Health Care Ctrs. v. Nolen***, 62 S.W.3d 813, 816 (Tex.App.—Waco 2001, no pet.). The date the trial court's plenary power expires becomes an issue when the trial court attempts to withdraw its order granting a new trial and to reinstate the judgment. Once plenary power expires, the trial court cannot re-enter the original judgment. The court does not have an additional 30 days after the 75 days to "ungrant" the motion. ***Luster***, 77 S.W.3d 334 n.1.

(4) PPE motion withdrawn. If the party who filed a PPE motion withdraws it, the trial court's plenary power reverts back to 30 days from the signing of the judgment. ***Rogers v. Clinton***, 794 S.W.2d 9, 11 (Tex.1990); ***In re Dilley ISD***, 23 S.W.3d 189, 191 (Tex.App.—San Antonio 2000, orig. proceeding). The withdrawal of a PPE motion is treated like a notice of nonsuit—it is effective immediately. ***Rogers***, 794 S.W.2d at 11. If the party withdraws the motion more than 30 days after the judgment is signed, the trial court cannot change the judgment; its plenary power has already expired, and it has no jurisdiction to change the judgment. ***Dilley ISD***, 23 S.W.3d at 191-92.

9-1. PLENARY POWER DEADLINES

SITUATION		DATE TRIAL COURT LOSES PLENARY POWER	
1	No PPE motion filed	Date judgment signed + 30 days	§6.5.2(1)
2	PPE motion overruled by court order	Date order signed overruling PPE motion + 30 days, but not later than 105 days from date judgment signed	§6.5.2(2)
3	PPE motion overruled by operation of law	Date judgment signed + 75 days + 30 days = 105 days	§6.5.2(2)
4	PPE motion granted by court order	Date judgment signed + 75 days	§6.5.2(3)
5	PPE motion withdrawn by party	Date judgment signed + 30 days	§6.5.2(4)

§7. POWER TO CHANGE JUDGMENT

§7.1 Changing judgment during plenary power. The trial court has the power to change its judgment for as long as it has plenary power over the judgment. See chart 9-1, above.

§7.2 Changing judgment after plenary power. Once the trial court loses plenary power, the court generally cannot change its judgment. There are two exceptions:

1. Correcting clerical errors. The trial court can correct clerical errors in the judgment. See "Motion for Judgment Nunc Pro Tunc," ch. 10-H, p. 659.

2. Retaxing costs. The trial court can retax costs after it loses plenary power as long as the request is made before the mandate in the case issues and costs are paid. ***Operation Rescue v. Planned Parenthood***, 937 S.W.2d 60, 87 (Tex.App.—Houston [14th Dist.] 1996), *modified on other grounds*, 975 S.W.2d 546 (Tex.1998). Taxing costs, as distinguished from adjudicating costs, is merely a ministerial duty of the clerk. An error in the clerk's tabulation of costs can be corrected after the court loses plenary power.

§8. POWER TO ENFORCE JUDGMENT

The trial court has the power to enforce its orders beyond the expiration of its plenary power. ***Katz v. Bianchi***, 848 S.W.2d 372, 374 (Tex.App.—Houston [14th Dist.] 1993, orig. proceeding). Enforcement orders cannot be inconsistent with the original judgment and cannot materially change a part of the judgment that was substantially adjudicated. ***Matz v. Bennion***, 961 S.W.2d 445, 452 (Tex.App.—Houston [1st Dist.] 1997, pet. denied).

§9. REVIEW

§9.1 Calculating appellate deadlines. Appellate deadlines are calculated from the date the court signs a final judgment or appealable order and depend on whether either party filed a motion extending the appellate deadlines. Motions extending the appellate deadlines include (1) a motion for new trial, (2) a motion to modify the judgment, (3) a motion to reinstate under TRCP 165a, (4) a request for findings of fact when findings either are required by the TRCPs or could properly be considered by the appellate court, and (5) any motion that seeks a substantive change in the judgment. TRAP 26.1(a); ***Lane Bank Equip. Co. v. Smith S. Equip., Inc.***, 10 S.W.3d 308, 314 (Tex.2000). See ***O'Connor's Texas Civil Appeals***, "Appellate Deadlines Extended," ch. 11-G, §3, p. 36 (2002-03).

9-2. APPELLATE DEADLINES

	Appeal from Final Judgment		Appeal from Interlocutory Order	
	Notice of appeal	Appellate record	Notice of appeal	Appellate record
When no ADE motion* filed—	30 days from judgment. TRAP 26.1	60 days from judgment. TRAP 35.1	20 days from order. TRAP 26.1(b)	10 days from notice of appeal. TRAP 35.1(b)
When ADE motion filed—	90 days from judgment. TRAP 26.1(a)	120 days from judgment. TRAP 35.1(a)	20 days from order. TRAP 26.1(b)	10 days from notice of appeal. TRAP 35.1(b)

* ADE motion = a timely filed appellate-deadline-extending motion.

§9.2 Accepting judgment. A party cannot treat a judgment as both right and wrong. ***Texas State Bank v. Amaro***, 87 S.W.3d 538, 544 (Tex.2002); ***Carle v. Carle***, 234 S.W.2d 1002, 1004 (Tex.1950); ***L.P.D. v. R.C.***, 959 S.W.2d 728, 731 (Tex.App.—Austin 1998, pet. denied).

1. Plaintiff.

(1) Acceptance of payment.

(a) Case moot. The general rule for a plaintiff (the judgment creditor) is that if it accepts the benefits of a judgment, it is estopped from challenging the judgment by appeal. ***Carle***, 234 S.W.2d at 1004; ***Rapp v.***

Mandell & Wright P.C., ___ S.W.3d ___ (Tex.App.—Houston [14th Dist.] 2003, n.p.h.) (No. 14-01-01047-CV; 8-28-03); ***Bloom v. Bloom***, 935 S.W.2d 942, 945 (Tex.App.—San Antonio 1996, no writ). In other words, the appeal becomes moot.

(b) Case not moot. There are two narrow exceptions to the rule that acceptance of payment renders the case moot.

[1] No effect of reversal. If the reversal of the judgment could not possibly affect the judgment creditor's right to the benefits it accepted under the judgment, the judgment creditor may appeal even though it accepted those benefits. ***Amaro***, 87 S.W.3d at 544; ***Carle***, 234 S.W.2d at 1004; ***Molina v. Moore***, 33 S.W.3d 323, 326 (Tex.App.—Amarillo 2000, no pet.); ***Briargrove Park Prop. Owners v. Riner***, 867 S.W.2d 58, 60 (Tex. App.—Texarkana 1993, writ denied).

[2] Involuntary acceptance of payment. If the economic circumstances were such that the judgment creditor benefits, the judgment creditor may appeal even though it accepted the benefits. ***Cooper v. Bushong***, 10 S.W.3d 20, 23-24 (Tex.App.—Austin 1999, pet. denied); ***Smith v. Texas Commerce Bank***, 822 S.W.2d 812, 814 (Tex.App.—Corpus Christi 1992, writ denied).

(2) Release of judgment. A judgment creditor who signs a release of judgment is estopped from challenging the judgment by appeal. ***Rapp***, ___ S.W.3d at ___. A release of judgment is itself a complete relinquishment by the judgment creditor of all its rights in the judgment. *Id.* When a judgment creditor accepts money in complete satisfaction and release of judgment, the judgment has no further force or authority. *Id.*; *see* ***Reames v. Logue***, 712 S.W.2d 802, 804-05 (Tex.App.—Dallas 1986, writ ref'd n.r.e.)

2. Defendant.

(1) Voluntary payment. The general rule for a defendant (the judgment debtor) is that if it pays the judgment, the appeal becomes moot. ***Continental Cas. Co. v. Huizar***, 740 S.W.2d 429, 430 (Tex.1987). In most cases, by paying the judgment, the judgment debtor waives its right to appeal. *Id.*

(2) Involuntary payment. If the judgment debtor does not pay the judgment voluntarily, the appeal is not moot. ***Riner v. Briargrove Park Prop. Owners***, 858 S.W.2d 370, 370-71 (Tex.1993) (judgment debtor did not waive appeal when he paid to prevent judgment creditor from executing on property); ***Highland Ch. of Christ v. Powell***, 640 S.W.2d 235, 236 (Tex.1982) (judgment debtor did not waive appeal when it paid to avoid execution). *But see* ***Hanna v. Godwin***, 876 S.W.2d 454, 456-57 (Tex.App.—El Paso 1994, no writ) (judgment debtor waived appeal when he paid disputed attorney fees to prevent execution of J). The mere fact that a judgment is paid "under protest" does not prevent the appeal from becoming moot upon payment. ***Continental Cas.***, 740 S.W.2d at 430.

D. RES JUDICATA & COLLATERAL ESTOPPEL

§1. GENERAL

§1.1 Rules. None.

§1.2 Purpose. Res judicata is sometimes used as a generic term for a group of related concepts concerning the conclusive effects given final judgments. ***Barr v. RTC***, 837 S.W.2d 627, 628 (Tex.1992). Res judicata is designed to promote judicial efficiency and protect litigants from multiple lawsuits. ***Sysco Food Servs. v. Trapnell***, 890 S.W.2d 796, 801 (Tex.1994).

§1.3 Forms. See ***O'Connor's Texas Civil Forms***, FORM 3E:11 (affirmative defenses), FORM 7B:02 (defendant's motion for summary judgment based on counterclaim or affirmative defense).

§1.4 Other references. Ratliff, *Offensive Collateral Estoppel & the Option Effect*, 67 Tex.L.Rev. 63 (1988).

§2. RES JUDICATA & COLLATERAL ESTOPPEL

§2.1 Comparison. Within the general doctrine of res judicata, there are two principal categories: (1) claim preclusion (also known as res judicata) and (2) issue preclusion (also known as collateral estoppel). ***Barr***, 837 S.W.2d at 628. In this book, res judicata refers only to claim preclusion and is not used as the generic term covering both categories.

1. Res judicata – claim preclusion. Res judicata bars the litigation of claims actually litigated as well as those arising from the same transaction that could have been litigated. ***Compania Financiara Libano v. Simmons***, 53 S.W.3d 365, 367 (Tex.2001); ***Barr***, 837 S.W.2d at 630. Thus, res judicata focuses on what could have been litigated. ***Van Dyke v. Boswell, O'Toole, Davis & Pickering***, 697 S.W.2d 381, 384 (Tex.1985). Res judicata requires mutuality of interests—the party invoking it and the party to be bound must have been parties in the earlier suit. See §3.2.2, below. Res judicata is broader than collateral estoppel. ***Van Dyke***, 697 S.W.2d at 384.

2. Collateral estoppel – issue preclusion. Collateral estoppel bars the litigation of specific issues already decided in an earlier case; it does not bar an entire cause of action or defense. Thus, collateral estoppel focuses on what was actually litigated and essential to the judgment. ***Van Dyke***, 697 S.W.2d at 384. Collateral estoppel does not require mutuality of interests—only the party against whom it is asserted or a person in privity with that party must have been a party in the earlier suit. See "Cast as adversaries," §4.2.3, p. 613.

§2.2 Preclusive effect. The policies behind res judicata and collateral estoppel reflect the need to bring litigation to an end, prevent vexatious litigation, maintain the stability of court decisions, promote judicial economy, and prevent double recovery. ***Barr***, 837 S.W.2d at 629. When a lawsuit is divided into separate parts, neither res judicata nor collateral estoppel prevents the litigation of the second part of the lawsuit after the litigation of the first part. *E.g.*, ***Van Dyke***, 697 S.W.2d at 384 (favorable resolution of claim for attorney fees did not preclude claim for legal malpractice because trial court severed the two issues); *see also* ***Finger v. Southern Refrigeration Servs.***, 881 S.W.2d 890, 895-96 (Tex.App.—Houston [1st Dist.] 1994, writ denied) (after directed verdict against one P was reversed on appeal, the unfavorable resolution of the rest of the suit did not preclude retrial by P who had been directed out of suit); ***Chandler v. Hendrick Mem'l Hosp.***, 317 S.W.2d 248, 251 (Tex.App.—Eastland 1958, writ ref'd n.r.e.) (judgment stated it did not resolve issue of hospital fees).

§2.3 Which jurisdiction's law. The preclusive effect of a judgment must be determined according to the law of the jurisdiction issuing the initial judgment. *See, e.g.*, ***Geary v. Texas Commerce Bank***, 967 S.W.2d 836, 839 (Tex.1998) (applied federal res judicata to determine preclusive effect of bankruptcy judgment); ***Purcell v. Bellinger***, 940 S.W.2d 599, 601 (Tex.1997) (applied NY res judicata to determine preclusive effect of NY judgment).

§3. RES JUDICATA – CLAIM PRECLUSION

§3.1 Purpose. Res judicata, or claim preclusion, prevents the relitigation of a claim or cause of action that was adjudicated and resolved by a final judgment, as well as related matters that with the use of diligence should have been litigated in the earlier suit. ***State & Cty. Mut. Fire Ins. Co. v. Miller***, 52 S.W.3d 693, 696 (Tex.2001); ***Amstadt v. U.S. Brass Corp.***, 919 S.W.2d 644, 652 (Tex.1996); ***Barr***, 837 S.W.2d at 628; ***Gracia v. RC Cola-7-Up Bottling Co.***, 667 S.W.2d 517, 519-20 (Tex.1984). Claim preclusion prevents splitting a cause of action. ***Barr***, 837 S.W.2d at 629; ***Jeanes v. Henderson***, 688 S.W.2d 100, 103 (Tex.1985); *see, e.g.*, ***Ingersoll-Rand Co. v. Valero Energy Corp.***, 997 S.W.2d 203, 212 (Tex.1999) (P could not "repackage" its tort claim as a contract claim after adverse judgment on tort claim). Texas applies the Restatement (2d) of Judgments' transactional test to determine whether two claims involve the same cause of action for res judicata purposes. ***Miller***, 52 S.W.3d at 696; ***Barr***, 837 S.W.2d at 631. Under that test, the critical issue is whether the two claims are based on the same nucleus of operative facts. ***Musgrave v. Owen***, 67 S.W.3d 513, 519 (Tex.App.—Texarkana 2002, no pet.). A transaction is determined pragmatically, "giving weight to such considerations as whether the facts are related in time, space, origin, or motivation, whether they form a convenient trial unit, and whether their treatment as a trial unit conforms with the parties' expectations or business understanding or usage." ***Barr***, 837 S.W.2d at 631 (partnership note & guarantee were part of a single transaction); *see* ***Southern Cty. Mut. Ins. Co. v. Ochoa***, 19 S.W.3d 452, 466-67 (Tex.App.—Corpus Christi 2000, no pet.) (breach of insurance contract claim should have been brought in ***Stowers*** suit).

§3.2 Elements of res judicata. A claim of res judicata requires proof of the following elements:

1. **Final judgment.** A court of competent jurisdiction rendered a final judgment on the merits in the first suit. ***Amstadt***, 919 S.W.2d at 652; *see, e.g.*, ***Martin v. Martin, Martin & Richards, Inc.***, 989 S.W.2d 357, 358-59 (Tex.1998) (dismissal with prejudice of a declaratory judgment action did not resolve issue of validity of contract); ***Glazer's Wholesale Distribs. v. Heineken USA***, 95 S.W.3d 286, 301-02 (Tex.App.—Dallas 2001, pet. granted w.r.m.) (res judicata applies to arbitration awards reduced to final judgment); ***Columbia Rio Grande Reg'l Hosp. v. Stover***, 17 S.W.3d 387, 394-95 (Tex.App.—Corpus Christi 2000, no pet.) (probate court had jurisdiction over executrix's motion to bar hospital's claim against estate).

2. **Same parties.** The parties in the first suit are the same as those in the second suit or, if not the same, are in privity with them. ***Amstadt***, 919 S.W.2d at 652-53; *see* ***State Farm Lloyds v. Borum***, 53 S.W.3d 877, 886 (Tex.App.—Dallas 2001, pet. denied) (doctrine did not apply; insurer & insured were not in privity in underlying liability suit where insurer reserved its rights to contest coverage); ***Southwest Guar. Trust Co. v. Providence Trust Co.***, 970 S.W.2d 777, 784 (Tex.App.—Austin 1998, pet. denied) (doctrine did not apply because parties were not the same). A party is in privity with another party when the party is a successor in interest to the other party and derives its claims through the other party. ***Montgomery First Corp. v. Caprock Inv. Corp.***, 89 S.W.3d 179, 186 (Tex.App.—Eastland 2002, no pet.); *see also* ***Mayes v. Stewart***, 11 S.W.3d 440, 449 (Tex.App.—Houston [14th Dist.] 2000, pet. denied) (privity is not established by mere fact persons happen to be interested in the same question or in proving the same facts). Due process requires that res judicata operate only against persons who have had their day in court, either as a party in the earlier suit or as a person in privity with a party. ***Benson v. Wanda Pet. Co.***, 468 S.W.2d 361, 363 (Tex.1971). For a party to be bound by a coparty, rather than an opposing party, res judicata acts as a bar only if the coparties had issues drawn between them in the first suit. ***Miller***, 52 S.W.3d at 696.

3. **Same or related claims.** The second suit is based on the same claims that were raised or that could have been raised in the first suit. ***Compania Financiara***, 53 S.W.3d at 367; ***Amstadt***, 919 S.W.2d at 652-53; *see* ***Robinson v. Garcia***, 5 S.W.3d 348, 352 (Tex.App.—Corpus Christi 1999, pet. denied) (P's claims, in both his tax suit and his fee suit, arose from his lawyer's representation of him in the same lawsuit). A claim must have existed at the time the original suit was filed; res judicata does not bar a claim that accrued after the original judgment. ***Hernandez v. Del Ray Chem. Int'l***, 56 S.W.3d 112, 116 (Tex.App.—Houston [14th Dist.] 2001, no pet.); *see, e.g.*, ***Compania Financiara***, 53 S.W.3d at 367 (res judicata did not bar P's suit to compel performance of settlement agreement after D breached agreement). When there is a legal relationship (*e.g.*, under a lease, contract, or marriage) all claims resulting from the relationship will arise from the same subject matter and be subject to res judicata. ***Genecov Group v. Roosth Prod. Co.***, ___ S.W.3d ___ (Tex.App.—Tyler 2003, pet. filed 8-8-03) (No. 12-02-00106-CV; 5-21-03); ***Pinebrook Props. v. Brookhaven Lake Prop. Owners Ass'n***, 77 S.W.3d 487, 497 (Tex.App.—Texarkana 2002, pet. denied). A defendant must bring as a counterclaim any claim arising out of the transaction that is the subject of the plaintiff's suit. ***Miller***, 52 S.W.3d at 696; ***Barr v. RTC***, 837 S.W.2d 627, 630 (Tex.1992). Res judicata applies to (1) the cause of action filed by the plaintiff, (2) any counterclaims actually filed by the defendant, and (3) all compulsory counterclaims the defendant should have filed but did not. *See* ***Musgrave***, 67 S.W.3d at 519; Restatement (2d) of Judgments §23 (1980). See "Compulsory-counterclaim rule," ch. 2-E, §6.1, p. 98.

§4. COLLATERAL ESTOPPEL – ISSUE PRECLUSION

§4.1 Purpose. Collateral estoppel, or issue preclusion, prevents a party from relitigating a particular fact issue the party already litigated and lost in an earlier suit. ***Miller***, 52 S.W.3d at 696; ***Quinney Elec. v. Kondos Entm't***, 988 S.W.2d 212, 213 (Tex.1999); ***Barr***, 837 S.W.2d at 628; ***Spera v. Fleming, Hovenkamp & Grayson***, 25 S.W.3d 863, 869 (Tex.App.—Houston [14th Dist.] 2000, no pet.). To invoke collateral estoppel, a party must establish (1) the same facts sought to be litigated in the second suit were fully litigated in the first suit, (2) those facts were essential to the judgment in the first suit, and (3) the parties were cast as adversaries in the first suit. ***Sysco Food Servs. v. Trapnell***, 890 S.W.2d 796, 801 (Tex.1994); ***Eagle Props. v. Scharbauer***, 807 S.W.2d 714, 721 (Tex. 1990).

§4.2 **Elements of collateral estoppel.** The claim of collateral estoppel requires proof of the following elements:

1. **Issues litigated.**

(1) **Same issue actually litigated.** Collateral estoppel applies only if the issue was actually litigated in the earlier proceeding. ***Texas DPS v. Petta***, 44 S.W.3d 575, 579 (Tex.2001) (issue of whether P reasonably believed she was in fear of imminent harm was litigated in P's criminal trial); ***Johnson & Higgins v. Kenneco Energy***, 962 S.W.2d 507, 522-23 (Tex.1998) (issue of contingency insurance was not litigated in federal court); ***Housing Auth. v. Massey***, 878 S.W.2d 624, 626-27 (Tex.App.—Corpus Christi 1994, no writ) (collateral estoppel did not bar litigation of issues arising after first suit). "Actually litigated" means an issue was raised by the pleadings or otherwise submitted for determination, and was determined by the fact-finder. ***Rexrode v. Bazar***, 937 S.W.2d 614, 617 (Tex.App.—Amarillo 1997, no writ). The issue decided in the first suit must be identical to the issue in the pending suit. ***Miller***, 52 S.W.3d at 696; ***Petta***, 44 S.W.3d at 579. Collateral estoppel may preclude relitigation of issues even though the later suit is based on a different cause of action. ***Johnson & Higgins***, 962 S.W.2d at 521.

(2) **Issue fully & fairly litigated.** Collateral estoppel applies when the issue sought to be precluded in the second suit was fully and fairly litigated in the first suit. ***State & Cty. Mut. Fire Ins. Co. v. Miller***, 52 S.W.3d 693, 696 (Tex.2001); ***Petta***, 44 S.W.3d at 579; ***Johnson & Higgins***, 962 S.W.2d at 522; ***Sysco Food***, 890 S.W.2d at 801; *e.g.*, ***Rexrode***, 937 S.W.2d at 617-20 (P who sued D and D's insurer nonsuited D during trial; insurer granted directed verdict; P could not sue D again); ***Phillips v. Allums***, 882 S.W.2d 71, 74-75 (Tex.App.—Houston [14th Dist.] 1994, writ denied) (D did not have a full and fair opportunity to litigate issue of wrongful foreclosure in summary judgment action); ***Robbins v. HNG Oil Co.***, 878 S.W.2d 351, 357-58 (Tex.App.—Beaumont 1994, writ dism'd) (in suit #1, 200 heirs sued Ds in federal court, based on interpretation of deed, which was resolved against heirs; in suit #2, another heir sued based on same deed; suit #2 precluded by collateral estoppel). An interlocutory order on matters collateral or incidental to the main suit does not operate as res judicata or collateral estoppel. ***Texacadian Energy v. Lone Star Energy Storage***, 829 S.W.2d 369, 373 (Tex.App.—Corpus Christi 1992, writ denied) (denial of motion to perpetuate testimony did not resolve merits of fraud claim).

2. **Essential to judgment.** Collateral estoppel applies only if the factual issues were essential to the first judgment. ***Miller***, 52 S.W.3d at 696; ***Sysco Food***, 890 S.W.2d at 801. To determine if the same facts were essential to the judgment in the first suit, a lawyer should subtract those facts from the first judgment to see if their absence changes the judgment. If it does, the facts were essential; if it does not, the facts were not essential. For example, if the first judgment is based on the determination of two issues, either of which is sufficient to support the judgment, the judgment is not conclusive with respect to either issue standing alone. ***Eagle Props.***, 807 S.W.2d at 722; Restatement (2d) of Judgments §27, cmt. i (1982); *see* ***Parker v. State Farm Mut. Auto. Ins. Co.***, 83 S.W.3d 179, 182 (Tex.App.—San Antonio 2002, no pet.) (when jury refuses to find D negligent, its damage findings were not essential to the outcome of the lawsuit; therefore, collateral estoppel does not bar relitigation of same damages in another suit). In other words, the general rule is there cannot be collateral estoppel by alternative holdings in a trial court's judgment. ***Johnson & Higgins***, 962 S.W.2d at 522. The rationale is when a judgment is based on alternative findings, each finding may not have been as rigorously considered as it would have been if only one was necessary for the result, and the losing party might have been dissuaded from appealing one issue because the other one might uphold the judgment. ***Eagle Props.***, 807 S.W.2d at 722. There is an exception to this rule. If the judgment based on alternative holdings was appealed and affirmed on both grounds, the judgment is conclusive on both. ***Johnson & Higgins***, 962 S.W.2d at 522; Restatement (2d) of Judgments §27, cmt. o (1982).

3. Cast as adversaries. Collateral estoppel precludes a party from relitigating an issue resolved in an earlier suit against the same party or someone in privity with that party or someone whose interest was actually and adequately represented in the earlier trial. ***Benson v. Wanda Pet. Co.***, 468 S.W.2d 361, 363 (Tex.1971). Strict mutuality of parties is not required. ***Petta***, 44 S.W.3d at 579; ***Sysco Food***, 890 S.W.2d at 801-02. The party asserting collateral estoppel need not have been a party or in privity with a party to the earlier litigation; only the party against whom the plea is being asserted must have been a party or in privity with a party. ***Eagle Props.***, 807 S.W.2d at 721; ***Logan v. McDaniel***, 21 S.W.3d 683, 687-88 (Tex.App.—Austin 2000, pet. denied).

(1) Defensive collateral estoppel. A defendant uses defensive collateral estoppel to prevent relitigation by a plaintiff of issues lost against another defendant. ***Johnson & Higgins***, 962 S.W.2d at 519; ***Texas Gen. Indem. Co. v. Texas Workers' Comp. Comm'n***, 36 S.W.3d 635, 638 (Tex.App.—Austin 2001, no pet.); *see, e.g.*, ***Hardy v. Fleming***, 553 S.W.2d 790, 792-93 (Tex.App.—El Paso 1977, writ ref'd n.r.e.) (in suit #1, P sued employer under workers' compensation for an on-the-job heart attack, but jury found he did not have a heart attack; in suit #2, P sued doctor for malpractice for advising him he could return to work just before the alleged heart attack; doctor used defense of collateral estoppel to prevent relitigation of whether P had a heart attack). If the party defending the claim prevailed in the first suit, the judgment acts as a bar to issues actually litigated and essential to the earlier suit. ***Eagle Props.***, 807 S.W.2d at 721-22.

(2) Offensive collateral estoppel. A plaintiff uses offensive collateral estoppel to assert liability against a party who previously litigated and lost a fact issue. ***Logan***, 21 S.W.3d at 687; ***Trapnell v. Sysco Food Servs. Inc.***, 850 S.W.2d 529, 536 (Tex.App.—Corpus Christi 1992), *aff'd*, 890 S.W.2d 796 (Tex.1994).

§4.3 Exceptions to collateral estoppel.

1. Unfairness. The trial court has discretion to refuse to apply collateral estoppel when it is unfair to do so. *See* ***Scurlock Oil Co. v. Smithwick***, 724 S.W.2d 1, 7 (Tex.1986); ***Tankersley v. Durish***, 855 S.W.2d 241, 245 (Tex.App.—Austin 1993, writ denied). In exercising its discretion, the trial court should consider the fairness factors discussed by the U.S. Supreme Court in ***Parklane Hosiery Co. v. Shore***, 439 U.S. 322, 330-31, 99 S.Ct. 645, 651 (1979). ***Scurlock Oil***, 724 S.W.2d at 7; *see* ***Goldstein v. Commission for Lawyer Discipline***, 109 S.W.3d 810, 813 (Tex.App.—Dallas 2003, pet. filed 9-11-03).

2. Restatement exceptions. The exceptions to the general rule of collateral estoppel listed in Restatement (2d) of Judgments §28 (1982) are the following:

1. The party against whom preclusion is sought could not, as a matter of law, have obtained review of the judgment in the initial action.

2. The issue is one of law, and either (1) the two actions involve claims substantially unrelated, or (2) a new determination is warranted to take account of an intervening change in the applicable legal context or otherwise to avoid inequitable administration of the laws. *See* ***Sysco Food***, 890 S.W.2d at 804-05 (P did not have full opportunity to litigate case against all Ds in federal court suit); *see also* ***Marino v. State Farm Fire & Cas. Ins. Co.***, 787 S.W.2d 948, 950 (Tex.1990) (cause of action for bad faith was not barred by res judicata because it was based on rights acquired after first lawsuit and was not part of that cause of action).

3. A new determination of the issue is warranted by differences in the quality or extensiveness of the procedures followed in the two courts or by factors relating to the allocation of jurisdiction between them.

4. The party against whom preclusion is sought had a significantly heavier burden of persuasion with respect to the issue in the initial action than in the later action; the burden has shifted to its adversary; or the adversary has a significantly heavier burden than it had in the first action.

5. There is a clear and convincing need for a new determination of the issue because of one of the following: (1) the potential adverse impact of the determination on the public interest or the interests of persons not parties in the initial action; (2) it was not sufficiently foreseeable at the time of the initial action that the issue

would arise in the context of a subsequent action; or (3) the party to be precluded, as a result of the conduct of its adversary or other special circumstances, did not have an adequate opportunity or incentive to obtain a full and fair adjudication in the initial action. *See, e.g.*, ***Finger v. Southern Refrigeration Servs.***, 881 S.W.2d 890, 895-96 (Tex. App.—Houston [1st Dist.] 1994, writ denied) (suit not barred because P, whom D sought to preclude, was improperly excluded from trial by D's motion for directed verdict on grounds P had no damages; D argued to jury not to consider any damages to P who was excluded).

§5. EFFECT OF PENDING APPEAL

A trial court's judgment is final for purposes of the preclusive effect of res judicata or collateral estoppel, even while the case is on appeal. ***Scurlock Oil***, 724 S.W.2d at 6; Restatement (2d) of Judgments §13 (1982). The exception to this rule is if the appeal is a trial de novo. ***Scurlock Oil***, 724 S.W.2d at 6.

COMMENTARIES

CHAPTER 10. POSTJUDGMENT MOTIONS
TABLE OF CONTENTS

COMMENTARIES

CHAPTER 10. POSTJUDGMENT MOTIONS

TABLE OF CONTENTS

A. INTRODUCTION

To preserve a complaint for appeal, a party must make an objection or present some motion to the trial court and obtain a ruling. TRAP 33 requires most appellate complaints to be presented first to the trial court. See "Preserving Error," ch. 1-F, §4, p. 31. Immediately after trial, the lawyer should mentally review the record and ask: Did the trial court do anything or refuse to do anything the party wants to complain about on appeal? The lawyer should make a list and check it against the record to see if, on each matter, there was a request, an objection, or a motion and a ruling or refusal to rule. If the lawyer did not make a request, make an objection, make a motion, or get a ruling, the lawyer may be able to preserve the complaint in a post-trial motion. As long as the trial court has plenary power over the case, a party may ask the trial court to make a written ruling on a issue raised during the trial.

Some complaints can be made for the first time only in a post-trial motion. Postjudgment motions, therefore, are the absolute last chance to preserve error for the appeal.

B. MOTION FOR NEW TRIAL

§1. GENERAL

§1.1 Rules. TRCP 306c, 320-329b; TRAP 33.1. See Gov't Code §51.317(b)(2) ($15 filing fee).

§1.2 Purpose. In a motion for new trial, a party asks the trial court to reconsider and rectify trial error—the court's rulings or the jury's findings—by granting a new trial. ***Smith v. Brock***, 514 S.W.2d 140, 142 (Tex.App.—Texarkana 1974, no writ). There are at least three reasons to file a motion for new trial: (1) to give the trial court one last chance to correct what the appellant will claim on appeal is reversible error, (2) to preserve that error for appeal, and (3) to extend the appellate deadlines. A party has the right to file a motion for new trial merely to extend time, even if there are no reasonable grounds for a new trial. ***Old Republic Ins. Co. v. Scott***, 846 S.W.2d 832, 833 (Tex.1993).

§1.3 Forms & timetable. ***O'Connor's Texas Civil Forms***, FORMS 10B; Timetable, this book, Appeal to the Court of Appeals, p. 1016.

§1.4 Other references. Copeland, Comment, *Room Without a View: Inquiries Into Jury Misconduct After the Adoption of Texas Rule of Evidence 606(b)*, 38 Baylor L.Rev. 965 (1986); O'Connor, *Appealing Jury Findings*, 12 Hous.L.Rev. 65 (1974).

§2. MOTION

§2.1 When MNT necessary. TRCP 324(b) lists most of the complaints that must be urged in a motion for new trial to preserve error for appeal. In the appeal of a jury trial, the party must file a motion for new trial in the following instances:

1. To preserve post-trial complaints on which evidence must be heard, for example: jury misconduct, TRCP 324(b)(1); newly discovered evidence, *id.*; failure to set aside a default judgment, *id.*; lack of consent to an agreed judgment, ***Newman v. Link***, 889 S.W.2d 288, 289 (Tex.1994); or a challenge to an award of fees to an attorney ad litem, ***Navistar Int'l Corp. v. Valles***, 740 S.W.2d 4, 6 (Tex.App.—El Paso 1987, no writ).

2. To preserve the complaint that the evidence is factually insufficient to support a jury finding or, the converse, that the jury finding is against the great weight and preponderance of the evidence. TRCP 324(b)(2), (3); ***Fredonia State Bank v. General Am. Life Ins. Co.***, 881 S.W.2d 279, 281 (Tex.1994); ***Cecil v. Smith***, 804 S.W.2d 509, 512 (Tex.1991).

3. To preserve the complaint that the jury's damages are inadequate or excessive. TRCP 324(b)(4); ***Hawthorne v. Guenther***, 917 S.W.2d 924, 937 (Tex.App.—Beaumont 1996, writ denied).

4. To preserve the complaint of incurable jury argument if the trial court did not already rule on it. TRCP 324(b)(5); ***Schindler Elevator Corp. v. Anderson***, 78 S.W.3d 392, 405 (Tex.App.—Houston [14th Dist.]

2001, pet. granted w.r.m.), *overruled on other grounds*, ***Roberts v. Williamson***, 111 S.W.3d 113 (Tex.2003); ***Austin v. Shampine***, 948 S.W.2d 900, 906-07 (Tex.App.—Texarkana 1997, no writ).

5. To preserve complaints not brought to the trial court's attention during the trial. *See* TRCP 324(a), (b); TRAP 33.1(a)(1); ***Luna v. Southern P.T. Co.***, 724 S.W.2d 383, 384 (Tex.1987).

§2.2 In writing. The motion for new trial must be in writing and signed by the attorney or the party. TRCP 320.

§2.3 Points of error. The motion for new trial must list the complaints in the points of error. TRCP 321. The complaints in the points must be specific. TRCP 322. The party should state what happened and why it was error. The points should cover the "who," "what," and "why" of the complaint. For example:

> *The trial court (who) erred in overruling the defendant's objections that jury question number 4 contained a comment on the evidence (what) because the question assumed as true that the defendant was negligent (why).*

On appeal, these points can be used as the statement of the issues presented in the brief. *See* TRAP 38.1(e) (in appellate briefs, parties must "state concisely all issues or points presented for review").

§2.4 Prayer. The motion for new trial must include a request to relitigate the case. ***Mercer v. Band***, 454 S.W.2d 833, 836 (Tex.App.—Houston [14th Dist.] 1970, no writ); *see* ***Finley v. J.C. Pace Ltd.***, 4 S.W.3d 319, 320 (Tex.App.—Houston [1st Dist.] 1999, order on mot.) (motion requesting rehearing sought to set aside judgment for purpose of litigating the issues). If the motion asks for other relief (*e.g.*, to enter a different judgment), it is not a motion for new trial. ***Mercer***, 454 S.W.2d at 836.

§2.5 Effect of MNT.

1. On plenary power. The filing of a motion for new trial extends the trial court's plenary power over the judgment. The exact date to which the plenary power is extended depends on whether the motion was denied or granted and the date the motion was denied or granted. If the motion was denied, plenary power is extended until 30 days after the motion was denied, either by written order or by operation of law, whichever occurred first, but in no event more than 105 days from the date the judgment was signed. If the motion was granted, plenary power is extended for 30 days after the order was signed, but in no event more than 75 days from the date the judgment was signed. See "When judgment becomes final," ch. 9-C, §6.5, p. 605; chart 9-1, "Plenary Power Deadlines," ch. 9-C, p. 607.

2. On appellate deadlines. See "Calculating appellate deadlines," ch. 9-C, §9.1, p. 608.

§3. VERIFICATION & AFFIDAVITS

It is not necessary to verify most motions for new trial or to attach affidavits. For example, sworn proof is not necessary to challenge the sufficiency of the evidence.

§3.1 When verification required. It is necessary to verify a motion for new trial and include affidavits when the motion is based on the grounds listed in TRCP 324(b)(1) (jury misconduct, newly discovered evidence, failure to set aside a default judgment), or any other ground that requires the presentation of evidence at a hearing. ***Zuniga v. Zuniga***, 13 S.W.3d 798, 803 n.4 (Tex.App.—San Antonio 1999, no pet.). See "Verification & affidavits," ch. 1-B, §4.14, p. 7. When in doubt, parties should verify the motion.

§3.2 Controverting affidavits. When the movant files a motion with affidavits, the nonmovant should consider filing controverting affidavits. On appeal, if there is no recorded hearing and no controverting affidavits, the appellate court will assume the movant's uncontroverted affidavit is true. ***Director v. Evans***, 889 S.W.2d 266, 268-69 (Tex.1994); ***Onyeanu v. Rivertree Apts. & Guar. Builders***, 920 S.W.2d 397, 398 (Tex.App.—Houston [1st Dist.] 1996, no writ).

§4. FILING FEE FOR MNT

§4.1 Amount & time for fee. A $15 filing fee must be paid at the time a motion for new trial is filed. Gov't Code §51.317(b)(2). Before filing, the lawyer should check with the clerk of the court because some counties add other fees. For example, the filing fee for a motion for new trial in Harris County is $26; Bexar County has two fees for civil cases—$20 for family law cases and $25 for other civil cases.

§4.2 MNT timely but fee late. If a motion for new trial is filed without the payment of the fee, the document is considered "conditionally filed" on the date it was tendered to the clerk. ***Jamar v. Patterson***, 868 S.W.2d 318, 319 (Tex.1993). When the filing fee is paid, the document is deemed filed on the date it was originally tendered. *Id.* The late payment of the filing fee for a motion for new trial can affect both the appellate deadlines and the preservation of error. Not all the issues of late payment have been resolved.

1. Paid before loss of jurisdiction.

(1) Effect on appellate deadlines. When the filing fee is paid before the trial court loses plenary power, the motion extends the appellate deadlines even if the fee was paid after the motion was denied. ***Tate v. E.I. DuPont de Nemours & Co.***, 934 S.W.2d 83, 84 (Tex.1996).

(2) Effect on preservation of error. In ***Tate***, the Supreme Court refused to decide whether payment of the filing fee before the loss of plenary power but after the motion is overruled by operation of law preserves error for appeal. ***Tate***, 934 S.W.2d at 84 n.1.

2. Paid after loss of jurisdiction. The courts of appeal disagree about the effect of payment of the filing fee after the trial court's loss of jurisdiction.

(1) Effect on appellate deadlines. Four courts of appeals have held that a timely motion for new trial extends the appellate deadlines even if the fee is paid after the trial court's loss of plenary power. ***Finley***, 4 S.W.3d at 321 (timely MNT extends appellate timetable regardless of when filing fee is paid); ***Polley v. Odom***, 937 S.W.2d 623, 625-26 (Tex.App.—Waco 1997, no writ) (fee paid 6 months late); ***Ramirez v. Get "N" Go #103***, 888 S.W.2d 29, 31 (Tex.App.—Corpus Christi 1994, writ denied) (fee paid 10 months late); ***Spellman v. Hoang***, 887 S.W.2d 480, 481 (Tex.App.—San Antonio 1994, no writ) (fee paid 7 months late). *Contra* ***Arndt v. Arndt***, 709 S.W.2d 281, 282 (Tex.App.—Houston [14th Dist.] 1986, no writ) (in dicta, court suggested deadlines would not be extended if filing fee paid after loss of jurisdiction). In ***Tate***, the Supreme Court refused to decide whether payment of the filing fee after the loss of plenary power extends appellate deadlines. ***Tate***, 934 S.W.2d at 84 n.1.

(2) Effect on preservation of error. One court of appeals has held that a timely motion for new trial does not preserve error for those issues that must be preserved in a motion for new trial if the fee is paid after the trial court loses plenary power. *See* ***Marathon Corp. v. Pitzner***, 55 S.W.3d 114, 123-25 (Tex.App.—Corpus Christi 2001) (appellate court refused to consider D's factual sufficiency points), *rev'd on other grounds*, 106 S.W.3d 724 (Tex.2003).

§5. DEADLINES FOR MNT

§5.1 Original MNT. A motion for new trial must be filed within 30 days of the date the judgment was signed. TRCP 329b(a); ***Padilla v. LaFrance***, 907 S.W.2d 454, 458 (Tex.1995); ***Jamar***, 868 S.W.2d at 319; ***Sadeghian v. Shaw***, 76 S.W.3d 229, 231 (Tex.App.—Texarkana 2002, no pet.); *see* ***Williams v. Flores***, 88 S.W.3d 631, 632 (Tex. 2002) (MNT timely filed on 32nd day after judgment because the 30th day was Sunday & 31st day was a legal holiday). A motion for new trial filed more than 30 days after judgment is a nullity and cannot be considered by the appellate courts. *See* ***Equinox Enters. v. Associated Media***, 730 S.W.2d 872, 875 (Tex.App.—Dallas 1987, no writ).

§5.2 No extensions. TRCP 5 prohibits the trial court from enlarging the time period "for taking any action under the rules relating to new trials." ***Moritz v. Preiss***, ___ S.W.3d ___ (Tex.2003) (No. 01-1270; 6-12-03); ***Lind v. Gresham***, 672 S.W.2d 20, 22 (Tex.App.—Houston [14th Dist.] 1984, no writ). Thus, the trial court cannot grant an extension of time to file the motion for new trial. ***Moritz***, ___ S.W.3d at ___; ***Lind***, 672 S.W.2d at 22. Although the court cannot grant an extension, if the court signs a modified judgment within its plenary power and changes the date, the modified judgment gives the parties another 30 days to file a motion. ***Check v. Mitchell***, 758 S.W.2d 755, 756 (Tex.1988); *see* TRCP 329b(h) (if a judgment is modified "in any respect, the time for appeal shall run" from the date of the modified judgment). See "Motion to Modify the Judgment," ch. 10-D, p. 639.

§5.3 Late MNT + plenary power. Even though the trial court cannot extend time to file the motion for new trial, it can grant a new trial on the grounds stated in a late motion if the motion is filed before the court loses plenary power. ***Moritz***, ___ S.W.3d at ___; ***Jackson v. Van Winkle***, 660 S.W.2d 807, 808 (Tex.1983); *see* TRCP 320. The court is not actually granting the late motion; it is granting a new trial on its own initiative. The late motion is meaningless for purposes of preserving error for appeal, but the grounds stated in the motion may convince the trial court a new trial is necessary. *See* ***Moritz***, ___ S.W.3d at ___; ***Kalteyer v. Sneed***, 837 S.W.2d 848, 851 (Tex. App.—Austin 1992, no writ).

§5.4 Premature MNT. A premature motion for new trial, filed before the judgment is signed, is deemed filed on the date of, but immediately after, the signing of the judgment. TRCP 306c; ***Padilla***, 907 S.W.2d at 458. TRAP 27.2 permits a premature motion to be treated as effective if the court later signs an appealable order relating to the premature motion. ***IPM Prods. Corp. v. Motor Parkway Rlty. Corp.***, 960 S.W.2d 879, 882 (Tex.App.—El Paso 1997, order on mot.); ***Miller v. Hernandez***, 708 S.W.2d 25, 27 (Tex.App.—Dallas 1986, order on mot.) (citing former TRAP 58(a)).

§5.5 Amended MNT. The last day a party may file an amended or supplemental motion for new trial is 30 days from the date the judgment was signed. ***Moritz***, ___ S.W.3d at ___ ; ***Ferguson v. Globe-Tex. Co.***, 35 S.W.3d 688, 690 (Tex.App.—Amarillo 2000, pet. denied); ***Voth v. Felderhoff***, 768 S.W.2d 403, 412 (Tex.App.—Fort Worth 1989, writ denied).

1. Without leave of court. Without leave of court, a party may amend a motion for new trial within 30 days after the date the judgment was signed, as long as the court has not overruled the earlier motion for new trial. TRCP 329b(b); ***Moritz***, ___ S.W.3d at ___; *see* ***Wirtz v. Massachusetts Mut. Life Ins. Co.***, 898 S.W.2d 414, 419 n.2 (Tex.App.—Amarillo 1995, no writ) (amended motion must be filed before original motion overruled).

2. With leave of court. With leave of court, a party may amend a motion for new trial within 30 days after the date the judgment was signed, even if the trial court has already overruled the earlier motion for new trial. *See* TRCP 329b(b); ***Cecil v. Smith***, 804 S.W.2d 509, 511 (Tex.1991) (dicta). Because TRCP 5 prohibits the trial court from enlarging the time to file a motion for new trial, the trial court cannot grant a party permission to file an amended or supplemental motion for new trial after the 30 days expire. ***Moritz***, ___ S.W.3d at ___ ; ***Kalteyer***, 837 S.W.2d at 851.

§5.6 Second judgment problems.

1. Preservation of error. When the trial court corrects the judgment by signing a second judgment, a motion for new trial filed to challenge the first judgment is effective for the second judgment if the substance of the motion challenges the second judgment. ***Fredonia State Bank v. General Am. Life Ins. Co.***, 881 S.W.2d 279, 281 (Tex.1994); *see* TRAP 27.3.

2. Extending appellate deadlines. A motion for new trial filed after the first judgment is a prematurely filed motion as to a second judgment, and it extends the appellate timetables from the signing of the second judgment if the grounds in the motion "assail" the second judgment. TRCP 306c; ***Gunnels v. City of Brownfield***, ___ S.W.3d ___ (Tex.App.—Amarillo 2002, order on mot.) (No. 07-02-0121-CV; 5-1-02); ***Harris Cty. Hosp. Dist. v. Estrada***, 831 S.W.2d 876, 878-79 (Tex.App.—Houston [1st Dist.] 1992, order on mot.); *see* TRAP 27.2; *see also* ***Padilla***, 907 S.W.2d at 458 (motion for reconsideration of 1st judgment, filed before 2nd judgment, extended deadlines).

§5.7 Late notice of judgment. If a party receives notice of the judgment between 20 and 90 days after the judgment was signed, the deadline for filing a motion for new trial is counted from the date the party actually learned or received notice of the judgment rather than the date the judgment was signed. TRCP 306a(4), (5). See "Motion to Extend Postjudgment Deadlines," ch. 10-G, p. 654.

§5.8 MNT after citation by publication. The defendant may file a motion for new trial within two years after the court signs a judgment signed after citation by publication. TRCP 329(a). The same is true if a judgment was signed after the citation was posted on the courthouse door. ***Gray v. PHI Res., Ltd.***, 710 S.W.2d 566, 568 (Tex. 1986). See "Attacking the Default Judgment," 7-A, §7, p. 452; "MNT After Service by Publication," §16, p. 634.

§5.9 After domesticated foreign judgment. When a plaintiff files an original petition in a Texas court to enforce a foreign judgment, the petition constitutes a final Texas judgment under the Uniform Enforcement of Foreign Judgments Act (UEFJA), CPRC §35.003. ***Walnut Equip. Leasing Co. v. Wu***, 920 S.W.2d 285, 286 (Tex.1996). The defendant must file a motion for new trial within 30 days of the filing of the petition. ***Walnut Equip.***, 920 S.W.2d at 286; ***Moncrief v. Harvey***, 805 S.W.2d 20, 23 (Tex.App.—Dallas 1991, no writ).

§6. RESPONSE

When the movant files an unsworn motion for new trial, it is probably not necessary for the nonmovant to file a response. However, because some local rules infer acquiescence when the nonmovant does not file a response, the lawyer should always check the local rules. When the movant files a sworn motion for new trial, the nonmovant should file a sworn response.

§7. HEARING

§7.1 Unsworn MNT – no hearing. Most motions for new trial do not require a hearing. The hearing on an unsworn motion is for argument only, and no evidence may be presented.

§7.2 Sworn MNT – hearing. If a motion for new trial requires sworn evidence to support it, it also requires a hearing to receive evidence. The types of motions for new trial that require a hearing are the following: jury misconduct, newly discovered evidence, failure to set aside a default judgment, and any other motion that must be supported by evidence. *See, e.g.*, ***Hensley v. Salinas***, 583 S.W.2d 617, 618 (Tex.1979) (hearing required for MNT challenging agreed judgment); ***Navistar Int'l Corp. v. Valles***, 740 S.W.2d 4, 6 (Tex.App.—El Paso 1987, no writ) (hearing required for MNT challenging attorney ad litem fees). A party is not entitled to a hearing unless it has filed a sworn motion with specific allegations. *See* ***Hatton v. Highlands Ins. Co.***, 631 S.W.2d 787, 789 (Tex.App.—Tyler 1982, no writ) (affidavit attached to MNT based on jury misconduct specified acts of misconduct and names of jurors who committed misconduct).

1. Setting. When a motion for new trial requires a hearing, the movant must ask the court for a setting and not allow its motion to be overruled by operation of law. ***Shamrock Roofing Sup. v. Mercantile Nat'l Bank***, 703 S.W.2d 356, 357 (Tex.App.—Dallas 1985, no writ).

2. Affidavits. When affidavits are filed as part of a motion for new trial, the proponent of the affidavits is not required to introduce them into evidence at the hearing on the motion. ***Director v. Evans***, 889 S.W.2d 266, 268 (Tex.1994). It is sufficient that the affidavits are attached to the motion for new trial and made part of the record. *Id.*

§8. ORDER

§8.1 In writing. The trial court's order on a motion for new trial must be in writing and signed by the trial court. TRCP 329b(c); ***In re Barber***, 982 S.W.2d 364, 366 (Tex.1998); ***Faulkner v. Culver***, 851 S.W.2d 187, 188 (Tex. 1993). See "In writing," ch. 1-G, §3.1, p. 34. The trial court's oral pronouncement and docket entry are not substitutes for a written order. ***Faulkner***, 851 S.W.2d at 188; ***Taack v. McFall***, 661 S.W.2d 923, 924 (Tex.1983); *see* ***In re J.H.***, 39 S.W.3d 688, 690 (Tex.App.—Houston [1st Dist.] 2001, no pet.) (docket entry & order setting case for new trial did not satisfy requirement for written order). See "Not an order," ch. 1-G, §3.3.1, p. 35.

§8.2 Grounds. The trial court has broad discretion in granting a new trial. ***Champion Int'l Corp. v. 12th Ct. of Appeals***, 762 S.W.2d 898, 899 (Tex.1988). A new trial may be granted "for good cause, on motion or on the court's own motion." TRCP 320. The court can grant a motion for new trial without stating any reason other than "in the interest of justice." ***Champion Int'l***, 762 S.W.2d at 899.

PRACTICE TIP

To avoid having an order for new trial subjected to a mandamus, you should include in the motion a request for a new trial "in the interest of justice and fairness." Make sure the same language is in the order granting the motion. ***Champion Int'l****, 762 S.W.2d at 899. If "the interest of justice" language is in the order, the appellate courts will deny mandamus.* ***Johnson v. 4th Ct. of Appeals****, 700 S.W.2d 916, 918 (Tex.1985).*

§8.3 Partial new trial. TRCP 320 permits the trial court to grant a new trial on part of the case under the following conditions:

1. Separable. The matter is clearly separable. TRCP 320; ***State Dept. of Highways & Pub. Transp. v. Cotner***, 845 S.W.2d 818, 819 (Tex.1993); *see also* ***Satellite Earth Stations E., Inc. v. Davis***, 756 S.W.2d 385, 387 (Tex.App.—Eastland 1988, writ denied) (when attorney fees are mandatory, they are clearly separable). To determine what is separable, consult TRCP 41 and 174(b). A partial new trial may be ordered despite the prohibition in TRCP 41 against post-submission severances; thus, TRCP 320 is an exception to TRCP 41. ***Cotner***, 845 S.W.2d at 819.

2. Not unfair. The matter is separable without unfairness to the parties. TRCP 320; *see* ***Cotner***, 845 S.W.2d at 819 (in PI suit, court could not grant partial new trial to one P and affirm as to other P).

3. Liquidated damages. The damages are liquidated, or the damages are unliquidated and liability is not contested. The court cannot grant a partial new trial on unliquidated damages if liability is contested. TRCP 320; *see* ***Redman Homes v. Ivy***, 920 S.W.2d 664, 669 (Tex.1996); ***Gramercy Ins. Co. v. Arcadia Fin. Ltd.***, 32 S.W.3d 402, 408 (Tex.App.—Houston [14th Dist.] 2000, no pet.).

§8.4 Deadline to sign order on MNT.

1. Deadline to grant new trial. To grant a motion for new trial, the court should sign a written order before the motion is overruled by operation of law, which is 75 days from the date the judgment was signed. TRCP 329b(c), (e); ***Thomas v. Oldham***, 895 S.W.2d 352, 356 (Tex.1995); *see* ***Lane Bank Equip. Co. v. Smith S. Equip., Inc.***, 10 S.W.3d 308, 310 (Tex.2000). However, the trial court can grant a motion for new trial as long as it has plenary power over the judgment, which can last as much as 105 days from the date the judgment was signed. *See* TRCP 329b(e); *see, e.g.*, ***Coinmach, Inc. v. Aspenwood Apt. Corp.***, 98 S.W.3d 377, 378-80 (Tex.App.—Houston [1st Dist.] 2003, no pet.) (court granted MNT 103 days after judgment signed). To determine when plenary power expires, see chart 9-1, "Plenary Power Deadlines," ch. 9-C, p. 607.

2. Deadline to deny new trial. To deny a motion for new trial, the court must sign an order within 75 days of the date the judgment was signed; if not, the motion will be overruled by operation of law on the 75th day after the judgment was signed. TRCP 329b(c); ***Clark & Co. v. Giles***, 639 S.W.2d 449, 450 (Tex.1982).

§8.5 Deadline to change order on MNT. The court can change its order on the motion for new trial as long as it has plenary power over the judgment. See chart 9-1, "Plenary Power Deadlines," ch. 9-C, p. 607.

1. When MNT granted. When the trial court grants a new trial but then decides it should not have, it has 30 days to "ungrant" the motion, counting from the date it signed the order granting the new trial. However, the court cannot "ungrant" the motion more than 75 days from the date it signed the judgment. See "PPE motion granted," ch. 9-C, §6.5.2(3), p. 607.

2. When MNT denied. When the motion for new trial is denied (either by written order or by operation of law), the court has the power to grant a new trial as long as it has plenary power over the judgment, that is, 30 days from the date the motion was denied, but in no event later than 105 days from the date the judgment was signed. ***In re Dickason***, 987 S.W.2d 570, 571 (Tex.1998). See "PPE motion denied," ch. 9-C, §6.5.2(2), p. 607.

§9. MNT TO CHALLENGE THE EVIDENCE

§9.1 Challenging sufficiency of evidence. Most motions for new trial after a jury trial are filed to complain about the sufficiency of the evidence. Because challenges to jury findings are some of the most important challenges a party can assert on appeal, it is important to preserve them in the motion for new trial. For a more detailed analysis on appealing jury findings and for additional flow charts about the process, see O'Connor, *Appealing Jury Findings*, 12 Hous.L.Rev. 65 (1974).

1. Legal & factual sufficiency. Each jury finding is susceptible to two challenges—legal sufficiency and factual sufficiency. Chart 10-1, below, shows how each adverse jury finding may be challenged.

10-1. GROUNDS FOR CHALLENGING ADVERSE JURY FINDINGS

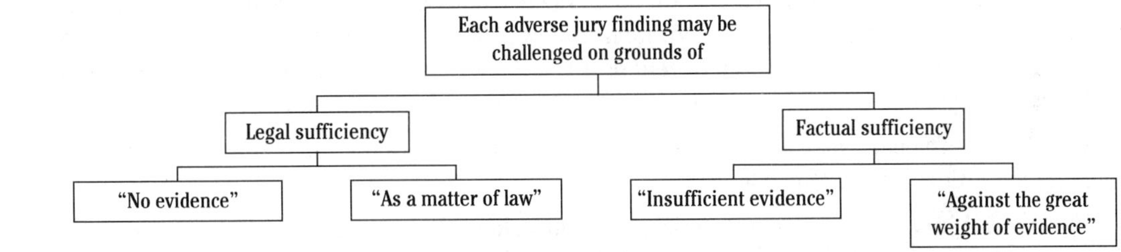

Choosing which terms to use to challenge a jury finding depends on who had the burden of proof on the issue at trial. If the movant had the burden of proof, and the jury returned an adverse finding, the movant challenges the jury finding by saying (1) the movant proved its issue as a matter of law, and (2) the jury's answer is against the great weight and preponderance of the evidence. If the movant did not have the burden of proof on the issues, it challenges an adverse finding by saying (1) there is no evidence to support the jury answer, and (2) there is insufficient evidence to support the jury answer.

2. Preserving factual sufficiency point. There is only one way to preserve the factual sufficiency challenges after a trial to a jury—in a motion for new trial. TRCP 324(b)(2); ***Cecil v. Smith***, 804 S.W.2d 509, 510 (Tex.1991).

3. Preserving legal sufficiency point. There are four ways to preserve the legal sufficiency challenges: (1) in a motion for directed verdict, (2) in an objection to the submission of a jury question, (3) in a motion for JNOV (or motion to disregard), and (4) in a motion for new trial. ***Cecil***, 804 S.W.2d at 510-11; ***Steves Sash & Door Co. v. Ceco Corp.***, 751 S.W.2d 473, 477 (Tex.1988). If the party properly preserves error in a motion for directed verdict, an objection to the charge, or a motion for JNOV, and if the appellate court sustains the challenge, the party may be entitled to rendition of judgment. However, if a party makes a legal sufficiency challenge for the first and only time in a motion for new trial, on appeal the party will not be entitled to rendition, only remand. ***Horrocks v. Texas DOT***, 852 S.W.2d 498, 499 (Tex.1993); ***Cecil***, 804 S.W.2d at 512; ***Ana, Inc. v. Lowry***, 31 S.W.3d 765, 772 (Tex.App.—Houston [1st Dist.] 2000, no pet.); *see* O'Connor, *Appealing Jury Findings*, 12 Hous.L.Rev. 65, 76 n.57 (1974) (challenges to adverse jury findings).

4. Standard challenges. The following are models for challenging jury findings on the evidence:

(1) When the party has burden of proof on jury question.

• The evidence proves conclusively as a matter of law that [*state what the evidence proves*]. The jury's answer to question number ___ is wrong, and the court erred in overruling [*the objections to the charge, the motion for directed verdict, or the motion for JNOV*].

• The jury's answer to question number ___ is against the great weight and preponderance of the evidence and is manifestly unjust.

(2) **When the party does not have burden of proof.**

• There is no evidence to support the jury's answer to question number ___, and the court erred in overruling [*the objections to the charge, the motion for directed verdict, or the motion for JNOV*].

• The evidence is insufficient to support the jury's answer to question number ___.

§9.2 Challenging broad-form jury question. The Supreme Court insists trial courts submit jury questions in broad form. ***Texas Dept. of Human Servs. v. E.B.***, 802 S.W.2d 647, 649 (Tex.1990). The submission of a broad-form jury question substantially reduces the losing party's ability to successfully challenge the evidence on appeal. To challenge a verdict when the charge asked separate questions for each element of a cause of action, the appellant can focus on the adverse findings. To challenge a verdict when the charge asked only a broad-form question, the appellant must assume the jury found against it on all the elements of the action and thus must challenge all the elements. *See, e.g.*, ***Prudential Ins. Co. v. Jefferson Assocs.***, 896 S.W.2d 156, 160 (Tex.1995) (court submitted one question for multiple theories of liability); ***GreenPoint Credit Corp. v. Perez***, 75 S.W.3d 40, 45-46 (Tex.App.—San Antonio 2002, pet. granted w.r.m.) (court submitted one damage question for multiple theories of damages).

§9.3 Remittitur. The party may ask for a remittitur in either the motion for new trial or a separate motion. See "Motion for Remittitur," ch. 10-C, p. 636.

§9.4 Immaterial jury answer. An immaterial jury finding should be challenged in the motion for new trial or in some other postverdict motion. The trial court may, with or without a motion, disregard the answer to an immaterial jury question. ***Clear Lake City Water Auth. v. Winograd***, 695 S.W.2d 632, 639 (Tex.App.—Houston [1st Dist.] 1985, writ ref'd n.r.e.). A question is immaterial when it should not have been submitted or, even though properly submitted, it was rendered immaterial by other findings. ***Spencer v. Eagle Star Ins. Co.***, 876 S.W.2d 154, 157 (Tex.1994). A jury's findings on a question of law may be deemed immaterial. ***Quick v. City of Austin***, 7 S.W.3d 109, 116 (Tex.1998); ***Spencer***, 876 S.W.2d at 157.

§10. MNT AFTER NONJURY TRIAL

§10.1 Not generally necessary. A party does not need to file a motion for new trial to preserve most errors in a nonjury trial. TRCP 324(a); ***Park v. Essa Tex. Corp.***, 311 S.W.2d 228, 229 (Tex.1958); *see* TRAP 33.1(a). In many cases, parties file a motion for new trial in a nonjury case just to extend the appellate deadlines.

1. **Not required.** There is no need to complain in a motion for new trial about factual insufficiency of the evidence ("insufficient evidence" or "against the great weight"), about legal insufficiency of the evidence ("no evidence" or "as a matter of law"), or that damages are too large or too small. TRCP 324(b)(2), (4); ***In re Parker***, 20 S.W.3d 812, 816 (Tex.App.—Texarkana 2000, no pet.); ***Strickland v. Coleman***, 824 S.W.2d 188, 191 (Tex.App.—Houston [1st Dist.] 1991, no writ). These issues can be raised for the first time in the appeal of a nonjury trial without a motion for new trial. *See* TRAP 33.1(d).

2. **Required.** If the complaint was not presented to the trial court during trial, or if the complaint is one on which evidence must be presented, the complaining party must file a motion for new trial. TRCP 324(b); *see* TRAP 33.1(a). Thus, the party must file a motion for new trial to complain about newly discovered evidence, any other matter on which evidence must be heard, and any other matter about which the party has not already objected. TRCP 324(b)(1). See "When MNT necessary," §2.1, p. 617.

§10.2 Verification. See "When verification required," §3.1, p. 618.

§11. MNT AFTER SUMMARY JUDGMENT

§11.1 Not generally necessary. In the appeal of a summary judgment, the appellant does not need to file a motion for new trial to preserve most errors. *See* TRCP 324(a); TRAP 33.1(a). The appellant may file a motion for new trial just to extend the appellate deadlines. ***Thomley v. Southwood-Driftwood Apts.***, 961 S.W.2d 6, 8 (Tex. App.—Amarillo 1996, order on mot.).

1. Not required. As a general rule, a motion for new trial is not necessary to preserve error about the merits of the summary judgment. ***Lee v. Braeburn Valley W. Civic Ass'n***, 786 S.W.2d 262, 263 (Tex.1990). In most cases, the objections to the motion for summary judgment are made in the response to the motion, a motion requesting more time for discovery, or a motion to file a late response. As long as the objections to the motion for summary judgment are preserved for appeal in some prejudgment motion or objection, a motion for new trial is not necessary. For example, if the nonmovant filed a motion for permission to file a late response, which the court overruled, the nonmovant is not required to file a motion for new trial; its motion to file a late response preserved the error. See "Secure ruling on objections," ch. 7-B, §6.8, p. 471.

2. Required.

(1) Newly discovered evidence. A party should file a motion for new trial to assert newly discovered evidence or any other matter on which evidence must be heard. TRCP 324(b)(1). See "When MNT necessary," §2.1.1, p. 617.

(2) No opportunity to file response. When the nonmovant did not have an opportunity to file a response or to seek a continuance or permission to file a late response, the nonmovant should file a sworn motion for new trial, probably relying on the factors from ***Craddock v. Sunshine Bus Lines***, 133 S.W.2d 124, 126 (Tex. 1939). *See* ***Carpenter v. Cimarron Hydrocarbons Corp.***, 98 S.W.3d 682, 686 (Tex.2002) (court said it did not decide whether ***Craddock*** applies when nonmovant discovers its mistake after SJ hearing or rendition of judgment). The motion for new trial should include the grounds the nonmovant would have included in a timely response. For a discussion of the ***Craddock*** factors, see "Failure to answer or appear after proper notice," §15.1.3, p. 632.

CAUTION

Do not confuse a motion for new trial filed when a nonmovant had an opportunity to file a motion for leave to file a late response or a motion to continue the summary judgment hearing with a motion for new trial when the nonmovant did not have a opportunity to file a response. In ***Carpenter****, the Supreme Court held that a motion for new trial establishing the* ***Craddock*** *factors is not appropriate to challenge the trial court's denial of permission to file a late response to a motion for summary judgment. See* ***Carpenter****, 98 S.W.3d at 686. Instead, the nonmovant must base its appeal on the trial court's abuse of discretion in denying the motion for permission to file a late response. See id. See "Motion for leave to file late SJ response," ch. 7-B, §6.6.6(3), p. 469.*

---

(3) Other matters. A party should file a motion for new trial to complain about any matter to which the party has not already objected or on which the court has not ruled. For example, if the trial court refused to rule on the nonmovant's objections to a motion for summary judgment, the nonmovant should file a motion for new trial reurging those objections and objecting to the court's earlier refusal to rule. When the motion for new trial is overruled, either by order or by operation of law, the objections will be preserved for appeal. See "Refusal to rule + objection," ch. 1-G, §2.2.3, p. 33.

§11.2 Verification. See "When verification required," §3.1, p. 618.

§12. MNT AFTER DISMISSAL

The type of motion (verified vs. unverified) and the grounds to challenge a dismissal order depend on the underlying reason for the dismissal.

§12.1 Dismissal for failure to prosecute. If the trial court dismissed the suit for failure to prosecute or failure to appear at trial, the party should follow the procedures for a verified motion outlined in "Motion to Reinstate After DWOP," ch. 10-F, p. 649.

§12.2 Other dismissals. To determine the grounds for a motion for new trial following other dismissals, check the grounds on which the dismissal was based (*e.g.*, for a motion for new trial following special exceptions, check "Special Exceptions—Challenging the Pleadings," ch. 3-G, p. 187).

1. Verified vs. unverified motion. As a general rule, if both the dismissal order and the motion for new trial are based on the pleadings, verification of the motion is not necessary; if either the dismissal order or the motion for new trial are based on evidence, verification is necessary. See "When verification required," §3.1, p. 618.

2. Inappropriate order of dismissal. If the trial court's order dismissed the suit with prejudice to refiling when the order should have dismissed without prejudice, the dismissal "with prejudice" must be challenged in a motion for new trial or a motion to reinstate; otherwise, the error is waived for appeal and the suit cannot be refiled. *See* ***El Paso Pipe & Sup. v. Mountain States Leasing***, 617 S.W.2d 189, 190 (Tex.1981). See "Challenge language of dismissal order," ch. 10-F, §3.5, p. 651.

§13. MNT BASED ON JURY OR BAILIFF MISCONDUCT

§13.1 Jury or bailiff misconduct. A new trial based on misconduct of the jury or the officer in charge of the jury (the bailiff) is controlled by TRCP 327 and TRE 606(b). *See also* TRCP 226a (general instructions to jury), TRCP 283 (instructions to bailiff), TRCP 285 (communications between jury & bailiff). Because of the restrictions on a juror's testimony in TRCP 327(b) and TRE 606(b), it is very difficult to prove jury misconduct. *See* ***Golden Eagle Archery, Inc. v Jackson***, 24 S.W.3d 362, 375 (Tex.2000) (restrictions on juror testimony in TRCP 327(b) and TRE 606(b) are constitutional).

§13.2 Who can testify about jury misconduct. Whether a person can testify about jury misconduct depends on two things: (1) the stage in the trial when the misconduct occurred and (2) the status of the person testifying about the misconduct.

1. Time of misconduct. A juror's misconduct can occur at any time between the beginning of voir dire and the jury's discharge. This time frame is divided in two parts: nondeliberation and deliberation. The nondeliberation stage of the trial begins with voir dire and ends with the beginning of deliberations; the deliberations stage begins when the jury is retired to deliberate on the jury charge and ends when the jury is discharged from its duties. *See* ***Golden Eagle***, 24 S.W.3d at 371-72.

2. Status of person testifying.

(1) Juror testimony. Whether a juror may testify about misconduct depends on the subject of the testimony and when the misconduct was said to have occurred.

(a) Deliberation. A juror cannot testify about any matter or statement that occurred during the jury's deliberations, or about the effect of anything on a juror's mental processes. TRCP 327(b); TRE 606(b); ***Golden Eagle***, 24 S.W.3d at 368; ***Weaver v. Westchester Fire Ins. Co.***, 739 S.W.2d 23, 24 (Tex.1987); *see* ***Chavarria v. Valley Transit Co.***, 75 S.W.3d 107, 111 (Tex.App.—San Antonio 2002, no pet.) (jurors' discussion of case during breaks in deliberation is same as deliberation itself). The only exception to this rule is that a juror may testify about an outside influence improperly brought to bear on a juror during deliberations. TRCP 327(b); TRE 606(b); ***Golden Eagle***, 24 S.W.3d at 368; ***Weaver***, 739 S.W.2d at 24. See "Jury misconduct during deliberations," §13.5.1, p. 628.

(b) Nondeliberation. A juror may testify about any conduct (her own, another juror's, a nonjuror's) if the conduct occurred during nondeliberations. ***Golden Eagle***, 24 S.W.3d at 370. A juror's testimony about conduct that occurred during nondeliberations is restricted by the general rules of evidence, but not by TRCP

327(b) or TRE 606(b). ***Golden Eagle***, 24 S.W.3d at 370. Some of the matters a juror can testify about include the following: improper contacts with individuals outside the jury; a conversation with another juror during a trial break; that another juror improperly viewed the scene of the event involved in the suit; and information showing another juror is disqualified as a juror, if the information was not acquired during deliberations. *Id.*

(2) Nonjuror testimony. A nonjuror may testify about any conduct (her own, another nonjuror's, a juror's) whether it occurred during nondeliberations or deliberations. ***Golden Eagle***, 24 S.W.3d at 369. A nonjuror's testimony is restricted by the general rules of evidence, but not by TRCP 327(b) or TRE 606(b). ***Golden Eagle***, 24 S.W.3d at 369. For example, although a nonjuror can testify about what she saw happen at trial, she cannot testify about the jury's deliberations because the information would be hearsay. *Id.*; *see, e.g.*, ***Mitchell v. Southern P.T. Co.***, 955 S.W.2d 300, 322 (Tex.App.—San Antonio 1997, no writ) (conversation with daughter-in-law of alternate juror about what happened in jury's deliberation was hearsay), *disapproved on other grounds*, ***Golden Eagle Archery, Inc. v Jackson***, 24 S.W.3d 362 (Tex.2000).

§13.3 Sworn motion. TRCP 324(b) and 327 govern the procedure for preserving error based on misconduct of the jury or the bailiff.

1. Allegations in MNT. The movant should allege (1) there was jury or bailiff misconduct, (2) it was material, and (3) it resulted in injury to the movant, based on the whole record. ***Redinger v. Living, Inc.***, 689 S.W.2d 415, 419 (Tex.1985). The allegations in the motion for new trial must be based on knowledge of misconduct, not just suspicion. ***American Home Assur. Co. v. Guevara***, 717 S.W.2d 381, 384-85 (Tex.App.—San Antonio 1986, no writ). The motion must describe the misconduct. TRCP 327(a) envisions four types of misconduct: jury misconduct, bailiff misconduct, an unauthorized communication to the jury, or an incorrect, material juror answer on voir dire. TRCP 327(a).

2. Affidavits. The motion must be supported by affidavits confirming the claim of misconduct. TRCP 327(a); ***Weaver v. Westchester Fire Ins. Co.***, 739 S.W.2d 23, 24 (Tex.1987). See "Verification & affidavits," §3, p. 618. The movant must attach one of the following types of affidavits:

(1) An affidavit by a juror describing the misconduct that occurred during nondeliberations or deliberations. See §13.2.2(1), above. If the misconduct occurred during deliberations, it must amount to an "outside influence" on the jury. TRE 606(b); ***Golden Eagle***, 24 S.W.3d at 369. See §13.5, below.

(2) An affidavit by a nonjuror describing misconduct. See §13.2.2(2), above.

(3) An affidavit by an attorney or other person explaining why affidavits are not available and describing the diligence used in attempting to procure affidavits. ***Roy Jones Lumber Co. v. Murphy***, 163 S.W.2d 644, 646 (Tex.1942); *see, e.g.*, ***Ramsey v. Lucky Stores***, 853 S.W.2d 623, 636 (Tex.App.—Houston [1st Dist.] 1993, writ denied) (statement describing improper contacts with jurors did not explain lack of affidavit by juror); ***American Home***, 717 S.W.2d at 384-85 (statement that jurors refused to sign affidavits was not enough to show diligence).

3. Request evidentiary hearing. In the motion for new trial, the movant should request a hearing to introduce evidence. The lawyer should check the provisions of the local rules on securing a hearing for the receipt of evidence.

§13.4 Hearing. To obtain a new trial on the basis of jury or bailiff misconduct, the movant must prove the following: (1) the misconduct occurred, (2) it was material, and (3) it probably resulted in injury to the movant, based on the record as a whole. ***Redinger***, 689 S.W.2d at 419; ***Flores v. Dosher***, 622 S.W.2d 573, 574 (Tex.1981). The trial court must conduct a hearing if the movant attached affidavits to the motion that either (1) described the misconduct or (2) stated a reasonable excuse for not filing affidavits alleging misconduct. *See* TRCP 327(a); ***Golden Eagle***, 24 S.W.3d at 369; ***Roy Jones***, 163 S.W.2d at 646; ***American Home***, 717 S.W.2d at 384-85. If the movant does not attach affidavits of misconduct and does not state in affidavits why it could not attach such affidavits, the court has discretion to grant a hearing. ***Roy Jones***, 163 S.W.2d at 646; ***American Home***, 717 S.W.2d at 385. The movant should request a court reporter to transcribe the hearing.

§13.5 Misconduct.

1. Jury misconduct during deliberations.

(1) Outside influence. To constitute outside influence, the information must have come from a source outside the jury (*i.e.*, a nonjuror who introduces information affecting the verdict). TRCP 327(b); ***Golden Eagle Archery, Inc. v. Jackson***, 24 S.W.3d 362, 370 (Tex.2000); ***Mitchell***, 955 S.W.2d at 321-22; ***Wooten v. Southern P.T. Co.***, 928 S.W.2d 76, 79 (Tex.App.—Houston [14th Dist.] 1995, no writ). Examples of outside influence include tampering with evidence, conversations between the judge and a juror, and threats to a juror. ***Clancy v. Zale Corp.***, 705 S.W.2d 820, 829 (Tex.App.—Dallas 1986, writ ref'd n.r.e.).

(2) Not outside influence. Broadly speaking, anything occurring during jury deliberations or as part of the jury's mental process is not an outside influence. ***Golden Eagle***, 24 S.W.3d at 370.

(a) Any matter in jury's deliberations. Since the 1984 amendment to TRCP 327, comments and statements made by a juror to the other jurors during deliberations are internal deliberations and are not outside influences. ***Golden Eagle***, 24 S.W.3d at 368; ***Kendall v. Whataburger***, 759 S.W.2d 751, 755-56 (Tex.App.—Houston [1st Dist.] 1988, no writ). The following are some matters that are considered part of the jury's deliberations and thus are not outside influences: • The jurors' speculation that the plaintiff had used alcohol and had received a settlement. ***Golden Eagle***, 24 S.W.3d at 370. • A juror's belief that the plaintiff had filed a workers' compensation claim to get someone to pay his medical bills. ***Weaver***, 739 S.W.2d at 24. • Information from the bailiff that the judge would require the jury to deliberate another day after reaching a deadlock, which motivated the jury to trade votes to reach a verdict. ***Rosell v. Central W. Motor Stages***, 89 S.W.3d 643, 661 (Tex.App.—Dallas 2002, pet. denied). • The jury's use of a discount formula from a juror's college textbook. ***Crowson v. Kansas City S. Ry.***, 11 S.W.3d 300, 304-05 (Tex.App.—Eastland 1999, no pet.). • A juror's statement to other jurors that he knew the railroad intersection was safe. ***Wooten***, 928 S.W.2d at 79. • The jurors' discussion about the effect the plaintiff's victory would have on the talc mine and their fear that similar suits might close it down, leaving many without jobs. ***Durbin v. Dal-Briar Corp.***, 871 S.W.2d 263, 272 (Tex.App.—El Paso 1994, writ denied), *disapproved on other grounds*, ***Golden Eagle Archery, Inc. v Jackson***, 24 S.W.3d 362 (Tex.2000). • The jury's improper voting procedures, such as the exclusion of jurors voting "no" from further deliberations. ***Moody v. EMC Servs.***, 828 S.W.2d 237, 243 (Tex.App.—Houston [14th Dist.] 1992, writ denied). • A juror's use of a published article mentioned during trial; reference to a dictionary; use of a juror's notes; coercive influence of one juror. ***Perry v. Safeco Ins. Co.***, 821 S.W.2d 279, 281 (Tex.App.—Houston [1st Dist.] 1991, writ denied). • A juror's statement that the plaintiff would still recover if they answered "no" to the negligence and proximate cause questions. ***Kendall***, 759 S.W.2d at 755. • A juror's discussion of personal experiences, insurance liability questions, and a newspaper article not in evidence. ***King v. Bauer***, 767 S.W.2d 197, 198 (Tex.App.—Corpus Christi 1989, writ denied); ***Moon v. Firestone Tire & Rubber Co.***, 742 S.W.2d 792, 792-93 (Tex.App.—Houston [14th Dist.] 1987, writ denied).

(b) Jury's mental process. The following are some matters that are considered part of the jury's mental process and thus are not outside influences: • The jurors' trading votes on two issues, in violation of court instructions. ***Golden Eagle***, 24 S.W.3d at 370. • The jurors' discussion about their impressions of the scene, in violation of court instructions. ***Soliz v. Saenz***, 779 S.W.2d 929, 932 (Tex.App.—Corpus Christi 1989, writ denied). • The jurors' misunderstanding or misinterpretation of the court's charge. ***Cortez v. Medical Protective Co.***, 560 S.W.2d 132, 137 (Tex.App.—Corpus Christi 1977, writ ref'd n.r.e.). • The jury's response to a verdict-urging "dynamite" or "Allen" charge. ***Shaw v. Greater Houston Transp. Co.***, 791 S.W.2d 204, 210 (Tex.App.—Corpus Christi 1990, no writ); ***Golden v. First City Nat'l Bank***, 751 S.W.2d 639, 644 (Tex.App.—Dallas 1988, no writ).

2. Erroneous juror answer on voir dire. When a juror responds to a question during voir dire with an answer that is untruthful, erroneous, or incomplete, it constitutes juror misconduct. TRCP 327(a); ***Doucet v.***

Owens-Corning Fiberglas Corp., 966 S.W.2d 161, 163 (Tex.App.—Beaumont 1998, pet. denied) (withheld information was material but did not cause injury); ***Missouri P. R.R. v. Cunningham***, 515 S.W.2d 678, 685 (Tex.App.—San Antonio 1974, writ dism'd) (withheld information was not material); *see* TRAP 44.1. A false answer on voir dire entitles a party to a new trial only if the juror's concealment was in response to a specific and direct question calling for disclosure. ***Wooten***, 928 S.W.2d at 79. Jurors and nonjurors may testify about voir dire. ***Golden Eagle***, 24 S.W.3d at 369; *see, e.g.*, ***Kiefer v. Continental Airlines***, 10 S.W.3d 34, 40 (Tex.App.—Houston [14th Dist.] 1999, pet. denied) (at MNT hearing, juror testified she may have seen in public one of the witnesses introduced by P's attorney at voir dire); ***Burton v. R.E. Hable Co.***, 852 S.W.2d 745, 746 (Tex.App.—Tyler 1993, no writ) (juror testified he misunderstood voir dire question). However, a juror cannot testify that another juror's voir dire response was untruthful if the juror learned of the untruthfulness during jury deliberations. *See* ***Golden Eagle***, 24 S.W.3d at 369-70.

3. Bailiff misconduct. TRCP 283 prohibits the bailiff from communicating with the jury except to inquire if they have agreed on a verdict or to make other communications as ordered by the court. ***Pharo v. Chambers Cty.***, 922 S.W.2d 945, 950 (Tex.1996); *see, e.g.*, ***OKC Corp. v. UPG, Inc.***, 798 S.W.2d 300, 303 (Tex.App.—Dallas 1990, writ denied) (error for bailiff to tell jury to use common meaning of the word when they had a question about it); ***Logan v. Grady***, 482 S.W.2d 313, 322 (Tex.App.—Fort Worth 1972, no writ) (reversible error for bailiff to tell jury, when it asked to rehear evidence, that it already had all it needed to answer jury question). To show probable injury, there must be some indication the bailiff's misconduct "most likely" caused a juror to vote differently on one or more issues vital to the judgment. ***Pharo***, 922 S.W.2d at 950; *see* ***OKC Corp.***, 798 S.W.2d at 304 (no probable injury). Determining the existence of probable injury is a question of law. ***Pharo***, 922 S.W.2d at 950.

4. Improper contact with jury. A juror is not permitted to accept any favors from any of the lawyers, parties, witnesses, or anyone who might be connected with or interested in the case, or to converse with them about the case. TRCP 226a (Instructions, Part I, ¶¶2, 3). A juror can testify about improper contacts with individuals outside the jury. ***Golden Eagle***, 24 S.W.3d at 370. When a party's contact with a juror is held improper, a judgment in favor of the party responsible for the improper contact will be reversed. *See, e.g.*, ***TEIA v. McCaslin***, 317 S.W.2d 916, 921 (Tex.1958) (party went to juror's office & asked her to do all she could for her); ***Texas Milk Prods. Co. v. Birtcher***, 157 S.W.2d 633, 634 (Tex.1941) (party purchased soft drink for juror); ***Gulf, C. & S.F. Ry. v. Mathews***, 66 S.W. 588, 592 (Tex.1902) (party's nephew, who managed the litigation, bought dinner for juror who was his friend); ***TEIA v. Brooks***, 414 S.W.2d 945, 946 (Tex.App.—Beaumont 1967, no writ) (juror requested ride home from party & brother-in-law); ***Occidental Life Ins. Co. v. Duncan***, 404 S.W.2d 52, 53-54 (Tex.App.—San Antonio 1966, writ ref'd n.r.e.) (party asked juror for an aspirin); ***Campbell v. Struve***, 30 S.W.2d 344, 346-47 (Tex.App.—San Antonio 1930, writ ref'd) (attorney drove juror home); *see also* ***TEIA v. Moore***, 549 S.W.2d 37, 39 (Tex.App.—El Paso 1977, no writ) (if jurors had drunk coffee supplied by one of the attorneys, it would have been reversible error). *But see* ***Pharo***, 922 S.W.2d at 950 (error not reversible even though court instructed jury not to have contact with persons associated with parties during trial, and juror visited D's office and dated D's employee); ***Mercado v. Warner-Lambert Co.***, 106 S.W.3d 393, 396 (Tex.App.—Houston [1st Dist.] 2003, no pet.) (not reversible error that D's shadow juror requested cigarette & quarter from actual juror); ***Ramsey v. Lucky Stores***, 853 S.W.2d 623, 635 (Tex.App.—Houston [1st Dist.] 1993, writ denied) (when attorney smoked cigarettes and talked with jurors who also were smoking, it gave rise to an appearance of impropriety, but did not show jury misconduct). If the contact was improper, the juror's disavowal of influence is not relevant. ***McCaslin***, 317 S.W.2d at 920.

§13.6 Burden.

1. Most cases. To obtain a new trial based on misconduct, the movant must prove (1) the misconduct occurred, (2) the misconduct was material, and (3) based on the entire record, the misconduct probably resulted in injury. TRCP 327(a); ***Golden Eagle***, 24 S.W.3d at 372; ***Pharo***, 922 S.W.2d at 950; ***Strauss v. Continental Airlines***, 67 S.W.3d 428, 446 (Tex.App.—Houston [14th Dist.] 2002, no pet.); *see* TRAP 44. To show probable injury, the record must indicate the misconduct probably caused a juror to vote differently on a question vital to the judgment.

Pharo, 922 S.W.2d at 950; ***Redinger v. Living, Inc.***, 689 S.W.2d 415, 419 (Tex.1985). Proof of misconduct is not proof of injury.

2. **Direct contact with juror.** Some acts are so inimical to fairness that proof of injury is met by simply showing the improper act occurred. ***McCaslin***, 317 S.W.2d at 921; ***Mercado***, 106 S.W.3d at 396. A favor requested by a party or given to a juror is considered reversible error without proof it influenced the juror. For example, a party's request to a juror for favorable treatment is reversible error. ***McCaslin***, 317 S.W.2d at 921. For other examples, see §13.5.4, above.

§14. MNT BASED ON NEWLY DISCOVERED EVIDENCE

Whether the court grants a motion for new trial based on newly discovered evidence is a matter within its discretion. ***Jackson v. Van Winkle***, 660 S.W.2d 807, 809 (Tex.1983).

§14.1 Motion. To make a claim for a new trial because of newly discovered evidence, the movant must allege the following:

1. The movant discovered admissible and competent evidence after the trial. ***Jackson***, 660 S.W.2d at 809. The knowledge of both the party and the attorney is relevant. *See* ***Dankowski v. Dankowski***, 922 S.W.2d 298, 305 (Tex.App.—Fort Worth 1996, writ denied) (evidence was not new).

2. The late discovery of the new evidence was not due to lack of diligence. ***Jackson***, 660 S.W.2d at 810. Generally, to establish this element the movant must show the evidence could not have been discovered sooner because (1) the movant had no notice of the existence of the evidence before trial, and (2) the movant used due diligence before trial to discover all available evidence. *See, e.g.*, ***Alvarez v. Anesthesiology Assocs.***, 967 S.W.2d 871, 882-83 (Tex.App.—Corpus Christi 1998, no pet.) (even though Ds requested documents, Ds did not file a motion to compel when P refused).

3. The evidence is not merely cumulative of other evidence. ***Jackson***, 660 S.W.2d at 809. Evidence is cumulative when it is of the same kind and tends to prove the same point as other evidence. ***In re Yarbrough***, 719 S.W.2d 412, 415 (Tex.App.—Amarillo 1986, no writ).

4. The evidence is not merely for impeachment. ***New Amsterdam Cas. Co. v. Jordan***, 359 S.W.2d 864, 866 (Tex.1962). When the only purpose of the new evidence is to impeach a witness, a new trial should not be granted. ***Eckert v. Smith***, 589 S.W.2d 533, 538 (Tex.App.—Amarillo 1979, writ ref'd n.r.e.). This element is sometimes considered a part of element 3. *See* ***New Amsterdam***, 359 S.W.2d at 866.

5. The evidence is material and would probably produce a different result at a new trial. ***Jackson***, 660 S.W.2d at 809. The new evidence must bring to light a new and independent truth so decisive it demonstrates justice was not obtained. ***New Amsterdam***, 359 S.W.2d at 867-68; *see, e.g.*, ***State Farm Lloyds v. Nicolau***, 951 S.W.2d 444, 452 (Tex.1997) (new evidence would not have resulted in different verdict).

§14.2 Sworn motion. The motion must be verified and should include affidavits supporting each element set out above. *See* ***Brown v. Hopkins***, 921 S.W.2d 306, 310-11 (Tex.App.—Corpus Christi 1996, no writ) (elements must be established by affidavit). *See generally* ***Jackson***, 660 S.W.2d at 809 (requisites for seeking a new trial on grounds of newly discovered evidence). See "Verification & affidavits," §3, p. 618.

§14.3 Hearing. The movant should request an evidentiary hearing and ask for a court reporter to transcribe it. If the motion and affidavits are in proper form and timely filed, the movant is entitled to a hearing. ***Hensley v. Salinas***, 583 S.W.2d 617, 618 (Tex.1979). *But see* ***Nicolau***, 951 S.W.2d at 452-53 (D not entitled to new trial hearing because no showing that new evidence would likely result in different verdict). At the hearing, the movant must introduce evidence to prove each allegation in the motion. ***Bell v. Showa Denko K.K.***, 899 S.W.2d 749, 757 (Tex.App.—Amarillo 1995, writ denied).

§15. MNT AFTER DEFAULT JUDGMENT

Most default judgments are granted because a defendant does not file an answer or does not appear for trial or other dispositive hearing. Challenges to these types of default judgments can be conveniently divided into two types: (1) the defendant was not properly served with notice of the suit, the trial, or the hearing, or (2) after receiving proper notice of the trial or hearing, the defendant did not appear because of a mistake or accident.

§15.1 Sworn motion. Before filing a motion for new trial to challenge a default judgment, the party should determine how and when the default was rendered. Was the default judgment rendered before or after service? Was the service defective? Did the defendant have notice of the hearing? How much time has passed since the default was rendered? A motion for new trial is not the only way to challenge a default judgment. For other ways, see "Attacking the Default Judgment," ch. 7-A, §7, p. 452.

1. Improper service + no-answer default. To challenge a no-answer default judgment rendered after improper service of citation, the motion for new trial should object to any deficiencies in the service documents and the plaintiff's petition. When a no-answer default judgment is rendered against a defendant after improper service, the defendant is not required to prove a meritorious defense to be entitled to a new trial. *See **Peralta v. Heights Med. Ctr.***, 485 U.S. 80, 85, 108 S.Ct. 896, 899 (1988). See ***O'Connor's*** FORM 10B:03, §C.

(1) Deficiencies in citation. The defendant should challenge defects in the citation. The citation must meet all the requirements of TRCP 15 and 99. See "Requirements for the Citation," ch. 2-H, §2, p. 118.

(2) Deficiencies in service. The defendant should challenge defects in the service of the citation. See "The No-Answer Default," ch. 7-A, §§3.3-3.5, pp. 444-45.

(3) Deficiencies in return. The defendant should challenge defects in the return of the service. The record must show that the officer or person who served the citation signed the return, and the return must state both when the citation was served and the manner of service. TRCP 107. See "Serving the Defendant with Suit," ch. 2-H, p. 118.

(4) Deficiencies in plaintiff's petition. The defendant should challenge all the defects in the plaintiff's petition. A plaintiff's petition will support a default judgment if it (a) attempts to state a cause of action against a defendant who is amenable to process, (b) gives fair notice to the defendant of its claim, and (c) does not affirmatively disclose the invalidity of its claim. ***Paramount Pipe & Sup. Co. v. Muhr***, 749 S.W.2d 491, 494 (Tex. 1988); ***Stoner v. Thompson***, 578 S.W.2d 679, 684-85 (Tex.1979). For cases on the sufficiency of the plaintiff's petition, see "Plaintiff's Original Petition," ch. 2-B, p. 66; "Sufficiency of plaintiff's petition," ch. 7-A, §3.2, p. 444. See ***O'Connor's*** FORM 10B:03, §D.

2. No notice of trial + post-answer default.

(1) Allege no notice. When a post-answer default is rendered without proper notice, the motion should allege and prove the defendant did not receive notice of the trial or dispositive hearing. See "Notice of the trial or dispositive hearing," ch. 7-A, §4.3, p. 450. Proof of lack of notice satisfies the first prong from ***Craddock v. Sunshine Bus Lines***, 133 S.W.2d 124, 126 (Tex.1939), because, without notice, a defendant cannot intentionally or with conscious indifference fail to appear. ***Texas Sting, Ltd. v. R.B. Foods***, 82 S.W.3d 644, 651-52 (Tex.App.—San Antonio, 2002, pet. denied). See §15.1.3, below. See ***O'Connor's*** FORM 10B:04, §C.

When a defendant proves lack of notice of the trial or hearing, the defendant does not need to establish the remaining ***Craddock*** factors to be entitled to a new trial. ***Lopez v. Lopez***, 757 S.W.2d 721, 722 (Tex.1988); ***Custom-Crete, Inc. v. K-Bar Servs.***, 82 S.W.3d 655, 660 (Tex.App.—San Antonio 2002, no pet.); ***Texas Sting***, 82 S.W.3d at 651-52. See §15.1.3, below. Once a defendant makes an appearance, it is entitled to notice of the trial setting as a matter of due process under the 14th Amendment to the U.S. Constitution. ***LBL Oil Co. v. Int'l Power Servs.***, 777 S.W.2d 390, 390-91 (Tex.1989).

(2) Allege Craddock factors in alternative. If the defendant is uncertain whether the court will sustain its argument that it did not receive proper service or notice, the defendant should allege and prove the three ***Craddock*** factors as an alternative ground for reversal. See §15.1.3, below. See ***O'Connor's*** FORM 10B:04, §D.

3. Failure to answer or appear after proper notice. When a default judgment is rendered against a defendant who had notice of the suit or hearing but did not file an answer to the suit or did not appear at a trial or hearing, the motion for new trial should allege the three elements listed below from ***Craddock***. *See* ***Director v. Evans***, 889 S.W.2d 266, 268 (Tex.1994); ***Old Republic Ins. Co. v. Scott***, 873 S.W.2d 381, 382 (Tex.1994). When the defendant has notice of trial and its lawyer appears but the defendant does not, the defendant is not entitled to argue the ***Craddock*** factors. ***In re K.C.***, 88 S.W.3d 277, 279 (Tex.App.—San Antonio 2002, pet. denied). When a defendant meets the ***Craddock*** test, the trial court must set aside the default judgment. ***Evans***, 889 S.W.2d at 268. See ***O'Connor's*** FORM 10B:04, §D.

(1) Not intentional, but accidental. The defendant must state its failure to file an answer or appear at a hearing was not intentional or the result of conscious indifference but was due to a mistake or accident. ***Estate of Pollack v. McMurrey***, 858 S.W.2d 388, 391 (Tex.1993); ***Bank One v. Moody***, 830 S.W.2d 81, 82-83 (Tex. 1992); ***Craddock***, 133 S.W.2d at 126. A mistake of law can satisfy this requirement. ***Bank One***, 830 S.W.2d at 85. The "not intentional" and "mistake or accident" are only one element, not two. ***Bank One***, 830 S.W.2d at 82-83. If the factual allegations in the defendant's motion and affidavits negate conscious indifference and the plaintiff does not controvert those allegations, the court must find the defendant's failure to answer was the result of a mistake or accident. *See* ***Strackbein v. Prewitt***, 671 S.W.2d 37, 38-39 (Tex.1984).

(a) Failure to answer or appear = accident. Default judgments in the following cases were reversed because the defendant pleaded and proved its failure to answer or appear was accidental. • Because the executors were unaware of the suit when the Secretary of State was served on their behalf, their failure to answer was not intentional. ***Pollack***, 858 S.W.2d at 391. • In a writ of garnishment proceeding, the bank president testified the bank did not file an answer because he thought the bank had complied with procedures. ***Bank One***, 830 S.W.2d at 84-85. • Defendant's office staff was to send the citation to the attorney but misplaced it. ***Strackbein***, 671 S.W.2d at 39; *see also* ***In re A.P.P.***, 74 S.W.3d 570, 574 (Tex.App.—Corpus Christi 2002, no pet.) (co-worker of D delivered notice & petition to attorney's office, where notice was inadvertently misfiled). • Defendant searched the house after receiving an inquiry about the lawsuit, found the citation, and took it to the insurance company the next day. ***Ward v. Nava***, 488 S.W.2d 736, 737-38 (Tex.1972). • Husband's letter to the court administrator requesting clarification of trial setting on belief he would get 45 days' notice negated conscious indifference. ***In re Parker***, 20 S.W.3d 812, 819 (Tex.App.—Texarkana 2000, no pet.). • The citation was lost in the mail when it was sent by the defendant's office in Michigan to a claims office in Texas for handling. ***K-Mart Corp. v. Armstrong***, 944 S.W.2d 59, 60 (Tex.App.—Amarillo 1997, writ denied). • The attorney's secretary made a mistake in getting a new trial setting, and the attorney was in another trial. ***Aero Mayflower Transit Co. v. Spoljaric***, 669 S.W.2d 158, 160 (Tex. App.—Fort Worth 1984, writ dism'd). • The party changed attorneys; the new attorney believed a bankruptcy stay was in effect. ***Martin v. Allman***, 668 S.W.2d 795, 799 (Tex.App.—Dallas 1984, no writ). • A corporate officer was served with two citations, one for each corporation; the officer thought the citations were copies, and only one corporation answered. ***National Rigging, Inc. v. City of San Antonio***, 657 S.W.2d 171, 172-73 (Tex.App.—San Antonio 1983, writ ref'd n.r.e.). • The attorney did not have notice of the trial setting; the attorney's actions in taking discovery and setting the case for trial were inconsistent with the notion of conscious indifference. ***Beard v. McKinney***, 456 S.W.2d 451, 454-55 (Tex.App.—Houston [1st Dist.] 1970, no writ).

(b) Failure to answer or appear = conscious indifference. Default judgments in the following cases were affirmed because the defendant did not plead and prove it was not consciously indifferent. • Reliance on an agent, such as an insurance carrier, to file an answer did not satisfy the test because there was no proof the agent was not guilty of conscious indifference. ***Holt Atherton Indus. v. Heine***, 835 S.W.2d 80, 83 (Tex. 1992); ***Memorial Hosp. Sys. v. Fisher Ins. Agency***, 835 S.W.2d 645, 652 (Tex.App.—Houston [14th Dist.] 1992, no writ). • Pro se's refusal to retrieve certified letter after notice by post office. ***Osborn v. Osborn***, 961 S.W.2d 408, 412-13 (Tex.App.—Houston [1st Dist.] 1997, pet. denied). • Defendant did not disprove its indifference with its affidavit containing only general statements without dates and other verifying information. ***Liberty Mut. Fire Ins. Co. v. Ybarra***, 751 S.W.2d 615, 617-18 (Tex.App.—El Paso 1988, no writ). • Mistaken belief about bankruptcy was not reason to reverse a default judgment. ***Novosad v. Cunningham***, 38 S.W.3d 767, 771 (Tex.App.—Houston [14th Dist.] 2001, no pet.); ***Dupnik v. Aransas Cty. Navigation Dist.***, 732 S.W.2d 780, 782 (Tex.App.—Corpus Christi 1987, no writ). • Defendant misunderstood the citation and thought he would get a notice of trial. ***Johnson v. Edmonds***, 712 S.W.2d 651, 652 (Tex.App.—Fort Worth 1986, no writ). • Bank president, who was served with a garnishment suit, gave the citation to the executive vice-president, who gave the citation to an auditor. ***First Nat'l Bank v. Peterson***, 709 S.W.2d 276, 278 (Tex.App.—Houston [14th Dist.] 1986, writ ref'd n.r.e.).

(2) Meritorious defense. The defendant must "set up" a meritorious defense. ***Ivy v. Carrell***, 407 S.W.2d 212, 214 (Tex.1966); ***Craddock v. Sunshine Bus Lines***, 133 S.W.2d 124, 126 (Tex.1939). The defendant is not required to prove a meritorious defense; the defendant is merely required to set one up. ***A.P.P.***, 74 S.W.3d at 574-75; *see* ***Evans***, 889 S.W.2d at 270. A meritorious defense is one that, if proved, would cause a different result on retrial, although not necessarily the opposite result. ***Liepelt v. Oliveira***, 818 S.W.2d 75, 77 (Tex.App.—Corpus Christi 1991, no writ). To set up a meritorious defense, the defendant must allege facts, supported by affidavits or other evidence, that in law would constitute a defense to the plaintiff's cause of action. *See* ***Pollack***, 858 S.W.2d at 392; ***Ivy***, 407 S.W.2d at 214; ***Wal-Mart Stores v. Kelley***, 103 S.W.3d 642, 644 (Tex.App.—Fort Worth 2003, no pet.); *see, e.g.*, ***Angelo v. Champion Rest. Equip. Co.***, 713 S.W.2d 96, 97 (Tex.1986) (in suit on open account, allegation that payment had been made, supported by canceled checks and affidavit, set up meritorious defense); ***Continental Carbon Co. v. Sea-Land Serv.***, 27 S.W.3d 184, 191 (Tex.App.—Dallas 2000, pet. denied) (in suit on sworn account, D's allegation that it did not owe debt was insufficient to set up meritorious defense). The trial court cannot consider controverting affidavits on the issue of a meritorious defense. ***Pollack***, 858 S.W.2d at 392; *see* ***Gotcher v. Barnett***, 757 S.W.2d 398, 403 (Tex.App.—Houston [14th Dist.] 1988, no writ) (P can establish lack of legal sufficiency of D's defenses but cannot controvert or negate those defenses).

(3) No delay or injury. The defendant must state that a new trial will not cause any delay or injury to the plaintiff. ***Craddock***, 133 S.W.2d at 126. The defendant should state it is ready for trial and willing to reimburse the plaintiff for all reasonable expenses incurred in getting the default. ***Evans***, 889 S.W.2d at 270 n.3; ***Tanknology/NDE Corp. v. Bowyer***, 80 S.W.3d 97, 103 (Tex.App.—Eastland 2002, pet. denied); ***A.P.P.***, 74 S.W.3d at 575. Failure to offer reimbursement does not necessarily preclude a new trial. ***Angelo***, 713 S.W.2d at 98; ***G.E. Capital Auto Fin. Leasing Servs. v. Stanfield***, 71 S.W.3d 351, 356 (Tex.App.—Tyler 2001, no pet.). Once the defendant alleges the granting of the motion will not cause delay or prejudice, the burden shifts to the plaintiff to prove injury. ***Evans***, 889 S.W.2d at 270; ***Pollack***, 858 S.W.2d at 393; ***Tanknology***, 80 S.W.3d at 103; ***A.P.P.***, 74 S.W.3d at 575-76. The purpose of this element is to protect the plaintiff against the sort of delay that would cause it to be disadvantaged in the trial of its case (*e.g.*, the loss of witnesses or other valuable evidence). ***Evans***, 889 S.W.2d at 270.

§15.2 Verification. The defaulting party must attach affidavits to support the factual allegations in the motion. See "Verification & affidavits," §3, p. 618. If the factual allegations in the affidavits are not controverted, the trial court must accept them as true. ***Evans***, 889 S.W.2d at 269; ***Old Republic Ins. Co. v. Scott***, 873 S.W.2d 381, 382 (Tex.1994); ***Litchfield v. Litchfield***, 794 S.W.2d 105, 106 (Tex.App.—Houston [1st Dist.] 1990, no writ). Not all the allegations in the motion for new trial must be supported by affidavits. The defendant is not required to file sworn proof to support its allegations of a meritorious defense or of no delay or injury. See §§15.1.3(2), 15.1.3(3), above.

1. No-answer default. The factual allegations that must be supported by affidavits when challenging a no-answer default judgment include the following: (1) facts regarding any defects in the service, citation, or return of service, or (2) facts supporting the defendant's allegation that its failure to file an answer was not intentional or the result of conscious indifference but was due to a mistake or accident.

2. **Post-answer default.** The factual allegations that must be supported by affidavits when challenging a post-answer default judgment include the following: (1) facts regarding lack of notice of the hearing or trial, or (2) facts supporting the defendant's allegations that its failure to appear was not intentional or the result of conscious indifference but was due to a mistake or accident.

§15.3 Request hearing. Because the hearing is for the receipt of evidence, the defendant should make a written request for a hearing. If the defendant requests a hearing but does not get one, the appellate court will accept all statements in the sworn pleadings and affidavits as true. ***Van Der Veken v. Joffrion***, 740 S.W.2d 28, 31 (Tex. App.—Texarkana 1987, no writ); *see, e.g.*, ***Ward v. Nava***, 488 S.W.2d 736, 737 (Tex.1972) (in reversing denial of new trial motion, court relied solely on affidavit of movant when no evidentiary hearing was held). The affidavits are considered for purposes of the ***Craddock*** test even if they are not introduced into evidence. ***Director v. Evans***, 889 S.W.2d 266, 268 (Tex.1994); ***McClure v. Landis***, 959 S.W.2d 679, 681 (Tex.App.—Austin 1997, pet. denied).

§15.4 Sworn response. In most cases, the plaintiff should file a response and object to the motion for new trial. When appropriate, the plaintiff should also file a controverting affidavit to prevent the court from assuming the facts stated in the defendant's motion are true. If the plaintiff does not file a controverting affidavit, the appellate courts will assume the facts in the defendant's affidavit are true. See §15.5.2, below.

§15.5 Hearing. When the court holds a hearing on the motion for new trial and evidence is introduced, the issues in the affidavits become fact questions for the court to resolve. ***Jackson v. Mares***, 802 S.W.2d 48, 50 (Tex. App.—Corpus Christi 1990, writ denied); *see* ***Young v. Kirsch***, 814 S.W.2d 77, 80 (Tex.App.—San Antonio 1991, no writ). The trial court is bound to accept as true the affidavits of the movant, unless the opponent requests a hearing. ***Averitt v. Bruton Paint & Floor Co.***, 773 S.W.2d 574, 576 (Tex.App.—Dallas 1989, no writ). When the court does not hold a hearing, the appellate court must limit its review to the affidavits. ***Ward***, 488 S.W.2d at 737.

1. **Controverted motion.** If any of the facts in the motion are controverted, the trial court ordinarily will conduct a hearing. ***Estate of Pollack v. McMurrey***, 858 S.W.2d 388, 392 (Tex.1993); ***Puri v. Mansukhani***, 973 S.W.2d 701, 715 (Tex.App.—Houston [14th Dist.] 1998, no pet.). At the hearing, it is not necessary to introduce the affidavits. ***Evans***, 889 S.W.2d at 268. If the facts are contested and the movant does not request a hearing, the movant will not be able to show it was entitled to a new trial on appeal. ***Puri***, 973 S.W.2d at 715; *see* ***Cocke v. Saks***, 776 S.W.2d 788, 789-90 (Tex.App.—Corpus Christi 1989, writ denied). Thus, when facts are contested, the defendant must ask for a hearing.

2. **Uncontroverted motion.** If the factual allegations in the motion for new trial are not controverted, the trial court must assume they are true; if the uncontroverted factual allegations support the movant's motion for new trial, the court should grant a new trial. *See* ***Scott***, 873 S.W.2d at 382; ***Holt Atherton Indus. v. Heine***, 835 S.W.2d 80, 82 (Tex.1992); ***Strackbein v. Prewitt***, 671 S.W.2d 37, 38-39 (Tex.1984); ***Van Der Veken***, 740 S.W.2d at 31; *see also* ***Liberty Mut. Fire Ins. Co. v. Ybarra***, 751 S.W.2d 615, 617-18 (Tex.App.—El Paso 1988, no writ) (trial court overruled MNT based on P's controverting affidavit).

§16. MNT AFTER SERVICE BY PUBLICATION

Service by publication is the method of notice that is least likely to bring the defendant's attention to the lawsuit. ***Mullane v. Central Hanover Bank & Trust Co.***, 339 U.S. 306, 315, 70 S.Ct. 652, 657-58 (1950); *see* ***Gray v. PHI Res., Ltd.***, 710 S.W.2d 566, 567-68 (Tex.1986) (posting a petition on the courthouse door is analogous to citation by publication). When the plaintiff serves the defendant by publication, special rules control the trial and the motion for new trial.

§16.1 Trial. When the plaintiff moves for judgment against a defendant who has not answered or appeared after service by publication, the trial court must appoint an attorney ad litem to defend the case. TRCP 244; ***Cahill v. Lyda***, 826 S.W.2d 932, 933 (Tex.1992); ***Isaac v. Westheimer Colony Ass'n***, 933 S.W.2d 588, 590-91 (Tex.App.—

Houston [1st Dist.] 1996, writ denied). The attorney must be paid a reasonable fee for services for the trial and appeal, which is taxed as part of the costs. ***J.D. Abrams, Inc. v. McIver***, 966 S.W.2d 87, 97 (Tex.App.—Houston [1st Dist.] 1998, pet. denied). After judgment is rendered, the court must approve and sign a statement of the evidence. TRCP 244.

§16.2 Sworn motion. A motion for new trial after service by publication is equivalent to an equitable bill of review. ***Stock v. Stock***, 702 S.W.2d 713, 714 (Tex.App.—San Antonio 1985, no writ). The motion must be verified by an affidavit. TRCP 329(a). The following are some of the allegations the defendant may make in a motion for new trial under TRCP 329. See ***O'Connor's*** FORM 10B:05.

1. The trial court did not appoint an attorney as required by TRCP 244. ***Isaac***, 933 S.W.2d at 591.

2. The trial court did not approve and sign the statement of evidence as required by TRCP 244.

3. The citation by publication was defective. For example, the citation did not contain a brief statement of the nature of the suit, as required by TRCP 114. ***Wiebusch v. Wiebusch***, 636 S.W.2d 540, 542 (Tex.App.—San Antonio 1982, no writ).

4. There was insufficient evidence adduced at the hearing to support the trial court's judgment.

5. The court made an error in the application of the law to the facts.

6. There is good cause to grant a new trial. TRCP 329(a).

7. The plaintiff procured the service and judgment by fraud. *See, e.g.*, ***Morris v. Morris***, 759 S.W.2d 707, 709 (Tex.App.—San Antonio 1988, writ denied) (wife committed fraud in procuring a divorce after citation by publication because she knew where husband was & could have served him with citation).

§16.3 Notice. The defendant must give notice of the motion for new trial to all parties to the trial court's judgment. *See* TRCP 329(a).

§16.4 Deadline. The defendant has two years after a judgment is signed and rendered on citation by publication to file a motion for new trial. TRCP 329(a); *see* ***Stock***, 702 S.W.2d at 714. When a motion for new trial challenging a judgment granted after citation by publication is filed more than 30 days after the judgment, the time period for determining the trial court's plenary power will be computed as if the judgment had been signed on the date the motion was filed. TRCP 306a(7), 329(d).

§16.5 Execution. The defendant can suspend the execution of the judgment during the pendency of the motion for new trial by filing a bond. TRCP 329(b). The amount for the bond is determined the same way supersedeas bonds are determined. *Id.*; *see also* TRAP 24.2 (supersedeas bonds). See ***O'Connor's Texas Civil Appeals***, "Superseding the Judgment," ch. 14-B, p. 137 (2002-03).

§16.6 Property sold. If property is sold under execution of the judgment before the defendant posts the bond, the defendant will not be able to recover the property. If the court grants a new trial, the defendant will be able to get a judgment equal to the proceeds of the sale. TRCP 329(c).

§16.7 Hearing. A hearing on the motion for new trial does not seem to be necessary. *See* TRCP 329(a) (court may grant a new trial upon petition supported by affidavits). If the plaintiff controverts any of the defendant's facts by filing an affidavit, the defendant should ask for a hearing. At the hearing, the defendant should introduce evidence to support all the facts in its motion for new trial.

§17. REVIEW

§17.1 Appellate deadlines. A motion for new trial extends the appellate deadlines. TRAP 26.1(a)(1). See "Calculating appellate deadlines," ch. 9-C, §9.1, p. 608.

§17.2 Standard of review. The standard of review of the trial court's ruling on a motion for new trial is abuse of discretion. ***Director v. Evans***, 889 S.W.2d 266, 268 (Tex.1994); ***Cliff v. Huggins***, 724 S.W.2d 778, 778-79 (Tex. 1987).

§17.3 Appellate record. If the movant filed a verified motion for new trial and the trial court conducted a hearing and received evidence, to appeal the court's denial of the motion, the movant must ask the court reporter to transcribe the hearing and include it in the reporter's record. *See* ***American Paging v. El Paso Paging***, 9 S.W.3d 237, 240 (Tex.App.—El Paso 1999, pet. denied). If no hearing was conducted on the motion, the appellate court can review a ruling based on the affidavits attached to a verified motion for new trial following a default judgment. ***Ward v. Nava***, 488 S.W.2d 736, 737 (Tex.1972).

§17.4 Order denying new trial. The order denying a new trial is appealable as part of the appeal from the final judgment. However, an order denying an untimely motion for new trial does not preserve issues for appellate review, even if the trial court acts within its plenary power period. ***Moritz v. Preiss***, ___ S.W.3d ___ (Tex.2003) (No. 01-1270; 6-12-03).

§17.5 Order granting new trial.

1. No appeal. As a rule, an order granting a new trial is an interlocutory order that is not reviewable on direct appeal from the order or from a final judgment. *See* ***Cummins v. Paisan Constr. Co.***, 682 S.W.2d 235, 236 (Tex.1984); ***Volkswagen v. Ramirez***, 79 S.W.3d 113, 128 (Tex.App.—Corpus Christi 2002, pet. granted 3-6-03). However, with the new interlocutory appeal procedures, an order granting a motion for new trial may be appealed before final judgment with permission of the court. See ***O'Connor's Texas Civil Appeals***, "Appealable orders by agreed motion," ch. 13-P, §2.2, p. 131. This new procedure may reduce the need for review by mandamus. See §17.5.2, below.

2. Mandamus. The trial court's order granting a new trial is subject to review by mandamus in only two situations. First, the trial court's order is reviewable by mandamus when it is wholly void. *See, e.g.*, ***In re Dickason***, 987 S.W.2d 570, 571 (Tex.1998) (mandamus granted to set aside void order granting MNT, which was signed after court lost plenary power); ***In re Dilley ISD***, 23 S.W.3d 189, 191 (Tex.App.—San Antonio 2000, orig. proceeding) (same; once counsel withdrew timely filed MNT, court lost its plenary power to consider new motion not filed within 30-day time limit). Second, the trial court's order is reviewable by mandamus when it states that the answers to jury questions are in fatal conflict, but they are not. ***Johnson v. 4th Ct. of Appeals***, 700 S.W.2d 916, 918 (Tex.1985).

C. MOTION FOR REMITTITUR

§1. GENERAL

§1.1 Rules. TRCP 315, 320; TRAP 46.

§1.2 Purpose. A request for remittitur asks the court to reduce the damages because they are excessive. Remittitur procedure is designed to discourage the expense and delay of appeals. Both the trial courts and the courts of appeals may suggest remittitur. TRAP 46.1, 46.3. The trial court's power to suggest a remittitur is derived from its power to grant a new trial. *See* TRCP 320. Although courts can reduce the amount of damages awarded by a jury by remittitur, they cannot increase the amount by additur. ***Ponce v. Sandoval***, 68 S.W.3d 799, 805 (Tex. App.—Amarillo 2001, no pet.).

§1.3 Forms. *O'Connor's Texas Civil Forms*, FORMS 10C.

§2. REQUEST

§2.1 Form. The request for remittitur is usually included in the motion for new trial, although it may be made in a separate motion. *See, e.g.*, ***Landmark Am. Ins. Co. v. Pulse Ambulance Serv.***, 813 S.W.2d 497, 499 (Tex.1991) (party filed "motion for new trial, and in the alternative, a motion for remittitur"); ***Brookshire Bros. v. Wagnon***, 979 S.W.2d 343, 354 (Tex.App.—Tyler 1998, pet. denied) (party filed "motion for remittitur"). See "Motion for New Trial," ch. 10-B, p. 617. See ***O'Connor's*** FORM 10C:01. If a party does not ask for a remittitur in a postjudgment motion, it waives the complaint. ***Hawthorne v. Guenther***, 917 S.W.2d 924, 937 (Tex.App.—Beaumont 1996, writ denied).

§2.2 Suggest amount. In the motion, the movant should suggest the amount by which the judgment should be reduced. ***Tidy Didy Wash, Inc. v. Barnett***, 246 S.W.2d 303, 306 (Tex.App.—Galveston 1952, writ ref'd n.r.e.); *see also* ***Marathon Oil Co. v. Sterner***, 777 S.W.2d 128, 132 (Tex.App.—Houston [14th Dist.] 1989, no writ) (because, at trial, D proposed reduction by $5,000, on appeal, it could not argue for reduction by $10,000).

§3. DEADLINE

Whether the request for remittitur is filed as part of the motion for new trial or separately, it must be filed within the time limits for a motion for new trial. *See* TRCP 320. See "Deadlines for MNT," ch. 10-B, §5, p. 619. If filed as a separate document, it must be filed before the motion for new trial is overruled and within 30 days of the date the judgment was signed. *See* TRCP 329b(b).

§4. ORDER

§4.1 Standard. The standard the trial court applies to a request for remittitur is the factual sufficiency of the evidence. ***Torrington Co. v. Stutzman***, 46 S.W.3d 829, 851 (Tex.2000); ***Larson v. Cactus Util. Co.***, 730 S.W.2d 640, 641 (Tex.1987). The court must examine all the evidence to determine if there is sufficient evidence to support the damages award, remitting only if some portion is so factually insufficient or against the great weight and preponderance of the evidence as to be manifestly unjust. ***Pope v. Moore***, 711 S.W.2d 622, 624 (Tex.1986); ***Gray v. Allen***, 41 S.W.3d 330, 332 (Tex.App.—Fort Worth 2001, no pet.); ***Gainsco Cty. Mut. Ins. Co. v. Martinez***, 27 S.W.3d 97, 108 (Tex.App.—San Antonio 2000, pet. granted w.r.m.).

NOTE

When damages are challenged on appeal with a no-evidence point and the court of appeals finds no evidence to support them, it should render a take-nothing judgment, not suggest a remittitur. ***Larson****, 730 S.W.2d at 641.*

§4.2 Must condition on new trial. The trial court cannot "order" a remittitur; it can only "suggest" a remittitur and condition it on a new trial. ***Snoke v. Republic Underwriters Ins. Co.***, 770 S.W.2d 777, 777 (Tex.1989). The trial court cannot reduce the damages unless it gives the plaintiff the choice between remitting part of the damages or trying the case again.

§5. RESPONSE

§5.1 Acceptance. A party who is awarded damages, generally the plaintiff, may remit any part of the judgment in open court or may execute and file with the court a written remittitur signed and acknowledged by the party or the attorney. TRCP 315. If the party files a remittitur, the court will reform the judgment and affirm it in accordance with the remittitur. ***Rose v. Doctors Hosp.***, 801 S.W.2d 841, 847 (Tex.1990) (remittitur suggested by court of appeals). See ***O'Connor's*** FORM 10C:04.

§5.2 Rejection. If the party rejects the suggestion of remittitur, the court will grant a new trial. *See* ***Rose***, 801 S.W.2d at 847. The party cannot appeal the order granting a new trial. ***Kolfeldt v. Thoma***, 822 S.W.2d 366, 368-69 (Tex.App.—Houston [14th Dist.] 1992, orig. proceeding).

§6. REVIEW

§6.1 Appellate timetable begins. The appellate timetable begins to run on the date the trial court signs the order granting the motion for remittitur. The order granting a motion for remittitur is a correction of the judgment that acts as a modified judgment for the purposes of appellate timetables. ***Landmark Am.***, 813 S.W.2d at 498-99.

§6.2 Right to appeal. If a party who benefited from the remittitur appeals, the remitting party is not barred from arguing on appeal that the remittitur should not have been ordered. TRAP 46.2; ***Rose***, 801 S.W.2d at 847-48.

§6.3 Standard of review. A court of appeals may vacate a damages award or suggest a remittitur only if the award is so factually insufficient or against the great weight and preponderance of the evidence as to be manifestly unjust. ***Maritime Overseas Corp. v. Ellis***, 971 S.W.2d 402, 407 (Tex.1998); ***Transportation Ins. Co. v. Moriel***, 879 S.W.2d 10, 30 (Tex.1994); ***Pope***, 711 S.W.2d at 624. Abuse of discretion is not the standard. ***Larson***, 730 S.W.2d at 641.

§6.4 Punitive damages award. When a punitive damages award is challenged on appeal, the court of appeals must detail the evidence supporting the award. ***Moriel***, 879 S.W.2d at 31; *see* ***Leonard & Harral Packing Co. v. Ward***, 937 S.W.2d 425, 425 (Tex.1996); ***Gray***, 41 S.W.3d at 334. Whether an award of punitive damages is impermissibly excessive involves a Fourteenth Amendment due process analysis. ***BMW v. Gore***, 517 U.S. 559, 568, 116 S.Ct. 1589, 1592 (1996).

§6.5 Remittitur in court of appeals.

1. Suggestion of remittitur. If the court of appeals believes that the trial court should have suggested a remittitur, the court of appeals may itself suggest one. TRAP 46.3; ***Isern v. Watson***, 942 S.W.2d 186, 200 (Tex. App.—Beaumont 1997, pet. denied); *see, e.g.*, ***America W. Airlines v. Tope***, 935 S.W.2d 908, 917 (Tex.App.—El Paso 1996, no writ) (court suggested reduction of mental anguish damages from $250,000 to $180,000); ***Johnson v. J. Hiram Moore, Ltd.***, 763 S.W.2d 496, 502-03 (Tex.App.—Austin 1988, writ denied) (court suggested reduction of exemplary damages from $463,202 to $134,649); ***Interfirst Bank Dallas v. Risser***, 739 S.W.2d 882, 909 (Tex.App.—Texarkana 1987, no writ) (court suggested reduction of exemplary damages from $10 million to $2.67 million).

(1) Plaintiff files remittitur. When the court of appeals suggests a remittitur and the plaintiff files a remittitur in compliance with the suggestion, the court will reform the judgment and affirm it. ***Rose***, 801 S.W.2d at 847.

(2) Plaintiff refuses to file remittitur. When the court of appeals suggests a remittitur and the plaintiff refuses to file one or does not timely file it, the court will reverse for a new trial. TRAP 46.3; ***Rose***, 801 S.W.2d at 847; *see* ***Missouri Pac. R.R. v. Alderete***, 945 S.W.2d 148, 153 (Tex.App.—San Antonio 1996, no writ).

2. Voluntary remittitur. If the court of appeals reverses the trial court's judgment because of a legal error affecting only a portion of the damages awarded, the affected party may, within 15 days after the court of appeals' judgment, voluntarily remit the amount it believes will cure the error. TRAP 46.5. If the court of appeals determines that remittitur is appropriate but that the voluntary remittitur is not sufficient to cure the error, the court must suggest an appropriate remittitur. See §6.5.1, above. If the court of appeals determines that the voluntary remittitur cures the reversible error, the court of appeals must accept the remittitur and reform and affirm the trial court judgment in accordance with the remittitur. TRAP 46.5.

§6.6 Remittitur in Supreme Court. Because the Supreme Court has no authority to review challenges to the factual sufficiency of the evidence, it cannot review challenges to remittitur. ***Maritime Overseas***, 971 S.W.2d at 407; ***Redman Homes v. Ivy***, 920 S.W.2d 664, 669 (Tex.1996). However, the Supreme Court can review the standard the court of appeals applied in its review of a remittitur point. ***Redman Homes***, 920 S.W.2d at 669; ***Pope***, 711 S.W.2d at 623-24. TRAP 46 does not authorize the Supreme Court to accept remittiturs. ***Formosa Plastics Corp. v. Presidio Eng'rs & Contractors***, 960 S.W.2d 41, 51 (Tex.1998); ***Redman Homes***, 920 S.W.2d at 669. However, in the past, the Court has accepted them. ***Moore v. Grantham***, 599 S.W.2d 287, 292 (Tex.1980); *see* ***Ogle v. Craig***, 464 S.W.2d 95, 98-99 (Tex.1971); ***TEIA v. Lightfoot***, 162 S.W.2d 929, 931 (Tex.1942).

D. MOTION TO MODIFY THE JUDGMENT

§1. GENERAL

§1.1 Rules. TRCP 329b; TRAP 26.1(a)(2).

§1.2 Purpose. A motion to modify the judgment is the procedure for asking the trial court to change the judgment.

§1.3 Forms. *O'Connor's Texas Civil Forms*, FORM 10D:01.

§2. MOTION

§2.1 Grounds. If the judgment did not award a party all the relief it was entitled to, or awarded the other party more relief than it was entitled to, the complaint must be brought to the attention of the trial court in a written motion. *See* TRCP 329b(g). Here are some examples of when a party should file a motion to modify the judgment.

1. Prejudgment interest. A party should file a motion to modify the judgment if the court did not award the correct amount of prejudgment interest. If a party does not bring the issue to the attention of the trial court in a motion to modify the judgment or make some other objection that appears on the record, the party cannot raise the issue on appeal. ***Bulgerin v. Bulgerin***, 724 S.W.2d 943, 946 (Tex.App.—San Antonio 1987, no writ), *overruled on other grounds*, ***Trinity Universal Ins. Co. v. Cowan***, 945 S.W.2d 819 (Tex.1997). However, in ***C&H Nationwide, Inc. v. Thompson***, 903 S.W.2d 315, 327-28 (Tex.1994), without addressing the issue of waiver, the Supreme Court reversed the court of appeals. The court of appeals had held the plaintiffs waived error in the calculation of interest because they did not file a motion to modify the judgment. *See* ***C&H Nationwide, Inc. v. Thompson***, 810 S.W.2d 259, 276 (Tex.App.—Houston [1st Dist.] 1991).

2. Attorney fees. A party should file a motion to modify the judgment when the trial court does not award attorney fees or does not award the correct amount of fees. *See* ***Texas Educ. Agency v. Maxwell***, 937 S.W.2d 621, 623 (Tex.App.—Eastland 1997, writ denied); ***American Bank v. Waco Airmotive, Inc.***, 818 S.W.2d 163, 178 (Tex.App.—Waco 1991, writ denied).

3. Costs. A party should file a motion to modify the judgment when the judgment does not award costs, awards costs to the wrong party, or does not award the correct amount of costs. *See* ***Portland S&L Ass'n v. Bernstein***, 716 S.W.2d 532, 541 (Tex.App.—Corpus Christi 1985, writ ref'd n.r.e.), *overruled on other grounds*, ***Dawson-Austin v. Austin***, 968 S.W.2d 319 (Tex.1998). To challenge the clerk's tabulation of the costs, the party should file a motion to retax costs. See ***O'Connor's Texas Causes of Action***, "Court Costs," ch. 37, p. 1033 (2004).

4. Any other error or omission in judgment. A party should file a motion to modify the judgment if there is any other error in the judgment. *See, e.g.*, ***L.M. Healthcare, Inc. v. Childs***, 929 S.W.2d 442, 443 (Tex.1996) (to change dismissal from "with prejudice" to "without prejudice"); ***Heard v. Houston Post Co.***, 684 S.W.2d 210, 214 (Tex.App.—Houston [1st Dist.] 1984, writ ref'd n.r.e.) (after court ordered sheriff to turn over all the information about a criminal investigation except the victim's name, the Houston Post filed a motion to modify the judgment to ask for the name).

§2.2 Not verified. A motion to modify the judgment should not be verified or supported with affidavits unless it presents facts not in the record.

§3. DEADLINES

The same rules apply to motions to modify judgments as to motions for new trial. See "Deadlines for MNT," ch. 10-B, §5, p. 619.

§3.1 Original or amended motion. The deadline to file a motion to modify, correct, or reform an error in the judgment is the same as for a motion for new trial—within 30 days of the date the judgment was signed. TRCP 329b(g); ***L.M. Healthcare***, 929 S.W.2d at 443; ***Padilla v. LaFrance***, 907 S.W.2d 454, 458 (Tex.1995). An amended motion to modify may be filed within 30 days of the date the judgment was signed as long as the original motion to modify has not been overruled by order of the trial court.

§3.2 After MNT overruled but within 30 days. A party can file a motion to modify the judgment even after the court has overruled a motion for new trial, as long as the motion to modify is filed within 30 days of the date the judgment was signed. ***L.M. Healthcare***, 929 S.W.2d at 443.

§3.3 Premature motion. A premature motion to modify the judgment, filed before the judgment is signed, is deemed to be filed on the date of, but immediately after, the signing of the judgment. ***Padilla***, 907 S.W.2d at 458 (motion to reconsider); *see* TRCP 306c, 329b(g); *see also* TRAP 27.2 (premature proceeding relating to an appeal is not ineffective).

§3.4 Late motion. If a party discovers an error in the judgment more than 30 days after the judgment was signed, it should still file a motion to modify the judgment. Although a late motion to modify will not preserve error or extend appellate deadlines, if the court still has plenary power over the judgment, the court has the authority to correct the error on its own initiative, even without a motion. See "Power to Change Judgment," ch. 9-C, §7, p. 608. If the court has lost plenary power, the party should name the motion a motion for judgment nunc pro tunc and argue that the error is clerical and can be corrected even after the court loses plenary power. See "Motion for Judgment Nunc Pro Tunc," ch. 10-H, p. 659.

§4. HEARING

The hearing on a motion to modify is for argument only, not evidence. If, however, a party files a motion to modify that for some reason must be supported by evidence, the party should both ask for a court reporter and present live testimony at the hearing.

§5. ORDER

§5.1 Granting motion. The court's order granting a motion to modify the judgment must be in writing and signed by the trial court no more than 74 days after the judgment was signed. TRCP 329b(c); *see* ***Faulkner v. Culver***, 851 S.W.2d 187, 188 (Tex.1993). The trial court's oral pronouncement and docket entry cannot substitute for a written order. ***Faulkner***, 851 S.W.2d at 188.

§5.2 Overruling motion. The trial court may overrule a motion to modify the judgment by written order, but if it does not, the motion is overruled by operation of law 75 days from the date the judgment was signed—just like a motion for new trial. TRCP 329b(c); ***Faulkner***, 851 S.W.2d at 188. See chart 9-1, "Plenary Power Deadlines," ch. 9-C, p. 607.

§6. REVIEW

§6.1 Motion to modify & postjudgment deadlines.

1. Appellate deadlines. The filing of a timely motion to modify the judgment seeking a substantive change in the judgment extends the same appellate deadlines as a motion for new trial. TRCP 329b(g); ***Lane Bank Equip. Co. v. Smith S. Equip., Inc.***, 10 S.W.3d 308, 310 (Tex.2000); ***L.M. Healthcare***, 929 S.W.2d at 444. A motion to modify the judgment extends appellate deadlines even if the motion is denied. See "Appellate deadlines," ch. 10-B, §17.1, p. 635.

2. Finality of judgment. A motion to modify the judgment delays the date the judgment becomes final—just like a motion for new trial. TRCP 329b(g); ***Home Owners Funding Corp. v. Scheppler***, 815 S.W.2d 884, 887 (Tex.App.—Corpus Christi 1991, no writ); *see* ***Lane Bank***, 10 S.W.3d at 313; ***Mackie v. McKenzie***, 890 S.W.2d 807, 808 (Tex.1994). See "When judgment becomes final," ch. 9-C, §6.5, p. 605.

§6.2 Modified judgment & postjudgment deadlines.

1. Restarts appellate timetable. Any modification to the judgment, whether material or not, made while the trial court has plenary power over the judgment, restarts the appellate timetables and extends the court's plenary power. TRCP 329b(h); TRAP 4.3(a), 27.3; ***Lane Bank***, 10 S.W.3d at 313; *e.g.*, ***Mackie***, 890 S.W.2d at 808 (addition of "Mother Hubbard" clause restarted deadlines); ***Old Republic Ins. Co. v. Scott***, 846 S.W.2d 832, 833 (Tex.1993) (order reinstating default judgment operated as modified judgment); ***Check v. Mitchell***, 758 S.W.2d 755, 756 (Tex.1988) (addition of correct docket number & statement that all writs could issue restarted deadlines); ***Quanaim v. Frasco Rest. & Catering***, 17 S.W.3d 30, 39-40 (Tex.App.—Houston [14th Dist.] 2000, pet. denied) (order identifying different grounds for summary judgment restarted deadlines); ***Crown Constr. Co. v. Huddleston***, 961 S.W.2d 552, 559-60 (Tex.App.—San Antonio 1997, no pet.) (order clarifying street address of property restarted deadlines); ***Owens-Corning Fiberglas Corp. v. Wasiak***, 883 S.W.2d 402, 405 (Tex.App.—Austin 1994, no writ) (change in signature date restarted deadlines); *see also* ***Naaman v. Grider***, ___ S.W.3d ___ (Tex.2003) (No. 02-0784; 10-31-03) (motion for judgment granted one month after final judgment was signed did not modify judgment; no restarting of appellate timetables). Even a clerical change to the judgment made while the court has plenary power will restart the deadlines. ***Lane Bank***, 10 S.W.3d at 313. Only when the face of the record shows that the trial court signed the modified judgment for the sole purpose of restarting the appellate deadlines are the deadlines not restarted. ***Mackie***, 890 S.W.2d at 808; ***Quanaim***, 17 S.W.3d at 38 n.5. *But see* ***Wang v. Hsu***, 899 S.W.2d 409, 411-12 (Tex.App.—Houston [14th Dist.] 1995, writ denied) (court held plenary power extended by second judgment that had different date from first judgment). See chart 9-1, "Plenary Power Deadlines," ch. 9-C, p. 607.

PRACTICE TIP

Any change to a judgment while the court retains plenary power will restart the appellate timetable under TRCP 329b(h), but only a motion that seeks a substantive change will extend the appellate deadlines and the court's plenary power under TRCP 329b(g). ***Lane Bank****, 10 S.W.3d at 313. See "When judgment becomes final," ch. 9-C, §6.5, p. 605.*

2. Extending appellate deadlines after 2nd judgment. To extend appellate deadlines after the second judgment, the party must file a motion to modify or other plenary-power-extending motion after the modified judgment is signed. See "PPE motions," ch. 9-C, §6.5.1(1), p. 605. A motion to modify a judgment filed after the first judgment does not extend appellate deadlines for the second judgment. *See* ***Trans-Continental Props. v. Taylor***, 717 S.W.2d 890, 891 (Tex.1986). If the complaint in the motion filed after the first judgment was not corrected by the second judgment and is still a viable complaint as to the second judgment, the motion extends the appellate deadlines for the second judgment. ***Maddox v. Cosper***, 25 S.W.3d 767, 770 n.3 (Tex.App.—Waco 2000, no pet.); ***Clark v. McFerrin***, 760 S.W.2d 822, 825 (Tex.App.—Corpus Christi 1988, writ denied). See "The second judgment problems," ch. 10-B, §5.6, p. 620.

E. REQUEST FOR FINDINGS OF FACT

§1. GENERAL

§1.1 Rules. TRCP 296-299a, 306c; TRAP 26.1(a)(4).

§1.2 Purpose. Findings of fact in a nonjury trial serve the same function as the jury's answers to jury questions—they resolve the factual disputes in the case. Conclusions of law are the court's statement of the legal principles it applied to the facts to resolve the case. For the purposes of appeal, findings of fact are more important than conclusions of law because appellate courts review findings of fact under the sufficiency of the evidence standards and review conclusions of law de novo. See "Review of conclusions of law," §6.5, p. 649.

§1.3 Forms & timetables. ***O'Connor's Texas Civil Forms***, FORMS 10E; Timetables, this book, Request for Findings of Fact, p. 1012, Appeal to the Court of Appeals, p. 1016.

§2. AVAILABILITY OF FINDINGS OF FACT

Throughout this section, findings of fact and conclusions of law will be referred to collectively as findings of fact.

§2.1 Findings of fact are necessary. In the following instances, parties should always ask the court to file findings of fact.

1. After nonjury trial of facts. Findings of fact may be requested in "any case tried in the district or county court without a jury." TRCP 296. A case is "tried" when there is a hearing before the court on conflicting evidence. ***Besing v. Moffitt***, 882 S.W.2d 79, 81-82 (Tex.App.—Amarillo 1994, no writ); ***Timmons v. Luce***, 840 S.W.2d 582, 586 (Tex.App.—Tyler 1992, no writ). Litigants are entitled to findings of fact only on the merits of the case. See "Only on controlling issues," §5.1.3, p. 647.

2. After motion for judgment in nonjury trial. Findings of fact should be requested in a nonjury case resolved by a judgment after the plaintiff rests. ***Qantel Bus. Sys. v. Custom Controls Co.***, 761 S.W.2d 302, 304 (Tex.1988).

3. After mandamus initiated in trial court. Findings of fact should be requested in an original mandamus proceeding in the trial court, which is a civil action subject to the TRCPs. ***Anderson v. City of Seven Points***, 806 S.W.2d 791, 792 n.1 (Tex.1991); *see* ***City of Beaumont v. Spivey***, 1 S.W.3d 385, 389 (Tex.App.—Beaumont 1999, pet. denied).

4. To supply omitted elements of an issue. When only some elements of an issue are submitted to a jury, the party should request findings on the omitted elements. *See* TRCP 299; *see also* ***Insurance Co. v. Bellah***, 373 S.W.2d 691, 692 (Tex.App.—Fort Worth 1963, no writ) (court required to file findings when certain issues were omitted from jury charge). See "Incomplete claim or defense submitted," ch. 8-I, §9.2, p. 577.

5. When part of case is decided by court. When part of a case is tried to a jury and part is decided by the court, findings of fact should be requested on the court-decided issues. ***IKB Indus. v. Pro-Line Corp.***, 938 S.W.2d 440, 443 (Tex.1997); *see, e.g.*, ***Awde v. Dabeit***, 938 S.W.2d 31, 33 (Tex.1997) (after dismissal & award of sanctions, hearing on attorney fees); ***Toles v. Toles***, 45 S.W.3d 252, 264 n.5 (Tex.App.—Dallas 2001, pet. denied) (in divorce case, division of property was decided by court); ***Schwartz v. Pinnacle Comm.***, 944 S.W.2d 427, 431 (Tex.App.—Houston [14th Dist.] 1997, no writ) (after no-answer default judgment rendered, hearing on damages); ***Heafner & Assocs. v. Koecher***, 851 S.W.2d 309, 313 (Tex.App.—Houston [1st Dist.] 1992, no writ) (issue of attorney fees was tried to court); ***Shenandoah Assocs. v. J & K Props.***, 741 S.W.2d 470, 484 (Tex.App.—Dallas 1987, writ denied) (same).

§2.2 Findings permitted after appealable orders. Specific rules permit the trial court to file findings of fact in the appeal of interlocutory orders. The request for findings of fact in an appeal of an interlocutory order does not extend the time to perfect appeal. *Cf.* TRAP 28.1 (filing a motion for new trial does not extend time to perfect appeal). See ***O'Connor's Texas Civil Appeals***, "Motion for Interlocutory Appeal & Stay of Trial," ch. 13-P, p. 131 (2002-03).

1. After TRO or temporary injunction. TRCP 683 requires each order granting a TRO or temporary injunction to include the reasons for its issuance in the order. ***Transport Co. v. Robertson Transps.***, 261 S.W.2d 549, 552-53 (Tex.1953). TRAP 28.1 permits, but does not require, the trial court to file separate findings of fact. ***Transport Co.***, 261 S.W.2d at 552-53; ***Operation Rescue v. Planned Parenthood***, 937 S.W.2d 60, 82 (Tex.App.—Houston [14th Dist.] 1996), *modified on other grounds*, 975 S.W.2d 546 (Tex.1998).

03 **2. After class action certification.** Implicit in TRCP 42(b)(3) is the requirement that the trial court make findings about TRCP 42's application to the facts of the case. TRCP 42 does not state whether the findings should be incorporated into the certification order or filed separately as findings of fact. *See* ***G.M. Corp. v. Bloyed***, 916 S.W.2d 949, 955-56 (Tex.1996) (trial court filed findings of fact); ***Texas Dept. of MHMR v. Petty***, 778 S.W.2d 156, 160 (Tex.App.—Austin 1989, writ dism'd) (trial court's findings were part of order certifying class). To award attorney fees in a class action certification, the trial court must state its findings in writing or orally on the record. TRCP 42(h)(3).

3. After other appealable orders. TRAP 28.1 permits, but does not require, the trial court to file findings of fact after rendering an interlocutory order. ***Mueller v. Beamalloy, Inc.***, 994 S.W.2d 855, 858-59 (Tex.App.—Houston [1st Dist.] 1999, no pet.) (appointment of receiver).

4. To review supersedeas bonds. TRAP 24.4(d) permits the appellate courts to remand the issue of the sufficiency of a supersedeas bond to the trial court to take evidence and file findings of fact. ***TransAmerican Nat. Gas Corp. v. Finkelstein***, 911 S.W.2d 153, 155 (Tex.App.—San Antonio 1995, order on mot.). See ***O'Connor's Texas Civil Appeals***, "Superseding the Judgment," ch. 14-B, p. 137.

§2.3 Findings of fact are helpful. Findings of fact are appropriate when (1) the trial court conducts an evidentiary hearing and (2) the findings could properly be considered by the appellate court. *See* ***IKB Indus.***, 938 S.W.2d at 442-43; ***Mocega v. Urquhart***, 79 S.W.3d 61, 63-64 (Tex.App.—Houston [14th Dist.] 2002, pet. denied). Findings in these instances are not given the same weight on appeal as findings made under TRCP 296 and 297. ***IKB Indus.*** 938 S.W.2d at 442. See "Review of FoF," §6.2, p. 648.

1. After hearing on sanctions under TRCP 215. In a case where judgment is rendered as a sanction for discovery abuse, findings supporting sanctions are helpful. ***IKB Indus.***, 938 S.W.2d at 442; ***Chrysler Corp. v. Blackmon***, 841 S.W.2d 844, 852 (Tex.1992); ***TransAmerican Nat. Gas Corp. v. Powell***, 811 S.W.2d 913, 919 n.9 (Tex.1991). The findings should be specifically tied to the appropriate legal standard. ***Chrysler Corp.***, 841 S.W.2d at 853.

2. After dismissal hearings.

(1) DWOP. Findings after a hearing on a motion to dismiss for failure to prosecute can help the appellate court understand the reasons the trial court refused to reinstate. *Cf.* ***Phillips v. Beavers***, 938 S.W.2d 446, 446-47 (Tex.1997) (hearing before dismissal for failure to prosecute).

PRACTICE TIP

If you decide to file a request for findings of fact and conclusions of law after a case is dismissed for want of prosecution, note that the request is due before the motion to reinstate. Compare TRCP 296 (20 days), with TRCP 165a(3) (30 days).

---

(2) Jurisdictional challenge. Findings can be helpful when the court rules on jurisdictional challenges after receiving evidence (*e.g.*, when the trial court rules on a special appearance challenging personal jurisdiction or on a plea to the jurisdiction challenging subject-matter jurisdiction). *See* ***Goodenbour v. Goodenbour***, 64 S.W.3d 69, 75 (Tex.App.—Austin 2001, pet. denied) (in special appearance, findings should be requested); ***Hernandez v. Texas Dept. of Ins.***, 923 S.W.2d 192, 194 (Tex.App.—Austin 1996, no writ) (plea to the jurisdiction).

(3) Groundless pleadings. It is not necessary to ask for separate findings when sanctions are imposed under TRCP 13 and CPRC §10.001; the court is required to include findings in the sanctions order. See "Order for Sanctions," ch. 5-J, §§11.2.4, 11.3.2(3), pp. 288-89. For sanctions under CPRC §9.012, separately filed findings of fact are helpful.

(4) Late report. In a medical malpractice case, findings are helpful when the court dismisses a plaintiff's suit for failure to file a timely report. *See* ***Mocega***, 79 S.W.3d at 63-64 (former TRCS art. 4590i, §13.01, now CPRC §74.351).

3. After hearing on venue. Findings can be helpful to review a venue ruling. *See* ***Coke v. Coke***, 802 S.W.2d 270, 278 (Tex.App.—Dallas 1990, writ denied); ***Gaston v. Chaney***, 734 S.W.2d 735, 737 (Tex.App.—Eastland 1987, no writ).

4. After judgment with exemplary damages. When the trial court awards exemplary damages, findings providing the reasons for refusing to disturb the jury's exemplary damages will "facilitate meaningful post-verdict review." ***Transportation Ins. Co. v. Moriel***, 879 S.W.2d 10, 33 (Tex.1994). Although it is optional for the trial court to make these findings, the courts of appeals are required to make them, whether they uphold, reduce, or eliminate the damages. *See* CPRC §41.013(a).

5. After hearing on remittitur. Findings stating the trial court's reasons for suggesting remittitur are helpful for appellate courts. ***Landon v. Jean-Paul Budinger, Inc.***, 724 S.W.2d 931, 940 (Tex.App.—Austin 1987, no writ).

6. After hearing to reinstate. Findings are helpful after a hearing on a motion to reinstate a case dismissed for want of prosecution. *Cf.* ***Phillips***, 938 S.W.2d at 446-47 (after dismissal for failure to prosecute). See "Motion to Reinstate After DWOP," ch. 10-F, p. 649.

7. After hearing on MNT. Findings are helpful after a motion for new trial hearing to receive evidence. *See, e.g.*, ***Higginbotham v. General Life & Acc. Ins. Co.***, 796 S.W.2d 695, 695 (Tex.1990) (motion for new trial after no-answer default judgment).

§2.4 Findings of fact are not appropriate. Findings of fact are not appropriate when they have no purpose. ***IKB Indus. v. Pro-Line Corp.***, 938 S.W.2d 440, 443 (Tex.1997). In such cases, findings should not be requested, made, or considered on appeal. *Id.* When findings of fact are not appropriate, a request for findings does not extend the time to perfect an appeal, as it does when they are appropriate. *Id.*; ***Linwood v. NCNB***, 885 S.W.2d 102, 103 (Tex.1994); ***Ford v. City of Lubbock***, 76 S.W.3d 795, 797-98 (Tex.App.—Amarillo 2002, no pet.). See "Review when findings not requested or filed," §6.3, p. 648.

1. After jury trial. Findings of fact are not appropriate on issues tried to a jury. ***IKB Indus.***, 938 S.W.2d at 443; ***Favaloro v. Commission for Lawyer Discipline***, 13 S.W.3d 831, 840 (Tex.App.—Dallas 2000, no pet.).

2. After summary judgment. Findings of fact are not appropriate after the court renders a summary judgment. ***IKB Indus.***, 938 S.W.2d at 441-42; ***Linwood***, 885 S.W.2d at 103; ***Eddins v. Borders***, 71 S.W.3d 368, 370 (Tex.App.—Tyler 2001, pet. denied).

3. After directed verdict. Findings of fact are not appropriate in a case resolved by a directed verdict. ***IKB Indus.***, 938 S.W.2d at 443; ***Ditto v. Ditto Inv. Co.***, 309 S.W.2d 219, 220 (Tex.1958).

4. After JNOV. Findings of fact are not appropriate when the court renders a judgment notwithstanding the verdict. ***IKB Indus.***, 938 S.W.2d at 443; ***Fancher v. Cadwell***, 314 S.W.2d 820, 822 (Tex.1958).

5. After trial of agreed case. Findings of fact are not appropriate when the court renders a judgment on an agreed statement of facts under TRCP 263. See "No findings of fact," ch. 7-D, §5.3, p. 493.

6. After default judgment on liquidated damages. Findings of fact are not appropriate when the court renders a default judgment based on liquidated damages. ***IKB Indus.***, 938 S.W.2d at 443.

7. After dismissal on pleadings without evidence. Findings of fact are not appropriate when the court dismisses a case for want of prosecution without a hearing to receive evidence, dismisses for want of subject-matter jurisdiction without sworn proof, dismisses after refusal to amend following an order on special exceptions, or renders any judgment without an evidentiary hearing. ***IKB Indus.***, 938 S.W.2d at 443 (dicta, listing inappropriate cases for findings of fact); *see, e.g.*, ***Awde v. Dabeit***, 938 S.W.2d 31, 33 (Tex.1997) (based on pleadings, suit dismissed for lack of subject-matter jurisdiction); ***CMS Partners v. Plumrose USA, Inc.***, 101 S.W.3d 730, 736-37 (Tex.App.—Texarkana 2003, no pet.) (suit dismissed under forum-selection clause); ***Ford***, 76 S.W.3d at 797-98 (based on pleadings, suit dismissed for lack of subject-matter jurisdiction).

§3. REQUESTING FINDINGS OF FACT

Either party may request that the court file findings of fact under TRCP 296. In cases governed by TRCP 296, the party who loses should always request findings of fact; otherwise, all findings are deemed in favor of the judgment.

Worford v. Stamper, 801 S.W.2d 108, 109 (Tex.1990); ***Roberson v. Robinson***, 768 S.W.2d 280, 281 (Tex.1989). Although the winning party probably does not want to ask for findings of fact, once the losing party makes a proper request for findings, the winning party should make sure they are filed. The rules provide for three requests for findings of fact.

§3.1 First request. TRCP 296 states that the original request must be entitled "Request for Findings of Fact and Conclusions of Law." See ***O'Connor's*** FORM 10E:01.

1. Deadline. The first request must be filed within 20 days of the date the judgment was signed. TRCP 296; ***Ohio Cas. Group v. Risinger***, 960 S.W.2d 708, 712 (Tex.App.—Tyler 1997, writ denied); ***Lopez v. Hansen***, 947 S.W.2d 587, 589 (Tex.App.—Houston [1st Dist.] 1997, no writ). If the request for findings is filed before the judgment is signed, it is considered a premature request and is deemed filed the day the judgment is signed. TRCP 306c; ***Pursley v. Ussery***, 982 S.W.2d 596, 599 (Tex.App.—San Antonio 1998, pet. denied); ***Vargas v. Texas Dept. of Protective & Regulatory Servs.***, 973 S.W.2d 423, 426 (Tex.App.—Austin 1998, pet. granted w.r.m.); *see* TRAP 27.2. The party requesting findings must send a copy of the request to the other party. TRCP 21a.

2. Clerk's duty. The clerk of the court must call the request immediately to the attention of the judge who tried the case. TRCP 296.

§3.2 Court's deadline to file findings. The trial court should file findings of fact within 20 days of the date the party requested findings. TRCP 297. The court is required to mail a copy of the findings of fact to all the parties. *Id.* Therefore, the party requesting findings should receive a copy in the mail. If it does not receive findings, the party should file a second request.

§3.3 Second request. If the trial court does not file findings of fact within 20 days after the first request is filed, the party who asked for findings has 30 days from the date it filed its original request to file a "Notice of Past Due Findings of Fact and Conclusions of Law." TRCP 297; ***Curtis v. Commission for Lawyer Discipline***, 20 S.W.3d 227, 231-32 (Tex.App.—Houston [14th Dist.] 2000, no pet.); ***Lopez***, 947 S.W.2d at 589. A party that does not file a notice of past due findings of fact waives the right to complain about the trial court's failure to file findings and conclusions. ***Curtis***, 20 S.W.3d at 232. In the notice of past due findings of fact, the party is required to state the date the original request was filed and the date the findings of fact were due. TRCP 297; ***Curtis***, 20 S.W.3d at 232. See ***O'Connor's*** FORM 10E:03.

PRACTICE TIP

Although all courts agree a premature first request for findings is considered timely, at least two courts have held that a premature notice of past due findings is not timely. ***Estate of Gorski v. Welch****, 993 S.W.2d 298, 301 (Tex.App.—San Antonio 1999, pet. denied);* ***Echols v. Echols****, 900 S.W.2d 160, 161 (Tex.App.—Beaumont 1995, writ denied). Those courts ignore TRCP 306c ("No … request for findings of fact … shall be held ineffective because prematurely filed….").*

§3.4 Court files findings & conclusions. Once a second request is filed, the trial court has 40 days from the day the first request was filed to file findings and conclusions. TRCP 297.

1. Not in judgment. The requirement for filing findings under TRCP 296-298 cannot be satisfied by statements of fact in the judgment. TRCP 299a prohibits the trial court from reciting findings of fact in the judgment. ***Frommer v. Frommer***, 981 S.W.2d 811, 814 (Tex.App.—Houston [1st Dist.] 1998, pet. dism'd).

2. Send findings to parties. Once the court makes findings, it must mail a copy of the findings to each party. TRCP 297. This gives the parties time to meet the deadline in TRCP 298 for requesting additional or amended findings within ten days after the filing of the original findings and conclusions.

§3.5 Third request – for additional or amended findings. Once the trial court files findings of fact, either party may ask the trial court to make additional findings.

1. Deadline to request. The request for additional findings must be filed within ten days of the trial court's initial findings. TRCP 298; ***SMI/USA v. Profile Technologies***, 38 S.W.3d 205, 209 (Tex.App.—Waco 2001, no pet.). If the request for additional findings is made before the trial court makes any findings, one court has said the premature request is ineffective. *See* ***Mohnke v. Greenwood***, 915 S.W.2d 585, 590 (Tex.App.—Houston [14th Dist.] 1996, no writ). *But see* TRCP 306c (no premature request for findings shall be ineffective).

2. Proposed findings. The party must submit specific proposed findings; a broad request for additional findings is not sufficient. ***Alvarez v. Espinoza***, 844 S.W.2d 238, 242 (Tex.App.—San Antonio 1992, writ dism'd). If the court omitted a finding on a material element, the party should ask the court to make the omitted finding; if the court made an error in a finding, the party should ask the court to amend the finding. See ***O'Connor's*** FORM 10E:04.

(1) By winner. The winning party should request additional or amended findings that support the judgment in its favor.

(2) By loser. The losing party's request for additional findings is difficult to make because a request for findings inconsistent with the judgment will be denied, and a request for findings consistent with the judgment might be considered a waiver. *See* ***In re Grossnickle***, 115 S.W.3d 238, 254 (Tex.App.—Texarkana 2003, n.p.h.) (trial court not required to make additional findings contrary to other findings); ***ASAI v. Vanco Insulation Abatement***, 932 S.W.2d 118, 122 (Tex.App.—El Paso 1996, no writ) (same). For the losing party to request additional findings properly, it should (1) inform the trial court that a material issue disputed during the trial was not addressed in any of the findings; (2) request specific, additional findings on that issue that are consistent with the judgment; (3) inform the trial court that the party does not agree with the additional findings it requests; and (4) state that the findings are necessary so that, on appeal, the party may challenge the findings or, if the additional findings are not entered, the lack of those findings. *See* ***Vickery v. Commission for Lawyer Discipline***, 5 S.W.3d 241, 254 (Tex.App.—Houston [14th Dist.] 1999, pet. denied) (appellant's request did not inform trial court that it had omitted two essential elements in its original findings).

§3.6 Court's deadline to file additional findings. The trial court has ten days to file additional or amended findings, counting from the date the request for additional findings is filed. TRCP 298. If the court refuses to make additional findings of fact requested by the losing party, the winning party cannot argue on appeal that findings should be deemed in support of the judgment. TRCP 299; ***Boy Scouts v. Responsive Terminal Sys.***, 790 S.W.2d 738, 742-43 (Tex.App.—Dallas 1990, writ denied). Thus, the party that won the judgment should encourage the court to make additional findings when they are necessary.

§3.7 Findings in child support cases. In a contested child support case, Family Code §154.130 requires the court to file findings of fact, when properly requested, "without regard to rules 296 through 299." The request for findings of fact under Family Code §154.130(a) may be made orally during the hearing or in writing, filed not more than ten days after the hearing. If the request is oral, it must be made on the record while the court reporter is transcribing the hearing. *See* Family Code §154.130(a)(2). Family Code §154.130(b) lists the specific findings the court must make.

§4. RESPONSE

The party that won the judgment should draft findings of fact when it receives notice the other party has requested findings of fact. In drafting the findings of fact, the party should include a finding on each element of the cause of action or defense. See generally ***O'Connor's Texas Causes of Action*** (2004).

§5. COURT'S FINDINGS OF FACT & CONCLUSIONS OF LAW

§5.1 Form & content. The findings of fact and conclusions of law are generally prepared by the prevailing party. ***Vickery***, 5 S.W.3d at 253; ***Grossnickle v. Grossnickle***, 935 S.W.2d 830, 837 n.1 (Tex.App.—Texarkana 1996, writ denied). The findings must be made in writing, not orally. ***Larry F. Smith, Inc. v. Weber Co.***, 110 S.W.3d 611, 615 (Tex.App.—Dallas 2003, n.p.h.).

1. Same document, separate headings. The findings and conclusions should be in the same document, but they should be stated under separate headings. When a finding of fact is mislabeled as a conclusion of law, the appellate court can treat it as a finding of fact. ***Ray v. Farmers' State Bank***, 576 S.W.2d 607, 608 n.1 (Tex. 1979); ***Lucas v. Texas Dept. of Protective & Regulatory Servs.***, 949 S.W.2d 500, 502 (Tex.App.—Waco 1997, pet. denied).

2. Not in the judgment. TRCP 299a requires the trial court to file findings of fact in a document separate from the judgment. TRCP 299a; ***Guridi v. Waller***, 98 S.W.3d 315, 316-17 (Tex.App.—Houston [1st Dist.] 2003, no pet.); ***Salinas v. Beaudrie***, 960 S.W.2d 314, 317 (Tex.App.—Corpus Christi 1997, no pet.). When factual findings in the judgment are in conflict with the findings in the findings of fact, the findings of fact will control. TRCP 299a. Most courts refuse to review findings that are included in the judgment. *See* ***Casino Magic Corp. v. King***, 43 S.W.3d 14, 19 n.6 (Tex.App.—Dallas 2001, pet. denied); ***Salinas***, 960 S.W.2d at 317; ***Sutherland v. Cobern***, 843 S.W.2d 127, 131 n.7 (Tex.App.—Texarkana 1992, writ denied). *But see* ***Tate v. Tate***, 55 S.W.3d 1, 8 n.4 (Tex.App.—El Paso 2000, no pet.) (party waived complaint that findings recited in divorce decree were invalid because party drafted decree); ***Hill v. Hill***, 971 S.W.2d 153, 157 (Tex.App.—Amarillo 1998, no pet.) (findings in a judgment have probative value as long as they do not conflict with those filed separately). When no findings are requested and no separate findings are filed, findings included in the judgment should not be considered. *See* ***Guridi***, 98 S.W.3d at 317.

3. Only on controlling issues. The trial court is required to make findings of fact only on controlling issues, not on matters of evidence. ***ASAI***, 932 S.W.2d at 122; ***Rafferty v. Finstad***, 903 S.W.2d 374, 376 (Tex.App.—Houston [1st Dist.] 1995, writ denied). An issue is controlling when it will support a basis for judgment for the proponent. ***Taylor v. Texas DPS***, 754 S.W.2d 464, 468 (Tex.App.—Fort Worth 1988, writ denied).

§5.2 Late findings of fact. The trial court can file findings of fact after the deadline to file them has expired. ***Jefferson Cty. Drainage Dist. v. Lower Neches Valley Auth.***, 876 S.W.2d 940, 959 (Tex.App.—Beaumont 1994, writ denied); ***Morrison v. Morrison***, 713 S.W.2d 377, 380 (Tex.App.—Dallas 1986, writ dism'd). The trial court can file additional findings even after it loses plenary power to affect the judgment. ***Morrison***, 713 S.W.2d at 380. The reason the appellate courts will consider late findings is that one of the remedies for not filing findings is for the appellate court to abate the case and remand to the trial court to make findings. *Id.* at 381.

§6. REVIEW

§6.1 Effect of request for FoF on appellate timetables. A timely request for findings of fact extends the time to perfect the appeal when (1) the findings and conclusions are required by TRCP 296, or (2) the trial court conducts an evidentiary hearing and the findings can properly be considered by the appellate court. TRAP 26.1(a)(4); ***IKB Indus. v. Pro-Line Corp.***, 938 S.W.2d 440, 443 (Tex.1997); ***Awde v. Dabeit***, 938 S.W.2d 31, 33 (Tex. 1997); ***Adams v. H & H Meat Prods.***, 41 S.W.3d 762, 769 (Tex.App.—Corpus Christi 2001, no pet.). See ***O'Connor's Texas Civil Appeals***, "Request for Findings of Fact," ch. 11-G, §§3.1.5, 3.2.3, p. 37 (2002-03).

1. Time extended. When a timely request for findings is made in a case in which findings are required (see list in §2.1, p. 642), or findings are helpful but not required (see list in §2.3, p. 643), the request extends the time to perfect an appeal. ***IKB Indus.***, 938 S.W.2d at 443.

2. Time not extended. A request for findings does not extend the time to perfect an appeal in the appeal of interlocutory orders (see list in §2.2, p. 642) or when findings are not appropriate (see list in §2.4, p. 644).

§6.2 Review of FoF.

1. When all necessary findings filed. An appellant should treat the findings of fact as if they were jury findings and challenge all findings with legal and factual sufficiency points of error. ***Catalina v. Blasdel***, 881 S.W.2d 295, 297 (Tex.1994); ***Krabbe v. Anadarko Pet. Corp.***, 46 S.W.3d 308, 314 (Tex.App.—Amarillo 2001, pet. denied). Findings of fact are not conclusive on appeal, even when unchallenged, when a reporter's record is part of the appellate record. ***Zac Smith & Co. v. Otis Elevator Co.***, 734 S.W.2d 662, 666 (Tex.1987); ***City of Beaumont v. Spivey***, 1 S.W.3d 385, 392 (Tex.App.—Beaumont 1999, pet. denied). Before reversing on a factual sufficiency point of error, the court of appeals must clearly state why the finding of fact is not supported by the evidence. ***Ortiz v. Jones***, 917 S.W.2d 770, 772 (Tex.1996).

2. When some findings omitted. When a party requests findings and the court files them, the court of appeals can presume that omitted findings support the judgment only when (1) an element of the ground of recovery was included in the findings of fact, (2) the omitted element was not properly requested, and (3) the omitted finding is supported by the evidence. TRCP 299; ***American Nat'l Ins. Co. v. Paul***, 927 S.W.2d 239, 245 (Tex.App.—Austin 1996, writ denied); ***Warehouse Partners v. Gardner***, 910 S.W.2d 19, 23 (Tex.App.—Dallas 1995, writ denied); *see, e.g.*, ***Tarrant Cty. Water Control & Imprv. Dist. v. Haupt, Inc.***, 854 S.W.2d 909, 913 (Tex. 1993) (because record contained some evidence of reasonableness, issue was deemed found in support of trial court's judgment). When a party does not request (and the trial court does not make) findings on an entire ground of recovery or defense, the appellate court cannot presume that specific ground of recovery or defense supports the judgment. TRCP 299; *see* ***F.R. Hernandez Constr. & Sup. Co. v. National Bank of Commerce***, 578 S.W.2d 675, 678-79 (Tex.1979). When findings are not requested or made, the party waives its claim or defense just as if, in a jury trial, the party did not request a jury question on a claim or defense.

3. When findings in conflict. If the trial court issues amended or additional findings in conflict with the original findings, the later findings control. ***Jefferson Cty. Drainage***, 876 S.W.2d at 960.

4. When no additional findings requested. If the appellant did not ask for additional findings, it cannot challenge the lack of findings on appeal. ***Smith v. Smith***, 22 S.W.3d 140, 149 (Tex.App.—Houston [14th Dist.] 2000, no pet.); ***Robles v. Robles***, 965 S.W.2d 605, 611 (Tex.App.—Houston [1st Dist.] 1998, pet. denied).

5. When findings are not required but are helpful.

(1) General rule. When findings of fact are not required by TRCP 296 or some other rule or statute but are helpful to the appellate court, they are not reviewed under the legal and factual sufficiency standard as are findings made under TRCP 296. ***Chrysler Corp. v. Blackmon***, 841 S.W.2d 844, 852 (Tex.1992). When findings of fact are not required but are helpful, they do not have the same weight on appeal as findings made under TRCP 296 and are not binding on the appellate court. ***IKB Indus.***, 938 S.W.2d at 442.

(2) Exception – special appearance. Even though findings of fact are not required by TRCP 296 or any other rule after a special appearance, when the trial court files findings after it denies a special appearance, those findings are reviewed for factual and legal sufficiency of the evidence. ***BMC Software v. Marchand***, 83 S.W.3d 789, 794 (Tex.2002).

§6.3 Review when findings not requested or filed. When no findings of fact are requested or filed, the trial court's judgment implies all findings of fact necessary to support it. ***Sixth RMA Partners v. Sibley***, 111 S.W.3d 46, 52 (Tex.2003); ***BMC Software***, 83 S.W.3d at 795; ***Worford v. Stamper***, 801 S.W.2d 108, 109 (Tex.1990). When a reporter's record is filed, the implied findings are not conclusive, and an appellant may challenge them by raising both legal and factual sufficiency points of error. ***Sixth RMA***, 111 S.W.3d at 52; ***BMC Software***, 83 S.W.3d at 795; ***Roberson v. Robinson***, 768 S.W.2d 280, 281 (Tex.1989).

§6.4 Review when findings requested but not filed. When properly requested, the trial court has a mandatory duty to file findings of fact. ***Cherne Indus. v. Magallanes***, 763 S.W.2d 768, 772 (Tex.1989); ***In re Davis***, 30 S.W.3d 609, 613 (Tex.App.—Texarkana 2000, no pet.). See "Findings of fact are necessary," §2.1, p. 642.

1. Presumed harmful. If the trial court does not file findings, it is presumed harmful unless the record affirmatively shows the appellant suffered no harm. ***Tenery v. Tenery***, 932 S.W.2d 29, 30 (Tex.1996); ***Cherne Indus.***, 763 S.W.2d at 772; ***Davis***, 30 S.W.3d at 613. In a complicated case with disputed facts where there are two or more grounds for recovery or defense, the inference of harm cannot be overcome. ***Larry F. Smith, Inc. v. Weber Co.***, 110 S.W.3d 611, 614 (Tex.App.—Dallas 2003, n.p.h.) (reversed for new trial); ***Randall v. Jennings***, 788 S.W.2d 931, 932 (Tex.App.—Houston [14th Dist.] 1990, no writ) (same). If the error is curable, the appellate court may abate the appeal and remand the case to the trial court to make findings. *See* TRAP 44.4; ***Cherne Indus.***, 763 S.W.2d at 773 (court noted trial judge was still on bench & could correct error); ***Brooks v. Housing Auth.***, 926 S.W.2d 316, 319-20 (Tex.App.—El Paso 1996, no writ) (appeal abated & trial judge given 30 days to file findings). If the error is not curable, the appellate court may reverse and remand the case for a new trial. *See* ***Weber Co.***, 110 S.W.3d at 616 (case reversed, trial judge no longer on bench). Oral findings made on the record are not a substitute for written findings. *Id.* at 615. *But see* ***Sagemont Plaza Shopping v. Harris Cty. Appr. Dist.***, 30 S.W.3d 425, 427 (Tex.App.—Corpus Christi 2000, pet. denied) (ruling announced in open court gave parties the reason for the ruling; no harm in court not filing findings); ***Texas Workers' Comp. Ins. Fund v. Ashy***, 972 S.W.2d 208, 212 (Tex. App.—Beaumont 1998, pet. denied) (same); ***Elizondo v. Gomez***, 957 S.W.2d 862, 865 (Tex.App.—San Antonio 1997, pet. denied) (same).

2. Harmless. If the trial court does not file findings, and the lack of findings is harmless, the appellate court will affirm. TRAP 44.1(a). Error is harmful if it prevents a party from properly presenting a case to the appellate court. TRAP 44.1(a)(2); ***Tenery***, 932 S.W.2d at 30. The issue is whether the circumstances of the particular case would require an appellant to guess at the reasons for the trial court's decision. ***Goggins v. Leo***, 849 S.W.2d 373, 379 (Tex.App.—Houston [14th Dist.] 1993, no writ).

§6.5 Review of conclusions of law. The legal conclusions of the trial court are not binding on an appellate court; instead, the appellate courts are free to draw their own legal conclusions. *See* ***Pegasus Energy Group v. Cheyenne Pet. Co.***, 3 S.W.3d 112, 121 (Tex.App.—Corpus Christi 1999, pet. denied); ***Austin Hardwoods, Inc. v. Vanden Berghe***, 917 S.W.2d 320, 322 (Tex.App.—El Paso 1995, writ denied). The review of conclusions of law is de novo. ***Hydrocarbon Mgmt. v. Tracker Expl.***, 861 S.W.2d 427, 431 (Tex.App.—Amarillo 1993, no writ).

F. MOTION TO REINSTATE AFTER DISMISSAL FOR WANT OF PROSECUTION

§1. GENERAL

§1.1 Rules. TRCP 165a; TRAP 26.1(a)(3).

§1.2 Purpose. TRCP 165a permits a plaintiff to ask the court to reinstate a case after it was dismissed for want of prosecution (DWOP).

§1.3 Forms & timetable. ***O'Connor's Texas Civil Forms***, FORMS 10F; Timetable, this book, Motion to Reinstate After DWOP, p. 1013.

§2. BEFORE DISMISSAL

The trial court's authority to dismiss for want of prosecution stems from two sources: TRCP 165a and the court's inherent power. See "Failure to prosecute," ch. 7-F, §2.2, p. 500.

§2.1 Notice case is on dismissal docket. See "Notice of Intent to Dismiss," ch. 7-F, §3, p. 501.

§2.2 Motion to retain. A plaintiff should file a motion to retain after it receives notice of the court's intent to dismiss and before the actual dismissal. See "Motion to retain," ch. 7-F, §4.1, p. 502.

§3. MOTION TO REINSTATE

§3.1 Court's initiative. A trial court can reinstate the case on its own initiative without a motion within 30 days of dismissal. ***Texas DPS v. Deck***, 954 S.W.2d 108, 111-12 (Tex.App.—San Antonio 1997, no writ); ***Neese v. Wray***, 893 S.W.2d 169, 170 (Tex.App.—Houston [1st Dist.] 1995, no writ).

§3.2 Plaintiff's motion. A motion to reinstate is not a prerequisite to appeal a dismissal for want of prosecution. ***Maida v. Fire Ins. Exch.***, 990 S.W.2d 836, 838 n.1 (Tex.App.—Fort Worth 1999, no pet.); ***Hosey v. County of Victoria***, 832 S.W.2d 701, 703 (Tex.App.—Corpus Christi 1992, no writ). However, the motion to reinstate gives the plaintiff one last chance to convince the trial court to restore the case to the docket, permits the plaintiff to make a record for appeal, and extends the court's plenary power and the appellate deadlines. *See* TRCP 165a(3) (timely filed motion to reinstate extends court's plenary power to reinstate case until 30 days after motion is overruled).

§3.3 Verified. The plaintiff must verify the motion to reinstate and, when necessary, attach affidavits. TRCP 165a(3); ***McConnell v. May***, 800 S.W.2d 194, 194 (Tex.1990); ***Kenley v. Quintana Pet. Corp.***, 931 S.W.2d 318, 321 (Tex.App.—San Antonio 1996, writ denied); *see* ***3V, Inc. v. JTS Enters.***, 40 S.W.3d 533, 538-39 (Tex.App.—Houston [14th Dist.] 2000, no pet.) (affidavits acted as substitute for verification). An unverified motion is a nullity and does not extend the trial court's plenary power or the deadlines for perfecting an appeal. ***McConnell***, 800 S.W.2d at 194; ***Butts v. Capitol City Nursing Home***, 705 S.W.2d 696, 697 (Tex.1986). Because the trial court can grant a motion to reinstate on its own motion, the court can grant an unverified motion if it signs a written order within 30 days of the date the judgment was signed. ***Dardari v. Texas Commerce Bank***, 961 S.W.2d 466, 469 (Tex.App.—Houston [1st Dist.] 1997, no pet.). See "Verification & affidavits," ch. 1-B, §4.14, p. 7.

§3.4 Grounds to reinstate. The motion to reinstate must address the grounds for dismissal stated in the trial court's order. ***Shook v. Gilmore & Tatge Mfg. Co.***, 951 S.W.2d 294, 296 (Tex.App.—Waco 1997, pet. denied). When the dismissal order does not identify the ground for dismissal, the motion must address and negate all possible grounds. ***Manning v. North***, 82 S.W.3d 706, 713 (Tex.App.—Amarillo 2002, no pet.). See ***O'Connor's*** FORM 10F:01.

1. Dismissal for failure to appear. When a court dismisses a suit for failure to appear at trial or other dispositive hearing under TRCP 165a(1), the plaintiff must establish by a verified motion that (1) it had no notice of the setting, (2) it had notice of a nondispostive hearing only, or (3) although it had notice, its failure to appear was due to an accident or mistake. See ***O'Connor's*** FORM 10F:01, §C.

(1) No notice of dispositive setting. If the plaintiff had no notice of the setting, the verified motion to reinstate should state the plaintiff did not appear at the trial or other dispositive hearing because it had no notice. The trial court cannot dismiss a suit for failure to appear unless the plaintiff was given proper notice of a trial or a dispositive hearing. TRCP 165a(1). See "Notice of Intent to Dismiss," ch. 7-F, §3, p. 501.

(2) Notice of nondispositive setting. If the plaintiff had notice of a nondispositive hearing only (*e.g.*, docket call), the verified motion to reinstate should state that the dismissal was rendered after notice, but that the plaintiff did not have notice its failure to appear could result in dismissal. ***Degen v. General Coatings, Inc.***, 705 S.W.2d 734, 735 (Tex.App.—Houston [14th Dist.] 1986, no writ). Dismissal is not appropriate for a failure to appear at a nondispositive hearing. See "Failure to appear," ch. 7-F, §2.2.1(1), p. 500.

(3) Notice of dispositive setting. If the plaintiff received notice of the trial or dispositive hearing, the verified motion should state its failure to appear was not intentional or the result of conscious indifference, but was the result of a mistake or accident, or is otherwise reasonably explained. TRCP 165a(3); ***Smith v. Babcock & Wilcox Constr. Co.***, 913 S.W.2d 467, 468 (Tex.1995). When the plaintiff received notice of the trial or hearing but did not appear, the standard of review is essentially the same as the ***Craddock*** standard for setting aside a default judgment. *Id.* at 468; *see* ***Craddock v. Sunshine Bus Lines***, 133 S.W.2d 124, 126 (Tex.1939). The failure to appear is not intentional or due to conscious indifference within the meaning of TRCP 165a(3) merely because it is deliberate; it must also be without adequate justification. ***Smith***, 913 S.W.2d at 468. Conscious indifference means more than just negligence. *See id.* (lawyer, in trial in one county, mistakenly thought a continuance would be granted in case in another county); ***Quita, Inc. v. Haney***, 810 S.W.2d 469, 470 (Tex.App.—Eastland 1991, no writ) (lawyer, in trial in one county, thought trial in other county would not be reached). Proof of justification (*i.e.*, accident, mistake, or other reasonable explanation) negates the intent or conscious indifference for which reinstatement can be denied. ***Smith***, 913 S.W.2d at 468. A mistake of law can satisfy this requirement. ***Bank One v. Moody***, 830 S.W.2d 81, 85 (Tex.1992).

2. Dismissal for failure to prosecute. A motion to reinstate a case dismissed for failure to diligently prosecute gives the plaintiff the opportunity to ask the court to reconsider the dismissal. ***Ellmossallamy v. Huntsman***, 830 S.W.2d 299, 302 (Tex.App.—Houston [14th Dist.] 1992, no writ).

(1) No notice of intent to dismiss. If the court dismissed the suit for failure to diligently prosecute without giving the plaintiff notice of its intent to dismiss, the plaintiff should file a verified motion to reinstate (1) proving lack of proper notice and (2) refuting the grounds for failure to prosecute. See "Notice of Intent to Dismiss," ch. 7-F, §3, p. 501. The court can overrule the motion if the plaintiff merely proves lack of notice and does not address the failure to prosecute. *See* ***Texas Sting, Ltd. v. R.B. Foods***, 82 S.W.3d 644, 649 (Tex.App.—San Antonio 2002, pet. denied). See ***O'Connor's*** FORM 10F:01, §E.

(2) Failure to comply with time standards. When a court dismisses a suit under TRCP 165a(2) for failure to comply with the Supreme Court's time standards, the plaintiff should file a verified motion to reinstate showing the following: (1) the suit was dismissed before the expiration of the appropriate time standard; (2) the plaintiff has a reasonable excuse for failing to prosecute the case within the time limits; or (3) there is good cause to maintain the case on the docket. *See, e.g.*, ***Johnson-Snodgrass v. KTAO***, 75 S.W.3d 84, 87 (Tex.App.—Fort Worth 2002, pet. filed 7-29-02) (dismissal reversed; case dismissed before it was 18-months old); ***Franklin v. Sherman ISD***, 53 S.W.3d 398, 404 (Tex.App.—Dallas 2001, pet. denied) (dismissal affirmed; P did not show excuse for failure to prosecute within time standards or good cause to maintain case). See "Failure to comply with time standards," ch. 7-F, §2.2.1(2), p. 500; ***O'Connor's*** FORM 10F:01, §D.

(3) Inherent power. When a court dismisses a suit under its inherent power for failure to prosecute, the plaintiff should file a verified motion to reinstate addressing the following issues: (1) the length the case was on file, (2) the extent of activity in the case (*i.e.*, showing plaintiff's diligence), (3) whether a trial setting was requested, and (4) a reasonable explanation for the delay. ***Maida***, 990 S.W.2d at 842; ***Bard v. Frank B. Hall & Co.***, 767 S.W.2d 839, 843 (Tex.App.—San Antonio 1989, writ denied). The purpose of the motion is to show that the plaintiff was "reasonably diligent" in prosecuting the suit. *See* ***MacGregor v. Rich***, 941 S.W.2d 74, 75 (Tex.1997); *see also* ***Veterans' Land Bd. v. Williams***, 543 S.W.2d 89, 90 (Tex.1976) ("due diligence"). A plaintiff is "reasonably diligent" if it acted as an ordinary, prudent person would have under the same or similar circumstances. ***Manning***, 82 S.W.3d at 713. The motion must prove the plaintiff took the steps necessary to prepare for trial. *See, e.g.*, ***Ellmossallamy***, 830 S.W.2d at 302 (P diligently pursued discovery, complied with D's requests, and was ready to proceed to trial). See "Inherent power," ch. 7-F, §2.2.2, p. 500; ***O'Connor's*** FORM 10F:01, §D.

§3.5 Challenge language of dismissal order. If the trial court's order mistakenly dismissed the suit "with prejudice" or stated that plaintiff "take nothing," that statement must be challenged in the motion to reinstate or in a motion for new trial; otherwise, the error is waived and the suit cannot be refiled. *See* ***El Paso Pipe & Sup. v. Mountain States Leasing***, 617 S.W.2d 189, 190 (Tex.1981); ***Almanara World Class Rest. v. Caspian Enters.***, ___ S.W.3d ___ (Tex.App.—Houston [14th Dist.] 2003, no pet.) (No. 14-02-00347-CV; 3-6-03). See "The Order of Dismissal," ch. 7-F, §6, p. 502. The wrong notation does not require reinstatement, just correction of the order.

§3.6 Request hearing. Even though the court is required to hold a hearing on a proper motion to reinstate, and a request for a hearing is not necessary, the plaintiff should ask for a hearing. See "Hearing Mandatory," §7.1, p. 653; ***O'Connor's*** FORM 10F:01, §F. Even when a plaintiff does not ask for a hearing, the trial court must conduct one unless the plaintiff actually waives it. *See* ***Thordson v. City of Houston***, 815 S.W.2d 550, 550 (Tex.1991). *But see* ***Rainbow Home Health v. Schmidt***, 76 S.W.3d 53, 57 (Tex.App.—San Antonio 2002, pet. denied) (relying on ***Cabrera***, court held it was necessary for P to alert the court of the need for a hearing); ***Cabrera v. Cedarapids Inc.***, 834 S.W.2d 615, 618 (Tex.App.—Houston [14th Dist.] 1992) (relying on cases predating 1983 version of TRCP 165a, court held P was required to ask for hearing), *writ denied*, 847 S.W.2d 247 (Tex.1993).

PRACTICE TIP

Always ask for a hearing for the motion to reinstate, attempt to get a setting for a hearing, and complain in writing if you don't get one.

§3.7 Amending the motion. The plaintiff must file an amended motion to reinstate within 30 days of the date the dismissal order was signed. *See, e.g.*, ***Mandujano v. Oliva***, 755 S.W.2d 512, 514 (Tex.App.—San Antonio 1988, writ denied) (P amended its petition to add verification before 30 days expired). If the court has already overruled the original motion, the plaintiff must seek leave of court to file an amended motion. TRCP 329b(b); *see also* ***Mandujano***, 755 S.W.2d at 513 (amended motion filed before trial court signed order overruling original motion). See "Amended MNT," ch. 10-B, §5.5, p. 620.

§4. DEADLINE

The deadline for filing a motion to reinstate depends on whether the plaintiff received timely notice of the dismissal. See "Notice of Dismissal Order," ch. 7-F, §8, p. 504; "Notice of Judgment," ch. 9-C, §5, p. 601.

§4.1 Timely notice of dismissal. If the plaintiff received timely notice of the dismissal of the suit, the plaintiff must file a motion to reinstate with the clerk within 30 days after the trial court signed the order of dismissal. ***Memorial Hosp. v. Gillis***, 741 S.W.2d 364, 365 (Tex.1987); ***In re Montemayor***, 2 S.W.3d 542, 545 (Tex.App.—San Antonio 1999, orig. proceeding). Timely notice of dismissal is notice within 20 days of the dismissal. ***Danforth Mem'l Hosp. v. Harris***, 573 S.W.2d 762, 763 (Tex.1978); *see* TRCP 306a(4); ***Montemayor***, 2 S.W.3d at 545.

§4.2 Late notice of dismissal. If the plaintiff received notice of the dismissal of the suit within 21 to 90 days after the date the judgment was signed, the plaintiff must file a motion to reinstate within 30 days of receiving notice of the dismissal and include the allegations required for a motion to extend postjudgment deadlines. TRCP 306a(4), (5); TRAP 4.2(a)(1); *see* ***Danforth Mem'l Hosp.***, 573 S.W.2d at 763. See "Motion to Extend Postjudgment Deadlines," ch. 10-G, p. 654.

§4.3 Premature motion. If a plaintiff filed a motion to reinstate after dismissal but before the judgment was signed, the premature motion should be treated as timely. ***In re Bokeloh***, 21 S.W.3d 784, 788 (Tex.App.—Houston [14th Dist.] 2000, orig. proceeding); ***Perez v. TEIA***, 926 S.W.2d 425, 427 (Tex.App.—Austin 1996, order on mot.); *see* TRAP 27.2 (premature motion is considered effective). *Contra* ***Brim Laundry Mach. Co. v. Washex Mach. Corp.***, 854 S.W.2d 297, 301 (Tex.App.—Fort Worth 1993, writ denied) (case ignored former TRAP 58, now TRAP 27, and applied TRCP 306c, which lists items that premature filing rule applies to; prematurely filed motion to reinstate was ineffective). A motion to retain cannot be treated as a prematurely filed motion to reinstate. ***Bokeloh***, 21 S.W.3d at 790-91.

§5. DUTY OF COURT

§5.1 Clerk. The clerk of the court is required to deliver a copy of the motion to reinstate to the trial court. TRCP 165a(3); ***Bush v. Ward***, 747 S.W.2d 43, 45 (Tex.App.—Beaumont 1988, no writ).

§5.2 Setting for hearing. When a timely motion to reinstate is filed, the trial court must set it for a hearing. See §7.1, below. The hearing must be at the earliest practicable time. TRCP 165a(3).

§5.3 Notice of hearing. The court must notify all parties of the date, time, and place of the hearing. *See* ***Rohus v. Licona***, 942 S.W.2d 111, 112 (Tex.App.—Houston [1st Dist.] 1997, no writ); ***Bush***, 747 S.W.2d at 45.

§6. RESPONSE

The defendant should file a response to a motion to reinstate and challenge the grounds in the motion, verifying any factual allegations in the response with affidavits.

§7. HEARING

The hearing on the motion to reinstate remedies any violations of the plaintiff's due process rights (*i.e.,* lack of notice of the hearing or the dismissal) that occurred before the dismissal. ***Manning v. North***, 82 S.W.3d 706, 715 (Tex.App.—Amarillo 2002, no pet.); ***Texas Sting, Ltd. v. R.B. Foods***, 82 S.W.3d 644, 648-49 (Tex.App.—San Antonio, 2002, pet. denied). See "Notice of Intent to Dismiss," ch. 7-F, §3, p. 501.

§7.1 Hearing mandatory. A hearing to receive evidence on a timely motion to reinstate is mandatory. ***Thordson v. City of Houston***, 815 S.W.2d 550, 550 (Tex.1991); ***Gulf Coast Inv. Corp. v. NASA 1 Bus. Ctr.***, 754 S.W.2d 152, 153 (Tex.1988); ***Matheson v. American Carbonics***, 867 S.W.2d 146, 148 (Tex.App.—Texarkana 1993, no writ). Whether the plaintiff requests a hearing on a motion to reinstate is irrelevant; a hearing is required unless affirmatively waived. ***Matheson***, 867 S.W.2d at 147-48 & n.2; *see, e.g.,* ***Kelly v. Cunningham***, 848 S.W.2d 370, 371 (Tex.App.—Houston [1st Dist.] 1993, no writ) (attorney set motion to reinstate for court's submission docket). However, if the court reinstates the case without a hearing, the order is valid. ***Eagle Signal Corp. v. Wittig***, 766 S.W.2d 390, 392-93 (Tex.App.—Houston [1st Dist.] 1989, orig. proceeding).

CAUTION

Although the 1983 amendment to TRCP 165a requires the trial court to hold a hearing, some opinions issued after 1983 have erroneously relied on pre-1983 cases to hold that the hearing is waivable. See "Request hearing," §3.6, p. 651.

§7.2 Evidence. The plaintiff must present all necessary evidence at the hearing in support of each element of the grounds to reinstate. *See* ***Bard v. Frank B. Hall & Co.***, 767 S.W.2d 839, 845 (Tex.App.—San Antonio 1989, writ denied). See "Grounds to reinstate," §3.4, p. 650. Both the plaintiff and its attorney should be sworn and formally present testimony about the reason for the dismissal, good cause to reinstate, and when necessary, the late notice of the dismissal. If no evidence is presented at the hearing, the dismissal will be affirmed on appeal. *See* ***MacGregor v. Rich***, 941 S.W.2d 74, 76 (Tex.1997); ***Balla v. Northeast Lincoln Mercury***, 717 S.W.2d 183, 185 (Tex. App.—Fort Worth 1986, no writ). The plaintiff should offer into evidence the affidavits attached to the motion, but it is not required. *Cf.* ***Director v. Evans***, 889 S.W.2d 266, 268 (Tex.1994) (motion for new trial challenging post-answer default judgment).

§8. REQUEST FOR FINDINGS OF FACT

If the trial court denied the motion to reinstate after receiving evidence, the plaintiff should ask the court to file findings of fact and conclusions of law. *See* ***Burns v. Drew Woods, Inc.***, 900 S.W.2d 128, 129-30 (Tex.App.—Waco 1995, writ denied) (in appeal from denial of motion to reinstate, court focuses on trial court's role in fact-finding process); *cf.* ***Phillips v. Beavers***, 938 S.W.2d 446, 447 (Tex.1997) (findings appropriate after hearing on motion to dismiss for want of prosecution). See "DWOP," ch. 10-E, §2.3.2(1), p. 643.

§9. ORDER

§9.1 In writing. An order granting a motion to reinstate must be in writing and signed. ***Emerald Oaks Hotel v. Zardenetta***, 776 S.W.2d 577, 578 (Tex.1989); ***Walker v. Harrison***, 597 S.W.2d 913, 915 (Tex.1980); ***In re Wal-Mart Stores***, 20 S.W.3d 734, 740 (Tex.App.—El Paso 2000, orig. proceeding). An oral order and docket entry are ineffective to reinstate, and the motion will be deemed overruled by operation of law. ***Emerald Oaks***, 776 S.W.2d at 578; ***Wal-Mart***, 20 S.W.3d at 740.

§9.2 Deadline to reinstate.

1. Timely notice of dismissal. If the plaintiff filed a proper, timely, and verified motion to reinstate (timely and verified), the court must sign an order on the motion to reinstate within 75 days from the date the judgment was signed, or the motion will be overruled by operation of law. TRCP 165a(3); ***Emerald Oaks***, 776 S.W.2d at 578. Once the motion is overruled, the trial court retains plenary power to change it for 30 more days. TRCP 165a(3); ***Nealy v. Home Indem. Co.***, 770 S.W.2d 592, 594 (Tex.App.—Houston [14th Dist.] 1989, no writ).

2. Late notice of dismissal. If the plaintiff received late notice that the case was dismissed, the provisions of TRCP 306a(4)-(5) apply to determine when the motion to reinstate must be filed and when the trial court must sign the order on the motion. If the trial court determines the plaintiff received notice of the dismissal within the 21- to 90-day window in TRCP 306a(4) and TRAP 4.2(a)(1), the reinstatement order must be signed no later than 75 days from the date of actual notice, or the motion will be overruled by operation of law. See "Motion to Extend Postjudgment Deadlines," ch. 10-G, below.

§10. REVIEW

§10.1 Effect of motion to reinstate. The filing of a proper motion to reinstate has the same effect on appellate deadlines and the court's plenary power as the filing of a motion for new trial. ***Butts v. Capitol City Nursing Home***, 705 S.W.2d 696, 697 (Tex.1986). See "Effect of MNT," ch. 10-B, §2.5, p. 618. If a motion is not verified or timely, it does not extend the deadlines or the court's plenary power. ***McConnell v. May***, 800 S.W.2d 194, 194 (Tex. 1990); ***Butts***, 705 S.W.2d at 697. If a motion to reinstate seeks more than reinstatement (*e.g.,* it challenges the order that the case was dismissed "with prejudice"), it can be classified as a motion for a new trial, and even an unverified motion will extend the appellate deadlines. ***State v. Martini***, 902 S.W.2d 138, 140-41 (Tex.App.—Houston [1st Dist.] 1995, no writ).

§10.2 Grounds for review. On appeal, the plaintiff may make either or both of the following arguments: (1) the trial court erred when it dismissed the case, and (2) the trial court erred when it refused to reinstate the case. ***Maida v. Fire Ins. Exch.***, 990 S.W.2d 836, 838 (Tex.App.—Fort Worth 1999, no pet.).

§10.3 Reporter's record. To appeal an order denying reinstatement, the plaintiff must file the reporter's record with the evidence from the hearing.

§10.4 Standard of review. To reverse a judgment of dismissal, the appellant must prove the trial court abused its discretion. *See* ***MacGregor v. Rich***, 941 S.W.2d 74, 75 (Tex.1997) (dismissal for failure to prosecute); ***State v. Rotello***, 671 S.W.2d 507, 509 (Tex.1984) (dismissal under local rule & court's inherent power for failure to prosecute); ***Johnson-Snodgrass v. KTAO***, 75 S.W.3d 84, 87 (Tex.App.—Fort Worth 2002, pet. filed 7-29-02) (dismissal under TRCP 165a). The standard of review for a motion to reinstate after failure to appear is essentially the same as for setting aside a default judgment—conscious indifference. See "Dismissal for failure to appear," §3.4.1, p. 650.

§10.5 Mandamus. If the trial court erroneously reinstated a case after it lost jurisdiction, the reinstatement order can be challenged by mandamus. ***Estate of Howley v. Haberman***, 878 S.W.2d 139, 140 (Tex.1994); ***In re Garcia***, 94 S.W.3d 832, 833 (Tex.App.—Corpus Christi 2002, orig. proceeding); ***In re Bokeloh***, 21 S.W.3d 784, 793 (Tex.App.—Houston [14th Dist.] 2000, orig. proceeding); *see, e.g.*, ***City of McAllen v. Ramirez***, 875 S.W.2d 702, 704-05 (Tex.App.—Corpus Christi 1994, orig. proceeding) (trial court erroneously granted unverified motion).

G. MOTION TO EXTEND POSTJUDGMENT DEADLINES

This is a motion in search of a name. TRCP 306a(4)-(5) and TRAP 4.2 describe the procedure for this motion without assigning it a name. In the last ten years this subchapter has been renamed five times. Beginning in 1991, it was called a "motion to amend date of judgment"; then, a "motion to extend the effective date of judgment"; then, a "motion to reopen the time for appeal"; then, a "motion for additional time to file documents," the name suggested in TRAP 4.2(a). In 2001, we adopted the name used by the Supreme Court in ***John v. Marshall Health Servs.***, 58 S.W.3d 738, 739 (Tex.2001)—"motion to extend postjudgment deadlines."

§1. GENERAL

§1.1 Rules. TRCP 306a(4), (5); TRAP 4.2.

§1.2 Purpose. A motion to extend postjudgment deadlines is the procedure used to ask the court to designate a new date for the judgment because the party did not receive timely notice of the judgment. The effect of a motion under TRCP 306a(5) is to extend the trial court's plenary power to consider postjudgment motions.

§1.3 Forms & timetable. ***O'Connor's Texas Civil Forms***, FORMS 10G; Timetable, this book, Motion to Extend Postjudgment Deadlines, p. 1014.

§2. NOTICE OF JUDGMENT

There are three rules requiring the clerk to notify the parties about the judgment: TRCP 165a(1) (notice of signing order of dismissal for failure to prosecute), TRCP 239a (notice of no-answer default judgment), and TRCP 306a(3) (notice of judgment). See "Notice of Judgment," ch. 9-C, §5, p. 601. If the clerk does not give the parties notice of the judgment as required by the rules, it does not affect the beginning of the time periods listed in TRCP 306a(1), except as provided by TRCP 306a(4). TRCP 306a(3).

§3. MOTION

When a party does not receive any notice of a judgment (official or actual) within 20 days after the judgment is signed, TRCP 306a(4) provides a limited time to request an extension before the judgment becomes final and the trial court loses plenary power. TRAP 4.2(a)(1); ***John v. State***, 826 S.W.2d 138, 140 n.2 (Tex.1992).

§3.1 Form. A motion to extend the postjudgment deadlines (MEPD) may be made as part of a motion for new trial or a motion to reinstate, or it may be filed as a separate motion. See "Motion for New Trial," ch. 10-B, p. 617; "Motion to Reinstate after DWOP," ch. 10-F, p. 649. An MEPD, whether made separately or as part of a motion for new trial or to reinstate, will extend the time to file post-trial motions, the trial court's plenary power, and the appellate deadlines. *See* ***In re Wal-Mart Stores***, 20 S.W.3d 734, 739 n.6 (Tex.App.—El Paso 2000, orig. proceeding) (court's plenary power could have been extended by either motion to reinstate or MEPD); ***University of Tex. v. Joki***, 735 S.W.2d 505, 506-07 (Tex.App.—Austin 1987, writ denied) (MNT extended time to perfect appeal); *cf.* ***Butts v. Capitol City Nursing Home***, 705 S.W.2d 696, 697 (Tex.1986) (motion to reinstate extends time to perfect appeal, just like MNT).

§3.2 Allegations. The MEPD should cover the following issues.

1. Date of first notice. The motion must state that (1) the first notice of the judgment was received by the movant (or its lawyer) on a specific date, and (2) the date was more than 20 days after the judgment was signed, but not more than 90 days after the judgment was signed ("date of actual notice"). TRCP 306a(4), (5); TRAP 4.2(a)(1); ***Levit v. Adams***, 850 S.W.2d 469, 470 (Tex.1993); *see* ***Gem Vending, Inc. v. Walker***, 918 S.W.2d 656, 657-58 (Tex.App.—Fort Worth 1996, orig. proceeding) (because notice received within 20 days of judgment, tolling provisions of TRCP 306a(4) did not apply). Notice to the party's lawyer is notice to the party. ***Gem Vending***, 918 S.W.2d at 658. Notice to the law firm is notice to the lawyer. *See* ***A. Copeland Enters. v. Tindall***, 683 S.W.2d 596, 599 (Tex.App.—Fort Worth 1985, writ ref'd n.r.e.).

2. Description of first notice. The motion must describe the notice, and include who gave it, who got it and when, the type of notice, and any other relevant information. *See* TRCP 306a(4), (5). The motion must identify the specific date the notice was received. *See, e.g.*, ***Womack-Humphreys Architects v. Barrasso***, 886 S.W.2d 809, 814 (Tex.App.—Dallas 1994, writ denied) ("after Dec. 25" was not sufficient), *overruled on other grounds*, ***John v. Marshall Health Servs.***, 58 S.W.3d 738 (Tex.2001). If the movant knows, it should state why the notice was late.

3. No earlier actual notice. The motion must state that neither the movant nor the lawyer acquired actual knowledge of the judgment before the date of first notice. TRCP 306a(5); ***Womack-Humphreys***, 886 S.W.2d at 815; *see, e.g.*, ***St. Louis Fed. S&L Ass'n v. Summerhouse Jt.V.***, 739 S.W.2d 441, 442 (Tex.App.—Corpus Christi 1987, no writ) (oral notice to lawyer within 20 days of judgment was actual notice of judgment).

4. No earlier notice from clerk. The motion must state that neither the movant nor the lawyer received from the clerk any notice of the judgment before the date of first notice. TRCP 306a(5); ***In re Jones***, 974 S.W.2d 766, 768 (Tex.App.—San Antonio 1998, orig. proceeding). TRCP 306a(4) requires the movant to negate timely receipt of the clerk's notice. ***Womack-Humphreys***, 886 S.W.2d at 814-15.

§3.3 Request hearing. The movant should request a hearing on the motion and comply with the requirements of the local rules for securing a hearing. ***Xu v. Davis***, 884 S.W.2d 916, 917-18 (Tex.App.—Waco 1994, orig. proceeding). The trial court is required to hold a hearing before ruling on the motion. *Id.* at 918. See "Hearing Required," §6.1, p. 658.

§3.4 Sworn motion. TRCP 306a(5) requires the movant to file a "sworn motion." An unverified motion with attached affidavits satisfies TRCP 306a(5) if the affidavits verify the facts in the motion. ***City of Laredo v. Schuble***, 943 S.W.2d 124, 126 (Tex.App.—San Antonio 1997, orig. proceeding); *see* ***Womack-Humphreys***, 886 S.W.2d at 814 n.4. To be safe, the motion should be verified separately from the affidavits.

1. Verification. The verification (or affidavit) should state directly and unequivocally that the facts in the motion are true and within the affiant's personal knowledge. ***Schuble***, 943 S.W.2d at 126 n.2. See "Verification & affidavits," ch. 1-B, §4.14, p. 7.

2. Affidavits. The motion should include the affidavits of the persons who should have learned about the judgment but did not—the lawyer and the party. The affidavits must be based on personal knowledge. See "Verification & affidavits," ch. 1-B, §4.14, p. 7.

(1) Lawyer. The lawyer should swear she did not receive timely notice of the judgment, state the exact date the notice was received, describe the type of notice received (notice from the clerk or actual knowledge elsewhere), and state that no earlier notice was received from the clerk. The lawyer might also describe the office procedures for processing notices from the court and state that a review of the process revealed that no notice was received before that date.

(2) Party. The party should swear it did not receive timely notice of the judgment, state the exact date that it received notice, and describe the type of notice received. *See* ***In re Simpson***, 932 S.W.2d 674, 678 (Tex. App.—Amarillo 1996, no writ) (motion did not negate possibility that party received notice within 20 days). When the party is a corporation or other legal entity, an employee or agent may file the affidavit on behalf of the entity. *See, e.g.*, ***Federal Ins. Co. v. Ticor Title Ins. Co.***, 774 S.W.2d 103, 104-05 (Tex.App.—Beaumont 1989, no writ) (affidavit filed by party's bond-claim attorney was sufficient).

(3) Clerk. If the court clerk has information about late notice, the attorney should prepare an affidavit for the clerk to execute. *See, e.g.*, ***Simpson***, 932 S.W.2d at 676-77.

§3.5 File notice of appeal. The party should file the notice of appeal with the trial court as soon as possible after learning of the judgment. The notice of appeal may be early, but it will perfect the appeal. *See* TRAP 27.1(a) (premature notice of appeal). See ***O'Connor's Texas Civil Appeals***, "Notice of Appeal," ch. 15-A, p. 160 (2002-03).

§4. DEADLINES FOR MOVANT

It is very difficult to determine the deadlines to file the MEPD and to rule on it. The ***John v. Marshall Health Services*** case clarified one issue regarding deadlines but created others.

§4.1 Plenary power limits. A motion to extend time to file postjudgment motions under TRCP 306a(5) can be filed only while the trial court has plenary power. ***John***, 58 S.W.3d at 741. The trial court's plenary power begins when it signs the judgment (or order disposing of the case) and ends 30 days later if no motion for new trial or other plenary-power-extending motion is filed. TRCP 306a(1), 329b(d). For a list of plenary-power-extending motions, see "PPE motions," ch. 9-C, §6.5.1(1), p. 605. For the effect of plenary-power-extending motions on the deadline to file a MEPD, see chart 9-1, "Plenary Power Deadlines," ch. 9-C, p. 607.

§4.2 TRCP 306a(4) limits.

1. Notice of judgment. A party that receives notice of the judgment between 20 and 90 days after the judgment is signed may file an MEPD.

(1) Earliest notice. The earliest notice of the judgment that entitles a party to file an MEPD is 21 days after the judgment is signed. TRCP 306a(4); TRAP 4.2(a)(1). When a party receives notice of a judgment within 20 days of the date the judgment is signed, the party cannot file an MEPD. ***In re Montemayor***, 2 S.W.3d 542, 545 (Tex.App.—San Antonio 1999, orig. proceeding) (party received notice 14 days after judgment); ***Greenspan v. Ross***, 949 S.W.2d 45, 46 (Tex.App.—Texarkana 1997, pet. denied) (party received notice 4 days after judgment). Notice of intent to enter judgment is not notice of the signing of the judgment. *See* ***Western Import Motors, Inc. v. Mechinus***, 739 S.W.2d 125, 126 (Tex.App.—San Antonio 1987, no writ).

(2) Latest notice. TRCP 306a does not address the deadline for receiving late notice of judgment. The courts have interpreted the statement in TRCP 306a(4), that "in no event shall such periods [in 306a(1)] begin more than 90 days after" the judgment, as precluding an MEPD when the notice of judgment is received more than 90 days after the judgment is signed. *See, e.g.*, ***Estate of Howley v. Haberman***, 878 S.W.2d 139, 140 (Tex. 1994) (too late to file MEPD because P learned of DWOP more than 90 days after dismissal); ***Levit v. Adams***, 850 S.W.2d 469, 470 (Tex.1993) (same, because P learned of DWOP 91 days after dismissal); ***Graham v. Fashing***, 928 S.W.2d 567, 569 (Tex.App.—El Paso 1996, orig. proceeding) (same, because D learned of default judgment 103 days after it was signed).

2. Deadline for motion. TRCP 306a does not address the deadline for filing an MEPD. ***John v. Marshall Health Servs.***, 58 S.W.3d 738, 741 (Tex.2001). A party may file an MEPD anytime within the trial court's plenary jurisdiction, measured from the date determined under TRCP 306a(4). ***John***, 58 S.W.3d at 741 (MEPD filed 71 days after notice, which was 93 days after J signed). See chart 9-1, "Plenary Power Deadlines," ch. 9-C, p. 607; Timetable, this book, Motion to Extend Postjudgment Deadlines, p. 1014.

(1) Short plenary power period. When no plenary-power-extending motions are filed, the court's plenary power expires 30 days after the party received late notice of the judgment. In these cases, the deadline to file an MEPD is 30 days from the date of the notice of judgment. ***John***, 58 S.W.3d at 741; *see, e.g.*, ***Green v. Guidry***, 34 S.W.3d 669, 670 (Tex.App.—Waco 2000, no pet.) (because no PPE motion filed, deadline to file MEPD was 30 days after notice of judgment).

(2) Long plenary power period. When a plenary-power-extending motion is filed within 30 days of the late notice of judgment, the court's plenary power expires 30 days after that motion is overruled by written order or by operation of law, but in no event more than 105 days after the notice of judgment. ***Green***, 34 S.W.3d at 670. A plenary-power-extending motion is one that seeks a substantive change in the judgment. ***Lane Bank Equip. Co. v. Smith S. Equip., Inc.***, 10 S.W.3d 308, 313 (Tex.2000). For a list of plenary-power-extending motions, see "PPE motions," ch. 9-C, §6.5.1(1), p. 605. When a plenary-power-extending motion is filed within 30 days of the late notice of judgment, that motion extends the time to file an MEPD, which can be filed as long as the court has plenary power. *See, e.g.*, ***John***, 58 S.W.3d at 741 (MNT filed 13 days after notice of judgment; MEPD filed 71 days after notice and within plenary power); ***Grondona v. Sutton***, 991 S.W.2d 90, 92 (Tex.App.—Austin 1998, pet. denied) (MNT filed 2 days after notice of judgment; MEPD filed 84 days after notice of judgment, within plenary power); ***Vineyard Bay Dev. Co. v. Vineyard on Lake Travis***, 864 S.W.2d 170, 172 (Tex.App.—Austin 1993, writ denied) (joint MNT & MEPD filed 24 days after notice of judgment, within plenary power). When a plenary-power-extending motion is overruled by operation of law, the absolute last day to file an MEPD is 105 days after the party received notice of the judgment. ***Green***, 34 S.W.3d at 670 n.1.

Assume the judgment was signed on day 0, P received notice of judgment on day 50, and P filed an MNT on day 60. The MNT will extend the time P has to file an MEPD because it was filed within 30 days of the notice of judgment. The time to file the MEPD is 30 days from the date the MNT is overruled, either by order or by operation of law. Thus, the deadline to file an MEPD depends on whether the MNT is overruled by written order or by operation of law. If the court overrules the MNT by written order on day 70, P has until day 100 to file the MEPD (70 + 30 = 100). If the court does not sign an order overruling the MNT, it is overruled by operation of law on day 125 (50 + 75 = 125); P has until day 155 to file an MEPD (125 + 30 = 155). If no MNT is filed, P has until day 80 to file an MEPD (50 + 30 = 80).

§5. RESPONSE

If the nonmovant objects to the allegations in the MEPD, the nonmovant should file a response challenging the motion. If the response contains factual recitations, it should be supported by affidavits.

§6. HEARING

§6.1 Hearing required. The trial court is required to hold a hearing on an MEPD. ***Cantu v. Longoria***, 878 S.W.2d 131, 132 (Tex.1994); ***In re Bokeloh***, 21 S.W.3d 784, 792 (Tex.App.—Houston [14th Dist.] 2000, orig. proceeding) (hearing is evidentiary in nature); ***Xu v. Davis***, 884 S.W.2d 916, 918 (Tex.App.—Waco 1994, orig. proceeding); *see* TRCP 306a(5); TRAP 4.2(c). As a result of the Supreme Court's holding in ***John***, an MEPD could conceivably be filed on the last day of the trial court's plenary jurisdiction, thereby precluding an opportunity for a hearing. *See* ***John***, 58 S.W.3d at 741; ***Green***, 34 S.W.3d at 670. If the trial court does not hold a hearing, the court of appeals may remand to the trial court for a hearing. ***Cantu***, 878 S.W.2d at 132. If the trial court does not hold a hearing, it must accept the movant's affidavits as true. ***Womack-Humphreys Architects v. Barrasso***, 886 S.W.2d 809, 816 n.9 (Tex.App.—Dallas 1994, writ denied), *overruled on other grounds*, ***John v. Marshall Health Servs.***, 58 S.W.3d 738, 741 (Tex.2001).

§6.2 Burden. At the hearing, the movant either (1) must prove the date it received actual notice of the judgment or (2) must prove it did not receive notice and did not know about the judgment until more than 20 days after the judgment was signed. TRCP 306a(5); TRAP 4.2(b); ***Sharm Inc. v. Martinez***, 885 S.W.2d 165, 166-67 (Tex. App.—Corpus Christi 1993, order on mot.).

§6.3 Deadline for hearing & ruling. TRCP 306a does not set a deadline for the court to conduct the hearing or make a ruling on the motion. The trial court should conduct a hearing and rule on the motion before its plenary power expires.

§6.4 Record. The movant should make sure the court reporter records the hearing on the motion so the movant can challenge an adverse ruling on appeal. If the court reporter does not record the evidence received at the hearing, the movant cannot offer proof of the late notice of the judgment in the appellate court. *See* ***Corro v. Southwestern Bell Media***, 784 S.W.2d 471, 474 (Tex.App.—Corpus Christi 1989, no writ).

§7. ORDER

TRAP 4.2(c) requires the trial court to sign a written order and to make a finding of the date of actual notice or knowledge of the judgment. ***Bokeloh***, 21 S.W.3d at 792; ***Sharm***, 885 S.W.2d at 166-67 (former TRAP 5(b)(5)). In the order denying or granting the motion, the court must state the date the movant received actual notice of the judgment. TRAP 4.2(c); *see* ***Hot Shot Messenger Serv. v. State***, 798 S.W.2d 413, 415 (Tex.App.—Austin 1990, writ denied). If the court grants the motion but does not identify the date of actual notice, the appellate court will look to the motion to supply the date. ***Gee v. Lewisville Mem'l Hosp.***, 849 S.W.2d 458, 460 (Tex.App.—Fort Worth 1993, writ denied).

§7.1 Court grants motion. If the trial court grants the MEPD, it will designate a new date for the judgment based on the date the movant received actual notice of the judgment. TRCP 306a(4); TRAP 4.2(c); *see* ***Levit v. Adams***, 850 S.W.2d 469, 469-70 (Tex.1993); *see also* ***Western Import Motors v. Mechinus***, 739 S.W.2d 125, 126 (Tex.App.—San Antonio 1987, no writ) (because movants learned of judgment on 59th day after it was signed, deadlines began to run on that date). Once the trial court establishes the new date for the judgment, if the motion for new trial and the notice of appeal are already filed, they will be considered timely filed. In no event can the period begin later than 90 days after the date the judgment or order was signed. TRCP 306a(4); TRAP 4.2(a)(1); ***Levit*** 850 S.W.2d at 470.

CAUTION

If the court establishes a new date for the judgment because one party received late notice of the judgment, the new date for that party does not restart the appeal for another party who received timely notice of the judgment. TRCP 306a(4) limits the reopening of the appellate time periods to the party who received late notice.

§7.2 Court denies motion. If the trial court denies the MEPD, the date of the judgment will not change from the date it was signed.

§8. REVIEW

§8.1 Appeal. The issue of late notice of judgment cannot be raised for the first time in an appellate court. ***In re Estate of Padilla***, 103 S.W.3d 563, 567 (Tex.App.—San Antonio 2003, n.p.h.).

1. **Court denied motion.** If the trial court refused to designate a new date of the judgment within the 20-to-90 day period provided in TRCP 306a(4), the movant may challenge the ruling by appeal. *See* ***Hot Shot***, 798 S.W.2d at 414-15; ***Jimmy Swaggart Ministries v. City of Arlington***, 718 S.W.2d 83, 84-85 (Tex.App.—Fort Worth 1986, no writ).

2. **Standard of review.** The trial court's ruling is reviewed on appeal for factual and legal sufficiency of the evidence. ***Hot Shot***, 798 S.W.2d at 414.

§8.2 Mandamus.

1. **Court grants late motion.** If the trial court grants a motion filed after 90 days, the order can be challenged by mandamus. ***Estate of Howley v. Haberman***, 878 S.W.2d 139, 140 (Tex.1994).

2. **No mandamus or regular appeal.** When the party received notice of the judgment after the 90-day period, it is too late to file an MEPD, and the party cannot attack the judgment by regular appeal. The party can, however, attack the judgment by a restricted appeal or a bill of review. *See* ***Levit*** 850 S.W.2d at 470. See "Attacking the Default Judgment," ch. 7-A, §7, p. 452.

H. MOTION FOR JUDGMENT NUNC PRO TUNC

§1. GENERAL

§1.1 Rules. TRCP 306a(6), 316, 329b; TRAP 4.3(b).

§1.2 Purpose. The purpose of a judgment nunc pro tunc is to correct a clerical error in the judgment after the court's plenary power has expired. ***Jenkins v. Jenkins***, 16 S.W.3d 473, 482 (Tex.App.—El Paso 2000, no pet.); ***Ferguson v. Naylor***, 860 S.W.2d 123, 126 (Tex.App.—Amarillo 1993, writ denied); ***West Tex. State Bank v. General Res. Mgmt. Corp.***, 723 S.W.2d 304, 306 (Tex.App.—Austin 1987, writ ref'd n.r.e.).

§1.3 Forms. ***O'Connor's Texas Civil Forms***, FORMS 10H.

§2. MOTION

§2.1 Grounds. The only ground for a motion for judgment nunc pro tunc is to correct a clerical error made in entering the judgment. ***Escobar v. Escobar***, 711 S.W.2d 230, 231 (Tex.1986) (contrasted with judicial error made in rendering judgment). If the court attempts to correct a judicial error by signing a judgment nunc pro tunc after the expiration of its plenary power, the judgment is void. *See* ***Dikeman v. Snell***, 490 S.W.2d 183, 186 (Tex.1973); ***In re Rollins Leasing***, 987 S.W.2d 633, 638 (Tex.App.—Houston [14th Dist.] 1999, orig. proceeding). The inquiry for a judgment nunc pro tunc proceeding is what judgment was rendered, not what judgment should have been rendered. ***Jenkins***, 16 S.W.3d at 482; ***Stuart v. City of Houston***, 419 S.W.2d 702, 703 (Tex.App.—Houston [14th Dist.] 1967, writ ref'd n.r.e.). When the error is judicial, it must be corrected by a timely motion to modify the judgment. See "Motion to Modify the Judgment," ch. 10-D, p. 639.

1. Test to determine type of error. To determine if an error was clerical or judicial, ask the following: Was the error the result of judicial reasoning and determination? ***Gonzalez v. Doctors Hosp.***, 814 S.W.2d 536, 537 (Tex.App.—Houston [1st Dist.] 1991, no writ). If the answer is no, the error was clerical, and the trial court can correct the error, even though the judgment is final, by signing a judgment nunc pro tunc. If the answer is yes, the error was a judicial error, and it cannot be corrected by the trial court after the judgment is final. ***Finlay v. Jones***, 435 S.W.2d 136, 138 (Tex.1968).

2. Difference between clerical & judicial errors. The decision whether an error is clerical or judicial is a question of law. ***Finlay***, 435 S.W.2d at 138; ***Dickens v. Willis***, 957 S.W.2d 657, 659 (Tex.App.—Austin 1997, no pet.).

(1) Clerical error. A clerical error is a discrepancy between the entry of a judgment in the official record and the judgment as it was actually rendered. ***Universal Underwriters Ins. Co. v. Ferguson***, 471 S.W.2d 28, 29-30 (Tex.1971); ***Butler v. Continental Airlines***, 31 S.W.3d 642, 647 (Tex.App.—Houston [1st Dist.] 2000, pet. denied). A clerical error does not result from judicial reasoning or determination. ***Andrews v. Koch***, 702 S.W.2d 584, 585 (Tex.1986); ***Butler***, 31 S.W.3d at 648. It is an error in entering or recording the decision of the court. ***Escobar***, 711 S.W.2d at 231. The following are examples of clerical errors (which can be corrected by judgment nunc pro tunc): • A discrepancy in the acreage description in land. *See* ***Escobar***, 711 S.W.2d at 232. • An unintended judgment of dismissal caused by the clerk. ***Knox v. Long***, 257 S.W.2d 289, 292-93 (Tex.1953). • An error in the date of signing of the judgment. ***Traylor Bros. v. Garcia***, 949 S.W.2d 368, 369 (Tex.App.—San Antonio 1997, no writ). • A variance between the judgment signed and the judgment the court intended to sign. *E.g.*, ***Andrews***, 702 S.W.2d at 586 (probate order to sell was different from order confirming sale); ***Delaup v. Delaup***, 917 S.W.2d 411, 413 (Tex.App.—Houston [14th Dist.] 1996, no writ) (judgment did not reflect settlement agreement made in open court). • A mathematical error in the amount of damages. ***Travelers Cos. v. Wolfe***, 838 S.W.2d 708, 710 n.2 (Tex.App.—Amarillo 1992, no writ). • A mistake in the party designations. *See, e.g.*, ***Dickens***, 957 S.W.2d at 659-60 ("respondent" should have been "petitioner"); ***Newsom v. Petrilli***, 919 S.W.2d 481, 483 (Tex.App.—Austin 1996, no writ) (same). • A mistake in a party's name in the judgment. *E.g.*, ***Gonzalez***, 814 S.W.2d at 537 (changed P's name from John to Juan). • A variance between the body of the judgment actually rendered and the title of the document. *See, e.g.*, ***Butler***, 31 S.W.3d at 647 (only reference to motion for sanctions was in title of order).

(2) Judicial error. A judicial error occurs when the court considers an issue and makes an erroneous decision. *See* ***Comet Aluminum Co. v. Dibrell***, 450 S.W.2d 56, 58-59 (Tex.1970). It is an error in rendering the judgment. ***Escobar***, 711 S.W.2d at 231; ***Lagoye v. Victoria Wood Condo Ass'n***, 112 S.W.3d 777, 783 (Tex.App.—Houston [14th Dist.] 2003, no pet.). The following are examples of judicial errors (which cannot be corrected by judgment nunc pro tunc): • Mistake in award of prejudgment interest. ***Comet Aluminum***, 450 S.W.2d at 59. • Erroneous recital that supported default judgment. *E.g.*, ***Lone Star Cement Corp. v. Fair***, 467 S.W.2d 402, 405-06 (Tex.1971) (that D failed to appear & answer); ***Finlay***, 435 S.W.2d at 138-39 (that D was served but did not answer). • An unintended judgment of dismissal. ***Love v. State Bank & Trust Co.***, 90 S.W.2d 819, 820-21 (Tex.1936); ***City of Marshall v. Gonzales***, 107 S.W.3d 799, 803-04 (Tex.App.—Texarkana 2003, no pet.). • Judgment that granted a nonsuit with prejudice, instead of without prejudice. ***In re Fuselier***, 56 S.W.3d 265, 268 (Tex.App.—Houston [1st Dist.] 2001, orig. proceeding) (drafting error made by attorney). *But see* ***Thompson v. Texas Dept. of Human Res.***, 859 S.W.2d 482, 485 (Tex.App.—San Antonio 1993, no writ) (court permitted nunc pro tunc 12 years after judgment to change dismissal from "with prejudice" to "without prejudice").

§2.2 Notice. The movant must give all interested parties notice of a motion for judgment nunc pro tunc. TRCP 316. If an interested party does not get notice, the judgment is a nullity. ***West Tex. State Bank***, 723 S.W.2d at 307; *see* TRCP 316.

§3. DEADLINE

Lawyers often confuse the purpose, the deadline, and the effect of motions to modify the judgment with motions for judgment nunc pro tunc. The purpose of the motion, whether it is to correct a judicial error or a clerical error, determines the deadline for the motion.

§3.1 For motion to modify the judgment. The deadline to file a motion to modify, correct, or reform an error in the judgment is 30 days after the trial court signs the judgment. TRCP 329b(a), (g). See "Deadlines," ch. 10-D, §3, p. 639. The motion to modify the judgment can correct both types of error, judicial and clerical. ***Riner v. Briargrove Park Prop. Owners***, 976 S.W.2d 680, 682 n.1 (Tex.App.—Houston [1st Dist.] 1997, no writ); *see* ***Lane Bank Equip. Co. v. Smith S. Equip., Inc.***, 10 S.W.3d 308, 313 (Tex.2000).

§3.2 For a motion for judgment nunc pro tunc. There is no deadline for filing a motion for judgment nunc pro tunc. *See* TRCP 316. The trial court can always correct a clerical error, even after it has lost plenary power over the case. The earliest date to file a motion for judgment nunc pro tunc is the day after the court loses plenary power over the judgment. *See* ***Riner***, 976 S.W.2d at 682 (judgment nunc pro tunc can only be rendered after court loses plenary power).

§4. RESPONSE

There is no requirement for the party opposing the motion for judgment nunc pro tunc to file a response. If a party believes the error was a judicial error and not a clerical one, it should file a motion citing authority to support its allegation that the error in the judgment was not a clerical error and cannot be changed because the court no longer has plenary power.

§5. HEARING

Because the decision whether the error was clerical or judicial is a legal decision, the hearing on the motion for judgment nunc pro tunc is not for the receipt of evidence but merely for argument. *See* ***Finlay***, 435 S.W.2d at 138. However, if it is necessary to introduce facts to prove the decision was clerical and not judicial, the movant should introduce sworn testimony and have the court reporter transcribe it.

§6. RULING

§6.1 Misnomer of judgment. If the court signs a corrected judgment while it still has plenary power, it is a modified judgment, not a judgment nunc pro tunc. ***Ferguson v. Naylor***, 860 S.W.2d 123, 128-29 (Tex.App.—Amarillo 1993, writ denied); ***Alford v. Whaley***, 794 S.W.2d 920, 922 (Tex.App.—Houston [1st Dist.] 1990, no writ). Even if the court mistakenly named the judgment a "judgment nunc pro tunc," the judgment is not a judgment nunc pro tunc. ***Mathes v. Kelton***, 569 S.W.2d 876, 878 (Tex.1978); ***Go Leasing, Inc. v. Groos Nat'l Bank***, 628 S.W.2d 143, 144-45 (Tex.App.—San Antonio 1982, no writ).

§6.2 Incorrect judgment nunc pro tunc. If the court attempts to correct a judicial error by signing a judgment nunc pro tunc after the expiration of its plenary power, the judgment is void. *See* ***Dikeman v. Snell***, 490 S.W.2d 183, 186 (Tex.1973); ***Wood v. Griffin & Brand***, 671 S.W.2d 125, 132 (Tex.App.—Corpus Christi 1984, no writ). After the expiration of the court's plenary power, the court cannot change the judgment by calling the correction of a judicial error a "judgment nunc pro tunc." *See* ***Dikeman***, 490 S.W.2d at 186.

NOTE

As long as the trial court has plenary power over the judgment, it can correct any error, clerical or judicial, and a motion to correct the judgment should be titled "Motion to Modify (or Correct or Reform) the Judgment Under TRCP 329b." A TRCP 329b motion eliminates the argument whether the error in the judgment was clerical or judicial. After the court loses plenary power over the judgment, a motion to correct a clerical mistake in the judgment should be titled "Motion for Judgment Nunc Pro Tunc Under TRCP 316."

§7. REVIEW

§7.1 Appeal from granting motion. If the trial court corrects a clerical error in the judgment, the time to appeal depends on whether the court still had plenary power over the judgment.

1. Correction made before losing plenary power – modified judgment. Any change made to the judgment before the trial court loses plenary power, even a clerical change, will restart the deadlines for the appeal. ***Lane Bank***, 10 S.W.3d at 313. See "When judgment becomes final," ch. 9-C, §6.5, p. 605.

2. Correction made after losing plenary power – judgment nunc pro tunc. If, after it has lost plenary power, the court signs a judgment nunc pro tunc that corrects a clerical error, the deadline to challenge the correction begins when the trial court signs the judgment nunc pro tunc. *See* TRCP 306a(6); TRAP 4.3(b).

(1) Does not extend appellate deadlines. A judgment nunc pro tunc does not extend the appellate timetable for any complaint about the original judgment. TRCP 306a(6); *e.g.*, ***Gonzalez v. Doctors Hosp.***, 814 S.W.2d 536, 537 (Tex.App.—Houston [1st Dist.] 1991, no writ) (correction of P's name from John to Juan 6 months after judgment was signed did not extend appellate timetable); ***Cavalier Corp. v. Store Enters.***, 742 S.W.2d 785, 787 (Tex.App.—Dallas 1987, writ denied) (correction of corporate P's name after expiration of plenary power did not extend appellate deadlines).

(2) Does extend appellate deadlines. A judgment nunc pro tunc extends the appellate deadlines for any complaint about a matter not in the original judgment. TRAP 4.3(b) states that if the trial court corrects or reforms a judgment under TRCP 316 after the expiration of the trial court's plenary power, all periods run from the date of the corrected judgment, but only for complaints that would not apply to the original judgment. TRCP 329b(h) states that if the trial court signs a corrected judgment after it loses plenary power over the judgment, on appeal no complaint will be heard that could have been presented in an appeal from the original judgment. Thus, if the trial court corrected a clerical error after it lost plenary power over the judgment, and that clerical correction requires some complaint not available before the trial court signed the judgment nunc pro tunc, the deadlines to complain about that issue are extended. For example, in ***Escobar v. Escobar***, 711 S.W.2d 230, 232 (Tex.1986), a complex adverse possession case with hundreds of claimants, the trial court awarded tract 34 to Ramon and tract 38 to Rodolfo. In the 1982 final judgment, tract 38 had the wrong acreage. ***Escobar***, 711 S.W.2d at 232. In 1983, Ramon, who was awarded the adjacent tract, filed a motion to correct the judgment, which reduced the acreage in Rodolfo's tract. *Id.* When the trial court entered the order correcting the acreage, on that issue alone the appellate deadlines were extended. *Id.* Rodolfo then filed an appeal from the corrected judgment on the issue of the acreage in his tract. *Id.*

§7.2 No appeal from denial of motion. The movant cannot appeal from the order denying a motion for judgment nunc pro tunc because the order is not an appealable, final judgment. ***Shadowbrook Apts. v. Abu-Ahmad***, 783 S.W.2d 210, 211 (Tex.1990).

§7.3 Mandamus. If the trial court denies a motion for judgment nunc pro tunc, the denial may be reviewable by mandamus. *See* ***In re Bridges***, 28 S.W.3d 191, 195-96 (Tex.App.—Fort Worth 2000, orig. proceeding) (court reasoned that, because Supreme Court in ***Shadowbrook Apts.*** held that a party cannot appeal denial of a motion for judgment nunc pro tunc, P lacked an adequate remedy at law; thus, mandamus relief was appropriate).

TEXAS RULES OF CIVIL PROCEDURE
ANNOTATED RULES
TABLE OF CONTENTS

PART I. GENERAL RULES

TRCP

TABLE OF CONTENTS

TABLE OF CONTENTS

TABLE OF CONTENTS

TABLE OF CONTENTS

TRCP

TABLE OF CONTENTS

TRCP

TEXAS RULES OF PROCEDURE

PART I. GENERAL RULES

TRCP 1. OBJECTIVE OF RULES

The proper objective of rules of civil procedure is to obtain a just, fair, equitable and impartial adjudication of the rights of litigants under established principles of substantive law. To the end that this objective may be attained with as great expedition and dispatch and at the least expense both to the litigants and to the state as may be practicable, these rules shall be given a liberal construction.

See *Commentaries*, "Introduction to the Texas Rules," ch. 1-A.

History of TRCP 1: Adopted eff. Sept. 1, 1941, by order of Oct. 29, 1940 (3 Tex.B.J. 525 [1940]). Source: New rule.

TRCP 2. SCOPE OF RULES

These rules shall govern the procedure in the justice, county, and district courts of the State of Texas in all actions of a civil nature, with such exceptions as may be hereinafter stated. Where any statute in effect immediately prior to September 1, 1941, prescribed a rule of procedure in lunacy, guardianship, or estates of decedents, or any other probate proceedings in the county court differing from these Rules, and not included in the "List of Repealed Statutes," such statute shall apply; and where any statute in effect immediately prior to September 1, 1941, and not included in the "List of Repealed Statutes," prescribed a rule of procedure in any special statutory proceeding differing from these rules, such statute shall apply. All statutes in effect immediately prior to September 1, 1941, prescribing rules of procedure in bond or recognizance forfeitures in criminal cases are hereby continued in effect as rules of procedure governing such cases, but where such statutes prescribed no rules of procedure in such cases, these rules shall apply. All statutes in effect immediately prior to September 1, 1941, prescribing rules of procedure in tax suits are hereby continued in effect as rules of procedure governing such cases, but where such statutes prescribed no rules of procedure in such cases, these rules shall apply; provided, however, that Rule 117a shall control with respect to citation in tax suits.

See *Commentaries*, "Introduction to the Texas Rules," ch. 1-A.

History of TRCP 2: Amended eff. Sept. 1, 1986, by order of Apr. 10, 1986 (705-06 S.W.2d [Tex.Cases] xxxii): Deleted reference to appellate procedure. Amended eff. Dec. 31, 1947, by order of Aug. 18, 1947 (10 Tex.B.J. 389 [1947]). Amended eff. Dec. 31, 1943, by order of June 16, 1943 (6 Tex.B.J. 327 [1943]). Amended eff. Dec. 31, 1941, by order of Sept. 20, 1941 (4 Tex.B.J. 489 [1941]). Adopted eff. Sept. 1, 1941, by order of Oct. 29, 1940 (3 Tex.B.J. 525 [1940]). Source: FRCP 1 (adapted).

TRCP 3. CONSTRUCTION OF RULES

Unless otherwise expressly provided, the past, present or future tense shall each include the other; the masculine, feminine, or neuter gender shall each include the other; and the singular and plural number shall each include the other.

See Gov't Code §312.003.

History of TRCP 3: Adopted eff. Sept. 1, 1941, by order of Oct. 29, 1940 (3 Tex.B.J. 525 [1940]). Source: TRCS art. 10(2)-(4) (repealed, now Gov't Code §312.003).

TRCP 3a. LOCAL RULES

Each administrative judicial region, district court, county court, county court at law, and probate court may make and amend local rules governing practice before such courts, provided:

(1) that any proposed rule or amendment shall not be inconsistent with these rules or with any rule of the administrative judicial region in which the court is located;

(2) no time period provided by these rules may be altered by local rules;

(3) any proposed local rule or amendment shall not become effective until it is submitted and approved by the Supreme Court of Texas;

(4) any proposed local rule or amendment shall not become effective until at least thirty days after its publication in a manner reasonably calculated to bring it to the attention of attorneys practicing before the court or courts for which it is made;

(5) all local rules or amendments adopted and approved in accordance herewith are made available upon request to the members of the bar;

(6) no local rule, order, or practice of any court, other than local rules and amendments which fully comply with all requirements of this Rule 3a, shall ever be applied to determine the merits of any matter.

See Gov't Code §51.807 (local rules for fax filing); Tex.R.Jud.Admin. 10; *Commentaries*, "Introduction to the Texas Rules," ch. 1-A.

History of TRCP 3a: Amended eff. Sept. 1, 1990, by order of Apr. 24, 1990 (785-86 S.W.2d [Tex.Cases] xxxiii): To make TRCP timetables mandatory and to preclude use of unpublished local rules or other "standing" orders or local practices to determine issues of substantive merit; title changed; added (2) and (6); sections renumbered; and changed "rules" to "local rules." Amended eff. Jan. 1, 1988, by order of July 15, 1987 (733-34 S.W.2d [Tex.Cases] xxxvi). Amended eff. Sept. 1, 1986, by order of Apr. 10, 1986 (705-06 S.W.2d [Tex.Cases] xxxii): Deleted reference to appellate procedure and the words "Court of Appeals, each." Amended eff. Apr. 1, 1984, by order of Dec. 5, 1983 (661-62 S.W.2d [Tex.Cases] xxxv): To emphasize the superiority of the general rules over local rules of procedure amendment moved TRCP 817 to TRCP 3a; and to achieve uniformity, local rules require Supreme Court approval.

TRCP 4. COMPUTATION OF TIME

In computing any period of time prescribed or allowed by these rules, by order of court, or by any applicable statute, the day of the act, event, or default after which the designated period of time begins to run is not to be included. The last day of the period so computed is to be included, unless it is a Saturday, Sunday or legal holiday, in which event the period runs until the end of the next day which is not a Saturday, Sunday or legal holiday. Saturdays, Sundays and legal holidays shall not be counted for any purpose in any time period of five days or less in these rules, except that Saturdays, Sundays and legal holidays shall be counted for purposes of the three-day periods in Rules 21 and 21a, extending other periods by three days when service is made by registered or certified mail or by telephonic document transfer, and for purposes of the five-day periods provided for under Rules 748, 749, 749a, 749b, and 749c.

See Gov't Code §311.014; ***Commentaries***, "Rules for Filing Documents," ch. 1-C; "Rules for Serving Documents," ch. 1-D; "Motion for Summary Judgment," ch. 7-B.

History of TRCP 4: Amended eff. Sept. 1, 1990, by order of Apr. 24, 1990 (785-86 S.W.2d [Tex.Cases] xxxiv): Changed title; added last sentence; and omits the counting of Saturdays, Sundays, and legal holidays in all periods of less than five days with certain exceptions. Amended eff. Jan. 1, 1961, by order of July 26, 1960 (23 Tex.B.J. 619 [Oct. 1960]): Added the word "Saturday" in second sentence. Adopted eff. Sept. 1, 1941, by order of Oct. 29, 1940 (3 Tex.B.J. 525 [1940]). Source: FRCP 6(a), with changes: Omitted the Federal provision excluding intermediate Sundays or holidays when the period of time is less than seven days and the Federal reference to half-holidays.

Sosa v. Central Power & Light, 909 S.W.2d 893, 895 (Tex.1995). Plaintiffs filed their amended petition 7 days before the hearing on the motion for summary judgment. "When [TRCP 4] is applied, the day on which [Ps] filed their amendment is not counted but the 7th day after it was filed is counted.... As we held in ***Lewis***, the last day counted from the date of the filing may be the date of the hearing. Therefore, [Ps] timely filed their second amended original petition."

Lewis v. Blake, 876 S.W.2d 314, 316 (Tex.1994). TRCP 4 "applies to *any* period of time prescribed by the rules of procedure.... Applying [TRCP] 4 to [TRCP] 166a(c), the ... hearing on a motion for summary judgment may be set as early as the 21st day after the motion is served, or the 24th day if the motion is served by mail."

Peacock v. Humble, 933 S.W.2d 341, 342 (Tex. App.—Austin 1996, no writ). "The Code Construction Act and [TRCP] 4 ... are not consistent in the manner in which they address Saturdays, Sundays, and legal holidays when computing time periods of 5 days or less. [¶] When a rule of procedure conflicts with a statute, the rule yields to the legislative enactment. *At 343:* Because the 3-day filing period in the present case is statutory, the Code Construction Act's method for computing time applies rather than the method contained in Rule 4."

TRCP 5. ENLARGEMENT OF TIME

When by these rules or by a notice given thereunder or by order of court an act is required or allowed to be done at or within a specified time, the court for cause shown may, at any time in its discretion (a) with or without motion or notice, order the period enlarged if application therefor is made before the expiration of the period originally prescribed or as extended by a previous order; or (b) upon motion permit the act to be done after the expiration of the specified period where good cause is shown for the failure to act. The court may not enlarge the period for taking any action under the rules relating to new trials except as stated in these rules.

If any document is sent to the proper clerk by first-class United States mail in an envelope or wrapper properly addressed and stamped and is deposited in the mail on or before the last day for filing same, the same, if received by the clerk not more than ten days tardily, shall be filed by the clerk and be deemed filed in time. A legible postmark affixed by the United States Postal Service shall be prima facie evidence of the date of mailing.

See TRAP 4; ***Commentaries***, "Rules for Filing Documents," ch. 1-C; "Motion for Continuance," ch. 5-D; "Requests for Admissions," ch. 6-G; "Motion for New Trial," ch. 10-B.

History of TRCP 5: Amended eff. Sept. 1, 1990, by order of Apr. 24, 1990 (785-86 S.W.2d [Tex.Cases] xxxiv): Amended to make the last date for mailing under TRCP 5 coincide with the last date for filing. Amended eff. Sept. 1, 1986, by order of Apr. 10, 1986 (705-06 S.W.2d [Tex.Cases] xxxiii): Deleted reference to appellate procedure and deleted the phrases "or motions for rehearing or the period for taking an appeal ... or the period for application for writ of error in the Supreme Court" and "motion for rehearing, any matter relating to taking an appeal ... or application for writ of error." Amended eff. Jan. 1, 1976, by order of July 22, 1975 (525-26 S.W.2d [Tex.Cases] xliv): A legible postmark shall be prima facie, not conclusive, evidence of date of mailing. Amended eff. Feb. 1, 1973, by order of Oct. 3, 1972 (483-484 S.W.2d [Tex.Cases] xxi): Inserted the words "affixed by the United States Postal Service" in the final proviso. Amended eff. Jan. 1, 1971, by order of July 21, 1970 (455-56 S.W.2d [Tex.Cases] xxiv): Changed to eliminate the requirement that the date of mailing be shown by a postmark on the envelope and added an additional proviso to make a legible postmark conclusive as to the date of mailing. Amended eff. Mar. 1, 1950, by order of Oct. 12, 1949 (12 Tex.B.J. 529 [1949]): Added the first proviso at the end of the rule. Adopted eff. Sept. 1, 1941, by order of Oct. 29, 1940 (3 Tex.B.J. 525 [1940]). Source: FRCP 6(b), with changes: The second clause in the Federal rule requires a showing that the failure to act "was the result of excusable neglect." Also, specific reference is made in this rule to the time limitations relating to motions for new trial and for rehearings and to appeals and writs of error, while in the Federal rule the cross reference to such subjects is by rule number.

Stokes v. Aberdeen Ins. Co., 917 S.W.2d 267, 268 (Tex.1996). "[W]e hold that mailing the document to the proper court address is *conditionally effective* as mailing it to the proper court clerk's address. [¶] The clerk still must receive the document within 10 days to perfect the filing."

Miller Brewing Co. v. Villarreal, 829 S.W.2d 770, 771-72 (Tex.1992). A "party who finds the courthouse closed on the last day that a document must be filed ... may mail the document that day, and if it is received by the clerk not more than ten days later it is timely filed. He may also locate the clerk or judge of the court and file the document with them. In some circumstances a party may also move for an enlargement of time."

Arnold v. Shuck, 24 S.W.3d 470, 472 (Tex.App.—Texarkana 2000, pet. denied). Under TRCP 5, "a document is deemed timely filed if (1) it is sent to the proper clerk, (2) by first-class United States mail, (3) in a properly addressed and stamped envelope, (4) on or before the last day for filing, and (5) it is received not more than ten days tardily. In addition, a legible postmark affixed by the U.S. Postal Service is prima facie evidence of the date of mailing."

Milam v. Miller, 891 S.W.2d 1, 2 (Tex.App.—Amarillo 1994, writ ref'd). "[O]nce the provisions of [TRCP] 5 are met, the post office becomes a branch of the district clerk's office for purposes of filing pleadings."

TRCP 6. SUITS COMMENCED ON SUNDAY

No civil suit shall be commenced nor process issued or served on Sunday, except in cases of injunction, attachment, garnishment, sequestration, or distress proceedings; provided that citation by publication published on Sunday shall be valid.

See *Commentaries*, "Serving the Defendant with Suit," ch. 2-H; "Default Judgment," ch. 7-A.

History of TRCP 6: Amended eff. Feb. 1, 1973, by order of Oct. 3, 1972 (483-84 S.W.2d [Tex.Cases] xxii): Added provision about publication of citation on Sunday. Adopted eff. Sept. 1, 1941, by order of Oct. 29, 1940 (3 Tex.B.J. 525 [1940]). Source: TRCS art. 1974 (repealed).

Nichols v. Nichols, 857 S.W.2d 657, 659 (Tex. App.—Houston [1st Dist.] 1993, no writ). Because Ms. Nichols was served on Sunday, service was invalid.

TRCP 7. MAY APPEAR BY ATTORNEY

Any party to a suit may appear and prosecute or defend his rights therein, either in person or by an attorney of the court.

See *Commentaries*, "Rules for Serving Documents," ch. 1-D; "The Lawyer," ch. 1-H; FORMS 1H.

History of TRCP 7: Adopted eff. Sept. 1, 1941, by order of Oct. 29, 1940 (3 Tex.B.J. 525 [1940]). Source: TRCS art. 1993 (repealed).

Kunstoplast v. Formosa Plastics Corp., 937 S.W.2d 455, 456 (Tex.1996). "Generally a corporation may be represented only by a licensed attorney.... We hold, however, that ... a nonlawyer [is not precluded] from performing the specific ministerial task of depositing cash with a clerk in lieu of a cost bond."

Ayres v. Canales, 790 S.W.2d 554, 557 (Tex.1990). "Ordering a party to be represented by an attorney violates [TRCP] 7."

Computize, Inc. v. NHS Comm. Group, 992 S.W.2d 608, 612 (Tex.App.—Texarkana 1999, no pet.). "[A] response to a motion for summary judgment by a corporation must be made through an attorney."

TRCP 8. ATTORNEY IN CHARGE

On the occasion of a party's first appearance through counsel, the attorney whose signature first appears on the initial pleadings for any party shall be the attorney in charge, unless another attorney is specifically designated therein. Thereafter, until such designation is changed by written notice to the court and all other parties in accordance with Rule 21a, said attorney in charge shall be responsible for the suit as to such party.

All communications from the court or other counsel with respect to a suit shall be sent to the attorney in charge.

See *Commentaries*, "Rules for Serving Documents," ch. 1-D; FORMS 1H.

History of TRCP 8: Amended eff. Jan. 1, 1988, by order of July 15, 1987 (733-34 S.W.2d [Tex.Cases] xxxvi). Adopted eff. Sept. 1, 1941, by order of Oct. 29, 1940 (3 Tex.B.J. 525 [1940]). Source: Tex. Rules for Dist. & Cty. Cts. 45.

Sunbeam Envtl. Servs. v. Texas Workers' Comp. Ins. Facility, 71 S.W.3d 846, 851 (Tex.App.—Austin 2002, no pet.). "[Ds] correctly assert that, by signing [P's] original petition, [P's lead attorney] became [P's] attorney in charge. The record plainly shows that attorneys other than [P's lead attorney] signed and filed documents without being designated as attorneys in charge. All attorneys ... were from the same firm as [P's lead attorney]. Though [Ds] were entitled to continue to correspond with the attorney in charge, they cite no authority ... that documents filed by other attorneys from his firm were invalidly filed. Most important, [Ds] have not shown how they were harmed by the filing of documents by co-counsel in the firm of the attorney in charge." *See also* ***Reichhold Chems. v. Puremco Mfg.***, 854 S.W.2d 240, 246 (Tex.App.—Waco 1993, writ denied) (service of discovery answers on co-counsel of attorney in charge did not comply with rules).

Gem Vending v. Walker, 918 S.W.2d 656, 658 (Tex. App.—Fort Worth 1996, orig. proceeding). "Notice to an attorney is notice to a party. [O]nce an attorney has entered an appearance in a case, all communications *must* be sent to that attorney."

Palmer v. Cantrell, 747 S.W.2d 39, 41 (Tex.App.—Houston [1st Dist.] 1988, no writ). "Where a single adverse party is represented by two attorneys who are not associated in a firm, we believe that it is sufficient to serve the attorney who is designated as lead counsel because he has 'control in the management of the cause....'"

TRCP 9. NUMBER OF COUNSEL HEARD

Not more than two counsel on each side shall be heard on any question or on the trial, except in important cases, and upon special leave of the court.

See ***Commentaries***, "The Defendant's Responses & Pleadings," ch. 3.

History of TRCP 9: Adopted eff. Sept. 1, 1941, by order of Oct. 29, 1940 (3 Tex.B.J. 525 [1940]). Source: Tex. Rules for Dist. & Cty. Cts. 44.

TRCP 10. WITHDRAWAL OF ATTORNEY

An attorney may withdraw from representing a party only upon written motion for good cause shown. If another attorney is to be substituted as attorney for the party, the motion shall state: the name, address, telephone number, telecopier number, if any, and State Bar of Texas identification number of the substitute attorney; that the party approves the substitution; and that the withdrawal is not sought for delay only. If another attorney is not to be substituted as attorney for the party, the motion shall state: that a copy of the motion has been delivered to the party; that the party has been notified in writing of his right to object to the motion; whether the party consents to the motion; the party's last known address and all pending settings and deadlines. If the motion is granted, the withdrawing attorney shall immediately notify the party in writing of any additional settings or deadlines of which the attorney has knowledge at the time of the withdrawal and has not already notified the party. The Court may impose further conditions upon granting leave to withdraw. Notice or delivery to a party shall be either made to the party in person or mailed to the party's last known address by both certified and regular first class mail. If the attorney in charge withdraws and another attorney remains or becomes substituted, another attorney in charge must be designated of record with notice to all other parties in accordance with Rule 21a.

See ***Commentaries***, "The Lawyer," ch. 1-H; FORMS 1H.

History of TRCP 10: Amended eff. Sept 1, 1990, by order of Apr. 24, 1990 (785-86 S.W.2d [Tex.Cases] xxxv): Rewrote rule; repealed the present rule; and clarified the requirements for withdrawal. Amended eff. Jan. 1, 1988, by order of July 15, 1987 (733-34 S.W.2d [Tex.Cases] xxxvii): Repealed the present rule; set forth requirements for withdrawal of counsel and withdrawal with substitution of counsel; and carried forward requirements of amended TRCP 8, regarding designation of attorney in charge. Adopted eff. Sept. 1, 1941, by order of Oct. 29, 1940 (3 Tex.B.J. 525 [1940]). Source: Tex. Rules for Dist. & Cty. Cts. 46.

Rogers v. Clinton, 794 S.W.2d 9, 10 n.1 (Tex.1990). "Although a client may discharge his attorney at any time even without cause, an attorney may withdraw from representation of a client only if he satisfies the requirements of [TRCP] 10."

Gillie v. Boulas, 65 S.W.3d 219, 221 (Tex.App.—Dallas 2001, pet. denied). "A trial court abuses its discretion when it grants a motion to withdraw that does not comply with the mandatory requirements of rule 10. However, 'such error may be harmless if the court allows the party time to secure new counsel and time for the new counsel to investigate the case and prepare for trial.'" *See also* ***Walton v. Canon, Short & Gaston, P.C.***, 23 S.W.3d 143, 148 (Tex.App.—El Paso 2000, no pet.).

TRCP 11. AGREEMENTS TO BE IN WRITING

Unless otherwise provided in these rules, no agreement between attorneys or parties touching any suit pending will be enforced unless it be in writing, signed and filed with the papers as part of the record, or unless it be made in open court and entered of record.

See TRCP 191.1 (agreements in discovery matters); ***Commentaries***, "The Lawyer," ch. 1-H; "Settlement of the Suit," ch. 7-H; FORMS 1H.

History of TRCP 11: Amended eff. Jan. 1, 1988, by order of July 15, 1987 (733-34 S.W.2d [Tex.Cases] xxxvii): The amendment makes it clear that TRCP 11 is subject to modification by any other rule of Civil Procedure. Adopted eff. Sept. 1, 1941, by order of Oct. 29, 1940 (3 Tex.B.J. 526 [1940]). Source: Tex. Rules for Dist. & Cty. Cts. 47.

Compania Financiara Libano v. Simmons, 53 S.W.3d 365, 368 (Tex.2001). It is not necessary for all the terms of a settlement agreement to be incorporated into the judgment. A settlement agreement is enforceable as a contract even though its terms are not incorporated in the judgment.

Padilla v. LaFrance, 907 S.W.2d 454, 461 (Tex. 1995). "The ... filing requirement [in TRCP 11] is satisfied so long as the agreement is filed before it is sought to be enforced."

London Mkt. Cos. v. Schattman, 811 S.W.2d 550, 552 (Tex.1991). TRCP 11 "requires agreements between attorneys or parties concerning a pending suit to be in writing, signed and filed in the record of the cause to be enforceable."

Cantu v. Moore, 90 S.W.3d 821, 824 (Tex.App.—San Antonio 2002, pet. denied). "[T]he requirements of Rule 11 were satisfied when the terms of the agreement were dictated before a certified shorthand reporter, and the record reflected who was present, the terms of the settlement, and the parties' acknowledgment of the settlement."

CherCo Props. v. Law, Snakard & Gambill, P.C., 985 S.W.2d 262, 265 (Tex.App.—Fort Worth 1999, no pet.). A TRCP 11 "settlement agreement is not enforceable unless it is complete ... as to every material detail and contains all the essential elements of the agreement so the contract can be ascertained from the writing, without resort to oral testimony."

Southwestern Bell Tel. Co. v. Perez, 904 S.W.2d 817, 821 (Tex.App.—San Antonio 1995, orig. proceeding). "[A]n oral agreement [to extend discovery deadlines] is unenforceable unless it is made in open court and entered of record."

TRCP 12. ATTORNEY TO SHOW AUTHORITY

A party in a suit or proceeding pending in a court of this state may, by sworn written motion stating that he believes the suit or proceeding is being prosecuted or defended without authority, cause the attorney to be cited to appear before the court and show his authority to act. The notice of the motion shall be served upon the challenged attorney at least ten days before the hearing on the motion. At the hearing on the motion, the burden of proof shall be upon the challenged attorney to show sufficient authority to prosecute or defend the suit on behalf of the other party. Upon his failure to show such authority, the court shall refuse to permit the attorney to appear in the cause, and shall strike the pleadings if no person who is authorized to prosecute or defend appears. The motion may be heard and determined at any time before the parties have announced ready for trial, but the trial shall not be unnecessarily continued or delayed for the hearing.

See *Commentaries*, "The Lawyer," ch. 1-H; FORMS 1H.

History of TRCP 12: Amended eff. Jan. 1, 1981, by order of June 10, 1980 (599-600 S.W.2d [Tex.Cases] xxxiv): Changed the rule to permit a challenge to a plaintiff's attorney, so that all attorneys are subject to a challenge that they are in court without authority. Adopted eff. Sept. 1, 1941, by order of Oct. 29, 1940 (3 Tex.B.J. 526 [1940]). Source: TRCS art. 320 (repealed), minor textual changes and added the requirement that notice be served at least 10 days before trial of the motion.

In re Users Sys. Servs., 22 S.W.3d 331, 335 (Tex. 1999). "[T]he procedure prescribed by [TRCP] 12 for requiring an attorney to show his authority to act for a party presupposes the possibility that an attorney can be counsel of record for a party he is not authorized to represent. The rules contemplate that authorization may not have existed or may cease before the attorney has withdrawn from the case."

Air Park-Dallas Zoning Comm. v. Crow-Billingsley Airpark, Ltd., 109 S.W.3d 900, 906 (Tex.App.—Dallas 2003, n.p.h.). A TRCP 12 "motion may be properly brought when a new and different attorney attempts to appear as attorney of record purporting to advance a motion for new trial after the trial has concluded."

City of San Antonio v. River City Cabaret, 32 S.W.3d 291, 293 (Tex.App.—San Antonio 2000, pet. denied). TRCP 12 "does not authorize the trial court to dismiss a lawsuit if an authorized person appears to prosecute or defend."

Coleson v. Bethan, 931 S.W.2d 706, 712 (Tex. App.—Fort Worth 1996, no writ). A challenge under TRCP 12 "would be appropriate where perhaps the attorney ad litem's duties had been fulfilled but the attorney ad litem continued to act and failed to seek his or her discharge...."

TRCP 13. EFFECT OF SIGNING OF PLEADINGS, MOTIONS & OTHER PAPERS; SANCTIONS

The signatures of attorneys or parties constitute a certificate by them that they have read the pleading, motion, or other paper; that to the best of their knowledge, information, and belief formed after reasonable inquiry the instrument is not groundless and brought in bad faith or groundless and brought for the purpose of harassment. Attorneys or parties who shall bring a fictitious suit as an experiment to get an opinion of the court, or who shall file any fictitious pleading in a cause for such a purpose, or shall make statements in pleading which they know to be groundless and false, for the purpose of securing a delay of the trial of the cause, shall be held guilty of a contempt. If a pleading, motion or other paper is signed in violation of this rule, the court, upon motion or upon its own initiative, after notice and hearing, shall impose an appropriate sanction available under Rule 215-2b, upon the person who signed it, a represented party, or both.

Courts shall presume that pleadings, motions, and other papers are filed in good faith. No sanctions under this rule may be imposed except for good cause, the particulars of which must be stated in the sanction order. "Groundless" for purposes of this rule means no basis in law or fact and not warranted by good faith argument for the extension, modification, or reversal of existing law. A general denial does not constitute a violation of this rule. The amount requested for damages does not constitute a violation of this rule.

See CPRC chs. 9 & 10; ***Commentaries***, "Groundless or Frivolous Pleadings," ch. 1-B, §5; "Motion for Sanctions," ch. 5-J.

History of TRCP 13: Amended eff. Sept. 1, 1990, by order of Apr. 24, 1990 (785-86 S.W.2d [Tex.Cases] xxxvi): Requires notice and hearing before a court determines to impose sanctions; specifies that any sanction imposed be appropriate; eliminates the 90-day "grace" period provided in the former version of the rule; and the last par. in the comment to the 1988 change was deleted. Amended eff. Jan. 1, 1988, by order of July 15, 1987 (733-34 S.W.2d [Tex.Cases] xxxvii): TRCP 13 contained the following as the last par. in the rule: "SB No. 5, art. 2. Trial; Judgment, Section 2.01. Subtitle A, Title 2, CPRC, Chapter 9 'Frivolous Pleadings and Claims' otherwise to be effective Sept. 2, 1987, insofar as it conflicts with this rule, is repealed pursuant to Tex.Const. art. 5, §31, and Tex. Gov't Code §22.004(c)." Adopted eff. Sept. 1, 1941, by order of Oct. 29, 1940 (3 Tex.B.J. 526 [1940]). Source: Tex. Rules for Dist. & Cty. Cts. 51.

Scott & White Mem'l Hosp. v. Schexnider, 940 S.W.2d 594, 596 (Tex.1996). "[A] trial court's plenary power to act in a case does not expire until 30 days after the court has signed the judgment. A trial court's power to decide a motion for sanctions pertaining to matters occurring before judgment is no different than its power to decide any other motion during its plenary jurisdiction."

GTE Comm. Sys. Corp. v. Tanner, 856 S.W.2d 725, 731 (Tex.1993). TRCP 13 "prescribes that courts presume that papers are filed in good faith. Thus, the burden is on the party moving for sanctions to overcome this presumption."

Griffin Indus. v. Grimes, ___ S.W.3d ___ (Tex. App.—San Antonio 2003, no pet.) (No. 04-02-00430-CV; 4-23-03). "In the context of [TRCP] 13, reasonable inquiry is defined as the amount of examination that is reasonable under the circumstances of the case."

In re A.C.B., 103 S.W.3d 570, 576 (Tex.App.—San Antonio 2003, no pet.). "Findings and conclusions filed after the issuance of a sanctions order can satisfy the particularity requirement of [TRCP] 13 if the findings and conclusions indicate the trial court has examined the facts available to the litigant and the circumstances existing when the litigant filed the pleading, motion, or other paper; inform the offending party of the particular conduct warranting sanctions for the purpose of deterring similar conduct in the future; and enable the appellate court to review the order in light of the particular findings made by the trial court." *See also* ***Murphy v. Friendswood Dev. Co.***, 965 S.W.2d 708, 709 (Tex. App.—Houston [1st Dist.] 1998, no pet.).

Appleton v. Appleton, 76 S.W.3d 78, 86-87 (Tex. App.—Houston [14th Dist.] 2002, no pet.). "One purpose of [TRCP 13] is to check abuses in the pleading process; that is, to ensure that at the time the challenged pleading was filed, the litigant's position was factually grounded and legally tenable. ... Bad faith does not exist when a party merely exercises bad judgment or is negligent; rather, 'it is the conscious doing of a wrong for dishonest, discriminatory, or malicious purposes.'"

TRCP 14. AFFIDAVIT BY AGENT

Whenever it may be necessary or proper for any party to a civil suit or proceeding to make an affidavit, it may be made by either the party or his agent or his attorney.

See TRCP 197.2(d); FORM 1B:07.

History of TRCP 14: Adopted eff. Sept. 1, 1941, by order of Oct. 29, 1940 (3 Tex.B.J. 526 [1940]). Source: TRCS art. 24 (repealed).

Cantu v. Holiday Inns, 910 S.W.2d 113, 116 (Tex. App.—Corpus Christi 1995, writ denied). "A party's attorney may verify the pleading where he has knowledge of the facts, but does not have authority to verify based merely on his status as counsel. Here, counsel does not show any basis in the pleading or in her affidavit for her personal knowledge of relevant facts."

TRCP 14a. REPEALED

Repealed eff. Sept. 1, 1986, by order of Apr. 10, 1986 (705-06 S.W.2d [Tex.Cases] xxxiii).

TRCP 14b. RETURN OR OTHER DISPOSITION OF EXHIBITS

The clerk of the court in which the exhibits are filed shall retain and dispose of the same as directed by the Supreme Court.

See TRCP 75b.

History of TRCP 14b: Amended eff. Jan. 1, 1988, by order of July 15, 1987 (733-34 S.W.2d [Tex.Cases] xxxviii). Adopted eff. Jan. 1, 1967, by order of July 20, 1966 (401-02 S.W.2d [Tex.Cases] xxxi). Source: New rule.

SUPREME COURT ORDER RELATING TO RETENTION & DISPOSITION OF EXHIBITS

In compliance with the provisions of Rule 14b, the Supreme Court hereby directs that exhibits offered or admitted into evidence shall be retained and disposed of by the clerk of the court in which the exhibits are filed upon the following basis.

This order shall apply only to: (1) those cases in which judgment has been rendered on service of process by publication and in which no motion for new trial was filed within two years after judgment was signed; and, (2) all other cases in which judgment has been signed for one year and in which no appeal was perfected or in which a perfected appeal was dismissed or concluded by a final judgment as to all parties and the issuance of the appellate court's mandate such that the case is no longer pending on appeal or in the trial court.

After first giving all attorneys of record thirty days written notice that they have an opportunity to claim and withdraw the trial exhibits, the clerk, unless otherwise directed by the court, may dispose of the exhibits. If any such exhibit is desired by more than one attorney, the clerk shall make the necessary copies and prorate the cost among all the attorneys desiring the exhibit.

If the exhibit is not a document or otherwise capable of reproduction, the party who offered the exhibit shall be entitled to claim same; provided, however, that the party claiming the exhibit shall provide a photograph of said exhibit to any other party upon request and payment of the reasonable cost thereof by the other party.

History of TRCP 14b order on exhibits: Supreme Court's order relating to exhibits eff. Jan. 1, 1988, by order of July 15, 1987 (733-34 S.W.2d [Tex.Cases] xxxviii).

TRCP 14c. DEPOSIT IN LIEU OF SURETY BOND

Wherever these rules provide for the filing of a surety bond, the party may in lieu of filing the bond deposit cash or other negotiable obligation of the government of the United States of America or any agency thereof, or with leave of court, deposit a negotiable obligation of any bank or savings and loan association chartered by the government of the United States of America or any state thereof that is insured by the government of the United States of America or any agency thereof, in the amount fixed for the surety bond, conditioned in the same manner as would be a surety bond for the protection of other parties. Any interest thereon shall constitute a part of the deposit.

History of TRCP 14c: Adopted eff. Jan. 1, 1981, by order of June 10, 1980 (599-600 S.W.2d [Tex.Cases] xxxiv): New rule authorizes various deposits in lieu of a surety bond. Source: New rule.

Southwestern States Gen. Corp. v. McKenzie, 658 S.W.2d 850, 852 (Tex.App.—Dallas 1983, writ dism'd). "Because we read [TRCP] 14c as requiring no more than that the issuing bank will be one whose deposits are insured by an agency of the U.S. government, and because we can take judicial notice that Mercantile Bank at Dallas is so insured, we hold [the debtor]'s complaints about the adequacy of insurance to be without merit."

PART II. RULES OF PRACTICE IN DISTRICT & COUNTY COURTS

SECTION 1. GENERAL RULES

TRCP 15. WRITS & PROCESS

The style of all writs and process shall be "The State of Texas;" and unless otherwise specially provided by law or these rules every such writ and process shall be directed to any sheriff or any constable within the State of Texas, shall be made returnable on the Monday next after expiration of twenty days from the date of service thereof, and shall be dated and attested by the clerk with the seal of the court impressed thereon; and the date of issuance shall be noted thereon.

See Local Gov't Code §86.021; ***Commentaries***, "Serving the Defendant with Suit," ch. 2-H; "Default Judgment," ch. 7-A; FORMS 2H.

History of TRCP 15: Adopted eff. Sept. 1, 1941, by order of Oct. 29, 1940 (3 Tex.B.J. 526 [1940]). Source: TRCS art. 2286 (repealed). Eliminated the requirement that the writ be addressed to the sheriff or any constable of a specific county and that the writ be returnable to a term of court. Compare to TRCP 101.

Barker CATV Constr. v. Ampro, Inc., 989 S.W.2d 789, 792 (Tex.App.—Houston [1st Dist.] 1999, no pet.). TRCP 15 "seems to conflict with [TRCP] 99(b), which states the citation shall (1) be styled The State of Texas, and (8) *be directed to the defendant*.... [¶] The citation ... in this case is a preprinted form addressed to the sheriff or any constable of Texas, as well as to the defendant. The requirements of rules 15 and 99(b) can be harmonized by allowing the citations to be directed to both the sheriff or constable, as the officer serving it, and the defendant, as the person being served." (Internal quotes omitted.)

TRCP 16. SHALL ENDORSE ALL PROCESS

Every officer or authorized person shall endorse on all process and precepts coming to his hand the day and hour on which he received them, the manner in which he executed them, and the time and place the process was served and shall sign the returns officially.

See TRCP 107; Local Gov't Code §§85.021, 86.021; *Commentaries*, "Serving the Defendant with Suit," ch. 2-H; "Default Judgment," ch. 7-A; "Motion for New Trial," ch. 10-B.

History of TRCP 16: Amended eff. Jan. 1, 1988, by order of July 15, 1987 (733-34 S.W.2d [Tex.Cases] xxxix): To conform with TRCS art. 3926a (eff. Sept. 1, 1981; repealed, now Local Gov't Code §118.131), which authorized the commissioner's court of each county to set a "reasonable" fee for service of process; mileage no longer authorized as an expense. Adopted eff. Sept. 1, 1941, by order of Oct. 29, 1940 (3 Tex.B.J. 526 [1940]). Source: TRCS art. 6875 (repealed).

Merritt v. Harris Cty., 775 S.W.2d 17, 23 (Tex. App.—Houston [14th Dist.] 1989, writ denied). "A constable is charged with the execution of all process, warrants, and precepts which are directed to him...."

TRCP 17. OFFICER TO EXECUTE PROCESS

Except where otherwise expressly provided by law or these rules, the officer receiving any process to be executed shall not be entitled in any case to demand his fee for executing the same in advance of such execution, but his fee shall be taxed and collected as other costs in the case.

See *Commentaries*, "Serving the Defendant with Suit," ch. 2-H; "Default Judgment," ch. 7-A; FORMS 2H.

History of TRCP 17: Adopted eff. Sept. 1, 1941, by order of Oct. 29, 1940 (3 Tex.B.J. 526 [1940]). Source: TRCS art. 3911 (repealed).

Rodeheaver v. Alridge, 601 S.W.2d 51, 54 (Tex. App.—Houston [1st Dist.] 1980, writ ref'd n.r.e.). "[T]here is no statutory authorization for the constable to require an advance deposit of fees for service of citation."

TRCP 18. WHEN JUDGE DIES DURING TERM, RESIGNS OR IS DISABLED

If the judge dies, resigns, or becomes unable to hold court during the session of court duly convened for the term, and the time provided by law for the holding of said court has not expired, such death, resignation, or inability on the part of the judge shall not operate to adjourn said court for the term, but such court shall be deemed to continue in session. If a successor to such judge shall qualify and assume office during the term, or if a judge be transferred to said district from some other judicial district, he may continue to hold said court for the term provided, and all motions undisposed of shall be heard and determined by him, and statements of facts and bills of exception shall be approved by him. If the time for holding such court expires before a successor shall qualify, and before a judge can be transferred to said district from some other judicial district, then all motions pending, including those for new trial, shall stand as continued in force until such successor has qualified and assumed office, or a judge has been transferred to said district who can hold said court, and thereupon such judge shall have power to act thereon at the succeeding term, or on an earlier day in vacation, on notice to all parties to the motion, and such orders shall have the same effect as if rendered in term time. The time for allowing statement of facts and bills of exception from such orders shall date from the time the motion was decided.

See Gov't Code §74.053.

History of TRCP 18: Amended eff. Dec. 31, 1943, by order of June 16, 1943 (6 Tex.B.J. 329 [1943]). Adopted eff. Sept. 1, 1941, by order of Oct. 29, 1940 (3 Tex.B.J. 527 [1940]). Source: TRCS art. 2288 (repealed).

W.C. Banks, Inc. v. Team, Inc., 783 S.W.2d 783, 786 (Tex.App.—Houston [1st Dist.] 1990, no writ). While TRCP 18 "specifically allows the successor judge to rule on motions pending, it does not allow rendition of judgment by a judge who has heard no evidence."

TRCP 18a. RECUSAL OR DISQUALIFICATION OF JUDGES

(a) At least ten days before the date set for trial or other hearing in any court other than the Supreme Court, the Court of Criminal Appeals or the court of appeals, any party may file with the clerk of the court a motion stating grounds why the judge before whom the case is pending should not sit in the case. The grounds may include any disability of the judge to sit in the case. The motion shall be verified and must state with particularity the grounds why the judge before whom the case is pending should not sit. The motion shall be made on

TRCP 18a

personal knowledge and shall set forth such facts as would be admissible in evidence provided that facts may be stated upon information and belief if the grounds of such belief are specifically stated.

(b) On the day the motion is filed, copies shall be served on all other parties or their counsel of record, together with a notice that movant expects the motion to be presented to the judge three days after the filing of such motion unless otherwise ordered by the judge. Any other party may file with the clerk an opposing or concurring statement at any time before the motion is heard.

(c) Prior to any further proceedings in the case, the judge shall either recuse himself or request the presiding judge of the administrative judicial district to assign a judge to hear such motion. If the judge recuses himself, he shall enter an order of recusal and request the presiding judge of the administrative judicial district to assign another judge to sit, and shall make no further orders and shall take no further action in the case except for good cause stated in the order in which such action is taken.

(d) If the judge declines to recuse himself, he shall forward to the presiding judge of the administrative judicial district, in either original form or certified copy, an order of referral, the motion, and all opposing and concurring statements. Except for good cause stated in the order in which further action is taken, the judge shall make no further orders and shall take no further action in the case after filing of the motion and prior to a hearing on the motion. The presiding judge of the administrative judicial district shall immediately set a hearing before himself or some other judge designated by him, shall cause notice of such hearing to be given to all parties or their counsel, and shall make such other orders including orders on interim or ancillary relief in the pending cause as justice may require.

(e) If within ten days of the date set for trial or other hearing a judge is assigned to a case, the motion shall be filed at the earliest practicable time prior to the commencement of the trial or other hearing.

(f) If the motion is denied, it may be reviewed for abuse of discretion on appeal from the final judgment. If the motion is granted, the order shall not be reviewable, and the presiding judge shall assign another judge to sit in the case.

(g) The Chief Justice of the Supreme Court may also appoint and assign judges in conformity with this rule and pursuant to statute.

(h) If a party files a motion to recuse under this rule and it is determined by the presiding judge or the judge designated by him at the hearing and on motion of the opposite party, that the motion to recuse is brought solely for the purpose of delay and without sufficient cause, the judge hearing the motion may, in the interest of justice, impose any sanction authorized by Rule 215(2)(b)*.

* Now TRCP 215.2(b).

See Gov't Code §§74.053, 74.059(c)(3); TRAP 16; ***Commentaries***, "Motion to Challenge the Judge," ch. 5-C; FORMS 5C.

History of TRCP 18a: Amended eff. Sept. 1, 1990, by order of Apr. 24, 1990 (785-86 S.W.2d [Tex.Cases] xxxvi): "Court Administration Act" in (g) was changed to "statute." Amended eff. Jan. 1, 1988, by order of July 15, 1987 (733-34 S.W.2d [Tex.Cases] xxxix): Amended par. (a), (g), (h). Amended eff. Sept. 1, 1986, by order of Apr. 10, 1986 (705-06 S.W.2d [Tex.Cases] xxxiii): Added words "the Court of Criminal Appeals" to (a); and subsec. (1) to (g). Amended eff. Apr. 1, 1984, by order of Dec. 5, 1983 (661-62 S.W.2d [Tex.Cases] xxxvi): Changed sec. (a) textually. Adopted eff. Jan. 1, 1981, by order of June 10, 1980 (599-600 S.W.2d [Tex.Cases] xxxiv). Source: New rule.

In re Perritt, 992 S.W.2d 444, 445 (Tex.1999). "[A] judge designated by the presiding judge of the administrative judicial district to hear a recusal motion under [TRCP] 18a is also an assigned judge subject to objection and mandatory disqualification under [Gov't Code] §74.053(b)...."

In re Union Pac. Res. Co., 969 S.W.2d 427, 428 (Tex.1998). Mandamus is not available to review the denial of a motion to recuse made under the TRCPs. TRCP 18a(f) "expressly provide[s] for appellate review from a final judgment after denial of a recusal motion. If the appellate court determines ... the trial judge should have been recused, the appellate court can reverse the trial court's judgment and remand for a new trial before a different judge."

Barron v. State Att'y Gen., 108 S.W.3d 379, 382-83 (Tex.App.—Tyler 2003, no pet.). "The procedural requisites for recusal in Rule 18a(a) are mandatory, and a party who fails to conform waives his right to complain of a judge's failure to recuse himself. Likewise, a party's failure to obey the ten-day notice provision of Rule 18a(a) bars any complaint on appeal of the denial of the motion to recuse. Thus, the provisions of Rule 18a obligating a trial judge to either recuse himself or refer the motion to the presiding judge of the administrative judicial district never come into play unless and until a formal timely, written and verified motion to recuse is filed."

Spigener v. Wallis, 80 S.W.3d 174, 181 (Tex.App.—Waco 2002, no pet.). "[A] party cannot create a constitutional disqualification by filing suit against the judge."

Johnson v. Pumjani, 56 S.W.3d 670, 672-73 (Tex. App.—Houston [14th Dist.] 2001, no pet.). "Even if [P] merely refiled his previously filed motion to recuse, 'the court does not have the option of doing nothing.' The fact that a motion to recuse has been filed previously does not affect the mandatory nature of Rule 18a."

Brosseau v. Ranzau, 28 S.W.3d 235, 238 (Tex. App.—Beaumont 2000, no pet.). "[T]he judge named in the motion [to recuse is] not ... permitted to act in *any* way other than the two options provided for in the rule. [I]f a trial court fails to comply with the strictures provided in Rule 18a, all actions taken by the judge subsequent to such violation are void."

In re Rio Grande Valley Gas Co., 987 S.W.2d 167, 179 (Tex.App.—Corpus Christi 1999, orig. proceeding). TRCP 18a(d) and (f) and Gov't Code §74.059(c)(3) "clearly contemplate a hearing will be held on a motion to recuse. A hearing affords the movants an opportunity to develop a record regarding the motions to recuse. "

TRCP 18b. GROUNDS FOR DISQUALIFICATION & RECUSAL OF JUDGES

(1) Disqualification. Judges shall disqualify themselves in all proceedings in which:

(a) they have served as a lawyer in the matter in controversy, or a lawyer with whom they previously practiced law served during such association as a lawyer concerning the matter; or

(b) they know that, individually or as a fiduciary, they have an interest in the subject matter in controversy; or

(c) either of the parties may be related to them by affinity or consanguinity within the third degree.

(2) Recusal. A judge shall recuse himself in any proceeding in which:

(a) his impartiality might reasonably be questioned;

(b) he has a personal bias or prejudice concerning the subject matter or a party, or personal knowledge of disputed evidentiary facts concerning the proceeding;

(c) he or a lawyer with whom he previously practiced law has been a material witness concerning it;

(d) he participated as counsel, adviser or material witness in the matter in controversy, or expressed an opinion concerning the merits of it, while acting as an attorney in government service;

(e) he knows that he, individually or as a fiduciary, or his spouse or minor child residing in his household, has a financial interest in the subject matter in controversy or in a party to the proceeding, or any other interest that could be substantially affected by the outcome of the proceeding;

(f) he or his spouse, or a person within the third degree of relationship to either of them, or the spouse of such a person:

(i) is a party to the proceeding, or an officer, director, or trustee of a party;

(ii) is known by the judge to have an interest that could be substantially affected by the outcome of the proceeding;

(iii) is to the judge's knowledge likely to be a material witness in the proceeding.

(g) he or his spouse, or a person within the first degree of relationship to either of them, or the spouse of such a person, is acting as a lawyer in the proceeding.

(3) A judge should inform himself about his personal and fiduciary financial interests, and make a reasonable effort to inform himself about the personal financial interests of his spouse and minor children residing in his household.

(4) In this rule:

(a) "proceeding" includes pretrial, trial, or other stages of litigation;

(b) the degree of relationship is calculated according to the civil law system;

(c) "fiduciary" includes such relationships as executor, administrator, trustee, and guardian;

(d) "financial interest" means ownership of a legal or equitable interest, however small, or a relationship as director, adviser, or other active participant in the affairs of a party, except that:

(i) ownership in a mutual or common investment fund that holds securities is not a "financial interest" in such securities unless the judge participates in the management of the fund;

(ii) an office in an educational, religious, charitable, fraternal, or civic organization is not a "financial interest" in securities held by the organization;

(iii) the proprietary interest of a policyholder in a mutual insurance company, of a depositor in a mutual savings association, or a similar proprietary interest, is a "financial interest" in the organization only if the outcome of the proceeding could substantially affect the value of the interest;

(iv) ownership of government securities is a "financial interest" in the issuer only if the outcome of the proceeding could substantially affect the value of the securities;

(v) an interest as a taxpayer or utility ratepayer, or any similar interest, is not a "financial interest" unless the outcome of the proceeding could substantially affect the liability of the judge or a person related to him within the third degree more than other judges.

(5) The parties to a proceeding may waive any ground for recusal after it is fully disclosed on the record.

(6) If a judge does not discover that he is recused under subparagraphs (2)(e) or (2)(f)(iii)* until after he has devoted substantial time to the matter, he is not required to recuse himself if he or the person related to him divests himself of the interest that would otherwise require recusal.

* Editor's Note: This should probably read "(2)(f)(ii)."

See Tex.Const. art. 5, §11; Gov't Code §§21.005, 74.053, 74.059(c)(3), 573.022-573.025; TRAP 16; ***Commentaries***, "Motion to Challenge the Judge," ch. 5-C; FORMS 5C.

History of TRCP 18b: Amended eff. Sept. 1, 1990, by order of Apr. 24, 1990 (785-86 S.W.2d [Tex.Cases] xxxvii): Rule entirely rewritten; expanded the grounds for a judge's mandatory recusal from those in earlier TRCP 18b(2). Adopted eff. Jan. 1, 1988, by order of July 15, 1987 (733-34 S.W.2d [Tex.Cases] xl). Source: New rule. Former TRCP 18b repealed eff. Sept. 1, 1986, by order of Apr. 10, 1986 (705-06 S.W.2d [Tex.Cases] xxxiv).

In re O'Connor, 92 S.W.3d 446, 449 (Tex.2002). "Rule 18b(1)(a) ... recognizes that a judge is vicariously disqualified under the Constitution as having 'been counsel in the case' if a lawyer with whom the judge previously practiced law served as counsel to a party concerning the matter during their association."

Sommers v. Concepcion, 20 S.W.3d 27, 42 (Tex. App.—Houston [14th Dist.] 2000, pet. denied). TRCP 18b(2)(c) "requires a judge to recuse himself in any proceeding in which he is called as a material witness. Here, ... the judge [was called] as a witness in another proceeding, a disciplinary proceeding."

Pena v. Pena, 986 S.W.2d 696, 700 (Tex.App.—Corpus Christi 1998), *pet. denied*, 8 S.W.3d 639 (Tex.1999). "[T]he interest of a judge, in order that he may be disqualified, must, in general, be a direct pecuniary or property interest in the subject matter of litigation. [¶] [W]e conclude that the trial judge's attorney-client relationship with opposing counsel does not amount to a constitutional disqualification."

Ludlow v. Deberry, 959 S.W.2d 265, 271 (Tex. App.—Houston [14th Dist.] 1997, no writ). "[J]udicial remarks during the course of a trial that are critical or disapproving or even hostile to counsel, parties, or their cases, ordinarily do not support recusal. Such remarks may do so if they reveal an opinion deriving from an extrajudicial source and such remarks will do so if they reveal such a high degree of favoritism or antagonism as to make fair judgment impossible."

TRCP 18c. RECORDING & BROADCASTING OF COURT PROCEEDINGS

A trial court may permit broadcasting, televising, recording, or photographing of proceedings in the courtroom only in the following circumstances:

(a) in accordance with guidelines promulgated by the Supreme Court for civil cases, or

(b) when broadcasting, televising, recording, or photographing will not unduly distract participants or impair the dignity of the proceedings and the parties have consented, and consent to being depicted or recorded is obtained from each witness whose testimony will be broadcast, televised, or photographed, or

(c) the broadcasting, televising, recording, or photographing of investiture, or ceremonial proceedings.

History of TRCP 18c: Adopted eff. Sept. 1, 1990, by order of Apr. 24, 1990 (785-86 S.W.2d [Tex.Cases] xxxix): New rule to provide guidelines for broadcasting, televising, recording, and photographing court proceedings. Source: New rule.

TRCP 19. NON-ADJOURNMENT OF TERM

Every term of court shall commence and convene by operation of law at the time fixed by statute without any act, order, or formal opening by a judge or other official thereof, and shall continue to be open at all times until and including the last day of the term unless sooner adjourned by the judge thereof.

History of TRCP 19: Amended eff. Dec. 31, 1943, by order of June 16, 1943 (6 Tex.B.J. 330 [1943]). Adopted eff. Sept. 1, 1941, by order of Oct. 29, 1940 (3 Tex.B.J. 527 [1940]). Source: TRCS art. 1922 (repealed).

TRCP 20. MINUTES READ & SIGNED

On the last day of the session, the minutes shall be read, corrected and signed in open court by the judge. Each special judge shall sign the minutes of such proceedings as were had by him.

History of TRCP 20: Adopted eff. Sept. 1, 1941, by order of Oct. 29, 1940 (3 Tex.B.J. 527 [1940]): Eliminated former requirement that minutes be signed daily; and extension of the rule to judges of both district and county courts. Source: TRCS art. 1918 (repealed).

TRCP 21. FILING & SERVING PLEADINGS & MOTIONS

Every pleading, plea, motion or application to the court for an order, whether in the form of a motion, plea or other form of request, unless presented during a hearing or trial, shall be filed with the clerk of the court in writing, shall state the grounds therefor, shall set forth the relief or order sought, and at the same time a true copy shall be served on all other parties, and shall be noted on the docket.

An application to the court for an order and notice of any hearing thereon, not presented during a hearing or trial, shall be served upon all other parties not less than three days before the time specified for the hearing unless otherwise provided by these rules or shortened by the court.

If there is more than one other party represented by different attorneys, one copy of such pleading shall be delivered or mailed to each attorney in charge.

The party or attorney of record, shall certify to the court compliance with this rule in writing over signature on the filed pleading, plea, motion or application.

After one copy is served on a party that party may obtain another copy of the same pleading upon tendering reasonable payment for copying and delivering.

See *Commentaries*, "Rules of Pleading," ch. 1-B; "Rules for Filing Documents," ch. 1-C; "Rules for Serving Documents," ch. 1-D; "Motion in Limine," ch. 5-E; "Motion to Seal Court Records," ch. 5-K.

History of TRCP 21: Amended eff. Sept. 1, 1990, by order of Apr. 24, 1990 (785-86 S.W.2d [Tex.Cases] xxxix): Rule entirely rewritten to require filing and service of all pleadings and motions on all parties and to consolidate notice and service TRCP 21, 72 and 73. Amended eff. Jan. 1, 1981, by order of June 10, 1980 (599-600 S.W.2d [Tex.Cases] xxxv): The rule is broadened to encompass matters other than motions and to require three-day notice unless the period is shortened. Amended eff. Jan. 1, 1978, by order of July 11, 1977 (553-54 S.W.2d [Tex.Cases] xlii): Deleted phrase "if it relates to a pending suit" from the end of the first sentence and phrase "If the motion does not relate to a pending suit" from the beginning of the second sentence. Amended eff. Dec. 31, 1947, by order of Aug. 18, 1947 (10 Tex.B.J. 390 [1947]). Amended eff. Dec. 31, 1941, by order of Sept. 20, 1941 (4 Tex.B.J. 491 [1991]). Adopted eff. Sept. 1, 1941, by order of Oct. 29, 1940 (3 Tex.B.J. 527 [1940]). Source: TRCS art. 2291 (repealed).

Tate v. E.I. du Pont de Nemours & Co., 934 S.W.2d 83, 84 (Tex.1996). "[T]he filing [of P's motion for new trial] became complete when she … paid the filing fee [after the motion was overruled by operation of law, but within the trial court's plenary jurisdiction]."

Jamar v. Patterson, 868 S.W.2d 318, 319 (Tex. 1993). "[T]he date of filing is when the document is first tendered to the clerk [even though no filing fee was paid]. The filing was completed … when Jamar paid the filing fee. *At n.3:* The filing is not completed until the fee is paid, and absent emergency or other rare circumstances, the court should not consider it before then."

Magnuson v. Mullen, 65 S.W.3d 815, 824 (Tex. App.—Fort Worth 2002, pet. denied). "Rule 21 requires that a party be afforded at least 3 days' notice of a hearing date. [T]he 3-day notice requirement did not apply when the March 23rd hearing was reset to March 24."

TRCP 21a. METHODS OF SERVICE

Every notice required by these rules, and every pleading, plea, motion, or other form of request required to be served under Rule 21, other than the citation to be served upon the filing of a cause of action and except as otherwise expressly provided in these rules, may be served by delivering a copy to the party to be served, or the party's duly authorized agent or attorney of record, as the case may be, either in person or by agent or by courier receipted delivery or by certified or registered mail, to the party's last known address, or by telephonic document transfer to the recipient's current telecopier number, or by such other manner as the court in its discretion may direct. Service by mail shall be complete upon deposit of the paper, enclosed in a postpaid, properly addressed wrapper, in a post office or official depository under the care and custody of the United States Postal Service. Service by telephonic document transfer after 5:00 p.m. local time of the recipient shall be deemed served on the following day. Whenever a party has the right or is required to do some act within a prescribed period after the service of a notice or other paper upon him and the notice or paper is served upon by mail or by telephonic document transfer, three days shall be added to the prescribed period. Notice may be served by a party to the suit, an attorney of record, a sheriff or constable, or by any other person competent to testify. The party or attorney of record shall certify to the court compliance with this rule in writing over signature and on the filed instrument. A certificate by a party or an attorney of record, or the return of an officer, or the affidavit of any person showing service of a notice shall be prima facie evidence of the fact of service. Nothing herein shall preclude any party from offering proof that the notice or instrument was not received, or, if service was by mail, that it was not received within three days from the date of deposit in a post office or official depository under the care and custody of the United States Postal Service, and upon so finding, the court may extend the time for taking the action required of such party or grant such other relief as it deems just. The provisions hereof relating to the method of service of notice are cumulative of all other methods of service prescribed by these rules.

See *Commentaries*, "Rules of Pleading," ch. 1-B; "Rules for Filing Documents," ch. 1-C; "Rules for Serving Documents," ch. 1-D; FORMS 1B:09-10.

History of TRCP 21a: Amended eff. Sept. 1, 1990, by order of Apr. 24, 1990 (785-86 S.W.2d [Tex.Cases] xl): To allow for service by current delivery means and technologies; title changed; expanded to include not just notice but "every pleading, plea, motion, or other form of request required to be served under Rule 21"; and allows service by telephonic document transfer. Amended eff. Apr. 1, 1984, by order of Dec. 5, 1983 (661-62 S.W.2d [Tex.Cases] xxxvii): This rule consolidates TRCP 21a and TRCP 21b. Amended eff. Jan. 1, 1981, by order of June 10, 1980 (599-600 S.W.2d [Tex.Cases] xxxvi): The next to last sentence from the end of the former rule requiring three-day notice is deleted because TRCP 21 is concurrently amended to require that notice. Amended eff. Jan. 1, 1978, by order of July 11, 1977 (553-54 S.W.2d [Tex.Cases] xlii): Deleted phrase "not relating to a pending suit" in the next to last sentence. Amended eff. Feb. 1, 1973, by order of Oct. 3, 1972 (483-84 S.W.2d [Tex.Cases] xxiii): Substituted words "Postal Service" for "Post Office Department" and inserted sentence authorizing the court to grant an extension of time or other relief upon finding that a notice or document was not received or, if service was by mail, was not received within three days from the date of deposit in the mail. Amended eff. Jan. 1, 1971, by order of July 21, 1970 (455-56 S.W.2d [Tex.Cases] xxv): The second and third sentences were added to make service by mail complete upon proper deposit in the mail and to enlarge the time for acting after service by mail; eliminated the sentence which provided for notice of a motion by filing and entry on the motion docket. Adopted eff. Dec. 31, 1947, by order of Aug. 18, 1947 (10 Tex.B.J. 390 [1947]). Source: New rule.

Wembley Inv. Co. v. Herrera, 11 S.W.3d 924, 928 (Tex.1999). "[W]hen the sender of a document relies on office routine or custom to support an inference that the document was mailed, the sender must provide corroborating evidence that the practice was actually carried out. ... At best, Upchurch's affidavit is only an 'opinion[] that the notice w[as] *probably* sent,' and does not controvert [D's] attorneys' affidavits attesting that the nonsuit motion was not received."

Thomas v. Ray, 889 S.W.2d 237, 238-39 (Tex.1994). "When a letter, properly addressed and postage prepaid, is mailed, there exists a presumption that the notice was duly received by the addressee. This presumption may be rebutted by an offer of proof of nonreceipt. [¶] [P] presented verified proof that the letter had been mailed and thereby raised the presumption of receipt. [¶] [D] failed to bring forward any verified proof that he did not receive [Ps'] designation of experts. [D], therefore, failed to rebut the presumption that the document was received."

Lewis v. Blake, 876 S.W.2d 314, 315 (Tex.1994). TRCP 21a "extends that minimum notice by 3 days when the motion is served by mail. *At 316:* [The] hearing on a motion for summary judgment may be set as early as the 21st day after the motion is served, or the 24th day if the motion is served by mail."

Gonzales v. Surplus Ins. Servs., 863 S.W.2d 96, 102 (Tex.App.—Beaumont 1993, writ denied), *overruled on other grounds*, ***Carpenter v. Cimarron Hydrocarbons***, 98 S.W.3d 682 (Tex.2002). "[W]here it is shown ... that a party has fully complied with the notice requirements set forth in [TRCP] 21a..., yet fails to establish actual receipt of notice upon opposing party or counsel, such notice shall be sufficient constructive notice where it is shown that the intended recipient engaged in instances of selective acceptance/refusal of certified mail relating to the case."

TRCP 21b. SANCTIONS FOR FAILURE TO SERVE OR DELIVER COPY OF PLEADINGS & MOTIONS

If any party fails to serve on or deliver to the other parties a copy of any pleading, plea, motion, or other application to the court for an order in accordance with Rules 21 and 21a, the court may in its discretion, after notice and hearing, impose an appropriate sanction available under Rule 215-2b*.

* Now TRCP 215.2(b).

See *Commentaries*, "Rules for Filing Documents," ch. 1-C; "Rules for Serving Documents," ch. 1-D; "Motion for Sanctions," ch. 5-J; FORMS 5J.

History of TRCP 21b: Adopted eff. Sept. 1, 1990, by order of Apr. 24, 1990 (785-86 S.W.2d [Tex.Cases] xl): Repealed provisions of TRCP 73, to the extent same are to remain operative, were moved to this new TRCP 21b to provide sanctions for the failure to serve any filed documents on all parties. Former TRCP 21b repealed eff. Apr. 1, 1984, by order of Dec. 5, 1983 (661-62 S.W.2d [Tex.Cases] xxxvii). Source: New rule.

Union City Body Co. v. Ramirez, 911 S.W.2d 196, 201 (Tex.App.—San Antonio 1995, orig. proceeding). "[A] complaint of inadequate notice under [TRCP] 21 or 21a is waived absent a timely and specific objection."

TRCP 21c. REPEALED

Repealed eff. Sept. 1, 1986, by order of Apr. 10, 1986 (705-06 S.W.2d [Tex.Cases] xxxiv).

SECTION 2. INSTITUTION OF SUIT

TRCP 22. COMMENCED BY PETITION

A civil suit in the district or county court shall be commenced by a petition filed in the office of the clerk.

See *Commentaries*, "Plaintiff's Original Petition," ch. 2-B; "Serving the Defendant with Suit," ch. 2-H; FORMS 2B.

History of TRCP 22: Adopted eff. Sept. 1, 1941, by order of Oct. 29, 1940 (3 Tex.B.J. 527 [1940]). Source: TRCS art. 1971 (repealed).

Billings v. Concordia Heritage Ass'n, 960 S.W.2d 688, 690 n.4 (Tex.App.—El Paso 1997, pet. denied). "In Texas an action is commenced in the district or county court by filing a petition in the office of the clerk. Judicial action without jurisdiction is void."

TRCP 23. SUITS TO BE NUMBERED CONSECUTIVELY

It shall be the duty of the clerk to designate the suits by regular consecutive numbers, called file numbers, and he shall mark on each paper in every case the file number of the cause.

See *Commentaries*, "Rules for Filing Documents," ch. 1-C.

History of TRCP 23: Adopted eff. Sept. 1, 1941, by order of Oct. 29, 1940 (3 Tex.B.J. 527 [1940]). Source: Tex. Rules for Dist. & Cty. Cts. 82.

TRCP 24. DUTY OF CLERK

When a petition is filed with the clerk he shall indorse thereon the file number, the day on which it was filed and the time of filing, and sign his name officially thereto.

See TRCP 74; *Commentaries*, "Rules for Filing Documents," ch. 1-C.

History of TRCP 24: Adopted eff. Sept. 1, 1941, by order of Oct. 29, 1940 (3 Tex.B.J. 527 [1940]). Source: TRCS art. 1972 (repealed).

Biffle v. Morton Rubber Indus., 785 S.W.2d 143, 144 (Tex.1990). "An instrument is deemed in law filed at the time it is delivered to the clerk, regardless of whether the instrument is filemarked."

TRCP 25. CLERK'S FILE DOCKET

Each clerk shall keep a file docket which shall show in convenient form the number of the suit, the names of the attorneys, the names of the parties to the suit, and the nature thereof, and, in brief form, the officer's return on the process, and all subsequent proceedings had in the case with the dates thereof.

See *Commentaries*, "Rules for Filing Documents," ch. 1-C.

History of TRCP 25: Adopted eff. Sept. 1, 1941, by order of Oct. 29, 1940 (3 Tex.B.J. 527 [1940]). Source: TRCS art. 1973 (repealed).

TRCP 26. CLERK'S COURT DOCKET

Each clerk shall also keep a court docket in a permanent record that shall include the number of the case and the names of parties, the names of the attorneys, the nature of the action, the pleas, the motions, and the ruling of the court as made.

See *Commentaries*, "Rules for Filing Documents," ch. 1-C.

History of TRCP 26: Amended eff. Sept. 1, 1990, by order of Apr. 24, 1990 (785-86 S.W.2d [Tex.Cases] xli): Changed "well-bound book" to "permanent record." Adopted eff. Sept. 1, 1941, by order of Oct. 29, 1940 (3 Tex.B.J. 528 [1940]). Source: Tex. Rules for Dist. & Cty. Cts. 79.

First Nat'l Life Ins. Co. v. Herring, 318 S.W.2d 119, 123 (Tex.App.—Waco 1958, no writ). "The making of entries on the docket sheet is primarily the duty of the clerk."

TRCP 27. ORDER OF CASES

The cases shall be placed on the docket as they are filed.

See *Commentaries*, "Rules for Filing Documents," ch. 1-C.

History of TRCP 27: Adopted eff. Sept. 1, 1941, by order of Oct. 29, 1940 (3 Tex.B.J. 528 [1940]). Source: Tex. Rules for Dist. & Cty. Cts. 80.

SECTION 3. PARTIES TO SUITS

TRCP 28. SUITS IN ASSUMED NAME

Any partnership, unincorporated association, private corporation, or individual doing business under an assumed name may sue or be sued in its partnership, assumed or common name for the purpose of enforcing for or against it a substantive right, but on a motion by any party or on the court's own motion the true name may be substituted.

See *Commentaries*, "Plaintiff's Original Petition," ch. 2-B; FORMS 2B. In 1995, the Legislature enacted the Texas Uniform Unincorporated Non-Profit Association Act, which makes unincorporated non-profit associations legal entities responsible for their contracts and torts and relieves their members from individual liability. TRCS art. 1396-70.01 §7.

History of TRCP 28: Amended eff. Jan. 1, 1971, by order of July 21, 1970 (455-56 S.W.2d [Tex.Cases] xxv): Added "an individual doing business under an assumed name," and partnership or common name to make the rule applicable to a private corporation and authorize the true name of the party to be substituted on motion. Adopted eff. Sept. 1, 1941, by order of Oct. 29, 1940 (3 Tex.B.J. 528 [1940]). Source: Part of FRCP 17(b).

Sixth RMA Partners v. Sibley, 111 S.W.3d 46, 53 (Tex.2003). TRCP 28 "requires that the correct legal name be substituted, but it does not mandate the procedural method by which substitution may be accomplished. ... Under [TRCP] 28, the 'true name' may be substituted 'on a motion by any party or on the court's own motion.' Therefore, the correct legal name may be substituted by filing either a motion requesting substitution or a pleading that substitutes the correct legal name for the assumed name." *See, e.g.,* ***Holberg & Co. v. Citizens Nat'l Assur. Co.***, 856 S.W.2d 515, 518 (Tex. App.—Houston [1st Dist.] 1993, no writ) (trial court had authority to substitute proprietor for unincorporated sole proprietorship).

Chilkewitz v. Hyson, 22 S.W.3d 825, 830 (Tex. 1999). Rule 28 "is not a tolling provision when a party is sued in the name under which it conducts business and that party has actual notice of the suit. Rule 28 allows suit directly against the correct party in its assumed name. To the extent that [earlier opinions] indicate that Rule 28 is a tolling provision, we disapprove of them."

Cox v. Thee Evergreen Ch., 836 S.W.2d 167, 171 (Tex.1992). TRCP 28 "treat[s] unincorporated associations as legal entities.... Rule 28 generally does not affect substantive rights."

TRCP 29. SUIT ON CLAIM AGAINST DISSOLVED CORPORATION

When no receiver has been appointed for a corporation which has dissolved, suit may be instituted on any claim against said corporation as though the same had not been dissolved, and service of process may be obtained on the president, directors, general manager, trustee, assignee, or other person in charge of the affairs of the corporation at the time it was dissolved, and judgment may be rendered as though the corporation had not been dissolved.

See Bus. Corp. Act art. 7.12; TRCP 160.

History of TRCP 29: Adopted eff. Sept. 1, 1941, by order of Oct. 29, 1940 (3 Tex.B.J. 528 [1940]). Source: TRCS art. 1391 (repealed).

TRCP 30. PARTIES TO SUITS

Assignors, endorsers and other parties not primarily liable upon any instruments named in the chapter of the Business and Commerce Code, dealing with commercial paper, may be jointly sued with their principal obligors, or may be sued alone in the cases provided for by statute.

See ***Commentaries***, "Plaintiff's Original Petition," ch. 2-B; FORMS 2B.

History of TRCP 30: Amended eff. Jan. 1, 1988, by order of July 15, 1987 (733-34 S.W.2d [Tex.Cases] xl). Adopted eff. Sept. 1, 1941, by order of Oct. 29, 1940 (3 Tex.B.J. 528 [1940]). Source: TRCS art. 572 (repealed).

Reed v. Buck, 370 S.W.2d 867, 872 (Tex.1963). "We hold that when a party signs a note in the capacity of a maker, the payee (or one standing in the shoes of a payee) may sue such maker singly and proceed to judgment upon the note without joining in the suit another or others who may also appear upon the note as co-makers."

TRCP 31. SURETY NOT TO BE SUED ALONE

No surety shall be sued unless his principal is joined with him, or unless a judgment has previously been rendered against his principal, except in cases otherwise provided for in the law and these rules.

See CPRC §17.001; ***Commentaries***, "Motion to Abate—Challenging the Suit," ch. 3-H.

History of TRCP 31: Adopted eff. Sept. 1, 1941, by order of Oct. 29, 1940 (3 Tex.B.J. 528 [1940]). Source: TRCS art. 6251 (repealed).

McGrath v. Bank of the W., 786 S.W.2d 754, 757 (Tex.App.—Houston [1st Dist.] 1990, no writ). "[T]he Bank acquired and perfected a valid and enforceable security interest in the certificate of deposit as security for Armstrong's debt. As such, the Bank was not required, under [TRCP] 31, to join Armstrong and attempt collection prior to exercising its rights in the collateral."

Hart v. First Fed. S&L Ass'n, 727 S.W.2d 723, 726 (Tex.App.—Austin 1987, no writ). "[T]he necessity of joining the principal debtor in the creditor's suit against the guarantor is subject to an exception for cases where the debtor is 'hopelessly insolvent.' *At n.1:* [TRCP] 31 incorporates, in effect, the provisions of [CPRC] §17.001."

TRCP 32. MAY HAVE QUESTION OF SURETYSHIP TRIED

When any suit is brought against two or more defendants upon any contract, any one or more of the defendants being surety for the other, the surety may cause the question of suretyship to be tried and determined upon the issue made for the parties defendant at the trial of the cause, or at any time before or after the trial or at a subsequent term. Such proceedings shall not delay the suit of the plaintiff.

See Bus. & Com. Code, ch. 34; ***Commentaries***, "Motion to Abate—Challenging the Suit," ch. 3-H.

History of TRCP 32: Adopted eff. Sept. 1, 1941, by order of Oct. 29, 1940 (3 Tex.B.J. 528 [1940]). Source: TRCS art. 6246 (repealed).

TRCP 33. SUITS BY OR AGAINST COUNTIES

Suits by or against a county or incorporated city, town or village shall be in its corporate name.

See ***Commentaries***, "Plaintiff's Original Petition," ch. 2-B.

History of TRCP 33: Adopted eff. Sept. 1, 1941, by order of Oct. 29, 1940 (3 Tex.B.J. 528 [1940]). Source: TRCS art. 1980 (repealed).

Scott v. Graham, 292 S.W.2d 324, 327 (Tex.1956). "A county is not made a party to a suit by joining the commissioners and other officials of the county as parties."

TRCP 34. AGAINST SHERIFF, ETC.

Whenever a sheriff, constable, or a deputy or either has been sued for damages for any act done in his official character, and has taken an indemnifying bond for the acts upon which the suit is based, he may make the principal and surety on such bond parties defendant in such suit, and the cause may be continued to obtain service on such parties.

History of TRCP 34: Adopted eff. Sept. 1, 1941, by order of Oct. 29, 1940 (3 Tex.B.J. 528 [1940]). Source: TRCS art. 1988 (repealed).

Agricultural Bond & Credit Corp. v. Shepherd, 69 S.W.2d 213, 215 (Tex.App.—Amarillo 1934, no writ). Under what is now TRCP 34, the sheriff has "a right to bring in the principal and surety on the indemnity bond given him."

TRCP 35. ON OFFICIAL BONDS

In suits brought by the State or any county, city, independent school district, irrigation district, or other political subdivision of the State, against any officer who has held an office for more than one term, or against any depository which has been such depository for more than one term, or has given more than one official bond, the sureties on each and all such bonds may be joined as defendants in the same suit whenever it is difficult to determine when the default sued for occurred and which set of sureties on such bonds is liable therefor.

History of TRCP 35: Amended eff. Dec. 31, 1943, by order of June 16, 1943 (6 Tex.B.J. 331 [1943]): Interpolated "irrigation district, or other political subdivision of the State"; omitted the second "or"; added a comma after "city." Adopted eff. Sept. 1, 1941, by order of Oct. 29, 1940 (3 Tex.B.J. 528 [1940]). Source: TRCS art. 1989 (repealed).

TRCP 36. DIFFERENT OFFICIALS & BONDSMEN

In suits by the State upon the official bond of a State officer, any subordinate officer who has given bond, payable either to the State or such superior officer, to cover all or part of the default sued for, together with the sureties on his official bond, may be joined as defendants with such superior officer and his bondsmen whenever it is alleged in the petition that both of such officers are liable for the money sued for.

History of TRCP 36: Adopted eff. Sept. 1, 1941, by order of Oct. 29, 1940 (3 Tex.B.J. 529 [1940]). Source: TRCS art. 1990 (repealed).

TRCP 37. ADDITIONAL PARTIES

Before a case is called for trial, additional parties, necessary or proper parties to the suit, may be brought in, either by the plaintiff or the defendant, upon such terms as the court may prescribe; but not at a time nor in a manner to unreasonably delay the trial of the case.

See ***Commentaries***, "Plaintiff's Original Petition," ch. 2-B; "The Answer—Denying Liability," ch. 3-E.

History of TRCP 37: Adopted eff. Sept. 1, 1941, by order of Oct. 29, 1940 (3 Tex.B.J. 529 [1940]). Source: TRCS art. 1992 (repealed).

Gomez v. Kestermeier, 924 S.W.2d 210, 212 (Tex. App.—Eastland 1996, writ denied). Defendants urge "that the trial court erred by rendering judgment without the joinder of ... the grantors. ... Even though they did raise the issue at trial, [Ds] did not preserve the issue for review because ... they made no effort themselves to join [the grantors] as parties."

TRCP 38. THIRD-PARTY PRACTICE

(a) When defendant may bring in third party. At any time after commencement of the action a defending party, as a third-party plaintiff, may cause a citation and petition to be served upon a person not a party to the action who is or may be liable to him or to the plaintiff for all or part of the plaintiff's claim against him. The third-party plaintiff need not obtain leave to make the service if he files the third-party petition not later than thirty (30) days after he serves his original answer. Otherwise, he must obtain leave on motion upon notice to all parties to the action. The person served, hereinafter called the third-party defendant, shall make his defenses to the third-party plaintiff's claim under the rules applicable to the defendant, and his counterclaims against the third-party plaintiff and cross-claims against other third-party defendants as provided in Rule 97. The third-party defendant may assert against the plaintiff any defenses which the third-party plaintiff has to the plaintiff's claim. The third-party defendant may also assert any claim against the plaintiff arising out of the transaction or occurrence that is the subject matter of the plaintiff's claim against the third-party plaintiff. The plaintiff may assert any claim against the third-party defendant arising out of the transaction or occurrence that is the subject matter of the plaintiff's claim against the third-party plaintiff, and the third-party defendant thereupon shall assert his defenses and his counterclaims and cross-claims. Any party may move to strike the third-party claim, or for its severance or separate trial. A third-party defendant may proceed under this rule against any person not a party to the action who is or who may be liable to him or to the third-party plaintiff for all or part of the claim made in the action against the third-party defendant.

(b) When plaintiff may bring in third party. When a counterclaim is asserted against a plaintiff, he may cause a third party to be brought in under circumstances which under this rule would entitle a defendant to do so.

(c) This rule shall not be applied, in tort cases, so as to permit the joinder of a liability or indemnity insurance company, unless such company is by statute or contract liable to the person injured or damaged.

(d) This rule shall not be applied so as to violate any venue statute, as venue would exist absent this rule.

See CPRC §33.004 (responsible third parties); ***Commentaries***, "Plaintiff's Original Petition," ch. 2-B; "The Answer—Denying Liability," ch. 3-E.

History of TRCP 38: Amended eff. Apr. 1, 1984, by order of Dec. 5, 1983 (661-62 S.W.2d [Tex.Cases] xxxvii): Removed need to secure leave of court to begin third-party action; made textual changes to clarify terminology. Amended eff. Sept. 1, 1941, by order of Mar. 31, 1941 (4 Tex.B.J. 169 [1941]): Added pars. (c) and (d). Adopted eff. Sept. 1, 1941, by order of Oct. 29, 1940 (3 Tex.B.J. 529 [1940]). Source: FRCP 14.

Smith v. Clary Corp., 917 S.W.2d 796, 797 (Tex. 1996). "[T]he legislature enacted Gov't Code §24.009, the aggregating statute, to allow multiple plaintiffs to aggregate their claims to achieve the minimum jurisdictional amount for a court, not to defeat jurisdiction for multiple defendants each of whose counterclaims is within the jurisdictional limit."

Heard v. Moore, 101 S.W.3d 726, 729 (Tex.App.—Texarkana 2003, pet. denied). TRCP 38(a) "allows [D] to bring third parties into a suit who may be liable for all or part of [P's] damages. Once joined, these third parties, known as third-party [Ds], may bring counterclaims against either [D] or [P]. [P] has a permissive right to assert a claim against the third-party [D], not a compulsory obligation [] as long as the third-party [D] has not asserted a claim against [P]."

Goose Creek Consol. ISD v. Jarrar's Plumbing, 74 S.W.3d 486, 492 (Tex.App.—Texarkana 2002, pet. denied). "A third-party action is not an independent cause of action, but is derivative of [P's] claim against the responsible third party. As such, an action for indemnification or contribution does not accrue for limitations purposes until [P] recovers damages or settles its suit against [D]."

TRCP 39. JOINDER OF PERSONS NEEDED FOR JUST ADJUDICATION

(a) Persons to be Joined if Feasible. A person who is subject to service of process shall be joined as a party in the action if (1) in his absence complete relief cannot be accorded among those already parties, or (2) he claims an interest relating to the subject of the action and is so situated that the disposition of the action in his absence may (i) as a practical matter impair or impede his ability to protect that interest or (ii) leave any of the persons already parties subject to a substantial risk of incurring double, multiple, or otherwise inconsistent obligations by reason of his claimed interest. If he has not been so joined, the court shall order that he be made a party. If he should join as a plaintiff but refuses to do so, he may be made a defendant, or, in a proper case, an involuntary plaintiff.

(b) Determination by Court Whenever Joinder Not Feasible. If a person as described in subdivision (a)(1)-(2) hereof cannot be made a party, the court shall determine whether in equity and good conscience the action should proceed among the parties before it, or should be dismissed, the absent person being thus regarded as indispensable. The factors to be considered by the court include: first, to what extent a judgment rendered in the person's absence might be prejudicial to him or those already parties; second, the extent to which, by protective provisions in the judgment, by the shaping of relief, or other measures, the prejudice can be lessened or avoided; third, whether a judgment rendered in the person's absence will be adequate; fourth, whether the plaintiff will have an adequate remedy if the action is dismissed for non-joinder.

(c) Pleading Reasons for Nonjoinder. A pleading asserting a claim for relief shall state the names, if known to the pleader, of any persons as described in subdivision (a)(1)-(2) hereof who are not joined, and the reasons why they are not joined.

(d) Exception of Class Actions. This rule is subject to the provisions of Rule 42.

See TRCP 40, 41, 51, 174; ***Commentaries***, "Plaintiff's Original Petition," ch. 2-B; "Parties & Claims," ch. 2-E; "The Answer—Denying Liability," ch. 3-E; "Motion to Abate—Challenging the Suit," ch. 3-H; "Motions for Severance & Separate Trials," ch. 5-H.

History of TRCP 39: Amended eff. Jan. 1, 1971, by order of July 21, 1970 (455-56 S.W.2d [Tex.Cases] xxxv): The rule was completely rewritten to adopt, with minor changes, the provisions of FRCP 19, as amended. Adopted eff. Sept. 1, 1941, by order of Oct. 29, 1940 (3 Tex.B.J. 529 [1940]). Source: FRCP 19.

Smith v. Clary Corp., 917 S.W.2d 796, 799 (Tex. 1996). "The courts have not and should not apply aggregation [in Gov't Code §24.009] to divest a court of jurisdiction on counterclaims asserted by multiple defendants, whose joinder normally is not voluntary, and who have not chosen the forum."

Cooper v. Texas Gulf Indus., 513 S.W.2d 200, 204 (Tex.1974). "Under the provisions of our present [TRCP] 39 it would be rare indeed if there were a person whose presence was so indispensable in the sense that his absence deprives the court of jurisdiction to adjudicate between the parties already joined."

Gilmer ISD v. Dorfman, ___ S.W.3d ___ (Tex. App.—Tyler 2003, n.p.h.) (No. 12-03-00111-CV; 8-29-03). "While such a situation is rare, there are parties whose presence is so indispensable to the resolution of a cause of action that their absence can deprive a court of jurisdiction. ... A state official primarily responsible for enforcement of a statute must be joined in any suit affecting the constitutionality of that statute. Failure to add a necessary and indispensable party to the constitutional challenge of a statute leaves the trial court without jurisdiction."

Sabre Oil & Gas Corp. v. Gibson, 72 S.W.3d 812, 815-16 (Tex.App.—Eastland 2002, pet. denied). D argues "that all royalty owners are necessary parties [under TRCP] 39. [The authority D relies on] was decided prior to the 1971 amendment to Rule 39. [¶] Rule 39(a) no longer speaks of 'necessary' and 'indispensable' parties, and Texas courts have begun to discard these terms. Moreover, Rule 39 focuses not so much upon whether the court has jurisdiction, but upon whether the court ought to proceed with the parties before it. Under Rule 39, any change should be to lessen the number of 'indispensable' parties."

TRCP 40. PERMISSIVE JOINDER OF PARTIES

(a) Permissive Joinder. All persons may join in one action as plaintiffs if they assert any right to relief jointly, severally, or in the alternative in respect of or arising out of the same transaction, occurrence, or series of transactions or occurrences and if any question of law or fact common to all of them will arise in the action. All persons may be joined in one action as defendants if there is asserted against them jointly, severally, or in the alternative any right to relief in respect of or arising out of the same transaction, occurrence, or series of transactions or occurrences and if any question of law or fact common to all of them will arise in the action. A plaintiff or defendant need not be interested in obtaining or defending against all the relief demanded. Judgment may be given for one or more of the plaintiffs according to their respective rights to relief, and against one or more defendants according to their respective liabilities.

(b) Separate Trials. The court may make such orders as will prevent a party from being embarrassed, delayed, or put to expense by the inclusion of a party against whom he asserts no claim and who asserts no claim against him, and may order separate trials or make other orders to prevent delay or prejudice.

See TRCP 39, 41, 51, 174; ***Commentaries***, "Plaintiff's Original Petition," ch. 2-B; "Parties & Claims," ch. 2-E; "The Answer—Denying Liability," ch. 3-E; "Motion to Abate—Challenging the Suit," ch. 3-H; "Motions for Severance & Separate Trials," ch. 5-H.

History of TRCP 40: Adopted eff. Sept. 1, 1941, by order of Oct. 29, 1940 (3 Tex.B.J. 530 [1940]). Source: FRCP 20.

Landers v. East Tex. Salt Water Disposal Co., 248 S.W.2d 731, 734 (Tex.1952). "Where the tortious acts of 2 or more wrongdoers join to produce an indivisible injury ... all of the wrongdoers will be held jointly and severally liable for the entire damages and the injured party may proceed to judgment against any one separately or against all in one suit. If fewer than the whole number of wrongdoers are joined as defendants..., those joined may by proper cross action ... bring in those omitted."

TRCP 41. MISJOINDER & NON-JOINDER OF PARTIES

Misjoinder of parties is not ground for dismissal of an action. Parties may be dropped or added, or suits filed separately may be consolidated, or actions which have been improperly joined may be severed and each ground of recovery improperly joined may be docketed as a separate suit between the same parties, by order of the court on motion of any party or on its own initiative at any stage of the action, before the time of submission to the jury or to the court if trial is without a jury, on such terms as are just. Any claim against a party may be severed and proceeded with separately.

See TRCP 39, 40, 51, 174; ***Commentaries***, "The Answer—Denying Liability," ch. 3-E.

History of TRCP 41: Amended eff. Sept. 1, 1941, by order of Mar. 31, 1941 (4 Tex.B.J. 169 [1941]): Eliminated the procedure "after judgment." Adopted eff. Sept. 1, 1941, by order of Oct. 29, 1940 (3 Tex.B.J. 530 [1940]): Added provision for adding and dropping parties, for consolidating suits, and for severing actions in case of misjoinder of parties or causes. Source: FRCP 21.

Liberty Nat'l Fire Ins. Co. v. Akin, 927 S.W.2d 627, 630 (Tex.1996). "A severance may ... be necessary in some bad faith cases. A trial court will undoubtedly confront instances in which evidence admissible only on the bad faith claim would prejudice the insurer to such an extent that a fair trial on the contract claim would become unlikely. One example would be when the insurer has made a settlement offer on the disputed contract claim."

State Dept. of Highways & Pub. Transp. v. Cotner, 845 S.W.2d 818, 819 (Tex.1993). TRCP 41 "does not 'permit a trial court to sever a case after it has been submitted to the trier of fact.' [¶] A partial new trial may be ordered notwithstanding the prohibition in Rule 41 against post-submission severances. [TRCP] 320 is thus an exception to [TRCP] 41."

Guaranty Fed. Sav. Bank v. Horseshoe Operating Co., 793 S.W.2d 652, 658 (Tex.1990). "A claim is properly severable if (1) the controversy involves more than one cause of action, (2) the severed claim is one that would be the proper subject of a lawsuit if independently asserted, and (3) the severed claim is not so interwoven with the remaining action that they involve the same facts and issues."

Arredondo v. City of Dallas, 79 S.W.3d 657, 665 (Tex.App.—Dallas 2002, pet. denied). "Although the trial court need not sever an interlocutory summary judgment, it has broad discretion in determining whether to grant a severance. If summary judgment in favor of one [D] is proper in a case with multiple [Ds], severance of that claim is proper so it can be appealed."

04 TRCP 42. CLASS ACTIONS

(a) Prerequisites to a Class Action. One or more members of a class may sue or be sued as representative parties on behalf of all only if (1) the class is so numerous that joinder of all members is impracticable, (2) there are questions of law or fact common to the class, (3) the claims or defenses of the representative parties are typical of the claims or defenses of the class, and (4) the representative parties will fairly and adequately protect the interests of the class.

(b) Class Actions Maintainable. An action may be maintained as a class action if the prerequisites of subdivision (a) are satisfied, and in addition:

(1) the prosecution of separate actions by or against individual members of the class would create a risk of

(A) inconsistent or varying adjudications with respect to individual members of the class which would establish incompatible standards of conduct for the party opposing the class, or

(B) adjudications with respect to individual members of the class which would as a practical matter be dispositive of the interests of the other members not parties to the adjudications or substantially impair or impede their ability to protect their interests; or

(2) the party opposing the class has acted or refused to act on grounds generally applicable to the class, thereby making appropriate final injunctive relief or corresponding declaratory relief with respect to the class as a whole; or

(3) the questions of law or fact common to the members of the class predominate over any questions affecting only individual members, and a class action is superior to other available methods for the fair and efficient adjudication of the controversy. The matters pertinent to these issues include:

(A) the interest of members of the class in individually controlling the prosecution or defense of separate actions;

(B) the extent and nature of any litigation concerning the controversy already commenced by or against members of the class;

(C) the desirability or undesirability of concentrating the litigation of the claims in the particular forum;

(D) the difficulties likely to be encountered in the management of a class action.

(c) Determining by Order Whether to Certify a Class Action; Notice and Membership in Class.

(1)(A) When a person sues or is sued as a representative of a class, the court must—at an early practicable time—determine by order whether to certify the action as a class action.

(B) An order certifying a class action must define the class and the class claims, issues, or defenses, and must appoint class counsel under Rule 42(g).

(C) An order under Rule 42(c)(1) may be altered or amended before final judgment. The court may order the naming of additional parties in order to insure the adequacy of representation.

(D) An order granting or denying certification under Rule 42(b)(3) must state:

(i) the elements of each claim or defense asserted in the pleadings;

(ii) any issues of law or fact common to the class members;

(iii) any issues of law or fact affecting only individual class members;

(iv) the issues that will be the object of most of the efforts of the litigants and the court;

(v) other available methods of adjudication that exist for the controversy;

(vi) why the issues common to the members of the class do or do not predominate over individual issues;

(vii) why a class action is or is not superior to other available methods for the fair and efficient adjudication of the controversy; and

(viii) If a class is certified, how the class claims and any issues affecting only individual members, raised by the claims or defenses asserted in the pleadings, will be tried in a manageable, time efficient manner.

(2)(A) For any class certified under Rule 42(b)(1) or (2), the court may direct appropriate notice to the class.

(B) For any class certified under Rule 42(b)(3), the court must direct to class members the best notice practicable under the circumstances, including individual notice to all members who can be identified through reasonable effort. The notice must concisely and clearly state in plain, easily understood language:

(i) the nature of the action;

(ii) the definition of the class certified;

(iii) the class claims, issues, or defenses;

(iv) that a class member may enter an appearance through counsel if the member so desires;

(v) that the court will exclude from the class any member who requests exclusion, stating when and how members may elect to be excluded; and

(vi) the binding effect of a class judgment on class members under Rule 42(c)(3).

(3) The judgment in an action maintained as a class action under subdivision (b)(1), or (b)(2), whether or not favorable to the class, shall include and describe those whom the court finds to be members of the class. The judgment in an action maintained as a class action under subdivision (b)(3), whether or not favorable to the class, shall include and specify or describe those to whom the notice provided in subdivision (c)(2) was directed, and who have not requested exclusion, and whom the court finds to be members of the class.

(d) Actions Conducted Partially as Class Actions; Multiple Classes and Subclasses. When appropriate (1) an action may be brought or maintained as a class action with respect to particular issues, or (2) a class may be divided into subclasses and each subclass treated as a class, and the provisions of this rule shall then be construed and applied accordingly.

(e) Settlement, Dismissal, or Compromise.

(1)(A) The court must approve any settlement, dismissal, or compromise of the claims, issues, or defenses of a certified class.

(B) Notice of the material terms of the proposed settlement, dismissal or compromise, together with an explanation of when and how the members may elect to be excluded from the class, shall be given to all members in such manner as the court directs.

(C) The court may approve a settlement, dismissal, or compromise that would bind class members only after a hearing and on finding that the settlement, dismissal, or compromise is fair, reasonable, and adequate.

(2) The parties seeking approval of a settlement, dismissal, or compromise under Rule 42(e)(1) must file a statement identifying any agreement made in connection with the proposed settlement, dismissal, or compromise.

(3) In an action previously certified as a class action under Rule 42(b)(3), the court may not approve a settlement unless it affords a new opportunity to request exclusion to individual class members who had an earlier opportunity to request exclusion but did not do so.

(4)(A) Any class member may object to a proposed settlement, dismissal, or compromise that requires court approval under Rule 42(e)(1)(A).

(B) An objection made under Rule 42(e)(4)(A) may be withdrawn only with the court's approval.

(f) Discovery. Unnamed members of a class action are not to be considered as parties for purposes of discovery.

(g) Class Counsel.

(1) *Appointing Class Counsel.*

(A) Unless a statute provides otherwise, a court that certifies a class must appoint class counsel.

(B) An attorney appointed to serve as class counsel must fairly and adequately represent the interests of the class.

(C) In appointing class counsel, the court

(i) must consider:

- the work counsel has done in identifying or investigating potential claims in the action;
- counsel's experience in handling class actions, other complex litigation, and claims of the type asserted in the action;
- counsel's knowledge of the applicable law; and
- the resources counsel will commit to representing the class;

(ii) may consider any other matter pertinent to counsel's ability to fairly and adequately represent the interests of the class;

(iii) may direct potential class counsel to provide information on any subject pertinent to the appointment and to propose terms for attorney fees and nontaxable costs; and

(iv) may make further orders in connection with the appointment.

(2) *Appointment Procedure.*

(A) The court may designate interim counsel to act on behalf of the putative class before determining whether to certify the action as a class action.

(B) When there is one applicant for appointment as class counsel, the court may appoint that applicant only if the applicant is adequate under Rule 42(g)(1)(B) and (C). If more than one adequate applicant seeks appointment as class counsel, the court must appoint the applicant or applicants best able to represent the interests of the class.

(C) The order appointing class counsel may include provisions about the award of attorney fees or nontaxable costs under Rule 42(h) and (i).

(h) Procedure for determining Attorney Fees Award. In an action certified as a class action, the court may award attorney fees in accordance with subdivision (i) and nontaxable costs authorized by law or by agreement of the parties as follows:

(1) *Motion for Award of Attorney Fees.* A claim for an award of attorney fees and nontaxable costs must be made by motion, subject to the provisions of this subdivision, at a time set by the court. Notice of the motion must be served on all parties and, for motions by class counsel, directed to class members in a reasonable manner.

(2) *Objections to Motion.* A class member, or a party from whom payment is sought, may object to the motion.

(3) *Hearing and Findings.* The court must hold a hearing in open court and must find the facts and state its conclusions of law on the motion. The court must state its findings and conclusions in writing or orally on the record.

(i) Attorney's fees award.

(1) In awarding attorney fees, the court must first determine a lodestar figure by multiplying the number of hours reasonably worked times a reasonable hourly rate. The attorney fees award must be in the range of 25% to 400% of the lodestar figure. In making these determinations, the court must consider the factors specified in Rule 1.04(b), Tex. Disciplinary R. Prof. Conduct.

(2) If any portion of the benefits recovered for the class are in the form of coupons or other noncash common benefits, the attorney fees awarded in the action must be in cash and noncash amounts in the same proportion as the recovery for the class.

(j) Effective date. Rule 42(i) applies only in actions filed after September 1, 2003.

Comments to 2003 amendments:

1. The second paragraph of subdivision (a) regarding derivative suits has been deleted because it is redundant of art. 5.14 of the Business Corporation Act, which sets forth detailed procedures for derivative suits.

2. Subparagraph (b)(3) is omitted as unnecessary.

3. The requirement that certification be decided "at an early practicable time" is a change from the previous Texas rule 42(c)(1) and federal rule 23(c)(1), which required the trial court to decide the certification issue "as soon as practicable after the commencement of [the suit]." The amended language is not intended to permit undue delay or permit excessive discovery unrelated to certification, but is designed to encourage good practices in making certification decisions only after receiving the information necessary to decide whether certification should be granted or denied and how to define the class if certification is granted.

See CPRC §51.014(a)(3); ***O'Connor's Texas Civil Appeals***, "Preliminary Issues to the Appeal," ch. 11 (2002-03).

History of TRCP 42: Amended eff. Jan. 1, 2004, by order of Oct. 9, 2003 (Tex.Sup.Ct. Order, Misc. Docket No. 03-9160). Amended eff. Apr. 1, 1984, by order of Dec. 5, 1983 (661-62 S.W.2d [Tex.Cases] xxxviii): The paragraph concerning a derivative suit was added to paragraph (a). Amended eff. Sept. 1, 1977, by order of May 9, 1977 (553-54 S.W.2d [Tex.Cases] xxxvi): Rewrote TRCP 42; copied (a) from revised FRCP 23(a), (b)(1) from revised FRCP 23(b)(2), and (b)(2) from revised FRCP 23(b)(2); added (b)(3) from present TRCP 42(a)(3), omitting the reference to the character of the right as "several"; adopted (b)(4) from revised FRCP 23(b)(3); adopted (c)(1) from revised FRCP (c)(1) with little change except in the choice of words; second sentence in (c)(1) is not found in the FRCP although the idea is implicit in it; and copied (d) from revised FRCP 23(c)(4), and (e) from revised FRCP 23(e). Amended eff. Dec. 31, 1941, by order of Sept. 20, 1941 (4 Tex.B.J. 494 [1941]). Adopted eff. Sept. 1, 1941, by order of Oct. 29, 1940 (3 Tex.B.J. 530 [1940]). Source:

FRCP 23, with change: In par. (b) deleted the requirement that the action is not collusive.

General

M.D. Anderson Cancer Ctr. v. Novak, 52 S.W.3d 704, 711 (Tex.2001). "[I]f the named plaintiff lacks individual standing, the court should dismiss the entire suit for want of jurisdiction. If the named plaintiff demonstrates individual standing, whether that plaintiff will then be permitted to represent the class depends on whether Rule 42's requirements are satisfied."

Southwestern Ref. Co. v. Bernal, 22 S.W.3d 425, 434 (Tex.2000). "Courts determine if common issues predominate by identifying the substantive issues of the case that will control the outcome of the litigation, assessing which issues will predominate, and determining if the predominating issues are, in fact, those common to the class. The test for predominance is not whether common issues outnumber uncommon issues but ... 'whether common or individual issues will be the object of most of the efforts of the litigants and the court.' If, after common issues are resolved, presenting and resolving individual issues is likely to be an overwhelming or unmanageable task for a single jury, then common issues do not predominate." *See also* ***Henry Schein, Inc. v. Stromboe***, 102 S.W.3d 675, 688 (Tex.2002).

Intratex Gas Co. v. Beeson, 22 S.W.3d 398, 403-04 (Tex.2000). "For a class to be sufficiently defined, it must be precise: the class members must be presently ascertainable by reference to objective criteria. This means that the class should not be defined by criteria that are subjective or that require an analysis of the merits of the case. ... We note, however, that a class definition will not fail merely because every potential class member cannot be identified at the suit's commencement."

Enron Oil & Gas Co. v. Joffrion, 116 S.W.3d 215, 219 (Tex.App.—Tyler 2003, n.p.h.). The "factors to consider in determining if the adequacy of representation element is satisfied [include]: 1) adequacy of counsel; 2) potential for conflicts of interest; 3) personal integrity of the plaintiffs; 4) whether the class is unmanageable because of geographic limitations; 5) whether the representative plaintiffs can afford to finance the class action; and 6) the representative plaintiffs' familiarity with the litigation and his or her belief in the legitimacy of the action."

Spera v. Fleming, Hovenkamp & Grayson, P.C., 4 S.W.3d 805, 809-10 (Tex.App.—Houston [14th Dist.] 1999, no pet.). "[W]hen the trial court makes a decision of class status at an early stage of the proceeding before supporting facts are fully developed, it should err in favor of, and not against, maintenance of the class action."

Appellate Review

Bally Total Fitness Corp. v. Jackson, 53 S.W.3d 352, 358 (Tex.2001). An order refusing to decertify a class action is not an appealable order because it does not change the status quo.

Ford Motor Co. v. Sheldon, 22 S.W.3d 444, 449 (Tex.2000). Unless the Supreme Court has specific statutory authority, it cannot review most interlocutory orders on class action certification.

Deloitte & Touche v. 14th Ct. of Appeals, 951 S.W.2d 394, 396 (Tex.1997). The Supreme Court has mandamus jurisdiction to review an interlocutory class certification order, over which it has no appellate jurisdiction.

De Los Santos v. Occidental Chem. Corp., 933 S.W.2d 493, 495 (Tex.1997). CPRC §51.014(a)(3) permits an interlocutory appeal to the court of appeals from an order that changes a class from opt-out to mandatory because "it alters the fundamental nature of the class."

Settlement

McAllen Med. Ctr. v. Cortez, 66 S.W.3d 227, 233 (Tex.2001). "Rule 42's typicality and adequacy-of-representation criteria ... demand heightened scrutiny when a settlement occurs. ... And when a settlement occurs, the potential for class representatives and counsel to ignore differences among class members, or even collude with defendants at absent class members' expense, mandates that the trial court rigorously scrutinize Rule 42's typicality and adequacy-of-representation criteria."

TRCP 43. INTERPLEADER

Persons having claims against the plaintiff may be joined as defendants and required to interplead when their claims are such that the plaintiff is or may be exposed to double or multiple liability. It is not ground for objection to the joinder that the claims of the several claimants or the titles on which their claims depend do not have a common origin or are not identical but are adverse to and independent of one another, or that the plaintiff avers that he is not liable in whole or in part to any or all of the claimants. A defendant exposed to similar liability may obtain such interpleader by way of cross-claim or counterclaim. The provisions of this rule supplement and do not in any way limit the joinder of parties permitted in any other rules.

History of TRCP 43: Adopted eff. Sept. 1, 1941, by order of Oct. 29, 1940 (3 Tex.B.J. 531 [1940]). Source: FRCP 22(1).

Great Am. Reserve Ins. Co. v. Sanders, 525 S.W.2d 956, 958 (Tex.1975). The insurance company "was entitled to maintain an interpleader suit if there existed a reasonable doubt, either of fact or law, as to which of the rival claimants was entitled to the proceeds of the policy."

Union Gas Corp. v. Gisler, ___ S.W.3d ___ (Tex. App.—Corpus Christi 2003, n.p.h.) (No. 13-01-734-CV; 8-29-03). "An interpleading party is entitled to interpleader relief if three elements are met: (1) he is either subject to, or has reasonable grounds to anticipate, rival claims to the same fund or property; (2) he has not unreasonably delayed filing his action for interpleader; and (3) he has unconditionally tendered the fund or property into the registry of the court. [F]ailure to meet any of these elements defeats an interpleader action."

TRCP 44. MAY APPEAR BY NEXT FRIEND

Minors, lunatics, idiots, or persons non compos mentis who have no legal guardian may sue and be represented by "next friend" under the following rules:

(1) Such next friend shall have the same rights concerning such suits as guardians have, but shall give security for costs, or affidavits in lieu thereof, when required.

(2) Such next friend or his attorney of record may with the approval of the court compromise suits and agree to judgments, and such judgments, agreements and compromises, when approved by the court, shall be forever binding and conclusive upon the party plaintiff in such suit.

See TRCP 173; *Commentaries*, "Guardians Ad Litem Under TRCP 173," ch. 1-I.

History of TRCP 44: Adopted eff. Sept. 1, 1941, by order of Oct. 29, 1940 (3 Tex.B.J. 531 [1940]). Source: TRCS art. 1994, now Prop. Code §142.002.

American Gen. Fire & Cas. Co. v. Vandewater, 907 S.W.2d 491, 492-93 (Tex.1995). A "court should evaluate whether the minor's interests have been properly protected and whether a deficiency in notice or due process has been shown to determine whether a trial court has obtained personal jurisdiction over a minor. In this case, the answer of [the mother] in her capacity as [the minor's] next friend was sufficient indication that [the minor's] legal representative knew about the proceedings and could therefore defend against them."

Urbish v. 127th Judicial Dist. Ct., 708 S.W.2d 429, 432 (Tex.1986). "[T]rial courts are authorized to replace next friends and attorneys when it appears to the court that either has an interest adverse to the minor."

Gracia v. RC Cola-7-Up Bottling Co., 667 S.W.2d 517, 519 (Tex.1984). "In a suit by a 'next friend,' the real party plaintiff is the child and not the next friend."

SECTION 4. PLEADING

A. GENERAL

TRCP 45. DEFINITION & SYSTEM

Pleadings in the district and county courts shall

(a) be by petition and answer;

(b) consist of a statement in plain and concise language of the plaintiff's cause of action or the defendant's grounds of defense. That an allegation be evidentiary or be of legal conclusion shall not be grounds for objection when fair notice to the opponent is given by the allegations as a whole;

(c) contain any other matter which may be required by any law or rule authorizing or regulating any particular action or defense;

(d) be in writing, on paper measuring approximately 8½ inches by 11 inches, and signed by the party or his attorney, and either the signed original together with any verification or a copy of said original and copy of any such verification shall be filed with the court. The use of recycled paper is strongly encouraged.

When a copy of the signed original is tendered for filing, the party or his attorney filing such copy is required to maintain the signed original for inspection by the court or any party incident to the suit, should a question be raised as to its authenticity.

All pleadings shall be construed so as to do substantial justice.

See *Commentaries*, "Rules of Pleading," ch. 1-B; "Rules for Filing Documents," ch. 1-C; "Plaintiff's Original Petition," ch. 2-B; "Special Exceptions—Challenging the Pleadings," ch. 3-G; "Default Judgment," ch. 7-A.

History of TRCP 45: Amended eff. Sept. 1, 1990 (retroactive), by order of Sept. 4, 1990 (793-94 S.W.2d [Tex.Cases] xxxii): To amend the Sept. 1, 1990 amendment by adding sentence regarding use of recycled paper to (d). Amended eff. Sept. 1, 1990, by order of Apr. 24, 1990 (785-86 S.W.2d [Tex.Cases] xli): Par. under (d) added and (d) changed to provide for filing of pleadings having either original or copies of signatures and verifications including documents telephonically transferred. Amended eff. Jan. 1, 1988, by order of July 15, 1987 (733-34 S.W.2d [Tex.Cases] xl). Adopted eff. Sept. 1, 1941, by order of Oct. 29, 1940 (3 Tex.B.J. 531 [1940]). Source: This rule embraces part of TRCS art. 1997 (repealed), Tex. Rules for Dist. & Cty. Cts. 1 & 32, and FRCP 8(f).

Perez v. Briercroft Serv. Corp., 809 S.W.2d 216, 218 (Tex.1991). "[T]he purpose of pleading is to give the adversary parties notice of each [party's] claims and defenses, as well as notice of the relief sought."

Paramount Pipe & Sup. Co. v. Muhr, 749 S.W.2d 491, 494-95 (Tex.1988). "The purpose of the fair notice requirement is to provide the opposing party with sufficient information to enable him to prepare a defense. [¶] [TRCP] 45 does not require that [P] set out in his pleadings the evidence upon which he relies to establish his asserted cause of action."

TRCP 46. PETITION & ANSWER; EACH ONE INSTRUMENT OF WRITING

The original petition, first supplemental petition, second supplemental petition, and every other, shall each be contained in one instrument of writing, and so with the original answer and each of the supplemental answers.

History of TRCP 46: Adopted eff. Sept. 1, 1941, by order of Oct. 29, 1940 (3 Tex.B.J. 531 [1940]). Source: Tex. Rules for Dist. & Cty. Cts. 9.

TRCP 47. CLAIMS FOR RELIEF

An original pleading which sets forth a claim for relief, whether an original petition, counterclaim, cross-claim, or third party claim, shall contain

(a) a short statement of the cause of action sufficient to give fair notice of the claim involved,

(b) in all claims for unliquidated damages only the statement that the damages sought are within the jurisdictional limits of the court, and

(c) a demand for judgment for all the other relief to which the party deems himself entitled.

Relief in the alternative or of several different types may be demanded; provided, further, that upon special exception the court shall require the pleader to amend so as to specify the maximum amount claimed.

See ***Commentaries***, "Rules of Pleading," ch. 1-B; "Plaintiff's Original Petition," ch. 2-B; "Special Exceptions—Challenging the Pleadings," ch. 3-G; "Default Judgment," ch. 7-A; FORMS 2B.

History of TRCP 47: Amended eff. Sept. 1, 1990, by order of Apr. 24, 1990 (785-86 S.W.2d [Tex.Cases] xli): Changed (b) to require damages to be within the court's jurisdictional limits. Amended eff. Jan. 1, 1978, by order of July 11, 1977 (553-54 S.W.2d [Tex.Cases] xliii): Changed first sentence, first sentence of (c), all of (b), and added the proviso in (c). Adopted eff. Sept. 1, 1941, by order of Oct. 29, 1940 (3 Tex.B.J. 531 [1940]). Source: FRCP 8(a).

Boyles v. Kerr, 855 S.W.2d 593, 601 (Tex.1993). "A court should uphold the petition as to a cause of action that may be reasonably inferred from what is specifically stated, even if an element of a cause of action is not specifically alleged."

Roark v. Allen, 633 S.W.2d 804, 810 (Tex.1982). "A petition is sufficient if it gives fair and adequate notice of the facts upon which the pleader bases his claim. The purpose of this rule is to give the opposing party information sufficient to enable him to prepare a defense."

TRCP 48. ALTERNATIVE CLAIMS FOR RELIEF

A party may set forth two or more statements of a claim or defense alternatively or hypothetically, either in one count or defense or in separate counts or defenses. When two or more statements are made in the alternative and one of them if made independently would be sufficient, the pleading is not made insufficient by the insufficiency of one or more of the alternative statements. A party may also state as many separate claims or defenses as he has regardless of consistency and whether based upon legal or equitable grounds or both.

See ***Commentaries***, "Rules of Pleading," ch. 1-B.

History of TRCP 48: Adopted eff. Sept. 1, 1941, by order of Oct. 29, 1940 (3 Tex.B.J. 531 [1940]). Source: FRCP 8(e), in part.

Regency Advantage L.P. v. Bingo Idea-Watauga, Inc., 936 S.W.2d 275, 278 (Tex.1996). "[O]ur rules expressly permit parties to proceed on alternative theories of relief."

Birchfield v. Texarkana Mem'l Hosp., 747 S.W.2d 361, 367 (Tex.1987). "[W]here the prevailing party fails to elect between alternative measures of damages, the court should utilize the findings affording the greater recovery and render judgment accordingly."

Household Credit Serv. v. Driscol, 989 S.W.2d 72, 80 (Tex.App.—El Paso 1998, pet. denied). "If a plaintiff pleads alternate theories of liability under [TRCP] 48, a judgment that awards damages based upon more than one theory does not amount to a double recovery if the theories of liability arise from two separate and distinct injuries, and there has been a separate and distinct finding of damages on both theories of liability."

TRCP 49. WHERE SEVERAL COUNTS

Where there are several counts in the petition, and entire damages are given, the verdict or judgment, as the case may be, shall be good, notwithstanding one or more of such counts may be defective.

History of TRCP 49: Adopted eff. Sept. 1, 1941, by order of Oct. 29, 1940 (3 Tex.B.J. 532 [1940]). Source: TRCS art. 2213 (repealed).

TRCP 50. PARAGRAPHS, SEPARATE STATEMENTS

All averments of claim or defense shall be made in numbered paragraphs, the contents of each of which shall be limited as far as practicable to a statement of a single set of circumstances; and a paragraph may be referred to by number in all succeeding pleadings, so long as the pleading containing such paragraph has not been superseded by an amendment as provided by Rule 65. Each claim founded upon a separate transaction or occurrence and each defense other than denials shall be stated in a separate count or defense whenever a separation facilitates the clear presentation of the matters set forth.

See ***Commentaries***, "Rules of Pleading," ch. 1-B; "Plaintiff's Original Petition," ch. 2-B.

History of TRCP 50: Adopted eff. Sept. 1, 1941, by order of Oct. 29, 1940 (3 Tex.B.J. 532 [1940]). Source: FRCP 10(b).

TRCP 51. JOINDER OF CLAIMS & REMEDIES

(a) Joinder of Claims. The plaintiff in his petition or in a reply setting forth a counterclaim and the defendant in an answer setting forth a counterclaim may join either as independent or as alternate claims as many claims either legal or equitable or both as he may have against an opposing party. There may be a like joinder of claims when there are multiple parties if the requirements of Rules 39, 40, and 43 are satisfied. There may be a like joinder of cross claims or third-party claims if the requirements of Rules 38 and 97, respectively, are satisfied.

(b) Joinder of Remedies. Whenever a claim is one heretofore cognizable only after another claim has been prosecuted to a conclusion, the two claims may be joined in a single action; but the court shall grant relief in that action only in accordance with the relative substantive rights of the parties. This rule shall not be applied in tort cases so as to permit the joinder of a liability or indemnity insurance company, unless such company is by statute or contract directly liable to the person injured or damaged.

See TRCP 39, 40, 41, 174.

History of TRCP 51: Amended eff. Jan. 1, 1961, by order of July 26, 1960 (23 Tex.B.J. 619 [Oct. 1960]): The word "statute" substituted for the word "law" in last sentence of par. (b). Amended eff. Dec. 31, 1941, by order of Sept. 20, 1941 (4 Tex.B.J. 496 [1941]): The last sentence was added. Adopted eff. Sept. 1, 1941, by order of Oct. 29, 1940 (3 Tex.B.J. 532 [1940]). Source: FRCP 18. Omitted reference to the right of plaintiff to join an action upon a claim for money and an action to set aside a fraudulent conveyance as unnecessary.

Allison v. Arkansas La. Gas Co., 624 S.W.2d 566, 568 (Tex.1981). "Under [TRCP] 51(a), [P] or [D] is permitted to join in the same proceeding 'as many claims either legal or equitable or both as he may have against an opposing party.'"

TRCP 52. ALLEGING A CORPORATION

An allegation that a corporation is incorporated shall be taken as true, unless denied by the affidavit of the adverse party, his agent or attorney, whether such corporation is a public or private corporation and however created.

See TRCP 93(6); ***Commentaries***, "The Defendant's Responses & Pleadings," ch. 3; "Motion to Abate—Challenging the Suit," ch. 3-H.

History of TRCP 52: Adopted eff. Sept. 1, 1941, by order of Oct. 29, 1940 (3 Tex.B.J. 532 [1940]). Source: TRCS art. 1999 (repealed).

Dr. Pepper Co. v. Crow, 621 S.W.2d 464, 465 (Tex. App.—Waco 1981, no writ). "[P] plead [D] was a corporation. [D] did not deny by verified pleading pursuant to [TRCP] 52 and 93 ... that it was not a corporation; thus, such fact was established."

TRCP 53. SPECIAL ACT OR LAW

A pleading founded wholly or in part on any private or special act or law of this State or of the Republic of Texas need only recite the title thereof, the date of its approval, and set out in substance so much of such act or laws as may be pertinent to the cause of action or defense.

History of TRCP 53: Adopted eff. Sept. 1, 1941, by order of Oct. 29, 1940 (3 Tex.B.J. 532 [1940]). Source: TRCS art. 2000 (repealed).

TRCP 54. CONDITIONS PRECEDENT

In pleading the performance or occurrence of conditions precedent, it shall be sufficient to aver generally that all conditions precedent have been performed or have occurred. When such performances or occurrences have been so plead, the party so pleading same shall be required to prove only such of them as are specifically denied by the opposite party.

See ***Commentaries***, "Plaintiff's Original Petition," ch. 2-B; "The Defendant's Responses & Pleadings," ch. 3; "The Answer—Denying Liability," ch. 3-E; FORMS 2B.

History of TRCP 54: Amended eff. Sept. 1, 1941, by order of Mar. 31, 1941 (4 Tex.B.J. 496 [1941]). Changed wording of last sentence to make it clearer. Adopted eff. Sept. 1, 1941, by order of Oct. 29, 1940 (3 Tex.B.J. 532 [1940]). Source: FRCP 9(c).

Associated Indem. Corp. v. CAT Contracting, 964 S.W.2d 276, 283 n.6 (Tex.1998). "Where a party avers generally that all conditions precedent have been performed or have occurred, he or she need only prove those that are specifically denied by the opposite party. This pleading rule, however, does not shift the burden of proof on those conditions which the opposite party denies."

Greathouse v. Charter Nat'l Bank-Southwest, 851 S.W.2d 173, 177 (Tex.1992). "[C]harter met its burden of pleading [that disposition of the collateral was commercially reasonable] by its general allegation that all conditions precedent had been performed. In answer, Greathouse did not specifically deny that Charter's disposition of the collateral was commercially unreasonable. Consequently, Charter was not required to prove commercial reasonableness at trial."

TRCP 55. JUDGMENT

In pleading a judgment or decision of a domestic or foreign court, judicial or quasi-judicial tribunal, or of a board or officer, it shall be sufficient to aver the judgment or decision without setting forth matter showing jurisdiction to render it.

See CPRC ch. 36.

History of TRCP 55: Adopted eff. Sept. 1, 1941, by order of Oct. 29, 1940 (3 Tex.B.J. 532 [1940]). Source: FRCP 9(e).

TRCP 56. SPECIAL DAMAGE

When items of special damage are claimed, they shall be specifically stated.

See ***Commentaries***, "Special damages," ch. 2-B, §8.3.1(2).

History of TRCP 56: Adopted eff. Sept. 1, 1941, by order of Oct. 29, 1940 (3 Tex.B.J. 532 [1940]). Source: FRCP 9(g).

Arthur Andersen & Co. v. Perry Equip. Corp., 945 S.W.2d 812, 816 (Tex.1997). "Consequential damages [also known as special damages] result naturally, but not necessarily, from the defendant's wrongful acts."

Naegeli Transp. v. Gulf Electroquip, Inc., 853 S.W.2d 737, 739 (Tex.App.—Houston [14th Dist.] 1993, writ denied). "Consequential damages are special damages and must be pleaded and proved separately."

TRCP 57. SIGNING OF PLEADINGS

Every pleading of a party represented by an attorney shall be signed by at least one attorney of record in his individual name, with his State Bar of Texas identification number, address, telephone number, and, if available, telecopier number. A party not represented by an attorney shall sign his pleadings, state his address, telephone number, and, if available, telecopier number.

See TRCP 191.3; ***Commentaries***, "Rules of Pleading," ch. 1-B; "Rules for Serving Documents," ch. 1-D; "Plaintiff's Original Petition," ch. 2-B; "Default Judgment," ch. 7-A; FORMS 1B.

History of TRCP 57: Amended eff. Sept. 1, 1990, by order of Apr. 24, 1990 (785-86 S.W.2d [Tex.Cases] xlii): To supply attorney telecopier information with other identifying information on pleadings; documents telephonically transferred are permitted to be filed under changes to TRCP 45. Amended eff. Jan. 1, 1981, by order of June 10, 1980 (599-600 S.W.2d [Tex.Cases] xxxvi): Rule changed to require statement on pleadings of attorney's State Bar of Texas identification number and telephone number and the telephone number of a party not represented by a lawyer. Adopted eff. Sept. 1, 1941, by order of Oct. 29, 1940 (3 Tex.B.J. 533 [1940]). Source: FRCP 11, first two sentences.

W.C. Turnbow Pet. Corp. v. Fulton, 194 S.W.2d 256, 257 (Tex.1946). "Counsel should sign their names to motions and pleadings 'to make themselves responsible for what is stated in them, and so as to leave no doubt as to the parties for whom they appear.' But ... the signature to a pleading is a formal requisite and ... failure to comply with the requirement is not fatal to the pleading."

TRCP 58. ADOPTION BY REFERENCE

Statements in a pleading may be adopted by reference in a different part of the same pleading or in another pleading or in any motion, so long as the pleading containing such statements has not been superseded by an amendment as provided by Rule 65.

See ***Commentaries***, "Rules of Pleading," ch. 1-B.

History of TRCP 58: Adopted eff. Sept. 1, 1941, by order of Oct. 29, 1940 (3 Tex.B.J. 533 [1940]). Source: FRCP 10(c), first sentence.

Texas Gas Utils. Co. v. Barrett, 460 S.W.2d 409, 416 (Tex.1970). Because "[t]he original petition had been superseded by [the] First Amended Original Petition ... statements in the former were not subject to adoption by reference in the supplemental petitions."

TRCP 59. EXHIBITS & PLEADING

Notes, accounts, bonds, mortgages, records, and all other written instruments, constituting, in whole or in part, the claim sued on, or the matter set up in defense, may be made a part of the pleadings by copies thereof, or the originals, being attached or filed and referred to as such, or by copying the same in the body of the pleading in aid and explanation of the allegations in the petition or answer made in reference to said instruments and shall be deemed a part thereof for all purposes. Such pleadings shall not be deemed defective because of the lack of any allegations which can be supplied from said exhibit. No other instrument of writing shall be made an exhibit in the pleading.

History of TRCP 59: Adopted eff. Sept. 1, 1941, by order of Oct. 29, 1940 (3 Tex.B.J. 533 [1940]). Source: Tex. Rules for Dist. & Cty. Cts. 19.

Houston Cmty. Coll. Sys. v. Schneider, 67 S.W.3d 241, 243 (Tex.App.—Houston [1st Dist.] 2000, pet. denied). "[A] pleading shall not be deemed defective because of the lack of any allegation that can be supplied from attached exhibits."

Skepnek v. Mynatt, 8 S.W.3d 377, 381 (Tex.App.—El Paso 1999, pet. denied). "[T]he statements found in the affidavit, having been incorporated into the special appearance motion, became part of the motion, which was then signed and tendered by [attorney]. Therefore, we hold that the trial court did not abuse its discretion in imposing sanctions against [attorney] under [CPRC] Chapter 10 [for filing a false affidavit]."

TRCP 60. INTERVENOR'S PLEADINGS

Any party may intervene by filing a pleading, subject to being stricken out by the court for sufficient cause on the motion of any party.

Comment to 1990 change: Rules 21 and 21a control notice and service of pleadings of intervenors.

See ***Commentaries***, "Joining an Ongoing Lawsuit," ch. 5-I; FORMS 5I.

History of TRCP 60: Amended eff. Sept. 1, 1990, by order of Apr. 24, 1990 (785-86 S.W.2d [Tex.Cases] xlii): Title changed; rule rewritten. Adopted eff. Sept. 1, 1941, by order of Oct. 29, 1940 (3 Tex.B.J. 533 [1940]). Source: TRCS art. 1998 (repealed).

Baker v. Monsanto Co., 111 S.W.3d 158, 160 (Tex. 2003). "Typically, an intervention involves a claim against persons who have already appeared. Under these circumstances, the plea in intervention is properly served by any of the methods provided in [TRCP] 21a. However, absent a subsequent appearance, service of citation is necessary against an original [D] when the intervenor seeks affirmative relief against a [D] who has not appeared at the time the intervention was filed. [¶] [I]ntervenors are required to serve citation on [D] when that [D] fails to appear and answer [P]'s petition. [A]n intervenor must serve citation on any third-party [D] it seeks to bring into the suit. And if the intervenor's claim is against [P], it must serve citation on [P], if [P] does not make any further appearance in the case after the intervention."

Guaranty Fed. Sav. Bank v. Horseshoe Operating Co., 793 S.W.2d 652, 657 (Tex.1990). "An intervenor is not required to secure the court's permission to intervene; the party who opposed the intervention has the burden to challenge it by a motion to strike. [¶] [I]t is an abuse of discretion to strike a plea in intervention if (1) the intervenor [could have brought some or all of the same action in its own name, or, if the action had been brought against it, it could defeat some or all of the recovery], (2) the intervention will not complicate the case by an excessive multiplication of the issues, and (3) the intervention is almost essential to effectively protect the intervenor's interest."

NCAA v. Yeo, 114 S.W.3d 584, 593 (Tex.App.—Austin 2003, n.p.h.). "Once an intervenor files its motion, any other party to the litigation may put the intervening party to the burden of proving its interest by filing a legally sufficient motion to strike. The motion to strike need not be accompanied by supporting evidence, but if evidence is attached the intervening party must have sufficient opportunity to explain and show proof of its interest in the lawsuit."

TRCP 61. TRIAL: INTERVENORS: RULES APPLY TO ALL PARTIES

These rules of pleading shall apply equally, so far as it may be practicable to intervenors and to parties, when more than one, who may plead separately.

History of TRCP 61: Adopted eff. Sept. 1, 1941, by order of Oct. 29, 1940 (3 Tex.B.J. 533 [1940]). Source: TRCS art. 1998 (repealed); and Tex. Rules for Dist. & Cty. Cts. 30.

TRCP 62. AMENDMENT DEFINED

The object of an amendment, as contra-distinguished from a supplemental petition or answer, is to add something to, or withdraw something from, that which has been previously pleaded so as to perfect that which is or may be deficient, or to correct that which has been incorrectly stated by the party making the amendment, or to plead new matter, additional to that formerly pleaded by the amending party, which constitutes an additional claim or defense permissible to the suit.

History of TRCP 62: Adopted eff. Sept. 1, 1941, by order of Oct. 29, 1940 (3 Tex.B.J. 533 [1940]). Source: Tex. Rules for Dist. & Cty. Cts. 12 & 15.

J.M. Huber Corp. v. Santa Fe Energy Res., 871 S.W.2d 842, 844 (Tex.App.—Houston [14th Dist.] 1994, no writ). "An amended petition ... adds or withdraws from that which was previously pleaded for correction or to plead new matter. An amended petition also supersedes all prior petitions and operates to dismiss parties and causes of action to the extent they are omitted from the amended pleading."

TRCP 63. AMENDMENTS & RESPONSIVE PLEADINGS

Parties may amend their pleadings, respond to pleadings on file of other parties, file suggestions of death and make representative parties, and file such other pleas as they may desire by filing such pleas with the clerk at such time as not to operate as a surprise to the opposite party; provided, that any pleadings, responses or pleas offered for filing within seven days of the date of trial or thereafter, or after such time as may be ordered by the judge under Rule 166, shall be filed only after leave of the judge is obtained, which leave shall be granted by the judge unless there is a showing that such filing will operate as a surprise to the opposite party.

See *Commentaries*, "Motion to Amend Pleadings—Pretrial," ch. 5-F; "Motion to Amend Pleadings—Trial and Post-Trial", ch. 8-F; FORMS 5F, 8F.

History of TRCP 63: Amended eff. Sept. 1, 1990, by order of Apr. 24, 1990 (785-86 S.W.2d [Tex.Cases] xlii): Changed title; added "respond to pleadings on file of other parties"; requires that all trial pleadings of all parties, except those permitted by TRCP 66, be on file at least seven days before trial unless leave of court permits later filing. Amended eff. Jan. 1, 1961, by order of July 26, 1960 (23 Tex.B.J. 620 [Oct. 1960]): Added language "or after such time as may be ordered by the judge under TRCP 166." Adopted eff. Sept. 1, 1941, by order of Oct. 29, 1940 (3 Tex.B.J. 533 [1940]). Source: TRCS art. 2001(1), (2) (repealed), with changes: Authorizes amendment without leave of court when filed seven days or more before the date of trial; requires leave to amend thereafter, which may be granted by the judge instead of by the court. Art. 2001(3) was superseded by TRCP 66 & 67.

Sosa v. Central Power & Light, 909 S.W.2d 893, 895 (Tex.1995). The plaintiffs "filed their second amended original petition exactly one week before a scheduled summary judgment hearing. [Under TRCP 4,] the day on which [Ps] filed their amendment is not counted but the seventh day after it was filed is counted. [T]he last day counted from the date of the filing may be the date of the hearing. Therefore, [Ps] timely filed their second amended original petition."

Chapin & Chapin, Inc. v. Texas Sand & Gravel Co., 844 S.W.2d 664, 665 (Tex.1992). Under TRCP "'63 and 66 a trial court has no discretion to refuse an amendment unless: 1) the opposing party presents evidence of surprise or prejudice; or 2) the amendment asserts a new cause of action or defense, and thus is prejudicial on its face....' [¶] [W]e conclude that the trial court's refusal to allow [D] to verify its denial [less than 7 days before trial] was an abuse of discretion."

Greenhalgh v. Service Lloyds Ins. Co., 787 S.W.2d 938, 940 (Tex.1990). "[A] party's right to amend under [TRCP] 63 is subject only to the opposing party's right to show surprise."

Goswami v. Metropolitan S&L Ass'n, 751 S.W.2d 487, 490 (Tex.1988). "[I]n the absence of a sufficient showing of surprise by the opposing party, the failure to obtain leave of court when filing a late pleading may be cured by the trial court's action in considering the amended pleading. [¶] A summary judgment proceeding is a trial within the meaning of [TRCP] 63."

TRCP 64. AMENDED INSTRUMENT

The party amending shall point out the instrument amended, as "original petition," or "plaintiff's first supplemental petition," or as "original answer," or "defendant's first supplemental answer" or other instrument filed by the party and shall amend by filing a substitute therefor, entire and complete in itself, indorsed "amended original petition," or "amended first supplemental petition," or "amended original answer," or "amended first supplemental answer," accordingly as said instruments of pleading are designated.

History of TRCP 64: Adopted eff. Sept. 1, 1941, by order of Oct. 29, 1940 (3 Tex.B.J. 533 [1940]). Source: Tex. Rules for Dist. & Cty. Cts. 13.

TRCP 65. SUBSTITUTED INSTRUMENT TAKES PLACE OF ORIGINAL

Unless the substituted instrument shall be set aside on exceptions, the instrument for which it is substituted shall no longer be regarded as a part of the pleading in the record of the cause, unless some error of the court in deciding upon the necessity of the amendment, or otherwise in superseding it, be complained of, and exception be taken to the action of the court, or unless it be necessary to look to the superseded pleading upon a question of limitation.

See *Commentaries*, "Amending the Pleadings," ch. 1-B, §7; "Nonsuit by amendment," ch. 7-E, §2.8.1.

History of TRCP 65: Adopted eff. Sept. 1, 1941, by order of Oct. 29, 1940 (3 Tex.B.J. 534 [1940]). Source: Tex. Rules for Dist. & Cty. Cts. 14.

Drake Ins. Co. v. King, 606 S.W.2d 812, 817 (Tex. 1980). The "original petition in intervention contained a judicial admission.... [H]owever ... a first and then a second amended petition [was filed]. [The original petition] was no longer a judicial admission, but must be introduced into evidence as any other admission before it may be considered as evidence."

Randolph v. Jackson Walker L.L.P., 29 S.W.3d 271, 274 (Tex.App.—Houston [14th Dist.] 2000, pet. denied). "When a party's name is omitted from an amended pleading, he is as effectively dismissed as where a formal order of dismissal is entered."

TRCP 66. TRIAL AMENDMENT

If evidence is objected to at the trial on the ground that it is not within the issues made by the pleading, or if during the trial any defect, fault or omission in a pleading, either of form or substance, is called to the attention of the court, the court may allow the pleadings to be amended and shall do so freely when the presentation of the merits of the action will be subserved thereby and the objecting party fails to satisfy the court that the allowance of such amendment would prejudice him in maintaining his action or defense upon the merits. The court may grant a postponement to enable the objecting party to meet such evidence.

See ***Commentaries***, "Motion to Amend Pleadings—Trial and Post-Trial," ch. 8-F; FORMS 8F.

History of TRCP 66: Amended eff. Sept. 1, 1941, by order of Mar. 31, 1941 (4 Tex.B.J. 498 [1941]). Adopted eff. Sept. 1, 1941, by order of Oct. 29, 1940 (3 Tex.B.J. 534 [1940]). Source: FRCP 15(b) (last two sentences).

City of Ft. Worth v. Zimlich, 29 S.W.3d 62, 73 (Tex. 2000). "A trial amendment must be filed as a written pleading; an oral statement at trial is insufficient to modify the pleadings. However, a party waives its complaint of any defect, omission, or fault in the pleadings if the party fails to specifically object before the submission of the charge to the jury."

State Bar v. Kilpatrick, 874 S.W.2d 656, 658 (Tex. 1994). "A court may not refuse a trial amendment unless (1) the opposing party presents evidence of surprise or prejudice, or (2) the amendment asserts a new cause of action or defense, and thus is prejudicial on its face. The burden of showing surprise or prejudice rests on the party resisting the amendment." *See also* ***Greenhalgh v. Service Lloyds Ins. Co.***, 787 S.W.2d 938, 941 (Tex.1990).

Deustch v. Hoover, Bax & Slovacek, L.L.P., 97 S.W.3d 179, 185-86 (Tex.App.—Houston [14th Dist.] 2002, no pet.). TRCP 66 "suggests a postponement may cure any prejudice from a trial amendment. [N]othing in the rule [suggests] an offer of a mistrial does so, especially when the trial is virtually completed. A party seeking leave to amend its pleadings after the trial has commenced should not be rewarded by forcing the judge, jury, and opposing party to either acquiesce in the tardy amendment or start over. [T]he mistrial was the trial court's suggestion. [D's] decision to refuse the trial court's offer ... did not amount to a relinquishment of his objection [to the trial amendment]."

In re Loftis, 40 S.W.3d 160, 163 (Tex.App.—Texarkana 2001, no pet.). "A party that opposes a trial amendment does not have to prove prejudice or surprise if the amendment is substantive, which would change the nature of the trial."

Weynand v. Weynand, 990 S.W.2d 843, 847 (Tex. App.—Dallas 1999, pet. denied). "An amendment that is prejudicial on its face has three defining characteristics. First, the pleading must assert new substantive matter that reshapes the nature of the trial itself. [¶] Second, the new matter asserted must be such that it could not have been anticipated by the opposing party in light of the development of the case. [¶] Finally, allowance of the amendment must not detrimentally affect the opposing party's case."

TRCP 67. AMENDMENTS TO CONFORM TO ISSUES TRIED WITHOUT OBJECTION

When issues not raised by the pleadings are tried by express or implied consent of the parties, they shall be treated in all respects as if they had been raised in the pleadings. In such case such amendment of the pleadings as may be necessary to cause them to conform to the evidence and to raise these issues may be made by leave of court upon motion of any party at any time up to the submission of the case to the Court or jury, but failure so to amend shall not affect the result of the trial of these issues; provided that written pleadings, before the time of submission, shall be necessary to the submission of questions, as is provided in Rules 277 and 279.

See ***Commentaries***, "Trial by Consent," ch. 1-B, §6.3.

History of TRCP 67: Amended eff. Sept. 1, 1990, by order of Apr. 24, 1990 (785-86 S.W.2d [Tex.Cases] xlii): Changed "special issues" to "questions." Amended eff. Sept. 1, 1941, by order of Mar. 31, 1941 (4 Tex.B.J. 498 [1941]). Adopted eff. Sept. 1, 1941, by order of Oct. 29, 1940 (3 Tex.B.J. 534 [1940]). Source: FRCP 15(b).

Bedgood v. Madalin, 600 S.W.2d 773, 775-76 (Tex. 1980). TRCP 67 "requires that written pleadings, before the time of submission, shall be necessary to the submission of special issues even where issues are tried by implied consent. Since there were no proper pleadings, the trial court erred in overruling [Ds'] objections to the introduction of evidence and the submission of special issues...."

Oil Field Haulers Ass'n v. Railroad Comm'n, 381 S.W.2d 183, 191 (Tex.1964). "[A] plaintiff may not sustain a favorable judgment on an unpleaded cause of action, in the absence of trial by consent...."

RE/MAX, Inc. v. Katar Corp., 961 S.W.2d 324, 328 (Tex.App.—Houston [1st Dist.] 1997), *pet. denied*, 989 S.W.2d 363 (Tex.1999). "Trial by consent is intended to cover the exceptional case where it clearly appears from the record as a whole that the parties tried the [unpled] issue."

TRCP 68. COURT MAY ORDER REPLEADER

The court, when deemed necessary in any case, may order a repleader on the part of one or both of the parties, in order to make their pleadings substantially conform to the rules.

History of TRCP 68: Adopted eff. Sept. 1, 1941, by order of Oct. 29, 1940 (3 Tex.B.J. 534 [1940]). Source: Tex. Rules for Dist. & Cty. Cts. 29.

Miller v. Kossey, 802 S.W.2d 873, 877 (Tex.App.—Amarillo 1991, writ denied). "[W]hen [P] failed to comply with the court's ... order to send a new notice establishing a necessary element of her cause of action, the court was authorized to dismiss her DTPA action. Consequently, the court did not err in dismissing the action."

TRCP 69. SUPPLEMENTAL PETITION OR ANSWER

Each supplemental petition or answer, made by either party, shall be a response to the last preceding pleading by the other party, and shall not repeat allegations formerly pleaded further than is necessary as an introduction to that which is stated in the pleading then being drawn up. These instruments, to wit, the original petition and its several supplements, and the original answer and its several supplements, shall respectively, constitute separate and distinct parts of the pleadings of each party; and the position and identity, by number and name, with the indorsement of each instrument, shall be preserved throughout the pleadings of either party.

History of TRCP 69: Adopted eff. Sept. 1, 1941, by order of Oct. 29, 1940 (3 Tex.B.J. 534 [1940]). Source: Tex. Rules for Dist. & Cty. Cts. 10.

Sixth RMA Partners v. Sibley, 111 S.W.3d 46, 53 (Tex.2003). TRCP 28 "requires that the correct legal name be substituted, but it does not mandate the procedural method by which substitution may be accomplished." The correct name may be substituted by motion of a party or the court, by amended pleading, and if no objection, by supplemental pleading.

J.M. Huber Corp. v. Santa Fe Energy Res., 871 S.W.2d 842, 844 (Tex.App.—Houston [14th Dist.] 1994, no writ). "A supplemental petition is a response to the last preceding pleading by the other party and does not repeat allegations previously pleaded unless such repetition is necessary."

TRCP 70. PLEADING: SURPRISE: COST

When either a supplemental or amended pleading is of such character and is presented at such time as to take the opposite party by surprise, the court may charge the continuance of the cause, if granted, to the party causing the surprise if the other party satisfactorily shows that he is not ready for trial because of the allowance of the filing of such supplemental or amended pleading, and the court may, in such event, in its discretion require the party filing such pleading to pay to the surprised party the amount of reasonable costs and expenses incurred by the other party as a result of the continuance, including attorney fees, or make such other order with respect thereto as may be just.

See ***Commentaries***, "Motion to Amend Pleadings—Pretrial," ch. 5-F; "Motion to Amend Pleadings—Trial and Post-Trial," ch. 8-F; FORMS 5F, 8F.

History of TRCP 70: Amended eff. Jan. 1, 1981, by order of June 10, 1980 (599-600 S.W.2d [Tex.Cases] xxxvii): This amendment enlarges the sanctions that may be applied in the discretion of the trial court for the filing of a pleading that takes the opposite party by surprise. Adopted eff. Sept. 1, 1941, by order of Oct. 29, 1940 (3 Tex.B.J. 534 [1940]). Source: Tex. Rules for Dist. & Cty. Cts. 16.

TRCP 71. MISNOMER OF PLEADING

When a party has mistakenly designated any plea or pleading, the court, if justice so requires, shall treat the plea or pleading as if it had been properly designated. Pleadings shall be docketed as originally designated and shall remain identified as designated, unless the court orders redesignation. Upon court order filed with the clerk, the clerk shall modify the docket and all other clerk records to reflect redesignation.

History of TRCP 71: Amended eff. Jan. 1, 1988, by order of July 15, 1987 (733-34 S.W.2d [Tex.Cases] xli). Adopted eff. Sept. 1, 1941, by order of Oct. 29,

1940 (3 Tex.B.J. 534 [1940]). Source: FRCP 8(c) last sentence. See TRCP 94 for balance of FRCP 8.

State Bar v. Heard, 603 S.W.2d 829, 833 (Tex. 1980). "We look to the substance of a plea for relief to determine the nature of the pleading, not merely at the form of title given to it."

Wilie v. Signature Geophysical Servs., 65 S.W.3d 355, 362 (Tex.App.—Houston [14th Dist.] 2001, pet. denied). "Generally, a misnamed pleading will not fail if it gives adequate notice to the opposing parties. The court will look to the substance of the pleading."

TRCP 72 - 73. REPEALED

TRCP 72 repealed eff. Sept. 1, 1990, by order of Apr. 24, 1990 (785-86 S.W.2d [Tex.Cases] xliii): The surviving provisions were moved to TRCP 21. TRCP 73 repealed eff. Sept. 1, 1990, by order of Apr. 24, 1990 (785-86 S.W.2d [Tex.Cases] xliii): The surviving provisions were moved to TRCP 21b.

TRCP 74. FILING WITH THE COURT DEFINED

The filing of pleadings, other papers and exhibits as required by these rules shall be made by filing them with the clerk of the court, except that the judge may permit the papers to be filed with him, in which event he shall note thereon the filing date and time and forthwith transmit them to the office of the clerk.

See TRCP 24; *Commentaries*, "Rules for Filing Documents," ch. 1-C.

History of TRCP 74: Amended eff. Jan. 1, 1967, by order of July 20, 1966 (401-02 S.W.2d [Tex.Cases] xxxii): Scope of rule expanded to include exhibits. Adopted eff. Sept. 1, 1941, by order of Oct. 29, 1940 (3 Tex.B.J. 535 [1940]). Source: FRCP 5(e), with changes: Permits the judge to accept instruments for filing and directs him, when he does so, to note thereon the date and time.

Miller Brewing Co. v. Villarreal, 829 S.W.2d 770, 771 (Tex.1992). "Under our current rules, a party who finds the courthouse closed on the last day that a document must be filed ... may also locate the clerk or judge of the court and file the document with them."

Standard Fire Ins. Co. v. LaCoke, 585 S.W.2d 678, 680 (Tex.1979). "The rule is traditionally stated to be that an instrument is deemed in law filed at the time it is left with the clerk, regardless of whether or not a file mark is placed on the instrument and regardless of whether the file mark gives some other date of filing."

TRCP 75. FILED PLEADINGS; WITHDRAWAL

All filed pleadings shall remain at all times in the clerk's office or in the court or in custody of the clerk, except that the court may by order entered on the minutes allow a filed pleading to be withdrawn for a limited time whenever necessary, on leaving a certified copy on file. The party withdrawing such pleading shall pay the costs of such order and certified copy.

History of TRCP 75: Adopted eff. Sept. 1, 1941, by order of Oct. 29, 1940 (3 Tex.B.J. 535 [1940]). Source: The 2d and 3d sentences of TRCS art. 2002a (repealed).

Trinity Indus. v. Rivera, 745 S.W.2d 525, 526 (Tex. App.—Corpus Christi 1988, no writ). A party cannot terminate a suit by withdrawing its pleadings. "Under our rules of civil procedure, a final order terminating a lawsuit may be accomplished by a judgment on the merits, a dismissal or a non-suit."

TRCP 75a. FILING EXHIBITS: COURT REPORTER TO FILE WITH CLERK

The court reporter or stenographer shall file with the clerk of the court all exhibits which were admitted in evidence or tendered on bill of exception during the course of any hearing, proceeding, or trial.

See TRAP 13.1(b), (c).

History of TRCP 75a: Adopted eff. Jan. 1, 1967, by order of July 20, 1966 (401-02 S.W.2d [Tex.Cases] xxxii). Source: New rule.

Walton v. Canon, Short & Gaston, P.C., 23 S.W.3d 143, 151 (Tex.App.—El Paso 2000, no pet.). TRCP 75a "provides that a court reporter shall file all exhibits admitted into evidence, so that a trial court may consider only evidence admitted at trial."

TRCP 75b. FILED EXHIBITS: WITHDRAWAL

All filed exhibits admitted in evidence or tendered on bill of exception shall, until returned or otherwise disposed of as authorized by Rule 14b, remain at all times in the clerk's office or in the court or in the custody of the clerk except as follows:

(a) The court may by order entered on the minutes allow a filed exhibit to be withdrawn by any party only upon such party's leaving on file a certified, photo, or other reproduced copy of such exhibit. The party withdrawing such exhibit shall pay the costs of such order and copy.

(b) The court reporter or stenographer of the court conducting the hearing, proceedings, or trial in which exhibits are admitted or offered in evidence, shall have the right to withdraw filed exhibits, upon giving the clerk proper receipt therefor, whenever necessary for the court reporter or stenographer to transmit such original exhibits to an appellate court under the provisions of Rule 379 or to otherwise discharge the duties imposed by law upon said court reporter or stenographer.

History of TRCP 75b: Adopted eff. Jan. 1, 1967, by order of July 20, 1966 (401-02 S.W.2d [Tex.Cases] xxxii). Source: New rule.

Perez v. Bagous, 833 S.W.2d 671, 674 (Tex.App.—Corpus Christi 1992, no writ). "Once a party has admitted an exhibit into evidence at trial, the exhibit may not be retrieved and used to create another during a jury recess without notifying opposing counsel or the court. It is wholly outside the scope of the rule to then enter this newly created exhibit into evidence without informing opposing counsel of the use of the entered exhibit."

TRCP 76. MAY INSPECT PAPERS

Each attorney at law practicing in any court shall be allowed at all reasonable times to inspect the papers and records relating to any suit or other matter in which he may be interested.

History of TRCP 76: Adopted eff. Sept. 1, 1941, by order of Oct. 29, 1940 (3 Tex.B.J. 535 [1940]). Source: TRCS art. 318 (repealed).

U.S. v. Marks, 949 S.W.2d 320, 326 (Tex.1997). "[T]here are exceptions [to TRCP 76], such as documents submitted *in camera* under a claim of privilege, documents subject to a protective order, or materials sealed under [TRCP] 76a. Rule 76 does not give [P] an absolute right to the transcript of the *in camera* hearing. *At 327:* However, the district court's order was overly broad in sealing the entire record rather than those portions that pertained to the grand jury proceeding."

Davenport v. Garcia, 834 S.W.2d 4, 24 (Tex.1992). "[A]ccess to [court records] is separately guaranteed to '[e]ach attorney at law practicing in any court....' A court may not escape the strict obligations of [TRCP 76 and 76a] by tacitly closing the record through an unwritten order."

TRCP 76a. SEALING COURT RECORDS

1. **Standard for Sealing Court Records.** Court records may not be removed from court files except as permitted by statute or rule. No court order or opinion issued in the adjudication of a case may be sealed. Other court records, as defined in this rule, are presumed to be open to the general public and may be sealed only upon a showing of all of the following:

(a) a specific, serious and substantial interest which clearly outweighs:

(1) this presumption of openness;

(2) any probable adverse effect that sealing will have upon the general public health or safety;

(b) no less restrictive means than sealing records will adequately and effectively protect the specific interest asserted.

2. **Court Records.** For purposes of this rule, court records means:

(a) all documents of any nature filed in connection with any matter before any civil court, except:

(1) documents filed with a court in camera, solely for the purpose of obtaining a ruling on the discoverability of such documents;

(2) documents in court files to which access is otherwise restricted by law;

(3) documents filed in an action originally arising under the Family Code.

(b) settlement agreements not filed of record, excluding all reference to any monetary consideration, that seek to restrict disclosure of information concerning matters that have a probable adverse effect upon the general public health or safety, or the administration of public office, or the operation of government.

(c) discovery, not filed of record, concerning matters that have a probable adverse effect upon the general public health or safety, or the administration of public office, or the operation of government, except discovery in cases originally initiated to preserve bona fide trade secrets or other intangible property rights.

3. **Notice.** Court records may be sealed only upon a party's written motion, which shall be open to public inspection. The movant shall post a public notice at the place where notices for meetings of county governmental bodies are required to be posted, stating: that a hearing will be held in open court on a motion to seal court records in the specific case; that any person may intervene and be heard concerning the sealing of court records; the specific time and place of the hearing; the style and number of the case; a brief but specific description of both the nature of the case and the records which are sought to be sealed; and the identity of the movant. Immediately after posting such notice, the movant shall file a verified copy of the posted notice with the clerk of the court in which the case is pending and with the Clerk of the Supreme Court of Texas.

4. **Hearing.** A hearing, open to the public, on a motion to seal court records shall be held in open court

as soon as practicable, but not less than fourteen days after the motion is filed and notice is posted. Any party may participate in the hearing. Non-parties may intervene as a matter of right for the limited purpose of participating in the proceedings, upon payment of the fee required for filing a plea in intervention. The court may inspect records in camera when necessary. The court may determine a motion relating to sealing or unsealing court records in accordance with the procedures prescribed by Rule 120a.

5. Temporary Sealing Order. A temporary sealing order may issue upon motion and notice to any parties who have answered in the case pursuant to Rules 21 and 21a upon a showing of compelling need from specific facts shown by affidavit or by verified petition that immediate and irreparable injury will result to a specific interest of the applicant before notice can be posted and a hearing held as otherwise provided herein. The temporary order shall set the time for the hearing required by paragraph 4 and shall direct that the movant immediately give the public notice required by paragraph 3. The court may modify or withdraw any temporary order upon motion by any party or intervenor, notice to the parties, and hearing conducted as soon as practicable. Issuance of a temporary order shall not reduce in any way the burden of proof of a party requesting sealing at the hearing required by paragraph 4.

6. Order on Motion to Seal Court Records. A motion relating to sealing or unsealing court records shall be decided by written order, open to the public, which shall state: the style and number of the case; the specific reasons for finding and concluding whether the showing required by paragraph 1 has been made; the specific portions of court records which are to be sealed; and the time period for which the sealed portions of the court records are to be sealed. The order shall not be included in any judgment or other order but shall be a separate document in the case; however, the failure to comply with this requirement shall not affect its appealability.

7. Continuing Jurisdiction. Any person may intervene as a matter of right at any time before or after judgment to seal or unseal court records. A court that issues a sealing order retains continuing jurisdiction to enforce, alter, or vacate that order. An order sealing or unsealing court records shall not be reconsidered on motion of any party or intervenor who had actual notice of the hearing preceding issuance of the order, without first showing changed circumstances materially affecting the order. Such circumstances need not be related to the case in which the order was issued. However, the burden of making the showing required by paragraph 1 shall always be on the party seeking to seal records.

8. Appeal. Any order (or portion of an order or judgment) relating to sealing or unsealing court records shall be deemed to be severed from the case and a final judgment which may be appealed by any party or intervenor who participated in the hearing preceding issuance of such order. The appellate court may abate the appeal and order the trial court to direct that further public notice be given, or to hold further hearings, or to make additional findings.

9. Application. Access to documents in court files not defined as court records by this rule remains governed by existing law. This rule does not apply to any court records sealed in an action in which a final judgment has been entered before its effective date. This rule applies to cases already pending on its effective date only with regard to:

(a) all court records filed or exchanged after the effective date;

(b) any motion to alter or vacate an order restricting access to court records, issued before the effective date.

For definitions of trade secret, see Tex. Penal Code §31.05(a)(4). See ***Commentaries***, "Motion to Seal Court Records," ch. 5-K; "Scope of Discovery," ch. 6-B; FORMS 5K.

History of TRCP 76a: Adopted eff. Sept. 1, 1990, by order of Apr. 24, 1990 (785-86 S.W.2d [Tex.Cases] xliv): To establish guidelines for sealing certain court records in compliance with Gov't Code §22.010. Source: New rule.

In re Continental Gen. Tire, 979 S.W.2d 609, 614 (Tex.1998). "[E]ven if a trade secret produced under a protective order is later determined to be a court record, this does not necessarily mean that the information must be made public. Rule 76a allows the information to remain sealed upon a showing that it meets the criteria specified in Rule 76a(1). That a document contains trade secret information is a factor to be considered in applying this sealing standard."

General Tire v. Kepple, 970 S.W.2d 520, 525 (Tex. 1998). "[W]e hold that when a party seeks a protective order under [TRCP] 166b(5)(c) [now 192.6] to restrict the dissemination of unfiled discovery, and no party or intervenor contends that the discovery is a 'court record,' a trial court need not conduct a hearing or render any findings on that issue. If a party or intervenor opposing a protective order claims that the discovery is a 'court record,' the court must make a threshold determination on that issue. However, public notice and a [TRCP] 76a hearing are mandated only if the court finds that the documents are court records."

U.S. v. Marks, 949 S.W.2d 320, 324-25 (Tex.1997). "To the extent the sealed record contained [grand jury] information protected by [FRCrP] 6(e), it is not a 'court record' under [TRCP] 76a(2)(a)(2), and thus sealing of those portions of the record does not violate [TRCP] 76a. ... The record [also] contains statements that are clearly not protected by [FRCrP] 6(e). The district court should have determined what statements were confidential before it sealed the record ... instead of simply sealing the entire transcription."

Dallas Morning News v. 5th Ct. of Appeals, 842 S.W.2d 655, 657 (Tex.1992). "The press and the public have a right to be present at all proceedings in the trial of the underlying case, and to report all that they observe."

Compaq Computer Corp. v. Lapray, 75 S.W.3d 669, 673 (Tex.App.—Beaumont 2002, no pet.). "Rule 76a contains no requirement that the trial court determine the discoverability of **court records** prior to determining whether to seal or unseal those records. Only under the 76a(2)(a)(1) exception—for documents filed in camera 'solely for the purpose of obtaining a ruling on the discoverability of such documents'—must the issue of discoverability be decided before the documents may become court records."

TRCP 77. LOST RECORDS & PAPERS

When any papers or records are lost or destroyed during the pendency of a suit, the parties may, with the approval of the judge, agree in writing on a brief statement of the matters contained therein; or either party may supply such lost records or papers as follows:

a. After three days' notice to the adverse party or his attorney, make written sworn motion before the court stating the loss or destruction of such record or papers, accompanied by certified copies of the originals if obtainable, or by substantial copies thereof.

b. If, upon hearing, the court be satisfied that they are substantial copies of the original, an order shall be made substituting such copies or brief statement for the originals.

c. Such substituted copies or brief statement shall be filed with the clerk, constitute a part of the cause, and have the force and effect of the originals.

See TRE 1003, 1004; TRAP 34.5(e), 34.6(f); ***Commentaries***, "Lost pleadings," ch. 1-C, §11.4.

History of TRCP 77: Amended eff. Dec. 31, 1943, by order of June 16, 1943 (3 Tex.B.J. 338 [1943]): Reworded par. (B). Adopted eff. Sept. 1, 1941, by order of Oct. 29, 1940 (3 Tex.B.J. 535 [1940]). Source: TRCS art. 2289 (repealed).

Coke v. Coke, 802 S.W.2d 270, 275 (Tex.App.—Dallas 1990, writ denied). The court overruled a party's objection to the trial court's reconstruction of the lost file from the other party's documents. The party "testified that as far as he could tell, the copies were true duplicates of the originals."

B. PLEADINGS OF PLAINTIFF

TRCP 78. PETITION; ORIGINAL & SUPPLEMENTAL; INDORSEMENT

The pleading of plaintiff shall consist of an original petition, and such supplemental petitions as may be necessary in the course of pleading by the parties to the suit. The original petition and the supplemental petitions shall be indorsed, so as to show their respective positions in the process of pleading, as "original petition," "plaintiff's first supplemental petition," "plaintiff's second supplemental petition," and so on, to be successively numbered, named, and indorsed.

History of TRCP 78: Adopted eff. Sept. 1, 1941, by order of Oct. 29, 1940 (3 Tex.B.J. 536 [1940]). Source: Tex. Rules for Dist. & Cty. Cts. 3.

TRCP 79. THE PETITION

The petition shall state the names of the parties and their residences, if known, together with the contents prescribed in Rule 47 above.

See ***Commentaries***, "Plaintiff's Original Petition," ch. 2-B; FORMS 2B.

History of TRCP 79: Adopted eff. Sept. 1, 1941, by order of Oct. 29, 1940 (3 Tex.B.J. 536 [1940]). Source: New rule.

Enserch Corp. v. Parker, 794 S.W.2d 2, 4-5 (Tex. 1990). "If [P] merely misnames the correct [D] (misnomer), limitations is tolled and a subsequent amendment ... relates back to the date of the original petition. If, however, [P] is mistaken as to which of two [Ds] is the correct one and there is ... a corporation with the name of the erroneously named [D] (misidentification), then [P] has sued the wrong party and limitations is not tolled."

TRCP 80. PLAINTIFF'S SUPPLEMENTAL PETITION

The plaintiff's supplemental petitions may contain special exceptions, general denials, and the allegations of new matter not before alleged by him, in reply to those which have been alleged by the defendant.

History of TRCP 80: Adopted eff. Sept. 1, 1941, by order of Oct. 29, 1940 (3 Tex.B.J. 536 [1940]). Source: Tex. Rules for Dist. & Cty. Cts. 5.

Moody-Rambin Interests v. Moore, 722 S.W.2d 790, 792 (Tex.App.—Houston [14th Dist.] 1987, no writ). The proper way to bring new parties into a suit is by an amended pleading, not a supplemental pleading. "An exception to this rule exists if the necessity for adding a new party arises from facts pled in [D's] answer."

TRCP 81. DEFENSIVE MATTERS

When the defendant sets up a counter claim, the plaintiff may plead thereto under rules prescribed for pleadings of defensive matter by the defendant, so far as applicable. Whenever the defendant is required to plead any matter of defense under oath, the plaintiff shall be required to plead such matters under oath when relied on by him.

History of TRCP 81: Adopted eff. Sept. 1, 1941, by order of Oct. 29, 1940 (3 Tex.B.J. 536 [1940]). Source: TRCS art. 2004 (repealed).

Greater Ft. Worth v. Mims, 627 S.W.2d 149, 152 (Tex.1982). "If [P] contesting the counterclaim does not intend to urge any defensive theory which must be verified or any affirmative defense under [TRCP] 94, he is not required to answer [D's] counterclaim."

TRCP 82. SPECIAL DEFENSES

The plaintiff need not deny any special matter of defense pleaded by the defendant, but the same shall be regarded as denied unless expressly admitted.

History of TRCP 82: Adopted eff. Sept. 1, 1941, by order of Oct. 29, 1940 (3 Tex.B.J. 536 [1940]). Source: TRCS art. 2005 (repealed).

Sanchez v. Matthews, 636 S.W.2d 455, 460 (Tex. App.—San Antonio 1982, writ ref'd n.r.e.). Under TRCP 82 [P] was not required to plead a special denial to the affirmative defense of release.

C. PLEADINGS OF DEFENDANT

TRCP 83. ANSWER; ORIGINAL & SUPPLEMENTAL; INDORSEMENT

The answer of defendant shall consist of an original answer, and such supplemental answers as may be necessary, in the course of pleading by the parties to the suit. The original answer and the supplemental answers shall be indorsed, so as to show their respective positions in the process of pleading, as "original answer," "defendant's first supplemental answer," "defendant's second supplemental answer," and so on, to be successively numbered, named and indorsed.

History of TRCP 83: Adopted eff. Sept. 1, 1941, by order of Oct. 29, 1940 (3 Tex.B.J. 536 [1940]). Source: Tex. Rules for Dist. & Cty. Cts. 6.

Smith v. Lippmann, 826 S.W.2d 137, 138 (Tex. 1992). "[A] defendant, who timely files a pro se answer by a signed letter that identifies the parties, the case, and the defendant's current address, has sufficiently appeared by answer and deserves notice of any subsequent proceedings in the case."

TRCP 84. ANSWER MAY INCLUDE SEVERAL MATTERS

The defendant in his answer may plead as many several matters, whether of law or fact, as he may think necessary for his defense, and which may be pertinent to the cause, and such matters shall be heard in such order as may be directed by the court, special appearance and motion to transfer venue, and the practice thereunder being excepted herefrom.

History of TRCP 84: Amended eff. Sept. 1, 1983, by order of June 15, 1983 (651-52 S.W.2d [Tex.Cases] xxxi): To conform to S.B. 898, 68th Legislature, 1983. Amended eff. Sept. 1, 1962, by order of Apr. 12, 1962 (25 Tex.B.J. 371 [1962]): Words "special appearance and" were inserted before "plea of privilege." Amended eff. Mar. 1, 1950, by order of Oct. 12, 1949 (2 Tex.B.J. 529 [1949]): The requirement that defensive matters must be filed at the same time and in due order of pleading was eliminated, and the provisions of the last clause were changed to allow pleas to be heard in such order as the court may direct, excepting a plea of privilege. Adopted eff. Sept. 1, 1941, by order of Oct. 29, 1940 (3 Tex.B.J. 536 [1940]). Source: TRCS arts. 2006 & 2012 (repealed). See TRCP 92 for balance of Art. 2006.

Glover v. Moser, 930 S.W.2d 940, 944 (Tex.App.—Beaumont 1996, writ denied). "We believe the clear intent of [TRCP] 84 was to prevent exactly what occurred in [this] case, i.e., the trial court proceeding on meritorious matters prior to its determination of whether venue is properly before it."

TRCP 85. ORIGINAL ANSWER; CONTENTS

The original answer may consist of motions to transfer venue, pleas to the jurisdiction, in abatement, or any other dilatory pleas; of special exceptions, of general denial, and any defense by way of avoidance or estoppel, and it may present a cross-action, which to that extent will place defendant in the attitude of a plaintiff. Matters in avoidance and estoppel may be stated together, or in several special pleas, each presenting a distinct defense, and numbered so as to admit of separate issues to be formed on them.

See *Commentaries*, "The Answer—Denying Liability," ch. 3-E; FORMS 3E.

History of TRCP 85: Amended eff. Sept. 1, 1983, by order of June 15, 1983 (651-52 S.W.2d [Tex.Cases] xxxii): To conform to S.B. 898, 68th Legislature, 1983. Adopted eff. Sept. 1, 1941, by order of Oct. 29, 1940 (3 Tex.B.J. 536 [1940]). Source: Tex. Rules for Dist. & Cty. Cts. 7.

Hines v. Hash, 843 S.W.2d 464, 469 (Tex.1992). "To be timely, [D's] request for an abatement [under the DTPA] must be made while the purpose of notice—settlement and avoidance of litigation expense—remains viable. Thus, [D] must request an abatement with the filing of an answer or very soon thereafter. If the trial court determines that [P] has failed to give notice as required by the [DTPA] statute, the action must be abated."

TRCP 86. MOTION TO TRANSFER VENUE

1. Time to File. An objection to improper venue is waived if not made by written motion filed prior to or concurrently with any other plea, pleading or motion except a special appearance motion provided for in Rule 120a. A written consent of the parties to transfer the case to another county may be filed with the clerk of the court at any time. A motion to transfer venue because an impartial trial cannot be had in the county where the action is pending is governed by the provisions of Rule 257.

2. How to File. The motion objecting to improper venue may be contained in a separate instrument filed concurrently with or prior to the filing of the movant's first responsive pleading or the motion may be combined with other objections and defenses and included in the movant's first responsive pleading.

3. Requisites of Motion. The motion, and any amendments to it, shall state that the action should be transferred to another specified county of proper venue because:

(a) The county where the action is pending is not a proper county; or

(b) Mandatory venue of the action in another county is prescribed by one or more specific statutory provisions which shall be clearly designated or indicated.

The motion shall state the legal and factual basis for the transfer of the action and request transfer of the action to a specific county of mandatory or proper venue. Verification of the motion is not required. The motion may be accompanied by supporting affidavits as provided in Rule 87.

4. Response and Reply. Except as provided in paragraph 3(a) of Rule 87, a response to the motion to transfer is not required. Verification of a response is not required.

5. Service. A copy of any instrument filed pursuant to Rule 86 shall be served in accordance with Rule 21a.

See CPRC ch. 15; *Commentaries*, "Motion to Transfer—Challenging Venue," ch. 3-C; FORMS 3C.

History of TRCP 86: Amended eff. Sept. 1, 1983, by order of June 15, 1983 (651-52 S.W.2d [Tex.Cases] xxxii): To conform to S.B. 898, 68th Legislature, 1983. Amended eff. Sept. 1, 1962, by order of Apr. 12, 1962 (25 Tex.B.J. 371 [1962]): Requisites of plea of privilege to be sued in county other than the county of one's residence prescribed, and note regarding 1943 amendment rewritten. Amended eff. Jan. 1, 1955, by order of July 20, 1954 (17 Tex.B.J. 566 [1954]): Copy of plea of privilege required to be served on the adverse party or his attorney by delivery to him in person or by registered mail, and requiring filing of controverting affidavit within ten days after receipt thereof. Amended eff. Dec. 31, 1943, by order of June 16, 1943 (6 Tex.B.J. 339 [1943]): Controverting affidavit required to be filed within ten days after appearance day if plea of privilege is filed in vacation, otherwise within ten days after appearance day or after the filing of the plea of privilege, whichever is the later date. Amended eff. Sept. 1, 1941, by order of Mar. 31, 1941 (4 Tex.B.J. 500 [1941]): The word "or" changed to read "of" between "service" and "process." Adopted eff. Sept. 1, 1941, by order of Oct. 29, 1940 (3 Tex.B.J. 537 [1940]). Source: TRCS art. 2007 (repealed). Changes: Requires the plea of privilege to state the post-office address of the defendant or attorney; increased time for filing a controverting affidavit to ten days.

GeoChem Tech Corp. v. Verseckes, 962 S.W.2d 541, 544 (Tex.1998). "[U]nder the current venue statutes, [P] has the 'first choice' of venue. However, the statutes do not say that [P] may choose venue only once."

Wichita Cty. v. Hart, 917 S.W.2d 779, 781 (Tex. 1996). "[D] raises the question of proper venue by objecting to [P]'s venue choice through a motion to transfer venue. The fact that mandatory venue lies in another county provides one ground for a motion to transfer venue. If [P]'s chosen venue rests on a permissive venue statute and [D] files a meritorious motion to transfer based on a mandatory venue provision, the trial court must grant the motion. A trial court's erroneous denial of a motion to transfer venue requires reversal of the judgment and remand for a new trial."

TRCP 87. DETERMINATION OF MOTION TO TRANSFER

1. **Consideration of Motion.** The determination of a motion to transfer venue shall be made promptly by the court and such determination must be made in a reasonable time prior to commencement of the trial on the merits. The movant has the duty to request a setting on the motion to transfer. Except on leave of court each party is entitled to at least 45 days notice of a hearing on the motion to transfer.

Except on leave of court, any response or opposing affidavits shall be filed at least 30 days prior to the hearing of the motion to transfer. The movant is not required to file a reply to the response but any reply and any additional affidavits supporting the motion to transfer must, except on leave of court, be filed not later than 7 days prior to the hearing date.

2. **Burden of Establishing Venue.**

(a) *In General.* A party who seeks to maintain venue of the action in a particular county in reliance upon Section 15.001* (General Rule), Sections 15.011-15.017 (Mandatory Venue), Sections 15.031-15.040 (Permissive Venue), or Sections 15.061 and 15.062 (Multiple Claims), Civil Practice and Remedies Code, has the burden to make proof, as provided in paragraph 3 of this rule, that venue is maintainable in the county of suit. A party who seeks to transfer venue of the action to another specified county under Section 15.001* (General Rule), Sections 15.011-15.017 (Mandatory Venue), Sections 15.031-15.040 (Permissive Venue), or Sections 15.061 and 15.062 (Multiple Claims), Civil Practice and Remedies Code, has the burden to make proof, as provided in paragraph 3 of this rule, that venue is maintainable in the county to which transfer is sought. A party who seeks to transfer venue of the action to another specified county under Sections 15.011-15.017, Civil Practice and Remedies Code on the basis that a mandatory venue provision is applicable and controlling has the burden to make proof, as provided in paragraph 3 of this rule, that venue is maintainable in the county to which transfer is sought by virtue of one or more mandatory venue exceptions.

(b) *Cause of Action.* It shall not be necessary for a claimant to prove the merits of a cause of action, but the existence of a cause of action, when pleaded properly, shall be taken as established as alleged by the pleadings. When the defendant specifically denies the venue allegations, the claimant is required, by prima facie proof as provided in paragraph 3 of this rule, to support such pleading that the cause of action taken as established by the pleadings, or a part of such cause of action, accrued in the county of suit. If a defendant seeks transfer to a county where the cause of action or a part thereof accrued, it shall be sufficient for the defendant to plead that if a cause of action exists, then the cause of action or part thereof accrued in the specific county to which transfer is sought, and such allegation shall not constitute an admission that a cause of action in fact exists. But the defendant shall be required to support his pleading by prima facie proof as provided in paragraph 3 of this rule, that, if a cause of action exists, it or a part thereof accrued in the county to which transfer is sought.

(c) *Other Rules.* A motion to transfer venue based on the written consent of the parties shall be determined in accordance with Rule 255. A motion to transfer venue on the basis that an impartial trial cannot be had in the county where the action is pending shall be determined in accordance with Rules 258 and 259.

3. **Proof.**

(a) *Affidavit and Attachments.* All venue facts, when properly pleaded, shall be taken as true unless specifically denied by the adverse party. When a venue fact is specifically denied, the party pleading the venue fact must make prima facie proof of that venue fact; provided, however, that no party shall ever be required for venue purposes to support by prima facie proof the existence of a cause of action or part thereof, and at the hearing the pleadings of the parties shall be taken as conclusive on the issues of existence of a cause of action. Prima facie proof is made when the venue facts are properly pleaded and an affidavit, and any duly proved attachments to the affidavit, are filed fully and specifically setting forth the facts supporting such pleading. Affidavits shall be made on personal knowledge, shall set forth specific facts as would be admissible in evidence, and shall show affirmatively that the affiant is competent to testify.

(b) *The Hearing.* The court shall determine the motion to transfer venue on the basis of the pleadings, any stipulations made by and between the parties and such affidavits and attachments as may be filed by the parties in accordance with the preceding subdivision of this paragraph 3 or of Rule 88.

(c) If a claimant has adequately pleaded and made prima facie proof that venue is proper in the county of suit as provided in subdivision (a) of paragraph 3, then the cause shall not be transferred but shall be retained in the county of suit, unless the motion to transfer is based on the grounds that an impartial trial cannot be had in the county where the action is pending as provided in Rules 257-259 or on an established ground of mandatory venue. A ground of mandatory venue is established when the party relying upon a mandatory exception to the general rule makes prima facie proof as provided in subdivision (a) of paragraph 3 of this rule.

(d) In the event that the parties shall fail to make prima facie proof that the county of suit or the specific county to which transfer is sought is a county of proper venue, then the court may direct the parties to make further proof.

4. No Jury. All venue challenges shall be determined by the court without the aid of a jury.

5. Motion for Rehearing. If venue has been sustained as against a motion to transfer, or if an action has been transferred to a proper county in response to a motion to transfer, then no further motions to transfer shall be considered regardless of whether the movant was a party to the prior proceedings or was added as a party subsequent to the venue proceedings, unless the motion to transfer is based on the grounds that an impartial trial cannot be had under Rules 257-259 or on the ground of mandatory venue, provided that such claim was not available to the other movant or movants.

Parties who are added subsequently to an action and are precluded by this rule from having a motion to transfer considered may raise the propriety of venue on appeal, provided that the party has timely filed a motion to transfer.

6. There shall be no interlocutory appeals from such determination.

* Now CPRC §15.002.

The Legislature enacted new venue provisions in 1995 which legislatively modified or overruled parts of TRCP 87. See CPRC ch. 15; ***Commentaries***, "Choosing the Court—Venue," ch. 2-G; "Motion to Transfer—Challenging Venue," ch. 3-C; FORMS 3C.

History of TRCP 87: Amended eff. Sept. 1, 1990, by order of Apr. 24, 1990 (785-86 S.W.2d [Tex.Cases] xlvi): Last phrase of TRCP 87(2)(b) was added; phrase in the second sentence of (3)(b) beginning "provided, however," was added; title to (5) changed; clarifies that no proof of any kind is required of any party to establish any element of a cause of action or part thereof; proof is restricted to place, if any, and the pleadings establish all other elements and may not be controverted for venue purposes as to the existence of a cause of action or part thereof. Amended eff. Jan. 1, 1988, by order of July 15, 1987 (733-34 S.W.2d [Tex.Cases] xli): Changes to 2(a). Amended eff. Sept. 1, 1983, by order of June 15, 1983 (651-52 S.W.2d [Tex.Cases] xxxiii): This rule was completely rewritten to conform to S.B. 898, 68th Legislature, 1983. Amended eff. Dec. 31, 1947, by order of Aug. 18, 1947 (10 Tex.B.J. 390 [1947]): The sentence commencing "If the defendant" and ending "at the same time" was added. Amended eff. Dec. 31, 1943, by order of June 16, 1943 (6 Tex.B.J. 340 [1943]): The words "or shall have been delivered to defendant or his attorney" were interpolated between the words "privilege" and "at." Amended eff. Dec. 31, 1941, by order of Sept. 20, 1941 (4 Tex.B.J. 501 [1941]): The second sentence was added. Adopted eff. Sept. 1, 1941, by order of Oct. 29, 1940 (3 Tex.B.J. 537 [1940]). Source: TRCS art. 2008 (repealed in part by TRCP). Change: Substituted service of notice of the controverting affidavit by registered mail for service by officer. The provisions for interlocutory appeals from orders sustaining or overruling pleas of privilege are included in art. 2008, which is deemed jurisdictional.

HCA Health Servs. v. Salinas, 838 S.W.2d 246, 247-48 (Tex.1992). "[I]t is an abuse of discretion, correctable by mandamus, for a trial court to rule on a motion to transfer venue without giving the parties the notice required by [TRCP 87(1)]."

Rodriguez v. Printone Color Corp., 982 S.W.2d 69, 71 (Tex.App.—Houston [1st Dist.] 1998, pet. denied). "[S]tatements such as '[D] specifically denies those venue facts pleaded in [P's] Petition' do not constitute a 'specific denial' as required by [TRCP] 87. Thus, [D] did not specifically deny [P's] allegations that he was a resident of Bexar County or that his injury occurred in Bexar County."

Bleeker v. Villarreal, 941 S.W.2d 163, 168 (Tex. App.—Corpus Christi 1997, writ dism'd). "The [Ps]' response to the motion to transfer venue did not comply with [TRCP] 87: neither an affidavit setting forth venue facts nor any duly proved attachments accompanied the response."

TRCP 88. DISCOVERY & VENUE

Discovery shall not be abated or otherwise affected by pendency of a motion to transfer venue. Issuing process for witnesses and taking depositions shall not constitute a waiver of a motion to transfer venue, but depositions taken in such case may be read in evidence in any subsequent suit between the same parties concerning the same subject matter in like manner as if taken in such subsequent suit. Deposition transcripts, responses to requests for admission, answers to interrogatories and other discovery products containing information relevant to a determination of proper venue may be considered by the court in making the venue determination when they are attached to, or incorporated by reference in, an affidavit of a party, a witness or an attorney who has knowledge of such discovery.

See ***Commentaries***, "Motion to Transfer—Challenging Venue," ch. 3-C.

History of TRCP 88: Amended eff. Jan. 1, 1988, by order of July 15, 1987 (733-34 S.W.2d [Tex.Cases] xlii). Amended eff. Sept. 1, 1983, by order of June 15, 1983 (651-52 S.W.2d [Tex.Cases] xxxv): To conform to S.B. 898, 68th

Legislature, 1983. Adopted eff. Sept. 1, 1941, by order of Oct. 29, 1940 (3 Tex.B.J. 537 [1940]). Source: TRCS art. 2018 (repealed).

Montalvo v. 4th Ct. of Appeals, 917 S.W.2d 1, 2 (Tex.1995). "[T]he trial court set a shortened schedule for completing discovery related to venue, filing [Ps]' response to the motions to transfer, and the hearing. [The Ps] offered no argument or evidence that the limitation on discovery or the abbreviated schedule deprived them of any ability to develop evidence pertinent to the venue issue. Without a showing of such harm, the record is wholly insufficient to establish that [Ps] lacked an adequate remedy by appeal."

Safety-Kleen Corp. v. Garcia, 945 S.W.2d 268, 270 (Tex.App.—San Antonio 1997, orig. proceeding). "[N]either the case law … nor the Texas Code of Judicial Conduct give Judge Garcia the discretion to refuse to hear or rule on [P's] motion [to compel discovery] within a reasonable period of time. [P's] right to discovery cannot be abated or otherwise affected by the pendency of a motion to transfer venue."

TRCP 89. TRANSFERRED IF MOTION IS SUSTAINED

If a motion to transfer venue is sustained, the cause shall not be dismissed, but the court shall transfer said cause to the proper court; and the costs incurred prior to the time such suit is filed in the court to which said cause is transferred shall be taxed against the plaintiff. The clerk shall make up a transcript of all the orders made in said cause, certifying thereto officially under the seal of the court, and send it with the original papers in the cause to the clerk of the court to which the venue has been changed. Provided, however, if the cause be severable as to parties defendant and shall be ordered transferred as to one or more defendants but not as to all, the clerk, instead of sending the original papers, shall make certified copies of such filed papers as directed by the court and forward the same to the clerk of the court to which the venue has been changed. After the cause has been transferred, as above provided for the clerk of the court to which the cause has been transferred shall mail notification to the plaintiff or his attorney that transfer of the cause has been completed, that the filing fee in the proper court is due and payable within thirty days from the mailing of such notification, and that the case may be dismissed if the filing fee is not timely paid; and if such filing fee is timely paid, the cause will be subject to trial at the expiration of thirty days after the mailing of notification to the parties or their attorneys by the clerk that the papers have been filed in the court to which the cause has been transferred; and if the filing fee is not timely paid, any court of the transferee county to which the case might have been assigned, upon its own motion or the motion of a party, may dismiss the cause without prejudice to the refiling of same.

See ***Commentaries***, "Motion to Transfer—Challenging Venue," ch. 3-C.

History of TRCP 89: Amended eff. Sept. 1, 1983, by order of June 15, 1983 (651-52 S.W.2d [Tex.Cases] xxxv): To conform to S.B. 898, 68th Legislature, 1983. Amended eff. Dec. 31, 1943, by order of June 16, 1943 (6 Tex.B.J. 340 [1943]). Adopted eff. Sept. 1, 1941, by order of Oct. 29, 1940 (3 Tex.B.J. 537 [1940]). Source: TRCS arts. 2019, 2020 (repealed).

WTFO, Inc. v. Braithwaite, 899 S.W.2d 709, 718 (Tex.App.—Dallas 1995, no writ). "Where a cause of action is against several [Ds] jointly and severally, the trial court shall transfer the action as to those [Ds] whose motions are sustained. Comakers on a note are jointly and severally liable. Accordingly, because venue was proper in Dallas County, the trial court did not abuse its discretion in severing [D's] cause of action and transferring it to Dallas County."

TRCP 90. WAIVER OF DEFECTS IN PLEADING

General demurrers shall not be used. Every defect, omission or fault in a pleading either of form or of substance, which is not specifically pointed out by exception in writing and brought to the attention of the judge in the trial court before the instruction or charge to the jury or, in a non-jury case, before the judgment is signed, shall be deemed to have been waived by the party seeking reversal on such account; provided that this rule shall not apply as to any party against whom default judgment is rendered.

See ***Commentaries***, "Special Exceptions—Challenging the Pleadings," ch. 3-G.

History of TRCP 90: Amended eff. Jan. 1, 1981, by order of June 10, 1980 (599-600 S.W.2d [Tex.Cases] xxxvii): The words "motion or" before "exception" are deleted, and "rendition of judgment" is changed to "judgment is signed." Adopted eff. Sept. 1, 1941, by order of Oct. 29, 1940 (3 Tex.B.J. 537 [1940]). Source: New rule.

Friesenhahn v. Ryan, 960 S.W.2d 656, 658 (Tex. 1998). "Special exceptions may be used to challenge the sufficiency of a pleading. When the trial court sustains special exceptions, it must give the pleader an opportunity to amend the pleading. If a party refuses to amend, or the amended pleading fails to state a cause of action, then summary judgment may be granted. Summary judgment may also be proper if a pleading deficiency is of the type that could not be cured by an amendment."

Shoemake v. Fogel, Ltd., 826 S.W.2d 933, 937 (Tex. 1992). The defendant "filed no special exceptions to clarify [P's claim]. Thus, [D] cannot now complain that [P's] pleading was insufficiently specific."

Steves Sash & Door Co. v. Ceco Corp., 751 S.W.2d 473, 476 (Tex.1988). "If [P] considered the pleading obscure or non-specific, [P] had the right to file special exceptions to clarify [D's] counterclaims. By failing to file special exceptions, [P] waived any defect in [D's] pleadings, and the pleadings must be construed in favor of the pleader." *See also* ***Roark v. Allen***, 633 S.W.2d 804, 809 (Tex.1982).

TRCP 91. SPECIAL EXCEPTIONS

A special exception shall not only point out the particular pleading excepted to, but it shall also point out intelligibly and with particularity the defect, omission, obscurity, duplicity, generality, or other insufficiency in the allegations in the pleading excepted to.

See ***Commentaries***, "Special Exceptions—Challenging the Pleadings," ch. 3-G; FORMS 3G.

History of TRCP 91: Amended eff. Sept. 1, 1941, by order of Mar. 31, 1941 (4 Tex.B.J. 501 [1941]). Adopted eff. Sept. 1, 1941, by order of Oct. 29, 1940 (3 Tex.B.J. 538 [1940]). Source: Tex. Rules for Dist. & Cty. Cts. 18.

Friesenhahn v. Ryan, 960 S.W.2d 656, 659 (Tex. 1998). "Before a court may grant a 'no cause of action' summary judgment..., it must give the parties an adequate opportunity to plead a viable cause of action."

Peek v. Equip. Serv. Co., 779 S.W.2d 802, 805 (Tex. 1989). "[T]he omission of any allegation regarding the amount in controversy from [P's] petition did not deprive the court of jurisdiction, but was instead a defect in pleading subject to special exception and amendment."

Humphreys v. Meadows, 938 S.W.2d 750, 753 (Tex. App.—Fort Worth 1996, writ denied). "No provision in the [TRCPs] permits a trial court to dismiss [P's] case because of insufficient pleadings. [¶] A trial court may not dismiss [P's] case for pleading defects unless an opportunity is first afforded to amend and cure the defect."

Villarreal v. Martinez, 834 S.W.2d 450, 451 (Tex. App.—Corpus Christi 1992, no writ). "The purpose of special exceptions is to furnish the adverse party a medium by which to force clarification of pleadings when they are not clear or sufficiently specific."

TRCP 92. GENERAL DENIAL

A general denial of matters pleaded by the adverse party which are not required to be denied under oath, shall be sufficient to put the same in issue. When the defendant has pleaded a general denial, and the plaintiff shall afterward amend his pleading, such original denial shall be presumed to extend to all matters subsequently set up by the plaintiff.

When a counterclaim or cross-claim is served upon a party who has made an appearance in the action, the party so served, in the absence of a responsive pleading, shall be deemed to have pleaded a general denial of the counterclaim or cross-claim, but the party shall not be deemed to have waived any special appearance or motion to transfer venue. In all other respects the rules prescribed for pleadings of defensive matter are applicable to answers to counterclaims and cross-claims.

See ***Commentaries***, "The Answer—Denying Liability," ch. 3-E.

History of TRCP 92: Amended eff. Apr. 1, 1985, by order of Dec. 19, 1984 (683-84 S.W.2d [Tex.Cases] xxxiv): The phrase "plea of privilege" was corrected to "motion to transfer venue." Amended eff. Apr. 1, 1984, by order of Dec. 5, 1983 (661-62 S.W.2d [Tex.Cases] xxxix): Added second paragraph to clarify ambiguity in the law and to codify the law. Adopted eff. Sept. 1, 1941, by order of Oct. 29, 1940 (3 Tex.B.J. 538 [1940]). Source: TRCS arts. 2006, 2012 (repealed). See TRCP 84 for balance of Art. 2006.

Shell Chem. Co. v. Lamb, 493 S.W.2d 742, 744 (Tex. 1973). "[A] general denial puts [P] on proof of every fact essential to his case and issue is joined on all material facts asserted by [P] except those which are required to be denied under oath."

Texas DPS v. Moran, 949 S.W.2d 523, 526 (Tex. App.—San Antonio 1997, no writ). [P] "contends he met his burden by filing a verified petition. Because [D] filed a general denial and appeared at the hearing, we disagree. ... Because a general denial was filed, the allegations in [P's] petition were not evidence; instead, the allegations were put into issue and [P] was required to prove he met the statutory conditions."

TRCP 93. CERTAIN PLEAS TO BE VERIFIED

A pleading setting up any of the following matters, unless the truth of such matters appear of record, shall be verified by affidavit.

1. That the plaintiff has not legal capacity to sue or that the defendant has not legal capacity to be sued.

2. That the plaintiff is not entitled to recover in the capacity in which he sues, or that the defendant is not liable in the capacity in which he is sued.

3. That there is another suit pending in this State between the same parties involving the same claim.

4. That there is a defect of parties, plaintiff or defendant.

5. A denial of partnership as alleged in any pleading as to any party to the suit.

6. That any party alleged in any pleading to be a corporation is not incorporated as alleged.

7. Denial of the execution by himself or by his authority of any instrument in writing, upon which any pleading is founded, in whole or in part and charged to have been executed by him or by his authority, and not alleged to be lost or destroyed. Where such instrument in writing is charged to have been executed by a person then deceased, the affidavit shall be sufficient if it states that the affiant has reason to believe and does believe that such instrument was not executed by the decedent or by his authority. In the absence of such a sworn plea, the instrument shall be received in evidence as fully proved.

8. A denial of the genuineness of the indorsement or assignment of a written instrument upon which suit is brought by an indorsee or assignee and in the absence of such a sworn plea, the indorsement or assignment thereof shall be held as fully proved. The denial required by this subdivision of the rule may be made upon information and belief.

9. That a written instrument upon which a pleading is founded is without consideration, or that the consideration of the same has failed in whole or in part.

10. A denial of an account which is the foundation of the plaintiff's action, and supported by affidavit.

11. That a contract sued upon is usurious. Unless such plea is filed, no evidence of usurious interest as a defense shall be received.

12. That notice and proof of loss or claim for damage has not been given as alleged. Unless such plea is filed such notice and proof shall be presumed and no evidence to the contrary shall be admitted. A denial of such notice or such proof shall be made specifically and with particularity.

13. In the trial of any case appealed to the court from the Industrial Accident Board the following, if pleaded, shall be presumed to be true as pleaded and have been done and filed in legal time and manner, unless denied by verified pleadings:

(a) Notice of injury.

(b) Claim for compensation.

(c) Award of the Board.

(d) Notice of intention not to abide by the award of the Board.

(e) Filing of suit to set aside the award.

(f) That the insurance company alleged to have been the carrier of the workers' compensation insurance at the time of the alleged injury was in fact the carrier thereof.

(g) That there was good cause for not filing claim with the Industrial Accident Board within the one year period provided by statute.

(h) Wage rate.

A denial of any of the matters set forth in subdivisions (a) or (g) of paragraph 13 may be made on information and belief.

Any such denial may be made in original or amended pleadings; but if in amended pleadings the same must be filed not less than seven days before the case proceeds to trial. In case of such denial the things so denied shall not be presumed to be true, and if essential to the case of the party alleging them, must be proved.

14. That a party plaintiff or defendant is not doing business under an assumed name or trade name as alleged.

15. In the trial of any case brought against an automobile insurance company by an insured under the provisions of an insurance policy in force providing protection against uninsured motorists, an allegation that the insured has complied with all the terms of the policy as a condition precedent to bringing the suit shall be presumed to be true unless denied by verified pleadings which may be upon information and belief.

16. Any other matter required by statute to be pleaded under oath.

See ***Commentaries***, "The Answer—Denying Liability," ch. 3-E; FORMS 3E.

History of TRCP 93: Amended eff. Apr. 1, 1984, by order of Dec. 5, 1983 (661-62 S.W.2d [Tex.Cases] xl): Section 10 was changed to conform to amended TRCP 185. Amended eff. Sept. 1, 1983, by order of June 15, 1983 (651-52 S.W.2d [Tex.Cases] xxxvi): To conform to S.B. 291 and 898, 68th Legislature, 1983. Amended eff. Jan. 1, 1976, by order of July 22, 1975 (525-26 S.W.2d [Tex.Cases] xlv): Par. (p) was adopted to simplify issues in uninsured motorist cases. Amended eff. Jan. 1, 1971, by order of July 21, 1970 (455-56 S.W.2d [Tex.Cases] xxvi): Final clause of par. (k) was changed to harmonize with TRCP 185 as amended; sec. (8) was added to subdivision (n). Amended eff. Mar. 1, 1950, by order of Oct. 12, 1949 (12 Tex.B.J. 530 [1949]): A new paragraph, designated (o), was added and the paragraph formerly lettered (o) was designated (p). Amended eff. Dec. 31, 1943 June 16, 1943 (6 Tex.B.J. 341 [1943]): Section (7) and the new sentence concerning secs. (1) and (7) were added to subdiv. (n) and minor textual changes were made in this par. Amended eff. Dec. 31, 1941, by order of Sept. 20, 1941 (4 Tex.B.J. 501 [1941]): Sec. (6) was added to par. (n). Amended eff. Sept. 1, 1941, by order of Mar. 31, 1941 (4 Tex.B.J. 501

[1941]): Pars. (m) and (n) added from TRCS art. 5546 (repealed eff. Sept. 1, 1985; now CPRC §16.071); par. (o) added. Adopted eff. Sept. 1, 1941, by order of Oct. 29, 1940 (3 Tex.B.J. 538 [1940]). Source: TRCS arts. 573, 1999, 2010, 3734, 5074 (repealed), with changes: The basic statute relating to sworn pleadings, Art. 2010, was combined with provisions from a number of other statutes which required sworn pleas. No change of meaning was intended by the combination. The scope of sworn denials, however, was broadened. Par. (b) includes the plea that "the defendant has not legal capacity to be sued." Par. (c) was extended to include a denial of defendant's liability in the capacity in which he is sued. In par. (d) the term "cause of action" was replaced by the word "claim." Par. (f) and (g) apply to allegations in any pleading, not merely to the petition as formerly stated in Art. 2010.

Sixth RMA Partners v. Sibley, 111 S.W.3d 46, 56 (Tex.2003). "When capacity is contested, [TRCP 93(1)] requires that a verified plea be filed unless the truth of the matter appears of record. [¶] An argument that an opposing party does not have the capacity to participate in a suit can be waived by [the] failure to properly raise the issue in the trial court. [P] never raised [D's] failure to file an assumed name certificate ... in the trial court. Therefore, [P] waived the complaint." *See also* ***Nootsie, Ltd. v. Williamson Cty. Appr. Dist.***, 925 S.W.2d 659, 662 (Tex.1996).

Werner v. Colwell, 909 S.W.2d 866, 870 (Tex.1995). "The failure to file [a verified] denial does waive any complaint of a judgment rendered in the capacity in which the party was sued. However, it does not allow the court to render judgment against the party in a capacity in which she was not sued."

Roark v. Stallworth Oil & Gas, 813 S.W.2d 492, 494 (Tex.1991). "[W]hen the defense is based on a claim enumerated in [TRCP] 93, [the party] must verify the pleading by affidavit."

Pledger v. Schoellkopf, 762 S.W.2d 145, 146 (Tex. 1988). "When capacity [to sue] is contested, [TRCP] 93(2) requires that a verified plea be filed anytime the record does not affirmatively demonstrate [P's] or [D's] right to bring suit or be sued in *whatever* capacity he is suing."

Miller v. Estate of Self, 113 S.W.3d 554, 556 (Tex. App.—Texarkana 2003, n.p.h.). "A suit seeking to establish the liability of an estate should be filed against the personal representative or, in certain circumstances, the heirs or beneficiaries. [P] maintains, however, [D's estate] waived this issue because the estate failed to plead by verified pleading under [TRCP] 93 that there was a defect in the parties. [¶] [D's estate] is not a legal entity. Because no legal entity had been named as defendant in the suit, there was no one to except to [P's] pleadings or to waive any defect found within them."

Gutierrez v. Rodriguez, 30 S.W.3d 558, 562 (Tex. App.—Texarkana 2000, no pet.). TRCP 93(7) "requires that a party denying the execution of a document must file a verified pleading of [its] contentions. Absent such a verified pleading, the document is received into evidence as fully proved." *See also* ***Boyd v. Diversified Fin. Sys.***, 1 S.W.3d 888, 891 (Tex.App.—Dallas 1999, no pet.).

TRCP 94. AFFIRMATIVE DEFENSES

In pleading to a preceding pleading, a party shall set forth affirmatively accord and satisfaction, arbitration and award, assumption of risk, contributory negligence, discharge in bankruptcy, duress, estoppel, failure of consideration, fraud, illegality, injury by fellow servant, laches, license, payment, release, res judicata, statute of frauds, statute of limitations, waiver, and any other matter constituting an avoidance or affirmative defense. Where the suit is on an insurance contract which insures against certain general hazards, but contains other provisions limiting such general liability, the party suing on such contract shall never be required to allege that the loss was not due to a risk or cause coming within any of the exceptions specified in the contract, nor shall the insurer be allowed to raise such issue unless it shall specifically allege that the loss was due to a risk or cause coming within a particular exception to the general liability; provided that nothing herein shall be construed to change the burden of proof on such issue as it now exists.

See ***Commentaries***, "The Answer—Denying Liability," ch. 3-E; FORMS 3E.

History of TRCP 94: Amended eff. Sept. 1, 1941, by order of Mar. 31, 1941 (4 Tex.B.J. 502 [1941]): Added second sentence. Adopted eff. Sept. 1, 1941, by order of Oct. 29, 1940 (3 Tex.B.J. 538 [1940]). Source: Part of FRCP 8(c).

Quantum Chem. Corp. v. Toennies, 47 S.W.3d 473, 481 (Tex.2001). "It is [D's] burden to plead and request instructions on an affirmative defense."

Kinnear v. Texas Comm'n on Human Rights, 14 S.W.3d 299, 300 (Tex.2000). "Because the Commission never pleaded sovereign immunity from liability as an affirmative defense to the requested attorney fees, it waived the defense, and the court of appeals erred in overturning the attorney fees award on sovereign immunity grounds." *See also* ***Davis v. City of San Antonio***, 752 S.W.2d 518, 519 (Tex.1988).

Texas Beef Cattle Co. v. Green, 921 S.W.2d 203, 212 (Tex.1996). "[A]n affirmative defense ... is one of confession and avoidance. An affirmative defense does not seek to defend by merely denying [P's] claims, but rather seeks to establish 'an independent reason why the plaintiff should not recover.'"

Dresser Indus. v. Page Pet., 853 S.W.2d 505, 508 (Tex.1993). "[Because a] release surrenders legal rights or obligations between the parties to an agreement [it] is expressly designated as an affirmative defense."

Shoemake v. Fogel, Ltd., 826 S.W.2d 933, 937 (Tex. 1992). "Rule 94's requirement of pleading is not absolute. [¶] [T]he defense of [parental] immunity ... is not waived by the failure to specifically plead it if it is apparent on the face of the petition and established as a matter of law."

Lewkowicz v. El Paso Apparel Corp., 625 S.W.2d 301, 303 (Tex.1981). TRCP 94 "requires that illegality as a defense must be affirmatively pleaded. However, if the illegal nature of the document ... sought to be enforced is apparent from [P's] pleadings, it is not necessary that illegality be specially pleaded by [D] in order to rely upon it as a defense."

Land Title Co. v. Stigler Inc., 609 S.W.2d 754, 756 (Tex.1980). "Ratification is a plea in avoidance and thus an affirmative defense which, absent trial by consent, is waived unless affirmatively pleaded."

TRCP 95. PLEAS OF PAYMENT

When a defendant shall desire to prove payment, he shall file with his plea an account stating distinctly the nature of such payment, and the several items thereof; failing to do so, he shall not be allowed to prove the same, unless it be so plainly and particularly described in the plea as to give the plaintiff full notice of the character thereof.

See ***Commentaries***, "The Answer—Denying Liability," ch. 3-E.

History of TRCP 95: Adopted eff. Sept. 1, 1941, by order of Oct. 29, 1940 (3 Tex.B.J. 539 [1940]). Source: TRCS art. 2014 (repealed).

Southwestern Fire & Cas. Co. v. Larue, 367 S.W.2d 162, 163 (Tex.1963). "Under [TRCP] 94 and [TRCP] 95, payment is ... an affirmative defense on which the defendant has the burden of proof, which must be specially pleaded, and may not be shown under a general denial." *See also* ***Sage St. Assoc. v. Northdale Constr. Co.***, 863 S.W.2d 438, 443 (Tex.1993).

TRCP 96. NO DISCONTINUANCE

Where the defendant has filed a counterclaim seeking affirmative relief, the plaintiff shall not be permitted by a discontinuance of his suit, to prejudice the right of the defendant to be heard on such counterclaim.

See TRCP 162; ***Commentaries***, "Voluntary Dismissal—Nonsuit," ch. 7-E.

History of TRCP 96: Adopted eff. Sept. 1, 1941, by order of Oct. 29, 1940 (3 Tex.B.J. 539 [1940]). Source: TRCS art. 2016 (repealed).

BHP Pet. Co. v. Millard, 800 S.W.2d 838, 840 (Tex. 1990). "The plaintiff's right to take a nonsuit is *unqualified and absolute* as long as the defendant has not made a claim for affirmative relief."

TRCP 97. COUNTERCLAIM & CROSS-CLAIM

(a) Compulsory Counterclaims. A pleading shall state as a counterclaim any claim within the jurisdiction of the court, not the subject of a pending action, which at the time of filing the pleading the pleader has against any opposing party, if it arises out of the transaction or occurrence that is the subject matter of the opposing party's claim and does not require for its adjudication the presence of third parties of whom the court cannot acquire jurisdiction; provided, however, that a judgment based upon a settlement or compromise of a claim of one party to the transaction or occurrence prior to a disposition on the merits shall not operate as a bar to the continuation or assertion of the claims of any other party to the transaction or occurrence unless the latter has consented in writing that said judgment shall operate as a bar.

(b) Permissive Counterclaims. A pleading may state as a counterclaim any claim against an opposing party whether or not arising out of the transaction or occurrence that is the subject matter of the opposing party's claim.

(c) Counterclaim Exceeding Opposing Claim. A counterclaim may or may not diminish or defeat the recovery sought by the opposing party. It may claim relief exceeding in amount or different in kind from that sought in the pleading of the opposing party, so long as the subject matter is within the jurisdiction of the court.

(d) Counterclaim Maturing or Acquired After Pleading. A claim which either matured or was acquired by the pleader after filing his pleading may be presented as a counterclaim by amended pleading.

(e) Cross-Claim Against Co-Party. A pleading may state as a cross-claim any claim by one party against a co-party arising out of the transaction or occurrence that is the subject matter either of the original action or of a counterclaim therein. Such cross-claim may include a claim that the party against whom it is asserted is or may be liable to the cross-claimant for all or part of a claim asserted in the action against the cross-claimant.

(f) Additional Parties. Persons other than those made parties to the original action may be made parties to a third party action, counterclaim or cross-claim in accordance with the provisions of Rules 38, 39 and 40.

(g) Tort shall not be the subject of set-off or counterclaim against a contractual demand nor a contractual demand against tort unless it arises out of or is incident to or is connected with same.

(h) Separate Trials; Separate Judgments. If the court orders separate trials as provided in Rule 174, judgment on a counterclaim or cross-claim may be rendered when the court has jurisdiction so to do, even if the claims of the opposing party have been dismissed or otherwise disposed of.

See CPRC §33.004 (responsible third parties); *Commentaries*, "The Answer—Denying Liability," ch. 3-E; FORMS 3E.

History of TRCP 97: Amended eff. Apr. 1, 1984, by order of Dec. 5, 1983 (661-62 S.W.2d [Tex.Cases] xl): Section (f) was rewritten. Amended eff. Jan. 1, 1971, by order of July 21, 1970 (455-56 S.W.2d [Tex.Cases] xxix): Proviso concerning effect of judgment based upon settlement or compromise of claim of one party to a transaction was added to par. (a). Amended eff. Sept. 1, 1941, by order of Mar. 31, 1941 (4 Tex.B.J. 503 [1941]): The proviso in par. (f) takes the place of the last sentence of par. (f) in original TRCP 97, and par. (g) was added. Par. (g) in original TRCP 97 was changed to (h). Adopted eff. Sept. 1, 1941, by order of Oct. 29, 1940 (3 Tex.B.J. 539 [1940]). Subdiv. (d), (e), (f), and (g) correspond to subdiv. (e), (g), (h), and (I) of FRCP 13. Limited the compulsory counterclaim to a claim within the jurisdiction of the court in TRCP 97(a) and (c). In section (f) a sentence was added to prevent any construction which would authorize the joinder of a liability or indemnity insurer in the original action to establish the obligation of the assured. Source: FRCP 13, with changes.

State & Cty. Mut. Fire Ins. Co. v. Miller, 52 S.W.3d 693, 696 (Tex.2001). "[W]hen the parties are co-parties rather than opposing parties, the compulsory counterclaim rule and res judicata only act as a bar to a co-party's claim in a subsequent action if the co-parties had 'issues drawn between them' in the first action. For the purposes of res judicata, co-parties have issues drawn between them and become adverse when one co-party files a cross-action against a second co-party." *See also* ***Getty Oil Co. v. Insurance Co. of N. Am.***, 845 S.W.2d 794, 800 (Tex.1992).

Ingersoll-Rand Comp. v. Valero Energy Corp., 997 S.W.2d 203, 207 (Tex.1999). "[A]counterclaim is compulsory only if: (1) it is within the jurisdiction of the court; (2) it is not at the time of filing the answer the subject of a pending action; (3) the claim is mature and owned by the defendant at the time of filing the answer; (4) it arose out of the same transaction or occurrence that is the subject matter of the opposing party's claim; (5) it is against an opposing party in the same capacity; and (6) it does not require the presence of third parties over whom the court cannot acquire jurisdiction. A claim having all of these elements must be asserted in the initial action and cannot be asserted in later actions."

Bard v. Charles R. Myers Ins. Agency, 839 S.W.2d 791, 796 (Tex.1992) The compulsory counterclaim rule is "designed to avoid piecemeal or duplicative litigation. Its purpose is to provide that a potential counterclaimant with a justifiable interest arising out of the same transaction or occurrence at issue in the opposing party's claim bring the counterclaim in the same proceeding or it will be deemed waived. The 'compelling interest' underlying the compulsory counterclaim rule is solely in judicial economy; its purpose it to prevent multiple suits arising out of the same transactions or occurrences."

Musgrave v. Owen, 67 S.W.3d 513, 519 (Tex. App.—Texarkana 2002, no pet.). "[W]here [D] interpose[s] a claim as a counterclaim and a valid and final judgment is rendered against him on the counterclaim, [D] becomes a counter-defendant for res judicata purposes and is required to assert all claims against [P] arising from the subject matter of the original claim."

TRCP 98. SUPPLEMENTAL ANSWERS

The defendant's supplemental answers may contain special exceptions, general denial, and the allegations of new matter not before alleged by him, in reply to that which has been alleged by the plaintiff.

History of TRCP 98: Amended eff. Sept. 1, 1941, by order of Mar. 31, 1941 (4 Tex.B.J. 504 [1941]). Adopted eff. Sept. 1, 1941, by order of Oct. 29, 1940 (3 Tex.B.J. 539 [1940]). Source: Tex. Rules for Dist. & Cty. Cts. 8.

Grimes Cty. Taxpayers Ass'n v. Texas Mun. Power Agency, 565 S.W.2d 258, 277 (Tex.App.—Houston [1st Dist.] 1978, writ dism'd). "A supplemental answer is properly filed in response to any pleading of [P], regardless of whether it is an amended petition or a supplemental petition."

SECTION 5. CITATION

TRCP 99. ISSUANCE & FORM OF CITATION

a. Issuance. Upon the filing of the petition, the clerk, when requested, shall forthwith issue a citation and deliver the citation as directed by the requesting party. The party requesting citation shall be responsible for obtaining service of the citation and a copy of the petition. Upon request, separate or additional citations shall be issued by the clerk.

b. Form. The citation shall (1) be styled "The State of Texas," (2) be signed by the clerk under seal of court, (3) contain name and location of the court, (4) show date of filing of the petition, (5) show date of issuance of citation, (6) show file number, (7) show names of parties, (8) be directed to the defendant, (9) show the name and address of attorney for plaintiff, otherwise the address of plaintiff, (10) contain the time within which these rules require the defendant to file a written answer with the clerk who issued citation, (11) contain address of the clerk, and (12) shall notify the defendant that in case of failure of defendant to file an answer, judgment by default may be rendered for the relief demanded in the petition. The citation shall direct the defendant to file a written answer to the plaintiff's petition on or before 10:00 a.m. on the Monday next after the expiration of twenty days after the date of service thereof. The requirement of subsections 10 and 12 of this section shall be in the form set forth in section c of this rule.

c. Notice. The citation shall include the following notice to the defendant: "You have been sued. You may employ an attorney. If you or your attorney do not file a written answer with the clerk who issued this citation by 10:00 a.m. on the Monday next following the expiration of twenty days after you were served this citation and petition, a default judgment may be taken against you."

d. Copies. The party filing any pleading upon which citation is to be issued and served shall furnish the clerk with a sufficient number of copies thereof for use in serving the parties to be served, and when copies are so furnished the clerk shall make no charge for the copies.

See ***Commentaries***, "Serving the Defendant with Suit," ch. 2-H; "Default Judgment," ch. 7-A; FORMS 2H.

History of TRCP 99: Amended eff. Jan. 1, 1988, by order of July 15, 1987 (733-34 S.W.2d [Tex.Cases] xlii). Amended eff. Feb. 1, 1946, by order of Oct. 10, 1945 (8 Tex.B.J. 532 [1945]). Adopted eff. Sept. 1, 1941, by order of Oct. 29, 1940 (3 Tex.B.J. 540 [1940]). Source: TRCS art. 2021 (repealed).

Primate Constr. v. Silver, 884 S.W.2d 151, 153 (Tex.1994). "It is the responsibility of the one requesting service, not the process server, to see that service is properly accomplished. This responsibility extends to seeing that service is properly reflected in the record."

Ingram Indus. v. U.S. Bolt Mfg., 121 S.W.3d 31, 35 (Tex.App.—Houston [1st Dist.] 2003, n.p.h.). "[A] party serving a citation is not required to list the operable rule of procedure or statute under which that party is given the authority to serve a citation."

Roberts v. Padre Island Brewing Co., 28 S.W.3d 618, 621-22 (Tex.App.—Corpus Christi 2000, pet. denied). "Reliance on the process server does not constitute due diligence in attempting service of process. A reasonable person … would have employed an alternate process server, a constable, or would have attempted service through other alternative court approved methods such as service through a court appointed third party. … Although the existence of diligence is usually a question of fact, a lack of diligence exists as a matter of law because it is clear that [P] did not exhaust all of the alternatives available to achieve proper service."

Boyattia v. Hinojosa, 18 S.W.3d 729, 734 (Tex. App.—Dallas 2000, pet. denied). "Although a party may ordinarily rely on the clerk to perform his duty within a reasonable amount of time, an unexplained three-month delay is not a reasonable time for the clerk to deliver a citation as directed by a party. [¶] We conclude [P's] failure to act during the clerk's three-month delay constitutes a lack of diligence as a matter of law."

Barker CATV Constr. v. Ampro, Inc., 989 S.W.2d 789, 792 (Tex.App.—Houston [1st Dist.] 1999, no pet.). TRCP 15 seems to conflict with TRCP 99(b), which states the citation shall (1) be styled The State of Texas, and (8) *be directed to the defendant.* [¶] The citation is a preprinted form addressed to the sheriff or any constable of Texas, as well as to the defendant. The requirements of TRCP 15 and 99(b) can be harmonized by allowing the citations to be directed to both the sheriff or constable, as the officer serving it, and the defendant, as the person being served.

TRCP 100 - 102. REPEALED

TRCP 100 to 102 repealed eff. Jan. 1, 1988, by order of July 15, 1987 (733-34 S.W.2d [Tex.Cases] xliii).

TRCP 103. WHO MAY SERVE

Citation and other notices may be served anywhere by (1) any sheriff or constable or other person authorized by law or, (2) by any person authorized by law or by written order of the court who is not less than eighteen years of age. No person who is a party to or interested in the outcome of a suit shall serve any process. Service by registered or certified mail and citation by publication shall, if requested, be made by the clerk of the court in which the case is pending. The order authorizing a person to serve process may be made without written motion and no fee shall be imposed for issuance of such order.

See ***Commentaries***, "Serving the Defendant with Suit," ch. 2-H; "Default Judgment," ch. 7-A.

History of TRCP 103: Amended eff. Jan. 1, 1988, by order of July 15, 1987 (733-34 S.W.2d [Tex.Cases] xliii): The amendment makes clear that the courts may authorize persons other than sheriffs or constables to serve citation. Further, sheriffs or constables are not restricted to service in their county. The last sentence is added to avoid the necessity of motions and fees. Amended eff. Jan. 1, 1981, by order of June 10, 1980 (599-600 S.W.2d [Tex.Cases] xxxviii): The rule is amended to permit service by mail by an officer of the county in which the case is pending or the party is found and also service by the clerk of the court. Adopted eff. Sept. 1, 1941, by order of Oct. 29, 1940 (3 Tex.B.J. 540 [1940]). Source: New rule.

Mayfield v. Dean Witter Fin. Servs., 894 S.W.2d 502, 505 (Tex.App.—Austin 1995, writ denied). "[S]ervice of process by a private process server in Texas ... requires authorization by law or a written order of the court. *At 506:* The parties do not dispute that pursuant to [TRCP] 103, a standing court order authorized ... the private process server[ ] to serve citation and other notices in any lawsuit filed in the district court of Travis County in which he was not an interested party."

TRCP 104. REPEALED

Repealed eff. Jan. 1, 1988, by order of July 15, 1987 (733-34 S.W.2d [Tex.Cases] xliv): TRCP 104 was rendered unnecessary because of amendments to TRCP 103.

TRCP 105. DUTY OF OFFICER OR PERSON RECEIVING

The officer or authorized person to whom process is delivered shall endorse thereon the day and hour on which he received it, and shall execute and return the same without delay.

See ***Commentaries***, "Serving the Defendant with Suit," ch. 2-H; "Default Judgment," ch. 7-A.

History of TRCP 105: Amended eff. Jan. 1, 1988, by order of July 15, 1987 (733-34 S.W.2d [Tex.Cases] xliv). Amended eff. Jan. 1, 1978, by order of July 11, 1977 (553-54 S.W.2d [Tex.Cases] xliv): Corrected spelling of the word "indorse" to "endorse." Adopted eff. Sept. 1, 1941, by order of Oct. 29, 1940 (3 Tex.B.J. 540 [1940]). Source: TRCS art. 2025 (repealed).

Melendez v. John R. Schatzman, Inc., 685 S.W.2d 137, 138 (Tex.App.—El Paso 1985, no writ). Service by certified mail "was attempted...; however, it does not appear that the officer receiving delivery of the process for service endorsed thereon the day and hour of receipt, nor was the return completed showing the execution by certified mail, all as required by Rule 105...."

TRCP 106. METHOD OF SERVICE

(a) Unless the citation or an order of the court otherwise directs, the citation shall be served by any person authorized by Rule 103 by

(1) delivering to the defendant, in person, a true copy of the citation with the date of delivery endorsed thereon with a copy of the petition attached thereto, or

(2) mailing to the defendant by registered or certified mail, return receipt requested, a true copy of the citation with a copy of the petition attached thereto.

(b) Upon motion supported by affidavit stating the location of the defendant's usual place of business or usual place of abode or other place where the defendant can probably be found and stating specifically the facts showing that service has been attempted under either (a)(1) or (a)(2) at the location named in such affidavit but has not been successful, the court may authorize service

(1) by leaving a true copy of the citation, with a copy of the petition attached, with anyone over sixteen years of age at the location specified in such affidavit, or

(2) in any other manner that the affidavit or other evidence before the court shows will be reasonably effective to give the defendant notice of the suit.

See ***Commentaries***, "Serving the Defendant with Suit," ch. 2-H.

History of TRCP 106: Amended eff. Sept. 1, 1990, by order of Apr. 24, 1990 (785-86 S.W.2d [Tex.Cases] xlvii). Par. (b) changed by deleting "or" and substituting "of" before "abode or other." Amended eff. Jan. 1, 1988, by order of July 15, 1987 (733-34 S.W.2d [Tex.Cases] xliv): Conforms to amended TRCP 103. Amended eff. Jan. 1, 1981, by order of June 10, 1980 (599-600 S.W.2d [Tex. Cases] xxxviii): The rule was reorganized to clarify its meaning. Alternate methods of service are authorized if either (a)(1) or (a)(2) are tried without success. Both methods are not required. Amended eff. Jan. 1, 1978, by order of July 11, 1977 (553-54 S.W.2d [Tex.Cases] xliv): Rewrote rule; added subsec. (b) and (e). Amended eff. Jan. 1, 1976, by order of July 22, 1975 (525-26 S.W.2d [Tex.Cases] xlv): Service "by registered or certified mail" is authorized in certain instances. Amended eff. Dec. 31, 1947, by orders of Aug. 18, 1947 (10

Tex.B.J. 391 [1947]). Adopted eff. Sept. 1, 1941, by order of Oct. 29, 1940 (3 Tex.B.J. 540 [1940]). Source: TRCS art. 2026 (repealed).

State Farm Fire & Cas. Co. v. Costley, 868 S.W.2d 298, 298-99 (Tex.1993). "Under [TRCP] 106(b) a court may authorize substituted service only after [P] has unsuccessfully tried to effect personal service or service by mail, return receipt requested, as required by Rule 106(a). ... Thus, to require proof of actual notice upon substituted service would frustrate Rule 106(b)'s purpose of providing alternate methods [of service]."

Wilson v. Dunn, 800 S.W.2d 833, 836 (Tex.1990). "[S]ubstitute service is not authorized under [TRCP] 106(b) without an affidavit which meets the requirements of the rule demonstrating the necessity for other than personal service."

Uvalde Country Club v. Martin Linen Sup. Co., 690 S.W.2d 884, 885 (Tex.1985). "There are no presumptions in favor of valid issuance, service, and return of citation in the face of a writ of error [now a restricted appeal] attack on a default judgment. Moreover, failure to affirmatively show strict compliance with the [TRCPs] renders the attempted service of process invalid and of no effect."

Coronado v. Norman, 111 S.W.3d 838, 842 (Tex. App.—Eastland 2003, n.p.h.). The process server's "affidavit does not contain sufficient facts to satisfy [TRCP] 106(b). While the cited cases do not specifically require the inclusion of the dates and times of attempted service, the cases suggest that the specific dates and times of attempted service are important to establish sufficient facts to uphold a default judgment under [TRCP] 106(b). Every attempt at personal service in this case may have been while [D] was at work. When told that [D] 'was not there,' the process server apparently did not try to find out where [D] could be located or when he would return."

TRCP 107. RETURN OF SERVICE

The return of the officer or authorized person executing the citation shall be endorsed on or attached to the same; it shall state when the citation was served and the manner of service and be signed by the officer officially or by the authorized person. The return of citation by an authorized person shall be verified. When the citation was served by registered or certified mail as authorized by Rule 106, the return by the officer or authorized person must also contain the return receipt with the addressee's signature. When the officer or authorized person has not served the citation, the return shall show the diligence used by the officer or authorized person to execute the same and the cause of failure to execute it, and where the defendant is to be found, if he can ascertain.

Where citation is executed by an alternative method as authorized by Rule 106, proof of service shall be made in the manner ordered by the court.

No default judgment shall be granted in any cause until the citation, or process under Rules 108 or 108a, with proof of service as provided by this rule or by Rules 108 or 108a, or as ordered by the court in the event citation is executed under Rule 106, shall have been on file with the clerk of the court ten days, exclusive of the day of filing and the day of judgment.

See TRCP 16; ***Commentaries***, "Serving the Defendant with Suit," ch. 2-H; FORMS 2H.

History of TRCP 107: Amended eff. Sept. 1, 1990, by order of Apr. 24, 1990 (785-86 S.W.2d [Tex.Cases] xlviii): References to TRCP 108 and 108a were added in the last par.; states more directly that a default judgment can be obtained when the defendant has been served with process in a foreign country pursuant to those provisions. Amended eff. Jan. 1, 1988, by order of July 15, 1987 (733-34 S.W.2d [Tex.Cases] xlv): Amended to conform to changes in TRCP 103. Amended eff. Jan. 1, 1981, by order of June 10, 1980 (599-600 S.W.2d [Tex.Cases] xxxix): The only changes are the references to TRCP 106. Amended eff. Jan. 1, 1978, by order of July 11, 1977 (553-54 S.W.2d [Tex.Cases] xlv): Changed to provide manner of return when service by mail or by an alternative method. Adopted eff. Sept. 1, 1941, by order of Oct. 29, 1940 (3 Tex.B.J. 540 [1940]). Source: TRCS arts. 2034, 2036 (repealed).

Primate Constr. v. Silver, 884 S.W.2d 151, 152-53 (Tex.1994). "The officer's return does not cease to be prima facie evidence of the facts of service simply because the facts are recited in a form rather than filled in by the officer. ... If the facts as recited in the sheriff's return, pre-printed or otherwise, are incorrect and do not show proper service, the one requesting service must amend the return prior to judgment."

Redwood Group v. Louiseau, 113 S.W.3d 866, 869 (Tex.App.—Austin 2003, n.p.h.). "While a return is prima facie evidence of the facts recited *therein*, this does not mean that the return is prima facie evidence of anything about which it is silent. For example, the two returns in question here contain nothing about the contents of the two lost citations; we cannot presume they conformed to the requirements of [TRCP 99] specifying the contents of a valid citation."

Vespa v. National Health Ins. Co., 98 S.W.3d 749, 752 (Tex.App.—Fort Worth 2003, no pet.). "[P] served

[D] using substitute service under [TRCP] 106. ... The trial court required the citation, petition, and a copy of the trial court's order to be placed on the front door of [D's] house. The return of service showed that the process server only placed the citation and petition on [D's] door. Because the return of service is prima facie evidence of how service was performed, it proves that the order was not placed on the door as instructed by the trial court."

All Commercial Floors v. Barton & Rasor, 97 S.W.3d 723, 727 (Tex.App.—Fort Worth 2003, no pet.). "[A] corporation is not a person capable of accepting process, and it must be served through its agents. Therefore, because the record shows on its face that the return was not signed by the addressee or registered agent and [D] is not capable of receiving service, [P] has failed to strictly comply with Rule 107."

Union Pac. Corp. v. Legg, 49 S.W.3d 72, 78 (Tex. App.—Austin 2001, no pet.). "The clerk's return of the citation directed to [D] and the accompanying certified-mail receipt do not bear a file mark or other indication that they were in fact filed with the clerk on a particular day, or that they were, indeed, filed at all. Consequently, they do not show they were 'on file' for the requisite ten days before default judgment was granted. We hold this violates the strict-compliance requirement."

Bautista v. Bautista, 9 S.W.3d 250, 251 (Tex.App.—San Antonio 1999, no pet.). "'Verified' for purposes of rule 107 has been defined as an acknowledgment of the instrument before a notary public."

Onyx TV v. TV Strategy Group, 990 S.W.2d 427, 431 (Tex.App.—Texarkana 1999, no pet.). "The Secretary of State's certificate of process, [showing proof of service under the long-arm statute,] does not place on file the information [required under TRCP 99 and] contained in the citation sent to [D]. We hold that the filing of the Secretary of State's certificate does not comply with the requirement of [TRCP] 107 that the citation be on file."

Seib v. Bekker, 964 S.W.2d 25, 28 (Tex.App.—Tyler 1997, no writ). "[A] return of service of citation by a private process server must contain the fact of service, the time of service, and manner of service, and shall be sworn to by the private process server before a notary public and filed with the papers in the cause."

TRCP 108. DEFENDANT WITHOUT STATE

Where the defendant is absent from the State, or is a nonresident of the State, the form of notice to such defendant of the institution of the suit shall be the same as prescribed for citation to a resident defendant; and such notice may be served by any disinterested person competent to make oath of the fact in the same manner as provided in Rule 106 hereof. The return of service in such cases shall be endorsed on or attached to the original notice, and shall be in the form provided in Rule 107, and be signed and sworn to by the party making such service before some officer authorized by the laws of this State to take affidavits, under the hand and official seal of such officer. A defendant served with such notice shall be required to appear and answer in the same manner and time and under the same penalties as if he had been personally served with a citation within this State to the full extent that he may be required to appear and answer under the Constitution of the United States in an action either in rem or in personam.

See *Commentaries*, "Serving the Defendant with Suit," ch. 2-H.

History of TRCP 108: Amended eff. Jan. 1, 1976, by order of July 22, 1975 (525-26 S.W.2d [Tex.Cases] xlv): The words after "State" in the last sentence were added to permit acquisition of in personam jurisdiction to the constitutional limits. Adopted eff. Sept. 1, 1941, by order of Oct. 29, 1940 (3 Tex.B.J. 541 [1940]). Source: TRCS arts. 2037, 2038 (repealed).

Paramount Pipe & Sup. Co. v. Muhr, 749 S.W.2d 491, 495-96 (Tex.1988). TRCP 108 "is a valid procedural alternative to service under the long-arm statute. ... So long as the allegations confronting [D] were sufficient to satisfy due process requirements, the trial court had jurisdiction to render judgment by default against him. The only question ... is whether the jurisdictional allegations in the petitions were sufficient, under the Constitution of the U.S., to require [D] to answer."

World Distribs. v. Knox, 968 S.W.2d 474, 479 (Tex.App.—El Paso 1998, no pet.). "We have ... found no authority for the Secretary of State to serve process. [N]umerous statutes require the Secretary of State to act as agent for service, but no statute authorizes him to serve process. [¶] We fail to perceive how the Secretary of State may act as [D's] agent for service and at the same time still qualify as a 'disinterested person.'"

TRCP 108a. SERVICE OF PROCESS IN FOREIGN COUNTRIES

(1) Manner. Service of process may be effected upon a party in a foreign country if service of the citation and petition is made: (a) in the manner prescribed by the law of the foreign country for service in that country in an action in any of its courts of general jurisdiction; or (b) as directed by the foreign authority in response to a letter rogatory or a letter of request; or (c) in the manner provided by Rule 106; or (d) pursuant to the terms and provisions of any applicable treaty or convention; or (e) by diplomatic or consular officials when authorized by the United States Department of State; or (f) by any other means directed by the court that is not prohibited by the law of the country where service is to be made. The method for service of process in a foreign country must be reasonably calculated, under all of the circumstances, to give actual notice of the proceedings to the defendant in time to answer and defend. A defendant served with process under this rule shall be required to appear and answer in the same manner and time and under the same penalties as if he had been personally served with citation within this state to the full extent that he may be required to appear and answer under the Constitution of the United States or under any applicable convention or treaty in an action either in rem or in personam.

(2) Return. Proof of service may be made as prescribed by the law of the foreign country, by order of the court, by Rule 107, or by a method provided in any applicable treaty or convention.

See CPRC §§17.044-17.045.

History of TRCP 108a: Adopted eff. Apr. 1, 1984, by order of Dec. 5, 1983 (661-62 S.W.2d [Tex.Cases] xli). Source: New rule.

Commission of Contracts v. Arriba, Ltd., 882 S.W.2d 576, 584 (Tex.App.—Houston [1st Dist.] 1994, no writ). "[Ps] argue that service on a resident of a foreign country under the long-arm statute is improper, and that a resident of a foreign country can only be served according to the methods of service prescribed in [TRCP] 108a. *At 585:* We find a party in a foreign country may be served under the long-arm statute."

TRCP 109. CITATION BY PUBLICATION

When a party to a suit, his agent or attorney, shall make oath that the residence of any party defendant is unknown to affiant, and to such party when the affidavit is made by his agent or attorney, or that such defendant is a transient person, and that after due diligence such party and the affiant have been unable to locate the whereabouts of such defendant, or that such defendant is absent from or is a nonresident of the State, and that the party applying for the citation has attempted to obtain personal service of nonresident notice as provided for in Rule 108, but has been unable to do so, the clerk shall issue citation for such defendant for service by publication. In such cases it shall be the duty of the court trying the case to inquire into the sufficiency of the diligence exercised in attempting to ascertain the residence or whereabouts of the defendant or to obtain service of nonresident notice, as the case may be, before granting any judgment on such service.

See *Commentaries*, "Serving the Defendant with Suit," ch. 2-H; "Motion for New Trial," ch. 10-B.

History of TRCP 109: Amended eff. Apr. 1, 1984, by order of Dec. 5, 1983 (661-62 S.W.2d [Tex.Cases] xli): The last sentence of the former rule was deleted. Amended eff. Jan. 1, 1976, by order of July 22, 1975 (525-26 S.W.2d [Tex.Cases] xlvi): Deleted the word "continental" before "United States" in the last sentence. Amended eff. Feb. 1, 1946, by order of Oct. 10, 1945 (8 Tex.B.J. 532 [1945]). Adopted eff. Sept. 1, 1941, by order of Oct. 29, 1940 (3 Tex.B.J. 541 [1940]). Source: TRCS art. 2039 (repealed), first sentence.

Wood v. Brown, 819 S.W.2d 799, 800 (Tex.1991). "In his affidavit, [P's] counsel stated that [D] had moved from his last known address in Oklahoma and that neighbors thought that [D] had moved to Florida. The affidavit, however, does not state that [D's] residence was unknown to [P's] attorney, that [D] was a transient person, that [D] was absent from Texas or that [D] did not reside in Texas. Therefore, the affidavit ... did not meet any of the requirements for service by publication under [TRCP] 109."

In re A.Y., 16 S.W.3d 387, 389 (Tex.App.—El Paso 2000, no pet.). TRCP "109 requires the trial court to determine the diligence used by [P] in trying to locate [D's] residence. If the trial court finds a lack of diligence, then [P] must undertake additional efforts to comply with Rule 109. If [P] is successful in his efforts to locate [D], then regular service of process is required."

TRCP 109a. OTHER SUBSTITUTED SERVICE

Whenever citation by publication is authorized, the court may, on motion, prescribe a different method of substituted service, if the court finds, and so recites in its order, that the method so prescribed would be as likely as publication to give defendant actual notice. When such method of substituted service is authorized, the return of the officer executing the citation shall state particularly the manner in which service is accomplished, and shall attach any return receipt, returned mail, or other evidence showing the result of such service. Failure of defendant to respond to such citation shall not render the service invalid. When such substituted service has been obtained and the defendant has not appeared, the provisions of Rules 244 and 329 shall apply as if citation had been served by publication.

See *Commentaries*, "Serving the Defendant with Suit," ch. 2-H.

History of TRCP 109a: Adopted eff. Jan. 1, 1976, by order of July 22, 1975 (525-26 S.W.2d [Tex.Cases] xlvi). Source: New rule.

Howell v. Homecraft Land Dev., 749 S.W.2d 103, 112 (Tex.App.—Dallas 1987, writ denied). "The rules require a strict showing of the need for substituted service, and the trial court must order the substituted service."

TRCP 110. EFFECT OF RULES ON OTHER STATUTES

Where by statute or these rules citation by publication is authorized and the statute or rules do not specify the requisites of such citation or the method of service thereof, or where they direct that such citation be issued or served as in other civil actions, the provisions of these rules shall govern. Where, however, the statute authorizing citation by publication provides expressly for requisites of such citation or service thereof, or both, differing from the provisions of Rules 114, 115, and 116, these rules shall not govern, but the special statutory procedure shall continue in force; provided, however, that Rule 117a shall control with respect to citation in tax suits.

History of TRCP 110: Amended eff. Dec. 31, 1947, by order of Aug. 18, 1947 (10 Tex.B.J. 391 [1947]). Adopted eff. Sept. 1, 1941, by order of Oct. 29, 1940 (3 Tex.B.J. 541 [1940]). Source: New rule.

TRCP 111. CITATION BY PUBLICATION IN ACTION AGAINST UNKNOWN HEIRS OR STOCKHOLDERS OF DEFUNCT CORPORATIONS

If the plaintiff, his agent, or attorney, shall make oath that the names of the heirs or stockholders against whom an action is authorized by Section 17.004, Civil Practice and Remedies Code, are unknown to the affiant, the clerk shall issue a citation for service by publication. Such citation shall be addressed to the defendants by a concise description of their classification, as "the Unknown Heirs of A.B., deceased," or "Unknown Stockholders of __________ Corporation," as the case may be, and shall contain the other requisites prescribed in Rules 114 and 115 and shall be served as provided by Rule 116.

See *Commentaries*, "Serving the Defendant with Suit," ch. 2-H.

History of TRCP 111: Amended eff. Jan. 1, 1988, by order of July 15, 1987 (733-34 S.W.2d [Tex.Cases] xlv). Adopted eff. Sept. 1, 1941, by order of Oct. 29, 1940 (3 Tex.B.J. 541 [1940]). Source: TRCS art. 2040 (repealed).

TRCP 112. PARTIES TO ACTIONS AGAINST UNKNOWN OWNERS OR CLAIMANTS OF INTEREST IN LAND

In suits authorized by Section 17.005, Civil Practice and Remedies Code, all persons claiming under such conveyance whose names are known to plaintiff shall be made parties by name and cited to appear, in the manner now provided by law as in other suits; all other persons claiming any interest in such land under such conveyance may be made parties to the suit and cited by publication under the designation "all persons claiming any title or interest in land under deed heretofore given to ______________ of ________________ as grantee" (inserting in the blanks the name and residence of grantee as given in such conveyance). It shall be permissible to join in one suit all persons claiming under two or more conveyances affecting title to the same tract of land.

See CPRC §17.005; TRCP 113; *Commentaries*, "Serving the Defendant with Suit," ch. 2-H.

History of TRCP 112: Amended eff. Jan. 1, 1988, by order of July 15, 1987 (733-34 S.W.2d [Tex.Cases] xlvi). Adopted eff. Sept. 1, 1941, by order of Oct. 29, 1940 (3 Tex.B.J. 542 [1940]). Source: TRCS art. 2040 (repealed).

TRCP 113. CITATION BY PUBLICATION IN ACTIONS AGAINST UNKNOWN OWNERS OR CLAIMANTS OF INTEREST IN LAND

In suits authorized by Section 17.005, Civil Practice and Remedies Code, plaintiff, his agent or attorney shall make and file with the clerk of the court an affidavit, stating

(a) the name of the grantee as set out in the conveyance constituting source of title of defendants, and

(b) stating that affiant does not know the names of any persons claiming title or interest under such conveyance other than as stated in plaintiff's petition and

(c) if the conveyance is to a company or association name as grantee, further stating whether grantee is incorporated or unincorporated, if such fact is known, and if such fact is unknown, so stating.

Said clerk shall thereupon issue a citation for service upon all persons claiming any title or interest in such land under such conveyance. The citation in such cases shall contain the requisites and be served in the manner provided by Rules 114, 115 and 116.

See CPRC §17.005; TRCP 112; *Commentaries*, "Serving the Defendant with Suit," ch. 2-H.

TRCP 113

History of TRCP 113: Amended eff. Sept. 1, 1990, by order of Apr. 24, 1990 (785-86 S.W.2d [Tex.Cases] xlviii): The letters "T.R.C.P." in last sentence were changed to "Rules." Amended eff. Jan. 1, 1988, by order of July 15, 1987 (733-34 S.W.2d [Tex.Cases] xlvi): The letters "T.R.S." in last sentence were changed to "T.R.C.P." Amended eff. Jan. 1, 1955, by order of July 20, 1954 (17 Tex.B.J. 567 [1954]). Adopted eff. Sept. 1, 1941, by order of Oct. 29, 1940 (3 Tex.B.J. 542 [1940]). Source: TRCS art. 2041a (repealed).

Quarles v. Champion Int'l Corp., 760 S.W.2d 792, 794 (Tex.App.—Beaumont 1988, writ denied). Service of citation by publication on a known party is improper, "[a]nd this notice requirement to a known party is of due process dimension."

TRCP 114. CITATION BY PUBLICATION; REQUISITES

Where citation by publication is authorized by these rules, the citation shall contain the requisites prescribed by Rules 15 and 99, in so far as they are not inconsistent herewith, provided that no copy of the plaintiff's petition shall accompany this citation, and the citation shall be styled "The State of Texas" and shall be directed to the defendant or defendants by name, if their names are known, or to the defendant or defendants as designated in the petition, if unknown, or such other classification as may be fixed by any statute or by these rules. Where there are two or more defendants or classes of defendants to be served by publication, the citation may be directed to all of them by name and classification, so that service may be completed by publication of the one citation for the required number of times. The citation shall contain the names of the parties, a brief statement of the nature of the suit (which need not contain the details and particulars of the claim) a description of any property involved and of the interest of the named or unknown defendant or defendants, and, where the suit involves land, the requisites of Rule 115. If issued from the district or county court, the citation shall command such parties to appear and answer at or before 10 o'clock a.m. of the first Monday after the expiration of 42 days from the date of issuance thereof, specifying the day of the week, the day of the month, and the time of day the defendant is required to answer. If issued from the justice of the peace court, such citation shall command such parties to appear and answer on or before the first day of the first term of court which convenes after the expiration of 42 days from the date of issue thereof, specifying the day of the week, and the day of the month, that such term will meet.

History of TRCP 114: Amended eff. Jan. 1, 1988, by order of July 15, 1987 (733-34 S.W.2d [Tex.Cases] xlvi). Amended eff. Dec. 31, 1941, by order of Sept. 20, 1941 (6 Tex.B.J. 506 [1941]). Adopted eff. Sept. 1, 1941, by order of Oct. 29, 1940 (3 Tex.B.J. 543 [1940]). Source: TRCS arts. 2041, 2092(6), (repealed).

Wiebusch v. Wiebusch, 636 S.W.2d 540, 542 (Tex. App.—San Antonio 1982, no writ). "[N]otice of the nature of the suit is essential to a valid citation by publication."

TRCP 115. FORM OF PUBLISHED CITATION IN ACTIONS INVOLVING LAND

In citations by publication involving land, it shall be sufficient in making the brief statement of the claim in such citation to state the kind of suit, the number of acres of land involved in the suit, or the number of the lot and block, or any other plat description that may be of record if the land is situated in a city or town, the survey on which and the county in which the land is situated, and any special pleas which are relied upon in such suit.

History of TRCP 115: Adopted eff. Sept. 1, 1941, by order of Oct. 29, 1940 (3 Tex.B.J. 543 [1940]). Source: TRCS art. 2041 (repealed).

TRCP 116. SERVICE OF CITATION BY PUBLICATION

The citation, when issued, shall be served by the sheriff or any constable of any county of the State of Texas or by the clerk of the court in which the case is pending, by having the same published once each week for four (4) consecutive weeks, the first publication to be at least twenty-eight (28) days before the return day of the citation. In all suits which do not involve the title to land or the partition of real estate, such publication shall be made in the county where the suit is pending, if there be a newspaper published in said county, but if not, then in an adjoining county where a newspaper is published. In all suits which involve the title to land or partition of real estate, such publication shall be made in the county where the land, or a portion thereof, is situated, if there be a newspaper in such county, but if not, then in an adjoining county to the county where the land or a part thereof is situated, where a newspaper is published.

History of TRCP 116: Amended eff. Apr. 1, 1984, by order of Dec. 5, 1983 (661-62 S.W.2d [Tex.Cases] xli): TRCP 116 was not amended when TRCP 103 was changed eff. Jan. 1, 1981; It was therefore inconsistent with TRCP 103. Adopted eff. Sept. 1, 1941, by order of Oct. 29, 1940 (3 Tex.B.J. 543 [1940]). Source: TRCS arts. 2042, 2092(6) (repealed).

In re A.Y., 16 S.W.3d 387, 389 (Tex.App.—El Paso 2000, no pet.). "The Family Code allows for citation by publication as in other civil cases. Therefore, ... Rule 116 makes citation by publication proper if published in the county where suit is pending."

Fleming v. Hernden, 564 S.W.2d 157, 159 (Tex. App.—El Paso 1978, writ ref'd n.r.e.). Citation by publication in San Antonio newspapers affecting title to land in Willacy County did not comply with TRCP 116.

TRCP 117. RETURN OF CITATION BY PUBLICATION

The return of the officer executing such citation shall be indorsed or attached to the same, and show how and when the citation was executed, specifying the dates of such publication, be signed by him officially and shall be accompanied by a printed copy of such publication.

History of TRCP 117: Adopted eff. Sept. 1, 1941, by order of Oct. 29, 1940 (3 Tex.B.J. 543 [1940]). Source: TRCS art. 2043, unchanged (repealed).

TRCP 117a. CITATION IN SUITS FOR DELINQUENT AD VALOREM TAXES

In all suits for collection of delinquent ad valorem taxes, the rules of civil procedure governing issuance and service of citation shall control the issuance and service of citation therein, except as herein otherwise specially provided.

1. **Personal Service: Owner and Residence Known, Within State.** Where any defendant in a tax suit is a resident of the State of Texas and is not subject to citation by publication under subdivision 3 below, the process shall conform substantially to the form hereinafter set out for personal service and shall contain the essential elements and be served and returned and otherwise regulated by the provisions of Rules 99 to 107, inclusive.

2. **Personal Service: Owner and Residence Known, Out of State.** Where any such defendant is absent from the State or is a nonresident of the State and is not subject to citation by publication under subdivision 3 below, the process shall conform substantially to the form hereinafter set out for personal service and shall contain the essential elements and be served and returned and otherwise regulated by the provisions of Rule 108.

3. **Service by Publication: Nonresident, Absent from State, Transient, Name Unknown, Residence Unknown, Owner Unknown, Heirs Unknown, Corporate Officers, Trustees, Receivers or Stockholders Unknown, Any Other Unknown Persons Owing or Claiming or Having an Interest.** Where any defendant in a tax suit is a nonresident of the State, or is absent from the State, or is a transient person, or the name or the residence of any owner of any interest in any property upon which a tax lien is sought to be foreclosed, is unknown to the attorney requesting the issuance of process or filing the suit for the taxing unit, and such attorney shall make affidavit that such defendant is a nonresident of the State, or is absent from the State, or is a transient person, or that the name or residence of such owner is unknown and cannot be ascertained after diligent inquiry, each such person in every such class above mentioned, together with any and all other persons, including adverse claimants, owning or claiming or having any legal or equitable interest in or lien upon such property, may be cited by publication. All unknown owners of any interest in any property upon which any taxing unit seeks to foreclose a lien for taxes, including stockholders of corporations—defunct or otherwise—their successors, heirs, and assigns, may be joined in such suit under the designation of "unknown owners" and citation be had upon them as such; provided, however, that record owners of such property or of any apparent interest therein, including, without limitation, record lien holders, shall not be included in the designation of "unknown owners"; and provided further that where any record owner has rendered the property involved within five years before the tax suit is filed, citation on such record owner may not be had by publication or posting unless citation for personal service has been issued as to such record owner, with a notation thereon setting forth the same address as is contained on the rendition sheet made within such five years, and the sheriff or other person to whom citation has been delivered makes his return thereon that he is unable to locate the defendant. Where any attorney filing a tax suit for a taxing unit, or requesting the issuance of process in such suit, shall make affidavit that a corporation is the record owner of any interest in any property upon which a tax lien is sought to be foreclosed, and that he does not know, and after diligent inquiry has been unable to ascertain, the location of the place of business, if any, of such corporation, or the name or place of residence of any officer of such corporation upon whom personal service may be had, such corporation may be cited by publication as herein provided. All defendants of the classes enumerated above may be joined in the same citation by publication.

TRCP 117a

An affidavit which complies with the foregoing requirements therefor shall be sufficient basis for the citation above mentioned in connection with it but shall be held to be made upon the criminal responsibility of affiant.

Such citation by publication shall be directed to the defendants by names or by designation as hereinabove provided, and shall be issued and signed by the clerk of the court in which such tax suit is pending. It shall be sufficient if it states the file number and style of the case, the date of the filing of the petition, the names of all parties by name or by designation as hereinabove provided, and the court in which the suit is pending; shall command such parties to appear and defend such suit at or before 10 o'clock a.m. of the first Monday after the expiration of forty-two days from the date of the issuance thereof, specifying such date when such parties are required to answer; shall state the place of holding the court, the nature of the suit, and the date of the issuance of the citation; and shall be signed and sealed by the clerk.

The citation shall be published in the English language one time a week for two weeks in some newspaper published in the county in which the property is located, which newspaper must have been in general circulation for at least one year immediately prior to the first publication and shall in every respect answer the requirements of the law applicable to newspapers which are employed for such a purpose, the first publication to be not less than twenty-eight days prior to the return day fixed in the citation; and the affidavit of the editor or publisher of the newspaper giving the date of publication, together with a printed copy of the citation as published, shall constitute sufficient proof of due publication when returned and filed in court. If there is no newspaper published in the county, then the publication may be made in a newspaper in an adjoining county, which newspaper shall in every respect answer the requirements of the law applicable to newspapers which are employed for such a purpose. The maximum fee for publishing the citation shall be the lowest published word or line rate of that newspaper for classified advertising. If the publication of the citation cannot be had for this fee, chargeable as costs and payable upon sale of the property, as provided by law, and this fact is supported by the affidavit of the attorney for the plaintiff or the attorney requesting the issuance of the process, then service of the citation may be made by posting a copy at the courthouse door of the county in which the suit is pending, the citation to be posted at least twenty-eight days prior to the return day fixed in the citation. Proof of the posting of the citation shall be made by affidavit of the attorney for the plaintiff, or of the person posting it. When citation is served as here provided it shall be sufficient, and no other form of citation or notice to the named defendants therein shall be necessary.

4. Citation in Tax Suits: General Provisions. Any process authorized by this rule may issue jointly in behalf of all taxing units who are plaintiffs or intervenors in any tax suit. The statement of the nature of the suit, to be set out in the citation, shall be sufficient if it contains a brief general description of the property upon which the taxes are due and the amount of such taxes, exclusive of interest, penalties, and costs, and shall state, in substance, that in such suit the plaintiff and all other taxing units who may set up their claims therein seek recovery of the delinquent ad valorem taxes due on said property, and the (establishment and foreclosure) of liens, if any, securing the payment of same, as provided by law; that in addition to the taxes all interest, penalties, and costs allowed by law up to and including the day of judgment are included in the suit; and that all parties to the suit, including plaintiff, defendants, and intervenors, shall take notice that claims for any taxes on said property becoming delinquent subsequent to the filing of the suit and up to the day of judgment, together with all interest, penalties, and costs allowed by law thereon, may, upon request therefor, be recovered therein without further citation or notice to any parties thereto. Such citation need not be accompanied by a copy of plaintiff's petition and no such copy need be served. Such citation shall also show the names of all taxing units which assess and collect taxes on said property not made parties to such suit, and shall contain, in substance, a recitation that each party to such suit shall take notice of, and plead and answer to, all claims and pleadings then on file or thereafter filed in said cause by all other parties therein, or who may intervene therein and set up their respective tax claims against said property. After citation or notice has been given on behalf of any plaintiff or intervenor taxing unit, the court shall have jurisdiction to hear and determine the tax claims of all taxing units who are parties plaintiff, intervenor or defendant at the time such process is issued and of all taxing units intervening after such process is issued, not only for the taxes, interest, penalties, and costs which may be due on said property at the time the suit is filed, but those becoming delinquent thereon at any time thereafter up to and including the day of judgment, without the necessity of further citation or notice to any party to said suit; and any taxing unit having a tax claim against said property may, by answer or intervention, set up and have determined its tax claim without the necessity of further citation or notice to any parties to such suit.

5. Form of Citation by Publication or Posting. The form of citation by publication or posting shall be sufficient if it is in substantially the following form, with proper changes to make the same applicable to personal property, where necessary, and if the suit includes or is for the recovery of taxes assessed on personal property, a general description of such personal property shall be sufficient:

THE STATE OF TEXAS §
COUNTY OF ___________ §

In the name and by the authority of the State of Texas

Notice is hereby given as follows:

To ______________________________________

____

and any and all other persons, including adverse claimants, owning or having or claiming any legal or equitable interest in or lien upon the following described property delinquent to Plaintiff herein, for taxes, to-wit:

____

____

Which said property is delinquent to Plaintiff for taxes in the following amounts:

$______, exclusive of interest, penalties, and costs, and there is included in this suit in addition to the taxes all said interest, penalties, and costs thereon, allowed by law up to and including the day of judgment herein.

You are hereby notified that suit has been brought by ______ as Plaintiffs, against _______ as Defendants, by petition filed on the ___ day of _____, 19___, in a certain suit styled __________ v. __________ for collection of the taxes on said property and that said suit is now pending in the District Court of _____ County, Texas, _____ Judicial District, and the file number of said suit is _____, that the names of all taxing units which assess and collect taxes on the property hereinabove described, not made parties to this suit, are _______________.

Plaintiff and all other taxing units who may set up their tax claims herein seek recovery of delinquent ad valorem taxes on the property hereinabove described, and in addition to the taxes all interest, penalties, and costs allowed by law thereon up to and including the day of judgment herein, and the establishment and foreclosure of liens, if any, securing the payment of same, as provided by law.

All parties to this suit, including plaintiff, defendants, and intervenors, shall take notice that claims not only for any taxes which were delinquent on said property at the time this suit was filed but all taxes becoming delinquent thereon at any time thereafter up to the day of judgment, including all interest, penalties, and costs allowed by law thereon, may, upon request therefor, be recovered herein without further citation or notice to any parties herein, and all said parties shall take notice of and plead and answer to all claims and pleadings now on file and which may hereafter be filed in said cause by all other parties herein, and all of those taxing units above named who may intervene herein and set up their respective tax claims against said property.

You are hereby commanded to appear and defend such suit on the first Monday after the expiration of forty-two (42) days from and after the date of issuance hereof, the same being the ____ day of _________, A.D., 19___ (which is the return day of such citation), before the honorable District Court of ______________ County, Texas, to be held at the courthouse thereof, then and there to show cause why judgment shall not be rendered for such taxes, penalties, interest, and costs, and condemning said property and ordering foreclosure of the constitutional and statutory tax liens thereon for taxes due the plaintiff and the taxing units parties hereto, and those who may intervene herein, together with all interest, penalties, and costs allowed by law up to and including the day of judgment herein, and all costs of this suit.

Issued and given under my hand and seal of said court in the City of _________, _______ County, Texas, this ___ day of _________, A.D., 19___.

____
Clerk of the District Court
____________ County, Texas,
____________ Judicial District.

6. Form of Citation by Personal Service in or out of State. The form of citation for personal service shall be sufficient if it is in substantially the following form, with proper changes to make the same applicable to personal property, where necessary, and if the suit includes or is for the recovery of taxes assessed on personal property, a general description of such personal property shall be sufficient:

THE STATE OF TEXAS

To ________, Defendant,

GREETING:

YOU ARE HEREBY COMMANDED to appear and answer before the Honorable District Court, _______ Judicial District, _____________ County, Texas, at the Courthouse of said county in _____________, Texas, at or before 10 o'clock a.m. of the Monday next after the expiration of 20 days from the date of service of this citation, then and there to answer the petition of _____________, Plaintiff, filed in said Court on the ___ day of ______, A.D., 19__, against __________, Defendant, said suit being number ________ on the docket of said Court, the nature of which demand is a suit to collect delinquent ad valorem taxes on the property hereinafter described.

The amount of taxes due Plaintiff, exclusive of interest, penalties, and costs, is the sum of $ __________, said property being described as follows, to-wit: ______

____

____

The names of all taxing units which assess and collect taxes on said property, not made parties to this suit, are: ____

____

Plaintiff and all other taxing units who may set up their tax claims herein seek recovery of delinquent ad valorem taxes on the property hereinabove described, and in addition to the taxes all interest, penalties, and costs allowed by law thereon up to and including the day of judgment herein, and the establishment and foreclosure of liens securing the payment of same, as provided by law.

All parties to this suit, including plaintiff, defendants, and intervenors, shall take notice that claims not only for any taxes which were delinquent on said property at the time this suit was filed but all taxes becoming delinquent thereon at any time thereafter up to the day of judgment, including all interest, penalties, and costs allowed by law thereon, may, upon request therefor, be recovered herein without further citation or notice to any parties herein, and all said parties shall take notice of and plead and answer to all claims and pleadings now on file and which may hereafter be filed in this cause by all other parties hereto, and by all of those taxing units above named, who may intervene herein and set up their respective tax claims against said property.

If this citation is not served within 90 days after the date of its issuance, it shall be returned unserved.

The officer executing this return shall promptly serve the same according to the requirements of law and the mandates hereof and make due return as the law directs.

Issued and given under my hand and seal of said Court at _____, Texas, this the ___ day of _______, A.D., 19__.

____

Clerk of the District Court

____________ County, Texas,

By ____________, Deputy

See *Commentaries*, "Serving the Defendant with Suit," ch. 2-H.

History of TRCP 117a: Amended eff. Jan. 1, 1988, by order of July 15, 1987 (733-34 S.W.2d [Tex.Cases] xlvii): Section 3. amended to update the fee schedule for service of citation of publications to an acceptable fee level for both litigants and the publications. Amended eff. Dec. 1, 1950, by order of July 17, 1950 (13 Tex.B.J. 423 [1950]). Amended eff. Oct. 1, 1948, by order of May 4, 1948 (11 Tex.B.J. 337 [1948]). Adopted eff. Dec. 31, 1947, by order of Aug. 18, 1947 (10 Tex.B.J. 391 [1947]). Source: New rule.

Anderson v. Collum, 514 S.W.2d 230, 231 (Tex. 1974). "[T]he failure to comply with [TRCP 117a] and the admitted lack of diligence to locate [Ds] renders the service by publication ineffective."

Conseco Fin. Serv. Corp. v. Klein ISD, 78 S.W.3d 666, 675 (Tex.App.—Houston [14th Dist.] 2002, no pet.). "The permissive language in Rule 117a(4) indicates an intent to give all other taxing units the discretion to join the suit, rather than giving the taxing unit instituting the suit discretion to exclude other taxing units, or cause them to have to obtain issuance of their own citations. ... Rule 117a does not require other taxing units to join a tax suit, but it clearly permits them to intervene without further service."

TRCP 118. AMENDMENT

At any time in its discretion and upon such notice and on such terms as it deems just, the court may allow any process or proof of service thereof to be amended, unless it clearly appears that material prejudice would result to the substantial rights of the party against whom the process issued.

See *Commentaries*, "Serving the Defendant with Suit," ch. 2-H.

History of TRCP 118: Adopted eff. Sept. 1, 1941, by order of Oct. 29, 1940 (3 Tex.B.J. 543 [1940]). Source: TRCS art. 2044 (repealed), FRCP 4(h).

Higginbotham v. General Life & Acc. Ins. Co., 796 S.W.2d 695, 697 (Tex.1990). Because a trial court's order holding that service was proper was "tantamount to formal amendment of the return of citation, the record was sufficient to show valid service."

Dawson v. Briggs, 107 S.W.3d 739, 745 (Tex.App.—Fort Worth 2003, no pet.). "[T]he filing of a notice of appeal by [D] did not deprive the trial court of jurisdiction to sign an order during its plenary power granting [P's] motion to amend the citation."

Union Pac. Corp. v. Legg, 49 S.W.3d 72, 77 (Tex. App.—Austin 2001, no pet.). "'If the facts as recited in the [officer's] return … are incorrect and do not show proper service, the one requesting service must amend the return prior to judgment.' [¶] [T]he rules allow for liberal amendment of 'any process or proof of service' before a default judgment is taken."

TRCP 119. ACCEPTANCE OF SERVICE

The defendant may accept service of process, or waive the issuance or service thereof by a written memorandum signed by him, or by his duly authorized agent or attorney, after suit is brought, sworn to before a proper officer other than an attorney in the case, and filed among the papers of the cause, and such waiver or acceptance shall have the same force and effect as if the citation had been issued and served as provided by law. The party signing such memorandum shall be delivered a copy of plaintiff's petition, and the receipt of the same shall be acknowledged in such memorandum. In every divorce action such memorandum shall also include the defendant's mailing address.

See CPRC §30.001; *Commentaries*, "Serving the Defendant with Suit," ch. 2-H; FORMS 2H.

History of TRCP 119: Amended eff. Jan. 1, 1961, by order of July 26, 1960 (23 Tex.B.J. 620 [Oct. 1960]): Requirement added that written memorandum constituting acceptance of process or waiver of issuance and service thereof be signed "after suit is brought." Amended eff. Jan. 1, 1955, by order of July 20, 1954 (17 Tex.B.J. 567 [1954]): Last sentence added. Amended eff. Dec. 31, 1941, by order of Sept. 20, 1941 (4 Tex.B.J. 507 [1941]): It is provided that the officer shall be "other than an attorney in the case," and the last sentence is added. Adopted eff. Sept. 1, 1941, by order of Oct. 29, 1940 (3 Tex.B.J. 543 [1940]). Source: TRCS art. 2045 (repealed). Change: Added requirement that the waiver of service be sworn to before an officer authorized to administer oaths.

Deen v. Kirk, 508 S.W.2d 70, 71 (Tex.1974). "Under the provisions of [TRCP] 119 [D] may waive the issuance and service of citation by filing among the papers of the cause a verified written memorandum 'signed by him, or by his duly authorized agent or attorney, after suit is brought.' Article 2224 [now CPRC §30.001] prohibits the waiver of process by an instrument executed prior to institution of suit." *See also* ***Tidwell v. Tidwell***, 604 S.W.2d 540, 541 (Tex.App.—Texarkana 1980, no writ).

TRCP 119a. COPY OF DECREE

The district clerk shall forthwith mail a certified copy of the final divorce decree or order of dismissal to the party signing a memorandum waiving issuance or service of process. Such divorce decree or order of dismissal shall be mailed to the signer of the memorandum at the address stated in such memorandum or to the office of his attorney of record.

History of TRCP 119a: Adopted eff. Jan. 1, 1955, by order of July 20, 1954 (17 Tex.B.J. 567 [1954]). Source: New rule.

TRCP 120. ENTERING APPEARANCE

The defendant may, in person, or by attorney, or by his duly authorized agent, enter an appearance in open court. Such appearance shall be noted by the judge upon his docket and entered in the minutes, and shall have the same force and effect as if the citation had been duly issued and served as provided by law.

See *Commentaries*, "Default Judgment," ch. 7-A.

History of TRCP 120: Adopted eff. Sept. 1, 1941, by order of Oct. 29, 1940 (3 Tex.B.J. 543 [1940]). Source: TRCS art. 2046 (repealed).

Mays v. Perkins, 927 S.W.2d 222, 225 (Tex.App.—Houston [1st Dist.] 1996, no writ). "A defendant's appearance before a court generally indicates a submission to the court's jurisdiction. However, the mere presence in court by an attorney, retained as counsel by a person formerly a party to the lawsuit, does not constitute a general appearance, unless the attorney seeks a judgment or an adjudication on some question."

Gonzalez v. Phoenix Frozen Foods, 884 S.W.2d 587, 589 (Tex.App.—Corpus Christi 1994, no writ). "A defendant's appearance in open court shall have the same force and effect as if the citation had been duly issued and served as provided by law."

TRCP 120a. SPECIAL APPEARANCE

1. Notwithstanding the provisions of Rules 121, 122 and 123, a special appearance may be made by any party either in person or by attorney for the purpose of objecting to the jurisdiction of the court over the person or property of the defendant on the ground that such party or property is not amenable to process issued by the courts of this State. A special appearance may be made as to an entire proceeding or as to any severable claim involved therein. Such special appearance shall be made by sworn motion filed prior to motion to transfer venue or any other plea, pleading or motion; provided however, that a motion to transfer venue and any other plea, pleading, or motion may be contained in the same instrument or filed subsequent thereto without waiver of such special appearance; and may be amended to cure defects. The issuance of process for witnesses, the taking of depositions, the serving of requests for admissions, and the use of discovery processes, shall not constitute a waiver of such special appearance. Every appearance, prior to judgment, not in compliance with this rule is a general appearance.

2. Any motion to challenge the jurisdiction provided for herein shall be heard and determined before a motion to transfer venue or any other plea or pleading may be heard. No determination of any issue of fact in connection with the objection to jurisdiction is a determination of the merits of the case or any aspect thereof.

3. The court shall determine the special appearance on the basis of the pleadings, any stipulations made by and between the parties, such affidavits and attachments as may be filed by the parties, the results of discovery processes, and any oral testimony. The affidavits, if any, shall be served at least seven days before the hearing, shall be made on personal knowledge, shall set forth specific facts as would be admissible in evidence, and shall show affirmatively that the affiant is competent to testify.

Should it appear from the affidavits of a party opposing the motion that he cannot for reasons stated present by affidavit facts essential to justify his opposition, the court may order a continuance to permit affidavits to be obtained or depositions to be taken or discovery to be had or may make such other order as is just.

Should it appear to the satisfaction of the court at any time that any of such affidavits are presented in violation of Rule 13, the court shall impose sanctions in accordance with that rule.

4. If the court sustains the objection to jurisdiction, an appropriate order shall be entered. If the objection to jurisdiction is overruled, the objecting party may thereafter appear generally for any purpose. Any such special appearance or such general appearance shall not be deemed a waiver of the objection to jurisdiction when the objecting party or subject matter is not amenable to process issued by the courts of this State.

See CPRC §§17.041-17.042, 51.014(a)(7); ***Commentaries***, "Special Appearance—Challenging Personal Jurisdiction," ch. 3-B; FORMS 3B.

History of TRCP 120a: Amended eff. Sept. 1, 1990, by order of Apr. 24, 1990 (785-86 S.W.2d [Tex.Cases] xlviii): Section 3 was added and former section 3 renumbered to section 4; provides for proof by affidavit at special appearance hearings, with safeguards to responding parties; and preserves Texas' prior practice to place the burden of proof on the party contesting jurisdiction. Amended eff. Sept. 1, 1983, by order of June 15, 1983 (651-52 S.W.2d [Tex.Cases] xxxviii): To conform to S.B. 898, 68th Legislature, 1983. Amended eff. Jan. 1, 1976, by order of July 22, 1975 (525-26 S.W.2d [Tex.Cases] xlvii): Words are added in the third sentence of par. 1 which permit amendments to the special appearance motion. Adopted eff. Sept. 1, 1962, by order of Apr. 12, 1962 (25 Tex.B.J. 372 [1962]). Source: New rule.

General

American Type Culture Collection v. Coleman, 83 S.W.3d 801, 809-10 (Tex.2002). "Although the quantity of [D's] contacts may suggest that [D] had a significant relationship with Texas, we are not concerned with the quantity of contacts. Instead, we must look to the quality of those contacts. [D] does not advertise in Texas, has no physical presence in Texas, performs all its business services outside Texas, and carefully constructs its contracts to ensure it does not benefit from Texas laws. Under these circumstances, we must conclude that [D's] contacts with Texas were not continuous and systematic."

BMC Software v. Marchand, 83 S.W.3d 789, 794 (Tex.2002). The "courts of appeals [should] review the trial court's factual findings for legal and factual sufficiency and review the trial court's legal conclusions *de novo*. [¶] Whether a court has personal jurisdiction over a defendant is a question of law. However, the trial court frequently must resolve questions of fact before deciding the jurisdiction question."

CMMC v. Salinas, 929 S.W.2d 435, 439 (Tex.1996). "[D's] mere knowledge that its winepress was to be sold and used in Texas and its wiring the machine for use in the U.S. were not sufficient to subject [D] to the jurisdiction of Texas courts. *At 440:* A manufacturer cannot fairly be expected to litigate in every part of the world where its products may end up; its contacts with the forum must be more purposeful ... before it can constitutionally be subjected to personal jurisdiction."

CSR Ltd. v. Link, 925 S.W.2d 591, 595-96 (Tex. 1996). "[D] should not be subject to the jurisdiction of a foreign court based upon 'random,' 'fortuitous,' or 'attenuated' contacts. Minimum contacts are particularly important when [D] is from a different country because of the unique and onerous burden placed on a party called upon to defend a suit in a foreign legal system. [¶] [T]he record contains no evidence that CSR [an Australian company] took any act purposefully directed toward selling or distributing the raw asbestos fiber in Texas."

Schlobohm v. Schapiro, 784 S.W.2d 355, 358 (Tex. 1990). The Texas standard for jurisdiction over a nonresident D requires: "(1) The nonresident [D] or foreign corporation must purposefully do some act or consummate some transaction in the forum state; (2) The cause of action must arise from, or be connected with, such act or transaction; and (3) The assumption of jurisdiction by the forum state must not offend traditional notions of fair play and substantial justice.... [¶] [However], we modify the second part ... to state that jurisdiction may also arise from the continuing and systematic contacts of [D] with Texas, even if the cause of action does not arise from a specific contact." *See also* ***Guardian Royal Exch. Assur. v. English China Clays***, 815 S.W.2d 223, 226 (Tex.1991).

Pleadings

Dawson-Austin v. Austin, 968 S.W.2d 319, 322-23 (Tex.1998). The Supreme Court held: (1) an unverified special appearance may be amended to cure the defect, even after the trial court has overruled it, as long as the amendment is filed before the D enters a general appearance; and (2) it is not necessary for the answer and other motions filed in the same instrument with the special appearance to contain "subject to" language.

Exito Elecs. Co. v. Trejo, 99 S.W.3d 360, 369 (Tex. App.—Corpus Christi 2003, pet. filed 5-7-03). "An unconditional [TRCP] 11 agreement filed prior to a special appearance is not filed in the same instrument or subsequent to the special appearance, and [TRCP] 120a(1) does not contemplate that it is considered subject to the special appearance. [A] nonresident defendant who files an unconditional [TRCP] 11 agreement prior to filing a special appearance enters a general appearance under the due-order-of-pleading requirement of [TRCP] 120a(1)."

Casino Magic Corp. v. King, 43 S.W.3d 14, 18 (Tex. App.—Dallas 2001, pet. denied). TRCP 120a "requires special appearances to be made by 'sworn motion.' Strict compliance with the rule is required. [¶] In this case, the special appearance was not sworn or verified. Although [D] attached an affidavit to the special appearance which set out various 'jurisdictional facts,' in that affidavit [D's] general counsel stated only that the allegations in the *affidavit* were true and correct, not that the facts set out in the *special appearance* were true and correct. [W]e conclude the affidavit did not strictly comply with rule 120a and it, therefore, could not serve to verify the special appearance."

Waiver

GFTA Trendanalysen v. Varme, 991 S.W.2d 785, 786 (Tex.1999). "[A] party [does not] waive[] a due process challenge for want of minimum contacts by challenging the method of service in the special appearance."

Case v. Grammar, 31 S.W.3d 304, 311 (Tex.App.—San Antonio 2000, no pet.), *overruled on other grounds*, ***BMC Software v. Marchand***, 83 S.W.3d 789 (Tex. 2002). "The trial court ... erred in determining that [Ds] waived their special appearances by using the discovery process to seek information pertaining to the merits of the case."

TRCP 121. ANSWER IS APPEARANCE

An answer shall constitute an appearance of the defendant so as to dispense with the necessity for the issuance or service of citation upon him.

History of TRCP 121: Adopted eff. Sept. 1, 1941, by order of Oct. 29, 1940 (3 Tex.B.J. 543 [1940]). Source: TRCS art. 2047 (repealed).

Torres v. Johnson, 91 S.W.3d 905, 910 (Tex.App.—Fort Worth 2002, no pet.). "[N]o new service was required because [D] entered an appearance in the suit by moving for summary judgment after [P] amended his pleadings."

Moody Nat'l Bank v. Riebschlager, 946 S.W.2d 521, 524 (Tex.App.—Houston [14th Dist.] 1997, writ denied). "In order for an act of the garnishee to constitute an appearance, it must seek a judgment or adjudication by the court on some issue.... When a garnishee appears for the purpose of filing a motion to quash the garnishment, such an appearance does not confer jurisdiction on the court for all purposes, and does not operate as a waiver of an objection as to jurisdiction."

TRCP 122. CONSTRUCTIVE APPEARANCE

If the citation or service thereof is quashed on motion of the defendant, such defendant shall be deemed to have entered his appearance at ten o'clock a.m. on the Monday next after the expiration of twenty (20) days after the day on which the citation or service is quashed, and such defendant shall be deemed to have been duly served so as to require him to appear and answer at that time, and if he fails to do so, judgment by default may be rendered against him.

See *Commentaries*, "Motion to Quash—Challenging the Service," ch. 3-I.

History of TRCP 122: Adopted eff. Sept. 1, 1941, by order of Oct. 29, 1940 (3 Tex.B.J. 543 [1940]). Source: TRCS arts. 2048, 2092(8) (repealed).

Kawasaki Steel Corp. v. Middleton, 699 S.W.2d 199, 202 (Tex.1985). "[A] non-resident [D], like any other [D], may move to quash the citation for defects in the process, but his only relief is additional time to answer rather than dismissal of the cause."

TRCP 123. REVERSAL OF JUDGMENT

Where the judgment is reversed on appeal or writ of error for the want of service, or because of defective service of process, no new citation shall be issued or served, but the defendant shall be presumed to have entered his appearance to the term of the court at which the mandate shall be filed.

See *Commentaries*, "Motion to Quash—Challenging the Service," ch. 3-I.

History of TRCP 123: Adopted eff. Sept. 1, 1941, by order of Oct. 29, 1940 (3 Tex.B.J. 544 [1940]). Source: TRCS art. 2049 (repealed).

Ackerly v. Ackerly, 13 S.W.3d 454, 458 (Tex.App.—Corpus Christi 2000, no pet.). "By attacking the judgment, [the husband] has submitted himself to the jurisdiction of the district court. Therefore, upon remand, [the husband] is presumed to have entered his appearance, and no new citation is required to be issued or served."

TRCP 124. NO JUDGMENT WITHOUT SERVICE

In no case shall judgment be rendered against any defendant unless upon service, or acceptance or waiver of process, or upon an appearance by the defendant, as prescribed in these rules, except where otherwise expressly provided by law or these rules.

When a party asserts a counterclaim or a cross-claim against another party who has entered an appearance, the claim may be served in any manner prescribed for service of citation or as provided in Rule 21a.

See *Commentaries*, "Serving the Defendant with Suit," ch. 2-H; "Default Judgment," ch. 7-A.

History of TRCP 124: Amended eff. Apr. 1, 1984, by order of Dec. 5, 1983 (661-62 S.W.2d [Tex.Cases] xlii): The last sentence clarifies the present uncertainty as to whether service of a counterclaim must be by citation; amendment is that service of a counterclaim may be done in any manner prescribed for service of citation and also pursuant to TRCP 21(a). Adopted eff. Sept. 1, 1941, by order of Oct. 29, 1940 (3 Tex.B.J. 544 [1940]). Source: TRCS art. 2050 (repealed).

Werner v. Colwell, 909 S.W.2d 866, 869-70 (Tex. 1995). "[M]erely appearing as a witness in a cause [does not serve] as a general appearance, subjecting one to the jurisdiction of the court."

Strawder v. Thomas, 846 S.W.2d 51, 62 (Tex. App.—Corpus Christi 1992, no writ). "Rules relating to service of process are mandatory, and a failure to comply therewith, if a judgment be rendered against a party who was not served in accordance with those rules (and who did not waive service of citation or appear voluntarily) renders the judgment void."

SECTION 6. COSTS & SECURITY THEREFOR

TRCP 125. PARTIES RESPONSIBLE

Each party to a suit shall be liable to the officers of the court for all costs incurred by himself.

History of TRCP 125: Adopted eff. Sept. 1, 1941, by order of Oct. 29, 1940 (3 Tex.B.J. 544 [1940]). Source: TRCS art. 2051 (repealed), 1st sentence.

Borg-Warner Protective Servs. Corp. v. Flores, 955 S.W.2d 861, 870 (Tex.App.—Corpus Christi 1997, no pet.). "[T]he right to costs is based entirely on statutes or procedural rules, and therefore the trial court is the proper authority to determine and award costs."

TRCP 126. FEE FOR EXECUTION OF PROCESS, DEMAND

No sheriff or constable shall be compelled to execute any process in civil cases coming from any county other than the one in which he is an officer, unless the fees allowed him by law for the service of such process shall be paid in advance; except when affidavit is filed, as provided by law or these rules. The clerk issuing the process shall indorse thereon the words "pauper oath filed," and sign his name officially below them; and the officer in whose hands such process is placed for service shall serve the same.

History of TRCP 126: Adopted eff. Sept. 1, 1941, by order of Oct. 29, 1940 (3 Tex.B.J. 544 [1940]). Source: TRCS art. 2051 (repealed), 2d sentence.

TRCP 127. PARTIES LIABLE FOR OTHER COSTS

Each party to a suit shall be liable for all costs incurred by him. If the costs cannot be collected from the party against whom they have been adjudged, execution may issue against any party in such suit for the amount of costs incurred by such party, but no more.

History of TRCP 127: Adopted eff. Sept. 1, 1941, by order of Oct. 29, 1940 (3 Tex.B.J. 544 [1940]). Source: TRCS art. 2052 (repealed).

TRCP 128. REPEALED

Repealed eff. Apr. 1, 1984, by order of Dec. 5, 1983 (661-62 S.W.2d [Tex.Cases] xlii): The rule was obsolete.

TRCP 129. HOW COSTS COLLECTED

If any party responsible for costs fails or refuses to pay the same within ten days after demand for payment, the clerk or justice of the peace may make certified copy of the bill of costs then due, and place the same in the hands of the sheriff or constable for collection. All taxes imposed on law proceedings shall be included in the bill of costs. Such certified bill of costs shall have the force and effect of an execution. The removal of a case by appeal shall not prevent the issuance of an execution for costs.

History of TRCP 129: Amended eff. Apr. 1, 1984, by order of Dec. 5, 1983 (661-62 S.W.2d [Tex.Cases] xlii): The words "at the end of the term" are dropped from the last sentence. Adopted eff. Sept. 1, 1941, by order of Oct. 29, 1940 (3 Tex.B.J. 544 [1940]). Source: TRCS art. 2054 (repealed).

TRCP 130. OFFICER TO LEVY

The sheriff or constable upon demand and failure to pay said bill of costs, may levy upon a sufficient amount of property of the person from whom said costs are due to satisfy the same, and sell such property as under execution. Where such party is not a resident of the county where such suit is pending, the payment of such costs may be demanded of his attorney of record; and neither the clerk nor justice of the peace shall be allowed to charge any fee for making out such certified bill of costs, unless he is compelled to make a levy.

History of TRCP 130: Adopted eff. Sept. 1, 1941, by order of Oct. 29, 1940 (3 Tex.B.J. 544 [1940]). Source: TRCS art. 2055 (repealed).

TRCP 131. SUCCESSFUL PARTY TO RECOVER

The successful party to a suit shall recover of his adversary all costs incurred therein, except where otherwise provided.

See CPRC §31.007; ***Commentaries***, "The Judgment," ch. 9-C.

History of TRCP 131: Adopted eff. Sept. 1, 1941, by order of Oct. 29, 1940 (3 Tex.B.J. 544 [1940]). Source: TRCS art. 2056 (repealed).

Furr's Supermkts. v. Bethune, 53 S.W.3d 375, 376 (Tex.2001). "Taxing costs against a successful party in the trial court ... generally contravenes Rule 131. Yet the trial court's ruling on costs under Rule 141 is permitted within its sound discretion, although that discretion is not unlimited. *At 378:* Rule 131's underlying purpose is to ensure that the prevailing party is freed of the burden of court costs and that the losing party pays those costs." *See also* ***Martinez v. Pierce***, 759 S.W.2d 114, 114 (Tex.1988).

Camarena v. TEC, 754 S.W.2d 149, 152 (Tex.1988). "[T]he court of appeals ordered that the costs of appeal be taxed equally between TEC and the farm workers.... We reverse the judgment of the court of appeals and order that all costs be assessed against the State. [TRCP] 131 provides that the successful party to a suit shall recover all costs incurred."

TRCP 132. REPEALED

Repealed eff. Apr. 1, 1984, by order of Dec. 5, 1983 (661-62 S.W.2d [Tex.Cases] xlii): The rule was obsolete.

TRCP 133. COSTS OF MOTION

The court may give or refuse costs on motions at its discretion, except where otherwise provided by law or these rules.

History of TRCP 133: Adopted eff. Sept. 1, 1941, by order of Oct. 29, 1940 (3 Tex.B.J. 544 [1940]). Source: TRCS art. 2058 (repealed).

TRCP 134 - 135. REPEALED

Repealed eff. Apr. 1, 1984, by order of Dec. 5, 1983 (661-62 S.W.2d [Tex.Cases] xlii-xliii): The rules were obsolete.

TRCP 136. DEMAND REDUCED BY PAYMENTS

Where the plaintiff's demand is reduced by payment to an amount which would not have been within the jurisdiction of the court, the defendant shall recover his costs.

History of TRCP 136: Adopted eff. Sept. 1, 1941, by order of Oct. 29, 1940 (3 Tex.B.J. 545 [1940]). Source: TRCS art. 2061 (repealed).

TRCP 137. IN ASSAULT & BATTERY, ETC.

In civil actions for assault and battery, slander and defamation of character, if the verdict or judgment shall be for the plaintiff, but for less than twenty dollars, the plaintiff shall not recover his costs, but each party shall be taxed with the costs incurred by him in such suit.

History of TRCP 137: Adopted eff. Sept. 1, 1941, by order of Oct. 29, 1940 (3 Tex.B.J. 545 [1940]). Source: TRCS art. 2062 (repealed).

Maass v. Sefcik, 138 S.W.2d 897, 900 (Tex.App.—Austin 1940, no writ). "We hold that the statements made by appellee are slanderous per se [and] costs ... should have been assessed under [TRCP 137]."

TRCP 138. COST OF NEW TRIALS

The costs of new trials may either abide the result of the suit or may be taxed against the party to whom the new trial is granted, as the court may adjudge when he grants such new trial.

History of TRCP 138: Adopted eff. Sept. 1, 1941, by order of Oct. 29, 1940 (3 Tex.B.J. 545 [1940]). Source: TRCS art. 2063 (repealed).

TRCP 139. ON APPEAL & CERTIORARI

When a case is appealed, if the judgment of the higher court be against the appellant, but for less amount than the original judgment, such party shall recover the costs of the higher court but shall be adjudged to pay the costs of the court below; if the judgment be against him for the same or a greater amount than in the court below, the adverse party shall recover the costs of both courts. If the judgment of the court above be in favor of the party appealing and for more than the original judgment, such party shall recover the costs of both courts; if the judgment be in his favor, but for the same or a less amount than in the court below, he shall recover the costs of the court below, and pay the costs of the court above.

History of TRCP 139: Adopted eff. Sept. 1, 1941, by order of Oct. 29, 1940 (3 Tex.B.J. 545 [1940]). Source: TRCS art. 2065 (repealed).

Keene Corp. v. Gardner, 837 S.W.2d 224, 232 (Tex. App.—Dallas 1992, writ denied). "Because the appellate relief given [D] is *de minimis* compared to [Ps'] overall award affirmed on appeal, we assess all costs of this appeal against [D]."

TRCP 140. NO FEE FOR COPY

No fee for a copy of a paper not required by law or these rules to be copied shall be taxed in the bill of costs.

History of TRCP 140: Adopted eff. Sept. 1, 1941, by order of Oct. 29, 1940 (3 Tex.B.J. 545 [1940]). Source: TRCS art. 3906 (repealed).

Crescendo Invs. v. Brice, 61 S.W.3d 465, 481 (Tex. App.—San Antonio 2001, pet. denied). "Awarding costs for certified copies of depositions which may be admitted at trial does not violate Rule 140."

TRCP 141. COURT MAY OTHERWISE ADJUDGE COSTS

The court may, for good cause, to be stated on the record, adjudge the costs otherwise than as provided by law or these rules.

History of TRCP 141: Adopted eff. Sept. 1, 1941, by order of Oct. 29, 1940 (3 Tex.B.J. 545 [1940]). Source: TRCS art. 2066 (repealed).

Roberts v. Williamson, 111 S.W.3d 113, 124 (Tex. 2003). The trial court "observed that because an ad litem is there for the benefit of all parties, it is 'fair' to split costs between the losing and prevailing parties. ... Certainly, fairness can be good cause, but the record must substantiate the connection. [¶] [T]he trial court's finding of good cause is premised on the perception that the prevailing party incidentally benefitted from the guardian ad litem's services. [TRCP] 141 still requires that the trial court state its reasons 'on the record' and with more specificity than the court's general notion of fairness here. Grounds of perceived fairness, without more, are insufficient to constitute good cause."

Furr's Supermkts. v. Bethune, 53 S.W.3d 375, 376-77 (Tex.2001). "Rule 141 has 2 requirements—that there be good cause and that it be stated on the record. 'Good cause' is an elusive concept that varies from case to case. Typically though, 'good cause' has meant that the prevailing party unnecessarily prolonged the proceedings, unreasonably increased costs, or otherwise did something that should be penalized." *See also* ***Rogers v. Walmart Stores, Inc.***, 686 S.W.2d 599, 601 (Tex. 1985).

TRCP 142. SECURITY FOR COSTS

The clerk shall require from the plaintiff fees for services rendered before issuing any process unless filing is requested pursuant to Rule 145 of these rules.

History of TRCP 142: Amended eff. Jan. 1, 1988, by order of July 15, 1987 (733-34 S.W.2d [Tex.Cases] xlviii). Amended eff. Sept. 1, 1941, by order of Mar. 31, 1941 (4 Tex.B.J. 509 [1941]): Added second sentence (deleted in 1988). Adopted eff. Sept. 1, 1941, by order of Oct. 29, 1940 (3 Tex.B.J. 545 [1940]). Source: TRCS art. 2067 (repealed).

TRCP 143. RULE FOR COSTS

A party seeking affirmative relief may be ruled to give security for costs at any time before final judgment, upon motion of any party, or any officer of the court interested in the costs accruing in such suit, or by the court upon its own motion. If such rule be entered against any party and he failed to comply therewith on or before twenty (20) days after notice that such rule has been entered, the claim for affirmative relief of such party shall be dismissed.

History of TRCP 143: Amended eff. Jan. 1, 1971, by order of July 21, 1970 (455-56 S.W.2d [Tex.Cases] xxx): Language was changed to provide that any party seeking affirmative relief may be ruled for costs upon motion of any party or by the court on its own motion and the words "knowledge or" which appeared before "notice" in last sentence were deleted. Adopted eff. Sept. 1, 1941, by order of Oct. 29, 1940 (3 Tex.B.J. 545 [1940]). Source: TRCS art. 2068 (repealed). Change: Substituted 20-day period for reference to next term of court.

Clanton v. Clark, 639 S.W.2d 929, 931 (Tex.1982). Under TRCP 143, the trial court may order a party to give security to cover accrued costs of the trial. If the party does not file the security, or files it late, the trial court may dismiss the suit.

TransAmerican Nat. Gas Corp. v. Mancias, 877 S.W.2d 840, 844 (Tex.App.—Corpus Christi 1994, orig. proceeding). TRCP 143 "generally allows the trial court to require a party to post security for costs that have already accrued, but not to fix a specific amount for anticipated costs which a party is required to pay or post security for prematurely." *See also* ***Hager v. Apollo Paper Corp.***, 856 S.W.2d 512, 515 (Tex.App.—Houston [1st Dist.] 1993, no writ).

TRCP 143a. COSTS ON APPEAL TO COUNTY COURT

If the appellant fails to pay the costs on appeal from a judgment of a justice of the peace or small claims court within twenty (20) days after being notified to do so by the county clerk, the appeal shall be deemed not perfected and the county clerk shall return all papers in said cause to the justice of the peace having original jurisdiction and the justice of the peace shall proceed as though no appeal had been attempted.

History of TRCP 143a: Adopted eff. Jan. 1, 1976, by order of July 22, 1975 (525-26 S.W.2d [Tex.Cases] xlvii). Rule requires the appellant to pay costs on appeal. Source: New rule.

Farmer v. McGee Servs., 704 S.W.2d 927, 929 (Tex. App.—Tyler 1986, no writ). "Since no notice [of costs] had been given, the trial court erred in applying [TRCP] 143a to dismiss [D's] appeal."

TRCP 144. JUDGMENT ON COST BOND

All bonds given as security for costs shall authorize judgment against all the obligors in such bond for the said costs, to be entered in the final judgment of the cause.

History of TRCP 144: Adopted eff. Sept. 1, 1941, by order of Oct. 29, 1940 (3 Tex.B.J. 545 [1940]): Source: TRCS art. 2069 (repealed).

Mosher v. Tunnell, 400 S.W.2d 402, 404 (Tex. App.—Houston [1st Dist.] 1966, writ ref'd n.r.e.). TRCP 144 "provides the bond shall authorize judgment against the obligors for said costs. This means such costs as shall be adjudged against the principal whatever be the amount."

TRCP 145. AFFIDAVIT OF INABILITY

In lieu of filing security for costs of an original action, a party who is unable to afford said costs shall file an affidavit as herein described. A "party who is unable to afford costs" is defined as a person who is presently receiving a governmental entitlement based on indigency or any other person who has no ability to pay costs. Said affidavit, and the party's action, shall be processed by the clerk in the manner prescribed by this rule.

1. **Procedure.** Upon the filing of the affidavit, the clerk shall docket the action, issue citation and provide such other customary services as are provided any party. After service of citation, the defendant may contest the affidavit by filing a written contest giving notice to all parties, provided that temporary hearings will not be continued pending the filing of the contest. If the court shall find at the first regular hearing in the course of the action that the party (other than a party receiving a governmental entitlement) is able to afford costs, the party shall pay the costs of the action. Reasons for such a finding shall be contained in an order. Except with leave of court, no further steps in the action will be taken by a party who is found able to afford costs until payment is made. If the party's action results in monetary award, and the court finds sufficient monetary

award to reimburse costs, the party shall pay the costs of the action. If the court finds that another party to the suit can pay the costs of the action, the other party shall pay the costs of the action.

2. **Affidavit.** The affidavit shall contain complete information as to the party's identity, nature and amount of governmental entitlement income, nature and amount of employment income, other income, (interest, dividends, etc.), spouse's income if available to the party, property owned (other than homestead), cash or checking account, dependents, debts, and monthly expenses. The affidavit shall contain the following statements: "I am unable to pay the court costs. I verify that the statements made in this affidavit are true and correct." The affidavit shall be sworn before a Notary Public.

3. **Attorney's Certification.** If the party is represented by an attorney who is providing free legal services, without contingency, because of the party's indigency, said attorney may file an affidavit to that effect to assist the court in understanding the financial condition of the party.

See CPRC chs. 13, 14; ***Commentaries***, "Suit by Indigent," ch. 2-I; FORMS 2I.

History of TRCP 145: Amended eff. Jan. 1, 1988, by order of July 15, 1987 (733-34 S.W.2d [Tex.Cases] xlviii): The purpose of the rule is to allow indigents to file suit and have citation issued based solely on an affidavit of indigency filed with the suit. Amended eff. Apr. 1, 1984, by order of Dec. 5, 1983 (661-62 S.W.2d [Tex.Cases] xliii): The requirement that the contest be tried at the term of court at which the affidavit is filed is deleted. Adopted eff. Sept. 1, 1941, by order of Oct. 29, 1940 (3 Tex.B.J. 545 [1940]). Source: TRCS art. 2070 (repealed).

Griffin Indus. v. 13th Ct. of Appeals, 934 S.W.2d 349, 354 (Tex.1996). When a contingency fee agreement "provides that the attorney is to pay or advance costs, and the [party] makes no further showing [at a hearing to determine indigency status], the agreement would be some evidence that the [party] has a source of funds from which to pay costs. But, when the facts establish that the attorney will not or cannot pay those costs, ... we cannot erect a legal fiction that an indigent has the ability to pay [costs]."

Equitable Gen. Ins. Co. v. Yates, 684 S.W.2d 669, 671 (Tex.1984). "An uncontested affidavit of inability to pay is conclusive as a matter of law."

Varkonyi v. Troche, 802 S.W.2d 63, 65 (Tex.App.—El Paso 1990, orig. proceeding). "The trial court's order of denial [of indigent status] failed to comply with [TRCP] 145 which requires that there should be contained in the denial order '*Reasons for such a finding....*'"

TRCP 146. DEPOSIT FOR COSTS

In lieu of a bond for costs, the party required to give the same may deposit with the clerk of court or the justice of the peace such sum as the court or justice from time to time may designate as sufficient to pay the accrued costs.

History of TRCP 146: Adopted eff. Sept. 1, 1941, by order of Oct. 29, 1940 (3 Tex.B.J. 546 [1940]). Source: TRCS art. 2071 (repealed).

Mosher v. Tunnell, 400 S.W.2d 402, 404-05 (Tex. App.—Houston [1st Dist.]1966, writ ref'd n.r.e.). "The deposit of court costs, as distinguished from a bond as security for costs, is provided for by [TRCP] 146 and clearly contemplates a deposit only for accrued costs."

TRCP 147. APPLIES TO ANY PARTY

The foregoing rules as to security and rule for costs shall apply to any party who seeks a judgment against any other party.

History of TRCP 147: Amended eff. Apr. 1, 1984, by order of Dec. 5, 1983 (661-62 S.W.2d [Tex.Cases] xliii): The rules for security and rule for costs are made applicable to any party. Adopted eff. Sept. 1, 1941, by order of Oct. 29, 1940 (3 Tex.B.J. 546 [1940]). Source: TRCS art. 2073 (repealed).

Ex parte Shaffer, 649 S.W.2d 300, 302 (Tex.1983). "[O]ne who involuntarily comes into court and does not seek any affirmative relief cannot be required to post a cost bond."

TRCP 148. SECURED BY OTHER BOND

No further security shall be required if the costs are secured by the provisions of an attachment or other bond filed by the party required to give security for costs.

History of TRCP 148: Adopted eff. Sept. 1, 1941, by order of Oct. 29, 1940 (3 Tex.B.J. 546 [1940]). Source: TRCS art. 2074 (repealed).

Buck v. Johnson, 495 S.W.2d 291, 298 (Tex.App.—Waco 1973, writ ref'd n.r.e.). "*[T]he option lies with the party ruled for costs, and not with the court,* as to whether a cost bond shall be furnished or a deposit in lieu of bond."

TRCP 149. EXECUTION FOR COSTS

When costs have been adjudged against a party and are not paid, the clerk or justice of the court in which the suit was determined may issue execution, accompanied by an itemized bill of costs, against such party to be levied and collected as in other cases; and said officer, on demand of any party to whom any such costs are due, shall issue execution for costs at once. This rule shall not apply to executors, administrators or guardians in cases where costs are adjudged against the estate of a deceased person or of a ward. No execution shall issue in any case for costs until after judgment rendered therefor by the court.

History of TRCP 149: Adopted eff. Sept. 1, 1941, by order of Oct. 29, 1940 (3 Tex.B.J. 546 [1940]). Source: TRCS art. 2077 (repealed).

SECTION 7. ABATEMENT & DISCONTINUANCE OF SUIT

TRCP 150. DEATH OF PARTY

Where the cause of action is one which survives, no suit shall abate because of the death of any party thereto before the verdict or decision of the court is rendered, but such suit may proceed to judgment as hereinafter provided.

See ***Commentaries***, "Plea to the Jurisdiction—Challenging the Court," ch. 3-F; "Motion to Abate—Challenging the Suit," ch. 3-H.

History of TRCP 150: Adopted eff. Sept. 1, 1941, by order of Oct. 29, 1940 (3 Tex.B.J. 546 [1940]). Source: TRCS art. 2078 (repealed).

Palomino v. Palomino, 960 S.W.2d 899, 900-01 (Tex.App.—El Paso 1997, pet. denied). "The general rule in Texas is that a cause of action for divorce ... becomes moot and abates upon the death of either spouse. ... However, when a trial court has rendered judgment on the merits in a divorce case, the cause does not abate when a party dies, and the cause cannot be dismissed."

TRCP 151. DEATH OF PLAINTIFF

If the plaintiff dies, the heirs, or the administrator or executor of such decedent may appear and upon suggestion of such death being entered of record in open court, may be made plaintiff, and the suit shall proceed in his or their name. If no such appearance and suggestion be made within a reasonable time after the death of the plaintiff, the clerk upon the application of defendant, his agent or attorney, shall issue a scire facias for the heirs or the administrator or executor of such decedent, requiring him to appear and prosecute such suit. After service of such scire facias, should such heir or administrator or executor fail to enter appearance within the time provided, the defendant may have the suit dismissed.

See ***Commentaries***, "Motion to Abate—Challenging the Suit," ch. 3-H.

History of TRCP 151: Amended eff. Apr. 1, 1984, by order of Dec. 5, 1983 (661-62 S.W.2d [Tex.Cases] xliii). Adopted eff. Sept. 1, 1941, by order of Oct. 29, 1940 (3 Tex.B.J. 546 [1940]). Source: TRCS art. 2078, 2079 (repealed).

Gracey v. West, 422 S.W.2d 913, 918 (Tex.1968). TRCP 151 "requires [D] to have a scire facias issued bringing in a deceased [P's] representative and his failure to appear before [D] can have the cause discontinued."

TRCP 152. DEATH OF DEFENDANT

Where the defendant shall die, upon the suggestion of death being entered of record in open court, or upon petition of the plaintiff, the clerk shall issue a scire facias for the administrator or executor or heir requiring him to appear and defend the suit and upon the return of such service, the suit shall proceed against such administrator or executor or heir.

See ***Commentaries***, "Motion to Abate—Challenging the Suit," ch. 3-H.

History of TRCP 152: Adopted eff. Sept. 1, 1941, by order of Oct. 29, 1940 (3 Tex.B.J. 547 [1940]). Source: TRCS art. 2080 (repealed).

Estate of Pollack v. McMurrey, 858 S.W.2d 388, 390 n.2 (Tex.1993). "*Scire facias* ... provides for substitution of any person or persons succeeding to the rights of the original party, whether executor, administrator, heir, or person holding the same practical relation."

Henson v. Estate of Crow, 734 S.W.2d 648, 649 (Tex.1987). After D died, P amended its petition naming D's estate as defendant. Even though an answer was filed on behalf of estate, court rendered take-nothing judgment because the estate was not a legal entity; the suit should have proceeded against personal representative of the estate.

TRCP 153. WHEN EXECUTOR, ETC., DIES

When an executor or administrator shall be a party to any suit, whether as plaintiff or as defendant, and shall die or cease to be such executor or administrator, the suit may be continued by or against the person succeeding him in the administration, or by or against the heirs, upon like proceedings being had as provided in the two preceding rules, or the suit may be dismissed, as provided in Rule 151.

History of TRCP 153: Amended eff. Apr. 1, 1984, by order of Dec. 5, 1983 (661-62 S.W.2d [Tex.Cases] xliii). Adopted eff. Sept. 1, 1941, by order of Oct. 29, 1940 (3 Tex.B.J. 547 [1940]). Source: TRCS art. 2081 (repealed).

TRCP 153

TRCP 154. REQUISITES OF SCIRE FACIAS

The scire facias and returns thereon, provided for in this section, shall conform to the requisites of citations and the returns thereon, under the provisions of these rules.

History of TRCP 154: Adopted eff. Sept. 1, 1941, by order of Oct. 29, 1940 (3 Tex.B.J. 547 [1940]). Source: TRCS art. 2091 (repealed).

Mackintosh v. State, 845 S.W.2d 361, 363 (Tex. App.—Houston [1st Dist.] 1992, no writ). "[T]here is a provision for amending the scire facias documents if necessary and the court is apprised of the necessity."

TRCP 155. SURVIVING PARTIES

Where there are two or more plaintiffs or defendants, and one or more of them die, upon suggestion of such death being entered upon the record, the suit shall at the instance of either party proceed in the name of the surviving plaintiffs or against the surviving defendants, as the case may be.

History of TRCP 155: Adopted eff. Sept. 1, 1941, by order of Oct. 29, 1940 (3 Tex.B.J. 547 [1940]). Source: TRCS art. 2082 (repealed).

First Nat'l Bank v. Hawn, 392 S.W.2d 377, 379 (Tex. App.—Dallas 1965, writ ref'd n.r.e.). "Having elected to proceed under [TRCP] 155 against the surviving [D], approving a judgment against that [D] ... and that judgment having become final [P] had no right to ... suggest [the other D's] death and endeavor to reinstate the suit as to his legal representative."

TRCP 156. DEATH AFTER VERDICT OR CLOSE OF EVIDENCE

When a party in a jury case dies between verdict and judgment, or a party in a non-jury case dies after the evidence is closed and before judgment is pronounced, judgment shall be rendered and entered as if all parties were living.

History of TRCP 156: Amended eff. Jan. 1, 1978, by order of July 11, 1977 (553-54 S.W.2d [Tex.Cases] xlv): The rule applies to non-jury as well as jury cases. Adopted eff. Sept. 1, 1941, by order of Oct. 29, 1940 (3 Tex.B.J. 547 [1940]). Source: TRCS art. 2083 (repealed).

Nacogdoches Mem'l Hosp. v. Justice, 694 S.W.2d 204, 206 (Tex.App.—Tyler 1985, writ ref'd n.r.e.). "The obvious purpose of [TRCP] 156 is merely to avoid a mistrial in a jury case upon the death of [a] party occurring *after* a jury has resolved all material disputed issues of fact."

TRCP 157. REPEALED

Repealed eff. Jan. 1, 1988, by order of July 15, 1987 (733-34 S.W.2d [Tex.Cases] xlix).

TRCP 158. SUIT FOR THE USE OF ANOTHER

When a plaintiff suing for the use of another shall die before verdict, the person for whose use such suit was brought, upon such death being suggested on the record in open court, may prosecute the suit in his own name, and shall be as responsible for costs as if he brought the suit.

History of TRCP 158: Adopted eff. Sept. 1, 1941, by order of Oct. 29, 1940 (3 Tex.B.J. 547 [1940]). Source: TRCS art. 2085 (repealed).

TRCP 159. SUIT FOR INJURIES RESULTING IN DEATH

In cases arising under the provisions of the title relating to injuries resulting in death, the suit shall not abate by the death of either party pending the suit, but in such case, if the plaintiff dies, where there is only one plaintiff, some one or more of the parties entitled to the money recovered may be substituted and the suit prosecuted to judgment in the name of such party or parties, for the benefit of the person entitled; if the defendant dies, his executor, administrator or heir may be made a party, and the suit prosecuted to judgment.

History of TRCP 159: Adopted eff. Sept. 1, 1941, by order of Oct. 29, 1940 (3 Tex.B.J. 547 [1940]). Source: TRCS art. 2086 (repealed).

TRCP 160. DISSOLUTION OF CORPORATION

The dissolution of a corporation shall not operate to abate any pending suit in which such corporation is a defendant, but such suit shall continue against such corporation and judgment shall be rendered as though the same were not dissolved.

See Bus. Corp. Act art. 7.12; TRCP 29.

History of TRCP 160: Adopted eff. Sept. 1, 1941, by order of Oct. 29, 1940 (3 Tex.B.J. 547 [1940]). Source: TRCS art. 1390 (repealed eff. Aug. 28, 1961, now Business Corp. Act art. 7.12).

TRCP 161. WHERE SOME DEFENDANTS NOT SERVED

When some of the several defendants in a suit are served with process in due time and others are not so served, the plaintiff may either dismiss as to those not so served and proceed against those who are, or he may take new process against those not served, or may obtain severance of the case as between those served and those not served, but no dismissal shall be allowed as to a principal obligor without also dismissing the parties secondarily liable except in cases provided by statute. No defendant against whom any suit may be so dismissed shall be thereby exonerated from any liability, but may at any time be proceeded against as if no such suit had been brought and no such dismissal ordered.

See TRCP 240.

History of TRCP 161: Amended eff. Jan. 1, 1988, by order of July 15, 1987 (733-34 S.W.2d [Tex.Cases] xlix). Amended eff. Oct. 1, 1984, by order of Apr. 24, 1984 (667-68 S.W.2d [Tex.Cases] xl). Amended eff. Apr. 1, 1984, by order of Dec. 5, 1983 (661-62 S.W.2d [Tex.Cases] xliv): Adopted eff. Sept. 1, 1941, by order of Oct. 29, 1940 (3 Tex.B.J. 547 [1940]). Source: TRCS art. 2087 (repealed).

Osborne v. St. Luke's Episcopal Hosp., 915 S.W.2d 906, 908 (Tex.App.—Houston [1st Dist.] 1996, writ denied). "Although the November 19 summary judgment did not explicitly dispose of the 8 nonappearing defendants that were not properly sued or served, such a judgment is normally considered final for purposes of appeal and the case stands as if there had been a discontinuance as to the parties not served."

Young v. Hunderup, 763 S.W.2d 611, 612-13 (Tex. App.—Austin 1989, no writ). "Where the judgment disposes of all named parties except those which have not been served and have not appeared ... the judgment is considered final for purposes of appeal and the case stands as if there had been a discontinuance as to those parties not served." *Contra* ***Reed v. Gum Keepsake Diamond Ctr.***, 657 S.W.2d 524, 525 (Tex.App.—Corpus Christi 1983, no writ) (judgment was not final because co-defendant was not served, did not waive the service, did not make an appearance, and was not dismissed).

TRCP 162. DISMISSAL OR NON-SUIT

At any time before the plaintiff has introduced all of his evidence other than rebuttal evidence, the plaintiff may dismiss a case, or take a non-suit, which shall be entered in the minutes. Notice of the dismissal or non-suit shall be served in accordance with Rule 21a on any party who has answered or has been served with process without necessity of court order.

Any dismissal pursuant to this rule shall not prejudice the right of an adverse party to be heard on a pending claim for affirmative relief or excuse the payment of all costs taxed by the clerk. A dismissal under this rule shall have no effect on any motion for sanctions, attorney's fees or other costs, pending at the time of dismissal, as determined by the court. Any dismissal pursuant to this rule which terminates the case shall authorize the clerk to tax court costs against dismissing party unless otherwise ordered by the court.

See TRCP 96; ***Commentaries***, "Voluntary Dismissal—Nonsuit," ch. 7-E; FORMS 7E.

History of TRCP 162: Amended eff. Jan. 1, 1988, by order of July 15, 1987 (733-34 S.W.2d [Tex.Cases] xlix): The purpose of this rule is to fix a definite time after which a party may not voluntarily dismiss or non-suit the cause of action. In addition, these amendments will not disturb any pending motions for sanctions or attorney's fees that were filed before the motion for non-suit or dismissal. Amended eff. Apr. 1, 1984, by order of Dec. 5, 1983 (661-62 S.W.2d [Tex.Cases] xliv): The rule is rewritten. Adopted eff. Sept. 1, 1941, by order of Oct. 29, 1940 (3 Tex.B.J. 548 [1940]). Source: TRCS art. 2089 (repealed).

In re Bennett, 960 S.W.2d 35, 38 (Tex.1997). "[Ps] have the right under [TRCP] 162 to take a nonsuit at any time until they have introduced all evidence other than rebuttal evidence. Such a nonsuit may have the effect of vitiating earlier interlocutory orders and of precluding further action by the trial court.... [¶] Appellate timetables do not run from the date a nonsuit is filed, but rather from the date the trial court signs an order of dismissal." *See also* ***Hyundai Motor Co. v. Alvarado***, 892 S.W.2d 853, 854-55 (Tex.1995).

Farmer v. Ben E. Keith Co., 907 S.W.2d 495, 496 (Tex.1995). "When a judgment is interlocutory because unadjudicated parties or claims remain before the court, and when one moves to have such unadjudicated claims or parties removed by severance, dismissal, or nonsuit, the appellate timetable runs from the signing of a judgment or order disposing of those claims or parties. The appellate timetable *does not* commence to run other than by signed, written order, even when the signing of such an order is purely ministerial."

TRCP 163. DISMISSAL AS TO PARTIES SERVED, ETC.

When it will not prejudice another party, the plaintiff may dismiss his suit as to one or more of several parties who were served with process, or who have answered, but no such dismissal shall in any case, be allowed as to a principal obligor, except in the cases provided for by statute.

See ***Commentaries***, "Voluntary Dismissal—Nonsuit," ch. 7-E.

History of TRCP 163: Amended eff. Jan. 1, 1988, by order of July 15, 1987 (733-34 S.W.2d [Tex.Cases] l). Amended eff. Apr. 1, 1984, by order of Dec. 5, 1983 (661-62 S.W.2d [Tex.Cases] xliv). Adopted eff. Sept. 1, 1941, by order of Oct. 29, 1940 (3 Tex.B.J. 548 [1940]). Source: TRCS art. 2090 (repealed eff. Sept. 1, 1985).

Texas Cab Co. v. Giles, 783 S.W.2d 695, 697 (Tex. App.—El Paso 1989, no writ). "Unless the settlement with the deleted defendant was properly presented to the trial court, there generally could have been no dismissal to that defendant under [TRCP] 162 or 163, as the dismissal would have prejudiced the codefendant...."

TRCP 164. REPEALED

Repealed eff. Jan. 1, 1988, by order of July 15, 1987 (733-34 S.W.2d [Tex.Cases] l).

TRCP 165. ABANDONMENT

A party who abandons any part of his claim or defense, as contained in the pleadings, may have that fact entered of record, so as to show that the matters therein were not tried.

See *Commentaries*, "Motion for Summary Judgment," ch. 7-B.

History of TRCP 165: Adopted eff. Sept. 1, 1941, by order of Oct. 29, 1940 (3 Tex.B.J. 548 [1940]). Source: Tex. Rules for Dist. & Cty. Cts. 33.

In re Shaw, 966 S.W.2d 174, 177 (Tex.App.—El Paso 1998, no pet.). "Whether a pleading has been abandoned is a question of law which we review de novo. Formal amendment of the pleadings is not required in order to show abandonment. Indeed, a stipulation may form the basis for abandonment."

In re R.G., 865 S.W.2d 504, 508 (Tex.App.—Corpus Christi 1993, no writ). TRCP 165 "permits the abandonment of claims; however, the rule has been interpreted to require abandonment '*before* but not *after* trial of the cause and entry of the judgment.' This is the same requirement as for the non-suit."

TRCP 165a. DISMISSAL FOR WANT OF PROSECUTION

1. Failure to Appear. A case may be dismissed for want of prosecution on failure of any party seeking affirmative relief to appear for any hearing or trial of which the party had notice. Notice of the court's intention to dismiss and the date and place of the dismissal hearing shall be sent by the clerk to each attorney of record, and to each party not represented by an attorney and whose address is shown on the docket or in the papers on file, by posting same in the United States Postal Service. At the dismissal hearing, the court shall dismiss for want of prosecution unless there is good cause for the case to be maintained on the docket. If the court determines to maintain the case on the docket, it shall render a pretrial order assigning a trial date for the case and setting deadlines for the joining of new parties, all discovery, filing of all pleadings, the making of a response or supplemental responses to discovery and other pretrial matters. The case may be continued thereafter only for valid and compelling reasons specifically determined by court order. Notice of the signing of the order of dismissal shall be given as provided in Rule 306a. Failure to mail notices as required by this rule shall not affect any of the periods mentioned in Rule 306a except as provided in that rule.

2. Non-Compliance With Time Standards. Any case not disposed of within time standards promulgated by the Supreme Court under its Administrative Rules may be placed on a dismissal docket.

3. Reinstatement. A motion to reinstate shall set forth the grounds therefor and be verified by the movant or his attorney. It shall be filed with the clerk within 30 days after the order of dismissal is signed or within the period provided by Rule 306a. A copy of the motion to reinstate shall be served on each attorney of record and each party not represented by an attorney whose address is shown on the docket or in the papers on file. The clerk shall deliver a copy of the motion to the judge, who shall set a hearing on the motion as soon as practicable. The court shall notify all parties or their attorneys of record of the date, time and place of the hearing.

The court shall reinstate the case upon finding after a hearing that the failure of the party or his attorney was not intentional or the result of conscious indifference but was due to an accident or mistake or that the failure has been otherwise reasonably explained.

In the event for any reason a motion for reinstatement is not decided by signed written order within seventy-five days after the judgment is signed, or, within such other time as may be allowed by Rule 306a, the motion shall be deemed overruled by operation of law. If a motion to reinstate is timely filed by any party, the trial court, regardless of whether an appeal has been perfected, has plenary power to reinstate the case until 30 days after all such timely filed motions are overruled, either by a written and signed order or by operation of law, whichever occurs first.

4. Cumulative Remedies. This dismissal and reinstatement procedure shall be cumulative of the rules and laws governing any other procedures available to the parties in such cases. The same reinstatement procedures and timetable are applicable to all dismissals for want of prosecution including cases which are dismissed pursuant to the court's inherent power, whether or not a motion to dismiss has been filed.

See *Commentaries*, "Notice of Intent to Dismiss," ch. 7-F, §3; "Motion to Reinstate after DWOP," ch. 10-F; FORM 7F:01.

History of TRCP 165a: Amended eff. Jan. 1, 1988, by order of July 15, 1987 (733-34 S.W.2d [Tex.Cases] l). Amended eff. Apr. 1, 1984, by order of Dec. 5, 1983 (661-62 S.W.2d [Tex.Cases] xliv): Rewrote to provide a statewide rule for dismissal and reinstatement of cases. Amended eff. Jan. 1, 1976, by order of July

22, 1975 (525-26 S.W.2d [Tex.Cases] xlviii): Deleted the words "or docket call" after the word "trial" in the first sentence. Adopted eff. Feb. 1, 1973, by order of Oct. 3, 1972 (483-84 S.W.2d [Tex.Cases] xxiv). Source: New rule.

Villarreal v. San Antonio Truck & Equip., 994 S.W.2d 628, 630 (Tex.1999). "The trial court's authority to dismiss for want of prosecution stems from two sources: (1) [TRCP] 165a ... and (2) the court's inherent power. The failure to provide adequate notice of the trial court's intent to dismiss for want of prosecution requires reversal."

Smith v. Babcock & Wilcox Constr. Co., 913 S.W.2d 467, 468 (Tex.1995). "A failure to appear is not intentional or due to conscious indifference within the meaning of the rule merely because it is deliberate; it must also be without adequate justification. Proof of such justification—accident, mistake or other reasonable explanation—negates the intent or conscious indifference for which reinstatement can be denied. Also, conscious indifference means more than mere negligence."

Thordson v. City of Houston, 815 S.W.2d 550, 550 (Tex.1991). Under the language in TRCP 165a(4), "it was not within the discretion of the trial court to fail to hold an oral hearing on the motion to reinstate."

McConnell v. May, 800 S.W.2d 194, 194 (Tex. 1990). "A proper motion to reinstate must be verified and filed with the clerk within 30 days of the signing of the order of dismissal."

Texas Sting, Ltd. v. R.B. Foods, 82 S.W.3d 644, 648-49 (Tex.App.—San Antonio 2002, pet. denied). "[T]he hearing on a motion to reinstate is the same hearing with the same burden of proof that [P] would receive before the trial court signs the order of dismissal. Therefore, a post-dismissal hearing ... remedies any violations to the litigant's due process rights occurring before dismissal."

In re Wal-Mart Stores, 20 S.W.3d 734, 740 (Tex. App.—El Paso 2000, orig. proceeding). "Rule 165a(3) requires that a case be reinstated by signed written order.... An oral pronouncement ... reinstating the case, even when accompanied by a docket entry, is ordinarily inadequate to reinstate the case."

Burton v. Hoffman, 959 S.W.2d 351, 353 (Tex. App.—Austin 1998, no pet.). Under TRCP 165a "a trial court may dismiss a case for failure to appear at trial or a hearing, and the clerk is required to send notice of the court's intention to dismiss and the date and the place of the dismissal hearing to the attorney of record."

Texas DPS v. Deck, 954 S.W.2d 108, 111 (Tex. App.—San Antonio 1997, no writ). "[A] court, on its own, can reinstate a case after dismissal."

SECTION 8. PRETRIAL PROCEDURE

TRCP 166. PRETRIAL CONFERENCE

In an appropriate action, to assist in the disposition of the case without undue expense or burden to the parties, the court may in its discretion direct the attorneys for the parties and the parties or their duly authorized agents to appear before it for a conference to consider:

(a) All pending dilatory pleas, motions and exceptions;

(b) The necessity or desirability of amendments to the pleadings;

(c) A discovery schedule;

(d) Requiring written statements of the parties' contentions;

(e) Contested issues of fact and simplification of the issues;

(f) The possibility of obtaining stipulations of fact;

(g) The identification of legal matters to be ruled on or decided by the court;

(h) The exchange of a list of direct fact witnesses, other than rebuttal or impeaching witnesses the necessity of whose testimony cannot reasonably be anticipated before the time of trial, who will be called to testify at trial, stating their address and telephone number, and the subject of the testimony of each such witness;

(i) The exchange of a list of expert witnesses who will be called to testify at trial, stating their address and telephone number, and the subject of the testimony and opinions that will be proffered by each expert witness;

(j) Agreed applicable propositions of law and contested issues of law;

(k) Proposed jury charge questions, instructions, and definitions for a jury case or proposed findings of fact and conclusions of law for a nonjury case;

(*l*) The marking and exchanging of all exhibits that any party may use at trial and stipulation to the authenticity and admissibility of exhibits to be used at trial;

(m) Written trial objections to the opposite party's exhibits, stating the basis for each objection;

(n) The advisability of a preliminary reference of issues to a master or auditor for findings to be used as evidence when the trial is to be by jury;

(o) The settlement of the case, and to aid such consideration, the court may encourage settlement;

(p) Such other matters as may aid in the disposition of the action.

The court shall make an order that recites the action taken at the pretrial conference, the amendments allowed to the pleadings, the time within which same may be filed, and the agreements made by the parties as to any of the matters considered, and which limits the issues for trial to those not disposed of by admissions, agreements of counsel, or rulings of the court; and such order when issued shall control the subsequent course of the action, unless modified at the trial to prevent manifest injustice. The court in its discretion may establish by rule a pretrial calendar on which actions may be placed for consideration as above provided and may either confine the calendar to jury actions or extend it to all actions.

03 Pretrial proceedings in multidistrict litigation may also be governed by Rules 11 and 13 of the Rules of Judicial Administration.

See Gov't Code §21.001(a); TRCP 248; Tex.R.Jud.Admin. 11, 13; ***Commentaries***, "The Pretrial Conference," ch. 5-A "Motion for Pretrial Consolidation," ch. 5-G; FORM 5A:01.

History of TRCP 166: Amended eff. Sept. 1, 2003, by order of Aug. 29, 2003 (114-15 S.W.3d [Tex.Cases] xx): added paragraph on multidistrict litigation. Amended eff. Sept. 1, 1990, by order of Apr. 24, 1990 (785-86 S.W.2d [Tex.Cases] xlix): First sentence amended to add "appropriate" and "to assist in the disposition of the case without undue expense or burden to the parties"; (a) amended to add "pending" and to change "all motions and exceptions relating to a suit pending" to "motions and exceptions"; (c) changed to (b); new (c) and (d) added; former (b) changed to (e) and "Contested issues of fact and" added; former (d) changed to (f) and "admissions" changed to "stipulations" and "and of documents which will avoid unnecessary proof" was deleted; (g)-(m) added; former (f) changed to (n); (o) added; former (g) changed to (p); last par. amended to add "or rulings of the court" and to change "entered" to "issued"; to broaden the scope of the rule and to confirm the ability of the trial courts at pretrial hearings to encourage settlement. Amended eff. Jan. 1, 1961, by order of July 26, 1960 (23 Tex.B.J. 620 [1961]): Requirement that court's order at pretrial conference allowing amendments show "the time within which same may be filed." Adopted eff. Sept. 1, 1941, by order of Oct. 29, 1940 (3 Tex.B.J. 548 [1940]). Source: FRCP 16. The rule gives the court the power to compel the appearance of the parties or their agents, as well as the attorneys; the case may be referred to an auditor.

Koslow's v. Mackie, 796 S.W.2d 700, 703 (Tex. 1990). TRCP 166 "includes the power to order the parties through their attorneys (or through themselves if appearing pro se) to confer to narrow the issues for the written pretrial conference report."

Provident Life & Acc. Ins. Co. v. Hazlitt, 216 S.W.2d 805, 807 (Tex.1949). "The purpose of [TRCP 166] is to simplify and shorten the trial.... [N]o controverted issues of fact could be adjudicated at [the pretrial] conference, but orders could be entered disposing of issues which are founded upon admitted or undisputed facts."

In re Bledsoe, 41 S.W.3d 807, 812 (Tex.App.—Fort Worth 2001, orig. proceeding). "Rule 166 of the [TRCPs] permits trial courts to hold pretrial conferences and to enter orders establishing the agreements of the parties as to any of the matters considered, which control the subsequent course of the case up to trial. The trial court has power, implicit under rule 166, to sanction a party for failing to obey its pretrial orders."

Lindley v. Johnson, 936 S.W.2d 53, 55 (Tex.App.—Tyler 1996, writ denied). "When a trial court's pretrial scheduling order changes the deadlines set forth in a procedural rule, the trial court's order prevails."

Masterson v. Cox, 886 S.W.2d 436, 439 (Tex.App.—Houston [1st Dist.] 1994, no writ). There is "no rule or caselaw that authorizes the trial court to hear evidence of both liability and unliquidated damages in a pretrial conference and to dispose of a case on the merits...."

TRCP 166a. SUMMARY JUDGMENT

(a) For Claimant. A party seeking to recover upon a claim, counterclaim, or cross-claim or to obtain a declaratory judgment may, at any time after the adverse party has appeared or answered, move with or without supporting affidavits for a summary judgment in his favor upon all or any part thereof. A summary judgment, interlocutory in character, may be rendered on the issue of liability alone although there is a genuine issue as to amount of damages.

(b) For Defending Party. A party against whom a claim, counterclaim, or cross-claim is asserted or a declaratory judgment is sought may, at any time, move with or without supporting affidavits for a summary judgment in his favor as to all or any part thereof.

(c) Motion and Proceedings Thereon. The motion for summary judgment shall state the specific grounds therefor. Except on leave of court, with notice to opposing counsel, the motion and any supporting affidavits shall be filed and served at least twenty-one days before the time specified for hearing. Except on leave of court, the adverse party, not later than seven days prior to the day of hearing may file and serve opposing affidavits or other written response. No oral testimony shall be received at the hearing. The judgment sought shall be rendered forthwith if (i) the deposition transcripts, interrogatory answers, and other discovery responses referenced or set forth in the motion or response, and (ii) the pleadings, admissions, affidavits, stipulations of the parties, and authenticated or certified public records, if any, on file at the time of the hearing, or filed thereafter and before judgment with permission of the court, show that, except as to the amount of damages, there is no genuine issue as to any material fact and the moving party is entitled to judgment as a matter of law on the issues expressly set out in the motion or in an answer or any other response. Issues not expressly presented to the trial court by written motion, answer or other response shall not be considered on appeal as grounds for reversal. A summary judgment may be based on uncontroverted testimonial evidence of an interested witness, or of an expert witness as to subject matter concerning which the trier of fact must be guided solely by the opinion testimony of experts, if the evidence is clear, positive and direct, otherwise credible and free from contradictions and inconsistencies, and could have been readily controverted.

(d) Appendices, References and Other Use of Discovery Not Otherwise on File. Discovery products not on file with the clerk may be used as summary judgment evidence if copies of the material, appendices containing the evidence, or a notice containing specific references to the discovery or specific references to other instruments, are filed and served on all parties together with a statement of intent to use the specified discovery as summary judgment proofs: (i) at least twenty-one days before the hearing if such proofs are to be used to support the summary judgment; or (ii) at least seven days before the hearing if such proofs are to be used to oppose the summary judgment.

(e) Case Not Fully Adjudicated on Motion. If summary judgment is not rendered upon the whole case or for all the relief asked and a trial is necessary, the judge may at the hearing examine the pleadings and the evidence on file, interrogate counsel, ascertain what material fact issues exist and make an order specifying the facts that are established as a matter of law, and directing such further proceedings in the action as are just.

(f) Form of Affidavits; Further Testimony. Supporting and opposing affidavits shall be made on personal knowledge, shall set forth such facts as would be admissible in evidence, and shall show affirmatively that the affiant is competent to testify to the matters stated therein. Sworn or certified copies of all papers or parts thereof referred to in an affidavit shall be attached thereto or served therewith. The court may permit affidavits to be supplemented or opposed by depositions or by further affidavits. Defects in the form of affidavits or attachments will not be grounds for reversal unless specifically pointed out by objection by an opposing party with opportunity, but refusal, to amend.

(g) When Affidavits Are Unavailable. Should it appear from the affidavits of a party opposing the motion that he cannot for reasons stated present by affidavit facts essential to justify his opposition, the court may refuse the application for judgment or may order a continuance to permit affidavits to be obtained or depositions to be taken or discovery to be had or may make such other order as is just.

(h) Affidavits Made in Bad Faith. Should it appear to the satisfaction of the court at any time that any of the affidavits presented pursuant to this rule are presented in bad faith or solely for the purpose of delay, the court shall forthwith order the party employing them to pay to the other party the amount of the reasonable expenses which the filing of the affidavits caused him to incur, including reasonable attorney's fees, and any offending party or attorney may be adjudged guilty of contempt.

(i) No-Evidence Motion. After adequate time for discovery, a party without presenting summary judgment evidence may move for summary judgment on the ground that there is no evidence of one or more essential elements of a claim or defense on which an adverse party would have the burden of proof at trial. The motion must state the elements as to which there is no evidence. The court must grant the motion unless the respondent produces summary judgment evidence raising a genuine issue of material fact.

By Texas Supreme Court Order dated Aug. 15, 1997, the amendments to TRCP 166a(e) & (i) take effect September 1, 1997, and apply to all motions for summary judgment filed on or after that date. Unlike other notes and comments in the TRCP, the Notes & Comments to TRCP 166a(i), below, is intended to inform the construction and application of the rule.

Notes & Comments to TRCP 166a(i): This comment is intended to inform the construction and application of the rule. Paragraph (i) authorizes a motion for summary judgment based on the assertion that, after adequate opportunity for discovery, there is no evidence to support one or more specified elements of an adverse party's claim or defense. A discovery period set by pretrial order should be adequate opportunity for discovery unless there is a showing to the contrary, and ordinarily a motion under paragraph (i) would be permitted after the period but not before. The motion must be specific in challenging the evidentiary support for an element of a claim or defense; paragraph (i) does not authorize conclusory motions or general no-evidence challenges to an opponent's case. Paragraph (i) does not apply to ordinary motions for summary judgment under paragraphs (a) or (b), in which the movant must prove it is entitled to judgment by establishing each element of its own claim or defense as a matter of law. To defeat a motion made under paragraph (i), the respondent is not required to marshal its proof; its response need only point out evidence that raises a fact issue on the challenged elements. The existing rules continue to govern the general requirements of summary judgment practice. A motion under paragraph (i) is subject to sanctions provided by existing law (CPRC §§9.001-10.006) and rules (TRCP 13). The denial of a motion under paragraph (i) is no more reviewable by appeal or mandamus than the denial of a motion under paragraph (c).

See ***Commentaries***, "Rules of Pleading," ch. 1-B; "Rules for Filing Documents," ch. 1-C; "Motion for Continuance," ch. 5-D; "Interrogatories," ch. 6-F; "Requests for Admissions," ch. 6-G; "Motion for Summary Judgment," ch. 7-B; FORMS 7B.

History of TRCP 166a: Amended effective Sept. 1, 1997, by order of Aug. 15, 1997 (60 Tex. B. J. 872 (Oct. 1997)): Amended (e) and added (i); see comment below. Amended eff. Sept. 1, 1990, by order of Apr. 24, 1990 (785-86 S.W.2d [Tex.Cases] l): Added (d); The amendment provides a mechanism for using previously non-filed discovery in summary judgment practice; such proofs must all be filed in advance of the hearing in accordance with TRCP 166a; renumbered (d) - (g) to (e) - (h). Amended eff. Jan. 1, 1988, by order of July 15, 1987 (733-34 S.W.2d [Tex.Cases] li): Amended sec. (c). Amended eff. Apr. 1, 1984, by order of Dec. 5, 1983 (661-62 S.W.2d [Tex.Cases] xlv): Amended sec. (c) to include stipulations and authenticated and certified public records as matters in support of a summary judgment. Amended eff. Jan. 1, 1981, by order of June 10, 1980 (599-600 S.W.2d [Tex.Cases] xxxix): Added in the second sentence the words "with notice to opposing counsel," "and any supporting affidavits," and "filed and"; added "file and" in third sentence. Amended eff. Jan. 1, 1978, by order of July 11, 1977 (553-54 S.W.2d [Tex.Cases] xlvi): Changed time requirements in (c); added third, fourth, and fifth sentences of (c), and the last sentence of (e). Amended eff. Jan. 1, 1971, by order of July 21, 1970 (455-56 S.W.2d [Tex.Cases] xxxi): Added first sentence of (c); inserted words "answers to interrogatories" in the fifth sentence of (c). Amended eff. Jan. 1, 1967, by order of July 20, 1966 (401-02 S.W.2d [Tex.Cases] xxxiii): Added third sentence of (c). Amended eff. Mar. 1, 1952, by order of Oct. 1, 1951 (14 Tex.B.J. 533 [1951]): Added last sentence to (a). Adopted eff. Mar. 1, 1950, by order of Oct. 12, 1949 (12 Tex.B.J. 531 [1949]). Source: FRCP 56, with changes: Substituted "adverse party has appeared or answered" for "pleading in answer thereto was served" in par. (a).

Traditional SJ

Huckabee v. Time Warner Entm't Co., 19 S.W.3d 413, 422 (Tex.2000). "Texas law has always emphasized that trial courts must not weigh the evidence at the summary judgment stage. [A] trial court's only duty at the summary judgment stage is to determine if a material question of fact exists."

Park Place Hosp. v. Estate of Milo, 909 S.W.2d 508, 510 (Tex.1995). For defendants "to prevail, they were required to prove that there was no genuine issue as to any material fact and that they were entitled to judgment as a matter of law. In reviewing a summary judgment, we must accept as true evidence favoring the nonmovant, indulging every reasonable inference and resolving all doubts in the nonmovant's favor."

Cathey v. Booth, 900 S.W.2d 339, 341 (Tex.1995). "A [D] who conclusively negates at least one of the essential elements of each of [P's] causes of action or who conclusively establishes all of the elements of an affirmative defense is entitled to summary judgment."

McConnell v. Southside ISD, 858 S.W.2d 337, 341 (Tex.1993). "In determining whether grounds are expressly presented, reliance may not be placed upon briefs or summary judgment evidence."

Rush v. Barrios, 56 S.W.3d 88, 98 (Tex.App.—Houston [14th Dist.] 2001, pet. denied). "A trial court may ... properly grant summary judgment after having previously denied [it] without a motion by or prior notice to the parties, as long as the court retains jurisdiction over the case."

Medlock v. Commission for Lawyer Discipline, 24 S.W.3d 865, 870 (Tex.App.—Texarkana 2000, no pet.). "The trial court may not grant a summary judgment motion by default for lack of an answer or response by the nonmovant when the summary judgment proof is legally insufficient. ... However, if the respondent fails to file a response, the only ground for reversal she may raise on appeal is the legal insufficiency of the movant's summary judgment motion or proof."

No-Evidence SJ

Forbes, Inc. v. Granada Biosciences, ___ S.W.3d ___ (Tex.2003) (No. 01-0788; 12-19-03). "A no-evidence summary judgment is improper if the respondent brings forth more than a scintilla of probative evidence to raise a genuine issue of material fact. Less than a scintilla of evidence exists when the evidence is so weak as to do no more than create a mere surmise or suspicion of a fact." (Internal quotes omitted.)

Restaurant Teams Int'l v. MG Sec. Corp., 95 S.W.3d 336, 339 (Tex.App.—Dallas 2002, no pet.). "To determine whether adequate time for discovery [under TRCP 166a(i)] has passed, we examine such factors as: (1) the nature of the case; (2) the nature of evidence necessary to controvert the no-evidence motion; (3) the length of time the case was active; (4) the amount of time the no-evidence motion was on file; (5) whether the movant had requested stricter deadlines for discovery; (6) the amount of discovery already taken place; and (7) whether the discovery deadlines in place were specific or vague."

Crocker v. Paulyne's Nursing Home, 95 S.W.3d 416, 419 (Tex.App.—Dallas 2002, no pet.). "A no-evidence summary judgment is essentially a pretrial directed verdict to which we apply the same legal sufficiency standard of review. [¶] [A] non-movant may challenge the legal sufficiency of a no-evidence motion for the first time on appeal."

Howell v. Hilton Hotels, 84 S.W.3d 708, 711-12 (Tex.App.—Houston [1st Dist.] 2002, pet. denied). "In a no-evidence motion for summary judgment, the movant must specifically state the elements as to which there is no evidence. The burden then shifts to the non-movant to produce evidence that raises a fact issue on the challenged elements." *See also* ***Harrill v. A.J.'s Wrecker Serv.***, 27 S.W.3d 191, 193 (Tex.App.—Dallas 2000, pet. dism'd).

Michael v. Dyke, 41 S.W.3d 746, 751 (Tex.App.—Corpus Christi 2001, no pet.). "When it is not readily apparent to the trial court that summary judgment is sought under rule 166a(i), the court should presume that it is filed under the traditional summary judgment rule and analyze it according to those well-recognized standards. [The] order granting summary judgment should clarify whether the motion is granted on no-evidence grounds or traditional grounds. When an order fails to so clarify, a motion requesting such clarification should be filed with the trial court."

Grant v. Southwestern Elec. Power Co., 20 S.W.3d 764, 768 (Tex.App.—Texarkana 2000), *rev'd in part on other grounds*, 73 S.W.3d 211 (Tex.2002). "[D's] motion contained both a no-evidence summary judgment motion ... and an ordinary summary judgment motion.... The rules do not prohibit such a hybrid motion, but the better practice is either to file two separate motions..., or to file one document containing both motions but with the arguments and authorities for each clearly delineated and separate from one another."

Brewer & Pritchard, P.C. v. Johnson, 7 S.W.3d 862, 869 (Tex.App.—Houston [1st Dist.] 1999), *aff'd*, 73 S.W.3d 193 (Tex.2002). "[A]lthough it is true that [P] globally stated facts to support its conclusions as it sees them and cited to the record in support of those facts, it made no effort to connect any of the facts to the challenged elements of the causes of action. We believe rule 166a(i) requires the non-movant to make that connection."

SJ Evidence

Morgan v. Anthony, 27 S.W.3d 928, 929 (Tex. 2000). "Generally, a party cannot rely on its own answer to an interrogatory as summary judgment evidence. However, [P] was questioned in one of her depositions about her seven-page interrogatory answer ... and the interrogatory answer was attached to her deposition as an exhibit. ... The interrogatory answer became competent summary judgment evidence when it became a deposition exhibit, [P] affirmed in her deposition that it was correct, and she was subject to cross-examination about the assertions in her interrogatory answer."

Wadewitz v. Montgomery, 951 S.W.2d 464, 466 (Tex.1997). "An expert's testimony will support summary judgment only if it is 'clear, positive and direct, otherwise credible and free from contradictions and inconsistencies, and could have been readily controverted.' Conclusory statements by an expert are insufficient to support or defeat summary judgment." *See also* ***United Blood Servs. v. Longoria***, 938 S.W.2d 29, 30 (Tex.1997).

Trico Tech. Corp. v. Montiel, 949 S.W.2d 308, 310 (Tex.1997). "The mere fact that the affidavit is self-serving does not necessarily make the evidence an improper basis for summary judgment. Summary judgment based on the uncontroverted affidavit of an interested witness is proper if the evidence is clear, positive, direct, otherwise credible, free from contradictions and inconsistencies, and could have been readily controverted. 'Could have been readily controverted' does not mean that the summary judgment evidence could have been easily and conveniently rebutted, but rather indicates that the testimony could have been effectively countered by opposing evidence."

Benchmark Bank v. Crowder, 919 S.W.2d 657, 663 (Tex.1996). "McCool's testimony is not part of the summary judgment record. [His] affidavit was filed 2 days before the summary judgment hearing. Summary judgment evidence may be filed late, but only with leave of court. There is no order in this record granting [Ps] leave to file [the] affidavit late."

McConathy v. McConathy, 869 S.W.2d 341, 341 (Tex.1994). "[D]eposition excerpts [and other discovery] submitted as summary judgment evidence need not be authenticated. *At 342:* All parties have ready access to depositions taken in a cause, and thus deposition excerpts submitted with a motion for summary judgment may be easily verified as to their accuracy."

Casso v. Brand, 776 S.W.2d 551, 558 (Tex.1989). "If the credibility of the affiant ... is likely to be a dispositive factor in the resolution of the case, then summary judgment is inappropriate. On the other hand, if the non-movant must, in all likelihood, come forth with independent evidence to prevail, then summary judgment may well be proper in the absence of such controverting proof."

Goss v. Bobby D. Assocs., 94 S.W.3d 65, 71 (Tex. App.—Tyler 2002, no pet.). "The trial court cannot consider affidavits offered by the non-movant to contradict deemed admissions in cases involving summary judgment."

Watts v. Hermann Hosp., 962 S.W.2d 102, 105 (Tex.App.—Houston [1st Dist.] 1997, no pet.). "Without a proper objection, defects in the authentication of attachments in support of a motion for summary judgment or response are waived."

Final vs. Partial SJ

Jacobs v. Satterwhite, 65 S.W.3d 653, 655 (Tex. 2001). "'[I]f [D] moves for summary judgment on only one of [multiple] claims asserted by [P], but the trial court renders judgment that [P] take nothing on all claims asserted, the judgment is final—erroneous, but final.'"

McNally v. Guevara, 52 S.W.3d 195, 196 (Tex. 2001). "Nothing in the trial court's judgment, other than its award of costs to the defendants, suggests that it intended to deny the defendants' claim for attorney fees. The award of costs, by itself, does not make the judgment final."

Lehmann v. Har-Con Corp., 39 S.W.3d 191, 192-93 (Tex.2001). "We no longer believe that a Mother Hubbard clause in an order or in a judgment issued without a full trial can be taken to indicate finality. We therefore hold that in cases in which only one final and appealable judgment can be rendered, a judgment issued without a conventional trial is final for purposes of appeal if and only if either it actually disposes of all claims and parties then before the court, regardless of its language, or it states with unmistakable clarity that it is a final judgment as to all claims and all parties." *See also* ***Page v. Geller***, 941 S.W.2d 101, 102 (Tex.1997).

Pleadings in SJ Cases

Sosa v. Central Power & Light, 909 S.W.2d 893, 895 (Tex.1995). "Because [Ps] timely filed their second amended original petition, it superseded their first amended original petition containing the statements on which [Ds] based their motion for summary judgment. Contrary to statements in live pleadings, those contained in superseded pleadings are not conclusive and indisputable judicial admissions. Therefore, the basis for [Ds'] motion no longer existed and summary judgment was improper."

Laidlaw Waste Sys. v. City of Wilmer, 904 S.W.2d 656, 660 (Tex.1995). "Generally, pleadings are not competent evidence, even if sworn or verified."

Natividad v. Alexsis, Inc., 875 S.W.2d 695, 699 (Tex.1994). "A review of the pleadings [when a summary judgment is based on the pleadings] is de novo, with the reviewing court taking all allegations, facts, and inferences in the pleadings as true and viewing them in a light most favorable to the pleader. The reviewing court will affirm the summary judgment only if the pleadings are legally insufficient."

In re B.I.V., 870 S.W.2d 12, 13 (Tex.1994). "A summary judgment should not be based on a pleading deficiency that could be cured by amendment."

Motion for Continuance

Carpenter v. Cimarron Hydrocarbons Corp., 98 S.W.3d 682, 688 (Tex.2002). "[A] motion for leave to file a late summary-judgment response should be granted when a litigant establishes good cause for failing to timely respond by showing that (1) the failure to respond was not intentional or the result of conscious indifference, but the result of accident or mistake, and (2) allowing the late response will occasion no undue delay or otherwise injure the party seeking summary judgment."

Tenneco, Inc. v. Enterprise Prods. Co., 925 S.W.2d 640, 647 (Tex.1996). "When a party contends that it has not had an adequate opportunity for discovery before a summary judgment hearing, it must file either an affidavit explaining the need for further discovery or a verified motion for continuance."

Carter v. MacFadyen, 93 S.W.3d 307, 310 (Tex. App.—Houston [14th Dist.] 2002, pet. denied). "A party seeking more time to oppose a summary judgment must file an affidavit describing the evidence sought, explaining its materiality, and showing the due diligence used to obtain the evidence. The affidavit must show why the continuance is necessary; conclusory allegations are not sufficient."

TRCP 166b - 166c. REPEALED

TRCP 166b and 166c were repealed eff. Jan. 1, 1999, by order of Nov. 9, 1998 (977-78 S.W.2d [Tex. Cases] xxxiii). For subject matter of former TRCP 166b, see TRCP 192. For subject matter of former TRCP 166c, see TRCP 191.1.

04

TRCP 167. OFFER OF SETTLEMENT; AWARD OF LITIGATION COSTS

167.1 Generally. Certain litigation costs may be awarded against a party who rejects an offer made substantially in accordance with this rule to settle a claim for monetary damages—including a counterclaim, crossclaim, or third-party claim—except in:

(a) a class action;

(b) a shareholder's derivative action;

(c) an action by or against the State, a unit of state government, or a political subdivision of the State;

(d) an action brought under the Family Code;

(e) an action to collect workers' compensation benefits under title 5, subtitle A of the Labor Code; or

(f) an action filed in a justice of the peace court or small claims court.

167.2 Settlement Offer.

(a) ***Defendant's declaration a prerequisite; deadline.*** A settlement offer under this rule may not be made until a defendant—a party against whom a claim for monetary damages is made—files a declaration invoking this rule. When a defendant files such a declaration, an offer or offers may be made under this rule to settle only those claims by and against that defendant. The declaration must be filed no later than 45 days before the case is set for conventional trial on the merits.

(b) ***Requirements of an offer.*** A settlement offer must:

(1) be in writing;

(2) state that it is made under Rule 167 and Chapter 42 of the Texas Civil Practice and Remedies Code;

(3) identify the party or parties making the offer and the party or parties to whom the offer is made;

(4) state the terms by which all monetary claims—including any attorney fees, interest, and costs that would be recoverable up to the time of the offer—between the offeror or offerors on the one hand and the offeree or offerees on the other may be settled;

(5) state a deadline—no sooner than 14 days after the offer is served—by which the offer must be accepted;

(6) be served on all parties to whom the offer is made.

(c) ***Conditions of offer.*** An offer may be made subject to reasonable conditions, including the execution of appropriate releases, indemnities, and other documents. An offeree may object to a condition by written notice served on the offeror before the deadline stated in the offer. A condition to which no such objection is made is presumed to have been reasonable. Rejection of an offer made subject to a condition determined by the trial court to have been unreasonable cannot be the basis for an award of litigation costs under this rule.

(d) ***Non-monetary and excepted claims not included.*** An offer must not include non-monetary claims and other claims to which this rule does not apply.

(e) ***Time limitations.*** An offer may not be made:

(1) before a defendant's declaration is filed;

(2) within 60 days after the appearance in the case of the offeror or offeree, whichever is later;

(3) within 14 days before the date the case is set for a conventional trial on the merits, except that an offer may be made within that period if it is in response to, and within seven days of, a prior offer.

(f) ***Successive offers.*** A party may make an offer after having made or rejected a prior offer. A rejection of an offer is subject to imposition of litigation costs under this rule only if the offer is more favorable to the offeree than any prior offer.

167.3 Withdrawal, Acceptance, and Rejection of Offer.

(a) ***Withdrawal of offer.*** An offer can be withdrawn before it is accepted. Withdrawal is effective when written notice of the withdrawal is served on the offeree. Once an unaccepted offer has been withdrawn, it cannot be accepted or be the basis for awarding litigation costs under this rule.

(b) ***Acceptance of offer.*** An offer that has not been withdrawn can be accepted only by written notice served on the offeror by the deadline stated in the offer. When an offer is accepted, the offeror or offeree may file the offer and acceptance and may move the court to enforce the settlement.

(c) ***Rejection of offer.*** An offer that is not withdrawn or accepted is rejected. An offer may also be rejected by written notice served on the offeror by the deadline stated in the offer.

(d) ***Objection to offer made before an offeror's joinder or designation of responsible third party.*** An offer made before an offeror joins another party or designates a responsible third party may not be the basis for awarding litigation costs under this rule against an offeree who files an objection to the offer within 15 days after service of the offeror's pleading or designation.

167.4 Awarding Litigation Costs.

(a) ***Generally.*** If a settlement offer made under this rule is rejected, and the judgment to be awarded on the monetary claims covered by the offer is significantly less favorable to the offeree than was the offer, the court must award the offeror litigation costs against the offeree from the time the offer was rejected to the time of judgment.

(b) ***"Significantly less favorable" defined.*** A judgment award on monetary claims is significantly less favorable than an offer to settle those claims if:

(1) the offeree is a claimant and the judgment would be less than 80 percent of the offer; or

(2) the offeree is a defendant and the judgment would be more than 120 percent of the offer.

(c) ***Litigation costs.*** Litigation costs are the expenditures actually made and the obligations actually incurred—directly in relation to the claims covered by a settlement offer under this rule—for the following:

(1) court costs;

(2) reasonable fees for not more than two testifying expert witnesses; and

(3) reasonable attorney fees.

(d) ***Limits on litigation costs.*** The litigation costs that may be awarded under this rule must not exceed the following amount:

(1) the sum of the noneconomic damages, the exemplary or additional damages, and one-half of the economic damages to be awarded to the claimant in the judgment; minus

(2) the amount of any statutory or contractual liens in connection with the occurrences or incidents giving rise to the claim.

(e) ***No double recovery permitted.*** A party who is entitled to recover attorney fees and costs under another law may not recover those same attorney fees and costs as litigation costs under this rule.

(f) ***Limitation on attorney fees and costs recovered by a party against whom litigation costs are awarded.*** A party against whom litigation costs are awarded may not recover attorney fees and costs under another law incurred after the date the party rejected the settlement offer made the basis of the award.

(g) ***Litigation costs to be awarded to defendant as a setoff.*** Litigation costs awarded to a defendant must be made a setoff to the claimant's judgment against the defendant.

167.5 Procedures.

(a) ***Modification of time limits.*** On motion, and for good cause shown, the court may—by written order made before commencement of trial on the merits—modify the time limits for filing a declaration under Rule 167.2(a) or for making an offer.

(b) ***Discovery permitted.*** On motion, and for good cause shown, a party against whom litigation costs are to be awarded may conduct discovery to ascertain the reasonableness of the costs requested. If the court determines the costs to be reasonable, it must order the party requesting discovery to pay all attorney fees and expenses incurred by other parties in responding to such discovery.

(c) ***Hearing required.*** The court must, upon request, conduct a hearing on a request for an award of litigation costs, at which the affected parties may present evidence.

167.6 Evidence Not Admissible. Evidence relating to an offer made under this rule is not admissible except for purposes of enforcing a settlement agreement or obtaining litigation costs. The provisions of this rule may not be made known to the jury by any means.

167.7 Other Settlement Offers Not Affected. This rule does not apply to any offer made in a mediation or arbitration proceeding. A settlement offer not made under this rule, or made in an action to which this rule does not apply, cannot be the basis for awarding litigation costs under this rule. This rule does not limit or affect a party's right to make a settlement offer that does not comply with this rule, or in an action to which this rule does not apply.

See *Commentaries*, "Offer of Settlement," ch. 7-G.

History of TRCP 167: Adopted eff. Jan. 1, 2004, by order of Oct. 9, 2003 (Tex.Sup.Ct. Order, Misc. Docket No. 03-9160). Source: New rule. Former TRCP

167 was repealed eff. Jan. 1, 1999, by order of Nov. 9, 1998 (977-78 S.W.2d [Tex.Cases] xxxiii). For subject matter of former TRCP 167, see TRCP 196.

TRCP 167a - 170. REPEALED

TRCP 167a, 168, and 169 were repealed eff. Jan. 1, 1999, by order of Nov. 9, 1998 (977-78 S.W.2d [Tex.Cases] xxxiii). TRCP 170 was repealed eff. Apr. 1, 1984, by order of Dec. 5, 1983 (661-62 S.W.2d [Tex.Cases] lvi): See TRCP 215. For subject matter of former TRCP 167a, see TRCP 204. For subject matter of former TRCP 168, see TRCP 197. For subject matter of former TRCP 169, see TRCP 198.

TRCP 171. MASTER IN CHANCERY

The court may, in exceptional cases, for good cause appoint a master in chancery, who shall be a citizen of this State, and not an attorney for either party to the action, nor related to either party, who shall perform all of the duties required of him by the court, and shall be under orders of the court, and have such power as the master of chancery has in a court of equity.

The order of reference to the master may specify or limit his powers, and may direct him to report only upon particular issues, or to do or perform particular acts, or to receive and report evidence only and may fix the time and place for beginning and closing the hearings, and for the filing of the master's report. Subject to the limitations and specifications stated in the order, the master has and shall exercise the power to regulate all proceedings in every hearing before him and to do all acts and take all measures necessary or proper for the efficient performance of his duties under the order. He may require the production before him of evidence upon all matters embraced in the reference, including the production of books, papers, vouchers, documents and other writings applicable thereto. He may rule upon the admissibility of evidence, unless otherwise directed by the order of reference and has the authority to put witnesses on oath, and may, himself, examine them, and may call the parties to the action and examine them upon oath. When a party so requests, the master shall make a record of the evidence offered and excluded in the same manner as provided for a court sitting in the trial of a case.

The clerk of the court shall forthwith furnish the master with a copy of the order of reference.

The parties may procure the attendance of witnesses before the master by the issuance and service of process as provided by law and these rules.

The court may confirm, modify, correct, reject, reverse or recommit the report, after it is filed, as the court may deem proper and necessary in the particular circumstances of the case. The court shall award reasonable compensation to such master to be taxed as costs of suit.

See *Commentaries*, "Master in Chancery," ch. 1-J.

History of TRCP 171: Amended eff. Dec. 31, 1941, by order of Sept. 20, 1941 (4 Tex.B.J. 513 [1941]). Adopted eff. Sept. 1, 1941, by order of Oct. 29, 1940 (3 Tex.B.J. 550 [1940]). Source: TRCS art. 2320 (repealed), FRCP 53.

Academy of Model Aeronautics v. Packer, 860 S.W.2d 419, 419 (Tex.1993). "[T]he trial court abused its discretion in entering an order referring all pending and future discovery matters to a master."

Republic Ins. Co. v. Davis, 856 S.W.2d 158, 160 (Tex.1993). "Republic did not have the opportunity to object [to the master's report before the trial court adopted it]. Consequently, without reaching the question of whether an objection is required, we conclude that Republic has not waived error...."

Simpson v. Canales, 806 S.W.2d 802, 811 (Tex. 1991). TRCP 171 "permits appointment of a master only 'in exceptional cases, for good cause'. [T]his requirement cannot be met merely by showing that a case is complicated or time-consuming, or that the court is busy."

AIU Ins. Co. v. Mehaffy, 942 S.W.2d 796, 803 (Tex. App.—Beaumont 1997, orig. proceeding). "The cases construing [TRCP] 171 provide that if a party timely and formally objects to a master's ruling, that party is entitled to a de novo hearing before a judge or jury. We conclude this right is automatic and not subject to a harmless error analysis."

TRCP 172. AUDIT

When an investigation of accounts or examination of vouchers appears necessary for the purpose of justice between the parties to any suit, the court shall appoint an auditor or auditors to state the accounts between the parties and to make report thereof to the court as soon as possible. The auditor shall verify his report by his affidavit stating that he has carefully examined the state of the account between the parties, and that his report contains a true statement thereof, so far as the same has come within his knowledge. Exceptions to such report or of any item thereof must be filed within 30 days of the filing of such report. The court shall award reasonable compensation to such auditor to be taxed as costs of suit.

See TRE 706.

History of TRCP 172: Amended eff. Jan. 1, 1988, by order of July 15, 1987 (733-34 S.W.2d [Tex.Cases] lvi). Adopted eff. Sept. 1, 1941, by order of Oct. 29, 1940 (3 Tex.B.J. 550 [1940]). Source: TRCS art. 2292 (repealed).

AIU Ins. Co. v. Mehaffy, 942 S.W.2d 796, 800-01 (Tex.App.—Beaumont 1997, orig. proceeding). "[T]he order does not state what authority the court relied upon in appointing the auditor. ... Although the word 'auditor' is used, it does not appear [TRCP] 172 was the basis since this was not 'an investigation of accounts or examination of vouchers.'"

Lovelace v. Sabine Consol., 733 S.W.2d 648, 656 (Tex.App.—Houston [14th Dist.] 1987, writ denied). "The audit report before this court contains no ... affidavit as is required by [TRCP] 172. ... Further, 6 days before trial [P] filed an objection to the audit. Therefore, the trial court did not err in admitting evidence that contradicted and supplemented the auditor's report."

TRCP 173. GUARDIAN AD LITEM

When a minor, lunatic, idiot or a non-compos mentis may be a defendant to a suit and has no guardian within this State, or where such person is a party to a suit either as plaintiff, defendant or intervenor and is represented by a next friend or a guardian who appears to the court to have an interest adverse to such minor, lunatic, idiot or non-compos mentis, the court shall appoint a guardian ad litem for such person and shall allow him a reasonable fee for his services to be taxed as a part of the costs.

See *Commentaries*, "Guardians Ad Litem Under TRCP 173," ch. 1-I.

History of TRCP 173: Adopted eff. Sept. 1, 1941, by order of Oct. 29, 1940 (3 Tex.B.J. 550 [1940]). Source: TRCS art. 2159 (repealed).

Garcia v. Martinez, 988 S.W.2d 219, 222 (Tex. 1998). "A guardian ad litem is entitled to a reasonable fee for his services to be taxed as a part of the costs. [¶] Generally, trial courts employ the same factors used to determine the reasonableness of attorney's fees to ascertain an appropriate guardian ad litem fee. These factors include: '(1) the time and labor required, the novelty and difficulty of the questions involved, and the skill required to perform the legal service properly; (2) the likelihood ... that the acceptance of the particular employment will preclude other employment by the lawyer; (3) the fee customarily charged in the locality for similar legal services; (4) the amount involved and the results obtained; (5) the time limitations imposed by the client or by the circumstances; (6) the nature and length of the professional relationship with the client; (7) the experience, reputation, and ability of the lawyer or lawyers performing the services; and (8) whether the fee is fixed or contingent on results obtained or uncertainty of collection before the legal services have been rendered.'"

American Gen. Fire & Cas. Co. v. Vandewater, 907 S.W.2d 491, 493 n.2 (Tex.1995). "A guardian ad litem is not an attorney for the child but an officer appointed by the court to assist in properly protecting the child's interests. A guardian ad litem is the personal representative of the minor appointed to protect the interests of the minor in a lawsuit in which the minor is a party. The guardian ad litem is required to participate in the case to the extent necessary to protect the minor."

Brownsville-Valley Reg'l Med. Ctr. v. Gamez, 894 S.W.2d 753, 755 (Tex.1995). "The trial court can appoint a guardian ad litem pursuant to [TRCP] 173 only when there is a conflict of interest between the minor and next friend. When the conflict of interest no longer exists, the trial court should remove the guardian ad litem." *See also* ***In re Fort Worth Children's Hosp.***, 100 S.W.3d 582, 590-91 (Tex.App.—Fort Worth 2003, orig. proceeding).

TRCP 174. CONSOLIDATION; SEPARATE TRIALS

(a) Consolidation. When actions involving a common question of law or fact are pending before the court, it may order a joint hearing or trial of any or all the matters in issue in the actions; it may order all the actions consolidated; and it may make such orders concerning proceedings therein as may tend to avoid unnecessary costs or delay.

(b) Separate Trials. The court in furtherance of convenience or to avoid prejudice may order a separate trial of any claim, cross-claim, counterclaim, or third-party claim, or of any separate issue or of any number of claims, cross-claims, counterclaims, third-party claims, or issues.

See TRCP 39, 40, 41, 51; *Commentaries*, "Motions for Severance & Separate Trials," ch. 5-H; "Joining an Ongoing Lawsuit," ch. 5-I.

History of TRCP 174: Adopted eff. Sept. 1, 1941, by order of Oct. 29, 1940 (3 Tex.B.J. 551 [1940]). Source: FRCP 42. Supersedes TRCS art. 2160 (repealed).

In re Ethyl Corp., 975 S.W.2d 606, 611-12 (Tex. 1998). "The maximum number of claims that can be aggregated is not an absolute, and the particular circumstances determine the outer limits beyond which trial courts cannot go. [¶] While considerations of judicial economy are a factor, '[c]onsiderations of convenience and economy must yield to a paramount concern for a fair and impartial trial.'"

Liberty Nat'l Fire Ins. Co. v. Akin, 927 S.W.2d 627, 630 (Tex.1996). "A severance may ... be necessary in some bad faith [and contract] cases. A trial court will ... confront instances in which evidence admissible only on the bad faith claim would prejudice the insurer to such an extent that a fair trial on the contract claim would become unlikely. One example would be when the insurer has made a settlement offer on the disputed contract claim."

Owens-Corning Fiberglas Corp. v. Martin, 942 S.W.2d 712, 716 (Tex.App.—Dallas 1997, no writ). TRCP 174 "gives the trial court broad discretion to consolidate cases with common issues of law or fact. [¶] In deciding whether to consolidate, the trial court must balance the judicial economy and convenience that may be gained by the consolidation against the risk of an unfair outcome because of prejudice or jury confusion. [¶] Even if the cases share common questions of law and fact, an abuse of discretion may be found if the consolidation results in prejudice to the complaining party."

TRCP 175. ISSUE OF LAW & DILATORY PLEAS

When a case is called for trial in which there has been no pretrial hearing as provided by Rule 166, the issues of law arising on the pleadings, all pleas in abatement and other dilatory pleas remaining undisposed of shall be determined; and it shall be no cause for postponement of a trial of the issues of law that a party is not prepared to try the issues of fact.

History of TRCP 175: Adopted eff. Sept. 1, 1941, by order of Oct. 29, 1940 (3 Tex.B.J. 551 [1940]). Source: TRCS art. 2166 (repealed).

Garcia v. TEIA, 622 S.W.2d 626, 630 n.3 (Tex. App.—Amarillo 1981, writ ref'd n.r.e.). "The language of [TRCP] 175 imposes on the party relying upon a dilatory plea a duty to demand action by the court thereon at the time the rule requires action by the court, and his failure to do so is a waiver of the plea."

SECTION 9. EVIDENCE & DISCOVERY

Explanatory Statement Accompanying the 1999 Amendments to the Rules of Civil Procedure Governing Discovery

The rules pertaining to discovery have been substantively revised and reorganized to clarify and streamline discovery procedures and to reduce costs and delays associated with discovery practice. The notes and comments appended to the rules, unlike most other notes and comments in the Rules of Civil Procedure, are intended to inform their construction and application by both courts and practitioners.

Discovery in civil cases is founded on the principle that justice is best served when litigants may obtain information not in their possession to prosecute and defend claims. Discovery provides access to that information, but at a price. Recent years' experience has shown that discovery may be misused to deny justice to parties by driving up the costs of litigation until it is unaffordable and stalling resolution of cases. As any litigant on a budget knows, the benefits to be gained by discovery in a particular case must be weighed against its costs. The rules of procedure must provide both adequate access to information and effective means of curbing discovery when appropriate to preserve litigation as a viable, affordable, and expeditious dispute resolution mechanism.

These revisions recognize the importance of discovery as well as the necessity for reasonable limits. The scope of discovery, always broad, is unchanged. All the forms of discovery under the prior rules are retained, and a new one—disclosure—is added. Disclosure is not required unless requested and thus does not burden cases in which it is not sought. When requested, it provides ready access to basic information without objection. At the same time, the necessity of a discovery control plan in each case, whether by rule or by order, is intended to focus courts and parties on both the need for discovery and its costs in each case. The Level 1 plan allows a party seeking recovery of no more than $50,000 to insist that discovery be minimal. The Level 2 plan will provide adequate discovery in most cases, and Level 3 is available for cases needing special attention. No single set of rules can address so diverse and changing a practice as discovery, and thus the rules maintain the ability of parties by agreement and courts by order to tailor discovery to individual cases.

Presentation of objections and assertions of privilege are streamlined under these rules. A party who objects to only part of a discovery request must usually comply with the rest of the request. Assertions of privilege are not to be made prophylactically against the threat of waiver, but only when information is actually withheld. Documents produced in discovery are now presumed to be authentic for use against the party producing them, thus avoiding the cost of proving authentication when there is no dispute. Procedures for oral depositions are revised to encourage focused examination by imposing time limits and to discourage colloquy between counsel.

An important aspect of these revisions has been the regrouping of provisions in a more logical sequence and the elimination of archaic and confusing language.

A. EVIDENCE

TRCP 176. SUBPOENAS

176.1 **Form.** Every subpoena must be issued in the name of "The State of Texas" and must:

(a) state the style of the suit and its cause number;

(b) state the court in which the suit is pending;

(c) state the date on which the subpoena is issued;

(d) identify the person to whom the subpoena is directed;

(e) state the time, place, and nature of the action required by the person to whom the subpoena is directed, as provided in Rule 176.2;

(f) identify the party at whose instance the subpoena is issued, and the party's attorney of record, if any;

(g) state the text of Rule 176.8(a); and

(h) be signed by the person issuing the subpoena.

176.2 **Required Actions.** A subpoena must command the person to whom it is directed to do either or both of the following:

(a) attend and give testimony at a deposition, hearing, or trial;

(b) produce and permit inspection and copying of designated documents or tangible things in the possession, custody, or control of that person.

176.3 **Limitations.**

(a) ***Range.*** A person may not be required by subpoena to appear or produce documents or other things in a county that is more than 150 miles from where the person resides or is served. However, a person whose appearance or production at a deposition may be compelled by notice alone under Rules 199.3 or 200.2 may be required to appear and produce documents or other things at any location permitted under Rules 199.2(b)(2).

(b) ***Use for discovery.*** A subpoena may not be used for discovery to an extent, in a manner, or at a time other than as provided by the rules governing discovery.

176.4 **Who May Issue.** A subpoena may be issued by:

(a) the clerk of the appropriate district, county, or justice court, who must provide the party requesting the subpoena with an original and a copy for each witness to be completed by the party;

(b) an attorney authorized to practice in the State of Texas, as an officer of the court; or

(c) an officer authorized to take depositions in this State, who must issue the subpoena immediately on a request accompanied by a notice to take a deposition under Rules 199 or 200, or a notice under Rule 205.3, and who may also serve the notice with the subpoena.

176.5 **Service.**

(a) ***Manner of service.*** A subpoena may be served at any place within the State of Texas by any sheriff or constable of the State of Texas, or any person who is not a party and is 18 years of age or older. A subpoena must be served by delivering a copy to the witness and tendering to that person any fees required by law. If the witness is a party and is represented by an attorney of record in the proceeding, the subpoena may be served on the witness's attorney of record.

(b) ***Proof of service.*** Proof of service must be made by filing either:

(1) the witness's signed written memorandum attached to the subpoena showing that the witness accepted the subpoena; or

(2) a statement by the person who made the service stating the date, time, and manner of service, and the name of the person served.

176.6 **Response.**

(a) ***Compliance required.*** Except as provided in this subdivision, a person served with a subpoena must comply with the command stated therein unless discharged by the court or by the party summoning such witness. A person commanded to appear and give testimony must remain at the place of deposition, hearing, or trial from day to day until discharged by the court or by the party summoning the witness.

(b) ***Organizations.*** If a subpoena commanding testimony is directed to a corporation, partnership, association, governmental agency, or other organization, and the matters on which examination is requested are described with reasonable particularity, the organization must designate one or more persons to testify on its behalf as to matters known or reasonably available to the organization.

(c) ***Production of documents or tangible things.*** A person commanded to produce documents or tangible things need not appear in person at the time and place of production unless the person is also commanded to attend and give testimony, either in the same subpoena or a separate one. A person must produce documents as they are kept in the usual course of business or must organize and label them to correspond with the categories in the demand. A person may withhold material or information claimed to be privileged but must comply with Rule 193.3. A nonparty's production of a document authenticates the document for use against the nonparty to the same extent as a party's production of a document is authenticated for use against the party under Rule 193.7.

(d) ***Objections.*** A person commanded to produce and permit inspection or copying of designated documents and things may serve on the party requesting issuance of the subpoena—before the time specified for compliance—written objections to producing any or all of the designated materials. A person need not comply with the part of a subpoena to which objection is made as provided in this paragraph unless ordered to do so by the court. The party requesting the subpoena may move for such an order at any time after an objection is made.

(e) ***Protective orders.*** A person commanded to appear at a deposition, hearing, or trial, or to produce and permit inspection and copying of designated documents and things, and any other person affected by the subpoena, may move for a protective order under Rule 192.6(b)—before the time specified for compliance—either in the court in which the action is pending or in a district court in the county where the subpoena was served. The person must serve the motion on all parties in accordance with Rule 21a. A person need not comply with the part of a subpoena from which protection is sought under this paragraph unless ordered to do so by the court. The party requesting the subpoena may seek such an order at any time after the motion for protection is filed.

(f) ***Trial subpoenas.*** A person commanded to attend and give testimony, or to produce documents or things, at a hearing or trial, may object or move for protective order before the court at the time and place specified for compliance, rather than under paragraphs (d) and (e).

176.7 Protection of Person from Undue Burden and Expense. A party causing a subpoena to issue must take reasonable steps to avoid imposing undue burden or expense on the person served. In ruling on objections or motions for protection, the court must provide a person served with a subpoena an adequate time for compliance, protection from disclosure of privileged material or information, and protection from undue burden or expense. The court may impose reasonable conditions on compliance with a subpoena, including compensating the witness for undue hardship.

176.8 Enforcement of Subpoena.

(a) ***Contempt.*** Failure by any person without adequate excuse to obey a subpoena served upon that person may be deemed a contempt of the court from which the subpoena is issued or a district court in the county in which the subpoena is served, and may be punished by fine or confinement, or both.

(b) ***Proof of payment of fees required for fine or attachment.*** A fine may not be imposed, nor a person served with a subpoena attached, for failure to comply with a subpoena without proof by affidavit of the party requesting the subpoena or the party's attorney of record that all fees due the witness by law were paid or tendered.

Comments to 1999 change:

1. This rule combines the former rules governing subpoenas for trial and discovery. When a subpoena is used for discovery, the protections from undue burden and expense apply, just as with any discovery.

2. Rule 176.3(b) prohibits the use of a subpoena to circumvent the discovery rules. Thus, for example, a deposition subpoena to a party is subject to the procedures of Rules 196, 199, and 200, and a deposition subpoena to a nonparty is subject to the procedures of Rule 205.

See CPRC §22.001; ***Commentaries***, "Subpoenas," ch. 1-K; "Depositions," ch. 6-E.

History of TRCP 176: Adopted eff. Jan. 1, 1999, by order of Nov. 9, 1998 (977-78 S.W.2d [Tex.Cases] xxxvi): Repealed former 176. Source: New rule.

Automatic Drilling Machs. v. Miller, 515 S.W.2d 256, 259 (Tex.1974). "On motion ... the court is authorized by Rule 177a [now TRCP 176.7] to quash or modify the subpoena if it is unreasonable or oppressive or condition denial of the motion on advancement of reasonable costs by the party in whose behalf the subpoena was issued."

In re Diversicare Gen. Partner, 41 S.W.3d 788, 794 (Tex.App.—Corpus Christi 2001, orig. proceeding). "[A] party may compel discovery from a nonparty by ... serving a notice on the nonparty and all parties pursuant to rule 205.2 and a subpoena compelling production of documents. The nonparty must then respond in accordance with rule 176 which provides the nonparty with an opportunity to make objections to the production and to move for a protective order."

St. Luke's Episcopal Hosp. v. Garcia, 928 S.W.2d 307, 310 (Tex.App.—Houston [14th Dist.] 1996, orig. proceeding). "In determining whether a deposition notice or subpoena duces tecum is unreasonable and oppressive, the following factors are relevant: '(1) the quantity of materials subpoenaed, (2) the ease or difficulty of collecting and transporting the materials, (3) the length of time before the deposition, (4) the availability of the information from other sources, and (5) the relevance of the materials.'"

TRCP 177-179. REPEALED

TRCP 177 to 179 were repealed eff. Jan. 1, 1999, by order of Nov. 9, 1998 (977-78 S.W.2d [Tex.Cases] xxxiii). For subject matter of former TRCP 177 to 179, see TRCP 176.

TRCP 180. REFUSAL TO TESTIFY

Any witness refusing to give evidence may be committed to jail, there to remain without bail until such witness shall consent to give evidence.

See TRCP 176; *Commentaries*, "Subpoenas," ch. 1-K; "Depositions," ch. 6-E.

History of TRCP 180: Adopted eff. Sept. 1, 1941, by order of Oct. 29, 1940 (3 Tex.B.J. 552 [1940]). Source: TRCS art. 3709 (repealed).

TRCP 181. PARTY AS WITNESS

Either party to a suit may examine the opposing party as a witness, and shall have the same process to compel his attendance as in the case of any other witness.

See TRCP 176, 199-201; *Commentaries*, "Subpoenas," ch. 1-K; "Depositions," ch. 6-E.

History of TRCP 181: Adopted eff. Sept. 1, 1941, by order of Oct. 29, 1940 (3 Tex.B.J. 552 [1940]). Source: TRCS art. 3711 (repealed). Note: Same as TRCP 176.

TRCP 182 - 182a. REPEALED

TRCP 182 repealed eff. Jan. 1, 1988, by order of July 15, 1987 (733-34 S.W.2d [Tex.Cases] lvii.): TRE 607 and TRE 610(c) fully satisfy the needs served by TRCP 182. TRCP 182a repealed eff. Jan. 1, 1988, by order of July 15, 1987 (733-34 S.W.2d [Tex.Cases] lvii): TRCP 182a, which was added to TRE 601(b), is no longer necessary.

TRCP 183. INTERPRETERS

The court may appoint an interpreter of its own selection and may fix the interpreter's reasonable compensation. The compensation shall be paid out of funds provided by law or by one or more of the parties as the court may direct, and may be taxed ultimately as costs, in the discretion of the court.

See TRCP 200.4; TRE 604; *Commentaries*, "Depositions," ch. 6-E.

History of TRCP 183: Amended eff. Sept. 1, 1990, by order of Apr. 24, 1990 (785-86 S.W.2d [Tex.Cases] lix): Rewrote to adopt procedures for the appointment and compensation of interpreters; source for amendment, FRCP 43(f); deleted provision regarding summoning interpreters and their conduct because it is covered by TRE 604. Adopted eff. Sept. 1, 1941, by order of Oct. 29, 1940 (3 Tex.B.J. 552 [1940]). Source: TRCS art. 3712 (repealed).

TRCP 184 - 184a. REPEALED

TRCP 184 repealed eff. Sept. 1, 1990, by order of Apr. 24, 1990 (785-86 S.W.2d [Tex.Cases] lx): Repealed TRCP 184 because it is covered by TRE 202. TRCP 184a repealed eff. Sept. 1, 1990, by order of Apr. 24, 1990 (785-86 S.W.2d [Tex.Cases] lx): Repealed TRCP 184a because it is covered by TRE 203.

TRCP 185. SUIT ON ACCOUNT

When any action or defense is founded upon an open account or other claim for goods, wares and merchandise, including any claim for a liquidated money demand based upon written contract or founded on business dealings between the parties, or is for personal service rendered, or labor done or labor or materials furnished, on which a systematic record has been kept, and is supported by the affidavit of the party, his agent or attorney taken before some officer authorized to administer oaths, to the effect that such claim is, within the knowledge of affiant, just and true, that it is due, and that all just and lawful offsets, payments and credits have been allowed, the same shall be taken as prima facie evidence thereof, unless the party resisting such claim shall file a written denial, under oath. A party resisting such a sworn claim shall comply with the rules of pleading as are required in any other kind of suit, provided, however, that if he does not timely file a written denial, under oath, he shall not be permitted to deny the claim, or any item therein, as the case may be. No particularization or description of the nature of the component parts of the account or claim is necessary unless the trial court sustains special exceptions to the pleadings.

See *Commentaries*, "Plaintiff's Original Petition," ch. 2-B; "The Answer—Denying Liability," ch. 3-E; FORMS 2B, 3E.

History of TRCP 185: Amended eff. Apr. 1, 1984, by order of Dec. 5, 1983 (661-62 S.W.2d [Tex.Cases] lvii): The rule is rewritten so that suits on accounts will be subject to ordinary rules of pleading and practice. Amended eff. Jan. 1, 1971, by order of July 21, 1970 (455-56 S.W.2d [Tex.Cases] xxxiii): Changed the language "stating that such claim is not just or true, in whole or in part, and if in part only, stating the items and particulars which are unjust" to "stating that each and every item is not just or true, or that some specified item or items are not just and true." Amended eff. Mar. 1, 1950, by order of Oct. 12, 1949 (12 Tex.B.J. 532 [1949]): The rule was extended to include a claim for "labor done or labor or materials furnished"; and the provision that when a counter-affidavit is filed on the day of the trial the party asserting the claim shall have the right to continue the cause until the next term of court was changed to the following: "the party asserting such verified claim shall have the right to postpone such cause for a reasonable time." Several textual changes not affecting the substance of the rule have also been made. Adopted eff. Sept. 1, 1941, by order of Oct. 29, 1940 (3 Tex.B.J. 552 [1940]). Source: TRCS art. 3736 (repealed).

Vance v. Holloway, 689 S.W.2d 403, 403-04 (Tex. 1985). "The petition and affidavit filed by [P] clearly met the requirements of [TRCP] 185. [D] answered by way of an unverified general denial only. He failed to meet the requirements of [TRCP] 185 and 93(10) which state that a written denial of the plaintiff's action must be verified. [¶] [D], therefore, waived his right to dispute the amount and ownership of the account."

Rizk v. Financial Guardian Ins. Agency, 584 S.W.2d 860, 862 (Tex.1979). "In the absence of a sworn denial meeting the requirements of the rule, the account is received as prima facie evidence as against a defendant sued thereon, and the defendant may not dispute the receipt of the items or services, or the correctness of the stated charges...."

Powers v. Adams, 2 S.W.3d 496, 498 (Tex.App.—Houston [14th Dist.] 1999, no pet.). "Under [TRCP 185], a [P's] petition on sworn account must contain a systematic, itemized statement of the goods or services sold, reveal offsets made to the account, and be supported by an affidavit stating the claim is within the affiant's knowledge, and that it is 'just and true.'"

Bird v. First Deposit Nat'l Bank, 994 S.W.2d 280, 282 (Tex.App.—El Paso 1999, pet. denied). "We find that a credit card issued by a financial institution does not create the sort of debtor-creditor relationship required in order to bring suit under [TRCP] 185."

Worley v. Butler, 809 S.W.2d 242, 245 (Tex.App.—Corpus Christi 1990, no writ). "To prevail in a cause of action on sworn account, a party must show: (1) that there was a sale and delivery of the merchandise or performance of the services; (2) that the amount of the account is just, that is, that the prices were charged in accordance with an agreement or in the absence of an agreement, they are the usual, customary and reasonable prices for that merchandise or services; and (3) that the amount is unpaid."

B. DISCOVERY

TRCP 186 - 189. REPEALED

TRCP 186, 186a, and 186b were repealed eff. Apr. 1, 1984, by order of Dec. 5, 1983 (661-62 S.W.2d [Tex.Cases] lvii). TRCP 187 and 188 were repealed eff. Jan. 1, 1999, by order of Nov. 9, 1998 (977-78 S.W.2d [Tex.Cases] xxxiii). TRCP 189 was repealed eff. Apr. 1, 1984, by order of Dec. 5, 1983 (661-62 S.W.2d [Tex.Cases] lix). For subject matter of former TRCP 186, see TRCP 199, 200, 202 and 252. For subject matter of former TRCP 186a and 186b, see TRCP 192 and 193. For subject matter of former TRCP 189, see TRCP 200. For subject matter of former TRCP 187, see TRCP 199 and 203. For subject matter of former TRCP 188, see TRCP 176 and 199.

TRCP 190. DISCOVERY LIMITATIONS

190.1 Discovery Control Plan Required. Every case must be governed by a discovery control plan as provided in this Rule. A plaintiff must allege in the first numbered paragraph of the original petition whether discovery is intended to be conducted under Level 1, 2, or 3 of this Rule.

190.2 Discovery Control Plan—Suits Involving $50,000 or Less (Level 1).

(a) ***Application.*** This subdivision applies to:

(1) any suit in which all plaintiffs affirmatively plead that they seek only monetary relief aggregating $50,000 or less, excluding costs, pre-judgment interest and attorneys' fees, and

(2) any suit for divorce not involving children in which a party pleads that the value of the marital estate is more than zero but not more than $50,000.

(b) ***Exceptions.*** This subdivision does not apply if:

(1) the parties agree that Rule 190.3 should apply;

(2) the court orders a discovery control plan under Rule 190.4; or

(3) any party files a pleading or an amended or supplemental pleading that seeks relief other than that to which this subdivision applies.

A pleading, amended pleading (including trial amendment), or supplemental pleading that renders this subdivision no longer applicable may not be filed without leave of court less than 45 days before the date set for trial. Leave may be granted only if good cause for filing the pleading outweighs any prejudice to an opposing party.

(c) ***Limitations.*** Discovery is subject to the limitations provided elsewhere in these rules and to the following additional limitations:

(1) *Discovery period.* All discovery must be conducted during the discovery period, which begins when

the suit is filed and continues until 30 days before the date set for trial.

(2) *Total time for oral depositions.* Each party may have no more than six hours in total to examine and cross-examine all witnesses in oral depositions. The parties may agree to expand this limit up to ten hours in total, but not more except by court order. The court may modify the deposition hours so that no party is given unfair advantage.

(3) *Interrogatories.* Any party may serve on any other party no more than 25 written interrogatories, excluding interrogatories asking a party only to identify or authenticate specific documents. Each discrete subpart of an interrogatory is considered a separate interrogatory.

(d) ***Reopening discovery.*** When the filing of a pleading or an amended or supplemental pleading renders this subdivision no longer applicable, the discovery period reopens, and discovery must be completed within the limitations provided in Rules 190.3 or 190.4, whichever is applicable. Any person previously deposed may be redeposed. On motion of any party, the court should continue the trial date if necessary to permit completion of discovery.

190.3 Discovery Control Plan—By Rule (Level 2).

(a) ***Application.*** Unless a suit is governed by a discovery control plan under Rules 190.2 or 190.4, discovery must be conducted in accordance with this subdivision.

(b) ***Limitations.*** Discovery is subject to the limitations provided elsewhere in these rules and to the following additional limitations:

(1) *Discovery period.* All discovery must be conducted during the discovery period, which begins when suit is filed and continues until:

(A) 30 days before the date set for trial, in cases under the Family Code; or

(B) in other cases, the earlier of

(i) 30 days before the date set for trial, or

(ii) nine months after the earlier of the date of the first oral deposition or the due date of the first response to written discovery.

(2) *Total time for oral depositions.* Each side may have no more than 50 hours in oral depositions to examine and cross-examine parties on the opposing side, experts designated by those parties, and persons who are subject to those parties' control. "Side" refers to all the litigants with generally common interests in the litigation. If one side designates more than two experts, the opposing side may have an additional six hours of total deposition time for each additional expert designated. The court may modify the deposition hours and must do so when a side or party would be given unfair advantage.

(3) *Interrogatories.* Any party may serve on any other party no more than 25 written interrogatories, excluding interrogatories asking a party only to identify or authenticate specific documents. Each discrete subpart of an interrogatory is considered a separate interrogatory.

190.4 Discovery Control Plan—By Order (Level 3).

(a) ***Application.*** The court must, on a party's motion, and may, on its own initiative, order that discovery be conducted in accordance with a discovery control plan tailored to the circumstances of the specific suit. The parties may submit an agreed order to the court for its consideration. The court should act on a party's motion or agreed order under this subdivision as promptly as reasonably possible.

(b) ***Limitations.*** The discovery control plan ordered by the court may address any issue concerning discovery or the matters listed in Rule 166, and may change any limitation on the time for or amount of discovery set forth in these rules. The discovery limitations of Rule 190.2, if applicable, or otherwise of Rule 190.3 apply unless specifically changed in the discovery control plan ordered by the court. The plan must include:

(1) a date for trial or for a conference to determine a trial setting;

(2) a discovery period during which either all discovery must be conducted or all discovery requests must be sent, for the entire case or an appropriate phase of it;

(3) appropriate limits on the amount of discovery; and

(4) deadlines for joining additional parties, amending or supplementing pleadings, and designating expert witnesses.

190.5 Modification of Discovery Control Plan. The court may modify a discovery control plan at any time and must do so when the interest of justice requires. The court must allow additional discovery:

(a) related to new, amended or supplemental pleadings, or new information disclosed in a discovery response or in an amended or supplemental response, if:

(1) the pleadings or responses were made after the deadline for completion of discovery or so nearly before that deadline that an adverse party does not have an adequate opportunity to conduct discovery related to the new matters, and

(2) the adverse party would be unfairly prejudiced without such additional discovery;

(b) regarding matters that have changed materially after the discovery cutoff if trial is set or postponed so that the trial date is more than three months after the discovery period ends.

190.6 Certain Types of Discovery Excepted. This rule's limitations on discovery do not apply to or include discovery conducted under Rule 202 ("Depositions Before Suit or to Investigate Claims"), or Rule 621a ("Discovery and Enforcement of Judgment"). But Rule 202 cannot be used to circumvent the limitations of this rule.

Comments to 1999 change:

1. This rule establishes three tiers of discovery plans and requires that every case be in one at all times. A case is in Level 1 if it is pleaded by the plaintiff so as to invoke application of Level 1, as provided by Rule 190.2(a). If a plaintiff does not or cannot plead the case in compliance with Rule 190.2(a) so as to invoke the application of Level 1, the case is automatically in Level 2. A case remains in Level 1 or Level 2, as determined by the pleadings, unless and until it is moved to Level 3. To be in Level 3, the court must order a specific plan for the case, either on a party's motion or on the court's own initiative. The plan may be one agreed to by the parties and submitted as an agreed order. A Level 3 plan may simply adopt Level 1 or Level 2 restrictions. Separate Level 3 plans for phases of the case may be appropriate. The initial pleading required by Rule 190.1 is merely to notify the court and other parties of the plaintiff's intention; it does not determine the applicable discovery level or bind the court or other parties. Thus, a plaintiff's failure to state in the initial pleading that the case should be in Level 1, as provided in Rule 190.1, does not alone make the case subject to Level 2 because the discovery level is determined by Rule 190.2. Likewise, a plaintiff's statement in the initial paragraph of the petition that the case is to be governed by Level 3 does not make Level 3 applicable, as a case can be in Level 3 only by court order. A plaintiff's failure to plead as required by Rule 190.1 is subject to special exception.

2. Rule 190.2 does not apply to suits for injunctive relief or divorces involving children. The requirement of an affirmative pleading of limited relief (*e.g.*: "Plaintiff affirmatively pleads that he seeks only monetary relief aggregating $50,000 or less, excluding costs, pre-judgment interest and attorneys' fees") does not conflict with other pleading requirements, such as Rule 47 and Tex. Rev. Civ. Stat. Ann. art. 4590i, §5.01. In a suit to which Rule 190.2 applies, the relief awarded cannot exceed the limitations of Level 1 because the purpose of the rule, unlike Rule 47, is to bind the pleader to a maximum claim. To this extent, the rule in *Greenhalgh v. Service Lloyds Ins. Co.*, 787 S.W.2d 938 (Tex. 1990), does not apply.

3. "Discrete subparts" of interrogatories are counted as single interrogatories, but not every separate factual inquiry is a discrete subpart. See FRCP 33(a). While not susceptible of precise definition, see *Braden v. Downey*, 811 S.W.2d 922, 927-928 (Tex.1991), a "discrete subpart" is, in general, one that calls for information that is not logically or factually related to the primary interrogatory. The number of sets of interrogatories is no longer limited to two.

4. As other rules make clear, unless otherwise ordered or agreed, parties seeking discovery must serve requests sufficiently far in advance of the end of the discovery period that the deadline for responding will be within the discovery period. The court may order a deadline for sending discovery requests in lieu of or in addition to a deadline for completing discovery.

5. Use of forms of discovery other than depositions and interrogatories, such as requests for disclosure, admissions, or production of documents, are not restricted in Levels 1 and 2. But depositions on written questions cannot be used to circumvent the limits on interrogatories.

6. The concept of "side" in Rule 190.3(b)(2) borrows from Rule 233, which governs the allocation of peremptory strikes, and from FRCP 30(a)(2). In most cases there are only two sides—plaintiffs and defendants. In complex cases, however, there may be more than two sides, such as when defendants have sued third parties not named by plaintiffs, or when defendants have sued each other. As an example, if P1 and P2 sue D1, D2, and D3, and D1 sues D2 and D3, Ps would together be entitled to depose Ds and others permitted by the rule (*i.e.*, Ds' experts and persons subject to Ds' control) for 50 hours, and Ds would together be entitled to depose Ps and others for 50 hours. D1 would also be entitled to depose D2 and D3 and others for 50 hours on matters in controversy among them, and D2 and D3 would together be entitled to depose D1 and others for 50 hours.

7. Any matter listed in Rule 166 may be addressed in an order issued under Rule 190.4. A pretrial order under Rule 166 may be used in individual cases regardless of the discovery level.

8. For purposes of defining discovery periods, "trial" does not include summary judgment.

See ***Commentaries***, "General Rules for Discovery," ch. 6-A.

History of TRCP 190: Amended eff. Jan. 1, 1999, by order of Dec. 31, 1998 (981-82 S.W.2d [Tex.Cases] xxxviii). Adopted eff. Jan. 1, 1999, by order of Nov. 9, 1998 (977-78 S.W.2d [Tex.Cases] xxxix). Applies to cases filed on or after Jan. 1, 1999. Source: New rule.

In re Van Waters & Rogers, Inc., 62 S.W.3d 197, 200 (Tex.2001). "[T]he [Ps] have failed to show why after 7 years of litigation they should not be required to provide the ... basic information regarding their individual injuries and the causative chemicals.... While ... a trial court must be given latitude in managing discovery..., that latitude is not unbounded. *At 201:* [T]he trial court's discovery order denies [Ds] 'discovery that goes to the heart of the litigation.'"

In re Alford Chevrolet-Geo, 997 S.W.2d 173, 181 (Tex.1999). "[C]ourts may limit discovery pending resolution of threshold issues like venue, jurisdiction, forum non conveniens, and official immunity."

In re SWEPI L.P., 103 S.W.3d 578, 589 (Tex.App.—San Antonio 2003, orig. proceeding). "A review of the interrogatories reveals none that have multiple 'discrete subparts.' Each question relates to a particular claim and asks [P] to provide certain details about the facts underlying that claim. The 'subparts' objected to by [P] simply identify the types of facts [D] would like to have disclosed so that it can understand the parameters of the claims and prepare its defenses. [T]he interrogatories do not exceed the number allowed by Rule 190.3(b)(3)...."

TRCP 191. MODIFYING DISCOVERY PROCEDURES & LIMITATIONS; CONFERENCE REQUIREMENT; SIGNING DISCLOSURES, DISCOVERY REQUESTS, RESPONSES, & OBJECTIONS; FILING REQUIREMENTS

191.1 Modification of Procedures. Except where specifically prohibited, the procedures and limitations set forth in the rules pertaining to discovery may be modified in any suit by the agreement of the parties or by court order for good cause. An agreement of the parties is enforceable if it complies with Rule 11 or, as it affects an oral deposition, if it is made a part of the record of the deposition.

191.2 Conference. Parties and their attorneys are expected to cooperate in discovery and to make any agreements reasonably necessary for the efficient disposition of the case. All discovery motions or requests for hearings relating to discovery must contain a certificate by the party filing the motion or request that a reasonable effort has been made to resolve the dispute without the necessity of court intervention and the effort failed.

191.3 Signing of Disclosures, Discovery Requests, Notices, Responses, and Objections.

(a) ***Signature required.*** Every disclosure, discovery request, notice, response, and objection must be signed:

(1) by an attorney, if the party is represented by an attorney, and must show the attorney's State Bar of Texas identification number, address, telephone number, and fax number, if any; or

(2) by the party, if the party is not represented by an attorney, and must show the party's address, telephone number, and fax number, if any.

(b) ***Effect of signature on disclosure.*** The signature of an attorney or party on a disclosure constitutes a certification that to the best of the signer's knowledge, information, and belief, formed after a reasonable inquiry, the disclosure is complete and correct as of the time it is made.

(c) ***Effect of signature on discovery request, notice, response, or objection.*** The signature of an attorney or party on a discovery request, notice, response, or objection constitutes a certification that to the best of the signer's knowledge, information, and belief, formed after a reasonable inquiry, the request, notice, response, or objection:

(1) is consistent with the rules of civil procedure and these discovery rules and warranted by existing law or a good faith argument for the extension, modification, or reversal of existing law;

(2) has a good faith factual basis;

(3) is not interposed for any improper purpose, such as to harass or to cause unnecessary delay or needless increase in the cost of litigation; and

(4) is not unreasonable or unduly burdensome or expensive, given the needs of the case, the discovery already had in the case, the amount in controversy, and the importance of the issues at stake in the litigation.

(d) ***Effect of failure to sign.*** If a request, notice, response, or objection is not signed, it must be stricken unless it is signed promptly after the omission is called to the attention of the party making the request, notice, response, or objection. A party is not required to take any action with respect to a request or notice that is not signed.

(e) ***Sanctions.*** If the certification is false without substantial justification, the court may, upon motion or its own initiative, impose on the person who made the certification, or the party on whose behalf the request, notice, response, or objection was made, or both, an appropriate sanction as for a frivolous pleading or motion under Chapter 10 of the Civil Practice and Remedies Code.

191.4 Filing of Discovery Materials.

(a) ***Discovery materials not to be filed.*** The following discovery materials must not be filed:

(1) discovery requests, deposition notices, and subpoenas required to be served only on parties;

(2) responses and objections to discovery requests and deposition notices, regardless on whom the requests or notices were served;

(3) documents and tangible things produced in discovery; and

(4) statements prepared in compliance with Rule 193.3(b) or (d).

(b) ***Discovery materials to be filed.*** The following discovery materials must be filed:

(1) discovery requests, deposition notices, and subpoenas required to be served on nonparties;

(2) motions and responses to motions pertaining to discovery matters; and

(3) agreements concerning discovery matters, to the extent necessary to comply with Rule 11.

(c) ***Exceptions.*** Notwithstanding paragraph (a)—

(1) the court may order discovery materials to be filed;

(2) a person may file discovery materials in support of or in opposition to a motion or for other use in a court proceeding; and

(3) a person may file discovery materials necessary for a proceeding in an appellate court.

(d) ***Retention requirement for persons.*** Any person required to serve discovery materials not required to be filed must retain the original or exact copy of the materials during the pendency of the case and any related appellate proceedings begun within six months after judgment is signed, unless otherwise provided by the trial court.

(e) ***Retention requirement for courts.*** The clerk of the court shall retain and dispose of deposition transcripts and depositions upon written questions as directed by the Supreme Court.

191.5 Service of Discovery Materials. Every disclosure, discovery request, notice, response, and objection required to be served on a party or person must be served on all parties of record.

Comments to 1999 change:

1. Rule 191.1 preserves the ability of parties by agreement and trial courts by order to adapt discovery to different circumstances. That ability is broad but not unbounded. Parties cannot merely by agreement modify a court order without the court's concurrence. Trial courts cannot simply "opt out" of these rules by form orders or approve or order a discovery control plan that does not contain the matters specified in Rule 190.4, but trial courts may use standard or form orders for providing discovery plans, scheduling, and other pretrial matters. In individual instances, courts may order, or parties may agree, to use discovery methods other than those prescribed in these rules if appropriate. Because the general rule is stated here, it is not repeated in each context in which it applies. Thus, for example, parties can agree to enlarge or shorten the time permitted for a deposition and to change the manner in which a deposition is conducted, notwithstanding Rule 199.5, although parties could not agree to be abusive toward a witness.

2. Rule 191.2 expressly states the obligation of parties and their attorneys to cooperate in conducting discovery.

3. The requirement that discovery requests, notices, responses, and objections be signed also applies to documents used to satisfy the purposes of such instruments. An example is a statement that privileged material or information has been withheld, which may be separate from a response to the discovery request but is nevertheless part of the response.

See CPRC §10.001; TRCP 11, 13, 57; ***Commentaries***, "General Rules for Discovery," ch. 6-A; "Requests for Disclosure," ch. 6-D; "Depositions," ch. 6-E; "Interrogatories," ch. 6-F.

History of TRCP 191: Adopted eff. Jan. 1, 1999, by order of Nov. 9, 1998 (977-78 S.W.2d [Tex.Cases] xliii). TRCP 191.3 and 191.4 apply only to discovery conducted after Jan. 1, 1999. Source: New rule.

In re Alford Chevrolet-Geo, 997 S.W.2d 173, 184 (Tex.1999). "[W]e expect class-action litigants to cooperate on discovery plans and make any agreements reasonably necessary for the efficient disposition of the case."

Groves v. Gabriel, 874 S.W.2d 660, 661 n.3 (Tex. 1994). "[P] complains that [D's] motion to compel discovery did not contain the certificate of conference required under [TRCP 191.2]. Because this rule is for the benefit of the trial court, the court's failure to require a certificate of conference does not justify mandamus relief."

USAA v. Thomas, 893 S.W.2d 628, 629 (Tex.App.—Corpus Christi 1994, writ denied). TRCP 191.2 "ensures that parties will make good faith efforts to settle discovery disputes before filing sanctions motions and that sanctions motions will be filed only when court intervention is absolutely necessary. *At 630:* We hold that the trial court abused its discretion by granting the motion for sanctions without the required certificate of conference."

TRCP 192. PERMISSIBLE DISCOVERY: FORMS & SCOPE; WORK PRODUCT; PROTECTIVE ORDERS; DEFINITIONS

192.1 Forms of Discovery. Permissible forms of discovery are:

(a) requests for disclosure;

(b) requests for production and inspection of documents and tangible things;

(c) requests and motions for entry upon and examination of real property;

(d) interrogatories to a party;

(e) requests for admission;

(f) oral or written depositions; and

(g) motions for mental or physical examinations.

192.2 Sequence of Discovery. The permissible forms of discovery may be combined in the same document and may be taken in any order or sequence.

192.3 Scope of Discovery.

(a) ***Generally.*** In general, a party may obtain discovery regarding any matter that is not privileged and is relevant to the subject matter of the pending action, whether it relates to the claim or defense of the party seeking discovery or the claim or defense of any other party. It is not a ground for objection that the information sought will be inadmissible at trial if the information sought appears reasonably calculated to lead to the discovery of admissible evidence.

(b) ***Documents and tangible things.*** A party may obtain discovery of the existence, description, nature, custody, condition, location, and contents of documents and tangible things (including papers, books, accounts, drawings, graphs, charts, photographs, electronic or videotape recordings, data, and data compilations) that constitute or contain matters relevant to the subject matter of the action. A person is required to produce a document or tangible thing that is within the person's possession, custody, or control.

(c) ***Persons with knowledge of relevant facts.*** A party may obtain discovery of the name, address, and telephone number of persons having knowledge of relevant facts, and a brief statement of each identified person's connection with the case. A person has knowledge of relevant facts when that person has or may have knowledge of any discoverable matter. The person need not have admissible information or personal knowledge of the facts. An expert is "a person with knowledge of relevant facts" only if that knowledge was obtained firsthand or if it was not obtained in preparation for trial or in anticipation of litigation.

(d) ***Trial witnesses.*** A party may obtain discovery of the name, address, and telephone number of any person who is expected to be called to testify at trial. This paragraph does not apply to rebuttal or impeaching witnesses the necessity of whose testimony cannot reasonably be anticipated before trial.

(e) ***Testifying and consulting experts.*** The identity, mental impressions, and opinions of a consulting expert whose mental impressions and opinions have not been reviewed by a testifying expert are not discoverable. A party may discover the following information regarding a testifying expert or regarding a consulting expert whose mental impressions or opinions have been reviewed by a testifying expert:

(1) the expert's name, address, and telephone number;

(2) the subject matter on which a testifying expert will testify;

(3) the facts known by the expert that relate to or form the basis of the expert's mental impressions and opinions formed or made in connection with the case in which the discovery is sought, regardless of when and how the factual information was acquired;

(4) the expert's mental impressions and opinions formed or made in connection with the case in which discovery is sought, and any methods used to derive them;

(5) any bias of the witness;

(6) all documents, tangible things, reports, models, or data compilations that have been provided to, reviewed by, or prepared by or for the expert in anticipation of a testifying expert's testimony;

(7) the expert's current resume and bibliography.

(f) ***Indemnity and insuring agreements.*** Except as otherwise provided by law, a party may obtain discovery of the existence and contents of any indemnity or insurance agreement under which any person may be liable to satisfy part or all of a judgment rendered in the action or to indemnify or reimburse for payments made to satisfy the judgment. Information concerning the indemnity or insurance agreement is not by reason of disclosure admissible in evidence at trial.

(g) ***Settlement agreements.*** A party may obtain discovery of the existence and contents of any relevant portions of a settlement agreement. Information concerning a settlement agreement is not by reason of disclosure admissible in evidence at trial.

(h) ***Statements of persons with knowledge of relevant facts.*** A party may obtain discovery of the statement of any person with knowledge of relevant facts—a "witness statement"—regardless of when the statement was made. A witness statement is (1) a written statement signed or otherwise adopted or approved in writing by the person making it, or (2) a stenographic, mechanical, electrical, or other type of recording of a witness's oral statement, or any substantially verbatim transcription of such a recording. Notes taken during a conversation or interview with a witness are not a witness statement. Any person may obtain, upon written request, his or her own statement concerning the lawsuit, which is in the possession, custody or control of any party.

(i) ***Potential parties.*** A party may obtain discovery of the name, address, and telephone number of any potential party.

(j) ***Contentions.*** A party may obtain discovery of any other party's legal contentions and the factual bases for those contentions.

192.4 Limitations on Scope of Discovery. The discovery methods permitted by these rules should be limited by the court if it determines, on motion or on its own initiative and on reasonable notice, that:

(a) the discovery sought is unreasonably cumulative or duplicative, or is obtainable from some other source that is more convenient, less burdensome, or less expensive; or

(b) the burden or expense of the proposed discovery outweighs its likely benefit, taking into account the needs of the case, the amount in controversy, the parties' resources, the importance of the issues at stake in the litigation, and the importance of the proposed discovery in resolving the issues.

192.5 Work Product.

(a) ***Work product defined.*** Work product comprises:

(1) material prepared or mental impressions developed in anticipation of litigation or for trial by or for a party or a party's representatives, including the party's attorneys, consultants, sureties, indemnitors, insurers, employees, or agents; or

(2) a communication made in anticipation of litigation or for trial between a party and the party's representatives or among a party's representatives, including the party's attorneys, consultants, sureties, indemnitors, insurers, employees, or agents.

(b) ***Protection of work product.***

(1) *Protection of core work product—attorney mental processes.* Core work product—the work product of an attorney or an attorney's representative that contains the attorney's or the attorney's representative's mental impressions, opinions, conclusions, or legal theories—is not discoverable.

(2) *Protection of other work product.* Any other work product is discoverable only upon a showing that the party seeking discovery has substantial need of the materials in the preparation of the party's case and that the party is unable without undue hardship to obtain the substantial equivalent of the material by other means.

(3) *Incidental disclosure of attorney mental processes.* It is not a violation of subparagraph (1) if disclosure ordered pursuant to subparagraph (2) incidentally discloses by inference attorney mental processes otherwise protected under subparagraph (1).

(4) *Limiting disclosure of mental processes.* If a court orders discovery of work product pursuant to subparagraph (2), the court must—insofar as possible—protect against disclosure of the mental impressions, opinions, conclusions, or legal theories not otherwise discoverable.

(c) ***Exceptions.*** Even if made or prepared in anticipation of litigation or for trial, the following is not work product protected from discovery:

(1) information discoverable under Rule 192.3 concerning experts, trial witnesses, witness statements, and contentions;

(2) trial exhibits ordered disclosed under Rule 166 or Rule 190.4;

(3) the name, address, and telephone number of any potential party or any person with knowledge of relevant facts;

(4) any photograph or electronic image of underlying facts (*e.g.*, a photograph of the accident scene) or a photograph or electronic image of any sort that a party intends to offer into evidence; and

(5) any work product created under circumstances within an exception to the attorney-client privilege in Rule 503(d) of the Rules of Evidence.

(d) ***Privilege.*** For purposes of these rules, an assertion that material or information is work product is an assertion of privilege.

192.6 Protective Orders.

(a) ***Motion.*** A person from whom discovery is sought, and any other person affected by the discovery request, may move within the time permitted for response to the discovery request for an order protecting that person from the discovery sought. A person should not move for protection when an objection to written discovery or an assertion of privilege is appropriate, but a motion does not waive the objection or assertion of privilege. If a person seeks protection regarding the time or place of discovery, the person must state a reasonable time and place for discovery with which the person will comply. A person must comply with a request to the extent protection is not sought unless it is unreasonable under the circumstances to do so before obtaining a ruling on the motion.

(b) ***Order.*** To protect the movant from undue burden, unnecessary expense, harassment, annoyance, or invasion of personal, constitutional, or property rights, the court may make any order in the interest of justice and may—among other things—order that:

(1) the requested discovery not be sought in whole or in part;

(2) the extent or subject matter of discovery be limited;

(3) the discovery not be undertaken at the time or place specified;

(4) the discovery be undertaken only by such method or upon such terms and conditions or at the time and place directed by the court;

(5) the results of discovery be sealed or otherwise protected, subject to the provisions of Rule 76a.

192.7 Definitions. As used in these rules—

(a) *Written discovery* means requests for disclosure, requests for production and inspection of documents and tangible things, requests for entry onto property, interrogatories, and requests for admission.

(b) *Possession, custody, or control* of an item means that the person either has physical possession of the item or has a right to possession of the item that is equal or superior to the person who has physical possession of the item.

(c) A *testifying expert* is an expert who may be called to testify as an expert witness at trial.

(d) A *consulting expert* is an expert who has been consulted, retained, or specially employed by a party in anticipation of litigation or in preparation for trial, but who is not a testifying expert.

Comments to 1999 change:

1. While the scope of discovery is quite broad, it is nevertheless confined by the subject matter of the case and reasonable expectations of obtaining information that will aid resolution of the dispute. The rule must be read and applied in that context. See *In re American Optical Corp.*, 988 S.W.2d 711 (Tex.1998) (per curiam); *K-Mart v. Sanderson*, 937 S.W.2d 429 (Tex.1996) (per curiam); *Dillard Dept. Stores v. Hall*, 909 S.W.2d 491 (Tex.1995) (per curiam); *Texaco, Inc. v. Sanderson*, 898 S.W.2d 813 (Tex.1995) (per curiam); *Loftin v. Martin*, 776 S.W.2d 145, 148 (Tex.1989).

2. The definition of documents and tangible things has been revised to clarify that things relevant to the subject matter of the action are within the scope of discovery regardless of their form.

3. Rule 192.3(c) makes discoverable a "brief statement of each identified person's connection with the case." This provision does not contemplate a narrative statement of the facts the person knows, but at most a few words describing the person's identity as relevant to the lawsuit. For instance: "treating physician," "eyewitness," "chief financial officer," "director," "plaintiff's mother and eyewitness to accident." The rule is intended to be consistent with *Axelson v. McIlhany*, 798 S.W.2d 550 (Tex.1990).

4. Rule 192.3(g) does not suggest that settlement agreements in other cases are relevant or irrelevant.

5. Rule 192.3(j) makes a party's legal and factual contentions discoverable but does not require more than a basic statement of those contentions and does not require a marshaling of evidence.

6. The sections in former Rule 166b concerning land and medical records are not included in this rule. They remain within the scope of discovery and are discussed in other rules.

7. The court's power to limit discovery based on the needs and circumstances of the case is expressly stated in Rule 192.4. The provision is taken from Rule 26(b)(2) of the Federal Rules of Civil Procedure. Courts should limit discovery under this rule only to prevent unwarranted delay and expense as stated more fully in the rule. A court abuses its discretion in unreasonably restricting a party's access to information through discovery.

8. Work product is defined for the first time, and its exceptions stated. Work product replaces the "attorney work product" and "party communication" discovery exemptions from former Rule 166b.

9. Elimination of the "witness statement" exemption does not render all witness statements automatically discoverable but subjects them to the same rules concerning the scope of discovery and privileges applicable to other documents or tangible things.

See ***Commentaries***, "Discovery," ch. 6; FORMS 6.

History of TRCP 192: Amended eff. Jan. 1, 1999, by order of Dec. 31, 1998 (981-82 S.W.2d [Tex.Cases] xxxviii). Adopted eff. Jan. 1, 1999, by order of Nov. 9, 1998 (977-78 S.W.2d [Tex.Cases] xlvi). This is former TRCP 166b, with modification. Source: New rule.

Definition

In re Kuntz, ___ S.W.3d ___ (Tex.2003) (No. 02-0375; 12-19-03). "[D] argues that he 'should not be ordered to produce documents in the physical possession of his corporate employer in this suit brought against him individually.' [¶] '[D's] access is strictly limited to use of the [documents] in furtherance of his employer's services....' [¶] [D]'s mere access to the [documents] does not constitute 'physical possession' of the documents under the definition of 'possession, custody, or control' set forth in [TRCP] 192.7(b)."

GTE Comm. Sys. Corp. v. Tanner, 856 S.W.2d 725, 729 (Tex.1993). "The phrase, 'possession, custody or control,' within the meaning of [TRCP 192.7(b)], includes not only actual physical possession, but constructive possession, and the right to obtain possession from a third party, such as an agent or representative."

Scope of Discovery

In re Alford Chevrolet-Geo, 997 S.W.2d 173, 182 (Tex.1999). "[I]t is within the trial court's discretion to schedule discovery and decide whether and how much discovery is warranted to determine any [class] certification questions. Factors in determining the scope of precertification discovery include the importance, benefit, burden, expense, and time needed to produce the proposed discovery."

K-Mart Corp. v. Sanderson, 937 S.W.2d 429, 431 (Tex.1996). No "discovery device can be used to 'fish.'"

Irving Healthcare Sys. v. Brooks, 927 S.W.2d 12, 18 (Tex.1996). "[R]outine business records of a health-care entity such as a patient's medical records do not become privileged and are not shielded from discovery simply because a medical peer review committee has reviewed or considered them."

Ford Motor Co. v. Leggat, 904 S.W.2d 643, 649 (Tex.1995). "Settlement agreements are discoverable, to the extent they are relevant. Settlement agreements themselves, of course, are not admissible at trial to prove liability."

Monsanto Co. v. May, 889 S.W.2d 274, 276 (Tex. 1994). "A party is entitled to discovery that is relevant to the subject matter of the claim, and which appears reasonably calculated to lead to the discovery of admissible evidence." *See also* ***Volkswagen, A.G. v. Valdez***, 909 S.W.2d 900, 902 (Tex.1995); ***Texaco, Inc. v. Sanderson***, 898 S.W.2d 813, 814 (Tex.1995).

Housing Auth. of El Paso v. Rodriguez-Yepez, 843 S.W.2d 475, 476 (Tex.1992). "The broad scope of discovery is tempered by the trial court's discretion, properly invoked under [TRCP 192.6], to narrow the scope of discovery on a case by case basis with a protective order."

Jampole v. Touchy, 673 S.W.2d 569, 573 (Tex. 1984), *overruled on other grounds*, ***Walker v. Packer***, 827 S.W.2d 833 (Tex.1992). "[T]he ultimate purpose of discovery is to seek the truth, so that disputes may be decided by what the facts reveal, not by what facts are concealed. For this reason, discovery is not limited to information that will be admissible at trial. To increase the likelihood that all relevant evidence will be disclosed and brought before the trier of fact, the law circumscribes a significantly larger class of discoverable evidence to include anything reasonably calculated to lead to the discovery of material evidence."

In re U-Haul Int'l, 87 S.W.3d 653, 656 (Tex.App.—San Antonio 2002, orig. proceeding). Ps "had the burden of proving [D] had constructive possession or the right to obtain possession of the requested documents from [D's insurer]. [D] presented evidence that it had requested the information from [insurer], but [insurer] refused to honor the request. Thus, even if [D] has the right to the files, [Ps] were still required to prove [D] had the ability to compel [insurer] to turn over its claims files."

Experts

In re City of Georgetown, 53 S.W.3d 328, 334 (Tex. 2001). "The [TRCPs] expressly provide that a party is not required to disclose the identity, mental impressions, and opinions of consulting experts. *At 337:* [I]f documents are privileged or confidential under the [TRCPs] or [TREs], they are within a 'category of information [that] is expressly made confidential under other law' within the meaning of [Gov't Code] §552.022 of the Public Information Act."

G.M. Corp. v. Gayle, 951 S.W.2d 469, 474 (Tex. 1997). "'The policy behind the consulting expert privilege is to encourage parties to seek expert advice in evaluating their case and to prevent a party from receiving undue benefit from an adversary's efforts and diligence.' [¶] Without the consulting-expert privilege, parties would be reluctant to test an uncertain theory, for fear that it would provide evidence for the other side. *At 476:* [W]e conclude that the trial court's crash-test order constitutes an abuse of discretion by infringing on General Motors' consulting-expert privilege."

Aluminum Co. of Am. v. Bullock, 870 S.W.2d 2, 4 (Tex.1994). TRCP 192.3(e) "provides for discovery of not only the identity, but also the expected substance of the testimony of expert witnesses who will testify at trial.... When [the expert's] opinion concerning [D's] negligence changed due to the review of additional facts, [Ps] then had a duty to supplement their discovery responses to disclose the material change."

Protective Orders

General Tire v. Kepple, 970 S.W.2d 520, 525 (Tex. 1998). "[W]e hold that when a party seeks a protective order under [TRCP 192.6] to restrict the dissemination of unfiled discovery, and no party or intervenor contends that the discovery is a 'court record,' a trial court need not conduct a hearing or render any findings on that issue. If a party or intervenor opposing a protective order claims that the discovery is a 'court record,' the court must make a threshold determination on that issue. However, public notice and a Rule 76a hearing are mandated only if the court finds that the documents are court records."

Crown Cent. Pet. Corp. v. Garcia, 904 S.W.2d 125, 128 (Tex.1995). "When a party seeks to depose a ... high level corporate official [apex deposition] and that official (or the corporation) files a motion for protective order ... denying any knowledge of relevant facts, the trial court should first determine whether the party seeking the deposition has arguably shown that the official has any unique or superior personal knowledge of discoverable information. If the party seeking the deposition cannot [so] show ... the trial court should grant the motion for protective order and first require the party seeking the deposition to attempt to obtain the discovery through less intrusive methods."

In re Amaya, 34 S.W.3d 354, 356-57 (Tex.App.—Waco 2001, orig. proceeding). "A trial judge may exercise some discretion in the granting of a protective order and in controlling the nature and form of discovery. ... A party seeking to avoid discovery must show particular, specific and demonstrable injury by facts sufficient to justify a protective order. [¶] Any party who seeks to exclude matters from discovery on grounds that the requested information is unduly burdensome, costly or harassing to produce, has the affirmative duty to plead and prove the work necessary to comply with discovery."

Work Product

Goode v. Shoukfeh, 943 S.W.2d 441, 449 (Tex. 1997). "Work product of counsel may not be considered by the factfinder unless the privilege has been waived or one of the [TRE] 503(d) exceptions applies."

Occidental Chem. Corp. v. Banales, 907 S.W.2d 488, 490 (Tex.1995). "The attorney work product privilege protects two related but different concepts. First, the privilege protects the attorney's thought process, which includes strategy decisions and issue formulation, and notes or writings evincing those mental processes. Second, the privilege protects the mechanical compilation of information to the extent such compilation reveals the attorney's thought processes. The work product exemption is of continuing duration."

National Un. Fire Ins. Co. v. Valdez, 863 S.W.2d 458, 461 (Tex.1993). "[N]o legitimate purpose is served by allowing a party to discover an opponent's litigation file. Our decision today does not prevent a party from requesting specific documents or categories of documents relevant to issues in a pending case, even though some or all of the documents may be contained in an attorney's files."

TRCP 193. WRITTEN DISCOVERY: RESPONSE; OBJECTION; ASSERTION OF PRIVILEGE; SUPPLEMENTATION & AMENDMENT; FAILURE TO TIMELY RESPOND; PRESUMPTION OF AUTHENTICITY

193.1 Responding to Written Discovery; Duty to Make Complete Response. A party must respond to written discovery in writing within the time provided by court order or these rules. When responding to written discovery, a party must make a complete response, based on all information reasonably available to the responding party or its attorney at the time the response is made. The responding party's answers, objections, and other responses must be preceded by the request to which they apply.

193.2 Objecting to Written Discovery.

(a) ***Form and time for objections.*** A party must make any objection to written discovery in writing—either in the response or in a separate document—within the time for response. The party must state specifically the legal or factual basis for the objection and the extent to which the party is refusing to comply with the request.

(b) ***Duty to respond when partially objecting; objection to time or place of production.*** A party must comply with as much of the request to which the party has made no objection unless it is unreasonable under the circumstances to do so before obtaining a ruling on the objection. If the responding party objects to the requested time or place of production, the responding party must state a reasonable time and place for complying with the request and must comply at that time and place without further request or order.

(c) ***Good faith basis for objection.*** A party may object to written discovery only if a good faith factual and legal basis for the objection exists at the time the objection is made.

(d) ***Amendment.*** An objection or response to written discovery may be amended or supplemented to state an objection or basis that, at the time the objection or response initially was made, either was inapplicable or was unknown after reasonable inquiry.

(e) ***Waiver of objection.*** An objection that is not made within the time required, or that is obscured by numerous unfounded objections, is waived unless the court excuses the waiver for good cause shown.

(f) ***No objection to preserve privilege.*** A party should not object to a request for written discovery on the grounds that it calls for production of material or information that is privileged but should instead comply with Rule 193.3. A party who objects to production of privileged material or information does not waive the privilege but must comply with Rule 193.3 when the error is pointed out.

193.3 Asserting a Privilege. A party may preserve a privilege from written discovery in accordance with this subdivision.

(a) ***Withholding privileged material or information.*** A party who claims that material or information responsive to written discovery is privileged may withhold the privileged material or information from the response. The party must state—in the response (or an amended or supplemental response) or in a separate document—that:

(1) information or material responsive to the request has been withheld,

(2) the request to which the information or material relates, and

(3) the privilege or privileges asserted.

(b) ***Description of withheld material or information.*** After receiving a response indicating that material or information has been withheld from production, the party seeking discovery may serve a written request that the withholding party identify the information and material withheld. Within 15 days of service of that request, the withholding party must serve a response that:

(1) describes the information or materials withheld that, without revealing the privileged information itself or otherwise waiving the privilege, enables other parties to assess the applicability of the privilege, and

(2) asserts a specific privilege for each item or group of items withheld.

(c) ***Exemption.*** Without complying with paragraphs (a) and (b), a party may withhold a privileged communication to or from a lawyer or lawyer's representative or a privileged document of a lawyer or lawyer's representative—

(1) created or made from the point at which a party consults a lawyer with a view to obtaining professional legal services from the lawyer in the prosecution or defense of a specific claim in the litigation in which discovery is requested, and

(2) concerning the litigation in which the discovery is requested.

(d) ***Privilege not waived by production.*** A party who produces material or information without intending to waive a claim of privilege does not waive that claim under these rules or the Rules of Evidence if—within ten days or a shorter time ordered by the court, after the producing party actually discovers that such production was made—the producing party amends the response, identifying the material or information produced and stating the privilege asserted. If the producing party thus amends the response to assert a privilege, the requesting party must promptly return the specified material or information and any copies pending any ruling by the court denying the privilege.

193.4 Hearing and Ruling on Objections and Assertions of Privilege.

(a) ***Hearing.*** Any party may at any reasonable time request a hearing on an objection or claim of privilege asserted under this rule. The party making the objection or asserting the privilege must present any evidence necessary to support the objection or privilege. The evidence may be testimony presented at the hearing or affidavits served at least seven days before the hearing or at such other reasonable time as the court permits. If the court determines that an *in camera* review of some or all of the requested discovery is necessary, that material or information must be segregated and produced to the court in a sealed wrapper within a reasonable time following the hearing.

(b) ***Ruling.*** To the extent the court sustains the objection or claim of privilege, the responding party has no further duty to respond to that request. To the extent the court overrules the objection or claim of privilege, the responding party must produce the requested material or information within 30 days after the court's ruling or at such time as the court orders. A party need not request a ruling on that party's own objection or assertion of privilege to preserve the objection or privilege.

(c) ***Use of material or information withheld under claim of privilege.*** A party may not use—at any hearing or trial—material or information withheld from discovery under a claim of privilege, including a claim sustained by the court, without timely amending or supplementing the party's response to that discovery.

193.5 Amending or Supplementing Responses to Written Discovery.

(a) ***Duty to amend or supplement.*** If a party learns that the party's response to written discovery was incomplete or incorrect when made, or, although complete and correct when made, is no longer complete and correct, the party must amend or supplement the response:

(1) to the extent that the written discovery sought the identification of persons with knowledge of relevant facts, trial witnesses, or expert witnesses, and

(2) to the extent that the written discovery sought other information, unless the additional or corrective information has been made known to the other parties in writing, on the record at a deposition, or through other discovery responses.

(b) ***Time and form of amended or supplemental response.*** An amended or supplemental response must be made reasonably promptly after the party discovers the necessity for such a response. Except as otherwise provided by these rules, it is presumed that an amended or supplemental response made less than 30 days before trial was not made reasonably promptly. An amended or supplemental response must be in the same form as the initial response and must be verified by the party if the original response was required to be verified by the party, but the failure to comply with this requirement does not make the amended or supplemental response untimely unless the party making the response refuses to correct the defect within a reasonable time after it is pointed out.

193.6 Failing to Timely Respond—Effect on Trial.

(a) ***Exclusion of evidence and exceptions.*** A party who fails to make, amend, or supplement a discovery response in a timely manner may not introduce in evidence the material or information that was not timely disclosed, or offer the testimony of a witness (other than a named party) who was not timely identified, unless the court finds that:

(1) there was good cause for the failure to timely make, amend, or supplement the discovery response; or

(2) the failure to timely make, amend, or supplement the discovery response will not unfairly surprise or unfairly prejudice the other parties.

(b) ***Burden of establishing exception.*** The burden of establishing good cause or the lack of unfair surprise or unfair prejudice is on the party seeking to introduce the evidence or call the witness. A finding of good cause or of the lack of unfair surprise or unfair prejudice must be supported by the record.

(c) ***Continuance.*** Even if the party seeking to introduce the evidence or call the witness fails to carry the burden under paragraph (b), the court may grant a continuance or temporarily postpone the trial to allow a response to be made, amended, or supplemented, and to allow opposing parties to conduct discovery regarding any new information presented by that response.

193.7 Production of Documents Self-Authenticating. A party's production of a document in response to written discovery authenticates the document for use against that party in any pretrial proceeding or at trial unless—within ten days or a longer or shorter time ordered by the court, after the producing party has actual notice that the document will be used—the party objects to the authenticity of the document, or any part of it, stating the specific basis for objection. An objection must be either on the record or in writing and must have a good faith factual and legal basis. An objection made to the authenticity of only part of a document does not affect the authenticity of the remainder. If objection is made, the party attempting to use the document should be given a reasonable opportunity to establish its authenticity.

Comments to 1999 change:

1. This rule imposes a duty upon parties to make a complete response to written discovery based upon all information reasonably available, subject to objections and privileges.

2. An objection to written discovery does not excuse the responding party from complying with the request to the extent no objection is made. But a party may object to a request for "all documents relevant to the lawsuit" as overly broad and not in compliance with the rule requiring specific requests for documents and refuse to comply with it entirely. See *Loftin v. Martin*, 776 S.W.2d 145 (Tex.1989). A party may also object to a request for a litigation file on the ground that it is overly broad and may assert that on its face the request seeks only materials protected by privilege. See *National Union Fire Ins. Co. v. Valdez*, 863 S.W.2d 458 (Tex.1993). A party who objects to production of documents from a remote time period should produce documents from a more recent period unless that production would be burdensome and duplicative should the objection be overruled.

3. This rule governs the presentation of all privileges including work product. It dispenses with objections to written discovery requests on the basis that responsive information or materials are protected by a specific privilege from discovery. Instead, the rule requires parties to state that information or materials have been withheld and to identify the privilege upon which the party relies. The statement should not be made prophylactically, but only when specific information and materials have been withheld. The party must amend or supplement the statement if additional privileged information or material is found subsequent to the initial response. Thus, when large numbers of documents are being produced, a party may amend the initial response when documents are found as to which the party claims privilege. A party need not state that material created by or for lawyers for the litigation has been withheld as it can be assumed that such material will be withheld from virtually any request on the grounds of attorney-client privilege or work product. However, the rule

does not prohibit a party from specifically requesting the material or information if the party has a good faith basis for asserting that it is discoverable. An example would be material or information described by Rule 503(d)(1) of the Rules of Evidence.

4. Rule 193.3(d) is a new provision that allows a party to assert a claim of privilege to material or information produced inadvertently without intending to waive the privilege. The provision is commonly used in complex cases to reduce costs and risks in large document productions. The focus is on the intent to waive the privilege, not the intent to produce the material or information. A party who fails to diligently screen documents before producing them does not waive a claim of privilege. This rule is thus broader than TRE 511 and overturns *Granada Corp. v. First Court of Appeals*, 844 S.W.2d 223 (Tex.1992), to the extent the two conflict. The ten-day period (which may be shortened by the court) allowed for an amended response does not run from the production of the material or information but from the party's first awareness of the mistake. To avoid complications at trial, a party may identify prior to trial the documents intended to be offered, thereby triggering the obligation to assert any overlooked privilege under this rule. A trial court may also order this procedure.

5. This rule imposes no duty to supplement or amend deposition testimony. The only duty to supplement deposition testimony is provided in Rule 195.6.

6. Any party can request a hearing in which the court will resolve issues brought up in objections or withholding statements. The party seeking to avoid discovery has the burden of proving the objection or privilege.

7. The self-authenticating provision is new. Authentication is, of course, but a condition precedent to admissibility and does not establish admissibility. See TRE 901(a). The ten-day period allowed for objection to authenticity (which period may be altered by the court in appropriate circumstances) does not run from the production of the material or information but from the party's actual awareness that the document will be used. To avoid complications at trial, a party may identify prior to trial the documents intended to be offered, thereby triggering the obligation to object to authenticity. A trial court may also order this procedure. An objection to authenticity must be made in good faith.

See ***Commentaries***, "General Rules for Discovery," ch. 6-A; "Scope of Discovery," ch. 6-B; "Requests for Disclosure," ch. 6-D; "Interrogatories," ch. 6-F; "Securing Documents & Tangible Things," ch. 6-H; "Medical Records," ch. 6-I; "Entry on Land," ch. 6-J.

History of TRCP 193: Amended eff. Jan. 1, 1999, by order of Dec. 31, 1998 (981-82 S.W.2d [Tex.Cases] xxxviii-ix). Adopted eff. Jan. 1, 1999, by order of Nov. 9, 1998 (977-78 S.W.2d [Tex.Cases] li): This is former TRCP 166b, with modification. Discovery responses, objections, amendments, assertions of privilege, and supplementations made prior to Jan. 1, 1999, are not subject to TRCP 193. Source: New rule.

193.2 – Objections

G.M. Corp. v. Tanner, 892 S.W.2d 862, 863 (Tex. 1995). "As the party objecting to the request, [P] was required to provide evidence in support of his objection."

193.3 – Privileges

In re Union Pac. Res. Co., 22 S.W.3d 338, 340 (Tex.1999) "'Any party who seeks to deny the production of evidence must claim a specific privilege against such production. The burden is on the party asserting a privilege from discovery to produce evidence *concerning the applicability of a particular privilege*.'"

In re Monsanto Co., 998 S.W.2d 917, 926 (Tex. App.—Waco 1999, orig. proceeding). "The mere listing of a specific privilege in a response or a privilege log does not prove that privilege. The response and log are the vehicles by which the privilege is claimed. Proof of the facts that justify the claim of privilege is necessary."

193.4 – Hearing

In re CI Host, 92 S.W.3d 514, 517 (Tex.2002). "Our discovery rules do not require notice to third parties so that they might have an opportunity to be heard on their own objections."

193.5 – Supplementing Discovery

Titus Cty. Hosp. Dist. v. Lucas, 988 S.W.2d 740, 740 (Tex.1998). TRCP 193.5 "requires supplementation of a response to a request for discovery. An interrogatory answer is a response to a request for discovery, but testimony in a deposition is not. A general duty to supplement deposition testimony (as opposed to a narrow duty for certain expert testimony, for example) would impose too great a burden on litigants. We therefore disapprove the court of appeals' holding that deposition testimony must be supplemented."

Exxon Corp. v. West Tex. Gathering Co., 868 S.W.2d 299, 304 (Tex.1993). "Our rules do not prevent experts from refining calculations and perfecting reports through the time of trial. The testimony of an expert should not be barred because a change in some minor detail of the person's work has not been disclosed a month before trial. The additional supplementation requirement of [TRCP 193.5] does require that opposing parties have sufficient information about an expert's opinion to prepare a rebuttal with their own experts and cross-examination, and that they be promptly and fully advised when further developments have rendered past information incorrect or misleading."

Snider v. Stanley, 44 S.W.3d 713, 715 (Tex.App.—Beaumont 2001, pet. denied). "'An amended or supplemental response must be made reasonably promptly after the party discovers the necessity for such a response.' It is presumed that response made within 30 days of trial is not reasonably promptly made. [D's] response, made 30 days before trial, is not subject to the presumption. [Ps] argue that the opposite presumption applies, that is, the supplementation was made reasonably promptly. We disagree. Had such a presumption been intended, it would have been incorporated into the rules."

193.6 – Effect of Failing to Respond

Norfolk S. Ry. v. Bailey, 92 S.W.3d 577, 581 (Tex. App.—Austin 2002, no pet.). "An expert ... may change an opinion without supplementation if the opinion is 'an expansion of an already disclosed subject.' However, a party may not present a material alteration of an expert's opinion at trial that would constitute a surprise attack. The purpose of requiring timely disclosure of a material change in an expert's opinion is to give the other party an opportunity to prepare a rebuttal."

Mares v. Ford Motor Co., 53 S.W.3d 416, 419 (Tex. App.—San Antonio 2001, no pet.). Even though [D] filed a general statement of the nature of the expert's opinions, the trial court did not abuse its discretion in permitting [D's] expert to testify because "the trial court limited the testimony of [D's] experts to the testimony provided at the earlier trial or in response to earlier discovery [and] the substance of that testimony had been fully disclosed to [Ps]."

193.7 – Self-Authenticating

Blanche v. First Nationwide Mortg. Corp., 74 S.W.3d 444, 451-52 (Tex.App.—Dallas 2002, no pet.). TRCP 193.7 "alleviate[s] the burden on a party receiving documents through discovery from proving the authenticity of those documents when they are used against the party who produced them. Rule 193.7 does not help [Ps] here because the documents attached to their summary judgment response were not produced to them by [D], the party against whom the documents were used. … A party cannot authenticate a document for use in its own favor by merely producing it in response to a discovery request."

TRCP 194. REQUESTS FOR DISCLOSURE

194.1 **Request.** A party may obtain disclosure from another party of the information or material listed in Rule 194.2 by serving the other party—no later than 30 days before the end of any applicable discovery period—the following request: "Pursuant to Rule 194, you are requested to disclose, within 30 days of service of this request, the information or material described in Rule [state rule, e.g., 194.2, or 194.2(a), (c), and (f), or 194.2(d)-(g)]."

194.2 **Content.** A party may request disclosure of any or all of the following:

(a) the correct names of the parties to the lawsuit;

(b) the name, address, and telephone number of any potential parties;

(c) the legal theories and, in general, the factual bases of the responding party's claims or defenses (the responding party need not marshal all evidence that may be offered at trial);

(d) the amount and any method of calculating economic damages;

(e) the name, address, and telephone number of persons having knowledge of relevant facts, and a brief statement of each identified person's connection with the case;

(f) for any testifying expert:

(1) the expert's name, address, and telephone number;

(2) the subject matter on which the expert will testify;

(3) the general substance of the expert's mental impressions and opinions and a brief summary of the basis for them, or if the expert is not retained by, employed by, or otherwise subject to the control of the responding party, documents reflecting such information;

(4) if the expert is retained by, employed by, or otherwise subject to the control of the responding party:

(A) all documents, tangible things, reports, models, or data compilations that have been provided to, reviewed by, or prepared by or for the expert in anticipation of the expert's testimony; and

(B) the expert's current resume and bibliography;

(g) any indemnity and insuring agreements described in Rule 192.3(f);

(h) any settlement agreements described in Rule 192.3(g);

(i) any witness statements described in Rule 192.3(h);

(j) in a suit alleging physical or mental injury and damages from the occurrence that is the subject of the case, all medical records and bills that are reasonably related to the injuries or damages asserted or, in lieu thereof, an authorization permitting the disclosure of such medical records and bills;

(k) in a suit alleging physical or mental injury and damages from the occurrence that is the subject of the case, all medical records and bills obtained by the responding party by virtue of an authorization furnished by the requesting party.

194.3 **Response.** The responding party must serve a written response on the requesting party within 30 days after service of the request, except that:

(a) a defendant served with a request before the defendant's answer is due need not respond until 50 days after service of the request, and

(b) a response to a request under Rule 194.2(f) is governed by Rule 195.

194.4 Production. Copies of documents and other tangible items ordinarily must be served with the response. But if the responsive documents are voluminous, the response must state a reasonable time and place for the production of documents. The responding party must produce the documents at the time and place stated, unless otherwise agreed by the parties or ordered by the court, and must provide the requesting party a reasonable opportunity to inspect them.

194.5 No Objection or Assertion of Work Product. No objection or assertion of work product is permitted to a request under this rule.

194.6 Certain Responses Not Admissible. A response to requests under Rule 194.2(c) and (d) that has been changed by an amended or supplemental response is not admissible and may not be used for impeachment.

Comments to 1999 change:

1. Disclosure is designed to afford parties basic discovery of specific categories of information, not automatically in every case, but upon request, without preparation of a lengthy inquiry, and without objection or assertion of work product. In those extremely rare cases when information ordinarily discoverable should be protected, such as when revealing a person's residence might result in harm to the person, a party may move for protection. A party may assert any applicable privileges other than work product using the procedures of Rule 193.3 applicable to other written discovery. Otherwise, to fail to respond fully to a request for disclosure would be an abuse of the discovery process.

2. Rule 194.2(c) and (d) permit a party further inquiry into another's legal theories and factual claims than is often provided in notice pleadings. So-called "contention interrogatories" are used for the same purpose. Such interrogatories are not properly used to require a party to marshal evidence or brief legal issues. Paragraphs (c) and (d) are intended to require disclosure of a party's basic assertions, whether in prosecution of claims or in defense. Thus, for example, a plaintiff would be required to disclose that he or she claimed damages suffered in a car wreck caused by defendant's negligence in speeding, and would be required to state how loss of past earnings and future earning capacity was calculated, but would not be required to state the speed at which defendant was allegedly driving. Paragraph (d) does not require a party, either a plaintiff or a defendant, to state a method of calculating non-economic damages, such as for mental anguish. In the same example, defendant would be required to disclose his or her denial of the speeding allegation and any basis for contesting the damage calculations.

3. Responses under Rule 194.2(c) and (d) that have been amended or supplemented are inadmissible and cannot be used for impeachment, but other evidence of changes in position is not likewise barred.

See ***Commentaries***, "General Rules for Discovery," ch. 6-A; "Securing Discovery from Experts," ch. 6-C; "Requests for Disclosure," ch. 6-D; FORMS 6C.

History of TRCP 194: Amended eff. Jan. 1, 1999, by order of Dec. 31, 1998 (981-82 S.W.2d [Tex.Cases] xxxix). Adopted eff. Jan. 1, 1999, by order of Nov. 9, 1998 (977-78 S.W.2d [Tex.Cases] lvi). Source: New rule.

Castellanos v. Littlejohn, 945 S.W.2d 236, 239 (Tex. App.—San Antonio 1997, orig. proceeding). "The issue presented … is whether a party who has inadvertently listed a consulting-only expert as a testifying expert may 'de-designate' him to reflect his proper status. We believe the party can do so, so long as the 'de-designation' does not constitute 'an offensive and unacceptable use of discovery mechanisms' or 'violate[ ] the clear purpose and policy underlying the rules of discovery.'"

TRCP 195. DISCOVERY REGARDING TESTIFYING EXPERT WITNESSES

195.1 Permissible Discovery Tools. A party may request another party to designate and disclose information concerning testifying expert witnesses only through a request for disclosure under Rule 194 and through depositions and reports as permitted by this rule.

195.2 Schedule for Designating Experts. Unless otherwise ordered by the court, a party must designate experts—that is, furnish information requested under Rule 194.2(f)—by the later of the following two dates: 30 days after the request is served, or—

(a) with regard to all experts testifying for a party seeking affirmative relief, 90 days before the end of the discovery period;

(b) with regard to all other experts, 60 days before the end of the discovery period.

195.3 Scheduling Depositions.

(a) ***Experts for party seeking affirmative relief.*** A party seeking affirmative relief must make an expert retained by, employed by, or otherwise in the control of the party available for deposition as follows:

(1) *If no report furnished.* If a report of the expert's factual observations, tests, supporting data, calculations, photographs, and opinions is not produced when the expert is designated, then the party must make the expert available for deposition reasonably promptly after the expert is designated. If the deposition cannot—due to the actions of the tendering party—reasonably be concluded more than 15 days before the deadline for designating other experts, that deadline must be extended for other experts testifying on the same subject.

(2) *If report furnished.* If a report of the expert's factual observations, tests, supporting data, calculations, photographs, and opinions is produced when the expert is designated, then the party need not make the expert available for deposition until reasonably promptly after all other experts have been designated.

(b) ***Other experts.*** A party not seeking affirmative relief must make an expert retained by, employed by, or otherwise in the control of the party available for deposition reasonably promptly after the expert is designated and the experts testifying on the same subject for the party seeking affirmative relief have been deposed.

195.4 Oral Deposition. In addition to disclosure under Rule 194, a party may obtain discovery concerning the subject matter on which the expert is expected to testify, the expert's mental impressions and opinions, the facts known to the expert (regardless of when the factual information was acquired) that relate to or form the basis of the testifying expert's mental impressions and opinions, and other discoverable matters, including documents not produced in disclosure, only by oral deposition of the expert and by a report prepared by the expert under this rule.

195.5 Court-Ordered Reports. If the discoverable factual observations, tests, supporting data, calculations, photographs, or opinions of an expert have not been recorded and reduced to tangible form, the court may order these matters reduced to tangible form and produced in addition to the deposition.

195.6 Amendment and Supplementation. A party's duty to amend and supplement written discovery regarding a testifying expert is governed by Rule 193.5. If an expert witness is retained by, employed by, or otherwise under the control of a party, that party must also amend or supplement any deposition testimony or written report by the expert, but only with regard to the expert's mental impressions or opinions and the basis for them.

195.7 Cost of Expert Witnesses. When a party takes the oral deposition of an expert witness retained by the opposing party, all reasonable fees charged by the expert for time spent in preparing for, giving, reviewing, and correcting the deposition must be paid by the party that retained the expert.

Comments to 1999 change:

1. This rule does not limit the permissible methods of discovery concerning consulting experts whose mental impressions or opinions have been reviewed by a testifying expert. See Rule 192.3(e). Information concerning purely consulting experts, of course, is not discoverable.

2. This rule and Rule 194 do not address depositions of testifying experts who are not retained by, employed by, or otherwise subject to the control of the responding party, nor the production of the materials identified in Rule 192.3(e)(5) and (6) relating to such experts. Parties may obtain this discovery, however, through Rules 176 and 205.

3. In scheduling the designations and depositions of expert witnesses, the rule attempts to minimize unfair surprise and undue expense. A party seeking affirmative relief must either produce an expert's report or tender the expert for deposition before an opposing party is required to designate experts. A party who does not wish to incur the expense of a report may simply tender the expert for deposition, but a party who wishes an expert to have the benefit of an opposing party's expert's opinions before being deposed may trigger designation by providing a report. Rule 191.1 permits a trial court, for good cause, to modify the order or deadlines for designating and deposing experts and the allocation of fees and expenses.

See ***Commentaries***, "General Rules for Discovery," ch. 6-A; "Scope of Discovery," ch. 6-B; "Securing Discovery from Experts," ch. 6-C; "Requests for Disclosure," ch. 6-D; "Depositions," ch. 6-E.

History of TRCP 195: Amended eff. Jan. 1, 1999, by order of Dec. 31, 1998 (981-82 S.W.2d [Tex.Cases] xxxix). Adopted eff. Jan. 1, 1999, by order of Nov. 9, 1998 (977-78 S.W.2d [Tex.Cases] lviii): New rule combines all provisions regarding discovery of expert witnesses by incorporating former TRCP 166b(e). Source: New rule.

Vaughn v. Ford Motor Co., 91 S.W.3d 387, 392 (Tex. App.—Eastland 2002, no pet.). When P designated 97 experts, narrowed the list to 6 experts only shortly before trial, did not make the experts available for deposition, and opposed D's motion to extend discovery, P violated her duty under Rule 195.3 and was properly sanctioned under TRCP 215.

Snider v. Stanley, 44 S.W.3d 713, 716 (Tex.App.—Beaumont 2001, pet. denied). Ds "did not designate [their expert] as soon as he was retained, employed, or otherwise in their control. Instead, they waited until 30 days before trial. We hold the trial court did not abuse its discretion in finding [Ds] did not supplement their discovery responses 'reasonably promptly.'"

TRCP 196. REQUESTS FOR PRODUCTION & INSPECTION TO PARTIES; REQUESTS & MOTIONS FOR ENTRY UPON PROPERTY

196.1 Request for Production and Inspection to Parties.

(a) ***Request.*** A party may serve on another party—no later than 30 days before the end of the discovery period—a request for production or for inspection, to inspect, sample, test, photograph and copy documents or tangible things within the scope of discovery.

(b) ***Contents of request.*** The request must specify the items to be produced or inspected, either by individual item or by category, and describe with reasonable particularity each item and category. The request must specify a reasonable time (on or after the date on which the response is due) and place for production. If the requesting party will sample or test the requested items, the means, manner and procedure for testing or sampling must be described with sufficient specificity to inform the producing party of the means, manner, and procedure for testing or sampling.

(c) ***Requests for production of medical or mental health records regarding nonparties.***

(1) *Service of request on nonparty.* If a party requests another party to produce medical or mental health records regarding a nonparty, the requesting party must serve the nonparty with the request for production under Rule 21a.

(2) *Exceptions.* A party is not required to serve the request for production on a nonparty whose medical records are sought if:

(A) the nonparty signs a release of the records that is effective as to the requesting party;

(B) the identity of the nonparty whose records are sought will not directly or indirectly be disclosed by production of the records; or

(C) the court, upon a showing of good cause by the party seeking the records, orders that service is not required.

(3) *Confidentiality.* Nothing in this rule excuses compliance with laws concerning the confidentiality of medical or mental health records.

196.2 Response to Request for Production and Inspection.

(a) ***Time for response.*** The responding party must serve a written response on the requesting party within 30 days after service of the request, except that a defendant served with a request before the defendant's answer is due need not respond until 50 days after service of the request.

(b) ***Content of response.*** With respect to each item or category of items, the responding party must state objections and assert privileges as required by these rules, and state, as appropriate, that:

(1) production, inspection, or other requested action will be permitted as requested;

(2) the requested items are being served on the requesting party with the response;

(3) production, inspection, or other requested action will take place at a specified time and place, if the responding party is objecting to the time and place of production; or

(4) no items have been identified—after a diligent search—that are responsive to the request.

196.3 Production.

(a) ***Time and place of production.*** Subject to any objections stated in the response, the responding party must produce the requested documents or tangible things within the person's possession, custody or control at either the time and place requested or the time and place stated in the response, unless otherwise agreed by the parties or ordered by the court, and must provide the requesting party a reasonable opportunity to inspect them.

(b) ***Copies.*** The responding party may produce copies in lieu of originals unless a question is raised as to the authenticity of the original or in the circumstances it would be unfair to produce copies in lieu of originals. If originals are produced, the responding party is entitled to retain the originals while the requesting party inspects and copies them.

(c) ***Organization.*** The responding party must either produce documents and tangible things as they are kept in the usual course of business or organize and label them to correspond with the categories in the request.

196.4 Electronic or Magnetic Data. To obtain discovery of data or information that exists in electronic or magnetic form, the requesting party must specifically request production of electronic or magnetic data and specify the form in which the requesting party wants it produced. The responding party must produce the electronic or magnetic data that is responsive to the request and is reasonably available to the responding party in its ordinary course of business. If the responding party cannot—through reasonable efforts—retrieve the data or information requested or produce it in the form requested, the responding party must state an objection complying with these rules. If the court orders the responding party to comply with the request, the court must also order that the requesting party pay the reasonable expenses of any extraordinary steps required to retrieve and produce the information.

196.5 Destruction or Alteration. Testing, sampling or examination of an item may not destroy or materially alter an item unless previously authorized by the court.

196.6 Expenses of Production. Unless otherwise ordered by the court for good cause, the expense of producing items will be borne by the responding party and the expense of inspecting, sampling, testing, photographing, and copying items produced will be borne by the requesting party.

196.7 Request or Motion for Entry Upon Property.

(a) ***Request or motion.*** A party may gain entry on designated land or other property to inspect, measure, survey, photograph, test, or sample the property or any designated object or operation thereon by serving—no later than 30 days before the end of any applicable discovery period—

(1) a request on all parties if the land or property belongs to a party, or

(2) a motion and notice of hearing on all parties and the nonparty if the land or property belongs to a nonparty. If the identity or address of the nonparty is unknown and cannot be obtained through reasonable diligence, the court must permit service by means other than those specified in Rule 21a that are reasonably calculated to give the nonparty notice of the motion and hearing.

(b) ***Time, place, and other conditions.*** The request for entry upon a party's property, or the order for entry upon a nonparty's property, must state the time, place, manner, conditions, and scope of the inspection, and must specifically describe any desired means, manner, and procedure for testing or sampling, and the person or persons by whom the inspection, testing, or sampling is to be made.

(c) ***Response to request for entry.***

(1) *Time to respond.* The responding party must serve a written response on the requesting party within 30 days after service of the request, except that a defendant served with a request before the defendant's answer is due need not respond until 50 days after service of the request.

(2) *Content of response.* The responding party must state objections and assert privileges as required by these rules, and state, as appropriate, that:

(A) entry or other requested action will be permitted as requested;

(B) entry or other requested action will take place at a specified time and place, if the responding party is objecting to the time and place of production; or

(C) entry or other requested action cannot be permitted for reasons stated in the response.

(d) ***Requirements for order for entry on nonparty's property.*** An order for entry on a nonparty's property may issue only for good cause shown and only if the land, property, or object thereon as to which discovery is sought is relevant to the subject matter of the action.

Comments to 1999 change:

1. "Document and tangible things" are defined in Rule 192.3(b).

2. A party requesting sampling or testing must describe the procedure with sufficient specificity to enable the responding party to make any appropriate objections.

3. A party requesting production of magnetic or electronic data must specifically request the data, specify the form in which it wants the data produced, and specify any extraordinary steps for retrieval and translation. Unless ordered otherwise, the responding party need only produce the data reasonably available in the ordinary course of business in reasonably usable form.

4. The rule clarifies how the expenses of production are to be allocated absent a court order to the contrary.

5. The obligation of parties to produce documents within their possession, custody or control is explained in Rule 192.3(b).

6. Parties may request production and inspection of documents and tangible things from nonparties under Rule 205.3.

7. Rule 196.3(b) is based on TRE 1003.

8. Rule 196.1(c) is merely a notice requirement and does not expand the scope of discovery of a nonparty's medical records.

See ***Commentaries***, "General Rules for Discovery," ch. 6-A; "Scope of Discovery," ch. 6-B; "Depositions," ch. 6-E; "Securing Documents & Tangible Things," ch. 6-H; "Medical Records," ch. 6-I; "Entry on Land," ch. 6-J; FORMS 6H-6J.

History of TRCP 196: Amended eff. Jan. 1, 1999, by order of Dec. 31, 1998 (981-82 S.W.2d [Tex.Cases] xxxix). Adopted eff. Jan. 1, 1999, by order of Nov. 9, 1998 (977-78 S.W.2d [Tex.Cases] lx): New rule combines former TRCP 167(1)(b) and 166(2)(c). Source: New rule.

In re Colonial Pipeline Co., 968 S.W.2d 938, 942 (Tex.1998). "While [Ps] may be entitled to production of any relevant discovery from the related cases 'as they are kept in the usual course of business,' [Ds] cannot be forced to prepare an inventory of the documents for [Ps]."

G.M. Corp. v. Gayle, 951 S.W.2d 469, 475-76 (Tex. 1997). "[Ps] rely on Rule 167(1)(b) [now TRCP 196.7(a)] to support their claim to attend [D's crash] testing. ... The rule allowing entry upon land does not render discoverable items which are privileged under [TRCP 193.3]. [TRCP 196.7(a)] does not authorize [Ps] to enter into testing facilities under [D's] control to view privileged tests."

Dillard Dept. Stores v. Hall, 909 S.W.2d 491, 492 (Tex.1995). "[P] admits that he wants the document production to explore whether he can in good faith allege racial discrimination. This is the very kind of 'fishing expedition' that is not allowable under [TRCP 196.1]."

Sears, Roebuck & Co. v. Ramirez, 824 S.W.2d 558, 559 (Tex.1992). The trial court ordered D to produce its annual reports and its federal income tax statements. The Supreme Court held there was "no justification for requiring [D] to produce the same information in different form."

In re SWEPI L.P., 103 S.W.3d 578, 584 (Tex.App.—San Antonio 2003, orig. proceeding). "It does not appear any Texas court has directly addressed what constitutes 'good cause' for a discovery order allowing entry onto land. Generally, 'good cause' for a discovery order is shown where … (1) the discovery sought is relevant and material, that is, the information will in some way aid the movant in the preparation or defense of the case; and (2) the substantial equivalent of the material cannot be obtained through other means."

In re Lincoln Elec. Co., 91 S.W.3d 432, 437 (Tex.App.—Beaumont 2002, orig. proceeding). "In keeping with the overall spirit of non-waiver apparent in the … discovery rules…, we believe [TRCP 196.2(b)] permits a responding party … to make 'objections' to such things as vagueness, overbreadth, [and] relevance…, have the[ ] 'objections' ruled upon, and then make any assertions of privilege … at a later time."

In re Diversicare Gen. Partner, 41 S.W.3d 788, 795 (Tex.App.—Corpus Christi 2001, orig. proceeding). "[W]hile rule 196.1(c) contemplates redaction of identifying information from nonparty medical records or a showing of good cause in order to avoid service on the nonparty, it is only a notice requirement rule and in no way addresses the parameters of the substantive confidentiality of the records."

TRCP 197. INTERROGATORIES TO PARTIES

197.1 Interrogatories. A party may serve on another party—no later than 30 days before the end of the discovery period—written interrogatories to inquire about any matter within the scope of discovery except matters covered by Rule 195. An interrogatory may inquire whether a party makes a specific legal or factual contention and may ask the responding party to state the legal theories and to describe in general the factual bases for the party's claims or defenses, but interrogatories may not be used to require the responding party to marshal all of its available proof or the proof the party intends to offer at trial.

197.2 Response to Interrogatories.

(a) ***Time for response.*** The responding party must serve a written response on the requesting party within 30 days after service of the interrogatories, except that a defendant served with interrogatories before the defendant's answer is due need not respond until 50 days after service of the interrogatories.

(b) ***Content of response.*** A response must include the party's answers to the interrogatories and may include objections and assertions of privilege as required under these rules.

(c) ***Option to produce records.*** If the answer to an interrogatory may be derived or ascertained from public records, from the responding party's business records, or from a compilation, abstract or summary of the responding party's business records, and the burden of deriving or ascertaining the answer is substantially the same for the requesting party as for the responding party, the responding party may answer the interrogatory by specifying and, if applicable, producing the records or compilation, abstract or summary of the records. The records from which the answer may be derived or ascertained must be specified in sufficient detail to permit the requesting party to locate and identify them as readily as can the responding party. If the responding party has specified business records, the responding party must state a reasonable time and place for examination of the documents. The responding party must produce the documents at the time and place stated, unless otherwise agreed by the parties or ordered by the court, and must provide the requesting party a reasonable opportunity to inspect them.

(d) ***Verification required; exceptions.*** A responding party—not an agent or attorney as otherwise permitted by Rule 14—must sign the answers under oath except that:

(1) when answers are based on information obtained from other persons, the party may so state, and

(2) a party need not sign answers to interrogatories about persons with knowledge of relevant facts, trial witnesses, and legal contentions.

197.3 Use. Answers to interrogatories may be used only against the responding party. An answer to an interrogatory inquiring about matters described in Rule 194.2(c) and (d) that has been amended or supplemented is not admissible and may not be used for impeachment.

Comments to 1999 change:

1. Interrogatories about specific legal or factual assertions—such as, whether a party claims a breach of implied warranty, or when a party contends that limitations began to run—are proper, but interrogatories that ask a party to state all legal and factual assertions are improper. As with requests for disclosure, interrogatories may be used to ascertain basic legal and factual claims and defenses but may not be used to force a party to marshal evidence. Use of the answers to such interrogatories is limited, just as the use of similar disclosures under Rule 194.6 is.

2. Rule 191's requirement that a party's attorney sign all discovery responses and objections applies to interrogatory responses and objections. In addition, the responding party must sign some interrogatory answers under oath, as specified by the rule. Answers in amended and supplemental responses must be signed by the party under oath only if the original answers were required to be signed under oath. The failure to sign or verify answers is only a formal defect that does not otherwise impair the answers unless the party refuses to sign or verify the answers after the defect is pointed out.

See *Commentaries*, "General Rules for Discovery," ch. 6-A; "Scope of Discovery," ch. 6-B; "Interrogatories," ch. 6-F; FORMS 6F.

History of TRCP 197: Amended eff. Jan. 1, 1999, by order of Dec. 31, 1998 (981-82 S.W.2d [Tex.Cases] xxxix). Adopted eff. Jan. 1, 1999, by order of Nov. 9, 1998 (977-78 S.W.2d [Tex.Cases] lxiv): This is former TRCP 168, with modification. Source: New rule.

Morgan v. Anthony, 27 S.W.3d 928, 929 (Tex. 2000). "Generally, a party cannot rely on its own answer to an interrogatory as summary judgment evidence. ... The interrogatory answer became competent summary judgment evidence when it became a deposition exhibit, [P] affirmed in her deposition that it was correct, and she was subject to cross-examination about [it]."

Ticor Title Ins. Co. v. Lacy, 803 S.W.2d 265, 266 (Tex.1991). "'A party must be able to rely on the interrogatories and answers of other parties in the same suit. Otherwise, a multi-party case would require redundant interrogatories with identical questions and answers.'"

Palmer v. Espey Huston & Assocs., 84 S.W.3d 345, 356 (Tex.App.—Corpus Christi 2002, pet. denied). "[I]nterrogatories may be used only against the responding party. [D] settled prior to trial and was not a party at the time [Ps] attempted to offer his answers to interrogatories. Therefore, [D's] answers were not admissible against the remaining [Ds]."

TRCP 198. REQUESTS FOR ADMISSIONS

198.1 Request for Admissions. A party may serve on another party—no later than 30 days before the end of the discovery period—written requests that the other party admit the truth of any matter within the scope of discovery, including statements of opinion or of fact or of the application of law to fact, or the genuineness of any documents served with the request or otherwise made available for inspection and copying. Each matter for which an admission is requested must be stated separately.

198.2 Response to Requests for Admissions.

(a) *Time for response.* The responding party must serve a written response on the requesting party within 30 days after service of the request, except that a defendant served with a request before the defendant's answer is due need not respond until 50 days after service of the request.

(b) *Content of response.* Unless the responding party states an objection or asserts a privilege, the responding party must specifically admit or deny the request or explain in detail the reasons that the responding party cannot admit or deny the request. A response must fairly meet the substance of the request. The responding party may qualify an answer, or deny a request in part, only when good faith requires. Lack of information or knowledge is not a proper response unless the responding party states that a reasonable inquiry was made but that the information known or easily obtainable is insufficient to enable the responding party to admit or deny. An assertion that the request presents an issue for trial is not a proper response.

(c) *Effect of failure to respond.* If a response is not timely served, the request is considered admitted without the necessity of a court order.

198.3 Effect of Admissions; Withdrawal or Amendment. Any admission made by a party under this rule may be used solely in the pending action and not in any other proceeding. A matter admitted under this rule is conclusively established as to the party making the admission unless the court permits the party to withdraw or amend the admission. The court may permit the party to withdraw or amend the admission if:

(a) the party shows good cause for the withdrawal or amendment; and

(b) the court finds that the parties relying upon the responses and deemed admissions will not be unduly prejudiced and that the presentation of the merits of the action will be subserved by permitting the party to amend or withdraw the admission.

See *Commentaries*, "General Rules for Discovery," ch. 6-A; "Scope of Discovery," ch. 6-B; "Requests for Admissions," ch. 6-G; FORMS 6G.

History of TRCP 198: Adopted eff. Jan. 1, 1999, by order of Nov. 9, 1998 (977-78 S.W.2d [Tex.Cases] lxv): This is former TRCP 169, with modification. Source: New rule.

Wal-Mart Stores v. Deggs, 968 S.W.2d 354, 356 (Tex.1998). "'Good cause' is established when the failure to respond is accidental or the result of a mistake, rather than intentional or the result of conscious indifference."

Vaughn v. Ford Motor Co., 91 S.W.3d 387, 395 (Tex.App.—Eastland 2002, no pet.). "A trial court has discretion ... to permit a party to withdraw an admission if the party shows good cause and if the trial court finds that the party relying on the admission will not be unduly prejudiced."

Payton v. Ashton, 29 S.W.3d 896, 898 (Tex.App.—Amarillo 2000, no pet.). "[A] party's duty to respond to requests for admission is dependent upon receipt of those requests. ... In short, the requests cannot be deemed admitted if service was not perfected."

TRCP 199. DEPOSITIONS UPON ORAL EXAMINATION

199.1 Oral Examination; Alternative Methods of Conducting or Recording.

(a) ***Generally.*** A party may take the testimony of any person or entity by deposition on oral examination before any officer authorized by law to take depositions. The testimony, objections, and any other statements during the deposition must be recorded at the time they are given or made.

(b) ***Depositions by telephone or other remote electronic means.*** A party may take an oral deposition by telephone or other remote electronic means if the party gives reasonable prior written notice of intent to do so. For the purposes of these rules, an oral deposition taken by telephone or other remote electronic means is considered as having been taken in the district and at the place where the witness is located when answering the questions. The officer taking the deposition may be located with the party noticing the deposition instead of with the witness if the witness is placed under oath by a person who is present with the witness and authorized to administer oaths in that jurisdiction.

(c) ***Nonstenographic recording.*** Any party may cause a deposition upon oral examination to be recorded by other than stenographic means, including videotape recording. The party requesting the nonstenographic recording will be responsible for obtaining a person authorized by law to administer the oath and for assuring that the recording will be intelligible, accurate, and trustworthy. At least five days prior to the deposition, the party must serve on the witness and all parties a notice, either in the notice of deposition or separately, that the deposition will be recorded by other than stenographic means. This notice must state the method of nonstenographic recording to be used and whether the deposition will also be recorded stenographically. Any other party may then serve written notice designating another method of recording in addition to the method specified, at the expense of such other party unless the court orders otherwise.

199.2 Procedure for Noticing Oral Deposition.

(a) ***Time to notice deposition.*** A notice of intent to take an oral deposition must be served on the witness and all parties a reasonable time before the deposition is taken. An oral deposition may be taken outside the discovery period only by agreement of the parties or with leave of court.

(b) ***Content of notice.***

(1) *Identity of witness; organizations.* The notice must state the name of the witness, which may be either an individual or a public or private corporation, partnership, association, governmental agency, or other organization. If an organization is named as the witness, the notice must describe with reasonable particularity the matters on which examination is requested. In response, the organization named in the notice must—a reasonable time before the deposition—designate one or more individuals to testify on its behalf and set forth, for each individual designated, the matters on which the individual will testify. Each individual designated must testify as to matters that are known or reasonably available to the organization. This subdivision does not preclude taking a deposition by any other procedure authorized by these rules.

(2) *Time and place.* The notice must state a reasonable time and place for the oral deposition. The place may be in:

(A) the county of the witness's residence;

(B) the county where the witness is employed or regularly transacts business in person;

(C) the county of suit, if the witness is a party or a person designated by a party under Rule 199.2(b)(1);

(D) the county where the witness was served with the subpoena, or within 150 miles of the place of service, if the witness is not a resident of Texas or is a transient person; or

(E) subject to the foregoing, at any other convenient place directed by the court in which the cause is pending.

(3) *Alternative means of conducting and recording.* The notice must state whether the deposition is to be taken by telephone or other remote electronic means and identify the means. If the deposition is to

be recorded by nonstenographic means, the notice may include the notice required by Rule 199.1(c).

(4) *Additional attendees.* The notice may include the notice concerning additional attendees required by Rule 199.5(a)(3).

(5) *Request for production of documents.* A notice may include a request that the witness produce at the deposition documents or tangible things within the scope of discovery and within the witness's possession, custody, or control. If the witness is a nonparty, the request must comply with Rule 205 and the designation of materials required to be identified in the subpoena must be attached to, or included in, the notice. The nonparty's response to the request is governed by Rules 176 and 205. When the witness is a party or subject to the control of a party, document requests under this subdivision are governed by Rules 193 and 196.

199.3 Compelling Witness to Attend. A party may compel the witness to attend the oral deposition by serving the witness with a subpoena under Rule 176. If the witness is a party or is retained by, employed by, or otherwise subject to the control of a party, however, service of the notice of oral deposition upon the party's attorney has the same effect as a subpoena served on the witness.

199.4 Objections to Time and Place of Oral Deposition. A party or witness may object to the time and place designated for an oral deposition by motion for protective order or by motion to quash the notice of deposition. If the motion is filed by the third business day after service of the notice of deposition, an objection to the time and place of a deposition stays the oral deposition until the motion can be determined.

199.5 Examination, Objection, and Conduct During Oral Depositions.

(a) ***Attendance.***

(1) *Witness.* The witness must remain in attendance from day to day until the deposition is begun and completed.

(2) *Attendance by party.* A party may attend an oral deposition in person, even if the deposition is taken by telephone or other remote electronic means. If a deposition is taken by telephone or other remote electronic means, the party noticing the deposition must make arrangements for all persons to attend by the same means. If the party noticing the deposition appears in person, any other party may appear by telephone or other remote electronic means if that party makes the necessary arrangements with the deposition officer and the party noticing the deposition.

(3) *Other attendees.* If any party intends to have in attendance any persons other than the witness, parties, spouses of parties, counsel, employees of counsel, and the officer taking the oral deposition, that party must give reasonable notice to all parties, either in the notice of deposition or separately, of the identity of the other persons.

(b) ***Oath; examination.*** Every person whose deposition is taken by oral examination must first be placed under oath. The parties may examine and cross-examine the witness. Any party, in lieu of participating in the examination, may serve written questions in a sealed envelope on the party noticing the oral deposition, who must deliver them to the deposition officer, who must open the envelope and propound them to the witness.

(c) ***Time limitation.*** No side may examine or cross-examine an individual witness for more than six hours. Breaks during depositions do not count against this limitation.

(d) ***Conduct during the oral deposition; conferences.*** The oral deposition must be conducted in the same manner as if the testimony were being obtained in court during trial. Counsel should cooperate with and be courteous to each other and to the witness. The witness should not be evasive and should not unduly delay the examination. Private conferences between the witness and the witness's attorney during the actual taking of the deposition are improper except for the purpose of determining whether a privilege should be asserted. Private conferences may be held, however, during agreed recesses and adjournments. If the lawyers and witnesses do not comply with this rule, the court may allow in evidence at trial statements, objections, discussions, and other occurrences during the oral deposition that reflect upon the credibility of the witness or the testimony.

(e) ***Objections.*** Objections to questions during the oral deposition are limited to "Objection, leading" and "Objection, form." Objections to testimony during the oral deposition are limited to "Objection, nonresponsive." These objections are waived if not stated as phrased during the oral deposition. All other objections need not be made or recorded during the oral deposition to be later raised with the court. The objecting party must give a clear and concise explanation of an objection if requested by the party taking the oral deposition, or the objection is waived. Argumentative or suggestive objections or explanations waive objection and may be grounds for terminating the oral deposition or assessing costs or other sanctions. The officer taking the oral deposition will not rule on objections but must record them for ruling by the court. The officer taking the oral deposition must not fail to record testimony because an objection has been made.

(f) ***Instructions not to answer.*** An attorney may instruct a witness not to answer a question during an oral deposition only if necessary to preserve a privilege, comply with a court order or these rules, protect a witness from an abusive question or one for which any answer would be misleading, or secure a ruling pursuant to paragraph (g). The attorney instructing the witness not to answer must give a concise, nonargumentative, nonsuggestive explanation of the grounds for the instruction if requested by the party who asked the question.

(g) ***Suspending the deposition.*** If the time limitations for the deposition have expired or the deposition is being conducted or defended in violation of these rules, a party or witness may suspend the oral deposition for the time necessary to obtain a ruling.

(h) ***Good faith required.*** An attorney must not ask a question at an oral deposition solely to harass or mislead the witness, for any other improper purpose, or without a good faith legal basis at the time. An attorney must not object to a question at an oral deposition, instruct the witness not to answer a question, or suspend the deposition unless there is a good faith factual and legal basis for doing so at the time.

199.6 Hearing on Objections. Any party may, at any reasonable time, request a hearing on an objection or privilege asserted by an instruction not to answer or suspension of the deposition; provided the failure of a party to obtain a ruling prior to trial does not waive any objection or privilege. The party seeking to avoid discovery must present any evidence necessary to support the objection or privilege either by testimony at the hearing or by affidavits served on opposing parties at least seven days before the hearing. If the court determines that an *in camera* review of some or all of the requested discovery is necessary to rule, answers to the deposition questions may be made in camera, to be transcribed and sealed in the event the privilege is sustained, or made in an affidavit produced to the court in a sealed wrapper.

Comments to 1999 change:

1. Rule 199.2(b)(5) incorporates the procedures and limitations applicable to requests for production or inspection under Rule 196, including the 30-day deadline for responses, as well as the procedures and duties imposed by Rule 193.

2. For purposes of Rule 199.5(c), each person designated by an organization under Rule 199.2(b)(1) is a separate witness.

3. The requirement of Rule 199.5(d) that depositions be conducted in the same manner as if the testimony were being obtained in court is a limit on the conduct of the lawyers and witnesses in the deposition, not on the scope of the interrogation permitted by Rule 192.

4. An objection to the form of a question includes objections that the question calls for speculation, calls for a narrative answer, is vague, is confusing, or is ambiguous. Ordinarily, a witness must answer a question at a deposition subject to the objection. An objection may therefore be inadequate if a question incorporates such unfair assumptions or is worded so that any answer would necessarily be misleading. A witness should not be required to answer whether he has yet ceased conduct he denies ever doing, subject to an objection to form (*i.e.*, that the question is confusing or assumes facts not in evidence) because any answer would necessarily be misleading on account of the way in which the question is put. The witness may be instructed not to answer. Abusive questions include questions that inquire into matters clearly beyond the scope of discovery or that are argumentative, repetitious, or harassing.

See CPRC §20.001; Gov't Code §§52.021, 52.031, 52.059 (imposes joint and several liability for the cost of the deposition on the lawyer who asks the first question and the lawyer's firm); TRE 603; ***Commentaries***, "General Rules for Discovery," ch. 6-A; "Scope of Discovery," ch. 6-B; "Depositions," ch. 6-E; FORMS 6E. Lawyers can find important information about the conduct of the deposition in the Supreme Court's rules regarding court reporters in the Uniform Format Manual for Texas Court Reporters §12 cmt., which can be found at www.supreme.courts.state.tx.us/rules/reporter.

History of TRCP 199: Adopted eff. Jan. 1, 1999, by order of Nov. 9, 1998 (977-78 S.W.2d [Tex.Cases] lxvi): This is former TRCP 200 and 201, with modification. Source: New rule.

Wal-Mart Stores v. Street, 754 S.W.2d 153, 154-55 (Tex.1988). The trial court abused its discretion when it ordered Sam Walton, the former president of the defendant corporation, to travel to Fort Worth from Arkansas to be deposed. TRCP 199 required the deposition to be taken in the Arkansas county where Walton lived.

Lindsey v. O'Neill, 689 S.W.2d 400, 402 (Tex.1985). TRCP 199.2(b)(1) "requires that a deposition notice of a corporation describe with reasonable particularity the matters on which examination is requested."

In re Harvest Cmtys., 88 S.W.3d 343, 346 (Tex. App.—San Antonio 2002, orig. proceeding). "[P's] counsel, who was taking the deposition, was repeatedly interrupted by long, argumentative objections by [D's counsel], some of which lasted several pages. ... The purpose of [TRCP 199.5] was to prevent [this] kind of obstructive behavior ... and to save substantive complaints for a later hearing before the trial court."

TRCP 200. DEPOSITIONS UPON WRITTEN QUESTIONS

200.1 Procedure for Noticing Deposition Upon Written Questions.

(a) *Who may be noticed; when.* A party may take the testimony of any person or entity by deposition on written questions before any person authorized by law to take depositions on written questions. A notice of intent to take the deposition must be served on the witness and all parties at least 20 days before the deposition is taken. A deposition on written questions may be taken outside the discovery period only by agreement of the parties or with leave of court. The party noticing the deposition must also deliver to the deposition officer a copy of the notice and of all written questions to be asked during the deposition.

(b) *Content of notice.* The notice must comply with Rules 199.1(b), 199.2(b), and 199.5(a)(3). If the witness is an organization, the organization must comply with the requirements of that provision. The notice also may include a request for production of documents as permitted by Rule 199.2(b)(5), the provisions of which will govern the request, service, and response.

200.2 Compelling Witness to Attend. A party may compel the witness to attend the deposition on written questions by serving the witness with a subpoena under Rule 176. If the witness is a party or is retained by, employed by, or otherwise subject to the control of a party, however, service of the deposition notice upon the party's attorney has the same effect as a subpoena served on the witness.

200.3 Questions and Objections.

(a) *Direct questions.* The direct questions to be propounded to the witness must be attached to the notice.

(b) *Objections and additional questions.* Within ten days after the notice and direct questions are served, any party may object to the direct questions and serve cross-questions on all other parties. Within five days after cross-questions are served, any party may object to the cross-questions and serve redirect questions on all other parties. Within three days after redirect questions are served, any party may object to the redirect questions and serve recross questions on all other parties. Objections to recross questions must be served within five days after the earlier of when recross questions are served or the time of the deposition on written questions.

(c) *Objections to form of questions.* Objections to the form of a question are waived unless asserted in accordance with this subdivision.

200.4 Conducting the Deposition Upon Written Questions. The deposition officer must: take the deposition on written questions at the time and place designated; record the testimony of the witness under oath in response to the questions; and prepare, certify, and deliver the deposition transcript in accordance with Rule 203. The deposition officer has authority when necessary to summon and swear an interpreter to facilitate the taking of the deposition.

Comments to 1999 change:

1. The procedures for asserting objections during oral depositions under Rule 199.5(e) do not apply to depositions on written questions.

2. Section 20.001 of the CPRC provides that a deposition on written questions of a witness who is alleged to reside or to be in this state may be taken by a clerk of a district court, a judge or clerk of a county court, or a notary public of this state.

See CPRC §20.001; Gov't Code §§52.021, 52.031; *Commentaries*, "General Rules for Discovery," ch. 6-A; "Scope of Discovery," ch. 6-B; "Depositions," ch. 6-E; FORMS 6E.

History of TRCP 200: Amended eff. Jan. 1, 1999, by order of Dec. 31, 1998 (981-82 S.W.2d [Tex.Cases] xxxix). Adopted eff. Jan. 1, 1999, by order of Nov. 9, 1998 (977-78 S.W.2d [Tex.Cases] lxxi): Repealed former TRCP 200. For subject matter of former TRCP 200, see TRCP 199. Source: New rule.

St. Luke's Episcopal Hosp. v. Garcia, 928 S.W.2d 307, 310 (Tex.App.—Houston [14th Dist.] 1996, orig. proceeding). "Because relator has no objection to the form of [the] written questions, relator claims the provision in [TRCP 200] regarding timeliness of objections is inapplicable. We agree. In its objections to the deposition notice and subpoena duces tecum, relator's primary objections are substantive objections relating to privilege. We hold that the ten-day limitation in [TRCP 200] is inapplicable to substantive objections."

Fibreboard Corp. v. Pool, 813 S.W.2d 658, 677 (Tex. App.—Texarkana 1991, writ denied). "[T]he trial court limited [Ds'] examination of [two witnesses] to 50 cross-questions.... [¶] Until [Ds] exhaust the number of questions allotted to them..., they cannot be heard to complain that they were denied the right to ask additional questions."

TRCP 201. DEPOSITIONS IN FOREIGN JURISDICTIONS FOR USE IN TEXAS PROCEEDINGS; DEPOSITIONS IN TEXAS FOR USE IN FOREIGN PROCEEDINGS

201.1 Depositions in Foreign Jurisdictions for Use in Texas Proceedings.

(a) ***Generally.*** A party may take a deposition on oral examination or written questions of any person or entity located in another state or a foreign country for use in proceedings in this State. The deposition may be taken by:

(1) notice;

(2) letter rogatory, letter of request, or other such device;

(3) agreement of the parties; or

(4) court order.

(b) ***By notice.*** A party may take the deposition by notice in accordance with these rules as if the deposition were taken in this State, except that the deposition officer may be a person authorized to administer oaths in the place where the deposition is taken.

(c) ***By letter rogatory.*** On motion by a party, the court in which an action is pending must issue a letter rogatory on terms that are just and appropriate, regardless of whether any other manner of obtaining the deposition is impractical or inconvenient. The letter must:

(1) be addressed to the appropriate authority in the jurisdiction in which the deposition is to be taken;

(2) request and authorize that authority to summon the witness before the authority at a time and place stated in the letter for examination on oral or written questions; and

(3) request and authorize that authority to cause the witness's testimony to be reduced to writing and returned, together with any items marked as exhibits, to the party requesting the letter rogatory.

(d) ***By letter of request or other such device.*** On motion by a party, the court in which an action is pending, or the clerk of that court, must issue a letter of request or other such device in accordance with an applicable treaty or international convention on terms that are just and appropriate. The letter or other device must be issued regardless of whether any other manner of obtaining the deposition is impractical or inconvenient. The letter or other device must:

(1) be in the form prescribed by the treaty or convention under which it is issued, as presented by the movant to the court or clerk; and

(2) must state the time, place, and manner of the examination of the witness.

(e) ***Objections to form of letter rogatory, letter of request, or other such device.*** In issuing a letter rogatory, letter of request, or other such device, the court must set a time for objecting to the form of the device. A party must make any objection to the form of the device in writing and serve it on all other parties by the time set by the court, or the objection is waived.

(f) ***Admissibility of evidence.*** Evidence obtained in response to a letter rogatory, letter of request, or other such device is not inadmissible merely because it is not a verbatim transcript, or the testimony was not taken under oath, or for any similar departure from the requirements for depositions taken within this State under these rules.

(g) ***Deposition by electronic means.*** A deposition in another jurisdiction may be taken by telephone, videoconference, teleconference, or other electronic means under the provisions of Rule 199.

201.2 Depositions in Texas for Use in Proceedings in Foreign Jurisdictions. If a court of record of any other state or foreign jurisdiction issues a mandate, writ, or commission that requires a witness's oral or written deposition testimony in this State, the witness may be compelled to appear and testify in the same manner and by the same process used for taking testimony in a proceeding pending in this State.

Comments to 1999 change:

1. Rule 201.1 sets forth procedures for obtaining deposition testimony of a witness in another state or foreign jurisdiction for use in Texas court proceedings. It does not, however, address whether any of the procedures listed are, in fact, permitted or recognized by the law of the state or foreign jurisdiction where the witness is located. A party must first determine what procedures are permitted by the jurisdiction where the witness is located before using this rule.

2. Section 20.001 of the CPRC provides a nonexclusive list of persons who are qualified to take a written deposition in Texas and who may take depositions (oral or written) in another state or outside the United States.

3. Rule 201.2 is based on Section 20.002 of the CPRC.

See CPRC §§20.001, 20.002; *Commentaries*, "General Rules for Discovery," ch. 6-A; "Scope of Discovery," ch. 6-B; "Depositions," ch. 6-E; FORMS 6E.

History of TRCP 201: Adopted eff. Jan. 1, 1999, by order of Nov. 9, 1998 (977-78 S.W.2d [Tex.Cases] lxxii): Repealed former TRCP 201. For subject matter of former TRCP 201, see TRCP 199. Source: New rule.

Kugle v. DaimlerChrysler Corp., 88 S.W.3d 355, 362 (Tex.App.—San Antonio 2002, pet. denied). "[Ps] contend that the trial court erred in admitting the deposition testimony of [three deponents] because the depositions were taken in Mexico but the witnesses were only sworn in by a Texas notary public. However, a foreign deposition may be taken by any notary public. [T]he trial court did not abuse its discretion in admitting the depositions."

Clone Component Distrib. v. State, 819 S.W.2d 593, 598 (Tex.App.—Dallas 1991, no writ). "[W]e hold that the requirement of [TRCP 201.1(b)] that the deposition be taken 'before' a person authorized to take oaths was satisfied by the court reporter's being in the vocal and aural presence of the deponent through the use of the telephone."

Latham v. Thornton, 806 S.W.2d 347, 349-50 (Tex. App.—Fort Worth 1991, orig. proceeding). "[A]s regards the person whose deposition is sought, if that person is not a party, the order may only be sought in the court where the deposition is to be taken. In this particular case under the authority of [TRCP] 201, that place is the county of the witness's residence...."

TRCP 202. DEPOSITIONS BEFORE SUIT OR TO INVESTIGATE CLAIMS

202.1 Generally. A person may petition the court for an order authorizing the taking of a deposition on oral examination or written questions either:

(a) to perpetuate or obtain the person's own testimony or that of any other person for use in an anticipated suit; or

(b) to investigate a potential claim or suit.

202.2 Petition. The petition must:

(a) be verified;

(b) be filed in a proper court of any county:

(1) where venue of the anticipated suit may lie, if suit is anticipated; or

(2) where the witness resides, if no suit is yet anticipated;

(c) be in the name of the petitioner;

(d) state either:

(1) that the petitioner anticipates the institution of a suit in which the petitioner may be a party; or

(2) that the petitioner seeks to investigate a potential claim by or against petitioner;

(e) state the subject matter of the anticipated action, if any, and the petitioner's interest therein;

(f) if suit is anticipated, either:

(1) state the names of the persons petitioner expects to have interests adverse to petitioner's in the anticipated suit, and the addresses and telephone numbers for such persons; or

(2) state that the names, addresses, and telephone numbers of persons petitioner expects to have interests adverse to petitioner's in the anticipated suit cannot be ascertained through diligent inquiry, and describe those persons;

(g) state the names, addresses and telephone numbers of the persons to be deposed, the substance of the testimony that the petitioner expects to elicit from each, and the petitioner's reasons for desiring to obtain the testimony of each; and

(h) request an order authorizing the petitioner to take the depositions of the persons named in the petition.

202.3 Notice and Service.

(a) ***Personal service on witnesses and persons named.*** At least 15 days before the date of the hearing on the petition, the petitioner must serve the petition and a notice of the hearing—in accordance with Rule 21a—on all persons petitioner seeks to depose and, if suit is anticipated, on all persons petitioner expects to have interests adverse to petitioner's in the anticipated suit.

(b) ***Service by publication on persons not named.***

(1) *Manner.* Unnamed persons described in the petition whom the petitioner expects to have interests adverse to petitioner's in the anticipated suit, if any, may be served by publication with the petition and notice of the hearing. The notice must state the place for the hearing and the time it will be held, which must be more than 14 days after the first publication of the notice. The petition and notice must be published once each week for two consecutive weeks in the newspaper of broadest circulation in the county in which the petition is filed, or if no such newspaper exists, in the newspaper of broadest circulation in the nearest county where a newspaper is published.

(2) *Objection to depositions taken on notice by publication.* Any interested party may move, in the proceeding or by bill of review, to suppress any deposition, in whole or in part, taken on notice by publication, and may also attack or oppose the deposition by any other means available.

(c) ***Service in probate cases.*** A petition to take a deposition in anticipation of an application for probate of a will, and notice of the hearing on the petition, may be served by posting as prescribed by Section 33(f)(2) of the Probate Code. The notice and petition must be directed to all parties interested in the testator's estate and must comply with the requirements of Section 33(c) of the Probate Code insofar as they may be applicable.

(d) ***Modification by order.*** As justice or necessity may require, the court may shorten or lengthen the notice periods under this rule and may extend the notice period to permit service on any expected adverse party.

202.4 Order.

(a) ***Required findings.*** The court must order a deposition to be taken if, but only if, it finds that:

(1) allowing the petitioner to take the requested deposition may prevent a failure or delay of justice in an anticipated suit; or

(2) the likely benefit of allowing the petitioner to take the requested deposition to investigate a potential claim outweighs the burden or expense of the procedure.

(b) ***Contents.*** The order must state whether a deposition will be taken on oral examination or written questions. The order may also state the time and place at which a deposition will be taken. If the order does not state the time and place at which a deposition will be taken, the petitioner must notice the deposition as required by Rules 199 or 200. The order must contain any protections the court finds necessary or appropriate to protect the witness or any person who may be affected by the procedure.

202.5 Manner of Taking and Use. Except as otherwise provided in this rule, depositions authorized by this rule are governed by the rules applicable to depositions of nonparties in a pending suit. The scope of discovery in depositions authorized by this rule is the same as if the anticipated suit or potential claim had been filed. A court may restrict or prohibit the use of a deposition taken under this rule in a subsequent suit to protect a person who was not served with notice of the deposition from any unfair prejudice or to prevent abuse of this rule.

Comments to 1999 change:

1. This rule applies to all discovery before suit covered by former rules governing depositions to perpetuate testimony and bills of discovery.

2. A deposition taken under this rule may be used in a subsequent suit as permitted by the rules of evidence, except that a court may restrict or prohibit its use to prevent taking unfair advantage of a witness or others. The bill of discovery procedure, which Rule 202 incorporates, is equitable in nature, and a court must not permit it to be used inequitably.

See CPRC §20.001; ***Commentaries***, "General Rules for Discovery," ch. 6-A; "Scope of Discovery," ch. 6-B; "Depositions," ch. 6-E; FORMS 6E.

History of TRCP 202: Adopted eff. Jan. 1, 1999, by order of Nov. 9, 1998 (977-78 S.W.2d [Tex.Cases] lxxiv): Repealed former TRCP 202. For subject matter of former TRCP 202, see TRCP 199. Source: New rule.

U.S. v. Marks, 949 S.W.2d 320, 322 (Tex.1997). TRCP 202 "authorizes a court to order the taking of a deposition to perpetuate testimony in anticipation of litigation."

Office Employees Int'l Un. v. Southwestern Drug Corp., 391 S.W.2d 404, 406 (Tex.1965). "[A] proceeding to perpetuate testimony is not of itself an independent suit, but is in aid of and incident to an anticipated suit."

In re Akzo Nobel Chem., 24 S.W.3d 919, 921 (Tex. App.—Beaumont 2000, orig. proceeding). "Neither by its language nor by implication can we construe [TRCP] 202 to authorize a trial court, before suit is filed, to order any form of discovery but deposition."

Removal

Texas v. Real Parties in Interest, 259 F.3d 387, 394 (5th Cir.2001). When TRCP 202 is used as an investigatory tool for potential claims, it is not a claim subject to removal. *See also* ***Mayfield-George v. Texas Rehab. Comm'n***, 197 F.R.D. 280, 283 (N.D. Tex.2000).

TRCP 203. SIGNING, CERTIFICATION & USE OF ORAL & WRITTEN DEPOSITIONS

203.1 Signature and Changes.

(a) ***Deposition transcript to be provided to witness.*** The deposition officer must provide the original deposition transcript to the witness for examination and signature. If the witness is represented by an attorney at the deposition, the deposition officer must provide the transcript to the attorney instead of the witness.

(b) ***Changes by witness; signature.*** The witness may change responses as reflected in the deposition transcript by indicating the desired changes, in writing, on a separate sheet of paper, together with a statement of the reasons for making the changes. No erasures or obliterations of any kind may be made to the original deposition transcript. The witness must then sign the transcript under oath and return it to the deposition officer. If the witness does not return the transcript to the deposition officer within 20 days of the

TRCP 203

date the transcript was provided to the witness or the witness's attorney, the witness may be deemed to have waived the right to make the changes.

(c) ***Exceptions.*** The requirements of presentation and signature under this subdivision do not apply:

(1) if the witness and all parties waive the signature requirement;

(2) to depositions on written questions; or

(3) to nonstenographic recordings of oral depositions.

203.2 **Certification.** The deposition officer must file with the court, serve on all parties, and attach as part of the deposition transcript or nonstenographic recording of an oral deposition a certificate duly sworn by the officer stating:

(a) that the witness was duly sworn by the officer and that the transcript or nonstenographic recording of the oral deposition is a true record of the testimony given by the witness;

(b) that the deposition transcript, if any, was submitted to the witness or to the attorney for the witness for examination and signature, the date on which the transcript was submitted, whether the witness returned the transcript, and if so, the date on which it was returned.

(c) that changes, if any, made by the witness are attached to the deposition transcript;

(d) that the deposition officer delivered the deposition transcript or nonstenographic recording of an oral deposition in accordance with Rule 203.3;

(e) the amount of time used by each party at the deposition;

(f) the amount of the deposition officer's charges for preparing the original deposition transcript, which the clerk of the court must tax as costs; and

(g) that a copy of the certificate was served on all parties and the date of service.

203.3 **Delivery.**

(a) ***Endorsement; to whom delivered.*** The deposition officer must endorse the title of the action and "Deposition of (name of witness)" on the original deposition transcript (or a copy, if the original was not returned) or the original nonstenographic recording of an oral deposition, and must return:

(1) the transcript to the party who asked the first question appearing in the transcript, or

(2) the recording to the party who requested it.

(b) ***Notice.*** The deposition officer must serve notice of delivery on all other parties.

(c) ***Inspection and copying; copies.*** The party receiving the original deposition transcript or nonstenographic recording must make it available upon reasonable request for inspection and copying by any other party. Any party or the witness is entitled to obtain a copy of the deposition transcript or nonstenographic recording from the deposition officer upon payment of a reasonable fee.

203.4 **Exhibits.** At the request of a party, the original documents and things produced for inspection during the examination of the witness must be marked for identification by the deposition officer and annexed to the deposition transcript or nonstenographic recording. The person producing the materials may produce copies instead of originals if the party gives all other parties fair opportunity at the deposition to compare the copies with the originals. If the person offers originals rather than copies, the deposition officer must, after the conclusion of the deposition, make copies to be attached to the original deposition transcript or nonstenographic recording, and then return the originals to the person who produced them. The person who produced the originals must preserve them for hearing or trial and make them available for inspection or copying by any other party upon seven days' notice. Copies annexed to the original deposition transcript or nonstenographic recording may be used for all purposes.

203.5 **Motion to Suppress.** A party may object to any errors and irregularities in the manner in which the testimony is transcribed, signed, delivered, or otherwise dealt with by the deposition officer by filing a motion to suppress all or part of the deposition. If the deposition officer complies with Rule 203.3 at least one day before the case is called to trial, with regard to a deposition transcript, or 30 days before the case is called to trial, with regard to a nonstenographic recording, the party must file and serve a motion to suppress before trial commences to preserve the objections.

203.6 **Use.**

(a) ***Nonstenographic recording; transcription.*** A nonstenographic recording of an oral deposition, or a written transcription of all or part of such a recording, may be used to the same extent as a deposition taken by stenographic means. However, the court, for good cause shown, may require that the party seeking to use a nonstenographic recording or written transcription first obtain a complete transcript of the deposition recording from a certified court reporter. The court reporter's transcription must be made from the original or a certified copy of the deposition recording. The court reporter must, to the extent applicable, comply with the provisions of this rule, except that the court reporter must deliver the original transcript to the attorney requesting the transcript, and the court reporter's certificate must include a statement that the transcript is a true record of the nonstenographic recording. The party to whom the court reporter delivers the original transcript must make the transcript available, upon reasonable request, for inspection and copying by the witness or any party.

(b) ***Same proceeding.*** All or part of a deposition may be used for any purpose in the same proceeding in which it was taken. If the original is not filed, a certified copy may be used. "Same proceeding" includes a proceeding in a different court but involving the same subject matter and the same parties or their representatives or successors in interest. A deposition is admissible against a party joined after the deposition was taken if:

(1) the deposition is admissible pursuant to Rule 804(b)(1) of the Rules of Evidence, or

(2) that party has had a reasonable opportunity to redepose the witness and has failed to do so.

(c) ***Different proceeding.*** Depositions taken in different proceedings may be used as permitted by the Rules of Evidence.

See Gov't Code §52.021; ***Commentaries***, "General Rules for Discovery," ch. 6-A; "Depositions," ch. 6-E. Lawyers can find important information about the conduct of the deposition in the Supreme Court's rules regarding court reporters in the Uniform Format Manual for Texas Court Reporters §12 cmt., which can be found at www.supreme.courts.state.tx.us/rules/reporter.

History of TRCP 203: Adopted eff. Jan. 1, 1999, by order of Nov. 9, 1998 (977-78 S.W.2d [Tex.Cases] lxxvi): Repealed former TRCP 203. For subject matter of former TRCP 203, see TRCP 176. New rule is former TRCP 206 and 207, with modification. Source: New rule.

Jones v. Colley, 820 S.W.2d 863, 866 (Tex.App.—Texarkana 1991, writ denied). "No rule requires that a deposition be read into the record or played before the jury in chronological order. A party, as a matter of trial strategy, is entitled to present his evidence in the order he believes constitutes the most effective presentation of his case, provided that it does not convey a *distinctly false* impression."

Klorer v. Block, 717 S.W.2d 754, 759 (Tex.App.—San Antonio 1986, writ ref'd n.r.e.). "The statement in [TRCP 203.5] that a deposition shall have been filed at least one entire day before the day of trial is a condition precedent to the filing of a *written* motion to suppress. This rule does not require that *all* depositions must be filed at least one entire day before the day of trial."

TRCP 204. PHYSICAL & MENTAL EXAMINATIONS

204.1 Motion and Order Required.

(a) ***Motion.*** A party may—no later than 30 days before the end of any applicable discovery period—move for an order compelling another party to:

(1) submit to a physical or mental examination by a qualified physician or a mental examination by a qualified psychologist; or

(2) produce for such examination a person in the other party's custody, conservatorship or legal control.

(b) ***Service.*** The motion and notice of hearing must be served on the person to be examined and all parties.

(c) ***Requirements for obtaining order.*** The court may issue an order for examination only for good cause shown and only in the following circumstances:

(1) when the mental or physical condition (including the blood group) of a party, or of a person in the custody, conservatorship or under the legal control of a party, is in controversy; or

(2) except as provided in Rule 204.4, an examination by a psychologist may be ordered when the party responding to the motion has designated a psychologist as a testifying expert or has disclosed a psychologist's records for possible use at trial.

(d) ***Requirements of order.*** The order must be in writing and must specify the time, place, manner, conditions, and scope of the examination and the person or persons by whom it is to be made.

204.2 Report of Examining Physician or Psychologist.

(a) ***Right to report.*** Upon request of the person ordered to be examined, the party causing the examination to be made must deliver to the person a copy of a detailed written report of the examining physician or psychologist setting out the findings, including results of all tests made, diagnoses and conclusions, together with like reports of all earlier examinations of the same condition. After delivery of the report, upon request of the party causing the examination, the party against whom the order is made must produce a like report of any examination made before or after the ordered examination of the same condition, unless the person examined is not a party and the party shows that the party is unable to obtain it. The court on motion may limit delivery of a report on such terms as are just. If a physician or psychologist fails or refuses to make a report the court may exclude the testimony if offered at the trial.

(b) *Agreements; relationship to other rules.* This subdivision applies to examinations made by agreement of the parties, unless the agreement expressly provides otherwise. This subdivision does not preclude discovery of a report of an examining physician or psychologist or the taking of a deposition of the physician or psychologist in accordance with the provisions of any other rule.

204.3 Effect of No Examination. If no examination is sought either by agreement or under this subdivision, the party whose physical or mental condition is in controversy must not comment to the court or jury concerning the party's willingness to submit to an examination, or on the right or failure of any other party to seek an examination.

204.4 Cases Arising Under Titles II or V, Family Code. In cases arising under Family Code Titles II or V, the court may—on its own initiative or on motion of a party—appoint:

(a) one or more psychologists or psychiatrists to make any and all appropriate mental examinations of the children who are the subject of the suit or of any other parties, and may make such appointment irrespective of whether a psychologist or psychiatrist has been designated by any party as a testifying expert;

(b) one or more experts who are qualified in paternity testing to take blood, body fluid, or tissue samples to conduct paternity tests as ordered by the court.

204.5 Definition. For the purpose of this rule, a psychologist is a person licensed or certified by a state or the District of Columbia as a psychologist.

See TRE 510(d)(5); ***Commentaries***, "General Rules for Discovery," ch. 6-A; "Scope of Discovery," ch. 6-B; "Medical Records," ch. 6-I; FORMS 6I.

History of TRCP 204: Adopted eff. Jan. 1, 1999, by order of Nov. 9, 1998 (977-78 S.W.2d [Tex.Cases] lxxix): Repealed former TRCP 204. For subject matter of former TRCP 204, see TRCP 199. New rule is former 167a, with modification. Source: New rule.

Coates v. Whittington, 758 S.W.2d 749, 751 (Tex. 1988). TRCP 204 "places an affirmative burden on the movant to meet a two pronged test: (1) the movant must show that the party's mental condition is 'in controversy'; and (2) the movant must demonstrate that there is 'good cause' for a compulsory mental examination. In the absence of an affirmative showing of both prongs of the test, a trial court may not order an examination pursuant to [TRCP 204.1]."

In re Transwestern Publ'g Relators Co., 96 S.W.3d 501, 506 (Tex.App.—Fort Worth 2002, orig. proceeding). "[E]ven if the person to be examined has designated a psychologist to testify regarding her mental condition, the party seeking the examination must still demonstrate 'good cause' for the examination. 'Good cause' is not assumed merely because a psychologist has been appointed to testify as an expert regarding the subject's mental condition."

In re Caballero, 36 S.W.3d 143, 145 (Tex.App.—Corpus Christi 2000, orig. proceeding). Good cause "requires an affirmative showing of three components: (1) that an examination is relevant to issues that are genuinely in controversy in the case; (2) that a reasonable nexus exists between the condition in controversy and the examination sought; and (3) that it is not possible to obtain the desired information through means that are less intrusive than a compelled examination."

In re Doe, 22 S.W.3d 601, 606 (Tex.App.—Austin 2000, orig. proceeding). "A court may compel [P] to submit to a mental examination only if *[P] asserts a mental injury that exceeds the common emotional reaction to an injury or loss.*"

TRCP 205. DISCOVERY FROM NONPARTIES

205.1 Forms of Discovery; Subpoena Requirement. A party may compel discovery from a nonparty—that is, a person who is not a party or subject to a party's control—only by obtaining a court order under Rules 196.7, 202, or 204, or by serving a subpoena compelling:

(a) an oral deposition;

(b) a deposition on written questions;

(c) a request for production of documents or tangible things, pursuant to Rule 199.2(b)(5) or Rule

200.1(b), served with a notice of deposition on oral examination or written questions; and

(d) a request for production of documents and tangible things under this rule.

205.2 Notice. A party seeking discovery by subpoena from a nonparty must serve, on the nonparty and all parties, a copy of the form of notice required under the rules governing the applicable form of discovery. A notice of oral or written deposition must be served before or at the same time that a subpoena compelling attendance or production under the notice is served. A notice to produce documents or tangible things under Rule 205.3 must be served at least 10 days before the subpoena compelling production is served.

205.3 Production of Documents and Tangible Things Without Deposition.

(a) ***Notice; subpoena.*** A party may compel production of documents and tangible things from a nonparty by serving—a reasonable time before the response is due but no later than 30 days before the end of any applicable discovery period—the notice required in Rule 205.2 and a subpoena compelling production or inspection of documents or tangible things.

(b) ***Contents of notice.*** The notice must state:

(1) the name of the person from whom production or inspection is sought to be compelled;

(2) a reasonable time and place for the production or inspection; and

(3) the items to be produced or inspected, either by individual item or by category, describing each item and category with reasonable particularity, and, if applicable, describing the desired testing and sampling with sufficient specificity to inform the nonparty of the means, manner, and procedure for testing or sampling.

(c) ***Requests for production of medical or mental health records of other nonparties.*** If a party requests a nonparty to produce medical or mental health records of another nonparty, the requesting party must serve the nonparty whose records are sought with the notice required under this rule. This requirement does not apply under the circumstances set forth in Rule 196.1(c)(2).

(d) ***Response.*** The nonparty must respond to the notice and subpoena in accordance with Rule 176.6.

(e) ***Custody, inspection and copying.*** The party obtaining the production must make all materials produced available for inspection by any other party on reasonable notice, and must furnish copies to any party who requests at that party's expense.

(f) ***Cost of production.*** A party requiring production of documents by a nonparty must reimburse the nonparty's reasonable costs of production.

Comments to 1999 change: Under this rule, a party may subpoena production of documents and tangible things from nonparties without need for a motion or oral or written deposition.

See ***Commentaries***, "General Rules for Discovery," ch. 6-A; "Scope of Discovery," ch. 6-B; "Depositions," ch. 6-E; "Securing Documents & Tangible Things," ch. 6-H.

History of TRCP 205: Amended eff. Jan. 1, 1999, by order of Dec. 31, 1998 (981-82 S.W.2d [Tex.Cases] xxxix-xl). Adopted eff. Jan. 1, 1999, by order of Nov. 9, 1998 (977-78 S.W.2d [Tex.Cases] lxxx): Repealed former TRCP 205. For subject matter of former TRCP 205, see TRCP 203. Source: New rule.

Automatic Drilling Machs. v. Miller, 515 S.W.2d 256, 259 (Tex.1974). "Under the general provisions of [TRCP 205], a subpoena may be issued in a proper case to require a witness to produce, at the time and place of giving his deposition, documents and other tangible things which constitute or contain evidence relating to any of the matters.... The subpoena is, however, subject to the provisions of [TRCP 176 & 192]."

In re Diversicare Gen. Partner, 41 S.W.3d 788, 794 (Tex.App.—Corpus Christi 2001, orig. proceeding). "[P]ersonal and clinical records do not have to be in the nonparty's possession to be described as nonparty records, they only have to be personal and clinical records *regarding* the nonparty."

TRCP 206 - 209. REPEALED

TRCP 206, 207, 208, and 209 were repealed eff. Jan. 1, 1999, by order of Nov. 9, 1998 (977-78 S.W.2d [Tex.Cases] xxxiii). TRCP 208a was repealed eff. Apr. 1, 1984, by order of Dec. 5, 1983 (661-62 S.W.2d [Tex.Cases] lxvii). For subject matter of former TRCP 206 and 207, see TRCP 203. For subject matter of former TRCP 208, see TRCP 200. For subject matter of former TRCP 208a, see TRCP 203.

TRCP 210 - 214. REPEALED

Repealed eff. Apr. 1, 1984, by order of Dec. 5, 1983 (661-62 S.W.2d [Tex.Cases] lxviii): For subject matter of former TRCP 210, see TRCP 203. For subject matter of former TRCP 211 to 213, see TRCP 203.

TRCP 215. ABUSE OF DISCOVERY; SANCTIONS

215.1 Motion for Sanctions or Order Compelling Discovery. A party, upon reasonable notice to other parties and all other persons affected thereby, may apply for sanctions or an order compelling discovery as follows:

(a) ***Appropriate court.*** On matters relating to a deposition, an application for an order to a party may be made to the court in which the action is pending, or to any district court in the district where the deposition is being taken. An application for an order to a deponent who is not a party shall be made to the court in the district where the deposition is being taken. As to all other discovery matters, an application for an order will be made to the court in which the action is pending.

(b) ***Motion.***

(1) If a party or other deponent which is a corporation or other entity fails to make a designation under Rules 199.2(b)(1) or 200.1(b); or

(2) if a party, or other deponent, or a person designated to testify on behalf of a party or other deponent fails:

(A) to appear before the officer who is to take his deposition, after being served with a proper notice; or

(B) to answer a question propounded or submitted upon oral examination or upon written questions; or

(3) if a party fails:

(A) to serve answers or objections to interrogatories submitted under Rule 197, after proper service of the interrogatories; or

(B) to answer an interrogatory submitted under Rule 197; or

(C) to serve a written response to a request for inspection submitted under Rule 196, after proper service of the request; or

(D) to respond that discovery will be permitted as requested or fails to permit discovery as requested in response to a request for inspection submitted under Rule 196;

the discovering party may move for an order compelling a designation, an appearance, an answer or answers, or inspection or production in accordance with the request, or apply to the court in which the action is pending for the imposition of any sanction authorized by Rule 215.2(b) without the necessity of first having obtained a court order compelling such discovery.

When taking a deposition on oral examination, the proponent of the question may complete or adjourn the examination before he applies for an order.

If the court denies the motion in whole or in part, it may make such protective order as it would have been empowered to make on a motion pursuant to Rule 192.6.

(c) ***Evasive or incomplete answer.*** For purposes of this subdivision an evasive or incomplete answer is to be treated as a failure to answer.

(d) ***Disposition of motion to compel: award of expenses.*** If the motion is granted, the court shall, after opportunity for hearing, require a party or deponent whose conduct necessitated the motion or the party or attorney advising such conduct or both of them to pay, at such time as ordered by the court, the moving party the reasonable expenses incurred in obtaining the order, including attorney fees, unless the court finds that the opposition to the motion was substantially justified or that other circumstances make an award of expenses unjust. Such an order shall be subject to review on appeal from the final judgment.

If the motion is denied, the court may, after opportunity for hearing, require the moving party or attorney advising such motion to pay to the party or deponent who opposed the motion the reasonable expenses incurred in opposing the motion, including attorney fees, unless the court finds that the making of the motion was substantially justified or that other circumstances make an award of expenses unjust.

If the motion is granted in part and denied in part, the court may apportion the reasonable expenses incurred in relation to the motion among the parties and persons in a just manner.

In determining the amount of reasonable expenses, including attorney fees, to be awarded in connection with a motion, the trial court shall award expenses which are reasonable in relation to the amount of work reasonably expended in obtaining an order compelling compliance or in opposing a motion which is denied.

(e) ***Providing person's own statement.*** If a party fails to comply with any person's written request for the person's own statement as provided in Rule 192.3(h), the person who made the request may move for an order compelling compliance. If the motion is granted, the movant may recover the expenses incurred in obtaining the order, including attorney fees, which are reasonable in relation to the amount of work reasonably expended in obtaining the order.

215.2 Failure to Comply with Order or with Discovery Request.

(a) ***Sanctions by court in district where deposition is taken.*** If a deponent fails to appear or to be sworn or to answer a question after being directed to do so by a district court in the district in which the deposition is being taken, the failure may be considered a contempt of that court.

(b) ***Sanctions by court in which action is pending.*** If a party or an officer, director, or managing agent of a party or a person designated under Rules 199.2(b)(1) or 200.1(b) to testify on behalf of a party fails to comply with proper discovery requests or to obey an order to provide or permit discovery, including an order made under Rules 204 or 215.1, the court in which the action is pending may, after notice and hearing, make such orders in regard to the failure as are just, and among others the following:

(1) an order disallowing any further discovery of any kind or of a particular kind by the disobedient party;

(2) an order charging all or any portion of the expenses of discovery or taxable court costs or both against the disobedient party or the attorney advising him;

(3) an order that the matters regarding which the order was made or any other designated facts shall be taken to be established for the purposes of the action in accordance with the claim of the party obtaining the order;

(4) an order refusing to allow the disobedient party to support or oppose designated claims or defenses, or prohibiting him from introducing designated matters in evidence;

(5) an order striking out pleadings or parts thereof, or staying further proceedings until the order is obeyed, or dismissing with or without prejudice the action or proceedings or any part thereof, or rendering a judgment by default against the disobedient party;

(6) in lieu of any of the foregoing orders or in addition thereto, an order treating as a contempt of court the failure to obey any orders except an order to submit to a physical or mental examination;

(7) when a party has failed to comply with an order under Rule 204 requiring him to appear or produce another for examination, such orders as are listed in paragraphs (1), (2), (3), (4) or (5) of this subdivision, unless the person failing to comply shows that he is unable to appear or to produce such person for examination.

(8) In lieu of any of the foregoing orders or in addition thereto, the court shall require the party failing to obey the order or the attorney advising him, or both, to pay, at such time as ordered by the court, the reasonable expenses, including attorney fees, caused by the failure, unless the court finds that the failure was substantially justified or that other circumstances make an award of expenses unjust. Such an order shall be subject to review on appeal from the final judgment.

(c) ***Sanction against nonparty for violation of Rules 196.7 or 205.3.*** If a nonparty fails to comply with an order under Rules 196.7 or 205.3, the court which made the order may treat the failure to obey as contempt of court.

215.3 Abuse of Discovery Process in Seeking, Making, or Resisting Discovery. If the court finds a party is abusing the discovery process in seeking, making or resisting discovery or if the court finds that any interrogatory or request for inspection or production is unreasonably frivolous, oppressive, or harassing, or that a response or answer is unreasonably frivolous or made for purposes of delay, then the court in which the action is pending may, after notice and hearing, impose any appropriate sanction authorized by paragraphs (1), (2), (3), (4), (5), and (8) of Rule 215.2(b). Such order of sanction shall be subject to review on appeal from the final judgment.

215.4 Failure to Comply with Rule 198.

(a) ***Motion.*** A party who has requested an admission under Rule 198 may move to determine the sufficiency of the answer or objection. For purposes of this subdivision an evasive or incomplete answer may be treated as a failure to answer. Unless the court determines that an objection is justified, it shall order that an answer be served. If the court determines that an answer does not comply with the requirements of Rule 198, it may order either that the matter is admitted or that an amended answer be served. The provisions of Rule 215.1(d) apply to the award of expenses incurred in relation to the motion.

(b) ***Expenses on failure to admit.*** If a party fails to admit the genuineness of any document or the truth of any matter as requested under Rule 198 and if the party requesting the admissions thereafter proves the genuineness of the document or the truth of the matter, he may apply to the court for an order requiring the other party to pay him the reasonable expenses incurred in making that proof, including reasonable attorney fees. The court shall make the order unless it finds that (1) the request was held objectionable pursuant to Rule 193, or (2) the admission sought was of no substantial importance, or (3) the party failing to admit had a reasonable ground to believe that he might prevail on the matter, or (4) there was other good reason for the failure to admit.

215.5 Failure of Party or Witness to Attend or to Serve Subpoena; Expenses.

(a) ***Failure of party giving notice to attend.*** If the party giving the notice of the taking of an oral deposition fails to attend and proceed therewith and another party attends in person or by attorney pursuant to the notice, the court may order the party giving the notice to pay such other party the reasonable expenses incurred by him and his attorney in attending, including reasonable attorney fees.

(b) ***Failure of witness to attend.*** If a party gives notice of the taking of an oral deposition of a witness and the witness does not attend because of the fault of the party giving the notice, if another party attends in person or by attorney because he expects the deposition of that witness to be taken, the court may order the party giving the notice to pay such other party the reasonable expenses incurred by him and his attorney in attending, including reasonable attorney fees.

215.6 Exhibits to Motions and Responses. Motions or responses made under this rule may have exhibits attached including affidavits, discovery pleadings, or any other documents.

Comments to 1999 change: The references in this rule to other discovery rules are changed to reflect the revisions in those rules, and former Rule 203 is added as Rule 215.5 in place of the former provision, which is superseded by Rule 193.6.

See CPRC ch. 10; ***Commentaries***, "Motion for Sanctions," ch. 5-J; "General Rules for Discovery," ch. 6-A; "Depositions," ch. 6-E; "Interrogatories," ch. 6-F; "Securing Documents & Tangible Things," ch. 6-H; FORMS 6A.

History of TRCP 215: Amended eff. Jan. 1, 1999, by order of Dec. 31, 1998 (981-82 S.W.2d [Tex.Cases] xl). Amended eff. Jan. 1, 1999, by order of Nov. 9, 1998 (977-78 S.W.2d [Tex.Cases] lxxxii). Source: Former 215, with modification. Amended eff. Sept. 1, 1990, by order of Apr. 24, 1990 (785-86 S.W.2d [Tex.Cases] lxiii): Requires notice and hearing in TRCP 215(3); adds "appropriate" before "sanction" in same par.; requires notice and hearing before an imposition of sanctions under par. 3, and to specify that such sanctions be appropriate. Amended eff. Jan. 1, 1988, by order of July 15, 1987 (733-34 S.W.2d [Tex.Cases] lxiv): Changed (5) & (6); this amendment states that the party offering the evidence has the burden of establishing good cause for any failure to supplement discovery before trial and provides a manner for making a record for discovery hearings. Added new rule eff. Apr. 1, 1984, by order of Dec. 5, 1983 (661-62 S.W.2d [Tex.Cases] lxviii): TRCP 170 was deleted because TRCP 215 covers conduct in violation of TRCP 167; purpose of revisions to TRCP 168, the deletion of TRCP 170, and the provisions of new TRCP 215 is to clarify when the most severe sanctions are authorized; TRCP 215 retains the conclusion reached in *Lewis v. Illinois Employers Ins. Co.*, 590 S.W.2d 119 (Tex.1979), and extends such rule to cover all discovery requests, except requests for admissions; TRCP 215 leaves to the discretion of the court whether to impose sanctions with or without an order compelling discovery, so that the court will be free to apply the proper sanction or order based upon the degree of the discovery abuse involved; the rule is rewritten to gather all discovery sanctions into a single rule; it includes specific provisions concerning the consequences of failing to comply with TRCP 169, and spells out penalties imposable upon a party who fails to supplement discovery responses; it provides for sanctions for those who seek to make discovery in an abusive manner. Adopted eff. Sept. 1, 1941, by order of Oct. 29, 1940 (3 Tex.B.J. 557 [1940]). Source: TRCS art. 3768 (repealed). Original TRCP 215 related to deposition of party.

Spohn Hosp. v. Mayer, 104 S.W.3d 878, 882 (Tex. 2003). For sanctions to be just, "there must be a direct nexus among the offensive conduct, the offender, and the sanction imposed. A just sanction must be directed against the abuse and toward remedying the prejudice caused to the innocent party, and the sanction should be visited upon the offender. The trial court must attempt to determine whether the offensive conduct is attributable to counsel only, to the party only, or to both."

Occidental Chem. Corp. v. Banales, 907 S.W.2d 488, 490 (Tex.1995). "The sanction imposed for discovery abuse should be no more severe than necessary to satisfy the legitimate purposes of the discovery process offended. The work product privilege is essential to the attorney-client relationship. Requiring the production of the attorney's notes from interviews of witnesses is a severe sanction and should receive an appropriately strict review. Piercing the work product privilege, like the 'death penalty' sanction, should apply only when lesser sanctions are inadequate to correct the discovery abuse that has occurred, i.e., when it is the only appropriate sanction. Here the record does not reflect why lesser traditional sanctions might not cure the discovery abuse."

Global Servs. v. Bianchi, 901 S.W.2d 934, 938 (Tex. 1995). "We recognize that it is often difficult to prove that a party has withheld documents from discovery. Direct evidence of such conduct is seldom available, and it may be necessary to rely entirely upon circumstantial evidence. But an imposition of sanctions cannot be based merely on a party's bald assertions. There must be some evidence to show an abuse of discovery before sanctions can be imposed. [The district] court ordered [D] to keep trying to produce all the documents requested, and prohibited [D] from conducting any discovery of its own until it complied."

DPS Officers Ass'n v. Denton, 897 S.W.2d 757, 760 (Tex.1995). "A trial court has limited authority to dismiss a cause of action on its own initiative."

Remington Arms Co. v. Caldwell, 850 S.W.2d 167, 170 (Tex.1993). "[I]f pretrial discovery abuse is not revealed until after the trial has begun, or even after trial, a party cannot be said to have waived a claim for sanctions." *See also* ***Cathey v. Meyer***, 115 S.W.3d 644, 672 (Tex.App.—Waco 2003, n.p.h.).

Chrysler Corp. v. Blackmon, 841 S.W.2d 844, 849 (Tex.1992). "Two factors mark the bounds of the trial court's discretion in order for sanctions to be just: first, a direct relationship between the offensive conduct and the sanction imposed must exist; and second, the sanction imposed must not be excessive. [¶] A permissible sanction should, therefore, be no more severe than required to satisfy legitimate purposes. This means that a court must consider relatively less stringent sanctions first to determine whether lesser sanctions will fully promote compliance, deterrence, and discourage further abuse." *See also* ***Hamill v. Level***, 917 S.W.2d 15, 16 (Tex.1996).

TransAmerican Nat. Gas Corp. v. Powell, 811 S.W.2d 913, 917 (Tex.1991). "The punishment [for discovery abuse] should fit the crime. *At 918:* Discovery sanctions cannot be used to adjudicate the merits of a party's claims or defenses unless a party's hindrance of the discovery process justifies a presumption that its claims or defenses lack merit."

TRCP 215a - 215c. REPEALED

Repealed eff. Apr. 1, 1984, by order of Dec. 5, 1983 (661-62 S.W.2d [Tex.Cases] lxviii): For subject matter of former TRCP 215a, see TRCP 215; for subject matter of former TRCP 215b, see TRCP 203; for subject matter of former TRCP 215c, see TRCP 202.

SECTION 10. THE JURY IN COURT

TRCP 216. REQUEST & FEE FOR JURY TRIAL

a. Request. No jury trial shall be had in any civil suit, unless a written request for a jury trial is filed with the clerk of the court a reasonable time before the date set for trial of the cause on the non-jury docket, but not less than thirty days in advance.

b. Jury Fee. Unless otherwise provided by law, a fee of ten dollars if in the district court and five dollars if in the county court must be deposited with the clerk of the court within the time for making a written request for a jury trial. The clerk shall promptly enter a notation of the payment of such fee upon the court's docket sheet.

See U.S. Const. amend. 7; Tex. Const. art. 1, §15; Gov't Code §51.604; ***Commentaries***, "Request for Jury Trial," ch. 5-B; FORMS 5B.

History of TRCP 216: Amended eff. Sept. 1, 1990, by order of Apr. 24, 1990 (785-86 S.W.2d [Tex.Cases] lxiv): (1) and (2) renumbered as letters (a) and (b); "Unless otherwise provided by law" added to the beginning of (b); additional fees for jury trials may be required by other law, *e.g.*, Texas Gov't Code §51.604. Amended eff. Jan. 1, 1988, by order of July 15, 1987 (733-34 S.W.2d [Tex.Cases] lxv). Amended eff. Mar. 1, 1950, by order of Oct. 12, 1949 (12 Tex.B.J. 534 [1949]). Amended eff. Dec. 31, 1941, by order of Sept. 20, 1941 (4 Tex.B.J. 520 [1941]). Amended eff. Sept. 1, 1941, by order of Mar. 31, 1941 (4 Tex.B.J. 172 [1941]). Adopted eff. Sept. 1, 1941, by order of Oct. 29, 1940 (3 Tex.B.J. 558 [1940]). Source: TRCS arts. 2124, 2125 (repealed).

G.M. Corp. v. Gayle, 951 S.W.2d 469, 476 (Tex. 1997). "Even where a party does not timely pay the jury fee, courts have held that a trial court should accord the right to jury trial if it can be done without interfering with the court's docket, delaying the trial, or injuring the opposing party. *At 477:* [D] established that a 30-day continuance to perfect [D's] jury trial demand would not cause [Ps] any injury or delay. [T]he trial court's seriatim trial schedule seems only a sham to hold [D] to its mistake in not paying the jury fee without penalizing the other side."

Ricardo N., Inc. v. Turcios de Argueta, 907 S.W.2d 423, 429 (Tex.1995). "Assuming [D's] request for a jury in advance of the first trial setting was not timely made, that request had certainly become timely when the case was remanded from federal court 4 years later."

Halsell v. DeHoyos, 810 S.W.2d 371, 371 (Tex. 1991). "A [jury] request in advance of the 30-day deadline [of TRCP 216] is presumed to have been made a reasonable time before trial."

Crittenden v. Crittenden, 52 S.W.3d 768, 769 (Tex. App.—San Antonio 2001, pet. denied). "[T]he party opposing the [jury] request may rebut the presumption by showing a jury trial will: (1) injure the party, (2) disrupt the trial court's docket, or (3) impede the ordinary handling of the court's business."

In re V.R.W., 41 S.W.3d 183, 194-95 (Tex.App.—Houston [14th Dist.] 2001, no pet.). "The refusal to grant a timely requested jury trial is harmless error only if the record shows that no material issues of fact exist[ ] and an instructed verdict would not have been justified. In the absence of a timely request, it is within the trial court's discretion to deny a jury trial."

Bell Helicopter Textron v. Abbott, 863 S.W.2d 139, 140 (Tex.App.—Texarkana 1993, writ denied). "As the first trial setting here gave only 24 days' notice [instead of the required 45 days], it did not comply with [TRCP] 245. *At 141:* [The error] was not harmless ... because it made it impossible for [D], after receiving notice of the setting, to comply with the time limit for paying the jury fee."

TRCP 217. OATH OF INABILITY

The deposit for a jury fee shall not be required when the party shall within the time for making such deposit, file with the clerk his affidavit to the effect that he is unable to make such deposit, and that he cannot, by the pledge of property or otherwise, obtain the money necessary for that purpose; and the court shall then order the clerk to enter the suit on the jury docket.

See *Commentaries*, "Request for Jury Trial," ch. 5-B.

History of TRCP 217: Adopted eff. Sept. 1, 1941, by order of Oct. 29, 1940 (3 Tex.B.J. 558 [1940]). Source: TRCS art. 2127 (repealed).

TRCP 218. JURY DOCKET

The clerks of the district and county courts shall each keep a docket, styled, "The Jury Docket," in which shall be entered in their order the cases in which jury fees have been paid or affidavit in lieu thereof has been filed as provided in the two preceding rules.

History of TRCP 218: Adopted eff. Sept. 1, 1941, by order of Oct. 29, 1940 (3 Tex.B.J. 558 [1940]). Source: TRCS art. 2128 (repealed).

Higginbotham v. Collateral Protection, 859 S.W.2d 487, 489 n.2 (Tex.App.—Houston [1st Dist.] 1993, writ denied). "The clerk is required to enter a notation on the court's docket sheet that the jury fee was paid."

TRCP 219. JURY TRIAL DAY

The court shall designate the days for taking up the jury docket and the trial of jury cases. Such order may be revoked or changed in the court's discretion.

History of TRCP 219: Amended eff. Apr. 1, 1984, by order of Dec. 5, 1983 (661-62 S.W.2d [Tex.Cases] lxxiii). Adopted eff. Sept. 1, 1941, by order of Oct. 29, 1940 (3 Tex.B.J. 558 [1940]). Source: TRCS art. 2129 (repealed).

TRCP 220. WITHDRAWING CAUSE FROM JURY DOCKET

When any party has paid the fee for a jury trial, he shall not be permitted to withdraw the cause from the jury docket over the objection of the parties adversely interested. If so permitted, the court in its discretion may by an order permit him to withdraw also his jury fee deposit. Failure of a party to appear for trial shall be deemed a waiver by him of the right to trial by jury.

See *Commentaries*, "Request for Jury Trial," ch. 5-B.

History of TRCP 220: Amended eff. Jan. 1, 1971, by order of July 21, 1970 (455-56 S.W.2d [Tex.Cases] xliii): Sentence added to provide that failure of a party to appear for trial is deemed a waiver of jury trial. Amended eff. Dec. 31, 1947, by order of Aug. 18, 1947 (8 Tex.B.J. 395 [1947]): The words "any party" were substituted for "one party"; "the cause" for "such cause"; and "over the objection" for "without the consent." Adopted eff. Sept. 1, 1941, by order of Oct. 29, 1940 (3 Tex.B.J. 558 [1940]). Source: TRCS art. 2130 (repealed).

Mercedes-Benz Credit Corp. v. Rhyne, 925 S.W.2d 664, 666 (Tex.1996). "Only when a party demands a jury *and* pays the fee can the opposing party rely on those actions. In such a case, the trial court may not remove the case from the jury docket over the objections of the opposing party."

Green v. Grace Mfg. Co., 422 S.W.2d 723, 726 (Tex. 1968). "We hold that a party, who does not timely demand a jury and pay the fee must object to the withdrawal of the case from the jury docket…."

In re J.N.F., 116 S.W.3d 426, 434-35 (Tex.App.—Houston [14th Dist.] 2003, n.p.h.). Unless "'an objection is made to the withdrawal of a case from the jury docket, the non-requesting party has no right to a jury trial.' If a party who has requested a jury trial in an initial pleading could effectively withdraw the request simply by omitting it in subsequent pleadings, the non-requesting party would be forced to scrutinize all such pleadings in order to avoid waiving a jury trial by failing to object to the withdrawal. [¶] [O]mitting a jury request from subsequent pleadings does not rise to the level of inaction that has been held to constitute the requesting party's waiver of a jury trial."

TRCP 221. CHALLENGE TO THE ARRAY

When the jurors summoned have not been selected by jury commissioners or by drawing the names from a jury wheel, any party to a suit which is to be tried by a jury may, before the jury is drawn challenge the array upon the ground that the officer summoning the jury has acted corruptly, and has wilfully summoned jurors known to be prejudiced against the party challenging or biased in favor of the adverse party. All such challenges must be in writing setting forth distinctly the grounds of such challenge and supported by the affidavit of the party or some other credible person. When such challenge is made, the court shall hear evidence and decide without delay whether or not the challenge shall be sustained.

See Gov't Code §62.001; *Commentaries*, "Jury Selection," ch. 8-A.

History of TRCP 221: Adopted eff. Sept. 1, 1941, by order of Oct. 29, 1940 (3 Tex.B.J. 558 [1940]). Source: TRCS art. 2131 (repealed).

Hightower v. Smith, 671 S.W.2d 32, 36 (Tex. 1984). "The courts of Smith County operate under the interchangeable jury system of [Gov't Code §62.016].

Objections to the jury panel therefore must be presented to the judge charged with organizing and impaneling the jurors for the week. [D's] motion to the trial judge after the panels were organized was not timely."

Mann v. Ramirez, 905 S.W.2d 275, 280 (Tex.App.—San Antonio 1995, writ denied). "It is undisputed that irregularities in the granting and documentation of exemptions and excuses occurred. *At 283:* We conclude that the trial court abused its discretion in denying a mistrial and erred in failing to grant a new trial, in light of the totality of the record and the evidence adduced at the posttrial hearings."

TRCP 222. WHEN CHALLENGE IS SUSTAINED

If the challenge be sustained, the array of jurors summoned shall be discharged, and the court shall order other jurors summoned in their stead, and shall direct that the officer who summoned the persons so discharged, and on account of whose misconduct the challenge has been sustained, shall not summon any other jurors in the case.

See Gov't Code §§62.101-62.110.

History of TRCP 222: Adopted eff. Sept. 1, 1941, by order of Oct. 29, 1940 (3 Tex.B.J. 558 [1940]). Source: TRCS art. 2132 (repealed).

Martinez v. City of Austin, 852 S.W.2d 71, 73 (Tex. App.—Austin 1993, writ denied). A challenge to the array "alleges a defect in the juror selection and summons procedure or a violation of the jury-wheel statute. If the movant is successful, the entire array is dismissed and a new array summoned. The challenge [to the array] must be presented in a written motion supported by affidavit to the particular judge in charge of the local jury system."

TRCP 223. JURY LIST IN CERTAIN COUNTIES

In counties governed as to juries by the laws providing for interchangeable juries, the names of the jurors shall be placed upon the general panel in the order in which they are randomly selected, and jurors shall be assigned for service from the top thereof, in the order in which they shall be needed, and jurors returned to the general panel after service in any of such courts shall be enrolled at the bottom of the list in the order of their respective return; provided, however, after such assignment to a particular court, the trial judge of such court, upon the demand prior to voir dire examination by any party or attorney in the case reached for trial in such court, shall cause the names of all members of such assigned jury panel in such case to be placed in a receptacle, shuffled, and drawn, and such names shall be transcribed in the order drawn on the jury list from which the jury is to be selected to try such case. There shall be only one shuffle and drawing by the trial judge in each case.

See Gov't Code §§62.016-62.017 (interchangeable juries in certain counties); ***Commentaries***, "Jury Selection," ch. 8-A.

History of TRCP 223: Amended eff. Sept. 1, 1990, by order of Apr. 24, 1990 (785-86 S.W.2d [Tex.Cases] lxiv): "Drawn from the wheel" changed to "randomly selected"; everything after "provided, however," is completely rewritten; to provide uniformity in jury shuffles. Adopted eff. Sept. 1, 1941, by order of Oct. 29, 1940 (3 Tex.B.J. 558 [1940]). Source: TRCS art. 2138 (repealed).

Rivas v. Liberty Mut. Ins. Co., 480 S.W.2d 610, 612 (Tex.1972). "The court of civil appeals recognized the listing and reshuffle provisions of [TRCP] 223 are designed to insure a random selection of jurors. While the method used here did not conform to the method prescribed by the rule, it did insure a degree of randomness in the listing of the jurors."

Carr v. Smith, 22 S.W.3d 128, 134 (Tex.App.—Fort Worth 2000, pet. denied). "After the venire panel has been sworn and once substantive inquiry begins and responses have been observed or made available to the parties or their counsel, whether verbally or in writing, voir dire has begun."

Whiteside v. Watson, 12 S.W.3d 614, 619 (Tex. App.—Eastland 2000, pet. denied). "[T]he first shuffle was not performed in compliance with the mandatory procedures set forth in [TRCP] 223. Whether it substantially complied with the underlying purpose of Rule 223 is irrelevant to the determination of whether it was error. Rule 223 sets forth a mandatory procedure for shuffling the jury panel, and failure to comply with that procedure is error. [¶] [However], even if the trial court erred by conducting the second shuffle, the error was harmless."

TRCP 224. PREPARING JURY LIST

In counties not governed as to juries by the laws providing for interchangeable juries, when the parties have announced ready for trial the clerk shall write the name of each regular juror entered of record for that week on separate slips of paper, as near the same size and appearance as may be, and shall place the slips in a box and mix them well. The clerk shall draw from the box, in the presence of the court, the names of twenty-four jurors, if in the district court, or so many as there may be, if there be a less number in the box; and the names of twelve jurors if in the county court, or so many as there may be, and write the names as drawn upon two slips of paper and deliver one slip to each party to the suit or his attorney.

See *Commentaries*, "Jury Selection," ch. 8-A.

History of TRCP 224: Adopted eff. Sept. 1, 1941, by order of Oct. 29, 1940 (3 Tex.B.J. 559 [1940]). Source: TRCS arts. 2139, 2140 (repealed).

Southwestern Pub. Serv. Co. v. Morris, 380 S.W.2d 648, 649 (Tex.App.—Amarillo 1964, no writ). "[E]rror was committed by the court in refusing condemnor's request that the jury panel be drawn before the selection of the jury." Such error may be harmless.

TRCP 225. SUMMONING TALESMAN

When there are not as many as twenty-four names drawn from the box, if in the district court, or as many as twelve, if in the county court, the court shall direct the sheriff to summon such number of qualified persons as the court deems necessary to complete the panel. The names of those thus summoned shall be placed in the box and drawn and entered upon the slips as provided in the preceding rules.

History of TRCP 225: Adopted eff. Sept. 1, 1941, by order of Oct. 29, 1940 (3 Tex.B.J. 559 [1940]). Source: TRCS art. 2141 (repealed).

TRCP 226. OATH TO JURY PANEL

Before the parties or their attorneys begin the examination of the jurors whose names have thus been listed, the jurors shall be sworn by the court or under its direction, as follows: "You, and each of you, do solemnly swear that you will true answers give to all questions propounded to you concerning your qualifications as a juror, so help you God."

See *Commentaries*, "Jury Selection," ch. 8-A.

History of TRCP 226: Adopted eff. Sept. 1, 1941, by order of Oct. 29, 1940 (3 Tex.B.J. 559 [1940]). Source: New rule.

Barron v. State, 378 S.W.2d 144, 147 (Tex.App.—San Antonio 1964, no writ). "[F]ailure to swear the jury panel prior to the voir dire examination as required by [TRCP] 226 ... was waived by [the] failure to timely complain of same."

TRCP 226a. ADMONITORY INSTRUCTIONS TO JURY PANEL & JURY

The court shall give such admonitory instructions to the jury panel and to the jury as may be prescribed by the Supreme Court in an order or orders entered for that purpose.

See *Commentaries*, "Jury Selection," ch. 8-A; FORMS 8A, 8I.

History of TRCP 226a: Amended eff. Jan. 1, 1988, by order of July 15, 1987 (733-34 S.W.2d [Tex.Cases] lxv). Adopted eff. Jan. 1, 1967, by order of July 20, 1966 (401-02 S.W.2d [Tex.Cases] xxxvi). Source: New rule.

APPROVED INSTRUCTIONS

Pursuant to the provisions of Rule 226a, Texas Rules of Civil Procedure, it is ordered [July 20, 1966] by the Supreme Court of Texas, effective January 1, 1967; January 1, 1971; February 1, 1973; December 5, 1983, effective April 1, 1984:

I.

That the following oral instructions, with such modifications as the circumstances of the particular case may require, shall be given by the court to the jurors after they have been sworn as provided in Rule 226 and before the voir dire examination:

Ladies and Gentlemen of the Jury Panel:

The case that is now on trial is _____ vs. _____. This is a civil action which will be tried before a jury. Your duty as jurors will be to decide the disputed facts. It is the duty of the judge to see that the case is tried in accordance with the rules of law. In this case, as in all cases, the actions of the judge, parties, witnesses, attorneys and jurors must be according to law. The Texas law permits proof of any violation of the rules of proper jury conduct. By this I mean that jurors and others may be called upon to testify in open court about acts of jury misconduct. I instruct you, therefore, to follow carefully all instructions which I am now going to give you, as well as others which you will receive while this case is on trial. If you do not obey the instructions I am about to give you, it may become necessary for another jury to re-try this case with all of the attendant waste of your time here and the expense to the litigants and the taxpayers of this county for another trial. These instructions are as follows:

1. Do not mingle with nor talk to the lawyers, the witnesses, the parties, or any other person who might be connected with or interested in this case, except for casual greetings. They have to follow these same instructions and you will understand it when they do.

2. Do not accept from, nor give to, any of those persons any favors however slight, such as rides, food or refreshments.

3. Do not discuss anything about this case, or even mention it to anyone whomsoever, including your wife or husband, nor permit anyone to mention it in your hearing until you are discharged as jurors or excused from this case. If anyone attempts to discuss the case, report it to me at once.

4. The parties through their attorneys have the right to direct questions to each of you concerning your qualifications, background, experiences and attitudes. In questioning you, they are not meddling in your personal affairs, but are trying to select fair and impartial jurors who are free from any bias or prejudice in this particular case.

a. Do not conceal information or give answers which are not true. Listen to the questions and give full and complete answers.

b. If the attorneys ask some questions directed to you as a group which require an answer on your part individually, hold up your hand until you have answered the questions.

Do you understand these instructions? If not, please let me know now.

Whether you are selected as a juror for this case or not, you are performing a significant service which only free people can perform. We shall try the case as fast as possible consistent with justice, which requires a careful and correct trial. If selected on the jury, unless I instruct you differently, you will be permitted to separate at recesses and for meals, and at night.

The attorneys will now proceed with their examination.

II.

That the following oral and written instructions, with such modifications as the circumstances of the particular case may require shall be given by the court to the jury immediately after the jurors are selected for the case:

ORAL INSTRUCTIONS

Ladies and Gentlemen:

By the oath which you take as jurors, you become officials of this court and active participants in the public administration of justice. I now give you further instructions which you must obey throughout this trial.

It is your duty to listen to and consider the evidence and to determine fact issues later submitted to you, but I, as judge, will decide matters of the law. You will now receive written instructions which you will observe during this trial, together with such other instructions as I may hereafter give, or as heretofore I have given to you.

(A copy of the written instructions set out below in this Section II shall thereupon be handed to each juror.)

As you examine the instructions which have just been handed to you, we will go over them briefly together. The first three instructions have previously been stated, and you will continue to observe them throughout the trial. These and the other instructions just handed to you are as follows:

(The written instructions set out below in this Section II shall thereupon be read by the court to the jury.)

Counsel, you may proceed.

WRITTEN INSTRUCTIONS

1. Do not mingle with nor talk to the lawyers, the witnesses, the parties, or any other person who might be connected with or interested in this case, except for casual greetings. They have to follow these same instructions and you will understand it when they do.

2. Do not accept from, nor give to, any of those persons any favors however slight, such as rides, food or refreshments.

3. Do not discuss anything about this case, or even mention it to anyone whomsoever, including your wife or husband nor permit anyone to mention it in your hearing until you are discharged as jurors or excused from this case. If anyone attempts to discuss the case, report it to me at once.

4. Do not even discuss this case among yourselves until after you have heard all of the evidence, the court's charge, the attorneys' arguments and until I have sent you to the jury room to consider your verdict.

5. Do not make any investigation about the facts of this case. Occasionally we have a juror who privately seeks out information about a case on trial. This is improper. All evidence must be presented in open court so that each side may question the witnesses and make proper objection. This avoids a trial based upon secret evidence. These rules apply to jurors the same as they apply to the parties and to me. If you know of, or learn anything about, this case except from the evidence admitted during the course of this trial, you should tell me about it at once. You have just taken an oath that you will render a verdict on the evidence submitted to you under my rulings.

6. Do not make personal inspections, observations, investigations, or experiments nor personally view premises, things or articles not produced in court. Do not let anyone else do any of these things for you.

7. Do not tell other jurors your own personal experiences nor those of other persons, nor relate any special information. A juror may have special knowledge of matters such as business, technical or professional matters or he may have expert knowledge or opinions, or he may know what happened in this or some other lawsuit. To tell the other jurors any of this information is a violation of these instructions.

8. Do not discuss or consider attorney's fees unless evidence about attorney's fees is admitted.

9. Do not consider, discuss, nor speculate whether or not any party is or is not protected in whole or in part by insurance of any kind.

10. Do not seek information contained in law books, dictionaries, public or private records or elsewhere, which is not admitted in evidence.

At the conclusion of all the evidence, I may submit to you a written charge asking you some specific questions. You will not be asked, and you should not consider, whether one party or the other should win. Since you will need to consider all of the evidence admitted by me, it is important that you pay close attention to the evidence as it is presented.

The Texas law permits proof of any violation of the rules of proper jury conduct. By this I mean that jurors and others may be called upon to testify in open court about acts of jury misconduct. I instruct you, therefore, to follow carefully all instructions which I have given you, as well as others which you later receive while this case is on trial.

You may keep these instructions and review them as the case proceeds. A violation of these instructions should be reported to me.

III.

That the following written instructions, with such modifications as the circumstances of the particular case may require, shall be given by the court to the jury as part of the charge:

Ladies and Gentlemen of the Jury:

This case is submitted to you by asking questions about the facts, which you must decide from the evidence you have heard in this trial. You are the sole judges of the credibility of the witnesses and the weight to be given their testimony, but in matters of law, you must be governed by the instructions in this charge. In discharging your responsibility on this jury, you will observe all the instructions which have previously been given you. I shall now give you additional instructions which you should carefully and strictly follow during your deliberations.

1. Do not let bias, prejudice or sympathy play any part in your deliberations.

2. In arriving at your answers, consider only the evidence introduced here under oath and such exhibits, if any, as have been introduced for your consideration under the rulings of the Court, that is, what you have seen and heard in this courtroom, together with the law as given you by the court. In your deliberations, you will not consider or discuss anything that is not represented by the evidence in this case.

3. Since every answer that is required by the charge is important, no juror should state or consider that any required answer is not important.

4. You must not decide who you think should win, and then try to answer the questions accordingly. Simply answer the questions, and do not discuss nor concern yourselves with the effect of your answers.

5. You will not decide the answer to a question by lot or by drawing straws, or by any other method of chance. Do not return a quotient verdict. A quotient verdict means that the jurors agree to abide by the result to be reached by adding together each juror's figures and dividing by the number of jurors to get an average. Do not do any trading on your answers; that is, one juror should not agree to answer a certain question one way if others will agree to answer another question another way.

6. You may render your verdict upon the vote of ten or more members of the jury. The same ten or more of you must agree upon all of the answers made and to the entire verdict. You will not, therefore, enter into an agreement to be bound by a majority or any other vote of less than ten jurors. If the verdict and all of the answers therein are reached by unanimous agreement, the presiding juror shall sign the verdict for the entire jury. If any juror disagrees as to any answer made by the verdict, those jurors who agree to all findings shall each sign the verdict.

These instructions are given you because your conduct is subject to review the same as that of the witnesses, parties, attorneys and the judge. If it should be found that you have disregarded any of these instructions, it will be jury misconduct and it may require another trial by another jury; then all of our time will have been wasted.

The presiding juror or any other who observes a violation of the court's instructions shall immediately warn the one who is violating the same and caution the juror not to do so again.

(Definitions, questions and special instructions given to the jury will be transcribed here.)

After you retire to the jury room, you will select your own presiding juror. The first thing the presiding juror will do is to have this complete charge read aloud and then you will deliberate upon your answers to the questions asked.

____

Judge Presiding

CERTIFICATE

We, the jury, have answered the above and foregoing questions as herein indicated, and herewith return same into court as our verdict.

(To be signed by the presiding juror if unanimous.)

____
Presiding Juror

(To be signed by those rendering the verdict if not unanimous.)

________________ ________________
________________ ________________
________________ ________________
________________ ________________
________________ ________________
________________ ________________

IV.

That the following oral instructions shall be given by the court to the jury after the verdict has been accepted by the court and before the jurors are discharged:

The court has previously instructed you that you should observe strict secrecy during the trial and during your deliberations, and that you should not discuss this case with anyone except other jurors during your deliberations. I am now about to discharge you. After your discharge, you are released from your secrecy. You will then be free to discuss the case and your deliberations with anyone. However, you are also free to decline to discuss the case and your deliberations if you wish.

After you are discharged, it is lawful for the attorneys or other persons to question you to determine whether any of the standards for jury conduct which I have given you in the course of this trial were violated and to ask you to give an affidavit to that effect. You are free to discuss or not to discuss these matters and to give or not to give an affidavit.

History of instructions to TRCP 226a: Amended instructions eff. Apr. 1, 1984, by orders of Dec. 5, 1983 (661-62 S.W.2d [Tex.Cases] lxxiii): The word "foreman" was changed to "presiding juror." Amended eff. Jan. 1, 1988, by order of July 15, 1987 (733-34 S.W.2d [Tex.Cases] lxv): Instructions from II., par. 10 to III, par. 6 changed. Amended eff. Jan. 1, 1988, by order of Jan. 28, 1988 (741-42 S.W.2d [Tex.Cases] xlv): Instructions from III, par. 6 to end were changed; corrected order of Dec. 16, 1987. Amended eff. Jan. 1, 1988, by order of Dec. 16, 1987 (741-42 S.W.2d [Tex.Cases] xliv): Instructions from III, par. 6 to end were changed to correct amendment of July 15, 1987, which had unintentionally included the last par. "The presiding juror ... the juror not to do so again"; that par. was deleted by this correction. Amended eff. Jan. 1, 1971, by order of July 21, 1970 (455-56 S.W.2d [Tex.Cases] xxii): Instructions from II, par. 9 changed. Amended eff. Feb. 1, 1973, by order of Oct. 3, 1972 (483-84 S.W.2d [Tex.Cases] xlvii): Instructions from III, par. 6 changed. Adopted eff. Jan. 1, 1967, by order of July 20, 1966 (401-02 S.W.2d [Tex.Cases] xxxvii). Source: New rule.

Pharo v. Chambers Cty., 922 S.W.2d 945, 949 (Tex. 1996). "[N]ot every employee of a county is automatically 'interested' in a case in which the county is a party. ... Collier, however, was a member of the Sheriff's Department, the division of county government whose conduct was being scrutinized at trial. [D]etermining whether [he] was connected with or interested in the case within the meaning of Rule 226a is a factually intensive inquiry, committed to the sound discretion of the trial court."

Woods v. Crane Carrier Co., 693 S.W.2d 377, 379 (Tex.1985). "[W]hen terms requiring definitions are used more than once in a charge, it is preferable that the definition or instruction occur immediately after the general instructions required by [TRCP] 226a...."

Phippen v. Deere & Co., 965 S.W.2d 713, 718 (Tex. App.—Texarkana 1998, no pet.). TRCP 226a "provides in relevant part that if a verdict is unanimous, it shall be signed by the presiding juror, and if not unanimous, then those jurors who agree with all of the findings shall sign the verdict. *At 719:* Because [Ds] failed to raise their objections to the exemplary damages verdict at trial before the jury was discharged, so that the trial court could have instructed the jury to enter a corrected verdict, we conclude that [Ds] waived their objection...."

TRCP 227. CHALLENGE TO JUROR

A challenge to a particular juror is either a challenge for cause or a peremptory challenge. The court shall decide without delay any such challenge, and if sustained, the juror shall be discharged from the particular case. Either such challenge may be made orally on the formation of a jury to try the case.

See Gov't Code §§62.101-62.110; ***Commentaries***, "Jury Selection," ch. 8-A.

History of TRCP 227: Adopted eff. Sept. 1, 1941, by order of Oct. 29, 1940 (3 Tex.B.J. 559 [1940]). Source: TRCS art. 2142 (repealed).

Lopez v. Southern P.T. Co., 847 S.W.2d 330, 333 (Tex.App.—El Paso 1993, no writ). "A party exercises its peremptory challenges by delivering its list of peremptory challenges to the court."

TRCP 228. "CHALLENGE FOR CAUSE" DEFINED

A challenge for cause is an objection made to a juror, alleging some fact which by law disqualifies him to serve as a juror in the case or in any case, or which in the opinion of the court, renders him an unfit person to sit on the jury. Upon such challenge the examination is not confined to the answers of the juror, but other evidence may be heard for or against the challenge.

See ***Commentaries***, "Jury Selection," ch. 8-A.

History of TRCP 228: Adopted eff. Sept. 1, 1941, by order of Oct. 29, 1940 (3 Tex.B.J. 559 [1940]). Source: TRCS art. 2144 (repealed).

Compton v. Henrie, 364 S.W.2d 179, 182 (Tex. 1963). "[T]he statutory disqualification of bias or prejudice extends not only to the litigant personally, but to the subject matter of the litigation as well."

TRCP 229. CHALLENGE FOR CAUSE

When twenty-four or more jurors, if in the district court, or twelve or more, if in the county court, are drawn, and the lists of their names delivered to the parties, if either party desires to challenge any juror for cause, the challenge shall then be made. The name of a juror challenged and set aside for cause shall be erased from such lists.

See Gov't Code §§62.101-62.110; *Commentaries*, "Jury Selection," ch. 8-A.
History of TRCP 229: Adopted eff. Sept. 1, 1941, by order of Oct. 29, 1940 (3 Tex.B.J. 559 [1940]). Source: TRCS art. 2143 (repealed).

Hallett v. Houston Northwest Med. Ctr., 689 S.W.2d 888, 890 (Tex.1985). To preserve error in the denial of challenges for cause, "[i]t was incumbent upon [P], prior to exercising her peremptory challenges, to advise the trial court of two things: (1) that she would exhaust her peremptory challenges; and, (2) that after exercising her peremptory challenges, specific objectionable jurors would remain on the jury list."

Lucas v. Titus Cty. Hosp. Dist., 964 S.W.2d 144, 157-58 (Tex.App.—Texarkana 1998), *pet. denied*, 988 S.W.2d 740 (Tex.1998). "[A] trial court's refusal to excuse an unqualified juror does not necessarily constitute harmful error. Harm occurs only if the party uses all of their peremptory challenges and is thus prevented from striking other objectionable jurors because he has no additional peremptory challenges. Additionally, the complaining party must inform the court that objectionable jurors will be chosen. Failure to notify the trial court of these two facts constitutes a waiver of the right to complain of the trial court's refusal to discharge a juror challenged for cause."

TRCP 230. CERTAIN QUESTIONS NOT TO BE ASKED

In examining a juror, he shall not be asked a question the answer to which may show that he has been convicted of an offense which disqualifies him, or that he stands charged by some legal accusation with theft or any felony.

See *Commentaries*, "Jury Selection," ch. 8-A.
History of TRCP 230: Adopted eff. Sept. 1, 1941, by order of Oct. 29, 1940 (3 Tex.B.J. 559 [1940]). Source: TRCS art. 2145 (repealed).

Palmer Well Servs. v. Mack Trucks, 776 S.W.2d 575, 576 (Tex.1989). Gov't Code §62.102 "disqualifies a person to serve as a petit juror if he is 'under indictment or other legal accusation of misdemeanor or felony theft, or any other felony.'"

TRCP 231. NUMBER REDUCED BY CHALLENGES

If the challenges reduce the number of jurors to less than twenty-four, if in the district court, or to less than twelve, if in the county court, the court shall order other jurors to be drawn from the wheel or from the central jury panel or summoned, as the practice may be in the particular county, and their names written upon the list instead of those set aside for cause. Such jurors so summoned may likewise be challenged for cause.

History of TRCP 231: Adopted eff. Sept. 1, 1941, by order of Oct. 29, 1940 (3 Tex.B.J. 559 [1940]). Source: TRCS art. 2146 (repealed).

Williams v. State, 631 S.W.2d 955, 957 (Tex.App.—Austin 1982, no writ). TRCP 231 "authorizes the calling of additional individuals to supplement a jury panel rendered insufficient (by disqualifications or peremptory strikes) to supply a jury of twelve."

TRCP 232. MAKING PEREMPTORY CHALLENGES

If there remain on such lists not subject to challenge for cause, twenty-four names, if in the district court, or twelve names, if in the county court, the parties shall proceed to make their peremptory challenges. A peremptory challenge is made to a juror without assigning any reason therefor.

See *Commentaries*, "Jury Selection," ch. 8-A.
History of TRCP 232: Adopted eff. Sept. 1, 1941, by order of Oct. 29, 1940 (3 Tex.B.J. 560 [1940]). Source: TRCS art. 2147 (repealed).

Goode v. Shoukfeh, 943 S.W.2d 441, 445-46 (Tex. 1997). "At the first step of the [***Batson***] process, the opponent of the peremptory challenge must establish a prima facie case of racial discrimination. [¶] During the second step of the process, the burden shifts to the party who has exercised the strike to come forward with a race-neutral explanation. ... The issue ... at this juncture is the facial validity of the explanation. ... It is not until the third step that the persuasiveness of the

TRCP 228

justification for the challenge becomes relevant. At the third step of the process, the trial court must determine if the party challenging the strike has proven purposeful racial discrimination, and the trial court may believe or not believe the explanation offered by the party who exercised the peremptory challenge. It is at this stage that implausible justifications for striking potential jurors 'may (and probably will) be found [by the trial court] to be pretexts for purposeful discrimination.'"

Powers v. Palacios, 813 S.W.2d 489, 491 (Tex. 1991). "We hold that equal protection is denied when race is a factor in counsel's exercise of a peremptory challenge to a prospective juror."

TRCP 233. NUMBER OF PEREMPTORY CHALLENGES

Except as provided below, each party to a civil action is entitled to six peremptory challenges in a case tried in the district court, and to three in the county court.

Alignment of the Parties. In multiple party cases, it shall be the duty of the trial judge to decide whether any of the litigants aligned on the same side of the docket are antagonistic with respect to any issue to be submitted to the jury, before the exercise of peremptory challenges.

Definition of Side. The term "side" as used in this rule is not synonymous with "party," "litigant," or "person." Rather, "side" means one or more litigants who have common interests on the matters with which the jury is concerned.

Motion to Equalize. In multiple party cases, upon motion of any litigant made prior to the exercise of peremptory challenges, it shall be the duty of the trial judge to equalize the number of peremptory challenges so that no litigant or side is given unfair advantage as a result of the alignment of the litigants and the award of peremptory challenges to each litigant or side. In determining how the challenges should be allocated the court shall consider any matter brought to the attention of the trial judge concerning the ends of justice and the elimination of an unfair advantage.

See ***Commentaries***, "Jury Selection," ch. 8-A.

History of TRCP 233: Amended eff. Apr. 1, 1984, by order of Dec. 5, 1983 (661-62 S.W.2d [Tex.Cases] lxxiv): The rule was adopted to conform with *Patterson Dental Co. v. Dunn*, 592 S.W.2d 914 (Tex.1979), and other Supreme Court decisions. Adopted eff. Sept. 1, 1941, by order of Oct. 29, 1940 (3 Tex.B.J. 560 [1940]). Source: TRCS art. 2148 (repealed).

Garcia v. Central Power & Light Co., 704 S.W.2d 734, 736 (Tex.1986). "The existence of antagonism [between litigants on the same side of a lawsuit] is a question of law. If no antagonism exists, each side must receive the same number of strikes. *At 737:* [I]n determining whether antagonism exists, the trial court must consider the pleadings, information disclosed by pretrial discovery, information and representations made during voir dire of the jury panel, and any other information brought to the attention of the trial court before the exercise of the strikes by the parties."

Van Allen v. Blackledge, 35 S.W.3d 61, 65 (Tex. App.—Houston [14th Dist.] 2000, pet. denied). "[W]hen defendants have collaborated on the exercise of their peremptory challenges such that no double strikes are made, this factor supports a finding that the defendants have used their ostensibly antagonistic positions unfairly."

TRCP 234. LISTS RETURNED TO THE CLERK

When the parties have made or declined to make their peremptory challenges, they shall deliver their lists to the clerk. The clerk shall, if the case be in the district court, call off the first twelve names on the lists that have not been erased; and if the case be in the county court, he shall call off the first six names on the lists that have not been erased; those whose names are called shall be the jury.

See ***Commentaries***, "Jury Selection," ch. 8-A.

History of TRCP 234: Adopted eff. Sept. 1, 1941, by order of Oct. 29, 1940 (3 Tex.B.J. 560 [1940]). Source: TRCS art. 2149 (repealed).

Lopez v. Southern P.T. Co., 847 S.W.2d 330, 333 (Tex.App.—El Paso 1993, no writ). To preserve error when the court refuses to strike a panelist for cause, the party must name the objectionable panelist before giving its peremptory strikes to the clerk.

TRCP 235. IF JURY IS INCOMPLETE

When by peremptory challenges the jury is left incomplete, the court shall direct other jurors to be drawn or summoned to complete the jury; and such other jurors shall be impaneled as in the first instance.

See ***Commentaries***, "Jury Selection," ch. 8-A.

History of TRCP 235: Adopted eff. Sept. 1, 1941, by order of Oct. 29, 1940 (3 Tex.B.J. 560 [1940]). Source: TRCS art. 2150 (repealed).

Thomas v. City of O'Donnell, 811 S.W.2d 757, 759 (Tex.App.—Amarillo, 1991, no writ). "Under the mandatory provisions of [TRCP 235], the onus is on the court to direct that additional prospective jurors be drawn or summoned. The trial court erred in overruling [P's] motion to call additional jurors...."

TRCP 236. OATH TO JURY

The jury shall be sworn by the court or under its direction, in substance as follows: "You, and each of you, do solemnly swear that in all cases between parties which shall be to you submitted, you will a true verdict render, according to the law, as it may be given you in charge by the court, and to the evidence submitted to you under the rulings of the court. So help you God."

History of TRCP 236: Adopted eff. Sept. 1, 1941, by order of Oct. 29, 1940 (3 Tex.B.J. 560 [1940]). Source: TRCS arts. 2151, 2179 (repealed).

Traders & Gen. Ins. Co. v. Diebel, 188 S.W.2d 411, 414 (Tex.App.—Dallas 1945, writ ref'd). "Jurors are sworn to render a verdict according to submitted evidence...."

SECTION 11. TRIAL OF CAUSES

A. APPEARANCE & PROCEDURE

TRCP 237. APPEARANCE DAY

If a defendant, who has been duly cited, is by the citation required to answer on a day which is in term time, such day is appearance day as to him. If he is so required to answer on a day in vacation, he shall plead or answer accordingly, and the first day of the next term is appearance day as to him.

See ***Commentaries***, "Default Judgment," ch. 7-A.

History of TRCP 237: Amended eff. Jan. 1, 1955, by order of July 20, 1954 (17 Tex.B.J. 568 [1954]): Second paragraph dealing with removal to Federal Court was eliminated. Amended eff. Sept. 1, 1941, by order of Mar. 31, 1941 (4 Tex.B.J. 172 [1941]): The last paragraph was added. Adopted eff. Sept. 1, 1941, by order of Oct. 29, 1940 (3 Tex.B.J. 560 [1940]). Source: TRCS art. 2152 (repealed). Change: Appearance day, where the answer is to be filed during the term, depends upon the date of service rather than on terms of court.

Texas Alco. Bev. Comm'n v. Wilson, 573 S.W.2d 832, 835 (Tex.App.—Beaumont 1978, writ ref'd n.r.e.). The TABC "had no valid notice that a hearing would be held prior to appearance day.... Any judgment entered before the time at which [D] is commanded by the citation to appear and answer is erroneous and must be set aside."

TRCP 237a. CASES REMANDED FROM FEDERAL COURT

When any cause is removed to the Federal Court and is afterwards remanded to the state court, the plaintiff shall file a certified copy of the order of remand with the clerk of the state court and shall forthwith give written notice of such filing to the attorneys of record for all adverse parties. All such adverse parties shall have fifteen days from the receipt of such notice within which to file an answer. No default judgment shall be rendered against a party in a removed action remanded from federal court if that party filed an answer in federal court during removal.

See ***Commentaries***, "Default Judgment," ch. 7-A.

History of TRCP 237a: Amended eff. Sept. 1, 1990, by order of Apr. 24, 1990 (785-86 S.W.2d [Tex.Cases] lxv): Added last sentence to expressly provide, consistent with existing law, that a default judgment cannot be taken in a case remanded from federal court if an answer was filed in federal court during removal. Amended eff. Apr. 1, 1984, by order of Dec. 5, 1983 (661-62 S.W.2d [Tex.Cases] lxxiv). Amended eff. Jan. 1, 1988, by order July 15, 1987 (733-34 S.W.2d [Tex.Cases] lxvii). Adopted eff. Jan. 1, 1955, by order of July 20, 1954 (17 Tex.B.J. 568 [1954]). Source: New rule.

Quaestor Invs. v. State of Chiapas, 997 S.W.2d 226, 229 (Tex.1999). "[W]e hold that jurisdiction revests in the state court when the federal district court executes the remand order and mails a certified copy to the state court. [¶] We are ... persuaded that nothing more is required to recommence the appellate timetable than the state court's reaquiring jurisdiction over a case. ... The court of appeals erred when it inferred from [TRCP] 237a ... that any further affirmative action was needed."

HBA East, Ltd. v. JEA Boxing Co., 796 S.W.2d 534, 538 (Tex.App.—Houston [1st Dist.] 1990, writ denied). "Reading [TRCP] 237a and 239 together, we conclude that a default judgment cannot be granted against [D] following remand of a case from federal to state court until 15 days have expired from [D's] receipt of the remand notice from [P]."

TRCP 238. CALL OF APPEARANCE DOCKET

On the appearance day of a particular defendant and at the hour named in the citation, or as soon thereafter as may be practicable, the court or clerk in open court shall call, in their order, all the cases on the docket in which such day is appearance day as to any defendant, or, the court or clerk failing therein, any such case shall be so called on request of the plaintiff's attorney.

See ***Commentaries***, "Default Judgment," ch. 7-A.

History of TRCP 238: Adopted eff. Sept. 1, 1941, by order of Oct. 29, 1940 (3 Tex.B.J. 560 [1940]). Source: TRCS art. 2153 (repealed).

TRCP 239. JUDGMENT BY DEFAULT

Upon such call of the docket, or at any time after a defendant is required to answer, the plaintiff may in term time take judgment by default against such defendant if he has not previously filed an answer, and provided that the citation with the officer's return thereon shall have been on file with the clerk for the length of time required by Rule 107.

See *Commentaries*, "Default Judgment," ch. 7-A; "Motion for New Trial," ch. 10-B; FORMS 7A.

History of TRCP 239: Amended eff. Sept. 1, 1962, by order of Apr. 12, 1962 (25 Tex.B.J. 428 [1962]): Final clause beginning with the words "and provided that" added. Adopted eff. Sept. 1, 1941, by order of Oct. 29, 1940 (3 Tex.B.J. 560 [1940]). Source: TRCS art. 2154 (repealed): "In term time" added.

LeBlanc v. LeBlanc, 778 S.W.2d 865, 865 (Tex. 1989). "***Craddock*** has general application to all judgments of default, both those 'entered on failure of a defendant to file an answer and those entered on failure to appear for trial.'"

Lopez v. Lopez, 757 S.W.2d 721, 723 (Tex.1988). "Because the record here establishes that [D] had no actual or constructive notice of the trial setting, the lower courts erred in requiring him to show that he had a meritorious defense as a condition to granting his motion for new trial."

Craddock v. Sunshine Bus Lines, 133 S.W.2d 124, 126 (Tex.1939). "A default judgment should be set aside and a new trial ordered in any case in which the failure of the defendant to answer before judgment was not intentional, or the result of conscious indifference on his part, but was due to a mistake or accident; provided the motion for new trial sets up a meritorious defense and is filed at a time when the granting thereof will occasion no delay or otherwise work an injury to the plaintiff."

TRCP 239a. NOTICE OF DEFAULT JUDGMENT

At or immediately prior to the time an interlocutory or final default judgment is rendered, the party taking the same or his attorney shall certify to the clerk in writing the last known mailing address of the party against whom the judgment is taken, which certificate shall be filed among the papers in the cause. Immediately upon the signing of the judgment, the clerk shall mail written notice thereof to the party against whom the judgment was rendered at the address shown in the certificate, and note the fact of such mailing on the docket. The notice shall state the number and style of the case, the court in which the case is pending, the names of the parties in whose favor and against whom the judgment was rendered, and the date of the signing of the judgment. Failure to comply with the provisions of this rule shall not affect the finality of the judgment.

See *Commentaries*, "Default Judgment," ch. 7-A; "The Judgment," ch. 9-C; "Motion to Extend Postjudgment Deadlines," ch. 10-G.

History of TRCP 239a: Amended eff. Jan. 1, 1988, by order of July 15, 1987 (733-34 S.W.2d [Tex.Cases] lxvii). Adopted eff. Jan. 1, 1967, by order of July 20, 1966 (401-02 S.W.2d [Tex.Cases] xlii). Source: New rule.

John v. State, 826 S.W.2d 138, 140 (Tex.1992). TRCP 239a "specifically states that 'failure to comply with the provisions of the rule shall not affect the finality of the judgment.'"

Campbell v. Fincher, 72 S.W.3d 723, 724 (Tex. App.—Waco 2002, no pet.). "Rule 239a is designed as an administrative convenience for the parties, and failure to give notice of the entry of a default judgment does not constitute reversible error."

TRCP 240. WHERE ONLY SOME ANSWER

Where there are several defendants, some of whom have answered or have not been duly served and some of whom have been duly served and have made default, an interlocutory judgment by default may be entered against those who have made default, and the cause may proceed or be postponed as to the others.

See TRCP 161; *Commentaries*, "Default Judgment," ch. 7-A; "The Judgment," ch. 9-C.

History of TRCP 240: Adopted eff. Sept. 1, 1941, by order of Oct. 29, 1940 (3 Tex.B.J. 560 [1940]). Source: TRCS art. 2155 (repealed).

Castano v. Foremost Cty. Mut. Ins. Co., 31 S.W.3d 387, 388 (Tex.App.—San Antonio 2000, no pet.). "Where [P's] petition names multiple [Ds], and [P] obtains a no-answer default judgment against one of [Ds], the default judgment is interlocutory and cannot be appealed until the trial court either renders a final judgment in the case, or signs an order of severance making the interlocutory default judgment final."

TRCP 241. ASSESSING DAMAGES ON LIQUIDATED DEMANDS

When a judgment by default is rendered against the defendant, or all of several defendants, if the claim is liquidated and proved by an instrument in writing, the damages shall be assessed by the court, or under its direction, and final judgment shall be rendered therefor, unless the defendant shall demand and be entitled to a trial by jury.

See *Commentaries*, "Default Judgment," ch. 7-A.

History of TRCP 241: Amended eff. Apr. 1, 1984, by order of Dec. 5, 1983 (661-62 S.W.2d [Tex.Cases] lxxv). Adopted eff. Sept. 1, 1941, by order of Oct. 29, 1940 (3 Tex.B.J. 560 [1940]). Source: TRCS art. 2156 (repealed).

Novosad v. Cunningham, 38 S.W.3d 767, 773 (Tex. App.—Houston [14th Dist.] 2001, no pet.). "Under

[TRCP] 241 ... proof is required only with respect to damages which are either unliquidated or not proven by a written instrument. A claim is liquidated if the amount of damages can be accurately calculated by the court from the factual, as opposed to the conclusory, allegations in the petition and an instrument in writing."

Hanners v. State Bar, 860 S.W.2d 903, 911 (Tex. App.—Dallas 1993, no writ). TRCP 241 "provides that when a default judgment is rendered against a defendant and the claim is liquidated or proven by a written instrument, the court shall assess the damages, unless the defendant is entitled to a jury trial."

TRCP 242. REPEALED

Repealed eff. Dec. 31, 1941, by order of Sept. 20, 1941 (4 Tex.B.J. 523 [1941]).

TRCP 243. UNLIQUIDATED DEMANDS

If the cause of action is unliquidated or be not proved by an instrument in writing, the court shall hear evidence as to damages and shall render judgment therefor, unless the defendant shall demand and be entitled to a trial by jury in which case the judgment by default shall be noted, a writ of inquiry awarded, and the cause entered on the jury docket.

See ***Commentaries***, "Motion for Sanctions," ch. 5-J; "Default Judgment," ch. 7-A.

History of TRCP 243: Amended eff. Sept. 1, 1941, by order of Mar. 31, 1941 (4 Tex.B.J. 172 [1941]): Substituted "cause of action" for "claim." Adopted eff. Sept. 1, 1941, by order of Oct. 29, 1940 (3 Tex.B.J. 561 [1940]). Source: TRCS art. 2157 (repealed).

Texas Commerce Bank v. New, 3 S.W.3d 515, 516 (Tex.1999). "We conclude that because unobjected-to hearsay is, as a matter of law, probative evidence, affidavits can be evidence for purposes of an unliquidated-damages hearing pursuant to [TRCP] 243."

Holt Atherton Indus. v. Heine, 835 S.W.2d 80, 86 (Tex.1992). "After a default judgment is granted, the trial court must hear evidence of unliquidated damages. ... Therefore, when an appellate court sustains a no evidence point after an *uncontested* hearing on unliquidated damages following a no-answer default judgment, the appropriate disposition is a remand for a new trial on the issue of unliquidated damages."

Ingram Indus. v. U.S. Bolt Mfg., 121 S.W.3d 31, 37 (Tex.App.—Houston [1st Dist.] 2003, n.p.h.). "A trial court may award unliquidated damages based on affidavit testimony. [T]he trial court based the award of damages on its consideration of 'the pleadings and evidence on file.' The evidence on file contained [the affidavit of P's general manager, which] set out [P's] damages. The trial court thus considered [the] affidavit to be proof of [P's] damages. Therefore, the trial court satisfied Rule 243's hearing requirement without the need of holding an evidentiary hearing."

TRCP 244. ON SERVICE BY PUBLICATION

Where service has been made by publication, and no answer has been filed nor appearance entered within the prescribed time, the court shall appoint an attorney to defend the suit in behalf of the defendant, and judgment shall be rendered as in other cases; but, in every such case a statement of the evidence, approved and signed by the judge, shall be filed with the papers of the cause as a part of the record thereof. The court shall allow such attorney a reasonable fee for his services, to be taxed as part of the costs.

See ***Commentaries***, "Motion for New Trial," ch. 10-B.

History of TRCP 244: Adopted eff. Sept. 1, 1941, by order of Oct. 29, 1940 (3 Tex.B.J. 561 [1940]). Source: TRCS art. 2158 (repealed).

Cahill v. Lyda, 826 S.W.2d 932, 933 (Tex.1992). TRCP 244 "requires that a trial court appoint an attorney ad litem to represent defendants served with citation by publication who fail to file an answer or appear before the court. [TRCP] 244 also requires that the attorney ad litem be paid a reasonable fee for his services, which is to be taxed as part of the costs. The attorney ad litem must exhaust all remedies available to his client and, if necessary, represent his client's interest on appeal."

Isaac v. Westheimer Colony Ass'n, 933 S.W.2d 588, 591 (Tex.App.—Houston [1st Dist.] 1996, writ denied). "[T]here is no evidence in the record of the trial court having appointed an attorney ad litem in [D's] behalf. Absent strict compliance with the essential requirements of [TRCP] 244, a trial court commits reversible error."

Barnes v. Domain, 875 S.W.2d 32, 33 (Tex.App.—Houston [14th Dist.] 1994, no writ). "Neither the case law nor the language of [TRCP 244] reveals any indication that the burden is on the attorney to move the court to make such appointment."

TRCP 245. ASSIGNMENT OF CASES FOR TRIAL

The Court may set contested cases on written request of any party, or on the court's own motion, with reasonable notice of not less than forty-five days to the parties of a first setting for trial, or by agreement of the parties; provided, however, that when a case previously has been set for trial, the Court may reset said contested case to a later date on any reasonable notice to the parties or by agreement of the parties. Noncontested cases may be tried or disposed of at any time whether set or not, and may be set at any time for any other time.

A request for trial setting constitutes a representation that the requesting party reasonably and in good faith expects to be ready for trial by the date requested, but no additional representation concerning the completion of pretrial proceedings or of current readiness for trial shall be required in order to obtain a trial setting in a contested case.

See Tex. Const. art. 1, §19; *Commentaries*, "Default Judgment," ch. 7-A; "Motion for New Trial," ch. 10-B.

History of TRCP 245: Amended eff. Sept. 1, 1990, by order of Apr. 24, 1990 (785-86 S.W.2d [Tex.Cases] lxv): First paragraph, to harmonize a first-time nonjury setting with the time for jury demand, and to set a more realistic notice for trial; second paragraph, to standardize the readiness requirement to obtain a trial setting. Amended eff. Apr. 1, 1984, by order of Dec. 5, 1983 (661-62 S.W.2d [Tex.Cases] lxxv): The last sentence of former TRCP 245 was deleted and moved to TRCP 306a. Amended eff. Jan. 1, 1976, by order of July 22, 1975 (525-26 S.W.2d [Tex.Cases] xlix): Rewritten to require notice of settings in county and district courts. Adopted eff. Sept. 1, 1941, by order of Oct. 29, 1940 (3 Tex.B.J. 561 [1940]). Source: FRCP 40.

Custom-Crete, Inc. v. K-Bar Servs., 82 S.W.3d 655, 659 (Tex.App.—San Antonio 2002, no pet.). "A trial court's failure to comply with Rule 245 in a contested case deprives a party of its constitutional right to be present at the hearing, to voice its objections in an appropriate manner, and results in a violation of fundamental due process. Failure to give the required notice constitutes lack of due process and is grounds for reversal."

In re Carter, 958 S.W.2d 919, 925 (Tex.App.—Amarillo 1997, orig. proceeding). TRCP 245 "indicates that once a written request for a trial setting has been filed no others need be proffered. [B]y making a written request ... the requesting party is implicitly telling the court that the cause will be ready to be tried on the dates suggested."

TRCP 246. CLERK TO GIVE NOTICE OF SETTINGS

The clerk shall keep a record in his office of all cases set for trial, and it shall be his duty to inform any nonresident attorney of the date of setting of any case upon request by mail from such attorney, accompanied by a return envelope properly addressed and stamped. Failure of the clerk to furnish such information on proper request shall be sufficient ground for continuance or for a new trial when it appears to the court that such failure has prevented the attorney from preparing or presenting his claim or defense.

History of TRCP 246: Adopted eff. Sept. 1, 1941, by order of Oct. 29, 1940 (3 Tex.B.J. 561 [1940]). Source: New rule.

Bruneio v. Bruneio, 890 S.W.2d 150, 156 n.2 (Tex. App.—Corpus Christi 1994, no writ). TRCP 246 "merely provides an additional vehicle for notice to any of the various attorneys who may be working on the case and want direct notification.... Accordingly, Rule 246 [expands] the requirements of notice to include nonresident attorneys who would not otherwise be entitled to direct notification of the setting under Rule 245 as the attorney in charge."

TRCP 247. TRIED WHEN SET

Every suit shall be tried when it is called, unless continued or postponed to a future day or placed at the end of the docket to be called again for trial in its regular order. No cause which has been set upon the trial docket of the court shall be taken from the trial docket for the date set except by agreement of the parties or for good cause upon motion and notice to the opposing party.

See *Commentaries*, "Motion for Continuance," ch. 5-D.

History of TRCP 247: Amended eff. Apr. 1, 1984, by order of Dec. 5, 1983 (661-62 S.W.2d [Tex.Cases] lxxv). Adopted eff. Sept. 1, 1941, by order of Oct. 29, 1940 (3 Tex.B.J. 561 [1940]). Source: TRCS art. 2162 (repealed): Added last sentence.

Brooks v. Brooks, 561 S.W.2d 949, 951 (Tex.App.—Tyler 1978, no writ). "It was the legal duty of the [the husband] to keep himself posted as to the setting of the case for trial, and to be present to testify and aid his counsel."

TRCP 248. JURY CASES

When a jury has been demanded, questions of law, motions, exceptions to pleadings, and other unresolved pending matters shall, as far as practicable, be heard and determined by the court before the trial commences, and jurors shall be summoned to appear on the day so designated.

See TRCP 166.

History of TRCP 248: Amended eff. Sept. 1, 1990, by order of Apr. 24, 1990 (785-86 S.W.2d [Tex.Cases] lxv): Adds "and other unresolved pending matters" after "pleadings,"; changes "before the day designated for the trial" to "before the trial commences."; to encourage resolution of matters prior to trial. Amended eff. Apr. 1, 1984, by order of Dec. 5, 1983 (661-62 S.W.2d [Tex.Cases] lxxv). Adopted eff. Sept. 1, 1941, by order of Oct. 29, 1940 (3 Tex.B.J. 561 [1940]). Source: TRCS art. 2164 (repealed).

Gaines v. Gaines, 677 S.W.2d 727, 730 (Tex.App.—Corpus Christi 1984, no writ). TRCP 166 and 248 "are directory procedures that are designed to help streamline the disposition of pre-trial issues."

STRCP 249. CALL OF NON-JURY DOCKET

The non-jury docket shall be taken up at such times as not unnecessarily to interfere with the dispatch of business on the jury docket.

History of TRCP 249: Adopted eff. Sept. 1, 1941, by order of Oct. 29, 1940 (3 Tex.B.J. 561 [1940]). Source: TRCS art. 2165 (repealed).

TRCP 250. REPEALED

Repealed eff. Dec. 31, 1941, by order of Sept. 20, 1941 (4 Tex.B.J. 524 [1941]).

B. CONTINUANCE & CHANGE OF VENUE

TRCP 251. CONTINUANCE

No application for a continuance shall be heard before the defendant files his defense, nor shall any continuance be granted except for sufficient cause supported by affidavit, or by consent of the parties, or by operation of law.

See *Commentaries*, "Motion for Continuance," ch. 5-D; FORMS 5D.

History of TRCP 251: Adopted eff. Sept. 1, 1941, by order of Oct. 29, 1940 (3 Tex.B.J. 562 [1940]). Source: TRCS art. 2167 (repealed).

Tenneco, Inc. v. Enterprise Prods. Co., 925 S.W.2d 640, 647 (Tex.1996). "When a party contends that it has not had an adequate opportunity for discovery before a summary judgment hearing, it must file either an affidavit explaining the need for further discovery or a verified motion for continuance."

Villegas v. Carter, 711 S.W.2d 624, 626 (Tex.1986). "Generally, when movants fail to comply with [TRCP] 251's requirement that the motion for continuance be 'supported by affidavit,' we presume that the trial court did not abuse its discretion in denying the motion." *See also* ***In re E.L.T.***, 93 S.W.3d 372, 375 (Tex.App.—Houston [14th Dist.] 2002, no pet.).

TRCP 252. APPLICATION FOR CONTINUANCE

If the ground of such application be the want of testimony, the party applying therefor shall make affidavit that such testimony is material, showing the materiality thereof, and that he has used due diligence to procure such testimony, stating such diligence, and the cause of failure, if known; that such testimony cannot be procured from any other source; and, if it be for the absence of a witness, he shall state the name and residence of the witness, and what he expects to prove by him; and also state that the continuance is not sought for delay only, but that justice may be done; provided that, on a first application for a continuance, it shall not be necessary to show that the absent testimony cannot be procured from any other source.

The failure to obtain the deposition of any witness residing within 100 miles of the courthouse of the county in which the suit is pending shall not be regarded as want of diligence when diligence has been used to secure the personal attendance of such witness under the rules of law, unless by reason of age, infirmity or sickness, or official duty, the witness will be unable to attend the court, or unless such witness is about to leave, or has left, the State or county in which the suit is pending and will not probably be present at the trial.

See *Commentaries*, "Rules for Filing Documents," ch. 1-C; "Motion for Continuance," ch. 5-D; "Motion for Summary Judgment," ch. 7-B; FORMS 5D.

History of TRCP 252: Amended eff. Apr. 1, 1984, by order of Dec. 5, 1983 (661-62 S.W.2d [Tex.Cases] lxxv): The second paragraph is added to the former rule. Adopted eff. Sept. 1, 1941, by order of Oct. 29, 1940 (3 Tex.B.J. 562 [1940]). Source: TRCS art. 2168 (repealed).

State v. Wood Oil Distrib., 751 S.W.2d 863, 865 (Tex.1988). "[T]he failure of a litigant to diligently utilize the rules of civil procedure for discovery purposes will not authorize the granting of a continuance."

Ramirez v. State, 973 S.W.2d 388, 391 (Tex.App.—El Paso 1998, no pet.). Defendant's continuance "motion failed to specify the information and testimony he sought or why it was material. [D] did not state the names of the witnesses from whom he sought testimony, nor did he state what he expected to prove from said witnesses."

Verkin v. Southwest Ctr. One, Ltd., 784 S.W.2d 92, 94 (Tex.App.—Houston [1st Dist.] 1989, writ denied). When a motion for continuance is: (1) in substantial compliance with the rule; (2) verified; and (3) uncontroverted, the court "must accept the statements in the motion as true."

TRCP 253. ABSENCE OF COUNSEL AS GROUND FOR CONTINUANCE

Except as provided elsewhere in these rules, absence of counsel will not be good cause for a continuance or postponement of the cause when called for trial, except it be allowed in the discretion of the court, upon cause shown or upon matters within the knowledge or information of the judge to be stated on the record.

See *Commentaries*, "Motion for Continuance," ch. 5-D; FORMS 5D.
History of TRCP 253: Adopted eff. Sept. 1, 1941, by order of Oct. 29, 1940 (3 Tex.B.J. 562 [1940]). Source: Tex. Rules for Dist. & Cty. Cts. 49.

Villegas v. Carter, 711 S.W.2d 624, 626 (Tex.1986). "[T]he trial court abused its discretion because the evidence shows that [P] was not negligent or at fault in causing his attorney's withdrawal. The court granted [P] attorney's motion to voluntarily withdraw 2 days before trial—too short a time for [P] to find a new attorney and for that new attorney to investigate the case and prepare for trial."

Rehabilitation Facility v. Cooper, 962 S.W.2d 151, 155-56 (Tex.App.—Austin 1998, no pet.). "In general, absence of counsel is not good cause for a continuance. The court does have the discretion, however, to allow a continuance if good cause is shown. [¶] [A]nother attorney from the same law firm ... had signed pleadings and conducted discovery in this case before trial. Nothing in the record suggests that attorney was incapable of rendering adequate representation."

TRCP 254. ATTENDANCE ON LEGISLATURE

In all civil actions, including matters of probate, and in all matters ancillary to such suits which require action by or the attendance of an attorney, including appeals but excluding temporary restraining orders, at any time within thirty days of a date when the legislature is to be in session, or at any time the legislature is in session, or when the legislature sits as a Constitutional Convention, it shall be mandatory that the court continue the cause if it shall appear to the court, by affidavit, that any party applying for continuance, or any attorney for any party to the cause, is a member of either branch of the legislature, and will be or is in actual attendance on a session of the same. If the member of the legislature is an attorney for a party to the cause, his affidavit shall contain a declaration that it is his intention to participate actively in the preparation and/or presentation of the case. Where a party to any cause, or an attorney for any party to a cause, is a member of the legislature, his affidavit need not be corroborated. On the filing of such affidavit, the court shall continue the cause until thirty days after adjournment of the legislature and the affidavit shall be proof of the necessity for the continuance, and the continuance shall be deemed one of right and shall not be charged against the movant upon any subsequent application for continuance.

The right to a continuance shall be mandatory, except only where the attorney was employed within ten days of the date the suit is set for trial, the right to continuance shall be discretionary.

See CPRC §30.003, for other requirements of a legislative continuance; *Commentaries*, "Motion for Continuance," ch. 5-D; FORMS 5D.
History of TRCP 254: Amended eff. Jan. 1, 1981, by order of June 10, 1980 (599-600 S.W.2d [Tex.Cases] xlvi): The rule was amended to conform with TRCS art. 2168a. Adopted eff. Sept. 1, 1941, by order of Oct. 29, 1940 (3 Tex.B.J. 562 [1940]). Source: TRCS art. 2168a (repealed).

Waites v. Sondock, 561 S.W.2d 772, 776 (Tex. 1977). "[A] legislative continuance is mandatory except in those cases in which the party opposing the continuance alleges that a substantial existing right will be defeated or abridged by delay. In cases of this type the trial court has a duty to conduct a hearing on the allegations. If the allegations are shown to be meritorious the court should deny the continuance."

TRCP 255. CHANGE OF VENUE BY CONSENT

Upon the written consent of the parties filed with the papers of the cause, the court, by an order entered on the minutes, may transfer the same for trial to the court of any other county having jurisdiction of the subject matter of such suit.

See CPRC §15.020; *Commentaries*, "Parties agreed to transfer," ch. 3-C, §2.3.1; FORMS 3C.
History of TRCP 255: Adopted eff. Sept. 1, 1941, by order of Oct. 29, 1940 (3 Tex.B.J. 562 [1940]). Source: TRCS art. 2169 (repealed).

Farris v. Ray, 895 S.W.2d 351, 352 (Tex.1995). "[A] signed written agreement filed in the record of the *transferee* court meets all the requirements of [TRCP] 11. Such an agreement, enforceable against the signatories under the terms of the rule, operates as an express waiver of any error there may have been in the initial transfer."

TRCP 256. REPEALED

Repealed eff. Sept. 1, 1941, by order of Mar. 31, 1941 (4 Tex.B.J. 173 [1941]).

TRCP 257. GRANTED ON MOTION

A change of venue may be granted in civil causes upon motion of either party, supported by his own affidavit and the affidavit of at least three credible persons, residents of the county in which the suit is pending, for any following cause:

(a) That there exists in the county where the suit is pending so great a prejudice against him that he cannot obtain a fair and impartial trial.

(b) That there is a combination against him instigated by influential persons, by reason of which he cannot expect a fair and impartial trial.

(c) That an impartial trial cannot be had in the county where the action is pending.

(d) For other sufficient cause to be determined by the court.

See *Commentaries*, "Motion to Transfer—Challenging Venue," ch. 3-C.

History of TRCP 257: Amended eff. Sept. 1, 1983, by order of June 15, 1983 (651-52 S.W.2d [Tex.Cases] xxxviii): To conform to S.B. 898, 68th Legislature, 1983. Adopted eff. Sept. 1, 1941, by order of Oct. 29, 1940 (3 Tex.B.J. 563 [1940]). Source: TRCS art. 2170 (repealed).

Acker v. Denton Publ'g Co., 937 S.W.2d 111, 118 (Tex.App.—Fort Worth 1996, no writ). "The inability to obtain a fair and impartial trial of a civil case may be grounds for a change of venue. A motion on those grounds must be supported by competent affidavits of the party seeking the transfer and 3 credible residents of the county where the suit is pending." *See also* ***Dorchester Gas Prod'g Co. v. Harlow Corp.***, 743 S.W.2d 243, 253 n.6 (Tex.App.—Amarillo 1987, no writ); ***Tenneco, Inc. v. Salyer***, 739 S.W.2d 448, 449 (Tex.App.—Corpus Christi 1987, orig. proceeding).

TRCP 258. SHALL BE GRANTED

Where such motion to transfer venue is duly made, it shall be granted, unless the credibility of those making such application, or their means of knowledge or the truth of the facts set out in the said application are attacked by the affidavit of a credible person; when thus attacked, the issue thus formed shall be tried by the judge; and the application either granted or refused. Reasonable discovery in support of, or in opposition to, the application shall be permitted, and such discovery as is relevant, including deposition testimony on file, may be attached to, or incorporated by reference in, the affidavit of a party, a witness, or an attorney who has knowledge of such discovery.

See *Commentaries*, "Motion to Transfer—Challenging Venue," ch. 3-C.

History of TRCP 258: Amended eff. Sept. 1, 1983, by order of June 15, 1983 (651-52 S.W.2d [Tex.Cases] xxxix): To conform to S.B. 898, 68th Legislature, 1983. Adopted eff. Sept. 1, 1941, by order of Oct. 29, 1940 (3 Tex.B.J. 563 [1940]). Source: TRCS art. 2171 (repealed).

City of Abilene v. Downs, 367 S.W.2d 153, 155 (Tex.1963). TRCP 258 "by its terms is mandatorily operative. It provides the only means by which issue can be joined."

Lone Star Steel Co. v. Scott, 759 S.W.2d 144, 146 (Tex.App.—Texarkana 1988, writ denied). "[I]f the motion for transfer is duly filed and is not challenged as provided in [TRCP 258] the trial judge is required to transfer the case."

TRCP 259. TO WHAT COUNTY

If the motion under Rule 257 is granted, the cause shall be removed:

(a) If from a district court, to any county of proper venue in the same or an adjoining district;

(b) If from a county court, to any adjoining county of proper venue;

(c) If (a) or (b) are not applicable, to any county of proper venue;

(d) If a county of proper venue (other than the county of suit) cannot be found, then if from

(1) A district court, to any county in the same or an adjoining district or to any district where an impartial trial can be had;

(2) A county court, to any adjoining county or to any district where an impartial trial can be had;

but the parties may agree that venue shall be changed to some other county, and the order of the court shall conform to such agreement.

See *Commentaries*, "Motion to Transfer—Challenging Venue," ch. 3-C.

History of TRCP 259: Amended eff. Sept. 1, 1983, by order of June 15, 1983 (651-52 S.W.2d [Tex.Cases] xxxix): To conform to S.B. 898, 68th Legislature, 1983. Adopted eff. Sept. 1, 1941, by order of Oct. 29, 1940 (3 Tex.B.J. 563 [1940]). Source: TRCS art. 2172 (repealed).

Dorchester Gas Prod'g Co. v. Harlow Corp., 743 S.W.2d 243, 253 (Tex.App.—Amarillo 1987, no writ). "[W]hen the trial court determined that [one party] could not obtain a fair and impartial trial in that county, the court had two options under [TRCP] 259(d)—either to remove the case to any county in the same or an adjoining district or to any district where an impartial trial could be had."

TRCP 260. REPEALED

Repealed eff. Sept. 1, 1990, by order of Apr. 24, 1990 (785-86 S.W.2d [Tex.Cases] lxvi): No longer needed.

TRCP 261. TRANSCRIPT ON CHANGE

When a change of venue has been granted, the clerk shall immediately make out a correct transcript of all the orders made in said cause, certifying thereto officially under the seal of the court, and send the same, with the original papers in the cause, to the clerk of the court to which the venue has been changed.

History of TRCP 261: Adopted eff. Sept. 1, 1941, by order of Oct. 29, 1940 (3 Tex.B.J. 563 [1940]). Source: TRCS art. 2174 (repealed).

C. THE TRIAL

TRCP 262. TRIAL BY THE COURT

The rules governing the trial of causes before a jury shall govern in trials by the court in so far as applicable.

History of TRCP 262: Adopted eff. Sept. 1, 1941, by order of Oct. 29, 1940 (3 Tex.B.J. 563 [1940]). Source: TRCS art. 2176 (repealed).

Qantel Bus. Sys. v. Custom Controls Co., 761 S.W.2d 302, 304 (Tex.1988). "When a plaintiff rests, he indicates that he does not desire to put on further evidence, except by rebuttal testimony, and that he has fully developed his case." In a nonjury case, the court is presumed to have ruled on the sufficiency of the evidence when it grants judgment for the defendant after the plaintiff rests.

TRCP 263. AGREED CASE

Parties may submit matters in controversy to the court upon an agreed statement of facts filed with the clerk, upon which judgment shall be rendered as in other cases; and such agreed statement signed and certified by the court to be correct and the judgment rendered thereon shall constitute the record of the cause.

See ***Commentaries***, "Motion for Judgment on Agreed Statement of Facts," ch. 7-D.

History of TRCP 263: Adopted eff. Sept. 1, 1941, by order of Oct. 29, 1940 (3 Tex.B.J. 563 [1940]). Source: TRCS art. 2177 (repealed).

Walker Eng'g v. Bracebridge Corp., 102 S.W.3d 837, 839 (Tex.App.—Dallas 2003, pet. denied). "An agreed statement of facts under [TRCP] 263 is similar to a special verdict; it is the parties' request for judgment under the applicable law. The only issue on appeal is whether the trial court properly applied the law to the agreed facts. The appellate court is limited to those facts unless other facts are necessarily implied from the express facts in the statement. In an appeal of an agreed case, there are no presumed findings in favor of the judgment, and the pleadings are immaterial."

Trevino & Gonzalez Co. v. R.F. Muller Co., 949 S.W.2d 39, 41 (Tex.App.—San Antonio 1997, no writ). "[P]arties to a lawsuit may submit matters in controversy to the court upon an agreed statement of facts. [N]o evidence is admitted or considered by the trial court and the trial court's decision is based upon the papers on file and the arguments of counsel. [W]e indulge no presumptions in favor of the judgment in such a case because the trial court had no factual issues to resolve."

City of Galveston v. Giles, 902 S.W.2d 167, 170 n.2 (Tex.App.—Houston [1st Dist.] 1995, no writ). "Findings of fact have no place in the trial of an agreed case. Once the parties stipulate to all the facts, the court may not make additional fact findings."

TRCP 264. VIDEOTAPE TRIAL

By agreement of the parties, the trial court may allow that all testimony and such other evidence as may be appropriate be presented at trial by videotape. The expenses of such videotape recordings shall be taxed as costs. If any party withdraws agreement to a videotape trial, the videotape costs that have accrued will be taxed against the party withdrawing from the agreement.

History of TRCP 264: Adopted eff. Jan. 1, 1988, by order of July 15, 1987 (733-34 S.W.2d [Tex.Cases] lxvii). Former TRCP 264 repealed eff. Jan. 1, 1988, by order of July 15, 1987 (733-34 S.W.2d [Tex.Cases] lxvii). Source: New rule.

TRCP 265. ORDER OF PROCEEDINGS ON TRIAL BY JURY

The trial of cases before a jury shall proceed in the following order unless the court should, for good cause stated in the record, otherwise direct:

(a) The party upon whom rests the burden of proof on the whole case shall state to the jury briefly the nature of his claim or defense and what said party expects to prove and the relief sought. Immediately thereafter, the adverse party may make a similar statement, and intervenors and other parties will be accorded similar rights in the order determined by the court.

(b) The party upon whom rests the burden of proof on the whole case shall then introduce his evidence.

(c) The adverse party shall briefly state the nature of his claim or defense and what said party expects to prove and the relief sought unless he has already done so.

(d) He shall then introduce his evidence.

(e) The intervenor and other parties shall make their statement, unless they have already done so, and shall introduce their evidence.

(f) The parties shall then be confined to rebutting testimony on each side.

(g) But one counsel on each side shall examine and cross-examine the same witness, except on leave granted.

History of TRCP 265: Amended eff. Jan. 1, 1978, by order of July 11, 1977 (553-54 S.W.2d [Tex.Cases] xlviii): Eliminated provisions in (a), (c), and (e) about the reading of pleadings. Amended eff. Jan. 1, 1967, by order of July 20, 1966 (401-02 S.W.2d [Tex.Cases] xlii): Rewrote rule to permit each party to either read his pleading or state the nature of his claim/defense to the jury, but not both. Amended eff. Sept. 1, 1941, by order of Mar. 31, 1941 (4 Tex.B.J. 173 [1941]): Added par. (j) from Tex. Rules for Dist. & Cty. Cts. 43. Adopted eff. Sept. 1, 1941, by order of Oct. 29, 1940 (3 Tex.B.J. 563 [1940]). Source: TRCS art. 2180 (repealed).

Producer's Constr. Co. v. Muegge, 669 S.W.2d 717, 719 (Tex.1984). "The trial court erred in rendering judgment before [D] had an opportunity to present evidence and rest its case."

TRCP 266. OPEN & CLOSE—ADMISSION

Except as provided in Rule 269 the plaintiff shall have the right to open and conclude both in adducing his evidence and in the argument, unless the burden of proof on the whole case under the pleadings rests upon the defendant, or unless the defendant or all of the defendants, if there should be more than one, shall, after the issues of fact are settled and before the trial commences, admit that the plaintiff is entitled to recover as set forth in the petition, except so far as he may be defeated, in whole or in part, by the allegations of the answer constituting a good defense, which may be established on the trial; which admission shall be entered of record, whereupon the defendant, or the defendants, if more than one, shall have the right to open and conclude in adducing the evidence and in the argument of the cause. The admission shall not serve to admit any allegation which is inconsistent with such defense, which defense shall be one that defendant has the burden of establishing, as for example, and without excluding other defenses: accord and satisfaction, adverse possession, arbitration and award, contributory negligence, discharge in bankruptcy, duress, estoppel, failure of consideration, fraud, release, res judicata, statute of frauds, statute of limitations, waiver, and the like.

See ***Commentaries***, "Opening Statement," ch. 8-B; "Final Argument," ch. 8-J.

History of TRCP 266: Adopted eff. Sept. 1, 1941, by order of Oct. 29, 1940 (3 Tex.B.J. 564 [1940]). Source: Tex. Rules for Dist. & Cty. Cts. 31.

4M Linen & Uniform Sup. Co. v. W.P. Ballard & Co., 793 S.W.2d 320, 324 (Tex.App.—Houston [1st Dist.] 1990, writ denied). TRCP 266 "provides that [P] has the right to open and close argument. There are two exceptions.... First, [D] has the right to open and close if the burden of proof for the entire case under the pleadings is on [D]. Second, [D] has the right to open and close if, before trial begins, [D] admits that [P] is entitled to recover, subject to proof of defensive allegations."

TRCP 267. WITNESSES PLACED UNDER RULE

a. At the request of either party, in a civil case, the witnesses on both sides shall be sworn and removed out of the courtroom to some place where they cannot hear the testimony as delivered by any other witness in the cause. This is termed placing witnesses under the rule.

b. This rule does not authorize exclusion of (1) a party who is a natural person or the spouse of such natural person, or (2) an officer or employee of a party that is not a natural person and who is designated as its representative by its attorney, or (3) a person whose presence is shown by a party to be essential to the presentation of the cause.

c. If any party be absent, the court in its discretion may exempt from the rule a representative of such party.

d. Witnesses, when placed under Rule 614 of the Texas Rules of Civil Evidence, shall be instructed by the court that they are not to converse with each other or with any other person about the case other than the attorneys in the case, except by permission of the court, and that they are not to read any report of or comment upon the testimony in the case while under the rule.

e. Any witness or other person violating such instructions may be punished for contempt of court.

See TRE 614; ***Commentaries***, "Objecting to Evidence," ch. 8-D.

History of TRCP 267: Amended eff. Jan. 1, 1988, by order of July 15, 1987 (733-34 S.W.2d [Tex.Cases] lxvii). Adopted eff. Sept. 1, 1941, by order of Oct. 29, 1940 (3 Tex.B.J. 564 [1940]). Source: Tex. Code Crim.P. arts. 644, 647 (repealed, now Tex. Code Crim.P. arts. 36.03, 36.06).

Drilex Sys. v. Flores, 1 S.W.3d 112, 118-19 (Tex. 1999). "Although an expert witness may *typically* be found exempt under the essential presence exception, experts are not *automatically* exempt. Instead, [TRE] 614 and [TRCP] 267 vest in trial judges broad discretion to determine whether a witness is essential. *At 120:* We acknowledge that the court never expressly placed [P's expert] under the Rule and never instructed him not to discuss the case with others. However, a court may, in its discretion, exclude the testimony of a prospective witness who technically violates the Rule even though the witness was never actually placed under the Rule."

TRCP 268. MOTION FOR INSTRUCTED VERDICT

A motion for directed verdict shall state the specific grounds therefor.

See *Commentaries*, "Motion for Directed Verdict," ch. 8-G; FORMS 8G.

History of TRCP 268: Adopted eff. Sept. 1, 1941, by order of Oct. 29, 1940 (3 Tex.B.J. 564 [1940]). Source: Last sentence of FRCP 50(a) unchanged.

S.V. v. R.V., 933 S.W.2d 1, 8 (Tex.1996). "In reviewing a directed verdict, we examine the evidence in the light most favorable to the person suffering an adverse judgment."

Szczepanik v. First S. Trust Co., 883 S.W.2d 648, 649 (Tex.1994). "In reviewing ... an instructed verdict, we must determine whether there is any evidence of probative force to raise a fact issue on the material questions presented. ... If there is any conflicting evidence of probative value on any theory of recovery, an instructed verdict is improper...."

Cano v. North Tex. Nephrology Assocs., 99 S.W.3d 330, 338 (Tex.App.—Fort Worth 2003, no pet.). "A directed verdict is proper only under limited circumstances: (1) the evidence conclusively establishes the right of the movant to judgment or negates the right of the opponent; or (2) the evidence is insufficient to raise a fact issue that must be established before the opponent is entitled to judgment." *See also* ***Mills v. Angel***, 995 S.W.2d 262, 266 (Tex.App.—Texarkana 1999, no pet.).

TRCP 269. ARGUMENT

(a) After the evidence is concluded and the charge is read, the parties may argue the case to the jury. The party having the burden of proof on the whole case, or on all matters which are submitted by the charge, shall be entitled to open and conclude the argument; where there are several parties having separate claims or defenses, the court shall prescribe the order of argument between them.

(b) In all arguments, and especially in arguments on the trial of the case, the counsel opening shall present his whole case as he relies on it, both of law and facts, and shall be heard in the concluding argument only in reply to the counsel on the other side.

(c) Counsel for an intervenor shall occupy the position in the argument assigned by the court according to the nature of the claim.

(d) Arguments on questions of law shall be addressed to the court, and counsel should state the substance of the authorities referred to without reading more from books than may be necessary to verify the statement. On a question on motions, exceptions to the evidence, and other incidental matters, the counsel will be allowed only such argument as may be necessary to present clearly the question raised, and refer to authorities on it, unless further discussion is invited by the court.

(e) Arguments on the facts should be addressed to the jury, when one is impaneled in a case that is being tried, under the supervision of the court. Counsel shall be required to confine the argument strictly to the evidence and to the arguments of opposing counsel. Mere personal criticism by counsel upon each other shall be avoided, and when indulged in shall be promptly corrected as a contempt of court.

(f) Side-bar remarks, and remarks by counsel of one side, not addressed to the court, while the counsel on the other side is examining a witness or arguing any question to the court, or addressing the jury, will be rigidly repressed by the court.

(g) The court will not be required to wait for objections to be made when the rules as to arguments are violated; but should they not be noticed and corrected by the court, opposing counsel may ask leave of the court to rise and present his point of objection. But the court shall protect counsel from any unnecessary interruption made on frivolous and unimportant grounds.

(h) It shall be the duty of every counsel to address the court from his place at the bar, and in addressing the court to rise to his feet; and while engaged in the trial of a case, he shall remain at his place in the bar.

See *Commentaries*, "Final Argument," ch. 8-J.

History of TRCP 269: Amended eff. Sept. 1, 1990, by order of Apr. 24, 1990 (785-86 S.W.2d [Tex.Cases] lxvi): Deleted "whether upon special issues or otherwise" in (a). Amended eff. Sept. 1, 1941, by order of Mar. 31, 1941 (4 Tex.B.J.

173 [1941]): Added pars. (b) - (h), from Tex. Rules for Dist. & Cty. Cts. 36 - 42. Adopted eff. Sept. 1, 1941, by order of Oct. 29, 1940 (3 Tex.B.J. 564 [1940]). Source of TRCP 269(a): TRCS art. 2183.

Standard Fire Ins. Co. v. Reese, 584 S.W.2d 835, 839 (Tex.1979). "There are only rare instances of incurable harm from improper argument."

Sanchez v. Espinoza, 60 S.W.3d 392, 395 (Tex. App.—Amarillo 2001, pet. denied). TRCP 269(e) "obligates counsel to confine his argument 'strictly to the evidence and to the arguments of opposing counsel.' [H]e may discuss the 'environments' or circumstances of the case, the reasonableness or unreasonableness of the evidence, and the probative effect (or lack thereof) of the evidence. So too does he have the leeway to 'present his case as to make the law contained in the charge applicable to the facts of the case.' This leeway also includes the opportunity to encourage the jury to weigh, evaluate, and test the evidence before it."

TEIA v. Guerrero, 800 S.W.2d 859, 867 (Tex.App.—San Antonio 1990, writ denied). TRCP 269 "commands courts to correct improper argument sua sponte…."

TRCP 270. ADDITIONAL TESTIMONY

When it clearly appears to be necessary to the due administration of justice, the court may permit additional evidence to be offered at any time; provided that in a jury case no evidence on a controversial matter shall be received after the verdict of the jury.

See *Commentaries*, "Motion to Reopen for Additional Evidence," ch. 8-H; FORM 8H:01.

History of TRCP 270: Amended eff. Apr. 1, 1984, by order of Dec. 5, 1983 (661-62 S.W.2d [Tex.Cases] lxxvi). Adopted eff. Sept. 1, 1941, by order of Oct. 29, 1940 (3 Tex.B.J. 564 [1940]). Source: TRCS art. 2181 (repealed).

In re S.L.M., 97 S.W.3d 224, 230 (Tex.App.—Amarillo 2002, no pet.). "[T]he trial court [may] permit evidence to be offered at any time when it clearly appears to be necessary to the administration of justice. Among factors the trial court may consider … are whether (1) due diligence was exercised by the parties in obtaining the evidence, (2) the additional evidence is decisive, (3) allowing additional evidence will cause undue delay and (4) allowing additional evidence will cause injustice."

D. CHARGE TO THE JURY

TRCP 271. CHARGE TO THE JURY

Unless expressly waived by the parties, the trial court shall prepare and in open court deliver a written charge to the jury.

See *Commentaries*, "The Charge," ch. 8 I.

History of TRCP 271: Amended eff. Jan. 1, 1988, by order of July 15, 1987 (733-34 S.W.2d [Tex.Cases] lxviii). Amended eff. Sept. 1, 1973, by order of May 25, 1973 (493-94 S.W.2d [Tex.Cases] xxiii): Last two sentences of the original rule were deleted. Adopted eff. Sept. 1, 1941, by order of Oct. 29, 1940 (3 Tex.B.J. 565 [1940]). Source: TRCS art. 2184 (repealed).

TRCP 272. REQUISITES

The charge shall be in writing, signed by the court, and filed with the clerk, and shall be a part of the record of the cause. It shall be submitted to the respective parties or their attorneys for their inspection, and a reasonable time given them in which to examine and present objections thereto outside the presence of the jury, which objections shall in every instance be presented to the court in writing, or be dictated to the court reporter in the presence of the court and opposing counsel, before the charge is read to the jury. All objections not so presented shall be considered as waived. The court shall announce its rulings thereon before reading the charge to the jury and shall endorse the rulings on the objections if written or dictate same to the court reporter in the presence of counsel. Objections to the charge and the court's rulings thereon may be included as a part of any transcript or statement of facts on appeal and, when so included in either, shall constitute a sufficient bill of exception to the rulings of the court thereon. It shall be presumed, unless otherwise noted in the record, that the party making such objections presented the same at the proper time and excepted to the ruling thereon.

See *Commentaries*, "The Charge," ch. 8-I.

History of TRCP 272: Amended eff. Jan. 1, 1988, by order of July 15, 1987 (733-34 S.W.2d [Tex.Cases] lxviii). Amended eff. Jan. 1, 1976, by order of July 22, 1975 (525-26 S.W.2d [Tex.Cases] xlix): The rule was rewritten. Amended eff. Sept. 1, 1973, by order of May 25, 1973 (493-94 S.W.2d [Tex.Cases] xxiii): Last sentence of the original rule was deleted. Amended eff. Dec. 31, 1941, by order of Sept. 20, 1941 (4 Tex.B.J. 527 [1941]). Adopted eff. Sept. 1, 1941, by order of Oct. 29, 1940 (3 Tex.B.J. 565 [1940]). Source: TRCS art. 2185 (repealed).

State Farm Life Ins. Co. v. Beaston, 907 S.W.2d 430, 440 (Tex.1995). "The failure to object to the conditional submission of the damages issue waives error as to form and substance of the submission."

City of Brownsville v. Alvarado, 897 S.W.2d 750, 752 (Tex.1995). "Submission of an improper jury question can be harmless error if the jury's answers to other questions render the improper question immaterial. A jury question is considered immaterial when its answer can be found elsewhere in the verdict or when its answer cannot alter the effect of the verdict."

State Dept. of Highways & Pub. Transp. v. Payne, 838 S.W.2d 235, 241 (Tex.1992). "The procedure for preparing and objecting to the charge has lost its philosophical moorings. There should be but one test for determining if a party has preserved error in the jury charge, and that is whether the party made the trial court aware of the complaint, timely and plainly, and obtained a ruling."

TRCP 273. JURY SUBMISSIONS

Either party may present to the court and request written questions, definitions, and instructions to be given to the jury; and the court may give them or a part thereof, or may refuse to give them, as may be proper. Such requests shall be prepared and presented to the court and submitted to opposing counsel for examination and objection within a reasonable time after the charge is given to the parties or their attorneys for examination. A request by either party for any questions, definitions, or instructions shall be made separate and apart from such party's objections to the court's charge.

See *Commentaries*, "The Charge," ch. 8-I.

History of TRCP 273: Amended eff. Jan. 1, 1988, by order of July 15, 1987 (733-34 S.W.2d [Tex.Cases] lxviii). Amended eff. Mar. 1, 1950, by order of Oct. 12, 1949 (12 Tex.B.J. 534 [1950]). Adopted eff. Sept. 1, 1941, by order of Oct. 29, 1940 (3 Tex.B.J. 565 [1940]). Source: TRCS art. 2186 (repealed).

Galveston Cty. Fair & Rodeo v. Glover, 940 S.W.2d 585, 586-87 (Tex.1996). "The court of appeals ... held that [D] 'did not separately request in writing any definitions or instructions on' 'what constitutes wrongful disqualification' as required by [TRCP] 273.... We disagree. [D's] written request was separate from its oral objection. This request fully complied with Rule 273."

Lester v. Logan, 907 S.W.2d 452, 453 (Tex.1995). Disapproved of the court of appeals' opinion that held a request on one piece of paper that included 5 related matters—one question, 2 instructions, and 2 definitions—was improper.

Alaniz v. Jones & Neuse, Inc., 907 S.W.2d 450, 451 (Tex.1995). TRCP 273 "does not prohibit including the request in a complete charge as long as it is not obscured."

Jarrin v. Sam White Oldsmobile Co., 929 S.W.2d 21, 25 (Tex.App.—Houston [1st Dist.] 1996, writ denied). "To complain of the trial court's omission of a requested instruction on appeal, a party is obliged to make a written request to the trial court.... Dictating a requested instruction to the court reporter is not sufficient to support an appeal based on the trial court's refusal to submit requested material."

TRCP 274. OBJECTIONS & REQUESTS

A party objecting to a charge must point out distinctly the objectionable matter and the grounds of the objection. Any complaint as to a question, definition, or instruction, on account of any defect, omission, or fault in pleading, is waived unless specifically included in the objections. When the complaining party's objection, or requested question, definition, or instruction is, in the opinion of the appellate court, obscured or concealed by voluminous unfounded objections, minute differentiations or numerous unnecessary requests, such objection or request shall be untenable. No objection to one part of the charge may be adopted and applied to any other part of the charge by reference only.

See *Commentaries*, "The Charge," ch. 8-I.

History of TRCP 274: Amended eff. Jan. 1, 1988, by order of July 15, 1987 (733-34 S.W.2d [Tex.Cases] lxix). Amended eff. Dec. 31, 1941, by order of Sept. 20, 1941 (4 Tex.B.J. 528 [1941]). Adopted eff. Sept. 1, 1941, by order of Oct. 29, 1940 (3 Tex.B.J. 566 [1940]). Source: New rule.

In re B.L.D., 113 S.W.3d 340, 351 (Tex.2003). "We are aware of no precedent in either our criminal or civil jurisprudence that informs the court of appeals' conclusion that 'core' jury charge issues in termination cases should be reviewed even when not preserved. Further, we cannot see any reasonable, practical, and consistent way of reviewing unpreserved complaints of charge error in termination cases that satisfies our narrow fundamental-error doctrine. [T]he fundamental-error doctrine does not permit appellate review of the complaint of unpreserved charge error in this case."

Holubec v. Brandenberger, 111 S.W.3d 32, 39 (Tex.2003) The defendants "plainly sought the submission of their statutory defense. Because the question actually submitted was defective, however, [Ds] did not have to submit their own substantially correct question. [D's] objection was sufficient to preserve error."

Harris Cty. v. Smith, 96 S.W.3d 230, 235-36 (Tex. 2002). If an element of damages in a broad-form submission is not supported by evidence, the party must object and ask the court to either (1) not include that element in the broad-form damage question or (2) submit the elements separately.

Universal Servs. Co. v. Ung, 904 S.W.2d 638, 640 (Tex.1995). A party cannot complain on appeal that the trial court did not submit an instruction or definition with the correct cluster if the party did not request it as part of that cluster.

General Chem. Corp. v. De La Lastra, 852 S.W.2d 916, 920 (Tex.1993). Defendant "requested the very issues that it now seeks to avoid. Parties may not invite error by requesting an issue and then objecting to its submission."

TRCP 275. CHARGE READ BEFORE ARGUMENT

Before the argument is begun, the trial court shall read the charge to the jury in the precise words in which it was written, including all questions, definitions, and instructions which the court may give.

See *Commentaries*, "The Charge," ch. 8-I.

History of TRCP 275: Amended eff. Jan. 1, 1988, by order of July 15, 1987 (733-34 S.W.2d [Tex.Cases] lxix). Adopted eff. Sept. 1, 1941, by order of Oct. 29, 1940 (3 Tex.B.J. 566 [1940]). Source: TRCS art. 2187 (repealed).

Board of Regents v. S&G Constr. Co., 529 S.W.2d 90, 98 (Tex.App.—Austin 1975, writ ref'd n.r.e.), *overruled on other grounds*, ***Federal Sign v. TSU***, 951 S.W.2d 401, 408 (Tex.1997). A trial court does not violate TRCP 275 by amending the written charge to correct errors after oral argument.

TRCP 276. REFUSAL OR MODIFICATION

When an instruction, question, or definition is requested and the provisions of the law have been complied with and the trial judge refuses the same, the judge shall endorse thereon "Refused," and sign the same officially. If the trial judge modifies the same the judge shall endorse thereon "Modified as follows: (stating in what particular the judge has modified the same) and given, and exception allowed" and sign the same officially. Such refused or modified instruction, question, or definition, when so endorsed shall constitute a bill of exceptions, and it shall be conclusively presumed that the party asking the same presented it at the proper time, excepted to its refusal or modification, and that all the requirements of law have been observed, and such procedure shall entitle the party requesting the same to have the action of the trial judge thereon reviewed without preparing a formal bill of exceptions.

See *Commentaries*, "The Charge," ch. 8-I.

History of TRCP 276: Amended eff. Jan. 1, 1988, by order of July 15, 1987 (733-34 S.W.2d [Tex.Cases] lxix). Adopted eff. Sept. 1, 1941, by order of Oct. 29, 1940 (3 Tex.B.J. 566 [1940]). Source: TRCS art. 2188 (repealed).

Dallas Mkt. Ctr. Dev. Co. v. Liedeker, 958 S.W.2d 382, 386-87 (Tex.1997), *overruled on other grounds*, ***Torrington Co. v. Stutzman***, 46 S.W.3d 829 (Tex. 2000). Although TRCP 276 requires the trial court to endorse refused requests "Refused," and sign them officially, that is not the only way to preserve error. The court can state on the record they are refused.

TRCP 277. SUBMISSION TO THE JURY

In all jury cases the court shall, whenever feasible, submit the cause upon broad-form questions. The court shall submit such instructions and definitions as shall be proper to enable the jury to render a verdict.

Inferential rebuttal questions shall not be submitted in the charge. The placing of the burden of proof may be accomplished by instructions rather than by inclusion in the question.

In any cause in which the jury is required to apportion the loss among the parties the court shall submit a question or questions inquiring what percentage, if any, of the negligence or causation, as the case may be, that caused the occurrence or injury in question is attributable to each of the persons found to have been culpable. The court shall also instruct the jury to answer the damage question or questions without any reduction because of the percentage of negligence or causation, if any, of the person injured. The court may predicate the damage question or questions upon affirmative findings of liability.

The court may submit a question disjunctively when it is apparent from the evidence that one or the other of the conditions or facts inquired about necessarily exists.

The court shall not in its charge comment directly on the weight of the evidence or advise the jury of the effect of their answers, but the court's charge shall not be objectionable on the ground that it incidentally constitutes a comment on the weight of the evidence or advises the jury of the effect of their answers when it is properly a part of an instruction or definition.

See *Commentaries*, "The Charge," ch. 8-I.

History of TRCP 277: Amended eff. Jan 1, 1988, by order July 15, 1987 (733-34 S.W.2d [Tex.Cases] lxx): The amendment to par. 1 of TRCP 277 will unify the practice of submitting broad form questions to the jury in the form approved by *Lemos v. Montez*, 680 S.W.2d 798 (Tex.1984); the amendment to the third par. includes a textual change and recognizes that damage issues may be predicated on affirmative liability findings. Amended eff. Apr. 1, 1984, by order Dec. 5, 1983 (661-62 S.W.2d [Tex.Cases] lxxvi). Amended eff. Sept. 1, 1973, by order of May 25, 1973 (493-94 S.W.2d [Tex.Cases] xxiv): The words "controlling the disposition of the case that are" were inserted in the first paragraph; the provisions of the former rule requiring issues to be submitted distinctly and separately, in the affirmative, and in plain and simple language, were deleted; the provision concerning placing the burden of proof was rewritten; the first three sentences of the second par. and all of the fourth, fifth and seventh par. were added; the last sentence of the original rule was deleted; and a number of minor textual changes were made. Amended eff. Sept. 1, 1941, by order of Mar. 31, 1941 (4 Tex.B.J. 173 [1941]). Adopted eff. Sept. 1, 1941, by order of Oct. 29, 1940 (3 Tex.B.J. 566 [1940]). Source: TRCS art. 2189 (repealed).

Crown Life Ins. Co. v. Casteel, 22 S.W.3d 378, 390 (Tex.1999). "Rule 277 is not absolute; rather, it mandates broad-form submission 'whenever feasible.' [W]hen the trial court is unsure whether it should submit a particular theory of liability, separating liability theories best serves the policy of judicial economy underlying Rule 277 by avoiding the need for a new trial when the basis for liability cannot be determined." *See also* ***Texas Dept. of Human Servs. v. Hinds***, 904 S.W.2d 629, 637 (Tex.1995); ***Texas Dept. of Human Servs. v. E.B.***, 802 S.W.2d 647, 649 (Tex.1990).

Hyundai Motor Co. v. Rodriguez, 995 S.W.2d 661, 664 (Tex.1999). "[S]ubmission of a single question relating to multiple theories may be necessary to avoid the risk that the jury will become confused and answer questions inconsistently. The goal of the charge is to submit to the jury the issues for decision logically, simply, clearly, fairly, correctly, and completely."

H.E. Butt Grocery Co. v. Bilotto, 985 S.W.2d 22, 24 (Tex.1998). "[W]hen an instruction merely directs the jury to answer a damages question only if some condition or conditions have been met, it does not directly instruct the jury about the legal effect of its answers."

State Farm Lloyds v. Nicolau, 951 S.W.2d 444, 451 (Tex.1997). TRCP 277 "affords the trial court considerable discretion in deciding what instructions are necessary and proper in submitting issues to the jury." *See also* ***Wichita Cty. v. Hart***, 917 S.W.2d 779, 783-84 (Tex. 1996).

H.E. Butt Grocery Co. v. Warner, 845 S.W.2d 258, 260 (Tex.1992). The trial court's "failure [to submit a properly requested broad-form question] was not harmful error. Although submitted in granulated form, the jury questions contained the proper elements of a premises liability action."

In re J.M.M., 80 S.W.3d 232, 247 (Tex.App.—Fort Worth 2002, pet. denied). "[W]hen a single broad-form liability question erroneously commingles valid and invalid theories and [D's] objection is timely and specific, the error is harmful and a new trial is required 'when the appellate court cannot determine whether the jury based its verdict on an improperly submitted invalid theory.'"

Toennies v. Quantum Chem. Corp., 998 S.W.2d 374, 377 (Tex.App.—Houston [1st Dist.] 1999), *aff'd*, 47 S.W.3d 473 (Tex.2001). "When liability is asserted based upon a provision of a statute or regulation, a jury charge should track the language of the provision as closely as possible."

TRCP 278. SUBMISSION OF QUESTIONS, DEFINITIONS, & INSTRUCTIONS

The court shall submit the questions, instructions and definitions in the form provided by Rule 277, which are raised by the written pleadings and the evidence. Except in trespass to try title, statutory partition proceedings, and other special proceedings in which the pleadings are specially defined by statutes or procedural rules, a party shall not be entitled to any submission of any question raised only by a general denial and not raised by affirmative written pleading by that party. Nothing herein shall change the burden of proof from what it would have been under a general denial. A judgment shall not be reversed because of the failure to submit other and various phases or different shades of the same question. Failure to submit a question shall not be deemed a ground for reversal of the judgment, unless its submission, in substantially correct wording, has been requested in writing and tendered by the party complaining of the judgment; provided, however, that objection to such failure shall suffice in such respect if the question is one relied upon by the opposing party. Failure to submit a definition or instruction shall not be deemed a ground for reversal of the judgment unless a substantially correct definition or instruction has been requested in writing and tendered by the party complaining of the judgment.

See *Commentaries*, "The Charge," ch. 8-I.

History of TRCP 278: Adopted eff. Jan. 1, 1988, by order of July 15, 1987 (733-34 S.W.2d [Tex.Cases] lxxi). Former TRCP 278 was repealed eff. Sept.

1941, by order of Mar. 31, 1941 (4 Tex.B.J. 174 [1941]). Source: New rule. See former TRCP 279, first par.

Union Pac. R.R. v. Williams, 85 S.W.3d 162, 166 (Tex.2002). "A party is entitled to a jury question, instruction, or definition if the pleadings and evidence raise an issue. An instruction is proper if it (1) assists the jury, (2) accurately states the law, and (3) finds support in the pleadings and evidence."

Texas Workers' Comp. Ins. Fund v. Mandlbauer, 34 S.W.3d 909, 912 (Tex.2000). "When a trial court refuses to submit a requested instruction, the question on appeal is whether the request was reasonably necessary to enable the jury to render a proper verdict."

Green Int'l v. Solis, 951 S.W.2d 384, 390 (Tex. 1997). "Assuming the trial court erred in failing to permit an amendment of the trial pleadings, the trial court did not err in failing to submit the accompanying jury questions. Each requested jury question must be supported by the evidence."

Texas Dept. of Human Servs. v. Hinds, 904 S.W.2d 629, 637-38 (Tex.1995). "[D] did not request the instruction that should have been given, but instead requested [another] instruction.... We believe this request nevertheless preserved error for 2 reasons. First, [D] took the instruction from the concurring opinion in ***Winters [v. Houston Chronicle Publ'g Co.***, 795 S.W.2d 723 (Tex.1990)]. Second, the request called the trial court's attention to the causation element missing in Question No. 2."

Triplex Comm. v. Riley, 900 S.W.2d 716, 718 (Tex. 1995). "If an issue is properly pleaded and is supported by some evidence, a litigant is entitled to have controlling questions submitted to the jury." *See also* ***Elbaor v. Smith***, 845 S.W.2d 240, 243 (Tex.1992).

Southwestern Bell Tel. Co. v. John Carlo Tex., Inc., 843 S.W.2d 470, 472 (Tex.1992). "The court of appeals ... held the error [in refusing to define justification] harmless. We disagree. Virtually the entire factual dispute between the parties has been over whether Bell's conduct was justified. To ask the jury to resolve this dispute without a proper legal definition to the essential legal issue was reversible error."

Robertson Cty. v. Wymola, 17 S.W.3d 334, 342 (Tex. App.—Austin 2000, pet. denied). "A fact issue that is established with uncontroverted evidence and is not in dispute should not be submitted to the jury."

Fairfield Estates L.P. v. Griffin, 986 S.W.2d 719, 724 (Tex.App.—Eastland 1999, no pet.). "[A]t the jury charge conference, [Ds] objected to the lack of an instruction on the measure of damages and [orally] requested an instruction on temporary damages. ... Because [Ds'] request was not made 'in writing,' it was waived."

TRCP 279. OMISSIONS FROM THE CHARGE

Upon appeal all independent grounds of recovery or of defense not conclusively established under the evidence and no element of which is submitted or requested are waived. When a ground of recovery or defense consists of more than one element, if one or more of such elements necessary to sustain such ground of recovery or defense, and necessarily referable thereto, are submitted to and found by the jury, and one or more of such elements are omitted from the charge, without request or objection, and there is factually sufficient evidence to support a finding thereon, the trial court, at the request of either party, may after notice and hearing and at any time before the judgment is rendered, make and file written findings on such omitted element or elements in support of the judgment. If no such written findings are made, such omitted element or elements shall be deemed found by the court in such manner as to support the judgment. A claim that the evidence was legally or factually insufficient to warrant the submission of any question may be made for the first time after verdict, regardless of whether the submission of such question was requested by the complainant.

See ***Commentaries***, "The Charge," ch. 8-I.

History of TRCP 279: Amended eff. Jan. 1, 1988, by order of July 15, 1987 (733-34 S.W.2d [Tex.Cases] lxxi): First par. transferred to TRCP 278. Amended eff. Sept. 1, 1941, by order of Mar. 31, 1941 (4 Tex.B.J. 174 [1941]). Adopted eff. Sept. 1, 1941, by order of Oct. 29, 1940 (3 Tex.B.J. 567 [1940]). Source: TRCS art. 2190 (repealed).

In re J.F.C., 96 S.W.3d 256, 262-63 (Tex.2002). Under TRCP 279 "when some but not all elements of a claim or cause of action are submitted to and found by a jury, and there is no request or objection with regard to the missing element, a trial court may expressly make a finding on the omitted element or, if it does not, the omitted element is deemed found by the court in a manner supporting the judgment if the deemed finding is supported by some evidence." *See also* ***State Farm Life Ins. Co. v. Beaston***, 907 S.W.2d 430, 437 (Tex.1995).

Gulf States Utils. Co. v. Low, 79 S.W.3d 561, 564 (Tex.2002). "Rule 279 may support a deemed finding only when it can be deemed found 'in such manner as to support the judgment.' ... The court of appeals misapplied Rule 279 to deem a finding, not to support the trial court's judgment, but to render a new judgment for actual damages in an amount nearly 15 times the trial court's award."

T.O. Stanley Boot Co. v. Bank of El Paso, 847 S.W.2d 218, 222-23 (Tex.1992). Plaintiff "failed to submit or request any element of its affirmative claim to the jury. Unless [P's] affirmative claim is conclusively established under the evidence, the ground of recovery is waived upon appeal."

State Dept. of Highways & Pub. Transp. v. Payne, 838 S.W.2d 235, 241 (Tex.1992). "To prevail on his premise defect theory, [P] was required to obtain a finding that he lacked knowledge of the culvert. This element of his claim was not included in the broad-form charge which the trial court submitted to the jury. A finding on this one element cannot be deemed in [P's] favor because [D] objected to the omission by requesting a jury question on that issue."

Ramos v. Frito-Lay, Inc., 784 S.W.2d 667, 668 (Tex. 1990). "Where ... issues are omitted which constitute only a part of a complete and independent ground and other issues necessarily referable to that ground are submitted and answered, the omitted elements are deemed found in support of the judgment if no objection is made and they are supported by some evidence."

E. CASE TO THE JURY

TRCP 280. PRESIDING JUROR OF JURY

Each jury shall appoint one of their body presiding juror.

History of TRCP 280: Amended eff. Apr. 1, 1984, by order of Dec. 5, 1983 (661-62 S.W.2d [Tex.Cases] lxxvii): Changed "foreman" to "presiding juror." Adopted eff. Sept. 1, 1941, by order of Oct. 29, 1940 (3 Tex.B.J. 568 [1940]). Source: TRCS art. 2192 (repealed).

TRCP 281. PAPERS TAKEN TO JURY ROOM

The jury may, and on request shall, take with them in their retirement the charges and instructions, general or special, which were given and read to them, and any written evidence, except the depositions of witnesses, but shall not take with them any special charges which have been refused. Where part only of a paper has been read in evidence, the jury shall not take the same with them, unless the part so read to them is detached from that which was excluded.

History of TRCP 281: Amended eff. Apr. 1, 1984, by order of Dec. 5, 1983 (661-62 S.W.2d [Tex.Cases] lxxvii). Adopted eff. Sept. 1, 1941, by order of Oct. 29, 1940 (3 Tex.B.J. 568 [1940]). Source: TRCS art. 2193 (repealed).

First Employees Ins. Co. v. Skinner, 646 S.W.2d 170, 172 (Tex.1983). TRCP 281 "is mandatory and ... the trial court is required to send all exhibits admitted into evidence to the jury room during the deliberations of the jury. Furthermore, this rule is self-operative and requires no request from the jurors or counsel."

Speier v. Webster Coll., 616 S.W.2d 617, 619 (Tex. 1981). "The fact that a chart happens to summarize testimony on damages does not remove its admissibility from the discretion of the trial court. The type of testimony summarized is only one of many factors a trial court must consider in exercising its discretion."

Harvey v. Culpepper, 801 S.W.2d 596, 601 (Tex. App.—Corpus Christi 1990, no writ). "The admission of depositions into evidence is prohibited. The trial court should not have allowed the jury to retire with the depositions."

TRCP 282. JURY KEPT TOGETHER

The jury may either decide a case in court or retire for deliberation. If they retire, they shall be kept together in some convenient place, under the charge of an officer, until they agree upon a verdict or are discharged by the court; but the court in its discretion may permit them to separate temporarily for the night and at their meals, and for other proper purposes.

History of TRCP 282: Adopted eff. Sept. 1, 1941, by order of Oct. 29, 1940 (3 Tex.B.J. 568 [1940]). Source: TRCS art. 2194 (repealed).

Union City Transfer v. Adams, 248 S.W.2d 256, 260 (Tex.App.—Fort Worth 1952, writ ref'd n.r.e.). "Permitting the jury to separate temporarily for their meal was within the discretion of the court."

TRCP 283. DUTY OF OFFICER ATTENDING JURY

The officer in charge of the jury shall not make nor permit any communication to be made to them, except to inquire if they have agreed upon a verdict, unless by order of the court; and he shall not before their verdict is rendered communicate to any person the state of their deliberations or the verdict agreed upon.

History of TRCP 283: Adopted eff. Sept. 1, 1941, by order of Oct. 29, 1940 (3 Tex.B.J. 568 [1940]). Source: TRCS art. 2195 (repealed).

Logan v. Grady, 482 S.W.2d 313, 322 (Tex.App.—Fort Worth 1972, no writ). "[T]he jury bailiff violated [TRCP] 283 and 285 … when he did not make the jury's wish as communicated to him known to the court and also when he instructed the jury that its members already had in the jury room all that it needed in order to answer Issue No. 14."

TRCP 284. JUDGE TO CAUTION JURY

If permitted to separate, either during the trial or after the case is submitted to them, the jury shall be admonished by the court that it is their duty not to converse with, or permit themselves to be addressed by any other person, on any subject connected with the trial.

History of TRCP 284: Adopted eff. Sept. 1, 1941, by order of Oct. 29, 1940 (3 Tex.B.J. 568 [1940]). Source: TRCS art. 2196 (repealed).

TRCP 285. JURY MAY COMMUNICATE WITH COURT

The jury may communicate with the court by making their wish known to the officer in charge, who shall inform the court, and they may then in open court, and through their presiding juror, communicate with the court, either verbally or in writing. If the communication is to request further instructions, Rule 286 shall be followed.

See *Commentaries*, "The Charge," ch. 8-I.

History of TRCP 285: Amended eff. Apr. 1, 1984, by order of Dec. 5, 1983 (661-62 S.W.2d [Tex.Cases] lxxvii): Changed word "foreman" to "presiding juror." Adopted eff. Sept. 1, 1941, by order of Oct. 29, 1940 (3 Tex.B.J. 569 [1940]). Source: TRCS art. 2197 (repealed). The last sentence was added.

Ross v. TEIA, 267 S.W.2d 541, 542 (Tex.1954). TRCP 285 "provides that the jury may communicate with the trial judge through its foreman in open court, and [TRCP] 286 provides that when the jury desires further instructions it shall appear in open court in a body, shall make a request in writing through its foreman, and, if additional instructions are given, they shall be in writing."

TRCP 286. JURY MAY RECEIVE FURTHER INSTRUCTIONS

After having retired, the jury may receive further instructions from the court touching any matter of law, either at their request or upon the court's own motion. For this purpose they shall appear before the judge in open court in a body, and if the instruction is being given at their request, they shall through their presiding juror state to the court, in writing, the particular question of law upon which they desire further instruction. The court shall give such instruction in writing, but no instruction shall be given except in conformity with the rules relating to the charge. Additional argument may be allowed in the discretion of the court.

See *Commentaries*, "The Charge," ch. 8-I.

History of TRCP 286: Amended eff. Jan. 1, 1988, by order of July 15, 1987 (733-34 S.W.2d [Tex.Cases] lxxi). Amended eff. Apr. 1, 1984, by order of Dec. 5, 1983 (661-62 S.W.2d [Tex.Cases] lxxviii): The word "foreman" was changed to "presiding juror." Adopted eff. Sept. 1, 1941, by order of Oct. 29, 1940 (3 Tex.B.J. 569 [1940]). Source: TRCS art. 2198 (repealed).

Stevens v. Travelers Ins. Co., 563 S.W.2d 223, 229 (Tex.1978). "[E]ven though there is a latent danger of coercion, supplemental, verdict-urging instructions are not, in and of themselves, erroneous, so long as the particular charge given is not otherwise objectionable. *At 226 n.1:* Under [TRCP] 286 the supplemental charge should have been given in writing and not orally."

Lochinvar Corp. v. Meyers, 930 S.W.2d 182, 187 (Tex.App.—Dallas 1996, no writ). "[TRCP] 286 allow[s] a court the opportunity to correct an error by modifying its charge. … The instruction was given to the jury in writing [but the trial court did not] reassemble the jury in the courtroom. [D waived the error because it] did not object to the court's failure to reassemble the jury and read the modified charge."

TRCP 287. DISAGREEMENT AS TO EVIDENCE

If the jury disagree as to the statement of any witness, they may, upon applying to the court, have read to them from the court reporter's notes that part of such witness' testimony on the point in dispute; but, if there be no such reporter, or if his notes cannot be read to the jury, the court may cause such witness to be again brought upon the stand and the judge shall direct him to repeat his testimony as to the point in dispute, and no other, as nearly as he can in the language used on the trial; and on their notifying the court that they disagree as to any portion of a deposition or other paper not permitted to be carried with them in their retirement, the court may, in like manner, permit such portion of said deposition or paper to be again read to the jury.

History of TRCP 287: Adopted eff. Sept. 1, 1941, by order of Oct. 29, 1940 (3 Tex.B.J. 569 [1940]). Source: TRCS art. 2199 (repealed), as amended.

Krishnan v. Ramirez, 42 S.W.3d 205, 225 (Tex. App.—Corpus Christi 2001, pet. denied). "The judge is given broad discretion in determining what portions of the testimony are relevant to the jury's request to have testimony re-read."

Steinberger v. Archer Cty., 621 S.W.2d 838, 843 (Tex.App.—Fort Worth 1981, no writ). Under TRCP 287 "the jury is entitled to hear only the specific part of the testimony relevant to the point in dispute, and only when the jury notifies the court, that it disagrees upon the statement made by the witness."

TRCP 288. COURT OPEN FOR JURY

The court, during the deliberations of the jury, may proceed with other business or recess from time to time, but shall be deemed open for all purposes connected with the case before the jury.

History of TRCP 288: Adopted eff. Sept. 1, 1941, by order of Oct. 29, 1940 (3 Tex.B.J. 569 [1940]). Source: TRCS art. 2201 (repealed).

TRCP 289. DISCHARGE OF JURY

The jury to whom a case has been submitted may be discharged by the court when they cannot agree and the parties consent to their discharge, or when they have been kept together for such time as to render it altogether improbable that they can agree, or when any calamity or accident may, in the opinion of the court, require it, or when by sickness or other cause their number is reduced below the number constituting the jury in such court.

The cause shall again be placed on the jury docket and shall again be set for trial as the court directs.

See ***Commentaries***, "The Charge," ch. 8-I.

History of TRCP 289: Amended eff. Apr. 1, 1984, by order of Dec. 5, 1983 (661-62 S.W.2d [Tex.Cases] lxxviii). Adopted eff. Sept. 1, 1941, by order of Oct. 29, 1940 (3 Tex.B.J. 569 [1940]). Source: TRCS art. 2200 (repealed).

Shaw v. Greater Houston Transp. Co., 791 S.W.2d 204, 205-10 (Tex.App.—Corpus Christi 1990, no writ). It was coercive for the trial court to refuse to release the jury after they stated three times they were deadlocked.

F. VERDICT

TRCP 290. DEFINITION & SUBSTANCE

A verdict is a written declaration by a jury of its decision, comprehending the whole or all the issues submitted to the jury, and shall be either a general or special verdict, as directed, which shall be signed by the presiding juror of the jury.

A general verdict is one whereby the jury pronounces generally in favor of one or more parties to the suit upon all or any of the issues submitted to it. A special verdict is one wherein the jury finds the facts only on issues made up and submitted to them under the direction of the court.

A special verdict shall, as between the parties, be conclusive as to the facts found.

History of TRCP 290: Amended eff. Apr. 1, 1984, by order of Dec. 5, 1983 (661-62 S.W.2d [Tex.Cases] lxxviii): Changed "foreman" to "presiding juror." Adopted eff. Sept. 1, 1941, by order of Oct. 29, 1940 (3 Tex.B.J. 569 [1940]). Source: TRCS art. 2202 (repealed).

Wal-Mart Stores v. Alexander, 868 S.W.2d 322, 328 (Tex.1993). "A jury's marginal notations generally may not be considered on appeal. They reflect the jury's mental processes, but they are not part of its verdict."

Houston Fire & Cas. Ins. Co. v. Gerhardt, 281 S.W.2d 176, 178 (Tex.App.—San Antonio 1955, orig. proceeding). "A verdict form reflecting answers to special issues but not signed by the foreman may or may not be a verdict, and presents a question which must be determined by the hearing of evidence."

TRCP 291. FORM OF VERDICT

No special form of verdict is required, and the judgment shall not be arrested or reversed for mere want of form therein if there has been substantial compliance with the requirements of the law in rendering a verdict.

History of TRCP 291: Amended eff. Feb. 1, 1973, by order of Oct. 3, 1972 (483-84 S.W.2d [Tex.Cases] xl): Deleted sentence requiring concurrence of all members of the jury in the verdict. Adopted eff. Sept. 1, 1941, by order of Oct. 29, 1940 (3 Tex.B.J. 570 [1940]). Source: TRCS art. 2203 (repealed).

TRCP 292. VERDICT BY PORTION OF ORIGINAL JURY

A verdict may be rendered in any cause by the concurrence, as to each and all answers made, of the same ten members of an original jury of twelve or of the same five members of an original jury of six. However, where as many as three jurors die or be disabled from sitting and there are only nine of the jurors remaining of an original jury of twelve, those remaining may render and return a verdict. If less than the original twelve or six jurors render a verdict, the verdict must be signed by each juror concurring therein.

See ***Commentaries***, "The Verdict," ch. 8-K.

History of TRCP 292: Amended eff. Feb. 1, 1973, by order of Oct. 3, 1972 (483-84 S.W.2d [Tex.Cases] xl): Inserted the first sentence, which provides for rendition of a verdict by 10 members of an original jury of 12 and by 5 members of an original jury of 6; and rewrote third sentence to require that any verdict rendered by less than the original 12 or 6 jurors be signed by each juror concurring in it. Adopted eff. Sept. 1, 1941, by order of Oct. 29, 1940 (3 Tex.B.J. 570 [1940]). Source: TRCS art. 2204 (repealed).

Yanes v. Sowards, 996 S.W.2d 849, 850 (Tex.1999). Trial courts have broad discretion in determining whether a juror is disabled from sitting when there is evidence of constitutional disqualification. But not just any inconvenience or delay is a disability. A constitutional disability must be in the nature of an actual physical or mental incapacity.

McDaniel v. Yarbrough, 898 S.W.2d 251, 253 (Tex. 1995). "No evidence of record suggests that [the juror] became 'disabled from sitting' within the [meaning of the constitution]. She was not mentally incompetent or sick, nor did she have some other physical or mental incapacity. On the contrary, she was temporarily detained by flooding caused by heavy rain, which is at most a transient physical barrier. Her dismissal from the jury as 'disabled' was improper. [¶] Depriving [Ps] of a full jury of 12 members, absent an exception authorized by the constitution or applicable rules, is a denial of the right to jury trial guaranteed by the Texas Constitution."

Schlafly v. Schlafly, 33 S.W.3d 863, 870 (Tex. App.—Houston [14th Dist.] 2000, pet. denied). "There is no reason to treat a jury comprised of 12 members, one of whom is an alternate, any differently than a jury comprised of 12 regular members. ... We find 'original jurors' means all the jurors empaneled, both regular members and alternates."

Fiore v. Fiore, 946 S.W.2d 436, 438 (Tex.App.—Fort Worth 1997, writ denied). "[W]hen a trial court dismisses a juror who is not 'disabled,' and there is no agreement to proceed with 11 jurors, it is an abuse of discretion to deny a motion for mistrial."

TRCP 293. WHEN THE JURY AGREE

When the jury agree upon a verdict, they shall be brought into court by the proper officer, and they shall deliver their verdict to the clerk; and if they state that they have agreed, the verdict shall be read aloud by the clerk. If the verdict is in proper form, no juror objects to its accuracy, no juror represented as agreeing thereto dissents therefrom, and neither party requests a poll of the jury, the verdict shall be entered upon the minutes of the court.

History of TRCP 293: Amended eff. Feb. 1, 1973, by order of Oct. 3, 1972 (483-84 S.W.2d [Tex.Cases] xl): In second sentence, inserted the words "objects to its accuracy, no juror represented as agreeing thereto," and made other minor changes. Adopted eff. Sept. 1, 1941, by order of Oct. 29, 1940 (3 Tex.B.J. 570 [1940]). Source: TRCS art. 2205 (repealed), with changes: Eliminated the requirement that the jurors' names be called by the clerk.

Thomas v. Oil & Gas Bldg., 582 S.W.2d 873, 880 (Tex.App.—Corpus Christi 1979, writ ref'd n.r.e.). TRCP 293, "in essence, provides that when a verdict is accurate and in proper form, that it 'shall be entered upon the minutes of the court.'"

TRCP 294. POLLING THE JURY

Any party shall have the right to have the jury polled. A jury is polled by reading once to the jury collectively the general verdict, or the questions and answers thereto consecutively, and then calling the name of each juror separately and asking the juror if it is the juror's verdict. If any juror answers in the negative when the verdict is returned signed only by the presiding juror as a unanimous verdict, or if any juror shown by the juror's signature to agree to the verdict should answer in the negative, the jury shall be retired for further deliberation.

See *Commentaries*, "Request to Poll the Jury," ch. 8-K, §5.

History of TRCP 294: Amended eff. Sept. 1, 1990, by order of Apr. 24, 1990 (785-86 S.W.2d [Tex.Cases] lxvii): Changed "his" to "the juror's," "him" to "the juror," "special issues" to "questions" and the first word from "Either" to "Any." Amended eff. Apr. 1, 1984, by order of Dec. 5, 1983 (661-62 S.W.2d [Tex.Cases] lxxviii): Changed "foreman" to "presiding juror." Amended eff. Feb. 1, 1973, by order of Oct. 3, 1972 (483-84 S.W.2d [Tex.Cases] xli): Rewrote last sentence to provide that the jury shall be retired for further deliberation if any juror answers in the negative where the verdict is returned as a unanimous verdict or if any juror shown by his signature to agree to the verdict answers in the negative. Adopted eff. Sept. 1, 1941, by order of Oct. 29, 1940 (3 Tex.B.J. 570 [1940]). Source: TRCS art. 2206 (repealed), with changes: Eliminated words "which is done by" and added the language of the second sentence through "and then."

Suggs v. Fitch, 64 S.W.3d 658, 660 (Tex.App.—Texarkana 2001, no pet.) "The right to poll the jury pursuant to [TRCP] 294 is a waivable right and must be requested in order to be invoked."

Pate v. Texline Feed Mills, 689 S.W.2d 238, 243 (Tex.App.—Amarillo 1985, writ ref'd n.r.e.). "Once the request is promptly made before the jury is discharged, the trial court has no discretion but to poll the jury, and the requesting party's motive is immaterial."

TRCP 295. CORRECTION OF VERDICT

If the purported verdict is defective, the court may direct it to be reformed. If it is incomplete, or not responsive to the questions contained in the court's charge, or the answers to the questions are in conflict, the court shall in writing instruct the jury in open court of the nature of the incompleteness, unresponsiveness, or conflict, provide the jury such additional instructions as may be proper, and retire the jury for further deliberations.

History of TRCP 295: Amended eff. Jan. 1, 1988, by order of July 15, 1987 (733-34 S.W.2d [Tex.Cases] lxxii): The amendment makes it clear that the court may direct a complete yet defective verdict to be reformed. The amendment also makes it clear that in the event the verdict is incomplete or otherwise improper, the court is limited to giving the jury additional instructions in writing. Adopted eff. Sept. 1, 1941, by order of Oct. 29, 1940 (3 Tex.B.J. 570 [1940]). Source: TRCS art. 2207 (repealed).

Archer Daniels Midland Co. v. Bohall, 114 S.W.3d 42, 46 (Tex.App.—Eastland 2003, n.p.h.). TRCP 295 "applies only to defective verdicts, not defective charges. Before [TRCP] 295 would authorize further instruction to the jury, the verdict must be incomplete, non-responsive to the questions contained in the court's charge, or contain answers which are in conflict." *See also* ***Elbar, Inc. v. Claussen***, 774 S.W.2d 45, 55 (Tex. App.—Dallas 1989, no writ).

G. FINDINGS BY COURT

TRCP 296. REQUESTS FOR FINDINGS OF FACTS & CONCLUSIONS OF LAW

In any case tried in the district or county court without a jury, any party may request the court to state in writing its findings of fact and conclusions of law. Such request shall be entitled "Request for Findings of Fact and Conclusions of Law" and shall be filed within twenty days after judgment is signed with the clerk of the court, who shall immediately call such request to the attention of the judge who tried the case. The party making the request shall serve it on all other parties in accordance with Rule 21a.

See ***Commentaries***, "Request for Findings of Fact," ch. 10-E; FORMS 10E.

History of TRCP 296: Amended eff. Sept. 1, 1990, by order of Apr. 24, 1990 (785-86 S.W.2d [Tex.Cases] lxvii): Rewrote rule and title to revise the practice and times for findings of fact and conclusions of law. [See TRCP 297 and 298]. Amended eff. April 1, 1984, by order of Dec. 5, 1983 (661-62 S.W.2d [Tex.Cases] lxxix): Changed time for filing the request for findings and conclusions so that it must be made within 10 days of the signing of the final judgment. Amended eff. Jan. 1, 1981, by order of June 10, 1990 (599-600 S.W.2d [Tex.Cases] xlvii): Amended to commence the running of time for filing findings and conclusions to the date the final judgment or order overruling a motion for new trial is signed or the motion is overruled by operation of law; the last sentence of former TRCP 296 becomes the second sentence of TRCP 297. Amended eff. Sept. 1, 1957, by order of Mar. 19, 1957 (20 Tex.B.J. 192 [1957]): Added provisions limiting time in which to request conclusions of fact and law and requiring notice to opposite party of filing of request. Adopted eff. Sept. 1, 1941, by order of Oct. 29, 1940 (3 Tex.B.J. 570 [1940]). Source: TRCS art. 2208 (repealed).

Tenery v. Tenery, 932 S.W.2d 29, 30 (Tex.1996). Under TRCP 296, "harm to the complaining party is presumed unless the contrary appears on the face of the record when the party makes a proper and timely request for findings and the trial court fails to comply. Error is harmful if it prevents an appellant from properly presenting a case to the appellate court." *See also* ***Cherne Indus., Inc. v. Magallanes***, 763 S.W.2d 768, 772 (Tex.1989).

Black v. Dallas Cty. Child Welfare Unit, 835 S.W.2d 626, 630 n.10 (Tex.1992). "If no findings of fact or conclusions of law are filed, the reviewing court must imply all necessary fact findings in support of the trial court's judgment."

Rutledge v. Staner, 9 S.W.3d 469, 470 (Tex.App.—Tyler 1999, pet. denied). "It is well-settled that an appellate court cannot construe comments the trial judge may have made at the conclusion of the bench trial as findings of fact and conclusions of law."

Kenedy Mem'l Found. v. Dewhurst, 994 S.W.2d 285, 308 (Tex.App.—Austin 1999), *rev'd on other grounds*, 90 S.W.3d 268 (Tex.2002). "Findings of fact set out in a trial-court memorandum are not findings of fact as contemplated by [TRCPs] 296-299. ... We do not review an opinion written by a trial court and it has no persuasive value for an appellate court."

TRCP 297. TIME TO FILE FINDINGS OF FACT & CONCLUSIONS OF LAW

The court shall file its findings of fact and conclusions of law within twenty days after a timely request is filed. The court shall cause a copy of its findings and conclusions to be mailed to each party in the suit.

If the court fails to file timely findings of fact and conclusions of law, the party making the request shall, within thirty days after filing the original request, file with the clerk and serve on all other parties in accordance with Rule 21a a "Notice of Past Due Findings of Fact and Conclusions of Law" which shall be immediately called to the attention of the court by the clerk. Such notice shall state the date the original request was filed and the date the findings and conclusions were due. Upon filing this notice, the time for the court to file findings of fact and conclusions of law is extended to forty days from the date the original request was filed.

See *Commentaries*, "Request for Findings of Fact," ch. 10-E.

History of TRCP 297: Amended eff. Sept. 1, 1990, by order of Apr. 24, 1990 (785-86 S.W.2d [Tex.Cases] lxvii): Rewrote rule and title to revise the practice and times for findings of fact and conclusion of law. [See TRCP 296 and 298]. Amended eff. Apr. 1, 1984, by order of Dec. 5, 1983 (661-62 S.W.2d [Tex.Cases] lxxix): Changed time for filing findings and conclusions so that the judge shall prepare them within 30 days after judgment. Amended eff. Jan. 1, 1981, by order of June 10, 1980 (599-600 S.W.2d [Tex.Cases] xlvii): Amended rule to commence the running of time for filing findings and conclusions from the date the final judgment or order overruling a motion for new trial is signed or the motion is overruled by operation of law. Adopted eff. Sept. 1, 1941, by order of Oct. 29, 1940 (3 Tex.B.J. 570 [1940]). Source: TRCS art. 2247 (repealed).

Curtis v. Commission for Lawyer Discipline, 20 S.W.3d 227, 232 (Tex.App.—Houston [14th Dist.] 2000, no pet.). "The failure to file a notice of past due findings of fact waives the right to complain about the trial court's failure to file findings of fact and conclusions of law." *See also* ***Salinas v. Beaudrie***, 960 S.W.2d 314, 317 (Tex.App.—Corpus Christi 1997, no pet.).

TRCP 298. ADDITIONAL OR AMENDED FINDINGS OF FACT & CONCLUSIONS OF LAW

After the court files original findings of fact and conclusions of law, any party may file with the clerk of the court a request for specified additional or amended findings or conclusions. The request for these findings shall be made within ten days after the filing of the original findings and conclusions by the court. Each request made pursuant to this rule shall be served on each party to the suit in accordance with Rule 21a.

The court shall file any additional or amended findings and conclusions that are appropriate within ten days after such request is filed, and cause a copy to be mailed to each party to the suit. No findings or conclusions shall be deemed or presumed by any failure of the court to make any additional findings or conclusions.

See *Commentaries*, "Request for Findings of Fact," ch. 10-E; FORMS 10E.

History of TRCP 298: Amended eff. Sept. 1, 1990, by order of Apr. 24, 1990 (785-86 S.W.2d [Tex.Cases] lxviii): Rewrote rule and title to revise the practice and times for findings of fact and conclusions of law. [See TRCP 296 and 297]. Amended eff. Sept. 1, 1957, by order of Mar. 19, 1957 (20 Tex.B.J. 192 [1957]): Added provision requiring that notice of request be given to opposite party. Adopted eff. Sept. 1, 1941, by order of Oct. 29, 1940 (3 Tex.B.J. 570 [1940]). Source: TRCS art. 2247a (repealed).

Jamestown Partners v. City of Ft. Worth, 83 S.W.3d 376, 386 (Tex.App.—Fort Worth 2002, pet. denied). "Additional findings are not required if the original findings of fact and conclusions of law 'properly and succinctly relate the ultimate findings of fact and law necessary to apprise [the party] of adequate information for the preparation of his or her appeal.' If the record indicates that a party did not suffer injury, the failure to make additional findings does not require a reversal."

Vickery v. Commission for Lawyer Discipline, 5 S.W.3d 241, 254 (Tex.App.—Houston [14th Dist.] 1999, pet. denied). "[B]efore the failure to grant additional findings will impede an appellate court from presuming implied findings, the omission must be made manifest to the trial court. ... If the trial court is not specifically made aware of the missing element, the omission is presumed to be inadvertent."

TRCP 299. OMITTED FINDINGS

When findings of fact are filed by the trial court they shall form the basis of the judgment upon all grounds of recovery and of defense embraced therein. The judgment may not be supported upon appeal by a presumed finding upon any ground of recovery or defense, no element of which has been included in the findings of fact; but when one or more elements thereof have been found by the trial court, omitted unrequested elements, when supported by evidence, will be supplied by presumption in support of the judgment. Refusal of the court to make a finding requested shall be reviewable on appeal.

See *Commentaries*, "Request for Findings of Fact," ch. 10-E.

History of TRCP 299: Amended eff. Sept. 1, 1990, by order of Apr. 24, 1990 (785-86 S.W.2d [Tex.Cases] lxviii): Changed "where" to "when," "presumption of finding" to "presumed finding" and "which has been found by the trial court" to "which has been included in the findings of fact." Amended eff. Dec. 31, 1941, by order of Sept. 20, 1941 (4 Tex.B.J. 532 [1941]). Adopted eff. Sept. 1, 1941, by order of Oct. 29, 1940 (3 Tex.B.J. 570 [1940]). Source: New rule.

Black v. Dallas Cty. Child Welfare Unit, 835 S.W.2d 626, 630 n.10 (Tex.1992). "[A]n omitted finding, supported by the evidence, may be supplied by a presumption that it supports the judgment."

Garcia v. Garza, 70 S.W.3d 362, 367 (Tex.App.—Corpus Christi 2002, pet. granted 10-10-02). "When findings of fact and conclusions of law are neither requested nor filed, the judgment of the trial court implies all findings necessary to support it, provided (1) the proposition is one raised by the pleadings and supported by the evidence, and (2) the trial court's decision can be sustained on any reasonable theory consistent with the evidence and the applicable law, after considering only the evidence that favors the decision."

Vickery v. Commission for Lawyer Discipline, 5 S.W.3d 241, 252 (Tex.App.—Houston [14th Dist.] 1999, pet. denied). "When a court makes findings of fact, but inadvertently omits an essential element of a ground of recovery or defense, the presumption of validity will supply the omitted element by implication. However, if the record demonstrates the trial judge deliberately omitted the element, the presumption is refuted and the element cannot logically be supplied by implication."

Boy Scouts v. Responsive Terminal Sys., 790 S.W.2d 738, 742 (Tex.App.—Dallas 1990, writ denied). "[T]he provisions of [TRCP 299] which allow omitted findings to be deemed to support the judgment of the trial court ... only apply to omitted *unrequested* elements. [¶] If a party makes a request for additional or amended findings of fact ... and the trial court fails to make such findings, its failure is tantamount to a refusal."

TRCP 299a. FINDINGS OF FACT TO BE SEPARATELY FILED & NOT RECITED IN A JUDGMENT

Findings of fact shall not be recited in a judgment. If there is a conflict between findings of fact recited in a judgment in violation of this rule and findings of fact made pursuant to Rules 297 and 298, the latter findings will control for appellate purposes. Findings of fact shall be filed with the clerk of the court as a document or documents separate and apart from the judgment.

See ***Commentaries***, "The Judgment," ch. 9-C; "Request for Findings of Fact," ch. 10-E.

History of TRCP 299a: Adopted eff. Sept. 1, 1990, by order of Apr. 24, 1990 (785-86 S.W.2d [Tex.Cases] lxix): To require that findings of fact be separate from the judgment and that such separate findings of fact are controlling on appeal. Source: New rule.

Sutherland v. Cobern, 843 S.W.2d 127, 131 n.7 (Tex.App.—Texarkana 1992, writ denied). "Findings of fact contained in the body of a judgment may not be considered on appeal. Therefore, for our purposes, we review this case as one in which no findings of fact were made."

H. JUDGMENTS

TRCP 300. COURT TO RENDER JUDGMENT

Where a special verdict is rendered, or the conclusions of fact found by the judge are separately stated the court shall render judgment thereon unless set aside or a new trial is granted, or judgment is rendered notwithstanding verdict or jury finding under these rules.

History of TRCP 300: Adopted eff. Sept. 1, 1941, by order of Oct. 29, 1940 (3 Tex.B.J. 571 [1940]). Source: TRCS art. 2209 (repealed).

Astec Indus. v. Suarez, 921 S.W.2d 794, 798 (Tex. App.—Fort Worth 1996, no writ). "In order for a judge's ministerial duty to render judgment under [TRCP] 300 to arise, the jury must first return a sufficient verdict for the judge to receive."

TRCP 301. JUDGMENTS

The judgment of the court shall conform to the pleadings, the nature of the case proved and the verdict, if any, and shall be so framed as to give the party all the relief to which he may be entitled either in law or equity. Provided, that upon motion and reasonable notice the court may render judgment non obstante veredicto if a directed verdict would have been proper, and provided further that the court may, upon like motion and notice, disregard any jury finding on a question that has no support in the evidence. Only one final judgment shall be rendered in any cause except where it is otherwise specially provided by law. Judgment may, in a proper case, be given for or against one or more of several plaintiffs, and for or against one or more of several defendants or intervenors.

See ***Commentaries***, "Motion for JNOV," ch. 9-B; "The Judgment," ch. 9-C; FORMS 9B, 9C.

History of TRCP 301: Amended eff. Sept. 1, 1990, by order of Apr. 24, 1990 (785-86 S.W.2d [Tex.Cases] lxix): Added last two sentences. Amended eff. Jan. 1, 1988, by order of July 15, 1987 (733-34 S.W.2d [Tex.Cases] lxxii). Adopted eff. Sept. 1, 1941, by order of Oct. 29, 1940 (3 Tex.B.J. 571 [1940]). Source: TRCS art. 2211 (repealed).

Holland v. Wal-Mart Stores, 1 S.W.3d 91, 95 (Tex. 1999). "[D] specifically challenged the availability of attorney's fees [in a motion for JNOV] before the error resulted. The court of appeals, therefore, erred in concluding that [D] waived its right to challenge the propriety of an award of attorney's fees...."

Wal-Mart Stores v. McKenzie, 997 S.W.2d 278, 280 (Tex.1999). "[D's] response to [P's] motion for judgment on the verdict was timely and sufficiently specific to give the trial court an opportunity to resolve the legal issue before rendering judgment."

Brown v. Bank of Galveston, 963 S.W.2d 511, 513 (Tex.1998). "A trial court may grant a judgment notwithstanding the verdict if there is no evidence to support one or more of the jury findings on issues necessary to liability. In determining whether [to] uphold the judgment n.o.v., we consider the evidence in the light most favorable to the verdict and reasonable inferences that tend to support it."

Stewart v. USA Custom Paint & Body Shop, 870 S.W.2d 18, 20 (Tex.1994). "A judgment must be sufficiently definite and certain to define and protect the rights of all litigants, or it should provide a definite means of ascertaining such rights, to the end that ministerial officers can carry the judgment into execution without ascertainment of facts not therein stated."

TRCP 302. ON COUNTERCLAIM

If the defendant establishes a demand against the plaintiff upon a counterclaim exceeding that established against him by the plaintiff, the court shall render judgment for defendant for such excess.

History of TRCP 302: Amended eff. Apr. 1, 1984, by order of Dec. 5, 1983 (661-62 S.W.2d [Tex.Cases] lxxix). Adopted eff. Sept. 1, 1941, by order of Oct. 29, 1940 (3 Tex.B.J. 571 [1940]). Source: TRCS art. 2215 (repealed).

Building Concepts, Inc. v. Duncan, 667 S.W.2d 897, 904 (Tex.App.—Houston [14th Dist.] 1984, writ ref'd n.r.e.). "[A]s a matter of law the court was required to offset the amount of damages established by [Ps] against the amount of [D's] counterclaim, and to render judgment in favor of [D] for the excess."

TRCP 303. ON COUNTERCLAIM FOR COSTS

When a counterclaim is pleaded, the party in whose favor final judgment is rendered shall also recover the costs, unless it be made to appear on the trial that the counterclaim of the defendant was acquired after the commencement of the suit, in which case, if the plaintiff establishes a claim existing at the commencement of the suit, he shall recover his costs.

See TRCP 131, 141.

History of TRCP 303: Amended eff. Apr. 1, 1984, by order of Dec. 5, 1983 (661-62 S.W.2d [Tex.Cases] lxxix). Adopted eff. Sept. 1, 1941, by order of Oct. 29, 1940 (3 Tex.B.J. 571 [1940]). Source: TRCS art. 2216 (repealed).

Reyna v. First Nat'l Bank, 55 S.W.3d 58, 74 (Tex. App.—Corpus Christi 2001, no pet.). "[O]n appeal, [P] asserts that since [D] did not prevail on its counterclaim, then some of the costs should be assessed against [D]. Given that the counterclaim was ... acquired before the suit, and [P] did not prevail on any of his claims, we conclude ... the trial court correctly assessed all costs against [P]."

TRCP 304. JUDGMENT UPON RECORD

Judgments rendered upon questions raised upon citations, pleadings, and all other proceedings, constituting the record proper as known at common law, must be entered at the date of each term when pronounced.

History of TRCP 304: Adopted eff. Sept. 1, 1941, by order of Oct. 29, 1940 (3 Tex.B.J. 571 [1940]). Source: Tex. Rules for Dist. & Cty. Cts. 65.

TRCP 305. PROPOSED JUDGMENT

Any party may prepare and submit a proposed judgment to the court for signature.

Each party who submits a proposed judgment for signature shall serve the proposed judgment on all other parties to the suit who have appeared and remain in the case, in accordance with Rule 21a.

Failure to comply with this rule shall not affect the time for perfecting an appeal.

See ***Commentaries***, "The Judgment," ch. 9-C.

History of TRCP 305: Amended eff. Sept. 1, 1990, by order of Apr. 24, 1990 (785-86 S.W.2d [Tex.Cases] lxix): Completely rewrote rule to clarify the practice for proposed judgments and notice to other parties. Adopted eff. Sept. 1, 1941, by order of Oct. 29, 1940 (3 Tex.B.J. 571 [1940]). Source: Tex. Rules for Dist. & Cty. Cts. 48.

First Nat'l Bank v. Fojtik, 775 S.W.2d 632, 633 (Tex.1989). A party's motion requesting the trial court to sign a judgment does not waive its right to complain about that judgment. "There must be a method by which a party who desires to initiate the appellate process may move the trial court to render judgment without being bound by its terms."

Dikeman v. Snell, 490 S.W.2d 183, 185-86 (Tex. 1973). Even when a judgment is prepared by a party, a mistake in the rendered judgment is a judicial error.

TRCP 306. RECITATION OF JUDGMENT

The entry of the judgment shall contain the full names of the parties, as stated in the pleadings, for and against whom the judgment is rendered.

See ***Commentaries***, "The Judgment," ch. 9-C.

History of TRCP 306: Amended eff. Jan. 1, 1971, by order of July 21, 1970 (455-56 S.W.2d [Tex.Cases] xliii): Eliminated language requiring judgment to recite findings of the jury. Adopted eff. Sept. 1, 1941, by order of Oct. 29, 1940 (3 Tex.B.J. 571 [1940]). Source: Tex. Rules for Dist. & Cty. Cts. 63 & 64.

Crystal City ISD v. Wagner, 605 S.W.2d 743, 747 (Tex.App.—San Antonio 1980, writ ref'd n.r.e.). "Undoubtedly, the better practice is to recite the names of all the parties in the judgment.... Nevertheless, when ... the names of all the parties and the relief each is entitled to is easily ascertainable from the record, it would be a useless thing to remand the entire cause for the purpose of amending the judgment to include the names of all the parties."

TRCP 306a. PERIODS TO RUN FROM SIGNING OF JUDGMENT

1. **Beginning of periods.** The date of judgment or order is signed as shown of record shall determine the beginning of the periods prescribed by these rules for the court's plenary power to grant a new trial or to vacate, modify, correct or reform a judgment or order and for filing in the trial court the various documents that these rules authorize a party to file within such periods including, but not limited to, motions for new trial, motions to modify judgment, motions to reinstate a case dismissed for want of prosecution, motions to vacate judgment and requests for findings of fact and conclusions of law; but this rule shall not determine what constitutes rendition of a judgment or order for any other purpose.

2. **Date to be shown.** Judges, attorneys and clerks are directed to use their best efforts to cause all judgments, decisions and orders of any kind to be reduced to writing and signed by the trial judge with the date of signing stated therein. If the date of signing is not recited in the judgment or order, it may be shown in the record by a certificate of the judge or otherwise; provided, however, that the absence of a showing of the date in the record shall not invalidate any judgment or order.

3. **Notice of judgment.** When the final judgment or other appealable order is signed, the clerk of the court shall immediately give notice to the parties or their attorneys of record by first-class mail advising that the judgment or order was signed. Failure to comply with the provisions of this rule shall not affect the periods mentioned in paragraph (1) of this rule, except as provided in paragraph (4).

4. **No notice of judgment.** If within twenty days after the judgment or other appealable order is signed, a party adversely affected by it or his attorney has neither received the notice required by paragraph (3) of this rule nor acquired actual knowledge of the order, then with respect to that party all the periods mentioned in paragraph (1) shall begin on the date that such party or his attorney received such notice or acquired actual knowledge of the signing, whichever occurred first, but in no event shall such periods begin more than ninety days after the original judgment or other appealable order was signed.

5. **Motion, notice and hearing.** In order to establish the application of paragraph (4) of this rule, the party adversely affected is required to prove in the trial court, on sworn motion and notice, the date on which the party or his attorney first either received a notice of the judgment or acquired actual knowledge of the signing and that this date was more than twenty days after the judgment was signed.

6. **Nunc pro tunc order.** When a corrected judgment has been signed after expiration of the court's plenary power pursuant to Rule 316, the periods mentioned in paragraph (1) of this rule shall run from the date of signing the corrected judgment with respect to any complaint that would not be applicable to the original document.

7. **When process served by publication.** With respect to a motion for new trial filed more than thirty days after the judgment was signed pursuant to Rule 329 when process has been served by publication, the periods provided by paragraph (1) shall be computed as if the judgment were signed on the date of filing the motion.

See *Commentaries*, "Default Judgment," ch. 7-A; "The Judgment," ch. 9-C; "Motion for New Trial," ch. 10-B; "Motion to Reinstate after DWOP" ch. 10-F; "Motion to Extend Postjudgment Deadlines," ch. 10-G; "Motion for Judgment Nunc Pro Tunc," ch. 10-H.

History of TRCP 306a: Amended eff. eff. Jan. 1, 1988, by order of July 15, 1987 (733-34 S.W.2d [Tex.Cases] lxxii): Changed (6); amended to reflect repeal of TRCP 317. Amended eff. Sept. 1, 1986, by order of Apr. 10, 1986 (705-06 S.W.2d [Tex.Cases] xxxiv): Amended to delete references to appellate procedure; deleted from (1) the words beginning with "in connection with an appeal, including but not limited to" and ending with "for filing in the appellate court of the transcript and statement of facts"; deleted from (4) the words, "except the period for filing a petition for writ of error"; and deleted from (7) the words "thirty days before." Amended eff. Apr. 1, 1984, by order of Dec. 5, 1983 (661-62 S.W.2d [Tex.Cases] lxxxix): The rule collects all provisions concerning the beginning of post-judgment periods that ordinarily run from the date the judgment is signed; par. 1 is the second par. of former TRCP 306a, with the addition of the period of the court's plenary power as defined by par. (d) and (e) of TRCP 329b; par. 2 is the first par. of former TRCP 306a; par. 3 changes former TRCP 306d by requiring notice by mail and incorporates that rule into this rule; par. 4 and 5 are new and apply when actual notice of the signing of the judgment is not received within twenty days after the judgment was signed; par. 6, with respect to nunc pro tunc orders, comes from former TRCP 306b and makes clear that par. 1 and 4 of this TRCP 306a do not revive the court's expired plenary power with respect to complaints that could have been made to the original judgment; par. 7 conforms TRCP 329 to the 1981 amendments to the appellate rules and eliminates the discrepancy created by those amendments in apparently providing for appeal that may expire before the time for filing a motion for new trial in cases of citation by publication. Amended eff. Jan. 1, 1981, by order of June 10, 1980 (599-600 S.W.2d [Tex.Cases] xlviii): Rewrote rule to eliminate the use of the term "rendition of judgment," and to make the period begin with the date the judgment is signed; a certificate by the judge is permitted to establish the date of signing; deleted reference to the notice of appeal and filing the statement of facts in the trial court, in view of amendments which omit these requirements; amended eff. Feb. 1, 1946, by order of Oct. 10, 1945 (8 Tex.B.J. 533 [1945]). Adopted eff. Dec. 31, 1943, by order of June 16, 1943 (6 Tex.B.J. 373 [1943]). Source: New rule.

Bastrop ISD v. Toungate, 958 S.W.2d 365, 367 (Tex.1997). "We note that the trial court should have submitted the modified judgment to the clerk immediately upon signing it to avoid the burden of a notification hearing."

Martinez v. Humble Sand & Gravel, 875 S.W.2d 311, 312 (Tex.1994). When "an otherwise final judgment fails to dispose of all parties, the court may make the judgment final for purposes of appeal by severing the causes and parties disposed of by the judgment into a different cause. *At 313:* When a severance order takes effect, the appellate timetable runs from the signing date of the order that made the judgment severed 'final' and appealable."

In re R.A.H., 117 S.W.3d 60, 63 (Tex.App.—Eastland 2003, pet. filed 8-25-03). "A judgment routinely goes through three stages: (1) rendition, (2) signing, and (3) entry. The judgment becomes effective once it is 'rendered.' A judgment is 'rendered' when the matter submitted to it for adjudication is officially announced either orally in open court or by memorandum filed with the clerk. The subsequent reduction of the pronouncement to a writing signed by the court is a ministerial act of the court provided for in [TRCP] 306a(2). ... A judgment is 'entered' when it is spread upon the minutes of the trial court by a purely ministerial act of the clerk of the court...." *See also* ***Burns v. Bishop***, 48 S.W.3d 459, 465 (Tex.App.—Houston [14th] Dist. 2001, no pet.).

Coinmach, Inc. v. Aspenwood Apt. Corp., 98 S.W.3d 377, 378 (Tex.App.—Houston [1st Dist.] 2003, no pet.). "The issue for this Court is whether the effective date of the order granting a new trial is (1) the date the trial court signs the order or (2) the date the trial court clerk file-stamps the signed order. ... We hold that the order granting a new trial became effective on the date signed by the trial court...."

Cannon v. ICO Tubular Servs., 905 S.W.2d 380, 388 (Tex.App.—Houston [1st Dist.] 1995, no writ). TRCP 306a "specifically require[s] the clerk of the court to send notice of the court's intent to dismiss a case for want of prosecution and order of dismissal to *each attorney of record.*"

No Notice of Judgment

John v. Marshall Health Servs., 58 S.W.3d 738, 741 (Tex.2001). Rule 306a(5) "does not prohibit a motion from being filed at any time within the trial court's plenary jurisdiction measured from the date determined under Rule 306a(4). [TRCP] 306a simply imposes no deadline, and none can be added by decision, other than the deadline of the expiration of the trial court's jurisdiction."

Estate of Howley v. Haberman, 878 S.W.2d 139, 140 (Tex.1994). "A party who does not have actual knowledge of an order of dismissal within 90 days of the date it is signed cannot move for reinstatement. Since [P] did not learn of the dismissal within this period, the order of dismissal for want of prosecution was final.... [P's] only possible recourse is a bill of review." *See also* ***Levit v. Adams***, 850 S.W.2d 469, 470 (Tex.1993).

TRCP 306b. REPEALED

Repealed eff. Apr. 1, 1984, by order of Dec. 5, 1983 (661-62 S.W.2d [Tex.Cases] lxxxi): See TRCP 306a(6), which supersedes this rule.

TRCP 306c. PREMATURELY FILED DOCUMENTS

No motion for new trial or request for findings of fact and conclusions of law shall be held ineffective because prematurely filed; but every such motion shall be deemed to have been filed on the date of but subsequent to the time of signing of the judgment the motion assails, and every such request for findings of fact and conclusions of law shall be deemed to have been filed on the date of but subsequent to the time of signing of the judgment.

See TRAP 27; ***Commentaries***, "Motion for New Trial," ch. 10-B.

History of TRCP 306c: Amended eff. Sept. 1, 1990, by order of Apr. 24, 1990 (785-86 S.W.2d [Tex.Cases] lxx): Changed "subsequent to the date of signing of the judgment" to "subsequent to the time of signing of the judgment. Amended eff. Sept. 1, 1986, by order of Apr. 10, 1986 (705-06 S.W.2d [Tex.Cases] xxxv): Deleted any reference to appellate procedure; deleted the phrases "appeal bond or affidavit in lieu thereof, notice of appeal, or notice of limitation of appeal", "and every such appeal bond or affidavit or notice of appeal or notice of limitation of appeal", and "or the date of the overruling of motion for new trial, if such a motion is filed." Amended eff. Apr. 1, 1984, by order of Dec. 5, 1983 (661-62 S.W.2d [Tex.Cases] lxxxi): Broadened rule to include prematurely filed request for findings of fact and conclusions of law. Amended eff. Jan. 1, 1976, by order of July 22, 1975 (525-26 S.W.2d [Tex.Cases] l): Added the words "or notice of limitation of appeal" in two places. Amended eff. Sept. 1, 1962, by order of Apr. 12, 1962 (25 Tex.B.J. 428 [1962]): Expanded scope of rule to include notice of appeal. Adopted eff. Feb. 1, 1946, by order of Oct. 10, 1945 (8 Tex.B.J. 534 [1945]). Source: New rule.

Fredonia State Bank v. General Am. Life Ins. Co., 881 S.W.2d 279, 281 (Tex.1994). "[A] motion for new trial relating to an earlier judgment may be considered applicable to a second judgment when the substance of the motion could properly be raised with respect to the corrected judgment."

Gunnels v. City of Brownfield, ___ S.W.3d ___ (Tex.App.—Amarillo 2002, order on mot.) (No. 07-02-0121-CV; 5-1-02). The court found P's prematurely filed motion for new trial extended the appellate timetable for perfecting appeal to 90 days after the amended summary judgment.

TRCP 306d. REPEALED

Repealed eff. Apr. 1, 1984, by order of Dec. 5, 1983 (661-62 S.W.2d [Tex.Cases] lxxxi): See TRCP 306a(3).

TRCP 307. EXCEPTIONS, ETC., TRANSCRIPT

In non-jury cases, where findings of fact and conclusions of law are requested and filed, and in jury cases, where a special verdict is returned, any party claiming that the findings of the court or the jury, as the case may be, do not support the judgment, may have noted in the record an exception to said judgment and thereupon take an appeal or writ of error, where such writ is allowed, without a statement of facts or further exceptions in the transcript, but the transcript in such cases shall contain the conclusions of law and fact or the special verdict and the judgment rendered thereon.

History of TRCP 307: Adopted eff. Sept. 1, 1941, by order of Oct. 29, 1940 (3 Tex.B.J. 571 [1940]). Source: TRCS art. 2210 (repealed).

TRCP 308. COURT SHALL ENFORCE ITS DECREES

The court shall cause its judgments and decrees to be carried into execution; and where the judgment is for personal property, and it is shown by the pleadings and evidence and the verdict, if any, that such property has an especial value to the plaintiff, the court may award a special writ for the seizure and delivery of such property to the plaintiff; and in such case may enforce its judgment by attachment, fine and imprisonment.

History of TRCP 308: Adopted eff. Sept. 1, 1941, by order of Oct. 29, 1940 (3 Tex.B.J. 571 [1940]). Source: TRCS art. 2217 (repealed).

Bridas Corp. v. Unocal Corp., 16 S.W.3d 887, 889 (Tex.App.—Houston [14th Dist.] 2000, pet. dism'd). "The trial court is vested with the inherent judicial authority to enforce its orders and decrees. Additionally, it is vested with explicit statutory authority to enforce its judgments, including the issuance of an injunction."

TRCP 308a. IN SUITS AFFECTING THE PARENT-CHILD RELATIONSHIP

When the court has ordered child support or possession of or access to a child and it is claimed that the order has been violated, the person claiming that a violation has occurred shall make this known to the court. The court may appoint a member of the bar to investigate the claim to determine whether there is reason to believe that the court order has been violated. If the attorney in good faith believes that the order has been violated, the attorney shall take the necessary action as provided under Chapter 14*, Family Code. On a finding of a violation, the court may enforce its order as provided in Chapter 14*, Family Code.

Except by order of the court, no fee shall be charged by or paid to the attorney representing the claimant. If the court determines that an attorney's fee should be paid, the fee shall be adjudged against the party who violated the court's order. The fee may be assessed as costs of court, or awarded by judgment, or both.

* Editor's Note: For current provisions of ch. 14, see ***O'Connor's Family Code***, Disposition Table, p. 1190 (2003-04).

History of TRCP 308a: Amended eff. Sept. 1, 1990, by order of Apr. 24, 1990 (785-86 S.W.2d [Tex.Cases] lxx): Completely rewrote rule to broaden its application to cover problems dealing with possession and access to a child as well as support. Amended eff. Jan. 1, 1988, by order of July 15, 1987 (733-34 S.W.2d [Tex.Cases] lxxiii). Amended eff. Mar. 1, 1952, by order of Oct. 10, 1951 (14 Tex.B.J. 634 [1951]). Added eff. Mar. 1, 1950, by order of Oct. 12, 1949 (12 Tex.B.J. 534 [1949]).

Ex parte Herring, 438 S.W.2d 801, 803 (Tex.1969). TRCP 308a "contemplates that service under any of the applicable portions of [TRCP] 21a including service upon the attorney would constitute a compliance with the rules. [¶] [I]t is a denial of due process to commit a person to prison for contempt who is not shown to be avoiding deliberately the service of process, and who has had *no* personal notice or knowledge of the show-cause hearing…." Relator discharged.

TRCP 309. IN FORECLOSURE PROCEEDINGS

Judgments for the foreclosure of mortgages and other liens shall be that the plaintiff recover his debt, damages and costs, with a foreclosure of the plaintiff's lien on the property subject thereto, and, except in judgments against executors, administrators and guardians, that an order of sale shall issue to any sheriff or any constable within the State of Texas, directing him to seize and sell the same as under execution, in satisfaction of the judgment; and, if the property cannot be found, or if the proceeds of such sale be insufficient to satisfy the judgment, then to take the money or any balance thereof remaining unpaid, out of any other property of the defendant, as in case of ordinary executions.

History of TRCP 309: Amended eff. Jan. 1, 1967, by order of July 20, 1966 (401-02 S.W.2d [Tex.Cases] xliii): Changed "of any county of the State" to "within the State of Texas." Adopted eff. Sept. 1, 1941, by order of Oct. 29, 1940 (3 Tex.B.J. 572 [1940]). Source: TRCS art. 2218 (repealed) except that the order of sale is to be directed to the sheriff or constable of any county of the State, in harmony with the rules relating to executions.

TRCP 310. WRIT OF POSSESSION

When an order foreclosing a lien upon real estate is made in a suit having for its object the foreclosure of such lien, such order shall have all the force and effect of a writ of possession as between the parties to the foreclosure suit and any person claiming under the defendant to such suit by any right acquired pending such suit; and the court shall so direct in the judgment providing for the issuance of such order. The sheriff or other officer executing such order of sale shall proceed by virtue of such order of sale to place the purchaser of the property sold thereunder in possession thereof within thirty days after the day of sale.

History of TRCP 310: Adopted eff. Sept. 1, 1941, by order of Oct. 29, 1940 (3 Tex.B.J. 572 [1940]). Source: TRCS art. 2219 (repealed).

TRCP 311. ON APPEAL FROM PROBATE COURT

Judgment on appeal or certiorari from any county court sitting in probate shall be certified to such county court for observance.

History of TRCP 311: Adopted eff. Sept. 1, 1941, by order of Oct. 29, 1940 (3 Tex.B.J. 572 [1940]). Source: TRCS art. 2220 (repealed).

TRCP 312. ON APPEAL FROM JUSTICE COURT

Judgments on appeal or certiorari from a justice court shall be enforced by the county or district court rendering the judgment.

History of TRCP 312: Adopted eff. Sept. 1, 1941, by order of Oct. 29, 1940 (3 Tex.B.J. 572 [1940]). Source: TRCS art. 2221 (repealed).

TRCP 313. AGAINST EXECUTORS, ETC.

A judgment for the recovery of money against an executor, administrator or guardian, as such, shall state that it is to be paid in the due course of administration. No execution shall issue thereon, but it shall be certified to the county court, sitting in matters of probate, to be there enforced in accordance with law, but judgment against an executor appointed and acting under a will dispensing with the action of the county court in reference to such estate shall be enforced against the property of the testator in the hands of such executor, by execution, as in other cases.

History of TRCP 313: Adopted eff. Sept. 1, 1941, by order of Oct. 29, 1940 (3 Tex.B.J. 572 [1940]). Source: TRCS art. 2222 (repealed).

TRCP 314. CONFESSION OF JUDGMENT

Any person against whom a cause of action exists may, without process, appear in person or by attorney, and confess judgment therefor in open court as follows:

(a) A petition shall be filed and the justness of the debt or cause of action be sworn to by the person in whose favor the judgment is confessed.

(b) If the judgment is confessed by attorney, the power of attorney shall be filed and its contents be recited in the judgment.

(c) Every such judgment duly made shall operate as a release of all errors in the record thereof, but such judgment may be impeached for fraud or other equitable cause.

See *Commentaries*, "Plaintiff's Original Petition," ch. 2-B; "The Answer—Denying Liability," ch. 3-E.

History of TRCP 314: Adopted eff. Sept. 1, 1941, by order of Oct. 29, 1940 (3 Tex.B.J. 572 [1940]). Source: TRCS art. 2225 (repealed).

I. REMITTITUR & CORRECTION

TRCP 315. REMITTITUR

Any party in whose favor a judgment has been rendered may remit any part thereof in open court, or by executing and filing with the clerk a written remittitur signed by the party or the party's attorney of record, and duly acknowledged by the party or the party's attorney. Such remittitur shall be a part of the record of the cause. Execution shall issue for the balance only of such judgment.

See *Commentaries*, "Motion for Remittitur," ch. 10-C; FORMS 10C.

History of TRCP 315: Amended eff. Jan. 1, 1988, by order of July 15, 1987 (733-34 S.W.2d [Tex.Cases] lxxiii). Adopted eff. Sept. 1, 1941, by order of Oct. 29, 1940 (3 Tex.B.J. 573 [1940]). Source: TRCS art. 2227 (repealed).

Larson v. Cactus Util. Co., 730 S.W.2d 640, 641 (Tex.1987). "A court of appeals should uphold a trial court remittitur only when the evidence is factually insufficient to support the verdict. [¶] If a court of appeals holds that there is no evidence to support a damages verdict, it should render a take nothing judgment as to that amount. If part of a damage verdict lacks sufficient evidentiary support, the proper course is to suggest a remittitur of that part of the verdict."

TRCP 316. CORRECTION OF CLERICAL MISTAKES IN JUDGMENT RECORD

Clerical mistakes in the record of any judgment may be corrected by the judge in open court according to the truth or justice of the case after notice of the motion therefor has been given to the parties interested in such judgment, as provided in Rule 21a, and thereafter the execution shall conform to the judgment as amended.

See *Commentaries*, "Motion for Judgment Nunc Pro Tunc," ch. 10-H.

History of TRCP 316: Amended eff. Jan. 1, 1988, by order of July 15, 1987 (733-34 S.W.2d [Tex.Cases] lxxiv). Amended eff. Dec. 31, 1943, by order of June 16, 1943 (10 Tex.B.J. 375 [1943]). Added the last sentence. Adopted eff. Sept. 1, 1941, by order of Oct. 29, 1940 (3 Tex.B.J. 573 [1940]). Source: TRCS art. 2228 (repealed).

Escobar v. Escobar, 711 S.W.2d 230, 231 (Tex. 1986). "After the trial court loses its jurisdiction over a judgment, it can correct only clerical errors in the judgment by judgment nunc pro tunc. In this regard, the trial court has plenary power to correct a clerical error made in *entering* final judgment. [¶] A judicial error is an error which occurs in the *rendering* as opposed to the *entering* of a judgment."

Andrews v. Koch, 702 S.W.2d 584, 585 (Tex.1986). "The salient distinction between 'clerical' and 'judicial' errors lies in the exercise of the judgmental offices of the court. A clerical error is one which does not result from judicial reasoning or determination."

In re Bridges, 28 S.W.3d 191, 195 (Tex.App.—Fort Worth 2000, orig. proceeding). "A trial court can enter a judgment nunc pro tunc to correct a clerical error at any time, even after it has lost jurisdiction over the case. [A] trial court commits a clerical error when it grants a motion for nonsuit and dismisses a defendant the plaintiff did not move to nonsuit. Such an order is void to the extent it purports or attempts to dismiss the lawsuit against a defendant who was not nonsuited."

TRCP 317 - 319. REPEALED

Repealed eff. Jan. 1, 1988, by order of July 15, 1987 (733-34 S.W.2d [Tex.Cases] lxxiv).

J. NEW TRIALS

TRCP 320. MOTION & ACTION OF COURT THEREON

New trials may be granted and judgment set aside for good cause, on motion or on the court's own motion on such terms as the court shall direct. New trials may be granted when the damages are manifestly too small or too large. When it appears to the court that a new trial should be granted on a point or points that affect only a part of the matters in controversy and that such part is clearly separable without unfairness to the parties, the court may grant a new trial as to that part only, provided that a separate trial on unliquidated damages alone shall not be ordered if liability issues are contested. Each motion for new trial shall be in writing and signed by the party or his attorney.

See *Commentaries*, "Motion for New Trial," ch. 10-B; FORMS 10B.

History of TRCP 320: Amended eff. Jan. 1, 1988, by order of July 15, 1987 (733-34 S.W.2d [Tex.Cases] lxxiv). Amended eff. Apr. 1, 1984, by order of Dec. 5, 1983 (661-62 S.W.2d [Tex.Cases] lxxxi): Rewrote rule to be consistent with TRCP 329b(d). Amended eff. Jan. 1, 1981, by order of June 10, 1980 (599-600 S.W.2d [Tex.Cases] xlviii): Substituted "point or points" for "ground or grounds." [See TRCP 321 and former TRCP 418(d), 458, 469(e), and 515]. Amended eff. Jan. 1, 1978, by order of July 11, 1977 (553-54 S.W.2d [Tex.Cases] xlix): Deleted the part requiring a specification of each ground from last sentence. Amended eff. Jan. 1, 1976, by order of July 22, 1975 (525-26 S.W.2d [Tex.Cases] l): Permits partial retrials in certain cases. Amended eff. Jan. 1, 1955, by order of July 20, 1954 (17 Tex.B.J. 568 [1954]): Eliminated par. (a) and (d) because they are covered in TRCP 329a and 329b. Adopted eff. Sept. 1, 1941, by order of Oct. 29, 1940 (3 Tex.B.J. 573 [1940]). Source: TRCS art. 2232 (repealed) with changes: exceptions were inserted to harmonize with provisions for special situations.

Old Republic Ins. Co. v. Scott, 846 S.W.2d 832, 833 (Tex.1993). "The **filing** of a motion for new trial in order to extend the appellate timetable is a matter of right, whether or not there is any sound or reasonable basis for the conclusion that a further motion is necessary."

State Dept. of Highways & Pub. Transp. v. Cotner, 845 S.W.2d 818, 819 (Tex.1993). "A partial new trial may be ordered notwithstanding the prohibition in [TRCP] 41 against post-submission severances. [TRCP] 320 is thus an exception to Rule 41."

TRCP 321. FORM

Each point relied upon in a motion for new trial or in arrest of judgment shall briefly refer to that part of the ruling of the court, charge given to the jury, or charge refused, admission or rejection of evidence, or other proceedings which are designated to be complained of, in such a way that the objection can be clearly identified and understood by the court.

See *Commentaries*, "Motion for New Trial," ch. 10-B; FORMS 10B.

History of TRCP 321: Amended eff. Jan. 1, 1981, by order of June 10, 1980 (599-600 S.W.2d [Tex.Cases] xlix): Substituted "point" for "ground." [See TRCP 320 and former TRCP 418(d), 458, 469(e), and 515]. Adopted eff. Sept. 1, 1941, by order of Oct. 29, 1940 (3 Tex.B.J. 573 [1940]). Source: Tex. Rules for Dist. & Cty. Cts. 67.

Marino v. Hartfield, 877 S.W.2d 508, 513 (Tex. App.—Beaumont 1994, writ denied). TRCP 321 "requires that the motion for new trial briefly refer to the ruling of the court, the charge, the evidence, or other proceedings complained of so that the objection can be identified and understood by the court."

TRCP 322. GENERALITY TO BE AVOIDED

Grounds of objections couched in general terms—as that the court erred in its charge, in sustaining or overruling exceptions to the pleadings, and in excluding or admitting evidence, the verdict of the jury is contrary to law, and the like—shall not be considered by the court.

See ***Commentaries***, "Motion for New Trial," ch. 10-B.

History of TRCP 322: Adopted eff. Sept. 1, 1941, by order of Oct. 29, 1940 (3 Tex.B.J. 573 [1940]). Source: Tex. Rules for Dist. & Cty. Cts. 68.

D/FW Commercial Roofing Co. v. Mehra, 854 S.W.2d 182, 189 (Tex.App.—Dallas 1993, no writ). "The purpose of a motion for new trial is to provide an opportunity for the trial court to cure any errors by granting a new trial. Therefore, the allegations in a motion for new trial must be sufficiently specific to enable the trial court to clearly understand what is being alleged as error."

TRCP 323. REPEALED

Repealed eff. Jan. 1, 1978, by order of July 11, 1977 (553-54 S.W.2d [Tex.Cases] xlix).

TRCP 324. PREREQUISITES OF APPEAL

(a) Motion for New Trial Not Required. A point in a motion for new trial is not a prerequisite to a complaint on appeal in either a jury or a nonjury case, except as provided in subdivision (b).

(b) Motion for New Trial Required. A point in a motion for new trial is a prerequisite to the following complaints on appeal:

(1) A complaint on which evidence must be heard such as one of jury misconduct or newly discovered evidence or failure to set aside a judgment by default;

(2) A complaint of factual insufficiency of the evidence to support a jury finding;

(3) A complaint that a jury finding is against the overwhelming weight of the evidence;

(4) A complaint of inadequacy or excessiveness of the damages found by the jury; or

(5) Incurable jury argument if not otherwise ruled on by the trial court.

(c) Judgment Notwithstanding Findings; Cross-Points. When judgment is rendered non obstante veredicto or notwithstanding the findings of a jury on one or more questions, the appellee may bring forward by cross-point contained in his brief filed in the Court of Appeals any ground which would have vitiated the verdict or would have prevented an affirmance of the judgment had one been rendered by the trial court in harmony with the verdict, including although not limited to the ground that one or more of the jury's findings have insufficient support in the evidence or are against the overwhelming preponderance of the evidence as a matter of fact, and the ground that the verdict and judgment based thereon should be set aside because of improper argument of counsel.

The failure to bring forward by cross-points such grounds as would vitiate the verdict shall be deemed a waiver thereof; provided, however, that if a cross-point is upon a ground which requires the taking of evidence in addition to that adduced upon the trial of the cause, it is not necessary that the evidentiary hearing be held until after the appellate court determines that the cause be remanded to consider such a cross-point.

See ***Commentaries***, "Motion in Limine," ch. 5-E; "Motion for JNOV," ch. 9-B; "Motion for New Trial," ch. 10-B.

History of TRCP 324: Amended eff. Jan. 1, 1988, by order of July 15, 1987 (733-34 S.W.2d [Tex.Cases] lxxiv): amended (c). Amended eff. Apr. 1, 1984, by order of Dec. 5, 1983 (661-62 S.W.2d [Tex.Cases] lxxxii): Added the requirement for a motion for new trial concerning factual complaints of jury findings, excessive and inadequacy of damages, and incurable jury argument. Amended eff. Jan. 1, 1981, by order of June 10, 1980 (599-600 S.W.2d [Tex.Cases] xlix): Rewrote third sentence; deleted the fourth sentence. Amended eff. Jan. 1, 1978, by order of July 11, 1977 (553-54 S.W.2d [Tex.Cases] xlix): Eliminated requirement for a motion for new trial in jury cases in most (though not all) instances. Amended eff. Sept. 1, 1962, by order of Apr. 12, 1962 (25 Tex.B.J. 428 [1962]): Rewrote the proviso in the first sentence to express more clearly its effect as declared in *Wagner v. Foster*, 341 S.W.2d 887 (Tex.1960). Deleted the words "in a case coming within the proviso of Rule 329-a" which formerly appeared after "non-jury case" in the first sentence; Rewrote the notes regarding original change and 1941 amendments. Amended eff. Sept. 1, 1957, by order of Mar. 19, 1957 (20 Tex.B.J. 192 [1957]): Expanded provisions dealing with cross-points of error of appellee when judgment is rendered JNOV to require cross-points as to any matter, not requiring the taking of evidence, which would vitiate the verdict; the amendment is intended to modify the holding in *De Winne v. Allen*, 277 S.W.2d 95, 99 (Tex.1955). Amended eff. Jan. 1, 1955, by order of July 20, 1954 (17 Tex.B.J. 568 [1954]): Rewrote and rearranged. Amended eff. Dec. 31, 1941, by order of Sept. 20, 1941 (4 Tex.B.J. 535 [1941]): Deleted reference to cross-assignments of error and motion for new trial from sentence dealing with appellee's right to complain of errors committed against him on the trial; added sentence providing that a motion for new trial shall not be necessary on behalf of appellee, except where he complains of the judgment or a part thereof; expanded provisions of par. dealing with right to complain on appeal without an assignment in a motion for new trial to include action of court "in withdrawing the case from the jury and rendering judgment." Amended eff. Sept. 1, 1941, by order of Mar. 31, 1941 (4 Tex.B.J. 175 [1941]): Added paragraph providing that an assignment in a motion for new trial shall not be a prerequisite to the right to complain on appeal of the action of the court in giving an instructed verdict, rendering or refusing to render judgment non obstante veredicto, or overruling appellant's motion for judgment on the verdict. Adopted eff. Sept. 1, 1941, by order of Oct. 29, 1940 (3 Tex.B.J. 574 [1940]). Source: Tex. Rules for Dist. &

Cty. Cts. 71a with changes: Eliminated reference to fundamental error as an exceptional situation not requiring motion for new trial; added proviso authorizing appellee, when judgment is rendered JNOV to complain of any prejudicial error committed against him over his objection on the trial by cross-assignments of error filed in the Court of Civil Appeals without having first presented such complaint in a motion for new trial.

State Farm Lloyds v. Nicolau, 951 S.W.2d 444, 452 (Tex.1997). Defendant was not entitled to a new trial based on newly discovered evidence because it "has not shown any likelihood that the new evidence, if introduced at trial, would have resulted in a different verdict on any of [Ps'] claims." *See also* ***Jackson v. Van Winkle***, 660 S.W.2d 807, 809 (Tex.1983).

Tate v. E.I. du Pont de Nemours & Co., 934 S.W.2d 83, 84 (Tex.1996). "[B]ecause the filing is not complete until the fee is paid, the trial court should not consider the motion [for new trial] before then, absent emergency or other rare circumstances. [T]he failure to pay the [filing] fee before the motion is overruled by operation of law may forfeit altogether the movant's opportunity to have the trial court consider the motion; it does not, however, retroactively invalidate the conditional filing for purposes of the appellate timetable."

Horrocks v. Dept. of Transp., 852 S.W.2d 498, 498-99 (Tex.1993). "The court of appeals erred in rendering judgment based on a no evidence point preserved solely in the State's motion for new trial. Ordinarily, an appellate court should render judgment after sustaining a complaint as to the legal sufficiency of the evidence. ... Here, the State ... failed to lay [the] predicate [for rendition]."

Cecil v. Smith, 804 S.W.2d 509, 510 (Tex.1991). "A point in a motion for new trial is a prerequisite to complain on appeal that the evidence is factually insufficient to support a jury finding and that a jury finding is against the overwhelming weight of the evidence."

Lee v. Braeburn Valley W. Civic Ass'n, 786 S.W.2d 262, 263 (Tex.1990). "[A] motion for new trial is not a prerequisite for an appeal of a summary judgment proceeding."

TRCP 325. REPEALED

Repealed eff. Jan. 1, 1978, by order of July 11, 1977 (553-54 S.W.2d [Tex.Cases] l).

TRCP 326. NOT MORE THAN TWO

Not more than two new trials shall be granted either party in the same cause because of insufficiency or weight of the evidence.

History of TRCP 326: Adopted eff. Sept. 1, 1941, by order of Oct. 29, 1940 (3 Tex.B.J. 574 [1940]). Source: TRCS art. 2233 (repealed).

TRCP 327. FOR JURY MISCONDUCT

a. When the ground of a motion for new trial, supported by affidavit, is misconduct of the jury or of the officer in charge of them, or because of any communication made to the jury, or that a juror gave an erroneous or incorrect answer on voir dire examination, the court shall hear evidence thereof from the jury or others in open court, and may grant a new trial if such misconduct proved, or the communication made, or the erroneous or incorrect answer on voir dire examination, be material, and if it reasonably appears from the evidence both on the hearing of the motion and the trial of the case and from the record as a whole that injury probably resulted to the complaining party.

b. A juror may not testify as to any matter or statement occurring during the course of the jury's deliberations or to the effect of anything upon his or any other juror's mind or emotions as influencing him to assent to or dissent from the verdict concerning his mental processes in connection therewith, except that a juror may testify whether any outside influence was improperly brought to bear upon any juror. Nor may his affidavit or evidence of any statement by him concerning a matter about which he would be precluded from testifying be received for these purposes.

See TRE 606(b); ***Commentaries***, "Rules of Pleading," ch. 1-B; "Jury Selection," ch. 8-A; "Motion for New Trial," ch. 10-B; FORMS 10B.

History of TRCP 327: Amended eff. Apr. 1, 1984, by order of Dec. 5, 1983 (661-62 S.W.2d [Tex.Cases] lxxxiii): Codified existing law that there must be affidavits before the trial judge need have a hearing; incorporates the provisions of TRE 606(b). Amended eff. Jan. 1, 1955, by order of July 20, 1954 (17 Tex.B.J. 568 [1954]): Inserted phrase "or that a juror gave an erroneous or incorrect answer on voir dire examination." Adopted eff. Sept. 1, 1941, by order of Oct. 29, 1940 (3 Tex.B.J. 574 [1940]). Source: TRCS art. 2234 (repealed), except to impose burden on complaining party to show probability of injury.

Golden Eagle Archery, Inc. v. Jackson, 24 S.W.3d 362, 370 (Tex.2000). "A juror may testify about jury misconduct provided it does not require delving into deliberations. [¶] [TRCP 327(b) and TRE 606(b)] contemplate that an 'outside influence' originates from sources other than the jurors themselves. *At 371:* [An] alleged conversation between [jurors] during a trial break ... should not be considered 'deliberations' and therefore barred by [TRE] 606(b) and [TRCP] 327(b)." *See also* ***Chavarria v. Valley Transit Co.***, 75 S.W.3d 107, 110 (Tex.App.—San Antonio 2002, no pet.).

Pharo v. Chambers Cty., 922 S.W.2d 945, 950 (Tex. 1996). The bailiff's misconduct justifies a new trial only if it reasonably appears from the record that injury probably resulted to the complaining party. To show probable injury, there must be some indication in the record that the alleged misconduct most likely caused a juror to vote differently than he would otherwise have done on one or more issues vital to the judgment.

Rosell v. Central W. Motor Stages, 89 S.W.3d 643, 660 (Tex.App.—Dallas 2002, pet. denied). "To warrant a new trial for jury misconduct, [Ps] had the burden to prove: (1) there was misconduct; (2) it was material; and (3) it probably caused injury. *At 661:* The essence of the 'outside influence' rule is to prevent outside information that affects the merits of the case from reaching the jury."

TRCP 328. REPEALED

Repealed eff. Jan. 1, 1988, by order of July 15, 1987 (733-34 S.W.2d [Tex.Cases] lxxv).

TRCP 329. MOTION FOR NEW TRIAL ON JUDGMENT FOLLOWING CITATION BY PUBLICATION

In cases in which judgment has been rendered on service of process by publication, when the defendant has not appeared in person or by attorney of his own selection:

(a) The court may grant a new trial upon petition of the defendant showing good cause, supported by affidavit, filed within two years after such judgment was signed. The parties adversely interested in such judgment shall be cited as in other cases.

(b) Execution of such judgment shall not be suspended unless the party applying therefor shall give a good and sufficient bond payable to the plaintiff in the judgment, in an amount fixed in accordance with Appellate Rule 47 relating to supersedeas bonds, to be approved by the clerk, and conditioned that the party will prosecute his petition for new trial to effect and will perform such judgment as may be rendered by the court should its decision be against him.

(c) If property has been sold under the judgment and execution before the process was suspended, the defendant shall not recover the property so sold, but shall have judgment against the plaintiff in the judgment for the proceeds of such sale.

(d) If the motion is filed more than thirty days after the judgment was signed, the time period shall be computed pursuant to Rule 306a(7).

See *Commentaries*, "Motion for New Trial," ch. 10-B.

History of TRCP 329: Amended eff. Jan. 1, 1988, by order of July 15, 1987 (733-34 S.W.2d [Tex.Cases] lxxv): Changed first par., (b), and (d). Amended eff. Apr. 1, 1984, by order of Dec. 5, 1983 (661-62 S.W.2d [Tex.Cases] lxxxiii): Conforms rule to the 1981 amendments to TRCP 329b, 356, 386, and other rules that make the periods for appeal begin to run from the signing of the judgment rather than from overruling the motion for new trial. Amended eff. Jan. 1, 1981, by order of June 10, 1980 (599-600 S.W.2d [Tex.Cases] l): Changed the word "rendered" in the first sentence of (a) to "signed." Adopted eff. Sept. 1, 1941, by order of Oct. 29, 1940 (3 Tex.B.J. 574 [1940]). Source: TRCS art. 2236 (repealed).

Stock v. Stock, 702 S.W.2d 713, 714 (Tex.App.—San Antonio 1985, no writ). "Because [the husband] was cited by publication for the modification hearing, he had 2 years in which to file the motion for new trial."

TRCP 329a. COUNTY COURT CASES

If a case or other matter is on trial or in the process of hearing when the term of the county court expires, such trial, hearing or other matter may be proceeded with at the next or any subsequent term of court and no motion or plea shall be considered as waived or overruled, because not acted upon at the term of court at which it was filed, but may be acted upon at any time the judge may fix or at which it may have been postponed or continued by agreement of the parties with leave of the court. This subdivision is not applicable to original or amended motions for new trial which are governed by Rule 329b.

History of TRCP 329a: Amended eff. Jan. 1, 1961, by order of July 26, 1960 (23 Tex.B.J. 681 [1961]): Completely rewrote rule. Amended eff. Sept. 1, 1957, by order of Mar. 19, 1957 (20 Tex.B.J. 193 [1957]): Changed time for filing motion from two (2) days to ten (10) days. Adopted eff. Jan. 1, 1955, by order of July 20, 1954 (17 Tex.B.J. 569 [1954]). Source: New rule.

TRCP 329b. TIME FOR FILING MOTIONS

The following rules shall be applicable to motions for new trial and motions to modify, correct, or reform judgments (other than motions to correct the record under Rule 316) in all district and county courts:

(a) A motion for new trial, if filed, shall be filed prior to or within thirty days after the judgment or other order complained of is signed.

(b) One or more amended motions for new trial may be filed without leave of court before any preceding motion for new trial filed by the movant is overruled and within thirty days after the judgment or other order complained of is signed.

(c) In the event an original or amended motion for new trial or a motion to modify, correct or reform a judgment is not determined by written order signed within seventy-five days after the judgment was signed, it shall be considered overruled by operation of law on expiration of that period.

(d) The trial court, regardless of whether an appeal has been perfected, has plenary power to grant a new trial or to vacate, modify, correct, or reform the judgment within thirty days after the judgment is signed.

(e) If a motion for new trial is timely filed by any party, the trial court, regardless of whether an appeal has been perfected, has plenary power to grant a new trial or to vacate, modify, correct, or reform the judgment until thirty days after all such timely-filed motions are overruled, either by a written and signed order or by operation of law, whichever occurs first.

(f) On expiration of the time within which the trial court has plenary power, a judgment cannot be set aside by the trial court except by bill of review for sufficient cause, filed within the time allowed by law; provided that the court may at any time correct a clerical error in the record of a judgment and render judgment nunc pro tunc under Rule 316, and may also sign an order declaring a previous judgment or order to be void because signed after the court's plenary power had expired.

(g) A motion to modify, correct, or reform a judgment (as distinguished from motion to correct the record of a judgment under Rule 316), if filed, shall be filed and determined within the time prescribed by this rule for a motion for new trial and shall extend the trial court's plenary power and the time for perfecting an appeal in the same manner as a motion for new trial. Each such motion shall be in writing and signed by the party or his attorney and shall specify the respects in which the judgment should be modified, corrected, or reformed. The overruling of such a motion shall not preclude the filing of a motion for new trial, nor shall the overruling of a motion for new trial preclude the filing of a motion to modify, correct, or reform.

(h) If a judgment is modified, corrected or reformed in any respect, the time for appeal shall run from the time the modified, corrected, or reformed judgment is signed, but if a correction is made pursuant to Rule 316 after expiration of the period of plenary power provided by this rule, no complaint shall be heard on appeal that could have been presented in an appeal from the original judgment.

See ***Commentaries***, "Rules for Filing Documents," ch. 1-C; "Motion for JNOV," ch. 9-B; "The Judgment," ch. 9-C; "Motion for New Trial," ch. 10-B; "Motion to Modify the Judgment," ch. 10-D; "Request for Findings of Fact," ch. 10-E; "Motion for Judgment Nunc Pro Tunc," ch. 10-H.

History of TRCP 329b: Amended eff. Jan. 1, 1988, by order of July 15, 1987 (733-34 S.W.2d [Tex.Cases] lxxv): Amended to conform with repeal of TRCP 317. Amended eff. Apr. 1, 1984, by order of Dec. 5, 1983 (661-62 S.W.2d [Tex.Cases] lxxxiii): Changed (c) to include a motion to modify, correct or reform a judgment; amended (h) to avoid opening a case for a general appeal after the time for appeal expired by the device of a corrected judgment nunc pro tunc pursuant to TRCP 316 or 317. Amended eff. Jan. 1, 1981, by order of June 10, 1980 (599-600 S.W.2d [Tex.Cases] l): Completely rewrote rule so appellate steps run from the date the judgment or order is signed; a motion for new trial may be filed and amended within thirty days from the date the judgment is signed, is overruled by operation of law seventy-five days after the judgment is signed, and the trial court has power over its judgment for thirty more days an amended motion for new trial gains no additional time; eliminated requirement of "presentment" and provision for an agreed postponement. Amended eff. Jan. 1, 1978, by order of July 11, 1977 (553-54 S.W.2d [Tex.Cases] l): Substituted words "if filed" for "when required" in par (1). Amended eff. Feb. 1, 1973, by order of Oct. 3, 1972 (483-84 S.W.2d [Tex.Cases] xxi, xli): Added par. (8). Amended eff. Jan. 1, 1967, by order of July 20, 1966 (401-02 S.W.2d [Tex.Cases] xliii): Substituted "without" for "by" in first sentence of par. (2). Amended eff. Jan. 1, 1961, by order of July 26, 1960 (23 Tex.B.J. 681 [1961]): Broadened rule to apply to county courts. Adopted eff. Jan. 1, 1955, by order of July 20, 1954 (17 Tex.B.J. 569 [1954]). Source: New rule. See TRCP 330(j), (k), & (*l*), before Jan. 1, 1955 changes to TRCP 330.

Plenary Power

Moritz v. Preiss, ___ S.W.3d ___ (Tex.2003) (No. 01-1270; 6-12-03). "[A]n amended motion for new trial filed more than thirty days after the trial court signs a final judgment is untimely. [T]he trial court may, at its discretion, consider the grounds raised in an untimely motion and grant a new trial under its inherent authority before the court loses plenary power. [¶] If the trial court ignores the tardy motion, it is ineffectual for any purpose. [I]f the court denies a new trial, the belated motion is a nullity and supplies no basis for consideration upon appeal of grounds which were required to be set forth in a timely motion. [A]n untimely amended motion for new trial does not preserve issues for appellate review, even if the trial court considers and denies the untimely motion within its plenary power period."

Lane Bank Equip. Co. v. Smith S. Equip., Inc., 10 S.W.3d 308, 312 (Tex.2000). A "motion made after judgment to incorporate a sanction as a part of the final judgment does propose a change to that judgment. Such a motion is, on its face, a motion to modify, correct or reform the existing judgment within the meaning of [TRCP] 329b(g). *At 314:* We ... hold that [such a motion] qualifies as a motion to modify under Rule

329b(g), thus extending the trial court's plenary jurisdiction and the appellate timetable."

Bastrop ISD v. Toungate, 958 S.W.2d 365, 367 (Tex. 1997). Plaintiff "filed a timely motion to modify or reform the judgment, and the trial court signed the modified judgment in favor of [P] well within its plenary power. Upon signing the modified judgment, the trial court then had plenary power to set aside or to further modify or reform that judgment within 30 days, absent another motion extending the time periods."

Scott & White Mem'l Hosp. v. Schexnider, 940 S.W.2d 594, 596 (Tex.1996). "A trial court's power to decide a motion for sanctions pertaining to matters occurring before judgment is no different than its power to decide any other motion during its plenary jurisdiction. [T]he time during which the trial court has authority to impose sanctions on such a motion is limited to when it retains plenary jurisdiction."

L.M. Healthcare v. Childs, 929 S.W.2d 442, 443 (Tex.1996). "That the trial court overruled [P's] motion for new trial does not shorten the trial court' plenary power to resolve a motion to modify the judgment. *At 444:* [TRCP 329b(g) & (e)] provide that a timely filed motion to modify judgment extends the trial court's plenary power, separate and apart from a motion for new trial."

Thomas v. Oldham, 895 S.W.2d 352, 356 (Tex. 1995). "Under Texas procedure, a plaintiff's suit does not end with rendition of judgment. Rather, the parties may file one or more motions for new trial within 30 days after rendition of judgment. The trial court may in its discretion grant such a motion within 75 days after the judgment is signed, continuing the action for a new trial. ... If a motion for new trial or motion to modify the judgment is overruled, the trial court still retains plenary power to vacate, modify, correct or reform the judgment for an additional 30 day period." *See also* ***Fruehauf Corp. v. Carrillo***, 848 S.W.2d 83, 84 (Tex.1993).

Written Order

Faulkner v. Culver, 851 S.W.2d 187, 188 (Tex. 1993). "A trial judge's oral pronouncement granting a motion for new trial or motion to modify, reform, or correct a judgment and a docket entry ... cannot substitute for a written order required by [TRCP] 329b."

Appellate Deadlines

Farmer v. Ben E. Keith Co., 907 S.W.2d 495, 496 (Tex.1995). "[T]he appellate timetable runs from the signing date of whatever order that makes a judgment final and appealable, i.e. whatever *order* disposes of any parties or issues remaining before the court. Further, the appellate timetable can begin yet again with the signing of an order or judgment where there is nothing on the face of the record to indicate it was signed for the sole purpose of *extending* the appellate timetable and the order is signed within the trial court's plenary power."

K. CERTAIN DISTRICT COURTS

TRCP 330. RULES OF PRACTICE & PROCEDURE IN CERTAIN DISTRICT COURTS

The following rules of practice and procedure shall govern and be followed in all civil actions in district courts in counties where the only district court of said county vested with civil jurisdiction, or all the district courts thereof having civil jurisdiction, have successive terms in said county throughout the year, without more than two days intervening between any of such terms, whether or not any one or more of such district courts include one or more other counties within its jurisdiction.

(a) Appealed Cases. In cases appealed to said district courts from inferior courts, the appeal, including transcript, shall be filed in the district court within thirty (30) days after the rendition of the judgment or order appealed from, and the appellee shall enter his appearance on the docket or answer to said appeal on or before ten o'clock a.m. of the Monday next after the expiration of twenty (20) days from the date the appeal is filed in the district court.

(b) Repealed by order of July 22, 1975, eff. Jan. 1, 1976 (525-526 S.W.2d (Tex.Cases) li).

(c) Postponement or Continuance. Cases may be postponed or continued by agreement with the approval of the court, or upon the court's own motion or for cause. When a case is called for trial and only one party is ready, the court may for good cause either continue the case for the term or postpone and reset it for a later day in the same or succeeding term.

(d) Cases May Be Reset. A case that is set and reached for trial may be postponed for a later day in the term or continued and reset for a day certain in the succeeding term on the same grounds as an application for continuance would be granted in other district courts. After any case has been set and reached in its due order and called for trial two (2) or more times and not tried, the court may dismiss the same unless the parties agree to a postponement or continuance but the court shall respect written agreements of counsel for postponement and continuance if filed in the case when or before it is called for trial unless to do so will unreasonably delay or interfere with other business of the court.

(e) Exchange and Transfer. Where in such county there are two or more district courts having civil jurisdiction, the judges of such courts may, in their discretion, exchange benches or districts from time to time, and may transfer cases and other proceedings from one court to another, and any of them may in his own courtroom try and determine any case or proceeding pending in another court without having the case transferred, or may sit in any other of said courts and there hear and determine any case there pending, and every judgment and order shall be entered in the minutes of the court in which the case is pending and at the time the judgment or order is rendered, and two (2) or more judges may try different cases in the same court at the same time, and each may occupy his own courtroom or the room of any other court. The judge of any such court may issue restraining orders and injunctions returnable to any other judge or court, and any judge may transfer any case or proceeding pending in his court to any other of said courts, and the judge of any court to which a case or proceeding is transferred shall receive and try the same, and in turn shall have power in his discretion to transfer any such case to any other of said courts and any other judge may in his courtroom try any case pending in any other of such courts.

(f) Cases Transferred to Judges Not Occupied. Where in such counties there are two or more district courts having civil jurisdiction, when the judge of any such court shall become disengaged, he shall notify the presiding judge, and the presiding judge shall transfer to the court of the disengaged judge the next case which is ready for trial in any of said courts. Any judge not engaged in his own court may try any case in any other court.

(g) Judge May Hear Only Part of Case. Where in such counties there are two or more district courts having civil jurisdiction, any judge may hear any part of any case or proceeding pending in any of said courts and determine the same, or may hear and determine any question in any case, and any other judge may complete the hearing and render judgment in the case.

(h) Any Judge May Hear Dilatory Pleas. Where in such county there are two or more district courts having civil jurisdiction, any judge may hear and determine motions, petitions for injunction, applications for appointment of receivers, interventions, pleas of privilege, pleas in abatement, all dilatory pleas and special exceptions, motions for a new trial and all preliminary matters, questions and proceedings and may enter judgment or order thereon in the court in which the case is pending without having the case transferred to the court of the judge acting, and the judge in whose court the case is pending may thereafter proceed to hear, complete and determine the case or other matter, or any part thereof, and render final judgment therein. Any judgment rendered or action taken by any judge in any of said courts in the county shall be valid and binding.

(i) Acts in Succeeding Terms. If a case or other matter is on trial, or in the process of hearing when the term of court expires, such trial, hearing or other matter may be proceeded with at the next or any subsequent term of court and no motion or plea shall be considered as waived or overruled, because not acted upon at the term of court at which it was filed, but may be acted upon at any time the judge may fix or at which it may have been postponed or continued by agreement of the parties with leave of the court. This subdivision is not applicable to original or amended motions for new trial which are governed by Rule 329b.

See Gov't Code §24.003; ***Commentaries***, "Default Judgment," ch. 7-A.

History of TRCP 330: Amended eff. Jan. 1, 1976, by order of July 22, 1975 (525-26 S.W.2d [Tex.Cases] li): Repealed TRCP 330(b), to avoid a conflict with amended TRCP 245. Amended eff. Feb. 1, 1973, by order of Oct. 3, 1972 (483-84 S.W.2d [Tex.Cases] xliii): Deleted former par. (i), which provided for the selection of a presiding judge; relettered former (j) as (i) [See TRCS art. 200b]. Amended eff. Jan. 1, 1961, by order of July 26, 1960 (23 Tex.B.J. 683 [1961]): Authorized court to proceed with hearing at "any subsequent term" of court. Adopted eff. Jan. 1, 1955, by order of July 20, 1954 (17 Tex.B.J. 570 [1954]). TRCP 329b incorporated the provisions of old TRCP 330(j), 330(k) and 330(*l*). Adopted eff. Sept. 1, 1941, by order of Oct. 29, 1940 (3 Tex.B.J. 575 [1940]). Source: TRCS art. 2092 (repealed).

Wilson v. Dunn, 800 S.W.2d 833, 835 n.6 (Tex. 1990). "The 236th District Court and the 67th District Court both sit in Tarrant County. They are permitted to, and do, hear each other's civil cases under [TRCP] 330."

In re Rio Grande Valley Gas Co., 987 S.W.2d 167, 173 (Tex.App.—Corpus Christi 1999, orig. proceeding). "[L]itigants do not have a protected proprietary interest in having their cases heard by a particular district judge or court within the county of filing."

Starnes v. Holloway, 779 S.W.2d 86, 96 (Tex.App.—Dallas 1989, writ denied). TRCP 330(e) is "consistent with [Tex. Const. art. 5, §11]. The rule ... make[s] each district judge the judge of any other district court in the county."

TRCP 331 - 351. REPEALED

Editor's Note: For a comprehensive history of the amendments and repealers to these rules, see *O'Connor's Texas Rules * Civil Trials*, p. 809 (2002).

PART III. RULES OF PROCEDURE FOR THE COURTS OF APPEALS

TRCP 352 - 473. REPEALED

Editor's Note: For a comprehensive history of the amendments and repealers to these rules, see *O'Connor's Texas Rules * Civil Trials*, p. 809 (2002).

PART IV. RULES OF PRACTICE FOR THE SUPREME COURT

TRCP 474 - 522. REPEALED

Editor's Note: For a comprehensive history of the amendments and repealers to these rules, see *O'Connor's Texas Rules * Civil Trials*, p. 809 (2002).

PART V. RULES OF PRACTICE IN JUSTICE COURTS

SECTION 1. GENERAL

TRCP 523. DISTRICT COURT RULES GOVERN

All rules governing the district and county courts shall also govern the justice courts, insofar as they can be applied, except where otherwise specifically provided by law or these rules.

History of TRCP 523: Adopted eff. Sept. 1, 1941, by order of Oct. 29, 1940 (3 Tex.B.J. 606 [1940]). Source: TRCS arts. 2381, 2410 (repealed).

Searcy v. Sagullo, 915 S.W.2d 595, 597 (Tex.App.—Houston [14th Dist.] 1996, no writ). TRCP 567 & 571 "specifically provide the procedures and time constraints to be used by justice courts in motions for new trial and appeals. Thus, [TRCP] 523 does not allow the justice court to grant new trials beyond the period provided in rule 567."

SECTION 2. INSTITUTION OF SUIT

TRCP 524. DOCKET

Each justice shall keep a civil docket in which he shall enter:

(a) The title of all suits commenced before him.

(b) The time when the first process was issued against the defendant, when returnable, and the nature thereof.

(c) The time when the parties, or either of them, appeared before him, either with or without a citation.

(d) A brief statement of the nature of the plaintiff's demand or claim, and the amount claimed, and a brief statement of the nature of the defense made by the defendant, if any.

(e) Every adjournment, stating at whose request and to what time.

(f) The time when the trial was had, stating whether the same was by a jury or by the justice.

(g) The verdict of the jury, if any.

(h) The judgment signed by the justice and the time of signing same.

(i) All applications for setting aside judgments or granting new trials and the order of the justice thereon, with the date thereof.

(j) The time of issuing execution, to whom directed and delivered, and the amount of debt, damages and costs; and, when any execution is returned, he shall note such return on said docket, with the manner in which it was executed.

(k) All stays and appeals that may be taken, and the time when taken, the amount of the bond and the names of the sureties.

(*l*) He shall also keep such other dockets, books and records as may be required by law or these rules, and shall keep a fee book in which shall be taxed all costs accruing in every suit commenced before him.

History of TRCP 524: Amended eff. Jan. 1, 1981, by order of June 10, 1980 (599-600 S.W.2d [Tex.Cases] lxxiv): The words "rendered" and "rendering" are changed to "signed" and "signing." Adopted eff. Sept. 1, 1941, by order of Oct. 29, 1940 (3 Tex.B.J. 607 [1940]). Source: TRCS art. 2382 (repealed).

Kahn v. Marik, 286 S.W.2d 639, 641 (Tex.App.—Galveston 1956, writ ref'd n.r.e.). "[T]he civil docket, which the law requires the justice of the peace to keep, is the proper place for the judgment to be entered and also serves as what we would call the execution docket in the county or district court."

TRCP 525. ORAL PLEADINGS

The pleadings shall be oral, except where otherwise specially provided; but a brief statement thereof may be noted on the docket; provided that after a case has been appealed and is docketed in the county (or district) court all pleadings shall be reduced to writing.

History of TRCP 525: Adopted eff. Sept. 1, 1941, by order of Oct. 29, 1940 (3 Tex.B.J. 607 [1940]). Source: TRCS art. 2388 (repealed).

TRCP 526. SWORN PLEADINGS

An answer or other pleading setting up any of the matters specified in Rule 93 shall be in writing and signed by the party or his attorney and verified by affidavit.

History of TRCP 526: Adopted eff. Sept. 1, 1941, by order of Oct. 29, 1940 (3 Tex.B.J. 607 [1940]). Source: TRCS art. 2389 (repealed).

TRCP 527. MOTION TO TRANSFER

A motion to transfer filed in the justice court shall contain the requisites prescribed in Rule 86; and in addition shall set forth the precinct to which transfer is sought.

History of TRCP 527: Amended eff. Sept. 1, 1983, by order of June 15, 1983 (651-52 S.W.2d [Tex.Cases] xl): To conform to S.B. 898, 68th Legislature, 1983. Adopted eff. Sept. 1, 1941, by order of Oct. 29, 1940 (3 Tex.B.J. 607 [1940]). Source: TRCS art. 2389(1) (repealed).

TRCP 528. VENUE CHANGED ON AFFIDAVIT

If any party to a suit before any justice shall make an affidavit supported by the affidavit of two other credible persons, citizens of the county, that they have good reason to believe, and do believe, that such party cannot have a fair and impartial trial before such justice or in such justice's precinct, the justice shall transfer such suit to the court of the nearest justice within the county not subject to the same or some other disqualification.

See CPRC §§15.081-15.100.

History of TRCP 528: Adopted eff. Sept. 1, 1941, by order of Oct. 29, 1940 (3 Tex.B.J. 607 [1940]). Source: TRCS art. 2394 (repealed).

Crowder v. Franks, 870 S.W.2d 568, 571-72 (Tex. App.—Houston [1st Dist.] 1993, no writ). TRCP 528 "incorporates in a single procedure the legislature's decision to give a civil litigant in a justice of the peace court an absolute right to the transfer of a case to avoid the alleged prejudice of a judge or potential jury. The affidavits ... are sufficient even though they may be only conclusionary, albeit sworn, allegations of impartiality and residency. There is no provision in the rule for the allegations to be factually contested, nor for an eventual fact-finding made by the justice of the peace as to their accuracy."

TRCP 529. "NEAREST JUSTICE" DEFINED

By the term "nearest justice," as used in this section, is meant the justice whose place of holding his court is nearest to that of the justice before whom the proceeding is pending or should have been brought.

History of TRCP 529: Adopted eff. Sept. 1, 1941, by order of Oct. 29, 1940 (3 Tex.B.J. 607 [1940]). Source: TRCS art. 2395 (repealed).

TRCP 530. BY CONSENT

The venue may also be changed to the court of any other justice of the county, upon the written consent of the parties or their attorneys, filed with the papers of the cause.

History of TRCP 530: Adopted eff. Sept. 1, 1941, by order of Oct. 29, 1940 (3 Tex.B.J. 607 [1940]). Source: TRCS art. 2396 (repealed).

TRCP 531. ORDER OF TRANSFER

The order of transfer in such cases shall state the cause of the transfer, and the name of the court to which the transfer is made, and shall require the parties and witnesses to appear before such court at its next ensuing term.

History of TRCP 531: Adopted eff. Sept. 1, 1941, by order of Oct. 29, 1940 (3 Tex.B.J. 607 [1940]). Source: TRCS art. 2397 (repealed).

TRCP 532. TRANSCRIPT

When such order of transfer is made, the justice who made the order shall immediately make out a true and correct transcript of all the entries made on his docket in the cause, certify thereto officially, and send it, with a certified copy of the bill of costs taken from his fee book, and the original papers in the cause, to the justice of the precinct to which the same has been transferred.

History of TRCP 532: Adopted eff. Sept. 1, 1941, by order of Oct. 29, 1940 (3 Tex.B.J. 607 [1940]). Source: TRCS art. 2398 (repealed).

TRCP 533. REQUISITES OF PROCESS

Every writ or process from the justice courts shall be issued by the justice, shall be in writing and signed by him officially. The style thereof shall be "The State of Texas." It shall, except where otherwise specially provided by law or these rules be directed to the person or party upon whom it is to be served, be made returnable to some regular term of court, and have noted thereon the date of its issuance.

History of TRCP 533: Adopted eff. Sept. 1, 1941, by order of Oct. 29, 1940 (3 Tex.B.J. 608 [1940]). Source: TRCS art. 2400 (repealed).

TRCP 534. ISSUANCE & FORM OF CITATION

a. Issuance. When a claim or demand is lodged with a justice for suit, the clerk when requested shall forthwith issue a citation and deliver the citation as directed by the requesting party. The party requesting citation shall be responsible for obtaining service of the citation and a copy of the petition if any is filed. Upon request, separate or additional citations shall be issued by the clerk.

b. Form. The citation shall (1) be styled "The State of Texas", (2) be signed by the clerk under seal of court or by the Justice of the Peace, (3) contain name and location of the court, (4) show date of filing of the petition if any is filed, (5) show date of issuance of citation, (6) show file number and names of parties, (7) state the nature of plaintiff's demand, (8) be directed to the defendant, (9) show name and address of attorney for plaintiff, otherwise the address of plaintiff, (10) contain the time within which these rules require defendant to file a written answer with the clerk who issued citation, (11) contain address of the clerk, and (12) shall notify defendant that in case of failure of defendant to file an answer, judgment by default may be rendered for the relief demanded in the petition. The citation shall direct defendant to file a written answer to plaintiff's petition on or before 10:00 a.m. on the Monday next after the expiration of ten days after the date of service thereof. The requirement of subsections 10 and 12 of this rule shall be in the form set forth in section c of this rule.

c. **Notice.** The citation shall include the following notice to defendant: "You have been sued. You may employ an attorney. If you or your attorney do not file a written answer with the clerk who issued this citation by 10:00 a.m. on the Monday next following the expiration of ten days after you were served this citation and petition, a default judgment may be taken against you."

d. **Copies.** The party filing any pleading upon which citation is to be issued and served shall furnish the clerk with a sufficient number of copies thereof for use in serving the parties to be served, and when copies are so furnished the clerk shall make no charge for the copies.

History of TRCP 534: Amended eff. Sept. 1, 1990, by order of Apr. 24, 1990 (785-86 S.W.2d [Tex.Cases] lxxi): Rule completely rewritten to conform justice court service of citation to the extent practicable to service of citation for other trial courts; sections b, c and d added. Amended eff. Dec. 31, 1947, by order of Aug. 18, 1947 (10 Tex.B.J. 399 [1947]). Adopted eff. Sept. 1, 1941, by order of Oct. 29, 1940 (3 Tex.B.J. 608 [1940]). Source: TRCS art. 2401 (repealed).

TRCP 535. ANSWER FILED

Where citation has been personally served at least ten days before appearance day, exclusive of the day of service and of return, the answer of the defendant shall be filed at or before ten o'clock a.m. on such day. Where citation has been served by publication, and the first publication has been made at least twenty-eight days before appearance day, the answer of the defendant shall be filed at or before ten o'clock a.m. on the first day of the first term which shall convene after the expiration of forty-two days from the date of issuance of such citation.

History of TRCP 535: Adopted eff. Sept. 1, 1941, by order of Oct. 29, 1940 (3 Tex.B.J. 608 [1940]). Source: TRCS arts. 2009, 2404 (repealed).

TRCP 536. WHO MAY SERVE & METHOD OF SERVICE

(a) Citation and other notices may be served anywhere by (1) any sheriff or constable or other person authorized by law or, (2) any person authorized by law or by written order of the court who is not less than eighteen years of age. No person who is a party to or interested in the outcome of a suit shall serve any process. Service by registered or certified mail and citation by publication shall, if requested, be made by the clerk of the court in which the case is pending. The order authorizing a person to serve process may be made without written motion and no fee shall be imposed for issuance of such order.

(b) Unless the citation or an order of the court otherwise directs, the citation shall be served by any person authorized by this rule by:

(1) delivering to the defendant, in person, a true copy of the citation with the date of delivery endorsed thereon with a copy of the petition attached thereto, or

(2) mailing to the defendant by registered or certified mail, return receipt requested, a true copy of the citation with a copy of the petition attached thereto if any is filed.

(c) Upon motion supported by affidavit stating the location of the defendant's usual place of business or usual place of abode or other place where the defendant can probably be found and stating specifically the facts showing that service has been attempted under either (a)(1) or (a)(2) at the location named in such affidavit but has not been successful, the court may authorize service:

(1) by leaving a true copy of the citation, with a copy of the petition attached, with anyone over sixteen years of age at the location specified in such affidavit, or

(2) in any other manner that the affidavit or other evidence before the court shows will be reasonably effective to give the defendant notice of the suit.

History of TRCP 536: Amended eff. Sept. 1, 1990, by order of Apr. 24, 1990 (785-86 S.W.2d [Tex.Cases] lxxii): Completely rewrote to conform justice court service of citation, to the extent practicable, to service of citation for other trial courts. Adopted eff. Sept. 1, 1941, by order of Oct. 29, 1940 (3 Tex.B.J. 608 [1940]). Source: TRCS art. 2402 (repealed).

TRCP 536a. DUTY OF OFFICER OR PERSON RECEIVING & RETURN OF CITATION

The officer or authorized person to whom process is delivered shall endorse thereon the day and hour on which he received it, and shall execute and return the same without delay.

The return of the officer or authorized person executing the citation shall be endorsed on or attached to the same; it shall state when the citation was served and the manner of service and be signed by the officer officially or by the authorized person. The return of citation by an authorized person shall be verified. When the citation was served by registered or certified mail as authorized by Rule 536, the return by the officer or authorized person must also contain the receipt with the addressee's signature. When the officer or authorized person has not served the citation, the return shall show the diligence used by the officer or authorized person to execute the same and the cause of failure to execute it, and where the defendant is to be found, if he can ascertain.

Where citation is executed by an alternative method as authorized by Rule 536, proof of service shall be made in the manner ordered by the court.

No default judgment shall be granted in any cause until the citation with proof of service as provided by this rule, or as ordered by the court in the event citation is executed under Rule 536, shall have been on file with the clerk of the court three (3) days, exclusive of the day of filing and the day of judgment.

History of TRCP 536a: Adopted eff. Sept. 1, 1990, by order of Apr. 24, 1990 (785-86 S.W.2d [Tex.Cases] lxxiii): Conforms justice court service of citation, to the extent practicable, to service of citation for other trial courts. Source: New rule.

SECTION 3. APPEARANCE & TRIAL

TRCP 537. APPEARANCE DAY

If a defendant who has been duly cited is required by the citation to answer on a day which is in term time, such day is appearance day as to him. If he is so required to answer on a day in vacation, the first day of the next term is appearance day as to him. Where service of citation has been had by publication, the first day of the term of court which convenes after the expiration of 42 days from the date of issuance of the citation shall be appearance day.

History of TRCP 537: Amended eff. Dec. 31, 1947, by order of Aug. 18, 1947 (8 Tex.B.J. 399 [1947]). Adopted eff. Sept. 1, 1941, by order of Oct. 29, 1940 (3 Tex.B.J. 608 [1940]). Source: TRCS art. 2404 (repealed).

TRCP 538. IF DEFENDANT FAILS TO APPEAR

If the defendant who has been duly served with a citation shall fail to appear at, or before, ten o'clock a.m. on appearance day, the justice shall proceed in the following manner:

(a) If the plaintiff's claim be liquidated and proved by an instrument of writing purporting to have been executed by the defendant, or be upon an open account duly verified by affidavit, the justice shall, whether the plaintiff appear or not, render judgment in his favor against the defendant for the amount of such written obligation or sworn account, after deducting all credits indorsed thereon.

(b) If the plaintiff's claim is not so liquidated, and the plaintiff appears in person or by attorney, the justice shall proceed to hear the testimony; and, if it appears therefrom that the plaintiff is entitled to recover, judgment shall be rendered against the defendant for such amount as the testimony shows the plaintiff entitled to; otherwise, judgment shall be rendered for the defendant.

History of TRCP 538: Adopted eff. Sept. 1, 1941, by order of Oct. 29, 1940 (3 Tex.B.J. 608 [1940]). Source: TRCS art. 2405 (repealed).

TRCP 539. APPEARANCE NOTED

If the defendant appear, the same shall be noted on the docket, and the cause shall stand for trial in its order.

History of TRCP 539: Adopted eff. Sept. 1, 1941, by order of Oct. 29, 1940 (3 Tex.B.J. 609 [1940]). Source: TRCS art. 2406, unchanged (repealed).

TRCP 540. IF NO DEMAND FOR JURY

If neither party shall demand and be entitled to a jury, the justice shall try the cause without a jury.

History of TRCP 540: Adopted eff. Sept. 1, 1941, by order of Oct. 29, 1940 (3 Tex.B.J. 609 [1940]). Source: TRCS art. 2407 (repealed).

TRCP 541. CONTINUANCE

The justice for good cause shown, supported by affidavit, may continue any suit pending before him to the next regular term of his court, or postpone the same to some other day of the term.

History of TRCP 541: Adopted eff. Sept. 1, 1941, by order of Oct. 29, 1940 (3 Tex.B.J. 609 [1940]). Source: TRCS art. 2403 (repealed).

TRCP 542. CALL OF NON-JURY DOCKET

The docket of cases to be tried by the justice shall be called regularly, and the cases shall be tried when called unless continued or postponed.

History of TRCP 542: Adopted eff. Sept. 1, 1941, by order of Oct. 29, 1940 (3 Tex.B.J. 609 [1940]). Source: TRCS art. 2408 (repealed).

TRCP 543. DISMISSAL

If the plaintiff shall fail to appear when the cause is called in its order for trial, the justice, on motion of the defendant, may dismiss the suit.

History of TRCP 543: Adopted eff. Sept. 1, 1941, by order of Oct. 29, 1940 (3 Tex.B.J. 609 [1940]). Source: TRCS art. 2409 (repealed).

TRCP 544. JURY TRIAL DEMANDED

Either party shall be entitled to a trial by jury. Except in forcible entry and detainer cases, the party desiring a jury shall before the case is called for trial not less than one day in advance of the date set for trial of the cause make a demand for a jury, and also deposit a jury fee of five dollars, which shall be noted on the docket; and the case shall be set down as a jury case.

History of TRCP 544: Amended eff. Jan. 1, 1988, by order of July 15, 1987 (733-34 S.W.2d [Tex.Cases] lxxvii). Adopted eff. Sept. 1, 1941, by order of Oct. 29, 1940 (3 Tex.B.J. 609 [1940]). Source: TRCS art. 2411 (repealed).

TRCP 545. JURY TRIAL DAY

The justice shall, on the first day of the term, fix a day for taking up the jury cases, if any, pending for trial at such term, and he may fix said first day of the term for that purpose.

History of TRCP 545: Adopted eff. Sept. 1, 1941, by order of Oct. 29, 1940 (3 Tex.B.J. 609 [1940]). Source: TRCS art. 2412 (repealed).

TRCP 546. CALL OF JURY DOCKET

When the required number of jurors is present, the jury cases set for trial shall be called.

History of TRCP 546: Adopted eff. Sept. 1, 1941, by order of Oct. 29, 1940 (3 Tex.B.J. 609 [1940]). Source: TRCS art. 2419 (repealed).

TRCP 547. CHALLENGE TO THE ARRAY

When the parties to a jury case have announced themselves for trial, either party may challenge the array of jurors. The cause and the manner of making such challenge, the decision thereof and the proceedings, when such challenge is sustained, shall be as provided for similar proceedings in the district and county courts.

History of TRCP 547: Adopted eff. Sept. 1, 1941, by order of Oct. 29, 1940 (3 Tex.B.J. 609 [1940]). Source: TRCS art. 2420 (repealed).

TRCP 548. DRAWING JURY

If no challenge to the array is made, the justice shall write the names of all the jurors present on separate slips of paper, as nearly alike as may be, and shall place them in a box and mix them well, and shall then draw the names one by one from the box, and write them down as they are drawn, upon several slips of paper, and deliver one slip to each of the parties, or their attorneys.

History of TRCP 548: Adopted eff. Sept. 1, 1941, by order of Oct. 29, 1940 (3 Tex.B.J. 610 [1940]). Source: TRCS art. 2421 (repealed).

TRCP 549. CHALLENGE FOR CAUSE

If either party desires to challenge any juror for cause, such challenge shall now be made. The causes of such challenge, and the manner of making it and the decision thereof, and the proceedings, when such challenge is sustained, shall be as provided for similar proceedings in the district and county courts.

History of TRCP 549: Adopted eff. Sept. 1, 1941, by order of Oct. 29, 1940 (3 Tex.B.J. 610 [1940]). Source: TRCS art. 2422 (repealed).

TRCP 550. PEREMPTORY CHALLENGE

When a juror has been challenged for cause, and the challenge has been sustained, his name shall be erased from the slips furnished to the parties; and, if as many as twelve names remain on such slips, the parties may make their peremptory challenges governed by the rules prescribed for the district and county courts. Each party shall be entitled to three peremptory challenges.

See *Commentaries*, "Jury Selection," ch. 8-A.

History of TRCP 550: Adopted eff. Sept. 1, 1941, by order of Oct. 29, 1940 (3 Tex.B.J. 610 [1940]). Source: TRCS art. 2423 (repealed).

TRCP 551. THE JURY

When the peremptory challenges are made, they shall deliver their slips to the justice, who shall call off the first six names on the slips that have not been erased, and these shall be the jury to try the case.

History of TRCP 551: Adopted eff. Sept. 1, 1941, by order of Oct. 29, 1940 (3 Tex.B.J. 610 [1940]). Source: TRCS art. 2424 (repealed).

TRCP 552. IF JURY IS INCOMPLETE

If the jury by peremptory challenges is left incomplete, the justice shall direct the sheriff or constable to summon others to complete the jury; and the same proceedings shall be had in selecting and impaneling such jurors as are had in the first instance.

History of TRCP 552: Adopted eff. Sept. 1, 1941, by order of Oct. 29, 1940 (3 Tex.B.J. 610 [1940]). Source: TRCS art. 2425 (repealed).

TRCP 553. JURY SWORN

When the jury has been selected, such of them as have not been previously sworn for the trial of civil cases shall be sworn by the justice. The form of the oath shall be in substance as follows: "You and each of you do solemnly swear that in all cases between parties which shall be to you submitted you will a true verdict render, according to the law and the evidence. So help you God."

History of TRCP 553: Adopted eff. Sept. 1, 1941, by order of Oct. 29, 1940 (3 Tex.B.J. 610 [1940]). Source: TRCS art. 2426 (repealed).

TRCP 554. JUSTICE SHALL NOT CHARGE JURY

The justice of the peace shall not charge the jury in any cause tried in his court before a jury.

History of TRCP 554: Adopted eff. Sept. 1, 1941, by order of Oct. 29, 1940 (3 Tex.B.J. 610 [1940]). Source: TRCS art. 2410 (repealed), part.

TRCP 555. VERDICT

When the suit is for the recovery of specific articles, the jury shall, if they find for the plaintiff, assess the value of each of such articles separately, according to the proof.

History of TRCP 555: Adopted eff. Sept. 1, 1941, by order of Oct. 29, 1940 (3 Tex.B.J. 610 [1940]). Source: TRCS art. 2427 (repealed).

SECTION 4. JUDGMENT

TRCP 556. JUDGMENT UPON VERDICT

Where the case has been tried by a jury and a verdict has been returned by them, the justice shall announce the same in open court and note it in his docket, and shall proceed to render judgment thereon.

History of TRCP 556: Adopted eff. Sept. 1, 1941, by order of Oct. 29, 1940 (3 Tex.B.J. 610 [1940]). Source: TRCS art. 2429 (repealed).

Pullin v. Parrish, 306 S.W.2d 241, 242 (Tex.App.—San Antonio 1957, writ ref'd). "A judgment is a prerequisite to an appeal from the justice court. [¶] An appeal from a docketed verdict, but not the judgment, is void. [¶] We do not hold that a judgment is inadequate if it is informal or merely noted on the docket sheet; ... the record must show that it is a judgment and not a verdict."

TRCP 557. CASE TRIED BY JUSTICE

When the case has been tried by the justice without a jury, he shall announce his decision in open court and note the same in his docket and render judgment thereon.

History of TRCP 557: Adopted eff. Sept. 1, 1941, by order of Oct. 29, 1940 (3 Tex.B.J. 610 [1940]). Source: TRCS art. 2430 (repealed).

TRCP 558. JUDGMENT

The judgment shall be recorded at length in the justice's docket, and shall be signed by the justice. It shall clearly state the determination of the rights of the parties in the subject matter in controversy and the party who shall pay the costs, and shall direct the issuance of such process as may be necessary to carry the judgment into execution.

History of TRCP 558: Adopted eff. Sept. 1, 1941, by order of Oct. 29, 1940 (3 Tex.B.J. 610 [1940]). Source: TRCS art. 2431 (repealed).

Housing Auth. v. Sanders, 693 S.W.2d 2, 2-3 (Tex. App.—Tyler 1985, writ ref'd n.r.e.). "A justice court judgment is a prerequisite to an appeal to the county court."

TRCP 559. COSTS

The successful party in the suit shall recover his costs, except in cases where it is otherwise expressly provided.

History of TRCP 559: Adopted eff. Sept. 1, 1941, by order of Oct. 29, 1940 (3 Tex.B.J. 611 [1940]). Source: TRCS art. 2432 (repealed).

TRCP 560. JUDGMENT FOR SPECIFIC ARTICLES

Where the judgment is for the recovery of specific articles, their value shall be separately assessed, and the judgment shall be that the plaintiff recover such specific articles, if they can be found, and if not, then their value as assessed with interest thereon at the rate of six per cent from the date of judgment.

History of TRCP 560: Adopted eff. Sept. 1, 1941, by order of Oct. 29, 1940 (3 Tex.B.J. 611 [1940]). Source: TRCS art. 2433 (repealed).

National Sur. Co. v. Odle, 40 S.W.2d 876, 877 (Tex. App.—Waco 1931, no writ). If the specific articles cannot be recovered under the judgment, the value to be given those articles is the value of the property at the date of judgment.

TRCP 561. TO ENFORCE JUDGMENT

The court shall cause its judgments to be carried into execution, and where the judgment is for personal property and the verdict, if any, is that such property has an especial value to the plaintiff the court may award a special writ for the seizure and delivery of such property to the plaintiff, and may, in addition to the other relief granted in such cases, enforce its judgment by attachment, fine and imprisonment.

History of TRCP 561: Adopted eff. Sept. 1, 1941, by order of Oct. 29, 1940 (3 Tex.B.J. 611 [1940]). Source: TRCS art. 2434 (repealed).

TRCP 562. NO JUDGMENT WITHOUT CITATION

No judgment, other than judgment by confession, shall be rendered by the justice of the peace against any party who has not entered an appearance or accepted service, unless such party has been duly cited.

History of TRCP 562: Adopted eff. Sept. 1, 1941, by order of Oct. 29, 1940 (3 Tex.B.J. 611 [1940]). Source: TRCS art. 2435 (repealed).

TRCP 563. CONFESSION OF JUDGMENT

Any party may appear in person, or by an agent or attorney, before any justice of the peace, without the issuance or service of process, and confess judgment for any amount within the jurisdiction of the justice court; and such judgment shall be entered on the justice's docket as in other cases; but, in such cases, the plaintiff, his agent or attorney shall make and file an affidavit signed by him, to the justness of his claim.

History of TRCP 563: Adopted eff. Sept. 1, 1941, by order of Oct. 29, 1940 (3 Tex.B.J. 611 [1940]). Source: TRCS art. 2436 (repealed).

TRCP 564. WARRANT OF ATTORNEY

Where such judgment is confessed by an agent or attorney, the warrant of attorney shall be in writing and filed with the justice and noted in the judgment.

History of TRCP 564: Adopted eff. Sept. 1, 1941, by order of Oct. 29, 1940 (3 Tex.B.J. 611 [1940]). Source: TRCS art. 2437 (repealed).

TRCP 565. RULES GOVERNING

The rules governing the district and county courts in relation to judgment and confession thereof, shall also apply to justice courts, insofar as they do not conflict with some provision of the rules applicable to justice courts.

History of TRCP 565: Adopted eff. Sept. 1, 1941, by order of Oct. 29, 1940 (3 Tex.B.J. 611 [1940]). Source: TRCS art. 2438 (repealed).

Triple T Inns v. Roberts, 800 S.W.2d 681, 683 (Tex. App.—Amarillo 1990, writ denied). "[P]roper application of [TRCP] 565 gives the justice [of the peace] the same right to instruct a verdict possessed by county and district judges."

SECTION 5. NEW TRIAL

TRCP 566. JUDGMENTS BY DEFAULT

A justice may within ten days after a judgment by default or of dismissal is signed, set aside such judgment, on motion in writing, for good cause shown, supported by affidavit. Notice of such motion shall be given to the opposite party at least one full day prior to the hearing thereof.

History of TRCP 566: Amended eff. Jan. 1, 1981, by order of June 10, 1980 (599-600 S.W.2d [Tex.Cases] lxxiv): Deleted, from first sentence, "the rendition of" following "after" and added "is signed" after "dismissal." Adopted eff. Sept. 1, 1941, by order of Oct. 29, 1940 (3 Tex.B.J. 611 [1940]). Source: TRCS art. 2439 (repealed).

TRCP 567. NEW TRIALS

The justice, within ten days after the rendition of a judgment in any suit tried before him, may grant a new trial therein on motion in writing showing that justice has not been done in the trial of the cause.

If the grounds of the motion be other than that the verdict or judgment is contrary to the law or the evidence, or that the justice erred in some matter of law, the motion shall be supported by affidavit.

History of TRCP 567: Amended eff. Jan. 1, 1988, by order of July 15, 1987 (733-34 S.W.2d [Tex.Cases] lxxvii). Adopted eff. Sept. 1, 1941, by order of Oct. 29, 1940 (3 Tex.B.J. 611 [1940]). Source: TRCS art. 2440 (repealed).

Searcy v. Sagullo, 915 S.W.2d 595, 596-97 (Tex. App.—Houston [14th Dist.] 1996, no writ). TRCP 567 "provides that a justice court may grant a new trial within 10 days of rendering judgment. [F]iling a motion for new trial in justice court does not enlarge the time period for filing an appeal bond. Because the justice court did not act on [P's] motion for new trial, it was overruled by operation of law ... 10 days after the justice court rendered judgment. [I]f a party files a motion for new trial in justice court, there is a **maximum** of 20 days to file an appeal bond. *At 596 n.2:* We note that rule 567 provides that the new trial time period begins when judgment is **rendered** rather than when the judgment is **signed** as is the case in district and county courts."

TRCP 568. REPEALED

Repealed eff. Jan. 1, 1988, by order of July 15, 1987 (733-34 S.W.2d [Tex.Cases] lxxvii): Former TRCP 568 merged with TRCP 567.

TRCP 569. NOTICE

All motions to set aside a judgment or to grant a new trial, under the two preceding rules, shall be made within five days after the rendition of judgment and one day's notice thereof shall be given the opposite party or his attorney.

History of TRCP 569: Adopted eff. Sept. 1, 1941, by order of Oct. 29, 1940 (3 Tex.B.J. 611 [1940]). Source: TRCS art. 2442 (repealed).

TRCP 570. BUT ONE NEW TRIAL

But one new trial may be granted to either party.

History of TRCP 570: Adopted eff. Sept. 1, 1941, by order of Oct. 29, 1940 (3 Tex.B.J. 611 [1940]). Source: TRCS art. 2444 (repealed).

SECTION 6. APPEAL

TRCP 571. APPEAL BOND

The party appealing, his agent or attorney, shall within ten days from the date a judgment or order overruling motion for new trial is signed, file with the justice a bond, with two or more good and sufficient sureties, to be approved by the justice, in double the amount of the judgment, payable to the appellee, conditioned that appellant shall prosecute his appeal to effect, and shall pay off and satisfy the judgment which may be rendered against him on appeal; or if the appeal is by the plaintiff by reason of judgment denying in whole or in part his claim, he shall file with the justice a bond in the same ten-day period, payable to the appellee, with two or more good and sufficient sureties, to be approved by the justice, in double the amount of the costs incurred in the justice court and estimated costs in the county court, less such sums as may have been paid by the plaintiff on the costs, conditioned that he shall prosecute his appeal to effect and shall pay off and satisfy such costs if judgment for costs be rendered against him on appeal. When such bond has been filed with the justice, the appeal shall be held to be thereby perfected and all parties to said suit or to any suit so appealed shall make their appearance at the next term of court to which said case has been appealed. Within five days following the filing of such appeal bond, the party appealing shall give notice as provided in Rule 21a of the filing of such bond to all parties to the suit who have not filed such bond. No judgment shall be taken by default against any party in the court to which the cause has been appealed without first showing that this rule has been complied with. The appeal shall not be dismissed for defects or irregularities in procedure, either of form or substance, without allowing appellant five days after notice within which to correct or amend same.

History of TRCP 571: Amended eff. Sept. 1, 1990, by order of Apr. 24, 1990 (785-86 S.W.2d [Tex.Cases] lxxiv): Deleted reference to TRCP 21b. Amended eff. Jan. 1, 1981, by order of June 10, 1980 (599-600 S.W.2d [Tex.Cases] lxxiv): Changed the first sentence to read: "The party appealing, his agent or attorney, shall within ten days from the date a judgment or order overruling motion for new trial is signed, file with the justice a bond...." Amended eff. Jan. 1, 1967, by order of July 20, 1966 (401-02 S.W.2d [Tex.Cases] xlvii): Added provision requiring the filing of an appeal bond by a plaintiff whose claim is denied in whole or in part. Amended eff. Sept. 1, 1962, by order of Apr. 12, 1962 (25 Tex.B.J. 435 [1962]): Added provision requiring notice of filing of appeal bond. Adopted eff. Sept. 1, 1941, by order of Oct. 29, 1940 (3 Tex.B.J. 612 [1940]). Source: TRCS arts. 2456, 2457 (repealed), with changes: Allows ten days from order overruling motion for new trial during which appeal bond may be filed.

TRCP 572. AFFIDAVIT OF INABILITY

Where appellant is unable to pay the costs of appeal, or give security therefor, he shall nevertheless be entitled to appeal by making strict proof of such inability within five days after the judgment or order overruling motion for new trial is signed, which shall consist of his affidavit filed with the justice of the peace stating his inability to pay such costs, or any part thereof, or to give security, which may be contested within five days after the filing of such affidavit and notice thereof to the opposite party or his attorney of record by any officer of court or party to the suit, whereupon it shall be the duty of the justice of the peace in whose court the suit is pending to hear evidence and determine the right of the party to appeal, and he shall enter his finding on the docket as a part of the record. It will be presumed prima facie that the affidavit speaks the truth, and, unless contested within five days after the filing and notice thereof, the presumption shall be deemed conclusive; but if a contest is filed, the burden shall then be on the appellant to prove his alleged inability by competent evidence other than by the affidavit above referred to. If the justice of the peace denies the right of appeal, appellant may, within five days thereafter, bring the matter before the county judge of the county for final decision, and, on request, the justice shall certify to the county judge appellant's affidavit, the contest thereof, and all documents and papers pertaining thereto. The county judge shall set a day for hearing, not later than ten days, and shall hear the contest de novo, and if the appeal is granted, shall direct the justice to transmit to the clerk of the county court, the transcript, records and papers of the case, as provided in these rules.

History of TRCP 572: Amended eff. Jan. 1, 1981, by order of June 10, 1980 (599-600 S.W.2d [Tex.Cases] lxxiv): Added in the first sentence the words "is signed" after the words "new trial." Adopted eff. Sept. 1, 1941, by order of Oct. 29, 1940 (3 Tex.B.J. 612 [1940]). Source: TRCS art. 2457 (repealed).

TRCP 573. APPEAL PERFECTED

When the bond, or the affidavit in lieu thereof, provided for in the rules applicable to justice courts, has been filed and the previous requirements have been complied with, the appeal shall be held to be perfected.

History of TRCP 573: Adopted eff. Sept. 1, 1941, by order of Oct. 29, 1940 (3 Tex.B.J. 612 [1940]). Source: TRCS art. 2458 (repealed).

Molina v. Negley, 425 S.W.2d 896, 898 (Tex.App.—San Antonio 1968, no writ). "We think a reasonable construction of the entire rule is that the filing of an appeal bond within 10 days perfects an appeal, as specifically provided for in [TRCP] 571 and 573 ... and that the failure to give this notice only prevents a default judgment."

TRCP 574. TRANSCRIPT

Whenever an appeal has been perfected from the justice court, the justice who made the order, or his successor, shall immediately make out a true and correct copy of all the entries made on his docket in the cause, and certify thereto officially, and immediately send it together with a certified copy of the bill of costs taken from his fee book, and the original papers in the cause, to the clerk of the county court of his county, or other court having jurisdiction.

History of TRCP 574: Adopted eff. Sept. 1, 1941, by order of Oct. 29, 1940 (3 Tex.B.J. 612 [1940]). Source: TRCS art. 2459 (repealed).

Advance Imports v. Gibson Prods. Co., 533 S.W.2d 168, 170 (Tex.App.—Dallas 1976, no writ). "[T]he duty of the justice to prepare a transcript of his docket entries and transmit it, along with the original papers, to the clerk of the county court, and the duty of the clerk to file the transcript and papers and collect the filing fee do not arise until the appeal 'has been perfected' by filing the bond or affidavit. Consequently, failure of the justice or clerk to perform any of these ministerial duties does not reinstate the judgment of the justice court. That judgment is vacated by filing the appeal bond."

TRCP 574a. NEW MATTER MAY BE PLEADED

Either party may plead any new matter in the county or district court which was not presented in the court below, but no new ground of recovery shall be set up by the plaintiff, nor shall any set-off or counterclaim be set up by the defendant which was not pleaded in the court below. The pleading thereof shall be in writing and filed in the cause before the parties have announced ready for trial.

See CPRC §31.005 (judgment or determination of fact or law in justice court proceeding is not res judicata in county or statutory county court, except that judgment rendered is binding on the parties as to recovery or denial of recovery).

History of TRCP 574a: Adopted eff. Jan. 1, 1988, by order of July 15, 1987 (733-34 S.W.2d [Tex.Cases] lxxvii). Source: New rule.

Harrill v. A.J.'s Wrecker Serv., 27 S.W.3d 191, 195 (Tex.App.—Dallas 2000, pet. dism'd). "[E]ven if [P's] additional causes of actions were 'new grounds of recovery' under rule 574a, [P] would not have been precluded from bringing these claims in a separate suit in county court. [I]n light of [CPRC] §31.005 and because of the unique nature of de novo appeals from justice court, rule 574a has little practical effect."

Crumpton v. Stevens, 936 S.W.2d 473, 476 (Tex. App.—Fort Worth 1996, no writ). "[A] statutory claim for attorney's fees that is dependent on a cause of action that was originally pleaded in the justice court may be asserted for the first time in a de novo appeal to the county court at law."

TRCP 574b. TRIAL DE NOVO

The cause shall be tried de novo in the county or district court; and judgment shall be rendered.

History of TRCP 574b: Adopted eff. Jan. 1, 1988, by order of July 15, 1987 (733-34 S.W.2d [Tex.Cases] lxxviii). Source: New rule.

In re Garza, 990 S.W.2d 372, 374 (Tex.App.—Corpus Christi 1999, orig. proceeding). "When an appeal from a justice court judgment is perfected in a county court, the judgment of the justice court is annulled. Once this occurs, the burden is on the appellee to obtain a new judgment."

SECTION 7. CERTIORARI

TRCP 575. ORDER FOR WRIT

The writ of certiorari shall be issued by order of the county court or the judge thereof (or district court or judge thereof, if jurisdiction is transferred to the district court) as provided in these rules.

History of TRCP 575: Adopted eff. Sept. 1, 1941, by order of Oct. 29, 1940 (3 Tex.B.J. 613 [1940]). Source: TRCS art. 942 (repealed).

TRCP 576. REQUISITES OF WRIT

The writ shall command the justice to immediately make and certify a copy of the entries in the cause on his docket, and immediately transmit the same, with the papers in his possession and a certified copy of the bill of costs to the proper court.

History of TRCP 576: Adopted eff. Sept. 1, 1941, by order of Oct. 29, 1940 (3 Tex.B.J. 613 [1940]). Source: TRCS arts. 943 (repealed), and 2460 (repealed eff. Sept. 1, 1985).

TRCP 577. AFFIDAVIT OF SUFFICIENT CAUSE

The writ shall not be granted unless the applicant or some person for him having knowledge of the facts, shall make affidavit setting forth sufficient cause to entitle him thereto.

See *Commentaries*, "The Answer—Denying Liability," ch. 3-E.

History of TRCP 577: Adopted eff. Sept. 1, 1941, by order of Oct. 29, 1940 (3 Tex.B.J. 613 [1940]). Source: TRCS art. 944 (repealed).

Centro Jurici De Instituto Tecnologico v. Intertravel, Inc., 2 S.W.3d 446, 449 (Tex.App.—San Antonio 1999, no pet.). "'Sufficient cause' includes a lack of jurisdiction."

TRCP 578. APPLICATION FOR CERTIORARI

To constitute a sufficient cause, the facts stated must show that either the justice of the peace had not jurisdiction, or that injustice was done to the applicant by the final determination of the suit or proceeding, and that such injustice was not caused by his own inexcusable neglect.

History of TRCP 578: Adopted eff. Sept. 1, 1941, by order of Oct. 29, 1940 (3 Tex.B.J. 613 [1940]). Source: TRCS art. 945 (repealed).

TRCP 579. WITHIN WHAT TIME GRANTED

Such writ shall not be granted after ninety days from the time the final judgment is signed.

History of TRCP 579: Amended eff. Jan. 1, 1981, by order of June 10, 1980 (599-600 S.W.2d [Tex.Cases] lxxv): Time will run from the time the judgment is signed. Adopted eff. Sept. 1, 1941, by order of Oct. 29, 1940 (3 Tex.B.J. 613 [1940]). Source: TRCS art. 946 (repealed).

TRCP 580. BOND WITH SURETIES REQUIRED

The writ shall not be issued unless the applicant shall first cause to be filed a bond with two or more good and sufficient sureties, to be approved by the clerk, payable to the adverse party, in such sum as the judge shall direct, to the effect that the party applying therefor will perform the judgment of the county or district court, if the same shall be against him.

History of TRCP 580: Adopted eff. Sept. 1, 1941, by order of Oct. 29, 1940 (3 Tex.B.J. 613 [1940]). Source: TRCS art. 947 (repealed).

TRCP 581. BOND, AFFIDAVIT & ORDER

The bond and affidavit, with the order of the judge, when made in vacation, shall be filed with the clerk of the court to which the same is returnable.

History of TRCP 581: Adopted eff. Sept. 1, 1941, by order of Oct. 29, 1940 (3 Tex.B.J. 613 [1940]). Source: TRCS art. 948 (repealed).

TRCP 582. WRIT TO ISSUE INSTANTER

As soon as such affidavit, order of the judge, and bond, shall have been filed, the clerk shall issue a writ of certiorari.

History of TRCP 582: Adopted eff. Sept. 1, 1941, by order of Oct. 29, 1940 (3 Tex.B.J. 613 [1940]). Source: TRCS art. 949 (repealed).

TRCP 583. JUSTICE SHALL STAY PROCEEDINGS

Upon service of such writ of certiorari being made upon the justice of the peace, he shall stay further proceedings on the judgment and forthwith comply with said writ.

History of TRCP 583: Adopted eff. Sept. 1, 1941, by order of Oct. 29, 1940 (3 Tex.B.J. 613 [1940]). Source: TRCS art. 950 (repealed).

TRCP 584. CITATION AS IN OTHER CASES

Whenever a writ of certiorari has been issued, the clerk shall forthwith issue a citation for the party adversely interested.

History of TRCP 584: Adopted eff. Sept. 1, 1941, by order of Oct. 29, 1940 (3 Tex.B.J. 613 [1940]). Source: TRCS art. 951 (repealed).

TRCP 585. CAUSE DOCKETED

The action shall be docketed in the name of the original plaintiff, as plaintiff, and of the original defendant, as defendant.

History of TRCP 585: Adopted eff. Sept. 1, 1941, by order of Oct. 29, 1940 (3 Tex.B.J. 613 [1940]). Source: TRCS art. 952 (repealed).

TRCP 586. MOTION TO DISMISS

Within thirty days after the service of citation on the writ of certiorari, the adverse party may move to dismiss the certiorari for want of sufficient cause appearing in the affidavit, or for want of sufficient bond.

History of TRCP 586: Adopted eff. Sept. 1, 1941, by order of Oct. 29, 1940 (3 Tex.B.J. 613 [1940]). Source: TRCS art. 953 (repealed).

TRCP 587. AMENDMENT OF BOND OR OATH

The affidavit or bond may be amended in the discretion of the court in which it is filed.

History of TRCP 587: Adopted eff. Sept. 1, 1941, by order of Oct. 29, 1940 (3 Tex.B.J. 614 [1940]). Source: TRCS art. 954 (repealed).

TRCP 588. JUDGMENT OF DISMISSAL

If the certiorari be dismissed, the judgment shall direct the justice to proceed with the execution of the judgment below.

History of TRCP 588: Adopted eff. Sept. 1, 1941, by order of Oct. 29, 1940 (3 Tex.B.J. 614 [1940]). Source: TRCS art. 955 (repealed).

TRCP 589. PLEADING

After the transcript of the proceedings in the justice court, together with the original papers and a bill of costs, have been filed in the county (or district) court, all pleadings in the cause which are not already written shall be reduced to writing.

History of TRCP 589: Adopted eff. Sept. 1, 1941, by order of Oct. 29, 1940 (3 Tex.B.J. 614 [1940]). Source: TRCS arts. 956, 957 (repealed).

TRCP 590. NEW MATTER MAY BE PLEADED

Either party may plead any new matter in the county or district court which was not presented in the court below, but no new ground of recovery shall be set up by the plaintiff, nor shall any set-off or counterclaim be set up by the defendant which was not pleaded in the court below. The pleading thereof shall be in writing and filed in the cause before the parties have announced ready for trial.

History of TRCP 590: Adopted eff. Sept. 1, 1941, by order of Oct. 29, 1940 (3 Tex.B.J. 614 [1940]). Source: TRCS art. 958 (repealed).

Hamby Co. v. Palmer, 631 S.W.2d 589, 591 (Tex. App.—Amarillo 1982, no writ). "[A]lthough set out in a section of the Rules dealing with certiorari proceedings, [TRCP 590] also applies to appeals from justice court[s] to higher courts."

TRCP 591. TRIAL DE NOVO

The cause shall be tried de novo in the county or district court; and judgment shall be rendered as in cases appealed from justice courts.

History of TRCP 591: Adopted eff. Sept. 1, 1941, by order of Oct. 29, 1940 (3 Tex.B.J. 614 [1940]). Source: TRCS art. 959 (repealed).

PART VI. RULES RELATING TO ANCILLARY PROCEEDINGS

SECTION 1. ATTACHMENT

TRCP 592. APPLICATION FOR WRIT OF ATTACHMENT & ORDER

Either at the commencement of a suit or at any time during its progress the plaintiff may file an application for the issuance of a writ of attachment. Such application shall be supported by affidavits of the plaintiff, his agent, his attorney, or other persons having knowledge of relevant facts. The application shall comply with all statutory requirements and shall state the grounds for issuing the writ and the specific facts relied upon by the plaintiff to warrant the required findings by the court. The writ shall not be quashed because two or more grounds are stated conjunctively or disjunctively. The application and any affidavits shall be made on personal knowledge and shall set forth such facts as would be admissible in evidence; provided that facts may be stated based upon information and belief if the grounds of such belief are specifically stated.

No writ shall issue except upon written order of the court after a hearing, which may be ex parte. The court, in its order granting the application, shall make specific findings of facts to support the statutory grounds found to exist, and shall specify the maximum value of property that may be attached, and the amount of bond required of plaintiff, and, further shall command that the attached property be kept safe and preserved subject to further orders of the court. Such bond shall be in an amount which, in the opinion of the court, will adequately compensate the defendant in the event plaintiff fails to prosecute his suit to effect, and to pay all damages and costs which may be adjudged against him for wrongfully suing out the writ of attachment. The court shall further find in its order the amount of bond required of defendant to replevy, which, unless the defendant chooses to exercise his option as provided in Rule 599, shall be the amount of plaintiff's claim, one year's accrual of interest if allowed by law on the claim, and the estimated costs of court. The order may direct the issuance of several writs at the same time, or in succession, to be sent to different counties.

History of TRCP 592: Adopted eff. Jan. 1, 1978, by order of July 11, 1977 (553-54 S.W.2d [Tex.Cases] lx): New rule added to meet the constitutional demands of due process in prejudgment remedies. Former TRCP 592 repealed and renumbered 592b eff. Jan. 1, 1978, by order of July 11, 1977 (553-54 S.W.2d [Tex.Cases] lx). Source: New rule.

TRCP 592a. BOND FOR ATTACHMENT

No writ of attachment shall issue until the party applying therefor has filed with the officer authorized to issue such writ a bond payable to the defendant in the amount fixed by the court's order, with sufficient surety or sureties as provided by statute to be approved by such officer, conditioned that the plaintiff will prosecute his suit to effect and pay to the extent of the penal amount of the bond all damages and costs as may be adjudged against him for wrongfully suing out such writ of attachment.

After notice to the opposite party, either before or after the issuance of the writ, the defendant or plaintiff may file a motion to increase or reduce the amount of such bond, or to question the sufficiency of the sureties thereon, in the court in which such suit is pending. Upon hearing, the court shall enter its order with respect to such bond and sufficiency of the sureties.

History of TRCP 592a: Adopted eff. Jan. 1, 1978, by order of July 11, 1977 (553-54 S.W.2d [Tex.Cases] lxi). Source: New rule.

TRCP 592b. FORM OF ATTACHMENT BOND

The following form of bond may be used:

"The State of Texas,

County of ________,

We, the undersigned, __________ as principal, and __________ and ___________ as sureties, acknowledge ourselves bound to pay to C.D. the sum of ___________ dollars, conditioned that the above bound plaintiff in attachment against the said C.D., defendant, will prosecute his said suit to effect, and that he will pay all such damages and costs to the extent of the penal amount of this bond as shall be adjudged against him for wrongfully suing out such attachment. Witness our hands this ___ day of ________, 19___."

History of TRCP 592b: Adopted eff. Jan. 1, 1978, by order of July 11, 1977 (553-54 S.W.2d [Tex.Cases] lxi): Renumbered from TRCP 592; added words "to the extent of the penal amount of this bond." Source: New rule. See former TRCP 592 repealed eff. Jan. 1, 1978, by order of July 11, 1977 (553-54 S.W.2d [Tex.Cases] lx).

TRCP 593. REQUISITES FOR WRIT

A writ of attachment shall be directed to the sheriff or any constable within the State of Texas. It shall command him to attach and hold, unless replevied, subject to the further order of the court, so much of the property of the defendant, of a reasonable value in approximately the amount fixed by the court, as shall be found within his county.

History of TRCP 593: Amended eff. Jan. 1, 1978, by order of July 11, 1977 (553-54 S.W.2d [Tex.Cases] lxii): Writ must be directed to the officer "within" the State of Texas; the writ recognizes the right to replevy, commands the officer to hold property of a reasonable value fixed by the court, and the attachment is subject to further orders of the court. Adopted eff. Sept. 1, 1941, by order of Oct. 29, 1940 (3 Tex.B.J. 615 [1940]). Source: TRCS art. 282 (repealed in part by TRCP).

TRCP 594. FORM OF WRIT

The following form of writ may be issued:

"The State of Texas.

"To the Sheriff or any Constable of any County of the State of Texas, greeting:

"We command you that you attach forthwith so much of the property of C.D., if it be found in your county, repleviable on security, as shall be of value sufficient to make the sum of ________ dollars, and the probable costs of suit, to satisfy the demand of A.B., and that you keep and secure in your hands the property so attached, unless replevied, that the same may be liable to further proceedings thereon to be had before our court in ________, County of ___________. You will true return make of this writ on or before 10 a.m. of Monday, the ________ day of ________, 19___, showing how you have executed the same."

History of TRCP 594: Adopted eff. Sept. 1, 1941, by order of Oct. 29, 1940 (3 Tex.B.J. 615 [1940]). Source: TRCS art. 284 (repealed).

TRCP 595. SEVERAL WRITS

Several writs of attachment may, at the option of the plaintiff, be issued at the same time, or in succession, and sent to different counties, until sufficient property shall be attached to satisfy the writ.

History of TRCP 595: Adopted eff. Sept. 1, 1941, by order of Oct. 29, 1940 (3 Tex.B.J. 615 [1940]). Source: TRCS art. 283 (repealed).

TRCP 596. DELIVERY OF WRIT

The writ of attachment shall be dated and tested as other writs, and may be delivered to the sheriff or constable by the officer issuing it, or he may deliver it to the plaintiff, his agent or attorney, for that purpose.

History of TRCP 596: Adopted eff. Sept. 1, 1941, by order of Oct. 29, 1940 (3 Tex.B.J. 615 [1940]). Source: TRCS art. 285 (repealed).

TRCP 597. DUTY OF OFFICER

The sheriff or constable receiving the writ shall immediately proceed to execute the same by levying upon so much of the property of the defendant subject to the writ, and found within his county, as may be sufficient to satisfy the command of the writ.

History of TRCP 597: Adopted eff. Sept. 1, 1941, by order of Oct. 29, 1940 (3 Tex.B.J. 615 [1940]). Source: TRCS art. 286 (repealed).

TRCP 598. LEVY, HOW MADE

The writ of attachment shall be levied in the same manner as is, or may be, the writ of execution upon similar property.

History of TRCP 598: Adopted eff. Sept. 1, 1941, by order of Oct. 29, 1940 (3 Tex.B.J. 615 [1940]). Source: TRCS art. 289 (repealed).

TRCP 598a. SERVICE OF WRIT ON DEFENDANT

The defendant shall be served in any manner prescribed for service of citation, or as provided in Rule 21a, with a copy of the writ of attachment, the application, accompanying affidavits, and orders of the court as soon as practicable following the levy of the writ. There shall be prominently displayed on the face of the copy of the writ served on the defendant, in ten-point type and in a manner calculated to advise a reasonably attentive person of its contents, the following:

To ________, Defendant:

You are hereby notified that certain properties alleged to be owned by you have been attached. If you claim any rights in such property, you are advised:

"YOU HAVE A RIGHT TO REGAIN POSSESSION OF THE PROPERTY BY FILING A REPLEVY BOND. YOU HAVE A RIGHT TO SEEK TO REGAIN POSSESSION OF THE PROPERTY BY FILING WITH THE COURT A MOTION TO DISSOLVE THIS WRIT."

History of TRCP 598a: Adopted eff. Jan. 1, 1978, by order of July 11, 1977 (553-54 S.W.2d [Tex.Cases] lxii): the new rule affords the defendant notice of the proceedings and informs him of some of his rights. Source: New rule.

TRCP 599. DEFENDANT MAY REPLEVY

At any time before judgment, should the attached property not have been previously claimed or sold, the defendant may replevy the same, or any part thereof, or the proceeds from the sale of the property if it has been sold under order of the court, by giving bond with sufficient surety or sureties as provided by statute, to be approved by the officer who levied the writ, payable to plaintiff, in the amount fixed by the court's order, or, at the defendant's option, for the value of the property sought to be replevied (to be estimated by the officer), plus one year's interest thereon at the legal rate from the date of the bond, conditioned that the defendant shall satisfy, to the extent of the penal amount of the bond, any judgment which may be rendered against him in such action.

On reasonable notice to the opposing party (which may be less than three days) either party shall have the right to prompt judicial review of the amount of bond required, denial of bond, sufficiency of sureties, and estimated value of the property, by the court which authorized issuance of the writ. The court's determination may be made upon the basis of affidavits, if uncontroverted, setting forth such facts as would be admissible in evidence; otherwise, the parties shall submit evidence. The court shall forthwith enter its order either approving or modifying the requirements of the officer or of the court's prior order, and such order of the court shall supersede and control with respect to such matters.

On reasonable notice to the opposing party (which may be less than three days) the defendant shall have the right to move the court for a substitution of property, of equal value as that attached, for the property attached. Provided that there has been located sufficient property of the defendants to satisfy the order of attachment, the court may authorize substitution of one or more items of defendant's property for all or for part of the property attached. The court shall first make findings as to the value of the property to be substituted. If property is substituted, the property released from attachment shall be delivered to defendant, if such property is personal property, and all liens upon such property from the original order of attachment or modification thereof shall be terminated. Attachment of substituted property shall be deemed to have existed from the date of levy on the original property attached, and no property on which liens have become affixed since the date of levy on the original property may be substituted.

History of TRCP 599: Amended eff. Jan. 1, 1978, by order of July 11, 1977 (553-54 S.W.2d [Tex.Cases] lxii): Permits the defendant to replevy the proceeds from a sale of property; changes the amount of bond from double the amount of plaintiff's debt to the amount fixed by the court; more clearly fixes the conditions of the replevy bond; affords a hearing to the parties; authorizes the substitution of property. Adopted eff. Sept. 1, 1941, by order of Oct. 29, 1940 (3 Tex.B.J. 616 [1940]). Source: TRCS art. 292 (repealed).

TRCP 600. SALE OF PERISHABLE PROPERTY

Whenever personal property which has been attached shall not have been claimed or replevied, the judge, or justice of the peace, out of whose court the writ was issued, may, either in term time or in vacation, order the same to be sold, when it shall be made to appear that such property is in danger of serious and immediate waste or decay, or that the keeping of the same until the trial will necessarily be attended with such expense or deterioration in value as greatly to lessen the amount likely to be realized therefrom.

History of TRCP 600: Adopted eff. Sept. 1, 1941, by order of Oct. 29, 1940 (3 Tex.B.J. 616 [1940]). Source: TRCS art. 293 (repealed).

TRCP 601. TO PROTECT INTERESTS

In determining whether the property attached is perishable, and the necessity or advantage of ordering a sale thereof, the judge or justice of the peace may act upon affidavits in writing or oral testimony, and may by a preliminary order entered of record, with or without notice to the parties as the urgency of the case in his opinion requires, direct the sheriff or constable to sell such property at public auction for cash, and thereupon the officer shall sell it accordingly.

History of TRCP 601: Adopted eff. Sept. 1, 1941, by order of Oct. 29, 1940 (3 Tex.B.J. 616 [1940]). Source: TRCS art. 294 (repealed).

TRCP 602. BOND OF APPLICANT FOR SALE

If the application for an order of sale be filed by any person or party other than the defendant from whose possession the property was taken by levy, the court shall not grant such order unless the applicant shall file with such court a bond payable to such defendant, with two or more good and sufficient sureties, to be approved by said court, conditioned that they will be responsible to the defendant for such damages as he may sustain in case such sale be illegally and unjustly applied for, or be illegally and unjustly made.

History of TRCP 602: Adopted eff. Sept. 1, 1941, by order of Oct. 29, 1940 (3 Tex.B.J. 616 [1940]). Source: New rule as applied to attachment proceedings. See TRCS art. 5233 (repealed).

TRCP 603. PROCEDURE FOR SALE

Such sale of attached perishable personal property shall be conducted in the same manner as sales of personal property under execution; provided, however, that the time of the sale, and at the time of advertisement thereof, may be fixed by the judge or justice of the peace at a time earlier than ten days, according to the exigency of the case, and in such event notice thereof shall be given in such manner as directed by the order.

History of TRCP 603: Adopted eff. Sept. 1, 1941, by order of Oct. 29, 1940 (3 Tex.B.J. 616 [1940]). Source: TRCS art. 295 (repealed).

TRCP 604. RETURN OF SALE

The officer making such sale of perishable property shall promptly pay the proceeds of such sale to the clerk of such court or justice of the peace, as the case may be, and shall make written return of the order of sale signed by him officially, stating the time and place of the sale, the name of the purchaser, and the amount of money received, with an itemized account of the expenses attending the sale. Such return shall be filed with the papers of the case.

History of TRCP 604: Adopted eff. Sept. 1, 1941, by order of Oct. 29, 1940 (3 Tex.B.J. 616 [1940]). Source: TRCS art. 296 (repealed).

TRCP 605. JUDGE MAY MAKE NECESSARY ORDERS

When the perishable personal property levied on under the attachment writ has not been claimed or replevied, the judge or justice of the peace may make such orders, either in term time or vacation, as may be necessary for its preservation or use.

History of TRCP 605: Adopted eff. Sept. 1, 1941, by order of Oct. 29, 1940 (3 Tex.B.J. 616 [1940]). Source: TRCS art. 297 (repealed).

TRCP 606. RETURN OF WRIT

The officer executing the writ of attachment shall return the writ, with his action endorsed thereon, or attached thereto, signed by him officially, to the court from which it issued, at or before 10 o'clock a.m. of the Monday next after the expiration of fifteen days from the date of issuance of the writ. Such return shall describe the property attached with sufficient certainty to identify it, and state when the same was attached, and whether any personal property attached remains still in his hands, and, if not, the disposition made of the same. When property has been replevied he shall deliver the replevy bond to the clerk or justice of the peace to be filed with the papers of the cause.

History of TRCP 606: Adopted eff. Sept. 1, 1941, by order of Oct. 29, 1940 (3 Tex.B.J. 617 [1940]). Source: TRCS art. 298 (repealed).

TRCP 607. REPORT OF DISPOSITION OF PROPERTY

When the property levied on is claimed, replevied or sold, or otherwise disposed of after the writ has been returned, the officer having the custody of the same shall immediately make a report in writing, signed by him officially, to the clerk, or justice of the peace, as the case may be, showing such disposition of the property. Such report shall be filed among the papers of the cause.

History of TRCP 607: Adopted eff. Sept. 1, 1941, by order of Oct. 29, 1940 (3 Tex.B.J. 617 [1940]). Source: TRCS art. 299 (repealed).

TRCP 608. DISSOLUTION OR MODIFICATION OF WRIT OF ATTACHMENT

A defendant whose property has been attached or any intervening party who claims an interest in such property, may by sworn written motion, seek to vacate, dissolve, or modify the writ, and the order directing its issuance, for any grounds or cause, extrinsic or intrinsic. Such motion shall admit or deny each finding of the order directing the issuance of the writ except where the movant is unable to admit or deny the finding, in which case movant shall set forth the reasons why he cannot admit or deny. Unless the parties agree to an extension of time, the motion shall be heard promptly, after reasonable notice to the plaintiff (which may be less than three days), and the issue shall be determined not later than ten days after the motion is filed. The filing of the motion shall stay any further proceedings under the writ, except for any orders concerning the care, preservation, or sale of perishable property, until a hearing is had and the issue is determined. The writ shall be dissolved unless at such hearing, the plaintiff shall prove the grounds relied upon for its issuance, but the court may modify its previous order granting the writ and the writ issued pursuant thereto. The movant shall, however, have the burden to prove that the reasonable value of the property attached exceeds the amount necessary to secure the debt, interest for one year, and probable costs. He shall also have the burden to prove the facts to justify substitution of property.

The court's determination may be made upon the basis of affidavits, if uncontroverted, setting forth such facts as would be admissible in evidence; otherwise, the parties shall submit evidence. The court may make all such orders, including orders concerning the care, preservation, or disposition of the property (or the proceeds therefrom if the same has been sold), as justice may require. If the movant has given a replevy bond, an order to vacate or dissolve the writ shall vacate the replevy bond and discharge the sureties thereon, and if the court modifies its order or the writ issued pursuant thereto, it shall make such further orders with respect to the bond as may be consistent with its modification.

History of TRCP 608: Amended eff. Jan. 1, 1978, by order of July 11, 1977 (553-54 S.W.2d [Tex.Cases] lxiii): To afford a prompt hearing, provide for the procedures, burden of proof, and the kind of proof. Adopted eff. Sept. 1, 1941, by order of Oct. 29, 1940 (3 Tex.B.J. 617 [1940]). Source: TRCS art. 303 (repealed).

TRCP 609. AMENDMENT

Clerical errors in the affidavit, bond, or writ of attachment, or the officer's return thereof, may upon application in writing to the judge or justice of the court in which the suit is filed, and after notice to the opponent, be amended in such manner and on such terms as the judge or justice shall authorize by an order entered in the minutes of the court or noted on the docket of the justice of the peace, provided the amendment does not change or add to the grounds of such attachment as stated in the affidavit, and provided such amendment appears to the judge or justice to be in furtherance of justice.

History of TRCP 609: Adopted eff. Sept. 1, 1941, by order of Oct. 29, 1940 (3 Tex.B.J. 617 [1940]). Source: New rule.

SECTION 2. DISTRESS WARRANT

TRCP 610. APPLICATION FOR DISTRESS WARRANT & ORDER

Either at the commencement of a suit or at any time during its progress the plaintiff may file an application for the issuance of a distress warrant with the justice of the peace. Such application may be supported by affidavits of the plaintiff, his agent, his attorney, or other persons having knowledge of relevant facts, but shall include a statement that the amount sued for is rent, or advances described by statute, or shall produce a writing signed by the tenant to that effect, and shall further swear that such warrant is not sued out for the purpose of vexing and harassing the defendant. The application shall comply with all statutory requirements and shall state the grounds for issuing the warrant and the specific facts relied upon by the plaintiff to warrant the required findings by the justice of the peace. The warrant shall not be quashed because two or more grounds are stated conjunctively or disjunctively. The application and any affidavits shall be made on personal knowledge and shall set forth such facts as would be admissible in evidence provided that facts may be stated based upon information and belief if the grounds of such belief are specifically stated.

No warrant shall issue before final judgment except on written order of the justice of the peace after a hearing, which may be ex parte. Such warrant shall be made returnable to a court having jurisdiction of the amount in controversy. The justice of the peace in his order granting the application shall make specific findings of fact to support the statutory grounds found to exist, and shall specify the maximum value of property that may be seized, and the amount of bond required of plaintiff, and, further shall command that property be kept safe and preserved subject to further orders of the court having jurisdiction. Such bond shall be in an amount which, in the opinion of the court, shall adequately compensate defendant in the event plaintiff fails to prosecute his suit to effect, and pay all damages and costs as shall be adjudged against him for wrongfully suing out the warrant. The justice of the peace shall further find in his order the amount of bond required to replevy, which, unless the defendant chooses to exercise his option as provided in Rule 614, shall be the amount of plaintiff's claim, one year's accrual of interest if allowed by law on the claim, and the estimated costs of court. The order may direct the issuance of several warrants at the same time, or in succession, to be sent to different counties.

History of TRCP 610: Adopted eff. Jan. 1, 1981, by order of June 10, 1980 (599-600 S.W.2d [Tex.Cases] lxxv): The rule was written to conform with the due process requirements of *Fuentes v. Shevin*, 407 U.S. 67 (1972), *Mitchell v. W.T. Grant Co.*, 416 U.S. 600 (1974), and *North Ga. Finishing, Inc. v. Di-Chem, Inc.*, 419 U.S. 601 (1975). Former TRCP 610 repealed eff. Jan. 1, 1981, by order of June 10, 1986 (599-600 S.W.2d [Tex.Cases] lxxvi). Source: New rule.

Lincoln Ten, Ltd. v. White, 706 S.W.2d 125, 128 (Tex.App.—Houston [14th Dist.] 1986, orig. proceeding). "According to [TRCP] 610, no distress warrant will issue before final judgment except on written order of a justice of the peace. This complies with the requirement that the writ must be issued by a judicial officer."

TRCP 611. BOND FOR DISTRESS WARRANT

No distress warrant shall issue before final judgment until the party applying therefor has filed with the justice of the peace authorized to issue such warrant a bond payable to the defendant in an amount approved by the justice of the peace, with sufficient surety or sureties as provided by statute, conditioned that the plaintiff will prosecute his suit to effect and pay all damages and costs as may be adjudged against him for wrongfully suing out such warrant.

After notice to the opposite party, either before or after the issuance of the warrant, the defendant or plaintiff may file a motion to increase or reduce the amount of such bond, or to question the sufficiency of the sureties thereon, in a court having jurisdiction of the subject matter. Upon hearing, the court shall enter its order with respect to such bond and sufficiency of the sureties.

History of TRCP 611: Adopted eff. Jan. 1, 1981, by order of June 10, 1980 (599-600 S.W.2d [Tex.Cases] lxxvi): The rule was written to conform with due process requirements. See history note to TRCP 610. Former TRCP 611 repealed eff. Jan. 1, 1981, by order of June 10, 1980 (599-600 S.W.2d [Tex.Cases] lxxvi). Source: New rule.

TRCP 612. REQUISITES FOR WARRANT

A distress warrant shall be directed to the sheriff or any constable within the State of Texas. It shall command him to attach and hold, unless replevied, subject to the further orders of the court having jurisdiction, so much of the property of the defendant, not exempt by statute, of reasonable value in approximately the amount fixed by the justice of the peace, as shall be found within his county.

History of TRCP 612: Adopted eff. Jan. 1, 1981, by order of June 10, 1980 (599-600 S.W.2d [Tex.Cases] lxxvi): The rule was written to conform with due process requirements. See history note to TRCP 610. Former TRCP 612 repealed eff. Jan. 1, 1981, by order of June 10, 1980 (599-600 S.W.2d [Tex.Cases] lxxvi). Source: New rule.

TRCP 613. SERVICE OF WARRANT ON DEFENDANT

The defendant shall be served in any manner prescribed for service of citation, or as provided in Rule 21a, with a copy of the distress warrant, the application, accompanying affidavits, and orders of the justice of the peace as soon as practicable following the levy of the warrant. There shall be prominently displayed on the face of the copy of the warrant served on the defendant, in 10-point type and in a manner calculated to advise a reasonably attentive person of its contents, the following:

To __________, Defendant: You are hereby notified that certain properties alleged to be owned by you have been seized. If you claim any rights in such property, you are advised: "YOU HAVE A RIGHT TO REGAIN POSSESSION OF THE PROPERTY BY FILING A REPLEVY BOND. YOU HAVE A RIGHT TO SEEK TO REGAIN POSSESSION OF THE PROPERTY BY FILING WITH THE COURT A MOTION TO DISSOLVE THIS WARRANT."

History of TRCP 613: Adopted eff. Jan. 1, 1981, by order of June 10, 1980 (599-600 S.W.2d [Tex.Cases] lxxvii): The rule was written to conform with due process requirements. See history note to TRCP 610. Former TRCP 613 repealed eff. Jan. 1, 1981, by order of June 10, 1980 (599-600 S.W.2d [Tex. Cases] lxxvii). Source: New rule.

TRCP 614. DEFENDANT MAY REPLEVY

At any time before judgment, should the seized property not have been previously claimed or sold, the defendant may replevy the same, or any part thereof, or the proceeds from the sale of the property if it has been sold under order of the court, by giving bond with sufficient surety or sureties as provided by statute, to be approved by a court having jurisdiction of the amount in controversy payable to plaintiff in double the amount of the plaintiff's debt, or, at the defendant's option for not less than the value of the property sought to be replevied, plus one year's interest thereon at the legal rate from the date of the bond, conditioned that the defendant shall satisfy to the extent of the penal amount of the bond any judgment which may be rendered against him in such action.

On reasonable notice to the opposing party (which may be less than three days) either party shall have the right to prompt judicial review of the amount of bond required, denial of bond, sufficiency of sureties, and estimated value of the property, by a court having jurisdiction of the amount in controversy. The court's determination may be made upon the basis of affidavits if uncontroverted setting forth such facts as would be admissible in evidence, otherwise the parties shall submit evidence. The court shall forthwith enter its order either approving or modifying the requirements of the order of the justice of the peace, and such order of the court shall supersede and control with respect to such matters.

On reasonable notice to the opposing party (which may be less than three days) the defendant shall have the right to move the court for a substitution of property, of equal value as that attached, for the property seized. Provided that there has been located sufficient property of the defendant's to satisfy the order of seizure, the court may authorize substitution of one or more items of defendant's property for all or part of the property seized. The court shall first make findings as to the value of the property to be substituted. If property is substituted, the property released from seizure shall be delivered to defendant, if such property is personal property, and all liens upon such property from the original order of seizure or modification thereof shall be terminated. Seizure of substituted property shall be deemed to have existed from the date of levy on the original property seized, and no property on which liens have become affixed since the date of levy on the original property may be substituted.

History of TRCP 614: Adopted eff. Jan. 1, 1981, by order of June 10, 1980 (599-600 S.W.2d [Tex.Cases] lxxvii): The rule was written to conform with due process requirements. See history note to TRCP 610. Former TRCP 614 repealed eff. Jan. 1, 1981, by order of June 10, 1980 (599-600 S.W.2d [Tex. Cases] lxxvii). Source: New rule.

TRCP 614a. DISSOLUTION OR MODIFICATION OF DISTRESS WARRANT

A defendant whose property has been seized or any intervening claimant who claims an interest in such property, may by sworn written motion, seek to vacate, dissolve, or modify the seizure, and the order directing its issuance, for any grounds or cause, extrinsic or intrinsic. Such motion shall admit or deny each finding of the order directing the issuance of the warrant except where the movant is unable to admit or deny the finding, in which case movant shall set forth the reasons why he cannot admit or deny. Unless the parties agree to an extension of time, the motion shall be heard promptly, after reasonable notice to the plaintiff (which may be less than three days), and the issue shall be determined not later than 10 days after the motion is filed. The filing of the motion shall stay any further proceedings under the warrant, except for any orders concerning the care, preservation, or sale of any perishable property, until a hearing is had, and the issue is determined. The warrant shall be dissolved unless, at such hearing, the plaintiff shall prove the specific facts alleged and the grounds relied upon for its issuance, but the court may modify the order of the justice of the peace granting the warrant and the warrant issued pursuant thereto. The movant shall however have the burden to prove that the reasonable value of the property seized exceeds the amount necessary to secure the debt, interest for one year, and probable costs. He shall also have the burden to prove the facts to justify substitution of property.

The court's determination may be made upon the basis of affidavits setting forth such facts as would be admissible in evidence, but additional evidence, if tendered by either party shall be received and considered. The court may make all such orders, including orders concerning the care, preservation, or disposition of the property (or the proceeds therefrom if the same has been sold), as justice may require. If the movant has given a replevy bond, an order to vacate or dissolve the warrant shall vacate the replevy bond and discharge the sureties thereon, and if the court modifies the order of the justice of the peace or the warrant issued pursuant thereto, it shall make such further orders with respect to the bond as may be consistent with its modification.

History of TRCP 614a: Adopted eff. Jan. 1, 1981, by order of June 10, 1980 (599-600 S.W.2d [Tex.Cases] lxxviii). The rule was written to conform with due process requirements. See history note to TRCP 610. Source: New rule.

TRCP 615. SALE OF PERISHABLE PROPERTY

Whenever personal property which has been levied on under a distress warrant shall not have been claimed or replevied, the judge, or justice of the peace, to whose court such writ is made returnable may, either in term time or in vacation, order the same to be sold, when it shall be made to appear that such property is in danger of serious and immediate waste or decay, or that the keeping of the same until the trial will necessarily be attended with such expense or deterioration in value as greatly to lessen the amount likely to be realized therefrom.

History of TRCP 615: Adopted eff. Sept. 1, 1941, by order of Oct. 29, 1940 (3 Tex.B.J. 619 [1940]). Source: TRCS art. 5233 (repealed).

TRCP 616. TO PROTECT INTERESTS

In determining whether the property levied upon is perishable, and the necessity or advantage of ordering a sale thereof, the judge or justice of the peace may act upon affidavits in writing or oral testimony, and may by a preliminary order entered of record with or without notice to the parties as the urgency of the case in his opinion requires, direct the sheriff or constable to sell such property at public auction for cash, and thereupon the sheriff or constable shall sell it accordingly. If the application for an order of sale be filed by any person or party other than the defendant from whose possession the property was taken by levy, the court shall not grant such order, unless the applicant shall file with such court a bond payable to such defendant, with two or more good and sufficient sureties, to be approved by said court, conditioned that they will be responsible to the defendant for such damages as he may sustain in case such sale be illegally and unjustly applied for, or be illegally and unjustly made.

History of TRCP 616: Adopted eff. Sept. 1, 1941, by order of Oct. 29, 1940 (3 Tex.B.J. 619 [1940]). Source: TRCS arts. 294, 5233 (repealed).

TRCP 617. PROCEDURE FOR SALE

Such sale of perishable personal property shall be conducted in the same manner as sales of personal property under execution; provided, however, that the time of the sale, and the time of advertisement thereof, may be fixed by the judge or justice of the peace at a time earlier than ten days, according to the exigency of the case, and in such event notice thereof shall be given in such manner as directed by the order.

History of TRCP 617: Adopted eff. Sept. 1, 1941, by order of Oct. 29, 1940 (3 Tex.B.J. 619 [1940]). Source: TRCS art. 295 (repealed).

TRCP 618. RETURN OF SALE

The officer making such sale of perishable property shall promptly pay the proceeds of such sale to the clerk of such court or to the justice of the peace, as the case may be, and shall make written return of the order of sale, signed by him officially, stating the time and place of the sale, the name of the purchaser, and the amount of money received, with an itemized account of the expenses attending the sale. Such return shall be filed with the papers of the case.

History of TRCP 618: Adopted eff. Sept. 1, 1941, by order of Oct. 29, 1940 (3 Tex.B.J. 619 [1940]). Source: TRCS art. 296 (repealed).

TRCP 619. CITATION FOR DEFENDANT

The justice at the time he issues the warrant shall issue a citation to the defendant requiring him to answer before such justice at the first day of the next succeeding term of court, stating the time and place of holding the same, if he has jurisdiction to finally try the cause, and upon its being returned served, to proceed to judgment as in ordinary cases; and, if he has not such jurisdiction, the citation shall require the defendant to answer before the court to which the warrant was made returnable at or before ten o'clock a.m. of the Monday next after the expiration of twenty days from the date of service thereof, stating the place of holding the court, and shall be returned with the other papers to such court. If the defendant has removed from the county without service, the proper officer shall state this fact in his return on the citation; and the court shall proceed to try the case ex parte, and may enter judgment.

History of TRCP 619: Adopted eff. Sept. 1, 1941, by order of Oct. 29, 1940 (3 Tex.B.J. 619 [1940]). Source: TRCS art. 5234 (repealed).

TRCP 620. PETITION

When the warrant is made returnable to the district or county court, the plaintiff shall file his petition within ten days from the date of the issuance of the writ.

History of TRCP 620: Adopted eff. Sept. 1, 1941, by order of Oct. 29, 1940 (3 Tex.B.J. 619 [1940]). Source: TRCS art. 5235 (repealed).

SECTION 3. EXECUTIONS

TRCP 621. ENFORCEMENT OF JUDGMENT

The judgments of the district, county, and justice courts shall be enforced by execution or other appropriate process. Such execution or other process shall be returnable in thirty, sixty, or ninety days as requested by the plaintiff, his agent or attorney.

History of TRCP 621: Adopted eff. Sept. 1, 1941, by order of Oct. 29, 1940 (3 Tex.B.J. 619 [1940]). Source: TRCS arts. 2445, 3784 (repealed).

TRCP 621a. DISCOVERY & ENFORCEMENT OF JUDGMENT

At any time after rendition of judgment, and so long as said judgment has not been suspended by a supersedeas bond or by order of a proper court and has not become dormant as provided by Article 3773, V.A.T.S., the successful party may, for the purpose of obtaining information to aid in the enforcement of such judgment, initiate and maintain in the trial court in the same suit in which said judgment was rendered any discovery proceeding authorized by these rules for pre-trial matters. Also, at any time after rendition of judgment, either party may, for the purpose of obtaining information relevant to motions allowed by Texas Rules of Appellate Procedure 47* and 49* initiate and maintain in the trial court in the same suit in which said judgment was rendered any discovery proceeding authorized by these rules for pre-trial matters. The rules governing and related to such pre-trial discovery proceedings shall apply in like manner to discovery proceedings after judgment. The rights herein granted to the parties shall inure to their successors or assignees, in whole or in part. Judicial supervision of such discovery proceedings after judgment shall be the same as that provided by law or these rules for pre-trial discovery and proceedings insofar as applicable.

* Now TRAP 24 (effective Sept. 1, 1997).

History of TRCP 621a: Amended eff. Jan. 1, 1988, by order of July 15, 1987 (733-34 S.W.2d [Tex.Cases] lxxviii). Adopted eff. Jan. 1, 1971, by order of July 21, 1970 (455-56 S.W.2d [Tex.Cases] xliv). Source: New rule.

Arndt v. Farris, 633 S.W.2d 497, 499 (Tex.1982). TRCP 621a "was adopted as a separate and independent rule applicable only to discovery in aid of enforcement of judgments. [¶] [T]he trial court has continuing jurisdiction over such matters as set forth in the rule."

Fisher v. P. M. Clinton Int'l Investigations, 81 S.W.3d 484, 486 (Tex.App.—Houston [1st Dist.] 2002, no pet.). "Because a post-judgment discovery order does not resolve all the disputes between the parties, a rule 621a order is not a final and appealable order."

TRCP 622. EXECUTION

An execution is a process of the court from which it is issued. The clerk of the district or county court or the justice of the peace, as the case may be, shall tax the costs in every case in which a final judgment has been rendered and shall issue execution to enforce such judgment and collect such costs. The execution and subsequent executions shall not be addressed to a particular county, but shall be addressed to any sheriff or any constable within the State of Texas.

History of TRCP 622: Amended eff. Dec. 31, 1941, by order of Sept. 20, 1941 (4 Tex.B.J. 580 [1941]). Adopted eff. Sept. 1, 1941, by order of Oct. 29, 1940 (3 Tex.B.J. 620 [1940]). Source: TRCS arts. 2446, 2447, 3770, 3780, 3781, 3782 (repealed).

TRCP 623. ON DEATH OF EXECUTOR

When an executor, administrator, guardian or trustee of an express trust dies, or ceases to be such executor, administrator, guardian or trustee after judgment, execution shall issue on such judgment in the name of his successor, upon an affidavit of such death or termination being filed with the clerk of the court or the justice of the peace, as the case may be, together with the certificate of the appointment of such successor under the hand and seal of the clerk of the court wherein the appointment was made.

History of TRCP 623: Adopted eff. Sept. 1, 1941, by order of Oct. 29, 1940 (3 Tex.B.J. 620 [1940]). Source: TRCS art. 3776 (repealed).

TRCP 624. ON DEATH OF NOMINAL PLAINTIFF

When a person in whose favor a judgment is rendered for the use of another dies after judgment, execution shall issue in the name of the party for whose use the suit was brought upon an affidavit of such death being filed with the clerk of the court or the justice of the peace.

History of TRCP 624: Adopted eff. Sept. 1, 1941, by order of Oct. 29, 1940 (3 Tex.B.J. 620 [1940]). Source: TRCS art. 3777 (repealed).

TRCP 625. ON MONEY OF DECEASED

If a sole defendant dies after judgment for money against him, execution shall not issue thereon, but the judgment may be proved up and paid in due course of administration.

History of TRCP 625: Adopted eff. Sept. 1, 1941, by order of Oct. 29, 1940 (3 Tex.B.J. 620 [1940]). Source: TRCS art. 3778 (repealed).

TRCP 626. ON PROPERTY OF DECEASED

In any case of judgment other than a money judgment, where the sole defendant, or one or more of several joint defendants, shall die after judgment, upon an affidavit of such death being filed with the clerk, together with the certificate of the appointment of a representative of such decedent under the hand and seal of the clerk of the court wherein such appointment was made, the proper process on such judgment shall issue against such representative.

History of TRCP 626: Adopted eff. Sept. 1, 1941, by order of Oct. 29, 1940 (3 Tex.B.J. 620 [1940]). Source: TRCS art. 3779 (repealed).

TRCP 627. TIME FOR ISSUANCE

If no supersedeas bond or notice of appeal, as required of agencies exempt from filing bonds, has been filed and approved, the clerk of the court or justice of the peace shall issue the execution upon such judgment upon application of the successful party or his attorney after the expiration of thirty days from the time a final judgment is signed. If a timely motion for new trial or in arrest of judgment is filed, the clerk shall issue the execution upon the judgment on application of the party or his attorney after the expiration of thirty days from the time the order overruling the motion is signed or from the time the motion is overruled by operation of law.

See CPRC §§65.013, 65.014.

History of TRCP 627: Amended eff. Apr. 1, 1984, by order of Dec. 5, 1983 (661-62 S.W.2d [Tex.Cases] cxv): Added, in the second sentence, the words, "from the time the motion" after the word "or." Amended eff. Jan. 1, 1981, by order of June 10, 1980 (599-600 S.W.2d [Tex.Cases] lxxix): Time will run from the time the judgment or order is signed or overruled by operation of law. Amended eff. Jan. 1, 1976, by order of July 22, 1975 (525-26 S.W.2d [Tex.Cases] lix): Changed the word "twenty" to "thirty." Adopted eff. Sept. 1, 1941, by order of Oct. 29, 1940 (3 Tex.B.J. 620 [1940]). Source: TRCS arts. 2448, 3771 (repealed).

Hood v. Amarillo Nat'l Bank, 815 S.W.2d 545, 548 (Tex.1991). "[A] writ of execution will not issue until after a final and appealable judgment is signed...."

Winkle v. Winkle, 951 S.W.2d 80, 89 (Tex.App.—Corpus Christi 1997, pet. denied). Under TRCP 627, "executions of final judgments from district courts may not issue until after 30 days have elapsed since the rendition of the final judgment or after the overruling of any motions for a new trial. A prematurely issued execution of judgment [is] voidable."

TRCP 628. EXECUTION WITHIN THIRTY DAYS

Such execution may be issued at any time before the thirtieth day upon the filing of an affidavit by the plaintiff in the judgment or his agent or attorney that the defendant is about to remove his personal property subject to execution by law out of the county, or is about to transfer or secrete such personal property for the purpose of defrauding his creditors.

See CPRC §§65.013, 65.014.

History of TRCP 628: Amended eff. Jan. 1, 1976, by order of July 22, 1975 (525-26 S.W.2d [Tex.Cases] lix): Changed the word "twentieth" to "thirtieth." Adopted eff. Sept. 1, 1941, by order of Oct. 29, 1940 (3 Tex.B.J. 620 [1940]). Source: TRCS arts. 2449, 3774 (repealed).

Perfection Casting Corp. v. Aluminum Alloys, Inc., 733 S.W.2d 385, 386 (Tex.App.—San Antonio 1987, no writ). It was proper for the trial court to allow immediate execution on a judgment, even if the affidavit did not allege sufficient facts to warrant immediate execution, where, after the affidavit was filed and execution was granted, the party received a hearing on the sufficiency of the affidavit.

TRCP 629. REQUISITES OF EXECUTION

The style of the execution shall be "The State of Texas." It shall be directed to any sheriff or any constable within the State of Texas. It shall be signed by the clerk or justice officially, and bear the seal of the court, if issued out of the district or county court, and shall require the officer to execute it according to its terms, and to make the costs which have been adjudged against the defendant in execution and the further costs of executing the writ. It shall describe the judgment, stating the court in which, and the time when, rendered, and the names of the parties in whose favor and against whom the judgment was rendered. A correct copy of the bill of costs taxed against the defendant in execution shall be attached to the writ. It shall require the officer to return it within thirty, sixty, or ninety days, as directed by the plaintiff or his attorney.

See CPRC §§65.013, 65.014.

History of TRCP 629: Amended eff. Dec. 20, 1941, by order of Sept. 20, 1941 (4 Tex.B.J. 580 [1941]). Adopted eff. Sept. 1, 1941, by order of Oct. 29, 1940 (3 Tex.B.J. 621 [1940]). Source: TRCS arts. 2446, 3783, 3784 (repealed).

TRCP 630. EXECUTION ON JUDGMENT FOR MONEY

When an execution is issued upon a judgment for a sum of money, or directing the payment simply of a sum of money, it must specify in the body thereof the sum recovered or directed to be paid and the sum actually due when it is issued and the rate of interest upon the sum due. It must require the officer to satisfy the judgment and costs out of the property of the judgment debtor subject to execution by law.

See CPRC §§65.013, 65.014.

History of TRCP 630: Adopted eff. Sept. 1, 1941, by order of Oct. 29, 1940 (3 Tex.B.J. 621 [1940]). Source: TRCS art. 3783(2) (repealed).

TRCP 631. EXECUTION FOR SALE OF PARTICULAR PROPERTY

An execution issued upon a judgment for the sale of particular chattels or personal property or real estate, must particularly describe the property, and shall direct the officer to make the sale by previously giving the public notice of the time and place of sale required by law and these rules.

See CPRC §§65.013, 65.014.

History of TRCP 631: Adopted eff. Sept. 1, 1941, by order of Oct. 29, 1940 (3 Tex.B.J. 621 [1940]). Source: TRCS art. 3783(3) (repealed).

TRCP 632. EXECUTION FOR DELIVERY OF CERTAIN PROPERTY

An execution issued upon a judgment for the delivery of the possession of a chattel or personal property, or for the delivery of the possession of real property, shall particularly describe the property, and designate the party to whom the judgment awards the possession. The writ shall require the officer to deliver the possession of the property to the party entitled thereto.

See CPRC §§65.013, 65.014.

History of TRCP 632: Adopted eff. Sept. 1, 1941, by order of Oct. 29, 1940 (3 Tex.B.J. 621 [1940]). Source: TRCS art. 3783(4) (repealed).

TRCP 633. EXECUTION FOR POSSESSION OR VALUE OF PERSONAL PROPERTY

If the judgment be for the recovery of personal property or its value, the writ shall command the officer, in case a delivery thereof cannot be had, to levy and collect the value thereof for which the judgment was recovered, to be specified therein, out of any property of the party against whom judgment was rendered, liable to execution.

See CPRC §§65.013, 65.014.

History of TRCP 633: Adopted eff. Sept. 1, 1941, by order of Oct. 29, 1940 (3 Tex.B.J. 621 [1940]). Source: TRCS art. 3783(5) (repealed).

TRCP 634. EXECUTION SUPERSEDED

The clerk or justice of the peace shall immediately issue a writ of supersedeas suspending all further proceedings under any execution previously issued when a supersedeas bond is afterward filed and approved within the time prescribed by law or these rules.

See CPRC §§65.013, 65.014.

History of TRCP 634: Adopted eff. Sept. 1, 1941, by order of Oct. 29, 1940 (3 Tex.B.J. 621 [1940]). Source: TRCS art. 3772 (repealed).

TRCP 635. STAY OF EXECUTION IN JUSTICE COURT

At any time within ten days after the rendition of any judgment in a justice court, the justice may grant a stay of execution thereof for three months from the date of such judgment, if the person against whom such judgment was rendered shall, with one or more good and sufficient sureties, to be approved by the justice, appear before him and acknowledge themselves and each of them bound to the successful party in such judgment for the full amount thereof, with interest and costs, which acknowledgment shall be entered in writing on the docket, and signed by the persons binding themselves as sureties; provided, no such stay of execution shall be granted unless the party applying therefor shall first file an affidavit with the justice that he has not the money with which to pay such judgment, and that the enforcement of same by execution prior to three months would be a hardship upon him and would cause a sacrifice of his property which would not likely be caused should said execution be stayed. Such acknowledgment shall be entered by the justice on his docket and shall constitute a judgment against the defendant and such sureties, upon which execution shall issue in case the same is not paid on or before the expiration of such day.

See CPRC §§65.013, 65.014.

History of TRCP 635: Adopted eff. Sept. 1, 1941, by order of Oct. 29, 1940 (3 Tex.B.J. 621 [1940]). Source: TRCS art. 2453 (repealed).

TRCP 636. INDORSEMENTS BY OFFICER

The officer receiving the execution shall indorse thereon the exact hour and day when he received it. If he receives more than one on the same day against the same person he shall number them as received.

History of TRCP 636: Adopted eff. Sept. 1, 1941, by order of Oct. 29, 1940 (3 Tex.B.J. 622 [1940]). Source: TRCS art. 3785 (repealed in part by TRCP), first sentence and first part of second sentence.

Diversified Ins. Mgmt. v. Phagan, 589 S.W.2d 854, 856 (Tex.App.—Fort Worth 1979, no writ). TRCP 636 "provides that when an officer receives more than one [execution] on the same day against the same person he shall number them as received. [¶] '[H]e must enforce them in the order that he received them.'"

TRCP 637. LEVY OF EXECUTION

When an execution is delivered to an officer he shall proceed without delay to levy the same upon the property of the defendant found within his county not exempt from execution, unless otherwise directed by the plaintiff, his agent or attorney. The officer shall first call upon the defendant, if he can be found, or, if absent, upon his agent within the county, if known, to point out property to be levied upon, and the levy shall first be made upon the property designated by the defendant, or his agent. If in the opinion of the officer the property so designated will not sell for enough to satisfy the execution and costs of sale, he shall require an additional designation by the defendant. If no property be thus designated by the defendant, the officer shall levy the execution upon any property of the defendant subject to execution.

History of TRCP 637: Adopted eff. Sept. 1, 1941, by order of Oct. 29, 1940 (3 Tex.B.J. 622 [1940]). Source: TRCS arts. 3788, 3789, 3790 (repealed).

Hickey v. Couchman, 797 S.W.2d 103, 109 (Tex. App.—Corpus Christi 1990, writ denied). "When the deputy learned that bankruptcy had not been filed [as alleged], he had a duty to execute immediately. We hold that where a sheriff is aware of the debtor's non-exempt assets and is able to seize them but does not, he willfully and intentionally violates [CPRC] §34.065."

Collum v. DeLoughter, 535 S.W.2d 390, 393 (Tex. App.—Texarkana 1976, writ ref'd n.r.e.). "[T]he failure of the officer to make any attempt to give [the debtor] an opportunity to designate property, as required by [TRCP] 637, was an irregularity. [That irregularity,] together with an inadequate price paid for the property, and the trial court's presumed finding that these irregularities were calculated to ... contribute to such inadequacy of price, [is] sufficient to avoid the sale."

TRCP 638. PROPERTY NOT TO BE DESIGNATED

A defendant in execution shall not point out property which he has sold, mortgaged or conveyed in trust, or property exempt from forced sale.

History of TRCP 638: Adopted eff. Sept. 1, 1941, by order of Oct. 29, 1940 (3 Tex.B.J. 622 [1940]). Source: TRCS art. 3791 (repealed).

TRCP 639. LEVY

In order to make a levy on real estate, it shall not be necessary for the officer to go upon the ground but it shall be sufficient for him to indorse such levy on the writ. Levy upon personal property is made by taking possession thereof, when the defendant in execution is entitled to the possession. Where the defendant in execution has an interest in personal property, but is not entitled to the possession thereof, a levy is made thereon by giving notice thereof to the person who is entitled to the possession, or one of them where there are several.

History of TRCP 639: Adopted eff. Sept. 1, 1941, by order of Oct. 29, 1940 (3 Tex.B.J. 622 [1940]). Source: TRCS art. 3793 (repealed).

Beaurline v. Sinclair Ref. Co., 191 S.W.2d 774, 777 (Tex.App.—San Antonio 1945, writ ref'd n.r.e.). "[W]here a levy is made on property ... which is so cumbersome that it may not be moved except at large expense and effort, it is sufficient if the officer goes upon the premises, points out the property, asserts dominion over it and forbids its removal by the person against whom the writ has been issued. The officer in making a levy on such property must do some act which would constitute a trespass except for the immunity furnished him by the writ."

TRCP 640. LEVY ON STOCK RUNNING AT LARGE

A levy upon livestock running at large in a range, and which cannot be herded and penned without great inconvenience and expense, may be made by designating by reasonable estimate the number of animals and describing them by their marks and brands, or either; such levy shall be made in the presence of two or more credible persons, and notice thereof shall be given in writing to the owner or his herder or agent, if residing within the county and known to the officer.

History of TRCP 640: Adopted eff. Sept. 1, 1941, by order of Oct. 29, 1940 (3 Tex.B.J. 622 [1940]). Source: TRCS art. 3794 (repealed).

TRCP 641. LEVY ON SHARES OF STOCK

A levy upon shares of stock of any corporation or joint stock company for which a certificate is outstanding is made by the officer seizing and taking possession of such certificate. Provided, however, that nothing herein shall be construed as restricting any rights granted under Section 8.317* of the Texas Uniform Commercial Code.

* Editor's Note: Deleted by Acts 1995, 74th Leg., ch. 962, §1 (eff. Sept. 1, 1995). See Bus. & Com. Code §8.112.

History of TRCP 641: Amended eff. Jan. 1, 1971, by order of July 21, 1970 (455-56 S.W.2d [Tex.Cases] xlv): Substituted the words "Section 8.317 of the Texas Uniform Commercial Code" for references to TRCS arts. 1358-13, 1358-14 (repealed, eff. Aug. 28, 1961). Amended eff. Dec. 31, 1947, by order of Aug. 18, 1947 (10 Tex.B.J. 399 [1947]): Materially altered the wording and meaning of the former rule. Adopted eff. Sept. 1, 1941, by order of Oct. 29, 1940 (3 Tex.B.J. 623 [1940]). Source: TRCS art. 3795 (repealed).

Benson v. Greenville Nat'l Exch. Bank, 253 S.W.2d 918, 928 (Tex.App.—Texarkana 1952, writ ref'd n.r.e.). "[W]hile the mere delivery of a stock certificate ... would not transfer title, yet the mere delivery of the stock would create a right in the bank as pledgee, by virtue of which it could resort to equity if its security was in any way threatened."

TRCP 642. REPEALED

TRCP 642 was repealed eff. Jan. 1, 1976, by order of July 22, 1975 (525-26 S.W.2d [Tex.Cases] lix). Former TRCS art. 6132b, §25(2)(c) and §28 superseded the repealed rule.

TRCP 643. LEVY ON GOODS PLEDGED OR MORTGAGED

Goods and chattels pledged, assigned or mortgaged as security for any debt or contract, may be levied upon and sold on execution against the person making the pledge, assignment or mortgage subject thereto; and the purchaser shall be entitled to the possession when it is held by the pledgee, assignee or mortgagee, on complying with the conditions of the pledge, assignment or mortgage.

History of TRCP 643: Adopted eff. Sept. 1, 1941, by order of Oct. 29, 1940 (3 Tex.B.J. 623 [1940]). Source: TRCS art. 3797 (repealed).

Conseco Fin. Servicing Corp. v. J&J Mobile Homes, 120 S.W.3d 878, 886 (Tex.App.—Fort Worth 2003, n.p.h.). P "reasons that under [TRCP] 643 a tax lien is the equivalent of a judicial lien created when an officer levies upon personal property under a writ of execution. [P] argues a tax lien is therefore subordinate to a security interest noted on the certificate of title. We disagree. [P] ignores the fact that tax liens are, by statute, given express priority status over security interests noted on certificates of title."

Grocers Sup. Co. v. Intercity Inv. Props., 795 S.W.2d 225, 227 (Tex.App.—Houston [14th Dist.] 1990, no writ). "[T]he right of ... a prior secured creditor, to take possession of its collateral was superior to the right of ... a mere judgment creditor, and [the prior secured creditor] could regain possession of the collateral from the constable who had levied on the property."

TRCP 644. MAY GIVE DELIVERY BOND

Any personal property taken in execution may be returned to the defendant by the officer upon the delivery by the defendant to him of a bond, payable to the plaintiff, with two or more good and sufficient sureties, to be approved by the officer, conditioned that the property shall be delivered to the officer at the time and place named in the bond, to be sold according to law, or for the payment to the officer of a fair value thereof, which shall be stated in the bond.

History of TRCP 644: Adopted eff. Sept. 1, 1941, by order of Oct. 29, 1940 (3 Tex.B.J. 623 [1940]). Source: TRCS art. 3801 (repealed).

TRCP 645. PROPERTY MAY BE SOLD BY DEFENDANT

Where property has been replevied, as provided in the preceding rule, the defendant may sell or dispose of the same, paying the officer the stipulated value thereof.

History of TRCP 645: Adopted eff. Sept. 1, 1941, by order of Oct. 29, 1940 (3 Tex.B.J. 623 [1940]). Source: TRCS art. 3802 (repealed).

TRCP 646. FORFEITED DELIVERY BOND

In case of the non-delivery of the property according to the terms of the delivery bond, and non-payment of the value thereof, the officer shall forthwith indorse the bond "Forfeited" and return the same to the clerk of the court or the justice of the peace from which the execution issued; whereupon, if the judgment remain unsatisfied in whole or in part, the clerk or justice shall issue execution against the principal debtor and the sureties on the bond for the amount due, not exceeding the stipulated value of the property, upon which execution no delivery bond shall be taken, which instruction shall be indorsed by the clerk or justice on the execution.

History of TRCP 646: Adopted eff. Sept. 1, 1941, by order of Oct. 29, 1940 (3 Tex.B.J. 623 [1940]). Source: TRCS art. 3803 (repealed).

TRCP 646a. SALE OF REAL PROPERTY

Real property taken by virtue of any execution shall be sold at public auction, at the courthouse door of the county, unless the court orders that such sale be at the place where the real property is situated, on the first Tuesday of the month, between the hours of ten o'clock, a.m. and four o'clock, p.m.

History of TRCP 646a: Adopted eff. Jan. 1, 1961, by order of July 26, 1960 (23 Tex.B.J. 684 [1961]): Court may order sale at place where real property is situated. Source: TRCS art. 3804 (repealed).

TRCP 647. NOTICE OF SALE OF REAL ESTATE

The time and place of sale of real estate under execution, order of sale, or venditioni exponas, shall be advertised by the officer by having the notice thereof published in the English language once a week for three consecutive weeks preceding such sale, in some newspaper published in said county. The first of said publications shall appear not less than twenty days immediately preceding the day of sale. Said notice shall contain a statement of the authority by virtue of which the sale is to be made, the time of levy, and the time and place of sale; it shall also contain a brief description of the property to be sold, and shall give the number of acres, original survey, locality in the county, and the name by which the land is most generally known, but it shall not be necessary for it to contain field notes. Publishers of newspapers shall charge the legal rate of Two (2) Cents per word for the first insertion of such publication and One (1) Cent per word for such subsequent insertions, or such newspapers shall be entitled to charge for such publication at a rate equal to but not in excess of the published word or line rate of that newspaper for such class of advertising. If there be no newspaper published in the county, or none which will publish the notice of sale for the compensation herein fixed, the officer shall then post such notice in writing in three public places in the county, one of which shall be at the courthouse door of such county, for at least twenty days successively next before the day of sale. The officer making the levy shall give the defendant, or his attorney, written notice of such sale, either in person or by mail, which notice shall substantially conform to the foregoing requirements.

History of TRCP 647: Amended eff. Dec. 31, 1941, by order of Sept. 20, 1941 (4 Tex.B.J. 583 [1941]). Adopted eff. Sept. 1, 1941, by order of Oct. 29, 1940 (3 Tex.B.J. 624 [1940]). Source: TRCS art. 3808 (repealed).

Collum v. DeLoughter, 535 S.W.2d 390, 392 (Tex. App.—Texarkana 1976, writ ref'd n.r.e.). "[T]he specific language of [TRCP] 21a imposes the requirement of registered mail upon the general provisions for 'mail' in [TRCP] 647."

TRCP 648. "COURTHOUSE DOOR" DEFINED

By the term "courthouse door" of a county is meant either of the principal entrances to the house provided by the proper authority for the holding of the district court. If from any cause there is no such house, the door of the house where the district court was last held in that county shall be deemed to be the courthouse door. Where the courthouse, or house used by the court, has been destroyed by fire or other cause, and another has not been designated by the proper authority, the place where such house stood shall be deemed to be the courthouse door.

History of TRCP 648: Adopted eff. Sept. 1, 1941, by order of Oct. 29, 1940 (3 Tex.B.J. 624 [1940]). Source: TRCS art. 3809 (repealed).

Micrea, Inc. v. Eureka Life Ins. Co., 534 S.W.2d 348, 358 (Tex.App.—Fort Worth 1976, writ ref'd n.r.e.). "In general the 'Courthouse Door' is either of the (several) entrances to the building provided for the holding of the district court."

TRCP 649. SALE OF PERSONAL PROPERTY

Personal property levied on under execution shall be offered for sale on the premises where it is taken in execution, or at the courthouse door of the county, or at some other place if, owing to the nature of the property, it is more convenient to exhibit it to purchasers at such place. Personal property susceptible of being exhibited shall not be sold unless the same be present and subject to the view of those attending the sale, except shares of stock in joint stock or incorporated companies, and in cases where the defendant in execution has merely an interest without right to the exclusive possession in which case the interest of defendant may be sold and conveyed without the presence or delivery of the property. When a levy is made upon livestock running at large on the range, it is not necessary that such stock, or any part thereof, be present at the place of sale, and the purchaser at such sale is authorized to gather and pen such stock and select therefrom the number purchased by him.

History of TRCP 649: Adopted eff. Sept. 1, 1941, by order of Oct. 29, 1940 (3 Tex.B.J. 624 [1940]). Source: TRCS arts. 3811, 3813, 3814 (repealed).

TRCP 650. NOTICE OF SALE OF PERSONAL PROPERTY

Previous notice of the time and place of the sale of any personal property levied on under execution shall be given by posting notice thereof for ten days successively immediately prior to the day of sale at the courthouse door of any county and at the place where the sale is to be made.

History of TRCP 650: Adopted eff. Sept. 1, 1941, by order of Oct. 29, 1940 (3 Tex.B.J. 624 [1940]). Source: TRCS art. 3812 (repealed).

TRCP 651. WHEN EXECUTION NOT SATISFIED

When the property levied upon does not sell for enough to satisfy the execution, the officer shall proceed anew, as in the first instance, to make the residue.

History of TRCP 651: Adopted eff. Sept. 1, 1941, by order of Oct. 29, 1940 (3 Tex.B.J. 624 [1940]). Source: TRCS art. 3815 (repealed).

TRCP 652. PURCHASER FAILING TO COMPLY

If any person shall bid off property at any sale made by virtue of an execution, and shall fail to comply with the terms of the sale, he shall be liable to pay the plaintiff in execution twenty per cent on the value of the property thus bid off, besides costs, to be recovered on motion, five days notice of such motion being given to such purchaser; and should the property on a second sale bring less than on the former, he shall be liable to pay to the defendant in execution all loss which he sustains thereby, to be recovered on motion as above provided.

History of TRCP 652: Adopted eff. Sept. 1, 1941, by order of Oct. 29, 1940 (3 Tex.B.J. 625 [1940]). Source: TRCS art. 3821 (repealed).

Jackson v. Universal Life Ins. Co., 582 S.W.2d 207, 209 (Tex.App.—Eastland 1979, writ ref'd n.r.e.). "[W]here a bidder fails to comply with the terms of an execution sale, he becomes liable under the express provisions of the rule, whether or not he acted in good faith."

TRCP 653. RESALE OF PROPERTY

When the terms of the sale shall not be complied with by the bidder the levying officer shall proceed to sell the same property again on the same day, if there be sufficient time; but if not, he shall readvertise and sell the same as in the first instance.

History of TRCP 653: Adopted eff. Sept. 1, 1941, by order of Oct. 29, 1940 (3 Tex.B.J. 625 [1940]). Source: TRCS art. 3822 (repealed).

TRCP 654. RETURN OF EXECUTION

The levying officer shall make due return of the execution, in writing and signed by him officially, stating concisely what such officer has done in pursuance of the requirements of the writ and of the law. The return shall be filed with the clerk of the court or the justice of the peace as the case may be. The execution shall be returned forthwith if satisfied by the collection of the money or if ordered by the plaintiff or his attorney indorsed thereon.

History of TRCP 654: Adopted eff. Sept. 1, 1941, by order of Oct. 29, 1940 (3 Tex.B.J. 625 [1940]). Source: TRCS art. 3828 (repealed).

Scott v. Wilson, 231 S.W.2d 912, 913 (Tex.App.—Amarillo 1950, no writ). "[A] sheriff's return upon an execution or order of sale may be amended."

TRCP 655. RETURN OF EXECUTION BY MAIL

When an execution is placed in the hands of an officer of a county other than the one in which the judgment is rendered, return may be made by mail; but money cannot be thus sent except by direction of the party entitled to receive the same or his attorney of record.

History of TRCP 655: Adopted eff. Sept. 1, 1941, by order of Oct. 29, 1940 (3 Tex.B.J. 625 [1940]). Source: TRCS art. 3823 (repealed).

TRCP 656. EXECUTION DOCKET

The clerk of each court shall keep an execution docket in which he shall enter a statement of all executions as they are issued by him, specifying the names of the parties, the amount of the judgment, the amount due thereon, the rate of interest when it exceeds six per cent, the costs, the date of issuing the execution, to whom delivered, and the return of the officer thereon, with the date of such return. Such docket entries shall be taken and deemed to be a record. The clerk shall keep an index and cross-index to the execution docket.

When execution is in favor or against several persons, it shall be indexed in the name of each person. Any clerk who shall fail to keep said execution docket and index thereto, or shall neglect to make the entries therein, shall be liable upon his official bond to any person injured for the amount of damages sustained by such neglect.

History of TRCP 656: Adopted eff. Sept. 1, 1941, by order of Oct. 29, 1940 (3 Tex.B.J. 626 [1940]). Source: TRCS art. 3831 (repealed).

SECTION 4. GARNISHMENT

TRCP 657. JUDGMENT FINAL FOR GARNISHMENT

In the case mentioned in subsection 3, section 63.001, Civil Practice and Remedies Code, the judgment whether based upon a liquidated demand or an unliquidated demand, shall be deemed final and subsisting for the purpose of garnishment from and after the date it is signed, unless a supersedeas bond shall have been approved and filed in accordance with Texas Rule of Appellate Procedure 47*.

* Now TRAP 24 (effective Sept. 1, 1997).

History of TRCP 657: Amended eff. Jan. 1, 1988, by order of July 15, 1987 (733-34 S.W.2d [Tex.Cases] lxxviii). Amended eff. Jan. 1, 1981, by order of June 10, 1980 (599-600 S.W.2d [Tex.Cases] lxxx): Finality of the judgment is counted from the time the judgment is signed. Adopted eff. Sept. 1, 1941, by order of Oct. 29, 1940 (3 Tex.B.J. 626 [1940]). Source: New rule.

Bank One v. Sunbelt Sav., 824 S.W.2d 557, 558 (Tex.1992). "Garnishment is a statutory proceeding whereby the property, money, or credits of a debtor in the possession of another are applied to the payment of the debt."

Westerman v. Comerica Bank-Tex., 928 S.W.2d 679, 682 (Tex.App.—San Antonio 1996, writ denied). "[T]he record contains conclusive summary judgment proof showing that when the garnishment action was actually finalized, the judgment was still a 'valid subsisting judgment'.... The fact that the underlying judgment was reversed 14 months after the garnishment judgment was rendered does not subsequently render the garnishment proceedings wrongful."

TRCP 658. APPLICATION FOR WRIT OF GARNISHMENT & ORDER

Either at the commencement of a suit or at any time during its progress the plaintiff may file an application for a writ of garnishment. Such application shall be supported by affidavits of the plaintiff, his agent, his attorney, or other person having knowledge of relevant facts. The application shall comply with all statutory requirements and shall state the grounds for issuing the writ and the specific facts relied upon by the plaintiff to warrant the required findings by the court. The writ shall not be quashed because two or more grounds are stated conjunctively or disjunctively. The application and any affidavits shall be made on personal knowledge and shall set forth such facts as would be admissible in evidence; provided that facts may be stated based upon information and belief if the grounds of such belief are specifically stated.

No writ shall issue before final judgment except upon written order of the court after a hearing, which may be ex parte. The court in its order granting the application shall make specific findings of facts to support the statutory grounds found to exist, and shall specify the maximum value of property or indebtedness that may be garnished and the amount of bond required of plaintiff. Such bond shall be in an amount which, in the opinion of the court, shall adequately compensate defendant in the event plaintiff fails to prosecute his suit to effect, and pay all damages and costs as shall be adjudged against him for wrongfully suing out the writ of garnishment. The court shall further find in its order the amount of bond required of defendant to replevy, which, unless defendant exercises his option as provided under Rule 664, shall be the amount of plaintiff's claim, one year's accrual of interest if allowed by law on the claim, and the estimated costs of court. The order may direct the issuance of several writs at the same time, or in succession, to be sent to different counties.

History of TRCP 658: Amended eff. Jan. 1, 1978, by order of July 11, 1977 (553-54 S.W.2d [Tex.Cases] lxiv): To require reliable proof of the grounds for issuance before judgment, findings, fixing value of property or indebtedness that may be garnished, fixing the amount of bond as well as the amount of a replevy bond, and for issuance of several writs. Amended eff. Dec. 31, 1947, by order of Aug. 18, 1947 (10 Tex.B.J. 399 [1947]). Adopted eff. Sept. 1, 1941, by order of Oct. 29, 1940 (3 Tex.B.J. 626 [1940]). Source: TRCS art. 4078 (repealed).

El Periodico, Inc. v. Parks Oil Co., 917 S.W.2d 777, 779 (Tex.1996). The garnishor's "application did not meet the requirements of [TRCP] 658.... [¶] The allegation of [the garnishee's] indebtedness to [the judgment defendant] is made on belief of counsel, and the grounds of such belief are not specifically stated."

TRCP 658a. BOND FOR GARNISHMENT

No writ of garnishment shall issue before final judgment until the party applying therefor has filed with the officer authorized to issue such writ a bond payable to the defendant in the amount fixed by the court's order, with sufficient surety or sureties as provided by statute, conditioned that the plaintiff will prosecute his suit to effect and pay to the extent of the penal amount of the bond all damages and costs as may be adjudged against him for wrongfully suing out such writ of garnishment.

After notice to the opposite party, either before or after the issuance of the writ, the defendant or plaintiff may file a motion to increase or reduce the amount of such bond, or to question the sufficiency of the sureties. Upon hearing, the court shall enter its order with respect to such bond and the sufficiency of the sureties.

Should it be determined from the garnishee's answer if such is not controverted that the garnishee is indebted to the defendant, or has in his hands effects belonging to the defendant, in an amount or value less than the amount of the debt claimed by the plaintiff, then after notice to the defendant the court in which such garnishment is pending upon hearing may reduce the required amount of such bond to double the sum of the garnishee's indebtedness to the defendant plus the value of the effects in his hands belonging to the defendant.

History of TRCP 658a: Amended eff. Jan. 1, 1978, by order of July 11, 1977 (553-54 S.W.2d [Tex.Cases] lxv): Rewrote first par. of the rule; amount of the bond is to be fixed by court order, amount will no longer be double the amount of the debt claimed; either party after notice and hearing may increase or reduce the amount of the bond. Adopted eff. Jan. 1, 1961, by order of July 26, 1960 (23 Tex.B.J. 684 [1961]). Source: TRCS art. 4077 (repealed).

TRCP 659. CASE DOCKETED

When the foregoing requirements of these rules have been complied with, the judge, or clerk, or justice of the peace, as the case may be, shall docket the case in the name of the plaintiff as plaintiff and of the garnishee as defendant; and shall immediately issue a writ of garnishment directed to the garnishee, commanding him to appear before the court out of which the same is issued at or before 10 o'clock a.m. of the Monday next following the expiration of twenty days from the date the writ was served, if the writ is issued out of the district or county court; or the Monday next after the expiration of ten days from the date the writ was served, if the writ is issued out of the justice court. The writ shall command the garnishee to answer under oath upon such return date what, if anything, he is indebted to the defendant, and was when the writ was served, and what effects, if any, of the defendant he has in his possession, and had when such writ was served, and what other persons, if any, within his knowledge, are indebted to the defendant or have effects belonging to him in their possession.

History of TRCP 659: Amended eff. Jan. 1, 1978, by order of July 11, 1977 (553-54 S.W.2d [Tex.Cases] lxvi): Deleted provision for compliance with art. 4077, which was repealed. Amended eff. Dec. 31, 1947, by order of Aug. 18, 1947 (10 Tex.B.J. 399 [1947]). Amended eff. Dec. 31, 1941, by order of Sept. 20, 1941 (4 Tex.B.J. 586 [1941]). Adopted eff. Sept. 1, 1941, by order of Oct. 29, 1940 (3 Tex.B.J. 626 [1940]). Source: TRCS art. 4079 (repealed).

Cloughly v. NBC Bank-Seguin, 773 S.W.2d 652, 658 (Tex.App.—San Antonio 1989, writ denied). "Although the statute contemplates a separate docketing, we do not find harm in proceeding with a garnishment action in the same cause number. Although this was an irregularity in procedure, the validity of the judgment was not affected."

TRCP 660. REPEALED

Repealed eff. Dec. 31, 1947, by order of Aug. 18, 1947 (10 Tex.B.J. 400 [1947]).

TRCP 661. FORM OF WRIT

The following form of writ may be used:

"The State of Texas.

To E.F., Garnishee, greeting:

Whereas, in the ______ Court of ____________ County (if a justice court, state also the number of the precinct), in a certain cause wherein A.B. is plaintiff and C.D. is defendant, the plaintiff, claiming an indebtedness against the said C.D. of ___________ dollars, besides interest and costs of suit, has applied for a writ of garnishment against you, E.F.; therefore you are hereby commanded to be and appear before said court at _________ in said county (if the writ is issued from the county or district court, here proceed: 'at 10 o'clock a.m. on the Monday next following the expiration of twenty days from the date of service hereof.' If the writ is issued from a justice of the peace court, here proceed: 'at or before 10 o'clock a.m. on the Monday next after the expiration of ten days from the date of service hereof.' In either event, proceed as follows:) then and there to answer upon oath what, if anything, you are indebted to the said C.D., and were when this writ was served upon you, and what effects, if any, of the said C.D. you have in your possession, and had when this writ was served, and what other persons, if any, within your knowledge, are indebted to the said C.D. or have effects belonging to him in their possession. You are further commanded NOT to pay to defendant any debt or to deliver to him any effects, pending further order of this court. Herein fail not, but make due answer as the law directs."

TRCP 661

History of TRCP 661: Amended eff. Jan. 1, 1978, by order of July 11, 1977 (553-54 S.W.2d [Tex.Cases] lxvi): Added next to the last sentence. Amended eff. Dec. 31, 1947, by order of Aug. 18, 1947 (10 Tex.B.J. 400 [1947]). Amended eff. Dec. 31, 1941, by order of Sept. 20, 1941 (4 Tex.B.J. 586 [1941]). Adopted eff. Sept. 1, 1941, by order of Oct. 29, 1940 (3 Tex.B.J. 627 [1940]). Source: TRCS art. 4081 (repealed).

Bank One v. Sunbelt Sav., 824 S.W.2d 557, 558 (Tex.1992). "When a creditor wants to challenge title to funds held by a third party, the creditor should seek a writ of garnishment naming the nominal owner not the true owner. The court is then responsible for determining true ownership."

TRCP 662. DELIVERY OF WRIT

The writ of garnishment shall be dated and tested as other writs, and may be delivered to the sheriff or constable by the officer who issued it, or he may deliver it to the plaintiff, his agent or attorney, for that purpose.

History of TRCP 662: Adopted eff. Sept. 1, 1941, by order of Oct. 29, 1940 (3 Tex.B.J. 627 [1940]). Source: TRCS art. 4082 (repealed).

Moody Nat'l Bank v. Riebschlager, 946 S.W.2d 521, 523 n.1 (Tex.App.—Houston [14th Dist.] 1997, writ denied). "Private process servers are prohibited from executing writs of garnishment as only a sheriff or constable may deliver the writs to a garnishee."

TRCP 663. EXECUTION & RETURN OF WRIT

The sheriff or constable receiving the writ of garnishment shall immediately proceed to execute the same by delivering a copy thereof to the garnishee, and shall make return thereof as of other citations.

History of TRCP 663: Adopted eff. Sept. 1, 1941, by order of Oct. 29, 1940 (3 Tex.B.J. 627 [1940]). Source: TRCS art. 4083 (repealed).

TRCP 663a. SERVICE OF WRIT ON DEFENDANT

The defendant shall be served in any manner prescribed for service of citation or as provided in Rule 21a with a copy of the writ of garnishment, the application, accompanying affidavits and orders of the court as soon as practicable following the service of the writ. There shall be prominently displayed on the face of the copy of the writ served on the defendant, in ten-point type and in a manner calculated to advise a reasonably attentive person of its contents, the following:

To __________, Defendant:

You are hereby notified that certain properties alleged to be owned by you have been garnished. If you claim any rights in such property, you are advised:

"YOU HAVE A RIGHT TO REGAIN POSSESSION OF THE PROPERTY BY FILING A REPLEVY BOND. YOU HAVE A RIGHT TO SEEK TO REGAIN POSSESSION OF THE PROPERTY BY FILING WITH THE COURT A MOTION TO DISSOLVE THIS WRIT."

History of TRCP 663a: Adopted eff. Jan. 1, 1978, by order of July 11, 1977 (553-54 S.W.2d [Tex.Cases] lxvii): Rule affords the defendant notice of the proceedings and informs him of some of his rights. Source: New rule.

Mendoza v. Luke Fruia Invs., 962 S.W.2d 650, 652 (Tex.App.—Corpus Christi 1998, no pet.). TRCP "663a requires *strict compliance*. [W]hen a judgment debtor voluntarily answers and appears in a garnishment proceeding, the debtor waives only irregularities in the writ of garnishment, such as defects in the affidavit or bond. Voluntary appearance does not waive the requirements of the writ itself. [¶] Rights under a writ of garnishment are determined by priority in time, which itself is determined by service of the writ. Without proper service of the writ on the debtor, no control or custody of his property can be gained by his answer."

TRCP 664. DEFENDANT MAY REPLEVY

At any time before judgment, should the garnished property not have been previously claimed or sold, the defendant may replevy the same, or any part thereof, or the proceeds from the sale of the property if it has been sold under order of the court, by giving bond with sufficient surety or sureties as provided by statute, to be approved by the officer who levied the writ, payable to plaintiff, in the amount fixed by the court's order, or, at the defendant's option, for the value of the property or indebtedness sought to be replevied (to be estimated by the officer), plus one year's interest thereon at the legal rate from the date of the bond, conditioned that the defendant, garnishee, shall satisfy, to the extent of the penal amount of the bond, any judgment which may be rendered against him in such action.

On reasonable notice to the opposing party (which may be less than three days) either party shall have the right to prompt judicial review of the amount of bond required, denial of bond, sufficiency of sureties, and estimated value of the property, by the court which authorized issuance of the writ. The court's determination may be made upon the basis of affidavits, if uncontroverted, setting forth such facts as would be admissible in evidence; otherwise, the parties shall submit evidence. The court shall forthwith enter its order either approving or modifying the requirements of the officer or of the court's prior order, and such order of the court shall supersede and control with respect to such matters.

On reasonable notice to the opposing party (which may be less than three days) the defendant shall have the right to move the court for a substitution of property, of equal value as that garnished, for the property garnished. Provided that there has been located sufficient property of the defendant's to satisfy the order of garnishment, the court may authorize substitution of one or more items of defendant's property for all or for part of the property garnished. The court shall first make findings as to the value of the property to be substituted. If property is substituted, the property released from garnishment shall be delivered to defendant, if such property is personal property, and all liens upon such property from the original order of garnishment or modification thereof shall be terminated. Garnishment of substituted property shall be deemed to have existed from date of garnishment on the original property garnished, and no property on which liens have become affixed since the date of garnishment of the original property may be substituted.

History of TRCP 664: Amended eff. Jan. 1, 1978, by order of July 11, 1977 (553-54 S.W.2d [Tex.Cases] lxvii): Rewrote rule - gives the defendant the right to replevy, including the proceeds from a sale of property; changes the amount of bond from double the amount of plaintiff's debt to the amount fixed by the court; clearly fixes the conditions of the replevy bond; gives the parties a hearing; authorizes the substitution of property. Adopted eff. Sept. 1, 1941, by order of Oct. 29, 1940 (3 Tex.B.J. 627 [1940]). Source: TRCS art. 4084 (repealed in part by TRCP), second and third sentences.

Woodall v. Clark, 802 S.W.2d 415, 418 (Tex.App.—Beaumont 1991, no writ). "[O]nce [D's] Replevy Bond was challenged by [P], a right provided to [P] by [TRCP] 664, the trial court was required to review, among other things, the sufficiency of the sureties."

TRCP 664a. DISSOLUTION OR MODIFICATION OF WRIT OF GARNISHMENT

A defendant whose property or account has been garnished or any intervening party who claims an interest in such property or account, may by sworn written motion, seek to vacate, dissolve or modify the writ of garnishment, and the order directing its issuance, for any grounds or cause, extrinsic or intrinsic. Such motion shall admit or deny each finding of the order directing the issuance of the writ except where the movant is unable to admit or deny the finding, in which case movant shall set forth the reasons why he cannot admit or deny. Unless the parties agree to an extension of time, the motion shall be heard promptly, after reasonable notice to the plaintiff (which may be less than three days), and the issue shall be determined not later than ten days after the motion is filed. The filing of the motion shall stay any further proceedings under the writ, except for any orders concerning the care, preservation or sale of any perishable property, until a hearing is had, and the issue is determined. The writ shall be dissolved unless, at such hearing, the plaintiff shall prove the grounds relied upon for its issuance, but the court may modify its previous order granting the writ and the writ issued pursuant thereto. The movant shall, however, have the burden to prove that the reasonable value of the property garnished exceeds the amount necessary to secure the debt, interest for one year, and probable costs. He shall also have the burden to prove facts to justify substitution of property.

The court's determination may be made upon the basis of affidavits, if uncontroverted, setting forth such facts as would be admissible in evidence; otherwise, the parties shall submit evidence. The court may make all such orders including orders concerning the care, preservation or disposition of the property (or the proceeds therefrom if the same has been sold), as justice may require. If the movant has given a replevy bond, an order to vacate or dissolve the writ shall vacate the replevy bond and discharge the sureties thereon, and if the court modifies its order or the writ issued pursuant thereto, it shall make such further orders with respect to the bond as may be consistent with its modification.

History of TRCP 664a: Adopted eff. Jan. 1, 1978, by order of July 11, 1977 (553-54 S.W.2d [Tex.Cases] lxviii): New rule affords a prompt hearing, provides for the procedures, burden of proof and the kind of proof. Source: New rule.

Swiderski v. Victoria Bank & Trust Co., 706 S.W.2d 676, 678 (Tex.App.—Corpus Christi 1986, writ ref'd n.r.e.). A TRCP 664a "hearing is a distinct proceeding from the writ of garnishment proceeding between the garnishor and garnishee. ... The issue to be determined in a Rule 664a hearing is that 'the plaintiff shall prove the ground relied upon for its (the writ of garnishment's) issuance.' [¶] Therefore, at a Rule 664a hearing, the plaintiff does not have to prove that the garnishee is indebted to the defendant debtor...."

TRCP 665. ANSWER TO WRIT

The answer of the garnishee shall be under oath, in writing and signed by him, and shall make true answers to the several matters inquired of in the writ of garnishment.

See ***Commentaries***, "The Answer—Denying Liability," ch. 3-E.

History of TRCP 665: Adopted eff. Sept. 1, 1941, by order of Oct. 29, 1940 (3 Tex.B.J. 628 [1940]). Source: TRCS art. 4085 (repealed).

TRCP 666. GARNISHEE DISCHARGED

If it appears from the answer of the garnishee that he is not indebted to the defendant, and was not so indebted when the writ of garnishment was served upon him, and that he has not in his possession any effects of the defendant and had not when the writ was served, and if he has either denied that any other persons within his knowledge are indebted to the defendant or have in their possession effects belonging to the defendant, or else has named such persons, should the answer of the garnishee not be controverted as hereinafter provided, the court shall enter judgment discharging the garnishee.

History of TRCP 666: Amended eff. Dec. 31, 1947, by order of Aug. 18, 1947 (10 Tex.B.J. 400 [1947]). Adopted eff. Sept. 1, 1941, by order of Oct. 29, 1940 (3 Tex.B.J. 628 [1940]). Source: TRCS art. 4086 (repealed).

TRCP 667. JUDGMENT BY DEFAULT

If the garnishee fails to file an answer to the writ of garnishment at or before the time directed in the writ, it shall be lawful for the court, at any time after judgment shall have been rendered against the defendant, and on or after appearance day, to render judgment by default, as in other civil cases, against such garnishee for the full amount of such judgment against the defendant together with all interest and costs that may have accrued in the main case and also in the garnishment proceedings. The answer of the garnishee may be filed as in any other civil case at any time before such default judgment is rendered.

History of TRCP 667: Adopted eff. Sept. 1, 1941, by order of Oct. 29, 1940 (3 Tex.B.J. 628 [1940]). Source: TRCS art. 4087 (repealed).

Falderbaum v. Lowe, 964 S.W.2d 744, 747 (Tex. App.—Austin 1998, no pet.). The garnishee "cannot now claim that the district court lacks subject-matter jurisdiction *to enforce* the garnishment order when she failed to properly challenge the trial court's jurisdiction when the writ of garnishment was originally issued."

TRCP 668. JUDGMENT WHEN GARNISHEE IS INDEBTED

Should it appear from the answer of the garnishee or should it be otherwise made to appear and be found by the court that the garnishee is indebted to the defendant in any amount, or was so indebted when the writ of garnishment was served, the court shall render judgment for the plaintiff against the garnishee for the amount so admitted or found to be due to the defendant from the garnishee, unless such amount is in excess of the amount of the plaintiff's judgment against the defendant with interest and costs, in which case, judgment shall be rendered against the garnishee for the full amount of the judgment already rendered against the defendant, together with interest and costs of the suit in the original case and also in the garnishment proceedings. If the garnishee fail or refuse to pay such judgment rendered against him, execution shall issue thereon in the same manner and under the same conditions as is or may be provided for the issuance of execution in other cases.

History of TRCP 668: Adopted eff. Sept. 1, 1941, by order of Oct. 29, 1940 (3 Tex.B.J. 628 [1940]). Source: TRCS art. 4088 (repealed).

Wrigley v. First Nat'l Sec. Corp., 104 S.W.3d 259, 264 (Tex.App.—Beaumont 2003, no pet.). "The funds captured by the writ of garnishment are those held by the garnishee in the account of the judgment debtor on the date the writ is served, and any additional funds deposited through the date the garnishee is required to answer. [P's] right to recover those funds from the garnishee is [not necessarily] fixed by whatever judgment [P] possesses on that date. The issuance and service of the writ of garnishment fixes the trial court's jurisdiction to determine whether the garnishee holds funds belonging to the judgment debtor, and necessarily that jurisdiction extends to a determination of title and ownership of the funds, regardless of how that ownership is placed in controversy. The garnishee may deposit the funds into the court, bring in all other claimants through interpleader, and the trial court may then adjudicate the conflicting claims of the parties."

Healy v. Wick Bldg. Sys., 560 S.W.2d 713, 717 (Tex. App.—Dallas 1977, writ ref'd n.r.e.). TRCP 668 "authorizes judgment only where the garnishee is indebted to [D] and then only to the extent of such indebtedness."

TRCP 669. JUDGMENT FOR EFFECTS

Should it appear from the garnishee's answer, or otherwise, that the garnishee has in his possession, or had when the writ was served, any effects of the defendant liable to execution, including any certificates of stock in any corporation or joint stock company, the court shall render a decree ordering sale of such effects under execution in satisfaction of plaintiff's judgment and directing the garnishee to deliver them, or so much thereof as shall be necessary to satisfy plaintiff's judgment, to the proper officer for that purpose.

History of TRCP 669: Amended eff. Dec. 31, 1947, by order of Aug. 18, 1947 (10 Tex.B.J. 400 [1947]). Adopted eff. Sept. 1, 1941, by order of Oct. 29, 1940 (3 Tex.B.J. 628 [1940]). Source: TRCS art. 4089 (repealed).

Healy v. Wick Bldg. Sys., 560 S.W.2d 713, 717 (Tex. App.—Dallas 1977, writ ref'd n.r.e.). TRCP 669 "provides for a sale of effects in the hands of the garnishee that may belong to [D] in order to satisfy the plaintiff's judgment against the defendant."

TRCP 670. REFUSAL TO DELIVER EFFECTS

Should the garnishee adjudged to have effects of the defendant in his possession, as provided in the preceding rule, fail or refuse to deliver them to the sheriff or constable on such demand, the officer shall immediately make return of such failure or refusal, whereupon on motion of the plaintiff, the garnishee shall be cited to show cause upon a date to be fixed by the court why he should not be attached for contempt of court for such failure or refusal. If the garnishee fails to show some good and sufficient excuse for such failure or refusal, he shall be fined for such contempt and imprisoned until he shall deliver such effects.

History of TRCP 670: Adopted eff. Sept. 1, 1941, by order of Oct. 29, 1940 (3 Tex.B.J. 628 [1940]). Source: TRCS art. 4090 (repealed).

Cohen v. Advance Imports, 597 S.W.2d 449, 451 (Tex.App.—Dallas 1980, writ ref'd n.r.e.). TRCP 670 "provides that if the garnishee fails to deliver [D's] effects to the officer on demand, and does not show a good excuse for such failure, he may be fined for contempt and imprisoned until he makes such delivery."

TRCP 671. REPEALED

Repealed eff. Dec. 31, 1947, by order of Aug. 18, 1947 (10 Tex.B.J. 400 [1947]).

TRCP 672. SALE OF EFFECTS

The sale so ordered shall be conducted in all respects as other sales of personal property under execution; and the officer making such sale shall execute a transfer of such effects or interest to the purchaser, with a brief recital of the judgment of the court under which the same was sold.

History of TRCP 672: Amended eff. Dec. 31, 1947, by order of Aug. 18, 1947 (10 Tex.B.J. 400 [1947]). Adopted eff. Sept. 1, 1941, by order of Oct. 29, 1940 (3 Tex.B.J. 629 [1940]). Source: TRCS art. 4092 (repealed).

TRCP 673. MAY TRAVERSE ANSWER

If the plaintiff should not be satisfied with the answer of any garnishee, he may controvert the same by his affidavit stating that he has good reason to believe, and does believe, that the answer of the garnishee is incorrect, stating in what particular he believes the same to be incorrect. The defendant may also, in like manner, controvert the answer of the garnishee.

History of TRCP 673: Adopted eff. Sept. 1, 1941, by order of Oct. 29, 1940 (3 Tex.B.J. 629 [1940]). Source: TRCS art. 4094 (repealed).

TRCP 674. TRIAL OF ISSUE

If the garnishee whose answer is controverted, is a resident of the county in which the proceeding is pending, an issue shall be formed under the direction of the court and tried as in other cases.

History of TRCP 674: Adopted eff. Sept. 1, 1941, by order of Oct. 29, 1940 (3 Tex.B.J. 629 [1940]). Source: TRCS art. 4095 (repealed).

First Nat'l Bank v. Steves Sash & Door Co., 468 S.W.2d 133, 138 (Tex.App.—San Antonio 1971, writ ref'd n.r.e.). When the garnishor filed an affidavit controverting the answer of the nonresident garnishee, the court of the county in which the garnishor resided "lost jurisdiction to proceed further, and any proceedings thereafter held were a nullity of no force and effect."

TRCP 675. DOCKET & NOTICE

The clerk of the court or the justice of the peace, on receiving certified copies filed in the county of the garnishee's residence under the provisions of the statutes, shall docket the case in the name of the plaintiff as plaintiff, and of the garnishee as defendant, and issue a notice to the garnishee, stating that his answer has been so controverted, and that such issue will stand for trial on the docket of such court. Such notice shall be directed to the garnishee, be dated and tested as other process from such court, and served by delivering a copy thereof to the garnishee. It shall be returnable, if issued from the district or county court, at ten o'clock a.m.

of the Monday next after the expiration of twenty days from the date of its service; and if issued from the justice court, to the next term of such court convening after the expiration of twenty days after the service of such notice.

History of TRCP 675: Amended eff. Dec. 31, 1941, by order of Sept. 20, 1941 (4 Tex.B.J. 588 [1941]). Adopted eff. Sept. 1, 1941, by order of Oct. 29, 1940 (3 Tex.B.J. 629 [1940]). Source: TRCS art. 4097 (repealed).

Atteberry, Inc. v. Standard Brass & Mfg. Co., 270 S.W.2d 252, 255 (Tex.App.—Waco 1954, writ ref'd n.r.e.). "[T]he issuance of the writ of garnishment must come from the court where the judgment was rendered, but where the garnishee is the resident of another county and is not entitled to be discharged on its answer the cause must be docketed and tried in the court having jurisdiction of the subject matter in the county of the residence of the garnishee...."

TRCP 676. ISSUE TRIED AS IN OTHER CASES

Upon the return of such notice served, an issue shall be formed under the direction of the court and tried as in other cases.

History of TRCP 676: Adopted eff. Sept. 1, 1941, by order of Oct. 29, 1940 (3 Tex.B.J. 629 [1940]). Source: TRCS art. 4098 (repealed).

TRCP 677. COSTS

Where the garnishee is discharged upon his answer, the costs of the proceeding, including a reasonable compensation to the garnishee, shall be taxed against the plaintiff; where the answer of the garnishee has not been controverted and the garnishee is held thereon, such costs shall be taxed against the defendant and included in the execution provided for in this section; where the answer is contested, the costs shall abide the issue of such contest.

History of TRCP 677: Adopted eff. Sept. 1, 1941, by order of Oct. 29, 1940 (3 Tex.B.J. 629 [1940]). Source: TRCS art. 4100 (repealed).

Rowley v. Lake Area Nat'l Bank, 976 S.W.2d 715, 721 (Tex.App.—Houston [1st Dist.] 1998, pet. denied). "[T]he term 'costs' has consistently been interpreted to include attorney's fees."

TRCP 678. GARNISHEE DISCHARGED ON PROOF

It shall be a sufficient answer to any claim of the defendant against the garnishee founded on an indebtedness of such garnishee, or on the possession by him of any effects, for the garnishee to show that such indebtedness has been paid, or such effects, including any certificates of stock in any incorporated or joint stock company, have been delivered to any sheriff or constable as provided for in Rule 669.

History of TRCP 678: Amended eff. Dec. 31, 1947, by order of Aug. 18, 1947 (10 Tex.B.J. 401 [1947]). Adopted eff. Sept. 1, 1941, by order of Oct. 29, 1940 (3 Tex.B.J. 630 [1940]). Source: TRCS art. 4101 (repealed).

TRCP 679. AMENDMENT

Clerical errors in the affidavit, bond, or writ of garnishment or the officer's return thereof, may upon application in writing to the judge or justice of the court in which the suit is filed, and after notice to the opponent, be amended in such manner and on such terms as the judge or justice shall authorize by an order entered in the minutes of the court (or noted on the docket of the justice of the peace), provided such amendment appears to the judge or justice to be in furtherance of justice.

History of TRCP 679: Adopted eff. Sept. 1, 1941, by order of Oct. 29, 1940 (3 Tex.B.J. 630 [1940]). Source: New rule.

Metroplex Factors, Inc. v. First Nat'l Bank, 610 S.W.2d 862, 866 (Tex.App.—Fort Worth 1980, writ ref'd n.r.e.). TRCP 679 "authorizes correction of clerical errors (such as the missing seal) but does not apply to substantive matters, such as the sufficiency of the required supporting affidavits or other deficiencies in the application for writ of garnishment."

SECTION 5. INJUNCTIONS

TRCP 680. TEMPORARY RESTRAINING ORDER

No temporary restraining order shall be granted without notice to the adverse party unless it clearly appears from specific facts shown by affidavit or by the verified complaint that immediate and irreparable injury, loss, or damage will result to the applicant before notice can be served and a hearing had thereon. Every temporary restraining order granted without notice shall be endorsed with the date and hour of issuance; shall be filed forthwith in the clerk's office and entered of record; shall define the injury and state why it is irreparable and why the order was granted without notice; and shall expire by its terms within such time after signing, not to exceed fourteen days, as the court fixes, unless within the time so fixed the order, for good cause shown, is extended for a like period or unless the party against whom the order is directed consents that it may be extended for a longer period. The reasons for the extension shall be entered of record. No more than one extension may be granted unless subsequent extensions are unopposed. In case a temporary restraining order is granted without notice, the application for a temporary injunction shall be set down for hearing at the earliest possible date and takes precedence of all matters except older matters of the same character; and when the application comes on for hearing the party who obtained the temporary restraining order shall proceed with the application for a temporary injunction and, if he does not do so, the court shall dissolve the temporary restraining order. On two days' notice to the party who obtained the temporary restraining order without notice or on such shorter notice to that party as the court may prescribe, the adverse party may appear and move its dissolution or modification and in that event the court shall proceed to hear and determine such motion as expeditiously as the ends of justice require.

Every restraining order shall include an order setting a certain date for hearing on the temporary or permanent injunction sought.

See CPRC ch. 65; ***Commentaries***, "Plaintiff's Pleadings for Injunctive Relief," ch. 2-C; FORMS 2C.

History of TRCP 680: Amended eff. Jan. 1, 1988, by order of July 15, 1987 (733-34 S.W.2d [Tex.Cases] lxxviii): Extends the length of the initial temporary restraining order from 10 days to 14 days. Amended eff. Apr. 1, 1984, by order of Dec. 5, 1983 (661-62 S.W.2d [Tex.Cases] cxvi): The rule was changed to avoid successive restraining orders and to require an order setting the date for hearing on the injunction. Adopted eff. Sept. 1, 1941, by order of Oct. 29, 1940 (3 Tex.B.J. 630 [1940]). Source: FRCP 65(b), superseding TRCS art. 4654.

In re Tex. Nat. Res. Conserv. Comm'n, 85 S.W.3d 201, 204-05 (Tex.2002). "[A]ll temporary restraining orders are subject to Rule 680's limitations on duration. ... Rule 680 provides the only method for extending a [TRO] beyond 14 days. [¶] [TRCP] 680 governs an extension of a [TRO], whether issued with or without notice, and permits but one extension for no longer than 14 days unless the restrained party agrees to a longer extension."

Ex Parte Lesikar, 899 S.W.2d 654, 654 (Tex.1995). "An oral extension of a TRO is ineffective, and the contemnor must have notice of the actual written extension before he can be charged with contempt."

Davis v. Huey, 571 S.W.2d 859, 862 (Tex.1978). "At a hearing upon the request for a temporary injunction the only question before the trial court is whether the applicant is entitled to preservation of the status quo of the subject matter of the suit pending trial on the merits."

TRCP 681. TEMPORARY INJUNCTIONS: NOTICE

No temporary injunction shall be issued without notice to the adverse party.

See CPRC §51.014(a)(4) (interlocutory appeal of temporary injunction).

History of TRCP 681: Adopted eff. Sept. 1, 1941, by order of Oct. 29, 1940 (3 Tex.B.J. 631 [1940]). Source: FRCP 65(a).

State v. Cook United, Inc., 469 S.W.2d 709, 712 (Tex.1971). "In the absence of notice to or service of citation upon the Attorney General ... the temporary injunction is hereby modified to enjoin only the county and district attorneys of Tarrant and McLennan Counties [who had notice], and shall have no effect on the Attorney General ... or the other district and county attorneys in this State."

PILF Invs. v. Arlitt, 940 S.W.2d 255, 260 (Tex. App.—San Antonio 1997, no writ). "[N]otice on a motion for injunctive relief is inadequate to the extent a non-movant party, who is ultimately enjoined, is not served with notice of the hearing."

TRCP 682. SWORN PETITION

No writ of injunction shall be granted unless the applicant therefor shall present his petition to the judge verified by his affidavit and containing a plain and intelligible statement of the grounds for such relief.

See ***Commentaries***, "Plaintiff's Pleadings for Injunctive Relief," ch. 2-C; FORMS 2C.

History of TRCP 682: Amended eff. Sept. 1, 1941, by order of Mar. 31, 1941 (4 Tex.B.J. 178 [1941]): Eliminated original rule and substituted this one. Adopted eff. Sept. 1, 1941, by order of Oct. 29, 1940 (3 Tex.B.J. 632 [1940]). Source: New rule. See TRCS art. 4647 (repealed).

Walling v. Metcalfe, 863 S.W.2d 56, 57 (Tex.1993). "A trial court may grant a temporary writ of injunction to preserve the status quo pending trial even though the applicant's prayer does not include a claim for equitable relief.... In such cases, however, a temporary injunction should only issue if the applicant establishes a probable right on final trial to the relief sought, and a probable injury in the interim."

Town of Palm Valley v. Johnson, 17 S.W.3d 281, 288 (Tex.App.—Corpus Christi 2000), *pet. denied*, 87 S.W.3d 110 (Tex.2001). "A verified petition for injunctive relief is not required ... when a full evidentiary hearing on evidence independent of the petition has been held."

Crystal Media v. HCI Acquisition Corp., 773 S.W.2d 732, 734 (Tex.App.—San Antonio 1989, no writ). "If the insufficiency of the verification is not objected to prior to the introduction of evidence the defect [is] waived."

TRCP 683. FORM & SCOPE OF INJUNCTION OR RESTRAINING ORDER

Every order granting an injunction and every restraining order shall set forth the reasons for its issuance; shall be specific in terms; shall describe in reasonable detail and not by reference to the complaint or other document, the act or acts sought to be restrained; and is binding only upon the parties to the action, their officers, agents, servants, employees, and attorneys, and upon those persons in active concert or participation with them who receive actual notice of the order by personal service or otherwise.

Every order granting a temporary injunction shall include an order setting the cause for trial on the merits with respect to the ultimate relief sought. The appeal of a temporary injunction shall constitute no cause for delay of the trial.

See ***Commentaries***, "Plaintiff's Original Petition," ch. 2-B; "Plaintiff's Pleadings for Injunctive Relief," ch. 2-C; "Request for Findings of Fact," ch. 10-E.

History of TRCP 683: Amended eff. Apr. 1, 1984, by order of Dec. 5, 1983 (661-62 S.W.2d [Tex.Cases] cxvi): The last paragraph was added. Adopted eff. Sept. 1, 1941, by order of Oct. 29, 1940 (3 Tex.B.J. 631 [1940]). Source: FRCP 65(d).

Qwest Comm. Corp. v. AT&T Corp., 24 S.W.3d 334, 337 (Tex.2000). "The [TRCPs] require that an order granting a temporary injunction set the cause for trial on the merits and fix the amount of security to be given by the applicant. These procedural requirements are mandatory, and an order granting a temporary injunction that does not meet them is subject to being declared void and dissolved." *See also* ***InterFirst Bank San Felipe v. Paz Constr. Co.***, 715 S.W.2d 640, 641 (Tex.1986).

Ex parte Slavin, 412 S.W.2d 43, 44 (Tex.1967). An injunction decree "must spell out the details of compliance in clear, specific and unambiguous terms so that such person will readily know exactly what duties or obligations are imposed upon him."

In re Marriage of Grossnickle, 115 S.W.3d 238, 244 (Tex.App.—Texarkana 2003, n.p.h.). TRCP 683 "does not expressly require that a trial date be set. [I]t simply provides that the injunction order set the cause for trial on the merits. This is effectively the same as requiring a specific trial date to be set in the order."

Fasken v. Darby, 901 S.W.2d 591, 593 (Tex.App.—El Paso 1995, no writ). "An injunction that fails to identify the harm that will be suffered if it does not issue must be declared void and be dissolved. This rule operates to invalidate an injunction even when the complaining party fails to bring the error to the trial court's attention." For cases that hold to the contrary, see "Waiver," ch. 2-C, §8.1.2, p. xxx.

TRCP 684. APPLICANT'S BOND

In the order granting any temporary restraining order or temporary injunction, the court shall fix the amount of security to be given by the applicant. Before the issuance of the temporary restraining order or temporary injunction the applicant shall execute and file with the clerk a bond to the adverse party, with two or more good and sufficient sureties, to be approved by the clerk, in the sum fixed by the judge, conditioned that the applicant will abide the decision which may be made in the cause, and that he will pay all sums of money and costs that may be adjudged against him if the restraining order or temporary injunction shall be dissolved in whole or in part.

Where the temporary restraining order or temporary injunction is against the State, a municipality, a State agency, or a subdivision of the State in its governmental capacity, and is such that the State, municipality, State agency, or subdivision of the State in its governmental capacity, has no pecuniary interest in the suit and no monetary damages can be shown, the bond shall be allowed in the sum fixed by the judge, and the liability of the applicant shall be for its face amount if the restraining order or temporary injunction shall be dissolved in whole or in part. The discretion of the trial court in fixing the amount of the bond shall be subject to review. Provided that under equitable circumstances and for good cause shown by affidavit or otherwise the court rendering judgment on the bond may allow recovery for less than its full face amount, the action of the court to be subject to review.

History of TRCP 684: Amended eff. Jan. 1, 1981, by order of June 10, 1980 (599-600 S.W.2d [Tex.Cases] lxxx): The rule was changed so that the amount of the bond may be left to the discretion of the court. Amended eff. Mar. 1, 1950, by order of Oct. 12, 1949 (12 Tex.B.J. 538 [1949]). Amended eff. Dec. 31, 1943, by order of June 16, 1943 (6 Tex.B.J. 434 [1943]). Adopted eff. Sept. 1, 1941, by order of Oct. 29, 1940 (3 Tex.B.J. 631 [1940]). Source: TRCS art. 4649 (repealed), harmonized with FRCP 65(d) by minor textual change.

DeSantis v. Wackenhut Corp., 793 S.W.2d 670, 685-86 (Tex.1990). "To prevail upon [a suit on a bond], the claimant must prove that the [TRO] or temporary injunction was issued or perpetuated when it should not have been, and that it was later dissolved. The claimant need not prove that the [TRO] or temporary injunction was obtained maliciously or without probable cause."

Ex parte Jordan, 787 S.W.2d 367, 368 (Tex.1990). The order for temporary injunction was void because it did not require a bond as required by TRCP 684. *See also* ***Ex parte Lesher***, 651 S.W.2d 734, 736 (Tex.1983).

TRCP 685. FILING & DOCKETING

Upon the grant of a temporary restraining order or an order fixing a time for hearing upon an application for a temporary injunction, the party to whom the same is granted shall file his petition therefor, together with the order of the judge, with the clerk of the proper court; and, if such orders do not pertain to a pending suit in said court, the cause shall be entered on the docket of the court in its regular order in the name of the party applying for the writ as plaintiff and of the opposite party as defendant.

History of TRCP 685: Adopted eff. Sept. 1, 1941, by order of Oct. 29, 1940 (3 Tex.B.J. 631 [1940]). Source: TRCS art. 4650 (repealed), harmonized with FRCP 65(d) by minor textual change.

TRCP 686. CITATION

Upon the filing of such petition and order not pertaining to a suit pending in the court, the clerk of such court shall issue a citation to the defendant as in other civil cases, which shall be served and returned in like manner as ordinary citations issued from said court; provided, however, that when a temporary restraining order is issued and is accompanied with a true copy of plaintiff's petition, it shall not be necessary for the citation in the original suit to be accompanied with a copy of plaintiff's petition, nor contain a statement of the nature of plaintiff's demand, but it shall be sufficient for said citation to refer to plaintiff's claim as set forth in a true copy of plaintiff's petition which accompanies the temporary restraining order; and provided further that the court may have a hearing upon an application for a temporary restraining order or temporary injunction at such time and upon such reasonable notice given in such manner as the court may direct.

History of TRCP 686: Amended eff. Dec. 31, 1947 Aug. 18, 1947 (10 Tex.B.J. 401 [1947]). Amended eff. Dec. 31, 1943, by order of June 16, 1943 (6 Tex.B.J. 434 [1943]). Adopted eff. Sept. 1, 1941, by order of Oct. 29, 1940 (3 Tex.B.J. 631 [1940]). Source: TRCS art. 4655 (repealed).

TRCP 687. REQUISITES OF WRIT

The writ of injunction shall be sufficient if it contains substantially the following requisites:

(a) Its style shall be, "The State of Texas."

(b) It shall be directed to the person or persons enjoined.

(c) It must state the names of the parties to the proceedings, plaintiff and defendant, and the nature of the plaintiff's application, with the action of the judge thereon.

(d) It must command the person or persons to whom it is directed to desist and refrain from the commission or continuance of the act enjoined, or to obey and execute such order as the judge has seen proper to make.

(e) If it is a temporary restraining order, it shall state the day and time set for hearing, which shall not exceed fourteen days from the date of the court's order granting such temporary restraining order; but if it is a temporary injunction, issued after notice, it shall be made returnable at or before ten o'clock a.m. of the Monday next after the expiration of twenty days from the date of service thereof, as in the case of ordinary citations.

(f) It shall be dated and signed by the clerk officially and attested with the seal of his office and the date of its issuance must be indorsed thereon.

History of TRCP 687: Amended eff. Sept. 1, 1990, by order of Apr. 24, 1990 (785-86 S.W.2d [Tex.Cases] lxxiv): Changed the time limit in (e) from 10 days to 14 days. Adopted eff. Sept. 1, 1941, by order of Oct. 29, 1940 (3 Tex.B.J. 632 [1940]). Source: TRCS art. 4651 (repealed).

TRCP 688. CLERK TO ISSUE WRIT

When the petition, order of the judge and bond have been filed, the clerk shall issue the temporary restraining order or temporary injunction, as the case may be, in conformity with the terms of the order, and deliver the same to the sheriff or any constable of the county of the residence of the person enjoined, or to the applicant, as the latter shall direct. If several persons are enjoined, residing in different counties, the clerk shall issue such additional copies of the writ as shall be requested by the applicant.

History of TRCP 688: Adopted eff. Sept. 1, 1941, by order of Oct. 29, 1940 (3 Tex.B.J. 632 [1940]). Source: TRCS art. 4652 (repealed).

Schliemann v. Garcia, 685 S.W.2d 690, 693 (Tex. App.—San Antonio 1984, orig. proceeding). The order was improper because the injunction was not properly issued or served.

TRCP 689. SERVICE & RETURN

The officer receiving a writ of injunction shall indorse thereon the date of its receipt by him, and shall forthwith execute the same by delivering to the party enjoined a true copy thereof. The original shall be returned to the court from which it issued on or before the return day named therein with the action of the officer indorsed thereon or annexed thereto showing how and when he executed the same.

History of TRCP 689: Adopted eff. Sept. 1, 1941, by order of Oct. 29, 1940 (3 Tex.B.J. 632 [1940]). Source: TRCS art. 4653 (repealed).

TRCP 690. THE ANSWER

The defendant to an injunction proceeding may answer as in other civil actions; but no injunction shall be dissolved before final hearing because of the denial of the material allegations of the plaintiff's petition, unless the answer denying the same is verified by the oath of the defendant.

See *Commentaries*, "The Answer—Denying Liability," ch. 3-E.

History of TRCP 690: Adopted eff. Sept. 1, 1941, by order of Oct. 29, 1940 (3 Tex.B.J. 632 [1940]). Source: TRCS art. 4657 (repealed).

Executive Tele-Comm. Sys. v. Buchbaum, 669 S.W.2d 400, 403 (Tex.App.—Dallas 1984, no writ). "The only prescribed response for a [D] to a temporary injunction proceeding is pronounced in [TRCP] 690, and the failure to answer does not impair [D's] right to a full hearing."

TRCP 691. BOND ON DISSOLUTION

Upon the dissolution of an injunction restraining the collection of money, by an interlocutory order of the court or judge, made in term time or vacation, if the petition be continued over for trial, the court or judge shall require of the defendant in such injunction proceedings a bond, with two or more good and sufficient sureties, to be approved by the clerk of the court, payable to the complainant in double the amount of the sum enjoined, and conditioned to refund to the complainant the amount of money, interest and costs which may be collected of him in the suit or proceeding enjoined if such injunction is made perpetual on final hearing. If such injunction is so perpetuated, the court, on motion of the complainant, may enter judgment against the principal and sureties in such bond for such amount as may be shown to have been collected from such defendant.

History of TRCP 691: Adopted eff. Sept. 1, 1941, by order of Oct. 29, 1940 (3 Tex.B.J. 632 [1940]). Source: TRCS art. 4659 (repealed).

TRCP 692. DISOBEDIENCE

Disobedience of an injunction may be punished by the court or judge, in term time or in vacation, as a contempt. In case of such disobedience, the complainant, his agent or attorney, may file in the court in which such injunction is pending or with the judge in vacation, his affidavit stating what person is guilty of such disobedience and describing the acts constituting the same; and thereupon the court or judge shall cause to be issued an attachment for such person, directed to the sheriff or any constable of any county, and requiring such officer to arrest the person therein named if found within his county and have him before the court or judge at the time and place named in such writ; or said court or judge may issue a show cause order, directing and requiring such person to appear on such date as may be designated and show cause why he should not be adjudged in contempt of court. On return of such attachment or show cause order, the judge shall proceed to hear proof; and if satisfied that such person has disobeyed the injunction, either directly or indirectly, may commit such person to jail without bail until he purges himself of such contempt, in such manner and form as the court or judge may direct.

History of TRCP 692: Amended eff. Dec. 31, 1943, by order of June 16, 1943 (6 Tex.B.J. 436 [1943]). Adopted eff. Sept. 1, 1941, by order of Oct. 29, 1940 (3 Tex.B.J. 633 [1940]). Source: TRCS art. 4661 (repealed).

City of San Antonio v. Singleton, 858 S.W.2d 411, 412 (Tex.1993). "A trial court generally retains jurisdiction to review, open, vacate or modify a permanent injunction upon a showing of changed conditions. The authority to exercise that jurisdiction, however, must be balanced against principles of res judicata. Whether right or wrong, an injunction 'is not subject to impeachment in its application to the conditions that existed at its making.'"

Ex parte Jackman, 663 S.W.2d 520, 524 (Tex. App.—Dallas 1983, orig. proceeding). "The injunction must be obeyed irrespective of the ultimate validity of the order, and [D] cannot avoid compliance with the commands, or excuse his violation, of the injunction by simply moving to dissolve it…."

TRCP 693. PRINCIPLES OF EQUITY APPLICABLE

The principles, practice and procedure governing courts of equity shall govern proceedings in injunctions when the same are not in conflict with these rules or the provisions of the statutes.

History of TRCP 693: Adopted eff. Sept. 1, 1941, by order of Oct. 29, 1940 (3 Tex.B.J. 633 [1940]). Source: TRCS art. 4663 (repealed).

State v. Texas Pet Foods, 591 S.W.2d 800, 804 (Tex. 1979). "[I]njunctive relief is proper when the trial court finds it justified under the rules of equity, notwithstanding [D's] cessation of the activity or solemn promises to cease the activity. *At 805:* When it is determined that [a] statute is being violated, it is within the province of the district court to restrain it."

TRCP 693a. BOND IN DIVORCE CASE

In a divorce case the court in its discretion may dispense with the necessity of a bond in connection with an ancillary injunction in behalf of one spouse against the other.

History of TRCP 693a: Adopted eff. Dec. 31, 1943, by order of June 16, 1943 (6 Tex.B.J. 436 [1943]). Source: New rule.

SECTION 6. MANDAMUS

TRCP 694. NO MANDAMUS WITHOUT NOTICE

No mandamus shall be granted by the district or county court on ex parte hearing, and any peremptory mandamus granted without notice shall be abated on motion.

History of TRCP 694: Adopted eff. Sept. 1, 1941, by order of Oct. 29, 1940 (3 Tex.B.J. 633 [1940]). Source: TRCS art. 2328 (repealed).

SECTION 7. RECEIVERS

TRCP 695. NO RECEIVER OF IMMOVABLE PROPERTY APPOINTED WITHOUT NOTICE

Except where otherwise provided by statute, no receiver shall be appointed without notice to take charge of property which is fixed and immovable. When an application for appointment of a receiver to take possession of property of this type is filed, the judge or court shall set the same down for hearing and notice of such hearing shall be given to the adverse party by serving notice thereof not less than three days prior to such hearing. If the order finds that the defendant is a nonresident or that his whereabouts is unknown, the notice may be served by affixing the same in a conspicuous manner and place upon the property or if that is impracticable it may be served in such other manner as the court or judge may require.

See *Commentaries*, "Motion for New Trial," ch. 10-B.

History of TRCP 695: Amended eff. Dec. 31, 1943, by order of June 16, 1943 (6 Tex.B.J. 436 [1943]). Adopted eff. Sept. 1, 1941, by order of Oct. 29, 1940 (3 Tex.B.J. 633 [1940]). Source: New rule.

Gray v. PHI Res., 710 S.W.2d 566, 567 (Tex.1986). "In this case, no citation was issued, but instead, notice was provided by a 3-day posting of the petition. [The Sept.] 7 order did not comply with the terms of [TRCP 695]. *At 568:* Nonetheless, the 3-day posting of the petition is analogous to citation by publication or other substituted service. Thus, the successors to [one of the D's] interest were entitled to bring their motion for new trial within two years from the date the judgment was signed."

Rusk v. Rusk, 5 S.W.3d 299, 309 (Tex.App.—Houston [14th Dist.] 1999, pet. denied). "We would hold that [TRCP] 695 is applicable to the appointment of receivers in marriage dissolution cases involving fixed and immovable property. Otherwise, every divorce proceeding could give rise to un-noticed, non-pled, last-second arguments for appointment of a receiver, as occurred in this case."

Continental Homes Co. v. Hilltown Prop. Owners Ass'n, 529 S.W.2d 293, 296 (Tex.App.—Fort Worth 1975, no writ). "Real estate is 'fixed and immovable property' within the meaning of [TRCP] 695, and the trial court committed reversible error in this case in appointing a receiver over the defendants' real estate ... without giving the defendants the notice required by Rule 695...."

TRCP 695a. BOND, & BOND IN DIVORCE CASE

No receiver shall be appointed with authority to take charge of property until the party applying therefor has filed with the clerk of the court a good and sufficient bond, to be approved by such clerk, payable to the defendant in the amount fixed by the court, conditioned for the payment of all damages and cost in such suit, in case it should be decided that such receiver was wrongfully appointed to take charge of such property. The amount of such bond shall be fixed at a sum sufficient to cover all such probable damages and costs. In a divorce case the court or judge, as a matter of discretion, may dispense with the necessity of a bond.

History of TRCP 695a: Adopted eff. Dec. 31, 1943, by order of June 16, 1940 (6 Tex.B.J. 436 [1943]). Source: New rule.

In re Herring, 983 S.W.2d 61, 64 (Tex.App.—Corpus Christi 1998, no pet.). "[T]he bond requirements of

Rule 695a do not apply to the appointment of a post-judgment receiver…."

Sclafani v. Sclafani, 870 S.W.2d 608, 609 (Tex. App.—Houston [1st Dist.] 1993, writ denied). The husband "contends that the trial court erred … in ordering the receiver to sell the property because [the wife] did not file an applicant's bond, in violation of [TRCP] 695a. *At n.2:* [W]hile this proceeding was pending in this Court, [the wife] filed an applicant's bond, making [the husband's] complaint about the lack of a bond moot."

SECTION 8. SEQUESTRATION

TRCP 696. APPLICATION FOR WRIT OF SEQUESTRATION & ORDER

Either at the commencement of a suit or at any time during its progress the plaintiff may file an application for a writ of sequestration. The application shall be supported by affidavits of the plaintiff, his agent, his attorney, or other persons having knowledge of relevant facts. The application shall comply with all statutory requirements and shall state the grounds for issuing the writ, including the description of the property to be sequestered with such certainty that it may be identified and distinguished from property of a like kind, giving the value of each article of the property and the county in which it is located, and the specific facts relied upon by the plaintiff to warrant the required findings by the court. The writ shall not be quashed because two or more grounds are stated conjunctively or disjunctively. The application and any affidavits shall be made on personal knowledge and shall set forth such facts as would be admissible in evidence; provided that facts may be stated based upon information and belief if the grounds of such belief are specifically stated.

No writ shall issue except upon written order of the court after a hearing, which may be ex parte. The court, in its order granting the application, shall make specific findings of facts to support the statutory grounds found to exist, and shall describe the property to be sequestered with such certainty that it may be identified and distinguished from property of a like kind, giving the value of each article of the property and the county in which it is located. Such order shall further specify the amount of bond required of plaintiff which shall be in an amount which, in the opinion of the court, shall adequately compensate defendant in the event plaintiff fails to prosecute his suit to effect and pay all damages and costs as shall be adjudged against him for wrongfully suing out the writ of sequestration including the elements of damages stated in Sections 62.044 and 62.045, Civil Practice and Remedies Code. The court shall further find in its order the amount of bond required of defendant to replevy, which shall be in an amount equivalent to the value of the property sequestered or to the amount of plaintiff's claim and one year's accrual of interest if allowed by law on the claim, whichever is the lesser amount, and the estimated costs of court. The order may direct the issuance of several writs at the same time, or in succession, to be sent to different counties.

See CPRC §62.001.

History of TRCP 696: Amended eff. Jan. 1, 1988, by order July 15, 1987 (733-34 S.W.2d [Tex.Cases] lxxix). Amended eff. Jan. 1, 1978, by order of July 11, 1977 (553-54 S.W.2d [Tex.Cases] lxix): Rewrote rule; the application must be supported by proof; no writ shall issue until after hearing, the court shall make findings, describe the property, fix the amount of bond, as well as the amount of a replevy bond, and may provide for the issuance of several writs. Adopted eff. Sept. 1, 1941, by order of Oct. 29, 1940 (3 Tex.B.J. 634 [1940]). Source: TRCS art. 6841 (repealed).

Marrs v. South Tex. Nat'l Bank, 686 S.W.2d 675, 678 (Tex.App.—San Antonio 1985, writ ref'd n.r.e.). A creditor may allege the value of the total inventory; it is not necessary to allege the value of each item.

Burnett Trailers, Inc. v. Polson, 387 S.W.2d 692, 695 (Tex.App.—San Antonio 1965, writ ref'd n.r.e.). To obtain exemplary damages, there must be "a finding that in bringing the suit and causing the writ of sequestration to issue [P] was activated by malice, or that [P] caused the writ of sequestration to issue without probable cause."

TRCP 697. PETITION

If the suit be in the district or county court, no writ of sequestration shall issue, unless a petition shall have been first filed therein, as in other suits in said courts.

History of TRCP 697: Adopted eff. Sept. 1, 1941, by order of Oct. 29, 1940 (3 Tex.B.J. 634 [1940]). Source: TRCS art. 6842 (repealed).

TRCP 698. BOND FOR SEQUESTRATION

No writ of sequestration shall issue until the party applying therefor has filed with the officer authorized to issue such writ a bond payable to the defendant in the amount fixed by the court's order, with sufficient surety or sureties as provided by statute to be approved by such officer, conditioned that the plaintiff will prosecute his suit to effect and pay to the extent of the penal amount of the bond all damages and costs as may be adjudged against him for wrongfully suing out such writ of sequestration, and plaintiff may further condition the bond pursuant to the provisions of Rule 708, in which case he shall not be required to give additional bond to replevy unless so ordered by the court.

After notice to the opposite party, either before or after the issuance of the writ, the defendant or plaintiff may file a motion to increase or reduce the amount of such bond, or to question the sufficiency of the sureties thereon, in the court in which such suit is pending. Upon hearing, the court shall enter its order with respect to such bond and sufficiency of the sureties as justice may require.

History of TRCP 698: Amended eff. Jan. 1, 1978, by order of July 11, 1977 (553-54 S.W.2d [Tex.Cases] lxx): To fix the amount of the bond by court order; no longer will the amount be double the amount of the value of the property sequestered; either party, after notice and hearing, may ask to change the amount of the bond. Adopted eff. Sept. 1, 1941, by order of Oct. 29, 1940 (3 Tex.B.J. 634 [1940]). Source: TRCS art. 6843 (repealed).

Kelso v. Hanson, 388 S.W.2d 396, 399 (Tex.1965). "It is apparent ... that the sequestration bond required by [TRCP] 698 and the replevy bond required by [TRCP] 708 serve two different purposes, and are conditioned against different contingencies. The sequestration bond guarantees the payment of damages and costs in case it is decided that the sequestration was wrongfully issued."

TRCP 699. REQUISITES OF WRIT

The writ of sequestration shall be directed "To the Sheriff or any Constable within the State of Texas" (not naming a specific county) and shall command him to take into his possession the property, describing the same as it is described in the application or affidavits, if to be found in his county, and to keep the same subject to further orders of the court, unless the same is replevied. There shall be prominently displayed on the face of the writ, in ten-point type and in a manner calculated to advise a reasonably attentive person of its contents, the following:

"YOU HAVE A RIGHT TO REGAIN POSSESSION OF THE PROPERTY BY FILING A REPLEVY BOND. YOU HAVE A RIGHT TO SEEK TO REGAIN POSSESSION OF THE PROPERTY BY FILING WITH THE COURT A MOTION TO DISSOLVE THIS WRIT."

See CPRC §§62.061-62.063.

History of TRCP 699: Amended eff. Jan. 1, 1978, by order of July 11, 1977 (553-54 S.W.2d [Tex.Cases] lxxi): To require the writ be directed to the officer "within" the State of Texas; the rule changes conform to art. 6840 and informs the party of some of his rights. Adopted eff. Sept. 1, 1941, by order of Oct. 29, 1940 (3 Tex.B.J. 634 [1940]). Source: TRCS art. 6845 (repealed).

Lindsey v. Williams, 228 S.W.2d 243, 248 (Tex. App.—Texarkana 1950, no writ). "The affidavit, the bond for sequestration, the writ, the seizure, and the officer's return are all to be read and considered together as parts of one proceeding. ... They constitute the 'face of the record' in the sequestration proceedings."

TRCP 700. AMENDMENT

Clerical errors in the affidavit, bond, or writ of sequestration or the officer's return thereof may upon application in writing to the judge of the court in which the suit is filed and after notice to the opponent, be amended in such manner and on such terms as the judge shall authorize by an order entered in the minutes of the court, provided the amendment does not change or add to the grounds of such sequestration as stated in the affidavit, and provided such amendment appears to the judge to be in furtherance of justice.

History of TRCP 700: Adopted eff. Sept. 1, 1941, by order of Oct. 29, 1940 (3 Tex.B.J. 634 [1940]). Source: New rule.

TRCP 700a. SERVICE OF WRIT ON DEFENDANT

The defendant shall be served in any manner provided for service of citation or as provided in Rule 21a, with a copy of the writ of sequestration, the application, accompanying affidavits, and orders of the court as soon as practicable following the levy of the writ. There shall also be prominently displayed on the face of the copy of the writ served on defendant, in ten-point type and in a manner calculated to advise a reasonably attentive person of its contents, the following:

To ____________________, Defendant:

You are hereby notified that certain properties alleged to be claimed by you have been sequestered. If you claim any rights in such property, you are advised:

"YOU HAVE A RIGHT TO REGAIN POSSESSION OF THE PROPERTY BY FILING A REPLEVY BOND. YOU HAVE A RIGHT TO SEEK TO REGAIN POSSESSION OF THE PROPERTY BY FILING WITH THE COURT A MOTION TO DISSOLVE THIS WRIT."

History of TRCP 700a: Adopted eff. Jan. 1, 1978, by order of July 11, 1977 (553-54 S.W.2d [Tex.Cases] lxxi): Rule affords the defendant notice of the proceedings and informs him of some of his rights. Source: New rule.

TRCP 701. DEFENDANT MAY REPLEVY

At any time before judgment, should the sequestered property not have been previously claimed, replevied, or sold, the defendant may replevy the same, or any part thereof, or the proceeds from the sale of the property if it has been sold under order of the court, by giving bond, with sufficient surety or sureties as provided by statute, to be approved by the officer who levied the writ, payable to plaintiff in the amount fixed by the court's order, conditioned as provided in Rule 702 or Rule 703.

On reasonable notice to the opposing party (which may be less than three days) either party shall have the right to prompt judicial review of the amount of bond required, denial of bond, sufficiency of sureties, and estimated value of the property, by the court which authorized issuance of the writ. The court's determination may be made upon the basis of affidavits, if uncontroverted, setting forth such facts as would be admissible in evidence; otherwise, the parties shall submit evidence. The court shall forthwith enter its order either approving or modifying the requirements of the officer or of the court's prior order, and such order of the court shall supersede and control with respect to such matters.

History of TRCP 701: Amended eff. Jan. 1, 1978, by order of July 11, 1977 (553-54 S.W.2d [Tex.Cases] lxxii): Rewrote rule - changed the amount of the replevy bond from double the amount of the value of the property to the amount fixed by the court and conditioned as provided in TRCP 702 or 703; the rule affords a hearing to the parties after notice about the bond. Adopted eff. Sept. 1, 1941, by order of Oct. 29, 1940 (3 Tex.B.J. 635 [1940]). Source: TRCS art. 6849 (repealed).

Commercial Sec. Co. v. Thompson, 239 S.W.2d 911, 914 (Tex.App.—Fort Worth 1951, no writ). "[T]he purpose of a replevy bond is to insure that the property will be forthcoming after judgment in the same condition as when replevied."

TRCP 702. BOND FOR PERSONAL PROPERTY

If the property to be replevied be personal property, the condition of the bond shall be that the defendant will not remove the same out of the county, or that he will not waste, ill-treat, injure, destroy, or dispose of the same, according to the plaintiff's affidavit, and that he will have such property, in the same condition as when it is replevied, together with the value of the fruits, hire or revenue thereof, forthcoming to abide the decision of the court, or that he will pay the value thereof, or the difference between its value at the time of replevy and the time of judgment and of the fruits, hire or revenue of the same in case he shall be condemned to do so.

History of TRCP 702: Adopted eff. Sept. 1, 1941, by order of Oct. 29, 1940 (3 Tex.B.J. 635 [1940]). Source: TRCS art. 6850 (repealed).

Associates Inv. Co. v. Soltes, 250 S.W.2d 593, 595 (Tex.App.—Dallas 1952, writ ref'd n.r.e.). "[T]he wording of [TRCP] 702 that [D] 'will have such property, in the same condition as when it is replevied,' excludes any ordinary depreciation in market value...."

TRCP 703. BOND FOR REAL ESTATE

If the property be real estate, the condition of such bond shall be that the defendant will not injure the property, and that he will pay the value of the rents of the same in case he shall be condemned so to do.

History of TRCP 703: Adopted eff. Sept. 1, 1941, by order of Oct. 29, 1940 (3 Tex.B.J. 635 [1940]). Source: TRCS art. 6851 (repealed).

TRCP 704. RETURN OF BOND & ENTRY OF JUDGMENT

The bond provided for in the three preceding rules shall be returned with the writ to the court from whence the writ issued. In case the suit is decided against the defendant, final judgment shall be rendered against all the obligors in such bond, jointly and severally, for the value of the property replevied as of the date of the execution of the replevy bond, and the value of the fruits, hire, revenue, or rent thereof, as the case may be.

History of TRCP 704: Amended eff. Jan. 1, 1981, by order of June 10, 1980 (599-600 S.W.2d [Tex.Cases] lxxx): Changed the word "entered" to "rendered." Adopted eff. Sept. 1, 1941, by order of Oct. 29, 1940 (3 Tex.B.J. 635 [1940]). Source: TRCS art. 6852 (repealed).

Transit Enters. v. Addicks Tire & Auto Sup., 725 S.W.2d 459, 463 (Tex.App.—Houston [1st Dist.] 1987, no writ). The "cost of replacement is not evidence of the value of the fruits, hire, revenue, or rent of the property replevied, as required by [TRCP] 704."

TRCP 705. DEFENDANT MAY RETURN SEQUESTERED PROPERTY

Within ten days after final judgment for personal property the defendant may deliver to the plaintiff, or to the officer who levied the sequestration or to his successor in office the personal property in question, and such officer shall deliver same to plaintiff upon his demand therefor; or such defendant shall deliver such property to the officer demanding same under execution issued therefor upon a judgment for the title or possession of the same; and such officer shall receipt the defendant for such property; provided, however, that such delivery to the plaintiff or to such officer shall be without prejudice to any rights of the plaintiff under the replevy bond given by the defendant. Where a mortgage or other lien of any kind is foreclosed upon personal property sequestered and replevied, the defendant shall deliver such property to the officer calling for same under order of sale issued upon a judgment foreclosing such mortgage or other lien, either in the county of defendant's residence or in the county where sequestered, as demanded by such officer; provided, however, that such delivery by the defendant shall be without prejudice to any rights of the plaintiff under the replevy bond given by the defendant.

History of TRCP 705: Amended eff. Dec. 31, 1941, by order of Sept. 20, 1941 (4 Tex.B.J. 594 [1941]). Adopted eff. Sept. 1, 1941, by order of Oct. 29, 1940 (3 Tex.B.J. 635 [1940]). Source: TRCS art. 6853 (repealed).

Shapiro v. Sampson Bros. & Cooper, Inc., 334 S.W.2d 200, 203 (Tex.App.—Eastland 1960, no writ). "The purpose of the finding of value at the time of the trial was to provide a basis for a credit on the judgment in the event the property was surrendered by the defendant in accordance with [TRCP] 705...."

TRCP 706. DISPOSITION OF THE PROPERTY BY OFFICER

When the property is tendered back by the defendant to the officer who sequestered the same or to the officer calling for same under an order of sale, such officer shall receive said property and hold or dispose of the same as ordered by the court; provided, however, that such return to and receipt of same by the officer and any sale or disposition of said property by the officer under order or judgment of the court shall not affect or limit any rights of the plaintiff under the bond provided for in Rule 702.

History of TRCP 706: Amended eff. Dec. 31, 1941, by order of Sept. 20, 1941 (4 Tex.B.J. 594 [1941]). Adopted eff. Sept. 1, 1941, by order of Oct. 29, 1940 (3 Tex.B.J. 635 [1940]). Source: TRCS art. 6854 (repealed).

TRCP 707. EXECUTION

If the property be not returned and received, as provided in the two preceding rules, execution shall issue upon said judgment for the amount due thereon, as in other cases.

History of TRCP 707: Adopted eff. Sept. 1, 1941, by order of Oct. 29, 1940 (3 Tex.B.J. 635 [1940]). Source: TRCS art. 6855 (repealed).

TRCP 708. PLAINTIFF MAY REPLEVY

When the defendant fails to replevy the property within ten days after the levy of the writ and service of notice on defendant, the officer having the property in possession shall at any time thereafter and before final judgment, deliver the same to the plaintiff upon his giving bond payable to defendant in a sum of money not less than the amount fixed by the court's order, with sufficient surety or sureties as provided by statute to be approved by such officer. If the property to be replevied be personal property, the condition of the bond shall be that he will have such property, in the same condition as when it is replevied, together with the value of the fruits, hire or revenue thereof, forthcoming to abide the decision of the court, or that he will pay the value thereof, or the difference between its value at the time of replevy and the time of judgment (regardless of the cause of such difference in value, and of the fruits, hire or revenue of the same in case he shall be condemned to do so). If the property be real estate, the condition of such bond shall be that the plaintiff will not injure the property, and that he will pay the value of the rents of the same in case he shall be condemned to do so.

On reasonable notice to the opposing party (which may be less than three days) either party shall have the right to prompt judicial review of the amount of bond required, denial of bond, sufficiency of sureties, and estimated value of the property, by the court which authorized issuance of the writ. The court's determination may be made upon the basis of affidavits, if uncontroverted, setting forth such facts as would be admissible in evidence; otherwise, the parties shall submit evidence. The court shall forthwith enter its order either approving or modifying the requirements of the officer or of the court's prior order, and such order of the court shall supersede and control with respect to such matters.

History of TRCP 708: Amended eff. Apr. 1, 1984, by order of Dec. 5, 1983 (661-62 S.W.2d [Tex.Cases] cxvii): To conform the amount of the bond with that required by TRCP 698. Amended eff. Jan. 1, 1978, by order of July 11, 1977 (553-54 S.W.2d [Tex.Cases] lxxii): To afford notice and hearing for the review of the bond and its terms; to provide for the nature of the hearing. Adopted eff. Sept. 1, 1941, by order of Oct. 29, 1940 (3 Tex.B.J. 636 [1940]). Source: TRCS art. 6856 (repealed).

Kelso v. Hanson, 388 S.W.2d 396, 399 (Tex.1965). "[T]he sequestration bond required by [TRCP] 698 and the replevy bond required by [TRCP] 708 serve two different purposes.... The sequestration bond guarantees the payment of damages and costs in case it is decided that the sequestration was wrongfully issued. The replevy bond guarantees that the replevisor will have the property in the same condition to abide the decision of the court."

TRCP 709. WHEN BOND FORFEITED

The bond provided for in the preceding rule shall be returned by the officer to the court issuing the writ immediately after he has approved same, and in case the suit is decided against the plaintiff, final judgment shall be entered against all the obligors in such bond, jointly and severally for the value of the property replevied as of the date of the execution of the replevy bond, and the value of the fruits, hire, revenue or rent thereof as the case may be. The same rules which govern the discharge or enforcement of a judgment against the obligors in the defendant's replevy bond shall be applicable to and govern in case of a judgment against the obligors in the plaintiff's replevy bond.

History of TRCP 709: Adopted eff. Sept. 1, 1941, by order of Oct. 29, 1940 (3 Tex.B.J. 636 [1940]). Source: TRCS art. 6857 (repealed), changed to harmonize with other rules.

Kelso v. Hanson, 388 S.W.2d 396, 399 (Tex.1965). "A [P] availing himself of the replevin proceeding, and those obligating themselves on the replevy bond guaranteeing the performance of its terms by [P], are bound to the conditions imposed by the rules governing the procedure."

TRCP 710. SALE OF PERISHABLE GOODS

If after the expiration of ten days from the levy of a writ of sequestration the defendant has failed to replevy the same, if the plaintiff or defendant shall make affidavit in writing that the property levied upon, or any portion thereof, is likely to be wasted or destroyed or greatly depreciated in value by keeping, and if the officer having possession of such property shall certify to the truth of such affidavit, it shall be the duty of the judge or justice of the peace to whose court the writ is returnable, upon the presentation of such affidavit and certificate, either in term time or vacation, to order the sale of said property or so much thereof as is likely to be so wasted, destroyed or depreciated in value by keeping, but either party may replevy the property at any time before such sale.

History of TRCP 710: Adopted eff. Sept. 1, 1941, by order of Oct. 29, 1940 (3 Tex.B.J. 636 [1940]). Source: TRCS art. 6859 (repealed).

TRCP 711. ORDER OF SALE FOR

The judge or justice granting the order provided for in the preceding rule shall issue an order directed to the officer having such property in possession, commanding such officer to sell such property in the same manner as under execution.

History of TRCP 711: Adopted eff. Sept. 1, 1941, by order of Oct. 29, 1940 (3 Tex.B.J. 636 [1940]). Source: TRCS art. 6860 (repealed).

TRCP 712. RETURN OF ORDER

The officer making such sale shall, within five days thereafter, return the order of sale to the court from whence the same issued, with his proceedings thereon, and shall, at the time of making such return, pay over to the clerk or justice of the peace the proceeds of such sale.

History of TRCP 712: Adopted eff. Sept. 1, 1941, by order of Oct. 29, 1940 (3 Tex.B.J. 636 [1940]). Source: TRCS art. 6861 (repealed).

TRCP 712a. DISSOLUTION OR MODIFICATION OF WRIT OF SEQUESTRATION

A defendant whose property has been sequestered or any intervening party who claims an interest in such property, may by sworn written motion, seek to vacate, dissolve, or modify the writ and the order directing its issuance, for any grounds or cause, extrinsic or intrinsic, including a motion to reduce the amount of property sequestered when the total amount described and authorized by such order exceeds the amount necessary to secure the plaintiff's claim, one year's interest if allowed by law on the claim, and costs. Such motion shall admit or deny each finding of the order directing the issuance of the writ except where the movant is unable to admit or deny the finding, in which case movant shall set forth the reasons why he cannot admit or deny. Unless the parties agree to an extension of time, the motion shall be heard promptly, after reasonable notice to the plaintiff (which may be less than three days), and the issue shall be determined not later than ten days after the motion is filed. The filing of the motion shall stay any further proceedings under the writ, except for any orders concerning the care, preservation, or sale of any perishable property, until a hearing is had, and the issue is determined. The writ shall be dissolved unless, at such hearing, the plaintiff shall prove the grounds relied upon for its issuance, but the court may modify its previous order granting the writ and the writ issued pursuant thereto. The movant shall, however, have the burden to prove that the reasonable value of the property sequestered exceeds the amount necessary to secure the debt, interest for one year, and probable costs.

The court's determination may be made upon the basis of affidavits, if uncontroverted, setting forth such facts as would be admissible in evidence; otherwise, the parties shall submit evidence. The court may make all such orders, including orders concerning the care, preservation, or disposition of the property (or the proceeds therefrom if the same has been sold) as justice may require. If the movant has given a replevy bond, an order to vacate or dissolve the writ shall vacate the replevy bond and discharge the sureties thereon, and if the court modifies its order or the writ issued pursuant thereto, it shall make such further orders with respect to the bond as may be consistent with its modification.

See CPRC §62.045.

History of TRCP 712a: Adopted eff. Jan. 1, 1978, by order of July 11, 1977 (553-54 S.W.2d [Tex.Cases] lxxiii): Rule affords a prompt hearing, provides for the procedures, the burden of proof and the kind of proof. Source: New rule.

B&W Cattle Co. v. First Nat'l Bank, 692 S.W.2d 946, 949 (Tex.App.—Amarillo 1985, no writ). "When the partners of [D] moved for the dissolution or modification of the writ of sequestration, the court ... was authorized to 'make all such orders, including orders concerning the care, preservation or disposition of the property (or the proceeds therefrom if the same has been sold) as justice may require....'"

Monroe v. GMAC, 573 S.W.2d 591, 594 (Tex.App.—Waco 1978, no writ). "Attorney's fees and damages against [P] are authorized only if the writ is dissolved."

TRCP 713. SALE ON DEBT NOT DUE

If the suit in which the sequestration issued be for a debt or demand not yet due, and the property sequestered be likely to be wasted, destroyed or greatly depreciated in value by keeping, the judge or justice of the peace shall, under the regulations hereinbefore provided, order the same to be sold, giving credit on such sale until such debt or demand shall become due.

See CPRC §62.003.

History of TRCP 713: Adopted eff. Sept. 1, 1941, by order of Oct. 29, 1940 (3 Tex.B.J. 636 [1940]). Source: TRCS art. 6862 (repealed).

TRCP 714. PURCHASER'S BOND

In the case of a sale as provided for in the preceding rule, the purchaser of the property shall execute his bond, with two or more good and sufficient sureties, to be approved by the officer making the sale, and payable to such officer, in a sum not less than double the amount of the purchase money, conditioned that such purchaser shall pay such purchase money at the expiration of the time given.

History of TRCP 714: Adopted eff. Sept. 1, 1941, by order of Oct. 29, 1940 (3 Tex.B.J. 637 [1940]). Source: TRCS art. 6863 (repealed).

TRCP 715. RETURN OF BOND

The bond provided for in the preceding rule shall be returned by the officer taking the same to the clerk or justice of the peace from whose court the order of sale issued, with such order, and shall be filed among the papers in the cause.

History of TRCP 715: Adopted eff. Sept. 1, 1941, by order of Oct. 29, 1940 (3 Tex.B.J. 637 [1940]). Source: TRCS art. 6864 (repealed).

TRCP 716. RECOVERY ON BOND

In case the purchaser does not pay the purchase money at the expiration of the time given, judgment shall be rendered against all the obligors in such bond for the amount of such purchase money, interest thereon and all costs incurred in the enforcement and collection of the same; and execution shall issue thereon in the name of the plaintiff in the suit, as in other cases, and the money when collected shall be paid to the clerk or justice of the peace to abide the final decision of the cause.

History of TRCP 716: Adopted eff. Sept. 1, 1941, by order of Oct. 29, 1940 (3 Tex.B.J. 637 [1940]). Source: TRCS art. 6864 (repealed).

SECTION 9. TRIAL OF RIGHT OF PROPERTY

TRCP 717. CLAIMANT MUST MAKE AFFIDAVIT

Whenever a distress warrant, writ of execution, sequestration, attachment, or other like writ is levied upon personal property, and such property, or any part thereof, shall be claimed by any claimant who is not a party to such writ, such claimant may make application that such claim is made in good faith, and file such application with the court in which such suit is pending. Such application may be supported by affidavits of the claimant, his agent, his attorney, or other persons having knowledge of relevant facts. The application shall comply with all statutory requirements and shall state the grounds for such claim and the specific facts relied upon by the claimant to warrant the required findings by the court.

The claim shall not be quashed because two or more grounds are stated conjunctively or disjunctively. The application and any affidavits shall be made on personal knowledge and shall set forth such facts as would be admissible in evidence; provided that facts may be stated based upon information and belief if the grounds of such belief are specifically stated.

No property shall be delivered to the claimant except on written order of the court after a hearing pursuant to Rule 718. The court in its order granting the application shall make specific findings of facts to support the statutory grounds found to exist and shall specify the amount of the bond required of the claimant.

History of TRCP 717: Adopted eff. Jan. 1, 1981, by order of June 10, 1980 (599-600 S.W.2d [Tex.Cases] lxxxi). TRCP 717 was rewritten to conform with due process requirements. See history note to TRCP 610. Former TRCP 717 repealed eff. Jan. 1, 1981, by order of June 10, 1980 (599-600 S.W.2d [Tex.Cases] lxxxi). Source: New rule.

Union Bank & Trust Co. v. Mireles, 697 S.W.2d 745, 747 (Tex.App.—Corpus Christi 1985, no writ). "The Trial of Right of Property is a statutory remedy made available to a third party claimant when personal property has been levied upon, and when the claimant is not a party to the writ under which the levy is made. It is intended to provide a means of giving a claimant a 'summary method of asserting his title or right of possession, without resort to an ordinary suit for a recovery of the property or its value.'"

TRCP 718. PROPERTY DELIVERED TO CLAIMANT

Any claimant who claims an interest in property on which a writ has been levied may, by sworn written motion, seek to obtain possession of such property. Such motion shall admit or deny each finding of the order directing the issuance of the writ except where the claimant is unable to admit or deny the finding, in which case claimant shall set forth the reasons why he cannot admit or deny. Such motion shall also contain the reasons why the claimant has superior right or title to the property claimed as against the plaintiff in the writ. Unless the parties agree to an extension of time, the motion shall be heard promptly, after reasonable notice to the plaintiff (which may be less than three days), and the issue shall be determined not later than 10 days after the motion is filed. The filing of the motion shall stay any further proceedings under the writ, except for any orders concerning the care, preservation, or sale of any perishable property, until a hearing is had, and the issue is determined. The claimant shall have the burden to show superior right or title to the property claimed as against the plaintiff and defendant in the writ.

The court's determination may be made upon the basis of affidavits, if uncontroverted, setting forth such facts as would be admissible in evidence, but additional evidence, if tendered by either party shall be received and considered. The court may make all such orders, including orders concerning the care, preservation, or disposition of the property, or the proceeds therefrom if the same has been sold, as justice may require, and if the court modifies its order or the writ issued pursuant thereto, it shall make such further orders with respect to the bond as may be consistent with its modification.

History of TRCP 718: Adopted eff. Jan. 1, 1981, by order of June 10, 1980 (599-600 S.W.2d [Tex.Cases] lxxxi): This new rule was written to conform with due process requirements. See history note to TRCP 610. Former TRCP 718 repealed eff. Jan. 1, 1981, by order of June 10, 1980 (599-600 S.W.2d [Tex. Cases] lxxxi). Source: New rule.

TRCP 719. BOND

No property shall be put in the custody of the claimant until the claimant has filed with the officer who made the levy, a bond in an amount fixed by the court's order equal to double the value of the property so claimed, payable to the plaintiff in the writ, with sufficient surety or sureties as provided by statute to be approved by such officer, conditioned that the claimant will return the same to the officer making the levy, or his successor, in as good condition as he received it, and shall also pay the reasonable value of the use, hire, increase and fruits thereof from the date of said bond, or, in case he fails so to return said property and pay for the use of the same, that he shall pay the plaintiff the value of said property, with legal interest thereon from the date of the bond, and shall also pay all damages and costs that may be awarded against him for wrongfully suing out such claim.

The plaintiff or claimant may file a motion to increase or reduce the amount of such bond, or to question the sufficiency of the sureties thereon, in the court in which such suit is pending. Upon hearing, the court shall enter its order with respect to such bond and sufficiency of the sureties.

History of TRCP 719: Adopted eff. Jan. 1, 1981, by order of June 10, 1980 (599-600 S.W.2d [Tex.Cases] lxxxii): TRCP 718 was rewritten to conform with due process requirements. See history note to TRCP 610. Former TRCP 719 repealed eff. Jan. 1, 1981, by order of June 10, 1980 (599-600 S.W.2d [Tex.Cases] lxxxii). Source: New rule.

TRCP 720. RETURN OF BOND

Whenever any person shall claim property and shall duly make the application and give the bond, if the writ under which the levy was made was issued by a justice of the peace or a court of the county where such levy was made, the officer receiving such application and bond shall endorse on the writ that such claim has been made and application and bond given, and by whom; and shall also endorse on such bond the value of the property as assessed by himself, and shall forthwith return such bond with a copy of the writ to the proper court having jurisdiction to try such claim.

History of TRCP 720: Adopted eff. Jan. 1, 1981, by order of June 10, 1980 (599-600 S.W.2d [Tex.Cases] lxxxiii): This new rule was written to conform with due process requirements. See history note to TRCP 610. Former TRCP 720 repealed eff. Jan. 1, 1981, by order of June 10, 1980 (599-600 S.W.2d [Tex.Cases] lxxxiii). Source: New rule.

Sandler v. Bufkor, Inc., 658 S.W.2d 289, 292 (Tex. App.—Houston [1st Dist.] 1983, no writ). "Having waived the right to establish that the property was of lesser value than that estimated by the officer fixing the amount of the bond, [the makers of the bond] became bound by the recitals of the assessed value appearing on the face of the bond they signed."

TRCP 721. OUT-COUNTY LEVY

Whenever any person shall claim property and shall make the application and give the bond as provided for herein, if the writ under which such levy was made was issued by a justice of the peace or a court of another county than that in which such levy was made, then the officer receiving such bond shall endorse on such bond the value of the property as assessed by himself, and shall forthwith return such bond with a copy of the writ, to the proper court having jurisdiction to try such claim.

History of TRCP 721: Adopted eff. Jan. 1, 1981, by order of June 10, 1980 (599-600 S.W.2d [Tex.Cases] lxxxiii): TRCP 722 was renumbered as TRCP 721 and rewritten to conform with due process requirements. See history note to TRCP 610. Former TRCP 721 repealed eff. Jan. 1, 1981, by order of June 10, 1980 (599-600 S.W.2d [Tex.Cases] lxxxiii). Source: New rule.

TRCP 722. RETURN OF ORIGINAL WRIT

The officer taking such bond shall also endorse on the original writ, if in his possession, that such claim has been made and application and bond given, stating by whom, the names of the surety or sureties, and to what justice or court the bond has been returned; and he shall forthwith return such original writ to the tribunal from which it issued.

History of TRCP 722: Adopted eff. Jan. 1, 1981, by order of June 10, 1980 (599-600 S.W.2d [Tex.Cases] lxxxiii): TRCP 723 was renumbered as TRCP 722 and rewritten to conform with due process requirements. See history note to TRCP 610. Former TRCP 722 repealed eff. Jan. 1, 1981, by order of June 10, 1980 (599-600 S.W.2d [Tex.Cases] lxxxiii). Source: New rule.

TRCP 723. DOCKETING CAUSE

Whenever any bond for the trial of the right of property shall be returned, the clerk of the court, or such justice of the peace, shall docket the same in the original writ proceeding in the name of the plaintiff in the writ as the plaintiff, and the claimant of the property as intervening claimant.

History of TRCP 723: Adopted eff. Jan. 1, 1981, by order of June 10, 1980 (599-600 S.W.2d [Tex.Cases] lxxxiv): This new rule was written to conform with due process requirements. See history note to TRCP 610. Former TRCP 723 repealed eff. Jan. 1, 1981, by order of June 10, 1980 (599-600 S.W.2d [Tex.Cases] lxxxiv). Source: New rule. See former TRCP 725 adopted eff. Sept. 1, 1941, by order of Oct. 29, 1940 (3 Tex.B.J. 638 [1940]). See TRCS art. 7410.

TRCP 724. ISSUE MADE UP

After the claim proceedings have been docketed, and on the hearing day set by the court, then the court, or the justice of the peace, as the case may be, shall enter an order directing the making and joinder of issues by the parties. Such issues shall be in writing and signed by each party or his attorney. The plaintiff shall make a brief statement of the authority and right by which he seeks to subject the property levied on to the process, and it shall be sufficient for the claimant and other parties to make brief statements of the nature of their claims thereto.

History of TRCP 724: Amended eff. Jan. 1, 1981, by order of June 10, 1980 (599-600 S.W.2d [Tex.Cases] lxxxiv): Former TRCP 726 was renumbered as TRCP 724 and rewritten to conform with due process requirements. See history note to TRCP 610. Source: See former TRCP 726 adopted eff. Sept. 1, 1941, by order of Oct. 29, 1940 (3 Tex.B.J. 638 [1940]). See TRCS art. 7411, 7412 (repealed).

TRCP 725. JUDGMENT BY DEFAULT

If the plaintiff appears and the claimant fails to appear or neglects or refuses to join issue under the direction of the court or justice within the time prescribed for pleading, the plaintiff shall have judgment by default.

History of TRCP 725: Adopted new rule eff. Jan. 1, 1981, by order of June 10, 1980 (599-600 S.W.2d [Tex.Cases] lxxxiv): The new rule is the same as former TRCP 727 except "defendant" in the first line was changed to "claimant." Former TRCP 725 repealed eff. Jan. 1, 1981, by order of June 10, 1980 (599-600 S.W.2d [Tex.Cases] lxxxiv). Source: New rule. See former TRCP 727 adopted eff. Sept. 1, 1941, by order of Oct. 29, 1940 (3 Tex.B.J. 638 [1940]). See TRCS art 7413 (repealed).

TRCP 726. JUDGMENT OF NON-SUIT

If the plaintiff does not appear, he shall be non-suited.

History of TRCP 726: Amended eff. Jan. 1, 1981, by order of June 10, 1980 (599-600 S.W.2d [Tex.Cases] lxxxv): Former TRCP 728 was renumbered as TRCP 726 and rewritten to conform with due process requirements. See history note to TRCP 610. Source: New rule. See former TRCP 728 adopted eff. Sept. 1, 1941, by order of Oct., 29, 1940 (3 Tex.B.J. 638 [1940]). See TRCS art. 7414 (repealed).

Union Bank & Trust Co. v. Mireles, 697 S.W.2d 745, 747 (Tex.App.—Corpus Christi 1985, no writ). "When [P is non suited after failing to appear,] the claimant has possession of the property and this specialized proceeding is ended."

TRCP 727. PROCEEDINGS

The proceedings and practice on the trial shall be as nearly as may be the same as in other cases before such court or justice.

History of TRCP 727: Amended eff. Jan. 1, 1981, by order of June 10, 1980 (599-600 S.W.2d [Tex.Cases] lxxxv): Same rule as former TRCP 729. Source: See former TRCP 729 adopted eff. Sept. 1, 1941, by order of Oct. 29, 1940 (3 Tex.B.J. 638 [1940]). See TRCS art. 7415 (repealed).

TRCP 728. BURDEN OF PROOF

If the property was taken from the possession of the claimant pursuant to the original writ, the burden of proof shall be on the plaintiff in the writ. If it was taken from the possession of the defendant in such writ, or any other person than the claimant, the burden of proof shall be on the claimant.

History of TRCP 728: Amended eff. Jan. 1, 1981, by order of June 10, 1980 (599-600 S.W.2d [Tex.Cases] lxxxv): Former TRCP 730 was renumbered as TRCP 728 and rewritten to conform with due process requirements. See history note to TRCP 610. Source: New rule. See former TRCP 730 adopted eff. Sept. 1, 1941, by order of Oct. 29, 1940 (3 Tex.B.J. 638). See TRCS art 7416 (repealed).

Peterson Sales Co. v. Mica, Inc., 623 S.W.2d 679, 682 (Tex.App.—Houston [1st Dist.] 1981, no writ). "The property at the time of the levying was in the possession of [D] and debtor. [The claimant], therefore, had the burden of proof of showing its ownership of the property."

TRCP 729. COPY OF WRIT EVIDENCE

In all trials of the right of property, under the provisions of this section in any county other than that in which the writ issued under which the levy was made, the copy of the writ herein required to be returned by the officer making the levy shall be received in evidence in like manner as the original could be.

History of TRCP 729: Amended eff. Jan. 1, 1981, by order of June 10, 1980 (599-600 S.W.2d [Tex.Cases] lxxxv). Same rule as former TRCP 731. Source: See former TRCP 731 adopted eff. Sept. 1, 1941, by order of Oct. 29, 1940 (3 Tex.B.J. 638 [1940]). See TRCS art. 7419 (repealed).

TRCP 730. FAILURE TO ESTABLISH TITLE

Where any claimant has obtained possession of property, and shall ultimately fail to establish his right thereto, judgment may be rendered against him and his sureties for the value of the property, with legal interest thereon from the date of such bond. Such judgment shall be rendered in favor of the plaintiff or defendant in the writ, or of the several plaintiffs or defendants, if more than one, and shall fix the amount of the claim of each.

History of TRCP 730: Adopted eff. Jan. 1, 1981, by order of June 10, 1980 (599-600 S.W.2d [Tex.Cases] lxxxv): This new rule was written to conform with due process requirements. See history note to TRCP 610. Former TRCP 730 repealed eff. Jan. 1, 1981, by order of June 20, 1980 (599-600 S.W.2d [Tex.Cases] lxxxv). Source: New rule. See former TRCP 732 adopted eff. Sept. 1, 1941, by order of Oct. 29, 1940 (3 Tex.B.J. 639 [1940]). See TRCS art. 7420 (repealed).

Sandler v. Bufkor, Inc., 658 S.W.2d 289, 292 (Tex. App.—Houston [1st Dist.] 1983, no writ). "Once [the claimant] failed to establish its right to the property protected by the bond, [Ps] were entitled to judgment against [the makers of the bond] and their surety for the value of the property."

TRCP 731. EXECUTION SHALL ISSUE

If such judgment should not be satisfied by a return of the property, then after the expiration of ten days from the date of the judgment, execution shall issue thereon in the name of the plaintiff or defendant for the amount of the claim, or of all the plaintiffs or defendants for the sum of their several claims, provided the amount of such judgment shall inure to the benefit of any person who shall show superior right or title to the property claimed as against the claimant; but if such judgment be for a less amount than the sum of the several plaintiffs' or defendants' claims, then the respective rights and priorities of the several plaintiffs or defendants shall be fixed and adjusted in the judgment.

History of TRCP 731: Adopted eff. Jan. 1, 1981, by order of June 10, 1980 (599-600 S.W.2d [Tex.Cases] lxxxvi): New rule written to conform with due process requirements. See history note to TRCP 610. Former TRCP 731 renumbered as TRCP 729 eff. Jan. 1, 1981, by order of June 10, 1980 (599-600 S.W.2d [Tex.Cases] lxxxvi). Source: New rule. See former TRCP 733 adopted eff. Sept. 1, 1941, by order of Oct. 29, 1940 (3 Tex.B.J. 639 [1940]). See TRCS art. 7421, 7422 (repealed).

TRCP 732. RETURN OF PROPERTY BY CLAIMANT

If, within ten days from the rendition of said judgment, the claimant shall return such property in as good condition as he received it, and pay for the use of the same together with the damages and costs, such delivery and payment shall operate as a satisfaction of such judgment.

History of TRCP 732: Adopted eff. Jan. 1, 1981, by order of June 10, 1980 (599-600 S.W.2d [Tex.Cases] lxxxvi): Same rule as former TRCP 734. Former TRCP 732 was repealed eff. Jan. 1, 1981, by order of June 10, 1980 (599-600 S.W.2d [Tex.Cases] lxxxvi). Source: See former TRCP 734 adopted eff. Sept. 1,

1941, by order of Oct. 29, 1940 (3 Tex.B.J. 639 [1940]). See TRCS art. 7423 (repealed).

Sandler v. Bufkor, Inc., 658 S.W.2d 289, 292-93 (Tex.App.—Houston [1st Dist.] 1983, no writ). "Although return of the property 'in as good condition as he received it' operates as a satisfaction of the judgment, partial tender and an offer to pay for missing property does not constitute such satisfaction. ... This is especially so where a 'substantial part' of the goods are missing."

TRCP 733. CLAIM IS A RELEASE OF DAMAGES

A claim made to the property, under the provisions of this section, shall operate as a release of all damages by the claimant against the officer who levied upon said property.

History of TRCP 733: Adopted eff. Jan. 1, 1981, by order of June 10, 1980 (599-600 S.W.2d [Tex.Cases] lxxxvi): Same rule as former TRCP 735. Former TRCP 733 was repealed eff. Jan. 1, 1981, by order of June 10, 1980 (599-600 S.W.2d [Tex.Cases] lxxxvi). Source: See former TRCP 735 adopted eff. Sept. 1, 1941, by order of Oct. 29, 1940 (3 Tex.B.J. 639 [1940]). See TRCS art. 7424 (repealed).

TRCP 734. LEVY ON OTHER PROPERTY

Proceedings for the trial of right of property under these rules shall in no case prevent the plaintiff in the writ from having a levy made upon any other property of the defendant.

History of TRCP 734: Adopted eff. Jan. 1, 1981, by order of June 10, 1980 (599-600 S.W.2d [Tex.Cases] lxxxvii): Same rule as former TRCP 736. Source: See former TRCP 736 adopted eff. Sept. 1, 1941, by order of Oct. 29, 1940 (3 Tex.B.J. 639 [1940]). See TRCS art. 7425 (repealed).

PART VII. RULES RELATING TO SPECIAL PROCEEDINGS

SECTION 1. PROCEDURES RELATED TO HOME EQUITY & CERTAIN REVERSE MORTGAGE FORECLOSURE

TRCP 735. PROCEDURES

A party seeking to foreclose a lien created under Tex. Const. art. XVI, §50(a)(6), for a home equity loan, or Tex. Const. art. XVI, §50(a)(7), for a reverse mortgage, that is to be foreclosed on grounds other than Tex. Const. art. XVI, §§50(k)(6)(A) or (B), may file: (1) a suit seeking judicial foreclosure; (2) a suit or counterclaim seeking a final judgment which includes an order allowing foreclosure under the security instrument and Tex. Prop. Code §51.002; or (3) an application under Rule 736 for an order allowing foreclosure.

Comment to 2000 change: Rules 735 and 736 do not change duties of a lender seeking foreclosure. These rules do not preclude a respondent from timely proceeding in district court to contest the right to foreclose or abate a Rule 736 proceeding.

See Tex. Const. art. XVI, §50; Prop. Code §51.002.

History of TRCP 735: Amended eff. Apr. 15, 2000, by order of Apr. 12, 2000 (15-16 S.W.3d [Tex.Cases] xxiii). Adopted eff. May 15, 1998, by order of Jan. 27, 1998 (961-62 S.W.2d [Tex.Cases] xxxiv): Written to adopt procedures for the foreclosure of home equity liens. Source: New rule.

TRCP 736. EXPEDITED FORECLOSURE PROCEEDING

1. **Application.** A party filing an application under Rule 736 seeking a court order allowing the foreclosure of a lien under Tex. Const. art. XVI, §50(a)(6)(D), for a home equity loan, or §50(k)(11), for a reverse mortgage, shall initiate such in rem proceeding by filing a verified application in the district court in any county where all or any part of the real property encumbered by the lien sought to be foreclosed (the "property") is located. The application shall:

(A) be styled: "In re: Order for Foreclosure Concerning (*Name of person to receive notice of foreclosure*) and (*Property Mailing Address*)";

(B) identify by name the party who, according to the records of the holder of the debt, is obligated to pay the debt secured by the property;

(C) identify the property by mailing address and legal description;

(D) identify the security instrument encumbering the property by reference to volume and page, clerk's file number or other identifying recording information found in the official real property records of the county where all or any part of the property is located or attach a legible copy of the security instrument;

(E) allege that:

(1) a debt exists;

(2) the debt is secured by a lien created under Tex. Const. art. XVI, §50(a)(6), for a home equity loan, or §50(a)(7), for a reverse mortgage;

(3) a default under the security instrument exists;

(4) the applicant has given the requisite notices to cure the default and accelerate the maturity of the debt under the security instrument, Tex. Prop. Code §51.002, Tex. Const. art. XVI, §50(k)(10), for a reverse mortgage, and applicable law;

(F) describe facts which establish the existence of a default under the security instrument; and

(G) state that the applicant seeks a court order required by Tex. Const. art. XVI, §50(a)(6)(D), for a home equity loan, or §50(k)(11), for a reverse mortgage, to sell the property under the security instrument and Tex. Prop. Code §51.002.

A notice required by Tex. Const. art. XVI, §50(k)(10), for a reverse mortgage, may be combined or incorporated in any other notice referenced in Rule 736(1)(E)(4). The verified application and any supporting affidavit shall be made on personal knowledge and shall set forth such facts as would be admissible in evidence, provided that facts may be stated based upon information and belief if the grounds of such belief are specifically stated.

2. Notice.

(A) *Service.* Every application filed with the clerk of the court shall be served by the party filing the application. Service of the application and notice shall be by delivery of a copy to the party to be served by certified and first class mail addressed to each party who, according to the records of the holder of the debt is obligated to pay the debt. Service shall be complete upon the deposit of the application and notice, enclosed in a postage prepaid and properly addressed wrapper, in a post office or official depository under the care and custody of the United States Postal Service. If the respondent is represented by an attorney and the applicant's attorney has knowledge of the name and address of the attorney, an additional copy of the application and notice shall be sent to respondent's attorney.

(B) *Certificate of Service.* The applicant or applicant's attorney shall certify to the court compliance with the service requirements of Rule 736. The applicant shall file a copy of the notice and the certificate of service with the clerk of the court. The certificate of service shall be prima facie evidence of the fact of service.

(C) *Form of Notice.* The notice shall be sufficient if it is in substantially the following form in at least ten point type:

Example 1: Form of Notice

Cause No. ____________

In re: Order for Foreclosure Concerning	In the District Court
____*(1)____	Of __________ County
and	
____*(2)____	______ Judicial District

NOTICE TO: ____*(3)____

____

____

An application has been filed by________, as Applicant, on ____*(4)____, in a proceeding described as:

"In re: Order for Foreclosure Concerning ___*(1)___ and ____*(2)____."

The attached application alleges that you, the Respondent, are in default under a security instrument creating a lien on your homestead under Tex. Const. art. XVI, §50(a)(6), for a home equity loan, or §50(a)(7), for a reverse mortgage. This application is now pending in this court.

Applicant seeks a court order, as required by Tex. Const. art. XVI, §50(a)(6)(D) or §50(k)(11), to allow it to sell at public auction the property described in the attached application under the security instrument and Tex. Prop. Code §51.002.

You may employ an attorney. If you or your attorney do not file a written response with the clerk of the court at ____*(5)____ on or before 10:00 a.m. on ____*(6)____ an order authorizing a foreclosure sale may be signed. If the court grants the application, the foreclosure sale will be conducted under the security instrument and Tex. Prop. Code §51.002.

You may file a response setting out as many matters, whether of law or fact, as you consider may be necessary and pertinent to contest the application. If a response is filed, the court will hold a hearing at the request of the applicant or respondent.

In your response to this application, you must provide your mailing address. In addition, you must send a copy of your response to ____*(7)____

ISSUED

By ______________________

(*Applicant or Applicant's Attorney*)

CERTIFICATE OF SERVICE

I certify that a true and correct copy of this notice with a copy of the application was sent certified and regular mail to ____*(3)____ on the ___ day of ____________________________.

____(*signature*)____

(*Applicant or Applicant's Applicant*)

*(1) name of respondent

*(2) mailing address of property

*(3) name and address of respondent

*(4) date application filed

*(5) address of clerk of court

*(6) response due date

*(7) name and address of applicant or applicant's attorney

(D) The applicant shall state in the notice the date the response is due in accordance with Rule 736(3).

(E) The application and notice may be accompanied by any other notice required by state or federal law.

3. Response Due Date. A response is due on or before 10:00 a.m. on the first Monday after the expiration of thirty-eight (38) days after the date of mailing of the application and notice to respondent, exclusive of the date of mailing, as set forth in the certificate of service.

4. Response.

(A) The respondent may file a response setting out as many matters, whether of law or fact, as respondent deems necessary or pertinent to contest the application. Such response and any supporting affidavit shall be made on personal knowledge and shall set forth such facts as would be admissible in evidence, provided that facts may be stated based upon information and belief if the grounds of such belief are specifically stated.

(B) The response shall state the respondent's mailing address.

(C) The response shall be filed with the clerk of the court. The respondent shall also send a copy of the response to the applicant or the applicant's attorney at the address set out in the notice.

5. Default. At any time after a response is due, the court shall grant the application without further notice or hearing if:

(A) the application complies with Rule 736(1);

(B) the respondent has not previously filed a response; and

(C) a copy of the notice and the certificate of service shall have been on file with the clerk of the court for at least ten days exclusive of the date of filing.

6. Hearing When Response Filed. On the filing of a response, the application shall be promptly heard after reasonable notice to the applicant and the respondent. No discovery of any kind shall be permitted in a proceeding under Rule 736. Unless the parties agree to an extension of time, the issue shall be determined by the court not later than ten business days after a request for hearing by either party. At the hearing, the applicant shall have the burden to prove by affidavits on file or evidence presented the grounds for the granting of the order sought in the application.

7. Only Issue. The only issue to be determined under Rule 736 shall be the right of the applicant to obtain an order to proceed with foreclosure under the security instrument and Tex. Prop. Code §51.002.

8. Order to Proceed with Notice of Sale and Sale.

(A) *Grant or denial.* The court shall grant the application if the court finds applicant has proved the elements of Rule 736(1)(E). Otherwise, the court shall deny the application. The granting or denial of the application is not an appealable order.

(B) *Form of order.* The order shall recite the mailing address and legal description of the property, direct that foreclosure proceed under the security instrument and Tex. Prop. Code §51.002, provide that a copy of the order shall be sent to respondent with the notice of sale, provide that applicant may communicate with the respondent and all third parties reasonably necessary to conduct the foreclosure sale, and, if respondent is represented by counsel, direct that notice of the foreclosure sale date shall also be mailed to counsel by certified mail.

(C) *Filing of order.* The applicant is to file a certified copy of the order in the real property records of the county where the property is located within ten business days of the entry of the order. Failure to timely record the order shall not affect the validity of the foreclosure or defeat the presumption of Tex. Const. art. XVI, §50(i).

9. Nonpreclusive Effect of Order. No order or determination of fact or law under Rule 736 shall be res judicata or constitute collateral estoppel or estoppel by judgment in any other proceeding or suit. The granting of an application under these rules shall be without prejudice to the right of the respondent to seek relief at law or in equity in any court of competent jurisdiction. The denial of an application under these rules shall be without prejudice to the right of the applicant to re-file the application or seek other relief at law or in equity in any court of competent jurisdiction.

10. Abatement and Dismissal. A proceeding under Rule 736 is automatically abated if, before the signing of the order, notice is filed with the clerk of the court in which the application is pending that respondent has filed a petition contesting the right to foreclose in a district court in the county where the application is pending. A proceeding that has been abated shall be dismissed.

Comment to 2000 changes: Rules 735 and 736 do not change duties of a lender seeking foreclosure. These rules do not preclude a respondent from timely proceeding in district court to contest the right to foreclose or abate a Rule 736 proceeding.

See Tex. Const. art. XVI, §50; Prop. Code §51.002.

History of TRCP 736: Amended eff. Apr. 15, 2000, by order of Apr. 12, 2000 (15-16 S.W.3d [Tex.Cases] xxiii). Adopted eff. May 15, 1998, by order of Jan. 27, 1998 (961-62 S.W.2d [Tex.Cases] xxxiv): Written to adopt procedures for the foreclosure of home equity liens. Source: New rule.

SECTION 2. BILL OF DISCOVERY

TRCP 737. REPEALED

TRCP 737 was repealed eff. Jan. 1, 1999, by order of Nov. 9, 1998 (61 Tex.B.J. 1140 [1998]). For subject matter of former TRCP 737, see TRCP 202.

SECTION 3. FORCIBLE ENTRY & DETAINER

TRCP 738. MAY SUE FOR RENT

A suit for rent may be joined with an action of forcible entry and detainer, wherever the suit for rent is within the jurisdiction of the justice court. In such case the court in rendering judgment in the action of forcible entry and detainer, may at the same time render judgment for any rent due the landlord by the renter; provided the amount thereof is within the jurisdiction of the justice court.

See CPRC §15.084; Prop. Code §24.004.

History of TRCP 738: Adopted eff. Sept. 1, 1941, by order of Oct. 29, 1940 (3 Tex.B.J. 640 [1940]). Source: TRCS art. 3976 (repealed).

Haginas v. Malbis Mem'l Found., 354 S.W.2d 368, 371 (Tex.1962). TRCP 738 "permits the plaintiff to join with his action of forcible entry and detainer, a suit for rent, but the rule specifically limits the amount of rent which may be recovered in the Justice Court to the jurisdictional limit placed on the Justice Court by [Tex. Const. art. 5, §16]."

TRCP 739. CITATION

When the party aggrieved or his authorized agent shall file his written sworn complaint with such justice, the justice shall immediately issue citation directed to the defendant or defendants commanding him to appear before such justice at a time and place named in such citation, such time being not more than ten days nor less than six days from the date of service of the citation.

The citation shall inform the parties that, upon timely request and payment of a jury fee no later than five days after the defendant is served with citation, the case shall be heard by a jury.

History of TRCP 739: Amended eff. Jan. 1, 1988, by order of July 15, 1987 (733-34 S.W.2d [Tex.Cases] lxxx). Adopted eff. Sept. 1, 1941, by order of Oct. 29, 1940 (3 Tex.B.J. 640 [1940]). Source: TRCS art. 3977 (repealed).

TRCP 740. COMPLAINANT MAY HAVE POSSESSION

The party aggrieved may, at the time of filing his complaint, or thereafter prior to final judgment in the justice court, execute and file a possession bond to be approved by the justice in such amount as the justice may fix as the probable amount of costs of suit and damages which may result to defendant in the event that the suit has been improperly instituted, and conditioned that the plaintiff will pay defendant all such costs and damages as shall be adjudged against plaintiff.

The defendant shall be notified by the justice court that plaintiff has filed a possession bond. Such notice shall be served in the same manner as service of citation and shall inform the defendant of all of the following rules and procedures:

(a) Defendant may remain in possession if defendant executes and files a counterbond prior to the expiration of six days from the date defendant is served with notice of the filing of plaintiff's bond. Said counterbond shall be approved by the justice and shall be in such amount as the justice may fix as the probable amount of costs of suit and damages which may result to plaintiff in the event possession has been improperly withheld by defendant;

(b) Defendant is entitled to demand and he shall be granted a trial to be held prior to the expiration of six days from the date defendant is served with notice of the filing of plaintiff's possession bond;

(c) If defendant does not file a counterbond and if defendant does not demand that trial be held prior to the expiration of said six-day period, the constable of the precinct or the sheriff of the county where the property is situated, shall place the plaintiff in possession of the property promptly after the expiration of six days from the date defendant is served with notice of the filing of plaintiff's possession bond; and

(d) If, in lieu of a counterbond, defendant demands trial within said six-day period, and if the justice of the peace rules after trial that plaintiff is entitled to possession of the property, the constable or sheriff shall place the plaintiff in possession of the property five days after such determination by the justice of the peace.

History of TRCP 740: Amended eff. Sept. 1, 1977, by order of May 9, 1977 (553-54 S.W.2d [Tex.Cases] xxxviii): Substituted "five days" for "immediately" to avoid conflict with TRCP 748. Amended eff. Jan. 1, 1976, by order of July 22, 1975 (525-26 S.W.2d [Tex.Cases] lix): Eliminated the requirement that the defendant execute a counterbond for double the amount of plaintiff's bond; rewritten to permit a possession bond and a counterbond in the probable amount of costs and damages; the new rule requires notice to the defendant of the rights and liabilities stated in secs. (a) through (d). Amended eff. Dec. 31, 1943, by order of June 16, 1943 (6 Tex.B.J. 443 [1943]): The regulations as to the bond of defendant were enlarged so as to include a case where an out-of-county officer effects service of citation and so as to make it clear that six days time will be allowed, before possession is given the aggrieved party, within which defendant may give such bond; and other relevant changes were made. Adopted eff. Sept. 1, 1941, by order of Oct. 29, 1940 (3 Tex.B.J. 640 [1940]). Source: TRCS art. 3978 (repealed).

TRCP 741. REQUISITES OF COMPLAINT

The complaint shall describe the lands, tenements or premises, the possession of which is claimed, with sufficient certainty to identify the same, and it shall also state the facts which entitled the complainant to the possession and authorize the action under Sections 24.001-24.004, Texas Property Code.

History of TRCP 741: Amended eff. Jan. 1, 1988, by order of July 15, 1987 (733-34 S.W.2d [Tex.Cases] lxxx). Amended eff. Apr. 1, 1984, by order of Dec. 5, 1983 (661-62 S.W.2d [Tex.Cases] cxvii): Adopted eff. Sept. 1, 1941, by order of Oct. 29, 1940 (3 Tex.B.J. 640 [1940]). Source: TRCS art. 3979 (repealed).

Family Inv. Co. v. Paley, 356 S.W.2d 353, 355-56 (Tex.App.—Houston [1st Dist.] 1962, writ dism'd). "An insufficient description in the complaint in forcible entry and detainer is not such a defect as to deprive the court of jurisdiction. The complaint can be amended in the Justice of the Peace Court."

TRCP 742. SERVICE OF CITATION

The officer receiving such citation shall execute the same by delivering a copy of it to the defendant, or by leaving a copy thereof with some person over the age of sixteen years, at his usual place of abode, at least six days before the return day thereof; and on or before the day assigned for trial he shall return such citation, with his action written thereon, to the justice who issued the same.

History of TRCP 742: Amended eff. Dec. 31, 1947, by order of Aug. 18, 1947 (10 Tex.B.J. 401 [1947]). Adopted eff. Sept. 1, 1941, by order of Oct. 29, 1940 (3 Tex.B.J. 640 [1940]). Source: TRCS art. 3980 (repealed).

American Spiritualist Ass'n v. Ravkind, 313 S.W.2d 121, 124 (Tex.App.—Dallas 1958, writ ref'd n.r.e.). "[T]he Justice Court judgment was fatally defective because of a lack of proper service of citation."

TRCP 742a. SERVICE BY DELIVERY TO PREMISES

If the sworn complaint lists all home and work addresses of the defendant which are known to the person filing the sworn complaint and if it states that such person knows of no other home or work addresses of the defendant in the county where the premises are located, service of citation may be by delivery to the premises in question as follows:

If the officer receiving such citation is unsuccessful in serving such citation under Rule 742, the officer shall no later than five days after receiving such citation execute a sworn statement that the officer has made diligent efforts to serve such citation on at least two occasions at all addresses of the defendant in the county where the premises are located as may be shown on the sworn complaint, stating the times and places of attempted service. Such sworn statement shall be filed by the officer with the justice who shall promptly consider the sworn statement of the officer. The justice may then authorize service according to the following:

(a) The officer shall place the citation inside the premises by placing it through a door mail chute or by slipping it under the front door; and if neither method is possible or practical, the officer shall securely affix the citation to the front door or main entry to the premises.

(b) The officer shall that same day or the next day deposit in the mail a true copy of such citation with a copy of the sworn complaint attached thereto, addressed to defendant at the premises in question and sent by first class mail;

(c) The officer shall note on the return of such citation the date of delivery under (a) above and the date of mailing under (b) above; and

(d) Such delivery and mailing to the premises shall occur at least six days before the return day of the citation; and on or before the day assigned for trial he shall return such citation with his action written thereon, to the justice who issued the same.

It shall not be necessary for the aggrieved party or his authorized agent to make request for or motion for alternative service pursuant to this rule.

History of TRCP 742a: Adopted eff. Aug. 15, 1982, by order of Apr. 15, 1982 (629-30 S.W.2d [Tex.Cases] xlii). Source: New rule.

Winrock Houston Assocs. v. Bergstrom, 879 S.W.2d 144, 151 (Tex.App.—Houston [14th Dist.] 1994, no writ). "[T]he Officer's Sworn Request for Alternative Service under [TRCP] 742a ... does not state that he ever attempted to serve [D] at his work address as shown on the sworn complaint and as required by Rule 742a. Therefore, the requirements of Rule 742a for substituted service by delivery to the premises were not strictly complied with, and [D] was not properly served with citation."

TRCP 743. DOCKETED

The cause shall be docketed and tried as other cases. If the defendant shall fail to enter an appearance upon the docket in the justice court or file answer before the case is called for trial, the allegations of the complaint may be taken as admitted and judgment by default entered accordingly. The justice shall have authority to issue subpoenas for witnesses to enforce their attendance, and to punish for contempt.

History of TRCP 743: Amended eff. Dec. 31, 1947, by order of Aug. 18, 1947 (10 Tex.B.J. 401 [1947]). Adopted eff. Sept. 1, 1941, by order of Oct. 29, 1940 (3 Tex.B.J. 640 [1940]). Source: TRCS art. 3981 (repealed).

TRCP 744. DEMANDING JURY

Any party shall have the right of trial by jury, by making a request to the court on or before five days from the date the defendant is served with citation, and by paying a jury fee of five dollars. Upon such request, a jury shall be summoned as in other cases in justice court.

History of TRCP 744: Amended eff. Jan. 1, 1988, by order of July 15, 1987 (733-34 S.W.2d [Tex.Cases] lxxx). Adopted eff. Sept. 1, 1941, by order of Oct. 29, 1940 (3 Tex.B.J. 640 [1940]). Source: TRCS art. 3982 (repealed).

Collins v. Cleme Manor Apts., 37 S.W.3d 527, 531 (Tex.App.—Texarkana 2001, no pet.). "We find the best reading of Rule 744 to be that it applies strictly to justice court proceedings, with the last phrase clarifying that although there exists a different procedure for requesting a jury in justice court forcible detainer proceedings, the procedures for summoning such jury are those prescribed for ordinary justice court actions."

TRCP 745. TRIAL POSTPONED

For good cause shown, supported by affidavit of either party, the trial may be postponed not exceeding six days.

History of TRCP 745: Adopted eff. Sept. 1, 1941, by order of Oct. 29, 1940 (3 Tex.B.J. 640 [1940]). Source: TRCS art. 3983 (repealed).

TRCP 746. ONLY ISSUE

In case of forcible entry or of forcible detainer under Sections 24.001-24.008, Texas Property Code, the only issue shall be as to the right to actual possession; and the merits of the title shall not be adjudicated.

History of TRCP 746: Amended eff. Jan. 1, 1988, by order of July 15, 1987 (733-34 S.W.2d [Tex.Cases] lxxxi). Amended eff. Apr. 1, 1984, by order of Dec. 5, 1983 (661-62 S.W.2d [Tex.Cases] cxvii). Adopted eff. Sept. 1, 1941, by order of Oct. 29, 1940 (3 Tex.B.J. 641 [1940]). Source: TRCS art. 3984 (repealed).

Lopez v. Sulak, 76 S.W.3d 597, 605 (Tex.App.—Corpus Christi 2002, no pet.). "[W]here the right to immediate possession necessarily requires resolution of a title dispute, the justice court has no jurisdiction to enter a judgment and may be enjoined from doing so. Because a forcible detainer action is not exclusive, but is cumulative of any other remedy a party may have in the courts of this state, the displaced party is entitled to bring a separate suit in district court to determine the issue of title."

Fandey v. Lee, 880 S.W.2d 164, 168-69 (Tex.App.—El Paso 1994, writ denied). "The principal purpose of a ... forcible entry and detainer action, is to determine who has the right to immediate possession of the premises. ... Where title to the property is directly involved in the suit, the justice and county courts lack jurisdiction."

TRCP 747. TRIAL

If no jury is demanded by either party, the justice shall try the case. If a jury is demanded by either party, the jury shall be empaneled and sworn as in other cases; and after hearing the evidence it shall return its verdict in favor of the plaintiff or the defendant as it shall find.

History of TRCP 747: Amended eff. Jan. 1, 1981, by order of June 10, 1980 (599-600 S.W.2d [Tex.Cases] lxxxvii): The last sentence of the former rule is deleted because it is the same provision as the second sentence of TRCP 743. Amended eff. Dec. 31, 1943, by order of June 16, 1943 (6 Tex.B.J. 444 [1943]). Adopted eff. Sept. 1, 1941, by order of Oct. 29, 1940 (3 Tex.B.J. 641 [1940]). Source: TRCS art. 3985 (repealed).

TRCP 747a. REPRESENTATION BY AGENTS

In forcible entry and detainer cases for non-payment of rent or holding over beyond the rental term, the parties may represent themselves or be represented by their authorized agents in justice court.

History of TRCP 747a: Adopted eff. Aug. 15, 1982, by order of Apr. 15, 1982 (629-30 S.W.2d [Tex.Cases] xliii). Source: New rule.

TRCP 748. JUDGMENT & WRIT

If the judgment or verdict be in favor of the plaintiff, the justice shall give judgment for plaintiff for possession of the premises, costs, and damages; and he shall award his writ of possession. If the judgment or verdict be in favor of the defendant, the justice shall give judgment for defendant against the plaintiff for costs and any damages. No writ of possession shall issue until the expiration of five days from the time the judgment is signed.

See *Commentaries*, "Rules for Filing Documents," ch. 1-C.

History of TRCP 748: Amended eff. Jan. 1, 1988, by order of July 15, 1987 (733-34 S.W.2d [Tex.Cases] lxxxi). Amended eff. Jan. 1, 1981, by order of June 10, 1980 (599-600 S.W.2d [Tex.Cases] lxxxvii): Time runs from the date judgment is signed. Amended eff. Jan. 1, 1976, by order of July 22, 1975 (525-26 S.W.2d [Tex.Cases] lx): The amendments authorize judgments for costs and damages, which TRCP 740 protects. Amended eff. Jan. 1, 1961, by order of July 26, 1960 (23 Tex.B.J. 685 [1961]): The time within which writ of restitution to issue changed from two days to five days. Adopted eff. Sept. 1, 1941, by order of Oct. 29, 1940 (3 Tex.B.J. 641 [1940]). Source: TRCS art. 3986 (repealed), modified by eliminating verdict of "guilty" or "not guilty."

Housing Auth. v. Sanders, 693 S.W.2d 2, 2-3 (Tex. App.—Tyler 1985, writ ref'd n.r.e.). "A justice court judgment is a prerequisite to an appeal to the county court."

TRCP 749. MAY APPEAL

In appeals in forcible entry and detainer cases, no motion for new trial shall be filed.

Either party may appeal from a final judgment in such case, to the county court of the county in which the judgment is rendered by filing with the justice within five days after the judgment is signed, a bond to be approved by said justice, and payable to the adverse party, conditioned that he will prosecute his appeal with effect, or pay all costs and damages which may be adjudged against him.

The justice shall set the amount of the bond to include the items enumerated in Rule 752.

Within five days following the filing of such bond, the party appealing shall give notice as provided in Rule 21a of the filing of such bond to the adverse party. No judgment shall be taken by default against the adverse party in the court to which the cause has been appealed without first showing substantial compliance with this rule.

See *Commentaries*, "Rules for Filing Documents," ch. 1-C.

History of TRCP 749: Amended eff. Jan. 1, 1988, by order of July 15, 1987 (733-34 S.W.2d [Tex.Cases] lxxxi): To give notice to the appellee that an appeal of the case from the justice court was perfected in the county court. Amended eff. Jan. 1, 1981, by order of June 10, 1980 (599-600 S.W.2d [Tex.Cases] lxxxvii): Time runs from the date judgment is signed. Amended eff. Jan. 1, 1976, by order of July 22, 1975 (525-26 S.W.2d [Tex.Cases] lxi): The first sentence was moved from within the rule. The amount of the appeal bond is to fixed by the justice as prescribed by TRCP 752. Amended eff. Dec. 31, 1947, by order of Aug. 18, 1947 (10 Tex.B.J. 401 [1947]). Adopted eff. Sept. 1, 1941, by order of Oct. 29, 1940 (3 Tex.B.J. 641 [1940]). Source: TRCS art. 3987 (repealed).

RCJ Liquidating Co. v. Village, Ltd., 670 S.W.2d 643, 644 (Tex.1984). TRCP 749 makes no provision for delay in the appeal when a motion for new trial is filed.

Mitchell v. Armstrong Capital Corp., 877 S.W.2d 480, 481 (Tex.App.—Houston [1st Dist.] 1994, no writ). TRCP 749 "does not provide that giving notice of the filing of an appeal bond is jurisdictional."

TRCP 749a. PAUPER'S AFFIDAVIT

If appellant is unable to pay the costs of appeal, or file a bond as required by Rule 749, he shall nevertheless be entitled to appeal by making strict proof of such inability within five days after the judgment is signed, which shall consist of his affidavit filed with the justice of the peace stating his inability to pay such costs, or any part thereof, or to give security, which may be contested within five days after the filing of such affidavit and notice thereof to the opposite party or his attorney of record by any officer of the court or party to the suit, whereupon it shall be the duty of the justice of the peace in whose court the suit is pending to hear evidence and determine the right of the party to appeal, and he shall enter his finding on the docket as part of the record. Upon the filing of a pauper's affidavit the justice of the peace or clerk of the court shall notice the opposing party of the filing of the affidavit of inability within one working day of its filing by written notification accomplished through first class mail. It will be presumed prima facie that the affidavit speaks the truth, and, unless contested within five days after the filing and notice thereof, the presumption shall be deemed conclusive; but if a contest is filed, the burden shall then be on the appellant to prove his alleged inability by competent evidence other than by the affidavit above referred to. When a pauper's affidavit is timely contested by the appellee, the justice shall hold a hearing and rule on the matter within five days.

If the justice of the peace disapproves the pauper's affidavit, appellant may, within five days thereafter bring the matter before the county judge for a final decision, and, on request, the justice shall certify to the county judge appellant's affidavit, the contest thereof, and all documents, and papers thereto. The county judge shall set a day for hearing, not later than five days, and shall hear the contest de novo. If the pauper's affidavit is approved by the county judge, he shall direct the justice to transmit to the clerk of the county court, the transcript, records and papers of the case.

A pauper's affidavit will be considered approved upon one of the following occurrences: (1) the pauper's affidavit is not contested by the other party; (2) the pauper's affidavit is contested by the other party and upon a hearing the justice determines that the pauper's affidavit is approved; or (3) upon a hearing by the justice disapproving of the pauper's affidavit the appellant appeals to the county judge who then, after a hearing, approves the pauper's affidavit.

No writ of possession may issue pending the hearing by the county judge of the appellant's right to appeal on a pauper's affidavit. If the county judge disapproves the pauper's affidavit, appellant may perfect his appeal by filing an appeal bond in the amount as required by Rule 749 within five days thereafter. If no appeal bond is filed within five days, a writ of possession may issue.

See *Commentaries*, "Rules for Filing Documents," ch. 1-C.

History of TRCP 749a: Amended eff. Sept. 1, 1990 (retroactive), by order of Sept. 4, 1990 (793-94 S.W.2d [Tex.Cases] xxxii): To amend the Sept. 1, 1990 amendment. Amended eff. Sept. 1, 1990, by order of Apr. 24, 1990 (785-86 S.W.2d [Tex.Cases] lxxv): Added second and last sentences to the first paragraph; added third paragraph; county judge must now set the hearing within five days rather than ten; and changed "writ of restitution" to "writ of possession"; revised the proceedings for pauper affidavits. Amended eff. Jan. 1, 1981, by order of June 10, 1980 (599-600 S.W.2d [Tex.Cases] lxxxviii): Time runs from the date judgment is signed. Adopted eff. Sept. 1, 1977, by order of May 9, 1977 (553-54 S.W.2d [Tex.Cases] xxxviii). TRCP 749a tracks TRCP 572. Source: New rule.

Hughes v. Habitat Apts., 860 S.W.2d 872, 872-73 (Tex.1993). Defendant "orally answered [P's] allegations in a [FED] action in the justice court. … Pursuant to [D's] appeal in the county court, she filed a pauper's affidavit but failed to file a written answer as required by [TRCP] 753. [¶] [B]ecause the pauper's affidavit supplied the type of information we found adequate for a pro se answer in [***Smith v. Lippmann***, 826 S.W.2d 137 (Tex.1992)], we hold that [D] was entitled to notice of the hearing on [P's] motion for default judgment."

Walker v. Blue Water Garden Apts., 776 S.W.2d 578, 581 (Tex.1989). TRCP 749a "requires that an affidavit of inability to pay costs made to perfect an appeal from the judgment of the justice court be filed within 5 days after the judgment is signed."

TRCP 749b. PAUPER'S AFFIDAVIT IN NONPAYMENT OF RENT APPEALS

In a nonpayment of rent forcible detainer case a tenant/appellant who has appealed by filing a pauper's affidavit under these rules shall be entitled to stay in possession of the premises during the pendency of the appeal, by complying with the following procedure:

(1) Within five days of the date that the tenant/appellant files his pauper's affidavit, he must pay into the justice court registry one rental period's rent under the terms of the rental agreement.

(2) During the appeal process as rent becomes due under the rental agreement, the tenant/appellant shall pay the rent into the county court registry within five days of the due date under the terms of the rental agreement.

(3) If the tenant/appellant fails to pay the rent into the court registry within the time limits prescribed by these rules, the appellee may file a notice of default in county court. Upon sworn motion by the appellee and a showing of default to the judge, the court shall issue a writ of restitution.

(4) Landlord/appellee may withdraw any or all rent in the county court registry upon a) sworn motion and hearing, prior to final determination of the case, showing just cause, b) dismissal of the appeal, or c) order of the court upon final hearing.

(5) All hearings and motions under this rule shall be entitled to precedence in the county court.

See *Commentaries*, "Rules for Filing Documents," ch. 1-C.

History of TRCP 749b: Adopted eff. Sept. 1, 1977, by order of May 9, 1977 (553-54 S.W.2d [Tex.Cases] xxxix). Source: New rule.

Kennedy v. Highland Hills Apts., 905 S.W.2d 325, 327 (Tex.App.—Dallas 1995, no writ). "The purpose of rule 749b is to permit an indigent appellant 'to stay in possession of the premises during the pendency of the appeal.' [¶] Rule 749b(3) does not expressly authorize the county court to enter a judgment by default."

Ibarra v. Housing Auth., 791 S.W.2d 224, 226 (Tex. App.—Corpus Christi 1990, writ denied). TRCP 749b(3) "does not provide for a hearing prior to a county court issuing a writ of restitution. The Due Process Clause requires only a single hearing before an impartial decision maker on the question of restitution. [D] had such a hearing.… [¶] [However] before [P] could withdraw the … rent from the court's registry, a hearing was required.…"

TRCP 749c. APPEAL PERFECTED

When an appeal bond has been timely filed in conformity with Rule 749 or a pauper's affidavit approved in conformity with Rule 749a, the appeal shall be perfected.

See *Commentaries*, "Rules for Filing Documents," ch. 1-C.
History of TRCP 749c: Amended eff. Sept. 1, 1990, by order of Apr. 24, 1990 (785-86 S.W.2d [Tex.Cases] lxxvi): Rewritten to dispense with the appellate requirement of payment of rent into the court registry. Amended eff. Aug. 15, 1982, by order of Apr. 15, 1982 (629-30 S.W.2d [Tex.Cases] xliii): Amended so that one month's rent need not be paid when an appeal bond is made. Adopted eff. Sept. 1, 1977, by order of May 9, 1977 (553-54 S.W.2d [Tex.Cases] xl). Source: New rule.

Walker v. Blue Water Garden Apts., 776 S.W.2d 578, 581-82 (Tex.1989). "The rules prescribe no deadline for making the deposit of one month's rent required by [TRCP] 749c. ... We choose not to imply a specific deadline in these rules where none exists expressly. Rather, we conclude that [D's] reasonably prompt efforts [50 days after judgment] to meet the requirements of Rule 749c were sufficient to perfect her appeal."

TRCP 750. FORM OF APPEAL BOND

The appeal bond authorized in the preceding article may be substantially as follows:

"The State of Texas,

"County of ________

"Whereas, upon a writ of forcible entry (or forcible detainer) in favor of A.B., and against C.D., tried before ________, a justice of the peace of _______ county, a judgment was rendered in favor of the said A.B. on the ___ day of ______, A.D. _____, and against the said C.D., from which the said C.D. has appealed to the county court; now, therefore, the said C.D. and ______ his sureties, covenant that he will prosecute his said appeal with effect and pay all costs and damages which may be adjudged against him, provided the sureties shall not be liable in an amount greater than $ _________, said amount being the amount of the bond herein.

"Given under our hands this ____ day of _______, A.D. ________."

History of TRCP 750: Amended eff. Jan. 1, 1976, by order of July 22, 1975 (525-26 S.W.2d [Tex.Cases] lxi): The form amended to state the limits of liability of the sureties. Adopted eff. Sept. 1, 1941, by order of Oct. 29, 1940 (3 Tex.B.J. 641 [1940]). Source: TRCS art. 3988 (repealed).

Pharis v. Culver, 677 S.W.2d 168, 170 (Tex.App.—Houston [1st Dist.] 1984, no writ). "While the form [of the FED appeal bond in TRCP 750] is not mandatory, the bond must substantially comply with Rule 750."

Family Inv. Co. v. Paley, 356 S.W.2d 353, 355 (Tex. App.—Houston [1st Dist.] 1962, writ dism'd). The trial court should have permitted amendment of the appeal bond because the defective bond was sufficient to confer jurisdiction over the appeal on the county court.

TRCP 751. TRANSCRIPT

When an appeal has been perfected, the justice shall stay all further proceedings on the judgment, and immediately make out a transcript of all the entries made on his docket of the proceedings had in the case; and he shall immediately file the same, together with the original papers and any money in the court registry, including sums tendered pursuant to Rule 749b(1), with the clerk of the county court of the county in which the trial was had, or other court having jurisdiction of such appeal. The clerk shall docket the cause, and the trial shall be de novo.

The clerk shall immediately notify both appellant and the adverse party of the date of receipt of the transcript and the docket number of the cause. Such notice shall advise the defendant of the necessity for filing a written answer in the county court when the defendant has pleaded orally in the justice court.

The trial, as well as all hearings and motions, shall be entitled to precedence in the county court.

History of TRCP 751: Amended eff. Sept. 1, 1990, by order of Apr. 24, 1990 (785-86 S.W.2d [Tex.Cases] lxxvi): Added "including sums tendered pursuant to TRCP 749b(1)" after "any money in the court registry" in the first paragraph; to provide for transfer of subject funds. Amended eff. Jan. 1, 1988, by order of July 15, 1987 (733-34 S.W.2d [Tex.Cases] lxxxi): Provides due process to pro se defendants by advising them of the necessity of filing a written answer in the county court if they did not file one in the justice court. Amended eff. Sept. 1, 1977, by order of May 9, 1977 (553-54 S.W.2d [Tex.Cases] xl): amended to require immediate filing of papers and money with clerk of county court; provided for precedence of trial, hearings, and motions. Adopted eff. Sept. 1, 1941, by order of Oct. 29, 1940 (3 Tex.B.J. 641 [1940]). Source: TRCS art. 3989 (repealed).

Polk v. Braddock, 864 S.W.2d 78, 80 (Tex.App.—Dallas 1992, no writ). TRCP 751 "makes it clear that the proper party for a mandamus proceeding concerning the failure to file appeal papers with the county court in an appeal from the justice court under rule 751 is the justice of the peace."

TRCP 752. DAMAGES

On the trial of the cause in the county court the appellant or appellee shall be permitted to plead, prove and recover his damages, if any, suffered for withholding or defending possession of the premises during the pendency of the appeal.

Damages may include but are not limited to loss of rentals during the pendency of the appeal and reasonable attorney fees in the justice and county courts provided, as to attorney fees, that the requirements of Section 24.006 of the Texas Property Code have been met. Only the party prevailing in the county court shall be entitled to recover damages against the adverse party. He shall also be entitled to recover court costs. He shall be entitled to recover against the sureties on the appeal bond in cases where the adverse party has executed such bond.

History of TRCP 752: Amended eff. Jan. 1, 1988, by order of July 15, 1987 (733-34 S.W.2d [Tex.Cases] lxxxii). Amended eff. Jan. 1, 1976, by order of July 22, 1975 (525-26 S.W.2d [Tex.Cases] lxi): Costs and damages are stated by this rule rather than by various other rules. Amended eff. Dec. 31, 1943, by order of June 16, 1943 (6 Tex.B.J. 445 [1943]): To extend, in a proper case, to appellant as well as to appellee; other relevant changes. Adopted eff. Sept. 1, 1941, by order of Oct. 29, 1940 (3 Tex.B.J. 641 [1940]). Source: TRCS art. 3990 (repealed).

RCJ Liquidating Co. v. Village, Ltd., 670 S.W.2d 643, 644 (Tex.1984). TRCP 752 "defines damages in a forcible detainer suit to include reasonable attorney fees in the justice and county courts."

Krull v. Somoza, 879 S.W.2d 320, 322 (Tex.App.—Houston [14th Dist.] 1994, writ denied). "Damage claims *related to* maintaining or obtaining possession of the premises may be joined with the detainer action and litigated in the county court. However, damages for other causes of action ... are *not* recoverable in a forcible entry and detainer action."

Mastermark Homebuilders v. Offenburger Constr., 857 S.W.2d 765, 768 (Tex.App.—Houston [14th Dist.] 1993, no writ). TRCP 752 "does not require that damages in the form of attorney's fees be plead in the justice court. The rule merely states that the requirements of §24.006 of the Property Code be satisfied."

TRCP 753. JUDGMENT BY DEFAULT

Said cause shall be subject to trial at any time after the expiration of eight full days after the date the transcript is filed in the county court. If the defendant has filed a written answer in the justice court, the same shall be taken to constitute his appearance and answer in the county court, and such answer may be amended as in other cases. If the defendant made no answer in writing in the justice court, and if he fails to file a written answer within eight full days after the transcript is filed in the county court, the allegations of the complaint may be taken as admitted and judgment by default may be entered accordingly.

History of TRCP 753: Amended eff. Jan. 1, 1988, by order of July 15, 1987 (733-34 S.W.2d [Tex.Cases] lxxxii). Amended eff. Dec. 31, 1947, by order of Aug. 18, 1947 (10 Tex.B.J. 401 [1947]). Amended eff. Dec. 31, 1943, by order of June 16, 1943 (6 Tex.B.J. 445 [1943]). Adopted eff. Sept. 1, 1941, by order of Oct. 29, 1940 (3 Tex.B.J. 641 [1940]). Source: TRCS art. 3991 (repealed).

Okpala v. Coleman, 964 S.W.2d 698, 700 (Tex. App.—Houston [14th Dist.] 1998, no pet.). "An answer ... must contain sufficient information to place in issue the claims made the basis of the suit. [¶] [W]e hold [D], while not filing a formal answer pursuant to [TRCP] 753, filed documents forming an answer sufficient to prevent the rendition of a default judgment."

TRCP 754. BLANK

TRCP 755. WRIT OF POSSESSION

The writ of possession, or execution, or both, shall be issued by the clerk of the county court according to the judgment rendered, and the same shall be executed by the sheriff or constable, as in other cases; and such writ of possession shall not be suspended or superseded in any case by appeal from such final judgment in the county court, unless the premises in question are being used as the principal residence of a party.

History of TRCP 755: Amended eff. Jan. 1, 1988, by order of July 15, 1987 (733-34 S.W.2d [Tex.Cases] lxxxiii). Adopted eff. Sept. 1, 1941, by order of Oct. 29, 1940 (3 Tex.B.J. 642 [1940]). Source: TRCS art. 3993 (repealed).

SECTION 4. PARTITION OF REAL ESTATE

TRCP 756. PETITION

The plaintiff's petition shall state:

(a) The names and residence, if known, of each of the other joint owners, or joint claimants, of such property.

(b) The share or interest which the plaintiff and the other joint owners, or joint claimants, of same own or claim so far as known to the plaintiff.

(c) The land sought to be partitioned shall be so described as that the same may be distinguished from any other and the estimated value thereof stated.

See Prop. Code §23.001.

History of TRCP 756: Adopted eff. Sept. 1, 1941, by order of Oct. 29, 1940 (3 Tex.B.J. 642 [1940]). Source: TRCS art. 6083 (repealed in part by TRCP).

Yoast v. Yoast, 649 S.W.2d 289, 292 (Tex.1983). "The court of appeals mischaracterized this case as a partition suit. [P's suit was for] trespass to try title. ... Partition issues may be resolved in a trespass to try title suit once the controversy as to title or right to possession is settled. That, however, does not convert the cause of action to a partition suit. [¶] A partition suit is based on the theory of common title, rather than disputed ownership."

TRCP 757. CITATION & SERVICE

Upon the filing of a petition for partition, the clerk shall issue citation for each of the joint owners, or joint claimants, named therein, as in other cases, and such citations shall be served in the manner and for the time provided for the service of citations in other cases.

History of TRCP 757: Adopted eff. Sept. 1, 1941, by order of Oct. 29, 1940 (3 Tex.B.J. 642 [1940]). Source: TRCS art. 6084 (repealed).

Carper v. Halamicek, 610 S.W.2d 556, 557 (Tex. App.—Tyler 1980, writ ref'd n.r.e.). "This rule and past cases indicate that the joinder of all owners is mandatory and that no valid, binding decree of partition can be made in their absence."

TRCP 758. WHERE DEFENDANT IS UNKNOWN OR RESIDENCE IS UNKNOWN

If the plaintiff, his agent or attorney, at the commencement of any suit, or during the progress thereof, for the partition of land, shall make affidavit that an undivided portion of the land described in plaintiff's petition in said suit is owned by some person unknown to affiant, or that the place of residence of any known party owning an interest in land sought to be partitioned is unknown to affiant, the Clerk of the Court shall issue citation for publication, conforming to the requirements of Rules 114 and 115, and served in accordance with the directions of Rule 116. In case of unknown residence or party, the affidavit shall include a statement that after due diligence plaintiff and the affiant have been unable to ascertain the name or locate the residence of such party, as the case may be, and in such case it shall be the duty of the court trying the action to inquire into the sufficiency of the diligence so stated before granting any judgment.

History of TRCP 758: Amended eff. Apr. 1, 1985, by order of Dec. 19, 1984 (683-84 S.W.2d [Tex.Cases] xxxix): Deleted reference to proviso in TRCP 109 which had been deleted. Amended eff. Jan. 1, 1955, by order of July 20, 1954 (17 Tex.B.J. 572 [1954]): Inserted the words "or that the place of residence of any known party owning an interest in the land sought to be partitioned is unknown to affiant" in first sentence, and added last sentence. Adopted eff. Sept. 1, 1941, by order of Oct. 29, 1940 (3 Tex.B.J. 642 [1940]). Source: TRCS art. 6085 (repealed), with changes: Eliminated specific declaration of requisites of citation by publication and service, and adopted (by reference) the general rules.

TRCP 759. JUDGMENT WHERE DEFENDANT CITED BY PUBLICATION

When the defendant has been duly cited by publication in accordance with the preceding rule, and no appearance is entered within the time prescribed for pleadings, the court shall appoint an attorney to defend in behalf of such owner or owners, and proceed as in other causes where service is made by publication. It shall be the special duty of the court in all cases to see that its decree protects the rights of the unknown parties thereto. The judge of the court shall fix the fee of the attorney so appointed, which shall be entered and collected as costs against said unknown owner or owners.

History of TRCP 759: Adopted eff. Sept. 1, 1941, by order of Oct. 29, 1940 (3 Tex.B.J. 642 [1940]). Caveat: This article was amended in 1939, eff. date after the enactment of the Rule Making Statute. See, however, *Garrett v. Mercantile Nat'l Bank*, 168 S.W.2d 636 (Tex.1943). Source: TRCS art. 6085 (repealed), last two sentences.

TRCP 760. COURT SHALL DETERMINE, WHAT

Upon the hearing of the cause, the court shall determine the share or interest of each of the joint owners or claimants in the real estate sought to be divided, and all questions of law or equity affecting the title to such land which may arise.

History of TRCP 760: Adopted eff. Sept. 1, 1941, by order of Oct. 29, 1940 (3 Tex.B.J. 643 [1940]). Source: TRCS art. 6086 (repealed).

Johnson v. Johnson-McHenry, 978 S.W.2d 142, 144 (Tex.App.—Austin 1998, no pet.). "[I]n a partition suit, the trial court determines whether the partition will be by sale or in kind, the share or interest of the joint owners or claimants, and all questions of law or equity affecting title. The court then allocates to the parties their rightful shares or tracts. A trial court may also exercise equitable powers in a partition suit."

Thomas v. McNair, 882 S.W.2d 870, 876 (Tex. App.—Corpus Christi 1994, no writ). "'In a partition suit two judgments are rendered. The first decree determines: the share or interest of each of the joint owners or claimants; all questions of law or equity affecting title; and appoints commissioners and gives them directions as may be necessary and appropriate. ... The rights and matters determined in the first decree are final, and it is appealable as a final judgment.'"

TRCP 761. APPOINTMENT OF COMMISSIONERS

The court shall determine before entering the decree of partition whether the property, or any part thereof, is susceptible of partition; and, if the court determines that the whole, or any part of such property is susceptible of partition, then the court for that part of such property held to be susceptible of partition shall enter a decree directing the partition of such real estate, describing the same, to be made in accordance with the respective shares or interests of each of such parties entitled thereto, specify in such decree the share or interest of each party, and shall appoint three or more competent and disinterested persons as commissioners to make such partition in accordance with such decree and the law, a majority of which commissioners may act.

History of TRCP 761: Adopted eff. Sept. 1, 1941, by order of Oct. 29, 1940 (3 Tex.B.J. 643 [1940]). Source: TRCS art. 6087 (repealed).

Spigener v. Wallis, 80 S.W.3d 174, 178 (Tex.App.—Waco 2002, no pet.). "[T]he court ... decides whether the property is 'susceptible to partition'; and if not, ... orders a sale of the property...."

Benson v. Fox, 589 S.W.2d 823, 826 (Tex.App.—Tyler 1979, no writ). "[TRCP] 761 employs the word 'partition' in a restricted sense as synonymous with the phrase 'partition in kind.'"

TRCP 762. WRIT OF PARTITION

The clerk shall issue a writ of partition, directed to the sheriff or any constable of the county, commanding such sheriff or constable to notify each of the commissioners of their appointment as such, and shall accompany such writ with a certified copy of the decree of the court directing the partition.

History of TRCP 762: Adopted eff. Sept. 1, 1941, by order of Oct. 29, 1940 (3 Tex.B.J. 643 [1940]). Source: TRCS art. 6088 (repealed).

TRCP 763. SERVICE OF WRIT OF PARTITION

The writ of partition shall be served by reading the same to each of the persons named therein as commissioners, and by delivering to any one of them the accompanying certified copy of the decree of the court.

History of TRCP 763: Adopted eff. Sept. 1, 1941, by order of Oct. 29, 1940 (3 Tex.B.J. 643 [1940]). Source: TRCS art. 6089 (repealed).

TRCP 764. MAY APPOINT SURVEYOR

The court may, should it be deemed necessary, appoint a surveyor to assist the commissioners in making the partition, in which case the writ of partition shall name such surveyor, and shall be served upon him by reading the same to him.

History of TRCP 764: Adopted eff. Sept. 1, 1941, by order of Oct. 29, 1940 (3 Tex.B.J. 643 [1940]). Source: TRCS art. 6090 (repealed).

TRCP 765. RETURN OF WRIT

A writ of partition, unless otherwise directed by the court, shall be made returnable twenty days from date of service on the commissioner last served; and the officer serving it shall endorse thereon the time and manner of such service.

History of TRCP 765: Adopted eff. Sept. 1, 1941, by order of Oct. 29, 1940 (3 Tex.B.J. 643 [1940]). Source: TRCS art. 6091 (repealed).

TRCP 766. SHALL PROCEED TO PARTITION

The commissioners, or a majority of them, shall proceed to partition the real estate described in the decree of the court, in accordance with the directions contained in such decree and with the provisions of law and these rules.

History of TRCP 766: Adopted eff. Sept. 1, 1941, by order of Oct. 29, 1940 (3 Tex.B.J. 643 [1940]). Source: TRCS art. 6092 (repealed).

Mansfield v. Davenport, 362 S.W.2d 912, 913 (Tex. App.—San Antonio 1962, writ ref'd n.r.e.). "By its first order or judgment in a partition suit, a court may properly give such directions as may be necessary and appropriate."

TRCP 767. MAY CAUSE SURVEY

If the commissioners deem it necessary, they may cause to be surveyed the real estate to be partitioned into several tracts or parcels.

History of TRCP 767: Adopted eff. Sept. 1, 1941, by order of Oct. 29, 1940 (3 Tex.B.J. 643 [1940]). Source: TRCS art. 6093 (repealed).

TRCP 768. SHALL DIVIDE REAL ESTATE

The commissioners shall divide the real estate to be partitioned into as many shares as there are persons entitled thereto, as determined by the court, each share to contain one or more tracts or parcels, as the commissioners may think proper, having due regard in the division to the situation, quantity and advantages of each share, so that the shares may be equal in value, as nearly as may be, in proportion to the respective interests of the parties entitled. The commissioners shall then proceed by lot to set apart to each of the parties entitled one of said shares, as determined by the decrees of the court.

History of TRCP 768: Adopted eff. Sept. 1, 1941, by order of Oct. 29, 1940 (3 Tex.B.J. 643 [1940]). Source: TRCS art. 6094 (repealed).

Grimes v. Hall, 211 S.W.2d 956, 958 (Tex.App.—Eastland 1948, no writ). "Where the interests of the parties in the realty to be partitioned are unequal, selection of owners of shares by lot is not required."

TRCP 769. REPORT OF COMMISSIONERS

When the commissioners have completed the partition, they shall report the same in writing and under oath to the court, which report shall show:

(a) The property divided, describing the same.

(b) The several tracts or parcels into which the same was divided by them, describing each particularly.

(c) The number of shares and the land which constitutes each share, and the estimated value of each share.

(d) The allotment of each share.

(e) The report shall be accompanied by such field notes and maps as may be necessary to make the same intelligible.

The clerk shall immediately mail written notice of the filing of the report to all parties.

History of TRCP 769: Amended eff. Sept. 1, 1990, by order of Apr. 24, 1990 (785-86 S.W.2d [Tex.Cases] lxxvii): Added last par. to require clerk notify the parties of the filing of the report. Adopted eff. Sept. 1, 1941, by order of Oct. 29, 1940 (3 Tex.B.J. 644 [1940]). Source: TRCS art. 6095 (repealed).

Thomas v. McNair, 882 S.W.2d 870, 876 (Tex. App.—Corpus Christi 1994, no writ). "'The second decree [in a partition suit] approves the report of the commissioners and allocates to the respective parties their separate shares or tracts.'"

TRCP 770. PROPERTY INCAPABLE OF DIVISION

Should the court be of the opinion that a fair and equitable division of the real estate, or any part thereof, cannot be made, it shall order a sale of so much as is incapable of partition, which sale shall be for cash, or upon such other terms as the court may direct, and shall be made as under execution or by private or public sale through a receiver, if the court so order, and the proceeds thereof shall be returned into court and be partitioned among the persons entitled thereto, according to their respective interests.

History of TRCP 770: Amended eff. Mar. 1, 1950, by order of Oct. 12, 1949 (12 Tex.B.J. 538 [1949]). Adopted eff. Sept. 1, 1941, by order of Oct. 29, 1940 (3 Tex.B.J. 644 [1940]). Source: TRCS art. 6096 (repealed).

Cecola v. Ruley, 12 S.W.3d 848, 853 (Tex.App.—Texarkana 2000, no pet.). "Whether a piece of land can fairly be partitioned in kind is a question of fact for the court or jury to decide. The law favors partition in kind over partition by sale. Therefore, at trial the burden of proof falls on the party opposing partitioning in kind and seeking a partition by sale."

Thomas v. McNair, 882 S.W.2d 870, 876 (Tex. App.—Corpus Christi 1994, no writ). "Pursuant to [TRCP] 770, a trial court must order the sale of property incapable of partition and determine the respective interests or shares of the persons entitled thereto. After the sale, the court enters an order of disbursement dividing the proceeds of the sale among the persons entitled thereto, according to their respective interests."

TRCP 771. OBJECTIONS TO REPORT

Either party to the suit may file objections to any report of the commissioners in partition within thirty days of the date the report is filed, and in such case a trial of the issues thereon shall be had as in other cases. If the report be found to be erroneous in any material respect, or unequal and unjust, the same shall be rejected, and other commissioners shall be appointed by the Court, and the same proceedings had as in the first instance.

History of TRCP 771: Amended eff. Sept. 1, 1990, by order of Apr. 24, 1990 (785-86 S.W.2d [Tex.Cases] lxxvii) (error showing Sup.Ct. order deleting phrase rather than adding it): Added phrase "within thirty days of the date the report is filed" to set a time within which objections to a commissioners report must be filed. Adopted eff. Sept. 1, 1941, by order of Oct. 29, 1940 (3 Tex.B.J. 644 [1940]). Source: TRCS art. 6097 (repealed).

Ellis v. First City Nat'l Bank, 864 S.W.2d 555, 557 (Tex.App.—Tyler 1993, no writ). "If the trial court finds the report of the commissioners is [erroneous or unequal] it must reject the report and appoint other commissioners. The party objecting to the commissioners' report had the burden of proving that it is materially erroneous or that it unequally and unjustly partitions the property."

SECTION 5. PARTITION OF PERSONAL PROPERTY

TRCP 772. PROCEDURE

An action seeking partition of personal property as authorized by Section 23.001, Texas Property Code, shall be commenced in the same manner as other civil suits, and the several owners or claimants of such property shall be cited as in other cases.

History of TRCP 772: Amended eff. Jan. 1, 1988, by order of July 15, 1987 (733-34 S.W.2d [Tex.Cases] lxxxiii). Adopted eff. Sept. 1, 1941, by order of Oct. 29, 1940 (3 Tex.B.J. 644 [1940]). Source: TRCS art. 6102 (repealed in part by TRCP), last clause.

TRCP 773. VALUE ASCERTAINED

The separate value of each article of such personal property, and the allotment in kind to which each owner is entitled, shall be ascertained by the court, with or without a jury.

History of TRCP 773: Adopted eff. Sept. 1, 1941, by order of Oct. 29, 1940 (3 Tex.B.J. 644 [1940]). Source: TRCS art. 6103 (repealed).

Price v. Price, 394 S.W.2d 855, 858 (Tex.App.—Tyler 1965, writ ref'd n.r.e.). "The fact that the property has now been transformed into personal property in the form of money would not alter the application rule, but would only make the property more susceptible to a partition in kind."

TRCP 774. DECREE OF COURT EXECUTED

When partition in kind of personal property is ordered by the judgment of the court, a writ shall be issued in accordance with such judgment, commanding the sheriff or constable of the county where the property may be to put the parties forthwith in possession of the property allotted to each respectively.

History of TRCP 774: Adopted eff. Sept. 1, 1941, by order of Oct. 29, 1940 (3 Tex.B.J. 644 [1940]). Source: TRCS art. 6104 (repealed).

TRCP 775. PROPERTY SOLD

When personal property will not admit of a fair and equitable partition, the court shall ascertain the proportion to which each owner thereof is entitled, and order the property to be sold, and execution shall be issued to the sheriff or any constable of the county where the property may be describing such property and commanding such officer to sell the same as in other cases of execution, and pay over the proceeds of sale to the parties entitled thereto, in the proportion ascertained by the judgment of the court.

History of TRCP 775: Adopted eff. Sept. 1, 1941, by order of Oct. 29, 1940 (3 Tex.B.J. 644 [1940]). Source: TRCS art. 6105 (repealed).

SECTION 6. PARTITION: MISCELLANEOUS PROVISIONS

TRCP 776. CONSTRUCTION

No provision of the statutes or rules relating to partition shall affect the mode of proceeding prescribed by law for the partition of estates of decedents among the heirs and legatees, nor preclude partition in any other manner authorized by the rules of equity, which rules shall govern in proceedings for partition in all respects not provided for by law or these rules.

History of TRCP 776: Adopted eff. Sept. 1, 1941, by order of Oct. 29, 1940 (3 Tex.B.J. 645 [1940]). Source: TRCS art. 6106 (repealed).

TRCP 777. PLEADING & PRACTICE

The same rules of pleading, practice and evidence which govern in other civil actions shall govern in suits for partition, when not in conflict with any provisions of the law or these rules relating to partition.

History of TRCP 777: Adopted eff. Sept. 1, 1941, by order of Oct. 29, 1940 (3 Tex.B.J. 645 [1940]). Source: TRCS art. 6107 (repealed).

Rayson v. Johns, 524 S.W.2d 380, 382 (Tex.App.—Texarkana 1975, writ ref'd n.r.e.). "[I]n whatever posture the question has arisen, the courts have treated disputed issues of fact in partition proceedings as being for the jury when one has been properly demanded. [¶] The law does not favor compelling an owner to sell his property against his will, but prefers a division in kind when such can be fairly and equitably made."

TRCP 778. COSTS

The court shall adjudge the costs in a partition suit to be paid by each party to whom a share has been allotted in proportion to the value of such share.

History of TRCP 778: Adopted eff. Sept. 1, 1941, by order of Oct. 29, 1940 (3 Tex.B.J. 645 [1940]). Source: TRCS art. 6109 (repealed).

Ellis v. First City Nat'l Bank, 864 S.W.2d 555, 557-58 (Tex.App.—Tyler 1993, no writ). TRCP 778 "provides that the court shall adjudge the costs in proportion to the *value* of each share. [Ds] concede that there was no testimony ... regarding the value of the several shares." Remanded to adjudge costs.

SECTION 7. QUO WARRANTO

TRCP 779. JOINDER OF PARTIES

When it appears to the court or judge that the several rights of diverse parties to the same office or franchise may properly be determined on one information, the court or judge may give leave to join all such persons in the same information in order to try their respective rights to such office or franchise.

History of TRCP 779: Adopted eff. Sept. 1, 1941, by order of Oct. 29, 1940 (3 Tex.B.J. 645 [1940]). Source: TRCS art. 6254 (repealed).

Newsom v. State, 922 S.W.2d 274, 277 (Tex.App.—Austin 1996, writ denied). "[T]he State uses quo warranto actions to challenge the authority to engage in certain practices specifically enumerated by statute. A quo warranto proceeding may be instituted by the attorney general or by a district or county attorney. The State is the real plaintiff and controls the litigation, even though in some instances the actions may be at the behest of private parties."

Beach City v. State, 473 S.W.2d 656, 659 (Tex. App.—Houston [14th Dist.] 1971, writ dism'd). "[Q]uo warranto proceedings are governed by the same ... rules of joinder of causes of action [as] apply ... in other civil cases."

TRCP 780. CITATION TO ISSUE

When such information is filed, the clerk shall issue citation as in civil actions, commanding the defendant to appear and answer the relator in an information in the nature of a quo warranto.

History of TRCP 780: Adopted eff. Sept. 1, 1941, by order of Oct. 29, 1940 (3 Tex.B.J. 645 [1940]). Source: TRCS art. 6255 (repealed).

TRCP 781. PROCEEDINGS AS IN CIVIL CASES

Every person or corporation who shall be cited as hereinbefore provided shall be entitled to all the rights in the trial and investigation of the matters alleged against him, as in cases of trial in civil cases in this State. Either party may prosecute an appeal or writ of error from any judgment rendered, as in other civil cases, subject, however, to the provisions of Rule 42*, Texas Rules of Appellate Procedure, and the appellate court shall give preference to such case, and hear and determine the same as early as practicable.

* Now TRAP 28 (effective Sept. 1, 1997).

History of TRCP 781: Amended eff. Sept. 1, 1990, by order of Apr. 24, 1990 (785-86 S.W.2d [Tex.Cases] lxxvii): Changed reference to Rule 384 to TRAP 42. Amended eff. Dec. 31, 1947, by order of Aug. 18, 1947 (10 Tex.B.J. 402 [1947]). Adopted eff. Sept. 1, 1941, by order of Oct. 29, 1940 (3 Tex.B.J. 645 [1940]). Source: TRCS art. 6256 (repealed).

State ex rel. Crawford v. Wagner, 203 S.W.2d 795, 798 (Tex.App.—San Antonio 1947, writ ref'd). "[E]ither party in a quo warranto proceeding is entitled to prosecute an appeal as in other civil cases, provided the transcript is filed in the Court of ... Appeals within 20 days after perfecting the appeal, and that the appellate court shall give preference to such cases and hear and determine them as early as practicable."

TRCP 782. REMEDY CUMULATIVE

The remedy and mode of procedure hereby prescribed shall be construed to be cumulative of any now existing.

History of TRCP 782: Adopted eff. Sept. 1, 1941, by order of Oct. 29, 1940 (3 Tex.B.J. 645 [1940]). Source: TRCS art. 6258 (repealed).

Derrick v. County Bd. of Educ., 374 S.W.2d 259, 262 (Tex.App.—Amarillo 1963, writ dism'd). "Even if it should be said that quo warranto was an appropriate method of contesting the elections here considered, such proceeding is only cumulative of other proper methods."

SECTION 8. TRESPASS TO TRY TITLE

TRCP 783. REQUISITES OF PETITION

The petition shall state:

(a) The real names of the plaintiff and defendant and their residences, if known.

(b) A description of the premises by metes and bounds, or with sufficient certainty to identify the same, so that from such description possession thereof may be delivered, and state the county or counties in which the same are situated.

(c) The interest which the plaintiff claims in the premises, whether it be a fee simple or other estate; and, if he claims an undivided interest, the petition shall state the same and the amount thereof.

(d) That the plaintiff was in possession of the premises or entitled to such possession.

(e) That the defendant afterward unlawfully entered upon and dispossessed him of such premises, stating the date, and withholds from him the possession thereof.

(f) If rents and profits or damages are claimed, such facts as show the plaintiff to be entitled thereto and the amount thereof.

(g) It shall conclude with a prayer for the relief sought.

History of TRCP 783: Adopted eff. Sept. 1, 1941, by order of Oct. 29, 1940 (3 Tex.B.J. 645 [1940]). Source: TRCS art. 7366 (repealed).

Yoast v. Yoast, 649 S.W.2d 289, 292 (Tex.1983). "A trespass to try title action is a procedure by which rival claims to title or right of possession may be adjudicated."

United Sav. Ass'n v. Villanueva, 878 S.W.2d 619, 621 (Tex.App.—Corpus Christi 1994, no writ). "While [P] by its petition asked for declaratory and injunctive relief it also properly alleged the elements of a trespass to try title action. We construe the pleadings as a trespass to try title action and a suit for possession."

Knupp v. Miller, 858 S.W.2d 945, 951 (Tex.App.—Beaumont 1993, writ denied). "[P] also pleaded that the acts of [Ds] in entering upon [P's] land and cutting the timber thereon were willful, wanton and in total disregard of the rights of [P]. [¶] The purpose of a trespass to try title action is to recover land and premises including timber when unlawfully withheld from owner and to which the owner has a right of immediate possession."

Smith v. Brooks, 825 S.W.2d 208, 210 (Tex.App.—Texarkana 1992, no writ). "In order to claim title by limitation based upon adverse possession, a party must plead it specifically."

TRCP 784. THE POSSESSOR SHALL BE DEFENDANT

The defendant in the action shall be the person in possession if the premises are occupied, or some person claiming title thereto in case they are unoccupied.

History of TRCP 784: Adopted eff. Sept. 1, 1941, by order of Oct. 29, 1940 (3 Tex.B.J. 646 [1940]). Source: TRCS art. 7370 (repealed).

Kennesaw Life & Acc. Ins. Co. v. Goss, 694 S.W.2d 115, 118 (Tex.App.—Houston [14th Dist.] 1985, writ ref'd n.r.e.). "The [D] would not have been a proper defendant ... since the defendant must be the person in possession of the premises or some person claiming title to the premises. By its pleadings [D] disclaimed all interest in the property, and was not in possession of the property, thus [Ps] would not have recovered any damages against [D] in a Trespass to Try Title action."

TRCP 785. MAY JOIN AS DEFENDANTS, WHEN

The plaintiff may join as a defendant with the person in possession, any other person who, as landlord, remainderman, reversioner or otherwise, may claim title to the premises, or any part thereof, adversely to the plaintiff.

History of TRCP 785: Adopted eff. Sept. 1, 1941, by order of Oct. 29, 1940 (3 Tex.B.J. 646 [1940]). Source: TRCS art. 7371 (repealed).

TRCP 786. WARRANTOR, ETC., MAY BE MADE A PARTY

When a party is sued for lands, the real owner or warrantor may make himself, or may be made, a party defendant in the suit, and shall be entitled to make such defense as if he had been the original defendant in the action.

History of TRCP 786: Adopted eff. Sept. 1, 1941, by order of Oct. 29, 1940 (3 Tex.B.J. 646 [1940]). Source: TRCS art. 7368 (repealed).

Williams v. Ballard, 722 S.W.2d 9, 11 (Tex.App.—Dallas 1986, no writ). TRCP 786 allows the mortgagor to intervene as a matter of right.

TRCP 787. LANDLORD MAY BECOME DEFENDANT

When such action shall be commenced against a tenant in possession, the landlord may enter himself as the defendant, or he may be made a party on motion of such tenant; and he shall be entitled to make the same defense as if the suit had been originally commenced against him.

History of TRCP 787: Adopted eff. Sept. 1, 1941, by order of Oct. 29, 1940 (3 Tex.B.J. 646 [1940]). Source: TRCS art. 7369 (repealed).

TRCP 788. MAY FILE PLEA OF "NOT GUILTY" ONLY

The defendant in such action may file only the plea of "not guilty," which shall state in substance that he is not guilty of the injury complained of in the petition filed by the plaintiff against him, except that if he claims an allowance for improvements, he shall state the facts entitling him to the same.

History of TRCP 788: Adopted eff. Sept. 1, 1941, by order of Oct. 29, 1940 (3 Tex.B.J. 646 [1940]). Source: TRCS art. 7372 (repealed).

Cox v. Olivard, 482 S.W.2d 682, 685 (Tex.App.—Dallas 1972, writ ref'd n.r.e.). "[D] in a trespass to try title action is not required to file a plea of 'not guilty' but that a plea of general denial has the effect of putting [P] upon proof of his right to recover the land in controversy."

TRCP 789. PROOF UNDER SUCH PLEA

Under such plea of "not guilty" the defendant may give in evidence any lawful defense to the action except the defense of limitations, which shall be specially pleaded.

History of TRCP 789: Adopted eff. Sept. 1, 1941, by order of Oct. 29, 1940 (3 Tex.B.J. 646 [1940]). Source: TRCS art. 7373 (repealed).

Walsh v. Austin, 590 S.W.2d 612, 616 (Tex.App.—Houston [1st Dist.] 1979, writ dism'd). "Where [P] has established a prima facie case, whether it be at a summary judgment hearing or upon a full trial, [D] then has the burden of introducing some defensive evidence to raise an issue of material fact in order to prevent the rendition of a summary judgment or an instructed verdict."

TRCP 790. ANSWER TAKEN AS ADMITTING POSSESSION

Such plea or any other answer to the merits shall be an admission by the defendant, for the purpose of that action, that he was in possession of the premises sued for, or that he claimed title thereto at the time of commencing the action, unless he states distinctly in his answer the extent of his possession or claim, in which case it shall be an admission to such extent only.

History of TRCP 790: Adopted eff. Sept. 1, 1941, by order of Oct. 29, 1940 (3 Tex.B.J. 646 [1940]). Source: TRCS art. 7374 (repealed).

Brohlin v. McMinn, 341 S.W.2d 420, 422 (Tex. 1960). "In an action in trespass to try title, the answer of [D] to the merits of the case by a plea of not guilty relieves [Ps] of the necessity of proving a trespass, since the plea constitutes an admission by [D] for the purpose of the action that he was in possession of or claimed title to the premises sued for by [Ps]."

TRCP 791. MAY DEMAND ABSTRACT OF TITLE

After answer filed, either party may, by notice in writing, duly served on the opposite party or his attorney of record, not less than ten days before the trial of the cause, demand an abstract in writing of the claim or title to the premises in question upon which he relies.

History of TRCP 791: Adopted eff. Sept. 1, 1941, by order of Oct. 29, 1940 (3 Tex.B.J. 646 [1940]). Source: TRCS art. 7376 (repealed).

Ramsey v. Jones Enters., 810 S.W.2d 902, 904 (Tex. App.—Beaumont 1991, writ denied). "We hold that the trial court erred in allowing [P] to prove up title ... by nothing more than the oral expert testimony of an attorney. [¶] [TRCP] 791 provides for the demanding of an abstract of title by either party.... *At 905:* [I]n trespass to try title actions where documents pertaining to title exist, ... testimony of an expert witness standing alone, constitutes no evidence of titles."

Corder v. Foster, 505 S.W.2d 645, 648 (Tex.App.—Houston [1st Dist.] 1973, writ ref'd n.r.e.). "The purpose of [TRCP] 791 and 792 ... is to enable the person demanding such abstract to investigate the records and thereby determine the character of the instruments upon which the opposing party relies, so that an informed defense may be prepared."

TRCP 792. TIME TO FILE ABSTRACT

Such abstract of title shall be filed with the papers of the cause that within thirty days after the service of the notice, or within such further time that the court on good cause shown may grant; and in default thereof, the court may, after notice and hearing prior to the beginning of trial, order that no written instruments which are evidence of the claim or title of such opposite party be given on trial.

History of TRCP 792: Amended eff. Sept. 1, 1990, by order of Apr. 24, 1990 (785-86 S.W.2d [Tex.Cases] lxxvii): Changed "order that no evidence of the claim" to "order that no written instruments which are evidence of the claim." Amended eff. Jan. 1, 1988, by order of July 15, 1987 (733-34 S.W.2d [Tex.Cases] lxxxiii). Adopted eff. Sept. 1, 1941, by order of Oct. 29, 1940 (3 Tex.B.J. 646 [1940]). Source: TRCS art. 7377 (repealed).

Hunt v. Heaton, 643 S.W.2d 677, 679 (Tex.1982). Plaintiff "sought to prove his title by a chain of instruments beginning with a patent from the State.... Because of the failure to file an abstract of the chain of title, the trial court properly excluded any offer of proof by [P] relating to his claim or title. [P] failed to prove his superior title and therefore, the correct judgment is that he take nothing."

Corder v. Foster, 505 S.W.2d 645, 648 (Tex.App.—Houston [1st Dist.] 1973, writ ref'd n.r.e.). "[T]he time for filing an abstract in response to a demand will be extended where the grant of additional time will not prejudice the party making the demand and the refusal of an extension would result in injustice."

TRCP 793. ABSTRACT SHALL STATE, WHAT

The abstract mentioned in the two preceding rules shall state:

(a) The nature of each document or written instrument intended to be used as evidence and its date; or

(b) If a contract or conveyance, its date, the parties thereto and the date of the proof of acknowledgment, and before what officer the same was made; and

(c) Where recorded, stating the book and page of the record.

(d) If not recorded in the county when the trial is had, copies of such instrument, with the names of the subscribing witnesses, shall be included. If such unrecorded instrument be lost or destroyed it shall be sufficient to state the nature of such instrument and its loss or destruction.

History of TRCP 793: Adopted eff. Sept. 1, 1941, by order of Oct. 29, 1940 (3 Tex.B.J. 647 [1940]). Source: TRCS art. 7378 (repealed).

Walker v. Barrow, 464 S.W.2d 480, 487 (Tex.App.—Houston [1st Dist.] 1971, writ ref'd n.r.e.). "[A]ny deficiency of the description contained in the abstract filed should have been called to the attention of [the receiver] by motion before trial. There was no error in its admission."

TRCP 794. AMENDED ABSTRACT

The court may allow either party to file an amended abstract of title, under the same rules, which authorize the amendment of pleadings so far as they are applicable; but in all cases the documentary evidence of title shall at the trial be confined to the matters contained in the abstract of title.

History of TRCP 794: Adopted eff. Sept. 1, 1941, by order of Oct. 29, 1940 (3 Tex.B.J. 647 [1940]). Source: TRCS art. 7379 (repealed).

Walker v. Barrow, 464 S.W.2d 480, 488 (Tex.App.—Houston [1st Dist.] 1971, writ ref'd n.r.e.). "[T]he court has authority to grant extensions of time to file an abstract and when one has, as here, been filed within the time allowed by the court, the court has discretion to allow amendments. The rule should be applied to promote justice."

TRCP 795. RULES IN OTHER CASES OBSERVED

The trial shall be conducted according to the rules of pleading, practice and evidence in other cases in the district court and conformable to the principles of trial by ejectment, except as otherwise provided by these rules.

History of TRCP 795: Adopted eff. Sept. 1, 1941, by order of Oct. 29, 1940 (3 Tex.B.J. 647 [1940]). Source: TRCS art. 7365 (repealed).

Ramsey v. Jones Enters., 810 S.W.2d 902, 905 (Tex. App.—Beaumont 1991, writ denied). TRE 702, 703 or 704 "do not excuse the necessity for the production and admission of documentary evidence regarding title to real property. [TRE] 1002 requires that if documentary evidence exist as to title to ... real property, that such documentary evidence must be produced and admitted."

TRCP 796. SURVEYOR APPOINTED, ETC.

The judge of the court may, either in term time or in vacation, at his own discretion, or on motion of either party to the action appoint a surveyor, who shall survey the premises in controversy pursuant to the order of the court, and report his action under oath to such court. If said report be not rejected for good cause shown, the same shall be admitted as evidence on the trial.

History of TRCP 796: Adopted eff. Sept. 1, 1941, by order of Oct. 29, 1940 (3 Tex.B.J. 647 [1940]). Source: TRCS art. 7380 (repealed).

Mayflower Inv. Co. v. Stephens, 345 S.W.2d 786, 796 (Tex.App.—Dallas 1960, writ ref'd n.r.e.). TRCP 796 "is applicable only in trespass to try title cases."

TRCP 797. SURVEY UNNECESSARY, WHEN

Where there is no dispute as to the lines or boundaries of the land in controversy, or where the defendant admits that he is in possession of the lands or tenements included in the plaintiff's claim, or title, an order of survey shall be unnecessary.

History of TRCP 797: Adopted eff. Sept. 1, 1941, by order of Oct. 29, 1940 (3 Tex.B.J. 647 [1940]). Source: TRCS art. 7381 (repealed).

TRCP 798. COMMON SOURCE OF TITLE

It shall not be necessary for the plaintiff to deraign title beyond a common source. Proof of a common source may be made by the plaintiff by certified copies of the deeds showing a chain of title to the defendant emanating from and under such common source. Before any such certified copies shall be read in evidence, they shall be filed with the papers of the suit three days before the trial, and the adverse party served with notice of such filing as in other cases. Such certified copies shall not be evidence of title in the defendant unless offered in evidence by him. The plaintiff may make any legal objection to such certified copies, or the originals thereof, when introduced by the defendant.

History of TRCP 798: Adopted eff. Sept. 1, 1941, by order of Oct. 29, 1940 (3 Tex.B.J. 647 [1940]). Source: TRCS art. 7382 (repealed).

Davis v. Gale, 330 S.W.2d 610, 612 (Tex.1960). "In a trespass to try title suit, where the parties agree as to a common source, it is incumbent upon [P] to discharge the burden of proof resting upon him to establish a superior title from such source."

Goggins v. Leo, 849 S.W.2d 373, 377 (Tex.App.—Houston [14th Dist.] 1993, no writ). TRCP 798 applies only to trespass to try title suits, not to forcible detainer cases.

TRCP 799. Judgment by Default

If the defendant, who has been personally served with citation according to law or these rules fails to appear and answer by himself or attorney within the time prescribed by law or these rules for other actions in the district court, then judgment by default may be entered against him and in favor of the plaintiff for the title to the premises, or the possession thereof, or for both, according to the petition, and for all costs, without any proof of title by the plaintiff.

History of TRCP 799: Adopted eff. Sept. 1, 1941, by order of Oct. 29, 1940 (3 Tex.B.J. 647 [1940]). Source: TRCS art. 7383 (repealed).

TRCP 800. Proof Ex Parte

If the defendant has been cited only by publication, and fails to appear and answer by himself, or by attorney of his own selection, or if any defendant, having answered, fails to appear by himself or attorney when the case is called for trial on its merits, the plaintiff shall make such proof as will entitle him prima facie to recover, whereupon the proper judgment shall be entered.

History of TRCP 800: Adopted eff. Sept. 1, 1941, by order of Oct. 29, 1940 (3 Tex.B.J. 647 [1940]). Source: TRCS art. 7384 (repealed).

TRCP 801. When Defendant Claims Part Only

Where the defendant claims part of the premises only, the answer shall be equivalent to a disclaimer of the balance.

History of TRCP 801: Adopted eff. Sept. 1, 1941, by order of Oct. 29, 1940 (3 Tex.B.J. 647 [1940]). Source: TRCS art. 7385 (repealed).

Salazar v. Garcia, 232 S.W.2d 685, 688 (Tex.App.—San Antonio 1950, writ ref'd). Because "[t]he answers filed by [Ds] in this cause do not claim title to [the real estate], but they limit their claim to an assertion of ownership of, or the right to fix a lien on the improvements[,] [t]he pleadings and evidence presented by [Ds] amount to a disclaimer by them of any title to the [real estate]."

TRCP 802. When Plaintiff Proves Part

Where the defendant claims the whole premises, and the plaintiff shows himself entitled to recover part, the plaintiff shall recover such part and costs.

History of TRCP 802: Adopted eff. Sept. 1, 1941, by order of Oct. 29, 1940 (3 Tex.B.J. 648 [1940]). Source: TRCS art. 7386 (repealed).

Southern Pine Lumber Co. v. Hart, 340 S.W.2d 775, 781 (Tex.1960). If the plaintiff sues for a larger tract, he can recover for the smaller tract for which he can prove title.

TRCP 803. May Recover a Part

When there are two or more plaintiffs or defendants any one or more of the plaintiffs may recover against one or more of the defendants the premises, or any part thereof, or any interest therein, or damages, according to the rights of the parties.

History of TRCP 803: Adopted eff. Sept. 1, 1941, by order of Oct. 29, 1940 (3 Tex.B.J. 648 [1940]). Source: TRCS art. 7387 (repealed).

TRCP 804. The Judgment

Upon the finding of the jury, or of the court where the case is tried by the court, in favor of the plaintiff for the whole or any part of the premises in controversy, the judgment shall be that the plaintiff recover of the defendant the title or possession, or both, as the case may be, of such premises, describing them, and where he recovers the possession, that he have his writ of possession.

History of TRCP 804: Adopted eff. Sept. 1, 1941, by order of Oct. 29, 1940 (3 Tex.B.J. 648 [1940]). Source: TRCS art. 7388 (repealed).

Logan v. First Bank, 736 S.W.2d 927, 931 (Tex.App.—Beaumont 1987, writ ref'd n.r.e.). TRCP 804 "provides that where [P] recovers possession of real property in a trespass to try title action, he is entitled to a writ of possession."

TRCP 805. Damages

Where it is alleged and proved that one of the parties is in possession of the premises, the court or jury, if they find for the adverse party, shall assess the damages for the use and occupation of the premises. If special injury to the property be alleged and proved, the damages for such injury shall also be assessed, and the proper judgment shall be entered therefor, on which execution may issue.

History of TRCP 805: Adopted eff. Sept. 1, 1941, by order of Oct. 29, 1940 (3 Tex.B.J. 648 [1940]). Source: TRCS art. 7389 (repealed in part by TRCP).

TRCP 806. CLAIM FOR IMPROVEMENTS

When the defendant or person in possession has claimed an allowance for improvements in accordance with Sections 22.021-22.024, Texas Property Code, the claim for use and occupation and damages mentioned in the preceding rule shall be considered and acted on in connection with such claim by the defendant or person in possession.

History of TRCP 806: Amended eff. Jan. 1, 1988, by order of July 15, 1987 (733-34 S.W.2d [Tex.Cases] lxxxiii). Amended eff. Apr. 1, 1984, by order of Dec. 5, 1983 (661-62 S.W.2d [Tex.Cases] cxviii). Adopted eff. Sept. 1, 1941, by order of Oct. 29, 1940 (3 Tex.B.J. 648 [1940]). Source: TRCS art. 7390 (repealed).

TRCP 807. JUDGMENT WHEN CLAIM FOR IMPROVEMENTS IS MADE

When a claim for improvements is successfully made under Sections 22.021-22.024, Texas Property Code, the judgment shall recite the estimated value of the premises without the improvements, and shall also include the conditions, stipulations and directions contained in Sections 22.021-22.024, Texas Property Code so far as applicable to the case before the court.

History of TRCP 807: Amended eff. Jan. 1, 1988, by order of July 15, 1987 (733-34 S.W.2d [Tex.Cases] lxxxiii). Amended eff. Apr. 1, 1984, by order of Dec. 5, 1983 (661-62 S.W.2d [Tex.Cases] cxviii). Adopted eff. Sept. 1, 1941, by order of Oct. 29, 1940 (3 Tex.B.J. 648 [1940]). Source: TRCS art. 7400 (repealed).

TRCP 808. THESE RULES SHALL NOT GOVERN, WHEN

Nothing in Sections 22.001-22.045, Texas Property Code, shall be so construed as to alter, impair or take away the rights of parties, as arising under the laws in force before the introduction of the common law, but the same shall be decided by the principles of the law under which the same accrued, or by which the same were regulated or in any manner affected.

History of TRCP 808: Amended eff. Jan. 1, 1988, by order of July 15, 1987 (733-34 S.W.2d [Tex.Cases] lxxxiii). Amended eff. Apr. 1, 1984, by order of Dec. 5, 1983 (661-62 S.W.2d [Tex.Cases] cxviii). Adopted eff. Sept. 1, 1941, by order of Oct. 29, 1940 (3 Tex.B.J. 648 [1940]). Source: TRCS art. 7392 (repealed eff. Jan. 1, 1984).

TRCP 809. THESE RULES SHALL NOT GOVERN, WHEN

Nothing in these rules relating to trespass to try title shall be so construed as to alter, impair or take away the rights of parties, as arising under the laws in force before the introduction of the common law, but the same shall be decided by the principles of the law under which the same accrued, or by which the same were regulated or in any manner affected.

History of TRCP 809: Adopted eff. Sept. 1, 1941, by order of Oct. 29, 1940 (3 Tex.B.J. 648 [1940]). Source: New rule.

SECTION 9. SUITS AGAINST NON-RESIDENTS

TRCP 810. REQUISITES OF PLEADINGS

The petition in actions authorized by Section 17.003, Civil Practice and Remedies Code, shall state the real names of the plaintiff and defendant, and shall describe the property involved with sufficient certainty to identify the same, the interest which the plaintiff claims, and such proceedings shall be had in such action as may be necessary to fully settle and determine the question of right or title in and to said property between the parties to said suit, and to decree the title or right of the party entitled thereto; and the court may issue the appropriate order to carry such decree, judgment or order into effect; and whenever such petition has been duly filed and citation thereon has been duly served by publication as required by Rules 114-116, the plaintiff may, at any time prior to entering the decree by leave of court first had and obtained, file amended and supplemental pleadings that do not subject additional property to said suit without the necessity of reciting the defendants so cited as aforesaid.

History of TRCP 810: Amended eff. Jan. 1, 1988, by order of July 15, 1987 (733-34 S.W.2d [Tex.Cases] lxxxiv). Amended eff. Apr. 1, 1984, by order of Dec. 5, 1983 (661-62 S.W.2d [Tex.Cases] cxviii). Adopted eff. Sept. 1, 1941, by order of Oct. 29, 1940 (3 Tex.B.J. 649 [1940]). Source: TRCS art. 1977 (repealed).

TRCP 811. SERVICE BY PUBLICATION IN ACTIONS UNDER SECTION 17.003, CIVIL PRACTICE & REMEDIES CODE

In actions authorized by Section 17.003, Civil Practice and Remedies Code, service on the defendant or defendants may be made by publication as is provided by Rules 114-116 or by service of notice of the character and in the manner provided by Rule 108.

History of TRCP 811: Amended eff. Jan. 1, 1988, by order of July 15, 1987 (733-34 S.W.2d [Tex.Cases] lxxxiv). Amended eff. Apr. 1, 1984, by order of Dec. 5, 1983 (661-62 S.W.2d [Tex.Cases] cxviii). Adopted eff. Sept. 1, 1941, by order of Oct. 29, 1940 (3 Tex.B.J. 649 [1940]). Source: TRCS art. 1976 (repealed in part by TRCP).

TRCP 812. NO JUDGMENT BY DEFAULT

No judgment by default shall be taken in such case when service has been had by publication, but in such case the facts entitling the plaintiff to judgment shall be exhibited to the court on the trial; and a statement of facts shall be filed as provided by law and these rules in suits against nonresidents of this State served by publication, where no appearance has been made by them.

History of TRCP 812: Amended eff. Mar. 1, 1950, by order of Oct. 12, 1949 (12 Tex.B.J. 538 [1949]). Adopted eff. Sept. 1, 1941, by order of Oct. 29, 1940 (3 Tex.B.J. 649 [1940]). Source: TRCS art. 1978 (repealed).

TRCP 813. SUIT TO EXTINGUISH LIEN

If said suit shall be for the extinguishment of a lien or claim for money on said property that may be held by the defendant, the amount thereof, with interest, shall be ascertained by the court; and the same deposited in the registry of the court, subject to be drawn by the parties entitled thereto; but in such case no decree shall be entered until said sum is deposited; which fact shall be noted in said decree.

History of TRCP 813: Adopted eff. Sept. 1, 1941, by order of Oct. 29, 1940 (3 Tex.B.J. 649 [1940]). Source: TRCS art. 1979 (repealed).

PART VIII. CLOSING RULES

TRCP 814. EFFECTIVE DATE

These rules shall take effect on September 1st, 1941. They shall govern all proceedings in actions brought after they take effect, and also all further proceedings in actions then pending, except to the extent that in the opinion of the court their application in a particular action pending when the rules take effect would not be feasible or would work injustice, in which event the former procedure shall apply. All things properly done under any previously existing rule or statutes prior to the taking effect of these rules shall be treated as valid. Where citation or other process is issued and served in compliance with existing rules or laws prior to the taking effect of these rules, the party upon whom such citation or other process has been served shall have the time provided for under such previously existing rules or laws in which to comply therewith.

History of TRCP 814: Adopted eff. Sept. 1, 1941, by order of Oct. 29, 1940 (3 Tex.B.J. 649 [1940]). Source: FRCP 86.

TRCP 815. SUBSTANTIVE RIGHTS UNAFFECTED

These rules shall not be construed to enlarge or diminish any substantive rights or obligations of any parties to any civil action.

See Gov't Code §22.004(a).

History of TRCP 815: Adopted eff. Sept. 1, 1941, by order of Oct. 29, 1940 (3 Tex.B.J. 649 [1940]). Source: TRCS art. 1731a (repealed, eff. Sept. 1, 1985), now Gov't Code §22.004(a).

McLendon v. McLendon, 847 S.W.2d 601, 608 (Tex. App.—Dallas 1992, writ denied). "[T]he supreme court's rulemaking power may not [adopt rules that] 'abridge, enlarge, or modify the substantive rights of a litigant.'"

TRCP 816. JURISDICTION & VENUE UNAFFECTED

These rules shall not be construed to extend or limit the jurisdiction of the courts of the State of Texas nor the venue of actions therein.

History of TRCP 816: Adopted eff. Sept. 1, 1941, by order of Oct. 29, 1940 (3 Tex.B.J. 649 [1940]). Source: FRCP 82.

TRCP 817. RENUMBERED

Repealed and renumbered as TRCP 3a eff. Apr. 1, 1984, by order of Dec. 5, 1983 (661-62 S.W.2d [Tex.Cases] cxix).

TRCP 818. REFERENCE TO FORMER STATUTES

Wherever any statute or rule refers to any practice or procedure in any law, laws, statute or statutes, or to a title, chapter, section, or article of the statutes, or contains any reference of any such nature, and the matter referred to has been supplanted in whole or in part by these rules, every such reference shall be deemed to be to the pertinent part or parts of these rules.

History of TRCP 818: Adopted eff. Sept. 1, 1941, by order of Oct. 29, 1940 (3 Tex.B.J. 650 [1940]). Source: New rule.

TRCP 819. PROCEDURE CONTINUED

All procedure prescribed by statutes of the State of Texas not specifically listed in the accompanying enumeration of repealed articles shall, insofar as the same is not inconsistent with the provisions of these rules, continue in accordance with the provisions of such statutes as rules of court. In case of inconsistency between the provisions of these rules and any statutory procedure not specifically listed as repealed, these rules shall apply.

History of TRCP 819: Adopted eff. Sept. 1, 1941, by order of Oct. 29, 1940 (3 Tex.B.J. 650 [1940]). Source: New rule.

Moore v. Johnson, 785 S.W.2d 176, 179 (Tex. App.—Waco 1990, orig. proceeding). TRCP 819 "clearly provides that in the event of an inconsistency between any statutory procedural matter which is given the effect of a court rule and a specific Rule of Civil Procedure, the Rule of Civil Procedure controls."

TRCP 820. WORKERS' COMPENSATION LAW

All portions of the Workers' Compensation Law, Articles 8306-8309-1, Revised Civil Statutes, and amendments thereto, which relate to matters of practice and procedure are hereby adopted and retained in force and effect as rules of court.

History of TRCP 820: Amended eff. Apr. 1, 1984, by order of Dec. 5, 1983 (661-62 S.W.2d [Tex.Cases] cxix). Adopted eff. Sept. 1, 1941, by order of Oct. 29, 1940 (3 Tex.B.J. 650 [1940]). Source: New rule.

TRCP 821. PRIOR COURT RULES REPEALED

These rules shall supersede all Court Rules heretofore promulgated for any court; and all of said prior Court Rules are hereby repealed; provided, however, any rules of procedure heretofore adopted by a particular county or district court or by any Court of Appeals which were not of general application but were solely to regulate procedure in the particular court promulgating such rules are to remain in force and effect insofar as they are not inconsistent with these rules.

History of TRCP 821: Amended eff. Apr. 1, 1984, by order of Dec. 5, 1983 (661-62 S.W.2d [Tex.Cases] cxix): Deleted "Civil" from Court of Civil Appeals. Adopted eff. Sept. 1, 1941, by order of Oct. 29, 1940 (3 Tex.B.J. 650 [1940]). Source: New rule.

TRCP 822. TITLE

These rules may be known and cited as the Texas Rules of Civil Procedure.

History of TRCP 822: Adopted eff. Sept. 1, 1941, by order of Oct. 29, 1940 (3 Tex.B.J. 650 [1940]). Source: FRCP 85.

Texas Rules of Evidence

Table of Contents

The annotated cases, reference notes, and history notes that follow the rules are not part of the official rules; they are copyrighted material included with the rules to assist in research.

TEXAS RULES OF EVIDENCE

ARTICLE I. GENERAL PROVISIONS

TRE 101. TITLE & SCOPE

(a) Title. These rules shall be known and cited as the Texas Rules of Evidence.

(b) Scope. Except as otherwise provided by statute, these rules govern civil and criminal proceedings (including examining trials before magistrates) in all courts of Texas, except small claims courts.

(c) Hierarchical Governance in Criminal Proceedings. Hierarchical governance shall be in the following order: the Constitution of the United States, those federal statutes that control states under the supremacy clause, the Constitution of Texas, the Code of Criminal Procedure and the Penal Code, civil statutes, these rules, and the common law. Where possible, inconsistency is to be removed by reasonable construction.

(d) Special Rules of Applicability in Criminal Proceedings.

(1) *Rules not applicable in certain proceedings.* These rules, except with respect to privileges, do not apply in the following situations:

(A) the determination of questions of fact preliminary to admissibility of evidence when the issue is to be determined by the court under Rule 104;

(B) proceedings before grand juries;

(C) proceedings in an application for habeas corpus in extradition, rendition, or interstate detainer;

(D) a hearing under Code of Criminal Procedure article 46.02, by the court out of the presence of a jury, to determine whether there is sufficient evidence of incompetency to require a jury determination of the question of incompetency;

(E) proceedings regarding bail except hearings to deny, revoke or increase bail;

(F) a hearing on justification for pretrial detention not involving bail;

(G) proceedings for the issuance of a search or arrest warrant; or

(H) proceedings in a direct contempt determination.

(2) *Applicability of privileges.* These rules with respect to privileges apply at all stages of all actions, cases, and proceedings.

(3) *Military justice hearings.* Evidence in hearings under the Texas Code of Military Justice, Tex. Gov't Code §432.001-432.195, shall be governed by that Code.

Comment to 1998 change: "Criminal proceedings" rather than "criminal cases" is used since that was the terminology used in the prior Rules of Criminal Evidence. In subpart (b), the reference to "trials before magistrates" comes from prior Criminal Rule 1101(a). In the prior Criminal Rules, both Rule 101 and Rule 1101 dealt with the same thing—the applicability of the rules. Thus, Rules 101(c) and (d) have been written to incorporate the provisions of former Criminal Rule 1101 and that rule is omitted.

See Cochran, ***Texas Rules of Evidence Handbook***, p. 65 (2003).

History of TRE 101 (civil): Amended eff. Mar. 1, 1998, by order of Feb. 25, 1998 (960 S.W.2d [Tex.Cases] xxxi). Amended eff. Jan. 1, 1988, by order of Nov. 10, 1986 (733-34 S.W.2d [Tex.Cases] lxxxvi): added "Civil" to title of rules in (a). Adopted eff. Sept. 1, 1983, by order of Nov. 23, 1982 (641-42 S.W.2d [Tex.Cases] xxxvi). Source: For TRE 101(a), see FRE 1103; for TRE 101(b), see FRE 101.

TRE 102. PURPOSE & CONSTRUCTION

These rules shall be construed to secure fairness in administration, elimination of unjustifiable expense and delay, and promotion of growth and development of the law of evidence to the end that the truth may be ascertained and proceedings justly determined.

See Cochran, ***Texas Rules of Evidence Handbook***, p. 79 (2003).

History of TRE 102 (civil): Amended eff. Mar. 1, 1998, by order of Feb. 25, 1998 (960 S.W.2d [Tex.Cases] xxxii). Adopted eff. Sept. 1, 1983, by order of Nov. 23, 1982 (641-42 S.W.2d [Tex.Cases] xxxvi). Source: FRE 102.

TRE 103. RULINGS ON EVIDENCE

(a) Effect of Erroneous Ruling. Error may not be predicated upon a ruling which admits or excludes evidence unless a substantial right of the party is affected, and

(1) *Objection.* In case the ruling is one admitting evidence, a timely objection or motion to strike appears of record, stating the specific ground of objection, if the specific ground was not apparent from the context. When the court hears objections to offered evidence out of the presence of the jury and rules that such evidence be admitted, such objections shall be deemed to apply to such evidence when it is admitted before the jury without the necessity of repeating those objections.

(2) *Offer of proof.* In case the ruling is one excluding evidence, the substance of the evidence was made known to the court by offer, or was apparent from the context within which questions were asked.

(b) Record of Offer and Ruling. The offering party shall, as soon as practicable, but before the court's charge is read to the jury, be allowed to make, in the absence of the jury, its offer of proof. The court may add any other or further statement which shows the character of the evidence, the form in which it was offered, the objection made, and the ruling thereon. The court may, or at the request of a party shall, direct the making of an offer in question and answer form.

(c) Hearing of Jury. In jury cases, proceedings shall be conducted, to the extent practicable, so as to prevent inadmissible evidence from being suggested to the jury by any means, such as making statements or offers of proof or asking questions in the hearing of the jury.

(d) Fundamental Error in Criminal Cases. In a criminal case, nothing in these rules precludes taking notice of fundamental errors affecting substantial rights although they were not brought to the attention of the court.

Comment to 1998 change: The exception to the requirement of an offer of proof for matters that were apparent from the context within which questions were asked, found in paragraph (a)(2), is now applicable to civil as well as criminal cases.

See TRAP 44.1; ***Commentaries***, "Motion in Limine," ch. 5-E; "Objecting to Evidence," ch. 8-D; "Offer of Proof & Bill of Exceptions," ch. 8-E; Cochran, ***Texas Rules of Evidence Handbook***, p. 81 (2003).

History of TRE 103 (civil): Amended eff. Mar. 1, 1998, by order of Feb. 25, 1998 (960 S.W.2d [Tex.Cases] xxxii). Amended eff. Jan. 1, 1988, by order of July 15, 1987 (733-34 S.W.2d [Tex.Cases] xciv): Added 2d sentence to (a)(1), to conform to TRAP 52(b); deleted the phrase "or was apparent from the context within which questions were asked" from (a)(2); and added 1st sentence to (b), requiring party make offer before jury is charged. Amended eff. Nov. 1, 1984, by order of June 25, 1984 (669-70 S.W.2d [Tex.Cases] xxx): Substituted the words "a party" for "counsel" in the last sentence of (b). Adopted eff. Sept. 1, 1983, by order of Nov. 23, 1982 (641-42 S.W.2d [Tex.Cases] xxxvi). Source: FRE 103, with changes: Party entitled to make offer in question-and-answer form.

In re N.R.C., 94 S.W.3d 799, 806 (Tex.App.—Houston [14th Dist.] 2002, pet. denied). "To adequately and effectively preserve error, an offer of proof must show the nature of the evidence specifically enough so that the reviewing court can determine its admissibility. ... The offer of proof may be made by counsel, who should reasonably and specifically summarize the evidence offered and state its relevance unless already apparent. If counsel does make such an offer, he must describe the actual content of the testimony and not merely comment on the reasons for it."

Norfolk S. Ry. v. Bailey, 92 S.W.3d 577, 583 (Tex. App.—Austin 2002, no pet.). A "denial of a motion in limine is not a final ruling on admission of evidence; a party must object at trial when the testimony is offered to preserve error."

Perez v. Lopez, 74 S.W.3d 60, 66 (Tex.App.—El Paso 2002, no pet.). "To preserve error concerning the exclusion of evidence, the complaining party must actually offer the evidence and secure an adverse ruling from the court. While the reviewing court may be able to discern from the record the nature of the evidence and the propriety of the trial court's ruling, without an offer of proof, we can never determine whether exclusion of the evidence was harmful. Thus, when evidence is excluded by the trial court, the proponent of the evidence must preserve the evidence in the record in order to complain of the exclusion on appeal."

Fletcher v. Minnesota Mining & Mfg. Co., 57 S.W.3d 602, 608 (Tex.App.—Houston [1st Dist.] 2001, pet. denied). "The excerpts from the pretrial hearing ... do not ... show a 'ruling,' as contemplated by [TRAP 33.1(a)(1)(A)], or any 'questions' that 'were asked,' as contemplated by [TRE 103(a)(2)]. Because the substance of [the expert's] testimony was not 'apparent from the context' and would not become apparent until [Ps] actually submitted his deposition testimony, we have no means to assess the harm, if any, arising from excluding that testimony."

Bean v. Baxter Healthcare Corp., 965 S.W.2d 656, 660 (Tex.App.—Houston [14th Dist.] 1998, no pet.). Plaintiff "preserved error after its initial offer of the videotape. If exclusion of evidence is based on the substance of the evidence, however, the offering party must reoffer it if it again becomes relevant. This may occur when the evidence is pertinent to rebuttal. Error is waived if the offering party fails to reoffer evidence for a limited purpose after it has been excluded pursuant to a general objection."

Hill v. Heritage Res., 964 S.W.2d 89, 136 (Tex. App.—El Paso 1997, pet. denied). "To obtain a reversal of judgment based upon a trial court's decision to admit or exclude evidence, [D] must show: (1) that the trial court abused its discretion in making the decision; and (2) that the error was reasonably calculated to cause and probably did cause rendition of an improper judgment. [¶] It has been held that when evidence is sharply conflicting and the case is hotly contested, any error of law by the trial court will be reversible...."

Chance v. Chance, 911 S.W.2d 40, 52 (Tex.App.—Beaumont 1995, writ denied). "[T]he rule requiring that proffered evidence be incorporated in a bill of exception does not apply to cross examination of an adverse witness. When cross-examination testimony is excluded, [D] need not show the answer to be expected but only need show that the substance of the evidence was apparent form the context within which the question was asked."

TRE 104. PRELIMINARY QUESTIONS

(a) Questions of Admissibility Generally. Preliminary questions concerning the qualification of a person to be a witness, the existence of a privilege, or the admissibility of evidence shall be determined by the court, subject to the provisions of subdivision (b). In making its determination the court is not bound by the rules of evidence except those with respect to privileges.

(b) Relevancy Conditioned on Fact. When the relevancy of evidence depends upon the fulfillment of a condition of fact, the court shall admit it upon, or subject to, the introduction of evidence sufficient to support a finding of the fulfillment of the condition.

(c) Hearing of Jury. In a criminal case, a hearing on the admissibility of a confession shall be conducted out of the hearing of the jury. All other civil or criminal hearings on preliminary matters shall be conducted out of the hearing of the jury when the interests of justice so require or in a criminal case when an accused is a witness and so requests.

(d) Testimony by Accused Out of the Hearing of the Jury. The accused in a criminal case does not, by testifying upon a preliminary matter out of the hearing of the jury, become subject to cross-examination as to other issues in the case.

(e) Weight and Credibility. This rule does not limit the right of a party to introduce before the jury evidence relevant to weight or credibility.

See ***Commentaries***, "Motion in Limine," ch. 5-E; "Objecting to Evidence," ch. 8-D; Cochran, ***Texas Rules of Evidence Handbook***, p. 105 (2003).

History of TRE 104 (civil): Amended eff. Mar. 1, 1998, by order of Feb. 25, 1998 (960 S.W.2d [Tex.Cases] xxxiii). Adopted eff. Sept. 1, 1983, by order of Nov. 23, 1982 (641-42 S.W.2d [Tex.Cases] xxxvi). Source: FRE 104.

Broders v. Heise, 924 S.W.2d 148, 151 (Tex.1996). "The qualification of a witness as an expert is within the trial court's discretion. [T]he party offering the expert's testimony bears the burden to prove that the witness is qualified under [TRE] 702.

E.I. du Pont de Nemours & Co. v. Robinson, 923 S.W.2d 549, 556 (Tex.1995). "The trial court is responsible for making the preliminary determination of whether the proffered testimony meets the standards set forth [for experts]."

Lofton v. Texas Brine Corp., 777 S.W.2d 384, 386 (Tex.1989). "Testimony by an interested witness may establish a fact as a matter of law only if the testimony could be readily contradicted if untrue, and is clear, direct and positive, and there are no circumstances tending to discredit or impeach it."

TRE 105. LIMITED ADMISSIBILITY

(a) Limiting Instruction. When evidence which is admissible as to one party or for one purpose but not admissible as to another party or for another purpose is admitted, the court, upon request, shall restrict the evidence to its proper scope and instruct the jury accordingly; but, in the absence of such request the court's action in admitting such evidence without limitation shall not be a ground for complaint on appeal.

(b) Offering Evidence for Limited Purpose. When evidence referred to in paragraph (a) is excluded, such exclusion shall not be a ground for complaint on appeal unless the proponent expressly offers the evidence for its limited, admissible purpose or limits its offer to the party against whom it is admissible.

See ***Commentaries***, "Request for limited admissibility," ch. 8-D, §7.1.3(1); Cochran, ***Texas Rules of Evidence Handbook***, p. 115 (2003).

History of TRE 105 (civil): Amended eff. Mar. 1, 1998, by order of Feb. 25, 1998 (960 S.W.2d [Tex.Cases] xxxiv). Adopted eff. Sept. 1, 1983, by order of Nov. 23, 1982 (641-42 S.W.2d [Tex.Cases] xxxvii). Source: FRE 105.

Horizon v. Auld, 34 S.W.3d 887, 906 (Tex.2000). Defendant "did not request a limiting instruction as to the general admission of the survey reports. Thus, if the survey reports were admissible by any party or for any purpose, the court of appeals did not err in affirming the trial court's admission of the reports."

Larson v. Cactus Util. Co., 730 S.W.2d 640, 642 (Tex.1987). "Where tendered evidence should be considered for only one purpose, it is the opponent's burden to secure a limiting instruction. Absent a requested limiting instruction, [the opponent of the evidence] waived his grounds for complaint."

TRE 106. REMAINDER OF OR RELATED WRITINGS OR RECORDED STATEMENTS

When a writing or recorded statement or part thereof is introduced by a party, an adverse party may at that time introduce any other part or any other writing or recorded statement which ought in fairness to be considered contemporaneously with it. "Writing or recorded statement" includes depositions.

See Cochran, ***Texas Rules of Evidence Handbook***, p. 120 (2003).

History of TRE 106 (civil): Amended eff. Mar. 1, 1998, by order of Feb. 25, 1998 (960 S.W.2d [Tex.Cases] xxxiv). Amended eff. Nov. 1, 1984, by order of June 25, 1984 (669-70 S.W.2d [Tex.Cases] xxxi): The title was changed; the last sentence added to the rule; and references to Tex. Code Crim.P. art. 38.24 and to TRCE 610(a) were added to the comment. Adopted eff. Sept. 1, 1983, by order of Nov. 23, 1982 (641-42 S.W.2d [Tex.Cases] xxxvii). Source: FRE 106. This rule is the same as FRE 106, with one modification. Under FRE 106, a party may require its opponent to introduce evidence contrary to the latter's own case. The Committee believed it was better to permit the party to introduce such evidence contemporaneously with the introduction of the incomplete evidence. TRCE 106 does not in any way circumscribe the right of a party to develop fully the matter on cross-examination or as part of his own case. *Cf.* Tex. Code Crim.P. art. 38.24. Nor does it alter the common law doctrine that the rule of optional completeness, as to writings, oral conversations, or other matters, may take precedence over exclusionary doctrines such as the hearsay or best evidence rule or the first-hand knowledge requirement.

Jones v. Colley, 820 S.W.2d 863, 866 (Tex.App.—Texarkana 1991, writ denied). TRE 106, the rule of optional completeness, "is not enforced by excluding the partial statement, but by allowing the opposing party to contemporaneously introduce any other part of the statement that should be considered with the portion introduced by the proponent."

TRE 107. RULE OF OPTIONAL COMPLETENESS

When part of an act, declaration, conversation, writing or recorded statement is given in evidence by one party, the whole on the same subject may be inquired into by the other, and any other act, declaration, writing or recorded statement which is necessary to make it fully understood or to explain the same may also be given in evidence, as when a letter is read, all letters on the same subject between the same parties may be given. "Writing or recorded statement" includes depositions.

Comment to 1998 change: This rule is the former Criminal Rule 107 except that the example regarding "when a letter is read" has been relocated in the rule so as to more accurately indicate the provision it explains. While this rule appeared only in the prior criminal rules, it is made applicable to civil cases because it accurately reflects the common law rule of optional completeness in civil cases.

See Cochran, ***Texas Rules of Evidence Handbook***, p. 123 (2003).

History of TRE 107 (criminal): Amended eff. Mar. 1, 1998, by order of Feb. 25, 1998 (960 S.W.2d [Tex.Cases] xxxiv). Adopted eff. Sept. 1, 1986 by order of Dec. 18, 1985 (701-02 S.W.2d [Tex.Cases] xxxiv).

ARTICLE II. JUDICIAL NOTICE

TRE 201. JUDICIAL NOTICE OF ADJUDICATIVE FACTS

(a) Scope of Rule. This rule governs only judicial notice of adjudicative facts.

(b) Kinds of Facts. A judicially noticed fact must be one not subject to reasonable dispute in that it is either (1) generally known within the territorial jurisdiction of the trial court or (2) capable of accurate and ready determination by resort to sources whose accuracy cannot reasonably be questioned.

(c) When Discretionary. A court may take judicial notice, whether requested or not.

(d) When Mandatory. A court shall take judicial notice if requested by a party and supplied with the necessary information.

(e) Opportunity to Be Heard. A party is entitled upon timely request to an opportunity to be heard as to the propriety of taking judicial notice and the tenor of the matter noticed. In the absence of prior notification, the request may be made after judicial notice has been taken.

(f) Time of Taking Notice. Judicial notice may be taken at any stage of the proceeding.

(g) Instructing Jury. In civil cases, the court shall instruct the jury to accept as conclusive any fact judicially noticed. In criminal cases, the court shall instruct the jury that it may, but is not required to, accept as conclusive any fact judicially noticed.

See CPRC §38.004; ***Commentaries***, "Motion for Judicial Notice," ch. 5-L; Cochran, ***Texas Rules of Evidence Handbook***, p. 130 (2003).

History of TRE 201 (civil): Amended eff. Mar. 1, 1998, by order of Feb. 25, 1998 (960 S.W.2d [Tex.Cases] xxxv). Adopted eff. Sept. 1, 1983, by order of Nov. 23, 1982 (641-42 S.W.2d [Tex.Cases] xxxvii). Source: FRE 201.

Office of Pub. Util. Counsel v. PUC, 878 S.W.2d 598, 600 (Tex.1994). "To be the proper subject of judicial notice, a fact must be 'capable of accurate and ready determination by resort to sources whose accuracy cannot reasonably be questioned.' Judicial notice is mandatory if 'requested by a party and [the court is] supplied with the necessary information.' A court of appeals has the power to take judicial notice for the first time on appeal. … The authenticity and contents of the PUC ratemaking order are capable of accurate and ready determination…."

Higginbotham v. General Life & Acc. Ins. Co., 796 S.W.2d 695, 696 (Tex.1990). "The trial court could properly take judicial notice that … March 18, 1986 … was not a statutory holiday."

Coward v. Gateway Nat'l Bank, 525 S.W.2d 857, 859 (Tex.1975). CPRC chapter 38 "applies only in suits on one or more of the claims described in [CPRC §38.001]. [¶] [T]he Legislature authorized the court, in non-jury cases, to take judicial notice of [attorney fees]. [T]he court may examine the case file and is to make a determination of the amount of attorney's fees even if no other evidence is offered. This responsibility may be discharged by the trial judge in his role of trier of fact in the conventional trial of a non-jury case but not in passing on a motion for summary judgment."

O'Quinn v. Hall, 77 S.W.3d 438, 447 (Tex.App.—Corpus Christi 2002, no pet.). "'[A]ssertions made by an individual, even under oath, are not the type of facts that are capable of accurate and ready determination by a source whose accuracy cannot reasonably be questioned.' Judicial notice applies only to facts which are beyond credible dispute."

Krishnan v. Ramirez, 42 S.W.3d 205, 222-23 (Tex. App.—Corpus Christi 2001, pet. denied). "Rule 201(b) allows a court to take judicial notice of a fact that is not subject to reasonable dispute. So long as a party provides proof of another court's records, a court can take judicial notice of another court's records."

Trimble v. Texas Dept. of Protective & Regulatory Servs., 981 S.W.2d 211, 215 (Tex.App.—Houston [14th Dist.] 1998, no pet.). "[A] trial court may take judicial notice of its own records in matters that are generally known, easily proven, and not reasonably disputed."

1.70 Acres v. State, 935 S.W.2d 480, 489 (Tex. App.—Beaumont 1996, no writ). "Although such variables as a vehicle's speed, road construction or repairs, weather, traffic, or accidents may be matters in someone's personal knowledge, they are not necessarily matters subject to judicial review. Personal knowledge is not judicial knowledge, and a judge may personally know a fact of which he cannot take judicial knowledge."

Tschirhart v. Tschirhart, 876 S.W.2d 507, 508 (Tex.App.—Austin 1994, no writ). "A court may not ... take judicial notice of the *truth* of allegations in its records."

Apostolic Ch. v. American Honda Motor Co., 833 S.W.2d 553, 555-56 (Tex.App.—Tyler 1992, writ denied). "Highway nomenclature and designations within the trial court's jurisdiction are matters of common knowledge and proper subjects for judicial notice. ... In matters involving geographical knowledge, it is not necessary that a formal request for judicial notice be made by a party."

TRE 202. DETERMINATION OF LAW OF OTHER STATES

A court upon its own motion may, or upon the motion of a party shall, take judicial notice of the constitutions, public statutes, rules, regulations, ordinances, court decisions, and common law of every other state, territory, or jurisdiction of the United States. A party requesting that judicial notice be taken of such matter shall furnish the court sufficient information to enable it properly to comply with the request, and shall give all parties such notice, if any, as the court may deem necessary, to enable all parties fairly to prepare to meet the request. A party is entitled upon timely request to an opportunity to be heard as to the propriety of taking judicial notice and the tenor of the matter noticed. In the absence of prior notification, the request may be made after judicial notice has been taken. Judicial notice of such matters may be taken at any stage of the proceeding. The court's determination shall be subject to review as a ruling on a question of law.

See ***Commentaries***, "Motion for Judicial Notice," ch. 5-L; Cochran, ***Texas Rules of Evidence Handbook***, p. 160 (2003).

History of TRE 202 (civil): Amended eff. Mar. 1, 1998, by order of Feb. 25, 1998 (960 S.W.2d [Tex.Cases] xxxv). Amended eff. Jan. 1, 1988, by order of Nov. 10, 1986 (733-34 S.W.2d [Tex.Cases] lxxxvi). Amended eff. Nov. 1, 1984, by order of June 25, 1984 (669-70 S.W.2d [Tex.Cases] xxxi): Language was added and deleted to make it clear that all parties are entitled to notice and hearing of the court's taking judicial notice of the law of other states; the last four sentences were added. Adopted eff. Sept. 1, 1983, by order of Nov. 23, 1982 (641-42 S.W.2d [Tex.Cases] xxxviii). Source: TRCP 184, 184a, TRCS art. 3731a (repealed). Former TRCP 184a, re judicial notice, was originally adopted eff. Feb. 1, 1946, by order of Oct. 10, 1945 (8 Tex.B.J. 533 [1945]).

Daugherty v. Southern P.T. Co., 772 S.W.2d 81, 83 (Tex.1989). "The failure to plead sister-state law does not preclude a court from judicially noticing that law. [TRE] 202 requires the moving party to furnish sufficient information to the trial court for it to determine the foreign law's applicability to the case and to furnish all parties any notice that the court finds necessary."

Pittsburgh Corning Corp. v. Walters, 1 S.W.3d 759, 769 (Tex.App.—Corpus Christi 1999, pet. denied). "The issue of a choice-of-law determination is distinct from the court's power to generally take judicial notice of a foreign state's law. [T]he mere fact that the court may take judicial notice of foreign laws does not mean that choice-of-law issues may be raised at any point in the proceeding. A preliminary motion is, therefore, necessary to assure the application of the laws of another jurisdiction. The court may undertake a choice of law analysis *sua sponte*, but [TRE] 202 does not compel this action."

TRE 203. DETERMINATION OF THE LAWS OF FOREIGN COUNTRIES

A party who intends to raise an issue concerning the law of a foreign country shall give notice in the pleadings or other reasonable written notice, and at least 30 days prior to the date of trial such party shall furnish all parties copies of any written materials or sources that the party intends to use as proof of the foreign law. If the materials or sources were originally written in a language other than English, the party intending to rely upon them shall furnish all parties both a copy of the foreign language text and an English translation. The court, in determining the law of a foreign nation, may consider any material or source, whether or not submitted by a party or admissible under the rules of evidence, including but not limited to affidavits, testimony, briefs, and treatises. If the court considers sources other than those submitted by a party, it shall give all parties notice and a reasonable opportunity to comment on the sources and to submit further materials for review by the court. The court, and not a jury, shall determine the laws of foreign countries. The court's determination shall be subject to review as a ruling on a question of law.

See ***Commentaries***, "Motion for Judicial Notice," ch. 5-L; Cochran, ***Texas Rules of Evidence Handbook***, p. 164 (2003).

History of TRE 203 (civil): Amended eff. Mar. 1, 1998, by order of Feb. 25, 1998 (960 S.W.2d [Tex.Cases] xxxvi). Amended eff. Nov. 1, 1984, by order of June 25, 1984 (669-70 S.W.2d [Tex.Cases] xxxii): The words "all parties" were substituted for "to the opposing party or counsel" in the first and second sentences; in the fourth sentence, "all" was substituted for "the"; in the last sentence, "The court's" was substituted for "It's"; and the words "on appeal" were deleted. Adopted eff. Sept. 1, 1983, by order of Nov. 23, 1982 (641-42 S.W.2d [Tex.Cases] xxxviii). Source: TRCS art. 3718; FRCP 44(a)(1), FRCrP 26(1).

Long Distance Int'l, Inc. v. Telefonos de Mexico, S.A., 49 S.W.3d 347, 351 (Tex.2001). "Rule 203 has been aptly characterized as a hybrid rule by which the presentation of the foreign law to the court resembles the presentment of evidence but which ultimately is decided as a question of law. Summary judgment is not precluded when experts disagree on the law's meaning if, as here, the parties do not dispute that all the pertinent foreign law was properly submitted in evidence. When experts disagree on how the foreign law applies to the facts, the court is presented with a question of law."

Exxon Corp. v. Breezevale Ltd., 82 S.W.3d 429, 437 (Tex.App.—Dallas 2002, pet. denied). Plaintiff "did not give notice and prove up Nigerian law in the trial court.... [P] told the court there was 'no need to invoke Nigerian law' and, consistent with that statement, did not submit any evidence of Nigerian law. [P] cannot now rely on Nigerian law to claim the conveyed interest was not an interest in real estate."

Reading & Bates Constr. Co. v. Baker Energy Res., 976 S.W.2d 702, 707 (Tex.App.—Houston [1st Dist.] 1998, pet. denied). TRE 203 "facilitates a trial court's determination of a particular law of a foreign country. Although it is contained within the article designated, 'Judicial Notice,' the rule itself does not refer to judicial notice. It sets forth the procedural mechanism for raising an issue concerning the law of a foreign country, for giving notice to the other parties, and for furnishing materials concerning the foreign law."

TRE 204. DETERMINATION OF TEXAS CITY & COUNTY ORDINANCES, THE CONTENTS OF THE TEXAS REGISTER, & THE RULES OF AGENCIES PUBLISHED IN THE ADMINISTRATIVE CODE

A court upon its own motion may, or upon the motion of a party shall, take judicial notice of the ordinances of municipalities and counties of Texas, of the contents of the Texas Register, and of the codified rules of the agencies published in the Administrative Code. Any party requesting that judicial notice be taken of such matter shall furnish the court sufficient information to enable it properly to comply with the request, and shall give all parties such notice, if any, as the court may deem necessary, to enable all parties fairly to prepare to meet the request. A party is entitled upon timely request to an opportunity to be heard as to the propriety of taking judicial notice and the tenor of the matter noticed. In the absence of prior notification, the request may be made after judicial notice has been taken. The court's determination shall be subject to review as a ruling on a question of law.

See ***Commentaries***, "Motion for Judicial Notice," ch. 5-L; Cochran, ***Texas Rules of Evidence Handbook***, p. 167 (2003).

History of TRE 204 (civil): Amended eff. Mar. 1, 1998, by order of Feb. 25, 1998 (960 S.W.2d [Tex.Cases] xxxvi). Amended eff. Jan. 1, 1988, by order of Nov. 10, 1986 (733-34 S.W.2d [Tex.Cases] lxxxvii): Judicial notice upon motion of a party is made mandatory rather than discretionary. Adopted eff. Nov. 1, 1984, by order of June 25, 1984 (669-70 S.W.2d [Tex.Cases] xxxii). Source: New rule.

Office of Pub. Util. Counsel v. PUC, 878 S.W.2d 598, 600 (Tex.1994). "The court of appeals ... erred by refusing to take judicial notice of the published order of the PUC. ... The authenticity and contents of the PUC ratemaking order are capable of accurate and ready determination by resort to a published record whose accuracy cannot reasonably be questioned."

Eckmann v. Des Rosiers, 940 S.W.2d 394, 399 (Tex. App.—Austin 1997, no writ). "[T]he duty [to take judicial notice is] mandatory, even in the absence of a request under [TRE] 204, respecting administrative agency regulations published in the Texas Register and Texas Administrative Code. ... They are legislative facts, or a part of the body of law a court is required to apply in reasoning toward a decision."

Fields v. City of Tex. City, 864 S.W.2d 66, 69 (Tex. App.—Houston [14th Dist.] 1993, writ denied). "[Ps] cite a portion of Article 21, §10 of the City Charter dealing with notice. Although [Ps] presented the same argument to the trial court, they did not ask the court to take judicial notice of §10. Instead, [Ds] have provided an unauthenticated copy of §10 and now ask this Court to take judicial notice of it. Courts may take judicial notice for the first time on appeal."

Metro Fuels, Inc. v. City of Austin, 827 S.W.2d 531, 532 (Tex.App.—Austin 1992, no writ). "Even if this Court were to take judicial notice of the ordinance [Ps] proffered, there is no showing that this is the version of the ordinance on which the district court rendered its judgment. To enable an appellate court to review a municipal or county ordinance, parties must both comply with the provisions of [TRE] 204 and make the ordinance a part of the trial-court record."

ARTICLE III. PRESUMPTIONS

[No rules adopted at this time.]

ARTICLE IV. RELEVANCY & ITS LIMITS

TRE 401. DEFINITION OF "RELEVANT EVIDENCE"

"Relevant evidence" means evidence having any tendency to make the existence of any fact that is of consequence to the determination of the action more probable or less probable than it would be without the evidence.

See Cochran, ***Texas Rules of Evidence Handbook***, p. 203 (2003).

History of TRE 401 (civil): Amended eff. Mar. 1, 1998, by order of Feb. 25, 1998 (960 S.W.2d [Tex.Cases] xxxvii). Amended eff. Nov. 1, 1984, by order of June 25, 1984 (669-70 S.W.2d [Tex.Cases] xxxiii): Title and entire rule were changed. Adopted eff. Sept. 1, 1983, by order of Nov. 23, 1982 (641-42 S.W.2d [Tex.Cases] xxxix). Source: FRE 401.

E.I. du Pont de Nemours & Co. v. Robinson, 923 S.W.2d 549, 556 (Tex.1995). "[T]o constitute scientific knowledge which will assist the trier of fact, the proposed [scientific] testimony must be relevant and reliable. [¶] The requirement that the proposed testimony be relevant incorporates traditional relevancy analysis under [TRE] 401 and 402.... To be relevant, the proposed testimony must be 'sufficiently tied to the facts of the case that it will aid the jury in resolving a factual dispute.'"

Transportation Ins. Co. v. Moriel, 879 S.W.2d 10, 24-25 (Tex.1994). "Simply because a piece or pieces of evidence are *material* in the sense that they make a 'fact that is of consequence to the determination of the action more ... or less probable' does not render the evidence *legally sufficient*. As Professor McCormick succinctly put it, 'a brick is not a wall.'"

Castillo v. State, 939 S.W.2d 754, 758 (Tex.App.—Houston [14th Dist.] 1997, writ ref'd). "The evidence need not prove or disprove a particular fact; the evidence is sufficiently relevant if it provides 'a small nudge' towards proving or disproving any fact of consequence. Furthermore, '[t]he motives which operate upon the mind of a witness when he testifies are never regarded as immaterial or collateral matters.'"

TRE 402. RELEVANT EVIDENCE GENERALLY ADMISSIBLE; IRRELEVANT EVIDENCE INADMISSIBLE

All relevant evidence is admissible, except as otherwise provided by Constitution, by statute, by these rules, or by other rules prescribed pursuant to statutory authority. Evidence which is not relevant is inadmissible.

See ***Commentaries***, "Objecting to Evidence," ch. 8-D; Cochran, ***Texas Rules of Evidence Handbook***, p. 203 (2003).

History of TRE 402 (civil): Amended eff. Mar. 1, 1998, by order of Feb. 25, 1998 (960 S.W.2d [Tex.Cases] xxxvii). Adopted eff. Sept. 1, 1983, by order of Nov. 23, 1982 (641-42 S.W.2d [Tex.Cases] xxxix). Source: FRE 402.

E.I. du Pont de Nemours & Co. v. Robinson, 923 S.W.2d 549, 556 (Tex.1995). "Evidence that has no relationship to any of the issues in the case is irrelevant and does not satisfy [TRE] 702's requirement that the testimony be of assistance to the jury. It is thus inadmissible under [TRE] 702 as well as under [TRE] 401 and 402."

Lunsford v. Morris, 746 S.W.2d 471, 473 (Tex. 1988). The rules of evidence do not "contemplate exclusion of otherwise relevant proof unless the evidence proffered is unfairly prejudicial, privileged, incompetent, or otherwise *legally* inadmissible."

Jampole v. Touchy, 673 S.W.2d 569, 573 (Tex. 1984), *overruled on other grounds*, ***Walker v. Packer***, 827 S.W.2d 833 (Tex.1992). "To increase the likelihood that all relevant evidence will be disclosed and brought before the trier of fact, the law circumscribes a significantly larger class of discoverable evidence [than admissible evidence] to include anything reasonably calculated to lead to the discovery of material evidence."

TRE 403. EXCLUSION OF RELEVANT EVIDENCE ON SPECIAL GROUNDS

Although relevant, evidence may be excluded if its probative value is substantially outweighed by the danger of unfair prejudice, confusion of the issues, or misleading the jury, or by considerations of undue delay, or needless presentation of cumulative evidence.

See *Commentaries,* "Objecting to Evidence," ch. 8-D; Cochran, *Texas Rules of Evidence Handbook*, p. 221 (2003).

History of TRE 403 (civil): Amended eff. Mar. 1, 1998, by order of Feb. 25, 1998 (960 S.W.2d [Tex.Cases] xxxvii). Adopted eff. Sept. 1, 1983, by order of Nov. 23, 1982 (641-42 S.W.2d [Tex.Cases] xxxix). Source: FRE 403.

Owens-Corning Fiberglas Corp. v. Malone, 972 S.W.2d 35, 41 (Tex.1998). "Evidence that is not relevant, or is unduly prejudicial, and thus, not admissible to mitigate punitive damages, includes actual damage amounts paid by settlements or by judgments; the number of pending claims filed against a [D] for the same conduct; the number of anticipated claims for the same conduct; insurance coverage; unpaid punitive damages awards for the same course of conduct; and evidence of punitive damages that may be levied in the future."

Ford Motor Co. v. Miles, 967 S.W.2d 377, 389 (Tex. 1998). "[R]elevant photographic evidence is admissible unless it is merely calculated to arouse the sympathy, prejudice or passion [of] the jury where the photographs do not serve to illustrate disputed issues or aid the jury in understanding the case. The videos were calculated to arouse the sympathy and passions of the jury." (Internal quotes omitted.)

In re N.R.C., 94 S.W.3d 799, 807 (Tex.App.—Houston [14th Dist.] 2002, pet. denied). The TREs "discourage 'needless presentation of cumulative evidence,' not cumulativeness in and of itself. The mere fact that another witness may have given the same or substantially the same testimony is not the decisive factor. Rather, we consider whether the excluded testimony would have added substantial weight to the complainant's case."

Pittsburgh Corning Corp. v. Walters, 1 S.W.3d 759, 772 (Tex.App.—Corpus Christi 1999, pet. denied). "The fact that evidence has some prejudicial effect is insufficient to warrant its exclusion. Instead, there must be a demonstration that introduction of the evidence would be *unfairly* prejudicial to the objecting party."

Boswell v. Brazos Elec. Power Coop., 910 S.W.2d 593, 602 n.3 (Tex.App.—Fort Worth 1995, pet. denied). "In making its determination under [TRE] 403, the trial court must: (i) identify the probative value of the proffered evidence; (ii) identify the costs of admitting the evidence; and (iii) weigh one against the other."

TRE 404. CHARACTER EVIDENCE NOT ADMISSIBLE TO PROVE CONDUCT; EXCEPTIONS; OTHER CRIMES

(a) Character Evidence Generally. Evidence of a person's character or character trait is not admissible for the purpose of proving action in conformity therewith on a particular occasion, except:

(1) *Character of accused.* Evidence of a pertinent character trait offered:

(A) by an accused in a criminal case, or by the prosecution to rebut the same, or

(B) by a party accused in a civil case of conduct involving moral turpitude, or by the accusing party to rebut the same;

(2) *Character of victim.* In a criminal case and subject to Rule 412, evidence of a pertinent character trait of the victim of the crime offered by an accused, or by the prosecution to rebut the same, or evidence of peaceable character of the victim offered by the prosecution in a homicide case to rebut evidence that the victim was the first aggressor; or in a civil case, evidence of character for violence of the alleged victim of assaultive conduct offered on the issue of self-defense by a party accused of the assaultive conduct, or evidence of peaceable character to rebut the same;

(3) *Character of witness.* Evidence of the character of a witness, as provided in rules 607, 608 and 609.

(b) Other Crimes, Wrongs or Acts. Evidence of other crimes, wrongs or acts is not admissible to prove the character of a person in order to show action in conformity therewith. It may, however, be admissible for other purposes, such as proof of motive, opportunity, intent, preparation, plan, knowledge, identity, or absence of mistake or accident, provided that upon timely request by the accused in a criminal case, reasonable notice is given in advance of trial of intent to introduce in the State's case-in-chief such evidence other than that arising in the same transaction.

See *Commentaries*, "Motion in Limine," ch. 5-E; Cochran, *Texas Rules of Evidence Handbook*, p. 254 (2003).

History of TRE 404 (civil): Amended eff. Mar. 1, 1998, by order of Feb. 25, 1998 (960 S.W.2d [Tex.Cases] xxxvii). Adopted eff. Sept. 1, 1983, by order of Nov. 23, 1982 (641-42 S.W.2d [Tex.Cases] xxxix). Source: FRE 404.

State Bar v. Evans, 774 S.W.2d 656, 658 (Tex. 1989). "Since [the attorney] was accused of conduct involving moral turpitude, he was allowed to offer evidence of a pertinent trait of his character, which he did; the State Bar was then allowed to offer rebuttal testimony, which it did."

In re M.R., 975 S.W.2d 51, 55 (Tex.App.—San Antonio 1998, pet. denied). "Rule 404(b) ... allows evidence of 'other' wrongs or acts to be admitted when they are not admitted to prove character in order to show that that person acted in conformity with the prior conduct. Here, the Family Code mandates that such evidence be admitted for another purpose—in order to establish what is in the best interest of the child. [The mother] was not trying to prove that [the father] committed acts in conformity with a prior act of violence. Instead, she was trying to establish that [his] violent act made it less in the best interest of the child that he be named sole managing conservator."

Bexar Cty. Appr. Review Bd. v. First Baptist Ch., 846 S.W.2d 554, 562 (Tex.App.—San Antonio 1993, writ denied). "[T]he court ... allowed the church to elicit ... testimony about several of [the company's] charitable works. [¶] No one contends that [the company's] character was an issue.... The church argues that it is 'just good lawyering' to humanize and personalize a corporate entity. ... Under such a system, trials would turn into contests about which party has the better charitable record. [T]he rules strictly limit the admissibility of evidence of good or bad character."

TRE 405. METHODS OF PROVING CHARACTER

(a) Reputation or Opinion. In all cases in which evidence of a person's character or character trait is admissible, proof may be made by testimony as to reputation or by testimony in the form of an opinion. In a criminal case, to be qualified to testify at the guilt stage of trial concerning the character or character trait of an accused, a witness must have been familiar with the reputation, or with the underlying facts or information upon which the opinion is based, prior to the day of the offense. In all cases where testimony is admitted under this rule, on cross-examination inquiry is allowable into relevant specific instances of conduct.

(b) Specific Instances of Conduct. In cases in which a person's character or character trait is an essential element of a charge, claim or defense, proof may also be made of specific instances of that person's conduct.

See *Commentaries*, "Motion in Limine," ch. 5-E; Cochran, *Texas Rules of Evidence Handbook*, p. 255 (2003).

History of TRE 405 (civil): Amended eff. Mar. 1, 1998, by order of Feb. 25, 1998 (960 S.W.2d [Tex.Cases] xxxviii). Adopted eff. Sept. 1, 1983, by order of Nov. 23, 1982 (641-42 S.W.2d [Tex.Cases] xl). Source: FRE 405.

In re G.M.P., 909 S.W.2d 198, 209 (Tex.App.—Houston [14th Dist.] 1995, no writ). "[W]hen a witness testifies as to the character of the accused, [TRE] 405(a) allows 'do you know' questions to be asked of the witness to test the basis for his personal opinion. Here, by making the statement 'My son wouldn't do that,' [the father of D] became a character witness, espousing his opinion about [D's] propensity to commit the crime."

International Sec. Life Ins. Co. v. Melancon, 463 S.W.2d 762, 767 (Tex.App.—Beaumont 1971, writ ref'd n.r.e.). In interrogating a witness on the subject of reputation, the only proper questions to ask are: "'Whether he knows the general character or reputation of the witness intended to be impeached in point of truth among his neighbors? If so, then what that character is, whether good or bad? We think the proper practice should be, that, after the impeaching witness has, prima facie, thus first qualified himself to speak of the general reputation of the other witness, ... then, before he answers the question as to what that reputation is, the opposite party, if he demands it, should have the right to cross-examine as to his means of knowledge....'"

TRE 406. HABIT; ROUTINE PRACTICE

Evidence of the habit of a person or of the routine practice of an organization, whether corroborated or not and regardless of the presence of eyewitnesses, is relevant to prove that the conduct of the person or organization on a particular occasion was in conformity with the habit or routine practice.

See Cochran, *Texas Rules of Evidence Handbook*, p. 310 (2003).

History of TRE 406 (civil): Amended eff. Mar. 1, 1998, by order of Feb. 25, 1998 (960 S.W.2d [Tex.Cases] xxxviii). Adopted eff. Sept. 1, 1983, by order of Nov. 23, 1982 (641-42 S.W.2d [Tex.Cases] xl). Source: FRE 406.

Acker v. Water Comm'n, 790 S.W.2d 299, 302 (Tex.1990). Both water commissioners who had been accused of holding an ex parte meeting in the restroom "testified by affidavit that they had no recollection of any conversation outside the hearing, and that considering their past behavior and habit at the Texas Water Commission, the occurrence of such a conversation was highly unlikely. The habit or custom of a person doing a particular act is relevant in determining his conduct on the occasion in question."

Oakwood Mobile Homes v. Cabler, 73 S.W.3d 363, 375 (Tex.App.—El Paso 2002, pet. denied). "For testimony of the routine practice of an organization to be admissible, it must show a regular response to a repeated specific situation."

McClure v. Landis, 959 S.W.2d 679, 681 (Tex. App.—Austin 1997, pet. denied). "The two instances suggested by [D about P's conduct] do not establish a habit or pattern and have, therefore, no probative force whatever as contradicting the testimony and affidavits supplied by [P]."

TRE 407. SUBSEQUENT REMEDIAL MEASURES; NOTIFICATION OF DEFECT

03 **(a) Subsequent Remedial Measures.** When, after an injury or harm allegedly caused by an event, measures are taken that, if taken previously, would have made the injury or harm less likely to occur, evidence of the subsequent remedial measures is not admissible to prove negligence, culpable conduct, a defect in a product, a defect in a product's design, or a need for a warning or instruction. This rule does not require the exclusion of evidence of subsequent remedial measures when offered for another purpose, such as proving ownership, control, or feasibility of precautionary measures, if controverted, or impeachment.

(b) Notification of Defect. A written notification by a manufacturer of any defect in a product produced by such manufacturer to purchasers thereof is admissible against the manufacturer on the issue of existence of the defect to the extent that it is relevant.

See *Commentaries*, "Motion in Limine," ch. 5-E; Cochran, ***Texas Rules of Evidence Handbook***, p. 318 (2003).

History of TRE 407 (civil): Amended eff. July 1, 2003, by order of Aug. 29, 2003 (114-15 S.W.3d [Tex.Cases] xxii). Amended eff. Mar. 1, 1998, by order of Feb. 25, 1998 (960 S.W.2d [Tex.Cases] xxxix). Adopted eff. Sept. 1, 1983, by order of Nov. 23, 1982 (641-42 S.W.2d [Tex.Cases] xl). Source: FRE 407.

Beavers v. Northrop Worldwide Aircraft Servs., 821 S.W.2d 669, 677 (Tex.App.—Amarillo 1991, writ denied). "[W]e hold the exclusion under [TRE] 407(a) does not apply to evidence of subsequent remedial measures taken by third parties when offered to show that a [D] was not the cause of [P's] injury."

E.V.R. II Assocs. v. Brundige, 813 S.W.2d 552, 556 (Tex.App.—Dallas 1991, no writ). "Evidence of subsequent remedial repair is inadmissible to establish negligence. The rule is one of policy and good sense to avoid discouraging safety measures. [T]he rule is inapplicable where the evidence would be valid as to other issues which also exist in the case."

TRE 408. COMPROMISE & OFFERS TO COMPROMISE

Evidence of (1) furnishing or offering or promising to furnish or (2) accepting or offering or promising to accept, a valuable consideration in compromising or attempting to compromise a claim which was disputed as to either validity or amount is not admissible to prove liability for or invalidity of the claim or its amount. Evidence of conduct or statements made in compromise negotiations is likewise not admissible. This rule does not require the exclusion of any evidence otherwise discoverable merely because it is presented in the course of compromise negotiations. This rule also does not require exclusion when the evidence is offered for another purpose, such as proving bias or prejudice or interest of a witness or a party, negativing a contention of undue delay, or proving an effort to obstruct a criminal investigation or prosecution.

See *Commentaries*, "Motion in Limine," ch. 5-E; Cochran, ***Texas Rules of Evidence Handbook***, p. 328 (2003).

History of TRE 408 (civil): Amended eff. Mar. 1, 1998, by order of Feb. 25, 1998 (960 S.W.2d [Tex.Cases] xxxix). Adopted eff. Sept. 1, 1983, by order of Nov. 23, 1982 (641-42 S.W.2d [Tex.Cases] xl). Source: FRE 408.

Ford Motor Co. v. Leggat, 904 S.W.2d 643, 649 (Tex. 1995). "Settlement agreements are discoverable to the extent they are relevant. Settlement agreements ... are not admissible at trial to prove liability." *See also* ***Birchfield v. Texarkana Mem. Hosp.***, 747 S.W.2d 361, 365 (Tex.1987).

Avary v. Bank of Am., 72 S.W.3d 779, 799 (Tex. App.—Dallas 2002, pet. denied). "[E]vidence of an offer to compromise is admissible to prove or disprove the extracontractual liability of an insurance company on a bad faith claim, even against the party making the offer.... [¶] Rule 408 does not prevent a party from proving a separate cause of action simply because some of the acts complained of took place during compromise negotiations."

Stam v. Mack, 984 S.W.2d 747, 752 (Tex.App.—Texarkana 1999, no pet.). "Settlement agreements may be admissible ... if offered for other purposes, such as proving bias or prejudice. ... These agreements are admissible to show the true alignment of the parties."

Tarrant Cty. v. English, 989 S.W.2d 368, 377 (Tex. App.—Fort Worth 1998, pet. denied). "The [TREs] prohibit the admission of settlement negotiations to prove a party's liability. But evidence of settlement negotiations may be admitted for other purposes, such as establishing that statements made during the negotiations were misrepresentations. In this case, the trial court admitted the letter for the limited purpose of showing [P's] state of mind."

TRE 409. PAYMENT OF MEDICAL & SIMILAR EXPENSES

Evidence of furnishing or offering or promising to pay medical, hospital, or similar expenses occasioned by an injury is not admissible to prove liability for the injury.

See ***Commentaries***, "Motion in Limine," ch. 5-E; Cochran, ***Texas Rules of Evidence Handbook***, p. 351 (2003).

History of TRE 409 (civil): Amended eff. Mar. 1, 1998, by order of Feb. 25, 1998 (960 S.W.2d [Tex.Cases] xxxix). Adopted eff. Sept. 1, 1983, by order of Nov. 23, 1982 (641-42 S.W.2d [Tex.Cases] xli). Source: FRE 409.

Port Neches ISD v. Soignier, 702 S.W.2d 756, 757 (Tex.App.—Beaumont 1986, writ ref'd n.r.e.). A letter from an insurance company authorizing medical expenses for a workers' compensation plaintiff and stating that all future medical bills should be sent to the insurance company goes beyond TRE 409 and actually admits coverage, and thus is admissible.

TRE 410. INADMISSIBILITY OF PLEAS, PLEA DISCUSSIONS & RELATED STATEMENTS

Except as otherwise provided in this rule, evidence of the following is not admissible against the defendant who made the plea or was a participant in the plea discussions:

(1) a plea of guilty that was later withdrawn;

(2) in civil cases, a plea of *nolo contendere*, and in criminal cases, a plea of *nolo contendere* that was later withdrawn;

(3) any statement made in the course of any proceedings under Rule 11 of the Federal Rules of Criminal Procedure or comparable state procedure regarding, in a civil case, either a plea of guilty that was later withdrawn or a plea of *nolo contendere*, or in a criminal case, either a plea of guilty that was later withdrawn or a plea of *nolo contendere* that was later withdrawn; or

(4) any statement made in the course of plea discussions with an attorney for the prosecuting authority, in a civil case, that do not result in a plea of guilty or that result in a plea of guilty later withdrawn, or in a criminal case, that do not result in a plea of guilty or a plea of *nolo contendere* or that results in a plea, later withdrawn, of guilty or *nolo contendere.*

However, such a statement is admissible in any proceeding wherein another statement made in the course of the same plea or plea discussions has been introduced and the statement ought in fairness be considered contemporaneously with it.

See ***Commentaries***, "Motion in Limine," ch. 5-E; Cochran, ***Texas Rules of Evidence Handbook***, p. 355 (2003).

History of TRE 410 (civil): Amended eff. Mar. 1, 1998, by order of Feb. 25, 1998 (960 S.W.2d [Tex.Cases] xxxix). Adopted eff. Sept. 1, 1983, by order of Nov. 23, 1982 (641-42 S.W.2d [Tex.Cases] xli). Source: FRE 410.

Cox v. Bohman, 683 S.W.2d 757, 758 (Tex.App.—Corpus Christi 1984, writ ref'd n.r.e.). "Unless a plea of guilty to a traffic offense was made in open court ... evidence of such guilty plea is not admissible in a civil suit for damages arising out of negligence giving rise to the charge. ... A plea of *nolo contendere* to a traffic violation cannot be admitted into evidence in a civil suit for damages arising out of the same incident."

TRE 411. LIABILITY INSURANCE

Evidence that a person was or was not insured against liability is not admissible upon the issue whether the person acted negligently or otherwise wrongfully. This rule does not require the exclusion of evidence of insurance against liability when offered for another issue, such as proof of agency, ownership, or control, if disputed, or bias or prejudice of a witness.

See Cochran, ***Texas Rules of Evidence Handbook***, p. 369 (2003).

History of TRE 411 (civil): Amended eff. Mar. 1, 1998, by order of Feb. 25, 1998 (960 S.W.2d [Tex.Cases] xl). Adopted eff. Sept. 1, 1983, by order of Nov. 23, 1982 (641-42 S.W.2d [Tex.Cases] xli). Source: FRE 411.

Brownsville Pediatric Ass'n v. Reyes, 68 S.W.3d 184, 193 (Tex.App.—Corpus Christi 2002, no pet.). Defendants "objected to the mention of insurance in the context of an insurance company issuing an annuity. The reference to insurance in this instance is not the type of injection of insurance into a case that is protected by [TRE 411]. Thus, the harm the rule was designed to prevent does not come into play."

Thornhill v. Ronnie's I-45 Truck Stop, 944 S.W.2d 780, 794 (Tex.App.—Beaumont 1997, writ dism'd). TRE 411 "only prohibits the admission of 'liability insurance,' not 'property insurance.' [¶] [TRE] 411 only prohibits the admission of evidence that a person was or was not insured against liability upon the issue of whether he acted negligently or otherwise wrongfully."

Beall v. Ditmore, 867 S.W.2d 791, 795 (Tex.App.—El Paso 1993, writ denied). "The mere mention of insurance during trial before a jury, though erroneous, does not result in an automatic mistrial or reversal."

TRE 412. EVIDENCE OF PREVIOUS SEXUAL CONDUCT IN CRIMINAL CASES

(a) Reputation or Opinion Evidence. In a prosecution for sexual assault or aggravated sexual assault, or attempt to commit sexual assault or aggravated sexual assault, reputation or opinion evidence of the past sexual behavior of an alleged victim of such crime is not admissible.

(b) Evidence of Specific Instances. In a prosecution for sexual assault or aggravated sexual assault, or attempt to commit sexual assault or aggravated sexual assault, evidence of specific instances of an alleged victim's past sexual behavior is also not admissible, unless:

(1) such evidence is admitted in accordance with paragraphs (c) and (d) of this rule;

(2) it is evidence:

(A) that is necessary to rebut or explain scientific or medical evidence offered by the State;

(B) of past sexual behavior with the accused and is offered by the accused upon the issue of whether the alleged victim consented to the sexual behavior which is the basis of the offense charged;

(C) that relates to the motive or bias of the alleged victim;

(D) is admissible under Rule 609; or

(E) that is constitutionally required to be admitted; and

(3) its probative value outweighs the danger of unfair prejudice.

(c) Procedure for Offering Evidence. If the defendant proposes to introduce any documentary evidence or to ask any question, either by direct examination or cross-examination of any witness, concerning specific instances of the alleged victim's past sexual behavior, the defendant must inform the court out of the hearing of the jury prior to introducing any such evidence or asking any such question. After this notice, the court shall conduct an in camera hearing, recorded by the court reporter, to determine whether the proposed evidence is admissible under paragraph (b) of this rule. The court shall determine what evidence is admissible and shall accordingly limit the questioning. The defendant shall not go outside these limits or refer to any evidence ruled inadmissible in camera without prior approval of the court without the presence of the jury.

(d) Record Sealed. The court shall seal the record of the in camera hearing required in paragraph (c) of this rule for delivery to the appellate court in the event of an appeal.

(e) Sexual Conduct of Child as Defense.* This rule does not limit the right of the accused to produce evidence of promiscuous sexual conduct of a child 14 years old or older as a defense to sexual assault, aggravated sexual assault, indecency with a child or an attempt to commit any of the foregoing crimes. If such evidence is admitted, the court shall instruct the jury as to the purpose of the evidence and as to its limited use.

* Editor's note: Former TRCrE 412(e), now TRE 412(e), was disapproved by the Texas Legislature in Acts 1993, 73rd Leg., ch. 900, §1.17 (eff. Sept. 1, 1994). *See* Gov't Code §22.109(b) (authority to disapprove rules of evidence in criminal cases).

See Cochran, ***Texas Rules of Evidence Handbook***, p. 377 (2003).

History of TRE 412 (criminal): Amended eff. Mar. 1, 1998, by order of Feb. 25, 1998 (960 S.W.2d [Tex.Cases] xl). Adopted eff. Sept. 1, 1986 by order of Dec. 18, 1985 (701-02 S.W.2d [Tex.Cases] xxxix).

In re Doe, 22 S.W.3d 601, 611-12 (Tex.App.—Austin 2000, orig. proceeding). "[P] argues that the 'rape victims shield laws,' incorporated in [TRE] 412, should apply despite the fact that the Rule specifically applies only in criminal cases. [¶] At this early stage of the litigation and considering the fact that [P] pleads that this was a forcible assault and the grand jury indicted [D's employee] under the criminal statutes for the crime of sexual assault, we hold that until the record is more fully developed and these issues are clarified the rape shield laws ought to protect the victim … at this time. We hold that the trial court abused its discretion by failing to issue a protective order preventing [D] from questioning [P] about her past and present sexual activity."

ARTICLE V. PRIVILEGES

TRE 501. PRIVILEGES RECOGNIZED ONLY AS PROVIDED

Except as otherwise provided by Constitution, by statute, by these rules, or by other rules prescribed pursuant to statutory authority, no person has a privilege to:

(1) refuse to be a witness;

(2) refuse to disclose any matter;

(3) refuse to produce any object or writing; or

(4) prevent another from being a witness or disclosing any matter or producing any object or writing.

See *Commentaries*, "Scope of Discovery," ch. 6-B; Cochran, *Texas Rules of Evidence Handbook*, p. 393 (2003).

History of TRE 501 (civil): Amended eff. Mar. 1, 1998, by order of Feb. 25, 1998 (960 S.W.2d [Tex.Cases] xli). Adopted eff. Sept. 1, 1983, by order of Nov. 23, 1982 (641-42 S.W.2d [Tex.Cases] xli). Source: Unif. R. Evid. 501 (1974). See TRCS arts. 41a-1, §26 (repealed); 3715 (repealed); 3715a (repealed); 4495b, §5.08 (repealed); 5561h (repealed). See also Tex. Code Crim.P. arts. 38.10, 38.11 (repealed).

Volkswagen, A.G. v. Valdez, 909 S.W.2d 900, 902-03 (Tex.1995). The trial court must weigh the following factors when evaluating a privilege of a foreign county: (1) the importance of the discovery request to the investigation or litigation; (2) the degree of specificity of the request; (3) whether the information originated in the U.S.; (4) the availability of alternative means of securing the information; and (5) the extent to which noncompliance with the request would undermine important interests of the U.S., or the extent to which compliance would undermine important interests of the foreign jurisdiction where the information is located.

State v. Lowry, 802 S.W.2d 669, 671 (Tex.1991). "Only in certain narrow circumstances is it appropriate to obstruct the search for truth by denying discovery. Very limited exceptions to the strongly preferred policy of openness are recognized in our state procedural rules and statutes."

Oyster Creek Fin. Corp. v. Richwood Invs., 957 S.W.2d 640, 646 (Tex.App.—Amarillo 1997, pet. denied). "[B]ecause evidence is presumed discoverable, the party resisting discovery … bears the burden of establishing the privilege and, therefore, must plead it and present evidence which establishes that the document(s) in question qualify for the privilege as a matter of law."

TRE 502. REQUIRED REPORTS PRIVILEGED BY STATUTE

A person, corporation, association, or other organization or entity, either public or private, making a return or report required by law to be made has a privilege to refuse to disclose and to prevent any other person from disclosing the return or report, if the law requiring it to be made so provides. A public officer or agency to whom a return or report is required by law to be made has a privilege to refuse to disclose the return or report if the law requiring it to be made so provides. No privilege exists under this rule in actions involving perjury, false statements, fraud in the return or report, or other failure to comply with the law in question.

See *Commentaries*, "Scope of Discovery," ch. 6-B; Cochran, *Texas Rules of Evidence Handbook*, p. 397 (2003).

History of TRE 502 (civil): Amended eff. Mar. 1, 1998, by order of Feb. 25, 1998 (960 S.W.2d [Tex.Cases] xlii). Adopted eff. Sept. 1, 1983, by order of Nov. 23, 1982 (641-42 S.W.2d [Tex.Cases] xlii). Source: New rule. See proposed FRE 502 (1972).

Star-Telegram, Inc. v. Schattman, 784 S.W.2d 109, 111 (Tex.App.—Fort Worth 1990, no writ). TRE 502 "only protects reports 'required by law to be made' if the law requiring the report to be made makes such report privileged. Reports are not required under the EEOC sexual harassment guidelines … and certainly are not made privileged…. Rule 502 thus provides no privilege here."

TRE 503. LAWYER-CLIENT PRIVILEGE

(a) Definitions. As used in this rule:

(1) A "client" is a person, public officer, or corporation, association, or other organization or entity, either public or private, who is rendered professional legal services by a lawyer, or who consults a lawyer with a view to obtaining professional legal services from that lawyer.

(2) A "representative of the client" is:

(A) a person having authority to obtain professional legal services, or to act on advice thereby rendered, on behalf of the client, or

(B) any other person who, for the purpose of effectuating legal representation for the client, makes or receives a confidential communication while acting in the scope of employment for the client.

(3) A "lawyer" is a person authorized, or reasonably believed by the client to be authorized, to engage in the practice of law in any state or nation.

(4) A "representative of the lawyer" is:

(A) one employed by the lawyer to assist the lawyer in the rendition of professional legal services; or

(B) an accountant who is reasonably necessary for the lawyer's rendition of professional legal services.

(5) A communication is "confidential" if not intended to be disclosed to third persons other than those to whom disclosure is made in furtherance of the rendition of professional legal services to the client or those reasonably necessary for the transmission of the communication.

(b) Rules of Privilege.

(1) *General rule of privilege.* A client has a privilege to refuse to disclose and to prevent any other person from disclosing confidential communications made for the purpose of facilitating the rendition of professional legal services to the client:

(A) between the client or a representative of the client and the client's lawyer or a representative of the lawyer;

(B) between the lawyer and the lawyer's representative;

(C) by the client or a representative of the client, or the client's lawyer or a representative of the lawyer, to a lawyer or a representative of a lawyer representing another party in a pending action and concerning a matter of common interest therein;

(D) between representatives of the client or between the client and a representative of the client; or

(E) among lawyers and their representatives representing the same client.

(2) *Special rule of privilege in criminal cases.* In criminal cases, a client has a privilege to prevent the lawyer or lawyer's representative from disclosing any other fact which came to the knowledge of the lawyer or the lawyer's representative by reason of the attorney-client relationship.

(c) Who May Claim the Privilege. The privilege may be claimed by the client, the client's guardian or conservator, the personal representative of a deceased client, or the successor, trustee, or similar representative of a corporation, association, or other organization, whether or not in existence. The person who was the lawyer or the lawyer's representative at the time of the communication is presumed to have authority to claim the privilege but only on behalf of the client.

(d) Exceptions. There is no privilege under this rule:

(1) *Furtherance of crime or fraud.* If the services of the lawyer were sought or obtained to enable or aid anyone to commit or plan to commit what the client knew or reasonably should have known to be a crime or fraud;

(2) *Claimants through same deceased client.* As to a communication relevant to an issue between parties who claim through the same deceased client, regardless of whether the claims are by testate or intestate succession or by inter vivos transactions;

(3) *Breach of duty by a lawyer or client.* As to a communication relevant to an issue of breach of duty by a lawyer to the client or by a client to the lawyer;

(4) *Document attested by a lawyer.* As to a communication relevant to an issue concerning an attested document to which the lawyer is an attesting witness; or

(5) *Joint clients.* As to a communication relevant to a matter of common interest between or among two or more clients if the communication was made by any of them to a lawyer retained or consulted in common, when offered in an action between or among any of the clients.

Comment to 1998 change: The addition of subsection (a)(2)(B) adopts a subject matter test for the privilege of an entity, in place of the control group test previously used. See *National Tank Co. v. Brotherton*, 851 S.W.2d 193, 197-98 (Tex.1993).

See ***Commentaries***, "Scope of Discovery," ch. 6-B; Cochran, ***Texas Rules of Evidence Handbook***, p. 399 (2003).

History of TRE 503 (civil): Amended eff. Mar. 1, 1998, by order of Feb. 25, 1998 (960 S.W.2d [Tex.Cases] xlii). Amended eff. Nov. 1, 1984, by order of June 25, 1984 (669-70 S.W.2d [Tex.Cases] xxxiii): Changed (a)(4); deleted (d); relettered (e) as (d); the language of former par. (d) was deleted because it was deemed unnecessary; the deletion was not intended to change the common law rule that communications privileged under this rule do not lose their privileged status by reason of the termination of the lawyer/client relationship; this rule governs only the lawyer/client privilege; it does not restrict the scope of the work product doctrine. See former TRCP 166b. Adopted eff. Sept. 1, 1983, by order of Nov. 23, 1982 (641-42 S.W.2d [Tex.Cases] xlii). Source: Codification of common law doctrine. See proposed FRE 503 (1972); Tex. Code Crim.P. art. 38.10 (repealed).

General

Duncan v. Board of Disciplinary Appeals, 898 S.W.2d 759, 762 (Tex.1995). "Our rules recognize that our system of justice relies on a client's privilege to speak frankly and candidly with his or her attorney."

In re Skiles, 102 S.W.3d 323, 327 (Tex.App.—Beaumont 2003, orig. proceeding) "A movant seeking to disqualify counsel based on an assertion of the joint defense privilege must show 1) that confidential information has been shared and 2) that the matter in which that information was shared is substantially related to the matter in which disqualification is sought."

Watson v. Kaminski, 51 S.W.3d 825, 827 (Tex. App.—Houston [1st Dist.] 2001, no pet.). "To be privileged, the communication must relate to pending or proposed litigation and must further the attorney's representation. [¶] The judge must consider the entire communication in its context and must extend the privilege to any statement that bears some relation to an existing or proposed judicial proceeding. All doubt should be resolved in favor of the communication's relation to the proceeding."

Boales v. Brighton Builders, Inc., 29 S.W.3d 159, 168 (Tex.App.—Houston [14th Dist.] 2000, pet. denied). "The [attorney-client] privilege extends to all matters concerning litigation or business transactions, regardless of whether the matters are pertinent to the matter for which the attorney was employed. The statements and advice of the attorney to the client are as protected as the communications of the client to the attorney."

Markowski v. City of Marlin, 940 S.W.2d 720, 726 (Tex.App.—Waco 1997, writ denied). "[A] governmental body has as much right as an individual to consult with its attorney without risking the disclosure of important confidential information."

Perez v. Kirk & Carrigan, 822 S.W.2d 261, 265 (Tex. App.—Corpus Christi 1991, writ denied). "An agreement to form an attorney-client relationship may be implied from the conduct of the parties. Moreover, the relationship does not depend upon the payment of a fee, but may exist as a result of rendering services gratuitously."

No Attorney-Client Privilege

In re Ford Motor Co., 988 S.W.2d 714, 719 (Tex. 1998). "The [Ps] assert that [the attorney-client] privilege extends to an insured's communication to its liability insurer concerning an incident possibly giving rise to liability covered by the policy, and, thus, protects communications by [P] contained in the claim file. However, at the time [P] made her statements, there was no attorney-client relationship between [P] and [her insurer]."

Huie v. DeShazo, 922 S.W.2d 920, 921 (Tex.1996). "The issue ... is whether the attorney-client privilege protects communications between a trustee and his or her attorney relating to trust administration from discovery by a trust beneficiary. We hold ... only the trustee, not the trust beneficiary, is the client of the trustee's attorney. The beneficiary therefore may not discover communications between the trustee and attorney otherwise protected under [TRE] 503."

In re Monsanto Co., 998 S.W.2d 917, 930 (Tex. App.—Waco 1999, orig. proceeding). "We recognize that it might be argued [under TRE 503(a)(2)(B)] that all communications between corporate representatives could be claimed as privileged on the basis that 'the legal department can better represent us if we keep them informed.' We reject that assertion. We do not believe that it is necessary for the legal department to be advised of every development out in the field, no matter how minute. Thus, we applied common sense to the contents of the documents."

In re Texas Farmers Ins., 990 S.W.2d 337, 340 (Tex. App.—Texarkana 1999, orig. proceeding). The attorney-client "privilege does not apply if the attorney is acting in a capacity other than that of an attorney. *At 341:* Based on the evidence presented at the hearing, the trial court did not abuse its discretion in determining that [the attorney] was acting as an investigator and was conducting a routine investigation of a fire of suspicious origin."

Exceptions to Privilege

Granada Corp. v. 1st Ct. of Appeals, 844 S.W.2d 223, 227 (Tex.1992). "The crime-fraud exception [to the attorney-client privilege in TRE 503(d)(1)] applies only if a prima facie case is made of contemplated fraud. Additionally, there must be a relationship between the document for which the privilege is challenged and the prima facie proof offered."

In re AEP Tex. Cent. Co., ___ S.W.3d ___ (Tex. App.—San Antonio 2003 orig. proceeding) (No. 04-03-00253-CV; 7-16-03) "'The prima facie case requirement [for the fraud exception] is met when the proponent offers evidence establishing the elements of fraud and that the fraud was ongoing or about to be committed when the document was prepared.' [M]ere allegations of fraud are insufficient: the fraud alleged to have occurred must have occurred at or during the time the document was prepared and in order to perpetrate the fraud. The fact that the plaintiff's cause of action involves fraudulent conduct is insufficient. The attorney-client privilege is lost only when the legal communications or services were obtained in order to commit or plan to commit a fraud."

Kugle v. DaimlerChrysler Corp., 88 S.W.3d 355, 363 (Tex.App.—San Antonio 2002, pet. denied). The investigator's testimony was not privileged because D received an anonymous report that the first inspection of the car revealed no steering problems. The report and the allegations in the petition relating to the defective steering decoupler were prima facie proof that D was being defrauded with regard to the cause of the accident, which was sufficient prima facie proof of a crime-fraud exception to defeat the assertion of the attorney-client privilege.

Vinson & Elkins v. Moran, 946 S.W.2d 381, 394 (Tex.App.—Houston [14th Dist.] 1997, writ dism'd). "When an attorney is sued by his own client, the attorney is permitted to reveal confidential information so far as necessary to defend himself."

Offensive Use

Republic Ins. Co. v. Davis, 856 S.W.2d 158, 163 (Tex. 1993). "In an instance in which the privilege is being used as a sword rather than a shield, the privilege may be waived. [T]he following factors should guide the trial court in determining whether a waiver has occurred. [¶] First, ... the party asserting the privilege must seek affirmative relief. Second, the privileged information sought must be such that, if believed by the fact finder, in all probability it would be outcome determinative of the cause of action asserted. Mere relevance is insufficient. A contradiction in position without more is insufficient. The confidential communication must go to the very heart of the affirmative relief sought. Third, disclosure of the confidential communication must be the only means by which the aggrieved party may obtain the evidence. If any one of these requirements is lacking, the trial court must uphold the privilege."

TRE 504. HUSBAND-WIFE PRIVILEGES

(a) Confidential Communication Privilege.

(1) *Definition.* A communication is confidential if it is made privately by any person to the person's spouse and it is not intended for disclosure to any other person.

(2) *Rule of privilege.* A person, whether or not a party, or the guardian or representative of an incompetent or deceased person, has a privilege during marriage and afterwards to refuse to disclose and to prevent another from disclosing a confidential communication made to the person's spouse while they were married.

(3) *Who may claim the privilege.* The confidential communication privilege may be claimed by the person or the person's guardian or representative, or by the spouse on the person's behalf. The authority of the spouse to do so is presumed.

(4) *Exceptions.* There is no confidential communication privilege:

(A) *Furtherance of crime or fraud.* If the communication was made, in whole or in part, to enable or aid anyone to commit or plan to commit a crime or fraud.

(B) *Proceeding between spouses in civil cases.* In (A)* a proceeding brought by or on behalf of one spouse against the other spouse, or (B)** a proceeding between a surviving spouse and a person who claims through the deceased spouse, regardless of whether the claim is by testate or intestate succession or by inter vivos transaction.

(C) *Crime against spouse or minor child.* In a proceeding in which the party is accused of conduct which, if proved, is a crime against the person of the spouse, any minor child, or any member of the household of either spouse.

(D) *Commitment or similar proceeding.* In a proceeding to commit either spouse or otherwise to place that person or that person's property, or both, under the control of another because of an alleged mental or physical condition.

(E) *Proceeding to establish competence.* In a proceeding brought by or on behalf of either spouse to establish competence.

(b) Privilege not to Testify in Criminal Case.

(1) *Rule of privilege.* In a criminal case, the spouse of the accused has a privilege not to be called as a witness for the state. This rule does not prohibit the spouse from testifying voluntarily for the state, even over objection by the accused. A spouse who testifies on behalf of an accused is subject to cross-examination as provided in rule 611(b).

(2) *Failure to call as witness.* Failure by an accused to call the accused's spouse as a witness, where other evidence indicates that the spouse could testify to relevant matters, is a proper subject of comment by counsel.

(3) *Who may claim the privilege.* The privilege not to testify may be claimed by the person or the person's

guardian or representative but not by that person's spouse.

(4) *Exceptions.* The privilege of a person's spouse not to be called as a witness for the state does not apply:

(A) *Certain criminal proceedings.* In any proceeding in which the person is charged with a crime against the person's spouse, a member of the household of either spouse, or any minor.

(B) *Matters occurring prior to marriage.* As to matters occurring prior to the marriage.

* Editor's Note: This should probably read "(i)."

** Editor's Note: This should probably read "(ii)."

Comment to 1998 change: The rule eliminates the spousal testimonial privilege for prosecutions in which the testifying spouse is the alleged victim of a crime by the accused. This is intended to be consistent with Code of Criminal Procedure art. 38.10, effective September 1, 1995.

See ***Commentaries***, "Scope of Discovery," ch. 6-B; Cochran, ***Texas Rules of Evidence Handbook***, p. 440 (2003).

History of TRE 504 (civil): Amended eff. Mar. 1, 1998, by order of Feb. 25, 1998 (960 S.W.2d [Tex.Cases] xliv). Adopted eff. Sept. 1, 1983, by order of Nov. 23, 1982 (641-42 S.W.2d [Tex.Cases] xliii). Source: TRCS art. 3715 (repealed); Tex. Code Crim.P. art. 38.11 (repealed).

Marshall v. Ryder Sys., 928 S.W.2d 190, 195 (Tex. App.—Houston [14th Dist.] 1996, writ denied). In civil cases, "[t]he marital privilege is limited to *confidential* communications between spouses. Only in criminal cases is there a broad, general privilege protecting a person from being a witness against his or her spouse."

Earthman's, Inc. v. Earthman, 526 S.W.2d 192, 206 (Tex.App.—Houston [1st Dist.] 1975, no writ). "We do not regard as error the trial court's ruling which allowed evidence of communications between [the parties] based on conversations prior to and after their divorce. This testimony insofar as relevant to the existing controversy between them was admissible notwithstanding the marital privilege."

TRE 505. COMMUNICATIONS TO MEMBERS OF THE CLERGY

(a) **Definitions.** As used in this rule:

(1) A "member of the clergy" is a minister, priest, rabbi, accredited Christian Science Practitioner, or other similar functionary of a religious organization or an individual reasonably believed so to be by the person consulting with such individual.

(2) A communication is "confidential" if made privately and not intended for further disclosure except to other persons present in furtherance of the purpose of the communication.

(b) General Rule of Privilege. A person has a privilege to refuse to disclose and to prevent another from disclosing a confidential communication by the person to a member of the clergy in the member's professional character as spiritual adviser.

(c) Who May Claim the Privilege. The privilege may be claimed by the person, by the person's guardian or conservator, or by the personal representative of the person if the person is deceased. The member of the clergy to whom the communication was made is presumed to have authority to claim the privilege but only on behalf of the communicant.

See ***Commentaries***, "Scope of Discovery," ch. 6-B; Cochran, ***Texas Rules of Evidence Handbook***, p. 464 (2003).

History of TRE 505 (civil): Amended eff. Mar. 1, 1998, by order of Feb. 25, 1998 (960 S.W.2d [Tex.Cases] xlv). Adopted eff. Sept. 1, 1983, by order of Nov. 23, 1982 (641-42 S.W.2d [Tex.Cases] xliv). Source: TRCS art. 3715a (repealed). See Unif. R. Evid. 505 (1974).

Simpson v. Tennant, 871 S.W.2d 301, 306 (Tex. App.—Houston [14th Dist.] 1994, orig. proceeding). "The real issue in this case is whether the scope of the communications-to-clergymen privilege encompasses the *identity* of the communicant. We hold, on the facts in this case, that it does."

Nicholson v. Wittig, 832 S.W.2d 681, 685 (Tex. App.—Houston [1st Dist.] 1992, orig. proceeding). The clergy-communicant "privilege attaches when a person makes a communication with a reasonable expectation of confidentiality to a member of the clergy acting in his or her professional or spiritual capacity. [¶] An individual may invoke a privilege regardless of the nature of the underlying proceeding. *At 686:* Rule 505 makes no reference to the content of the communication; rather, the rule focuses on the counseling opportunity."

TRE 506. POLITICAL VOTE

Every person has a privilege to refuse to disclose the tenor of the person's vote at a political election conducted by secret ballot unless the vote was cast illegally.

See ***Commentaries***, "Scope of Discovery," ch. 6-B; Cochran, ***Texas Rules of Evidence Handbook***, p. 469 (2003).

History of TRE 506 (civil): Amended eff. Mar. 1, 1998, by order of Feb. 25, 1998 (960 S.W.2d [Tex.Cases] xlvi). Adopted eff. Sept. 1, 1983, by order of Nov. 23, 1982 (641-42 S.W.2d [Tex.Cases] xliv). Source: Tex. Election Code §221.009(a) (1986). See proposed FRE 507 (1972).

Oliphint v. Christy, 299 S.W.2d 933, 939 (Tex. 1957). "The privilege of nondisclosure belongs only to the legal voter and the individual who votes illegally cannot be considered a 'voter' for any purpose."

Simmons v. Jones, 838 S.W.2d 298, 300 (Tex. App.—El Paso 1992, no writ). "[L]egal voters may not be compelled to disclose how they voted, but ... an illegal voter can be compelled to disclose for whom he voted...."

TRE 507. TRADE SECRETS

A person has a privilege, which may be claimed by the person or the person's agent or employee, to refuse to disclose and to prevent other persons from disclosing a trade secret owned by the person, if the allowance of the privilege will not tend to conceal fraud or otherwise work injustice. When disclosure is directed, the judge shall take such protective measure as the interests of the holder of the privilege and of the parties and the furtherance of justice may require.

See Penal Code §31.05(a)(4); TRCP 193; ***Commentaries***, "Scope of Discovery," ch. 6-B; Cochran, ***Texas Rules of Evidence Handbook***, p. 470 (2003).

History of TRE 507 (civil): Amended eff. Mar. 1, 1998, by order of Feb. 25, 1998 (960 S.W.2d [Tex.Cases] xlvi). Adopted eff. Sept. 1, 1983, by order of Nov. 23, 1982 (641-42 S.W.2d [Tex.Cases] xliv). Source: Common law. See proposed FRE 508 (1972).

In re Bass, 113 S.W.3d 735, 739-40 (Tex.2003) The following factors are used to "determine whether a trade secret exists ...: (1) the extent to which the information is known outside of his business; (2) the extent to which it is known by employees and others involved in his business; (3) the extent of the measures taken by him to guard the secrecy of the information; (4) the value of the information to him and to his competitors; (5) the amount of effort or money expended by him in developing the information; (6) the ease or difficulty with which the information could be properly acquired or duplicated by others. [¶] Texas courts ... are split on whether the six-factors should be weighed as relevant criteria or whether a person claiming trade secret privilege must satisfy all six factors before trade secret status applies. [¶] We agree ... that the party claiming a trade secret should not be required to satisfy all six factors because trade secrets do not fit neatly into each factor every time."

In re Continental Gen. Tire, 979 S.W.2d 609, 610 (Tex.1998). "[W]hen a party resisting discovery establishes that the requested information is a trade secret under Rule 507, the burden shifts to the requesting party to establish that the information is necessary for a fair adjudication of its claim or defense."

Computer Assocs. Int'l v. Altai, Inc., 918 S.W.2d 453, 455 (Tex.1996). "A trade secret is any formula, pattern, device or compilation of information which is used in one's business and presents an opportunity to obtain an advantage over competitors who do not know or use it."

Jampole v. Touchy, 673 S.W.2d 569, 574-75 (Tex. 1984), *overruled on other grounds*, ***Walker v. Packer***, 827 S.W.2d 833 (Tex.1992). "Although a valid proprietary interest may justify denying or limiting discovery requested by a direct competitor, this is not such a case. ... We hold that discovery cannot be denied ... when a protective order would sufficiently preserve that interest."

TRE 508. IDENTITY OF INFORMER

(a) Rule of Privilege. The United States or a state or subdivision thereof has a privilege to refuse to disclose the identity of a person who has furnished information relating to or assisting in an investigation of a possible violation of a law to a law enforcement officer or member of a legislative committee or its staff conducting an investigation.

(b) Who May Claim. The privilege may be claimed by an appropriate representative of the public entity to which the information was furnished, except the privilege shall not be allowed in criminal cases if the state objects.

(c) Exceptions.

(1) *Voluntary disclosure; informer a witness.* No privilege exists under this rule if the identity of the informer or the informer's interest in the subject matter of the communication has been disclosed to those who would have cause to resent the communication by a holder of the privilege or by the informer's own action, or if the informer appears as a witness for the public entity.

(2) *Testimony on merits.* If it appears from the evidence in the case or from other showing by a party that an informer may be able to give testimony necessary to a fair determination of a material issue on the merits in a civil case to which the public entity is a party, or on guilt or innocence in a criminal case, and the public entity invokes the privilege, the court shall give the public entity an opportunity to show in camera facts relevant to determining whether the informer can, in fact, supply that testimony. The showing will ordinarily be in the

form of affidavits, but the court may direct that testimony be taken if it finds that the matter cannot be resolved satisfactorily upon affidavit. If the court finds that there is a reasonable probability that the informer can give the testimony, and the public entity elects not to disclose the informer's identity, the court in a civil case may make any order that justice requires, and in a criminal case shall, on motion of the defendant, and may, on the court's own motion, dismiss the charges as to which the testimony would relate. Evidence submitted to the court shall be sealed and preserved to be made available to the appellate court in the event of an appeal, and the contents shall not otherwise be revealed without consent of the public entity. All counsel and parties shall be permitted to be present at every stage of proceedings under this subdivision except a showing in camera, at which no counsel or party shall be permitted to be present.

(3) *Legality of obtaining evidence.* If information from an informer is relied upon to establish the legality of the means by which evidence was obtained and the court is not satisfied that the information was received from an informer reasonably believed to be reliable or credible, it may require the identity of the informer to be disclosed. The court shall, on request of the public entity, direct that the disclosure be made in camera. All counsel and parties concerned with the issue of legality shall be permitted to be present at every stage of proceedings under this subdivision except a disclosure in camera, at which no counsel or party shall be permitted to be present. If disclosure of the identity of the informer is made in camera, the record thereof shall be sealed and preserved to be made available to the appellate court in the event of an appeal, and the contents shall not otherwise be revealed without consent of the public entity.

See ***Commentaries***, "Scope of Discovery," ch. 6-B; Cochran, ***Texas Rules of Evidence Handbook***, p. 572 (2003).

History of TRE 508 (civil): Amended eff. Mar. 1, 1998, by order of Feb. 25, 1998 (960 S.W.2d [Tex.Cases] xlvi). Adopted eff. Sept. 1, 1983, by order of Nov. 23, 1982 (641-42 S.W.2d [Tex.Cases] xlv). Source: Proposed FRE 510 (1972) and Unif. R. Evid. 509 (1974).

State v. Lowry, 802 S.W.2d 669, 673 (Tex.1991). "To establish the informant privilege, the State must initially show that the person has provided to a law enforcement officer information assisting in the investigation of a possible violation of the law."

In re Bates, 555 S.W.2d 420, 430 (Tex.1977). Where the "role of the informer was very minor and occurred quite early in the [bribery] investigation; and absent other evidence concerning the relevance of the identity of the informer; the disclosure [of the informer's identity] is not required."

Warford v. Childers, 642 S.W.2d 63, 66-67 (Tex. App.—Amarillo 1982, no writ). The rule blocking disclosure "is a recognition of the fact that most informants relay rumor, gossip and street talk of no evidentiary value and the exceptions [to the rule] are designed for the rare case where the informant can give eyewitness testimony about the alleged crime or arrest."

TRE 509. PHYSICIAN-PATIENT PRIVILEGE

(a) Definitions. As used in this rule:

(1) A "patient" means any person who consults or is seen by a physician to receive medical care.

(2) A "physician" means a person licensed to practice medicine in any state or nation, or reasonably believed by the patient so to be.

(3) A communication is "confidential" if not intended to be disclosed to third persons other than those present to further the interest of the patient in the consultation, examination, or interview, or those reasonably necessary for the transmission of the communication, or those who are participating in the diagnosis and treatment under the direction of the physician, including members of the patient's family.

(b) Limited Privilege in Criminal Proceedings. There is no physician-patient privilege in criminal proceedings. However, a communication to any person involved in the treatment or examination of alcohol or drug abuse by a person being treated voluntarily or being examined for admission to treatment for alcohol or drug abuse is not admissible in a criminal proceeding.

(c) General Rule of Privilege in Civil Proceedings. In a civil proceeding:

(1) Confidential communications between a physician and a patient, relative to or in connection with any professional services rendered by a physician to the patient are privileged and may not be disclosed.

(2) Records of the identity, diagnosis, evaluation, or treatment of a patient by a physician that are created or maintained by a physician are confidential and privileged and may not be disclosed.

(3) The provisions of this rule apply even if the patient received the services of a physician prior to the enactment of the Medical Liability and Insurance Improvement Act, Tex. Rev. Civ. Stat. art. 4590i.

(d) Who May Claim the Privilege in a Civil Proceeding. In a civil proceeding:

(1) The privilege of confidentiality may be claimed by the patient or by a representative of the patient acting on the patient's behalf.

(2) The physician may claim the privilege of confidentiality, but only on behalf of the patient. The authority to do so is presumed in the absence of evidence to the contrary.

(e) Exceptions in a Civil Proceeding. Exceptions to confidentiality or privilege in administrative proceedings or in civil proceedings in court exist:

(1) when the proceedings are brought by the patient against a physician, including but not limited to malpractice proceedings, and in any license revocation proceeding in which the patient is a complaining witness and in which disclosure is relevant to the claims or defense of a physician;

(2) when the patient or someone authorized to act on the patient's behalf submits a written consent to the release of any privileged information, as provided in paragraph (f);

(3) when the purpose of the proceedings is to substantiate and collect on a claim for medical services rendered to the patient;

(4) as to a communication or record relevant to an issue of the physical, mental or emotional condition of a patient in any proceeding in which any party relies upon the condition as a part of the party's claim or defense;

(5) in any disciplinary investigation or proceeding of a physician conducted under or pursuant to the Medical Practice Act, Tex. Rev. Civ. Stat. art. 4495b*, or of a registered nurse under or pursuant to Tex. Rev. Civ. Stat. arts. 4525**, 4527a**, 4527b**, and 4527c**, provided that the board shall protect the identity of any patient whose medical records are examined, except for those patients covered under subparagraph (e)(1) or those patients who have submitted written consent to the release of their medical records as provided by paragraph (f);

(6) in an involuntary civil commitment proceeding, proceeding for court-ordered treatment, or probable cause hearing under Tex. Health & Safety Code ch. 462; tit. 7, subtit. C; and tit. 7, subtit. D;

(7) in any proceeding regarding the abuse or neglect, or the cause of any abuse or neglect, of the resident of an "institution" as defined in Tex. Health & Safety Code §242.002.

(f) Consent.

(1) Consent for the release of privileged information must be in writing and signed by the patient, or a parent or legal guardian if the patient is a minor, or a legal guardian if the patient has been adjudicated incompetent to manage personal affairs, or an attorney ad litem appointed for the patient, as authorized by Tex. Health & Safety Code tit. 7, subtits. C and D; Tex. Prob. Code ch. V; and Tex. Fam. Code §107.011; or a personal representative if the patient is deceased, provided that the written consent specifies the following:

(A) the information or medical records to be covered by the release;

(B) the reasons or purposes for the release; and

(C) the person to whom the information is to be released.

(2) The patient, or other person authorized to consent, has the right to withdraw consent to the release of any information. Withdrawal of consent does not affect any information disclosed prior to the written notice of the withdrawal.

(3) Any person who received information made privileged by this rule may disclose the information to others only to the extent consistent with the authorized purposes for which consent to release the information was obtained.

* Now Occupations Code, title 3, subtitle B-C.

** Now Occupations Code, chapter 301.

Comment to 1998 change: This comment is intended to inform the construction and application of this rule. Prior Criminal Rules of Evidence 509 and 510 are now in subparagraph (b) of this Rule. This rule governs disclosures of patient-physician communications only in judicial or administrative proceedings. Whether a physician may or must disclose such communications in other circumstances is governed by TRCS art. 4495b, §5.08 [now Occ. Code ch. 159]. Former subparagraph (d)(6) of the Civil Evidence Rules, regarding disclosures in a suit affecting the parent-child relationship, is omitted, not because there should be no exception to the privilege in suits affecting the parent-child relationship, but because the exception in such suits is properly considered under subparagraph (e)(4) of the new rule (formerly subparagraph (d)(4)), as construed in *R.K. v. Ramirez*, 887 S.W.2d 836 (Tex.1994). In determining the proper application of an exception in such suits, the trial court must ensure that the precise need for the information is not outweighed by legitimate privacy interests protected by the privilege. Subparagraph (e) of the new rule does not except from the privilege information relating to a nonparty patient who is or may be a consulting or testifying expert in the suit.

See ***Commentaries***, "Scope of Discovery," ch. 6-B; "Medical Records," ch. 6-I; Cochran, ***Texas Rules of Evidence Handbook***, p. 481 (2003).

History of TRE 509 (civil): Amended eff. Mar. 1, 1998, by order of Feb. 25, 1998 (960 S.W.2d [Tex.Cases] xlvii). Amended eff. Jan. 1, 1988, by order of Nov. 10, 1986 (733-34 S.W.2d [Tex.Cases] lxxxvii): Re-wrote (d)(4); added references to statutes relating to registered nurses in (d)(5). Amended eff. Nov. 1, 1984, by order of June 25, 1984 (669-70 S.W.2d [Tex.Cases] xxxiii): In (a)(2) added the words "in any state or nation, or reasonably believed by the patient so to be", in (b)(3) substituted the word "provisions" for "prohibitions"; substituted the word "rule" for "section continue to", deleted the phrase "to confidential communications or records concerning any patient irrespective", substituted "even if" for "of when"; in (b)(3) added the phrase "prior to the enactment of the Medical Practice Act, TRCS art. 4590i (Vernon Supp.1984)"; in (c)(1) substituted the words "by a representative of the patient" for the word "physician"; and in (d)(7) deleted the words "when the disclosure is relevant to" and substituted the words "proceeding, proceeding for court-ordered treatment, or probable cause hearing" for "or hospitalization proceeding." Adopted eff. Sept. 1, 1983, by order of Nov. 23, 1982 (641-42 S.W.2d [Tex.Cases] xlvi). Source: TRCS art. 4495b, §5.08 (repealed).

R.K. v. Ramirez, 887 S.W.2d 836, 842 (Tex.1994). "[T]he patient-litigant exception to the [TRE 509 & 510] privileges applies when a party's condition relates in a significant way to a party's claim or defense. *At 843 n.7:* Whether a condition is a part of a claim or defense should be determined on the face of the pleadings, without reference to the evidence that is allegedly privileged. *At 843:* [T]he exceptions to the medical and mental health privileges apply when (1) the records sought to be discovered are relevant to the condition at issue, and (2) the condition is relied upon as a part of a party's claim or defense, meaning that the condition itself is a fact that carries some legal significance."

Groves v. Gabriel, 874 S.W.2d 660, 661 (Tex.1994). "[A] trial court's order compelling release of medical records should be restrictively drawn so as to maintain the privilege with respect to records or communications not relevant to the underlying suit. The global release in this case does not meet the ***Mutter*** standard."

Mutter v. Wood, 744 S.W.2d 600, 601 (Tex.1988). "Even in the interest of broad discovery directed at seeking the truth, no privilege should be totally ignored." A court order requiring the plaintiffs to waive the physician-patient privilege was too broad.

In re Fort Worth Children's Hosp., 100 S.W.3d 582, 589 (Tex.App.—Fort Worth 2003, orig. proceeding). "[T]he record contains no proof that the [patients' admittance papers] are completed and maintained by physicians rather than hospital employees. Because [D] did not present any evidence that the [admittance papers] are records created or maintained by a physician, it failed to carry its burden to prove that the documents are subject to the physician-patient privilege under [TRE] 509.... [D] has no standing to assert the privilege on behalf of the nonparty patients."

In re Whiteley, 79 S.W.3d 729, 732-34 (Tex.App.—Corpus Christi 2002, orig. proceeding). Doctor, as D in a medical malpractice case, created the TRCP 509(e)(4) exception to physician-patient privilege, when he testified on deposition that he successfully performed the same surgical procedure on nonparty patients; thus, nonparty patients medical records became discoverable by P.

James v. Kloos, 75 S.W.3d 153, 160 (Tex.App.—Fort Worth 2002, no pet.). "[A] party can be prejudiced when his doctor meets with opposing counsel, but ... such prejudice may not be severe enough to disallow the doctor's testimony. [P]rejudice due to an improper meeting does not necessarily mean prejudice at trial, and, therefore, does not mean that an improper verdict necessarily results when a doctor is allowed to testify after such a meeting. [T]here must be a showing that the ruling probably caused the rendition of an improper judgment."

Durst v. Hill Country Mem'l Hosp., 70 S.W.3d 233, 237 (Tex.App.—San Antonio 2001, no pet.). "[T]here is no specific rule prohibiting ex parte communications between a plaintiff's treating physician and defense counsel. *At 238:* [A] reason to permit ex parte communication is that, in a practical sense, a doctor bears the burden of refraining from revealing irrelevant (and thus privileged) matters when responding to requests for discovery pursuant to a malpractice claim.... [¶] There is nothing in this record to indicate that the ex parte contact with a physician four years after he had given a second opinion on the plaintiff's condition delved into areas of privilege or irrelevant personal matters."

TRE 510. CONFIDENTIALITY OF MENTAL HEALTH INFORMATION IN CIVIL CASES

(a) Definitions. As used in this rule:

(1) "Professional" means any person:

(A) authorized to practice medicine in any state or nation;

(B) licensed or certified by the State of Texas in the diagnosis, evaluation or treatment of any mental or emotional disorder;

(C) involved in the treatment or examination of drug abusers; or

(D) reasonably believed by the patient to be included in any of the preceding categories.

(2) "Patient" means any person who:

(A) consults, or is interviewed by, a professional for purposes of diagnosis, evaluation, or treatment of any mental or emotional condition or disorder, including alcoholism and drug addiction; or

(B) is being treated voluntarily or being examined for admission to voluntary treatment for drug abuse.

(3) A representative of the patient is:

(A) any person bearing the written consent of the patient;

(B) a parent if the patient is a minor;

(C) a guardian if the patient has been adjudicated incompetent to manage the patient's personal affairs; or

(D) the patient's personal representative if the patient is deceased.

(4) A communication is "confidential" if not intended to be disclosed to third persons other than those present to further the interest of the patient in the diagnosis, examination, evaluation, or treatment, or those reasonably necessary for the transmission of the communication, or those who are participating in the diagnosis, examination, evaluation, or treatment under the direction of the professional, including members of the patient's family.

(b) General Rule of Privilege.

(1) Communication between a patient and a professional is confidential and shall not be disclosed in civil cases.

(2) Records of the identity, diagnosis, evaluation, or treatment of a patient which are created or maintained by a professional are confidential and shall not be disclosed in civil cases.

(3) Any person who received information from confidential communications or records as defined herein, other than a representative of the patient acting on the patient's behalf, shall not disclose in civil cases the information except to the extent that disclosure is consistent with the authorized purposes for which the information was first obtained.

(4) The provisions of this rule apply even if the patient received the services of a professional prior to the enactment of Tex. Rev. Civ. Stat. art. 5561h (Vernon Supp. 1984) (now codified as Tex. Health & Safety Code §§611.001-611.008).

(c) Who May Claim the Privilege.

(1) The privilege of confidentiality may be claimed by the patient or by a representative of the patient acting on the patient's behalf.

(2) The professional may claim the privilege of confidentiality but only on behalf of the patient. The authority to do so is presumed in the absence of evidence to the contrary.

(d) Exceptions. Exceptions to the privilege in court or administrative proceedings exist:

(1) when the proceedings are brought by the patient against a professional, including but not limited to malpractice proceedings, and in any license revocation proceedings in which the patient is a complaining witness and in which disclosure is relevant to the claim or defense of a professional;

(2) when the patient waives the right in writing to the privilege of confidentiality of any information, or when a representative of the patient acting on the patient's behalf submits a written waiver to the confidentiality privilege;

(3) when the purpose of the proceeding is to substantiate and collect on a claim for mental or emotional health services rendered to the patient;

(4) when the judge finds that the patient after having been previously informed that communications would not be privileged, has made communications to a professional in the course of a court-ordered examination relating to the patient's mental or emotional condition or disorder, providing that such communications shall not be privileged only with respect to issues involving the patient's mental or emotional health. On granting of the order, the court, in determining the extent to which any disclosure of all or any part of any communication is necessary, shall impose appropriate safeguards against unauthorized disclosure;

(5) as to a communication or record relevant to an issue of the physical, mental or emotional condition of a patient in any proceeding in which any party relies upon the condition as a part of the party's claim or defense;

(6) in any proceeding regarding the abuse or neglect, or the cause of any abuse or neglect, of the resident of an institution as defined in Tex. Health and Safety Code §242.002.

Comment to 1998 change: This comment is intended to inform the construction and application of this rule. This rule governs disclosures of patient-professional communications only in judicial or administrative proceedings. Whether a professional may or must disclose such communications in other circumstances is governed by Tex. Health & Safety Code §§611.001-611.008. Former subparagraph (d)(6) of the Civil Evidence Rules, regarding disclosures in a suit affecting the parent-child relationship, is omitted, not because there should be no exception to the privilege in suits affecting the parent-child relationship, but because the exception in such suits is properly considered under subparagraph (d)(5), as construed in *R.K. v. Ramirez*, 887 S.W.2d 836 (Tex.1994). In determining the proper application of an exception in such suits, the trial court must ensure that the precise need for the information is not outweighed by legitimate privacy interests protected by the privilege. Subparagraph (d) does not except from the privilege information relating to a nonparty patient who is or may be a consulting or testifying expert in the suit.

See ***Commentaries***, "Scope of Discovery," ch. 6-B; "Medical Records," ch. 6-I; Cochran, ***Texas Rules of Evidence Handbook***, p. 500 (2003).

History of TRE 510 (civil): Amended eff. Mar. 1, 1998, by order of Feb. 25, 1998 (960 S.W.2d [Tex.Cases] l). Amended eff. Nov. 1, 1984, by order of June 25, 1984 (669-70 S.W.2d [Tex.Cases] xxxiv): In the phrase "patient/client" the word "client" was deleted throughout rule; in (a)(2)(A) the word "other" was deleted; in (b)(4) the word "provisions" was substituted for the "prohibitions" and the words "continue to" "to confidential communications or records concerning any patient/client irrespective of when" were deleted; in (d)(5) the entire language has been substituted; in (d)(7) the words "TRCS art. 4442c, §2 (Vernon Supp. 1984)" were substituted for the "Sec. 1, ch. 684, Acts of the 67th Legislature, Regular Session 1981 (Art. 4442c, §2, Vernon's Texas Civil Statutes)." Amended eff. Jan. 1, 1988, by order of Nov. 10, 1986 (733-34 S.W.2d [Tex.Cases] lxxxviii). Re-wrote (d)(5). Adopted eff. Sept. 1, 1983, by order of Nov. 23, 1982 (641-42 S.W.2d [Tex.Cases] xlviii). Source: TRCS art. 5561h (repealed); Tex. Code Crim.P. art. 38.101.

R.K. v. Ramirez, 887 S.W.2d 836, 843 (Tex.1994). "As a general rule, a mental condition will be a 'part' of a claim or defense if the pleadings indicate that the jury must make a factual determination concerning the condition itself. *At n.7:* Whether a condition is a party of a claim or defense should be determined on the face of the pleadings, without reference to the evidence that is allegedly privileged."

Groves v. Gabriel, 874 S.W.2d 660, 661 (Tex.1994). "Because [P] alleges severe emotional damages, including 'post-traumatic stress disorder,' [she] waived the privilege as to any medical records relevant to her claim for emotional damages." *See also* ***Ginsberg v. 5th Ct. of Appeals***, 686 S.W.2d 105, 107 (Tex.1985).

TRE 511. WAIVER OF PRIVILEGE BY VOLUNTARY DISCLOSURE

A person upon whom these rules confer a privilege against disclosure waives the privilege if:

(1) the person or a predecessor of the person while holder of the privilege voluntarily discloses or consents to disclosure of any significant part of the privileged matter unless such disclosure itself is privileged; or

(2) the person or a representative of the person calls a person to whom privileged communications have been made to testify as to the person's character or character trait insofar as such communications are relevant to such character or character trait.

See ***Commentaries***, "Waiver of objections & privileges," ch. 6-A, §23.3; Cochran, ***Texas Rules of Evidence Handbook***, p. 529 (2003).

History of TRE 511 (civil): Amended eff. Mar. 1, 1998, by order of Feb. 25, 1998 (960 S.W.2d [Tex.Cases] lii). Amended eff. Nov. 1, 1984, by order of June 25, 1984 (669-70 S.W.2d [Tex.Cases] xxxvii): Numbers (1) and (2) were added; the words "unless such disclosure itself is privileged, or (2) he or his representative calls a person to whom privileged communications have been made to testify as to his character or a trait of his character, insofar as such communications are relevant to such character or character trait" were added; the last sentence was deleted. Adopted eff. Sept. 1, 1983, by order of Nov. 23, 1982 (641-42 S.W.2d [Tex.Cases] l). Source: See Unif. R. Evid. 510 (1980).

Axelson, Inc. v. McIlhany, 798 S.W.2d 550, 553-54 (Tex.1990). "[D] resists discovery based on the attorney-client privilege under [TRE] 503(b) and the work product privilege under [TRCP 166b(3) now TRCP 192.5]. Since there was evidence that the investigation was disclosed to the FBI, IRS, and the *Wall Street Journal*, the court of appeals properly held that these privileges had been waived."

Jordan v. 4th Ct. of Appeals, 701 S.W.2d 644, 649 (Tex.1985). "If the matter for which a privilege is sought has been disclosed to a third party, thus raising the question of waiver of the privilege, the party asserting the privilege has the burden of proving that no waiver has occurred."

TRE 512. PRIVILEGED MATTER DISCLOSED UNDER COMPULSION OR WITHOUT OPPORTUNITY TO CLAIM PRIVILEGE

A claim of privilege is not defeated by a disclosure which was (1) compelled erroneously or (2) made without opportunity to claim the privilege.

See ***Commentaries***, "General Rules for Discovery," ch. 6-A; Cochran, ***Texas Rules of Evidence Handbook***, p. 539 (2003).

History of TRE 512 (civil): Amended eff. Mar. 1, 1998, by order of Feb. 25, 1998 (960 S.W.2d [Tex.Cases] lii). Adopted eff. Sept. 1, 1983, by order of Nov. 23, 1982 (641-42 S.W.2d [Tex.Cases] l). Source: Unif. R. Evid. 511 (1980).

TRE 513. COMMENT UPON OR INFERENCE FROM CLAIM OF PRIVILEGE; INSTRUCTION

(a) Comment or Inference Not Permitted. Except as permitted in Rule 504(b)(2), the claim of a privilege, whether in the present proceeding or upon a prior occasion, is not a proper subject of comment by judge or counsel, and no inference may be drawn therefrom.

(b) Claiming Privilege Without Knowledge of Jury. In jury cases, proceedings shall be conducted, to the extent practicable, so as to facilitate the making of claims of privilege without the knowledge of the jury.

(c) Claim of Privilege Against Self-Incrimination in Civil Cases. Paragraphs (a) and (b) shall not apply with respect to a party's claim, in the present civil proceeding, of the privilege against self-incrimination.

(d) Jury Instruction. Except as provided in Rule 504(b)(2) and in paragraph (c) of this Rule, upon request any party against whom the jury might draw an adverse inference from a claim of privilege is entitled to an instruction that no inference may be drawn therefrom.

Comment to 1998 change: Subdivision (d) regarding a party's entitlement to a jury instruction about a claim of privilege is made applicable to civil cases.

See Cochran, ***Texas Rules of Evidence Handbook***, p. 543 (2003).

History of TRE 513 (civil): Amended eff. Mar. 1, 1998, by order of Feb. 25, 1998 (960 S.W.2d [Tex.Cases] lii). Adopted eff. Sept. 1, 1983, by order of Nov. 23, 1982 (641-42 S.W.2d [Tex.Cases] l). Source: Unif. R. Evid. 512 (1980); proposed FRE 513.

In re L.S., 748 S.W.2d 571, 575 (Tex.App.—Amarillo 1988, no writ). TRE 513(b) "reflects a desire to protect the parties from any adverse inference drawn by the jurors who witness the invocation of the privilege against self-incrimination. 'It is reasonable to anticipate that in most instances, planned reliance upon the privilege will be known in advance and the mandate of rule 513(b) can be implemented through the use of motions in limine.'"

ARTICLE VI. WITNESSES

TRE 601. COMPETENCY & INCOMPETENCY OF WITNESSES

(a) General Rule. Every person is competent to be a witness except as otherwise provided in these rules. The following witnesses shall be incompetent to testify in any proceeding subject to these rules:

(1) *Insane persons.* Insane persons who, in the opinion of the court, are in an insane condition of mind at the time when they are offered as a witness, or who, in the opinion of the court, were in that condition when the events happened of which they are called to testify.

(2) *Children.* Children or other persons who, after being examined by the court, appear not to possess sufficient intellect to relate transactions with respect to which they are interrogated.

(b) "Dead Man's Rule" in Civil Actions. In civil actions by or against executors, administrators, or guardians, in which judgment may be rendered for or against them as such, neither party shall be allowed to testify against the others as to any oral statement by the testator, intestate or ward, unless that testimony to the oral statement is corroborated or unless the witness is called at the trial to testify thereto by the opposite party; and, the provisions of this article shall extend to and include all actions by or against the heirs or legal representatives of a decedent based in whole or in part on such oral statement. Except for the foregoing, a witness is not precluded from giving evidence of or concerning any transaction with, any conversations with, any admissions of, or statement by, a deceased or insane party or person merely because the witness is a party to the action or a person interested in the event thereof. The trial court shall, in a proper case, where this rule prohibits an interested party or witness from testifying, instruct the jury that such person is not permitted by the law to give evidence relating to any oral statement by the deceased or ward unless the oral statement is corroborated or unless the party or witness is called at the trial by the opposite party.

See ***Commentaries***, "Motion in Limine," ch. 5-E; "Objecting to Evidence," ch. 8-D; Cochran, ***Texas Rules of Evidence Handbook***, p. 551 (2003).

History of TRE 601 (civil): Amended eff. Mar. 1, 1998, by order of Feb. 25, 1998 (960 S.W.2d [Tex.Cases] liii). Amended eff. Jan. 1, 1988, by order of July 15, 1987 (733-34 S.W.2d [Tex.Cases] xcv): In (a)(2) deleted "or who do not understand the obligation of an oath"; in (b) added last sentence "The trial court shall ... opposite party." Amended eff. Nov. 1, 1984, by order of June 25, 1984 (669-70 S.W.2d [Tex.Cases] xxxvii): Added the words "at the trial" in the first sentence. Adopted eff. Sept. 1, 1983, by order of Nov. 23, 1982 (641-42 S.W.2d [Tex.Cases] li). Source: For (a), FRE 601; Tex. Code Crim.P. art. 38.06 (repealed); for (b), TRCS arts. 3714, 3716 (repealed).

Lunsford v. Morris, 746 S.W.2d 471, 473 (Tex. 1988). "[T]he rules of evidence [do not] contemplate exclusion of otherwise relevant proof unless the evidence proffered is unfairly prejudicial, privileged, incompetent, or otherwise *legally* inadmissible."

Quitta v. Fossati, 808 S.W.2d 636, 641 (Tex.App.—Corpus Christi 1991, writ denied). Because "the [Ps] are neither heirs nor legal representatives of [the deceased], but [are successors in interest to the deceased, t]he Dead Man's Statute ... does not apply to prevent the [Ds] from testifying to their conversations with [the deceased] concerning the modification."

TRE 602. LACK OF PERSONAL KNOWLEDGE

A witness may not testify to a matter unless evidence is introduced sufficient to support a finding that the witness has personal knowledge of the matter. Evidence to prove personal knowledge may, but need not, consist of the testimony of the witness. This rule is subject to the provisions of Rule 703, relating to opinion testimony by expert witnesses.

See ***Commentaries***, "Introducing Evidence," ch. 8-C; "Objecting to Evidence," ch. 8-D; Cochran, ***Texas Rules of Evidence Handbook***, p. 562 (2003).

History of TRE 602 (civil): Amended eff. Mar. 1, 1998, by order of Feb. 25, 1998 (960 S.W.2d [Tex.Cases] liv). Adopted eff. Sept. 1, 1983, by order of Nov. 23, 1982 (641-42 S.W.2d [Tex.Cases] li). Source: FRE 602.

Anderson Prod'g v. Koch Oil Co., 929 S.W.2d 416, 425 (Tex.1996). Defendant "argues that the trial court erred [because P's attorney] failed to demonstrate personal knowledge supporting the testimony. The record reflects that [P's attorney's] testimony was based on his review of the documents executed by [D], and that [D] had ample opportunity to cross-examine [him] regarding the basis of his conclusion. Under these circumstances, the trial court did not abuse its discretion in failing to strike the testimony."

Radio Station KSCS v. Jennings, 750 S.W.2d 760, 762 (Tex.1988). The affidavit of an inmate confined to TDC "fails to show how [the inmate] became familiar with the facts in the affidavit. [The inmate] does not claim to have worked for any radio station or record company. [¶] We hold that the [inmate's] affidavit controverting the [D's] motion for summary judgment fails to establish personal knowledge of the business practices of record companies or of the radio station."

TRE 603. OATH OR AFFIRMATION

Before testifying, every witness shall be required to declare that the witness will testify truthfully, by oath or affirmation administered in a form calculated to awaken the witness' conscience and impress the witness' mind with the duty to do so.

See Cochran, ***Texas Rules of Evidence Handbook***, p. 566 (2003).

History of TRE 603 (civil): Amended eff. Mar. 1, 1998, by order of Feb. 25, 1998 (960 S.W.2d [Tex.Cases] liv). Adopted eff. Sept. 1, 1983, by order of Nov. 23, 1982 (641-42 S.W.2d [Tex.Cases] li). Source: FRE 603. See Tex. Const. art. I, §5.

Glenn v. C&G Elec., 977 S.W.2d 686, 689 (Tex. App.—Fort Worth 1998, pet. denied). "Th[e] requirement [to testify truthfully under oath] applies not only to those who will testify in person in the courtroom, but also to those whose testimony at the trial will be presented by deposition."

TRE 604. INTERPRETERS

An interpreter is subject to the provisions of these rules relating to qualification as an expert and the administration of an oath or affirmation to make a true translation.

See TRCP 183, regarding appointment and compensation of interpreters; Cochran, ***Texas Rules of Evidence Handbook***, p. 568 (2003).

History of TRE 604 (civil): Amended eff. Mar. 1, 1998, by order of Feb. 25, 1998 (960 S.W.2d [Tex.Cases] liv). Amended eff. Sept. 1, 1990, by order of Apr. 24, 1990 (785-86 S.W.2d [Tex.Cases] cvi): Added comment with reference to TRCP 183, regarding appointment and compensation of interpreters. Adopted eff. Sept. 1, 1983, by order of Nov. 23, 1982 (641-42 S.W.2d [Tex.Cases] li). Source: FRE 604.

International Commercial Bank v. Hall-Fuston Corp., 767 S.W.2d 259, 261 (Tex.App.—Beaumont 1989, no writ). Where a foreign company attempts to introduce into evidence business records that are not written in English, it may have one of its corporate representatives orally interpret the documents under oath after being qualified as an expert.

TRE 605. COMPETENCY OF JUDGE AS A WITNESS

The judge presiding at the trial may not testify in that trial as a witness. No objection need be made in order to preserve the point.

See Cochran, ***Texas Rules of Evidence Handbook***, p. 570 (2003).

History of TRE 605 (civil): Amended eff. Mar. 1, 1998, by order of Feb. 25, 1998 (960 S.W.2d [Tex.Cases] liv). Adopted eff. Sept. 1, 1983, by order of Nov. 23, 1982 (641-42 S.W.2d [Tex.Cases] lii). Source: FRE 605.

In re M.S., 115 S.W.3d 534, 538 (Tex.2003). "A judge's findings of fact are not technically the same as testimony.... In this case, the orders submitted into evidence, containing findings based on pretrial evidence by the very judge presiding over the termination proceeding, could be, like a judicial comment on the weight of the evidence, a form of judicial influence no less proscribed than judicial testimony. [T]he jury was permitted to see findings of fact made by the very judge presiding over the trial, and those facts were the very ones that the jury itself was being asked to find. The fact-finding present in the orders admitted as evidence comes far too close to indicating the opinion of the trial judge as to the verity or accuracy of the facts in inquiry...."

O'Quinn v. Hall, 77 S.W.3d 438, 448 (Tex.App.—Corpus Christi 2002, no pet.). TRE 605 "applies not only to members of the judiciary, 'but also to those performing judicial functions that conflict with a witness's role.' [¶] 'The judge is a neutral arbiter in the courtroom, and the rule seeks to preserve his posture of impartiality before the parties....'"

In re M.E.C., 66 S.W.3d 449, 457 (Tex.App.—Waco 2001, no pet.). TRE 605 "prohibit[s] not only direct testimony by the judge but also that which 'is the functional equivalent of witness testimony.'"

TRE 606. COMPETENCY OF JUROR AS A WITNESS

(a) At the Trial. A member of the jury may not testify as a witness before that jury in the trial of the case in which the juror is sitting as a juror. If the juror is called so to testify, the opposing party shall be afforded an opportunity to object out of the presence of the jury.

(b) Inquiry Into Validity of Verdict or Indictment. Upon an inquiry into the validity of a verdict or indictment, a juror may not testify as to any matter or statement occurring during the jury's deliberations, or to the effect of anything on any juror's mind or emotions or mental processes, as influencing any juror's assent to or dissent from the verdict or indictment. Nor may a juror's affidavit or any statement by a juror concerning any matter about which the juror would be precluded from testifying be admitted in evidence for any of these purposes. However, a juror may testify: (1) whether any outside influence was improperly brought to bear upon any juror; or (2) to rebut a claim that the juror was not qualified to serve.

See TRCP 327(b); *Commentaries*, "MNT Based on Jury or Bailiff Misconduct," ch. 10-B, §13; Cochran, ***Texas Rules of Evidence Handbook***, p. 573 (2003).

History of TRE 606 (civil): Amended eff. Mar. 1, 1998, by order of Feb. 25, 1998 (960 S.W.2d [Tex.Cases] liv). Adopted eff. Sept. 1, 1983, by order of Nov. 23, 1982 (641-42 S.W.2d [Tex.Cases] lii). Source: FRE 606.

Golden Eagle Archery, Inc. v. Jackson, 24 S.W.3d 362, 371 (Tex.2000). An "alleged conversation between [jurors] during a trial break ... should not be considered 'deliberations' and therefore barred by [TRE] 606(b) and [TRCP] 327(b). [TRCPs] use the term 'deliberations' as meaning formal jury deliberations—when the jury weighs the evidence to arrive at a verdict."

Rosell v. Central W. Motor Stages, Inc., 89 S.W.3d 643, 661 (Tex.App.—Dallas 2002, pet. denied). "The essence of the 'outside influence' rule is to prevent outside information that affects the merits of the case from reaching the jury. The only evidence here is that the jury was told that they probably would be required to deliberate another day. ... Thus, the bailiff informing the jury of the court's schedule was not misconduct. Further, the juror testimony that jurors traded answers on issues is testimony about deliberations and is not evidence of outside influences."

Chavarria v. Valley Transit Co., 75 S.W.3d 107, 110 (Tex.App.—San Antonio 2002, no pet.). TRE 606(b) does "not bar juror testimony about conversations during a trial break. *At 111:* [However, we] believe that jurors discussing the case on breaks during deliberations is the same as deliberations themselves."

Perry v. Safeco Ins. Co., 821 S.W.2d 279, 281 (Tex. App.—Houston [1st Dist.] 1991, writ denied). "Information gathered by a juror and introduced to other jurors by that juror—even if it were introduced to prejudice the vote—does not constitute outside influence. [¶] Further, the coercive influence of one juror upon the rest of the panel is not 'outside influence.' Proof of coercive statements and their effect on the jury is barred by the rules."

TRE 607. WHO MAY IMPEACH

The credibility of a witness may be attacked by any party, including the party calling the witness.

See *Commentaries*, "Introducing Evidence," ch. 8-C; Cochran, ***Texas Rules of Evidence Handbook***, p. 588 (2003).

History of TRE 607 (civil): Amended eff. Mar. 1, 1998, by order of Feb. 25, 1998 (960 S.W.2d [Tex.Cases] lv). Adopted eff. Sept. 1, 1983, by order of Nov. 23, 1982 (641-42 S.W.2d [Tex.Cases] lii). Source: FRE 607.

Allied Chem. Co. v. DeHaven, 824 S.W.2d 257, 265 (Tex.App.—Houston [14th Dist.] 1992, no writ). TRE 607 "allows the credibility of a witness to be attacked by the party calling him." *See also* ***Loyd Elec. Co. v. Millett***, 767 S.W.2d 476, 479 (Tex.App.—San Antonio 1989, no writ).

TRE 608. EVIDENCE OF CHARACTER & CONDUCT OF A WITNESS

(a) Opinion and Reputation Evidence of Character. The credibility of a witness may be attacked or supported by evidence in the form of opinion or reputation, but subject to these limitations:

(1) the evidence may refer only to character for truthfulness or untruthfulness; and

(2) evidence of truthful character is admissible only after the character of the witness for truthfulness has been attacked by opinion or reputation evidence or otherwise.

(b) Specific Instances of Conduct. Specific instances of the conduct of a witness, for the purpose of attacking or supporting the witness' credibility, other than conviction of crime as provided in Rule 609, may not be inquired into on cross-examination of the witness nor proved by extrinsic evidence.

See *Commentaries*, "Motion in Limine," ch. 5-E; "Introducing Evidence," ch. 8-C; Cochran, ***Texas Rules of Evidence Handbook***, p. 594 (2003).

History of TRE 608 (civil): Amended eff. Mar. 1, 1998, by order of Feb. 25, 1998 (960 S.W.2d [Tex.Cases] lv). Adopted eff. Sept. 1, 1983, by order of Nov. 23, 1982 (641-42 S.W.2d [Tex.Cases] lii). Source: FRE 608(a).

Closs v. Goose Creek Consol. ISD, 874 S.W.2d 859, 870 n.7 (Tex.App.—Texarkana 1994, no writ). "The credibility of a witness may be attacked by evidence in the form of an opinion or reputation. Specific instances of the conduct of a witness, other than conviction for a crime, may not be inquired into nor proved by extrinsic evidence for purposes of attacking the credibility of the witness."

Service Lloyds Ins. Co. v. Martin, 855 S.W.2d 816, 823 (Tex.App.—Dallas 1993, no writ). "Under [TRE] 608(a), a witness's credibility can be attacked by either opinion or reputation evidence. The evidence, however, must relate only to the witness's character for truthfulness or untruthfulness."

Rose v. Intercontinental Bank, 705 S.W.2d 752, 757 (Tex.App.—Houston [1st Dist.] 1986, writ ref'd n.r.e.). Under TRE 608(a), "the witness' reputation for truthfulness must first be attacked before [the party] can offer rehabilitating evidence."

TRE 609. IMPEACHMENT BY EVIDENCE OF CONVICTION OF CRIME

(a) General Rule. For the purpose of attacking the credibility of a witness, evidence that the witness has been convicted of a crime shall be admitted if elicited from the witness or established by public record but only if the crime was a felony or involved moral turpitude, regardless of punishment, and the court determines that the probative value of admitting this evidence outweighs its prejudicial effect to a party.

(b) Time Limit. Evidence of a conviction under this rule is not admissible if a period of more than ten years has elapsed since the date of the conviction or of the release of the witness from the confinement imposed for that conviction, whichever is the later date, unless the court determines, in the interests of justice, that the probative value of the conviction supported by specific facts and circumstances substantially outweighs its prejudicial effect.

(c) Effect of Pardon, Annulment, or Certificate of Rehabilitation. Evidence of a conviction is not admissible under this rule if:

(1) based on the finding of the rehabilitation of the person convicted, the conviction has been the subject of a pardon, annulment, certificate of rehabilitation, or other equivalent procedure, and that person has not been convicted of a subsequent crime which was classified as a felony or involved moral turpitude, regardless of punishment;

(2) probation has been satisfactorily completed for the crime for which the person was convicted, and that person has not been convicted of a subsequent crime which was classified as a felony or involved moral turpitude, regardless of punishment; or

(3) based on a finding of innocence, the conviction has been the subject of a pardon, annulment, or other equivalent procedure.

(d) Juvenile Adjudications. Evidence of juvenile adjudications is not admissible, except for proceedings conducted pursuant to Title III, Family Code, in which the witness is a party, under this rule unless required to be admitted by the Constitution of the United States or Texas.

(e) Pendency of Appeal. Pendency of an appeal renders evidence of a conviction inadmissible.

(f) Notice. Evidence of a conviction is not admissible if after timely written request by the adverse party specifying the witness or witnesses, the proponent fails to give to the adverse party sufficient advance written notice of intent to use such evidence to provide the adverse party with a fair opportunity to contest the use of such evidence.

See ***Commentaries***, "Motion in Limine," ch. 5-E; "Introducing Evidence," ch. 8-C; Cochran, ***Texas Rules of Evidence Handbook***, p. 603 (2003).

History of TRE 609 (civil): Amended eff. Mar. 1, 1998, by order of Feb. 25, 1998 (960 S.W.2d [Tex.Cases] lv). Adopted eff. Sept. 1, 1983, by order of Nov. 23, 1982 (641-42 S.W.2d [Tex.Cases] lii). Source: FRE 609.

U.S.A. Precision Mach. Co. v. Marshall, 95 S.W.3d 407, 410 (Tex.App.—Houston [1st Dist.] 2002, pet. denied). A conviction is not final for purposes of impeachment under TRE 609 if it was reversed, it is pending on appeal, or the case was dismissed after a new trial was granted.

In re M.R., 975 S.W.2d 51, 55 (Tex.App.—San Antonio 1998, pet. denied). TRE 609 "exists to establish when and within what parameters a prior conviction may be introduced. It does not *require* a conviction in order to admit some testimony. [¶] [T]he Family Code itself does not require a conviction in order to introduce evidence of family violence. Instead, it requires that the evidence be 'credible.'"

Porter v. Nemir, 900 S.W.2d 376, 382 (Tex.App.—Austin 1995, no writ). "[T]he danger of unfair prejudice was particularly great because the extraneous conduct involved sexual abuse of a child. [¶] [D's] conviction for sexual abuse of a child was not admissible under [TRE] 609 [, and] the court did not abuse its discretion in concluding that the probative value *was substantially outweighed* by the danger of unfair prejudice...."

Borden, Inc. v. Rios, 850 S.W.2d 821, 834 (Tex. App.—Corpus Christi 1993), *writ granted w.r.m.*, 859 S.W.2d 70 (Tex.1993). "Evidence of a conviction is not admissible under [TRE] 609 if the person successfully completes probation for the crime and has not been convicted for a subsequent crime."

TRE 610. RELIGIOUS BELIEFS OR OPINIONS

Evidence of the beliefs or opinions of a witness on matters of religion is not admissible for the purpose of showing that by reason of their nature the witness' credibility is impaired or enhanced.

Comment to 1998 change: This is prior Rule of Criminal Evidence 615.

See ***Commentaries***, "Motion in Limine," ch. 5-E; "Objecting to Evidence," ch. 8-D; Cochran, ***Texas Rules of Evidence Handbook***, p. 621 (2003).

History of TRE 610 (civil): Amended eff. Mar. 1, 1998, by order of Feb. 25, 1998 (960 S.W.2d [Tex.Cases] lvi). Adopted eff. Jan. 1, 1988, by order of Nov. 10, 1986 (733-34 S.W.2d [Tex.Cases] lxxxviii): While the rule forecloses inquiry into the religious beliefs or opinions of a witness for the purpose of showing that his character for truthfulness is affected by their nature, an inquiry for the purpose of showing interest or bias because of them is not within the prohibition; thus disclosure of affiliation with a church which is a party to the litigation is allowed under the rule. Former TRCE 610 renumbered TRCE 611. Source: New rule. See FRE 610.

TRE 611. MODE & ORDER OF INTERROGATION & PRESENTATION

(a) Control by Court. The court shall exercise reasonable control over the mode and order of interrogating witnesses and presenting evidence so as to (1) make the interrogation and presentation effective for the ascertainment of the truth, (2) avoid needless consumption of time, and (3) protect witnesses from harassment or undue embarrassment.

(b) Scope of Cross-Examination. A witness may be cross-examined on any matter relevant to any issue in the case, including credibility.

(c) Leading Questions. Leading questions should not be used on the direct examination of a witness except as may be necessary to develop the testimony of the witness. Ordinarily leading questions should be permitted on cross-examination. When a party calls a hostile witness, an adverse party, or a witness identified with an adverse party, interrogation may be by leading questions.

See ***Commentaries***, "Introducing Evidence," ch. 8-C; Cochran, ***Texas Rules of Evidence Handbook***, p. 623 (2003).

History of TRE 611 (civil): Amended eff. Mar. 1, 1998, by order of Feb. 25, 1998 (960 S.W.2d [Tex.Cases] lvi). Amended eff. Jan. 1, 1988, by order of Nov. 10, 1986 (733-34 S.W.2d [Tex.Cases] lxxxix): This is former TRCE 610; the purpose of the amendment is to permit the court in it's discretion the use of leading questions on preliminary or introductory matters, refreshing memory, questions to ignorant or illiterate persons or children; the rule also conforms to tradition in making the use of leading questions on cross-examination a matter of right; the purpose of the qualification "ordinarily" is to furnish a basis for denying the use of leading questions when the cross-examination is only in the form of cross-examination and not in fact, e.g., the "cross-examination" of a party by his own counsel after being called by the opponent or of an insured defendant who is friendly to the plaintiff. Adopted as TRCE 610 eff. Sept. 1, 1983, by order of Nov. 23, 1982 (641-42 S.W.2d [Tex.Cases] liv). Source: FRE 611.

National Family Care Life Ins. Co. v. Fletcher, 57 S.W.3d 662, 669-70 (Tex.App.—Beaumont 2001, pet. denied). "[D] had the right to test the credibility of the party bringing the suit on the elements of that party's cause of action. If, upon cross-examination, the party is found to be equivocal or less than truthful, the jury weighs that response and draws its own conclusion. In short, '[t]he right to cross examination is a vital element in a fair adjudication of disputed facts[,]' and it includes 'the right to cross examine adverse witnesses and to examine and rebut all evidence[.]'"

Stam v. Mack, 984 S.W.2d 747, 752 (Tex.App.—Texarkana 1999, no pet.). "The trial court interrupted [P's] cross-examination because it felt that [P] was questioning the witness on immaterial issues and he was going into areas that were improper. The trial court's interruption of the cross-examination was not improper, but was a proper action to maintain control and promote expedition."

Cecil v. T.M.E. Invs., 893 S.W.2d 38, 47 (Tex.App.—Corpus Christi 1994, no writ). D, in cross-examining its own witness who had been called by P, should not have been able to "lead" the witness. See comment to TRE 611, in the history note. The error was harmless.

GAB Bus. Servs. v. Moore, 829 S.W.2d 345, 351 (Tex.App.—Texarkana 1992, no writ). TRE 611 "gives the trial judge the discretion to limit the use of leading questions in cross-examining a friendly witness. [¶] A question framed so that a yes or no answer will enable the witness to merely echo the words of counsel is leading."

TRE 612. WRITING USED TO REFRESH MEMORY

If a witness uses a writing to refresh memory for the purpose of testifying either

(1) while testifying;

(2) before testifying, in civil cases, if the court in its discretion determines it is necessary in the interests of justice; or

(3) before testifying, in criminal cases;

an adverse party is entitled to have the writing produced at the hearing, to inspect it, to cross-examine the witness thereon, and to introduce in evidence those portions which relate to the testimony of the witness. If it is claimed that the writing contains matters not related to the subject matter of the testimony the court shall examine the writing in camera, excise any portion not so related, and order delivery of the remainder to the party entitled thereto. Any portion withheld over objections shall be preserved and made available to the appellate court in the event of an appeal. If a writing is not produced or delivered pursuant to order under this rule, the court shall make any order justice requires, except that in criminal cases when the prosecution elects not to comply, the order shall be one striking the testimony or, if the court in its discretion determines that the interests of justice so require, declaring a mistrial.

See Cochran, ***Texas Rules of Evidence Handbook***, p. 630 (2003).

History of TRE 612 (civil): Amended eff. Mar. 1, 1998, by order of Feb. 25, 1998 (960 S.W.2d [Tex.Cases] lvii). Amended eff. Jan. 1, 1988, by order of July 15, 1987 (733-34 S.W.2d [Tex.Cases] xcv): This is former TRCE 611; former TRCE 612 was amended and renumbered as TRCE 613. Adopted as TRCE 611 eff. Sept. 1, 1983, by order of Nov. 23, 1982 (641-42 S.W.2d [Tex.Cases] liv). Source: FRE 612.

Goode v. Shoukfeh, 943 S.W.2d 441, 449 (Tex. 1997). "If a witness uses the writing while testifying the adverse party must be given access to it, but if the writing is used before the witness testifies, the court has the discretion to order the writing disclosed to the adverse party."

TRE 613. PRIOR STATEMENTS OF WITNESSES: IMPEACHMENT & SUPPORT

(a) Examining Witness Concerning Prior Inconsistent Statement. In examining a witness concerning a prior inconsistent statement made by the witness, whether oral or written, and before further cross-examination concerning, or extrinsic evidence of, such statement may be allowed, the witness must be told the contents of such statement and the time and place and the person to whom it was made, and must be afforded an opportunity to explain or deny such statement. If written, the writing need not be shown to the witness at that time, but on request the same shall be shown to opposing counsel. If the witness unequivocally admits having made such statement, extrinsic evidence of same shall not be admitted. This provision does not apply to admissions of a party-opponent as defined in Rule 801(e)(2).

(b) Examining Witness Concerning Bias or Interest. In impeaching a witness by proof of circumstances or statements showing bias or interest on the part of such witness, and before further cross-examination concerning, or extrinsic evidence of, such bias or interest may be allowed, the circumstances supporting such claim or the details of such statement, including the contents and where, when and to whom made, must be made known to the witness, and the witness must be given an opportunity to explain or to deny such circumstances or statement. If written, the writing need not be shown to the witness at that time, but on request the same shall be shown to opposing counsel. If the witness unequivocally admits such bias or interest, extrinsic evidence of same shall not be admitted. A party shall be permitted to present evidence rebutting any evidence impeaching one of said party's witnesses on grounds of bias or interest.

(c) Prior Consistent Statements of Witnesses. A prior statement of a witness which is consistent with the testimony of the witness is inadmissible except as provided in Rule 801(e)(1)(B).

See ***Commentaries***, "Introducing Evidence," ch. 8-C; Cochran, ***Texas Rules of Evidence Handbook***, p. 637 (2003).

History of TRE 613 (civil): Amended eff. Mar. 1, 1998, by order of Feb. 25, 1998 (960 S.W.2d [Tex.Cases] lvii). Amended eff. Jan. 1, 1988, by order of July 15, 1987 (733-34 S.W.2d [Tex.Cases] xcvi): This is former TRCE 612, with change - in first sentence of (b) deleted the comma after "interest"; former TRCE 613 was amended and renumbered as TRCE 614. Former TRCE 612 amended eff. Nov. 1, 1984, by order of June 25, 1984 (669-70 S.W.2d [Tex.Cases] xxxvii): Added "If written, the writing need not be shown to him at that time, but on request the same shall be shown to opposing counsel" to (a) and (b). Adopted as TRCE 612 eff. Sept. 1, 1983, by order of Nov. 23, 1982 (641-42 S.W.2d [Tex.Cases] liv). Source: FRE 613.

Walker v. Packer, 827 S.W.2d 833, 839 n.5 (Tex. 1992). "Evidence of bias is not admissible if the witness 'unequivocally admits such bias or interest' at trial. ... [Because D's witness] flatly denied [bias], such evidence should be discoverable."

Downen v. Texas Gulf Shrimp Co., 846 S.W.2d 506, 512 (Tex.App.—Corpus Christi 1993, writ denied). "[T]o impeach a witness with a prior statement, a proper foundation must be established [, which] includes establishing where, when, and to whom the statement was made. Additionally, the party ... must allow the witness to admit or deny making the prior statement. If ... the witness admits unequivocally having made the statement the impeachment is complete and the prior statement is not admissible."

TRE 614. EXCLUSION OF WITNESSES

At the request of a party the court shall order witnesses excluded so that they cannot hear the testimony of other witnesses, and it may make the order of its own motion. This rule does not authorize exclusion of:

(1) a party who is a natural person or in civil cases the spouse of such natural person;

(2) an officer or employee of a party in a civil case or a defendant in a criminal case that is not a natural person designated as its representative by its attorney;

(3) a person whose presence is shown by a party to be essential to the presentation of the party's cause; or

(4) the victim in a criminal case, unless the victim is to testify and the court determines that the victim's testimony would be materially affected if the victim hears other testimony at the trial.

See TRCP 267; ***Commentaries***, "Introducing Evidence," ch. 8-C; Cochran, ***Texas Rules of Evidence Handbook***, p. 650 (2003).

History of TRE 614 (civil): Amended eff. Mar. 1, 1998, by order of Feb. 25, 1998 (960 S.W.2d [Tex.Cases] lviii). Amended eff. Jan. 1, 1988, by order of July 15, 1987 (733-34 S.W.2d [Tex.Cases] xcvii): This is former TRCE 613. Adopted as TRCE 613 eff. Sept. 1, 1983, by order of Nov. 23, 1982 (641-42 S.W.2d [Tex.Cases] lv). Source: FRE 615.

Drilex Systems, Inc. v. Flores, 1 S.W.3d 112, 118-19 (Tex.1999). "Although an expert witness may *typically* be found exempt under the essential presence exception, experts are not *automatically* exempt. Instead, Rules 614 and 267 vest in trial judges broad discretion to determine whether a witness is essential."

Elbar, Inc. v. Claussen, 774 S.W.2d 45, 51 (Tex. App.—Dallas 1989, writ dism'd). TRE 614, "commonly referred to as 'the rule,' provides for the exclusion of witnesses from the courtroom so that they cannot hear and be influenced by the testimony of other witnesses."

TRE 615. PRODUCTION OF STATEMENTS OF WITNESSES IN CRIMINAL CASES

(a) Motion for Production. After a witness other than the defendant has testified on direct examination, the court, on motion of a party who did not call the witness, shall order the attorney for the state or the defendant and defendant's attorney, as the case may be, to produce, for the examination and use of the moving party, any statement of the witness that is in their possession and that relates to the subject matter concerning which the witness has testified.

(b) Production of Entire Statement. If the entire contents of the statement relate to the subject matter concerning which the witness has testified, the court shall order that the statement be delivered to the moving party.

(c) Production of Excised Statement. If the other party claims that the statement contains matter that does not relate to the subject matter concerning which the witness has testified, the court shall order that it be delivered to the court in camera. Upon inspection, the court shall excise the portions of the statement that do not relate to the subject matter concerning which the witness has testified, and shall order that the statement, with such material excised, be delivered to the moving party. Any portion withheld over objection shall be preserved and made available to the appellate court in the event of appeal.

(d) Recess for Examination of Statement. Upon delivery of the statement to the moving party, the court, upon application of that party, shall recess proceedings in the trial for a reasonable examination of such statement and for preparation for its use in the trial.

(e) Sanction for Failure to Produce Statement. If the other party elects not to comply with an order to deliver a statement to the moving party, the court shall order that the testimony of the witness be stricken from the record and that the trial proceed, or, if it is the attorney for the state who elects not to comply, shall declare a mistrial if required by the interest of justice.

(f) Definition. As used in this rule, a "statement" of a witness means:

(1) a written statement made by the witness that is signed or otherwise adopted or approved by the witness;

(2) a substantially verbatim recital of an oral statement made by the witness that is recorded contemporaneously with the making of the oral statement and that is contained in a stenographic, mechanical, electrical, or other recording or a transcription thereof; or

(3) a statement, however taken or recorded, or a transcription thereof, made by the witness to a grand jury.

Comment to 1998 change: This is prior Rule of Criminal Evidence 614.

See Cochran, ***Texas Rules of Evidence Handbook***, p. 657 (2003).

History of TRE 615 (criminal): Amended eff. Mar. 1, 1998, by order of Feb. 25, 1998 (960 S.W.2d [Tex.Cases] lviii). Adopted eff. Sept. 1, 1986 by order of Dec. 18, 1985 (701-02 S.W.2d [Tex.Cases] l).

ARTICLE VII. OPINIONS & EXPERT TESTIMONY

TRE 701. OPINION TESTIMONY BY LAY WITNESSES

If the witness is not testifying as an expert, the witness' testimony in the form of opinions or inferences is limited to those opinions or inferences which are (a) rationally based on the perception of the witness and (b) helpful to a clear understanding of the witness' testimony or the determination of a fact in issue.

See Cochran, ***Texas Rules of Evidence Handbook***, p. 668 (2003).

History of TRE 701 (civil): Amended eff. Mar. 1, 1998, by order of Feb. 25, 1998 (960 S.W.2d [Tex.Cases] lix). Adopted eff. Sept. 1, 1983, by order of Nov. 23, 1982 (641-42 S.W.2d [Tex.Cases] lv). Source: FRE 701.

Porras v. Craig, 675 S.W.2d 503, 505 (Tex.1984). "[F]or a property owner to qualify as a witness to the damages to his property, his testimony must show that it refers to market, rather than intrinsic or some other value of the property. This requirement is usually met by asking the witness if he is familiar with the market value of his property."

Texas DPS v. Struve, 79 S.W.3d 796, 803 (Tex. App.—Corpus Christi 2002, pet. denied). "A police officer does not need to be an expert to express an opinion as to whether a person he observed is intoxicated. However, if the officer bases his opinion not only on observations, but also on his training and experience, then his qualifications must be established under rule 702."

Whalen v. Condominium Consulting & Mgmt. Servs., 13 S.W.3d 444, 448 (Tex.App.—Corpus Christi 2000, pet. denied). "Lay opinion is adequate to prove causation where general experience and common sense enables a laymen to determine, with reasonable probability, the causal relationship between the event and the condition."

Coker v. Burghardt, 833 S.W.2d 306, 309 (Tex. App.—Dallas 1992, writ denied). "A witness who familiarizes himself with the reasonable car repair costs in a given county can give his opinion about what those costs might be."

City of San Antonio v. Vela, 762 S.W.2d 314, 321 (Tex.App.—San Antonio 1988, writ denied). "'In general, a witness need not be an expert in medical matters to state an opinion as to his own physical health.'"

TRE 702. TESTIMONY BY EXPERTS

If scientific, technical, or other specialized knowledge will assist the trier of fact to understand the evidence or to determine a fact in issue, a witness qualified as an expert by knowledge, skill, experience, training, or education may testify thereto in the form of an opinion or otherwise.

See ***Commentaries***, "Motion to Exclude Expert," ch. 5-M; "Introducing Evidence," ch. 8-C; "Objecting to Evidence," ch. 8-D; Cochran, ***Texas Rules of Evidence Handbook***, p. 682 (2003).

History of TRE 702 (civil): Amended eff. Mar. 1, 1998, by order of Feb. 25, 1998 (960 S.W.2d [Tex.Cases] lix). Adopted eff. Sept. 1, 1983, by order of Nov. 23, 1982 (641-42 S.W.2d [Tex.Cases] lv). Source: FRE 702.

Qualification of Expert

Broders v. Heise, 924 S.W.2d 148, 152 (Tex.1996). "[E]very licensed medical doctor [is not] automatically qualified to testify as an expert on every medical question. *At 153:* [T]he offering party [must] establish that the expert has 'knowledge, skill, experience, training, or education' regarding the specific issue before the court which would qualify the expert to give an opinion on that particular subject." *See also* ***Roberts v. Williamson***, 111 S.W.3d 113, 121 (Tex.2003).

Havner v. E-Z Mart Stores, 825 S.W.2d 456, 460 n.4 (Tex.1992). "An investigating officer may properly testify as to causation."

Schindler Elevator Corp. v. Anderson, 78 S.W.3d 392, 402 (Tex.App.—Houston [14th Dist.] 2001, pet. granted w.r.m.). "[A] witness need not have a college degree to qualify as an expert. Nor is it a prerequisite that an expert witness be an escalator designer to testify about escalator safety and foot entrapment."

Gainsco Cty. Mut. Ins. Co. v. Martinez, 27 S.W.3d 97, 104 (Tex.App.—San Antonio 2000, pet. granted w.r.m.). "Generally, a law enforcement officer is not qualified to render an expert opinion regarding an accident simply by virtue of his position. However, an officer may offer expert testimony in accident cases if the party proffering the testimony demonstrates that the officer is trained in the science about which he will testify and possesses the high degree of knowledge sufficient to qualify him as an expert."

Reliability of Opinion

Exxon Pipeline Co. v. Zwahr, 88 S.W.3d 623, 629 (Tex.2002). TRE 702's "reliability requirement focuses on the principles, research, and methodology underlying an expert's conclusions. [E]xpert testimony is unreliable if it is not grounded in the methods and procedures of science and is no more than subjective belief or unsupported speculation[; or] if there is too great an analytical gap between the data the expert relies upon and the opinion offered. [T]he trial court does not decide whether the expert's conclusions are correct; rather, [it] determines whether the analysis used to reach those conclusions is reliable." (Internal quotes omitted.) *See also* ***Tamez v. Mack Trucks***, 100 S.W.3d 549, 555 (Tex.App.—Corpus Christi 2003, no pet.).

Guadalupe-Blanco River Auth. v. Kraft, 77 S.W.3d 805, 807 (Tex.2002). "To preserve a complaint that an expert's testimony is unreliable, a party must object to the testimony before trial or when it is offered. *See also* ***Maritime Overseas Corp. v. Ellis***, 971 S.W.2d 402, 409 (Tex.1998).

Gammill v. Jack Williams Chevrolet, 972 S.W.2d 713, 726 (Tex.1998). "Nothing in the language of [TRE 702] suggests that opinions based on scientific knowledge should be treated any differently than opinions based on technical or other specialized knowledge. It would be an odd rule of evidence that insisted that some expert opinions be reliable but not others. All expert testimony should be shown to be reliable before it is admitted." *See also* ***Helena Chem. Co. v. Wilkins***, 47 S.W.3d 486, 499 (Tex.2001).

Merrell Dow Pharms. v. Havner, 953 S.W.2d 706, 714 (Tex.1997). "If the foundational data underlying opinion testimony are unreliable, ... any opinion drawn from that data is likewise unreliable. Further, an expert's testimony is unreliable even when the underlying data are sound if the expert draws conclusions from that data based on flawed methodology. A flaw in the expert's reasoning from the data may render reliance on a study unreasonable and render the inferences drawn therefrom dubious. Under that circumstance, the expert's scientific testimony is unreliable and, legally, no evidence."

E.I. du Pont de Nemours & Co. v. Robinson, 923 S.W.2d 549, 557 (Tex.1995). "[The] factors [to consider in determining the admissibility of scientific knowledge include], but are not limited to: (1) the extent to which the theory has been or can be tested; (2) the extent to which the technique relies upon the subjective interpretation of the expert; (3) whether the theory has been subjected to peer review and/or publication; (4) the technique's potential rate of error; (5) whether the underlying theory or technique has been generally accepted as valid by the relevant scientific community; and (6) the non-judicial uses which have been made of the theory or technique."

Common Knowledge

GTE Southwest, Inc. v. Bruce, 998 S.W.2d 605, 620 (Tex.1999). "Except in highly unusual circumstances, expert testimony concerning extreme and outrageous conduct would not meet [the standards of TRE 702]. Where ... the issue involves only general knowledge and experience rather than expertise, it is within the province of the jury to decide...." *See also* ***K-Mart Corp. v. Honeycutt***, 24 S.W.3d 357, 360 (Tex.2000).

In re G.M.P., 909 S.W.2d 198, 206 (Tex.App.—Houston [14th Dist.] 1995, no writ). "A determination of who is telling the truth is the sole province of the jury. [T]he trial court erred in allowing [the expert] to testify that, in his expert opinion [the witness] was telling the truth."

TRE 703. BASES OF OPINION TESTIMONY BY EXPERTS

The facts or data in the particular case upon which an expert bases an opinion or inference may be those perceived by, reviewed by, or made known to the expert at or before the hearing. If of a type reasonably relied upon by experts in the particular field in forming opinions or inferences upon the subject, the facts or data need not be admissible in evidence.

Comment to 1998 change: The former Civil Rule referred to facts or data "perceived by or reviewed by" the expert. The former Criminal Rule referred to facts or data "perceived by or made known to" the expert. The terminology is now conformed, but no change in meaning is intended.

See ***Commentaries***, "Motion to Exclude Expert," ch. 5-M; "Introducing Evidence," ch. 8-C; "Objecting to Evidence," ch. 8-D; Cochran, ***Texas Rules of Evidence Handbook***, p. 717 (2003).

History of TRE 703 (civil): Amended eff. Mar. 1, 1998, by order of Feb. 25, 1998 (960 S.W.2d [Tex.Cases] lx). Amended eff. Sept. 1, 1990, by order of Apr. 24, 1990 (785-86 S.W.2d [Tex.Cases] cvii): Changed the words "made known to him" to "reviewed by the expert."; this amendment conforms TRE 703 to the rules of discovery by using the term "reviewed by the expert." See former TRCP

166b. Adopted eff. Sept. 1, 1983, by order of Nov. 23, 1982 (641-42 S.W.2d [Tex.Cases] lv). Source: FRE 703.

Merrell Dow Pharms. v. Havner, 953 S.W.2d 706, 711 (Tex.1997). "The substance of the [expert's] testimony must be considered. *At 712:* [A]n expert's bald assurance of validity is not enough. *At 713:* The underlying data should be independently evaluated in determining if the opinion itself is reliable."

Stam v. Mack, 984 S.W.2d 747, 750 (Tex.App.—Texarkana 1999, no pet.). TRE 703 and 705 "allow a testifying expert to relate on direct examination the reasonably reliable facts and data on which he relied in forming his opinion, subject to an objection under [TRE] 403 that the probative value of such facts and data is outweighed by the risk of undue prejudice. ... The details of those facts and data may be brought out on cross-examination pursuant to [TRE] 705(a), 705(b), and 705(d). Moreover, the opponent of such evidence may ask for a limiting instruction if he fears the evidence may be used for a purpose other than support for the testifying expert's opinion."

Sosa ex rel. Grant v. Koshy, 961 S.W.2d 420, 427 (Tex.App.—Houston [1st Dist.] 1997, pet. denied). "Under rule 703, Officer Null, as an expert on accident reconstruction, properly relied on hearsay evidence provided by eyewitnesses to the accident if experts in his field would reasonably rely on such evidence."

TRE 704. OPINION ON ULTIMATE ISSUE

Testimony in the form of an opinion or inference otherwise admissible is not objectionable because it embraces an ultimate issue to be decided by the trier of fact.

See ***Commentaries***, "Objecting to Evidence," ch. 8-D; Cochran, ***Texas Rules of Evidence Handbook***, p. 790 (2003).

History of TRE 704 (civil): Amended eff. Mar. 1, 1998, by order of Feb. 25, 1998 (960 S.W.2d [Tex.Cases] lx). Adopted eff. Sept. 1, 1983, by order of Nov. 23, 1982 (641-42 S.W.2d [Tex.Cases] lv). Source: FRE 704.

Birchfield v. Texarkana Mem'l Hosp., 747 S.W.2d 361, 365 (Tex.1987). "Fairness and efficiency dictate that an expert may state an opinion on a mixed question of law and fact as long as the opinion is confined to the relevant issues and is based on proper legal concepts." An expert may testify that conduct constituted "negligence" and "gross negligence," and that certain acts were "proximate causes" of P's injuries.

Dickerson v. DeBarbieris, 964 S.W.2d 680, 690 (Tex.App.—Houston [14th Dist.] 1998, no pet.). "Although rule 704 allows an expert to state an opinion on a mixed question of law and fact, it does not permit an expert to state an opinion or conclusion on a pure question of law because such a question is exclusively for the court to decide...."

Isern v. Watson, 942 S.W.2d 186, 193 (Tex.App.—Beaumont 1997, pet. denied). "[B]efore a testifying expert's opinion can be rendered [on negligence, gross negligence, or proximate cause], a predicate must be laid showing that the expert is familiar with the proper legal definition in question."

TRE 705. DISCLOSURE OF FACTS OR DATA UNDERLYING EXPERT OPINION

(a) Disclosure of Facts or Data. The expert may testify in terms of opinion or inference and give the expert's reasons therefor without prior disclosure of the underlying facts or data, unless the court requires otherwise. The expert may in any event disclose on direct examination, or be required to disclose on cross-examination, the underlying facts or data.

(b) Voir dire. Prior to the expert giving the expert's opinion or disclosing the underlying facts or data, a party against whom the opinion is offered upon request in a criminal case shall, or in a civil case may, be permitted to conduct a *voir dire* examination directed to the underlying facts or data upon which the opinion is based. This examination shall be conducted out of the hearing of the jury.

(c) Admissibility of opinion. If the court determines that the underlying facts or data do not provide a sufficient basis for the expert's opinion under Rule 702 or 703, the opinion is inadmissible.

(d) Balancing test; limiting instructions. When the underlying facts or data would be inadmissible in evidence, the court shall exclude the underlying facts or data if the danger that they will be used for a purpose other than as explanation or support for the expert's opinion outweighs their value as explanation or support or are unfairly prejudicial. If otherwise inadmissible facts or data are disclosed before the jury, a limiting instruction by the court shall be given upon request.

Comment to 1998 change: Paragraphs (b), (c), and (d) are based on the former Criminal Rule and are made applicable to civil cases. This rule does not preclude a party in any case from conducting a *voir dire* examination into the qualifications of an expert.

See *Commentaries,* "Motion to Exclude Expert," ch. 5-M; Cochran, ***Texas Rules of Evidence Handbook***, p. 738 (2003).

History of TRE 705 (civil): Amended eff. Mar. 1, 1998, by order of Feb. 25, 1998 (960 S.W.2d [Tex.Cases] lx). Amended eff. Nov. 1, 1984, by order of June 25, 1984 (669-70 S.W.2d [Tex.Cases] xxxviii): Added "disclose on direct examination, or" and "on cross-examination" to last sentence. Adopted eff. Sept. 1, 1983, by order of Nov. 23, 1982 (641-42 S.W.2d [Tex.Cases] lv). Source: FRE 705.

Weiss v. Mechanical Assoc. Servs., 989 S.W.2d 120, 124-25 (Tex.App.—San Antonio 1999, pet. denied). "The non-exclusive list of factors the court may consider in deciding admissibility [under TRE 705(c)] includes the extent to which the theory has been or can be tested, the extent to which the technique relies upon the subjective interpretation of the expert, whether the theory has been subjected to peer review and/or publication, the technique's potential rate of error, whether the underlying theory or technique has been generally accepted as valid by the relevant scientific community, and the non-judicial uses that have been made of the theory or technique."

Stam v. Mack, 984 S.W.2d 747, 750 (Tex.App.—Texarkana 1999, no pet.). See annotation under TRE 703.

TRE 706. AUDIT IN CIVIL CASES

Despite any other evidence rule to the contrary, verified reports of auditors prepared pursuant to Rule of Civil Procedure 172, whether in the form of summaries, opinions, or otherwise, shall be admitted in evidence when offered by any party whether or not the facts or data in the reports are otherwise admissible and whether or not the reports embrace the ultimate issues to be decided by the trier of fact. Where exceptions to the reports have been filed, a party may contradict the reports by evidence supporting the exceptions.

See Cochran, ***Texas Rules of Evidence Handbook***, p. 753 (2003).

History of TRE 706 (civil): Amended eff. Mar. 1, 1998, by order of Feb. 25, 1998 (960 S.W.2d [Tex.Cases] lxi). Adopted eff. Jan. 1, 1988, by order of July 15, 1987 (733-34 S.W.2d [Tex.Cases] xcvii): To conform to TRCP 172. Source: New rule.

Lovelace v. Sabine Consol., Inc., 733 S.W.2d 648, 656 (Tex.App.—Houston [14th Dist.] 1987, writ denied). "The audit report ... contains no such affidavit as is required by [TRCP] 172. ... Further, 6 days before trial [P] filed an objection to the audit. Therefore, the trial court did not err in admitting evidence that contradicted and supplemented the auditor's report."

ARTICLE VIII. HEARSAY

TRE 801. DEFINITIONS

The following definitions apply under this article:

(a) Statement. A "statement" is (1) an oral or written verbal expression or (2) nonverbal conduct of a person, if it is intended by the person as a substitute for verbal expression.

(b) Declarant. A "declarant" is a person who makes a statement.

(c) Matter Asserted. "Matter asserted" includes any matter explicitly asserted, and any matter implied by a statement, if the probative value of the statement as offered flows from declarant's belief as to the matter.

(d) Hearsay. "Hearsay" is a statement, other than one made by the declarant while testifying at the trial or hearing, offered in evidence to prove the truth of the matter asserted.

(e) Statements Which Are Not Hearsay. A statement is not hearsay if:

(1) *Prior statement by witness.* The declarant testifies at the trial or hearing and is subject to cross-examination concerning the statement, and the statement is:

(A) inconsistent with the declarant's testimony, and was given under oath subject to the penalty of perjury at a trial, hearing, or other proceeding except a grand jury proceeding in a criminal case, or in a deposition;

(B) consistent with the declarant's testimony and is offered to rebut an express or implied charge against the declarant of recent fabrication or improper influence or motive;

(C) one of identification of a person made after perceiving the person; or

(D) taken and offered in a criminal case in accordance with Code of Criminal Procedure article 38.071.

(2) *Admission by party-opponent.* The statement is offered against a party and is:

(A) the party's own statement in either an individual or representative capacity;

(B) a statement of which the party has manifested an adoption or belief in its truth;

(C) a statement by a person authorized by the party to make a statement concerning the subject;

(D) a statement by the party's agent or servant concerning a matter within the scope of the agency or employment, made during the existence of the relationship; or

(E) a statement by a co-conspirator of a party during the course and in furtherance of the conspiracy.

(3) *Depositions.* In a civil case, it is a deposition taken in the same proceeding, as same proceeding is defined in Rule of Civil Procedure 203.6(b). Unavailability of deponent is not a requirement for admissibility.

See ***Commentaries***, "Depositions," ch. 6-E; "Requests for Admissions," ch. 6-G; Cochran, ***Texas Rules of Evidence Handbook***, p. 763 (2003).

History of TRE 801 (civil): Amended eff. Jan. 1, 1999, by order of Dec. 31, 1998 (981-82 S.W.2d [Tex.Cases] xxxviii). Amended eff. Mar. 1, 1998, by order of Feb. 25, 1998 (960 S.W.2d [Tex.Cases] lxi). Amended eff. Jan. 1, 1988, by order of Nov. 10, 1986 (733-34 S.W.2d [Tex.Cases] xc): Amended (c)(3). Adopted eff. Sept. 1, 1983, by order of Nov. 23, 1982 (641-42 S.W.2d [Tex.Cases] lvi): The definitions in TRCE 801(a), (b), (c) and (d) combined bring within the hearsay rule four categories of conduct; these are described and illustrated below.

(1) A verbal (oral or written) explicit assertion. Illustration. Witness testifies that declarant said "A shot B." Declarant's conduct is a statement because it is an oral expression. Because it is an explicit assertion, the matter asserted is that A shot B. Finally, the statement is hearsay because it was not made while testifying at the trial and is offered to prove the truth of the matter asserted.

(2) A verbal (oral or written) explicit assertion, not offered to prove the matter explicitly asserted, but offered for the truth of a matter implied by the statement, the probative value of the statement flowing from declarant's belief as to the matter. Illustration. The only known remedy for X disease is medicine Y and the only known use of medicine Y is to cure X disease. To prove that Oglethorpe had X disease, witness testifies that declarant, a doctor, stated, "The best medicine for Oglethorpe is Y." The testimony is to a statement because it was a verbal expression. The matter asserted was that Oglethorpe had X disease because that matter is implied from the statement, the probative value of the statement as offered flowing from declarant's belief as to the matter. Finally, the statement is hearsay because it was not made while testifying at the trial and is offered to prove the truth of the matter asserted.

(3) Non-assertive verbal conduct offered for the truth of a matter implied by the statement, the probative value of the statement flowing from declarant's belief as to the matter. Illustration. In a rape prosecution to prove that Richard, the defendant, was in the room at the time of the rape, W testifies that declarant knocked on the door to the room and shouted, "Open the door, Richard." The testimony is to a statement because it was a verbal expression. The matter asserted was that Richard was in the room because that matter is implied from the statement, the probative value of the statement as offered flowing from declarant's belief as to the matter. Finally, the statement is hearsay because it was not made while testifying at the trial and is offered to prove the truth of the matter asserted.

(4) Nonverbal assertive conduct intended as a substitute for verbal expression. Illustration. W testifies that A asked declarant "Which way did X go?" and declarant pointed north. This nonverbal conduct of declarant was intended by him as a substitute for verbal expression and so is a statement. The matter asserted is that X went north because that is implied from the statement and the probative value of the statement as offered flows from declarant's belief that X went north. Finally, the statement is hearsay because it was not made at trial and is offered to prove the truth of the matter asserted.

Source: FRE 801.

TRE 801(d)

In re M.S., 115 S.W.3d 534, 543 (Tex.2003). "[T]he Agreement [between D and Child Protective Services] was not offered as proof of [D's] inability to care for her children, or as proof that her parental rights should be terminated, or as proof that termination was in the children's best interest. Rather, the Agreement was offered to show that an agreement had been made and what its terms were. The Agreement was not hearsay."

McCraw v. Maris, 828 S.W.2d 756, 757 (Tex.1992). "Out-of-court statements are not hearsay if offered for a purpose other than to prove the truth of the matter asserted. Since the duplicate beneficiary designation form was offered only to prove its existence, we conclude that it was not hearsay."

City of Austin v. H.L. & P. Co., 844 S.W.2d 773, 791 (Tex.App.—Dallas 1992, writ denied). "Generally, Texas courts consider newspaper articles inadmissible hearsay. [N]ewspaper articles not offered for the truth of the matters asserted but used merely to show notice of those matters are not hearsay."

TRE 801(e)

Tome v. U.S., 513 U.S. 150, 156, 115 S.Ct. 696, 701 (1995) (criminal case interpreting federal rule). If a witness was cross-examined about the statement, a party may introduce a earlier consistent statement to rebut the charge of recent fabrication or improper influence by proving through another witness, that (1) before testifying, the testifying witness made out-of-court statement consistent with testimony, and (2) the statement was made before the testifying witness had reason to fabricate.

Trencor, Inc. v. Cornech Mach. Co., 115 S.W.3d 145, 151 (Tex.App.—Fort Worth 2003, pet. denied). "A statement by a party's agent or servant concerning a matter within the scope of his agency or employment and made during the existence of the relationship may be offered as an admission by the party itself. The fact of agency must, however, be established before the declaration can be admitted."

Worley v. Butler, 809 S.W.2d 242, 245 (Tex.App.—Corpus Christi 1990, no writ). TRE 801(e)(2) "provides that a statement is not hearsay if it is offered against a party and is his own statement in either his individual or representative capacity. [D's] prior testimony concerning his employment agreement and fee arrangement is being offered against him as a party-opponent. Further, [D] made these statements in his individual capacity."

Reviea v. Marine Drilling Co., 800 S.W.2d 252, 257 (Tex.App.—Corpus Christi 1990, writ denied). D's witness "testified at trial and was subject to cross-examination concerning his statement about [P's] prior knee injury. Thus, his statement to [the claims investigator] was consistent with his trial testimony regarding [P's] prior knee injury. We find that the prior consistent statement of [D's witness] concerning [P's] admission of a prior injury was not hearsay, as it was offered to rebut [P's] implied charge of recent fabrication."

TRE 802. HEARSAY RULE

Hearsay is not admissible except as provided by statute or these rules or by other rules prescribed pursuant to statutory authority. Inadmissible hearsay admitted without objection shall not be denied probative value merely because it is hearsay.

See Cochran, ***Texas Rules of Evidence Handbook***, p. 808 (2003).

History of TRE 802 (civil): Amended eff. Mar. 1, 1998, by order of Feb. 25, 1998 (960 S.W.2d [Tex.Cases] lxii). Adopted eff. Sept. 1, 1983, by order of Nov. 23, 1982 (641-42 S.W.2d [Tex.Cases] lvii). Source: FRE 802.

Texas Commerce Bank v. New, 3 S.W.3d 515, 517 (Tex.1999). "Nothing in [TRE] 802 limits its application to contested hearings. The rule is not ambiguous and requires no explication." Thus, an affidavit containing unobjected-to hearsay can establish facts in a default judgment case.

Birchfield v. Texarkana Mem'l Hosp., 747 S.W.2d 361, 365 (Tex.1987). "Ordinarily an expert witness should not be permitted to recount a hearsay conversation with a third person, even if that conversation forms part of the basis of his opinion."

Schleuter v. City of Ft. Worth, 947 S.W.2d 920, 930 (Tex.App.—Fort Worth 1997, pet. denied). "[D] timely objected to admission of the affidavits as hearsay [but the] court overruled the objection.... Admission of these out-of-court statements without a showing that the declarants were unavailable or that a hearsay exception applied was error."

TRE 803. HEARSAY EXCEPTIONS; AVAILABILITY OF DECLARANT IMMATERIAL

The following are not excluded by the hearsay rule, even though the declarant is available as a witness:

(1) Present Sense Impression. A statement describing or explaining an event or condition made while the declarant was perceiving the event or condition, or immediately thereafter.

(2) Excited Utterance. A statement relating to a startling event or condition made while the declarant was under the stress of excitement caused by the event or condition.

(3) Then Existing Mental, Emotional, or Physical Condition. A statement of the declarant's then existing state of mind, emotion, sensation, or physical condition (such as intent, plan, motive, design, mental feeling, pain, or bodily health), but not including a statement of memory or belief to prove the fact remembered or believed unless it relates to the execution, revocation, identification, or terms of declarant's will.

(4) Statements for Purposes of Medical Diagnosis or Treatment. Statements made for purposes of medical diagnosis or treatment and describing medical history, or past or present symptoms, pain, or sensations, or the inception or general character of the cause or external source thereof insofar as reasonably pertinent to diagnosis or treatment.

(5) Recorded Recollection. A memorandum or record concerning a matter about which a witness once had personal knowledge but now has insufficient recollection to enable the witness to testify fully and accurately, shown to have been made or adopted by the witness when the matter was fresh in the witness' memory and to reflect that knowledge correctly, unless the circumstances of preparation cast doubt on the document's trustworthiness. If admitted, the memorandum or record may be read into evidence but may not itself be received as an exhibit unless offered by an adverse party.

(6) Records of Regularly Conducted Activity. A memorandum, report, record, or data compilation, in any form, of acts, events, conditions, opinions, or diagnoses, made at or near the time by, or from information transmitted by, a person with knowledge, if kept in the course of a regularly conducted business activity, and if it was the regular practice of that business activity to make the memorandum, report, record, or data compilation, all as shown by the testimony of the custodian or other qualified witness, or by affidavit that complies with Rule 902(10), unless the source of information or the method or circumstances of preparation indicate lack of trustworthiness. "Business" as used in this paragraph includes any and every kind of regular organized activity whether conducted for profit or not.

(7) Absence of Entry in Records Kept in Accordance With the Provisions of Paragraph (6). Evidence that a matter is not included in the memoranda, reports, records, or data compilations, in any form, kept in accordance with the provisions of paragraph (6), to prove the nonoccurrence or nonexistence of the matter, if the matter was of a kind of which a memorandum, report, record, or data compilation was regularly made and preserved, unless the sources of information or other circumstances indicate lack of trustworthiness.

(8) Public Records and Reports. Records, reports, statements, or data compilations, in any form, of public offices or agencies setting forth:

(A) the activities of the office or agency;

(B) matters observed pursuant to duty imposed by law as to which matters there was a duty to report, excluding in criminal cases matters observed by police officers and other law enforcement personnel; or

(C) in civil cases as to any party and in criminal cases as against the state, factual findings resulting from an investigation made pursuant to authority granted by law;

unless the sources of information or other circumstances indicate lack of trustworthiness.

(9) Records of Vital Statistics. Records or data compilations, in any form, of births, fetal deaths, deaths, or marriages, if the report thereof was made to a public office pursuant to requirements of law.

(10) Absence of Public Record or Entry. To prove the absence of a record, report, statement, or data compilation, in any form, or the nonoccurrence or nonexistence of a matter of which a record, report, statement, or data compilation, in any form, was regularly made and preserved by a public office or agency, evidence in the form of a certification in accordance with Rule 902, or testimony, that diligent search failed to disclose the record, report statement, or data compilation, or entry.

(11) Records of Religious Organizations. Statements of births, marriages, divorces, deaths, legitimacy, ancestry, relationship by blood or marriage, or other similar facts of personal or family history, contained in a regularly kept record of a religious organization.

(12) Marriage, Baptismal, and Similar Certificates. Statements of fact contained in a certificate that the maker performed a marriage or other ceremony or administered a sacrament, made by a member of the clergy, public official, or other person authorized by the rules or practices of a religious organization or by law to perform the act certified, and purporting to have been issued at the time of the act or within a reasonable time thereafter.

(13) Family Records. Statements of fact concerning personal or family history contained in family Bibles, genealogies, charts, engravings on rings, inscriptions on family portraits, engravings on urns, crypts, or tombstones, or the like.

(14) Records of Documents Affecting an Interest in Property. The record of a document purporting to establish or affect an interest in property, as proof of the content of the original recorded document and its execution and delivery by each person by whom it purports to have been executed, if the record is a record of a public office and an applicable statute authorizes the recording of documents of that kind in that office.

(15) Statements in Documents Affecting an Interest in Property. A statement contained in a document purporting to establish or affect an interest in property if the matter stated was relevant to the purpose of the document, unless dealings with the property since the document was made have been inconsistent with the truth of the statement or the purport of the document.

(16) Statements in Ancient Documents. Statements in a document in existence twenty years or more the authenticity of which is established.

(17) Market Reports, Commercial Publications. Market quotations, tabulations, lists, directories, or other published compilations, generally used and relied upon by the public or by persons in particular occupations.

(18) Learned Treatises. To the extent called to the attention of an expert witness upon cross-examination or relied upon by the expert in direct examination, statements contained in published treatises, periodicals, or pamphlets on a subject of history, medicine, or other science or art established as a reliable authority by the testimony or admission of the witness or by other expert testimony or by judicial notice. If admitted, the statements may be read into evidence but may not be received as exhibits.

(19) Reputation Concerning Personal or Family History. Reputation among members of a person's family by blood, adoption, or marriage, or among a person's associates, or in the community, concerning a person's birth, adoption, marriage, divorce, death, legitimacy, relationship by blood, adoption, or marriage, ancestry, or other similar fact of personal or family history.

(20) Reputation Concerning Boundaries or General History. Reputation in a community, arising before the controversy, as to boundaries of or customs affecting lands in the community, and reputation as to events of general history important to the community or state or nation in which located.

(21) Reputation as to Character. Reputation of a person's character among associates or in the community.

(22) Judgment of Previous Conviction. In civil cases, evidence of a judgment, entered after a trial or upon a plea of guilty (but not upon a plea of *nolo contendere*), judging a person guilty of a felony, to prove any fact essential to sustain the judgment of conviction. In criminal cases, evidence of a judgment, entered after a trial or upon a plea of guilty or nolo contendere, adjudging a person guilty of a criminal offense, to prove any fact essential to sustain the judgment of conviction, but not including, when offered by the state for purposes other than impeachment, judgments against persons other than the accused. In all cases, the pendency of an appeal renders such evidence inadmissible.

(23) Judgment as to Personal, Family, or General History, or Boundaries. Judgments as proof of matters of personal, family or general history, or boundaries, essential to the judgment, if the same would be provable by evidence of reputation.

(24) Statement Against Interest. A statement which was at the time of its making so far contrary to the declarant's pecuniary or proprietary interest, or so far tended to subject the declarant to civil or criminal liability, or to render invalid a claim by the declarant against another, or to make the declarant an object of hatred, ridicule, or disgrace, that a reasonable person in declarant's position would not have made the statement unless believing it to be true. In criminal cases, a statement tending to expose the declarant to criminal liability is not admissible unless corroborating circumstances clearly indicate the trustworthiness of the statement.

See Family Code §54.031, for statutory exceptions to hearsay rule for testimony of a child in a juvenile proceeding; Cochran, ***Texas Rules of Evidence Handbook***, p. 810 (2003).

History of TRE 803 (civil): Amended eff. Mar. 1, 1998, by order of Feb. 25, 1998 (960 S.W.2d [Tex.Cases] lxii). Amended eff. Jan. 1, 1988, by order of Nov. 10, 1986 (733-34 S.W.2d [Tex.Cases] xc): To (6), added "or by affidavit that complies with Rule 902(10)." Amended eff. Nov. 1, 1984, by order of order of June 25, 1984 (669-70 S.W.2d [Tex.Cases] xxxviii): Added the following comment: The provision in par. (6) rejects the doctrine of *Loper v. Andrews*, 404 S.W.2d 300, 305 (Tex.1966), which required that an entry of a medical opinion or diagnosis meet a test of "reasonable medical certainty." Adopted eff. Sept. 1, 1983, by order of Nov. 23, 1982 (641-42 S.W.2d [Tex.Cases] lvii). Source: FRE 803. See TRCS arts. 3718-3737e (repealed).

Generally

Robinson v. Harkins & Co., 711 S.W.2d 619, 621 (Tex.1986). "All hearsay exceptions require a showing of trustworthiness."

TRE 803(1)

1.70 Acres v. State, 935 S.W.2d 480, 488 (Tex. App.—Beaumont 1996, no writ). "Present sense impressions are those comments made at the time the declarant is receiving the impression or immediately thereafter. They possess the following safeguards which render them reliable: 1) the report at the moment of the thing then seen, heard, etc. is safe from any error from defect of memory of the declarant; 2) there is little or no time for a calculated misstatement; 3) the statement will usually be made to another—the witness who reports it—who would have equal opportunity to observe and hence to check a misstatement."

TRE 803(2)

Felix v. Gonzalez, 87 S.W.3d 574, 578-79 (Tex. App.—San Antonio 2002, pet. denied). "The core of [TRE 803(2)] is reliability—a statement made by an out-of-court declarant during a state of excitement is more reliable than a statement made after time for reflection upon a startling event. Once the timing of the state of excitement is demonstrated, so long as the statement made *relates to* the startling event, it falls within the purview of the excited utterance exception."

Almaraz v. Burke, 827 S.W.2d 80, 83 (Tex.App.—Fort Worth 1992, writ denied). "Although [***First Southwest Lloyds***, see below] states that the witness's statement was a narrative account, given after he had returned to the scene of the fire, the opinion does not reflect whether the witness was still excited from the fire and the chase at the time the statement was given, nor does it state whether that mattered in reaching the result. If the witness in that case were still excited from the event at the time he told the fire marshall what had just happened, we would have held that the evidence qualified as an exception to the hearsay rule in accordance with rule 803(2). On the other hand, if there were no evidence that the witness was still under the excitement of the preceding events, we would agree with the opinion."

First Southwest Lloyds Ins. Co. v. MacDowell, 769 S.W.2d 954, 959 (Tex.App.—Texarkana 1989, writ denied). "A statement that is simply a narrative of past acts or events, as distinguished from a spontaneous utterance, does not qualify as an excited utterance regardless of how soon after the event that it is made. The circumstances must show that it was the event speaking through the person and not the person speaking about the event."

TRE 803(3)

Power v. Kelley, 70 S.W.3d 137, 141 (Tex.App.—San Antonio 2001, pet. denied). "'Statements admitted under [TRE 803(3)] are usually spontaneous remarks about pain or some other sensation, made by the declarant while the sensation, not readily observable by a third party, is being experienced.' 'The exception does not extend to statements of past external facts or conditions.'"

TRE 803(4)

In re L.S., 748 S.W.2d 571, 576 (Tex.App.—Amarillo 1988, no writ). "The crucial issue under [TRE 803(4)] is whether the out-of-court statement was reasonably pertinent to diagnosis or treatment. [¶] [A] statement made by a victim of child abuse identifying the alleged perpetrator is pertinent to both physical and psychological diagnosis and treatment."

TRE 803(6)

Burroughs Wellcome Co. v. Crye, 907 S.W.2d 497, 500 (Tex.1995). "The diagnoses contained in [P's] medical and hospital records are admissible. However, to constitute evidence of causation, an expert opinion must rest in reasonable medical probability. [¶] The context of the opinions contained in the medical records ... indicates that these statements are merely recitations of medical history or opinion as to causation provided by other records, [P], or [her doctor]." Held: no evidence of causation.

Freeman v. American Motorists Ins. Co., 53 S.W.3d 710, 715 (Tex.App.—Houston [1st Dist.] 2001, no pet.) The letter from P's physician "to [P's] attorney was dated ... over 10 years after the cause of action accrued and a mere 10 days before the summary judgment hearing. This time frame indicates a lack of trustworthiness. In the absence of [P's physician's] remaining records, it appears that he wrote the letter solely in response to a request from [P's] attorney. [The letter] does not qualify as a routine entry in [P's] medical history; therefore, it is inadmissible as a business record under rule 803(6)."

Rodriguez-Narrera v. Ridinger, 19 S.W.3d 531, 532 (Tex.App.—Fort Worth 2000, no pet.). "[P's] medical bills and expenses, verified by custodians' affidavits, were admissible as business records. ... However, those exhibits would have been admissible solely to prove the amount, not the reasonableness or necessity, of the expenses. Proof of amounts charged or paid is not proof of reasonableness...."

GT & MC, Inc. v. Texas City Ref., Inc., 822 S.W.2d 252, 258 (Tex.App.—Houston [1st Dist.] 1991, writ denied). D claimed evidence admitted as P's business records were not business records because they were invoices created by another entity and sent to P. "Though the documents in question were initially authored by outside vendors, employees of [P] placed numerous markings on the invoices after receipt by [P]. ... Thus, the invoices became [P's] primary record of information about the underlying transaction."

TRE 803(7)

Coleman v. United Sav. Ass'n, 846 S.W.2d 128, 131 (Tex.App.—Fort Worth 1993, no writ). "Testimony that is offered as evidence that a matter is not included in records to prove the nonoccurrence or nonexistence of the matter is inadmissible hearsay evidence unless [TRE] 803(7) is satisfied. The initial foundational predicate of rule 803(7) is that the records that would include the matter, if it were not absent from those records, are kept in accordance with the provisions of rule 803(6). [D's] affidavit does not even attempt to satisfy the requirements of rule 803(6) and therefore cannot support the summary judgment."

TRE 803(8)

Robinson v. Warner-Lambert, 998 S.W.2d 407, 412 (Tex.App.—Waco 1999, no pet.). "[T]he evidence at issue here is an article and not a record, report, statement, or data compilation of a public office or agency. The information contained within the article may summarize a study, but cannot be said to be a report of an agency. Thus, the article is not admissible under [TRE] 803(8)(C)."

TRE 803(10)

Towne Square Assocs. v. Angelina Cty. Appr. Dist., 709 S.W.2d 776, 777 (Tex.App.—Beaumont 1986, no writ). "[Ds'] affidavits stated that, after a diligent search, [Ds] could find no notice of appeal filed in the records. [Ps] assert these affidavits are insufficient in that they contain hearsay and do not have some of the predicate language required for a business record in accordance with [TRE] 902. [Ps'] complete reliance on this rule is misplaced. The affidavits are controlled by [TRE] 803(10).... While it is true the affidavits do not meet the authentication requirements of Rule 902, they do contain testimony that a diligent search failed to disclose the notice of appeal."

TRE 803(14) & (15)

Compton v. WWV Enters., 679 S.W.2d 668, 671 (Tex.App.—Eastland 1984, no writ). "Hearsay exceptions [TRE 803(14) & (15)] must ... be construed to relate to recitals or statements made in deeds, leases, mortgages and other such 'documents affecting an interest in property' and not to affidavits of heirship which more properly fall within the hearsay exception stated under [TRE] 804(b)(3)."

TRE 803(16)

Guthrie v. Suiter, 934 S.W.2d 820, 825 (Tex.App.—Houston [1st Dist.] 1996, no writ). "Statements contained in documents 20 years old or older qualify as an exception to the hearsay rule, provided the documents are properly authenticated. To qualify for this exception, the document must be shown (1) in such condition as to create no suspicion concerning its authenticity; (2) that it was in a place where it would likely be if it were authentic; and (3) that it has been in existence 20 years or more at the time it is offered."

TRE 803(17)

New Braunfels Factory Outlet Ctr. v. IHOP Rlty. Corp., 872 S.W.2d 303, 310 (Tex.App.—Austin 1994, no writ). "The hearsay exception provided by [TRE] 803(17) permits the admission of certain objective data.... At common law, survey results were also admissible *provided* that the party opposing admission was given the opportunity to cross-examine the person who had conducted the survey."

TRE 803(18)

King v. Bauer, 767 S.W.2d 197, 199-200 (Tex.App.—Corpus Christi 1989, writ denied). Under TRE 803(18), P introduced a medical textbook that was published two years after P's therapy, but the earlier edition of which was recognized by D as a learned treatise. "The fact that the 3rd edition [of the textbook] was not published until 1980 does not serve to disqualify the evidence which was aimed at illustrating an appropriate treatment plan for [P] in 1978. Treatises which directly refer to the standard of care in use at the time of the occurrence are material, relevant and therefore admissible."

TRE 803(19)

Akers v. Stevenson, 54 S.W.3d 880, 885 (Tex.App.—Beaumont 2001, pet. denied). The hearsay exception for evidence concerning personal or family history arises "from necessity and [is] founded on the general reliability of statements by family members about family affairs when the statements by deceased persons regarding family history were made at a time when no pecuniary interest or other biased reason for the statements were present."

TRE 803(20)

Roberts v. Allison, 836 S.W.2d 185, 191 (Tex. App.—Tyler 1992, writ denied). "A reason for the exception [in TRE 803(20)] is '[t]he fact that a prolonged observation and discussion of certain matters of *general interest by a whole community will sift possible errors and bring the result down to us in a fairly trustworthy form furnishes a guarantee of correctness.*' [Ps'] proposed testimony pertains to an individual family's assertion of an easement; there is no contention of the ... community's knowledge of [Ps'] claim to access [D's] property. ... There was no proof of the recognized 'vehicles of reputation', such as 'declarations of residents, old maps, surveys, deeds and leases' of the claimed easement. ... The trial court did not abuse its discretion in excluding [the] testimony of a claimed oral agreement granting an easement to [Ps] over the subject property."

TRE 803(22)

McCormick v. Texas Commerce Bank, 751 S.W.2d 887, 890 (Tex.App.—Houston [14th Dist.] 1988, writ denied). "Where (i) the issue at stake was identical to that in the criminal case, (ii) the issue had been actually litigated, and (iii) determination of the issue was a critical and necessary part of the prior judgment, the judgment is established by offensive collateral estoppel and is within the hearsay exception of [FRE] 803(22). [¶] Applying the standards of the federal judiciary to [TRE] 803(22), we hold that the trial court did not err in refusing to permit [D] to explain the circumstances of his criminal conviction."

TRE 803(24)

State v. Arnold, 778 S.W.2d 68, 69 (Tex.1989). Under TRE 803(24), a "statement may be self-serving in one respect but contrary to another interest. The court must balance these competing interests to determine their predominant nature and ultimately the level of trustworthiness to be accorded."

Green v. Reyes, 836 S.W.2d 203, 213 (Tex.App.—Houston [14th Dist.] 1992, no writ). "[A]ffidavits of persons who ... admit under oath an action which can subject them to criminal liability may be properly admitted at trial as an exception to the hearsay rule as statements against their interest."

TRE 804. HEARSAY EXCEPTIONS; DECLARANT UNAVAILABLE

(a) Definition of Unavailability. "Unavailability as a witness" includes situations in which the declarant:

(1) is exempted by ruling of the court on the ground of privilege from testifying concerning the subject matter of the declarant's statement;

(2) persists in refusing to testify concerning the subject matter of the declarant's statement despite an order of the court to do so;

(3) testifies to a lack of memory of the subject matter of the declarant's statement;

(4) is unable to be present or to testify at the hearing because of death or then existing physical or mental illness or infirmity; or

(5) is absent from the hearing and the proponent of the declarant's statement has been unable to procure the declarant's attendance or testimony by process or other reasonable means.

A declarant is not unavailable as a witness if the declarant's exemption, refusal, claim of lack of memory, inability, or absence is due to the procurement or wrong-doing of the proponent of the declarant's statement for the purpose of preventing the witness from attending or testifying.

(b) Hearsay Exceptions. The following are not excluded if the declarant is unavailable as a witness:

(1) *Former testimony.* In civil cases, testimony given as a witness at another hearing of the same or a different proceeding, or in a deposition taken in the course of another proceeding, if the party against whom the testimony is now offered, or a person with a similar interest, had an opportunity and similar motive to develop the testimony by direct, cross, or redirect examination. In criminal cases, testimony given as a witness at another hearing of the same or a different proceeding, if the party against whom the testimony is now offered had an opportunity and similar motive to develop the testimony by direct, cross, or redirect examination. In criminal cases the use of depositions is controlled by Chapter 39 of the Code of Criminal Procedure.

(2) *Dying declarations.* A statement made by a declarant while believing that the declarant's death was imminent, concerning the cause or circumstances of what the declarant believed to be impending death.

(3) *Statement of personal or family history.*

(A) A statement concerning the declarant's own birth, adoption, marriage, divorce, legitimacy, relationship by blood, adoption, or marriage, ancestry, or other similar fact of personal or family history even though declarant had no means of acquiring personal knowledge of the matter stated; or

(B) A statement concerning the foregoing matters, and death also, of another person, if the declarant was related to the other by blood, adoption, or marriage or was so intimately associated with the other's family as to be likely to have accurate information concerning the matter declared.

See *Commentaries*, "Depositions," ch. 6-E; Cochran, ***Texas Rules of Evidence Handbook***, p. 804 (2003).

History of TRE 804 (civil): Amended eff. Mar. 1, 1998, by order of Feb. 25, 1998 (960 S.W.2d [Tex.Cases] lxvi). Amended eff. Jan. 1, 1988, by order of Nov. 10, 1986 (733-34 S.W.2d [Tex.Cases] xc): To TRCE 804(b)(1), deleted "the same or" before "another proceeding."; in some circumstances, a deposition may be admissible without regard to unavailability of the deponent. See former TRCE 801(e)(3) and former TRCP 207. Adopted eff. Sept. 1, 1983, by order of Nov. 23, 1982 (641-42 S.W.2d [Tex.Cases] lx). Source: FRE 804.

Fuller-Austin Insulation Co. v. Bilder, 960 S.W.2d 914, 921 (Tex.App.—Beaumont 1998, pet. dism'd). "[T]he fact that [the witness] was uncooperative in attending trial did not mean he could not give his deposition.... Although [the witness] may have been beyond the subpoena power of the court, [D] did not establish it was unable to take his deposition or otherwise procure his testimony in this cause."

Thompson v. Mayes, 707 S.W.2d 951, 957 (Tex. App.—Eastland 1986, writ ref'd n.r.e.). Under TRE 804(b)(2), "dying declarations which concern the cause or the circumstances of what the declarant believed to be his impending death are admissible as exceptions to the hearsay rule."

TRE 805. HEARSAY WITHIN HEARSAY

Hearsay included within hearsay is not excluded under the hearsay rule if each part of the combined statements conforms with an exception to the hearsay rule provided in these rules.

See Cochran, ***Texas Rules of Evidence Handbook***, p. 884 (2003).

History of TRE 805 (civil): Amended eff. Mar. 1, 1998, by order of Feb. 25, 1998 (960 S.W.2d [Tex.Cases] lxvii). Adopted eff. Sept. 1, 1983, by order of Nov. 23, 1982 (641-42 S.W.2d [Tex.Cases] lxi). Source: FRE 805.

H.L. & P. Co. v. Klein ISD, 739 S.W.2d 508, 519 (Tex.App.—Houston [14th Dist.] 1987, writ denied). "[C]harts summarizing studies of power lines and health effects [were] objected to ... as hearsay because the underlying studies were hearsay. [T]he error [in admitting the charts did not] cause the rendition of an improper verdict."

TRE 806. ATTACKING & SUPPORTING CREDIBILITY OF DECLARANT

When a hearsay statement, or a statement defined in Rule 801(e)(2)(C), (D), or (E), or in civil cases a statement defined in Rule 801(e)(3), has been admitted in evidence, the credibility of the declarant may be attacked, and if attacked may be supported by any evidence which would be admissible for those purposes if declarant had testified as a witness. Evidence of a statement or conduct by the declarant at any time, offered to impeach the declarant, is not subject to any requirement that the declarant may have been afforded an opportunity to deny or explain. If the party against whom a hearsay statement has been admitted calls the declarant as a witness, the party is entitled to examine the declarant on the statement as if under cross-examination.

See Cochran, ***Texas Rules of Evidence Handbook***, p. 886 (2003).

History of TRE 806 (civil): Amended eff. Mar. 1, 1998, by order of Feb. 25, 1998 (960 S.W.2d [Tex.Cases] lxvii). Adopted eff. Sept. 1, 1983, by order of Nov. 23, 1982 (641-42 S.W.2d [Tex.Cases] lxi). Source: FRE 806.

Anthony Pools, Inc. v. Charles & David, Inc., 797 S.W.2d 666, 676 (Tex.App.—Houston [14th Dist.] 1990, writ denied). "Texas courts long have allowed the use of affidavits to impeach a witness. The jury could have been allowed to consider any inconsistencies between the affidavit and the deposition as damaging to the credibility of [the witness'] deposition, but not as substantive evidence. [¶] Upon timely request and objection ... the court was required to instruct the jury of the limited use to be made of the affidavit."

Victor M. Solis Underground Util. & Paving Co. v. City of Laredo, 751 S.W.2d 532, 537 (Tex.App.—San Antonio 1988, writ denied). "If a declarant is unavailable as a witness, [TRE] 806 ... provides that testimony by that person at a former hearing is not excluded as hearsay if the party against whom the testimony is offered, 'or a person with similar interest, had an opportunity and similar motive to develop the testimony by direct, cross, or redirect examination.'"

ARTICLE IX. AUTHENTICATION & IDENTIFICATION

TRE 901. REQUIREMENT OF AUTHENTICATION OR IDENTIFICATION

(a) General Provision. The requirement of authentication or identification as a condition precedent to admissibility is satisfied by evidence sufficient to support a finding that the matter in question is what its proponent claims.

(b) Illustrations. By way of illustration only, and not by way of limitation, the following are examples of authentication or identification conforming with the requirements of this rule:

(1) *Testimony of witness with knowledge.* Testimony that a matter is what it is claimed to be.

(2) *Nonexpert opinion on handwriting.* Nonexpert opinion as to the genuineness of handwriting, based upon familiarity not acquired for purposes of the litigation.

(3) *Comparison by trier or expert witness.* Comparison by the trier of fact or by expert witness with specimens which have been found by the court to be genuine.

(4) *Distinctive characteristics and the like.* Appearance, contents, substance, internal patterns, or other distinctive characteristics, taken in conjunction with circumstances.

(5) *Voice identification.* Identification of a voice, whether heard firsthand or through mechanical or electronic transmission or recording, by opinion based upon hearing the voice at anytime under circumstances connecting it with the alleged speaker.

(6) *Telephone conversations.* Telephone conversations, by evidence that a call was made to the number assigned at the time by the telephone company to a particular person or business, if:

(A) in the case of a person, circumstances, including self-identification, show the person answering to be the one called; or

(B) in the case of a business, the call was made to a place of business and the conversation related to business reasonably transacted over the telephone.

(7) *Public records or reports.* Evidence that a writing authorized by law to be recorded or filed and in fact recorded or filed in a public office, or a purported public record, report, statement, or data compilation, in any form, is from the public office where items of this nature are kept.

(8) *Ancient documents or data compilation.* Evidence that a document or data compilation, in any form, (A) is in such condition as to create no suspicion concerning its authenticity, (B) was in a place where it, if authentic, would likely be, and (C) has been in existence twenty years or more at the time it is offered.

(9) *Process or system.* Evidence describing a process or system used to produce a result and showing that the process or system produces an accurate result.

(10) *Methods provided by statute or rule.* Any method of authentication or identification provided by statute or by other rule prescribed pursuant to statutory authority.

See ***Commentaries***, "Introducing Evidence," ch. 8-C; Cochran, ***Texas Rules of Evidence Handbook***, p. 892 (2003).

History of TRE 901 (civil): Amended eff. Mar. 1, 1998, by order of Feb. 25, 1998 (960 S.W.2d [Tex.Cases] lxvii). Adopted eff. Sept. 1, 1983, by order of Nov. 23, 1982 (641-42 S.W.2d [Tex.Cases] lxii). Source: FRE 901. See TRCS arts. 3725, 3737b (repealed).

G.M. Corp. v. Gayle, 951 S.W.2d 469, 475 (Tex. 1997). "Any tests that a party ... offer[s] at trial will be admissible only if the trial court determines that there is a substantial similarity between the test conditions and the accident conditions."

In re G.F.O., 874 S.W.2d 729, 731 (Tex.App.—Houston [1st Dist.] 1994, no writ). TRE 901(a) "requires the authentication or identification as a condition precedent to admissibility; the requirement is satisfied by evidence sufficient to support a finding that the matter in question is what its proponent claims. [¶] A document is considered authentic if a sponsoring witness vouches for its authenticity or if the document meets the requirements of self-authentication."

Durkay v. Madco Oil Co., 862 S.W.2d 14, 24 (Tex. App.—Corpus Christi 1993, writ denied). "Even if the report was admissible ... the report was still subject to the requirement of authentication. [No] witness testified to the completeness of the report, how it was prepared, its accuracy, or the basis for the calculations contained within it. The report is not a self authenticating document under the provisions of [TRE] 902 and must be authenticated in some other manner."

TRE 902. SELF-AUTHENTICATION

Extrinsic evidence of authenticity as a condition precedent to admissibility is not required with respect to the following:

(1) Domestic Public Documents Under Seal. A document bearing a seal purporting to be that of the United States, or of any State, district, Commonwealth, territory, or insular possession thereof, or the Panama Canal Zone, or the Trust Territory of the Pacific Islands, or of a political subdivision, department, officer, or agency thereof, and a signature purporting to be an attestation or execution.

(2) Domestic Public Documents Not Under Seal. A document purporting to bear the signature in the official capacity of an officer or employee of any entity included in paragraph (1) hereof, having no seal, if a public officer having a seal and having official duties in the district or political subdivision of the officer or employee certifies under seal that the signer has the official capacity and that the signature is genuine.

(3) Foreign Public Documents. A document purporting to be executed or attested in an official capacity by a person, authorized by the laws of a foreign country to make the execution or attestation, and accompanied by a final certification as to the genuineness of the signature and official position (A) of the executing or attesting person, or (B) of any foreign official whose certificate of genuineness of signature and official position relates to the execution or attestation or is in a chain of certificates of genuineness of signature and official position relating to the execution or attestation. A final certification may be made by a secretary of embassy or legation, consul general, consul, vice consul, or consular agent of the United States, or a diplomatic or consular official of the foreign country assigned or accredited to the United States. If reasonable opportunity has been given to all parties to investigate the authenticity and accuracy of official documents, the court may, for good cause shown, order that they be treated as presumptively authentic without final certification or permit them to be evidenced by an attested summary with or without final certification. The final certification shall be dispensed with whenever both the United

States and the foreign country in which the official record is located are parties to a treaty or convention that abolishes or displaces such requirement, in which case the record and the attestation shall be certified by the means provided in the treaty or convention.

(4) Certified Copies of Public Records. A copy of an official record or report or entry therein, or of a document authorized by law to be recorded or filed and actually recorded or filed in a public office, including data compilations in any form certified as correct by the custodian or other person authorized to make the certification, by certificate complying with paragraph (1), (2) or (3) of this rule or complying with any statute or other rule prescribed pursuant to statutory authority.

(5) Official Publications. Books, pamphlets, or other publications purporting to be issued by public authority.

(6) Newspapers and Periodicals. Printed materials purporting to be newspapers or periodicals.

(7) Trade Inscriptions and the Like. Inscriptions, signs, tags, or labels purporting to have been affixed in the course of business and indicating ownership, control, or origin.

(8) Acknowledged Documents. Documents accompanied by a certificate of acknowledgment executed in the manner provided by law by a notary public or other officer authorized by law to take acknowledgments.

(9) Commercial Paper and Related Documents. Commercial paper, signatures thereon, and documents relating thereto to the extent provided by general commercial law.

(10) Business Records Accompanied by Affidavit.

(a) *Records or photocopies; admissibility; affidavit; filing.* Any record or set of records or photographically reproduced copies of such records, which would be admissible under Rule 803(6) or (7) shall be admissible in evidence in any court in this state upon the affidavit of the person who would otherwise provide the prerequisites of Rule 803(6) or (7), that such records attached to such affidavit were in fact so kept as required by Rule 803(6) or (7), provided further, that such record or records along with such affidavit are filed with the clerk of the court for inclusion with the papers in the cause in which the record or records are sought to be used as evidence at least fourteen days prior to the day upon which trial of said cause commences, and provided the other parties to said cause are given prompt notice by the party filing same of the filing of such record or records and affidavit, which notice shall identify the name and employer, if any, of the person making the affidavit and such records shall be made available to the counsel for other parties to the action or litigation for inspection and copying. The expense for copying shall be borne by the party, parties or persons who desire copies and not by the party or parties who file the records and serve notice of said filing, in compliance with this rule. Notice shall be deemed to have been promptly given if it is served in the manner contemplated by Rule of Civil Procedure 21a fourteen days prior to commencement of trial in said cause.

(b) *Form of affidavit.* A form for the affidavit of such person as shall make such affidavit as is permitted in paragraph (a) above shall be sufficient if it follows this form though this form shall not be exclusive, and an affidavit which substantially complies with the provisions of this rule shall suffice, to-wit:

No.__________

John Doe	§	IN THE ________
(Name of Plaintiff)	§	COURT IN AND FOR
v.	§	
John Roe	§	______ COUNTY,
(Name of Defendant)	§	TEXAS

AFFIDAVIT

Before me, the undersigned authority, personally appeared ____________, who, being by me duly sworn, deposed as follows:

My name is __________, I am of sound mind, capable of making this affidavit, and personally acquainted with the facts herein stated:

I am the custodian of the records of ____________. Attached hereto are _____ pages of records from ______. These said ____ pages of records are kept by ________ in the regular course of business, and it was the regular course of business of __________ for an employee or representative of ________, with knowledge of the act, event, condition, opinion, or diagnosis, recorded to make the record or to transmit information thereof to be included in such record; and the record was made at or near the time or reasonably soon thereafter. The records attached hereto are the original or exact duplicates of the original.

____
Affiant

SWORN TO AND SUBSCRIBED before me on the ________ day of _________, 19 ____.

____
Notary Public, State of Texas
Notary's printed name:

____
My commission expires:

____

(11) Presumptions Under Statutes or Other Rules. Any signature, document, or other matter declared by statute or by other rules prescribed pursuant to statutory authority to be presumptively or prima facie genuine or authentic.

See *Commentaries*, "Motion for Summary Judgment," ch. 7-B; "Introducing Evidence," ch. 8-C; Cochran, *Texas Rules of Evidence Handbook*, p. 918 (2003).

History of TRE 902 (civil): Amended eff. Mar. 1, 1998, by order of Feb. 25, 1998 (960 S.W.2d [Tex.Cases] lxix). Amended eff. Jan. 1, 1988, by order of Nov. 10, 1986 (733-34 S.W.2d [Tex.Cases] xci). Adopted eff. Sept. 1, 1983, by order of Nov. 23, 1982 (641-42 S.W.2d [Tex.Cases] lxiii). Source: FRE 902. See TRCS arts. 3718-3737e (repealed). TRCE 902(10) was based on portions of the affidavit authentication provisions of TRCS art. 3737e. It was intended that this method of authentication would be available for any kind of regularly kept record that satisfies the requirements of TRCE 803(6) and (7), including X-rays, hospital records, or any other kind of regularly kept medical record.

In re N.C.M., 66 S.W.3d 417, 419 (Tex.App.—Tyler 2001, no pet.). "The plain language of Rule 902(10)(a) does not require that the affidavit be attached to a business record when the exhibit is offered into evidence."

Texas DPS v. Silva, 988 S.W.2d 873, 877 (Tex. App.—San Antonio 1999, pet. denied). D "cites no authority, nor have we found any requirement that the stamp state what the document is certifying or that the stamp be from the county where the documents were prepared."

Mathis v. State, 930 S.W.2d 203, 206 (Tex.App.—Houston [14th Dist.] 1996, no writ). "Certified copies have traditionally been permitted to prove public records because of reluctance to remove originals from their proper custody and the inconvenience of requiring testimony of the custodian in order to authenticate either an original or a copy."

Fullick v. City of Baytown, 820 S.W.2d 943, 945 (Tex.App.—Houston [1st Dist.] 1991, no writ). Although "the tax statements were not self-authenticating under [TRE] 902(4)[ ] because [they] did not bear a seal [, they] were properly self-authenticated under [TRE] 902(10)."

March v. Victoria Lloyds Ins. Co., 773 S.W.2d 785, 789 (Tex.App.—Fort Worth 1989, writ denied). "[T]he requirements for authentication under [TRE] 803(6) and 902(10) do not require the sponsoring witness or affiant to testify as to the trustworthiness of the report. The witness or affiant is to set forth the facts upon which an assessment of trustworthiness can be made by the court."

TRE 903. SUBSCRIBING WITNESS' TESTIMONY UNNECESSARY

The testimony of a subscribing witness is not necessary to authenticate a writing unless required by the laws of the jurisdiction whose laws govern the validity of the writing.

See Cochran, *Texas Rules of Evidence Handbook*, p. 938 (2003).

History of TRE 903 (civil): Amended eff. Mar. 1, 1998, by order of Feb. 25, 1998 (960 S.W.2d [Tex.Cases] lxxi). Adopted eff. Sept. 1, 1983, by order of Nov. 23, 1982 (641-42 S.W.2d [Tex.Cases] lxvi). Source: FRE 903. See TRCS art. 3734a (repealed).

ARTICLE X. CONTENTS OF WRITINGS, RECORDINGS, & PHOTOGRAPHS

TRE 1001. DEFINITIONS

For purposes of this article the following definitions are applicable:

(a) Writings and Recordings. "Writings" and "recordings" consist of letters, words, or numbers or their equivalent, set down by handwriting, typewriting, printing, photostating, photographing, magnetic impulse, mechanical or electronic recording, or other form of data compilation.

(b) Photographs. "Photographs" include still photographs, X-ray films, video tapes, and motion pictures.

(c) Original. An "original" of a writing or recording is the writing or recording itself or any counterpart intended to have the same effect by a person executing or issuing it. An "original" of a photograph includes the negative or any print therefrom. If data are stored in a computer or similar device, any printout or other output readable by sight, shown to reflect the data accurately, is an "original."

(d) Duplicate. A "duplicate" is a counterpart produced by the same impression as the original, or from the same matrix, or by means of photography, including enlargements and miniatures, or by mechanical or electronic re-recording, or by chemical reproduction, or by other equivalent techniques which accurately reproduce the original.

See *Commentaries*, "Introducing Evidence," ch. 8-C; Cochran, *Texas Rules of Evidence Handbook*, p. 944 (2003).

History of TRE 1001 (civil): Amended eff. Mar. 1, 1998, by order of Feb. 25, 1998 (960 S.W.2d [Tex.Cases] lxxii). Adopted eff. Sept. 1, 1983, by order of Nov. 23, 1982 (641-42 S.W.2d [Tex.Cases] lxvi). Source: FRE 1001.

S.D.G. v. State, 936 S.W.2d 371, 381 (Tex.App.—Houston [14th Dist.] 1996, writ denied). "The predicate for introduction of a photograph and a videotape not accompanied by a sound recording requires proof of (1) its accuracy as a correct representation of the subject at a given time, and (2) its relevance to a material issue. ... Any witness who observed the object or the scene depicted in the photograph may lay the predicate."

TRE 1002. REQUIREMENT OF ORIGINALS

To prove the content of a writing, recording, or photograph, the original writing, recording, or photograph is required except as otherwise provided in these rules or by law.

See Cochran, *Texas Rules of Evidence Handbook*, p. 944 (2003).

History of TRE 1002 (civil): Amended eff. Mar. 1, 1998, by order of Feb. 25, 1998 (960 S.W.2d [Tex.Cases] lxxii). Adopted eff. Sept. 1, 1983, by order of Nov. 23, 1982 (641-42 S.W.2d [Tex.Cases] lxvi). Source: FRE 1002.

White v. Bath, 825 S.W.2d 227, 231 (Tex.App.—Houston [14th Dist.] 1992, writ denied). "[O]nly when one seeks to prove the contents of a document [does] the best evidence rule [apply]. When the document and its contents are only collaterally related to the issues in the case, the best evidence rule does not apply."

Ramsey v. Jones Enters., 810 S.W.2d 902, 905 (Tex. App.—Beaumont 1991, writ denied). "The best evidence of the content of documents is the documents themselves. The trial court erred in admitting hearsay testimony to prove up the content of documents without a proper showing that the subject documents were unavailable through no fault or failure on the part of the party offering same."

TRE 1003. ADMISSIBILITY OF DUPLICATES

A duplicate is admissible to the same extent as an original unless (1) a question is raised as to the authenticity of the original or (2) in the circumstances it would be unfair to admit the duplicate in lieu of the original.

See *Commentaries*, "Introducing Evidence," ch. 8-C; Cochran, *Texas Rules of Evidence Handbook*, p. 945 (2003).

History of TRE 1003 (civil): Amended eff. Mar. 1, 1998, by order of Feb. 25, 1998 (960 S.W.2d [Tex.Cases] lxxii). Adopted eff. Sept. 1, 1983, by order of Nov. 23, 1982 (641-42 S.W.2d [Tex.Cases] lxvi). Source: FRE 1003.

Ford Motor Co. v. Leggat, 904 S.W.2d 643, 646 (Tex.1995). "[I]n the absence of a challenge to the authenticity of the affidavit, submission of a copy is not grounds for rejecting it."

Closs v. Goose Creek Consol. ISD, 874 S.W.2d 859, 868 (Tex.App.—Texarkana 1994, no writ). "A duplicate is admissible to the same extent as the original unless a question is raised as to the authenticity of the original or it would otherwise be unfair to submit the duplicate in lieu of the original."

TRE 1004. ADMISSIBILITY OF OTHER EVIDENCE OF CONTENTS

The original is not required, and other evidence of the contents of a writing, recording, or photograph is admissible if:

(a) Originals Lost or Destroyed. All originals are lost or have been destroyed, unless the proponent lost or destroyed them in bad faith;

(b) Original Not Obtainable. No original can be obtained by any available judicial process or procedure;

(c) Original Outside the State. No original is located in Texas;

(d) Original in Possession of Opponent. At a time when an original was under the control of the party against whom offered, that party was put on notice, by the pleadings or otherwise, that the content would be a subject of proof at the hearing, and that party does not produce the original at the hearing; or

(e) Collateral Matters. The writing, recording or photograph is not closely related to a controlling issue.

See TRCP 77; *Commentaries*, "Rules for Filing Documents," ch. 1-C; "Introducing Evidence," ch. 8-C; Cochran, *Texas Rules of Evidence Handbook*, p. 960 (2003).

History of TRE 1004 (civil): Amended eff. Mar. 1, 1998, by order of Feb. 25, 1998 (960 S.W.2d [Tex.Cases] lxxii). Adopted eff. Sept. 1, 1983, by order of Nov. 23, 1982 (641-42 S.W.2d [Tex.Cases] lxvii). Source: FRE 1004.

Coke v. Coke, 802 S.W.2d 270, 275 (Tex.App.—Dallas 1990, writ denied). "Under [TRE] 1004, an original document is not required if the original is lost or destroyed without the fault of the proponent. Copies are admissible if 'there is a reasonable account for [the originals'] absence or if there is no question of their authenticity.'"

TRE 1005. PUBLIC RECORDS

The contents of an official record or of a document authorized to be recorded or filed and actually recorded or filed, including data compilations in any form, if otherwise admissible, may be proved by copy, certified as correct in accordance with Rule 902 or testified to be correct by a witness who has compared it with the original. If a copy which complies with the foregoing cannot be obtained by the exercise of reasonable diligence, then other evidence of the contents may be given.

See ***Commentaries***, "Introducing Evidence," ch. 8-C; Cochran, ***Texas Rules of Evidence Handbook***, p. 965 (2003).

History of TRE 1005 (civil): Amended eff. Mar. 1, 1998, by order of Feb. 25, 1998 (960 S.W.2d [Tex.Cases] lxxiii). Adopted eff. Sept. 1, 1983, by order of Nov. 23, 1982 (641-42 S.W.2d [Tex.Cases] lxvii). Source: FRE 1005.

ESIS, Inc. v. Johnson, 908 S.W.2d 554, 561 (Tex. App.—Fort Worth 1995, writ denied). "A copy of a public record is considered authentic if a sponsoring witness vouches for its authenticity or if the document meets the certification requirements for self-authentication contained in [TRE] 902."

TRE 1006. SUMMARIES

The contents of voluminous writings, recordings, or photographs, otherwise admissible, which cannot conveniently be examined in court may be presented in the form of a chart, summary, or calculation. The originals, or duplicates, shall be made available for examination or copying, or both, by other parties at a reasonable time and place. The court may order that they be produced in court.

See Cochran, ***Texas Rules of Evidence Handbook***, p. 969 (2003).

History of TRE 1006 (civil): Amended eff. Mar. 1, 1998, by order of Feb. 25, 1998 (960 S.W.2d [Tex.Cases] lxxiii). Adopted eff. Sept. 1, 1983, by order of Nov. 23, 1982 (641-42 S.W.2d [Tex.Cases] lxvii). Source: FRE 1006.

Aquamarine Assocs. v. Burton Shipyard, Inc., 659 S.W.2d 820, 821 (Tex.1983). "In cases involving voluminous records, the trial court has discretion to relax the best evidence rule and allow the admission of summaries.... The party sponsoring the summary must, however, lay the proper predicate for its admission."

Welder v. Welder, 794 S.W.2d 420, 429 (Tex.App.—Corpus Christi 1990, no writ). "In order to bring a summary within the guidelines of [TRE] 1006, the party sponsoring the summary must lay the proper predicate for its admission, by demonstrating that the underlying records were voluminous, were made available to the opposing party for inspection and use in cross examination, and were admissible under the Texas Business Records Act."

TRE 1007. TESTIMONY OR WRITTEN ADMISSION OF PARTY

Contents of writings, recordings, or photographs may be proved by the testimony or deposition of the party against whom offered or by that party's written admission, without accounting for the nonproduction of the original.

See Cochran, ***Texas Rules of Evidence Handbook***, p. 973 (2003).

History of TRE 1007 (civil): Amended eff. Mar. 1, 1998, by order of Feb. 25, 1998 (960 S.W.2d [Tex.Cases] lxxiii). Amended eff. Jan. 1, 1988, by order of Nov. 10, 1986 (733-34 S.W.2d [Tex.Cases] xcii): In title, deleted "Permission" and added "Admission." Adopted eff. Sept. 1, 1983, by order of Nov. 23, 1982 (641-42 S.W.2d [Tex.Cases] lxvii). Source: FRE 1007.

TRE 1008. FUNCTIONS OF COURT & JURY

When the admissibility of other evidence of contents of writings, recordings, or photographs under these rules depends upon the fulfillment of a condition of fact, the question whether the condition has been fulfilled is ordinarily for the court to determine in accordance with the provisions of Rule 104. However, when an issue is raised (a) whether the asserted writing ever existed, or (b) whether another writing, recording, or photograph produced at the trial is the original, or (c) whether other evidence of contents correctly reflects the contents, the issue is for the trier of fact to determine as in the case of other issues of fact.

See Cochran, ***Texas Rules of Evidence Handbook***, p. 974 (2003).

History of TRE 1008 (civil): Amended eff. Mar. 1, 1998, by order of Feb. 25, 1998 (960 S.W.2d [Tex.Cases] lxxiii). Adopted eff. Sept. 1, 1983, by order of Nov. 23, 1982 (641-42 S.W.2d [Tex.Cases] lxvii). Source: FRE 1008.

TRE 1009. TRANSLATION OF FOREIGN LANGUAGE DOCUMENTS

(a) Translations. A translation of foreign language documents shall be admissible upon the affidavit of a qualified translator setting forth the qualifications of the translator and certifying that the translation is fair and accurate. Such affidavit, along with the translation and the underlying foreign language documents, shall be served upon all parties at least 45 days prior to the date of trial.

(b) Objections. Any party may object to the accuracy of another party's translation by pointing out the specific inaccuracies of the translation and by stating with specificity what the objecting party contends is a fair and accurate translation. Such objection shall be served upon all parties at least 15 days prior to the date of trial.

(c) Effect of Failure to Object or Offer Conflicting Translation. If no conflicting translation or objection is timely served, the court shall admit a translation submitted under paragraph (a) without need of proof, provided however that the underlying foreign language documents are otherwise admissible under the Texas Rules of Evidence. Failure to serve a conflicting translation under paragraph (a) or failure to timely and properly object to the accuracy of a translation under paragraph (b) shall preclude a party from attacking or offering evidence contradicting the accuracy of such translation at trial.

(d) Effect of Objections or Conflicting Translations. In the event of conflicting translations under paragraph (a) or if objections to another party's translation are served under paragraph (b), the court shall determine whether there is a genuine issue as to the accuracy of a material part of the translation to be resolved by the trier of fact.

(e) Expert Testimony of Translator. Except as provided in paragraph (c), this Rule does not preclude the admission of a translation of foreign language documents at trial either by live testimony or by deposition testimony of a qualified expert translator.

(f) Varying of Time Limits. The court, upon motion of any party and for good cause shown, may enlarge or shorten the time limits set forth in this Rule.

(g) Court Appointment. The court, if necessary, may appoint a qualified translator, the reasonable value of whose services shall be taxed as court costs.

Comment to 1998 change: This is a new rule.

See Cochran, ***Texas Rules of Evidence Handbook***, p. 976 (2003).

History of TRE 1009 (civil): Adopted eff. Mar. 1, 1998, by order of Feb. 25, 1998 (960 S.W.2d [Tex.Cases] lxxiv). Source: New rule.

TEXAS RULES OF APPELLATE PROCEDURE

TABLE OF CONTENTS

To save space, we have eliminated the TRAPs relating to criminal appellate procedure and the TRAP history notes. See ***O'Connor's Texas Civil Appeals*** for the complete set of the TRAPs.

TEXAS RULES OF APPELLATE PROCEDURE

SECTION ONE: GENERAL PROVISIONS

TRAP 1. SCOPE OF RULES; LOCAL RULES OF COURTS OF APPEALS

1.1 **Scope.** These rules govern procedure in appellate courts and before appellate judges and post-trial procedure in trial courts in criminal cases.

1.2 **Local Rules.**

(a) ***Promulgation.*** A court of appeals may promulgate rules governing its practice that are not inconsistent with these rules. Local rules governing civil cases must first be approved by the Supreme Court. Local rules governing criminal cases must first be approved by the Court of Criminal Appeals.

(b) ***Copies.*** The clerk must provide a copy of the court's local rules to anyone who requests it.

(c) ***Party's noncompliance.*** A court must not dismiss an appeal for noncompliance with a local rule without giving the noncomplying party notice and a reasonable opportunity to cure the noncompliance.

TRAP 2. SUSPENSION OF RULES

On a party's motion or on its own initiative an appellate court may—to expedite a decision or for other good cause—suspend a rule's operation in a particular case and order a different procedure; but a court must not construe this rule to suspend any provision in the Code of Criminal Procedure or to alter the time for perfecting an appeal in a civil case.

TRAP 3. DEFINITIONS; UNIFORM TERMINOLOGY

3.1 **Definitions.**

(a) *Appellant* means a party taking an appeal to an appellate court.

(b) *Appellate court* means the courts of appeals, the Court of Criminal Appeals, and the Supreme Court.

(c) *Appellee* means a party adverse to an appellant.

(d) *Applicant* means a person seeking relief by a habeas corpus in a criminal case.

(e) *Petitioner* means a party petitioning the Supreme Court or the Court of Criminal Appeals for review.

(f) *Relator* means a person seeking relief in an original proceeding in an appellate court other than by habeas corpus in a criminal case.

(g) *Reporter* or *court reporter* means the court reporter or court recorder.

(h) *Respondent* means:

(1) a party adverse to a petitioner in the Supreme Court or the Court of Criminal Appeals; or

(2) a party against whom relief is sought in an original proceeding in an appellate court.

3.2 **Uniform Terminology in Criminal Cases.**

TRAP 4. TIME & NOTICE PROVISIONS

4.1 **Computing Time.**

(a) ***In general.*** The day of an act, event, or default after which a designated period begins to run is not included when computing a period prescribed or allowed by these rules, by court order, or by statute. The last day of the period is included, but if that day is a Saturday, Sunday, or legal holiday, the period extends to the end of the next day that is not a Saturday, Sunday, or legal holiday.

(b) ***Clerk's office closed or inaccessible.*** If the act to be done is filing a document, and if the clerk's office where the document is to be filed is closed or inaccessible during regular hours on the last day for filing the document, the period for filing the document extends to the end of the next day when the clerk's office is open and accessible. The closing or inaccessibility of the clerk's office may be proved by a certificate of the clerk or counsel, by a party's affidavit, or by other satisfactory proof, and may be controverted in the same manner.

4.2 **No Notice of Trial Court's Judgment in Civil Case.**

(a) ***Additional time to file documents.***

(1) ***In general.*** If a party affected by a judgment or other appealable order has not—within 20 days after the judgment or order was signed—either received the notice required by Texas Rule of Civil Procedure 306a.3 or acquired actual knowledge of the signing, then a period that, under these rules, runs from the signing will begin for that party on the earlier of the date when the party receives notice or acquires actual knowledge of the signing. But in no event may the period begin more than 90 days after the judgment or order was signed.

(2) ***Exception for restricted appeal.*** Subparagraph (1) does not extend the time for perfecting a restricted appeal.

(b) ***Procedure to gain additional time.*** The procedure to gain additional time is governed by Texas Rule of Civil Procedure 306a.5.

(c) ***The court's order.*** After hearing the motion, the trial court must sign a written order that finds the date when the party or the party's attorney first either received notice or acquired actual knowledge that the judgment or order was signed.

4.3 Periods Affected by Modified Judgment in Civil Case.

(a) ***During plenary-power period.*** If a judgment is modified in any respect while the trial court retains plenary power, a period that, under these rules, runs from the date when the judgment is signed will run from the date when the modified judgment is signed.

(b) ***After plenary power expires.*** If the trial court corrects or reforms the judgment under Texas Rule of Civil Procedure 316 after expiration of the trial court's plenary power, all periods provided in these rules that run from the date the judgment is signed run from the date the corrected judgment is signed for complaints that would not apply to the original judgment.

4.4 Periods Affected When Process Served by Publication. If process was served by publication and if a motion for new trial was filed under Texas Rule of Civil Procedure 329 more than 30 days after the judgment was signed, a period that, under these rules, runs from the date when the judgment is signed will be computed as if the judgment were signed on the date when the motion for new trial was filed.

4.5 No Notice of Judgment or Order of Appellate Court; Effect on Time to File Certain Documents.

(a) ***Additional time to file documents.*** A party may move for additional time to file a motion for rehearing in the court of appeals, a petition for review, or a petition for discretionary review, if the party did not—until after the time expired for filing the document—either receive notice of the judgment or order from the clerk or acquire actual knowledge of the rendition of the judgment or order.

(b) ***Procedure to gain additional time.*** The motion must state the earliest date when the party or the party's attorney received notice or acquired actual knowledge that the judgment or order had been rendered. The motion must be filed within 15 days of that date but in no event more than 90 days after the date of the judgment or order.

(c) ***Where to file.***

(1) A motion for additional time to file a motion for rehearing in the court of appeals must be filed in and ruled on by the court of appeals in which the case is pending.

(2) A motion for additional time to file a petition for review must be filed in and ruled on by the Supreme Court.

(3) A motion for additional time to file a petition for discretionary review must be filed in and ruled on by the Court of Criminal Appeals.

(d) ***Order of the court.*** If the court finds that the motion for additional time was timely filed and the party did not—within the time for filing the motion for rehearing, petition for review, or petition for discretionary review, as the case may be—receive the notice or have actual knowledge of the judgment or order, the court must grant the motion. If the court grants the motion, the time for filing the document will begin to run on the date when the court grants the motion.

TRAP 5. FEES IN CIVIL CASES

A party who is not excused by statute or these rules from paying costs must pay—at the time an item is presented for filing—whatever fees are required by statute or Supreme Court order. The appellate court may enforce this rule by any order that is just.

TRAP 6. REPRESENTATION BY COUNSEL

6.1 Lead Counsel.

(a) ***For appellant.*** Unless another attorney is designated, lead counsel for an appellant is the attorney whose signature first appears on the notice of appeal.

(b) ***For a party other than appellant.*** Unless another attorney is designated, lead counsel for a party other than an appellant is the attorney whose signature first appears on the first document filed in the appellate court on that party's behalf.

(c) ***How to designate.*** The original or a new lead counsel may be designated by filing a notice stating that attorney's name, mailing address, telephone number, fax number, if any, and State Bar of Texas identification number. If a new lead counsel is being designated, both the new attorney and either the party or the former lead counsel must sign the notice.

6.2 Appearance of Other Attorneys. An attorney other than lead counsel may file a notice stating that the attorney represents a specified party to the proceeding and giving that attorney's name, mailing address, telephone number, fax number, if any, and State Bar of Texas identification number. The clerk will note on the docket the attorney's appearance. When a brief or motion is filed, the clerk will note on the docket the name of each attorney, if not already noted, who appears on the document.

6.3 To Whom Communications Sent. Any notice, copies of documents filed in an appellate court, or other communications must be sent to:

(a) each party's lead counsel on appeal;

(b) a party's lead counsel in the trial court if:

(1) that party was represented by counsel in the trial court;

(2) lead counsel on appeal has not yet been designated for that party; and

(3) lead counsel in the trial court has not filed a nonrepresentation notice or been allowed to withdraw;

(c) a party if the party is not represented by counsel.

6.4 Nonrepresentation Notice.

(a) ***In general.*** If, in accordance with paragraph 6.3(b), the lead counsel in the trial court is being sent notices, copies of documents, or other communications, that attorney may file a nonrepresentation notice in the appellate court. The notice must:

(1) state that the attorney is not representing the party on appeal;

(2) state that the court and other counsel should communicate directly with the party in the future;

(3) give the party's name and last known address and telephone number; and

(4) be signed by the party.

(b) ***Appointed counsel.*** In a criminal case, an attorney appointed by the trial court to represent an indigent party cannot file a nonrepresentation notice.

6.5 Withdrawal. An appellate court may, on appropriate terms and conditions, permit an attorney to withdraw from representing a party in the appellate court.

(a) ***Contents of motion.*** A motion for leave to withdraw must contain the following:

(1) a list of current deadlines and settings in the case;

(2) the party's name and last known address and telephone number;

(3) a statement that a copy of the motion was delivered to the party; and

(4) a statement that the party was notified in writing of the right to object to the motion.

(b) ***Delivery to party.*** The motion must be delivered to the party in person or mailed—both by certified and by first-class mail—to the party at the party's last known address.

(c) ***If motion granted.*** If the court grants the motion, the withdrawing attorney must immediately notify the party, in writing, of any deadlines or settings that the attorney knows about at the time of withdrawal but that were not previously disclosed to the party. The withdrawing attorney must file a copy of that notice with the court clerk.

(d) ***Exception for substitution of counsel.*** If an attorney substitutes for a withdrawing attorney, the motion to withdraw need not comply with (a) but must state only the substitute attorney's name, mailing address, telephone number, fax number, if any, and State Bar of Texas identification number. The withdrawing attorney must comply with (b) but not (c).

6.6 Agreements of Parties or Counsel. To be enforceable, an agreement of parties or their counsel concerning an appellate court proceeding must be in writing and signed by the parties or their counsel. Such an agreement is subject to any appellate court order necessary to ensure that the case is properly presented.

TRAP 7. SUBSTITUTING PARTIES

7.1 Parties Who Are Not Public Officers.

(a) ***Death of a Party.***

(1) ***Civil cases.*** If a party to a civil case dies after the trial court renders judgment but before the case has been finally disposed of on appeal, the appeal may be perfected, and the appellate court will proceed to adjudicate the appeal as if all parties were alive. The appellate court's judgment will have the same force and

effect as if rendered when all parties were living. The decedent party's name may be used on all papers.

(2) ***Criminal cases.*** If the appellant in a criminal case dies after an appeal is perfected but before the appellate court issues the mandate, the appeal will be permanently abated.

(b) ***Substitution for Other Reasons.*** If substitution of a party in the appellate court is necessary for a reason other than death, the appellate court may order substitution on any party's motion at any time.

7.2 Public Officers.

(a) ***Automatic Substitution of Officer.*** When a public officer is a party in an official capacity to an appeal or original proceeding, and if that person ceases to hold office before the appeal or original proceeding is finally disposed of, the public officer's successor is automatically substituted as a party if appropriate. Proceedings following substitution are to be in the name of the substituted party, but any misnomer that does not affect the substantial rights of the parties may be disregarded. Substitution may be ordered at any time, but failure to order substitution of the successor does not affect the substitution.

(b) ***Abatement.*** If the case is an original proceeding under Rule 52, the court must abate the proceeding to allow the successor to reconsider the original party's decision. In all other cases, the suit will not abate, and the successor will be bound by the appellate court's judgment or order as if the successor were the original party.

TRAP 8. BANKRUPTCY IN CIVIL CASES

8.1 Notice of Bankruptcy. Any party may file a notice that a party is in bankruptcy. The notice must contain:

(a) the bankrupt party's name;

(b) the court in which the bankruptcy proceeding is pending;

(c) the bankruptcy proceeding's style and case number;

(d) the date when the bankruptcy petition was filed; and

(e) an authenticated copy of the page or pages of the bankruptcy petition that show when the petition was filed.

8.2 Effect of Bankruptcy. A bankruptcy suspends the appeal and all periods in these rules from the date when the bankruptcy petition is filed until the appellate court reinstates or severs the appeal in accordance with federal law. A period that began to run and had not expired at the time the proceeding was suspended begins anew when the proceeding is reinstated or severed under 8.3. A document filed by a party while the proceeding is suspended will be deemed filed on the same day, but after, the court reinstates or severs the appeal and will not be considered ineffective because it was filed while the proceeding was suspended.

8.3 Motion to Reinstate or Sever Appeal Suspended by Bankruptcy.

(a) ***Motion to reinstate.*** If a case has been suspended by a bankruptcy filing, a party may move that the appellate court reinstate the appeal if permitted by federal law or the bankruptcy court. If the bankruptcy court has lifted or terminated the stay a certified copy of the order must be attached to the motion.

(b) ***Motion to sever.*** A party may move to sever the appeal with respect to the bankrupt party and to reinstate the appeal with respect to the other parties. The motion must show that the case is severable and must comply with applicable federal law regarding severance of a bankrupt party. The court may proceed under this paragraph on its own initiative.

TRAP 9. PAPERS GENERALLY

9.1 Signing.

(a) ***Represented parties.*** If a party is represented by counsel, a document filed on that party's behalf must be signed by at least one of the party's attorneys. For each attorney whose name appears on a document as representing that party, the document must contain that attorney's State Bar of Texas identification number, mailing address, telephone number, and fax number, if any.

(b) ***Unrepresented parties.*** A party not represented by counsel must sign any document that the party files and give the party's mailing address, telephone number, and fax number, if any.

9.2 Filing.

(a) ***With whom.*** A document is filed in an appellate court by delivering it to:

(1) the clerk of the court in which the document is to be filed; or

(2) a justice or judge of that court who is willing to accept delivery. A justice or judge who accepts delivery must note on the document the date and time of delivery, which will be considered the time of filing, and must promptly send it to the clerk.

(b) ***Filing by mail.***

(1) ***Timely filing.*** A document received within ten days after the filing deadline is considered timely filed if:

(A) it was sent to the proper clerk by United States Postal Service first-class, express, registered, or certified mail;

(B) it was placed in an envelope or wrapper properly addressed and stamped; and

(C) it was deposited in the mail on or before the last day for filing.

(2) ***Proof of mailing.*** Though it may consider other proof, the appellate court will accept the following as conclusive proof of the date of mailing:

(A) a legible postmark affixed by the United States Postal Service;

(B) a receipt for registered or certified mail if the receipt is endorsed by the United States Postal Service; or

(C) a certificate of mailing by the United States Postal Service.

(c) ***Electronic filing.*** A court of appeals may by local rule permit documents to be filed, signed, or verified by electronic means that are consistent with technological standards, if any, that the Supreme Court establishes.

9.3 Number of Copies.

(a) ***Courts of appeals.***

(1) A party must file:

(A) the original and three copies of all documents in an original proceeding;

(B) the original and two copies of all motions in an appellate proceeding; and

(C) the original and five copies of all other documents.

(2) A court of appeals may by local rule require the filing of more or fewer copies of any document other than a petition for discretionary review.

(b) ***Supreme Court and Court of Criminal Appeals.*** A party must file the original and 11 copies of any document addressed to either the Supreme Court or the Court of Criminal Appeals, except that only the original of the following must be filed in the Court of Criminal Appeals:

(1) a motion for extension of time or a response to the motion; or

(2) a pleading under Code of Criminal Procedure article 11.07.

(c) ***Exception for record.*** Only the original record need be filed in any proceeding.

9.4 Form. Except for the record, a document filed with an appellate court must—unless the court accepts another form in the interest of justice—be in the following form:

(a) ***Printing.*** A document may be produced by standard typographic printing or by any duplicating process that produces a distinct black image. Printing may be on both sides of the paper.

(b) ***Paper type and size.*** The paper on which the document is produced must be white or nearly white, and opaque. Paper must be 8 1/2 by 11 inches.

(c) ***Margins.*** Papers must have at least one-inch margins on both sides and at the top and bottom.

(d) ***Spacing.*** Text must be double-spaced, but footnotes, block quotations, short lists, and issues or points of error may be single-spaced.

(e) ***Typeface.*** A document must be printed in standard 10-character-per-inch (cpi) nonproportionally spaced Courier typeface or in 13-point or larger proportionally spaced typeface. But if the document is printed in a proportionally spaced typeface, footnotes may be printed in typeface no smaller than 10-point.

(f) ***Binding and covering.*** A document must be bound so as to ensure that it will not lose its cover or fall apart in regular use. A document should be stapled once in the top left-hand corner or be bound so that it will lie flat when open. A petition or brief should have durable front and back covers which must not be plastic or be red, black, or dark blue.

(g) ***Contents of cover.*** A document's front cover, if any, must contain the case style, the case number, the title of the document being filed, the name of the party filing the document, and the name, mailing address, telephone number, fax number, if any, and State Bar of Texas identification number of the lead counsel for the filing party. If a party requests oral argument in the court of appeals, the request must appear on the front cover of that party's first brief.

(h) ***Appendix.*** An appendix may be bound either with the document to which it is related or separately. If separately bound, the appendix must comply with paragraph (f). An appendix should be tabbed and indexed.

(i) ***Nonconforming documents.*** Unless every copy of a document conforms to these rules, the court may strike the document and return all nonconforming copies to the filing party. The court must identify the error to be corrected and state a deadline for the party to resubmit the document in a conforming format. If another nonconforming document is filed, the court may strike the document and prohibit the party from filing further documents of the same kind. The use of footnotes, smaller or condensed typeface, or compacted or compressed printing features to avoid the limits of these rules are grounds for the court to strike a document.

9.5 **Service.**

(a) ***Service of all documents required.*** At or before the time of a document's filing, the filing party must serve a copy on all parties to the proceeding. But a party need not serve a copy of the record.

(b) ***Manner of service.*** Service on a party represented by counsel must be made on that party's lead counsel. Service may be personal, by mail, by commercial delivery service, or by fax. Personal service includes delivery to any responsible person at the office of the lead counsel for the party served.

(c) ***When complete.***

(1) Service by mail is complete on mailing.

(2) Service by commercial delivery service is complete when the document is placed in the control of the delivery service.

(3) Service by fax is complete on receipt.

(d) ***Proof of service.*** A document presented for filing must contain a proof of service in the form of either an acknowledgment of service by the person served or a certificate of service. Proof of service may appear on or be affixed to the filed document. The clerk may permit a document to be filed without proof of service, but will require the proof to be filed promptly.

(e) ***Certificate requirements.*** A certificate of service must be signed by the person who made the service and must state:

(1) the date and manner of service;

(2) the name and address of each person served; and

(3) if the person served is a party's attorney, the name of the party represented by that attorney.

9.6 **Communications with the Court.** Parties and counsel may communicate with the appellate court about a case only through the clerk.

9.7 **Adoption by Reference.** Any party may join in or adopt by reference all or any part of a brief, petition, response, motion, or other document filed in an appellate court by another party in the same case.

TRAP 10. MOTIONS IN THE APPELLATE COURTS

10.1 **Contents of Motions; Response.**

(a) ***Motion.*** Unless these rules prescribe another form, a party must apply by motion for an order or other relief. The motion must:

(1) contain or be accompanied by any matter specifically required by a rule governing such a motion;

(2) state with particularity the grounds on which it is based;

(3) set forth the order or relief sought;

(4) be served and filed with any brief, affidavit, or other paper filed in support of the motion; and

(5) in civil cases, contain or be accompanied by a certificate stating that the filing party conferred, or made a reasonable attempt to confer, with all other parties about the merits of the motion and whether those parties oppose the motion.

(b) ***Response.*** A party may file a response to a motion at any time before the court rules on the motion or by any deadline set by the court. The court may determine a motion before a response is filed.

10.2 **Evidence on Motions.** A motion need not be verified unless it depends on the following types of facts, in which case the motion must be supported by affidavit or other satisfactory evidence. The types of facts requiring proof are those that are:

(a) not in the record;

(b) not within the court's knowledge in its official capacity; or

(c) not within the personal knowledge of the attorney signing the motion.

10.3 Determining Motions.

(a) ***Time for determination.*** A court should not hear or determine a motion until 10 days after the motion was filed, unless:

(1) the motion is to extend time to file a brief, a petition for review, or a petition for discretionary review;

(2) the motion states that the parties have conferred and that no party opposes the motion; or

(3) the motion is an emergency.

(b) ***Reconsideration.*** If a motion is determined prematurely, any party adversely affected may request the court to reconsider its order.

10.4 Power of Panel or Single Justice or Judge to Entertain Motions.

(a) ***Single justice.*** In addition to the authority expressly conferred by these rules or by law, a single justice or judge of an appellate court may grant or deny a request for relief that these rules allow to be sought by motion. But in a civil case, a single justice should not do the following:

(1) act on a petition for an extraordinary writ; or

(2) dismiss or otherwise determine an appeal or a motion for rehearing.

(b) ***Panel.*** An appellate court may provide, by order or rule, that a panel or the full court must act on any motion or class of motions.

10.5 Particular Motions.

(a) ***Motions relating to informalities in the record.*** A motion relating to informalities in the manner of bringing a case into court must be filed within 30 days after the record is filed in the court of appeals. The objection, if waivable, will otherwise be deemed waived.

(b) ***Motions to extend time.***

(1) ***Contents of motion in general.*** All motions to extend time, except a motion to extend time for filing a notice of appeal, must state:

(A) the deadline for filing the item in question;

(B) the length of the extension sought;

(C) the facts relied on to reasonably explain the need for an extension; and

(D) the number of previous extensions granted regarding the item in question.

(2) ***Contents of motion to extend time to file notice of appeal.*** A motion to extend the time for filing a notice of appeal must:

(A) comply with (1)(A) and (C);

(B) identify the trial court;

(C) state the date of the trial court's judgment or appealable order; and

(D) state the case number and style of the case in the trial court.

(3) ***Contents of motion to extend time to file petition for review or petition for discretionary review.*** A motion to extend time to file a petition for review or petition for discretionary review must also specify:

(A) the court of appeals;

(B) the date of the court of appeals' judgment; and

(C) the case number and style of the case in the court of appeals.

(c) ***Motions to postpone argument.*** Unless all parties agree, or unless sufficient cause is apparent to the court, a motion to postpone argument of a case must be supported by sufficient cause.

TRAP 11. AMICUS CURIAE BRIEFS

An appellate clerk may receive, but not file, an amicus curiae brief. But the court for good cause may refuse to consider the brief and order that it be returned. An amicus curiae brief must:

(a) comply with the briefing rules for parties;

(b) identify the person or entity on whose behalf the brief is tendered;

(c) disclose the source of any fee paid or to be paid for preparing the brief; and

(d) certify that copies have been served on all parties.

TRAP 12. DUTIES OF APPELLATE CLERK

12.1 Docketing the Case. On receiving a copy of the notice of appeal, the petition for review, the petition for discretionary review, the petition in an original proceeding, or a certified question, the appellate clerk must:

(a) endorse on the document the date of receipt;

(b) collect any filing fee;

(c) docket the case;

(d) notify all parties of the receipt of the document; and

(e) if the document filed is a petition for review filed in the Supreme Court, notify the court of appeals clerk of the filing of the petition.

12.2 Docket Numbers. The clerk must put the case's docket number on each item received in connection with the case and must put the docket number on the envelope in which the record is stored.

(a) ***Numbering system.*** Each case filed in a court of appeals must be assigned a docket number consisting of the following four parts, separated by hyphens:

(1) the number of the court of appeals district;

(2) the last two digits of the year in which the case is filed;

(3) the number assigned to the case; and

(4) the designation "CV" for a civil case or "CR" for a criminal case.

(b) ***Numbering order.*** Each case must be docketed in the order of its filing.

(c) ***Multiple notices of appeal.*** All notices of appeal filed in the same case must be given the same docket number.

(d) ***Appeals not yet filed.*** A motion relating to an appeal that has been perfected but not yet filed must be docketed and assigned a docket number that will also be assigned to the appeal when it is filed.

12.3 Custody of Papers. The clerk must safeguard the record and every other item filed in a case. If the record or any part of it or any other item is missing, the court will make an order for the replacement of the record or item that is just under the circumstances.

12.4 Withdrawing Papers. The clerk may permit the record or other filed item to be taken from the clerk's office at any time, on the following conditions:

(a) the clerk must have a receipt for the record or item;

(b) the clerk should make reasonable conditions to ensure that the withdrawn record or item is preserved and returned;

(c) the clerk may demand the return of the record or item at any time;

(d) after the case is submitted to the court and before the court's decision, the record cannot be withdrawn;

(e) after the court's decision, the losing party must be given priority in withdrawing the record;

(f) the clerk may not allow original documents filed under Rule 34.5(f) or original exhibits filed under Rule 34.6(g) to be taken from the clerk's office;

(g) if the court allows an original document or exhibit to be taken by a party and it is not returned, the court may accept the opposing party's statement concerning the document's or exhibit's nature and contents;

(h) withdrawn material must not be removed from the court's jurisdiction; and

(i) the court may, on the motion of any party or its own initiative, modify any of these conditions.

12.5 Clerk's Duty to Account. The clerk of an appellate court who receives money due another court must promptly pay the money to the court to whom it is due. This rule is enforceable by the Supreme Court.

12.6 Notices of Court's Judgments and Orders. In any proceeding, the clerk of an appellate court must promptly send a notice of any judgment, mandate, or other court order to all parties to the proceeding.

TRAP 13. COURT REPORTERS & COURT RECORDERS

13.1 Duties of Court Reporters and Recorders. The official court reporter or court recorder must:

(a) unless excused by agreement of the parties, attend court sessions and make a full record of the proceedings;

(b) take all exhibits offered in evidence during a proceeding and ensure that they are marked;

(c) file all exhibits with the trial court clerk after a proceeding ends;

(d) perform the duties prescribed by Rules 34.6 and 35; and

(e) perform other acts relating to the reporter's or recorder's official duties, as the trial court directs.

13.2 Additional Duties of Court Recorder. The official court recorder must also:

(a) ensure that the recording system functions properly throughout the proceeding and that a complete, clear, and transcribable recording is made;

(b) make a detailed, legible log of all proceedings being recorded, showing:

(1) the number and style of the case before the court;

(2) the name of each person speaking;

(3) the event being recorded such as the voir dire, the opening statement, direct and cross-examinations, and bench conferences;

(4) each exhibit offered, admitted, or excluded;

(5) the time of day of each event; and

(6) the index number on the recording device showing where each event is recorded;

(c) after a proceeding ends, file with the clerk the original log;

(d) have the original recording stored to ensure that it is preserved and is accessible; and

(e) ensure that no one gains access to the original recording without the court's written order.

13.3 Priorities of Reporters. The trial court must help ensure that the court reporter's work is timely accomplished by setting work priorities. The reporter's duties relating to proceedings before the court take preference over other work.

13.4 Report of Reporters. To aid the trial court in setting priorities under 13.3, each court reporter must give the trial court a monthly written report showing the amount and nature of the business pending in the reporter's office. A copy of this report must be filed with the appellate clerk of each district in which the court sits.

13.5 Appointing Deputy Reporter. When the official court reporter is unable to perform the duties in 13.1 or 13.2 because of illness, press of official work, or unavoidable absence or disability, the trial court may designate a deputy reporter. If the court appoints a deputy reporter, that person must file with the trial court clerk a document stating:

(a) the date the deputy worked;

(b) the court in which the deputy worked; and

(c) the number and style of the case on which the deputy worked.

13.6 Filing of Notes in a Criminal Case.

TRAP 14. RECORDING & BROADCASTING COURT PROCEEDINGS

14.1 Recording and Broadcasting Permitted. An appellate court may permit courtroom proceedings to be broadcast, televised, recorded, or photographed in accordance with this rule.

14.2 Procedure.

(a) ***Request to cover court proceeding.***

(1) A person wishing to broadcast, televise, record, or photograph a court proceeding must file with the court clerk a request to cover the proceeding. The request must state:

(A) the case style and number;

(B) the date and time when the proceeding is to begin;

(C) the name of the requesting person or organization;

(D) the type of coverage requested (for example, televising or photographing); and

(E) the type and extent of equipment to be used.

(2) A request to cover argument of a case must be filed no later than five days before the date the case is set for argument and must be served on all parties to the case. A request to cover any other proceeding must be filed no later than two days before the date when the proceeding is to begin.

(b) ***Response.*** Any party may file a response to the request. If the request is to cover argument, the response must be filed no later than two days before the date set for argument. If a party objects to coverage of the argument, the response should state the injury that will allegedly result from coverage.

(c) ***Court may shorten time.*** The court may, in the interest of justice, shorten the time for filing a document under this rule if no party or interested person would be unduly prejudiced.

(d) ***Decision of court.*** In deciding whether to allow coverage, the court may consider information known *ex parte* to the court. The court may allow, deny, limit, or terminate coverage for any reason the court considers necessary or appropriate, such as protecting the parties' rights or the dignity of the court and ensuring the orderly conduct of the proceedings.

14.3 **Equipment and Personnel.** The court may, among other things:

(a) require that a person seeking to cover a proceeding demonstrate or display the equipment that will be used;

(b) prohibit equipment that produces distracting sound or light;

(c) prohibit signal lights or devices showing when equipment is operating, or require their concealment;

(d) prohibit moving lights, flash attachments, or sudden lighting changes;

(e) require the use of the courtroom's existing video, audio, and lighting systems, if any;

(f) specify the placement of personnel and equipment;

(g) determine the number of cameras to be allowed in the courtroom; and

(h) require pooling of equipment if more than one person wishes to cover a proceeding.

14.4 **Enforcement.** The court may sanction a violation of this rule by measures that include barring a person or organization from access to future coverage of proceedings in that court for a defined period.

TRAP 15. ISSUANCE OF WRIT OR PROCESS BY APPELLATE COURT

15.1 **In General.**

(a) ***Signature under seal.*** A writ or process issuing from an appellate court must bear the court's seal and be signed by the clerk.

(b) ***To whom directed; by whom served.*** Unless a rule or statute provides otherwise, the writ or process must be directed to the person or court to be served. The writ or process may be served by the sheriff, constable, or other peace officer whose jurisdiction includes the county in which the person or court to be served may be found.

(c) ***Return; lack of execution; simultaneous writs.*** The writ or process must be returned to the issuing court according to the writ's direction. If the writ or process is not executed, the clerk may issue another writ or process if requested by the party who requested the former writ or process. At a party's request, the clerk may issue two or more writs simultaneously.

15.2 **Appearance Without Service; Actual Knowledge.** A party who appears in person or by attorney in an appellate court proceeding—or who has actual knowledge of the court's opinion, judgment, or order related to a writ or process—is bound by the opinion, judgment, or order to the same extent as if personally served under 15.1.

TRAP 16. DISQUALIFICATION OR RECUSAL OF APPELLATE JUDGES

16.1 **Grounds for Disqualification.** The grounds for disqualification of an appellate court justice or judge are determined by the Constitution and laws of Texas.

16.2 **Grounds for Recusal.** The grounds for recusal of an appellate court justice or judge are the same as those provided in the Rules of Civil Procedure. In addition, a justice or judge must recuse in a proceeding if it presents a material issue which the justice or judge participated in deciding while serving on another court in which the proceeding was pending.

16.3 **Procedure for Recusal.**

(a) ***Motion.*** A party may file a motion to recuse a justice or judge before whom the case is pending. The motion must be filed promptly after the party has reason to believe that the justice or judge should not participate in deciding the case.

(b) ***Decision.*** Before any further proceeding in the case, the challenged justice or judge must either remove himself or herself from all participation in the case or certify the matter to the entire court, which will decide the motion by a majority of the remaining judges sitting en banc. The challenged justice or judge must not sit with the remainder of the court to consider the motion as to him or her.

(c) ***Appeal.*** An order of recusal is not reviewable, but the denial of a recusal motion is reviewable.

TRAP 17. COURT OF APPEALS UNABLE TO TAKE IMMEDIATE ACTION

17.1 **Inability to Act.** A court of appeals is unable to take immediate action if it cannot—within the time when action must be taken—assemble a panel because members of the court are ill, absent, or unavailable. A justice who is disqualified or recused is unavailable. A court of appeals' inability to act immediately may be established by certificate of the clerk, a member of the court, or a party's counsel, or by affidavit of a party.

17.2 Nearest Available Court of Appeals. If a court of appeals is unable to take immediate action, the nearest court of appeals that is able to take immediate action may do so with the same effect as the other court. The nearest court of appeals is the one whose courthouse is nearest—measured by a straight line—the courthouse of the trial court.

17.3 Further Proceedings. After acting or refusing to act, the nearest court of appeals must promptly send a copy of its order, and the original or a copy of any document presented to it, to the other court, which will conduct any further proceedings in the matter.

TRAP 18. MANDATE

18.1 Issuance. The clerk of the appellate court that rendered the judgment must issue a mandate in accordance with the judgment and send it to the clerk of the court to which it is directed and to all parties to the proceeding when one of the following periods expires:

(a) *In the court of appeals.*

(1) Ten days after the time has expired for filing a motion to extend time to file a petition for review or a petition for discretionary review if:

(A) no timely petition for review or petition for discretionary review has been filed;

(B) no timely filed motion to extend time to file a petition for review or petition for discretionary review is pending; and

(C) in a criminal case, the Court of Criminal Appeals has not granted review on its own initiative.

(2) Ten days after the time has expired for filing a motion to extend time to file a motion for rehearing of a denial, refusal, or dismissal of a petition for review, or a refusal or dismissal of a petition for discretionary review, if no timely filed motion for rehearing or motion to extend time is pending.

(b) ***In the Supreme Court and the Court of Criminal Appeals.*** Ten days after the time has expired for filing a motion to extend time to file a motion for rehearing if no timely filed motion for rehearing or motion to extend time is pending.

(c) ***Agreement to issue.*** The mandate may be issued earlier if the parties so agree, or for good cause on the motion of a party.

18.2 Stay of Mandate. A party may move to stay issuance of the mandate pending the United States Supreme Court's disposition of a petition for writ of certiorari. The motion must state the grounds for the petition and the circumstances requiring the stay. The appellate court authorized to issue the mandate may grant a stay if it finds that the grounds are substantial and that the petitioner or others would incur serious hardship from the mandate's issuance if the United States Supreme Court were later to reverse the judgment. In a criminal case, the stay will last for no more than 90 days, to permit the timely filing of a petition for writ of certiorari. After that period and others mentioned in this rule expire, the mandate will issue.

18.3 Trial Court Case Number. The mandate must state the trial court case number.

18.4 Filing of Mandate. The clerk receiving the mandate will file it with the case's other papers and note it on the docket.

18.5 Costs. The mandate will be issued without waiting for costs to be paid. If the Supreme Court declines to grant review, Supreme Court costs must be included in the court of appeals' mandate.

18.6 Mandate in Accelerated Appeals. The appellate court's judgment on an appeal from an interlocutory order takes effect when the mandate is issued. The court may issue the mandate with its judgment or delay the mandate until the appeal is finally disposed of. If the mandate is issued, any further proceeding in the trial court must conform to the mandate.

18.7 Recall of Mandate. If an appellate court vacates or modifies its judgment or order after issuing its mandate, the appellate clerk must promptly notify the clerk of the court to which the mandate was directed and all parties. The mandate will have no effect and a new mandate may be issued.

TRAP 19. PLENARY POWER OF THE COURTS OF APPEALS & EXPIRATION OF TERM

19.1 Plenary Power of Courts of Appeals. A court of appeals' plenary power over its judgment expires:

(a) 60 days after judgment if no timely filed motion to extend time or motion for rehearing is then pending; or

(b) 30 days after the court overrules all timely filed motions for rehearing, including motions or en banc reconsideration of a panel's decision under Rule 49.7, and motions to extend time to file a motion for rehearing.

19.2 Plenary Power Continues After Petition Filed. In a civil case, the court of appeals retains plenary power to vacate or modify its judgment during the periods prescribed in 19.1 even if a party has filed a petition for review in the Supreme Court.

19.3 Proceedings After Plenary Power Expires. After its plenary power expires, the court cannot vacate or modify its judgment. But the court may:

(a) correct a clerical error in its judgment or opinion;

(b) issue and recall its mandate as these rules provide;

(c) enforce or suspend enforcement of its judgment as these rules or applicable law provide;

(d) order or modify the amount and type of security required to suspend a judgment, and decide the sufficiency of the sureties, under Rule 24; and

(e) order its opinion published in accordance with Rule 47.

19.4 Expiration of Term. The expiration of the appellate court's term does not affect the court's plenary power or its jurisdiction over a case that is pending when the court's term expires.

TRAP 20. WHEN PARTY IS INDIGENT

20.1 Civil Cases.

(a) ***Establishing indigence.*** A party who cannot pay the costs in an appellate court may proceed without advance payment of costs if:

(1) the party files an affidavit of indigence in compliance with this rule;

(2) the claim of indigence is not contested or, if contested, the contest is not sustained by written order; and

(3) the party timely files a notice of appeal.

(b) ***Contents of affidavit.*** The affidavit of indigence must identify the party filing the affidavit and must state what amount of costs, if any, the party can pay. The affidavit must also contain complete information about:

(1) the nature and amount of the party's current employment income, government-entitlement income, and other income;

(2) the income of the party's spouse and whether that income is available to the party;

(3) real and personal property the party owns;

(4) cash the party holds and amounts on deposit that the party may withdraw;

(5) the party's other assets;

(6) the number and relationship to the party of any dependents;

(7) the nature and amount of the party's debts;

(8) the nature and amount of the party's monthly expenses;

(9) the party's ability to obtain a loan for court costs;

(10) whether an attorney is providing free legal services to the party without a contingent fee; and

(11) whether an attorney has agreed to pay or advance court costs.

(c) ***When and where affidavit filed.***

(1) ***Appeals.*** An appellant must file the affidavit of indigence in the trial court with or before the notice of appeal. An appellee who is required to pay part of the cost of preparation of the record under Rule 34.5(b)(3) or 34.6(c)(3) must file an affidavit of indigence in the trial court within 15 days after the date when the appellee becomes responsible for paying that cost.

(2) ***Other proceedings.*** In any other appellate court proceeding, a petitioner must file the affidavit of indigence in the court in which the proceeding is filed, with or before the document seeking relief. A respondent who requests preparation of a record in connection with an appellate court proceeding must file an affidavit of indigence in the appellate court within 15 days after the date when the respondent requests preparation of the record.

(3) ***Extension of time.*** The appellate court may extend the time to file an affidavit of indigence if, within 15 days after the deadline for filing the affidavit, the party files in the appellate court a motion complying with Rule 10.5(b).

(d) ***Duty of clerk.***

(1) ***Trial court clerk.*** If the affidavit of indigence is filed with the trial court clerk under (c)(1), the clerk must promptly send a copy of the affidavit to the appropriate court reporter.

(2) ***Appellate court clerk.*** If the affidavit of indigence is filed with the appellate court clerk under (c)(2) and if the filing party is requesting the preparation of a record, the appellate court clerk must:

(A) send a copy of the affidavit to the trial court clerk and the appropriate court reporter; and

(B) send to the trial court clerk, the court reporter, and all parties, a notice stating the deadline for filing a contest to the affidavit of indigence.

(e) ***Contest to affidavit.*** The clerk, the court reporter, or any party may challenge the claim of indigence by filing—in the court in which the affidavit was filed—a contest to the affidavit. The contest must be filed on or before the date set by the clerk if the affidavit was filed in the appellate court, or within 10 days after the date when the affidavit was filed if the affidavit was filed in the trial court. The contest need not be sworn.

(f) ***No contest filed.*** Unless a contest is timely filed, no hearing will be conducted, the affidavit's allegations will be deemed true, and the party will be allowed to proceed without advance payment of costs.

(g) ***Burden of proof.*** If a contest is filed, the party who filed the affidavit of indigence must prove the affidavit's allegations. If the indigent party is incarcerated at the time the hearing on a contest is held, the affidavit must be considered as evidence and is sufficient to meet the indigent party's burden to present evidence without the indigent party's attending the hearing.

(h) ***Decision in appellate court.*** If the affidavit of indigence is filed in an appellate court and a contest is filed, the court may:

(1) conduct a hearing and decide the contest;

(2) decide the contest based on the affidavit and any other timely filed documents;

(3) request the written submission of additional evidence and, without conducting a hearing, decide the contest based on the evidence; or

(4) refer the matter to the trial court with instructions to hear evidence and grant the appropriate relief.

(i) ***Hearing and decision in the trial court.***

(1) ***Notice required.*** If the affidavit of indigence is filed in the trial court and a contest is filed, or if the appellate court refers a contest to the trial court, the trial court must set a hearing and notify the parties and the appropriate court reporter of the setting.

(2) ***Time for hearing.*** The trial court must either conduct a hearing or sign an order extending the time to conduct a hearing:

(A) within 10 days after the contest was filed, if initially filed in the trial court; or

(B) within 10 days after the trial court received a contest referred from the appellate court.

(3) ***Extension of time for hearing.*** The time for conducting a hearing on the contest must not be extended for more than 20 days from the date the order is signed.

(4) ***Time for written decision; effect.*** Unless—within the period set for the hearing—the trial court signs an order sustaining the contest, the affidavit's allegations will be deemed true, and the party will be allowed to proceed without advance payment of costs.

(j) ***Record to be prepared without prepayment.*** If a party establishes indigence, the trial court clerk and the court reporter must prepare the appellate record without prepayment.

(k) ***Partial payment of costs.*** If the party can pay or give security for some of the costs, the court must order the party, in writing, to pay or give security, or both, to the extent of the party's ability. The court will allocate the payment among the officials to whom payment is due.

(*l*) ***Later ability to pay.*** If a party who has proceeded in the appellate court without having to pay all the costs is later able to pay some or all of the costs, the appellate court may order the party to pay costs to the extent of the party's ability.

(m) ***Costs defined.*** As used in this rule, *costs* means:

(1) a filing fee relating to the case in which the affidavit of inability is filed; and

(2) the charges for preparing the appellate record in that case.

20.2 Criminal Cases.

SECTION TWO: APPEALS FROM TRIAL COURT JUDGMENTS & ORDERS

TRAP 21. NEW TRIALS IN CRIMINAL CASES

TRAP 22. ARREST OF JUDGMENT IN CRIMINAL CASES

TRAP 23. NUNC PRO TUNC PROCEEDINGS IN CRIMINAL CASES

TRAP 24. SUSPENSION OF ENFORCEMENT OF JUDGMENT PENDING APPEAL IN CIVIL CASES

24.1 Suspension of Enforcement.

(a) ***Methods.*** Unless the law or these rules provide otherwise, a judgment debtor may supersede the judgment by:

(1) filing with the trial court clerk a written agreement with the judgment creditor for suspending enforcement of the judgment;

(2) filing with the trial court clerk a good and sufficient bond;

(3) making a deposit with the trial court clerk in lieu of a bond; or

(4) providing alternate security ordered by the court.

(b) ***Bonds.***

(1) A bond must be:

(A) in the amount required by 24.2;

(B) payable to the judgment creditor;

(C) signed by the judgment debtor or the debtor's agent;

(D) signed by a sufficient surety or sureties as obligors; and

(E) conditioned as required by (d).

(2) To be effective a bond must be approved by the trial court clerk. On motion of any party, the trial court will review the bond.

(c) ***Deposit in lieu of bond.***

(1) ***Types of deposits.*** Instead of filing a surety bond, a party may deposit with the trial court clerk:

(A) cash;

(B) a cashier's check payable to the clerk, drawn on any federally insured and federally or state-chartered bank or savings-and-loan association; or

(C) with leave of court, a negotiable obligation of the federal government or of any federally insured and federally or state-chartered bank or savings-and-loan association.

(2) ***Amount of deposit.*** The deposit must be in the amount required by 24.2.

(3) ***Clerk's duties.*** The clerk must promptly deposit any cash or a cashier's check in accordance with law. The clerk must hold the deposit until the conditions of liability in (d) are extinguished. The clerk must then release any remaining funds in the deposit to the judgment debtor.

(d) ***Conditions of liability.*** The surety or sureties on a bond, any deposit in lieu of a bond, or any alternate security ordered by the court is subject to liability for all damages and costs that may be awarded against the debtor—up to the amount of the bond, deposit, or security—if:

(1) the debtor does not perfect an appeal or the debtor's appeal is dismissed, and the debtor does not perform the trial court's judgment;

(2) the debtor does not perform an adverse judgment final on appeal; or

(3) the judgment is for the recovery of an interest in real or personal property, and the debtor does not pay the creditor the value of the property interest's rent or revenue during the pendency of the appeal.

(e) ***Orders of trial court.*** The trial court may make any order necessary to adequately protect the judgment creditor against loss or damage that the appeal might cause.

(f) ***Effect of supersedeas.*** Enforcement of a judgment must be suspended if the judgment is superseded. Enforcement begun before the judgment is superseded must cease when the judgment is superseded. If execution has been issued, the clerk will promptly issue a writ of supersedeas.

03 24.2 Amount of Bond, Deposit or Security.

(a) ***Type of judgment.***

(1) ***For recovery of money.*** When the judgment is for money, the amount of the bond, deposit, or security must equal the sum of compensatory damages awarded in the judgment, interest for the estimated duration of the appeal, and costs awarded in the judgment. But the amount must not exceed the lesser of:

(A) 50 percent of the judgment debtor's current net worth; or

(B) 25 million dollars.

(2) ***For recovery of property.*** When the judgment is for the recovery of an interest in real or personal property, the trial court will determine the type of security that the judgment debtor must post. The amount of that security must be at least:

(A) the value of the property interest's rent or revenue, if the property interest is real; or

(B) the value of the property interest on the date when the court rendered judgment, if the property interest is personal.

(3) ***Other judgment.*** When the judgment is for something other than money or an interest in property, the trial court must set the amount and type of security that the judgment debtor must post. The security must adequately protect the judgment creditor against loss or damage that the appeal might cause. But the trial court may decline to permit the judgment to be superseded if the judgment creditor posts security ordered by the trial court in an amount and type that will secure the judgment debtor against any loss or damage caused by the relief granted the judgment creditor if an appellate court determines, on final disposition, that that relief was improper.

(4) ***Conservatorship or custody.*** When the judgment involves the conservatorship or custody of a minor or other person under legal disability, enforcement of the judgment will not be suspended, with or without security, unless ordered by the trial court. But upon a proper showing, the appellate court may suspend enforcement of the judgment with or without security.

(5) ***For a governmental entity.*** When a judgment in favor of a governmental entity in its governmental capacity is one in which the entity has no pecuniary interest, the trial court must determine whether to suspend enforcement, with or without security, taking into account the harm that is likely to result to the judgment debtor if enforcement is not suspended, and the harm that is likely to result to others if enforcement is suspended. The appellate court may review the trial court's determination and suspend enforcement of the judgment, with or without security, or refuse to suspend the judgment. If security is required, recovery is limited to the governmental entity's actual damages resulting from suspension of the judgment.

(b) ***Lesser amount.*** The trial court must lower the amount of security required by (a) to an amount that will not cause the judgment debtor substantial economic harm if, after notice to all parties and a hearing, the court finds that posting a bond, deposit, or security in the amount required by (a) is likely to cause the judgment debtor substantial economic harm.

(c) ***Determination of Net Worth.***

(1) ***Judgment Debtor's Affidavit Required; Contents; Prima Facie Evidence.*** A judgment debtor who provides a bond, deposit, or security under (a)(1)(A) in an amount based on the debtor's net worth must simultaneously file an affidavit that states the debtor's net worth and states complete, detailed information concerning the debtor's assets and liabilities from which net worth can be ascertained. The affidavit is prima facie evidence of the debtor's net worth.

(2) ***Contest; Discovery.*** A judgment creditor may file a contest to the debtor's affidavit of net worth. The contest need not be sworn. The creditor may conduct reasonable discovery concerning the judgment debtor's net worth.

(3) ***Hearing; Burden of Proof; Findings.*** The trial court must hear a judgment creditor's contest promptly after any discovery has been completed. The judgment debtor has the burden of proving net worth. The trial court must issue an order that states the debtor's net worth and states with particularity the factual basis for that determination.

(d) ***Injunction.*** The trial court may enjoin the judgment debtor from dissipating or transferring assets to avoid satisfaction of the judgment, but the trial court may not make any order that interferes with the judgment debtor's use, transfer, conveyance, or dissipation of assets in the normal course of business.

24.3 Continuing Trial Court Jurisdiction; Duties of Judgment Debtor.

(a) ***Continuing jurisdiction.*** Even after the trial court's plenary power expires, the trial court has continuing jurisdiction to do the following:

(1) order the amount and type of security and decide the sufficiency of sureties; and

(2) if circumstances change, modify the amount or type of security required to continue the suspension of a judgment's execution.

(b) ***Duties of judgment debtor.*** If, after jurisdiction attaches in an appellate court, the trial court orders or modifies the security or decides the sufficiency of sureties, the judgment debtor must notify the appellate court of the trial court's action.

24.4 **Appellate Review.**

(a) ***Motions; review.*** On a party's motion to the appellate court, that court may review:

03 (1) the sufficiency or excessiveness of the amount of security, but when the judgment is for money, the appellate court must not modify the amount of security to exceed the limits imposed by rule 24.2(a)(1);

(2) the sureties on any bond;

(3) the type of security;

(4) the determination whether to permit suspension of enforcement; and

(5) the trial court's exercise of discretion under 24.3(a).

(b) ***Grounds of review.*** Review may be based both on conditions as they existed at the time the trial court signed an order and on changes in those conditions afterward.

(c) ***Temporary orders.*** The appellate court may issue any temporary orders necessary to preserve the parties' rights.

(d) ***Action by appellate court.*** The motion must be heard at the earliest practicable time. The appellate court may require that the amount of a bond, deposit, or other security be increased or decreased, and that another bond, deposit, or security be provided and approved by the trial court clerk. The appellate court may require other changes in the trial court order. The appellate court may remand to the trial court for entry of findings of fact or for the taking of evidence.

(e) ***Effect of ruling.*** If the appellate court orders additional or other security to supersede the judgment, enforcement will be suspended for 20 days after the appellate court's order. If the judgment debtor does not comply with the order within that period, the judgment may be enforced. When any additional bond, deposit, or security has been filed, the trial court clerk must notify the appellate court. The posting of additional security will not release the previously posted security or affect any alternative security arrangements that the judgment debtor previously made unless specifically ordered by the appellate court.

2003 change: Amended eff. Sept. 10, 2003, by order of Sept. 10, 2003 (Tex.Sup.Ct. Order, Misc. Docket No. 03-9150): amended incorrect cross reference in Rule 24.2(c)(1). Amended eff. Sept. 1, 2003, by order of Aug. 29, 2003 (114-15 S.W.3d [Tex.Cases] xx).

TRAP 25. PERFECTING APPEAL

25.1 **Civil Cases.**

(a) ***Notice of appeal.*** An appeal is perfected when a written notice of appeal is filed with the trial court clerk. If a notice of appeal is mistakenly filed with the appellate court, the notice is deemed to have been filed the same day with the trial court clerk, and the appellate clerk must immediately send the trial court clerk a copy of the notice.

(b) ***Jurisdiction of appellate court.*** The filing of a notice of appeal by any party invokes the appellate court's jurisdiction over all parties to the trial court's judgment or order appealed from. Any party's failure to take any other step required by these rules, including the failure of another party to perfect an appeal under (c), does not deprive the appellate court of jurisdiction but is ground only for the appellate court to act appropriately, including dismissing the appeal.

(c) ***Who must file notice.*** A party who seeks to alter the trial court's judgment or other appealable order must file a notice of appeal. Parties whose interests are aligned may file a joint notice of appeal. The appellate court may not grant a party who does not file a notice of appeal more favorable relief than did the trial court except for just cause.

(d) ***Contents of notice.*** The notice of appeal must:

(1) identify the trial court and state the case's trial court number and style;

(2) state the date of the judgment or order appealed from;

(3) state that the party desires to appeal;

(4) state the court to which the appeal is taken unless the appeal is to either the First or Fourteenth Court of Appeals, in which case the notice must state that the appeal is to either of those courts;

(5) state the name of each party filing the notice;

(6) in an accelerated appeal, state that the appeal is accelerated; and

(7) in a restricted appeal:

(A) state that the appellant is a party affected by the trial court's judgment but did not participate—either in person or through counsel—in the hearing that resulted in the judgment complained of;

(B) state that the appellant did not timely file either a postjudgment motion, request for findings of fact and conclusions of law, or notice of appeal; and

(C) be verified by the appellant if the appellant does not have counsel.

(e) ***Service of notice; copy filed with appellate court.*** The notice of appeal must be served on all parties to the trial court's final judgment or, in an interlocutory appeal, on all parties to the trial court proceeding. A copy of the notice of appeal must be filed with the appellate court clerk.

(f) ***Amending the notice.*** An amended notice of appeal correcting a defect or omission in an earlier filed notice may be filed in the appellate court at any time before the appellant's brief is filed. The amended notice is subject to being struck for cause on the motion of any party affected by the amended notice. After the appellant's brief is filed, the notice may be amended only on leave of the appellate court and on such terms as the court may prescribe.

(g) ***Enforcement of judgment not suspended by appeal.*** The filing of a notice of appeal does not suspend enforcement of the judgment. Enforcement of the judgment may proceed unless:

(1) the judgment is superseded in accordance with Rule 24, or

(2) the appellant is entitled to supersede the judgment without security by filing a notice of appeal.

25.2 Criminal Cases.

TRAP 26. TIME TO PERFECT APPEAL

26.1 Civil Cases. The notice of appeal must be filed within 30 days after the judgment is signed, except as follows:

(a) the notice of appeal must be filed within 90 days after the judgment is signed if any party timely files:

(1) a motion for new trial;

(2) a motion to modify the judgment;

(3) a motion to reinstate under Texas Rule of Civil Procedure 165a; or

(4) a request for findings of fact and conclusions of law if findings and conclusions either are required by the Rules of Civil Procedure or, if not required, could properly be considered by the appellate court;

(b) in an accelerated appeal, the notice of appeal must be filed within 20 days after the judgment or order is signed;

(c) in a restricted appeal, the notice of appeal must be filed within six months after the judgment or order is signed; and

(d) if any party timely files a notice of appeal, another party may file a notice of appeal within the applicable period stated above or 14 days after the first filed notice of appeal, whichever is later.

26.2 Criminal Cases.

26.3 Extension of Time. The appellate court may extend the time to file the notice of appeal if, within 15 days after the deadline for filing the notice of appeal, the party:

(a) files in the trial court the notice of appeal; and

(b) files in the appellate court a motion complying with Rule 10.5(b).

TRAP 27. PREMATURE FILINGS

27.1 Prematurely Filed Notice of Appeal.

(a) ***Civil cases.*** In a civil case, a prematurely filed notice of appeal is effective and deemed filed on the day of, but after, the event that begins the period for perfecting the appeal.

(b) ***Criminal cases.*** In a criminal case, a prematurely filed notice of appeal is effective and deemed filed on the same day, but after, sentence is imposed or suspended in open court, or the appealable order is signed by the trial court. But a notice of appeal is not effective if filed before the trial court makes a finding of guilt or receives a jury verdict.

27.2 Other Premature Actions. The appellate court may treat actions taken before an appealable order is signed as relating to an appeal of that order and give them effect as if they had been taken after the order was signed. The appellate court may allow an appealed order that is not final to be modified so as to be made final and may allow the modified order and all proceedings relating to it to be included in a supplemental record.

27.3 If Appealed Order Modified or Vacated. After an order or judgment in a civil case has been appealed, if the trial court modifies the order or judgment, or if the trial court vacates the order or judgment and replaces it with another appealable order or judgment, the appellate court must treat the appeal as from the subsequent order or judgment and may treat actions relating to the appeal of the first order or judgment as relating to the appeal of the subsequent order or judgment. The subsequent order or judgment and actions relating to it may be included in the original or supplemental record. Any party may nonetheless appeal from the subsequent order or judgment.

TRAP 28. ACCELERATED APPEALS IN CIVIL CASES

28.1 Interlocutory Orders. An appeal from an interlocutory order, when allowed, will be accelerated. Filing a motion for new trial will not extend the time to perfect the appeal. The trial court need not, but may—within 30 days after the order is signed—file findings of fact and conclusions of law.

28.2 Quo Warranto. An appeal in a quo warranto proceeding will be accelerated. In such a proceeding, filing a motion for new trial will not extend the time to perfect the appeal. But the trial court may grant a timely filed motion for new trial until 50 days after the judgment or appealable order is signed. If not determined by written order within that period, the motion for new trial will be deemed overruled.

28.3 Record and Briefs. In lieu of the clerk's record, the appellate court may hear an accelerated appeal on the original papers forwarded by the trial court or on sworn and uncontroverted copies of those papers. The appellate court may allow the case to be submitted without briefs.

TRAP 29. ORDERS PENDING INTERLOCUTORY APPEAL IN CIVIL CASES

29.1 Effect of Appeal. Perfecting an appeal from an order granting interlocutory relief does not suspend the order appealed from unless:

(a) the order is superseded in accordance with 29.2; or

(b) the appellant is entitled to supersede the order without security by filing a notice of appeal.

29.2 Security. The trial court may permit an order granting interlocutory relief to be superseded pending an appeal from the order, in which event the appellant may supersede the order in accordance with Rule 24. If the trial court refuses to permit the appellant to supersede the order, the appellant may move the appellate court to review that decision for abuse of discretion.

29.3 Temporary Orders of Appellate Court. When an appeal from an interlocutory order is perfected, the appellate court may make any temporary orders necessary to preserve the parties' rights until disposition of the appeal and may require appropriate security. But the appellate court must not suspend the trial court's order if the appellant's rights would be adequately protected by supersedeas or another order made under Rule 24.

29.4 Enforcement of Temporary Orders. While an appeal from an interlocutory order is pending, only the appellate court in which the appeal is pending may enforce the order. But the appellate court may refer any enforcement proceeding to the trial court with instructions to:

(a) hear evidence and grant appropriate relief; or

(b) make findings and recommendations and report them to the appellate court.

29.5 Further Proceedings in Trial Court. While an appeal from an interlocutory order is pending, the trial court retains jurisdiction of the case and may make further orders, including one dissolving the order appealed from, and if permitted by law, may proceed with a trial on the merits. But the court must not make an order that:

(a) is inconsistent with any appellate court temporary order; or

(b) interferes with or impairs the jurisdiction of the appellate court or effectiveness of any relief sought or that may be granted on appeal.

29.6 Review of Further Orders.

(a) ***Motion to review further orders.*** While an appeal from an interlocutory order is pending, on a party's motion or on the appellate court's own initiative, the appellate court may review the following:

(1) a further appealable interlocutory order concerning the same subject matter; and

(2) any interlocutory order that interferes with or impairs the effectiveness of the relief sought or that may be granted on appeal.

(b) ***Record.*** The party filing the motion may rely on the original record or may file a supplemental record with the motion.

TRAP 30. RESTRICTED APPEAL TO COURT OF APPEALS IN CIVIL CASES

A party who did not participate—either in person or through counsel—in the hearing that resulted in the judgment complained of and who did not timely file a postjudgment motion or request for findings of fact and conclusions of law, or a notice of appeal within the time permitted by Rule 26.1(a), may file a notice of appeal within the time permitted by Rule 26.1(c). Restricted appeals replace writ of error appeals to the court of appeals. Statutes pertaining to writ of error appeals to the court of appeals apply equally to restricted appeals.

TRAP 31. APPEALS IN HABEAS CORPUS, BAIL, & EXTRADITION PROCEEDINGS IN CRIMINAL CASES

TRAP 32. DOCKETING STATEMENT

32.1 Civil Cases. Upon perfecting the appeal in a civil case, the appellant must file in the appellate court a docketing statement that includes the following information:

(a)(1) if the appellant filing the statement has counsel, the name of that appellant and the name, address, telephone number, fax number, if any, and State Bar of Texas identification number of the appellant's lead counsel; or

(2) if the appellant filing the statement is not represented by an attorney, that party's name, address, telephone number, and fax number, if any;

(b) the date the notice of appeal was filed in the trial court and, if mailed to the trial court clerk, the date of mailing;

(c) the trial court's name and county, the name of the judge who tried the case, and the date the judgment or order appealed from was signed;

(d) the date of filing of any motion for new trial, motion to modify the judgment, request for findings of fact, motion to reinstate, or other filing that affects the time for perfecting the appeal;

(e) the names of all other parties to the trial court's judgment or the order appealed from, and:

(1) if represented by counsel, their lead counsel's names, addresses, telephone numbers, and fax numbers, if any; or

(2) if not represented by counsel, the name, address, and telephone number of the party, or a statement that the appellant diligently inquired but could not discover that information;

(f) the general nature of the case—for example, personal injury, breach of contract, or temporary injunction;

(g) whether the appeal's submission should be given priority or whether the appeal is an accelerated one under Rule 28 or another rule or statute;

(h) whether the appellant has requested or will request a reporter's record, and whether the trial was electronically recorded;

(i) the name of the court reporter;

(j) whether the appellant intends to seek temporary or ancillary relief while the appeal is pending;

(k)(1) the date of filing of any affidavit of indigence;

(2) the date of filing of any contest;

(3) the date of any order on the contest; and

(4) whether the contest was sustained or overruled;

(*l*) whether the appellant has filed or will file a supersedeas bond; and

(m) any other information the appellate court requires.

32.2 Criminal Cases.

32.3 Supplemental Statements. Any party may file a statement supplementing or correcting the docketing statement.

32.4 Purpose of Statement. The docketing statement is for administrative purposes and does not affect the appellate court's jurisdiction.

TRAP 33. PRESERVATION OF APPELLATE COMPLAINTS

33.1 Preservation; How Shown.

(a) ***In general.*** As a prerequisite to presenting a complaint for appellate review, the record must show that:

(1) the complaint was made to the trial court by a timely request, objection, or motion that:

(A) stated the grounds for the ruling that the complaining party sought from the trial court with sufficient specificity to make the trial court aware of the complaint, unless the specific grounds were apparent from the context; and

(B) complied with the requirements of the Texas Rules of Civil or Criminal Evidence or the Texas Rules of Civil or Appellate Procedure; and

(2) the trial court:

(A) ruled on the request, objection, or motion, either expressly or implicitly; or

(B) refused to rule on the request, objection, or motion, and the complaining party objected to the refusal.

(b) ***Ruling by operation of law.*** In a civil case, the overruling by operation of law of a motion for new trial or a motion to modify the judgment preserves for appellate review a complaint properly made in the motion, unless taking evidence was necessary to properly present the complaint in the trial court.

(c) ***Formal exception and separate order not required.*** Neither a formal exception to a trial court ruling or order nor a signed, separate order is required to preserve a complaint for appeal.

(d) ***Sufficiency of evidence complaints in nonjury Cases.*** In a nonjury case, a complaint regarding the legal or factual insufficiency of the evidence—including a complaint that the damages found by the court are excessive or inadequate, as distinguished from a complaint that the trial court erred in refusing to amend a fact finding or to make an additional finding of fact—may be made for the first time on appeal in the complaining party's brief.

33.2 Formal Bills of Exception. To complain on appeal about a matter that would not otherwise appear in the record, a party must file a formal bill of exception.

(a) ***Form.*** No particular form of words is required in a bill of exception. But the objection to the court's ruling or action, and the ruling complained of, must be stated with sufficient specificity to make the trial court aware of the complaint.

(b) ***Evidence.*** When the appellate record contains the evidence needed to explain a bill of exception, the bill itself need not repeat the evidence, and a party may attach and incorporate a transcription of the evidence certified by the court reporter.

(c) ***Procedure.***

(1) The complaining party must first present a formal bill of exception to the trial court.

(2) If the parties agree on the contents of the bill of exception, the judge must sign the bill and file it with the trial court clerk. If the parties do not agree on the contents of the bill, the trial judge must—after notice and hearing—do one of the following things:

(A) sign the bill of exception and file it with the trial court clerk if the judge finds that it is correct;

(B) suggest to the complaining party those corrections to the bill that the judge believes are necessary to make it accurately reflect the proceedings in the trial court, and if the party agrees to the corrections, have the corrections made, sign the bill, and file it with the trial court clerk; or

(C) if the complaining party will not agree to the corrections suggested by the judge, return the bill to the complaining party with the judge's refusal written on it, and prepare, sign, and file with the trial court clerk such bill as will, in the judge's opinion, accurately reflect the proceedings in the trial court.

(3) If the complaining party is dissatisfied with the bill of exception filed by the judge under (2)(C), the party may file with the trial court clerk the bill that was rejected by the judge. That party must also file the affidavits of at least three people who observed the matter to which the bill of exception is addressed. The affidavits must attest to the correctness of the bill as presented by the party. The matters contained in that bill of exception may be controverted and maintained by additional affidavits filed by any party within ten days after the filing of that bill. The truth of the bill of exception will be determined by the appellate court.

(d) ***Conflict.*** If a formal bill of exception conflicts with the reporter's record, the bill controls.

(e) ***Time to file.***

(1) ***Civil cases.*** In a civil case, a formal bill of exception must be filed no later than 30 days after the filing party's notice of appeal is filed.

(2) ***Criminal cases.*** In a criminal case, a formal bill of exception must be filed:

(A) no later than 60 days after the trial court pronounces or suspends sentence in open court; or

(B) if a motion for new trial has been timely filed, no later than 90 days after the trial court pronounces or suspends sentence in open court.

(3) ***Extension of time.*** The appellate court may extend the time to file a formal bill of exception if, within 15 days after the deadline for filing the bill, the party files in the appellate court a motion complying with Rule 10.5(b).

(f) ***Inclusion in clerk's record.*** When filed, a formal bill of exception should be included in the appellate record.

TRAP 34. APPELLATE RECORD

34.1 Contents. The appellate record consists of the clerk's record and, if necessary to the appeal, the reporter's record. Even if more than one notice of appeal is filed, there should be only one appellate record in a case.

34.2 Agreed Record. By written stipulation filed with the trial court clerk, the parties may agree on the contents of the appellate record. An agreed record will be presumed to contain all evidence and filings relevant to the appeal. To request matter to be included in the agreed record, the parties must comply with the procedures in Rules 34.5 and 34.6.

34.3 Agreed Statement of the Case. In lieu of a reporter's record, the parties may agree on a brief statement of the case. The statement must be filed with the trial court clerk and included in the appellate record.

34.4 Form. The Supreme Court and Court of Criminal Appeals will prescribe the form of the appellate record.

34.5 Clerk's Record.

(a) ***Contents.*** Unless the parties designate the filings in the appellate record by agreement under Rule 34.2, the record must include copies of the following:

(1) in civil cases, all pleadings on which the trial was held;

(2) in criminal cases, the indictment or information, any special plea or defense motion that was presented to the court and overruled, any written waiver, any written stipulation, and, in cases in which a plea of guilty or nolo contendere has been entered, any documents executed for the plea;

(3) the court's docket sheet;

(4) the court's charge and the jury's verdict, or the court's findings of fact and conclusions of law;

(5) the court's judgment or other order that is being appealed;

(6) any request for findings of fact and conclusions of law, any post-judgment motion, and the court's order on the motion;

(7) the notice of appeal;

(8) any formal bill of exception;

(9) any request for a reporter's record, including any statement of points or issues under Rule 34.6(c);

(10) any request for preparation of the clerk's record;

(11) in civil cases, a certified bill of costs, including the cost of preparing the clerk's record, showing credits for payments made; and

(12) in criminal cases, the trial court's certification of the defendant's right of appeal under Rule 25.2; and

(13) subject to (b), any filing that a party designates to have included in the record.

(b) ***Request for additional items.***

(1) ***Time for request.*** At any time before the clerk's record is prepared, any party may file with the trial court clerk a written designation specifying items to be included in the record.

(2) ***Request must be specific.*** A party requesting that an item be included in the clerk's record must specifically describe the item so that the clerk can readily identify it. The clerk will disregard a general designation, such as one for "all papers filed in the case."

(3) ***Requesting unnecessary items.*** In a civil case, if a party requests that more items than necessary be included in the clerk's record or any supplement, the appellate court may—regardless of the appeal's outcome—require that party to pay the costs for the preparation of the unnecessary portion.

(4) ***Failure to timely request.*** An appellate court must not refuse to file the clerk's record or a supplemental clerk's record because of a failure to timely request items to be included in the clerk's record.

(c) ***Supplementation.***

(1) If a relevant item has been omitted from the clerk's record, the trial court, the appellate court, or any party may by letter direct the trial court clerk to prepare, certify, and file in the appellate court a supplement containing the omitted item.

(2) If the appellate court in a criminal case orders the trial court to prepare and file findings of fact and conclusions of law as required by law or certification of the defendant's right of appeal as required by these rules, the trial court clerk must prepare, certify, and file in the appellate court a supplemental clerk's record containing those findings and conclusions.

(3) Any supplemental clerk's record will be part of the appellate record.

(d) *Defects or inaccuracies.* If the clerk's record is defective or inaccurate, the appellate clerk must inform the trial court clerk of the defect or inaccuracy and instruct the clerk to make the correction.

(e) *Clerk's record lost or destroyed.* If a filing designated for inclusion in the clerk's record has been lost or destroyed, the parties may, by written stipulation, deliver a copy of that item to the trial court clerk for inclusion in the clerk's record or a supplement. If the parties cannot agree, the trial court must—on any party's motion or at the appellate court's request—determine what constitutes an accurate copy of the missing item and order it to be included in the clerk's record or a supplement.

(f) *Original documents.* If the trial court determines that original documents filed with the trial court clerk should be inspected by the appellate court or sent to that court in lieu of copies, the trial court must make an order for the safekeeping, transportation, and return of those original documents. The order must list the original documents and briefly describe them. All the documents must be arranged in their listed sequence and bound firmly together. On any party's motion or its own initiative, the appellate court may direct the trial court clerk to send it any original document.

(g) *Additional copies of clerk's record in criminal cases.* In a criminal case, the clerk's record must be made in duplicate, and in a case in which the death penalty was assessed, in triplicate. The trial court clerk must retain the copy or copies for the parties to use with the court's permission.

(h) *Clerk may consult with parties.* The clerk may consult with the parties concerning the contents of the clerk's record.

34.6 Reporter's Record.

(a) *Contents.*

(1) ***Stenographic recording.*** If the proceedings were stenographically recorded, the reporter's record consists of the court reporter's transcription of so much of the proceedings, and any of the exhibits, that the parties to the appeal designate.

(2) ***Electronic recording.*** If the proceedings were electronically recorded, the reporter's record consists of certified copies of all tapes or other audio-storage devices on which the proceedings were recorded, any of the exhibits that the parties to the appeal designate, and certified copies of the logs prepared by the court recorder under Rule 13.2.

(b) *Request for preparation.*

(1) ***Request to court reporter.*** At or before the time for perfecting the appeal, the appellant must request in writing that the official reporter prepare the reporter's record. The request must designate the exhibits to be included. A request to the court reporter—but not the court recorder—must also designate the portions of the proceedings to be included.

(2) ***Filing.*** The appellant must file a copy of the request with the trial court clerk.

(3) ***Failure to timely request.*** An appellate court must not refuse to file a reporter's record or a supplemental reporter's record because of a failure to timely request it.

(c) *Partial reporter's record.*

(1) ***Effect on appellate points or issues.*** If the appellant requests a partial reporter's record, the appellant must include in the request a statement of the points or issues to be presented on appeal and will then be limited to those points or issues.

(2) ***Other parties may designate additions.*** Any other party may designate additional exhibits and portions of the testimony to be included in the reporter's record.

(3) ***Costs; requesting unnecessary matter.*** Additions requested by another party must be included in the reporter's record at the appellant's cost. But if the trial court finds that all or part of the designated additions are unnecessary to the appeal, the trial court may order the other party to pay the costs for the preparation of the unnecessary additions. This paragraph does not affect the appellate court's power to tax costs differently.

(4) ***Presumptions.*** The appellate court must presume that the partial reporter's record designated by the parties constitutes the entire record for purposes of reviewing the stated points or issues. This presumption applies even if the statement includes a point or issue complaining of the legal or factual insufficiency of the evidence to support a specific factual finding identified in that point or issue.

(5) ***Criminal cases.*** In a criminal case, if the statement contains a point complaining that the evidence is insufficient to support a finding of guilt, the

record must include all the evidence admitted at the trial on the issue of guilt or innocence and punishment.

(d) ***Supplementation.*** If anything relevant is omitted from the reporter's record, the trial court, the appellate court, or any party may by letter direct the official court reporter to prepare, certify, and file in the appellate court a supplemental reporter's record containing the omitted items. Any supplemental reporter's record is part of the appellate record.

(e) ***Inaccuracies in the Reporter's Record.***

(1) ***Correction of Inaccuracies by Agreement.*** The parties may agree to correct an inaccuracy in the reporter's record, including an exhibit, without the court reporter's recertification.

(2) ***Correction of Inaccuracies by Trial Court.*** If the parties cannot agree on whether or how to correct the reporter's record so that the text accurately discloses what occurred in the trial court and the exhibits are accurate, the trial court must—after notice and hearing—settle the dispute. If the court finds any inaccuracy, it must order the court reporter to conform the reporter's record (including text and any exhibits) to what occurred in the trial court, and to file certified corrections in the appellate court.

(3) ***Correction After Filing in Appellate Court.*** If the dispute arises after the reporter's record has been filed in the appellate court, that court may submit the dispute to the trial court for resolution. The trial court must then proceed as under subparagraph (e)(2).

(f) ***Reporter's Record Lost or Destroyed.*** An appellant is entitled to a new trial under the following circumstances:

(1) if the appellant has timely requested a reporter's record;

(2) if, without the appellant's fault, a significant exhibit or a significant portion of the court reporter's notes and records has been lost or destroyed or—if the proceedings were electronically recorded—a significant portion of the recording has been lost or destroyed or is inaudible;

(3) if the lost, destroyed, or inaudible portion of the reporter's record, or the lost or destroyed exhibit, is necessary to the appeal's resolution; and

(4) if the lost, destroyed or inaudible portion of the reporter's record cannot be replaced by agreement of the parties, or the lost or destroyed exhibit cannot be replaced either by agreement of the parties or with a copy determined by the trial court to accurately duplicate with reasonable certainty the original exhibit.

(g) ***Original exhibits.***

(1) ***Reporter may use in preparing reporter's record.*** At the court reporter's request, the trial court clerk must give all original exhibits to the reporter for use in preparing the reporter's record. Unless ordered to include original exhibits in the reporter's record, the court reporter must return the original exhibits to the clerk after copying them for inclusion in the reporter's record. If someone other than the trial court clerk possesses an original exhibit, either the trial court or the appellate court may order that person to deliver the exhibit to the trial court clerk.

(2) ***Use of original exhibits by appellate court.*** If the trial court determines that original exhibits should be inspected by the appellate court or sent to that court in lieu of copies, the trial court must make an order for the safekeeping, transportation, and return of those exhibits. The order must list the exhibits and briefly describe them. To the extent practicable, all the exhibits must be arranged in their listed order and bound firmly together before being sent to the appellate clerk. On any party's motion or its own initiative, the appellate court may direct the trial court clerk to send it any original exhibit.

(h) ***Additional copies of reporter's record in criminal cases.*** In a criminal case in which a party requests a reporter's record, the court reporter must prepare a duplicate of the reporter's record and file it with the trial court clerk. In a case where the death penalty was assessed, the court reporter must prepare two duplicates of the reporter's record.

(i) ***Supreme Court and Court of Criminal Appeals may set fee.*** From time to time, the Supreme Court and the Court of Criminal Appeals may set the fee that the court reporters may charge for preparing the reporter's record.

TRAP 35. TIME TO FILE RECORD; RESPONSIBILITY FOR FILING RECORD

35.1 **Civil Cases.** The appellate record must be filed in the appellate court within 60 days after the judgment is signed, except as follows:

TRAP 34

(a) if Rule 26.1(a) applies, within 120 days after the judgment is signed;

(b) if Rule 26.1(b) applies, within 10 days after the notice of appeal is filed; or

(c) if Rule 26.1(c) applies, within 30 days after the notice of appeal is filed.

35.2 Criminal Cases.

35.3 Responsibility for Filing Record.

(a) ***Clerk's record.*** The trial court clerk is responsible for preparing, certifying, and timely filing the clerk's record if:

(1) a notice of appeal has been filed; and

(2) the party responsible for paying for the preparation of the clerk's record has paid the clerk's fee, has made satisfactory arrangements with the clerk to pay the fee, or is entitled to appeal without paying the fee.

(b) ***Reporter's record.*** The official or deputy reporter is responsible for preparing, certifying, and timely filing the reporter's record if:

(1) a notice of appeal has been filed;

(2) the appellant has requested that the reporter's record be prepared; and

(3) the party responsible for paying for the preparation of the reporter's record has paid the reporter's fee, or has made satisfactory arrangements with the reporter to pay the fee, or is entitled to appeal without paying the fee.

(c) ***Courts to ensure record timely filed.*** The trial and appellate courts are jointly responsible for ensuring that the appellate record is timely filed. The appellate court must allow the record to be filed late when the delay is not the appellant's fault, and may do so when the delay is the appellant's fault. The appellate court may enter any order necessary to ensure the timely filing of the appellate record.

TRAP 36. AGENCY RECORD IN ADMINISTRATIVE APPEALS

36.1 Scope. This rule applies only to cases involving judicial review of state agency decisions in contested cases under the Administrative Procedure Act.

36.2 Inclusion in Appellate Record. The record of an agency proceeding filed in the trial court may be included in either the clerk's record or the reporter's record.

36.3 Correcting the Record.

(a) ***Correction by agreement.*** At any stage of the proceeding, the parties may agree to correct an agency record filed under Section 2001.175(b) of the Government Code to ensure that the agency record accurately reflects the contested case proceedings before the agency. The court reporter need not recertify the agency record.

(b) ***Correction by trial court.*** If the parties cannot agree to a correction to the agency record, the appellate court must—on any party's motion or its own incentive—send the question to the trial court. After notice and hearing, the trial court must determine what constitutes an accurate copy of the agency record and order the agency to send an accurate copy to the clerk of the court in which the case is pending.

TRAP 37. DUTIES OF THE APPELLATE CLERK ON RECEIVING THE NOTICE OF APPEAL & RECORD

37.1 On Receiving the Notice of Appeal. If the appellate clerk determines that the notice of appeal or certification of defendant's right of appeal in a criminal case is defective, the clerk must notify the parties of the defect so that it can be remedied, if possible. If a proper notice of appeal or certification of defendant's right of appeal is not filed in the trial court within 30 days of the date of the clerk's notice, the clerk must refer the matter to the appellate court, which will make an appropriate order under this rule or Rule 34.5(c)(2).

37.2 On Receiving the Record. On receiving the clerk's record from the trial court clerk or the reporter's record from the reporter, the appellate clerk must determine whether each complies with the Supreme Court's and Court of Criminal Appeals' order on preparation of the record. If so, the clerk must endorse on each the date of receipt, file it, and notify the parties of the filing and the date. If not, the clerk must endorse on the clerk's record or reporter's record—whichever is defective—the date of receipt and return it to the official responsible for filing it. The appellate court clerk must specify the defects and instruct the official to correct the defects and return the record to the appellate court by a specified date.

37.3 **If No Record Filed.**

(a) ***Notice of late record.***

(1) ***Civil cases.*** If the clerk's record or reporter's record has not been timely filed, the appellate clerk must send notice to the official responsible for filing it, stating that the record is late and requesting that the record be filed within 30 days if an ordinary or restricted appeal, or 10 days if an accelerated appeal. The appellate clerk must send a copy of this notice to the parties and the trial court. If the clerk does not receive the record within the stated period, the clerk must refer the matter to the appellate court. The court must make whatever order is appropriate to avoid further delay and to preserve the parties' rights.

(2) ***Criminal cases.*** If the clerk's record or reporter's record has not been timely filed, the appellate court clerk must refer the matter to the appellate court. The court must make whatever order is appropriate to avoid further delay and to preserve the parties' rights.

(b) ***If no clerk's record filed due to appellant's fault.*** If the trial court clerk failed to file the clerk's record because the appellant failed to pay or make arrangements to pay the clerk's fee for preparing the clerk's record, the appellate court may—on a party's motion or its own initiative—dismiss the appeal for want of prosecution unless the appellant was entitled to proceed without payment of costs. The court must give the appellant a reasonable opportunity to cure before dismissal.

(c) ***If no reporter's record filed due to appellant's fault.*** Under the following circumstances, and if the clerk's record has been filed, the appellate court may—after first giving the appellant notice and a reasonable opportunity to cure—consider and decide those issues or points that do not require a reporter's record for a decision. The court may do this if no reporter's record has been filed because:

(1) the appellant failed to request a reporter's record; or

(2)(A) appellant failed to pay or make arrangements to pay the reporter's fee to prepare the reporter's record; and

(B) the appellant is not entitled to proceed without payment of costs.

TRAP 38. REQUISITES OF BRIEFS

38.1 **Appellant's Brief.** The appellant's brief must, under appropriate headings and in the order here indicated, contain the following:

(a) ***Identity of parties and counsel.*** The brief must give a complete list of all parties to the trial court's judgment or order appealed from, and the names and addresses of all trial and appellate counsel.

(b) ***Table of contents.*** The brief must have a table of contents with references to the pages of the brief. The table of contents must indicate the subject matter of each issue or point, or group of issues or points.

(c) ***Index of authorities.*** The brief must have an index of authorities arranged alphabetically and indicating the pages of the brief where the authorities are cited.

(d) ***Statement of the case.*** The brief must state concisely the nature of the case (e.g., whether it is a suit for damages, on a note, or involving a murder prosecution), the course of proceedings, and the trial court's disposition of the case. The statement should be supported by record references, should seldom exceed one-half page, and should not discuss the facts.

(e) ***Issues presented.*** The brief must state concisely all issues or points presented for review. The statement of an issue or point will be treated as covering every subsidiary question that is fairly included.

(f) ***Statement of facts.*** The brief must state concisely and without argument the facts pertinent to the issues or points presented. In a civil case, the court will accept as true the facts stated unless another party contradicts them. The statement must be supported by record references.

(g) ***Summary of the argument.*** The brief must contain a succinct, clear, and accurate statement of the arguments made in the body of the brief. This summary must not merely repeat the issues or points presented for review.

(h) ***Argument.*** The brief must contain a clear and concise argument for the contentions made, with appropriate citations to authorities and to the record.

(i) ***Prayer.*** The brief must contain a short conclusion that clearly states the nature of the relief sought.

(j) ***Appendix in civil cases.***

(1) ***Necessary contents.*** Unless voluminous or impracticable, the appendix must contain a copy of:

(A) the trial court's judgment or other appealable order from which relief is sought;

(B) the jury charge and verdict, if any, or the trial court's findings of fact and conclusions of law, if any; and

(C) the text of any rule, regulation, ordinance, statute, constitutional provision, or other law (excluding case law) on which the argument is based, and the text of any contract or other document that is central to the argument.

(2) ***Optional contents.*** The appendix may contain any other item pertinent to the issues or points presented for review, including copies or excerpts of relevant court opinions, laws, documents on which the suit was based, pleadings, excerpts from the reporter's record, and similar material. Items should not be included in the appendix to attempt to avoid the page limits for the brief.

38.2 Appellee's Brief.

(a) ***Form of brief.***

(1) An appellee's brief must conform to the requirements of Rule 38.1, except that:

(A) the list of parties and counsel is not required unless necessary to supplement or correct the appellant's list;

(B) the appellee's brief need not include a statement of the case, a statement of the issues presented, or a statement of facts, unless the appellee is dissatisfied with that portion of the appellant's brief; and

(C) the appendix to the appellee's brief need not contain any item already contained in an appendix filed by the appellant.

(2) When practicable, the appellee's brief should respond to the appellant's issues or points in the order the appellant presented those issues or points.

(b) ***Cross-points.***

(1) ***Judgment notwithstanding the verdict.*** When the trial court renders judgment notwithstanding the verdict on one or more questions, the appellee must bring forward by cross-point any issue or point that would have vitiated the verdict or that would have prevented an affirmance of the judgment if the trial court had rendered judgment on the verdict. Failure to bring forward by cross-point an issue or point that would vitiate the verdict or prevent an affirmance of the judgment waives that complaint. Included in this requirement is a point that:

(A) the verdict or one or more jury findings have insufficient evidentiary support or are against the overwhelming preponderance of the evidence as a matter of fact; or

(B) the verdict should be set aside because of improper argument of counsel.

(2) ***When evidentiary hearing needed.*** The appellate court must remand a case to the trial court to take evidence if:

(A) the appellate court has sustained a point raised by the appellant; and

(B) the appellee raised a cross-point that requires the taking of additional evidence.

38.3 Reply Brief. The appellant may file a reply brief addressing any matter in the appellee's brief. However, the appellate court may consider and decide the case before a reply brief is filed.

38.4 Length of Briefs. An appellant's brief or an appellee's brief must be no longer than 50 pages, exclusive of pages containing the identity of parties and counsel, the table of contents, the index of authorities, the statement of the case, the issues presented, the signature, the proof of service, and the appendix. A reply brief must be no longer than 25 pages, exclusive of the items stated above. But in a civil case, the aggregate number of pages of all briefs filed by a party must not exceed 90, exclusive of the items stated above. The court may, on motion, permit a longer brief.

38.5 Appendix for Cases Recorded Electronically. In cases where the proceedings were electronically recorded, the following rules apply:

(a) ***Appendix.***

(1) ***In general.*** At or before the time a party's brief is due, the party must file one copy of an appendix containing a transcription of all portions of the recording that the party considers relevant to the appellate issues or points. Unless another party objects, the transcription will be presumed accurate.

(2) ***Repetition not required.*** A party's appendix need not repeat evidence included in any previously filed appendix.

(3) ***Form.*** The form of the appendix and transcription must conform to any specifications of the

Supreme Court and Court of Criminal Appeals concerning the form of the reporter's record except that it need not have the reporter's certificate.

(4) ***Notice.*** At the time the appendix is filed, the party must give written notice of the filing to all parties to the trial court's judgment or order. The notice must specify, by referring to the index numbers in the court recorder's logs, those parts of the recording that are included in the appendix. The filing party need not serve a copy of the appendix but must make a copy available to all parties for inspection and copying.

(b) ***Presumptions.*** The same presumptions that apply to a partial reporter's record under Rule 34.6(c)(4) apply to the parties' appendixes. The appellate court need not review any part of the electronic recording.

(c) ***Supplemental appendix.*** The appellate court may direct or allow a party to file a supplemental appendix containing a transcription of additional portions of the recording.

(d) ***Inability to pay.*** A party who cannot pay the cost of an appendix must file the affidavit provided for by Rule 20. The party must also state in the affidavit or a supplemental affidavit that the party has neither the access to the equipment necessary nor the skill necessary to prepare the appendix. If a contest to the affidavit is not sustained by written order, the court recorder must transcribe or have transcribed those portions of the recording that the party designates and must file the transcription as that party's appendix, along with all exhibits.

(e) ***Inaccuracies.***

(1) ***Correction by agreement.*** The parties may agree to correct an inaccuracy in the transcription of the recording.

(2) ***Correction by appellate or trial court.*** If the parties dispute whether an electronic recording or transcription accurately discloses what occurred in the trial court but cannot agree on corrections, the appellate court may:

(A) settle the dispute by reviewing the recording; or

(B) submit the dispute to the trial court, which must—after notice and hearing—settle the dispute and ensure that the recording or transcription is made to conform to what occurred in the trial court.

(f) ***Costs.*** The actual expense of preparing the appendixes or the amount prescribed for official reporters, whichever is less, is taxed as costs. The appellate court may disallow the cost of any portion of the appendixes that it considers surplusage or that does not conform to any specifications prescribed by the Supreme Court or Court of Criminal Appeals.

38.6 Time to File Briefs.

(a) ***Appellant's filing date.*** Except in a habeas corpus or bail appeal, which is governed by Rule 31, an appellant must file a brief within 30 days—20 days in an accelerated appeal—after the later of:

(1) the date the clerk's record was filed; or

(2) the date the reporter's record was filed.

(b) ***Appellee's filing date.*** The appellee's brief must be filed within 30 days—20 days in an accelerated appeal—after the date the appellant's brief was filed. In a civil case, if the appellant has not filed a brief as provided in this rule, an appellee may file a brief within 30 days—20 days in an accelerated appeal—after the date the appellant's brief was due.

(c) ***Filing date for reply brief.*** A reply brief, if any, must be filed within 20 days after the date the appellee's brief was filed.

(d) ***Modifications of filing time.*** On motion complying with Rule 10.5(b), the appellate court may extend the time for filing a brief and may postpone submission of the case. A motion to extend the time to file a brief may be filed before or after the date the brief is due. The court may also, in the interests of justice, shorten the time for filing briefs and for submission of the case.

38.7 Amendment or Supplementation. A brief may be amended or supplemented whenever justice requires, on whatever reasonable terms the court may prescribe.

38.8 Failure of Appellant to File Brief.

(a) ***Civil cases.*** If an appellant fails to timely file a brief, the appellate court may:

(1) dismiss the appeal for want of prosecution, unless the appellant reasonably explains the failure and the appellee is not significantly injured by the appellant's failure to timely file a brief;

(2) decline to dismiss the appeal and give further direction to the case as it considers proper; or

(3) if an appellee's brief is filed, the court may regard that brief as correctly presenting the case and may affirm the trial court's judgment upon that brief without examining the record.

(b) ***Criminal cases.***

(1) ***Effect.*** An appellant's failure to timely file a brief does not authorize either dismissal of the appeal or, except as provided in (4), consideration of the appeal without briefs.

(2) ***Notice.*** If the appellant's brief is not timely filed, the appellate clerk must notify counsel for the parties and the trial court of that fact. If the appellate court does not receive a satisfactory response within ten days, the court must order the trial court to immediately conduct a hearing to determine whether the appellant desires to prosecute his appeal, whether the appellant is indigent, or, if not indigent, whether retained counsel has abandoned the appeal, and to make appropriate findings and recommendations.

(3) ***Hearing.*** In accordance with (2), the trial court must conduct any necessary hearings, make appropriate findings and recommendations, and have a record of the proceedings prepared, which record—including any order and findings—must be sent to the appellate court.

(4) ***Appellate court action.*** Based on the trial court's record, the appellate court may act appropriately to ensure that the appellant's rights are protected, including initiating contempt proceedings against appellant's counsel. If the trial court has found that the appellant no longer desires to prosecute the appeal, or that the appellant is not indigent but has not made the necessary arrangements for filing a brief, the appellate court may consider the appeal without briefs, as justice may require.

38.9 Briefing Rules to be Construed Liberally. Because briefs are meant to acquaint the court with the issues in a case and to present argument that will enable the court to decide the case, substantial compliance with this rule is sufficient, subject to the following.

(a) ***Formal defects.*** If the court determines that this rule has been flagrantly violated, it may require a brief to be amended, supplemented, or redrawn. If another brief that does not comply with this rule is filed, the court may strike the brief, prohibit the party from filing another, and proceed as if the party had failed to file a brief.

(b) ***Substantive defects.*** If the court determines, either before or after submission, that the case has not been properly presented in the briefs, or that the law and authorities have not been properly cited in the briefs, the court may postpone submission, require additional briefing, and make any other order necessary for a satisfactory submission of the case.

TRAP 39. ORAL ARGUMENT; DECISION WITHOUT ARGUMENT

39.1 Right to Oral Argument. Except as provided in 39.8, any party who has filed a brief and who has timely requested oral argument may argue the case to the court when the case is called for argument.

39.2 Purpose of Argument. Oral argument should emphasize and clarify the written arguments in the briefs. Counsel should not merely read from prepared text. Counsel should assume that all members of the court have read the briefs before oral argument and counsel should be prepared to respond to questions. A party should not refer to or comment on matters not involved in or pertaining to what is in the record.

39.3 Time Allowed. The court will set the time that will be allowed for argument. Counsel must complete argument in the time allotted and may continue after the expiration of the allotted time only with permission of the court. Counsel is not required to use all the allotted time. The appellant must be allowed to conclude the argument.

39.4 Number of Counsel. Generally, only one counsel should argue for each side. Except on leave of court, no more than two counsel on each side may argue. Only one counsel may argue in rebuttal.

39.5 Argument by Amicus. With leave of court obtained before the argument and with a party's consent, an amicus curiae may share allotted time with that party. Otherwise, counsel for amicus may not argue.

39.6 When Only One Party Files a Brief. If counsel for only one party has filed a brief, the court may allow that party to argue.

39.7 Request and Waiver. A party desiring oral argument must note that request on the front cover of the party's brief. A party's failure to request oral argument waives the party's right to argue. But even if a party has waived oral argument, the court may direct the party to appear and argue.

39.8 Cases Advanced Without Oral Argument. In its discretion, the court of appeals may decide a case without oral argument if argument would not significantly aid the court in determining the legal and factual issues presented in the appeal.

39.9 Clerk's Notice. The clerk must send to the parties—at least 21 days before the date the case is set for argument or submission without argument—a notice telling the parties:

(a) whether the court will allow oral argument or will submit the case without argument;

(b) the date of argument or submission without argument;

(c) if argument is allowed, the time allotted for argument; and

(d) the names of the members of the panel to which the case will be argued or submitted, subject to change by the court.

A party's failure to receive the notice does not prevent a case's argument or submission on the scheduled date.

TRAP 40. ORDER OF DECISION

40.1 Civil Cases. The court of appeals may determine the order in which civil cases will be decided. But the following types of cases have precedence over all others:

(a) a case given precedence by law;

(b) an accelerated appeal; and

(c) a case that the court determines should be given precedence in the interest of justice.

40.2 Criminal Cases.

TRAP 41. PANEL & EN BANC DECISION

41.1 Decision by Panel.

(a) ***Constitution of panel.*** Unless a court of appeals with more than three justices votes to decide a case en banc, a case must be assigned for decision to a panel of the court consisting of three justices, although not every member of the panel must be present for argument. If the case is decided without argument, three justices must participate in the decision. A majority of the panel, which constitutes a quorum, must agree on the judgment. Except as otherwise provided in these rules, a panel's opinion constitutes the court's opinion, and the court must render a judgment in accordance with the panel opinion.

(b) ***When panel cannot agree on judgment.*** After argument, if for any reason a member of the panel cannot participate in deciding a case, the case may be decided by the two remaining justices. If they cannot agree on a judgment, the chief justice of the court of appeals must designate another justice of the court to sit on the panel to consider the case, request the assignment of a retired or former justice or judge to sit on the panel to consider the case, or convene the court en banc to consider the case. The reconstituted panel or the en banc court may order the case reargued.

(c) ***When court cannot agree on judgment.*** After argument, if for any reason a member of a court consisting of only three justices cannot participate in deciding a case, the case may be decided by the two remaining justices. If they cannot agree on a judgment, that fact must be certified to the Chief Justice of the Supreme Court. The Chief Justice may then temporarily assign a justice of another court of appeals or a qualified retired or former justice or judge to sit with the court of appeals to consider the case. The reconstituted court may order the case reargued.

41.2 Decision by En Banc Court.

(a) ***Constitution of en banc court.*** An en banc court consists of all members of the court who are not disqualified or recused and—if the case was originally argued before or decided by a panel—any members of the panel who are not members of the court but remain eligible for assignment to the court. A majority of the en banc court constitutes a quorum. A majority of the en banc court must agree on a judgment.

(b) ***When en banc court cannot agree on judgment.*** If a majority of an en banc court cannot agree on a judgment, that fact must be certified to the Chief Justice of the Supreme Court. The Chief Justice may then temporarily assign a justice of another court of appeals or a qualified retired or former justice or judge to sit with the court of appeals to consider the case. The reconstituted court may order the case reargued.

(c) ***En banc consideration disfavored.*** En banc consideration of a case is not favored and should not be ordered unless necessary to secure or maintain uniformity of the court's decisions or unless extraordinary circumstances require en banc consideration. A vote to determine whether a case will be heard or reheard en banc need not be taken unless a justice of the court requests a vote. If a vote is requested and a majority of the court's members vote to hear or rehear the case en banc, the en banc court will hear or rehear the case. Otherwise, a panel of the court will consider the case.

TRAP 42. DISMISSAL; SETTLEMENT

42.1 Voluntary Dismissal and Settlement in Civil Cases.

(a) ***On Motion or by Agreement.*** The appellate court may dispose of an appeal as follows:

(1) On Motion of Appellant. In accordance with a motion of appellant, the court may dismiss the appeal or affirm the appealed judgment or order unless such disposition would prevent a party from seeking relief to which it would otherwise be entitled.

(2) By agreement. In accordance with an agreement signed by the parties or their attorneys and filed with the clerk, the court may:

(A) render judgment effectuating the parties' agreement;

(B) set aside the trial court's judgment without regard to the merits and remand the case to the trial court for rendition of judgment in accordance with the agreement; or

(C) abate the appeal and permit proceedings in the trial court to effectuate the agreement.

(b) ***Partial Disposition.*** A severable portion of the proceeding may be disposed of under (a) if it will not prejudice the remaining parties.

(c) ***Effect on Court's Opinion.*** In dismissing a proceeding, the appellate court will determine whether to withdraw any opinion it has already issued. An agreement or motion for dismissal cannot be conditioned on withdrawal of the opinion.

(d) ***Costs.*** Absent agreement of the parties, the court will tax costs against the appellant.

42.2 Voluntary Dismissal in Criminal Cases.

42.3 Involuntary Dismissal in Civil Cases. Under the following circumstances, on any party's motion—or on its own initiative after giving ten days' notice to all parties—the appellate court may dismiss the appeal or affirm the appealed judgment or order. Dismissal or affirmance may occur if the appeal is subject to dismissal:

(a) for want of jurisdiction;

(b) for want of prosecution; or

(c) because the appellant has failed to comply with a requirement of these rules, a court order, or a notice from the clerk requiring a response or other action within a specified time.

42.4 Involuntary Dismissal in Criminal Cases.

TRAP 43. JUDGMENT OF THE COURT OF APPEALS

43.1 Time. The court of appeals should render its judgment promptly after submission of a case.

43.2 Types of Judgment. The court of appeals may:

(a) affirm the trial court's judgment in whole or in part;

(b) modify the trial court's judgment and affirm it as modified;

(c) reverse the trial court's judgment in whole or in part and render the judgment that the trial court should have rendered;

(d) reverse the trial court's judgment and remand the case for further proceedings;

(e) vacate the trial court's judgment and dismiss the case; or

(f) dismiss the appeal.

43.3 Rendition Appropriate Unless Remand Necessary. When reversing a trial court's judgment, the court must render the judgment that the trial court should have rendered, except when:

(a) a remand is necessary for further proceedings; or

(b) the interests of justice require a remand for another trial.

43.4 Judgment for Costs in Civil Cases. In a civil case, the court of appeals' judgment should award to the prevailing party the appellate costs—including preparation costs for the clerk's record and the reporter's record—that were incurred by that party. But the court of appeals may tax costs otherwise as required by law or for good cause.

43.5 Judgment Against Sureties in Civil Cases. When a court of appeals affirms the trial court judgment, or modifies that judgment and renders judgment against the appellant, the court of appeals must render judgment against the sureties on the appellant's supersedeas bond, if any, for the performance of the judgment and for any costs taxed against the appellant.

43.6 Other Orders. The court of appeals may make any other appropriate order that the law and the nature of the case require.

TRAP 44. REVERSIBLE ERROR

44.1 Reversible Error in Civil Cases.

(a) ***Standard for reversible error.*** No judgment may be reversed on appeal on the ground that the trial court made an error of law unless the court of appeals concludes that the error complained of:

(1) probably caused the rendition of an improper judgment; or

(2) probably prevented the appellant from properly presenting the case to the court of appeals.

(b) ***Error affecting only part of case.*** If the error affects part of, but not all, the matter in controversy and that part is separable without unfairness to the parties, the judgment must be reversed and a new trial ordered only as to the part affected by the error. The court may not order a separate trial solely on unliquidated damages if liability is contested.

44.2 Reversible Error in Criminal Cases.

44.3 Defects in Procedure. A court of appeals must not affirm or reverse a judgment or dismiss an appeal for formal defects or irregularities in appellate procedure without allowing a reasonable time to correct or amend the defects or irregularities.

44.4 Remediable Error of the Trial Court.

(a) ***Generally.*** A court of appeals must not affirm or reverse a judgment or dismiss an appeal if:

(1) the trial court's erroneous action or failure or refusal to act prevents the proper presentation of a case to the court of appeals; and

(2) the trial court can correct its action or failure to act.

(b) ***Court of appeals direction if error remediable.*** If the circumstances described in (a) exist, the court of appeals must direct the trial court to correct the error. The court of appeals will then proceed as if the erroneous action or failure to act had not occurred.

TRAP 45. DAMAGES FOR FRIVOLOUS APPEALS IN CIVIL CASES

If the court of appeals determines that an appeal is frivolous, it may—on motion of any party or on its own initiative, after notice and a reasonable opportunity for response—award each prevailing party just damages. In determining whether to award damages, the court must not consider any matter that does not appear in the record, briefs, or other papers filed in the court of appeals.

TRAP 46. REMITTITUR IN CIVIL CASES

46.1 Remittitur After Appeal Perfected. If the trial court suggests a remittitur but the case is appealed before the remittitur is filed, the party who would make the remittitur may do so in the court of appeals in the same manner as in the trial court. The court of appeals must then render the judgment that the trial court should have rendered if the remittitur had been made in the trial court.

46.2 Appeal on Remittitur. If a party makes the remittitur at the trial judge's suggestion and the party benefiting from the remittitur appeals, the remitting party is not barred from contending in the court of appeals that all or part of the remittitur should not have been required, but the remitting party must perfect an appeal to raise that point. If the court of appeals sustains the remitting party's contention that remittitur should not have been required, the court must render the judgment that the trial court should have rendered.

46.3 Suggestion of Remittitur by Court of Appeals. The court of appeals may suggest a remittitur. If the remittitur is timely filed, the court must reform and affirm the trial court's judgment in accordance with the remittitur. If the remittitur is not timely filed, the court must reverse the trial court's judgment.

46.4 Refusal to Remit Must Not Be Mentioned in Later Trial. If the court of appeals suggests a remittitur but no remittitur is filed, evidence of the court's determination regarding remittitur is inadmissible in a later trial of the case.

46.5 Voluntary Remittitur. If a court of appeals reverses the trial court's judgment because of a legal error that affects only part of the damages awarded by the judgment, the affected party may—within 15 days after the court of appeals' judgment—voluntarily remit the amount that the affected party believes will cure the reversible error. A party may include in a motion for rehearing—without waiving any complaint that the court of appeals erred—a conditional request that the court accept the remittitur and affirm the trial court's judgment as reduced. If the court of appeals determines that the voluntary remittitur is not sufficient to cure the reversible error, but that remittitur is appropriate, the court must suggest a remittitur in accordance with Rule 46.3. If the remittitur is timely filed and the court of appeals determines that the voluntary remittitur cures the reversible error, then the court must accept the remittitur and reform and affirm the trial court judgment in accordance with the remittitur.

TRAP 47. OPINIONS, DISTRIBUTION, PUBLICATION, & CITATION

47.1 Written Opinions. The court of appeals must hand down a written opinion that is as brief as practicable but that addresses every issue raised and necessary to final disposition of the appeal.

47.2 Designation and Signing of Opinions; Participating Justices.

(a) ***Civil and Criminal Cases.*** Each opinion of the court must be designated either an "Opinion" or a "Memorandum Opinion." A majority of the justices who participate in considering the case must determine whether the opinion will be signed by a justice or will be per curiam and whether it will be designated an opinion or memorandum opinion. The names of the participating justices must be noted on all written opinions or orders of the court or a panel of the court.

(b) ***Criminal Cases.*** In addition, each opinion in a criminal case must bear the notation "publish" or "do not publish" as determined—before the opinion is handed down—by a majority of the justices who participate in considering the case. Any party may move the appellate court to change the notation, but the court of appeals must not change the notation after the Court of Criminal Appeals has acted on any party's petition for discretionary review or other request for relief. The Court of Criminal Appeals may, at any time, order that a "do not publish" notation be changed to "publish."

47.3 Distribution of Opinions. All opinions of the courts of appeals are open to the public and must be made available to public reporting services, print or electronic.

47.4 Memorandum Opinions. If the issues are settled, the court should write a brief memorandum opinion no longer than necessary to advise the parties of the court's decision and the basic reasons for it. An opinion may not be designated a memorandum opinion if the author of a concurrence or dissent opposes that designation. An opinion must be designated a memorandum opinion unless it does any of the following:

(a) establishes a new rule of law, alters or modifies an existing rule, or applies an existing rule to a novel fact situation likely to recur in future cases;

(b) involves issues of constitutional law or other legal issues important to the jurisprudence of Texas;

(c) criticizes existing law; or

(d) resolves an apparent conflict of authority.

47.5 Concurring and Dissenting Opinions. Only a justice who participated in the decision of a case may file or join in an opinion concurring in or dissenting from the judgment of the court of appeals. Any justice on the court may file an opinion in connection with a denial of a hearing or rehearing en banc.

47.6 Change in Designation by En Banc Court. A court en banc may change a panel's designation of an opinion.

47.7 Citation of Unpublished Opinions. Opinions not designated for publication by the court of appeals under these or prior rules have no precedential value but may be cited with the notation, "(not designated for publication)."

TRAP 48. COPY OF OPINION & JUDGMENT TO INTERESTED PARTIES & OTHER COURTS

48.1 Mailing Opinion and Judgment in All Cases. On the date when an appellate court's opinion is handed down, the appellate clerk must mail or deliver copies of the opinion and judgment to the following persons:

(a) the trial judge;

(b) the trial court clerk;

(c) the regional administrative judge; and

(d) all parties to the appeal.

48.2 **Additional Recipients in Criminal Cases.**

48.3 **Filing Opinion and Judgment.** The trial court clerk must file a copy of the opinion and judgment among the papers of the case in that court.

TRAP 49. MOTION & FURTHER MOTION FOR REHEARING

49.1 **Motion for Rehearing.** A motion for rehearing may be filed within 15 days after the court of appeals' judgment or order is rendered. The motion must clearly state the points relied on for the rehearing.

49.2 **Response.** No response to a motion for rehearing need be filed unless the court so requests. A motion will not be granted unless a response has been filed or requested by the court.

49.3 **Decision on Motion.** A motion for rehearing may be granted by a majority of the justices who participated in the decision of the case. Otherwise, it must be denied. If rehearing is granted, the court or panel may dispose of the case with or without rebriefing and oral argument.

49.4 **Accelerated Appeals.** In an accelerated appeal, the appellate court may deny the right to file a motion for rehearing or shorten the time to file such a motion.

49.5 **Further Motion for Rehearing.** After a motion for rehearing is decided, a further motion for rehearing may be filed within 15 days of the court's action if the court:

(a) modifies its judgment;

(b) vacates its judgment and renders a new judgment; or

(c) issues an opinion in overruling a motion for rehearing.

49.6 **Amendments.** A motion for rehearing may be amended as a matter of right anytime before the 15-day period allowed for filing the motion expires, and with leave of the court, anytime before the court of appeals decides the motion.

49.7 **En Banc Reconsideration.** While the court of appeals has plenary jurisdiction, a majority of the en banc court may, with or without a motion, order en banc reconsideration of a panel's decision. If a majority orders reconsideration, the panel's judgment or order does not become final, and the case will be resubmitted to the court for en banc review and disposition.

49.8 **Extensions of Time.** A court of appeals may extend the time for filing a motion or a further motion for rehearing if a party files a motion complying with Rule 10.5(b) no later than 15 days after the last date for filing the motion for rehearing.

49.9 **Not Required for Review.** A motion for rehearing is not a prerequisite to filing a petition for review in the Supreme Court or a petition for discretionary review in the Court of Criminal Appeals nor is it required to preserve error.

49.10 **Length of Motion and Response.** A motion or response must be no longer than 15 pages.

TRAP 50. RECONSIDERATION ON PETITION FOR DISCRETIONARY REVIEW

Within 30 days after a petition for discretionary review has been filed with the clerk of the court of appeals that delivered the decision, a majority of the justices who participated in the decision may summarily reconsider and correct or modify the court's opinion or judgment. If the court's opinion or judgment is corrected or modified, the original opinion or judgment must be withdrawn and the modified or corrected opinion or judgment must be substituted as the opinion or judgment of the court. The original petition for discretionary review is dismissed by operation of law. Any party may then file with the court of appeals a petition for discretionary review seeking review of the corrected or modified opinion or judgment under Rule 68.2.

TRAP 51. ENFORCEMENT OF JUDGMENTS AFTER MANDATE

51.1 **Civil Cases.**

(a) ***Statement of costs.*** The appellate clerk must prepare, and send to the trial court clerk with the mandate, a statement of costs showing:

(1) the preparation costs for the appellate record, and any court of appeals filing fees, with a notation of those items that have been paid and those that are owing; and

(2) the party or parties against whom costs have been adjudged.

(b) ***Enforcement of judgment.*** When the trial court clerk receives the mandate, the appellate court's judgment must be enforced. Appellate court costs must be included with the trial court costs in any process to enforce the judgment. If all or part of the costs are collected, the trial court clerk must immediately remit to the appellate court clerk any amount due to that clerk. The trial court need not make any further order in the case, and the appellate court's judgment may be enforced as in other cases, when the appellate judgment:

(1) affirms the trial court's judgment;

(2) modifies the trial court's judgment and, as so modified, affirms that judgment; or

(3) renders the judgment the trial court should have rendered.

51.2 Criminal Cases.

SECTION THREE: ORIGINAL PROCEEDINGS IN THE SUPREME COURT & THE COURTS OF APPEALS

TRAP 52. ORIGINAL PROCEEDINGS

52.1 Commencement. An original appellate proceeding seeking extraordinary relief—such as a writ of habeas corpus, mandamus, prohibition, injunction, or quo warranto—is commenced by filing a petition with the clerk of the appropriate appellate court. The petition must be captioned "*In re* [name of relator]."

52.2 Designation of Parties. The party seeking the relief is the relator. In original proceedings other than habeas corpus, the person against whom relief is sought—whether a judge, court, tribunal, officer, or other person—is the respondent. A person whose interest would be directly affected by the relief sought is a real party in interest and a party to the case.

52.3 Form and Contents of Petition. All factual statements in the petition must be verified by affidavit made on personal knowledge by an affiant competent to testify to the matters stated. The petition must, under appropriate headings and in the order here indicated, contain the following:

(a) ***Identity of parties and counsel.*** The petition must give a complete list of all parties, and the names, and addresses of all counsel.

(b) ***Table of contents.*** The petition must include a table of contents with references to the pages of the petition. The table of contents must indicate the subject matter of each issue or point, or group of issues or points.

(c) ***Index of authorities.*** The petition must include an index of authorities arranged alphabetically and indicating the pages of the petition where the authorities are cited.

(d) ***Statement of the case.*** The petition must contain a statement of the case that should seldom exceed one page and should not discuss the facts. The statement must contain the following:

(1) a concise description of the nature of any underlying proceeding (e.g., a suit for damages, a contempt proceeding for failure to pay child support, or the certification of a candidate for inclusion on an election ballot);

(2) if the respondent is a judge, the name of the judge, the designation of the court in which the judge was sitting, and the county in which the court is located; and if the respondent is an official other than a judge, the designation and location of the office held by the respondent;

(3) a concise description of the respondent's action from which the relator seeks relief;

(4) if the relator seeks a writ of habeas corpus, a statement describing how and where the relator is being deprived of liberty;

(5) if the petition is filed in the Supreme Court after a petition requesting the same relief was filed in the court of appeals:

(A) the date the petition was filed in the court of appeals;

(B) the district of the court of appeals and the names of the justices who participated in the decision;

(C) the author of any opinion for the court of appeals and the author of any separate opinion;

(D) the citation of the court's opinion, if available, or a statement that the opinion was unpublished;

(E) the disposition of the case by the court of appeals, and the date of the court of appeals' order.

(e) ***Statement of jurisdiction.*** The petition must state, without argument, the basis of the court's jurisdiction. If the Supreme Court and the court of appeals have concurrent jurisdiction, the petition must be presented first to the court of appeals unless there is a compelling reason not to do so. If the petition is filed in the Supreme Court without first being presented to the court of appeals, the petition must state the compelling reason why the petition was not first presented to the court of appeals.

(f) ***Issues presented.*** The petition must state concisely all issues or points presented for relief. The statement of an issue or point will be treated as covering every subsidiary question that is fairly included.

(g) ***Statement of facts.*** The petition must state concisely and without argument the facts pertinent to the issues or points presented. The statement must be supported by references to the appendix or record.

(h) ***Argument.*** The petition must contain a clear and concise argument for the contentions made, with appropriate citations to authorities and to the appendix or record.

(i) ***Prayer.*** The petition must contain a short conclusion that clearly states the nature of the relief sought.

(j) ***Appendix.***

(1) ***Necessary contents.*** The appendix must contain:

(A) a certified or sworn copy of any order complained of, or any other document showing the matter complained of;

(B) any order or opinion of the court of appeals, if the petition is filed in the Supreme Court;

(C) unless voluminous or impracticable, the text of any rule, regulation, ordinance, statute, constitutional provision, or other law (excluding case law) on which the argument is based; and

(D) if a writ of habeas corpus is sought, proof that the relator is being restrained.

(2) ***Optional contents.*** The appendix may contain any other item pertinent to the issues or points presented for review, including copies or excerpts of relevant court opinions, statutes, constitutional provisions, documents on which the suit was based, pleadings, and similar material. Items should not be included in the appendix to attempt to avoid the page limits for the petition. The appendix should not contain any evidence or other item that is not necessary for a decision.

52.4 Response. Any party may file a response to the petition, but it is not mandatory. The court must not grant relief—other than temporary relief—before a response has been filed or requested by the court. The response must conform to the requirements of 52.3, except that:

(a) the list of parties and counsel is not required unless necessary to supplement or correct the list contained in the petition;

(b) the response need not include a statement of the case, a statement of the issues presented, or a statement of the facts unless the responding party is dissatisfied with that portion of the petition;

(c) a statement of jurisdiction should be omitted unless the petition fails to assert valid grounds for jurisdiction, in which case the reasons why the court lacks jurisdiction must be concisely stated;

(d) the argument must be confined to the issues or points presented in the petition; and

(e) the appendix to the response need not contain any item already contained in an appendix filed by the relator.

52.5 Relator's Reply to Response. The relator may file a reply addressing any matter in the response. However, the court may consider and decide the case before a reply brief is filed.

52.6 Length of Petition, Response, and Reply. Excluding those pages containing the identity of parties and counsel, the table of contents, the index of authorities, the statement of the case, the statement of jurisdiction, the issues presented, the signature, the proof of service, and the appendix, the petition and response must not exceed 50 pages each if filed in the court of appeals, or 15 pages each if filed in the Supreme Court. A reply may be no longer than 8 pages, exclusive of the items stated above. The court may, on motion, permit a longer petition, response, or reply.

52.7 Record.

(a) ***Filing by relator required.*** Relator must file with the petition:

(1) a certified or sworn copy of every document that is material to the relator's claim for relief and that was filed in any underlying proceeding; and

(2) a properly authenticated transcript of any relevant testimony from any underlying proceeding, including any exhibits offered in evidence, or a statement that no testimony was adduced in connection with the matter complained.

(b) ***Supplementation permitted.*** After the record is filed, relator or any other party to the proceeding may file additional materials for inclusion in the record.

(c) ***Service of record on all parties.*** Relator and any party who files materials for inclusion in the record must—at the same time—serve on each party:

(1) those materials not previously served on that party as part of the record in another original appellate proceeding in the same or another court; and

(2) an index listing the materials filed and describing them in sufficient detail to identify them.

52.8 Action on Petition.

(a) ***Relief denied.*** If the court determines from the petition and any response and reply that the relator is not entitled to the relief sought, the court must deny the petition. If the relator in a habeas corpus proceeding has been released on bond, the court must remand the relator to custody and issue an order of commitment. If the relator is not returned to custody, the court may declare the bond to be forfeited and render judgment against the surety.

(b) ***Interim action.*** If the court is of the tentative opinion that relator is entitled to the relief sought or that a serious question concerning the relief requires further consideration:

(1) the court must request a response if one has not been filed;

(2) the Supreme Court may request full briefing under Rule 55;

(3) in a habeas corpus proceeding, the court may order that relator be discharged on execution and filing of a bond in an amount set by the court; and

(4) the court may set the case for oral argument.

(c) ***Relief granted.*** If the court determines that relator is entitled to relief, it must make an appropriate order. The court may grant relief without hearing oral argument.

(d) ***Opinion.*** When denying relief, the court may hand down an opinion but is not required to do so. When granting relief, the court must hand down an opinion as in any other case. Rule 47 is applicable to an order or opinion by a court of appeals except that the court of appeals may not order an unpublished opinion published after the Supreme Court or Court of Criminal Appeals has acted on any party's petition for extraordinary relief addressing the same issues.

52.9 Motion for Rehearing.

Any party may file a motion for rehearing within 15 days after the final order is rendered. The motion must clearly state the points relied on for the rehearing. No response to a motion for rehearing need be filed unless the court so requests. The court will not grant a motion for rehearing unless a response has been filed or requested. A motion or response must be no longer than 15 pages.

52.10 Temporary Relief.

(a) ***Motion for temporary relief; certificate of compliance.*** The relator may file a motion to stay any underlying proceedings or for any other temporary relief pending the court's action on the petition. The relator must notify or make a diligent effort to notify all parties by expedited means (such as by telephone or fax) that a motion for temporary relief has been or will be filed and must certify to the court that the relator has complied with this paragraph before temporary relief will be granted.

(b) ***Grant of temporary relief.*** The court—on motion of any party or on its own initiative—may without notice grant any just relief pending the court's action on the petition. As a condition of granting temporary relief, the court may require a bond to protect the parties who will be affected by the relief. Unless vacated or modified, an order granting temporary relief is effective until the case is finally decided.

(c) ***Motion to reconsider.*** Any party may move the court at any time to reconsider a grant of temporary relief.

52.11 Groundless Petition or Misleading Statement or Record.

On motion of any party or on its own initiative, the court may—after notice and a reasonable opportunity to respond—impose just sanctions on a party or attorney who is not acting in good faith as indicated by any of the following:

(a) filing a petition that is clearly groundless;

(b) bringing the petition solely for delay of an underlying proceeding;

(c) grossly misstating or omitting an obviously important and material fact in the petition or response; or

(d) filing an appendix or record that is clearly misleading because of the omission of obviously important and material evidence or documents.

SECTION FOUR: PROCEEDINGS IN THE SUPREME COURT

TRAP 53. PETITION FOR REVIEW

53.1 Method of Review. The Supreme Court may review a court of appeals' final judgment on a petition for review addressed to "The Supreme Court of Texas." A party who seeks to alter the court of appeals' judgment must file a petition for review. The petition for review procedure replaces the writ of error procedure. Statutes pertaining to the writ of error in the Supreme Court apply equally to the petition for review.

53.2 Contents of Petition. The petition for review must, under appropriate headings and in the order here indicated, contain the following items:

(a) ***Identity of parties and counsel.*** The petition must give a complete list of all parties to the trial court's final judgment, and the names and addresses of all trial and appellate counsel.

(b) ***Table of contents.*** The petition must have a table of contents with references to the pages of the petition. The table of contents must indicate the subject matter of each issue or point, or group of issues or points.

(c) ***Index of authorities.*** The petition must have an index of authorities arranged alphabetically and indicating the pages of the petition where the authorities are cited.

(d) ***Statement of the case.*** The petition must contain a statement of the case that should seldom exceed one page and should not discuss the facts. The statement must contain the following:

(1) a concise description of the nature of the case (e.g., whether it is a suit for damages, on a note, or in trespass to try title);

(2) the name of the judge who signed the order or judgment appealed from;

(3) the designation of the trial court and the county in which it is located;

(4) the disposition of the case by the trial court;

(5) the parties in the court of appeals;

(6) the district of the court of appeals;

(7) the names of the justices who participated in the decision in the court of appeals, the author of the opinion for the court, and the author of any separate opinion;

(8) the citation for the court of appeals' opinion, if available, or a statement that the opinion was unpublished; and

(9) the disposition of the case by the court of appeals.

(e) ***Statement of jurisdiction.*** The petition must state, without argument, the basis of the Court's jurisdiction.

(f) ***Issues presented.*** The petition must state concisely all issues or points presented for review. The statement of an issue or point will be treated as covering every subsidiary question that is fairly included. If the matter complained of originated in the trial court, it should have been preserved for appellate review in the trial court and assigned as error in the court of appeals.

(g) ***Statement of facts.*** The petition must affirm that the court of appeals correctly stated the nature of the case, except in any particulars pointed out. The petition must state concisely and without argument the facts and procedural background pertinent to the issues or points presented. The statement must be supported by record references.

(h) ***Summary of the argument.*** The petition must contain a succinct, clear, and accurate statement of the arguments made in the body of the petition. This summary must not merely repeat the issues or points presented for review.

(i) ***Argument.*** The petition must contain a clear and concise argument for the contentions made, with appropriate citations to authorities and to the record. The argument need not address every issue or point included in the statement of issues or points. Any issue or point not addressed may be addressed in the brief on the merits if one is requested by the Court. The argument should state the reasons why the Supreme Court should exercise jurisdiction to hear the case with specific reference to the factors listed in Rule 56.1(a). The petition need not quote at length from a matter included in the appendix; a reference to the appendix is sufficient. The Court will consider the court of appeals' opinion along with the petition, so statements in that opinion need not be repeated.

(j) ***Prayer.*** The petition must contain a short conclusion that clearly states the nature of the relief sought.

(k) ***Appendix.***

(1) ***Necessary contents.*** Unless voluminous or impracticable, the appendix must contain a copy of:

(A) the judgment or other appealable order of the trial court from which relief in the court of appeals was sought;

(B) the jury charge and verdict, if any, or the trial court's findings of fact and conclusions of law, if any;

(C) the opinion and judgment of the court of appeals; and

(D) the text of any rule, regulation, ordinance, statute, constitutional provision, or other law on which the argument is based (excluding case law), and the text of any contract or other document that is central to the argument.

(2) ***Optional contents.*** The appendix may contain any other item pertinent to the issues or points presented for review, including copies or excerpts of relevant court opinions, statutes, constitutional provisions, documents on which the suit was based, pleadings, and similar material. Items should not be included in the appendix to attempt to avoid the page limits for the petition.

53.3 Response to Petition for Review. Any other party to the appeal may file a response to the petition for review, but it is not mandatory. If no response is timely filed, or if a party files a waiver of response, the Court will consider the petition without a response. A petition will not be granted before a response has been filed or requested by the Court. The response must conform to the requirements of 53.2, except that:

(a) the list of parties and counsel is not required unless necessary to supplement or correct the list contained in the petition;

(b) a statement of the case and a statement of the facts need not be made unless the respondent is dissatisfied with that portion of the petition;

(c) a statement of the issues presented need not be made unless:

(1) the respondent is dissatisfied with the statement made in the petition;

(2) the respondent is asserting independent grounds for affirmance of the court of appeals' judgment; or

(3) the respondent is asserting grounds that establish the respondent's right to a judgment that is less favorable to the respondent than the judgment rendered by the court of appeals but more favorable to the respondent than the judgment that might be awarded to the petitioner (e.g., a remand for a new trial rather than a rendition of judgment in favor of the petitioner);

(d) a statement of jurisdiction should be omitted unless the petition fails to assert valid grounds for jurisdiction, in which case the reasons why the Supreme Court lacks jurisdiction must be concisely stated;

(e) the respondent's argument must be confined to the issues or points presented in the petition or asserted by the respondent in the respondent's statement of issues; and

(f) the appendix to the response need not contain any item already contained in an appendix filed by the petitioner.

53.4 Points Not Considered in Court of Appeals. To obtain a remand to the court of appeals for consideration of issues or points briefed in that court but not decided by that court, or to request that the Supreme Court consider such issues or points, a party may raise those issues or points in the petition, the response, the reply, any brief, or a motion for rehearing.

53.5 Petitioner's Reply to Response. The petitioner may file a reply addressing any matter in the response. However, the Court may consider and decide the case before a reply brief is filed.

53.6 Length of Petition, Response, and Reply. The petition and any response must be no longer than 15 pages each, exclusive of pages containing the identity of parties and counsel, the table of contents, the index of authorities, the statement of the case, the statement of jurisdiction, the issues presented, the signature, the proof of service, and the appendix. A reply may be no longer than 8 pages, exclusive of the items stated above. The Court may, on motion, permit a longer petition, response, or reply.

53.7 Time and Place of Filing.

(a) ***Petition.*** The petition must be filed with the Supreme Court clerk within 45 days after the following:

(1) the date the court of appeals rendered judgment, if no motion for rehearing is timely filed; or

(2) the date of the court of appeals' last ruling on all timely filed motions for rehearing.

(b) ***Premature filing.*** A party may not file a motion for rehearing in the court of appeals after that party has filed a petition for review in the Supreme Court unless the court of appeals modifies its opinion or judgment after the petition for review is filed. The filing of a petition for review does not preclude another party from filing a motion for rehearing or the court of appeals from ruling on the motion. If a motion for rehearing is timely filed after a petition for review is filed, the petitioner must immediately notify the Supreme Court clerk of the filing of the motion, and must notify the clerk when the last timely filed motion is overruled by the court of appeals. A petition filed before the last ruling on all timely filed motions for rehearing is treated as having been filed on the date of, but after, the last ruling on any such motion.

(c) ***Petitions filed by other parties.*** If a party files a petition for review within the time specified in 53.7(a)—or within the time specified by the Supreme Court in an order granting an extension of time to file a petition—any other party required to file a petition may do so within 45 days after the last timely motion for rehearing is overruled or within 30 days after any preceding petition is filed, whichever date is later.

(d) ***Response.*** Any response must be filed with the Supreme Court clerk within 30 days after the petition is filed.

(e) ***Reply.*** Any reply must be filed with the Supreme Court clerk within 15 days after the response is filed.

(f) ***Extension of time.*** The Supreme Court may extend the time to file a petition for review if a party files a motion complying with Rule 10.5(b) no later than 15 days after the last day for filing the petition. The Supreme Court may extend the time to file a response or reply if a party files a motion complying with Rule 10.5(b) either before or after the response or reply is due.

(g) ***Petition filed in court of appeals.*** If a petition is mistakenly filed in the court of appeals, the petition is deemed to have been filed the same day with the Supreme Court clerk, and the court of appeals clerk must immediately send the petition to the Supreme Court clerk.

53.8 Amendment. On motion showing good cause, the Court may allow the petition, response, or reply to be amended on such reasonable terms as the Court may prescribe.

53.9 Court May Require Revision. If a petition, response, or reply does not conform with these rules, the Supreme Court may require the document to be revised or may return the document to the party who filed it and consider the case without allowing the document to be revised.

TRAP 54. FILING THE RECORD

54.1 Request for Record. With or without granting the petition for review, the Supreme Court may request that the record from the court of appeals be filed with the clerk of the Supreme Court.

54.2 Duty of Court of Appeals Clerk.

(a) ***Request for record.*** The court of appeals clerk must not send the record to the Supreme Court unless it is requested. Upon receiving the Supreme Court clerk's request for the record, the court of appeals clerk must promptly send to the Supreme Court clerk all of the following:

(1) the original record;

(2) any motion filed in the court of appeals;

(3) copies of all orders of the court of appeals; and

(4) copies of all opinions and the judgment of the court of appeals.

(b) ***Nondocumentary exhibits.*** The clerk should not send any nondocumentary exhibits unless the Supreme Court specifically requests.

54.3 Expenses. The petitioner must pay to the court of appeals clerk a sum sufficient to pay the cost of mailing or shipping the record to and from the Supreme Court clerk.

54.4 Duty of Supreme Court Clerk. Upon receiving the record, the Supreme Court clerk must file it and enter the filing on the docket. The clerk may refuse the record if the charges for mailing or shipping have not been paid.

TRAP 55. BRIEFS ON THE MERITS

55.1 Request by Court. A brief on the merits must not be filed unless requested by the Court. With or without granting the petition for review, the Court may request the parties to file briefs on the merits. In appropriate cases, the Court may realign parties and direct that parties file consolidated briefs.

55.2 Petitioner's Brief on the Merits. The petitioner's brief on the merits must be confined to the issues or points stated in the petition for review and must, under appropriate headings and in the order here indicated, contain the following items:

(a) ***Identity of parties and counsel.*** The brief must give a complete list of all parties to the trial court's final judgment, and the names and addresses of all trial and appellate counsel.

(b) ***Table of contents.*** The brief must have a table of contents with references to the pages of the brief. The table of contents must indicate the subject matter of each issue or point, or group of issues or points.

(c) ***Index of authorities.*** The brief must have an index of authorities arranged alphabetically and indicating the pages of the brief where the authorities are cited.

(d) ***Statement of the case.*** The brief must contain a statement of the case that should seldom exceed one page and should not discuss the facts. The statement must contain the following:

(1) a concise description of the nature of the case (e.g., whether it is a suit for damages, on a note, or in trespass to try title);

(2) the name of the judge who signed the order or judgment appealed from;

(3) the designation of the trial court and the county in which it is located;

(4) the disposition of the case by the trial court;

(5) the parties in the court of appeals;

(6) the district of the court of appeals;

(7) the names of the justices who participated in the decision in the court of appeals, the author of the opinion for the court, and the author of any separate opinion;

(8) the citation for the court of appeals' opinion, if available, or a statement that the opinion was unpublished; and

(9) the disposition of the case by the court of appeals.

(e) ***Statement of jurisdiction.*** The brief must state, without argument, the basis of the Court's jurisdiction.

(f) ***Issues presented.*** The brief must state concisely all issues or points presented for review. The statement of an issue or point will be treated as covering every subsidiary question that is fairly included. The phrasing of the issues or points need not be identical to the statement of issues or points in the petition for review, but the brief may not raise additional issues or points or change the substance of the issues or points presented in the petition.

(g) ***Statement of facts.*** The brief must affirm that the court of appeals correctly stated the nature of the case, except in any particulars pointed out. The brief must state concisely and without argument the facts and procedural background pertinent to the issues or points presented. The statement must be supported by record references.

(h) ***Summary of the argument.*** The brief must contain a succinct, clear, and accurate statement of the arguments made in the body of the brief. This summary must not merely repeat the issues or points presented for review.

(i) ***Argument.*** The brief must contain a clear and concise argument for the contentions made, with appropriate citations to authorities and to the record.

(j) ***Prayer.*** The brief must contain a short conclusion that clearly states the nature of the relief sought.

55.3 Respondent's Brief. If the petitioner files a brief on the merits, any other party to the appeal may file a brief in response, which must conform to 55.2, except that:

(a) the list of parties and counsel is not required unless necessary to supplement or correct the list contained in the petitioner's brief;

(b) a statement of the case and a statement of the facts need not be made unless the respondent is dissatisfied with that portion of the petitioner's brief; and

(c) a statement of the issues presented need not be made unless:

(1) the respondent is dissatisfied with the statement made in the petitioner's brief;

(2) the respondent is asserting independent grounds for affirmance of the court of appeals' judgment; or

(3) the respondent is asserting grounds that establish the respondent's right to a judgment that is

less favorable to the respondent than the judgment rendered by the court of appeals but more favorable to the respondent than the judgment that might be awarded to the petitioner (e.g., a remand for a new trial rather than a rendition of judgment in favor of the petitioner);

(d) a statement of jurisdiction should be omitted unless the petition fails to assert valid grounds for jurisdiction; and

(e) the respondent's argument must be confined to the issues or points presented in the petitioner's brief or asserted by the respondent in the respondent's statement of issues.

55.4 Petitioner's Brief in Reply. The petitioner may file a reply brief addressing any matter in the brief in response. However, the Court may consider and decide the case before a reply brief is filed.

55.5 Reliance on Prior Brief. As a brief on the merits or a brief in response, a party may file the brief that the party filed in the court of appeals.

55.6 Length of Briefs. A brief on the merits or brief in response must not exceed 50 pages, exclusive of pages containing the identity of parties and counsel, the table of contents, the index of authorities, the statement of the case, the statement of jurisdiction, the issues presented the signature, and the proof of service. A brief in reply may be no longer than 25 pages, exclusive of the items stated above. The Court may, on motion, permit a longer brief.

55.7 Time and Place of Filing; Extension of Time. Briefs must be filed with the Supreme Court clerk in accordance with the schedule stated in the clerk's notice that the Court has requested briefs on the merits. If no schedule is stated in the notice, petitioner must file a brief on the merits within 30 days after the date of the notice, respondent must file a brief in response within 20 days after receiving petitioner's brief, and petitioner must file any reply brief within 15 days after receiving respondent's brief. On motion complying with Rule 10.5(b) either before or after the brief is due, the Supreme Court may extend the time to file a brief.

55.8 Amendment. On motion showing good cause, the Court may allow a party to amend a brief on such reasonable terms as the Court may prescribe.

55.9 Court May Require Revision. If a brief does not conform with these rules, the Supreme Court may require the brief to be revised or may return it to the party who filed it and consider the case without further briefing by that party.

TRAP 56. ORDERS ON PETITION FOR REVIEW

56.1 Orders on Petition for Review.

(a) ***Considerations in granting review.*** Whether to grant review is a matter of judicial discretion. Among the factors the Supreme Court considers in deciding whether to grant a petition for review are the following:

(1) whether the justices of the court of appeals disagree on an important point of law;

(2) whether there is a conflict between the courts of appeals on an important point of law;

(3) whether a case involves the construction or validity of a statute;

(4) whether a case involves constitutional issues;

(5) whether the court of appeals appears to have committed an error of law of such importance to the state's jurisprudence that it should be corrected; and

(6) whether the court of appeals has decided an important question of state law that should be, but has not been, resolved by the Supreme Court.

(b) ***Petition denied or dismissed.*** When the petition has been on file in the Supreme Court for 30 days, the Court may deny or dismiss the petition—whether or not a response has been filed—with one of the following notations:

(1) ***"Denied."*** If the Supreme Court is not satisfied that the opinion of the court of appeals has correctly declared the law in all respects, but determines that the petition presents no error that requires reversal or that is of such importance to the jurisprudence of the state as to require correction, the Court will deny the petition with the notation "Denied."

(2) ***"Dismissed w.o.j."*** If the Supreme Court lacks jurisdiction, the Court will dismiss the petition with the notation "Dismissed for Want of Jurisdiction."

(c) ***Petition refused.*** If the Supreme Court determines—after a response has been filed or requested—

that the court of appeals' judgment is correct and that the legal principles announced in the opinion are likewise correct, the Court will refuse the petition with the notation "Refused." The court of appeals' opinion in the case has the same precedential value as an opinion of the Supreme Court.

(d) ***Improvident grant.*** If the Court has granted review but later decides that review should not have been granted, the Court may, without opinion, set aside the order granting review and dismiss the petition or deny or refuse review as though review had never been granted.

56.2 **Moot Cases.** If a case is moot, the Supreme Court may, after notice to the parties, grant the petition and, without hearing argument, dismiss the case or the appealable portion of it without addressing the merits of the appeal.

56.3 **Settled Cases.** If a case is settled by agreement of the parties and the parties so move, the Supreme Court may grant the petition if it has not already been granted and, without hearing argument or considering the merits, render a judgment to effectuate the agreement. The Supreme Court's action may include setting aside the judgment of the court of appeals or the trial court without regard to the merits and remanding the case to the trial court for rendition of a judgment in accordance with the agreement. The Supreme Court may abate the case until the lower court's proceedings to effectuate the agreement are complete. A severable portion of the proceeding may be disposed of if it will not prejudice the remaining parties. In any event, the Supreme Court's order does not vacate the court of appeals' opinion unless the order specifically provides otherwise. An agreement or motion cannot be conditioned on vacating the court of appeals' opinion.

56.4 **Notice to Parties.** When the Supreme Court grants, denies, refuses, or dismisses a petition for review, the Supreme Court clerk must send a written notice of the disposition to the court of appeals, the trial court, and all parties to the appeal.

56.5 **Return of Documents to Court of Appeals.** When the Supreme Court denies, refuses, or dismisses a petition for review, the clerk will retain the petition, together with the record and accompanying papers, for 30 days after the order is rendered. If no motion for rehearing has been filed by the end of that period or when any motion for rehearing of the order has been overruled, the clerk must send a certified copy of its order to the court of appeals and return the record and all papers (except for documents filed in the Supreme Court) to the court of appeals clerk.

TRAP 57. DIRECT APPEALS TO THE SUPREME COURT

57.1 **Application.** This rule governs direct appeals to the Supreme Court that are authorized by the Constitution and by statute. Except when inconsistent with a statute or this rule, the rules governing appeals to courts of appeals also apply to direct appeals to the Supreme Court.

57.2 **Jurisdiction.** The Supreme Court may not take jurisdiction over a direct appeal from the decision of any court other than a district court or county court, or over any question of fact. The Supreme Court may decline to exercise jurisdiction over a direct appeal of an interlocutory order if the record is not adequately developed, or if its decision would be advisory, or if the case is not of such importance to the jurisprudence of the state that a direct appeal should be allowed.

57.3 **Statement of Jurisdiction.** Appellant must file with the record a statement fully but plainly setting out the basis asserted for exercise of the Supreme Court's jurisdiction. Appellee may file a response to appellant's statement of jurisdiction within ten days after the statement is filed.

57.4 **Preliminary Ruling on Jurisdiction.** If the Supreme Court notes probable jurisdiction over a direct appeal, the parties must file briefs under Rule 38 as in any other case. If the Supreme Court does not note probable jurisdiction over a direct appeal, the appeal will be dismissed.

57.5 **Direct Appeal Exclusive While Pending.** If a direct appeal to the Supreme Court is filed, the parties to the appeal must not, while that appeal is pending, pursue an appeal to the court of appeals. But if the direct appeal is dismissed, any party may pursue any other appeal available at the time when the direct appeal was filed. The other appeal must be perfected within ten days after dismissal of the direct appeal.

TRAP 58. CERTIFICATION OF QUESTIONS OF LAW BY UNITED STATES COURTS

58.1 Certification. The Supreme Court of Texas may answer questions of law certified to it by any federal appellate court if the certifying court is presented with determinative questions of Texas law having no controlling Supreme Court precedent. The Supreme Court may decline to answer the questions certified to it.

58.2 Contents of the Certification Order. An order from the certifying court must set forth:

(a) the questions of law to be answered; and

(b) a stipulated statement of all facts relevant to the questions certified, showing fully the nature of the controversy in which the questions arose.

58.3 Transmission of Certification Order. The clerk of the certifying court must send to the clerk of the Supreme Court of Texas the following:

(a) the certification order under the certifying court's official seal;

(b) a list of the names of all parties to the pending case, giving the address and telephone number, if known, of any party not represented by counsel; and

(c) a list of the names, addresses, and telephone numbers of counsel for each party.

58.4 Transmission of Record. The certifying court should not send the Supreme Court of Texas the record in the pending case with the certification order. The Supreme Court may later require the original or copies of all or part of the record before the certifying court to be filed with the Supreme Court clerk.

58.5 Fees and Costs. Unless the certifying court orders otherwise in its certification order, the parties must bear equally the fees under Rule 5.

58.6 Notice. If the Supreme Court agrees to answer the questions certified to it, the Court will notify all parties and the certifying court. The Supreme Court clerk must also send a notice to the Attorney General of Texas if:

(a) the constitutionality of a Texas statute is the subject of a certified question that the Supreme Court has agreed to answer; and

(b) the State of Texas or an officer, agency, or employee of the state is not a party to the proceeding in the certifying court.

58.7 Briefs and Oral Argument.

(a) ***Briefs.*** The appealing party in the certifying court must file a brief with the Supreme Court clerk within 30 days after the date of the notice. Opposing parties must file an answering brief within 20 days after receiving the opening brief. Briefs must comply with Rule 55 to the extent its provisions apply. On motion complying with Rule 10.5(b), either before or after the brief is due, the Supreme Court may extend the time to file a brief.

(b) ***Oral Argument.*** Oral argument may be granted either on a party's request or on the Court's own initiative. Argument is governed by Rule 59.

58.8 Intervention by the State. If the constitutionality of a Texas statute is the subject of a certified question that the Supreme Court has agreed to answer the State of Texas may intervene at any reasonable time for briefing and oral argument (if argument is allowed), on the question of constitutionality.

58.9 Opinion on Certified Questions. If the Supreme Court has agreed to answer a certified question, it will hand down an opinion as in any other case.

58.10 Answering Certified Questions. After all motions for rehearing have been overruled, the Supreme Court clerk must send to the certifying court the written opinion on the certified questions. The opinion must be under the Supreme Court's seal.

TRAP 59. SUBMISSION & ARGUMENT

59.1 Submission Without Argument. If at least six members of the Court so vote, a petition may be granted and an opinion handed down without oral argument.

59.2 Submission With Argument. If the Supreme Court decides that oral argument would aid the Court, the Court will set the case for argument. The clerk will notify all parties of the submission date.

59.3 Purpose of Argument. Oral argument should emphasize and clarify the written arguments in the briefs. Counsel should not merely read from a prepared text. Counsel should assume that all Justices have read the briefs before oral argument and should be prepared to respond to the Justices' questions.

59.4 Time for Argument. Each side is allowed only as much time as the Court orders. Counsel is not required to use all the allotted time. On motion filed before the day of argument, the Court may extend the time for argument. The Court may also align the parties for purposes of presenting argument.

59.5 Number of Counsel. Generally, only one counsel should argue for each side. Except on leave of court, no more than two counsel on each side may argue. Only one counsel may argue in rebuttal.

59.6 Argument by Amicus Curiae. With leave of court obtained before the argument and with a party's consent, an amicus may share allotted time with that party. Otherwise, counsel for amicus curiae may not argue.

TRAP 60. JUDGMENTS IN THE SUPREME COURT

60.1 Announcement of Judgments. The Court's judgments will be announced by the clerk.

60.2 Types of Judgment. The Supreme Court may:

(a) affirm the lower court's judgment in whole or in part;

(b) modify the lower court's judgment and affirm it as modified;

(c) reverse the lower court's judgment in whole or in part and render the judgment that the lower court should have rendered;

(d) reverse the lower court's judgment and remand the case for further proceedings;

(e) vacate the judgments of the lower courts and dismiss the case; or

(f) vacate the lower court's judgment and remand the case for further proceedings in light of changes in the law.

60.3 Remand in the Interest of Justice. When reversing the court of appeals' judgment, the Supreme Court may, in the interest of justice, remand the case to the trial court even if a rendition of judgment is otherwise appropriate.

60.4 Judgment for Costs. The Supreme Court's judgment will award to the prevailing party the costs incurred by that party in the Supreme Court. If appropriate, the judgment may also award the prevailing party the costs—including preparation costs for the record—incurred by that party in the court of appeals and in the trial court. But the Court may tax costs otherwise as required by law or for good cause.

60.5 Judgment Against Sureties. When affirming, modifying, or rendering a judgment against the party who was the appellant in the court of appeals, the Supreme Court must render judgment against the sureties on that party's supersedeas bond, if any, for the performance of the judgment. If the Supreme Court taxes costs against the party who was the appellant in the court of appeals, the Court must render judgment for those costs against the sureties on that party's supersedeas bond, if any.

60.6 Other Orders. The Supreme Court may make any other appropriate order required by the law and the nature of the case.

TRAP 61. REVERSIBLE ERROR

61.1 Standard for Reversible Error. No judgment may be reversed on appeal on the ground that the trial court made an error of law unless the Supreme Court concludes that the error complained of:

(a) probably caused the rendition of an improper judgment; or

(b) probably prevented the petitioner from properly presenting the case to the appellate courts.

61.2 Error Affecting Only Part of the Case. If the error affects a part, but not all, of the matter in controversy, and that part is separable without unfairness to the parties, the judgment must be reversed and a new trial ordered only as to the part affected by the error. The Court may not order a separate trial solely on unliquidated damages if liability is contested.

61.3 Defects in Procedure. The Supreme Court will not affirm or reverse a judgment or dismiss a petition for review for formal defects or irregularities in appellate procedure without allowing a reasonable time to correct or amend the defects or irregularities.

61.4 Remediable Error of the Trial Court or Court of Appeals.

(a) ***Generally.*** The Supreme Court will not affirm or reverse a judgment or dismiss a petition for review if:

(1) the trial court's or court of appeals' erroneous action or failure or refusal to act prevents the proper presentation of a case to the Supreme Court; and

(2) the trial court or court of appeals can correct its action or failure to act.

(b) ***Supreme Court direction if error remediable.*** If the circumstances described in (a) exist, the Supreme Court will direct the trial court or court of appeals to correct the error. The Supreme Court will then proceed as if the error had not occurred.

TRAP 62. DAMAGES FOR FRIVOLOUS APPEALS

If the Supreme Court determines that a direct appeal or a petition for review is frivolous, it may—on motion of any party or on its own initiative, after notice and a reasonable opportunity for response—award to each prevailing party just damages. In determining whether to award damages, the Court must not consider any matter that does not appear in the record, briefs, or other papers filed in the court of appeals or the Supreme Court.

TRAP 63. OPINIONS; COPY OF OPINION & JUDGMENT TO INTERESTED PARTIES & OTHER COURTS

The Supreme Court will hand down a written opinion in all cases in which it renders a judgment. The clerk will send a copy of the opinion and judgment to the court of appeals clerk, the trial court clerk, the regional administrative judge, and all parties to the appeal.

TRAP 64. MOTION FOR REHEARING

64.1 **Time for Filing.** A motion for rehearing may be filed with the Supreme Court clerk within 15 days from the date when the Court renders judgment or makes an order disposing of a petition for review. In exceptional cases, if justice requires, the Court may shorten the time within which the motion may be filed or even deny the right to file it altogether.

64.2 **Contents.** The motion must specify the points relied on for the rehearing.

64.3 **Response and Decision.** No response to a motion for rehearing need be filed unless the Court so requests. A motion will not be granted unless a response has been filed or requested by the Court. But in exceptional cases, if justice so requires, the Court may deny the right to file a response and act on a motion any time after it is filed.

64.4 **Second Motion.** The Court will not consider a second motion for rehearing.

64.5 **Extensions of Time.** The Court may extend the time to file a motion for rehearing in the Supreme Court, if a motion complying with Rule 10.5(b) is filed with the Court no later than 15 days after the last date for filing a motion for rehearing.

64.6 **Length of Motion and Response.** A motion or response must be no longer than 15 pages.

TRAP 65. ENFORCEMENT OF JUDGMENT AFTER MANDATE

65.1 **Statement of Costs.** The Supreme Court clerk will prepare, and send to the clerk to whom the mandate is directed, a statement of costs showing:

(a) the costs that were incurred in the Supreme Court, with a notation of those items that have been paid and those that are owing; and

(b) the party or parties against whom costs have been adjudged.

65.2 **Enforcement of Judgment.** If the Supreme Court renders judgment, the trial court need not make any further order. Upon receiving the Supreme Court's mandate, the trial court clerk must proceed to enforce the judgment of the Supreme Court's as in any other case. Appellate court costs must be included with the trial court costs in any process to enforce the judgment. If all or part of the costs are collected, the trial court clerk must immediately remit to the appellate court clerk any amount due to that clerk.

SECTION FIVE: PROCEEDINGS IN THE COURT OF CRIMINAL APPEALS

TIMETABLES

TABLE OF CONTENTS

1. SPECIAL APPEARANCE

STEP	ACTION/FORM	RULE	DEADLINE	DUE	DONE
1	Plaintiff files suit; FORMS 2B, 2C, 2D	TRCP 45-59, 78-82	Before statute of limitations expires		
2	Defendant is served; FORMS 2H	TRCP 99, 119	Before statute of limitations expires		
3	Deadline for defendant's answer	TRCP 99(b)	By 10:00 a.m. on the next Monday, 20 days after Step 2		
4	Defendant files special appearance; FORMS 3B:01-02	TRCP 120a	By Step 3 & before Step 5		
5	Defendant files answer—general denial; FORMS 3E	TRCP 85, 92	By Step 3, but after Step 4		
6	Plaintiff files response to special appearance; FORM 3B:03	TRCP 120a(3)	As soon as possible, at least 7 days before Step 10		
7	Plaintiff files sworn motion for continuance to secure affidavits or discovery; FORM 5D:01	TRCP 120a(3)	As necessary, but no later than Step 9		
8	File discovery & stipulations	TRCP 120a(3)	As soon as possible, but no later than Step 9		
9	File affidavits; FORM 1B:07	TRCP 120a(3)	At least 7 days before Step 10		
10	Hearing on special appearance, oral testimony permitted	TRCP 120a(2), (3)	Before Steps 13 & 14		
11	Order sustains special appearance; FORM 3B:04	TRCP 120a(4)	Suit is dismissed		
12	Order overrules special appearance; FORM 3B:04	TRCP 120a(4)	Suit continues		
13	Hearing on other pending motions (*e.g.*, venue)	TRCP 87	After Step 12, but before Step 14		
14	The trial	TRCP 262-265			

Legend:
FORMS *O'Connor's Texas Civil Forms* (2002)
TRCP Texas Rules of Civil Procedure

2. MOTION TO TRANSFER VENUE—WRONG OR INCONVENIENT COUNTY

STEP	ACTION/FORM	RULE	DEADLINE	DUE	DONE
1	Plaintiff files suit; FORMS 2B, 2C, 2D	TRCP 45-59, 78-82	Before statute of limitations expires		
2	Defendant is served; FORMS 2H	TRCP 99, 119	Before statute of limitations expires		
3	Deadline for defendant's answer	TRCP 99(b)	By 10:00 a.m. on the next Monday, 20 days after Step 2		
4	Defendant files motion to transfer venue to another county; FORMS 3C:01-03	TRCP 86(1); CPRC §15.063	By Step 3, but after filing special appearance and before Step 5		
5	Defendant files answer—general denial; FORMS 3E	TRCP 85, 92	By Step 3, but after Step 4		
6	Notice of hearing; FORM 1E:01	TRCP 87(1)	45 days before Step 10		
7	Plaintiff files response to motion to transfer; FORMS 3C:05, 07	TRCP 87(1)	30 days before Step 10		
8	Plaintiff files affidavits with discovery attached; FORM 1B:07	TRCP 87(1), 87(3)(a), 88	30 days before Step 10		
9	Defendant files reply & affidavits to plaintiff's response; FORMS 1B:07, 3C:09	TRCP 87(1)	7 days before Step 10		
10	Hearing on pending motions in due order: special appearance, then venue	TRCP 84, 87(1), 120a(2)	Promptly & a reasonable time before Step 13		
11	Order grants motion to transfer; FORM 3C:11	TRCP 89	Suit transferred to other county		
12	Order denies motion to transfer; FORM 3C:11	TRCP 87(3)(c)	Suit continues		
13	The trial	TRCP 262-265			

Legend:

CPRC Civil Practice & Remedies Code
FORMS ***O'Connor's Texas Civil Forms*** (2002)
TRCP Texas Rules of Civil Procedure

3. MOTION TO CHANGE VENUE—LOCAL PREJUDICE

STEP	ACTION/FORM	RULE	DEADLINE	DUE	DONE
1	Plaintiff files suit; FORMS 2B, 2C, 2D	TRCP 45-59, 78-82	Before statute of limitations expires		
2	Defendant is served; FORMS 2H	TRCP 99, 119	Before statute of limitations expires		
3	Deadline for defendant's answer	TRCP 99(b)	By 10:00 a.m. on the next Monday, 20 days after Step 2		
4	Defendant files answer—general denial; FORMS 3E	TRCP 85, 92	By Step 3		
5	Movant (defendant/plaintiff) files motion to change venue because of local prejudice & affidavits; FORMS 1B:07, 3C:04	TRCP 257	As soon as prejudice becomes known		
6	Nonmovant files response & controverting affidavit; FORM 3C:08	TRCP 258			
7	Motion for continuance to secure discovery; FORM 5D:01	TRCP 252, 258	As necessary		
8	Hearing on motions in due order: special appearance, motion to transfer venue, then motion to change venue	TRCP 84, 87(1), 120a(2), 258	Promptly & a reasonable time before Step 9 or 10		
9	Order grants motion to change venue; FORM 3C:11	TRCP 259, 261	Suit transferred to another county		
10	Order denies motion to change venue; FORM 3C:11	TRCP 258	Suit continues		
11	The trial	TRCP 262-265			

Legend:

FORMS *O'Connor's Texas Civil Forms* (2002)
TRCP Texas Rules of Civil Procedure

4. MOTION TO DISMISS—CODE FORUM NON CONVENIENS

STEP	ACTION/FORM	RULE	DEADLINE	DUE	DONE
1	Plaintiff files suit; FORMS 2B, 2C, 2D	TRCP 45-59, 78-82	Before statute of limitations expires		
2	Defendant is served; FORMS 2H	TRCP 99, 119	Before statute of limitations expires		
3	Deadline for defendant's answer	TRCP 99(b)	By 10:00 a.m. on the next Monday, 20 days after Step 2		
4	Defendant files code motion to dismiss on grounds of FNC; FORMS 3D:01-02	CPRC §71.051(d)	Step 3 + 180 days		
5	Defendant files answer—general denial; FORMS 3E	TRCP 85, 92	By Step 3, but after filing special appearance or motion to transfer venue		
6	Plaintiff files response to motion to dismiss, with evidence to support pleadings; FORM 3D:04	No rule or statute	Reasonable time before Step 9		
7	Motion for continuance, for good cause; FORMS 5D:01-02	CPRC §71.051(g)	As necessary, but before Step 9		
8	Notice of hearing; FORM 1E:01	CPRC §71.051(d)	21 days before Step 9		
9	Hearing on pending motions in due order: special appearance, venue, then Code FNC motion	TRCP 84, 87 120a(2); CPRC §71.051(d)	30 days before Step 12		
10	Order grants motion to dismiss or to stay; court has continuing jurisdiction if defendant violates court's order; FORM 3D:07	CPRC §71.051(c)	Suit transferred to other forum		
11	Order denies motion to dismiss; FORM 3D:07	CPRC §71.051(e), (f)	Suit continues		
12	The trial	TRCP 262-265			

Legend:

CPRC Civil Practice & Remedies Code
FNC Forum Non Conveniens
FORMS *O'Connor's Texas Civil Forms* (2002)
TRCP Texas Rules of Civil Procedure

5. MOTION TO DISMISS—COMMON-LAW FORUM NON CONVENIENS

STEP	ACTION/FORM	RULE	DEADLINE	DUE	DONE
1	Plaintiff files suit; FORMS 2B, 2C, 2D	TRCP 45-59, 78-82	Before statute of limitations expires		
2	Defendant is served; FORMS 2H	TRCP 99, 119	Before statute of limitations expires		
3	Deadline for defendant's answer	TRCP 99(b)	By 10:00 a.m. on the next Monday, 20 days after Step 2		
4	Defendant files answer—general denial; FORMS 3E	TRCP 85, 92	By Step 3		
5	Defendant files motion to dismiss on grounds of common-law FNC; FORM 3D:03	No rule or statute	As soon as ground becomes apparent, but after filing special appearance or motion to change venue		
6	Defendant should file stipulation		At Step 5		
7	Plaintiff files response to motion to dismiss, with evidence; FORM 3D:05		Before Step 10		
8	Motion for continuance, for good cause; FORMS 5D:01-02		Before Step 10		
9	Notice of hearing; FORM 1E:01		Before Step 10		
10	Hearing on pending motions in due order: special appearance, venue, then common-law FNC motion	TRCP 84, 87, 120a(2)	Before Step 13		
11	Order grants motion to dismiss or to stay; FORM 3D:07		Suit transferred to other forum		
12	Order denies motion to dismiss or to stay; FORM 3D:07		Suit continues		
13	The trial	TRCP 262-265			

Legend:

FNC Forum Non Conveniens
FORMS ***O'Connor's Texas Civil Forms*** (2002)
TRCP Texas Rules of Civil Procedure

6. MOTION TO ABATE

STEP	ACTION/FORM	RULE	DEADLINE	DUE	DONE
1	Plaintiff files suit; FORMS 2B, 2C, 2D	TRCP 45-59, 78-82	Before statute of limitations expires		
2	Defendant is served; FORMS 2H	TRCP 99, 119	Before statute of limitations expires		
3	Deadline for defendant's answer	TRCP 99(b)	By 10:00 a.m. on the next Monday, 20 days after Step 2		
4	Defendant files (as appropriate) special appearance, motion to transfer venue, & answer; FORMS 3B:01-02, 3C:01-04, 3E	TRCP 86, 92, 120a	By Step 3		
5	Defendant files motion to abate; FORMS 3H:01-02	TRCP 21, 85, 150-156, 158-160, 175	After Step 4, at least 3 days before Step 7, & while purpose of motion remains viable		
6	Plaintiff files response to motion to abate; FORM 3H:03		Before Step 7		
7	Hearing on pending motions in due order: special appearance, venue, then motion to abate	TRCP 84, 87, 120a(2)	Before Step 12		
8	Order grants motion to abate		Suit abated until obstacle to its prosecution is removed		
9	Order denies motion to abate		Suit continues		
10	Plaintiff files motion to revive suit—plaintiff cures defect		After Step 8, when obstacle to suit is removed		
11	Defendant files motion to dismiss suit; FORM 7F:01		After Step 8, if defect is not cured		
12	The trial	TRCP 262-265			

Legend:

CPRC Civil Practice & Remedies Code
FORMS ***O'Connor's Texas Civil Forms*** (2002)
TRCP Texas Rules of Civil Procedure

7. PRETRIAL MOTIONS

STEP	ACTION/FORM	RULE	DEADLINE	DUE	DONE
1	Plaintiff files suit; FORMS 2B, 2C, 2D	TRCP 45-59, 78-82	Before statute of limitations expires		
2	Jury request by either party; FORM 5B:01	TRCP 216-220	At least 30 days before Step 31		
3	Hearing on TRO, if requested	TRCP 680	Immediately		
4	Court grants TRO; FORM 2C:02	TRCP 680			
5	TRO expires	TRCP 680	By its own terms or 14 days from Step 4		
6	Hearing on temporary injunction	TRCP 680, 681	Earliest possible time; takes precedence		
7	Defendant is served; FORMS 2H	TRCP 99, 119	Before statute of limitations expires		
8	Return filed with court	TRCP 107	As soon as defendant served		
9	Deadline for defendant's answer	TRCP 99(b)	By 10:00 a.m. on the next Monday, 20 days after Step 7		
10	Plaintiff files motion for a no-answer default judgment; Timetable No. 11; FORM 7A:01	TRCP 107, 239	After Step 9 & at least 10 days after Step 8, but before defendant files answer		
11	Defendant files notice of removal to federal court; FEDFRMS 4A:01	12 USC §1819(b), 28 USC §1446	30 days from Step 7 or receipt of a copy of the initial pleading; if FDIC a party, 90 days from Step 7		
12	Plaintiff files motion to remand to state court; FEDFRM 4B:01	28 USC §1447(c)	Step 11 + 30 days		
13	Defendant files special appearance; Timetable No. 1; FORMS 3B:01-02	TRCP 120a	By Step 9 & before any other pleadings below		
14	Defendant files motion to transfer venue to another county; Timetable No. 2; FORMS 3C:01-02	TRCP 86(1)	By Step 9, after Step 13, & before Steps 15-17		
15	Defendant files Code FNC motion to dismiss; Timetable No. 4; FORMS 3D:01-02	CPRC §71.051(d)	Step 9 + 180 days		
16	Defendant files common-law FNC motion to dismiss; Timetable No. 5; FORM 3D:03	No rule or statute	As soon as ground becomes apparent, but after Steps 13 & 14		
17	Defendant files motion to change venue because of local prejudice; Timetable No. 3; FORM 3C:04	TRCP 257	As soon as prejudice becomes known		

PRETRIAL MOTIONS (CONT'D)

STEP	ACTION/FORM	RULE	DEADLINE	DUE	DONE
18	Defendant files answer—general denial; FORMS 3E	TRCP 85, 92	By Step 9, but after Steps 13 & 14		
19	Defendant/Plaintiff files special exceptions; FORM 3G:01	TRCP 91	At or after Step 18; it must be ruled on before Step 31		
20	Defendant/Plaintiff files motion to abate; Timetable No. 6; FORMS 3H:01-02	TRCP 85	At or after Step 18; it must be ruled on before Step 31		
21	Defendant files plea to the court's jurisdiction; FORM 3F:01	TRCP 85	As soon as it becomes known		
22	Objection to visiting judge; FORM 5C:01	Gov't Code §74.053(c)	Before first hearing at which visiting judge to preside		
23	Motion to disqualify a judge; FORM 5C:03	Tex.Const. art. 5, §11; TRCP 18a, 18b(1)	As soon as ground becomes known		
24	Motion to recuse a judge; FORM 5C:04	TRCP 18a, 18b(2)	At least 10 days before date set for hearing or trial		
25	Plaintiff/Defendant serves MSJ; Timetable No. 12; FORMS 7B:01-02, 7C:01	TRCP 166a(c), (i)	If regular SJ, after Step 7, and 21 days before SJ hearing If no-evidence SJ, after adequate time for discovery, and 21 days before SJ hearing		
26	Hearings on pending motions in due order: special appearance, venue, FNC, abate, etc.	TRCP 84, 87, 120a(2); CPRC §71.051	30 days before Step 31		
27	Trial setting	TRCP 245	45 days before Step 31		
28	Motion in limine; FORM 5E:01	No rule	Before voir dire		
29	Plaintiff files nonsuit; FORM 7E:01	TRCP 162	Before plaintiff rests its case		
30	Offer of proof	TRE 103(b)	Before the jury is charged		
31	The trial	TRCP 262-265			

PRETRIAL MOTIONS (CONT'D)

Legend:

CPRC	Civil Practice & Remedies Code
FEDFRMS	***O'Connor's Federal Civil Forms*** (2003-04)
FNC	Forum Non Conveniens
FORMS	***O'Connor's Texas Civil Forms*** (2002)
MSJ	Motion for Summary Judgment
TRAP	Texas Rules of Appellate Procedure
TRCP	Texas Rules of Civil Procedure
TRO	Temporary Restraining Order
USC	United States Code

8. DISCOVERY SCHEDULE FOR LEVEL 1

STEP	ACTION/FORM	RULE	DEADLINE		DUE	DONE
1	Plaintiff files suit; FORMS 2B, 2C, 2D	TRCP 45-59, 78-82	Before statute of limitations expires			
2	Discovery period begins	TRCP 190.2(c)(1)	At Step 1			
3	Defendant is served; FORMS 2H	TRCP 99, 119	Before statute of limitations expires			
4	Deadline for defendant's answer	TRCP 99(b)	By 10:00 a.m. on the next Monday, 20 days after Step 3			
5	Plaintiff serves discovery requests on defendant; FORMS 6D-6J	TRCP 190.2(c)(1)	No later than 30 days before Step 16	RFD		
				INT		
				RFP		
				RFA		
				RFE		
6	Defendant's deadline to respond to plaintiff's discovery requests; FORMS 6D-6J	TRCP 194.3, 196.2(a), 196.7(c)(1), 197.2(a), 198.2(a)	If request served before Step 4, Step 5 + 50-54 days, depending on type of service If request served after Step 4, Step 5 + 30-34 days, depending on type of service	RFD		
				INT		
				RFP		
				RFA		
				RFE		
7	Defendant serves discovery requests on plaintiff; FORMS 6D-6J	TRCP 190.2(c)(1)	No later than 30 days before Step 16	RFD		
				INT		
				RFP		
				RFA		
				RFE		
8	Plaintiff's deadline to respond to defendant's discovery requests; FORMS 6D-6J	TRCP 194.3, 196.2(a), 196.7(c)(1), 197.2(a), 198.2(a)	Step 7 + 30-34 days, depending on type of service	RFD		
				INT		
				RFP		
				RFA		
				RFE		
9	Plaintiff designates its testifying experts	TRCP 194.2(f), 195.2	At Step 8, when plaintiff responds to RFD about experts, or 90 days before Step 16			
10	Plaintiff furnishes its retained testifying expert's report; FORM 6C:01	TRCP 194.2(f)(4), 195.5	At Step 9, or as ordered by the court			

DISCOVERY SCHEDULE FOR LEVEL 1 (CONT'D)

STEP	ACTION/FORM	RULE	DEADLINE	DUE	DONE
11	Plaintiff tenders its retained testifying expert for deposition	TRCP 195.3(a)	If plaintiff furnished expert report—reasonably promptly after Step 12 If plaintiff did not furnish expert report—reasonably promptly after Step 9		
12	Defendant designates its testifying experts	TRCP 194.2(f), 195.2	At Step 6, when defendant responds to RFD about experts, or 60 days before Step 16		
13	Defendant furnishes its retained testifying expert's report; FORM 6C:01	TRCP 194.2(f)(4), 195.5	At Step 12, or as ordered by the court		
14	Defendant tenders its retained testifying expert for deposition	TRCP 195.3(b)	Reasonably promptly after Step 12 and after plaintiff's experts testifying on the same subject have been deposed		
15	Deadline to supplement discovery responses; FORMS 6A:22-23	TRCP 193.5(b)	Reasonably promptly after discovering need and no later than 30 days before Step 20		
16	Discovery period ends	TRCP 190.2(c)(1)	30 days before Step 20		
17	Deadline for MSJ; Timetable No. 12	TRCP 166a(c), (i)	If date not set by court: For regular MSJ, after Step 4 but 21 days before Step 19 For no-evidence MSJ, after adequate time for discovery but 21 days before Step 19		
18	Pretrial conference	TRCP 166	Date set by court		
19	Hearing on MSJ	TRCP 166a	At least 21 days after Step 17		
20	The trial	TRCP 262-265	Date set by court		

Legend:

ADR	Alternative Dispute Resolution
CPRC	Civil Practice & Remedies Code
FORMS	***O'Connor's Texas Civil Forms*** (2002)
INT	Interrogatories
MSJ	Motion for summary judgment
RFA	Requests for admission
RFD	Requests for disclosure
RFE	Request for entry on land
RFP	Requests for production of documents or things
TRCP	Texas Rules of Civil Procedure

9. DISCOVERY SCHEDULE FOR LEVEL 2

STEP	ACTION/FORM	RULE	DEADLINE		DUE	DONE
1	Plaintiff files suit; FORMS 2B, 2C, 2D	TRCP 45-59, 78-82	Before statute of limitations expires			
2	Discovery period begins	TRCP 190.3(b)(1)(B)	At Step 1			
3	Defendant is served; FORMS 2H	TRCP 99, 119	Before statute of limitations expires			
4	Deadline for defendant's answer	TRCP 99(b)	By 10:00 a.m. on the next Monday, 20 days after Step 3			
5	Plaintiff serves discovery requests on defendant; FORMS 6D-6J	TRCP 190.3(b)(1)	No later than 30 days before Step 17	RFD		
				INT		
				RFP		
				RFA		
				RFE		
6	Defendant's deadline to respond to plaintiff's discovery requests; FORMS 6D-6J	TRCP 194.3, 196.2(a), 196.7(c)(1), 197.2(a), 198.2(a)	If request served before Step 4, Step 5 + 50-54 days, depending on type of service If request served after Step 4, Step 5 + 30-34 days, depending on type of service	RFD		
				INT		
				RFP		
				RFA		
				RFE		
7	Beginning of 9-month limitation for discovery in non-Family Code cases	TRCP 190.3(b)(1)(B)	Earlier of date of first oral deposition or due date for first response to written discovery			
8	Defendant serves discovery requests on plaintiff; FORMS 6D-6J	TRCP 190.3(b)(1)	No later than 30 days before Step 17	RFD		
				INT		
				RFP		
				RFA		
				RFE		
9	Plaintiff's deadline to respond to defendant's discovery requests; FORMS 6D-6J	TRCP 194.3, 196.2(a), 196.7(c)(1), 197.2(a), 198.2(a)	Step 8 + 30-34 days, depending on type of service	RFD		
				INT		
				RFP		
				RFA		
				RFE		
10	Plaintiff designates its testifying experts	TRCP 194.2(f)(1), 195.2	At Step 9, when plaintiff responds to RFD about experts, or 90 days before Step 17			
11	Plaintiff furnishes its retained testifying expert's report; FORM 6C:01	TRCP 194.2(f)(4), 195.5	At Step 10, or as ordered by the court			

DISCOVERY SCHEDULE FOR LEVEL 2 (CONT'D)

STEP	ACTION/FORM	RULE	DEADLINE	DUE	DONE
12	Plaintiff tenders its retained testifying expert for deposition	TRCP 195.3(a)	If plaintiff furnished expert report—reasonably promptly after Step 13 If plaintiff did not furnish expert report—reasonably promptly after Step 10		
13	Defendant designates its testifying experts	TRCP 194.2(f)(1) 195.2	At Step 6, when defendant responds to RFD about experts, or 60 days before Step 17		
14	Defendant furnishes its retained testifying expert's report; FORM 6C:01	TRCP 194.2(f)(4), 195.5	At Step 13, or as ordered by the court		
15	Defendant tenders its retained testifying expert for deposition	TRCP 195.3(b)	Reasonably promptly after Step 13 and after plaintiff's experts testifying on the same subject have been deposed		
16	Deadline to supplement discovery responses; FORMS 6A:22-23	TRCP 193.5(b)	Reasonably promptly after discovering need and no later than 30 days before Step 21		
17	Discovery period ends	TRCP 190.3(b)(1)	Family Code cases: 30 days before Step 21 Other cases: Earlier of 30 days before Step 21, or Step 7 + 9 months		
18	Deadline for MSJ; Timetable No. 12	TRCP 166a(c), (i)	If date not set by court: For regular MSJ, after Step 4 but 21 days before Step 20 For no-evidence MSJ, after adequate time for discovery but 21 days before Step 20		
19	Pretrial conference	TRCP 166	Date set by court		
20	Hearing on MSJ	TRCP 166a	At least 21 days after Step 18		
21	The trial	TRCP 262-265	Date set by court		

Legend:

ADR Alternative Dispute Resolution
CPRC Civil Practice & Remedies Code
FORMS ***O'Connor's Texas Civil Forms*** (2002)
INT Interrogatories
MSJ Motion for summary judgment
RFA Requests for admission
RFD Requests for disclosure
RFE Request for entry on land
RFP Requests for production of documents or things
TRCP Texas Rules of Civil Procedure

10. OFFER OF PROOF & BILL OF EXCEPTIONS

STEP	ACTION/FORM	RULE	DEADLINE	DUE	DONE
1	Offer of proof	TRE 103(b)	Before Step 2		
2	Court reads charge to the jury	TRCP 277	After close of evidence		
3	Jury returns verdict	TRCP 290-293			
4	Trial court signs judgment	TRCP 306a(1)	After Step 3		
5	Judgment becomes final & court loses plenary power	TRCP 329b(d), (e)	Step 4 + 30 days, if no MNT; if MNT, Step 4 + 30 days after MNT is overruled by written order or by operation of law		
6	Movant presents formal bill of exceptions to judge for signature; T-FORM 8E:01	TRAP 33.2(c)(1), (e)(1)	As soon as possible after Step 5, but not later than Step 16 + 30 days		
7	If parties agree to contents, judge signs & files bill with clerk; T-FORM 8E:04	TRAP 33.2(c)(2), (e)(1)	Immediately after Step 6, but not later than Step 16 + 30 days		
8	If parties do not agree, judge notifies parties & holds a hearing	TRAP 33.2(c)(2)	As soon as possible after Step 6		
9	If bill is approved, judge signs & files bill with clerk; T-FORM 8E:04	TRAP 33.2(c)(2)(A), (e)(1)	Immediately after Step 8, but not later than Step 16 + 30 days		
10	If bill is disapproved, judge suggests changes	TRAP 33.2(c)(2) (B) & (C)	Immediately after Step 8		
11	If movant agrees to judge's changes, bill is corrected & judge signs & files bill with clerk; T-FORM 8E:04	TRAP 33.2(c)(2)(B), (e)(1)	Immediately after Step 10, but not later than Step 16 + 30 days		
12	If movant refuses to agree to changes, judge notes bill is refused & returns to movant; T-FORM 8E:04	TRAP 33.2(c)(2)(C)	Immediately after Step 10		
13	Judge prepares a bill of exceptions that accurately reflects court proceedings & files it with clerk	TRAP 33.2(c)(2)(C), (e)(1)	Immediately after Step 12, but not later than Step 16 + 30 days		
14	If movant disagrees with judge's bill, movant may file refused bill & affidavits of 3 bystanders with the clerk; T-FORMS 8E:02-03	TRAP 33.2(c)(3), (e)(1)	Immediately after Step 13, but not later than Step 16 + 30 days		

OFFER OF PROOF & BILL OF EXCEPTIONS (CONT'D)

STEP	ACTION/FORM	RULE	DEADLINE	DUE	DONE
15	If nonmovant disagrees with movant's affidavits, nonmovant may file affidavits of bystanders with the clerk; T-FORMS 8E:02-03	TRAP 33.2(c)(3)	Step 14 + 10 days		
16	Movant perfects appeal: (1) files notice of appeal in trial court, (2) sends copy to CA, (3) serves copies on all parties to final judgment; A-FORM 15A:01	TRAP 25.1, 26.1	Step 4 + 30 days if no MNT; Step 4 + 90 days if MNT		
17	Movant files in CA motion for extension of time to file formal bill of exceptions	TRAP 10.5(b), 33.2(e)(3)	Last day for filing formal bill (Step 16 + 30 days) + 15 days		

Legend:

CA Court of Appeals
FORMS A-FORM – appeal form in ***O'Connor's Texas Civil Appeals*** (2002-03)
T-FORM – trial form in ***O'Connor's Texas Civil Forms*** (2002)
MNT Motion for New Trial
TRAP Texas Rules of Appellate Procedure
TRCP Texas Rules of Civil Procedure
TRE Texas Rules of Evidence

11. DEFAULT JUDGMENT

STEP	ACTION/FORM	RULE	DEADLINE	DUE	DONE
1	Plaintiff files suit; FORMS 2B, 2C, 2D	TRCP 45-59, 78-82	Before statute of limitations expires		
2	If suit against the State, plaintiff must send copy of petition to Attorney General by certified mail	CPRC §30.004(b)	At Step 1		
3	Defendant is served; FORMS 2H	TRCP 99, 119	Before statute of limitation expires		
4	Return filed with the court	TRCP 105, 107	After Step 3		
5	Deadline for defendant's answer	TRCP 99(b)	By 10:00 a.m. on the next Monday, 20 days after Step 3		
6	Plaintiff files motion for default judgment; FORM 7A:01	TRCP 107, 239	After Step 5 & at least 10 days after Step 4		
7	If suit against the State, plaintiff sends notice of intent to take default to Attorney General	CPRC §39.001	No later than 11 days before entry of the default judgment		
8	Plaintiff files certificate of last known address & military affidavit; FORMS 7A:02-03	TRCP 239a; 50 USC app. §520(1)	By Step 10		
9	Hearing on motion for default judgment—unliquidated damages; FORM 7A:04	TRCP 243	At or before Step 10		
10	Default judgment signed	TRCP 239	After Step 9		
11	Clerk sends defendant notice of the default judgment	TRCP 239a	After Step 10		

Legend:

CPRC Civil Practice & Remedies Code
FORMS *O'Connor's Texas Civil Forms* (2002)
TRCP Texas Rules of Civil Procedure
USC United States Code

12. MOTION FOR SUMMARY JUDGMENT

STEP	ACTION/FORM	RULE	DEADLINE	DUE	DONE
1	Plaintiff files suit; FORMS 2B, 2C, 2D	TRCP 45-59, 78-82	Before statute of limitations expires		
2	Defendant is served; FORMS 2H	TRCP 99, 119	Before statute of limitations expires		
3	Deadline for defendant's answer	TRCP 99(b)	By 10:00 a.m. on the next Monday, 20 days after Step 2		
4	Defendant files answer; FORMS 3E	TRCP 83-98	At or before Step 3		
5	Movant files MSJ; FORMS 7B:01-02, 7C:01	TRCP 166a(a)-(c), (i)	After adequate time for discovery, and 21 days before Step 15		
6	Movant serves notice of date of SJ hearing	TRCP 166a(c)	At or after Step 5, and 21 days before Step 15		
7	If regular SJ, movant files evidence to support MSJ	TRCP 166a(c), (d)	21 days before Step 15		
8	Nonmovant files response & objections to MSJ; FORMS 7B:04-05, 7B:11-13, 7C:02	TRCP 166a(c), (i)	7 days before Step 15		
9	Nonmovant files evidence to support response to MSJ	TRCP 166a(c), (d), (i)	7 days before Step 15		
10	Nonmovant files motion for continuance; FORM 7B:09	TRCP 166a(g)	As soon as possible, but before Step 15		
11	Nonmovant files special exceptions to challenge vague or unclear MSJ; FORM 7B:06	TRCP 166a(c)	7 days before Step 15		
12	Nonmovant files amended pleading (petition or answer) adding new claims or defenses; FORMS 2B, 3E	TRCP 63	Before Step 15		
13	Movant files special exceptions to challenge vague or unclear response to MSJ; FORM 7B:06	TRCP 90, 91	3 days before Step 15		
14	Order on special exceptions signed; FORM 3G:02		At or before Step 15		
15	Hearing on MSJ	TRCP 166a(c)	At least 21 days after Step 6		
16	Summary judgment signed; FORM 7B:14	TRCP 166a	As soon as practical after Step 15		
17	MNT filed; FORM 10B:06	TRCP 329b	Step 16 + 30 days		

MOTION FOR SUMMARY JUDGMENT (CONT'D)

STEP	ACTION/FORM	RULE	DEADLINE	DUE	DONE
18	MNT overruled; FORM 10B:08	TRCP 329b(c)	Step 16 + 75 days by operation of law, or earlier by written order		
19	Judgment becomes final & court loses plenary power	TRCP 329b(d), (e)	Step 16 or Step 18 + 30 days		

Legend:

FORMS *O'Connor's Texas Civil Forms* (2002)
MNT Motion for New Trial
MSJ Motion for Summary Judgment
TRCP Texas Rules of Civil Procedure

13. OFFER OF SETTLEMENT

STEP	ACTION	RULE	DEADLINE	DUE	DONE
1	Plaintiff files suit; FORMS 2B, 2C, 2D	TRCP 45-59, 78-82	Before statute of limitations expires		
2	Defendant is served; FORMS 2H	TRCP 99, 119	Before statute of limitations expires		
3	Deadline for defendant's answer	TRCP 99(b)	By 10:00 a.m. on the next Monday, 20 days after Step 2		
4	Defendant files answer; FORMS 3E	TRCP 83-98	At or before Step 3		
5	Defendant files TRCP 167 declaration with court	TRCP 167.2(a)	45 days before Step 17		
6	Offeror (either party) serves settlement offer on offeree	TRCP 167.2(e)	At least 60 days after Step 4 & after Step 5 & at least 14 days before Step 17		
7	Deadline for offeree to accept	TRCP 167.2(b)(5)	As stated in offer, but at least 14 days after Step 6		
8	Offeree serves objections to unreasonable conditions of offer	TRCP 167.2(c)	By Step 7		
9	Offeror serves withdrawal of offer	TRCP 167.3(a)	Before Step 10		
10	Offeree serves acceptance of offer	TRCP 167.2(b)(5), 167.3(b)	Before Step 7 & Step 9		
11	Offeree serves rejection of offer	TRCP 167.3(c)	Before Step 7 & Step 9		
12	Offeree serves counteroffer	TRCP 167.2(e)(3), 167.2(f)	Within 7 days of Step 6 or at least 14 days before Step 17, whichever is later		
13	Offeror joins third party or designates RTP	CPRC §33.004; TRCP 38, 97	As permitted by TRCP & CPRC		
14	Offeree serves objections to offer based on joinder or designation	TRCP 167.3(d)	Within 15 days of Step 13		
15	Motion to modify deadlines for Step 5 & Step 6	TRCP 167.5(a)	Before Step 16		
16	Order modifying deadlines	TRCP 167.5(a)	Before Step 18		

OFFER OF SETTLEMENT (CONT'D)

STEP	ACTION	RULE	DEADLINE	DUE	DONE
17	Case set for trial on the merits	TRCP 167.2(a)			
18	Commencement of trial on the merits	TRCP 167.5(a)			

Legend:
FORMS *O'Connor's Texas Civil Forms* (2002)
CPRC Civil Practice & Remedies Code
TRCP Texas Rules of Civil Procedure
RTP Responsible third party

14. REQUEST FOR FINDINGS OF FACT

STEP	ACTION	RULE	DEADLINE	DUE	DONE
1	Trial court signs judgment; T-FORMS 9C	TRCP 306a(1)			
2	Trial court clerk sends notice that court signed judgment	TRCP 306a(3)	Immediately after Step 1		
3	Appellant files request for FoF	TRCP 296; TRAP 26.1(a)(4)	Step 1 + 20 days		
4	Appellant files notice of past due FoF	TRCP 297; TRAP 26.1(a)(4)	Step 3 + 30 days		
5	Trial court files FoF	TRCP 297	Step 3 + 20 days, or Step 3 + 40 days, if Step 4		
6	Appellant files request for additional or amended FoF	TRCP 298	Step 5 + 10 days		
7	Trial court files additional or amended FoF	TRCP 298	Step 6 + 10 days		
8	Optional – appellant files MNT; T-FORMS 10B:01-06	TRCP 324, 329b(a)	Step 1 + 30 days		
9	MNT overruled	TRCP 329b(c)	Step 1 + 75 days by operation of law, or earlier by written order		
10	Appellant perfects appeal in trial court & files docketing statement in CA; A-FORMS 15A:01, 15B:01	TRAP 25.1, 26.1(a)	Step 1 + 30 days if no MNT or request for FoF; Step 1 + 90 days if MNT or request for FoF		
11	Trial court loses plenary power over judgment	TRCP 329b(d), (e)	Step 1 + 30 days if no MNT; Step 9 + 30 days if MNT		

For the deadlines for filing an appeal, see Timetable 17, "Appeal to the Court of Appeals," p. 1016. From this Timetable, insert into Timetable 17 the dates that apply to the appeal: the date the trial court signed the judgment, the date the appeal was perfected, the date trial court lost plenary power.

Legend:

CA	Court of Appeals
FoF	Findings of fact & conclusions of law
FORMS	A-FORM – appeal form in ***O'Connor's Texas Civil Appeals*** (2002-03)
	T-FORM – trial form in ***O'Connor's Texas Civil Forms*** (2002)
MNT	Motion for new trial
TRAP	Texas Rules of Appellate Procedure
TRCP	Texas Rules of Civil Procedure

15. MOTION TO REINSTATE AFTER DISMISSAL FOR WANT OF PROSECUTION

STEP	ACTION	RULE	DEADLINE	DUE	DONE
1	Clerk sends notice of date case will be dismissed	TRCP 165a(1)			
2	Plaintiff files motion to retain on docket	TRCP 165a(1)	Before Step 4		
3	Date set for hearing on dismissal	TRCP 165a(1)	Set by trial court		
4	Trial court signs order dismissing case	TRCP 165a(1), 306a(1)			
5	Clerk sends notice of dismissal order	TRCP 165a(1), 306a(3)	Immediately after Step 4		
6	Plaintiff files VMR & affidavits; T-FORM 10F:01	TRCP 165a(3), 306a	Step 4 + 30 days		
7	Trial court sets date for hearing, with notice to parties	TRCP 165a(3)	As soon as possible & before Step 4 + 75 days		
8	Hearing on VMR	TRCP 165a(3)	When set by court		
9	VMR overruled	TRCP 165a(1), 306a	Step 4 + 75 days by operation of law, or earlier by written order		
10	Plaintiff perfects appeal in trial court & files docketing statement in CA; A-FORMS 15A:01, 15B:01	TRAP 25.1, 26.1(a)	Step 4 + 30 days if no VMR; Step 4 + 90 days if VMR		
11	Trial court loses plenary power over judgment	TRCP 329b(d), (e)	Step 4 + 30 days if no VMR; Step 9 + 30 days if VMR		
For the deadlines for filing an appeal, see Timetable 17, "Appeal to the Court of Appeals," p. 1016. From this Timetable, insert into Timetable 17 the dates that apply to the appeal: the date of the order of dismissal, the date the appeal was perfected, the date trial court lost plenary power.					

Legend:

CA	Court of Appeals
FoF	Findings of fact & conclusions of law
FORMS	A-FORM – appeal form in ***O'Connor's Texas Civil Appeals*** (2002-03)
	T-FORM – trial form in ***O'Connor's Texas Civil Forms*** (2002)
TRAP	Texas Rules of Appellate Procedure
TRCP	Texas Rules of Civil Procedure
VMR	Verified motion to reinstate the case

16. MOTION TO EXTEND POSTJUDGMENT DEADLINES

STEP	ACTION	RULE	DEADLINE	DUE	DONE
1	Trial court signs judgment, T-FORMS 9C	TRCP 306a(1)			
2	Trial court clerk sends notice that court signed judgment	TRCP 306a(3)	After Step 1		
3	Appellant receives late notice of judgment	TRCP 306a(4); TRAP 4.2	Step 1 + 20 to 90 days		
4	Appellant perfects appeal conditionally in trial court to be effective if court grants MEPJD & files docketing statement in CA; A-FORMS 15A:01, 15B:01	TRAP 25.1, 26.1(a)	As soon as possible, but no later than Step 3 + 30 days if no MNT, or Step 3 + 90 days if MNT		
5	Appellant files MNT, T-FORMS 10B:01-06	TRCP 324, 329b(a)	Step 3 + 30 days		
6	MNT overruled	TRCP 306a(3), 329b(c)	Step 3 + 75 days by operation of law, or earlier by written order		
7	Appellant files MEPJD with affidavits, T-FORMS 10G:01-03	TRCP 306a(4), (5), 329b(d)	Before Step 11		
8	Trial court conducts hearing on MEPJD	TRCP 306a(4), (5)	As soon as possible but before Step 11		
9	Court overrules MEPJD; all appellate deadlines run from Step 1	TRCP 306a(1)	Enter date for judgment from Step 1		
10	Court grants MEPJD & makes finding of date appellant received actual notice of judgment; all appellate deadlines run from Step 10	TRCP 306a(5); TRAP 4.2(c)	Enter new date for judgment, which is the same as Step 3		
11	Judgment becomes final & court loses plenary power	TRCP 329b(d), (e)	Step 1 + 30 days if no MNT; Step 6 + 30 days if MNT		

For the deadlines for filing an appeal, see Timetable 17, "Appeal to the Court of Appeals," p. 1016. From this Timetable, insert into Timetable 17 the dates that apply to the appeal: the new date for the judgment, the date appeal was perfected, the date trial court lost plenary power.

MOTION TO EXTEND POSTJUDGMENT DEADLINES (CONT'D)

Legend:

CA	Texas Court of Appeals
FORMS	A-FORM – appeal form in ***O'Connor's Texas Civil Appeals*** (2002-03) T-FORM – trial form in ***O'Connor's Texas Civil Forms*** (2002)
MEPJD	Motion to extend postjudgment deadlines
MNT	Motion for new trial
TRAP	Texas Rules of Appellate Procedure
TRCP	Texas Rules of Civil Procedure

17. APPEAL TO THE COURT OF APPEALS

STEP	ACTION/FORM	RULE	DEADLINE	DUE	DONE
1	Trial court signs judgment, T-FORMS 9C	TRCP 306a(1)	As soon as possible after the jury returns the verdict		
2	Appellant files MNT, T-FORMS 10B:01-06	TRCP 324, 329b(a)	Step 1 + 30 days		
3	MNT is overruled	TRCP 329b(c)	Step 1 + 75 days by operation of law, or earlier by written order		
4	Appellant perfects appeal: (1) files notice of appeal in trial court, (2) sends copy to CA, (3) serves copies on other parties; A-FORM 15A:01	TRAP 25.1, 26.1(a)	Step 1 + 30 days if no MNT; Step 1 + 90 days if MNT		
5	Appellant files docketing statement in CA; A-FORM 15B:01	TRAP 32.1	Step 4		
6	Optional – file formal bill of exceptions, T-FORM 8E:01	TRAP 33.2(e)(1)	Step 4 + 30 days		
7	Optional – file motion to stay execution of judgment in trial court; A-FORMS 14B	TRAP 24.1, 24.2; TRCP 627	Before execution of judgment		
8	Appellant must arrange to pay trial court clerk for clerk's record	TRAP 35.3(a)(2)	Before clerk's record is prepared		
9	Optional – file request with trial court clerk to include additional matters in clerk's record; A-FORM 16B:02	TRAP 34.5(b)	Before clerk's record is prepared		
10	Appellant must: (1) arrange to pay court reporter for reporter's record, (2) send written request to court reporter requesting record & list of exhibits, (3) file copy of request in trial court; A-FORMS 16C	TRAP 34.6(b), 35.3(b)(3)	Step 4		
11	Judgment becomes final & court loses plenary power	TRCP 329b(d), (e)	Step 1 + 30 days if no MNT; Step 3 + 30 days if MNT		
12	Trial court clerk files clerk's record in the CA	TRAP 35.1, 35.3	Step 1 + 60 days if no MNT; Step 1 + 120 days if MNT		
13	Court reporter files reporter's record in the CA				
14	CA clerk must notify parties of dates the clerk's & reporter's record are filed	TRAP 37.2	At Steps 12 & 13		

APPEAL TO THE COURT OF APPEALS (CONT'D)

STEP	ACTION/FORM	RULE	DEADLINE	DUE	DONE
15	Appellant files brief in CA; A-FORMS 17B	TRAP 38.4, 38.6(a), 39.7	Whichever is later – 30 days after later of Step 12 or 13		
16	Appellee files brief in CA; A-FORMS 17C	TRAP 38.4, 38.6(b), 39.7	Step 15 + 30 days		
17	Optional – appellant files reply brief in CA	TRAP 38.4, 38.6(c)	Step 16 + 20 days		
18	CA clerk sends notice to parties re: oral argument	TRAP 39.9	21 days before Step 19		
19	Date for oral argument or written submission in CA	TRAP 39.9	As set by CA		
20	CA renders judgment & issues opinion	TRAP 43.1, 47.1	Promptly		
21	Optional – file MReh in CA; A-FORMS 17H	TRAP 49.1, 49.10	Step 20 + 15 days		
22	CA rules on MReh	TRAP 49.3			
23	CA may order en banc rehearing with or without a motion	TRAP 49.7	Before Step 24		
24	CA loses plenary power over judgment	TRAP 19.1	Step 22 + 30 days if MReh or motion to extend time; Step 20 + 60 days if no MReh or motion to extend time		
25	For deadlines for filing a petition for review in the Texas Supreme Court, see ***O'Connor's Texas Civil Appeals***, Timetable, "Petition for Review to Texas Supreme Court," p. 987 (2002-03).				
26	Mandate issues	TRAP 18.1(a)	If no MReh or petition for review filed, 10 days after deadline to file motion to extend time to file MReh		

Legend:

CA Texas Court of Appeals
FORMS A-FORM – appeal form in ***O'Connor's Texas Civil Appeals*** (2002-03)
T-FORM – trial form in ***O'Connor's Texas Civil Forms*** (2002)
MNT Motion for new trial
MReh Motion for rehearing
TRAP Texas Rules of Appellate Procedure
TRCP Texas Rules of Civil Procedure

See ***O'Connor's Texas Civil Appeals***, "Perfecting the Appeal," ch. 15, p. 159; "The Court of Appeals," ch. 17, p. 203 (2002-03).

INDEX

INDEX

NUMBERS IN EMPHASIZED TYPE REPRESENT PAGES IN THE COMMENTARY SECTION

INDEX

INDEX

NUMBERS IN EMPHASIZED TYPE REPRESENT PAGES IN THE COMMENTARY SECTION

INDEX

NUMBERS IN EMPHASIZED TYPE REPRESENT PAGES IN THE COMMENTARY SECTION

INDEX

INDEX

INDEX

NUMBERS IN EMPHASIZED TYPE REPRESENT PAGES IN THE COMMENTARY SECTION

INDEX

NUMBERS IN EMPHASIZED TYPE REPRESENT PAGES IN THE COMMENTARY SECTION

INDEX

NUMBERS IN EMPHASIZED TYPE REPRESENT PAGES IN THE COMMENTARY SECTION

INDEX

NUMBERS IN EMPHASIZED TYPE REPRESENT PAGES IN THE COMMENTARY SECTION

INDEX

INDEX

NUMBERS IN EMPHASIZED TYPE REPRESENT PAGES IN THE COMMENTARY SECTION

INDEX

NUMBERS IN EMPHASIZED TYPE REPRESENT PAGES IN THE COMMENTARY SECTION

INDEX

INDEX

INDEX

NUMBERS IN EMPHASIZED TYPE REPRESENT PAGES IN THE COMMENTARY SECTION

INDEX

NUMBERS IN EMPHASIZED TYPE REPRESENT PAGES IN THE COMMENTARY SECTION

NUMBERS IN EMPHASIZED TYPE
REPRESENT PAGES IN THE COMMENTARY SECTION

INDEX

NUMBERS IN EMPHASIZED TYPE
REPRESENT PAGES IN THE COMMENTARY SECTION

Notes

Notes

NOTES

Notes

Notes

Notes